Master the NCERT

Line by Line MCQs from Latest NCERT Books

for JEE/CUET

MATHEMATICS XII

BL Sharma

Co-authored by

Naveen Chandra Joshi

Alokmani Tripathi

Priyanka Sharma

arihant

SUCCESS AND NOTHING LESS

arihant
SUCCESS AND NOTHING LESS

Arihant Prakashan (Series), Meerut

卐 **Administrative & Production Offices**

Regd. Office
'Ramchhaya' 4577/15, Agarwal Road, Darya Ganj, New Delhi -110002
Tele: 011- 47630600, 43518550

Head Office
Kalindi, TP Nagar, Meerut (UP) - 250002
Tel: 0121-7156203, 7156204

卐 **Sales & Support Offices**
Agra, Ahmedabad, Bengaluru, Bareilly, Chennai, Delhi, Guwahati, Hyderabad, Jaipur, Jhansi, Kolkata, Lucknow, Nagpur & Pune.

卐 **PRICE** ₹695.00

卐 **PO No :** TXT-XX-XXXXXXX-X-XX

Published by Arihant Publications (India) Ltd.

For further information about the books published by Arihant, log on to www.arihantbooks.com or e-mail at info@arihantbooks.com

Follow us on

Preface...

In the present dynamic scenario of competitions, NCERT Books are gaining importance day by day. Most of the questions asked in various competitions are from NCERT. Similarly with the incorporation of Board weightage in competitions the necessity of dual synchronous preparation *i.e.,* to study NCERT for School Exams and for Competitive Exams, is increasing day by day. **Arihant's Master the NCERT Series** is framed with the philosophy of such synchronous preparation in mind.

The book consists of 13 chapters in each of which Questions are framed in Two Categories; First category has questions divided topically while Second category has Miscellaneous Questions from the chapter as a whole. The questions in first category i.e., Topical Questions have been prepared in the same order as in NCERT.

Some special points associated with the distribution of the questions are

- The Questions of First Category have been divided into Two Levels; Level I Questions are directly in patch up with the theory of NCERT especially in flow. The solutions of these problems are framed in such a way to give the maximum exposure of NCERT theory.
- Thus, in Level I questions of the book we have tried to connect the student with the theory of NCERT.
- Questions of Level II are compiled to provide the insight of competitions regarding the topic concerned. This set contains elevated levelwise questions *i.e.,* more difficult questions as compared to level I.
- The questions of Second Category i.e., Miscellaneous, are the toughest one and are arranged in random manner to provide tough testing to a student's learning.

Hence, while level one question's are related to learning, the questions of rest of the levels are framed for exposure and practice.

The variety in types of questions framed will be helpful in analysis of self-performance, and exposures to face tough problems of competitions. **Previous Years' Engineering Entrance Questions** have also been incorporated at both the levels so that the students get the exposure of type of questions asked in various competitions on the same topic.

We are thankful to Mr. Ashwani and Mr. Manish for their valuable support in the making of this book.

Huge efforts have been made from our side to make this book error free. Any suggestions for further improvement and pointing out mistakes and misprints in the book are welcome.

AUTHORS

Key Features

3 Level Chapter Analysis

On the first page of each chapter, JEE Analysis of 3 years is given on following 3 basis -
(i) Topics
(ii) Special format Questions
(iii) Chapter weightage

Topicwise No. of Ques asked in 3 Years (JEE Main)

Topics	No. of Questions		
	2024	2023	2022
Sets, Their Representations and Type of Sets	–	–	–
Venn Diagram and Operations on Sets	2	1	2
Practical problems on Union and Intersection of Two Sets	4	5	6

Special Type of Ques Asked In 3 Years (JEE Main)

Types	Years		
	2024	2023	2022
A-R	–	–	–
Statement Based	–	–	–
Numerical Value Type	2	2	5

Last 3 Years Weightage (JEE Main)

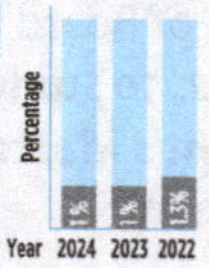

Marks Maximizer

Number of different types of relation

Let R be a relation on set A, $n(A) = m$, then

- Number of different possible relation on set $A = 2^{m^2}$ **[JEE Main 2022, 2023]**
- Number of reflexive relation $= 2^{m(m-1)}$
- Number of symmetric relation $= 2^{\frac{m(m+1)}{2}}$
- Number of relation which are both symmetric and reflexive $= 2^{\frac{m(m-1)}{2}}$

Marks Maximiser

Specialised box matter with JEE exclusive important information which may or may not be present in NCERT.

Operations on Matrices

Addition of Matrices

Let A and B be two matrices each of same order $m \times n$. Then, the sum of matrices $A + B$ is a matrix whose elements are obtained by adding the corresponding elements of A and B.

i.e. if $A = [a_{ij}]_{m \times n}$ and $B = [b_{ij}]_{m \times n}$

Then, $A + B = [a_{ij} + b_{ij}]_{m \times n}$

Multiplication of a Matrix by a Scalar

Let $A = [a_{ij}]_{m \times n}$ be a matrix and k be any scalar. Then, kA is another matrix which is obtained by multiplying each element of A by k, i.e. $kA = k[a_{ij}]_{m \times n} = [k(a_{ij})]_{m \times n}$.

Mathematics Through Concept Master

Unique video support to explain difficult Topics/Concept of NCERT in simple and easy to understand language.

Key Features

PYQ Notes

Let A and B be finite sets having m and n elements respectively. Then,

1. Number of function from A to $B = n^m$. **[JEE Main 2024]**
2. Number of one to one function from A to B
$$= \begin{cases} {}^nP_m, & n \geq m \\ 0, & n < m \end{cases}$$ **[JEE Main 2024]**
3. Number of many to one function from A and B
$$= \begin{cases} n^m - {}^nP_m, & \text{if } n \geq m \\ n^m, & \text{if } n < m \end{cases}$$
4. Number of onto (surjective) function from A to B
$$= \begin{cases} n^m - {}^nC_1(n-1)^m - {}^nC_2(n-2)^m \ldots & n < m \\ n!\,, & n = m \\ 0\,, & n > m \end{cases}$$
5. Number of into function from A to B
$$= \begin{cases} {}^nC_1(n-1)^m - {}^nC_2(n-2)^m \ldots, & n \leq m \\ n^m, & n > m \end{cases}$$
6. Number of one-one and onto (bijective) fun
$$= \begin{cases} n!, & \text{if } n = m \\ 0, & \text{if } n > m \text{ or } n < m \end{cases}$$

PYQ Notes

JEE specific important points, which were asked in past years but not incorporated in present Rationalised NCERT .

Step by Step

Mastering NCERT

- Concept Builders
- Topical Questions
- Numerical Type Questions
- Assertion and Reason Questions
- Case or Paragraph Type Questions
- Past Years Questions
- Skill Boosters

Concept Builders

1 If A and B are finite sets consisting of m and n elements respectively, then $A \times B$ has .... ordered pairs and hence .... relations can be defined from A to B.

2 The set of first components of the ordered pairs belong to R is called the .... (domain/range) of R and the set of second components of the ordered pairs belonging to R is called the .... (domain/range) of relation R.

3 Let A be a set. Then, the relation $I_A = \{(a, a) : a \in A\}$ is called the ....

9 The total number of function from the set $A = \{1, 2, 3, 4, 5\}$ to the set $B = \{a, b, c, d\}$ is ....

10 The number of one to one function from the set $A = \{1, 2, 3\}$ to set $B = \{a, b, c, d\}$ is ....

11 The domain of the real function $f(x) = \frac{x}{\sqrt{9 - x^2}}$ is ....

12 A function $f : A \to B$ is an onto function or a surjection, if range (f) is the proper subset of co-domain (f). (T/F)

Step by Step Mastering NCERT

The scientifically designed practice exercise with all possible type of questions to be asked in competition like JEE.

Concept Builders

1 If A and B are finite sets consisting of m and n elements respectively, then $A \times B$ has .... ordered pairs and hence .... relations can be defined from A to B.

2 The set of first components of the ordered pairs belong to R is called the .... (domain/range) of R and the set of second components of the ordered pairs belonging to R is called the .... (domain/range) of relation R.

3 Let A be a set. Then, the relation $I_A = \{(a, a) : a \in A\}$ is called the ....

4 The identity relation on a set A is always reflexive but a reflexive relation on A need not be the identity relation. (T/F)

5 The smallest equivalence relation on the set $A = \{a, b, c, d\}$ is ....

Concept Builders

These are present as simple teasers like T/F, Fill ups and one word question. Thus, structured to build foundation stone of NCERT concepts.

Key Features

Topical Questions

JEE like MCQs from line by line text of NCERT with complete tagging of pages. All these MCQs are arranged as per the Topic headings of NCERT.

Topical Questions

Types of Relations

Level I

1 If $(a, b) \in R$, where R is a relation, then NCERT Pg. 1
(a) (a, b) is not an ordered pair
(b) $a = b$ only
(c) $ab = 1$ only
(d) a is related to b under the relation R

2 A relation in a set A is a subset of NCERT Pg. 2
(a) $A \times A$ (b) A
(c) $A \cdot A$ (d) None of these

Numerical Type Questions

1 Let A and B two sets containing 2 elements and 4 elements respectively, then number of subsets of $A \times B$ having 3 or more elements is ...... NCERT Pg. 6

2 Let $x = \{1, 2, 3, 4, 5\}$. The number of different ordered pairs (y, z) that can be formed such that $Y \subseteq X, Z \subseteq X$ and $Y \cap z = \phi$, is .... NCERT Pg. 6

3 Let $A = \{a, b, c\}$ and $B = \{1, 2, 3, 4\}$. Then, the number of elements in the set $C = \{f : A \to \frac{B}{2} \in f(A)$ and f is not one-one$\}$ is .... NCERT Pg. 11

Numerical Type Questions

Most Important special format numerical category. All of these are also tagged with NCERT page numbers as well .

A-R Questions

Most Important special format MCQs category. All of these are also tagged with NCERT page numbers as well .

Assertion and Reason Questions

Direction (Q. Nos. 1-13) The following questions consist of two statements, one labelled as "Assertion (A) and the other labelled as Reason (R)". You are to examine these two statements carefully true and it so, where the Reason (R) is the correct explanation a for the given Assertion (A). Select your answer from following options.

(a) Both Assertion and Reason are correct and Reason is the correct explanation of Assertion.
(b) Both Assertion and Reason are correct but Reason is not the correct explanation of Assertion.
(c) Assertion is correct but Reason is incorrect.
(d) Assertion is incorrect but Reason is correct.

1 **Assertion (A)** The relation R in the set $A = \{1, 2, 3, 4, 5, 6\}$ defined as $R = \{(x, y) : y$ is divisible by $x\}$ is not an equivalence relation.

Reason (R) The relation R will be an equivalence relation, if it is reflexive, symmetric and transitive. NCERT Pg. 6

Case or Paragraph Type Questions

Direction (Q. Nos. 1-3) *If A_1, A_2 and A_3 are subsets of Z, whose union is Z, defined by*

$A_1 = \{x \in Z : x$ is a multiple of 3$\}$
$A_2 = \{x \in Z : x - 1$ is a multiple of 3$\}$
$A_3 = \{x \in Z : x - 2$ is a multiple of 3$\}$
and R is a relation in Z given by
$R = \{(a, b) : 3$ divides $a - b\}$. NCERT Pg. 4

1 The relation R is
(a) reflexive (b) symmetric
(c) transitive (d) an equivalence relation

Case or Paragraph Type

JEE Mathematics paper such types of case or paragraph based questions are asked. Such Type of Questions are covered in step by step practice with NCERT page tagging.

Key Features

Past Year's Questions

Selected PYQs with NCERT page tagging are present as the final check of preparation.

Past Years Questions

Single Correct Type

1 Let $[t]$ be the greatest integer less than or equal to t. Let A be the set of all prime factors of 2310 and $f: A \to Z$ be the function $f(x) = \left[\log_2\left(x^2 + \left[\frac{x^3}{5}\right]\right)\right]$. The number of one-to-one functions from A to the range of f is

NCERT Pg. 7, JEE Main 2024, 8 April Shift-I

(a) 20 (b) 25 (c) 24 (d) 120

2 Let $f(x) = \begin{cases} -a & \text{if } -a \le x \le 0 \\ x + a & \text{if } 0 < x \le a \end{cases}$, where $a > 0$ and $g(x) = (f(|x|) - |f(x)|)/2$.

Then, the function $g: [-a, a] \to [-a, a]$ is

NCERT Pg. 7, 8, JEE Main 2024, 8 April Shift-II

(a) one-one. (b) onto.
(c) both one-one and onto. (d) neither one-one nor onto.

Skill Boosters

1 Let N be the set of natural numbers and a relation R on N defined by
$R = \{(x, y) \in N \times N\ ;\ x^3 - 3x^2y - xy^2 + 3y^3 = 0\}$. Then, the relation R is

(a) reflexive but neither symmetric nor transitive
(b) On equivalence relation
(c) reflexive and symmetric, but not transitive
(d) symmetric but neither reflexive nor transitive

2 Let $R = \{(1, 3), (4, 2), (2, 4), (2, 3), (3, 1)\}$ be a relation on the set $A = \{1, 2, 3, 4\}$. The relation R is

(a) not symmetric (b) transitive
(c) a function (d) reflexive

3 Let Z be the set of integers if
$A = \{x \in Z: 2^{(x+2)(x^2-5x+6)} = 1\}$ and
$B = \{x \in Z: -3 < 2x - 1 < 9\}$, then the number of subsets of the set $A \times B$ is

(a) 2^{15} (b) 2^{14} (c) 2^{16} (d) 2^{13}

Skill Boosters

Brain Teasers present at the end of step by step practice to provide extra edge for preparation.

Step by Step

Decoding the Questions

Concept Builders

1 $m \times n, 2^{m \times n}$
2 Domain, Range
3 Identity function
4 True
5 $\{(a, a), (b, b), (c, c), (d, d)\}$
6 Symmetric
7 $n^2, 2^{n^2-n}, 2^{\frac{n^2+n}{2}}$
8 True
9 4^5

4 (c) A relation R in a set A is called universal relation, if each element of A is related to every element of A, i.e. $R = A \times A$.

5 (c) Both the empty relation and the universal relation are sometimes called trivial relations.

6 (b) A relation R in a set A is called reflexive, if $(a, a) \in R$ for every $a \in A$.

7 (a) A relation R in a set A is called symmetric, if $(a_1, a_2) \in R$ implies that $(a_2, a_1) \in R$, for all $a_1, a_2 \in A$.

C. We have, $A = \{4, 6, 8\}$ and a relation R in A defined as
$R = \{(4, 4), (6, 6), (8, 8), (4, 6), (6, 4), (6, 8), (8, 6)\}$

Relation R is reflexive, since for every $a \in A, (a, a) \in R$ i.e. $(4, 4), (6, 6), (8, 8) \in A$.

Relation R is symmetric since $(a, b) \in R \Rightarrow (b, a) \in R$ for all $a, b \in A$.

Relation R is not transitive, since $(4, 6), (6, 8) \in R$ but $(4, 8) \notin R$.

Decoding the Questions

Answers and explanatory solutions of selected questions for better gripping of NCERT concepts.

Contents

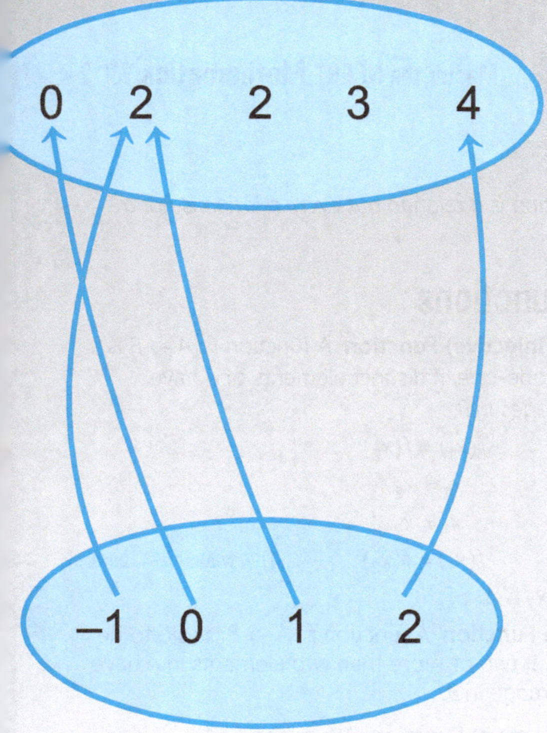

01

Relations and Functions

Topicwise No. of Ques asked in 3 Years (JEE Main)

Topics	No. of Questions		
	2024	2023	2022
Types of Relations	11	16	5
Types of Functions	6	2	5
Composite Functions and Invertible Functions	7	5	7

Special Type of Ques Asked in 3 Years (JEE Main)

Types	Years		
	2024	2023	2022
A-R	–	–	–
Statement Based	–	–	–
Numerical Value Type	5	10	5

Last 3 Years Weightage (JEE Main)

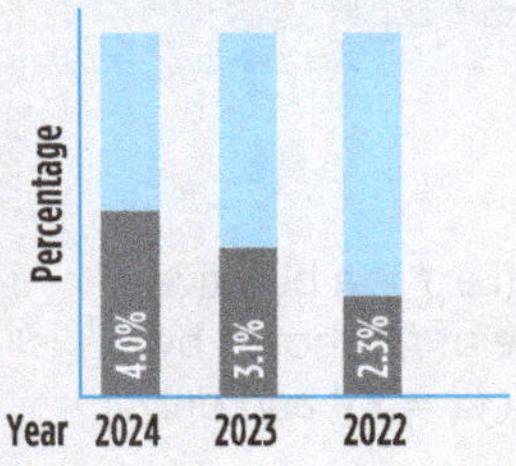

Introduction and Types of Relation

Let A be a non-empty set and $R \subseteq A \times A$. Then, R is called a relation on A. If $(a, b) \in R$, then we say that a is related to b and we write aRb and if $(a, b) \notin R$, then we write $a \not R b$.

Domain, Range and Codomain of a Relation

- Let R be a relation from set A to set B, such that $R = \{(a, b): a \in A$ and $b \in B\}$. Domain is a set of elements of set A which are related to elements of set B.
- Range is a set of elements of set B which are related to elements of set A. i.e. Domain $(R) = \{a : (a, b) \in R\}$ and Range $(R) = \{b : (a, b) \in R\}$. The set B is called the codomain of relation R. Range is subset of codomain.

Types of Relations

(i) **Empty (void) Relation** A relation R on a set A is called empty relation, if no element of A is related to any element of A, i.e. $R = \phi \subset A \times A$.

(ii) **Universal Relation** A relation R on a set A is called universal relation, if each element of A is related to every element of A, i.e. $R = A \times A$.

(iii) **Identity Relation** A relation R on a set A is called an identity relation, if each element of A is related to **itself only.** It is denoted by I_A, i.e. $I_A = R = \{(x, x): a \in A\}$.

(iv) **Reflexive Relation** A relation R defined on set A is said to be reflexive, if $(x, x) \in R, \forall\, x \in A$ i.e. $xRx, \forall\, x \in A$.

Note *Every identity relation is a reflexive relation but every reflexive relation need not to be an identity relation.*

(v) **Symmetric Relation** A relation R defined on set A is said to be symmetric, if $(x, y) \in R \Rightarrow (y, x) \in R$, $\forall\, x, y \in A$ i.e. $xRy \Rightarrow yRx, \forall\, x, y \in A$. [JEE Main 2024]

(vi) **Transitive Relation** A relation R defined on set A is said to be transitive, if $(x, y) \in R$ and $(y, z) \in R$ $\Rightarrow (x, z) \in R$, $\forall\, x, y$ and $z \in A$ [JEE Main 2024]

i.e. xRy and $yRz \Rightarrow xRz, \forall\, x, y$ and $z \in A$.

(vii) **Anti Symmetric Relation** A relation R on a set A is called anti-symmetric relation, if $(x, y) \in R$ $\Rightarrow x = y\ \forall\, x, y \in A$.

Equivalence Relation

A relation R on a set A is called an equivalence relation, if it is reflexive, symmetric and transitive. [JEE Main 2024, 2023, 2022]

Concept Master Video

Marks Maximizer

Number of different types of relation

Let R be a relation on set A, $n(A) = m$, then

- Number of different possible relation on set $A = 2^{m^2}$ [JEE Main 2022, 2023]
- Number of reflexive relation $= 2^{m(m-1)}$
- Number of symmetric relation $= 2^{\frac{m(m+1)}{2}}$
- Number of relation which are both symmetric and reflexive $= 2^{\frac{m(m-1)}{2}}$

Equivalence Classes

Consider an arbitrary equivalence relation R on an arbitrary set X, R divides X into mutually disjoint subsets A_i, called partitions or subdivisions of X, satisfying

(i) for each i all elements of A_i are related to each other i.e. $A_i \cup A_j = X, i \neq j$.

(ii) no element of A_i is related to any element of A_j, i.e. $A_i \cap A_j = \phi$, for $i \neq j$.

(iii) $\cup A_i = X$ and $A_i \cap A_j = \phi$, for $i \neq j$.

Here, subset A_i's are also called equivalence classes.

Function

Let A and B be two non-empty sets. Then, a rule f from A to B which associates each element $x \in A$, to a unique element of $f(x) \in B$ is called a function or mapping from A to B and we write $f : A \to B$. Here, elements of A is called the domain of f and elements of B is called the codomain of f.

Also, $\{f(x) : x \in A\} \subseteq B$ is called the range of f.

Note *Every function is a relation but every relation is not a function.*

Types of Functions

(i) **One-one (Injective) Function** A function $f : A \to B$ is said to be one-one, if distinct elements of A have distinct images in B,

i.e. $\quad f(x_1) = f(x_2)$

$\Rightarrow \quad x_1 = x_2$

or $\quad x_1 \neq x_2$

$\Rightarrow \quad f(x_1) \neq f(x_2)$ [JEE Main 2024, 2022]

where, $x_1, x_2 \in A$.

(ii) **Many-one Function** A function $f : A \to B$ is said to be many-one, if two or more than two elements in A have the same image in B.

(iii) **Onto (Surjective) Function** A function $f : A \to B$ is said to be onto or surjective, if every element in B has atleast one pre-image in A, i.e. if for each $y \in B$, there exists an element $x \in A$, such that $f(x) = y$. [JEE Main 2024, 2022]

(iv) **Into Function** A function $f : A \to B$ is said to be into, if atleast one element of B does not have a pre-image in A.

(v) **One-one and Onto (Bijective) Function** A function $f : X \to Y$ is said to be bijective, if f is both one-one and onto.

Composite Function

Let $f : A \to B$ and $g : B \to C$ be two functions, then a function $gof : A \to C$ defined by $(gof)(x) = g[f(x)], \forall\, x \in A$. [JEE Main 2024]

Marks Maximizer

- If f and g are injective, then fog and gof are injective.
- If f and g are surjective, then fog and gof are surjective.
- If f and g are bijective, then fog and gof are bijective.
- Domain (f^{-1}) = Range (f)
- Range (f^{-1}) = Domain (f)
- If $f(x) = y$, then $f^{-1}(y) = x$ and *vice-verse*.

Inverse Function

Let f be a one-one and onto function (i.e. f is a bijective function) from A to B. Then, the inverse of f denoted by f^{-1}, is the function from B to A defined as $f^{-1}(y) = x$ if and only if $f(x) = y$.

Note that if f is not bijective function then f^{-1} does not exist.

Caution Points

- Domain of a relation from A to B is a subset of A and its range is a subset of B.
- The universal relation on a non-void set A is equivalence relation.
- The relation R on a set A is symmetric if $R = R^{-1}$.
- The identity and the universal relations on a non-void set are transitive.
- The union of two equivalence relations on a set is not necessarily an equivalence relation on a set.
- Function cannot be multivalued.
- Any function will be either one-one or many-one.
- If range is same as co-domain, then function is onto.
- If range of a function f is proper subset of co-domain, then function f is into.
- The composition of function is not commutative, but its associative.
- Inverse of bijective function is also bijective and composition of two bijective functions is also a bijective function.

PYQ Notes

Let A and B be finite sets having m and n elements respectively. Then,

1. Number of function from A to $B = n^m$. **[JEE Main 2024]**
2. Number of one to one function from A to B
$$= \begin{cases} {}^nP_m, & n \geq m \\ 0, & n < m \end{cases}$$
[JEE Main 2024]
3. Number of many to one function from A and B
$$= \begin{cases} n^m - {}^nP_m, & \text{if } n \geq m \\ n^m, & \text{if } n < m \end{cases}$$
4. Number of onto (surjective) function from A to B
$$= \begin{cases} n^m - {}^nC_1(n-1)^m - {}^nC_2(n-2)^m \dots & n < m \\ n! \quad , & n = m \\ 0 \quad , & n > m \end{cases}$$
5. Number of into function from A to B
$$= \begin{cases} {}^nC_1(n-1)^m - {}^nC_2(n-2)^m \dots, & n \leq m \\ n^m, & n > m \end{cases}$$
6. Number of one-one and onto (bijective) function
$$= \begin{cases} n!, & \text{if } n = m \\ 0, & \text{if } n > m \text{ or } n < m \end{cases}$$

Step by Step

Mastering NCERT

- Concept Builders
- Topical Questions
- Numerical Type Questions
- Assertion and Reason Questions
- Case or Paragraph Type Questions
- Past Years Questions
- Skill Boosters

Concept Builders

1 If A and B are finite sets consisting of m and n elements respectively, then $A \times B$ has .... ordered pairs and hence .... relations can be defined from A to B.

2 The set of first components of the ordered pairs belong to R is called the .... (domain/range) of R and the set of second components of the ordered pairs belonging to R is called the .... (domain/range) of relation R.

3 Let A be a set. Then, the relation $I_A = \{(a, a) : a \in A\}$ is called the ....

4 The identity relation on a set A is always reflexive but a reflexive relation on A need not be the identity relation. (T/F)

5 The smallest equivalence relation on the set $A = \{a, b, c, d\}$ is ....

6 A relation R on a set A is called a .... relation, if $(a_1, a_2) \in R$ implies $(a_2, a_1) \in R$ for all $a_1\ a_2 \in A$.

7 Let $A = \{a_1, a_2, a_3, \ldots, a_n\}$ be a finite set containing of n distinct elements. Then, $A \times A$ has .... ordered pairs, the number of reflexive relation on A is .... and the number of symmetric relation on A is ....

8 A subset f of $A \times B$ is a function from A to B, if each element of A appears in same ordered pair in f and no two ordered pairs in f have the same first elements. (T/F)

9 The total number of function from the set $A = \{1, 2, 3, 4, 5\}$ to the set $B = \{a, b, c, d\}$ is ....

10 The number of one to one function from the set $A = \{1, 2, 3\}$ to set $B = \{a, b, c, d\}$ is ....

11 The domain of the real function $f(x) = \dfrac{x}{\sqrt{9 - x^2}}$ is ....

12 A function $f : A \to B$ is an onto function or a surjection, if range (f) is the proper subset of co-domain (f). (T/F)

13 The total number of onto function from the set $A = \{1, 2, 3\}$ to the set $B = \{x, y\}$ is ....

14 Let $f : R \to R$ and $g : R \to R$ be function defined by $f(x) = 5 - x^2$ and $g(x) = 3x - 4$. Then, the value of $fog(-1)$ is ....

15 Let $f = \{(1, 2), (3, 5), (4, 1)\}$ and $g = \{(2, 3), (5, 1), (1, 3)\}$, then $gof =$ .... and $fog =$ ....

16 A curve in a plane represents the graph of a real function if and only if no vertical line (parallel to Y-axis) intersects it more than once. (T/F)

17 Let $f : A \to B$ and $g : B \to A$ be two functions

(i) If $gof = I_A$ and f is an injection, then g is a surjective. (T/F)

(ii) If $fog = I_B$ and f is a surjection, then g is also a surjection. (T/F)

Topical Questions

Types of Relations

Level I

1 If $(a, b) \in R$, where R is a relation, then NCERT Pg. 1
(a) (a, b) is not an ordered pair
(b) $a = b$ only
(c) $ab = 1$ only
(d) a is related to b under the relation R

2 A relation in a set A is a subset of NCERT Pg. 2
(a) $A \times A$ (b) A
(c) $A \cdot A$ (d) None of these

3 A relation R in set A is called empty relation, if NCERT Pg. 2
(a) no element of A is related to any element of A
(b) every element of A is related to every element of A
(c) some elements of A are related to some elements of A
(d) None of the above

4 A relation R in a set A is called universal relation, if NCERT Pg. 2
(a) each element of A is not related to every element of A
(b) no element of A is related to any element of A
(c) each element of A is related to every element of A
(d) None of the above

5 The trivial relation(s) is/are NCERT Pg. 2
(a) empty relation only
(b) universal relation only
(c) empty relation and universal relation
(d) None of the above

6 If R is a relation in a set A such that $(a, a) \in R$ for every $a \in A$, then the relation R is called NCERT Pg. 2
(a) symmetric (b) reflexive
(c) transitive (d) symmetric or transitive

7 A relation R in a set A is called symmetric, if for all $a_1, a_2 \in A$ NCERT Pg. 2
(a) $(a_1, a_2) \in R \Rightarrow (a_2, a_1) \in R$
(b) $(a_1, a_2) \in R \Rightarrow (a_1, a_1) \in R$
(c) $(a_1, a_2) \in R \Rightarrow (a_2, a_2) \in R$
(d) None of the above

8 A relation R in a set A is called transitive, if for all $a_1, a_2, a_3 \in A$, $(a_1, a_2) \in R$ and $(a_2, a_3) \in R$ implies NCERT Pg. 2
(a) $(a_2, a_1) \in R$ (b) $(a_1, a_3) \in R$
(c) $(a_3, a_1) \in R$ (d) $(a_3, a_2) \in R$

9 Match the terms of Column I with the terms of Column II and choose the correct option from the codes given below. NCERT Pg. 2

Column I	Column II
A. $R = \{(5, 6), (6, 5)\}$ in $A = \{5, 6, 7\}$	1. Symmetric and transitive but not reflexive.
B. $R = \{(a, b) : a < b\}$ in R	2. Reflexive and transitive but not symmetric.
C. $R = \{(4, 4), (6, 6), (8, 8), (4, 6), (6, 4), (6, 8), (8, 6)\}$ in $A = \{4, 6, 8\}$	3. Reflexive and symmetric but not transitive.
D. $R = \{a, b) : a^3 \geq b^3$ in R	4. Transitive but neither reflexive nor symmetric.
E. $R = \{(1, 1), (1, 2), (2, 2), (2, 1)\}$ in $A = \{1, 2, 3\}$	5. Symmetric but neither reflexive nor transitive.

Codes

	A	B	C	D	E
(a)	3	5	4	2	1
(b)	2	3	5	4	1
(c)	5	4	3	2	1
(d)	5	1	3	4	2

10 A relation R in a set A is said to be an equivalence relation, if R is NCERT Pg. 3
(a) symmetric only (b) reflexive only
(c) transitive only (d) All of these

11 Let T be the set of all triangles in a plane with R a relation in T given by $R = \{(T_1, T_2) : T_1$ is congruent to $T_2\}$.
Then, R is NCERT Pg. 3
(a) reflexive only (b) not transitive
(c) an equivalence relation (d) symmetric only

12 Let R be the relation in the set Z of all integers defined by $R = \{(x, y) : x - y$ is an integer$\}$. Then R is NCERT Pg. 5
(a) reflexive (b) symmetric
(c) transitive (d) an equivalence relation

13 Let R be the relation in the set R of real numbers. Now, match the terms of column I with the terms of column II and choose the correct option from the codes given below. NCERT Pg. 5

Column I	Column II
A. $R = \{(a, b) : a \leq b^2\}$	1. Reflexive
B. $R = \{(a, b) : a \leq b\}$	2. Symmetric
C. $R = \{(a, b) : a \leq b^3\}$	3. Transitive
	4. Neither reflexive nor symmetric
	5. Neither reflexive nor symmetric nor transitive

Codes

	A	B	C
(a)	5	4	3
(b)	1,3	5, 1	2
(c)	5	1, 3	5
(d)	5	5	5

14 If R is the relation defined in the set {1, 2, 3, 4, 5, 6} as $R = \{(a, b) : b = a + 1\}$, then R is **NCERT Pg. 5**
(a) reflexive (b) symmetric
(c) transitive (d) None of these

15 The relation R in the set {1, 2, 3} given by $R = \{(1, 2), (2, 1)\}$ is
(a) reflexive (b) symmetric **NCERT Pg. 6**
(c) transitive (d) reflexive and symmetric

16 Let R be the relation in the set A of all books in a library of a college given by $R = \{(x, y) : x$ and y have same number of pages$\}$. Then, R is **NCERT Pg. 6**
(a) not reflexive (b) not symmetric
(c) not transitive (d) an equivalence relation

17 If R is the relation in the set $A = \{1, 2, 3, 4, 5\}$ given by $R = \{(a, b) : |a - b|$ is even$\}$, then consider the following statements. **NCERT Pg. 6**

I. R is an equivalence relation.
II. All elements of {1, 3, 5} are related to each other and all elements of {2, 4} are related to each other.
III. All elements of {1, 3, 5} are related to all elements of {2, 4}.

Choose the correct option.
(a) Only I is true (b) Only III is true
(c) Both I and II are true (d) Neither I nor II is true

18 If $A = \{x \in Z : 0 \le x \le 12\}$ and R is the relation in A given by $R = \{(a, b): |a - b|$ is a multiple of 4$\}$. Then, the set of all elements related to 1 is **NCERT Pg. 6**
(a) {1, 4, 6} (b) {1, 5, 9}
(c) {2, 4, 6} (d) {1, 3, 9}

19 If $A = \{x \in Z : 0 \le x \le 12\}$ and R is the relation in A given by $R = \{(a, b) : a = b\}$. Then, the set of all elements related to 1 is **NCERT Pg. 6**
(a) {1, 2} (b) {2, 3} (c) {1} (d) {2}

20 If the relation R in the set A of points in a plane given by $R = \{(P, Q)$: distance of the point P from the origin is same as the distance of the point Q from the origin$\}$ is an equivalence relation, then the set of all points related to a point $P \ne (0, 0)$ is the **NCERT Pg. 6**
(a) circle
(b) ellipse
(c) parabola
(d) hyperbola

21 Let R be the relation defined in the set A of all triangles as $R = \{(T_1, T_2): T_1$ is similar to $T_2\}$. If R is an equivalence relation and there are three right angled triangles T_1 with sides 3, 4, 5; T_2 with sides 5, 12, 13 and T_3 with sides 6, 8, 10. Then, **NCERT Pg. 6**
(a) T_1 is related to T_2
(b) T_2 is related to T_3
(c) T_1 is related to T_3
(d) None of the above

22 If an equivalence relation R defined in the set A of all polygons as $R = \{(P_1, P_2): P_1$ and P_2 have same number of sides$\}$. Then, the set of all elements in A related to the right angled triangle T with sides 3, 4 and 5 is **NCERT Pg. 6**
(a) right angled triangle (b) triangle
(c) square (d) circle

23 Let L be the set of all lines in XY-plane and R be the relation in L defined as $R = \{(L_1, L_2) : L_1$ is parallel to $L_2\}$. If R is an equivalence relation, then the set of all lines related to the line $y = 2x + 4$ is **NCERT Pg. 6**
(a) $y = 2x + c, c \in R$ (b) $y = 4x$
(c) $y = 4$ (d) $y = -2x$

24 Let R be the relation in the set {1, 2, 3, 4} given by $R = \{(1, 2), (2, 2), (1, 1), (4, 4), (1, 3), (3, 3), (3, 2)\}$. Choose the correct answer. **NCERT Pg. 7**
(a) R is reflexive and symmetric but not transitive
(b) R is reflexive and transitive but not symmetric
(c) R is symmetric and transitive but not reflexive
(d) R is an equivalence relation

25 Let R be the relation in the set N given by $R = \{(a, b) : a = b - 2, b > 6\}$. Choose the correct answer. **NCERT Pg. 7**
(a) $(2, 4) \in R$ (b) $(3, 8) \in R$
(c) $(6, 8) \in R$ (d) $(8, 7) \in R$

Level II

26 Let R be the relation on the set R of real numbers defined by $R = \{(a, b) : 1 + ab > 0\}$. Then, R is **NCERT Pg. 6**
(a) reflexive, symmetric but not transitive
(b) reflexive, transitive but not symmetric
(c) transitive but not symmetric and reflexive
(d) an equivalence relation

27 For the set $A = \{1, 2, 3\}$, define a relation R in the set A as follows $R = \{(1, 1), (2, 2), (3, 3), (1, 3)\}$.
Then, the ordered pair to be added to R to make it the smallest equivalence relation is **NCERT Pg. 3**
(a) (1, 3) (b) (3, 1)
(c) (2, 1) (d) (1, 2)

28 Let S be the set of all points in a plane and R be a relation on S defined as

$R = \{(P, Q)$: distance between P and Q is less than 2 units$\}$. **NCERT Pg. 6**

Then, R is

(a) reflexive but not symmetric
(b) symmetric and transitive
(c) reflexive and transitive
(d) reflexive and symmetric but not transitive

29 Let $A = \{1, 2, 3\}$ and $R = \{(1, 2), (2, 3)\}$ be a relation in A. Then, the minimum number of ordered pairs may be added, so that R becomes an equivalence relation, is **NCERT Pg. 6**

(a) 7 (b) 5 (c) 1 (d) 4

30 If R_1 and R_2 are equivalence relation in a set A, then $R_1 \cap R_2$ is **NCERT Pg. 13**

(a) symmetric
(b) reflexive
(c) transitive
(d) an equivalence relation

31 Let $A = \{1, 2, 3\}$. Then, number of relations containing (1, 2) and (1, 3), which are reflexive and symmetric but not transitive, is **NCERT Pg. 6**

(a) 1 (b) 2 (c) 3 (d) 4

32 Let R be a relation from R to R the set of real numbers defined by $R = \{(x, y) : x, y \in R$ and $x - y + \sqrt{3}$ is an irrational number$\}$. Then, R is **NCERT Pg. 6**

(a) an equivalence relation
(b) reflexive
(c) transitive
(d) symmetric

33 On the set N of all natural numbers, define the relation R by aRb, iff GCD of a and b is 2. Then, R is **NCERT Pg. 6**

(a) reflexive, but not symmetric
(b) symmetric only
(c) reflexive and transitive
(d) reflexive, transitive and symmetric

34 Let R be a relation in the set N of natural numbers defined by nRm, if n divides m. Then, R is **NCERT Pg. 6**

(a) reflexive and symmetric
(b) transitive and symmetric
(c) equivalence
(d) reflexive, transitive but not symmetric

35 Consider the non-empty set consisting of children in a family and a relation R defined as aRb, if a is brother of b. Then, R is **NCERT Pg. 6**

(a) symmetric but not transitive
(b) transitive but not symmetric
(c) neither symmetric nor transitive
(d) both symmetric and transitive

36 Given a non-empty set X, consider $P(X)$ which is the set of all subsets of X.

Define the relation R in $P(X)$ as follows.

For subsets A and B in $P(X)$, ARB, if and only if $A \subset B$. Then, R is **NCERT Pg. 6**

(a) reflexive
(b) transitive
(c) not symmetric
(d) an equivalence relation

Types of Functions

Level I

1 Consider the function f_1, f_2, f_3 and f_4 given by the following diagrams. **NCERT Pg. 8**

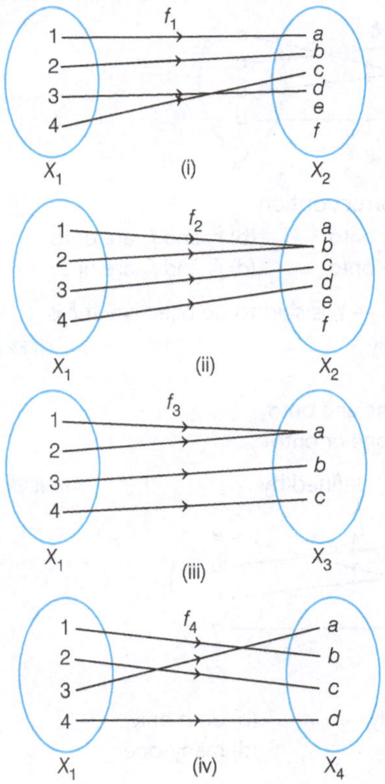

Choose the correct option.

(a) f_1 and f_2 are one-one and f_3 and f_4 are many-one
(b) f_1 and f_4 are one-one and f_2 and f_3 are many-one
(c) f_1 and f_3 are one-one and f_2 and f_4 are many-one
(d) f_2 and f_3 are one-one and f_1 and f_4 are many-one

2 Consider the four functions f_1, f_2, f_3 and f_4 as follows. **NCERT Pg. 8**

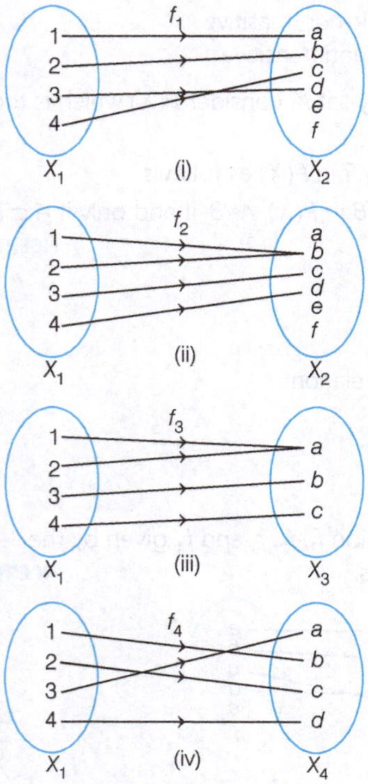

Choose the correct option.

(a) f_1 and f_2 are onto (b) f_2 and f_4 are onto
(c) f_2 and f_3 are onto (d) f_3 and f_4 are onto

3 A function $f: X \to Y$ is said to be bijective, if f is **NCERT Pg. 8**

(a) one-one only
(b) onto only
(c) both one-one and onto
(d) either one-one or onto

4 The function f_4 defined by **NCERT Pg. 8**

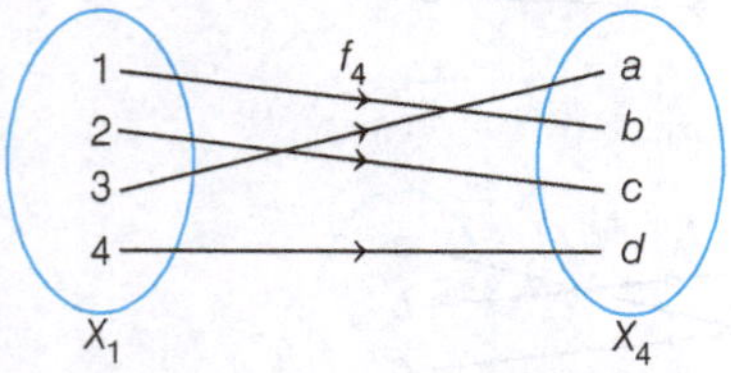

(a) one-one only (b) onto only
(c) bijective (d) many-one

5 The function $f: N \to N$ given by $f(x) = 2x$ is **NCERT Pg. 8**

(a) surjective (b) bijective
(c) injective (d) many-one

6 The function $f: R \to R$ given by $f(x) = 2x$ is **NCERT Pg. 9**

(a) injective (b) surjective
(c) many-one (d) bijective

7 The function $f: N \to N$ given by **NCERT Pg. 9**

$$f(x) = \begin{cases} x+1, & \text{if } x \text{ is odd} \\ x-1, & \text{if } x \text{ is even} \end{cases} \text{ is}$$

(a) injective (b) surjective
(c) bijective (d) many-one

8 Match the terms of column I with the terms of column II and choose the correct option from the codes given below. **NCERT Pg. 10**

Column I	Column II
A. $f: N \to N$ given by $f(x) = x^2$	1. One-one
B. $f: Z \to Z$ given by $f(x) = x^2$	2. Onto
C. $f: R \to R$ given by $f(x) = x^2$	3. Bijectiive
D. $f: N \to N$ given by $f(x) = x^3$	4. Neither one-one nor onto
E. $f: Z \to Z$ given by $f(x) = x^3$	
F. $f: R \to R$ defined by $f(x) = 3 - 4x$	
G. $f: R \to R$ given by $f(x) = 1 + x^2$	

Codes

	A	B	C	D	E	F	G
(a)	1	2	4	4	3	2	1
(b)	3	4	2	1	1	4	3
(c)	4	3	3	1	2	2	1
(d)	1	4	4	1	1	3	4

9 The greatest integer function $f: R \to R$, given by $f(x) = [x]$ is **NCERT Pg. 10**

(a) one-one
(b) onto
(c) both one-one and onto
(d) neither one-one nor onto

10 Let $f: R \to R$ be defined as $f(x) = x^4$. **NCERT Pg. 11**
Choose the correct option.

(a) f is one-one onto
(b) f is many-one onto
(c) f is one-one but not onto
(d) f is neither one-one nor onto

11 Let $f: R \to R$ be defined as $f(x) = 3x$. Choose the correct option. **NCERT Pg. 11**

(a) f is one-one onto
(b) f is many-one onto
(c) f is one-one but not onto
(d) f is neither one-one nor onto

12 Let $A = \{1, 2, 3\}$ and $B = \{4, 5, 6, 7\}$ and let $f = \{(1, 4), (2, 5), (3, 6)\}$ be a function from A to B. Then, f is **NCERT Pg. 11**

(a) one-one (b) onto
(c) many-one (d) bijective

13 Let $A = R - \{3\}$ and $B = R - \{1\}$. Consider the function $f : A \to B$ defined by $f(x) = \left(\frac{x-2}{x-3}\right)$. Then, f is **NCERT Pg. 11**

(a) injective (b) bijective
(c) surjective (d) many-one

14 Consider the following statements. **NCERT Pg. 11**

I. The modulus function $f : R \to R$ given by $f(x) = |x|$ is neither one-one nor onto.

II. The signum function $f : R \to R$ given by

$$f(x) = \begin{cases} 1, & \text{if } x > 0 \\ 0, & \text{if } x = 0 \\ -1, & \text{if } x < 0 \end{cases}$$ is bijective.

III. The function $f : N \to N$ defined by

$$f(n) = \begin{cases} \frac{n+1}{2}, & \text{if } n \text{ is odd} \\ \frac{n}{2}, & \text{if } n \text{ is even} \end{cases}$$ for all $n \in N$ is not bijective.

Choose the correct option.

(a) I and II are true (b) II and III are true
(c) I and III are true (d) All are true

Level II

15 The function $f : R \to R$ defined by $f(x) = \frac{x}{x^2+1}, \forall x \in R$, is **NCERT Pg. 11**

(a) one-one (b) onto
(c) both one-one and onto (d) neither one-one nor onto

16 The function $f : R \to R$ defined by $f(x) = x^2 + x$ is **NCERT Pg. 11**

(a) one-one (b) onto
(c) many-one (d) None of these

17 Let N be the set of natural numbers and the function $f : N \to N$ be defined by $f(n) = 2n + 3, \forall n \in N$. Then, f is **NCERT Pg. 11**

(a) surjective (b) injective
(c) bijective (d) None of these

18 On the set of integers Z, define $f : Z \to Z$ as

$$f(n) = \begin{cases} \frac{n}{2}, & n \text{ is even} \\ 0, & n \text{ is odd} \end{cases}.$$ Then, f is **NCERT Pg. 11**

(a) injective but not surjective
(b) neither injective nor surjective
(c) surjective but not injective
(d) bijective

19 Which of the following function is one-one? **NCERT Pg. 11**

(a) $f(x) = \sin x, x \in [-\pi, \pi]$
(b) $f(x) = \sin x, x \in \left[-\frac{3\pi}{2}, -\frac{\pi}{4}\right]$
(c) $f(x) = \cos x, x \in \left[-\frac{\pi}{2}, \frac{\pi}{2}\right]$
(d) $f(x) = \cos x, x \in \left[\pi, \frac{3\pi}{2}\right]$

20 The number of all one-one functions from set $A = \{1, 2, 3\}$ to itself is **NCERT Pg. 11**

(a) 2 (b) 6 (c) 3 (d) 1

21 The domain of the function $f : R \to R$ defined by $f(x) = \sqrt{x^2 - 3x + 2}$ is **NCERT Pg. 11**

(a) $(-\infty, 1]$ (b) $[2, \infty)$
(c) $(-\infty, 1] \cup [2, \infty)$ (d) $[1, 2]$

22 Match the terms of column I with the terms of column II and choose the correct option from the codes given below. **NCERT Pg. 11**

Column I	Column II
A. $f : C \to R$ defined by $f(z) = \lvert z \rvert \ \forall z \in C$	1. One-one
B. $f : R \to R$ defined by $f(x) = \cos x \ \forall x \in R$	2. Onto
C. $f : [-1, 1] \to [-1, 1]$ defined by $f(x) = \frac{x}{2}$	3. Bijective
D. $g : [-1, 1] \to [-1, 1]$ defined by $g(x) = \lvert x \rvert$	4. Neither one-one nor onto
E. $h : [-1, 1] \to [-1, 1]$ defined by $h(x) = x\lvert x \rvert$	
F. $k : [-1, 1] \to [-1, 1]$ defined by $k(x) = x^2$	

Codes

	A	B	C	D	E	F
(a)	4	1	1	4	3	4
(b)	4	4	1	4	3	4
(c)	3	2	4	4	3	4
(d)	4	4	1	3	3	4

23 Let $A = \{1, 2, 3, 4\}$ and $B = = \{1, 2, 3, 4, 5, 6\}$ are two sets and function $f : A \to B$ is defined by $f(x) = x + 2 \ \forall x \in A$. Then, the function f is **NCERT Pg. 11**

(a) bijective (b) onto
(c) one-one (d) many-one

24 Let $n(A) = 4$ and $n(B) = 6$. Then, the number of one-one functions from A to B is **NCERT Pg. 11**

(a) 24 (b) 60 (c) 120 (d) 360

25 If $f, g : R \to R$ defined as NCERT Pg. 11

$$f(x) = \begin{cases} x, & \text{if } x \text{ is rational} \\ 0, & \text{if } x \text{ is irrational} \end{cases}$$

and $g(x) = \begin{cases} 0, & \text{if } x \text{ is rational} \\ x, & \text{if } x \text{ is irrational} \end{cases}$

Then, $f - g$ is

(a) one-one (b) neither one-one nor onto
(c) many-one (d) one-one and onto

26 The function $f : X \to Y$ defined by $f(x) = \sin x$ is one-one but not onto, if X and Y respectively equal to NCERT Pg. 11

(a) R and R (b) $[0, \pi]$ and $[0, 1]$
(c) $\left[0, \frac{\pi}{2}\right]$ and $[-1, 1]$ (d) $\left[-\frac{\pi}{2}, \frac{\pi}{2}\right]$ and $[-1, 1]$

27 Let $A = \{1, 2, 3, \cdots, n\}$ and $B = \{a, b\}$. Then, the number of surjections from A into B is NCERT Pg. 11

(a) ${}^nP_2$ (b) $2^n - 2$
(c) $2^n - 1$ (d) None of these

28 Which of the following functions from Z into Z is bijective? NCERT Pg. 11

(a) $f(x) = x^3$ (b) $f(x) = x + 2$
(c) $f(x) = 2x + 1$ (d) $f(x) = x^2 + 1$

Composition of Functions and Invertible Functions

Level I

1 If $f : A \to B$ and $g : B \to C$ be two functions, then the composition of functions f and g is given by NCERT Pg. 12

(a) $gof(x) = g(f(x))$
(b) $gof(x) = g(x)f(x)$
(c) $fog(x) = g(f(x))$
(d) None of the above

2 If $f : R \to R$ and $g : R \to R$ are given by $f(x) = \cos x$ and $g(x) = 3x^2$, then NCERT Pg. 12

(a) $gof(x) = \cos^2 x$ (b) $fog(x) = \cos x^2$
(c) $gof \neq fog$ (d) $fog = gof$

3 If $f : B \to A$ is defined by $f(x) = \dfrac{3x + 4}{5x - 7}$ and $g : A \to B$ is defined by $g(x) = \dfrac{7x + 4}{5x - 3}$, where $A = R - \left\{\frac{3}{5}\right\}$ and $B = R - \left\{\frac{7}{5}\right\}$ and I_A is an identity function on A and I_B is identity function on B, then NCERT Pg. 12

(a) $fog = I_A$ and $gof = I_A$
(b) $fog = I_A$ and $gof = I_B$
(c) $fog = I_B$ and $gof = I_B$
(d) $fog = I_B$ and $gof = I_A$

4 Consider the following statements.

I. If $f : A \to B$ and $g : B \to C$ are one-one, then $gof : A \to C$ is also one-one.
II. If $f : A \to B$ and $g : B \to C$ are onto, then $gof : A \to C$ is not onto. NCERT Pg. 12

Choose the correct option.

(a) Only I is true
(b) Only II is true
(c) Both I and II are true
(d) Neither I nor II is true

5 If the function gof is defined and is one-one, then NCERT Pg. 12

(a) neither f nor g is one-one
(b) f and g both are necessarily one-one
(c) g must be one-one
(d) None of the above

6 If the function gof is defined and onto, then NCERT Pg. 12

(a) neither f nor g is onto
(b) f and g both are necessarily onto
(c) f must be onto
(d) None of the above

7 Which of the following options is correct? NCERT Pg. 12

(a) gof is one one $\Rightarrow g$ is one-one
(b) gof is one-one $\Rightarrow f$ is one-one
(c) gof is onto $\Rightarrow g$ is not onto
(d) gof is onto $\Rightarrow f$ is onto

8 Let $X = \{1, 2, 3\}$ and $Y = \{a, b, c\}$ and $f : X \to Y$ be one-one and onto function given by $f(1) = a$, $f(2) = b$, $f(3) = c$. Then, the function $g : Y \to X$ such that $fog = I_Y$ and $gof = I_X$ is given by NCERT Pg. 12

(a) $g(a) = 2, g(b) = 1, g(c) = 3$
(b) $g(a) = 1, g(b) = 2, g(c) = 3$
(c) $g(a) = 1, g(b) = 3, g(c) = 2$
(d) $g(a) = 3, g(b) = 2, g(c) = 1$

9 If $f : X \to Y$ is a function such that there exists a function $g : Y \to X$ such that $gof = I_X$ and $fog = I_Y$, then f must be NCERT Pg. 12

(a) one-one (b) onto
(c) one-one and onto (d) None of these

10 A function $f : X \to Y$ is said to be invertible, if there exists a function $g : Y \to X$ such that NCERT Pg. 12

(a) $gof = I_X$ and $fog = I_X$ (b) $gof = I_Y$ and $fog = I_Y$
(c) $gof = I_Y$ and $fog = I_X$ (d) $gof = I_X$ and $fog = I_Y$

11 Consider the following statements. NCERT Pg. 12

I. If f is invertible, then f must be one-one and onto.
II. If f is one-one and onto, then f must be invertible.

Choose the correct option.

(a) Only I is true (b) Only II is true
(c) Both I and II are true (d) Neither I nor II is true

12 Let $f:\{1,3,4\}\rightarrow\{1,2,5\}$ and $g:\{1,2,5\}\rightarrow\{1,3\}$ be given by $f=\{(1,2),(3,5),(4,1)\}$ and $g=\{(1,3),(2,3),(5,1)\}$. Then, gof is **NCERT Pg. 12**

(a) $\{(1,3),(3,1),(4,3)\}$ (b) $\{(1,3),(4,3)\}$
(c) $\{(3,1),(4,3)\}$ (d) $\{(3,1),(1,3)\}$

13 Let f, g and h be functions from R to R. Then, **NCERT Pg. 12**

(a) $(f+g)oh=fog+goh$ (b) $(f+g)oh=foh+goh$
(c) $(f\cdot g)oh=(foh)+(goh)$ (d) $(f\cdot g)oh=(fog)\cdot(goh)$

14 If $f(x)=|x|$ and $g(x)=|5x-2|$, then **NCERT Pg. 12**

(a) $gof(x)=|5x-2|$ (b) $gof=|5|x|-2|$
(c) $fog(x)=|5|x|-2|$ (d) $fog=|5x+2|$

15 If $f(x)=8x^3$ and $g(x)=x^{1/3}$, then **NCERT Pg. 12**

(a) $fog(x)=2x$ (b) $fog=8x$
(c) $gof(x)=2x^{1/3}$ (d) $gof(x)=x^{1/3}$

16 If $f:R\rightarrow R$ be given by $f(x)=(3-x^3)^{\frac{1}{3}}$, then $fof(x)$ is **NCERT Pg. 12**

(a) $x^{\frac{1}{3}}$ (b) x^3
(c) x (d) $(3-x^3)$

Level II

17 Let $f:R\rightarrow R$ be defined as $f(x)=10x+7$. Then, the function $g:R\rightarrow R$ such that $fog=gof=I_R$ is **NCERT Pg. 12**

(a) $\frac{y+7}{10}$ (b) $\frac{7-y}{10}$
(c) $\frac{y-7}{10}$ (d) $10y-7$

18 Which of the following functions is inverse of itself? **NCERT Pg. 12**

(a) $f(x)=\frac{1-x}{1+x}$ (b) $f(x)=5^{\log x}$
(c) $f(x)=2^{x(x-1)}$ (d) None of these

19 If $f=\{(5,2),(6,3)\}$ and $g=\{(2,5),(3,6)\}$, then fog is **NCERT Pg. 12**

(a) $\{(2,2),(3,3)\}$ (b) $\{(5,3),(6,2)\}$
(c) $\{(2,2),(5,5)\}$ (d) $\{(6,6),(3,3)\}$

20 If $f(x)=e^x$ and $g(x)=\log_e x$, then which of the following is true? **NCERT Pg. 12**

(a) $f\{g(x)\}\neq g\{f(x)\}$ (b) $f\{g(x)\}=g\{f(x)\}$
(c) $f\{g(x)\}+g\{f(x)\}=0$ (d) $f\{g(x)\}-g\{f(x)\}=1$

21 If $f:R\rightarrow R$ and $g:R\rightarrow R$ are defined by $f(x)=x-3$ and $g(x)=x^2+1$, then the values of x for which $g\{f(x)\}=10$, are **NCERT Pg. 12**

(a) 0, – 6 (b) 2, – 2 (c) 1, – 1 (d) 0, 6

22 Let $f:R\rightarrow R$ and $g:R\rightarrow R$ be the function defined by $f(x)=x^2+3x+1$ and $g(x)=2x-3$. Now, match the terms of column I with the terms of column II and choose the correct option from the codes given below. **NCERT Pg. 12**

	Column I		Column II
A.	fog	1.	$x^4+6x^3+14x^2+15x+5$
B.	gof	2.	$4x-9$
C.	fof	3.	$2x^2+6x-1$
D.	gog	4.	$4x^2-6x+1$

Codes

	A	B	C	D
(a)	4	1	2	3
(b)	4	3	1	2
(c)	3	4	2	1
(d)	2	1	3	4

23 If for two functions g and f, gof is both injective and surjective, then which of the following is true? **NCERT Pg. 12**

(a) f and g should be injective and surjective respectively
(b) g should be injective and surjective
(c) f should be injective and surjective
(d) None of them may be surjective and injective

24 If $f:R\rightarrow R$ is defined by $f(x)=x^2-3x+2$, then $f\{f(x)\}$ is **NCERT Pg. 12**

(a) $x^4-6x^3-10x^2+3x$ (b) $x^4-6x^3-10x^2-3x$
(c) $x^4+6x^3+10x^2-3x$ (d) $x^4-6x^3+10x^2-3x$

25 If $f(x)=\frac{\alpha x}{x+1}$, $x\neq-1$, then for what value of α, $f\{f(x)\}=x$? **NCERT Pg. 12**

(a) $\sqrt{2}$ (b) $-\sqrt{2}$ (c) – 1 (d) 2

Miscellaneous Exercise

1 Let R and S be two non-void relations on a set A. Which of the following statements is false? **NCERT Pg. 13**

(a) R and S are transitive implies $R\cap S$ is transitive.
(b) R and S are transitive implies $R\cup S$ is transitive.
(c) R and S are symmetric implies $R\cup S$ is symmetric.
(d) R and S are reflexive implies $R\cap S$ is reflexive.

2 Let R be a relation on the set A of ordered pairs of positive integers defined by $(x, y)\ R\ (u, v)$, if and only if $xv=yu$. Then, R is **NCERT Pg. 13**

(a) reflexive (b) symmetric
(c) transitive (d) an equivalence relation

3 The function $f:R\rightarrow R$ defined by $f(x)=e^x$ is **NCERT Pg. 11**

(a) onto (b) one-one
(c) one-one and onto (d) many-one and onto

4 The function $f:R\rightarrow R$ defined by $f(x)=(x-1)(x-2)(x-3)$ is **NCERT Pg. 11**

(a) one-one but not onto
(b) onto but not one-one
(c) both one-one and onto
(d) neither one-one nor onto

5 Let $f(x) = \dfrac{ax+b}{cx+d}$. Then, $fof(x) = x$ provided that **NCERT Pg. 12**

(a) $d = -a$ (b) $d = a$
(c) $a = b = c = d = 1$ (d) $a = b = 1$

6 Let $f: R \to R$ and $g: R \to R$ be defined by $f(x) = x^2$ and $g(x) = x + 5$. Then, gof is **NCERT Pg. 12**

(a) $x + 5$ (b) $x + 5^2$ (c) $x^2 + 5$ (d) $(x + 5)^2$

7 The function $f: R \to \{x \in R: -1 < x < 1\}$ defined by $f(x) = \dfrac{x}{1+|x|}$, $x \in R$ is **NCERT Pg. 15**

(a) one-one (b) onto
(c) one-one and onto (d) None of these

8 The value of parameter α, for which the function $f: R \to R$ given by $f(x) = 1 + \alpha x$, $\alpha \neq 0$ is the inverse of itself, is **NCERT Pg. 12**

(a) -2 (b) -1 (c) 1 (d) 2

9 Let W denote the words in the English dictionary. Define the relation R as follows.
$R = \{(x, y) \in W \times W$: the words x and y have atleast one letter in common$\}$. **NCERT Pg. 6**
Then, R is

(a) not reflexive, symmetric and transitive
(b) reflexive, symmetric and not transitive
(c) reflexive, not symmetric and transitive
(d) reflexive, symmetric and transitive

10 Let the set A has 3 elements and B has 4 elements. Then, the number of injections that can be defined from A to B, is **NCERT Pg. 7**

(a) 144 (b) 12 (c) 24 (d) 64

11 Let $f: [2, \infty) \to R$ be the function defined by $f(x) = x^2 - 4x + 5$. Then, the range of f is **NCERT Pg. 11**

(a) R (b) $[1, \infty)$
(c) $[4, \infty)$ (d) $[5, \infty)$

12 Let $f: N \to R$ be the function defined by $f(x) = \dfrac{2x-1}{2}$ and $g: Q \to R$ be another function defined by $g(x) = x + 2$. Then, $gof\left(\dfrac{3}{2}\right)$ is **NCERT Pg. 12**

(a) -1 (b) 1 (c) $\dfrac{7}{2}$ (d) None of these

13 The number of equivalence relations in the set $\{1, 2, 3\}$ containing $(1, 2)$ and $(2, 1)$ is **NCERT Pg. 16**

(a) 2 (b) 3 (c) 1 (d) 4

Numerical Type Questions

1 Let A and B two sets containing 2 elements and 4 elements respectively, then number of subsets of $A \times B$ having 3 or more elements is ...... **NCERT Pg. 6**

2 Let $x = \{1, 2, 3, 4, 5\}$. The number of different ordered pairs (y, z) that can be formed such that $Y \subseteq X, Z \subseteq X$ and $Y \cap z = \phi$, is .... **NCERT Pg. 6**

3 Let $A = \{a, b, c\}$ and $B = \{1, 2, 3, 4\}$. Then, the number of elements in the set $C = \{f: A \to \frac{B}{2} \in f(A)$ and f is not one-one$\}$ is .... **NCERT Pg. 11**

4 Let $A = \{1, 2, 3\}$. Then, the number of relation containing $(1, 2)$ and $(1, 3)$ which are reflexive and symmetric is .... **NCERT Pg. 6**

5 Function $f: R \to R^+, f(x) = x^2 + 2$ and $g: R^+ \to R$, $g(x) = \left(1 - \dfrac{1}{1-x}\right)$. If $gof(2)$ is λ, then 5λ is .... **NCERT Pg. 12**

6 If $f(x) = |x|$ and $g(x) = [x]$; then $fog\left(-\dfrac{1}{4}\right) + gof\left(\dfrac{1}{4}\right)$ is ...... **NCERT Pg. 12**

7 Let Z be the set of all integers. **NCERT Pg. 12**
$A = \{(x, y) \in Z \times Z : (x-2)^2 + y^2 \leq 4\}$
$B = \{(x, y) \in Z \times Z : x^2 + y^2 \leq 4\}$ and
$C = \{(x, y) \in Z \times Z : (x-2)^2 + (y-2)^2 \leq 4\}$
If the total number of relation from $A \cap B$ and $A \cap C$ is 2^p, then p is .... **NCERT Pg. 1**

Assertion and Reason Questions

Direction (Q. Nos. 1-13) The following questions consist of two statements, one labelled as "Assertion (A) and the other labelled as Reason (R)". You are to examine these two statements carefully true and it so, where the Reason (R) is the correct explanation a for the given Assertion (A). Select your answer from following options.

(a) Both Assertion and Reason are correct and Reason is the correct explanation of Assertion.
(b) Both Assertion and Reason are correct but Reason is not the correct explanation of Assertion.
(c) Assertion is correct but Reason is incorrect.
(d) Assertion is incorrect but Reason is correct.

1 **Assertion (A)** The relation R in the set $A = \{1, 2, 3, 4, 5, 6\}$ defined as $R = \{(x, y) : y$ is divisible by $x\}$ is not an equivalence relation.

Reason (R) The relation R will be an equivalence relation, if it is reflexive, symmetric and transitive. **NCERT Pg. 6**

2 **Assertion (A)** The relation R on the set $N \times N$ defined by $(a, b)\ R\ (c, d) \Leftrightarrow a + d = b + c$, for all (a, b), $(c, d) \in N \times N$ is an equivalence relation.

Reason (R) Any relation R is an equivalence relation, if it is reflexive, symmetric and transitive. **NCERT Pg. 6**

3 **Assertion (A)** Let A and B be sets. Then, the function $f : A \times B \to B \times A$ such that $f(a, b) = (b, a)$ is bijective.

Reason (R) A function f is said to be bijective, if it is both one-one and onto. **NCERT Pg. 11**

4 **Assertion (A)** The function $f : R \to R$ given by $f(x) = x^3$ is injective.

Reason (R) The function $f : X \to Y$ is injective, if $f(x) = f(y) \Rightarrow x = y$ for all $x, y \in X$. **NCERT Pg. 15**

5 **Assertion (A)** If the function $f : R \to R$ is defined by $f(x) = 4x + 5$, then f is invertible and $f^{-1}(x) = \frac{x-5}{4}$.

Reason (R) If for a function $f : X \to Y$, there exists a function $g : Y \to X$ such that $fog = I_Y$ and $gof = I_X$, then f is invertible and $f^{-1} = g$. **NCERT Pg. 12**

6 **Assertion (A)** The relation R on the set $N \times N$ defined by $(a, b)\ R(c, d) \Leftrightarrow a + d = b + c$ for all $a, b, c, d \in N$ is an equivalence relation.

Reason (R) The intersection of two equivalence relations on a set A is an equivalence relation. **NCERT Pg. 13**

7 Let R be the set of real numbers.

Assertion (A) $A = \{(x, y) \in R \times R : y - x$ is an integer$\}$ is an equivalence relation on R.

Reason (R) $B = \{(x, y) \in R \times R : x = \alpha y$ for some rational number $\alpha\}$ is an equivalence relation on R. **NCERT Pg. 6**

8 Let $X = \{0, 2, 4, 6, 8\}$ and P be a relation on X defined by $P = \{(0, 2), (4, 2), (4, 6), (8, 6), (2, 4), (0, 4)\}$.

Assertion (A) The relation P on set X is a transtive relation.

Reason (R) The relation P has a subset $\{(a, b), (b, c), (a, c)\}$ where $a, b, c \in X$. **NCERT Pg. 2**

9 **Assertion (A)** If A and B are two sets having 3 and 5 element respectively, then the total number of functions that can be defined from A to B is 5^3.

Reason (R) A function from set A to set B relates elements of set A to elements of set B. **NCERT Pg. 11**

10 **Assertion (A)** If $f : R \to R$ and $g : R \to R$ be two functions such that $f(x) = x^2$ and $g(x) = x^3$, then $fog(x) = gof(x)$.

Reason (R) The composition of functions is commutative. **NCERT Pg. 12**

11 Let $f : A \to A$ and $g : A \to A$ be two function such that $fog(x) = gof(x) = x \ \forall \ x \in A$.

Assertion (A) $\{x \in A : f(x) = f(x)\} = \{x \in A : f(x) = x\} = \{x \in A : g(x) = x\}$

Reason (R) $f : A \to A$ is bijection. **NCERT Pg. 12**

12 **Assertion (A)** The function $f : R \to R$ defined by $f(x) = x^3 + 4x - 5$ is a bijection.

Reason (R) Every odd degree polynomial has atleast one real root. **NCERT Pg. 11**

13 Shown below is the graph of function $f : R - \{0\} \to R$

defined by $f(x) = \begin{cases} \dfrac{9 - x^2}{9x - x^3}, & x \neq \pm 3 \\ \dfrac{1}{x}, & x = \pm 3 \end{cases}$

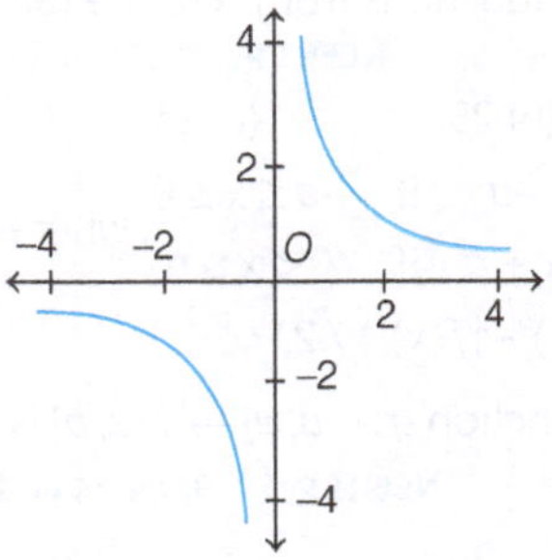

Assertion (A) The function is not onto.

Reason (R) $3 \in R$ (codomain of f) has no preimage in the domain f. **NCERT Pg. 11**

Case or Paragraph Type Questions

Direction (Q. Nos. 1-3) *If A_1, A_2 and A_3 are subsets of Z, whose union is Z, defined by*

$A_1 = \{x \in Z : x \text{ is a multiple of } 3\}$
$A_2 = \{x \in Z : x-1 \text{ is a multiple of } 3\}$
$A_3 = \{x \in Z : x-2 \text{ is a multiple of } 3\}$
and R is a relation in Z given by
$R = \{(a, b) : 3 \text{ divides } a-b\}$. **NCERT Pg. 4**

1 The relation R is
(a) reflexive (b) symmetric
(c) transitive (d) an equivalence relation

2 A_1 coincides with the set of all integers in Z which are related to ...A..., A_2 coincides with the set of all integers which are related to ...B... and A_3 coincides with the set of all integers in Z which are related to ...C... . Here, A, B and C are respectively
(a) one, zero, two (b) zero, one, two
(c) two, one, zero (d) one, two, zero

3 If $A_1 = [0]$, $A_2 = [1]$ and $A_3 = [2]$, then
(a) $A_1 = [3r]$, $A_2 = [3r+1]$, $A_3 = [3r+2]$, $\forall\, r \in Z$
(b) $A_1 = [3r+1]$, $A_2 = [3r]$, $A_3 = [3r+2]$, $\forall\, r \in Z$
(c) $A_1 = [3r+2]$, $A_2 = [3r]$, $A_3 = [3r+1]$, $\forall\, r \in Z$
(d) $A_1 = [3r]$, $A_2 = [3r+2]$, $A_3 = [3r+1]$, $\forall\, r \in Z$

Direction (Q. Nos. 4-7) *Let R be any relation in the set A of human beings in a town at a particular time.* **NCERT Pg. 3**

4 If $R = \{(x, y) : x \text{ and } y \text{ work at the same place}\}$, then R is
(a) reflexive
(b) symmetric
(c) transitive
(d) an equivalence relation

5 If $R = \{(x, y) : x \text{ and } y \text{ live in the same locality}\}$, then R is
(a) not reflexive
(b) not transitive
(c) not symmetric
(d) an equivalence relation

6 If $R = \{(x, y) : x \text{ is exactly 7cm taller than } y\}$, then R is
(a) not symmetric
(b) reflexive
(c) symmetric but not transitive
(d) an equivalence relation

7 If $R = \{(x, y) : x \text{ is wife of } y\}$, then R is
(a) reflexive
(b) symmetric
(c) transitive
(d) an equivalence relation

Past Years Questions

Single Correct Type

1 Let $[t]$ be the greatest integer less than or equal to t. Let A be the set of all prime factors of 2310 and $f : A \to Z$ be the function $f(x) = \left[\log_2\left(x^2 + \left[\frac{x^3}{5}\right]\right)\right]$. The number of one-to-one functions from A to the range of f is
NCERT Pg. 7, JEE Main 2024, 8 April Shift-I
(a) 20 (b) 25 (c) 24 (d) 120

2 Let $f(x) = \begin{cases} -a & \text{if } -a \le x \le 0 \\ x+a & \text{if } 0 < x \le a \end{cases}$, where $a > 0$ and
$g(x) = (f(|x|) - |f(x)|)/2$.
Then, the function $g : [-a, a] \to [-a, a]$ is
NCERT Pg. 7, 8, JEE Main 2024, 8 April Shift-II
(a) one-one.
(b) onto.
(c) both one-one and onto.
(d) neither one-one nor onto.

3 Let $A = \{1, 2, 3, 4, 5\}$. Let R be a relation on A defined by xRy if and only if $4x \le 5y$. Let m be the number of elements in R and n be the minimum number of elements from $A \times A$ that are required to be added to R to make it a symmetric relation. Then, $m+n$ is equal to
NCERT Pg. 2, JEE Main 2024, 6 April Shift-II
(a) 26 (b) 23 (c) 24 (d) 25

4 Let a relation R on $N \times N$ be defined as:
$(x_1, y_1) R (x_2, y_2)$ if and only if $x_1 \le x_2$ or $y_1 \le y_2$.
Consider the two statements :
I : R is reflexive but not symmetric.
II : R is transitive
Then, which one of the following is true?
NCERT Pg. 2, JEE Main 2024, 4 April Shift-II
(a) Only I is correct.
(b) Only II is correct.
(c) Neither I nor II is correct.
(d) Both I and II are correct.

5 If $f(x)=\dfrac{4x+3}{6x-4}, x \neq \dfrac{2}{3}$ and $(fof)(x)=g(x)$, where $g: R-\left\{\dfrac{2}{3}\right\} \rightarrow R-\left\{-\dfrac{2}{3}\right\}$, then $(gogog)(4)$ is equal to
NCERT Pg. 12, JEE Main 2024, 31 Jan Shift-I

(a) $\dfrac{19}{20}$ (b) -4 (c) $-\dfrac{19}{20}$ (d) 4

6 Let $A=\{2,3,4\}$ and $B=\{8,9,12\}$. Then, the number of elements in the relation $R=\{((a_1, b_1),(a_2, b_2)) \in(A \times B, A \times B): a_1$ divides b_2 and a_2 divides $b_1\}$ is
NCERT Pg. 2, JEE Main 2023, 10 April Shift-II

(a) 24 (b) 18 (c) 36 (d) 12

7 Let R be the relation over the set A of all straight lines in a plane such that, $l_1 R l_2 \Leftrightarrow l_1$ is parallel to l_2. Then R is
NCERT Pg. 7, CUET 2024, 16 May

(a) symmetric (b) an equivalence relation
(c) transitive (d) reflexive

8 If the function $f: \mathrm{N} \times \mathrm{N}$ is defined as

$$f(n)=\begin{cases} n-1, & \text{if } n \text{ is even} \\ n+1, & \text{if } n \text{ is odd} \end{cases}, \text{ then}$$

A. f is injective B. f is into
C. f is surjective D. f is invertible

Choose the correct answer from the options given below :
NCERT Pg. 11, CUET 2024, 16 May

(a) B (b) A, B and D
(c) A and C (d) A, C and D

9 Let $f: R \rightarrow R$ be defined as $f(x)=x-1$ and $g: R-\{1,-1\} \rightarrow R$ be defined as $g(x)=\dfrac{x^2}{x^2-1}$.

Then, the function fog is
NCERT Pg. 12, JEE Main 2022, 26 June Shift-II

(a) one-one but not onto function
(b) onto but not one-one function
(c) Both one-one and onto function
(d) Neither one-one nor onto function

10 Let $f(x)=\dfrac{x-1}{x+1}, x \in R-\{0,-1,1\}$. If $f^{n+1}(x)=f\left(f^n(x)\right)$, $\forall n \in N$, then $f^6(6)+f^7(7)$ is equal to
NCERT Pg. 12, JEE Main 2022, 26 June Shift-I]

(a) $\dfrac{7}{6}$ (b) $-\dfrac{3}{2}$ (c) $\dfrac{7}{12}$ (d) $-\dfrac{11}{12}$

Numerical Value Type

11 Let $A=\{(x, y): 2x+3y=23, x, y \in N\}$ and $B=\{x:(x, y) \in A\}$. Then, the number of one-one functions from A to B is equal to ....
NCERT Pg. 7, JEE Main 2024, 9 April Shift-II

12 Let $A=\{1,2,3, \ldots, 100\}$. Let R be a relation on A defined by $(x, y) \in R$ if and only if $2x=3y$. Let R_1 be a symmetric relation on A such that $R \subset R_1$ and the number of elements in R_1 is n. Then, the minimum value of n is ... .
NCERT Pg. 2, JEE Main 2024, 31 Jan Shift-II

13 The number of relations, on the set $\{1,2,3\}$ containing $(1,2)$ and $(2,3)$, which are reflexive and transitive but not symmetric, is ....
NCERT Pg. 2, JEE Main 2023, 12 April Shift-I

14 Let $f(x)$ be a quadratic polynomial with leading coefficient 1 such that $f(0)=p, p \neq 0$ and $f(1)=\dfrac{1}{3}$. If the equation $f(x)=0$ and $fofofof(x)=0$ have a common real root, then $f(-3)$ is equal to ....
NCERT Pg. 12, JEE Main 2022, 25 July Shift-II

15 Let $S=\{1,2,3,4,5,6,7,8,9,10\}$. Define $f: S \rightarrow S$ as

$$f(n)=\begin{cases} 2n, & \text{if } n=1,2,3,4,5 \\ 2n-11, & \text{if } 6,7,8,9,10 \end{cases}$$

Let $g: S \rightarrow S$ be a function such that

$$fog(n)=\begin{cases} n+1, & \text{if } n \text{ is odd} \\ n-1, & \text{if } n \text{ is even} \end{cases}$$

$g(10)((g(1)+g(2)+g(3)+g(4)+g(5))$ is equal to ....
NCERT Pg. 12, JEE Main 2022, 27 June Shift-II

Skill Boosters

1 Let N be the set of natural numbers and a relation R on N defined by $R=\{(x, y) \in N \times N ; x^3-3x^2y-xy^2+3y^3=0\}$. Then, the relation R is

(a) reflexive but neither symmetric nor transitive
(b) On equivalence relation
(c) reflexive and symmetric, but not transitive
(d) symmetric but neither reflexive nor transitive

2 Let $R=\{(1,3),(4,2),(2,4),(2,3),(3,1)\}$ be a relation on the set $A=\{1,2,3,4\}$. The relation R is

(a) not symmetric (b) transitive
(c) a function (d) reflexive

3 Let Z be the set of integers if $A=\{x \in Z: 2^{(x+2)(x^2-5x+6)}=1\}$ and $B=\{x \in Z:-3<2x-1<9\}$, then the number of subsets of the set $A \times B$ is

(a) 2^{15} (b) 2^{14} (c) 2^{16} (d) 2^{13}

Correct Codes

Topical Questions

Introduction and Types Relations

1 (d)	2 (a)	3 (a)	4 (c)	5 (c)	6 (b)	7 (a)	8 (b)	9 (c)	10 (d)
11 (c)	12 (d)	13 (c)	14 (d)	15 (b)	16 (d)	17 (c)	18 (b)	19 (c)	20 (a)
21 (c)	22 (b)	23 (a)	24 (b)	25 (c)	26 (a)	27 (b)	28 (d)	29 (a)	30 (d)
31 (a)	32 (b)	33 (b)	34 (d)	35 (b)	36 (c)				

Types of Functions

1 (b)	2 (d)	3 (c)	4 (c)	5 (c)	6 (d)	7 (c)	8 (d)	9 (d)	10 (d)
11 (a)	12 (a)	13 (b)	14 (c)	15 (d)	16 (c)	17 (b)	18 (c)	19 (d)	20 (b)
21 (c)	22 (b)	23 (c)	24 (d)	25 (d)	26 (c)	27 (b)	28 (b)		

Composition of Functions and Invertible Functions

1 (a)	2 (c)	3 (b)	4 (a)	5 (d)	6 (d)	7 (b)	8 (b)	9 (c)	10 (d)
11 (c)	12 (a)	13 (b)	14 (b)	15 (b)	16 (c)	17 (c)	18 (a)	19 (a)	20 (b)
21 (d)	22 (b)	23 (a)	24 (d)	25 (c)					

Miscellaneous Exercise

1 (b)	2 (d)	3 (b)	4 (b)	5 (a)	6 (c)	7 (c)	8 (b)	9 (b)	10 (c)
11 (b)	12 (d)	13 (a)							

Numberical Type Questions

1 (219)	2 (243)	3 (19)	4 (1)	5 (6)	6 (1)	7 (25)

Assertion and Reason Questions

1 (a)	2 (a)	3 (a)	4 (a)	5 (a)	6 (b)	7 (c)	8 (d)	9 (c)	10 (c)
11 (a)	12 (a)	13 (c)							

Case or Paragraph Type Questions

1 (d)	2 (b)	3 (a)	4 (d)	5 (d)	6 (a)	7 (c)

Past Years Questions

1 (d)	2 (d)	3 (d)	4 (d)	5 (d)	6 (c)	7 (b)	8 (d)	9 (d)	10 (b)
11 (24)	12 (66)	13 (3)	14 (25)	15 (190)					

Skill Boosters

1 (a)	2 (a)	3 (a)

Step by Step

Decoding the Questions

Concept Builders

1 $m \times n, 2^{m \times n}$

2 Domain, Range

3 Identity function

4 True

5 $\{(a, a), (b, b), (c, c), (d, d)\}$

6 Symmetric

7 $n^2, 2^{n^2-n}, 2^{\frac{n^2+n}{2}}$

8 True

9 4^5

10 ${}^4C_3 \times 3!$

11 $(-3, 3)$

12 False

13 $2^3 - 2 = 6$

14 -44

15 $\{(1, 3), (3, 1), (4, 3)\}$

$\{(2, 5), (5, 2), (1, 5)\}$

16 True

17 (i) True

(ii) False

Topical Questions

Introduction and Types of Relations

1 (*d*) If $(a, b) \in R$, we say that a is related to b under the relation R and we write as $a\,R\,b$. In general, $(a, b) \in R$, we do not bother whether there is a recognisable connection or link between a and b.

2 (*a*) A relation in a set A is a subset of $A \times A$.

3 (*a*) A relation R in a set A is called empty relation, if no element of A is related to any element of A, i.e. $R = \phi \subset A \times A$.

4 (*c*) A relation R in a set A is called universal relation, if each element of A is related to every element of A, i.e. $R = A \times A$.

5 (*c*) Both the empty relation and the universal relation are sometimes called trivial relations.

6 (*b*) A relation R in a set A is called reflexive, if $(a, a) \in R$ for every $a \in A$.

7 (*a*) A relation R in a set A is called symmetric, if $(a_1, a_2) \in R$ implies that $(a_2, a_1) \in R$, for all $a_1, a_2 \in A$.

8 (*b*) A relation R is a set A is called transitive, if $(a_1, a_2) \in R$ and $(a_2, a_3) \in R$, implies that $(a_1, a_3) \in R$, for all $a_1, a_2, a_3 \in A$.

9 (*c*)

A. We have, $A = \{5, 6, 7\}$ and a relation R in A defined as $R = \{(5, 6), (6, 5)\}$.

Relation R is not reflexive as $(5, 5), (6, 6), (7, 7) \notin R$.

Now, as $(5, 6) \in R$ and also $(6, 5) \in R$. So, R is symmetric.

Now, $(5, 6), (6, 5) \in R$ but $(5, 5) \notin R$.

Therefore, R is not transitive.

B. Consider a relation R in R defined as

$$R = \{(a, b): a < b\}$$

For any $a \in R$, we have $(a, a) \notin R$, since a cannot be strictly less than by itself.

Therefore, R is not reflexive.

Now, $(1, 2) \in R$ (as $1 < 2$)

But $(2,1) \notin R$ as 2 is not less than 1.

Therefore, R is not symmetric.

Now, let $(a, b), (b, c) \in R$

$\Rightarrow \quad a < b$ and $b < c$

$\Rightarrow \quad a < c \Rightarrow (a, c) \in R$

Therefore, R is transitive.

C. We have, $A = \{4, 6, 8\}$ and a relation R in A defined as

$$R = \{(4, 4), (6, 6), (8, 8), (4, 6), (6, 4), (6, 8), (8, 6)\}$$

Relation R is reflexive, since for every $a \in A, (a, a) \in R$ i.e. $(4, 4), (6, 6), (8, 8) \in A$.

Relation R is symmetric since $(a, b) \in R \Rightarrow (b, a) \in R$ for all $a, b \in A$.

Relation R is not transitive, since $(4, 6), (6, 8) \in R$ but $(4, 8) \notin R$.

D. We have a relation R in R defined as

$R = \{(a, b) : a^3 \geq b^3\}$

Clearly, $(a, a) \in R$ as $a^3 = a^3$.

Therefore, R is reflexive.

Now, $(2,1) \in R$ (as $2^3 \geq 1^3$)

But $(1, 2) \notin R$ (as $1^3 < 2^3$)

Therefore, R is not symmetric.

Now, let $(a, b), (b, c) \in R$

$\Rightarrow a^3 \geq b^3$ and $b^3 \geq c^3$

$\Rightarrow a^3 \geq c^3 \Rightarrow (a, c) \in R$.

Therefore, R is transitive.

E. We have, $A = \{1, 2, 3\}$ and a relation R in A defined as $R = \{(1, 1), (1, 2), (2, 2), (2, 1)\}$

Relation R is not reflexive as $(2\,2) \notin R$.

Relation R is symmetric as $(1, 2) \in R$ and $(2, 1) \in R$.

Relation R is transitive as $(1, 2) \in R, (2, 1) \in R \Rightarrow (1, 1) \in R$, $(1, 1) \in R, (1, 2) \in R \Rightarrow (1, 2) \in R$, $(2, 1) \in R, (1, 1) \in R$

$\Rightarrow (2, 1) \in R$.

$(2, 1) \in R, (1, 2) \in R$

$\Rightarrow (2, 2) \in R$

10 (*d*) A relation R in a set A is said to be an equivalence relation, if R is reflexive, symmetric and transitive.

11 (*c*) R is reflexive, since every triangle is congruent to itself.
Further, $(T_1, T_2) \in R$
i.e. T_1 is congruent to T_2
$\Rightarrow T_2$ is congruent to T_1
$\Rightarrow (T_2, T_1) \in R$.
Hence, R is symmetric.

Moreover, $(T_1, T_2), (T_2, T_3) \in R$
i.e. T_1 is congruent to T_2 and T_2 is congruent to T_3
$\Rightarrow T_1$ is congruent to T_3
$\Rightarrow (T_1, T_3) \in R$. Therefore, R is an equivalence relation.

12 (*d*) Here, $R = \{(x, y) : x - y$ is an integer$\}$ is a relation in the set of integers.

For reflexivity, put $y = x, x - x = 0$ which is an integer for all $x \in Z$. So, R is reflexive in Z.

For symmetry, let $(x, y) \in R$, then $(x - y)$ is an integer λ (say) and also $y - x = -\lambda$.
$[\because \lambda \in Z \Rightarrow -\lambda \in Z]$

$\therefore$ $y - x$ is an integer $\Rightarrow (y, x) \in R$.
So, R is symmetric.

For transitivity, let $(x, y) \in R$ and $(y, z) \in R$, so $x - y =$ integer and $y - z =$ integers, then $x - z$ is also an integer.
$\therefore$ $(x, z) \in R$. So, R is transitive.

13 (*c*)

A. We have, relation $R = \{(a, b) : a \le b^2\}$, where $a, b \in R$ (set of real number).

For reflexivity, we observe that $\frac{1}{2} \le \left(\frac{1}{2}\right)^2$ is not true.

So, R is not reflexive as $\left(\frac{1}{2}, \frac{1}{2}\right) \notin R$.

For symmetry, we observe that $-1 \le 3^2$ but $3 \not\le (-1)^2$.

$\therefore$ $(-1, 3) \in R$ but $(3, -1) \notin R$
So, R is not symmetric.

For transitivity, we observe that $2 \le (-3)^2$ and $-3 \le (1)^2$ but $2 \not\le (1)^2$
$\therefore$ $(2, -3) \in R$ and $(-3, 1) \in R$ but $(2, 1) \notin R$. So, R is not transitive.

B. We have, relation $R = \{(a, b) : a \le b\}$. Let $a, b \in R$.

For reflexivity, for any $a \in R$ we have $a \le a$. So, R is reflexive.

For symmetry, we observe that $(2, 3) \in R$ but $(3, 2) \notin R$. So, R is not symmetric.

Fot transitivity, $(a, b) \in R$ and $(b, c) \in R \Rightarrow a \le b$ and $b \le c \Rightarrow a \le c \Rightarrow (a, c) \in R$

So, R is transitive. Hence, R is reflexive and transitive but not symmetric.

C. Given that, $R = \{(a, b) : a \le b^3\}$.

It is observed that $\left(\frac{1}{2}, \frac{1}{2}\right) \notin R$ as $\frac{1}{2} \not\le \left(\frac{1}{2}\right)^3 = \frac{1}{8}$.

So, R is not reflexive.

Now, $(1, 2) \in R$ [as $1 < 2^3 = 8$]
But $(2, 1) \notin R$ [as $2 > 1^3$]
So, R is not symmetric.

We have, $\left(3, \frac{3}{2}\right), \left(\frac{3}{2}, \frac{6}{5}\right) \in R$ as $3 < \left(\frac{3}{2}\right)^3$ and $\frac{3}{2} < \left(\frac{6}{5}\right)^3$

But $\left(3, \frac{6}{5}\right) \notin R$ as $3 > \left(\frac{6}{5}\right)^3$

Therefore, R is not transitive.

14 (*d*) Let $A = \{1, 2, 3, 4, 5, 6\}$
A relation R is defined on set A is $R = \{(a, b) : b = a + 1\}$.
Therefore,
$R = \{(1, 2), (2, 3) (3, 4), (4, 5), (5, 6)\}$
Now, $6 \in A$ but $(6, 6) \notin R$.
Therefore, R is not reflexive.
It can be observed that $(1, 2) \in R$ but $(2, 1) \notin R$. Therefore, R is not symmetric.
Now, $(1, 2), (2, 3) \in R$ but $(1, 3) \notin R$.
Therefore, R is not transitive.

15 (*b*) Given that $A = \{1, 2, 3\}$.
A relation R on A is defined as $R = \{(1, 2), (2, 1)\}$.
It is seen that $(1, 1), (2, 2), (3, 3) \notin R$.
Therefore, R is not reflexive.
Since, $(1, 2) \in R$ and $(2, 1) \in R$. So, R is symmetric.
Now, $(1, 2)$ and $(2, 1) \in R$ but $(1, 1) \notin R$. So, R is not transitive.

16 (*d*) Here, A is the set of all books in the library of a college, and $R = \{(x, y) : x$ and y have the same number of pages$\}$.
Now, R is reflexive, since $(x, x) \in R$ $\forall\, x \in A$, as x and x has the same number of pages.
Let $(x, y) \in R$.
$\Rightarrow$ x and y have the same number of pages.
$\Rightarrow$ y and x have the same number of pages.
$\Rightarrow (y, x) \in R$. So, R is symmetric.
Now, let $(x, y) \in R$ and $(y, z) \in R$.
$\Rightarrow$ x and y and have the same number of pages and y and z have the same number of pages.
$\Rightarrow$ x and z have the same number of pages
$\Rightarrow$ $(x, z) \in R$

17 (*c*)

I. Given that, $A = \{1, 2, 3, 4, 5\}$, $R = \{(a, b) : |a - b|$ is even$\}$.
Let $a \in A \Rightarrow |a - a| = 0$ (which is even), $\forall\, a$
So, R is reflexive.
Let $(a, b) \in R \Rightarrow |a - b|$ is even.
$\Rightarrow |a - b| = |-(b - a)| = |b - a|$, therefore $|b - a|$ is also even.
$\Rightarrow (b, a) \in R$. So, R is symmetric.
Now, let $(a, b) \in R$ and $(b, c) \in R$.
$\Rightarrow |a - b|$ is even and $|b - c|$ is even.

$\Rightarrow (a-b)$ is even and $(b-c)$ is even.

$\Rightarrow (a-c)=(a-b)+(b-c)$ is even

[$\because$ sum of two even integers is even]

$\Rightarrow \quad |a-c|$ is even $\Rightarrow (a,c)\in R$.

II. Now, all elements of the set {1, 3, 5} are related to each other, as all the elements of this set are odd. So, the modulus of the difference between any two elements will be even.
Similarly, all elements of the set {2, 4} are related to each other, as all the elements of this set are even. So, the modulus of the difference between any two elements will be even.

III. Also, no element of the {1, 3, 5} can be related to any element of {2, 4}, as all elements of {1, 3, 5} are odd and all elements of {2, 4} are even. So, the modulus of the difference between the two elements (from each of these two subsets) will not be even.

18 (b) $R=\{(a,b):|a-b|$ is a multiple of $4\}$

For any element $a\in A$, we have $(a,a)\in R$ as $|a-a|=0$ is a multiple of 4. Therefore, R is reflexive.

Now , let $(a,b)\in R$

$\Rightarrow |a-b|$ is a multiple of 4.

$|b-a|=|-(a-b)|=|a-b|$ is multiple of 4.

$\Rightarrow (b,a)\in R$. Therefore, R is symmetric.

Now, let $(a,b),(b,c)\in R$

So, $|a-b|$ and $|b-c|$ are multiples of 4.

$\Rightarrow (a-b)$ and $(b-c)$ are multiples of 4.

Now, since

$(a-c)=(a-b)+(b-c)$

$\therefore (a-c)$ is also a multiple of 4.

$\Rightarrow |a-c|$ is a multiple of 4.

$\Rightarrow (a,c)\in R$

Therefore, R is transitive.

Hence, R is an equivalence relation (which is already given).

$\Rightarrow$ The set of elements related to 1 is {1, 5, 9}, since

$|1-1|=0$ is multiple of 4

$|5-1|=4$ is a multiple of 4

and $|9-1|=8$ is a multiple of 4 .

19 (c) $R=\{(a,b):a=b\}$

For any element $a\in A$, we have $(a,a)\in R$, as $a=a$.

Therefore, R is reflexive.

Now, let $(a,b)\in R$

$\Rightarrow \quad a=b \Rightarrow b=a$

$\Rightarrow \quad (b,a)\in R$

Therefore, R is symmetric.

Now, let $(a,b)\in R$ and $(b,c)\in R$

$\Rightarrow \quad a=b$ and $b=c$

$\Rightarrow \quad a=c$

$\Rightarrow (a,c)\in R$. Therefore, R is transitive.

Hence, R is an equivalence relation (which is already given).

The elements that are related to 1 will be those elements from set A which are equal to 1.

20 (a) Here, $R=\{(P,Q)$: distance of point P from the origin is same as the distance of point Q from the origin$\}$. Clearly, $(P,P)\in R$, since the distance of point P from the origin is always the same as the distance of the same point P from the origin.

Therefore, R is reflexive.

Now, let $(P,Q)\in R$.

$\Rightarrow$ The distance of point P from the origin is same as the distance of point Q from the origin.

$\Rightarrow$ The distance of point Q from the origin is same as the distance of point P from the origin.

$\Rightarrow \quad (Q,P)\in R$

Therefore, R is symmetric.

Now, let $(P,Q),(Q,S)\in R$

The distance of points P and Q from the origin is same and also the distance of points Q and S from the origin is same.

$\Rightarrow$ The distance of points P and S from the origin is same.

$\Rightarrow \quad (P,S)\in R$

Therefore, R is transitive. Hence, R is an equivalence relation (which is already given). The set of all points related to $P\neq(0,0)$ will be those points whose distance from the origin is the same as the distance of point P from the origin.

In other words, if $O(0,0)$ is the origin and $OP=k$, then the set of all points related to P is the set of those points which are at a distance of k from the origin.

21 (c) Here, $R=\{(T_1,T_2):T_1$ is similar to $T_2\}$

R is reflexive; since every triangle is similar to itself.

Further, if $(T_1,T_2)\in R$, then T_1 is similar to T_2.

$\Rightarrow T_2$ is similar to T_1

$\Rightarrow \quad (T_2,T_1)\in R$

Therefore, R is symmetric.

Now, let $(T_1,T_2),(T_2,T_3)\in R$.

$\Rightarrow T_1$ is similar to T_2 and T_2 is similar to T_3.

$\Rightarrow T_1$ is similar to $T_3 \Rightarrow (T_1,T_3)\in R$

Therefore, R is transitive. Thus, R is an equivalence relation (which is already given).

Now, we can observe that

$$\frac{3}{6}=\frac{4}{8}=\frac{5}{10}=\left(\frac{1}{2}\right)$$

i.e. The corresponding sides of triangles T_1 and T_3 are in the same ratio.Therefore, triangle T_1 is similar to triangle T_3.

22 (b) Here, $R=\{(P_1,P_2)$; P_1 and P_2 have the same number of sides$\}$.

R is reflexive, since $(P_1,P_1)\in R$ as the same polygon has the same number of sides with itself.

Let $(P_1,P_2)\in R$

$\Rightarrow P_1$ and P_2 have the same number of sides

$\Rightarrow P_2$ and P_1 have the same number of sides.

$\Rightarrow \quad (P_2, P_1) \in R$

Therefore, R is symmetric.

Now, let $(P_1, P_2), (P_2, P_3) \in R$

$\Rightarrow P_1$ and P_2 have the same number of sides. Also, P_2 and P_3 have the same number of sides. Therefore, P_1 and P_3 have the same number of sides.

$\Rightarrow \quad (P_1, P_3) \in R$

Therefore, R is transitive. Hence, R is an equivalence relation (which is already given).

The elements in A related to the right-angled triangle (T) with sides 3, 4 and 5 are those polygons which have 3 sides (since, T is a polygon with 3 sides).

23 (a) Here, $R = \{(L_1, L_2) : L_1$ is parallel to $L_2\}$

R is reflexive as any line L_1 is parallel to itself i.e. $(L_1, L_1) \in R$.

Now, let $(L_1, L_2) \in R$

$\Rightarrow \quad L_1$ is parallel to L_2.

$\Rightarrow \quad L_2$ is parallel to L_1.

$\Rightarrow \quad (L_2, L_1) \in R$

Therefore, R is symmetric.

Now, let $(L_1, L_2), (L_2, L_3) \in R$

$\Rightarrow \quad L_1$ is parallel to L_2 and L_2 is parallel to L_3.

$\Rightarrow \quad L_1$ is parallel to L_3.

$\Rightarrow \quad (L_1, L_3) \in R$

Therefore, R is transitive.

Hence, R is an equivalence relation (which is already given).

The set of all lines related to the line $y = 2x + 4$ is the set of those lines that are parallel to the line $y = 2x + 4$.

Slope of line $y = 2x + 4$ is $m = 2$.

It is known that parallel lines have the same slope.

The lines parallel to the given line is of the form $y = 2x + c$, where $c \in R$.

24 (b) Here, $R = \{(1, 2), (2, 2), (1, 1), (4, 4), (1, 3), (3, 3), (3, 2)\}$

Since, $(a, a) \in R$, for every $a \in \{1, 2, 3, 4\}$. Therefore, R is reflexive.

Now, since $(1, 2) \in R$ but $(2, 1) \notin R$. Therefore, R is not symmetric.

Also, it is observed that $(a, b), (b, c) \in R$

$\Rightarrow (a, c) \in R$ for all $a, b, c \in \{1, 2, 3, 4\}$

25 (c) Given, $R = \{(a, b) : a = b - 2, b > 6\}$

Now, since, $b > 6$ so $(2, 4) \notin R$.

Also, as $3 \neq 8 - 2$, so $(3, 8) \notin R$ and as $8 \neq 7 - 2$

Therefore, $(8, 7) \notin R$

Now, consider $(6, 8)$. We have, $8 > 6$ and also $6 = 8 - 2$

Therefore, $(6, 8) \in R$.

26 (a) Let $a \in R$ be any element.

Then, $1 + a \cdot a = 1 + a^2 > 0$ $\quad [\because a^2 \geq 0, \forall a \in R]$

$\Rightarrow \quad (a, a) \in R$

Hence, R is reflexive.

Let $(a, b) \in R$. Then,

$1 + ab > 0$

$\Rightarrow \quad 1 + ba > 0$

$\Rightarrow \quad (b, a) \in R$

$\because \quad (a, b) \in R$

$\Rightarrow \quad (b, a) \in R$

Hence, R is symmetric.

Now, $\quad \left(1, \frac{1}{2}\right) \in R$

and $\quad \left(\frac{1}{2}, -1\right) \in R$

As $\quad 1 + \frac{1}{2} = \frac{3}{2} > 0$

and $\quad 1 - \frac{1}{2} = \frac{1}{2} > 0$

but $(1, -1) \notin R$, as

$1 + (1)(-1) = 1 - 1 = 0 \not> 0$

Hence, R is not transitive.

27 (b) The given relation is $R = \{(1, 1), (2, 2), (3, 3), (1, 3)\}$ on the set $A = \{1, 2, 3\}$.

Clearly, R is reflexive and transitive.

To make R symmetric, we need $(3, 1)$ as $(1, 3) \in R$.

$\therefore$ If $(3, 1) \in R$, then R will be an equivalence relation. Hence, $(3,1)$ is the single ordered pair which needs to be added to R to make it the smallest equivalence relation.

28 (d) Given that, S is the set of all points in a plane and R is the relation on S defined as

$R = \{(P, Q)$: Distance between P and Q is less than 2 units$\}$

Now, for any point P in set S, the distance between P and P is 0 which is less than 2 units.

$\therefore \quad (P, P) \in R$

$\Rightarrow \quad (P, P) \in R$ for all $P \in S$

So, R is reflexive in S.

Let P and Q be two points in S such that $(P, Q) \in R$.

$\because \quad (P, Q) \in R$

Then, distance between P and Q is less than 2 units.

$\Rightarrow$ Distance between Q and P is less than 2 units.

$\Rightarrow \quad (Q, P) \in R$

$\Rightarrow \quad R$ is symmetric.

Now, consider points P', Q' and R' having coordinates (0,0) (1.5, 0) and (3.2, 0). The distance between P' and Q' is 1.5 units which is less than 2 units and the distance between Q' and R' is 1.7 units which is also less than 2 units.

But the distance between P' and R' is 3.2, which is not less than 2 units.

$\Rightarrow \quad (P', Q') \in R$

and $(Q', R') \in R$ but $(P', R') \notin R$

$\Rightarrow \quad R$ is not transitive on S.

29 (a) The given relation is $R = \{(1, 2), (2, 3)\}$ in the set $A = \{1, 2, 3\}$.

Now, R is reflexive, if $(1, 1), (2, 2), (3, 3) \in R$.

R is symmetric, if $(2, 1), (3, 2) \in R$.

R is transitive, if $(1, 3)$ and $(3, 1) \in R$.

Thus, the minimum number of ordered pairs which are to be added, so that R becomes an equivalence relation, is 7.

30 (*d*) Since, R_1 and R_2 are equivalence relations, therefore $(a, a) \in R_1, (a, a) \in R_2, \forall a \in A$. This implies that $(a, a) \in R_1 \cap R_2, \forall a$, showing $R_1 \cap R_2$ is reflexive.

Further, $(a, b) \in R_1 \cap R_2$

$\Rightarrow (a, b) \in R_1$ and $(a, b) \in R_2$

$\Rightarrow (b, a) \in R_1$ and $(b, a) \in R_2$

$\Rightarrow (b, a) \in R_1 \cap R_2$, hence, $R_1 \cap R_2$ is symmetric. Similarly,

$(a, b) \in R_1 \cap R_2$ and $(b, c) \in R_1 \cap R_2$

$\Rightarrow (a, c) \in R_1$ and $(a, c) \in R_2$

$\Rightarrow (a, c) \in R_1 \cap R_2$.

This shows that $R_1 \cap R_2$ is transitive. Thus, $R_1 \cap R_2$ is an equivalence relation.

31 (*a*) Let R be a relation containing $(1, 2)$ and $(1, 3)$, R is reflexive, if $(1, 1), (2, 2), (3, 3) \in R$.

Relation R is symmetric, if $(2, 1) \in R$ and $(3, 1) \in R$.

But relation R is not transitive as $(3, 1), (1, 2) \in R$ but $(3, 2) \notin R$.

Now, if we add the pair $(3, 2)$ and $(2, 3)$ to relation R, then relation R will become transitive.

Hence, the total number of desired relations is one.

32 (*b*) The given relation is $R = \{(x, y) : x, y \in R \text{ and } x - y + \sqrt{3}$ is an irrational number$\}$.

Then, $x R x \Rightarrow x - x + \sqrt{3} = \sqrt{3}$ which is an irrational number.

$\Rightarrow R$ is reflexive.

Now, $2R\sqrt{3}$

$\Rightarrow \quad 2 - \sqrt{3} + \sqrt{3} = 2$

which is not an irrational number.

and $\sqrt{3}\ R2$

$\Rightarrow \sqrt{3} - 2 + \sqrt{3} = 2\sqrt{3} - 2$

which is an irrational number.

$\therefore \quad 2R\sqrt{3}$ but $\sqrt{3}\ R\ 2$

$\Rightarrow R$ is not symmetric.

Also, $-\sqrt{3}\ R\sqrt{5}$ and $\sqrt{5}\ R\ 2$

As $-\sqrt{3} - \sqrt{5} + \sqrt{3} = -\sqrt{5}$ is an irrational number and $\sqrt{5} - 2 + \sqrt{3}$ is an irrational number.

But $-\sqrt{3} - 2 + \sqrt{3} = -2$ is a rational number.

$\therefore -\sqrt{3}$ is not related with 2.

$\Rightarrow R$ is not transitive.

33 (*b*) aRa, then GCD of a and a is a.

$\therefore$ R is not reflexive.

Now, $\quad aRb \Rightarrow bRa$

If GCD of a and b is 2, then GCD of b and a is 2.

$\therefore$ R is symmetric.

Now, $\quad aRb, bRc \nRightarrow aRc$

If GCD of a and b is 2 and GCD of b and c is 2, then it need not be GCD of a and c is 2.

$\therefore$ R is not transitive.

e.g. $6R2, 2\not{R}12$ but $6R12$.

34 (*d*) Since, n divides $n, \forall\ n \in N$, R is reflexive. R is not symmetric since for $3, 6 \in N, 3R6, 6\not{R}3$. R is transitive since for n, m, r whenever n/m and $m/r \Rightarrow n/r$, i.e. whenever n divides m and m divides r, then n will divide r.

35 (*b*) Given that, $a\ Rb$

$\Rightarrow a$ is brother of b.

$\therefore\ a\ Ra \Rightarrow a$ is brother of a, which is not true.

$\therefore$ R is not reflexive.

$a\ Rb \Rightarrow a$ is brother of b.

This does not mean b is also brother of a as b can be a sister of a.

$\therefore$ R is not symmetric.

Now, $aRb \Rightarrow a$ is brother of b and $bRc \Rightarrow b$ is brother of c.

$\Rightarrow a$ is brother of c.

$\Rightarrow R$ is transitive.

36 (*c*) Since, every set is a subset of itself, ARA for all $A \in P(X)$.

Therefore, R is reflexive.

Let $\quad ARB \Rightarrow A \subset B$

This cannot be implied to $B \subset A$.

For instance, if $A = \{1, 2\}$ and $B = \{1, 2, 3\}$, then it cannot be implied that B is related to A.

Therefore, R is not symmetric.

Further, if ARB and BRC, then $A \subset B$ and $B \subset C$.

$\Rightarrow \quad A \subset C \Rightarrow ARC$

Therefore, R is transitive.

Types of Functions

1 (*b*) The function f_1 and f_4 in (i) and (iv) are one-one and the function f_2 and f_3 in (ii) and (iii) are many-one.

2 (*d*) The function f_3 and f_4 in (iii), (iv) are onto and the function f_1 in (i) is not onto as elements e, f in X_2 are not the image of any element in X_1 under f_1. Similarly, f_2 is not onto.

3 (*c*) A function $f : X \to Y$ is said to be one-one and onto (or bijective), if f is both one-one and onto.

4 (*c*) Since, distinct elements of X_1 have distinct images in X_4 and every element in X_4 has a unique pre image in X_1.

$\therefore$ The function f_4 is both one-one and onto $\Rightarrow f_4$ is bijective.

5 (*c*) The function f is one-one, as

$$f(x_1) = f(x_2)$$

$$\Rightarrow \quad 2x_1 = 2x_2 \Rightarrow x_1 = x_2.$$

Further, f is not onto, as for $1 \in N$, there does not exist any x in N such that $f(x) = 2x = 1$.

6 (*d*) f is one-one, as $f(x_1) = f(x_2)$

$$\Rightarrow \quad 2x_1 = 2x_2$$

$$\Rightarrow \quad x_1 = x_2$$

Also, given any real number y in R, there exists $\frac{y}{2}$ in R such that

$$f\left(\frac{y}{2}\right) = 2\left(\frac{y}{2}\right) = y$$

Hence, f is onto.

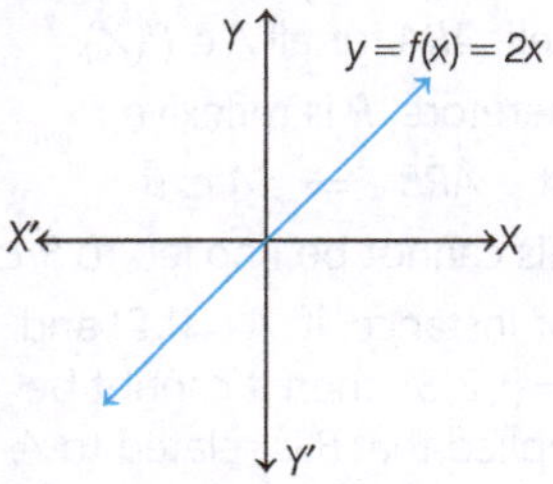

7 (c) Suppose $f(x_1) = f(x_2)$. Note that, if x_1 is odd and x_2 is even, then we will have $x_1 + 1 = x_2 - 1$, i.e. $x_2 - x_1 = 2$ which is impossible. Similarly, the possibility of x_1 being even and x_2 being odd can also be ruled out, using the similar argument. Therefore, both x_1 and x_2 must be either odd or even.

Suppose both x_1 and x_2 are odd.

Then, $f(x_1) = f(x_2)$

$\Rightarrow x_1 + 1 = x_2 + 1$

$\Rightarrow x_1 = x_2$.

Similarly, if both x_1 and x_2 are even, then also $f(x_1) = f(x_2)$

$\Rightarrow x_1 - 1 = x_2 - 1 \Rightarrow x_1 = x_2$.

Thus, f is one-one. Also, any odd number $2r + 1$ in the codomain N is the image of $2r + 2$ in the domain N and any even number $2r$ in the codomain N is the image of $2r - 1$ in the domain N. Thus, f is onto.

8 (d)

A. $f : N \to N$ is given by $f(x) = x^2$

It is seen that for $x, y \in N$,

$f(x) = f(y)$

$\Rightarrow x^2 = y^2 \Rightarrow x = y$

[$\because x$ and y are positive numbers]

Therefore, f is injective.

Now, $2 \in N$, but there does not exist any x in N such that $f(x) = x^2 = 2$.

It means there are some elements in codomain which do not have any pre images.

Therefore, f is not surjective.

B. $f : Z \to Z$ is given by $f(x) = x^2$

It is seen that $f(-1) = f(1) = 1$ but $-1 \neq 1$.

Therefore f is not injective.

Now, $-2 \in Z$. But there does not exist any element $x \in Z$ such that $f(x) = x^2 = -2$

Therefore, f is not surjective.

C. $f : R \to R$ is given by $f(x) = x^2$.

It is seen that $f(-1) = f(1) = 1$ but $-1 \neq 1$.

Therefore, f is not injective.

Now, $-2 \in R$. But there does not exist any element $x \in R$ such that $f(x) = x^2 = -2$.

Therefore, f is not surjective.

D. $f : N \to N$ given by, $f(x) = x^3$

It is seen that for

$x, y \in N$,

$f(x) = f(y)$

$\Rightarrow x^3 = y^3$

$\Rightarrow x^3 - y^3 = 0$

$\Rightarrow (x - y)(x^2 + y^2 + xy) = 0$

$\Rightarrow x = y \quad [\because x^2 + y^2 + xy \neq 0]$

Therefore, f is injective. Now, $2 \in N$. But, there does not exist any element x in domain N such that $f(x) = x^3 = 2$.

Therefore, f is not surjective.

E. $f : Z \to Z$ is given by, $f(x) = x^3$

It is seen that for $x, y \in Z$,

$f(x) = f(y)$

$\Rightarrow x^3 = y^3$

$\Rightarrow x^3 - y^3 = 0$

$(x - y)(x^2 + y^2 + xy) = 0$

$$\Rightarrow (x - y)\left[\left(x + \frac{y}{2}\right)^2 + 3\left(\frac{y}{2}\right)^2\right] = 0$$

$\Rightarrow x = y$

$$\left[\because \left(x + \frac{y}{2}\right)^2 + 3\left(\frac{y}{2}\right)^2 \neq 0\right]$$

Therefore, f is injective.

Now, $2 \in Z$. But, there does not exist any element x in domain Z such that $f(x) = x^3 = 2$.

Therefore, f is not surjective.

F. Here, $f : R \to R$ is defined by $f(x) = 3 - 4x$

Let $x_1, x_2 \in R$ such that

$f(x_1) = f(x_2)$

$\Rightarrow 3 - 4x_1 = 3 - 4x_2$

$\Rightarrow -4x_1 = -4x_2 \Rightarrow x_1 = x_2$

Therefore, f is one-one.

For any real number y in R, there exists $\frac{3-y}{4}$ in R such that

$$f\left(\frac{3-y}{4}\right) = 3 - 4\left(\frac{3-y}{4}\right) = y$$

Therefore, f is onto. Hence, f is bijective.

G. Here, $f : R \to R$ is defined as

$f(x) = 1 + x^2$

Let $x_1, x_2 \in R$ such that

$f(x_1) = f(x_2)$

$\Rightarrow 1 + x_1^2 = 1 + x_2^2$

$\Rightarrow x_1^2 = x_2^2$

$\Rightarrow x_1 = \pm x_2$

For instance, $f(1) = f(-1) = 2$

Therefore, $f(x_1) = f(x_2)$ does not imply that $x_1 = x_2$

Therefore, f is not one-one.

Consider an element -2 in codomain R.

It is seen that $f(x) = 1 + x^2$ is positive for all $x \in R$.

Thus, there does not exist any x in domain R such that $f(x) = -2$.

9 (d) Here, $f : R \to R$ is given by $f(x) = [x]$

It is seen that

$f(1.2) = [1.2] = 1$, $f(1.9) = [1.9] = 1$

Therefore, $f(1.2) = f(1.9)$, but $1.2 \neq 1.9$

Therefore, f is not one-one.

Now, consider $0.7 \in R$. It is known that $f(x) = [x]$ is always an integer. Thus, there does not exist any element $x \in R$ such that $f(x) = 0.7$.

Therefore, f is not onto.

Hence, the greatest integer function is neither one-one nor onto.

10 (*d*) Function $f : R \to R$ is defined as $f(x) = x^4$.

Let $x, y \in R$ such that $f(x) = f(y)$

$\Rightarrow \quad x^4 = y^4 \Rightarrow x = \pm y$

[considering only real values]

Therefore, $f(x_1) = f(x_2)$ does not imply that $x_1 = x_2$.

For instance, $f(1) = f(-1) = 1$

Therefore, f is not one-one.

Consider an element -2 in codomain R. It is clear that there does not exist any x in domain R such that $f(x) = -2$.

11 (*a*) $f : R \to R$ is defined as $f(x) = 3x$

Let $x, y \in R$ such that $f(x) = f(y)$.

$\Rightarrow \quad 3x = 3y \quad \Rightarrow \quad x = y$

Therefore, f is one-one.

Also, for any real number (y) in codomain R, there exists $\frac{y}{3}$ in domain R such that

$$f\left(\frac{y}{3}\right) = 3\left(\frac{y}{3}\right) = y$$

12 (*a*) Given that,

$A = \{1, 2, 3\}$ and $B = \{4, 5, 6, 7\}$

Now, $f : A \to B$ is defined as $f = \{(1, 4), (2, 5), (3, 6)\}$

Therefore,

$$f(1) = 4, f(2) = 5, f(3) = 6$$

It can be seen that the images of distinct elements of A under f are distinct.

Hence, function f is one-one. But, f is not onto, as $7 \in B$ does not have a pre image in A.

13 (*b*)Here, $A = R - \{3\}, B = R - \{1\}$ and $f : A \to B$ is defined as

$$f(x) = \left(\frac{x-2}{x-3}\right)$$

Let $x, y \in A$ such that $f(x) = f(y)$

$$\Rightarrow \quad \frac{x-2}{x-3} = \frac{y-2}{y-3}$$

$\Rightarrow (x-2)(y-3) = (y-2)(x-3)$

$\Rightarrow xy - 3x - 2y + 6 = xy - 3y - 2x + 6$

$\Rightarrow \quad -3x - 2y = -3y - 2x$

$\Rightarrow \quad 3x - 2x = 3y - 2y \Rightarrow x = y$

Therefore, f is one- one. Let $y \in B = R - \{1\}$. Then, $y \neq 1$

The function f is onto, if there exists $x \in A$ such that $f(x) = y$.

Now, $\quad f(x) = y \Rightarrow \frac{x-2}{x-3} = y$

$\Rightarrow \quad x - 2 = xy - 3y$

$\Rightarrow \quad x(1-y) = -3y + 2$

$\Rightarrow \quad x = \frac{2-3y}{1-y} \in A$

$$\left[\because y \neq 1 \text{ and } \frac{2-3y}{1-y} \neq 3\right]$$

Thus, for any $y \in B$, there exists $\frac{2-3y}{1-y} \in A$ such that

$$f\left(\frac{2-3y}{1-y}\right) = \frac{\left(\frac{2-3y}{1-y}\right) - 2}{\left(\frac{2-3y}{1-y}\right) - 3}$$

$$= \frac{2-3y-2+2y}{2-3y-3+3y} = \frac{-y}{-1} = y$$

14 (*c*)

I. Here, $f : R \to R$ is given by

$$f(x) = |x| = \begin{cases} x, & \text{if } x \geq 0 \\ -x, & \text{if } x < 0 \end{cases}$$

It is seen that

$$f(-1) = |-1| = 1$$
$$f(1) = |1| = 1$$

Therefore, $f(-1) = f(1)$ but $-1 \neq 1$.

Therefore, f is not one-one.

Now, consider $-1 \in R$

It is known that $f(x) = |x|$ is always non-negative.

Thus, there does not exist any element x in domain R such that

$$f(x) = |x| = -1.$$

Therefore, f is not onto.

Hence, the modulus function is neither one-one nor onto.

II. $f : R \to R, f(x) = \begin{cases} 1, & \text{if } \quad x > 0 \\ 0, & \text{if } \quad x = 0 \\ -1, & \text{if } \quad x < 0 \end{cases}$

It is seen that $f(1) = f(2) = 1$ but $1 \neq 2$. Therefore, f is not one-one.

Now, as $f(x)$ takes only three values (1, 0 or -1), therefore for the element -2 in codomain R, there does not exist any x in domain R such that $f(x) = -2$.

Therefore, f is not onto.

Hence, the Signum function is neither one-one nor onto.

III. Here, $f : N \to N$ is defined as

$$f(n) = \begin{cases} \frac{n+1}{2}, & \text{if } n \text{ is odd} \\ \frac{n}{2}, & \text{if } n \text{ is even} \end{cases} \text{ for}$$

all $n \in N$. It can be observed that

$$f(1) = \frac{1+1}{2} = 1 \text{ and } f(2) = \frac{2}{2} = 1$$

[by definition of f]

$\therefore \; f(1) = f(2)$, where $1 \neq 2$.

Case I When n is odd.

Therefore, $n = 2r + 1$ for some $r \in W$.

Then, there exists $4r + 1 \in N$ such that

$$f(4r + 1) = \frac{4r + 1 + 1}{2} = 2r + 1$$

Therefore, f is onto.

Case II When n is even.

Therefore, $n = 2r$ for some $r \in N$.

Then, there exists $4r \in N$ such that $f(4r) = \frac{4r}{2} = 2r$

Therefore, f is onto. Hence, f is not a bijective function.

15 (*d*) The given function is

$$f(x) = \frac{x}{x^2 + 1}, \forall \, x \in R$$

For $x_1, x_2 \in R$, consider

$$f(x_1) = f(x_2)$$

$\Rightarrow \quad \frac{x_1}{x_1^2 + 1} = \frac{x_2}{x_2^2 + 1}$

$\Rightarrow \quad x_1x_2^2 + x_1 = x_2x_1^2 + x_2$

$\Rightarrow x_1x_2(x_2 - x_1) = x_2 - x_1$

$\Rightarrow \quad x_1 = x_2$ or $x_1x_2 = 1$

We note that there are points x_1 and x_2 with $x_1 \neq x_2$ and

$f(x_1) = f(x_2)$, for instance, if we take $x_1 = 2$ and $x_2 = \frac{1}{2}$, then we have $f(x_1) = \frac{2}{5}$ and $f(x_2) = \frac{2}{5}$ but $2 \neq \frac{1}{2}$. Hence, f is not one-one.

Also, f is not onto. As, if f is onto, then for $1 \in R\ \exists\ x \in R$ such that $f(x) = 1$ which gives $\frac{x}{x^2+1} = 1$. But there is no such x in the domain R, since the equation $x^2 - x + 1 = 0$ does not give any real value of x.

16 (c) The given function $f : R \to R$ defined by $f(x) = x^2 + x$

Now, for $x = 0$ and -1

We have, $f(0) = 0$ and $f(-1) = 0$

Hence, $f(0) = f(-1)$ but $0 \neq -1$

$\Rightarrow f$ is not one-one.

$\Rightarrow f$ is many-one.

17 (b) Given that, $f: N \to N$ defined by $f(n) = 2n + 3\ \forall n \in N$

Now, let $n_1, n_2 \in N$

Then, $f(n_1) = f(n_2)$

$\Rightarrow 2n_1 + 3 = 2n_2 + 3$

$\Rightarrow 2n_1 = 2n_2 \Rightarrow n_1 = n_2$

$\Rightarrow f$ is injective

Now, let $y \in N$ such that $y = f(n)$

$\Rightarrow y = 2n + 3 \Rightarrow \frac{y-3}{2} = n$

But $\frac{y-3}{2} \notin N$, for some y

For instance, $y = 3 \Rightarrow \frac{y-3}{2} \notin N$.

Thus, for $y = 3$, there does not exist any $x \in N$ (domain) such that $f(x) = 3$.

18 (c) Given, $f(n) = \begin{cases} \frac{n}{2}, & \text{if } n \text{ is even} \\ 0, & \text{if } n \text{ is odd} \end{cases}$

Here, we see that for every odd values of n, it will give zero. It means that it is many-one function.

For every even values of n, we will get a set of integers. So, it is onto. Hence, it is surjective but not injective.

19 (d) Any function $f(x)$ will be a one-one function, if the line parallel to X-axis (i.e. horizontal line) cuts the graph of $f(x)$ only at one point. Otherwise, it is said to be many-one function.

Now, consider the graph of $\sin x$ and $\cos x$ as follows.

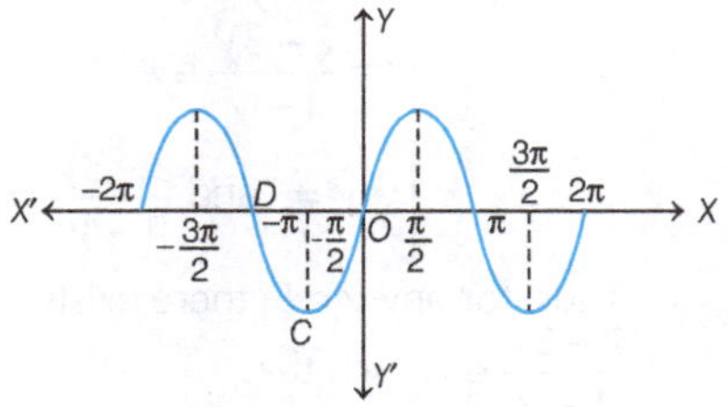

Graph of sin x

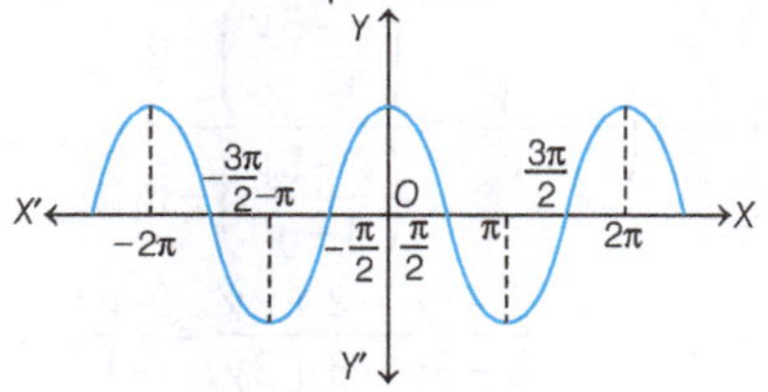

Graph of cos x

Now, in the graph of $\sin x$, if we draw the horizontal line,it will cut the $\sin x$ at two points in the intervals $[-\pi, \pi]$ and $\left[\frac{-3\pi}{2}, \frac{-\pi}{4}\right]$.

Also, in the graph of $\cos x$, if we draw the horizontal line, it will cut the $\cos x$ at two points in the interval $\left[\frac{-\pi}{2}, \frac{\pi}{2}\right]$, but in the interval $\left[\pi, \frac{3\pi}{2}\right]$, it will cut the $\cos x$ at only one point.

$\therefore$ The function $f(x) = \cos x$, $x \in \left[\pi, \frac{3\pi}{2}\right]$ is one-one.

20 (b) One-one function from {1, 2, 3} to itself is simply a permutation on three symbols 1, 2, 3. Therefore, total number of one-one maps from {1, 2, 3} to itself is same as total number of permutations on symbols 1, 2, 3, which is $3! = 6$.

21 (c) $\because f : R \to R$ defined by $f(x) = \sqrt{x^2 - 3x + 2}$

Here, $x^2 - 3x + 2 \geq 0$

$\Rightarrow (x-1)(x-2) \geq 0$

$\Rightarrow x \leq 1$ or $x \geq 2$

Hence, the domain of $f = (-\infty, 1] \cup [2, \infty)$.

22 (b) A. Here, $|-1| = |1| = 1$

i.e. Two distinct elements of domain have same image.

$\therefore$ It is many-one, and it is clear that $|z| \in [0, \infty)$, which is a subset of R. Hence, it is not onto.

B. The given function is $f(x) = \cos x, \forall x \in R$. This function is not one-one, since $f\left(\frac{\pi}{2}\right) = f\left(\frac{3\pi}{2}\right) = 0$ but $\frac{\pi}{2} \neq \frac{3\pi}{2}$.

Also, $f(x) = \cos x, \forall x \in R$ is not onto as the range of $f = [-1, 1]$ and codomain is R.

$\Rightarrow [-1, 1] \neq R$

C. Now, $f : [-1, 1] \to [-1, 1]$ is given by $f(x) = \frac{x}{2}$.

Let $f(x_1) = f(x_2)$, $x_1, x_2 \in [-1, 1]$

$\Rightarrow \frac{x_1}{2} = \frac{x_2}{2}$

$\Rightarrow x_1 = x_2$

$\Rightarrow f$ is one-one.

Let $y \in [-1, 1]$ such that $y = f(x)$

$\Rightarrow y = \frac{x}{2}$

$\because -1 \leq x \leq 1$

$\Rightarrow -\frac{1}{2} \leq \frac{x}{2} \leq \frac{1}{2}$

$\Rightarrow \frac{-1}{2} \leq f(x) \leq \frac{1}{2}$

$\because$ Range is subset of $[-1, 1]$.

Then, f is not onto function.

D. The given function is $g : [-1, 1] \to [-1, 1]$ given by $g(x) = |x|$.

Then, let $g(x_1) = g(x_2)$ for $x_1, x_2 \in [-1, 1]$.

$\Rightarrow |x_1| = |x_2|$

$\Rightarrow x_1 = \pm x_2$

$\Rightarrow g$ is many-one.

$\Rightarrow g$ is not one-one.

Also, the range of g is the set $[0, 1]$, since $|x|$ gives all the positive values of $x \in [-1, 1]$ and $[0, 1] \neq [-1, 1]$

$\therefore$ g is not onto.

E. Given that $h : [-1, 1] \to [-1, 1]$ is a function defined by $h(x) = x|x|$

Let $x > 0$. Then, for $x_1, x_2 \in [-1, 1]$,

$$h(x_1) = h(x_2)$$

$$\Rightarrow \quad x_1 |x_1| = x_2 |x_2|$$

$$\Rightarrow \quad x_1 \cdot x_1 = x_2 \cdot x_2$$

$$[\because x > 0 \Rightarrow x_1, x_2 > 0]$$

$$\Rightarrow \quad x_1^2 - x_2^2 = 0$$

$$\Rightarrow \quad (x_1 + x_2)(x_1 - x_2) = 0$$

$$\Rightarrow \quad x_1 = x_2$$

$$[\because x_1 \neq -x_2 \text{ as } x_1, x_2 > 0] \quad \text{...(i)}$$

Now, let $x < 0$.

Then, $h(x) = -x \cdot x = -x^2$

$$\therefore \quad h(x_1) = h(x_2)$$

$$\Rightarrow \quad -x_1^2 = -x_2^2$$

$$\Rightarrow \quad x_1^2 - x_2^2 = 0$$

$$\Rightarrow \quad (x_1 - x_2)(x_1 + x_2) = 0$$

$$\Rightarrow \quad x_1 = x_2 \quad \text{...(ii)}$$

$$[\because x_1 \neq -x_2, x_2 < 0 \Rightarrow -x_2 > 0 \text{ and } x_1 < 0]$$

Now, if $x_1 > 0$ and $x_2 < 0$, then we have

$$h(x_1) = h(x_2)$$

$$\Rightarrow \quad x_1^2 = -x_2^2$$

$$\Rightarrow \quad x_1^2 + x_2^2 = 0$$

which is not possible.

$$\Rightarrow \quad x_1 \neq x_2$$

$$\Rightarrow \quad h(x_1) \neq h(x_2) \quad \text{...(iii)}$$

Similarly, we can prove that when $x_1 < 0$ and $x_2 > 0$

So, from Eqs. (i), (ii) and (iii), we get h is one-one.

Now, let $y \in [-1, 1]$ such that

$$y = h(x)$$

$$\Rightarrow \quad y = x|x|$$

$$\Rightarrow \quad y = \begin{cases} x^2, & x \geq 0 \\ -x^2, & x < 0 \end{cases}$$

Now, for $x \geq 0$,

$$0 \leq x \leq 1$$

$$\Rightarrow \quad 0 \leq x^2 \leq 1 \quad \text{... (iv)}$$

Also, when $x < 0$

$$\Rightarrow \quad -1 \leq x < 0$$

$$\Rightarrow \quad 0 < x^2 \leq 1$$

$$\Rightarrow \quad -1 \leq -x^2 < 0 \quad \text{...(v)}$$

From Eqs. (iv) and (v), we have

$$0 \leq x^2 \leq 1, \; -1 \leq -x^2 < 0$$

$\Rightarrow$ The range of $h(x) = [-1, 1]$ $=$ Codomain of $h(x)$

$\Rightarrow$ $h(x)$ is an onto function.

$\Rightarrow$ $h(x)$ is bijective.

Alternate Method

The graph of $h(x)$ is given by

When we draw a horizontal line, then it cuts $h(x)$ at only one point.

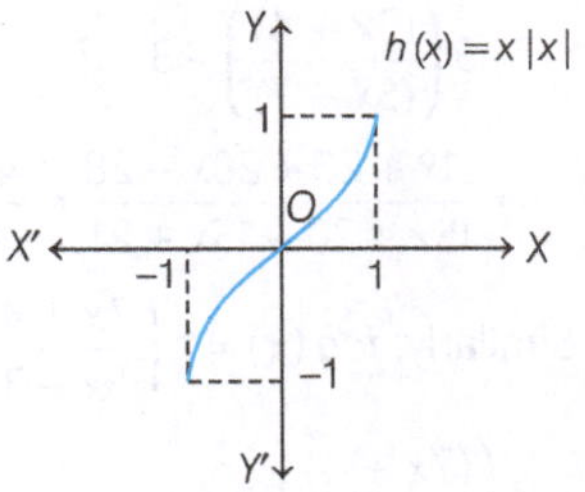

$\therefore$ $h(x)$ is one-one.

Also, when $x = -1$, then $h(x) = -1$ and when $x = 1$, $h(x) = 1$.

$\therefore$ Range of $h(x) = [-1, 1]$ $=$ Codomain of $h(x)$

$\Rightarrow h(x)$ is onto.

Hence, $h(x)$ is bijective.

F. The given function is $k : [-1, 1] \to [-1, 1]$ defined by

$$k(x) = x^2$$

Then, for $x_1, x_2 \in [-1, 1]$,

$$k(x_1) = k(x_2)$$

$$\Rightarrow \quad x_1^2 = x_2^2$$

$$\Rightarrow \quad x_1 = \pm x_2$$

$\Rightarrow$ $k(x)$ is many-one.

$\Rightarrow$ $k(x)$ is not one-one.

Now, let $y \in [-1, 1]$ such that

$$y = k(x)$$

$$\Rightarrow \quad y = x^2 \Rightarrow x = \pm\sqrt{y}$$

Now, since, $-1 \in [-1, 1]$ (the codomain of k)

But $\pm\sqrt{-1} \notin [-1, 1]$ (domain of k)

$\therefore$ $x = \pm\sqrt{y} \notin$ domain of $k = [-1, 1]$ for some values of y

$\Rightarrow$ k is not onto.

$\Rightarrow$ k is neither one-one nor onto.

23 (c) Given that, $A = \{1, 2, 3, 4\}$ and $B = \{1, 2, 3, 4, 5, 6\}$. Then, $f : A \to B$ is a function defined by $f(x) = x + 2, \forall x \in A$.

Now, for $x_1, x_2 \in A$,

Consider, $f(x_1) = f(x_2)$

$$\Rightarrow \quad x_1 + 2 = x_2 + 2$$

$$\Rightarrow \quad x_1 = x_2$$

$\Rightarrow f$ is one-one.

Let $y \in B$ such that

$$y = f(x)$$

$$\Rightarrow \quad y = x + 2 \Rightarrow x = y - 2$$

Now, for $1 \in B$,

$$x = 1 - 2 = -1 \notin A$$

$$\Rightarrow \quad x = y - 2 \notin A \text{ for } y = 1$$

$\Rightarrow$ f is not onto.

24 (d) Given, $n(A) = 4$ and $n(B) = 6$

Here, $n(B) > n(A)$

Then, the number of one-one functions $= {}^6P_4 = \dfrac{6!}{2!} = 360$

25 (d) Let $\phi(x) = f(x) - g(x)$

$$= \begin{cases} x, & x \in Q \\ -x, & x \notin Q \end{cases}$$

Then, any straight line parallel to X-axis will cut $\phi(x)$ only at one point.

$\therefore$ $\phi(x)$ is one-one.

$\phi(x) = x$ for rational values and $\phi(x) = -x$ for irrational values

$\Rightarrow$ $\phi(x) \in$ real numbers

$\therefore$ Range $=$ Codomain

$\Rightarrow$ $\phi(x)$ is onto.

$\Rightarrow$ $f - g$ is one-one and onto.

26 (c) Since, $f: X \rightarrow Y$ and $f(x) = \sin x$
Now, take option (c).

$$\text{Domain} = \left[0, \frac{\pi}{2}\right]$$

and $\quad \text{Range} = [-1, 1]$

For every value of x, we get unique value of y. But the value of y in $[-1, 0)$ does not have any pre image.

$\therefore$ Function is one-one but not onto.

27 (b) Here, $A = \{1, 2, 3, \cdots, n\}$ and $B = \{a, b\}$
Since, every element of domain A has two choices i.e. a or b.

$\therefore$ Number of functions will be 2^n.

Also, there will be a case when all the elements of A will map to a only then, since b is left which do not have pre image in A.

$\therefore$ In such a case, the function from A to B is not onto.

Similarly, when all elements of A will map to b only, then also the function from A to B is not onto.

$\therefore$ Total number of onto functions is $2^n - 2$.

28 (b) The function $f(x) = x + 2$ is one-one as for $x_1, x_2 \in Z$.
Consider, $\quad f(x_1) = f(x_2)$

$\Rightarrow \quad x_1 + 2 = x_2 + 2$

$\Rightarrow \quad x_1 = x_2$

Also, let $y \in$ codomain of $f = Z$ such that

$$y = f(x)$$

$\Rightarrow \quad y = x + 2$

$\Rightarrow \quad x = y - 2 \in Z$ for all $y \in Z$

$\therefore$ f is onto.

Hence, $f(x) = x + 2$ is bijective.

Composition of Functions and Invertible Functions

1 (a) We have $f: A \rightarrow B$ and $g: B \rightarrow C$ be two functions.

Then, the composition of f and g, denoted by gof, is defined as the function $gof: A \rightarrow C$ given by

$$gof\,(x) = g(f(x)), \forall\, x \in A$$

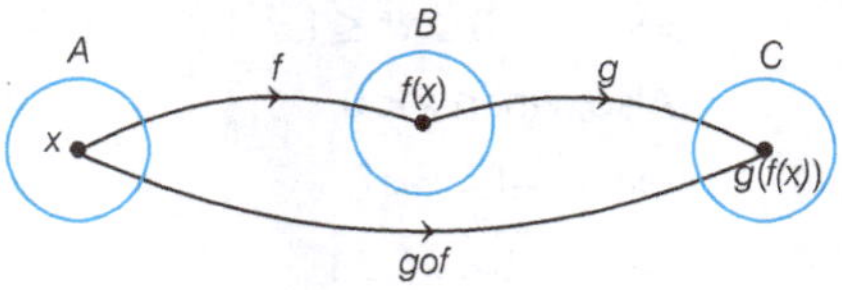

2 (c) We have,

$$gof(x) = g[f(x)] = g(\cos x)$$
$$= 3(\cos x)^2 = 3\cos^2 x$$

Similarly,
$fog(x) = f(g(x)) = f(3x^2) = \cos(3x^2)$

Note that $3\cos^2 x \neq \cos 3x^2$, for $x = 0$.

Hence, $gof \neq fog$.

3 (b) We have, $gof(x) = g\left(\dfrac{3x+4}{5x-7}\right)$

$$= \frac{7\left(\dfrac{(3x+4)}{(5x-7)}\right) + 4}{5\left(\dfrac{(3x+4)}{(5x-7)}\right) - 3}$$

$$= \frac{21x + 28 + 20x - 28}{15x + 20 - 15x + 21} = \frac{41\,x}{41} = x$$

Similarly, $fog\,(x) = f\left(\dfrac{7x+4}{5x-3}\right)$

$$= \frac{3\left(\dfrac{(7x+4)}{(5x-3)}\right) + 4}{5\left(\dfrac{(7x+4)}{(5x-3)}\right) - 7}$$

$$= \frac{21x + 12 + 20x - 12}{35\,x + 20 - 35x + 21} = \frac{41x}{41} = x$$

Thus, $gof(x) = x, \forall\, x \in B$ and $fog(x) = x, \forall\, x \in A$, which implies that $gof = I_B$ and $fog = I_A$.

4 (a)

I. Suppose $gof(x_1) = gof(x_2)$

$\Rightarrow \quad g[f(x_1)] = g[f(x_2)]$

$\Rightarrow f(x_1) = f(x_2)$, as g is one-one

$\Rightarrow x_1 = x_2$, as f is one-one

Hence, gof is one-one.

II. Given an arbitrary element $z \in C$, there exists a pre image y of z under g such that $g(y) = z$, since g is onto.

Further, for $y \in B$, there exists an element x in A with $f(x) = y$, since f is onto. Therefore, $gof(x) = g(f(x)) = g(y) = z$, showing that gof is onto.

5 (d) Consider
$f: \{1, 2, 3, 4\} \rightarrow \{1, 2, 3, 4, 5, 6\}$ defined as $f(x) = x, \forall x$ and $g: \{1, 2, 3, 4, 5, 6\} \rightarrow \{1, 2, 3, 4, 5, 6\}$ as $g(x) = x$, for $x = 1, 2, 3, 4$ and $g(5) = g(6) = 5$. Then, $gof(x) = x, \forall x$ which shows that gof is one-one. But g is clearly not one-one.

6 (d) Consider
$f: \{1, 2, 3, 4\} \rightarrow \{1, 2, 3, 4\}$ and $g: \{1, 2, 3, 4\} \rightarrow \{1, 2, 3\}$ defined as $f(1) = 1, f(2) = 2, f(3) = f(4) = 3$, $g(1) = 1, g(2) = 2$ and $g(3) = g(4) = 3$. It can be seen that gof is onto but f is not onto.

7 (b) In general, gof is one-one implies that f is one-one. Similarly, gof is onto implies that g is onto.

8 (b) Consider $g: \{a, b, c\} \rightarrow \{1, 2, 3\}$ as $g(a) = 1, g(b) = 2$ and $g(c) = 3$. It is easy to verify that the composite $gof = I_X$ is the identify function on X and the composite $fog = I_Y$ is the identity function on Y.

9 (c) If $f: X \rightarrow Y$ is a function such that there exists a function $g: Y \rightarrow X$ such that $gof = I_X$ and $fog = I_Y$, then f must be one-one and onto.

10 (d) A function $f: X \rightarrow Y$ is defined to be invertible, if there exists a function $g: Y \rightarrow X$ such that $gof = I_X$ and $fog = I_Y$. The function g is called the inverse of f and is denoted by f^{-1}.

Note *$fog = I_Y$, and $gof = I_X$, shows that f and g are inverse of each other.*

11 (c) Inverse of function is possible only when it is one-one and onto.

Thus, if f is invertible, then f must be one-one and onto and conversely, if f is one-one and onto, then f must be invertible.

12 (*a*) The functions $f:\{1,3,4\}\to\{1,2,5\}$ and $g:\{1,2,5\}\to\{1,3\}$ are defined as $f=\{(1,2),(3,5),(4,1)\}$

and $g=\{(1,3),(2,3),(5,1)\}$.

$\therefore\ gof(1)=g(f(1))=g(2)=3$ $[\because f(1)=2 \text{ and } g(2)=3]$

$gof(3)=g(f(3))=g(5)=1$ $[\because f(3)=5 \text{ and } g(5)=1]$

$gof(4)=g(f(4))=g(1)=3$ $[\because f(4)=1 \text{ and } g(1)=3]$

$\therefore\ gof=\{(1,3),(3,1),(4,3)\}$

13 (*b*) Consider $((f.g)oh)(x)$

$=(f.g)(h(x))$

$=f(h(x)).g(h(x))$

$=(foh)(x).(goh)(x)$

$=\{(foh).(goh)\}(x)$

$\therefore\ ((f.g)oh)(x)=\{(foh).(goh)\}(x),\ \forall x\in R$

Hence, $(f.g)oh=(foh).(goh)$

Now, consider

$((f+g)oh)(x)=(f+g)(h(x))$

$=f(h(x))+g(h(x))$

$=(foh)(x)+(goh)(x)$

$=\{(foh)+(goh)\}(x)$

$\therefore ((f+g)oh)(x)=\{(foh)+(goh)\}(x),\ \forall x\in R$

Hence, $(f+g)oh=foh+goh$

14 (*b*) $f(x)=|x|$ and $g(x)=|5x-2|$

$\therefore\ fog(x)=f(g(x))$

$=f(|5x-2|)=||5x-2||=|5x-2|$

and $(gof)(x)=g(f(x))=g(|x|)$

$=|5|x|-2|$

15 (*b*) $f(x)=8x^3$ and $g(x)=x^{1/3}$

$\therefore\ (gof)(x)=g(f(x))=g(8x^3)$

$=(8x^3)^{1/3}=2x$

and $fog(x)=f(g(x))=f(x^{1/3})$

$=8(x^{1/3})^3=8x$

16 (*c*) Here, function $f:R\to R$ is given as $f(x)=(3-x^3)^{1/3}$

$\therefore\ fof(x)=f(f(x))=f((3-x^3)^{1/3})$

$=[3-((3-x^3)^{1/3})^3]^{1/3}$

$=[3-(3-x^3)]^{1/3}$

$=(x^3)^{1/3}=x$

$\therefore\ fof(x)=x$

17 (*c*) It is given that $f:R\to R$ defined as $f(x)=10x+7$.

For one-one,

Let $f(x)=f(y)$, where $x,y\in R$

$\Rightarrow\ 10x+7=10y+7$

$\Rightarrow\ x=y$

Therefore, f is a one-one function.

For onto,

For $y\in R$, let $y=10x+7$

$\Rightarrow\ x=\dfrac{y-7}{10}\in R$

Therefore, for any $y\in R$, there exists $x=\dfrac{y-7}{10}\in R$ such that

$f(x)=f\left(\dfrac{y-7}{10}\right)=10\left(\dfrac{y-7}{10}\right)+7$

$=y-7+7=y$

Therefore, f is onto.

Now, since f is one-one and onto.

Therefore, f is an invertible function.

Let us define $g:R\to R$ as

$g(y)=\dfrac{y-7}{10}$

Now, we have

$gof(x)=g(f(x))=g(10x+7)$

$=\dfrac{(10x+7)-7}{10}=\dfrac{10x}{10}=x$

and $fog(y)=f(g(y))=f\left(\dfrac{y-7}{10}\right)$

$=10\left(\dfrac{y-7}{10}\right)+7$

$=y-7+7=y$

$\therefore\ gof=I_R$

and $fog=I_R$

Hence, the required function $g:R\to R$ is defined as

$g(y)=\dfrac{y-7}{10}$.

18 (*a*) For $f(x)=\dfrac{1-x}{1+x}$, consider

$fof(x)=f(f(x))$

$=f\left(\dfrac{1-x}{1+x}\right)=\dfrac{1-\dfrac{1-x}{1+x}}{1+\dfrac{1-x}{1+x}}$

$=\dfrac{1+x-1+x}{1+x+1-x}=x$

$\because\ fof(x)=x$

$\Rightarrow\ f$ is the inverse of itself

19 (*a*) The given functions are

$f=\{(5,2),(6,3)\}$

and $g=\{(2,5),(3,6)\}$

$\Rightarrow\ f(5)=2,\ f(6)=3$

and $g(2)=5$

and $g(3)=6$

Now, $fog(2)=f(g(2))=f(5)=2$

$fog(3)=f(g(3))=f(6)=3$

$\therefore\ fog=\{(2,2),(3,3)\}$

20 (*b*) Given, $f(x)=e^x$

and $g(x)=\log_e x$

Now, $f\{g(x)\}=e^{\log_e x}=x$

and $g\{f(x)\}=\log_e e^x=x$

$\therefore\ f\{g(x)\}=g\{f(x)\}$

21 (*d*) Given, $f(x)=x-3$, $g(x)=x^2+1$

$\therefore\ g\{f(x)\}=g(x-3)$

$\Rightarrow\ 10=(x-3)^2+1$

$\Rightarrow\ 10=x^2+10-6x$

$\Rightarrow\ x(x-6)=0$

$\Rightarrow\ x=0,6$

22 (*b*) The given functions are

$f(x)=x^2+3x+1$

and $g(x)=2x-3$

Now,

A. $fog(x)=f(g(x))$

$=f(2x-3)$

$=(2x-3)^2+3(2x-3)+1$

$=4x^2+9-12x+6x-9+1$

$=4x^2-6x+1$

B. $gof(x)=g(f(x))$

$=g(x^2+3x+1)$

$=2(x^2+3x+1)-3$

$=2x^2+6x+2-3$

$=2x^2+6x-1$

C. $fof(x)=f(f(x))$

$=f(x^2+3x+1)$

$=(x^2+3x+1)^2+3$

$(x^2+3x+1)+1$

$= x^4 + 9x^2 + 1 + 6x^3 + 6x + 2x^2 + 3x^2 + 9x + 3 + 1$

$= x^4 + 6x^3 + 14x^2 + 15x + 5$

D. $gog(x) = g(g(x))$

$= g(2x - 3)$

$= 2(2x - 3) - 3$

$= 4x - 6 - 3 = 4x - 9$

23 (*a*) Given that *gof* is both injective and surjective.

Now, *gof* is injective

$\Rightarrow f$ is injective and *gof* is surjective

$\Rightarrow$ So, *g* is surjective.

24 (*d*) It is given that $f: R \to R$ is defined as

$$f(x) = x^2 - 3x + 2$$

Now, $f(f(x)) = f(x^2 - 3x + 2)$

$= (x^2 - 3x + 2)^2 - 3(x^2 - 3x + 2) + 2$

$= x^4 + 9x^2 + 4 - 6x^3 - 12x + 4x^2 - 3x^2 + 9x - 6 + 2$

$= x^4 - 6x^3 + 10x^2 - 3x$

25 (*c*) $\because f(f(x)) = f\left(\frac{\alpha x}{x+1}\right)$

$$= \frac{\alpha\left(\frac{\alpha x}{x+1}\right)}{\left(\frac{\alpha x}{x+1}\right) + 1} = \frac{\alpha^2 x}{\alpha x + x + 1}$$

$\Rightarrow \frac{\alpha^2 x}{\alpha x + x + 1} = x$ [given]

$\Rightarrow \alpha^2 = \alpha x + x + 1$

$\Rightarrow \alpha^2 - 1 = (\alpha + 1)x$

$\Rightarrow (\alpha + 1)(\alpha - 1 - x) = 0$

$\Rightarrow \alpha + 1 = 0$ [$\because \alpha - 1 - x \neq 0$]

$\Rightarrow \alpha = -1$

Miscellaneous Exercise

1 (*b*) Let $A = \{1, 2, 3\}$

Let two transitive relations on the set *A* are

$R = \{(1, 1), (1, 2)\}$

$S = \{(2, 2), (2, 3)\}$

Now,

$R \cup S = \{(1, 1), (1, 2), (2, 2), (2, 3)\}$

Here, $(1, 2), (2, 3) \in R \cup S$

But $(1, 3) \notin R \cup S$

$\therefore$ $R \cup S$ is not transitive.

2 (*d*) Clearly,

$(x, y) R (x, y), \forall (x, y) \in A$, since $xy = yx$. This shows that *R* is reflexive.

Further $(x, y) R (u, v)$

$\Rightarrow xv = yu$

$\Rightarrow uy = vx$ and hence $(u, v) R (x, y)$. This shows that *R* is symmetric. Similarly, $(x, y) R (u, v)$ and $(u, v) R (a, b)$

$\Rightarrow xv = yu$ and $ub = va$

$\Rightarrow xv\frac{a}{u} = yu\frac{a}{u} \Rightarrow xv\frac{b}{v} = yu\frac{a}{u}$

$\Rightarrow xb = ya$ and hence $(x, y) R (a, b)$. Therefore, *R* is transitive. Thus, *R* is an equivalence relation.

3 (*b*) Let $f: R \to R$ be the function defined by $f(x) = e^x$.

Now, let $x_1, x_2 \in R$ such that

$f(x_1) = f(x_2)$

$\Rightarrow e^{x_1} = e^{x_2}$

$\Rightarrow x_1 = x_2$

$\Rightarrow f$ is one-one.

Now, let $y \in R$ such that

$f(x) = y$

$\Rightarrow e^x = y$

$\Rightarrow x = \log y$ [taking log on both sides]

For zero and negative real number in the codomain of *f*, there does not exist any pre image in the domain of *f*.

$\therefore$ The function *f* is not onto.

4 (*b*) Given,

$f(x) = (x - 1)(x - 2)(x - 3)$

$\Rightarrow f(1) = f(2) = f(3) = 0$

$\Rightarrow f(x)$ is not one-one.

Since, degree of $f(x)$ is odd, therefore the range of *f* is *R*.

$\because$ Codomain of f = Range of f

$\therefore$ For each $y \in R$, there exists $x \in R$ such that $f(x) = y$.

Thus, *f* is onto.

5 (*a*) Given, $f(x) = \frac{ax + b}{cx + d}$

and $fof(x) = x$

$\Rightarrow f\left(\frac{ax+b}{cx+d}\right) = x$

$\Rightarrow \frac{a\left(\frac{ax+b}{cx+d}\right) + b}{c\left(\frac{ax+b}{cx+d}\right) + d} = x$

$\Rightarrow \frac{x(a^2 + bc) + ab + bd}{x(ac + cd) + bc + d^2} = x$

$\Rightarrow a^2 + bc = bc + d^2, ab + bd = 0$

and $ac + cd = 0$

$\Rightarrow d = -a$

6 (*c*) The given functions are $f: R \to R$ and $g: R \to R$ defined as $f(x) = x^2$ and $g(x) = x + 5$.

Now, $gof(x) = g(f(x))$

$= g(x^2) = x^2 + 5$

7 (*c*) It is given that $f: R \to \{x \in R : -1 < x < 1\}$ is defined as $f(x) = \frac{x}{1+|x|}, x \in R$.

Suppose $f(x) = f(y)$, where $x, y \in R$

It can be observed that, if *x* is positive and *y* is negative, then we have

$$\frac{x}{1+x} = \frac{y}{1-y}$$

[as $x > 0$ and $y < 0$]

$\Rightarrow 2xy = x - y$

Since *x* is positive and *y* is negative, then

$x > y \Rightarrow x - y > 0$

8 (*b*) It is given that $f: R \to R$ given by $f(x) = 1 + \alpha x, \alpha \neq 0$ is inverse of itself.

$\therefore fof(x) = x, \forall x \in R$

$\Rightarrow f(f(x)) = x, \forall x \in R$

$\Rightarrow f(1 + \alpha x) = x, \forall x \in R$

$\Rightarrow 1 + \alpha(1 + \alpha x) = x, \forall x \in R$

$\Rightarrow x(\alpha^2 - 1) + (\alpha + 1) = 0, \forall x \in R$

$\Rightarrow \alpha^2 - 1 = 0$

and $\alpha + 1 = 0$

$\Rightarrow \alpha = \pm 1$ and $\alpha = -1$

$\Rightarrow \alpha = -1$

9 (*b*) The given set W which denotes the words in the English dictionary.

The relation R is defined as

$R = \{(x, y) \in W \times W$: the words x and y have atleast one letter in common$\}$.

Then, clearly $(x, x) \in R, \forall x \in W$

$\Rightarrow$ R is reflexive.

Let $(x, y) \in R$.

Then, x and y have atleast one letter in common.

$\Rightarrow$ y and x have atleast one letter in common.

$\Rightarrow$ $(y, x) \in R$

$\Rightarrow$ R is symmetric.

R is not transitive because, the words 'DELHI' and 'DWARKA' have one letter common. Also, 'DWARKA' and 'PATNA' have one letter common. But 'DELHI' and 'PATNA' have no common letter.

10 (*c*) The total number of injective functions from a set A containing 3 elements to a set B containing 4 elements is equal to the total number of arrangements of 4 elements by taking 3 elements at a time i.e. ${}^4P_3 = 24$.

11 (*b*) The given function $f : [2, \infty) \to R$ are defined by

$$f(x) = x^2 - 4x + 5$$

Now, let $y = f(x)$

$\Rightarrow \quad y = x^2 - 4x + 5$

$\Rightarrow x^2 - 4x + 4 + 1 = y$

$\Rightarrow \quad (x-2)^2 = y - 1$

$\Rightarrow \quad x - 2 = \sqrt{y-1} \quad [\because x - 2 \geq 0]$

$\Rightarrow \quad x = 2 + \sqrt{y-1}$

$\therefore \quad y - 1 \geq 0 \Rightarrow y \geq 1$

$\therefore$ Range of f is $[1, \infty)$.

12 (*d*) The given function $f : N \to R$ and $g : Q \to R$ are defined by

$f(x) = \dfrac{2x-1}{2}$ and $g(x) = x + 2$

Now, $gof\left(\dfrac{3}{2}\right) = g\left(f\left(\dfrac{3}{2}\right)\right)$

$$= g\left(\frac{2 \times \frac{3}{2} - 1}{2}\right)$$

$$= g\left(\frac{3-1}{2}\right) = g\left(\frac{2}{2}\right)$$

$$= g(1) = 1 + 2$$

$\therefore \quad (gof)\left(\dfrac{3}{2}\right) = 3$

13 (*a*) The smallest equivalence relation R_1 containing (1, 2) and (2, 1) is {(1, 1), (2, 2), (3, 3), (1, 2), (2, 1)}. Now, we are left with only 4 pairs namely (2, 3), (3, 2), (1, 3) and (3, 1). If we add any one, say (2, 3) to R_1, then for symmetry we must add (3, 2) also and now for transitivity we are forced to add (1, 3) and (3, 1).

Thus, the only equivalence relation bigger than R_1 is the universal relation. This shows that the total number of equivalence relations containing (1, 2) and (2, 1) is two.

Numerical Type Questions

1 (219) $n(A \times B) = 2 \times 4 = 8$

Now, subsets of $A \times B$ having 3 or more elements are

$${}^8C_3 + {}^8C_4 + {}^8C_5 + \ldots + {}^8C_8$$

$$= 2^8 - {}^8C_0 - {}^8C_1 - {}^8C_2$$

$$= 256 - 1 - 8 - 28 = 219$$

2 (243) Every element can be selected by three ways of set A.

So answer is $3^5 = 243$.

3 (19) We have,

$C = \{f : A \to B \mid 2 \in f(A)$ and f is not one-one$\}$

Case I If $f(x) = 2 \; \forall \; x \in A$, then number of many functions = 1.

Case II If $f(x) = 2$ for exactly two elements.

Then, total number of many-one functions $= {}^3C_2 \cdot {}^3C_1 = 9$.

Case III If $f(x) = 2$ for exactly one element.

Then, total number of many-one functions $= {}^3C_1 \cdot {}^3C_3 = 9$.

Total number of functions

$1 + 9 + 9 = 19$

4 (1) Relation R is reflexive as (1, 1), (2, 2), (3, 3) $\in R$. Relations R is symmetric since (1, 2), (2, 1) $\in R$ and (1, 3), (3, 1) $\in R$.

But relation R is not transitive as (3, 1), (1, 2) $\in R$ but (3, 2) $\notin R$.

Now, if we add any one of the two pairs (3, 2) and (2, 3) (or both) to relation R, then relation R will become transitive.

hence, the total number of desired relations is one.

5 (6) $f(x) = x^2 + 2$

$$g(x) = \left(1 - \frac{1}{1-x}\right)$$

$$gof(2) = g(f(2)) = g(6)$$

$$= 1 - \frac{1}{1-6} = \frac{6}{5}$$

So, $\quad 5\lambda = 5 \times \dfrac{6}{5} = 6$

6 (1) If $f(x) = |x|$ and $g(x) = [x]$

$$fog\left(-\frac{1}{4}\right) + gof\left(\frac{1}{4}\right)$$

$$= f\left(g\left(-\frac{1}{4}\right)\right) + g\left(f\left(\frac{1}{4}\right)\right)$$

$$= f(-1) + g\left(\frac{1}{4}\right) = 1 + 0 = 1$$

7 (25) We have,

$A = \{x, y) \in Z \times Z : (x-2)^2 + y^2 \leq 4\}$, $B = \{(x, y) \in Z \times Z : x^2 + y^2 \leq 4\}$ and $C = \{(x, y) \in Z \times Z : (x-2)^2 + (y-2)^2 \leq 4\}$

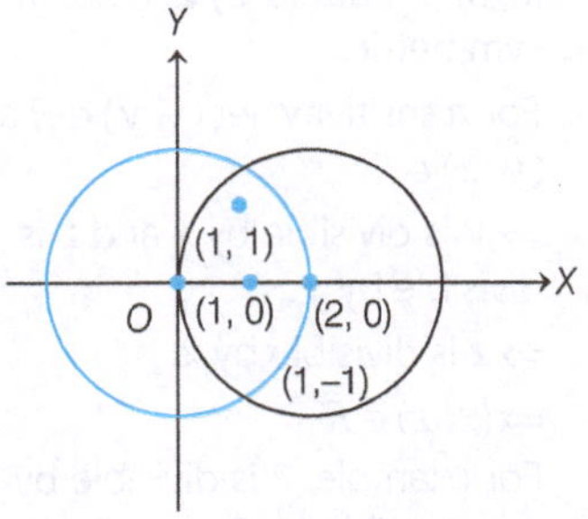

Intersection of A and B is shown by graph as given.

So, $A \cap B = \{(0, 0), (1, 0), (2, 0), (1, 1), (1, -1)\}$

$\therefore \quad n(A \cap B) = 5$

Also, intersection of A and C is shown by graph as given.

So, $A \cap C = \{(1, 1), (2, 0), (2, 1), (2, 2), (3, 1)\}$

$\Rightarrow \quad n(A \cap C) = 5$

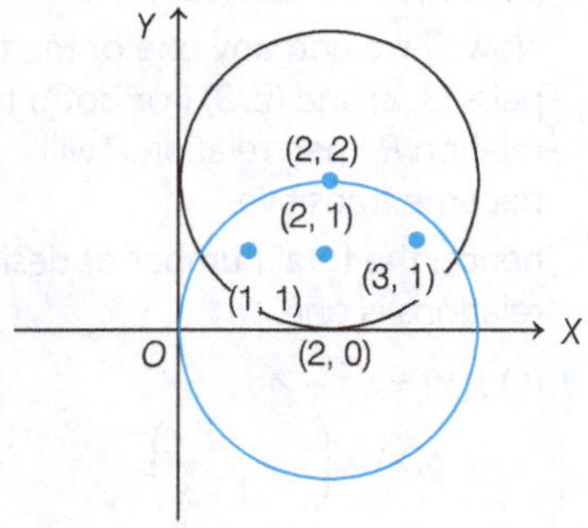

Number of relations from $(A \cap B)$ to $(A \cap C)$

$= 2^{5 \times 5} = 2^{25} = 2^p$

$\Rightarrow \quad p = 25$

Assertion and Reason Questions

1 (a) Here, $R = \{(x, y) : y$ is divisible by $x\}$ is a relation in the set $A = \{1, 2, 3, 4, 5, 6\}$.

For reflexive, we know that x is divisible by x, which is true for all $x \in A$.

$\therefore (x, x) \in R$ for all $x \in A$. So, R is reflexive.

For symmetry, we observe that 6 is divisible by 2. This means that $(2, 6) \in R$ but $(6, 2) \notin R$. So, R is not symmetric.

For transitivity, let $(x, y) \in R$ and $(y, z) \in R$

$\Rightarrow y$ is divisible by x and z is divisible by y.

$\Rightarrow z$ is divisible by x.

$\Rightarrow (x, z) \in R$

For example, 2 is divisible by 1 and 4 is divisible by 2.

Hence, 4 is divisible by 1. So, R is transitive.

2 (a) Let (a, b) be an arbitrary element of $N \times N$. Then,

$(a, b) \in N \times N$

$\Rightarrow \quad a, b \in N$

$\Rightarrow \quad a + b = b + a$

[by commutativity of addition in N]

$\Rightarrow \quad (a, b) R (a, b)$

$\Rightarrow \quad R$ is reflexive on $N \times N$.

Let $(a, b), (c, d) \in N \times N$ be such that $(a, b) R (c, d)$.

$\Rightarrow \quad a + d = b + c$

$\Rightarrow \quad b + c = a + d$

$\Rightarrow \quad c + b = d + a$

$\Rightarrow \quad (c, d) R (a, b)$

$\Rightarrow \quad R$ is symmetric on $N \times N$.

Now, let $(a, b), (c, d), (e, f) \in N \times N$ such that $(a, b) R (c, d)$ and $(c, d) R (e, f)$.

$\because \quad (a, b) R (c, d)$

$\Rightarrow \quad a + d = b + c$

$\because \quad (c, d) R (e, f)$

$\Rightarrow \quad c + f = d + e$

$\Rightarrow (a + d) + (c + f) = (b + c) + (d + e)$

$\Rightarrow \quad a + f = b + e$

$\Rightarrow \quad (a, b) R (e, f)$

Thus, $(a, b) R (c, d)$ and $(c, d) R (e, f)$

$\Rightarrow \quad (a, b) R (e, f)$ for all $(a, b), (c, d), (e, f) \in N \times N$

$\Rightarrow R$ is transitive on $N \times N$.

$\Rightarrow R$ is an equivalence relation on $N \times N$.

3 (a) Here, $f : A \times B \to B \times A$ is defined as $f(a, b) = (b, a)$.

Let $(a_1, b_1), (a_2, b_2) \in A \times B$ such that

$f(a_1, b_1) = f(a_2, b_2)$

$\Rightarrow \quad (b_1, a_1) = (b_2, a_2)$

$\Rightarrow \quad b_1 = b_2$

and $\quad a_1 = a_2$

$\Rightarrow \quad (a_1, b_1) = (a_2, b_2)$

Therefore, f is one-one.

Now, let $(b, a) \in B \times A$ be any element.

Then, there exists $(a, b) \in A \times B$ such that $f(a, b) = (b, a)$

[definition of f]

Therefore, f is onto. Hence, f is bijective.

4 (a) Here, $f : R \to R$ is given as $f(x) = x^3$.

Suppose $f(x) = f(y)$

where $\quad x, y \in R \Rightarrow x^3 = y^3$ ...(i)

Now, we try to show that $x = y$.

Suppose $x \neq y$, their cubes will also be not equal.

$x^3 \neq y^3$

However, this will be a contradiction to Eq. (i).

Therefore, $x = y$. Hence, f is injective.

5 (a) Here, the function $f : R \to R$ is defined as $f(x) = 4x + 5 = y$(say).

Then, $4x = y - 5$ or $x = \dfrac{y-5}{4}$.

This leads to a function $g : R \to R$ defined as $g(y) = \dfrac{y-5}{4}$

Therefore,

$(gof)(x) = g(f(x)) = g(4x + 5)$

$= \dfrac{4x + 5 - 5}{4} = x$ or $gof = I_R$

Similarly, $(fog)(y) = f(g(y))$

$= f\left(\dfrac{y-5}{4}\right)$

$= 4\left(\dfrac{y-5}{4}\right) + 5 = y$

or $\quad fog = I_R$.

Hence, f is invertible and $f^{-1} = g$ which is given by $f^{-1}(x) = \dfrac{x-5}{4}$

6 (b) **Reflexivity** Let $(a, b) \in N \times N$

$(a, b) R (a, b) \Leftrightarrow a + b = b + a$

$\Leftrightarrow a + b = a + b$

$\Rightarrow$ Given relationis reflexive

Symmetry Let $(a, b) \in R$

$\Rightarrow (a, b) R (c, d) \Leftrightarrow a + d = b + c$

$\Leftrightarrow c + b = d + a$

$(a, b) R (c, d) \Leftrightarrow (c, d) R (a, b)$

$\Rightarrow$ Given relation is symmetric.

Transtivity Let $(a, b), (c, d)$ and $(e, f) \in N \times N$

$\Rightarrow (a, b) R (c, d) \Leftrightarrow a + d = b + c$ ...(i)

and $(c, d) R (e, f) \Leftrightarrow c + f = d + e$ ...(ii)

By Eqs. (i) and (ii) we get,

$\Leftrightarrow \quad a+f=b+e$

$\Leftrightarrow \quad (a, b)\, R\, (e, f)$

$\Rightarrow$ Given relation is transitive.

Hence, given relation is an equivalence relation on $N \times N$.

7 (*c*) **Reflexivity** For any $x \in R$, we have $x - x = 0$, which is an integer.

$\therefore \quad (x, x) \in A \;\forall x \in R$

$\Rightarrow A$ is reflexive relation on R.

Symmetry Let $(x, y) \in A$.

Then, $x - y$ is an integer

$\Rightarrow y - x$ is an integer

$\Rightarrow \quad (y, x) \in A$

A is symmetric relation an R.

Transitivity Let $(x, y) \in A$ and $(y, z) \in A$. Then,

$x - y$ is an integer and $y - z$ is an integer $\Rightarrow x - z$ is an integer

$\Rightarrow \quad (x, z) \in A$

$\therefore A$ is transitive relation on R.

Hence, A is an equivalence relation on R. So, Assertion is true.

We find that $0 = 0 \times 2$, where 0 is a rational number $\Rightarrow (0, 2) \in B$ but $(2, 0) \notin B$. So, B is not an equivalence relation on R.

Hence, Reason is not true.

8 (*d*) We find that $(4, 2) \in R$ and $(2, 4) \in$ but $(4, 4) \notin R$.

So, R is not transitive.

Consequently, Assertion is not true.

Reason is true as a relation on X in a subset of $X \times X$.

9 (*c*) A function from set A to set B relates every element of set A to a element in set B. So, Reason is not correct.

Since, each element of set A can be associated to any one of five elements in B and there are 3 elements in set A.

Total number of functions from A to $B = 5 \times 5 \times 5 = 5^3$.

So, Assertion is true.

10 (*c*) We have,

$fog(x) = f(g(x)) = f(x^3) = (x^3)^2 = x^6$

and $\quad gof(x) = g(f(x))$

$= g(x^2) = (x^2)^3 = x^6$

$fog(x) = gof(x)$

So, Assertion is true, but in general $fog \neq gof$, if $f(x) = x^2$ and $g(x) = \sin x$, then $fog(x) = \sin^2 x$ and $gof(x) = \sin(x^2)$

So, the composition of function is not commutative in general.

Hence, Reason is false.

11 (*a*) We have $fog(x) = gof(x)$

$= x \;\forall\; x \in R$

$\Rightarrow fog(x) = gof(x) = I_x \;\forall\; x \in A$.

$fog = gof = I \Rightarrow f$ is invertible such that $g = f^{-1}$

$\Rightarrow f$ is a bijective.

$\Rightarrow$ Curve $g = f(x)$ and $y = g(x)$ meet at $y = x$.

$\Rightarrow \{x \in A : f(x) = g(x)\}$

$= \{x \in A : f(x) = x\}$

$= \{x \in A : g(x) = x\}$

12 (*a*) For any $x, y \in R$

$f(x) = f(y)$

$\Rightarrow \quad x^3 + 4x - 5 = y^3 + 4y - 5$

$\Rightarrow \quad x^3 - y^3 + 4(x - y) = 0$

$\Rightarrow (x - y)(x^2 + y^2 + xy + 4) = 0$

$$\left[\because x^2 + y^2 + xy + 4 = \left(x + \frac{y}{2}\right)^2 + \frac{3y^2}{4} + 4 > 0 \;\forall\; x, y \in R\right]$$

$\Rightarrow \quad x = y$

$\therefore \; f : R \to R$ is an injective function.

Let y be an arbitrary element in R (co-domain of f), then

$f(x) = y$

$\Rightarrow \quad x^3 + 4x - (5 + y) = 0$

For given value of y, this equation has atleast one real root, say α, as every odd degree equation has atleast are real root.

$\therefore \quad \alpha^3 + 4\alpha - (5 + y) = 0$

$\Rightarrow \quad f(\alpha) = y$

Thus, for each $y \in R$ (co-domain) there exists $\alpha \in$ (domain f) such that $f(\alpha) = y$. So $f : R \to R$ is a surjection. Hence, f is a bijection.

Also, Reason is a correct explanation for Assertion.

13 (*c*) It is evident from the graph of $f(x)$ that Range $(f(x)) = R - \{0\} \neq R$ (co-domain). So, it is not onto.

Consequently, Assertion is true.

We find

$$f(x) = \begin{cases} \dfrac{9 - x^2}{9x - x^3} = \dfrac{1}{x}; & x \neq \pm 3 \\ \dfrac{1}{x}; & x = \pm 3 \end{cases}$$

$f\left(\dfrac{1}{3}\right) = 3$ i.e. the pre image of 3 in $\dfrac{1}{3}$.

So, Reason is not true.

Case or Paragraph Type Questions

Sol. (Q. Nos. 1-3) *Consider a subdivision of the set Z given by three mutually disjoint subsets A_1, A_2 and A_3 whose union is Z with*

$A_1 = \{x \in Z : x$ is a multiple of 3$\}$

$= \{\ldots -6 -3, 0, 3, 6, \ldots\}$

$A_2 = \{x \in Z : x - 1$ is a multiple of 3$\}$

$= \{\ldots -5 -2, 1, 4, 7, \ldots\}$

$A_3 = \{x \in Z : x - 2$ is a multiple of 3$\}$

$= \{\ldots -4 -1, 2, 5, 8, \ldots\}$

Define a relation R in Z given by $R = \{(a, b) : 3$ divides $a - b\}$.

1 (*d*) R is reflexive as 3 divides $(a - a) = 0$ for all $a \in Z$.

Further, if $(a, b) \in R$, then 3 divides $a - b$.

$\therefore$ 3 divides $b - a$

$\Rightarrow (b, a) \in R$.

$\Rightarrow R$ is symmetric.

Similarly, if $(a, b) \in R$, $(b, c) \in R$.

$\Rightarrow a - b$ and $b - c$ are divisible by 3.

Now, $a - c = a - b + b - c$ is a multiple of 3 as $a - b$ is a multiple of 3 and $b - c$ is a multiple of 3.

[$\because$ 3 divides $a - b$ and 3 divides $b - c$]

$\therefore$ 3 divides $a-c$ also.
$\therefore$ R is transitive also.
Hence, R is an equivalence relation.

2 (*b*) A_1 coincides with the set of all integers in Z which are related to zero, A_2 coincides with the set of all integers which are related to 1 and A_3 coincides with the set of all integers in Z which are related to 2.

3 (*a*) Here, A_1, A_2 and A_3 are sets of those integers which are related to 0,1 and 2, respectively.
$A_1 = [0], A_2 = [1]$ and $A_3 = [2]$
Infact, $A_1 = [3r], A_2 = [3r+1]$ and $A_3 = [3r+2]$, for all $r \in Z$.

4 (*d*) Here, $R = \{(x, y): x$ and y work at the same place$\}$. Then, R is reflexive as x works at same place of x.
$\Rightarrow \quad (x, x) \in R, \forall\, x \in A$
If x and y work at same place, then y and x work at same place i.e. if
$$(x, y) \in R$$
$$\Rightarrow \quad (y, x) \in R$$
$\Rightarrow R$ is symmetric.
Let $(x, y) \in R, (y, z) \in R$
$\Rightarrow x$ and y work at same place and y and z work at same place.
Since, all three work at same place.
$\Rightarrow x$ and z work at same place.
$$\Rightarrow \quad (x, z) \in R$$
$\Rightarrow R$ is transitive.
$\Rightarrow R$ is an equivalence relation.

5 (*d*) Here, $R = \{(x, y): x$ and y live in the same locality$\}$
R is reflexive, as x lives in the same locality of x.
$\therefore \quad (x, x) \in R, \forall\, x \in A$
Let $\quad (x, y) \in R$
$\Rightarrow x$ and y live in same locality.
$\Rightarrow y$ and x live in same locality.
$\Rightarrow (y, x) \in R$
Thus, R is symmetric.
Now, let (x, y) and $(y, z) \in R$
$\Rightarrow \quad x$ and y live in same locality and y and z live in same locality.
$\Rightarrow$ All three live in same locality.
$\therefore$ x and z live in same locality.
$$\Rightarrow \quad (x, z) \in R$$
$\Rightarrow R$ is transitive.
Hence, R is an equivalence relation.

6 (*a*) Here, R is not reflexive as x is not 7 cm taller than x.
R is not symmetric as if x is exactly 7 cm taller than y, then y cannot be 7 cm taller than x and R is not transitive as if x is exactly 7 cm taller than y and y is exactly 7 cm taller than z, then x is exactly 14 cm taller than z.

7 (*c*) Here, R is not reflexive; as x cannot wife of x, R is not symmetric, as if x is wife of y, then y is husband (not wife) of x and R is transitive as transitivity is not contradicted in this case.
Whenever $(x, y) \in R$, then $(y, z) \notin R$ for any z as if x is wife of y, then y is a male and a male cannot be a wife.

Past Years Questions

1 (*d*) Prime factors of 2310
$$= 2 \times 3 \times 5 \times 7 \times 11$$
$$= 2, 3, 5, 7, 11$$
and $f(x) = \left[\log_2 \left(x^2 + \left[\dfrac{x^3}{3}\right]\right)\right]$

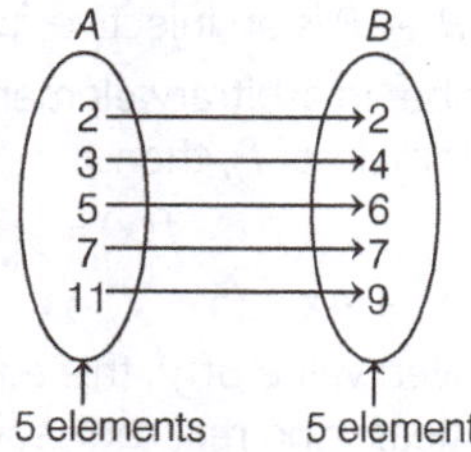

[put the values of x and find the values of $f(x)$]
{$\because$ [ ] is a greatest function}

So, number of one-to-one function $= {}^5P_5 = 5! = 120$

2 (*d*) $f(x) = \begin{cases} -a, & -a \le x \le 0 \\ x + a, & 0 < x \le a \end{cases}$

So, $y = f(x) \Rightarrow$
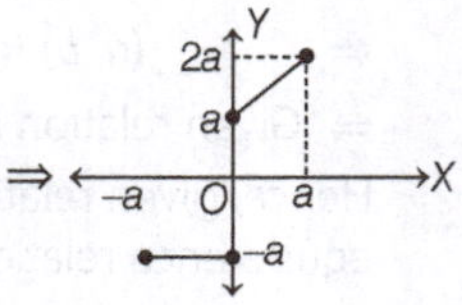

$y = f(|x|) \Rightarrow$
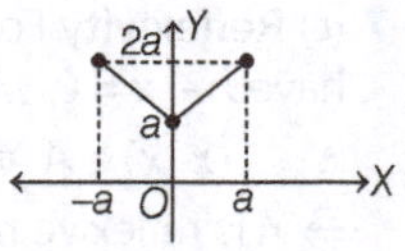

$y = |f(x)| \Rightarrow$
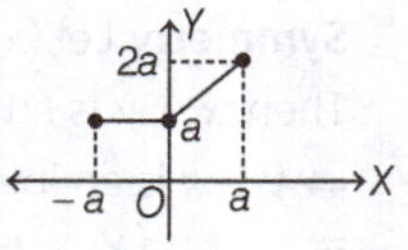

Now, $g(x) = \dfrac{f|x| - |f(x)|}{2}$

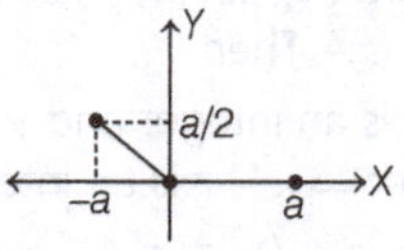

Hence, $g(x)$ is neither one-one nor onto.

3 (*d*) Given, $A = \{1, 2, 3, 4, 5\}$
Relation R on A is defined as xRy iff $4x \le 5y$
Now, for $x = 1, y \ge \dfrac{4}{5}$
$x = 2, y \ge \dfrac{8}{5}$ ... so on.
$\therefore R = \{(1, 1), (1, 2), (1, 3), (1, 4), (1, 5), (2, 2), (2, 3), (2, 4), (2, 5), (3, 3), (3, 4), (3, 5), (4, 4), (4, 5), (5, 4), (5, 5)\}$
According to the question, $m = 16$
Now, for R to be symmetric, we will have to add
For $(1, 2) \in R$, $(2, 1)$ has to be added
For $(1, 3) \in R$, $(3, 1)$ has to be added
For $(1, 4) \in R$, $(4, 1)$ has to be added
For $(1, 5) \in R$, $(5, 1)$ has to be added
For $(2, 3) \in R$, $(3, 2)$ has to be added
For $(2, 4) \in R$, $(4, 2)$ has to be added
For $(2, 5) \in R$, $(5, 2)$ has to be added
For $(3, 4) \in R$, $(4, 3)$ has to be added
For $(3, 5) \in R$, $(5, 3)$ has to be added
$$n = 9 \Rightarrow m + n = 25$$

4 (d) $(x_1, y_1) R(x_2, y_2)$
$\Rightarrow x_1 \leq x_2$ or $y_1 \leq y_2$
For $(x_1, y_1), (x_1, y_1)$
$\Rightarrow x_1 \leq x_1$ or $y_1 \leq y_1$ which is true for all natural number.
$\therefore R$ is reflexive.
$(1,1)R(2,3)$ but $((2,3),(1,1)) \notin R$
$\therefore R$ is not symmetric.
For transitive $x_1 < x_2, y_1 < y_2$
$x_2 < x_3, y_2 < y_3$
$\therefore x_1 < x_3$ and $y_1 < y_3$
R is transitive.

5 (d) $f(x) = \dfrac{4x+3}{6x-4}\ x \neq \dfrac{2}{3}$
$fof(x) = g(x)$
$\Rightarrow \quad g(x) = fof(x)$
$$= \frac{4\left(\frac{4x+3}{6x-4}\right)+3}{6\left(\frac{4x+3}{6x-4}\right)-4} = \frac{34x}{34} = x$$
$g(x) = x$
$gogog(x) = x$
$gogog(4) = 4$

6 (c) We have, $A = \{2,3,4\}, B = \{8,9,12\}$

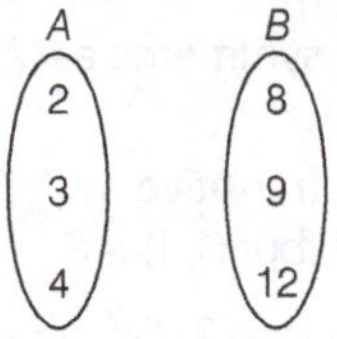

$R = \{((a_1, b_1),(a_2, b_2)) \in (A \times B, A \times B)$
a_1 divides b_2 and a_2 divides $b_1\}$
2 divides 8 and 12, 3 divides 9 and 12, and 4 divides 8 and 12.
$\therefore$ Each element in A divides exactly 2 element is B.
The number of cases that a_1 divides $b_2 = 3 \times 2 = 6$
[$\because$ each element has 2 choices]
Similarly, the number of cases that a_2 divides $b_1 = 3 \times 2 = 6$
Hence, the required number of cases $= 6 \times 6 = 36$

7 (b) Let l be any straight line in the plane.
For reflexive relation:
Since, l is parallel to itself, lRl
Therefore, the relation is reflexive.
For symmetric relation:
Let l_1 and l_2 be any two straight lines in the plane such that l_1Rl_2.
Since, l_1 is parallel to l_2.
So, l_2 is parallel to l_1, l_2Rl_1
Therefore, the relation is symmetric.
For transitive relation,
Let l_1, l_2 and l_3 be any three straight lines in the plane such that l_1Rl_2 and l_2Rl_3.
Since, l_1 is parallel to l_2 and l_2 is parallel to l_3. So, l_1 is parallel to l_3, l_1Rl_3.
Therefore, the relation is transitive.
$\therefore$ The relation is reflexive, symmetric and transitive.
Hence, it is an equivalence relation.

8 (d) **Injective**
Let n, m be any two even natural numbers.
Then, $f(n) = f(m) \Rightarrow n-1 = m-1$
$\Rightarrow n = m.$
If n, m are any two odd natural numbers. Then,
$f(n) = f(m) \Rightarrow n+1 = m+1$
$\Rightarrow n = m.$
If n is even and m is odd, then $n \neq m$.
$\therefore f(n) \neq f(m)$
Thus, f is injective.
Surjective
Let n be an arbitrary natural number.
If n is an odd natural number.
Then, there exist and even natural number $(n+1)$ such that $f(n+1) = n+1-1 = n.$
If n is an even natural number, there exists an odd natural number $(n-1)$ such that $f(n-1) = n-1+1 = n$. Thus, every $n \in N$ has its pre-image in N.
So, f is surjective.
Hence, f is **bijective** and thus **invertible.**

9 (d) $f(x) = x-1$ and $g(x) = \dfrac{x^2}{x^2-1}$
$$fog(x) = f(g(x)) = \frac{x^2}{x^2-1} - 1$$
$$= \frac{1}{x^2-1}$$
$fog(x) = \dfrac{1}{x^2-1}$ is an even function,
$x \neq \pm 1$
$\Rightarrow$ It is many one function.
Now, $y = \dfrac{1}{x^2-1} \Rightarrow x^2 = \dfrac{1}{y} + 1$
$\dfrac{y+1}{y} \geq 0 \qquad [\because x^2 \geq 0]$
Here, $y > 0$ or $y+1 \geq 0 \Rightarrow y \geq -1$
$y \in (0, \infty)$
Range $\neq$ codomain $\Rightarrow fog(x)$ is into function.

Concept Enhancer
A function f is even, if the following equations hold for all x and $-x$ in the domain of $f: f(x) = f(-x)$.

10 (b) Given, $f(x) = \dfrac{x-1}{x+1}$
$$f(f(x)) = f\left(\frac{x-1}{x+1}\right) = \frac{\frac{x-1}{x+1} - 1}{\frac{x-1}{x+1} + 1}$$
$\therefore \quad f^2(x) = -\dfrac{1}{x}$
Then, $f^3(x) = f(f^2(x)) = f\left(-\dfrac{1}{x}\right)$
$$\Rightarrow \quad f^3(x) = \frac{-\frac{1}{x} - 1}{-\frac{1}{x} + 1}$$
$\therefore \quad f^3(x) = \dfrac{x+1}{1-x}$
So, $f^6(x) = f^3(f^3(x))$
$$= \frac{\frac{x+1}{1-x} + 1}{1 - \frac{x+1}{1-x}} = -\frac{1}{x}$$
and $f^7(x) = f(f^6(x))$
$$= f\left(-\frac{1}{x}\right) = \frac{x+1}{1-x}$$

Then, $f^6(6)+f^7(7)$

$$=-\frac{1}{6}+\left(\frac{8}{-6}\right)=-\frac{3}{2}$$

$\therefore\ f^6(6)+f^7(7)=-\frac{3}{2}$

11 (24) $2x+3y=23$

$x=1 \quad y=7$
$x=4 \quad y=5$
$x=7 \quad y=3$
$x=10 \quad y=1$

A	B
(1, 7)	1
(4, 5)	4
(7, 3)	7
(10, 1)	10

$\therefore$ Number of one-one function $=4!=24$

12 (66) $A=\{1,2,3,\ldots,100\}$

$(x,y)\in R$ and $2x=3y$

Then, $R=\{(3,2),(6,4),(9,6),(12,8),\ldots,(99,66)\}$

Number of elements in $R=33$

R_1 be a symmetric relation on A such that $R\subset R_1$

$\therefore\ R_1=\{(3,2),(2,3),(6,4),(4,6),\ldots(99,66),(66,99)\}$

So minimum number of elements in $R_1=66$

So, $n=66$

13 (3) Given, set $A=\{1, 2, 3\}$

For relation R to be reflexive,

$\Rightarrow (1,1),(2,2),(3,3)\in R$

$\therefore\ R=\{(1,1),(2,2),(3,3),(1,2),(2,3),\ldots\}$

Since, $(1,2),(2,3)\in R$

$\Rightarrow (1,3)\in R$ to be transitive

$\therefore\ R_1=\{(1,1),(2,,2),(3,3),(1,2),(2,3),(1,3)\}$ is a required relation.

Now, $R_2=\{R_1,(2,1)\}$ is reflexive, transitive but not symmetric

$R_3=\{R_1,(3,2)\}$ and $R_4=\{R_1,(3,1),(2,1)\}$ are total 3 such possible relations.

14 (25) Let the roots of quadratic polynomial are t and s.

Then, $f(x)=(x-t)(x-s)$

$f(0)=p$

$\Rightarrow\ st=p$ [given]

and $f(1)=1/3$

$\Rightarrow\ (1-t)(1-s)=\frac{1}{3}$

Now, assume that t is the common root of $f(x)=0$ and $fofofo(x)=0$

Take, $fofofof(x)=0$

$\Rightarrow\ fofof(0)=0$

$\Rightarrow\ fof(p)=0$

So, $f(p)$ is either t or s

$(p-t)(p-s)=t$

$(ts-t)(ts-s)=t$

$\Rightarrow\ (s-1)(t-1)s=1 \quad [\because t\neq 0]$

So, $s=3$

$$(1-t)(1-3)=\frac{1}{3}\Rightarrow t=\frac{7}{6}$$

$$f(x)=\left(x-\frac{7}{6}\right)(x-3)$$

$$f(-3)=\left(-3-\frac{7}{6}\right)(-3-3)=25$$

15 (190) From given

$$f(n)=\begin{cases}2n, & \text{if } n=1,2,3,4,5\\ 2n-11, & \text{if } n=6,7,\ldots,10\end{cases}$$

Put $n=1, 2, 3, 4, \ldots, 10$

$f(1)=2, f(2)=4, f(3)=6,$
$f(4)=8, \ldots f(6)=1, f(7)=3,$
$f(8)=5\ldots f(10)=9.$

Take, $fog(n)=\begin{cases}(n+1), & \text{if } n \text{ is odd}\\ (n-1), & \text{if } n \text{ is even}\end{cases}$

Put $n=1, 2, 3, 4, \ldots, 10$

$f(g(1))=2, f(g(2))=1, f(g(3))=4,$
$f(g(4))=3, f(g(5))=6, f(g(10))=9$

As, $f(g(10))=9$, and $f(10)=9$, then $g(10)=10$

Similarly, $g(1)=1, g(2)=6, g(3)=2, g(4)=7, g(5)=3$

Put the values in the expression,

$g(10)(g(1)+g(2)+g(3)+g(4)+g(5)$

$\Rightarrow 10(1+6+2+7+3)$

$\Rightarrow\ 10\times(19)=190$

Skill Boosters

1 (a) $x^3-3x^2y-xy^2+3y^3=0$

$\Rightarrow x^2(x-3y)-y^2(x-3y)=0$

$\Rightarrow\ (x-y)(x+y)(x-3y)=0$ ...(i)

$\because$ (i) holds for all (x,x)

$\therefore\ R$ is reflexive

If (x,y) holds, then (y,x) may or may not hold for factor $(x-3y)$.

For example (3, 1)

$\therefore R$ is not symmetric

Similarly factor $(x-3y)$ does not hold for transitive.

For example $(9,3)\in R$ and $(3,1)\in R$ but $(9,1)\notin R$

Hence, relation R is reflexive but neither symmetric nor transitive.

2 (a) $\because R$ is not a function as $A=\{1,2,3,4\}$ and $(2,4),(2,3)\in R$

R is not reflexive as $(1,1)\notin R$.

R is not symmetric as $(2,3)\in R$ but $(3,2)\notin R$.

R is not transitive as $(1,3)\in R$ and $(3,1)\in R$ but $(1,1)\notin R$.

3 (a) $A=(x+2)(x^2-5x+6)=0$

$\Rightarrow\ (x+2)(x-2)(x-3)=0$

$\Rightarrow\ x=2,3,-2$

$\therefore\ n(A)=3$

and $B=\frac{-3+1}{2}<x<\frac{9+1}{2}$

$\Rightarrow\ -1<x<5$

$\Rightarrow\ x=0,1,2,3,4$

$\therefore n(B)=5$

$\Rightarrow\ n(A\times B)=3\times 5$

$\therefore$ Subsets of $A\times B=2^{3\times 5}=2^{15}$

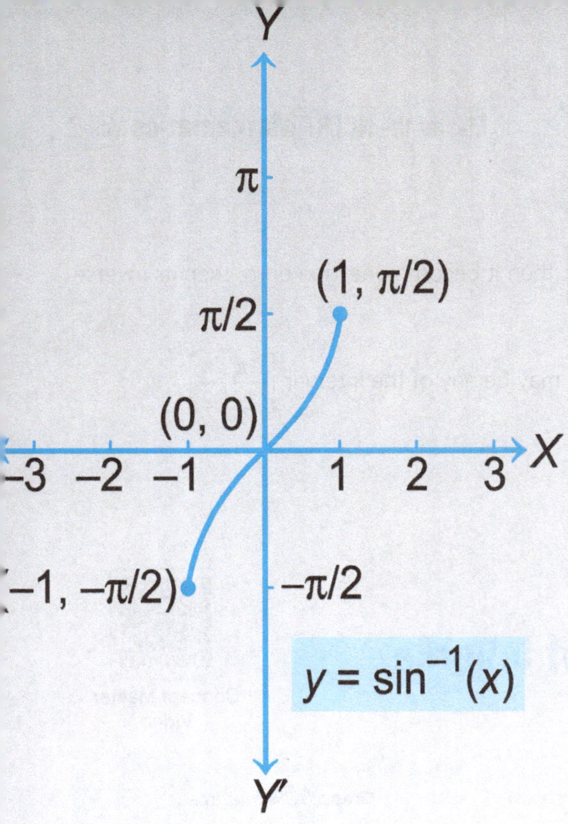

02

Inverse Trigonometric Functions

Topicwise No. of Ques asked in 3 Years (JEE Main)

Topics	No. of Questions		
	2024	2023	2022
Basic Concepts	7	3	8
Properties of Inverse Trigonometric Function	3	7	5

Special Type of Ques Asked in 3 Years (JEE Main)

Types	Years		
	2024	2023	2022
A-R	–	–	–
Statement Based	–	–	–
Numerical Value Type	2	4	3

Last 3 Years Weightage (JEE Main)

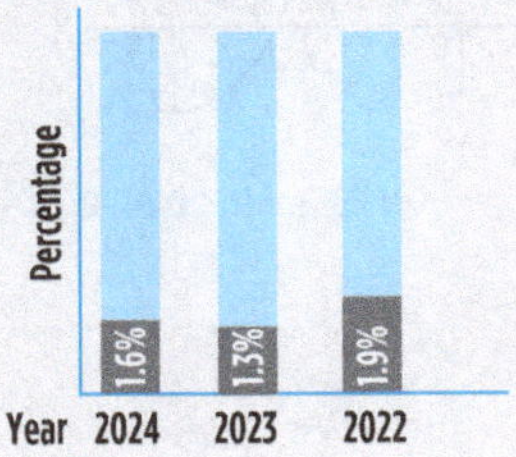

Basic Concepts

Trigonometric functions are not one-one on their natural domains, so their inverse does not exist in all values but their inverse may exists in some interval of their restricted domains. Thus, we can say that inverse of trigonometric functions are defined within restricted domains of corresponding trigonometric functions. Inverse of f is denoted by f^{-1}.

- Let $f : A \to B$ is a one-one and onto function from A to B, then its inverse function will be $f^{-1} : B \to A$. i.e. image of x under f is $y \Leftrightarrow$ image of y under f^{-1} is x.
- If domain and range of function f is A and B respectively, then domain and range of f^{-1} will be B and A respectively.

  Domain of f^{-1} = Range of f and Range of f^{-1} = Domain of f
- Inverse of a function exists if and only if, it is one-one onto. Here, one-one function means that function never takes the same value twice.
- Trigonometric functions are periodic function i.e. they take same value periodically, so their inverse does not exist. But if we restrict their domain and range, then their inverse may exist.

Inverse of Sine Function

- Value of sine function varies from – 1 to 1 i.e. its range is [– 1, 1]. For $\frac{-\pi}{2}$ value of sine is – 1 and for $\pi/2$ value of sine is 1. Similarly, for $-3\pi/2, \frac{-\pi}{2}$ and $\pi/2, 3\pi/2$ value of sine is also in the range [–1, 1].

- If we restrict sine function to any of the interval $\left[\frac{-\pi}{2}, \frac{\pi}{2}\right], \left[\frac{-3\pi}{2}, \frac{-\pi}{2}\right], \left[\frac{\pi}{2}, \frac{3\pi}{2}\right]$, then it become one-one onto, then its inverse can be found.
- Inverse of sine function ($\sin^{-1}$) is a function whose domain is $[-1, 1]$ and range may be any of the interval $\left[\frac{-\pi}{2}, \frac{\pi}{2}\right]$, $\left[\frac{-3\pi}{2}, \frac{-\pi}{2}\right], \left[\frac{\pi}{2}, \frac{3\pi}{2}\right]$, for each such interval a branch of $\sin^{-1}$ is obtained.
- The branch $\left[\frac{-\pi}{2}, \frac{\pi}{2}\right]$ is called **principal value branch.**
- The value of function in this branch is called **principal value.**

Concept Master Video

Domain, Principal Value, Range and Graph of Inverse Trigonometric Functions

Function	Domain	Principal value branch (Range)	Other possible range	Graph (By interchanging axes)	Graph (As mirror image)
$y = \sin^{-1} x$	$[-1, 1]$	$\left[-\frac{\pi}{2}, \frac{\pi}{2}\right]$	$\left[\frac{-3\pi}{2}, \frac{-\pi}{2}\right]$, $\left[\frac{\pi}{2}, \frac{3\pi}{2}\right]$ etc.	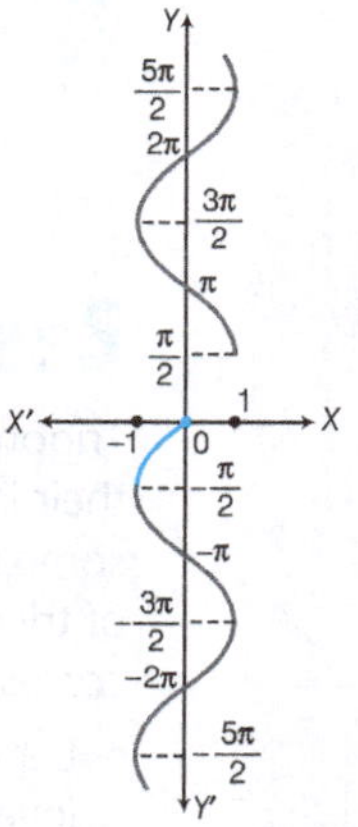	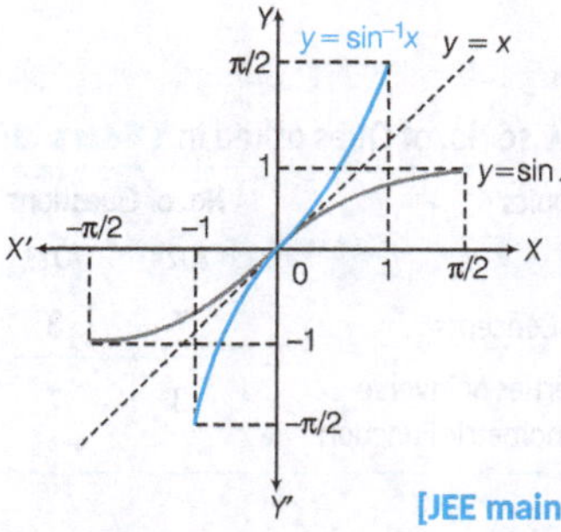 [JEE main 2024]
$y = \cos^{-1} x$	$[-1, 1]$	$[0, \pi]$	$[-\pi, 0]$, $[\pi, 2\pi]$, etc.	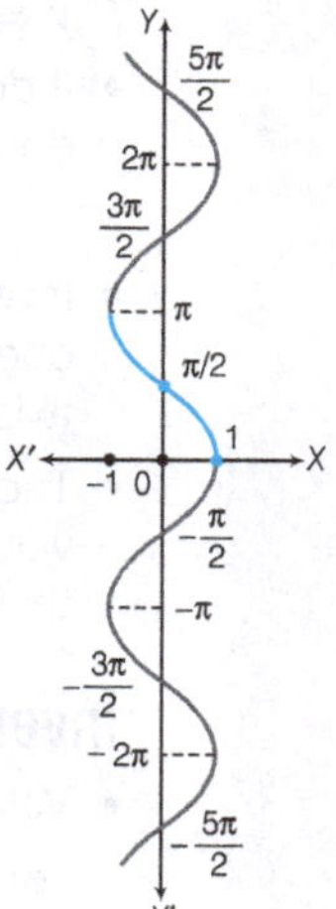	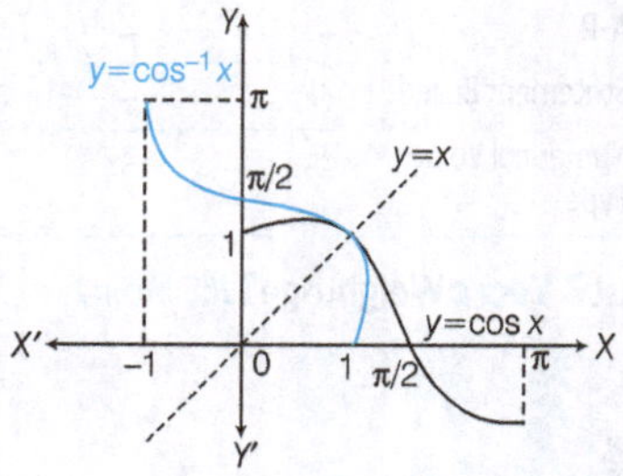 [JEE main 2024, 2022]

Function	Domain	Principal value branch (Range)	Other possible range	Graph (By interchanging axes)	Graph (As mirror image)
$y = \tan^{-1}x$	R	$\left(-\frac{\pi}{2}, \frac{\pi}{2}\right)$	$\left(\frac{-3\pi}{2}, \frac{-\pi}{2}\right)$, $\left(\frac{\pi}{2}, \frac{3\pi}{2}\right)$ etc.	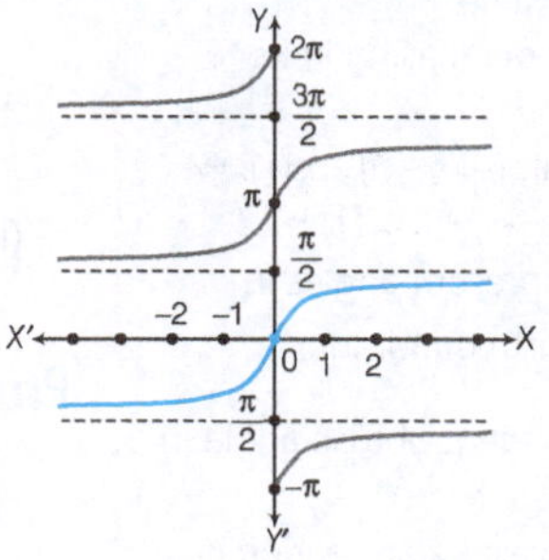	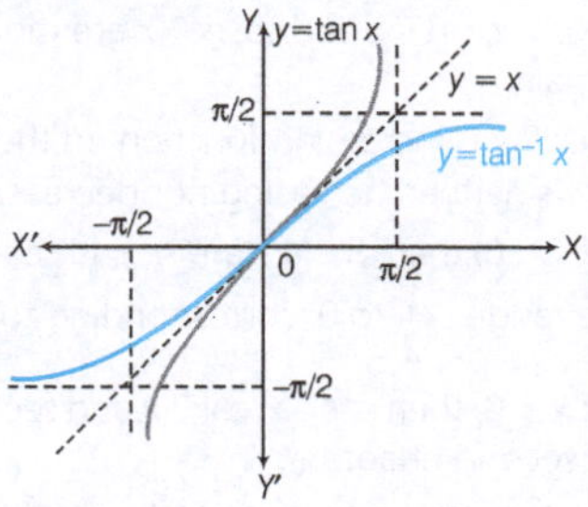
$y = \sec^{-1}x$	$R-(-1, 1)$ or $(-\infty, -1] \cup [1, \infty)$	$[0, \pi]-\left\{\frac{\pi}{2}\right\}$	$[-\pi, 0]-\left\{-\frac{\pi}{2}\right\}$, $[\pi, 2\pi]-\left\{\frac{3\pi}{2}\right\}$ etc.	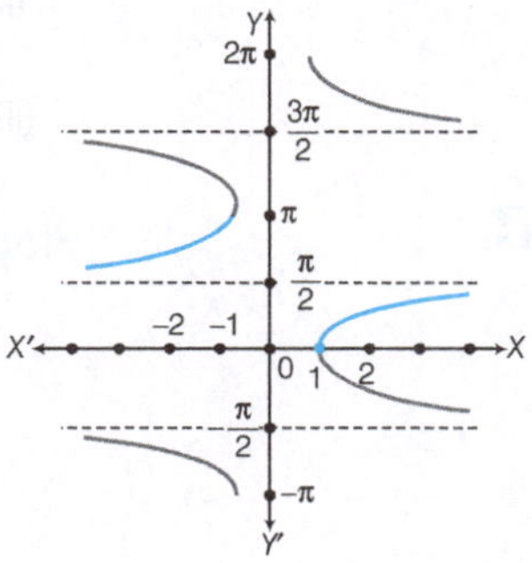	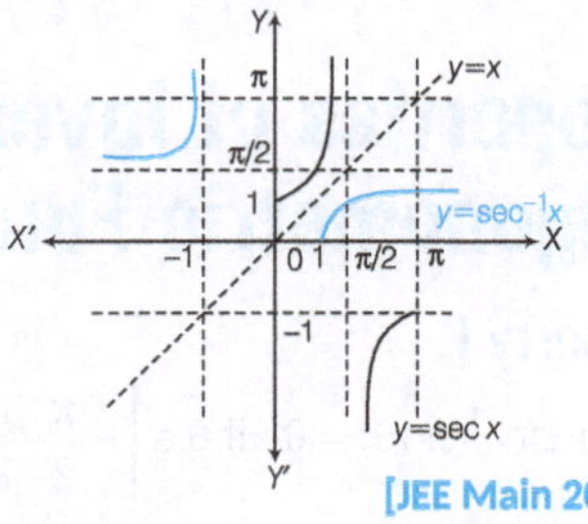 **[JEE Main 2023]**
$y = \text{cosec}^{-1}x$	$R-(-1, 1)$ or $(-\infty, -1] \cup [1, \infty)$	$\left[\frac{-\pi}{2}, \frac{\pi}{2}\right]-\{0\}$	$\left[\frac{-3\pi}{2}, \frac{-\pi}{2}\right]-\{-\pi\}$, $\left[\frac{\pi}{2}, \frac{3\pi}{2}\right]-\{\pi\}$ etc.	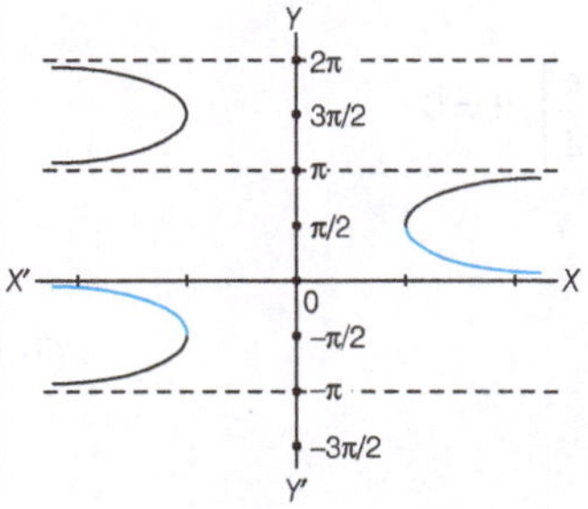	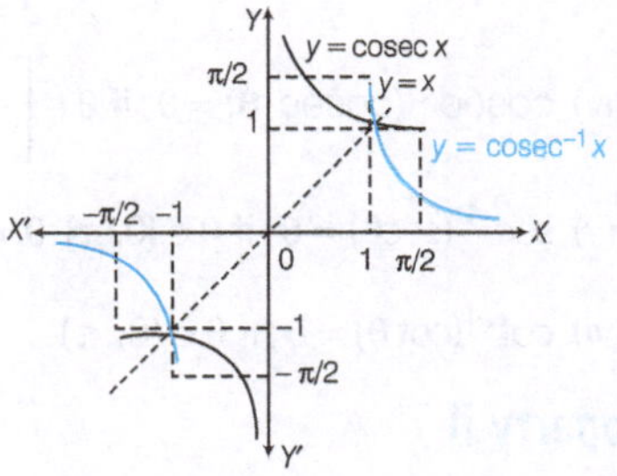
$y = \cot^{-1}x$	R	$(0, \pi)$	$(-\pi, 0), (\pi, 2\pi)$ etc.	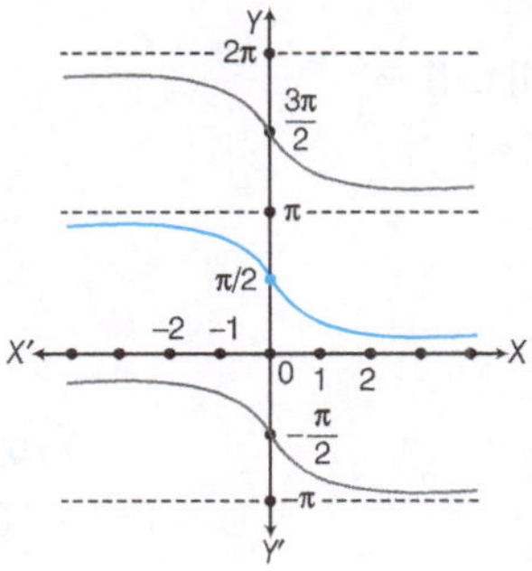	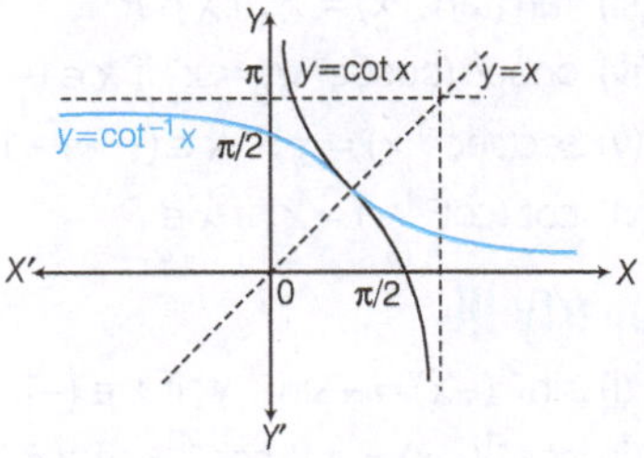

Marks Maximizer

- $\sin^{-1}x$ and $\tan^{-1}x$ are monotonic increasing function in its domain.
- $\cos^{-1}x, \cot^{-1}x$ and $\text{cosec}^{-1}x$ are monotonic decreasing in its domain.
- $\sec^{-1}x$ is increasing function on the intervals $(-\infty, -1]$ and $[1, \infty)$ but its neither increasing nor decreasing on $(-\infty, -1] \cup [1, \infty)$.
- If $x < 0$, then $\sin^{-1}x, \tan^{-1}x$ and $\text{cosec}^{-1}x$ represent angles in the range $-\frac{\pi}{2}$ to 0, corresponding to the fourth quadrant.
- If $x < 0$, then $\cos^{-1}x, \cot^{-1}x$ and $\sec^{-1}x$ represent obtuse angle in the second quadrant.
- $\sin^{-1}x, \cos^{-1}x, \tan^{-1}x, \cot^{-1}x, \sec^{-1}x$ and $\text{cosec}^{-1}x$ are periodic and bounded function.

Properties of Inverse Trigonometric Function

Property I

(i) $\sin^{-1}(\sin\theta) = \theta$; if $\theta \in \left[-\frac{\pi}{2}, \frac{\pi}{2}\right]$

(ii) $\cos^{-1}(\cos\theta) = \theta$; if $\theta \in [0, \pi]$

(iii) $\tan^{-1}(\tan\theta) = \theta$; if $\theta \in \left(-\frac{\pi}{2}, \frac{\pi}{2}\right)$

(iv) $\text{cosec}^{-1}(\text{cosec }\theta) = \theta$; if $\theta \in \left[-\frac{\pi}{2}, \frac{\pi}{2}\right]; \theta \neq 0$

(v) $\sec^{-1}(\sec\theta) = \theta$; if $\theta \in [0, \pi], \theta \neq \frac{\pi}{2}$

(vi) $\cot^{-1}(\cot\theta) = \theta$; if $\theta \in (0, \pi)$

Property II

(i) $\sin(\sin^{-1}x) = x$; if $x \in [-1, 1]$

(ii) $\cos(\cos^{-1}x) = x$; if $x \in [-1, 1]$

(iii) $\tan(\tan^{-1}x) = x$; if $x \in R$

(iv) $\text{cosec}(\text{cosec}^{-1}x) = x$; if $x \in (-\infty, -1] \cup [1, \infty)$

(v) $\sec(\sec^{-1}x) = x$; if $x \in (-\infty, -1] \cup [1, \infty)$

(vi) $\cot(\cot^{-1}x) = x$; if $x \in R$

Property III

(i) $\sin^{-1}(-x) = -\sin^{-1}x$; if $x \in [-1, 1]$

(ii) $\cos^{-1}(-x) = \pi - \cos^{-1}x$; if $x \in [-1, 1]$

(iii) $\tan^{-1}(-x) = -\tan^{-1}x$; if $x \in R$

(iv) $\text{cosec}^{-1}(-x) = -\text{cosec}^{-1}x$; if $|x| \geq 1$ or $x \in (-\infty, -1] \cup [1, \infty)$

(v) $\sec^{-1}(-x) = \pi - \sec^{-1}x$; if $|x| \geq 1$ or $x \in (-\infty, -1] \cup [1, \infty)$

(vi) $\cot^{-1}(-x) = \pi - \cot^{-1}x$; if $x \in R$

Property IV

(i) $\sin^{-1}\left(\frac{1}{x}\right) = \text{cosec}^{-1}x$; if $x \in (-\infty, -1] \cup [1, \infty)$

(ii) $\cos^{-1}\left(\frac{1}{x}\right) = \sec^{-1}x$; if $x \in (-\infty, -1] \cup [1, \infty)$

(iii) $\tan^{-1}\left(\frac{1}{x}\right) = \begin{cases} \cot^{-1}x; & \text{if } x > 0 \\ -\pi + \cot^{-1}x; & \text{if } x < 0 \end{cases}$ **[JEE Main 2023]**

Property V

(i) $\sin^{-1}x + \cos^{-1}x = \frac{\pi}{2}$; if $x \in [-1, 1]$ **[JEE Main 2022]**

(ii) $\tan^{-1}x + \cot^{-1}x = \frac{\pi}{2}$; if $x \in R$

(iii) $\sec^{-1}x + \text{cosec}^{-1}x = \frac{\pi}{2}$; if $x \in (-\infty, -1] \cup [1, \infty)$ or $|x| \geq 1$

Property VI

(i) $\sin^{-1}x + \sin^{-1}y =$

$$\begin{cases} \sin^{-1}\{x\sqrt{1-y^2} + y\sqrt{1-x^2}\}; & \text{if } -1 \leq x, y \leq 1 \text{ and } x^2 + y^2 \leq 1 \\ & \text{or if } xy < 0 \text{ and } x^2 + y^2 > 1 \\ \pi - \sin^{-1}\{x\sqrt{1-y^2} + y\sqrt{1-x^2}\}; & \text{if } 0 < x, y \leq 1 \text{ and } x^2 + y^2 > 1 \\ -\pi - \sin^{-1}\{x\sqrt{1-y^2} + y\sqrt{1-x^2}\}; & \text{if } -1 \leq x, y < 0 \text{ and } x^2 + y^2 > 1 \end{cases}$$

(ii) $\sin^{-1}x - \sin^{-1}y =$

$$\begin{cases} \sin^{-1}\{x\sqrt{1-y^2} - y\sqrt{1-x^2}\}; & \text{if } -1 \leq x, y \leq 1 \text{ and } x^2 + y^2 \leq 1 \\ & \text{or if } xy > 0 \text{ and } x^2 + y^2 > 1 \\ \pi - \sin^{-1}\{x\sqrt{1-y^2} - y\sqrt{1-x^2}\}; & \text{if } 0 < x \leq 1, -1 \leq y \leq 0 \text{ and } x^2 + y^2 > 1 \\ -\pi - \sin^{-1}\{x\sqrt{1-y^2} - y\sqrt{1-x^2}\}; & \text{if } -1 \leq x < 0, 0 < y \leq 1 \text{ and } x^2 + y^2 > 1 \end{cases}$$

[JEE Main 2023]

Property VII

(i) $\cos^{-1}x + \cos^{-1}y =$

$$\begin{cases} \cos^{-1}\{xy - \sqrt{1-x^2}\sqrt{1-y^2}\}; & \text{if } -1 \leq x, y \leq 1 \text{ and } x + y \geq 0 \\ 2\pi - \cos^{-1}\{xy - \sqrt{1-x^2}\sqrt{1-y^2}\}; & \text{if } -1 \leq x, y \leq 1 \text{ and } x + y \leq 0 \end{cases}$$

(ii) $\cos^{-1} x - \cos^{-1} y = \begin{cases} \cos^{-1}\{xy + \sqrt{1-x^2}\sqrt{1-y^2}\}; & \text{if } -1 \le x, y \le 1 \text{ and } x \le y \\ -\cos^{-1}\{xy + \sqrt{1-x^2}\sqrt{1-y^2}\}; & \text{if } -1 \le y \le 0, 0 < x \le 1 \text{ and } x \ge y \end{cases}$

Property VIII

(i) $\sin^{-1} x = \cos^{-1}\sqrt{1-x^2} = \tan^{-1}\dfrac{x}{\sqrt{1-x^2}} = \cot^{-1}\dfrac{\sqrt{1-x^2}}{x}$

$= \sec^{-1}\left(\dfrac{1}{\sqrt{1-x^2}}\right) = \text{cosec}^{-1}\left(\dfrac{1}{x}\right), x \in (0, 1)$

(ii) $\cos^{-1} x = \sin^{-1}\sqrt{1-x^2} = \tan^{-1}\dfrac{\sqrt{1-x^2}}{x}$

$= \cot^{-1}\dfrac{x}{\sqrt{1-x^2}} = \sec^{-1}\left(\dfrac{1}{x}\right)$

$= \text{cosec}^{-1}\left(\dfrac{1}{\sqrt{1-x^2}}\right), x \in (0, 1)$

(iii) $\tan^{-1} x = \sin^{-1}\left(\dfrac{x}{\sqrt{1+x^2}}\right) = \cos^{-1}\left(\dfrac{1}{\sqrt{1+x^2}}\right)$

$= \cot^{-1}\left(\dfrac{1}{x}\right)$

$= \text{cosec}^{-1}\left(\dfrac{\sqrt{1+x^2}}{x}\right)$

$= \sec^{-1}(\sqrt{1+x^2}), x \in (0, \infty)$

Property IX

(i) $2\sin^{-1} x = \begin{cases} \sin^{-1}(2x\sqrt{1-x^2}); & \text{if } -\dfrac{1}{\sqrt{2}} \le x \le \dfrac{1}{\sqrt{2}} \\ \pi - \sin^{-1}(2x\sqrt{1-x^2}); & \text{if } \dfrac{1}{\sqrt{2}} \le x \le 1 \\ -\pi - \sin^{-1}(2x\sqrt{1-x^2}); & \text{if } -1 \le x \le -\dfrac{1}{\sqrt{2}} \end{cases}$

(ii) $2\cos^{-1} x = \begin{cases} \cos^{-1}(2x^2 - 1); & \text{if } 0 \le x \le 1 \\ 2\pi - \cos^{-1}(2x^2 - 1); & \text{if } -1 \le x \le 0 \end{cases}$

(iii) $2\tan^{-1} x = \begin{cases} \tan^{-1}\left(\dfrac{2x}{1-x^2}\right); & \text{if } -1 < x < 1 \\ \pi + \tan^{-1}\left(\dfrac{2x}{1-x^2}\right); & \text{if } x > 1 \\ -\pi + \tan^{-1}\left(\dfrac{2x}{1-x^2}\right); & \text{if } x < -1 \end{cases}$

Property X

(i) $3\sin^{-1} x = \begin{cases} \sin^{-1}(3x - 4x^3); & \text{if } -\dfrac{1}{2} \le x \le \dfrac{1}{2} \\ \pi - \sin^{-1}(3x - 4x^3); & \text{if } \dfrac{1}{2} < x \le 1 \\ -\pi - \sin^{-1}(3x - 4x^3); & \text{if } -1 \le x < -\dfrac{1}{2} \end{cases}$

(ii) $3\cos^{-1} x = \begin{cases} \cos^{-1}(4x^3 - 3x); & \text{if } \dfrac{1}{2} \le x \le 1 \\ 2\pi - \cos^{-1}(4x^3 - 3x); & \text{if } -\dfrac{1}{2} \le x \le \dfrac{1}{2} \\ 2\pi + \cos^{-1}(4x^3 - 3x); & \text{if } -1 \le x \le -\dfrac{1}{2} \end{cases}$

(iii) $3\tan^{-1} x = \begin{cases} \tan^{-1}\left(\dfrac{3x - x^3}{1 - 3x^2}\right); & \text{if } -\dfrac{1}{\sqrt{3}} < x < \dfrac{1}{\sqrt{3}} \\ \pi + \tan^{-1}\left(\dfrac{3x - x^3}{1 - 3x^2}\right); & \text{if } x > \dfrac{1}{\sqrt{3}} \\ -\pi + \tan^{-1}\left(\dfrac{3x - x^3}{1 - 3x^2}\right); & \text{if } x < -\dfrac{1}{\sqrt{3}} \end{cases}$

Property XI

(i) $2\tan^{-1} x = \begin{cases} \sin^{-1}\left(\dfrac{2x}{1+x^2}\right); & \text{if } -1 \le x \le 1 \\ \pi - \sin^{-1}\left(\dfrac{2x}{1+x^2}\right); & \text{if } x > 1 \\ -\pi - \sin^{-1}\left(\dfrac{2x}{1+x^2}\right); & \text{if } x < -1 \end{cases}$

(ii) $2\tan^{-1} x = \begin{cases} \cos^{-1}\left(\dfrac{1-x^2}{1+x^2}\right); & \text{if } 0 \le x < \infty \\ -\cos^{-1}\left(\dfrac{1-x^2}{1+x^2}\right); & \text{if } -\infty < x < 0 \end{cases}$

Caution Points

- $\sin^{-1} x$ is the inverse (arc sine) of sine, while $(\sin x)^{-1} = \frac{1}{\sin x}$ is the reciprocal (i.e. cosecant).
- If $f(x)$ is increasing function, then $f^{-1}(x)$ is also increasing function, vice versa.
- The principal value of an inverse trigonometric function lies within defined range ensuring a unique and specific output.
- $\sin^{-1} x, \tan^{-1} x$ and $\text{cosec}^{-1} x$ are the odd functions.
- $\cos^{-1} x, \cot^{-1} x$ and $\sec^{-1} x$ are neither even nor odd function.
- If $x \geq 0$, the inverse trigonometric function $\sin^{-1} x, \cos^{-1} x, \tan^{-1} x, \sec^{-1} x, \text{cosec}^{-1} x, \cot^{-1} x$ typically return an angle in first quadrant which is acute angle.
- The third quadrant is never used in inverse trigonometric function.

PYQ Notes

1. $\tan^{-1} x_1 + \tan^{-1} x_2 + \ldots + \tan^{-1} x_n$

$$= \tan^{-1}\left(\frac{S_1 - S_3 + S_5 - \ldots}{1 - S_2 + S_4 - S_6 + \ldots}\right),$$

[JEE Main 2022]

where S_k denotes the sum of the products of $x_1, x_2, \ldots, x_n$ takes k at a time.

2. $\tan^{-1} x - \tan^{-1} y$

$$= \begin{cases} \tan^{-1}\left(\frac{x-y}{1+xy}\right); & \text{if } xy > -1 \\ \pi + \tan^{-1}\left(\frac{x-y}{1+xy}\right); & \text{if } x > 0, y < 0 \text{ and } xy < -1 \\ -\pi + \tan^{-1}\left(\frac{x-y}{1+xy}\right); & \text{if } x < 0, y > 0 \text{ and } xy < -1 \end{cases}$$

[JEE Main 2024]

3. $\tan^{-1} x + \tan^{-1} y$

$$= \begin{cases} \tan^{-1}\left(\frac{x+y}{1-xy}\right); & \text{if } xy < 1 \\ \pi + \tan^{-1}\left(\frac{x+y}{1-xy}\right); & \text{if } x > 0, y > 0 \text{ and } xy > 1 \\ -\pi + \tan^{-1}\left(\frac{x+y}{1-xy}\right); & \text{if } x < 0, y < 0 \text{ and } xy > 1 \end{cases}$$

[JEE Main 2023]

Step by Step

Mastering NCERT

- Concept Builders
- Topical Questions
- Numerical Type Questions
- Assertion and Reason Questions
- Case or Paragraph Type Questions
- Past Years Questions
- Skill Boosters

Concept Builders

1 The value of $\sin\left(\tan^{-1}2+\tan^{-1}\frac{1}{2}\right)$ is .....

2 If $\sin^{-1}x+\sin^{-1}y=\pi$, then value of $(x+y)^2$ is ....

3 $\cos(\tan^{-1}x)$ in terms of x only is .....

4 If $x<0$, then $\cot^{-1}x-\tan^{-1}\frac{1}{x}$ is .....

5 The value of $\tan^{-1}(1)+\cos^{-1}\left(-\frac{1}{2}\right)$ is ....

6 If $x\le 0$ and $\cos^{-1}\left(\frac{1-x^2}{1+x^2}\right)=\lambda\tan^{-1}x$, then λ is equal to ....

7 The range of $\sin^{-1}x+\cos^{-1}x+\tan^{-1}x$ is ....

8 If $\sin^{-1}x-\cos^{-1}x=\frac{\pi}{6}$, then x is equal to .....

9 If $x>0, y>0, xy>1$, then
$\tan^{-1}x+\tan^{-1}y=\tan^{-1}\left(\frac{x+y}{1-xy}\right)$ (T/F)

10 The result $\tan^{-1}x-\tan^{-1}y=\tan^{-1}\left(\frac{x-y}{1+xy}\right)$, when
$xy>-1$ (T/F)

11 Every trigonometric function is one-one in its natural domain and range. (T/F)

12 The inverse of trigonometric functions exist in their natural domain and range. (T/F)

13 The inverse of sine function is defined is the interval $[-\pi, 0]$, $[0, \pi]$ etc. (T/F)

14 If (a, b) is a point on the graph of sine function, then (a, b) is also the corresponding point on the graph of inverse of sine function. (T/F)

15 $\sec^{-1}x$ can be defined as a function, if the domain is R and range is $[0, \pi]$- $\left\{\frac{\pi}{2}\right\}$. (T/F)

16 The principal value branch of the $\sec^{-1}x$ is $[0, \pi]-\left\{\frac{\pi}{2}\right\}$. (T/F)

17 Find the domain of the function $f(x)=\sin^{-1}\sqrt{x-1}$.

18 Write the domain of the function $\cos^{-1}(2x-1)$.

19 Find the value of $\tan^{-1}\left(\tan\frac{9\pi}{8}\right)$.

20 If $\tan^{-1}(\tan x)=x$, then $x\in(a, b)$, Write the value of a and b.

Topical Questions

Basic Concepts

Level I

1 If $f: X\to Y$ such that $f(x)=y$ is one-one and onto, then we can define a unique function $g: Y\to X$ such that $g(y)=x$, where $x\in X$ and $y\in Y$. Then, which of the following is/are true? **NCERT Pg. 19**

(a) Domain of g = Range of f
(b) Range of g = Domain of f
(c) $g=f^{-1}$
(d) All of the above

2 The domain in which sine function will be one-one, is **NCERT Pg. 19**

(a) $\left[\frac{-\pi}{2}, \frac{\pi}{2}\right]$ (b) $\left[\frac{\pi}{2}, \frac{3\pi}{2}\right]$
(c) $[0, \pi]$ (d) Both (a) and (b)

3 The principal value branch of $\sin^{-1}x$ is **NCERT Pg. 19**

(a) $\left[\frac{-3\pi}{2}, \frac{-\pi}{2}\right]$ (b) $\left[\frac{-\pi}{2}, \frac{\pi}{2}\right]$
(c) $\left[\frac{\pi}{2}, \frac{3\pi}{2}\right]$ (d) None of these

4 If $\sin^{-1} x : [-1, 1] \to \left[\frac{-\pi}{2}, \frac{\pi}{2}\right]$ is a function, then **NCERT Pg. 19**

(a) $\sin(\sin^{-1} x) = \pi - x, -1 \le x \le 1$
(b) $\sin^{-1}(\sin x) = x, -1 \le x \le 1$
(c) $\sin^{-1}(\sin x) = x, \frac{-\pi}{2} \le x \le \frac{\pi}{2}$
(d) None of the above

5 Which of the following is the graph of $\sin^{-1} x$? **NCERT Pg. 20**

(a) 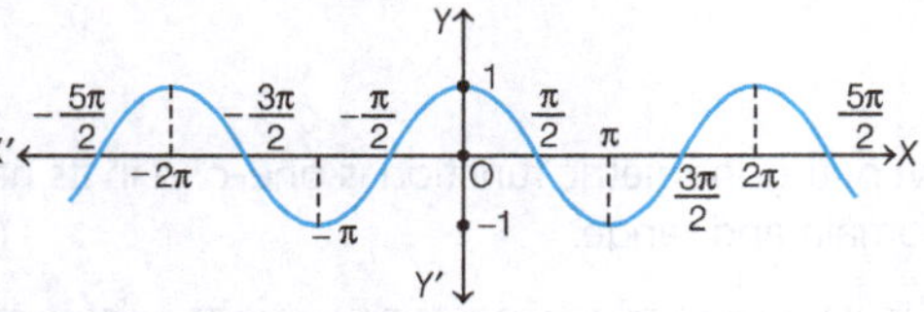

(b) 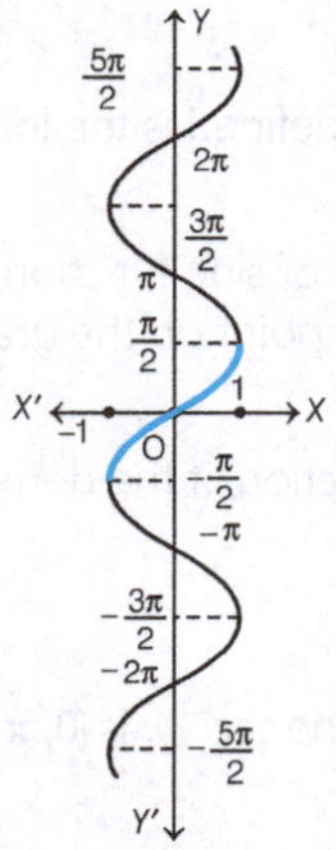

(c) 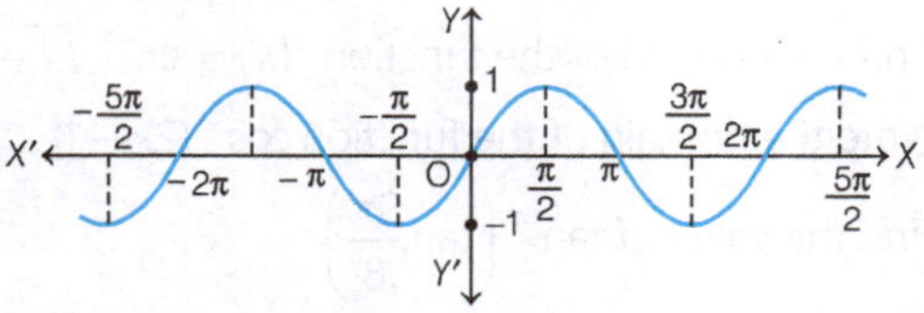

(d) 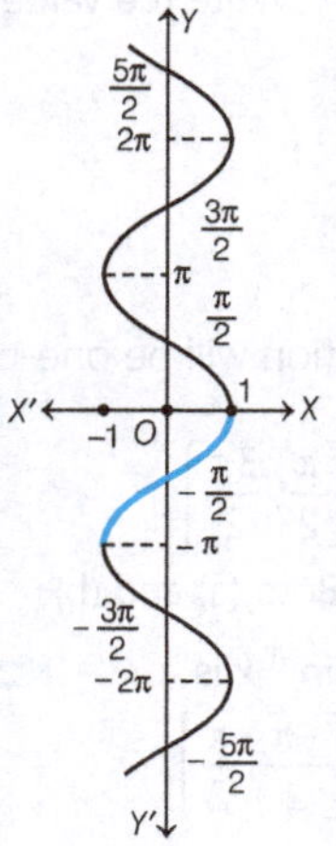

6 The graph of $\sin^{-1} x$ is the mirror image of the graph of $\sin x$ along the line **NCERT Pg. 20**

(a) $y = x$
(b) $y = -x$
(c) $y = x - 1$
(d) None of these

7 If the domain and range of cosine function are $[0, \pi]$ and $[-1, 1]$ respectively, then it is **NCERT Pg. 20**

(a) one-one
(b) onto
(c) both one-one and onto
(d) None of these

8 The inverse of cosine function is defined in the intervals **NCERT Pg. 21**

(a) $[-\pi, 0]$ (b) $\left[\frac{-\pi}{2}, 0\right]$ (c) $\left[0, \frac{\pi}{2}\right]$ (d) $\left[\frac{\pi}{2}, \pi\right]$

9 The principal value branch of $\cos^{-1} x$ function is **NCERT Pg. 21**

(a) $\left[\frac{-\pi}{2}, \frac{\pi}{2}\right]$
(b) $\left[0, \frac{\pi}{2}\right]$
(c) $[-\pi, \pi]$
(d) $[0, \pi]$

10 The principal value branch of $\text{cosec}^{-1} x$ is ...*A*... Here, *A* refers to **NCERT Pg. 22**

(a) $\left(\frac{-\pi}{2}, \frac{\pi}{2}\right)$
(b) $\left[\frac{-\pi}{2}, \frac{\pi}{2}\right]$
(c) $\left[\frac{-\pi}{2}, \frac{\pi}{2}\right] - \{0\}$
(d) $\left(\frac{-\pi}{2}, \frac{\pi}{2}\right) - \{0\}$

11 Which of the following is true? **NCERT Pg. 22**

(a) The graph of $\text{cosec}\, x$ is

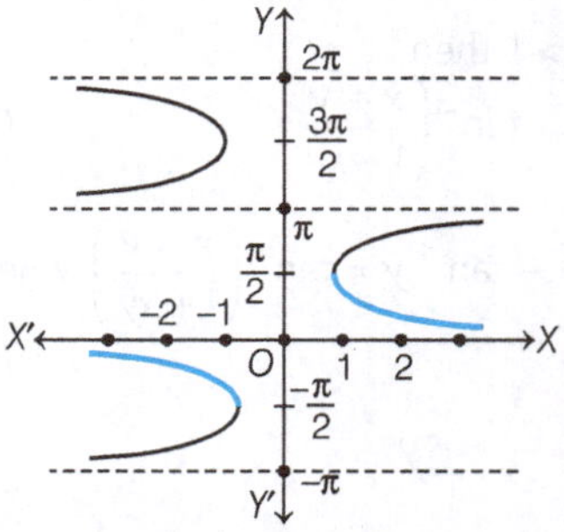

(b) The graph of the $\text{cosec}^{-1} x$ is

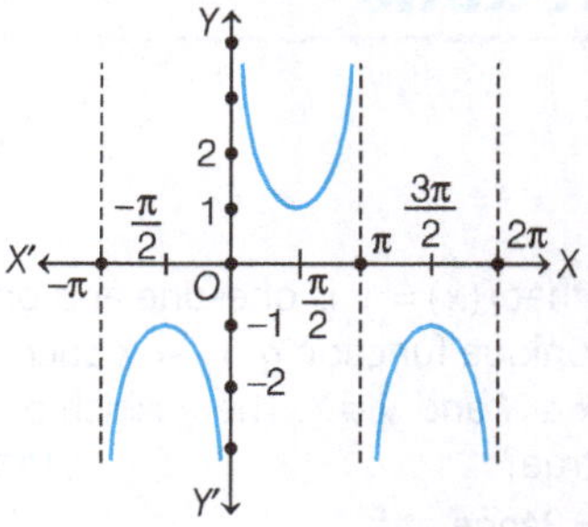

(c) Both (a) and (b)
(d) None of these

12 Sec function (secant function) is not defined for **NCERT Pg. 22**

(a) even multiples of $\frac{\pi}{2}$.

(b) odd multiples of $\frac{\pi}{2}$.

(c) even multiples of π.

(d) odd multiples of π.

13 Secant function is bijective when its domain and range are ..*A*.. and $R - (-1, 1)$, respectively. Here *A* refers to **NCERT Pg. 23**

(a) $[0, \pi]$ (b) $\left[0, \frac{\pi}{2}\right]$

(c) $[0, \pi] - \left\{\frac{\pi}{2}\right\}$ (d) None of these

14

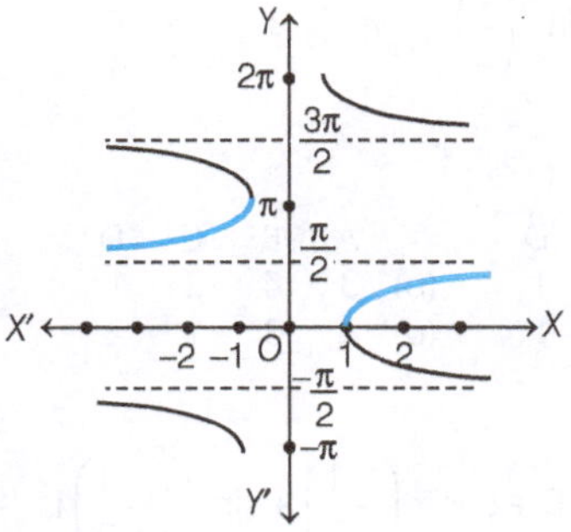

NCERT Pg. 23

Which of the following represents the above graph?

(a) $\sec^{-1} x$ (b) $\tan^{-1} x$

(c) $\text{cosec}^{-1} x$ (d) None of these

15 Tan function (tangent function) is not defined for ...*A*... Here, *A* refers to **NCERT Pg. 24**

(a) odd multiple of $\frac{\pi}{2}$.

(b) even multiple of $\frac{\pi}{2}$.

(c) an integral multiple of π

(d) None of the above

16 The graph of $\tan^{-1} x$ is **NCERT Pg. 24**

(a)

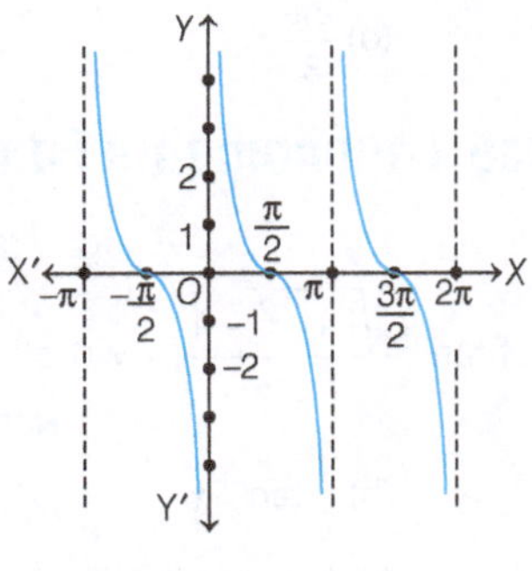

(b)

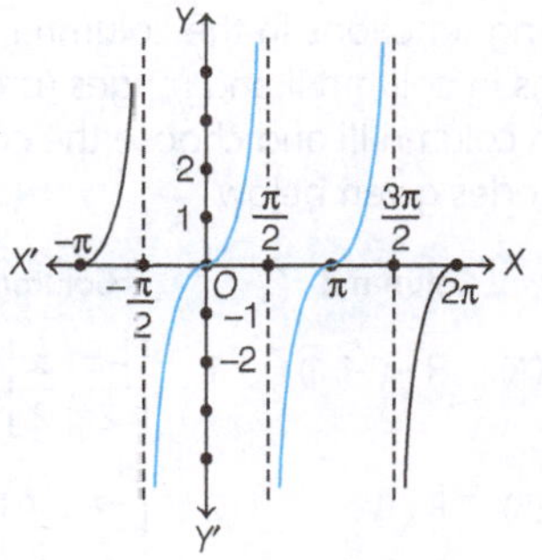

(c)

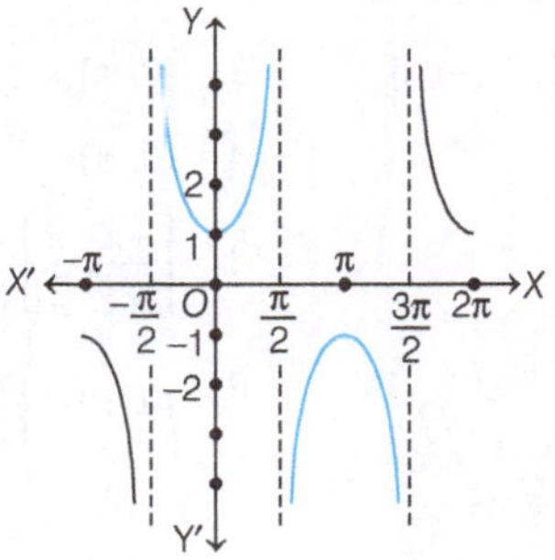

(d)

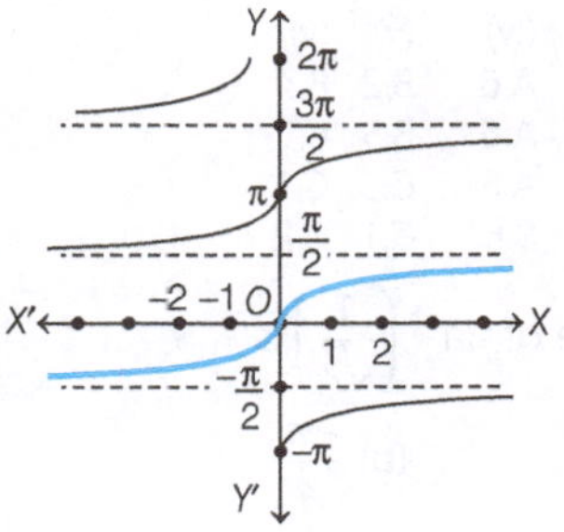

17 Which of the following is true? **NCERT Pg. 24**

(a) Cotangent function is not defined for odd multiples of $\frac{\pi}{2}$.

(b) Cotangent function is bijective when its range is R^+.

(c) Both (a) and (b)

(d) None of the above

18 Which of the following represents the given graph?

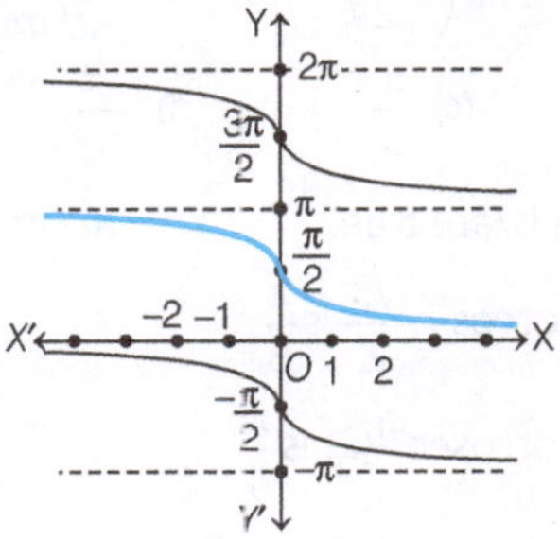

NCERT Pg. 25

(a) $\sec^{-1} x$ (b) $\tan^{-1} x$

(c) $\cot^{-1} x$ (d) $\text{cosec}^{-1} x$

19 Match the following functions in the column I along with their domains in column II and ranges (principal value branches) in column III and choose the correct option from the codes given below. NCERT Pg. 25

Column I	Column II	Column III
(i) $\sin^{-1}$	(A) $R-(-1, 1)$	1. $\left[\frac{-\pi}{2}, \frac{\pi}{2}\right]-\{0\}$
(ii) $\cos^{-1}$	(B) R	2. $\left(\frac{-\pi}{2}, \frac{\pi}{2}\right)$
(iii) cosec^{-1}	(C) $[-1, 1]$	3. $[0, \pi]$
(iv) $\sec^{-1}$		4. $(0, \pi)$
(v) $\tan^{-1}$		5. $\left[\frac{-\pi}{2}, \frac{\pi}{2}\right]$
(vi) $\cot^{-1}$		6. $[0, \pi]-\left\{\frac{\pi}{2}\right\}$

Codes

	(i)	(ii)	(iii)	(iv)	(v)	(vi)
(a)	C,5	C,3	A,1	A,6	B,2	B,4
(b)	C,4	C,3	A,2	A,6	B,5	B,1
(c)	B,4	B,3	A,2	A,6	C,5	C,1
(d)	A,4	A,3	A,5	B,6	C,1	C,2

20 The principal value of $\sin^{-1}\left(\frac{1}{\sqrt{2}}\right)$ is NCERT Pg. 26

(a) $\frac{\pi}{4}$ (b) $\frac{-\pi}{4}$

(c) $\frac{3\pi}{4}$ (d) None of these

21 The principal value of $\cot^{-1}\left(\frac{-1}{\sqrt{3}}\right)$ is ..*A*.. Here, *A* refers to NCERT Pg. 26

(a) $\frac{\pi}{3}$ (b) $\frac{-\pi}{3}$ (c) $\frac{2\pi}{3}$ (d) $\frac{4\pi}{3}$

22 The principal value of $\sin^{-1}\left(-\frac{1}{2}\right)$ is NCERT Pg. 26

(a) $\frac{-\pi}{6}$ (b) $\frac{\pi}{6}$ (c) $\frac{\pi}{3}$ (d) $\frac{-\pi}{3}$

23 Which of the following is/are true? NCERT Pg. 26

(i) The principal value of $\cos^{-1}\frac{\sqrt{3}}{2}$ is $\frac{\pi}{6}$.

(ii) The principal value of $\text{cosec}^{-1}(2)$ is $\frac{\pi}{4}$.

(iii) The principal value of $\tan^{-1}(-\sqrt{3})$ is $\frac{-\pi}{3}$.

(a) (i), (ii) (b) (ii), (iii)

(c) (i), (iii) (d) (i), (ii), (iii)

24 The principal value of $\sec^{-1}\frac{2}{\sqrt{3}}$ is ..*A*.. Here, *A* refers to NCERT Pg. 27

(a) $\frac{\pi}{3}$ (b) $\frac{\pi}{6}$ (c) $\frac{-\pi}{3}$ (d) $\frac{2\pi}{3}$

25 Match the inverse functions in column I with their principal values in column II and choose the correct option from the codes given below. NCERT Pg. 27

Column I		Column II
A. $\cot^{-1}(\sqrt{3})$	1.	$\frac{2\pi}{3}$
B. $\cos^{-1}\left(-\frac{1}{\sqrt{2}}\right)$	2.	$-\frac{\pi}{4}$
C. $\text{cosec}^{-1}(-\sqrt{2})$	3.	$\frac{3\pi}{4}$
D. $\cos^{-1}\left(\frac{1}{2}\right)+2\sin^{-1}\left(\frac{1}{2}\right)$	4.	$\frac{\pi}{6}$

Codes

	A	B	C	D		A	B	C	D
(a)	4	3	2	1	(b)	3	4	2	1
(c)	2	3	4	1	(d)	4	3	1	2

Level II

26 The value of $\tan^{-1}(1)+\cos^{-1}\left(-\frac{1}{2}\right)+\sin^{-1}\left(-\frac{1}{2}\right)$ is NCERT Pg. 27

(a) $\frac{\pi}{2}$ (b) $\frac{\pi}{4}$

(c) $\frac{3\pi}{4}$ (d) $\frac{2\pi}{3}$

27 If $\sin^{-1} x = y$, then NCERT Pg. 27

(a) $0 \le y \le \pi$ (b) $\frac{-\pi}{2} \le y \le \frac{\pi}{2}$

(c) $0 < y < \pi$ (d) $\frac{-\pi}{2} < y < \frac{\pi}{2}$

28 $\tan^{-1}\sqrt{3}-\sec^{-1}(-2)$ is equal to NCERT Pg. 27

(a) π (b) $\frac{\pi}{3}$

(c) $\frac{-\pi}{3}$ (d) $\frac{2\pi}{3}$

Properties of Inverse Trigonometric Functions

Level I

1 The simplest form of $\tan^{-1}\frac{\sqrt{1+x^2}-1}{x}, x \ne 0$ is NCERT Pg. 29

(a) $\tan^{-1} x$ (b) $\frac{1}{2}\tan^{-1} x$

(c) $2\tan^{-1} x$ (d) None of these

2 The function $\tan^{-1}\left(\sqrt{\frac{1-\cos x}{1+\cos x}}\right), 0<x<\pi$ in the simplest form is ...A... Here, A refers to **NCERT Pg. 29**

(a) x (b) $\frac{x}{2}$ (c) $\frac{x}{4}$ (d) $\frac{1}{2x}$

3 The function $\tan^{-1}\left(\frac{\cos x-\sin x}{\cos x+\sin x}\right), 0<x<\pi$ can be written as ...B... Here, B refers to **NCERT Pg. 29**

(a) $\frac{\pi}{2}-x$ (b) $\frac{\pi}{4}-x$ (c) $\pi-x$ (d) $-x$

4 The value of $\tan^{-1}\left[2\cos\left(2\sin^{-1}\frac{1}{2}\right)\right]$ is **NCERT Pg. 29**

(a) π (b) $\frac{\pi}{2}$ (c) $\frac{\pi}{4}$ (d) $\frac{\pi}{3}$

5 The value of the function $\tan\frac{1}{2}\left[\sin^{-1}\frac{2x}{1+x^2}+\cos^{-1}\frac{1-y^2}{1+y^2}\right], |x|<1, y>0$ and $xy<1$ is **NCERT Pg. 29**

(a) $x-y$ (b) $\frac{x-y}{1+xy}$ (c) $x+y$ (d) $\frac{x+y}{1-xy}$

6 Which of the following is the simplest form of $\cot^{-1}\left(\frac{1}{\sqrt{x^2-1}}\right), x>1$? **NCERT Pg. 29**

(a) $\cos^{-1}x$ (b) $\sec^{-1}x$ (c) $\tan x$ (d) $\cot x$

7 The value of $\sin^{-1}\left[\cos\left(\sin^{-1}\frac{\sqrt{3}}{2}\right)\right]$ is **NCERT Pg. 30**

(a) $\frac{\pi}{3}$ (b) $\frac{\pi}{6}$

(c) $\frac{-\pi}{3}$ (d) $\frac{-\pi}{6}$

8 The value of $\tan^{-1}\left(\tan\frac{7\pi}{6}\right)$ is **NCERT Pg. 30**

(a) $\frac{\pi}{6}$ (b) $\frac{-\pi}{6}$ (c) $\frac{\pi}{3}$ (d) $\frac{7\pi}{6}$

9 If $\frac{\pi}{2}\le x\le\frac{3\pi}{2}$, then $\sin^{-1}(\sin x)$ is equal to **NCERT Pg. 30**

(a) x (b) $-x$

(c) $\pi+x$ (d) $\pi-x$

10 The value of $\cos^{-1}\left(\cos\frac{14\pi}{3}\right)$ is ..A.. Here, A refers to **NCERT Pg. 30**

(a) $\frac{2\pi}{3}$ (b) $\frac{-\pi}{3}$

(c) $\frac{\pi}{6}$ (d) None of these

11 The value of $\tan^{-1}\left\{\tan\left(\frac{3\pi}{5}\right)\right\}$ is **NCERT Pg. 30**

(a) $\frac{3\pi}{5}$ (b) $\frac{-3\pi}{5}$

(c) $\frac{2\pi}{5}$ (d) $\frac{-2\pi}{5}$

12 The principal value of $\sin^{-1}\left[\sin\left(\frac{2\pi}{3}\right)\right]$ is **NCERT Pg. 30**

(a) $\frac{-2\pi}{3}$ (b) $\frac{2\pi}{3}$

(c) $\frac{4\pi}{3}$ (d) None of these

13 The value of $\tan^{-1}\left[2\sin\left(2\cos^{-1}\frac{\sqrt{3}}{2}\right)\right]$ is **NCERT Pg. 30**

(a) $\frac{\pi}{3}$ (b) $\frac{2\pi}{3}$ (c) $\frac{-\pi}{3}$ (d) $\frac{\pi}{6}$

14 The value of $\tan\left(\sin^{-1}\frac{3}{5}+\cot^{-1}\frac{3}{2}\right)$ is ...Y... . Here, Y refers to **NCERT Pg. 30**

(a) $\frac{6}{17}$ (b) $\frac{17}{6}$ (c) $\frac{17}{24}$ (d) $\frac{5}{7}$

15 $\cos^{-1}\left(\cos\frac{7\pi}{6}\right)$ is equal to **NCERT Pg. 30**

(a) $\frac{7\pi}{6}$ (b) $\frac{5\pi}{6}$

(c) $\frac{\pi}{3}$ (d) $\frac{\pi}{6}$

16 $\sin\left(\frac{\pi}{3}-\sin^{-1}\left(-\frac{1}{2}\right)\right)$ is equal to **NCERT Pg. 30**

(a) $\frac{1}{2}$ (b) $\frac{1}{3}$

(c) $\frac{1}{4}$ (d) 1

17 $\tan^{-1}\sqrt{3}-\cot^{-1}(-\sqrt{3})$ is equal to **NCERT Pg. 30**

(a) π (b) $-\frac{\pi}{2}$

(c) 0 (d) $2\sqrt{3}$

18 Which of the following is/are true? **Old NCERT Pg. 43**

(i) If $x\in[-1,1]$, then $\sin^{-1}(-x)=\pi-\sin^{-1}x$

(ii) $\tan^{-1}(-x)=-\tan^{-1}x, \forall x\in R$

(iii) $\text{cosec}^{-1}(-x)=-\text{cosec}^{-1}x, |x|\ge 1$

(a) (i) and (ii)

(b) (ii) and (iii)

(c) (i) and (iii)

(d) (i), (ii) and (iii)

19 Match the terms of column I with the terms of column II and choose the correct option from the codes given below. **Old NCERT Pg. 43**

Column I	Column II
A. $\cos^{-1}(-x)$	1. $\pi - \sec^{-1}x, \|x\| \geq 1$
B. $\sec^{-1}(-x)$	2. $\pi - \cot^{-1}x, x \in R$
C. $\cot^{-1}(-x)$	3. $\pi - \cos^{-1}x, x \in [-1, 1]$

Codes

	A	B	C		A	B	C
(a)	1	2	3	(b)	3	1	2
(c)	2	1	3	(d)	3	2	1

20 Which of the following is/are true? **Old NCERT Pg. 43**

(i) $\sin^{-1}x + \cos^{-1}x = \frac{\pi}{2}, x \in [-1, 1]$

(ii) $\tan^{-1}x + \cot^{-1}x = \frac{\pi}{2}, x \in R$

(iii) $\text{cosec}^{-1}x + \sec^{-1}x = \frac{\pi}{2}, |x| \geq 1$

(a) (i), (ii) (b) (ii), (iii)
(c) (i), (iii) (d) (i), (ii), (iii)

21 The value of $2\tan^{-1}x$ is **Old NCERT Pg. 44**

(a) $\sin^{-1}\frac{2x}{1+x^2}, |x| \leq 1$ (b) $\cos^{-1}\frac{1-x^2}{1+x^2}, x \geq 0$

(c) $\tan^{-1}\frac{2x}{1-x^2}, -1 < x < 1$ (d) All of these

22 The value of $\tan^{-1}\frac{1}{2} + \tan^{-1}\frac{2}{11}$ is **Old NCERT Pg. 45**

(a) $\tan^{-1}\frac{3}{4}$ (b) $\tan^{-1}\frac{1}{4}$

(c) $\tan^{-1}\frac{1}{2}$ (d) None of these

23 Match the terms of column I with the terms of column II and choose the correct option from the codes given below. **Old NCERT Pg. 47**

Column I	Column II
A. $\sin^{-1}(3x - 4x^3), x \in \left[-\frac{1}{2}, \frac{1}{2}\right]$	1. $\tan^{-1}\frac{31}{17}$
B. $\tan^{-1}\frac{2}{11} + \tan^{-1}\frac{7}{24}$	2. $3\sin^{-1}x$
C. $\cos^{-1}(4x^3 - 3x), x \in \left[\frac{1}{2}, 1\right]$	3. $\tan^{-1}\frac{1}{2}$
D. $2\tan^{-1}\frac{1}{2} + \tan^{-1}\frac{1}{7}$	4. $3\cos^{-1}x$

Codes

	A	B	C	D		A	B	C	D
(a)	2	1	4	3	(b)	3	1	4	2
(c)	3	4	2	1	(d)	2	3	4	1

24 $\tan^{-1}\frac{1}{\sqrt{x^2-1}}, |x| > 1$ can be written as **Old NCERT Pg. 47**

(a) $\sec^{-1}x$ (b) $\cos^{-1}x$

(c) $\frac{\pi}{2} - \sec^{-1}x$ (d) $\frac{\pi}{2} - \cos^{-1}x$

25 The value of $\cot(\tan^{-1}a + \cot^{-1}a)$ is **Old NCERT Pg. 48**

(a) 0 (b) 1 (c) -1 (d) ∞

26 The value of x for which $\sin\left(\sin^{-1}\frac{1}{5} + \cos^{-1}x\right) = 1$, is **Old NCERT Pg. 48**

(a) $\frac{2}{5}$ (b) $\frac{1}{5}$ (c) $-\frac{1}{5}$ (d) -1

Level II

27 The value of

$$\tan^{-1}\left(\frac{-1}{\sqrt{3}}\right) + \cot^{-1}\left(\frac{1}{\sqrt{3}}\right) + \tan^{-1}\left(\sin\left(-\frac{\pi}{2}\right)\right)$$ is **NCERT Pg. 29**

(a) $\frac{\pi}{6}$ (b) $\frac{\pi}{12}$ (c) $-\frac{\pi}{12}$ (d) $\frac{\pi}{3}$

28 The value of $\sin^{-1}\left(\cos\left(\frac{33\pi}{5}\right)\right)$ is **NCERT Pg. 30**

(a) $\frac{3\pi}{5}$ (b) $\frac{-7\pi}{5}$ (c) $\frac{\pi}{10}$ (d) $-\frac{\pi}{10}$

29 The principal value of the expression $\cos^{-1}[\cos(-680°)]$ is **NCERT Pg. 27**

(a) $\frac{2\pi}{9}$ (b) $\frac{-2\pi}{9}$ (c) $\frac{34\pi}{9}$ (d) $\frac{\pi}{9}$

30 The value of $\cos(\tan^{-1}x)$ is **NCERT Pg. 42**

(a) $\sqrt{1+x^2}$ (b) $\frac{1}{\sqrt{1+x^2}}$

(c) $1 + x^2$ (d) None of these

31 If $\sin^{-1}\frac{1}{3} + \sin^{-1}\frac{2}{3} = \sin^{-1}x$, then x is equal to **Old NCERT Pg. 42**

(a) 0 (b) $\frac{\sqrt{5} - 4\sqrt{2}}{9}$

(c) $\frac{\sqrt{5} + 4\sqrt{2}}{9}$ (d) $\frac{\pi}{2}$

32 If $\tan^{-1}x + \tan^{-1}y = \frac{\pi}{4}$, $xy < 1$, then the value of $x + y + xy$ is **Old NCERT Pg. 44**

(a) 0 (b) -1 (c) 1 (d) 2

33 If $\tan^{-1}\sqrt{3} + \cot^{-1}x = \frac{\pi}{2}$, then the value of x is **Old NCERT Pg. 43**

(a) $\frac{1}{\sqrt{3}}$ (b) $-\sqrt{3}$ (c) $\sqrt{3}$ (d) $-\frac{1}{\sqrt{3}}$

34. The value of $\cos\left[\sin^{-1}\frac{1}{4}+\sec^{-1}\frac{4}{3}\right]$ is **NCERT Pg. 28**

(a) $\frac{3\sqrt{5}-\sqrt{7}}{16}$ (b) $\frac{3\sqrt{15}-\sqrt{7}}{16}$

(c) $\frac{3\sqrt{15}+\sqrt{7}}{16}$ (d) None of these

35 The solution of the equation $\sin^{-1}6x+\sin^{-1}6\sqrt{3}x=-\frac{\pi}{2}$ is ...*A*... Here, *A* refers to **NCERT Pg. 27**

(a) $\frac{1}{12}$ (b) $-\frac{1}{12}$ (c) 3 (d) –3

36 The greatest and least value of $(\sin^{-1}x)^2+(\cos^{-1}x)^2$ are, respectively **Old NCERT Pg. 43**

(a) $\frac{5\pi^2}{4}$ and $\frac{\pi^2}{8}$ (b) $\frac{\pi}{2}$ and $-\frac{\pi}{2}$

(c) $\frac{\pi^2}{4}$ and $-\frac{\pi^2}{4}$ (d) $\frac{\pi^2}{4}$ and 0

37 The value of $\tan\left(\cos^{-1}\frac{3}{5}+\tan^{-1}\frac{1}{4}\right)$ is **Old NCERT Pg. 44**

(a) $\frac{19}{8}$ (b) $\frac{8}{19}$ (c) $\frac{19}{12}$ (d) $\frac{3}{4}$

38 The value of $\sin\left(2\tan^{-1}\frac{2}{3}\right)+\cos(\tan^{-1}\sqrt{3})$ is **Old NCERT Pg. 44**

(a) $\frac{26}{37}$ (b) $\frac{37}{26}$ (c) $\frac{12}{13}$ (d) $\frac{13}{15}$

39 If $\cot^{-1}\left(\frac{1+x}{1-x}\right)=\frac{1}{2}\cot^{-1}\left(\frac{1}{x}\right)$, $x>0$, then the value of x is **Old NCERT Pg. 43**

(a) $\sqrt{3}$ (b) $\frac{1}{\sqrt{3}}$

(c) $-\frac{1}{\sqrt{3}}$ (d) None of these

40 If $\sin(\cot^{-1}(x+1))=\cos(\tan^{-1}x)$, then the value of x is **Old NCERT Pg. 43**

(a) $-\frac{1}{2}$ (b) $\frac{1}{2}$ (c) 0 (d) $\frac{9}{4}$

41 If $\tan^{-1}2x+\tan^{-1}3x=\frac{\pi}{4}$, then x is equal to **Old NCERT Pg. 44**

(a) –1 (b) $-1, \frac{1}{10}$

(c) $\frac{1}{6}$ (d) None of these

42 If $\sin^{-1}\left(\frac{2a}{1+a^2}\right)+\cos^{-1}\left(\frac{1-a^2}{1+a^2}\right)=\tan^{-1}\frac{2x}{1-x^2}$, where $a, x\in[0,1]$, then the value of x is **Old NCERT Pg. 44**

(a) 0 (b) $\frac{a}{2}$ (c) a (d) $\frac{2a}{1-a^2}$

Miscellaneous Exercise

1 If $2\sin^{-1}\frac{3}{5}=\tan^{-1}x$, then x is equal to **Old NCERT Pg. 51**

(a) $\frac{24}{5}$ (b) $\frac{24}{7}$

(c) $\frac{3}{4}$ (d) $\frac{24}{25}$

2 The simplest form of $\tan^{-1}\left[\frac{a\cos x-b\sin x}{b\cos x+a\sin x}\right]$, if $\frac{a}{b}\tan x>-1$ is **Old NCERT Pg. 50**

(a) $\tan^{-1}\frac{a}{b}$ (b) $\tan^{-1}\frac{a}{b}+x$

(c) $\tan^{-1}\frac{a}{b}-x$ (d) $-x$

3 If $\cos^{-1}\frac{12}{13}+\sin^{-1}\frac{3}{5}=\sin^{-1}x$, then the value of x is **NCERT Pg. 31**

(a) $\frac{5}{13}$ (b) $\frac{63}{65}$ (c) $\frac{56}{65}$ (d) $\frac{56}{63}$

4 $\tan^{-1}\ldots A\ldots=\sin^{-1}\frac{5}{13}+\cos^{-1}\frac{3}{5}$. Here, *A* refers to **NCERT Pg. 31**

(a) $\frac{63}{16}$ (b) $\frac{63}{65}$ (c) $\frac{12}{13}$ (d) $\frac{25}{63}$

5 $\tan^{-1}\frac{1}{5}+\tan^{-1}\frac{1}{7}+\tan^{-1}\frac{1}{3}+\tan^{-1}\frac{1}{8}$ is equal to **Old NCERT Pg. 51**

(a) 0 (b) $\frac{\pi}{2}$ (c) $\frac{\pi}{4}$ (d) π

6 If $x\in[0,1]$, then $\frac{1}{2}\cos^{-1}\left(\frac{1-x}{1+x}\right)=\ldots A\ldots$

Here, *A* stands for **NCERT Pg. 31**

(a) $\tan^{-1}x$ (b) $\tan^{-1}x^2$

(c) $\tan^{-1}\sqrt{x}$ (d) $\tan^{-1}\frac{1}{x}$

7 If $\frac{9\pi}{8}-\frac{9}{4}\sin^{-1}\frac{1}{3}=\frac{9}{4}\sin^{-1}x$, then the value of x is **Old NCERT Pg. 52**

(a) $\frac{\sqrt{2}}{3}$ (b) $\frac{2\sqrt{2}}{3}$ (c) $2\sqrt{2}$ (d) $\frac{2}{3}$

8 $\sin(\tan^{-1}x), |x|<1$ is equal to **NCERT Pg. 31**

(a) $\frac{x}{\sqrt{1-x^2}}$ (b) $\frac{1}{\sqrt{1-x^2}}$

(c) $\frac{1}{\sqrt{1+x^2}}$ (d) $\frac{x}{\sqrt{1+x^2}}$

9 $\tan^{-1}\left(\frac{x}{y}\right)-\tan^{-1}\left(\frac{x-y}{x+y}\right)$ is equal to **Old NCERT Pg. 52**

(a) $\frac{\pi}{2}$ (b) $\frac{\pi}{3}$ (c) $\frac{\pi}{4}$ (d) $\frac{-3\pi}{4}$

10 $\sin^{-1}(1-x)-2\sin^{-1}x=\frac{\pi}{2}$, then x is equal to **NCERT Pg. 31**

(a) $0, \frac{1}{2}$ (b) $1, \frac{1}{2}$

(c) 0 (d) $\frac{1}{2}$

11 If $\cos^{-1}x>\sin^{-1}x$, then **NCERT Pg. 20**

(a) $\frac{1}{\sqrt{2}}<x<1$ (b) $0\le x<\frac{1}{\sqrt{2}}$

(c) $-1\le x<\frac{1}{\sqrt{2}}$ (d) $x>0$

12 The value of $\tan^{-1}\frac{\sqrt{1+x^2}+\sqrt{1-x^2}}{\sqrt{1+x^2}-\sqrt{1-x^2}}$ is equal to **Old NCERT Pg. 52**

(a) $\frac{\pi}{4}+\cos^{-1}x^2$ (b) $\frac{\pi}{2}+\frac{1}{2}\cos^{-1}x^2$

(c) $\frac{\pi}{4}+\frac{1}{2}\cos^{-1}x^2$ (d) $\cos^{-1}x^2$

13 The domain of the function $y=\sin^{-1}(-x^2)$ is **NCERT Pg. 20**

(a) [0, 1] (b) [0, 2]
(c) [−1, 1] (d) ϕ

14 The number of real solutions of the equation $\tan^{-1}\sqrt{x(x+1)}+\sin^{-1}\sqrt{x^2+x+1}=\frac{\pi}{2}$ is **NCERT Pg. 20, 22**

(a) 0 (b) 1
(c) 2 (d) 3

15 The domain of $y=\cos^{-1}(x^2-4)$ is **NCERT Pg. 21**

(a) [3, 5]
(b) $[0, \pi]$
(c) $[-\sqrt{5},-\sqrt{3}]\cap[-\sqrt{5},\sqrt{3}]$
(d) $[-\sqrt{5},-\sqrt{3}]\cup[\sqrt{3},\sqrt{5}]$

16 The value of $\sin[2\sin^{-1}(0.6)]$ is **Old NCERT Pg. 42**

(a) 0.48 (b) 0.96
(c) 1.2 (d) sin 1.2

17 The value of $\tan\left(\frac{\pi}{4}+\frac{1}{2}\cos^{-1}\frac{a}{b}\right)+\tan\left(\frac{\pi}{4}-\frac{1}{2}\cos^{-1}\frac{a}{b}\right)$ is **Old NCERT Pg. 42**

(a) $\frac{a}{b}$ (b) $\frac{b}{a}$

(c) $\frac{2a}{b}$ (d) $\frac{2b}{a}$

18 Which of the following is true? **NCERT Pg. 24**

(a) $\tan^{-1}1=\tan 1$ (b) $\tan 1>\tan^{-1}1$

(c) $\tan 1<\tan^{-1}1$ (d) None of these

19 If $\sin^{-1}x+\sin^{-1}y=\frac{\pi}{2}$, then the value of $\cos^{-1}x+\cos^{-1}y$ is **Old NCERT Pg. 43**

(a) $\frac{\pi}{2}$ (b) π

(c) 0 (d) $\frac{2\pi}{3}$

20 The domain of the function defined by $f(x)=\sin^{-1}x+\cos x$ is **NCERT Pg. 20**

(a) [−1, 1] (b) $[-1, \pi+1]$
(c) $(-\infty, \infty)$ (d) ϕ

21 If $a_1, a_2, a_3, \cdots, a_n$ is an arithmetic progression with common difference d, then the value of the expression,

$$\tan\left[\tan^{-1}\left(\frac{d}{1+a_1a_2}\right)+\tan^{-1}\left(\frac{d}{1+a_2a_3}\right)+\cdots+\tan^{-1}\left(\frac{d}{1+a_{n-1}a_n}\right)\right]$$ is **Old NCERT Pg. 44**

(a) a_n-a_1 (b) $\frac{a_n-a_1}{a_1a_n}$

(c) $\frac{a_n-a_1}{1+a_na_1}$ (d) Does not exist

22 The value of $\sin(2\tan^{-1}(0.75))$ is equal to **NCERT Pg. 27**

(a) 0.75 (b) 1.5
(c) 0.96 (d) sin 1.5

23 The equation $\tan^{-1}x-\cot^{-1}x=\tan^{-1}\left(\frac{1}{\sqrt{3}}\right)$ has **Old NCERT Pg. 44**

(a) no solution.
(b) unique solution.
(c) infinite number of solutions.
(d) two solutions.

24 If $\alpha\le 2\sin^{-1}x+\cos^{-1}x\le\beta$, then **NCERT Pg. 27**

(a) $\alpha=-\frac{\pi}{2}, \beta=\frac{\pi}{2}$ (b) $\alpha=0, \beta=\pi$

(c) $\alpha=-\frac{\pi}{2}, \beta=\frac{3\pi}{2}$ (d) $\alpha=0, \beta=2\pi$

25 The value of $\tan^2(\sec^{-1}2)+\cot^2(\text{cosec}^{-1}3)$ is **NCERT Pg. 27**

(a) 5 (b) 13
(c) 11 (d) 15

26 The simplest form of $\sin^{-1}[x\sqrt{1-x}-\sqrt{x}\sqrt{1-x^2}]$ is **Old NCERT Pg. 42**

(a) $\sin^{-1}x+\sin^{-1}\sqrt{x}$ (b) $\sin^{-1}x-\sin^{-1}\sqrt{x}$
(c) $\sin^{-1}\sqrt{x}-\sin^{-1}x$ (d) None of these

27 The number of real solutions of the equation $\sqrt{1+\cos 2x}=\sqrt{2}\cos^{-1}(\cos x)$ in $\left[\frac{\pi}{2},\pi\right]$ is **NCERT Pg. 27**

(a) 0 (b) 1
(c) 2 (d) infinite

28 The value of $x^2 + y^2 + z^2 + 2xyz$, if $\sin^{-1} x + \sin^{-1} y + \sin^{-1} z = \frac{\pi}{2}$ is **Old NCERT Pg. 42**

(a) 0 (b) 1 (c) 2 (d) 3

29 The value of $\cos\left[2\cos^{-1}\frac{1}{5} + \sin^{-1}\frac{1}{5}\right]$ is **Old NCERT Pg. 48**

(a) $\frac{2\sqrt{6}}{5}$ (b) $\frac{-2\sqrt{6}}{5}$ (c) $\frac{1}{5}$ (d) $-\frac{1}{5}$

30 The value of $\tan\left[\cos^{-1}\frac{4}{5} + \tan^{-1}\frac{2}{3}\right]$ is **Old NCERT Pg. 44**

(a) $\frac{6}{17}$ (b) $\frac{17}{6}$ (c) $\frac{7}{16}$ (d) $\frac{16}{7}$

31 If $\tan^{-1}\left(\frac{a+x}{a}\right) + \tan^{-1}\left(\frac{a-x}{a}\right) = \frac{\pi}{6}$, then x^2 is **Old NCERT Pg. 44**

(a) $2\sqrt{3}\ a$
(b) $\sqrt{3}\ a$
(c) $2\sqrt{3}\ a^2$
(d) None of the above

32 The value of $\cos[\tan^{-1}\{\sin(\cot^{-1} x)\}]$ is **Old NCERT Pg. 52**

(a) $\frac{1}{\sqrt{x^2+2}}$ (b) $\sqrt{\frac{x^2+2}{x^2+1}}$

(c) $\sqrt{\frac{x^2+1}{x^2+2}}$ (d) $\frac{1}{\sqrt{x^2+1}}$

Numerical Type Questions

1 The value of $\sec^2(\tan^{-1} 2) + \text{cosec}^2(\cot^{-1} 3)$ is ...... **NCERT Pg. 30**

2 If the domain of the function $f(x) = \sin^{-1}\left(\frac{x+1}{3x+2}\right)$ is $R - (\alpha, \beta)$, then the value of $8\alpha\beta$ is ...... **NCERT Pg. 20**

3 If the range of $y = \sin^{-1}\sqrt{x^2+x+1}$ is $\left[\frac{\pi}{\alpha}, \frac{\pi}{2}\right]$, then the value of α is equal to ...... **NCERT Pg. 20**

4 If $\sin^{-1}(\sin 3) + \sin^{-1}(\sin 4) + \sin^{-1}(\sin 5) = -k$, then the value of k is ...... **NCERT Pg. 30**

5 The number of positive integer solution of $\tan^{-1} x + \tan^{-1} y = \tan^{-1} 3$ is ...... **Old NCERT Pg. 44**

6 If $\tan^{-1}\left(\frac{x-1}{x+1}\right) + \tan^{-1}\left(\frac{2x-1}{2x+1}\right) = \tan^{-1}\left(\frac{23}{36}\right)$, then the value of $3x$ is ...... **Old NCERT Pg. 44**

7 If $\cot\left[\tan^{-1}\left(\frac{4}{1+3\cdot 4}\right) + \tan^{-1}\left(\frac{6}{1+8\cdot 9}\right) + \tan^{-1}\left(\frac{8}{1+15\cdot 16}\right) + \ldots\infty\right] = \lambda$

Then, λ is equal to ...... **Old NCERT Pg. 44**

8 The product of all values of x satisfying the equation

$$\sin^{-1}\left[\cos\left(\frac{2x^2+10|x|+4}{x^2+5|x|+3}\right)\right] = \cot\left[\cot^{-1}\left(\frac{2-18|x|}{9|x|}\right)\right] + \frac{\pi}{2}$$

is ...... **Old NCERT Pg. 43**

9 If $3\sin^{-1}(\log_2 x) + \cos^{-1}(\log_2 y) = \frac{\pi}{2}$ and $\sin^{-1}(\log_2 x) + 2\cos^{-1}(\log_2 y) = \frac{11\pi}{6}$, then the value of $\frac{1}{x^2} + \frac{1}{y^2}$ is ...... **Old NCERT Pg. 51**

10 The total number of solution of the equation $\sin[2\cos^{-1}\{\cot(2\tan^{-1} x)\}] = 0$ is ...... **Old NCERT Pg. 48**

11 If $f(x) = \tan^{-1}\left(\frac{x-2}{x^2+2x+2}\right)$, then the value of $26f'(1)$ is ...... **Old NCERT Pg. 44**

12 If $\sum_{n=0}^{\infty} 2\,\text{arccot}\left(\frac{n^2+n+4}{2}\right) = k\pi$, then the value of k is ...... **Old NCERT Pg. 44**

13 If $\sin(30° + \text{arc}\tan x) = \frac{13}{14}$ and $0 < x < 1$, the value of x is $\frac{a\sqrt{3}}{b}$, where a and b are positive integers with no common factors, then the value of $\left(\frac{a+b}{2}\right)$ is ...... **NCERT Pg. 27**

Assertion and Reason Questions

Direction (Q. Nos. 1-13) In the questions given below are to statements labelled as Assertion (A) and Reason (R). In the context on the two statements, which one of the following is correct?

(a) Both Assertion and Reason are correct and Reason is the correct explanation of Assertion.
(b) Both Assertion and Reason are correct but Reason is not the correct explanation of Assertion.
(c) Assertion is correct but Reason is incorrect.
(d) Assertion is incorrect but Reason is correct.

1 **Assertion (A)** $\operatorname{cosec}^{-1}$ is define as a function whose domain is $R-(-1,1)$ and range could be any of the intervals $\left[\frac{-\pi}{2},\frac{\pi}{2}\right]-\{0\},\left[\frac{-3\pi}{2},\frac{-\pi}{2}\right]-\{-\pi\}$, $\left[\frac{\pi}{2},\frac{3\pi}{2}\right]-\{\pi\}$ etc.

Reason (R) If cosec function is bijective, then the intervals $\left[\frac{-3\pi}{2},\frac{-\pi}{2}\right]-\{-\pi\},\left[\frac{-\pi}{2},\frac{\pi}{2}\right]-\{0\}$, $\left[\frac{\pi}{2},\frac{3\pi}{2}\right]-\{\pi\}$ etc., are the domain and range is the set of all real numbers $R-(-1, 1)$. NCERT Pg. 21

2 **Assertion (A)** $\tan^{-1}$ is defined as a function if the domain is R and range is any of the intervals $\left(\frac{-3\pi}{2},\frac{-\pi}{2}\right),\left(\frac{-\pi}{2},\frac{\pi}{2}\right)\left(\frac{\pi}{2},\frac{3\pi}{2}\right)$ and so on.

Reason (R) The principal value branch of $\tan^{-1}$ is $\left(\frac{-\pi}{2},\frac{\pi}{2}\right)$.

NCERT Pg. 24

3 **Assertion (A)** The value of $\cos^{-1}\left[\cos\left(\frac{13\pi}{6}\right)\right]$ is $\frac{\pi}{6}$.

Reason (R) $\cos^{-1}(\cos x)=x\,;\,x\in[0,\pi]$. NCERT Pg. 30

4 **Assertion (A)** If $\tan^{-1}\frac{x-1}{x-2}+\tan^{-1}\frac{x+1}{x+2}=\frac{\pi}{4}$, then the value of x is $\pm\frac{1}{\sqrt{2}}$.

Reason (R) The value of $\tan^{-1}\left(\tan\frac{3\pi}{4}\right)$ is $\frac{\pi}{4}$.

Old NCERT Pg. 44

5 **Assertion (A)** $\cot^{-1}\left(\frac{\sqrt{1+\sin x}+\sqrt{1-\sin x}}{\sqrt{1+\sin x}-\sqrt{1-\sin x}}\right)=\frac{x}{2}, x\in\left(0,\frac{\pi}{4}\right)$.

Reason (R) $\tan^{-1}\left(\frac{\sqrt{1+x}-\sqrt{1-x}}{\sqrt{1+x}+\sqrt{1-x}}\right)=\frac{\pi}{4},-\frac{1}{\sqrt{2}}\le x\le 1$.

NCERT Pg. 27

6 **Assertion (A)** $\tan^{-1}x+\cot^{-1}(x+1)=\tan^{-1}(x^2+x)$.

Reason (R) $\cot^{-1}\frac{xy+1}{x-y}+\cot^{-1}\frac{yz+1}{y-z}+\cot^{-1}\frac{zx+1}{z-x}=\pi$.

Old NCERT Pg. 44

7 **Assertion (A)** The value of $\sin^{-1}(\sin 10)$ is $3\pi-10$

Reason (R) The value of $\cos^{-1}(\cos 10)$ is $4\pi-10$

NCERT Pg. 20

8 **Assertion (A)** If $\sin^{-1}x+\sin^{-1}y+\sin^{-1}z=\frac{3\pi}{2}$.Then

$x^{2020}+y^{2021}+z^{2022}-\frac{9}{x^{2022}+y^{2024}+z^{2026}}=0$.

Reason (R) The greatest value of $\sin^{-1}x$ is $\frac{\pi}{2}$ at $x=1$.

NCERT Pg. 20

9 **Assertion (A)** If $\frac{1}{2}\le x\le 1$, then

$\cos^{-1}x-\sin^{-1}\left\{\frac{x}{2}+\frac{\sqrt{3-3x^2}}{2}\right\}$ is equal to $-\frac{\pi}{6}$.

Reason (R) $\sin^{-1}(2x\sqrt{1-x^2})=2\sin^{-1}x$, if $x\in\left[-\frac{1}{\sqrt{2}},\frac{1}{\sqrt{2}}\right]$.

NCERT Pg. 27

10 **Assertion (A)** $\sin^{-1}\left\{x-\frac{x^2}{2}+\frac{x^3}{2}-......\right\}$

$=\frac{\pi}{2}-\cos^{-1}\left\{x^2-\frac{x^4}{2}+\frac{x^6}{4}-......\right\}$

for $0<|x|<\sqrt{2}$ has a unique solution.

Reason (R) $\tan^{-1}\sqrt{x(x+1)}+\sin^{-1}\sqrt{x^2+x+1}=\frac{\pi}{2}$ has no solution for $-\sqrt{2}<x<0$. Old NCERT Pg. 43

11 **Assertion (A)** If $a^2+b^2=c^2, c\ne 0, ab\ne 0$, then the non zero solution of the equation,

$\sin^{-1}\left(\frac{ax}{c}\right)+\sin^{-1}\left(\frac{bx}{c}\right)=\sin^{-1}x$ is ± 1.

Reason (R) $\sin^{-1}x+\sin^{-1}y=\sin^{-1}(x+y)$. NCERT Pg. 27

12 **Assertion (A)** All trigonometric functions have their inverses over the respective principal domain.

Reason (R) The inverse of $\tan^{-1}x: R\to\left(-\frac{\pi}{2},\frac{\pi}{2}\right)$ exists.

NCERT Pg. 25

13 **Assertion (A)** $\tan^{-1}2+\tan^{-1}3=\frac{3\pi}{4}$

Reason (R) $\tan^{-1}x+\tan^{-1}y=\pi+\tan^{-1}\left(\frac{x-y}{1-xy}\right)$; if $x>0, y>0$ and $xy>1$ Old NCERT Pg. 44

Case or Paragraph Type Questions

Direction (Q. Nos. 1-4) Two men on either side of a Tower of 30 m high observe its top at the angles of elevation α and β, respectively (as shown in figure). The distance between two men is $40\sqrt{3}$ m and the distance between the first person A and the tower is $30\sqrt{3}$ m. Based upon the above information, answer the following. NCERT Pg. 20

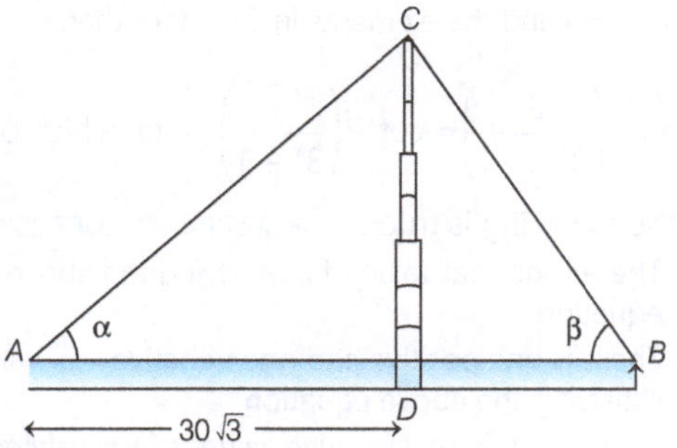

1 $\angle CAB =$

(a) $\sin^{-1}\left(\frac{2}{\sqrt{3}}\right)$

(b) $\sin^{-1}\left(\frac{1}{2}\right)$

(c) $\sin^{-1} 2$

(d) $\sin^{-1} \frac{\sqrt{3}}{2}$

2 The domain and Range of the function $f(x) = \sin^{-1} x$

(a) $(-1, 1)$ and $[0, \pi]$

(b) $[-1, 1]$ and $\left[-\frac{\pi}{2}, \frac{\pi}{2}\right]$

(c) $[-1, 1]$ and $\left[0, \frac{\pi}{2}\right]$

(d) $(-1, 1)$ and $\left[-\frac{\pi}{2}, \frac{\pi}{2}\right]$

3 $\angle CBA = ?$

(a) $\tan^{-1} \frac{1}{2}$

(b) $\tan^{-1} 2$

(c) $\tan^{-1} \frac{1}{\sqrt{3}}$

(d) $\tan^{-1} \sqrt{3}$

4 The domain and Range of $f(x) = \tan^{-1} x$ are

(a) $(-\infty, \infty)$ and $\left(-\frac{\pi}{2}, \frac{\pi}{2}\right)$

(b) $(0, \infty)$ and $\left(-\frac{\pi}{2}, \frac{\pi}{2}\right)$

(c) $(-\infty, \infty)$ and $\left[-\frac{\pi}{2}, \frac{\pi}{2}\right]$

(d) $(-\infty, \infty)$ and $(0, \pi)$

Direction (Q. Nos. 5-7) We know $\sin^{-1}: [-1, 1] \to \left[-\frac{\pi}{2}, \frac{\pi}{2}\right]$,

$\cos^{-1} [-1, 1] \to [0, \pi]$,

and $\sin^{-1} x + \cos^{-1} x = \pi / 2$

Answer the following by using above information. NCERT Pg. 20, 21

5 The domain and Range of the function $f(x) = \sin^{-1}(x) + \cos^{-1}(x)$ are

(a) $[-1, 0]$ and $\left[-\frac{\pi}{0}, 0\right]$

(b) $[-1, 1]$ and $\left[0, \frac{\pi}{2}\right]$

(c) $[-1, 1]$ and $\left[\frac{\pi}{2}\right]$

(d) None of the above

6 The Range of the function $f(x) = (\sin^{-1} x)^2 + (\cos^{-1} x)^2$

(a) $\left[\frac{\pi^2}{4}, \frac{5\pi^2}{4}\right]$

(b) $\left[\frac{\pi^2}{8}, \frac{5\pi^2}{8}\right]$

(c) $\left[\frac{\pi^2}{8}, \frac{5\pi^2}{4}\right]$

(d) None of these

7 If $\sin^{-1} x + \sin^{-1} y = \frac{\pi}{2}$, then the value of $\cos^{-1} x + \cos^{-1} y$ is

(a) $\frac{\pi}{2}$

(b) π

(c) 0

(d) $\frac{2\pi}{3}$

Past Years Questions

Single Correct Type

1 Considering only the principal values of inverse trigonometric functinos, the number of positive real values of x satisfying $\tan^{-1}(x)+\tan^{-1}(2x)=\frac{\pi}{4}$ is

Old NCERT Pg. 51, JEE Main 2024, 27 Jan Shift-II

(a) 2 (b) 0
(c) more than 2 (d) 1

2 For $\alpha, \beta, \gamma = \theta$, if $\sin^{-1}\alpha+\sin^{-1}\beta+\sin^{-1}\gamma=\pi$ and $(\alpha+\beta+\gamma)(\alpha-\gamma+\beta)=3\alpha\beta$, then γ equals

NCERT Pg. 27, JEE Main 2023 Jan Shift-I

(a) $\frac{\sqrt{3}-1}{2\sqrt{2}}$ (b) $\sqrt{3}$ (c) $\frac{\sqrt{3}}{2}$ (d) $\frac{1}{\sqrt{2}}$

3 If the domain of the function $f(x)=\sin^{-1}\left(\frac{x-1}{2x+3}\right)$ is $R-(\alpha,\beta)$, then $12\alpha\beta$ is equal to

NCERT Pg. 20, JEE Main 2024, 9 April Shift-I

(a) 36 (b) 32 (c) 40 (d) 24

4 If the domain of the function $f(x)=\log_e\left(\frac{2x+3}{4x^2+x-3}\right)+\cos^{-1}\left(\frac{2x-1}{x+2}\right)$ is $(\alpha,\beta]$, then the value of $5\beta-4\alpha$ is equal to

NCERT Pg. 21, JEE Main 2024, 30 Jan Shift-II

(a) 11 (b) 9 (c) 12 (d) 10

5 Given that the inverse trigonometric function assumes principal values only. Let x, y be any two real numbers in $[-1, 1]$ such that $\cos^{-1}x-\sin^{-1}y=\alpha$, $\frac{-\pi}{2}\le\alpha\le\pi$. Then, the minimum value of $x^2+y^2+2x\sin\alpha$ is

Old NCERT Pg. 43, JEE Main 2024, 4 April Shift-II

(a) 0 (b) $\frac{-1}{2}$ (c) $\frac{1}{2}$ (d) -1

6 Let $a_1=1, a_2, a_3, a_4, \ldots\ldots$ be consecutive natural numbers. Then, $\tan^{-1}\left(\frac{1}{1+a_1a_2}\right)+\tan^{-1}\left(\frac{1}{1+a_2a_3}\right)+\ldots+\tan^{-1}\left(\frac{1}{1+a_{2021}\,a_{2022}}\right)$ is equal to

Old NCERT Pg. 43, JEE Main 2023, 30 Jan Shift-II

(a) $\frac{\pi}{4}-\cot^{-1}(2022)$ (b) $\tan^{-1}(2022)-\frac{\pi}{4}$
(c) $\frac{\pi}{4}-\tan^{-1}(2022)$ (d) $\cot^{-1}(2022)-\frac{\pi}{4}$

7 Let $S=\left\{x\in R: 0<x<1 \text{ and } 2\tan^{-1}\left(\frac{1-x}{1+x}\right)=\cos^{-1}\left(\frac{1-x^2}{1+x^2}\right)\right\}$.

If $n(S)$ denotes the number of elements in S, then

Old NCERT Pg. 30, JEE Main 2023, 1 Feb Shift-II

(a) $n(S)=1$ and the element in S is less than $\frac{1}{2}$
(b) $n(S)=2$ and only one element in S is less than $\frac{1}{2}$
(c) $n(S)=0$
(d) $n(S)=1$ and the elements in S is more than $\frac{1}{2}$

8 If $\tan^{-1}\left(\frac{2}{3^{-x}+1}\right)=\cot^{-1}\left(\frac{3}{3^x+1}\right)$, then which one of the following is true ?

NCERT Pg. 23, CUET 2024, 16 May

(a) There is no real value of x satisfying the above equation
(b) There is one positive and one negative real value of x satisfying the above equation
(c) There are two real positive values of x satisfying the above equation
(d) There are two real negative values of x satisfying the above equation

9 The domain of the function $f(x)=\sin^{-1}\left(\frac{x^2-3x+2}{x^2+2x+7}\right)$ is

Old NCERT Pg. 30, JEE Main 2022, July Shift-II

(a) $[1,\infty)$ (b) $(-1, 2]$ (c) $[-1,\infty)$ (d) $(-\infty, 2]$

Numerical Value Type

10 For $n\in N$, if $\cot^{-1}3+\cot^{-1}4+\cot^{-1}5+\cot^{-1}n=\frac{\pi}{4}$, then n is equal to ....

Old NCERT Pg. 43, JEE Main 2024, 6 April Shift-I

11 Let the inverse trigonometric function take principal values. The number of real solutions of the equation $2\sin^{-1}x+3\cos^{-1}x=\frac{2\pi}{5}$, is ....

Old NCERT, Pg. 43, JEE Main 2024, 9 April Shift-II

12 If the domain of the function $f(x)=\sec^{-1}\left(\frac{2x}{5x+3}\right)$ is $[\alpha,\beta)\cup(\gamma,\delta]$, then $|3\alpha+10(\beta+\gamma)+21\delta|$ is equal to .... Old NCERT, Pg. 38, JEE Main 2023, 10 April Shift-II

13 For $k\in R$, let the solution of the equation $\cos(\sin^{-1}(x\cot(\tan^{-1}(\cos(\sin^{-1}x)))))=k, 0<|x|<\frac{1}{\sqrt{2}}$ be α and β, where the inverse trigonometric functions take only principal values. If the solutions of the equation $x^2-bx-5=0$ are $\frac{1}{\alpha^2}+\frac{1}{\beta^2}$ and $\frac{\alpha}{\beta}$, then $\frac{b}{k^2}$ is equal to .... Old NCERT, Pg. 35, 39, JEE Main, 2022, 27 July Shift-I

Skill Boosters

1 Find the number of solution of the equation $\tan^{-1} x + \tan^{-1} 2x + \tan^{-1} 3x = \pi$.

(a) 1 (b) 0
(c) −1 (d) $\frac{1}{2}$

2 If $\cot^{-1}\sqrt{\cos\alpha} - \tan^{-1}\sqrt{\cos\alpha} = x$, then $\sin x =$

(a) $\sin^2\frac{\alpha}{2}$ (b) $\cos^2\frac{\alpha}{2}$
(c) $\cot^2\frac{\alpha}{2}$ (d) $\tan^2\frac{\alpha}{2}$

3 If m and M are the least and greatest values of $(\cos^{-1} x)^2 - (\sin^{-1} x)^2$, then the value of $\frac{M}{m} =$

(a) 3 (b) 1
(c) −3 (d) −1

4 If x_1, x_2, x_3, x_4 are the roots of $x^4 - x^3\sin 2\alpha + x^2\cos 2\alpha - x\cos\alpha - \sin\alpha = 0$, then $\sum_{i=1}^{4}\tan^{-1}(x_i) =$

(a) $\frac{\pi}{4}-\alpha$ (b) $\frac{\pi}{2}-\alpha$ (c) $\frac{\pi}{4}-2\alpha$ (d) $\frac{\pi}{2}+2\alpha$

5 If $\cos(\theta-\alpha) = a$, $\sin(\theta-\beta) = b$, then $\cos^2(\alpha-\beta) + 2ab\sin(\alpha-\beta) =$

(a) $a^2 - b^2$ (b) $a - b$ (c) $a + b$ (d) $a^2 + b^2$

6 Let a, b, c be positive and

$$\theta = \tan^{-1}\sqrt{\frac{a(a+b+c)}{bc}} + \tan^{-1}\sqrt{\frac{b(a+b+c)}{ac}} + \tan^{-1}\sqrt{\frac{c(a+b+c)}{ab}},$$

then $\tan\theta$ is equal to

(a) 0 (b) 1
(c) 2 (d) 3

7 Let $A = 2\tan^{-1}(2\sqrt{2}-1)$ and $B = 3\sin^{-1}\frac{1}{3} - \sin^{-1}\left(\frac{3}{5}\right)$, then

(a) $A \geq B$ (b) $A > B$
(c) $A \leq B$ (d) $A < B$

8 If $\sum_{r=1}^{n}\tan^{-1}\left(\frac{1}{2r^2}\right) = \tan^{-1}(\lambda)$, then find the value of λ.

(a) $\frac{n+1}{n}$ (b) $\frac{n}{n+1}$
(c) $\frac{n-1}{n}$ (d) $\frac{n}{n-1}$

Correct Codes

Topical Questions

Basic Concepts

1 (d)	2 (d)	3 (b)	4 (c)	5 (b)	6 (a)	7 (c)	8 (a)	9 (d)	10 (c)
11 (d)	12 (b)	13 (c)	14 (a)	15 (a)	16 (d)	17 (d)	18 (c)	19 (a)	20 (a)
21 (c)	22 (a)	23 (c)	24 (b)	25 (a)	26 (c)	27 (b)	28 (c)		

Properties of Inverse Trigonometric Functions

1 (b)	2 (b)	3 (b)	4 (c)	5 (d)	6 (b)	7 (b)	8 (a)	9 (d)	10 (a)
11 (d)	12 (d)	13 (a)	14 (b)	15 (b)	16 (d)	17 (b)	18 (b)	19 (b)	20 (d)
21 (d)	22 (a)	23 (d)	24 (c)	25 (a)	26 (b)	27 (c)	28 (d)	29 (a)	30 (b)
31 (c)	32 (c)	33 (c)	34 (b)	35 (b)	36 (a)	37 (a)	38 (b)	39. (b)	40 (a)
41 (c)	42 (d)								

Miscellaneous Exercise

1 (b)	2 (c)	3 (c)	4 (a)	5 (c)	6 (c)	7 (b)	8 (d)	9 (c)	10 (c)
11 (c)	12 (c)	13 (c)	14 (c)	15 (d)	16 (b)	17 (d)	18 (b)	19 (a)	20 (a)
21 (c)	22 (c)	23 (b)	24 (b)	25 (c)	26 (b)	27 (a)	28 (b)	29 (b)	30 (b)
31 (c)	32 (c)								

Numerical Type Questions

1 (15)	2 (3)	3 (3)	4 (2)	5 (0)	6 (4)	7 (2)	8 (9)	9 (6)	10 (6)
11 (9)	12 (1)	13 (8)							

Assertion and Reason Questions

1 (a)	2 (b)	3 (a)	4 (c)	5 (c)	6 (d)	7 (b)	8 (a)	9 (b)	10 (c)
11 (c)	12 (b)	13 (a)							

Case or Paragraph Type Questions

1 (b)	2 (b)	3 (d)	4 (a)	5 (c)	6 (c)	7 (a)

Past Years Questions

1 (d)	2 (c)	3 (b)	4 (c)	5 (a)	6 (b)	7 (a)	8 (b)	9 (c)	10 (47)
11 (0)	12 (24)	13 (12)							

Skill Boosters

1 (a)	2 (d)	3 (c)	4 (b)	5 (d)	6 (a)	7 (b)	8 (b)

Step by Step

Decoding the Questions

Concept Builders

1 (1) $\left[\because \tan^{-1}\left(\frac{1}{2}\right) = \cot^{-1} 2\right.$

and $\tan^{-1} x + \cot^{-1} x = \pi / 2]$

2 (4) The greatest value of $\sin^{-1} x$ is $\pi / 2$.

So, $\sin^{-1} x = \sin^{-1} y = \pi / 2$

$\Rightarrow x = y = 1$

$(x + y)^2 = (1 + 1)^2 = 4$

3 $\left(\frac{1}{\sqrt{1+x^2}}\right)$ Let $\tan^{-1} x = \theta$

$\Rightarrow x = \tan\theta$

$\Rightarrow x^2 = \tan^2\theta$

$\Rightarrow x^2 = \sec^2\theta - 1$

$\Rightarrow \sec^2\theta = 1 + x^2$

$\Rightarrow \cos^2\theta = \frac{1}{1+x^2}$

$\Rightarrow \cos\theta = \frac{1}{\sqrt{1+x^2}}$

4 (π) $x < 0$

$\Rightarrow \tan^{-1}\left(\frac{1}{x}\right) = -\pi + \cot^{-1} x$

So, $\cot^{-1} x - \tan^{-1}\frac{1}{x}$

$= \cot^{-1} x - (-\pi + \cot^{-1} x) = \pi$

5 $\left(\frac{11\pi}{12}\right)$ $\tan^{-1}(1) + \cos^{-1}\left(-\frac{1}{2}\right)$

$= \frac{\pi}{4} + \pi - \cos^{-1}\left(\frac{1}{2}\right)$

$= \frac{\pi}{4} + \pi - \frac{\pi}{3}$

$= \frac{3\pi + 12\pi - 4\pi}{12} = \frac{11\pi}{12}$

6 (– 2) Let $x = \tan\theta$

since $x < 0 \Rightarrow -\frac{\pi}{2} < \theta \le 0$

$\Rightarrow -\pi < 2\theta \le 0 \Rightarrow 0 \le -2\theta < \pi$

Now,

$\cos^{-1}\left(\frac{1 - \tan^2\theta}{1 + \tan^2\theta}\right) = \cos^{-1}(\cos 2\theta)$

$= \cos^{-1}(\cos(-2\theta)) = -2\theta$

$= -2\tan^{-1} x$

$\therefore \lambda = -2$

7 $\left[\frac{\pi}{4}, \frac{3\pi}{4}\right]$ $\sin^{-1} x + \cos^{-1} x + \tan^{-1} x$

Since domain of the above expression is $[-1, 1]$

So, $\frac{\pi}{2} + \tan^{-1} x$ is least at $x = -1$

and greatest at $x = 1$

So, Range of it is equal to $\left[\frac{\pi}{4}, \frac{3\pi}{4}\right]$

8 $\left(\frac{\sqrt{3}}{2}\right)$ $\sin^{-1} x - \cos^{-1} x = \pi / 6$

$\frac{\pi}{2} - \cos^{-1} x - \cos^{-1} x = \pi / 6$

$[\because \sin^{-1} x + \cos^{-1} x = \pi / 2]$

$\Rightarrow \cos^{-1} x = \pi / 6$

$\Rightarrow x = \sqrt{3} / 2$

9 (False)

$\left[\because \tan^{-1} x + \tan^{-1} y = \pi + \tan^{-1}\left(\frac{x+y}{1-xy}\right)\right.$

when $xy > 1, x > 0, y > 0$]

when $xy > 1$.

10 True **11** False

12 False **13** False

14 False **15** False

16 True

17 [1, 2] $x - 1 \ge 0$ and $-1 \le \sqrt{x-1} \le 1$

So, $0 \le x - 1 \le 1$

$\Rightarrow 1 \le x \le 2$

Therefore, domain is $[1, 2]$.

18 [0, 1] Since $-1 \le 2x - 1 \le 1$

$\Rightarrow x \in [0, 1]$

19 $\left(\frac{\pi}{8}\right)$ $\tan^{-1}\left(\tan\frac{9\pi}{8}\right)$

$= \tan^{-1}\left(\tan\left(\pi + \frac{\pi}{8}\right)\right)$

$= \tan^{-1}\left(\tan\frac{\pi}{8}\right) = \pi / 8$

20 $\left(a = -\frac{\pi}{2}; b = \frac{\pi}{2}\right)$

Topical Questions

Basic Concepts

1 (*d*) As we know that when a function f i.e. $f : X \to Y$ such that $f(x) = y$ is one-one and onto, then we can define a unique function $g : Y \to X$ such that $g(y) = x$, where $x \in X$ and $y = f(x), y \in Y$.

Here, the domain of g = range of f and the range of g = domain of f.

The function g is called the inverse of f and is denoted by f^{-1}.

2 (*d*) Since, the domain of sine function is the set of all real numbers and range is the closed interval [–1, 1]. If we restrict its domain to $\left[\frac{-\pi}{2}, \frac{\pi}{2}\right]$, then it becomes one-one and onto with range [–1, 1]. Actually, sine function restricted to any of the intervals $\left[\frac{-3\pi}{2}, -\frac{\pi}{2}\right], \left[\frac{-\pi}{2}, \frac{\pi}{2}\right], \left[\frac{\pi}{2}, \frac{3\pi}{2}\right]$ etc. is one-one and its range is [–1, 1].

3 (*b*) The branch with range $\left[\frac{-\pi}{2}, \frac{\pi}{2}\right]$ is called the principal value branch, whereas other intervals as range give different branches of $\sin^{-1} x$.

4 (*c*) $\sin^{-1} x : [-1, 1] \to \left[\frac{-\pi}{2}, \frac{\pi}{2}\right]$.

From the definition of the inverse functions, it follows that $\sin(\sin^{-1} x) = x$, if $-1 \le x \le 1$ and $\sin^{-1}(\sin x) = x$, if $-\frac{\pi}{2} \le x \le \frac{\pi}{2}$. In other words, if $y = \sin^{-1} x$, then $\sin y = x$.

5 (*b*) We know that the graph of $\sin x$ is

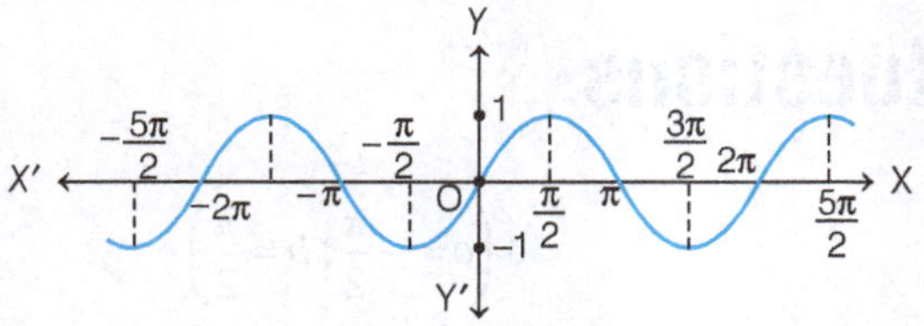

$y = \sin x$

Therefore, the graph of $\sin^{-1} x$ is

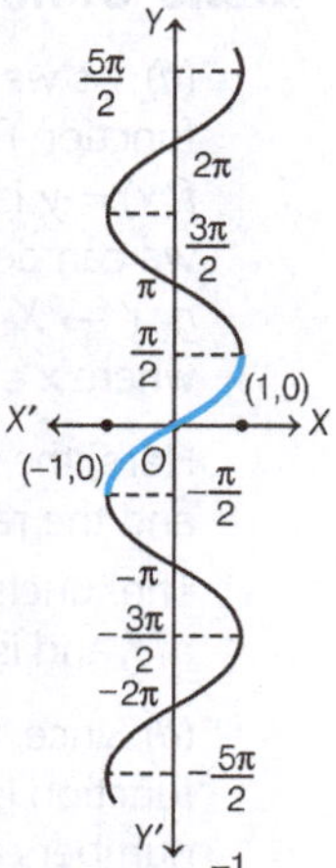

$y = \sin^{-1} x$

6 (*a*) The graph of $\sin^{-1} x$ is the mirror image of the graph of $\sin x$ along the line $y = x$ as shown in the figure given below.

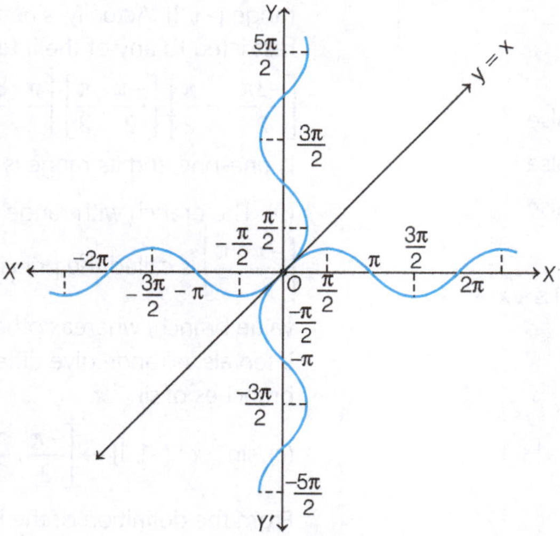

$y = \sin x$ and $x = \sin^{-1} y$

7 (*c*) The cosine function is a function whose domain is the set of all real numbers and range is the set [–1, 1]. If we restrict the domain of cosine function to $[0, \pi]$, then it becomes one-one and onto with range [–1, 1].

8 (*a*) Cosine function restricted to any of the intervals $[-\pi, 0]$, $[0, \pi]$, $[\pi, 2\pi]$ etc. is bijective with range as [–1, 1]. We can, therefore, define the inverse of cosine function in each of these intervals.

9 (*d*) $\cos^{-1} x$ is a function whose domain is [–1, 1] and range could be any of the intervals $[-\pi, 0]$, $[0, \pi]$ or $[\pi, 2\pi]$ etc. Corresponding to each such interval, we get a branch of the function $\cos^{-1} x$. The branch with range $[0, \pi]$ is called the principal value branch of the function $\cos^{-1} x$ and we write.

$$\cos^{-1} x : [-1, 1] \longrightarrow [0, \pi]$$

10 (*c*) $\text{cosec}^{-1} x$ is a function whose domain is $R - (-1, 1)$ and range could be any of the intervals $[-\pi/2, \pi/2] - \{0\}$, $[-3\pi/2, -\pi/2] - \{-\pi\}$, $[\pi/2, 3\pi/2] - \{\pi\}$ etc. corresponding to each such interval, we get a branch of the function $\text{cosec}^{-1} x$. The branch with range $\left[-\frac{\pi}{2}, \frac{\pi}{2}\right] - \{0\}$ is called the principal value branch of $\text{cosec}^{-1} x$.

11 (*d*) $\text{cosec}^{-1} x : R - (-1, 1) \to \left[\frac{-\pi}{2}, \frac{\pi}{2}\right] - \{0\}$

The graphs of $y = \text{cosec}\, x$ and $y = \text{cosec}^{-1} x$ are given below.

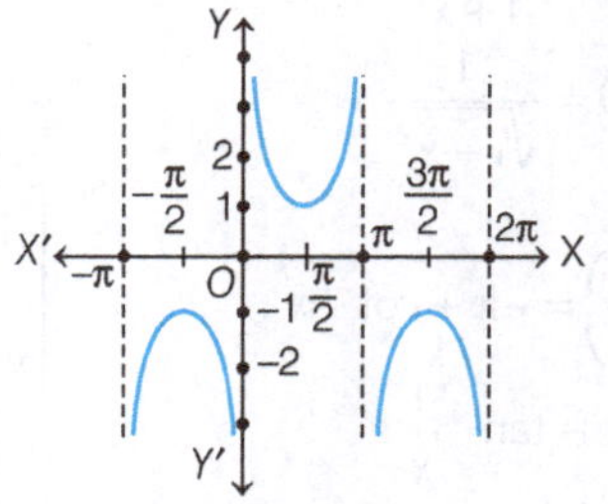

$y = \text{cosec}\, x$

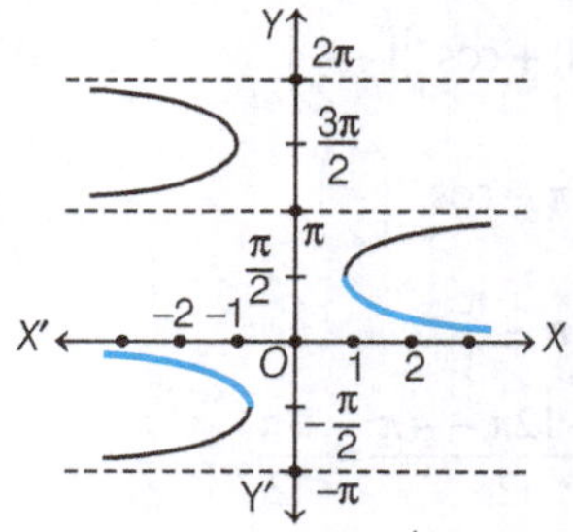

$y = \text{cosec}^{-1} x$

12 (*b*) Since, $\sec x = \dfrac{1}{\cos x}$, the domain of $y = \sec x$ is the set $R - \{x : x = (2n + 1)\frac{\pi}{2}, n \in Z\}$ and range is the set $R - (-1, 1)$. It means that sec (secant function) assumes all real values except $-1 < y < 1$ and is not defined for odd multiples of $\frac{\pi}{2}$.

13 (*c*) If we restrict the domain of secant function to $[0, \pi] - \left\{\frac{\pi}{2}\right\}$, then it is one-one and onto with its range as the set $R - (-1, 1)$. Actually, secant function restricted to any of the intervals $[-\pi, 0] - \left\{\frac{-\pi}{2}\right\}$, $[0, \pi] - \left\{\frac{\pi}{2}\right\}$, $[\pi, 2\pi] - \left\{\frac{3\pi}{2}\right\}$ etc. is bijective and its range is $R - (-1, 1)$.

14 (*a*) We know that the graph of $\sec x$.

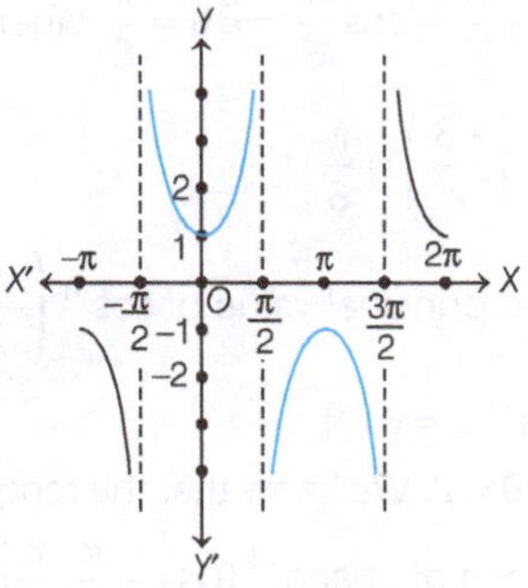

$y = \sec x$

Now, by interchanging X and Y-axes, we get the given graph.

Hence, the given graph is the graph of $\sec^{-1} x$.

15 (*a*) We know that the domain of the tan function (tangent function) is the set $\{x : x \in R \text{ and } x \neq (2n+1)\frac{\pi}{2}, n \in Z\}$ and the range is R. It means that tan function is not defined for odd multiples of $\frac{\pi}{2}$.

16 (*d*) $\tan^{-1} x : R \rightarrow \left(\frac{-\pi}{2}, \frac{\pi}{2}\right)$. Since, the graph of $\tan^{-1} x$ is the mirror image of the graph of $\tan x$ along $y = x$. Therefore, the graphs of the function $y = \tan x$ and $y = \tan^{-1} x$ are given as

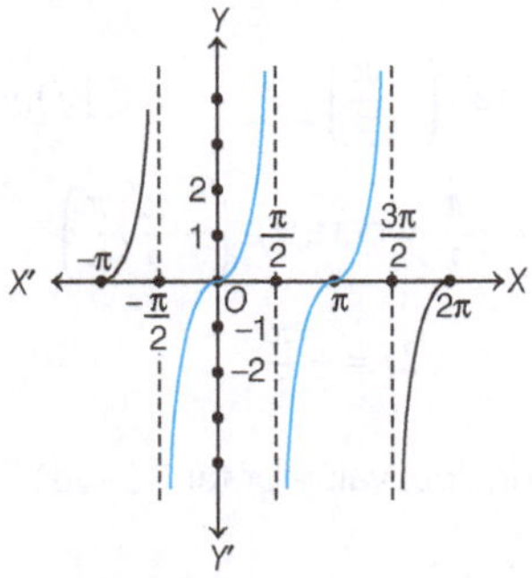

$y = \tan x$

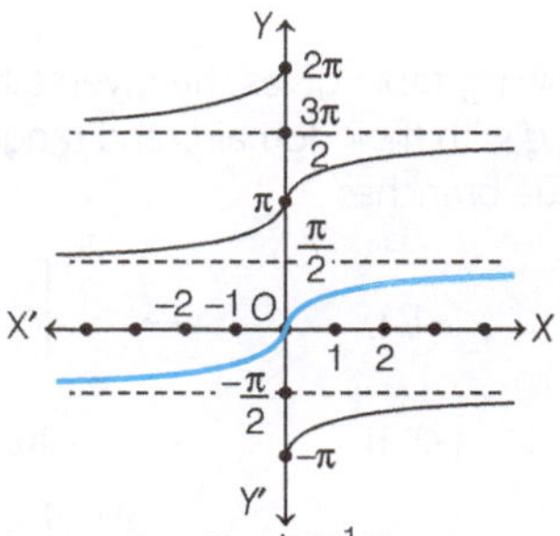

$y = \tan^{-1} x$

17 (*d*) We know that domain of the cot function (cotangent function) is the set $\{x : x \in R \text{ and } x \neq n\pi, n \in Z\}$ and range is R. It means that cotangent function is not defined for integral multiples of π.

If we restrict the domain of cotangent function to $(0, \pi)$, then it is bijective with its range as R. Infact, cotangent function restricted to any of the intervals $(-\pi, 0)$, $(0, \pi)$, $(\pi, 2\pi)$ etc. is bijective and its range is R.

18 (*c*) We know that graph of $y = \cot x$ is

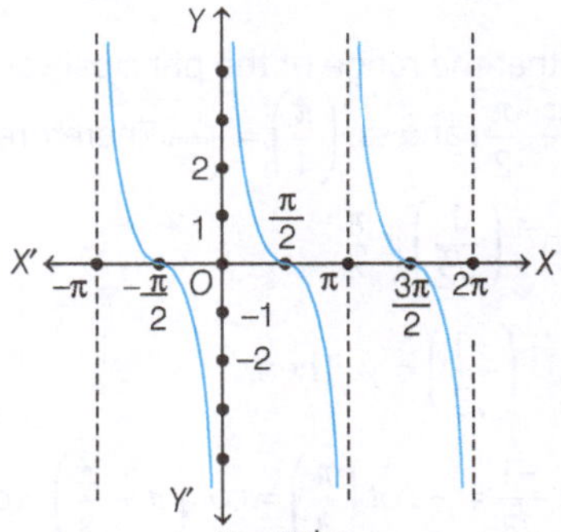

$y = \cot x$

Now, $\cot^{-1} x : R \rightarrow (0, \pi), (-\pi, 0), (\pi, 2\pi)$ etc. give different branch of the function $\cot^{-1} x$.

The mirror image of the graph of $\cot x$ along the line $y = x$ is given by

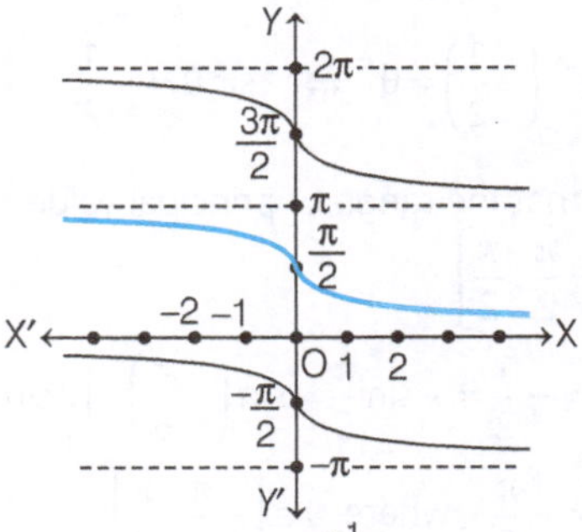

$y = \cot^{-1} x$

So, the given graph is the graph of $\cot^{-1} x$.

19 (*a*) The following table gives the inverse trigonometric function along with their domains and ranges (principal value branches).

$\sin^{-1}$	:	$[-1, 1]$	$\rightarrow$	$\left[-\frac{\pi}{2}, \frac{\pi}{2}\right]$
$\cos^{-1}$	:	$[-1, 1]$	$\rightarrow$	$[0, \pi]$
cosec^{-1}	:	$R-(-1, 1)$	$\rightarrow$	$\left[-\frac{\pi}{2}, \frac{\pi}{2}\right]-\{0\}$
$\sec^{-1}$	:	$R-(-1, 1)$	$\rightarrow$	$[0, \pi]-\left\{\frac{\pi}{2}\right\}$
$\tan^{-1}$	:	R	$\rightarrow$	$\left(\frac{-\pi}{2}, \frac{\pi}{2}\right)$
$\cot^{-1}$	:	R	$\rightarrow$	$(0, \pi)$

20 (*a*) Let $\sin^{-1}\left(\frac{1}{\sqrt{2}}\right)=y$. Then, $\sin y=\frac{1}{\sqrt{2}}$.

We know that the range of the principal value branch of $\sin^{-1}$ is $\left[\frac{-\pi}{2}, \frac{\pi}{2}\right]$ and $\sin\left(\frac{\pi}{4}\right)=\frac{1}{\sqrt{2}}$. Therefore, principal value of $\sin^{-1}\left(\frac{1}{\sqrt{2}}\right)$ is $\frac{\pi}{4}$.

21 (*c*) Let $\cot^{-1}\left(\frac{-1}{\sqrt{3}}\right)=y$. Then,

$$\cot y=\frac{-1}{\sqrt{3}}=-\cot\left(\frac{\pi}{3}\right)=\cot\left(\pi-\frac{\pi}{3}\right)=\cot\left(\frac{2\pi}{3}\right)$$

We know that the range of principal value branch of $\cot^{-1}$ is $(0, \pi)$ and $\cot\left(\frac{2\pi}{3}\right)=\frac{-1}{\sqrt{3}}$. Hence, principal value branch of $\cot^{-1}\left(\frac{-1}{\sqrt{3}}\right)$ is $\frac{2\pi}{3}$.

22 (*a*) Let $\sin^{-1}\left(-\frac{1}{2}\right)=\theta \Rightarrow \sin\theta=-\frac{1}{2}$

We know that the range of principal value branch of $\sin^{-1}\theta$ is $\left[-\frac{\pi}{2}, \frac{\pi}{2}\right]$.

$$\because \quad \sin\theta=-\frac{1}{2}=-\sin\frac{\pi}{6}=\sin\left(-\frac{\pi}{6}\right) \quad [\because \sin(-\theta)=-\sin\theta]$$

$$\Rightarrow \quad \theta=-\frac{\pi}{6} \quad \text{where, } \theta\in\left[-\frac{\pi}{2}, \frac{\pi}{2}\right]$$

$$\Rightarrow \sin^{-1}\left(-\frac{1}{2}\right)=-\frac{\pi}{6}$$

Hence, the principal value of branch $\sin^{-1}\left(-\frac{1}{2}\right)$ is $-\frac{\pi}{6}$.

23 (*c*)

(i) Let $\cos^{-1}\left(\frac{\sqrt{3}}{2}\right)=\theta$

$$\Rightarrow \quad \cos\theta=\frac{\sqrt{3}}{2}$$

We know that the range of principal value branch of $\cos^{-1}\theta$ is $[0, \pi]$.

$$\because \cos\theta=\frac{\sqrt{3}}{2}=\cos\frac{\pi}{6} \Rightarrow \theta=\frac{\pi}{6}, \text{ where } \theta\in[0, \pi]$$

$$\Rightarrow \quad \cos^{-1}\left(\frac{\sqrt{3}}{2}\right)=\frac{\pi}{6}$$

Hence, the principal value of $\cos^{-1}\left(\frac{\sqrt{3}}{2}\right)$ is $\frac{\pi}{6}$.

(ii) Let $\text{cosec}^{-1} 2=\theta$

$\Rightarrow \text{cosec}\,\theta=2$. We know that the range of principal value branch of $\text{cosec}^{-1}\theta$ is $\left[-\frac{\pi}{2}, \frac{\pi}{2}\right]-\{0\}$.

$$\because \quad \text{cosec}\,\theta=2=\text{cosec}\,\frac{\pi}{6}$$

$$\Rightarrow \quad \theta=\frac{\pi}{6}, \text{ where } \theta\in\left[-\frac{\pi}{2}, \frac{\pi}{2}\right]-\{0\}$$

$$\Rightarrow \quad \text{cosec}^{-1}(2)=\frac{\pi}{6}$$

Hence, the principal value of $\text{cosec}^{-1}(2)$ is $\frac{\pi}{6}$.

(iii) Let $\tan^{-1}(-\sqrt{3})=\theta$

$$\Rightarrow \quad \tan\theta=-\sqrt{3}$$

We know that the range of principal value branch of $\tan^{-1}\theta$ is $\left(-\frac{\pi}{2}, \frac{\pi}{2}\right)$.

$$\because \tan\theta=-\sqrt{3}=-\tan\frac{\pi}{3}$$

$$=\tan\left(-\frac{\pi}{3}\right) \quad [\because \tan(-\theta)=-\tan\theta]$$

$$\Rightarrow \quad \theta=-\frac{\pi}{3}, \text{ where } \theta\in\left(-\frac{\pi}{2}, \frac{\pi}{2}\right)$$

$$\Rightarrow \quad \tan^{-1}(-\sqrt{3})=-\frac{\pi}{3}$$

Hence, principal value of $\tan^{-1}(-\sqrt{3})$ is $-\frac{\pi}{3}$.

24 (*b*) Let $\sec^{-1}\left(\frac{2}{\sqrt{3}}\right)=\theta$

$$\Rightarrow \quad \sec\theta=\frac{2}{\sqrt{3}}$$

We know that the range of principal value branch of $\sec^{-1}\theta$ is $[0, \pi] - \left\{\frac{\pi}{2}\right\}$.

$\because \sec\theta = \frac{2}{\sqrt{3}} = \sec\frac{\pi}{6} \Rightarrow \theta = \frac{\pi}{6}$

where, $\theta \in [0, \pi] - \left\{\frac{\pi}{2}\right\}$

$\Rightarrow \quad \sec^{-1}\left(\frac{2}{\sqrt{3}}\right) = \frac{\pi}{6}$

Hence, the principal value of $\sec^{-1}\left(\frac{2}{\sqrt{3}}\right)$ is $\frac{\pi}{6}$.

25 (*a*)

A. Let $\cot^{-1}(\sqrt{3}) = \theta$

$\Rightarrow \quad \cot\theta = \sqrt{3}$

We know that the range of principal value branch of $\cot^{-1}\theta$ is $(0, \pi)$.

$\because \quad \cot\theta = \sqrt{3} = \cot\frac{\pi}{6}$

$\Rightarrow \quad \theta = \frac{\pi}{6}$ where, $\theta \in (0, \pi)$

$\Rightarrow \quad \cot^{-1}(\sqrt{3}) = \frac{\pi}{6}$

Hence, the principal value of $\cot^{-1}(\sqrt{3})$ is $\frac{\pi}{6}$.

B. Let $\cos^{-1}\left(-\frac{1}{\sqrt{2}}\right) = \theta$

$\Rightarrow \quad \cos\theta = -\frac{1}{\sqrt{2}}$

We know that the range of principal value branch of $\cos^{-1}\theta$ is $[0, \pi]$.

$\because \quad \cos\theta = -\frac{1}{\sqrt{2}} = -\cos\frac{\pi}{4}$

$= \cos\left(\pi - \frac{\pi}{4}\right)$

$[\because \cos(\pi - \theta) = -\cos\theta)]$

$\Rightarrow \quad \theta = \frac{3\pi}{4}$ where, $\theta \in [0, \pi]$

$\Rightarrow \quad \cos^{-1}\left(-\frac{1}{\sqrt{2}}\right) = \frac{3\pi}{4}$

Hence, the principal value of $\cos^{-1}\left(-\frac{1}{\sqrt{2}}\right)$ is $\frac{3\pi}{4}$.

C. Let $\text{cosec}^{-1}(-\sqrt{2}) = \theta$

$\Rightarrow \quad \text{cosec}\,\theta = -\sqrt{2}$

We know that the range of principal value branch of $\text{cosec}^{-1}\theta$ is $\left[-\frac{\pi}{2}, \frac{\pi}{2}\right] - \{0\}$.

$\because \text{cosec}\,\theta = -\sqrt{2} = -\text{cosec}\,\frac{\pi}{4}$

$= \text{cosec}\left(-\frac{\pi}{4}\right)$

$[\because \text{cosec}(-\theta) = -\text{cosec}\,\theta]$

$\Rightarrow \quad \theta = -\frac{\pi}{4}$

where, $\theta \in \left[-\frac{\pi}{2}, \frac{\pi}{2}\right] - \{0\}$

$\Rightarrow \quad \text{cosec}^{-1}(-\sqrt{2}) = -\frac{\pi}{4}$

Hence, the principal value of $\text{cosec}^{-1}(-\sqrt{2})$ is $-\frac{\pi}{4}$.

D. Let $\cos^{-1}\left(\frac{1}{2}\right) = x$

$\Rightarrow \quad \cos x = \frac{1}{2} = \cos\frac{\pi}{3}$

$\Rightarrow \quad x = \frac{\pi}{3} \in [0, \pi]$

[principal value branch]

Again, let $\sin^{-1}\left(\frac{1}{2}\right) = y$

$\Rightarrow \quad \sin y = \frac{1}{2} = \sin\frac{\pi}{6}$

$\Rightarrow \quad y = \frac{\pi}{6} \in \left[-\frac{\pi}{2}, \frac{\pi}{2}\right]$

[principal value branch]

$\therefore \cos^{-1}\left(\frac{1}{2}\right) + 2\sin^{-1}\left(\frac{1}{2}\right)$

$= x + 2y$

$= \frac{\pi}{3} + 2 \times \frac{\pi}{6} = \frac{2\pi}{3}$

26 (*c*) Let $\tan^{-1}(1) = x$

$\Rightarrow \tan x = 1 = \tan\frac{\pi}{4} \Rightarrow x = \frac{\pi}{4}$,

where, principal value $x \in \left(-\frac{\pi}{2}, \frac{\pi}{2}\right)$

$\therefore \quad \tan^{-1}(1) = \frac{\pi}{4}$

Let $\cos^{-1}\left(-\frac{1}{2}\right) = y$

$\Rightarrow \quad \cos y = -\frac{1}{2}$

$= -\cos\left(\frac{\pi}{3}\right) = \cos\left(\pi - \frac{\pi}{3}\right)$

$= \cos\left(\frac{2\pi}{3}\right)$

$[\because \cos(\pi - \theta) = -\cos\theta]$

$\Rightarrow \quad y = \frac{2\pi}{3}$,

where, principal value $y \in [0, \pi]$

$\therefore \quad \cos^{-1}\left(-\frac{1}{2}\right) = \frac{2\pi}{3}$

Let $\sin^{-1}\left(-\frac{1}{2}\right) = z$

$\Rightarrow \quad \sin z = -\frac{1}{2} = -\sin\left(\frac{\pi}{6}\right)$

$= \sin\left(-\frac{\pi}{6}\right)$

$\Rightarrow \quad z = -\frac{\pi}{6}$

where, principal value $z \in \left[-\frac{\pi}{2}, \frac{\pi}{2}\right]$

$\therefore \quad \sin^{-1}\left(-\frac{1}{2}\right) = -\frac{\pi}{6}$

$\therefore$

$\tan^{-1}(1) + \cos^{-1}\left(-\frac{1}{2}\right) + \sin^{-1}\left(-\frac{1}{2}\right)$

$= x + y + z$

$= \frac{\pi}{4} + \frac{2\pi}{3} - \frac{\pi}{6}$

$= \frac{3\pi + 8\pi - 2\pi}{12} = \frac{9\pi}{12} = \frac{3\pi}{4}$

27 (*b*) As range of $\sin^{-1}x$ is $\left[-\frac{\pi}{2}, \frac{\pi}{2}\right]$, therefore $-\frac{\pi}{2} \le y \le \frac{\pi}{2}$.

28 (*c*) Let $\tan^{-1}\sqrt{3} = x$

$\Rightarrow \tan x = \sqrt{3} \Rightarrow \tan x = \tan\frac{\pi}{3}$

$\Rightarrow \quad x = \frac{\pi}{3} \in \left(-\frac{\pi}{2}, \frac{\pi}{2}\right)$

[principal value branch]

Let $\sec^{-1}(-2) = y$

$\Rightarrow \quad \sec y = -2$

$\Rightarrow \quad \sec y = -\sec\frac{\pi}{3}$

$\Rightarrow \quad \sec y = \sec\left(\pi - \frac{\pi}{3}\right)$

$[\because \sec(\pi - \theta) = -\sec\theta]$

$\Rightarrow \quad \sec y = \sec\left(\frac{2\pi}{3}\right)$

$\Rightarrow \quad y = \frac{2\pi}{3} \in [0, \pi] - \left(\frac{\pi}{2}\right)$

[principal value branch]

$\therefore \tan^{-1}\sqrt{3} - \sec^{-1}(-2) = x - y$

$= \frac{\pi}{3} - \frac{2\pi}{3} = -\frac{\pi}{3}$

Properties of Inverse Trigonometric Functions

1 (*b*) Let $x = \tan\theta$, then

$\theta = \tan^{-1} x \quad \text{...(i)}$

$\therefore \tan^{-1}\frac{\sqrt{1+x^2}-1}{x}$

$= \tan^{-1}\frac{\sqrt{1+\tan^2\theta}-1}{\tan\theta}$

$= \tan^{-1}\frac{\sqrt{\sec^2\theta - 1}}{\tan\theta}$

$[\because 1 + \tan^2\theta = \sec^2\theta]$

$= \tan^{-1}\left[\frac{\sec\theta - 1}{\tan\theta}\right]$

$= \tan^{-1}\left[\frac{\frac{1}{\cos\theta} - 1}{\frac{\sin\theta}{\cos\theta}}\right]$

$= \tan^{-1}\left[\frac{\frac{1-\cos\theta}{\cos\theta}}{\frac{\sin\theta}{\cos\theta}}\right]$

$= \tan^{-1}\left[\frac{1-\cos\theta}{\cos\theta} \times \frac{\cos\theta}{\sin\theta}\right]$

$= \tan^{-1}\left[\frac{1-\cos\theta}{\sin\theta}\right]$

$= \tan^{-1}\left[\frac{2\sin^2\frac{\theta}{2}}{2\sin\frac{\theta}{2}\cos\frac{\theta}{2}}\right]$

$\left[\because 1 - \cos\theta = 2\sin^2\frac{\theta}{2} \text{ and } \sin\theta = 2\sin\frac{\theta}{2}\cos\frac{\theta}{2}\right]$

$= \tan^{-1}\left[\frac{2\sin\frac{\theta}{2}}{2\cos\frac{\theta}{2}}\right]$

$= \tan^{-1}\left[\tan\frac{\theta}{2}\right]$

$= \frac{\theta}{2} = \frac{\tan^{-1} x}{2} \quad$ [from Eq. (i)]

$\therefore \tan^{-1}\frac{\sqrt{1+x^2}-1}{x} = \frac{1}{2}\tan^{-1} x$

2 (*b*) $\tan^{-1}\left(\sqrt{\frac{1-\cos x}{1+\cos x}}\right)$

$= \tan^{-1}\left(\sqrt{\frac{2\sin^2(x/2)}{2\cos^2(x/2)}}\right)$

$\left[\because \begin{array}{l} 1-\cos x = 2\sin^2(x/2) \\ \text{and } 1+\cos x = 2\cos^2(x/2) \end{array}\right]$

$= \tan^{-1}\left(\sqrt{\tan^2\frac{x}{2}}\right)$

$= \tan^{-1}\left(\tan\frac{x}{2}\right) = \frac{x}{2}$

Note *If x is positive, then* $\sqrt{\tan^2\frac{x}{2}} = \tan\frac{x}{2}$ and if x is negative, then $\sqrt{\tan^2\frac{x}{2}} = -\tan\frac{x}{2}$.

3 (*b*) We have, $\tan^{-1}\left(\frac{\cos x - \sin x}{\cos x + \sin x}\right)$

$= \tan^{-1}\left(\frac{\frac{\cos x}{\cos x} - \frac{\sin x}{\cos x}}{\frac{\cos x}{\cos x} + \frac{\sin x}{\cos x}}\right)$

[divide numerator and denominator by $\cos x$]

$= \tan^{-1}\left(\frac{1-\tan x}{1+\tan x}\right)$

$= \tan^{-1}\left[\tan\left(\frac{\pi}{4} - x\right)\right]$

$\left[\because \tan\left(\frac{\pi}{4} - x\right) = \frac{\tan\frac{\pi}{4} - \tan x}{1 + \tan\frac{\pi}{4}\cdot\tan x} = \frac{1-\tan x}{1+\tan x}\right]$

$= \frac{\pi}{4} - x$

4 (*c*) We have,

$\tan^{-1}\left[2\cos\left(2\sin^{-1}\frac{1}{2}\right)\right]$

$= \tan^{-1}\left[2\cos\left\{2\sin^{-1}\left(\sin\frac{\pi}{6}\right)\right\}\right]$

$\left[\because \sin\frac{\pi}{6} = \frac{1}{2}\right]$

$= \tan^{-1}\left[2\cos\left(2 \times \frac{\pi}{6}\right)\right]$

$= \tan^{-1}\left[2\cos\frac{\pi}{3}\right]$

$= \tan^{-1}\left[2 \times \frac{1}{2}\right] = \tan^{-1}(1)$

$\left[\because \cos\frac{\pi}{3} = \frac{1}{2}\right]$

$= \tan^{-1}\left(\tan\frac{\pi}{4}\right) = \frac{\pi}{4} \quad \left[\because \tan\frac{\pi}{4} = 1\right]$

5 (*d*) We have,

$\tan\frac{1}{2}\left[\sin^{-1}\frac{2x}{1+x^2} + \cos^{-1}\frac{1-y^2}{1+y^2}\right]$

$\left[\begin{array}{l} \because 2\tan^{-1} x = \sin^{-1}\left(\frac{2x}{1+x^2}\right) \\ \text{and } 2\tan^{-1} y = \cos^{-1}\left(\frac{1-y^2}{1+y^2}\right) \end{array}\right]$

$= \tan\left(\frac{1}{2}(2\tan^{-1} x + 2\tan^{-1} y)\right)$

$= \tan\left[\frac{1}{2} \times 2(\tan^{-1} x + \tan^{-1} y)\right]$

$= \tan(\tan^{-1} x + \tan^{-1} y)$

$= \tan\left[\tan^{-1}\left(\frac{x+y}{1-xy}\right)\right] = \frac{x+y}{1-xy}$

$\left[\because \tan^{-1} x + \tan^{-1} y = \tan^{-1}\frac{x+y}{1-xy}\right]$

6 (*b*) Let $x = \sec\theta$, then

$\sqrt{x^2 - 1} = \sqrt{\sec^2\theta - 1} = \tan\theta$

Therefore,

$\cot^{-1}\left(\frac{1}{\sqrt{x^2-1}}\right) = \cot^{-1}(\cot\theta) = \theta$

$= \sec^{-1} x,$

which is the simplest form.

7 (*b*) Let $\theta = \sin^{-1}\left[\cos\left(\sin^{-1}\frac{\sqrt{3}}{2}\right)\right]$

$= \sin^{-1}\left[\cos\frac{\pi}{3}\right]$

$= \sin^{-1}\left[\frac{1}{2}\right] = \frac{\pi}{6}$

$\left[\because \text{range of } \sin^{-1}x \text{ is } \left[-\frac{\pi}{2}, \frac{\pi}{2}\right]\right]$

8 (*a*) Let $\theta = \tan^{-1}\left(\tan\frac{7\pi}{6}\right)$

$= \tan^{-1}\left[\tan\left(\pi + \frac{\pi}{6}\right)\right]$

$\left[\because \text{range of } \tan^{-1}x \text{ is } \left(-\frac{\pi}{2}, \frac{\pi}{2}\right)\right]$

$= \tan^{-1}\left[\tan\frac{\pi}{6}\right]$

$[\because \tan(\pi + x) = \tan x]$

$= \frac{\pi}{6}$

$\left[\because \tan^{-1}(\tan x) = x, x \in \left(-\frac{\pi}{2}, \frac{\pi}{2}\right)\right]$

9 (*d*) $\because \quad \frac{\pi}{2} \le x \le \frac{3\pi}{2}$

$\Rightarrow \frac{-3\pi}{2} \le -x \le -\frac{\pi}{2}$

$\Rightarrow \pi - \frac{3\pi}{2} \le \pi - x \le \pi - \frac{\pi}{2}$

$\frac{-\pi}{2} \le \pi - x \le \frac{\pi}{2}$

Now, let $\theta = \sin^{-1}(\sin x)$

$= \sin^{-1}[\sin(\pi - x)]$

Since, range of $\sin^{-1}x$ is $\left[-\frac{\pi}{2}, \frac{\pi}{2}\right]$

$\therefore \quad \theta = \pi - x$

10 (*a*) We have, $\cos^{-1}\left(\cos\frac{14\pi}{3}\right)$

$= \cos^{-1}\left[\cos\left(4\pi + \frac{2\pi}{3}\right)\right]$

$\left[\because \frac{2\pi}{3} \in [0, \pi]\right]$

$= \cos^{-1}\left(\cos\frac{2\pi}{3}\right)$

$= \frac{2\pi}{3}$

$[\because \cos^{-1}(\cos x) = x, x \in [0, \pi]]$

11 (*d*) We have, $\tan^{-1}\left\{\tan\left(\frac{3\pi}{5}\right)\right\}$

$= \tan^{-1}\left\{\tan\left(\pi - \frac{2\pi}{5}\right)\right\}$

$= \tan^{-1}\left\{\tan\left(\frac{-2\pi}{5}\right)\right\}$

$= \frac{-2\pi}{5}$

$\left[\because \tan^{-1}(\tan x) = x, x \in \left(-\frac{\pi}{2}, \frac{\pi}{2}\right)\right]$

12 (*d*) We have, $\sin^{-1}\left[\sin\left(\frac{2\pi}{3}\right)\right]$

$= \sin^{-1}\left[\sin\left(\pi - \frac{\pi}{3}\right)\right]$

$= \sin^{-1}\left[\sin\left(\frac{\pi}{3}\right)\right]$

$[\because \sin(\pi - \theta) = \sin\theta]$

$= \frac{\pi}{3}$

$\left[\because \sin^{-1}(\sin x) = x, x \in \left[-\frac{\pi}{2}, \frac{\pi}{2}\right]\right]$

13 (*a*) Given,

$\tan^{-1}\left[2\sin\left(2\cos^{-1}\left(\frac{\sqrt{3}}{2}\right)\right)\right]$

$= \tan^{-1}\left[2\sin\left(2 \times \frac{\pi}{6}\right)\right]$

$= \tan^{-1}\left[2\sin\left(\frac{\pi}{3}\right)\right]$

$= \tan^{-1}\left[2 \times \frac{\sqrt{3}}{2}\right]$

$= \tan^{-1}\sqrt{3} = \frac{\pi}{3}$

14 (*b*) $\tan\left(\sin^{-1}\frac{3}{5} + \cot^{-1}\frac{3}{2}\right)$

$= \tan\left[\tan^{-1}\frac{\frac{3}{5}}{\sqrt{1-\left(\frac{3}{5}\right)^2}} + \tan^{-1}\frac{2}{3}\right]$

$\left[\because \sin^{-1}x = \tan^{-1}\frac{x}{\sqrt{1-x^2}} \text{ and } \cot^{-1}\frac{x}{y} = \tan^{-1}\frac{y}{x}\right]$

$= \tan\left[\tan^{-1}\frac{3}{4} + \tan^{-1}\frac{2}{3}\right]$

$= \tan\left[\tan^{-1}\frac{\frac{3}{4}+\frac{2}{3}}{1-\frac{3}{4}\times\frac{2}{3}}\right]$

$= \tan\left[\tan^{-1}\frac{\frac{17}{12}}{\frac{1}{2}}\right]$

$\left[\because \tan^{-1}x + \tan^{-1}y = \tan^{-1}\left(\frac{x+y}{1-xy}\right)\right]$

$= \tan\left[\tan^{-1}\frac{17}{6}\right] = \frac{17}{6}$

15 (*b*) $\cos^{-1}\left(\cos\frac{7\pi}{6}\right) = \cos^{-1}\left[\cos\left(2\pi - \frac{5\pi}{6}\right)\right]$

where, $\frac{5\pi}{6} \in [0, \pi]$

$\Rightarrow \cos^{-1}\left(\cos\frac{7\pi}{6}\right)$

$= \cos^{-1}\left[\cos\left(\frac{5\pi}{6}\right)\right] = \frac{5\pi}{6}$

$[\because \cos(2\pi - \theta) = \cos\theta]$

16 (*d*) $\sin\left[\frac{\pi}{3} - \sin^{-1}\left(-\frac{1}{2}\right)\right]$

$= \sin\left[\frac{\pi}{3} - \sin^{-1}\left(-\sin\frac{\pi}{6}\right)\right]$

$\left[\because \sin\frac{\pi}{6} = \frac{1}{2}\right]$

$= \sin\left[\frac{\pi}{3} - \sin^{-1}\left\{\sin\left(-\frac{\pi}{6}\right)\right\}\right]$

$[\because \sin(-x) = -\sin x]$

$= \sin\left[\frac{\pi}{3} - \left(-\frac{\pi}{6}\right)\right]$

$= \sin\left[\frac{\pi}{3} + \frac{\pi}{6}\right] = \sin\frac{\pi}{2} = 1$

17 (*b*) $\tan^{-1}\sqrt{3} - \cot^{-1}(-\sqrt{3})$

$= \tan^{-1}\sqrt{3} - [\pi - \cot^{-1}\sqrt{3}]$

$[\because \cot^{-1}(-x) = \pi - \cot^{-1}x]$

$= \tan^{-1}\sqrt{3} - \pi + \cot^{-1}\sqrt{3}$

$= \tan^{-1}\sqrt{3} - \pi + \tan^{-1}\frac{1}{\sqrt{3}}$

$\left[\because \tan^{-1}\frac{1}{x} = \cot^{-1}x\right]$

$= \left[\tan^{-1}\sqrt{3} + \tan^{-1}\frac{1}{\sqrt{3}}\right] - \pi$

$= \tan^{-1}\frac{\left(\sqrt{3}+\frac{1}{\sqrt{3}}\right)}{1-\left(\sqrt{3}\times\frac{1}{\sqrt{3}}\right)} - \pi$

$\left[\because \tan^{-1}x + \tan^{-1}y = \tan^{-1}\left(\frac{x+y}{1-xy}\right)\right]$

$= \tan^{-1}(\infty) - \pi$

$= \frac{\pi}{2} - \pi \quad \left[\because \tan\frac{\pi}{2} = \infty\right]$

$= -\frac{\pi}{2}$

18 (*b*) (i) $\sin^{-1}(-x) = -\sin^{-1}x, x \in [-1, 1]$

(ii) $\tan^{-1}(-x) = -\tan^{-1}x, x \in R$

(iii) $\text{cosec}^{-1}(-x) = -\text{cosec}^{-1}x, |x| \geq 1$

Let $\sin^{-1}(-x) = y$, i.e. $-x = \sin(y)$

So that $x = -\sin y$, i.e. $x = \sin(-y)$

Therefore,

$\sin^{-1}x = -y = -\sin^{-1}(-x)$

Hence, $\sin^{-1}(-x) = -\sin^{-1}x$

Similarly, we can prove the other parts.

19 (*b*)

(i) $\cos^{-1}(-x) = \pi - \cos^{-1}x$, $x \in [-1, 1]$

(ii) $\sec^{-1}(-x) = \pi - \sec^{-1}x, |x| \geq 1$

(iii) $\cot^{-1}(-x) = \pi - \cot^{-1}x, x \in R$

Let $\cos^{-1}(-x) = y$ i.e. $-x = \cos y$, so that $x = -\cos y = \cos(\pi - y)$

Therefore,

$\cos^{-1}x = \pi - y = \pi - \cos^{-1}(-x)$

Hence, $\cos^{-1}(-x) = \pi - \cos^{-1}x$

Similarly, we can prove the other parts.

20 (*d*)

(i) $\sin^{-1}x + \cos^{-1}x = \frac{\pi}{2}, x \in [-1, 1]$

(ii) $\tan^{-1}x + \cot^{-1}x = \frac{\pi}{2}, x \in R$

(iii) $\text{cosec}^{-1}x + \sec^{-1}x = \frac{\pi}{2}, |x| \geq 1$

Let $\sin^{-1}x = y$.

Then, $x = \sin y = \cos\left(\frac{\pi}{2} - y\right)$

Therefore,

$\cos^{-1}x = \frac{\pi}{2} - y = \frac{\pi}{2} - \sin^{-1}x$

Hence, $\sin^{-1}x + \cos^{-1}x = \frac{\pi}{2}$

Similarly, we can prove the other parts.

21 (*d*)

(a) $2\tan^{-1}x = \sin^{-1}\frac{2x}{1+x^2}, |x| \leq 1$

(b) $2\tan^{-1}x = \cos^{-1}\frac{1-x^2}{1+x^2}, x \geq 0$

(c) $2\tan^{-1}x = \tan^{-1}\frac{2x}{1-x^2}, -1 < x < 1$

Let $\tan^{-1}x = y$, then $x = \tan y$.

Now, $\sin^{-1}\frac{2x}{1+x^2} = \sin^{-1}\frac{2\tan y}{1+\tan^2 y}$

$= \sin^{-1}(\sin 2y) = 2y = 2\tan^{-1}x$

Also, $\cos^{-1}\frac{1-x^2}{1+x^2} = \cos^{-1}\frac{1-\tan^2 y}{1+\tan^2 y}$

$= \cos^{-1}(\cos 2y)$

$= 2y = 2\tan^{-1}x$

$\therefore$ (iii) can be worked out similarly.

22 (*a*) $\tan^{-1}\frac{1}{2} + \tan^{-1}\frac{2}{11}$

$= \tan^{-1}\frac{\frac{1}{2}+\frac{2}{11}}{1-\frac{1}{2}\times\frac{2}{11}} = \tan^{-1}\frac{15}{20}$

$= \tan^{-1}\frac{3}{4}$

23 (*d*)

A. Let $\sin^{-1}x = \theta \Rightarrow x = \sin\theta$, then

$\sin^{-1}(3x - 4x^3)$

$= \sin^{-1}[3\sin\theta - 4\sin^3\theta]$

$= \sin^{-1}[\sin 3\theta] = 3\theta$

$[\because \sin 3\theta = 3\sin\theta - 4\sin^3\theta]$

$= 3\sin^{-1}x$

B. $\tan^{-1}\left(\frac{2}{11}\right) + \tan^{-1}\left(\frac{7}{24}\right)$

$= \tan^{-1}\left(\frac{\frac{2}{11}+\frac{7}{24}}{1-\frac{2}{11}\cdot\frac{7}{24}}\right)$

$\left[\because \tan^{-1}x + \tan^{-1}y = \tan^{-1}\left(\frac{x+y}{1-xy}\right)\right]$

$= \tan^{-1}\left(\frac{\frac{48+77}{264}}{1-\frac{14}{264}}\right) = \tan^{-1}\left(\frac{\frac{125}{264}}{\frac{264-14}{264}}\right)$

$= \tan^{-1}\frac{\frac{125}{264}}{\frac{250}{264}}$

$= \tan^{-1}\left(\frac{125}{264}\times\frac{264}{250}\right) = \tan^{-1}\left(\frac{1}{2}\right)$

C. Let $x = \cos\theta$

$\Rightarrow \theta = \cos^{-1}x$,

then $\cos^{-1}(4x^3 - 3x)$

$= \cos^{-1}[4\cos^3\theta - 3\cos\theta]$

$= \cos^{-1}[\cos 3\theta] = 3\theta$

$= 3\cos^{-1}x$

$[\because \cos 3\theta = 4\cos^3\theta - 3\cos\theta]$

D. $2\tan^{-1}\left(\frac{1}{2}\right) + \tan^{-1}\left(\frac{1}{7}\right)$

$= \tan^{-1}\left(\frac{2\times\frac{1}{2}}{1-\left(\frac{1}{2}\right)^2}\right) + \tan^{-1}\left(\frac{1}{7}\right)$

$\left[\because 2\tan^{-1}x = \tan^{-1}\left(\frac{2x}{1-x^2}\right)\right]$

$= \tan^{-1}\frac{1}{1-\frac{1}{4}} + \tan^{-1}\frac{1}{7}$

$= \tan^{-1}\left(\frac{4}{3}\right) + \tan^{-1}\left(\frac{1}{7}\right)$

$= \tan^{-1}\left(\frac{\frac{4}{3}+\frac{1}{7}}{1-\frac{4}{3}\times\frac{1}{7}}\right)$

$\left[\because \tan^{-1}x + \tan^{-1}y = \tan^{-1}\left(\frac{x+y}{1-xy}\right)\right]$

$= \tan^{-1}\left(\frac{\frac{28+3}{21}}{1-\frac{4}{21}}\right) = \tan^{-1}\left(\frac{\frac{31}{21}}{\frac{17}{21}}\right)$

$= \tan^{-1}\left(\frac{31}{21}\times\frac{21}{17}\right) = \tan^{-1}\left(\frac{31}{17}\right)$

24 (c) Let $x = \sec\theta$, then

$$\theta = \sec^{-1} x \quad ...(i)$$

$$\therefore \tan^{-1}\frac{1}{\sqrt{x^2-1}}$$

$$= \tan^{-1}\left(\frac{1}{\sqrt{\sec^2\theta - 1}}\right)$$

$$= \tan^{-1}\left(\frac{1}{\sqrt{\tan^2\theta}}\right) \quad [\because \sec^2\theta - \tan^2\theta = 1]$$

$$= \tan^{-1}\left(\frac{1}{\tan\theta}\right)$$

$$= \tan^{-1}(\cot\theta) = \tan^{-1}\left(\tan\left(\frac{\pi}{2}-\theta\right)\right)$$

$$\left[\because \tan\left(\frac{\pi}{2}-\theta\right) = \cot\theta\right]$$

$$= \frac{\pi}{2} - \theta = \frac{\pi}{2} - \sec^{-1} x$$

25 (a) We have,

$$\cot(\tan^{-1} a + \cot^{-1} a) = \cot\frac{\pi}{2} = 0$$

$$\left[\because \tan^{-1} x + \cot^{-1} x = \frac{\pi}{2}\right]$$

26 (b) Given, $\sin\left(\sin^{-1}\frac{1}{5} + \cos^{-1} x\right) = 1$

$$\Rightarrow \sin^{-1}\frac{1}{5} + \cos^{-1} x = \sin^{-1} 1$$

$$[\because \sin\theta = x \Rightarrow \theta = \sin^{-1} x]$$

$$\Rightarrow \sin^{-1}\frac{1}{5} + \cos^{-1} x = \sin^{-1}\left(\sin\frac{\pi}{2}\right)$$

$$\left[\because \sin\left(\frac{\pi}{2}\right) = 1\right]$$

$$\Rightarrow \sin^{-1}\frac{1}{5} + \cos^{-1} x = \frac{\pi}{2}$$

$$\Rightarrow \sin^{-1}\frac{1}{5} = \frac{\pi}{2} - \cos^{-1} x$$

$$\Rightarrow \sin^{-1}\frac{1}{5} = \sin^{-1} x$$

$$\left[\because \sin^{-1} x + \cos^{-1} x = \frac{\pi}{2}\right]$$

$$\Rightarrow \frac{1}{5} = x$$

27 (c) Given, $\tan^{-1}\left(-\frac{1}{\sqrt{3}}\right) + \cot^{-1}\left(\frac{1}{\sqrt{3}}\right) + \tan^{-1}\left[\sin\left(\frac{-\pi}{2}\right)\right]$

$$= \tan^{-1}\left(-\frac{1}{\sqrt{3}}\right) + \cot^{-1}\left(\frac{1}{\sqrt{3}}\right) + \tan^{-1}\left(-\sin\frac{\pi}{2}\right)$$

$$[\because \sin(-\theta) = -\sin\theta]$$

$$= \frac{-\pi}{6} + \frac{\pi}{3} - \tan^{-1}\left(\sin\frac{\pi}{2}\right)$$

$$[\because \tan^{-1}(-x) = -\tan^{-1} x]$$

$$= \frac{\pi}{6} - \tan^{-1}(1)$$

$$= \frac{\pi}{6} - \frac{\pi}{4} = -\frac{\pi}{12}$$

28 (d) Given, $\sin^{-1}\left(\cos\left(\frac{33\pi}{5}\right)\right)$

$$= \sin^{-1}\left(\cos\left(6\pi + \frac{3\pi}{5}\right)\right)$$

$$= \sin^{-1}\left(\cos\frac{3\pi}{5}\right)$$

$$[\because \cos(6\pi + x) = \cos x]$$

$$= \sin^{-1}\left(\sin\left(\frac{\pi}{2} - \frac{3\pi}{5}\right)\right)$$

$$\left[\because \sin\left(\frac{\pi}{2} - x\right) = \cos x\right]$$

$$= \sin^{-1}\left(\sin\left(-\frac{\pi}{10}\right)\right)$$

$$= -\frac{\pi}{10}$$

$$\left[\because \sin^{-1}(\sin x) = x, \text{ if } x \in \left[-\frac{\pi}{2}, \frac{\pi}{2}\right]\right]$$

29 (a) Given, $\cos^{-1}[\cos(-680°)]$

$$= \cos^{-1}[\cos 680°]$$

$$[\because \cos(-x) = \cos x]$$

$$= \cos^{-1}[\cos(720° - 40°)]$$

$$= \cos^{-1}[\cos 40°]$$

$$[\because \cos(720° - x) = \cos x]$$

$$= 40°$$

$$[\because \cos^{-1}(\cos x) = x, \text{ if } x \in [0, \pi]]$$

$$= 40 \times \frac{\pi}{180} = \frac{2\pi}{9}$$

30 (b) Let $\tan^{-1} x = \theta$

$$\Rightarrow x = \tan\theta$$

We know that

$$1 + \tan^2\theta = \sec^2\theta$$

$$\Rightarrow 1 + x^2 = \sec^2\theta$$

$$\Rightarrow \sec\theta = \sqrt{1+x^2}$$

$$\Rightarrow \cos\theta = \frac{1}{\sqrt{1+x^2}}$$

$$\Rightarrow \cos(\tan^{-1} x) = \frac{1}{\sqrt{1+x^2}}$$

31 (c) Let $\sin^{-1}\frac{1}{3} = \alpha$

and $\sin^{-1}\frac{2}{3} = \beta$

$$\Rightarrow \sin\alpha = \frac{1}{3}$$

and $\sin\beta = \frac{2}{3}$

$$\Rightarrow \cos\alpha = \sqrt{1 - \left(\frac{1}{3}\right)^2}$$

and $\cos\beta = \sqrt{1 - \left(\frac{2}{3}\right)^2}$

$$[\because \cos x = \sqrt{1 - \sin^2 x}]$$

$$\Rightarrow \cos\alpha = \frac{2\sqrt{2}}{3}$$

and $\cos\beta = \frac{\sqrt{5}}{3}$

Now, $\sin(\alpha + \beta) = \sin\alpha\cos\beta + \cos\alpha\sin\beta$

$$= \frac{1}{3} \times \frac{\sqrt{5}}{3} + \frac{2\sqrt{2}}{3} \times \frac{2}{3}$$

$$= \frac{\sqrt{5} + 4\sqrt{2}}{9}$$

$$\therefore \sin\left[\sin^{-1}\left(\frac{1}{3}\right) + \sin^{-1}\left(\frac{2}{3}\right)\right] = \frac{\sqrt{5} + 4\sqrt{2}}{9}$$

$$\Rightarrow \sin[\sin^{-1} x] = \frac{\sqrt{5} + 4\sqrt{2}}{9}$$

$$\Rightarrow x = \frac{\sqrt{5} + 4\sqrt{2}}{9}$$

32 (c) Given, $\tan^{-1} x + \tan^{-1} y = \frac{\pi}{4}$

$$\Rightarrow \tan^{-1}\left(\frac{x+y}{1-xy}\right) = \frac{\pi}{4}$$

$$\Rightarrow \frac{x+y}{1-xy} = \tan\frac{\pi}{4}$$

$$\Rightarrow \frac{x+y}{1-xy} = 1$$

$$\Rightarrow x + y = 1 - xy$$

$$\Rightarrow x + y + xy = 1$$

33 (c) Given, $\tan^{-1}\sqrt{3}+\cot^{-1}x=\frac{\pi}{2}$

$\Rightarrow \tan^{-1}\sqrt{3}=\frac{\pi}{2}-\cot^{-1}x$

$\Rightarrow \tan^{-1}\sqrt{3}=\tan^{-1}x \quad \left[\because \tan^{-1}x+\cot^{-1}x=\frac{\pi}{2}\right]$

$\Rightarrow x=\sqrt{3}$

34 (b) Let $\alpha=\sin^{-1}\frac{1}{4}$

and $\beta=\sec^{-1}\frac{4}{3}$

$\Rightarrow \sin\alpha=\frac{1}{4}$

and $\sec\beta=\frac{4}{3}$

$\Rightarrow \sin\alpha=\frac{1}{4}$

and $\cos\beta=\frac{3}{4}$

$\Rightarrow \cos\alpha=\sqrt{1-\frac{1}{16}}$

and $\sin\beta=\sqrt{1-\frac{9}{16}}$

$[\because \sin^2x+\cos^2x=1]$

$\Rightarrow \cos\alpha=\frac{\sqrt{15}}{4}$

and $\sin\beta=\frac{\sqrt{7}}{4}$

$\therefore \cos(\alpha+\beta)=\cos\alpha\cos\beta-\sin\alpha\sin\beta$

$\Rightarrow \cos\left[\sin^{-1}\frac{1}{4}+\sec^{-1}\frac{4}{3}\right]$

$=\frac{\sqrt{15}}{4}\times\frac{3}{4}-\frac{1}{4}\times\frac{\sqrt{7}}{4}$

$=\frac{3\sqrt{15}-\sqrt{7}}{16}$

35 (b) Given,

$\sin^{-1}6x+\sin^{-1}6\sqrt{3}x=-\frac{\pi}{2}$ ...(i)

$\Rightarrow \sin^{-1}6x=\frac{-\pi}{2}-\sin^{-1}6\sqrt{3}x$

$\Rightarrow \sin(\sin^{-1}6x)=\sin\left(-\frac{\pi}{2}-\sin^{-1}6\sqrt{3}x\right)$

$\Rightarrow 6x=-\sin\left(\frac{\pi}{2}+\sin^{-1}6\sqrt{3}x\right)$

$\Rightarrow 6x=-\cos(\sin^{-1}6\sqrt{3}x)$

$\Rightarrow 6x=-\cos(\cos^{-1}\sqrt{1-108x^2})$

$\left[\begin{array}{l}\because \theta=\sin^{-1}6\sqrt{3}x\\ \Rightarrow \sin\theta=6\sqrt{3}x\\ \Rightarrow \cos\theta=\sqrt{1-108x^2}\\ \Rightarrow \theta=\cos^{-1}\sqrt{1-108x^2}\end{array}\right]$

$\Rightarrow 6x=-\sqrt{1-108x^2}$

On squaring both sides, we get

$36x^2=1-108x^2$

$\Rightarrow 144x^2=1$

$\Rightarrow x^2=\frac{1}{144} \Rightarrow x=\pm\frac{1}{12}$

Now, $x=\frac{1}{12}$ does not satisfy Eq. (i).

So, $x=-\frac{1}{12}$ is the only root of the equation.

36 (a) We have, $(\sin^{-1}x)^2+(\cos^{-1}x)^2$

$=(\sin^{-1}x+\cos^{-1}x)^2-2\sin^{-1}x\cos^{-1}x$

$=\frac{\pi^2}{4}-2\sin^{-1}x\left(\frac{\pi}{2}-\sin^{-1}x\right)$

$=\frac{\pi^2}{4}-\pi\sin^{-1}x+2(\sin^{-1}x)^2$

$=2\left[(\sin^{-1}x)^2-\frac{\pi}{2}\sin^{-1}x+\frac{\pi^2}{8}\right]$

$=2\left[\left(\sin^{-1}x-\frac{\pi}{4}\right)^2+\frac{\pi^2}{16}\right]$

Thus, the least value is $2\left(\frac{\pi^2}{16}\right)$

i.e. $\frac{\pi^2}{8}$ and the greatest value is

$2\left[\left(\frac{-\pi}{2}-\frac{\pi}{4}\right)^2+\frac{\pi^2}{16}\right]$ i.e. $\frac{5\pi^2}{4}$.

37 (a) Let $x=\cos^{-1}\frac{3}{5}$

$\Rightarrow \cos x=\frac{3}{5}$

$\Rightarrow \sin x=\sqrt{1-\frac{9}{25}}$

$[\because \sin x=\sqrt{1-\cos^2x}]$

$\Rightarrow \sin x=\frac{4}{5}$

$\Rightarrow \tan x=\frac{4}{3} \quad \left[\because \tan x=\frac{\sin x}{\cos x}\right]$

Now, $\tan\left(\cos^{-1}\frac{3}{5}+\tan^{-1}\frac{1}{4}\right)$

$=\tan\left(\tan^{-1}\frac{4}{3}+\tan^{-1}\frac{1}{4}\right)$

$=\tan\left(\tan^{-1}\frac{\frac{4}{3}+\frac{1}{4}}{1-\frac{4}{3}\times\frac{1}{4}}\right)$

$=\tan\left(\tan^{-1}\frac{19}{8}\right)=\frac{19}{8}$

38 (b) Let $\tan^{-1}\frac{2}{3}=x$ and

$\tan^{-1}\sqrt{3}=y$

$\Rightarrow \tan x=\frac{2}{3}$ and $\tan y=\sqrt{3}$

$\therefore \sin\left(2\tan^{-1}\frac{2}{3}\right)+\cos(\tan^{-1}\sqrt{3})$

$=\sin(2x)+\cos y$

$=\frac{2\tan x}{1+\tan^2x}+\frac{1}{\sec y}$

$\left[\because \sin 2x=\frac{2\tan x}{1+\tan^2x}\right]$

$=\frac{2\times\frac{2}{3}}{1+\left(\frac{2}{3}\right)^2}+\frac{1}{\sqrt{1+(\sqrt{3})^2}}$

$[\because \sec y=\sqrt{1+\tan^2y}]$

$=\frac{12}{13}+\frac{1}{2}=\frac{24+13}{26}=\frac{37}{26}$

39 (b) We have,

$\cot^{-1}\left(\frac{1+x}{1-x}\right)=\frac{1}{2}\cot^{-1}\left(\frac{1}{x}\right)$

$\Rightarrow \tan^{-1}\left(\frac{1-x}{1+x}\right)=\frac{1}{2}\tan^{-1}x$

$\Rightarrow 2\tan^{-1}\left(\frac{1-x}{1+x}\right)=\tan^{-1}x$

$\Rightarrow 2[\tan^{-1}1-\tan^{-1}x]=\tan^{-1}x$

$\Rightarrow 2\left(\frac{\pi}{4}-\tan^{-1}x\right)=\tan^{-1}x$

$\Rightarrow \frac{\pi}{2}-2\tan^{-1}x=\tan^{-1}x$

$\Rightarrow 3\tan^{-1}x=\frac{\pi}{2}$

$\Rightarrow \tan^{-1}x=\frac{\pi}{6}$

$\Rightarrow x=\tan\frac{\pi}{6}$

$\Rightarrow x=\frac{1}{\sqrt{3}}$

40 (*a*) Let $\cot^{-1}(x+1)=\alpha$

and $\tan^{-1}x=\beta$

$\Rightarrow x+1=\cot\alpha$ and $x=\tan\beta$

$\Rightarrow \operatorname{cosec}\alpha=\sqrt{1+(x+1)^2}$

and $\sec\beta=\sqrt{1+x^2}$

$\Rightarrow \sin\alpha=\dfrac{1}{\sqrt{x^2+2x+2}}$

and $\cos\beta=\dfrac{1}{\sqrt{1+x^2}}$

$\Rightarrow \alpha=\sin^{-1}\dfrac{1}{\sqrt{x^2+2x+2}}$

and $\beta=\cos^{-1}\left(\dfrac{1}{\sqrt{1+x^2}}\right)$

Now, $\sin(\cot^{-1}(x+1))=\cos(\tan^{-1}x)$

$$\Rightarrow \sin\left(\sin^{-1}\frac{1}{\sqrt{x^2+2x+2}}\right)=\cos\left(\cos^{-1}\frac{1}{\sqrt{1+x^2}}\right)$$

$$\Rightarrow \frac{1}{\sqrt{x^2+2x+2}}=\frac{1}{\sqrt{1+x^2}}$$

$\Rightarrow x^2+2x+2=1+x^2$

$\Rightarrow 2x=-1 \Rightarrow x=-\dfrac{1}{2}$

41 (*c*) Given,

$$\tan^{-1}2x+\tan^{-1}3x=\frac{\pi}{4} \quad ...(i)$$

$\Rightarrow \tan^{-1}\left(\dfrac{2x+3x}{1-2x\cdot 3x}\right)=\dfrac{\pi}{4}$

$\Rightarrow \tan^{-1}\left(\dfrac{5x}{1-6x^2}\right)=\dfrac{\pi}{4}$

$\Rightarrow \dfrac{5x}{1-6x^2}=\tan\dfrac{\pi}{4}$

$\Rightarrow \dfrac{5x}{1-6x^2}=1$

$\Rightarrow 5x=1-6x^2$

$\Rightarrow 6x^2+5x-1=0$

$\Rightarrow 6x^2+6x-x-1=0$

$\Rightarrow 6x(x+1)-1(x+1)=0$

$\Rightarrow (x+1)(6x-1)=0$

$\Rightarrow x=\dfrac{1}{6},-1$

But $x=-1$ does not satisfy Eq. (i).
Since, here RHS > 0 and $\tan^{-1}(x)<0$ for $x<0$.

So, $x=\dfrac{1}{6}$ is the only solution for given equation.

42 (*d*) Given,

$$\sin^{-1}\left(\frac{2a}{1+a^2}\right)+\cos^{-1}\left(\frac{1-a^2}{1+a^2}\right)=\tan^{-1}\left(\frac{2x}{1-x^2}\right)$$

$$\Rightarrow 2\tan^{-1}a+2\tan^{-1}a=\tan^{-1}\left(\frac{2x}{1-x^2}\right)$$

$$\left[\because \sin^{-1}\left(\frac{2x}{1+x^2}\right)=2\tan^{-1}x \text{ and } \cos^{-1}\left(\frac{1-x^2}{1+x^2}\right)=2\tan^{-1}x\right]$$

$$\Rightarrow 4\tan^{-1}a=\tan^{-1}\left(\frac{2x}{1-x^2}\right)$$

$$\Rightarrow 2\tan^{-1}\left(\frac{2a}{1-a^2}\right)=\tan^{-1}\left(\frac{2x}{1-x^2}\right)$$

$$\left[\because 2\tan^{-1}x=\tan^{-1}\frac{2x}{1-x^2}\right]$$

$$\Rightarrow 2\tan^{-1}\left(\frac{2a}{1-a^2}\right)=2\tan^{-1}x$$

On comparing, we get

$$x=\frac{2a}{1-a^2}$$

Miscellaneous Exercise

1 (*b*) Let,

$$2\sin^{-1}\frac{3}{5}=\sin^{-1}\left[2\times\frac{3}{5}\sqrt{1-\left(\frac{3}{5}\right)^2}\right]$$

$$[\because 2\sin^{-1}y=\sin^{-1}(2y\sqrt{1-y^2})]$$

$$=\sin^{-1}\left[2\times\frac{3}{5}\times\frac{4}{5}\right]=\sin^{-1}\left(\frac{24}{25}\right)$$

$$=\tan^{-1}\left[\frac{\frac{24}{25}}{\sqrt{1-\left(\frac{24}{25}\right)^2}}\right]$$

$$\left[\because \sin^{-1}y=\tan^{-1}\frac{y}{\sqrt{1-y^2}}\right]$$

$$=\tan^{-1}\left[\frac{\frac{24}{25}}{\sqrt{1-\frac{576}{625}}}\right]$$

$$=\tan^{-1}\left[\frac{24}{25}\times\frac{25}{7}\right]=\tan^{-1}\left[\frac{24}{7}\right]$$

Hence, $x=\dfrac{24}{7}$

2 (*c*) We have,

$$\tan^{-1}\left[\frac{a\cos x-b\sin x}{b\cos x+a\sin x}\right]$$

$$=\tan^{-1}\left[\frac{\frac{a\cos x-b\sin x}{b\cos x}}{\frac{b\cos x+a\sin x}{b\cos x}}\right]$$

$$=\tan^{-1}\left[\frac{\frac{a}{b}-\tan x}{1+\frac{a}{b}\tan x}\right]$$

$$=\tan^{-1}\frac{a}{b}-\tan^{-1}(\tan x)$$

$$=\tan^{-1}\frac{a}{b}-x$$

3 (*c*) $\cos^{-1}\dfrac{12}{13}=\theta \Rightarrow \cos\theta=\dfrac{12}{13}$

$\therefore \sin\theta=\sqrt{1-\left(\dfrac{12}{13}\right)^2}$

$\Rightarrow \sin\theta=\sqrt{\dfrac{25}{169}}=\dfrac{5}{13}$

$\Rightarrow \theta=\sin^{-1}\dfrac{5}{13}$

Now, LHS $=\cos^{-1}\dfrac{12}{13}+\sin^{-1}\dfrac{3}{5}$

$$=\sin^{-1}\frac{5}{13}+\sin^{-1}\frac{3}{5}$$

$$=\sin^{-1}\left(\frac{5}{13}\sqrt{1-\left(\frac{3}{5}\right)^2}+\frac{3}{5}\sqrt{1-\left(\frac{5}{13}\right)^2}\right)$$

$$[\because \sin^{-1}x+\sin^{-1}y=\sin^{-1}(x\sqrt{1-y^2}+y\sqrt{1-x^2})]$$

$$=\sin^{-1}\left(\frac{5}{13}\sqrt{\frac{16}{25}}+\frac{3}{5}\sqrt{\frac{144}{169}}\right)$$

$$=\sin^{-1}\left(\frac{5}{13}\times\frac{4}{5}+\frac{3}{5}\times\frac{12}{13}\right)=\sin^{-1}\left(\frac{56}{65}\right)$$

$\therefore \sin^{-1}x=\sin^{-1}\dfrac{56}{65}\Rightarrow x=\dfrac{56}{65}$

4 (*a*) RHS $= \sin^{-1}\frac{5}{13} + \cos^{-1}\frac{3}{5}$

Let $\sin^{-1}\left(\frac{5}{13}\right) = x$

$\Rightarrow \sin x = \frac{5}{13}$

$\because 1 - \sin^2 x = \cos^2 x$

$\Rightarrow 1 - \left(\frac{5}{13}\right)^2 = \cos^2 x$

$\Rightarrow \frac{169-25}{169} = \cos^2 x$

$\Rightarrow \frac{144}{169} = \cos^2 x$

$\Rightarrow \frac{12}{13} = \cos x$

$\therefore \tan x = \frac{\sin x}{\cos x}$

$\Rightarrow \tan x = \frac{\frac{5}{13}}{\frac{12}{13}} = \frac{5}{12}$

$\Rightarrow x = \tan^{-1}\frac{5}{12}$

Let $\cos^{-1}\frac{3}{5} = y$

$\Rightarrow \cos y = \frac{3}{5}$

$\because 1 - \cos^2 y = \sin^2 y$

$\Rightarrow 1 - \left(\frac{3}{5}\right)^2 = \sin^2 y$

$\Rightarrow \frac{25-9}{25} = \sin^2 y$

$\Rightarrow \frac{16}{25} = \sin^2 y$

$\Rightarrow \frac{4}{5} = \sin y$

$\therefore \tan y = \frac{\sin y}{\cos y}$

$\Rightarrow \tan y = \frac{\frac{4}{5}}{\frac{3}{5}}$

$\Rightarrow y = \tan^{-1}\frac{4}{3}$

$\therefore$ Given equation becomes

$\tan^{-1} A = x + y$

$\Rightarrow \tan^{-1} A = \tan^{-1}\left(\frac{5}{12}\right) + \tan^{-1}\left(\frac{4}{3}\right)$

Consider, RHS

$= \tan^{-1}\left(\frac{5}{12}\right) + \tan^{-1}\left(\frac{4}{3}\right)$

$= \tan^{-1}\left[\frac{\frac{5}{12}+\frac{4}{3}}{1-\frac{5}{12}\times\frac{4}{3}}\right]$

$\left[\because \tan^{-1} x + \tan^{-1} y = \tan^{-1}\left(\frac{x+y}{1-xy}\right)\right]$

$= \tan^{-1}\left[\frac{\frac{15+48}{12\times 3}}{\frac{12\times 3-20}{12\times 3}}\right]$

$= \tan^{-1}\left[\frac{63}{36}\times\frac{36}{36-20}\right]$

$= \tan^{-1}\left[\frac{63}{16}\right]$

$\therefore \tan^{-1} A = \tan^{-1}\left(\frac{63}{16}\right)$

$\Rightarrow A = \frac{63}{16}$

5 (*c*) We have,

$\left(\tan^{-1}\frac{1}{5} + \tan^{-1}\frac{1}{7}\right) + \left(\tan^{-1}\frac{1}{3} + \tan^{-1}\frac{1}{8}\right)$

$= \tan^{-1}\left(\frac{\frac{1}{5}+\frac{1}{7}}{1-\frac{1}{5}\times\frac{1}{7}}\right) + \tan^{-1}\left(\frac{\frac{1}{3}+\frac{1}{8}}{1-\frac{1}{3}\times\frac{1}{8}}\right)$

$\left[\because \tan^{-1} x + \tan^{-1} y = \tan^{-1}\left(\frac{x+y}{1-xy}\right)\right]$

$= \tan^{-1}\left(\frac{\frac{7+5}{35}}{\frac{35-1}{35}}\right) + \tan^{-1}\left(\frac{\frac{8+3}{24}}{\frac{24-1}{24}}\right)$

$= \tan^{-1}\left(\frac{6}{17}\right) + \tan^{-1}\left(\frac{11}{23}\right)$

$= \tan^{-1}\left(\frac{\frac{6}{17}+\frac{11}{23}}{1-\frac{6}{17}\times\frac{11}{23}}\right)$

$= \tan^{-1}\left(\frac{6\times 23 + 11\times 17}{17\times 23 - 6\times 11}\right)$

$= \tan^{-1}\left(\frac{325}{325}\right)$

$= \tan^{-1}(1) = \frac{\pi}{4}$

6 (*c*) We have, $\frac{1}{2}\cos^{-1}\left(\frac{1-x}{1+x}\right), x \in [0, 1]$

Let $\sqrt{x} = \tan\theta$

$\Rightarrow \theta = \tan^{-1}\sqrt{x}$

So, $\frac{1}{2}\cos^{-1}\left(\frac{1-\tan^2\theta}{1+\tan^2\theta}\right)$

$= \frac{1}{2}\cos^{-1}[\cos 2\theta]$

$\left[\because \cos 2x = \frac{1-\tan^2 x}{1+\tan^2 x}\right]$

$= \frac{1}{2}\times 2\theta = \theta = \tan^{-1}\sqrt{x}$

7 (*b*) LHS $= \frac{9\pi}{8} - \frac{9}{4}\sin^{-1}\left(\frac{1}{3}\right)$

$= \frac{9}{4}\left(\frac{\pi}{2} - \sin^{-1}\left(\frac{1}{3}\right)\right) = \frac{9}{4}\left(\cos^{-1}\left(\frac{1}{3}\right)\right)$

$\left[\because \sin^{-1} x + \cos^{-1} x = \frac{\pi}{2}\right]$

$= \frac{9}{4}\sin^{-1}\sqrt{1-\left(\frac{1}{3}\right)^2}$

$[\because \cos^{-1} x = \sin^{-1}\sqrt{1-x^2}]$

$= \frac{9}{4}\sin^{-1}\sqrt{1-\frac{1}{9}} = \frac{9}{4}\sin^{-1}\frac{2\sqrt{2}}{3}$

$\therefore \frac{9}{4}\sin^{-1} x = \frac{9}{4}\sin^{-1}\frac{2\sqrt{2}}{3}$

$\Rightarrow x = \frac{2\sqrt{2}}{3}$

8 (*d*) Let $\tan^{-1} x = \theta$

$\Rightarrow x = \tan\theta$

$\Rightarrow \sec\theta = \sqrt{1+x^2}$

$[\because \sec\theta = \sqrt{1+\tan^2\theta}]$

$\Rightarrow \cos\theta = \frac{1}{\sqrt{1+x^2}}$

$\therefore \sin\theta = \sqrt{1-\frac{1}{1+x^2}}$

$[\because \sin\theta = \sqrt{1-\cos^2\theta}]$

$= \sqrt{\frac{1+x^2-1}{1+x^2}} = \frac{x}{\sqrt{1+x^2}}$

$\therefore \sin(\tan^{-1} x) = \sin\left(\sin^{-1}\frac{x}{\sqrt{1+x^2}}\right)$

$= \frac{x}{\sqrt{1+x^2}}$

9 (c) We have,

$$\tan^{-1}\left(\frac{x}{y}\right)-\tan^{-1}\left(\frac{x-y}{x+y}\right)$$

$$=\tan^{-1}\left(\frac{x}{y}\right)-\tan^{-1}\left(\frac{\frac{x}{y}-1}{\frac{x}{y}+1}\right)$$

$$=\tan^{-1}\left(\frac{x}{y}\right)-\left\{\tan^{-1}\frac{x}{y}-\tan^{-1}(1)\right\}$$

$$\left[\because \tan^{-1}x-\tan^{-1}y=\tan^{-1}\left(\frac{x-y}{1+xy}\right)\right]$$

$$=\tan^{-1}1=\frac{\pi}{4}$$

10 (c) Given, $\sin^{-1}(1-x)-2\sin^{-1}x=\frac{\pi}{2}$

Let $x=\sin\theta$

$\Rightarrow \theta=\sin^{-1}x$, then

$$\sin^{-1}(1-\sin\theta)-2\theta=\frac{\pi}{2}$$

$$\Rightarrow \sin^{-1}(1-\sin\theta)=\frac{\pi}{2}+2\theta$$

$$\Rightarrow 1-\sin\theta=\sin\left(\frac{\pi}{2}+2\theta\right)$$

$$\Rightarrow 1-\sin\theta=\cos 2\theta$$

$$\left[\because \sin\left(\frac{\pi}{2}+\theta\right)=\cos\theta\right]$$

$$\Rightarrow 1-\sin\theta=1-2\sin^2\theta$$

$$[\because \cos 2\theta=1-2\sin^2\theta]$$

$$\Rightarrow 2\sin^2\theta-\sin\theta=0$$

$$\Rightarrow \sin\theta\,(2\sin\theta-1)=0$$

$$\Rightarrow \sin\theta=0$$

or $\quad 2\sin\theta-1=0$

$$\Rightarrow x=0 \text{ or } 2x-1=0$$

$$[\because \sin\theta=x]$$

$$\Rightarrow x=0 \text{ or } x=\frac{1}{2}$$

But $x=\frac{1}{2}$ does not satisfy the given equation.

So, $x=0$

To check your answer put $x=0$ in the given equation,

$$\therefore \sin^{-1}(1-0)-2\sin^{-1}0=\frac{\pi}{2}$$

$$\Rightarrow \frac{\pi}{2}-2\times 0=\frac{\pi}{2}\Rightarrow\frac{\pi}{2}=\frac{\pi}{2}$$

11 (c) Given that $\cos^{-1}x>\sin^{-1}x$

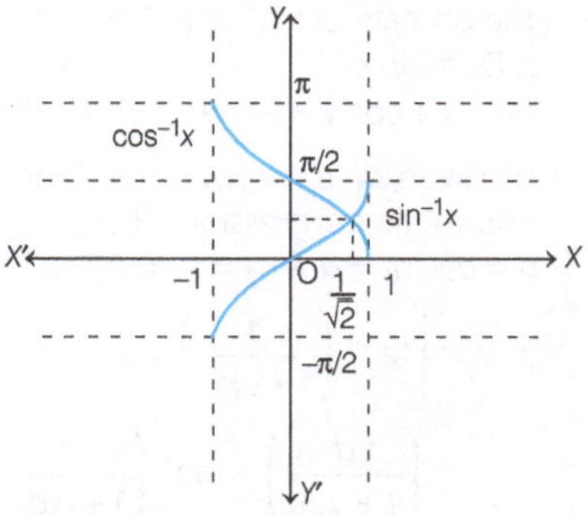

Then, $\sin^{-1}x=\cos^{-1}x\Rightarrow x=\frac{1}{\sqrt{2}}$

From the figure, it is clear that $-1\le x<\frac{1}{\sqrt{2}}$.

12 (c) We have,

$$\tan^{-1}\left(\frac{\sqrt{1+x^2}+\sqrt{1-x^2}}{\sqrt{1+x^2}-\sqrt{1-x^2}}\right)$$

Let $x^2=\cos 2\theta$. Then, we get

Given expression

$$=\tan^{-1}\left(\frac{\sqrt{1+\cos 2\theta}+\sqrt{1-\cos 2\theta}}{\sqrt{1+\cos 2\theta}-\sqrt{1-\cos 2\theta}}\right)$$

$$=\tan^{-1}\left(\frac{\sqrt{2}\cos\theta+\sqrt{2}\sin\theta}{\sqrt{2}\cos\theta-\sqrt{2}\sin\theta}\right)$$

$$\left[\begin{array}{l}\because 1+\cos 2\theta=2\cos^2\theta\\ \text{and } 1-\cos 2\theta=2\sin^2\theta\end{array}\right]$$

$$=\tan^{-1}\left(\frac{\cos\theta+\sin\theta}{\cos\theta-\sin\theta}\right)$$

$$=\tan^{-1}\left(\frac{1+\tan\theta}{1-\tan\theta}\right)$$

[divide numerator and denominator inside the bracket by $\cos\theta$]

$$=\tan^{-1}\left(\frac{\tan\frac{\pi}{4}+\tan\theta}{1-\left(\tan\frac{\pi}{4}\right)(\tan\theta)}\right)$$

$$=\tan^{-1}\left[\tan\left(\frac{\pi}{4}+\theta\right)\right]$$

$$\left[\because \tan(\theta+\phi)=\frac{\tan\theta+\tan\phi}{1-\tan\theta\tan\phi}\right]$$

$$=\frac{\pi}{4}+\theta=\frac{\pi}{4}+\frac{1}{2}\cos^{-1}x^2$$

$$\left[\because x^2=\cos 2\theta\Rightarrow\theta=\frac{1}{2}\cos^{-1}x^2\right]$$

13 (c) Given, $\quad y=\sin^{-1}(-x^2)$

$$\Rightarrow \sin y=-x^2$$

We know that

$$-1\le\sin y\le 1$$

$$\Rightarrow -1\le -x^2\le 1\Rightarrow -1\le x^2\le 1$$

$$\Rightarrow 0\le x^2\le 1\Rightarrow |x|\le 1$$

$$\Rightarrow -1\le x\le 1$$

14 (c) $\tan^{-1}\sqrt{x(x+1)}$

$$+\sin^{-1}\sqrt{x^2+x+1}=\frac{\pi}{2}$$

$$\Rightarrow \tan^{-1}\sqrt{x^2+x}$$

$$+\sin^{-1}\sqrt{x^2+x+1}=\frac{\pi}{2}$$

This equation holds, if

$$x^2+x\ge 0$$

and $\quad 0\le x^2+x+1\le 1$

Now, $\quad x^2+x\ge 0$

and $\quad 0\le x^2+x+1\le 1$

$$\Rightarrow x^2+x\ge 0$$

and $\quad x^2+x+1\le 1$

$$[\because x^2+x+1>0, \text{ for all } x]$$

$$\Rightarrow x^2+x\ge 0$$

and $\quad x^2+x\le 0$

$$\Rightarrow x^2+x=0$$

$$\Rightarrow x=0,-1$$

Clearly, these two values satisfy the given equation. Hence, $x=0,-1$ are the solutions of the given equation.

15 (d) Given, $y=\cos^{-1}(x^2-4)$

$$\Rightarrow \cos y=x^2-4$$

$$\because -1\le\cos y\le 1$$

$$\Rightarrow -1\le x^2-4\le 1$$

$$\Rightarrow 3\le x^2\le 5$$

$$\Rightarrow \sqrt{3}\le|x|\le\sqrt{5}$$

$$\Rightarrow x\in[-\sqrt{5},-\sqrt{3}]\cup[\sqrt{3},\sqrt{5}]$$

16 (b) Let $\sin^{-1}(0.6)=\theta$

$$\Rightarrow \sin\theta=0.6$$

$$\Rightarrow \cos\theta=\sqrt{1-0.36}$$

$$=\sqrt{0.64}=0.8$$

$$\therefore \sin 2\theta=2\sin\theta\cdot\cos\theta$$

$$=2\times 0.6\times 0.8$$

$$=0.96$$

17 (*d*) Given, $\tan\left(\frac{\pi}{4}+\frac{1}{2}\cos^{-1}\frac{a}{b}\right)+\tan\left(\frac{\pi}{4}-\frac{1}{2}\cos^{-1}\frac{a}{b}\right)$

Let $\frac{1}{2}\cos^{-1}\frac{a}{b}=x$

$\Rightarrow \quad \cos 2x=\frac{a}{b}$

So, $\tan\left(\frac{\pi}{4}+x\right)+\tan\left(\frac{\pi}{4}-x\right)$

$=\frac{1+\tan x}{1-\tan x}+\frac{1-\tan x}{1+\tan x}$

$=\frac{1+\tan^2 x+2\tan x+1+\tan^2 x-2\tan x}{1-\tan^2 x}$

$=\frac{2(1+\tan^2 x)}{1-\tan^2 x}=\frac{2}{\cos 2x}$

$=\frac{2}{\frac{a}{b}}=\frac{2b}{a}$

18 (*b*) From figure, we note that $\tan x$ is an increasing function in the interval $\left(-\frac{\pi}{2},\frac{\pi}{2}\right)$, since $1>\frac{\pi}{4}$.

This gives

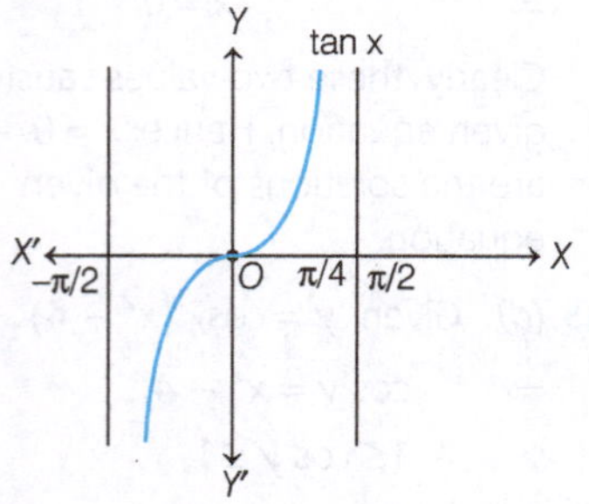

$\tan 1>1$

$\Rightarrow \quad \tan 1>1>\frac{\pi}{4}$

$\Rightarrow \quad \tan 1>1>\tan^{-1}(1)$

19 (*a*) Given, $\sin^{-1}x+\sin^{-1}y=\frac{\pi}{2}$

$\Rightarrow \quad \frac{\pi}{2}-\cos^{-1}x+\frac{\pi}{2}-\cos^{-1}y=\frac{\pi}{2}$

$\left[\because \sin^{-1}x+\cos^{-1}x=\frac{\pi}{2}\right]$

$\Rightarrow \quad \cos^{-1}x+\cos^{-1}y=\frac{\pi}{2}$

20 (*a*) The domain of $\cos x$ is R and the domain of $\sin^{-1}$ is $[-1,1]$.

$\therefore$ Domain of

$\sin^{-1}x+\cos x=[-1,1]\cap R=[-1,1]$

21 (*c*) Given, $a_1, a_2, a_3, a_4, \ldots, a_n$ is an arithmetic progression. Then,

$d=a_2-a_1=a_3-a_2=\cdots=a_n-a_{n-1}$

$\therefore \quad \tan\left[\tan^{-1}\left(\frac{d}{1+a_1a_2}\right)+\tan^{-1}\left(\frac{d}{1+a_2a_3}\right)+\tan^{-1}\left(\frac{d}{1+a_3a_4}\right)+\ldots.+\tan^{-1}\left(\frac{d}{1+a_{n-1}a_n}\right)\right]$

$=\tan\left[\tan^{-1}\left(\frac{a_2-a_1}{1+a_1a_2}\right)+\tan^{-1}\left(\frac{a_3-a_2}{1+a_2a_3}\right)+\tan^{-1}\left(\frac{a_4-a_3}{1+a_3a_4}\right)+\ldots.+\tan^{-1}\left(\frac{a_n-a_{n-1}}{1+a_{n-1}a_n}\right)\right]$

$=\tan[\tan^{-1}a_2-\tan^{-1}a_1+\tan^{-1}a_3-\tan^{-1}a_2+\tan^{-1}a_4-\tan^{-1}a_3+\ldots..+\tan^{-1}a_n-\tan^{-1}a_{n-1}]$

$\left[\because \tan^{-1}\left[\frac{x-y}{1+xy}\right]=\tan^{-1}x-\tan^{-1}y\right]$

$=\tan[\tan^{-1}a_n-\tan^{-1}a_1]$

$=\tan\left[\tan^{-1}\left(\frac{a_n-a_1}{1+a_na_1}\right)\right]=\frac{a_n-a_1}{1+a_1a_n}$

22 (*c*) We have, $\sin(2\tan^{-1}(0.75))$

$=\sin\left[\sin^{-1}\frac{2\times(0.75)}{1+(0.75)^2}\right]$

$\left[\because 2\tan^{-1}x=\sin^{-1}\frac{2x}{1+x^2}\right]$

$=\sin\left[\sin^{-1}\frac{1.5}{1.5625}\right]$

$=\sin[\sin^{-1}0.96]=0.96$

23 (*b*) Given,

$\tan^{-1}x-\cot^{-1}x=\tan^{-1}\left(\frac{1}{\sqrt{3}}\right)$

$\Rightarrow \quad \tan^{-1}x-\cot^{-1}x=\frac{\pi}{6}$ ...(i)

But $\quad \tan^{-1}x+\cot^{-1}x=\frac{\pi}{2}$ ...(ii)

On adding Eqs. (i) and (ii), we get

$2\tan^{-1}x=\frac{\pi}{6}+\frac{\pi}{2}=\frac{2\pi}{3}$

$\Rightarrow \quad \tan^{-1}x=\frac{\pi}{3}$

$\Rightarrow \quad x=\tan\frac{\pi}{3}\Rightarrow x=\sqrt{3}$

Thus, the equation has unique solution.

24 (*b*) We have, $-\frac{\pi}{2}\le\sin^{-1}x\le\frac{\pi}{2}$

$-\frac{\pi}{2}+\frac{\pi}{2}\le\sin^{-1}x+\frac{\pi}{2}\le\frac{\pi}{2}+\frac{\pi}{2}$

$0\le\sin^{-1}x+\sin^{-1}x+\cos^{-1}x\le\pi$

$0\le 2\sin^{-1}x+\cos^{-1}x\le\pi$

25 (*c*) $\tan^2(\sec^{-1}2)+\cot^2(\operatorname{cosec}^{-1}3)$

$=\sec^2(\sec^{-1}2)-1+\operatorname{cosec}^2(\operatorname{cosec}^{-1}3)-1$

$=(2)^2+(3)^2-2=4+9-2=11$

26 (*b*) Let $x=\sin\alpha$ and $\sqrt{x}=\sin\beta$

Hence, $\sin^{-1}\left(x\sqrt{1-x}-\sqrt{x}\sqrt{1-x^2}\right)$

$=\sin^{-1}\left(\sin\alpha\sqrt{1-\sin^2\beta}-\sin\beta\sqrt{1-\sin^2\alpha}\right)$

$=\sin^{-1}(\sin\alpha\cos\beta-\cos\alpha\sin\beta)$

$=\sin^{-1}(\sin(\alpha-\beta))=\alpha-\beta$

$=\sin^{-1}x-\sin^{-1}\sqrt{x}$

27 (*a*) Given,

$\sqrt{1+\cos 2x}=\sqrt{2}\cos^{-1}(\cos x)$

$\Rightarrow \quad \sqrt{2\cos^2 x}=\sqrt{2}x$

$\Rightarrow \quad \sqrt{2}|\cos x|=\sqrt{2}x$

$\Rightarrow \quad -\cos x=x \quad [\because x\in[\pi/2,\pi]]$

which is not true for any real value of x.

28 (*b*) Let $\sin^{-1}x=\alpha$, $\sin^{-1}y=\beta$ and $\sin^{-1}z=\gamma$

$\therefore \quad \alpha+\beta+\gamma=\frac{\pi}{2}$ [given]

$\Rightarrow \quad \alpha+\beta=\frac{\pi}{2}-\gamma$

$\Rightarrow \cos(\alpha+\beta)=\cos\left(\frac{\pi}{2}-\gamma\right)$

$\Rightarrow \cos\alpha\cos\beta-\sin\alpha\sin\beta=\sin\gamma$ ...(i)

We have, $\quad \sin\alpha=x$

$\Rightarrow \quad \cos\alpha=\sqrt{1-x^2}$

$$\sin\beta = y$$
$$\Rightarrow \quad \cos\beta = \sqrt{1-y^2}$$
$\therefore$ From Eq. (i), we get
$$\sqrt{1-x^2}\sqrt{1-y^2} - xy = z$$
$$\Rightarrow \quad \sqrt{1-x^2}\sqrt{1-y^2} = xy + z$$
Squaring on both sides, we get
$$\Rightarrow \quad (1-x^2)(1-y^2) = (xy+z)^2$$
$$\Rightarrow 1 - x^2 - y^2 + x^2y^2 = x^2y^2 + z^2 + 2xyz$$
$$\Rightarrow \quad x^2 + y^2 + z^2 + 2xyz = 1$$

29 (*b*) We have,
$$\cos\left[2\cos^{-1}\frac{1}{5} + \sin^{-1}\frac{1}{5}\right]$$
$$= \cos\left[\cos^{-1}\frac{1}{5} + \cos^{-1}\frac{1}{5} + \sin^{-1}\frac{1}{5}\right]$$
$$= \cos\left[\frac{\pi}{2} + \cos^{-1}\frac{1}{5}\right] \quad \left[\because \sin^{-1}x + \cos^{-1}x = \frac{\pi}{2}\right]$$
$$= -\sin\left(\cos^{-1}\frac{1}{5}\right)$$
$$= -\sin\left[\sin^{-1}\sqrt{1-\frac{1}{25}}\right]$$
$$= -\sin\left[\sin^{-1}\frac{2\sqrt{6}}{5}\right] = -\frac{2\sqrt{6}}{5}$$

30 (*b*) Let $\cos^{-1}\frac{4}{5} = x$
$$\Rightarrow \quad \cos x = \frac{4}{5} \Rightarrow \sec x = \frac{5}{4}$$
$$\Rightarrow \quad \tan x = \sqrt{\frac{25}{16} - 1}$$
$$\Rightarrow \quad \tan x = \frac{3}{4} \Rightarrow x = \tan^{-1}\frac{3}{4}$$
Hence, $\tan\left[\cos^{-1}\frac{4}{5} + \tan^{-1}\frac{2}{3}\right]$
$$= \tan\left[\tan^{-1}\frac{3}{4} + \tan^{-1}\frac{2}{3}\right]$$
$$= \tan\left[\tan^{-1}\frac{\frac{3}{4}+\frac{2}{3}}{1-\frac{3}{4}\times\frac{2}{3}}\right]$$
$$= \tan\left[\tan^{-1}\frac{9+8}{12-6}\right]$$
$$= \tan\left[\tan^{-1}\frac{17}{6}\right] = \frac{17}{6}$$

31 (*c*) Given,
$$\tan^{-1}\frac{a+x}{a} + \tan^{-1}\frac{a-x}{a} = \frac{\pi}{6}$$
$$\Rightarrow \tan^{-1}\left[\frac{\frac{a+x}{a} + \frac{a-x}{a}}{1 - \left(\frac{a+x}{a}\right)\left(\frac{a-x}{a}\right)}\right] = \frac{\pi}{6}$$
$$\left[\because \tan^{-1}x + \tan^{-1}y = \tan^{-1}\left(\frac{x+y}{1-xy}\right)\right]$$
$$\Rightarrow \tan^{-1}\left[\frac{\frac{a+x+a-x}{a}}{\frac{a^2-a^2+x^2}{a^2}}\right] = \frac{\pi}{6}$$
$$\Rightarrow \quad \frac{2a^2}{x^2} = \tan\frac{\pi}{6}$$
$$\Rightarrow \quad \frac{2a^2}{x^2} = \frac{1}{\sqrt{3}} \Rightarrow x^2 = 2\sqrt{3}a^2$$

32 (*c*) We have, $\cos[\tan^{-1}\{\sin(\cot^{-1}x)\}]$

Let $\quad \cot^{-1}x = \alpha$
$$\Rightarrow \quad \cot\alpha = x$$
$$\Rightarrow \quad \operatorname{cosec}\alpha = \sqrt{1+x^2}$$
$$\Rightarrow \quad \sin\alpha = \frac{1}{\sqrt{1+x^2}}$$
$$\Rightarrow \quad \alpha = \sin^{-1}\frac{1}{\sqrt{1+x^2}}$$
Hence, $\cos[\tan^{-1}\{\sin(\cot^{-1}x)\}]$
$$= \cos\left[\tan^{-1}\left\{\sin\left(\sin^{-1}\frac{1}{\sqrt{1+x^2}}\right)\right\}\right]$$
$$= \cos\left[\tan^{-1}\frac{1}{\sqrt{1+x^2}}\right]$$
$$= \cos\left[\cos^{-1}\sqrt{\frac{x^2+1}{x^2+2}}\right]$$
$$\left[\begin{array}{l}\because \text{If we let } \tan^{-1}\frac{1}{\sqrt{1+x^2}} = \beta \\ \tan\beta = \frac{1}{\sqrt{1+x^2}} \\ \sec\beta = \sqrt{1+\frac{1}{1+x^2}} = \sqrt{\frac{x^2+2}{x^2+1}} \\ \cos\beta = \sqrt{\frac{x^2+1}{x^2+2}}\end{array}\right]$$
$$= \sqrt{\frac{x^2+1}{x^2+2}}$$

Numerical Type Questions

1 (15) $\sec^2(\tan^{-1}2) + \operatorname{cosec}^2(\cot^{-1}3)$
$$= 1 + \tan^2(\tan^{-1}2) + 1 + \cot^2(\cot^{-1}3)$$
$$= 2 + 4 + 9 = 15$$

2 (3) For $f(x)$ to be defined,
$$3x + 2 \neq 0 \Rightarrow x \neq -\frac{2}{3}$$
and $\quad -1 \le \frac{x+1}{3x+2} \le 1$

and $\quad \frac{x+1}{3x+2} \ge -1$
$$\Rightarrow \quad \frac{x+1+3x+2}{3x+2} \ge 0$$
$$\Rightarrow \quad \frac{4x+3}{3x+2} \ge 0$$
$$x \in \left(-\infty, -\frac{3}{4}\right) \cup \left(-\frac{2}{3}, \infty\right)$$
$$\frac{x+1}{3x+2} \le 1$$
$$\frac{x+1-3x-2}{3x+2} \le 0$$
$$\frac{2x+1}{3x+2} \ge 0$$
$$x \in \left(-\infty, -\frac{2}{3}\right) \cup \left[-\frac{1}{2}, \infty\right)$$
$$\therefore \quad x \in \left(-\infty, -\frac{3}{4}\right] \cup \left[-\frac{1}{2}, \infty\right)$$
$$R - \left(\frac{-3}{4}, -\frac{1}{2}\right)$$
$$\therefore \quad \alpha = -\frac{3}{4} \Rightarrow \beta = -\frac{1}{2}$$
$$8\alpha\beta = 8\left(-\frac{3}{4}\right)\left(-\frac{1}{2}\right) = 3$$

3 (3) Let $f(x) = x^2 + x + 1$
$$= \left(x + \frac{1}{2}\right)^2 + \frac{3}{4}$$
$$f(x) \ge \frac{3}{4}$$
So, $\frac{3}{4} \le f(x) \le 1$
$$[\because \sin^{-1}x, -1 \le x \le 1 \text{ and } \sqrt{f(x)} \ge 0]$$
$$\Rightarrow \quad \sin^{-1}\left(\frac{\sqrt{3}}{2}\right) \le \sin^{-1}(\sqrt{f(x)}) \le \sin^{-1}(1)$$
$$\text{Range} = \left[\frac{\pi}{3}, \frac{\pi}{2}\right]$$
So that $\alpha = 3$

4 (2) The graph of $y = \sin^{-1}(\sin x)$ is

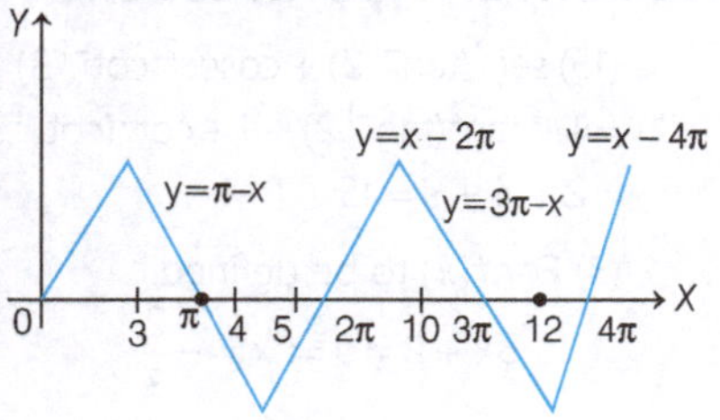

$$y(3) + y(4) + y(5) = (\pi - 3) + (\pi - 4) + (5 - 2\pi) = -2$$

$$-k = -2 \Rightarrow k = 2$$

5 (0) $\tan^{-1} x + \tan^{-1} y = \tan^{-1} 3$

$$\tan^{-1}\left(\frac{x+y}{1-xy}\right) = \tan^{-1} 3$$

$$\Rightarrow \frac{x+y}{1-xy} = 3,$$

$$x + y = 3 - 3xy$$

$$\Rightarrow y = \frac{3-x}{1+3x}, x, y \text{ are positive}$$

$$\Rightarrow x < 3$$

$$\Rightarrow x = 1, y = \frac{1}{2}, x = 2, y = \frac{1}{7}$$

$\therefore$ There are no integer pairs (x, y).

6 (4) Taking tan, both side

$$\frac{\frac{x-1}{x+1} + \frac{2x-1}{2x+1}}{1 - \frac{(x-1)(2x-1)}{(x+1)(2x+1)}} = \frac{23}{36}$$

$$\Rightarrow \frac{2x^2 - x - 1 + 2x^2 + x - 1}{2x^2 + 3x + 1 - 2x^2 + 3x - 1} = \frac{23}{36}$$

$$\Rightarrow \frac{4x^2 - 2}{6x} = \frac{23}{36}$$

$$\Rightarrow 24x^2 - 12 = 23x$$

$$\Rightarrow 24x^2 - 23x - 12 = 0$$

$$\Rightarrow x = \frac{4}{3}, -\frac{3}{8}$$

$x = -3/8$ makes the left hand side negative.

$$\therefore \quad x = 4/3$$

$$\therefore \quad 3x = 4$$

7 (2) $S_n = \tan^{-1}\left(\frac{4}{1+2\cdot 6}\right) + \tan^{-1}\left(\frac{6}{1+6\cdot 12}\right) + \tan^{-1}\left(\frac{6}{1+12\times 20}\right) + \ldots\ldots \text{ upto } n$

$$S_n = \tan^{-1}\left(\frac{6-2}{1+2\times 6}\right) + \tan^{-1}\left(\frac{12-6}{1+6\cdot 12}\right) + \tan^{-1}\left(\frac{20-12}{1+12\times 20}\right) + \ldots + \tan^{-1}\frac{2(n+1)}{1+[n(n+1)][(n+1)(n+2)]}$$

$$S_n = (\tan^{-1} 6 - \tan^{-1} 2) + (\tan^{-1} 12 - \tan^{-1} 6) + (\tan^{-1} 20 - \tan^{-1} 12) + \ldots + \tan^{-1}((n+1)(n+2) - \tan^{-1}(n(n+1))$$

$$S_n = \tan^{-1}[(n+1)(n+2) - \tan^{-1} 2]$$

$$S_n = \tan^{-1}\left[\frac{(n+1)(n+2) - 2}{1 + 2\cdot(n+1)(n+2)}\right]$$

$$S_n = \tan^{-1}\left(\frac{n^2 + 3n}{2n^2 + 6n + 5}\right)$$

$$S_\infty = \lim_{n\to\infty} S_n = \lim_{n\to\infty} \tan^{-1}\left(\frac{n^2 + 3n}{2n^2 + 6n + 5}\right)$$

$$= \lim_{n\to\infty} \tan^{-1}\left(\frac{1 + \frac{3}{n}}{2 + \frac{6}{n} + \frac{5}{n^2}}\right)$$

$$= \tan^{-1}\left(\frac{1}{2}\right)$$

$$S_\infty = \cot^{-1}(2)$$

Therefore, $\cot(\cot^{-1} 2) = 2$.

8 (9) Given,

$$\sin^{-1}\left[\cos\left(\frac{2x^2 + 10|x| + 4}{x^2 + 5|x| + 3}\right)\right] = \cot\left[\cot^{-1}\left(\frac{2 - 18|x|}{9|x|}\right) + \frac{\pi}{2}\right]$$

$$\Rightarrow \frac{\pi}{2} - \cos^{-1}\left[\cos\left(\frac{2(x^2 + 5|x| + 3) - 2}{x^2 + 5|x| + 3}\right)\right] = \cot\left[\cot^{-1}\left(\frac{2}{9|x|} - 2\right)\right] + \frac{\pi}{2}$$

$$\Rightarrow \frac{\pi}{2} - 2 + \frac{2}{x^2 + 5|x| + 3} = \frac{2}{9|x|} - 2 + \frac{\pi}{2}$$

$$\Rightarrow |x|^2 - 4|x| + 3 = 0$$

$$\Rightarrow |x| = 1 \text{ or } 3 \Rightarrow x = \pm 1, \pm 3$$

$\therefore$ Product $= (1)(-1)(3)(-3) = 9$.

9 (6) Let $\sin^{-1}(\log_2 x) = u$ ...(i)

and $\cos^{-1}(\log_2 y) = v$ ...(ii)

So, given equation becomes

$$3u + v = \frac{\pi}{2} \quad \text{...(iii)}$$

$$\text{and} \quad u + 2v = \frac{11\pi}{6} \quad \text{...(iv)}$$

On solving Eqs. (iii) and (iv), we get

$$u = -\frac{\pi}{6} \text{ and } v = \pi$$

Hence, $x = \frac{1}{\sqrt{2}}$ and $y = \frac{1}{2}$

[from Eqs. (i) and (ii)]

$$\Rightarrow \frac{1}{x^2} + \frac{1}{y^2} = 6$$

10 (6) Given,

$$\sin[2\cos^{-1}\{\cot(2\tan^{-1} x)\}] = 0$$

$$\Rightarrow 2\cos^{-1}\{\cot(2\tan^{-1} x)\} = n\pi, n \in I$$

$$\Rightarrow \cos^{-1}(\cot(2\tan^{-1} x)) = \frac{n\pi}{2}, n \in I$$

$$\Rightarrow \cos^{-1}(\cot(2\tan^{-1} x)) = \begin{cases} 0, & n = 0 \\ \frac{\pi}{2}, & n = 1 \\ \pi, & n = 2 \end{cases}$$

$$\Rightarrow \cot(2\tan^{-1} x) = \begin{cases} 1, & n = 0 \\ 0, & n = 1 \\ -1, & n = 2 \end{cases}$$

$$\Rightarrow 2\tan^{-1} x = \begin{cases} k\pi + \frac{\pi}{4} \\ k\pi + \frac{\pi}{2}, \text{ where } k \in I \\ k\pi - \frac{\pi}{4} \end{cases}$$

$$\Rightarrow \tan^{-1} x = \begin{cases} \frac{k\pi}{2} + \frac{\pi}{8} \\ \frac{k\pi}{2} + \frac{\pi}{4}, \text{ where } k \in I \\ \frac{k\pi}{2} - \frac{\pi}{8}, \end{cases}$$

$$\Rightarrow \tan^{-1} x = \begin{cases} \frac{\pi}{8}, \frac{-3\pi}{8} \\ \frac{\pi}{4}, \frac{-\pi}{4} \\ \frac{-\pi}{8}, \frac{3\pi}{8} \end{cases}$$

$$\Rightarrow x = \pm 1, \pm(\sqrt{2} - 1), \pm(\sqrt{2} + 1)$$

Hence, the total number of solutions is 6.

11 (9) $f(x) = \tan^{-1}\left(\dfrac{\left(\dfrac{x}{2}-1\right)}{1+x\left(\dfrac{x}{2}+1\right)}\right)$

$= \tan^{-1}(x) - \tan^{-1}\left(\dfrac{x}{2}+1\right)$

$\Rightarrow f'(x) = \dfrac{1}{(1+x^2)} - \dfrac{1}{\left(1+\left(\dfrac{x}{2}+1\right)^2\right)} \times \dfrac{1}{2}$

$\Rightarrow f'(1) = \dfrac{1}{2} - \dfrac{1}{2\left(1+\dfrac{9}{4}\right)}$

$= \dfrac{1}{2} - \dfrac{2}{13} = \dfrac{9}{26}$

$\Rightarrow \quad 26 f'(1) = 9$

12 (1) We have,

$T_n = 2 \operatorname{arc} \cot \left(\dfrac{n^2+n+4}{2}\right)$

$= 2\tan^{-1}\left(\dfrac{2}{n^2+n+4}\right)$

$T_n = 2\tan^{-1}\left(\dfrac{\dfrac{1}{2}}{1+\dfrac{(n(n+1))}{2\cdot 2}}\right)$

$= 2\left(\tan^{-1}\left(\dfrac{n+1}{2}\right) - \tan^{-1}\left(\dfrac{n}{2}\right)\right)$

Hence, $S_n = \sum_{n=0}^{n} T_n = 2\sum_{n=0}^{n} \left(\tan^{-1}\left(\dfrac{n+1}{2}\right) - \tan^{-1}\left(\dfrac{n}{2}\right)\right)$

$S_n = \tan^{-1}\left(\dfrac{1}{2}\right) - \tan^{-1}(0) + \tan^{-1}(1) - \tan^{-1}\left(\dfrac{1}{2}\right) + \ldots\ldots + \tan^{-1}\left(\dfrac{n+1}{2}\right) - \tan^{-1}\left(\dfrac{n}{2}\right)$

$\Rightarrow \quad S_n = 2\tan^{-1}\left(\dfrac{n+1}{2}\right)$

$\therefore \lim_{n\to\infty} S_n = 2\cdot\left(\dfrac{\pi}{2}\right)$

$= \pi = k\pi$ [given]

$\Rightarrow \quad k = 1$

13 (8) $\sin(30° + \tan^{-1} x) = \dfrac{13}{14}$

$\Rightarrow \dfrac{1}{2}\cos(\tan^{-1} x) + \dfrac{\sqrt{3}}{2}\sin(\tan^{-1} x) = \dfrac{13}{14}$

$\Rightarrow \quad 7(1+\sqrt{3}x) = 13\sqrt{1+x^2}$

$\Rightarrow 11x^2 - 49\sqrt{3}x + 60 = 0$

[on squaring]

$\Rightarrow \quad x = \dfrac{49\sqrt{3} \pm 39\sqrt{3}}{22} = \dfrac{5\sqrt{3}}{11}, 4\sqrt{3}$

[reject]

$\therefore \quad x = \dfrac{5\sqrt{3}}{11}$

Given, $x = \dfrac{a\sqrt{3}}{b}$

Therefore, $a = 5$ and $b = 11$

$\Rightarrow \quad \dfrac{a+b}{2} = 8$

Assertion and Reason Questions

1 (*a*) If we restrict the domain of cosec function to $\left[\dfrac{-\pi}{2}, \dfrac{\pi}{2}\right] - \{0\}$, then it is one-one and onto and its range is the set $R-(-1, 1)$. Actually, cosec function restricted to any of the intervals $\left[\dfrac{-3\pi}{2}, \dfrac{-\pi}{2}\right] - \{-\pi\}$, $\left[\dfrac{-\pi}{2}, \dfrac{\pi}{2}\right] - \{0\}$, $\left[\dfrac{\pi}{2}, \dfrac{3\pi}{2}\right] - \{\pi\}$ etc. is bijective and its range is the set of all real numbers $R-(-1, 1)$.

Thus, $\operatorname{cosec}^{-1}$ can be defined as a function whose domain is $R-(-1, 1)$ and range could be any of the intervals $\left[\dfrac{-\pi}{2}, \dfrac{\pi}{2}\right] - \{0\}$, $\left[\dfrac{-3\pi}{2}, \dfrac{-\pi}{2}\right] - \{-\pi\}$, $\left[\dfrac{\pi}{2}, \dfrac{3\pi}{2}\right] - \{\pi\}$ etc.

2 (*b*) $\tan^{-1}$ can be defined as a function whose domain is R and range could be any of the intervals $\left(\dfrac{-3\pi}{2}, \dfrac{-\pi}{2}\right)$, $\left(\dfrac{-\pi}{2}, \dfrac{\pi}{2}\right)$, $\left(\dfrac{\pi}{2}, \dfrac{3\pi}{2}\right)$ and so on.

These intervals give different branches of the function $\tan^{-1}$. The branch with range $\left(\dfrac{-\pi}{2}, \dfrac{\pi}{2}\right)$ is called the principal value branch of the function $\tan^{-1}$.

3 (*a*) Let $\theta = \cos^{-1}\left[\cos\left(\dfrac{13\pi}{6}\right)\right] \neq \dfrac{13\pi}{6}$

$\left[\because \dfrac{13\pi}{6} \notin [0, \pi]\right]$

Now, $\theta = \cos^{-1}\left[\cos\left(2\pi + \dfrac{\pi}{6}\right)\right]$

[$\because$ range of $\cos^{-1} x$ is $[0, \pi]$]

$= \cos^{-1}\left[\cos\dfrac{\pi}{6}\right]$

[$\because \cos[2\pi + x] = \cos x$]

$= \dfrac{\pi}{6}$

[$\because \cos^{-1}(\cos x) = x$, if $x \in [0, \pi]$]

$\therefore$ Both A and R are correct; R is correct explanation of A.

4 (*c*) Given,

$\tan^{-1}\dfrac{x-1}{x-2} + \tan^{-1}\dfrac{x+1}{x+2} = \dfrac{\pi}{4}$

$\Rightarrow \tan^{-1}\left(\dfrac{\dfrac{x-1}{x-2} + \dfrac{x+1}{x+2}}{1-\left(\dfrac{x-1}{x-2}\right)\left(\dfrac{x+1}{x+2}\right)}\right) = \dfrac{\pi}{4}$

$\left[\because \tan^{-1} x + \tan^{-1} y = \tan^{-1}\left(\dfrac{x+y}{1-xy}\right)\right]$

$\Rightarrow \tan^{-1}\left(\dfrac{\dfrac{(x-1)(x+2)+(x+1)(x-2)}{(x-2)(x+2)}}{\dfrac{(x-2)(x+2)-(x-1)(x+1)}{(x-2)(x+2)}}\right) = \dfrac{\pi}{4}$

$\Rightarrow \dfrac{(x-1)(x+2)+(x+1)(x-2)}{(x-2)(x+2)-(x-1)(x+1)} = \tan\dfrac{\pi}{4}$

$\Rightarrow \quad \dfrac{2x^2-4}{(x^2-4)-(x^2-1)} = 1$

$\left[\because \tan\dfrac{\pi}{4} = 1\right]$

$\Rightarrow \quad 2x^2 - 4 = -3$

$\Rightarrow \quad 2x^2 = 1$

$\Rightarrow \quad x^2 = \frac{1}{2}$

$\Rightarrow \quad x = \pm\frac{1}{\sqrt{2}}$

Now, $\tan^{-1}\left(\tan\frac{3\pi}{4}\right)$

$= \tan^{-1}\left[\tan\left(\pi - \frac{\pi}{4}\right)\right]$

$= \tan^{-1}\left(-\tan\frac{\pi}{4}\right)$

$[\because \tan(\pi - \theta) = -\tan\theta]$

$= \tan^{-1}\left[\tan\left(-\frac{\pi}{4}\right)\right]$

$[\because -\tan\theta = \tan(-\theta)]$

$= -\frac{\pi}{4}$

which lies in the range $\left(-\frac{\pi}{2}, \frac{\pi}{2}\right)$.

5 (c) LHS

$= \cot^{-1}\left(\frac{\sqrt{1+\sin x} + \sqrt{1-\sin x}}{\sqrt{1+\sin x} - \sqrt{1-\sin x}}\right)$ ...(i)

Now, we can write $\sqrt{1+\sin x}$

$= \sqrt{\sin^2\frac{x}{2} + \cos^2\frac{x}{2} + 2\sin\frac{x}{2}\cos\frac{x}{2}}$

$= \sqrt{\left(\sin\frac{x}{2} + \cos\frac{x}{2}\right)^2}$

$\left[\because \sin^2\frac{x}{2} + \cos^2\frac{x}{2} = 1 \text{ and } \sin x = 2\sin\frac{x}{2}\cos\frac{x}{2}\right]$

$\Rightarrow \sqrt{1+\sin x} = \left(\sin\frac{x}{2} + \cos\frac{x}{2}\right)$

$\left[\because x \in \left(0, \frac{\pi}{4}\right)\right]$

Similarly, we can get

$\sqrt{1-\sin x} = \cos\frac{x}{2} - \sin\frac{x}{2}$

On substituting above two values in Eq. (i), we get

LHS $= \cot^{-1}\left(\frac{\sin\frac{x}{2} + \cos\frac{x}{2} + \cos\frac{x}{2} - \sin\frac{x}{2}}{\sin\frac{x}{2} + \cos\frac{x}{2} + \sin\frac{x}{2} - \cos\frac{x}{2}}\right)$

$= \cot^{-1}\left(\frac{2\cos\frac{x}{2}}{2\sin\frac{x}{2}}\right)$

$= \cot^{-1}\left(\cot\frac{x}{2}\right) = \frac{x}{2} = \text{RHS}$

Let $x = \cos\theta$ so that $\cos^{-1}x = \theta$

$\therefore \quad \tan^{-1}\left(\frac{\sqrt{1+x} - \sqrt{1-x}}{\sqrt{1+x} + \sqrt{1-x}}\right)$

$= \tan^{-1}\left(\frac{\sqrt{1+\cos\theta} - \sqrt{1-\cos\theta}}{\sqrt{1+\cos\theta} + \sqrt{1-\cos\theta}}\right)$

$= \tan^{-1}\left(\frac{\sqrt{2}\cos\frac{\theta}{2} - \sqrt{2}\sin\frac{\theta}{2}}{\sqrt{2}\cos\frac{\theta}{2} + \sqrt{2}\sin\frac{\theta}{2}}\right)$

$\left[\because 1+\cos\theta = 2\cos^2\frac{\theta}{2} \text{ and } 1-\cos\theta = 2\sin^2\frac{\theta}{2}\right]$

$= \tan^{-1}\left(\frac{\cos\frac{\theta}{2} - \sin\frac{\theta}{2}}{\cos\frac{\theta}{2} + \sin\frac{\theta}{2}}\right)$

$= \tan^{-1}\left(\frac{1-\tan\frac{\theta}{2}}{1+\tan\frac{\theta}{2}}\right)$

[inside the bracket divide, numerator and denominator by $\cos\frac{\theta}{2}$]

$= \tan^{-1}\left(\tan\left(\frac{\pi}{4} - \frac{\theta}{2}\right)\right)$

$\left[\because \tan(A-B) = \frac{\tan A - \tan B}{1 + \tan A \tan B}\right]$

$= \frac{\pi}{4} - \frac{\theta}{2} = \frac{\pi}{4} - \frac{1}{2}\cos^{-1}x$

6 (d) We have, $\tan^{-1}x + \cot^{-1}(x+1)$

$= \tan^{-1}x + \tan^{-1}\frac{1}{x+1}$

$= \tan^{-1}\left(\frac{x + \frac{1}{x+1}}{1 - x\left(\frac{1}{x+1}\right)}\right)$

$= \tan^{-1}\left(\frac{x^2+x+1}{x+1-x}\right)$

$= \tan^{-1}(x^2+x+1)$

Hence, A is incorrect.

Now, $\cot^{-1}\frac{xy+1}{x-y} + \cot^{-1}\frac{yz+1}{y-z} + \cot^{-1}\frac{zx+1}{z-x}$

$= \tan^{-1}\frac{x-y}{1+xy} + \tan^{-1}\frac{y-z}{1+yz} + \tan^{-1}\frac{z-x}{1+zx} + \pi$

$= \tan^{-1}x - \tan^{-1}y + \tan^{-1}y - \tan^{-1}z + \tan^{-1}z - \tan^{-1}x + \pi$

$= \pi$

In this, we can consider

$x > y$ and $y > z$

$\Rightarrow \quad x > z$

$\Rightarrow \quad z - x < 0$

$\cot^{-1}x = \pi + \tan^{-1}\frac{1}{x}$, when $x < 0$

$\therefore$ R is correct

7 (b) We know that $\sin^{-1}(\sin\theta) = \theta$, if $-\frac{\pi}{2} < \theta < \frac{\pi}{2}$. Here, $\theta = 10°$ does not lie between $-\frac{\pi}{2}$ and $\frac{\pi}{2}$. But $3\pi - 10°$ lies between $-\pi/2$ and $\pi/2$. Also $\sin(3\pi - 10) = \sin 10$. Therefore,

$\sin^{-1}(\sin 10) = \sin^{-1}(\sin(3\pi - 10))$

$= 3\pi - 10.$

So, assertion is correct.

$\cos^{-1}(\cos\theta) = \theta$, if $0 \le \theta \le \pi$, we find that $4\pi - 10$ lies between 0 and π. Also, $\cos(4\pi - 10) = \cos 10$ Therefore, Reason is correct but it is not a correct explanation for Assertion.

8 (a) $\sin^{-1} : [-1, 1] \to \left[-\frac{\pi}{2}, \frac{\pi}{2}\right]$ is a bijection and the greatest value of $\sin^{-1}x$ is $\frac{\pi}{2}$ at $x = 1$

So, Reason is correct.

Now, $\sin^{-1}x + \sin^{-1}y + \sin^{-1}z = \frac{3\pi}{2}$

$\Rightarrow \sin^{-1}x = \sin^{-1}y = \sin^{-1}z = \frac{\pi}{2}$

$\Rightarrow \quad x = y = z = 1$

Hence, $x^{2020}+y^{2021}+z^{2022}-\dfrac{9}{x^{2022}+x^{2024}+x^{2026}}$

$=3-\dfrac{9}{3}=0$

So, Assertion is also true. Clearly, Reason is correct explanation for Assertion.

9 (*b*) Let $x=\cos\theta$, then $\frac{1}{2}\le x\le 1$

$\Rightarrow \quad \frac{1}{2}\le\cos\theta\le 1$

$\Rightarrow \quad 0\le\theta\le\frac{\pi}{3}$

$\therefore \cos^{-1}x-\sin^{-1}\left\{\frac{x}{2}+\frac{\sqrt{3-3x^2}}{2}\right\}$

$=\theta-\sin^{-1}\left\{\frac{1}{2}\cos\theta+\frac{\sqrt{3}}{2}\sin\theta\right\}$

$=\theta-\sin^{-1}\left(\sin\left(\frac{\pi}{6}+\theta\right)\right)$

$\left[\because 0\le\theta\le\frac{\pi}{3}\Rightarrow\frac{\pi}{6}\le\theta+\frac{\pi}{6}\le\frac{\pi}{2}\right]$

$=\theta-\frac{\pi}{6}-\theta=-\pi/6$

Therefore, Assertion is true.

Now, $x=\sin\theta$ (let)

Then, $-\frac{1}{\sqrt{2}}\le\sin\theta\le\frac{1}{\sqrt{2}}$

$-\frac{\pi}{4}\le\theta\le\frac{\pi}{4}$

$\therefore \sin^{-1}(2x\sqrt{1-x^2})=\sin^{-1}(\sin 2\theta)$

$\left[-\frac{\pi}{4}\le\theta\le\frac{\pi}{4}\Rightarrow-\frac{\pi}{2}\le 2\theta\le\frac{\pi}{2}\right]$

$=2\theta=2\sin^{-1}x$

So, Reason is true.

10 (c) In Assertion, we use

$\sin^{-1}x+\cos^{-1}x=\frac{\pi}{2}$

$\Rightarrow \quad x-\frac{x^2}{2}+\frac{x^3}{4}-\ldots..$

$=x^2-\frac{x^4}{2}+\frac{x^6}{6}\ldots$

$\Rightarrow \quad \dfrac{x}{1+\frac{x}{2}}=\dfrac{x^2}{1+\frac{x^2}{2}}$

$\Rightarrow \quad x=1 \qquad [\because 0<|x|<\sqrt{2}]$

Therefore, Assertion is true.

Now, in Reason if $x^2+x\ge 0$,

$x^2+x+1\ge 0$

and $0\le\sqrt{x^2+x+1}\le 1$

$\Rightarrow \quad x^2+x\ge 0$ and $x^2+x\le 0$

$\Rightarrow \quad x^2+x=0$

$\Rightarrow \quad x=0,-1$

$\Rightarrow \quad x=-1\ [\because -\sqrt{2}<x<0]$

So, $x=-1$ is a solution.

So, Reason is not true.

11 (c) Clearly, Reason is not true.

We have, $c^2=a^2+b^2$

So, $\quad a=c\cos\alpha$

and $\quad b=c\sin\alpha$

Then, $\sin^{-1}(x\cos\alpha)+\sin^{-1}(x\sin\alpha)=\sin^{-1}x$

$\Rightarrow \sin^{-1}\{x\cos\alpha\sqrt{1-x^2\sin^2\alpha}+x\sin\alpha\sqrt{1-x^2\cos^2\alpha}\}=\sin^{-1}x$

$\Rightarrow \cos\alpha\sqrt{1-x^2\sin^2\alpha}+\sin\alpha\sqrt{1-x^2\cos^2\alpha}=1$

So, $x=\pm 1$ satisfies the above equation

12 (*b*) We know that

$\sin:\left[-\frac{\pi}{2},\frac{\pi}{2}\right]\to[-1,1];$

$\cos:[0,\pi]\to[-1,1]$

$\tan:\left(-\frac{\pi}{2},\frac{\pi}{2}\right)\to R,$

$\operatorname{cosec}:\left[-\frac{\pi}{2},0\right)\cup\left(0,\frac{\pi}{2}\right]\to(-\infty,-1)\cup(1,\infty)$

$\sec:\left[0,\frac{\pi}{2}\right)\cup\left(\frac{\pi}{2},\pi\right]\to(-\infty,-1)\cup(1,\infty)$

$\cot:(0,\pi)\to R$ are invertible over their respective principal domains.

So, Assertion is true.

Now, we know that

$\tan^{-1}:R\to\left(-\frac{\pi}{2},\frac{\pi}{2}\right)$ invertible.

So, inverse of $\tan^{-1}x$ exists for all $x\in R$.

Thus, both A and R are correct.

Hence option (b) is correct.

13 (*a*) Reason (R) is a standard result. So, it is correct and using it, we obtain

$\tan^{-1}2+\tan^{-1}3=\pi+\tan^{-1}\left(\frac{2+3}{1-6}\right)$

$=\pi+\tan^{-1}(-1)$

$=\pi-\pi/4=3\pi/4$

Thus, both A and R are true and R is correct explation for A.

Hence, option (a) is correct.

Case or Paragraph Type Questions

1 (*b*) $\tan(\angle CAB)=\frac{CD}{AD}=\frac{30}{30\sqrt{3}}$

$\tan(\angle CAB)=\frac{1}{\sqrt{3}}$

$\sin(\angle CAB)=\left(\frac{1}{2}\right)$

$\angle CAB=\sin^{-1}\left(\frac{1}{2}\right)$

2 (*b*) Domain of $\sin^{-1}x$ is $[-1,1]$

and range is $\left[-\frac{\pi}{2},\frac{\pi}{2}\right]$.

3 (*d*) $\tan(\angle CBA)$

$=\tan\beta$

$=\dfrac{\text{Height of Tower}}{\text{Distance of } B \text{ from the tower}}$

$=\frac{30}{10\sqrt{3}}=\sqrt{3}$

$\beta=\tan^{-1}\sqrt{3}$

4 (*a*) Range of $\tan^{-1}x$ is $\left(-\frac{\pi}{2},\frac{\pi}{2}\right)$

and domain is $(-\infty,\infty)$.

5 (c) The domain of $\sin^{-1}x$ is $[-1,1]$

Domain of $\cos^{-1}x$ is $[-1,1]$

So $[-1,1]\cap[-1,1]$ is $[-1,1]$

$\therefore$ Domain of $\sin^{-1}x+\cos^{-1}x$ is $[-1,1]$

Range of $\sin^{-1}x+\cos^{-1}x=\frac{\pi}{2}$

6 (c) Domain of $f(x)$ is $[-1,1]$.

$(\sin^{-1}x)^2+(\cos^{-1}x)^2$

$=(\sin^{-1}x+\cos^{-1}x)^2-2\sin^{-1}x\cdot\cos^{-1}x$

$= \left(\frac{\pi}{2}\right)^2 - 2\left(\frac{\pi}{2} - \cos^{-1} x\right)(\cos^{-1} x)$

$= 2(\cos^{-1} x)^2 - \pi(\cos^{-1} x) + \frac{\pi^2}{4}$

On perfect squaring,

$2\left[\left(\cos^{-1} x - \frac{\pi}{4}\right)^2\right] + \frac{\pi^2}{8}$

So, the least value of $f(x)$ is $\frac{\pi^2}{8}$

and the greatest value is

$2 \cdot \frac{9\pi^2}{16} + \frac{\pi^2}{8} = \frac{10\pi^2}{8} = \frac{5\pi^2}{4}$

Hence, range is $\frac{\pi^2}{8}, \frac{5\pi^2}{4}$.

7 (a) Let $\cos^{-1} x + \cos^{-1} y = k$ ...(i)

$\sin^{-1} x + \sin^{-1} y = \frac{\pi}{2}$ ... (ii)

On adding Eqs. (i) and (ii),

$\cos^{-1} x + \cos^{-1} y + \sin^{-1} x + \sin^{-1} y = k + \frac{\pi}{2}$

$\Rightarrow \frac{\pi}{2} + \frac{\pi}{2} = k + \frac{\pi}{2} \Rightarrow k = \pi/2$

Past Years Questions

1 (d) Given, $\tan^{-1} x + \tan^{-1}(2x) = \frac{\pi}{4}$

$\Rightarrow \tan^{-1}\left(\frac{3x}{1-2x^2}\right) = \frac{\pi}{4}$

$\Rightarrow \frac{3x}{1-2x^2} = 1 \Rightarrow 3x = 1 - 2x^2$

$\Rightarrow 2x^2 + 3x - 1 = 0$

$\Rightarrow x = \frac{-3 \pm \sqrt{9+8}}{4}$

$\Rightarrow x = \frac{-3 \pm \sqrt{17}}{4}$

$\Rightarrow x = \frac{-3 - \sqrt{17}}{4} < 0$

or $x = \frac{-3 + \sqrt{17}}{4} > 0$

Hence, total number of positive real values of $x = 1$.

2 (c) Let $\sin^{-1} \alpha = A, \sin^{-1} \beta = B$ and $\sin^{-1} \gamma = C$

$\because \sin^{-1} \alpha + \sin^{-1} \beta + \sin^{-1} \gamma = \pi$

$\Rightarrow A + B + C = \pi$

Given, $(\alpha + \beta + \gamma)(\alpha - \gamma + \beta) = 3\alpha\beta$

$(\alpha + \beta)^2 - \gamma^2 = 3\alpha\beta$

$\alpha^2 + \beta^2 - \gamma^2 = \alpha\beta$

$\frac{\alpha^2 + \beta^2 - \gamma^2}{2\alpha\beta} = \frac{1}{2}$

$\therefore \cos C = \frac{1}{2}$

$\Rightarrow \sqrt{1 - \sin^2 C} = \frac{1}{2}$

$\Rightarrow \sqrt{1 - \gamma^2} = \frac{1}{2}$

$\Rightarrow \gamma = \frac{\sqrt{3}}{2}$

3 (b) Given, $f(x) = \sin^{-1}\left(\frac{x-1}{2x+3}\right)$

For $f(x)$ to be defined

$2x + 3 \neq 0$ and $\left|\frac{x-1}{2x+3}\right| \leq 1$

$\Rightarrow x \neq -\frac{3}{2}$ and $|x - 1| \leq |2x + 3|$

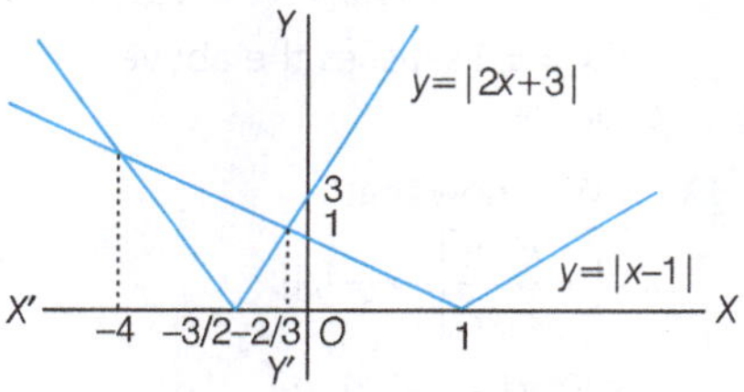

From above graph i.e. graph of $y = |2x + 3|$ and $y = |x - 1|$, we observe that, for $|2x + 3| \geq |x - 1|$

$\Rightarrow x \in (-\infty, -4] \cup \left[-\frac{2}{3}, \infty\right)$

i.e. $R - \left(-4, -\frac{2}{3}\right)$

So, $\alpha = -4$ and $\beta = -\frac{2}{3}$

Hence, $12\alpha\beta = 32$

4 (c) $f(x) = \log_e\left(\frac{2x+3}{4x^2 + x - 3}\right) + \cos^{-1}\left(\frac{2x-1}{x+2}\right)$

Domain of $f(x)$

$\frac{2x+3}{4x^2 + x - 3} > 0$ and $-1 \leq \frac{2x-1}{x+2} \leq 1$

$\frac{2x+3}{(4x-3)(x+1)} > 0$

and $\frac{2x-1}{x+2} + 1 \geq 0$

and $\frac{2x-1}{x+2} - 1 \leq 0$

$\frac{2x+3}{(4x-3)(x+1)} > 0,$	$\frac{3x+1}{x+2} \geq 0,$	$\frac{x-3}{x+2} \leq 0$
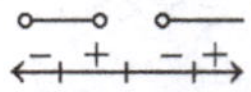 −3/2 −1 3/4	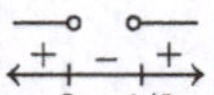 −2 −1/3	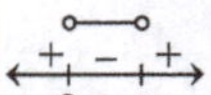 −2 3

Common of all soutions.

We get $x \in \left(\frac{3}{4}, 3\right]$

$\therefore \alpha = \frac{3}{4}, \beta = 3$

$\therefore 5\beta - 4\alpha \Rightarrow 15 - 3 = 12$

5 (a) $\cos^{-1} x - \sin^{-1} y = \alpha;$

$-\frac{\pi}{2} \leq \alpha \leq \pi$

$\Rightarrow \cos^{-1} x - \frac{\pi}{2} + \cos^{-1} y = \alpha$

$\Rightarrow \cos^{-1} x + \cos^{-1} y = \frac{\pi}{2} + \alpha$

$\Rightarrow \cos^{-1}(xy - \sqrt{1-x^2}\sqrt{1-y^2}) = \frac{\pi}{2} + \alpha$

$\Rightarrow xy - \sqrt{1-x^2}\sqrt{1-y^2} = -\sin\alpha$

$(xy + \sin\alpha)^2 = (1 - x^2)(1 - y^2)$

$x^2y^2 + \sin^2\alpha + 2xy$

$\sin\alpha = 1 + x^2y^2 - x^2 - y^2$

$x^2 + y^2 + 2xy \sin\alpha = 1 - \sin^2\alpha = \cos^2\alpha$

$\therefore$ Minimum value of $x^2 + y^2 + 2xy \sin\alpha = 0$

6 (b) Given that

$a_1 = 1, a_2 = 2, \ldots, a_{2022} = 2022,$

Now,

$\tan^{-1}\left(\frac{1}{1 + a_1a_2}\right) + \tan^{-1}\left(\frac{1}{1 + a_2a_3}\right) + \ldots + \tan^{-1}\left(\frac{1}{1 + a_{2021}a_{2022}}\right)$

On putting $a_1 = 1, a_2 = 2, \ldots, a_{2021} = 2021$ and $a_{2022} = 2022$, we get

$$\tan^{-1}\left[\frac{1}{1+1\cdot 2}\right]+\tan^{-1}\left[\frac{1}{1+2\cdot 3}\right]+\ldots+\tan^{-1}\left[\frac{1}{1+2021\cdot 2022}\right]$$

$$=\tan^{-1}\left[\frac{2-1}{1+2\cdot 1}\right]+\tan^{-1}\left[\frac{3-2}{1+3\cdot 2}\right]+\ldots+\tan^{-1}\left[\frac{2022-2021}{1+2022\cdot 2021}\right]$$

$$=\tan^{-1}(2)-\tan^{-1}(1)+\tan^{-1}(3)-\tan^{-1}(2)+\ldots+\tan^{-1}(2022)-\tan^{-1}(2021)$$

$$=\tan^{-1}(2022)-\tan^{1}(1)$$

$$\left[\because \tan^{-1}x-\tan^{-1}y=\tan^{-1}\left(\frac{x-y}{1+x\cdot y}\right)\right]$$

$$=\tan^{-1}(2022)-\frac{\pi}{4}$$

7 (*a*) We have,

$$2\tan^{-1}\left(\frac{1-x}{1+x}\right)=\cos^{-1}\left(\frac{1-x^2}{1+x^2}\right)$$

On putting $x=\tan\theta$.

Also, $0<x<1$

$\Rightarrow 0<\theta<\frac{\pi}{4}$

Now, $2\tan^{-1}\left(\frac{1-\tan\theta}{1+\tan\theta}\right)=\cos^{-1}\left(\frac{1-\tan^2\theta}{1+\tan^2\theta}\right)$

$\Rightarrow 2\tan^{-1}\tan\left(\frac{\pi}{4}-\theta\right)=\cos^{-1}\cos 2\theta$

$\Rightarrow 2\left(\frac{\pi}{4}-\theta\right)=2\theta$

$\Rightarrow \frac{\pi}{4}-\theta=\theta \Rightarrow \theta=\frac{\pi}{8}$

$\Rightarrow \tan^{-1}x=\frac{\pi}{8}$

$\Rightarrow x=\tan\frac{\pi}{8}=\sqrt{2}-1\approx 0.414$

$\therefore x<\frac{1}{2}$

So, $n(S)=1$ and the element in S is less than $\frac{1}{2}$.

8 (*b*) Given that,

$$\tan^{-1}\left(\frac{2}{3^{-x}+1}\right)=\cot^{-1}\left(\frac{3}{3^x+1}\right)$$

Since, $\tan^{-1}\left(\frac{1}{x}\right)=\cot^{-1}(x)$

So,

$$\tan^{-1}\left(\frac{2}{3^{-x}+1}\right)=\cot^{-1}\left(\frac{3^{-x}+1}{2}\right)$$

Thus,

$$\cot^{-1}\left(\frac{3^{-x}+1}{2}\right)=\cot^{-1}\left(\frac{3}{3^x+1}\right)$$

$$\Rightarrow \frac{3^{-x}+1}{2}=\frac{3}{3^x+1}$$

On simplifying, we get

$$3^{2x}-4\cdot 3^x+1=0$$

Let $3^x=y$, then $y^2-4y+1=0$

On solving this quadratic equation on y, we get

$$y=2\pm\sqrt{3}$$

We have, $3^x=y$

So, $3^x=2\pm\sqrt{3}$

Since, 3^x is always positive, we need $2-\sqrt{3}>0$.

Which is true because, $2-\sqrt{3}\approx 0.268$.

So, both values are valid for 3^x.

Now, number of solutions,

For $3^x=2+\sqrt{3}$, corresponds to one real value of x (positive).

For $3^x=2-\sqrt{3}$, corresponds to one real value of x (negative, since $2-\sqrt{3}<1$)

Thus, there are one positive and one negative real value of x that satisfy the equation.

9 (*c*) $f(x)=\sin^{-1}\left(\frac{x^2-3x+2}{x^2+2x+7}\right)$

Now, take domain of $\sin^{-1}x$ as $x\in[-1,1]$

$$\frac{x^2-3x+2}{x^2+2x+7}\geq -1$$

and $$\frac{x^2-3x+2}{x^2+2x+7}\leq 1$$

$2x^2-x+9\geq 0$ and $5x\geq -5$

$\Rightarrow x\geq -1$ where, $x\in R$.

Hence, Domain $x\in[-1,\infty)$.

10 (47) According to the question,

$$\cos^{-1}3+\cot^{-1}4+\cot^{-1}5+\cot^{-1}n=\frac{\pi}{4}$$

$$\Rightarrow \tan^{-1}\left(\frac{1}{3}\right)+\tan^{-1}\left(\frac{1}{4}\right)+\tan^{-1}\left(\frac{1}{5}\right)+\tan^{-1}\left(\frac{1}{n}\right)=\frac{\pi}{4}$$

$$\left[\because \cot^{-1}(x)=\tan^{-1}\left(\frac{1}{x}\right)\right]$$

$$\Rightarrow \tan^{-1}\left(\frac{\frac{1}{3}+\frac{1}{4}}{1-\frac{1}{3}\times\frac{1}{4}}\right)+\tan^{-1}\left(\frac{\frac{1}{5}+\frac{1}{n}}{1-\frac{1}{5}\times\frac{1}{n}}\right)=\frac{\pi}{4}$$

$$\left[\because \tan^{-1}x+\tan^{-1}y=\tan^{-1}\frac{x+y}{1-xy}\right]$$

$$\Rightarrow \tan^{-1}\left(\frac{7}{11}\right)+\tan^{-1}\left(\frac{n+5}{5n-1}\right)=\frac{\pi}{4}$$

$$\Rightarrow \tan^{-1}\left(\frac{\frac{7}{11}+\frac{(n+5)}{5n-1}}{1-\left(\frac{7}{11}\right)\left(\frac{n+5}{5n-1}\right)}\right)=\frac{\pi}{4}$$

$$\Rightarrow \frac{35n-7+11n+55}{11(5n-1)-7(n+5)}=1\Rightarrow n=47$$

11 (0) $2\sin^{-1}x+3\cos^{-1}x=\frac{2\pi}{5}$

$$\pi+\cos^{-1}x=\frac{2\pi}{5}$$

$$\cos^{-1}x=\frac{-3\pi}{5}$$

Not possible.

Thus, there is zero solution.

12 (24) We have $f(x)=\sec^{-1}\left(\frac{2x}{5x+3}\right)$

$$\frac{2x}{5x+3}\leq -1 \text{ or } \frac{2x}{5x+3}\geq 1$$

$$\frac{2x+5x+3}{5x+3}\leq 0 \text{ or } \frac{2x-5x-3}{5x+3}\geq 0$$

$$\frac{7x+3}{5x+3}\leq 0 \text{ or } \frac{-3(x+1)}{5x+3}\geq 0$$

Case I $7x+3\leq 0$ and $5x+3>0$

$$x\leq -\frac{3}{7} \text{ or } x>-\frac{3}{5}\Rightarrow -\frac{3}{5}<x\leq -\frac{3}{7}$$

Case II $7x+3\geq 0$ and $5x+3<0$

$$x\geq -\frac{3}{7} \text{ and } x<-\frac{3}{5}$$

which is not possible.

Case III $x+1\ge 0$ and $5x+3<0$

$x\ge -1$ and $x<-\frac{3}{5} \Rightarrow -1\le x<-\frac{3}{5}$

Case IV $x+1\le 0$ and $5x+3\ge 0$

$x\le -1$ and $x\ge -\frac{3}{5}$

which is not possible.

$\therefore$ Domain is

$$\left[-1,-\frac{3}{5}\right)\cup\left(-\frac{3}{5},-\frac{3}{7}\right]$$

$\therefore \alpha=-1, \beta=-\frac{3}{5}, \gamma=-\frac{3}{5}, \delta=-\frac{3}{7}$

$$|3\alpha+10(\beta+\gamma)+21\delta|$$

$$=\left|-3+10\left(-\frac{3}{5}-\frac{3}{5}\right)+21\left(-\frac{3}{7}\right)\right|$$

$=24$

13 (12) $\cos(\sin^{-1}(x\cot(\tan^{-1}(\cos(\sin^{-1}x)))))$

$$=k, 0<|x|<\frac{1}{\sqrt{2}}$$

$$\Rightarrow \cos(\sin^{-1}(x\cot(\tan^{-1}(\sqrt{1-x^2})))) = k$$

$$\Rightarrow \cos\left(\sin^{-1}\left(\frac{x}{\sqrt{1-x^2}}\right)\right)=k$$

$$\Rightarrow \sqrt{1-\frac{x^2}{1-x^2}}=k \Rightarrow \frac{1-2x^2}{1-x^2}=k^2$$

$$\therefore (k^2-2)x^2=k^2-1 \Rightarrow x^2=\frac{k^2-1}{k^2-2}$$

$$\therefore \quad \alpha^2=\beta^2=\frac{k^2-1}{k^2-2}$$

$$\Rightarrow \frac{1}{\alpha^2}+\frac{1}{\beta^2}=2\left(\frac{k^2-2}{k^2-1}\right) \text{ and } \frac{\alpha}{\beta}=-1$$

As $\frac{1}{\alpha^2}+\frac{1}{\beta^2}$ and $\frac{\alpha}{\beta}$ are roots of

$x^2-bx-5=0$

$$b=\frac{1}{\alpha^2}+\frac{1}{\beta^2}+\frac{\alpha}{\beta}$$

$$=\frac{2k^2-4}{k^2-1}-1=\frac{k^2-3}{k^2-1}$$

$$\text{Also } \left(\frac{1}{\alpha^2}+\frac{1}{\beta^2}\right)\times\left(\frac{\alpha}{\beta}\right)=-5$$

$$\Rightarrow \quad 2\left(\frac{k^2-2}{k^2-1}\right)=5 \Rightarrow k^2=\frac{1}{3}$$

$$\therefore \quad b=\frac{\frac{1}{3}-3}{\frac{1}{3}-1}=4 \Rightarrow \frac{b}{k^2}=\frac{4}{1/3}=12$$

Skill Boosters

1 (a) $\tan^{-1}x+\tan^{-1}2x=\pi-\tan^{-1}3x$

Taking tan on both sides, we get

$$\frac{x+2x}{1-2x^2}=-3x$$

$$\Rightarrow \quad 6x^3-6x=0 \Rightarrow x=0,1,-1$$

$x=0$, makes left hand side zero

$x=-1$ makes left hand side negative

Therefore, $x=1$ is only and one solution.

2 (d) $x=\frac{\pi}{2}-2\tan^{-1}\sqrt{\cos\alpha}$

$$\therefore \quad \sin x=\cos(2\tan^{-1}\sqrt{\cos\alpha})$$

$$=\frac{1-\cos\alpha}{1+\cos\alpha}=\tan^2\frac{\alpha}{2}$$

3 (c) $(\cos^{-1}x)^2-(\sin^{-1}x)^2$

$$=(\cos^{-1}x-\sin^{-1}x)(\cos^{-1}x+\sin^{-1}x)$$

$$=\frac{\pi}{2}\left(2\cos^{-1}x-\frac{\pi}{2}\right)$$

Now, simply we can say $m=-\frac{\pi^2}{4}$

[$\because$ least value of $\cos^{-1}x=0$]

and $M=\frac{\pi}{2}\left(2\pi-\frac{\pi}{2}\right)=\frac{3\pi^2}{4}$

[$\because$ greatest value of $\cos^{-1}x=\pi$]

$$\Rightarrow \quad \frac{M}{m}=-3$$

4 (b) $\sum x_i=\sin 2\alpha$

$$\sum_{i<j}x_i x_j=\cos 2\alpha$$

$$\sum_{i<j<k}x_i x_j x_k=\cos\alpha$$

$$x_1,x_2,x_3,x_4=-\sin\alpha$$

$$\sum_{i=1}^{4}\tan^{-1}(x_i)$$

$$=\tan^{-1}\frac{\sum x_i-\sum x_i x_j x_k}{1-\sum x_i x_j+x_1x_2x_3x_4}$$

$$=\tan^{-1}\left(\frac{\sin 2\alpha-\cos\alpha}{1-\cos 2\alpha-\sin\alpha}\right)$$

$$=\tan^{-1}(\cot\alpha)$$

$$=\tan^{-1}\left(\tan\left(\frac{\pi}{2}-\alpha\right)\right)=\frac{\pi}{2}-\alpha$$

5 (d) $\theta-\alpha=\cos^{-1}a$

$$\theta-\beta=\sin^{-1}b$$

$$\Rightarrow \quad \alpha-\beta=\sin^{-1}b-\cos^{-1}a$$

$$\cos(\alpha-\beta)=a\sqrt{1-b^2}+b\sqrt{1-a^2}$$

$$\Rightarrow \cos^2(\alpha-\beta)=a^2+b^2-2a^2b^2 +2ab\sqrt{1-a^2}\sqrt{1-b^2} \quad \ldots(i)$$

and $\sin(\alpha-\beta)=ab-\sqrt{1-a^2}\sqrt{1-b^2} \quad \ldots(ii)$

From Eqs (i) and (ii),

$$\cos^2(\alpha-\beta)+2ab\cdot\sin(\alpha-\beta)=a^2+b^2$$

6 (a) $\tan(\tan^{-1}p+\tan^{-1}q+\tan^{-1}r)$

$$=\frac{p+q+r-pqr}{1-(pq+qr+rp)}$$

$$p+q+r=\sqrt{a+b+c}\left(\sqrt{\frac{a}{bc}}+\sqrt{\frac{b}{ac}}+\sqrt{\frac{c}{ab}}\right)$$

$$=\sqrt{a+b+c}\cdot\frac{1}{\sqrt{abc}}(a+b+c)$$

$$=\frac{(a+b+c)^{3/2}}{\sqrt{abc}}=pqr$$

$\therefore \tan\theta=0$

7 (b) $2\sqrt{2}-1=2.828-1=1.828>\sqrt{3}$

$A=2\tan^{-1}(2\sqrt{2}-1)>2\tan^{-1}\sqrt{3}$

$\Rightarrow A>120°$

$$B=3\sin^{-1}\left(\frac{1}{3}\right)+\sin^{-1}\left(\frac{3}{5}\right)$$

$$=3\tan^{-1}\left(\frac{1}{2\sqrt{2}}\right)+\tan^{-1}\left(\frac{3}{4}\right)$$

$$\left(\frac{1}{2\sqrt{2}}=0.353<\sqrt{2}-1 \text{ and } \frac{3}{4}<1\right)$$

Now, $B<3\times(22.5)+45$

$B<67.5+45$

$B<\left(112\frac{1}{2}\right)°$

$\therefore \quad A>B$

8 (b) $\tan^{-1}\frac{1}{2r^2}=\tan^{-1}\left(\frac{2}{4r^2}\right)$

$$=\tan^{-1}\frac{(2r+1)-(2r-1)}{1+(4r^2-1)}$$

$$=\tan^{-1}(2r+1)-\tan^{-1}(2r-1)$$

$$\sum_{r=1}^{n}\tan^{-1}\left(\frac{1}{2r^2}\right)=\sum_{r=1}^{n}\tan^{-1}(2r+1)-\tan^{-1}(2r-1)$$

$$=\tan^{-1}(2n+1)-\tan^{-1}1$$

$$=\tan^{-1}\frac{2n+1-1}{1+2n+1}$$

$$=\tan^{-1}\left(\frac{2n}{2n+2}\right)=\tan^{-1}\left(\frac{n}{n+1}\right)$$

$$\therefore \quad \lambda=\frac{n}{n+1}$$

03

Matrices

Topicwise No. of Ques asked in 3 Years (JEE Main)

Topics	No. of Questions 2024	2023	2022
Matrix and Order of Matrix	–	1	–
Types of Matrices	–	–	–
Operations on Matrices	1	7	10
Transpose of a Matrix	1	4	2
Symmetric and Skew-symmetric Matrices	–	3	2
Invertible Matrices	–	–	–

Special Type of Ques Asked in 3 Years (JEE Main)

Types	Years 2024	2023	2022
A-R	–	–	–
Statement Based	0	–	–
Numerical Value Type	0	3	9

Last 3 Years Weightage (JEE Main)

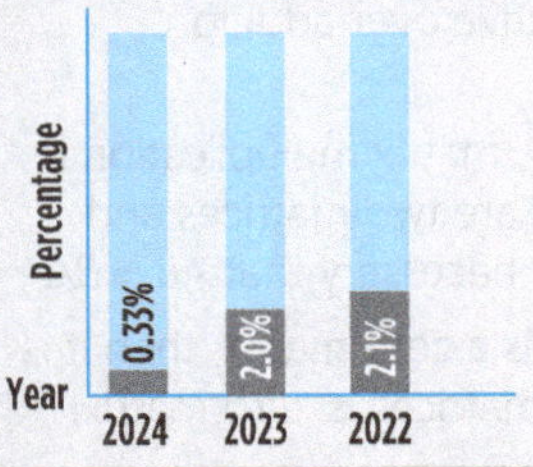

Matrix

A matrix is an ordered rectangular array of numbers or functions. The number or functions are called the elements or the entries of the matrix.

Order of Matrix

A matrix of order $m \times n$ is of the form

$$A = \begin{bmatrix} a_{11} & a_{12} & a_{13} & \dots & a_{1n} \\ a_{21} & a_{22} & a_{23} & \dots & a_{2n} \\ \vdots & \vdots & \vdots & \vdots & \vdots \\ a_{m1} & a_{m2} & a_{m3} & \dots & a_{mn} \end{bmatrix}$$

where, m represents number of rows and n represents number of columns.

In notation form, it can be rewritten as $A = [a_{ij}]_{m \times n}$

where, $1 \le i \le m, 1 \le j \le n$ and $i, j \in N$.

Here, a_{ij} is an element lying in the ith row and jth column.

Types of Matrices

(i) **Row matrix** A matrix having only one row, is called a row matrix.

(ii) **Column matrix** A matrix having only one column, is called a column matrix.

(iii) **Zero or Null matrix** If all the elements of a matrix are zero, then it is called a zero matrix or null matrix. It is denoted by symbol O.

(iv) **Square matrix** A matrix in which number of rows and number of columns are equal, is called a square matrix. **JEE Main 2024, 2023, 2022**

(v) **Diagonal matrix** A square matrix is said to be a diagonal matrix, if all the elements lying outside the diagonal elements are zero.

(vi) **Scalar matrix** A diagonal matrix in which all diagonal elements are equal, is called a scalar matrix.

Note *A scalar matrix is a diagonal matrix but a diagonal matrix may or may not be a scalar matrix.*

(vii) **Unit or Identity matrix** A diagonal matrix in which all the diagonal elements are equal to unity (one), is called an identity matrix. It is denoted by I.

Marks Maximizer

- If a square matrix of order n (i.e. $n \times n$), then number of elements above diagonal or number of elements below diagonal is $\frac{n(n-1)}{2}$.
- In a square matrix of order n, a_{ij} and a_{ji} are called conjugate elements.
- A matrix has $m \times n$ order,
  If $n > m$, it is called horizontal matrix.
  If $m > n$, it is called vertical matrix.
- In a square matrix,
  If $a_{ij} = 0 \, \forall \, i > j$, then it is called upper triangular matrix.
  If $a_{ij} = 0 \, \forall \, i < j$, then it is called lower triangular matrix.
- Minimum number of zeroes in a diagonal matrix is given by $n^2 - n$, where n is the order of the matrix.

Equality of Matrices

Two matrices are said to be equal, if their order are same and their corresponding elements are also equal, i.e. $a_{ij} = b_{ij}, \forall \, i, j$.

Operations on Matrices

Addition of Matrices

Let A and B be two matrices each of same order $m \times n$. Then, the sum of matrices $A + B$ is a matrix whose elements are obtained by adding the corresponding elements of A and B.

Concept Master Video

i.e. if $A = [a_{ij}]_{m \times n}$ and $B = [b_{ij}]_{m \times n}$

Then, $A + B = [a_{ij} + b_{ij}]_{m \times n}$

Multiplication of a Matrix by a Scalar

Let $A = [a_{ij}]_{m \times n}$ be a matrix and k be any scalar. Then, kA is another matrix which is obtained by multiplying each element of A by k, i.e. $kA = k[a_{ij}]_{m \times n} = [k(a_{ij})]_{m \times n}$.

Negative of a Matrix

If we multiply a matrix A by a scalar quantity (-1), then the negative of a matrix (i.e. $-A$) is obtained.

In negative of A, each element is multiplied by (-1).

Difference (or Subtraction) of Matrices

If $A = [a_{ij}]$ and $B = [b_{ij}]$ are two matrices of the same order $m \times n$, then difference of these matrices $A - B$ is defined as a matrix $D = [d_{ij}]$, where $d_{ij} = a_{ij} - b_{ij}, \forall \, i, j$.

Properties of Matrix Addition

Let A, B and C be three matrices of same order $m \times n$, then

(i) Matrix addition is commutative,
i.e. $A + B = B + A$

(ii) Matrix addition is associative,
i.e. $(A + B) + C = A + (B + C)$

(iii) **Existence of additive identity** Zero matrix (O) of order $m \times n$ (same as of A) is called additive identity, as $A + O = A = O + A$.

(iv) **Existence of additive inverse** For the square matrix, the matrix $(-A)$ is called additive inverse, if

$$A + (-A) = O = (-A) + A.$$

Note *If A and B are not of same order, then A + B is not defined.*

Properties of Scalar Multiplication of a Matrix

Let A and B be two matrices of same order, then

(i) $k(A + B) = kA + kB$, where k is scalar.

(ii) $(k_1 + k_2)A = k_1A + k_2A$, where k_1 and k_2 are scalars.

(iii) $(kl)A = k(lA) = l(kA)$, where l and k are scalars.

Multiplication of Matrices

Let $A = [a_{ij}]_{m \times n}$ and $B = [b_{jk}]_{n \times p}$ be two matrices such that the number of columns of A is equal to the number of rows of B, then multiplication of A and B is denoted by AB and it is given by $c_{ik} = \sum_{j=1}^{n} a_{ij} b_{jk}$, where c_{ik} is the (i, k) th element of matrix C of order $m \times p$, where $C = AB$.

Note *Generally, multiplication of matrices is not commutative, i.e. $AB \neq BA$.*

Properties of Multiplication of Matrices

(i) Let A, B and C be three matrices of same order.
Then, matrix multiplication is associative.
i.e. $(AB)C = A(BC)$

(ii) **Existence of multiplicative identity** For every square matrix A, there exists an identity matrix I of same order, such that

$$A \cdot I = A = I \cdot A$$

(iii) Matrix multiplication is distributive over addition.
i.e. $A(B + C) = AB + AC$

(iv) **Non-commutativity** Generally, matrix multiplication is not commutative i.e. if A and B are two matrices and AB, BA both exist, then it is not necessary that $AB = BA$.

(v) If the product of two matrices is a zero matrix, then it is not necessary that one of the matrices is zero matrix.

Marks Maximizer

- If $A = [a_{ij}]_{n\times n}$ be a square matrix. Then, the sum of all diagonal elements of A is called trace of matrix.

$$tr(A) = \sum_{i=1}^{n} a_{ii} = a_{11} + a_{22} + \dots a_{nn}.$$

- **Properties of trace** [A and B are two square matrix]

$$tr(A+B) = tr(A) + tr(B)$$
$$tr(AB) = tr(BA)$$
$$tr(kA) = ktr(A), \text{ where } k \text{ is a constant.}$$
$$tr(A^T) = tr(A)$$ [JEE Main 2024]

- **Cancellation law**

$$A + B = A + C \Rightarrow B = C$$ [Left cancellation law]

$$B + A = C + A \Rightarrow B = C$$ [Right cancellation law]

- Let A be the square matrix. Then,
  (i) $A^{n+1} = A^n \cdot A$, where $n \in N$
  (ii) $A^m \cdot A^n = A^{m+n}$
  (iii) $(A^m)^n = A^{mn}\ \forall\ m, n \in N$ [JEE Main 2023]

Transpose of a Matrix

The matrix obtained by interchanging the rows and columns of a given matrix A, is called transpose of a matrix A.

It is denoted by A' or A^T or A^c.

Properties of Transpose of Matrix

(i) $(A')' = A$

(ii) $(A \pm B)' = A' \pm B'$

(iii) $(kA)' = kA'$, where k is any constant.

(iv) $(AB)' = B'A'$ [reversal law]

(v) $(ABC)' = C'B'A'$

(vi) $(A^n)' = (A')^n$

Symmetric and Skew-symmetric Matrices

A square matrix A is called symmetric matrix, if $A' = A$ and a square matrix A is called skew-symmetric, if $A' = -A$.

Properties of Symmetric and Skew-symmetric Matrices

(i) For a square matrix A with real number entries, $A + A'$ is a symmetric matrix and $A - A'$ is a skew-symmetric matrix.

(ii) Any square matrix A can be expressed as the sum of a symmetric and a skew-symmetric matrices.

i.e. $A = \frac{1}{2}(A + A') + \frac{1}{2}(A - A')$ [JEE Main 2023]

(iii) Elements of principal diagonals of a skew-symmetric matrix are all zero. i.e. $a_{ii} = -a_{ii} \Rightarrow 2a_{ii} = 0$ or $a_{ii} = 0$, for all values of i.

(iv) If A and B are two symmetric (or skew-symmetric) matrices of same order, then $A + B$ is also symmetric (or skew-symmetric) matrix.

(v) If A is symmetric (or skew-symmetric), then kA (k is any scalar) is also symmetric (or skew-symmetric) matrix.

(vi) If A and B are symmetric matrices of the same order, then the product AB is symmetric, iff $BA = AB$.

(vii) The matrix $B'AB$ is symmetric or skew-symmetric according as A is symmetric or skew-symmetric matrix.

(xiii) For a square matrix A, AA' and $A'A$ are symmetric matrices.

Invertible Matrix

- A square matrix A of order m is said to be invertible, if there exists another square matrix B of same order m, such that $AB = BA = I$, where I is a unit matrix of same order m. The matrix B, is called the inverse of matrix A and is denoted by A^{-1}.
- A rectangular matrix does not possess inverse matrix. Since, for the products BA and AB to be defined and to be equal, it is necessary that matrices A and B are square matrices of the same order.
- If B is the inverse of A, then A is also the inverse of B.

Theorem 1

(Uniqueness of Inverse) Inverse of a square matrix, if it exists, is unique.

Theorem 2

If A and B are invertible matrices of the same order, then $(AB)^{-1} = B^{-1}A^{-1}$, where A and B are matrices of the same order.

Marks Maximizer

- All positive integral power of a symmetric matrix are symmetric. [JEE Main 2024]
- All positive odd integral power of a skew-symmetric matrix are skew-symmetric and positive even integral power of a skew-symmetric matrix are symmetric. [JEE Main 2024]
- Maximum number of distinct entries in a symmetric matrix of order n is $\frac{n(n+1)}{2}$.
- Maximum number of distinct entries in a skew-symmetric matrix of order n is $\frac{n(n-1)}{2}$.

Caution Points

- If A and B matrices are not of same order, then $A + B$ is not defined.
- When a matrix is multiplied by a scalar k, every element of the matrix is multiplied by k likewise to factor out a common term, it must be taken from each element of the matrix.
- We can multiply two matrices when the number of columns in matrix A is equal the number of rows in matrix B, $A_{m\times n} \times B_{n\times q} = C_{m\times q}$
- Matrix multiplication is associative but not commutative i.e. $(AB)\,C = A\,(BC)$ but $AB \neq BA$.

PYQ Notes

1. If A and B are symmetric matrices of the same order then,
   (i) $(AB - BA)$ is a skew-symmetric matrix.
   (ii) $(AB + BA)$ is a symmetric matrix. **[JEE Main 2022]**
2. If matrix $A = \begin{bmatrix} 1 & x \\ 0 & 1 \end{bmatrix}^n = \begin{bmatrix} 1 & nx \\ 0 & 1 \end{bmatrix}$

   or $A = \begin{bmatrix} 1 & 0 \\ x & 1 \end{bmatrix}^n = \begin{bmatrix} 1 & 0 \\ nx & 1 \end{bmatrix}$ **[JEE Main 2023]**
3. If A and B are square matrices of same order and commute each other $(AB = BA)$, then
   $(A + B)^n = {}^nC_0 A^n + {}^nC_1 A^{n-1} B + {}^nC_2 A^{n-2} B^2 + \ldots + {}^nC_n B^n$. **[JEE Main 2023]**

Step by Step

Mastering NCERT

- Concept Builders
- Topical Questions
- Numerical Type Questions
- Assertion and Reason Questions
- Case or Paragraph Type Questions
- Past Years Questions
- Skill Boosters

Concept Builders

1 Let A be any matrix of order 3×4, then number of elements in A?

2 A matrix having only one row is known as ....

3 A matrix having 4 row and 1 column, then the matrix is known as ....

4 What is the sum of all elements of null matrix?

5 Let A be any $n \times n$ diagonal matrix whose diagonal element is 3, then sum of all diagonal elemnets of A is equal to ....

6 A matrix having same number of rows and columns is known as ....

7 Addition of matrices not hold commutative property. (T/F)

8 Multiplication of matrices hold commulative property. (T/F)

9 Let A be $m \times n$ matrix, then order of transpose of A is ....

10 If A, B, C are three matrices of same order, then $(ABC)^T =$

11 If $A = \dfrac{B + B^T}{2}$, where B is a square matrix with real number entries, then A is .... matrix.

12 If P and Q are two skew-symmetric matrices, then PQ is symmetric matrix if ....

13 If A and B are matrices of same order, then $(2B - 3A)'$ is equal to ....

14 Substraction of matrices is defined if order of the matrices is ....

15 If B is skew-symmetric matrix, then B^{2024} is ....

16 If matrix $PQ = 0$, then $P = 0$ or $Q = 0$ or both P and Q are null matrices. (T/F)

17 Transpose of row matrix is column matrix. (T/F)

18 If A and B are skew-symmetric matrix, then $(AB + BA)'$ is .... matrix.

19 If $A = \dfrac{B - B^T}{2}$, where B is a square matrix with real number entries, then A is .... matrix.

20 If A and B are symmetric matrices and $AB = BA$, then $(AB' - BA)^T$ is .... matrix.

Topical Questions

Matrix

Level I

1 If $B = \begin{bmatrix} 2+i & 3 & -1/2 \\ 3.5 & -1 & 2 \\ \sqrt{3} & 5 & 5/7 \end{bmatrix}$

and $C = \begin{bmatrix} 1+x & x^3 & 3 \\ \cos x & \sin x + 2 & \tan x \end{bmatrix}$ are two matrices.

Then, consider the following statements.

I. B has 3 rows and 3 columns.

II. C has 2 rows and 3 columns.

Choose the correct option. **NCERT Pg. 36**

(a) Both I and II are false
(b) Only II is false
(c) Both I and II are true
(d) Only I is false

2 If A is a 3×2 matrix, B is a 3×3 matrix and C is a 2×3 matrix, then the elements in A, B and C are, respectively **NCERT Pg. 36**

(a) 6, 9, 8 (b) 6, 9, 6
(c) 9, 6, 6 (d) 6, 6, 9

3 If a matrix has 8 elements, then which of the following will not be a possible order of the matrix? **NCERT Pg. 38**

(a) 1×8 (b) 2×4
(c) 4×2 (d) 4×4

4 Consider the matrix $A=\begin{bmatrix} 2 & 5 & 19 & -7 \\ 35 & -2 & 5/2 & 12 \\ \sqrt{3} & 1 & -5 & 17 \end{bmatrix}$.

Now, consider the following statements.

I. The order of the matrix is 4×3 and number of elements is 12.

II. The elements a_{13}, a_{21}, a_{33} are respectively 19, 35, –5.

Choose the correct option. **NCERT Pg. 42**

(a) Only I is true
(b) Only II is true
(c) Both I and II are true
(d) Neither I nor II is true

5 Consider the following statements.

I. If a matrix has 24 elements, then all the possible orders it can have are $24 \times 1, 1 \times 24, 2 \times 4, 4 \times 2, 2 \times 12, 12 \times 2, 3 \times 8, 8 \times 3, 4 \times 6$ and 6×4.

II. For a matrix having 13 elements, all possible orders are 1×13 and 13×1.

III. For a matrix having 18 elements, all possible orders are $18 \times 1, 1 \times 18, 2 \times 9, 9 \times 2, 3 \times 6, 6 \times 3$.

IV. For a matrix having 5 elements, all possible orders are 1×5 and 5×1.

Choose the correct option. **NCERT Pg. 42**

(a) Only I is false
(b) Only II is false
(c) Only III is false
(d) All are true

6 [A] is a 2×2 matrix $A = [a_{ij}]$, whose elements are given by $a_{ij} = \frac{i}{j}$, is **NCERT Pg. 42**

(a) $\begin{bmatrix} 1 & 1/2 \\ 2 & 1 \end{bmatrix}$ (b) $\begin{bmatrix} 1 & 2 \\ 1/2 & 1 \end{bmatrix}$ (c) $\begin{bmatrix} 1/2 & 1 \\ 2 & 1 \end{bmatrix}$ (d) $\begin{bmatrix} 1/2 & 1 \\ 1 & 2 \end{bmatrix}$

7 Match the terms of column I with the terms of column II and choose the correct option from the codes given below. **NCERT Pg. 42**

	Column I		Column II
A.	If $A = [a_{ij}]_{2 \times 2}$ is a matrix, where $a_{ij} = \frac{(i+j)^2}{2}$, then a_{21} is	1.	$\frac{49}{2}$
B.	If $B = [b_{ij}]_{2 \times 3}$ is a matrix, where $b_{ij} = \frac{(i+2j)^2}{2}$, then b_{13} is	2.	1
C.	If $C = [c_{ij}]_{3 \times 4}$ is a matrix, where $c_{ij} = \frac{1}{2}\lvert -3i + j \rvert$, then c_{11} is	3.	2
D.	If $D = [d_{ij}]_{3 \times 4}$ is a matrix, where $d_{ij} = 2i - j$, then d_{34} is	4.	$\frac{9}{2}$

Codes

	A	B	C	D
(a)	1	4	2	3
(b)	2	4	3	1
(c)	4	2	1	3
(d)	4	1	2	3

8 The number of all possible matrices of order 3×3 with each entry 0 or 1 is **NCERT Pg. 43**

(a) 27
(b) 18
(c) 81
(d) 512

9 Matrix A has x rows and $(x+5)$ columns. Matrix B has y rows and $(11-y)$ columns. If both AB and BA exist, then the respective values of x and y are **NCERT Pg. 43**

(a) 3, 9
(b) 8, 3
(c) 3, 8
(d) 4, 8

Level II

10 If $A = [a_{ij}]_{2 \times 2}$, where $a_{ij} = e^{2ix} \sin jx$. Then, A is equal to **NCERT Exemplar Pg. 46**

(a) $\begin{bmatrix} e^{2x}\sin x & e^{2x}\sin 2x \\ e^{4x}\sin x & e^{4x}\sin x \end{bmatrix}$

(b) $\begin{bmatrix} e^{x}\sin x & e^{2x}\sin x \\ e^{2x}\sin x & e^{x}\sin x \end{bmatrix}$

(c) $\begin{bmatrix} e^{2x}\sin x & e^{2x}\sin 2x \\ e^{4x}\sin x & e^{4x}\sin 2x \end{bmatrix}$

(d) None of the above

11 If $A = [a_{ij}]_{3 \times 4}$ is matrix given by

$$A=\begin{bmatrix} 4 & -2 & 1 & 3 \\ 5 & 7 & 9 & 6 \\ 21 & 15 & 18 & -25 \end{bmatrix}.$$

Then, $a_{23} + a_{24}$ will be equal to the element **NCERT Pg. 36**

(a) a_{14}
(b) a_{44}
(c) a_{13}
(d) a_{32}

12 If A is a matrix defined by

$$A = [a_{ij}] = [\sin j\, x^i]; 1 \le i \le 3, 1 \le j \le 3$$

and B is a matrix defined by

$$B = [b_{ij}] = [\cos i\, x^j]; 1 \le i \le 3, 1 \le j \le 3.$$

Then, the value of $\frac{a_{22}}{b_{12}}$ is **NCERT Exemplar Pg. 53**

(a) $2\cos x^2$
(b) $2\sin^2 x$
(c) $2\sin x^2$
(d) None of these

13 How many matrices are possible of order 2×2 with the numbers 0, 1 and 2 such that each element of the matrix is non-zero? **NCERT Pg. 43**

(a) 3^4 (b) 2^4 (c) 4^2 (d) 4^3

Types of Matrices

Level I

1 A matrix is said to be a column matrix, if it has only
(a) two columns (b) one column **NCERT Pg. 39**
(c) three columns (d) None of these

2 A matrix is said to be a row matrix, if it has only
(a) three rows (b) two rows **NCERT Pg. 39**
(c) one row (d) None of these

3 Consider the following statements

I. $B = \begin{bmatrix} -\frac{1}{2} & \sqrt{5} & 2 & 3 \end{bmatrix}_{1\times 4}$ is a row matrix.

II. If $B = [b_{ij}]_{1\times n}$ is a row matrix, then its order is $1 \times n$.

Choose the correct option. **NCERT Pg. 39**
(a) Only I is true
(b) Only II is true
(c) Both I and II are true
(d) Neither I nor II is true

4 The matrix $A = \begin{bmatrix} 3 & -1 & 0 \\ 3/2 & 3\sqrt{2} & 1 \\ 4 & 3 & -1 \end{bmatrix}$ is a **NCERT Pg. 39**
(a) column matrix of order 3×1
(b) rectangular matrix of order 3
(c) row matrix of order 1×3
(d) square matrix of order 3

5 If A is a square matrix of order m with elements a_{ij}, then **NCERT Pg. 39**
(a) $A = [a_{ij}]_{n\times n}$ (b) $A = [a_{ji}]_{m\times n}$
(c) $A = [a_{ij}]_{m\times m}$ (d) $A = [a_{ji}]_{n\times n}$

6 If $A = [a_{ij}]$ is a square matrix of order n, then elements (entries) $a_{11}, a_{22}, a_{33}, \ldots a_{nn}$ are said to constitute the diagonal of the matrix A. Thus, if $A = \begin{bmatrix} 1 & -3 & 1 \\ 2 & 4 & -1 \\ 3 & 5 & 6 \end{bmatrix}$, then the elements of the diagonal are **NCERT Pg. 39**
(a) 1, 4, 6 (b) 1, 4, 3
(c) 1, 4, 5 (d) 1, 4, 1

7 A square matrix $B = [b_{ij}]_{m\times m}$ is said to be a diagonal matrix, if **NCERT Pg. 40**
(a) all its non-diagonal elements are non-zero i.e. $b_{ji} \neq 0$; $i \neq j$
(b) all its diagonal elements are zero i.e. $b_{ii} = 0, i = j$
(c) all its non-diagonal elements are zero i.e. $b_{ij} = 0$ when $i \neq j$
(d) None of the above

8 Let $A = [4]$, $B = \begin{bmatrix} -1 & 0 \\ 0 & 2 \end{bmatrix}$ and $C = \begin{bmatrix} -1.1 & 0 & 0 \\ 0 & 2 & 0 \\ 0 & 0 & 3 \end{bmatrix}$ are the matrices.

Consider the following statements
I. The matrices A, B and C are diagonal matrices.
II. The matrices A, B and C are of order 1, 3 and 2, respectively.

Choose the correct option. **NCERT Pg. 40**
(a) I is true and II is false
(b) I is false and II is true
(c) Both I and II are true
(d) Both I and II are false

9 If the diagonal elements of a diagonal matrix are all equal, then the matrix is called **NCERT Pg. 40**
(a) row matrix (b) scalar matrix
(c) rectangular matrix (d) None of these

10 Choose the incorrect statement. **NCERT Pg. 40**
(a) A matrix $A = [3]$ is a scalar matrix of order 1.
(b) A matrix $B = \begin{bmatrix} -1 & 0 \\ 0 & -1 \end{bmatrix}$ is a scalar matrix of order 2.
(c) A matrix $C = \begin{bmatrix} \sqrt{3} & 0 & 0 \\ 0 & \sqrt{3} & 0 \\ 0 & 0 & \sqrt{3} \end{bmatrix}$ of order 3 is not a scalar matrix.
(d) None of the above

11 A square matrix $A = [a_{ij}]_{n\times n}$ is an identity matrix, if **NCERT Pg. 40**
(a) $a_{ij} = \begin{cases} 1, & \text{if } i = j \\ 0, & \text{if } i \neq j \end{cases}$ (b) $a_{ij} = \begin{cases} 0, & \text{if } i = j \\ 1, & \text{if } i \neq j \end{cases}$
(c) $a_{ij} = \begin{cases} k, & \text{if } i \neq j \\ 0, & \text{if } i = j \end{cases}$ (d) $a_{ij} = \begin{cases} 0, & \text{if } i \neq j \\ k, & \text{if } i = j \end{cases}$

12 Which of the following is correct? **NCERT Pg. 40**
(a) [1] is the identity matrix of order 2.
(b) $\begin{bmatrix} 1 & 0 \\ 0 & 1 \end{bmatrix}$ is the identity matrix of order 2.
(c) $\begin{bmatrix} 1 & 0 & 0 \\ 0 & 1 & 0 \\ 0 & 0 & 1 \end{bmatrix}$ is the identity matrix of order 2.
(d) None of the above

13 Consider the following statements
I. Scalar matrix $A = [a_{ij}] = \begin{cases} k; & i = j \\ 0; & i \neq j \end{cases}$
where k is a scalar, in an identity matrix when $k = 1$.
II. Every identity matrix is not a scalar matrix.

Choose the correct option. **NCERT Pg. 40**

(a) Only I is true

(b) Only II is true

(c) Both I and II are true

(d) Both I and II are false

14 Choose the correct statement. **NCERT Pg. 40**

(a) Zero matrix is always a square matrix.

(b) Zero matrix is only a rectangular matrix.

(c) Zero matrix cannot be a row matrix.

(d) Zero matrix can be of any order.

15 Two matrices $A = [a_{ij}]$ and $B = [b_{ij}]$ are said to be equal, if they are of same order and for all i and j **NCERT Pg. 41**

(a) $a_{ij} = b_{ji}$ (b) $a_{ij} = b_{ij}$

(c) $a_{ij} = -b_{ij}$ (d) $a_{ij} + b_{ij} = 0$

16 Consider the following statements.

I. The matrices $\begin{bmatrix} 2 & 3 \\ 0 & 1 \end{bmatrix}$ and $\begin{bmatrix} 2 & 3 \\ 0 & 1 \end{bmatrix}$ are not equal.

II. The matrices $\begin{bmatrix} 3 & 2 \\ 0 & 1 \end{bmatrix}$ and $\begin{bmatrix} 2 & 3 \\ 0 & 1 \end{bmatrix}$ are equal.

Choose the correct option. **NCERT Pg. 41**

(a) I is true and II is false (b) I is false and II is true

(c) Both I and II are true (d) Both I and II are false

17 If two matrices A and B are equal, we write $A = B$. Now, if $\begin{bmatrix} x & y \\ z & a \\ b & c \end{bmatrix} = \begin{bmatrix} -1.5 & 0 \\ 2 & \sqrt{6} \\ 3 & 2 \end{bmatrix}$, then the values of x, y, z, a, b, c are **NCERT Pg. 41**

(a) $x = -1.5, y = \sqrt{6}, z = 2, a = 0, b = 2, c = 3$

(b) $x = -1.5, y = 0, z = \sqrt{6}, a = 2, b = 2, c = 3$

(c) $x = -1.5, y = 2, z = 2, a = \sqrt{6}, b = 3, c = 0$

(d) $x = -1.5, y = 0, z = 2, a = \sqrt{6}, b = 3, c = 2$

18 If $\begin{bmatrix} x+3 & z+4 & 2y-7 \\ -6 & a-1 & 0 \\ b-3 & -21 & 0 \end{bmatrix} = \begin{bmatrix} 0 & 6 & 3y-2 \\ -6 & -3 & 2c+2 \\ 2b+4 & -21 & 0 \end{bmatrix}$, then find the values of x, y, z, a, b, c. **NCERT Pg. 41**

(a) $x = -3, y = -5, z = 2, a = -2, b = -7, c = -1$

(b) $x = -2, y = -7, z = -1, a = -3, b = -5, c = 2$

(c) $x = -3, y = -5, z = 2, a = 2, b = 7, c = 1$

(d) $x = 3, y = 5, z = 2, a = 2, b = 7, c = 1$

19 The values of a, b, c and d from the following equation are

$$\begin{bmatrix} 2a+b & a-2b \\ 5c-d & 4c+3d \end{bmatrix} = \begin{bmatrix} 4 & -3 \\ 11 & 24 \end{bmatrix}$$ **NCERT Pg. 41**

(a) $a = 1, b = 2, c = 3, d = 4$

(b) $a = 2, b = 1, c = 3, d = 4$

(c) $a = 1, b = 2, c = 4, d = 3$

(d) $a = 4, b = 2, c = 1, d = 3$

20 Find the values of a, b, c and d from the equation

$$\begin{bmatrix} a-b & 2a+c \\ 2a-b & 3c+d \end{bmatrix} = \begin{bmatrix} -1 & 5 \\ 0 & 13 \end{bmatrix}.$$ **NCERT Pg. 42**

(a) $a = 1, b = 3, c = 4, d = 2$

(b) $a = 2, b = 1, c = 4, d = 3$

(c) $a = 1, b = 2, c = 3, d = 4$

(d) $a = 1, b = 3, c = 2, d = 4$

21 Which of the given values of x and y make the following pair of matrices equal?

$$\begin{bmatrix} 3x+7 & 5 \\ y+1 & 2-3x \end{bmatrix}, \begin{bmatrix} 0 & y-2 \\ 8 & 4 \end{bmatrix}$$ **NCERT Pg. 43**

(a) $x = -\frac{1}{3}, y = 7$ (b) Not possible to find

(c) $y = 7, x = -\frac{2}{3}$ (d) $x = \frac{1}{3}, y = \frac{2}{3}$

22 Match the terms of column I with the terms of column II and choose the correct option from the codes given below. **NCERT Pg. 42**

Column I (Equal matrices)	Column II (Values of x, y, z)
A. $\begin{bmatrix} 4 & 3 \\ x & 5 \end{bmatrix} = \begin{bmatrix} y & z \\ 1 & 5 \end{bmatrix}$	1. $x = 2, y = 4, z = 0$
B. $\begin{bmatrix} x+y & 2 \\ 5+z & xy \end{bmatrix} = \begin{bmatrix} 6 & 2 \\ 5 & 8 \end{bmatrix}$	2. $x = 2, y = 4, z = 3$
C. $\begin{bmatrix} x+y+z \\ x+z \\ y+z \end{bmatrix} = \begin{bmatrix} 9 \\ 5 \\ 7 \end{bmatrix}$	3. $x = 1, y = 4, z = 3$

Codes

	A	B	C		A	B	C
(a)	1	2	3	(b)	3	2	1
(c)	2	1	3	(d)	3	1	2

Level II

23 Let $A = [4]$ be a matrix of order 1×1. Consider the following statements

I. The matrix A is a square matrix.

II. The matrix A is both row and column matrix.

Choose the correct option. **NCERT Pg. 39**

(a) Only I is true (b) Only II is true

(c) Both I and II are true (d) Neither I nor II is true

24 If $A = [a_{ij}]$ is a matrix of order 4×5, then the diagonal elements of A are **NCERT Pg. 39**

(a) $a_{11}, a_{22}, a_{33}, a_{44}$
(b) $a_{55}, a_{44}, a_{33}, a_{22}, a_{11}$
(c) a_{11}, a_{22}, a_{33}
(d) Do not exist

25 Which of the following is correct statement? **NCERT Pg. 40**

(a) Diagonal matrix is also a scalar matrix.
(b) Identity matrix is a particular case of scalar matrix.
(c) Scalar matrix is not a diagonal matrix.
(d) Null matrix cannot be a square matrix.

26 From the following matrix equation, the value of x is

$$\begin{bmatrix} x+y & 4 \\ 5 & 3y \end{bmatrix} = \begin{bmatrix} 3 & 4 \\ 5 & 6 \end{bmatrix}$$

NCERT Pg. 41

(a) 2 (b) 1 (c) 3 (d) −1

27 If $\begin{bmatrix} x-y-z \\ -y+z \\ z \end{bmatrix} = \begin{bmatrix} 0 \\ 5 \\ 3 \end{bmatrix}$, then the values of x, y and z are, respectively **NCERT Pg. 41**

(a) 5, 2, 2 (b) 1, −2, 3
(c) 0, −3, 3 (d) 11, 8, 3

Operations on Matrices

Level I

1 If $A = [a_{ij}]$ and $B = [b_{ij}]$ are two matrices of the same order, say $m \times n$, then the sum of the two matrices A and B is defined as a matrix $C = [c_{ij}]_{m \times n}$, where for all possible values of i and j **NCERT Pg. 44**

(a) $c_{ij} = a_{ij} + b_{ji}$
(b) $c_{ij} = a_{ji} + b_{ij}$
(c) $c_{ji} = a_{ij} + b_{ij}$
(d) $c_{ij} = a_{ij} + b_{ij}$

2 For the given matrices $A = \begin{bmatrix} \sqrt{3} & 1 & -1 \\ 2 & 3 & 0 \end{bmatrix}$ and $B = \begin{bmatrix} 2 & \sqrt{5} & 1 \\ -2 & 3 & 1/2 \end{bmatrix}$, $A+B$ is given by **NCERT Pg. 44**

(a) $\begin{bmatrix} 2+\sqrt{3} & \sqrt{5} & -1 \\ 0 & 3 & 0 \end{bmatrix}$

(b) $\begin{bmatrix} \sqrt{3} & 1+\sqrt{5} & 1 \\ 2 & 6 & 1/2 \end{bmatrix}$

(c) $\begin{bmatrix} 2+\sqrt{3} & 1+\sqrt{5} & 0 \\ 0 & 6 & 1/2 \end{bmatrix}$

(d) $\begin{bmatrix} 2+\sqrt{3} & 1+\sqrt{5} & 1 \\ 0 & 6 & 1/2 \end{bmatrix}$

3 Match the terms of column I with the terms of column II and choose the correct option from the codes given below. **NCERT Pg. 58**

Column I	Column II
A. $\begin{bmatrix} a & b \\ -b & a \end{bmatrix} + \begin{bmatrix} a & b \\ b & a \end{bmatrix}$	1. $\begin{bmatrix} (a+b)^2 & (b+c)^2 \\ (a-c)^2 & (a-b)^2 \end{bmatrix}$
B. $\begin{bmatrix} a^2+b^2 & b^2+c^2 \\ a^2+c^2 & a^2+b^2 \end{bmatrix} + \begin{bmatrix} 2ab & 2bc \\ -2ac & -2ab \end{bmatrix}$	2. $\begin{bmatrix} 1 & 1 \\ 1 & 1 \end{bmatrix}$
C. $\begin{bmatrix} \cos^2 x & \sin^2 x \\ \sin^2 x & \cos^2 x \end{bmatrix} + \begin{bmatrix} \sin^2 x & \cos^2 x \\ \cos^2 x & \sin^2 x \end{bmatrix}$	3. $\begin{bmatrix} 2a & 2b \\ 0 & 2a \end{bmatrix}$

Codes

	A	B	C		A	B	C
(a)	3	2	1	(b)	1	3	2
(c)	2	1	3	(d)	3	1	2

4 Consider the following statements.

I. Let $A = [a_{ij}]$ be a $m \times n$ matrix and O be a $m \times n$ zero matrix, then $A + O = O + A = A$. In other words, O is the additive identity for matrix addition.

II. Let $A = [a_{ij}]_{m \times n}$ be any matrix, then we have another matrix $-A = [-a_{ij}]_{m \times n}$ such that $A + (-A) = (-A) + A = 0$. Then, $-A$ is the additive inverse of A or negative of A.

Choose the correct option. **NCERT Pg. 46**

(a) Only I is true (b) Only II true
(c) Both I and II are true (d) Neither I nor II are true

5 Let $A = \begin{bmatrix} 1 & 2 & -3 \\ 5 & 0 & 2 \\ 1 & -1 & 1 \end{bmatrix}$, $B = \begin{bmatrix} 3 & -1 & 2 \\ 4 & 2 & 5 \\ 2 & 0 & 3 \end{bmatrix}$ and $C = \begin{bmatrix} 4 & 1 & 2 \\ 0 & 3 & 2 \\ 1 & -2 & 3 \end{bmatrix}$ be three matrices of order 3.

Now, consider the following statements.

I. $A + B = \begin{bmatrix} 4 & 1 & -1 \\ 9 & 2 & 7 \\ 3 & -1 & 4 \end{bmatrix}$ and $B - C = \begin{bmatrix} -1 & -2 & 0 \\ 4 & -1 & 3 \\ 1 & 2 & 0 \end{bmatrix}$

II. $A + (B - C) = (A + B) - C$

Choose the correct option. **NCERT Pg. 59**

(a) Only I is true (b) Only II is true
(c) Both I and II are true (d) Neither I nor II is true

6 If $X + Y = \begin{bmatrix} 7 & 0 \\ 2 & 5 \end{bmatrix}$ and $X - Y = \begin{bmatrix} 3 & 0 \\ 0 & 3 \end{bmatrix}$, then X and Y are, respectively **NCERT Pg. 59**

(a) $\begin{bmatrix} 2 & 0 \\ 1 & 1 \end{bmatrix}$ and $\begin{bmatrix} 5 & 0 \\ 1 & 4 \end{bmatrix}$ (b) $\begin{bmatrix} 5 & 0 \\ 1 & 4 \end{bmatrix}$ and $\begin{bmatrix} 2 & 0 \\ 1 & 1 \end{bmatrix}$

(c) $\begin{bmatrix} 5 & 1 \\ 0 & 4 \end{bmatrix}$ and $\begin{bmatrix} 2 & 1 \\ 0 & 1 \end{bmatrix}$ (d) $\begin{bmatrix} 2 & 1 \\ 0 & 1 \end{bmatrix}$ and $\begin{bmatrix} 5 & 1 \\ 0 & 4 \end{bmatrix}$

7 If $A = [a_{ij}]$ and $B = [b_{ij}]$ are two matrices of the same order, (say $m \times n$). Also, k and l are scalars. Then, consider the following statements

I. $k(A + B) = kA + kB$

II. $(k + l)A = kA + lA$

Choose the correct option. **NCERT Pg. 47**

(a) Only I is true
(b) Only II is true
(c) Both I and II are true
(d) Neither I nor II is true

8 $\cos\theta \begin{bmatrix} \cos\theta & \sin\theta \\ -\sin\theta & \cos\theta \end{bmatrix} + \sin\begin{bmatrix} \sin\theta & -\cos\theta \\ \cos\theta & \sin\theta \end{bmatrix}$ equals to **NCERT Pg. 59**

(a) $\begin{bmatrix} 0 & 1 \\ 1 & 0 \end{bmatrix}$ (b) $\begin{bmatrix} 1 & 0 \\ 0 & 1 \end{bmatrix}$

(c) $\begin{bmatrix} 1 & 0 \\ 1 & 0 \end{bmatrix}$ (d) $\begin{bmatrix} 0 & 1 \\ 0 & 1 \end{bmatrix}$

9 If $2\begin{bmatrix} 1 & 3 \\ 0 & x \end{bmatrix} + \begin{bmatrix} y & 0 \\ 1 & 2 \end{bmatrix} = \begin{bmatrix} 5 & 6 \\ 1 & 8 \end{bmatrix}$, then the values of x and y are **NCERT Pg. 59**

(a) $x = -3, y = 3$ (b) $x = 3, y = -3$
(c) $x = -3, y = -3$ (d) $x = 3, y = 3$

10 If $2\begin{bmatrix} x & z \\ y & t \end{bmatrix} + 3\begin{bmatrix} 1 & -1 \\ 0 & 2 \end{bmatrix} = 3\begin{bmatrix} 3 & 5 \\ 4 & 6 \end{bmatrix}$, then x, y, z and t are, respectively **NCERT Pg. 59**

(a) 3, 6, 9, 6 (b) 3, 9, 6, 6
(c) 3, 6, 6, 9 (d) 6, 9, 3, 6

11 If $x\begin{bmatrix} 2 \\ 3 \end{bmatrix} + y\begin{bmatrix} -1 \\ 1 \end{bmatrix} = \begin{bmatrix} 10 \\ 5 \end{bmatrix}$, then x and y are **NCERT Pg. 59**

(a) $x = 3, y = 4$ (b) $x = 3, y = -4$
(c) $x = 4, y = 3$ (d) $x = -4, y = 3$

12 The values of x, y, z and w from the matrix equation

$$3\begin{bmatrix} x & y \\ z & w \end{bmatrix} = \begin{bmatrix} x & 6 \\ -1 & 2w \end{bmatrix} + \begin{bmatrix} 4 & x + y \\ z + w & 3 \end{bmatrix}$$

are, respectively **NCERT Pg. 59**

(a) 1, 4, 2, 3 (b) 1, 2, 3, 4
(c) 2, 4, 1, 3 (d) 4, 2, 3, 1

13 Consider the following statements.

I. For multiplication of two matrices A and B, the number of columns in A should be less than the number of rows in B.

II. For getting the elements of the product matrix, we take rows of A and column of B, multiply them elementwise and take the sum.

Choose the correct option. **NCERT Pg. 57**

(a) Only I is true
(b) Only II is true
(c) Both I and II are true
(d) Neither I nor II is true

14 Let $A = [a_{ij}]$ be an $m \times n$ matrix and $B = [b_{jk}]$ be an $n \times p$ matrix. Then, the product of the matrices A and B is the matrix C of order **NCERT Pg. 57**

(a) $n \times m$ (b) $m \times n$
(c) $p \times m$ (d) $m \times p$

15 The matrix $C = [c_{ik}]_{m \times p}$ is the product of $A = [a_{ij}]_{m \times n}$ and $B = [b_{jk}]_{n \times p}$, where c_{ik} is **NCERT Pg. 57**

(a) $c_{ik} = \sum_{j=1}^{n} b_{jk}\, a_{ij}$ (b) $c_{ik} = \sum_{k=1}^{p} a_{ij}\, b_{jk}$

(c) $c_{ik} = \sum_{j=1}^{n} a_{ij} b_{jk}$ (d) $c_{ik} = \sum_{j=1}^{n} a_{ij} b_{jk}$

16 If $A = \begin{bmatrix} 6 & 9 \\ 2 & 3 \end{bmatrix}$ and $B = \begin{bmatrix} 2 & 6 & 0 \\ 7 & 9 & 8 \end{bmatrix}$, then AB is **NCERT Pg. 52**

(a) $\begin{bmatrix} 75 & 25 & 117 \\ 72 & 39 & 24 \end{bmatrix}$ (b) $\begin{bmatrix} 75 & 117 & 72 \\ 25 & 39 & 24 \end{bmatrix}$

(c) $\begin{bmatrix} 72 & 29 & 24 \\ 75 & 25 & 117 \end{bmatrix}$ (d) not defined

17 If AB is defined, then BA need not be defined.

Now, let $A = \begin{bmatrix} 6 & 9 \\ 2 & 3 \end{bmatrix}$ and $B = \begin{bmatrix} 2 & 6 & 0 \\ 7 & 9 & 8 \end{bmatrix}$, then BA is **NCERT Pg. 53**

(a) $\begin{bmatrix} 12 & 25 \\ 39 & 72 \end{bmatrix}$ (b) $\begin{bmatrix} 72 & 29 & 24 \\ 75 & 25 & 117 \end{bmatrix}$

(c) $\begin{bmatrix} 75 & 117 & 72 \\ 25 & 39 & 24 \end{bmatrix}$ (d) not defined

18 If A and B are respectively $m \times n$, $k \times l$ matrices, then both AB and BA are defined, if and only if **NCERT Pg. 53**

(a) $n = k$ only (b) $l = m$ only
(c) $n = k$ and $l = m$ (d) $m = n$

19 If A and B are square matrices of the same order, then **NCERT Pg. 54**

(a) only AB is defined
(b) only BA is defined
(c) both AB and BA are defined
(d) None of the above

20 Consider the following statements.

I. If AB and BA are both defined, then they must be equal i.e. $AB = BA$.

II. If AB and BA are both defined, it is not necessary that $AB = BA$.

Choose the correct option. NCERT Pg. 53

(a) Only I is true
(b) Only II is true
(c) Both I and II are true
(d) None of the above

21 If $A = \begin{bmatrix} 1 & -2 & 3 \\ -4 & 2 & 5 \end{bmatrix}$ and $B = \begin{bmatrix} 2 & 3 \\ 4 & 5 \\ 2 & 1 \end{bmatrix}$, then NCERT Pg. 53

(a) AB is not defined (b) BA is not defined
(c) $AB = BA$ (d) $AB \neq BA$

22 If $A = \begin{bmatrix} 1 & 0 \\ 0 & -1 \end{bmatrix}$ and $B = \begin{bmatrix} 0 & 1 \\ 1 & 0 \end{bmatrix}$, then NCERT Pg. 53

(a) $AB = \begin{bmatrix} 0 & -1 \\ 1 & 0 \end{bmatrix}$ (b) $BA = \begin{bmatrix} 0 & 1 \\ -1 & 0 \end{bmatrix}$
(c) $AB = BA$ (d) $AB \neq BA$

23 If the product of two matrices is a zero matrix, then NCERT Pg. 54

(a) atleast one of the matrix is a zero matrix
(b) both the matrices are zero matrices
(c) it is not necessary that one of the matrices is a zero matrix
(d) None of the above

24 Match the terms of column I with the terms of column II and choose the correct option from the codes given below. NCERT Pg. 58

Column I (Matrices)	Column II (Their product)
A. $\begin{bmatrix} 2 & 4 \\ 3 & 2 \end{bmatrix}\begin{bmatrix} 1 & 3 \\ -2 & 5 \end{bmatrix}$	1. $\begin{bmatrix} 11 & 10 \\ 11 & 2 \end{bmatrix}$
B. $\begin{bmatrix} 1 & 3 \\ -2 & 5 \end{bmatrix}\begin{bmatrix} 2 & 4 \\ 3 & 2 \end{bmatrix}$	2. $\begin{bmatrix} 2 & 3 & 4 \\ 4 & 6 & 8 \\ 6 & 9 & 12 \end{bmatrix}$
C. $\begin{bmatrix} 1 \\ 2 \\ 3 \end{bmatrix}[2 \ 3 \ 4]$	3. $\begin{bmatrix} -6 & 26 \\ -1 & 19 \end{bmatrix}$

Codes

	A	B	C		A	B	C
(a)	2	1	3	(b)	3	2	1
(c)	3	1	2	(d)	1	3	2

25 The product $\begin{bmatrix} a & b \\ -b & a \end{bmatrix}\begin{bmatrix} a & -b \\ b & a \end{bmatrix}$ is equal to NCERT Pg. 58

(a) $\begin{bmatrix} a^2+b^2 & 0 \\ 0 & a^2+b^2 \end{bmatrix}$ (b) $\begin{bmatrix} (a+b)^2 & 0 \\ (a+b)^2 & 0 \end{bmatrix}$
(c) $\begin{bmatrix} a^2+b^2 & 0 \\ a^2+b^2 & 0 \end{bmatrix}$ (d) $\begin{bmatrix} a & 0 \\ 0 & b \end{bmatrix}$

26 Match the terms of column I with the terms of column II and choose the correct option from the codes given below. NCERT Pg. 58

Column I	Column II
A. $\begin{bmatrix} 1 & -2 \\ 2 & 3 \end{bmatrix}\begin{bmatrix} 1 & 2 & 3 \\ 2 & 3 & 1 \end{bmatrix}$	1. $\begin{bmatrix} 1 & 2 & 3 \\ 1 & 4 & 5 \\ -2 & 2 & 0 \end{bmatrix}$
B. $\begin{bmatrix} 2 & 3 & 4 \\ 3 & 4 & 5 \\ 4 & 5 & 6 \end{bmatrix}\begin{bmatrix} 1 & -3 & 5 \\ 0 & 2 & 4 \\ 3 & 0 & 5 \end{bmatrix}$	2. $\begin{bmatrix} 14 & 0 & 42 \\ 18 & -1 & 56 \\ 22 & -2 & 70 \end{bmatrix}$
C. $\begin{bmatrix} 2 & 1 \\ 3 & 2 \\ -1 & 1 \end{bmatrix}\begin{bmatrix} 1 & 0 & 1 \\ -1 & 2 & 1 \end{bmatrix}$	3. $\begin{bmatrix} 14 & -6 \\ 4 & 5 \end{bmatrix}$
D. $\begin{bmatrix} 3 & -1 & 3 \\ -1 & 0 & 2 \end{bmatrix}\begin{bmatrix} 2 & -3 \\ 1 & 0 \\ 3 & 1 \end{bmatrix}$	4. $\begin{bmatrix} -3 & -4 & 1 \\ 8 & 13 & 9 \end{bmatrix}$

Codes

	A	B	C	D
(a)	4	2	1	3
(b)	3	1	2	4
(c)	1	4	3	2
(d)	2	1	4	3

27 Consider the following statements.

I. $\begin{bmatrix} 5 & -1 \\ 6 & 7 \end{bmatrix}\begin{bmatrix} 2 & 1 \\ 3 & 4 \end{bmatrix} = \begin{bmatrix} 2 & 1 \\ 3 & 4 \end{bmatrix}\begin{bmatrix} 5 & -1 \\ 6 & 7 \end{bmatrix}$

II. $\begin{bmatrix} 1 & 2 & 3 \\ 0 & 1 & 0 \\ 1 & 1 & 0 \end{bmatrix}\begin{bmatrix} -1 & 1 & 0 \\ 0 & -1 & 1 \\ 2 & 3 & 4 \end{bmatrix} \neq \begin{bmatrix} -1 & 1 & 0 \\ 0 & -1 & 1 \\ 2 & 3 & 4 \end{bmatrix}\begin{bmatrix} 1 & 2 & 3 \\ 0 & 1 & 0 \\ 1 & 1 & 0 \end{bmatrix}$

Choose the correct option. NCERT Pg. 60

(a) Only I is true
(b) Only II is true
(c) Both I and II are true
(d) Neither I nor II is true

28 For every square matrix A, there exists an identity matrix of same order such that NCERT Pg. 54

(a) $IA = A$ only (b) $AI = A$ only
(c) $IA = AI = A$ (d) None of these

29 If $A=\begin{bmatrix}2&0&1\\2&1&3\\1&-1&3\end{bmatrix}$, then $A^2-5A+6I$ is equal to **NCERT Pg. 60**

(a) $\begin{bmatrix}0&1&0\\1&0&0\\0&1&0\end{bmatrix}$ (b) $\begin{bmatrix}0&0&0\\0&0&0\\0&0&0\end{bmatrix}$

(c) $\begin{bmatrix}1&-1&-3\\-1&-1&-10\\-5&4&4\end{bmatrix}$ (d) $\begin{bmatrix}1&0&0\\1&0&1\\0&1&0\end{bmatrix}$

30 If $A=\begin{bmatrix}1&0&2\\0&2&1\\2&0&3\end{bmatrix}$, then $A^3-6A^2+7A+2I$ is equal to **NCERT Pg. 60**

(a) $\begin{bmatrix}1&0&0\\0&1&0\\1&0&1\end{bmatrix}$ (b) $\begin{bmatrix}0&0&0\\0&0&0\\0&0&0\end{bmatrix}$

(c) $\begin{bmatrix}-1&-1&1\\2&3&-1\\5&-6&0\end{bmatrix}$ (d) $\begin{bmatrix}2&0&0\\0&2&0\\0&0&1\end{bmatrix}$

31 If $A=\begin{bmatrix}3&-2\\4&-2\end{bmatrix}$ and $I=\begin{bmatrix}1&0\\0&1\end{bmatrix}$, then the value of k such that $A^2=kA-2I$, is **NCERT Pg. 60**

(a) -1 (b) 2 (c) -2 (d) 1

32 If $A=\begin{bmatrix}0&-\tan\frac{\alpha}{2}\\\tan\frac{\alpha}{2}&0\end{bmatrix}$ and I is the identity matrix of order 2, then $(I-A)\begin{bmatrix}\cos\alpha&-\sin\alpha\\\sin\alpha&\cos\alpha\end{bmatrix}$ is equal to **NCERT Pg. 60**

(a) $I+A$ (b) $I-A$
(c) $A-I$ (d) A

33 Assume X, Y, Z, W and P are matrices of order $2\times n$, $3\times k$, $2\times p$, $n\times 3$ and $p\times k$, respectively.

Now, consider the following statements.

I. $PY+WY$ will be defined for $k=3$ and $p=n$.

II. The order of the matrix $7X-5Z$ is $n\times 2$ (if $p=n$).

Choose the correct option. **NCERT Pg. 61**

(a) Only I is true (b) Only II is true
(c) Both I and II are true (d) Neither I nor II is true

Level II

34 If $A=\begin{bmatrix}2&3\\1&2\end{bmatrix}, B=\begin{bmatrix}1&3&2\\4&3&1\end{bmatrix}, C=\begin{bmatrix}1\\2\end{bmatrix}$ and $D=\begin{bmatrix}4&6&8\\5&7&9\end{bmatrix}$, then which of the options is defined? **NCERT Pg. 58**

(a) $A+B$ (b) $B+C$
(c) $C+D$ (d) $B+D$

35 If $\begin{bmatrix}1&2\\-2&-b\end{bmatrix}+\begin{bmatrix}a&4\\3&2\end{bmatrix}=\begin{bmatrix}5&6\\1&0\end{bmatrix}$, then a^2+b^2 is equal to **NCERT Pg. 58**

(a) 20 (b) 22 (c) 12 (d) 10

36 If $A=\begin{bmatrix}2&4\\3&2\end{bmatrix}$ and $B=\begin{bmatrix}1&3\\-2&5\end{bmatrix}$, then $A-B$ is **NCERT Pg. 59**

(a) $\begin{bmatrix}3&7\\5&7\end{bmatrix}$ (b) $\begin{bmatrix}1&1\\5&-3\end{bmatrix}$

(c) $\begin{bmatrix}7&5\\7&1\end{bmatrix}$ (d) $\begin{bmatrix}3&1\\5&-3\end{bmatrix}$

37 If $A=[a_{ij}]_{m\times n}$ is a matrix and k is a scalar, then kA (multiplication of a matrix by a scalar k) is another matrix which is obtained by ... B... each element of A by the scalar k. Here, B refers to **NCERT Pg. 45**

(a) adding (b) subtracting
(c) multiplying (d) None of these

38 If $A=[a_{ij}]_{m\times n}$ is a matrix and k is any scalar, then $kA=k[a_{ij}]_{m\times n}=[k(a_{ij})]_{m\times n}$ i.e. $(i, j)^{\text{th}}$ element of kA is **NCERT Pg. 45**

(a) $k+a_{ij}$ (b) ka_{ji}
(c) ka_{ij} (d) $k+a_{ji}$

39 If $A=\begin{bmatrix}3&1&1.5\\\sqrt{5}&7&-3\\2&0&5\end{bmatrix}$, then $3A$ is **NCERT Pg. 45**

(a) $\begin{bmatrix}9&3&4.5\\\sqrt{5}&21&-9\\2&0&5\end{bmatrix}$ (b) $\begin{bmatrix}9&3&4.5\\3\sqrt{5}&21&-9\\6&0&15\end{bmatrix}$

(c) $\begin{bmatrix}9&3&1.5\\3\sqrt{5}&21&-3\\6&0&5\end{bmatrix}$ (d) $\begin{bmatrix}3&1&4.5\\\sqrt{5}&21&-6\\2&0&15\end{bmatrix}$

40 If $A=\begin{bmatrix}2&4\\3&2\end{bmatrix}$ and $C=\begin{bmatrix}-2&5\\3&4\end{bmatrix}$, then $3A-C$ is **NCERT Pg. 58**

(a) $\begin{bmatrix}8&2\\6&7\end{bmatrix}$ (b) $\begin{bmatrix}8&5\\6&4\end{bmatrix}$ (c) $\begin{bmatrix}8&7\\6&2\end{bmatrix}$ (d) $\begin{bmatrix}2&7\\3&2\end{bmatrix}$

41 Find X, if $Y=\begin{bmatrix}3&2\\1&4\end{bmatrix}$ and $2X+Y=\begin{bmatrix}1&0\\-3&2\end{bmatrix}$. **NCERT Pg. 59**

(a) $\begin{bmatrix}1&1\\-2&-1\end{bmatrix}$ (b) $\begin{bmatrix}-1&-1\\2&-1\end{bmatrix}$

(c) $\begin{bmatrix}1&1\\2&1\end{bmatrix}$ (d) $\begin{bmatrix}-1&-1\\-2&-1\end{bmatrix}$

42 If $A=\begin{bmatrix}\frac{2}{3}&1&\frac{5}{3}\\\frac{1}{3}&\frac{2}{3}&\frac{4}{3}\\\frac{7}{3}&2&\frac{2}{3}\end{bmatrix}$ and $B=\begin{bmatrix}\frac{2}{5}&\frac{3}{5}&1\\\frac{1}{5}&\frac{2}{5}&\frac{4}{5}\\\frac{7}{5}&\frac{6}{5}&\frac{2}{5}\end{bmatrix}$, then $3A-5B$ is **NCERT Pg. 59**

(a) $\begin{bmatrix}1&0&0\\0&0&0\\0&1&0\end{bmatrix}$ (b) $\begin{bmatrix}0&0&0\\0&0&0\\0&0&0\end{bmatrix}$

(c) $\begin{bmatrix}0&1&0\\1&0&0\\0&0&0\end{bmatrix}$ (d) $\begin{bmatrix}0&0&1\\0&0&1\\1&0&0\end{bmatrix}$

43 The value of $y-x$ from the equation

$$2\begin{bmatrix}x&5\\7&y-3\end{bmatrix}+\begin{bmatrix}3&-4\\1&2\end{bmatrix}=\begin{bmatrix}7&6\\15&14\end{bmatrix}$$ is **NCERT Pg. 48**

(a) -5 (b) 5 (c) -7 (d) 7

44 If A and B are two matrices of the order $3\times m$ and $3\times n$ respectively and $m=n$, then the order of the matrix $(5A-2B)$ is **NCERT Pg. 46**

(a) $m\times 3$ (b) 3×3
(c) $m\times n$ (d) $3\times n$

45 If $2X+3Y=\begin{bmatrix}2&3\\4&0\end{bmatrix}$ and $3X+2Y=\begin{bmatrix}2&-2\\-1&5\end{bmatrix}$. Then, X and Y are, respectively **NCERT Pg. 59**

(a) $\begin{bmatrix}-2/5&12/5\\11/5&-3\end{bmatrix}$ and $\begin{bmatrix}2/5&13/5\\14/5&2\end{bmatrix}$

(b) $\begin{bmatrix}-2/5&-13/5\\14/5&2\end{bmatrix}$ and $\begin{bmatrix}2/5&12/5\\11/5&3\end{bmatrix}$

(c) $\begin{bmatrix}2/5&13/5\\14/5&-2\end{bmatrix}$ and $\begin{bmatrix}2/5&-12/5\\-11/5&3\end{bmatrix}$

(d) $\begin{bmatrix}2/5&-12/5\\-11/5&3\end{bmatrix}$ and $\begin{bmatrix}2/5&13/5\\14/5&-2\end{bmatrix}$

46 The additive inverse of the matrix $A=\begin{bmatrix}3&-1\\2&5\end{bmatrix}$ is **NCERT Pg. 47**

(a) $\begin{bmatrix}-3&0\\-2&0\end{bmatrix}$ (b) $\begin{bmatrix}-3&1\\-2&-5\end{bmatrix}$ (c) $\begin{bmatrix}3&1\\5&2\end{bmatrix}$ (d) $\begin{bmatrix}-3&1\\2&-5\end{bmatrix}$

47 The value of x and y such that

$$x\begin{bmatrix}2\\1\end{bmatrix}+y\begin{bmatrix}3\\5\end{bmatrix}+\begin{bmatrix}-8\\-11\end{bmatrix}=0$$ are **NCERT Pg. 59**

(a) $x=1, y=2$ (b) $x=2, y=1$
(c) $x=-2, y=-1$ (d) $x=-1, y=-1$

48 If $A=\begin{bmatrix}0&2\\3&-4\end{bmatrix}$ and $kA=\begin{bmatrix}0&3a\\2b&24\end{bmatrix}$, then the values of k, a, b are, respectively **NCERT Pg. 45**

(a) $-6, -12, -18$ (b) $-6, 4, 9$
(c) $-6, -4, -9$ (d) $-6, 12, 18$

49 If $F(x)=\begin{bmatrix}\cos x&-\sin x&0\\\sin x&\cos x&0\\0&0&1\end{bmatrix}$, then $F(x)\cdot F(y)$ is equal to **NCERT Pg. 60**

(a) $F(xy)$ (b) $F(x)+F(y)$
(c) $F(x+y)$ (d) $F(x-y)$

50 If $A=\begin{bmatrix}2&1&2\\1&2&4\end{bmatrix}$ and $B=\begin{bmatrix}4&1\\2&3\\1&2\end{bmatrix}$, then **NCERT Pg. 52**

(a) AB is not defined
(b) BA is not defined
(c) AB and BA both are defined
(d) None of the above

51 Conisder the matrices **NCERT Pg. 53**

$$A=\begin{bmatrix}2&1&3\\3&-2&1\\-1&0&1\end{bmatrix}, B=\begin{bmatrix}1&-2\\2&1\\4&3\end{bmatrix}, C=[1\ \ 2\ \ 6]$$

Then, which of the following is not defined?

(a) CA (b) BA (c) AB (d) CB

52 The value of x such that

$$[1\ \ 2\ \ 1]\begin{bmatrix}1&2&0\\2&0&1\\1&0&2\end{bmatrix}\begin{bmatrix}0\\2\\x\end{bmatrix}=O,$$ is **NCERT Pg. 72**

(a) 1 (b) 0 (c) -1 (d) 3

53 If $A=\begin{bmatrix}3&1\\-1&2\end{bmatrix}$, then $A^2-5A+7I$ is equal to **NCERT Pg. 60**

(a) $\begin{bmatrix}0&0\\1&1\end{bmatrix}$ (b) $\begin{bmatrix}0&0\\0&0\end{bmatrix}$

(c) $\begin{bmatrix}-1&1\\-2&1\end{bmatrix}$ (d) $\begin{bmatrix}1&0\\0&1\end{bmatrix}$

54 If $[2x\ \ 3]\begin{bmatrix}1&2\\-3&0\end{bmatrix}\begin{bmatrix}x\\8\end{bmatrix}=O$, then value of x is **NCERT Pg. 54**

(a) $-\dfrac{23}{2}$ (b) $\dfrac{23}{2}$ (c) 23 (d) 2

55 If A and B are square matrices of same order, then $(A+B)(A-B)$ is equal to **NCERT Pg. 54**

(a) A^2-B^2 (b) $A^2-BA-AB-B^2$
(c) $A^2-B^2+BA-AB$ (d) A^2-BA+B^2+AB

56 Let A, B, and C be three matrices of same order. Now, consider the following statements.

I. If $A=B$, then $AC=BC$.
II. If $AC=BC$, then $A=B$.

Choose the correct option. **NCERT Exemplar Pg. 64**

(a) Only I is true (b) Only II is true
(c) Both I and II are true (d) Neither I nor II is true

57 If $A\cdot A=A^2, A\cdot A\cdot A=A^3$ and so on, then A is **NCERT Pg. 54**

(a) rectangular matrix (b) row matrix
(c) square matrix (d) column matrix

58 If A and B are square matrices such that $AB = BA$, then $(A+B)^2$ is equal to **NCERT Pg. 54**

(a) $A^2 + B^2 + AB$
(b) $A^2 + B^2 + BA - AB$
(c) $A^2 + B^2 - BA + AB$
(d) $A^2 + 2AB + B^2$

59 If $A = \begin{bmatrix} \alpha & 0 \\ 1 & 1 \end{bmatrix}$ and $B = \begin{bmatrix} 1 & 0 \\ 5 & 1 \end{bmatrix}$, then the value of α for which $A^2 = B$, is **NCERT Pg. 54**

(a) 1
(b) −1
(c) 4
(d) No real value

60 The value of x, if $[x \quad -5 \quad -1] \begin{bmatrix} 1 & 0 & 2 \\ 0 & 2 & 1 \\ 2 & 0 & 3 \end{bmatrix} \begin{bmatrix} x \\ 4 \\ 1 \end{bmatrix} = 0$, is **NCERT Pg. 72**

(a) $14\sqrt{3}$
(b) $\pm 4\sqrt{3}$
(c) $-\sqrt{3}$
(d) $\sqrt{3}$

61 The matrix X such that $X \begin{bmatrix} 1 & 2 & 3 \\ 4 & 5 & 6 \end{bmatrix} = \begin{bmatrix} -7 & -8 & -9 \\ 2 & 4 & 6 \end{bmatrix}$ is **NCERT Pg. 54**

(a) $\begin{bmatrix} 1 & 2 \\ 2 & 0 \end{bmatrix}$
(b) $\begin{bmatrix} 1 & -2 \\ 2 & 0 \end{bmatrix}$
(c) $\begin{bmatrix} 1 & 2 \\ -2 & 0 \end{bmatrix}$
(d) $\begin{bmatrix} 1 & 2 \\ 0 & -2 \end{bmatrix}$

Transpose of a Matrix

Level I

1 Let $A = [a_{ij}]$ be a $m \times n$ matrix, then the transpose of a matrix A, denoted by A' (or A^T) is the matrix obtained by **NCERT Pg. 61**

(a) deleting last row from the matrix A
(b) adding a row in the matrix A
(c) interchanging the rows and columns of A
(d) deleting last column from the matrix A

2 If $A = [a_{ij}]_{m \times n}$, then A' is equal to **NCERT Pg. 61**

(a) $[a_{ji}]_{n \times m}$
(b) $[a_{ij}]_{m \times n}$
(c) $[a_{ji}]_{m \times n}$
(d) $[a_{ij}]_{n \times m}$

3 If $A = \begin{bmatrix} 3 & 5 \\ \sqrt{3} & 1 \\ 0 & -\frac{1}{5} \end{bmatrix}_{3 \times 2}$, then A' is equal to **NCERT Pg. 61**

(a) $\begin{bmatrix} 3 & \sqrt{3} & 10 \\ 5 & 1 & -\frac{1}{5} \end{bmatrix}_{3 \times 2}$
(b) $\begin{bmatrix} 3 & \sqrt{3} & 0 \\ 5 & 1 & -\frac{1}{5} \end{bmatrix}_{2 \times 3}$
(c) $\begin{bmatrix} 3 & 5 \\ \sqrt{3} & 1 \\ 0 & -\frac{1}{5} \end{bmatrix}_{2 \times 3}$
(d) None of these

4 Match the terms of column I with the terms of column II and choose the correct option from the codes given below. **NCERT Pg. 61**

Column I		Column II
A. $(A')'$	1.	$B'A'$
B. $(kA)'$, where k is any constant.	2.	A
C. $(A+B)'$	3.	kA'
D. $(AB)'$	4.	$A'+B'$
	5	$A'B'$

Codes

	A	B	C	D		A	B	C	D
(a)	2	4	3	5	(b)	1	4	3	2
(c)	3	1	4	2	(d)	2	3	4	1

5 The transpose of the matrix $\begin{bmatrix} 5 \\ 1/2 \\ -1 \end{bmatrix}$ is given by **NCERT Pg. 66**

(a) $[5 \quad 1/2 \quad -1]$
(b) $[-1 \quad 1/2 \quad 5]$
(c) $[1/2 \quad 5 \quad -1]$
(d) $[5 \quad -1 \quad 1/2]$

6 The transpose of the matrix $\begin{bmatrix} -1 & 5 & 6 \\ \sqrt{3} & 5 & 6 \\ 2 & 3 & -1 \end{bmatrix}$ is given by **NCERT Pg. 66**

(a) $\begin{bmatrix} \sqrt{3} & 5 & 6 \\ -1 & 5 & 6 \\ 2 & 3 & -1 \end{bmatrix}$
(b) $\begin{bmatrix} -1 & 5 & 6 \\ \sqrt{3} & 3 & -1 \\ 2 & 5 & 6 \end{bmatrix}$
(c) $\begin{bmatrix} -1 & \sqrt{3} & 2 \\ 5 & 5 & 3 \\ 6 & 6 & -1 \end{bmatrix}$
(d) $\begin{bmatrix} 2 & 3 & -1 \\ \sqrt{3} & 5 & 6 \\ -1 & 5 & 6 \end{bmatrix}$

7 If $A = \begin{bmatrix} -1 & 2 & 3 \\ 5 & 7 & 9 \\ -2 & 1 & 1 \end{bmatrix}$ and $B = \begin{bmatrix} -4 & 1 & -5 \\ 1 & 2 & 0 \\ 1 & 3 & 1 \end{bmatrix}$, then **NCERT Pg. 66**

(a) $(A+B)' = A' + B'$ and $(A-B)' = A' - B'$
(b) $(A+B)' = A' - B'$
(c) $(A-B)' = A' + B'$
(d) None of the above

8 For the matrices $A' = \begin{bmatrix} 3 & 4 \\ -1 & 2 \\ 0 & 1 \end{bmatrix}$ and $B = \begin{bmatrix} -1 & 2 & 1 \\ 1 & 2 & 3 \end{bmatrix}$.

Consider the following statements.

I. $(A+B)' = A' - B'$
II. $(A-B)' = A' - B'$

Choose the correct option. NCERT Pg. 67

(a) Only I is true

(b) Only II is true

(c) Both I and II are true

(d) Neither I nor II is true

9 If $A=\begin{bmatrix}1\\-4\\3\end{bmatrix}$ and $B=[-1 \quad 2 \quad 1]$, then $(AB)'$ is equal to NCERT Pg. 67

(a) $B'A'=\begin{bmatrix}-1 & 4 & -3\\ 2 & -8 & 6\\ 1 & -4 & 3\end{bmatrix}$ (b) $B'A'=\begin{bmatrix}-1 & 2 & 1\\ 4 & -8 & -4\\ -3 & 6 & 3\end{bmatrix}$

(c) $B'A'=\begin{bmatrix}1 & 4 & -3\\ 2 & -8 & 6\\ 1 & 4 & 3\end{bmatrix}$ (d) $B'A'=\begin{bmatrix}-1 & 4 & -3\\ 2 & 8 & 6\\ 1 & -4 & 3\end{bmatrix}$

10 If $A=\begin{bmatrix}\cos\alpha & \sin\alpha\\ -\sin\alpha & \cos\alpha\end{bmatrix}$, then NCERT Pg. 67

(a) $A'A=I$

(b) $A'A=O$

(c) $A'A=2I$

(d) $A'A=-I$

Level II

11 If $A=\begin{bmatrix}\cos\alpha & -\sin\alpha\\ \sin\alpha & \cos\alpha\end{bmatrix}$ and $A+A'=I$. Then, the value of α is NCERT Pg. 67

(a) $\frac{\pi}{6}$ (b) $\frac{\pi}{3}$

(c) π (d) $\frac{3\pi}{2}$

12 If A and B are matrices of same order, then NCERT Pg. 61

(a) $AB=BA$ always

(b) $AB=-BA$

(c) $(AB)'=B'A'$

(d) $(A+B)(A-B)=A^2-B^2$

13 If $A'=\begin{bmatrix}-2 & 3\\ 1 & 2\end{bmatrix}$ and $B=\begin{bmatrix}-1 & 0\\ 1 & 2\end{bmatrix}$, then $(A+2B)'$ is NCERT Pg. 66

(a) $\begin{bmatrix}-4 & 1\\ 5 & 6\end{bmatrix}$ (b) $\begin{bmatrix}-4 & 6\\ 1 & 5\end{bmatrix}$

(c) $\begin{bmatrix}1 & -4\\ 6 & 5\end{bmatrix}$ (d) $\begin{bmatrix}-4 & 5\\ 1 & 6\end{bmatrix}$

14 If $A=\begin{bmatrix}0 & 2y & z\\ x & y & -z\\ x & -y & z\end{bmatrix}$ satisfies the equation $A'A=I$, then the values of x, y and z are NCERT Pg. 72

(a) $x=\pm\frac{1}{\sqrt{3}}, y=+\frac{1}{\sqrt{6}}, z=\pm\frac{1}{\sqrt{2}}$

(b) $x=\pm\frac{1}{\sqrt{2}}, y=\pm\frac{1}{\sqrt{3}}, z=\pm\frac{1}{\sqrt{6}}$

(c) $x=\pm\frac{1}{\sqrt{6}}, y=\pm\frac{1}{\sqrt{6}}, z=\pm\frac{1}{\sqrt{2}}$

(d) $x=\pm\frac{1}{\sqrt{2}}, y=\pm\frac{1}{\sqrt{6}}, z=\pm\frac{1}{\sqrt{3}}$

Symmetric and Skew-symmetric Matrices

Level I

1 A square matrix $A=[a_{ij}]$ is said to be symmetric if for all possible values of i and j NCERT Pg. 63

(a) $[a_{ij}]=[a_{ji}]$ (b) $[a_{ij}]=-[a_{ij}]+1$

(c) $[a_{ij}]+[a_{ji}]=0$ (d) $[a_{ij}]=2[a_{ji}]$

2 If $A=\begin{bmatrix}\sqrt{3} & 2 & 3\\ 2 & -1.5 & -1\\ 3 & -1 & 1\end{bmatrix}$, then NCERT Pg. 63

(a) $A'=-A$ (b) $A'=A$

(c) $A'=2A$ (d) $A'=-2A$

3 A square matrix $A=[a_{ij}]$ is said to be skew-symmetric matrix, if $A'=-A$. Then, for all possible values of i and j, which is true for skew-symmetric matrix? NCERT Pg. 63

(a) $[a_{ij}]=[a_{ji}]$ (b) $[a_{ij}]=[a_{ij}]$

(c) $[a_{ij}]=-[a_{ji}]$ (d) None of these

4 If $A=[a_{ij}]$ is a skew-symmetric matrix, then the diagonal elements of A are NCERT Pg. 63

(a) 1 (b) -1

(c) zero (d) 2

5 The matrix $B=\begin{bmatrix}0 & e & f\\ -e & 0 & g\\ -f & -g & 0\end{bmatrix}$ is NCERT Pg. 64

(a) skew-symmetric matrix (b) symmetric matrix

(c) diagonal matrix (d) None of these

6 For any square matrix A with real number entries, consider the following statements.

I. $A+A'$ is a symmetric matrix.

II. $A-A'$ is a skew-symmetric matrix.

Choose the correct option. NCERT Pg. 64

(a) Only I is true (b) Only II is true

(c) Both I and II are true (d) Neither I nor II is true

7 Any square matrix can be expressed as the ...B... of a symmetric and a skew-symmetric matrix. Here, B refers to NCERT Pg. 64

(a) difference (b) product

(c) sum (d) None of these

8 The matrix $A=\begin{bmatrix}1 & -1 & 5\\ -1 & 2 & 1\\ 5 & 1 & 3\end{bmatrix}$ is a **NCERT Pg. 63**

(a) skew-symmetric matrix (b) symmetric matrix
(c) diagonal matrix (d) identity matrix

9 The matrix $A=\begin{bmatrix}0 & 1 & -1\\ -1 & 0 & 1\\ 1 & -1 & 0\end{bmatrix}$ is a **NCERT Pg. 63**

(a) symmetric matrix (b) skew-symmetric matrix
(c) identity matrix (d) diagonal matrix

10 For the matrix $A=\begin{bmatrix}1 & 5\\ 6 & 7\end{bmatrix}$, $A-A'$ is a **NCERT Pg. 64**

(a) skew-symmetric matrix (b) symmetric matrix
(c) diagonal matrix (d) scalar matrix

11 For a matrix $A=\begin{bmatrix}0 & a & b\\ -a & 0 & c\\ -b & -c & 0\end{bmatrix}$, $\frac{1}{2}(A-A')$ is **NCERT Pg. 64**

(a) zero matrix (b) A
(c) diagonal matrix (d) identity matrix

12 If A and B are symmetric matrices of same order, then $AB-BA$ is a **NCERT Pg. 63**

(a) skew-symmetric matrix (b) symmetric matrix
(c) zero matrix (d) identity matrix

13 We know any square matrix can be expressed as sum of symmetric and skew-symmetric matrices. Thus, match the terms of column I with the terms of column II and choose the correct option from the codes given below. **NCERT Pg. 64**

Column I (Matrices)	Column II (Their symmetric parts)
A. $\begin{bmatrix}3 & 5\\ 1 & -1\end{bmatrix}$	1. $\begin{bmatrix}3 & 1/2 & -5/2\\ 1/2 & -2 & -2\\ -5/2 & -2 & 2\end{bmatrix}$
B. $\begin{bmatrix}1 & 5\\ -1 & 2\end{bmatrix}$	2. $\begin{bmatrix}6 & -2 & 2\\ -2 & 3 & -1\\ 2 & -1 & 3\end{bmatrix}$
C. $\begin{bmatrix}6 & -2 & 2\\ -2 & 3 & -1\\ 2 & -1 & 3\end{bmatrix}$	3. $\begin{bmatrix}1 & 2\\ 2 & 2\end{bmatrix}$
D. $\begin{bmatrix}3 & 3 & -1\\ -2 & -2 & 1\\ -4 & -5 & 2\end{bmatrix}$	4. $\begin{bmatrix}3 & 3\\ 3 & -1\end{bmatrix}$

Codes

	A	B	C	D		A	B	C	D
(a)	4	3	2	1	(b)	3	4	1	2
(c)	1	4	3	2	(d)	2	3	1	4

Level II

14 Consider the following statements.

I. If A is symmetric, then $B'AB$ is symmetric.
II. If A is skew-symmetric, then $B'AB$ is skew-symmetric.

Choose the correct option. **NCERT Pg. 72**

(a) Only I is true
(b) Only II is true
(c) Both I and II are true
(d) Neither I nor II is true

15 If A and B are symmetric matrices of the same order, then $AB'-BA'$ is a **NCERT Pg. 72**

(a) skew-symmetric matrix
(b) null matrix
(c) symmetric matrix
(d) None of the above

16 For any matrix A, **NCERT Pg. 61**

(a) $A'A$ and AA' are both symmetric matrices
(b) $A'A$ is symmetric matrix but AA' is skew-symmetric matrix
(c) $A'A$ is skew-symmetric matrix but AA' is symmetric matrix
(d) $A'A$ and AA' are both skew-symmetric matrices

17 If a matrix A is both symmetric and skew-symmetric matrix, then **NCERT Exemplar Pg. 62**

(a) A is a diagonal matrix
(b) A is zero square matrix
(c) A is a square matrix
(d) None of the above

18 If A is a symmetric matrix and $n \in N$, then A^n is **NCERT Exemplar Pg. 62**

(a) symmetric matrix (b) a diagonal matrix
(c) skew-symmetric matrix (d) None of these

19 The square matrix $A=[a_{ij}]$ given by $a_{ij}=(i-j)^3$, is a **NCERT Pg. 63**

(a) symmetric matrix (b) skew-symmetric matrix
(c) diagonal matrix (d) None of the above

20 If $A=[a_{ij}]$ is a skew-symmetric matrix of order n, then a_{ii} is equal to **NCERT Pg. 63**

(a) 0 for some i (b) 0 for all $i=1,2,\ldots,n$
(c) 1 for some i (d) 1 for all $i=1,2,\ldots,n$

Invertible Matrices

Level I

1 If A is a square matrix of order m, then the matrix B of same order is called the inverse of the matrix A, if **NCERT Pg. 68**

(a) $AB=A$ (b) $BA=A$
(c) $AB=BA=I$ (d) $AB=-BA$

2 The inverse of A is denoted by NCERT Pg. 68
(a) A^{-1} (b) A^2
(c) $-A$ (d) $A-1$

3 **Statement I** If $A=\begin{bmatrix}2 & 3\\1 & 2\end{bmatrix}$ and $B=\begin{bmatrix}2 & -3\\-1 & 2\end{bmatrix}$, then B is the inverse of A.

Statement II If A is a square matrix of order m and if there exists another square matrix B of the same order m, such that $AB=BA=I$, then B is called the inverse of A.

Choose the correct option. NCERT Pg. 69
(a) Both statements are correct
(b) Both statements are incorect
(c) Statement I is correct; Statement II is incorrect
(d) Statement I is incorrect; Statement II is correct.

4 Consider the following statements.
I. A rectangular matrix possesses inverse matrix.
II. If B is the inverse of A, then A is also the inverse of B.
III. Inverse of a square matrix, if it exists, is not unique.
IV. If A and B are invertible matrices of the same order, then $(AB)^{-1}=B^{-1}A^{-1}$.

Choose the correct option. NCERT Pg. 69
(a) I and III are correct
(b) II and IV are correct
(c) I and II are correct
(d) III and IV are correct

Level II

5 Matrices A and B will be inverse of each other, if and only if NCERT Pg. 69
(a) $AB=BA$
(b) $AB=BA=0$
(c) $AB=0, BA=I$
(d) $AB=BA=I$

6 If A and B are square matrices of the same order and $AB=3I$, then A^{-1} is equal to NCERT Pg. 69
(a) $3B$ (b) $\frac{1}{3}B$
(c) $3B^{-1}$ (d) $\frac{1}{3}B^{-1}$

Miscellaneous Exercise

Level I

1 The value of x and y that satisfy the equation $\begin{bmatrix}3 & -2\\3 & 0\\2 & 4\end{bmatrix}\begin{bmatrix}y & y\\x & x\end{bmatrix}=\begin{bmatrix}3 & 3\\3y & 3y\\10 & 10\end{bmatrix}$ are, respectively NCERT Pg. 41, 50
(a) $\frac{3}{2}, 1$ (b) $\frac{3}{2}, 2$
(c) $2, \frac{3}{2}$ (d) None of these

2 If X and Y are 2×2 matrices such that $2X+3Y=0$ and $X+2Y=I$, where O and I denote the 2×2 zero matrix and the 2×2 identity matrix respectively, then X is equal to NCERT Pg. 43
(a) $\begin{bmatrix}1 & 0\\0 & 1\end{bmatrix}$ (b) $\begin{bmatrix}2 & 0\\0 & 2\end{bmatrix}$ (c) $\begin{bmatrix}-3 & 0\\0 & -3\end{bmatrix}$ (d) $\begin{bmatrix}3 & 0\\0 & 3\end{bmatrix}$

3 Consider the following statements.
I. Addition of matrices is defined, if order of matrices is same.
II. $AB=AC \Rightarrow B=C$, for any three matrices of same order.
III. If A and B are matrices of same order, then $(3A-2B)'=3A'+2B'$.
IV. If $A=\begin{bmatrix}3 & 1 & 1\\5 & 2 & 3\end{bmatrix}$ and $B=\begin{bmatrix}2 & 1\\7 & 2\\4 & -1\end{bmatrix}$, then the product AB is a matrix of order 2×2.

Choose the correct option. NCERT Pg. 43, 61
(a) I and IV are true (b) II and III are true
(c) I and III are true (d) All are true

4 If $[1 \;\; x \;\; 1]\begin{bmatrix}1 & 2 & 3\\0 & 5 & 1\\0 & 3 & 2\end{bmatrix}\begin{bmatrix}x\\1\\-2\end{bmatrix}=0$, then the value of x is NCERT Pg. 72
(a) 0 (b) $\frac{2}{3}$ (c) $\frac{5}{4}$ (d) $-\frac{4}{5}$

5 If $A=\begin{bmatrix}1 & 2 & 2\\2 & 1 & 2\\2 & 2 & 1\end{bmatrix}$, then A^2-4A is equal to NCERT Pg. 72
(a) $2I_3$ (b) $3I_3$ (c) $4I_3$ (d) $5I_3$

6 If $A=[3 \;\; 5]$ and $B=[7 \;\; 3]$, then the order of a non-zero matrix C such that AC and BC are defined, is NCERT Pg. 50
(a) $1\times n$ (b) $2\times n$ (c) 1×2 (d) 3×1

7 If $m[-3 \;\; 4]+n[4 \;\; -3]=[10 \;\; -11]$, then $3m+7n$ is equal to NCERT Pg. 43
(a) 3 (b) 5 (c) 10 (d) 1

8 Which among the following is matrix X, if $2X+\begin{bmatrix}1 & 2\\3 & 4\end{bmatrix}=\begin{bmatrix}3 & 8\\7 & 2\end{bmatrix}$? NCERT Pg. 71
(a) $\begin{bmatrix}1 & 3\\2 & -1\end{bmatrix}$ (b) $\begin{bmatrix}1 & -3\\2 & -1\end{bmatrix}$
(c) $\begin{bmatrix}2 & 6\\4 & -2\end{bmatrix}$ (d) $\begin{bmatrix}2 & -6\\4 & -2\end{bmatrix}$

9 Let $A=\begin{bmatrix}1 & 2\\ 3 & 4\end{bmatrix}$ and $B=\begin{bmatrix}a & 0\\ 0 & b\end{bmatrix}$, $a, b \in N$. Then, **NCERT Pg. 50**

(a) there exists more than one but finite number of B's such that $AB = BA$
(b) there exists exactly one B such that $AB = BA$
(c) there exists infinitely many B's such that $AB = BA$
(d) there cannot exist any B such that $AB = BA$

10 If $A=\begin{bmatrix}6 & 8 & 5\\ 4 & 2 & 3\\ 9 & 7 & 1\end{bmatrix}$ is the sum of a symmetric matrix B and skew-symmetric matrix C, then B is equal to **NCERT Pg. 64**

(a) $\begin{bmatrix}6 & 6 & 7\\ 6 & 2 & 5\\ 7 & 5 & 1\end{bmatrix}$ (b) $\begin{bmatrix}0 & 2 & -2\\ -2 & 5 & -2\\ 2 & 2 & 0\end{bmatrix}$

(c) $\begin{bmatrix}6 & 6 & 7\\ -6 & 2 & -5\\ -7 & 5 & 1\end{bmatrix}$ (d) $\begin{bmatrix}0 & 6 & -2\\ 2 & 0 & -2\\ -2 & -2 & 0\end{bmatrix}$

11 If $A=\begin{bmatrix}0 & 3 & 3\\ -3 & 0 & -4\\ -3 & 4 & 0\end{bmatrix}$ and $B=\begin{bmatrix}x\\ y\\ z\end{bmatrix}$, then $B'(AB)$ is **NCERT Pg. 50**

(a) symmetric matrix (b) zero matrix
(c) singular matrix (d) unit matrix

12 Let A and B be square matrices of the same order such that $AB = BA$. Now, consider the following statements.

I. For all $n \in N$, $AB^n = B^nA$.
II. For all $n \in N$, $(AB)^n = A^nB^n$.

Choose the correct option. **NCERT Pg. 50**

(a) Only I is true
(b) Only II is true
(c) Both I and II are true
(d) Neither I nor II is true

13 Consider the following statements.

I. If $\begin{bmatrix}xy & 4\\ z+5 & x+y\end{bmatrix}=\begin{bmatrix}4 & w\\ 0 & 4\end{bmatrix}$, then $x=2, y=2$, $z=-5$ and $w=4$.

II. Two matrices are equal, if their orders are same and their corresponding elements are equal.

Choose the correct option. **NCERT Pg. 41**

(a) Only I is true
(b) Only II is true
(c) Both I and II are true
(d) Neither I nor II is true

14 If A and B are symmetric matrices of the same order, then AB is symmetric, if and only if **NCERT Exemplar Pg. 63**

(a) $AB = BA$ (b) $AB = -BA$
(c) $AB = 0$ (d) $AB = I$

15 If $A=\begin{bmatrix}\cos^2\alpha & \cos\alpha\sin\alpha\\ \cos\alpha\sin\alpha & \sin^2\alpha\end{bmatrix}$ and $B=\begin{bmatrix}\cos^2\beta & \cos\beta\sin\beta\\ \cos\beta\sin\beta & \sin^2\beta\end{bmatrix}$ are two matrices such that $AB = 0$, then $\alpha-\beta$ is equal to **NCERT Pg. 68**

(a) 0 (b) π
(c) $\frac{\pi}{2}$ (d) None of these

16 If $A=\begin{bmatrix}0 & 1\\ 0 & 0\end{bmatrix}$, then $(aI+bA)^n$, where I is an identity matrix, is equal to **NCERT Pg. 50**

(a) $a^nI + a^{n-1}bA$ (b) $a^nI - a^{n-1}bA$
(c) $a^nI + na^{n-1}bA$ (d) $a^nI - na^{n-1}bA$

17 If $A=\begin{bmatrix}1 & 1 & 1\\ 1 & 1 & 1\\ 1 & 1 & 1\end{bmatrix}$, then A^n, $n \in N$, is **NCERT Pg. 50**

(a) $\begin{bmatrix}3^n & 3^n & 3^n\\ 3^n & 3^n & 3^n\\ 3^n & 3^n & 3^n\end{bmatrix}$ (b) $\begin{bmatrix}3n & 3n & 3n\\ 3n & 3n & 3n\\ 3n & 3n & 3n\end{bmatrix}$

(c) $\begin{bmatrix}3^{n+1} & 3^{n+1} & 3^{n+1}\\ 3^{n+1} & 3^{n+1} & 3^{n+1}\\ 3^{n+1} & 3^{n+1} & 3^{n+1}\end{bmatrix}$ (d) $\begin{bmatrix}3^{n-1} & 3^{n-1} & 3^{n-1}\\ 3^{n-1} & 3^{n-1} & 3^{n-1}\\ 3^{n-1} & 3^{n-1} & 3^{n-1}\end{bmatrix}$

18 Consider the following statements.

I. Matrices of different orders cannot be subtracted.
II. A square matrix in which every element is unity, is called an identity matrix.
III. Transpose of a column matrix is a column matrix.
IV. If A and B are diagonal matrices of same order, then $AB = BA$.

Choose the correct option. **NCERT Pg. 40, 43, 61**

(a) II and IV are true (b) I and IV are true
(c) I and II are true (d) III and IV are true

19 If $A=\begin{bmatrix}1 & 2 & -2\\ 1 & 1 & 1\\ 1 & 3 & -1\end{bmatrix}$, then $A^3 - A^2 - 4A$ is equal to **NCERT Pg. 60**

(a) -4 (b) $-4I$ (c) $2I$ (d) $-2I$

20 If the matrix $A=\begin{bmatrix}\alpha & \beta\\ \gamma & -\alpha\end{bmatrix}$ is such that $A^2 = I$, then **NCERT Pg. 60**

(a) $1+\alpha^2+\beta\gamma=0$ (b) $1-\alpha^2+\beta\gamma=0$
(c) $1-\alpha^2-\beta\gamma=0$ (d) $1+\alpha^2-\beta\gamma=0$

21 If A is a square matrix such that $A^2 = A$, then $(I + A)^3 - 7A$ is equal to NCERT Pg. 73

(a) A (b) $I - A$
(c) I (d) $3A$

22 If A and B are two matrices such that both $A + B$ and $A \times B$ are defined, then NCERT Pg. 43, 50

(a) A and B are of same order
(b) A is of order $m \times m$ and B is of order $n \times n$, $m \neq n$
(c) both A and B are of same order $n \times n$
(d) A is of order $m \times n$ and B is of order $n \times m$

23 Total number of possible matrices of order 3×3 with each entry 2 or 0 is NCERT Pg. 43

(a) 9 (b) 27 (c) 81 (d) 512

24 If $A = \begin{bmatrix} 3 & -4 \\ 1 & -1 \end{bmatrix}$, then for $n \in N$, A^n is equal to NCERT Pg. 50

(a) $\begin{bmatrix} 1+2n & -4n \\ n & 1-2n \end{bmatrix}$
(b) $\begin{bmatrix} 1-2n & 4n \\ n & 1+2n \end{bmatrix}$
(c) $\begin{bmatrix} 1+2n & 4n \\ -n & 1+2n \end{bmatrix}$
(d) $\begin{bmatrix} 1-2n & -4n \\ -n & -1+2n \end{bmatrix}$

25 If A is a square matrix such that $A^2 = I$, then $(A - I)^3 + (A + I)^3 - 7A$ is equal to NCERT Pg. 73

(a) A (b) $I - A$ (c) $I + A$ (d) $3A$

Numerical Type Questions

1 If $[2x \quad 3] \begin{bmatrix} 1 & 3 \\ -3 & 0 \end{bmatrix} \begin{bmatrix} x \\ 8 \end{bmatrix} = 0$, then find the value of x (x is an integer) .... NCERT Pg. 72

2 Let $A = \begin{bmatrix} 2 & -1 \\ 1 & 1 \end{bmatrix}$. If the sum of the diagonal elements of A^{13} is 3^n, then n is equal to .... NCERT Pg. 50

3 The number of square matrices of order 4 with entriers from the set {0, 1}, such that the sum of all the elements in each row is 1 and the sum of all the elements in each column is also 1 is .... NCERT Pg. 43

4 If $A = \begin{bmatrix} \alpha & 0 \\ 1 & 1 \end{bmatrix}$, $B = \begin{bmatrix} 1 & 0 \\ 2 & 1 \end{bmatrix}$, then the value of α for which $A^2 = B$ is .... NCERT Pg. 50

5 If $[m \quad n] \begin{bmatrix} m \\ n \end{bmatrix} = [25]$ and $m < n$, then $(m + n) =$ .... NCERT Pg. 50

6 If $M = \begin{bmatrix} 1 & 2 \\ 2 & 3 \end{bmatrix}$ and $M^2 - rM - I_2 = 0$, then r .... NCERT Pg. 60

7 Let $A = \begin{bmatrix} 1 & 0 & 0 \\ 0 & 1 & 1 \\ 1 & 0 & 0 \end{bmatrix}$, then the value of a_{21} element of $A^{2025} - A^{2020}$ is .... NCERT Pg. 50

8 If $A = \begin{bmatrix} 0 & 2 & 0 \\ 0 & 0 & 3 \\ -2 & 2 & 0 \end{bmatrix}$ and $B = \begin{bmatrix} 1 & 2 & 3 \\ 3 & 4 & 5 \\ 5 & -4 & 0 \end{bmatrix}$, then the element of 3rd row and 3rd column in AB will be .... NCERT Pg. 50

9 Let $A = \begin{bmatrix} 1/2 & 3/4 \\ 1 & -1/2 \end{bmatrix}$, then the sum of all the elements of A^{100} is .... NCERT Pg. 50

10 Let I_2 be an identity matrix of order 2×2 and $S = \begin{bmatrix} 2 & -1 \\ 5 & -3 \end{bmatrix}$, then the value of n, where $n \in N$ for which $S^n = 5I - 8S$, is equal to .... NCERT Pg. 60

11 If p, q, r are integers, then the number of matrices $A = \begin{bmatrix} p & q & r \\ q & r & p \\ r & p & q \end{bmatrix}$, which are possible such that $AA' = I$, is ...... NCERT Pg. 41, 50

12 Let $A = \begin{bmatrix} 1 & 0 & 0 \\ 3 & 1 & 0 \\ 9 & 3 & 1 \end{bmatrix}$ and $B = [a_{ij}]$ be two 3×3 matrices such that $B - A^5 = I_3$, then $\frac{a_{21} + a_{31}}{a_{32}}$ is equal to .... NCERT Pg. 50

Assertion and Reason Questions

Direction (Q. Nos. 1-9) In the questions given below are to statements labelled as Assertion (A) and Reason (R). In the context on the two statements, which one of the following is correct?

(a) Both Assertion and Reason are correct and Reason is the correct explanation of Assertion.
(b) Both Assertion and Reason are correct but Reason is not the correct explanation of Assertion.
(c) Assertion is correct but Reason is incorrect.
(d) Assertion is incorrect but Reason is correct.

1 Assertion (A) $\begin{bmatrix} 0 & 0 & 1 \\ 0 & 1 & 0 \\ 1 & 0 & 0 \end{bmatrix}$ is an identity matrix.

Reason (R) A matrix $P = [a_{ij}]$ is an identity matrix if $a_{ij} = \begin{cases} 1 & \text{if } i = j \\ 0 & \text{if } i \neq j \end{cases}$.

NCERT Pg. 40

2 Assertion (A) Matrix $A = \begin{bmatrix} 0 \\ \sqrt{3} \\ -1 \\ 1/2 \end{bmatrix}$ is a column matrix of order 4×1.

Reason (R) If $A = [a_{ij}]_{m \times 1}$ is a column matrix, then its order is $m \times 1$.

NCERT Pg. 40

3 Assertion (A) Matrix $\begin{bmatrix} 1 & 2 & 3 \\ 2 & 4 & 5 \\ 3 & 5 & 6 \end{bmatrix}$ is a symmetric matrix.

Reason (R) A matrix A is symmetric if $A' = -A$.

NCERT Pg. 63

4 Assertion (A) If A is a symmetric matrix, then $B'AB$ is also symmetric.

Reason (R) $(PQR)' = R'Q'P'$ for three matrices P, Q and R.

NCERT Pg. 63

5 Let A, B and C be three symmetric matrices of order 3.

Assertion (A) $B(CB)$ and $(BC)B$ are symmetric matrices.

Reason (R) AB is symmetric matrix, if matrix multiplication of A with B is commutative.

NCERT Pg. 63

6 Assertion (A) If the matrix $A = \begin{bmatrix} 0 & 2a & -2 \\ 3 & 1 & 3 \\ 3b & 3 & 3 \end{bmatrix}$ is a symmetrix matrix, then $b = \frac{-2}{3}$ and $a = \frac{3}{2}$.

Reason (R) If B is a symmetric matrix, then $B' = -B$.

NCERT Pg. 63

7 Assertion (A) If $A = \begin{bmatrix} 2 & 3 & -1 \\ 1 & 4 & 2 \end{bmatrix}$ and $B = \begin{bmatrix} 2 & 3 \\ 4 & 5 \\ 2 & 1 \end{bmatrix}$, then AB and BA both are defined.

Reason (R) For two matrices A and B, then product AB is defined, if number of columns in A is equal to the number of rows in B.

NCERT Pg. 53

8 Assertion (A) For two matrices $A = \begin{bmatrix} 4 & 0 \\ 0 & 3 \end{bmatrix}$ and $B = \begin{bmatrix} 2 & 0 \\ 0 & 0 \end{bmatrix}$, $(A+B)^2 = A^2 + 2AB + B^2$.

Reason (R) For two matrices A and B, $AB = BA$.

NCERT Pg. 54

9 Assertion (A) If $A = \begin{bmatrix} 3 & -1 \\ -5 & x \end{bmatrix}$, then $(-A)$ is given by $\begin{bmatrix} -3 & 1 \\ 5 & -x \end{bmatrix}$.

Reason (R) The negative of a matrix is denoted by $-A$ and is defined as $-A = (-1)A$.

NCERT Pg. 44

Case or Paragraph Type Questions

Direction (Q. Nos. 1-3) If a manufacturer produces three types of bolts, p, q and r which he sells in two markets. Annual sales (in ₹) are indicated below. NCERT Pg. 72

Markets	Products		
	p	q	r
I	6000	20000	8000
II	10000	2000	18000

If unit sales prices of p, q and r are ₹ 2.50, ₹ 1.50 and ₹ 1.00 respectively, then answer the following questions using the concept of matrices.

1 Find the total revenue collected from the market I.
(a) ₹ 44000 (b) ₹ 48000
(c) ₹ 46000 (d) ₹ 53000

2 Find the total revenue collected from the market II.
(a) ₹ 51000 (b) ₹ 53000
(c) ₹ 46000 (d) ₹ 49000

3 If the unit costs of the above three commodities are ₹ 2.00, ₹ 1.00 and ₹ 0.50 respectively, then find the gross profit from both the markets.
(a) ₹ 53000 (b) ₹ 46000
(c) ₹ 34000 (d) ₹ 32000

Direction (Q. Nos. 4-6) Consider families A and B. Suppose there are 3 men 5 women and 2 children in family A and 1 man, 3 women, and 4 children in family B. The recommended daily amount of calories is 2500 for a man, 2000 for a woman and 1700 for a child. The recommended daily amount of protiens is 50 grams for a man, 60 grams for a woman, and 35 grams for a child.

Based on the given information, answer the following questions. NCERT Pg. 72

4 The requirement of calories and protiens for each person in matrix form can be represented as

(a) $\begin{matrix} \text{Man} \\ \text{Woman} \\ \text{Child} \end{matrix} \overset{\begin{matrix}\text{Calories} & \text{Proteins}\end{matrix}}{\begin{bmatrix} 2500 & 50 \\ 2000 & 60 \\ 1700 & 35 \end{bmatrix}}$

(b) $\begin{matrix} \text{Man} \\ \text{Woman} \\ \text{Child} \end{matrix} \overset{\begin{matrix}\text{Calories} & \text{Proteins}\end{matrix}}{\begin{bmatrix} 2000 & 60 \\ 2500 & 35 \\ 1700 & 50 \end{bmatrix}}$

(c) $\begin{matrix} \text{Man} \\ \text{Woman} \\ \text{Child} \end{matrix} \overset{\begin{matrix}\text{Calories} & \text{Proteins}\end{matrix}}{\begin{bmatrix} 1700 & 50 \\ 2000 & 60 \\ 2500 & 35 \end{bmatrix}}$

(d) $\begin{matrix} \text{Man} \\ \text{Woman} \\ \text{Child} \end{matrix} \overset{\begin{matrix}\text{Calories} & \text{Proteins}\end{matrix}}{\begin{bmatrix} 2500 & 35 \\ 1700 & 60 \\ 2000 & 50 \end{bmatrix}}$

5 What is the total daily requirement of calories and protiens for family A?
(a) 28200 calories, 490 grams of proteins.
(b) 28700 calories, 510 grams of proteins.
(c) 20900 calories, 520 grams of proteins.
(d) 29800 calories, 530 grams of proteins.

6 Requirement of proteins for family B is
(a) 370 (b) 420 (c) 290 (d) 450

Past Years Questions

Single Correct Type

1 Let $A = \begin{bmatrix} 2 & a & 0 \\ 1 & 3 & 1 \\ 0 & 5 & b \end{bmatrix}$. If $A^3 = 4A^2 - A - 21I$, where I is the identity matrix of order 3×3. Then, $2a + 3b$ is equal to
NCERT Pg. 56, JEE Main 2024, 8 April Shift-I
(a) -10 (b) -9 (c) -13 (d) -12

2 If A and B are symmetric matrices of the same order, then $AB - BA$ is a NCERT Pg. 68, CUET 2024, 16 May
(a) symmetric matrix (b) zero matrix
(c) skew symmetric matrix (d) identity matrix

3 If $[A]_{3\times 2}[B]_{x\times y} = [C]_{3\times 1}$, then
NCERT Pg. 36, CUET 2024, 16 May
(a) $x = 1, y = 3$ (b) $x = 2, y = 1$
(c) $x = 3, y = 3$ (d) $x = 3, y = 1$

4 Let α and β be real numbers. Consider a 3×3 matrix A such that $A^2 = 3A + \alpha I$. If $A^4 = 21A + \beta I$, then
NCERT Pg. 56, JEE Main 2023, 29 Jan Shift-I
(a) $\alpha = 1$ (b) $\alpha = 4$ (c) $\beta = 8$ (d) $\beta = -8$

5 If A is a square matrix and I is an identity matrix such that $A^2 = A$, then $A(I - 2A)^3 + 2A^3$ is equal to
NCERT Pg. 64, CUET 2024, 16 May
(a) $I + A$ (b) $I + 2A$ (c) $I - A$ (d) A

6 The matrix $\begin{bmatrix}1 & 0 & 0\\0 & 1 & 0\\0 & 0 & 1\end{bmatrix}$ is a

A. scalar matrix B. diagonal matrix
C. skew-symmetric matrix D. symmetric matrix

Choose the correct answer from the options given below. NCERT Pg. 63, CUET 2024, 16 May

(a) A, B and D (b) A, B and C
(c) A, B, C and D (d) B, C and D

7 Let P be a square matrix such that $P^2 = I - P$. For α, β, γ and $\delta \in N$. If $P^\alpha + P^\beta = \gamma I - 29P$ and $P^\alpha - P^\beta = \delta I - 13P$, then $\alpha + \beta + \gamma - \delta$ is equal to NCERT Pg. 56, JEE Main 2023, 6 April Shift-II

(a) 22 (b) 18 (c) 24 (d) 40

8 Let $P = \begin{bmatrix}\frac{\sqrt{3}}{2} & \frac{1}{2}\\ -\frac{1}{2} & \frac{\sqrt{3}}{2}\end{bmatrix}$, $A = \begin{bmatrix}1 & 1\\0 & 1\end{bmatrix}$ and $Q = PAP^T$. If $P^TQ^{2007}P = \begin{bmatrix}a & b\\c & d\end{bmatrix}$, then $2a + b - 3c - 4d$ is equal to NCERT Pg. 61, JEE Main 2023, 8 April Shift-I

(a) 2007 (b) 2004 (c) 2005 (d) 2006

9 Let $A = \begin{bmatrix}1\\1\\1\end{bmatrix}$ and $B = \begin{bmatrix}9^2 & -10^2 & 11^2\\12^2 & 13^2 & -14^2\\-15^2 & 16^2 & 17^2\end{bmatrix}$, then the value of $A'BA$ is NCERT Pg. 61, JEE Main 2022, 26 July Shift-II

(a) 1224 (b) 1042
(c) 540 (d) 539

10 Let A and B be any two 3×3 symmetric and skew-symmetric matrices, respectively. Then, which of the following is not true? NCERT Pg. 63, JEE Main 2022, 28 July Shift-II

(a) $A^4 - B^4$ is a symmetric matrix
(b) $AB - BA$ is a symmetric matrix
(c) $B^5 - A^5$ is a skew-symmetric matrix
(d) $AB + BA$ is a skew-symmetric matrix

Numerical Value Type

11 Let $A = \begin{bmatrix}1 & a & a\\0 & 1 & b\\0 & 0 & 1\end{bmatrix}$, $a, b \in R$.

If for some $n \in N$, $A^n = \begin{bmatrix}1 & 48 & 2160\\0 & 1 & 96\\0 & 0 & 1\end{bmatrix}$, then $n + a + b$ is equal to .... NCERT Pg. 50, JEE Main 2022, 25 July Shift-II

12 Let $M = \begin{bmatrix}0 & -\alpha\\ \alpha & 0\end{bmatrix}$, where α is a non-zero real number and $N = \sum_{k=1}^{49} M^{2k}$. If $(I - M^2)N = -2I$, then the positive integral value of α is .... NCERT Pg. 51, JEE Main 2022, 29 June Shift-II

Skill Boosters

1 Let B be a square matrix such that $BB^T = I$, then $\frac{1}{2}B[(B + B^T)^2 + (B - B^T)^2]$ is equal to

(a) $(B^2 + I)$ (b) $(B^3 + I)$
(c) $(B^2 + B^T)$ (d) $(B^3 + B^T)$

2 Let P, Q and R be 3×3 matrices such that P is symmetric and Q and R are skew-symmetric matrices. Consider the statements.

I. $P^{13}Q^{26} - Q^{26}P^{13}$ is symmetric matrices.
II. $P^{26}R^{13} - R^{13}P^{26}$ is symmetric matrices.

Then,
(a) Only I is true
(b) Only II is true
(c) Both I and II are false
(d) Both I and II are true

3 Let $A = \begin{bmatrix}1/\sqrt{5} & 2/\sqrt{5}\\ -2/\sqrt{5} & 1/\sqrt{5}\end{bmatrix}$ and $B = \begin{bmatrix}1 & -i\\0 & 1\end{bmatrix}$, where $i = \sqrt{-1}$.

If $P = A^TBA$, then find $AP^{2023}P^T$.

(a) $\begin{bmatrix}1 & -2023i\\0 & 1\end{bmatrix}$ (b) $\begin{bmatrix}1 & 0\\-2023 & 1\end{bmatrix}$
(c) $\begin{bmatrix}1 & 0\\2023i & 1\end{bmatrix}$ (d) $\begin{bmatrix}1 & 2023i\\0 & 1\end{bmatrix}$

4 If $A = \begin{bmatrix}1/\sqrt{2} & 1/\sqrt{2}\\ -1/\sqrt{2} & 1/\sqrt{2}\end{bmatrix}$, then

(a) $A^{28} - A^{20} = 2I$ (b) $A^{16} - A^9 = I$
(c) $A^{16} = A^{20}$ (d) $A^{16} - I = 0$

5 The number of diagonal matrix B of order n for which $B^3 = B$ is

(a) 1 (b) 0 (c) 2^n (d) 3^n

Correct Codes

Topical Questions

Matrix

1 (c)	2 (b)	3 (d)	4 (b)	5 (a)	6 (a)	7 (d)	8 (d)	9 (c)	10 (c)
11 (d)	12 (c)	13 (b)							

Types of Matrices

1 (b)	2 (c)	3 (c)	4 (d)	5 (c)	6 (a)	7 (c)	8 (a)	9 (b)	10 (c)
11 (a)	12 (b)	13 (a)	14 (d)	15 (b)	16 (d)	17 (d)	18 (a)	19 (a)	20 (c)
21 (b)	22 (d)	23 (c)	24 (d)	25 (b)	26 (b)	27 (b)			

Operations on Matrices

1 (d)	2 (c)	3 (d)	4 (c)	5 (c)	6 (b)	7 (c)	8 (b)	9 (d)	10 (a)
11 (b)	12 (c)	13 (b)	14 (d)	15 (c)	16 (b)	17 (d)	18 (c)	19 (c)	20 (b)
21 (d)	22 (d)	23 (c)	24 (c)	25 (a)	26 (a)	27 (b)	28 (c)	29 (c)	30 (b)
31 (d)	32 (a)	33 (a)	34 (d)	35 (a)	36 (b)	37 (c)	38 (c)	39 (b)	40 (c)
41 (d)	42 (b)	43 (d)	44 (d)	45 (d)	46 (b)	47 (a)	48 (c)	49 (c)	50 (c)
51 (b)	52 (c)	53 (b)	54 (a)	55 (c)	56 (a)	57 (c)	58 (d)	59 (d)	60 (b)
61 (b)									

Transpose of a Matrix

1 (c)	2 (a)	3 (b)	4 (d)	5 (a)	6 (c)	7 (a)	8 (b)	9 (a)	10 (a)
11 (b)	12 (c)	13 (d)	14 (d)						

Symmetric and Skew-symmetric Matrices

1 (a)	2 (b)	3 (c)	4 (c)	5 (a)	6 (c)	7 (c)	8 (b)	9 (b)	10 (a)
11 (b)	12 (a)	13 (a)	14 (c)	15 (a)	16 (a)	17 (b)	18 (a)	19 (b)	20 (b)

Invertible Matrices

1 (c)	2 (a)	3 (a)	4 (b)	5 (d)	6 (b)

Miscellaneous Exercise

1 (b)	2 (c)	3 (a)	4 (c)	5 (d)	6 (b)	7 (d)	8 (a)	9 (c)	10 (a)
11 (b)	12 (c)	13 (c)	14 (a)	15 (c)	16 (c)	17 (d)	18 (b)	19 (b)	20 (c)
21 (c)	22 (c)	23 (d)	24 (a)	25 (a)					

Numerical Type Questions

1 (0)	2 (7)	3 (24)	4 (1)	5 (7)	6 (4)	7 (5)	8 (4)	9 (2)	10 (6)
11 (6)	12 (10)								

Assertion and Reason Questions

1 (d)	2 (a)	3 (c)	4 (a)	5 (b)	6 (c)	7 (a)	8 (c)	9 (a)

Case or Paragraph Type Questions

1 (d)	2 (c)	3 (d)	4 (a)	5 (c)	6 (a)

Past Years Questions

1 (c)	2 (c)	3 (b)	4 (d)	5 (d)	6 (a)	7 (c)	8 (c)	9 (d)	10 (c)
11 (24)	12 (1)								

Skill Boosters

1 (d)	2 (b)	3 (a)	4 (d)	5 (d)

Step by Step

Decoding the Questions

Concept Builders

1 12

2 Row matrix

3 Vertical matrix

4 0

5 $3n$

6 Square matrix

7 False

8 False

9 $n \times m$

10 $C^T B^T A^T$

11 symmetric

12 $PQ = QP$

13 $2B' - 3A'$

14 Same

15 Symmetric matrix

16 False

17 True

18 Symmetric

19 Skew-symmetric

20 Zero

Topical Questions

Matrix

1 (c) The matrix B has 3 rows and 3 columns and the matrix C has 2 rows and 3 columns.

2 (b) If A is a 3×2 matrix, then A has $3 \times 2 = 6$ elements.

Similarly, if B is a 3×3 matrix, then B has $3 \times 3 = 9$ elements and C has $2 \times 3 = 6$ elements.

3 (d) We know that, if a matrix is of order $m \times n$, then it has mn elements. Thus, to find all possible orders of a matrix with 8 elements, we will find all ordered pairs of natural numbers, whose product is 8. Thus, all possible ordered pair are (1, 8), (8, 1), (2, 4), (4, 2).
Hence, possible orders are $1 \times 8, 8 \times 1, 4 \times 2, 2 \times 4$.

4 (b) The given matrix is

$$A = \begin{bmatrix} 2 & 5 & 19 & -7 \\ 35 & -2 & 5/2 & 12 \\ \sqrt{3} & 1 & -5 & 17 \end{bmatrix}$$

Since, A has 3 rows and 4 columns.
$\therefore$ The order of A is 3×4 and the number of elements in A is 12.
Also, a_{13} is the element lying in the first row and third column

$\Rightarrow \quad a_{13} = 19$

Similarly, $a_{21} = 35$ and $a_{33} = -5$.

5 (a) If a matrix is of order $m \times n$, then it has mn elements.

I. Thus, to find the all possible orders of a matrix with 24 elements, we will find all ordered pairs of natural numbers, whose product is 24.
Thus, all possible ordered pairs are (1, 24), (24, 1), (2, 12), (12, 2), (3, 8), (8, 3), (4, 6), (6, 4).
$\therefore$ All possible orders are
$1 \times 24, 24 \times 1, 2 \times 12, 12 \times 2, 3 \times 8, 8 \times 3, 4 \times 6, 6 \times 4$

II. Similarly, if a matrix has 13 elements, then all its possible orders are 1×13 and 13×1.

III. If a matrix has 18 elements, then all its possible orders are $18 \times 1, 1 \times 18, 2 \times 9, 9 \times 2, 3 \times 6, 6 \times 3$

IV. A matrix have 5 elements, then its possible orders are 1×5 and 5×1.

6 (a) In general, the matrix A of order 2×2 is given by

$$A = \begin{bmatrix} a_{11} & a_{12} \\ a_{21} & a_{22} \end{bmatrix}$$

Now, $a_{ij} = \dfrac{i}{j}$; $i = 1, 2$ and $j = 1, 2$

$\therefore a_{11} = 1, a_{12} = \dfrac{1}{2}, a_{21} = 2, a_{22} = 1$

Thus, matrix A is $\begin{bmatrix} 1 & 1/2 \\ 2 & 1 \end{bmatrix}$.

7 (d)

A. Here, $A = [a_{ij}]_{2 \times 2}$ is a matrix with $a_{ij} = \dfrac{(i+j)^2}{2}$.

$\therefore \quad a_{21} = \dfrac{(2+1)^2}{2} = \dfrac{9}{2}$

B. Here, $B = [b_{ij}]_{2 \times 3}$ is a matrix with $b_{ij} = \dfrac{(i+2j)^2}{2}$.

$\therefore \quad b_{13} = \dfrac{(1 + 2 \times 3)^2}{2} = \dfrac{49}{2}$

C. Given that, $C = [C_{ij}]_{3 \times 4}$ is a matrix with $C_{ij} = \dfrac{1}{2}|-3i + j|$.

$\therefore \quad C_{11} = \dfrac{1}{2}|-3 \times 1 + 1| = 1$

D. Here, $D = [d_{ij}]$ is a matrix with $d_{ij} = 2i - j$.

$\therefore \quad d_{34} = 2 \times 3 - 4 = 2$

8 (d) In a 3×3 matrix, there are 9 elements and it is given that each element can take two values. So, the total number of matrices having 0 and 1 as their elements is $2^9 = 512$.

9 (c) Since, AB is defined.
$\therefore$ Numer of columns in A = Number of rows in B

$\Rightarrow \quad x + 5 = y$

or $\quad x - y = -5 \qquad$ ...(i)

Also, BA is defined.
$\therefore$ Number of columns in B = number of rows in A

$\Rightarrow \quad x = 11 - y$

or $\quad x + y = 11 \qquad$ ...(ii)

From Eqs. (i) and (ii), we get

$x = 3, y = 8$

10 (c) Given that $A = [a_{ij}]_{2\times 2}$,

where $a_{ij} = e^{2ix} \sin jx$

In general, matrix $A = \begin{bmatrix} a_{11} & a_{12} \\ a_{21} & a_{22} \end{bmatrix}$

Now, $a_{11} = e^{2x} \sin x$,

$a_{12} = e^{2x} \sin 2x$,

$a_{21} = e^{4x} \sin x$,

$a_{22} = e^{4x} \sin 2x$

$\therefore \quad A = \begin{bmatrix} e^{2x} \sin x & e^{2x} \sin 2x \\ e^{4x} \sin x & e^{4x} \sin 2x \end{bmatrix}$

11 (d) The given matrix is

$$A = \begin{bmatrix} 4 & -2 & 1 & 3 \\ 5 & 7 & 9 & 6 \\ 21 & 15 & 18 & -25 \end{bmatrix}.$$

Here, $a_{23} = 9$ and $a_{24} = 6$

$\therefore \quad a_{23} + a_{24} = 15$

Also, 15 lies in 3rd row and 2nd column.

$\therefore \quad 15 = a_{32}$

12 (c) The given matrix is

$$A = [a_{ij}] = [\sin jx^i]\,; 1 \le i, j \le 3$$

$\therefore \quad a_{22} = \sin 2x^2$

Also, given that matrix

$B = [b_{ij}] = [\cos i x^j]\,; 1 \le i, j \le 3$

$\therefore \quad b_{12} = \cos x^2$

Now, $\dfrac{a_{22}}{b_{12}} = \dfrac{\sin 2x^2}{\cos x^2}$

$= \dfrac{2 \sin x^2 \cos x^2}{\cos x^2} = 2 \sin x^2$

13 (b) Since, we need the matrices of order 2×2 such that none of the element is zero.

So, the required matrices will have either 1 or 2 or both as their elements.

Since, the matrix of order 2×2 has 4 elements and each element has 2 choices i.e. 1 or 2.

$\therefore$ The possible number of matrices is 2^4.

Types of Matrices

1 (b) A matrix is said to be a column matrix, if it has only one column.

2 (c) A matrix is said to be a row matrix, if it has only one row.

3 (c) $B = \begin{bmatrix} -\frac{1}{2} & \sqrt{5} & 2 & 3 \end{bmatrix}_{1\times 4}$ is a row matrix. In general, $B = [b_{ij}]_{1\times n}$ is a row matrix of order $1 \times n$.

4 (d) $A = \begin{bmatrix} 3 & -1 & 0 \\ \frac{3}{2} & 3\sqrt{2} & 1 \\ 4 & 3 & -1 \end{bmatrix}$ is a square matrix of order 3.

5 (c) In general, $A = [a_{ij}]_{m\times m}$ is a square matrix of order m.

6 (a) If $A = [a_{ij}]$ is a square matrix of order n, then elements (entries) $a_{11}, a_{22}, \cdots, a_{nn}$ are said to be constitute the diagonal of the matrix A. Thus, if $A = \begin{bmatrix} 1 & -3 & 1 \\ 2 & 4 & -1 \\ 3 & 5 & 6 \end{bmatrix}$, then the elements of the diagonal of A are 1,4 and 6.

7 (c) A square matrix $B = [b_{ij}]_{m\times m}$ is said to be a diagonal matrix, if all its non-diagonal elements are zero, that is a matrix $B = [b_{ij}]_{m\times m}$ is said to be a diagonal matrix, if $b_{ij} = 0$, when $i \ne j$.

8 (a) $A = [4], B = \begin{bmatrix} -1 & 0 \\ 0 & 2 \end{bmatrix}$,

$$C = \begin{bmatrix} -1\cdot 1 & 0 & 0 \\ 0 & 2 & 0 \\ 0 & 0 & 3 \end{bmatrix},$$

are diagonal matrices of order 1, 2 and 3, respectively.

9 (b) A diagonal matrix is said to be a scalar matrix, if its diagonal elements are equal.

10 (c) $A = [3], B = \begin{bmatrix} -1 & 0 \\ 0 & -1 \end{bmatrix}$,

$$C = \begin{bmatrix} \sqrt{3} & 0 & 0 \\ 0 & \sqrt{3} & 0 \\ 0 & 0 & \sqrt{3} \end{bmatrix}$$

are scalar matrices of order 1, 2 and 3, respectively.

11 (a) A square matrix in which elements in the diagonal are all 1 and rest are all zero, is called an identity matrix. In other words, the square matrix $A = [a_{ij}]_{n\times n}$ is an identity matrix, if $a_{ij} = \begin{cases} 1, & \text{if } i = j \\ 0 & \text{if } i \ne j \end{cases}$

12 (b) $[1], \begin{bmatrix} 1 & 0 \\ 0 & 1 \end{bmatrix}$ and $\begin{bmatrix} 1 & 0 & 0 \\ 0 & 1 & 0 \\ 0 & 0 & 1 \end{bmatrix}$ are identity matrices of order 1, 2 and 3, respectively.

13 (a) A scalar matrix

$A = [a_{ij}] = \begin{cases} k, & i = j \\ 0, & i \ne j \end{cases}$ is an identity matrix when, $k = 1$. But every identity matrix is clearly a scalar matrix.

14 (d) $[0], \begin{bmatrix} 0 & 0 \\ 0 & 0 \end{bmatrix}, \begin{bmatrix} 0 & 0 & 0 \\ 0 & 0 & 0 \end{bmatrix}, [0, 0]$ are all zero matrices.

Hence, zero matrix can be of any order.

We denote zero matrix by O.

15 (b) Two matrices $A = [a_{ij}]$ and $B = [b_{ij}]$ are said to be equal, if

(i) they are of the same order.

(ii) each element of A is equal to the corresponding element of B, i.e. $a_{ij} = b_{ij}$ for all i and j.

16 (d) $\begin{bmatrix} 2 & 3 \\ 0 & 1 \end{bmatrix}$ and $\begin{bmatrix} 2 & 3 \\ 0 & 1 \end{bmatrix}$ are equal matrices but $\begin{bmatrix} 3 & 2 \\ 0 & 1 \end{bmatrix}$ and $\begin{bmatrix} 2 & 3 \\ 0 & 1 \end{bmatrix}$ are not equal matrices.

17 (d) Symbolically, if two matrices A and B are equal, we write $A = B$. If

$\begin{bmatrix} x & y \\ z & a \\ b & c \end{bmatrix} = \begin{bmatrix} -1.5 & 0 \\ 2 & \sqrt{6} \\ 3 & 2 \end{bmatrix}$, then

$x = -1.5, y = 0, z = 2, a = \sqrt{6}$,

$b = 3, c = 2$

18 (a) As the given matrices are equal, therefore their corresponding elements must be equal.

Comparing the corresponding elements, we get

$$x+3=0,\quad z+4=6,\quad 2y-7=3y-2,\quad a-1=-3,\quad 0=2c+2,\quad b-3=2b+4,$$

On simplifying, we get

$a=-2, b=-7, c=-1, x=-3$

$y=-5, z=2$

19 (*a*) By equality of two matrices, equating the corresponding elements, we get

$$2a+b=4,\quad 5c-d=11,\quad a-2b=-3,\quad 4c+3d=24$$

On solving these equations, we get $a=1, b=2, c=3$ and $d=4$

20 (*c*) The given equation is

$$\begin{bmatrix} a-b & 2a+c \\ 2a-b & 3c+d \end{bmatrix} = \begin{bmatrix} -1 & 5 \\ 0 & 13 \end{bmatrix}$$

On equating the corresponding elements, we get

$$a-b=-1,\quad 2a+c=5,\quad 2a-b=0,\quad 3c+d=13$$

On simplifying, we get

$a=1, b=2, c=3, d=4$

21 (*b*) The given pair of matrices will be equal, if

$$\begin{bmatrix} 3x+7 & 5 \\ y+1 & 2-3x \end{bmatrix} = \begin{bmatrix} 0 & y-2 \\ 8 & 4 \end{bmatrix}$$

On equating corresponding elements, we have

$3x+7=0 \Rightarrow x=-7/3$

$y-2=5 \Rightarrow y=7$

$y+1=8 \Rightarrow y=7$

$2-3x=4 \Rightarrow x=-\dfrac{2}{3}$

Since, the values of x are different.

$\therefore$ It is not possible to find the values of x and y for which the given pairs of matrices are equal.

22. (*d*)

A. $\begin{bmatrix} 4 & 3 \\ x & 5 \end{bmatrix} = \begin{bmatrix} y & z \\ 1 & 5 \end{bmatrix}$

On equating the corresponding elements, we have

$x=1, y=4$

and $z=3$

B. $\begin{bmatrix} x+y & 2 \\ 5+z & xy \end{bmatrix} = \begin{bmatrix} 6 & 2 \\ 5 & 8 \end{bmatrix}$

On equating the corresponding elements, we have

$5+z=5$

$\Rightarrow z=0,$

$x+y=6$

and $xy=8$

$\Rightarrow x+\dfrac{8}{x}=6$

$\Rightarrow x^2-6x+8=0$

$\Rightarrow (x-4)(x-2)=0$

$\Rightarrow x=4$ or $x=2$

$\Rightarrow y=2$ or $y=4$

Thus, we have

$x=4, y=2, z=0$

or $x=2, y=4$

and $z=0$

C. $\begin{bmatrix} x+y+z \\ x+z \\ y+z \end{bmatrix} = \begin{bmatrix} 9 \\ 5 \\ 7 \end{bmatrix}$

On equating the corresponding elements, we get

$x+y+z=9,$

$x+z=5,$

$y+z=7$

$\Rightarrow x+7=9$

$\Rightarrow x=2$

Also, $2+z=5$

$\Rightarrow z=3$

and $y+3=7$

$\Rightarrow y=4$

$\therefore x=2, y=4$ and $z=3$

23 (*c*) The given matrix is $A=[4]$.

Since, its order is 1×1.

$\Rightarrow$ Number of rows is equal to the number of columns.

$\Rightarrow$ Matrix A is a square matrix.

Also, since matrix A has only 1 row and 1 column.

$\therefore$ This is a both row and column matrix.

24 (*d*) The given matrix $A=[a_{ij}]$ is a matrix of order 4×5, which is not a square matrix.

$\therefore$ The diagonal elements of A do not exist.

25 (*b*) Scalar matrix is a particular case of a diagonal matrix, where all the diagonal elements are same. Thus, every diagonal matrix is not a scalar matrix.

Identity matrix is a particular case of scalar matrix, since all diagonal elements are same and have the value 1.

By definition of scalar matrix, it is a diagonal matrix.

Null matrix is a matrix in which all elements are zero. Such a matrix can be of any order and any type.

26 (*b*) The given matrix equation is

$$\begin{bmatrix} x+y & 4 \\ 5 & 3y \end{bmatrix} = \begin{bmatrix} 3 & 4 \\ 5 & 6 \end{bmatrix}$$

On equating the corresponding elements, we get

$x+y=3, 3y=6$

$\Rightarrow y=2$

and $x+2=3$

$\Rightarrow x=1$

and $y=2$

27 (*b*) The given matrix equation is

$$\begin{bmatrix} x-y-z \\ -y+z \\ z \end{bmatrix} = \begin{bmatrix} 0 \\ 5 \\ 3 \end{bmatrix}$$

On equating the corresponding elements, we get

$x-y-z=0, -y+z=5$

and $z=3$

$\Rightarrow -y+3=5$

$\Rightarrow y=-2$

and $x-(-2)-3=0$

$\Rightarrow x=1$

$\therefore x=1, y=-2, z=3$

Operations on Matrices

1 (*d*) In general, if $A=[a_{ij}]$ and $B=[b_{ij}]$ are two matrices of the same order, say $m\times n$, then the sum of the two matrices A and B is defined as a matrix $C=[c_{ij}]_{m\times n}$, where $c_{ij}=a_{ij}+b_{ij}$, for all possible values of i and j.

2 (*c*) Since, A and B are of the same order 2×3.

Therefore, addition of A and B is defined and is given by

$$A+B=\begin{bmatrix}2+\sqrt{3} & 1+\sqrt{5} & 1-1\\ 2-2 & 3+3 & 0+\frac{1}{2}\end{bmatrix}=\begin{bmatrix}2+\sqrt{3} & 1+\sqrt{5} & 0\\ 0 & 6 & \frac{1}{2}\end{bmatrix}$$

3 (*d*) A. $\begin{bmatrix}a & b\\ -b & a\end{bmatrix}+\begin{bmatrix}a & b\\ b & a\end{bmatrix}$

$$=\begin{bmatrix}a+a & b+b\\ -b+b & a+a\end{bmatrix}=\begin{bmatrix}2a & 2b\\ 0 & 2a\end{bmatrix}$$

B. $\begin{bmatrix}a^2+b^2 & b^2+c^2\\ a^2+c^2 & a^2+b^2\end{bmatrix}+\begin{bmatrix}2ab & 2bc\\ -2ac & -2ab\end{bmatrix}$

$$=\begin{bmatrix}a^2+b^2+2ab & b^2+c^2+2bc\\ a^2+c^2-2ac & a^2+b^2-2ab\end{bmatrix}$$

$$=\begin{bmatrix}(a+b)^2 & (b+c)^2\\ (a-c)^2 & (a-b)^2\end{bmatrix}$$

$$\left[\because (a+b)^2=a^2+2ab+b^2 \text{ and } (a-b)^2=a^2-2ab+b^2\right]$$

C. $\begin{bmatrix}\cos^2 x & \sin^2 x\\ \sin^2 x & \cos^2 x\end{bmatrix}+\begin{bmatrix}\sin^2 x & \cos^2 x\\ \cos^2 x & \sin^2 x\end{bmatrix}$

$$=\begin{bmatrix}\cos^2 x+\sin^2 x & \sin^2 x+\cos^2 x\\ \sin^2 x+\cos^2 x & \cos^2 x+\sin^2 x\end{bmatrix}$$

$$=\begin{bmatrix}1 & 1\\ 1 & 1\end{bmatrix} \quad [\because \sin^2 x+\cos^2 x=1]$$

4 (*c*) **Existence of additive identity**

Let $A=[a_{ij}]$ be a $m\times n$ matrix and O be a $m\times n$ zero matrix, then $A+O=O+A=A$. In other words, O is the additive identity for matrix addition.

The existence of additive inverse

Let $A=[a_{ij}]_{m\times n}$ be any matrix, then we have another matrix $-A=[-a_{ij}]_{m\times n}$ such that $A+(-A)=(-A)+A=O$. So, $-A$ is the additive inverse of A or negative of A.

5 (*c*)

$$A+B=\begin{bmatrix}1 & 2 & -3\\ 5 & 0 & 2\\ 1 & -1 & 1\end{bmatrix}+\begin{bmatrix}3 & -1 & 2\\ 4 & 2 & 5\\ 2 & 0 & 3\end{bmatrix}=\begin{bmatrix}4 & 1 & -1\\ 9 & 2 & 7\\ 3 & -1 & 4\end{bmatrix}$$

$$B-C=\begin{bmatrix}3 & -1 & 2\\ 4 & 2 & 5\\ 2 & 0 & 3\end{bmatrix}-\begin{bmatrix}4 & 1 & 2\\ 0 & 3 & 2\\ 1 & -2 & 3\end{bmatrix}=\begin{bmatrix}-1 & -2 & 0\\ 4 & -1 & 3\\ 1 & 2 & 0\end{bmatrix}$$

$$\therefore (A+B)-C=\begin{bmatrix}4 & 1 & -1\\ 9 & 2 & 7\\ 3 & -1 & 4\end{bmatrix}-\begin{bmatrix}4 & 1 & 2\\ 0 & 3 & 2\\ 1 & -2 & 3\end{bmatrix}=\begin{bmatrix}0 & 0 & -3\\ 9 & -1 & 5\\ 2 & 1 & 1\end{bmatrix}$$

and $A+(B-C)=\begin{bmatrix}1 & 2 & -3\\ 5 & 0 & 2\\ 1 & -1 & 1\end{bmatrix}+\begin{bmatrix}-1 & -2 & 0\\ 4 & -1 & 3\\ 1 & 2 & 0\end{bmatrix}=\begin{bmatrix}0 & 0 & -3\\ 9 & -1 & 5\\ 2 & 1 & 1\end{bmatrix}$

Hence, $(A+B)-C=A+(B-C)$ is verified.

6 (*b*) Given, $X+Y=\begin{bmatrix}7 & 0\\ 2 & 5\end{bmatrix}$ ...(i)

and $X-Y=\begin{bmatrix}3 & 0\\ 0 & 3\end{bmatrix}$ ...(ii)

On adding Eqs. (i) and (ii), we get

$$2X=\begin{bmatrix}7 & 0\\ 2 & 5\end{bmatrix}+\begin{bmatrix}3 & 0\\ 0 & 3\end{bmatrix}=\begin{bmatrix}10 & 0\\ 2 & 8\end{bmatrix}$$

$$\Rightarrow X=\frac{1}{2}\begin{bmatrix}10 & 0\\ 2 & 8\end{bmatrix}=\begin{bmatrix}5 & 0\\ 1 & 4\end{bmatrix}$$

On subtracting Eq. (ii) from Eq. (i), we get

$$2Y=\begin{bmatrix}7 & 0\\ 2 & 5\end{bmatrix}-\begin{bmatrix}3 & 0\\ 0 & 3\end{bmatrix}=\begin{bmatrix}4 & 0\\ 2 & 2\end{bmatrix}$$

$$\Rightarrow Y=\frac{1}{2}\begin{bmatrix}4 & 0\\ 2 & 2\end{bmatrix}=\begin{bmatrix}2 & 0\\ 1 & 1\end{bmatrix}$$

7 (*c*) If $A=[a_{ij}]$ and $B=[b_{ij}]$ are two matrices of the same order (say $m\times n$) and k and l are scalars, then

(i) $k(A+B)=k([a_{ij}]+[b_{ij}])$
$=k[a_{ij}+b_{ij}]=[k(a_{ij}+b_{ij})]$
$=[(k\,a_{ij})+(k\,b_{ij})]$
$=[k\,a_{ij}]+[k\,b_{ij}]=k[a_{ij}]+k[b_{ij}]$
$=kA+kB$

(ii) $(k+l)A=(k+l)[a_{ij}]$
$=[(k+l)a_{ij}]=[ka_{ij}]+[l\,a_{ij}]$
$=k[a_{ij}]+l[a_{ij}]=kA+lA$

8 (*b*) Consider,

$$\cos\theta\begin{bmatrix}\cos\theta & \sin\theta\\ -\sin\theta & \cos\theta\end{bmatrix}+\sin\theta\begin{bmatrix}\sin\theta & -\cos\theta\\ \cos\theta & \sin\theta\end{bmatrix}$$

$$=\begin{bmatrix}\cos^2\theta & \sin\theta\cos\theta\\ -\sin\theta\cos\theta & \cos^2\theta\end{bmatrix}+\begin{bmatrix}\sin^2\theta & -\cos\theta\sin\theta\\ \cos\theta\sin\theta & \sin^2\theta\end{bmatrix}$$

$$=\begin{bmatrix}\cos^2\theta+\sin^2\theta & \sin\theta\cos\theta-\cos\theta\sin\theta\\ -\sin\theta\cos\theta+\cos\theta\sin\theta & \cos^2\theta+\sin^2\theta\end{bmatrix}$$

$$=\begin{bmatrix}1 & 0\\ 0 & 1\end{bmatrix} \quad [\because \sin^2\theta+\cos^2\theta=1]$$

9 (*d*) Given,

$$2\begin{bmatrix}1 & 3\\0 & x\end{bmatrix}+\begin{bmatrix}y & 0\\1 & 2\end{bmatrix}=\begin{bmatrix}5 & 6\\1 & 8\end{bmatrix}$$

$$\Rightarrow \begin{bmatrix}2+y & 6+0\\0+1 & 2x+2\end{bmatrix}=\begin{bmatrix}5 & 6\\1 & 8\end{bmatrix}$$

By definition of equality of matrices, as the given matrices are equal, their corresponding elements are equal.

Comparing the corresponding elements, we get

$$2+y=5 \quad ...(i)$$

and $$2x+2=8 \quad ...(ii)$$

$$\Rightarrow y=5-2=3$$

and $2x=8-2$

$$x=\frac{6}{2}=3$$

10 (*a*) Given,

$$2\begin{bmatrix}x & z\\y & t\end{bmatrix}+3\begin{bmatrix}1 & -1\\0 & 2\end{bmatrix}=3\begin{bmatrix}3 & 5\\4 & 6\end{bmatrix}$$

$$\Rightarrow \begin{bmatrix}2x & 2z\\2y & 2t\end{bmatrix}+\begin{bmatrix}3 & -3\\0 & 6\end{bmatrix}=\begin{bmatrix}9 & 15\\12 & 18\end{bmatrix}$$

$$\Rightarrow \begin{bmatrix}2x+3 & 2z-3\\2y+0 & 2t+6\end{bmatrix}=\begin{bmatrix}9 & 15\\12 & 18\end{bmatrix}$$

By definition of equality of matrices, as the given matrices are equal, their corresponding elements are equal.

Comparing the corresponding elements, we get

$$2x+3=9,\ 2y+0=12,$$
$$2z-3=15 \text{ and } 2t+6=18$$

$$\Rightarrow x=\frac{9-3}{2},\ y=\frac{12}{2},\ z=\frac{15+3}{2}$$

and $t=\frac{18-6}{2}$

$$\Rightarrow x=3,\ y=6,\ z=9 \text{ and } t=6$$

11 (*b*) If $x\begin{bmatrix}2\\3\end{bmatrix}+y\begin{bmatrix}-1\\1\end{bmatrix}=\begin{bmatrix}10\\5\end{bmatrix}$

$$\Rightarrow \begin{bmatrix}2x+y(-1)\\3x+y\end{bmatrix}=\begin{bmatrix}10\\5\end{bmatrix}$$

By definition of equality of matrices, as the given matrices are equal, their corresponding elements are equal.

Comparing the corresponding elements, we get

$$2x-y=10 \quad ...(i)$$

and $$3x+y=5 \quad ...(ii)$$

On adding Eqs. (i) and (ii), we get

$$5x=15 \Rightarrow x=3$$

On substituting $x=3$ in Eq. (i), we get

$$2\times 3-y=10$$

$$\Rightarrow y=6-10=-4$$

12 (*c*) Given, $3\begin{bmatrix}x & y\\z & w\end{bmatrix}=\begin{bmatrix}x & 6\\-1 & 2w\end{bmatrix}+\begin{bmatrix}4 & x+y\\z+w & 3\end{bmatrix}$

$$\Rightarrow \begin{bmatrix}3x & 3y\\3z & 3w\end{bmatrix}=\begin{bmatrix}x+4 & 6+x+y\\-1+z+w & 2w+3\end{bmatrix}$$

By definition of equality of matrices, as the given matrices are equal, then their corresponding elements will be equal.

Comparing the corresponding elements, we get

$$3x=x+4$$
$$\Rightarrow 2x=4$$
$$\Rightarrow x=2$$

and $$3y=6+x+y$$
$$\Rightarrow 2y=6+x$$
$$\Rightarrow y=\frac{6+x}{2}$$

On putting the value of x, we get

$$y=\frac{6+2}{2}=\frac{8}{2}=4$$

Also, $3z=-1+z+w,$
$$\Rightarrow 2z=-1+w$$
$$\Rightarrow z=\frac{-1+w}{2} \quad ...(i)$$

Also, $3w=2w+3 \Rightarrow w=3$

On putting the value of w in Eq. (i), we get

$$z=\frac{-1+3}{2}=\frac{2}{2}=1$$

Hence, the values of x, y, z and w are 2, 4, 1 and 3.

13 (*b*) For multiplication of two matrices A and B, the number of columns in A must be equal to the number of rows in B. Furthermore, for getting the elements of the product matrix, we take rows of A and columns of B, multiply corresponding element and add them.

14 (*d*) Let $A=[a_{ij}]$ be a $m\times n$ matrix and $B=[b_{jk}]$ be a $n\times p$ matrix. Then, the product of the matrices A and B is the matrix C of order $m\times p$.

15 (*c*) If $A=[a_{ij}]_{m\times n}, B=[b_{jk}]_{n\times p}$, then the ith row of A is $[a_{i1}\ a_{i2} \cdots a_{in}]$ and the kth column of B is $\begin{bmatrix}b_{1k}\\b_{2k}\\\vdots\\b_{nk}\end{bmatrix}$, then

$$c_{ik}=a_{i1}\,b_{1k}+a_{i2}\,b_{2k}+a_{i3}\,b_{3k}+\cdots+a_{in}\,b_{nk}=\sum_{j=1}^{n}a_{ij}\,b_{jk}.$$

The matrix $C=[c_{ik}]_{m\times p}$ is the product of A and B.

16 (*b*) The matrix A has 2 columns which is equal to the number of rows of B. Hence, AB is defined. Now,

$$AB=\begin{bmatrix}6(2)+9(7) & 6(6)+9(9) & 6(0)+9(8)\\2(2)+3(7) & 2(6)+3(9) & 2(0)+3(8)\end{bmatrix}$$

$$=\begin{bmatrix}12+63 & 36+81 & 0+72\\4+21 & 12+27 & 0+24\end{bmatrix}$$

$$=\begin{bmatrix}75 & 117 & 72\\25 & 39 & 24\end{bmatrix}$$

17 (*d*) Here, $A=\begin{bmatrix}6 & 9\\2 & 3\end{bmatrix}$

and $B=\begin{bmatrix}2 & 6 & 0\\7 & 9 & 8\end{bmatrix}$

Here, AB is defined but BA is not defined because B has 3 columns, while A has only 2 (not 3) rows.

18 (*c*) If A and B are respectively $m \times n$, $k \times l$ order matrices, then both AB and BA are defined, if and only if $n = k$ and $l = m$.

19 (*c*) If both A and B are square matrices of the same order, then both AB and BA are defined.

20 (*b*) **Non-commutativity of multiplication of matrices**

If AB and BA are both defined, it is not necessary that $AB = BA$.

21 (*d*) Since, A is a 2×3 matrix and B is 3×2 matrix. Hence, AB and BA are both defined and are matrices of order 2×2 and 3×3, respectively. Note that

$$AB = \begin{bmatrix} 1 & -2 & 3 \\ -4 & 2 & 5 \end{bmatrix} \begin{bmatrix} 2 & 3 \\ 4 & 5 \\ 2 & 1 \end{bmatrix}$$

$$= \begin{bmatrix} 2-8+6 & 3-10+3 \\ -8+8+10 & -12+10+5 \end{bmatrix}$$

$$= \begin{bmatrix} 0 & -4 \\ 10 & 3 \end{bmatrix}$$

and $$BA = \begin{bmatrix} 2 & 3 \\ 4 & 5 \\ 2 & 1 \end{bmatrix} \begin{bmatrix} 1 & -2 & 3 \\ -4 & 2 & 5 \end{bmatrix}$$

$$= \begin{bmatrix} 2-12 & -4+6 & 6+15 \\ 4-20 & -8+10 & 12+25 \\ 2-4 & -4+2 & 6+5 \end{bmatrix}$$

$$= \begin{bmatrix} -10 & 2 & 21 \\ -16 & 2 & 37 \\ -2 & -2 & 11 \end{bmatrix}$$

Clearly, $AB \neq BA$.

Note that, here AB and BA are of different orders.

22 (*d*) If $A = \begin{bmatrix} 1 & 0 \\ 0 & -1 \end{bmatrix}$ and $B = \begin{bmatrix} 0 & 1 \\ 1 & 0 \end{bmatrix}$,

then $AB = \begin{bmatrix} 0 & 1 \\ -1 & 0 \end{bmatrix}$, $BA = \begin{bmatrix} 0 & -1 \\ 1 & 0 \end{bmatrix}$.

Clearly, $AB \neq BA$.

Thus, matrix multiplication is not commutative.

This shows that even if AB and BA are of same order, then they may not be same.

23 (*c*) If $A = \begin{bmatrix} 0 & -1 \\ 0 & 2 \end{bmatrix}$, $B = \begin{bmatrix} 3 & 5 \\ 0 & 0 \end{bmatrix}$, then

$AB = \begin{bmatrix} 0 & 0 \\ 0 & 0 \end{bmatrix}$.

Thus, if the product of two matrices is a zero matrix, it is not necessary that one of the matrices is a zero matrix.

24 (*c*) A. $\begin{bmatrix} 2 & 4 \\ 3 & 2 \end{bmatrix} \begin{bmatrix} 1 & 3 \\ -2 & 5 \end{bmatrix}$

$$= \begin{bmatrix} 2 \times 1 + 4 \times (-2) & 2 \times 3 + 4 \times 5 \\ 3 \times 1 + 2 \times (-2) & 3 \times 3 + 2 \times 5 \end{bmatrix}$$

$$= \begin{bmatrix} -6 & 26 \\ -1 & 19 \end{bmatrix}$$

B. $\begin{bmatrix} 1 & 3 \\ -2 & 5 \end{bmatrix} \begin{bmatrix} 2 & 4 \\ 3 & 2 \end{bmatrix}$

$$= \begin{bmatrix} 1 \times 2 + 3 \times 3 & 1 \times 4 + 3 \times 2 \\ (-2) \times 2 + 5 \times 3 & (-2) \times 4 + 5 \times 2 \end{bmatrix}$$

$$= \begin{bmatrix} 11 & 10 \\ 11 & 2 \end{bmatrix}$$

C. $\begin{bmatrix} 1 \\ 2 \\ 3 \end{bmatrix}_{3 \times 1} \begin{bmatrix} 2 & 3 & 4 \end{bmatrix}_{1 \times 3}$

$$= \begin{bmatrix} 1 \times 2 & 1 \times 3 & 1 \times 4 \\ 2 \times 2 & 2 \times 3 & 2 \times 4 \\ 3 \times 2 & 3 \times 3 & 3 \times 4 \end{bmatrix}_{3 \times 3}$$

$$= \begin{bmatrix} 2 & 3 & 4 \\ 4 & 6 & 8 \\ 6 & 9 & 12 \end{bmatrix}$$

25 (*a*) $\begin{bmatrix} a & b \\ -b & a \end{bmatrix} \begin{bmatrix} a & -b \\ b & a \end{bmatrix}$

$$= \begin{bmatrix} a \times a + b \times b & a \times (-b) + b \times a \\ (-b) \times a + a \times b & (-b) \times (-b) + a \times a \end{bmatrix}$$

$$= \begin{bmatrix} a^2 + b^2 & -ab + ab \\ -ab + ab & b^2 + a^2 \end{bmatrix}$$

$$= \begin{bmatrix} a^2 + b^2 & 0 \\ 0 & b^2 + a^2 \end{bmatrix}$$

26 (*a*) A. $\begin{bmatrix} 1 & -2 \\ 2 & 3 \end{bmatrix} \begin{bmatrix} 1 & 2 & 3 \\ 2 & 3 & 1 \end{bmatrix}$

$$= \begin{bmatrix} 1 \times 1 + (-2) \times 2 & 1 \times 2 + (-2) \times 3 & 1 \times 3 + (-2) \times 1 \\ 2 \times 1 + 3 \times 2 & 2 \times 2 + 3 \times 3 & 2 \times 3 + 3 \times 1 \end{bmatrix}$$

$$= \begin{bmatrix} -3 & -4 & 1 \\ 8 & 13 & 9 \end{bmatrix}$$

B. $\begin{bmatrix} 2 & 3 & 4 \\ 3 & 4 & 5 \\ 4 & 5 & 6 \end{bmatrix} \begin{bmatrix} 1 & -3 & 5 \\ 0 & 2 & 4 \\ 3 & 0 & 5 \end{bmatrix}$

$$= \begin{bmatrix} 2+0+12 & -6+6+0 & 10+12+20 \\ 3+0+15 & -9+8+0 & 15+16+25 \\ 4+0+18 & -12+10+0 & 20+20+30 \end{bmatrix}$$

$$= \begin{bmatrix} 14 & 0 & 42 \\ 18 & -1 & 56 \\ 22 & -2 & 70 \end{bmatrix}$$

C. $\begin{bmatrix} 2 & 1 \\ 3 & 2 \\ -1 & 1 \end{bmatrix} \begin{bmatrix} 1 & 0 & 1 \\ -1 & 2 & 1 \end{bmatrix}$

$$= \begin{bmatrix} 2-1 & 0+2 & 2+1 \\ 3-2 & 0+4 & 3+2 \\ -1-1 & 0+2 & -1+1 \end{bmatrix}$$

$$= \begin{bmatrix} 1 & 2 & 3 \\ 1 & 4 & 5 \\ -2 & 2 & 0 \end{bmatrix}$$

D. $\begin{bmatrix} 3 & -1 & 3 \\ -1 & 0 & 2 \end{bmatrix} \begin{bmatrix} 2 & -3 \\ 1 & 0 \\ 3 & 1 \end{bmatrix}$

$$= \begin{bmatrix} 6-1+9 & -9+0+3 \\ -2+0+6 & 3+0+2 \end{bmatrix}$$

$$= \begin{bmatrix} 14 & -6 \\ 4 & 5 \end{bmatrix}$$

27 (*b*) $\begin{bmatrix} 5 & -1 \\ 6 & 7 \end{bmatrix} \begin{bmatrix} 2 & 1 \\ 3 & 4 \end{bmatrix}$

$$= \begin{bmatrix} 10-3 & 5-4 \\ 12+21 & 6+28 \end{bmatrix}$$

$$= \begin{bmatrix} 7 & 1 \\ 33 & 34 \end{bmatrix}$$

$\begin{bmatrix} 2 & 1 \\ 3 & 4 \end{bmatrix} \begin{bmatrix} 5 & -1 \\ 6 & 7 \end{bmatrix}$

$$= \begin{bmatrix} 10+6 & -2+7 \\ 15+24 & -3+28 \end{bmatrix}$$

$$= \begin{bmatrix} 16 & 5 \\ 39 & 25 \end{bmatrix}$$

Hence,

$$\begin{bmatrix}5&-1\\6&7\end{bmatrix}\begin{bmatrix}2&1\\3&4\end{bmatrix}\neq\begin{bmatrix}2&1\\3&4\end{bmatrix}\begin{bmatrix}5&-1\\6&7\end{bmatrix}.$$

Now, $\begin{bmatrix}1&2&3\\0&1&0\\1&1&0\end{bmatrix}\begin{bmatrix}-1&1&0\\0&-1&1\\2&3&4\end{bmatrix}$

$$=\begin{bmatrix}-1+0+6&1-2+9&0+2+12\\0+0+0&0+(-1)+0&0+1+0\\-1+0+0&1-1+0&0+1+0\end{bmatrix}$$

$$=\begin{bmatrix}5&8&14\\0&-1&1\\-1&0&1\end{bmatrix}$$

and $\begin{bmatrix}-1&1&0\\0&-1&1\\2&3&4\end{bmatrix}\begin{bmatrix}1&2&3\\0&1&0\\1&1&0\end{bmatrix}$

$$=\begin{bmatrix}-1+0+0&-2+1+0&-3+0+0\\0+0+1&0-1+1&0+0+0\\2+0+4&4+3+4&6+0+0\end{bmatrix}$$

$$=\begin{bmatrix}-1&-1&-3\\1&0&0\\6&11&6\end{bmatrix}$$

Hence,

$$\begin{bmatrix}1&2&3\\0&1&0\\1&1&0\end{bmatrix}\begin{bmatrix}-1&1&0\\0&-1&1\\2&3&4\end{bmatrix}\neq\begin{bmatrix}-1&1&0\\0&-1&1\\2&3&4\end{bmatrix}\begin{bmatrix}1&2&3\\0&1&0\\1&1&0\end{bmatrix}.$$

28 (*c*) **The existence of multiplicative identity** For every square matrix A, there exists an identity matrix of same order such that $IA = AI = A$.

29 (*c*) Here,

$$A^2 = A\times A=\begin{bmatrix}2&0&1\\2&1&3\\1&-1&0\end{bmatrix}\begin{bmatrix}2&0&1\\2&1&3\\1&-1&0\end{bmatrix}$$

$$=\begin{bmatrix}4+0+1&0+0-1&2+0+0\\4+2+3&0+1-3&2+3+0\\2-2+0&0-1+0&1-3+0\end{bmatrix}$$

$$=\begin{bmatrix}5&-1&2\\9&-2&5\\0&-1&-2\end{bmatrix}$$

$\therefore \quad A^2-5A+6I$

$$=\begin{bmatrix}5&-1&2\\9&-2&5\\0&-1&-2\end{bmatrix}-5\begin{bmatrix}2&0&1\\2&1&3\\1&-1&0\end{bmatrix}+6\begin{bmatrix}1&0&0\\0&1&0\\0&0&1\end{bmatrix}$$

$$=\begin{bmatrix}5&-1&2\\9&-2&5\\0&-1&-2\end{bmatrix}-\begin{bmatrix}10&0&5\\10&5&15\\5&-5&0\end{bmatrix}+\begin{bmatrix}6&0&0\\0&6&0\\0&0&6\end{bmatrix}$$

$$=\begin{bmatrix}5-10+6&-1+0+0&2-5+0\\9-10+0&-2-5+6&5-15+0\\0-5+0&-1+5+0&-2+0+6\end{bmatrix}$$

$$=\begin{bmatrix}1&-1&-3\\-1&-1&-10\\-5&4&4\end{bmatrix}$$

30 (*b*) $A^2 = A\times A=\begin{bmatrix}1&0&2\\0&2&1\\2&0&3\end{bmatrix}\begin{bmatrix}1&0&2\\0&2&1\\2&0&3\end{bmatrix}$

$$=\begin{bmatrix}1+0+4&0+0+0&2+0+6\\0+0+2&0+4+0&0+2+3\\2+0+6&0+0+0&4+0+9\end{bmatrix}$$

$$=\begin{bmatrix}5&0&8\\2&4&5\\8&0&13\end{bmatrix}$$

$$A^3=A^2\times A=\begin{bmatrix}5&0&8\\2&4&5\\8&0&13\end{bmatrix}\begin{bmatrix}1&0&2\\0&2&1\\2&0&3\end{bmatrix}$$

$$=\begin{bmatrix}5+0+16&0+0+0&10+0+24\\2+0+10&0+8+0&4+4+15\\8+0+26&0+0+0&16+0+39\end{bmatrix}$$

$$=\begin{bmatrix}21&0&34\\12&8&23\\34&0&55\end{bmatrix}$$

$$\therefore A^3-6A^2+7A+2I=\begin{bmatrix}21&0&34\\12&8&23\\34&0&55\end{bmatrix}-6\begin{bmatrix}5&0&8\\2&4&5\\8&0&13\end{bmatrix}+7\begin{bmatrix}1&0&2\\0&2&1\\2&0&3\end{bmatrix}+2\begin{bmatrix}1&0&0\\0&1&0\\0&0&1\end{bmatrix}$$

$$=\begin{bmatrix}21&0&34\\12&8&23\\34&0&55\end{bmatrix}-\begin{bmatrix}30&0&48\\12&24&30\\48&0&78\end{bmatrix}+\begin{bmatrix}7&0&14\\0&14&7\\14&0&21\end{bmatrix}+\begin{bmatrix}2&0&0\\0&2&0\\0&0&2\end{bmatrix}$$

$$=\begin{bmatrix}21-30+7+2&0-0+0+0&34-48+14+0\\12-12+0+0&8-24+14+2&23-30+7+0\\34-48+14+0&0-0+0+0&55-78+21+2\end{bmatrix}$$

$$=\begin{bmatrix}0&0&0\\0&0&0\\0&0&0\end{bmatrix}=O$$

31 (*d*) Given, $A^2 = kA-2I$

$\Rightarrow \quad AA = kA-2I$

$$\Rightarrow \begin{bmatrix}3&-2\\4&-2\end{bmatrix}\begin{bmatrix}3&-2\\4&-2\end{bmatrix}=k\begin{bmatrix}3&-2\\4&-2\end{bmatrix}-2\begin{bmatrix}1&0\\0&1\end{bmatrix}$$

$$\Rightarrow \begin{bmatrix}9-8&-6+4\\12-8&-8+4\end{bmatrix}=\begin{bmatrix}3k&-2k\\4k&-2k\end{bmatrix}-\begin{bmatrix}2&0\\0&2\end{bmatrix}$$

$$\Rightarrow \begin{bmatrix}1&-2\\4&-4\end{bmatrix}=\begin{bmatrix}3k-2&-2k\\4k&-2k-2\end{bmatrix}$$

By definition of equality of matrix, as the given matrices are equal, their corresponding elements are equal.

Comparing the corresponding elements, we get

$3k-2=1 \Rightarrow k=1$

$-2k=-2 \Rightarrow k=1$

$4k=4 \Rightarrow k=1$

$-4=-2k-2 \Rightarrow k=1$

Hence, $k=1$.

32 (*a*) Here, $A=\begin{bmatrix}0 & -t\\ t & 0\end{bmatrix}$, where $t=\tan\left(\frac{\alpha}{2}\right)$.

Now, $\cos\alpha=\dfrac{1-\tan^2\left(\frac{\alpha}{2}\right)}{1+\tan^2\left(\frac{\alpha}{2}\right)}=\dfrac{1-t^2}{1+t^2}$

and $\sin\alpha=\dfrac{2\tan\left(\frac{\alpha}{2}\right)}{1+\tan^2\left(\frac{\alpha}{2}\right)}=\dfrac{2t}{1+t^2}$

Consider, $(I-A)\begin{bmatrix}\cos\alpha & -\sin\alpha\\ \sin\alpha & \cos\alpha\end{bmatrix}$

$$=\left(\begin{bmatrix}1 & 0\\ 0 & 1\end{bmatrix}-\begin{bmatrix}0 & -t\\ t & 0\end{bmatrix}\right)\begin{bmatrix}\frac{1-t^2}{1+t^2} & \frac{-2t}{1+t^2}\\ \frac{2t}{1+t^2} & \frac{1-t^2}{1+t^2}\end{bmatrix}$$

$$=\begin{bmatrix}1 & t\\ -t & 1\end{bmatrix}\begin{bmatrix}\frac{1-t^2}{1+t^2} & \frac{-2t}{1+t^2}\\ \frac{2t}{1+t^2} & \frac{1-t^2}{1+t^2}\end{bmatrix}$$

$$=\begin{bmatrix}\frac{1-t^2+2t^2}{1+t^2} & \frac{-2t+t(1-t^2)}{1+t^2}\\ \frac{-t(1-t^2)+2t}{1+t^2} & \frac{2t^2+1-t^2}{1+t^2}\end{bmatrix}$$

$$=\begin{bmatrix}\frac{1+t^2}{1+t^2} & \frac{-2t+t-t^3}{1+t^2}\\ \frac{-t+t^3+2t}{1+t^2} & \frac{2t^2+1-t^2}{1+t^2}\end{bmatrix}$$

$$=\begin{bmatrix}\frac{1+t^2}{1+t^2} & \frac{-t(1+t^2)}{1+t^2}\\ \frac{t(1+t^2)}{1+t^2} & \frac{1+t^2}{1+t^2}\end{bmatrix}=\begin{bmatrix}1 & -t\\ t & 1\end{bmatrix}$$

Also, $I+A=\begin{bmatrix}1 & 0\\ 0 & 1\end{bmatrix}+\begin{bmatrix}0 & -t\\ t & 0\end{bmatrix}$

$$=\begin{bmatrix}0+1 & -t+0\\ t+0 & 0+1\end{bmatrix}$$

$$=\begin{bmatrix}1 & -t\\ t & 1\end{bmatrix}$$

$$=(I-A)\begin{bmatrix}\cos\alpha & -\sin\alpha\\ \sin\alpha & \cos\alpha\end{bmatrix}$$

33 (*a*)

I. Matrices P and Y are of the orders $p\times k$ and $3\times k$, respectively.

Therefore, matrix PY will be defined, if $k=3$. Consequently, PY will be of the order $p\times k$. Matrices W and Y are of the orders $n\times 3$ and $3\times k$, respectively.

Since, the number of columns in W is equal to the number of rows in Y, matrix WY is well-defined and is of the order $n\times k$.

Matrices PY and WY can be added only when their orders are same. However, PY is of the order $p\times k$ and WY is of the order $n\times k$, therefore we must have $p=n$. Thus, $k=3$ and $p=n$ are the restrictions on n, k and p, so that $PY+WY$ will be defined.

II. Matrix X is of the order $2\times n$.

Therefore, matrix $7X$ is also of the same order.

Matrix Z is of the order $2\times p$ i.e. $2\times n$. $[\because n=p]$

Therefore, matrix $5Z$ is also of the same order.

Now, both the matrices $7X$ and $5Z$ are of the order $2\times n$.

Thus, matrix $7X-5Z$ is well-defined and is of the order $2\times n$.

34 (*d*) Only $B+D$ is defined, since the matrices B and D are of same order.

35 (*a*) Given that,

$$\begin{bmatrix}1 & 2\\ -2 & -b\end{bmatrix}+\begin{bmatrix}a & 4\\ 3 & 2\end{bmatrix}=\begin{bmatrix}5 & 6\\ 1 & 0\end{bmatrix}$$

$$\Rightarrow \begin{bmatrix}1+a & 6\\ -2+3 & -b+2\end{bmatrix}=\begin{bmatrix}5 & 6\\ 1 & 0\end{bmatrix}$$

$$\Rightarrow \begin{bmatrix}1+a & 6\\ 1 & 2-b\end{bmatrix}=\begin{bmatrix}5 & 6\\ 1 & 0\end{bmatrix}$$

On equating the corresponding elements, we have

$$1+a=5$$
$$\Rightarrow a=4$$

and $2-b=0$

$\Rightarrow b=2$

$\therefore a^2+b^2=4^2+2^2$

$=16+4=20$

36 (*b*) $A-B=\begin{bmatrix}2 & 4\\ 3 & 2\end{bmatrix}-\begin{bmatrix}1 & 3\\ -2 & 5\end{bmatrix}$

$$=\begin{bmatrix}2-1 & 4-3\\ 3-(-2) & 2-5\end{bmatrix}=\begin{bmatrix}1 & 1\\ 5 & -3\end{bmatrix}$$

37 (*c*) In general, we may define multiplication of a matrix by a scalar as follows :

If $A=[a_{ij}]_{m\times n}$ is a matrix and k is a scalar, then kA is another matrix which is obtained by multiplying each element of A by the scalar k.

38 (*c*) In other words, $kA=k\,[a_{ij}]_{m\times n}=[k(a_{ij})]_{m\times n}$, i.e. $(i, j)^{th}$ element of kA is ka_{ij} for all possible values of i and j.

39 (*b*) We have $A=\begin{bmatrix}3 & 1 & 1.5\\ \sqrt{5} & 7 & -3\\ 2 & 0 & 5\end{bmatrix}$, then

$$3A=3\begin{bmatrix}3 & 1 & 1.5\\ \sqrt{5} & 7 & -3\\ 2 & 0 & 5\end{bmatrix}$$

$$=\begin{bmatrix}9 & 3 & 4.5\\ 3\sqrt{5} & 21 & -9\\ 6 & 0 & 15\end{bmatrix}$$

40 (*c*) $3A-C=3\begin{bmatrix}2 & 4\\ 3 & 2\end{bmatrix}-\begin{bmatrix}-2 & 5\\ 3 & 4\end{bmatrix}$

$$=\begin{bmatrix}6 & 12\\ 9 & 6\end{bmatrix}-\begin{bmatrix}-2 & 5\\ 3 & 4\end{bmatrix}$$

$$=\begin{bmatrix}6-(-2) & 12-5\\ 9-3 & 6-4\end{bmatrix}$$

$$=\begin{bmatrix}8 & 7\\ 6 & 2\end{bmatrix}$$

41 (*d*) Given, $2X+Y=\begin{bmatrix}1 & 0\\ -3 & 2\end{bmatrix}$

and $Y=\begin{bmatrix}3 & 2\\ 1 & 4\end{bmatrix}$

$\Rightarrow 2X=\begin{bmatrix}1 & 0\\ -3 & 2\end{bmatrix}-Y$

$$= \begin{bmatrix} 1 & 0 \\ -3 & 2 \end{bmatrix} - \begin{bmatrix} 3 & 2 \\ 1 & 4 \end{bmatrix}$$

$$= \begin{bmatrix} 1-3 & 0-2 \\ -3-1 & 2-4 \end{bmatrix}$$

$$= \begin{bmatrix} -2 & -2 \\ -4 & -2 \end{bmatrix}$$

$$\therefore \quad X = \frac{1}{2}\begin{bmatrix} -2 & -2 \\ -4 & -2 \end{bmatrix} = \begin{bmatrix} -1 & -1 \\ -2 & -1 \end{bmatrix}$$

42 (*b*) $3A - 5B = 3\begin{bmatrix} 2/3 & 1 & 5/3 \\ 1/3 & 2/3 & 4/3 \\ 7/3 & 2 & 2/3 \end{bmatrix} - 5\begin{bmatrix} 2/5 & 3/5 & 1 \\ 1/5 & 2/5 & 4/5 \\ 7/5 & 6/5 & 2/5 \end{bmatrix}$

$$= \begin{bmatrix} 2 & 3 & 5 \\ 1 & 2 & 4 \\ 7 & 6 & 2 \end{bmatrix} - \begin{bmatrix} 2 & 3 & 5 \\ 1 & 2 & 4 \\ 7 & 6 & 2 \end{bmatrix}$$

$$= \begin{bmatrix} 0 & 0 & 0 \\ 0 & 0 & 0 \\ 0 & 0 & 0 \end{bmatrix}$$

43 (*d*) The given equation is

$$2\begin{bmatrix} x & 5 \\ 7 & y-3 \end{bmatrix} + \begin{bmatrix} 3 & -4 \\ 1 & 2 \end{bmatrix} = \begin{bmatrix} 7 & 6 \\ 15 & 14 \end{bmatrix}$$

$$\Rightarrow \begin{bmatrix} 2x & 10 \\ 14 & 2y-6 \end{bmatrix} + \begin{bmatrix} 3 & -4 \\ 1 & 2 \end{bmatrix} = \begin{bmatrix} 7 & 6 \\ 15 & 14 \end{bmatrix}$$

$$\Rightarrow \begin{bmatrix} 2x+3 & 6 \\ 15 & 2y-4 \end{bmatrix} = \begin{bmatrix} 7 & 6 \\ 15 & 14 \end{bmatrix}$$

On equating the corresponding elements, we have

$2x + 3 = 7$ and $2y - 4 = 14$

$\Rightarrow$ $2x = 4$ and $2y = 18$

$\Rightarrow$ $x = 2$ and $y = 9$

$\therefore$ $y - x = 9 - 2 = 7$

44 (*d*) Given that, A and B are two matrices of order $3 \times m$ and $3 \times n$ and $m = n$.

$\Rightarrow$ The order of $5A$ is $3 \times m$ and $2B$ is $3 \times n$, where $m = n$.

$\Rightarrow$ The order of $5A - 2B$ is $3 \times m$ or $3 \times n$. $[\because m = n]$

45 (*d*) Given, $2X + 3Y = \begin{bmatrix} 2 & 3 \\ 4 & 0 \end{bmatrix}$ ...(i)

and $3X + 2Y = \begin{bmatrix} 2 & -2 \\ -1 & 5 \end{bmatrix}$ ...(ii)

On multiplying Eq. (i) by 2 and Eq. (ii) by 3 and then subtracting, we get

$$2(2X + 3Y) - 3(3X + 2Y) = 2\begin{bmatrix} 2 & 3 \\ 4 & 0 \end{bmatrix} - 3\begin{bmatrix} 2 & -2 \\ -1 & 5 \end{bmatrix}$$

$$\Rightarrow 4X + 6Y - 9X - 6Y = \begin{bmatrix} 4 & 6 \\ 8 & 0 \end{bmatrix} - \begin{bmatrix} 6 & -6 \\ -3 & 15 \end{bmatrix}$$

$$\Rightarrow -5X = \begin{bmatrix} 4-6 & 6+6 \\ 8+3 & 0-15 \end{bmatrix} = \begin{bmatrix} -2 & 12 \\ 11 & -15 \end{bmatrix}$$

$$\Rightarrow X = -\frac{1}{5}\begin{bmatrix} -2 & 12 \\ 11 & -15 \end{bmatrix} = \begin{bmatrix} 2/5 & -12/5 \\ -11/5 & 3 \end{bmatrix}$$

Then, from Eq. (i), we get

$$3Y = \begin{bmatrix} 2 & 3 \\ 4 & 0 \end{bmatrix} - 2X$$

$$= \begin{bmatrix} 2 & 3 \\ 4 & 0 \end{bmatrix} - 2\begin{bmatrix} 2/5 & -12/5 \\ -11/5 & 3 \end{bmatrix}$$

$$= \begin{bmatrix} 2-\frac{4}{5} & 3+\frac{24}{5} \\ 4+\frac{22}{5} & 0-6 \end{bmatrix}$$

$$= \begin{bmatrix} 6/5 & 39/5 \\ 42/5 & -6 \end{bmatrix}$$

$$\therefore \quad Y = \frac{1}{3}\begin{bmatrix} 6/5 & 39/5 \\ 42/5 & -6 \end{bmatrix} = \begin{bmatrix} 2/5 & 13/5 \\ 14/5 & -2 \end{bmatrix}$$

46 (*b*) The given matrix is $A = \begin{bmatrix} 3 & -1 \\ 2 & 5 \end{bmatrix}$.

Then, its additive inverse is $-A$.

$$\Rightarrow \quad -A = (-1)A = (-1)\begin{bmatrix} 3 & -1 \\ 2 & 5 \end{bmatrix} = \begin{bmatrix} -3 & 1 \\ -2 & -5 \end{bmatrix}$$

47 (*a*) Consider,

$x\begin{bmatrix} 2 \\ 1 \end{bmatrix} + y\begin{bmatrix} 3 \\ 5 \end{bmatrix} + \begin{bmatrix} -8 \\ -11 \end{bmatrix} = O$, where O is a null matrix.

$$\Rightarrow \begin{bmatrix} 2x \\ x \end{bmatrix} + \begin{bmatrix} 3y \\ 5y \end{bmatrix} + \begin{bmatrix} -8 \\ -11 \end{bmatrix} = O$$

$$\Rightarrow \begin{bmatrix} 2x+3y-8 \\ x+5y-11 \end{bmatrix} = \begin{bmatrix} 0 \\ 0 \end{bmatrix}$$

On equating the corresponding elements, we get

$2x + 3y - 8 = 0$

$\Rightarrow$ $2x + 3y = 8$ ...(i)

and $x + 5y - 11 = 0$

$\Rightarrow$ $x + 5y = 11$ ...(ii)

On solving Eqs. (i) and (ii), we get

$x = 1$ and $y = 2$

48 (*c*) The given matrix is $A = \begin{bmatrix} 0 & 2 \\ 3 & -4 \end{bmatrix}$.

Now, $kA = k\begin{bmatrix} 0 & 2 \\ 3 & -4 \end{bmatrix} = \begin{bmatrix} 0 & 2k \\ 3k & -4k \end{bmatrix}$

Also, it is given that

$$kA = \begin{bmatrix} 0 & 3a \\ 2b & 24 \end{bmatrix}$$

$$\therefore \begin{bmatrix} 0 & 2k \\ 3k & -4k \end{bmatrix} = \begin{bmatrix} 0 & 3a \\ 2b & 24 \end{bmatrix}$$

On equating corresponding elements, we get

$2k = 3a, 3k = 2b$ and $-4k = 24$

$\Rightarrow$ $k = -6, a = -4, b = -9$

49 (*c*) $F(x)F(y) = \begin{bmatrix} \cos x & -\sin x & 0 \\ \sin x & \cos x & 0 \\ 0 & 0 & 1 \end{bmatrix}\begin{bmatrix} \cos y & -\sin y & 0 \\ \sin y & \cos y & 0 \\ 0 & 0 & 1 \end{bmatrix}$

$$= \begin{bmatrix} \cos x\cos y - \sin x\sin y & -\sin y\cos x - \sin x\cos y & 0 \\ \sin x\cos y + \cos x\sin y & -\sin x\sin y + \cos x\cos y & 0 \\ 0 & 0 & 1 \end{bmatrix}$$

$$= \begin{bmatrix} \cos(x+y) & -\sin(x+y) & 0 \\ \sin(x+y) & \cos(x+y) & 0 \\ 0 & 0 & 1 \end{bmatrix}$$

$$\begin{bmatrix} \because \cos(A+B) = \cos A \cos B - \sin A \sin B, \\ \sin(A+B) = \sin A \cos B + \sin B \cos A \end{bmatrix}$$

Now, replacing x by $(x+y)$ in $F(x)$, we get

$$F(x+y) = \begin{bmatrix} \cos(x+y) & -\sin(x+y) & 0 \\ \sin(x+y) & \cos(x+y) & 0 \\ 0 & 0 & 1 \end{bmatrix}$$

$\therefore \quad F(x)\,F(y) = F(x+y)$

50 (*c*) Given that, $A = \begin{bmatrix} 2 & 1 & 2 \\ 1 & 2 & 4 \end{bmatrix}$

and $B = \begin{bmatrix} 4 & 1 \\ 2 & 3 \\ 1 & 2 \end{bmatrix}$

Now, the order of $A = 2 \times 3$

and the order of $B = 3 \times 2$

$\because$ The number of columns in A is equal to the number of rows in B.

$\therefore AB$ is well-defined.

Also, the number of columns in B is equal to the number of rows in A.

$\therefore BA$ is also well-defined.

51 (*b*) The given matrices are

$A = \begin{bmatrix} 2 & 1 & 3 \\ 3 & -2 & 1 \\ -1 & 0 & 1 \end{bmatrix}, B = \begin{bmatrix} 1 & -2 \\ 2 & 1 \\ 4 & 3 \end{bmatrix}$ and

$C = [1 \ \ 2 \ \ 6]$

The order of A is 3×3, order of B is 3×2 and order of C is 1×3.

$\therefore CA$, AB and CB are all defined.

But BA is not defined as number of columns in B is not equal to the number of rows in A.

52 (*c*) Given,

$$[1 \ \ 2 \ \ 1] \begin{bmatrix} 1 & 2 & 0 \\ 2 & 0 & 1 \\ 1 & 0 & 2 \end{bmatrix} \begin{bmatrix} 0 \\ 2 \\ x \end{bmatrix} = O$$

$$\Rightarrow [1 \ \ 2 \ \ 1] \left(\begin{bmatrix} 1 & 2 & 0 \\ 2 & 0 & 1 \\ 1 & 0 & 2 \end{bmatrix} \begin{bmatrix} 0 \\ 2 \\ x \end{bmatrix} \right) = O$$

[$\because$ matrix multiplication is associative]

$$\Rightarrow \quad [1 \ \ 2 \ \ 1] \begin{bmatrix} 0+4+0 \\ 0+0+x \\ 0+0+2x \end{bmatrix} = O$$

$$\Rightarrow [1 \ \ 2 \ \ 1] \begin{bmatrix} 4 \\ x \\ 2x \end{bmatrix} = O$$

$$\Rightarrow [4 + 2x + 2x] = O$$

$$\Rightarrow \quad 4 + 4x = 0 \Rightarrow x = -1$$

53 (*b*) Given, $A = \begin{bmatrix} 3 & 1 \\ -1 & 2 \end{bmatrix}$.

Now, $A^2 = AA = \begin{bmatrix} 3 & 1 \\ -1 & 2 \end{bmatrix} \begin{bmatrix} 3 & 1 \\ -1 & 2 \end{bmatrix}$

$$= \begin{bmatrix} 9-1 & 3+2 \\ -3-2 & -1+4 \end{bmatrix} = \begin{bmatrix} 8 & 5 \\ -5 & 3 \end{bmatrix}$$

$$\therefore A^2 - 5A + 7I = \begin{bmatrix} 8 & 5 \\ -5 & 3 \end{bmatrix} - 5\begin{bmatrix} 3 & 1 \\ -1 & 2 \end{bmatrix} + 7\begin{bmatrix} 1 & 0 \\ 0 & 1 \end{bmatrix}$$

$$= \begin{bmatrix} 8 & 5 \\ -5 & 3 \end{bmatrix} - \begin{bmatrix} 15 & 5 \\ -5 & 10 \end{bmatrix} + \begin{bmatrix} 7 & 0 \\ 0 & 7 \end{bmatrix}$$

$$= \begin{bmatrix} 8-15+7 & 5-5+0 \\ -5+5+0 & 3-10+7 \end{bmatrix}$$

$$= \begin{bmatrix} 0 & 0 \\ 0 & 0 \end{bmatrix} = O$$

54 (*a*) We have,

$$[2x \ \ 3] \begin{bmatrix} 1 & 2 \\ -3 & 0 \end{bmatrix} \begin{bmatrix} x \\ 8 \end{bmatrix} = O$$

$$\Rightarrow [2x - 9 \ \ 4x] \begin{bmatrix} x \\ 8 \end{bmatrix} = [0]$$

$$[2x^2 - 9x \ + 32x] = [0]$$

$$\Rightarrow \quad 2x^2 + 23x = 0$$

$$\Rightarrow \quad x(2x + 23) = 0$$

$$\Rightarrow \quad x = 0, x = \frac{-23}{2}$$

55 (*c*) We have,

$$(A+B)(A-B) = A(A-B) + B(A-B)$$

$$= A^2 - AB + BA - B^2$$

Note *We cannot cancel AB and BA, because in general* $AB \neq BA$.

56 (*a*) For three matrices A, B and C of the same order, if $A = B$, then $AC = BC$, but the converse is not true.

57 (*c*) We have,

$A \cdot A = A^2, A \cdot A \cdot A = A^3$ and so on.

Then, A is a square matrix. Since, if the number of columns of A will always be equal to the number of rows of A, then $A \cdot A$ will be defined and so on.

58 (*d*) Let A and B are square matrices such that $AB = BA$.

Consider,

$$(A+B)^2 = (A+B)(A+B)$$
$$= A(A+B) + B(A+B)$$
$$= A^2 + AB + BA + B^2$$
$$= A^2 + AB + AB + B^2$$

[$\because AB = BA$]

$$= A^2 + 2AB + B^2$$

Hence, $(A+B)^2 = A^2 + 2AB + B^2$

59 (*d*) Consider the matrix $A = \begin{bmatrix} \alpha & 0 \\ 1 & 1 \end{bmatrix}$.

$$\therefore \quad A^2 = A \cdot A = \begin{bmatrix} \alpha & 0 \\ 1 & 1 \end{bmatrix} \begin{bmatrix} \alpha & 0 \\ 1 & 1 \end{bmatrix}$$

$$= \begin{bmatrix} \alpha^2 & 0 \\ \alpha + 1 & 1 \end{bmatrix}$$

Also, it is given that $A^2 = B$, where

$$B = \begin{bmatrix} 1 & 0 \\ 5 & 1 \end{bmatrix}.$$

$$\Rightarrow \begin{bmatrix} \alpha^2 & 0 \\ \alpha + 1 & 1 \end{bmatrix} = \begin{bmatrix} 1 & 0 \\ 5 & 1 \end{bmatrix}$$

On equating the corresponding elements, we get

$$\alpha^2 = 1 \ \text{ and } \ \alpha + 1 = 5$$

$$\Rightarrow \quad \alpha = \pm 1 \ \text{ and } \ \alpha = 4$$

Since, there is no common solution.

$\therefore$ No real value of α exists.

60 (*b*) Here,

$$[x \ \ -5 \ \ -1] \begin{bmatrix} 1 & 0 & 2 \\ 0 & 2 & 1 \\ 2 & 0 & 3 \end{bmatrix} \begin{bmatrix} x \\ 4 \\ 1 \end{bmatrix} = 0$$

$$\Rightarrow [x \ \ -5 \ \ -1] \left(\begin{bmatrix} 1 & 0 & 2 \\ 0 & 2 & 1 \\ 2 & 0 & 3 \end{bmatrix} \begin{bmatrix} x \\ 4 \\ 1 \end{bmatrix} \right) = 0$$

$$\Rightarrow \quad [x \ \ -5 \ \ -1] \begin{bmatrix} x+0+2 \\ 0+8+1 \\ 2x+0+3 \end{bmatrix} = 0$$

$$\Rightarrow [x(x+2)+(-5)(9)+(-1)(2x+3)]=0$$
$$\Rightarrow x^2-48=0 \Rightarrow x^2=48$$
$$\therefore \quad x=\pm\sqrt{48}=\pm 4\sqrt{3}$$

61 (*b*) Here,

$$X\begin{bmatrix}1 & 2 & 3\\ 4 & 5 & 6\end{bmatrix}=\begin{bmatrix}-7 & -8 & -9\\ 2 & 4 & 6\end{bmatrix}$$

The matrix given on the RHS of the equation is a 2×3 matrix and the one given on the LHS of the equation is a 2×3 matrix.

Therefore, X has to be a 2×2 matrix.

Now, let $X=\begin{bmatrix}a & c\\ b & d\end{bmatrix}$.

Therefore, we have

$$\begin{bmatrix}a & c\\ b & d\end{bmatrix}\begin{bmatrix}1 & 2 & 3\\ 4 & 5 & 6\end{bmatrix}=\begin{bmatrix}-7 & -8 & -9\\ 2 & 4 & 6\end{bmatrix}$$
$$\Rightarrow \begin{bmatrix}a+4c & 2a+5c & 3a+6c\\ b+4d & 2b+5d & 3b+6d\end{bmatrix}=\begin{bmatrix}-7 & -8 & -9\\ 2 & 4 & 6\end{bmatrix}$$

On equating the corresponding elements of the two matrices, we get

$$a+4c=-7, 2a+5c=-8, 3a+6c=-9$$

and $b+4d=2, 2b+5d=4, 3b+6d=6$

Now, $a+4c=-7$

$\Rightarrow a=-7-4c$

and $2a+5c=-8$

$\Rightarrow -14-8c+5c=-8$

$\Rightarrow -3c=6$

$\Rightarrow c=-2$

$\therefore a=-7-4(-2)=-7+8=1$

Now, $b+4d=2$

$\Rightarrow b=2-4d$

and $2b+5d=4$

$\Rightarrow 4-8d+5d=4$

$\Rightarrow -3d=0 \Rightarrow d=0$

$\therefore b=2-4(0)=2$

Thus, $a=1, b=2, c=-2, d=0$

Hence, the required matrix X is

$$\begin{bmatrix}1 & -2\\ 2 & 0\end{bmatrix}$$

Transpose of a Matrix

1 (*c*) If $A=[a_{ij}]$ is a $m\times n$ matrix, then the matrix obtained by interchanging the rows and columns of A is called the transpose of A. Transpose of the matrix A is denoted by A' or (A^T).

2 (*a*) If $A=[a_{ij}]_{m\times n}$, then $A'=[a_{ji}]_{n\times m}$.

3 (*b*) If $A=\begin{bmatrix}3 & 5\\ \sqrt{3} & 1\\ 0 & \frac{-1}{5}\end{bmatrix}_{3\times 2}$, then

$$A'=\begin{bmatrix}3 & \sqrt{3} & 0\\ 5 & 1 & \frac{-1}{5}\end{bmatrix}_{2\times 3}$$

4 (*d*) For any matrices A and B of suitable orders, we have

A. $(A')'=A$,

B. $(kA)'=kA'$ (where, k is any constant)

C. $(A+B)'=A'+B'$

D. $(AB)'=B'A'$

5 (*a*) Let $A=\begin{bmatrix}5\\ 1/2\\ -1\end{bmatrix}_{3\times 1}$.

Since, A' is obtained by interchanging rows and columns.

$\therefore \quad A'=[5 \quad 1/2 \quad -1]_{1\times 3}$

6 (*c*) Let $A=\begin{bmatrix}-1 & 5 & 6\\ \sqrt{3} & 5 & 6\\ 2 & 3 & -1\end{bmatrix}$, then

$$A'=\begin{bmatrix}-1 & \sqrt{3} & 2\\ 5 & 5 & 3\\ 6 & 6 & -1\end{bmatrix}$$

7 (a) Here, $A+B=\begin{bmatrix}-1 & 2 & 3\\ 5 & 7 & 9\\ -2 & 1 & 1\end{bmatrix}+\begin{bmatrix}-4 & 1 & -5\\ 1 & 2 & 0\\ 1 & 3 & 1\end{bmatrix}=\begin{bmatrix}-5 & 3 & -2\\ 6 & 9 & 9\\ -1 & 4 & 2\end{bmatrix}$

$$\Rightarrow (A+B)'=\begin{bmatrix}-5 & 6 & -1\\ 3 & 9 & 4\\ -2 & 9 & 2\end{bmatrix} \quad \text{...(i)}$$

Also, $A'+B'=\begin{bmatrix}-1 & 2 & 3\\ 5 & 7 & 9\\ -2 & 1 & 1\end{bmatrix}'+\begin{bmatrix}-4 & 1 & -5\\ 1 & 2 & 0\\ 1 & 3 & 1\end{bmatrix}'$

$$=\begin{bmatrix}-1 & 5 & -2\\ 2 & 7 & 1\\ 3 & 9 & 1\end{bmatrix}+\begin{bmatrix}-4 & 1 & 1\\ 1 & 2 & 3\\ -5 & 0 & 1\end{bmatrix}$$
$$=\begin{bmatrix}-5 & 6 & -1\\ 3 & 9 & 4\\ -2 & 9 & 2\end{bmatrix} \quad \text{...(ii)}$$

From Eqs. (i) and (ii), it is verified that $(A+B)'=A'+B'$.

Here,

$$A-B=\begin{bmatrix}-1 & 2 & 3\\ 5 & 7 & 9\\ -2 & 1 & 1\end{bmatrix}-\begin{bmatrix}-4 & 1 & -5\\ 1 & 2 & 0\\ 1 & 3 & 1\end{bmatrix}$$
$$=\begin{bmatrix}-1+4 & 2-1 & 3+5\\ 5-1 & 7-2 & 9-0\\ -2-1 & 1-3 & 1-1\end{bmatrix}=\begin{bmatrix}3 & 1 & 8\\ 4 & 5 & 9\\ -3 & -2 & 0\end{bmatrix}$$
$$\Rightarrow (A-B)'=\begin{bmatrix}3 & 4 & -3\\ 1 & 5 & -2\\ 8 & 9 & 0\end{bmatrix} \quad \text{...(iii)}$$

Also, $A'-B'=\begin{bmatrix}-1 & 5 & -2\\ 2 & 7 & 1\\ 3 & 9 & 1\end{bmatrix}-\begin{bmatrix}-4 & 1 & 1\\ 1 & 2 & 3\\ -5 & 0 & 1\end{bmatrix}$

$$=\begin{bmatrix}-1+4 & 5-1 & -2-1\\ 2-1 & 7-2 & 1-3\\ 3-(-5) & 9-0 & 1-1\end{bmatrix}$$
$$=\begin{bmatrix}3 & 4 & -3\\ 1 & 5 & -2\\ 8 & 9 & 0\end{bmatrix} \quad \text{...(iv)}$$

From Eqs. (iii) and (iv), we have $(A-B)'=A'-B'$.

8 (b) $A = (A')' = \begin{bmatrix} 3 & 4 \\ -1 & 2 \\ 0 & 1 \end{bmatrix}' = \begin{bmatrix} 3 & -1 & 0 \\ 4 & 2 & 1 \end{bmatrix}$

Here,
$$A + B = \begin{bmatrix} 3 & -1 & 0 \\ 4 & 2 & 1 \end{bmatrix} + \begin{bmatrix} -1 & 2 & 1 \\ 1 & 2 & 3 \end{bmatrix} = \begin{bmatrix} 2 & 1 & 1 \\ 5 & 4 & 4 \end{bmatrix}$$

$$\therefore \quad (A+B)' = \begin{bmatrix} 2 & 1 & 1 \\ 5 & 4 & 4 \end{bmatrix}' = \begin{bmatrix} 2 & 5 \\ 1 & 4 \\ 1 & 4 \end{bmatrix}$$

$$B' = \begin{bmatrix} -1 & 2 & 1 \\ 1 & 2 & 3 \end{bmatrix}' = \begin{bmatrix} -1 & 1 \\ 2 & 2 \\ 1 & 3 \end{bmatrix}$$

Also, $A' = \begin{bmatrix} 3 & 4 \\ -1 & 2 \\ 0 & 1 \end{bmatrix}$

Thus, $A' + B' = \begin{bmatrix} 3 & 4 \\ -1 & 2 \\ 0 & 1 \end{bmatrix} + \begin{bmatrix} -1 & 1 \\ 2 & 2 \\ 1 & 3 \end{bmatrix} = \begin{bmatrix} 2 & 5 \\ 1 & 4 \\ 1 & 4 \end{bmatrix}$

So, verified that

$(A+B)' = A' + B'$.

Here, $A' - B' = \begin{bmatrix} 3 & 4 \\ -1 & 2 \\ 0 & 1 \end{bmatrix} - \begin{bmatrix} -1 & 1 \\ 2 & 2 \\ 1 & 3 \end{bmatrix}$

$$= \begin{bmatrix} 3+1 & 4-1 \\ -1-2 & 2-2 \\ 0-1 & 1-3 \end{bmatrix} = \begin{bmatrix} 4 & 3 \\ -3 & 0 \\ -1 & -2 \end{bmatrix}$$

Also, $A - B = \begin{bmatrix} 3 & -1 & 0 \\ 4 & 2 & 1 \end{bmatrix} - \begin{bmatrix} -1 & 2 & 1 \\ 1 & 2 & 3 \end{bmatrix}$

$$= \begin{bmatrix} 3+1 & -1-2 & 0-1 \\ 4-1 & 2-2 & 1-3 \end{bmatrix}$$

$$(A-B)' = \begin{bmatrix} 4 & -3 & -1 \\ 3 & 0 & -2 \end{bmatrix}' = \begin{bmatrix} 4 & 3 \\ -3 & 0 \\ -1 & -2 \end{bmatrix}$$

$\Rightarrow \quad (A-B)' = A' - B'$

9 (a) Here, $AB = \begin{bmatrix} 1 \\ -4 \\ 3 \end{bmatrix} [-1 \ \ 2 \ \ 1]$

$$= \begin{bmatrix} -1 & 2 & 1 \\ 4 & -8 & -4 \\ -3 & 6 & 3 \end{bmatrix}$$

$$(AB)' = \begin{bmatrix} -1 & 2 & 1 \\ 4 & -8 & -4 \\ -3 & 6 & 3 \end{bmatrix}' = \begin{bmatrix} -1 & 4 & -3 \\ 2 & -8 & 6 \\ 1 & -4 & 3 \end{bmatrix} \quad \text{...(i)}$$

Also, $B'A' = [-1 \ \ 2 \ \ 1]' \begin{bmatrix} 1 \\ -4 \\ 3 \end{bmatrix}'$

$$= \begin{bmatrix} -1 \\ 2 \\ 1 \end{bmatrix} [1 \ \ -4 \ \ 3] = \begin{bmatrix} -1 & 4 & -3 \\ 2 & -8 & 6 \\ 1 & -4 & 3 \end{bmatrix} \quad \text{...(ii)}$$

From Eqs. (i) and (ii),we find that $(AB)' = B'A'$.

10 (a) Here, $A = \begin{bmatrix} \cos\alpha & \sin\alpha \\ -\sin\alpha & \cos\alpha \end{bmatrix}$

$$\Rightarrow \quad A' = \begin{bmatrix} \cos\alpha & \sin\alpha \\ -\sin\alpha & \cos\alpha \end{bmatrix}^T = \begin{bmatrix} \cos\alpha & -\sin\alpha \\ \sin\alpha & \cos\alpha \end{bmatrix}$$

$$\therefore \quad A'A = \begin{bmatrix} \cos\alpha & -\sin\alpha \\ \sin\alpha & \cos\alpha \end{bmatrix} \begin{bmatrix} \cos\alpha & \sin\alpha \\ -\sin\alpha & \cos\alpha \end{bmatrix}$$

$$= \begin{bmatrix} (\cos\alpha)(\cos\alpha) + (\sin\alpha)(\sin\alpha) & (\cos\alpha)(\sin\alpha) + (-\sin\alpha)(\cos\alpha) \\ (\sin\alpha)(\cos\alpha) + (\cos\alpha)(-\sin\alpha) & \sin^2\alpha + \cos^2\alpha \end{bmatrix}$$

$$= \begin{bmatrix} \cos^2\alpha + \sin^2\alpha & \cos\alpha\sin\alpha - \sin\alpha\cos\alpha \\ \sin\alpha\cos\alpha - \cos\alpha\sin\alpha & \sin^2\alpha + \cos^2\alpha \end{bmatrix}$$

$$= \begin{bmatrix} 1 & 0 \\ 0 & 1 \end{bmatrix} = I$$

$[\because \sin^2\alpha + \cos^2\alpha = 1]$

11 (b) Here, $A = \begin{bmatrix} \cos\alpha & -\sin\alpha \\ \sin\alpha & \cos\alpha \end{bmatrix}$

and $A' = \begin{bmatrix} \cos\alpha & -\sin\alpha \\ \sin\alpha & \cos\alpha \end{bmatrix}^T = \begin{bmatrix} \cos\alpha & \sin\alpha \\ -\sin\alpha & \cos\alpha \end{bmatrix}$

[interchanging rows and columns]

Given, $A + A' = I$.

$$\therefore \begin{bmatrix} \cos\alpha & -\sin\alpha \\ \sin\alpha & \cos\alpha \end{bmatrix} + \begin{bmatrix} \cos\alpha & \sin\alpha \\ -\sin\alpha & \cos\alpha \end{bmatrix} = \begin{bmatrix} 1 & 0 \\ 0 & 1 \end{bmatrix}$$

$$\Rightarrow \begin{bmatrix} 2\cos\alpha & 0 \\ 0 & 2\cos\alpha \end{bmatrix} = \begin{bmatrix} 1 & 0 \\ 0 & 1 \end{bmatrix}$$

On comparing the corresponding elements of the above matrices, we get

$$2\cos\alpha = 1$$

$$\Rightarrow \quad \cos\alpha = \frac{1}{2} = \cos\frac{\pi}{3}$$

$$\Rightarrow \quad \alpha = \frac{\pi}{3}$$

So, correct option is (b).

12 (c) Since, A and B are two matrices of same order.

Then, $(AB)' = B'A'$

Also, $AB \neq BA$ and $AB \neq -BA$.

and $(A+B)(A-B) = A^2 - B^2$, if $AB = BA$.

13 (d) $A' = \begin{bmatrix} -2 & 3 \\ 1 & 2 \end{bmatrix}$

and $B = \begin{bmatrix} -1 & 0 \\ 1 & 2 \end{bmatrix}$

$$\Rightarrow \quad A = \begin{bmatrix} -2 & 1 \\ 3 & 2 \end{bmatrix}$$

$$\therefore \ A + 2B = \begin{bmatrix} -2 & 1 \\ 3 & 2 \end{bmatrix} + 2\begin{bmatrix} -1 & 0 \\ 1 & 2 \end{bmatrix}$$

$$= \begin{bmatrix} -2 & 1 \\ 3 & 2 \end{bmatrix} + \begin{bmatrix} -2 & 0 \\ 2 & 4 \end{bmatrix} = \begin{bmatrix} -4 & 1 \\ 5 & 6 \end{bmatrix}$$

$$\Rightarrow \quad (A+2B)' = \begin{bmatrix} -4 & 5 \\ 1 & 6 \end{bmatrix}$$

14 (*d*) Given, $A'A = I$.

$$\therefore \begin{bmatrix} 0 & 2y & z \\ x & y & -z \\ x & -y & z \end{bmatrix}' \begin{bmatrix} 0 & 2y & z \\ x & y & -z \\ x & -y & z \end{bmatrix} = I$$

$$\Rightarrow \begin{bmatrix} 0 & x & x \\ 2y & y & -y \\ z & -z & z \end{bmatrix} \begin{bmatrix} 0 & 2y & z \\ x & y & -z \\ x & -y & z \end{bmatrix} = \begin{bmatrix} 1 & 0 & 0 \\ 0 & 1 & 0 \\ 0 & 0 & 1 \end{bmatrix}$$

$$\Rightarrow \begin{bmatrix} 0+x^2+x^2 & 0+xy-xy & 0-xz+xz \\ 0+yx-yx & 4y^2+y^2+y^2 & 2yz-yz-yz \\ 0-zx+zx & 2yz-yz-yz & z^2+z^2+z^2 \end{bmatrix} = \begin{bmatrix} 1 & 0 & 0 \\ 0 & 1 & 0 \\ 0 & 0 & 1 \end{bmatrix}$$

$$\Rightarrow \begin{bmatrix} 2x^2 & 0 & 0 \\ 0 & 6y^2 & 0 \\ 0 & 0 & 3z^2 \end{bmatrix} = \begin{bmatrix} 1 & 0 & 0 \\ 0 & 1 & 0 \\ 0 & 0 & 1 \end{bmatrix}$$

On comparing the corresponding elements, we get

$2x^2 = 1, 6y^2 = 1, 3z^2 = 1$

$\Rightarrow x^2 = \frac{1}{2}, y^2 = \frac{1}{6}, z^2 = \frac{1}{3}$

$\Rightarrow x = \pm\frac{1}{\sqrt{2}}, y = \pm\frac{1}{\sqrt{6}}, z = \pm\frac{1}{\sqrt{3}}$

Symmetric and Skew-symmetric Matrices

1 (*a*) A square matrix $A = [a_{ij}]$ is said to be symmetric, if

$A' = A$, i.e. $[a_{ij}] = [a_{ji}]$ for all possible values of i and j.

2 (*b*) We have,

$$A = \begin{bmatrix} \sqrt{3} & 2 & 3 \\ 2 & -1.5 & -1 \\ 3 & -1 & 1 \end{bmatrix}$$

$$A' = \begin{bmatrix} \sqrt{3} & 2 & 3 \\ 2 & -1.5 & -1 \\ 3 & -1 & 1 \end{bmatrix} = A$$

$A' = A$

Thus, A is a symmetric matrix.

3 (*c*) For a square matrix $A = [a_{ij}]$ to be skew-symmetric,

$$a_{ij} = -a_{ji} \ \forall\ i, j$$

4 (*c*) Now, if we put $i = j$, we get $a_{ii} = -a_{ii}$.

Therefore, $2a_{ii} = 0$

or $a_{ii} = 0$ for all i's.

This means that all the diagonal elements of a skew-symmetric matrix are zero.

5 (*a*) The matrix $B = \begin{bmatrix} 0 & e & f \\ -e & 0 & g \\ -f & -g & 0 \end{bmatrix}$ is a skew-symmetric matrix as $B' = -B$.

$$B' = \begin{bmatrix} 0 & -e & -f \\ e & 0 & -g \\ f & g & 0 \end{bmatrix} = -\begin{bmatrix} 0 & e & f \\ -e & 0 & g \\ -f & -g & 0 \end{bmatrix} = -B$$

Thus, B is skew-symmetric matrix.

6 (*c*) Let $B = A + A'$, then

$B' = (A + A')'$

$= A' + (A')'$ $[\because (A+B)' = A' + B']$

$= A' + A$ $[\because (A')' = A]$

$= A + A'$ $[\because A + B = B + A]$

$= B$

Therefore, $B = A + A'$ is a symmetric matrix.

Now, let $C = A - A'$

$C' = (A - A')' = A' - (A')'$

$= A' - A$

$= -(A - A') = -C$

Therefore, $C = A - A'$ is a skew-symmetric matrix.

7 (*c*) Let A be a square matrix, then we can write

$$A = \frac{1}{2}(A + A') + \frac{1}{2}(A - A')$$

We know that, $(A + A')$ is a symmetric matrix and $(A - A')$ is a skew-symmetric matrix. Since, for any matrix A, $(kA)' = kA'$, it follows that $\frac{1}{2}(A + A')$ is symmetric matrix and $\frac{1}{2}(A - A')$ is skew-symmetric matrix. Thus, any square matrix can be expressed as the sum of a symmetric and a skew-symmetric matrix.

8 (*b*) Here, $A' = \begin{bmatrix} 1 & -1 & 5 \\ -1 & 2 & 1 \\ 5 & 1 & 3 \end{bmatrix}' = \begin{bmatrix} 1 & -1 & 5 \\ -1 & 2 & 1 \\ 5 & 1 & 3 \end{bmatrix} = A$

$\therefore$ $A' = A$

Hence, A is a symmetric matrix.

9 (*b*) Now, $A' = \begin{bmatrix} 0 & 1 & -1 \\ -1 & 0 & 1 \\ 1 & -1 & 0 \end{bmatrix}' = \begin{bmatrix} 0 & -1 & 1 \\ 1 & 0 & -1 \\ -1 & 1 & 0 \end{bmatrix}$

$$= -\begin{bmatrix} 0 & 1 & -1 \\ -1 & 0 & 1 \\ 1 & -1 & 0 \end{bmatrix} = -A$$

$\therefore$ $A' = -A$

Hence, A is skew-symmetric matrix.

10 (*a*) $A - A' = \begin{bmatrix} 1 & 5 \\ 6 & 7 \end{bmatrix} - \begin{bmatrix} 1 & 5 \\ 6 & 7 \end{bmatrix}'$

$= \begin{bmatrix} 1 & 5 \\ 6 & 7 \end{bmatrix} - \begin{bmatrix} 1 & 6 \\ 5 & 7 \end{bmatrix} = \begin{bmatrix} 0 & -1 \\ 1 & 0 \end{bmatrix}$

$\Rightarrow A - A' = \begin{bmatrix} 0 & -1 \\ 1 & 0 \end{bmatrix}$

and $(A - A')' = \begin{bmatrix} 0 & 1 \\ -1 & 0 \end{bmatrix}$

$= -\begin{bmatrix} 0 & -1 \\ 1 & 0 \end{bmatrix} = -(A - A')$

$[\because A' = -A$, so A is a skew-symmetric matrix$]$

Hence, $(A - A')$ is skew-symmetric matrix.

11 (*b*) $\frac{1}{2}(A - A') = \frac{1}{2}$

$$\left(\begin{bmatrix} 0 & a & b \\ -a & 0 & c \\ -b & -c & 0 \end{bmatrix} - \begin{bmatrix} 0 & a & b \\ -a & 0 & c \\ -b & -c & 0 \end{bmatrix}'\right)$$

$$= \frac{1}{2}\left(\begin{bmatrix} 0 & a & b \\ -a & 0 & c \\ -b & -c & 0 \end{bmatrix} - \begin{bmatrix} 0 & -a & -b \\ a & 0 & -c \\ b & c & 0 \end{bmatrix}\right)$$

$$= \frac{1}{2}\begin{bmatrix} 0 & 2a & 2b \\ -2a & 0 & 2c \\ -2b & -2c & 0 \end{bmatrix}$$

$$= \begin{bmatrix} 0 & a & b \\ -a & 0 & c \\ -b & -c & 0 \end{bmatrix} = A$$

$\therefore \quad \frac{1}{2}(A - A') = A$

12 (*a*) Given, A and B are symmetric matrices.

$\Rightarrow \quad A' = A$ and $B' = B$

$(AB - BA)' = (AB)' - (BA)'$ $\quad [\because (A - B)' = A' - B']$

$= B'A' - A'B'$ $\quad [\because (AB)' = B'A']$

$= BA - AB$ $\quad [\because A' = A \text{ and } B' = B]$

$= -(AB - BA)$

$\Rightarrow (AB - BA)' = -(AB - BA)$

Thus, $(AB - BA)$ is a skew-symmetric matrix.

13 (*a*)

A. Let $A = \begin{bmatrix} 3 & 5 \\ 1 & -1 \end{bmatrix}$, then $A = P + Q$

where, $P = \frac{1}{2}(A + A')$

and $Q = \frac{1}{2}(A - A')$

Now, $P = \frac{1}{2}(A + A')$

$$= \frac{1}{2}\left(\begin{bmatrix} 3 & 5 \\ 1 & -1 \end{bmatrix} + \begin{bmatrix} 3 & 1 \\ 5 & -1 \end{bmatrix}\right)$$

$$= \frac{1}{2}\begin{bmatrix} 6 & 6 \\ 6 & -2 \end{bmatrix} = \begin{bmatrix} 3 & 3 \\ 3 & -1 \end{bmatrix}$$

$$\therefore P' = \begin{bmatrix} 3 & 3 \\ 3 & -1 \end{bmatrix}' = \begin{bmatrix} 3 & 3 \\ 3 & -1 \end{bmatrix} = P$$

$\because P' = P$, so P is a symmetric matrix.

Thus, $P = \frac{1}{2}(A + A')$ is symmetric matrix.

B. Let $A = \begin{bmatrix} 1 & 5 \\ -1 & 2 \end{bmatrix}$, then

$$A' = \begin{bmatrix} 1 & 5 \\ -1 & 2 \end{bmatrix}' = \begin{bmatrix} 1 & -1 \\ 5 & 2 \end{bmatrix}$$

Now,

$$A + A' = \begin{bmatrix} 1 & 5 \\ -1 & 2 \end{bmatrix} + \begin{bmatrix} 1 & -1 \\ 5 & 2 \end{bmatrix} = \begin{bmatrix} 2 & 4 \\ 4 & 4 \end{bmatrix}$$

Let $\quad P = \frac{1}{2}(A + A')$

$$= \frac{1}{2}\begin{bmatrix} 2 & 4 \\ 4 & 4 \end{bmatrix} = \begin{bmatrix} 1 & 2 \\ 2 & 2 \end{bmatrix}.$$

$$\text{Now, } P' = \begin{bmatrix} 1 & 2 \\ 2 & 2 \end{bmatrix}' = \begin{bmatrix} 1 & 2 \\ 2 & 2 \end{bmatrix} = P$$

Thus, $P = \frac{1}{2}(A + A')$ is a symmetric matrix.

C. Let $\quad A = \begin{bmatrix} 6 & -2 & 2 \\ -2 & 3 & -1 \\ 2 & -1 & 3 \end{bmatrix}$.

$$\text{Then, } A' = \begin{bmatrix} 6 & -2 & 2 \\ -2 & 3 & -1 \\ 2 & -1 & 3 \end{bmatrix}' = \begin{bmatrix} 6 & -2 & 2 \\ -2 & 3 & -1 \\ 2 & -1 & 3 \end{bmatrix} = A$$

$$\text{Now, } A + A' = \begin{bmatrix} 6 & -2 & 2 \\ -2 & 3 & -1 \\ 2 & -1 & 3 \end{bmatrix} + \begin{bmatrix} 6 & -2 & 2 \\ -2 & 3 & -1 \\ 2 & -1 & 3 \end{bmatrix}$$

$$= \begin{bmatrix} 12 & -4 & 4 \\ -4 & 6 & -2 \\ 4 & -2 & 6 \end{bmatrix}$$

Let $P = \frac{1}{2}(A + A')$

$$= \frac{1}{2}\begin{bmatrix} 12 & -4 & 4 \\ -4 & 6 & -2 \\ 4 & -2 & 6 \end{bmatrix} = \begin{bmatrix} 6 & -2 & 2 \\ -2 & 3 & -1 \\ 2 & -1 & 3 \end{bmatrix}$$

$$\text{Now, } P' = \begin{bmatrix} 6 & -2 & 2 \\ -2 & 3 & -1 \\ 2 & -1 & 3 \end{bmatrix}' = \begin{bmatrix} 6 & -2 & 2 \\ -2 & 3 & -1 \\ 2 & -1 & 3 \end{bmatrix} = P$$

Thus, $P = \frac{1}{2}(A + A')$ is a symmetric matrix.

D. Let $A = \begin{bmatrix} 3 & 3 & -1 \\ -2 & -2 & 1 \\ -4 & -5 & 2 \end{bmatrix}$.

$$\text{Then, } A' = \begin{bmatrix} 3 & -2 & -4 \\ 3 & -2 & -5 \\ -1 & 1 & 2 \end{bmatrix}$$

$$\text{Now, } A + A' = \begin{bmatrix} 3 & 3 & -1 \\ -2 & -2 & 1 \\ -4 & -5 & 2 \end{bmatrix} + \begin{bmatrix} 3 & -2 & -4 \\ 3 & -2 & -5 \\ -1 & 1 & 2 \end{bmatrix}$$

$$= \begin{bmatrix} 6 & 1 & -5 \\ 1 & -4 & -4 \\ -5 & -4 & 4 \end{bmatrix}$$

$P = \frac{1}{2}(A + A')$

$$= \frac{1}{2}\begin{bmatrix} 6 & 1 & -5 \\ 1 & -4 & -4 \\ -5 & -4 & 4 \end{bmatrix} = \begin{bmatrix} 3 & 1/2 & -5/2 \\ 1/2 & -2 & 2 \\ -5/2 & -2 & 2 \end{bmatrix}$$

$$\text{Now, } P' = \begin{bmatrix} 3 & 1/2 & -5/2 \\ 1/2 & -2 & -2 \\ -5/2 & -2 & 2 \end{bmatrix}' = \begin{bmatrix} 3 & 1/2 & -5/2 \\ 1/2 & -2 & -2 \\ -5/2 & -2 & 2 \end{bmatrix} = P$$

Thus, $P = \frac{1}{2}(A + A')$ is a symmetric matrix.

14 (c)

I. We suppose that A is a symmetric matrix, then $A' = A$.

Consider,
$(B'AB)' = \{B'(AB)\}' = (AB)'(B')'$
$= B'A'(B)$
$[\because (AB)' = B'A' \text{ and } (B')' = B]$
$= B'(A'B) = B'(AB)$
$[\because A' = A]$

$\therefore \ (B'AB)' = B'AB$

which shows that $B'AB$ is a symmetric matrix.

II. Now, we suppose that A is a skew-symmetric matrix.
Then, $A' = -A$.

Consider,
$(B'AB)' = [B'(AB)]' = (AB)'(B')'$
$[\because (AB)' = B'A' \text{ and } (A')' = A]$
$= (B'A')B$
$= B'(-A)B = -B'AB$
$[\because A' = -A]$

$\therefore \ (B'AB)' = -B'AB$

which shows that $B'AB$ is a skew-symmetric matrix.

15 (a) $(AB' - BA')' = (AB')' - (BA')'$
$= (BA' - AB') = -(AB' - BA')$

$\therefore \ (AB' - BA')' = -(AB' - BA')$

Thus, $AB' - BA'$ is a skew-symmetric matrix.

16 (a) For $A'A$, consider
$(A'A)' = (A)'(A')' [\because (AB)' = B'A']$
$= A'A \qquad [\because (X')' = X]$

Hence, $A'A$ is symmetric for any matrix A.

Also, $(AA')' = (A')'(A)' = AA'$

Hence, AA' is also symmetric for any matrix A.

17 (b) Let A be a square matrix such that A is both symmetric and skew-symmetric matrix.

$\Rightarrow \ A' = A \qquad [\because A \text{ is symmetric}]$

and $A' = -A$
$[\because A \text{ is skew-symmetric}]$

$\therefore \qquad A = -A$

$\Rightarrow \qquad A + A = 0$

$\Rightarrow \qquad 2A = 0$

$\therefore \qquad A = 0$

18 (a) Since, A is symmetric $\Rightarrow A' = A$.

Now, $(A^n)' = (A')^n = A^n$

Therefore, A^n is a symmetric matrix.

19 (b) We have, $a_{ij} = (i - j)^3$

$\Rightarrow \quad a_{ji} = (j - i)^3 = -(i - j)^3$
$= -a_{ij}$ for all i and j

Thus, A is a skew-symmetric matrix.

20 (b) Since, the diagonal elements of a skew-symmetric matrix are all zero.

$\therefore \ a_{ii} = 0$ for all $i = 1, 2, \ldots, n$.

Invertible Matrices

1 (c) If A is a square matrix of order m, and if there exists another square matrix B of the same order m, such that $AB = BA = I$, then B is called the inverse matrix of A. In this case, A is said to be invertible.

2 (a) The inverse of A is denoted by A^{-1}.

3 (a) Let $A = \begin{bmatrix} 2 & 3 \\ 1 & 2 \end{bmatrix}$ and

$B = \begin{bmatrix} 2 & -3 \\ -1 & 2 \end{bmatrix}$ be two matrices.

Now, $AB = \begin{bmatrix} 2 & 3 \\ 1 & 2 \end{bmatrix}\begin{bmatrix} 2 & -3 \\ -1 & 2 \end{bmatrix}$

$= \begin{bmatrix} 4-3 & -6+6 \\ 2-2 & -3+4 \end{bmatrix}$

$= \begin{bmatrix} 1 & 0 \\ 0 & 1 \end{bmatrix} = I$

Also, $BA = \begin{bmatrix} 1 & 0 \\ 0 & 1 \end{bmatrix} = I$

Thus, B is the inverse of A, in other words $B = A^{-1}$ and A is inverse of B i.e. $A = B^{-1}$.

4 (b)

I. A rectangular matrix does not possess inverse matrix, since for products BA and AB to be defined and to be equal, it is necessary that matrices A and B should be square matrices of the same order.

II. If B is the inverse of A, then A is also the inverse of B.

III. **Uniqueness of inverse** Inverse of a square matrix, if it exists, is unique.

Let $A = [a_{ij}]$ be a square matrix of order m. If possible, let B and C be two inverses of A. We shall show that $B = C$.

Since, B is the inverse of A.

$\Rightarrow \qquad AB = BA = I \qquad \ldots(i)$

Since, C is also the inverse of A.

$\Rightarrow \qquad AC = CA = I \qquad \ldots(ii)$

Thus, $\quad B = BI = B(AC)$
$= (BA)C = IC = C$

IV. From the definition of inverse of a matrix, we have

$(AB)(AB)^{-1} = I$

or $A^{-1}(AB)(AB)^{-1} = A^{-1}I$
[multiplying both sides by A^{-1}]

or $(A^{-1}A)B(AB)^{-1} = A^{-1}$
$[\because A^{-1}I = A^{-1}]$

or $\quad IB(AB)^{-1} = A^{-1}$

or $\quad B(AB)^{-1} = A^{-1}$

or $\quad B^{-1}B(AB)^{-1} = B^{-1}A^{-1}$

or $\quad I(AB)^{-1} = B^{-1}A^{-1}$

5 (d) We know that, if A is a square matrix of order m and if there exists another square matrix B of the same order m, such that $AB = BA = I$, then B is said to be the inverse of A.

In this case, it is clear that A is the inverse of B.

Thus, matrices A and B will be inverse of each other only, if $AB = BA = I$.

6 (b) Since, $AB = 3I$.

$\Rightarrow \ A^{-1}AB = 3A^{-1}I$
[multiplying both sides by A^{-1}]

$\Rightarrow \qquad B = 3A^{-1} \quad [\because AA^{-1} = I]$

$\therefore \qquad A^{-1} = \frac{B}{3}$

Miscellaneous Exercise

1 (*b*) Given,

$$\begin{bmatrix}3 & -2\\3 & 0\\2 & 4\end{bmatrix}\begin{bmatrix}y & y\\x & x\end{bmatrix}=\begin{bmatrix}3 & 3\\3y & 3y\\10 & 10\end{bmatrix}$$

$$\Rightarrow \begin{bmatrix}3y-2x & 3y-2x\\3y & 3y\\2y+4x & 2y+4x\end{bmatrix}=\begin{bmatrix}3 & 3\\3y & 3y\\10 & 10\end{bmatrix}$$

Comparing the elements, we have

$$3y-2x=3 \quad \text{...(i)}$$
$$2y+4x=10 \quad \text{...(ii)}$$

On solving Eqs. (i) and (ii), we get

$$x=\frac{3}{2} \text{ and } y=2$$

2 (*c*) Given that, $2X+3Y=O$ and $X+2Y=I$, where

$$O=\begin{bmatrix}0 & 0\\0 & 0\end{bmatrix} \text{ and } I=\begin{bmatrix}1 & 0\\0 & 1\end{bmatrix}$$

On multiplying $2X+3Y=O$ by 2 and $X+2Y=I$ by 3, we get

$4X+6y=O$ by 2 and $3X+6Y=3I$

On subtracting these two equations, we get

$$X=-3I$$
$$=-3\begin{bmatrix}1 & 0\\0 & 1\end{bmatrix}=\begin{bmatrix}-3 & 0\\0 & -3\end{bmatrix}$$

3 (*a*)

I. Addition of matrices is defined, if order of matrices is same since matrices of different order cannot be added.

II. Also, $B=C \Rightarrow AB=AC$ but converse is not true.

III. $\because$ For two matrices A and B of same order, $(A-B)'=A'-B'$ and $(kA)=kA'$, where k is non-zero scalar.

$\therefore (3A-2B)'=3A'-2B'$

IV. The given matrices are

$$A=\begin{bmatrix}3 & 1 & 1\\5 & 2 & 3\end{bmatrix} \text{ and } B=\begin{bmatrix}2 & 1\\7 & 2\\4 & -1\end{bmatrix}$$

Since, the order of A is 2×3 and order of B is 3×2.

$\therefore$ The product AB is defined and is of order 2×2.

4 (*c*) Given,

$$[1 \quad x \quad 1]\begin{bmatrix}1 & 2 & 3\\0 & 5 & 1\\0 & 3 & 2\end{bmatrix}\begin{bmatrix}x\\1\\-2\end{bmatrix}=0$$

$$\Rightarrow [1 \quad x \quad 1]\begin{bmatrix}x+2-6\\0+5-2\\0+3-4\end{bmatrix}=0$$

$$\Rightarrow [1 \quad x \quad 1]\begin{bmatrix}x-4\\3\\-1\end{bmatrix}=0$$

$$\Rightarrow x-4+3x-1=0 \Rightarrow x=\frac{5}{4}$$

5 (*d*) The given matrix is

$$A=\begin{bmatrix}1 & 2 & 2\\2 & 1 & 2\\2 & 2 & 1\end{bmatrix}$$

$$\text{Now, } A^2=\begin{bmatrix}1 & 2 & 2\\2 & 1 & 2\\2 & 2 & 1\end{bmatrix}\begin{bmatrix}1 & 2 & 2\\2 & 1 & 2\\2 & 2 & 1\end{bmatrix}$$
$$=\begin{bmatrix}9 & 8 & 8\\8 & 9 & 8\\8 & 8 & 9\end{bmatrix}$$

$$\text{Now, } A^2-4A=\begin{bmatrix}9 & 8 & 8\\8 & 9 & 8\\8 & 8 & 9\end{bmatrix}-\begin{bmatrix}4 & 8 & 8\\8 & 4 & 8\\8 & 8 & 4\end{bmatrix}$$
$$=\begin{bmatrix}5 & 0 & 0\\0 & 5 & 0\\0 & 0 & 5\end{bmatrix}=5I_3$$

6 (*b*) The given matrices are

$$A=[3 \quad 5] \text{ and } B=[7 \quad 3]$$

$\because$ AC is defined and A has 2 columns.

$\therefore$ C has 2 rows.

Also, BC is defined and B has 2 columns.

$\therefore$ C has 2 rows.

Also, this matrix can have any numbers of columns, since AC and BC are defined.

$\therefore$ Order of $C=2\times n, n\in N$

7 (*d*) $m[-3 \quad 4]+n[4 \quad -3]=[10 \quad -11]$

$$\Rightarrow [-3m+4n \quad 4m-3n]=[10 \quad -11]$$

On equating the corresponding elements, we get

$$-3m+4n=10 \quad \text{...(i)}$$
$$\text{and} \quad 4m-3n=-11 \quad \text{...(ii)}$$

On solving Eqs. (i) and (ii), we get

$$n=1, m=-2$$

Now, $3m+7n=3(-2)+7(1)=1$

8 (*a*) The given matrix equation is

$$2X+\begin{bmatrix}1 & 2\\3 & 4\end{bmatrix}=\begin{bmatrix}3 & 8\\7 & 2\end{bmatrix}$$

$$\Rightarrow 2X=\begin{bmatrix}3 & 8\\7 & 2\end{bmatrix}-\begin{bmatrix}1 & 2\\3 & 4\end{bmatrix}$$

$$\Rightarrow 2X=\begin{bmatrix}2 & 6\\4 & -2\end{bmatrix}=2\begin{bmatrix}1 & 3\\2 & -1\end{bmatrix}$$

$$\Rightarrow X=\begin{bmatrix}1 & 3\\2 & -1\end{bmatrix}$$

9 (*c*) Given that,

$$A=\begin{bmatrix}1 & 2\\3 & 4\end{bmatrix}$$

$$\text{and} \quad B=\begin{bmatrix}a & 0\\0 & b\end{bmatrix}$$

$$\text{Now, } AB=\begin{bmatrix}1 & 2\\3 & 4\end{bmatrix}\begin{bmatrix}a & 0\\0 & b\end{bmatrix}=\begin{bmatrix}a & 2b\\3a & 4b\end{bmatrix}$$

$$\text{and} \quad BA=\begin{bmatrix}a & 0\\0 & b\end{bmatrix}\begin{bmatrix}1 & 2\\3 & 4\end{bmatrix}=\begin{bmatrix}a & 2a\\3b & 4b\end{bmatrix}$$

If $AB=BA$, then $a=b$.

Hence, $AB=BA$ is possible for infinitely many values of B.

10 (*a*) We have, $A=\begin{bmatrix}6 & 8 & 5\\4 & 2 & 3\\9 & 7 & 1\end{bmatrix}$

$$\Rightarrow A'=\begin{bmatrix}6 & 4 & 9\\8 & 2 & 7\\5 & 3 & 1\end{bmatrix}$$

$$\because \quad A=\left(\frac{A+A'}{2}\right)+\left(\frac{A-A'}{2}\right)$$

Here, $\frac{A+A'}{2}$ is the symmetric part of A and $\frac{A-A'}{2}$ is the skew-symmetric part of A.

$\therefore$ We have, symmetric matrix,

$$B=\frac{A+A'}{2}$$

$$=\frac{1}{2}\left\{\begin{bmatrix}6&8&5\\4&2&3\\9&7&1\end{bmatrix}+\begin{bmatrix}6&4&9\\8&2&7\\5&3&1\end{bmatrix}\right\}$$

$$=\frac{1}{2}\begin{bmatrix}12&12&14\\12&4&10\\14&10&2\end{bmatrix}=\begin{bmatrix}6&6&7\\6&2&5\\7&5&1\end{bmatrix}$$

11 (*b*) The given matrices are

$$A=\begin{bmatrix}0&3&3\\-3&0&-4\\-3&4&0\end{bmatrix}$$

and $B=\begin{bmatrix}x\\y\\z\end{bmatrix}\Rightarrow B'=[x\quad y\quad z]$

$$\text{Now, } AB=\begin{bmatrix}0&3&3\\-3&0&-4\\-3&4&0\end{bmatrix}\begin{bmatrix}x\\y\\z\end{bmatrix}=\begin{bmatrix}3y+3z\\-3x-4z\\-3x+4y\end{bmatrix}$$

$$\text{Now, } B'(AB)=[x\ y\ z]\begin{bmatrix}3y+3z\\-3x-4z\\-3x+4y\end{bmatrix}$$

$$=[3xy+3zx-3xy-4\,yz-3xz+4\,yz]=[0]$$

$\therefore$ $B'(AB)$ is a null matrix.

12 (*c*)

I. Given that, $AB=BA$. ...(i)

We want to prove that

$AB^n=B^nA$ ...(ii)

For $n=1$, Eq. (ii) is obviously true.

Let Eq. (ii) be true for a positive integer $n=m$.

i.e. $AB^m=B^mA$ ...(iii)

Then, for $n=m+1$,

$AB^{m+1}=A(B^mB)=(AB^m)B$ (associative law of matrix multiplication)

$=(B^mA)B$ [using Eq. (iii)]

$=B^m(AB)=B^m(BA)$ [using Eq. (i)]

$=(B^mB)A=B^{m+1}A$

Hence, by induction, Eq. (ii) is true for all $n\in N$.

II. Here, given that,

$AB=BA$ ...(i)

We want to prove that

$(AB)^n=A^nB^n$ ...(ii)

For $n=1$, Eq. (ii) is obviously true. [from Eq. (i)]

Let Eq. (ii) be true for a positive integer $n=m$

i.e. $(AB)^m=A^mB^m$ ...(iii)

Then, for $n=m+1$, $(AB)^{m+1}$

$=(AB)^m(AB)=(A^mB^m)(AB)$ [using Eq. (iii)]

$=A^m(B^mA)B=A^m(AB^m)B$ [$\because AB^n=B^nA$ for all $n\in N$ whenever $AB=BA$]

$=(A^mA)(B^mB)=A^{m+1}B^{m+1}$

Hence, by induction, Eq. (ii) is true for all $n\in N$.

13 (*c*)

I. The given matrices are

$$\begin{bmatrix}xy&4\\z+5&x+y\end{bmatrix}\text{ and }\begin{bmatrix}4&w\\0&4\end{bmatrix}.$$

Also, given that,

$$\begin{bmatrix}xy&4\\z+5&x+y\end{bmatrix}=\begin{bmatrix}4&w\\0&4\end{bmatrix}$$

On equating the corresponding elements, we get

$xy=4, w=4, z+5=0$

and $x+y=4$

$\Rightarrow z=-5, w=4$

and $x=4-y$

$\Rightarrow (4-y)y=4$

$\Rightarrow y^2-4y+4=0$

$\Rightarrow (y-2)^2=0\Rightarrow y=2$

$\therefore$ $x=2$

Hence, we get

$x=2, y=2, z=-5$ and $w=4$.

II. Also, the two matrices are equal, if their orders are same and their corresponding elements are same.

14 (*a*) Since, A and B are both symmetric matrices, therefore $A'=A$ and $B'=B$.

Let AB be symmetric, then

$(AB)'=AB$ ...(i)

But $(AB)'=B'A'=BA$

Therefore, $BA=AB$. [using Eq. (i)]

Conversely, if $AB=BA$, then we shall show that AB is symmetric.

Now, $(AB)'=B'A'=BA$ [$\because A$ and B are symmetric]

$=AB$

Hence, AB is symmetric.

15 (*c*) The given matrices are

$$A=\begin{bmatrix}\cos^2\alpha&\cos\alpha\sin\alpha\\\cos\alpha\sin\alpha&\sin^2\alpha\end{bmatrix}$$

$$\text{and } B=\begin{bmatrix}\cos^2\beta&\cos\beta\sin\beta\\\cos\beta\sin\beta&\sin^2\beta\end{bmatrix}$$

It is given that $AB=0$.

$$\Rightarrow\begin{bmatrix}\cos^2\alpha&\cos\alpha\sin\alpha\\\cos\alpha\sin\alpha&\sin^2\alpha\end{bmatrix}\begin{bmatrix}\cos^2\beta&\cos\beta\sin\beta\\\cos\beta\sin\beta&\sin^2\beta\end{bmatrix}=\begin{bmatrix}0&0\\0&0\end{bmatrix}$$

$$\Rightarrow\begin{bmatrix}\cos^2\alpha\cos^2\beta+\cos\alpha\sin\alpha\cos\beta\sin\beta&\cos^2\alpha\cos\beta\sin\beta+\cos\alpha\sin\alpha\sin^2\beta\\\cos\alpha\sin\alpha\cos^2\beta+\sin^2\alpha\cos\beta\sin\beta&\cos\alpha\sin\alpha\cos\beta\sin\beta+\sin^2\alpha\sin^2\beta\end{bmatrix}=\begin{bmatrix}0&0\\0&0\end{bmatrix}$$

$$\Rightarrow\begin{bmatrix}\cos\alpha\cos\beta\cdot\cos(\alpha-\beta)&\cos\alpha\sin\beta\cos(\alpha-\beta)\\\cos\beta\sin\alpha\cos(\alpha-\beta)&\sin\alpha\sin\beta\cos(\alpha-\beta)\end{bmatrix}=\begin{bmatrix}0&0\\0&0\end{bmatrix}$$

On equating the corresponding elements, we get

$\cos\alpha\cdot\cos\beta\cos(\alpha-\beta)=0,$

$\cos\beta\sin\alpha\cos(\alpha-\beta)=0,$

$\cos\alpha\sin\beta\cos(\alpha-\beta)=0$

and $\sin\alpha\sin\beta\cos(\alpha-\beta)=0$

$\Rightarrow \cos(\alpha-\beta)=0$

$\therefore \alpha-\beta=\frac{\pi}{2}$

16 (c) Given, $A=\begin{bmatrix}0 & 1\\0 & 0\end{bmatrix}$.

Let $P(n):(aI+bA)^n$
$=a^nI+na^{n-1}bA$

We shall prove the result by principle of mathematical induction.

Putting $n=1$,

$P(1):(aI+bA)^1=a^1I+1\cdot a^{1-1}bA$
$aI+bA=aI+bA$

which is true for $n=1$.

Let the result be true for $n=k$.

$\therefore\quad P(k):(aI+bA)^k$
$=a^kI+k\cdot a^{k-1}bA$ ...(i)

Now, we prove that the result is true for $n=k+1$.

$\therefore\quad P(k+1):(aI+bA)^{k+1}=a^{k+1}I$
$+(k+1)\cdot a^{k+1-1}bA$

Now, taking LHS $=(aI+bA)^{k+1}$
$=(aI+bA)^k(aI+bA)$
$(\because a^{x+y}=a^x\times a^y)$
$=(a^kI+k\cdot a^{k-1}bA)(aI+bA)$
[$\because$ using Eq. (i), putting $(aI+bA)^k=a^kI+k\,a^{k-1}bA$]
$=a^{k+1}I+ka^kIbA+a^kIbA$
$+ka^{k-1}b^2A^2$
$=a^{k+1}I+ka^k\,b(IA)+a^k\,b(IA)$
$+ka^{k-1}b^2(A^2)$
$=a^{k+1}I+ka^kbA+a^kbA$
$+ka^{k-1}b^2\times 0$

$$\left\{\begin{array}{l}\because AI=A \text{ and } A^2=AA\\ =\begin{bmatrix}0 & 1\\0 & 0\end{bmatrix}\\ \begin{bmatrix}0 & 1\\0 & 0\end{bmatrix}=\begin{bmatrix}0 & 0\\0 & 0\end{bmatrix}=0\end{array}\right\}$$

$=a^{k+1}I+(k+1)\cdot a^kbA$

Therefore, the result is true for $n=k+1$, whenever it is true for $n=k$. So, by principle of mathematical induction, it is true for all $n\in N$.

17 (d) Here, $A=\begin{bmatrix}1 & 1 & 1\\1 & 1 & 1\\1 & 1 & 1\end{bmatrix}$.

Let $P(n):A^n=\begin{bmatrix}3^{n-1} & 3^{n-1} & 3^{n-1}\\3^{n-1} & 3^{n-1} & 3^{n-1}\\3^{n-1} & 3^{n-1} & 3^{n-1}\end{bmatrix}$

We shall prove the result by principle of mathematical induction.

Putting $n=1$,

$$P(1):A^1=\begin{bmatrix}3^{1-1} & 3^{1-1} & 3^{1-1}\\3^{1-1} & 3^{1-1} & 3^{1-1}\\3^{1-1} & 3^{1-1} & 3^{1-1}\end{bmatrix}$$

$$=\begin{bmatrix}3^0 & 3^0 & 3^0\\3^0 & 3^0 & 3^0\\3^0 & 3^0 & 3^0\end{bmatrix}=\begin{bmatrix}1 & 1 & 1\\1 & 1 & 1\\1 & 1 & 1\end{bmatrix} \quad \text{...(i)}$$

which is true for $n=1$. Let the result be true for $n=k$.

$$\therefore\quad P(k):A^k=\begin{bmatrix}3^{k-1} & 3^{k-1} & 3^{k-1}\\3^{k-1} & 3^{k-1} & 3^{k-1}\\3^{k-1} & 3^{k-1} & 3^{k-1}\end{bmatrix} \quad \text{...(ii)}$$

Putting $n=k+1$,

$$P(k+1):A^{k+1}=\begin{bmatrix}3^k & 3^k & 3^k\\3^k & 3^k & 3^k\\3^k & 3^k & 3^k\end{bmatrix}$$

Now, LHS $=A^{k+1}=A^k\cdot A^1$

$$A^k\cdot A^1=\begin{bmatrix}3^{k-1} & 3^{k-1} & 3^{k-1}\\3^{k-1} & 3^{k-1} & 3^{k-1}\\3^{k-1} & 3^{k-1} & 3^{k-1}\end{bmatrix}\begin{bmatrix}1 & 1 & 1\\1 & 1 & 1\\1 & 1 & 1\end{bmatrix} \quad \text{[using Eqs. (i) and (ii)]}$$

$$=\begin{bmatrix}3^{k-1}+3^{k-1}+3^{k-1} & 3^{k-1}+3^{k-1}+3^{k-1} & 3^{k-1}+3^{k-1}+3^{k-1}\\3^{k-1}+3^{k-1}+3^{k-1} & 3^{k-1}+3^{k-1}+3^{k-1} & 3^{k-1}+3^{k-1}+3^{k-1}\\3^{k-1}+3^{k-1}+3^{k-1} & 3^{k-1}+3^{k-1}+3^{k-1} & 3^{k-1}+3^{k-1}+3^{k-1}\end{bmatrix}$$

$$\begin{bmatrix}3\cdot 3^{k-1} & 3\cdot 3^{k-1} & 3\cdot 3^{k-1}\\3\cdot 3^{k-1} & 3\cdot 3^{k-1} & 3\cdot 3^{k-1}\\3\cdot 3^{k-1} & 3\cdot 3^{k-1} & 3\cdot 3^{k-1}\end{bmatrix}$$

$$\Rightarrow\quad A^{k+1}=\begin{bmatrix}3^k & 3^k & 3^k\\3^k & 3^k & 3^k\\3^k & 3^k & 3^k\end{bmatrix}$$

Hence, by principle of mathematical induction, $P(n)$ is true for all $n\in N$.

18 (b) Matrices of same order can be subtracted. Also, identity matrix is a diagonal matrix in which all the diagonal elements are 1. Transpose of a column matrix is a row matrix.

Also, the matrix multiplication is commutative for the diagonal matrix.

Thus, if A and B are diagonal matrices, then $AB=BA$.

19 (b) We have, $A^2=A\cdot A$

$$=\begin{bmatrix}1 & 2 & -2\\1 & 1 & 1\\1 & 3 & -1\end{bmatrix}\begin{bmatrix}1 & 2 & -2\\1 & 1 & 1\\1 & 3 & -1\end{bmatrix}$$

$$=\begin{bmatrix}1 & -2 & 2\\3 & 6 & -2\\3 & 2 & 2\end{bmatrix}$$

and $A^3=A^2\cdot A$

$$=\begin{bmatrix}1 & -2 & 2\\3 & 6 & -2\\3 & 2 & 2\end{bmatrix}\begin{bmatrix}1 & 2 & -2\\1 & 1 & 1\\1 & 3 & -1\end{bmatrix}$$

$$=\begin{bmatrix}1 & 6 & -6\\7 & 6 & 2\\7 & 14 & -6\end{bmatrix}$$

Thus, A^3-A^2-4A

$$=\begin{bmatrix}1 & 6 & -6\\7 & 6 & 2\\7 & 14 & -6\end{bmatrix}-\begin{bmatrix}1 & -2 & 2\\3 & 6 & -2\\3 & 2 & 2\end{bmatrix}-4\begin{bmatrix}1 & 2 & -2\\1 & 1 & 1\\1 & 3 & -1\end{bmatrix}$$

$=-4I$

20 (c) Given, $A^2=I$.

$\therefore\quad AA=I$

$$\Rightarrow\quad \begin{bmatrix}\alpha & \beta\\\gamma & -\alpha\end{bmatrix}\begin{bmatrix}\alpha & \beta\\\gamma & -\alpha\end{bmatrix}=\begin{bmatrix}1 & 0\\0 & 1\end{bmatrix}$$

$$\Rightarrow\quad \begin{bmatrix}\alpha^2+\beta\gamma & \alpha\beta-\alpha\beta\\\alpha\gamma-\gamma\alpha & \gamma\beta+\alpha^2\end{bmatrix}=\begin{bmatrix}1 & 0\\0 & 1\end{bmatrix}$$

On comparing the corresponding elements, we have

$$\alpha^2+\beta\gamma=1$$
$$\Rightarrow\quad \alpha^2+\beta\gamma-1=0$$
$$\Rightarrow\quad 1-\alpha^2-\beta\gamma=0$$

21 (c) Here, $A^2 = A$.

$\therefore (I + A)^3 - 7A = I^3 + A^3 + 3I^2A + 3A^2I - 7A$

$[\because (a+b)^3 = a^3 + b^3 + 3ab^2 + 3a^2b]$

$= I + A^3 + 3A + 3A^2 - 7A$

$= I + A^2 \cdot A + 3A + 3A - 7A$ $\quad [\because A^2 = A]$

$= I + A \cdot A - A = I + A - A$ $\quad [\because A^2 = A]$

$= I$

$\therefore \quad (I + A)^3 - 7A = I$

22 (c) Since, $A + B$ is defined.

$\therefore$ The matrices A and B are of same order.

Also, let A is of order $m \times n$.

Then, B is of order $m \times n$.

Since, AB is defined.

$\therefore \quad m = n$

Thus, A and B are the square matrices of same order $m \times m$ or $n \times n$.

23 (d) The number of places in a 3×3 matrix is 9.

Also, each place has two choices i.e. either 2 or 0.

$\therefore$ The number of possible matrices of order 3×3 with each entry 2 or 0 is 2^9 i.e. 512.

24 (a) We are required to prove that for all $n \in N$,

$$P(n) : A^n = \begin{bmatrix} 1+2n & -4n \\ n & 1-2n \end{bmatrix}$$

Let $\quad n = 1$.

$$P(1) : A^1 = \begin{bmatrix} 1+2(1) & -4(1) \\ 1 & 1-2(1) \end{bmatrix}$$

$$= \begin{bmatrix} 3 & -4 \\ 1 & -1 \end{bmatrix} \quad \text{...(i)}$$

which is true for $n = 1$.

Let the result be true for $n = k$.

$$P(k) : A^k = \begin{bmatrix} 1+2k & -4k \\ k & 1-2k \end{bmatrix} \quad \text{...(ii)}$$

For $n = k + 1$,

$$P(k+1) : \quad A^{k+1} = \begin{bmatrix} 1+2(k+1) & -4(k+1) \\ k+1 & 1-2(k+1) \end{bmatrix}$$

$$= \begin{bmatrix} 2k+3 & -4k-4 \\ k+1 & -2k-1 \end{bmatrix}$$

Now, LHS $= A^{k+1} = A^k A^1$

$$= \begin{bmatrix} 1+2k & -4k \\ k & 1-2k \end{bmatrix} \begin{bmatrix} 3 & -4 \\ 1 & -1 \end{bmatrix}$$

[using Eqs. (i) and (ii)]

$$= \begin{bmatrix} (1+2k) \cdot 3 + (-4k) \cdot 1 & (1+2k) \cdot (-4) + (-4k) \cdot (-1) \\ k \cdot 3 + (1-2k) \cdot 1 & k \cdot (-4) + (1-2k) \cdot (-1) \end{bmatrix}$$

$$= \begin{bmatrix} 3+2k & -4-4k \\ k+1 & -1-2k \end{bmatrix}$$

$$= \begin{bmatrix} 1+2(k+1) & -4(k+1) \\ k+1 & 1-2(k+1) \end{bmatrix}$$

Therefore, the result is true for $n = k + 1$, whenever it is true for $n = k$. So, by principle of mathematical induction, it is true for all $n \in N$.

25 (a) Given that, $A^2 = I$.

Consider, $\quad (A - I)^3 + (A + I)^3 - 7A$

$= A^3 - I^3 - 3A^2I + 3AI^2 + A^3 + I^3 + 3A^2I + 3AI^2 - 7A$

$$\begin{bmatrix} \because (a+b)^3 = a^3 + b^3 + 3a^2b + 3ab^2 \\ \text{and } (a-b)^3 = a^3 - b^3 - 3a^2 b + 3ab^2 \end{bmatrix}$$

$= 2A^3 + 6AI^2 - 7A$

$= 2A^2 \cdot A + 6AI - 7A$ $\quad [\because A^3 = A^2 \cdot A \text{ and } I^2 = I]$

$= 2I \cdot A + 6A - 7A$ $\quad [\because A^2 = I]$

$= 2A + 6A - 7A$

$= 8A - 7A = A$

Numerical Type Questions

1 (0) $[2x \quad 3] \begin{bmatrix} 1 & 3 \\ -3 & 0 \end{bmatrix} \begin{bmatrix} x \\ 8 \end{bmatrix} = 0$

$$[2x - 9 \quad 6x] \begin{bmatrix} x \\ 8 \end{bmatrix} = 0$$

$\Rightarrow \quad 2x^2 - 9x + 48x = 0$

$\Rightarrow \quad 2x^2 + 39x = 0$

$\Rightarrow \quad x(2x + 39) = 0$

$\Rightarrow \quad x = 0, \quad x = \dfrac{-39}{2}$

2 (7) Given, $A = \begin{bmatrix} 2 & -1 \\ 1 & 1 \end{bmatrix}$

$$A^2 = \begin{bmatrix} 2 & -1 \\ 1 & 1 \end{bmatrix} \begin{bmatrix} 2 & -1 \\ 1 & 1 \end{bmatrix} = \begin{bmatrix} 3 & -3 \\ 3 & 0 \end{bmatrix}$$

$$A^3 = A^2 \cdot A = \begin{bmatrix} 3 & -3 \\ 3 & 0 \end{bmatrix} \begin{bmatrix} 2 & -1 \\ 1 & 1 \end{bmatrix}$$

$$= \begin{bmatrix} 3 & -6 \\ 6 & -3 \end{bmatrix}$$

$$A^4 = \begin{bmatrix} 3 & -6 \\ 6 & -3 \end{bmatrix} \begin{bmatrix} 2 & -1 \\ 1 & 1 \end{bmatrix} = \begin{bmatrix} 0 & -9 \\ 9 & -9 \end{bmatrix}$$

$$A^5 = \begin{bmatrix} 0 & -9 \\ 9 & -9 \end{bmatrix} \begin{bmatrix} 2 & -1 \\ 1 & 1 \end{bmatrix} = \begin{bmatrix} -9 & -9 \\ 9 & -18 \end{bmatrix}$$

$$A^6 = \begin{bmatrix} -9 & -9 \\ 9 & -18 \end{bmatrix} \begin{bmatrix} 2 & -1 \\ 1 & 1 \end{bmatrix}$$

$$= \begin{bmatrix} -27 & 0 \\ 0 & -27 \end{bmatrix}$$

$$A^7 = \begin{bmatrix} -27 & 0 \\ 0 & -27 \end{bmatrix} \begin{bmatrix} 2 & -1 \\ 1 & 1 \end{bmatrix}$$

$$= \begin{bmatrix} -54 & 27 \\ -27 & -27 \end{bmatrix}$$

$$A^{13} = \begin{bmatrix} -54 & 27 \\ -27 & -27 \end{bmatrix} \begin{bmatrix} -27 & 0 \\ 0 & -27 \end{bmatrix}$$

$$= \begin{bmatrix} 3^6 \times 2 & -27^2 \\ 27^2 & 3^6 \end{bmatrix}$$

Sum of diagonal elements of A^{13}

$= 3^6 \times 2 + 3^6 = 3^6 (2 + 1) = 3^7$

It is given that sum of diagonal elemnet is 3^n.

$\Rightarrow \quad 3^n = 3^7 \Rightarrow n = 7$

3 (24)

$$\begin{bmatrix} 0 & 0 & 1 & 0 \\ 0 & 1 & 0 & 0 \\ 0 & 0 & 0 & 1 \\ 1 & 0 & 0 & 0 \end{bmatrix} \begin{matrix} \text{— 4 ways} \\ \text{— 3 ways} \\ \text{— 2 ways} \\ \text{— 1 way} \end{matrix}$$

Select any 1 place for 1's in row 1. Automatically, some columns will get filled with 0's.

Now, select 1 place for 1's.

Automatically, some columns will get filled with 0's.

$\Rightarrow$ Each time one less place will be available for putting 1's.

Repeat this till last row.

$\therefore$ Required number of matrices

$= 4 \times 3 \times 2 \times 1 = 24.$

4 (1) $A=\begin{bmatrix}\alpha & 0\\1 & 1\end{bmatrix}, B=\begin{bmatrix}1 & 0\\2 & 1\end{bmatrix}$

Given, $A^2 = B$.

$$A^2=\begin{bmatrix}\alpha & 0\\1 & 1\end{bmatrix}\begin{bmatrix}\alpha & 0\\1 & 1\end{bmatrix}=\begin{bmatrix}\alpha^2 & 0\\\alpha+1 & 1\end{bmatrix}$$

$$\therefore \begin{bmatrix}\alpha^2 & 0\\\alpha+1 & 1\end{bmatrix}=\begin{bmatrix}1 & 0\\2 & 1\end{bmatrix}$$

$\Rightarrow \quad \alpha^2=1$ and $\alpha+1=2$

$\Rightarrow \quad \alpha=1 \Rightarrow \alpha=\pm 1$

$\alpha=-1$ is rejected because it does not satisfy the equation $A^2=B$.

Hence, $\alpha=1$.

5 (7) $[m \quad n]\begin{bmatrix}m\\n\end{bmatrix}=[25]$

$\Rightarrow \quad m^2+n^2=25$

$(3)^2+(4)^2=25$

$\Rightarrow m=3$ and $n=4$ or $(m,n)=(3,4)$

Thus, $m+n=7$.

6 (4) $M^2-rM-I_2=0$

$$\begin{bmatrix}1 & 2\\2 & 3\end{bmatrix}\begin{bmatrix}1 & 2\\2 & 3\end{bmatrix}-r\begin{bmatrix}1 & 2\\2 & 3\end{bmatrix}-\begin{bmatrix}1 & 0\\0 & 1\end{bmatrix}=0$$

$$\Rightarrow \begin{bmatrix}5 & 8\\8 & 13\end{bmatrix}-\begin{bmatrix}r & 2r\\2r & 3r\end{bmatrix}=\begin{bmatrix}1 & 0\\0 & 1\end{bmatrix}$$

$$\Rightarrow \begin{bmatrix}5-r & 8-2r\\8-2r & 13-3r\end{bmatrix}=\begin{bmatrix}1 & 0\\0 & 1\end{bmatrix}$$

$\Rightarrow \quad 5-r=1,\ 8-2r=0,$

$\Rightarrow 8-2r=0,\ 13-3r=1 \Rightarrow r=4$

[satisfies all 4 equations]

7 (5) $$A=\begin{bmatrix}1 & 0 & 0\\0 & 1 & 1\\1 & 0 & 0\end{bmatrix}$$

$$A^2=\begin{bmatrix}1 & 0 & 0\\1 & 1 & 1\\1 & 0 & 0\end{bmatrix}$$

$$A^3=\begin{bmatrix}1 & 0 & 0\\2 & 1 & 1\\1 & 0 & 0\end{bmatrix}$$

$$A^4=\begin{bmatrix}1 & 0 & 0\\3 & 1 & 1\\1 & 0 & 0\end{bmatrix}$$

$$A^5=\begin{bmatrix}1 & 0 & 0\\4 & 1 & 1\\1 & 0 & 0\end{bmatrix}$$

$$A^n=\begin{bmatrix}1 & 0 & 0\\n-1 & 1 & 1\\1 & 0 & 0\end{bmatrix}$$

$$A^{2025}-A^{2020}=\begin{bmatrix}1 & 0 & 0\\2024 & 1 & 1\\1 & 0 & 0\end{bmatrix}-\begin{bmatrix}1 & 0 & 0\\2019 & 1 & 1\\1 & 0 & 0\end{bmatrix}$$

$$\Rightarrow A^{2025}-A^{2020}=\begin{bmatrix}0 & 0 & 0\\5 & 0 & 0\\0 & 0 & 0\end{bmatrix}$$

Thus, $a_{21}=5$.

8 (4) $$A\cdot B=\begin{bmatrix}0 & 2 & 0\\0 & 0 & 3\\-2 & 2 & 0\end{bmatrix}\begin{bmatrix}1 & 2 & 3\\3 & 4 & 5\\5 & -4 & 0\end{bmatrix}$$

$$=\begin{bmatrix}6 & 8 & 10\\15 & -12 & 0\\4 & 4 & 4\end{bmatrix}$$

$\therefore \quad a_{33}=4.$

9 (2) $A=\begin{bmatrix}1/2 & 3/4\\1 & -1/2\end{bmatrix}$

$$A^2=\begin{bmatrix}1/2 & 3/4\\1 & -1/2\end{bmatrix}\begin{bmatrix}1/2 & 3/4\\1 & -1/2\end{bmatrix}=\begin{bmatrix}1 & 0\\0 & 1\end{bmatrix}$$

$$A^{100}=\begin{bmatrix}1 & 0\\0 & 1\end{bmatrix}$$

$\therefore$ Sum of all elements of $A^{100}=2$.

10 (6) $S=\begin{bmatrix}2 & -1\\5 & -3\end{bmatrix}$

$$5I-8S=\begin{bmatrix}5 & 0\\0 & 5\end{bmatrix}-\begin{bmatrix}16 & -8\\40 & -24\end{bmatrix}=\begin{bmatrix}-11 & 8\\-40 & 29\end{bmatrix}$$

$$S^2=\begin{bmatrix}-1 & 1\\-5 & 4\end{bmatrix}, S^3=\begin{bmatrix}3 & -2\\10 & -7\end{bmatrix}$$

$$\Rightarrow \quad S^6=\begin{bmatrix}-11 & 8\\-40 & 29\end{bmatrix}=S^n$$

$\Rightarrow \quad n=6$

11 (6) $AA^T=I$

$$\Rightarrow \begin{bmatrix}p & q & r\\q & r & p\\r & p & q\end{bmatrix}\begin{bmatrix}p & q & r\\q & r & p\\r & p & q\end{bmatrix}=\begin{bmatrix}1 & 0 & 0\\0 & 1 & 0\\0 & 0 & 1\end{bmatrix}$$

$$\Rightarrow \begin{bmatrix}p^2+q^2+r^2 & pq+qr+rp & pr+qp+rq\\qp+rq+pr & q^2+r^2+p^2 & qr+rp+pq\\rp+pq+qr & rq+pr+qp & r^2+p^2+q^2\end{bmatrix}=\begin{bmatrix}1 & 0 & 0\\0 & 1 & 0\\0 & 0 & 1\end{bmatrix}$$

$\Rightarrow \quad p^2+q^2+r^2=1$

and $\quad pq+qr+pr=0$

This is possible, when

(i) $p=\pm 1, q=0=r=0$

(ii) $q=\pm 1, p=r=0$

(iii) $r=\pm 1, p=q=0.$

So, there are 6 such matrices A.

12 (10) $$A^2=\begin{bmatrix}1 & 0 & 0\\3 & 1 & 0\\9 & 3 & 1\end{bmatrix}\begin{bmatrix}1 & 0 & 0\\3 & 1 & 0\\9 & 3 & 1\end{bmatrix}=\begin{bmatrix}1 & 0 & 0\\6 & 1 & 0\\27 & 6 & 1\end{bmatrix}$$

Similarly,

$$A^4=\begin{bmatrix}1 & 0 & 0\\6 & 1 & 0\\27 & 6 & 1\end{bmatrix}\begin{bmatrix}1 & 0 & 0\\6 & 1 & 0\\27 & 6 & 1\end{bmatrix}=\begin{bmatrix}1 & 0 & 0\\12 & 1 & 0\\90 & 12 & 1\end{bmatrix}$$

$$A^5=\begin{bmatrix}1 & 0 & 0\\12 & 1 & 0\\90 & 12 & 1\end{bmatrix}\begin{bmatrix}1 & 0 & 0\\3 & 1 & 0\\9 & 3 & 1\end{bmatrix}=\begin{bmatrix}1 & 0 & 0\\15 & 1 & 0\\135 & 15 & 1\end{bmatrix}$$

Given, $B-A^5=I_3$.

$\Rightarrow \quad B=I_3+A^5$

$$B=\begin{bmatrix}1 & 0 & 0\\0 & 1 & 0\\0 & 0 & 1\end{bmatrix}+\begin{bmatrix}1 & 0 & 0\\15 & 1 & 0\\135 & 15 & 1\end{bmatrix}=\begin{bmatrix}2 & 0 & 0\\15 & 2 & 0\\135 & 15 & 2\end{bmatrix}$$

$$\therefore \quad \frac{a_{21}+a_{31}}{a_{32}}=\frac{15+135}{15}=\frac{150}{15}=10$$

Assertion and Reason Questions

1 (*d*) We know that, $A = \begin{bmatrix} 1 & 0 & 0 \\ 0 & 1 & 0 \\ 0 & 0 & 1 \end{bmatrix}$ is an identity matrix.

$\therefore$ Assertion (A) is false

If $a_{ij} \begin{cases} 1 & \text{if } i = j \\ 0 & \text{if } i \neq j \end{cases}$, then $P = [a_{ij}]$ is an identity matrix.

$\therefore$ Reason (R) is true.

2 (*a*) $A = \begin{bmatrix} 0 \\ \sqrt{3} \\ -1 \\ 1/2 \end{bmatrix}$ is a column matrix of order 4×1.

$\therefore$ Assertion (A) is true.

In general, $A = [a_{ij}]_{m \times 1}$ is a column matrix of order $m \times 1$.

$\therefore$ Reason (R) is true.

3 (*c*) $A = \begin{bmatrix} 1 & 2 & 3 \\ 2 & 4 & 5 \\ 3 & 5 & 6 \end{bmatrix}$

$A' = \begin{bmatrix} 1 & 2 & 3 \\ 2 & 4 & 5 \\ 3 & 5 & 6 \end{bmatrix}$

$A' = A \Rightarrow A$ is symmetric matrix.

$\therefore$ Assertion is true and Reason is false.

4 (*a*) Given that, A is symmetric matrix

$\therefore A' = A$

Now, $(B'AB)' = B'A'(B')'$

$\Rightarrow \quad (B'AB)' = B'AB$

Hence, A is true.

For three matrices P, Q and R if PQR is defined, then

$(PQR)' = R'Q'P'$

5 (*b*) **Assertion** Since, A, B and C are symmetric matrices.

$\therefore \quad B^T = B$ and $C^T = C$

Now to check $B(CB)$ is symmetric.

Consider

$[B(CB)]^T = (CB)^T B^T = (B^T C^T) B^T$

$= BCB$

So, $\quad (B(CB))^T = B(CB)$

$\Rightarrow B(CB)$ is symmetric.

Similarly,

$[(BC)B]^T = B^T (BC)^T = B^T C^T B^T$

$= BCB$

$\Rightarrow (BC)B$ is symmetric.

So, Assertion is true.

Reason Now, $(AB)' = B'A' = BA$.

This will be symmetric, if A and B are commutative i.e. $AB = BA$.

So, both Assertion and Reason are true but Reason is not the correct explanation of Assertion.

6 (*c*) **Assertion** A is a symmetric matrix, then $A' = A$.

$\therefore \begin{bmatrix} 0 & 3 & 3b \\ 2a & 1 & 3 \\ -2 & 3 & -1 \end{bmatrix} = \begin{bmatrix} 0 & 2a & -2 \\ 3 & 1 & 3 \\ 3b & 3 & 3 \end{bmatrix}$

$\therefore$ By equality of matrices,

$2a = 3$ and $3b = -2$

$\Rightarrow \quad a = \frac{3}{2}$ and $b = \frac{-2}{3}$

Hence, Assertion is true.

Reason (R) If B is a symmetric matrix, then $B' = B$.

Hence, Reason is false.

7 (*a*) The given matrices are

$A = \begin{bmatrix} 2 & 3 & -1 \\ 1 & 4 & 2 \end{bmatrix}$ and $B = \begin{bmatrix} 2 & 3 \\ 4 & 5 \\ 2 & 1 \end{bmatrix}$

Order of $A = 2 \times 3$

Order of $B = 3 \times 2$

Since, number of columns in A is equal to the number of rows in B.

$\Rightarrow AB$ is defined.

Also number of columns in B is equal to the number of rows in A.

$\therefore$ The product BA is also defined.

8 (*c*) Given, $A = \begin{bmatrix} 4 & 0 \\ 0 & 3 \end{bmatrix}$ and $B = \begin{bmatrix} 2 & 0 \\ 0 & 0 \end{bmatrix}$.

$AB = \begin{bmatrix} 4 & 0 \\ 0 & 3 \end{bmatrix} \begin{bmatrix} 2 & 0 \\ 0 & 0 \end{bmatrix} = \begin{bmatrix} 8 & 0 \\ 0 & 0 \end{bmatrix}$

$BA = \begin{bmatrix} 2 & 0 \\ 0 & 0 \end{bmatrix} \begin{bmatrix} 4 & 0 \\ 0 & 3 \end{bmatrix} = \begin{bmatrix} 8 & 0 \\ 0 & 0 \end{bmatrix}$

$\Rightarrow \quad AB = BA$

Now, $(A + B)^2 = (A + B)(A + B)$

$= A^2 + AB + BA + B^2$

$= A^2 + 2AB + B^2 \quad [\because AB = BA]$

$(A + B)^2 = A^2 + 2AB + B^2$

$\therefore$ Given, Assertion is correct and Reason is incorrect.

9 (*a*) **Negative of a matrix** The negative of a matrix is denoted by $-A$. We define $-A = (-1)A$.

If $A = \begin{bmatrix} 3 & -1 \\ -5 & x \end{bmatrix}$, then $-A$ is given by

$-A = (-1)A$

$= (-1) \begin{bmatrix} 3 & -1 \\ -5 & x \end{bmatrix} = \begin{bmatrix} -3 & 1 \\ 5 & -x \end{bmatrix}$

Case or Paragraph Type Questions

Solution (Q. Nos. 1-3) Let A be 2×3 matrix representing the annual sales of products in two markets.

$$\therefore A = \begin{array}{c} \\ \\ \end{array} \overset{\begin{matrix} p & \quad q & \quad r \end{matrix}}{\begin{bmatrix} 6000 & 20000 & 8000 \\ 10000 & 2000 & 18000 \end{bmatrix}} \begin{matrix} \text{Market I} \\ \text{Market II} \end{matrix}$$

Let B be the column matrix representing the sale price of each unit of products p, q and r.

$\therefore \quad B = \begin{bmatrix} 2.5 \\ 1.5 \\ 1 \end{bmatrix}$

Now, revenue = Sale price × Number of items sold.

$= \begin{bmatrix} 6000 & 20000 & 8000 \\ 10000 & 2000 & 18000 \end{bmatrix} \begin{bmatrix} 2.5 \\ 1.5 \\ 1 \end{bmatrix}$

$= \begin{bmatrix} 15000 + 30000 + 8000 \\ 25000 + 3000 + 18000 \end{bmatrix}$

$= \begin{bmatrix} 53000 \\ 46000 \end{bmatrix}$

$\therefore$ The revenue collected from market I = ₹ 53000

and revenue collected from market II = ₹ 46000

1 (*d*)

2 (*c*)

3 (*d*) Let C be the column matrix representing cost price of each unit of products p, q and r.

$\therefore$ Total cost in each market is given by

$$AC = \begin{bmatrix} 6000 & 20000 & 8000 \\ 10000 & 2000 & 18000 \end{bmatrix} \begin{bmatrix} 2 \\ 1 \\ 0.5 \end{bmatrix}$$

$$= \begin{bmatrix} 12000 & +20000 & +4000 \\ 20000 & +2000 & +9000 \end{bmatrix}$$

$$= \begin{bmatrix} 36000 \\ 31000 \end{bmatrix}$$

Now, profit matrix = Revenue matrix − Cost matrix.

$$= \begin{bmatrix} 53000 \\ 46000 \end{bmatrix} - \begin{bmatrix} 36000 \\ 31000 \end{bmatrix} = \begin{bmatrix} 17000 \\ 15000 \end{bmatrix}$$

$\therefore$ The gross profit from both the markets $= 15000 + 17000 = 32000$

4 (*a*) Let F be the matrix representing the number of family members and R be the matrix representing the requirement of calories and proteins for each person, then

$$F = \begin{matrix} \text{Family } A \\ \text{Family } B \end{matrix} \overset{\begin{matrix}\text{Men} & \text{Women} & \text{Children}\end{matrix}}{\begin{bmatrix} 3 & 5 & 2 \\ 1 & 3 & 4 \end{bmatrix}}$$

$$R = \begin{matrix} \text{Man} \\ \text{Woman} \\ \text{Child} \end{matrix} \overset{\begin{matrix}\text{Calories} & \text{Protien}\end{matrix}}{\begin{bmatrix} 2500 & 50 \\ 2000 & 60 \\ 1700 & 35 \end{bmatrix}}$$

5 (*c*) The requirement of calories and proteins for each of the two familes is given by product matrix .

$$FR = \begin{bmatrix} 3 & 5 & 2 \\ 1 & 3 & 4 \end{bmatrix} \begin{bmatrix} 2500 & 50 \\ 2000 & 60 \\ 1700 & 35 \end{bmatrix}$$

$$= \begin{bmatrix} 7500 + 10000 + 3400 & 150 + 300 + 70 \\ 2500 + 6000 + 6800 & 50 + 180 + 140 \end{bmatrix}$$

$$= \begin{bmatrix} 20900 & 520 \\ 15300 & 370 \end{bmatrix}$$

$$FR = \overset{\begin{matrix}\text{Calories} & \text{Proteins}\end{matrix}}{\begin{bmatrix} 20900 & 520 \\ 15300 & 370 \end{bmatrix}} \begin{matrix} \text{Family } A \\ \text{Family } B \end{matrix}$$

6 (*a*)

Past Years Questions

1 (*c*) $A = \begin{bmatrix} 2 & a & 0 \\ 1 & 3 & 1 \\ 0 & 5 & b \end{bmatrix}$

and $A^3 = 4A^2 - A - 21I$

So, $x^3 - 4x^2 + x + 21 = 0$ is the characteristic equation of matrix A.

So, sum of roots $= T_r(A)$

$\Rightarrow \quad -(-4) = 2 + 3 + b$

$\Rightarrow \quad 5 + b = 4 \Rightarrow b = -1 \quad$ ...(i)

Product of roots $= |A|$

$\Rightarrow \quad -21 = 2(3b - 5) - a(b)$

Put $b = -1$ from Eq. (i), we get

$-21 = 2(-8) + a$

$\Rightarrow \quad a = -21 + 16 = -5$

Therefore,

$2a + 3b = 2(-5) + 3(-1) = -13$

2 (*c*) **Given** A and B are symmetric matrices.

So, $A' = A$ and $B' = B$

Now, $(AB - BA)' = (AB)' - (BA)'$

$= B'A' - A'B'$

$= -(A'B' - B'A')$

$= -(AB - BA)$

$\therefore \quad (AB - BA)' = -(AB - BA)$

Hence, $(AB - BA)$ is skew symmetric matrix.

3 (*b*) We have,

$A_{3\times 2} \times B_{x \times y} = C_{3\times 1}$

For multiplication column of A = Row of B

$\therefore \quad x = 2$

Now, $A_{3\times 2} \times B_{x\times y} = C_{3\times 1}$

$\Rightarrow \quad A_{3\times 2} \times B_{2\times y} = C_{3\times 1}$

$\Rightarrow \quad D_{3\times y} = C_{3\times 1}$

$\therefore \quad y = 1$

4 (*d*) We have, $\alpha, \beta \in R$ and 3×3 matrix A such that

$A^2 = 3A + \alpha I \quad$ ... (i)

and $\quad A^4 = 21A + \beta I \quad$ ... (ii)

Consider, $A^4 = A^2 \cdot A^2$

$= (3A + \alpha I)(3A + \alpha I)$ [from Eq. (i)]

$= 9A^2 + 6\alpha A + \alpha^2 I$

From Eq. (i),

$A^4 = 9(3A + \alpha I) + 6\alpha A + \alpha^2 I$

$= (27 + 6\alpha)A + (\alpha^2 + 9\alpha)I \quad$ ...(iii)

From Eqs. (ii) and (iii), we get

$21A + \beta I = (27 + 6\alpha)A + (\alpha^2 + 9\alpha)I$

$\Rightarrow (\beta - \alpha^2 - 9\alpha)I = (6 + 6\alpha)A$

For a general 3×3 matrix A, we get

$6 + 6\alpha = 0$

$\Rightarrow \quad 6\alpha = -6$

$\Rightarrow \quad \alpha = -1 \quad$ ...(iv)

and $\beta - \alpha^2 - 9\alpha = 0$

$\Rightarrow \quad \beta = \alpha^2 + 9\alpha = (-1)^2 + 9(-1)$

$= 1 - 9 = -8$

$\therefore \quad \beta = -8$

5 (*d*) We know that,

$(I - 2A)^3 = (I - 2A)(I - 2A)(I - 2A)$

$= (I \cdot I - 2I \cdot A - 2A \cdot I + 4A \cdot A)(I - 2A)$

$= (I - 2A - 2A + 4A)(I - 2A)$ $[\because A^2 = A]$

$= I(I - 2A)$

$= I - 2A$

$\therefore \; A(I - 2A)^3 + 2A^3 = A(I - 2A) + 2A^2 \cdot A$

$= A \cdot I - 2A \cdot A + 2A \cdot A$

$= A - 2A^2 + 2A^2$

$= A$

6 (*a*) Let $A = \begin{bmatrix} 1 & 0 & 0 \\ 0 & 1 & 0 \\ 0 & 0 & 1 \end{bmatrix} = I$

Thus, A is identify matrix. Hence, it is scalar, diagonal and symmetric.

7 (*c*) We have, $P^2 = I - P \quad$ ...(i)

$\Rightarrow \quad P^4 = (I - P)^2 = I + P^2 - 2P$

$= 2I - 3P \quad$ [using Eq. (i)]

$\Rightarrow \quad P^8 = (2I - 3P)^2$

$= 4I + 9P^2 - 12P$

$= 13I - 21P \quad$ [using Eq. (i)]

and $P^6 = (I - P)(2I - 3P)$

$= 2I - 3P - 2P + 3P^2$

$= 5I - 8P \quad$ [using Eq. (i)]

Now, $P^8 + P^6 = 18I - 29P$

and $\quad P^8 - P^6 = 8I - 13P$

$\therefore \quad \alpha = 8, \beta = 6, \gamma = 18, \delta = 8$

$\therefore \; \alpha + \beta + \gamma - \delta = 8 + 6 + 18 - 8 = 24$

8 (c) Given,

$$A=\begin{bmatrix}1&1\\0&1\end{bmatrix},\quad P=\begin{bmatrix}\frac{\sqrt{3}}{2}&\frac{1}{2}\\\frac{-1}{2}&\frac{\sqrt{3}}{2}\end{bmatrix}$$

$$\Rightarrow A^2=\begin{bmatrix}1&2\\0&1\end{bmatrix},\quad P^T=\begin{bmatrix}\frac{\sqrt{3}}{2}&\frac{-1}{2}\\\frac{1}{2}&\frac{\sqrt{3}}{2}\end{bmatrix}$$

$$\Rightarrow A^3=\begin{bmatrix}1&2\\0&1\end{bmatrix}\begin{bmatrix}1&1\\0&1\end{bmatrix}=\begin{bmatrix}1&3\\0&1\end{bmatrix}$$

$$\therefore A^n=\begin{bmatrix}1&n\\0&1\end{bmatrix}$$

$$PP^T=\begin{bmatrix}\frac{\sqrt{3}}{2}&\frac{1}{2}\\\frac{-1}{2}&\frac{\sqrt{3}}{2}\end{bmatrix}\begin{bmatrix}\frac{\sqrt{3}}{2}&-\frac{1}{2}\\\frac{1}{2}&\frac{\sqrt{3}}{2}\end{bmatrix}$$

$$=\begin{bmatrix}1&0\\0&1\end{bmatrix}=I$$

Now, $\begin{bmatrix}a&b\\c&d\end{bmatrix}=P^TQ^{2007}P$

$$=P^T(PAP^T)(PAP^T)(PAP^T)\ldots(PAP^T)P$$

$$=IAIA\ldots IAI=A^{2007}$$

$$\Rightarrow\begin{bmatrix}a&b\\c&d\end{bmatrix}=\begin{bmatrix}1&2007\\0&1\end{bmatrix}\quad\left[\because A^n=\begin{bmatrix}1&n\\0&1\end{bmatrix}\right]$$

On comparing both sides, we get

$a=1, b=2007, c=0, d=1$

$\therefore\ 2a+b-3c-4d=2005$

9 (d) Given, $A=\begin{bmatrix}1\\1\\1\end{bmatrix}$

and $B=\begin{bmatrix}9^2&-10^2&11^2\\12^2&13^2&-14^2\\-15^2&16^2&17^2\end{bmatrix}$

Now, $A'BA=$

$$[1\ \ 1\ \ 1]\begin{bmatrix}81&-100&121\\144&169&-196\\-225&256&289\end{bmatrix}\begin{bmatrix}1\\1\\1\end{bmatrix}$$

$$=[1\ \ 1\ \ 1]\begin{bmatrix}81-100+121\\144+169-196\\-225+256+289\end{bmatrix}$$

$$=[1\ \ 1\ \ 1]\begin{bmatrix}102\\117\\320\end{bmatrix}=539$$

10 (c) Given, A and B are any two 3×3 symmetric and skew-symmetric matrix, respectively.

$\Rightarrow\ A^T=A, B^T=-B$

Let $C=A^4-B^4$.

$$C^T=(A^4-B^4)^T=(A^4)^T-(B^4)^T$$
$$=(A^T)^4-(B^T)^4=A^4-(-B)^4$$
$$[\because A^T=A \text{ and } B^T=-B]$$
$$=A^4-B^4\quad[\because(-B)^4=B^4]$$
$$=C$$

$\therefore$ C is a symmetric matrix.

Let $D=AB-BA$.

$$D^T=(AB-BA)^T=(AB)^T-(BA)^T$$
$$=B^TA^T-A^TB^T\quad[\because(AB)^T=B^TA^T]$$
$$=-BA+AB\quad[\because A^T=A \text{ and } B^T=-B]$$
$$=D$$

$\therefore$ D is a symmetric matrix.

Let $E=B^5-A^5$.

$$E^T=(B^5-A^5)^T=(B^5)^T-(A^5)^T$$
$$=(B^T)^5-(A^T)^5=(-B)^5-A^5$$
$$[\because A^T=A, B^T=-B]$$
$$=-B^5-A^5=-[B^5+A^5]\neq-E$$

$\therefore$ E is neither symmetric nor skew-symmetric matrix.

Let $F=AB+BA$.

$$F^T=(AB+BA)^T=(AB)^T+(BA)^T$$
$$=B^TA^T+A^TB^T=-BA-AB$$
$$=-(AB+BA)=-F$$

$\therefore$ F is a skew-symmetric matrix.

11 (24) Given, $A=\begin{bmatrix}1&a&a\\0&1&b\\0&0&1\end{bmatrix}, a, b\in R$

$$=\begin{bmatrix}1&0&0\\0&1&0\\0&0&1\end{bmatrix}+\begin{bmatrix}0&a&a\\0&0&b\\0&0&0\end{bmatrix}=I+B$$

where, $B=\begin{bmatrix}0&a&a\\0&0&b\\0&0&0\end{bmatrix}$

$$B^2=\begin{bmatrix}0&a&a\\0&0&b\\0&0&0\end{bmatrix}\begin{bmatrix}0&a&a\\0&0&b\\0&0&0\end{bmatrix}$$
$$=\begin{bmatrix}0&0&ab\\0&0&0\\0&0&0\end{bmatrix}$$

and $B^3=\begin{bmatrix}0&0&ab\\0&0&0\\0&0&0\end{bmatrix}\begin{bmatrix}0&a&a\\0&0&b\\0&0&0\end{bmatrix}$

$$=\begin{bmatrix}0&0&0\\0&0&0\\0&0&0\end{bmatrix}$$

Now, $A^n=(I+B)^n={}^nC_0I+{}^nC_1B+{}^nC_2B^2+{}^nC_3B^3+\ldots+{}^nC_nB^n$

$$=\begin{bmatrix}1&0&0\\0&1&0\\0&0&1\end{bmatrix}+\begin{bmatrix}0&na&na\\0&0&nb\\0&0&0\end{bmatrix}+\begin{bmatrix}0&0&\frac{n(n-1)}{2}ab\\0&0&0\\0&0&0\end{bmatrix}$$

$$=\begin{bmatrix}1&na&na+\frac{n(n-1)}{2}ab\\0&1&nb\\0&0&1\end{bmatrix}$$

$$=\begin{bmatrix}1&48&2160\\0&1&96\\0&0&1\end{bmatrix}\quad\text{[Given]}$$

Now, comparing above matrices, we get

$na=48$ and $nb=96$

and $na+\dfrac{n(n-1)ab}{2}=2160$

$\Rightarrow\ 48+48(n-1)a=2160$

$\Rightarrow\ 1+na-a=45$

$\Rightarrow\ a=4$

$\therefore\ n=12.$

Also, $nb=96\Rightarrow b=8$

$\therefore\ n+a+b=12+4+8=24$

12 (1) $M = \begin{bmatrix} 0 & -\alpha \\ \alpha & 0 \end{bmatrix}$

$$N = \sum_{k=1}^{49} M^{2k} \text{ and } (I - M^2)N = -2I$$

$$M^2 = \begin{bmatrix} 0 & -\alpha \\ \alpha & 0 \end{bmatrix}\begin{bmatrix} 0 & -\alpha \\ \alpha & 0 \end{bmatrix}$$

$$= \begin{bmatrix} -\alpha^2 & 0 \\ 0 & -\alpha^2 \end{bmatrix} = -\alpha^2 I$$

$$N = \sum_{k=1}^{49} M^{2k} = \sum_{k=1}^{49} (M^2)^k$$

$$= (M^2)^1 + (M^2)^2 + (M^2)^3 + \ldots + (M^2)^{49}$$

$$= [-\alpha^2 + \alpha^4 - \alpha^6 + \ldots . - \alpha^{98}] I$$

$$= -\frac{\alpha^2[1 - (-\alpha^2)^{49}]}{1 - (-\alpha^2)} I$$

$$= \frac{-\alpha^2[1 + \alpha^{98}]}{1 + \alpha^2} I$$

Given, $(I - M^2) N = -2I$

$$(1 + 2^2)\left[\frac{-\alpha^2(1 + \alpha^{98})}{(1 + \alpha^2)}\right] I = -2I$$

$$\Rightarrow \quad \alpha^2(1 + \alpha^{98}) = 2$$

$$\Rightarrow \quad \alpha^2 = 1 \Rightarrow \alpha = \pm 1$$

$$\therefore \quad \alpha = 1$$

Skill Boosters

1 (*d*) $BB^T = I = B^T B$.

Now, $\frac{1}{2} B[(B + B^T)^2 + (B - B^T)^2]$

$$= \frac{1}{2} B[(B + B^T)(B + B^T) + (B - B^T)(B - B^T)]$$

$$= \frac{B}{2}[B^2 + BB^T + B^T B + (B^T)^2 + B^2 + (B^T)^2 - B^T B - BB^T]$$

$$= \frac{B}{2}[2(B^2 + (B^T)^2] = B[B^2 + (B^T)^2]$$

$$= B^3 + B \cdot (B^T)^2 = B^3 + B \cdot B^T \cdot B^T$$

$$= B^3 + B^T$$

Hence, option (d) is correct.

2 (*b*)

I. Given, $P^T = P$, $Q^T = -Q$ and $R^T = -R$.

Let $A = P^{13} Q^{26} - Q^{26} P^{13}$

Then, $A^T = (P^{13} Q^{26} - Q^{26} P^{13})^T$

$$= (P^{13} Q^{26})^T - (Q^{26} P^{13})^T$$

$$= (Q^{26})^T (P^{13})^T - (P^{13})^T (Q^{26})^T$$

$$= (Q^T)^{26} (P^T)^{13} - (P^T)^{13} (Q^T)^{26}$$

$$= (-Q)^{26} P^{13} - (P)^{13} (Q^T)^{26}$$

$$= Q^{26} P^{13} - P^{13} Q^{26}$$

$$= -(P^{13} Q^{26} - Q^{26} P^{13})$$

$$\therefore A^T = -A$$

Hence, A is skew-symmetric.

II. Let $B = P^{26} R^{13} - R^{13} P^{26}$

Then, $B^T = (P^{26} R^{13} - R^{13} P^{26})^T$

$$= (P^{26} R^{13})^T - (R^{13} P^{26})^T$$

$$= (R^{13})^T (P^{26})^T - (P^{26})^T (R^{13})^T$$

$$= (R^T)^{13} (P^T)^{26} - (P^T)^{26} (R^T)^{13}$$

$$= (-R)^{13} P^{26} - P^{26}(-R^{13})$$

$$= -R^{13} P^{26} + P^{26} R^{13}$$

$$= P^{26} R^{13} - R^{13} P^{26} = B$$

$$\Rightarrow B^T = B$$

$\Rightarrow P^{26} R^{13} - R^{13} P^{26}$ is symmetric.

Hence, option (b) is correct.

3 (*a*) $A = \begin{bmatrix} 1/\sqrt{5} & 2/\sqrt{5} \\ -2/\sqrt{5} & 1/\sqrt{5} \end{bmatrix}$

$$AA^T = \begin{bmatrix} 1/\sqrt{5} & 2/\sqrt{5} \\ -2/\sqrt{5} & 1/\sqrt{5} \end{bmatrix}\begin{bmatrix} 1/\sqrt{5} & -2/\sqrt{5} \\ 2/\sqrt{5} & 1/\sqrt{5} \end{bmatrix}$$

$$= \begin{bmatrix} 1 & 0 \\ 0 & 1 \end{bmatrix}$$

$$B = \begin{bmatrix} 1 & -i \\ 0 & 1 \end{bmatrix}$$

$$B^2 = \begin{bmatrix} 1 & -i \\ 0 & 1 \end{bmatrix}\begin{bmatrix} 1 & -i \\ 0 & 1 \end{bmatrix} = \begin{bmatrix} 1 & -2i \\ 0 & 1 \end{bmatrix}$$

$$B^3 = \begin{bmatrix} 1 & -3i \\ 0 & 1 \end{bmatrix}$$

$$B^{2023} = \begin{bmatrix} 1 & -2023i \\ 0 & 1 \end{bmatrix}$$

$$P = A^T BA$$

$$P^2 = P \cdot P = (A^T BA)(A^T BA)$$

$$= A^T BAA^T BA = A^T B^2 A$$

$$P^3 = P^2 \cdot P = (A^T B^2 A)(A^T BA)$$

$$P^3 = A^T B^3 A$$

$$P^{2023} = A^T B^{2023} A$$

$$AP^{2023} A^T = AA^T B^{2023} AA^T$$

$$AP^{2023} A^T = B^{2023}$$

$$AP^{2023} A^T = \begin{bmatrix} 1 & -2023i \\ 0 & 1 \end{bmatrix}$$

Hence, option (a) is correct.

4 (*d*) $A = \begin{bmatrix} 1/\sqrt{2} & 1/\sqrt{2} \\ -1/\sqrt{2} & 1/\sqrt{2} \end{bmatrix}$

$$\Rightarrow A = \begin{bmatrix} \cos 45° & \sin 45° \\ -\sin 45° & \cos 45° \end{bmatrix}$$

If $A = \begin{bmatrix} \cos x & \sin x \\ -\sin x & \cos x \end{bmatrix}$, then $x = \frac{\pi}{4}$.

$$A^2 = \begin{bmatrix} \cos x & \sin x \\ -\sin x & \cos x \end{bmatrix}\begin{bmatrix} \cos x & \sin x \\ -\sin x & \cos x \end{bmatrix}$$

$$A^2 = \begin{bmatrix} \cos 2x & \sin 2x \\ -\sin 2x & \cos 2x \end{bmatrix}$$

$$\Rightarrow A^{28} = \begin{bmatrix} \cos 28x & \sin 28x \\ -\sin 28x & \cos 28x \end{bmatrix}$$

$$= \begin{bmatrix} \cos 28 \times \frac{\pi}{4} & \sin 28 \times \frac{\pi}{4} \\ -\sin 28 \times \frac{\pi}{4} & \cos 28 \times \frac{\pi}{4} \end{bmatrix}$$

$$= \begin{bmatrix} -1 & 0 \\ 0 & -1 \end{bmatrix}$$

$$A^{20} = \begin{bmatrix} -1 & 0 \\ 0 & -1 \end{bmatrix}; A^{28} - A^{20} = \begin{bmatrix} 0 & 0 \\ 0 & 0 \end{bmatrix}$$

So, option (a) is incorrect.

$$A^{16} - A^9 = \begin{bmatrix} 1 & 0 \\ 0 & 1 \end{bmatrix} - \begin{bmatrix} 1/\sqrt{2} & 1/\sqrt{2} \\ -1/\sqrt{2} & 1/\sqrt{2} \end{bmatrix}$$

$$= \begin{bmatrix} 1 - 1/\sqrt{2} & -1/\sqrt{2} \\ 1/\sqrt{2} & 1 - 1/\sqrt{2} \end{bmatrix} \neq I$$

Hence, option (b) is incorrect.

$A^{16} \neq A^{20}$, option (c) is incorrect.

$$A^{16} = \begin{bmatrix} 1 & 0 \\ 0 & 1 \end{bmatrix} - \begin{bmatrix} 1 & 0 \\ 0 & 1 \end{bmatrix} = \begin{bmatrix} 0 & 0 \\ 0 & 0 \end{bmatrix}$$

Hence, option (d) is correct.

5 (*d*) $B = \text{diag}(d_1, d_2, \ldots d_n)$

Given, $B^3 = B$.

$\Rightarrow \text{diag}(d_1^3, d_2^3, \ldots d_n^3) = \text{diag}(d_1, d_2, \ldots d_n)$

$\Rightarrow d_1^3 = d_1, d_2^3 = d_2, \ldots d_n^3 = d_n$

Hence, all $d_1, d_2, \ldots d_n$ have 3 possible values $\pm 1, 0$. Each diagonal element can be selected in three ways. Hence, the number of different matrices is 3^n.

Hence, option (d) is correct.

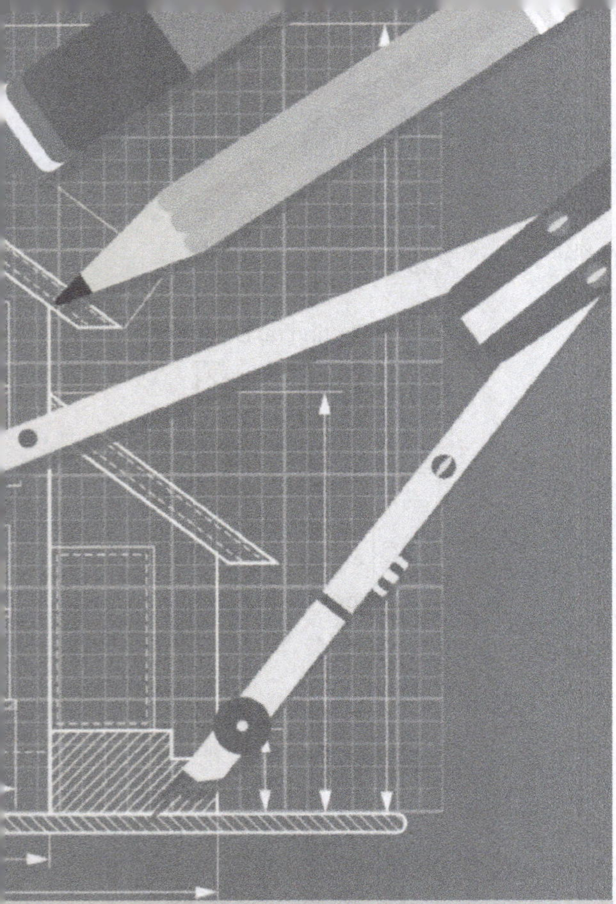

04

Determinants

Topicwise Number of Ques asked in 3 Years (JEE Main)

Topics	Number of Questions		
	2024	2023	2022
Determinant	4	5	4
Area of Triangle	–	–	–
Minors and Cofactors	2	1	1
Adjoint and Inverse of a Matrix	7	10	6
Application of Determinants and Matrices	10	12	10

Special Type of Ques Asked in 3 Years (JEE Main)

Types	Years		
	2024	2023	2022
A-R	–	–	–
Statement Based	1	–	–
Numerical Value Type	6	4	3

Last 3 Years Weightage (JEE Main)

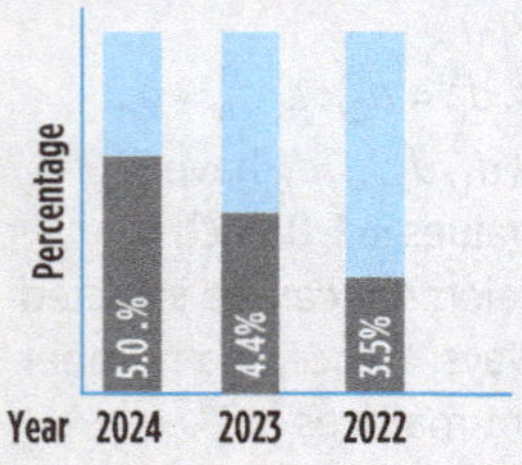

Determinant

Every square matrix A of order n is associated with a number, called its determinant and it is denoted by det(A) or $|A|$.

Determinant of Matrix of Order 1

Let $A = [a]$ be a square matrix of order 1, then $|A| = |a| = a$ i.e. element itself is the determinant.

Determinant of Matrix of Order 2

$$\det(A) \text{ or } |A| = \begin{vmatrix} a_{11} & a_{12} \\ a_{21} & a_{22} \end{vmatrix} = a_{11}a_{22} - a_{12}a_{21}$$

Determinant of Matrix of Order 3

$$\det(A) = |A| = \begin{vmatrix} a_{11} & a_{12} & a_{13} \\ a_{21} & a_{22} & a_{23} \\ a_{31} & a_{32} & a_{33} \end{vmatrix}$$

$$= a_{11}(a_{22}a_{33} - a_{32}a_{23}) - a_{12}(a_{21}a_{33} - a_{31}a_{23}) + a_{13}(a_{21}a_{32} - a_{31}a_{22}) \text{ [expanding along } R_1]$$

Note *We can expand the above determinant corresponding to any row or column. If A is $n \times n$ matrix, then $|kA| = k^n|A|$.* **[JEE Main 2023]**

Area of Triangle

Let $A(x_1, y_1)$, $B(x_2, y_2)$ and $C(x_3, y_3)$ be the vertices of a ΔABC. Then, its area is given by

$$\Delta = \frac{1}{2}\left\| \begin{matrix} x_1 & y_1 & 1 \\ x_2 & y_2 & 1 \\ x_3 & y_3 & 1 \end{matrix} \right\| = \frac{1}{2} \cdot |[x_1(y_2 - y_3) + x_2(y_3 - y_1) + x_3(y_1 - y_2)]|$$

Note
- *Area is a positive quantity. So, we always take the absolute value of the determinant.*
- *If area is given, then use both positive and negative values of the determinant for calculation.*

Condition of Collinearity for Three Points

Three points $A(x_1, y_1)$, $B(x_2, y_2)$ and $C(x_3, y_3)$ are collinear if and only if the area of triangle formed by these three points is zero

i.e. $$\begin{vmatrix} x_1 & y_1 & 1 \\ x_2 & y_2 & 1 \\ x_3 & y_3 & 1 \end{vmatrix} = 0$$

Marks Maximizer

- If any two rows or columns of a determinant are identical (all corresponding elements are same), then the value of determinant is zero.
- The determinant of triangular, diagonal, scalar and identity matrices is equal to the product of its diagonal entries.
- **Some special determinants**

(i) $$\begin{vmatrix} 1 & x & x^2 \\ 1 & y & y^2 \\ 1 & z & z^2 \end{vmatrix} = (x-y)(y-z)(z-x)$$

(ii) $$\begin{vmatrix} 1 & x & x^3 \\ 1 & y & y^3 \\ 1 & z & z^3 \end{vmatrix} = (x-y)(y-z)(z-x)(x+y+z)$$

(iii) $$\begin{vmatrix} 1 & x^2 & x^3 \\ 1 & y^2 & y^3 \\ 1 & z^2 & z^3 \end{vmatrix} = (x-y)(y-z)(z-x)(xy+yz+zx)$$

- A skew-symmetric matrix ($a_{ij} = -a_{ji}$) of odd order has determinant value zero.
- Cyclic determinant

$$\Delta = \begin{vmatrix} a & b & c \\ b & c & a \\ c & a & b \end{vmatrix}$$
$$= -(a+b+c)(a^2+b^2+c^2-ab-bc-ca)$$
$$= 3abc - a^3 - b^3 - c^3$$
$$= -(a+b+c)\frac{1}{2}[(a-b)^2+(b-c)^2+(c-a)^2]$$

If a, b, c are not equal, then
  - if $a+b+c>0$, then $\Delta<0$.
  - if $a+b+c<0$, then $\Delta>0$.

- If $z_1 = x_1 + iy_1$, $z_2 = x_2 + iy_2$ and $z_3 = x_3 + iy_3$ are three complex numbers then the condition for three complex numbers to be collinear is

$$\begin{vmatrix} z_1 & \bar{z}_1 & 1 \\ z_2 & \bar{z}_2 & 1 \\ z_3 & \bar{z}_3 & 1 \end{vmatrix} = 0$$

Minors and Cofactors

Minors

Concept Master Video

Minor of an element a_{ij} of a determinant is the determinant obtained by deleting ith row and jth column in which element a_{ij} lies. It is denoted by M_{ij}.

e.g. If $A = \begin{vmatrix} a_{11} & a_{12} & a_{13} \\ a_{21} & a_{22} & a_{23} \\ a_{31} & a_{32} & a_{33} \end{vmatrix}$, then minor of elements of A are

$$M_{11} = \begin{vmatrix} a_{22} & a_{23} \\ a_{32} & a_{33} \end{vmatrix}, M_{12} = \begin{vmatrix} a_{21} & a_{23} \\ a_{31} & a_{33} \end{vmatrix} \text{ and } M_{13} = \begin{vmatrix} a_{21} & a_{22} \\ a_{31} & a_{32} \end{vmatrix}, \text{ etc.}$$

Note *The minor of an element of a matrix of order n $(n \geq 2)$ is a determinant of order $n-1$.*

Cofactors

If M_{ij} is the minor of an element a_{ij}, then the cofactor of a_{ij} is denoted by C_{ij} or A_{ij} and defined as follows

$$A_{ij} \text{ or } C_{ij} = (-1)^{i+j} M_{ij}$$ **[JEE Main 2024]**

Note *If elements of a row (column) are multiplied with cofactors of any other row (column), then their sum is zero.*

Adjoint and Inverse of a Matrix

Singular and Non-singular Matrices

A square matrix A is said to be a singular matrix, if $|A| = 0$ and if $|A| \neq 0$, then matrix A is said to be non-singular matrix. **[JEE Main 2024]**

Adjoint of a Matrix

The adjoint of a square matrix A is defined as the transpose of the matrix formed by cofactors of elements of A.

Let $A = [a_{ij}]_{n \times n}$ be a square matrix, then adjoint of A

i.e. $\text{adj}(A) = C^T$,

where, $C = [c_{ij}]$ is the cofactor matrix of A.

Properties of Adjoint of Square Matrix

[JEE Main 2024, 23, 22]

If A and B are two square matrices of order n, then

(i) $\text{adj}(A^T) = (\text{adj } A)^T$

(ii) $\text{adj}(kA) = k^{n-1}(\text{adj } A), k \in R$

(iii) $(\text{adj } AB) = (\text{adj } B)(\text{adj } A)$

(iv) $|\text{adj } A| = |A|^{n-1}$, if $|A| \neq 0$

(v) $|\text{adj}[\text{adj}(A)]| = |A|^{(n-1)^2}$, if $|A| \neq 0$

(vi) $\text{adj}(\text{adj } A) = |A|^{n-2} \cdot A$

Inverse of a Matrix

Suppose A is a non-zero square matrix of order n and there exists matrix B of same order n such that $AB = BA = I_n$, then such matrix B is called an inverse of matrix A. It is denoted by A^{-1} and is given by $A^{-1} = \frac{1}{|A|}[\text{adj}(A)]$.

Properties of Inverse of a Matrix [JEE Main 2024]

(i) $(A^{-1})^{-1} = A$ (ii) $(AB)^{-1} = B^{-1}A^{-1}$

(iii) $(A^T)^{-1} = (A^{-1})^T$ (iv) $|A^{-1}| = |A|^{-1}$

(v) $AA^{-1} = A^{-1}A = I$

(vi) $(kA)^{-1} = \frac{1}{k}A^{-1}$, where $k \neq 0$

Application of Determinants and Matrices

Solution of System of Linear Equations by Inverse of a Matrix (or by Matrix Method)

Let the system of linear equations be

$$a_1x + b_1y + c_1z = d_1,\ a_2x + b_2y + c_2z = d_2$$

and $\quad a_3x + b_3y + c_3z = d_3$.

If $d_1 = d_2 = d_3 = 0$, then system of equation is called a system of homogeneous linear equations and if atleast one of d_1, d_2 and d_3 is non-zero, then it is called a system of non-homogeneous linear equations.

We can write the above system of linear equations in matrix form as $AX = B$, where

$$A = \begin{bmatrix} a_1 & b_1 & c_1 \\ a_2 & b_2 & c_2 \\ a_3 & b_3 & c_3 \end{bmatrix}, X = \begin{bmatrix} x \\ y \\ z \end{bmatrix} \text{ and } B = \begin{bmatrix} d_1 \\ d_2 \\ d_3 \end{bmatrix}$$

$$\Rightarrow \quad X = A^{-1}B = \frac{(\text{adj}\,A)\,B}{|A|}$$

(1) **When system of equations is non-homogeneous**

(i) If $|A| \neq 0$, then the system of equations is consistent and has a unique solution given by $X = A^{-1}B$.

(ii) If $|A| = 0$ and $(\text{adj}A) \cdot B \neq O$, then the system of equations is inconsistent and has no solution.

(iii) If $|A| = 0$ and $(\text{adj}A) \cdot B = O$, then the system of equations is consistent and has an infinite number of solutions.

(2) **When system of equations is homogeneous**

(i) If $|A| \neq 0$, then the system of equations has only trivial solution and it has one solution.

(ii) If $|A| = 0$, then the system of equations has non-trivial solution and it has infinite solutions.

(iii) If number of equations < number of unknowns, then it has non-trivial solution.

Marks Maximizer

- **Summation of determinants** (when one row or column elements are functions of r).

Let $\Delta(r) = \begin{vmatrix} f_1(r) & f_2(r) & f_3(r) \\ a & b & c \\ d & e & f \end{vmatrix}$, where $f_1(r), f_2(r)$ and $f_3(r)$ are functions of r and a, b, c, d, e and f are constants.

Then, $\sum_{r=1}^{n} \Delta(r) = \begin{vmatrix} \sum_{r=1}^{n} f_1(r) & \sum_{r=1}^{n} f_2(r) & \sum_{r=1}^{n} f_3(r) \\ a & b & c \\ d & e & f \end{vmatrix}$

[JEE Main 2024]

- If the elements of more than one column or row are functions of r, then summation can be done only after expansion of the determinant.

Caution Points

- For square matrix A, $|A|$ is read as determinant of A and not modulus of A.
- Determinant is defined only for square matrices.
- We prefer to expand the determinant along the row or column with the most zeroes.
- We can expand a determinant in 6 ways, 3 along rows and 3 along columns.

PYQ Notes

1. If A and B are square matrices of same order, then

$$|A^n| = |A|^n$$
$$|AB| = |A|\,|B|$$ [JEE Main 2024]

2. The characteristic equation of any square matrix A is $|A - \lambda I| = 0$ and for 2×2 square matrix, the characteristic equation can also be written as $\lambda^2 - (\text{trace of } A)\lambda + |A| = 0$. [JEE Main 2024, 22]

Step by Step

Mastering NCERT

- Concept Builders
- Topical Questions
- Numerical Type Questions
- Assertion and Reason Questions
- Case or Paragraph Type Questions
- Past Years Questions
- Skill Boosters

Concept Builders

1 If A is 3×3 scalar matrix and a_{11} element = 2, then $|A| =$

2 If $|PQ| = 5$, then find $|Q^T P|$.

3 If $|A| = 5$, then $|A^{-1}| =$ ....

4 $\det(A^n) = (\det(A))^n$. (T/F)

5 Let P and Q be the matrices of order 2×2 and $|P| = -1$ and $|Q| = 2$. Then, find $|2PQ^{-1}|$.

6 Let A be 2×2 matrix and $|A| = 3$. Then, $|\text{adj } A| =$ ....

7 $\det(PQ) = \det(QP) = \det(Q^T P)$. (T/F)

8 If $|A| = 2$, then $|A^T| =$ ....

9 Let A be 3×3 upper triangular matrix whose diagonal entries are $(1, -1, 2)$. Then, $|A| =$ ....

10 Let A be 3×3 matrix and $|A| = -1$. Then, $|2A| =$ ....

11 A matrix whose determinant is equal to zero. Then, given matrix is known as ......

12 If A is any triangular matrix, then (adj A) is ......

13 Let A be a matrix of order 2 whose determinant is 3. Then, $|(2A)^{-1}| =$ ....

14 For a square matrix A in matrix equation $AX = B$, if $|A| = 0$ and (adj $A)B \neq 0$, then given system is ...... (consistent/inconsistent).

15 $(kA)^{-1} = \frac{1}{k} A^{-1}$, where k is any real number and $k \neq 0$. (T/F)

16 Let A be any diagonal matrix of order 3 and whose diagonal entries are $1, -1$ and 2. Then $|A| =$ ....

17 If A is singular matrix, then $|\text{adj } A| =$ ....

18 If A is any $n \times n$ matrix, then $|\text{adj (adj } (A))| =$ ....

19 $(ABCD)^{-1} = C^{-1}D^{-1}B^{-1}A^{-1}$. (T/F)

20 $(A^T)^{-1} =$ ...... $(A^{-T} / (A^{-1})^T)$

Topical Questions

Determinant

Level I

1 Consider the following statements

I. To every rectangular matrix $A = [a_{ij}]$ of order $m \times n$, we can associate a number (real or complex) called determinant of A.

II. Determinant is a function which associates each square matrix with a unique number (real or complex).

Choose the correct option **NCERT Pg. 76**

(a) Only I is true (b) Only II is true
(c) Both I and II are true (d) Neither I nor II is true

2 If M is the set of square matrices, K is the set of numbers (real or complex) and $f : M \longrightarrow K$ is defined by $f(A) = k$, where $A \in M$ and $k \in K$, then $f(A)$ is called **NCERT Pg. 77**

(a) determinant of A (b) matrix A
(c) square matrix A
(d) determinant of rectangular matrix A

3 Let $A = [a]$ be the matrix of order 1, then determinant of A is equal to **NCERT Pg. 77**

(a) $-a$ (b) a (c) a^n (d) a^2

4 If $A = \begin{bmatrix} a_{11} & a_{12} \\ a_{21} & a_{22} \end{bmatrix}$ is a matrix of order 2×2, then $|A|$ is equal to **NCERT Pg. 77**

(a) $a_{11}a_{22} - a_{12}a_{21}$ (b) $a_{11}a_{12} - a_{21}a_{22}$
(c) $a_{11}a_{21} - a_{12}a_{22}$ (d) $a_{11}a_{22} + a_{12}a_{21}$

5 The value of the determinant $\begin{vmatrix} x & x+1 \\ x-1 & x \end{vmatrix}$ is **NCERT Pg. 77**

(a) 1 (b) -1 (c) 2 (d) 0

6 Determinant of a matrix of order 3 can be determined by expressing it in terms of ...A... order determinants. This is known as expansion of a determinant along a row (or column). Here, A refers to **NCERT Pg. 77**

(a) first (b) second
(c) third (d) None of these

7 In how many ways, the determinant of order 3 can be expanded? NCERT Pg. 77

(a) 5 (b) 4 (c) 3 (d) 6

8 The value of determinant of a square matrix

$$A = [a_{ij}]_{3\times 3} = \begin{bmatrix} a_{11} & a_{12} & a_{13} \\ a_{21} & a_{22} & a_{23} \\ a_{31} & a_{32} & a_{33} \end{bmatrix} \text{ is}$$

NCERT Pg. 80

(a) $a_{11}a_{22}a_{33} - a_{11}a_{32}a_{23} - a_{12}a_{31}a_{23} + a_{12}a_{21}a_{33} + a_{13}a_{21}a_{32} - a_{13}a_{31}a_{22}$

(b) $a_{11}a_{22}a_{33} - a_{11}a_{32}a_{23} - a_{12}a_{21}a_{33} + a_{13}a_{31}a_{22} - a_{12}a_{31}a_{23} + a_{13}a_{21}a_{32}$

(c) $a_{11}a_{22}a_{33} - a_{11}a_{32}a_{23} - a_{12}a_{21}a_{33} + a_{12}a_{31}a_{23} + a_{13}a_{21}a_{32} - a_{13}a_{31}a_{22}$

(d) $a_{11}a_{32}a_{23} - a_{11}a_{22}a_{33} - a_{12}a_{21}a_{33} + a_{12}a_{31}a_{23} + a_{13}a_{21}a_{32} - a_{13}a_{31}a_{22}$

9 While expanding the determinant, instead of multiplying by $(-1)^{i+j}$, we can multiply by +1 or −1 according as $i + j$ is NCERT Pg. 80

(a) odd or even (b) even or odd

(c) even (d) odd

10 If $A = \begin{bmatrix} 2 & 2 \\ 4 & 0 \end{bmatrix}$ and $B = \begin{bmatrix} 1 & 1 \\ 2 & 0 \end{bmatrix}$, then NCERT Pg. 80

(a) $|A| = |B|$ (b) $|A| = 2|B|$

(c) $|A| = 2^2|B|$ (d) $|A| = -|B|$

11 If $A = kB$, where A and B are square matrices of order n, then for $n = 1, 2, 3,$ NCERT Pg. 80

(a) $|A| = k|B|$ (b) $|A| = nk|B|$

(c) $|A| = n + k|B|$ (d) $|A| = k^n|B|$

12 The value of the determinant $\Delta = \begin{vmatrix} 1 & 2 & 4 \\ -1 & 3 & 0 \\ 4 & 1 & 0 \end{vmatrix}$ is NCERT Pg. 80

(a) − 52 (b) 52 (c) 44 (d) − 44

13 If $\Delta = \begin{vmatrix} 0 & \sin\alpha & -\cos\alpha \\ -\sin\alpha & 0 & \sin\beta \\ \cos\alpha & -\sin\beta & 0 \end{vmatrix}$, then Δ is equal to NCERT Pg. 80

(a) −1 (b) 1 (c) 0 (d) −2

14 Match the terms of column I with the terms of column II and choose the correct option from the codes given below. NCERT Pg. 81

	Column I	Column II
A.	$\begin{vmatrix} 2 & 4 \\ -5 & -1 \end{vmatrix}$	1. 1
B.	$\begin{vmatrix} \cos\theta & -\sin\theta \\ \sin\theta & \cos\theta \end{vmatrix}$	2. $x^3 - x^2 + 2$
C.	$\begin{vmatrix} x^2 - x + 1 & x - 1 \\ x + 1 & x + 1 \end{vmatrix}$	3. 18

Codes

	A	B	C		A	B	C
(a)	3	1	2	(b)	2	1	3
(c)	1	3	2	(d)	3	2	1

15 If $A = \begin{bmatrix} 1 & 2 \\ 4 & 2 \end{bmatrix}$, then $|2A|$ is equal to NCERT Pg. 81

(a) $2|A|$ (b) $6|A|$

(c) $4|A|$ (d) $-2|A|$

16 If $A = \begin{bmatrix} 1 & 0 & 1 \\ 0 & 1 & 2 \\ 0 & 0 & 4 \end{bmatrix}$, then $|3A|$ is equal to NCERT Pg. 81

(a) $6|A|$ (b) $3|A|$

(c) $9|A|$ (d) $27|A|$

17 Match the terms of column I with the terms of column II and choose the correct option from the codes given below. NCERT Pg. 81

	Column I	Column II
A.	$\begin{vmatrix} 3 & -1 & -2 \\ 0 & 0 & -1 \\ 3 & -5 & 0 \end{vmatrix}$	1. 0
B.	$\begin{vmatrix} 3 & -4 & 5 \\ 1 & 1 & -2 \\ 2 & 3 & 1 \end{vmatrix}$	2. 5
C.	$\begin{vmatrix} 0 & 1 & 2 \\ -1 & 0 & -3 \\ -2 & 3 & 0 \end{vmatrix}$	3. −12
D.	$\begin{vmatrix} 2 & -1 & -2 \\ 0 & 2 & -1 \\ 3 & -5 & 0 \end{vmatrix}$	4. 46

Codes

	A	B	C	D		A	B	C	D
(a)	2	1	3	4	(b)	4	3	1	2
(c)	3	4	2	1	(d)	3	4	1	2

18 If $A = \begin{bmatrix} 1 & 1 & -2 \\ 2 & 1 & -3 \\ 5 & 4 & -9 \end{bmatrix}$, then $|A|$ is equal to NCERT Pg. 82

(a) 0 (b) 6 (c) 3 (d) − 3

19 If $\begin{vmatrix} 2 & 4 \\ 5 & 1 \end{vmatrix} = \begin{vmatrix} 2x & 4 \\ 6 & x \end{vmatrix}$, then the value(s) of x is/are NCERT Pg. 82

(a) $\pm\sqrt{3}$ (b) ±3 (c) 3 (d) $\pm 3\sqrt{3}$

20 If $\begin{vmatrix} 2 & 3 \\ 4 & 5 \end{vmatrix} = \begin{vmatrix} x & 3 \\ 2x & 5 \end{vmatrix}$, then the value(s) of x is/are NCERT Pg. 82

(a) ±2 (b) 2

(c) −2 (d) $\pm\sqrt{2}$

Level II

21 The value of the determinant $\begin{vmatrix} x^2+xy+y^2 & x+y \\ x^2-xy+y^2 & x-y \end{vmatrix}$ is NCERT Pg. 81

(a) $2y^3$ (b) $-2y^3$ (c) $2y^2$ (d) $-2y^2$

22 If $\Delta = \begin{vmatrix} 1 & \log_b a \\ \log_a b & 1 \end{vmatrix}$, then Δ is equal to NCERT Pg. 77

(a) 1 (b) -1 (c) 0 (d) 2

23 Evaluate $\Delta = \begin{vmatrix} 2 & 3 & -2 \\ 1 & 2 & 3 \\ -2 & 1 & -3 \end{vmatrix}$. NCERT Pg. 78

(a) -37 (b) 37 (c) 26 (d) -26

24 Consider the following statements

I. Matrix cannot be reduced to a number.

II. Determinant can be reduced to a number.

Choose the correct option NCERT Pg. 76

(a) Only I is true (b) Only II is true
(c) Both I and II are true (d) Neither I nor II is true

25 The determinant $\begin{vmatrix} x & \sin\theta & \cos\theta \\ -\sin\theta & -x & 1 \\ \cos\theta & 1 & x \end{vmatrix}$ is NCERT Pg. 99

(a) independent of θ only
(b) independent of x only
(c) independent of both θ and x
(d) None of the above

26 The value of $\begin{vmatrix} \sin 10° & -\cos 10° \\ \sin 80° & \cos 80° \end{vmatrix}$ is NCERT Pg. 77

(a) -1 (b) 1 (c) 2 (d) 0

27 If $\Delta = \begin{vmatrix} a+ib & c+id \\ -c+id & a-ib \end{vmatrix}$, then Δ is equal to NCERT Pg. 77

(a) $a^2+b^2+c^2+d^2$ (b) $a^2-b^2-c^2-d^2$
(c) $a^2-b^2+c^2-d^2$ (d) $a^2-b^2-c^2+d^2$

28 If $\begin{vmatrix} x & 2 \\ 18 & x \end{vmatrix} = \begin{vmatrix} 6 & 2 \\ 18 & 6 \end{vmatrix}$, then x is equal to NCERT Pg. 81

(a) 6 (b) ± 6
(c) -6 (d) 0

Area of Triangle

Level I

1 The area of a triangle whose vertices are $(x_1, y_1), (x_2, y_2)$ and (x_3, y_3), is NCERT Pg. 82

(a) $\frac{1}{2}|x_1(y_2-y_1)+x_2(y_3-y_2)+x_3(y_1-y_3)|$
(b) $\frac{1}{2}|x_1(y_2-y_3)+x_2(y_3-y_1)+x_3(y_1-y_2)|$
(c) $|x_1(y_2-y_3)+x_2(y_3-y_1)+x_3(y_1-y_2)|$
(d) $2|x_1(y_2-y_3)+x_2(y_3-y_1)+x_3(y_1-y_2)|$

2 The area of triangle with vertices (x_1, y_1), (x_2, y_2) and (x_3, y_3) in the form of a determinant is NCERT Pg. 82

(a) $\Delta = \frac{1}{2}\begin{vmatrix} x_1 & y_1 & 1 \\ x_2 & y_2 & 1 \\ x_3 & y_3 & 1 \end{vmatrix}$ (b) $\Delta = \frac{1}{2}\begin{vmatrix} x_1 & y_1 & 1 \\ y_1 & y_2 & 1 \\ x_3 & y_3 & 1 \end{vmatrix}$

(c) $\Delta = \begin{vmatrix} x_1 & y_1 & 1 \\ x_2 & y_2 & 1 \\ x_3 & y_3 & 1 \end{vmatrix}$ (d) None of these

3 The area of the triangle formed by three collinear points is NCERT Pg. 82

(a) 1 (b) 2 (c) 0 (d) 4

4 The area of the triangle, whose vertices are (3, 8), (−4, 2) and (5, 1), is NCERT Pg. 82

(a) 60 (b) 61 (c) $\frac{61}{2}$ (d) 30

5 If the area of a ΔABD is 3 sq units with vertices A (1, 3), B (0, 0) and D $(k, 0)$, then k is equal to NCERT Pg. 83

(a) 3 (b) ± 3
(c) 2 (d) ± 2

6 Match the terms of column I with the terms of column II and choose the correct option from the codes given below. NCERT Pg. 83

Column I (Vertices)		Column II (Area of triangle)
A. (1, 0), (6, 0), (4, 3)	1.	15
B. (2, 7), (1, 1), (10, 8)	2.	0
C. (−2, −3), (3, 2), (− 1, −8)	3.	$\frac{47}{2}$
	4.	$\frac{15}{2}$

Codes

	A	B	C		A	B	C
(a)	2	1	3	(b)	4	3	1
(c)	4	1	3	(d)	3	1	2

7 The equation of line joining (1, 2) and (3, 6) is NCERT Pg. 83

(a) $y = 4x$ (b) $x = 4y$
(c) $x = 2y$ (d) $y = 2x$

8 The equation of line joining (3, 1) and (9, 3) is NCERT Pg. 83

(a) $x = 3y$ (b) $y = 3x$
(c) $x = y + 3$ (d) $y = x + 3$

9 If area of triangle is 4 sq units with vertices $(k, 0)$, $(4, 0)$ and $(0, 2)$, then values of k are NCERT Pg. 83

(a) 0, 8 (b) 0, –8 (c) 0, 6 (d) 0, –6

Level II

10 Area of the triangle whose vertices are $(a, b+c)$, $(b, c+a)$ and $(c, a+b)$, is NCERT Pg. 83

(a) 2 sq units (b) 3 sq units
(c) zero (d) None of these

11 If the points (a_1, b_1), (a_2, b_2) and (a_1+a_2, b_1+b_2) are collinear, then NCERT Pg. 83

(a) $a_1b_1 = a_2b_2$ (b) $a_1b_2 = a_2b_1$
(c) $a_1a_2 = b_1b_2$ (d) $a_1 - b_2 = a_2 - b_1$

12 The area of a triangle with vertices $(-3, 0)$, $(3, 0)$ and $(0, k)$ is 9 sq units. Then the value of k will be NCERT Exemplar Pg. 80

(a) 9 (b) 3 (c) –9 (d) 6

13 If the points $(2, -3)$, $(\lambda, -1)$ and $(0, 4)$ are collinear, then the value of λ is NCERT Pg. 83

(a) $\frac{-10}{7}$ (b) $\frac{10}{7}$ (c) $\frac{2}{7}$ (d) $\frac{7}{2}$

Minors and Cofactors

Level I

1 Minor of an element of a determinant of order $n (n \geq 2)$ is a determinant of order NCERT Pg. 84

(a) n (b) $n-1$ (c) $n-2$ (d) $n+1$

2 The minor of element 6 in the determinant $\Delta = \begin{vmatrix} 1 & 2 & 3 \\ 4 & 5 & 6 \\ 7 & 8 & 9 \end{vmatrix}$ is NCERT Pg. 84

(a) –6 (b) 6 (c) 22 (d) –22

3 Cofactor of an element a_{ij}, denoted by A_{ij} is equal to NCERT Pg. 84

(a) M_{ij} (b) $(-1) M_{ij}$
(c) $(-1) M_{ji}$ (d) $(-1)^{i+j} M_{ij}$

4 For $\Delta = \begin{vmatrix} a_{11} & a_{12} & a_{13} \\ a_{21} & a_{22} & a_{23} \\ a_{31} & a_{32} & a_{33} \end{vmatrix}$, if $\Delta = a_{11}A_{21} + a_{12}A_{22} + a_{13}A_{23}$, where A_{ij} is a cofactor of a_{ij}, then Δ is equal to NCERT Pg. 85

(a) 1 (b) –1 (c) 0 (d) 2

5 Consider the following statements

I. For $\Delta = \begin{vmatrix} 2 & -4 \\ 0 & 3 \end{vmatrix}$, $A_{11} = 3$, $A_{12} = 0$, $A_{21} = 4$ and $A_{22} = 2$.

II. For $\Delta = \begin{vmatrix} a & c \\ b & d \end{vmatrix}$, $A_{11} = d$, $A_{12} = -b$, $A_{21} = -c$ and $A_{22} = a$.

Choose the correct option NCERT Pg. 87

(a) Only I is true (b) Only II is true
(c) Both I and II are true (d) Neither I nor II is true

6 If $\Delta = \begin{vmatrix} 1 & 0 & 0 \\ 0 & 1 & 0 \\ 0 & 0 & 1 \end{vmatrix}$, then NCERT Pg. 87

(a) $M_{23} = 0, A_{13} = 0, A_{33} = 1$
(b) $M_{21} = 0, M_{22} = -1, A_{31} = 0$
(c) $M_{11} = -1, A_{12} = 0, A_{32} = 0$
(d) $M_{22} = -1, A_{11} = -1, A_{31} = 1$

7 If $\Delta = \begin{vmatrix} 1 & 0 & 4 \\ 3 & 5 & -1 \\ 0 & 1 & 2 \end{vmatrix}$, then NCERT Pg. 87

(a) $A_{11} = -11, A_{22} = 2, A_{31} = 20$
(b) $M_{21} = 6, M_{12} = 6, M_{31} = 20$
(c) $A_{33} = 5, A_{21} = 4, A_{13} = 3$
(d) $M_{11} = -11, M_{22} = 2, M_{32} = 13$

8 The value of $\Delta = \begin{vmatrix} 5 & 3 & 8 \\ 2 & 0 & 1 \\ 1 & 2 & 3 \end{vmatrix}$ using cofactors of elements of second row is NCERT Pg. 87

(a) –14 (b) 14
(c) –7 (d) 7

9 The value of $\Delta = \begin{vmatrix} 1 & x & yz \\ 1 & y & zx \\ 1 & z & xy \end{vmatrix}$ using cofactors of elements of third column is NCERT Pg. 87

(a) 0 (b) $(x-y)(y-z)(z-x)$
(c) $x+y+z$ (d) xyz

10 If $\Delta = \begin{vmatrix} a_{11} & a_{12} & a_{13} \\ a_{21} & a_{22} & a_{23} \\ a_{31} & a_{32} & a_{33} \end{vmatrix}$ and A_{ij} is cofactor of a_{ij}, then value of Δ is NCERT Pg. 87

(a) $a_{11}A_{31} + a_{12}A_{32} + a_{13}A_{33}$
(b) $a_{11}A_{11} + a_{12}A_{21} + a_{13}A_{31}$
(c) $a_{21}A_{11} + a_{22}A_{12} + a_{23}A_{13}$
(d) $a_{11}A_{11} + a_{21}A_{21} + a_{31}A_{31}$

Level II

11 If $M_{11} = -40$, $M_{12} = -10$ and $M_{13} = 35$ of the determinant $\Delta = \begin{vmatrix} 1 & 3 & -2 \\ 4 & -5 & 6 \\ 3 & 5 & 2 \end{vmatrix}$, then the value of Δ is NCERT Pg. 87

(a) –80 (b) 60
(c) 70 (d) 100

12 If $\Delta = \begin{vmatrix} a & h & g \\ h & b & f \\ g & f & c \end{vmatrix}$, then the cofactor A_{21} is NCERT Pg. 87

(a) $-(hc+fg)$ (b) $fg-hc$
(c) $fg+hc$ (d) $hc-fg$

13 If $\Delta = \begin{vmatrix} 1 & a & bc \\ 1 & b & ca \\ 1 & c & ab \end{vmatrix}$, then the minor M_{31} is NCERT Pg. 87

(a) $-c(a^2-b^2)$ (b) $c(b^2-a^2)$
(c) $c(a^2+b^2)$ (d) $c(a^2-b^2)$

Adjoint *and* Inverse *of* a Matrix

Level I

1 If $A=[a_{ij}]_{n\times n}$ is a square matrix of order n, then adjoint of A is the transpose of the matrix NCERT Pg. 87

(a) $[a_{ji}]_{n\times n}$ (b) $[A_{ji}]_{n\times n}$ (c) $[A_{ij}]_{n\times n}$ (d) $[a_{ij}]_{n\times n}$

2 If $A = \begin{bmatrix} a_{11} & a_{12} & a_{13} \\ a_{21} & a_{22} & a_{23} \\ a_{31} & a_{32} & a_{33} \end{bmatrix}$, where A_{ij} is the cofactor of a_{ij}, then adj A is NCERT Pg. 88

(a) $\begin{bmatrix} A_{11} & A_{12} & A_{13} \\ A_{21} & A_{22} & A_{23} \\ A_{31} & A_{32} & A_{33} \end{bmatrix}$ (b) $\begin{bmatrix} A_{11} & A_{21} & A_{31} \\ A_{12} & A_{22} & A_{32} \\ A_{13} & A_{23} & A_{33} \end{bmatrix}$

(c) $\begin{bmatrix} -A_{11} & A_{12} & -A_{13} \\ A_{21} & -A_{22} & A_{23} \\ -A_{31} & A_{32} & -A_{33} \end{bmatrix}$ (d) None of these

3 If $A = \begin{bmatrix} 2 & 3 \\ 1 & 4 \end{bmatrix}$, then adj A is NCERT Pg. 88

(a) $\begin{bmatrix} 2 & 1 \\ 4 & 3 \end{bmatrix}$ (b) $\begin{bmatrix} 4 & 3 \\ 2 & 1 \end{bmatrix}$ (c) $\begin{bmatrix} 4 & -3 \\ 1 & 2 \end{bmatrix}$ (d) $\begin{bmatrix} 4 & -3 \\ -1 & 2 \end{bmatrix}$

4 If A is a square matrix of order 2 given by $A = \begin{bmatrix} a_{11} & a_{12} \\ a_{21} & a_{22} \end{bmatrix}$, then adj A is NCERT Pg. 88

(a) $\begin{bmatrix} a_{22} & -a_{12} \\ -a_{21} & a_{11} \end{bmatrix}$ (b) $\begin{bmatrix} a_{22} & a_{12} \\ a_{21} & a_{11} \end{bmatrix}$

(c) $\begin{bmatrix} a_{12} & a_{22} \\ a_{11} & a_{21} \end{bmatrix}$ (d) $\begin{bmatrix} a_{11} & -a_{12} \\ -a_{21} & a_{22} \end{bmatrix}$

5 If A is any square matrix of order n, then NCERT Pg. 88, 89

(a) $A(\text{adj } A) = |A| I$ only
(b) $(\text{adj} A) A = |A| I$ only
(c) $A(\text{adj } A) = (\text{adj } A) A = |A| I$
(d) $(\text{adj } A) A = -|A| I$

6 A square matrix A is said to be singular, if NCERT Pg. 89

(a) $|A|=0$ (b) $|A|\neq 0$ (c) $|A|=1$ (d) $|A|=-1$

7 A square matrix A is said to be non-singular, if NCERT Pg. 89

(a) $|A|=0$ (b) $|A|\neq 0$
(c) $|A|=-1$ (d) $|A|=1$

8 If $A = \begin{bmatrix} 1 & 2 \\ 3 & 4 \end{bmatrix}$, then A is NCERT Pg. 89

(a) non-singular (b) singular
(c) diagonal matrix (d) scalar matrix

9 Let A and B are non-singular matrices of same order. Now, consider the following statements

I. AB is also non-singular matrix.
II. BA is also non-singular matrix.

Choose the correct option NCERT Pg. 89

(a) Only I is true (b) Only II is true
(c) Both I and II are true (d) Neither I nor II is true

10 If A and B are square matrices of same order, then NCERT Pg. 89

(a) $|AB| = |A|\cdot|B|$ (b) $|AB| \neq |A|\cdot|B|$
(c) $|AB| = \dfrac{|A|}{|B|}, |B|\neq 0$ (d) $|AB| = \dfrac{|B|}{|A|}, |A|\neq 0$

11 If A is a non-singular square matrix of order 3, then NCERT Pg. 90

(a) $|(\text{adj } A)| = |A|^3$ (b) $|(\text{adj } A)| = |A|^2$
(c) $|(\text{adj } A)| = |A|$ (d) $|(\text{adj } A)| = 2|A|$

12 If A is a non-singular square matrix of order n, then $|(\text{adj } A)|$ is NCERT Pg. 90

(a) $|A|^{n-1}$ (b) $-|A|^{n-1}$
(c) $n|A|$ (d) $|A|^n$

13 A square matrix A is invertible, if and only if NCERT Pg. 90

(a) A is singular matrix i.e. $|A|\neq 0$
(b) A is non-singular matrix i.e. $|A|\neq 0$
(c) A is non-singular matrix i.e. $|A|=0$
(d) A is singular matrix i.e. $|A|=0$

14 The adjoint of the matrix $A = \begin{bmatrix} 1 & 2 \\ 3 & 4 \end{bmatrix}$ is NCERT Pg. 92

(a) $\begin{bmatrix} 4 & 2 \\ 3 & 1 \end{bmatrix}$ (b) $\begin{bmatrix} -4 & 2 \\ 3 & -1 \end{bmatrix}$ (c) $\begin{bmatrix} 4 & -2 \\ -3 & 1 \end{bmatrix}$ (d) $\begin{bmatrix} 1 & -2 \\ -3 & 4 \end{bmatrix}$

15 The adjoint of the matrix $A = \begin{bmatrix} 1 & -1 & 2 \\ 2 & 3 & 5 \\ -2 & 0 & 1 \end{bmatrix}$ is NCERT Pg. 92

(a) $\begin{bmatrix} 3 & 1 & -11 \\ -12 & 5 & -1 \\ 6 & 2 & 5 \end{bmatrix}$ (b) $\begin{bmatrix} 3 & -12 & 6 \\ 1 & 5 & 2 \\ -11 & -1 & 5 \end{bmatrix}$

(c) $\begin{bmatrix} 3 & 1 & 11 \\ 12 & 5 & 1 \\ 6 & 2 & 5 \end{bmatrix}$ (d) $\begin{bmatrix} 3 & 1 & -11 \\ 12 & 5 & -1 \\ 6 & 2 & 5 \end{bmatrix}$

16 If $A=\begin{bmatrix}2 & 3\\ -4 & -6\end{bmatrix}$, then which of the following is true? NCERT Pg. 92

(a) $A\,(\text{adj}\,A)\neq |A|\,I$
(b) $A\,(\text{adj}\,A)\neq (\text{adj}\,A)\,A$
(c) $A\,(\text{adj}\,A)=(\text{adj}\,A)\,A=|A|\,I=\begin{bmatrix}0 & 0\\ 0 & 0\end{bmatrix}$
(d) None of the above

17 If $A=\begin{bmatrix}1 & -1 & 2\\ 3 & 0 & -2\\ 1 & 0 & 3\end{bmatrix}$, then NCERT Pg. 92

(a) $A\,(\text{adj}\,A)=(\text{adj}\,A)\,A=|A|\,I=\begin{bmatrix}11 & 0 & 0\\ 0 & 11 & 0\\ 0 & 0 & 11\end{bmatrix}$
(b) $A\,(\text{adj}\,A)\neq (\text{adj}\,A)\,A$
(c) $A\,(\text{adj}\,A)=-|A|\,I$
(d) $(\text{adj}\,A)\,A=-|A|\,I$

18 Consider the following statements

I. If $A=\begin{bmatrix}2 & -2\\ 4 & 3\end{bmatrix}$, then $A^{-1}=\begin{bmatrix}3 & -2\\ 4 & 3\end{bmatrix}$.

II. If $A=\begin{bmatrix}-1 & 5\\ -3 & 2\end{bmatrix}$, then $A^{-1}=\begin{bmatrix}\frac{2}{13} & -\frac{5}{13}\\ \frac{3}{13} & -\frac{1}{13}\end{bmatrix}$.

Choose the correct option. NCERT Pg. 92

(a) Only I is true
(b) Only II is true
(c) Both I and II are true
(d) Neither I nor II is true

19 The inverse of the matrix $A=\begin{bmatrix}1 & 0 & 0\\ 0 & \cos\alpha & \sin\alpha\\ 0 & \sin\alpha & -\cos\alpha\end{bmatrix}$ is NCERT Pg. 93

(a) $\begin{bmatrix}1 & 0 & 0\\ 0 & \cos\alpha & -\sin\alpha\\ 0 & \sin\alpha & -\cos\alpha\end{bmatrix}$

(b) $\begin{bmatrix}1 & 0 & 0\\ 0 & \cos\alpha & \sin\alpha\\ 0 & \sin\alpha & -\cos\alpha\end{bmatrix}$

(c) $\begin{bmatrix}1 & 0 & 0\\ 0 & \sin\alpha & \cos\alpha\\ 0 & \cos\alpha & -\sin\alpha\end{bmatrix}$

(d) Does not exist

20 Match the terms of column I with the terms of column II and choose the correct option from the codes given below. NCERT Pg. 92, 93

Column I	Column II (Inverse of matrices)
A. $\begin{bmatrix}1 & 2 & 3\\ 0 & 2 & 4\\ 0 & 0 & 5\end{bmatrix}$	1. $\begin{bmatrix}1 & 0 & 0\\ -1 & 1/3 & 0\\ 3 & 2/3 & -1\end{bmatrix}$
B. $\begin{bmatrix}1 & 0 & 0\\ 3 & 3 & 0\\ 5 & 2 & -1\end{bmatrix}$	2. $\begin{bmatrix}1 & -1 & 1/5\\ 0 & 1/2 & -2/5\\ 0 & 0 & 1/5\end{bmatrix}$
C. $\begin{bmatrix}2 & 1 & 3\\ 4 & -1 & 0\\ -7 & 2 & 1\end{bmatrix}$	3. $\begin{bmatrix}-2 & 0 & 1\\ 9 & 2 & -3\\ 6 & 1 & -2\end{bmatrix}$
D. $\begin{bmatrix}1 & -1 & 2\\ 0 & 2 & -3\\ 3 & -2 & 4\end{bmatrix}$	4. $\begin{bmatrix}1/3 & -5/3 & -1\\ 4/3 & -23/3 & -4\\ -1/3 & 11/3 & 2\end{bmatrix}$
	5. Does not exist

Codes

	A	B	C	D		A	B	C	D
(a)	5	5	4	3	(b)	2	1	5	4
(c)	2	1	4	3	(d)	3	4	5	1

21 If $A=\begin{bmatrix}2 & -1 & 1\\ -1 & 2 & -1\\ 1 & -1 & 2\end{bmatrix}$ satisfies the equation $A^3-6A^2+9A-4I=0$, then A^{-1} is NCERT Pg. 93

(a) $\frac{1}{4}\begin{bmatrix}3 & 1 & -1\\ 1 & 3 & 1\\ -1 & 1 & 3\end{bmatrix}$
(b) $\begin{bmatrix}3 & 1 & -1\\ 1 & 3 & 1\\ -1 & 1 & 3\end{bmatrix}$

(c) $\frac{1}{4}\begin{bmatrix}3 & 1 & 1\\ 1 & 3 & 1\\ 1 & 1 & 3\end{bmatrix}$
(d) $\frac{1}{4}\begin{bmatrix}3 & 1 & -1\\ -1 & 3 & 1\\ 1 & 1 & 3\end{bmatrix}$

22 If the matrix $A=\begin{bmatrix}3 & 2\\ 1 & 1\end{bmatrix}$ satisfies the equation $A^2+aA+bI=0$, then a and b are respectively NCERT Pg. 93

(a) -4 and 1
(b) 1 and 4
(c) -1 and -4
(d) -4 and -1

23 If $A=\begin{bmatrix}3 & 7\\ 2 & 5\end{bmatrix}$ and $B=\begin{bmatrix}6 & 8\\ 7 & 9\end{bmatrix}$, then $B^{-1}A^{-1}$ is equal to NCERT Pg. 93

(a) $(BA)^{-1}=\begin{bmatrix}-\frac{61}{2} & \frac{87}{2}\\ \frac{47}{2} & -\frac{67}{2}\end{bmatrix}$
(b) $(AB)^{-1}=\begin{bmatrix}-\frac{61}{2} & \frac{87}{2}\\ \frac{47}{2} & -\frac{67}{2}\end{bmatrix}$

(c) $(AB)^{-1}=\begin{bmatrix}\frac{61}{2} & \frac{87}{2}\\ \frac{47}{2} & -\frac{67}{2}\end{bmatrix}$
(d) $(BA)^{-1}=\begin{bmatrix}-\frac{61}{2} & \frac{87}{2}\\ -\frac{47}{2} & \frac{67}{2}\end{bmatrix}$

24 If $A=\begin{bmatrix}3 & 1\\-1 & 2\end{bmatrix}$ satisfies $A^2-5A+7I=0$, then A^{-1} is **NCERT Pg. 93**

(a) $\frac{1}{7}\begin{bmatrix}2 & -1\\1 & 3\end{bmatrix}$ (b) $\frac{1}{7}\begin{bmatrix}2 & 1\\1 & 3\end{bmatrix}$

(c) $\frac{1}{7}\begin{bmatrix}3 & 1\\1 & 2\end{bmatrix}$ (d) Does not exist

25 If A is an invertible matrix of order 2, then $\det(A^{-1})$ is equal to **NCERT Pg. 93**

(a) $\det(A)$ (b) $\frac{1}{\det(A)}$

(c) 1 (d) 0

26 If the matrix $A=\begin{bmatrix}1 & 1 & 1\\1 & 2 & -3\\2 & -1 & 3\end{bmatrix}$ satisfies the equation $A^3-6A^2+5A+11I=0$, then A^{-1} is **NCERT Pg. 93**

(a) $\frac{1}{11}\begin{bmatrix}-3 & 4 & 5\\9 & 1 & 4\\5 & 3 & -1\end{bmatrix}$ (b) $\frac{1}{11}\begin{bmatrix}-3 & 4 & 5\\9 & 1 & 4\\5 & -3 & -1\end{bmatrix}$

(c) $\frac{1}{11}\begin{bmatrix}-3 & 4 & -5\\-9 & 1 & -4\\5 & 3 & -1\end{bmatrix}$ (d) $\frac{1}{11}\begin{bmatrix}-3 & 4 & 5\\9 & -1 & -4\\5 & -3 & -1\end{bmatrix}$

Level II

27 If A is a non-singular 3×3 matrix and B is its adjoint such that $|B|=64$, then $|A|$ is **NCERT Pg. 90**

(a) 64 (b) ± 64

(c) ± 8 (d) 18

28 If $A^{-1}=\begin{bmatrix}3 & -1 & 1\\-15 & 6 & -5\\5 & -2 & 2\end{bmatrix}$ and $B=\begin{bmatrix}1 & 2 & -2\\-1 & 3 & 0\\0 & -2 & 1\end{bmatrix}$, then $(AB)^{-1}$ is **NCERT Pg. 99**

(a) $\begin{bmatrix}9 & -3 & 5\\-2 & 1 & 0\\1 & 0 & 2\end{bmatrix}$ (b) $\begin{bmatrix}9 & -2 & 1\\-3 & 1 & 0\\5 & 0 & 2\end{bmatrix}$

(c) $\begin{bmatrix}9 & 3 & 5\\-2 & 1 & 0\\1 & 0 & 2\end{bmatrix}$ (d) Does not exist

29 If the adjoint of a 3×3 non-singular matrix P is $\begin{bmatrix}1 & 4 & 4\\2 & 1 & 7\\1 & 1 & 3\end{bmatrix}$, then the possible values of the determinant of P are **NCERT Pg. 90**

(a) ± 2 (b) ± 1

(c) ± 3 (d) ± 4

30 If A is an invertible matrix, then $(A^{-1})'$ is equal to **NCERT Exemplar Pg. 82**

(a) $-(A^{-1})$

(b) $(A^{-1})^2$

(c) $(A')^{-1}$

(d) Does not exist

31 If $A=\begin{bmatrix}2 & \lambda & -3\\0 & 2 & 5\\1 & 1 & 3\end{bmatrix}$, then A^{-1} exists if **NCERT Pg. 90**

(a) $\lambda=2$

(b) $\lambda=-\frac{8}{5}$

(c) $\lambda\neq -2$

(d) Both (a) and (b)

32 If x, y and z are non-zero real numbers, then the inverse of matrix $A=\begin{bmatrix}x & 0 & 0\\0 & y & 0\\0 & 0 & z\end{bmatrix}$ is **NCERT Pg. 100**

(a) $\begin{bmatrix}x^{-1} & 0 & 0\\0 & y^{-1} & 0\\0 & 0 & z^{-1}\end{bmatrix}$

(b) $\frac{1}{xyz}\begin{bmatrix}x^{-1} & 0 & 0\\0 & y^{-1} & 0\\0 & 0 & z^{-1}\end{bmatrix}$

(c) $\frac{1}{xyz}\begin{bmatrix}x & 0 & 0\\0 & y & 0\\0 & 0 & z\end{bmatrix}$

(d) $\frac{1}{xyz}\begin{bmatrix}1 & 0 & 0\\0 & 1 & 0\\0 & 0 & 1\end{bmatrix}$

33 If A is an invertible matrix of order 3 and $|A|=5$, then $|\text{adj } A|$ is **NCERT Pg. 90**

(a) 10 (b) 25 (c) -5 (d) 15

34 Let $A=\begin{bmatrix}1 & -2 & 1\\-2 & 3 & 1\\1 & 1 & 5\end{bmatrix}$. Then, consider the following statements **NCERT Pg. 99**

I. $[\text{adj } A]^{-1}=(\text{adj } A^{-1})$

II. $(A^{-1})^{-1}=A$

Choose the correct option

(a) Only I is true

(b) Only II is true

(c) Both I and II are true

(d) Neither I nor II is true

Application of Determinants and Matrices

Level I

1 Consider the system of equations

$$2x+5y=1$$

and $$3x+2y=7$$

Then, its solution is **NCERT Pg. 95**

(a) $x=-3, y=1$ (b) $x=3, y=1$
(c) $x=3, y=-1$ (d) $x=-3, y=-1$

2 The sum of three numbers is 6. If we multiply third number by 3 and add second number to it, we get 11. By adding first and third numbers, we get double of the second number. Then, numbers are **NCERT Pg. 96**

(a) 3, 6, −3 (b) 5, −2, 3
(c) 1, 2, 3 (d) 4, 1, 1

3 Match the terms of column I with the terms of column II and choose the correct option from the codes given below. **NCERT Pg. 97**

Column I	Column II
A. $x+2y=2, 2x+3y=3$	
B. $2x-y=5, x+y=4$	1. Consistent
C. $x+3y=5, 2x+6y=8$	2. Inconsistent
D. $x+y+z=1$, $2x+3y+2z=2$, $ax+ay+2az=4$	
E. $3x-y-2z=2$, $2y-z=-1$, $3x-5y=3$	
F. $5x-y+4z=5$, $2x+3y+5z=2$, $5x-2y+6z=-1$	

Codes

	A	B	C	D	E	F
(a)	1	2	1	1	2	1
(b)	2	2	1	1	2	1
(c)	1	1	2	2	1	1
(d)	1	1	2	1	2	1

4 For the system of equations

$$5x+2y=4;\ 7x+3y=5,$$

the values of x and y are respectively **NCERT Pg. 97**

(a) $x=2$ and $y=-3$ (b) $x=2$ and $y=3$
(c) $x=-2$ and $y=-3$ (d) $x=-2$ and $y=3$

5 If the system of equations

$$4x-3y=3;\ 3x-5y=7$$

has unique solution, then **NCERT Pg. 97**

(a) $x=\frac{6}{11}$ and $y=\frac{19}{11}$ (b) $x=-\frac{6}{11}$ and $y=-\frac{19}{11}$
(c) $x=-\frac{6}{11}$ and $y=\frac{19}{11}$ (d) $x=\frac{6}{11}$ and $y=-\frac{9}{11}$

6 If the system of equations

$$2x+y+z=1$$
$$x-2y-z=\frac{3}{2}$$
$$3y-5z=9$$

has unique solution, then **NCERT Pg. 97**

(a) $x=1, y=2, z=-3$
(b) $x=1, y=\frac{1}{2}, z=\frac{3}{2}$
(c) $x=1, y=\frac{1}{2}, z=-\frac{3}{2}$
(d) $x=1, y=-\frac{1}{2}, z=\frac{3}{2}$

7 Consider the following statements

I. For the system of equations

$$x-y+z=4$$
$$2x+y-3z=0$$
$$x+y+z=2$$

the values of x, y and z are 2, −1 and 1, respectively.

II. If the system of equations is

$$2x+3y+3z=5$$
$$x-2y+z=-4$$
$$3x-y-2z=3$$

then $x=1$, $y=2$ and $z=-1$.

III. For the system of equations

$$x-y+2z=7$$
$$3x+4y-5z=-5$$
$$2x-y+3z=12$$

the system has a unique solution and is given by $x=2$, $y=3$ and $z=1$.

Choose the correct option. **NCERT Pg. 97**

(a) I and II are true (b) I and III are true
(c) II and III are true (d) All are true

8 If $A=\begin{bmatrix}2 & -3 & 5\\ 3 & 2 & -4\\ 1 & 1 & -2\end{bmatrix}$ and A^{-1} exists, then the solution of the system of equations

$$2x-3y+5z=11$$
$$3x+2y-4z=-5$$
$$x+y-2z=-3$$ is **NCERT Pg. 98**

(a) $x=1, y=2, z=3$ (b) $x=-1, y=2, z=3$
(c) $x=1, y=-2, z=3$ (d) $x=1, y=2, z=-3$

9 The cost of 4 kg onion, 3 kg wheat and 2 kg riceis ₹ 60. The cost of 2 kg onion, 4 kg wheat and 6 kg rice is ₹ 90. The cost of 6 kg onion, 2 kg wheat and 3 kg rice is ₹ 70. The costs (in ₹) of onion, wheat and rice per kilogram are respectively **NCERT Pg. 98**

(a) 5, 9, 10 (b) 5, 8, 8
(c) 8, 5, 8 (d) 8, 8, 5

Level II

10 Consider the system of equations in x, y and z as $x \sin 3\theta - y + z = 0$, $x \cos 2\theta + 4y + 3z = 0$ and $2x + 7y + 7z = 0$. If this system has a non-trivial solution, then for integer n, values of θ are given by **NCERT Exemplar Pg. 78**

(a) $\pi\left(n + \frac{(-1)^n}{3}\right)$ (b) $\pi\left(n + \frac{(-1)^n}{4}\right)$
(c) $\pi\left(n + \frac{(-1)^n}{6}\right)$ (d) $\frac{n\pi}{2}$

11 The system of equations

$$x + y + z = 8$$
$$x - y + 2z = 6$$
$$3x + 5y - 7z = 14 \text{ has}$$

NCERT Pg. 97

(a) no solution
(b) unique solution
(c) infinitely many solutions
(d) None of the above

12 If the system of equations is given by

$$\frac{2}{x} + \frac{3}{y} + \frac{10}{z} = 4$$
$$\frac{4}{x} - \frac{6}{y} + \frac{5}{z} = 1$$
$$\frac{6}{x} + \frac{9}{y} - \frac{20}{z} = 2$$

then values of x, y and z are respectively **NCERT Pg. 100**

(a) 2, 3 and 5 (b) $\frac{1}{2}, \frac{1}{3}$ and $\frac{1}{5}$
(c) $2, \frac{1}{3}$ and 5 (d) 2, 3 and $\frac{1}{5}$

Miscellaneous Exercise

1 The value of $\begin{vmatrix} 1 & \log_x y & \log_x z \\ \log_y x & 1 & \log_y z \\ \log_z x & \log_z y & 1 \end{vmatrix}$ is equal to **NCERT Pg. 81**

(a) 1 (b) 0
(c) $\log xyz$ (d) xyz

2 If for any matrix M, M^{-1} exists, then which of the following is not true? **NCERT Pg. 90**

(a) $|M^{-1}| = |M|^{-1}$ (b) $(M^2)^{-1} \neq (M^{-1})^2$
(c) $(M')^{-1} = (M^{-1})'$ (d) $(M^{-1})^{-1} = M$

3 For what value of k, the following system of linear equations will have infinite solutions?

$$x - y + z = 3$$
$$2x + y - z = 2$$
$$-3x - 2ky + 6z = 3$$

NCERT Pg. 97

(a) $k \neq 2$ (b) $k = 0$
(c) $k = 3$ (d) $k \in [2, 3]$

4 Let A be a square matrix, all of whose entries are integers. Then, which of the following is true? **NCERT Pg. 90**

(a) If det $(A) = \pm 1$, then A^{-1} does not exist.
(b) If det $(A) = \pm 1$, then A^{-1} exists but all its entries are non-integers.
(c) If det $(A) \neq \pm 1$, then A^{-1} exists and all its entries are non-integers.
(d) If det $(A) = \pm 1$, then A^{-1} exists and all its entries are integers.

5 If the coordinates of the vertices of an equilateral triangle with sides of length a are (x_1, y_1), (x_2, y_2) and (x_3, y_3), then $\begin{vmatrix} x_1 & y_1 & 1 \\ x_2 & y_2 & 1 \\ x_3 & y_3 & 1 \end{vmatrix}^2$ is equal to **NCERT Exemplar Pg. 78**

(a) $-\frac{3a^4}{4}$ (b) $\frac{3a^4}{4}$ (c) $3a^4$ (d) $4a^4$

6 If $A = \begin{bmatrix} 1 & \sin\theta & 1 \\ -\sin\theta & 1 & \sin\theta \\ -1 & -\sin\theta & 1 \end{bmatrix}$, where $0 \leq \theta \leq 2\pi$, then **NCERT Pg. 100**

(a) det $(A) = 0$ (b) det $(A) \in (2, \infty)$
(c) det $(A) \in (2, 4)$ (d) det $(A) \in [2, 4]$

7 An amount of ₹ 5000 is put into three investments at the rates of interest 6%, 7% and 8% per annum, respectively. The total annual income is ₹ 358. If the combined income from the first two investments is ₹ 70 more than the income from the third, then the amount of each investment (in ₹) is **NCERT Pg. 98**

(a) 1000, 2200, 180 (b) 1000, 2200, 1100
(c) 1000, 2200, 1800 (d) 2200, 1800, 1100

8 The simultaneous equations

$$kx + 2y - z = 1$$
$$(k-1)y - 2z = 2$$
$$(k+2)z = 3$$

have only one solution when **NCERT Pg. 97**

(a) $k = -2$ (b) $k = -1$
(c) $k = 0$ (d) $k = 1$

9 The system of equations

$$3x - y + 4z = 3$$
$$x + 2y - 3z = -2$$
$$6x + 5y + \lambda z = -3$$

has atleast one solution if **NCERT Pg. 97**

(a) $\lambda = -5$ (b) $\lambda = 5$
(c) $\lambda = 3$ (d) $\lambda = -13$

10 Match the terms of column I with the terms of column II and choose the correct option from the codes given below. **NCERT Pg. 99**

Column I	Column II
A. $\begin{vmatrix} \cos\alpha\cos\beta & \cos\alpha\sin\beta & -\sin\alpha \\ -\sin\beta & \cos\beta & 0 \\ \sin\alpha\cos\beta & \sin\alpha\sin\beta & \cos\alpha \end{vmatrix}$	1. xy
B. $\begin{vmatrix} x & y & x+y \\ y & x+y & x \\ x+y & x & y \end{vmatrix}$	2. 1
C. $\begin{vmatrix} 1 & x & y \\ 1 & x+y & y \\ 1 & x & x+y \end{vmatrix}$	3. $-2(x^3 + y^3)$

Codes

	A	B	C
(a)	2	2	1
(b)	1	3	2
(c)	2	3	1
(d)	3	1	2

11 If $\begin{vmatrix} -12 & 0 & \lambda \\ 0 & 2 & -1 \\ 2 & 1 & 15 \end{vmatrix} = -360$, then the value of λ is **NCERT Exemplar Pg. 82**

(a) -1 (b) -2
(c) -3 (d) -4

12 The solution of the equation $\begin{vmatrix} x & 2 & -1 \\ 2 & 5 & x \\ -1 & 2 & x \end{vmatrix} = 0$ is **NCERT Pg. 82**

(a) $3, -1$ (b) $-3, 1$
(c) $3, 13$ (d) $-3, -1$

13 If $\begin{vmatrix} 6i & -3i & 1 \\ 4 & 3i & -1 \\ 40 & 3 & i \end{vmatrix} = x + iy$, then **NCERT Pg. 82**

(a) $x = 3, y = 1$ (b) $x = 1, y = 3$
(c) $x = 0, y = 3$ (d) $x = 0, y = 0$

14 If $f(x) = \begin{vmatrix} (1+x)^{17} & (1+x)^{19} & (1+x)^{23} \\ (1+x)^{23} & (1+x)^{29} & (1+x)^{34} \\ (1+x)^{41} & (1+x)^{43} & (1+x)^{47} \end{vmatrix}$

$= A + Bx + Cx^2 + \ldots$, then A is equal to **NCERT Exemplar Pg. 84**

(a) 1 (b) 0 (c) x (d) x^2

15 If A is a 3×3 non-singular matrix, then $|A^{-1} \text{ adj } A|$ is **NCERT Pg. 90**

(a) $|A|$ (b) 1 (c) $|A|^2$ (d) $|A|^{-1}$

16 If $A = \begin{bmatrix} 0 & 0 & -1 \\ 0 & -1 & 0 \\ -1 & 0 & 0 \end{bmatrix}$, then the only correct statement about the matrix A is **NCERT Pg. 90**

(a) A is a zero matrix
(b) $A = (-1) I$, where I is a unit matrix
(c) A^{-1} does not exist
(d) $A^2 = I$

17 If A, B and C are angles of a triangle, then the determinant $\begin{vmatrix} -1 & \cos C & \cos B \\ \cos C & -1 & \cos A \\ \cos B & \cos A & -1 \end{vmatrix}$ is equal to **NCERT Exemplar Pg. 81**

(a) 0 (b) -1
(c) 1 (d) None of these

18 The maximum value of

$\Delta = \begin{vmatrix} 1 & 1 & 1 \\ 1 & 1+\sin\theta & 1 \\ 1+\cos\theta & 1 & 1 \end{vmatrix}$ is (θ is real number) **NCERT Exemplar Pg. 81**

(a) $\frac{1}{2}$ (b) $\frac{\sqrt{3}}{2}$
(c) $\sqrt{2}$ (d) $\frac{2\sqrt{3}}{4}$

Numerical Type Questions

1 If $\begin{vmatrix} p^n & p^{n+1} & p^{n+2} \\ q^n & q^{n+1} & q^{n+2} \\ r^n & r^{n+1} & r^{n+2} \end{vmatrix} = (p-q)(q-r)(r-p)$, then n is equal to, where $(p \neq q \neq r)$ **NCERT Pg. 82**

2 Let $B = [b_{ij}]$ be 2×2 matrix, where

$$b_{ij} = \begin{cases} 1 & , \text{ if } i = j \\ -2x^2 + 1 & , \text{ if } |i - j| = 1 \\ 2x + 1 & , \text{ otherwise} \end{cases}$$

Let a function $f : R \to R$ be defined as $f(x) = \det(A)$. Then, the sum of maximum and minimum values of f on R is equal to ...... **NCERT Pg. 82**

3 Let $A = \begin{bmatrix} 2 & 1 & 0 \\ 0 & 2 & -4 \\ 0 & 0 & 1 \end{bmatrix}$. If $|\text{adj}(\text{adj}(\text{adj}(2A)))| = 4^n$, then n is equal to ...... **NCERT Pg. 90**

4 If $B = \begin{bmatrix} 1 & \alpha & 3 \\ 2 & 3 & 4 \\ 2 & 1 & 3 \end{bmatrix}$ is the adjoint of a 3×3 matrix A and $|A| = 6$, then $2\alpha (\alpha \in R)$ is equal to ...... **NCERT Pg. 90**

5 Let $A = \begin{bmatrix} 1 & 3 \\ 2 & 7 \end{bmatrix}$. If $A^{-1} = xI + yA$, $x, y \in R$ and I is a 2×2 identity matrix, then $3(x + y)$ is equal to ...... **NCERT Pg. 90**

6 Let the area of the triangle with vertices $A(x, 1)$, $B(0, x)$ and $C(x, 0)$ be 9 sq. units such that the points $(x, -x)$, $(-x, x)$ and (x^2, y) are collinear then $\left|\dfrac{y}{18}\right|$ is ...... **NCERT Pg. 83**

7 If a and b are the cofactors of -3 and 3 respectively in the determinant $\begin{vmatrix} 2 & -3 & 1 \\ 0 & 2 & 4 \\ 3 & 1 & 2 \end{vmatrix}$ then $|a + b|$ is .... **NCERT Pg. 84**

8 Let $A = \begin{bmatrix} 1 & 3 \\ 2 & 7 \end{bmatrix}$ and B be a 2×2 matrix such that $BA^{-1} = B^{-1}$. If $\bar{A}CA^{-1} = B$ and $C^4 + aC^2 + bI = 0$. Then, $2b - a$ is equal to .... **NCERT Pg. 94**

9 If $A = \begin{bmatrix} 1 & 2a & 3 \\ 2 & 1 & 3 \\ 4 & 2 & a \end{bmatrix}$ is the inverse of a 3×3 matrix B, then 4 times the sum of all values of a for which $\det(B) + 1 = 0$ is .... **NCERT Pg. 90**

Assertion and Reason Questions

Direction (Q. Nos. 1-6) In the questions given below are the statements labelled as Assertion (A) and Reason (R). In the context on the two statements, which one of the following is correct?

(a) Both Assertion and Reason are correct and Reason is the correct explanation of Assertion.
(b) Both Assertion and Reason are correct but Reason is not the correct explanation of Assertion.
(c) Assertion is correct but Reason is incorrect.
(d) Assertion is incorrect but Reason is correct.

1 Let $A = [a_{ij}]$ be a matrix of order 3×3.

Assertion (A) Expansion of determinant of A along second row and first column gives the same value.

Reason (R) Expanding a determinant along any row or column gives the same value. **NCERT Pg. 78**

2 **Assertion (A)** The points $A(a, b + c)$, $B(b, c + a)$ and $C(c, a + b)$ are collinear.

Reason (R) Area of a triangle with three collinear points is zero. **NCERT Pg. 83**

3 **Assertion (A)** $\Delta = a_{11}A_{11} + a_{12}A_{12} + a_{13}A_{13}$ where, A_{ij} is cofactor of a_{ij}.

Reason (R) $\Delta =$ Sum of the products of elements of any row (or column) with their corresponding cofactors. **NCERT Pg. 85**

4 **Assertion (A)** The system of equations

$2x - y = -2;\ 3x + 4y = 3$

has unique solution and $x = -\dfrac{5}{11}$ and $y = \dfrac{12}{11}$.

Reason (R) The system of equation $AX = B$ has a unique solution, if $|A| \neq 0$. **NCERT Pg. 95**

5 **Assertion (A)** Let $A = \begin{bmatrix} 2 & 5 \\ 6 & x \end{bmatrix}$ is singular if $x = 15$.

Reason (R) A matrix A is singular if $|A| \neq 0$. **NCERT Pg. 89**

6 **Assertion (A)** For a matrix $A = [a_{ij}]_{3 \times 3}$, if $\det(\text{adj } A) = 25$, then $|A| = \pm 5$.

Reason (R) For a square matrix A of order n, $|\text{adj } A| = |A|^{n-1}$. **NCERT Pg. 90**

Case or Paragraph Type Questions

Direction (Q. Nos. 1-3) Consider the system of equations

$$a_1x + b_1y + c_1z = d_1;\ a_2x + b_2y + c_2z = d_2$$
$$a_3x + b_3y + c_3z = d_3$$

This system of equations can be written as $AX = B$, where $A = \begin{bmatrix} a_1 & b_1 & c_1 \\ a_2 & b_2 & c_2 \\ a_3 & b_3 & c_3 \end{bmatrix}$, $X = \begin{bmatrix} x \\ y \\ z \end{bmatrix}$ and $B = \begin{bmatrix} d_1 \\ d_2 \\ d_3 \end{bmatrix}$. NCERT Pg. 94

1 If A is non-singular, then its solution is
(a) $X = A^{-1}B$ (b) $X = AB$
(c) $X = B^{-1}A$ (d) $X = A^{-1}B^{-1}$

2 If A is singular matrix and (adj A) $B \neq 0$, then
(a) there is unique solution
(b) solution does not exist
(c) there are infinitely many solutions
(d) None of the above

3 If A is singular and (adj A) $B = 0$, then the system $AX = B$ has
(a) infinitely many solution or no solution
(b) no solution only
(c) unique solution
(d) None of the above

Direction (Q. Nos. 4-6) Let $A = \begin{bmatrix} 2 & 0 \\ 3 & 2 \end{bmatrix}$ and X and Y be first and second columns respectively of a 2×2 matrix B. Also, let the column matrices X and Y satisfy $AX = \begin{bmatrix} 2 \\ 3 \end{bmatrix}$ and $AY = \begin{bmatrix} 4 \\ 0 \end{bmatrix}$.

Based on the above information, answer the following questions. NCERT Pg. 84

4 The matrix $X - Y$ is equal to
(a) $\begin{bmatrix} -1 \\ 3 \end{bmatrix}$ (b) $\begin{bmatrix} 2 \\ 3 \end{bmatrix}$ (c) $\begin{bmatrix} 1 \\ 3 \end{bmatrix}$ (d) $\begin{bmatrix} 0 \\ 2 \end{bmatrix}$

5 The value of $|B|$ is
(a) 2 (b) -3 (c) -1(d) 1

6 If $B = [a_{ij}]_{2 \times 2}$, then the value of $A_{11} + A_{22}$ where A_{ij}, denotes the cofactor of a_{ij}, is
(a) 2 (b) 3 (c) -3 (d) -2

Past Years Questions

Single Correct Type

1 If $\alpha \neq a, \beta \neq b, \gamma \neq c$ and $\begin{vmatrix} \alpha & b & c \\ a & \beta & c \\ a & b & \gamma \end{vmatrix} = 0$, then $\dfrac{a}{\alpha - a} + \dfrac{b}{\beta - b} + \dfrac{\gamma}{\gamma - c}$ is equal to
NCERT Pg. 82, JEE Main 2024, 8 April Shift-II
(a) 0 (b) 3 (c) 2 (d) 1

2 Let $A = \begin{bmatrix} 2 & a & 0 \\ 1 & 3 & 1 \\ 0 & 5 & b \end{bmatrix}$. If $A^3 = 4A^2 - A - 21I$, where I is the identity matrix of order 3×3. Then, $2a + 3b$ is equal to
NCERT Pg. 95, JEE Main 2024, 8 April Shift-I
(a) -10 (b) -9 (c) -13 (d) -12

3 For $\alpha, \beta \in R$ and a natural number n. Let
$$A_r = \begin{vmatrix} r & 1 & \dfrac{n^2}{2} + \alpha \\ 2r & 2 & n^2 - \beta \\ 3r - 2 & 3 & \dfrac{n(3n-1)}{2} \end{vmatrix}.$$ Then, $2A_{10} - A_8$ is
NCERT Pg. 82, JEE Main 2024, 6 April Shift-I
(a) $4\alpha + 2\beta$ (b) $2\alpha + 4\beta$ (c) 0 (d) $2n$

4 If $A = \begin{bmatrix} \sqrt{2} & 1 \\ -1 & \sqrt{2} \end{bmatrix}$, $B = \begin{bmatrix} 1 & 0 \\ 1 & 1 \end{bmatrix}$, $C = ABA^T$ and $X = A^TC^2A$, then det X is equal to
NCERT Pg. 81, JEE Main 2024, 1 Feb Shift-I
(a) 243 (b) 729 (c) 891 (d) 27

5 The values of α, for which $\begin{vmatrix} 1 & \dfrac{3}{2} & \alpha + \dfrac{3}{2} \\ 1 & \dfrac{1}{3} & \alpha + \dfrac{1}{3} \\ 2\alpha + 3 & 3\alpha + 1 & 0 \end{vmatrix} = 0$, lie in the interval
NCERT Exemplar Pg. 74, JEE Main 2024, 27 Jan Shift-II
(a) $(-2, 1)$ (b) $(-3, 0)$ (c) $\left(-\dfrac{3}{2}, \dfrac{3}{2}\right)$ (d) $(0, 3)$

6 If A is a square matrix of order 4 and $|A| = 4$, then $|2A|$ will be
NCERT Pg. 80, CUET 2024
(a) 8 (b) 64 (c) 16 (d) 4

7 For a square matrix $A_{n \times n}$
(a) $|\text{adj } A| = |A|^{n-1}$ (b) $|A| = |\text{adj } A|^{n-1}$
(c) $A(\text{adj } A) = |A|$ (d) $|A^{-1}| = \dfrac{1}{|A|}$

Choose the correct answer from the options given below. NCERT Pg. 88, CUET 2024

(a) B and D (b) A and D
(c) A, C and D (d) B, C and D

8 $\Delta = \begin{vmatrix} 1 & \cos x & 1 \\ -\cos x & 1 & \cos x \\ -1 & -\cos x & 1 \end{vmatrix}$

A. $\Delta = 2(1-\cos^2 x)$

B. $\Delta = 2(2-\sin^2 x)$

C. Minimum value of Δ is 2

D. Maximum value of Δ is 4

Choose the correct answer from the options given below. NCERT Pg. 78, CUET 2024

(a) A, C and D (b) A, B and C
(c) A, B, C and D (d) B, C and D

9 Let $A = \begin{bmatrix} 2 & 1 & 0 \\ 1 & 2 & -1 \\ 0 & -1 & 2 \end{bmatrix}$. If $|\text{adj}(\text{adj}(\text{adj}\,2A))| = (16)^n$, then n is equal to NCERT Pg. 90, JEE Main 2023, 8 April Shift-I

(a) 8 (b) 10 (c) 12 (d) 9

10 If P is a 3×3 real matrix such that $P^T = aP + (a-1)I$, where $a > 1$, then NCERT Pg. 89, JEE Main 2023, 30 Jan Shift-II

(a) P is a singular matrix (b) $|\text{Adj } P| = 1$
(c) $|\text{Adj } P| > 1$ (d) $|\text{Adj } P| = 1/2$

11 Let $x, y, z > 1$ and $A = \begin{bmatrix} 1 & \log_x y & \log_x z \\ \log_y x & 2 & \log_y z \\ \log_z x & \log_z y & 3 \end{bmatrix}$. Then, $|\text{adj}(\text{adj } A^2)|$ is equal to NCERT Pg. 82, JEE Main 2023, 25 Jan Shift-I

(a) 6^4 (b) 4^8 (c) 2^8 (d) 2^4

Numerical Value Type Questions

12 Let A be a non-singular matrix of order 3. If det (3 adj (2 adj (det A))) $= 3^{-13} \cdot 2^{-10}$ and det (3 adj (2 A)) $= 2^m \cdot 3^n$, then $|3m + 2n|$ is equal to .... NCERT Pg. 90 2024, 9 April Shift-II

13 Let A be a 2×2 symmetric matrix such that $A\begin{bmatrix}1\\1\end{bmatrix} = \begin{bmatrix}3\\7\end{bmatrix}$ and the determinant of A be 1.

If $A^{-1} = \alpha A + \beta I$, where I is an identity matrix of order 2×2, then $\alpha + \beta$ equals .... NCERT Pg. 95 2024, 4 April Shift-II

14 Let A be an $n \times n$ matrix such that $|A| = 2$. If the determinant of the matrix Adj $(2 \cdot \text{Adj}(2A^{-1}))$ is 2^{84}, then n is equal to .... NCERT Pg. 90 2023, 31 Jan Shift-II

15 The number of matrices $A = \begin{bmatrix} a & b \\ c & d \end{bmatrix}$, where a, b, c and $d \in \{-1, 0, 1, 2, 3, \ldots, 10\}$, such that $A = A^{-1}$, is .... NCERT Pg. 92 2022, 26 July Shift-II

Skill Boosters

1 If $0 \le [a] < 2, -1 \le [b] < 1$ and $1 \le [c] < 3$, where $[\cdot]$ denotes the greatest integer function, then the maximum value of the determinant

$$\Delta = \begin{vmatrix} [a]+1 & [b] & [c] \\ [a] & [b]+1 & [c] \\ [a] & [b] & [c]+1 \end{vmatrix} \text{ is}$$

(a) 2 (b) 4 (c) 6 (d) 8

2 Let the sum of roots be α and product of roots be β of the equation $\begin{vmatrix} x & -2 & -1 \\ 1 & -3x & x-1 \\ 2 & x & x+1 \end{vmatrix} = 0$ is equal to

(a) $\alpha + \beta = \frac{1}{2}$ (b) $\alpha + \beta = 1$
(c) $\alpha + \beta = 1$ (d) $\alpha + \beta = 4$

3 The values of Ω and μ for which the system of linear equations $x + 2y + 3z = 1, 3y + z = 2$ and $x + 2y + \Omega z = \mu$ has more than 2 solutions are respectively.

(a) $\Omega = 2$ and $\mu = 1$ (b) $\Omega = 9$ and $\mu = 1$
(c) $\Omega = 3$ and $\mu = 1$ (d) $\Omega = 1$ and $\mu = 9$

4 If $B = \begin{bmatrix} 2a & b \\ 1 & 3 \end{bmatrix}$ and adj $B = BB^T$, then $2a - b$ is equal to

(a) 2 (b) 4 (c) 5 (d) 6

5 If $A = \begin{bmatrix} \cos\theta & -\sin\theta \\ \sin\theta & \cos\theta \end{bmatrix}$, then the determinants of A^{-36} when $\theta = \frac{\pi}{6}$ is equal to

(a) $\frac{1}{2}$ (b) 2 (c) 1 (d) 4

Correct Codes

Topical Questions

Determinants

1 (b) 2 (a) 3 (b) 4 (a) 5 (a) 6 (b) 7 (d) 8 (c) 9 (b) 10 (c)
11 (d) 12 (a) 13 (c) 14 (a) 15 (c) 16 (d) 17 (d) 18 (a) 19 (a) 20 (b)
21 (b) 22 (c) 23 (a) 24 (c) 25 (a) 26 (b) 27 (a) 28 (b)

Area of Triangle

1 (b) 2 (a) 3 (c) 4 (c) 5 (d) 6 (b) 7 (d) 8 (a) 9 (a) 10 (c)
11 (b) 12 (b) 13 (b)

Minors and Cofactors

1 (b) 2 (a) 3 (d) 4 (c) 5 (c) 6 (a) 7 (c) 8 (d) 9 (b) 10 (d)
11 (a) 12 (b) 13 (d)

Adjoint and Inverse of a Matrix

1 (c) 2 (b) 3 (d) 4 (a) 5 (c) 6 (a) 7 (b) 8 (a) 9 (c) 10 (a)
11 (b) 12 (a) 13 (b) 14 (c) 15 (a) 16 (c) 17 (a) 18 (b) 19 (b) 20 (c)
21 (a) 22 (a) 23 (b) 24 (a) 25 (b) 26 (d) 27 (c) 28 (a) 29 (a) 30 (c)
31 (d) 32 (a) 33 (b) 34 (c)

Application of Determinants and Matrices

1 (c) 2 (c) 3 (d) 4 (a) 5 (b) 6 (c) 7 (a) 8 (a) 9 (b) 10 (c)
11 (b) 12 (a)

Miscellaneous Exercise

1 (b) 2 (b) 3 (c) 4 (d) 5 (b) 6 (d) 7 (c) 8 (b) 9 (a) 10 (c)
11 (c) 12 (a) 13 (d) 14 (b) 15 (a) 16 (d) 17 (a) 18 (a)

Numerical Type Questions

1 (0) 2 (1) 3 (20) 4 (43) 5 (21) 6 (18) 7 (2) 8 (10) 9 (25)

Assertion and Reason Questions

1 (a) 2 (a) 3 (a) 4 (a) 5 (c) 6 (a)

Case or Paragraph Type Questions

1 (a) 2 (b) 3 (a) 4 (a) 5 (b) 6 (d)

Past Years Questions

1 (a) 2 (c) 3 (a) 4 (b) 5 (b) 6 (b) 7 (b) 8 (d) 9 (b) 10 (b)
11 (c) 12 (14) 13 (5) 14 (5) 15 (50)

Skill Boosters

1 (b) 2 (b) 3 (c) 4 (b) 5 (c).

Step by Step

Decoding the Questions

Concept Builders

1 8	2 5
3 $\frac{1}{5}$	4 True
5 −2	6 3
7 True	8 2
9 −2	10 −8
11 Singular matrix	
12 Triangular matrix	
13 $\frac{1}{12}$	
14 Inconsistent	
15 True	16 −2
17 0	18 $\lvert A\rvert^{(n-1)^2}$
19 False	20 $(A^{-1})^T$

Topical Questions

Determinant

1 (*b*) To every square matrix $A=[a_{ij}]$ of order *n*, we can associate a number (real or complex), called determinant of the square matrix *A*, where $a_{ij}=(i,\ j)$th element of *A*.

Determinant is a function, which associates each square matrix with a unique number.

2 (*a*) If *M* is the set of square matrices, *K* is the set of numbers (real or complex) and $f: M \to K$ is defined by $f(A)=k$, where $A \in M$ and $k \in K$, then $f(A)$ is called the determinant of *A*.

3 (*b*) We have, $A=[a]$ is the matrix of order 1, then determinant of *A* is equal to *a* i.e. $|A|=a$.

4 (*a*) Let $A=\begin{bmatrix} a_{11} & a_{12} \\ a_{21} & a_{22}\end{bmatrix}$ be a matrix of order 2×2, then the determinant of *A* is defined as

$$\det(A)=|A|=\Delta=\begin{vmatrix} a_{11} & a_{12} \\ a_{21} & a_{22}\end{vmatrix}$$
$$=a_{11}a_{22}-a_{21}a_{12}$$

5 (*a*) We have,

$$\begin{vmatrix} x & x+1 \\ x-1 & x\end{vmatrix}=x(x)-(x+1)(x-1)$$
$$=x^2-(x^2-1)$$
$$=x^2-x^2+1=1$$

6 (*b*) Determinant of a matrix of order three can be determined by expressing it in terms of second order determinants. This is known as expansion of a determinant along a row (or a column).

7 (*d*) There are six ways of expanding a determinant of order 3 corresponding to each of three rows (R_1, R_2 and R_3) and three columns (C_1, C_2 and C_3).

8 (*c*) Consider the determinant of square matrix $A=[a_{ij}]_{3\times 3}$

i.e. $|A|=\begin{vmatrix} a_{11} & a_{12} & a_{13} \\ a_{21} & a_{22} & a_{23} \\ a_{31} & a_{32} & a_{33}\end{vmatrix}$

Expansion along first row (R_1)

Step I Multiply first element a_{11} of R_1 by $(-1)^{(1+1)}[(-1)^{\text{sum of suffixes in } a_{11}}]$ and with the second order determinant obtained by deleting the elements of first row R_1 and first column C_1 of $|A|$ as a_{11} lies in R_1 and C_1

i.e. $(-1)^{1+1}a_{11}\begin{vmatrix} a_{22} & a_{23} \\ a_{32} & a_{33}\end{vmatrix}$

Step II Multiply second element a_{12} of R_1 by $(-1)^{(1+2)}[(-1)^{\text{sum of suffixes in } a_{12}}]$ and the second order determinant obtained by deleting elements of first row R_1 and second column C_2 of $|A|$ as a_{12} lies in R_1 and C_2

i.e. $(-1)^{1+2}a_{12}\begin{vmatrix} a_{21} & a_{23} \\ a_{31} & a_{33}\end{vmatrix}$

Step III Multiply third element a_{13} of R_1 by $(-1)^{(1+3)}[(-1)^{\text{sum of suffixes in } a_{13}}]$ and the second order determinant obtained by deleting elements of first row R_1 and third column C_3 of $|A|$ as a_{13} lies in R_1 and C_3

i.e. $(-1)^{1+3}a_{13}\begin{vmatrix} a_{21} & a_{22} \\ a_{31} & a_{32}\end{vmatrix}$

Step IV Now, the expansion of determinant of *A*, i.e. $|A|$ written as sum of all three terms obtained in steps I, II and III above, is given by

$$\det A=|A|=(-1)^{1+1}a_{11}\begin{vmatrix} a_{22} & a_{23} \\ a_{32} & a_{33}\end{vmatrix}+(-1)^{1+2}a_{12}\begin{vmatrix} a_{21} & a_{23} \\ a_{31} & a_{33}\end{vmatrix}+(-1)^{1+3}a_{13}\begin{vmatrix} a_{21} & a_{22} \\ a_{31} & a_{32}\end{vmatrix}$$

or $|A|=a_{11}(a_{22}a_{33}-a_{32}a_{23})-a_{12}(a_{21}a_{33}-a_{31}a_{23})+a_{13}(a_{21}a_{32}-a_{31}a_{22})$

$$=a_{11}a_{22}a_{33}-a_{11}a_{32}a_{23}-a_{12}a_{21}a_{33}+a_{12}a_{31}a_{23}+a_{13}a_{21}a_{32}-a_{13}a_{31}a_{22} \quad \text{...(i)}$$

Expansion along second row (R_2)

$$|A|=\begin{vmatrix} a_{11} & a_{12} & a_{13} \\ a_{21} & a_{22} & a_{23} \\ a_{31} & a_{32} & a_{33}\end{vmatrix}$$

By expanding along R_2, we get

$$|A|=(-1)^{2+1}a_{21}\begin{vmatrix} a_{12} & a_{13} \\ a_{32} & a_{33}\end{vmatrix}+(-1)^{2+2}a_{22}\begin{vmatrix} a_{11} & a_{13} \\ a_{31} & a_{33}\end{vmatrix}+(-1)^{2+3}a_{23}\begin{vmatrix} a_{11} & a_{12} \\ a_{31} & a_{32}\end{vmatrix}$$

(applying all steps together)

$$= -a_{21}(a_{12}a_{33} - a_{32}a_{13}) + a_{22}(a_{11}a_{33} - a_{31}a_{13}) - a_{23}(a_{11}a_{32} - a_{31}a_{12})$$

$$|A| = -a_{21}a_{12}a_{33} + a_{21}a_{32}a_{13} + a_{22}a_{11}a_{33} - a_{22}a_{31}a_{13} - a_{23}a_{11}a_{32} + a_{23}a_{31}a_{12}$$

$$= a_{11}a_{22}a_{33} - a_{11}a_{23}a_{32} - a_{12}a_{21}a_{33} + a_{12}a_{23}a_{31} + a_{13}a_{21}a_{32} - a_{13}a_{31}a_{22} \quad ...(ii)$$

$$|A| = \begin{vmatrix} a_{11} & a_{12} & a_{13} \\ a_{21} & a_{22} & a_{23} \\ a_{31} & a_{32} & a_{33} \end{vmatrix}$$

By expanding along C_1, we get

$$|A| = a_{11}(-1)^{1+1}\begin{vmatrix} a_{22} & a_{23} \\ a_{32} & a_{33} \end{vmatrix} + a_{21}(-1)^{2+1}\begin{vmatrix} a_{12} & a_{13} \\ a_{32} & a_{33} \end{vmatrix} + a_{31}(-1)^{3+1}\begin{vmatrix} a_{12} & a_{13} \\ a_{22} & a_{23} \end{vmatrix}$$

$$= a_{11}(a_{22}a_{33} - a_{23}a_{32}) - a_{21}(a_{12}a_{33} - a_{13}a_{32}) + a_{31}(a_{12}a_{23} - a_{13}a_{22})$$

$$|A| = a_{11}a_{22}a_{33} - a_{11}a_{23}a_{32} - a_{21}a_{12}a_{33} + a_{21}a_{13}a_{32} + a_{31}a_{12}a_{23} - a_{31}a_{13}a_{22}$$

$$= a_{11}a_{22}a_{23} - a_{11}a_{23}a_{32} - a_{12}a_{21}a_{33} + a_{12}a_{23}a_{31} + a_{13}a_{21}a_{32} - a_{13}a_{31}a_{22} \quad ...(iii)$$

Clearly, the values of $|A|$ in Eqs. (i), (ii) and (iii) are equal. Also, it can be easily verified that the values of $|A|$ by expanding along R_3, C_2 and C_3 are equal to the value of $|A|$ obtained in Eqs. (i), (ii) and (iii). Hence, expanding a determinant along any row or column gives same value.

9 (*b*) While expanding the determinant instead of multiplying by $(-1)^{i+j}$, we can multiply by $+1$ or -1 according as $(i + j)$ is even or odd.

10 (*c*) Let $A = \begin{bmatrix} 2 & 2 \\ 4 & 0 \end{bmatrix}$ and $B = \begin{bmatrix} 1 & 1 \\ 2 & 0 \end{bmatrix}$.

Then, it is easy to verify that

$$A = 2B.$$

Also, $|A| = 0 - 8 = -8$ and $|B| = 0 - 2 = -2$.

Observe that $|A| = 4(-2) = 2^2|B|$ or $|A| = 2^n|B|$, where $n = 2$ is the order of square matrices A and B.

11 (*d*) In general, if $A = kB$, where A and B are square matrices of order n, then $|A| = k^n|B|$, where $n = 1, 2, 3$.

12 (*a*) For easier calculations, we shall expand the determinant along that row or column which contains maximum number of zeroes.

Note that In the third column, two entries are zero. So, expanding along third column C_3, we get

$$\Delta = 4\begin{vmatrix} -1 & 3 \\ 4 & 1 \end{vmatrix} - 0\begin{vmatrix} 1 & 2 \\ 4 & 1 \end{vmatrix} + 0\begin{vmatrix} 1 & 2 \\ -1 & 3 \end{vmatrix}$$

$$= 4(-1 - 12) - 0 + 0 = -52$$

13 (*c*) By expanding along R_1, we get

$$\Delta = 0\begin{vmatrix} 0 & \sin\beta \\ -\sin\beta & 0 \end{vmatrix} - \sin\alpha\begin{vmatrix} -\sin\alpha & \sin\beta \\ \cos\alpha & 0 \end{vmatrix} - \cos\alpha\begin{vmatrix} -\sin\alpha & 0 \\ \cos\alpha & -\sin\beta \end{vmatrix}$$

$$= 0 - \sin\alpha(0 - \sin\beta\cos\alpha) - \cos\alpha(\sin\alpha\sin\beta - 0)$$

$$= \sin\alpha\sin\beta\cos\alpha - \cos\alpha\sin\alpha\sin\beta$$

$$= 0$$

14 (*a*)

A. $\begin{vmatrix} 2 & 4 \\ -5 & -1 \end{vmatrix} = 2(-1) - 4(-5)$

$$= -2 + 20 = 18$$

B. $\begin{vmatrix} \cos\theta & -\sin\theta \\ \sin\theta & \cos\theta \end{vmatrix}$

$$= (\cos\theta)(\cos\theta) - (\sin\theta)(-\sin\theta)$$

$$= \cos^2\theta + \sin^2\theta$$

$$= 1 \quad [\because \cos^2\theta + \sin^2\theta = 1]$$

C. $\begin{vmatrix} x^2 - x + 1 & x - 1 \\ x + 1 & x + 1 \end{vmatrix}$

$$= (x^2 - x + 1)(x + 1) - (x + 1)(x - 1)$$

$$= x^3 + x^2 - x^2 - x + x + 1 - (x^2 - 1)$$

$$= x^3 + 1 - x^2 + 1 = x^3 - x^2 + 2$$

15 (*c*) We have, $A = \begin{bmatrix} 1 & 2 \\ 4 & 2 \end{bmatrix}$

$$\because 2A = 2\begin{bmatrix} 1 & 2 \\ 4 & 2 \end{bmatrix} = \begin{bmatrix} 2\times 1 & 2\times 2 \\ 2\times 4 & 2\times 2 \end{bmatrix} = \begin{bmatrix} 2 & 4 \\ 8 & 4 \end{bmatrix}$$

$$\therefore |2A| = \begin{vmatrix} 2 & 4 \\ 8 & 4 \end{vmatrix}$$

$$= 2\times 4 - 8\times 4 = -24 \quad ...(i)$$

Also, $|A| = \begin{vmatrix} 1 & 2 \\ 4 & 2 \end{vmatrix} = 1\times 2 - 4\times 2$

$$= -6$$

$$\Rightarrow 4|A| = 4\times(-6) = -24 \quad ...(ii)$$

From Eqs. (i) and (ii), we get

$$|2A| = 4|A|$$

Alternate Method

$\because$ A is a square matrix of order 2.

$$\therefore \quad |2A| = 2^2|A| = 4|A|$$

$[|kA| = k^n|A|$, if A is square matrix of order $n]$

16 (*d*) Given, $A = \begin{bmatrix} 1 & 0 & 1 \\ 0 & 1 & 2 \\ 0 & 0 & 4 \end{bmatrix}$

It can be observed that in the first column, two entries are zero. Therefore, we expand the determinant of matrix A along the first column C_1.

$$\therefore \quad |A| = 1\begin{vmatrix} 1 & 2 \\ 0 & 4 \end{vmatrix} - 0\begin{vmatrix} 0 & 1 \\ 0 & 4 \end{vmatrix} + 0\begin{vmatrix} 0 & 1 \\ 1 & 2 \end{vmatrix}$$

$$= 1(1\times 4 - 0\times 2) = 4$$

$$\therefore \quad 27|A| = 27\times 4 = 108 \quad ...(i)$$

Now, $|3A| = 3\begin{vmatrix} 1 & 0 & 1 \\ 0 & 1 & 2 \\ 0 & 0 & 4 \end{vmatrix}$

$$\therefore \quad |3A| = \begin{vmatrix} 3 & 0 & 3 \\ 0 & 3 & 6 \\ 0 & 0 & 12 \end{vmatrix}$$

It can be observed that in the first column, two entries are zero.

Therefore, we expand the determinant along the first column C_1 for easier calculation.

$$|3A|=3\begin{vmatrix}3&6\\0&12\end{vmatrix}-0\begin{vmatrix}0&3\\0&12\end{vmatrix}+0\begin{vmatrix}0&3\\3&6\end{vmatrix}$$

$$=3(3\times12-0\times6)$$

$\Rightarrow\ |3A|=3(36)=108$ ...(ii)

From Eqs. (i) and (ii), we get

$$|3A|=27|A|.$$

Alternate Method

$\because$ A is a square matrix of order 3.

$\therefore\quad |3A|=3^3|A|=27|A|$

($|kA|=k^n|A|$, if A is a square matrix of order n)

17 (*d*)

A. Let $|A|=\begin{vmatrix}3&-1&-2\\0&0&-1\\3&-5&0\end{vmatrix}$

It can be observed that in the second row, two entries are zero. Therefore, we expand the determinant along the second row for easier calculation.

$$|A|=-0\begin{vmatrix}-1&-2\\-5&0\end{vmatrix}+0\begin{vmatrix}3&-2\\3&0\end{vmatrix}-(-1)\begin{vmatrix}3&-1\\3&-5\end{vmatrix}$$

$=\{3\times(-5)-3\times(-1)\}$

$=-15+3=-12$

B. Let $|B|=\begin{vmatrix}3&-4&5\\1&1&-2\\2&3&1\end{vmatrix}$

By expanding along R_1 (first row), we get

$$|B|=3\begin{vmatrix}1&-2\\3&1\end{vmatrix}-(-4)\begin{vmatrix}1&-2\\2&1\end{vmatrix}+5\begin{vmatrix}1&1\\2&3\end{vmatrix}$$

$=3(1+6)+4(1+4)+5(3-2)$

$=3(7)+4(5)+5(1)$

$=21+20+5=46$

C. Let $|C|=\begin{vmatrix}0&1&2\\-1&0&-3\\-2&3&0\end{vmatrix}$

By expanding along R_1 (first row), we get

$$|C|=0\begin{vmatrix}0&-3\\3&0\end{vmatrix}-1\begin{vmatrix}-1&-3\\-2&0\end{vmatrix}+2\begin{vmatrix}-1&0\\-2&3\end{vmatrix}$$

$=-1(0-6)+2(-3-0)$

$=-1(-6)+2(-3)=6-6=0$

D. Let $|D|=\begin{vmatrix}2&-1&-2\\0&2&-1\\3&-5&0\end{vmatrix}$

By expanding along R_2 (second row), we get

$$|D|=-0\begin{vmatrix}-1&-2\\-5&0\end{vmatrix}+2\begin{vmatrix}2&-2\\3&0\end{vmatrix}-(-1)\begin{vmatrix}2&-1\\3&-5\end{vmatrix}$$

$=0+2(0+6)+(-10+3)$

$=12-7=5$

18 (*a*) The given matrix is

$$A=\begin{bmatrix}1&1&-2\\2&1&-3\\5&4&-9\end{bmatrix}$$

Then, $|A|=\begin{vmatrix}1&1&-2\\2&1&-3\\5&4&-9\end{vmatrix}$

By expanding along R_1 (first row), we get

$$|A|=1\begin{vmatrix}1&-3\\4&-9\end{vmatrix}-1\begin{vmatrix}2&-3\\5&-9\end{vmatrix}+(-2)\begin{vmatrix}2&1\\5&4\end{vmatrix}$$

$=1(-9+12)-1(-18+15)-2(8-5)$

$=1(3)-1(-3)-2(3)$

$=3+3-6=0$

19 (*a*) Given, $\begin{vmatrix}2&4\\5&1\end{vmatrix}=\begin{vmatrix}2x&4\\6&x\end{vmatrix}$

On expanding both determinants, we get

$2\times1-5\times4=2x\times x-6\times4$

$\Rightarrow\quad 2-20=2x^2-24$

$\Rightarrow\quad 2x^2=-18+24$

$\Rightarrow\quad x^2=\frac{6}{2}=3$

$\Rightarrow\quad x=\pm\sqrt{3}$

20 (*b*) Given, $\begin{vmatrix}2&3\\4&5\end{vmatrix}=\begin{vmatrix}x&3\\2x&5\end{vmatrix}$

On expanding both determinants, we get

$2\times5-4\times3=5\times x-3\times 2x$

$\Rightarrow\quad 10-12=5x-6x$

$\Rightarrow\quad -2=-x$

$\Rightarrow\quad x=2$

21 (*b*) Consider

$$\begin{vmatrix}x^2+xy+y^2&x+y\\x^2-xy+y^2&x-y\end{vmatrix}$$

$=(x^2+xy+y^2)(x-y)-(x^2-xy+y^2)(x+y)$

$=x^3-y^3-(x^3+y^3)$

$=x^3-y^3-x^3-y^3$

$=-2y^3$

22 (*c*) Consider

$$\Delta=\begin{vmatrix}1&\log_b a\\\log_a b&1\end{vmatrix}$$

$=1-\log_b a\cdot\log_a b$

$=1-1\quad\left[\because \log_b a=\frac{1}{\log_a b}\right]$

$=0$

23 (*a*) The given determinant is

$$\Delta=\begin{vmatrix}2&3&-2\\1&2&3\\-2&1&-3\end{vmatrix}$$

By expanding along second row, we get

$$\Delta=-1\begin{vmatrix}3&-2\\1&-3\end{vmatrix}+2\begin{vmatrix}2&-2\\-2&-3\end{vmatrix}-3\begin{vmatrix}2&3\\-2&1\end{vmatrix}$$

$=-(-9+2)+2(-6-4)-3(2+6)$

$=7-20-24$

$=-37$

24 (*c*) Matrix cannot be reduced to a number because it is just an arrangement of numbers, while if $A=[a_{ij}]_{n\times n}$ be a square matrix of order n, then the expression $|A|=|a_{ij}|$ is called determinant of A which can be reduced to a number.

25 (*a*) Let $\Delta = \begin{vmatrix} x & \sin\theta & \cos\theta \\ -\sin\theta & -x & 1 \\ \cos\theta & 1 & x \end{vmatrix}$

By expanding along first row, we get

$$\Delta = x\begin{vmatrix} -x & 1 \\ 1 & x \end{vmatrix} - \sin\theta \begin{vmatrix} -\sin\theta & 1 \\ \cos\theta & x \end{vmatrix} + \cos\theta \begin{vmatrix} -\sin\theta & -x \\ \cos\theta & 1 \end{vmatrix}$$

$= x(-x^2 - 1) - \sin\theta(-x\sin\theta - \cos\theta) + \cos\theta(-\sin\theta + x\cos\theta)$

$= -x^3 - x + x\sin^2\theta + \sin\theta\cos\theta - \sin\theta\cos\theta + x\cos^2\theta$

$= -x^3 - x + x(\sin^2\theta + \cos^2\theta)$

$= -x^3 - x + x$ $\quad [\because \sin^2\theta + \cos\theta^2 = 1]$

$= -x^3$

Hence, Δ is independent of θ.

26 (*b*) Consider

$$\Delta = \begin{vmatrix} \sin 10° & -\cos 10° \\ \sin 80° & \cos 80° \end{vmatrix}$$

$= \sin 10° \cos 80° + \sin 80° \cos 10°$

$= \sin(10° + 80°)$ $\quad [\because \sin(A+B) = \sin A\cos B + \cos A \sin B]$

$= \sin(90°) = 1$ $\quad [\because \sin 90° = 1]$

27 (*a*) Consider

$$\Delta = \begin{vmatrix} a+ib & c+id \\ -c+id & a-ib \end{vmatrix}$$

$= (a+ib)(a-ib) - (c+id)(-c+id)$

$= a^2 - iab + iab + b^2 - [-c^2 + icd - icd - d^2]$ $\quad [\because i^2 = -1]$

$= a^2 + b^2 + c^2 + d^2$

28 (*b*) Consider $\begin{vmatrix} x & 2 \\ 18 & x \end{vmatrix} = \begin{vmatrix} 6 & 2 \\ 18 & 6 \end{vmatrix}$

On expanding both determinants, we get

$x^2 - 36 = 36 - 36$

$\Rightarrow \quad x^2 = 36$

$\Rightarrow \quad x = \pm 6$

Area of Triangle

1 (*b*) The area of a triangle with vertices $(x_1, y_1), (x_2, y_2)$ and (x_3, y_3) is given by the expression

$$\frac{1}{2}|x_1(y_2 - y_3) + x_2(y_3 - y_1) + x_3(y_1 - y_2)|.$$

2 (*a*) We know that, the area of triangle with vertices $(x_1, y_1), (x_2, y_2)$ and (x_3, y_3) is $\frac{1}{2}|x_1(y_2 - y_3) + x_2(y_3 - y_1) + x_3(y_1 - y_2)|$

and this expression can be written in the form of determinant as

$$\Delta = \frac{1}{2}\begin{vmatrix} x_1 & y_1 & 1 \\ x_2 & y_2 & 1 \\ x_3 & y_3 & 1 \end{vmatrix}$$

3 (*c*) The area of the triangle formed by three collinear points is zero.

4 (*c*) The area of triangle is given by

$$\Delta = \frac{1}{2}\begin{vmatrix} 3 & 8 & 1 \\ -4 & 2 & 1 \\ 5 & 1 & 1 \end{vmatrix}$$

$= \frac{1}{2}[3(2-1) - 8(-4-5) + 1(-4-10)]$

$= \frac{1}{2}(3 + 72 - 14) = \frac{61}{2}$ sq units

Note *Since, area is a positive quantity, so we always take the absolute value of the determinant.*

5 (*d*) Since, the area of the ΔABD is 3 sq units, then we have

$$\frac{1}{2}\begin{vmatrix} 1 & 3 & 1 \\ 0 & 0 & 1 \\ k & 0 & 1 \end{vmatrix} = \pm 3$$

This gives $\frac{3k}{2} = \pm 3$, i.e. $k = \pm 2$.

Note *If area is given, then use both positive and negative values of the determinant for calculation.*

6 (*b*) We know that the area of triangle with vertices $(x_1, y_1), (x_2, y_2)$ and (x_3, y_3) is given by

$$\Delta = \frac{1}{2}\begin{vmatrix} x_1 & y_1 & 1 \\ x_2 & y_2 & 1 \\ x_3 & y_3 & 1 \end{vmatrix}$$

Thus,

A. Required area $= \frac{1}{2}\begin{vmatrix} 1 & 0 & 1 \\ 6 & 0 & 1 \\ 4 & 3 & 1 \end{vmatrix}$

$= \frac{1}{2}|1(0-3) - 0(6-4) + 1(18-0)|$

$= \frac{1}{2}|-3 + 18| = \frac{15}{2}$ sq units

B. Required area $= \frac{1}{2}\begin{vmatrix} 2 & 7 & 1 \\ 1 & 1 & 1 \\ 10 & 8 & 1 \end{vmatrix}$

$= \frac{1}{2}|2(1-8) - 7(1-10) + 1(8-10)|$

$= \frac{1}{2}|2(-7) - 7(-9) + 1(-2)|$

$= \frac{1}{2}|-14 + 63 - 2|$

$= \frac{47}{2}$ sq units

C. Required area $= \frac{1}{2}\begin{vmatrix} -2 & -3 & 1 \\ 3 & 2 & 1 \\ -1 & -8 & 1 \end{vmatrix}$

$= \frac{1}{2}|-2(2+8) + 3(3+1) + 1(-24+2)|$

$= \frac{1}{2}|-20 + 12 - 22|$

$= \frac{1}{2}|-30| = 15$ sq units

7 (*d*) Let $P(x, y)$ be any point on the line joining $A(1, 2)$ and $B(3, 6)$. Since, the points A, B and P are collinear, therefore area of ΔABP will be zero.

i.e. $\frac{1}{2}\begin{vmatrix} 1 & 2 & 1 \\ 3 & 6 & 1 \\ x & y & 1 \end{vmatrix} = 0$

$\Rightarrow \frac{1}{2}[1(6-y)-2(3-x)$
$+1(3y-6x)]=0$

$\Rightarrow 6-y-6+2x+3y-6x=0$

$\Rightarrow 2y-4x=0$

$\Rightarrow y=2x$

Hence, the equation of the line joining the given points is $y=2x$.

8 (a) Let $P(x, y)$ be any point on the line joining $A(3,1)$ and $B(9,3)$. Then, the points A, B and P are collinear. Therefore, the area of the ΔABP will be zero.

$$\therefore \frac{1}{2}\begin{vmatrix} 3 & 1 & 1 \\ 9 & 3 & 1 \\ x & y & 1 \end{vmatrix}=0$$

$\Rightarrow \frac{1}{2}|3(3-y)-1(9-x)$
$+1(9y-3x)|=0$

$\Rightarrow 9-3y-9+x+9y-3x=0$

$\Rightarrow 6y-2x=0$

$\Rightarrow x-3y=0$

Hence, the equation of the line joining the given points is $x-3y=0$ i.e. $x=3y$.

9 (a) Area of triangle

$$=\frac{1}{2}\begin{vmatrix} x_1 & y_1 & 1 \\ x_2 & y_2 & 1 \\ x_3 & y_3 & 1 \end{vmatrix}$$

Given, $\frac{1}{2}\begin{vmatrix} k & 0 & 1 \\ 4 & 0 & 1 \\ 0 & 2 & 1 \end{vmatrix}=4$

$\Rightarrow |k(0-2)+1(8-0)|=8$

$\Rightarrow k(0-2)+1(8-0)=\pm 8$

On taking positive sign,

$\Rightarrow -2k=0 \Rightarrow k=0$

On taking negative sign,

$\Rightarrow -2k=-16 \Rightarrow k=8$

$\therefore k=0, 8$

10 (c) The given points are $(a, b+c), (b, c+a)$ and $(c, a+b)$.

Area of triangle,

$$\Delta=\frac{1}{2}\begin{vmatrix} a & b+c & 1 \\ b & c+a & 1 \\ c & a+b & 1 \end{vmatrix}$$

$=\frac{1}{2}[a(c+a-a-b)$
$-b(b+c-a-b)$
$+c(b+c-c-a)]$

$=\frac{1}{2}[ac-ab-bc+ab+bc-ac]$

$=\frac{1}{2}\times 0=0$

$\therefore \Delta=0$

Thus, area of triangle is zero. Hence, the three given points are collinear.

11 (b) Given that the three points are collinear.

$$\therefore \frac{1}{2}\begin{vmatrix} a_1 & b_1 & 1 \\ a_2 & b_2 & 1 \\ a_1+a_2 & b_1+b_2 & 1 \end{vmatrix}=0$$

$$\Rightarrow \begin{vmatrix} a_1 & b_1 & 1 \\ a_2 & b_2 & 1 \\ a_1+a_2 & b_1+b_2 & 1 \end{vmatrix}=0$$

$\Rightarrow a_1(b_2-b_1-b_2)-a_2(b_1-b_1-b_2)$
$+(a_1+a_2)(b_1-b_2)=0$

$\Rightarrow -a_1b_1+a_2b_2+a_1b_1-a_1b_2$
$+a_2b_1-a_2b_2=0$

$\therefore a_1b_2=a_2b_1$

12 (b) Given that the area of a triangle with vertices $(-3,0), (3,0)$ and $(0,k)$ is 9 sq units.

$$\therefore \frac{1}{2}\begin{vmatrix} -3 & 0 & 1 \\ 3 & 0 & 1 \\ 0 & k & 1 \end{vmatrix}=\pm 9$$

$$\Rightarrow \begin{vmatrix} -3 & 0 & 1 \\ 3 & 0 & 1 \\ 0 & k & 1 \end{vmatrix}=\pm 18$$

By expanding along C_2, we get

$$-k\begin{vmatrix} -3 & 1 \\ 3 & 1 \end{vmatrix}=\pm 18$$

$\Rightarrow +6k=\pm 18$

$\therefore k=\pm 3$

13 (b) Given that, the points $(2,-3), (\lambda,-1)$ and $(0,4)$ are collinear.

$$\therefore \frac{1}{2}\begin{vmatrix} 2 & -3 & 1 \\ \lambda & -1 & 1 \\ 0 & 4 & 1 \end{vmatrix}=0$$

$$\Rightarrow \begin{vmatrix} 2 & -3 & 1 \\ \lambda & -1 & 1 \\ 0 & 4 & 1 \end{vmatrix}=0$$

$\Rightarrow 2(-1-4)-\lambda(-3-4)=0$

$\Rightarrow -10+7\lambda=0$

$\Rightarrow \lambda=\frac{10}{7}$

Minors and Cofactors

1 (b) Minor of an element of a determinant of order $n(n\geq 2)$ is a determinant of order $n-1$.

2 (a) Since, 6 lies in the second row and third column, therefore its minor M_{23} is given by

$$M_{23}=\begin{vmatrix} 1 & 2 \\ 7 & 8 \end{vmatrix}$$

$=8-14=-6$

[obtained by deleting R_2 and C_3 in Δ]

3 (d) Cofactor of an element a_{ij} denoted by A_{ij} is defined by $A_{ij}=(-1)^{i+j}M_{ij}$, where M_{ij} is minor of a_{ij}.

4 (c) If elements of a row (or column) are multiplied with cofactors of any other row (or column), then their sum is zero.

$\therefore \Delta=a_{11}A_{21}+a_{12}A_{22}+a_{13}A_{23}$

$$=a_{11}(-1)^{2+1}\begin{vmatrix} a_{12} & a_{13} \\ a_{32} & a_{33} \end{vmatrix}+a_{12}(-1)^{2+2}\begin{vmatrix} a_{11} & a_{13} \\ a_{31} & a_{33} \end{vmatrix}+a_{13}(-1)^{2+3}\begin{vmatrix} a_{11} & a_{12} \\ a_{31} & a_{32} \end{vmatrix}$$

$$=\begin{vmatrix} a_{11} & a_{12} & a_{13} \\ a_{11} & a_{12} & a_{13} \\ a_{31} & a_{32} & a_{33} \end{vmatrix}=0$$

Similarly, we can try for other rows and columns.

5 (c)

I. Here, $\Delta = \begin{vmatrix} 2 & -4 \\ 0 & 3 \end{vmatrix}$

$\therefore$ Minors,

$M_{11} = 3, M_{12} = 0, M_{21} = -4$

and $M_{22} = 2$

Also, cofactors

$A_{11} = (-1)^{1+1} M_{11} = 1 \times 3 = 3$

$A_{12} = (-1)^{1+2} M_{12} = (-1) \times 0 = 0$

$A_{21} = (-1)^{2+1} M_{21} = (-1)(-4) = 4$

and $A_{22} = (-1)^{2+2} M_{22} = 1 \times 2 = 2$

II. Here, $\Delta = \begin{vmatrix} a & c \\ b & d \end{vmatrix}$

$\therefore$ Minors,

$M_{11} = d, M_{12} = b, M_{21} = c$

and $M_{22} = a$

Also, cofactors

$A_{11} = (-1)^{1+1} M_{11} = 1 \times d = d$

$A_{12} = (-1)^{1+2} M_{12} = (-1) \times b = -b$

$A_{21} = (-1)^{2+1} M_{21} = (-1) \times c = -c$

$A_{22} = (-1)^{2+2} M_{22} = 1 \times a = a$

6 (a) Here, $\Delta = \begin{vmatrix} 1 & 0 & 0 \\ 0 & 1 & 0 \\ 0 & 0 & 1 \end{vmatrix}$

Minors of elements of first row are

$M_{11} = \begin{vmatrix} 1 & 0 \\ 0 & 1 \end{vmatrix} = 1 - 0 = 1$

$M_{12} = \begin{vmatrix} 0 & 0 \\ 0 & 1 \end{vmatrix} = 0 - 0 = 0$

and $M_{13} = \begin{vmatrix} 0 & 1 \\ 0 & 0 \end{vmatrix} = 0 - 0 = 0$

Minors of elements of second row are

$M_{21} = \begin{vmatrix} 0 & 0 \\ 0 & 1 \end{vmatrix} = 0 - 0 = 0$

$M_{22} = \begin{vmatrix} 1 & 0 \\ 0 & 1 \end{vmatrix} = 1 - 0 = 1$

and $M_{23} = \begin{vmatrix} 1 & 0 \\ 0 & 0 \end{vmatrix} = 0 - 0 = 0$

Minors of elements of third row are

$M_{31} = \begin{vmatrix} 0 & 0 \\ 1 & 0 \end{vmatrix} = 0 - 0 = 0$

$M_{32} = \begin{vmatrix} 1 & 0 \\ 0 & 0 \end{vmatrix} = 0 - 0 = 0$

and $M_{33} = \begin{vmatrix} 1 & 0 \\ 0 & 1 \end{vmatrix} = 1 - 0 = 1$

Hence, cofactors of elements of first row are

$A_{11} = (-1)^{1+1} M_{11} = 1 \times 1 = 1$

$A_{12} = (-1)^{1+2} M_{12} = -1 \times 0 = 0$

and $A_{13} = (-1)^{1+3} M_{13} = 1 \times 0 = 0$

Cofactors of elements of second row are

$A_{21} = (-1)^{2+1} M_{21} = -1 \times 0 = 0$

$A_{22} = (-1)^{2+2} M_{22} = 1 \times 1 = 1$

and $A_{23} = (-1)^{2+3} M_{23} = -1 \times 0 = 0$

Cofactors of elements of third row are

$A_{31} = (-1)^{3+1} M_{31} = 1 \times 0 = 0,$

$A_{32} = (-1)^{3+2} M_{32} = -1 \times 0 = 0$

and $A_{33} = (-1)^{3+3} M_{33} = 1 \times 1 = 1$

7 (c) Here, $\Delta = \begin{vmatrix} 1 & 0 & 4 \\ 3 & 5 & -1 \\ 0 & 1 & 2 \end{vmatrix}$

Minors of elements of first row are

$M_{11} = \begin{vmatrix} 5 & -1 \\ 1 & 2 \end{vmatrix} = 10 + 1 = 11$

$M_{12} = \begin{vmatrix} 3 & -1 \\ 0 & 2 \end{vmatrix} = 6 - 0 = 6$

and $M_{13} = \begin{vmatrix} 3 & 5 \\ 0 & 1 \end{vmatrix} = 3 - 0 = 3$

Minors of elements of second row are

$M_{21} = \begin{vmatrix} 0 & 4 \\ 1 & 2 \end{vmatrix} = 0 - 4 = -4$

$M_{22} = \begin{vmatrix} 1 & 4 \\ 0 & 2 \end{vmatrix} = 2 - 0 = 2$

and $M_{23} = \begin{vmatrix} 1 & 0 \\ 0 & 1 \end{vmatrix} = 1 - 0 = 1$

Minors of elements of third row are

$M_{31} = \begin{vmatrix} 0 & 4 \\ 5 & -1 \end{vmatrix} = 0 - 20 = -20,$

$M_{32} = \begin{vmatrix} 1 & 4 \\ 3 & -1 \end{vmatrix} = -1 - 12 = -13$

and $M_{33} = \begin{vmatrix} 1 & 0 \\ 3 & 5 \end{vmatrix} = 5 - 0 = 5$

Hence, cofactors of elements of first row are

$A_{11} = (-1)^{1+1} M_{11} = 1 \times 11 = 11,$

$A_{12} = (-1)^{1+2} M_{12} = -1 \times 6 = -6$

and $A_{13} = (-1)^{1+3} M_{13} = 1 \times 3 = 3$

Cofactors of elements of second row are

$A_{21} = (-1)^{2+1} M_{21} = -1 \times -4 = 4,$

$A_{22} = (-1)^{2+2} M_{22} = 1 \times 2 = 2$

and $A_{23} = (-1)^{2+3} M_{23} = -1 \times 1 = -1$

Cofactors of elements of third row are

$A_{31} = (-1)^{3+1} M_{31} = 1 \times -20 = -20$

$A_{32} = (-1)^{3+2} M_{32} = -1 \times (-13) = 13$

and $A_{33} = (-1)^{3+3} M_{33} = 1 \times 5 = 5$

8 (d) Given, $\Delta = \begin{vmatrix} 5 & 3 & 8 \\ 2 & 0 & 1 \\ 1 & 2 & 3 \end{vmatrix}$

Cofactors of the elements of second row are

$A_{21} = (-1)^{2+1} \begin{vmatrix} 3 & 8 \\ 2 & 3 \end{vmatrix}$

$= -(9 - 16) = 7$ $\quad [\because A_{ij} = (-1)^{i+j} M_{ij}]$

$A_{22} = (-1)^{2+2} \begin{vmatrix} 5 & 8 \\ 1 & 3 \end{vmatrix}$

$= 15 - 8 = 7$

and $A_{23} = (-1)^{2+3} \begin{vmatrix} 5 & 3 \\ 1 & 2 \end{vmatrix}$

$= -(10 - 3) = -7$

Now, expansion of Δ using cofactors of elements of second row is given by

$\Delta = a_{21}A_{21} + a_{22}A_{22} + a_{23}A_{23}$

$= 2 \times 7 + 0 \times 7 + 1(-7)$

$= 14 - 7 = 7$

9 (*b*) Given, $\Delta = \begin{vmatrix} 1 & x & yz \\ 1 & y & zx \\ 1 & z & xy \end{vmatrix}$

Cofactors of the elements of third column are

$$A_{13} = (-1)^{1+3}\begin{vmatrix} 1 & y \\ 1 & z \end{vmatrix}$$
$$= 1(z - y) = z - y$$
$$A_{23} = (-1)^{2+3}\begin{vmatrix} 1 & x \\ 1 & z \end{vmatrix}$$
$$= -1(z - x) = x - z$$
and $A_{33} = (-1)^{3+3}\begin{vmatrix} 1 & x \\ 1 & y \end{vmatrix}$
$$= 1(y - x) = y - x$$

Now, expansion of Δ using cofactors of elements of third column is given by

$$\Delta = a_{13}A_{13} + a_{23}A_{23} + a_{33}A_{33}$$
$$= yz(z - y) + zx(x - z) + xy(y - x)$$
$$= yz^2 - y^2z + zx^2 - z^2x + xy^2 - x^2y$$
$$= x^2(z - y) + x(y^2 - z^2) + yz(z - y)$$
$$= (z - y)\{x^2 - x(y + z) + yz\}$$
$$= (z - y)\{x^2 - xy - zx + yz\}$$
$$= (z - y)[x(x - y) - z(x - y)]$$
$$= (y - z)(x - y)(z - x)$$
$$= (x - y)(y - z)(z - x)$$

10 (*d*) Δ is equal to the sum of the products of the elements of a row (or a column) with their corresponding cofactors.

$\therefore \Delta = a_{11}A_{11} + a_{12}A_{12} + a_{13}A_{13}$

or $a_{21}A_{21} + a_{22}A_{22} + a_{23}A_{23}$

or $a_{31}A_{31} + a_{32}A_{32} + a_{33}A_{33}$

or $a_{11}A_{11} + a_{21}A_{21} + a_{31}A_{31}$

or $a_{12}A_{12} + a_{22}A_{22} + a_{32}A_{32}$

or $a_{13}A_{13} + a_{23}A_{23} + a_{33}A_{33}$

Sum of the products of the elements of first column with their corresponding cofactors is $\Delta = a_{11}A_{11} + a_{21}A_{21} + a_{31}A_{31}$.

11 (*a*) Given that, $\Delta = \begin{vmatrix} 1 & 3 & -2 \\ 4 & -5 & 6 \\ 3 & 5 & 2 \end{vmatrix}$

Also, $M_{11} = -40, M_{12} = -10$

and $M_{13} = 35$

$\therefore \quad A_{11} = (-1)^{1+1}M_{11} = -40$

$A_{12} = (-1)^{1+2}M_{12} = 10$

and $A_{13} = (-1)^{1+3}M_{13} = 35$

$$\therefore \Delta = a_{11}A_{11} + a_{12}A_{12} + a_{13}A_{13}$$
$$= 1 \times (-40) + 3(10) + (-2)(35)$$
$$= -40 + 30 - 70 = -80$$

12 (*b*) We have, $\Delta = \begin{vmatrix} a & h & g \\ h & b & f \\ g & f & c \end{vmatrix}$.

Now, minor of a_{21} is

$$M_{21} = \begin{vmatrix} h & g \\ f & c \end{vmatrix} = hc - fg$$
$$\therefore \quad A_{21} = (-1)^{2+1}M_{21}$$
$$= -(hc - fg) = fg - hc$$

13 (*d*) We have, $\Delta = \begin{vmatrix} 1 & a & bc \\ 1 & b & ca \\ 1 & c & ab \end{vmatrix}$.

Then, minor M_{31} is given by

$$M_{31} = \begin{vmatrix} a & bc \\ b & ca \end{vmatrix}$$
$$= a^2c - b^2c = c(a^2 - b^2)$$

Adjoint and Inverse of a Matrix

1 (*c*) The adjoint of a square matrix $A = [a_{ij}]_{n \times n}$ is defined as the transpose of the matrix $[A_{ij}]_{n \times n}$, where A_{ij} is the cofactor of the element a_{ij}.

2 (*b*) Let $A = \begin{bmatrix} a_{11} & a_{12} & a_{13} \\ a_{21} & a_{22} & a_{23} \\ a_{31} & a_{32} & a_{33} \end{bmatrix}$

Then, adj A = Transpose of

$$\begin{bmatrix} A_{11} & A_{12} & A_{13} \\ A_{21} & A_{22} & A_{23} \\ A_{31} & A_{32} & A_{33} \end{bmatrix}$$
$$= \begin{bmatrix} A_{11} & A_{21} & A_{31} \\ A_{12} & A_{22} & A_{32} \\ A_{13} & A_{23} & A_{33} \end{bmatrix}$$

3 (*d*) We have,

$A_{11} = 4, A_{12} = -1, A_{21} = -3, A_{22} = 2$

Hence, adj $A = \begin{bmatrix} A_{11} & A_{21} \\ A_{12} & A_{22} \end{bmatrix}$

$$= \begin{bmatrix} 4 & -3 \\ -1 & 2 \end{bmatrix}$$

4 (*a*) For a square matrix of order 2, given by

$$A = \begin{bmatrix} a_{11} & a_{12} \\ a_{21} & a_{22} \end{bmatrix}$$

The adj A can also be obtained by interchanging a_{11} and a_{22} and by changing signs of a_{12} and a_{21} i.e.

$$\text{adj } A = \begin{bmatrix} a_{22} & -a_{12} \\ -a_{21} & a_{11} \end{bmatrix}$$

Change sign Interchange

5 (*c*) If A be any given square matrix of order n, then

$$A(\text{adj } A) = (\text{adj } A)A = |A| I,$$

where I is the identity matrix of order n.

Verification

Let $A = \begin{bmatrix} a_{11} & a_{12} & a_{13} \\ a_{21} & a_{22} & a_{23} \\ a_{31} & a_{32} & a_{33} \end{bmatrix}$

Then, adj $A = \begin{bmatrix} A_{11} & A_{21} & A_{31} \\ A_{12} & A_{22} & A_{32} \\ A_{13} & A_{23} & A_{33} \end{bmatrix}$

Since, sum of products of elements of a row (or a column) with corresponding cofactors is equal to $|A|$ and otherwise zero.

$\therefore$ We have,

$$A(\text{adj } A) = \begin{bmatrix} |A| & 0 & 0 \\ 0 & |A| & 0 \\ 0 & 0 & |A| \end{bmatrix}$$
$$= |A|\begin{bmatrix} 1 & 0 & 0 \\ 0 & 1 & 0 \\ 0 & 0 & 1 \end{bmatrix} = |A| I$$

Similarly, we can show $(\text{adj } A)A = |A| I$.

Hence, $A(\text{adj } A) = (\text{adj } A)A = |A| I$

6 (*a*) A square matrix A is said to be singular, if $|A| = 0$.

7 (*b*) A square matrix A is said to be non-singular, if $|A| \neq 0$.

8 (*a*) If $A = \begin{bmatrix} 1 & 2 \\ 3 & 4 \end{bmatrix}$, then

$$|A| = \begin{vmatrix} 1 & 2 \\ 3 & 4 \end{vmatrix} = 4 - 6 = -2 \neq 0$$

Hence, A is non-singular matrix.

9 (*c*) If A and B are non-singular matrices of the same order, then AB and BA are also non-singular matrices of the same order.

10 (*a*) The determinant of the product of matrices is equal to product of their respective determinants, i.e. $|AB| = |A| \cdot |B|$, where A and B are square matrices of the same order.

11 (*b*) We know that

$$(\text{adj } A)\, A = |A|\, I = \begin{bmatrix} |A| & 0 & 0 \\ 0 & |A| & 0 \\ 0 & 0 & |A| \end{bmatrix}$$

Writing determinants of matrices on both sides, we get

$$|(\text{adj } A)\, A| = \begin{vmatrix} |A| & 0 & 0 \\ 0 & |A| & 0 \\ 0 & 0 & |A| \end{vmatrix}$$

i.e. $|(\text{adj } A)|\,|A| = |A|^3 \begin{vmatrix} 1 & 0 & 0 \\ 0 & 1 & 0 \\ 0 & 0 & 1 \end{vmatrix}$

i.e. $|(\text{adj } A)|\,|A| = |A|^3$ (1)

i.e. $|(\text{adj } A)| = |A|^2$ $[\because |A| \neq 0]$

12 (*a*) In general, if A is a non-singular square matrix of order n, then $|\text{adj } A| = |A|^{n-1}$.

13 (*b*) A square matrix A is invertible, if and only if A is non-singular matrix i.e. $|A| \neq 0$.

Justification Let A be invertible matrix of order n and I be the identity matrix of order n.

Then, there exists a square matrix B of order n such that $AB = BA = I$.

Now, $AB = I$.

So, $|AB| = |I|$ or $|A|\,|B| = 1$

$[\because |I| = 1, |AB| = |A|\,|B|]$

This gives $|A| \neq 0$.

Hence, A is non-singular.

Conversely, let A be non-singular. Then, $|A| \neq 0$.

Now, $A(\text{adj } A) = (\text{adj } A)\, A = |A|\, I$

or $A\left(\dfrac{1}{|A|}\text{adj } A\right) = \left(\dfrac{1}{|A|}\text{adj } A\right) A = I$

or $AB = BA = I$,

where $B = \dfrac{1}{|A|}\text{adj } A$

Thus, A is invertible and

$A^{-1} = \dfrac{1}{|A|}\text{adj } A$.

14 (*c*) Let $A = \begin{bmatrix} 1 & 2 \\ 3 & 4 \end{bmatrix}$

Then, $A_{11} = 4, A_{12} = -3, A_{21} = -2$ and $A_{22} = 1$

$\therefore$ $\text{adj } A = \begin{bmatrix} A_{11} & A_{12} \\ A_{21} & A_{22} \end{bmatrix}'$

$= \begin{bmatrix} 4 & -3 \\ -2 & 1 \end{bmatrix}' = \begin{bmatrix} 4 & -2 \\ -3 & 1 \end{bmatrix}$

15 (*a*) Let $A = \begin{bmatrix} 1 & -1 & 2 \\ 2 & 3 & 5 \\ -2 & 0 & 1 \end{bmatrix}$

Cofactors of elements of first row are

$A_{11} = \begin{vmatrix} 3 & 5 \\ 0 & 1 \end{vmatrix} = 3 - 0 = 3$,

$A_{12} = -\begin{vmatrix} 2 & 5 \\ -2 & 1 \end{vmatrix} = -(2 + 10) = -12$,

and $A_{13} = \begin{vmatrix} 2 & 3 \\ -2 & 0 \end{vmatrix} = 0 - (-6) = 6$

Cofactors of elements of second row are

$A_{21} = -\begin{vmatrix} -1 & 2 \\ 0 & 1 \end{vmatrix} = -(-1 - 0) = 1$,

$A_{22} = \begin{vmatrix} 1 & 2 \\ -2 & 1 \end{vmatrix} = 1 + 4 = 5$

and $A_{23} = -\begin{vmatrix} 1 & -1 \\ -2 & 0 \end{vmatrix}$

$= -(0 - 2) = 2$

Cofactors of elements of third row are

$A_{31} = \begin{vmatrix} -1 & 2 \\ 3 & 5 \end{vmatrix} = (-5 - 6) = -11$,

$A_{32} = -\begin{vmatrix} 1 & 2 \\ 2 & 5 \end{vmatrix} = -(5 - 4) = -1$

and $A_{33} = \begin{vmatrix} 1 & -1 \\ 2 & 3 \end{vmatrix} = 3 + 2 = 5$

Hence, $\text{adj }(A) = \begin{bmatrix} 3 & -12 & 6 \\ 1 & 5 & 2 \\ -11 & -1 & 5 \end{bmatrix}'$

$= \begin{bmatrix} 3 & 1 & -11 \\ -12 & 5 & -1 \\ 6 & 2 & 5 \end{bmatrix}$

16 (*c*) Let $A = \begin{bmatrix} 2 & 3 \\ -4 & -6 \end{bmatrix}$,

$|A| = \begin{vmatrix} 2 & 3 \\ -4 & -6 \end{vmatrix}$

$= -12 - (-12)$

$= -12 + 12 = 0$

$|A|\, I = 0 \begin{bmatrix} 1 & 0 \\ 0 & 1 \end{bmatrix} = \begin{bmatrix} 0 & 0 \\ 0 & 0 \end{bmatrix}$

Cofactors of A are

$A_{11} = -6, A_{12} = 4$,

$A_{21} = -3$ and $A_{22} = 2$.

$\therefore$ $\text{adj }(A) = \begin{bmatrix} -6 & 4 \\ -3 & 2 \end{bmatrix}'$

$= \begin{bmatrix} -6 & -3 \\ 4 & 2 \end{bmatrix}$

Now,

$(\text{adj } A)\, A = \begin{bmatrix} -6 & -3 \\ 4 & 2 \end{bmatrix}\begin{bmatrix} 2 & 3 \\ -4 & -6 \end{bmatrix}$

$= \begin{bmatrix} -12 + 12 & -18 + 18 \\ 8 - 8 & 12 - 12 \end{bmatrix}$

$= \begin{bmatrix} 0 & 0 \\ 0 & 0 \end{bmatrix}$

Also,

$A(\text{adj } A) = \begin{bmatrix} 2 & 3 \\ -4 & -6 \end{bmatrix}\begin{bmatrix} -6 & -3 \\ 4 & 2 \end{bmatrix}$

$= \begin{bmatrix} -12 + 12 & -6 + 6 \\ 24 - 24 & 12 - 12 \end{bmatrix}$

$= \begin{bmatrix} 0 & 0 \\ 0 & 0 \end{bmatrix}$

Hence,

$A(\text{adj } A) = (\text{adj } A)A = |A|\, I_2 = \begin{bmatrix} 0 & 0 \\ 0 & 0 \end{bmatrix}$

17 (*a*) Let $A=\begin{bmatrix}1 & -1 & 2\\3 & 0 & -2\\1 & 0 & 3\end{bmatrix}$

Now, $|A|=\begin{vmatrix}1 & -1 & 2\\3 & 0 & -2\\1 & 0 & 3\end{vmatrix}$

$=1(0-0)-(-1)(9+2)+2(0-0)$
$=0+11+0=11$

$\therefore |A|I=11\begin{bmatrix}1 & 0 & 0\\0 & 1 & 0\\0 & 0 & 1\end{bmatrix}=\begin{bmatrix}11 & 0 & 0\\0 & 11 & 0\\0 & 0 & 11\end{bmatrix}$

Cofactors of A are
$A_{11}=0, A_{12}=-(9+2)=-11, A_{13}=0,$
$A_{21}=-(-3-0)=3,$
$A_{22}=3-2=1, A_{23}=-(0+1)=-1,$
$A_{31}=2-0=2,$
$A_{32}=-(-2-6)=8, A_{33}=0+3=3$

$\therefore \quad \text{adj}(A)=\begin{bmatrix}0 & -11 & 0\\3 & 1 & -1\\2 & 8 & 3\end{bmatrix}'$

$=\begin{bmatrix}0 & 3 & 2\\-11 & 1 & 8\\0 & -1 & 3\end{bmatrix}$

Now, $A(\text{adj}\,A)$

$=\begin{bmatrix}1 & -1 & 2\\3 & 0 & -2\\1 & 0 & 3\end{bmatrix}\begin{bmatrix}0 & 3 & 2\\-11 & 1 & 8\\0 & -1 & 3\end{bmatrix}$

$=\begin{bmatrix}0+11+0 & 3-1-2 & 2-8+6\\0+0+0 & 9+0+2 & 6+0-6\\0+0+0 & 3+0-3 & 2+0+9\end{bmatrix}$

$=\begin{bmatrix}11 & 0 & 0\\0 & 11 & 0\\0 & 0 & 11\end{bmatrix}$

Also, $(\text{adj}\,A)\,A$

$=\begin{bmatrix}0 & 3 & 2\\-11 & 1 & 8\\0 & -1 & 3\end{bmatrix}\begin{bmatrix}1 & -1 & 2\\3 & 0 & -2\\1 & 0 & 3\end{bmatrix}$

$=\begin{bmatrix}0+9+2 & 0+0+0 & 0-6+6\\-11+3+8 & 11+0+0 & -22-2+24\\0-3+3 & 0+0+0 & 0+2+9\end{bmatrix}$

$=\begin{bmatrix}11 & 0 & 0\\0 & 11 & 0\\0 & 0 & 11\end{bmatrix}$

Hence, $A(\text{adj}A)=(\text{adj}\,A)\,A=|A|\,I_3$

18 (*b*)

I. Let $A=\begin{bmatrix}2 & -2\\4 & 3\end{bmatrix}$.

We have,
$|A|=\begin{vmatrix}2 & -2\\4 & 3\end{vmatrix}=6-(-8)=14$

Cofactors of $A_{11}=3, A_{12}=-4,$
$A_{21}=2$ and $A_{22}=2.$

$\therefore \quad \text{adj}(A)=\begin{bmatrix}3 & -4\\2 & 2\end{bmatrix}'$

$=\begin{bmatrix}3 & 2\\-4 & 2\end{bmatrix}$

Now, $A^{-1}=\dfrac{1}{|A|}(\text{adj}\,A)$

$=\dfrac{1}{14}\begin{bmatrix}3 & 2\\-4 & 2\end{bmatrix}$

$\Rightarrow A^{-1}=\begin{bmatrix}\frac{3}{14} & \frac{2}{14}\\-\frac{4}{14} & \frac{2}{14}\end{bmatrix}=\begin{bmatrix}\frac{3}{14} & \frac{1}{7}\\-\frac{2}{7} & \frac{1}{7}\end{bmatrix}$

II. Let $A=\begin{bmatrix}-1 & 5\\-3 & 2\end{bmatrix}$.

We have,
$|A|=\begin{vmatrix}-1 & 5\\-3 & 2\end{vmatrix}=-2-(-15)=13$

Now, cofactors of A are
$A_{11}=2, A_{12}=3, A_{21}=-5$
and $A_{22}=-1$

$\therefore \text{adj}(A)=\begin{bmatrix}2 & 3\\-5 & -1\end{bmatrix}'=\begin{bmatrix}2 & -5\\3 & -1\end{bmatrix}$

Now, $A^{-1}=\dfrac{1}{|A|}(\text{adj}\,A)$

$=\dfrac{1}{13}\begin{bmatrix}2 & -5\\3 & -1\end{bmatrix}$

$=\begin{bmatrix}\frac{2}{13} & -\frac{5}{13}\\\frac{3}{13} & -\frac{1}{13}\end{bmatrix}$

19 (*b*) We have,

$A=\begin{bmatrix}1 & 0 & 0\\0 & \cos\alpha & \sin\alpha\\0 & \sin\alpha & -\cos\alpha\end{bmatrix}$

Clearly, $|A|=\begin{vmatrix}1 & 0 & 0\\0 & \cos\alpha & \sin\alpha\\0 & \sin\alpha & -\cos\alpha\end{vmatrix}$

$=1(-\cos^2\alpha-\sin^2\alpha)$

$=-(\cos^2\alpha+\sin^2\alpha)=-1$
$[\because \cos^2\theta+\sin^2\theta=1]$

Cofactors of A are
$A_{11}=-\cos^2\alpha-\sin^2\alpha=-1,$
$A_{12}=-(0-0)=0,$
$A_{13}=0-0=0,$
$A_{21}=-(0-0)=0,$
$A_{22}=-\cos\alpha-0=-\cos\alpha,$
$A_{23}=-(\sin\alpha-0)=-\sin\alpha,$
$A_{31}=0-0=0$
$A_{32}=-(\sin\alpha-0)=-\sin\alpha$
and $A_{33}=\cos\alpha-0=\cos\alpha$

$\therefore \text{adj}(A)=\begin{bmatrix}-1 & 0 & 0\\0 & -\cos\alpha & -\sin\alpha\\0 & -\sin\alpha & \cos\alpha\end{bmatrix}'$

$=\begin{bmatrix}-1 & 0 & 0\\0 & -\cos\alpha & -\sin\alpha\\0 & -\sin\alpha & \cos\alpha\end{bmatrix}$

Now, $A^{-1}=\dfrac{1}{|A|}(\text{adj}\,A)$

$=\dfrac{1}{-1}\begin{bmatrix}-1 & 0 & 0\\0 & -\cos\alpha & -\sin\alpha\\0 & -\sin\alpha & \cos\alpha\end{bmatrix}$

$=\begin{bmatrix}1 & 0 & 0\\0 & \cos\alpha & \sin\alpha\\0 & \sin\alpha & -\cos\alpha\end{bmatrix}$

20 (*c*)

A. Let $A=\begin{bmatrix}1 & 2 & 3\\0 & 2 & 4\\0 & 0 & 5\end{bmatrix}$

We have,
$|A|=1(10-0)-2(0-0)$
$+3(0-0)=10$

Now, cofactors of A are
$A_{11}=10-0=10, A_{12}=-(0-0)=0,$
$A_{13}=0-0=0,$
$A_{21}=-(10-0)=-10,$
$A_{22}=5-0=5, A_{23}=-(0-0)=0$
$A_{31}=8-6=2, A_{32}=-(4-0)=-4$
and $A_{33}=2-0=2$

$\therefore \text{adj}(A)=\begin{bmatrix}10 & 0 & 0\\-10 & 5 & 0\\2 & -4 & 2\end{bmatrix}'$

$=\begin{bmatrix}10 & -10 & 2\\0 & 5 & -4\\0 & 0 & 2\end{bmatrix}$

Now, $A^{-1} = \frac{1}{|A|} \cdot (\text{adj } A)$

$$= \frac{1}{10}\begin{bmatrix} 10 & -10 & 2 \\ 0 & 5 & -4 \\ 0 & 0 & 2 \end{bmatrix}$$

$$= \begin{bmatrix} 1 & -1 & \frac{1}{5} \\ 0 & \frac{1}{2} & -\frac{2}{5} \\ 0 & 0 & \frac{1}{5} \end{bmatrix}$$

B. Let $A = \begin{bmatrix} 1 & 0 & 0 \\ 3 & 3 & 0 \\ 5 & 2 & -1 \end{bmatrix}$

We have, $|A| = \begin{vmatrix} 1 & 0 & 0 \\ 3 & 3 & 0 \\ 5 & 2 & -1 \end{vmatrix}$

$= 1(-3-0) - 0 + 0 = -3$

Cofactors of A are

$A_{11} = -3 - 0 = -3,$

$A_{12} = -(-3-0) = 3,$

$A_{13} = 6 - 15 = -9$

$A_{21} = -(0-0) = 0,$

$A_{22} = -1 - 0 = -1,$

$A_{23} = -(2-0) = -2$

$A_{31} = 0 - 0 = 0,$

$A_{32} = -(0-0) = 0$

and $A_{33} = 3 - 0 = 3$

$$\therefore \quad \text{adj}(A) = \begin{bmatrix} -3 & 3 & -9 \\ 0 & -1 & -2 \\ 0 & 0 & 3 \end{bmatrix}'$$

$$= \begin{bmatrix} -3 & 0 & 0 \\ 3 & -1 & 0 \\ -9 & -2 & 3 \end{bmatrix}$$

Now, $A^{-1} = \frac{1}{|A|}(\text{adj } A)$

$$= \frac{1}{-3}\begin{bmatrix} -3 & 0 & 0 \\ 3 & -1 & 0 \\ -9 & -2 & 3 \end{bmatrix}$$

$$= \begin{bmatrix} 1 & 0 & 0 \\ -1 & \frac{1}{3} & 0 \\ 3 & \frac{2}{3} & -1 \end{bmatrix}$$

C. Let $A = \begin{bmatrix} 2 & 1 & 3 \\ 4 & -1 & 0 \\ -7 & 2 & 1 \end{bmatrix}$

We have, $|A| = \begin{vmatrix} 2 & 1 & 3 \\ 4 & -1 & 0 \\ -7 & 2 & 1 \end{vmatrix}$

$= 2(-1-0) - 1(4-0) + 3(8-7)$

$= -2 - 4 + 3 = -3$

Cofactors of A are

$A_{11} = -1,$

$A_{12} = -(4-0) = -4,$

$A_{13} = 8 - 7 = 1$

$A_{21} = -(1-6) = 5,$

$A_{22} = 2 + 21 = 23,$

$A_{23} = -(4+7) = -11$

$A_{31} = 0 + 3 = 3,$

$A_{32} = -(0-12) = 12$

and $A_{33} = -2 - 4 = -6$

$$\therefore \quad \text{adj}(A) = \begin{bmatrix} -1 & -4 & 1 \\ 5 & 23 & -11 \\ 3 & 12 & -6 \end{bmatrix}'$$

$$= \begin{bmatrix} -1 & 5 & 3 \\ -4 & 23 & 12 \\ 1 & -11 & -6 \end{bmatrix}$$

Now, $A^{-1} = \frac{1}{|A|}(\text{adj } A)$

$$= \frac{1}{-3}\begin{bmatrix} -1 & 5 & 3 \\ -4 & 23 & 12 \\ 1 & -11 & -6 \end{bmatrix}$$

$$= \begin{bmatrix} \frac{1}{3} & -\frac{5}{3} & -1 \\ \frac{4}{3} & -\frac{23}{3} & -4 \\ -\frac{1}{3} & \frac{11}{3} & 2 \end{bmatrix}$$

D. Let $A = \begin{bmatrix} 1 & -1 & 2 \\ 0 & 2 & -3 \\ 3 & -2 & 4 \end{bmatrix}$

We have, $|A| = \begin{vmatrix} 1 & -1 & 2 \\ 0 & 2 & -3 \\ 3 & -2 & 4 \end{vmatrix}$

$= 1(8-6) - (-1)(0+9) + 2(0-6)$

$= 2 + 9 - 12 = -1$

Cofactors of A are

$A_{11} = 8 - 6 = 2,$

$A_{12} = -(0+9) = -9,$

$A_{13} = 0 - 6 = -6$

$A_{21} = -(-4+4) = 0,$

$A_{22} = 4 - 6 = -2,$

$A_{23} = -(-2+3) = -1$

$A_{31} = 3 - 4 = -1,$

$A_{32} = -(-3-0) = 3$

and $A_{33} = 2 - 0 = 2$

$$\therefore \quad \text{adj}(A) = \begin{bmatrix} 2 & -9 & -6 \\ 0 & -2 & -1 \\ -1 & 3 & 2 \end{bmatrix}'$$

$$= \begin{bmatrix} 2 & 0 & -1 \\ -9 & -2 & 3 \\ -6 & -1 & 2 \end{bmatrix}$$

Now, $A^{-1} = \frac{1}{|A|}(\text{adj } A)$

$$= \frac{1}{-1}\begin{bmatrix} 2 & 0 & -1 \\ -9 & -2 & 3 \\ -6 & -1 & 2 \end{bmatrix}$$

$$= \begin{bmatrix} -2 & 0 & 1 \\ 9 & 2 & -3 \\ 6 & 1 & -2 \end{bmatrix}$$

21 (a) Given, $A = \begin{bmatrix} 2 & -1 & 1 \\ -1 & 2 & -1 \\ 1 & -1 & 2 \end{bmatrix}$

$\therefore \quad A^2 = A \cdot A$

$$= \begin{bmatrix} 2 & -1 & 1 \\ -1 & 2 & -1 \\ 1 & -1 & 2 \end{bmatrix}\begin{bmatrix} 2 & -1 & 1 \\ -1 & 2 & -1 \\ 1 & -1 & 2 \end{bmatrix}$$

$$= \begin{bmatrix} 4+1+1 & -2-2-1 & 2+1+2 \\ -2-2-1 & 1+4+1 & -1-2-2 \\ 2+1+2 & -1-2-2 & 1+1+4 \end{bmatrix}$$

$$= \begin{bmatrix} 6 & -5 & 5 \\ -5 & 6 & -5 \\ 5 & -5 & 6 \end{bmatrix}$$ and $A^3 = A^2 \cdot A$

$$= \begin{bmatrix} 6 & -5 & 5 \\ -5 & 6 & -5 \\ 5 & -5 & 6 \end{bmatrix}\begin{bmatrix} 2 & -1 & 1 \\ -1 & 2 & -1 \\ 1 & -1 & 2 \end{bmatrix}$$

$$= \begin{bmatrix} 12+5+5 & -6-10-5 & 6+5+10 \\ -10-6-5 & 5+12+5 & -5-6-10 \\ 10+5+6 & -5-10-6 & 5+5+12 \end{bmatrix}$$

$$= \begin{bmatrix} 22 & -21 & 21 \\ -21 & 22 & -21 \\ 21 & -21 & 22 \end{bmatrix}$$

$\therefore\ A^3 - 6A^2 + 9A - 4I$

$$= \begin{bmatrix} 22 & -21 & 21 \\ -21 & 22 & -21 \\ 21 & -21 & 22 \end{bmatrix} - 6\begin{bmatrix} 6 & -5 & 5 \\ -5 & 6 & -5 \\ 5 & -5 & 6 \end{bmatrix} + 9\begin{bmatrix} 2 & -1 & 1 \\ -1 & 2 & -1 \\ 1 & -1 & 2 \end{bmatrix} - 4\begin{bmatrix} 1 & 0 & 0 \\ 0 & 1 & 0 \\ 0 & 0 & 1 \end{bmatrix}$$

$$= \begin{bmatrix} 22 & -21 & 21 \\ -21 & 22 & -21 \\ 21 & -21 & 22 \end{bmatrix} - \begin{bmatrix} 36 & -30 & 30 \\ -30 & 36 & -30 \\ 30 & -30 & 36 \end{bmatrix} + \begin{bmatrix} 18 & -9 & 9 \\ -9 & 18 & -9 \\ 9 & -9 & 18 \end{bmatrix} - \begin{bmatrix} 4 & 0 & 0 \\ 0 & 4 & 0 \\ 0 & 0 & 4 \end{bmatrix}$$

$$= \begin{bmatrix} 22-36+18-4 & -21+30-9-0 & 21-30+9-0 \\ -21+30-9-0 & 22-36+18-4 & -21+30-9-0 \\ 21-30+9-0 & -21+30-9-0 & 22-36+18-4 \end{bmatrix}$$

$$= \begin{bmatrix} 0 & 0 & 0 \\ 0 & 0 & 0 \\ 0 & 0 & 0 \end{bmatrix} = 0$$

$\therefore\ A^3 - 6A^2 + 9A - 4I = 0$

$\Rightarrow (AAA)A^{-1} - 6(AA)A^{-1} + 9AA^{-1} - 4IA^{-1} = 0$

[post-multiplying by A^{-1} as

$$|A| = \begin{vmatrix} 2 & -1 & 1 \\ -1 & 2 & -1 \\ 1 & -1 & 2 \end{vmatrix} = 2(4-1) + 1(-2+1) + 1(1-2) = 6 - 1 - 1 = 4 \neq 0]$$

$\Rightarrow\ AA(AA^{-1}) - 6A(AA^{-1}) + 9(AA^{-1}) - (4IA^{-1}) = 0$

$\Rightarrow\ AAI - 6AI + 9I - 4A^{-1} = 0$

[using $AA^{-1} = I$ and $IA^{-1} = A^{-1}$]

$\Rightarrow\ A^2 - 6A + 9I = 4A^{-1}$

[using $A^2I = A^2$ and $AI = A$]

$\Rightarrow\ A^{-1} = \frac{1}{4}(A^2 - 6A + 9I)$

$$= \frac{1}{4}\left\{\begin{bmatrix} 6 & -5 & 5 \\ -5 & 6 & -5 \\ 5 & -5 & 6 \end{bmatrix} - 6\begin{bmatrix} 2 & -1 & 1 \\ -1 & 2 & -1 \\ 1 & -1 & 2 \end{bmatrix} + 9\begin{bmatrix} 1 & 0 & 0 \\ 0 & 1 & 0 \\ 0 & 0 & 1 \end{bmatrix}\right\}$$

$$= \frac{1}{4}\left\{\begin{bmatrix} 6 & -5 & 5 \\ -5 & 6 & -5 \\ 5 & -5 & 6 \end{bmatrix} - \begin{bmatrix} 12 & -6 & 6 \\ -6 & 12 & -6 \\ 6 & -6 & 12 \end{bmatrix} + \begin{bmatrix} 9 & 0 & 0 \\ 0 & 9 & 0 \\ 0 & 0 & 9 \end{bmatrix}\right\}$$

$$= \frac{1}{4}\begin{bmatrix} 6-12+9 & -5+6+0 & 5-6+0 \\ -5+6+0 & 6-12+9 & -5+6+0 \\ 5-6+0 & -5+6+0 & 6-12+9 \end{bmatrix}$$

$$= \frac{1}{4}\begin{bmatrix} 3 & 1 & -1 \\ 1 & 3 & 1 \\ -1 & 1 & 3 \end{bmatrix}$$

22 (*a*) Given, $A = \begin{bmatrix} 3 & 2 \\ 1 & 1 \end{bmatrix}$

$\therefore\ A^2 = AA = \begin{bmatrix} 3 & 2 \\ 1 & 1 \end{bmatrix}\begin{bmatrix} 3 & 2 \\ 1 & 1 \end{bmatrix} = \begin{bmatrix} 9+2 & 6+2 \\ 3+1 & 2+1 \end{bmatrix} = \begin{bmatrix} 11 & 8 \\ 4 & 3 \end{bmatrix}$

Also, we have $A^2 + aA + bI = 0$

Now, putting the values of A^2, A and I, we get

$$\begin{bmatrix} 11 & 8 \\ 4 & 3 \end{bmatrix} + a\begin{bmatrix} 3 & 2 \\ 1 & 1 \end{bmatrix} + b\begin{bmatrix} 1 & 0 \\ 0 & 1 \end{bmatrix} = 0$$

$$\Rightarrow \begin{bmatrix} 11+3a+b & 8+2a+0 \\ 4+a+0 & 3+a+b \end{bmatrix} = 0$$

$$\Rightarrow \begin{bmatrix} 11+3a+b & 8+2a \\ 4+a & 3+a+b \end{bmatrix} = \begin{bmatrix} 0 & 0 \\ 0 & 0 \end{bmatrix}$$

We know that if two matrices are equal, then their corresponding elements are also equal

$\Rightarrow\ 11 + 3a + b = 0$ ...(i)

$8 + 2a = 0$ ...(ii)

$4 + a = 0$ ...(iii)

and $3 + a + b = 0$ ...(iv)

On solving Eqs. (iii) and (iv), we get

$4 + a = 0 \Rightarrow a = -4$

and $3 + a + b = 0$

$\Rightarrow\ 3 - 4 + b = 0 \Rightarrow b = 1$

Thus, $a = -4$ and $b = 1$

23 (*b*) Given, $A = \begin{bmatrix} 3 & 7 \\ 2 & 5 \end{bmatrix}$,

$|A| = \begin{vmatrix} 3 & 7 \\ 2 & 5 \end{vmatrix} = 15 - 14 = 1$

Cofactors of A are

$A_{11} = 5, A_{12} = -2,$

$A_{21} = -7$ and $A_{22} = 3.$

$\therefore\ \text{adj}(A) = \begin{bmatrix} 5 & -2 \\ -7 & 3 \end{bmatrix}' = \begin{bmatrix} 5 & -7 \\ -2 & 3 \end{bmatrix}$

Now, $A^{-1} = \frac{1}{|A|}(\text{adj } A)$

$= \frac{1}{1}\begin{bmatrix} 5 & -7 \\ -2 & 3 \end{bmatrix}$

Here, $B = \begin{bmatrix} 6 & 8 \\ 7 & 9 \end{bmatrix}$

$\therefore |B| = \begin{vmatrix} 6 & 8 \\ 7 & 9 \end{vmatrix} = 54 - 56 = -2$

Cofactors of B are $B_{11} = 9, B_{12} = -7,$ $B_{21} = -8$ and $B_{22} = 6$

$\text{adj}(B) = \begin{bmatrix} 9 & -7 \\ -8 & 6 \end{bmatrix}' = \begin{bmatrix} 9 & -8 \\ -7 & 6 \end{bmatrix}$

$\therefore\ B^{-1} = \frac{1}{|B|}(\text{adj } B) = \frac{1}{-2}\begin{bmatrix} 9 & -8 \\ -7 & 6 \end{bmatrix}$

Now, $B^{-1}A^{-1}$

$$= \frac{1}{-2}\begin{bmatrix} 9 & -8 \\ -7 & 6 \end{bmatrix}\begin{bmatrix} 5 & -7 \\ -2 & 3 \end{bmatrix}$$

$$= \frac{1}{-2}\begin{bmatrix} 45+16 & -63-24 \\ -35-12 & 49+18 \end{bmatrix}$$

$$= \frac{1}{-2}\begin{bmatrix} 61 & -87 \\ -47 & 67 \end{bmatrix} = \begin{bmatrix} -\frac{61}{2} & \frac{87}{2} \\ \frac{47}{2} & -\frac{67}{2} \end{bmatrix} \quad \text{...(i)}$$

and $AB = \begin{bmatrix} 3 & 7 \\ 2 & 5 \end{bmatrix}\begin{bmatrix} 6 & 8 \\ 7 & 9 \end{bmatrix}$

$$= \begin{bmatrix} 18+49 & 24+63 \\ 12+35 & 16+45 \end{bmatrix}$$

$$= \begin{bmatrix} 67 & 87 \\ 47 & 61 \end{bmatrix}$$

$$\therefore \ |AB| = \begin{vmatrix} 67 & 87 \\ 47 & 61 \end{vmatrix}$$

$$= 67 \times 61 - 47 \times 87$$

$$= 4087 - 4089 = -2$$

Cofactors of AB are $A_{11} = 61$, $A_{12} = -47$, $A_{21} = -87$ and $A_{22} = 67$.

$$\therefore \ \text{adj}\,(AB) = \begin{bmatrix} 61 & -47 \\ -87 & 67 \end{bmatrix}'$$

$$= \begin{bmatrix} 61 & -87 \\ -47 & 67 \end{bmatrix}$$

Now, $(AB)^{-1} = \dfrac{1}{|AB|}(\text{adj}\,AB)$

$$= \frac{1}{-2}\begin{bmatrix} 61 & -87 \\ -47 & 67 \end{bmatrix}$$

$$= \begin{bmatrix} -\frac{61}{2} & \frac{87}{2} \\ \frac{47}{2} & -\frac{67}{2} \end{bmatrix} \quad \text{...(ii)}$$

From Eqs. (i) and (ii), we get

$$(AB)^{-1} = B^{-1}A^{-1}$$

24 (*a*) Given, $A = \begin{bmatrix} 3 & 1 \\ -1 & 2 \end{bmatrix}$

$$\therefore \ A^2 = AA = \begin{bmatrix} 3 & 1 \\ -1 & 2 \end{bmatrix}\begin{bmatrix} 3 & 1 \\ -1 & 2 \end{bmatrix}$$

$$= \begin{bmatrix} 9-1 & 3+2 \\ -3-2 & -1+4 \end{bmatrix} = \begin{bmatrix} 8 & 5 \\ -5 & 3 \end{bmatrix}$$

Now, $A^2 - 5A + 7I$

$$= \begin{bmatrix} 8 & 5 \\ -5 & 3 \end{bmatrix} - 5\begin{bmatrix} 3 & 1 \\ -1 & 2 \end{bmatrix} + 7\begin{bmatrix} 1 & 0 \\ 0 & 1 \end{bmatrix}$$

$$= \begin{bmatrix} 8 & 5 \\ -5 & 3 \end{bmatrix} - \begin{bmatrix} 15 & 5 \\ -5 & 10 \end{bmatrix} + \begin{bmatrix} 7 & 0 \\ 0 & 7 \end{bmatrix}$$

$$= \begin{bmatrix} 8-15+7 & 5-5+0 \\ -5+5+0 & 3-10+7 \end{bmatrix}$$

$$= \begin{bmatrix} 0 & 0 \\ 0 & 0 \end{bmatrix} = 0$$

$$\therefore \quad A^2 - 5A + 7I = 0$$

$$\because \ |A| = \begin{vmatrix} 3 & 1 \\ -1 & 2 \end{vmatrix} = 6 + 1 = 7 \neq 0.$$

$\therefore \quad A^{-1}$ exists.

Now, $A \cdot A - 5A = -7I$

Post-multiply by A^{-1} on both sides, we get

$$A \cdot A\,(A^{-1}) - 5AA^{-1} = -7IA^{-1}$$

$$\Rightarrow \quad AI - 5I = -7A^{-1}$$

[using $AA^{-1} = I$ and $IA^{-1} = A^{-1}$]

$$\Rightarrow \quad A^{-1} = -\frac{1}{7}(A - 5I)$$

$$\Rightarrow \quad A^{-1} = \frac{1}{7}(5I - A)$$

$$= \frac{1}{7}\left\{\begin{bmatrix} 5 & 0 \\ 0 & 5 \end{bmatrix} - \begin{bmatrix} 3 & 1 \\ -1 & 2 \end{bmatrix}\right\}$$

$$= \frac{1}{7}\begin{bmatrix} 2 & -1 \\ 1 & 3 \end{bmatrix}$$

$$\therefore \quad A^{-1} = \frac{1}{7}\begin{bmatrix} 2 & -1 \\ 1 & 3 \end{bmatrix}$$

25 (*b*) We know that $AA^{-1} = I$

$$\therefore |AA^{-1}| = |I| \ \Rightarrow \ |A||A^{-1}| = 1$$

[using $|AA^{-1}| = |A||A^{-1}|$ and $|I| = 1$]

$$\Rightarrow \ |A^{-1}| = \frac{1}{|A|} = \frac{1}{\det(A)}$$

26 (*d*) Given, $A = \begin{bmatrix} 1 & 1 & 1 \\ 1 & 2 & -3 \\ 2 & -1 & 3 \end{bmatrix}$

$$\therefore \ A^2 = AA$$

$$= \begin{bmatrix} 1 & 1 & 1 \\ 1 & 2 & -3 \\ 2 & -1 & 3 \end{bmatrix}\begin{bmatrix} 1 & 1 & 1 \\ 1 & 2 & -3 \\ 2 & -1 & 3 \end{bmatrix}$$

$$= \begin{bmatrix} 1+1+2 & 1+2-1 & 1-3+3 \\ 1+2-6 & 1+4+3 & 1-6-9 \\ 2-1+6 & 2-2-3 & 2+3+9 \end{bmatrix}$$

$$= \begin{bmatrix} 4 & 2 & 1 \\ -3 & 8 & -14 \\ 7 & -3 & 14 \end{bmatrix}$$

Now, $A^3 = A^2A$

$$= \begin{bmatrix} 4 & 2 & 1 \\ -3 & 8 & -14 \\ 7 & -3 & 14 \end{bmatrix}\begin{bmatrix} 1 & 1 & 1 \\ 1 & 2 & -3 \\ 2 & -1 & 3 \end{bmatrix}$$

$$= \begin{bmatrix} 4+2+2 & 4+4-1 & 4-6+3 \\ -3+8-28 & -3+16+14 & -3-24-42 \\ 7-3+28 & 7-6-14 & 7+9+42 \end{bmatrix}$$

$$= \begin{bmatrix} 8 & 7 & 1 \\ -23 & 27 & -69 \\ 32 & -13 & 58 \end{bmatrix}$$

$$\therefore \quad A^3 - 6A^2 + 5A + 11I$$

$$= \begin{bmatrix} 8 & 7 & 1 \\ -23 & 27 & -69 \\ 32 & -13 & 58 \end{bmatrix} - 6\begin{bmatrix} 4 & 2 & 1 \\ -3 & 8 & -14 \\ 7 & -3 & 14 \end{bmatrix} + 5\begin{bmatrix} 1 & 1 & 1 \\ 1 & 2 & -3 \\ 2 & -1 & 3 \end{bmatrix} + 11\begin{bmatrix} 1 & 0 & 0 \\ 0 & 1 & 0 \\ 0 & 0 & 1 \end{bmatrix}$$

$$= \begin{bmatrix} 8 & 7 & 1 \\ -23 & 27 & -69 \\ 32 & -13 & 58 \end{bmatrix} - \begin{bmatrix} 24 & 12 & 6 \\ -18 & 48 & -84 \\ 42 & -18 & 84 \end{bmatrix} + \begin{bmatrix} 5 & 5 & 5 \\ 5 & 10 & -15 \\ 10 & -5 & 15 \end{bmatrix} + \begin{bmatrix} 11 & 0 & 0 \\ 0 & 11 & 0 \\ 0 & 0 & 11 \end{bmatrix}$$

$$= \begin{bmatrix} 8-24+5+11 & 7-12+5+0 & 1-6+5+0 \\ -23+18+5+0 & 27-48+10+11 & -69+84-15+0 \\ 32-42+10+0 & -13+18-5+0 & 58-84+15+11 \end{bmatrix}$$

$$= \begin{bmatrix} 0 & 0 & 0 \\ 0 & 0 & 0 \\ 0 & 0 & 0 \end{bmatrix} = 0$$

Now, $A^3 - 6A^2 + 5A + 11I = 0$

$$\Rightarrow (AAA)\,A^{-1} - 6(AA)\,A^{-1} + 5AA^{-1} + 11IA^{-1} = 0$$

[post-multiply by A^{-1} as

$$|A| = \begin{vmatrix} 1 & 1 & 1 \\ 1 & 2 & -3 \\ 2 & -1 & 3 \end{vmatrix} = 1(6-3) - 1(3+6) + 1(-1-4) = 3 - 9 - 5 = -11 \neq 0]$$

$$\Rightarrow AA(AA^{-1}) - 6A\,(AA^{-1}) + 5(AA^{-1}) + 11(IA^{-1}) = 0$$

$$\Rightarrow \quad AAI - 6AI + 5I + 11A^{-1} = 0$$

[using $AA^{-1} = I$ and $IA^{-1} = A^{-1}$]

$\Rightarrow \quad A^2 - 6A + 5I = -11A^{-1}$

[using $AAI = A^2$ and $AI = A$]

$\Rightarrow \quad A^{-1} = -\frac{1}{11}(A^2 - 6A + 5I)$

$\Rightarrow \quad A^{-1} = \frac{1}{11}(-A^2 + 6A - 5I)$

$$= \frac{1}{11}\left\{-\begin{bmatrix} 4 & 2 & 1 \\ -3 & 8 & -14 \\ 7 & -3 & 14 \end{bmatrix} + 6\begin{bmatrix} 1 & 1 & 1 \\ 1 & 2 & -3 \\ 2 & -1 & 3 \end{bmatrix} - 5\begin{bmatrix} 1 & 0 & 0 \\ 0 & 1 & 0 \\ 0 & 0 & 1 \end{bmatrix}\right\}$$

$$= \frac{1}{11}\left\{\begin{bmatrix} -4 & -2 & -1 \\ 3 & -8 & 14 \\ -7 & 3 & -14 \end{bmatrix} + \begin{bmatrix} 6 & 6 & 6 \\ 6 & 12 & -18 \\ 12 & -6 & 18 \end{bmatrix} - \begin{bmatrix} 5 & 0 & 0 \\ 0 & 5 & 0 \\ 0 & 0 & 5 \end{bmatrix}\right\}$$

$$= \frac{1}{11}\begin{bmatrix} -4+6-5 & -2+6-0 & -1+6-0 \\ 3+6-0 & -8+12-5 & 14-18-0 \\ -7+12-0 & 3-6-0 & -14+18-5 \end{bmatrix}$$

$$= \frac{1}{11}\begin{bmatrix} -3 & 4 & 5 \\ 9 & -1 & -4 \\ 5 & -3 & -1 \end{bmatrix}$$

27 (*c*) Given that A is a square matrix of order 3 and B is its adjoint such that $|B| = 64$

$\Rightarrow \quad |\text{adj } A| = 64$

$\because |\text{adj } A| = |A|^{n-1}$ for any non-singular square matrix A of order n.

$\therefore$ For given matrix A of order 3×3, we have,

$|\text{adj } A| = |A|^{3-1} = |A|^2$

$\Rightarrow \quad |A|^2 = 64 \Rightarrow |A| = \pm 8$

28 (*a*) We know that $(AB)^{-1} = B^{-1}A^{-1}$ and A^{-1} is known, therefore we proceed to find B^{-1}.

Here, $|B| = \begin{vmatrix} 1 & 2 & -2 \\ -1 & 3 & 0 \\ 0 & -2 & 1 \end{vmatrix}$

$= 1(3-0) - 2(-1-0) - 2(2-0)$

$= 3 + 2 - 4 = 1 \neq 0$

$\therefore \; B^{-1}$ exists.

Cofactors of B are

$B_{11} = (3-0) = 3,$

$B_{12} = -(-1-0) = 1,$

$B_{13} = (2-0) = 2,$

$B_{21} = -(2-4) = 2, \quad B_{22} = 1 - 0 = 1,$

$B_{23} = -(-2-0) = 2,$

$B_{31} = (0+6) = 6, B_{32} = -(0-2) = 2$

and $B_{33} = 3 + 2 = 5$

$\therefore \quad (\text{adj } B) = \begin{bmatrix} 3 & 1 & 2 \\ 2 & 1 & 2 \\ 6 & 2 & 5 \end{bmatrix}' = \begin{bmatrix} 3 & 2 & 6 \\ 1 & 1 & 2 \\ 2 & 2 & 5 \end{bmatrix}$

$\therefore \quad B^{-1} = \frac{1}{|B|}(\text{adj } B)$

$= \frac{1}{1}\begin{bmatrix} 3 & 2 & 6 \\ 1 & 1 & 2 \\ 2 & 2 & 5 \end{bmatrix} = \begin{bmatrix} 3 & 2 & 6 \\ 1 & 1 & 2 \\ 2 & 2 & 5 \end{bmatrix}$

Now, $(AB)^{-1} = B^{-1}A^{-1}$

$$= \begin{bmatrix} 3 & 2 & 6 \\ 1 & 1 & 2 \\ 2 & 2 & 5 \end{bmatrix}\begin{bmatrix} 3 & -1 & 1 \\ -15 & 6 & -5 \\ 5 & -2 & 2 \end{bmatrix}$$

$$= \begin{bmatrix} 9-30+30 & -3+12-12 & 3-10+12 \\ 3-15+10 & -1+6-4 & 1-5+4 \\ 6-30+25 & -2+12-10 & 2-10+10 \end{bmatrix}$$

$$= \begin{bmatrix} 9 & -3 & 5 \\ -2 & 1 & 0 \\ 1 & 0 & 2 \end{bmatrix}$$

29 (*a*) Given that adjoint of 3×3 matrix P is $\begin{bmatrix} 1 & 4 & 4 \\ 2 & 1 & 7 \\ 1 & 1 & 3 \end{bmatrix}$.

$\therefore \quad \begin{vmatrix} 1 & 4 & 4 \\ 2 & 1 & 7 \\ 1 & 1 & 3 \end{vmatrix} = |P|^2$

[$\because |\text{adj } A| = |A|^2$ for n non-singular square matrix A of order 3]

$\Rightarrow |P|^2 = 1\begin{vmatrix} 1 & 7 \\ 1 & 3 \end{vmatrix} - 4\begin{vmatrix} 2 & 7 \\ 1 & 3 \end{vmatrix} + 4\begin{vmatrix} 2 & 1 \\ 1 & 1 \end{vmatrix}$

$= (3-7) - 4(6-7) + 4(2-1)$

$= -4 + 4 + 4 = 4$

$\Rightarrow \quad |P| = \pm 2$

30 (*c*) Since, A is an invertible matrix, so it is non-singular.

We know that $|A| = |A'|$. But $|A| \neq 0$. So, $|A'| \neq 0$ i.e. A' is invertible matrix.

Also, we know that

$AA^{-1} = A^{-1}A = I.$

On taking transpose on both sides, we get

$(A^{-1})'A' = A'(A^{-1})' = (I)' = I$

Hence, $(A^{-1})'$ is inverse of A' i.e. $(A')^{-1} = (A^{-1})'$.

31 (*d*) The given matrix is

$A = \begin{bmatrix} 2 & \lambda & -3 \\ 0 & 2 & 5 \\ 1 & 1 & 3 \end{bmatrix}$.

Now, A^{-1} exists, if $|A| \neq 0$.

$\therefore \quad \begin{vmatrix} 2 & \lambda & -3 \\ 0 & 2 & 5 \\ 1 & 1 & 3 \end{vmatrix} \neq 0$

$\Rightarrow 2\begin{vmatrix} 2 & 5 \\ 1 & 3 \end{vmatrix} - \lambda\begin{vmatrix} 0 & 5 \\ 1 & 3 \end{vmatrix} - 3\begin{vmatrix} 0 & 2 \\ 1 & 1 \end{vmatrix} \neq 0$

$\Rightarrow 2(6-5) - \lambda(0-5) - 3(0-2) \neq 0$

$\Rightarrow \quad 2 + 5\lambda + 6 \neq 0$

$\Rightarrow \quad 5\lambda \neq -8$

$\Rightarrow \quad \lambda \neq -\frac{8}{5}$

32 (*a*) Given, $A = \begin{bmatrix} x & 0 & 0 \\ 0 & y & 0 \\ 0 & 0 & z \end{bmatrix}$

$|A| = \begin{vmatrix} x & 0 & 0 \\ 0 & y & 0 \\ 0 & 0 & z \end{vmatrix}$

$= x(yz - 0) = xyz \neq 0$

[$\because x, y$ and z are all non-zero]

Cofactors of A are

$A_{11} = (yz - 0) = yz$,

$A_{12} = -(0-0) = 0$, $A_{13} = 0 - 0 = 0$,

$A_{21} = -(0-0) = 0$,

$A_{22} = xz - 0 = xz$,

$A_{23} = -(0-0) = 0$,

$A_{31} = 0 - 0 = 0$, $A_{32} = -(0-0) = 0$

and $A_{33} = (xy - 0) = xy$

$$\therefore \text{ adj}(A) = \begin{bmatrix} yz & 0 & 0 \\ 0 & xz & 0 \\ 0 & 0 & xy \end{bmatrix}' = \begin{bmatrix} yz & 0 & 0 \\ 0 & xz & 0 \\ 0 & 0 & xy \end{bmatrix}$$

Now, $A^{-1} = \dfrac{1}{|A|}(\text{adj } A)$

$$= \frac{1}{xyz}\begin{bmatrix} yz & 0 & 0 \\ 0 & xz & 0 \\ 0 & 0 & xy \end{bmatrix} = \begin{bmatrix} \frac{1}{x} & 0 & 0 \\ 0 & \frac{1}{y} & 0 \\ 0 & 0 & \frac{1}{z} \end{bmatrix}$$

$$= \begin{bmatrix} x^{-1} & 0 & 0 \\ 0 & y^{-1} & 0 \\ 0 & 0 & z^{-1} \end{bmatrix}$$

33 (*b*) Given that A is an invertible matrix of order 3 and $|A| = 5$.

Now, $|\text{adj } A| = |A|^{3-1} = |A|^2$

$= 5^2 = 25$

34 (*c*) Given, $A = \begin{bmatrix} 1 & -2 & 1 \\ -2 & 3 & 1 \\ 1 & 1 & 5 \end{bmatrix}$

$$\Rightarrow \quad |A| = \begin{vmatrix} 1 & -2 & 1 \\ -2 & 3 & 1 \\ 1 & 1 & 5 \end{vmatrix}$$

$= 1(15-1) - (-2)(-10-1) + (-2-3)$

$= 14 - 22 - 5 = -13 \neq 0$

Cofactors of A are

$A_{11} = 15 - 1 = 14$,

$A_{12} = -(-10-1) = 11$,

$A_{13} = -2 - 3 = -5$,

$A_{21} = -(-10-1) = 11$,

$A_{22} = 5 - 1 = 4$,

$A_{23} = -(1+2) = -3$,

$A_{31} = (-2-3) = -5$,

$A_{32} = -(1+2) = -3$

and $A_{33} = 3 - 4 = -1$

$$\text{adj}(A) = \begin{bmatrix} 14 & 11 & -5 \\ 11 & 4 & -3 \\ -5 & -3 & -1 \end{bmatrix}' = \begin{bmatrix} 14 & 11 & -5 \\ 11 & 4 & -3 \\ -5 & -3 & -1 \end{bmatrix}$$

$$\therefore \quad A^{-1} = \frac{1}{|A|}(\text{adj } A) = \begin{bmatrix} \frac{-14}{13} & \frac{-11}{13} & \frac{5}{13} \\ \frac{-11}{13} & \frac{-4}{13} & \frac{3}{13} \\ \frac{5}{13} & \frac{3}{13} & \frac{1}{13} \end{bmatrix}$$

I. Here,

$$\text{adj}(A) = \begin{bmatrix} 14 & 11 & -5 \\ 11 & 4 & -3 \\ -5 & -3 & -1 \end{bmatrix} = B \text{ (let)}$$

$$\therefore |B| = |\text{adj } A| = \begin{vmatrix} 14 & 11 & -5 \\ 11 & 4 & -3 \\ -5 & -3 & -1 \end{vmatrix}$$

$= 14(-4-9) - 11(-11-15) - 5(-33+20)$

$= -182 + 286 + 65 = 169 \neq 0$

Cofactors of B are

$B_{11} = (-4-9) = -13$,

$B_{12} = -(-11-15) = 26$,

$B_{13} = (-33+20) = -13$,

$B_{21} = -(-11-15) = 26$,

$B_{22} = -14 - 25 = -39$,

$B_{23} = -(-42+55) = -13$,

$B_{31} = (-33+20) = -13$,

$B_{32} = -(-42+55) = -13$

and $B_{33} = 56 - 121 = -65$

adj (B) = adj (adj A)

$$= \begin{bmatrix} -13 & 26 & -13 \\ 26 & -39 & -13 \\ -13 & -13 & -65 \end{bmatrix}' = \begin{bmatrix} -13 & 26 & -13 \\ 26 & -39 & -13 \\ -13 & -13 & -65 \end{bmatrix}$$

$\therefore \quad B^{-1} = (\text{adj } A)^{-1}$

$= \dfrac{1}{|\text{adj } A|}[\text{adj}(\text{adj } A)]$

$\Rightarrow [\text{adj } A]^{-1}$

$$= \frac{1}{169}\begin{bmatrix} -13 & 26 & -13 \\ 26 & -39 & -13 \\ -13 & -13 & -65 \end{bmatrix} = \frac{1}{13}\begin{bmatrix} -1 & 2 & -1 \\ 2 & -3 & -1 \\ -1 & -1 & -5 \end{bmatrix} \quad \text{...(i)}$$

Cofactors of A^{-1} are

$A_{11} = \dfrac{-13}{169}$, $A_{12} = \dfrac{26}{169}$,

$A_{13} = \dfrac{-13}{169}$,

$A_{21} = \dfrac{26}{169}$, $A_{22} = \dfrac{-39}{169}$,

$A_{23} = \dfrac{-13}{169}$, $A_{31} = \dfrac{-13}{169}$,

$A_{32} = -\dfrac{13}{169}$ and $A_{33} = -\dfrac{65}{169}$

Now, adj (A^{-1})

$$= \begin{bmatrix} -\frac{13}{169} & \frac{26}{169} & -\frac{13}{169} \\ \frac{26}{169} & -\frac{39}{169} & -\frac{13}{169} \\ -\frac{13}{169} & -\frac{13}{169} & -\frac{65}{169} \end{bmatrix}' = \begin{bmatrix} -\frac{13}{169} & \frac{26}{169} & -\frac{13}{169} \\ \frac{26}{169} & -\frac{39}{169} & -\frac{13}{169} \\ -\frac{13}{169} & -\frac{13}{169} & -\frac{65}{169} \end{bmatrix}$$

$$\Rightarrow \text{adj}(A^{-1}) = \frac{1}{13}\begin{bmatrix} -1 & 2 & -1 \\ 2 & -3 & -1 \\ -1 & -1 & -5 \end{bmatrix} \quad \text{...(ii)}$$

From Eqs. (i) and (ii), we get

adj $(A^{-1}) = (\text{adj } A)^{-1}$

II. $|A^{-1}| = -\dfrac{14}{13}\left(-\dfrac{4}{169} - \dfrac{9}{169}\right) + \dfrac{11}{13}\left(-\dfrac{11}{169} - \dfrac{15}{169}\right) + \dfrac{5}{13}\left(-\dfrac{33}{169} + \dfrac{20}{169}\right)$

$= -\dfrac{14}{13}\left(-\dfrac{13}{169}\right) + \dfrac{11}{13}\left(-\dfrac{26}{169}\right) + \dfrac{5}{13}\left(-\dfrac{13}{169}\right)$

$$= \frac{14}{169} - \frac{22}{169} - \frac{5}{169}$$

$$= -\frac{13}{169} = -\frac{1}{13}$$

$$\text{adj}(A^{-1}) = \frac{1}{13}\begin{bmatrix} -1 & 2 & -1 \\ 2 & -3 & -1 \\ -1 & -1 & -5 \end{bmatrix}$$

$$\therefore \quad (A^{-1})^{-1} = \frac{1}{|A^{-1}|}(\text{adj}\, A^{-1})$$

$$= \frac{1}{-\frac{1}{13}} \times \frac{1}{13}\begin{bmatrix} -1 & 2 & -1 \\ 2 & -3 & -1 \\ -1 & -1 & -5 \end{bmatrix}$$

$$= \begin{bmatrix} 1 & -2 & 1 \\ -2 & 3 & 1 \\ 1 & 1 & 5 \end{bmatrix} = A$$

Application of Determinants and Matrices

1 (c) The system of equations can be written in the form $AX = B$, where

$$A = \begin{bmatrix} 2 & 5 \\ 3 & 2 \end{bmatrix}, X = \begin{bmatrix} x \\ y \end{bmatrix} \text{ and } B = \begin{bmatrix} 1 \\ 7 \end{bmatrix}$$

Now, $|A| = -11 \neq 0$, Hence, A is non-singular matrix and so it has a unique solution.

$$A^{-1} = -\frac{1}{11}\begin{bmatrix} 2 & -5 \\ -3 & 2 \end{bmatrix}$$

Therefore,

$$X = A^{-1}B = -\frac{1}{11}\begin{bmatrix} 2 & -5 \\ -3 & 2 \end{bmatrix}\begin{bmatrix} 1 \\ 7 \end{bmatrix}$$

i.e. $\begin{bmatrix} x \\ y \end{bmatrix} = -\frac{1}{11}\begin{bmatrix} -33 \\ 11 \end{bmatrix} = \begin{bmatrix} 3 \\ -1 \end{bmatrix}$

Hence, $x = 3$ and $y = -1$

2 (c) Let first, second and third numbers are denoted by x, y and z, respectively. Then, according to given conditions, we have

$$x + y + z = 6 \quad \text{...(i)}$$

$$y + 3z = 11 \quad \text{...(ii)}$$

$$x + z = 2y$$

or $\quad x - 2y + z = 0 \quad$ ...(iii)

This system can be written as $AX = B$, where

$$A = \begin{bmatrix} 1 & 1 & 1 \\ 0 & 1 & 3 \\ 1 & -2 & 1 \end{bmatrix}, X = \begin{bmatrix} x \\ y \\ z \end{bmatrix}$$

and $\quad B = \begin{bmatrix} 6 \\ 11 \\ 0 \end{bmatrix}$

Here, $|A| = 1(1+6) - (0-3) + (0-1) = 9 \neq 0.$

Now, we find adj (A).

Cofactors of A are $A_{11} = (1+6) = 7$,
$A_{12} = -(0-3) = 3$, $A_{13} = -1$,
$A_{21} = -(1+2) = -3$, $A_{22} = 0$,
$A_{23} = -(-2-1) = 3$,
$A_{31} = (3-1) = 2$,
$A_{32} = -(3-0) = -3$
and $A_{33} = (1-0) = 1$

$$\text{Hence, adj}(A) = \begin{bmatrix} 7 & -3 & 2 \\ 3 & 0 & -3 \\ -1 & 3 & 1 \end{bmatrix}$$

$$\text{Thus,} \quad A^{-1} = \frac{1}{|A|}\text{adj}(A)$$

$$= \frac{1}{9}\begin{bmatrix} 7 & -3 & 2 \\ 3 & 0 & -3 \\ -1 & 3 & 1 \end{bmatrix}$$

Since, $X = A^{-1}B$

$$\Rightarrow \quad X = \frac{1}{9}\begin{bmatrix} 7 & -3 & 2 \\ 3 & 0 & -3 \\ -1 & 3 & 1 \end{bmatrix}\begin{bmatrix} 6 \\ 11 \\ 0 \end{bmatrix}$$

$$\text{or} \quad \begin{bmatrix} x \\ y \\ z \end{bmatrix} = \frac{1}{9}\begin{bmatrix} 42 - 33 + 0 \\ 18 + 0 + 0 \\ -6 + 33 + 0 \end{bmatrix}$$

$$= \frac{1}{9}\begin{bmatrix} 9 \\ 18 \\ 27 \end{bmatrix} = \begin{bmatrix} 1 \\ 2 \\ 3 \end{bmatrix}$$

Thus, $x = 1$, $y = 2$ and $z = 3$.

3 (d)

A. The given system can be written as $AX = B$, where

$$A = \begin{bmatrix} 1 & 2 \\ 2 & 3 \end{bmatrix}, X = \begin{bmatrix} x \\ y \end{bmatrix} \text{ and } B = \begin{bmatrix} 2 \\ 3 \end{bmatrix}$$

$$|A| = \begin{vmatrix} 1 & 2 \\ 2 & 3 \end{vmatrix} = 1(3) - 2(2)$$

$$= 3 - 4 = -1 \neq 0$$

$\therefore$ A is non-singular.
Therefore, A^{-1} exists.
Hence, the given system of equations is consistent.

B. The given system can be written as $AX = B$, where

$$A = \begin{bmatrix} 2 & -1 \\ 1 & 1 \end{bmatrix}, X = \begin{bmatrix} x \\ y \end{bmatrix} \text{ and } B = \begin{bmatrix} 5 \\ 4 \end{bmatrix}$$

Here,

$$|A| = \begin{vmatrix} 2 & -1 \\ 1 & 1 \end{vmatrix} = 2(1) - (-1)(1)$$

$$= 2 + 1 = 3 \neq 0$$

$\therefore$ A is non-singular.
Therefore, A^{-1} exists.
Hence, the given system of equations is consistent.

C. The given system can be written as $AX = B$, where

$$A = \begin{bmatrix} 1 & 3 \\ 2 & 6 \end{bmatrix}, X = \begin{bmatrix} x \\ y \end{bmatrix} \text{ and } B = \begin{bmatrix} 5 \\ 8 \end{bmatrix}$$

$$\text{Here, } |A| = \begin{vmatrix} 1 & 3 \\ 2 & 6 \end{vmatrix} = 1(6) - 3(2)$$

$$= 6 - 6 = 0$$

$\therefore$ A is singular matrix.
Nothing can be said about consistency yet.
We compute
(adj A) B

$$= \begin{bmatrix} 6 & -3 \\ -2 & 1 \end{bmatrix}\begin{bmatrix} 5 \\ 8 \end{bmatrix} = \begin{bmatrix} 30 - 24 \\ -10 + 8 \end{bmatrix}$$

$$= \begin{bmatrix} 6 \\ -2 \end{bmatrix} \neq 0$$

Thus, the solution of the given system of equations does not exist. Hence, the system of equations is inconsistent.

D. The given system can be written as $AX = B$, where

$$A = \begin{bmatrix} 1 & 1 & 1 \\ 2 & 3 & 2 \\ a & a & 2a \end{bmatrix}, X = \begin{bmatrix} x \\ y \\ z \end{bmatrix}$$

and $B = \begin{bmatrix} 1 \\ 2 \\ 4 \end{bmatrix}$

$$\text{Here, } |A| = \begin{vmatrix} 1 & 1 & 1 \\ 2 & 3 & 2 \\ a & a & 2a \end{vmatrix}$$

$$= 1(6a - 2a) - 1(4a - 2a) + 1(2a - 3a)$$

$$= 4a - 2a - a = 4a - 3a = a \neq 0$$

$\therefore A$ is non-singular.

Therefore, A^{-1} exists.

Hence, the given system of equations is consistent.

E. The given system of equations is $\quad 3x - y - 2z = 2,$

$0x + 2y - z = -1$

and $3x - 5y + 0z = 3$

which can be written as $AX = B$, where

$$A = \begin{bmatrix} 3 & -1 & -2 \\ 0 & 2 & -1 \\ 3 & -5 & 0 \end{bmatrix}, X = \begin{bmatrix} x \\ y \\ z \end{bmatrix}$$

and $B = \begin{bmatrix} 2 \\ -1 \\ 3 \end{bmatrix}$

Here, $|A| = \begin{vmatrix} 3 & -1 & -2 \\ 0 & 2 & -1 \\ 3 & -5 & 0 \end{vmatrix}$

$= 3(0-5) + 1(0+3) - 2(0-6)$

$= -15 + 3 + 12 = 0$

$\therefore$ A is a singular matrix

Therefore, nothing can be said about consistency yet.

So, we compute (adj A) B.

Cofactors of A are $A_{11} = -5$, $A_{12} = -3, A_{13} = -6,$ $A_{21} = 10, A_{22} = 6, A_{23} = 12,$ $A_{31} = 5, A_{32} = 3$ and $A_{33} = 6$

$$\text{adj}(A) = \begin{bmatrix} -5 & -3 & -6 \\ 10 & 6 & 12 \\ 5 & 3 & 6 \end{bmatrix}' = \begin{bmatrix} -5 & 10 & 5 \\ -3 & 6 & 3 \\ -6 & 12 & 6 \end{bmatrix}$$

$$\therefore (\text{adj } A)B = \begin{bmatrix} -5 & 10 & 5 \\ -3 & 6 & 3 \\ -6 & 12 & 6 \end{bmatrix}\begin{bmatrix} 2 \\ -1 \\ 3 \end{bmatrix} = \begin{bmatrix} -10-10+15 \\ -6-6+9 \\ -12-12+18 \end{bmatrix} = \begin{bmatrix} -5 \\ -3 \\ -6 \end{bmatrix} \neq 0$$

Thus, the solution of the given system of equations does not exist. Hence, the system of equations is inconsistent.

F. The given system can be written as $AX = B$, where

$$A = \begin{bmatrix} 5 & -1 & 4 \\ 2 & 3 & 5 \\ 5 & -2 & 6 \end{bmatrix}, X = \begin{bmatrix} x \\ y \\ z \end{bmatrix}$$

and $\quad B = \begin{bmatrix} 5 \\ 2 \\ -1 \end{bmatrix}$

Here, $\quad |A| = \begin{vmatrix} 5 & -1 & 4 \\ 2 & 3 & 5 \\ 5 & -2 & 6 \end{vmatrix}$

$= 5(18+10) - (-1)(12-25) + 4(-4-15)$

$= 140 - 13 - 76 = 51 \neq 0$

$\therefore A$ is non-singular.

Therefore, A^{-1} exists.

Hence, the given system of equations is consistent.

4 (*a*) The given system can be written as $AX = B$, where

$$A = \begin{bmatrix} 5 & 2 \\ 7 & 3 \end{bmatrix}, X = \begin{bmatrix} x \\ y \end{bmatrix} \text{ and } B = \begin{bmatrix} 4 \\ 5 \end{bmatrix}$$

Here, $|A| = \begin{vmatrix} 5 & 2 \\ 7 & 3 \end{vmatrix} = 15 - 14 = 1 \neq 0$

Thus, A is non-singular. Therefore, its inverse exists.

Therefore, the given system is consistent and has unique solution given by

$$A^{-1}(AX) = A^{-1}B$$

$$\Rightarrow \quad X = A^{-1}B$$

Cofactors of A are $A_{11} = 3, A_{12} = -7,$ $A_{21} = -2$ and $A_{22} = 5.$

$$\therefore \quad \text{adj}(A) = \begin{bmatrix} 3 & -7 \\ -2 & 5 \end{bmatrix}' = \begin{bmatrix} 3 & -2 \\ -7 & 5 \end{bmatrix}$$

Now, $A^{-1} = \dfrac{1}{|A|}(\text{adj } A)$

$$= \frac{1}{1}\begin{bmatrix} 3 & -2 \\ -7 & 5 \end{bmatrix} = \begin{bmatrix} 3 & -2 \\ -7 & 5 \end{bmatrix}$$

$$X = A^{-1}B = \begin{bmatrix} 3 & -2 \\ -7 & 5 \end{bmatrix}\begin{bmatrix} 4 \\ 5 \end{bmatrix} = \begin{bmatrix} 3 \times 4 + (-2) \times 5 \\ -7 \times 4 + 5 \times 5 \end{bmatrix} = \begin{bmatrix} 2 \\ -3 \end{bmatrix}$$

$$\Rightarrow \begin{bmatrix} 2 \\ -3 \end{bmatrix} = \begin{bmatrix} x \\ y \end{bmatrix}$$

Hence, $x = 2$ and $y = -3$.

5 (*b*) The given system can be written as $AX = B$, where

$$A = \begin{bmatrix} 4 & -3 \\ 3 & -5 \end{bmatrix}, X = \begin{bmatrix} x \\ y \end{bmatrix}, B = \begin{bmatrix} 3 \\ 7 \end{bmatrix}$$

Here,

$|A| = \begin{vmatrix} 4 & -3 \\ 3 & -5 \end{vmatrix} = 4(-5) - 3(-3)$

$= -20 + 9 = -11 \neq 0$

Thus, A is non-singular.

Therefore, its inverse exists.

Therefore, the given system is consistent and has a unique solution given by $X = A^{-1}B$.

Cofactors of A are $A_{11} = -5$, $A_{12} = -3, A_{21} = 3$ and $A_{22} = 4$.

$$\therefore \quad \text{adj}(A) = \begin{bmatrix} -5 & -3 \\ 3 & 4 \end{bmatrix}' = \begin{bmatrix} -5 & 3 \\ -3 & 4 \end{bmatrix}$$

$$\therefore \quad A^{-1} = \frac{1}{|A|}(\text{adj } A) = \frac{1}{-11}\begin{bmatrix} -5 & 3 \\ -3 & 4 \end{bmatrix}$$

Now, $X = A^{-1}B = \dfrac{1}{-11}\begin{bmatrix} -5 & 3 \\ -3 & 4 \end{bmatrix}\begin{bmatrix} 3 \\ 7 \end{bmatrix}$

$$= \frac{1}{-11}\begin{bmatrix} -15+21 \\ -9+28 \end{bmatrix} = \frac{1}{-11}\begin{bmatrix} 6 \\ 19 \end{bmatrix}$$

$$\Rightarrow \begin{bmatrix} x \\ y \end{bmatrix} = \begin{bmatrix} -\dfrac{6}{11} \\ -\dfrac{19}{11} \end{bmatrix}$$

$\therefore \quad x = -\dfrac{6}{11}$ and $y = -\dfrac{19}{11}$

6 (c) The given system can be written as $AX = B$, where

$$A = \begin{bmatrix} 2 & 1 & 1 \\ 2 & -4 & -2 \\ 0 & 3 & -5 \end{bmatrix}, X = \begin{bmatrix} x \\ y \\ z \end{bmatrix}$$

and $B = \begin{bmatrix} 1 \\ 3 \\ 9 \end{bmatrix}$

Here, $|A| = \begin{vmatrix} 2 & 1 & 1 \\ 2 & -4 & -2 \\ 0 & 3 & -5 \end{vmatrix}$

$= 2(20+6) - 1(-10-0) + 1(6-0)$
$= 52 + 10 + 6 = 68 \neq 0$

Thus, A is non-singular.
Therefore, its inverse exists.

Therefore, the given system is consistent and has a unique solution given by $X = A^{-1}B$.

Cofactors of A are

$A_{11} = 20 + 6 = 26$,
$A_{12} = -(-10+0) = 10$,
$A_{13} = 6 + 0 = 6$,
$A_{21} = -(-5-3) = 8$,
$A_{22} = -10 - 0 = -10$,
$A_{23} = -(6-0) = -6$,
$A_{31} = (-2+4) = 2$,
$A_{32} = -(-4-2) = 6$
and $A_{33} = -8 - 2 = -10$

$$\text{adj}(A) = \begin{bmatrix} 26 & 10 & 6 \\ 8 & -10 & -6 \\ 2 & 6 & -10 \end{bmatrix}'$$

$$= \begin{bmatrix} 26 & 8 & 2 \\ 10 & -10 & 6 \\ 6 & -6 & -10 \end{bmatrix}$$

$$\therefore A^{-1} = \frac{1}{|A|}(\text{adj } A)$$

$$= \frac{1}{68}\begin{bmatrix} 26 & 8 & 2 \\ 10 & -10 & 6 \\ 6 & -6 & -10 \end{bmatrix}$$

Now, $X = A^{-1}B$

$$\Rightarrow \begin{bmatrix} x \\ y \\ z \end{bmatrix} = \frac{1}{68}\begin{bmatrix} 26 & 8 & 2 \\ 10 & -10 & 6 \\ 6 & -6 & -10 \end{bmatrix}\begin{bmatrix} 1 \\ 3 \\ 9 \end{bmatrix}$$

$$\Rightarrow \begin{bmatrix} x \\ y \\ z \end{bmatrix} = \frac{1}{68}\begin{bmatrix} 26+24+18 \\ 10-30+54 \\ 6-18-90 \end{bmatrix}$$

$$= \frac{1}{68}\begin{bmatrix} 68 \\ 34 \\ -102 \end{bmatrix}$$

$$\Rightarrow \begin{bmatrix} x \\ y \\ z \end{bmatrix} = \begin{bmatrix} 1 \\ \frac{1}{2} \\ \frac{-3}{2} \end{bmatrix}$$

Hence, $x = 1, y = \frac{1}{2}$ and $z = \frac{-3}{2}$.

7 (a)

I. The given system can be written as $AX = B$, where

$$A = \begin{bmatrix} 1 & -1 & 1 \\ 2 & 1 & -3 \\ 1 & 1 & 1 \end{bmatrix}, X = \begin{bmatrix} x \\ y \\ z \end{bmatrix}$$

and $B = \begin{bmatrix} 4 \\ 0 \\ 2 \end{bmatrix}$

Here, $|A| = \begin{vmatrix} 1 & -1 & 1 \\ 2 & 1 & -3 \\ 1 & 1 & 1 \end{vmatrix}$,

$= 1(1+3) - (-1)(2+3) + 1(2-1)$
$= 4 + 5 + 1$
$= 10 \neq 0$

Thus, A is non-singular.
Therefore, its inverse exists.
Therefore, the given system is consistent and has a unique solution given by $X = A^{-1}B$.
Cofactors of A are

$A_{11} = 1 + 3 = 4$,
$A_{12} = -(2+3) = -5$,
$A_{13} = 2 - 1 = 1$,
$A_{21} = -(-1-1) = 2$,
$A_{22} = 1 - 1 = 0$,
$A_{23} = -(1+1) = -2$,
$A_{31} = 3 - 1 = 2$,
$A_{32} = -(-3-2) = 5$
and $A_{33} = 1 + 2 = 3$

$$\therefore \text{adj}(A) = \begin{bmatrix} 4 & -5 & 1 \\ 2 & 0 & -2 \\ 2 & 5 & 3 \end{bmatrix}'$$

$$= \begin{bmatrix} 4 & 2 & 2 \\ -5 & 0 & 5 \\ 1 & -2 & 3 \end{bmatrix}$$

$$\therefore A^{-1} = \frac{1}{|A|}(\text{adj } A)$$

$$= \frac{1}{10}\begin{bmatrix} 4 & 2 & 2 \\ -5 & 0 & 5 \\ 1 & -2 & 3 \end{bmatrix}$$

Now, $X = A^{-1}B$

$$\Rightarrow \begin{bmatrix} x \\ y \\ z \end{bmatrix} = \frac{1}{10}\begin{bmatrix} 4 & 2 & 2 \\ -5 & 0 & 5 \\ 1 & -2 & 3 \end{bmatrix}\begin{bmatrix} 4 \\ 0 \\ 2 \end{bmatrix}$$

$$\Rightarrow \begin{bmatrix} x \\ y \\ z \end{bmatrix} = \frac{1}{10}\begin{bmatrix} 16+0+4 \\ -20+0+10 \\ 4+0+6 \end{bmatrix}$$

$$\Rightarrow \begin{bmatrix} x \\ y \\ z \end{bmatrix} = \frac{1}{10}\begin{bmatrix} 20 \\ -10 \\ 10 \end{bmatrix} = \begin{bmatrix} 2 \\ -1 \\ 1 \end{bmatrix}$$

Hence, $x = 2, y = -1$ and $z = 1$.

II. The given system can be written as $AX = B$, where

$$A = \begin{bmatrix} 2 & 3 & 3 \\ 1 & -2 & 1 \\ 3 & -1 & -2 \end{bmatrix}, X = \begin{bmatrix} x \\ y \\ z \end{bmatrix}$$

and $B = \begin{bmatrix} 5 \\ -4 \\ 3 \end{bmatrix}$

Here, $|A| = \begin{vmatrix} 2 & 3 & 3 \\ 1 & -2 & 1 \\ 3 & -1 & -2 \end{vmatrix}$

$= 2(4+1) - 3(-2-3) + 3(-1+6)$
$= 10 + 15 + 15 = 40 \neq 0$

Thus, A is non-singular.
Therefore, its inverse exists.
Therefore, the given system is consistent and has a unique solution given by $X = A^{-1}B$.
Cofactors of A are

$A_{11} = 4 + 1 = 5$,
$A_{12} = -(-2-3) = 5$,
$A_{13} = (-1+6) = 5$,
$A_{21} = -(-6+3) = 3$,
$A_{22} = (-4-9) = -13$,
$A_{23} = -(-2-9) = 11$,

$A_{31} = 3 + 6 = 9,$
$A_{32} = -(2 - 3) = 1$
and $A_{33} = -4 - 3 = -7$

$$\therefore \quad \text{adj}(A) = \begin{bmatrix} 5 & 5 & 5 \\ 3 & -13 & 11 \\ 9 & 1 & -7 \end{bmatrix}' = \begin{bmatrix} 5 & 3 & 9 \\ 5 & -13 & 1 \\ 5 & 11 & -7 \end{bmatrix}$$

$$\therefore \quad A^{-1} = \frac{1}{|A|}(\text{adj } A) = \frac{1}{40}\begin{bmatrix} 5 & 3 & 9 \\ 5 & -13 & 1 \\ 5 & 11 & -7 \end{bmatrix}$$

Now, $\quad X = A^{-1}B$

$$\Rightarrow \begin{bmatrix} x \\ y \\ z \end{bmatrix} = \frac{1}{40}\begin{bmatrix} 5 & 3 & 9 \\ 5 & -13 & 1 \\ 5 & 11 & -7 \end{bmatrix}\begin{bmatrix} 5 \\ -4 \\ 3 \end{bmatrix} = \frac{1}{40}\begin{bmatrix} 25 - 12 + 27 \\ 25 + 52 + 3 \\ 25 - 44 - 21 \end{bmatrix} = \frac{1}{40}\begin{bmatrix} 40 \\ 80 \\ -40 \end{bmatrix} = \begin{bmatrix} 1 \\ 2 \\ -1 \end{bmatrix}$$

Hence, $x = 1, y = 2$ and $z = -1$.

III. The given system can be written as $AX = B$, where

$$A = \begin{bmatrix} 1 & -1 & 2 \\ 3 & 4 & -5 \\ 2 & -1 & 3 \end{bmatrix}, X = \begin{bmatrix} x \\ y \\ z \end{bmatrix}$$

and $B = \begin{bmatrix} 7 \\ -5 \\ 12 \end{bmatrix}$

Here, $|A| = \begin{vmatrix} 1 & -1 & 2 \\ 3 & 4 & -5 \\ 2 & -1 & 3 \end{vmatrix}$

$= 1(12 - 5) - (-1)(9 + 10) + 2(-3 - 8)$

$= 7 + 19 - 22 = 4 \neq 0$

Thus, A is non-singular.

Therefore, its inverse exists.

Therefore, the given system is consistent and has a unique solution given by $X = A^{-1}B$.

Cofactors of A are

$A_{11} = 12 - 5 = 7,$
$A_{12} = -(9 + 10) = -19,$
$A_{13} = -3 - 8 = -11,$
$A_{21} = -(-3 + 2) = 1,$
$A_{22} = 3 - 4 = -1,$
$A_{23} = -(-1 + 2) = -1,$
$A_{31} = 5 - 8 = -3,$
$A_{32} = -(-5 - 6) = 11$
and $A_{33} = 4 + 3 = 7$

$$\text{adj}(A) = \begin{bmatrix} 7 & -19 & -11 \\ 1 & -1 & -1 \\ -3 & 11 & 7 \end{bmatrix}' = \begin{bmatrix} 7 & 1 & -3 \\ -19 & -1 & 11 \\ -11 & -1 & 7 \end{bmatrix}$$

$$\therefore A^{-1} = \frac{1}{|A|}(\text{adj } A) = \frac{1}{4}\begin{bmatrix} 7 & 1 & -3 \\ -19 & -1 & 11 \\ -11 & -1 & 7 \end{bmatrix}$$

Now, $X = A^{-1}B$

$$\Rightarrow \begin{bmatrix} x \\ y \\ z \end{bmatrix} = \frac{1}{4}\begin{bmatrix} 7 & 1 & -3 \\ -19 & -1 & 11 \\ -11 & -1 & 7 \end{bmatrix}\begin{bmatrix} 7 \\ -5 \\ 12 \end{bmatrix} = \frac{1}{4}\begin{bmatrix} 49 - 5 - 36 \\ -133 + 5 + 132 \\ -77 + 5 + 84 \end{bmatrix}$$

$$\Rightarrow \begin{bmatrix} x \\ y \\ z \end{bmatrix} = \frac{1}{4}\begin{bmatrix} 8 \\ 4 \\ 12 \end{bmatrix} = \begin{bmatrix} 2 \\ 1 \\ 3 \end{bmatrix}$$

Hence, $x = 2, y = 1$ and $z = 3$.

8 (*a*) The given system can be written as $AX = B$, where

$$A = \begin{bmatrix} 2 & -3 & 5 \\ 3 & 2 & -4 \\ 1 & 1 & -2 \end{bmatrix}, X = \begin{bmatrix} x \\ y \\ z \end{bmatrix}$$

and $\quad B = \begin{bmatrix} 11 \\ -5 \\ -3 \end{bmatrix}$

Here, $|A| = \begin{vmatrix} 2 & -3 & 5 \\ 3 & 2 & -4 \\ 1 & 1 & -2 \end{vmatrix}$

$= 2(-4 + 4) - (-3)(-6 + 4) + 5(3 - 2)$

$= 0 - 6 + 5 = -1 \neq 0$

Thus, A is non-singular.

Therefore, its inverse exists.

Therefore, the given system is consistent and has a unique solution given by $X = A^{-1}B$.

Cafactors of A are

$A_{11} = -4 + 4 = 0,$
$A_{12} = -(-6 + 4) = 2,$
$A_{13} = 3 - 2 = 1,$
$A_{21} = -(6 - 5) = -1,$
$A_{22} = -4 - 5 = -9,$
$A_{23} = -(2 + 3) = -5,$
$A_{31} = (12 - 10) = 2,$
$A_{32} = -(-8 - 15) = 23$
and $A_{33} = 4 + 9 = 13$

$$\text{adj}(A) = \begin{bmatrix} 0 & 2 & 1 \\ -1 & -9 & -5 \\ 2 & 23 & 13 \end{bmatrix}' = \begin{bmatrix} 0 & -1 & 2 \\ 2 & -9 & 23 \\ 1 & -5 & 13 \end{bmatrix}$$

$$\therefore A^{-1} = \frac{1}{|A|}(\text{adj } A) = \frac{1}{-1}\begin{bmatrix} 0 & -1 & 2 \\ 2 & -9 & 23 \\ 1 & -5 & 13 \end{bmatrix} = \begin{bmatrix} 0 & 1 & -2 \\ -2 & 9 & -23 \\ -1 & 5 & -13 \end{bmatrix}$$

$$\therefore X = A^{-1}B = \begin{bmatrix} x \\ y \\ z \end{bmatrix} = \begin{bmatrix} 0 & 1 & -2 \\ -2 & 9 & -23 \\ -1 & 5 & -13 \end{bmatrix}\begin{bmatrix} 11 \\ -5 \\ -3 \end{bmatrix}$$

$$\Rightarrow \begin{bmatrix} x \\ y \\ z \end{bmatrix} = \begin{bmatrix} 0 - 5 + 6 \\ -22 - 45 + 69 \\ -11 - 25 + 39 \end{bmatrix} = \begin{bmatrix} 1 \\ 2 \\ 3 \end{bmatrix}.$$

Hence, $x = 1, y = 2$ and $z = 3$.

9 (*b*) Let the prices (per kg) of onion, wheat and rice be ₹ x, ₹ y and ₹ z, respectively.

Then, $4x + 3y + 2z = 60$
$2x + 4y + 6z = 90$
$6x + 2y + 3z = 70$

This system of equations can be written as $AX = B$, where

$$A = \begin{bmatrix} 4 & 3 & 2 \\ 2 & 4 & 6 \\ 6 & 2 & 3 \end{bmatrix}, X = \begin{bmatrix} x \\ y \\ z \end{bmatrix}$$

and $B = \begin{bmatrix} 60 \\ 90 \\ 70 \end{bmatrix}$

Here, $|A| = \begin{vmatrix} 4 & 3 & 2 \\ 2 & 4 & 6 \\ 6 & 2 & 3 \end{vmatrix}$

$= 4(12-12) - 3(6-36) + 2(4-24)$

$= 0 + 90 - 40 = 50 \neq 0$

Thus, A is non-singular. Therefore, its inverse exists. Therefore, the given system is consistent and has a unique solution given by $X = A^{-1}B$.

Cofactors of A are

$A_{11} = 12 - 12 = 0$,
$A_{12} = -(6-36) = 30$,
$A_{13} = 4 - 24 = -20$,
$A_{21} = -(9-4) = -5$,
$A_{22} = 12 - 12 = 0$,
$A_{23} = -(8-18) = 10$,
$A_{31} = (18-8) = 10$,
$A_{32} = -(24-4) = -20$
and $A_{33} = 16 - 6 = 10$

$$\text{adj}(A) = \begin{bmatrix} 0 & 30 & -20 \\ -5 & 0 & 10 \\ 10 & -20 & 10 \end{bmatrix}' = \begin{bmatrix} 0 & -5 & 10 \\ 30 & 0 & -20 \\ -20 & 10 & 10 \end{bmatrix}$$

$$\therefore A^{-1} = \frac{1}{|A|}(\text{adj } A) = \frac{1}{50}\begin{bmatrix} 0 & -5 & 10 \\ 30 & 0 & -20 \\ -20 & 10 & 10 \end{bmatrix}$$

Now, $X = A^{-1}B$

$$\Rightarrow \begin{bmatrix} x \\ y \\ z \end{bmatrix} = \frac{1}{50}\begin{bmatrix} 0 & -5 & 10 \\ 30 & 0 & -20 \\ -20 & 10 & 10 \end{bmatrix}\begin{bmatrix} 60 \\ 90 \\ 70 \end{bmatrix}$$

$$= \frac{1}{50}\begin{bmatrix} 0 - 450 + 700 \\ 1800 + 0 - 1400 \\ -1200 + 900 + 700 \end{bmatrix}$$

$$\Rightarrow \begin{bmatrix} x \\ y \\ z \end{bmatrix} = \frac{1}{50}\begin{bmatrix} 250 \\ 400 \\ 400 \end{bmatrix} = \begin{bmatrix} 5 \\ 8 \\ 8 \end{bmatrix}$$

$$\Rightarrow \begin{bmatrix} x \\ y \\ z \end{bmatrix} = \begin{bmatrix} 5 \\ 8 \\ 8 \end{bmatrix}$$

$\therefore x = 5, y = 8$ and $z = 8$.

Hence, price of onion per kg is ₹ 5, price of wheat per kg is ₹ 8 and price of rice per kg is ₹ 8.

10 (*c*) Given, $x \sin 3\theta - y + z = 0$

$x \cos 2\theta + 4y + 3z = 0$

and $2x + 7y + 7z = 0$

For non-trivial solution,

$$\begin{vmatrix} \sin 3\theta & -1 & 1 \\ \cos 2\theta & 4 & 3 \\ 2 & 7 & 7 \end{vmatrix} = 0$$

$\Rightarrow \sin 3\theta(28-21) - \cos 2\theta(-7-7) + 2(-3-4) = 0$

$\Rightarrow 7\sin 3\theta + 14\cos 2\theta - 14 = 0$

$\Rightarrow 7(3\sin\theta - 4\sin^3\theta) + 14(1 - 2\sin^2\theta) - 14 = 0$

$\left[\because \sin 3\theta = 3\sin\theta - 4\sin^3\theta \text{ and } \cos 2\theta = 1 - 2\sin^2\theta\right]$

$\Rightarrow -28\sin^3\theta - 28\sin^2\theta + 21\sin\theta = 0$

$\Rightarrow -7\sin\theta(4\sin^2\theta + 4\sin\theta - 3) = 0$

$\Rightarrow \sin\theta = 0, \sin\theta = \frac{1}{2} \quad \left[\because \sin\theta \neq -\frac{3}{2}\right]$

$\therefore \quad \theta = n\pi, n\pi + (-1)^n \frac{\pi}{6}$

Hence, (c) is the correct answer.

11 (*b*) The given system of equations is

$x + y + z = 8$

$x - y + 2z = 6$

$3x + 5y - 7z = 14$

This can be written as

$$\begin{bmatrix} 1 & 1 & 1 \\ 1 & -1 & 2 \\ 3 & 5 & -7 \end{bmatrix}\begin{bmatrix} x \\ y \\ z \end{bmatrix} = \begin{bmatrix} 8 \\ 6 \\ 14 \end{bmatrix}$$

$\Rightarrow AX = B$, where $A = \begin{bmatrix} 1 & 1 & 1 \\ 1 & -1 & 2 \\ 3 & 5 & -7 \end{bmatrix}$

$X = \begin{bmatrix} x \\ y \\ z \end{bmatrix}$ and $B = \begin{bmatrix} 8 \\ 6 \\ 14 \end{bmatrix}$

Now, $|A| = \begin{vmatrix} 1 & 1 & 1 \\ 1 & -1 & 2 \\ 3 & 5 & -7 \end{vmatrix}$

$= 1(7-10) - 1(-7-6) + 1(5+3)$

$= -3 + 13 + 8$

$= 18 \neq 0$

$\because \quad |A| \neq 0$

Hence, the system has unique solution.

12 (*a*) Let $\frac{1}{x} = p, \frac{1}{y} = q$ and $\frac{1}{z} = r$

Then, the given equations become

$2p + 3q + 10r = 4$

$4p - 6q + 5r = 1$

$6p + 9q - 20r = 2$

This system can be written as $AX = B$, where

$$A = \begin{bmatrix} 2 & 3 & 10 \\ 4 & -6 & 5 \\ 6 & 9 & -20 \end{bmatrix}, X = \begin{bmatrix} p \\ q \\ r \end{bmatrix}$$

and $B = \begin{bmatrix} 4 \\ 1 \\ 2 \end{bmatrix}$

Here, $|A| = \begin{vmatrix} 2 & 3 & 10 \\ 4 & -6 & 5 \\ 6 & 9 & -20 \end{vmatrix}$

$= 2(120 - 45) - 3(-80 - 30) + 10(36 + 36)$

$= 150 + 330 + 720 = 1200$

$\because \quad |A| \neq 0$

Thus, the system has unique solution given by $X = A^{-1}B$.

The cofactors of A are

$A_{11} = \begin{vmatrix} -6 & 5 \\ 9 & -20 \end{vmatrix} = 75$,

$$A_{12} = -\begin{vmatrix} 4 & 5 \\ 6 & -20 \end{vmatrix} = 110,$$

$$A_{13} = \begin{vmatrix} 4 & -6 \\ 6 & 9 \end{vmatrix} = 72,$$

$$A_{21} = -\begin{vmatrix} 3 & 10 \\ 9 & -20 \end{vmatrix} = 150,$$

$$A_{22} = \begin{vmatrix} 2 & 10 \\ 6 & -20 \end{vmatrix} = -100,$$

$$A_{23} = -\begin{vmatrix} 2 & 3 \\ 6 & 9 \end{vmatrix} = 0,$$

$$A_{31} = \begin{vmatrix} 3 & 10 \\ -6 & 5 \end{vmatrix} = 75,$$

$$A_{32} = -\begin{vmatrix} 2 & 10 \\ 4 & 5 \end{vmatrix} = 30$$

and $A_{33} = \begin{vmatrix} 2 & 3 \\ 4 & -6 \end{vmatrix} = -24$

$$\therefore \text{adj}(A) = \begin{bmatrix} 75 & 110 & 72 \\ 150 & -100 & 0 \\ 75 & 30 & -24 \end{bmatrix}' = \begin{bmatrix} 75 & 150 & 75 \\ 110 & -100 & 30 \\ 72 & 0 & -24 \end{bmatrix}$$

Now, $A^{-1} = \dfrac{1}{|A|}(\text{adj } A)$

$$= \frac{1}{1200}\begin{bmatrix} 75 & 150 & 75 \\ 110 & -100 & 30 \\ 72 & 0 & -24 \end{bmatrix}$$

$\therefore \quad X = A^{-1}B$

$$\therefore X = \frac{1}{1200}\begin{bmatrix} 75 & 150 & 75 \\ 110 & -100 & 30 \\ 72 & 0 & -24 \end{bmatrix}\begin{bmatrix} 4 \\ 1 \\ 2 \end{bmatrix}$$

$$= \frac{1}{1200}\begin{bmatrix} 300+150+150 \\ 440-100+60 \\ 288+0-48 \end{bmatrix}$$

$$= \frac{1}{1200}\begin{bmatrix} 600 \\ 400 \\ 240 \end{bmatrix} = \begin{bmatrix} \frac{1}{2} \\ \frac{1}{3} \\ \frac{1}{5} \end{bmatrix}$$

$\Rightarrow \; p = \dfrac{1}{2}, q = \dfrac{1}{3}, r = \dfrac{1}{5}$

Hence, $x = 2$, $y = 3$ and $z = 5$.

Miscellaneous Exercise

1 (*b*) Consider,

$$\begin{vmatrix} 1 & \log_x y & \log_x z \\ \log_y x & 1 & \log_y z \\ \log_z x & \log_z y & 1 \end{vmatrix}$$

$= 1(1 - \log_y z \log_z y) - \log_x y (\log_y x - \log_z x \log_y z) + \log_x z (\log_z y \log_y x - \log_z x)$

$= (1 - \log_y y) - \log_x y [\log_y x - \log_y x] + \log_x z (\log_z x - \log_z x)$

$= (1-1) - 0 + 0 = 0$

$$\left[\because \log_a b = \frac{1}{\log_b a}\right]$$

2 (*b*) All are true but

$(M^2)^{-1} \neq (M^{-1})^2$ is not true.

Since, $(M^2)^{-1} = (M \cdot M)^{-1}$ $\quad [\because M^2 = M \cdot M]$

$= M^{-1} \cdot M^{-1}$ $\quad [(AB)^{-1} = B^{-1}A^{-1}]$

$= (M^{-1})^2$

$\therefore \quad (M^2)^{-1} = (M^{-1})^2$

3 (*c*) Given system of equations is

$$x - y + z = 3$$
$$2x + y - z = 2$$

and $\; -3x - 2ky + 6z = 3$

$\because$ The given system will have infinite solutions.

$$\therefore \begin{vmatrix} 1 & -1 & 1 \\ 2 & 1 & -1 \\ -3 & -2k & 6 \end{vmatrix} = 0$$

$\Rightarrow \quad 6k - 18 = 0 \Rightarrow k = 3$

Also, for this value of k, (adj A) $B = 0$.

4 (*d*) If det $(A) = \pm 1$, A^{-1} exists and

$A^{-1} = \dfrac{1}{\det(A)}(\text{adj } A) = \pm(\text{adj } A)$

All entries in adj (A) are integers.

$\therefore$ A^{-1} has integer entries.

5 (*b*) If (x_1, y_1), (x_2, y_2) and (x_3, y_3) are the vertices of a triangle, then

$$\text{Area} = \frac{1}{2}\begin{vmatrix} x_1 & y_1 & 1 \\ x_2 & y_2 & 1 \\ x_3 & y_3 & 1 \end{vmatrix} \quad \text{...(i)}$$

Also, we know that, if a be the length of side of an equilateral triangle, then

$$\text{Area} = \frac{\sqrt{3}}{4}a^2 \quad \text{...(ii)}$$

From Eqs. (i) and (ii), we get

$$\frac{\sqrt{3}}{4}a^2 = \frac{1}{2}\begin{vmatrix} x_1 & y_1 & 1 \\ x_2 & y_2 & 1 \\ x_3 & y_3 & 1 \end{vmatrix}$$

$$\Rightarrow \frac{\sqrt{3}}{2}a^2 = \begin{vmatrix} x_1 & y_1 & 1 \\ x_2 & y_2 & 1 \\ x_3 & y_3 & 1 \end{vmatrix}$$

On squaring both sides, we get

$$\frac{3}{4}a^4 = \begin{vmatrix} x_1 & y_1 & 1 \\ x_2 & y_2 & 1 \\ x_3 & y_3 & 1 \end{vmatrix}^2$$

6 (*d*) Given,

$$A = \begin{bmatrix} 1 & \sin\theta & 1 \\ -\sin\theta & 1 & \sin\theta \\ -1 & -\sin\theta & 1 \end{bmatrix}$$

$$|A| = \begin{vmatrix} 1 & \sin\theta & 1 \\ -\sin\theta & 1 & \sin\theta \\ -1 & -\sin\theta & 1 \end{vmatrix}$$

$= 1(1 + \sin^2\theta) - \sin\theta(-\sin\theta + \sin\theta) + 1(\sin^2\theta + 1)$

$= 2 + 2\sin^2\theta$

For $0 \leq \theta \leq 2\pi, -1 \leq \sin\theta \leq 1$

$\Rightarrow \quad 0 \leq \sin^2\theta \leq 1$

$\Rightarrow \quad 1 \leq 1 + \sin^2\theta \leq 2$

$\Rightarrow \quad 2 \leq 2(1 + \sin^2\theta) \leq 4$

$\therefore \quad \det(A) \in [2, 4]$

7 (*c*) Let ₹ x, ₹ y, and ₹ z be the investments at the rates of interest of 6%, 7% and 8% per annum, respectively. Then,

Total investment = ₹ 5000

$\Rightarrow \quad x + y + z = 5000$

Now, income from first investment

$= ₹ \dfrac{6x}{100}$

Income from second investment

$= ₹ \dfrac{7y}{100}$

Income from third investment

$= ₹ \dfrac{8z}{100}$

$\therefore$ Total annual income

$$= ₹\left(\frac{6x}{100}+\frac{7y}{100}+\frac{8z}{100}\right)$$

$$\Rightarrow \frac{6x}{100}+\frac{7y}{100}+\frac{8z}{100}=358$$

$$\Rightarrow 6x+7y+8z=35800$$

It is given that the combined income from the first two investments is ₹ 70 more than the income from the third.

$$\therefore \frac{6x}{100}+\frac{7y}{100}=70+\frac{8z}{100}$$

$$\Rightarrow 6x+7y-8z=7000$$

Thus, the system of equations is

$$x+y+z=5000$$
$$6x+7y+8z=35800$$
$$6x+7y-8z=7000$$

or $AX=B$,

where $A=\begin{bmatrix}1&1&1\\6&7&8\\6&7&-8\end{bmatrix}, X=\begin{bmatrix}x\\y\\z\end{bmatrix}$

and $B=\begin{bmatrix}5000\\35800\\7000\end{bmatrix}$

Now, $|A|=\begin{vmatrix}1&1&1\\6&7&8\\6&7&-8\end{vmatrix}$

$$=1(-56-56)-1(-48-48)+1(42-42)$$

$$=-16\neq 0$$

$\therefore$ The solution of the system $AX=B$ exists and is given by

$$X=A^{-1}B$$

Now, the cofactors of A are

$A_{11}=-112, A_{12}=96, A_{13}=0,$

$A_{21}=15, A_{22}=-14,$

$A_{23}=-1, A_{31}=1$

and $A_{32}=-2, A_{33}=1$

$$\therefore \text{adj}(A)=\begin{bmatrix}-112&96&0\\15&-14&-1\\1&-2&1\end{bmatrix}'$$

$$=\begin{bmatrix}-112&15&1\\96&-14&-2\\0&-1&1\end{bmatrix}$$

$$\therefore A^{-1}=\frac{1}{|A|}(\text{adj } A)$$

$$=\frac{-1}{16}\begin{bmatrix}-112&15&1\\96&-14&-2\\0&-1&1\end{bmatrix}$$

Hence, solution is given by

$X=A^{-1}B$

$$=-\frac{1}{16}\begin{bmatrix}-112&15&1\\96&-14&-2\\0&-1&1\end{bmatrix}\begin{bmatrix}5000\\35800\\7000\end{bmatrix}$$

$$=-\frac{1}{16}\begin{bmatrix}-560000+537000+7000\\480000-501200-14000\\0-35800+7000\end{bmatrix}$$

$$\Rightarrow \begin{bmatrix}x\\y\\z\end{bmatrix}=\begin{bmatrix}1000\\2200\\1800\end{bmatrix}$$

$$\Rightarrow x=1000$$
$$y=2200$$
and $z=1800$

Hence, three investments are of ₹ 1000, ₹ 2200 and ₹ 1800, respectively.

8 (*b*) The system of given equations is

$$kx+2y-z=1$$
$$(k-1)y-2z=2$$
and $(k+2)z=3$

This system of equations has unique solution, if

$$\begin{vmatrix}k&2&-1\\0&k-1&-2\\0&0&k+2\end{vmatrix}\neq 0$$

$$\Rightarrow (k+2)(k)(k-1)\neq 0$$

$$\Rightarrow k\neq -2,0,1$$

i.e. $k=-1$ is the required answer.

9 (*a*) The given system of equations is

$$3x-y+4z=3$$
$$x+2y-3z=-2$$
$$6x+5y+\lambda z=-3$$

This can be written as $AX=B$, where

$$A=\begin{bmatrix}3&-1&4\\1&2&-3\\6&5&\lambda\end{bmatrix}, X=\begin{bmatrix}x\\y\\z\end{bmatrix}$$

and $B=\begin{bmatrix}3\\-2\\-3\end{bmatrix}$

The given system of equations has atleast one solution, if

$$\begin{vmatrix}3&-1&4\\1&2&-3\\6&5&\lambda\end{vmatrix}=0$$

$$\Rightarrow 3(2\lambda+15)+1(\lambda+18)+4(5-12)=0$$

$$\Rightarrow 7\lambda=-35$$

$$\therefore \lambda=-5$$

Also, for this value of λ, $(\text{adj } A)B=0$.

10 (*c*)

A. Given determinant is

$$\begin{vmatrix}\cos\alpha\cos\beta&\cos\alpha\sin\beta&-\sin\alpha\\-\sin\beta&\cos\beta&0\\\sin\alpha\cos\beta&\sin\alpha\sin\beta&\cos\alpha\end{vmatrix}$$

By expanding corresponding to R_1, we get

$$=\cos\alpha\cos\beta(\cos\alpha\cos\beta-0)-\cos\alpha\sin\beta(-\cos\alpha\sin\beta-0)$$
$$-\sin\alpha(-\sin^2\beta\sin\alpha-\cos^2\beta\sin\alpha)$$
$$=\cos^2\alpha\cos^2\beta+\cos^2\alpha\sin^2\beta+\sin^2\alpha(\sin^2\beta+\cos^2\beta)$$
$$=\cos^2\alpha(\cos^2\beta+\sin^2\beta)+\sin^2\alpha(\sin^2\beta+\cos^2\beta)$$
$$=\cos^2\alpha(1)+\sin^2\alpha(1)$$
$$=\cos^2\alpha+\sin^2\alpha=1$$
$$[\because \sin^2\theta+\cos^2\theta=1]$$

B. Let $|A|=\begin{vmatrix}x&y&x+y\\y&x+y&x\\x+y&x&y\end{vmatrix}$

$$=x[(x+y)y-x^2]-y[y^2-x(x+y)]+(x+y)[(xy-(x+y)^2]$$
$$=x[(xy+y^2-x^2]-y[y^2-x^2-xy]+(x+y)[xy-x^2-y^2-2xy]$$
$$=x^2y+xy^2-x^3-y^3+x^2y+xy^2+x^2y-x^3-xy^2-2x^2y+xy^2-x^2y-y^3-2xy^2$$
$$=-2(x+y)(x^2-xy+y^2)$$

$\Rightarrow |A| = -2(x^3 + y^3)$

C. Let $|A| = \begin{vmatrix} 1 & x & y \\ 1 & x+y & y \\ 1 & x & x+y \end{vmatrix}$

$= 1[(x+y)^2 - xy] - 1$
$[x(x+y) - xy] + 1[xy - y(x+y)]$
$= x^2 + y^2 + xy - x^2 - xy + xy$
$+ xy - xy - y^2$

$= xy$

11 (c) $\begin{vmatrix} -12 & 0 & \lambda \\ 0 & 2 & -1 \\ 2 & 1 & 15 \end{vmatrix} = -360$

$\Rightarrow -12(30+1) - 4\lambda = -360$
$\Rightarrow \quad -372 + 360 = 4\lambda$
$\therefore \quad \lambda = -\dfrac{12}{4} = -3$

12 (a) Given, $\begin{vmatrix} x & 2 & -1 \\ 2 & 5 & x \\ -1 & 2 & x \end{vmatrix} = 0$

$\Rightarrow x(5x - 2x) - 2(2x + x)$
$- 1(4+5) = 0$
$\Rightarrow 3x^2 - 6x + 9 = 0$
$\Rightarrow \quad x^2 - 2x - 3 = 0$
$\therefore \quad x = 3, -1$

13 (d) $x + iy = -3i \begin{vmatrix} 6i & 1 & 1 \\ 4 & -1 & -1 \\ 40 & i & i \end{vmatrix} = 0$

$\Rightarrow \quad x = 0, y = 0$

14 (b) Given that

$f(x) = \begin{vmatrix} (1+x)^{17} & (1+x)^{19} & (1+x)^{23} \\ (1+x)^{23} & (1+x)^{29} & (1+x)^{34} \\ (1+x)^{41} & (1+x)^{43} & (1+x)^{47} \end{vmatrix}$

$= A + Bx + Cx^2 + \ldots$

On putting $x = 0$, we get

$f(1) = \begin{vmatrix} 1 & 1 & 1 \\ 1 & 1 & 1 \\ 1 & 1 & 1 \end{vmatrix} = A$

$\Rightarrow \quad A = 0$

15 (a) $|A^{-1} \text{adj } A| = |A^{-1}| \cdot |\text{adj } A|$
$[\because |AB| = |A||B|]$
$= |A|^{-1} |\text{adj } A| \quad [\because |A^{-1}| = |A|^{-1}]$
$= |A|^{-1} \cdot |A|^2$

[$\because A$ is a 3×3 non-singular matrix, so $|\text{adj } A| = |A|^2$]

$= |A|$

16 (d)
$A^2 = \begin{bmatrix} 0 & 0 & -1 \\ 0 & -1 & 0 \\ -1 & 0 & 0 \end{bmatrix} \begin{bmatrix} 0 & 0 & -1 \\ 0 & -1 & 0 \\ -1 & 0 & 0 \end{bmatrix}$

$\Rightarrow \quad A^2 = \begin{bmatrix} 1 & 0 & 0 \\ 0 & 1 & 0 \\ 0 & 0 & 1 \end{bmatrix}$

$\Rightarrow \quad A^2 = I$

17 (a) Given A, B and C are the angles of a triangle.

$\therefore \quad A + B + C = \pi$
$\Rightarrow \quad A + B = \pi - C$

Now, $\cos(A+B) = \cos(\pi - C)$
$= -\cos C$
$\Rightarrow \cos A \cos B - \sin A \sin B$
$= -\cos C$
$\Rightarrow \cos A \cos B + \cos C = \sin A \sin B$ ...(i)

Similarly, $\cos A \cos C + \cos B$
$= \sin A \sin C$ ...(ii)

and $\sin(B + C) = \sin(\pi - A)$
$= \sin A$ ...(iii)

Now, let

$\Delta = \begin{vmatrix} -1 & \cos C & \cos B \\ \cos C & -1 & \cos A \\ \cos B & \cos A & -1 \end{vmatrix}$

By expanding along R_1, we get
$\Delta = -1(1 - \cos^2 A) + \cos C$
$(\cos C + \cos A \cos B)$
$+ \cos B(\cos B + \cos A \cos C)$
$= -\sin^2 A + \cos C(\sin A \sin B)$
$+ \cos B(\sin A \sin C)$
[using Eqs. (i) and (ii); and $\cos^2 A + \sin^2 A = 1$]
$= -\sin^2 A + \sin A(\sin B \cos C$
$+ \cos B \sin C)$
$= -\sin^2 A + \sin A \sin(B + C)$
[$\because \sin(x + y) = \sin x \cos y + \cos x \sin y$]
$= -\sin^2 A + \sin^2 A = 0$
[using Eq. (iii)]

18 (a) Given,
$\Delta = \begin{vmatrix} 1 & 1 & 1 \\ 1 & 1+\sin\theta & 1 \\ 1+\cos\theta & 1 & 1 \end{vmatrix}$

$= 1(1 + \sin\theta - 1) - 1(1 - 1 - \cos\theta)$
$+ 1(1 - 1 - \sin\theta - \cos\theta - \sin\theta\cos\theta)$
$= \sin\theta + \cos\theta - \sin\theta - \cos\theta$
$- \sin\theta\cos\theta$
$= -\sin\theta\cos\theta = -\dfrac{1}{2}\sin 2\theta$

$\because$ For maximum value of Δ, $\sin(2\theta)$ will be minimum

$\therefore \quad \Delta = \dfrac{-1}{2} \times (-1) = \dfrac{1}{2}$

[$\because$ minimum value of $\sin(2\theta)$ is -1]

Numerical Type Questions

1 (0) $\begin{vmatrix} p^n & p^{n+1} & p^{n+2} \\ q^n & q^{n+1} & q^{n+2} \\ r^n & r^{n+1} & r^{n+2} \end{vmatrix}$
$= (p-q)(q-r)(r-p)$
$\Rightarrow p^n(q^{n+1}r^{n+2} - r^{n+1}q^{n+2})$
$- q^n(p^{n+1}r^{n+2} - r^{n+1}p^{n+2})$
$+ r^n(p^{n+1}q^{n+2} - q^{n+1}p^{n+2})$
$= (p-q)(q-r)(r-p)$
$\Rightarrow p^n q^n r^n (p-q)(q-r)(r-p)$
$= (p-q)(r-r)(r-p)$
$(pqr)^n = 1$
$\Rightarrow \quad (pqr)^n = (pqr)^0$
$\Rightarrow \quad n = 0 \quad [\because p \neq q \neq r]$

2 (1) Given,
$b_{ij} = \begin{cases} 1, & \text{if } i = j \\ -2x^2 + 1, & \text{if } |i - j| = 1 \\ 2x + 1, & \text{otherwise} \end{cases}$

Let $B = [b_{ij}]$ be 2×2 matrix.

$\therefore \quad B = \begin{bmatrix} 1 & -2x^2 + 1 \\ -2x^2 + 1 & 1 \end{bmatrix}$

$|B| = 1 - (-2x^2 + 1)(-2x^2 + 1)$
$= 1 - (1 - 2x^2)^2$
$= 1 - (1 + 4x^4 - 4x^2)$
$|B| = 4x^2 - 4x^4$

Let $f(x) = 4x^2 - 4x^4$
$\Rightarrow f'(x) = 8x - 16x^3$

Now, $f'(x) = 0$

$8x - 16x^3 = 0$

$8x(1 - 2x^2) = 0$

$x = 0, x = \pm\frac{1}{\sqrt{2}}$

Now, $f''(x) = 8 - 48x^2$

$f''(0) = 0 \Rightarrow f$ is minimum at $x = 0$.

$$f''\left(\frac{1}{\sqrt{2}}\right) = 8 - 48\left(\frac{1}{\sqrt{2}}\right)^2$$

$$= 8 - 24 = -16$$

$\Rightarrow f$ is maximum at $x = \pm\frac{1}{\sqrt{2}}$

$\therefore \quad f(0) = 0$

and $f\left(\pm\frac{1}{\sqrt{2}}\right) = 4\left(\pm\frac{1}{\sqrt{2}}\right)^2 - 4\left(\pm\frac{1}{\sqrt{2}}\right)^4$

$$f\left(\pm\frac{1}{\sqrt{2}}\right) = 4 \times \frac{1}{2} - 4 \times \frac{1}{4}$$

$$f\left(\pm\frac{1}{\sqrt{2}}\right) = 2 - 1 = 1$$

Hence, sum of maximum and minimum values of $f(x)$ is 1.

3 (20) $|\text{adj}(\text{adj}(\text{adj}(2A)))| = |2A|^{(n-1)^3}$

$$= |2A|^{(3-1)^3}$$

$$= |2A|^8 = (2^3 |A|)^8$$

Now, $A = \begin{bmatrix} 2 & 1 & 0 \\ 0 & 2 & -4 \\ 0 & 0 & 1 \end{bmatrix}$

$\Rightarrow \quad |A| = 4$

$$|\text{adj}(\text{adj}(\text{adj}(2A)))| = 2^{24} \cdot (4)^8 = 2^{24} \cdot (2^2)^8 = 2^{24} \cdot 2^{16} = 2^{40}$$

It is given $|\text{adj}(\text{adj}(\text{adj}(2A)))| = 4^n$

$\Rightarrow \quad 2^{40} = 4^n$

$\Rightarrow \quad (2^2)^{20} = 4^n$

$\Rightarrow \quad 4^{20} = 4^n$

$\Rightarrow \quad n = 20$

4 (43) $B = \begin{bmatrix} 1 & \alpha & 3 \\ 2 & 3 & 4 \\ 2 & 1 & 3 \end{bmatrix}$

$\therefore |B| = 1(9 - 4) - \alpha(6 - 8) + 3(2 - 6)$

$$= 5 + 2\alpha - 12$$

$$= 2\alpha - 7$$

It is given that $B = \text{adj}\, A$.

$$|B| = |\text{adj}\, A| = |A|^{3-1}$$

$$= |A|^2 = (6)^2 = 36$$

$\therefore \quad 2\alpha - 7 = 36$

$\Rightarrow \quad 2\alpha = 43$

5 (21) Given, $A = \begin{bmatrix} 1 & 3 \\ 2 & 7 \end{bmatrix}$

$A^{-1} = xI + yA, x, y \in R$

Now, we know that $A^{-1} = \frac{\text{adj}\, A}{|A|}$

and we know that $B = \begin{bmatrix} a & b \\ c & d \end{bmatrix}$, then

$$\text{adj}\, B = \begin{bmatrix} d & -b \\ -c & a \end{bmatrix}$$

Similarly, $\text{adj}\, A = \begin{bmatrix} 7 & -3 \\ -2 & 1 \end{bmatrix}$,

and $\quad |A| = 7 - 6 = 1$

$\therefore \quad A^{-1} = \begin{bmatrix} 7 & -3 \\ -2 & 1 \end{bmatrix}$

$$x\begin{bmatrix} 1 & 0 \\ 0 & 1 \end{bmatrix} + y\begin{bmatrix} 1 & 3 \\ 2 & 7 \end{bmatrix} = \begin{bmatrix} 7 & -3 \\ -2 & 1 \end{bmatrix}$$

$$\begin{bmatrix} x & 0 \\ 0 & x \end{bmatrix} + \begin{bmatrix} y & 3y \\ 2y & 7y \end{bmatrix} = \begin{bmatrix} 7 & -3 \\ -2 & 1 \end{bmatrix}$$

$$\begin{bmatrix} x + y & 3y \\ 2y & x + 7y \end{bmatrix} = \begin{bmatrix} 7 & -3 \\ -3 & 1 \end{bmatrix}$$

$$3y = -3 \Rightarrow y = -1$$

$$x + y = 7 \Rightarrow x = 7 - y$$

$\Rightarrow \quad x = 7 + 1 \Rightarrow x = 8$

$\therefore \quad 3(x + y) = 3(8 - 1) = 3 \times 7 = 21.$

6 (18) Given that area of the triangle whose vertices are $A(x, 1)$, $B(0, x)$ and $C(x, 0)$ is 9 sq. units.

Thus, $\frac{1}{2}\begin{vmatrix} x & 1 & 1 \\ 0 & x & 1 \\ x & 0 & 1 \end{vmatrix} = 9$

$\Rightarrow |x(x - 0) - 1(0 - x) + 1(-x^2)| = 18$

$\Rightarrow \quad |x^2 + x - x^2| = 18$

$\Rightarrow \quad x = \pm 18$

Take $\quad x = 18$

Thus, $(18, -18)$, $(-18, 18)$ and $(324, y)$ are collinear.

Then, $\begin{vmatrix} 18 & -18 & 1 \\ -18 & 18 & 1 \\ 324 & y & 1 \end{vmatrix} = 0$

$18(18 - y) + 18(-18 - 324) + 1(-18y - 18 \times 324) = 0$

On dividing by 18 both sides, we get

$(18 - y) + (-18 - 324) + (-y - 324) = 0$

$\Rightarrow 18 - y - 18 - 324 - y - 324 = 0$

$\Rightarrow \quad -2y - 648 = 0$

$\Rightarrow \quad y = -324$

$\therefore \quad \left|\frac{y}{18}\right| = \left|\frac{-324}{18}\right| = 18$

7 (2) $\begin{vmatrix} 2 & -3 & 1 \\ 0 & 2 & 4 \\ 3 & 1 & 2 \end{vmatrix}$, here a and b are the co-factors of -3 and 3.

$\therefore \quad a = (-1)^3 \begin{vmatrix} 0 & 4 \\ 3 & 2 \end{vmatrix} = (-1)(-12) = 12$

and $b = (-1)^4 \begin{vmatrix} -3 & 1 \\ 2 & 4 \end{vmatrix}$

$$= -12 - 2 = -14.$$

$\therefore \quad |a + b| = |12 - 14| = 2$

8 (10) $A = \begin{bmatrix} 1 & 3 \\ 2 & 7 \end{bmatrix}$

$$ACA^{-1} = B$$

and $\quad (ACA^{-1})(ACA^{-1}) = B^2$

$$AC^2 A^{-1} = B^2 \quad \text{...(i)}$$

and $\quad BA^{-1} = B^{-1}$

$$A^{-1} = B^{-1}B^{-1}$$

Pre-multiply by A^{-1} in Eq. (i) and post-multiply by A, we get

$$C^2 = A^{-1} B^2 A$$

$$= B^{-1} B^{-1} BBA$$

$\Rightarrow \quad C^2 = A$

Now, $C^4 + aC^2 + bI = 0$

$\Rightarrow \quad A^2 + aA + bI = 0 \quad \text{...(ii)}$

which is characteristic equation of A.

i.e. $\quad |A - B| = 0$

Now, $\quad A^2 - 8A + I = 0 \quad \text{...(iii)}$

On comparing Eqs. (ii) and (iii), we get

$$a = -8 \text{ and } b = 1$$

$\therefore \quad 2b - a = 2(1) - (-8) = 2 + 8 = 10$

9 (25) $A=\begin{bmatrix}1 & 2a & 3\\ 2 & 1 & 3\\ 4 & 2 & a\end{bmatrix}$ is the inverse of B.

It is given that $\det(B)+1=0$

and $\det(B)=\dfrac{1}{\det(A)}$

$\Rightarrow \quad \dfrac{1}{\det(A)}+1=0 \Rightarrow 1+\det(A)=0$

$\Rightarrow \quad \det(A)=-1$. ...(i)

and $|A|=1(a-6)-2a(2a-12)+3(4-4)$

$=a-6-4a^2+24a$

$=-4a^2+25a-6$ ...(ii)

From Eqs. (i) and (ii), we get

$-4a^2+25a-6=-1$

$4a^2-25a+6=1$

$4a^2-25a-5=0$

$a=\dfrac{25\pm\sqrt{625-80}}{8}$

$a=\dfrac{25\pm\sqrt{545}}{8}$

$a=\dfrac{25+\sqrt{545}}{8}$ or $a=\dfrac{25-\sqrt{545}}{8}$

$\therefore$ 4 times sum of all values of

$a=4\left(\dfrac{25}{8}\times 2\right)=25$

Assertion and Reason Questions

1 (a) Expansion along second row (R_2)

$$|A|=\begin{vmatrix}a_{11} & a_{12} & a_{13}\\ a_{21} & a_{22} & a_{23}\\ a_{31} & a_{32} & a_{33}\end{vmatrix}$$

By expanding along R_2, we get

$$|A|=(-1)^{2+1}a_{21}\begin{vmatrix}a_{12} & a_{13}\\ a_{32} & a_{33}\end{vmatrix}+(-1)^{2+2}a_{22}\begin{vmatrix}a_{11} & a_{13}\\ a_{31} & a_{33}\end{vmatrix}+(-1)^{2+3}a_{23}\begin{vmatrix}a_{11} & a_{12}\\ a_{31} & a_{32}\end{vmatrix}$$

[applying all steps together]

$=-a_{21}(a_{12}a_{33}-a_{32}a_{13})+a_{22}(a_{11}a_{33}-a_{31}a_{13})-a_{23}(a_{11}a_{32}-a_{31}a_{12})$

$|A|=-a_{21}a_{12}a_{33}+a_{21}a_{32}a_{13}+a_{22}a_{11}a_{33}-a_{22}a_{31}a_{13}-a_{23}a_{11}a_{32}+a_{23}a_{31}a_{12}$

$=a_{11}a_{22}a_{33}-a_{11}a_{23}a_{32}-a_{12}a_{21}a_{33}+a_{12}a_{23}a_{31}+a_{13}a_{21}a_{32}-a_{13}a_{31}a_{22}$ ...(i)

Expansion along first column (C_1)

$$|A|=\begin{vmatrix}a_{11} & a_{12} & a_{13}\\ a_{21} & a_{22} & a_{23}\\ a_{31} & a_{32} & a_{33}\end{vmatrix}$$

By expanding along C_1, we get

$$|A|=a_{11}(-1)^{1+1}\begin{vmatrix}a_{22} & a_{23}\\ a_{32} & a_{33}\end{vmatrix}+a_{21}(-1)^{2+1}\begin{vmatrix}a_{12} & a_{13}\\ a_{32} & a_{33}\end{vmatrix}+a_{31}(-1)^{3+1}\begin{vmatrix}a_{12} & a_{13}\\ a_{22} & a_{23}\end{vmatrix}$$

$=a_{11}(a_{22}a_{33}-a_{23}a_{32})-a_{21}(a_{12}a_{33}-a_{13}a_{32})+a_{31}(a_{12}a_{23}-a_{13}a_{22})$

$|A|=a_{11}a_{22}a_{33}-a_{11}a_{23}a_{32}-a_{21}a_{12}a_{33}+a_{21}a_{13}a_{32}+a_{31}a_{12}a_{23}-a_{31}a_{13}a_{22}$

$=a_{11}a_{22}a_{23}-a_{11}a_{23}a_{32}-a_{12}a_{21}a_{33}+a_{12}a_{23}a_{31}+a_{13}a_{21}a_{32}-a_{13}a_{31}a_{22}$ ...(ii)

Clearly, the values of $|A|$ in Eqs. (i) and (ii) are equal.

Also, it can be easily verified that the values of $|A|$ by expanding along R_1, R_3, C_2 and C_3 are equal to the value of $|A|$ obtained in Eqs. (i) and (ii).

Hence, expanding a determinant along any row or column gives same value.

2 (a) We know that the area of triangle with three collinear points is zero.

Now, consider

$$\text{area of } \Delta ABC=\frac{1}{2}\begin{vmatrix}a & b+c & 1\\ b & c+a & 1\\ c & a+b & 1\end{vmatrix}$$

$=\dfrac{1}{2}|a\{(c+a)\times 1-(a+b)\times 1\}-(b+c)\{b\times 1-1\times c\}+1\{b\times(a+b)-(c+a)\times c\}|$

$=\dfrac{1}{2}|a(c+a-a-b)-(b+c)(b-c)+1(ab+b^2-c^2-ac)|$

$=\dfrac{1}{2}|ac-ab-b^2+c^2+ab+b^2-c^2-ac|$

$=\dfrac{1}{2}\times 0=0$

Since, area of $\Delta ABC=0$.

Hence, points $A(a,b+c)$, $B(b,c+a)$ and $C(c,a+b)$ are collinear.

3 (a) By expanding the determinant $\Delta=\begin{vmatrix}a_{11} & a_{12} & a_{13}\\ a_{21} & a_{22} & a_{23}\\ a_{31} & a_{32} & a_{33}\end{vmatrix}$ along R_1, we get

$$\Delta=(-1)^{1+1}a_{11}\begin{vmatrix}a_{22} & a_{23}\\ a_{32} & a_{33}\end{vmatrix}+(-1)^{1+2}a_{12}\begin{vmatrix}a_{21} & a_{23}\\ a_{31} & a_{33}\end{vmatrix}+(-1)^{1+3}a_{13}\begin{vmatrix}a_{21} & a_{22}\\ a_{31} & a_{32}\end{vmatrix}$$

$=a_{11}A_{11}+a_{12}A_{12}+a_{13}A_{13}$, where A_{ij} is cofactor of a_{ij}.

= Sum of products of elements of R_1 with their corresponding cofactors

Similarly, Δ can be calculated by other five ways of expansion that is along R_2, R_3, C_1, C_2 and C_3.

Hence, Δ = sum of the products of elements of any row (or column) with their corresponding cofactors.

4 (a) The given system can be written as $AX=B$, where

$A=\begin{bmatrix}2 & -1\\ 3 & 4\end{bmatrix}$, $X=\begin{bmatrix}x\\ y\end{bmatrix}$ and $B=\begin{bmatrix}-2\\ 3\end{bmatrix}$

Here, $|A|=\begin{vmatrix}2 & -1\\ 3 & 4\end{vmatrix}$

$=2\times 4-(-3)=11\neq 0$

Thus, A is non-singular.

Therefore, its inverse exists.

Therefore, the given system is consistent and has a unique solution given by $X=A^{-1}B$.

Cofactors of A are

$A_{11}=4$, $A_{12}=-3$,

$A_{21}=1$ and $A_{22}=2$.

$$\text{adj}(A) = \begin{bmatrix} 4 & -3 \\ 1 & 2 \end{bmatrix}' = \begin{bmatrix} 4 & 1 \\ -3 & 2 \end{bmatrix}$$

$$\therefore A^{-1} = \frac{1}{|A|}(\text{adj} A) = \frac{1}{11}\begin{bmatrix} 4 & 1 \\ -3 & 2 \end{bmatrix}$$

Now, $X = A^{-1}B = \frac{1}{11}\begin{bmatrix} 4 & 1 \\ -3 & 2 \end{bmatrix}\begin{bmatrix} -2 \\ 3 \end{bmatrix}$

$$= \frac{1}{11}\begin{bmatrix} -8+3 \\ 6+6 \end{bmatrix} = \frac{1}{11}\begin{bmatrix} -5 \\ 12 \end{bmatrix} = \begin{bmatrix} -\frac{5}{11} \\ \frac{12}{11} \end{bmatrix}$$

$$\Rightarrow \begin{bmatrix} x \\ y \end{bmatrix} = \begin{bmatrix} -\frac{5}{11} \\ \frac{12}{11} \end{bmatrix}$$

Hence, $x = \frac{-5}{11}$ and $y = \frac{12}{11}$.

5 (*c*) $|A| = 2x - 30$ If A is singular matrix, then $|A| = 0$.

$\Rightarrow \quad 2x - 30 = 0 \Rightarrow x = 15$

$\therefore$ Assertion is correct and Reason is incorrect.

6 (*a*) det (adj A) = 25

We know that $|\text{adj} A| = |A|^2$

$|A|^2 = 25 \Rightarrow |A| = \pm 5.$

$\therefore$ Assertion is correct.

For any square matrix of order n,

$|\text{adj} A| = |A|^{n-1}$

$\therefore$ Reason is correct.

Case or Paragraph Type Questions

1 (*a*) Consider the system of equations

$$a_1 x + b_1 y + c_1 z = d_1$$
$$a_2 x + b_2 y + c_2 z = d_2$$
$$a_3 x + b_3 y + c_3 z = d_3$$

Let $A = \begin{bmatrix} a_1 & b_1 & c_1 \\ a_2 & b_2 & c_2 \\ a_3 & b_3 & c_3 \end{bmatrix}, X = \begin{bmatrix} x \\ y \\ z \end{bmatrix}$

and $B = \begin{bmatrix} d_1 \\ d_2 \\ d_3 \end{bmatrix}$

Then, the system of equations can be written as

$$AX = B$$

i.e. $\begin{bmatrix} a_1 & b_1 & c_1 \\ a_2 & b_2 & c_2 \\ a_3 & b_3 & c_3 \end{bmatrix}\begin{bmatrix} x \\ y \\ z \end{bmatrix} = \begin{bmatrix} d_1 \\ d_2 \\ d_3 \end{bmatrix}$

If A is a non-singular matrix, then its inverse exists.

Now, $\quad AX = B$

$\Rightarrow \quad A^{-1}(AX) = A^{-1}B$ [pre-multiplying by A^{-1}]

$\Rightarrow \quad (A^{-1}A)X = A^{-1}B$ [by associative property]

$\Rightarrow \quad IX = A^{-1}B$

$\therefore \quad X = A^{-1}B$

This matrix equation provides unique solution for the given system of equations as inverse of a matrix is unique. This method of solving system of equations is known as matrix method.

2 (*b*) If A is a singular matrix, then $|A| = 0$.

In this case, we calculate (adj A) B.

If (adj A) $B \neq 0$, (0 being zero matrix), then solution does not exist and the system of equation is called inconsistent.

3 (*a*) If A is a singular matrix, then $|A| = 0$ and if (adj A)$B = 0$, then the system may be either consistent or inconsistent according as the system have either infinitely many solutions or no solution.

Solution (Q. Nos. 4-6) We have,

$A = \begin{bmatrix} 2 & 0 \\ 3 & 2 \end{bmatrix}$

Let $X = \begin{bmatrix} a \\ b \end{bmatrix}$. Then, $AX = \begin{bmatrix} 2 \\ 3 \end{bmatrix}$

$$\Rightarrow \begin{bmatrix} 2 & 0 \\ 3 & 2 \end{bmatrix}\begin{bmatrix} a \\ b \end{bmatrix} = \begin{bmatrix} 2 \\ 3 \end{bmatrix}$$

$\Rightarrow a = 1$ and $3a + 2b = 3 \Rightarrow b = 0$

$\therefore \quad X = \begin{bmatrix} 1 \\ 0 \end{bmatrix}$

Let $Y = \begin{bmatrix} c \\ d \end{bmatrix}$. Then, $AY = \begin{bmatrix} 4 \\ 0 \end{bmatrix}$

$$\begin{bmatrix} 2 & 0 \\ 3 & 2 \end{bmatrix}\begin{bmatrix} c \\ d \end{bmatrix} = \begin{bmatrix} 4 \\ 0 \end{bmatrix}$$

$2c = 4 \Rightarrow c = 2$

and $\quad 3c + 2d = 0 \Rightarrow d = -3$

$\therefore \quad Y = \begin{bmatrix} 2 \\ -3 \end{bmatrix}$

4 (*a*) Thus, $X - Y = \begin{bmatrix} 1 \\ 0 \end{bmatrix} - \begin{bmatrix} 2 \\ -3 \end{bmatrix} = \begin{bmatrix} -1 \\ 3 \end{bmatrix}$

5 (*b*) $B = [X \quad Y] = \begin{bmatrix} 1 & 2 \\ 0 & -3 \end{bmatrix}$

$|B| = -3$

6 (*d*) $A_{11} = -3$ and $A_{22} = 1$

$\therefore \quad A_{11} + A_{22} = -3 + 1 = -2$

Past Years Questions

1 (*a*) $\begin{vmatrix} \alpha & b & c \\ a & \beta & c \\ a & b & \gamma \end{vmatrix} = 0$

$\Rightarrow \alpha(\beta\gamma - bc) - b(a\gamma - ac) + c(ab - a\beta) = 0$

$\Rightarrow \alpha\beta\gamma - bc\alpha - ba\gamma + abc + abc - ca\beta = 0$

$\Rightarrow \gamma(\alpha - a)(\beta - b) - b(\alpha - a)(c - \gamma) + a(b - \beta)(c - \gamma) = 0$

Divide and multiply by $(\alpha - a)(\beta - b)(\gamma - c)$, we get

$$\Rightarrow \frac{\gamma}{(\gamma - c)} + \frac{b}{(\beta - b)} + \frac{a}{(\alpha - a)} = 0$$

2 (*c*) **Key Idea** *Use, if A is* 3×3 *matrices, then*

$A^3 - \text{Tr}(A)(A)^2 + \Sigma A_{ii}(A) + |A| I = 0$

where A_{ii} = *cofactor of* a_{ii} *to solve the questions.*

$$A = \begin{bmatrix} 2 & a & 0 \\ 1 & 3 & 1 \\ 0 & 5 & b \end{bmatrix}$$

and $A^3 = 4A^2 - A - 21I$

So, $x^3 - 4x^2 + x + 21 = 0$ is the characteristic equation of matrix A.

So, sum of roots = $T_r(A)$

$\Rightarrow \quad -(-4) = 2 + 3 + b$

$\Rightarrow \quad 5 + b = 4 \Rightarrow b = -1 \qquad \ldots(i)$

Product of roots = $|A|$

$\Rightarrow \quad -21 = 2(3b - 5) - a(b)$

Put $b = -1$ from Eq. (i),

$-21 = 2(-8) + a$

$\Rightarrow \quad a = -21 + 16 = -5$

Therefore,

$2a + 3b = 2(-5) + 3(-1) = -13$

3 (a) According to the question,

$$A_r = \begin{vmatrix} r & 1 & \frac{n^2}{2}+\alpha \\ 2r & 2 & n^2-\beta \\ 3r-2 & 3 & \frac{n(3n-1)}{2} \end{vmatrix}$$

$$= r[3n^2 - n - 3n^2 + 3\beta] - 2r\left[\frac{3}{2}n^2 - \frac{n}{2} - \frac{3n^2}{2} - 3\alpha\right] + (3r-2)(n^2-\beta-n^2-2\alpha)$$

$$= -nr + 3\beta r + nr + 6\alpha r - 3\beta r - 6\alpha r + 2\beta + 4\alpha$$

$$= 2\beta + 4\alpha$$

$$A_r = 2[2\alpha+\beta]$$

$\therefore$ A_r is independent of r.

So, $2A_{10} - A_8$

$$= 4[2\alpha+\beta] - 2[2\alpha+\beta]$$

$$= 2[2\alpha+\beta] = 4\alpha + 2\beta$$

4 (b) Given,

$$A = \begin{bmatrix} \sqrt{2} & 1 \\ -1 & \sqrt{2} \end{bmatrix},$$

$$B = \begin{bmatrix} 1 & 0 \\ 1 & 1 \end{bmatrix}$$

$$A^T = \begin{bmatrix} \sqrt{2} & -1 \\ 1 & \sqrt{2} \end{bmatrix}$$

$$AA^T = \begin{bmatrix} \sqrt{2} & 1 \\ -1 & \sqrt{2} \end{bmatrix}\begin{bmatrix} \sqrt{2} & -1 \\ 1 & \sqrt{2} \end{bmatrix}$$

$$= \begin{bmatrix} 3 & 0 \\ 0 & 3 \end{bmatrix} = 3I$$

$$C = ABA^T$$

$$C^2 = (ABA^T)(ABA^T)$$

$$C^2 = ABA^TABA^T$$

$$C^2 = AB3IBA^T = 3AB^2A^T$$

$$X = A^TC^2A$$

$$= 3A^TAB^2A^TA = 27B^2$$

$$\left[B^2 = \begin{bmatrix} 1 & 0 \\ 1 & 1 \end{bmatrix}\begin{bmatrix} 1 & 0 \\ 1 & 1 \end{bmatrix} = \begin{bmatrix} 1 & 0 \\ 2 & 1 \end{bmatrix}\right]$$

$$X = \begin{bmatrix} 27 & 0 \\ 54 & 27 \end{bmatrix}$$

$$|X| = \begin{vmatrix} 27 & 0 \\ 54 & 27 \end{vmatrix}$$

$$|X| = 27 \times 27$$

$$= 729$$

5 (b) Given determinant is

$$\begin{vmatrix} 1 & \frac{3}{2} & \alpha+\frac{3}{2} \\ 1 & \frac{1}{3} & \alpha+\frac{1}{3} \\ 2\alpha+3 & 3\alpha+1 & 0 \end{vmatrix} = 0$$

$$\Rightarrow -(3\alpha+1)\left(\alpha+\frac{1}{3}\right) + (3\alpha+1)\left(\alpha+\frac{3}{2}\right) + (2\alpha+3)\left[\frac{3}{2}\left(\alpha+\frac{1}{3}\right)+\left(\alpha+\frac{3}{2}\right)\right]$$

$$\Rightarrow -3\alpha^2 - \alpha - \alpha - \frac{1}{3} + 3\alpha^2 + \frac{9}{2}\alpha + \alpha + \frac{3}{2} + \frac{7}{3}\alpha^2 + \frac{7}{2}\alpha = 0$$

$$\Rightarrow \frac{7}{6}(2\alpha^2 + 6\alpha + 1) = 0$$

$$\Rightarrow 2\alpha^2 + 6\alpha + 1 = 0$$

$$\Rightarrow \alpha = \frac{-6 \pm \sqrt{36 - 4\times 2\times 1}}{2\times 2}$$

$$\Rightarrow \alpha = \frac{-6\pm\sqrt{28}}{4}$$

$$\Rightarrow \alpha = \frac{-3\pm\sqrt{7}}{2} = \frac{-3\pm 2.65}{2}$$

$$[\because \sqrt{7} \cong 2.645]$$

$$\Rightarrow \alpha = (-0.175) \text{ or } (-2.82)$$

$$\Rightarrow \alpha \in (-3, 0)$$

Alternate Solution

Given determinant is

$$\begin{vmatrix} 1 & \frac{3}{2} & \alpha+\frac{3}{2} \\ 1 & \frac{1}{3} & \alpha+\frac{1}{3} \\ 2\alpha+3 & 3\alpha+1 & 0 \end{vmatrix} = 0$$

$$\Rightarrow \left(\alpha+\frac{3}{2}\right)\left[3\alpha+1-\frac{2\alpha}{3}-1\right] - \left(\alpha+\frac{1}{3}\right)\left[3\alpha+1-3\alpha-\frac{9}{2}\right] = 0$$

$$\Rightarrow \left(\alpha+\frac{3}{2}\right)\left[\frac{7\alpha}{3}\right] - \left(\alpha+\frac{1}{3}\right)\left[-\frac{7}{2}\right] = 0$$

$$\Rightarrow \frac{7\alpha^2}{3} + \frac{7\alpha}{2} + \frac{7}{2}\alpha + \frac{7}{6} = 0$$

$$\Rightarrow \frac{7\alpha^2}{3} + 14\alpha + \frac{7}{6} = 0$$

$$\Rightarrow 14\alpha^2 + 84\alpha + 7 = 0$$

$$\Rightarrow 2\alpha^2 + 6\alpha + 1 = 0$$

$$\Rightarrow \alpha = \frac{-6\pm\sqrt{36-4\times 2\times 1}}{2\times 2}$$

$$\Rightarrow \alpha = \frac{-6\pm\sqrt{28}}{4}$$

$$\Rightarrow \alpha = \frac{-3\pm\sqrt{7}}{2} = \frac{-3\pm 2.65}{2}$$

$$[\because \sqrt{7} \cong 2.645]$$

$$\Rightarrow \alpha = (-0.175) \text{ or } (-2.82) \in (-3, 0)$$

6 (b) **Given** A is a square matrix of order 4 and $|A| = 4$. We know that if A is an $n\times n$ matrix and C is a scalar, then $|CA| = C^n|A|$.

So, $|2A| = 2^4|A| = 16\times 4 = 64$

7 (b) We know that,

$$|\text{adj } A| = |A|^{n-1}$$

$$A(\text{adj } A) = |A| I_n$$

$$|A^{-1}| = \frac{1}{|A|}$$

So, (A) and (D) are only correct.

8 (d) $\Delta = \begin{vmatrix} 1 & \cos x & 1 \\ -\cos x & 1 & \cos x \\ -1 & -\cos x & 1 \end{vmatrix}$

$$\Delta = 1(1+\cos^2 x) - \cos x(-\cos x + \cos x) + 1\cdot(\cos^2 x + 1)$$

$$\Delta = 1 + \cos^2 x - 0 + \cos^2 x + 1$$

$$\Delta = 2(1+\cos^2 x)$$

$$\Delta = 2(1 + 1 - \sin^2 x)$$

$$\Rightarrow \Delta = 2(2 - \sin^2 x)$$

Again, $-1 \le \cos x \le 1$

$$\Rightarrow 0 \le \cos^2 x \le 1$$

$$\Rightarrow 1 \le 1 + \cos^2 x \le 2$$

$$\Rightarrow 2 \le 2(1+\cos^2 x) \le 4 \Rightarrow 2 \le \Delta \le 4$$

So, $\Delta_{min} = 2, \Delta_{max} = 4$

9 (b) $|\text{adj}(\text{adj}(\text{adj } 2A))|$

$$= |2A|^{(n-1)^3} = |2A|^8$$

$$= (2^3|A|)^8 = 2^{24}|A|^8$$

Now, $A = \begin{bmatrix} 2 & 1 & 0 \\ 1 & 2 & -1 \\ 0 & -1 & 2 \end{bmatrix} \Rightarrow |A| = 4$

$$\therefore |\text{adj}(\text{adj}(\text{adj } 2A))| = 2^{24}\cdot 4^8$$

$$= 2^{24}\cdot 2^{16}$$

$$= 2^{40} = (16)^{10} = (16)^n \quad \text{[given]}$$

$$\therefore n = 10$$

10 (*b*) Given that $P^T = aP + (a-1)I$ ...(i)

$\Rightarrow (P^T)^T = aP^T + (a-1)I^T$

$\Rightarrow \quad P = aP^T + (a-1)I$ ...(ii)

$[\because (A^T)^T = A \text{ and } I^T = I]$

From Eq. (i), putting the value of P^T in Eq. (ii), we get

$P = a[aP + (a-1)I] + (a-1)I$

$\Rightarrow P = a^2P + a(a-1)I + (a-1)I$

$\Rightarrow (1-a^2)P = (a-1)(a+1)I$

$\Rightarrow \quad (1-a^2)P = (a^2-1)I$

$\therefore \quad P = -I$

So, $\text{adj } P = I \Rightarrow |\text{adj } P| = 1$

11 (*c*) Given,

$$A = \begin{bmatrix} 1 & \log_x y & \log_x z \\ \log_y x & 2 & \log_y z \\ \log_z x & \log_z y & 3 \end{bmatrix}$$

$$|A| = \begin{vmatrix} 1 & \dfrac{\log y}{\log x} & \dfrac{\log z}{\log x} \\ \dfrac{\log x}{\log y} & 2 & \dfrac{\log z}{\log y} \\ \dfrac{\log x}{\log z} & \dfrac{\log y}{\log z} & 3 \end{vmatrix}$$

Expanding along R_1, we get

$$|A| = 1(6-1) - \frac{\log y}{\log x}\left(\frac{3\log x}{\log y} - \frac{\log x}{\log y}\right) + \frac{\log z}{\log x}\left(\frac{\log x}{\log z} - \frac{2\log x}{\log z}\right)$$

$|A| = 5 - 2 - 1 = 2$

We know that

$|\text{adj}(\text{adj}(A))| = |A|^{(n-1)^2}$

So, $|\text{adj}(\text{adj } A^2)| = |A^2|^{(3-1)^2}$

$= |A^2|^4 = |A|^8 = 2^8$

12 (*14*) $|3 \text{ adj}(2 \text{ adj}(|A|A)|$

$= |3 \text{ adj}(2|A|^2 \text{ adj} A|$

$= |3 \cdot 2^2 |A|^4 \text{ adj}(\text{adj} A)|$

$= 2^6 \cdot 3^3 |A|^{12} |A|^4$

$= 2^6 \cdot 3^3 \cdot |A|^{16} = 2^{-10} \cdot 3^{-13}$ [given]

So, $|A|^{16} = 2^{-16} \cdot 3^{-16}$

$\Rightarrow |A| = 2^{-1} \cdot 3^{-1}$ ...(i)

Now, $|3 \text{ adj}(2A)| = |3 \cdot 2^2 \text{ adj}(A)|$

$= 2^6 \cdot 3^3 |A|^2 = 2^m \cdot 3^n$ [given]

$\Rightarrow 2^6 \cdot 3^3 \cdot 2^{-2} \cdot 3^{-2} = 2^m \cdot 3^n$

[from Eq. (i)]

$\Rightarrow 2^m \cdot 3^n = 2^4 \, 3^1$

$\therefore \quad m = 4, n = 1$

Hence, $|3m + 2n| = |12 + 2|$

$= |14| = 14$

13 (*5*) Let $A = \begin{bmatrix} a & b \\ b & d \end{bmatrix}$

$\begin{bmatrix} a & b \\ b & d \end{bmatrix}\begin{bmatrix} 1 \\ 1 \end{bmatrix} = \begin{bmatrix} 3 \\ 7 \end{bmatrix}$ and $|A| = 1$

$ad - b^2 = 1, a + b = 3, b + d = 7$

$a = 3 - b, d = 7 - b$

Now, $ad - b^2 = 1$

$(3-b)(7-b) - b^2 = 1$

$\Rightarrow \quad 21 - 10b = 1$

$\therefore \quad b = 2, a = 1$ and $d = 5$

$\therefore \quad A = \begin{bmatrix} 1 & 2 \\ 2 & 5 \end{bmatrix}$

$A^{-1} = \alpha A + \beta I$

$\Rightarrow \begin{bmatrix} 5 & -2 \\ -2 & 1 \end{bmatrix} = \begin{bmatrix} \alpha & 2\alpha \\ 2\alpha & 5\alpha \end{bmatrix} + \begin{bmatrix} \beta & 0 \\ 0 & \beta \end{bmatrix}$

$\alpha + \beta = 5 \Rightarrow 2\alpha = -2$

$\alpha = -1, \beta = 6$

$\therefore \quad \alpha + \beta = 5$

14 (*5*) We have, $|\text{adj}(2 \text{ adj}(2A^{-1}))| = 2^{84}$

$\Rightarrow \quad |2 \text{ adj}(2A^{-1})|^{n-1} = 2^{84}$

$\Rightarrow \quad (2^n |\text{adj}(2A^{-1})|)^{n-1} = 2^{84}$

$\Rightarrow 2^{n(n-1)}(|2A^{-1}|^{(n-1)})^{n-1} = 2^{84}$

$\Rightarrow 2^{n(n-1)}(2^n|A^{-1}|)^{(n-1)^2} = 2^{84}$

$\Rightarrow \quad 2^{n(n-1)}\left(2^n \dfrac{1}{|A|}\right)^{(n-1)^2} = 2^{84}$

$\Rightarrow \quad 2^{n(n-1)}\left(\dfrac{2^n}{2}\right)^{(n-1)^2} = 2^{84}$

$\Rightarrow \quad 2^{n(n-1)+(n-1)^3} = 2^{84}$

$\Rightarrow \quad n(n-1) + (n-1)^3 = 84$

$\Rightarrow \quad (n-1)[n + n^2 - 2n + 1] = 84$

$\Rightarrow \quad (n-1)(n^2 - n + 1) = 84$

$\Rightarrow \quad n = 5$

15 (*50*) Given, $A = \begin{bmatrix} a & b \\ c & d \end{bmatrix}$

$$|A| = \begin{vmatrix} a & b \\ c & d \end{vmatrix} = ad - bc$$

A^{-1} exist if $ad - bc \neq 0$

If $A = A^{-1}$, then $A^2 = I$

$$\begin{bmatrix} a & b \\ c & d \end{bmatrix}\begin{bmatrix} a & b \\ c & d \end{bmatrix} = \begin{bmatrix} 1 & 0 \\ 0 & 1 \end{bmatrix}$$

$\Rightarrow \begin{bmatrix} a^2 + bc & ab + bd \\ ac + cd & bc + d^2 \end{bmatrix} = \begin{bmatrix} 1 & 0 \\ 0 & 1 \end{bmatrix}$

$\Rightarrow \begin{bmatrix} a^2 + bc & b(a+d) \\ c(a+d) & bc + d^2 \end{bmatrix} = \begin{bmatrix} 1 & 0 \\ 0 & 1 \end{bmatrix}$

$ab + bd = 0$ ...(i)

$ac + cd = 0$ ...(ii)

$a^2 + bc = 1$ ...(iii)

$bc + d^2 = 1$ ...(iv)

On subtracting Eq. (iv) from Eq. (iii), we get

$a^2 - d^2 = 0$

$(a+d)(a-d) = 0$

$\Rightarrow \quad a + d = 0$ or $a - d = 0$

Case I When, $a + d = 0$ or $a = -d$

(a, d) can be $(-1, 1)$, $(0, 0)$ and $(1, -1)$

(a) When, $(a, d) = (-1, 1)$

$a^2 + bc = 1$

$1 + bc = 1$

$bc = 0$

When, $b = 0$, then possibility of c is 12.

When, $c = 0$, then possibility of b is 12.

$\therefore$ Total number of possibility

$= 24 - 1$

$= 23$

as $(0, 0)$ is repeated.

(b) When, $(a, d) = (0, 0)$

$a^2 + bc = 1 \Rightarrow bc = 1$

Possible value of (b, c) is $(1, 1)$, $(-1, -1)$

(c) When, $(a, d) = (1, -1)$

There are 23 possible value

Case II When $a - d = 0$, then $a = d$

From Eq. (ii),

$ac + cd = 0 \Rightarrow 2ac = 0$

$a \neq 0, c = 0$

From Eq. (i),

$d \neq 0, b = 0$

From Eq. (iii),

$a^2 = 1 \Rightarrow a = \pm 1$

There are only 2 possible values.

Total number of possible values

$= 23 + 23 + 2 + 2 = 50$

Skill Boosters

1 (b) $0 \le [a] < 2 \Rightarrow [a] = 0, 1$

$-1 \le [b] < 1 \Rightarrow [b] = -1, 0$

$1 \le [c] < 3 \Rightarrow [c] = 1, 2$

$$\Delta = \begin{vmatrix} [a]+1 & [b] & [c] \\ [a] & [b]+1 & [c] \\ [a] & [b] & [c]+1 \end{vmatrix}$$

$$= ([a]+1)(([b]+1)([c]+1) - [b][c]) - [a]([b][c] + [b] - [b][c]) + [a]([b][c] - [b][c] - [c])$$

$$= ([a]+1)([b]+[c]+1) - [a][b] - [a][c]$$

Expanding the Δ from R_3, we get

$D = (-1)(0 - [c]) - 0 + 1([a] + 1 + [b])$

$\Rightarrow \Delta = 1 + [a] + [b] + [c]$

For maximum value of Δ, take maximum values of $[a]$, $[b]$ and $[c]$ i.e. 1, 0 and 2.

$\Delta = 1 + 1 + 0 + 2 = 4$

$\therefore \quad \Delta = 4.$

2 (b) Given equation

$$\begin{vmatrix} x & -2 & -1 \\ 1 & -3x & x-1 \\ 2 & x & x+1 \end{vmatrix} = 0$$

Expanding the above determinant along R_1, we get

$$x(-3x(x+1) - x(x-1)) + 2((x+1) - 2(x-1)) - 1(x+6x) = 0$$

$$\Rightarrow x(-3x^2 - 3x - x^2 + x) + 2(x + 1 - 2x + 2) - (7x) = 0$$

$$\Rightarrow -4x^3 - 2x^2 - 2x + 6 - x - 6x = 0$$

$$\Rightarrow \quad -4x^3 - 2x^2 - 9x + 6 = 0$$

$$\Rightarrow \quad 4x^3 + 2x^2 + 9x - 6 = 0$$

Now, sum of roots

$$\alpha = -\frac{\text{Coefficient of } x^2}{\text{Coefficient of } x^3} = \frac{-2}{4} = \frac{-1}{2}$$

and Product of roots,

$$\beta = -\frac{\text{Coefficient of constant term}}{\text{Coefficient of } x^3} = \frac{-(-6)}{4} = \frac{3}{2}$$

$$\therefore \quad (\alpha + \beta) = \frac{-1}{2} + \frac{3}{2} = 1$$

3 (c) If a given system of equation has more than one solution, then given system has infinitely many solutions.

$$\therefore \quad \begin{vmatrix} 1 & 2 & 3 \\ 0 & 3 & 1 \\ 1 & 2 & \Omega \end{vmatrix} = 0$$

$$1(3\Omega - 2) - 2(-1) + 3(0 - 3) = 0$$

$$3\Omega - 2 + 2 - 9 = 0$$

$$3\Omega = 9$$

$$\Omega = 3$$

$$\text{and also} \begin{vmatrix} 1 & 2 & 1 \\ 0 & 3 & 2 \\ 1 & 2 & \mu \end{vmatrix} = 0$$

$$1(3\mu - 4) - 2(-2) + 1(0 - 3) = 0$$

$$3\mu - 4 + 4 - 3 = 0$$

$$3\mu = 3$$

$$\mu = 1$$

4 (b) Given, $B = \begin{bmatrix} 2a & b \\ 1 & 3 \end{bmatrix}$

and $B \text{ adj } B = BB^T$

We know that $A = \begin{bmatrix} a_{11} & a_{12} \\ a_{21} & a_{22} \end{bmatrix}$.

Then, $\quad \text{adj } A = \begin{bmatrix} a_{22} & -a_{12} \\ -a_{21} & a_{11} \end{bmatrix}$

and also we know that

$$A \text{ adj } A = |A| I_2$$

$$\therefore \quad |B| = 6a - b$$

$$B \text{ adj } B = \begin{bmatrix} (6a-b) & 0 \\ 0 & (6a-b) \end{bmatrix}$$

$$BB^T = \begin{bmatrix} 2a & b \\ 1 & 3 \end{bmatrix} \begin{bmatrix} 2a & 1 \\ b & 3 \end{bmatrix} = \begin{bmatrix} 4a^2 + b^2 & 2a + 3b \\ 2a + 3b & 10 \end{bmatrix}$$

According to question,

$$B \text{ adj } B = BB^T$$

$$\begin{bmatrix} 6a-b & 0 \\ 0 & 6a-b \end{bmatrix} = \begin{bmatrix} 4a^2 + b^2 & 2a + 3b \\ 2a + 3b & 10 \end{bmatrix}$$

$$4a^2 + b^2 = 6a - b$$

$$2a + 3b = 0$$

$$\Rightarrow \quad a = \frac{-3}{2} b$$

$$6a - b = 10$$

$$6 \times \frac{-3}{2} b - b = 10$$

$$-10b = 10$$

$$b = -1$$

If $b = -1$, then $a = \frac{-3}{2} \times (-1)$

$$a = \frac{3}{2}$$

$$\therefore \quad 2a - b = 2 \times \frac{3}{2} + 1 = 4$$

5 (c) $A = \begin{bmatrix} \cos\theta & -\sin\theta \\ \sin\theta & \cos\theta \end{bmatrix}$

$|A| = \cos^2\theta + \sin^2\theta = 1$

$|A| = 1$

Now, $A^{-1} = \frac{\text{adj } A}{|A|}$

and $\text{adj } A = \begin{bmatrix} \cos\theta & \sin\theta \\ -\sin\theta & \cos\theta \end{bmatrix}$

$$A^{-1} = \begin{bmatrix} \cos\theta & \sin\theta \\ -\sin\theta & \cos\theta \end{bmatrix} = B \quad \text{(let)}$$

$$B^2 = \begin{bmatrix} \cos\theta & \sin\theta \\ -\sin\theta & \cos\theta \end{bmatrix} \begin{bmatrix} \cos\theta & \sin\theta \\ -\sin\theta & \cos\theta \end{bmatrix} = \begin{bmatrix} \cos 2\theta & \sin 2\theta \\ -\sin 2\theta & \cos 2\theta \end{bmatrix}$$

$$A^{-36} = B^{36} = \begin{bmatrix} \cos 36\theta & \sin 36\theta \\ -\sin 36\theta & \cos 36\theta \end{bmatrix}$$

$$(A^{-36})_{\theta = \frac{\pi}{6}} = \begin{bmatrix} \cos 36 \times \frac{\pi}{6} & \sin 36 \times \frac{\pi}{6} \\ -\sin 36 \times \frac{\pi}{6} & \cos 36 \times \frac{\pi}{6} \end{bmatrix} = \begin{bmatrix} \cos 6\pi & \sin 6\pi \\ -\sin 6\pi & \cos 6\pi \end{bmatrix} = \begin{bmatrix} 1 & 0 \\ 0 & 1 \end{bmatrix}$$

$$\therefore |A^{-36}| = 1$$

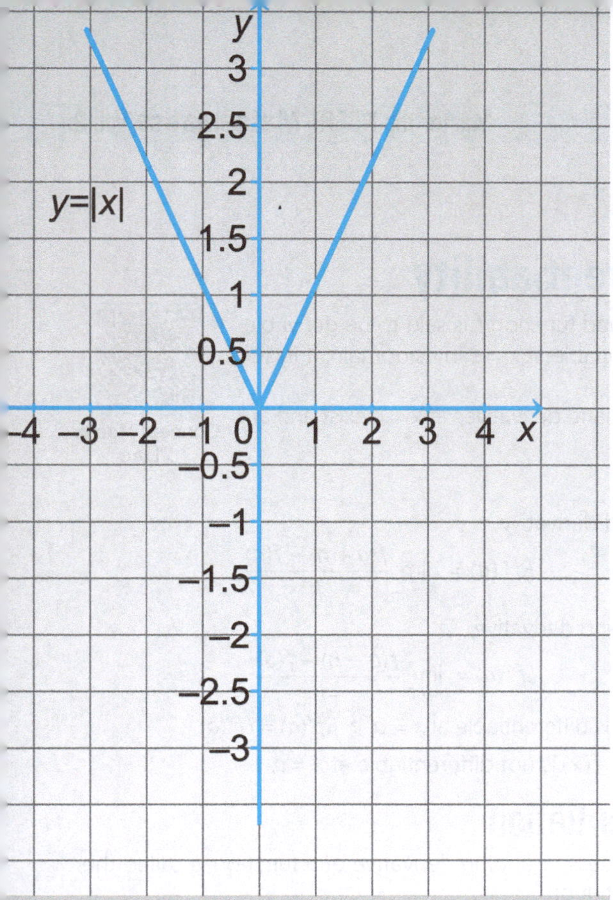

05

Continuity and Differentiability

Topicwise No. of Ques asked in 3 Years (JEE Main)

Topics	No. of Questions		
	2024	2023	2022
Continuity	8	3	7
Differentiability and Derivatives	7	7	5
Exponential and Logarithmic Functions	–	–	–
Logarithmic Differentiation and Derivatives of Function in Parametric Forms	10	3	2
Second Order Derivatives	6	2	3

Special Type of Ques Asked in 3 Years (JEE Main)

Types	Years		
	2024	2023	2022
A-R	–	–	–
Statement Based	–	–	–
Numerical Value Type	7	4	5

Last 3 Years Weightage (JEE Main)

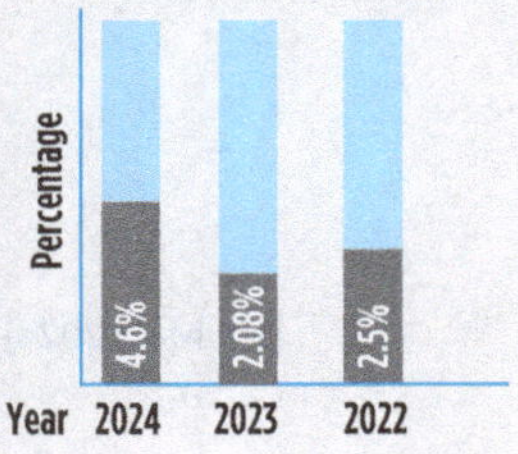

Continuity

Continuous Function

A real valued function f is said to be continuous, if it is continuous at every point in the domain of f.

Continuity of a Function at a Point

Suppose, f is a real valued function on a subset of the real numbers and let c be a point in the domain of f.

Then, f is continuous at $x = c$, if $\lim_{x \to c} f(x) = f(c)$

i.e. if $f(c) = \lim_{x \to c^+} f(x) = \lim_{x \to c^-} f(x)$, then $f(x)$ is continuous at $x = c$.

Otherwise, $f(x)$ is discontinuous at $x = c$. **[JEE Main 2024, 2023, 2022]**

Some Basic Continuous Function

(i) Every constant function is continuous.

(ii) Every identity function is continuous.

(iii) Every rational function is always continuous.

(iv) Every polynomial function is continuous.

(v) Modulus function $f(x) = |x|$ is continuous. **[JEE Main 2024]**

(vi) All trigonometric functions are continuous in their domain.

Algebra of Continuous Function

Let f and g be two real functions continuous at a real number c, then

(i) $(f+g)$ is continuous at $x=c$.

(ii) $(f-g)$ is continuous at $x=c$.

(iii) fg is continuous at $x=c$.

(iv) $\frac{f}{g}$ is continuous at $x=c$ provided that $g(x)\neq 0$.

Marks Maximizer

- Graphically, a function $f(x)$ is said to be continuous at a point, if graph of the function has no break either on the left or on the right, in the neighourbhood of a point i.e. if at $(x=a)$

  LHL = RHL = $f(a)$ = finite value

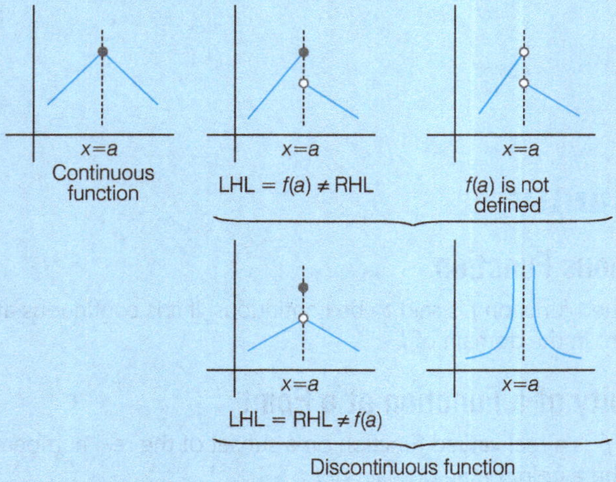

- $[x]$ and $\{x\}$ function are discontinuous at every integer. **[JEE Main 2024]**
- If f is continuous in its domain, then $|f|$ is also continuous in its domain. **[JEE Main 2023]**
- The sum and difference of a continuous and discontinuous function is always discontinuous [Continuous function ± Discontinuous function = Always discontinuous]
- If $g(x)$ is continuous function at $x=a$ and $f(x)$ is continuous function at $x=g(a)$, then $f(g(x))$ is continuous at $x=a$. **[JEE Main 2022]**
- If $f(x)$ is continuous on $x\in[a,b]$ and $f(a)\neq f(b)$, then for any value $k\in(f(a),f(b))$, there exist ($\exists$) at least one number $c\in(a,b)$ for whcih $f(c)=k$.
- If function $f(x)$ is continuous in the interval $[\alpha,\beta]$ and $f(\alpha)$ and $f(\beta)$ have opposite sign, then $f(x)$ will have at least one root in (α,β). **[JEE Main 2023]**

Differentiability

A real valued function f is said to be derivable or differentiable at $x=c$ in its domain, if its left hand and right hand derivatives at $x=c$ exist and are equal.

Concept Master Video

At $x=a$,

Right hand derivative,

$$Rf'(a)=\lim_{h\to 0}\frac{f(a+h)-f(a)}{h}$$

and left hand derivative,

$$Lf'(a)=\lim_{h\to 0}\frac{f(a-h)-f(a)}{-h}$$

Thus, $f(x)$ is differentiable at $x=a$, if $Rf'(a)=Lf'(a)$.

Otherwise, $f(x)$ is not differentiable at $x=a$.

Differentiation

- The process of finding derivative of a function is called the differentiation.
- Derivative is the instantaneous rate change of a function w.r.t. independent variable.

Derivatives of Some Standard Functions

(i) $\frac{d}{dx}(\text{constant})=0$

(ii) $\frac{d}{dx}(x^n)=nx^{n-1}$

(iii) $\frac{d}{dx}(cx^n)=cn\,x^{n-1}$, where c is a constant.

(iv) $\frac{d}{dx}(\sin x)=\cos x$

(v) $\frac{d}{dx}(\cos x)=-\sin x$

(vi) $\frac{d}{dx}(\tan x)=\sec^2 x$

(vii) $\frac{d}{dx}(\operatorname{cosec} x)=-\operatorname{cosec} x\cot x$

(viii) $\frac{d}{dx}(\sec x)=\sec x\tan x$

(ix) $\frac{d}{dx}(\cot x)=-\operatorname{cosec}^2 x$

(x) $\frac{d}{dx}(e^x)=e^x$

(xi) $\frac{d}{dx}(a^x)=a^x\log_e a, a>0$

(xii) $\frac{d}{dx}(\log_e x)=\frac{1}{x}, x>0$ **[JEE Main 2024]**

Algebra of Derivatives

(i) $\frac{d}{dx}(u \pm v) = \frac{du}{dx} \pm \frac{dv}{dx}$ [sum and difference rule]

(ii) $\frac{d}{dx}(u \cdot v) = u\frac{d}{dx}(v) + v\frac{d}{dx}(u)$ [product rule]

(iii) $\frac{d}{dx}\left(\frac{u}{v}\right) = \frac{v\frac{d}{dx}(u) - u\frac{d}{dx}(v)}{v^2}$ [quotient rule]

Where, u and v are functions of x.

Derivatives of Implicit Functions

Let $f(x, y) = 0$ be an implicit function of x. Then, to find $\frac{dy}{dx}$ we first differentiate both sides of equation w.r.t. x and then take all terms involving $\frac{dy}{dx}$ on LHS and remaining terms on RHS to get required value.

$$\frac{dy}{dx} = -\frac{\text{Differentiation of } f \text{ w.r.t. } x \text{ keeping } y \text{ constant}}{\text{Differentiation of } f \text{ w.r.t. } y \text{ keeping } x \text{ constant}}$$

Derivatives of Inverse Trigonometric Functions

(i) $\frac{d}{dx}(\sin^{-1} x) = \frac{1}{\sqrt{1-x^2}}, -1 < x < 1$

(ii) $\frac{d}{dx}(\cos^{-1} x) = \frac{-1}{\sqrt{1-x^2}}, -1 < x < 1$

(iii) $\frac{d}{dx}(\tan^{-1} x) = \frac{1}{1+x^2}$

(iv) $\frac{d}{dx}(\cot^{-1} x) = \frac{-1}{1+x^2}$

(v) $\frac{d}{dx}(\sec^{-1} x) = \frac{1}{x\sqrt{x^2-1}}, |x| > 1$

(vi) $\frac{d}{dx}(\text{cosec}^{-1} x) = \frac{-1}{x\sqrt{x^2-1}}, |x| > 1$

Derivative of a Function with Respect to Another Function

Let $y = f(x)$ and $z = g(x)$ be two given functions, we firstly differentiate both functions with respect to x separately and then put these values in the following formulae.

$$\frac{dy}{dz} = \frac{dy/dx}{dz/dx} \text{ or } \frac{dz}{dy} = \frac{dz/dx}{dy/dx}$$

Marks Maximizer

- If $f'(a^+) = f'(a^-)$ and finite, then $f(x)$ at $x = a$ is continuous and differentiable.
- If $f'(a^+) \neq f'(a^-)$ but both are finite, then $f(x)$ at $x = a$ is continuous but not differentiable (also called sharp corner). **[JEE Main 2024]**
- If among $f'(a^+)$ and $f'(a^-)$ atleast one is non-finite, then $f(x)$ at $x = a$ is non-differentiable but continuity need to be checked.
- Graphically, a point is said to be differentiable if a unique "TANGENT" with finite slope can be drawn at that point.

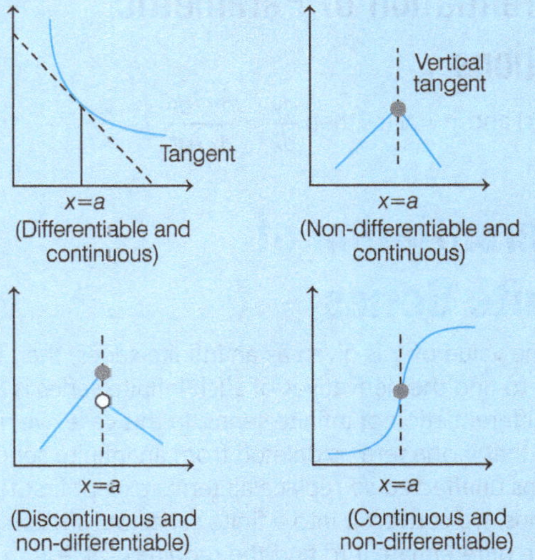

- Sum and difference of a differentiable and non-differentiable functions is always non-differentiable. **[JEE Main 2024, 2023]**
- If a functions $f(x)$ differentiable at $x = a$ and function $g(x)$ continuous at $x = a$, then $y = f(x) \cdot g(x)$ ia always differentiable at $x = a$.
- If a function $f(x)$ at $x = a$ has repeated roots, then $f(x)$ is differentiable at $x = a$. **[JEE Main 2022]**
- The function obtained by algebraic operations of two non-differentiable functions $f(x)$ and $g(x)$, may or may not be differentiable at $x = a$.

Exponential and Logarithmic Functions

- Exponential function is given by $y = f(x) = a^x$, where $a > 0$, $a \neq 1$. The graph of the function is increasing if $a > 1$ and decreasing if $0 < a < 1$.
  Domain of $f(x) = R$ and range of $f(x) = (0, \infty)$.
- Logarithmic function may be given by $y = f(x) = \log_a x$, where $a > 0$, $a \neq 1$ and $x > 0$. If $a > 1$ graph is increasing and if $0 < a < 1$, graph is decreasing.
  Domain of $f(x) = R^+$ and range of $f(x) = R$.

Differentiation of Logarithmic Functions

Suppose, given function is of the form $[u(x)]^{v(x)}$, where $u(x)$ and $v(x)$ are functions of x. In such cases, we take logarithm on both sides and use properties of logarithm to simplify it and then differentiate it.

$$y = [u(x)]^{v(x)}$$

$\Rightarrow$ $y = e^{v(x)\log u(x)}$ **[JEE Main 2024]**

$\Rightarrow$ $\ln y = v(x)\ln u(x)$

Differentiation of Parametric Functions

If $x = \phi(t)$ and $y = \psi(t)$, then $\frac{dy}{dx} = \frac{dy/dt}{dx/dt}$.

Differentiation of Infinite Series

When the value of y is given as an infinite series, then the process to find the derivatives of such infinite series is called differentiation of infinite series. In this case, we use the fact that if one term is deleted from an infinite series, it remains unaffected so replace all terms except first term by y. Thus, we convert it into a finite series or function. Then, we differentiate it to find the required value.

Second Order Derivative

Let $y = f(x)$ be a given function, then $\frac{dy}{dx} = f'(x)$ is called the first derivative of y or $f(x)$ and $\frac{d}{dx}\left(\frac{dy}{dx}\right)$ is called the second order derivative of y w.r.t. x and it is denoted by $\frac{d^2y}{dx^2}$ or y'' or y_2.

Marks Maximizer

- **Derivatives of Special Types of Functions**

(i) If $y = f(x)^{\{f(x)\}^{\cdots\infty}}$, then $\frac{dy}{dx} = \frac{y^2 f'(x)}{f(x)\{1 - y\log f(x)\}}$

(ii) If $y = \sqrt{f(x) + \sqrt{f(x) + \sqrt{f(x) + \ldots\infty}}}$, then $\frac{dy}{dx} = \frac{f'(x)}{2y - 1}$

(iii) If $\{f(x)\}^{g(y)} = \{g(y)\}^{f(x)}$, then

$$\frac{dy}{dx} = \frac{g(y)}{f(x)} \cdot \frac{f'(x)}{g'(y)}\left[\frac{f(x)\log g(y) - g(y)}{g(y)\log f(x) - f(x)}\right]$$

- **Differentiation of a Determinant** If $y = \begin{vmatrix} p & q & r \\ u & v & w \\ l & m & n \end{vmatrix}$, where all elements of determinant are functions of x, then

$$\frac{dy}{dx} = \begin{vmatrix} \frac{dp}{dx} & \frac{dq}{dx} & \frac{dr}{dx} \\ u & v & w \\ l & m & n \end{vmatrix} + \begin{vmatrix} p & q & r \\ \frac{du}{dx} & \frac{dv}{dx} & \frac{dw}{dx} \\ l & m & n \end{vmatrix} + \begin{vmatrix} p & q & r \\ u & v & w \\ \frac{dl}{dx} & \frac{dm}{dx} & \frac{dn}{dx} \end{vmatrix}$$

Caution Points

- If $f(x)$ is continuous and $g(x)$ is discontinuous at $x = a$, then the product function $\phi(x) = f(x) \cdot g(x)$ is not necessarily be discontinuous at $x = a$.
- A real function f is continuous if it is continuous at every point in its domain.
- The function $f(x)$ is differentiable at a point P iff there exists a unique tangent at point P.
- If the curve has no break point and no sharp edge, then it is differentiable.
- If a function f is differentiable at a point C, then it is also continuous at that point but the converse is not necessarily true.
- Sum, product, difference and division of two differentiable functions is always differentiable.
- Polynomial, rational, trigonometric, exponential logarithmic, inverse trigonometric functions are differentiable in their respective domains.
- Derivative of continuous and differentiable function need not to be continuous.
- Always simplify given function before differentiation.
- Differentiation of equation or inequality is not valid but any identity is differentiable.

PYQ Notes

1. The product and division of one continuous and one discontinuous function may be continuous or may be discontinuous. **[JEE Main 2023]**
2. The function $g(x)$ given by $g(x) = |x - \lambda_1| + |x - \lambda_2| + |x - \lambda_3| \ldots + |x - \lambda_n|$ is not differentiable at $x = \lambda_1, \lambda_2, \lambda_3 \ldots \lambda_n$. However, it is continuous at these points. **[JEE Main 2024, 2023]**
3. If $f\left(\frac{x}{y}\right) = \frac{f(x)}{f(y)}$, then partially differntiating w.r.t. x, $f'\left(\frac{x}{y}\right) = y \cdot \frac{1}{f(y)} f'(x)$. **[JEE Main 2024]**
4. If $y = [f(x)]^{g(x)}$, then $\frac{dy}{dx}$ = Differentiation of y treating $f(x)$ as constant + differentiation of y treating $g(x)$ as constant.

Step by Step

Mastering NCERT

- Concept Builders
- Topical Questions
- Numerical Type Questions
- Assertion and Reason Questions
- Case or Paragraph Type Questions
- Past Years Questions
- Skill Boosters

Concept Builders

1 Function $f(x)=\begin{cases}\frac{|x|}{x}, & x\neq 0\\ 1, & x=0\end{cases}$ is continuous at the origin. (T/F)

2 The function $f(x)=4x-|x|$ is discontinuous at $x=0$. (T/F)

3 The greatest integer function $[x]$ is continuous at all points except at .... points.

4 The value of k for which of the function $f(x)=\begin{cases}\frac{\sin 7x}{5x}, & x\neq 0\\ k, & x=0\end{cases}$ is continuous at $x=0$ is $\frac{7}{5}$. (T/F)

5 If $f(x)=\begin{cases}\frac{1-\cos 4kx}{x^2}, & \text{if } x\neq 0\\ 8, & \text{if } x=0\end{cases}$ is continuous at $x=0$, then the value of k is ± 1. (T/F)

6 The function $f(x)=|1+x-|x||$, where x is any real number, is a continuous function. (T/F)

7 If $y=\tan^{-1}\{\sqrt{1+x^2}-x\}, x\in R$, then $\frac{dy}{dx}=\frac{1}{2(1+x^2)}$. (T/F)

8 The derivative of $\sin^{-1}(e^{2x})$ is $\frac{2e^{2x}}{\sqrt{1-e^{4x^2}}}$. (T/F)

9 The derivative of $x^{\cos x}, x>0$ is $x\cos x\left(\frac{\cos x}{x}+\sin x\log x\right)$. (T/F)

10 The derivative of $\log_5(\log x)$ is $\frac{1}{\log 5\,(x\log x)}$. (T/F)

11 If $y=x^4+\tan x$, then second derivative of y is $12x^2+2\sec^2 x\tan x$. (T/F)

12 The function $f(x)=|\log_e|x||$, for $x>0$ is differentiable at $x=1$. (T/F)

Topical Questions

Continuity

Level I

1 Consider the function $f(x)=\begin{cases}1, \text{if } x\neq 0\\ 2, \text{if } x=0\end{cases}$

some statements are given below based on the above function. Identify the correct combination of true (T) and false (F) of the given statements. NCERT Pg. 104

(i) Left and right hand limit of the function is equal at $x=0$.

(ii) Limit of the function does not exist at $x=0$.

(iii) The left and right hand limit of f at 0 is 1 and 2, respectively.

(a) T T T (b) T F T (c) F T T (d) T T F

2 Fill in the blanks. NCERT Pg. 104

(i) If we cannot draw the graph of a function in one stroke i.e. without lifting pen from the plane of the paper, the function is said to be ...A.... .

(ii) If we need to lift the pen when we come to 0 from left, while drawing the graph of the function $f(x)=\begin{cases}1, & \text{if } x\leq 0\\ 2, & \text{if } x>0\end{cases}$, then $f(x)$ is not continuous at ...B.... .

Here, A and B refer to

(a) continuous, $x=0$ (b) not continuous, $x=1$
(c) continuous, $x=1$ (d) not continuous, $x=0$

3 If we can draw the graph of the function around a point without lifting the pen from the plane of the paper, then the function is said to be NCERT Pg. 104

(a) not continuous (b) continuous
(c) not defined (d) None of these

4 The function $f(x)=\begin{cases}1, & \text{if } x\neq 0\\ 2, & \text{if } x=0\end{cases}$ is not continuous at NCERT Pg. 105

(a) $x=0$ (b) $x=1$
(c) $x=-1$ (d) None of these

5 Suppose f is a real function on a subset of the real numbers and let c be a point in the domain of f. Then, f is ...A... at c, if $\lim_{x \to c} f(x) =$ ...B... . Here, A and B refer to **NCERT Pg. 105**

(a) not continuous, $f(c)$ (b) not continuous, 0
(c) continuous, $f(c)$ (d) None of these

6 Identify the correct combination of true (T) and false (F) of the given statements. **NCERT Pg. 105**

(i) If the left hand limit, right hand limit and the value of the function at $x = c$ exist and are equal to each other, then f is said to be continuous at $x = c$.
(ii) If left and right hand limits coincide at $x = c$ and their common value is not equal to value of the function at $x = c$, then $f(x)$ is not continuous at $x = c$.
(iii) If the right hand and left hand limits at $x = c$ coincide, then common value is the limit of the function at $x = c$.

(a) T T F (b) T F T
(c) F F T (d) T T T

7 A real function f is said to be continuous, if it is continuous at every point in the **NCERT Pg. 105**

(a) domain of f
(b) codomain of f
(c) range of f
(d) None of the above

8 If a function f is defined on $[a, b]$, then for f to be continuous, it needs to be continuous at every point in $[a, b]$ **NCERT Pg. 105**

(a) including a and b (b) excluding a and b
(c) including only a (d) excluding only a

9 If the domain of f is singleton (f is defined only at one point), then f is **NCERT Pg. 105**

(a) continuous at the point.
(b) discontinuous at the point.
(c) defined on R.
(d) None of the above

10 If $f(x) = 2x + 3$, then **NCERT Pg. 106**

(a) f is not continuous at $x = 1$.
(b) f is not defined at $x = 1$.
(c) f is continuous at $x = 1$.
(d) None of the above

11 If $f(x) = x^2$, then **NCERT Pg. 106**

(a) f is continuous at $x = 0$
(b) f is discontinuous at $x = 0$
(c) f is not defined at $x = 0$
(d) None of the above

12 Every polynomial function is ...A... and greatest integer function defined by $f(x) = [x]$ is ...B... at every integral point. Here, A and B refer to **NCERT Pg. 106**

(a) discontinuous, continuous
(b) continuous in the domain of f, discontinuous
(c) continuous, discontinuous
(d) None of the above

13 Continuity of a function at a point is entirely dictated by the ...A... of the function at that point. Here, A refers to

(a) limit (b) value **NCERT Pg. 106**
(c) Both (a) and (b) (d) None of these

14 Identify the correct combination of true (T) and false (F) of the given statements. **NCERT Pg. 107**

(i) $f(x) = |x|$ is continuous at all $x \in R$.
(ii) $f(x) = x^3 + x^2 - 1$ is not continuous at all $x \in R$.
(iii) $f(x) = \frac{1}{x}$ is continuous everywhere except at $x = 0$.

(a) T T F (b) T F T (c) F T T (d) T T T

15 If $f(x) = \frac{1}{x}$, then which of the following statements is/are true? **NCERT Pg. 107**

I. $\lim_{x \to 0^+} f(x) = +\infty$ II. $\lim_{x \to 0^-} f(x) = -\infty$
III. $\lim_{x \to 0} f(x)$ does not exist.

(a) Only I is true (b) Only II is true
(c) Only III is true (d) All are true

16 Suppose f and g be two real functions continuous at a real number c. Then, which of the following statements is /are true? **NCERT Pg. 113**

I. $f + g$ is continuous at $x = c$.
II. $f - g$ is continuous at $x = c$.
III. $f \cdot g$ is discontinuous at $x = c$.
IV. $\left(\frac{f}{g}\right)$ is continuous at $x = c$ (provided $g(c) \neq 0$)

(a) II and III are true (b) III and IV are true
(c) I, II and IV are true (d) All are true

17 Which of the following function(s) is/are continuous?

I. Every rational function in its domain. **NCERT Pg. 113**
II. Sine function.
III. Cosine function.
IV. Tangent function is continuous in their domain.

(a) Only I is continuous (b) Only II is continuous
(c) I and II are continuous (d) All are continuous

18 Suppose f and g are real valued functions such that (fog) is defined at c. If g is continuous at c and f is continuous at ...A..., then (fog) is ...B... c. Here, A and B refer to **NCERT Pg. 113**

(a) c, continuous (b) $f(c)$, continuous
(c) $g(c)$, discontinuous (d) $g(c)$, continuous

19 The function $f(x) = 5x - 3$ is discontinuous at **NCERT Pg. 116**

(a) $x = 0$ (b) $x = -3$
(c) $x = 5$ (d) None of these

20 Examine the continuity of the given functions at the indicated points in column I and accordingly match with the options in column II. Choose the correct code from the options given below. **NCERT Pg. 116**

Column I	Column II
A. $f(x) = 2x^2 - 1$ at $x = 3$	1. Continuous
B. $f(x) = x - 5, x \in R$	2. Discontinuous
C. $f(x) = \frac{1}{x-5}, x \neq 5$	
D. $f(x) = \frac{x^2 - 25}{x+5}, x \neq -5$	
E. $f(x) = \lvert x - 5 \rvert$ at $x = 5$	

Codes

	A	B	C	D	E
(a)	1	1	1	2	2
(b)	1	2	1	2	1
(c)	1	1	1	1	1
(d)	1	2	2	1	1

21. The function $f(x) = x^n$, where n is a positive integer, is **NCERT Pg. 116**

(a) continuous at $x = n$
(b) limit of f at $x = n$ does not exist
(c) limit of f at $x = n$ exists and not equal to $f(x)$
(d) None of the above

22 The function f defined by $f(x) = \begin{cases} x, \text{ if } x \leq 1 \\ 5, \text{ if } x > 1 \end{cases}$ is **NCERT Pg. 116**

I. continuous at $x = 0$.
II. discontinuous at $x = 1$.
III. continuous at $x = 2$.

Then, which of the following is/are true?

(a) Only I is true (b) Only II is true
(c) I and II are true (d) All are true

23 The point of discontinuity of the function $f(x) = \begin{cases} 2x + 3, & \text{if } x \leq 2 \\ 2x - 3, & \text{if } x > 2 \end{cases}$ is **NCERT Pg. 116**

(a) $x = 0$ (b) $x = 1$
(c) $x = 2$ (d) None of these

24 The function $f(x) = \begin{cases} \lvert x \rvert + 3, & \text{if } x \leq -3 \\ -2x, & \text{if } -3 < x < 3 \\ 6x + 2, & \text{if } x \geq 3 \end{cases}$ is continuous at $x = $ ...A... and discontinuous at $x = $ ...B... . Here, A and B refer to **NCERT Pg. 116**

(a) $-3, 3$ (b) $3, -3$
(c) $3, 0$ (d) $0, 3$

25 Examine the continuity of the given functions at the indicated points in column I and accordingly match with the options in column II. Choose the correct code from the options given below. **NCERT Pg. 116**

Column I	Column II
A. $f(x) = \begin{cases} \frac{\lvert x \rvert}{x}, \text{ if } x \neq 0 \\ 0, \text{ if } x = 0 \end{cases}$ at $x = 0$	1. Continuous at $x = 2$
B. $f(x) = \begin{cases} \frac{x}{\lvert x \rvert}, \text{ if } x < 0 \\ -1, \text{ if } x \geq 0 \end{cases}$ at $x = 0$	2. Discontinuous at $x = 0$.
C. $f(x) = \begin{cases} x + 1, & \text{if } x \geq 1 \\ x^2 + 1, & \text{if } x < 1 \end{cases}$, at $x = 1$	3. Continuous at $x = 0$.
D. $f(x) = \begin{cases} x^3 - 3, \text{ if } x \leq 2 \\ x^2 + 1, \text{ if } x > 2 \end{cases}$, at $x = 2$	4. Continuous at $x = 1$.
E. $f(x) = \begin{cases} x^{10} - 1, \text{ if } x \leq 1 \\ x^2, \quad \text{if } x > 1 \end{cases}$ at $x = 1$	5. Discontinuous at $x = 1$

Codes

	A	B	C	D	E
(a)	5	4	1	2	3
(b)	4	1	5	2	3
(c)	2	5	3	4	1
(d)	2	3	4	1	5

26 The function defined by $f(x) = \begin{cases} x + 5, \text{ if } x \leq 1 \\ x - 5, \text{ if } x > 1 \end{cases}$ is discontinuous at **NCERT Pg. 116**

(a) $x = 0$ (b) $x = 1$
(c) $x = 2$ (d) None of these

27 All the points of discontinuity of the function f defined by $f(x) = \begin{cases} 3, & \text{if } 0 \leq x \leq 1 \\ 4, & \text{if } 1 < x < 3 \\ 5, & \text{if } 3 \leq x \leq 10 \end{cases}$ are **NCERT Pg. 117**

(a) 1, 3 (b) 3, 10
(c) 1, 3, 10 (d) 0, 1, 3

28 The relationship between a and b, so that the function f defined by $f(x) = \begin{cases} ax + 1, \text{ if } x \leq 3 \\ bx + 3, \text{ if } x > 3 \end{cases}$ is continuous at $x = 3$, is **NCERT Pg. 117**

(a) $a = b + \frac{2}{3}$ (b) $a - b = \frac{3}{2}$
(c) $a + b = \frac{2}{3}$ (d) $a + b = 2$

29 If $f(x) = \begin{cases} \lambda(x^2 - 2x), & \text{if } x \le 0 \\ 4x + 1, & \text{if } x > 0 \end{cases}$, then which one of the following is correct? **NCERT Pg. 117**

(a) $f(x)$ is continuous at $x = 0$ for any value of λ
(b) $f(x)$ is discontinuous at $x = 0$ for any value of λ
(c) $f(x)$ is discontinuous at $x = 1$ for any value of λ
(d) None of the above

30 The function defined by $g(x) = x - [x]$ is discontinuous (where, $[\cdot]$ is greatest integer function) at **NCERT Pg. 117**

(a) all rational points
(b) all irrational points
(c) all integral points
(d) None of the above

31 The function $f(x) = x^2 - \sin x + 5$, then **NCERT Pg. 117**

(a) $f(x)$ is continuous at all points
(b) $f(x)$ is discontinuous at $x = \pi$
(c) It is discontinuous $x = \frac{\pi}{2}$
(d) None of the above

32 Match the terms of column I with the terms of column II and choose the correct option from the codes given below. **NCERT Pg. 117**

Column I		Column II	
A.	$f(x) = \cos x$	1.	$f(x)$ is continuous at all points except $x = n\pi, n \in Z$.
B.	$f(x) = \operatorname{cosec} x$	2.	$f(x)$ is continuous at all points except $x = (2n+1)\frac{\pi}{2}, n \in Z$.
C.	$f(x) = \sec x$	3.	$f(x)$ is continuous at all points.
D.	$f(x) = \cot x$		

Codes

	A	B	C	D		A	B	C	D
(a)	2	3	1	1	(b)	1	2	3	1
(c)	3	1	2	1	(d)	1	3	1	2

33 The given function $f(x) = \begin{cases} \frac{\sin x}{x}, & x < 0 \\ x + 1, & x \ge 0 \end{cases}$ is/has **NCERT Pg. 117**

(a) discontinuous at $x = 0$
(b) discontinuous at $x = 1$
(c) no point of discontinuity
(d) None of the above

34 Identify the correct combination of true (T) and false (F) of the given statements. **NCERT Pg. 118**

(i) The function $f(x) = \sin x + \cos x$ is continuous at all points.

(ii) The function $f(x) = \sin x - \cos x$ is continuous at all points.

(iii) The function $f(x) = \sin x \cdot \cos x$ is discontinuous at all points.

(a) T F T (b) T T F
(c) F F T (d) F T F

35 Which of the following statement(s) is/are true? **NCERT Pg. 118**

Statement I A function $f(x) = \begin{cases} x^2 \sin \frac{1}{x}, & \text{if } x \ne 0 \\ 0, & \text{if } x = 0 \end{cases}$ is discontinuous at $x = 0$.

Statement II The function $f(x) = \begin{cases} \sin x - \cos x, & \text{if } x \ne 0 \\ -1, & \text{if } x = 0 \end{cases}$ is continuous for all value of x.

(a) Only I is true (b) Only II is true
(c) Both I and II are true (d) Neither I nor II is true

36 The function $f(x) = \begin{cases} \frac{k \cos x}{\pi - 2x}, & \text{if } x \ne \frac{\pi}{2} \\ 3, & \text{if } x = \frac{\pi}{2} \end{cases}$ is continuous at $x = \frac{\pi}{2}$, then k is equal to **NCERT Pg. 118**

(a) -6 (b) 6 (c) 5 (d) -5

37 Identify the correct combination of true (T) and false (F) of the given statements. **NCERT Pg. 118**

(i) The function is defined by $f(x) = \begin{cases} kx^2, & \text{if } x \le 2 \\ 3, & \text{if } x > 2 \end{cases}$ is continuous at $x = 2$ for $k = \frac{4}{3}$.

(ii) The function is defined by $f(x) = \begin{cases} kx + 1, & \text{if } x \le \pi \\ \cos x, & \text{if } x > \pi \end{cases}$ is continuous at $x = \pi$ for $k = \frac{-2}{\pi}$.

(iii) The function is defined by $f(x) = \begin{cases} kx + 1, & \text{if } x \le 5 \\ 3x - 5, & \text{if } x > 5 \end{cases}$ is continuous at $x = 5$ for $k = \frac{9}{5}$.

(a) T T F (b) T F T (c) F T T (d) T T T

38 If $f(x) = \begin{cases} 5, & x \le 2 \\ ax + b, & 2 < x < 10 \\ 21, & x \ge 10 \end{cases}$ is a continuous function, then the values of a and b are **NCERT Pg. 118**

(a) 1, 2 (b) 2, 1 (c) 1, 1 (d) 2, 2

39 **Statement I** The function defined by $f(x) = \cos(x^2)$ is a continuous function.

Statement II The cosine function is continuous in its domain i.e. $x \in R$. **NCERT Pg. 118**

(a) Both statements are true.
(b) Both statement are false.
(c) Statement I is true; Statement II is false.
(d) Statement I is false; Statement II is true.

40 Which of the following statements is/are true?

Statement I The function $f(x) = |\cos x|$ is continuous function.

Statement II The function $f(x) = \sin|x|$ is a continuous function. NCERT Pg. 118

(a) Both statements are true.
(b) Both statement are false.
(c) Statement I is true; Statement II is false.
(d) Statement I is false; Statement II is true.

41 All the points of discontinuity of f defined by $f(x) = |x| - |x+1|$ is/are NCERT Pg. 118

(a) 0, 1
(b) 1, 0, 2
(c) no point of discontinuity
(d) None of the above

Level II

42 $f(x) = \begin{cases} |x|\cos\left(\frac{1}{x}\right), & \text{if } x \neq 0 \\ 0, & \text{if } x = 0 \end{cases}$ is NCERT Pg. 118

(a) discontinuous at $x = 0$
(b) continuous at $x = 0$
(c) Does not exist
(d) None of the above

43 The number of points at which the function $f(x) = \frac{1}{x - [x]}$, (where $[\cdot]$ denotes the greatest integer function) is not continuous, at NCERT Pg. 118

(a) 1 (b) 2
(c) 3 (d) None of these

44 If $f(x) = 2x$ and $g(x) = \frac{x^2}{2} + 1$, then which of the following can be a discontinuous function? NCERT Pg. 118

(a) $f(x) + g(x)$ (b) $f(x) - g(x)$
(c) $f(x) \cdot g(x)$ (d) $\frac{g(x)}{f(x)}$

45 If $f(x) = \frac{\sin 2x + A\sin x + B\cos x}{x^3}$ is continuous at $x = 0$, then the value of A, B and $f(0)$ are NCERT Pg. 118

(a) $A = -2, B = 0$ and $f(0) = -1$
(b) $A = 0, B = -2$ and $f(0) = 1$
(c) $A = 1, B = -1$ and $f(0) = 1$
(d) None of the above

46 Identify the correct combination of true (T) and false (F) statements given below. NCERT Pg. 118

(i) If f is continuous on its domain D, then $|f|$ is also continuous on D.
(ii) The composition of two continuous functions is a continuous function.
(iii) If $f \cdot g$ is continuous at $x = a$, then f and g are separately continuous at $x = a$.

(a) T F T (b) T T F (c) F T T (d) T T T

47 If $f(x) = \begin{cases} \frac{\sqrt{1+kx} - \sqrt{1-kx}}{x}, & \text{for } -1 \le x < 0 \\ 2x^2 + 3x - 2, & \text{for } 0 \le x \le 1 \end{cases}$ NCERT Pg. 118

is continuous at $x = 0$, then k is equal to

(a) -4 (b) -3 (c) -2 (d) -1

48 If $f(x) = \begin{cases} \frac{\sin^3(\sqrt{x})\log(1+3x)}{(\tan^{-1}\sqrt{x})^2(e^{5\sqrt{x}} - 1)x}, & x \neq 0 \\ a, & x = 0 \end{cases}$

is continuous in [0, 1], then NCERT Pg. 118

(a) $a = 0$ (b) $a = \frac{3}{5}$
(c) $a = 2$ (d) $a = \frac{5}{3}$

49 If $f : R \to R$ is defined by

$$f(x) = \begin{cases} \frac{x+2}{x^2+3x+2}, & \text{if } x \in R - \{-1, -2\} \\ -1, & \text{if } x = -2 \\ 0, & \text{if } x = -1 \end{cases}$$

then f is continuous on the set NCERT Pg. 118

(a) R
(b) $R - \{-2\}$
(c) $R - \{-1\}$
(d) $R - \{-1, -2\}$

50 Let $f(x) = \frac{1 - \tan x}{4x - \pi}$, $x \neq \frac{\pi}{4}$, $x \in \left[0, \frac{\pi}{2}\right]$.

If $f(x)$ is continuous in $\left[0, \frac{\pi}{2}\right]$, then $f\left(\frac{\pi}{4}\right)$ is NCERT Pg. 118

(a) 1 (b) $\frac{1}{2}$ (c) $-\frac{1}{2}$ (d) -1

51 The value of $f(0)$, so that the function

$$f(x) = \frac{\sqrt{a^2 - ax + x^2} - \sqrt{a^2 + ax + x^2}}{\sqrt{a+x} - \sqrt{a-x}}$$ becomes

continuous for all x, is given by NCERT Pg. 118

(a) $a^{3/2}$ (b) $a^{1/2}$
(c) $-a^{1/2}$ (d) $-a^{3/2}$

52 If $f: R \rightarrow R$ is defined by

$$f(x)=\begin{cases}\dfrac{2\sin x-\sin 2x}{2x\cos x}, & \text{if } x\neq 0\\ a, & \text{if } x=0\end{cases}$$

then the value of a, so that f is continuous at 0, is **NCERT Pg. 117**

(a) 2 (b) 1 (c) −1 (d) 0

53 The function $f: R-\{0\}\rightarrow R$ given by $f(x)=\dfrac{1}{x}-\dfrac{2}{e^{2x}-1}$ can be made continuous at $x=0$ by defining $f(0)$ as **NCERT Pg. 117**

(a) 2 (b) −1 (c) 0 (d) 1

54 If $f(x)=\begin{cases}\dfrac{1-\sqrt{2}\sin x}{\pi-4x}, & \text{if } x\neq\dfrac{\pi}{4}\\ a, & \text{if } x=\dfrac{\pi}{4}\end{cases}$ is continuous at $\dfrac{\pi}{4}$, then a is equal to **NCERT Pg. 118**

(a) 4 (b) 2 (c) 1 (d) $\dfrac{1}{4}$

55 If the function $f(x)=\begin{cases}x+a^2\sqrt{2}\sin x, & 0\leq x\leq\dfrac{\pi}{4}\\ x\cot x+b, & \dfrac{\pi}{4}\leq x\leq\dfrac{\pi}{2}\\ b\sin 2x-a\cos 2x, & \dfrac{\pi}{2}<x\leq\pi\end{cases}$

is continuous in the interval $[0, \pi]$, then the values of (a, b) are **NCERT Pg. 118**

I. $(-1, -1)$ II. $(0, 0)$

III. $(-1, 1)$ IV. $(1, 1)$

(a) I and II are correct (b) II and IV are correct
(c) III and IV are correct (d) None of these

56 The number of points at which the function $f(x)=\dfrac{1}{\log|x|}$ is discontinuous, is ...A... . Here, A refers to **NCERT Pg. 117**

(a) 2 (b) 3 (c) 4 (d) None of these

57 If $f(x)=\begin{cases}ax+1, & \text{if } x\geq 1\\ x+2, & \text{if } x<1\end{cases}$ is continuous, then a should be equal to ...A... . Here, A refers to **NCERT Pg. 118**

(a) 2 (b) 3 (c) 4 (d) None of these

58 If $f(x)=\begin{cases}\dfrac{\sin 5x}{x^2+2x}, & x\neq 0\\ k+\dfrac{1}{2}, & x=0\end{cases}$ is continuous at $x=0$, then the value of k is **NCERT Pg. 117**

(a) 1 (b) −2 (c) 2 (d) $\dfrac{1}{2}$

Differentiability, Derivatives of Composite Functions, Derivatives of Implicit Functions and Derivatives of Inverse Trigonometric Functions

Level I

1 Whenever we define derivative at a point $x=c$, then at that point $\lim_{h\to 0}\dfrac{f(c+h)-f(c)}{h}$ **NCERT Pg. 118**

(a) does not exist
(b) exists
(c) function is not defined
(d) None of the above

2 If both $\lim_{h\to 0^-}\dfrac{f(c+h)-f(c)}{h}$ and $\lim_{h\to 0^+}\dfrac{f(c+h)-f(c)}{h}$ are finite and equal, then **NCERT Pg. 118**

(a) f is continuous at a point c
(b) f is not continuous at c
(c) f is differentiable at a point c in its domain
(d) None of the above

3 A function is said to be differentiable in an interval $[a, b]$, if it is differentiable at every point of $[a, b]$ **NCERT Pg. 118**

(a) including a and b (b) excluding a and b
(c) including a but not b (d) including b but not a

4 A function is said to be differentiable in an interval (a, b), if it is ...A... at ...B... point of (a, b). Here, A and B refer to **NCERT Pg. 118**

(a) differentiable, one
(b) differentiable, two
(c) not differentiable, every
(d) differentiable, every

5 The function defined by $f'(x)=\lim_{h\to 0}\dfrac{f(x+h)-f(x)}{h}$ (wherever the limit exists) is defined to be **NCERT Pg. 119**

(a) the derivative of f (b) limit of f
(c) value of f (d) None of these

6 Identify the correct combination of true (T) or false (F) statements given below. **NCERT Pg. 119**

(i) The phrase differentiate $f(x)$ with respect to x is to find $f'(x)$.
(ii) $(u\pm v)'=u'\pm v'$.
(iii) $(u\cdot v)'=u'v+uv'$ (Leibnitz or product rule).
(iv) $\left(\dfrac{u}{v}\right)'=\dfrac{u'v+uv'}{v^2}$, wherever, $v\neq 0$ (quotient rule).

(a) T T F F (b) T F T F
(c) F F T T (d) T T T F

7 Match the terms of column I with the terms of column II and choose the correct option from the codes given below. **NCERT Pg. 119**

	Column I		Column II
A.	$f(x) = x^n$	1.	$f'(x) = \cos x$
B.	$f(x) = \sin x$	2.	$f'(x) = nx^{n-1}$
C.	$f(x) = \cos x$	3.	$f'(x) = \sec^2 x$
D.	$f(x) = \tan x$	4.	$f'(x) = -\sin x$

Codes

	A	B	C	D
(a)	4	3	2	1
(b)	1	2	3	4
(c)	2	1	4	3
(d)	3	4	1	2

8 If a function f is differentiable at c, then it is **NCERT Pg. 120**

(a) discontinuous at c (b) continuous at c
(c) not defined at c (d) None of these

9 The derivative of $f(x) = (2x+1)^3$ is **NCERT Pg. 120**

(a) $3(2x+1)^2$
(b) $6(2x+1)^2$
(c) $3(2x+1)$
(d) None of the above

10 Let f be a real valued function such that $f = vou$ and $t = u(x)$. If $\frac{dt}{dx} \cdot \frac{du}{dt}$ exists, then **NCERT Pg. 121**

(a) $\frac{df}{du} = \frac{dt}{dv} \cdot \frac{dt}{du}$ (b) $\frac{df}{du} = \frac{du}{dt} \cdot \frac{dx}{dt}$
(c) $\frac{df}{dx} = \frac{dv}{dt} \cdot \frac{dt}{dx}$ (d) None of these

11 Suppose f is a real valued functions which is a composition of three functions u, v and w i.e. $f = (wou)ov$. If ...A... and ...B... provided all the derivatives in the statement exist, then $\frac{df}{dx} = \ldots C \ldots$. Here, A, B and C refer to **NCERT Pg. 121**

(a) $t = u(t)$ and $s = u(x)$, $\frac{df}{dx} = \frac{dw}{ds} \cdot \frac{ds}{dt} \cdot \frac{dt}{dx}$
(b) $t = v(x)$ and $s = u(t)$, $\frac{df}{dx} = \frac{dw}{ds} \cdot \frac{ds}{dt} \cdot \frac{dt}{dx}$
(c) $t = v(x)$ and $s = u(t)$, $\frac{df}{dx} = \frac{dw}{ds} \cdot \frac{ds}{dt} \cdot \frac{dx}{dt}$
(d) None of the above

12 The differential coefficient of $\sin(\cos(x^2))$ with respect to x is. **NCERT Pg. 121**

(a) $-2x \sin x^2 \cos(\cos x^2)$
(b) $2x \sin(x^2) \cos(x^2)$
(c) $2x \sin(x^2) \cos(x^2) \cos x$
(d) None of the above

13 Match the terms of column I with the terms of column II and choose the correct option from the codes given below. **NCERT Pg. 122**

	Column I		Column II
A.	$f(x) = \sin(x^2+5)$	1.	$f'(x) = a\cos(ax+b)$
B.	$f(x) = \cos(\sin x)$	2.	$f'(x) = \frac{1}{2\sqrt{x}} \sec(\tan\sqrt{x})$ $\tan(\tan\sqrt{x})\sec^2\sqrt{x}$
C.	$f(x) = \sin(ax+b)$	3.	$f'(x) = 2x\cos(x^2+5)$
D.	$f(x) = \sec(\tan\sqrt{x})$	4.	$f'(x) = -\cos x \sin(\sin x)$

Codes

	A	B	C	D
(a)	3	4	1	2
(b)	1	2	3	4
(c)	2	1	4	3
(d)	2	4	1	3

14 Which of the following statement(s) is/are true?

Statement I If $f(x) = \cos x^3 \sin^2(x^5)$, then $f'(x) = 10x^4 \sin x^5 \cos x^5 \cos x^3 - 3x^2 \sin x^3 \sin^2 x^5$.

Statement II $\frac{d}{dx}[2\sqrt{\cot(x^2)}] = \frac{-2x\cos^2(x^2)}{\sqrt{\cot(x^2)}}$. **NCERT Pg. 122**

(a) Both statements are true.
(b) Both statement are false.
(c) Statement I is true; Statement II is false.
(d) Statement I is false; Statement II is true.

15 Identify the correct combination of true (T) and false (F) statements given below. **NCERT Pg. 122**

(i) $\frac{d}{dx}\cos(\sqrt{x}) = \frac{-\sin\sqrt{x}}{2\sqrt{x}}$
(ii) $f(x) = |x-1|, x \in R$ is not differentiable at $x = 1$.
(iii) $f(x) = [x], 0 < x < 3$ is differentiable at $x = 1$ and $x = 2$.

(a) T F T (b) T T F (c) F T T (d) T T T

16 Which of the following function(s) is/are implicit?

I. $x - y - \pi = 0$ II. $x + \sin xy - y = 0$ **NCERT Pg. 122**

(a) Only I (b) Only II
(c) Both I and II (d) Neither I nor II

17 If $y + \sin y = \cos x$, then $\frac{dy}{dx}$ is equal to **NCERT Pg. 123**

(a) $-\frac{\sin x}{1+\cos y}$, $y = (2n+1)\pi$
(b) $\frac{\sin x}{1+\cos y}$, $y \neq (2n+1)\pi$
(c) $-\frac{\sin x}{1+\cos y}$, $y \neq (2n+1)y$
(d) None of the above

18 Match the functions given in column I with their derivatives in column II and choose the correct option from the codes given below. NCERT Pg. 124

Column I	Column II
A. $f(x) = \sin^{-1} x$	1. $\frac{1}{1+x^2}, x \in R$
B. $f(x) = \tan^{-1} x$	2. $\frac{1}{\sqrt{1-x^2}}, x \in (-1, 1)$
C. $f(x) = \cos^{-1} x$	3. $-\frac{1}{\sqrt{1-x^2}}, x \in (-1, 1)$
D. $f(x) = \cot^{-1} x$	4. $-\frac{1}{1+x^2}, x \in R$

Codes

	A	B	C	D		A	B	C	D
(a)	3	1	2	4	(b)	2	1	3	4
(c)	1	4	3	2	(d)	1	2	3	4

19 If $2x + 3y = \sin x$, then $\frac{dy}{dx}$ is equal to NCERT Pg. 125

(a) $\frac{\cos x + 2}{3}$ (b) $\frac{\cos x - 2}{3}$

(c) $\cos x + 2$ (d) None of these

20 The derivative of $2x + 3y = \sin y$ is NCERT Pg. 125

(a) $\frac{2}{\cos y}$ (b) $\frac{2}{\cos y + 3}$

(c) $\frac{2}{\cos y - 3}$ (d) None of these

21 The differential coefficient of the implicit function $ax + by^2 = \cos y$ is ...A... and of $xy + y^2 = \tan x + y$ is ...B... . Here, A and B refer to NCERT Pg. 125

(a) $\left(\frac{-a}{2by + \sin y}\right), \frac{\sec^2 x - y}{x + 2y - 1}$ (b) $\frac{\sec^2 x - y}{x + 2y + 1}, \left(\frac{-a}{2by + \sin y}\right)$

(c) $\frac{\sec^2 x - y}{x + 2y + 1}, \frac{a}{2by + \sin y}$ (d) None of these

22 Match the terms of column I with the terms of column II and choose the correct option from the codes given below. NCERT Pg. 125

Column I	Column II
A. $f(x, y) = x^2 + xy + y^2 - 100$	1. $f'(x, y) = \frac{\sin 2x}{\sin 2y}$
B. $f(x, y) = x^3 + x^2 y + xy^2 + y^3 - 81$	2. $f'(x, y) = \frac{y \sin(xy)}{\sin 2y - x \sin xy}$
C. $f(x, y) = \sin^2 y + \cos xy - k$	3. $f'(x, y) = \frac{-(3x^2 + 2xy + y^2)}{x^2 + 2xy + 3y^2}$
D. $f(x, y) = \sin^2 x + \cos^2 y - 1$	4. $f'(x, y) = \frac{-(2x + y)}{x + 2y}$

Codes

	A	B	C	D		A	B	C	D
(a)	4	1	2	3	(b)	2	1	4	3
(c)	1	2	3	4	(d)	4	3	2	1

23 If $y = \sin^{-1}\left(\frac{2x}{1+x^2}\right)$, then $\frac{dy}{dx}$ is equal to NCERT Pg. 125

(a) $\frac{1}{1+x^2}$ (b) $\frac{2}{1+x^2}$ (c) $\frac{2}{1-x^2}$ (d) $\frac{-2}{1+x^2}$

24 If $y = \tan^{-1}\left(\frac{3x - x^3}{1 - 3x^2}\right), -\frac{1}{\sqrt{3}} < x < \frac{1}{\sqrt{3}}$, then $\frac{dy}{dx}$ is NCERT Pg. 125

(a) $\frac{3}{1+x^2}$ (b) $\frac{1}{1+x^2}$ (c) $\frac{-3}{1+x^2}$ (d) $\frac{3}{1-x^2}$

25 Which of the following statement(s) is/are true?

Statement I If $y = \cos^{-1}\left(\frac{1-x^2}{1+x^2}\right), 0 < x < 1$, then $y' = \frac{2}{1+x^2}$. NCERT Pg. 125

Statement II The derivative of $\cos^{-1} x$ is $\frac{-1}{\sqrt{1-x^2}}$.

(a) Both statements are true.
(b) Both statements are false.
(c) Statement I is true; Statement II is false.
(d) Statement I is false; Statement II is true.

26 Match the functions given in column I with their derivatives in column II and choose the correct option from the codes given below. NCERT Pg. 125

Column I	Column II
A. $y = \sin^{-1}\left(\frac{1-x^2}{1+x^2}\right), 0 < x < 1$	1. $y' = \frac{-2}{1+x^2}$
B. $y = \cos^{-1}\left(\frac{2x}{1+x^2}\right), -1 < x < 1$	2. $y' = \frac{2}{\sqrt{1-x^2}}$
C. $y = \sin^{-1}(2x\sqrt{1-x^2}), \frac{1}{\sqrt{2}} < x < \frac{1}{\sqrt{2}}$	3. $y' = \frac{-2}{\sqrt{1-x^2}}$
D. $y = \sec^{-1}\left(\frac{1}{2x^2 - 1}\right), 0 < x < \frac{1}{\sqrt{2}}$	

Codes

	A	B	C	D
(a)	1	2	1	3
(b)	2	1	2	3
(c)	1	1	2	3
(d)	3	1	2	1

Level II

27 The set of points, where the function f given by $f(x) = |2x - 1|\sin x$ is differentiable, is **NCERT Pg. 125**

(a) R (b) $R - \left\{\frac{1}{2}\right\}$

(c) $(0, \infty)$ (d) None of these

28 If $f(x) = |\sin x|$, then **NCERT Pg. 122**

(a) f is everywhere differentiable

(b) f is everywhere continuous but not differentiable at $x = n\pi$, $n \in Z$

(c) f is everywhere continuous but not differentiable at $x = (2n+1)\frac{\pi}{2}$, $n \in Z$

(d) None of the above

29 The function $f(x) = \begin{cases} x[x], & \text{if } 0 \le x < 2 \\ (x-1)x, & \text{if } 2 \le x < 3 \end{cases}$ is **NCERT Pg. 122**

(a) differentiable at $x = 2$ (b) not differentiable at $x = 2$

(c) continuous at $x = 2$ (d) None of these

30 A function $f: R \to R$ satisfies the equation $f(x + y) = f(x) f(y)$ for all $x, y \in R$, $f(x) \ne 0$. Suppose that the function is differentiable at $x = 0$ and $f'(0) = 2$. Then, **NCERT Pg. 122**

(a) $f'(x) = f(x)$ (b) $f'(x) = 2f(x)$

(c) $2f'(x) = f(x)$ (d) None of these

31 Let $f(x) = \begin{cases} (x-1)\sin\dfrac{1}{(x-1)} & , \text{if } x \ne 1 \\ 0 & , \text{if } x = 1 \end{cases}$. Then, which of the following is true? **NCERT Pg. 122**

(a) f is differentiable at $x = 1$ but not at $x = 0$.

(b) f is neither differentiable at $x = 0$ nor at $x = 1$.

(c) f is differentiable at $x = 0$ and at $x = 1$.

(d) f is differentiable at $x = 0$ but not at $x = 1$.

32 If $y = \tan^{-1} x + \cot^{-1} x + \sec^{-1} x + \operatorname{cosec}^{-1} x$, then $\frac{dy}{dx}$ is equal to **NCERT Pg. 125**

(a) $\frac{x^2 - 1}{x^2 + 1}$ (b) π (c) 0 (d) 1

33 If $y = \sin^{-1}\sqrt{1-x}$, then $\frac{dy}{dx}$ is equal to **NCERT Pg. 125**

(a) $\frac{1}{\sqrt{1-x}}$ (b) $\frac{-1}{2\sqrt{1-x}}$

(c) $\frac{1}{\sqrt{x}}$ (d) $\frac{-1}{2\sqrt{x}\sqrt{1-x}}$

34 If $f: (-1, 1) \to R$ be a differentiable function with $f(0) = -1$ and $f'(0) = 1$. Let $g(x) = [f(2f(x) + 2)]^2$. Then, $g'(0)$ is equal to **NCERT Pg. 122**

(a) 4 (b) -4 (c) 0 (d) -2

Exponential *and* Logarithmic Functions

Level I

1 If $f(x) = ae^{|x|} + b|x|^2$, $a\ b \in R$ and $f(x)$ is differentiable at $x = 0$. Then, a and b are **NCERT Pg. 126**

(a) $a = 0, b \in R$ (b) $a = 1, b = 2$

(c) $b = 0, a \in R$ (d) $a = 4, b = 5$

2 Identify the correct combination of true (T) and false (F) statements given below. **NCERT Pg. 126**

(i) Domain of the exponential function is R, the set of all real numbers.

(ii) Range of the exponential function is the set of all positive real numbers.

(iii) The point (0, 1) is always on the graph of the exponential function.

(a) T F T (b) F F T (c) T T F (d) T T T

3 The sum of the series $1 + \frac{1}{1!} + \frac{1}{2!} + \ldots\ldots = e$. Then, e lies between **NCERT Pg. 126**

(a) 1 and 2 (b) 2 and 3

(c) 3 and 4 (d) None of these

4 Exponential function with base 10 is called ...A... and with base e is called ...B... . Here, A and B refer to **NCERT Pg. 126**

(a) natural exponential function, common exponential function

(b) common exponential function, natural exponential function

(c) particular exponential function, general exponential function

(d) None of the above

5 Let $b > 1$ be a real number. Then, logarithm of a to the base b is x, if **NCERT Pg. 126**

(a) $b^a = x$ (b) $a^b = x$

(c) $b^x = a$ (d) None of these

6 The logarithm function with base $b > 1$ from positive real number to all real numbers is defined by **NCERT Pg. 126**

(a) $\log_b : R^+ \to R$ $\quad x \to \log_b x = y$, if $b^y = x$

(b) $\log_b ; R^+ \to R$ $\quad x \to \log_b y = x$, if $b^y = x$

(c) $\log_b : R^+ \to R$ $\quad y \to \log_b x = y$, if $b^y = x$

(d) None of the above

7 In $\log_b x$, if $b = 10$, then it is ...A... and if $b = e$, then it is ...B... . Here, A and B refer to **NCERT Pg. 126**

(a) natural logarithm, common logarithm

(b) common logarithm, natural logarithm

(c) nepier logarithm, common logarithm

(d) None of the above

8 Identify the correct combination of true (T) and false (F) statements given below. **NCERT Pg. 126**

(i) We cannot make a meaningful definition of logarithm of non-positive numbers and hence the domain of log function is R^+.

(ii) The range of log function is the set of all real numbers.

(iii) The point (1, 0) is always on the graph of the log function.

(iv) The log function with base $b (b > 1)$ is ever increasing i.e. as we move from left to right the graph rises above.

(a) T F T F (b) T T F F (c) F T F T (d) T T T T

9 $\log_a p$ is shifted to the base b is equal to **NCERT Pg. 128**

(a) $\dfrac{\log_a p}{\log_b a}$ (b) $\dfrac{\log_b p}{\log_a b}$

(c) $\dfrac{\log_b p}{\log_b a}$ (d) None of these

10 Match the terms of column I with terms of column II and choose the correct option from the codes given below. **NCERT Pg. 128**

Column I	Column II
A. $\log_b pq,\ b \neq 1, b > 0, p > 0, q > 0$	1. $\log_b p + \log_b p = 2\log_b p$
B. $\log_b p^2,\ b \neq 1, b > 0, p > 0$	2. $n \log_b p$
C. $\log_b p^n,\ b \neq 1, b > 0, p > 0$	3. $\log_b x - \log_b y$
D. $\log_b \dfrac{x}{y},\ b \neq 1, b > 0, x > 0, y > 0$	4. $\log_b p + \log_b q$

Codes

	A	B	C	D
(a)	4	1	2	3
(b)	2	3	1	4
(c)	1	2	3	4
(d)	3	4	2	1

11 Which of the following is/are true? **NCERT Pg. 129**

I. $\dfrac{d}{dx} e^{-x} = -e^{-x}$

II. $\dfrac{d}{dx} \sin(\log x) = \dfrac{\cos(\log x)}{x}, x > 0$

(a) Only I is true (b) Only II is true

(c) Both I and II are true (d) Neither I nor II is true

12 The derivative of $\cos^{-1}(e^x)$ is **NCERT Pg. 129**

(a) $\dfrac{2e^x}{\sqrt{1-e^{2x}}}$ (b) $\dfrac{e^x}{\sqrt{1-e^{2x}}}$

(c) $\dfrac{-e^x}{\sqrt{1-e^{2x}}}$ (d) None of these

13 Match the functions in column I with their derivatives in column II and choose the correct option from the codes given below. **NCERT Pg. 130**

Column I	Column II
A. $f(x) = \dfrac{e^x}{\sin x}$	1. $f'(x) = 3x^2 e^{x^3}$
B. $f(x) = e^{\sin^{-1} x}$	2. $f'(x) = \dfrac{e^{\sin^{-1} x}}{\sqrt{1-x^2}}, x \in (-1, 1)$
C. $f(x) = e^{x^3}$	3. $f'(x) = \dfrac{-e^{-x} \cos(\tan^{-1} e^{-x})}{1+e^{-2x}}$
D. $f(x) = \sin(\tan^{-1} e^{-x})$	4. $f'(x) = \dfrac{e^x(\sin x - \cos x)}{\sin^2 x}, x \neq n\pi\ n \in Z$

Codes

	A	B	C	D		A	B	C	D
(a)	4	2	1	3	(b)	1	3	2	4
(c)	3	1	2	4	(d)	1	2	3	4

14 The derivative of $\log(\cos e^x)$ is **NCERT Pg. 130**

(a) $-\tan(e^x)$ (b) $e^x \tan e^x$

(c) $-e^x \tan(e^x)$ (d) None of these

15 $\dfrac{d}{dx}(e^x + e^{x^2} + \ldots + e^{x^5})$ is equal to **NCERT Pg. 130**

(a) $e^x + 2e^x + \ldots\ldots\ldots + 5e^x$

(b) $e^x + 2xe^x + 3xe^{x^2} + 4e^{x^3} + 5xe^{x^4}$

(c) $e^x + 2x e^{x^2} + 3x^2 e^{x^3} + 4x^3 e^{x^4} + 5x^4 e^{x^5}$

(d) None of the above

16 Which of the following is/are true? **NCERT Pg. 130**

Statement I $\dfrac{d}{dx}(\sqrt{e^{\sqrt{x}}}) = \dfrac{e^{\sqrt{x}}}{4\sqrt{xe^{\sqrt{x}}}}$.

Statement II $\dfrac{d}{dx}[\log(\log(x))] = \dfrac{1}{x \log x}, x > 1$

(a) Both statements are true.

(b) Both statements are false.

(c) Statement I is true; Statement II is false.

(d) Statement I is false; Statement II is true.

17 Which of the following is/are true? **NCERT Pg. 130**

I. $\dfrac{d}{dx}\left[\dfrac{\cos x}{\log x}\right] = \dfrac{x \sin x \log x + \cos x}{x(\log x)^2}, x > 0$

II. $\dfrac{d}{dx}[\cos(\log x + e^x)] = \dfrac{-(xe^x + 1)\sin(\log x + e^x)}{x}$

(a) Only I is true (b) Only II is true

(c) Both I and II are true (d) Neither I nor II is true

Level II

18 $\frac{d}{dx}\left[\log\left\{e^x\left(\frac{x-2}{x+2}\right)\right\}^{3/4}\right]$ is equal to **NCERT Pg. 130**

(a) 1 (b) $\frac{x^2+1}{x^2-4}$ (c) $\frac{x^2-1}{x^2-4}$ (d) $e^x\frac{x^2-1}{x^2-4}$

19 Derivative of $\log[\log(\log x^5)]$ with respect to x is **NCERT Pg. 130**

(a) $\frac{1}{x\log x\cdot\log(\log x^5)}$ (b) $\frac{1}{x\log(\log x^5)}$

(c) $\frac{5}{x\log(\log x^5)}$ (d) None of these

20 If $y=\log\left(\frac{1-x^2}{1+x^2}\right)$, then $\frac{dy}{dx}$ is equal to **NCERT Pg. 130**

(a) $\frac{4x^3}{1-x^4}$ (b) $\frac{-4x}{1-x^4}$ (c) $\frac{1}{4-x^4}$ (d) $\frac{-4x^3}{1-x^4}$

21 If $f(x)=\log_x(\log_e x)$, then $f'(x)$ at $x=e$ is equal to **NCERT Pg. 130**

(a) 1 (b) 2 (c) 0 (d) $\frac{1}{e}$

22 Let $f(x)=e^x$, $g(x)=\sin^{-1}x$ and $h(x)=f[g(x)]$, then $\frac{h'(x)}{h(x)}$ is equal to **NCERT Pg. 130**

(a) $e^{\sin^{-1}x}$ (b) $\frac{1}{\sqrt{1-x^2}}$ (c) $\sin^{-1}x$ (d) $\frac{1}{1-x^2}$

23 If $y=\log x\,.\,e^{(\tan x+x^2)}$, then $\frac{dy}{dx}$ is equal to **NCERT Pg. 130**

(a) $e^{(\tan x+x^2)}\left[\frac{1}{x}+(\sec^2 x+x)\log x\right]$

(b) $e^{(\tan x+x^2)}\left[\frac{1}{x}+(\sec^2 x-x)\log x\right]$

(c) $e^{(\tan x+x^2)}\left[\frac{1}{x}+(\sec^2 x+2x)\log x\right]$

(d) $e^{(\tan x+x^2)}\left[\frac{1}{x}+(\sec^2 x-2x)\log x\right]$

24 If $y=\log_{\sin x}(\tan x)$, then $\frac{dy}{dx}$ at $x=\frac{\pi}{4}$ is **NCERT Pg. 130**

(a) $\frac{4}{\log 2}$ (b) $\frac{-4}{\log 2}$

(c) $\frac{1}{\log 2}$ (d) None of these

25 If $y=\log x^x$, then the value of $\frac{dy}{dx}$ is **NCERT Pg. 130**

(a) $x^x(1+\log x)$ (b) $\log(ex)$

(c) $\log\frac{e}{x}$ (d) $\log\left(\frac{x}{e}\right)$

26 If $y=\log_a x+\log_x a+\log_x x+\log_a a$, then $\frac{dy}{dx}$ is equal to **NCERT Pg. 130**

(a) $\frac{1}{x}+x\log a$ (b) $\frac{\log a}{x}+\frac{x}{\log a}$

(c) $\frac{1}{x\log a}+x\log a$ (d) None of these

27 If $y=2^{\log x}$, then $\frac{dy}{dx}$ is **NCERT Pg. 130**

(a) $\frac{2^{\log x}}{\log_e 2}$ (b) $2^{\log x}\cdot\log_e 2$

(c) $\frac{2^{\log x}}{x}$ (d) $\frac{2^{\log x}\log_e 2}{x}$

28 If $y=5^x\cdot x^5$, then $\frac{dy}{dx}$ is **NCERT Pg. 134**

(a) $5^x(x^5\log 5-5x^4)$ (b) $x^5\log 5-5x^4$

(c) $x^5\log 5+5x^4$ (d) $5^x(x^5\log 5+5x^4)$

29 Match the terms of column I with terms of column II and choose the correct option from the codes given below. **NCERT Pg. 134**

Column I	Column II
A. $f(x)=2^{\cos^2 x}$	1. $f'(x)=\frac{1}{\sqrt{x^2+a}}$
B. $f(x)=\frac{8^x}{x^8}$	2. $f'(x)=\frac{8^x}{x^8}\left[\log 8-\frac{8}{x}\right]$
C. $f(x)=\log(x+\sqrt{x^2+a})$	3. $f'(x)=-2^{\cos^2 x}\sin 2x\log 2$
D. $f(x)=\log[\log(\log\sin x)]$	4. $f'(x)=\frac{\cot x}{\log(\log\sin x)(\log\sin x)}$

Codes

	A	B	C	D
(a)	1	2	3	4
(b)	3	2	1	4
(c)	2	1	3	4
(d)	1	4	3	2

30 Let $f(x)=2^{2x-1}$ and $\phi(x)=-2^x+2x\log 2$. If $f'(x)>\phi'(x)$, then **NCERT Pg. 134**

(a) $0<x<1$ (b) $0\le x<1$

(c) $x>0$ (d) $x\ge 0$

31 If $y=\log_2[\log_2(x)]$, then $\frac{dy}{dx}$ is equal to **NCERT Pg. 134**

(a) $\frac{\log_2 e}{\log_e x}$ (b) $\frac{\log_2 e}{x\log_x 2}$

(c) $\frac{\log_2 x}{\log_e 2}$ (d) $\frac{\log_2 e}{x\log_e x}$

Logarithmic Differentiation and Derivatives of Functions in Parametric Forms

Level I

1 The derivative of $y = f(x) = [u(x)]^{v(x)}$ is NCERT Pg. 130

(a) $y\left[\frac{v(x)}{u(x)}u'(x) - v'(x)\log[u(x)]\right]$

(b) $y\left[\frac{u(x)}{v(x)}u'(x) - v'(x)\log[v(x)]\right]$

(c) $y\left[\frac{v(x)}{u(x)}u'(x) + v'(x)\log[u(x)]\right]$

(d) None of the above

2 The derivative of $\sqrt{\frac{(x-3)(x^2+4)}{3x^2+4x+5}}$ with respect to x is NCERT Pg. 131

(a) $\frac{1}{2}\sqrt{\frac{(x-3)(x^2+4)}{3x^2+4x+5}}\left[\frac{1}{x-3} + \frac{2x}{x^2+4} - \frac{6x+4}{3x^2+4x+5}\right]$

(b) $\frac{1}{2}\sqrt{\frac{(x-3)(x^2+4)}{3x^2+4x+5}}\left[\frac{1}{x-3} - \frac{2x}{x^2+4} + \frac{6x+4}{3x^2+4x+5}\right]$

(c) $\frac{1}{2}\sqrt{\frac{(x-3)(x^2+4)}{3x^2+4x+5}}\left[\frac{1}{x-3} - \frac{2x}{x^2+4} - \frac{6x+4}{3x^2+4x+5}\right]$

(d) None of the above

3 Match the functions in column I with their derivatives in column II and choose the correct option from the codes given below. NCERT Pg. 132

Column I	Column II
A. $f(x) = a^x$	1. $f'(x) = x^{\sin x - 1}\cdot\sin x + x^{\sin x}\cdot\cos x\log x$
B. $f(x) = x^{\sin x}, x > 0$	2. $f'(x) = a^x\log a$
C. $y^x + x^y + x^x = a^b$	3. $f'(x) = -\cos x\cos 2x\cos 3x\{\tan x + 2\tan 2x + 3\tan 3x\}$
D. $f(x) = \cos x\cdot\cos 2x\cdot\cos 3x$	4. $y' = \frac{-\left[y^x\log y + y\cdot x^{y-1} + x^x(1+\log x)\right]}{x\cdot y^{x-1} + x^y\log x}$

Codes

	A	B	C	D
(a)	2	1	4	3
(b)	2	4	1	3
(c)	1	2	4	3
(d)	3	1	2	4

4 If $y = \sqrt{\frac{(x-1)(x-2)}{(x-3)(x-4)(x-5)}}$, then $\frac{dy}{dx}$ is equal to NCERT Pg. 134

(a) $\frac{1}{2}\sqrt{\frac{(x-1)(x-2)}{(x-3)(x-4)(x-5)}}\left\{\frac{1}{x-1} + \frac{1}{x-2} - \frac{1}{x-3} - \frac{1}{x-4} - \frac{1}{x-5}\right\}$

(b) $\frac{1}{2}\sqrt{\frac{(x-1)(x-2)}{(x-3)(x-4)(x-5)}}\left\{\frac{1}{x-1} - \frac{1}{x-2} + \frac{1}{x-3} + \frac{1}{x-4} + \frac{1}{x-5}\right\}$

(c) $\sqrt{-\frac{(x-1)(x-2)}{(x-3)(x-4)(x-5)}}\left\{\frac{1}{x-1} - \frac{1}{x-2} + \frac{1}{x-3} - \frac{1}{x-4} + \frac{1}{x-5}\right\}$

(d) None of the above

5 Which of the following is/are true?

Statement I $y = (\log x)^{\cos x}$,

$\frac{dy}{dx} = (\log x)^{\cos x}\left\{\frac{\cos x}{x\log x} - \sin x(\log x)\right\}$

Statement II $f(x) = x^x - 2^{\sin x}$,

$f'(x) = x^x(1 + \log x) - 2^{\sin x}(\cos x\log 2)$ NCERT Pg. 134

(a) Both statements are true.

(b) Both statements are false.

(c) Statement I is true; Statement II is false.

(d) Statement I is false; Statement II is true.

6 Derivative of $(x+3)^2(x+4)^3(x+5)^4$ with respect to x is NCERT Pg. 134

(a) $(x+3)(x+4)(x+5)^2(9x^2+70x+133)$

(b) $(x+3)(x+4)^2(x+5)^3(9x^2+70x+133)$

(c) $(x+3)(x+4)^2(x+5)(9x^2-70x-133)$

(d) None of the above

7 If $y = \left(x + \frac{1}{x}\right)^x + x^{\left(1+\frac{1}{x}\right)}$, then $\frac{dy}{dx}$ is equal to NCERT Pg. 134

(a) $\left(x+\frac{1}{x}\right)^x\left[\frac{(x^2-1)}{(x^2+1)} + \log\left(x+\frac{1}{x}\right)\right] + x^{\left(1+\frac{1}{x}\right)}\left[\frac{x+1-\log x}{x^2}\right]$

(b) $\left(x+\frac{1}{x}\right)^x\left[\frac{x^2-1}{x^2+1} - \log\left(x+\frac{1}{x}\right)\right] - x^{\left(1+\frac{1}{x}\right)}\left[\frac{x+1-\log x}{x^2}\right]$

(c) $\left(x+\frac{1}{x}\right)^x\left[\frac{x^2-1}{x^2+1} - \log\left(x+\frac{1}{x}\right) - x^{\left(1+\frac{1}{x}\right)}(x+\log x)\right]$

(d) None of the above

8 Match the terms of column I with terms of column II and choose the correct option from the codes given below. NCERT Pg. 134

Column I	Column II
A. $f(x)=(\log x)^x + x^{\log x}$	1. $f'(x)=x^{\sin x}\left[\frac{\sin x}{x}+\cos x\log x\right] + (\sin x)^{\cos x}\left[\cot x\cos x - \sin x\log\sin x\right]$
B. $f(x)=(\sin x)^x + \sin^{-1}\sqrt{x}$	2. $f'(x)=(\log x)^{x-1}[1+\log x\log(\log x)] + 2x^{\log x - 1}\log x$
C. $f(x)=x^{\sin x}+(\sin x)^{\cos x}$	3. $f'(x)=(\sin x)^x[x\cot x+\log\sin x]+\frac{1}{2\sqrt{x-x^2}}$
D. $f(x)=x^{x\cos x}+\frac{x^2+1}{x^2-1}$	4. $f'(x)=x^{x\cos x}[\cos x(1+\log x)-x\sin x\log x] - \frac{4x}{(x^2-1)^2}$

Codes

	A	B	C	D
(a)	2	1	3	4
(b)	2	3	1	4
(c)	1	2	4	3
(d)	3	1	2	4

9 Which of the following is/are true?

Statement I If $f(x)=(x\cos x)^x+(x\sin x)^{1/x}$, then

$$f'(x)=(x\cos x)^x[-x\tan x+1+\log(x\cos x)] + (x\sin x)^{1/x}\left[\frac{x\cot x+1-\log(x\sin x)}{x^2}\right].$$

Statement II If $x^y+y^x=1$, then

$$\frac{dy}{dx}=-\frac{y^x\log y+yx^{y-1}}{x^y\log x+xy^{x-1}}.$$ NCERT Pg. 134

(a) Both statements are true.
(b) Both statements are false.
(c) Statement I is true; Statement II is false.
(d) Statement I is false; Statement II is true.

10 If $y^x=x^y$, then $\frac{dy}{dx}$ is equal to NCERT Pg. 134

(a) $\frac{y}{x}\left(\frac{y+x\log y}{x-y\log x}\right)$ (b) $\frac{y}{x}\left(\frac{y-x\log y}{x-y\log x}\right)$
(c) $\frac{x}{y}\left(\frac{y+x\log y}{x+y\log x}\right)$ (d) None of these

11 If $(\cos x)^y=(\cos y)^x$, then $\frac{dy}{dx}$ is equal to NCERT Pg. 134

(a) $\frac{\log(\cos y)+y(\tan x)}{\log(\cos x)+x\tan y}$ (b) $\frac{\log(\cos y)-y(\tan x)}{\log(\cos x)-x(\tan y)}$
(c) $\frac{\log(\tan x)+y(\cos x)}{\log(\cos x)+x(\tan y)}$ (d) None of these

12 If $f(x)=(1+x)(1+x^2)(1+x^4)(1+x^8)$, then $f'(1)$ is NCERT Pg. 134

(a) 130 (b) 120
(c) 110 (d) None of these

13 The derivative of $(x^2-5x+8)(x^3+7x+9)$ can be obtained NCERT Pg. 134

(i) by using product rule.
(ii) by expanding the product to obtain a single polynomial.
(iii) by logarithmic differentiation.

(a) Only by (i) (b) Only by (ii)
(c) By (i), (ii) and (iii) (d) None of these

14 If $x=a\cos\theta$, $y=a\sin\theta$, then $\frac{dy}{dx}$ is equal to NCERT Pg. 135

(a) $-\sin\theta$ (b) $-\cos\theta$ (c) $-\cot\theta$ (d) $\tan\theta$

15 If $x=at^2$ and $y=2at$, then $\frac{dy}{dx}$ is equal to NCERT Pg. 135

(a) t (b) $\frac{1}{t}$ (c) $\frac{-1}{t^2}$ (d) None of these

16 $\frac{dy}{dx}$ is expressed in terms of ...A... only without directly involving the main variable ...B... .Here, A and B refer to NCERT Pg. 135

(a) parameter, $f(t)$, $g(t)$ (b) $f(t)$, $g(t)$, parameter
(c) parameter, x and y (d) None of these

17 If $x^{2/3}+y^{2/3}=a^{2/3}$, then $\frac{dy}{dx}$ is equal to NCERT Pg. 136

(a) $-\sqrt[3]{\frac{y}{x}}$ (b) $\sqrt[3]{y/x}$
(c) $\frac{y}{x}$ (d) None of these

18 Match the terms of column I with terms of column II and choose the correct option from the codes given below. NCERT Pg. 137

Column I	Column II
A. $x=2at^2,\ y=at^4$	1. $\frac{dy}{dx}=-\frac{1}{t^2}$
B. $x=a\cos\theta,\ y=b\cos\theta$	2. $\frac{dy}{dx}=t^2$
C. $x=\sin t,\ y=\cos 2t$	3. $\frac{dy}{dx}=\frac{b}{a}$
D. $x=4t,\ y=\frac{4}{t}$	4. $\frac{dy}{dx}=-4\sin t$
E. $x=\cos\theta-\cos 2\theta,$ $y=\sin\theta-\sin 2\theta$	5. $\frac{dy}{dx}=\frac{\cos\theta-2\cos 2\theta}{2\sin 2\theta-\sin\theta}$

Codes

	A	B	C	D	E
(a)	2	3	4	1	5
(b)	1	2	4	3	5
(c)	3	1	4	2	5
(d)	4	5	1	2	3

19 Which of the following is/are true? NCERT Pg. 137

Statement I If $x = a(\theta - \sin\theta)$, $y = a(1 + \cos\theta)$, then $\frac{dy}{dx} = -\cot\frac{\theta}{2}$.

Statement II If $x = \frac{\sin^3 t}{\sqrt{\cos 2t}}$, $y = \frac{\cos^3 t}{\sqrt{\cos 2t}}$, then derivative of y with respect to x is $-\cot 3t$.

(a) Both statements are true.
(b) Both statements are false.
(c) Statement I is true; Statement II is false.
(d) Statement I is false; Statement II is true.

20 If $x = a(\cos t + \log\tan t/2)$ and $y = a\sin t$, then $\frac{dy}{dx}$ is equal to NCERT Pg. 137

(a) $\cot t$ (b) $\tan t$ (c) $\sec t$ (d) $\operatorname{cosec} t$

21 If $x = a(\cos\theta + \theta\sin\theta)$ and $y = a(\sin\theta - \theta\cos\theta)$, then $\frac{dy}{dx}$ is equal to NCERT Pg. 137

(a) $\tan\theta$ (b) $\cot\theta$ (c) $\sin\theta$ (d) $\cos\theta$

22 If $x = \sqrt{a^{\sin^{-1} t}}$ and $y = \sqrt{a^{\cos^{-1} t}}$, then NCERT Pg. 137

(a) $x\frac{dy}{dx} + y = 0$ (b) $x\frac{dy}{dx} = y$
(c) $y\frac{dy}{dx} = x$ (d) None of these

Level II

23 If $y^x = e^{y-x}$, then $\frac{dy}{dx}$ is equal to NCERT Pg. 134

(a) $\frac{1+\log y}{y\log y}$ (b) $\frac{(1+\log y)^2}{y\log y}$
(c) $\frac{1+\log y}{(\log y)^2}$ (d) $\frac{(1+\log y)^2}{\log y}$

24 If $x = e^{x/y}$, then $\frac{dy}{dx}$ is equal to NCERT Pg. 134

(a) $\frac{x-y}{x\log x}$ (b) $\frac{y-x}{\log x}$ (c) $\frac{y-x}{x\log x}$ (d) $\frac{x-y}{\log x}$

25 If $y = (\cos x)^{(\cos x)^{(\cos x)\ldots\infty}}$, then $\frac{dy}{dx}$ is equal to NCERT Pg. 134

(a) $\frac{y\tan x}{y\log\cos x - 1}$ (b) $\frac{y^2\tan x}{y\log\cos x - 1}$
(c) $\frac{y\tan x}{1 + y\log\cos x}$ (d) None of these

26 If $x = \exp\left\{\tan^{-1}\left(\frac{y-x^2}{x^2}\right)\right\}$, then $\frac{dy}{dx}$ is equal to NCERT Pg. 134

(a) $2x[1+\tan(\log x)] + x\sec^2(\log x)$
(b) $x[1+\tan(\log x)] + \sec^2(\log x)$
(c) $2x[1+\tan(\log x)] + x^2\sec^2(\log x)$
(d) $2x[1+\tan(\log x)] + \sec^2(\log x)$

27 If $\cos\frac{x}{2}\cos\frac{x}{2^2}\cos\frac{x}{2^3}\ldots\cos\frac{x}{2^n} = f(x)$, then $\frac{1}{2}\tan\frac{x}{2} + \frac{1}{2^2}\tan\frac{x}{2^2} + \ldots + \frac{1}{2^n}\tan\frac{x}{2^n}$ is equal to NCERT Pg. 134

(a) $\frac{f'(x)}{f(x)}$ (b) $\frac{f(x)}{f'(x)}$ (c) $\frac{-f'(x)}{f(x)}$ (d) 0

28 If $f(x) = \cos x\cos 2x\cos 4x\cos 8x\cos 16x$, then the value of $f'\left(\frac{\pi}{4}\right)$ is NCERT Pg. 137

(a) 1 (b) $\sqrt{2}$ (c) $\frac{1}{\sqrt{2}}$ (d) 0

29 Given, $x = a\cos t\sqrt{\cos 2t}$ and $y = a\sin t\sqrt{\cos 2t}$ $(a > 0)$, then $\left|\frac{\left[1+\left(\frac{dy}{dx}\right)^2\right]^{3/2}}{\frac{d^2y}{dx^2}}\right|$ at $\frac{\pi}{6}$ is given by NCERT Pg. 137

(a) $\frac{a}{3}$ b) $a\sqrt{2}$ (c) $\frac{\sqrt{2}}{3a}$ (d) $\frac{-\sqrt{2}a}{3}$

30 If $y = (1+x)(1+x^2)(1+x^4)\ldots(1+x^{2^n})$, then the value of $\frac{dy}{dx}$ at $x = 0$ is NCERT Pg. 134

(a) 0 (b) -1
(c) 1 (d) None of these

31 If $y = |\sin x|^{|x|}$, then the value of $\frac{dy}{dx}$ at $x = -\frac{\pi}{6}$ is NCERT Pg. 134

(a) $\frac{2^{-\frac{\pi}{6}}}{6}[6\log 2 - \sqrt{3}\pi]$ (b) $\frac{2^{\frac{\pi}{6}}}{6}[6\log 2 + \sqrt{3}\pi]$
(c) $\frac{2^{-\frac{\pi}{6}}}{6}[6\log 2 + \sqrt{3}\pi]$ (d) None of these

32 If $x^y = y^x$, then $x(x - y\log x)\frac{dy}{dx}$ is equal to NCERT Pg. 134

(a) $y(y - x\log y)$ (b) $y(y + x\log y)$
(c) $x(x + y\log x)$ (d) $x(y - x\log y)$

33 If $f(x) = (x-2)(x-4)(x-6)\ldots(x-2n)$, then $f'(2)$ is equal to NCERT Pg. 134

(a) $(-1)^n 2^{n-1}(n-1)!$ (b) $(-2)^{n-1}(n-1)!$
(c) $(-2)^n n!$ (d) $(-1)^{n-1}2^n(n-1)!$

34 If $y = a\sin^3\theta$ and $x = a\cos^3\theta$, then at $\theta = \frac{\pi}{3}$, $\frac{dy}{dx}$ is equal to NCERT Pg. 137

(a) $\frac{1}{\sqrt{3}}$ (b) $-\sqrt{3}$ (c) $-\frac{1}{\sqrt{3}}$ (d) $\sqrt{3}$

35 If $x = \log(1+t^2)$ and $y = t - \tan^{-1} t$, then $\frac{dy}{dx}$ is equal to **NCERT Pg. 137**

(a) $e^x - 1$ (b) $t^2 - 1$

(c) $\frac{\sqrt{e^x - 1}}{2}$ (d) $e^x - y$

36 Which of the following statements is/are true?

Statement I The first derivative of the function $\left[\cos^{-1}\left(\sin\sqrt{\frac{1+x}{2}}\right) + x^x\right]$ with respect to x at $x = 1$ is $\frac{3}{4}$.

Statement II If $y = (1+x)^x$, then $\frac{dy}{dx} = (1+x)^x\left[\frac{x}{1+x} - \log(1+x)\right]$. **NCERT Pg. 137**

(a) Both statements are true.
(b) Both statements are false.
(c) Statement I is true; Statement II is false.
(d) Statement I is false; Statement II is true.

Second Order Derivatives

Level I

1 Match the terms of column I with terms of column II and choose the correct option from the codes given below. **NCERT Pg. 138**

Column I	Column II
A. $y = x^3 + \tan x$	1. $\frac{d^2y}{dx^2} + y = 0$
B. $y = A\sin x + B\cos x$	2. $\frac{d^2y}{dx^2} - \frac{5dy}{dx} + 6y = 0$
C. $y = 3e^{2x} + 2e^{3x}$	3. $(1-x^2)\frac{d^2y}{dx^2} - x\frac{dy}{dx} = 0$
D. $y = \sin^{-1} x$	4. $\frac{d^2y}{dx^2} = 6x + 2\sec^2 x \tan x$

Codes

	A	B	C	D
(a)	4	1	2	3
(b)	1	3	2	4
(c)	2	1	4	3
(d)	3	2	1	4

2 If $y = x\cos x$, then $\frac{d^2y}{dx^2}$ is **NCERT Pg. 139**

(a) $-x\cos x - 2\sin x$ (b) $x\cos x + 2\sin x$

(c) $x\sin x + \cos x$ (d) None of these

3 $\frac{d^2}{dx^2}(e^x \cdot \sin 5x)$ is equal to **NCERT Pg. 139**

(a) $2e^x(5\sin 5x - 12\cos 5x)$

(b) $2e^x(5\cos 5x - 12\sin 5x)$

(c) $2e^x(12\cos 5x - 5\sin 5x)$

(d) None of the above

4 Match the terms of column I with the terms of column II and choose the correct option from the codes given below. **NCERT Pg. 139**

Column I	Column II
A. $y = \tan^{-1} x$	1. $\frac{d^2y}{dx^2} = \frac{-(1+\log x)}{(x\log x)^2}$
B. $y = \log(\log x)$	2. $\frac{d^2y}{dx^2} = \frac{-2x}{(1+x^2)^2}$
C. $y = \sin(\log x)$	3. $\frac{d^2y}{dx^2} + y = 0$
D. $y = 5\cos x - 3\sin x$	4. $\frac{d^2y}{dx^2} = -\frac{\sin(\log x) + \cos(\log x)}{x^2}$

Codes

	A	B	C	D		A	B	C	D
(a)	1	3	2	4	(b)	3	2	1	4
(c)	2	1	4	3	(d)	4	3	1	2

5 If $y = \cos^{-1} x$, then the value of $\frac{d^2y}{dx^2}$ in terms of y alone is **NCERT Pg. 140**

(a) $-\cot y \operatorname{cosec}^2 y$ (b) $\operatorname{cosec} y \cot^2 y$

(c) $-\cot y \operatorname{cosec} y$ (d) None of these

Level II

6 If $y = 3\cos(\log x) + 4\sin(\log x)$, then **NCERT Pg. 140**

(a) $xy_2 + y_1 + y = 0$ (b) $xy_2 + y_1 - y = 0$

(c) $x^2y_2 + xy_1 + y = 0$ (d) None of these

7 If $y = Ae^{mx} + Be^{nx}$, then $\frac{d^2y}{dx^2}$ is equal to **NCERT Pg. 140**

(a) $(m+n)\frac{dy}{dx} + mny$ (b) $(m+n)\frac{dy}{dx} - mny$

(c) $-(m+n)\frac{dy}{dx} + mny$ (d) None of these

8 Which of the following statement(s) is/are true?

Statement I If $y = 500e^{7x} + 600e^{-7x}$, then $\frac{d^2y}{dx^2} = 49y$.

Statement II If $e^y(x+1) = 1$, then $\frac{d^2y}{dx^2} = \left(\frac{dy}{dx}\right)^2$. **NCERT Pg. 140**

(a) Both statements are true.
(b) Both statements are false.
(c) Statement I is true; Statement II is false.
(d) Statement I is false; Statement II is true.

9 If $y = (\tan^{-1} x)^2$, then the value of $(x^2+1)^2 y_2 + 2x(x^2+1)\, y_1$ is NCERT Pg. 140

(a) 2 (b) 3 (c) 4 (d) None of these

Miscellaneous Exercise

1 If $y = \sqrt{3x+2} + \dfrac{1}{\sqrt{2x^2+4}}$, then $\dfrac{dy}{dx}$ is equal to NCERT Pg. 140

(a) $\dfrac{3}{2\sqrt{3x+2}} - \dfrac{2x}{(2x^2+4)^{3/2}}$

(b) $\dfrac{3}{2\sqrt{3x+2}} + \dfrac{2x}{(2x^2+4)^{3/2}}$

(c) $\dfrac{3}{2\sqrt{3x+2}} + \dfrac{2}{(2x^2+4)^{3/2}}$

(d) None of the above

2 If $y = \log_7(\log x)$, then $\dfrac{dy}{dx}$ is equal to NCERT Pg. 140

(a) $\dfrac{1}{x \log x \log 7}$ (b) $\dfrac{-1}{x \log x \log 7}$

(c) $\dfrac{1}{x \log x}$ (d) None of these

3 Match the terms of column I with terms of column II and choose the correct option from the codes given below. NCERT Pg. 141

Column I	Column II
A. $f(x) = \cos^{-1}(\sin x)$	1. $f'(x) = (\sin x)^{\sin x} \cos x\,[1+\log(\sin x)]$
B. $f(x) = \tan^{-1}\left(\dfrac{\sin x}{1+\cos x}\right)$	2. $f'(x) = \dfrac{2^{x+1}\log 2}{1+4^x}$
C. $f(x) = \sin^{-1}\left(\dfrac{2^{x+1}}{1+4^x}\right)$	3. $f'(x) = -1$
D. $f(x) = (\sin x)^{\sin x}, 0 < x < \pi$	4. $f'(x) = 1/2$

Codes

	A	B	C	D		A	B	C	D
(a)	3	4	2	1	(b)	2	3	1	4
(c)	1	2	4	3	(d)	4	1	3	2

4 If $y = a^{t+\frac{1}{t}}$ and $x = \left(t+\dfrac{1}{t}\right)^a$, then $\dfrac{dy}{dx}$ is equal to NCERT Pg. 143

(a) $\dfrac{a^{\left(1+\frac{1}{t}\right)} \log a}{\left(t+\frac{1}{t}\right)^{a-1}}$ (b) $\dfrac{a^{\left(1+\frac{1}{t}\right)}}{\left(t+\frac{1}{t}\right)^{a-1}}$

(c) $\dfrac{a^{\left(t+\frac{1}{t}\right)} \log a}{a\left(t+\frac{1}{t}\right)^{a-1}}$ (d) None of these

5 The derivative of $\sin^2 x$ with respect to $e^{\cos x}$ is NCERT Pg. 144

(a) $\dfrac{2\cos x}{e^{\cos x}}$ (b) $-\dfrac{2\cos x}{e^{\cos x}}$

(c) $\dfrac{2}{e^{\cos x}}$ (d) None of these

6 If $f(x) = (3x^2 - 9x + 5)^9$, then $f'(x)$ is equal to NCERT Pg. 144

(a) $(2x-3)(3x^2-9x+5)^8$

(b) $9(3x^2-9x+5)^8$

(c) $27(2x-3)(3x^2-9x+5)^8$

(d) None of the above

7 Match the terms to column I with terms of column II and choose the correct option from the codes given below. NCERT Pg. 144

Column I	Column II
A. $f(x) = \sin^3 x + \cos^6 x$	1. $f'(x) = \dfrac{3}{2}\dfrac{\sqrt{x}}{\sqrt{1-x^3}}$
B. $f(x) = (5x)^{3\cos 2x}$	2. $f'(x) = -\left[\dfrac{1}{\sqrt{4-x^2}\sqrt{2x+7}} + \dfrac{\cos^{-1} x/2}{(2x+7)^{3/2}}\right]$
C. $f(x) = \sin^{-1}(x\sqrt{x}), 0 \le x \le 1$	3. $f'(x) = (5x)^{3\cos 2x}\left\{\dfrac{3\cos 2x}{x} - 6\sin 2x \log 5x\right\}$
D. $f(x) = \dfrac{\cos^{-1} x/2}{\sqrt{2x+7}}, -2 < x < 2$	4. $f'(x) = 3\sin x \cos x (\sin x - 2\cos^4 x)$

Codes

	A	B	C	D
(a)	4	3	1	2
(b)	3	4	2	1
(c)	2	1	3	4
(d)	1	2	4	3

8 Derivative of $\cot^{-1}\left[\dfrac{\sqrt{1+\sin x}+\sqrt{1-\sin x}}{\sqrt{1+\sin x}-\sqrt{1-\sin x}}\right], 0 < x < \dfrac{\pi}{2}$ is NCERT Pg. 144

(a) $\dfrac{1}{2}$ (b) 1 (c) 2 (d) None of these

9 Which of the following statement(s) is/are true?

Statement I If $y = (\log x)^{\log x}$, then $\dfrac{dy}{dx} = (\log x)^{\log x}\left[\dfrac{1}{x} + \dfrac{\log(\log x)}{x}\right]$.

Statement II If $y = \cos(a\cos x + b\sin x)$ for some constants a and b, then
$y' = (a\sin x - b\cos x)\sin(a\cos x + b\sin x)$ **NCERT Pg. 144**
(a) Both statements are true.
(b) Both statements are false.
(c) Statement I is true; Statement II is false.
(d) Statement I is false; Statement II is true.

10 Derivative of $(\sin x - \cos x)^{(\sin x - \cos x)}$ is **NCERT Pg. 144**
(a) $(\cos x + \sin x)(\sin x - \cos x)^{(\sin x - \cos x)}$ $\{1 + \log(\sin x - \cos x)\}$
(b) $(\sin x - \cos x)^{(\sin x - \cos x)}\{1 + \log(\sin x - \cos x)\}$
(c) $(\sin x - \cos x)^{(\sin x - \cos x)}\{1 - \log(\sin x - \cos x)\}$
(d) None of the above

11 If $y = 12(1 - \cos t)$, $x = 10(t - \sin t)$, $-\frac{\pi}{2} < t < \frac{\pi}{2}$, then $\frac{dy}{dx}$ is equal to **NCERT Pg. 145**
(a) $\frac{5}{6}\cot(t/2)$ (b) $\frac{6}{5}\cot(t/2)$
(c) $\cot t$ (d) None of these

12 If $y = \sin^{-1} x + \sin^{-1}\sqrt{1-x^2}, -1 \le x < 1$, then $\frac{dy}{dx}$ is equal to **NCERT Pg. 145**
(a) 0 (b) 1 (c) 2 (d) 3

13 If $x\sqrt{1+y} + y\sqrt{1+x} = 0$ for $-1 < x < 1$, then $\frac{dy}{dx}$ is equal to **NCERT Pg. 145**
(a) $\frac{1}{(1+x^2)}$ (b) $\frac{y}{x}\sqrt{\frac{1+y}{1+x}}$
(c) $\frac{-1}{(1+x)^2}$ (d) None of these

14 If $(x-a)^2 + (y-b)^2 = c^2$ for some $c > 0$, then the value of $\frac{\left[1 + \left(\frac{dy}{dx}\right)^2\right]^{3/2}}{\frac{d^2y}{dx^2}}$ is **NCERT Pg. 145**
(a) independent of a and b
(b) dependent of a and b
(c) depend on a only
(d) depend on b only

15 If $\cos y = x\cos(a + y)$ with $\cos a \ne 1$, then $\frac{dy}{dx}$ is equal to **NCERT Pg. 145**
(a) $\frac{\sin^2(a+y)}{\sin a}$ (b) $\frac{\cos^2(a+y)}{\sin a}$
(c) $\sin^2(a+y)\sin a$ (d) None of these

Numerical Type Question

1 The function $f(x) = \begin{cases} \dfrac{\frac{\pi}{2} - x}{\cos x}, & x \ne \frac{\pi}{2} \\ 1, & x = \frac{\pi}{2} \end{cases}$ is continuous at $t =$ .... **NCERT Pg. 116**

2 The value of $9k$ for which the function $f(x) = \begin{cases} \dfrac{\sin 2x}{6x}, & \text{if } x \ne 0 \\ 3k, & \text{if } x = 0 \end{cases}$ is continuous at $x = 0$ is ...... **NCERT Pg. 119**

3 If $f(3) = 5$ and $f'(3) = 1$, the value of $\lim_{x \to 3} \frac{x\,f(3) - 3f(x)}{x - 3}$ is .... **NCERT Pg. 119**

4 If $y = \cos^{-1} x + \cos^{-1}\sqrt{1-x^2}, x \in (0, 1)$, then $\frac{dy}{dx}$ is equal to .... **NCERT Pg. 144**

5 If $x = a\tan^3\theta$ and $y = a\sec^3\theta$, then the value of $\frac{dy}{dx}$ at $\theta = \frac{\pi}{2}$ is .... **NCERT Pg. 135**

6 The function $f(x)\begin{cases} 6x - 5, & 0 < x \le 1 \\ 5x^3 - 4x, & 1 < x < 2 \end{cases}$ is continuous at $x =$ .... **NCERT Pg. 116**

7 The value of k for which the function $f(x) = \begin{cases} \dfrac{k\cos x}{\pi - 2x}, & x \ne \frac{\pi}{2} \\ 5, & x = \frac{\pi}{2} \end{cases}$ is continuous at $x = \frac{\pi}{2}$ is .... **NCERT Pg. 116**

8 Let $f(x) = x^2 + 3x + 8$, then the value of $f'(4)$ is .... **NCERT Pg. 119**

Assertion and Reason Questions

Direction (Q. Nos. 1-11) In the questions given below are to statements labelled as Assertion (A) and Reason (R). In the context on the two statements, which one of the following is correct?

(a) Both Assertion and Reason are correct and Reason is the correct explanation of Assertion.
(b) Both Assertion and Reason are correct but Reason is not the correct explanation of Assertion.
(c) Assertion is correct but Reason is incorrect.
(d) Assertion is incorrect but Reason is correct.

1 Assertion (A) The function f defined by

$f(x)=\begin{cases} x+2, & x<0 \\ -x+2, & x>0 \end{cases}$ is continuous at all points in the domain of f.

Reason (R) The function $f(x)=\begin{cases} x, \text{ if } x\geq 0 \\ x^2, \text{ if } x<0 \end{cases}$ is a discontinuous function. **NCERT Pg. 116**

2 Assertion (A) The function $f(x)=\begin{cases} 2x, \text{ if } x<0 \\ 0, \text{ if } 0\leq x\leq 1 \\ 4x, \text{ if } x>1 \end{cases}$ is continuous everywhere except at $x=1$.

Reason (R) The function $f(x)=\begin{cases} -2, \text{ if } x\leq -1 \\ 2x, \text{ if } -1<x\leq 1 \\ 2, \text{ if } x>1 \end{cases}$ is continuous for every value of x. **NCERT Pg. 116**

3 Assertion (A) Every differentiable function is continuous but converse is not true.

Reason (R) Function $f(x)=|x|$ is continuous. **NCERT Pg. 120**

4 Assertion (A) If $f(x)=\dfrac{\sin(ax+b)}{\cos(cx+d)}$, then

$f'(x)=a\cos(ax+b)\sec(cx+d)$
$+c\sin(ax+b)\tan(cx+d)\sec(cx+d)$.

Reason (R) If $f(x)=\dfrac{u}{v}$, then $f'(x)=\dfrac{vu'-uv'}{v^2}$. **NCERT Pg. 119**

5 Let $f(x)=x|x|$ and $g(x)=\sin x$ **NCERT Pg. 124**

Assertion (A) gof is differentiable at $x=0$ and its derivative is continuous at that point.

Reason (R) gof is twice differentiable at $x=0$.

6 Assertion (A) The set of all points, where the function

$f(x)=\begin{cases} 0, & x=0 \\ \dfrac{x}{1+e^{1/x}}, & x\neq 0 \end{cases}$ is differentiable, is $(-\infty,\infty)-\{0\}$.

Reason (R) $Lf'(0)=1$, $Rf'(0)=0$ and

$f'(x)=\dfrac{1+e^{1/x}+e^{1/x}\dfrac{1}{x}}{(1+e^{1/x})^2}$ which exists when $x\neq 0$. **NCERT Pg. 120**

7 Assertion (A) $\dfrac{d}{dx}e^{\cos x}=e^{\cos x}(-\sin x)$

Reason (R) $\dfrac{d}{dx}e^x=e^x$ **NCERT Pg. 130**

8 Consider for $f(x,y)=0$, $\dfrac{d}{dx}f(x,y)=\dfrac{-\partial f/\partial x}{\partial f/\partial y}$.

Assertion (A) If $e^{xy}+\log(xy)+\cos(xy)+5=0$, then $\dfrac{dy}{dx}=-\dfrac{y}{x}$. **NCERT Pg. 130**

Reason (R) $\dfrac{d}{dx}(xy)=0\Rightarrow\dfrac{dy}{dx}=-\dfrac{y}{x}$

9 Assertion (A) If $xy=e^{x-y}$, then $\dfrac{dy}{dx}=\dfrac{y}{x}\dfrac{(x-1)}{(1+y)}$.

Reason (R) $\dfrac{d}{dx}(u\cdot v)=u\dfrac{d}{dx}v+v\dfrac{d}{dx}u$ **NCERT Pg. 130**

10 Assertion (A) If $x=a\sec\theta$, $y=b\tan\theta$, then derivative of y with respect to x is $\dfrac{b}{a}\operatorname{cosec}\theta$.

Reason (R) If $x=f(t)$ and $y=g(t)$, then $\dfrac{dy}{dx}=\dfrac{g'(t)}{f'(t)}$ **NCERT Pg. 137**

11 Assertion (A) If $x=\dfrac{2at}{1+t^3}$ and $y=\dfrac{2at^2}{(1+t^3)^2}$, then $\dfrac{dy}{dx}=\dfrac{x}{a}$.

Reason (R) If $x=f(t)$ and $y=g(t)$, then $\dfrac{dy}{dx}=\dfrac{\frac{dy}{dt}}{\frac{dx}{dt}}$. **NCERT Pg. 135**

Case or Paragraph Type Questions

Direction (Q. No. 1-4) Logarithmic differentiation allows us to differentiate functions of the form $f(x) = [u(x)]^{v(x)}$, where both $u(x)$ and $v(x)$ are differentiable functions and f and u need to be positive functions.

Let function $y = f(x) = (u(x))^{v(x)}$, then

$$y' = y\left[\frac{v(x)}{u(x)}u'(x) + v'(x)\log(u(x))\right].$$

On the basis of above information, answer the following questions. NCERT Pg. 134

1 if $x = e^{x/y}$, then find $\frac{dy}{dx}$.

(a) $\frac{x-y}{x\log x}$ (b) $\frac{x+y}{x\log x}$ (c) $\frac{x+y}{\log x}$ (d) $\frac{x-y}{\log x}$

2 If $y = (2-x)^3(3+2x)^5$, then find $\frac{dy}{dx}$.

(a) $\left[\frac{10}{(3-2x)} + \frac{3}{(2+x)}\right]y$

(b) $(2-x)^3(3+2x)^5\left[\frac{10}{3+2x} - \frac{3}{2-x}\right]$

(c) $\left[\frac{10}{(3-2x)} - \frac{3}{(2-x)}\right]y$

(d) $\left[\frac{10}{(3-2x)} + \frac{3}{(2-x)}\right]y$

3 Differentiate $(\sin x)^{\log x}$ w.r.t. x.

(a) $\frac{\log x(\cos x)}{x} + \tan x\log x$

(b) $\frac{\log(\sin x)}{x} + \tan x\log x$

(c) $\frac{\log(\cos x)}{x} + \cot x\log x$

(d) $(\sin x)\log x\left[\frac{\log(\sin x)}{x} + \cot x\log x\right]$

4 If $x^m y^n = (x+y)^{m+n}$, then find $\frac{dy}{dx}$.

(a) $\frac{-y}{x}$ (b) $\frac{-x}{y}$ (c) $\frac{y}{x}$ (d) $\frac{x}{y}$

Direction (Q. No. 5-8) Let $f : A \to B$ and $g : B \to C$ be two functions defined on non-empty sets A, B, C then $gof : A \to C$ is called the composition of f and g defined as $gof(x) = g(f(x)), \forall\, x \in A$.

Consider the functions $f(x) = \begin{cases} \sin x, & x \ge 0 \\ 1-\cos x, & x < 0 \end{cases}$, $g(x) = e^x$.

Based on the above information, answer the following questions. NCERT Pg. 121

5 If $x \ge 0$, then function $gof(x)$ is defined as

(a) $e^{(1-\cos x)}$ (b) $e^{\sin x}$ (c) $e^{-(1-\cos x)}$ (d) $e^{-\sin x}$

6 If $x < 0$, then $\frac{d}{dx}[gof(x)]$.

(a) $\sin x\, e^{1-\cos x}$ (b) $\cos x\, e^{1-\cos x}$

(c) $e^{\cos x - 1}$ (d) $\cos x\, e^{\cos x - 1}$

7 LHD of $gof(x)$ at $x = 0$ is

(a) 2 (b) –2 (c) 1 (d) –1

8 RHD of $gof(x)$ at $x = 0$ is

(a) 2 (b) $\frac{1}{2}$ (c) 1 (d) $\frac{3}{4}$

Past Years Questions

Single Correct Type

1 If $\sin y = x\sin(a+y)$, then $\frac{dy}{dx}$ is NCERT Pg. 145, CUET 2024

(a) $\frac{\sin^2 a}{\sin(a+y)}$ (b) $\frac{\sin(a+y)}{\sin^2 a}$

(c) $\frac{\sin(a+y)}{\sin a}$ (d) $\frac{\sin^2(a+y)}{\sin a}$

2 Let : $R \to R$ be a function given by

$$f(x) = \begin{cases} \frac{1-\cos 2x}{x^2}, & x<0 \\ \alpha, & x=0, \\ \frac{\beta\sqrt{1-\cos x}}{x}, & x>0 \end{cases}$$

where $\alpha, \beta \in R$. If f is continuous at $x=0$, then $\alpha^2+\beta^2$ is equal to NCERT Pg. 116, JEE Main 2024, 4 April Shift-I

(a) 3 (b) 12

(c) 48 (d) 6

3 Let $f(x) = [x^2 - x] + |-x + [x]|$, where $x \in R$ and $[t]$ denotes the greatest integer less than or equal to t. Then, f is NCERT Pg. 112, JEE Main 2023, 11 April Shift-I

(a) continuous at $x=0$ and $x=1$.

(b) continuous at $x=1$ but not continuous at $x=0$

(c) not continuous at $x=0$ and $x=1$.

(d) continuous at $x=0$ but not continuous at $x=1$.

4 Let $f:(-\infty,\infty)-\{0\} \to R$ be a differentiable function such that $f'(1) = \lim_{a\to\infty} a^2 f\left(\frac{1}{a}\right)$. Then,

$$\lim_{a\to\infty} \frac{a(a+1)}{2}\tan^{-1}\left(\frac{1}{a}\right) + a^2 - 2\log_e a$$

is equal to NCERT Pg. 144, JEE Main 2024, 6 April Shift-I

(a) $\frac{5}{2}+\frac{\pi}{8}$ (b) $\frac{3}{2}+\frac{\pi}{4}$

(c) $\frac{3}{4}+\frac{\pi}{8}$ (d) $\frac{3}{8}+\frac{\pi}{4}$

5 Let $[x]$ denote the greatest integer function. Then match List-I with List-II.

	List-I		List-II
A.	$\lvert x-1\rvert + \lvert x-2\rvert$	(i)	is differentiable everywhere except at $x=0$
B.	$x - \lvert x\rvert$	(ii)	is continuous everywhere
C.	$x-[x]$	(iii)	is not differentiable at $x=1$
D.	$x\lvert x\rvert$	(iv)	is differentiable at $x=1$

Choose the correct answer from the options given below : NCERT Pg. 118, CUET 2024

	A	B	C	D
(a)	(i)	(ii)	(iii)	(iv)
(b)	(i)	(iii)	(ii)	(iv)
(c)	(ii)	(i)	(iii)	(iv)
(d)	(ii)	(iv)	(iii)	(i)

6 Let $f: R-\{0\} \to R$ be a function satisfying $f\left(\frac{x}{y}\right) = \frac{f(x)}{f(y)}$ for all $x, y, f(y) = 0$. If $f'(1) = 2024$, then NCERT Pg. 144, JEE Main 2024, 30 Jan Shift-II

(a) $xf'(x) + f(x) = 2024$ (b) $xf'(x) - 2023f(x) = 0$

(c) $xf'(x) + 2024f(x) = 0$ (d) $xf'(x) - 2024f(x) = 0$

7 Let $f(x) = \frac{\sin x + \cos x - \sqrt{2}}{\sin x - \cos x}$, $x \in [0,\pi] - \left\{\frac{\pi}{4}\right\}$. Then, $f\left(\frac{7\pi}{12}\right)f''\left(\frac{7\pi}{12}\right)$ is equal to NCERT Pg. 144, JEE Main 2023, 8 April Shift-I

(a) $\frac{2}{9}$ (b) $\frac{-1}{3\sqrt{3}}$ (c) $\frac{-2}{3}$ (d) $\frac{2}{3\sqrt{3}}$

8 Let $y = f(x) = \sin^3\left(\frac{\pi}{3}\left(\cos\left(\frac{\pi}{3\sqrt{2}}(-4x^3+5x^2+1)^{\frac{3}{2}}\right)\right)\right)$.

Then, at $x=1$, NCERT Pg. 144, JEE Main 2023, 31 Jan Shift-I

(a) $2y' + 3\pi^2 y = 0$ (b) $2y' + \sqrt{3}\pi^2 y = 0$

(c) $y' + 3\pi^2 y = 0$ (d) $\sqrt{2}y' - 3\pi^2 y = 0$

9 If for $p \neq q \neq 0$, the function $f(x) = \frac{\sqrt[7]{p(729+x)}-3}{\sqrt[3]{729+qx}-9}$ is continuous at $x=0$, then NCERT Pg. 116, JEE Main 2022, 27 July Shift-II

(a) $7pq\,f(0) - 1 = 0$ (b) $63\,q\,f(0) - p^2 = 0$

(c) $21\,q\,f(0) - p^2 = 0$ (d) $7pq\,f(0) - 9 = 0$

10 If $f(x) = \begin{cases} x+a, & x \le 0 \\ |x-4|, & x>0 \end{cases}$ and

$g(x) = \begin{cases} x+1, & x<0 \\ (x-4)^2+b, & x \ge 0 \end{cases}$ are continuous on R, then

$(gof)(2) + (fog)(-2)$ is equal to NCERT Pg. 121, JEE Main 2022, 26 July Shift-I

(a) –10 (b) 10 (c) 8 (d) –8

11 If $f(x)$, defined by $f(x) = \begin{cases} kx+1, & \text{if } x \le \pi \\ \cos x, & \text{if } x > \pi \end{cases}$ is continuous at $x=\pi$, then the value of k is NCERT Pg. 118, CUET 2024

(a) 0 (b) π (c) $\frac{2}{\pi}$ (d) $-\frac{2}{\pi}$

12 For the differentiable function $f : R - \{0\} \to R$, let $3f(x) + 2f\left(\frac{1}{x}\right) = \frac{1}{x} - 10$, then $\left| f(3) + f'\left(\frac{1}{4}\right) \right|$ is equal to

NCERT Pg. 144, JEE Main 2023, 13 April Shift-I

(a) $\frac{33}{5}$ (b) $\frac{29}{5}$

(c) 7 (d) 13

Numerical Value Type

13 Let $[t]$ denote the greatest integer less than or equal to t. Let $f : [0, \infty] \to R$ be a function defined by $f(x) = \left[\frac{x}{2} + 3\right] - [\sqrt{x}]$. Let S be the set of all points in the interval $[0, 8]$ at which f is not continuous.

Then, $\sum_{a \in S} a$ is equal to .... NCERT Pg. 144 JEE Main 2024, 6 April Shift-II

14 If the function $f(x) = \begin{cases} \frac{1}{|x|}, & |x| \geq 2 \\ ax^2 + 2b, & |x| < 2 \end{cases}$ is differentiable on R, then $48(a + b)$ is equal to ....

NCERT Pg. 144 JEE Main 2024, 24 Jan Shift-I

15 Let $f(x) = \sum_{k=1}^{10} kx^k, x \in R$. If $2f(2) + f'(2) = 119(2)^n + 1$, then n is equal to ..... . NCERT Pg. 144 JEE Main 2023, 13 April Shift-II

16 For the curve $C : (x^2 + y^2 - 3) + (x^2 - y^2 - 1)^5 = 0$, the value of $3y' - y^3y''$, at the point (α, α), $\alpha > 0$, on C is equal to .... [2022, 27 July Shift-II]

Skill Boosters

1 Let $f(x) = x \cdot \left[\frac{x}{2}\right]$, for $-8 < x < 8$, where $[t]$ denotes greatest integer function. Then, the points discontinuity of f is equal to .... NCERT Pg. 117

(a) $\pm 2, \pm 4, \pm 6$ (b) ± 3

(c) $\pm 8, \pm 9$ (d) $\pm 10, \pm 11, \pm 12$

2 If the function f defined on $\left(\frac{-1}{4}, \frac{1}{4}\right)$ by $f(x) = \begin{cases} \frac{1}{x} \log_e \left(\frac{1+4x}{1-3x}\right), & x \neq 0 \\ k, & x = 0 \end{cases}$ is continuous, then k is equal to .... NCERT Pg. 116

(a) 8 (b) 7

(c) 12 (d) 14

3 The value of k for whcih the function $f(x) = \begin{cases} \left(\frac{2}{3}\right)^{\frac{\tan 2x}{\tan 3x}}, & 0 < x < \frac{\pi}{2} \\ k + \frac{3}{5}, & x = \frac{\pi}{2} \end{cases}$ is continuous at $x = \frac{\pi}{2}$, is .... NCERT Pg. 117

(a) $\frac{7}{8}$ (b) $\frac{5}{6}$

(c) $\frac{2}{5}$ (d) $\frac{8}{9}$

4 If $x = e^{y + e^{y + \dots \text{ to } \infty}}, x > 0$, then $\frac{dy}{dx}$ is .... NCERT Pg. 144

(a) $\frac{1-x}{x}$ (b) $\frac{x-1}{x^2}$

(c) $\frac{x^2}{1+x}$ (d) $\frac{x^3-1}{x-1}$

5 If $f(x + y) = f(x) \cdot f(y) \forall x, y$ and $f(5) = 3, f'(0) = 4$, then $f'(5)$ is .... NCERT Pg. 144

(a) 7 (b) 8

(c) 12 (d) 14

6 Let f and g be differentiable functions on R such that fog is the identify function. If for some $a, b \in R, g'(a) = 4$ and $g(a) = p$, then $f'(p)$ is equal to .... NCERT Pg. 121

(a) $\frac{1}{4}$ (b) $\frac{7}{8}$

(c) $\frac{2}{8}$ (d) $\frac{7}{15}$

Correct Codes

Topical Questions

Continuity

1 (c)	2 (d)	3 (b)	4 (a)	5 (c)	6 (d)	7 (a)	8 (a)	9 (a)	10 (c)
11 (a)	12 (c)	13 (c)	14 (b)	15 (d)	16 (c)	17 (d)	18 (d)	19 (d)	20 (c)
21 (a)	22 (d)	23 (c)	24 (a)	25 (d)	26 (b)	27 (a)	28 (a)	29 (b)	30 (c)
31 (a)	32 (c)	33 (c)	34 (b)	35 (b)	36 (b)	37 (c)	38 (b)	39 (a)	40 (a)
41 (c)	42 (b)	43 (d)	44 (d)	45 (a)	46 (b)	47 (c)	48 (b)	49 (c)	50 (c)
51 (c)	52 (d)	53 (d)	54 (d)	55 (b)	56 (b)	57 (a)	58 (c)		

Differentiability, Derivatives of Composite Functions, Derivatives of Implicit Functions and Derivatives of Inverse Trigonometric Functions

1 (b)	2 (c)	3 (a)	4 (d)	5 (a)	6 (d)	7 (c)	8 (b)	9 (b)	10 (c)
11 (b)	12 (a)	13 (a)	14 (a)	15 (b)	16 (b)	17 (c)	18 (b)	19 (b)	20 (c)
21 (a)	22 (d)	23 (b)	24 (a)	25 (a)	26 (c)	27 (b)	28 (b)	29 (b)	30 (b)
31 (d)	32 (c)	33 (d)	34 (b)						

Exponential and Logarithmic Functions

1 (a)	2 (d)	3 (b)	4 (b)	5 (c)	6 (a)	7 (b)	8 (d)	9 (c)	10 (a)
11 (c)	12 (c)	13 (a)	14 (c)	15 (c)	16 (a)	17 (b)	18 (c)	19 (a)	20 (b)
21 (d)	22 (b)	23 (c)	24 (b)	25 (b)	26 (d)	27 (d)	28 (d)	29 (b)	30 (c)
31 (d)									

Logarithmic Differentiation and Derivatives of Functions in Parametric Form

1 (c)	2 (a)	3 (a)	4 (a)	5 (d)	6 (b)	7 (a)	8 (b)	9 (a)	10 (b)
11 (a)	12 (b)	13 (c)	14 (c)	15 (b)	16 (c)	17 (a)	18 (a)	19 (a)	20 (b)
21 (a)	22 (a)	23 (d)	24 (a)	25 (b)	26 (a)	27 (c)	28 (b)	29 (d)	30 (c)
31 (a)	32 (a)	33 (b)	34 (b)	35 (c)	36 (c)				

Second Order Derivative

1 (a)	2 (a)	3 (b)	4 (c)	5 (a)	6 (c)	7 (b)	8 (a)	9 (a)

Miscellaneous Exercise

1 (a)	2 (a)	3 (a)	4 (c)	5 (b)	6 (c)	7 (a)	8 (a)	9 (a)	10 (a)
11 (b)	12 (a)	13 (c)	14 (a)	15 (b)					

Numerical Type Questions

1 (1.57)	2 (1)	3 (2)	4 (0)	5 (1)	6 (1)	7 (10)	8 (11)

Assertion and Reason Questions

1 (c)	2 (b)	3 (b)	4 (a)	5 (c)	6 (a)	7 (b)	8 (a)	9 (b)	10 (a)
11 (a)									

Case or Paragraph Type Questions

1 (a)	2 (b)	3 (d)	4 (c)	5 (b)	6 (a)	7 (c)	8 (c)

Past Years Questions

1 (d)	2 (b)	3 (b)	4 (a)	5 (c)	6 (d)	7 (a)	8 (a)	9 (b)	10 (d)
11 (d)	12 (d)	13 (17)	14 (15)	15 (10)	16 (16)				

Skill Boosters

1 (a)	2 (b)	3 (c)	4 (a)	5 (c)	6 (a)

Step by Step

Decoding the Questions

Concept Builders

1 (*False*)

$$\text{LHL} = \lim_{x\to 0^-} f(x) = \lim_{h\to 0} \frac{|-h|}{-h} = -1$$

$$\text{RHL} = \lim_{x\to 0^+} f(x) = \lim_{h\to 0} \frac{|h|}{h} = 1$$

Thus, $\lim_{x\to 0^-} f(x) \neq \lim_{x\to 0^+} f(x)$

Hence, $f(x)$ is not continuous at the origin.

2 (*False*)

$$f(x) = \begin{cases} 4x - x, & \text{if } x \geq 0 \\ 4x-(-x), & \text{if } x < 0 \end{cases}$$

$$= \begin{cases} 3x, & \text{if } x \geq 0 \\ 5x, & \text{if } x < 0 \end{cases}$$

$$\text{LHL} = \lim_{x\to 0^-} f(x) = \lim_{x\to 0^-} 5x = 0$$

$$\text{RHL} = \lim_{x\to 0^+} f(x) = \lim_{x\to 0^+} 3x = 0$$

$\therefore$ LHL = RHL

Hence, $f(x)$ is continuous at $x = 0$.

3 (*Integral*)

4 (*True*)

Since, $f(x)$ is continuous at $x = 0$.

$$\therefore \quad \lim_{x\to 0} f(x) = f(0)$$

$$\Rightarrow \quad \lim_{x\to 0} \frac{\sin 7x}{5x} = k$$

$$\Rightarrow \quad \frac{1}{5} \lim_{x\to 0} \frac{7\sin 7x}{7x} = k$$

$$\Rightarrow \quad \frac{7}{5} \lim \frac{\sin 7x}{7x} = k$$

$$\therefore \quad k = \frac{7}{5}$$

5 (*True*)

Since, $f(x)$ is continuous at $x = 0$.

$$\therefore \quad \lim_{x\to 0^-} f(x) = f(0)$$

$$\Rightarrow \quad \lim_{x\to 0^-} \frac{1-\cos 4kx}{x^2} = 8$$

$$\Rightarrow \lim_{h\to 0} \frac{1-\cos 4k(0-h)}{(0-h)^2} = 8$$

$$\Rightarrow \quad \lim_{h\to 0} \frac{1-\cos 4kh}{h^2} = 8$$

$$\Rightarrow \quad \lim_{h\to 0} \frac{8k^2 \sin^2 2kh}{(2kh)^2} = 8$$

$$\Rightarrow \quad k^2 = 1$$

$$\therefore \quad k = \pm 1$$

6 (*True*)

7 (*False*)

Let $x = \cot\theta$, then we get

$$y = \tan^{-1}(\operatorname{cosec}\theta - \cot\theta)$$

$$\Rightarrow y = \tan^{-1}\left(\frac{1-\cos\theta}{\sin\theta}\right)$$

$$= \tan^{-1}\left(\frac{2\sin^2\frac{\theta}{2}}{2\sin\frac{\theta}{2}\cos\frac{\theta}{2}}\right)$$

$$\Rightarrow \quad y = \tan^{-1}\left(\tan\frac{\theta}{2}\right)$$

$$= \frac{1}{2}\theta = \frac{1}{2}\cot^{-1} x$$

$$\therefore \quad \frac{dy}{dx} = \frac{1}{2}\left(-\frac{1}{1+x^2}\right) = -\frac{1}{2(1+x^2)}$$

8 (*True*)

Let $y = \sin^{-1}(e^{2x})$

$$\Rightarrow \frac{dy}{dx} = \frac{1}{\sqrt{1-(e^{2x})^2}} \cdot \frac{d}{dx}(e^{2x})$$

$$= \frac{2e^{2x}}{\sqrt{1-e^{4x^2}}}$$

9 (*False*)

Let $y = x^{\cos x}$, then $y = e^{\cos x \log x}$, then

$$\Rightarrow \quad \frac{dy}{dx} = e^{\cos x \log x} \frac{d}{dx}(\cos x \log x)$$

$$\Rightarrow \frac{dy}{dx} = x^{\cos x} \left(\log x(-\sin x) + \frac{\cos x}{x}\right)$$

$$= x^{\cos x}\left(\frac{\cos x}{x} - \sin x \log x\right)$$

10 (*True*)

Let $y = \log_5(\log x)$

$$\Rightarrow \quad y = \frac{\log(\log x)}{\log 5}$$

$$\Rightarrow \quad \frac{dy}{dx} = \frac{1}{\log 5}\left(\frac{1}{\log x}\frac{d}{dx}(\log x)\right)$$

$$\therefore \quad \frac{dy}{dx} = \frac{1}{\log 5\,(x \log x)}$$

11 (*True*)

$$y = x^4 + \tan x$$

$$\therefore \quad \frac{dy}{dx} = 4x^3 + \sec^2 x$$

$$\text{So,} \quad \frac{d^2y}{dx^2} = 12x^2 + 2\sec x \cdot \sec x \tan x$$

$$= 12x^2 + 2\sec^2 x \cdot \tan x$$

12 (*False*)

We have, $f(x) = |\log_e |x||$

$$= \begin{cases} -\log_e x, & 0 < x < 1 \\ \log_e x, & x > 1 \end{cases}$$

$$\text{LHD} = \lim_{x\to 1^-} \frac{-\log x - \log 1}{x-1} = -1$$

$$\text{RHD} = \lim_{x\to 1^+} \frac{\log x - \log 1}{x-1} = 1$$

$\therefore$ LHD $\neq$ RHD

Hence, $f(x)$ is not differentiable at $x = 1$.

Topical Questions

Continuity

1 (*c*) Using the definition of left and right hand limits, we may say that the left (respectively right) hand limit of f at 0 is 1 (respectively 2).

In particular the left and right hand limits do not coincide thus the limit of the function does not exist at $x = 0$.

2 (*d*)

(i) If we cannot draw the graph of a function in one stroke i.e. without lifting pen from the plane of the paper the function is said to be not continuous.

(ii) Infact, we need to lift the pen when we come to 0 from left of function $f(x)$. Thus, $f(x)$ is not continuous at $x = 0$.

3 (*b*) We may say that a function is continuous at a fixed point, if we can draw the graph of the function around that point without lifting the pen from the plane of the paper.

4 (*a*) This function is defined at every point. The left and right hand limits at $x = 0$ are both equal to 1. But the value of the function at $x = 0$ equals to 2 which does not coincide with the common value of the left and right hand limits. Again, we note that we cannot draw the graph of the function without lifting the pen. This is yet another instance of a function being not continuous at $x = 0$.

5 (*c*) Suppose f is a real function on a subset of the real numbers and let c be a point in the domain of f. Then, f is continuous at c, if

$$\lim_{x \to c} f(x) = f(c)$$

6 (*d*) If the left hand limit, right hand limit and the value of the function at $x = c$ exist and are equal to each other, then f is said to be continuous at $x = c$. If the right and left hand limits at $x = c$ coincide, then we say that the common value is the limit of the function at $x = c$. Also, if left and right hand limits at $x = c$ coincide and their common value is not equal to value of function at $x = c$, then $f(x)$ is not continuous at $x = c$.

7 (*a*) A real function f is said to be continuous, if it is continuous at every point in the domain of f.

8 (*a*) A function defined on a closed interval $[a, b]$, then for f to be continuous, it needs to be continuous at every point in $[a, b]$ including the end points a and b.

Continuity of f at point a means

$$\lim_{x \to a^+} f(x) = f(a)$$

and continuity of f at point b means

$$\lim_{x \to b^-} f(x) = f(b)$$

Observe that $\lim_{x \to a^-} f(x)$ and $\lim_{x \to b^+} f(x)$ do not make sense.

9 (*a*) If f is defined only at one point, it is continuous there i.e. if the domain of f is a singleton set, f is a continuous function.

10 (*c*) First note that the function is defined at the given point, $x = 1$ and its value is 5.

Then, find the limit of the function at $x = 1$.

Clearly,

$$\lim_{x \to 1} f(x) = \lim_{x \to 1} (2x + 3) = 2(1) + 3 = 5$$

Thus, $\lim_{x \to 1} f(x) = 5 = f(1)$

Hence, f is continuous at $x = 1$.

11 (*a*) First note that the function is defined at the given point $x = 0$ and its value is 0.

Then, find the limit of the function at $x = 0$. Clearly,

$$\lim_{x \to 0} f(x) = \lim_{x \to 0} x^2 = 0^2 = 0$$

Thus, $\lim_{x \to 0} f(x) = 0 = f(0)$

Hence, f is continuous at $x = 0$.

12 (*c*) Recall that a function $p(x)$ is a polynomial function if it is defined by $p(x) = a_0 + a_1 x + \dots + a_n x^n$ for some natural number n, $a_n \neq 0$ and $a_i \in R$. Clearly, this function is defined for every real number. For a fixed real number c, we have

$$\lim_{x \to c} p(x) = p(c)$$

By definition, p is continuous at c. Since, c is any real number, p is continuous at every real number and hence p is a continuous function.

For $f(x) = [x]$, first observe that f is defined for all real numbers. Graph of the function is given in figure. From the graph it looks like that f is discontinuous at every integral point. Below we explore, if this is true.

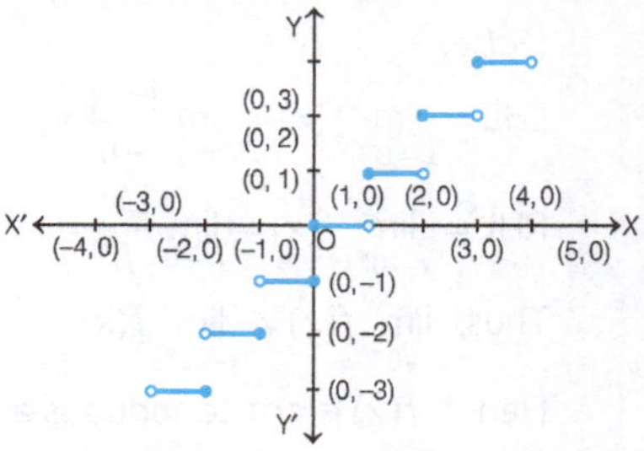

Case I Let c be a real number which is not equal to any integer. It is evident from the graph that for all real numbers *close* to c the value of the function is equal to $[c]$ i.e. $\lim_{x \to c} f(x) = \lim_{x \to c} [x] = [c]$ and hence the function is continuous at all real numbers not equal to integers.

Case II Let c be an integer. Then, we can find a sufficiently small real number $r > 0$ such that $[c - r] = c - 1$ whereas $[c + r] = c$.

This, in terms of limits, we have

$$\lim_{x \to c^-} f(x) = c - 1, \quad \lim_{x \to c^+} f(x) = c$$

Since, these limits cannot be equal to each other for any c, the function is discontinuous at every integral point.

13 (*c*) Continuity of a function at a point is dictated by the limit and value of the function at that point.

14 (*b*)

(i) For $f(x) = |x|$

We may rewrite f as

$$f(x) = \begin{cases} -x, & \text{if } x < 0 \\ x, & \text{if } x \geq 0 \end{cases}$$

Here, $f(0) = 0$

$$\lim_{x \to 0^-} f(x) = \lim_{x \to 0^-} (-x) = 0$$

$$\lim_{x \to 0^+} f(x) = \lim_{x \to 0^+} (x) = 0$$

$$\therefore \lim_{x \to 0^-} f(x) = \lim_{x \to 0^+} f(x) = f(0)$$

Thus, f is continuous at $x = 0$.

Case I Let c be a real number such that $c < 0$. Then, $f(c) = -c$.

Also,
$$\lim_{x \to c} f(x) = \lim_{x \to c}(-x) = -c$$

Since, $\lim_{x \to c} f(x) = f(c)$.

f is continuous at all negative real numbers.

Case II

Now, let c be a real number such that $c > 0$.

Then, $f(c) = c$.

Also, $\lim_{x \to c} f(x) = \lim_{x \to c} x = c$

Since, $\lim_{x \to c} f(x) = f(c)$, f is continuous at all positive real numbers. Hence, f is continuous at all points.

(ii) $f(x) = x^3 + x^2 - 1$

Clearly, f is defined at every real number c and its value at c is $c^3 + c^2 - 1$. We also know that
$$\lim_{x \to c} f(x) = \lim_{x \to c}(x^3 + x^2 - 1)$$
$$= c^3 + c^2 - 1$$

Thus, $\lim_{x \to c} f(x) = f(c)$, and hence

f is continuous at every real number. This means f is a continuous function.

(iii) $f(x) = \dfrac{1}{x}$

Fix any non-zero real number c, we have
$$\lim_{x \to c} f(x) = \lim_{x \to c} \frac{1}{x} = \frac{1}{c}$$

Also, since for $c \neq 0$, $f(c) = \dfrac{1}{c}$.

We have $\lim_{x \to c} f(x) = f(c)$ and hence, f is continuous at every point in the domain of f. Thus, f is a continuous function.

15 (*d*) To analyse the function $f(x) = \dfrac{1}{x}$ near $x = 0$. We follow the usual trick of finding the value of the function at real numbers close to 0. Essentially we are trying to find the right hand limit of f at 0. We tabulate this in the following table.

Table I

x	1	0.3	0.2	0.1 $= 10^{-1}$	0.01 $= 10^{-2}$	0.001 $= 10^{-3}$	10^{-n}
$f(x)$	1	3.333	5	10	100 $= 10^2$	1000 $= 10^3$	10^n

We observe that as x gets closer to 0 from the right, the value of $f(x)$ shoots up higher. This may be rephrased as the value of $f(x)$ may be made larger than any given number by choosing a positive real number very close to 0.

In symbols, we write
$$\lim_{x \to 0^+} f(x) = +\infty$$

(to be read as the right hand limit of $f(x)$ at 0 is plus infinity). We wish to emphasise that $+\infty$ is not a real number and hence the right hand limit of f at 0 does not exist (as a real number).

Similarly, the left hand limit of f at 0 may be found. The following table is self explanatory.

Table II

x	-1	-0.3	-0.2	-10^{-1}	-10^{-2}	-10^{-3}	-10^{-n}
$f(x)$	-1	$-3.333\ldots$	-5	-10	-10^2	-10^3	-10^n

From the Table II, we deduce that the value of $f(x)$ may be made smaller than any given number by choosing a negative real number very close to 0. In symbols, we write
$$\lim_{x \to 0^-} f(x) = -\infty$$

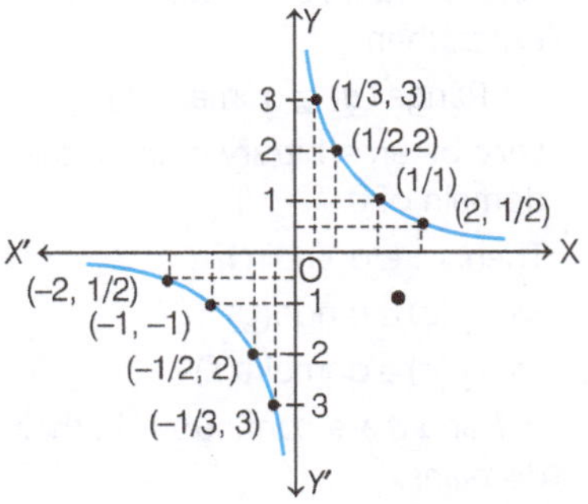

(to be read as the left hand limit of $f(x)$ at 0 is $-\infty$). Again, we wish to emphasise that $-\infty$ is not a real number and hence the left hand limit of f at 0 does not exist (as a real number). The graph of the reciprocal function given in figure is a geometric representation of the above mentioned facts.

16 (*c*)

I. We are investigating continuity of $(f + g)$ at $x = c$. Clearly, it is defined at $x = c$. We have
$$\lim_{x \to c}(f + g)(x) = \lim_{x \to c}[f(x) + g(x)]$$
[by definition of $f + g$]
$$= \lim_{x \to c} f(x) + \lim_{x \to c} g(x)$$
[by the theorem on limits]
$$= f(c) + g(c)$$
[as f and g are continuous]
$$= (f + g)(c)$$
[by definition of $f + g$]

Hence, $f + g$ is continuous at $x = c$.

II. We have,
$$\lim_{x \to c}(f - g)x = \lim_{x \to c}[f(x) - g(x)]$$
$$= \lim_{x \to c} f(x) - \lim_{x \to c} g(x) = f(c) - g(c)$$
$$\Rightarrow \lim_{x \to c}(f - g)x = (f - g)(c)$$

$\therefore$ $f - g$ is continuous at $x = c$.

III. We have,
$$\lim_{x \to c}(f \cdot g)(x) = \lim_{x \to c}\{f(x) \cdot g(x)\}$$
$$= \lim_{x \to c} f(x) \cdot \lim_{x \to c} g(x) = f(c) \cdot g(c)$$

$\therefore$ $f \cdot g$ is continuous $x = c$.

IV. $$\lim_{x \to c} \frac{f}{g}(x) = \lim_{x \to c}\left(\frac{f}{g}\right)(x)$$
$$= \lim_{x \to c}\left\{\frac{f(x)}{g(x)}\right\}$$
$$= \frac{\lim_{x \to c} f(x)}{\lim_{x \to c} g(x)}$$
$$= \frac{f(c)}{g(c)} = \frac{f}{g}(c)$$

$\therefore$ $\left(\dfrac{f}{g}\right)$ is continuous at $x = c$ provided $g(c) \neq 0$.

17 (*d*)

(i) Recall that every rational function f is given by

$$f(x)=\frac{p(x)}{q(x)},\ q(x)\neq 0,$$

where p and q are polynomial functions. The domain of f is all real numbers except those points at which q is zero. Since, polynomial functions are continuous, f is continuous.

(ii) To see this, we use the following facts.

$$\lim_{x\to 0}\sin x=0$$

We have not proved it, but is intuitively clear from the graph of $\sin x$ near 0.

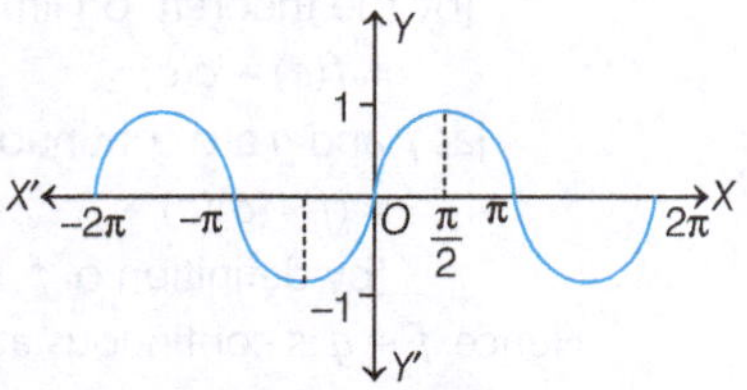

Now, observe that $f(x)=\sin x$ is defined for every real number.

Let c be a real number.

Put $x=c+h$.

If $x\to c$ we know that $h\to 0$.

Therefore,

$$\lim_{x\to c} f(x)=\lim_{x\to c}\sin x$$

$$=\lim_{h\to 0}\sin(c+h)$$

$$=\lim_{h\to 0}(\sin c\cos h+\cos c\sin h)$$

$$=\lim_{h\to 0}(\sin c\cos h)+\lim_{h\to 0}(\cos c\sin h)$$

$$=\sin c+0=\sin c=f(c)$$

Thus, $\lim_{x\to c} f(x)=f(c)$ and hence f is a continuous function.

(iii) Let $f(x)=\cos x$ and let c be any real number.

Then, $\lim_{x\to c^+} f(x)=\lim_{h\to 0} f(c+h)$

$\Rightarrow \quad \lim_{x\to c^+} f(x)=\lim_{h\to 0}\cos(c+h)$

$\Rightarrow \quad \lim_{x\to c^+} f(x)=\lim_{h\to 0}(\cos c\cos h-\sin c\sin h)$

$\Rightarrow \lim_{x\to c^+} f(x)=\cos c\lim_{h\to 0}\cos h-\sin c\lim_{h\to 0}\sin h$

$$=\cos c\times 1-\sin c\times 0$$

$$\lim_{x\to c^+} f(x)=\cos c$$

$$\left[\because \lim_{h\to 0}\cos h=1 \text{ and } \lim_{h\to 0}\sin h=0\right]$$

Similarly, we have

$$\lim_{x\to c^-} f(x)=f(c)$$

$$\therefore \lim_{x\to c^-} f(x)=\lim_{x\to c^+} f(x)=f(c)$$

$f(x)$ is continuous at $x=c$.

$\because c$ is arbitrary real number, so $f(x)$ is everywhere continuous.

(iv) Let $f(x)=\tan x$

Clearly, domain of f

$$=R-\left\{(2n+1)\frac{\pi}{2},\ n\in Z\right\}$$

We have,

$$f(x)=\tan x=\frac{\sin x}{\cos x}$$

$\because \sin x$ and $\cos x$ are everywhere continuous.

Therefore, $f(x)=\tan x$ is continuous for all $x\in R$ such that $\cos x\neq 0$.

But $\cos x\neq 0$.

$$\Rightarrow \qquad x\neq(2n+1)\frac{\pi}{2},\ n\in Z$$

Hence, $f(x)=\tan x$ is continuous for all

$$x\in R-\left\{(2n+1)\frac{\pi}{2},\ n\in Z\right\}.$$

18 (*d*) Suppose, f and g are real valued functions such that (fog) is defined at c. If g is continuous at c and if f is continuous at $g(c)$, then (fog) is continuous at c.

Because if f and g are two real valued functions such that fog exists, then

Range $(g)\subseteq$ domain (f)

Let c be an arbitrary point in the domain of g.

Then, $c\in$ domain g

$\Rightarrow \quad g(c)\in \text{range}(g)$

$\Rightarrow \quad g(c)\in \text{domain}(f)$

$\because f$ and g are continuous in their domains.

$\therefore\ c\in$ domain g and $g(c)\in$ domain (f)

g is continuous at $x=c$ and f is continuous at $g(c)$.

$\Rightarrow \qquad \lim_{x\to c} g(x)=g(c)$

and $\qquad \lim_{y\to g(c)} f(y)=f[g(c)]$

$\Rightarrow \qquad \lim_{x\to c} g(x)=g(c)$

and $\qquad \lim_{g(x)\to g(c)} f[g(x)]=f[g(c)]$

where, $\qquad y=g(x)$

$\Rightarrow \qquad \lim_{x\to c} f[g(x)=f[g(c)]$

$[\because x\to c\Rightarrow g(x)\to g(c)]$

$\Rightarrow \qquad \lim_{x\to c} fog(x)=fog(c)$

$\Rightarrow fog$ is continuous at $x=c$.

$\because c$ is an arbitrary point in its domain.

Hence, fog is continuous.

19 (*d*) Here, $f(x)=5x-3$

At $x=0$, $\lim_{x\to 0} f(x)=\lim_{x\to 0}(5x-3)$

$$=5\times 0-3=0-3=-3$$

$f(0)=5\times 0-3=-3$

$\therefore \qquad \lim_{x\to 0} f(x)=f(0)$

Thus, $f(x)$ is continuous at $x=0$.

At $x=-3$,

$$\lim_{x\to -3} f(x)=\lim_{x\to -3}(5x-3)$$

$$=5\times(-3)-3$$

$$=-15-3=-18$$

and $\quad f(-3)=5\times -3-3=-18$

$\therefore \quad \lim_{x\to -3} f(x)=f(-3).$

Thus, $f(x)$ is continuous at $x=-3$.

At $x=5$,

$$\lim_{x\to 5} f(x)=\lim_{x\to 5}(5x-3)$$

$$=5\times 5-3=25-3=22$$

and $f(5)=5\times 5-3=25-3=22$

$\therefore \qquad \lim_{x\to 5} f(x)=f(5)$

Thus, $f(x)$ is continuous at $x=5$.

20 (c) A. Here, $f(x)=2x^2-1$

$\therefore \qquad \lim_{x\to 3} f(x)=\lim_{x\to 3}(2x^2-1)$

$$=2\times(3)^2-1=18-1=17$$

$f(3)=2\times(3)^2-1=18-1=17$

$\therefore \lim_{x\to 3} f(x)=f(3).$

Thus, $f(x)$ is continuous at $x=3$.

B. $f(x) = x - 5$ is a polynomial function, so $f(x)$ is continuous for all values of x.

C. $f(x) = \dfrac{1}{x-5}$ is a rational function of two polynomial functions, so $f(x)$ is continuous for all values of x provided $x \neq 5$.

D. $f(x) = \dfrac{x^2 - 25}{x+5}$

$$= \frac{(x+5)(x-5)}{x+5} = x - 5$$

$\therefore f(x) = x - 5$ is a polynomial function, so $f(x)$ is continuous at all values of x in domain of $f(x)$.

E. $f(x) = |x - 5|$

$$= \begin{cases} x - 5, & \text{for } x \geq 5 \\ 5 - x, & \text{for } x < 5 \end{cases}$$

For $x \to 5^+$,

$$\lim_{x\to 5^+} f(x) = \lim_{x\to 5^+} (x-5) = 5 - 5 = 0$$

For $x \to 5^-$,

$$\lim_{x\to 5^-} f(x) = \lim_{x\to 5^-} (5-x) = 5 - 5 = 0$$

Also, $f(5) = 5 - 5 = 0$

$\because$ LHL = RHL = $f(5)$

Therefore, the function is continuous at $x = 5$.

21 (*a*) Here, $f(x) = x^n$

$\therefore \lim_{x\to n} f(x) = \lim_{x\to n} x^n = n^n$

and $f(n) = n^n$ $[\because f(x) = x^n]$

$\therefore \lim_{x\to n} f(x) = f(n) = n^n$

Thus, $f(x)$ is continuous at $x = n$, where n is a positive integer.

22 (*d*) Here, $f(x) = \begin{cases} x, \text{if } x \leq 1 \\ 5, \text{if } x > 1 \end{cases}$

At $x = 0$,

LHL $= \lim_{x\to 0^-} f(x) = \lim_{x\to 0^-} (x)$

Putting $x = 0 - h$ as $x \to 0$, $h \to 0$

LHL $= \lim_{h\to 0} (0 - h) = 0 - 0 = 0$

RHL $= \lim_{x\to 0^+} f(x) = \lim_{x\to 0^+} (x)$

Putting $x = 0 + h$ as $x \to 0$, $h \to 0$

RHL $= \lim_{h\to 0} (0 + h) = 0 + 0 = 0$

Also, $f(0) = 0$ $[\because f(x) = x]$

$\therefore$ LHL = RHL = $f(0)$

Thus, $f(x)$ is continuous at $x = 0$.

At $x = 1$,

LHL $= \lim_{x\to 1^-} f(x) = \lim_{x\to 1^-} (x)$

Putting $x = 1 - h$ as $x \to 1^-$, $h \to 0$

LHL $= \lim_{h\to 0} (1 - h) = 1 - 0 = 1$

RHL $= \lim_{x\to 1^+} f(x) = 5$

$\therefore$ LHL $\neq$ RHL

Thus, $f(x)$ is discontinuous at $x = 1$.

At $x = 2$, $\lim_{x\to 2^+} f(x) = \lim_{x\to 2^-} f(x) = 5$

Also, $f(2) = 5$

$\therefore$ LHL = RHL = $f(2)$

Thus, $f(x)$ is continuous at $x = 2$.

23 (*c*) Here, $f(x) = \begin{cases} 2x + 3, \text{if } x \leq 2 \\ 2x - 3, \text{if } x > 2 \end{cases}$

LHL $= \lim_{x\to 2^-} f(x) = \lim_{x\to 2^-} (2x + 3)$

Putting $x = 2 - h$ as $x \to 2^-$ when $h \to 0$

$\therefore \lim_{h\to 0} [2(2-h) + 3] = \lim_{h\to 0} (7 - 2h) = 7 - 2 \times 0 = 7$

RHL $= \lim_{x\to 2^+} f(x) = \lim_{x\to 2^+} (2x - 3)$

Putting $x = 2 + h$ as $x \to 2^+$ when $h \to 0$

$\therefore \lim_{h\to 0} [2(2+h) - 3] = \lim_{h\to 0} (1 + 2h) = 1 + 2 \times 0 = 1$

$\therefore$ LHL $\neq$ RHL

Thus, $f(x)$ is discontinuous at $x = 2$.

24 (*a*) Here,

$$f(x) = \begin{cases} |x| + 3, \text{if } & x \leq -3 \\ -2x, \text{if } & -3 < x < 3 \\ 6x + 2, \text{if } & x \geq 3 \end{cases}$$

For $x < -3$, $f(x) = |x| + 3$; sum of modulus and constant function, thus continuous.

For $-3 < x < 3$, $f(x) = -2x$

and for $x > 3$,

$f(x) = 6x + 2$

is a polynomial function, so it is continuous in a given interval. So, we have to check the continuity only at $x = -3$ and 3.

At $x = -3$,

LHL $= \lim_{x\to -3^-} f(x) = \lim_{x\to -3^-} (|x| + 3)$

Putting $x = (-3 - h)$, as $x \to -3^-$, $h \to 0$

$\lim_{h\to 0} [|-3 - h| + 3] = \lim_{h\to 0} [6 + h] = 6 + 0 = 6$

$\therefore$ RHL $= \lim_{x\to -3^+} f(x) = \lim_{x\to -3^+} (-2x)$

Putting $x = -3 + h$ as $x \to -3^+$ when $h \to 0$

$\lim_{h\to 0} -2(-3 + h) = \lim_{h\to 0} (6 - 2h) = 6 - 2 \times 0 = 6$

Also, $f(-3) = |-3| + 3 = 3 + 3 = 6$ $[\because f(x) = |x| + 3]$

$\therefore$ LHL = RHL = $f(-3)$

Thus, $f(x)$ is continuous at $x = -3$.

At $x = 3$,

LHL $= \lim_{x\to 3^-} f(x) = \lim_{x\to 3^-} (-2x)$

Putting $x = 3 - h$, as $x \to 3^-$, $h \to 0$

LHL $= \lim_{h\to 0} -2(3 - h) = \lim_{h\to 0} (-6 + 2h) = -6 + 2 \times 0 = -6$

RHL $= \lim_{x\to 3^+} f(x) = \lim_{x\to 3^+} (6x + 2)$

Putting $x = 3 + h$, as $x \to 3^+$, $h \to 0$

$\lim_{h\to 0} [6(3 + h) + 2] = \lim_{h\to 0} (18 + 6h + 2)$

$= \lim_{h\to 0} (20 + 6h) = 20 + 6 \times 0 = 20$

$\therefore$ LHL $\neq$ RHL

Thus, $f(x)$ is discontinuous at $x = 3$.

25 (*d*) A. Here, $f(x) = \begin{cases} \dfrac{|x|}{x}, & \text{if } x \neq 0 \\ 0, & \text{if } x = 0 \end{cases}$

LHL $= \lim_{x\to 0^-} f(x) = \lim_{x\to 0^-} \dfrac{|x|}{x}$

Putting $x = 0 - h$, as $x \to 0^-$, $h \to 0$

$\therefore \lim_{h\to 0} \dfrac{|0 - h|}{0 - h} = \lim_{h\to 0} \dfrac{h}{-h} = -1$ $[\because |-h| = h]$

RHL $= \lim_{x\to 0^+} f(x) = \lim_{x\to 0^+} \dfrac{|x|}{x}$

Putting $x = 0 + h$ as $x \to 0^+$, $h \to 0$

$\therefore \lim_{h\to 0} \frac{|0+h|}{0+h} = \lim_{h\to 0} \frac{h}{h} = 1$

$\therefore$ LHL $\neq$ RHL.

Thus, $f(x)$ is discontinuous at $x = 0$.

B. Here, $f(x) = \begin{cases} \frac{x}{|x|}, \text{if } x < 0 \\ -1, \text{ if } x \geq 0 \end{cases}$

LHL $= \lim_{x\to 0^-} f(x) = \lim_{x\to 0^-} \frac{x}{|x|}$

Putting $x = 0 - h$ as $x \to 0^-$, when $h \to 0$

$\therefore \lim_{h\to 0} \frac{0-h}{|0-h|} = \lim_{h\to 0} \frac{-h}{h} = -1$ $[\because |-h| = h]$

RHL $= \lim_{x\to 0^+} f(x) = -1$

Also, $f(0) = -1$

$\therefore$ LHL = RHL = $f(0)$

Thus, $f(x)$ is continuous at $x = 0$.

C. Here,

$f(x) = \begin{cases} x+1, \text{ if } x \geq 1 \\ x^2+1, \text{if } x < 1 \end{cases}$

For $x > 1$, $f(x) = x + 1$ and for $x < 1$, $f(x) = x^2 + 1$ is a polynomial function, so $f(x)$ is a continuous in the given interval. Therefore, we have to check the continuity at $x = 1$.

LHL $= \lim_{x\to 1^-} f(x) = \lim_{x\to 1^-} (x^2+1)$

Putting $x = 1 - h$ as $x \to 1^-$, when $h \to 0$

$\therefore \lim_{h\to 0} [(1-h)^2 + 1]$

$= \lim_{h\to 0} [1 + h^2 - 2h + 1]$

$= \lim_{h\to 0} [2 + h^2 - 2h]$

$= 2 + 0 - 0 = 2$

RHL $= \lim_{x\to 1^+} f(x) = \lim_{x\to 1^+} (x+1)$

Putting $x = 1 + h$ as $x \to 1^+$, when $h \to 0$

$\therefore \lim_{h\to 0} (1 + h + 1) = \lim_{h\to 0} (2 + h)$

$= 2 + 0 = 2$

Also, $f(1) = 1 + 1 = 2$ $[\because f(x) = x + 1]$

$\therefore$ LHL = RHL = $f(1)$

Thus, $f(x)$ is continuous at $x = 1$.

D. Here,

$f(x) = \begin{cases} x^3 - 3, \text{if } x \leq 2 \\ x^2 + 1, \text{if } x > 2 \end{cases}$

For $x < 2$, $f(x) = x^3 - 3$ and for $x > 2$, $f(x) = x^2 + 1$ is a polynomial function, so f is continuous in the above interval. Therefore, we have to check the continuity at $x = 2$.

LHL $= \lim_{x\to 2^-} f(x) = \lim_{x\to 2^-} (x^3 - 3)$

Putting $x = 2 - h$ as $x \to 2^-$, when $h \to 0$

$\therefore \lim_{h\to 0} [(2-h)^3 - 3]$

$= \lim_{h\to 0} (8 - h^3 - 12h + 6h^2 - 3)$

$= \lim_{h\to 0} (5 - h^3 - 12h + 6h^2) = 5$

RHL $= \lim_{x\to 2^+} f(x) = \lim_{x\to 2^+} (x^2+1)$

Putting $x = 2 + h$ as $x \to 2^+$, when $h \to 0$

$\therefore \lim_{h\to 0} [(2+h)^2 + 1]$

$= \lim_{h\to 0} (4 + h^2 + 4h + 1)$

$= \lim_{h\to 0} (5 + h^2 + 4h) = 5$

Also, $f(2) = (2)^3 - 3$

$= 8 - 3 = 5$ $[\because f(x) = x^3 - 3]$

$\therefore$ LHL = RHL = $f(2)$

Thus, $f(x)$ is continuous at $x = 2$.

E. Here, $f(x) = \begin{cases} x^{10} - 1, \text{if } x \leq 1 \\ x^2, \quad \text{if } x > 1 \end{cases}$

For $x < 1$, $f(x) = x^{10} - 1$ and $x > 1$, $f(x) = x^2$ is a polynomial function, so f is continuous in the above interval. Therefore, we have to check the continuity at $x = 1$.

LHL $= \lim_{x\to 1^-} f(x) = \lim_{x\to 1^-} (x^{10} - 1)$

Putting $x = 1 - h$ as $x \to 1^-$, when $h \to 0$

$\therefore \lim_{h\to 0} [(1-h)^{10} - 1]$

$= (1-0)^{10} - 1 = 1 - 1 = 0$

RHL $= \lim_{x\to 1^+} f(x) = \lim_{x\to 1^+} (x^2)$

Putting $x = 1 + h$ as $x \to 1^+$, $h \to 0$

$\therefore \lim_{h\to 0} (1+h)^2$

$= \lim_{h\to 0} (1 + h^2 + 2h) = 1$

$\therefore$ LHL $\neq$ RHL

Thus, $f(x)$ is discontinuous at $x = 1$.

26 (*b*) Here, $f(x) = \begin{cases} x+5, \text{if } x \leq 1 \\ x-5, \text{if } x > 1 \end{cases}$

LHL $= \lim_{x\to 1^-} f(x) = \lim_{x\to 1^-} (x+5)$

Putting $x = 1 - h$ as $x \to 1^-$, $h \to 0$

$\therefore \lim_{h\to 0} [1 - h + 5] = \lim_{h\to 0} (6 - h)$

$= 6 - 0 = 6$

RHL $= \lim_{x\to 1^+} f(x) = \lim_{x\to 1^+} (x-5)$

Putting $x = 1 + h$ as $x \to 1^+$ when $h \to 0$

$\therefore \lim_{h\to 0} (1 + h - 5) = \lim_{h\to 0} (h - 4)$

$= 0 - 4 = -4$

$\therefore$ LHL $\neq$ RHL

Thus, $f(x)$ is not continuous at $x = 1$.

27 (*a*) Here, $f(x) = \begin{cases} 3, \text{if } 0 \leq x \leq 1 \\ 4, \text{if } 1 < x < 3 \\ 5, \text{if } 3 \leq x \leq 10 \end{cases}$

For $0 \leq x \leq 1$, $f(x) = 3$; $1 < x < 3$; $f(x) = 4$ and $3 \leq x \leq 10$, $f(x) = 5$ are constant functions, so it is continuous in the above interval. So we have to check the continuity at $x = 1$ and 3.

At $x = 1$,

LHL $= \lim_{x\to 1^-} f(x) = \lim_{x\to 1^-} (3) = 3$,

RHL $= \lim_{x\to 1^+} f(x) = \lim_{x\to 1^+} (4) = 4$

$\therefore$ LHL $\neq$ RHL

Thus, $f(x)$ is discontinuous at $x = 1$.

At $x = 3$,

LHL $= \lim_{x\to 3^-} f(x) = \lim_{x\to 3^-} (4) = 4$,

RHL $= \lim_{x\to 3^+} f(x) = \lim_{x\to 3^+} (5) = 5$

$\therefore$ LHL $\neq$ RHL

Thus, $f(x)$ is continuous everywhere except at $x = 1, 3$.

28 (a) Here, $f(x)=\begin{cases} ax+1, \text{if } x\le 3 \\ bx+3, \text{if } x>3 \end{cases}$

LHL $= \lim_{x\to 3^-} f(x) = \lim_{x\to 3^-} (ax+1)$

Putting $x=3-h$ as $x\to 3^-$, $h\to 0$

$\therefore \lim_{h\to 0} [a(3-h)+1]$

$= \lim_{h\to 0} (3a-ah+1) = 3a+1$

RHL $= \lim_{x\to 3^+} f(x) = \lim_{x\to 3^+} (bx+3)$

Putting $x=3+h$ as $x\to 3^+$, $h\to 0$

$\therefore \lim_{h\to 0} [b(3+h)+3]$

$= \lim_{h\to 0} (3b+bh+3) = 3b+3$

Also, $f(3)=3a+1$ $[\because f(x)=ax+1]$

Since, $f(x)$ is continuous at $x=3$.

$\therefore$ LHL = RHL = $f(3)$

$\Rightarrow 3a+1=3b+3$

$\Rightarrow 3a=3b+2 \Rightarrow a=b+\frac{2}{3}$

29 (b) Here,

$f(x)=\begin{cases} \lambda(x^2-2x), \text{if } x\le 0 \\ 4x+1, \quad \text{if } x>0 \end{cases}$

At $x=0$,

LHL $= \lim_{x\to 0^-} f(x) = \lim_{x\to 0^-} \lambda(x^2-2x)$

Putting $x=0-h$ as $x\to 0^-$, when $h\to 0$.

$\therefore \lim_{h\to 0} \lambda[(0-h)^2-2(0-h)]$

$= \lim_{h\to 0} [\lambda(h^2+2h)] = 0$

RHL $= \lim_{x\to 0^+} f(x) = \lim_{x\to 0^+} (4x+1)$

Putting $x=0+h$ as $x\to 0^+$, when $h\to 0$.

$\therefore \lim_{h\to 0} [4(0+h)+1] = \lim_{h\to 0} [4h+1]$

$=0+1=1$

$\therefore$ LHL $\neq$ RHL

Thus, $f(x)$ is not continuous at $x=0$ for any value of λ.

At $x=1$,

LHL $= \lim_{x\to 1^-} f(x)$

$= \lim_{x\to 1^-} (4x+1)$

Putting $x=1-h$ as $x\to 1^-$, when $h\to 0$.

$\therefore \lim_{h\to 0} [4(1-h)+1] = \lim_{h\to 0} [5-4h]$

$=5-0=5$

RHL $= \lim_{x\to 1^+} f(x) = \lim_{x\to 1^+} (4x+1)$

Putting $x=1+h$ as $x\to 1^+$, when $h\to 0$.

$\therefore \lim_{h\to 0} [4(1+h)+1] = \lim_{h\to 0} (5+4h)$

$=5+0=5$

Also, $f(1)=4\times 1+1=5$

$[\because f(x)=4x+1]$

Thus, $f(x)$ is continuous at $x=1$ for all values of λ.

30 (c) Here, $g(x)=x-[x]$.

Let a be an integer. Then, $[a-h]=a-1$, $[a+h]=a$ and $[a]=a$ for $h\to D$.

At $x=a$,

LHL $= \lim_{x\to a^-} g(x) = \lim_{x\to a^-} (x-[x])$

Putting $x=a-h$, as $x\to a^-$, $h\to 0$.

$\therefore \lim_{h\to 0} (a-h-[a-h])$

$= \lim_{h\to 0} (a-h-(a-1))$

$= \lim_{h\to 0} (-h+1)=1$

$[\because [a-h]=a-1]$

RHL $= \lim_{x\to a^+} g(x) = \lim_{x\to a^+} (x-[x])$

Putting $x=a+h$ as $x\to a^+$, when $h\to 0$.

$\lim_{h\to 0} (a+h-[a+h])$

$= \lim_{h\to 0} (a+h-a)$

$= \lim_{h\to 0} h=0$ $[\because [a+h]=a]$

$\therefore$ LHL $\neq$ RHL

Thus, $g(x)$ is discontinuous at all integral points.

31 (a) Since, $f(x)$ is a sum of a polynomial function (x^2-5) and $\sin x$, both of which are continuous functions everywhere. Thus, $f(x)$ is continuous everywhere.

32 (c)

A. Here, $f(x)=\cos x$.

At $x=a$, where $a\in R$,

$\lim_{x\to a} f(x) = \lim_{x\to a} \cos x = \cos a$

$[\because f(x)=\cos x]$

and $f(a)=\cos a$

$\therefore \lim_{x\to a} f(x)=f(a)$

Thus, $f(x)$ is continuous at $x=a$. But a is an arbitrary point, so $f(x)$ is continuous at all points.

B. Here, $f(x)=\operatorname{cosec} x=\frac{1}{\sin x}$.

Since, $f(x)$ is not defined at $x=n\pi$, $n\in Z$.

Thus, $f(x)$ is continuous at all points except $x=n\pi$, $n\in Z$.

[as 1 and $\sin x$ are continuous functions]

C. Here, $f(x)=\sec x=\frac{1}{\cos x}$.

Since, $f(x)$ is not defined at $x=(2n+1)\frac{\pi}{2}$, $n\in Z$.

Thus, $f(x)$ is continuous at all points except $x=(2n+1)\frac{\pi}{2}$, $n\in Z$.

[as 1 and $\cos x$ are continuous functions]

D. Here, $f(x)=\cot x=\frac{\cos x}{\sin x}$.

Since, $f(x)$ is not defined at $x=n\pi$, $n\in Z$.

Thus, $f(x)$ is continuous at all points excepts $x=n\pi$, $n\in Z$.

[as $\cos x$ and $\sin x$ are continuous functions]

33 (c) Here, $f(x)=\begin{cases} \frac{\sin x}{x}, & \text{if } x<0 \\ x+1, & \text{if } x\ge 0 \end{cases}$.

LHL $= \lim_{x\to 0^-} f(x) = \lim_{x\to 0^-} \frac{\sin x}{x}$

Putting $x=0-h$ as $x\to 0^-$, when $h\to 0$.

$\therefore \lim_{h\to 0} \frac{\sin(0-h)}{(0-h)} = \lim_{h\to 0} \frac{-\sin h}{-h}$

$= \lim_{h\to 0} \frac{\sin h}{h} = 1$

RHL $= \lim_{x\to 0^+} f(x) = \lim_{x\to 0^+} (x+1)$

Putting $x=0+h$ as $x\to 0^+$, when $h\to 0$.

$\therefore \lim_{h\to 0} (0+h+1)=0+1=1$

$f(0)=0+1=1$ $[\because f(x)=x+1]$

$\therefore$ LHL = RHL = $f(0)$

Thus, $f(x)$ is continuous at $x=0$.
When $x<0$, $\sin x$ and x both are continuous. Therefore, $\frac{\sin x}{x}$ is also continuous.

When $x>0$, $f(x)=x+1$ is a polynomial. Therefore, f is continuous.

34 (b)

(i) $f(x)=\sin x+\cos x$

$$=\sqrt{2}\left(\frac{1}{\sqrt{2}}\sin x+\frac{1}{\sqrt{2}}\cos x\right)$$

$$=\sqrt{2}\left(\sin x\cos\frac{\pi}{4}+\cos x\sin\frac{\pi}{4}\right)$$

$$=\sqrt{2}\sin\left(x+\frac{\pi}{4}\right)$$

At $x=a$, where $a\in R$

$$\text{LHL}=\lim_{x\to a^-}f(x)$$

$$=\lim_{x\to a^-}\sqrt{2}\sin\left(x+\frac{\pi}{4}\right)$$

$$=\lim_{h\to 0}\sqrt{2}\sin\left(a-h+\frac{\pi}{4}\right)$$

$$=\sqrt{2}\lim_{h\to 0}\left[\sin\left(a+\frac{\pi}{4}\right)\cos h-\cos\left(a+\frac{\pi}{4}\right)\sin h\right]$$

$[\because \sin(A-B)=\sin A\cos B-\cos A\sin B]$

$$=\sqrt{2}\sin\left(a+\frac{\pi}{4}\right)\cos 0-\sqrt{2}\cos\left(a+\frac{\pi}{4}\right)\sin 0$$

$$=\sqrt{2}\sin\left(a+\frac{\pi}{4}\right)$$

$$\text{RHL}=\lim_{x\to a^+}f(x)$$

$$=\lim_{x\to a^+}\sqrt{2}\sin\left(x+\frac{\pi}{4}\right)$$

$$=\lim_{h\to 0}\sqrt{2}\sin\left(a+h+\frac{\pi}{4}\right)$$

$$=\sqrt{2}\lim_{h\to 0}\left[\sin\left(a+\frac{\pi}{4}\right)\cos h+\sin h\cos\left(a+\frac{\pi}{4}\right)\right]$$

$[\because \sin(A+B)=\sin A\cos B+\cos A\sin B]$

$$=\sqrt{2}\sin\left(a+\frac{\pi}{4}\right)\cos 0+\sqrt{2}\sin 0\cos\left(a+\frac{\pi}{4}\right)$$

$$=\sqrt{2}\sin\left(a+\frac{\pi}{4}\right)$$

Also, $f(a)=\sqrt{2}\sin\left(a+\frac{\pi}{4}\right)$

$\therefore$ LHL = RHL = $f(a)$

Hence, $f(x)$ is continuous at all points.

(ii) Here, $f(x)=\sin x-\cos x$

$$=\sqrt{2}\left(\frac{1}{\sqrt{2}}\sin x-\frac{1}{\sqrt{2}}\cos x\right)$$

$$=\sqrt{2}\left(\sin x\cos\frac{\pi}{4}-\cos x\sin\frac{\pi}{4}\right)$$

$$=\sqrt{2}\sin\left(x-\frac{\pi}{4}\right)$$

At $x=a$, where $a\in R$,

$$\text{LHL}=\lim_{x\to a^-}f(x)$$

$$=\lim_{x\to a^-}\sqrt{2}\sin\left(x-\frac{\pi}{4}\right)$$

$$=\lim_{h\to 0}\sqrt{2}\sin\left(a-h-\frac{\pi}{4}\right)$$

$$=\lim_{h\to 0}\sqrt{2}\left[\sin\left(a-\frac{\pi}{4}\right)\cos h-\cos\left(a-\frac{\pi}{4}\right)\sin h\right]$$

[using formula of $\sin(A-B)$]

$$=\sqrt{2}\left[\sin\left(a-\frac{\pi}{4}\right)\right]\cos 0-\sqrt{2}\cos\left(a-\frac{\pi}{4}\right)\sin 0$$

$$=\sqrt{2}\sin\left(a-\frac{\pi}{4}\right)$$

$$\text{RHL}=\lim_{x\to a^+}\sqrt{2}\sin\left(x-\frac{\pi}{4}\right)$$

$$=\lim_{h\to 0}\sqrt{2}\sin\left(a+h-\frac{\pi}{4}\right)$$

$$=\lim_{h\to 0}\sqrt{2}\left[\sin\left(a-\frac{\pi}{4}\right)\cos h+\cos\left(a-\frac{\pi}{4}\right)\sin h\right]$$

[using formula of $\sin(A+B)$]

$$=\sqrt{2}\left[\sin\left(a-\frac{\pi}{4}\right)\right]\cos 0+\sqrt{2}\cos\left(a-\frac{\pi}{4}\right)\sin 0$$

$$=\sqrt{2}\sin\left(a-\frac{\pi}{4}\right)$$

Also, $f(a)=\sqrt{2}\sin\left(a-\frac{\pi}{4}\right)$

$\therefore$ LHL = RHL = $f(a)$

Hence, $f(x)$ is continuous at all points.

(iii) Here, $f(x)=\sin x\cos x$

$$=\frac{1}{2}\times 2\sin x\cos x$$

$$=\frac{1}{2}\sin 2x$$

At $x=a$, where a belongs to domain of f.

$$\text{LHL}=\lim_{x\to a^-}f(x)$$

$$=\lim_{x\to a^-}\frac{1}{2}\sin 2x$$

$$=\lim_{h\to 0}\frac{1}{2}\sin 2(a-h)$$

$$=\lim_{h\to 0}\frac{1}{2}[\sin 2a\cos 2h-\cos 2a\sin 2h]$$

$$=\frac{1}{2}[\sin 2a\cos 0-\cos 2a\sin 0]$$

$$=\frac{1}{2}\sin 2a$$

$$\text{RHL}=\lim_{x\to a^+}f(x)$$

$$=\lim_{x\to a^+}\frac{1}{2}\sin 2x$$

$$=\lim_{h\to 0}\frac{1}{2}\sin 2(a+h)$$

$$=\lim_{h\to 0}\frac{1}{2}[\sin 2a\cos 2h+\cos 2a\sin 2h]$$

[using formula of $\sin(A+B)$]

$$=\frac{1}{2}[\sin 2a\cos 0+\cos 2a\sin 0]$$

$$=\frac{1}{2}\sin 2a$$

Also, $f(a)=\frac{1}{2}\sin 2a$

$\therefore$ LHL = RHL = $f(a)$

Hence, $f(x)$ is continuous at all points.

35 (*b*) I. Here,

$$f(x)=\begin{cases} x^2\sin\frac{1}{x}, & \text{if } x\neq 0\\ 0, & \text{if } x=0\end{cases}$$

$$\text{LHL}=\lim_{x\to 0^-} f(x)$$
$$=\lim_{x\to 0^-} x^2\sin\frac{1}{x}$$

Putting $x=0-h$ as $x\to 0^-$, $h\to 0$.

$$\therefore \lim_{h\to 0}(0-h)^2\sin\left(\frac{1}{0-h}\right)$$
$$=\lim_{h\to 0}\left(-h^2\sin\frac{1}{h}\right)$$
$$[\because \sin(-\theta)=-\sin\theta]$$
$$=-0\times\sin(\infty)$$
$=-0\times$ (a finite value between -1 and 1)
$$=0$$

$$\text{RHL}=\lim_{x\to 0^+} f(x)$$
$$=\lim_{x\to 0^+} x^2\sin\frac{1}{x}$$

Putting $x=0+h$, as $x\to 0^+$, $h\to 0$.

$$\therefore \lim_{h\to 0}(0+h)^2\sin\left(\frac{1}{0+h}\right)$$
$$=\lim_{h\to 0} h^2\sin\frac{1}{h}$$
$$=0\times\sin(\infty)$$
$=0\times$ (a finite value between -1 and 1)
$$=0$$

Also, $f(0)=0$

$\therefore$ LHL = RHL = $f(0)$. Thus, $f(x)$ is continuous at $x=0$.

II. Here,

$$f(x)=\begin{cases}\sin x-\cos x, \text{if } x\neq 0\\ -1, \quad \text{if } x=0\end{cases}$$

$$\text{LHL}=\lim_{x\to 0^-} f(x)$$
$$=\lim_{x\to 0^-}(\sin x-\cos x)$$

Putting $x=0-h$ as $x\to 0^-$ when $h\to 0$.

$$\therefore \lim_{h\to 0}[\sin(0-h)-\cos(0-h)]$$
$$=\lim_{h\to 0}(-\sin h-\cos h)$$
$$=0-1=-1$$

$$\text{RHL}=\lim_{x\to 0^+} f(x)$$
$$=\lim_{x\to 0^+}(\sin x-\cos x)$$

Putting $x=0+h$ as $x\to 0^+$ when $h\to 0$.

$$\therefore \lim_{h\to 0}[\sin(0+h)-\cos(0+h)]$$
$$=\lim_{h\to 0}(\sin h-\cos h)$$
$$=0-1=-1$$

Also, $f(0)=-1$

$\therefore$ LHL = RHL = $f(0)$

Thus, $f(x)$ is continuous at $x=0$.

We know at $x<0$, $f(x)=\sin x-\cos x$ is continuous and at $x>0$, $f(x)=\sin x-\cos x$ is also continuous.

Hence, $f(x)$ is continuous for all values of x.

36 (*b*) Here, $f(x)=\begin{cases}\dfrac{k\cos x}{\pi-2x}, & \text{if } x\neq\dfrac{\pi}{2}\\ 3, & \text{if } x=\dfrac{\pi}{2}\end{cases}$

$$\therefore \text{LHL}=\lim_{x\to\frac{\pi}{2}^-} f(x)$$
$$=\lim_{x\to\frac{\pi}{2}^-}\frac{k\cos x}{\pi-2x}$$

Putting $x=\dfrac{\pi}{2}-h$ as $x\to\dfrac{\pi}{2}$, when $h\to 0$.

$$\therefore \lim_{h\to 0}\frac{k\cos\left(\frac{\pi}{2}-h\right)}{\pi-2\left(\frac{\pi}{2}-h\right)}=\lim_{h\to 0}\frac{k\sin h}{2h}$$
$$=\lim_{h\to 0}\frac{k}{2}\times\frac{\sin h}{h}=\frac{k}{2}\times 1=\frac{k}{2}$$
$$\left[\because \lim_{x\to 0}\frac{\sin x}{x}=1\right]$$

$$\text{RHL}=\lim_{x\to\frac{\pi}{2}^+} f(x)$$
$$=\lim_{x\to\frac{\pi}{2}^+}\frac{k\cos x}{\pi-2x}$$

Putting $x=\dfrac{\pi}{2}+h$ as $x\to\dfrac{\pi}{2}^+$, when $h\to 0$.

$$\therefore \lim_{h\to 0}\frac{k\cos\left(\frac{\pi}{2}+h\right)}{\pi-2\left(\frac{\pi}{2}+h\right)}=\lim_{h\to 0}\frac{-k\sin h}{-2h}$$
$$=\lim_{h\to 0}\frac{k}{2}\times\frac{\sin h}{h}=\frac{k}{2}\times 1=\frac{k}{2}$$
$$\left[\because \lim_{x\to 0}\frac{\sin x}{x}=1\right]$$

Also, $f\left(\dfrac{\pi}{2}\right)=3$.

Since, $f(x)$ is continuous at $x=\dfrac{\pi}{2}$.

$$\therefore \quad \text{LHL}=\text{RHL}=f\left(\frac{\pi}{2}\right)$$
$$\Rightarrow \quad \frac{k}{2}=3$$
$$\therefore \quad k=6$$

37 (*c*)

(i) Here, $f(x)=\begin{cases}kx^2, \text{if } x\leq 2\\ 3, \ \text{if } x>2\end{cases}$

$$\text{LHL}=\lim_{x\to 2^-} f(x)=\lim_{x\to 2^-} kx^2$$

Putting $x=2-h$, as $x\to 2^-$, $h\to 0$.

$$\therefore \lim_{h\to 0} k(2-h)^2$$
$$=\lim_{h\to 0} k(4+h^2-4h)=4k$$

$$\text{RHL}=\lim_{x\to 2^+} f(x)$$
$$=\lim_{x\to 2^+}(3)=3$$

Also, $f(2)=k\times(2)^2=4k$

$$[\because f(x)=kx^2]$$

Since, $f(x)$ is continuous at $x=2$.

$\therefore$ LHL = RHL = $f(2)$

$\Rightarrow \quad 4k=3$

$\Rightarrow \quad k=\dfrac{3}{4}$

(ii) Here, $f(x)=\begin{cases}kx+1, \text{if } x\leq\pi\\ \cos x, \text{if } x>\pi\end{cases}$

$$\text{LHL}=\lim_{x\to\pi^-} f(x)=\lim_{x\to\pi^-}(kx+1)$$

Putting $x=\pi-h$, as $x\to\pi^-$, then $h\to 0$.

$$\therefore \lim_{h\to 0} k(\pi-h)+1$$
$$=\lim_{h\to 0} k\pi-kh+1=k\pi+1$$

$$\text{RHL}=\lim_{x\to\pi^+} f(x)=\lim_{x\to\pi^+}\cos x$$

Putting $x = \pi + h$ as $x \to \pi^+$, then $h \to 0$.

$\therefore \lim_{h\to 0} \cos(\pi + h)$

$= \cos \pi = -1$

Also, $f(\pi) = k\pi + 1$ $[\because f(x) = kx + 1]$

Since, $f(x)$ is continuous at $x = \pi$.

$\therefore$ LHL = RHL = $f(\pi)$

$\Rightarrow k\pi + 1 = -1$

$\therefore k = \frac{-2}{\pi}$

(iii) Here, $f(x) = \begin{cases} kx+1, \text{ if } x \le 5 \\ 3x-5, \text{ if } x > 5 \end{cases}$

LHL $= \lim_{x\to 5^-} f(x) = \lim_{x\to 5^-} (kx+1)$

Putting $x = 5 - h$, as $x \to 5^-$, then $h \to 0$.

$\therefore \lim_{h\to 0} [k(5-h)+1]$

$= \lim_{h\to 0} [5k - kh + 1] = 5k + 1$

RHL $= \lim_{x\to 5^+} f(x)$

$= \lim_{x\to 5^+} (3x-5)$

Putting $x = 5 + h$, as $x \to 5^+$, then $h \to 0$.

$\therefore \lim_{h\to 0} [3(5+h) - 5]$

$= \lim_{h\to 0} (10 + 3h) = 10$

Also, $f(5) = 5k + 1$ $[\because f(x) = kx + 1]$

Since, $f(x)$ is continuous at $x = 5$.

$\therefore$ LHL = RHL = $f(5)$

$\Rightarrow 5k + 1 = 10$

$\therefore k = \frac{9}{5}$

38 (*b*) Here, $f(x) = \begin{cases} 5, & \text{if } x \le 2 \\ ax+b, & \text{if } 2 < x < 10 \\ 21, & \text{if } x \ge 10 \end{cases}$

At $x = 2$,

LHL $= \lim_{x\to 2^-} f(x) = \lim_{x\to 2^-} (5) = 5$

RHL $= \lim_{x\to 2^+} f(x) = \lim_{x\to 2^+} (ax+b)$

Putting $x = 2 + h$, as $x \to 2^+$, then $h \to 0$.

$\therefore \lim_{h\to 0} [a(2+h)+b]$

$= \lim_{h\to 0} (2a + ah + b) = 2a + b$

Also, $f(2) = 5$

Since, $f(x)$ is continuous at $x = 2$.

$\therefore$ LHL = RHL = $f(2)$

$\Rightarrow 2a + b = 5$ ...(i)

At $x = 10$,

LHL $= \lim_{x\to 10^-} f(x) = \lim_{x\to 10^-} (ax+b)$

Putting $x = 10 - h$, as $x \to 10^-$, then $h \to 0$.

$\therefore \lim_{h\to 0} [a(10-h)+b]$

$= \lim_{h\to 0} (10a - ah + b) = 10a + b$

RHL $= \lim_{x\to 10^+} f(x) = \lim_{x\to 10^+} (21) = 21$

Also, $f(10) = 21$.

Since, $f(x)$ is continuous at $x = 10$.

$\therefore$ LHL = RHL = $f(10)$

$\Rightarrow 10a + b = 21$ ...(ii)

Subtracting Eq. (i) from Eq. (ii), we get

$8a = 16 \Rightarrow a = 2$

Putting $a = 2$ in Eq. (i), we get

$2 \times 2 + b = 5$

$\Rightarrow b = 1$

39 (*a*) Let $h(x) = x^2$ and $g(x) = \cos x$

Now, $h(x)$ is a polynomial function, so it is continuous for all $x \in R$.

$g(x)$ is a cosine function, so it is continuous function in its domain i.e. $x \in R$.

$\therefore (goh)(x) = g[h(x)]$

$= g(x^2) = \cos x^2$

We know, if g is continuous at c and if f is continuous at $g(c)$, then fog is continuous at c.

Since, $g(x)$ and $h(x)$ are both continuous functions for all $x \in R$, so composition of $g(x)$ and $h(x)$ is also a continuous function for all $x \in R$.

Thus, $f(x) = \cos(x^2)$ is a continuous function for all $x \in R$.

40 (*a*)

I. Let $g(x) = \cos x$ and $h(x) = |x|$.

Now, $g(x)$ is a cosine function, so it is continuous function in its domain i.e. $x \in R$.

$h(x) = |x|$ is the absolute value function, so it is continuous function for all $x \in R$.

$\therefore (hog)(x) = h[g(x)] = h(\cos x)$

$= |\cos x|$

Since, $g(x)$ and $h(x)$ are both continuous functions for all $x \in R$, so composition of $g(x)$ and $h(x)$ is also a continuous function for all $x \in R$.

Thus, $f(x) = |\cos x|$ is a continuous function for all $x \in R$.

II. Let $g(x) = |x|$ and $h(x) = \sin x$.

Now, $g(x) = |x|$ is the absolute value function, so it is continuous function for all $x \in R$.

$h(x) = \sin x$ is the sine function, so it is a continuous function for all $x \in R$.

$\therefore (hog)(x) = h[g(x)] = h(|x|)$

$= \sin |x|$

Since, $g(x)$ and $h(x)$ are both continuous functions for all $x \in R$, so composition of $g(x)$ and $h(x)$ is also a continuous function for all $x \in R$.

Thus, $f(x) = \sin |x|$ is a continuous function.

41 (*c*) Let $g(x) = |x|$ and $h(x) = |x+1|$.

Now, $g(x) = |x|$ is the absolute value function, so it is a continuous function for all $x \in R$.

$h(x) = |x+1|$ is the absolute value function, so it is a continuous function for all $x \in R$.

Since, $g(x)$ and $h(x)$ are both continuous functions for all $x \in R$, so difference of two continuous function is a continuous function for all $x \in R$.

Thus, $f(x) = |x| - |x+1|$ is a continuous function at all points.

Hence, there is no point at which $f(x)$ is discontinuous.

42 (*b*) To check the continuity at $x=0$.

$$\text{LHL} = \lim_{x\to 0^-} f(x) = \lim_{h\to 0} f(0-h)$$

$$= \lim_{h\to 0} |-h| \cos\left(\frac{1}{-h}\right)$$

$$= \lim_{h\to 0} h\cos\left(\frac{1}{h}\right)$$

$[\because -1 \le \cos x \le 1, \forall\, x \in R]$

$= 0 \times$ (an oscillating value between -1 and 1) $= 0$

$$\text{RHL} = \lim_{x\to 0^+} f(x) = \lim_{h\to 0} (0+h)$$

$$\lim_{h\to 0} h\cos\frac{1}{h} = 0$$

$\times$ (an oscillating number between -1 and 1) $= 0$

and $f(0) = 0$

Thus, LHL $=$ RHL $= f(0) = 0$.

Hence, function is continuous at $x = 0$.

43 (*d*) $x - [x] = 0$, when x is an integer.

Hence, $f(x)$ is discontinuous for all $x \in I$ i.e. $f(x)$ is discontinuous at infinite number of points.

44 (*d*) We know that, sum, product and difference of two polynomials is a polynomial, and polynomial function is everywhere continuous.

Now, we check the continuity of $\frac{g(x)}{f(x)}$.

$$\frac{g(x)}{f(x)} = \frac{\frac{x^2}{2}+1}{2x}$$

Clearly, $\frac{g(x)}{f(x)}$ is not defined at $x = 0$.

$\therefore$ It is discontinuous at $x = 0$.

45 (*a*) As $f(x)$ is continuous at $x = 0$.

$\therefore \lim_{x\to 0} f(x) = f(0)$ and both $f(0)$ and $\lim_{x\to 0} f(x)$ are finite.

$$\Rightarrow f(0) = \lim_{x\to 0} \frac{\sin 2x + A\sin x + B\cos x}{x^3}$$

As denominator $\to 0$, when $x \to 0$.

$\therefore \sin 2(0) + A\sin(0) + B\cos(0) = 0$

$\Rightarrow \quad B = 0$

$$\therefore f(0) = \lim_{x\to 0} \frac{\sin 2x + A\sin x}{x^3}$$

$$\Rightarrow f(0) = \lim_{x\to 0} \left(\frac{\sin x}{x}\right)\left(\frac{2\cos x + A}{x^2}\right)$$

$$= \lim_{x\to 0} \left(\frac{2\cos x + A}{x^2}\right)$$

Again, we can see that denominator $\to 0$ as $x \to 0$.

$\therefore$ Numerator should also approach 0 as $x \to 0$

$2\cos 0 + A = 0 \Rightarrow A = -2$

$$\Rightarrow f(0) = \lim_{x\to 0} \left(\frac{2\cos x - 2}{x^2}\right)$$

$$= \lim_{x\to 0} \left(\frac{-4\sin^2 \frac{x}{2}}{x^2}\right)$$

$$= \lim_{x\to 0} \left(\frac{-\sin^2 \frac{x}{2}}{\frac{x^2}{4}}\right) = -1$$

So, we get $A = -2$, $B = 0$ and $f(0) = -1$.

46 (*b*)

(i) True, because modulus of a continuous functions is also continuous.

(ii) True, because composition of two continuous functions is continuous.

(iii) False, because

Let $f(x) = \sin x$ and $g(x) = \cot x$

Clearly, $f(x) \cdot g(x) = \sin x \cdot \cot x$

$$= \sin x \cdot \frac{\cos x}{\sin x} = \cos x$$

which is continuous at $x = 0$.

But $\cot x$ is not continuous at $x = 0$.

47 (*c*) $$\text{LHL} = \lim_{x\to 0^-} \frac{\sqrt{1+kx} - \sqrt{1-kx}}{x}$$

$$= \lim_{x\to 0^-} \frac{2kx}{x(\sqrt{1+kx} + \sqrt{1-kx})} = k$$

$$\text{RHL} = \lim_{x\to 0^+} (2x^2 + 3x - 2) = -2$$

$f(0) = -2$

$\because$ It is given that $f(x)$ is continuous.

$\therefore \quad$ LHL $=$ RHL $= f(0)$

$\therefore \quad k = -2$

48 (*b*) We have,

$$f(x) = \begin{cases} \dfrac{\sin^3(\sqrt{x})\log(1+3x)}{(\tan^{-1}\sqrt{x})^2(e^{5\sqrt{x}}-1)x}, & x \ne 0 \\ a, & x = 0 \end{cases}$$

For continuity in [0, 1],

$$f(0) = f(0^+)$$

$$\therefore \quad \lim_{x\to 0^+} \frac{\sin^3\sqrt{x}\log(1+3x)}{x(\tan^{-1}\sqrt{x})^2(e^{5\sqrt{x}}-1)} = a$$

$$\Rightarrow \lim_{x\to 0^+} \left[\frac{3}{5}\frac{\sin^3\sqrt{x}}{(\sqrt{x})^3} \cdot \frac{(\sqrt{x})^2}{(\tan^{-1}\sqrt{x})^2} \times \frac{\log(1+3x)}{3x} \cdot \frac{5\sqrt{x}}{(e^{5\sqrt{x}}-1)}\right] = a$$

$$\therefore \quad a = \frac{3}{5}$$

49 (*c*) Since, $f(x)$ is continuous for every value of R except $\{-1, -2\}$. Now, we have to check at these points.

At $x = -2$,

$$\text{LHL} = \lim_{h\to 0} \frac{(-2-h)+2}{(-2-h)^2 + 3(-2-h) + 2}$$

$$= \lim_{h\to 0} \frac{-h}{h^2+h} = -1$$

$$\text{RHL} = \lim_{h\to 0} \frac{(-2+h)+2}{(-2+h)^2 + 3(-2+h) + 2}$$

$$= \lim_{h\to 0} \frac{h}{h^2-h} = -1$$

$\Rightarrow$ LHL $=$ RHL $= f(-2)$

$\therefore$ It is continuous at $x = -2$.

Now, check for $x = -1$,

$$\text{LHL} = \lim_{h\to 0} \frac{(-1-h)+2}{(-1-h)^2 + 3(-1-h) + 2}$$

$$= \lim_{h\to 0} \frac{1-h}{h^2-h} = \infty$$

$$\text{RHL} = \lim_{h\to 0} \frac{(-1+h)+2}{(-1+h)^2 + 3(-1+h) + 2}$$

$$= \lim_{h\to 0} \frac{1+h}{h^2+h} = \infty$$

$f(-1) = 0$

$\Rightarrow \quad$ LHL $\ne$ RHL $\ne f(-1)$

$\therefore$ It is not continuous at $x = -1$.

The required function is continuous in $R - \{-1\}$.

50 (c) Since, $f(x)=\dfrac{1-\tan x}{4x-\pi}$.

Now, $\lim_{x\to\frac{\pi}{4}} f(x)=\lim_{x\to\frac{\pi}{4}}\left(\dfrac{1-\tan x}{4x-\pi}\right)$ $\left[\dfrac{0}{0}\text{ form}\right]$

Putting $x=\dfrac{\pi}{4}+h$, as $x\to\dfrac{\pi}{4}$, then $h\to 0$.

$$\therefore \lim_{h\to 0}\frac{1-\tan\left(\frac{\pi}{4}+h\right)}{4\left(\frac{\pi}{4}+h\right)-\pi}$$

$$=\lim_{h\to 0}\frac{1-\left(\frac{1+\tan h}{1-\tan h}\right)}{\pi+4h-\pi}$$

$$=\lim_{h\to 0}\frac{(1-\tan h)-(1+\tan h)}{4h(1-\tan h)}$$

$$=\lim_{h\to 0}-\frac{2\tan h}{4h(1-\tan h)}$$

$$=-\frac{1}{2}$$

Since, $f(x)$ is continuous at $x=\dfrac{\pi}{4}$.

$$\therefore \lim_{x\to\frac{\pi}{4}} f(x)=f\left(\frac{\pi}{4}\right)=-\frac{1}{2}$$

51 (c)

$$f(x)=\frac{\sqrt{a^2-ax+x^2}-\sqrt{a^2+ax+x^2}}{\sqrt{a+x}-\sqrt{a-x}}\times\frac{\sqrt{a^2-ax+x^2}+\sqrt{a^2+ax+x^2}}{\sqrt{a^2-ax+x^2}+\sqrt{a^2+ax+x^2}}\times\frac{\sqrt{a+x}+\sqrt{a-x}}{\sqrt{a+x}+\sqrt{a-x}}$$

$$\Rightarrow \lim_{x\to 0} f(x)=\lim_{x\to 0}\frac{-2ax(\sqrt{a+x}+\sqrt{a-x})}{2x(\sqrt{a^2-ax+x^2}+\sqrt{a^2+ax+x^2})}$$

$$=\frac{-a(2\sqrt{a})}{a+a}=-\sqrt{a}$$

52 (d) Given,

$$f(x)=\begin{cases}\dfrac{2\sin x-\sin 2x}{2x\cos x}, & x\neq 0\\ a, & x=0\end{cases}$$

Now, $\lim_{x\to 0} f(x)=\lim_{x\to 0}\dfrac{2\sin x-\sin 2x}{2x\cos x}$ $\left(\dfrac{0}{0}\text{ form}\right)$

$$=\lim_{x\to 0}\frac{2\sin x(1-\cos x)}{2x\cos x}$$

$$=\lim_{x\to 0}\frac{\tan x}{x}\cdot\lim_{x\to 0}(1-\cos x)$$

$$=1\cdot 0=0$$

Since, $f(x)$ is continuous at $x=0$.

$$\therefore f(0)=\lim_{x\to 0} f(x)$$

$$\Rightarrow a=0$$

53 (d) $\lim_{x\to 0}\dfrac{e^{2x}-1-2x}{x(e^{2x}-1)}$

$$=\lim_{x\to 0}\frac{2e^{2x}-2}{(e^{2x}-1)+2xe^{2x}}$$

[using L' Hospital rule]

$$=\lim_{x\to 0}\frac{4e^{2x}}{4e^{2x}+4xe^{2x}}=1$$

[using L' Hospital rule]

Since, $f(x)$ is continuous at $x=0$, then

$$\lim_{x\to 0} f(x)=f(0)$$

$$\Rightarrow 1=f(0)$$

54 (d) $\lim_{x\to\frac{\pi}{4}} f(x)=\lim_{x\to\frac{\pi}{4}}\dfrac{1-\sqrt{2}\sin x}{\pi-4x}$

$$=\lim_{x\to\frac{\pi}{4}}\frac{-\sqrt{2}\cos x}{-4}=\frac{1}{4}$$

[by L' Hospital rule]

Since, $f(x)$ is continuous at $x=\dfrac{\pi}{4}$.

$$\therefore \lim_{x\to\frac{\pi}{4}} f(x)=f\left(\frac{\pi}{4}\right)$$

$$\Rightarrow \frac{1}{4}=a$$

55 (b) At $x=\dfrac{\pi}{4}$,

$$\text{LHL}=\lim_{x\to\frac{\pi}{4}^-} f(x)$$

$$=\lim_{x\to\frac{\pi}{4}^-}(x+a^2\sqrt{2}\sin x)=a^2+\frac{\pi}{4}$$

$$\text{RHL}=\lim_{x\to\frac{\pi}{4}^+} f(x)$$

$$=\lim_{x\to\frac{\pi}{4}^+}(x\cot x+b)=b+\frac{\pi}{4}$$

Since, $f(x)$ is continuous at $x=\dfrac{\pi}{4}$.

$$\therefore a^2+\frac{\pi}{4}=b+\frac{\pi}{4}$$

$$\therefore a^2=b \quad \text{...(i)}$$

At $x=\dfrac{\pi}{2}$,

$$\text{LHL}=\lim_{x\to\frac{\pi}{2}^-} f(x)$$

$$=\lim_{x\to\frac{\pi}{2}^-}(x\cot x+b)=b$$

$$\text{RHL}=\lim_{x\to\frac{\pi}{2}^+} f(x)$$

$$=\lim_{x\to\frac{\pi}{2}^+}(b\sin 2x-a\cos 2x)=a$$

$\because f(x)$ is continuous at $x=\dfrac{\pi}{2}$.

$$\therefore a=b \quad \text{...(ii)}$$

Solving Eqs. (i) and (ii), we get

$$a^2-a=0$$

$$\Rightarrow a=0,1$$

When $a=0, b=0$

and when $a=1, b=1$.

56 (b) Given, $f(x)=\dfrac{1}{\log|x|}$.

The given function is defined only when $\log|x|\neq 0$

and is not defined at $\log|x|=0$

$$\Rightarrow |x|=e^0$$

$$\Rightarrow |x|=1$$

$$\Rightarrow x=\pm 1$$

and also $\log|x|$ is not defined at $x=0$.

$\therefore$ The number of points of discontinuity is 3.

57 (a) Given, $f(x)=\begin{cases}ax+1, & x\geq 1\\ x+2, & x<1\end{cases}$

$$\text{LHL}=\lim_{x\to 1^-}(x+2)$$

$$=\lim_{h\to 0}(1-h)+2=3$$

$$\text{RHL}=\lim_{x\to 1^+} ax+1$$

$$=\lim_{h\to 0} a(1+h)+1=a+1$$

Also, $f(1) = a \times 1 + 1 = a + 1$

$\because f(x)$ is continuous.

$\therefore \quad a + 1 = 3 \Rightarrow a = 2$

58 (c) LHL $= \lim_{h \to 0} f(0-h)$

$$= \lim_{h \to 0} \frac{\sin 5(0-h)}{(0-h)^2 + 2(0-h)}$$

$$= -\lim_{h \to 0} \frac{\frac{\sin 5h}{5h}}{\frac{1}{5}(h-2)} = \frac{5}{2}$$

$$\text{RHL} = \lim_{x \to 0^+} \frac{\sin 5x}{x^2 + 2x}$$

$$= \lim_{x \to 0^+} \frac{\sin 5x}{5x} \cdot \lim_{x \to 0^+} \frac{1}{(x+2)}$$

$$= \frac{5}{2}$$

$$f(0) = k + \frac{1}{2}$$

Since, it is continuous at $x = 0$.

$\therefore \quad$ LHL = RHL $= f(0)$

$\Rightarrow \quad \frac{5}{2} = k + \frac{1}{2}$

$\therefore \quad k = 2$

Differentiability, Derivatives of Composite Functions, Derivatives of Implicit Functions and Derivatives of Inverse Trigonometric Functions

1 (b) Whenever we define derivative at a point $x = c$, then

$\lim_{h \to 0} \frac{f(c+h) - f(c)}{h}$ exists finitely.

2 (c) We say that a function f is differentiable at a point c in its domain if both $\lim_{h \to 0^-} \frac{f(c+h) - f(c)}{h}$ and $\lim_{h \to 0^+} \frac{f(c+h) - f(c)}{h}$ are finite and equal.

3 (a) A function is said to be differentiable in an interval $[a, b]$ if it is differentiable at every point of $[a, b]$ including a and b.

4 (d) A function is said to be differentiable in an interval (a, b) if it is differentiable at every point of (a, b).

5 (a) The function defined by

$$f'(x) = \lim_{h \to 0} \frac{f(x+h) - f(x)}{h}$$

(wherever the limit exist) is defined to be derivative of f.

6 (d) We use the phrase differentiate $f(x)$ with respect to x to find $f'(x)$.

The following rules were established as a part of algebra of derivatives.

1. $(u \pm v)' = u' \pm v'$
2. $(uv)' = u'v + uv'$ [Leibnitz or product rule]
3. $\left(\frac{u}{v}\right)' = \frac{u'v - uv'}{v^2}$, wherever $v \neq 0$ [quotient rule]

7 (c) The following table gives a list of derivatives of functions.

$f(x)$	x^n	$\sin x$	$\cos x$	$\tan x$
$f'(x)$	nx^{n-1}	$\cos x$	$-\sin x$	$\sec^2 x$

8 (b) Since, f is differentiable at c, we have

$$\lim_{x \to c} \frac{f(x) - f(c)}{x - c} = f'(c)$$

But for $x \neq c$, we have

$$f(x) - f(c) = \frac{f(x) - f(c)}{x - c} \cdot (x - c)$$

Therefore, $\lim_{x \to c} [f(x) - f(c)]$

$$= \lim_{x \to c} \left[\frac{f(x) - f(c)}{x - c} \cdot (x - c)\right]$$

or $\quad \lim_{x \to c} [f(x)] - \lim_{x \to c} [f(c)]$

$$= \lim_{x \to c} \left[\frac{f(x) - f(c)}{x - c}\right] \cdot \lim_{x \to c} [(x - c)]$$

$$= f'(c) \cdot 0 = 0$$

or $\quad \lim_{x \to c} f(x) = f(c)$

Hence, f is continuous at $x = c$.

9 (b) One way is to expand $(2x+1)^3$ using binomial theorem and find the derivative as a polynomial function as illustrated below.

$$\frac{d}{dx} f(x) = \frac{d}{dx}[(2x+1)^3]$$

$$= \frac{d}{dx}(8x^3 + 12x^2 + 6x + 1)$$

$$= 24x^2 + 24x + 6$$

$$= 6(2x+1)^2$$

Now, observe that $f(x) = (hog)(x)$, where, $g(x) = 2x + 1$ and $h(x) = x^3$.

Putting $t = g(x) = 2x + 1$.

Then, $\quad f(x) = h(t) = t^3$.

Thus $\quad \frac{df}{dx} = \frac{dh}{dt} \cdot \frac{dt}{dx}$

$$= 3t^2 \cdot 2$$

$$= 3(2x+1)^2 \cdot 2$$

$$= 6(2x+1)^2$$

10 (c) Let f be a real valued function which is composition of two functions u and v i.e. $f = v\,o\,u$.

Suppose $t = u(x)$ and if both $\frac{dt}{dx}$ and $\frac{dv}{dt}$ exist, we have $\frac{df}{dx} = \frac{dv}{dt} \cdot \frac{dt}{dx}$.

11 (b) Suppose f is a real valued function which is a composite of three functions u, v and w i.e. $f = (w\,o\,u)\,o\,v$. If $t = v(x)$ and $s = u(t)$, then

$$\frac{df}{dx} = \frac{d(w\,o\,u)}{dt} \cdot \frac{dt}{dx} = \frac{dw}{ds} \cdot \frac{ds}{dt} \cdot \frac{dt}{dx}$$

provided all the derivatives in the statement exist.

12 (a) The function $f(x) = \sin[\cos(x^2)]$ is a composition $f(x) = (w\,o\,v\,o\,u)(x)$ of the three functions u, v and w, where $u(x) = x^2$, $v(t) = \cos t$ and $w(s) = \sin s$.

Putting $t = u(x) = x^2$ and $s = v(t) = \cos t$.

Observe that $\frac{dw}{ds} = \cos s$, $\frac{ds}{dt} = -\sin t$

and $\frac{dt}{dx} = 2x$ exist for all real x.

Hence, by chain rule, we have

$$\frac{df}{dx} = \frac{dw}{ds} \cdot \frac{ds}{dt} \cdot \frac{dt}{dx}$$

$$= (\cos s)(-\sin t)\,2x$$

$$= -2x \sin x^2 \cos(\cos x^2)$$

Alternate Method

We can proceed as follows.

$y=\sin(\cos x^2)$

Therefore, $\dfrac{dy}{dx}=\dfrac{d}{dx}\sin(\cos x^2)$

$=\cos(\cos x^2)\dfrac{d}{dx}(\cos x^2)$

$=\cos(\cos x^2)(-\sin x^2)\dfrac{d}{dx}(x^2)$

$=-\sin x^2\cos(\cos x^2)(2x)$

$=-2x\sin x^2\cos(\cos x^2)$

13 (*a*) A. Let $y=\sin(x^2+5)$.

On differentiating both sides w.r.t. x, we get

$\dfrac{dy}{dx}=\dfrac{d}{dx}(\sin(x^2+5))$

$=\cos(x^2+5)\dfrac{d}{dx}(x^2+5)$ [by chain rule]

$=\cos(x^2+5)(2x+0)$

$=2x\cos(x^2+5)$

B. Let $y=\cos(\sin x)$.

On differentiating both sides w.r.t. x, we get

$\dfrac{dy}{dx}=\dfrac{d}{dx}(\cos(\sin x))$

$=-\sin(\sin x)\dfrac{d}{dx}(\sin x)$ [by chain rule]

$=-\sin(\sin x)\cos x$

$=-\cos x\sin(\sin x)$

C. Let $y=\sin(ax+b)$.

On differentiating both sides w.r.t. x, we get

$\dfrac{dy}{dx}=\dfrac{d}{dx}\sin(ax+b)$

$=\cos(ax+b)\dfrac{d}{dx}(ax+b)$ [by chain rule]

$=\cos(ax+b)\{a\times 1+0\}$

$=a\cos(ax+b)$

D. Let $y=\sec(\tan\sqrt{x})$.

On differentiating both sides w.r.t. x, we get

$\dfrac{dy}{dx}=\dfrac{d}{dx}(\sec(\tan\sqrt{x}))$

$=\sec(\tan\sqrt{x})\tan(\tan\sqrt{x})\dfrac{d}{dx}(\tan\sqrt{x})$ [by chain rule]

$=\sec(\tan\sqrt{x})\tan(\tan\sqrt{x})\sec^2\sqrt{x}\dfrac{d}{dx}(\sqrt{x})$

$=\sec(\tan\sqrt{x})\tan(\tan\sqrt{x})(\sec^2\sqrt{x})\left(\dfrac{1}{2\sqrt{x}}\right)$

$=\dfrac{1}{2\sqrt{x}}\sec(\tan\sqrt{x})\tan(\tan\sqrt{x})(\sec^2\sqrt{x})$

14 (*a*)

I. Let $y=\cos x^3\sin^2(x^5)$.

On differentiating both sides w.r.t. x, we get

$\dfrac{dy}{dx}=\dfrac{d}{dx}\{\cos x^3\sin^2(x^5)\}$

$=\cos x^3\dfrac{d}{dx}\sin^2(x^5)+\sin^2(x^5)\dfrac{d}{dx}(\cos x^3)$

$\left[\text{using product rule, } \dfrac{d}{dx}(uv)=u\dfrac{d}{dx}v+v\dfrac{d}{dx}u\right]$

$=(\cos x^3)(2\sin x^5)\dfrac{d}{dx}(\sin x^5)+\sin^2(x^5)(-\sin x^3)\dfrac{d}{dx}(x^3)$

$\left[\text{using chain rule, } \dfrac{d}{dx}f(g(x))=f'(g(x))\dfrac{d}{dx}g(x)\right]$

$=(\cos x^3)(2\sin x^5)(\cos x^5)\dfrac{d}{dx}(x^5)+\sin^2(x^5)(-\sin x^3)(3x^2)$ [using chain rule]

$=(\cos x^3)(2\sin x^5)(\cos x^5)(5x^4)-\sin^2(x^5)(\sin x^3)(3x^2)$

$=10x^4(\sin x^5)(\cos x^5)(\cos x^3)-3x^2\sin x^3\sin^2 x^5$

II. Let $y=2\sqrt{\cot(x^2)}$.

On differentiating both sides w.r.t. x, we get

$\dfrac{dy}{dx}=\dfrac{d}{dx}2(\cot x^2)^{1/2}$

$=2.\dfrac{1}{2}\{\cot(x^2)\}^{\frac{1}{2}-1}\dfrac{d}{dx}\cot(x^2)$

$\left[\text{using chain rule, } \dfrac{d}{dx}f(g(x))=f'(g(x))\dfrac{d}{dx}g(x)\right]$

$=\dfrac{1}{\sqrt{\cot(x^2)}}[-\operatorname{cosec}^2 x^2]\dfrac{d}{dx}(x^2)$ [using chain rule]

$=-\dfrac{\operatorname{cosec}^2(x^2)\,2x}{\sqrt{\cot(x^2)}}=\dfrac{-2x\operatorname{cosec}^2(x^2)}{\sqrt{\cot(x^2)}}$

15 (*b*)

I. Let $y=\cos(\sqrt{x})$.

On differentiating both sides w.r.t. x, we get

$\dfrac{dy}{dx}=\dfrac{d}{dx}\cos(\sqrt{x})$

$=-\sin\sqrt{x}\dfrac{d}{dx}(\sqrt{x})$

$\left[\text{using chain rule, } \dfrac{d}{dx}f(g(x))=f'(g(x))\dfrac{d}{dx}g(x)\right]$

$=-\sin\sqrt{x}\dfrac{1}{2\sqrt{x}}=-\dfrac{\sin\sqrt{x}}{2\sqrt{x}}$

(ii) Given, $f(x)=|x-1|$

$=\begin{cases} x-1, & \text{if } x-1\ge 0\\ -(x-1), & \text{if } x-1<0\end{cases}$

We have to check the differentiability at $x=1$.

Here, $f(1)=1-1=0$

$Lf'(1)=\lim\limits_{h\to 0^-}\dfrac{f(1-h)-f(1)}{-h}$

$=\lim\limits_{h\to 0^-}\dfrac{|1-(1-h)|-0}{-h}$

$=\lim\limits_{h\to 0^-}\dfrac{+h}{-h}=-1$

$[\because$ when $x<1\Rightarrow f(x)=1-x]$

and $Rf'(1)=\lim\limits_{h\to 0^+}\dfrac{f(1+h)-f(1)}{h}$

$=\lim\limits_{h\to 0^+}\dfrac{|(1+h)-1|-0}{h}$

$=\lim\limits_{h\to 0^+}\dfrac{h}{h}=1$

$[\because$ when $x>1\Rightarrow f(x)=x-1]$

$\therefore Lf'(1)\ne Rf'(1)$.

Hence, $f(x)$ is not differentiable at $x=1$.

(iii) Given, $f(x)=[x]$,

RHD of $f(x)$ at $x=1$;

Putting $x=1+h$, as $x \to 1^+$, then $h \to 0$

$$Rf'(1)=\lim_{h\to 0}\frac{[1+h]-[1]}{h}$$

$$=\lim_{h\to 0}\frac{1-1}{h}=0$$

$$\left[\because Rf'(x)=\lim_{h\to 0}\frac{f(x+h)-f(x)}{h}\right]$$

LHD of $f(x)$ at $x=1$;

Putting $x=1-h$, as $x\to 1^-$ then $h\to 0$

$$Lf'(1)=\lim_{h\to 0}\frac{[1-h]-[1]}{-h}$$

$$=\lim_{h\to 0}\frac{0-1}{-h}$$

$$=\lim_{h\to 0}\frac{1}{h}=\infty$$

$$\left[\because Lf'(x)=\lim_{h\to 0}\frac{f(x-h)-f(x)}{-h}\right]$$

$\therefore$ LHD $\neq$ RHD

Thus, $f(x)$ is not differentiable at $x=1$.

At $x=2$,

RHD $=Rf'(2)$

$$=\lim_{h\to 0}\frac{f(2+h)-f(2)}{h}$$

$$\left[\because Rf'(x)=\lim_{h\to 0}\frac{f(x+h)-f(x)}{h}\right]$$

$$=\lim_{h\to 0}\frac{[2+h]-2}{h}$$

$$=\lim_{h\to 0}\frac{2-2}{h}=0$$

LHD $=Lf'(2)$

$$=\lim_{h\to 0}\frac{f(2-h)-f(2)}{-h}$$

$$\left[\because Lf'(x)=\lim_{h\to 0}\frac{f(x-h)-f(x)}{-h}\right]$$

$$=\lim_{h\to 0}\frac{[2-h]-[2]}{-h}$$

$$=\lim_{h\to 0}\frac{1-2}{-h}=\infty$$

$\therefore$ RHD $\neq$ LHD

Thus, $f(x)$ is not differentiable at $x=2$.

16 (*b*) Consider one of the following relationships between x and y.

$$x-y-\pi=0$$

$$x+\sin xy-y=0$$

In the first case, we can solve for y and rewrite the relationship as $y=x-\pi$. In the second case, it does not seem that there is an easy way to solve for y. Nevertheless, there is no doubt about the dependence of y on x in either of the cases.

When a relationship between x and y is expressed in a way that it is easy to solve for y and write $y=f(x)$, we say that y is given as an explicit function of x. In the latter case, it is implicit that y is a function of x and we say that the relationship of the second type above, gives function implicitly.

17 (*c*) We differentiate the relationship directly with respect to x, we get

$$\frac{dy}{dx}+\frac{d}{dx}(\sin y)=\frac{d}{dx}(\cos x)$$

which implies

$$\frac{dy}{dx}+\cos y\cdot\frac{dy}{dx}=-\sin x$$

This gives $\dfrac{dy}{dx}=-\dfrac{\sin x}{1+\cos y}$

Where, $\quad y\neq(2n+1)\pi$

18 (*b*)

A. Let $y=\sin^{-1}x$. Then, $x=\sin y$.

On differentiating both sides w.r.t. x, we get

$$1=\cos y\frac{dy}{dx}$$

which implies that

$$\frac{dy}{dx}=\frac{1}{\cos y}=\frac{1}{\cos(\sin^{-1}x)}$$

Observe that this is defined only for $\cos y\neq 0$, i.e. $\sin^{-1}x\neq-\frac{\pi}{2},\frac{\pi}{2}$, i.e. $x\neq-1,1$, i.e. $x\in(-1,1)$.

To make this result a bit more attractive, we carry out the following manipulation. Recall that for $x\in(-1,1)$, $\sin(\sin^{-1}x)=x$ and hence

$$\cos^2 y=1-(\sin y)^2$$
$$=1-(\sin(\sin^{-1}x))^2=1-x^2$$

Also, since $y\in\left(-\frac{\pi}{2},\frac{\pi}{2}\right)$, $\cos y$ is positive and hence $\cos y=\sqrt{1-x^2}$.

Thus, for $x\in(-1,1)$.

$$\frac{dy}{dx}=\frac{1}{\cos y}=\frac{1}{\sqrt{1-x^2}}$$

B. Let $y=\tan^{-1}x$. Then, $x=\tan y$.

On differentiating both sides with respect to x, we get

$$1=\sec^2 y\frac{dy}{dx}$$

which implies that

$$\frac{dy}{dx}=\frac{1}{\sec^2 y}=\frac{1}{1+\tan^2 y}$$

$$=\frac{1}{1+(\tan(\tan^{-1}x))^2}=\frac{1}{1+x^2}$$

C. $\cos^{-1}x=y$, $\cos y=x$

On differentiating both sides with respect to x, we get

$$-\sin y\frac{dy}{dx}=1$$

$$\frac{dy}{dx}=-\frac{1}{\sin y}=\frac{1}{\sin(\cos^{-1}x)}$$

$$=\frac{-1}{\sin(\sin^{-1}\sqrt{1-x^2})}$$

$$=\frac{-1}{\sqrt{1-x^2}}\qquad[\because x\in(-1,1)]$$

D. Let $\cot^{-1}x=y$, $\cot y=x$.

On differentiating both sides w.r.t. x, we get

$$-\operatorname{cosec}^2 y\frac{dy}{dx}=1$$

$$\Rightarrow \frac{dy}{dx}=-\frac{1}{\operatorname{cosec}^2 y}$$

$$=-\frac{1}{1+\cot^2 y}$$

$$=-\frac{1}{1+\{\cot(\cot^{-1}x)\}^2}$$

$$=-\frac{1}{1+x^2}$$

19 (*b*) Given, $2x + 3y = \sin x$

On differentiating both sides with respect to *x*, we get

$$\frac{d}{dx}(2x+3y) = \frac{d}{dx}(\sin x)$$

$$2 + 3\frac{dy}{dx} = \cos x$$

$$\Rightarrow \quad 3\frac{dy}{dx} = \cos x - 2$$

$$\therefore \quad \frac{dy}{dx} = \frac{\cos x - 2}{3}$$

20 (*c*) Given, $2x + 3y = \sin y$

On differentiating both sides with respect to *x*, we get

$$\frac{d}{dx}(2x+3y) = \frac{d}{dx}(\sin y)$$

$$\Rightarrow \quad 2 + 3\frac{dy}{dx} = \cos y \frac{dy}{dx}$$

$$\Rightarrow \quad 3\frac{dy}{dx} - \cos y \frac{dy}{dx} = -2$$

$$\Rightarrow \quad (3 - \cos y)\frac{dy}{dx} = -2$$

$$\therefore \quad \frac{dy}{dx} = \frac{2}{\cos y - 3}$$

21 (*a*) Given, $ax + by^2 = \cos y$

On differentiating both sides with respect to *x*, we get

$$\frac{d}{dx}(ax + by^2) = \frac{d}{dx}(\cos y)$$

$$\Rightarrow \quad a + 2by\frac{dy}{dx} = -\sin y\frac{dy}{dx}$$

$$\Rightarrow 2by\frac{dy}{dx} + \sin y\frac{dy}{dx} = -a$$

$$\Rightarrow \quad \frac{dy}{dx}(2by + \sin y) = -a$$

$$\Rightarrow \quad \frac{dy}{dx} = \frac{-a}{2\,by + \sin y}$$

Given, $xy + y^2 = \tan x + y$

On differentiating both sides w.r.t. *x*, we get

$$\frac{d}{dx}(xy + y^2) = \frac{d}{dx}(\tan x + y)$$

$$\Rightarrow \frac{d}{dx}(xy) + \frac{d}{dx}(y^2) = \sec^2 x + \frac{dy}{dx}$$

$$\Rightarrow x\frac{dy}{dx} + y.1 + 2y\frac{dy}{dx} = \sec^2 x + \frac{dy}{dx}$$

$$\left[\text{using product rule, } \frac{d}{dx}(u \cdot v) = u\frac{d}{dx}v + v\frac{d}{dx}u\right]$$

$$\Rightarrow x\frac{dy}{dx} + 2y\frac{dy}{dx} - \frac{dy}{dx} = \sec^2 x - y$$

$$\Rightarrow \quad (x + 2y - 1)\frac{dy}{dx} = \sec^2 x - y$$

$$\therefore \quad \frac{dy}{dx} = \frac{\sec^2 x - y}{x + 2y - 1}$$

22 (*d*)

A. Given, $x^2 + xy + y^2 = 100$

On differentiating both sides w.r.t. *x*, we get

$$\frac{d}{dx}(x^2 + xy + y^2) = 0$$

$$\Rightarrow 2x + \left(x\frac{dy}{dx} + y \cdot 1\right) + 2y\frac{dy}{dx} = 0$$

$$\left[\text{using product rule, } \frac{d}{dx}(u \cdot v) = u\frac{d}{dx}v + v\frac{d}{dx}u\right]$$

$$\Rightarrow \frac{dy}{dx}(x + 2y) = -2x - y$$

$$\therefore \quad \frac{dy}{dx} = -\frac{(2x + y)}{x + 2y}$$

B. Given, $x^3 + x^2y + xy^2 + y^3 = 81$

On differentiating both sides w.r.t *x*, we get

$$\frac{d}{dx}(x^3 + x^2y + xy^2 + y^3) = \frac{d}{dx}(81)$$

$$3x^2 + \frac{d}{dx}(x^2\,y) + \frac{d}{dx}(xy^2) + 3y^2\frac{dy}{dx} = 0$$

$$\Rightarrow 3x^2 + x^2\frac{dy}{dx} + y(2x) + x\left(2y\frac{dy}{dx}\right) + y^2.1 + 3y^2\frac{dy}{dx} = 0$$

$$\left[\text{using product rule } \frac{d}{dx}(u \cdot v) = u\frac{d}{dx}v + v\frac{d}{dx}u\right]$$

$$\Rightarrow \quad (x^2 + 2xy + 3y^2)\frac{dy}{dx} = -3x^2 - 2xy - y^2$$

$$\therefore \quad \frac{dy}{dx} = -\frac{(3x^2 + 2xy + y^2)}{x^2 + 2xy + 3y^2}$$

C. Given, $\sin^2 y + \cos xy = k$

On differentiating both sides w.r.t. *x*, we get

$$\frac{d}{dx}(\sin^2 y + \cos xy) = \frac{d}{dx}(k)$$

$$\Rightarrow \frac{d}{dx}(\sin^2 y) + \frac{d}{dx}(\cos xy) = 0$$

$$\Rightarrow 2\sin y \cos y\frac{dy}{dx} + (-\sin xy)\frac{d}{dx}(xy) = 0$$

$$\left[\text{using chain rule, } \frac{d}{dx}f(g(x)) = f'(g(x))\frac{d}{dx}g(x)\right]$$

$$\Rightarrow \sin 2y\frac{dy}{dx} - \sin xy\left(x\frac{dy}{dx} + y \cdot 1\right) = 0$$

$$\Rightarrow \sin 2y\frac{dy}{dx} - x\sin xy\frac{dy}{dx} = y\sin xy$$

$$\therefore \quad \frac{dy}{dx} = \frac{y\sin(xy)}{\sin 2y - x\sin(xy)}$$

D. Given, $\sin^2 x + \cos^2 y = 1$

On differentiating both sides w.r.t. *x*, we get

$$\frac{d}{dx}(\sin^2 x + \cos^2 y) = \frac{d}{dx}(1)$$

$$2\sin x\cos x + 2\cos y\left(-\sin y\frac{dy}{dx}\right) = 0$$

$$\left[\text{using chain rule, } \frac{d}{dx}f(g(x)) = f'(g(x))\frac{d}{dx}g(x)\right]$$

$$\Rightarrow \quad -2\sin y\cos y\frac{dy}{dx} = -2\sin x\cos x$$

$$\Rightarrow \quad \frac{dy}{dx} = \frac{-\sin 2x}{-\sin 2y} = \frac{\sin 2x}{\sin 2y}$$

$$[\because \sin 2\theta = 2\sin\theta\cos\theta]$$

23 (*b*) Given, $y = \sin^{-1}\left(\frac{2x}{1+x^2}\right)$

Putting $\theta = \tan^{-1} x$ i.e. $x = \tan\theta$

Then, $y = \sin^{-1}\left(\frac{2\tan\theta}{1+\tan^2\theta}\right)$

$$= \sin^{-1}(\sin 2\theta) = 2\theta = 2\tan^{-1} x$$

$$\left[\because \sin 2A = \frac{2\tan A}{1 + \tan^2 A}\right]$$

On differentiating both sides w.r.t. *x*, we get

$$\frac{dy}{dx} = \frac{d}{dx}(2\tan^{-1} x)$$

$$\frac{dy}{dx} = 2 \cdot \frac{1}{1+x^2} = \frac{2}{1+x^2}$$

$$\left[\because \frac{d}{dx}\tan^{-1} x = \frac{1}{1+x^2}\right]$$

24 (*a*) Putting $x = \tan\theta$

$$\therefore \quad y = \tan^{-1}\left(\frac{3x - x^3}{1-3x^2}\right)$$

$$= \tan^{-1}\left(\frac{3\tan\theta - \tan^3\theta}{1-3\tan^2\theta}\right)$$

$$\left[\because \tan 3x = \frac{3\tan x - \tan^3 x}{1-3\tan^2 x}\right]$$

$$\Rightarrow \quad y = \tan^{-1}(\tan 3\theta) = 3\theta$$

$$= 3\tan^{-1} x$$

On differentiating both sides w.r.t. *x*, we get

$$\Rightarrow \quad \frac{dy}{dx} = 3\frac{d}{dx}(\tan^{-1} x)$$

$$= \frac{3}{1+x^2}$$

$$\left[\because \frac{d}{dx}\tan^{-1} x = \frac{1}{1+x^2}\right]$$

25 (*a*) I. Let $\tan^{-1} x = \theta$ i.e. $x = \tan\theta$

$$\therefore \quad y = \cos^{-1}\left(\frac{1-x^2}{1+x^2}\right)$$

$$= \cos^{-1}\left(\frac{1-\tan^2\theta}{1+\tan^2\theta}\right)$$

$$\left[\because \frac{1-\tan^2\theta}{1+\tan^2\theta} = \cos 2\theta\right]$$

$$\Rightarrow y = \cos^{-1}(\cos 2\theta)$$

$$= 2\theta = 2\tan^{-1} x$$

On differentiating both sides w.r.t. *x*, we get

$$\frac{dy}{dx} = 2\frac{d}{dx}(\tan^{-1} x) = \frac{2}{1+x^2}$$

$$\left[\because \frac{d}{dx}\tan^{-1} x = \frac{1}{1+x^2}\right]$$

II. $\frac{d}{dx}(\cos^{-1} x) = -\frac{1}{\sqrt{1-x^2}}$

26 (*c*)

A. Substituting $x = \tan\theta$

$$\Rightarrow \tan^{-1} x = \theta$$

$$\therefore \quad y = \sin^{-1}\left(\frac{1-\tan^2\theta}{1+\tan^2\theta}\right)$$

$$= \sin^{-1}(\cos 2\theta)$$

$$\Rightarrow \quad y = \sin^{-1}\left[\sin\left(\frac{\pi}{2} - 2\theta\right)\right]$$

$$\Rightarrow \quad y = \frac{\pi}{2} - 2\theta$$

$$\Rightarrow \quad y = \frac{\pi}{2} - 2\tan^{-1} x$$

On differentiating w.r.t. *x* both sides, we get

$$\frac{dy}{dx} = \frac{d}{dx}\left(\frac{\pi}{2}\right) - 2\frac{d}{dx}(\tan^{-1} x)$$

$$\Rightarrow \frac{dy}{dx} = 0 - \frac{2}{1+x^2}$$

$$\Rightarrow \frac{dy}{dx} = \frac{-2}{1+x^2}$$

$$\left[\because \frac{d}{dx}\tan^{-1}\theta = \frac{1}{1+\theta^2}\right]$$

B. Substituting $x = \tan\theta$

$$\Rightarrow \quad \theta = \tan^{-1} x$$

$$y = \cos^{-1}\left(\frac{2\tan\theta}{1+\tan^2\theta}\right)$$

$$\Rightarrow \quad y = \cos^{-1}(\sin 2\theta)$$

$$\left[\because \sin 2x = \frac{2\tan x}{1+\tan^2 x}\right]$$

$$\Rightarrow \quad y = \cos^{-1}\left[\cos\left(\frac{\pi}{2} - 2\theta\right)\right]$$

$$\left[\because \sin 2\theta = \cos\left(\frac{\pi}{2} - 2\theta\right)\right]$$

$$\Rightarrow \quad y = \frac{\pi}{2} - 2\theta$$

$$\Rightarrow \quad y = \frac{\pi}{2} - 2\tan^{-1} x$$

$$[\because \theta = \tan^{-1} x]$$

On differentiating both sides w.r.t. *x*, we get

$$\frac{dy}{dx} = 0 - \frac{2}{1+x^2}$$

$$\left[\because \frac{d}{dx}\tan^{-1} x = \frac{1}{1+x^2}\right]$$

$$\therefore \quad \frac{dy}{dx} = \frac{-2}{1+x^2}$$

C. Let $\sin^{-1} x = \theta$, then $x = \sin\theta$

$$\therefore \quad y = \sin^{-1}(2x\sqrt{1-x^2})$$

$$\Rightarrow \quad y = \sin^{-1}(2\sin\theta\sqrt{1-\sin^2\theta})$$

$$[\because 1 - \sin^2\theta = \cos^2\theta]$$

$$\Rightarrow \quad y = \sin^{-1}(2\sin\theta\cos\theta)$$

$$= \sin^{-1}(\sin 2\theta)$$

$$\Rightarrow y = 2\theta$$

$$\Rightarrow y = 2\sin^{-1} x$$

On differentiating both sides w.r.t. *x*, we get

$$\Rightarrow \frac{dy}{dx} = \frac{2}{\sqrt{1-x^2}}$$

$$\left[\because \frac{d}{dx}\sin^{-1} x = \frac{1}{\sqrt{1-x^2}}\right]$$

D. Let $\cos^{-1} x = \theta$ i.e. $x = \cos\theta$

$$\therefore \quad y = \sec^{-1}\left(\frac{1}{2x^2-1}\right)$$

$$\Rightarrow \quad y = \sec^{-1}\left(\frac{1}{2\cos^2\theta - 1}\right)$$

$$\Rightarrow y = \sec^{-1}\left(\frac{1}{\cos 2\theta}\right)$$

$$[\because \cos 2\theta = 2\cos^2\theta - 1]$$

$$\Rightarrow y = \sec^{-1}(\sec 2\theta)$$

$$\Rightarrow y = 2\theta$$

$$\Rightarrow y = 2\cos^{-1} x$$

On differentiating both sides w.r.t. *x*, we get

$$\Rightarrow \frac{dy}{dx} = 2\frac{d}{dx}(\cos^{-1} x)$$

$$= \frac{-2}{\sqrt{1-x^2}}$$

$$\left[\because \frac{d}{dx}\cos^{-1}\theta = \frac{-1}{\sqrt{1-\theta^2}}\right]$$

27 (*b*)

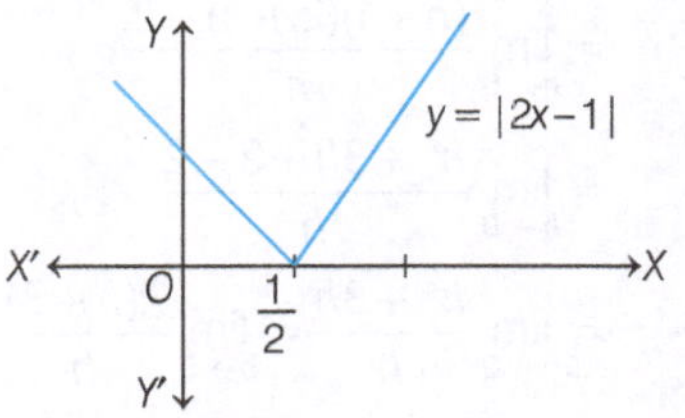

$\because$ At $x = \frac{1}{2}$, curve have two tangents at that point. Therefore, from the graph, it is clear that $y = |2x - 1|$ is not differentiable at $x = \frac{1}{2}$.

$\therefore$ $f(x)$ is differentiable in $R - \left\{\frac{1}{2}\right\}$.

28 (b) Let $u(x) = \sin x$

$v(x) = |x|$

$\therefore \quad f(x) = vou(x) = v(u(x))$

$= v(\sin x)$

$= |\sin x|$

$\because u(x) = \sin x$ is a continuous function and $v(x) = |x|$ is a continuous function.

$\therefore f(x) = vou(x)$ is also continuous everywhere but $v(x)$ is not differentiable at $x = 0$.

$\Rightarrow f(x)$ is not differentiable, where $\sin x = 0$ i.e. $x = n\pi,\ n \in Z$.

Hence, $f(x)$ is continuous everywhere but not differentiable at $x = n\pi,\ n \in Z$.

29 (b) Here,

$$f(x) = \begin{cases} x[x], & \text{if } 0 \le x < 2 \\ (x-1)x, & \text{if } 2 \le x < 3 \end{cases}$$

At $x = 2$

$$\text{LHD} = Lf'(2) = \lim_{h\to 0} \frac{f(2-h) - f(2)}{-h}$$

$$= \lim_{h\to 0} \frac{(2-h)[2-h] - (2-1)2}{-h}$$

$$= \lim_{h\to 0} \frac{(2-h)(1) - 2}{-h} \quad [\because [2-h] = 1]$$

$$= \lim_{h\to 0} \frac{2-h-2}{-h} = \lim_{h\to 0} \frac{-h}{-h} = 1$$

$$\text{RHD} = Rf'(2) = \lim_{h\to 0} \frac{f(2+h) - f(2)}{h}$$

$$= \lim_{h\to 0} \frac{(2+h-1)(2+h) - (2-1)(2)}{h}$$

$$= \lim_{h\to 0} \frac{(h+1)(2+h) - 2}{h}$$

$$= \lim_{h\to 0} \frac{h^2 + 3h + 2 - 2}{h}$$

$$= \lim_{h\to 0} \frac{h^2 + 3h}{h} = \lim_{h\to 0} \frac{h(h+3)}{h} = 3$$

$\because$ LHD $\neq$ RHD

$\therefore f(x)$ is not differentiable at $x = 2$.

30 (b) $f'(x) = \lim_{h\to 0} \dfrac{f(x+h) - f(x)}{h}$

$$f'(x) = \lim_{h\to 0} \frac{f(x)\cdot f(h) - f(x)}{h}$$

$[\because f(x+y) = f(x)f(y)]$

$$f'(x) = \lim_{h\to 0} \frac{f(x)[f(h) - 1]}{h} \quad \text{...(i)}$$

and $f(x+y) = f(x)f(y)\ \forall x, y \in R$ [given]

$f(0+0) = f(0)\,f(0)$

$f(0) = f(0)^2$

$\Rightarrow \quad f(0)^2 - f(0) = 0$

$\Rightarrow \quad f(0)[f(0) - 1] = 0$

$f(0) \neq 0$

$\Rightarrow \quad f(0) = 1 \quad [\because f(x) \neq 0]$

$$\text{Now, } f'(0) = \lim_{x\to 0} \frac{f(x+0) - f(0)}{x-0}$$

$$2 = \lim_{x\to 0} \frac{f(x)\cdot f(0) - f(0)}{x-0}$$

$$2 = \lim_{x\to 0} \frac{f(0)[f(x) - 1]}{x-0} \quad [\because f(0) = 1]$$

$$2 = \lim_{h\to 0} \frac{f(0+h) - 1}{h}$$

$$2 = \lim_{h\to 0} \frac{f(0)\cdot f(h) - 1}{h} \quad [\because f(0) = 1]$$

$$2 = \lim_{h\to 0} \frac{f(h) - 1}{h} \quad \text{...(ii)}$$

From Eqs. (i) and (ii), we have

$f'(x) = 2f(x)$

31 (d) $f'(1^-) = \lim_{h\to 0} \dfrac{f(1-h) - f(1)}{-h}$

$$= \lim_{h\to 0} \frac{(1-h-1)\cdot \sin\left(\frac{1}{1-h-1}\right) - 0}{-h}$$

$$= -\lim_{h\to 0} \sin\frac{1}{h}$$

$$\text{and } f'(1^+) = \lim_{h\to 0} \frac{f(1+h) - f(1)}{h}$$

$$= \lim_{h\to 0} \frac{(1+h-1)\sin\left(\frac{1}{1+h-1}\right) - 0}{h}$$

$$= \lim_{h\to 0} \sin\frac{1}{h}$$

$\therefore \quad f'(1^-) \neq f'(1^+)$

$\Rightarrow f$ is not differentiable at $x = 1$.

Again, $f'(0^+)$

$$= \lim_{h\to 0} \frac{(0+h-1)\sin\left(\frac{1}{0+h-1}\right) - \sin 1}{h}$$

$$= \lim_{h\to 0} \frac{\left[\left\{(h-1)\cos\left(\frac{1}{h-1}\right) \times \left(\frac{-1}{(h-1)^2}\right)\right\} + \sin\left(\frac{+1}{h-1}\right)\right]}{1}$$

[using L' Hospital rule]

$= \cos 1 - \sin 1$

and $f'(0^-)$

$$= \lim_{h\to 0} \frac{(0-h-1)\sin\left(\frac{1}{0-h-1}\right) - \sin 1}{-h}$$

$$= \lim_{h\to 0} \frac{(-h-1)\cos\left(\frac{1}{-h-1}\right)\left(\frac{-1}{(-h-1)^2}\right)(-1) - \sin\left(\frac{1}{-h-1}\right)}{-1}$$

[using L' Hospital rule]

$= \cos 1 - \sin 1$

$\Rightarrow \quad f'(0^-) = f'(0^+)$

$\therefore f$ is differentiable at $x = 0$.

32 (c) $y = \tan^{-1} x + \cot^{-1} x + \sec^{-1} x + \text{cosec}^{-1} x$

$$= \frac{\pi}{2} + \frac{\pi}{2}$$

$$\left[\because \tan^{-1}\theta + \cot^{-1}\theta = \frac{\pi}{2} \text{ and } \sec^{-1}\theta + \text{cosec}^{-1}\theta = \frac{\pi}{2}\right]$$

$\therefore \quad y = \pi \Rightarrow \dfrac{dy}{dx} = 0$

33 (d) $y = \sin^{-1}\sqrt{1-x}$

$$\Rightarrow \frac{dy}{dx} = \frac{1}{\sqrt{1-(1-x)}}\cdot\frac{1}{2\sqrt{1-x}}(-1)$$

$$= \frac{-1}{2\sqrt{x}\sqrt{1-x}}$$

34 (b) Given, $g(x) = [f(2f(x) + 2]^2$

$\therefore \ g'(x) = 2f(2f(x) + 2) \cdot f'(2f(x) + 2)\cdot 2f'(x)$

$= 4f(2f(x) + 2)f'(2f(x) + 2)f'(x)$

$g'(0) = 4f(2f(0) + 2)\, f'(2f(0) + 2)f'(0)$

$= 4f(0)f'(0)f'(0)$

$= -4$

$\therefore \ g'(0) = -4$

Exponential and Logarithmic Functions

1 (*a*) Given, $f(x) = ae^{|x|} + b|x|^2$

We know, $e^{|x|}$ is not differentiable at $x = 0$ and $|x|^2$ is differentiable at $x = 0$.

$\therefore$ $f(x)$ is differentiable at $x = 0$, if $a = 0$ and $b \in R$.

2 (*d*)

(i) Domain of the exponential function is R, the set of all real numbers.

(ii) Range of the exponential function is the set of all positive real numbers.

(iii) The point $(0, 1)$ is always on the graph of the exponential function (this is a restatement of the fact that $b^0 = 1$ for any real $b > 1$).

3 (*b*) It was observed that the sum of the series $1 + \frac{1}{1!} + \frac{1}{2!} + \ldots$

is a number between 2 and 3 and is denoted by e.

4 (*b*) Exponential function with base 10 is called common exponential function and with base e is called natural exponential function.

5 (*c*) Let $b > 1$ be a real number. Then, we say logarithm of a to base b is x, if $b^x = a$.

Logarithm of a to base b is denoted by $\log_b a$.

Thus, $\log_b a = x$, if $b^x = a$. Let us work with a few explicit examples to get a feel for this. We know, $2^3 = 8$. In terms of logarithms, we may rewrite this as $\log_2 8 = 3$. Similarly, $10^4 = 10000$ is equivalent to saying $\log_{10} 10000 = 4$. Also, $625 = 5^4 = 25^2$ is equivalent to saying $\log_5 625 = 4$ or $\log_{25} 625 = 2$.

6 (*a*) Fixing a base $b > 1$, we may look at logarithm as a function from positive real number to all real numbers.

This function, called the logarithmic function, is defined by

$$\log_b R^+ \to R$$
$$x \to \log_b x = y, \text{ if } b^y = x$$

7 (*b*) In $\log_b x$, if $b = 10$, then it is common logarithm and if $b = e$, then it is natural logarithm.

8 (*d*)

(i) We cannot make a meaningful definition of logarithm of non-positive numbers and hence the domain of log function is R^+.

(ii) The range of log function is the set of all real numbers.

(iii) The point $(1, 0)$ is always on the graph of the log function.

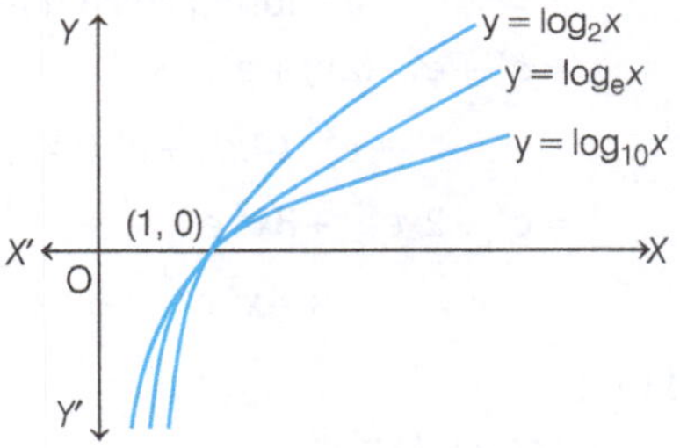

(iv) The log function with base $b(b > c)$ is ever increasing i.e. as we move from the left to right the graph rises above.

9 (*c*) There is a standard change of base rule to obtain $\log_a P$ in terms of $lob_b\, p$. Let $\log_a p = \alpha$, $\log_a p = \beta$ and $\log_b a = \gamma$. This means $a^\alpha = p$, $b^\beta = p$ and $b^\gamma = a$.

Substituting the third equation in the first one, we have

$$(b^\gamma)^\alpha = b^{\gamma\alpha} = p$$

Using this in the second equation , we get

$$b^\beta = p = b^{\gamma\alpha}$$

which implies $\beta = \alpha\gamma$ or $\alpha = \dfrac{\beta}{\gamma}$.

But then $\log_a p = \dfrac{\log_b p}{\log_b a}$

10 (*a*) Let $\log_b pq = \alpha$. Then, $b^\alpha = pq$. If $\log_b p = \beta$ and $\log_b q = \gamma$, then $b^\beta = p$ and $b^\gamma = q$. But, then

$b^\alpha = pq = b^\beta\, b^\gamma = b^{\beta + \gamma}$

which implies $\alpha = \beta + \gamma$ i.e.

$$\log_b pq = \log_b p + \log_b q$$

A particularly interesting and important consequence of this is when $p = q$. In this case, the above may be rewritten as

$$\log_b p^2 = \log_b p + \log_p p = 2\log p$$

An easy generalisation of this (left as an exercise) is

$$\log_b p^n = n \log p$$

For any positive integer n. In fact this is true for any real number n, but we will not attempt to prove this. On the similar lines, the reader is invited to verify

$$\log_b \frac{x}{y} = \log_b x - \log_b y$$

11 (*c*)

(i) Let $y = e^{-x}$.

Using chain rule, we have

$$\frac{dy}{dx} = e^{-x} \cdot \frac{d}{dx}(-x) = -e^{-x}$$

(ii) Let $y = \sin(\log x)$.

Using chain rule, we have

$$\frac{dy}{dx} = \cos(\log x) \cdot \frac{d}{dx}(\log x)$$
$$= \frac{\cos(\log x)}{x}$$

12 (*c*) Let $y = \cos^{-1}(e^x)$.

Using chain rule, we have

$$\frac{dy}{dx} = \frac{-1}{\sqrt{1-(e^x)^2}} \cdot \frac{d}{dx}(e^x) = \frac{-e^x}{\sqrt{1-e^{2x}}}$$

13 (*a*)

A. Let $y = \dfrac{e^x}{\sin x}$.

On differentiating both sides w.r.t. x, we get

$$\frac{dy}{dx} = \frac{d}{dx}\left(\frac{e^x}{\sin x}\right)$$
$$= \frac{\sin x \frac{d}{dx} e^x - e^x \frac{d}{dx} \sin x}{\sin^2 x}$$
$$= \frac{\sin x\, e^x - e^x \cos x}{\sin^2 x}$$
$$= \frac{e^x(\sin x - \cos x)}{\sin^2 x}, x \neq n\pi, n \in Z.$$

B. Let $y = e^{\sin^{-1}x}$

On differentiating both sides w.r.t. x, we get

$$\Rightarrow \frac{dy}{dx} = \frac{d}{dx}(e^{\sin^{-1}x})$$

$$= e^{\sin^{-1}x}\frac{d}{dx}\sin^{-1}x$$

$$\left[\text{using chain rule, } \frac{d}{dx}e^{ax} = e^{ax}\frac{d}{dx}(ax)\right]$$

$$= e^{\sin^{-1}x}\frac{1}{\sqrt{1-x^2}} = \frac{e^{\sin^{-1}x}}{\sqrt{1-x^2}}, \quad x \in (-1, 1)$$

$$\left[\because \frac{1}{\sqrt{1-x^2}} \text{ is defined for } x \in (-1, 1)\right]$$

C. Let $y = e^{x^3}$

On differentiating both sides w.r.t. x, we get

$$\Rightarrow \frac{dy}{dx} = \frac{d}{dx}(e^{x^3}) = e^{x^3}\frac{d}{dx}(x^3)$$

$$= e^{x^3}(3x^2) = 3x^2 e^{x^3}$$

$$\left[\text{using chain rule, } \frac{d}{dx}e^{ax} = e^{ax}\frac{d}{dx}(ax)\right]$$

D. Let $y = \sin(\tan^{-1}e^{-x})$

On differentiating both sides w.r.t. x, we get

$$\Rightarrow \frac{dy}{dx} = \frac{d}{dx}[\sin(\tan^{-1}(e^{-x})]$$

$$= \cos\{\tan^{-1}(e^{-x})\}\frac{d}{dx}\{\tan^{-1}(e^{-x})\}$$

[using chain rule]

$$= \cos\{\tan^{-1}(e^{-x})\}\frac{1}{1+(e^{-x})^2}\frac{d}{dx}(e^{-x})$$

$$= \cos(\tan^{-1}(e^{-x}))\frac{1}{1+e^{-2x}}\cdot(-e^{-x})$$

$$= -\frac{e^{-x}\cos(\tan^{-1}e^{-x})}{1+e^{-2x}}$$

14 (c) Let $y = \log(\cos e^x)$

On differentiating both sides w.r.t. x, we get

$$\frac{dy}{dx} = \frac{d}{dx}[\log\{\cos(e^x)\}]$$

$$= \frac{1}{\cos(e^x)}\frac{d}{dx}\{\cos(e^x)\}$$

[using chain rule]

$$= \frac{1}{\cos(e^x)}\{-\sin(e^x)\}\frac{d}{dx}(e^x)$$

[using chain rule]

$$= -\tan(e^x)\cdot e^x = -e^x\tan(e^x)$$

15 (c) Let $y = e^x + e^{x^2} + \ldots\ldots + e^{x^5}$

On differentiating both sides with respect to x, we get

$$\frac{d}{dx}y = \frac{d}{dx}\{e^x + e^{x^2} + e^{x^3} + e^{x^4} + e^{x^5}\}$$

$$= \frac{d}{dx}(e^x) + \frac{d}{dx}(e^{x^2}) + \frac{d}{dx}(e^{x^3}) + \frac{dv}{dx}(e^{x^4}) + \frac{d}{dx}(e^{x^5})$$

$$= e^x + e^{x^2}\frac{d}{dx}x^2 + e^{x^3}\frac{d}{dx}x^3 + e^{x^4}\frac{d}{dx}(x^4) + e^{x^5}\frac{d}{dx}(x^5)$$

[using chain rule]

$$= e^x + e^{x^2}(2x) + e^{x^3}(3x^2) + e^{x^4}(4x^3) + e^x(5x^4)$$

$$= e^x + 2xe^{x^2} + 3x^2e^{x^3} + 4x^3e^{x^4} + 5x^4e^{x^5}$$

16 (a)

I. Let $y = (e^{\sqrt{x}})^{1/2}$

On differentiating both sides w.r.t. x, we get

$$\frac{dy}{dx} = \frac{1}{2}(e^{\sqrt{x}})^{\frac{1}{2}-1}\frac{d}{dx}e^{\sqrt{x}}$$

$$\Rightarrow \frac{dy}{dx} = \frac{1}{2}(e^{\sqrt{x}})^{-\frac{1}{2}}.e^{\sqrt{x}}.\frac{d}{dx}(\sqrt{x})$$

$$\Rightarrow \frac{dy}{dx} = \frac{1}{2}\frac{e^{\sqrt{x}}}{\sqrt{e^{\sqrt{x}}}} \times \frac{1}{2\sqrt{x}}$$

$$= \frac{e^{\sqrt{x}}}{4\sqrt{x}\sqrt{e^{\sqrt{x}}}} = \frac{e^{\sqrt{x}}}{4\sqrt{xe^{\sqrt{x}}}}$$

II. Let $y = \log(\log x)$

On differentiating both sides w.r.t. x, we get

$$\frac{dy}{dx} = \frac{d}{dx}(\log(\log x))$$

$$= \frac{1}{\log x}\left\{\frac{d}{dx}(\log x)\right\}$$

$$\Rightarrow \frac{dy}{dx} = \frac{1}{\log x}\cdot\frac{1}{x}$$

$$= \frac{1}{x\log x}, x > 1$$

17 (b) I. Let $y = \frac{\cos x}{\log x}$

On differentiating both sides w.r.t. x, we get

$$\frac{dy}{dx} = \frac{d}{dx}\left(\frac{\cos x}{\log x}\right), x > 0$$

$$\Rightarrow \frac{dy}{dx} = \frac{(\log x)\frac{d}{dx}(\cos x) - \cos x\frac{d}{dx}(\log x)}{(\log x)^2}$$

$$\left[\because \frac{d}{dx}\left(\frac{u}{v}\right) = \frac{v\frac{d}{dx}(u) - u\frac{d}{dx}(v)}{v^2}\right]$$

$$\Rightarrow \frac{dy}{dx} = \frac{(\log x)(-\sin x) - (\cos x)\frac{1}{x}}{(\log x)^2}$$

$$\therefore \frac{dy}{dx} = -\left(\frac{x\sin x\log x + \cos x}{x(\log x)^2}\right), \quad x > 0$$

II. Let $y = \cos(\log x + e^x)$

On differentiating both sides w.r.t. x, we get

$$\frac{dy}{dx} = \frac{d}{dx}\{\cos(\log x + e^x)\}$$

$$\Rightarrow \frac{dy}{dx} = -\sin(\log x + e^x)\frac{d}{dx}(\log x + e^x)$$

[using chain rule]

$$\Rightarrow \frac{dy}{dx} = -\sin(\log x + e^x)\left(\frac{1}{x} + e^x\right)$$

$$\Rightarrow \frac{dy}{dx} = \frac{-(xe^x + 1)\sin(\log x + e^x)}{x}$$

18 (c) Let $y = \left[\log\left\{e^x\left(\frac{x-2}{x+2}\right)^{3/4}\right\}\right]$

$$= \log e^x + \log\left(\frac{x-2}{x+2}\right)^{3/4}$$

$$\Rightarrow y = x + \frac{3}{4}[\log(x-2) - \log(x+2)]$$

On differentiating with respect to x, we get

$$\frac{dy}{dx} = \frac{d}{dx}\left[x + \frac{3}{4}\{\log(x-2) - \log(x+2)\}\right]$$

$$= 1 + \frac{3}{4}\left[\frac{1}{x-2} - \frac{1}{x+2}\right]$$

$$= 1 + \frac{3}{x^2-4}$$

$$\therefore \frac{dy}{dx} = \frac{x^2-1}{x^2-4}$$

19 (a) Let $y = \log[\log(\log x^5)]$

On differentiating w.r.t. x, we get

$$\frac{dy}{dx} = \frac{1}{\log(\log x^5)} \cdot \frac{d}{dx}[\log(\log x^5)]$$

$$= \frac{1}{\log(\log x^5)} \cdot \frac{1}{\log x^5} \cdot \frac{d}{dx}(\log x^5)$$

$$= \frac{1}{\log(\log x^5)} \cdot \frac{1}{(\log x^5)} \cdot \frac{1}{x^5} \cdot \frac{d}{dx}(x^5)$$

$$= \frac{5x^4}{x^5 \log x^5 \log(\log x^5)}$$

$$= \frac{5}{x \cdot 5\log x \cdot \log(\log x^5)}$$

$$= \frac{1}{x \log x \cdot \log(\log x^5)}$$

20 (b) $y = \log\left(\frac{1-x^2}{1+x^2}\right)$

$$\frac{dy}{dx} = \frac{1}{\frac{1-x^2}{1+x^2}} \frac{d}{dx}\left(\frac{1-x^2}{1+x^2}\right)$$

$$\frac{dy}{dx} = \frac{1+x^2}{1-x^2} \times \left[\frac{(1+x^2)(-2x) - (1-x^2)(2x)}{(1+x^2)^2}\right]$$

$$= \frac{1+x^2}{1-x^2} \times \frac{2x(-1-x^2-1+x^2)}{(1+x^2)^2}$$

$$= \frac{1+x^2}{1-x^2} \times \frac{-4x}{(1+x^2)^2} = \frac{-4x}{1-x^4}$$

21 (d) Given,

$$f(x) = \log_x(\log_e x) = \frac{\log_e(\log_e x)}{\log_e x}$$

On differentiating w.r.t. x, we get

$$f'(x) = \frac{\log_e x \cdot \frac{1}{\log_e x} \cdot \frac{1}{x} - \log_e(\log_e x) \cdot \frac{1}{x}}{(\log_e x)^2}$$

$$\Rightarrow f'(x) = \frac{1 - \log_e(\log_e x)}{x(\log_e x)^2}$$

$$\Rightarrow f'(e) = \frac{1 - \log_e(\log_e e)}{e(\log_e e)^2} = \frac{1 - \log_e 1}{e} = \frac{1}{e}$$

22 (b) $f(x) = e^x$ and $g(x) = \sin^{-1} x$ and $h(x) = f[g(x)]$

$$\Rightarrow h(x) = f(\sin^{-1} x) = e^{\sin^{-1} x}$$

$$\therefore h(x) = e^{\sin^{-1} x}$$

$$\Rightarrow h'(x) = e^{\sin^{-1} x} \frac{1}{\sqrt{1-x^2}}$$

$$\therefore \frac{h'(x)}{h(x)} = \frac{1}{\sqrt{1-x^2}}$$

23 (c) Given, $y = \log x \cdot e^{(\tan x + x^2)}$

$$\therefore \frac{dy}{dx} = e^{(\tan x + x^2)} \cdot \frac{1}{x} + \log x \cdot e^{(\tan x + x^2)}(\sec^2 x + 2x)$$

$$= e^{(\tan x + x^2)}\left[\frac{1}{x} + (\sec^2 x + 2x)\log x\right]$$

24 (b) We have,

$$y = \log_{\sin x}(\tan x) = \frac{\log \tan x}{\log \sin x}$$

$$\therefore \frac{dy}{dx} = \frac{\log \sin x \cdot \frac{1}{\tan x} \cdot \sec^2 x - \log \tan x \times \frac{1}{\sin x}\cos x}{(\log \sin x)^2}$$

At $x = \frac{\pi}{4}$,

$$\left(\frac{dy}{dx}\right)_{x=\frac{\pi}{4}} = \frac{\left(\log \frac{1}{\sqrt{2}}\right)(\sqrt{2})^2}{\left[\log\left(\frac{1}{\sqrt{2}}\right)\right]^2}$$

$$= \frac{(\sqrt{2})^2}{\log\left(\frac{1}{\sqrt{2}}\right)} = \frac{-2 \times 2}{\log 2} = \frac{-4}{\log 2}$$

25 (b) Given, $y = x \log x$

$$\frac{dy}{dx} = \frac{x}{x} + \log x$$

$$\Rightarrow \frac{dy}{dx} = \log e + \log x$$

$$\therefore \frac{dy}{dx} = \log(ex)$$

26 (d) Given, $y = \frac{\log x}{\log a} + \frac{\log a}{\log x} + 1 + 1$

$$\Rightarrow \frac{dy}{dx} = \frac{1}{x \log a} - \frac{\log a}{x(\log x)^2}$$

27 (d) Given, $y = 2^{\log x}$

$$\frac{dy}{dx} = 2^{\log x} \times \frac{1}{x} \log_e 2$$

$$\therefore \frac{dy}{dx} = \frac{2^{\log x} \log_e 2}{x}$$

28 (d) Given, $y = 5^x x^5$

$$\frac{dy}{dx} = 5^x \log 5 \cdot x^5 + 5^x\, 5x^4$$

$$= 5^x(x^5 \log 5 + 5x^4)$$

29 (b)

A. $f(x) = 2^{\cos^2 x}$

$$\frac{d}{dx} f(x) = f'(x)$$

$$= 2^{\cos^2 x} \frac{d}{dx}(\cos^2 x) \cdot \log_e 2$$

$$= 2^{\cos^2 x} \log_e 2(-2\cos x \sin x)$$

$$= -2^{\cos^2 x} \sin 2x \log_e 2$$

B. $f(x) = \frac{8^x}{x^8}$

$$f'(x) = \frac{x^8 \cdot \frac{d}{dx} 8^x - 8^x \frac{d}{dx}(x^8)}{(x^8)^2}$$

$$= \frac{x^8\, 8^x \cdot \log_e 8 - 8^x \cdot 8x^7}{x^{16}}$$

$$= \frac{8^x}{x^{16}}[x^8 \log_e 8 - 8x^7]$$

$$= \frac{8^x}{x^8}\left[\log_e 8 - \frac{8}{x}\right]$$

C. $f(x) = \log(x + \sqrt{x^2 + a})$

$$f'(x) = \frac{1}{x + \sqrt{x^2+a}} \cdot \frac{d}{dx}(x + \sqrt{x^2+a})$$

$$= \frac{1}{x + \sqrt{x^2+a}} \times \left[1 + \frac{1}{2\sqrt{x^2+a}} 2x\right]$$

$$= \frac{1}{x + \sqrt{x^2+a^2}}\left[\frac{\sqrt{x^2+a^2} + x}{\sqrt{x^2+a}}\right]$$

$$= \frac{1}{\sqrt{x^2+a}}$$

D. $f(x) = \log[\log(\log \sin x)]$

$$f'(x) = \frac{1}{\log(\log \sin x)} \cdot \frac{d}{dx}(\log \log \sin x)$$

$$= \frac{1}{\log(\log \sin x)} \times \frac{1}{\log \sin x} \times \frac{d}{dx}(\log \sin x)$$

$$= \frac{1}{\log(\log \sin x)} \times \frac{1}{\log \sin x} \times \frac{1}{\sin x}\frac{d}{dx}(\sin x)$$

$$= \frac{1}{\log(\log \sin x)} \times \frac{1}{\log \sin x} \times \frac{\cos x}{\sin x}$$

$$f'(x) = \frac{\cot x}{\log(\log \sin x)(\log \sin x)}$$

30 (c) Since, $f'(x) > \phi'(x)$

$$2^{2x-1}(2\log 2) > -2^x \log 2 + 2\log 2$$

$\Rightarrow \quad 2^{2x} > -2^x + 2$

$\Rightarrow \quad 2^{2x} + 2^x - 2 > 0$

$\Rightarrow (2^x - 1)(2^x + 2) > 0$

$\Rightarrow \quad 2^x - 1 > 0$ $\quad [\because 2^x + 2 > 0 \text{ for all } x]$

$\Rightarrow \quad 2^x > 1$

$\therefore \quad x > 0$

31 (d) Given, $y = \log_2[\log_2(x)]$

$$= \frac{\log_e(\log_2 x)}{\log_e 2} = \frac{\log\left[\frac{\log_e x}{\log_e 2}\right]}{\log_e 2}$$

$$\Rightarrow y = \frac{\log(\log_e x) - \log_e(\log_e 2)}{\log_e 2}$$

On differentiating w.r.t. x, we get

$$\frac{dy}{dx} = \frac{1}{\log_e 2}\left[\frac{1}{x \log_e x} - 0\right]$$

$$= \frac{\log_2 e}{x \log_e x}$$

Logarithmic Differentiation and Derivatives of Functions in Parametric Form

1 (c) $y = f(x) = [u(x)]^{v(x)}$

On taking logarithm (to base e) the above equation can be rewritten as

$$\log y = v(x)\log[u(x)]$$

Using chain rule, we may differentiate this to get

$$\frac{1}{y} \cdot \frac{dy}{dx} = v(x) \cdot \frac{1}{u(x)} \cdot u'(x) + v'(x) \cdot \log[u(x)]$$

which implies that

$$\frac{dy}{dx} = y\left[\frac{v(x)}{u(x)} \cdot u'(x) + v'(x) \cdot \log[u(x)]\right]$$

2 (a) Let $y = \sqrt{\frac{(x-3)(x^2+4)}{(3x^2+4x+5)}}$

Taking log on both sides, we have

$$\log y = \frac{1}{2}[\log(x-3) + \log(x^2+4) - \log(3x^2+4x+5)]$$

Now, on differentiating both sides with respect to x, we get

$$\frac{1}{y} \cdot \frac{dy}{dx} = \frac{1}{2}\left[\frac{1}{x-3} + \frac{2x}{x^2+4} - \frac{6x+4}{3x^2+4x+5}\right]$$

or $$\frac{dy}{dx} = \frac{y}{2}\left[\frac{1}{x-3} + \frac{2x}{x^2+4} - \frac{6x+4}{3x^2+4x+5}\right]$$

$$= \frac{1}{2}\sqrt{\frac{(x-3)(x^2+4)}{3x^2+4x+5}}\left[\frac{1}{(x-3)} + \frac{2x}{x^2+4} - \frac{6x+4}{3x^2+4x+5}\right]$$

3 (a) A. Let $y = a^x$.

Then, $\log y = x \log a$

On differentiating both sides w.r.t. x, we get

$$\frac{1}{y}\frac{dy}{dx} = \log a$$

or $$\frac{dy}{dx} = y \log a$$

Thus, $$\frac{d}{dx}(a^x) = a^x \log a$$

Alternate Method

$$\frac{d}{dx}(a^x) = \frac{d}{dx}e^{(x\log a)}$$

$$= e^{x\log a}\frac{d}{dx}(x \log a)$$

$$= e^{x\log a} \cdot \log a = a^x \log a$$

B. Let $y = x^{\sin x}$.

Taking log on both sides, we have

$$\log y = \sin x \log x$$

$$\therefore \quad \frac{1}{y} \cdot \frac{dy}{dx} = \sin x \frac{d}{dx}(\log x) + \log x \frac{d}{dx}(\sin x)$$

or $$\frac{1}{y} \cdot \frac{dy}{dx} = (\sin x)\frac{1}{x} + \log x \cos x$$

$$\Rightarrow \frac{dy}{dx} = y\left[\frac{\sin x}{x} + \cos x \log x\right]$$

$$= x^{\sin x}\left[\frac{\sin x}{x} + \cos x \log x\right]$$

$$\frac{dy}{dx} = x^{\sin x - 1} \cdot \sin x + x^{\sin x} \cdot \cos x \log x$$

C. Given that $y^x + x^y + x^x = a^b$

Putting $u = y^x$, $v = x^y$ and $w = x^x$, we get

$$u + v + w = a^b$$

Therefore, $$\frac{du}{dx} + \frac{dv}{dx} + \frac{dw}{dx} = 0 \quad \text{...(i)}$$

Now, $u = y^x$.

Taking log on both sides, we get

$$\log u = x \log y$$

On differentiating both sides w.r.t. x, we get

$$\frac{1}{w} \cdot \frac{dw}{dx} = x\frac{d}{dx}(\log x) + \log x \cdot \frac{d}{dx}(x)$$

$$= x \cdot \frac{1}{x} + \log x \cdot 1$$

i.e. $$\frac{dw}{dx} = w(1 + \log x)$$

$$= x^x(1 + \log x) \quad \text{...(iv)}$$

From Eqs. (i), (ii), (iii) and (iv), we get

$$y^x\left(\frac{x}{y}\frac{dy}{dx} + \log y\right) + x^y\left(\frac{y}{x} + \log x \frac{dy}{dx}\right) + x^x(1 + \log x) = 0$$

or $$(x \cdot y^{x-1} + x^y \cdot \log x)\frac{dy}{dx} = -x^x(1 + \log x) - y \cdot x^{y-1} - y^x \log y$$

Therefore, $$\frac{dy}{dx} = -\frac{[y^x \log y + y \cdot x^{y-1} + x^x(1 + \log x)}{x \cdot y^{x-1} + x^y \log x}$$

D. Let $y = \cos x \cos 2x \cos 3x$.

Taking log on both sides, we get

$\log y = \log (\cos x \cos 2x \cos 3x)$

$[\because \log m \times n \times l = \log m + \log n + \log l]$

or $\log y = \log (\cos x) + \log (\cos 2x) + \log (\cos 3x)$

On differentiating both sides w.r.t. x, we get

$$\frac{d}{dx}\log y = \frac{d}{dx}\log(\cos x) + \frac{d}{dx}\log(\cos 2x) + \frac{d}{dx}\log(\cos 3x)$$

$$\frac{1}{y}\frac{dy}{dx} = \frac{1}{\cos x}(-\sin x) + \frac{1}{\cos 2x}\left(-\sin 2x \frac{d}{dx}(2x)\right) + \frac{1}{\cos 3x}(-\sin 3x)\cdot\frac{d}{dx}(3x)$$

$$\Rightarrow \frac{dy}{dx} = y\{-\tan x - 2\tan 2x - 3\tan 3x\}$$

$$= -y\{\tan x + 2\tan 2x + 3\tan 3x\}$$

$$= -\cos x \cos 2x \cos 3x\{\tan x + 2\tan 2x + 3\tan 3x\}$$

4 (*a*) Let $y = \sqrt{\dfrac{(x-1)(x-2)}{(x-3)(x-4)(x-5)}}$

Taking log on both sides, we get

$$\log y = \log\left\{\frac{(x-1)(x-2)}{(x-3)(x-4)(x-5)}\right\}^{1/2}$$

$$= \frac{1}{2}[\log (x-1)(x-2) - \log(x-3)(x-4)(x-5)]$$

$$= \frac{1}{2}\{\log (x-1) + \log (x-2) - \log(x-3) - \log(x-4) - \log (x-5)\}$$

On differentiating both sides w.r.t. x, we get

$$\frac{1}{y}\frac{dy}{dx} = \frac{1}{2}\left[\frac{d}{dx}\log(x-1) + \frac{d}{dx}\log(x-2) - \frac{d}{dx}\log(x-3) - \frac{d}{dx}\log(x-4) - \frac{d}{dx}\log(x-5)\right]$$

$$= \frac{1}{2}\left\{\frac{1}{x-1}(1-0) + \frac{1}{x-2}(1-0) - \frac{1}{x-3}(1-0) - \frac{1}{x-4}(1-0) - \frac{1}{x-5}(1-0)\right\}$$

$$\frac{dy}{dx} = \frac{y}{2}\left\{\left(\frac{1}{x-1} + \frac{1}{x-2}\right) - \left(\frac{1}{x-3} + \frac{1}{x-4} + \frac{1}{x-5}\right)\right\}$$

$$= \frac{1}{2}\sqrt{\frac{(x-1)(x-2)}{(x-3)(x-4)(x-5)}}\left\{\frac{1}{x-1} + \frac{1}{x-2} - \frac{1}{x-3} - \frac{1}{x-4} - \frac{1}{x-5}\right\}$$

5 (*d*)

I. Let $y = (\log x)^{\cos x}$

Taking log on both sides, we get

$$\log y = \log\{(\log x)^{\cos x}\}$$

$$\Rightarrow \log y = \cos x \log(\log x) \quad [\because \log m^n = n\log m]$$

On differentiating both sides with respect to x, we get

$$\frac{1}{y}\frac{dy}{dx} = \frac{d}{dx}\{\cos x \log(\log x)\}$$

$$\Rightarrow \frac{1}{y}\frac{dy}{dx} = \cos x\,\frac{1}{\log x}\cdot\frac{1}{x} + \log(\log x)(-\sin x)$$

$$\left[\text{using product rule, } \frac{d}{dx}(u\cdot v) = u\frac{dv}{dx} + v\frac{du}{dx}\right]$$

$$\Rightarrow \frac{dy}{dx} = y\left\{\frac{\cos x}{x\log x} - \sin x \log(\log x)\right\}$$

$$= (\log x)^{\cos x}\cdot\left\{\frac{\cos x}{x\log x} - \sin x\log(\log x)\right\}$$

Note *In log function, if base is not given, then base is consider as e, then* $\dfrac{d}{dx}(\log x) = \dfrac{1}{x}$.

If base is other than *e*.

Then, $\dfrac{d}{dx}(\log_a x) = \log_a e\cdot\dfrac{1}{x}$

II. Let $y = x^x - 2^{\sin x}$

Let $u = x^x$ and $v = 2^{\sin x}$

$\therefore \quad y = u - v$

On differentiating both sides with respect to x, we get

$$\frac{dy}{dx} = \frac{du}{dx} - \frac{dv}{dx}$$

Now, $\quad u = x^x \quad$ ...(i)

Taking log on both sides, we get

$$\Rightarrow \log u = \log x^x$$

$$\Rightarrow \log u = x\log x$$

$$\Rightarrow \frac{1}{u}\frac{du}{dx} = x\frac{d}{dx}\log x + \log x\frac{d}{dx}x$$

[differentiate with respect to x]

$$\Rightarrow \frac{1}{u}\frac{du}{dx} = x\times\frac{1}{x} + \log x$$

$$\Rightarrow \frac{1}{u}\frac{du}{dx} = 1 + \log x$$

$$\Rightarrow \frac{du}{dx} = x^x(1+\log x)$$

Now, $\quad v = 2^{\sin x}$

Taking log on both sides, we get

$$\Rightarrow \log v = \log(2^{\sin x})$$

$$\Rightarrow \log v = (\sin x)\log 2$$

$$\Rightarrow \frac{1}{v}\frac{dv}{dx} = \cos x(\log 2)$$

[differentiate with respect to x]

$$\Rightarrow \frac{dv}{dx} = v[\cos x\log 2]$$

$$= 2^{\sin x}[\cos x\log 2]$$

Now, putting the values of $\dfrac{du}{dx}$ and $\dfrac{dv}{dx}$ in Eq. (i), we get

$$\frac{dy}{dx} = x^x[1+\log x] - 2^{\sin x}[\cos x\log 2]$$

6 (*b*) Let $y = (x+3)^2(x+4)^3(x+5)^4$

Taking log on both sides, we get

$$\log y = \log\{(x+3)^2(x+4)^3(x+5)^4\}$$

or $\log y = 2\log(x+3) + 3\log(x+4) + 4\log(x+5)$

$[\because \log(lmn) = \log l + \log m + \log n]$

On differentiating both sides with respect to x, we get

$$\frac{d}{dx}(\log y) = 2\frac{d}{dx}\log(x+3) + 3\frac{d}{dx}\log(x+4) + 4\frac{d}{dx}\log(x+5)$$

$$\frac{1}{y}\frac{dy}{dx} = 2\left(\frac{1}{x+3}\right)(1+0) + 3\left(\frac{1}{x+4}\right)(1+0) + 4\left(\frac{1}{x+5}\right)(1+0)$$

$$\Rightarrow \frac{dy}{dx} = y\left\{\left(\frac{2}{x+3}\right)+\left(\frac{3}{x+4}\right)+\left(\frac{4}{x+5}\right)\right\}$$

$$\Rightarrow \frac{dy}{dx} = (x+3)^2(x+4)^3(x+5)^4\left\{\left(\frac{2}{x+3}\right)+\left(\frac{3}{x+4}\right)+\left(\frac{4}{x+5}\right)\right\}$$

$$= (x+3)^2(x+4)^3(x+5)^4\left\{\frac{2(x+4)(x+5)+3(x+3)(x+5)+4(x+3)(x+4)}{(x+3)(x+4)(x+5)}\right\}$$

$$= (x+3)(x+4)^2(x+5)^3(9x^2+70x+133)$$

7 *(a)* Given $y = \left(x+\frac{1}{x}\right)^x + x^{\left(1+\frac{1}{x}\right)}$

Again, let $u = \left(x+\frac{1}{x}\right)^x$, $v = x^{\left(1+\frac{1}{x}\right)}$

$\therefore \quad y = u + v$

On differentiating with respect to x, we get

$$\Rightarrow \frac{dy}{dx} = \frac{du}{dx} + \frac{dv}{dx} \quad \text{...(i)}$$

Now, $u = \left(x+\frac{1}{x}\right)^x$

Taking log on both sides, we get

$$\Rightarrow \log u = \log\left(x+\frac{1}{x}\right)^x$$

$$\Rightarrow \log u = x\log\left(x+\frac{1}{x}\right) \quad [\because \log m^n = n\log m]$$

On differentiating with respect to x, we get

$$\Rightarrow \frac{1}{u}\frac{du}{dx} = x\frac{d}{dx}\log\left(x+\frac{1}{x}\right) + \log\left(x+\frac{1}{x}\right)\frac{d}{dx}(x) \quad \text{[using chain rule]}$$

$$\Rightarrow \frac{1}{u}\frac{du}{dx} = \frac{x\times 1}{\left(x+\frac{1}{x}\right)}\left[1-\frac{1}{x^2}\right] + \log\left(x+\frac{1}{x}\right)$$

$$\Rightarrow \frac{1}{u}\frac{du}{dx} = \frac{x}{\frac{(x^2+1)}{x}}\left[\frac{x^2-1}{x^2}\right] + \log\left(x+\frac{1}{x}\right)$$

$$\Rightarrow \frac{1}{u}\frac{du}{dx} = \left[\frac{(x^2-1)}{(x^2+1)} + \log\left(x+\frac{1}{x}\right)\right]$$

$$\Rightarrow \frac{du}{dx} = u\left[\frac{(x^2-1)}{(x^2+1)} + \log\left(x+\frac{1}{x}\right)\right]$$

$$\Rightarrow \frac{du}{dx} = \left(x+\frac{1}{x}\right)^x\left[\frac{(x^2-1)}{(x^2+1)} + \log\left(x+\frac{1}{x}\right)\right]$$

Now, $v = x^{\left(1+\frac{1}{x}\right)}$

Taking log on both sides, we get

$$\Rightarrow \log v = \log x^{\left(1+\frac{1}{x}\right)}$$

$$\Rightarrow \log v = \left(1+\frac{1}{x}\right)\log x$$

On differentiating with respect to x, we get

$$\Rightarrow \frac{1}{v}\frac{dv}{dx} = \left(1+\frac{1}{x}\right)\frac{d}{dx}(\log x) + \log x\frac{d}{dx}\left(1+\frac{1}{x}\right) \quad \text{[using chain rule]}$$

$$\Rightarrow \frac{1}{v}\frac{dv}{dx} = \left(1+\frac{1}{x}\right)\times\frac{1}{x} + \log x\left[0-\frac{1}{x^2}\right]$$

$$\Rightarrow \frac{1}{v}\frac{dv}{dx} = \left[\frac{x+1}{x^2}\right] - \frac{1}{x^2}\log x$$

$$\Rightarrow \frac{1}{v}\frac{dv}{dx} = \left[\frac{x+1-\log x}{x^2}\right]$$

$$\Rightarrow \frac{dv}{dx} = v\left[\frac{x+1-\log x}{x^2}\right]$$

$$\Rightarrow \frac{dv}{dx} = x^{\left(1+\frac{1}{x}\right)}\left[\frac{x+1-\log x}{x^2}\right]$$

Putting the values of $\frac{du}{dx}$ and $\frac{dv}{dx}$ in Eq. (i), we get

$$\therefore \frac{dy}{dx} = \left(x+\frac{1}{x}\right)^x\left[\frac{(x^2-1)}{(x^2+1)} + \log\left(x+\frac{1}{x}\right)\right] + x^{\left(1+\frac{1}{x}\right)}\left[\frac{x+1-\log x}{x^2}\right]$$

8 *(b)*

A. Let $y = (\log x)^x + x^{\log x}$

Let $u = (\log x)^x$, $v = x^{\log x}$

$\therefore \quad y = u + v$

On differentiating with respect to x, we get

$$\frac{dy}{dx} = \frac{du}{dx} + \frac{dv}{dx} \quad \text{...(i)}$$

Now, $u = (\log x)^x$

Taking log on both sides, we get

$$\Rightarrow \log u = \log(\log x)^x$$

$$\Rightarrow \log u = x\log(\log x)$$

On differentiating with respect to x, we get

$$\Rightarrow \frac{1}{u}\frac{du}{dx} = x\frac{d}{dx}\log(\log x) + \log(\log x)\frac{d}{dx}(x) \quad \text{[using chain rule]}$$

$$\Rightarrow \frac{1}{u}\frac{du}{dx} = \frac{x}{\log x}\times\frac{1}{x} + \log(\log x)$$

$$\Rightarrow \frac{du}{dx} = u\left[\frac{1}{\log x} + \log(\log x)\right]$$

$$\Rightarrow \frac{du}{dx} = (\log x)^x\left[\frac{1}{\log x} + \log(\log x)\right]$$

Again, $v = x^{\log x}$

Taking log on both sides, we get

$\Rightarrow \log v = \log x^{\log x}$

$\Rightarrow \log v = (\log x)(\log x)$

$\Rightarrow \log v = (\log x)^2$

On differentiating w.r.t. x, we get

$$\Rightarrow \frac{1}{v}\frac{dv}{dx} = 2\log x \frac{d}{dx}(\log x)$$

$$= 2\log x \times \frac{1}{x}$$

$$\left[\because \frac{d}{dx}[f(x)]^2 = 2f(x)\frac{d}{dx}f(x)\right]$$

$$\Rightarrow \frac{dv}{dx} = v\left[\frac{2\log x}{x}\right]$$

$$\Rightarrow \frac{dv}{dx} = x^{\log x}\left[\frac{2\log x}{x}\right]$$

Now, putting the values of $\frac{du}{dx}$ and $\frac{dv}{dx}$ in Eq. (i), we get

$$\frac{dy}{dx} = (\log x)^x\left[\frac{1}{\log x} + \log(\log x)\right] + x^{\log x}\left[\frac{2\log x}{x}\right]$$

$$\frac{dy}{dx} = (\log x)^{x-1}[1 + \log x \log(\log x)] + 2x^{\log x - 1}\cdot \log x$$

B. $y = (\sin x)^x + \sin^{-1}\sqrt{x}$

Let $u = (\sin x)^x, v = \sin^{-1}\sqrt{x}$

$\therefore \quad y = u + v$

On differentiating w.r.t. x, we get

$$\Rightarrow \frac{dy}{dx} = \frac{du}{dx} + \frac{dv}{dx} \quad \text{...(i)}$$

Now, $u = (\sin x)^x$

Taking log on both sides, we get

$\log u = \log(\sin x)^x$

$\Rightarrow \log u = x\log(\sin x)$

On differentiating w.r.t. x, we get

$$\Rightarrow \frac{1}{u}\frac{du}{dx} = x\frac{d}{dx}\log(\sin x) + \log(\sin x)\frac{d}{dx}(x)$$

[using product rule]

$$= \frac{x}{\sin x}\cos x + \log(\sin x)$$

$$\frac{du}{dx} = u[x\cot x + \log\sin x]$$

$$= (\sin x)^x[x\cot x + \log\sin x]$$

Again, $v = \sin^{-1}\sqrt{x}$

On differentiating w.r.t. x, we get

Now, $v = \sin^{-1}\sqrt{x}$

$$\frac{dv}{dx} = \frac{1}{\sqrt{1-(\sqrt{x})^2}}\frac{d}{dx}x^{1/2}$$

$$= \frac{1}{\sqrt{1-x}}\frac{1}{2}x^{-1/2}$$

[using chain rule]

$$\Rightarrow \frac{dv}{dx} = \frac{1}{\sqrt{1-x}} \times \frac{1}{2\sqrt{x}}$$

$$\Rightarrow = \frac{1}{2\sqrt{x}\sqrt{1-x}}$$

$$\Rightarrow \frac{dv}{dx} = \frac{1}{2\sqrt{x-x^2}}$$

Putting the values of $\frac{du}{dx}$ and $\frac{dv}{dx}$ in Eq. (i), we get

$$\frac{dy}{dx} = (\sin x)^x[x\cot x + \log\sin x] + \frac{1}{2\sqrt{x-x^2}}$$

C. Let $y = x^{\sin x} + (\sin x)^{\cos x}$

Let $u = x^{\sin x}, v = (\sin x)^{\cos x}$

$\therefore \quad y = u + v$

On differentiating w.r.t. x, we get

$$\Rightarrow \frac{dy}{dx} = \frac{du}{dx} + \frac{dv}{dx} \quad \text{...(i)}$$

Now, $u = x^{\sin x}$

Taking log on both sides, we get

$\log u = (\sin x)\log x$

On differentiating w.r.t. x, we get

$$\frac{d}{dx}(\log u) = \sin x\frac{d}{dx}(\log x) + \log x\frac{d}{dx}(\sin x)$$

[using product rule]

$$\Rightarrow \frac{1}{u}\frac{du}{dx} = \left[\sin x \times \frac{1}{x} + \log x\cos x\right]$$

$$\Rightarrow \frac{du}{dx} = u\left[\frac{\sin x}{x} + \cos x\log x\right]$$

$$\Rightarrow \frac{du}{dx} = x^{\sin x}\left[\frac{\sin x}{x} + \cos x\log x\right]$$

Now, $v = (\sin x)^{\cos x}$

Taking log on both sides, we get

$\log v = \cos x\log(\sin x)$

On differentiating w.r.t. x, we get

$$\frac{d}{dx}(\log v) = \cos x\frac{d}{dx}\log(\sin x) + \log\sin x\frac{d}{dx}\cos x$$

$$\Rightarrow \frac{1}{v}\frac{dv}{dx} = \left[\cos x \times \frac{1}{\sin x} \times \cos x + \log\sin x(-\sin x)\right]$$

$$\Rightarrow \frac{dv}{dx} = v[\cot x\cos x - \sin x\log(\sin x)]$$

$$\Rightarrow \frac{dv}{dx} = \sin x^{\cos x}[\cot x\cos x - \sin x\log(\sin x)]$$

Now, putting the values of $\frac{du}{dx}$ and $\frac{dv}{dx}$ in Eq.(i), we get

$$\frac{dy}{dx} = x^{\sin x}\left[\frac{\sin x}{x} + \cos x\log x\right] + (\sin x)^{\cos x}[\cot x\cos x - \sin x\log(\sin x)]$$

D. Let $y = x^{x\cos x} + \frac{x^2+1}{x^2-1}$

Let $u = x^{x\cos x}, v = \frac{x^2+1}{x^2-1}$

$\therefore \quad y = u + v$

On differentiating w.r.t. x, we get

$$\frac{dy}{dx} = \frac{du}{dx} + \frac{dv}{dx}$$

Now, $u = x^{x\cos x}$

Taking log on both sides, we get

$\log u = x\cos x\log x$

On differentiating w.r.t. x, we get

$$\frac{d}{dx}(\log u) = x\cos x \frac{d}{dx}(\log x) + \log x \frac{d}{dx}(x\cos x)$$

$$= x\cos x \times \frac{1}{x} + \log x \left[x\frac{d}{dx}\cos x + \cos x \frac{d}{dx}(x)\right]$$

$$\Rightarrow \frac{1}{u}\frac{du}{dx} = x\cos x \times \frac{1}{x} + \log x [(-x\sin x) + \cos x]$$

$$\Rightarrow \frac{du}{dx} = u[\cos x - x\sin x \log x + \cos x . \log x]$$

$$\Rightarrow \frac{du}{dx} = x^{x\cos x}[\cos x - x\sin x \log x + \cos x . \log x]$$

Again, $v = \frac{x^2+1}{x^2-1}$

Taking log on both sides, we get

$\log v = \log(x^2+1) - \log(x^2-1)$

On differentiating w.r.t. x, we get

$$\Rightarrow \frac{d}{dx}\log v = \frac{d}{dx}\log(x^2+1) - \frac{d}{dx}\log(x^2-1)$$

$$\Rightarrow \frac{1}{v}\frac{dv}{dx} = \frac{1}{(x^2+1)}\frac{d}{dx}(x^2+1) - \frac{1}{(x^2-1)}\frac{d}{dx}(x^2-1)$$

$$\Rightarrow \frac{1}{v}\frac{dv}{dx} = \frac{2x}{(x^2+1)} - \frac{2x}{(x^2-1)}$$

$$= 2x\left[\frac{(x^2-1)-(x^2+1)}{(x^2+1)(x^2-1)}\right]$$

$$\Rightarrow \frac{dv}{dx} = v\left[\frac{-4x}{x^4-1}\right]$$

$$= \frac{x^2+1}{x^2-1}\left[\frac{-4x}{x^4-1}\right]$$

Now, putting the values of $\frac{du}{dx}$ and $\frac{dv}{dx}$ in Eq. (i), we get

$$\therefore \frac{dy}{dx} = x^{x\cos x}[\cos x - x\sin x \log x + \cos x.\log x] + \frac{x^2+1}{x^2-1}\left[\frac{-4x}{x^4-1}\right]$$

$$= x^{x\cos x}[\cos x.(1+\log x) - x\sin x \log x] - \frac{4x}{(x^2-1)^2}$$

9 (a)

I. Let $y = (x\cos x)^x + (x\sin x)^{1/x}$,

Let $u = (x\cos x)^x, v = (x\sin x)^{1/x}$

$\therefore \quad y = u + v$

On differentiating w.r.t. x, we get

$$\frac{dy}{dx} = \frac{du}{dx} + \frac{dv}{dx} \quad ...(i)$$

Now, $\quad u = (x\cos x)^x$

Taking log on both sides,

$\log u = x\log(x\cos x)$

On differentiating w.r.t. x, we get

$$\frac{d}{dx}(\log u) = x\frac{d}{dx}\log(x\cos x) + \log(x\cos x)\frac{d}{dx}(x)$$

$$\Rightarrow \frac{1}{u}\frac{du}{dx} = x \times \frac{1}{x\cos x}\frac{d}{dx}(x\cos x) + \log(x\cos x) \times 1$$

$$\Rightarrow \frac{1}{u}\frac{du}{dx} = \frac{1}{\cos x}\left(x\frac{d}{dx}\cos x + \cos x\frac{d}{dx}x\right) + \log(x\cos x)$$

$$\Rightarrow \frac{1}{u}\frac{du}{dx} = \frac{1}{\cos x}[x(-\sin x) + \cos x] + \log(x\cos x)$$

$$= \frac{1}{\cos x}[-x\sin x + \cos x] + \log(x\cos x)$$

$$\Rightarrow \frac{1}{u}\frac{du}{dx} = -x\tan x + 1 + \log(x\cos x)$$

$$\Rightarrow \frac{du}{dx} = u[-x\tan x + 1 + \log(x\cos x)]$$

$$\Rightarrow \frac{du}{dx} = (x\cos x)^x[-x\tan x + 1 + \log(x\cos x)]$$

Now, $\quad v = (x\sin x)^{1/x}$

Taking log on both sides, we get

$$\log v = \frac{1}{x}\log(x\sin x)$$

On differentiating w.r.t. x, we get

$$\frac{1}{v}\frac{d}{dx}\log v = \frac{1}{x}\frac{d}{dx}(\log(x\sin x)) + \log(x\sin x)\frac{d}{dx}\left(\frac{1}{x}\right)$$

$$\frac{1}{v}\frac{dv}{dx} = \frac{1}{x}\left[\frac{1}{x\sin x}\frac{d}{dx}(x\sin x)\right] + \log(x\sin x)\left(-\frac{1}{x^2}\right)$$

$$= \frac{1}{x} \times \left[\frac{1}{x\sin x}\left\{x\frac{d}{dx}\sin x + \sin x\frac{d}{dx}x\right\}\right] - \left(\frac{1}{x^2}\right)\log(x\sin x)$$

$$\Rightarrow \frac{1}{v}\frac{dv}{dx} = \frac{1}{x}\frac{1}{x\sin x}[x\cos x + \sin x] + \log(x\sin x)\left(\frac{-1}{x^2}\right)$$

$$= \frac{x\cos x}{x^2\sin x} + \frac{\sin x}{x^2\sin x} + \left(\frac{-1}{x^2}\right)\log(x\sin x)$$

$$\Rightarrow \frac{dv}{dx} = v\left[\frac{\cot x}{x} + \frac{1}{x^2} - \frac{1}{x^2}\log(x\sin x)\right]$$

$$\Rightarrow \frac{dv}{dx} = v\left[\frac{x\cot x + 1 - \log(x\sin x)}{x^2}\right]$$

$$\Rightarrow \frac{dv}{dx} = (x\sin x)^{1/x}\left[\frac{x\cot x + 1 - \log(x\sin x)}{x^2}\right]$$

Now, on putting the values of $\frac{du}{dx}$ and $\frac{dv}{dx}$ in Eq.(i), we get

$$\frac{dy}{dx} = (x\cos x)^x[-x\tan x + 1 + \log(x\cos x)] + (x\sin x)^{1/x}\left[\frac{x\cot x + 1 - \log(x\sin x)}{x^2}\right]$$

II. Given, $x^y + y^x = 1$

Let $\quad u = x^y, v = y^x$

$\therefore \quad u + v = 1$

On differentiating w.r.t. x, we get

$$\frac{du}{dx} + \frac{dv}{dx} = 0 \quad ...(i)$$

Now, $u = x^y$

Taking log on both sides, we get

$$\log u = y \log x$$

On differentiating w.r.t. x, we get

$$\Rightarrow \frac{1}{u}\frac{du}{dx} = y \times \frac{1}{x} + \log x \frac{dy}{dx}$$

[using product rule]

$$\Rightarrow \frac{du}{dx} = u\left[\frac{y}{x} + \log x \frac{dy}{dx}\right]$$

$$\Rightarrow \frac{du}{dx} = x^y\left[\frac{y}{x} + \log x \frac{dy}{dx}\right]$$

$$\Rightarrow \frac{du}{dx} = yx^{y-1} + x^y.\log x \frac{dy}{dx}$$

Now, $v = y^x$

Taking log on both sides, we get

$$\Rightarrow \log v = x \log y$$

On differentiating w.r.t. x, we get

$$\Rightarrow \frac{1}{v}\frac{dv}{dx} = x \times \frac{1}{y}\frac{dy}{dx} + \log y$$

[using product rule]

$$\Rightarrow \frac{dv}{dx} = v\left[\frac{x}{y}\frac{dy}{dx} + \log y\right]$$

$$\Rightarrow \frac{dv}{dx} = y^x\left[\frac{x}{y}\frac{dy}{dx} + \log y\right]$$

$$\Rightarrow \frac{dv}{dx} = xy^{x-1}\frac{dy}{dx} + y^x \log y$$

Now, putting the values of $\frac{du}{dx}$ and $\frac{dv}{dx}$ in Eq. (i), we get

$$yx^{y-1} + x^y.\log x \frac{dy}{dx} + xy^{x-1}\frac{dy}{dx} + y^x \log y = 0$$

$$\Rightarrow \frac{dy}{dx}[x^y \log x + xy^{x-1}] = -y^x \log y - yx^{y-1}$$

$$\therefore \frac{dy}{dx} = -\frac{y^x \log y + yx^{y-1}}{x^y \log x + xy^{x-1}}$$

10 (*b*) Given, $y^x = x^y$

Taking log on both sides, we get

$$\log y^x = \log x^y$$

$$\Rightarrow x \log y = y \log x$$

On differentiating both sides w.r.t. x, we get

$$\frac{d}{dx}(x \log y) = \frac{d}{dx}(y \log x)$$

$$\Rightarrow x\left(\frac{1}{y}\right)\frac{dy}{dx} + (\log y) = y\frac{1}{x} + (\log x)\frac{dy}{dx}$$

[using product rule]

$$\Rightarrow \frac{x}{y}\frac{dy}{dx} - (\log x)\frac{dy}{dx} = \frac{y}{x} - \log y$$

$$\Rightarrow \left(\frac{x}{y} - \log x\right)\frac{dy}{dx} = \frac{y}{x} - \log y$$

$$\Rightarrow \left(\frac{x - y\log x}{y}\right)\frac{dy}{dx} = \frac{y - x\log y}{x}$$

$$\therefore \frac{dy}{dx} = \frac{y}{x}\left(\frac{y - x\log y}{x - y\log x}\right)$$

11 (*a*) Given, $(\cos x)^y = (\cos y)^x$.

Taking log on both sides, we get

$$\log [(\cos x)^y] = \log [(\cos y)^x]$$

or $\quad y \log (\cos x) = x \log (\cos y)$

On differentiating both sides with respect to x, we get

$$y\frac{d}{dx}(\log \cos x) + \log \cos x \frac{d}{dx}y = x\frac{d}{dx}(\log \cos y) + \log \cos y \frac{d}{dx}x$$

[using product rule]

$$y\left(\frac{1}{\cos x}\right)(-\sin x) + \log(\cos x)\frac{dy}{dx} = x\left(\frac{1}{\cos y}\right)(-\sin y)\frac{dy}{dx} + \log(\cos y).1$$

$$\Rightarrow \log(\cos x)\frac{dy}{dx} + x\tan y\frac{dy}{dx} = \log(\cos y) + y\tan x$$

$$\Rightarrow (\log(\cos x) + x\tan y)\frac{dy}{dx} = \log(\cos y) + y\tan x$$

$$\therefore \frac{dy}{dx} = \frac{\log(\cos y) + y(\tan x)}{\log(\cos x) + x\tan y}$$

12 (*b*) Given,

$$f(x) = (1+x)(1+x^2)(1+x^4)(1+x^8)$$

Taking log on both sides, we get

$$\log(f(x)) = \log\{(1+x)(1+x^2)(1+x^4)(1+x^8)\}$$

$$\Rightarrow \log(f(x)) = \log(1+x) + \log(1+x^2) + \log(1+x^4) + \log(1+x^8)$$

On differentiating both sides with respect to x, we get

$$\frac{d}{dx}\log(f(x)) = \frac{d}{dx}\log(1+x) + \frac{d}{dx}\log(1+x^2) + \frac{d}{dx}\log(1+x^4) + \frac{d}{dx}\log(1+x^8)$$

$$\Rightarrow \frac{1}{f(x)}f'(x) = \frac{1}{1+x}(1+0) + \frac{1}{1+x^2}(0+2x) + \frac{1}{1+x^4}(0+4x^3) + \frac{1}{1+x^8}(0+8x^7)$$

$$\Rightarrow f'(x) = f(x)\left\{\frac{1}{1+x} + \frac{2x}{1+x^2} + \frac{4x^3}{1+x^4} + \frac{8x^7}{1+x^8}\right\}$$

$$= (1+x)(1+x^2)(1+x^4)(1+x^8)\left\{\frac{1}{1+x} + \frac{2x}{1+x^2} + \frac{4x^3}{1+x^4} + \frac{8x^7}{1+x^8}\right\}$$

$$\therefore f'(1) = (1+1)(1+1)(1+1)(1+1)\left\{\frac{1}{1+1} + \frac{2}{1+1} + \frac{4}{1+1} + \frac{8}{1+1}\right\}$$

$$= 2^4\left\{\frac{1}{2} + 1 + 2 + 4\right\}$$

$$= 16\left(\frac{15}{2}\right) = 120$$

13 (*c*) Let $y = (x^2 - 5x + 8)(x^3 + 7x + 9)$ ...(i)

(a) Using product rule,

$$\frac{dy}{dx} = (x^2 - 5x + 8)\frac{d}{dx}(x^3 + 7x + 9) + (x^3 + 7x + 9)\frac{d}{dx}(x^2 - 5x + 8)$$

$= (x^2 - 5x + 8)(3x^2 + 7) + (x^3 + 7x + 9)(2x - 5)$

$= 3x^4 - 15x^3 + 24x^2 + 7x^2 - 35x + 56 + 2x^4 + 14x^2 + 18x - 5x^3 - 35x - 45$

$= 5x^4 - 20x^3 + 45x^2 - 52x + 11$ ...(ii)

(b) Writing y as a single polynomial,

$y = (x^2 - 5x + 8)(x^3 + 7x + 9)$

$= x^5 - 5x^4 + 15x^3 - 26x^2 + 11x + 72$

On differentiating both sides with respect to x, we get

$\therefore \frac{dy}{dx} = \frac{d}{dx}(x^5 - 5x^4 + 15x^3 - 26x^2 + 11x + 72)$

$= 5x^4 - 20x^3 + 45x^2 - 52x + 11$ ...(iii)

(c) Taking logarithms on both sides of Eq. (i), we get

$\log y = \log\{(x^2 - 5x + 8)(x^3 + 7x + 9)\}$

$\Rightarrow \log y = \log(x^2 - 5x + 8) + \log(x^3 + 7x + 9)$

On differentiating both sides with respect to x, we get

$\frac{1}{y}\frac{dy}{dx} = \frac{1}{x^2 - 5x + 8}\frac{d}{dx}(x^2 - 5x + 8) + \frac{1}{x^3 + 7x + 9}\frac{d}{dx}(x^3 + 7x + 9)$

[using chain rule]

$\frac{1}{y}\frac{dy}{dx} = \frac{2x - 5}{x^2 - 5x + 8} + \frac{3x^2 + 7}{x^3 + 7x + 9}$

$\Rightarrow \frac{dy}{dx} = y\left(\frac{2x - 5}{x^2 - 5x + 8} + \frac{3x^2 + 7}{x^3 + 7x + 9}\right)$

$= (x^2 - 5x + 8)(x^3 + 7x + 9)\left(\frac{2x - 5}{x^2 - 5x + 8} + \frac{3x^2 + 7}{x^3 + 7x + 9}\right)$

$= (2x - 5)(x^3 + 7x + 9) + (3x^2 + 7)(x^2 - 5x + 8)$

$= 2x^4 + 14x^2 + 18x - 5x^3 - 35x - 45 + 3x^4 - 15x^3 + 24x^2 + 7x^2 - 35x + 56$

$= 5x^4 - 20x^3 + 45x^2 - 52x + 11$ ...(iv)

From Eqs. (ii), (iii) and (iv), we find that result is same in every case.

14 (*c*) Given that

$x = a\cos\theta$

$y = a\sin\theta$

$\therefore \frac{dx}{d\theta} = -a\sin\theta$

$\frac{dy}{d\theta} = a\cos\theta$

Hence, $\frac{dy}{dx} = \frac{\frac{dy}{d\theta}}{\frac{dx}{d\theta}} = \frac{a\cos\theta}{-a\sin\theta} = -\cot\theta$

15 (*b*) Given that $x = at^2$, $y = 2at$

So, $\frac{dx}{dt} = 2at$ and $\frac{dy}{dt} = 2a$

Therefore, $\frac{dy}{dx} = \frac{\frac{dy}{dt}}{\frac{dx}{dt}} = \frac{2a}{2at} = \frac{1}{t}$

16 (*c*) It may be noted here that $\frac{dy}{dx}$ is expressed in terms of parameter only without directly involving the main variables x and y.

17 (*a*) Let $x = a\cos^3\theta$, $y = a\sin^3\theta$.

Then, $x^{\frac{2}{3}} + y^{\frac{2}{3}} = (a\cos^3\theta)^{\frac{2}{3}} + (a\sin^3\theta)^{\frac{2}{3}}$

$= a^{\frac{2}{3}}[(\cos^2\theta + (\sin^2\theta)] = a^{\frac{2}{3}}$

Hence, $x = a\cos^3\theta$, $y = a\sin^3\theta$ are parametric equation of

$x^{\frac{2}{3}} + y^{\frac{2}{3}} = a^{\frac{2}{3}}$

Now, $\frac{dx}{d\theta} = -3a\cos^2\theta\sin\theta$

and $\frac{dy}{d\theta} = 3a\sin^2\theta\cos\theta$

$\frac{dy}{dx} = \frac{\frac{dy}{d\theta}}{\frac{dx}{d\theta}} = \frac{3a\sin^2\theta\cos\theta}{-3a\cos^2\theta\sin\theta}$

$= -\tan\theta = -\sqrt[3]{\frac{y}{x}}$

18 (*a*)

A. Given, $x = 2at^2$, $y = at^4$

On differentiating with respect to t, we get

$\frac{dx}{dt} = (2a)(2t)$ and $\frac{dy}{dt} = a(4t^3)$

$\therefore \frac{dy}{dx} = \frac{\frac{dy}{dt}}{\frac{dx}{dt}} = \frac{dy}{dt} \times \frac{dt}{dx}$

$= \frac{4at^3}{4at} = \frac{t^3}{t} = t^2$

B. Given, $x = a\cos\theta$, $y = b\cos\theta$

On differentiating with respect to θ, we get

$\frac{dx}{d\theta} = a(-\sin\theta)$

and $\frac{dy}{d\theta} = b(-\sin\theta)$

$\therefore \frac{dy}{dx} = \frac{\frac{dy}{d\theta}}{\frac{dx}{d\theta}} = \frac{dy}{d\theta} \times \frac{d\theta}{dx}$

$= \frac{-b\sin\theta}{-a\sin\theta} = \frac{b}{a}$

C. Given, $x = \sin t$, $y = \cos 2t$

On differentiating with respect to t, we get

$\therefore \frac{dx}{dt} = \cos t$

and $\frac{dy}{dt} = -(\sin 2t)2$

$\therefore \frac{dy}{dx} = \frac{\frac{dy}{dt}}{\frac{dx}{dt}} = \frac{dy}{dt} \times \frac{dt}{dx}$

$= \frac{-2\sin 2t}{\cos t} = \frac{-2(2\sin t\cos t)}{\cos t}$

$[\because \sin 2\theta = 2\sin\theta\cos\theta]$

$= -4\sin t$

D. Given, $x = 4t$, $y = \frac{4}{t}$

On differentiating with respect to t, we get

$\frac{dx}{dt} = 4$ and $\frac{dy}{dt} = 4(-1)t^{-2}$

$\therefore \frac{dy}{dx} = \frac{\frac{dy}{dt}}{\frac{dx}{dt}} = \frac{-4t^{-2}}{4} = -\frac{1}{t^2}$

$\left[\because \frac{dy}{dx} = \frac{dy/dt}{dx/dt}\right]$

E. Given, $x = \cos\theta - \cos 2\theta$,
$y = \sin\theta - \sin 2\theta$

On differentiating with respect to θ, we get

$$\therefore \frac{dx}{d\theta} = \frac{d}{d\theta}(\cos\theta - \cos 2\theta)$$
$$= -\sin\theta - (-\sin 2\theta)\,2$$
$$= -\sin\theta + 2\sin 2\theta$$

and $\frac{dy}{d\theta} = \frac{d}{d\theta}(\sin\theta - \sin 2\theta)$
$$= \cos\theta - (\cos 2\theta)2$$
$$= \cos\theta - 2\cos 2\theta$$
$$\Rightarrow \frac{dy}{dx} = \frac{\frac{dy}{d\theta}}{\frac{dx}{d\theta}} = \frac{dy}{d\theta} \times \frac{d\theta}{dx}$$
$$= \frac{\cos\theta - 2\cos 2\theta}{2\sin 2\theta - \sin\theta}$$

19 (*a*)

I. Given, $x = a(\theta - \sin\theta)$,
$y = a(1 + \cos\theta)$

On differentiating with respect to θ, we get

$$\therefore \frac{dx}{d\theta} = \frac{d}{d\theta}a(\theta - \sin\theta)$$
$$= a(1 - \cos\theta)$$

and $\frac{dy}{d\theta} = \frac{d}{d\theta}a(1 + \cos\theta)$
$$= a(0 - \sin\theta)$$
$$\Rightarrow \frac{dy}{dx} = \frac{\frac{dy}{d\theta}}{\frac{dx}{d\theta}} = \frac{dy}{d\theta} \times \frac{d\theta}{dx}$$
$$= \frac{-a\sin\theta}{a(1 - \cos\theta)}$$
$$= \frac{-2\sin\frac{\theta}{2}\cos\frac{\theta}{2}}{2\sin^2\left(\frac{\theta}{2}\right)}$$
$$\left[\because \sin x = 2\sin\frac{x}{2}\cos\frac{x}{2} \text{ and } 1 - \cos x = 2\sin^2\frac{x}{2}\right]$$
$$= -\cot\left(\frac{\theta}{2}\right)$$

II. Given, $x = \frac{\sin^3 t}{\sqrt{\cos 2t}}$

and $y = \frac{\cos^3 t}{\sqrt{\cos 2t}}$

On differentiating with respect to *t*, we get

$$\therefore \frac{dx}{dt} = \frac{d}{dt}\left(\frac{\sin^3 t}{\sqrt{\cos 2t}}\right)$$
$$= \frac{\sqrt{\cos 2t}\,(3\sin^2 t\cos t) - \sin^3 t\left(\frac{-2\sin 2t}{2\sqrt{\cos 2t}}\right)}{(\sqrt{\cos 2t})^2}$$
$$\left[\text{using quotient rule, } \frac{d}{dx}\left(\frac{u}{v}\right) = \frac{v\frac{du}{dx} - u\frac{dv}{dx}}{v^2}\right]$$
$$= \frac{3(\cos 2t)\sin^2 t\cos t + \sin 2t\sin^3 t}{\cos 2t\sqrt{\cos 2t}}$$
$$= \frac{3(1 - 2\sin^2 t)\sin^2 t\cos t + (2\sin t\cos t)\sin^3 t}{\cos 2t\sqrt{\cos 2t}}$$
$$[\because \cos 2\theta = 1 - 2\sin^2\theta \text{ and } \sin 2\theta = 2\sin\theta\cos\theta]$$
$$= \frac{3\sin^2 t\cos t - 4\sin^4 t\cos t}{\cos 2t\sqrt{\cos 2t}}$$

and $\frac{dy}{dt} = \frac{d}{dt}\left(\frac{\cos^3 t}{\sqrt{\cos 2t}}\right)$
$$= \frac{\sqrt{\cos 2t}\,(-3\cos^2 t\sin t) - \cos^3 t\left(\frac{-2\sin 2t}{2\sqrt{\cos 2t}}\right)}{(\sqrt{\cos 2t})^2}$$
[using quotient rule]
$$= \frac{-3(\cos 2t)\cos^2 t\sin t + \sin 2t\cos^3 t}{\cos 2t\sqrt{\cos 2t}}$$
$$= \frac{-3(2\cos^2 t - 1)\cos^2 t\sin t + \cos^3 t(2\sin t\cos t)}{\cos 2t\sqrt{\cos 2t}}$$
$$\left[\because \cos 2\theta = 2\cos^2\theta - 1,\ \sin 2\theta = 2\sin\theta\cos\theta\right]$$
$$= \frac{3\cos^2 t\sin t - 4\cos^4 t\sin t}{\cos 2t\sqrt{\cos 2t}}$$
$$\Rightarrow \frac{dy}{dx} = \frac{\frac{dy}{dt}}{\frac{dx}{dt}} = \frac{dy}{dt} \times \frac{dt}{dx}$$
$$= \frac{3\cos^2 t\sin t - 4\cos^4 t\sin t}{3\sin^2 t\cos t - 4\sin^4 t\cos t}$$
$$= \frac{\cos^2 t\sin t(3 - 4\cos^2 t)}{\sin^2 t\cos t\,(3 - 4\sin^2 t)}$$
$$= \frac{\cos t\,(3 - 4\cos^2 t)}{\sin t\,(3 - 4\sin^2 t)}$$
$$= \frac{3\cos t - 4\cos^3 t}{3\sin t - 4\sin^3 t}$$
$$= \frac{-\cos 3t}{\sin 3t} = -\cot 3t$$
$$\left[\because \cos 3\theta = 4\cos^3\theta - 3\cos\theta \text{ and } \sin 3\theta = 3\sin\theta - 4\sin^3\theta\right]$$

20 (*b*) Given, $x = a\left(\cos t + \log\tan\frac{t}{2}\right)$

On differentiating with respect to *t*, we get

$$\frac{dx}{dt} = a\left\{-\sin t + \frac{1}{\tan\frac{t}{2}}.\sec^2\frac{t}{2}.\frac{1}{2}\right\}$$
$$\left[\because \frac{d}{dx}(\log|x|) = \frac{1}{x}\right]$$
$$= a\left\{-\sin t + \frac{1}{2\sin\frac{t}{2}\cos\frac{t}{2}}\right\}$$
$$= a\left\{-\sin t + \frac{1}{\sin t}\right\} = a\left\{\frac{1 - \sin^2 t}{\sin t}\right\}$$
$$\left[\because \sin t = 2\sin\frac{t}{2}\cos\frac{t}{2}\right]$$
$$\Rightarrow \frac{dx}{dt} = \frac{a\cos^2 t}{\sin t}$$
$$[\because 1 - \sin^2 t = \cos^2 t] \quad \text{...(i)}$$

Also, $y = a\sin t$
$$\Rightarrow \frac{dy}{dt} = a\cos t \quad \text{...(ii)}$$

From Eqs. (i) and (ii), we get

$$\therefore \frac{dy}{dx} = \frac{\frac{dy}{dt}}{\frac{dx}{dt}} \Rightarrow \frac{dy}{dx} = \frac{a\cos t}{\frac{a\cos^2 t}{\sin t}} = \tan t$$

21 (*a*) Given, $x = a(\cos\theta + \theta\sin\theta)$,
$y = a(\sin\theta - \theta\cos\theta)$

On differentiating with respect to θ, we get

$$\therefore \frac{dx}{d\theta} = a\frac{d}{d\theta}(\cos\theta + \theta\sin\theta)$$
$$= a\left(\frac{d}{d\theta}(\cos\theta) + \frac{d}{d\theta}(\theta\sin\theta)\right)$$

$$= a\{-\sin\theta + (\theta\cos\theta + \sin\theta\cdot 1)\}$$
$$= a\theta\cos\theta$$
[using product rule in $\frac{d}{d\theta}(\theta\sin\theta)$]

and $\frac{dy}{d\theta} = a\frac{d}{d\theta}(\sin\theta - \theta\cos\theta)$
$$= a\left\{\frac{d}{d\theta}(\sin\theta) - \frac{d}{d\theta}(\theta\cos\theta)\right\}$$
$$= a[\cos\theta - \{\theta(-\sin\theta) + \cos\theta.1\}]$$
$$= a\theta\sin\theta$$
[using product rule in $\frac{d}{d\theta}(\theta\cos\theta)$]
$$\Rightarrow \frac{dy}{dx} = \frac{\frac{dy}{d\theta}}{\frac{dx}{d\theta}} = \frac{a\theta\sin\theta}{a\theta\cos\theta} = \tan\theta$$

22 (*a*) Given, $x = \sqrt{a^{\sin^{-1}t}}$,
$$y = \sqrt{a^{\cos^{-1}t}} \text{ i.e. } x = a^{\frac{1}{2}\sin^{-1}t}$$
and $y = a^{\frac{1}{2}\cos^{-t}t}$ $[\because (a^b)^c = a^{bc}]$

On differentiating with respect to t, we get
$$\frac{dx}{dt} = a^{\frac{1}{2}\sin^{-1}t}\log a\frac{d}{dt}\left(\frac{1}{2}\sin^{-1}t\right)$$
$$\left[\because \frac{d}{dx}a^x = a^x\log a\right]$$
$$= a^{\frac{1}{2}\sin^{-1}t}\log a\left(\frac{1}{2\sqrt{1-t^2}}\right)$$
$$= \frac{a^{\frac{1}{2}\sin^{-1}t}\log a}{2\sqrt{1-t^2}}$$
$$\frac{dy}{dt} = a^{\frac{1}{2}\cos^{-1}t}\log a\frac{d}{dt}\left(\frac{1}{2}\cos^{-1}t\right)$$
[using chain rule]
$$= a^{\frac{1}{2}\cos^{-1}t}\log a\left(\frac{-1}{2\sqrt{1-t^2}}\right)$$
$$= \frac{-a^{\frac{1}{2}\cos^{-1}t}\log a}{2\sqrt{1-t^2}}$$
$$\Rightarrow \frac{dy}{dx} = \frac{\frac{dy}{dt}}{\frac{dx}{dt}} = \frac{-a^{\frac{1}{2}\cos^{-1}t}}{a^{\frac{1}{2}\sin^{-1}t}}$$
$$= -\frac{\sqrt{a^{\cos^{-1}t}}}{\sqrt{a^{\sin^{-1}t}}} = -\frac{y}{x}$$

Alternate Method 1
$$x = \sqrt{a^{\sin^{-1}t}}$$
Taking log on both sides, we get
$$\log x = \log(a^{\sin^{-1}t})^{1/2}$$
$$\Rightarrow \log x = \frac{1}{2}\log a^{\sin^{-1}t}$$
$$\Rightarrow \log x = \frac{1}{2}\sin^{-1}t\log a$$
$$\Rightarrow \log x = \frac{1}{2}\log a\sin^{-1}t$$
On differentiating with respect to t, we get
$$\frac{1}{x}.\frac{dx}{dt} = \frac{1}{2}\log a\frac{d}{dt}(\sin^{-1}t)$$
$$= \frac{1}{2}\log a\frac{1}{\sqrt{1-t^2}}$$
$$\Rightarrow \frac{dx}{dt} = \frac{x\log a}{2}\times\frac{1}{\sqrt{1-t^2}}$$
Again, $y = \sqrt{a^{\cos^{-1}t}}$

Taking log on both sides, we get
$$\log y = \log(a^{\cos^{-1}t})^{1/2}$$
$$\Rightarrow \log y = \frac{1}{2}\log a^{\cos^{-1}t}$$
$$\Rightarrow \log y = \frac{1}{2}\cos^{-1}t\log a$$
On differentiating with respect to t, we get
$$\frac{1}{y}.\frac{dy}{dt} = \frac{1}{2}\log a\times\left[\frac{-1}{\sqrt{1-t^2}}\right]$$
$$\Rightarrow \frac{dy}{dt} = -\frac{y\log a}{2}\times\frac{1}{\sqrt{1-t^2}}$$
We know that
$$\frac{dy}{dx} = \frac{dy}{dt}\times\frac{dt}{dx}$$
$$\Rightarrow \frac{dy}{dx} = \frac{-y\log a}{2}\times\frac{1}{\sqrt{1-t^2}}\times\frac{2\times\sqrt{1-t^2}}{x\log a}$$
$$\therefore \frac{dy}{dx} = \frac{-y}{x}$$

Alternate Method 2
$$x = \sqrt{a^{\sin^{-1}t}} \quad \text{...(i)}$$
and $y = \sqrt{a^{\cos^{-1}t}}$ ...(ii)

Multiplying Eqs. (i) and (ii), we get
$$\Rightarrow xy = \sqrt{a^{\sin^{-1}t}}\times\sqrt{a^{\cos^{-1}t}}$$
$$\Rightarrow xy = \sqrt{a^{\sin^{-1}t}.a^{\cos^{-1}t}}$$
$$\Rightarrow xy = \sqrt{a^{\sin^{-1}t+\cos^{-1}t}}$$
$$\left[\because \sin^{-1}x + \cos^{-1}x = \frac{\pi}{2}\right]$$
$$\Rightarrow xy = \sqrt{a^{\frac{\pi}{2}}}$$
On differentiating with respect to x, we get
$$x\frac{dy}{dx} + y = 0 \Rightarrow x\frac{dy}{dx} = -y$$
$$\therefore \frac{dy}{dx} = \frac{-y}{x}$$

23 (*d*) Here, $y^x = e^{y-x}$

Taking log on both sides, we get
$$\log y^x = \log e^{y-x}$$
$$\Rightarrow x\log y = (y-x)\log e$$
$[\because \log a^b = b\log a \text{ and } \log e = 1]$
$$\Rightarrow x\log y = y - x \quad \text{...(i)}$$
On differentiating w.r.t x, we get
$$\frac{d}{dx}(x\log y) = \frac{d}{dx}(y-x)$$
[using product rule]
$$\Rightarrow \left[x\frac{d}{dx}(\log y) + \log y\frac{d}{dx}(x)\right] = \frac{dy}{dx} - 1$$
$$\Rightarrow x\left(\frac{1}{y}\right)\frac{dy}{dx} + \log y(1) = \frac{dy}{dx} - 1$$
$$\Rightarrow \frac{dy}{dx}\left(\frac{x}{y} - 1\right) = -1 - \log y$$
$$\Rightarrow \frac{dy}{dx}\left[\frac{y}{(1+\log y)y} - 1\right] = -(1+\log y)$$
$$\left[\because \text{from Eq. (i), } x = \frac{y}{(1+\log y)}\right]$$
$$\Rightarrow \frac{dy}{dx}\left[\frac{1-1-\log y}{1+\log y}\right] = -(1+\log y)$$
$$\Rightarrow \frac{dy}{dx} = -\frac{(1+\log y)^2}{-\log y}$$
$$\therefore \frac{dy}{dx} = \frac{(1+\log y)^2}{\log y}$$

24 (*a*) Given that $x = e^{\frac{x}{y}}$

Taking log on both sides, we get

$$\log x = \frac{x}{y} \cdot \log e = \frac{x}{y}$$

$$\Rightarrow \quad x = y \log x$$

Now, on differentiating with respect to x, we get

$$\Rightarrow \quad 1 = y \cdot \frac{1}{x} + \log x \cdot \frac{dy}{dx}$$

$$\therefore \quad \frac{dy}{dx} = \frac{x-y}{x \log x}$$

25 (*b*) Given that

$$y = (\cos x)^{(\cos x)^{(\cos x)^{\cdots\infty}}}$$

$$\Rightarrow \quad y = (\cos x)^y$$

Taking log on both sides, we get

$$\log y = y \log(\cos x)$$

Now, on differentiating with respect to x, we get

$$\frac{1}{y} \cdot \frac{dy}{dx} = y \cdot \frac{1}{\cos x}(-\sin x) + \log(\cos x) \cdot \frac{dy}{dx}$$

$$\Rightarrow \frac{dy}{dx} = y \left\{ -y \tan x + \log \cos x \cdot \frac{dy}{dx} \right\}$$

$$\Rightarrow (1 - y \log \cos x) \frac{dy}{dx} = -y^2 \tan x$$

$$\Rightarrow \quad \frac{dy}{dx} = \frac{y^2 \tan x}{(y \log \cos x - 1)}$$

26 (*a*) Given that

$$x = \exp\left\{ \tan^{-1}\left[\frac{y-x^2}{x^2} \right] \right\}$$

$$x = e^{\tan^{-1}\left(\frac{y-x^2}{x^2}\right)}$$

Taking log on both sides, we get

$$\log x = \tan^{-1}\left(\frac{y-x^2}{x^2} \right)$$

$$\Rightarrow \quad \frac{y-x^2}{x^2} = \tan(\log x)$$

$$\Rightarrow \quad y = x^2 \tan(\log x) + x^2$$

On differentiating with respect to x, we get

$$\frac{dy}{dx} = 2x \tan(\log x) + x^2 \frac{\sec^2(\log x)}{x} + 2x$$

$$\Rightarrow \frac{dy}{dx} = 2x \tan(\log x) + x \sec^2(\log x) + 2x$$

$$\Rightarrow \frac{dy}{dx} = 2x\,[1 + \tan(\log x)] + x \sec^2(\log x)$$

27 (*c*) $f(x) = \cos \frac{x}{2} \cos \frac{x}{2^2} \cos \frac{x}{x_3} \ldots \cos \frac{x}{2^n}$

Taking log on both sides, we get

$$\log f(x) = \log \cos \frac{x}{2} + \log \cos \frac{x}{2^2} + \ldots \log \cos \frac{x}{2^n}$$

On differentiating with respect to x, we get

$$\frac{f'(x)}{f(x)} = -\left(\frac{1}{2} \tan \frac{x}{2} + \frac{1}{2^2} \tan\left(\frac{x}{2^2}\right) + \ldots + \frac{1}{2^n} \tan \frac{x}{2^n} \right)$$

$$\Rightarrow -\frac{f'(x)}{f(x)} = \frac{1}{2} \tan \frac{x}{2} + \frac{1}{2^2} \tan \frac{x}{2^2} + \ldots + \frac{1}{2^n} \tan \frac{x}{2^n}$$

28 (*b*) **Trick** $\cos A \cos 2A \cos 2^2 A \ldots \cos 2^{n-1} A$

$$= \frac{\sin(2^n A)}{2^n \sin A}$$

$\therefore \cos x \cos 2x \cos 4x \cos 8x \cos 16x$

$$= \frac{\sin 32x}{32 \sin x}$$

$$\Rightarrow \quad f(x) = \frac{1}{32} \cdot \frac{\sin 32x}{\sin x}$$

$$\therefore \quad f'(x) = \frac{1}{32} \times \frac{\sin x\,(32 \cos 32x) - \sin 32x \cos x}{\sin^2 x}$$

$$\Rightarrow f'\left(\frac{\pi}{4}\right) = \frac{1}{\sin \frac{\pi}{4}} = \sqrt{2}$$

29 (*d*) We have,

$$\frac{dx}{dt} = a\left[\frac{-\sin t \cos 2t - \cos t \cdot \sin 2t}{\sqrt{\cos 2t}} \right] = \frac{-a \sin 3t}{\sqrt{\cos 2t}}$$

and $$\frac{dy}{dt} = a \left[\frac{\cos t(\cos 2t) - \sin t \cdot \sin 2t}{\sqrt{\cos 2t}} \right] = \frac{a \cos 3t}{\sqrt{\cos 2t}}$$

$$\therefore \quad \frac{dy}{dx} = \frac{dy/dt}{dx/dt} = -\cot 3t$$

$$\Rightarrow \frac{d^2y}{dx^2} = 3 \operatorname{cosec}^2 3t \, \frac{dt}{dx} = \frac{-3 \operatorname{cosec}^2 3t \cdot \sqrt{\cos 2t}}{a \sin 3t} = -\left(\frac{3}{a}\right) \operatorname{cosec}^3 3t \cdot \sqrt{\cos 2t}$$

$$\therefore \quad \frac{\left[1 + \left(\frac{dy}{dx}\right)^2\right]^{3/2}}{\frac{d^2y}{dx^2}} = \frac{(1 + \cot^2 3t)^{3/2}}{\left(\frac{-3}{a}\right) \operatorname{cosec}^3 3t \sqrt{\cos 2t}}$$

$$\Rightarrow \left| \frac{\left[1 + \left(\frac{dy}{dx}\right)^2\right]^{3/2}}{\frac{d^2y}{dx^2}} \right| \text{ at } t = \frac{\pi}{6} \text{ is } \frac{-a}{3\sqrt{\cos \frac{\pi}{3}}} = \frac{-\sqrt{2}a}{3}$$

30 (*c*) Since, $y = (1+x)(1+x^2)(1+x^4) \ldots (1+x^{2^n})$

$$\Rightarrow (1-x)\,y = (1-x^2)(1+x^2)(1+x^4)\ldots(1+x^{2^n})$$

$$= (1-x^4)(1+x^4)\ldots(1+x^{2^n})$$

$\ldots \ldots \ldots \ldots \ldots$

$\ldots \ldots \ldots \ldots \ldots$

$$= (1-x^{2^n})(1+x^{2^n})$$

$$= 1 - x^{2^{n+1}}$$

$\therefore \quad y = \dfrac{1 - x^{2^{2n+1}}}{(1-x)}$

$\dfrac{dy}{dx} = \dfrac{(1-x)(2^{2^n+1}) \cdot x^{2^{2n+1}} - 1 - (1 - x^{2^{n+1}})(-1)}{(1-x)^2}$

$\therefore \left(\dfrac{dy}{dx}\right)_{x=0} = \dfrac{(1-0)(-2^{2^n+1} \cdot 0) - (1-0)(-1)}{1} = 1$

31 (*a*) Given, $y = |\sin x|^{|x|}$

In the neighbourhood of $-\dfrac{\pi}{6}$, $|x|$ and $|\sin x|$ both are negative

i.e. $\quad y = (-\sin x)^{(-x)}$

Taking log on both sides, we get

$\log y = (-x) \cdot \log(-\sin x)$

On differentiating with respect to x, we get

$\dfrac{1}{y}\dfrac{dy}{dx} = (-x)\left(\dfrac{1}{-\sin x}\right) \cdot (-\cos x) + \log(-\sin x) \cdot (-1)$

$= -x \cot x - \log(-\sin x)$

$= -[x \cot x + \log(-\sin x)]$

$\Rightarrow \dfrac{dy}{dx} = -y[x \cot x + \log(-\sin x)]$

$\left(\dfrac{dy}{dx}\right)$ at $x = \dfrac{-\pi}{6} = \dfrac{(2)^{\frac{-\pi}{6}}[6\log 2 - \sqrt{3}\pi]}{6}$

32 (*a*) Since, $x^y = y^x$

$\Rightarrow \quad y \log x = x \log y$

On differentiating with respect to x, we get

$\Rightarrow y \cdot \dfrac{1}{x} + \log x \dfrac{dy}{dx} = \dfrac{x}{y}\dfrac{dy}{dx} + \log y$

$\Rightarrow \dfrac{dy}{dx}\left(\dfrac{x}{y} - \log x\right) = \dfrac{y}{x} - \log y$

$\therefore x(x - y\log x)\dfrac{dy}{dx} = y(-x\log y + y)$

33 (*b*) $\because f(x) = (x-2)(x-4)(x-6) \ldots\ldots (x-2n)$

Taking log on both sides of the given equation, we get

$\log f(x) = \log(x-2) + \log(x-4) + \ldots\ldots + \log(x-2n)$

On differentiating with respect to x, we get

$\dfrac{1}{f(x)} f'(x) = \dfrac{1}{x-2} + \dfrac{1}{x-4} + \ldots + \dfrac{1}{(x-2n)}$

$\Rightarrow f'(x) = (x-4)(x-6) \ldots\ldots (x-2n) + (x-2)(x-6) \ldots (x-2n) + \ldots + (x-2)(x-4) \ldots\ldots (x-(2x-2))$

$\therefore \quad f'(2) = (-2)(-4) \ldots (2-2n)$

$= (-2)^{n-1}(1.2 \ldots\ldots (n-1)$

$= (-2)^{n-1}(n-1)!$

34 (*b*) Given, $y = a\sin^3\theta$ and $x = a\cos^3\theta$

On differentiating with respect to θ, we get

$\dfrac{dy}{d\theta} = 3a\sin^2\theta\cos\theta$

and $\dfrac{dx}{d\theta} = -3a\cos^2\theta \cdot \sin\theta$

$\therefore \quad \dfrac{dy}{dx} = \dfrac{dy/d\theta}{dx/d\theta} = -\dfrac{3a\sin^2\theta\cos\theta}{3a\cos^2\theta\sin\theta}$

$= -\tan\theta$

At $\theta = \dfrac{\pi}{3}, \dfrac{dy}{dx} = -\tan\dfrac{\pi}{3} = -\sqrt{3}$

35 (*c*) Given, $x = \log(1+t^2)$

and $\quad y = t - \tan^{-1} t$

$\dfrac{dx}{dt} = \dfrac{1}{1+t^2} 2t$

$\dfrac{dy}{dt} = 1 - \dfrac{1}{1+t^2} = \dfrac{t^2}{1+t^2}$

$\therefore \quad \dfrac{dy}{dx} = \dfrac{t^2/1+t^2}{2t/1+t^2} = t/2 \quad \ldots(i)$

Also, $x = \log(1+t^2) \Rightarrow t^2 = e^x - 1$

From Eqs. (i) and (ii), we get

$\dfrac{dy}{dx} = \dfrac{\sqrt{e^x - 1}}{2}$

36 (*c*)

I. $f(x) = \cos^{-1}\left[\cos\left(\dfrac{\pi}{2} - \sqrt{\dfrac{1+x}{2}}\right)\right] + x^x$

$f(x) = \dfrac{\pi}{2} - \sqrt{\dfrac{1+x}{2}} + x^x$

$\therefore f'(x) = -\dfrac{1}{\sqrt{2}} \cdot \dfrac{1}{2\sqrt{1+x}} + x^x(1 + \log x)$

$f'(1) = -\dfrac{1}{4} + 1 = \dfrac{3}{4}$

II. $y = (1+x)^x$

Taking log on both sides, we get

$\log y = x\log(1+x)$

On differentiating with respect to x, we have

$\dfrac{1}{y}\dfrac{dy}{dx} = \log(1+x) + x \times \dfrac{1}{1+x}$

Thus, $\dfrac{dy}{dx} = (1+x)^x \left[\dfrac{x}{1+x} + \log(1+x)\right]$

Second Order Derivatives

1 (*a*)

A. Given that $y = x^3 + \tan x$, Then,

$\dfrac{dy}{dx} = 3x^2 + \sec^2 x$

$\therefore \dfrac{d^2y}{dx^2} = \dfrac{d}{dx}(3x^2 + \sec^2 x)$

$= 6x + 2\sec x \sec x \tan x$

$= 6x + 2\sec^2 x \tan x$

B. We have,

$\dfrac{dy}{dx} = A\cos x - B\sin x$

$\dfrac{d^2y}{dx^2} = \dfrac{d}{dx}(A\cos x - B\sin x)$

$= -A\sin x - B\cos x = -y$

Hence, $\dfrac{d^2y}{dx^2} + y = 0$

C. Given that $y = 3e^{2x} + 2e^{3x}$.

Then, $\quad \dfrac{dy}{dx} = 6e^{2x} + 6e^{3x}$

$= 6(e^{2x} + e^{3x})$

$\therefore \quad \dfrac{d^2y}{dx^2} = 12e^{2x} + 18e^{3x}$

$= 6(2e^{2x} + 3e^{3x})$

Hence, $\dfrac{d^2y}{dx^2} - 5\dfrac{dy}{dx} + 6y$

$= 6(2e^{2x} + 3e^{3x}) - 30(e^{2x} + e^{3x}) + 6(3e^{2x} + 2e^{3x})$

$= 0$

D. We have, $y=\sin^{-1}x$.

Then, $\frac{dy}{dx}=\frac{1}{\sqrt{(1-x^2)}}$

$\Rightarrow \quad \sqrt{(1-x^2)}\frac{dy}{dx}=1$

So, $\frac{d}{dx}\left(\sqrt{1-x^2},\frac{dy}{dx}\right)=0$

$\Rightarrow \sqrt{(1-x^2)}\cdot\frac{d^2y}{dx^2}+\frac{dy}{dx}\cdot\frac{d}{dx}\sqrt{(1-x^2)}=0$

$\Rightarrow \sqrt{(1-x^2)}\cdot\frac{d^2y}{dx^2}-\frac{dy}{dx}\cdot\frac{2x}{2\sqrt{(1-x^2)}}=0$

Hence, $(1-x^2)\frac{d^2y}{dx^2}-x\frac{dy}{dx}=0$

Alternate Method

Given that $y=\sin^{-1}x$, we have

$y_1=\frac{1}{\sqrt{(1-x^2)}}$

i.e. $(1-x^2)\,y_1^2=1$

So,

$(1-x^2)\cdot 2y_1\,y_2+y_1^2(0-2x)=0$

Hence, $\quad (1-x^2)\,y_2-xy_1=0$

2 (a) Let $y=x\cos x$

On differentiating w.r.t. x, we get

$\frac{dy}{dx}=\frac{d}{dx}(x\cos x)$

$=x\frac{d}{dx}(\cos x)+\cos x\frac{d}{dx}(x)$

$=x(-\sin x)+\cos x\cdot 1$

$=-x\sin x+\cos x$

and $\frac{d^2y}{dx^2}=\frac{d}{dx}(-x\sin x+\cos x)$

$=-\frac{d}{dx}(x\sin x)+\frac{d}{dx}\cos x$

$=-\{x\cos x+\sin x\}-\sin x$

$=-x\cos x-2\sin x$

3 (b) Let $y=e^x\sin 5x$

On differentiating twice with respect to x, we get

$\frac{dy}{dx}=\frac{d}{dx}(e^x\sin 5x)=e^x\frac{d}{dx}(\sin 5x)+\sin 5x\frac{d}{dx}(e^x)$

$=e^x\cos 5x.5+\sin 5x\,e^x$ [using product rule]

$=e^x(5\cos 5x+\sin 5x)$

and $\frac{d^2y}{dx^2}=\frac{d}{dx}\{e^x(5\cos 5x+\sin 5x)\}$

$=e^x\frac{d}{dx}(5\cos 5x+\sin 5x)+(5\cos 5x+\sin 5x)\frac{d}{dx}e^x$

$=e^x\{-5\sin 5x.(5)+\cos 5x.5\}+(5\cos 5x+\sin 5x)\,e^x$

$=e^x\{10\cos 5x-24\sin 5x\}$

$=2e^x(5\cos 5x-12\sin 5x)$

4 (c)

A. Let $y=\tan^{-1}x$

On differentiating twice w.r.t. x, we get

$\frac{dy}{dx}=\frac{d}{dx}(\tan^{-1}x)=\frac{1}{1+x^2}$

and $\frac{d^2y}{dx^2}=\frac{d}{dx}\left(\frac{1}{1+x^2}\right)$

$=\frac{d}{dx}(1+x^2)^{-1}$

$=-1(1+x^2)^{-2}\frac{d}{dx}(1+x^2)$

$=-1(1+x^2)^{-2}(0+2x)$

$=\frac{-2x}{(1+x^2)^2}$

B. Let $y=\log(\log x)$

On differentiating twice w.r.t. x, we get

$\frac{dy}{dx}=\frac{1}{\log x}\frac{d}{dx}(\log x)$

$=\frac{1}{\log x}\cdot\frac{1}{x}=\frac{1}{x\log x}$

and $\frac{d^2y}{dx^2}=\frac{d}{dx}\left(\frac{1}{x\log x}\right)$

$=\frac{d}{dx}(x\log x)^{-1}$

$=-1(x\log x)^{-2}\frac{d}{dx}(x\log x)$

$=-\frac{1}{(x\log x)^2}\left[x\frac{d}{dx}\log x+\log x\frac{d}{dx}(x)\right]$

$=\frac{-1}{(x\log x)^2}\left(x\cdot\frac{1}{x}+\log x\cdot 1\right)$

$=\frac{-(1+\log x)}{(x\log x)^2}$

C. Let $y=\sin(\log x)$

On differentiating twice w.r.t. x, we get

$\frac{dy}{dx}=\cos(\log x)\frac{d}{dx}(\log x)$

$=\cos(\log x)\frac{1}{x}$

$=\frac{\cos(\log x)}{x}$

and $\frac{d^2y}{dx^2}=\frac{d}{dx}\left(\frac{\cos(\log x)}{x}\right)$

$=\frac{x\frac{d}{dx}(\cos(\log x))-\cos(\log x)\frac{d}{dx}(x)}{x^2}$

$=\frac{x\left\{-\sin(\log x)\cdot\frac{1}{x}\right\}-\cos(\log x).1}{x^2}$

(using quotient rule)

$=-\frac{\sin(\log x)+\cos(\log x)}{x^2}$

D. Given, $y=5\cos x-3\sin x$

On differentiating twice w.r.t. x, we get

$\frac{dy}{dx}=-5\sin x-3\cos x$

and $\frac{d^2y}{dx^2}=\frac{d}{dx}(-5\sin x-3\cos x)$

$=-5\cos x+3\sin x$

$=-(5\cos x-3\sin x)=-y$

$\therefore \frac{d^2y}{dx^2}+y=0$

5 (a) Given, $y=\cos^{-1}x$

$\Rightarrow \quad x=\cos y$

On differentiating w.r.t. y, we get

$\frac{dx}{dy}=-\sin y$

$\Rightarrow \quad \frac{dy}{dx}=-\text{cosec}\ y$ ...(i)

Again, on differentiating with respect to x, we get

$\frac{d^2y}{dx^2}=\frac{d}{dx}(-\text{cosec}\ y)$

$=-(-\text{cosec}\ y\cot y)\frac{dy}{dx}$

$=\text{cosec}\ y\cot y(-\text{cosec}\ y)$

$=-\cot y\cdot\text{cosec}^2\ y$ [from Eq. (i)]

6 (*c*) Given,
$y = 3\cos(\log x) + 4\sin(\log x)$ ...(i)

On differentiating with respect to x, we get

$$\frac{dy}{dx} = y_1 = -3\sin(\log x)\frac{d}{dx}(\log x) + 4\cos(\log x)\frac{d}{dx}\log x$$

$$= -3\sin(\log x)\frac{1}{x} + 4\cos(\log x)\frac{1}{x}$$

Multiplying by x, we get

$xy_1 = -3\sin(\log x) + 4\cos(\log x)$ ...(ii)

Again, on differentiating w.r.t. x, we obtain

$$xy_2 + y_1 . 1 = -3\cos(\log x)\frac{d}{dx}(\log x) - 4\sin(\log x)\frac{d}{dx}\log x$$

$$= -3\cos(\log x)\frac{1}{x} - 4\sin(\log x)\frac{1}{x}$$

Multiplying throughout by x, we have

$x^2 y_2 + xy_1 = -(3\cos(\log x) + 4\sin(\log x))$ [from Eq. (i)]

$\Rightarrow \quad x^2y_2 + xy_1 = -y$

$\Rightarrow \quad x^2y_2 + xy_1 + y = 0$

7 (*b*) Given, $y = Ae^{mx} + Be^{nx}$ ...(i)

On differentiating twice w.r.t. x, we get

$$\frac{dy}{dx} = Ae^{mx}\frac{d}{dx}(mx) + Be^{nx}\frac{d}{dx}(nx)$$

$= Ae^{mx}\, m + Be^{nx}\, n$ ...(ii)

$\Rightarrow \dfrac{d^2y}{dx^2} = m^2 Ae^{mx} + n^2Be^{nx}$ ...(iii)

Using Eqs. (i), (ii) and (iii), we have

$$\frac{d^2y}{dx^2} - (m+n)\frac{dy}{dx} + mny$$

$$= m^2 Ae^{mx} + n^2 Be^{nx} - (m+n)\{Ame^{mx} + nBe^{nx}\} + mn\{Ae^{mx} + Be^{nx}\}$$

i.e. $\dfrac{d^2y}{dx^2} - (m+n)\dfrac{dy}{dx} + mny = 0.$

$\therefore \quad \dfrac{d^2y}{dx^2} = (m+n)\dfrac{dy}{dx} - mny$

8 (*a*)

I. Given,

$y = 500e^{7x} + 600e^{-7x}$ ...(i)

On differentiating twice w.r.t. x, we get

$$\frac{dy}{dx} = 500e^{7x}\frac{d}{dx}(7x) + 600e^{-7x}\frac{d}{dx}(-7x)$$

$$= 500e^{7x}(\cdot 7) + 600e^{-7x}\cdot(-7)$$

and $\dfrac{d^2y}{dx^2} = (7\times 500)e^{7x}\cdot 7 - (7\times 600)e^{-7x}(-7)$

$= 49\{500e^{7x} + 600e^{-7x}\}$

$\Rightarrow \quad \dfrac{d^2y}{dx^2} = 49y$

Hence, given Statement I is true.

II. Given, $e^y(x+1) = 1$ ...(i)

$\Rightarrow \quad e^y = \dfrac{1}{x+1}$

On differentiating both sides with respect to x, we get

$$e^y\frac{dy}{dx} = -\frac{1}{(x+1)^2}$$

$$\Rightarrow \left(\frac{1}{x+1}\right)\frac{dy}{dx} = -\frac{1}{(x+1)^2} \quad \left[\because e^y = \frac{1}{x+1}\right]$$

$\Rightarrow \dfrac{dy}{dx} = -\dfrac{x+1}{(x+1)^2} = -\dfrac{1}{x+1}$ ...(ii)

On differentiating again w.r.t. x, we get

$$\frac{d^2y}{dx^2} = \frac{1}{(x+1)^2}$$

or $\dfrac{d^2y}{dx^2} = \left(-\dfrac{1}{x+1}\right)^2 = \left(\dfrac{dy}{dx}\right)^2$

9 (*a*) Given, $y = (\tan^{-1}x)^2$

On differentiating w.r.t. x, we get

$$\frac{dy}{dx} = 2\tan^{-1}x\frac{d}{dx}(\tan^{-1}x)$$

$$= 2(\tan^{-1}x)\frac{1}{1+x^2}$$

or $\quad (1+x^2)\,y_1 = 2\tan^{-1}x \quad \left[\because \dfrac{dy}{dx} = y_1\right]$

Again, on differentiating with respect to x, we get

$$(1+x^2)\frac{dy_1}{dx} + y_1\frac{d}{dx}(1+x^2) = \frac{2}{1+x^2}$$

$$\Rightarrow (1+x^2)y_2 + y_1(0+2x) = \frac{2}{1+x^2}$$

$$\Rightarrow (1+x^2)^2y_2 + 2x(1+x^2)y_1 = 2 \quad \left[\because \frac{d}{dx}y_1 = y_2\right]$$

Miscellaneous Exercise

1 (*a*) Let $y = \sqrt{3x+2} + \dfrac{1}{\sqrt{2x^2+4}}$

$$= (3x+2)^{\frac{1}{2}} + (2x^2+4)^{-\frac{1}{2}}$$

Note that this function is defined at all real numbers $x > -\dfrac{2}{3}$.

Therefore,

$$\frac{dy}{dx} = \frac{1}{2}(3x+2)^{\frac{1}{2}-1}\cdot\frac{d}{dx}(3x+2) + \left(-\frac{1}{2}\right)(2x^2+4)^{-\frac{1}{2}-1}\cdot\frac{d}{dx}(2x^2+4)$$

$$= \frac{1}{2}(3x+2)^{-\frac{1}{2}}\cdot(3) - \left(\frac{1}{2}\right)(2x^2+4)^{-3/2}(4x)$$

$$= \frac{3}{2\sqrt{3x+2}} - \frac{2x}{(2x^2+4)^{\frac{3}{2}}}$$

This is defined for all real numbers $x > -\dfrac{2}{3}$.

2 (*a*)

A. Let $y = \log_7(\log x) = \dfrac{\log(\log x)}{\log 7}$

[by change of base formula]

The function is defined for all real numbers $x > 1$.

Therefore,

$$\frac{dy}{dx} = \frac{1}{\log 7}\frac{d}{dx}(\log(\log x))$$

$$= \frac{1}{\log 7}\frac{1}{\log x}\cdot\frac{d}{dx}(\log x)$$

$$= \frac{1}{x\log x\log 7}$$

3 (*a*)

A. Let $f(x)=\cos^{-1}(\sin x)$. Observe that this function is defined for all real numbers. We may rewrite this function as

$$f(x)=\cos^{-1}(\sin x)$$
$$=\cos^{-1}\left[\cos\left(\frac{\pi}{2}-x\right)\right]=\frac{\pi}{2}-x$$

Thus, $f'(x)=-1$.

B. Let $f(x)=\tan^{-1}\left(\frac{\sin x}{1+\cos x}\right)$.

Observe that this function is defined for all real numbers, where $\cos x\neq-1$, i.e. at all odd multiples of π. We may rewrite this function as

$$f(x)=\tan^{-1}\left(\frac{\sin x}{1+\cos x}\right)$$
$$=\tan^{-1}\left[\frac{2\sin\left(\frac{x}{2}\right)\cos\left(\frac{x}{2}\right)}{2\cos^2\left(\frac{x}{2}\right)}\right]$$
$$=\tan^{-1}\left[\tan\left(\frac{x}{2}\right)\right]=\frac{x}{2}$$

Observe that we could cancel $\cos\left(\frac{x}{2}\right)$ in both numerator and denominator as it is not equal to zero. Thus, $f'(x)=\frac{1}{2}$.

C. Let $f(x)=\sin^{-1}\left(\frac{2^{x+1}}{1+4^x}\right)$. To find the domain of this function, we need to find all x such that $-1\leq\frac{2^{x+1}}{1+4^x}\leq1$. Since, the quantity in the middle is always positive. We need to find all x such that $\frac{2^{x+1}}{1+4^x}\leq1$, i.e. all x such that $2^{x+1}\leq1+4^x$. We may rewrite this as $2\leq\frac{1}{2^x}+2^x$, which is true for all x. Hence, the function is defined at every real number. By putting $2^x=\tan\theta$, this function may be rewritten as

$$f(x)=\sin^{-1}\left[\frac{2^{x+1}}{1+4^x}\right]$$
$$=\sin^{-1}\left[\frac{2^x\cdot2}{1+(2^x)^2}\right]$$
$$=\sin^{-1}\left[\frac{2\tan\theta}{1+\tan^2\theta}\right]$$
$$=\sin^{-1}[\sin2\theta]$$
$$=2\theta=2\tan^{-1}(2^x)$$

Thus, $f'(x)=2\cdot\frac{1}{1+(2^x)^2}\cdot\frac{d}{dx}(2^x)$

$$=\frac{2}{1+4^x}\cdot(2^x)\log2=\frac{2^{x+1}\log2}{1+4^x}$$

D. The function $y=(\sin x)^{\sin x}$ is defined for all positive real numbers. Taking logarithm, we have

$$\log y=\log(\sin x)^{\sin x}$$
$$=\sin x\log(\sin x)$$

Then, $\frac{1}{y}\frac{dy}{dx}=\frac{d}{dx}(\sin x\log(\sin x))$

$$=\cos x\log(\sin x)+\sin x\cdot\frac{1}{\sin x}\cdot\frac{d}{dx}(\sin x)$$
$$=\cos x\log(\sin x)+\cos x$$
$$=(1+\log(\sin x))\cos x$$

Thus, $\frac{dy}{dx}=y[(1+\log(\sin x))(\cos x)$

$$=[1+\log(\sin x)](\sin x)^{\sin x}\cos x$$

4 (*c*) Observe that both y and x are defined for all real $t\neq0$. Clearly,

$$\frac{dy}{dt}=\frac{d}{dt}\left(a^{t+\frac{1}{t}}\right)$$
$$=a^{t+\frac{1}{t}}\frac{d}{dt}\left(t+\frac{1}{t}\right)\cdot\log a$$
$$=a^{t+\frac{1}{t}}\left(1-\frac{1}{t^2}\right)\log a$$

Similarly,

$$\frac{dx}{dt}=a\left[t+\frac{1}{t}\right]^{a-1}\cdot\frac{d}{dt}\left(t+\frac{1}{t}\right)$$
$$=a\left[t+\frac{1}{t}\right]^{a-1}\cdot\left(1-\frac{1}{t^2}\right)$$

$\therefore\quad\frac{dx}{dt}\neq0$ only if $t\neq\pm1$

Thus, for $t\neq\pm1$,

$$\frac{dy}{dx}=\frac{\frac{dy}{dt}}{\frac{dx}{dt}}=\frac{a^{t+\frac{1}{t}}\left(1-\frac{1}{t^2}\right)\log a}{a\left[t+\frac{1}{t}\right]^{a-1}\cdot\left(1-\frac{1}{t^2}\right)}$$
$$=\frac{a^{t+\frac{1}{t}}\log a}{a\left(t+\frac{1}{t}\right)^{a-1}}$$

5 (*b*) Let $u(x)=\sin^2x$ and $v(x)=e^{\cos x}$. We want to find $\frac{du}{dv}=\frac{du/dx}{dv/dx}$.

Clearly, $\frac{du}{dx}=2\sin x\cos x$ and

$$\frac{dv}{dx}=e^{\cos x}(-\sin x)=-(\sin x)e^{\cos x}$$
$$\frac{du}{dv}=\frac{2\sin x\cos x}{-\sin xe^{\cos x}}=-\frac{2\cos x}{e^{\cos x}}$$

6 (*c*) Let $y=(3x^2-9x+5)^9$

On differentiating with respect to x, we get

$$\frac{dy}{dx}=9(3x^2-9x+5)^8\frac{d}{dx}(3x^2-9x+5)$$
$$=9(3x^2-9x+5)^8(6x-9)$$
$$=9\times3(2x-3)(3x^2-9x+5)^8$$
$$=27(2x-3)(3x^2-9x+5)^8$$

7 (*a*)

A. Let $y=\sin^3x+\cos^6x$

On differentiating with respect to x, we get

$$\frac{dy}{dx}=\frac{d}{dx}(\sin^3x+\cos^6x)$$
$$=\frac{d}{dx}(\sin x)^3+\frac{d}{dx}(\cos x)^6$$
$$=3(\sin x)^{3-1}\frac{d}{dx}(\sin x)+6(\cos x)^{6-1}\frac{d}{dx}(\cos x)$$
$$=3\sin^2x\cos x+6\cos^5x(-\sin x)$$
$$=3\sin^2x\cos x-6\sin x\cos^5x$$
$$=3\sin x\cos x(\sin x-2\cos^4x)$$

B. Let $y=(5x)^{3\cos2x}$

Taking log on both sides, we get

$$\log y=\log(5x)^{3\cos2x}$$
$$=3\cos2x(\log5x)$$

On differentiating with respect to x, we get

$$\frac{1}{y}\frac{dy}{dx} = 3\cos 2x \frac{d}{dx}(\log 5x) + \log 5x \frac{d}{dx}(3\cos 2x)$$

$$= (3\cos 2x)\left(\frac{1}{5x}5\right) + (\log 5x)\{3(-\sin 2x)2\}$$

$$\left[\text{using product rule, } \frac{d}{dx}(uv) = u\frac{d}{dx}v + v\frac{d}{dx}u\right]$$

$$\Rightarrow \frac{dy}{dx} = y\left\{\frac{3\cos 2x}{x} - 6(\sin 2x)(\log 5x)\right\}$$

$$\Rightarrow \frac{dy}{dx} = (5x)^{3\cos 2x}\left\{\frac{3\cos 2x}{x} - 6\sin 2x \log 5x\right\}$$

C. Let $y = \sin^{-1}(x\sqrt{x})$

On differentiating with respect to x, we get

$$\frac{dy}{dx} = \frac{d}{dx}(\sin^{-1} x\sqrt{x}),\ 0 \le x \le 1$$

$$\Rightarrow \frac{dy}{dx} = \frac{\frac{d}{dx}(x^{3/2})}{\sqrt{1-(x\sqrt{x})^2}}$$

$$\Rightarrow \frac{dy}{dx} = \frac{\frac{3}{2}x^{1/2}}{\sqrt{1-x^3}}$$

$$\therefore \frac{dy}{dx} = \frac{3}{2}\frac{\sqrt{x}}{\sqrt{1-x^3}}$$

D. Let $y = \dfrac{\cos^{-1}\frac{x}{2}}{\sqrt{2x+7}}, -2 < x < 2$

On differentiating with respect to x, we get

$$\frac{dy}{dx} = \frac{\sqrt{2x+7}\frac{d}{dx}\left(\cos^{-1}\frac{x}{2}\right) - \cos^{-1}\frac{x}{2}\frac{d}{dx}(\sqrt{2x+7})}{2x+7}$$

$$\left[\because \frac{d}{dx}\left(\frac{u}{v}\right) = \frac{v\frac{d}{dx}(u) - u\frac{d}{dx}(v)}{v^2}\right]$$

$$= \frac{\sqrt{2x+7}\dfrac{-1}{\sqrt{1-\left(\frac{x^2}{4}\right)}}\dfrac{1}{2} - \cos^{-1}\left(\frac{x}{2}\right)\dfrac{2}{2\sqrt{2x+7}}}{2x+7}$$

$$= \frac{-\dfrac{\sqrt{2x+7}}{\sqrt{4-x^2}} - \dfrac{\cos^{-1}\left(\frac{x}{2}\right)}{\sqrt{2x+7}}}{2x+7}$$

$$= \frac{-\left\{2x+7+\cos^{-1}\left(\frac{x}{2}\right)\sqrt{4-x^2}\right\}}{\sqrt{4-x^2}\,(2x+7)^{3/2}}$$

$$= -\left[\frac{1}{\sqrt{4-x^2}\sqrt{2x+7}} + \frac{\cos^{-1}\frac{x}{2}}{(2x+7)^{3/2}}\right]$$

8 (a) Let

$$y = \cot^{-1}\left[\frac{\sqrt{1+\sin x}+\sqrt{1-\sin x}}{\sqrt{1+\sin x}-\sqrt{1-\sin x}}\right]$$

$$= \cot^{-1}\left[\frac{\left(\sin\frac{x}{2}+\cos\frac{x}{2}\right)+\left(\cos\frac{x}{2}-\sin\frac{x}{2}\right)}{\left(\sin\frac{x}{2}+\cos\frac{x}{2}\right)-\left(\cos\frac{x}{2}-\sin\frac{x}{2}\right)}\right]$$

$$\left[\begin{array}{l}\because 1+\sin x = \sin^2\frac{x}{2}+\cos^2\frac{x}{2} \\ +2\sin\frac{x}{2}\cos\frac{x}{2} = \left(\sin\frac{x}{2}+\cos\frac{x}{2}\right)^2 \\ \text{and } 1-\sin x = \sin^2\frac{x}{2}+\cos^2\frac{x}{2} \\ -2\sin\frac{x}{2}\cos\frac{x}{2} = \left(\cos\frac{x}{2}-\sin\frac{x}{2}\right)^2\end{array}\right]$$

$$= \cot^{-1}\left(\frac{2\cos(x/2)}{2\sin(x/2)}\right)$$

$$= \cot^{-1}\left(\cot\left(\frac{x}{2}\right)\right) = \frac{x}{2}$$

$$\Rightarrow \frac{dy}{dx} = \frac{1}{2}$$

Note *If* $\frac{\pi}{2} < x < \pi$, *then*

$$\sqrt{1-\sin x} = \sin\frac{x}{2} - \cos\frac{x}{2}.$$

9 (a)

I. Let $y = (\log x)^{\log x}$

Taking log on both sides, we get

$$\log y = \log[(\log x)^{\log x}]$$

$$\Rightarrow \log y = \log x \log(\log x)$$

$$[\because \log m^n = n\log m]$$

On differentiating both sides with respect to x, we have

$$\frac{1}{y}\frac{dy}{dx} = (\log x)\frac{d}{dx}\{\log(\log x)\} + \log(\log x)\frac{d}{dx}\log(x)$$

$$= (\log x)\frac{1}{\log x}\frac{1}{x} + \log(\log x)\frac{1}{x}$$

$$= \frac{1}{x}\{1+\log(\log x)\}$$

$$\Rightarrow \frac{dy}{dx} = \frac{y}{x}\{1+\log(\log x)\}$$

$$= \frac{(\log x)^{\log x}}{x}(1+\log(\log x))$$

$$= (\log x)^{\log x}\left[\frac{1}{x} + \frac{\log(\log x)}{x}\right]$$

II. Let $y = \cos(a\cos x + b\sin x)$

On differentiating with respect to x, we get

$$\frac{d}{dx}\{\cos(a\cos x + b\sin x)\}$$

$$= -\sin(a\cos x + b\sin x)\frac{d}{dx}(a\cos x + b\sin x)$$

$$= -\sin(a\cos x + b\sin x)\{-a\sin x + b\cos x\}$$

$$= \{a\sin x - b\cos x\}\sin(a\cos x + b\sin x)$$

10 (a) Let $y = (\sin x - \cos x)^{(\sin x - \cos x)}$

Taking log on both sides, we get

$$\log y = \log\{(\sin x - \cos x)^{(\sin x - \cos x)}\}$$

or $\log y = (\sin x - \cos x)\log(\sin x - \cos x)$

$$[\because \log m^n = n\log m]$$

On differentiating both sides with respect to x, we get

$$\frac{1}{y}\frac{dy}{dx} = (\sin x - \cos x)\frac{\cos x + \sin x}{\sin x - \cos x} + \{\log(\sin x - \cos x)\}(\cos x + \sin x)$$

$$\Rightarrow \frac{dy}{dx} = y(\cos x + \sin x)\{1 + \log(\sin x - \cos x)\}$$
$$= (\cos x + \sin x)(\sin x - \cos x)^{(\sin x - \cos x)}\{1 + \log(\sin x - \cos x)\}$$

11 (b) $\because \frac{dy}{dt} = 12(0 + \sin t)$

and $\frac{dx}{dt} = 10(1 - \cos t)$

$$\frac{dy}{dx} = \frac{\frac{dy}{dt}}{\frac{dx}{dt}} = \frac{dy}{dt} \times \frac{dt}{dx}$$
$$= \frac{12\sin t}{10(1 - \cos t)}$$
$$= \frac{12 \times 2\sin(t/2)\cos(t/2)}{10\{2\sin^2(t/2)\}}$$
$$= \frac{6}{5}\cot\left(\frac{t}{2}\right)$$
$$\left[\because \sin\theta = 2\sin\frac{\theta}{2}\cos\frac{\theta}{2} \text{ and } \cos\theta = 1 - 2\sin^2\frac{\theta}{2}\right]$$

12 (a) Given, $y = \sin^{-1} x + \sin^{-1}\sqrt{1 - x^2}$

Putting $\sin^{-1} x = \theta \Rightarrow x = \sin\theta$

$$\Rightarrow y = \theta + \sin^{-1}\sqrt{1 - \sin^2\theta}$$
$$\Rightarrow y = \theta + \sin^{-1}(\cos\theta) \quad [\because 1 - \sin^2\theta = \cos^2\theta]$$
$$\Rightarrow y = \theta + \sin^{-1}\sin\left(\frac{\pi}{2} - \theta\right)$$
$$\Rightarrow y = \theta + \frac{\pi}{2} - \theta = \frac{\pi}{2} \quad \left[\because \sin\left(\frac{\pi}{2} - \theta\right) = \cos\theta\right]$$
$$\Rightarrow y = \frac{\pi}{2}$$

On differentiating with respect to x, we get $\frac{dy}{dx} = 0$

13 (c) Given, $x\sqrt{1 + y} + y\sqrt{1 + x} = 0$

$$\Rightarrow x\sqrt{1 + y} = -y\sqrt{1 + x} \quad \text{...(i)}$$

On squaring on both sides of Eq.(i), we get

$$x^2(1 + y) = y^2(1 + x)$$
$$\Rightarrow x^2 - y^2 + x^2y - y^2x = 0$$
$$\Rightarrow (x - y)(x + y) + xy(x - y) = 0$$
$$\Rightarrow (x - y)\{x + y + xy\} = 0$$
$$\Rightarrow x - y = 0 \text{ or } x + y + xy = 0$$
$$\Rightarrow y = x \text{ or } y \cdot (1 + x) = -x$$
$$\Rightarrow y = x \text{ or } y = \frac{-x}{1 + x}$$

But $y = x$ does not satisfy the given equation.

So, we consider only $y = \frac{-x}{1 + x}$

On differentiating with respect to x, we get

$$\frac{dy}{dx} = \frac{d}{dx}\left(\frac{-x}{1 + x}\right)$$
$$= -\left[\frac{(1 + x)\frac{d}{dx}(x) - x\frac{d}{dx}(1 + x)}{(1 + x)^2}\right]$$
$$= -\left[\frac{(1 + x)1 - x(0 + 1)}{(1 + x)^2}\right]$$
$$= -\frac{1}{(1 + x)^2}$$

14 (a) Given,

$$(x - a)^2 + (y - b)^2 = c^2 \quad \text{...(i)}$$

On differentiating with respect to x, we get

$$2(x - a) + 2(y - b)\frac{dy}{dx} = 0$$
$$\Rightarrow \frac{dy}{dx} = -\frac{x - a}{y - b} \quad \text{...(ii)}$$

Again, on differentiating with respect to x, we get

$$\frac{d^2y}{dx^2} = -\frac{(y - b)1 - (x - a)\frac{dy}{dx}}{(y - b)^2}$$
$$\left[\because \frac{d}{dx}\left(\frac{u}{v}\right) = \frac{v\frac{du}{dx} - u\frac{dv}{dx}}{v^2}\right]$$
$$= -\frac{(y - b).1 - (x - a)\left(-\frac{x - a}{y - b}\right)}{(y - b)^2} \quad \text{[using Eq. (ii)]}$$
$$= -\frac{(y - b)^2 + (x - a)^2}{(y - b)^3} = -\frac{c^2}{(y - b)^3}$$

Now,

$$\frac{\left[1 + \left(\frac{dy}{dx}\right)^2\right]^{3/2}}{\frac{d^2y}{dx^2}} = \frac{\left[1 + \left(\frac{x - a}{y - b}\right)^2\right]^{3/2}}{-\frac{c^2}{(y - b)^3}}$$
$$= \frac{\{(y - b)^2 + (x - a)^2\}^{3/2}}{\{(y - b)^2\}^{3/2}\frac{(-c^2)}{(y - b)^3}}$$
$$= \frac{(c^2)^{3/2}}{-c^2} = \frac{c^3}{-c^2} = -c,$$

which is independent of a and b.

15 (b) Given, $\cos y = x\cos(a + y)$

$$\Rightarrow x = \frac{\cos y}{\cos(a + y)}$$

On differentiating both sides w.r.t. y, we get

$$\frac{dx}{dy} = \frac{d}{dy}\left\{\frac{\cos y}{\cos(a + y)}\right\}$$
$$= \frac{\cos(a + y)(-\sin y) - \cos y(-\sin(a + y)1)}{\cos^2(a + y)}$$
$$\left[\text{using quotient rule, } \frac{d}{dy}\left(\frac{u}{v}\right) = \frac{v\frac{d}{dy}u - u\frac{d}{dy}v}{v^2}\right]$$
$$= \frac{\sin(a + y)\cos y - \cos(a + y)\sin y}{\cos^2(a + y)}$$
$$= \frac{\sin(a + y - y)}{\cos^2(a + y)} = \frac{\sin a}{\cos^2(a + y)}$$
$$[\because \sin(A - B) = \sin A\cos B - \cos A\sin B]$$
$$\therefore \frac{dy}{dx} = \frac{1}{\frac{dx}{dy}} = \frac{\cos^2(a + y)}{\sin a}$$

Numerical Type Questions

1 (1.57) Given, $f(x) = \begin{cases} \frac{\frac{\pi}{2} - x}{\cos x}, & x \neq \frac{\pi}{2} \\ 1, & x = \frac{\pi}{2} \end{cases}$

$$\text{LHL}\left(\text{at } x = \frac{\pi}{2}\right) = \lim_{x \to \frac{\pi}{2}^-} f(x)$$
$$= \lim_{h \to 0} f\left(\frac{\pi}{2} - h\right)$$

$$= \lim_{h\to 0} \frac{\frac{\pi}{2} - \left(\frac{\pi}{2} - h\right)}{\cos\left(\frac{\pi}{2} - h\right)}$$

$$= \lim_{h\to 0} \frac{h}{\sin h} = 1$$

$$\text{RHL}\left(\text{at } x = \frac{\pi}{2}\right) = \lim_{x\to \frac{\pi}{2}^+} f(x)$$

$$= \lim_{h\to 0} f\left(\frac{\pi}{2} + h\right)$$

$$= \lim_{h\to 0} \frac{\frac{\pi}{2} - \left(\frac{\pi}{2} + h\right)}{\cos\left(\frac{\pi}{2} + h\right)}$$

$$= \lim_{h\to 0} \frac{-h}{\sin h} = 1$$

Also, $f\left(\frac{\pi}{2}\right) = 1$

$$\therefore \lim_{x\to \frac{\pi}{2}^-} f(x) = \lim_{x\to \frac{\pi}{2}^+} = f\left(\frac{\pi}{2}\right)$$

Hence, $f(x)$ continuous at $t = \frac{\pi}{2}$ or $t = 1.57$

2 (1) Given, $f(x) = \begin{cases} \frac{\sin 2x}{6x}, & \text{if } x \neq 0 \\ 3k, & \text{if } x = 0 \end{cases}$ is continuous at $x = 0$.

$$\therefore \lim_{x\to 0} f(x) = f(0)$$

$$\Rightarrow \lim_{x\to 0} \frac{\sin 2x}{6x} = 3k$$

$$\Rightarrow \frac{1}{6}\lim_{x\to 0} \frac{2\sin 2x}{2x} = 3k$$

$$\Rightarrow \frac{2}{6}\lim_{x\to 0} \frac{\sin 2x}{2x} = 3k$$

$$\Rightarrow \frac{2}{6} = 3k \Rightarrow k = \frac{1}{9}$$

Hence, $9k = 1$

3 (2) We have, $\lim_{x\to 3} \frac{x\,f(3) - 3f(x)}{x-3}$

$$= \lim_{x\to 3} \frac{xf(3) - 3f(3) + 3f(3) - 3f(x)}{x-3}$$

$$= \lim_{x\to 3} \frac{(x-3)f(3) - 3(f(x) - f(3))}{x-3}$$

$$= \lim_{x\to 3} \frac{(x-3)\,f(3)}{x-3} - 3\lim_{x\to 3} \frac{f(x) - f(3)}{x-3}$$

$$= f(3) - 3f'(3)$$

$$= 5 - 3\times 1 = 2$$

4 (0) Putting $x = \cos\theta$, we get

$y = \cos^{-1}(\cos\theta) + \cos^{-1}(\cos\theta)$

We have,

$$x \in (0, 1) \text{ and } x = \cos\theta$$

$$\Rightarrow 0 < \cos\theta < 1$$

$$\Rightarrow 0 < \theta < \frac{\pi}{2}$$

$$\Rightarrow 0 < \frac{\pi}{2} - \theta < \frac{\pi}{2}$$

$$\therefore y = \cos^{-1}(\cos\theta) + \cos^{-1}(\sin\theta)$$

$$\Rightarrow y = \cos^{-1}(\cos\theta) + \cos^{-1}\left(\cos\left(\frac{\pi}{2} - \theta\right)\right)$$

$$\Rightarrow y = \theta + \frac{\pi}{2} - \theta$$

$$\Rightarrow y = \frac{\pi}{2}$$

$$\therefore \frac{dy}{dx} = 0$$

5 (1) Given, $x = a\tan^3\theta$

and $y = a\sec^3\theta$

On differentiating w.r.t. θ, we get

$$\frac{dx}{d\theta} = 3a\tan^2\theta\,\frac{d}{d\theta}(\tan\theta)$$

$$\text{and } \frac{dy}{d\theta} = 3a\sec^2\theta\,\frac{d}{d\theta}(\sec\theta)$$

$$\Rightarrow \frac{dx}{d\theta} = 3a\tan^2\theta\sec^2\theta$$

$$\text{and } \frac{dy}{d\theta} = 3a\sec^3\theta\tan\theta$$

$$\therefore \frac{dy}{dx} = \frac{dy/d\theta}{dx/d\theta}$$

$$= \frac{3a\sec^3\theta\tan\theta}{3a\tan^2\theta\sec^2\theta}$$

$$= \frac{\sec\theta}{\tan\theta}$$

$$= \operatorname{cosec}\theta$$

$$\Rightarrow \left(\frac{dy}{dx}\right)_{\theta=\frac{\pi}{2}} = \operatorname{cosec}\frac{\pi}{2} = 1$$

6 (1) Given,

$$f(x) = \begin{cases} 6x - 5, & 0 < x \le 1 \\ 5x^3 - 4x, & 1 < x < 2 \end{cases}$$

We have,

$$\text{LHL (at } x = 1) = \lim_{x\to 1^-} f(x)$$

$$= \lim_{x\to 1^-} 6x - 5$$

$$= 6\times 1 - 5 = 1$$

$$\text{RHL (at } x = 1) = \lim_{x\to 1^+} 5x^3 - 4x$$

$$= 5(1)^3 - 4(1) = 1$$

and $f(1) = 5\times 1 - 4 = 1$

$$\therefore \lim_{x\to 1^-} f(x) = f(1) = \lim_{x\to 1^+} f(x)$$

Hence, $f(x)$ is continuous at $x = 1$.

7 (10) Given, $f(x) = \begin{cases} \frac{k\cos x}{\pi - 2x}, & x \neq \frac{\pi}{2} \\ 5, & x = \frac{\pi}{2} \end{cases}$

Since, $f(x)$ is continuous at $x = \frac{\pi}{2}$.

$$\therefore \lim_{x\to \frac{\pi}{2}} f(x) = f\left(\frac{\pi}{2}\right)$$

$$\Rightarrow \lim_{x\to \frac{\pi}{2}} \frac{k\cos x}{\pi - 2x} = 5$$

$$\Rightarrow k\lim_{x\to \frac{\pi}{2}} \frac{\sin\left(\frac{\pi}{2} - x\right)}{2\left(\frac{\pi}{2} - x\right)} = 5$$

$$\Rightarrow \frac{k}{2} = 5$$

$$\Rightarrow k = 10$$

8 (11) Given, $f(x) = x^2 + 3x + 8$

We know that a polynomial function is everywhere differentiable.

Therefore, $f(x)$ is differentiable at $x = 4$.

$$\therefore f'(4) = \lim_{h\to 0} \frac{f(4+h) - f(4)}{h}$$

$$= \lim_{h\to 0} \frac{\{(4+h)^2 + 3(4+h) + 8\} - \{16 + 12 + 8\}}{h}$$

$$= \lim_{h\to 0} \frac{16 + h^2 + 8h + 12 + 3h + 8 - 36}{h}$$

$$= \lim_{h\to 0} \frac{h^2 + 11h}{h}$$

$$= \lim_{h\to 0} (h + 11) = 11$$

Assertion and Reason Questions

1 (c) Observe that the function is defined at all real numbers except at 0. Domain of definition of this function is

$D_1 \cup D_2$, where $D_1 = \{x \in R : x < 0\}$ and $D_2 = \{x \in R : x > 0\}$

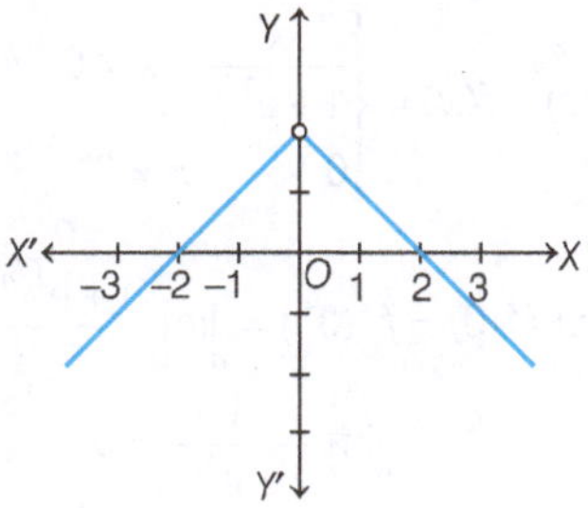

Case I If $c \in D_1$, then

$\lim\limits_{x \to c} f(x) = \lim\limits_{x \to c} (x+2) = c + 2 = f(c)$

and hence f is continuous in D_1.

Case II If $c \in D_2$, then

$\lim\limits_{x \to c} f(x) = \lim\limits_{x \to c} (-x+2)$

$= -c + 2 = f(c)$

and hence f is continuous in D_2.

Since, f is continuous at all points in the domain of f, we deduce that f is continuous. Graph of this function is given in the adjoining figure. Note that to graph this function we need to lift the pen from the plane of the paper, but we need to do that only for those points where the function in not defined.

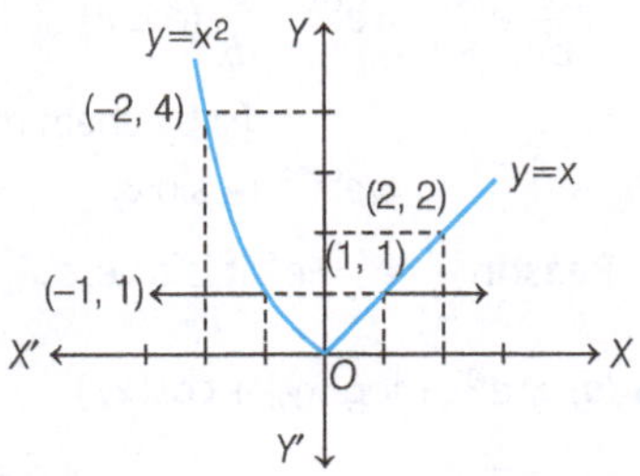

Clearly, the function is defined at every real number. Graph of the function is given in figure. By inspection, it seems prudent to partition the domain of definition of f into three disjoint subsets of the real line.

Let $D_1 = \{x \in R : x < 0\}$, $D_2 = \{0\}$ and $D_3 = \{x \in R : x > 0\}$

Case I At any point in D_1, we have $f(x) = x^2$ and it is easy to see that it is continuous there.

Let $x = -c < 0$, where $c > 0$

$\therefore \quad \lim\limits_{x \to -c} f(x) = \lim\limits_{x \to -c} x^2$

$= \lim\limits_{x \to -c} (-c)^2 = c^2$

$f(-c) = (-c)^2 = c^2$

$\because \quad \lim\limits_{x \to -c} f(x) = f(-c) = c^2$

$\therefore \quad \lim\limits_{x \to -c} f(x) = f(-c)$

$\therefore$ f is continuous in D_1.

Case II At any point in D_3, we have $f(x) = x$ and it is easy to see that it is continuous there.

Let $x = c$

$\lim\limits_{x \to c} f(x) = \lim\limits_{x \to c} x = c$

and $f(c) = c$

$\because \quad \lim\limits_{x \to c} f(x) = f(c) = c$

$\therefore$ f is continuous in D_3.

Case III Now, we analyse the function at $x = 0$. The value of the function at 0 is $f(0) = 0$.

The left hand limit of f at 0 is

$\lim\limits_{x \to 0^-} f(x) = \lim\limits_{x \to 0^-} x^2 = 0^2 = 0$

The right hand limit of f at 0 is

$\lim\limits_{x \to 0^+} f(x) = \lim\limits_{x \to 0^+} x = 0$

Thus, $\lim\limits_{x \to 0} f(x) = 0 = f(0)$ and hence f is continuous at 0. This means that f is continuous at every point in its domain and hence, f is a continuous function.

2 (b)

A. Here, $f(x) = \begin{cases} 2x, \text{if } & x < 0 \\ 0, \text{ if } 0 \le x \le 1 \\ 4x, \text{if } & x > 1 \end{cases}$

For $x < 0$, $f(x) = 2x$; $0 \le x < 1$, $f(x) = 0$ and $x > 1$, $f(x) = 4x$ are polynomial and constant function, so it is continuous in the given interval. So, we have to check the continuity at $x = 0$ and 1.

At $x = 0$,

$\text{LHL} = \lim\limits_{x \to 0^-} f(x) = \lim\limits_{x \to 0^-} (2x)$

Putting $x = 0 - h$ as $x \to 0^-$, $h \to 0$

$\therefore \lim\limits_{h \to 0} [2(0-h)] = \lim\limits_{h \to 0} (-2h)$

$= -2 \times 0 = 0$

$\text{RHL} = \lim\limits_{x \to 0^+} f(x) = \lim\limits_{x \to 0^+} (0) = 0$.

Also, $f(0) = 0$

$\therefore \quad \text{LHL} = \text{RHL} = f(0)$

Thus, $f(x)$ is continuous at $x = 0$

At $x = 1$,

$\text{LHL} = \lim\limits_{x \to 1^-} f(x) = \lim\limits_{x \to 1^-} (0) = 0$,

$\text{RHL} = \lim\limits_{x \to 1^+} f(x) = \lim\limits_{x \to 1^+} (4x)$

Putting $x = 1 + h$ as $x \to 1^+$ when, $h \to 0$

$\lim\limits_{h \to 0} [4(1+h)] = \lim\limits_{h \to 0} (4 + 4h)$

$= 4 + 4 \times 0 = 4$

$\therefore \quad \text{LHL} \ne \text{RHL}$.

Thus, $f(x)$ is continuous everywhere except at $x = 1$.

B. Here, $f(x) = \begin{cases} -2, \text{if } & x \le -1 \\ 2x, \text{if } -1 < x \le 1 \\ 2, \text{ if } & x > 1 \end{cases}$

for $x < -1$, $f(x) = -2$; $-1 < x < 1$, $f(x) = 2x$

and for $x > 1$, $f(x) = 2$, a constant and polynomial function, thus continuous.

We have to check the continuity only at $x = -1$ and 1.

At $x = -1$,

$\text{LHL} = \lim\limits_{x \to -1^-} f(x)$

$= \lim\limits_{x \to -1^-} (-2)$

$= -2$

$\text{RHL} = \lim\limits_{x \to -1^+} f(x) = \lim\limits_{x \to -1^+} (2x)$

Putting $x = -1 + h$ as $x \to -1^+$, $h \to 0$

$\therefore \lim\limits_{h \to 0} 2(-1+h) = \lim\limits_{h \to 0} (-2 + 2h)$

$= -2 + 0 = -2$

Also, $f(-1) = -2$

$\therefore$ LHL = RHL = $f(-1)$

Thus, $f(x)$ is continuous at $x = -1$.

At $x = 1$,

$$\text{LHL} = \lim_{x \to 1^-} f(x) = \lim_{x \to 1^-} (2x)$$

Putting $x = 1 - h$ as $h \to 1^-$, $h \to 0$

$$\therefore \lim_{h \to 0} [2(1-h)] = \lim_{h \to 0} (2 - 2h)$$
$$= 2 - 2 \times 0 = 2$$

$$\text{RHL} = \lim_{x \to 1^+} f(x) = \lim_{x \to 1^+} (2) = 2$$

Also, $f(1) = 2 \times 1 = 2$

$[\because f(x) = 2x]$

$\therefore$ LHL = RHL = $f(1)$

Thus, $f(x)$ is continuous at $x = 1$.

Hence, $f(x)$ is continuous for every value of x.

3 (*b*) In given solution we have proved that, every differentiable function is continuous.

But the converse of the above statement is not true.

We know that, $f(x) = |x|$ is a continuous function. Consider the left hand limit

$$\lim_{h \to 0^-} \frac{f(0+h) - f(0)}{h} = \frac{-h}{h} = -1$$

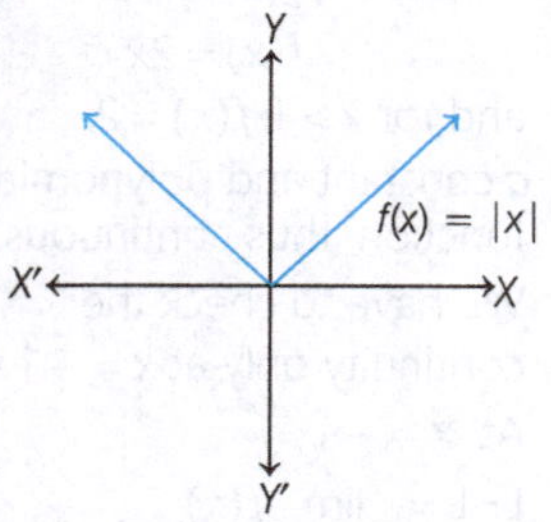

The right hand limit

$$\lim_{h \to 0^+} \frac{f(0+h) - f(0)}{h} = \frac{h}{h} = 1$$

Since, the above left and right hand limits at 0 are not equal.

$\lim_{h \to 0} \frac{f(0+h) - f(0)}{h}$ does not exist and hence f is not differentiable at 0.

4 (*a*) Let $y = \frac{\sin(ax+b)}{\cos(cx+d)}$

On differentiating both sides w.r.t. x, we get

$$\frac{dy}{dx} = \frac{d}{dx}\left(\frac{\sin(ax+b)}{\cos(cx+d)}\right)$$

$$= \frac{\cos(cx+d)\frac{d}{dx}\{\sin(ax+b)\} - \sin(ax+b)\frac{d}{dx}\cos(cx+d)}{[\cos(cx+d)]^2}$$

[by quotient rule]

$$= \frac{\cos(cx+d)\cos(ax+b).(a+0) + \sin(ax+b)\sin(cx+d)(c+0)}{\cos^2(cx+d)}$$

[by chain rule,

$\frac{d}{dx}\sin(ax+b) = \cos(ax+b)\frac{d}{dx}(ax+b)$
$= \cos(ax+b) \times (a \times 1 + 0)$

$\frac{d}{dx}\cos(cx+d) = -\sin(cx+d)\frac{d}{dx}(cx+d)$
$= -\sin(cx+d) \times (c \times 1 + 0)$]

$$= \frac{a\cos(cx+d)\cos(ax+b) + c\sin(ax+b)\sin(cx+d)}{\cos^2(cx+d)}$$

$$= \frac{a\cos(cx+d)\cos(ax+b)}{\cos^2(cx+d)} + \frac{c\sin(ax+b)\sin(cx+d)}{\cos^2(cx+d)}$$

$$= \frac{a\cos(ax+b)}{\cos(cx+d)} + \frac{c\sin(ax+b)\sin(cx+d)}{\cos(cx+d)\cos(cx+d)}$$

$$= a\cos(ax+b)\sec(cx+d) + c\sin(ax+b)\tan(cx+d)\sec(cx+d)$$

5 (*c*) $f(x) = x|x|$ and $g(x) = \sin x$

$$gof(x) = \sin(x|x|) = \begin{cases} -\sin x^2, & x < 0 \\ \sin x^2, & x \ge 0 \end{cases}$$

$$\therefore (gof)'(x) = \begin{cases} -2x\cos x^2, & x < 0 \\ 2x\cos x^2, & x \ge 0 \end{cases}$$

Clearly, $L(gof)'(0) = 0 = R(gof)'(0)$

$\therefore$ gof is differentiable at $x = 0$ and also its derivative is continuous at $x = 0$.

Now, $(gof)''(x)$

$$= \begin{cases} -2\cos x^2 + 4x^2\sin x^2, & x < 0 \\ 2\cos x^2 - 4x^2\sin x^2, & x > 0 \end{cases}$$

$\therefore$ $L(gof)''(0) = -2$

and $R(gof)''(0) = 2$

$\therefore$ $L(gof)''(0) \ne R(gof)''(0)$

$\therefore$ $gof(x)$ is not twice differentiable at $x = 0$

6 (*a*) $f(x) = \begin{cases} \frac{x}{1+e^{1/x}}, & x \ne 0 \\ 0, & x = 0 \end{cases}$

$$\therefore Rf'(0) = f'(0^+) = \lim_{h \to 0} \frac{\frac{h}{1+e^{1/h}} - 0}{h}$$

$$= \lim_{h \to 0} \frac{1}{1+e^{1/h}} = 0$$

$$Lf'(0) = f'(0^-) = \lim_{h \to 0} \frac{\frac{-h}{1+e^{-\frac{1}{h}}} - 0}{-h}$$

$$= \lim_{h \to 0} \frac{1}{1+\frac{1}{e^{1/h}}} = \frac{1}{1+0} = 1$$

$\therefore$ $f'(0^+) = 0$ and $f'(0^-) = 1$

For $x \ne 0$, $f(x) = \frac{x}{1+e^{1/x}}$, clearly differentiable

Also,

$$f'(x) = \frac{(1+e^{1/x}) - xe^{1/x}(-1/x^2)}{(1+e^{1/x})^2}$$

$$= \frac{1+e^{1/x} + \frac{e^{1/x}}{x}}{(1+{}^{1/x})^2}$$

7 (*b*) **Assertion**

$$\frac{d}{dx}e^{\cos x} = e^{\cos x}\frac{d}{dx}(\cos x)$$

$[\because$ by chain rule$]$

$$= e^{\cos x}(-\sin x)$$

Reason $\frac{d}{dx}e^x = e^x$ it is true.

8 (*a*) $\because e^{xy} + \log(xy) + \cos(xy) + 5 = 0$

Then, $e^{xy}\frac{d}{dx}(xy) + \frac{1}{xy}\frac{d}{dx}(xy) - \sin xy\frac{d}{dx}(xy) = 0$

$$\Rightarrow \frac{d}{dx}(xy)\left\{e^{xy}+\frac{1}{xy}-\sin(xy)\right\}=0$$

$\because \quad e^{xy}+\frac{1}{xy}-\sin(xy)\neq 0$

$\therefore \quad \frac{d}{dx}(xy)=0 \Rightarrow x\frac{dy}{dx}+y=0$

$\therefore \quad \frac{dy}{dx}=\frac{-y}{x}$

9 (*b*) Given, $xy=e^{(x-y)}$

On differentiating both sides with respect to x, we get

$$\frac{d}{dx}(xy)=\frac{d}{dx}(e^{x-y})$$

$$\Rightarrow x\frac{dy}{dx}+y.1=e^{x-y}\frac{d}{dx}(x-y)$$

[using product rule in LHS and chain rule in RHS]

$$\Rightarrow x\frac{dy}{dx}+y=e^{x-y}\left(1-\frac{dy}{dx}\right)$$

$$\Rightarrow x\frac{dy}{dx}+e^{x-y}\frac{dy}{dx}=e^{x-y}-y$$

$$\Rightarrow (x+e^{x-y})\frac{dy}{dx}=e^{x-y}-y$$

$$\Rightarrow \frac{dy}{dx}=\frac{e^{x-y}-y}{x+e^{x-y}}=\frac{xy-y}{x+xy}$$

$[\because e^{x-y}=xy$ is given$]$

$$=\frac{y(x-1)}{x(1+y)}$$

10 (*a*) Given, $x=a\sec\theta$, $y=b\tan\theta$

On differentiating w.r.t. θ, we get

$$\frac{dx}{d\theta}=a\sec\theta\tan\theta$$

and $\frac{dy}{d\theta}=b\sec^2\theta$

$$\therefore \quad \frac{dy}{dx}=\frac{\frac{dy}{d\theta}}{\frac{dx}{d\theta}}=\frac{dy}{d\theta}\times\frac{d\theta}{dx}$$

$$=\frac{b\sec^2\theta}{a\sec\theta\tan\theta}=\frac{b}{a}\left(\frac{\sec\theta}{\tan\theta}\right)$$

$$=\frac{b}{a}\operatorname{cosec}\theta$$

11 (*a*) $\because \quad x=\frac{2at}{1+t^3}, y=\frac{2at^2}{(1+t^3)^2}$

$\therefore \quad 2ay=x^2 \Rightarrow \frac{dy}{dx}=\frac{x}{a}$

Case or Paragraph Type Questions

1 (*a*) Given, $x=e^{x/y}$

$$\log x=\frac{x}{y}\log e$$

$\Rightarrow \quad y\log x=x$

On differentiating with respect to x, we get

$$y\frac{1}{x}+(\log x)\frac{dy}{dx}=1$$

$$\Rightarrow \frac{dy}{dx}=\left(1-\frac{y}{x}\right)\frac{1}{\log x}$$

$$\Rightarrow \frac{dy}{dx}=\frac{1}{x\log x}(x-y)$$

2 (*b*) Given, $y=(2-x)^3(3+2x)^5$

$$\Rightarrow \log y=\log(2-x)^3+\log(3+2x)^5$$

$$=3\log(2-x)+5\log(3+2x)$$

On differentiating both sides with respect to x, we get

$$\frac{1}{y}\frac{dy}{dx}=\frac{3\times(-1)}{2-x}+\frac{5}{3+2x}\times(2)$$

$$\Rightarrow \frac{dy}{dx}=(2-x)^3(3+2x)^5\left[\frac{10}{3+2x}-\frac{3}{2-x}\right]$$

3 (*d*) Let $y=(\sin x)^{\log x}$

Then, $y=e^{\log x\cdot\log(\sin(x))}$

On differentiating both sides w.r.t. x, we get

$$\frac{dy}{dx}=e^{\log x\log(\sin(x))}\frac{d}{dx}\{\log x\log(\sin x)\}$$

$$\Rightarrow \frac{dy}{dx}=(\sin x)^{\log x}\left\{\log(\sin x)\cdot\frac{1}{x}+\log x\frac{1}{\sin x}\cos x\right\}$$

$$\Rightarrow \frac{dy}{dx}=(\sin x)^{\log x}\left\{\frac{\log(\sin x)}{x}+\cot x\log x\right\}$$

4 (*c*) Given, $x^m\cdot y^n=(x+y)^{m+n}$

Taking log on both sides, we get

$$m\log x+n\log y=(m+n)\log(x+y)$$

On differentiating both sides w.r.t. x, we get

$$m\frac{1}{x}+n\frac{1}{y}\frac{dy}{dx}=\frac{m+n}{x+y}\left(\frac{d}{dx}(x+y)\right)$$

$$\Rightarrow \frac{m}{x}+\frac{n}{y}\frac{dy}{dx}=\frac{m+n}{x+y}\left(1+\frac{dy}{dx}\right)$$

$$\Rightarrow \left\{\frac{n}{y}-\frac{m+n}{x+y}\right\}\frac{dy}{dx}=\frac{m+n}{x+y}-\frac{m}{x}$$

$$\Rightarrow \left\{\frac{nx+ny-my-ny}{y(x+y)}\right\}\frac{dy}{dx}=\left\{\frac{mx+nx-mx-my}{(x+y)x}\right\}$$

$$\Rightarrow \frac{nx-my}{y(x+y)}\cdot\frac{dy}{dx}=\frac{nx-my}{(x+y)x}$$

$$\therefore \quad \frac{dy}{dx}=\frac{y}{x}$$

5 (*b*) We have,

$$f(x)=\begin{cases}\sin x, & x\geq 0\\ 1-\cos x, & x\leq 0\end{cases}$$

and $g(x)=e^x$

$$\text{Then, } gof(x)=\begin{cases}e^{\sin x}, & x\geq 0\\ e^{1-\cos x}, & x<0\end{cases}$$

6 (a) $\frac{d}{dx}[gof(x)]$

$$=\begin{cases}\frac{d}{dx}(e^{\sin x}), & x<0\\ \frac{d}{dx}(e^{1-\cos x}), & x<0\end{cases}$$

$$=\begin{cases}\cos x e^{\sin x}, & x\geq 0\\ \sin x e^{1-\cos x}, & x<0\end{cases}$$

7 (c) LHD at $x=0$

$$=\lim_{x\to 0^-}\left(\frac{gof(x)-gof(0)}{f(x)-0}\right)$$

$$=\lim_{x\to 0^-}\left(\frac{e^{1-\cos x}-1}{1-\cos x-0}\right)$$

$$=\lim_{x\to 0^-}\left(\frac{\left(1+\frac{(1-\cos x)}{1!}+\frac{(1-\cos x)^2}{2!}+\ldots\right)}{1-\cos x}\right)$$

$$= \lim_{x\to 0^-} \frac{(1-\cos x)\left(1+\dfrac{1-\cos x}{2!}+\ldots\right)}{1-\cos x}$$

$=1$

8 (c) RHD at $x=0$

$$= \lim_{x\to 0^+}\left(\frac{gof(x)-gof(0)}{f(x)-0}\right)$$

$$= \lim_{x\to 0^+}\left(\frac{e^{\sin x}-1}{\sin x - 0}\right)$$

$$= \lim_{x\to 0^+}\left(\frac{\left(1+\dfrac{\sin x}{1!}+\dfrac{(\sin x)^2}{2!}+\ldots\right)}{\sin x}\right)$$

$$= \lim_{x\to 0^+}\left(\frac{\sin x\left(1+\dfrac{\sin x}{2!}+\ldots\right)}{\sin x}\right)=1$$

Past Years Questions

1 (*d*) Given, $\sin y = x\sin(a+y)$

Now, differentiate on both sides w.r.t. x, we get

$$\frac{d}{dx}(\sin y)=\frac{d}{dx}\{x\cdot\sin(a+y)\}$$

$$\Rightarrow \cos y\frac{dy}{dx}=\sin(a+y) + x\cdot\cos(a+y)\frac{dy}{dx}$$

$$\Rightarrow \{\cos y - x\cos(a+y)\}\frac{dy}{dx}=\sin(a+y)$$

$$\Rightarrow \frac{dy}{dx}=\frac{\sin(a+y)}{\cos y - x\cdot\cos(a+y)}$$

$$=\frac{\sin(a+y)}{\cos y - \dfrac{\sin y}{\sin(a+y)}\cos(a+y)}$$

$$\left\{\because x=\frac{\sin y}{\sin(a+y)}\right\}$$

$$=\frac{\sin^2(a+y)}{\cos y\cdot\sin(a+y)-\sin y\cos(a+y)}$$

$$=\frac{\sin^2(a+y)}{\sin(a+y-y)}$$

$$\left[\begin{array}{l}\because \cos A\sin B-\sin A\cos B\\ =\sin(A-B)\end{array}\right]$$

$$\frac{dy}{dx}=\frac{\sin^2(a+y)}{\sin a}$$

2 (*b*) Given,

$$f(x)=\begin{cases}\dfrac{1-\cos 2x}{x^2}, & x<0\\ \alpha, & x=0\\ \dfrac{\beta\sqrt{1-\cos x}}{x}, & x>0\end{cases}$$

Where, $\alpha,\beta\in R$

Since, $f(x)$ is continuous at $x=0$.

So, LHL = RHL

= Value of function ... (i)

Now, $f(0^-)=\lim_{x\to 0^-}\dfrac{2\sin^2 x}{x^2}=2$

[using $1-\cos 2x = 2\sin^2 x$]

$$f(0^+)=\lim_{x\to 0^+}\beta\times\sqrt{2}\,\frac{\sin\frac{x}{2}}{2.\frac{x}{2}}=\frac{\beta}{\sqrt{2}}$$

[$\because x\to 0^+; |\sin x/2| = \sin x/2$]

and $f(0)=\alpha$

From Eq. (i),

$\alpha = 2$

and $\beta = 2\sqrt{2}$

Hence, $\alpha^2+\beta^2 = 4+8=12$

3 (*b*) We have,

$f(x)=[x^2-x]+|-x+[x]|$

$=[x(x-1)]+\{x\}$

$$f(x)=\begin{cases}x+1, & -0.5<x<0\\ 0, & x=0\\ -1+x, & 0<x<1\\ 0, & x=1\\ x-1, & 1<x<1.5\end{cases}$$

At $x=0$,

LHL $=\lim_{x\to 0^-}f(x)=1$

RHL $=\lim_{x\to 0^+}f(x)=-1$

$f(0)=0$

$\therefore f(x)$ is not continuous at $x=0$.

At $x=1$,

LHL $=\lim_{x\to 1^-}f(x)=-1+1=0$

RHL $=\lim_{x\to 1^+}f(x)=1-1=0$

$f(1)=0$

$\therefore f(x)$ is continuous at $x=1$.

Hence, $f(x)$ is continuous at $x=1$, but not continuous at $x=0$.

4 (*a*) Given, $f:(-\infty,\infty)-\{0\}\to R$

$$f'(1)=\lim_{a\to\infty}a^2 f\left(\frac{1}{a}\right)$$

Now, we have to find

$$\lim_{a\to\infty}\frac{a(a+1)}{2}\tan^{-1}\left(\frac{1}{a}\right)+a^2-2\ln(a)$$

$$=\lim_{a\to\infty}a^2\left(\frac{\left(1+\frac{1}{a}\right)}{2}\tan^{-1}\left(\frac{1}{a}\right)+1+\frac{2}{a^2}\ln\frac{1}{a}\right)$$

$$\Rightarrow f(x)=\frac{1}{x^2}(1+x)\tan^{-1}x+1+2x^2\ln(x)$$

$$f'(x)=\frac{1}{x^2}\left(\frac{1+x}{1+x^2}+\tan^{-1}x\right)+4x\ln x+2x$$

$$f'(1)=\frac{1}{2}\left(1+\frac{\pi}{4}\right)+2$$

$$\therefore f'(1)=\frac{5}{2}+\frac{\pi}{8}$$

5 (*c*) Let $f(x)=|x-1|+|x-2|$

$$=\begin{cases}-2x+3, & x<1\\ 1, & 1\le x<2\\ 2x-3, & x\ge 2\end{cases}$$

$$\Rightarrow f'(x)=\begin{cases}-2, & x<1\\ 0, & 1\le x<2\\ 2, & x\ge 2\end{cases}$$

So, $f(x)$ is continuous everywhere, but not differentiable at $x=1,2$

Let $g(x)=x-|x|=\begin{cases}2x, & x<0\\ 0, & x\ge 0\end{cases}$

$$\Rightarrow g'(x)=\begin{cases}2, & x<0\\ 0, & x\ge 0\end{cases}$$

So, $g(x)$ is continuous everywhere, but not differentiable at $x=0$.

Let $h(x)=x-[x]$, Since $[x]$ is discontinuous at integers and hence not differentiable. So, $h(x)$ is not differentiable at $x=1$.

Let $k(x)=x|x|=\begin{cases}-x^2, & x<0\\ x^2, & x\ge 0\end{cases}$

$$\Rightarrow k'(x)=\begin{cases}-2x, & x<0\\ 2x, & x\ge 0\end{cases}$$

So, $k(x)$ is continuous and differentiable at all values of x.

So, correct option is (c).

6 (d) $f\left(\frac{x}{y}\right)=\frac{f(x)}{f(y)}, f'(1)=2024$

Putting $x=y$, $f(1)=1$

On differentiating w.r.t. x, taking y as constant, we get

$$f'\left(\frac{x}{y}\right)\cdot\frac{1}{y}=\frac{f'(x)}{f(y)}$$

Putting $\quad x=y$

$$f'(1)\frac{1}{x}=\frac{f'(x)}{f(x)}$$

$$\Rightarrow \quad \frac{2024}{x}=\frac{f'(x)}{f(x)}$$

$$\Rightarrow \quad 2024f(x)=xf'(x)$$

$$\therefore\ xf'(x)-2024f(x)=0$$

7 (a) $f(x)=\frac{\sin x+\cos x-\sqrt{2}}{\sin x-\cos x}$

On dividing numerator and denominator by $\sqrt{2}$, we get

$$\frac{\frac{1}{\sqrt{2}}\sin x+\frac{1}{\sqrt{2}}\cos x-1}{\frac{1}{\sqrt{2}}\sin x-\frac{1}{\sqrt{2}}\cos x}$$

$$f(x)=\frac{\sin\left(x+\frac{\pi}{4}\right)-1}{\sin\left(x-\frac{\pi}{4}\right)}$$

On differentiating $f(x)$ w.r.t. x, we get

$$f'(x)=\frac{\sin\left(x-\frac{\pi}{4}\right)\cos\left(x+\frac{\pi}{4}\right)-\cos\left(x-\frac{\pi}{4}\right)\left(\sin\left(x+\frac{\pi}{4}\right)-1\right)}{\sin^2\left(x-\frac{\pi}{4}\right)}$$

$$=\frac{\cos\left(x-\frac{\pi}{4}\right)-1}{\sin^2\left(x-\frac{\pi}{4}\right)}$$

$$=\frac{-1}{1+\cos\left(x-\frac{\pi}{4}\right)}$$

Again, on differentiating $f(x)$ w.r.t. x, we get

$$f''(x)=\frac{-\sin\left(x-\frac{\pi}{4}\right)}{\left[1+\cos\left(x-\frac{\pi}{4}\right)\right]^2}$$

Now, $\quad f\left(\frac{7\pi}{12}\right)=-\frac{1}{\sqrt{3}}$

and $\quad f''\left(\frac{7\pi}{12}\right)=-\frac{2\sqrt{3}}{9}$

$$\therefore\quad f\left(\frac{7\pi}{12}\right)f''\left(\frac{7\pi}{12}\right)=\frac{2}{9}$$

8 (a) We have,

$$y=f(x)=\sin^3\left(\frac{\pi}{3}\left(\cos\left(\frac{\pi}{3\sqrt{2}}(-4x^3+5x^2+1)^{3/2}\right)\right)\right)$$

$$=\sin^3\left(\frac{\pi}{3}\left(\cos\left(\frac{\pi}{3\sqrt{2}}(-4x^3+5x^2+1)^{3/2}\right)\right)\right).$$

$$\frac{dy}{dx}=-3\sin^2\left(\frac{\pi}{3}\left(\cos\left(\frac{\pi}{3\sqrt{2}}(-4x^3+5x^2+1)^{3/2}\right)\right)\right)$$

$$\cos\left(-\cos\left(\frac{\pi}{3\sqrt{2}}(-4x^3+5x^2+1)^{3/2}\right)\right)$$

$$\frac{\pi}{3}\sin\left[\frac{\pi}{3\sqrt{2}}(-4x^3+5x^2+1)\frac{3}{2}\right]$$

$$\times\frac{\pi}{3\sqrt{2}}\times\frac{3}{2}\times$$

$$(-4x^3+5x^2+1)^{1/2}\times(-12x^2+10x)$$

Now, at $x=1$, $y=f(1)=\sin^3\left(\frac{\pi}{3}\left(\cos\left(\frac{\pi}{3\sqrt{2}}(-4+5+1)^{3/2}\right)\right)\right)$

$$=\sin^3\left(\frac{\pi}{3}\left(\cos\frac{2\pi}{3}\right)\right)$$

$$=\sin^3\left(\frac{\pi}{3}\times\left(-\frac{1}{2}\right)\right)=\left(-\frac{1}{2}\right)^3=-\frac{1}{8}$$

and $y'=3\left(-\frac{1}{2}\right)^2\cdot\left(\cos\frac{\sqrt{3}}{2}\right)$

$$\left(-\frac{\pi}{3}\right)\left(\frac{\sqrt{3}}{2}\right)\cdot\frac{\pi}{3\sqrt{2}}\left(\frac{3}{2}\sqrt{2}\right)(-2)=\frac{3\pi^2}{16}$$

Now, $2y'+3\pi^2y$

$$=2\left(\frac{3\pi^2}{16}\right)+3\pi^2\left(-\frac{1}{8}\right)$$

$$=\frac{3\pi^2}{8}-\frac{3\pi^2}{8}=0$$

9 (b) $f(x)=\frac{\sqrt[7]{p(729+x)}-3}{\sqrt[3]{729+qx}-9}$

$\lim_{x\to 0} f(x)$ is finite and equal to $f(0)$.

$$\therefore\ \sqrt[7]{p(729)}-3=0 \Rightarrow p=3$$

Now,

$$\lim_{x\to 0} f(x)=\lim_{x\to 0}\frac{\sqrt[7]{3(729+x)}-3}{\sqrt[3]{729+qx}-9}$$

$$=\lim_{x\to 0}\frac{1}{3}\times\frac{\left(1+\frac{x}{3^6}\right)^{1/7}-1}{\left(1+\frac{qx}{9^3}\right)^{\frac{1}{3}}-1}\quad\left[\because \frac{0}{0}\text{ form}\right]$$

$$=\frac{1}{3}\times\frac{\frac{1}{7}\times\frac{1}{3^6}}{\frac{1}{3}\times\frac{q}{9^3}}\Rightarrow\frac{1}{7q}=f(0)$$

$$\Rightarrow\quad 7q\,f(0)=1$$

$$\Rightarrow\quad 63q\,f(0)=9=p^2\quad[\because p=3]$$

$$\therefore\quad 63q\,f(0)-p^2=0$$

10 (d) Given, $f(x)=\begin{cases}x+a, & x\le 0\\ |x-4|, & x>0\end{cases}$

and $g(x)=\begin{cases}x+1, & x<0\\ (x-4)^2+b, & x\ge 0\end{cases}$

As, $f(x)$ is continuous on R.

$$\therefore\ \lim_{x\to 0^-} f(x)=\lim_{x\to 0^+} f(x)=f(0)$$

$$\Rightarrow\quad 0+a=|0-4|\Rightarrow a=4$$

As, $g(x)$ is continuous on R.

$$\therefore\ \lim_{x\to 0^-} g(x)=\lim_{x\to 0^+} g(x)=g(0)$$

$$\Rightarrow\quad 0+1=(0-4)^2+b$$

$$\Rightarrow\quad 1=16+b\Rightarrow b=-15$$

$$\therefore\ f(x)=\begin{cases}x+4, & x\le 0\\ |x-4|, & x>0\end{cases}$$

and $g(x)=\begin{cases}x+1, & x<0\\ (x-4)^2-15, & x\ge 0\end{cases}$

$gof(2)+fog(-2)$

$$=g[f(2)]+f[g(-2)]$$

$$=g(2)+f(-1)$$

$$=(2-4)^2-15+(-1+4)$$

$$=8-16=-8$$

11 (*d*) We have,

$$f(x)=\begin{cases}kx+1, & \text{if } x\le\pi\\ \cos x, & \text{if } x>\pi\end{cases}$$

LHL at $x=\pi$

$$\lim_{x\to\pi^-} f(x)=\lim_{x\to\pi^-}(kx+1)$$
$$=\lim_{h\to 0} k(\pi-h)+1$$
$$=k\pi+1 \quad \text{...(i)}$$

RHL at $x=\pi$

$$\lim_{x\to\pi^-} f(x)=\lim_{x\to\pi^+}\cos x$$
$$=\lim_{h\to 0}\cos(\pi+h)$$
$$=-\lim_{h\to 0}\cos h$$
$$=-\cos 0=-1 \quad \text{...(ii)}$$

Since, $f(x)$ is continuous at $x=\pi$.

$\therefore$ LHL = RHL = $f(\pi)$

Using Eqs. (i) and (ii), we get

$$k\pi+1=-1$$
$$\Rightarrow k\pi=-2$$
$$\therefore k=-\frac{2}{\pi}$$

12 (*d*) Given,

$$3f(x)+2f\left(\frac{1}{x}\right)=\frac{1}{x}-10 \quad \text{...(i)}$$

Change x by $1/x$, we get

$$3f\left(\frac{1}{x}\right)+2f(x)=x-10$$
$$\Rightarrow \frac{3}{2}\left[\frac{1}{x}-10-3f(x)\right]+2f(x)=x-10$$

[from Eq. (i)]

$$\Rightarrow \frac{3}{2x}-15-\frac{9}{2}f(x)+2f(x)=x-10$$
$$\Rightarrow -\frac{5}{2}f(x)-15+\frac{3}{2x}=x-10$$
$$\Rightarrow -\frac{5}{2}f(x)=x-\frac{3}{2x}+5$$
$$\Rightarrow f(x)=-\frac{2}{5}x+\frac{3}{5x}-2$$
$$\Rightarrow f'(x)=\frac{-2}{5}-\frac{3}{5x^2}$$
$$\therefore f(3)=-3$$

and $f'\left(\frac{1}{4}\right)=-10$

$$\left|f(3)+f'\left(\frac{1}{4}\right)\right|=|-3+(-10)|$$
$$=|-3-10|$$
$$=|-13|=13$$

13 (17) $\left[\frac{x}{2}+3\right]$ is discontinuous at

$x=2,4,6,8$

$\sqrt{x}$ is discontinuous at $x=1,4$

$f(x)$ is discontinuous at $x=1,2,6,8$

$\Sigma a=1+2+6+8=17$

14 (15) Given,

$$f(x)=\begin{cases}\dfrac{1}{|x|}, & |x|\ge 2\\ ax^2+2b, & |x|<2\end{cases}$$

$$\Rightarrow f(x)=\begin{cases}-\dfrac{1}{x}, & x<-2\\ ax^2+2b, & -2<x<2\\ 1/x, & x\ge 2\end{cases}$$

Given that $f(x)$ is differentiable on R.

$\Rightarrow f(x)$ also continuious on R.

Now, we check continuity on -2.

Now, $\lim_{x\to -2^-} f(x)=\lim_{x\to -2^+} f(x)$

$$\Rightarrow \lim_{x\to -2}-\frac{1}{x}=\lim_{x\to -2^+}(ax^2+2b)$$
$$\Rightarrow 4a+2b=\frac{1}{2} \quad \text{...(i)}$$

Now, LHD = RHD at $x=-2$

$$f'(x)=\begin{cases}-1/x^2, & x\le -2\\ 2ax, & -2<x<2\\ -1/x^2, & x\ge 2\end{cases}$$

$$\lim_{x\to 2^-} f'(x)=\lim_{x\to 2^+} f'(x)$$
$$\Rightarrow \lim_{x\to -2^-}\left(\frac{1}{x^2}\right)=\lim_{x\to -2^+}(2ax)$$
$$\Rightarrow \frac{1}{4}=-4a$$
$$\Rightarrow a=-1/16$$

Putting $a=-1/16$ in Eq. (i),

$$4\left(-\frac{1}{16}\right)+2b=\frac{1}{2}$$
$$\Rightarrow b=3/8$$

Now, $48(a+b)=48\left(-\frac{1}{16}+\frac{3}{8}\right)$

$$=15$$

15 (10) Given, $f(x)=\sum_{k=1}^{10} k\cdot x^k, x\in R$

Now, $f(x)=x+2x^2+\ldots+10x^{10}$

$$\Rightarrow x\cdot f(x)=x^2+2x^3+\ldots+9x^{10}+10x^{11}$$
$$\Rightarrow (1-x)f(x)=(x+2x^2+\ldots+10x^{10})-(x^2+2x^3+\ldots+9x^{10}+10x^{11})$$
$$=x+x^2+x^3+\ldots+x^{10}-10x^{11}$$
$$=\frac{x(1-x^{10})}{(1-x)}-10x^{11}$$
$$\Rightarrow f(x)=\frac{x(1-x^{10})}{(1-x)^2}-\frac{10x^{11}}{(1-x)}$$
$$=\frac{x-x^{11}-10x^{11}+10x^{12}}{(1-x)^2}$$
$$=\frac{10x^{12}-11x^{11}+x}{(1-x)^2}$$

$$f'(x)=\frac{(10x^{12}-11x^{11}+x)\cdot 2\cdot(1-x)+(120x^{11}-121x^{10}+1)\cdot(1-x)^2}{(1-x)^4}$$
$$=\frac{20x^{12}-22x^{11}+2x+(120x^{11}-121x^{10}+1)(1-x)}{(1-x)^3}$$

Thus, $2f(2)+f'(2)=119\cdot 2^{10}+1$

So, $n=10$.

16 (16) Given,

$$C\,(x^2+y^2-3)+(x^2-y^2-1)^5=0$$

Point (α,α) lies on C and $\alpha>0$.

$$\therefore 2\alpha^2-3-1=0$$
$$\Rightarrow \alpha=\sqrt{2}$$

On differentiating w.r.t. x

$$C:(x^2+y^2-3)+(x^2-y^2-1)^5=0$$
$$\Rightarrow 2x+2yy'+5(x^2-y^2-1)^4(2x-2yy')=0$$

On putting $x=\alpha, y=\alpha, \alpha=\sqrt{2}$,

$$\sqrt{2}+\sqrt{2}y'+5(\sqrt{2}-\sqrt{2}y')=0$$
$$\Rightarrow 6\sqrt{2}=4\sqrt{2}y'$$
$$\Rightarrow y'=\frac{3}{2}$$

Again differentiating C,

$$2+2((y')^2+yy'')+20(x^2-y^2-1)^3(2x-2yy')^2+5(x^2-y^2-1)^4(2-2((y')^2+yy''))=0$$

On putting $x = y = \sqrt{2}, y' = \frac{3}{2}$,

$$2 + \frac{9}{2} + 2\sqrt{2}y'' - 40 + 10$$

$$-\frac{45}{2} - 10\sqrt{2}y'' = 0$$

$$\Rightarrow \quad y'' = \frac{-23}{4\sqrt{2}}$$

$\therefore$ $3y' - y^3y''$ at $(\sqrt{2}, \sqrt{2})$

$$3 \times \frac{3}{2} - 2\sqrt{2} \times \left(\frac{-23}{4\sqrt{2}}\right) = 16$$

Skill Boosters

1 (*a*) We know that $[x]$ is discontinuous for $x \in Z$.

So, $f(x) = x\left[\frac{x}{2}\right]$ may be discontinuous, where $\frac{x}{2}$ is an integer.

$\therefore$ Points of discontinuity are $x = \pm 2, \pm 4, \pm 6$ and 0.

But at $x = 0$

$$\lim_{x \to 0^+} f(x) = f(x) = \lim_{x \to 0^-} f(x) = 0.$$

Hence, $f(x)$ will be discontinuous at $x = \pm 2, \pm 4$ and ± 6.

2 (*b*) Given, $f(x)$ is continuous at $x = 0$

$$\therefore \lim_{x \to 0} f(x) = f(0)$$

$$\Rightarrow \lim_{x \to 0}\left(\frac{1}{x}\ln\left(\frac{1+4x}{1-3x}\right)\right) = k$$

$$\Rightarrow \lim_{x \to 0}\left(\frac{\ln(1+4x)}{x} - \frac{\ln(1-3x)}{x}\right) = k$$

$$\Rightarrow \lim_{x \to 0}\left(\frac{4\ln(1+4x)}{4x} - \frac{3\ln(1-3x)}{-3x}\right) = k$$

$$\Rightarrow \quad 4 + 3 = k \Rightarrow k = 7$$

3 (*c*) Since, $f(x)$ is continuous at $x = \frac{\pi}{2}$.

$$\therefore \quad \lim_{x \to \frac{\pi}{2}} f(x) = f\left(\frac{\pi}{2}\right)$$

$$\Rightarrow \quad \lim_{x \to \frac{\pi}{2}} \left(\frac{2}{3}\right)^{\frac{\tan 2x}{\tan 3x}} = k + \frac{3}{5}$$

$$\Rightarrow \quad 1 = k + \frac{3}{5}$$

$$\Rightarrow \quad k = 1 - \frac{3}{5} \Rightarrow k = \frac{2}{5}$$

4 (*a*) Given that $x = e^{y + e^{y + \dots \text{ to } \infty}}$

$$\Rightarrow \quad x = e^{y+x}$$

Taking log on both sides, we get

$$\log x = \log e^{y+x}$$

$$\Rightarrow \quad \log x = y + x$$

On differentiating both sides w.r.t. x, we get

$$\frac{1}{x} = \frac{dy}{dx} + 1$$

$$\Rightarrow \quad \frac{dy}{dx} = \frac{1}{x} - 1$$

$$\Rightarrow \quad \frac{dy}{dx} = \frac{1-x}{x}$$

5 (*c*) Given, $f(x + y) = f(x) \times f(y)$

On differentiating w.r.t. x, treating y as constant, we get

$$f'(x + y) = f'(x) f(y)$$

On putting $x = 0$ and $y = x$, we get

$$f'(x) = f'(0) f(x)$$

$$\Rightarrow \quad f'(5) = 4f(5)$$

$$\Rightarrow \quad f'(5) = 4 \times 3 = 12$$

6 (*a*) If is given that functions f and g are differentiable and fog is identify function.

$\therefore$ $(fog)(x) = x \Rightarrow f(g(x)) = x$

On differentiating both sides, we get

$$f'(g(x)) \cdot g'(x) = 1$$

Now, on putting $x = a$, we get

$$f'(g(a)) \cdot g'(a) = 1$$

$$\Rightarrow \quad f'(p) \cdot 4 = 1$$

$$\therefore \quad f'(p) = \frac{1}{4}$$

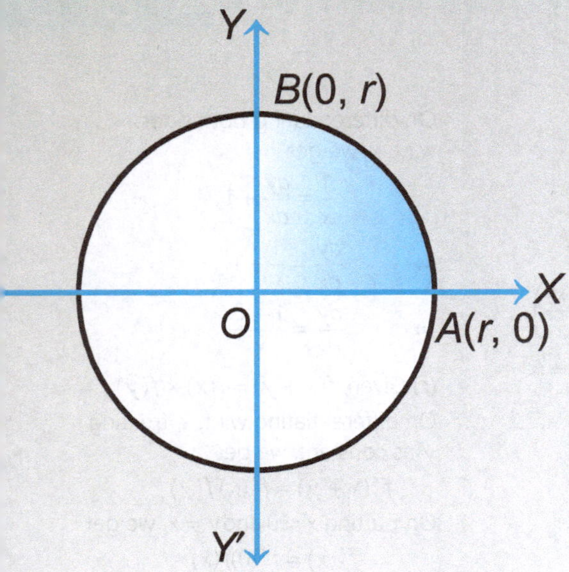

Topicwise No. of Ques asked in 3 Years (JEE Main)

Topics	No. of Questions 2024	2023	2022
Rate of Change of Quantities	–	1	2
Increasing and Decreasing Functions	9	4	4
Maxima and Minima	13	9	13

Special Type of Ques Asked in 3 Years (JEE Main)

Types	Years 2024	2023	2022
A-R	–	–	–
Statement Based	2	1	–
Numerical Value Type	5	2	2

Last 3 Years Weightage (JEE Main)

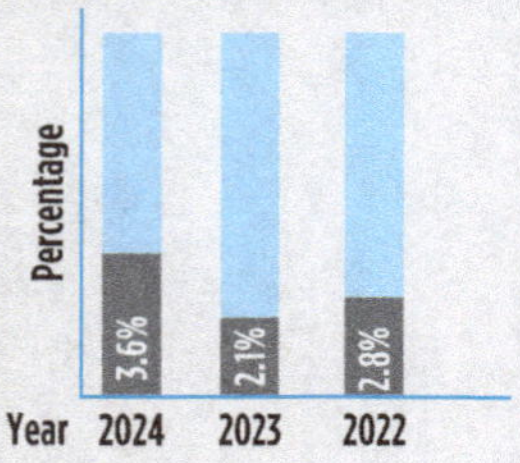

06

Application of Derivatives

Rate of Change of Quantities

- The **rate of change** of y with respect to x at point $x = x_0$ is given by $\left(\frac{dy}{dx}\right)_{x=x_0}$ or $f'(x_0)$.
- Suppose $y = f(t)$ and $x = g(t)$. Then, **rate of change** of y with respect to x is given by
$$\frac{dy}{dx} = \frac{dy/dt}{dx/dt} \text{ provided } \frac{dx}{dt} \neq 0 \text{ or } \frac{dy}{dx} = \frac{dy}{dt} \cdot \frac{dt}{dx}.$$
[JEE Main 2022]

Increasing and Decreasing Functions

Concept Master Video

[JEE Main 2024, 2023, 2022]

(i) **Increasing functions** Let I be an interval contained in the domain of a real valued function f. Then, f is said to be

(a) Increasing on I, if $x_1 < x_2$
$\Rightarrow f(x_1) \leq f(x_2), \forall\ x_1, x_2 \in I$

(b) strictly increasing on I, if $x_1 < x_2$
$\Rightarrow f(x_1) < f(x_2), \forall x_1, x_2 \in I$

(ii) **Decreasing functions** Let I be an interval contained in the domain of a real valued function f. Then, f is said to be

(a) decreasing on I, if $x_1 < x_2$
$\Rightarrow \quad f(x_1) \geq f(x_2), \forall\ x_1, x_2 \in I$

(b) strictly decreasing on I, if $x_1 < x_2$
$\Rightarrow \quad f(x_1) > f(x_2), \forall x_1, x_2 \in I$

Theorem Let f be continuous on $[a, b]$ and differentiable on (a, b).

- If $f'(x) > 0$ for each $x \in (a, b)$, then $f(x)$ is said to be increasing in $[a, b]$ and strictly increasing in (a, b).

- If $f'(x) < 0$ for each $x \in (a, b)$, then $f(x)$ is said to be decreasing in $[a, b]$ and strictly decreasing in (a, b).
- If $f'(x) = 0$ for each $x \in (a, b)$, then f is said to be a constant function in $[a, b]$.

Marks Maximizer

- $\frac{dy}{dx}$ is positive, if y increases as x increases and $\frac{dy}{dx}$ is negative, if y decreases as x increases.
- A function $f(x)$ is said to be increasing (decreasing) at point x_0, if there is an interval $(x_0 - h, x_0 + h)$ containing x_0 such that $f(x)$ is increasing (decreasing) on $(x_0 - h, x_0 + h)$.
- Let f be a function defined on (a, b).
  (i) If $f'(x) > 0 \ \forall x \in (a, b)$ except for a finite number of points, where $f'(x) = 0$, then $f(x)$ is increasing on (a, b).
  (ii) If $f'(x) < 0 \ \forall x \in (a, b)$ except for a finite number of points, where $f'(x) = 0$, then $f(x)$ is decreasing on (a, b).
- If $f(x)$ and $g(x)$ are strictly increasing (or decreasing) function on $[a, b]$, then $gof(x)$ is strictly increasing function on $[a, b]$.
- If one of the two functions $f(x)$ and $g(x)$ is strictly increasing and other a strictly decreasing, then $gof(x)$ is strictly decreasing on $[a, b]$.

Maxima and Minima

- **Maxima and Minima** Let f be a real valued function and c be an interior point in the domain of f. Then,
  (i) point c is called a point of **local maxima**, if there is a $h > 0$ such that $f(c) > f(x), \forall x$ in $(c - h, c + h)$.
  Here, value $f(c)$ is called the **local maximum value** of function.
  (ii) point c is called a point of **local minima**, if there is a $h > 0$ such that $f(c) < f(x), \forall x$ in $(c - h, c + h)$. Here, value $f(c)$ is called the **local minimum value** of function. **[JEE Main 2024]**
- **Critical Point** A point c in the domain of a function f at which either $f'(c) = 0$ or f is not differentiable, is called a critical point of function. If function is continuous at c and $f'(c) = 0$, then there exists $h > 0$ such that function is differentiable in the interval $(c - h, c + h)$.
- **First Derivative Test** Let f be a function defined on an open interval I and let f be continuous at a critical point c in I. Then,
  (i) if $f'(x)$ changes sign from positive to negative as x increases through point c, then c is a point of local maxima.
  (ii) if $f'(x)$ changes sign from negative to positive as x increases through point c, then c is a point of local minima.
  (iii) if $f'(x)$ does not change sign as x increases through c, then c is neither a point of local maxima nor a point of local minima. Infact, such a point is called **point of inflection**. **[JEE Main 2024, 2023, 2022]**
- **Second Derivative Test** Let f be a function defined on an interval I and $c \in I$. Let f be twice differentiable at c, then
  (i) $x = c$ is a point of local maxima, if $f'(c) = 0$ and $f''(c) < 0$. The value $f(c)$ is local maximum value of function.
  (ii) $x = c$ is a point of local minima, if $f'(c) = 0$ and $f''(c) > 0$. Then, the value $f(c)$ is local minimum value of function.
  (iii) The test fails, if $f'(c) = 0$ and $f''(c) = 0$. **[JEE Main 2024, 2023, 2022]**
- **Absolute Maxima and Absolute Minima** Let f be a continuous function on $[a, b]$ and c be a point in $[a, b]$ such that $f'(c) = 0$. Then, find $f(a)$, $f(b)$ and $f(c)$. The maximum of these values gives a maxima or absolute maxima and minimum of these values gives a minima or absolute minima. **[JEE Main 2024, 2023]**

Marks Maximizer

- If $f(x) \to \infty$ as $x \to a$ or b and $f'(x) = 0$ only for one value of x (say c) between a and b, then $f(c)$ is necessarily the minimum and the least value.
- If $f(x) \to -\infty$ as $x \to a$ or b and $f'(x) = 0$ only for one value of x (say c) between a and b, then $f(c)$ is necessarily the maximum and the greatest value.
- If $f(x)$ be a differentiable functions, then $f'(x)$ vanishes at every local maximum and at every local minimum.
- The converse of above is not true i.e. every point at which $f'(x)$ vanishes need not be a local maximum or minimum. e.g. if $f(x) = x^3$, then $f'(0) = 0$. At $x = 0$, the function has neither maximum nor minimum. In general, these points are point of inflection.
- A function may attain an extreme value at a point without being derivable at that point e.g. $f(x) = |x|$ has a minima at $x = 0$ but $f'(0)$ does not exist.
- A function $f(x)$ can has several local maximum and local minimum values in an interval. Thus, the maximum and minimum values of $f(x)$ defined above are not necessarily the greatest and the least values of $f(x)$ in a given interval.
- A minimum value at some point may even be greater than a maximum values at some other point.
- The sign of the 2nd derivative determines the concavity of the curve.
  (a) If $f''(x) \ge 0, \forall x \in (a, b)$, then graph of $f(x)$ is concave upward in (a, b).
  (b) If $f''(x) \le 0, \forall x \in (a, b)$, then graph of $f(x)$ is concave downward in (a, b).

Caution Points

- If a function is either strictly increasing or strictly decreasing on an interval (a, b), then it is said to be a monotonic function.
- If $f(x)$ is increasing in some intervals and decreasing in some intervals, then that function is not monotonic function.
- If $f(x)$ is increasing function on an interval $[a, b]$, then f^{-1} exist and also a strictly increasing function.
- If $f(x)$ is continuous function in its domain, then at least one maxima and one minima must lie between two equal values of x.
- Maxima and Minima occur alternately i.e. between two maxima, there is one minima and *vice-versa*.
- A function may attain an extreme value at a point without being derivable at that point. e.g. $f(x) = |x|$ has a minima at $x = 0$ but $f'(0)$ does not exist.
- **To Find Range of a Continuous Function** Let $f(x)$ be a continuous function on $[a, b]$, such that its least value in $[a, b]$ is m and the greatest value in $[a, b]$ is M. Then, range of value of $f(x)$ for $x \in [a, b]$ is $[m, M]$.
- **To Check for the Injectivity of a Function** A strictly monotonic function is always one-one (injective). Hence, a function $f(x)$ is one-one in the interval $[a, b]$, if $f'(x) > 0, \forall x \in [a, b]$ or $f'(x) < 0, \forall x \in [a, b]$.
- A necessary condition for $f(a)$ to be an extreme value of a function $f(x)$ is that $f'(a) = 0$ in case if exists. It is not sufficient. i.e. $f'(a) = 0$ does not necessarily imply that $x = a$ is an extreme point. There are functions for which the derivatives vanish at a point but do not have an extreme value. e.g. the function $f(x) = x^3$, $f'(0) = 0$ but at $x = 0$ the function does not attain an extreme value.
- Geometrically the above condition means that the tangent to the curve $y = f(x)$ at a point where the ordinate is maximum or minimum is parallel to the X-axis.
- All x, for which $f'(x) = 0$, do not give us the extreme values. The values of x for which $f'(x) = 0$ are called stationary values or critical values of x and the corresponding values of $f(x)$ are called stationary or turning values of $f(x)$.

PYQ Notes

1. Let f be a differentiable real valued function defined on (a, b). **[JEE Main 2024]**
   (a) If $f'(x) > 0, \forall x \in (a, b)$, then $f(x)$ increasing on (a, b).
   (b) If $f'(x) < 0, \forall x \in (a, b)$, then $f(x)$ is decreasing on (a, b).

Step by Step

Mastering NCERT

- Concept Builders
- Topical Questions
- Numerical Type Questions
- Assertion and Reason Questions
- Case or Paragraph Type Questions
- Past Years Questions
- Skill Boosters

Concept Builders

1 If the side of a square increases at the rate of $\frac{1}{8}$ cm/sec, then the rate of increase of its perimeter is ....

2 The rate of change of the surface area of a sphere of radius r, when the radius is increasing at the rate of 4 cm/sec in ....

3 The distance S described by a particle in t seconds is given by $S = a \cdot e^t + \frac{b}{e^t}$. Then, the acceleration of the particle at time t is equal to ....

4 State whether $\tan x - x$ is increasing or decreasing function in its domain ....

5 Find the increasing interval of the function $f(x) = \sin^4 x + \cos^4 x$, if $x \in \left[0, \frac{\pi}{2}\right]$.

6 Derivative can be used to determine the rate of change of quantities. (T/F)

7 Derivatives help us to locate that points at which a function is having its largest and smallest value (locally). (T/F)

8 Two men A and B start with velocity v at the same time from the junction of two roads inclined at 45° to each other if they travel by different roads, then the rate at which they are being separated is $\sqrt{2-\sqrt{2}}\ v$ unit/sec. (T/F)

9 The function $f(x) = x^2 - 4x + 6$ is strictly increasing in the interval $(2, \infty)$. (T/F)

10 The natural logarithm function is strictly increasing on $(0, \infty)$. (T/F)

11 The function given by $f(x) = x^2 - x + 1$ is neither increasing nor decreasing strictly on $(-1, 1)$. (T/F)

12 The function given by $f(x) = \log(\sin x)$ is strictly decreasing on $\left(0, \frac{\pi}{2}\right)$. (T/F)

13 Local minimum value of the function $f(x) = x^2$ is 0. (T/F)

14 Local maximum value and local minimum value of the the function $f(x) = x^3 - 3x$ are 2 and -2, respectively. (T/F)

15 Maximum value of $3x^4 - 8x^3 + 12x^2 - 48x + 25$ on the interval $[0, 3]$ is ....

16 Explain necessary condition for a point $x = c$ to be an extreme point of the function $f(x)$.

17 If $f(x)$ attains a local maxima at $x = c$, then write the values of $f'(c)$ and $f''(c)$.

18 Find the maximum and minimum values of the function given by $f(x) = 5 + \sin 2x$.

19 Write the maximum value of $f(x) = \frac{\ln x}{x}$, if it exists.

20 The function $f(x) = \frac{x}{2} + \frac{2}{x}$ has a local minimum at $x =$ ....

21 What are the values of a for which $f(x) = a^x$ is increasing on R?

22 If $g(x)$ is a decreasing function on R and $f(x) = \tan^{-1}\{g(x)\}$. State whether $f(x)$ is increasing or decreasing on R.

Topical Questions

Rate of Change of Quantities

Level I

1 The rate of change of the area of a circle with respect to its radius r at **NCERT Pg. 150**

(a) $r = 3$ cm is $6\pi^2$ cm^2 / cm

(b) $r = 4$ cm is 4π cm^2 / cm

(c) Both (a) and (b) are correct

(d) Both (a) and (b) are incorrect

2 The volume of a cube is increasing at the rate of 8 cm^3/s. If the length of an edge is 12 cm, then the surface area is increasing at the rate of **NCERT Pg. 150**

(a) $\frac{4}{3}$ cm^2 / s (b) $\frac{8}{3}$ cm^2 / s

(c) $\frac{2}{3}$ cm^2 / s (d) None of these

3 The radius of a circle is increasing uniformly at the rate of 3 cm/s. At radius of 10 cm, the area of the circle is increasing at the rate of **NCERT Pg. 150**

(a) 40π cm^2 / s (b) 45π cm^2 / s

(c) 35π cm^2 / s (d) 60π cm^2 / s

4 A stone is dropped into a quiet lake and waves move in circles at the speed of 5 cm/s. If at an instant, the radius of the circular wave is 8 cm, then the rate at which enclosed area is increasing, is **NCERT Pg. 150**

(a) 20π cm^2 / s (b) 40π cm^2 /s

(c) 60π cm^2 / s (d) 80π cm^2 / s

5 Match the terms of column I with the terms of column II and choose the correct option from the codes given below. **NCERT Pg. 150, 151**

	Column I		Column II
A.	An edge of a variable cube is increasing at the rate of 3 cm/s. The volume of the cube, if the edge is 10 cm long, is increasing at the rate of	1.	$\frac{27}{8}\pi(2x+1)^2$
B.	The radius of a circle is increasing at the rate of 0.7 cm/s. The rate of increase of its circumference is	2.	900 cm^3 /s
C.	The radius of an air bubble is increasing at the rate of $\frac{1}{2}$ cm/s. At the radius of 1 cm, its volume is increasing at the rate of	3.	1.4π cm/s
D.	A balloon, which always remains spherical, has a variable diameter $\frac{3}{2}(2x+1)$. The rate of change of its volume with respect to x is	4.	2π cm^3 /s

Codes

	A	B	C	D		A	B	C	D
(a)	2	4	3	1	(b)	1	3	4	2
(c)	2	3	4	1	(d)	1	4	3	2

6 The length x of a rectangle is decreasing at the rate of 5cm/min and the width y is increasing at the rate of 4 cm/min. If $x = 8$ cm and $y = 6$ cm, then which of the following is correct? **NCERT Pg. 151**

I. The rate of change of the perimeter is -2 cm/min.

II. The rate of change of the area of the rectangle is 12 cm^2/min.

(a) Only I is correct

(b) Only II is correct

(c) Both I and II are correct

(d) Both I and II are incorrect

7 A balloon which always remains spherical on inflation, is being inflated by pumping in 900 cm^3 of gas per second. The rate at which the radius of the balloon increases when the radius is 15 cm, is **NCERT Pg. 151**

(a) $\frac{2}{\pi}$ cm/s (b) $\frac{3}{\pi}$ cm/s

(c) $\frac{1}{\pi}$ cm/s (d) None of these

8 A ladder 5m long is leaning against a wall. The bottom of the ladder is pulled along the ground, away from the wall at the rate of 2 cm/s. If the foot of the ladder is 4 m away from the wall, then its height on the wall is decreasing at the rate of **NCERT Pg. 151**

(a) $\frac{3}{8}$ cm/s (b) $\frac{3}{8}$ m/s

(c) $\frac{8}{3}$ cm/s (d) $\frac{8}{3}$ m/s

9 The rate of change of the area of a circle with respect to its radius r at $r = 6$ cm is **NCERT Pg. 151**

(a) 10π cm^2 / cm (b) 12π cm^2 / cm

(c) 8π cm^2 / cm (d) 11π cm^2 / cm

10 A particle moves along the curve $6y = x^3 + 2$. The point P on the curve at which the y-coordinate is changing 8 times as fast as the x-coordinate, are (4, 11) and $\left(-4, -\frac{31}{3}\right)$. **NCERT Pg. 151**

(a) x-coordinates of the point P are ± 4.

(b) y-coordinates of the point P are 11 and $\frac{-31}{3}$.

(c) Both (a) and (b)

(d) None of the above

11 Sand is pouring from a pipe at the rate of 12 cm^3/s. The falling sand forms a cone on the ground in such a way that the height of the cone is always one-sixth of the radius of the base. The rate at which the height of the sand cone increasing when the height is 4 cm, is **NCERT Pg. 151**

(a) 48π cm/s (b) 24π cm/s
(c) $\frac{1}{48\pi}$ cm/s (d) $\frac{7}{48\pi}$ cm/s

12 The total cost $C(x)$ (in ₹) associated with the production of x units of an item is given by

$$C(x) = 0.007x^3 - 0.003x^2 + 15x + 4000$$

The marginal cost when 17 units are produced, is where by marginal cost, we mean the instantaneous rate of change of total cost at any level of output. **NCERT Pg. 151**

(a) ₹ 20.967 (b) ₹ 21.967 (c) ₹ 81.968 (d) ₹ 11.967

13 The total revenue (in ₹) received from the sales of x units of a product is given by

$$R(x) = 13x^2 + 26x + 15$$

The marginal revenue when $x = 7$, is **NCERT Pg. 151**

(a) ₹ 200 (b) ₹ 350
(c) ₹ 208 (d) None of these

14 The total revenue (in ₹) received from the sale of x units of a product is given by $R(x) = 3x^2 + 36x + 5$.
The marginal revenue when $x = 15$, is where by marginal revenue we mean the rate of change of total revenue with respect to the number of items sold at an instant. **NCERT Pg. 152**

(a) ₹ 116 (b) ₹ 96 (c) ₹ 90 (d) ₹ 126

Level II

15 For the curve $y = 5x - 2x^3$, if x increases at the rate of 2 units/s, then the rate at which the slope of curve is changing when $x = 3$, is **NCERT Exemplar Pg. 119**

(a) – 78 units/s (b) – 72 units/s
(c) –36 units/s (d) – 18 units/s

16 Water is dripping out from a conical funnel of semi-vertical angle $\frac{\pi}{4}$ at the uniform rate of $2\ cm^2/s$ in the surface area through a tiny hole at the vertex of the bottom. When the slant height of cone is 4cm, then rate of decrease of the slant height of water is **NCERT Exemplar Pg. 120**

(a) $\frac{\sqrt{2}}{3\pi}$ cm/s (b) $\frac{\sqrt{2}}{\pi}$ cm/s
(c) $\frac{\sqrt{2}}{4\pi}$ cm/s (d) None of these

17 The rate of change of volume of a sphere with respect to its surface area when the radius is 2 cm, is **NCERT Exemplar Pg. 135**

(a) $2\ cm^3/cm^2$ (b) $3\ cm^3/cm^2$
(c) $1\ cm^3/cm^2$ (d) None of these

18 Water is dripping out at a steady rate of $1\ cm^3/s$ through a tiny hole at the vertex of the conical vessel whose axis is vertical. If the slant height of water in the vessel is 4 cm, then the rate of decrease of slant height where the vertical angle of the conical vessel is $\frac{\pi}{3}$, is **NCERT Exemplar Pg. 124**

(a) $\frac{1}{2\sqrt{3}\pi}$ cm/s (b) $2\sqrt{3}\pi$ cm/s
(c) $\sqrt{3}\pi$ cm/s (d) None of these

19 A kite is moving horizontally at a height of 151.5 m. If the speed of kite is 10 m/s, then the rate at which the string is being let out when the kite is 250 m away from the boy who is flying the kite and the height of the boy is 1.5 m, is **NCERT Exemplar Pg. 135**

(a) 4 m/s (b) 6 m/s (c) 7 m/s (d) 8 m/s

20 The diagonal of a square is changing at the rate of 0.5 cm/s . Then, the rate of change of area when the area is $400\ cm^2$, is equal to **NCERT Pg. 151**

(a) $20\sqrt{2}\ cm^2/s$ (b) $10\sqrt{2}\ cm^2/s$
(c) $\frac{1}{10\sqrt{2}}\ cm^2/s$ (d) $\frac{10}{\sqrt{2}}\ cm^2/s$

21 For $0 < \theta < \frac{\pi}{2}$, the value of θ, if it increases twice as fast as its sine, is **NCERT Exemplar Pg. 135**

(a) $\frac{\pi}{2}$ (b) $\frac{\pi}{3}$
(c) $\frac{\pi}{6}$ (d) None of these

22 The distance covered by a particle in time t is given by $x = 3 + 8t - 4t^2$. After 1s, its velocity will be **NCERT Pg. 150**

(a) 0 unit/s (b) 3 units/s
(c) 4 units/s (d) 7 units/s

23 An edge of a variable cube is increasing at the rate of 10 cm/s. How fast the volume of the cube will increase when the edge is 5 cm long? **NCERT Pg. 150**

(a) $750\ cm^3/s$ (b) $75\ cm^3/s$
(c) $300\ cm^3/s$ (d) $150\ cm^3/s$

24 The radius of a cylinder is increasing at the rate of 3m/s and its altitude is decreasing at the rate of 4m/s. The rate of change of volume when radius is 4m and altitude is 6m, is **NCERT Pg. 151**

(a) $20\pi\ m^3/s$ (b) $40\pi\ m^3/s$
(c) $60\pi\ m^3/s$ (d) None of these

Increasing and Decreasing Functions

Level I

1 Consider the information given below.

The function f is given by $f(x) = x^2, x \in R$. The graph of this function is a parabola as shown below.

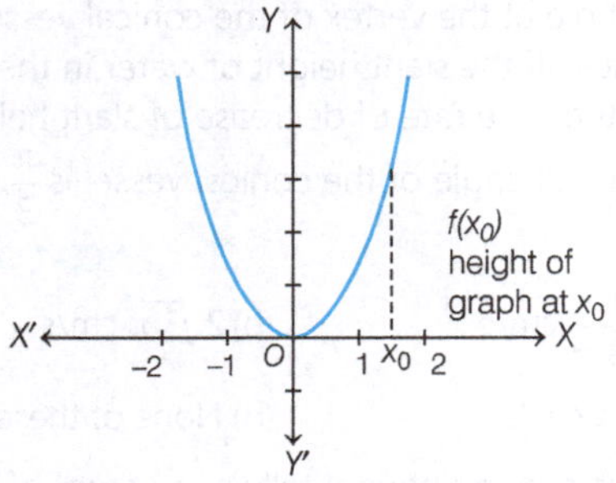

Based on above information, choose the statement which is correct? **NCERT Pg. 152**

(a) For the values left to origin on moving from left to right, the height of the graph increases.

(b) For the values right to origin on moving from left to right, the height of the graph decreases.

(c) The given function is called decreasing for the real numbers $x > 0$.

(d) The given function is said to be decreasing for the real numbers $x < 0$.

2 If I be an open interval contained in the domain of a real valued function f and if $x_1 < x_2$ in I, then which of the following statements is true? **NCERT Pg. 152**

(a) f is said to be increasing on I, if $f(x_1) \le f(x_2)$ for all $x_1, x_2 \in I$.

(b) f is said to be strictly increasing on I, if $f(x_1) < f(x_2)$ for all $x_1, x_2 \in I$.

(c) Both (a) and (b) are true.

(d) Both (a) and (b) are false.

3 If I be an open interval contained in the domain of a real valued function f and if $x_1 < x_2$ in I, then which of the following statements is true? **NCERT Pg. 153**

(a) f is said to be decreasing on I, if $f(x_1) > f(x_2)$ for all $x_1, x_2 \in I$.

(b) f is said to be strictly decreasing on I, if $f(x_1) \ge f(x_2)$ for all $x_1, x_2 \in I$.

(c) Both (a) and (b) are true.

(d) Both (a) and (b) are false.

4 Which of the following can be said true for a function f to be increasing at x_0, in an interval $I = (x_0 - h, x_0 + h), h > 0$ such that $x_1, x_2 \in R$? **NCERT Pg. 153**

(a) $x_1 < x_2$ in $I \Rightarrow f(x_1) \le f(x_2)$

(b) $x_1 > x_2$ in $I \Rightarrow f(x_1) \le f(x_2)$

(c) $x_1 < x_2$ in $I \Rightarrow f(x_1) \ge f(x_2)$

(d) None of the above

5 Which of the following is true for the function $f(x) = 7x - 3$? **NCERT Pg. 153**

(a) $f(x)$ is strictly increasing on R

(b) $f(x)$ is strictly decreasing on R

(c) Both (a) and (b) are false

(d) $f(x)$ is decreasing on R

6 If f is continuous on $[a, b]$ and differentiable on the open interval (a, b), then which of the following is/are correct? **NCERT Pg. 154**

(a) f is strictly increasing in $[a, b]$, if $f'(x) > 0$ for each $x \in (a, b)$.

(b) f is strictly decreasing in $[a, b]$, if $f'(x) < 0$ for each $x \in (a, b)$.

(c) f is a constant function in $[a, b]$, if $f'(x) = 0$ for each $x \in (a, b)$.

(d) All the above are correct

7 If the function f is given by

$f(x) = x^3 - 3x^2 + 4x, x \in R$, then **NCERT Pg. 154**

(a) f is strictly increasing on R

(b) f is decreasing on R

(c) f is neither increasing nor decreasing on R

(d) f is strictly decreasing on R

8 If $f(x) = \cos x$, then **NCERT Pg. 154**

(a) $f(x)$ is strictly decreasing in $(0, \pi)$.

(b) $f(x)$ is strictly increasing in $(0, 2\pi)$.

(c) $f(x)$ is neither increasing nor decreasing in $(\pi, 2\pi)$.

(d) All the above are correct

9 Which of the following statements is true for $f(x) = 4x^3 - 6x^2 - 72x + 30$? **NCERT Pg. 155**

I. f is strictly increasing in the interval $(-\infty, -2)$.

II. f is strictly increasing in the interval $(3, \infty)$.

III. f is strictly decreasing in the interval $(-2, 3)$.

IV. f is neither increasing nor decreasing in R.

(a) I and II are true
(b) II and III are true
(c) II and IV are true
(d) All are true

10 Which among the following is correct? **NCERT Pg. 156**

(a) The function given by $f(x) = \sin 3x, x \in \left[0, \frac{\pi}{2}\right]$ is increasing in $\left[0, \frac{\pi}{6}\right]$.

(b) The function given by $f(x) = \sin 3x, x \in \left[0, \frac{\pi}{2}\right]$ is decreasing in $\left[\frac{\pi}{6}, \frac{\pi}{2}\right]$.

(c) Both (a) and (b) are correct

(d) Both (a) and (b) are incorrect

11 Consider the information given below.
The function f is given by $f(x) = \sin x + \cos x, 0 \le x \le 2\pi$.
Based on above information, choose the correct statement from the following. **NCERT Pg. 157**

(a) f is strictly increasing in $\left[0, \frac{\pi}{4}\right)$.

(b) f is strictly decreasing in $\left(\frac{\pi}{4}, \frac{5\pi}{4}\right)$.

(c) f is strictly increasing in $\left(\frac{5\pi}{4}, 2\pi\right]$.

(d) All the above are correct

12 The function f given by $f(x) = 3x + 17$ is **NCERT Pg. 158**

(a) strictly increasing on R (b) strictly decreasing on R
(c) decreasing on R (d) Both (b) and (c) are correct

13 The function $f(x) = \sin x$ is **NCERT Pg. 158**

I. strictly increasing in $\left[0, \frac{\pi}{2}\right]$.

II. strictly decreasing in $\left(\frac{\pi}{2}, \pi\right)$.

III. neither increasing nor decreasing in $[0, \pi]$.

(a) I and II are true (b) I, II and III are true
(c) Only II is true (d) Only III is true

14 The function given $f(x) = e^{2x}$ is ...A... on R. Here, A refers to **NCERT Pg. 158**

(a) strictly increasing (b) strictly decreasing
(c) neither increasing nor decreasing
(d) decreasing

15 The function f given by $f(x) = 2x^2 - 3x$, is **NCERT Pg. 158**

(a) strictly increasing in the interval $\left(\frac{3}{4}, \infty\right)$.

(b) strictly decreasing in the interval $\left(-\infty, \frac{3}{4}\right)$.

(c) Both (a) and (b) are true
(d) Both (a) and (b) are false

16 Match the terms of column I with the terms of column II and choose the correct option from the codes given below. **NCERT Pg. 158**

Column I	Column II
A. $f(x) = x^2 + 2x - 5$ is	1. strictly decreasing in $(-\infty, -1)$ and strictly increasing in $(-1, \infty)$.
B. $f(x) = 10 - 6x - 2x^2$ is	2. strictly increasing in $(-\infty, -9/2)$ and strictly decreasing in $\left(-\frac{9}{2}, \infty\right)$
C. $f(x) = -2x^3 - 9x^2 - 12x + 1$ is	3. strictly decreasing in $(-\infty, -2)$ and $(-1, \infty)$ and strictly increasing in $(-2, -1)$.
D. $f(x) = 6 - 9x - x^2$ is	4. strictly increasing in $(-\infty, -3/2)$ and strictly decreasing in $\left(-\frac{3}{2}, \infty\right)$
E. $f(x) = (x + 1)^3 (x - 3)^3$ is	5. strictly increasing in $(1, 3)$ and $(3, \infty)$ and strictly decreasing in $(-\infty, -1)$ and $(-1, 1)$.

Codes

	A	B	C	D	E
(a)	1	2	3	4	5
(b)	2	3	4	1	5
(c)	1	4	3	2	5
(d)	5	4	3	2	1

17 If $y = \log(1 + x) - \frac{2x}{2 + x}$ is an increasing function of x throughout **NCERT Pg. 158**

(a) $x < -1$ as its domain (b) $x > -1$ as its domain
(c) $x = -1$ (d) $x > 2$ as its domain

18 The values of x for which $y = [x(x - 2)]^2$ is an increasing function, are **NCERT Pg. 158**

(a) $0 < x < 1$ and $x > 2$ (b) $0 < x < 2$ and $x > 3$
(c) $0 < x < \frac{1}{2}$ and $x > \frac{3}{2}$ (d) $0 < x < \frac{3}{2}$ and $x > 4$

19 The function $y = \frac{4 \sin \theta}{(2 + \cos \theta)} - \theta$ is increasing on θ in the interval **NCERT Pg. 158**

(a) $[0, \pi]$ (b) $\left[0, \frac{\pi}{2}\right]$
(c) $\left(0, \frac{\pi}{2}\right)$ (d) None of these

20 If $f(x) = \cos x$, $g(x) = \cos 2x$, $h(x) = \cos 3x$ and $l(x) = \tan x$, then which of the following option is correct? **NCERT Pg. 159**

(a) $f(x)$ and $g(x)$ are strictly decreasing in $(0, \pi/2)$.
(b) $h(x)$ is neither increasing nor decreasing in $(0, \pi/2)$.
(c) $l(x)$ is strictly increasing in $(0, \pi/2)$.
(d) All above are correct

21 On which of the following intervals is the function f given by $f(x) = x^{100} + \sin x - 1$ strictly decreasing? **NCERT Pg. 159**

(a) $(0, 1)$ (b) $\left(\frac{\pi}{2}, \pi\right)$ (c) $\left(0, \frac{\pi}{2}\right)$ (d) None of these

22 The least value of a such that the function f given by $f(x)=x^2+ax+1$ is strictly increasing on (1, 2), is **NCERT Pg. 159**

(a) -1 (b) -2 (c) 0 (d) 1

23 If I be any interval disjoint from $[-1,1]$, then the function f given by $f(x)=x+\frac{1}{x}$ is **NCERT Pg. 159**

(a) strictly decreasing on I
(b) strictly increasing on I
(c) decreasing on I
(d) Only (a) and (c) are true

24 Which of the following statements is/are true? **NCERT Pg. 159**

(a) $f(x)=\log\cos x$ is strictly decreasing on $\left(0,\frac{\pi}{2}\right)$.
(b) $f(x)=\log\cos x$ is strictly decreasing on $(0,\pi)$.
(c) Both (a) and (b) are true
(d) Both (a) and (b) are false

25 The function given by $f(x)=x^3-3x^2+3x-100$ is **NCERT Pg. 159**

(a) increasing on R (b) decreasing on R
(c) strictly decreasing on R (d) None of these

26 The interval in which $y=x^2e^{-x}$ is increasing, is **NCERT Pg. 159**

(a) $(-\infty,\infty)$ (b) $(-2,0)$
(c) $(2,\infty)$ (d) $(0,2)$

Level II

27 The function $f(x)=\tan x-4x$ is strictly decreasing on **NCERT Exemplar Pg. 121**

(a) $\left(-\frac{\pi}{3},\frac{\pi}{3}\right)$ (b) $\left(\frac{\pi}{3},\frac{\pi}{2}\right)$ (c) $\left(-\frac{\pi}{3},\frac{\pi}{2}\right)$ (d) $\left(\frac{\pi}{2},\pi\right)$

28 The interval of increasing of the function $f(x)=x-e^x+\tan\left(\frac{2\pi}{7}\right)$ is **NCERT Pg. 159**

(a) $(-\infty,0)$ (b) $(0,\infty)$ (c) $(1,\infty)$ (d) $(-\infty,1)$

29 $f(x)=\left(\frac{e^{2x}-1}{e^{2x}+1}\right)$ is **NCERT Pg. 158**

(a) a decreasing function (b) an increasing function
(c) Both (a) and (b) are true (d) None of these

30 If the function f be given by $f(x)=xe^{1-x}$, then choose the correct statement from the following. **NCERT Pg. 158**

(a) f is strictly increasing in $\left(\frac{1}{2},2\right)$.
(b) f is decreasing in $(0,2)$.
(c) f is increasing in $(0,\infty)$.
(d) f is strictly decreasing in $(1,\infty)$.

31 The function $f(x)=\tan^{-1}(\sin x+\cos x)$ is an increasing function in **NCERT Exemplar Pg. 137**

(a) $\left(\frac{\pi}{4},\frac{\pi}{2}\right)$ (b) $\left(-\frac{\pi}{2},\frac{\pi}{4}\right)$ (c) $\left(0,\frac{\pi}{2}\right)$ (d) $\left(-\frac{\pi}{2},\frac{\pi}{2}\right)$

32 For what value of a, $f(x)=-x^3+4ax^2+2x-5$ is decreasing for all? **NCERT Pg. 159**

(a) (1, 2) (b) (3 , 4)
(c) R (d) No value of a

33 The interval on which the function $f(x)=2x^3+9x^2+12x-1$ is decreasing, is **NCERT Exemplar Pg. 140**

(a) $[-1,\infty)$ (b) $[-2,-1]$
(c) $(-\infty,-2]$ (d) $[-1,1]$

34 The function

$f(x)=4\sin^3x-6\sin^2x+12\sin x+100$

is strictly **NCERT Exemplar Pg. 140**

(a) increasing in $\left(\pi,\frac{3\pi}{2}\right)$ (b) decreasing in $\left(\frac{\pi}{2},\pi\right)$
(c) decreasing in $\left[-\frac{\pi}{2},\frac{\pi}{2}\right]$ (d) decreasing in $\left[0,\frac{\pi}{2}\right]$

35 Which of the following functions is decreasing on $\left(0,\frac{\pi}{2}\right)$? **NCERT Exemplar Pg. 140**

(a) $\sin 2x$ (b) $\tan x$ (c) $\cos x$ (d) $\cos 3x$

36 If the function f be given by $f(x)=(x+2)e^{-x}$, then **NCERT Pg. 159**

(a) f is increasing in $(-\infty,-1)$.
(b) f is decreasing in $[-1,\infty]$.
(c) Both (a) and (b) are true
(d) Both (a) and (b) are false

Maxima and Minima

Level I

1 If f be a function defined on an interval I and there exists a point c in I such that $f(c)>f(x),\forall\, x\in I$, then **NCERT Pg. 160**

(a) function f is said to have a maximum value in I.
(b) the number $f(c)$ is called the maximum value of f in I.
(c) the point c is called a point of maximum value of f in I.
(d) All the above are true

2 If f be a function defined on an interval I and there exists a point c in I such that **NCERT Pg. 160**

$f(c)<f(x),\forall\, x\in I$, then

(a) function f is said to have a minimum value in I.
(b) the number $f(c)$ is called the global value of f in I.
(c) the point c is called a global point.
(d) All the above are correct

3 Consider the graph given below.

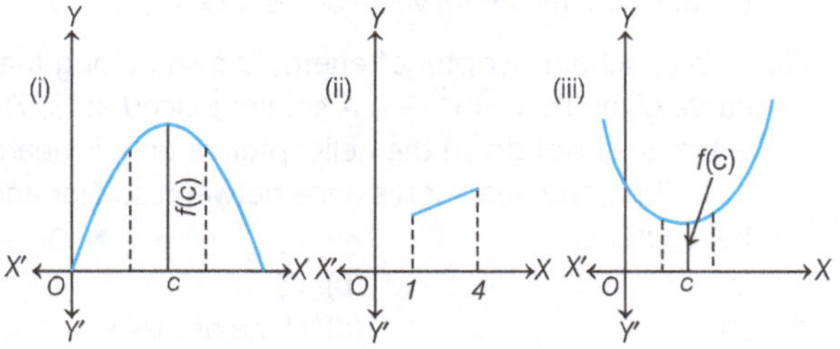

Choose the graph which represents differentiable function? NCERT Pg. 161

(a) Only I (b) Only II
(c) Both I and II (d) All of these

4 If the function f is given by $f(x) = x^2$, $x \in R$, then

(a) minimum value of f is 0. NCERT Pg. 161
(b) the point of minimum value of f is $x = 0$.
(c) f has no maximum value and hence no point of maximum value of f in R.
(d) All the above are true

5 If the function is given by $f(x) = |x|$, $x \in R$, then

(a) point of minimum value of f is $x = 1$. NCERT Pg. 161
(b) f has no point of maximum value in R.
(c) Both (a) and (b) are true
(d) Both (a) and (b) are not true

6 If f be any function given by $f(x) = x$, $x \in (0, 1)$, then which of the following is true for the given interval? NCERT Pg. 162

(a) The maximum value of the given function is 1.
(b) The minimum value of the given function is zero.
(c) Both (a) and (b) are correct
(d) Both (a) and (b) are incorrect

7 A point at which the derivative vanishes need not be a point of NCERT Pg. 164

(a) local maxima or local minima
(b) global maxima or global minima
(c) Both (a) and (b)
(d) Neither (a) nor (b)

8 A point c in the domain of a function f is called a critical point of f if NCERT Pg. 164

(i) $f'(c) = 0$.
(ii) f is not differentiable at c.

(a) Either (i) or (ii) (b) Only (i)
(c) Only (ii) (d) Neither (i) nor (ii)

9 If the function f be given by $f(x) = x^3 - 3x + 3$, then NCERT Pg. 165

(i) $x = \pm 2$ are the only critical points for local maxima or local minima.
(ii) $x = 1$ is a point of local minima.
(iii) local minimum value is 2.
(iv) local maximum value is 5.

(a) Only (i) and (ii) are true
(b) Only (ii) and (iii) are true
(c) Only (i), (ii) and (iii) are true
(d) Only (ii) and (iv) are true

10 If the function f be given by $f(x) = 2x^3 - 6x^2 + 6x + 5$, then NCERT Pg. 166

(a) $x = 0$ is the only critical point of f
(b) $x = 1$ is the point of local minima
(c) $x = 1$ is the point of local maxima
(d) $x = 1$ is a point of inflection

11 The local minimum value of the function f given by $f(x) = 3 + |x|$, $x \in R$ is NCERT Pg. 166

(a) 1 (b) 2 (c) 3 (d) 0

12 If the function f be given by $f(x) = 3x^4 + 4x^3 - 12x^2 + 12$, then NCERT Pg. 167

(a) local maximum value of f is 12
(b) local minimum values of f are 7 and -20
(c) Both (a) and (b) are correct
(d) Both (a) and (b) are incorrect

13 The two positive numbers whose sum is 15 and the sum of whose squares is minimum, are NCERT Pg. 167

(a) $\frac{15}{2}, \frac{13}{2}$ (b) $\frac{13}{2}, \frac{11}{2}$ (c) $\frac{15}{2}, \frac{15}{2}$ (d) $\frac{17}{2}, \frac{13}{2}$

14 The shortest distance of the point $(0, c)$ from the parabola $y = x^2$, where $0 \le c \le 5$ is NCERT Pg. 168

(a) $\frac{\sqrt{2c-1}}{2}$ (b) $\frac{\sqrt{4c-1}}{2}$
(c) $\frac{\sqrt{3c-1}}{2}$ (d) None of these

15 Let AP and BQ be two vertical poles at points A and B, respectively. If $AP = 16$ m, $BQ = 22$ m and $AB = 20$ m, then the distance of a point R on AB from the point A such that $RP^2 + RQ^2$ is minimum, is NCERT Pg. 169

(a) 5 m (b) 10 m (c) 15 m (d) 20 m

16 If a right circular cylinder of greatest curved surface area is inscribed in a given cone, then the ratio of the radius of the circular cylinder to the radius of cone is NCERT Pg. 170

(a) 2 : 1 (b) 1 : 2 (c) 1 : 3 (d) 3 : 1

17 If f be given by $f(x) = x + 2$, $x \in (0, 1)$, then NCERT Pg. 171

(a) the function f has not a local maximum value.
(b) the function f has not a local minimum value.
(c) Both (a) and (b) are true
(d) Both (a) and (b) are false

18 Consider the function f given by $f(x) = x + 2, x \in [0, 1]$, then the NCERT Pg. 171

(a) the maximum value 3 of f at $x = 1$ is called the absolute maximum value of f on [0, 1].
(b) the minimum value 2 of f at $x = 0$ is called the absolute minimum value of f on [0, 1].
(c) Both (a) and (b) are incorrect
(d) Both (a) and (b) are correct

19 Consider the figure given below. NCERT Pg. 172

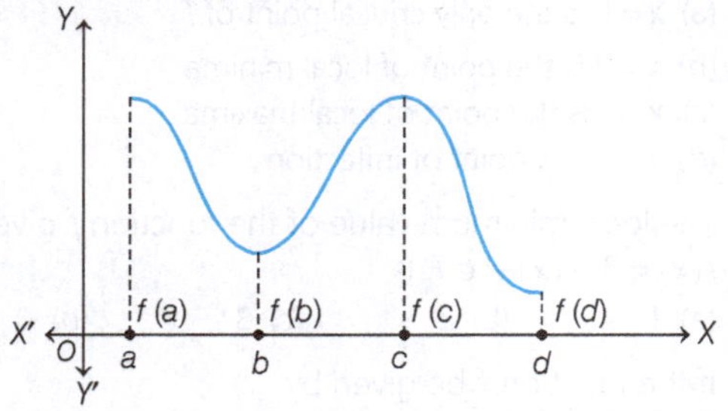

Here, graph of a continuous function defined on a closed interval $[a, d]$.
Based on above information, which of the following is correct?

(a) The function f has a local minimum value as $f(b)$ and local maximum value as $f(c)$.
(b) f has absolute maximum value $f(a)$ and absolute minimum value $f(d)$.
(c) Both (a) and (b) are correct
(d) Both (a) and (b) are incorrect

20 If f be a continuous function on an closed interval $I = [a, b]$, then NCERT Pg. 172

(a) f has the absolute maximum value.
(b) f attains its absolute maximum value atleast once in I.
(c) f has the absolute minimum value and attains it atleast once in I.
(d) All the above are true

21 If f be a differentiable function on a closed interval I and let c be any interior point of I, then which of the following is correct? NCERT Pg. 172

(i) If f attains its absolute maximum value at c, then $f'(c) = 0$.
(ii) If f attains its absolute minimum value at c, then $f'(c) = 0$.

(a) Only (i) is true (b) Only (ii) is true
(c) Both (i) and (ii) are true (d) Both (i) and (ii) are false

22 If the function f be given by $f(x) = 2x^3 - 15x^2 + 36x + 1$ on the interval [1, 5], then NCERT Pg. 173

(a) absolute maximum value of the function f is 24.
(b) absolute minimum value of the function f is 20.
(c) absolute maximum value of f is on $x = 5$.
(d) absolute minimum value of f is on $x = 2$.

23 If an apache helicopter of enemy is flying along the curve given by $y = x^2 + 7$. A soldier placed at (3, 7) wants to shoot down the helicopter when it is nearest to him. Then, the nearest distance between soldier and the helicopter is NCERT Pg. 174

(a) $\sqrt{3}$ (b) $\sqrt{5}$
(c) $\sqrt{7}$ (d) None of these

24 The maximum and minimum values of the following functions are given in column II, where as in column I functions are given. You have to match the functions of column I with the maximum and minimum values in the column II and choose the correct option from the codes given below. NCERT Pg. 174

Column I	Column II
A. $f(x) = (2x - 1)^2 + 3$ has	1. does not have a particular minimum value but it has its maximum value as 10.
B. $f(x) = 9x^2 + 12x + 2$ has	2. minimum value is 3 but does not have a particular maximum value.
C. $f(x) = -(x - 1)^2 + 10$ has	3. no maximum and minimum value.
D. $f(x) = x^3 + 1$ has	4. minimum value is –2 but does not have a particular maximum value.

Codes

	A	B	C	D
(a)	1	2	3	4
(b)	2	4	1	3
(b)	4	3	2	1
(c)	2	1	4	3

25 Match the terms of column I with the terms of column II and choose the correct option from the codes given below. NCERT Pg. 175

Column I (Function)	Column II (Maximum and minimum values respectively)
A. $f(x) = \|x + 2\| - 1$ has	1. no maximum value and –1 as minimum value
B. $g(x) = -\|x + 1\| + 3$ has	2. 3 as maximum value, but it has no minimum value
C. $h(x) = \sin(2x) + 5$ has	3. 6 as maximum value, and 4 as minimum value
D. $F(x) = \|\sin 4x + 3\|$ has	4. 4 as maximum value and 2 as minimum value
E. $h(x) = x + 1, x \in (-1, 1)$ has	5. neither a maximum value nor a minimum value

Codes

	A	B	C	D	E
(a)	1	2	3	4	5
(b)	2	3	4	1	5
(c)	1	3	2	4	5
(d)	3	1	2	5	4

26 Which of the following functions do not have maxima or minima? NCERT Pg. 175

(a) $f(x) = e^x$ (b) $g(x) = \log x$

(c) $h(x) = x^3 + x^2 + x + 1$ (d) All of these

27 Match the terms of column I with terms of column II and choose the correct option from the codes given below. NCERT Pg. 175

Column I (Functions with the given interval)	Column II (Absolute maximum and absolute minimum value respectively)
A. $f(x) = x^3$, $x \in [-2, 2]$	1. 8, −8
B. $f(x) = \sin x + \cos x$, $x \in [0, \pi]$	2. 8, −10
C. $f(x) = 4x - \frac{1}{2}x^2$, $x \in \left[-2, \frac{9}{2}\right]$	3. 19, 3
D. $f(x) = (x-1)^2 + 3$, $x \in [-3, 1]$	4. $\sqrt{2}, -1$

Codes

	A	B	C	D		A	B	C	D
(a)	1	4	2	3	(b)	1	2	4	3
(c)	2	1	3	4	(d)	2	3	1	4

28 The maximum profit that a company can make, if the profit function is given by $p(x) = 41 - 72x - 18x^2$, is NCERT Pg. 175

(a) 111 (b) 101

(c) 113 (d) None of these

29 The function $\sin 2x$ in the interval $[0, 2\pi]$ attain its maximum value at NCERT Pg. 175

(a) $\frac{\pi}{4}$ (b) $\frac{3\pi}{2}$ (c) $\frac{7\pi}{2}$ (d) $\frac{3\pi}{4}$

30 Which of the following statement is correct? NCERT Pg. 175

(a) If $f(x) = x^3 - 6x^2 + 9x + 15$, then its maximum and minimum value are 15 and 19.

(b) If $g(x) = \frac{x}{2} + \frac{2}{x}$, $x > 0$, then its minimum value is 1.

(c) If $g(x) = \frac{1}{x^2 + 2}$, then its maximum value is $\frac{1}{2}$.

(d) If $f(x) = x\sqrt{1-x}$, $0 < x < 1$, it has maximum value as $\frac{\sqrt{3}}{9}$.

31 The maximum value of the function $\sin x + \cos x$ is

(a) 1 (b) $\sqrt{2}$ NCERT Pg. 175

(c) 2 (d) None of these

32 If at $x = 1$, the function $x^4 - 62x^2 + ax + 9$ attains its maximum value on the interval [0, 2], then the value of a is NCERT Pg. 176

(a) 110 (b) 10

(c) 55 (d) None of these

33 For the function $x + \sin 2x$ on $[0, 2\pi]$, which of the following is not true? NCERT Pg. 176

(a) The maximum value of the function is 2π.

(b) The maximum value of the function is at $x = \frac{\pi}{3}$.

(c) The minimum value of the function is 0.

(d) The minimum value of the function is at $x = 0$.

34 If sum of two numbers is 24 and their product is as large as possible, then one of the number is NCERT Pg. 176

(a) 23 (b) 20

(c) 18 (d) None of these

35 If two positive numbers x and y are such that $x + y = 60$ and xy^3 is maximum, then the numbers x and y are respectively NCERT Pg. 176

(a) 13, 47

(b) 28, 32

(c) 12, 48

(d) 15, 45

36 A square piece of tin of side 18 cm is to be made into a box without top, by cutting a square from each corner and folding up the flaps to form the box. The side of the square that should be cutoff, so that the volume of the box is maximum possible, is NCERT Pg. 176

(a) 2 cm (b) 3 cm

(c) 4 cm (d) None of these

37 A rectangular sheet of tin 45 cm by 24 cm is to be made into a box without top, by cutting off square from each corner and folding up the flaps. The side of the square, which should be cutoff so that the volume of the box is maximum, is NCERT Pg. 176

(a) 2 cm (b) 3 cm

(c) 4 cm (d) None of these

38 For all the rectangles inscribed in a given fixed circle, the maximum area is possible only for a NCERT Pg. 176

(a) rhombus

(b) parallelogram

(c) square

(d) None of the above

39 For all the closed cylindrical cans (right circular), of a given volume of 100 cm^3, the dimensions of the cane, which has the minimum surface area, are **NCERT Pg. 176**

(a) $2\left(\frac{50}{\pi}\right)^{1/3}$ cm, $\left(\frac{50}{\pi}\right)^{1/3}$ cm

(b) $2\left(\frac{25}{\pi}\right)^{1/3}$ cm, $\left(\frac{25}{\pi}\right)^{1/3}$ cm

(c) $\left(\frac{13}{\pi}\right)^{1/3}$ cm, $\left(\frac{15}{\pi}\right)^{1/3}$ cm

(d) $\left(\frac{17}{2\pi}\right)^{1/3}$ cm, $\left(\frac{21}{2\pi}\right)^{1/3}$ cm

40 A wire of length 28m is to be cut into two pieces. One of the pieces is to be made into a square and the other into a circle. The length of the two pieces, so that the combined area of the square and the circle is minimum, are **NCERT Pg. 176**

(a) $\frac{28\pi}{4+\pi}, \frac{112}{6+\pi}$ (b) $\frac{128\pi}{14+\pi}, \frac{112}{4+\pi}$

(c) $\frac{28\pi}{4+\pi}, \frac{112}{4+\pi}$ (d) $\frac{112}{6+\pi}, \frac{128\pi}{14+\pi}$

41 The right circular cone of least curved surface and given volume has an altitude equal to **NCERT Pg. 176**

(a) $\sqrt{3}$ times the radius of the base.
(b) $\sqrt{5}$ times the radius of the base.
(c) $\sqrt{2}$ times the radius of the base.
(d) None of the above

42 The point on the curve $x^2 = 2y$, which is nearest to the point (0, 5) is **NCERT Pg. 177**

(a) $(2\sqrt{2}, 4)$ (b) $(2\sqrt{2}, 0)$
(c) (0, 0) (d) (2, 2)

43 For all real values of x, then the minimum value of $\frac{1-x+x^2}{1+x+x^2}$ is **NCERT Pg. 177**

(a) zero (b) 1
(c) 3 (d) $\frac{1}{3}$

44 The maximum value of $[x(x-1)+1]^{1/3}, 0 \le x \le 1$ is **NCERT Pg. 177**

(a) $\left(\frac{1}{3}\right)^{1/3}$ (b) $\frac{1}{2}$
(c) 1 (d) zero

Level II

45 The minimum value of $f(x) = e^{(x^4 - x^3 + x^2)}$ is **NCERT Pg. 175**

(a) e (b) $\frac{e}{2}$ (c) 1 (d) -1

46 If a and b are positive numbers such that $a > b$, then the minimum value of $a\sec\theta - b\tan\theta$, $\left(0<\theta<\frac{\pi}{2}\right)$ is **NCERT Pg. 175**

(a) $\sqrt{a^2-b^2}$ (b) $\sqrt{a^2+b^2}$
(c) $\frac{1}{\sqrt{a^2-b^2}}$ (d) $\frac{1}{\sqrt{a^2+b^2}}$

47 The point in the interval $[0, 2\pi]$, where $f(x) = e^x \sin x$ has maximum slope, is **NCERT Pg. 175**

(a) $\frac{\pi}{4}$ (b) $\frac{\pi}{2}$
(c) $\frac{3\pi}{2}$ (d) π

48 For the function $f(x) = 4x^3 - 18x^2 + 27x - 7$, which of the following is true? **NCERT Exemplar Pg. 122**

(a) $f(x)$ has no maxima.
(b) $f(x)$ has no minima.
(c) Both (a) and (b) are true.
(d) Both (a) and (b) are false

49 The function $f(x) = x^3 + ax^2 + bx + c, a^2 \le 3b$ has **NCERT Pg. 175**

(a) one maximum value
(b) one maximum and one minimum value
(c) one minimum value
(d) no extreme value

50 If $y = \frac{\sin(x+a)}{\sin(x+b)}, a \ne b$, then y is **NCERT Pg. 175**

(a) minima at $x = 0$.
(b) maxima at $x = 0$.
(c) Neither minima nor maxima at $x = 0$.
(d) None of the above

51 If $f(x) = \frac{-3}{4}x^4 - 8x^3 - \frac{45}{2}x^2 + 105$, then which of the following holds? **NCERT Exemplar Pg. 123**

(i) $f(x)$ has local maxima at $x = 2$.
(ii) $f(x)$ has local maxima at $x = 5$.
(iii) $f(x)$ has local minima at $x = -3$.

(a) Only (i) is true.
(b) Only (iii) is true.
(c) Both (i) and (ii) are true.
(d) All (i), (ii) and (iii) are true.

52. The maximum value of the function $f(x) = \sin x\,(1+\cos x), x \in R$ is **NCERT Pg. 175**

(a) $\frac{3^{3/2}}{4}$ (b) $\frac{3^{5/8}}{4}$
(c) $\frac{3}{2}$ (d) $\frac{3^{5/3}}{4}$

53 If f be defined as $f(x) = x + \frac{1}{x}$, then which of following is true? NCERT Exemplar Pg. 124

(a) Local maximum value of $f(x)$ is -2.
(b) Local minimum value of $f(x)$ is 2.
(c) Local maximum value of $f(x)$ is less than local minimum value of $f(x)$.
(d) All the above are true

54 The maximum value of $\frac{\ln x}{x}$ in $(2, \infty)$ is NCERT Pg. 175

(a) 1 (b) e
(c) $2/e$ (d) $1/e$

55 The minimum value of $e^{(2x^2 - 2x + 1)\sin^2 x}$ is NCERT Pg. 175

(a) 0 (b) 1
(c) 2 (d) 3

56 If 12 is divided into two parts such that the product of the square on one part and the fourth power of the second part is maximum, then its parts are NCERT Pg. 176

(a) 5, 7 (b) 6, 6
(c) 3, 9 (d) 4, 8

57 If $y = a\log x + bx^2 + x$ has its extremum at $x = -1$ and $x = 2$, then NCERT Pg. 175

(a) $a = 2, b = \frac{1}{2}$ (b) $a = 2, b = \frac{-1}{2}$
(c) $a = \frac{-1}{2}, b = 2$ (d) $a = \frac{1}{2}, b = 2$

58 Suppose the cubic $x^3 - px + q$ has three distinct real roots, where $p > 0$ and $q > 0$. Then, which one of the following holds? NCERT Pg. 176

(a) The cubic has maxima at both $\sqrt{\frac{p}{3}}$ and $-\sqrt{\frac{p}{3}}$.
(b) The cubic has minima at $\sqrt{\frac{p}{3}}$ and maxima at $-\sqrt{\frac{p}{3}}$.
(c) The cubic has minima at $-\sqrt{\frac{p}{3}}$ and maxima at $\sqrt{\frac{p}{3}}$.
(d) The cubic has minima at both $\sqrt{\frac{p}{3}}$ and $-\sqrt{\frac{p}{3}}$.

59 The area of greatest rectangle that can be inscribed in an ellipse $\frac{x^2}{a^2} + \frac{y^2}{b^2} = 1$, is NCERT Exemplar Pg. 129

(a) ab sq units (b) $\frac{ab}{2}$ sq units
(c) $2ab$ sq units (d) $3ab$ sq units

60 If the function $f(x) = 2x^3 - 9ax^2 + 12a^2x + 1$ attains its maximum and minimum at p and q, respectively such that $p^2 = q$, then a is equals to NCERT Pg. 176

(a) 1 (b) 2
(c) 0 (d) None of these

61 The greatest value of $\sin^3 x + \cos^3 x$ is NCERT Pg. 175

(a) 1 (b) 2 (c) $\sqrt{2}$ (d) $\sqrt{3}$

62 The difference between the greatest and least values of the function $f(x) = \sin 2x - x$, on $\left[\frac{-\pi}{2}, \frac{\pi}{2}\right]$ is NCERT Exemplar Pg. 130

(a) $\frac{\pi}{2}$ (b) π (c) $\frac{3\pi}{2}$ (d) $\frac{\pi}{4}$

63 On the interval $[0, 1]$ the function $x^{25}(1-x)^{75}$ takes its maximum value at the point NCERT Pg. 177

(a) 0 (b) $\frac{1}{4}$ (c) $\frac{1}{2}$ (d) $\frac{1}{3}$

64 The maximum value of $x^{1/x}$ is NCERT Pg. 177

(a) $\frac{1}{e^e}$ (b) e (c) $\frac{1}{e}$ (d) $e^{1/e}$

Miscellaneous Exercise

1 A car starts from a point P at time $t = 0$ s and stops at point Q. If the distance x, (in metres), covered by it, in t s is given by $x = t^2\left(2 - \frac{t}{3}\right)$. NCERT Pg. 177

Statement I The time taken by car to reach Q is 4 s.
Statement II The distance travelled from P to Q is 32 m.

(a) Statement I is true.
(b) Statement II is true.
(c) Both the statements are true.
(d) Both the statements are false.

2 A water tank has the shape of an inverted right circular cone with its axis vertical and vertex lowermost. Its semi-vertical angle is $\tan^{-1}(0.5)$.

Water is poured into it at a constant rate of 5 cubic meter per hour. The rate at which the level of the water is rising at the instant when the depth of water in tank is 4m, is NCERT Pg. 178

(a) 35 m/h (b) 37 m/h
(c) 88 m/h (d) None of these

3 A man of height 2 m walks at a uniform speed of 5 km/h away from a lamp post which is 6 m high. The rate at which the length of his shadow increases, is NCERT Pg. 178

(a) $\frac{3}{2}$ km/h (b) $\frac{5}{2}$ km/h (c) 7 km/h (d) 8 km/h

4 If the function f be given by

$$f(x) = \frac{3}{10}x^4 - \frac{4}{5}x^3 - 3x^2 + \frac{36}{5}x + 11$$

Statement I The intervals in which f is strictly increasing are $(-\infty, -2)$ and $(1, 3)$.

Statement II The intervals in which f is strictly decreasing are $(-2, 1)$ and $(3, \infty)$. NCERT Pg. 179

(a) Statement I is true.
(b) Statement II is true.
(c) Both the statements are true.
(d) Both the statements are false.

5 If the function f is given by

$$f(x) = \tan^{-1}(\sin x + \cos x), x > 0.$$

Then, f is always an strictly increasing function in the interval. **NCERT Pg. 180**

(a) $\left[0, \frac{\pi}{6}\right]$ (b) $\left(0, \frac{\pi}{4}\right)$
(c) $\left[0, \frac{\pi}{2}\right]$ (d) None of these

6 A circular disc of radius 3 cm is being heated. Due to expansion, its radius increases at the rate of 0.05 cm/s. The rate, at which its area is increasing when its radius is 3.2 cm, is **NCERT Pg. 181**

(a) $0.320\,\pi\ \text{cm}^2/\text{s}$
(b) $0.160\,\pi\ \text{cm}^2/\text{s}$
(c) $0.260\,\pi\ \text{cm}^2/\text{s}$
(d) $1.2\,\pi\ \text{cm}^2/\text{s}$

7 An open topped box is to be constructed by removing equal squares from each corner of a 3 m by 8 m rectangular sheet of aluminium and folding up the sides. The largest volume of such a box is **NCERT Pg. 181**

(a) $\frac{200}{27}\ \text{m}^3$ (b) $\frac{100}{27}\ \text{m}^3$
(c) $\frac{90}{31}\ \text{m}^3$ (d) $\frac{81}{28}\ \text{m}^3$

8 The function given by $f(x) = \frac{\log x}{x}$ has maximum at **NCERT Pg. 183**

(a) $x = e$ (b) $x = 1$
(c) $x = 2$ (d) None of these

9 The two equal sides of an isosceles triangle with fixed base b are decreasing at the rate of 3 cm/s. If the two equal sides are equal to the base, then the rate at which its area is decreasing, is **NCERT Pg. 183**

(a) $\frac{b}{3}\ \text{cm}^2/\text{s}$
(b) $b^2\ \text{cm}^2/\text{s}$
(c) $\frac{b}{\sqrt{3}}\ \text{cm}^2/\text{s}$
(d) $b\sqrt{3}\ \text{cm}^2/\text{s}$

10 If the function f be given by $f(x) = x^3 + \frac{1}{x^3}, x \neq 0$, then **NCERT Pg. 183**

(a) f is increasing in $(-\infty, -1) \cup (1, \infty)$.
(b) f is decreasing in $(-1, 1)$.
(c) Both (a) and (b) are true.
(d) Both (a) and (b) are false.

11 The maximum area of an isosceles triangle inscribed in the ellipse $\frac{x^2}{a^2} + \frac{y^2}{b^2} = 1$ with its vertex at one end of the major axis is **NCERT Pg. 184**

(a) $\frac{3\sqrt{3}}{4}ab$ (b) $\frac{\sqrt{3}}{4}ab$
(c) $\frac{\sqrt{3}}{2}ab$ (d) $\frac{3\sqrt{3}}{2}ab$

12 A tank with rectangular base and rectangular sides, open at the top is to be constructed so that its depth is 2m and volume is 8 m^3. If building of tank costs ₹ 70 per sq m for the base and ₹ 45 per sq m for sides, then the cost of least expensive tank is **NCERT Pg. 184**

(a) ₹ 1000 (b) ₹ 500
(c) ₹ 800 (d) None of these

13 If the sum of the perimeter of a circle and square is k, where k is some constant, then which of the following is true? **NCERT Pg. 184**

(a) The sum of their areas is least when the side of square is triple the radius of the circle.
(b) The sum of their areas is maximum when the side of square is double the radius of the circle.
(c) The sum of their areas is least when the side of square is double the radius of the circle.
(d) None of the above

14 A window is in the form of a rectangle surmounted by a semi-circular opening. The total perimeter of the window is 10 m.

Statement I One of the dimension of the window to admit maximum light through the whole opening is $\frac{20}{\pi + 4}$ m.

Statement II One of the dimension of the window to admit maximum light through the whole opening is $\frac{10}{\pi + 4}$ m. **NCERT Pg. 184**

(a) Statement I is true.
(b) Statement II is true.
(c) Both the statements are true.
(d) None of the above.

15 If a point on the hypotenuse of a triangle is at distance a and b from the sides of triangle, then the minimum length of the hypotenuse is **NCERT Pg. 184**

(a) $\left(a^{\frac{2}{3}} + b^{\frac{2}{3}}\right)$ (b) $\left(a^{\frac{2}{3}} + b^{\frac{2}{3}}\right)^{\frac{3}{2}}$
(c) $\left(a^{\frac{1}{3}} + b^{\frac{1}{3}}\right)^{\frac{3}{2}}$ (d) None of these

Numerical Type Questions

1 A despatch rider is in open country at a distance of 6 km from the nearest point P of a straight road. He wishes to proceed as quickly as possible to a point Q on the road 20 km from P. If his maximum speed across country is 40 km/h, 50 km/h on road, then at what distance from P, he should touch the road? NCERT Pg. 160

2 The minimum value of $\dfrac{\tan\left(x+\dfrac{\pi}{6}\right)}{\tan x}$ is ....

NCERT Pg. 160

3 The least value of a for which the equation, $\dfrac{4}{\sin x}+\dfrac{1}{1-\sin x}=a$ has atleast one solution in the interval $\left(0, \dfrac{\pi}{2}\right)$ is ....

NCERT Pg. 175

4 A particular substance is being cooled by a stream of cold air (temperature of the air is constant and is 5°C), where rate of cooling is directly proportional to square of difference of temperature of the substance and the air. If the substance is cooled from 40°C to 30°C in 15 min and temperature after 1 h is T°C, then find the value of $[T]/2$, where $[\cdot]$ represents the greatest integer function. NCERT Pg. 151

5 Let $f(x)=\begin{cases} x^{3/5}, & \text{if } x \le 1 \\ -(x-2)^3, & \text{if } x>1 \end{cases}$, then the number of critical points on the graph of the function are ....

NCERT Pg. 172

6 The graph of $y=f''(x)$ for a function f is shown. Number of points of inflection for $y=f'(x)$ is ....

NCERT Pg. 164

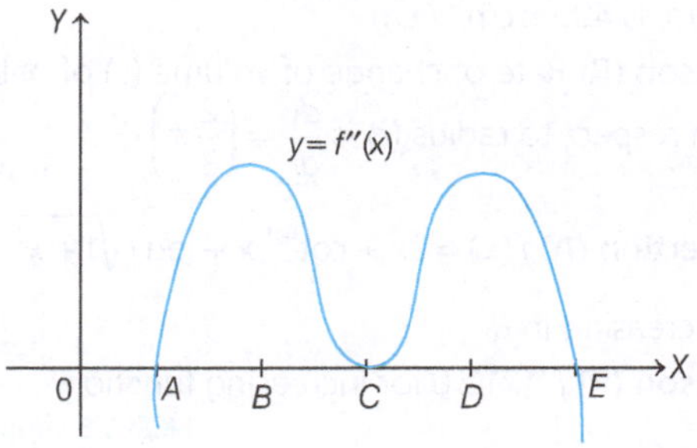

7 If the function $f(x)=\dfrac{t+3x-x^2}{x-4}$, where t is parameter, has a minimum and a maximum, then the greatest value of t is .... NCERT Pg. 173

8 If the surface area of a cube is increasing at the rate of 3.6 cm^2/sec, retaining its shape, then find the rate of change of its volume (in cm^3/sec) when the length of a side of the cube is 10 cm. NCERT Pg. 151

9 The surface area of a balloon of spherical shape being inflated, increases at a constant rate. If initially, the radius of balloon in 3 units and after 5 sec, it becomes 7 units, then find its radius after 9 sec is NCERT Pg. 151

10 A water tank has the shape of an inverted right circular cone, whose semi-vertical angle is $\tan^{-1}\left(\dfrac{1}{2}\right)$.

Water is poured into it at a constant rate of 5 cubic meter per minute. Then, the rate (in m/min), at which the level of water is rising at the instant when the depth of water in the tank is 10 m is λ. Then, the value of $20\pi\lambda$ is .... NCERT Pg. 178

Assertion and Reason Questions

Direction (Q. No. 1-14) In the questions given below are to statements labelled as Assertion (A) and Reason (R). In the context on the two statements, which one of the following is correct?

(a) Both Assertion and Reason are correct and Reason is the correct explanation of Assertion.

(b) Both Assertion and Reason are correct but Reason is not the correct explanation of Assertion.

(c) Assertion is correct but Reason is incorrect.

(d) Assertion is incorrect but Reason is correct.

1 **Assertion (A)** If two variables x and y are varying with respect to another variable t, i.e. if $x=f(t)$ and $y=g(t)$, then the rate of change of y with respect to x can be calculated using the rate of change of y and that of x both with respect to t.

Reason (R) By Chain rule, we have

$$\frac{dy}{dx}=\frac{dy}{dt}\Big/\frac{dx}{dt}, \text{ if } \frac{dx}{dt}\ne 0$$

NCERT Pg. 147

2 Assertion (A) A balloon, which always remains spherical, has a variable radius. The rate, at which its volume is increasing with the radius when the radius is 10 cm, is 400 π cm^3 / cm.

Reason (R) Rate of change of volume (v) of balloon with respect to radius (r) is $\frac{dv}{dr} = \left(\frac{2}{3}\pi\right) \cdot 3r^2$ **NCERT Pg. 151**

3 Assertion (A) $f(x) = 2x + \cot^{-1} x + \log(\sqrt{1+x^2} - x)$ is increasing in R.

Reason (R) $f'(x) \geq 0$ for increasing function. **NCERT Exemplar Pg. 136**

4 Observe the following statements

Assertion (A) $f(x) = 2x^3 - 9x^2 + 12x - 3$ is increasing outside the interval (1, 2).

Reason (R) $f'(x) < 0$ for $x \in (1, 2)$. **NCERT Pg. 158**

5 Assertion (A) If the length of three sides of a trapezium other than base are equal to 10 cm, then the area of trapezium when it is maximum, is $75\sqrt{3}$ cm^2.

Reason (R) Area of trapezium is maximum at $x = 5$. **NCERT Pg. 169**

6 The function f be given by $f(x) = 12x^{4/3} - 6x^{1/3}, x \in [-1, 1]$

Assertion (A) The absolute maximum value of f is 18.

Reason (R) The absolute minimum value of f is $\frac{-9}{4}$. **NCERT Pg. 173**

7 Assertion (A) If two positive numbers x and y are such that $x + y = 35$ and x^2y^5 is maximum, then the numbers are 10 and 25.

Reason (R) If f be a function defined on an interval I and $c \in I$ and also, if f be twice differentiable at c, then $x = c$ is a point of local maxima if $f'(c) = 0$ and $f''(c) < 0$ and the value $f(c)$ is local maximum value of f. **NCERT Pg. 176**

8 Assertion (A) If two positive numbers are such that sum is 16 and sum of their cubes is minimum, then numbers are 8, 8.

Reason (R) If f be a function defined on an interval I and $c \in I$ and let f be twice differentiable at c, then $x = c$ is a point of local minima if $f'(c) = 0$ and $f''(c) > 0$ and $f(c)$ is local minimum value of f. **NCERT Pg. 176**

9 The function f be given by $f(x) = 2x^3 - 6x^2 + 6x + 5$.

Assertion (A) $x = 1$ is not a point of local maxima.

Reason (R) $x = 1$ is not a point of local minima. **NCERT Pg. 175**

10 Assertion (A) If manufacturer can sell x items at a price of ₹ $\left(5 - \frac{x}{100}\right)$ each. The cost price of x items is ₹ $\left(\frac{x}{5} + 500\right)$. Then, the number of items he should sell to earn maximum profit is 240 items.

Reason (R) The profit for selling x items is given by $\frac{24}{5}x - \frac{x^2}{100} - 300$. **NCERT Pg. 182**

11 Consider the function f be given by

$f(x) = \frac{4\sin x - 2x - x\cos x}{2 + \cos x}$ **NCERT Pg. 183**

Assertion (A) f is increasing in the interval $\left(\frac{3\pi}{2}, 2\pi\right)$.

Reason (R) f is decreasing in the interval $\left(\frac{\pi}{2}, \frac{3\pi}{2}\right)$.

12 Assertion (A) The maximum value of the function $f(x) = x^5, x \in [-1, 1]$, is not attained at its critical point $x = 0$.

Reason (R) The maximum of a function can only occur at points, where derivative is zero. **NCERT Pg. 175**

13 Assertion (A) If m and M respectively are the minimum and maximum values of $f(x) = x^2 - 2x + 4$ for $x \in [-3, 1]$, then $(m, M) = (f(1), f(-3))$.

Reason (R) $f(x)$ is strictly decreasing on [–3, 1]. **NCERT Pg. 175**

14 Assertion (A) The number of critical points of $f(x) = \frac{|x-1|}{x^2}$ is 3.

Reason (R) A point $x = \alpha$ is a critical point of a function f, if $f'(\alpha) = 0$ or $f'(\alpha)$ does not. **NCERT Pg. 164**

Case or Paragraph Type Questions

Direction (Q. No. 1-3) Examine the graph of a function as shown below.

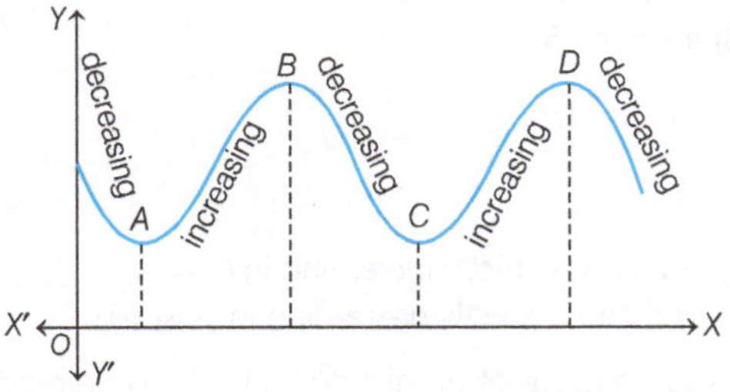

Based on above graph, answer the questions given below.
NCERT Pg. 163

1 The points of local minimum value (or relative minimum value) are
(a) A and B (b) A and C
(c) B and C (d) C and D

2 The local maximum value (or relative maximum value) for the given function are
(a) B and C (b) A and B
(c) B and D (d) A and C

3 The local maximum value and local minimum value of the function are referred to as respectively
(a) local maxima and local minima
(b) global maxima and global minima
(c) Both (a) and (b) are correct
(d) Both (a) and (b) are incorrect

Direction (Q. No. 4-7) A tank as shown in the figure below, formed using a combination of a cylinder and a cone, offers better drainage as compared to a flat bottomed tank.

A tap is connected to such a tank whose conical part is full of water. Water is dripping out from a tap at the bottom at the uniform rate of 2 cm^3/s. The semi-vertical angle of the conical tank is 45°.

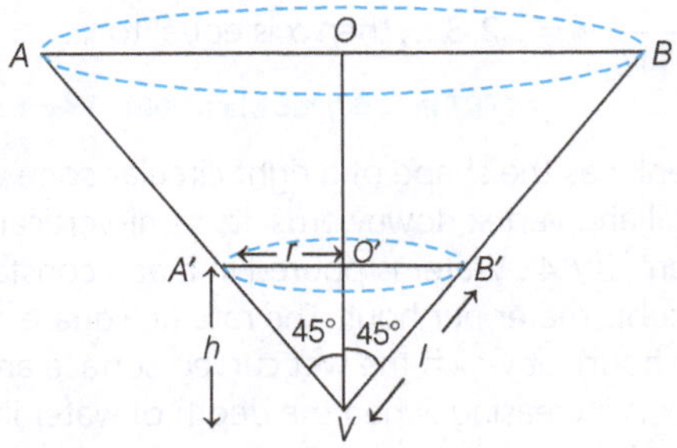

On the basis of given information, answer the following questions.
NCERT Pg. 178

4 The rate of change of volume (cm^3/s) of water in the tank in terms of its radius r is
(a) $\pi r^2 \dfrac{dr}{dt}$ (b) $\pi^2 r \dfrac{dr}{dt}$ (c) $\pi r^2 \dfrac{dt}{dr}$ (d) $\pi^2 r^2 \dfrac{dr}{dt}$

5 The rate of change of radius (cm/s) at an instant when $r = 2\sqrt{2}$ cm, is
(a) $\dfrac{1}{4\pi}$ (b) $-\dfrac{1}{4\pi}$ (c) 4π (d) -4π

6 The rate at which the wet surface (cm^2/s) of the conical tank is decreasing at an instant when radius $r = 2\sqrt{2}$ cm is
(a) $\dfrac{1}{2}$ (b) $-\dfrac{1}{2}$ (c) -2 (d) 2

7 Find the rate of change of height 'h' (m) at an instant when slant height is 4 cm is
(a) 4π (b) -4π (c) $\dfrac{1}{4\pi}$ (d) $-\dfrac{1}{4\pi}$

Direction (Q. Nos. 8-11) Engine displacement is the measure of the cylinder volume swept by all the pistons of a piston engine. The piston moves inside the cylinder bore.

The cylinder bore in the form of circular cylinder open at the top is to be made from a metal sheet of area 75 π cm^2.

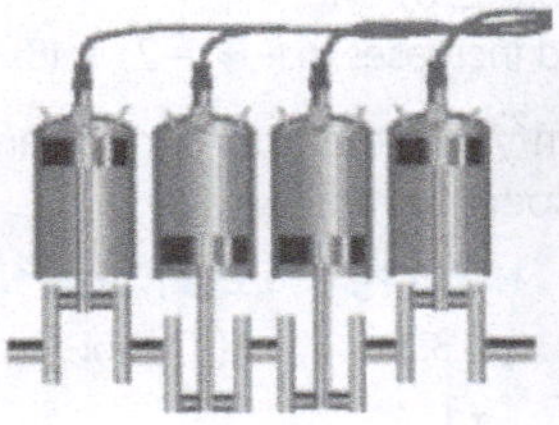

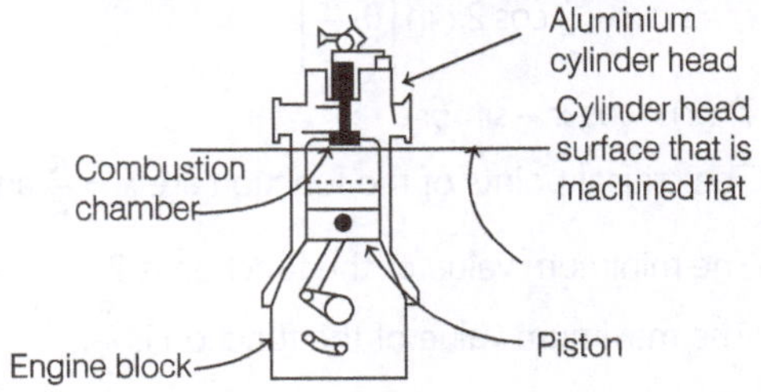

Base on the above information, answer the following questions.
NCERT Pg. 184

8 If the radius of cylinder is r cm and height is h cm, then the volume V of cylinder in term of radius r is
(a) $\dfrac{\pi}{2}(75r - r^3)$ (b) $\dfrac{\pi}{2}(75\,r^2 - r^3)$
(c) $\dfrac{\pi}{4}(75r^2 - r^3)$ (d) $\dfrac{\pi}{4}(75r - r^4)$

9 Find the value of $\dfrac{d^2V}{dr^2}$

(a) $3\pi r$ (b) $-3\pi r$ (c) $\dfrac{3}{2}\pi r$ (d) $-\dfrac{3}{2}\pi r$

10 The radius of cylinder when its volume is maximum is

(a) 2 (b) 9 (c) 5 (d) 15

11 Which of the following condition is correct for maximum volume,

(a) $h=2, r=5$
(b) $h=5, r=2$
(c) $h=2, r=2$
(d) $h=5, r=5$

Past Years Questions

Single Correct Type

1 For the function $f(x)=(\cos x)-x+1, x\in R$, between the following two statements

S1 $f(x)=0$ for only one value of x in $[0,\pi]$.

S2 $f(x)$ is decreasing in $\left[0,\dfrac{\pi}{2}\right]$ and increasing in $\left[\dfrac{\pi}{2},\pi\right]$.

NCERT Pg. 154, JEE Main 2024, 8 April Shift-I

(a) Only S2 is correct.
(b) Both S1 and S2 are correct.
(c) Both S1 and S2 are incorrect.
(d) Only S1 is correct.

2 The function $f(x)=\dfrac{x}{x^2-6x-16}, x\in R-\{-2,8\}$

NCERT Pg. 158, JEE Main 2024, 29 Jan Shift-II

(a) decreases in $(-\infty,-2)$ and increases in $(8,\infty)$.
(b) increases in $(-\infty,-2)\cup(-2,8)\cup(8,\infty)$.
(c) decreases in $(-\infty,-2)\cup(-2,8)\cup(8,\infty)$.
(d) decreases in $(-2,8)$ and increases in $(-\infty,-2)\cup(8,\infty)$.

3 The rate of change (in cm^2/s) of the total surface area of a hemisphere with respect to radius r at $r=\sqrt[3]{1.331}$ cm is NCERT Pg. 150, CUET 2024, 16 May

(a) 66π (b) 6.6π (c) 3.3π (d) 4.4π

4 $f(x)=\sin x+\dfrac{1}{2}\cos 2x$ in $\left[0,\dfrac{\pi}{2}\right]$

A. $f'(x)=\cos x-\sin 2x$

B. The critical points of the function are $x=\dfrac{\pi}{6}$ and $x=\dfrac{\pi}{2}$

C. The minimum value of the function is 2.

D. The maximum value of the function is $\dfrac{3}{4}$.

Choose the correct answer from the options given below: NCERT Pg. 184, CUET 2024, 16 May

(a) A, B and D (b) A, B and C
(c) A, B, C and D (d) B, C and D

5 If $f(x)=2\left(\tan^{-1}(e^x)-\dfrac{\pi}{4}\right)$, then $f(x)$ is

NCERT Pg. 158, CUET 2024, 16 May

(a) even and is strictly increasing in $(0,\infty)$
(b) even and is strictly decreasing in $(0,\infty)$
(c) odd and is strictly increasing in $(-\infty,\infty)$
(d) odd and is strictly decreasing in $(-\infty,\infty)$

6 A square piece of tin of side 30 cm is to be made into a box without top by cutting a square from each corner and folding up the flaps to form a box. If the volume of the box is maximum, then its surface area (in cm^2) is equal to NCERT Pg. 176, JEE Main 2023, 10 April Shift-I

(a) 800 (b) 900 (c) 1025 (d) 675

7 The function $f(x)=xe^{x(1-x)}, x\in R$ is

NCERT Pg. 159, JEE Main 2022, 28 July Shift-II

(a) increasing in $\left(-\dfrac{1}{2},1\right)$ (b) decreasing in $\left(\dfrac{1}{2},2\right)$

(c) increasing in $\left(-1,-\dfrac{1}{2}\right)$ (d) decreasing in $\left(-\dfrac{1}{2},\dfrac{1}{2}\right)$

Numerical Value Type

8 Let the set of all values of p, for which $f(x)=(p^2-6p+8)(\sin^2 2x-\cos^2 2x)+2(2-p)x+7$ does not have any critical point, be the interval (a,b). Then, $16ab$ is equal to ....

NCERT Pg. 164, JEE Main 2024, 9 April Shift-II

9 Let $S=\{\sin^2 2\theta : (\sin^4\theta+\cos^4\theta)x^2+(\sin 2\theta)x+(\sin^6\theta+\cos^6\theta)=0$ has real roots$\}$.

If α and β are the smallest and largest elements of the set S, respectively, then $3((\alpha-2)^2+(\beta-1)^2)$ equals ....

NCERT Pg. 184, JEE Main 2024, 4 April Shift-II

10 If a_α is the greatest term in the sequence $a_n=\dfrac{n^3}{n^4+147}\cdot n=1,2,3\ldots$, then α is equal to ....

NCERT Pg. 160, JEE Main 2023, 8 April Shift-I

11 A water tank has the shape of a right circular cone with axis vertical and vertex downwards. Its semi-vertical angle is $\tan^{-1}3/4$. Water is poured in it at a constant rate of 6 cubic meter per hour. The rate (in square metre per hour), at which the wet curved surface area of the tank is increasing, when the depth of water in the tank is 4 m, is ....

NCERT Pg. 178, JEE Main 2022, 27 July Shift-II

Skill Boosters

1 The range of the function $f(x) = x \sin x - \frac{1}{2}\sin^2 x$ for $x \in \left(0 \frac{\pi}{2}\right)$ is

(a) $\left(0, \frac{\pi - 1}{2}\right)$ (b) $\left(\frac{\pi - 1}{2}, 0\right)$

(c) $\left(0, \pi - \frac{1}{2}\right)$ (d) $\left(\pi - \frac{1}{2}, 0\right)$

2 Let $f(x)$ be a differentiable function and $g(x) = (f(x))^3 - 3(f(x))^2 + 4f(x) + 5x + 3\sin x + 4\cos x$ for all $x \in R$, then

(a) $g(x)$ is increasing whenever f is decreasing.

(b) $g(x)$ is increasing whenever f is increasing.

(c) $g(x)$ is decreasing whenever f is increasing.

(d) $g(x)$ is decreasing whenever f is decreasing.

3 If the function $f(x) = x^3 - 3(a-2)x^2 + 3ax + 7$, for some $a \in R$ increasing in (0, 1] and decreasing in [1, 5) then a root of the equation $\frac{f(x) - 14}{(x-1)^2} = 0\, (x \neq 1)$ is

(a) 7 (b) 14

(c) –7 (d) –14

4 A spherical balloon is filled with 4500 π cubic metres of helium gas. If a leak in the balloon cause the gas to escape at the rate of 72π cubic metres per minutes, then the rate (in metres per min) at which the radius of the balloon decreases 49 min after the leakage began is

(a) 2/9 (b) 9/2

(c) 9/7 (d) 7/9

5 Let $f(x)$ be a polynomial of degree four having extreme values at $x = 1$ and $x = 2$. If $\lim_{x \to 0}\left[1 + \frac{f(x)}{x^2}\right] = 3$, then $f(2)$ is equal to

(a) 0 (b) 4 (c) –8 (d) –4

6 Let $f : R \to R$ be defined by $f(x) = \begin{cases} k - 2x, & \text{if } x \leq -1 \\ 2x + 3, & \text{if } x > -1 \end{cases}$. If $f(x)$ has a local minimum at $x = -1$, then a possible value of k is

(a) 1 (b) 0 (c) –1/2 (d) –1

7 The least value of the expression $x^2 + 4y^2 + 3z^2 - 2x - 12y - 6z + 14$. x, y and $z \in R$ is

(a) 1 (b) 2

(c) 0 (d) 3

8 The radius of a right circular cylinder increases at a constant rate. Its altitude is a linear function of the radius and increases three time as fast as radius. When the radius is 1 cm and the altitude is 6 cm. When the radius is 6 cm, the volume in increasing at the rate of 1 cubic cm/sec. When the radius is 36 cm, the volume is increasing at a rate of n cm^3/sec. Then value of $\frac{n}{11}$ is ......

(a) 2 (b) 1 (c) 3 (d) 4

9 If $f(x) = x^{1/x}, x > 0$ then,

(a) $e^\pi > \pi^e$ (b) $e^\pi > \frac{1}{\pi^e}$

(c) $e^\pi < \pi^2$ (d) $e^\pi < \frac{1}{\pi^e}$

Correct Codes

Topical Questions

Rate of Change of Quantities

1 (d)	2 (b)	3 (d)	4 (d)	5 (c)	6 (a)	7 (c)	8 (c)	9 (b)	10 (c)
11 (c)	12 (a)	13 (c)	14 (d)	15 (b)	16 (c)	17 (c)	18 (a)	19 (d)	20 (b)
21 (b)	22 (a)	23 (a)	24 (d)						

Increasing and Decreasing Functions

1 (d)	2 (c)	3 (d)	4 (a)	5 (a)	6 (d)	7 (a)	8 (a)	9 (d)	10 (c)
11 (d)	12 (a)	13 (b)	14 (a)	15 (c)	16 (c)	17 (b)	18 (a)	19 (b)	20 (d)
21 (d)	22 (b)	23 (b)	24 (a)	25 (a)	26 (d)	27 (a)	28 (a)	29 (b)	30 (d)
31 (b)	32 (d)	33 (b)	34 (b)	35 (c)	36 (c)				

Maxima and Minima

1 (d)	2 (a)	3 (d)	4 (d)	5 (b)	6 (d)	7 (a)	8 (a)	9 (d)	10 (d)
11 (c)	12 (c)	13 (c)	14 (b)	15 (b)	16 (b)	17 (c)	18 (d)	19 (c)	20 (d)
21 (c)	22 (c)	23 (b)	24 (b)	25 (a)	26 (d)	27 (a)	28 (c)	29 (a)	30 (c)
31 (b)	32 (d)	33 (b)	34 (d)	35 (d)	36 (b)	37 (d)	38 (c)	39 (a)	40 (c)
41 (c)	42 (a)	43 (d)	44 (c)	45 (c)	46 (a)	47 (b)	48 (c)	49 (d)	50 (c)
51 (b)	52 (a)	53 (d)	54 (d)	55 (b)	56 (d)	57 (b)	58 (b)	59 (c)	60 (b)
61 (a)	62 (b)	63 (b)	64 (d)						

Miscellaneous Exercise

1 (a)	2 (d)	3 (b)	4 (d)	5 (b)	6 (a)	7 (a)	8 (a)	9 (d)	10 (c)
11 (a)	12 (a)	13 (c)	14 (c)	15 (b)					

Numerical Type Questions

1 (8)	2 (3)	3 (9)	4 (9)	5 (3)	6 (0)	7 (3)	8 (9)	9 (9)	10 (4)

Assertion and Reason Questions

1 (a)	2 (c)	3 (a)	4 (b)	5 (a)	6 (b)	7 (a)	8 (a)	9 (b)	10 (c)
11 (b)	12 (c)	13 (a)	14 (a)						

Case or Paragraph Type Questions

1 (b)	2 (c)	3 (a)	4 (a)	5 (b)	6 (c)	7 (d)	8 (a)	9 (b)	10 (c)
11 (d)									

Past Years Questions

1 (d)	2 (c)	3 (b)	4 (a)	5 (c)	6 (a)	7 (a)	8 (252)	9 (4)	10 (5)
11 (5)									

Skill Boosters

1 (a)	2 (b)	3 (a)	4 (a)	5 (a)	6 (d)	7 (a)	8 (c)	9 (a)

Step by Step

Decoding the Questions

Concept Builders

1 $\frac{1}{2}$ cm/sec   2 $32\pi r$ cm^2/s

3 S 4 decreasing

5 $\left(\frac{\pi}{4}, \frac{\pi}{2}\right)$ 6 True

7 True   8 True

9 True   10 True

11 True   12 False

13 True   14 True

15 25   16 $f'(c) = 0$

17 $f'(0) = 0$ and $f''(0) < 0$

18 6, 4   19 $1/e$

20 $x = 2$ 21 $a \in (1, \infty)$

22 decreasing

Topical Questions

Rate of Change of Quantities

1 (*d*) Let A denote the area of the circle when its radius is r, then $A = \pi r^2$.

Now, the rate of change of the area with respect to its radius is given by

$$\frac{dA}{dr} = \frac{d}{dr}(\pi r^2) = 2\pi r$$

(a) When

$$r = 3\text{ cm}, \left(\frac{dA}{dr}\right)_{r=3} = 2\pi(3)$$

$$= 6\pi \text{ cm}^2/\text{cm}.$$

Hence, the area of the circle is changing at the rate of 6π cm^2 / cm when its radius is 3 cm.

(b) When

$$r = 4\text{ cm}, \left(\frac{dA}{dt}\right)_{r=4} = 2\pi(4)$$

$$= 8\pi \text{ cm}^2 \text{ per cm}$$

Hence, the area of the circle is changing at the rate of 8π cm^2 / cm when its radius is 4 cm.

2 (*b*) Let x be the length of a side (edge), V be the volume and S be the surface area of the cube.

$V = x^3$ and $S = 6x^2$

[$\because$ cube has six square faces, each of side x]

Where, x is a function of time t.

It is given that $\frac{dV}{dt} = 8$ cm^3/s.

Then, by using the chain rule, we have

$$8 = \frac{dV}{dt} = \frac{d}{dt}(x^3) = 3x^2 \cdot \frac{dx}{dt}$$

$$\Rightarrow \frac{dx}{dt} = \frac{8}{3x^2} \quad \text{... (i)}$$

$$\text{Now, } \frac{dS}{dt} = \frac{d}{dt}(6x^2) = 12x\frac{dx}{dt}$$

$$= 12x\left(\frac{8}{3x^2}\right) = \frac{32}{x}$$

[from Eq. (i)]

Thus, when

$$x = 12\text{ cm}, \frac{dS}{dt} = \frac{32}{12}\text{ cm}^2/\text{s}$$

$$= \frac{8}{3}\text{ cm}^2/\text{ s}.$$

Hence, if the length of the edge of a cube is 12 cm, then the surface area is increasing at the rate of $\frac{8}{3}$ cm^2 / s.

3 (*d*) Let r be the radius of circle and A be the area of circle at any time t. Area of circle, $A = \pi r^2$.

Now, the rate of change of area A w.r.t. time t is given by

$$\frac{dA}{dt} = \frac{d}{dt}(\pi r^2) = 2\pi r\frac{dr}{dt}$$

[by Chain rule]

It is given that radius of circle is increasing at the rate of 3 cm / s,

so $\frac{dr}{dt} = 3$ cm / s.

$$\therefore \frac{dA}{dt} = 2\pi r(3) = 6\pi r \text{ cm}^2/\text{ s}$$

Thus, when

$$r = 10\text{ cm}, \frac{dA}{dt} = 6\pi(10)$$

$$= 60\pi \text{ cm}^2/\text{ s}$$

Hence, the rate at which the area of the circle is increasing, when the radius is 10 cm, is 60π cm^2 / s.

4 (*d*) Let r be the radius of the circular wave and A be the area, then $A = \pi r^2$

Therefore, the rate of change of area (A) with respect to time (t) is given by

$$\frac{dA}{dt} = \frac{d}{dt}(\pi r^2)$$

$$\Rightarrow \frac{dA}{dt} = 2\pi r\frac{dr}{dt} \quad \text{[by Chain rule]}$$

It is given that waves move in circles at the speed of 5 cm/s.

So, $dr/dt = 5$ cm/s

$$\therefore \frac{dA}{dt} = 2\pi r \times 5 = 10\pi r \text{ cm}^2/\text{s}$$

Thus, when $r = 8$ cm,

$$\frac{dA}{dt} = 10\pi(8) = 80\pi \text{ cm}^2/\text{s}$$

Hence, when the radius of the circular wave is 8 cm, the enclosed area is increasing at the rate of 80π cm^2/s.

5 (*c*)

A. Let x be the length of an edge of cube and V be the volume of the cube.

Then, $V = x^3$

$\therefore$ Rate of change of volume w.r.t. t time,

$$\frac{dV}{dt} = \frac{d}{dt}(x^3) = 3x^2\frac{dx}{dt}$$

[by Chain rule]

It is given that edge of the cube is increasing at the rate of 3 cm / s, so $\frac{dx}{dt} = 3$ cm / s.

$\therefore \quad \frac{dV}{dt} = 3x^2 (3)$

$= 9x^2$ cm^3/s

Thus, when $x = 10$ cm,

$\frac{dv}{dt} = 9(10)^2 = 900$ cm^3/s.

Hence, the volume of the cube is increasing at the rate of 900 cm^3 / s when the edge is 10 cm long.

B. At any instant of time t, let the radius of the circle be r and its circumference be C, then

$C = 2\pi r$

$\Rightarrow$ Rate of increase of circumference $\frac{dC}{dt} = 2\pi \frac{dr}{dt}$

[differentiating w.r.t. t, by chain rule]

where, $\frac{dr}{dt}$ is rate of increase of radius, so $\frac{dr}{dt} = 0.7$ cm/s

$\therefore \quad \frac{dC}{dt} = 2\pi (0.7)$ cm/s

$= 1.4\pi$ cm/s

$\left[\because \frac{dr}{dt} = 0.7 \text{ cm / s (given)}\right]$

Hence, rate of increase of circumference is 1.4π cm/s.

C. The air bubble is in the shape of a sphere.

Let r be the radius of bubble and V be the volume of bubble at any time t.

Then, rate of change of radius

$\frac{dr}{dt} = \frac{1}{2}$ cm/s

and $\quad r = 1$ cm [given]

Now, volume of the bubble

$V = \frac{4}{3}\pi r^3$

On differentiating w.r.t. t, we get

Rate of increase of volume

$\frac{dV}{dt} = \left(\frac{4}{3}\pi\right)\left(3r^2 \frac{dr}{dt}\right)$

$= 4\pi r^2 \frac{dr}{dt} = 4\pi(1)^2 \frac{1}{2}$

$\left[\text{on putting } r = 1 \text{ and } \frac{dr}{dt} = \frac{1}{2}\right]$

$= 2\pi$ cm^3/s

Hence, the rate at which the volume of the bubble increases is 2π cm^3/s.

D. Given, the diameter of the balloon $= \frac{3}{2}(2x + 1)$

$\therefore$ Radius of the balloon

$= \frac{\text{Diameter}}{2} = \frac{1}{2}\left[\frac{3}{2}(2x + 1)\right]$

$= \frac{3}{4}(2x + 1)$

For the volume V, the balloon is given by

$V = \frac{4}{3}\pi \text{ (radius)}^3$

$= \frac{4}{3}\pi\left[\frac{3}{4}(2x + 1)\right]^3$

$= \frac{9\pi}{16}(2x + 1)^3$

For the rate of change of volume, differentiate w.r.t. x, we get

$\frac{dV}{dx} = \frac{9\pi}{16} \times 3(2x + 1)^2 \times 2$

$= \frac{27\pi}{8}(2x + 1)^2$

Thus, rate of change of volume is $\frac{27\pi}{8}(2x + 1)^2$.

A $\rightarrow$ 2, B $\rightarrow$ 3, C $\rightarrow$ 4, D $\rightarrow$ 1

6 (*a*) At any instant of time t, let length, breadth, perimeter and area of the rectangle are x, y, P and A respectively, then

$P = 2(x + y)$ and $A = xy$ ...(i)

[$\because$ perimeter of rectangle = 2(length + breadth) and area = length $\times$ breadth]

It is given that $\frac{dx}{dt} = -5$ cm/min

and $\quad \frac{dy}{dt} = 4$ cm/min

[negative sign shows that the length is decreasing]

I. Now, $P = 2(x + y)$. On differentiating w.r.t. t, we get

Rate of change of perimeter,

$\frac{dP}{dt} = 2\left(\frac{dx}{dt} + \frac{dy}{dt}\right)$

$= 2\{-5 + 4\}$ cm/min

$= -2$ cm/min

$\left[\because \frac{dx}{dt} = -5 \text{ and } \frac{dy}{dt} = 4\right]$

Hence, perimeter of the rectangle is decreasing at the rate of 2 cm/min.

II. Here, area of rectangle, $A = xy$. On differentiating w.r.t. t, we get

Rate of change of area,

$\frac{dA}{dt} = x\frac{dy}{dt} + y\frac{dx}{dt}$

$= 8 \times 4 + 6 \times (-5)$

$\left[\because \frac{dx}{dt} = -5 \text{ and } \frac{dy}{dt} = 4\right]$

$= 32 - 30 = 2$ cm^2/min

Hence, area of the rectangle is increasing at the rate of 2 cm^2/min.

7 (*c*) At any instant of time t let the radius of the balloon be r and its volume be V, then volume of balloon, $V = (4/3)\pi r^3$

The balloon is being inflated at 900 cubic cm/s i.e. the rate of change of volume with respect to time is 900 cm^3/s.

On differentiating w.r.t. t, we get

Rate of change of volume,

$\frac{dV}{dt} = \left(\frac{4}{3}\pi\right)\left(3r^2 \frac{dr}{dt}\right)$

Given, $\quad r = 15$ cm

$\Rightarrow \quad 900 = \left(\frac{4}{3}\pi\right)\left\{3(15)^2 \frac{dr}{dt}\right\}$

$\Rightarrow \quad \frac{dr}{dt} = \frac{900}{3 \times (15)^2} \times \frac{3}{4\pi}$

$\Rightarrow$ Rate of change of radius r,

$\frac{dr}{dt} = \frac{900}{4\pi \times (15)^2}$

$= \frac{225}{\pi \times 225} = \frac{1}{\pi}$ cm/s

8 (c) Let $AB = 5$ m be the ladder and y be the height of the wall at which the ladder touches. Also, let the foot of the ladder be at B whose distance from the wall is x.

Given that the bottom of ladder is pulled along the ground at 2 cm/s, so $\frac{dx}{dt} = 2$ cm/s

As we know that ΔABC is right angled, so by Pythagoras theorem, we have $x^2 + y^2 = 5^2$ ...(i)

When $x = 4$, then

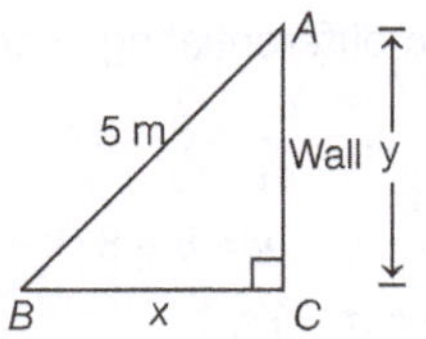

$$y^2 = 5^2 - 4^2$$
$$\Rightarrow \quad y = \sqrt{25 - 16}$$
$$\Rightarrow \quad y = 3 \text{ m}$$

On differentiating Eq. (i) w.r.t. time t on both sides, we get

$$2x\frac{dx}{dt} + 2y\frac{dy}{dt} = 0$$
$$\Rightarrow \quad x\frac{dx}{dt} + y\frac{dy}{dt} = 0$$
$$\Rightarrow \quad 4 \times 2 + 3 \times \frac{dy}{dt} = 0$$
$$\left[\because x = 4, y = 3 \text{ and } \frac{dx}{dt} = 2\right]$$

$\Rightarrow$ The rate of fall of height on the wall $\frac{dy}{dt} = -\frac{8}{3}$ cm/s

[negative sign shows that height of ladder on the wall is decreasing at the rate of $\frac{8}{3}$ cm/s.]

9 (b) If A is the area of the circle corresponding to radius r, then $A = \pi r^2$

On differentiating w.r.t. r, we get

$$\frac{dA}{dr} = 2\pi r$$

On putting $r = 6$, we get

$$\left(\frac{dA}{dr}\right) = 2\pi(6) = 12\pi \text{ cm}^2/\text{cm}$$

10 (c) Given, $6y = x^3 + 2$

On differentiating w.r.t. t, we get

$$6\frac{dy}{dt} = 3x^2\frac{dx}{dt}$$
$$\Rightarrow \quad 6 \times 8\frac{dx}{dt} = 3x^2\frac{dx}{dt}$$
$$\Rightarrow \quad 3x^2 = 48$$
$$\Rightarrow \quad x^2 = 16 \Rightarrow x = \pm 4$$

When $x = 4$, then $6y = (4)^3 + 2$

$$\Rightarrow \quad 6y = 64 + 2$$
$$\Rightarrow \quad y = \frac{66}{6} = 11$$

When $x = -4$, then $6y = (-4)^3 + 2$

$$\Rightarrow \quad 6y = -64 + 2$$
$$\Rightarrow \quad y = \frac{-62}{6} = \frac{-31}{3}$$

11 (c) Let r be the radius, h be the height and V be the volume of sand cone at any time t.

It is given that $\frac{dV}{dt} = 12\text{cm}^3/\text{s}$

and $\quad h = \frac{1}{6}r$

$$\Rightarrow \quad r = 6h$$
$$\therefore \quad V = \frac{1}{3}\pi r^2 h = \frac{1}{3}\pi(6h)^2 h$$
$$= 12\pi h^3$$

On differentiating w.r.t. t, we get

$$\frac{dV}{dt} = (12\pi)\left(3h^2\frac{dh}{dt}\right)$$
$$= 36\pi h^2\frac{dh}{dt}$$
$$\Rightarrow \quad 12 = 36\pi(4)^2\frac{dh}{dt}$$
$$\left[\because h = 4 \text{ cm and } \frac{dV}{dt} = 12 \text{ cm}^3/\text{s}\right]$$
$$\Rightarrow \quad \frac{dh}{dt} = \frac{12}{36\pi \times 16} = \frac{1}{48\pi} \text{ cm/s}$$

12 (a) Marginal Cost (MC)

$$= \frac{dC}{dx} = 0.007(3x^2) - 0.003(2x) + 15$$
$$= 0.021x^2 - 0.006x + 15$$

When $x = 17$,

$$MC = 0.021(17)^2 - 0.006(17) + 15$$
$$= 0.021(289) - 0.006(17) + 15$$
$$= 6.069 - 0.102 + 15 = 20.967$$

Hence, when 17 units are produced, the marginal cost is ₹ 20.967.

13 (c) Marginal Revenue (MR)

$$= \frac{dR}{dx} = \frac{d}{dx}(13x^2 + 26x + 15)$$
$$= 13 \times 2x + 26 = 26x + 26$$

When $x = 7$,

$$MR = 26(7) + 26$$
$$= 182 + 26 = 208$$

14 (d) Given, $R(x) = 3x^2 + 36x + 5$

$\therefore$ Marginal Revenue (MR)

$$= \frac{dR}{dx} = \frac{d}{dx}(3x^2 + 36x + 5)$$
$$= 6x + 36$$

When $x = 15$,

$$MR = 6 \times 15 + 36 = 126$$

15 (b) Slope of curve $= \frac{dy}{dx} = 5 - 6x^2$

$$\Rightarrow \quad \frac{d}{dt}\left(\frac{dy}{dx}\right) = -12x \,.\, \frac{dx}{dt}$$
$$= -12 \,.\, (3) \,.\, (2)$$
$$= -72 \text{ units/s}$$

Thus, slope of curve is decreasing at the rate of 72 units/s when x is increasing at the rate of 2 units/s.

16 (c) If s represents the surface area, then

$$\frac{ds}{dt} = 2 \text{ cm}^2/\text{s}$$
$$s = \pi r . l = \pi l \,.\, \sin\frac{\pi}{4} l = \frac{\pi}{\sqrt{2}} l^2$$
$$\left[\because r = l \sin\frac{\pi}{4}\right]$$

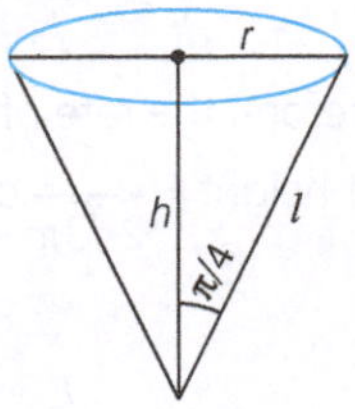

Therefore,

$$\frac{ds}{dt} = \frac{2\pi}{\sqrt{2}} l \cdot \frac{dl}{dt} = \sqrt{2}\pi l \cdot \frac{dl}{dt}$$

When $\frac{ds}{dt} = 2 \text{ cm}^2/\text{s}, l = 4$ cm,

$$\frac{dl}{dt} = \frac{1}{\sqrt{2}\pi \cdot 4} \cdot 2 = \frac{1}{2\sqrt{2}\pi} = \frac{\sqrt{2}}{4\pi} \text{ cm/s}$$

17 (c) $V = \frac{4}{3}\pi r^3 \Rightarrow \frac{dV}{dr} = 4\pi r^2$

$S = 4\pi r^2$

$\Rightarrow \frac{dS}{dr} = 8\pi r$

$\Rightarrow \frac{dV}{dS} = \frac{r}{2} = 1$ at $r = 2$

$\therefore \frac{dV}{dS} = 1\,\text{cm}^3/\text{cm}^2$

18 (a) Given that $\frac{dV}{dt} = -1\,\text{cm}^3/\text{s}$,

where V is the volume of water in the conical vessel.

From the figure,

$l = 4$ cm, $h = l\cos\frac{\pi}{6} = \frac{\sqrt{3}}{2}l$

and $r = l\sin\frac{\pi}{6} = \frac{l}{2}$

Therefore,

$V = \frac{1}{3}\pi r^2 h = \frac{1\cdot\pi}{3}\left(\frac{l}{2}\right)^2 \cdot \left(\frac{\sqrt{3}}{2}l\right)$

$= \frac{\sqrt{3}}{24} l^3 \pi$

$\frac{dV}{dt} = \frac{\sqrt{3}\pi}{8} l^2 \frac{dl}{dt}$

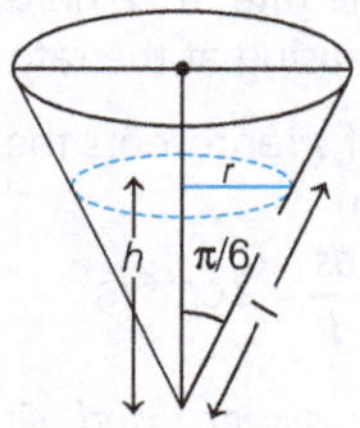

Therefore, $-1 = \frac{\sqrt{3}\pi}{8} 16 . \frac{dl}{dt}$

$\Rightarrow \frac{dl}{dt} = \frac{-1}{2\sqrt{3}\pi}$ cm/s.

Therefore, the rate of decrease of slant height $= \frac{1}{2\sqrt{3}\pi}$ cm / s.

19 (d)

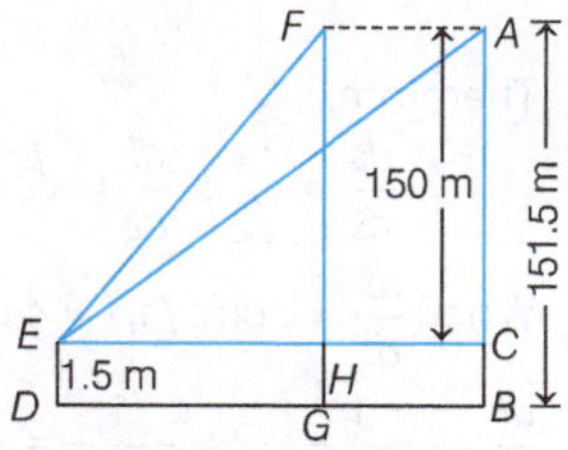

Let AB be the height of the kite and DE be the height of the boy.

Let $DB = x = EC$

$\therefore \frac{dx}{dt} = 10$ m / s

Let $AE = y$

$\because AB = 151.5$ m

$\therefore AC = AB - BC$

$= 151.5$ m $- 1.5$ m

$= 150$ m

Also, $AC^2 + EC^2 = AE^2$

[by Pythagoras theorem]

$\Rightarrow 150^2 + x^2 = y^2$

On differentiating both sides w.r.t. t, we have

$0 + 2x\frac{dx}{dt} = 2y\frac{dy}{dt}$

$\Rightarrow x\frac{dx}{dt} = y\frac{dy}{dt}$

Now, when $y = 250$ m

$x = \sqrt{y^2 - (150)^2}$

$= \sqrt{62500 - 22500}$

$= \sqrt{40000} = 200$ m

$\therefore 200 \times 10 = 250 \times \frac{dy}{dt}$

$\therefore \frac{dy}{dt} = \frac{2000}{250} = 8$ m/s

20 (b) Let D denote the diagonal of the square.

Given, $\frac{dD}{dt} = 0.5$ cm/s ... (i)

Since, $A = 400 = \frac{1}{2}D^2$

$\Rightarrow D = 20\sqrt{2}$ $[\because A = D^2/2]$

On differentiating w.r.t. t, we get

$\frac{dA}{dt} = \frac{d}{dt}\left(\frac{D^2}{2}\right) = D\frac{dD}{dt}$

$= 20\sqrt{2} \times 0.5$

$= 10\sqrt{2}\,\text{cm}^2/\text{s}$

21 (b) Since, θ increases twice as fast as its sine.

$\therefore \theta = 2\sin\theta$

On differentiating both sides w.r.t. t, we have

$\frac{d\theta}{dt} = 2\cos\theta\frac{d\theta}{dt}$

$\left[\because \frac{d}{d\theta}(\sin\theta) = \cos\theta\right]$

$\Rightarrow 1 = 2\cos\theta$

$\Rightarrow \cos\theta = \frac{1}{2} = \cos\left(\frac{\pi}{3}\right)$

$[\because 0 < \theta < \pi/2]$

$\Rightarrow \theta = \frac{\pi}{3}$

$\therefore$ Required angle is $\frac{\pi}{3}$.

22 (a) Since, $x = 3 + 8t - 4t^2$

On differentiating w.r.t. t, we get

$\therefore \frac{dx}{dt} = 8 - 8t$

$\Rightarrow v = 8 - 8t$

$\therefore$ At $t = 1$ s,

$v = 8 - 8$

$= 0$ unit/s

23 (a) Let l be the length of an edge and V be the volume of cube at any time t.

$\because V = l^3$

$\therefore \frac{dV}{dt} = 3l^2\frac{dl}{dt}$

$= 3 \times 5^2 \times 10\,\text{cm}^3/\text{s}$

$= 750\,\text{cm}^3/\text{s}$

24 (d) Let h and r be the height and radius of cylinder.

Given that $\frac{dr}{dt} = 3$ m/s,

$\frac{dh}{dt} = -4$ m/s

Let volume of cylinder,

$V = \pi r^2 h$

$\Rightarrow \frac{dV}{dt} = \pi\left[r^2\frac{dh}{dt} + h.2r\frac{dr}{dt}\right]$

At $r = 4$ m

and $h = 6$ m

$\therefore \frac{dV}{dt} = \pi[-64 + 144]$

$= 80\,\pi\,\text{m}^3/\text{s}$

Increasing and Decreasing Functions

1 (*d*) For the function f given by $f(x) = x^2, x \in R$, we get the graph of this function, a parabola as given below.

Values left to origin

x	$f(x) = x^2$
-2	4
$-\frac{3}{2}$	$\frac{9}{4}$
-1	1
$-\frac{1}{2}$	$\frac{1}{4}$
0	0

as we move from left to right, the height of the graph decreases

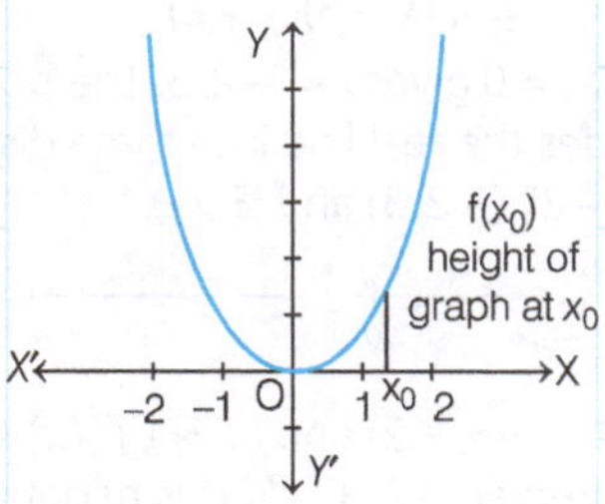

Values right to origin

x	$f(x) = x^2$
0	0
$\frac{1}{2}$	$\frac{1}{4}$
1	1
$\frac{3}{2}$	$\frac{9}{4}$
2	4

as we move from left to right, the height of the graph increases

First considering the graph to the right of the origin. We see that as we move from left to right along the graph, the height of the graph continuously increases. For this reason, the function is said to be increasing for the real numbers $x > 0$.

Now, considering the graph to the left of the origin. We observe here that as we move from left to right along the graph, the height of the graph continuously decreases. Consequently, the function is said to be decreasing for the real numbers $x < 0$.

Thus, we see that only option (d) is correct.

2 (*c*) If I be an open interval contained in the domain of a real valued function f. Then, f is said to be

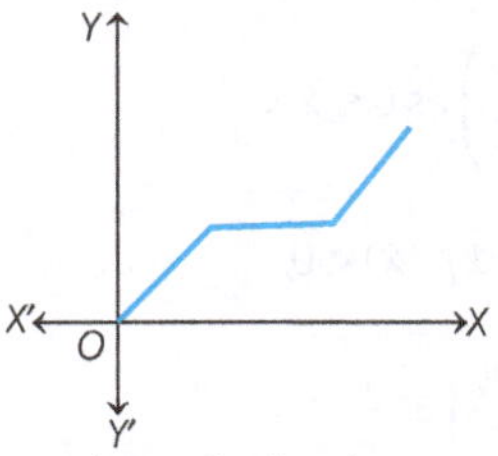

Increasing function
(i)

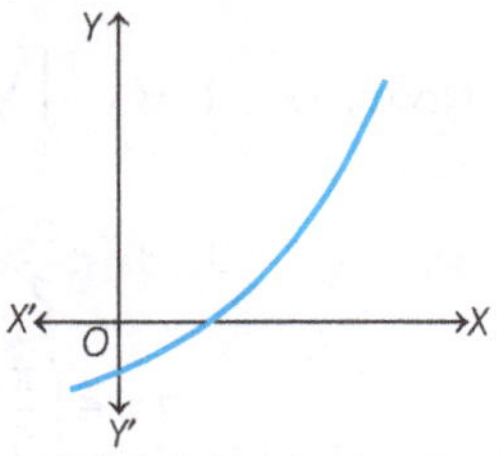

Strictly increasing function
(ii)

(a) Increasing on I, if $x_1 < x_2$ in I

$\Rightarrow \quad f(x_1) \le f(x_2), \forall x_1, x_2 \in I.$

(b) Strictly increasing on I, if $x_1 < x_2$ in I

$\Rightarrow \quad f(x_1) < f(x_2), \forall x_1, x_2 \in I$

3 (*d*) If I be an open interval contained in the domain of a real valued function f, then f is said to be

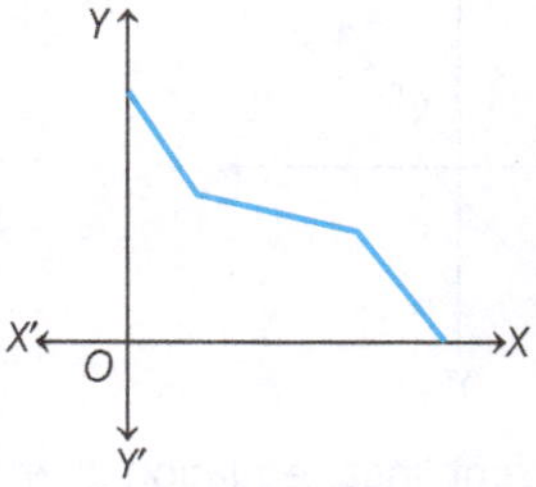

Decreasing function
(i)

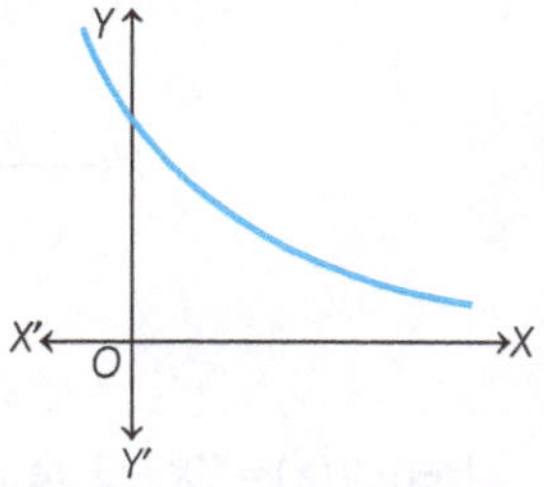

Strictly decreasing function
(ii)

(a) Decreasing on I, if $x_1 < x_2$ in I

$\Rightarrow \quad f(x_1) \ge f(x_2), \forall x_1, x_2 \in I.$

(b) Strictly decreasing on I, if $x_1 < x_2$ in I

$\Rightarrow \quad f(x_1) > f(x_2), \forall x_1, x_2 \in I.$

Note *Figure given below shows that function is neither increasing nor decreasing.*

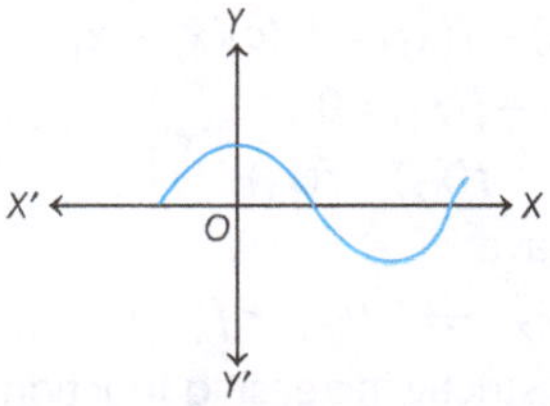

Neither increasing nor decreasing function

4 (*a*) For a function to be increasing or decreasing at a point, we follow the definition given below.

If x_0 be a point in the domain of definition of a real valued function f.

Then, f is said to be increasing, strictly increasing, decreasing or strictly decreasing at x_0 if there exists an open interval I containing x_0 such that f is increasing, strictly increasing, decreasing or strictly decreasing, respectively in I.

Let us clarify this definition for the case of increasing function.

A function f is said to be increasing at x_0 if there exists an interval, $I = (x_0 - h, x_0 + h), h > 0$ such that for $x_1, x_2 \in I$

$$x_1 < x_2 \text{ in } I$$

$$\Rightarrow \quad f(x_1) \le f(x_2)$$

Similarly, the other cases can be clarified.

5 (*a*) Let x_1 and x_2 be any two numbers in R. Then,

$x_1 < x_2 \Rightarrow 7x_1 < 7x_2 \Rightarrow 7x_1 - 3 < 7x_2 - 3 \Rightarrow f(x_1) < f(x_2)$

Thus, f is strictly increasing on R.

Alternate Method

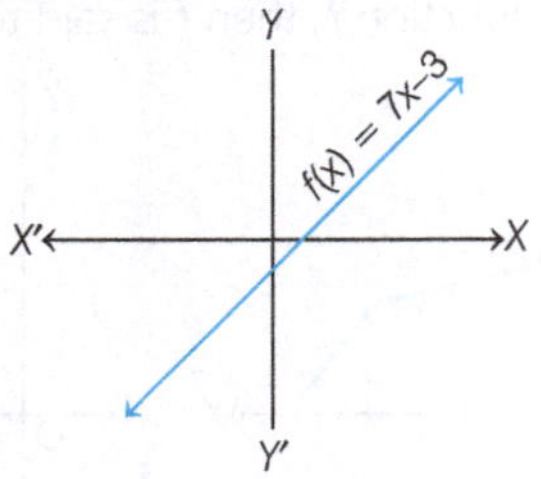

Here, $f(x)=7x-3$ represent linear equation, then by graph it is clear that $f(x)$ is strictly increasing.

6 (*d*) Mean value theorem, which states that if $f:[a,b]\to R$ be a continuous function on $[a,b]$ and differentiable on (a,b), then there exists some c in (a,b) such that

$$f'(c)=\frac{f(b)-f(a)}{b-a}$$

Let $x_1,x_2\in[a,b]$ be such that $x_1<x_2$, then there exists a point c between x_1 and x_2 such that

$$f(x_2)-f(x_1)=f'(c)(x_2-x_1)$$

i.e. $f(x_2)-f(x_1)>0$ [as $f'(c)>0$ (given)]

i.e. $f(x_2)>f(x_1)$

Thus, we have

$$x_1<x_2 \Rightarrow f(x_1)<f(x_2),\ \forall\, x_1,x_2\in[a,b]$$

Hence, f is strictly increasing function in $[a,b]$.

The proofs of part (b) and (c) are similar.

Hence, option (d) is correct.

Remarks

(i) f is strictly increasing in (a,b) if $f'(x)>0$ for each $x\in(a,b)$.

(ii) f is strictly decreasing in (a,b) if $f'(x)<0$ for each $x\in(a,b)$.

(iii) If a function is strictly increasing or strictly decreasing in an interval I, then it is necessarily increasing or decreasing in I. However, converse need not be true.

7 (*a*) We have, $f(x)=x^3-3x^2+4x,\ x\in R$

$$\therefore\quad f'(x)=3x^2-6x+4$$
$$=3(x^2-2x+1)+1$$
$$=3(x-1)^2+1>0 \text{ in every interval of } R.$$

Therefore, the function f is strictly increasing on R.

8 (*a*) We have, $f(x)=\cos x$.

$$f'(x)=-\sin x$$

(a) Since, for each $x\in(0,\pi)$, $\sin x>0$, we have $f'(x)<0$ and so f is strictly decreasing in $(0,\pi)$.

(b) Since, for each $x\in(\pi,2\pi)$, $\sin x<0$, we have $f'(x)>0$ and so f is strictly increasing in $(\pi,2\pi)$.

(c) Clearly, by (a) and (b) above, f is neither increasing nor decreasing in $(0,2\pi)$.

Note *However, since the function is continuous at the end points 0 and π, by theorem stated in solution 7, f is increasing in $[\pi,2\pi]$ and decreasing in $[0,\pi]$.*

9 (*d*) We have, $f(x)=4x^3-6x^2-72x+30$

or $f'(x)=12x^2-12x-72$
$$=12(x^2-x-6)$$
$$=12(x-3)(x+2)$$

Therefore, $f'(x)=0$ gives $x=-2,3$. The points $x=-2$ and $x=3$ divides the real line into three disjoint intervals, namely $(-\infty,-2)$, $(-2,3)$ and $(3,\infty)$.

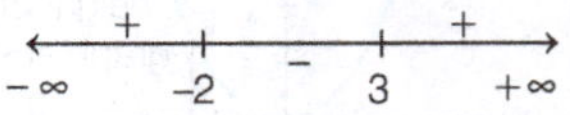

In the intervals $(-\infty,-2)$ and $(3,\infty)$, $f'(x)$ is positive while in the interval $(-2,3)$, $f'(x)$ is negative. Consequently, the function f is strictly increasing in the intervals $(-\infty,-2)$ and $(3,\infty)$ while the function is strictly decreasing in the interval $(-2,3)$. However, f is neither increasing nor decreasing in R.

Interval	Sign of $f'(x)$	Nature of function f
$(-\infty,-2)$	$(-)(-)>0$	f is strictly increasing
$(-2,3)$	$(-)(+)<0$	f is strictly decreasing
$(3,\infty)$	$(+)(+)>0$	f is strictly increasing

10 (*c*) We have, $f(x)=\sin 3x$ or $f'(x)=3\cos 3x$

Therefore, $f'(x)=0$ gives $\cos 3x=0$ which in turn gives

$$3x=\frac{\pi}{2},\frac{3\pi}{2}\left(\text{as } x\in\left[0,\frac{\pi}{2}\right] \text{ implies } 3x\in\left[0,\frac{3\pi}{2}\right]\right).$$

So, $x=\frac{\pi}{6}$ and $\frac{\pi}{2}$. The point $x=\frac{\pi}{6}$ divides the interval $\left[0,\frac{\pi}{2}\right]$ into two disjoint intervals $\left[0,\frac{\pi}{6}\right)$ and $\left(\frac{\pi}{6},\frac{\pi}{2}\right]$.

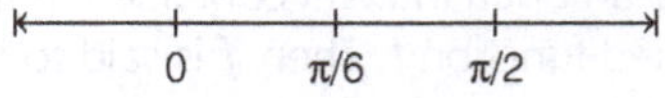

Now, $f'(x)>0,\ \forall\, x\in\left[0,\frac{\pi}{6}\right)$ as $0\le x<\frac{\pi}{6}$

$$\Rightarrow\quad 0\le 3x<\frac{\pi}{2} \text{ and } f'(x)<0,$$

$$\forall\, x\in\left(\frac{\pi}{6},\frac{\pi}{2}\right) \text{ as } \frac{\pi}{6}<x<\frac{\pi}{2}$$

$$\Rightarrow\quad \frac{\pi}{2}<3x<\frac{3\pi}{2}.$$

Therefore, f is strictly increasing in $\left[0,\frac{\pi}{6}\right)$ and strictly decreasing in $\left(\frac{\pi}{6},\frac{\pi}{2}\right)$. Also, the given function is continuous at $x = 0$ and $x = \frac{\pi}{6}$. Therefore, by theorem, f is increasing on $\left[0, \frac{\pi}{6}\right]$ and decreasing on $\left[\frac{\pi}{6}, \frac{\pi}{2}\right]$.

11 (*d*) We have, $f(x) = \sin x + \cos x$,

or $\quad f'(x) = \cos x - \sin x$

Now $f'(x) = 0$ gives $\sin x = \cos x$ which gives that

$x = \frac{\pi}{4}, \frac{5\pi}{4}$ as $0 \le x \le 2\pi$

The points $x = \frac{\pi}{4}$ and $x = \frac{5\pi}{4}$ divide the interval $[0, 2\pi]$ into three disjoint intervals, namely,

$\left[0, \frac{\pi}{4}\right), \left(\frac{\pi}{4}, \frac{5\pi}{4}\right)$ and $\left(\frac{5\pi}{4}, 2\pi\right]$.

Note that $f'(x) > 0$ if $x \in \left[0, \frac{\pi}{4}\right) \cup \left(\frac{5\pi}{4}, 2\pi\right]$

or f is strictly increasing in the intervals

$\left[0, \frac{\pi}{4}\right)$ and $\left(\frac{5\pi}{4}, 2\pi\right]$

Also, $f'(x) < 0$ if $x \in \left(\frac{\pi}{4}, \frac{5\pi}{4}\right)$ or f is strictly decreasing in $\left(\frac{\pi}{4}, \frac{5\pi}{4}\right)$.

Interval	Sign of $f'(x)$	Nature of function
$\left[0, \frac{\pi}{4}\right)$	>0	f is strictly increasing
$\left(\frac{\pi}{4}, \frac{5\pi}{4}\right)$	<0	f is strictly decreasing
$\left(\frac{5\pi}{4}, 2\pi\right]$	>0	f is strictly increasing

12 (*a*) Let x_1 and x_2 be any two numbers in R, where $x_1 < x_2$.

Then, we have $f(x_1) = 3x_1 + 17$

and $\quad f(x_2) = 3x_2 + 17 \quad [\because f(x) = 3x + 17, \text{given}]$

$x_1 < x_2 \Rightarrow 3x_1 < 3x_2$

$\Rightarrow \quad 3x_1 + 17 < 3x_2 + 17$

$\Rightarrow \quad f(x_1) < f(x_2)$

Now, we see that $f(x_1) < f(x_2)$.

Hence, f is strictly increasing on R.

Alternate Method

Given, $f(x) = 3x + 17$. On differentiating w.r.t. x, we get $f'(x) = 3 > 0$ in every interval of R.

Thus, the function is strictly increasing on R.

13 (*b*) The given function is $f(x) = \sin x$

On differentiating w.r.t. x, we get $f'(x) = \cos x$

I. Since, for each $x \in \left(0, \frac{\pi}{2}\right)$, $\cos x > 0$, we have $f'(x) > 0$

[$\because \cos x$ in Ist quadrant is positive]

Hence, f is strictly increasing in $\left(0, \frac{\pi}{2}\right)$

II. Since, for each $x \in \left(\frac{\pi}{2}, \pi\right)$, $\cos x < 0$, we have

$f'(x) < 0 \quad$ [$\because \cos x$ in IInd quadrant is negative]

Hence, f is strictly decreasing in $\left(\frac{\pi}{2}, \pi\right)$.

III. When $x \in (0, \pi)$. We see that $f'(x) > 0$ in $\left(0, \frac{\pi}{2}\right)$ and

$f'(x) < 0$ in $\left(\frac{\pi}{2}, \pi\right)$.

So, $f'(x)$ is positive and negative in $(0, \pi)$.

Thus, $f(x)$ is neither increasing nor decreasing in $(0, \pi)$.

14 (*a*) Let x_1 and x_2 be any two numbers in R, where $x_1 < x_2$.

Given, $f(x) = e^{2x}$

Then, we have $x_1 < x_2$

$\Rightarrow \quad 2x_1 < 2x_2$

$\Rightarrow \quad e^{2x_1} < e^{2x_2}$

[$\because x_1 < x_2$ then $a^{x_1} < a^{x_2}$, when $a > 1$]

$\Rightarrow \quad f(x_1) < f(x_2)$.

Hence, f is strictly increasing on R.

Alternate Method

Given, $f(x) = e^{2x}$

On differentiating both sides w.r.t. x, we get

$$\frac{d}{dx} f(x) = \frac{d}{dx}(e^{2x})$$

$$\Rightarrow \quad f'(x) = 2e^{2x}$$

(i) When $x > 0$, then $2e^{2x} = 2\left[1 + 2x + \frac{(2x)^2}{2!} + \ldots\ldots\right] > 0$

$\therefore \quad f'(x) > 0$

(ii) When $x = 0$, then $2e^{2x} = 2 \cdot 1 = 2 > 0$

$\therefore \quad f'(x) > 0$

(iii) When $x < 0$, then $2e^{2x} = 2 \times e^{2(-z)} = \frac{2}{e^{2z}}$

[here, $x = -z$, where $z > 0$]

$$= \frac{2}{\left[1 + 2z + \frac{(2z)^2}{2!} + \ldots\ldots\right]} > 0$$

$\therefore f'(x) > 0$

Thus, for all values of x, $f'(x) > 0$. So, $f(x)$ is strictly increasing function on R.

15 (c) Given, $f(x) = 2x^2 - 3x$

On differentiating w.r.t. x, $f'(x) = 4x - 3$

On putting $f'(x) = 0$, we get $4x - 3 = 0$

$\Rightarrow \quad x = 3/4$

The point $x = 3/4$ divides the real line into two disjoint intervals namely

$$\left(-\infty, \frac{3}{4}\right) \text{ and } \left(\frac{3}{4}, \infty\right).$$

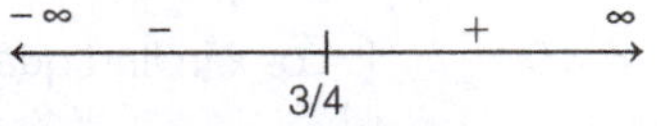

Intervals	Sign of $f'(x)$	Nature of $f(x)$
$\left(-\infty, \frac{3}{4}\right)$	(–) negative [$\because x < 3/4$]	Strictly decreasing
$\left(\frac{3}{4}, \infty\right)$	(+) positive [$\because x > 3/4$]	Strictly increasing

Hence, $f(x)$ is strictly increasing on $\left(\frac{3}{4}, \infty\right)$ and strictly decreasing on $\left(-\infty, \frac{3}{4}\right)$.

16 (c) A. Let $f(x) = x^2 + 2x - 5$

$\Rightarrow f'(x) = 2x + 2$ [by differentiating w.r.t. x]

On putting $f'(x) = 0$, we get $2x + 2 = 0$

$\Rightarrow \quad 2x = -2$

$\Rightarrow \quad x = -1$

$x = -1$ divides real line into two intervals namely $(-\infty, -1)$ and $(-1, \infty)$.

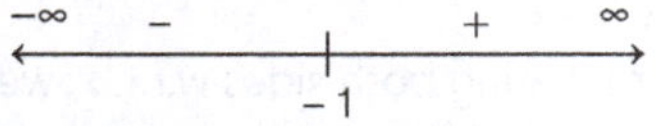

Intervals	Sign of $f'(x)$	Nature of $f(x)$
$(-\infty, -1)$	–ve	Strictly decreasing
$(-1, \infty)$	+ve	Strictly increasing

Therefore, $f(x)$ is strictly increasing when $x > -1$ and strictly decreasing when $x < -1$.

B. Let $\quad f(x) = 10 - 6x - 2x^2$

$\Rightarrow \quad f'(x) = 0 - 6 - 2 \cdot 2x = -6 - 4x$

On putting $f'(x) = 0$, we get $-6 - 4x = 0$

$\Rightarrow \quad x = \frac{-3}{2}$

which divides real line into two intervals namely $\left(-\infty, \frac{-3}{2}\right)$ and $\left(\frac{-3}{2}, \infty\right)$.

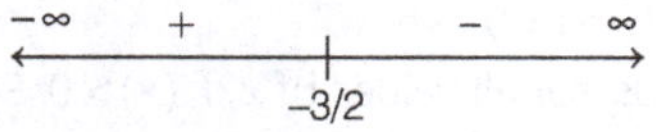

Intervals	Sign of $f'(x)$	Nature of $f(x)$
$(-\infty, -3/2)$	+ ve	Strictly increasing
$(-3/2, \infty)$	– ve	Strictly decreasing

Hence, f is strictly increasing for $x < -\frac{3}{2}$ and strictly decreasing for $x > -\frac{3}{2}$.

C. Given, $f(x) = -2x^3 - 9x^2 - 12x + 1$,

$\Rightarrow \quad f'(x) = -2 \cdot 3x^2 - 9 \cdot 2x - 12$

$= -6x^2 - 18x - 12$

On putting $f'(x) = 0$, we get $-6x^2 - 18x - 12 = 0$

$\Rightarrow \quad -6(x + 2)(x + 1) = 0$

$\Rightarrow \quad x = -2, -1$

which divides real line into three intervals $(-\infty, -2)$, $(-2, -1)$ and $(-1, \infty)$

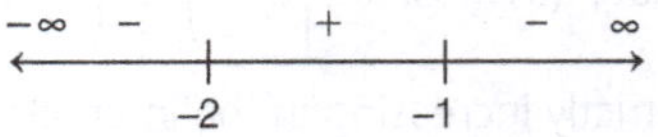

Intervals	Sign of $f'(x)$	Nature of $f(x)$
$(-\infty, -2)$	$(-)(-)(-) = -$ ve	Strictly decreasing
$(-2, -1)$	$(-)(-)(+) = +$ ve	Strictly increasing
$(-1, \infty)$	$(-)(+)(+) = -$ ve	Strictly decreasing

Therefore, $f(x)$ is strictly increasing in $-2 < x < -1$ and strictly decreasing for $x < -2$ and $x > -1$.

D. Given, $f(x) = 6 - 9x - x^2 \Rightarrow f'(x) = -9 - 2x$

On putting $f'(x) = 0$, we get $-9 - 2x = 0 \Rightarrow x = -\frac{9}{2}$

which divides the real line in two disjoint intervals $\left(-\infty, \frac{-9}{2}\right)$ and $\left(-\frac{9}{2}, \infty\right)$.

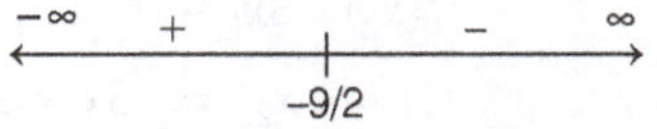

Intervals	Sign of $f'(x)$	Nature of $f(x)$
$(-\infty, -9/2)$	+ ve	Strictly increasing
$(-9/2, \infty)$	– ve	Strictly decreasing

Therefore, $f(x)$ is strictly increasing when $x < -\frac{9}{2}$ and strictly decreasing when $x > -\frac{9}{2}$.

E. Given, $f(x) = (x+1)^3 (x-3)^3$

On differentiating, we get

$$f'(x) = (x+1)^3 \cdot 3(x-3)^2 \cdot 1 + (x-3)^3 \cdot 3(x+1)^2 \cdot 1$$
$$= 3(x-3)^2 (x+1)^2 \{(x+1) + (x-3)\}$$
$$= 3(x-3)^2 (x+1)^2 (2x-2)$$
$$= 6(x-3)^2 (x+1)^2 (x-1)$$

On putting $f'(x) = 0$, we get $x = -1, 1, 3$.

which divides real line into four disjoint intervals namely $(-\infty, -1)$, $(-1, 1)$, $(1, 3)$ and $(3, \infty)$.

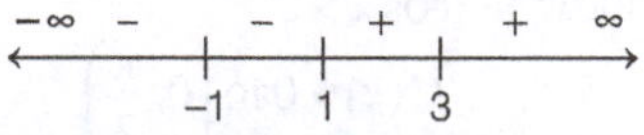

Intervals	Sign of $f'(x)$	Nature of $f(x)$
$-\infty < x < -1$	(+) (+) (−) = − ve	Strictly decreasing
$-1 < x < 1$	(+) (+) (−) = − ve	Strictly decreasing
$1 < x < 3$	(+) (+) (+) = + ve	Strictly increasing
$3 < x < \infty$	(+) (+) (+) = + ve	Strictly increasing

Therefore, $f(x)$ is strictly increasing in $(1, 3)$ and $(3, \infty)$ and strictly decreasing in $(-\infty, -1)$ and $(-1, 1)$.

17 (*b*) Given, $y = \log(1+x) - \dfrac{2x}{(2+x)}$.

On differentiating, we get

$$\frac{dy}{dx} = \frac{d}{dx}\left[\log(1+x) - \frac{2x}{2+x}\right]$$
$$= \frac{1}{1+x} - \frac{(2+x)\frac{d}{dx}(2x) - 2x\frac{d}{dx}(2+x)}{(2+x)^2}$$
$$= \frac{1}{1+x} - \frac{4+2x-2x}{(2+x)^2} = \frac{1}{1+x} - \frac{4}{(2+x)^2}$$
$$= \frac{(2+x)^2 - 4(1+x)}{(1+x)(2+x)^2} = \frac{4+x^2+4x-4-4x}{(1+x)(2+x)^2}$$
$$= \frac{x^2}{(1+x)(2+x)^2}$$

When $x \in (-1, \infty)$, then $\dfrac{x^2}{(2+x)^2} > 0$ and $(1+x) > 0$

$\therefore$ $y' > 0$ when $x > -1$.

Hence, y is an increasing function throughout $(x > -1)$ as its domain.

18 (*a*) Given function is $y = [x(x-2)]^2 = [x^2 - 2x]^2$

On differentiating w.r.t. x, we get

$$\frac{dy}{dx} = 2(x^2 - 2x)\frac{d}{dx}(x^2 - 2x)$$
$$= 2(x^2 - 2x)(2x - 2) = 4x(x-2)(x-1)$$

On putting $\dfrac{dy}{dx} = 0$, we get $x = 0, 1$ and 2

which divides real line in disjoint intervals $(-\infty, 0)$, $(0, 1)$, $(1, 2)$ and $(2, \infty)$.

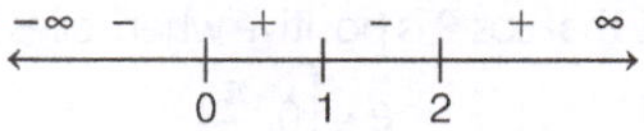

Intervals	Sign of $f'(x)$	Nature of $f(x)$
$(-\infty, 0)$	(−) (−) (−) = − ve	Strictly decreasing
$(0, 1)$	(+) (−) (−) = + ve	Strictly increasing
$(1, 2)$	(+) (−) (+) = − ve	Strictly decreasing
$(2, \infty)$	(+) (+) (+) = + ve	Strictly increasing

Therefore, y is increasing in $(0, 1)$ and $(2, \infty)$.

19 (*b*) We have, $y = \dfrac{4\sin\theta}{(2+\cos\theta)} - \theta$

On differentiating w.r.t. θ, we get

$$\frac{dy}{d\theta} = \frac{d}{d\theta}\left[\frac{4\sin\theta}{2+\cos\theta} - \theta\right]$$
$$= \frac{(2+\cos\theta)\frac{d}{d\theta}(4\sin\theta) - 4\sin\theta\frac{d}{d\theta}(2+\cos\theta)}{(2+\cos\theta)^2} - 1$$
$$= \frac{4\cos\theta(2+\cos\theta) - 4\sin\theta(-\sin\theta)}{(2+\cos\theta)^2} - 1$$
$$= \frac{8\cos\theta + 4\cos^2\theta + 4\sin^2\theta}{(2+\cos\theta)^2} - 1$$
$$= \frac{8\cos\theta + 4(\cos^2\theta + \sin^2\theta)}{(2+\cos\theta)^2} - 1$$
$$= \frac{8\cos\theta + 4}{(2+\cos\theta)^2} - 1 = \frac{8\cos\theta + 4 - (2+\cos\theta)^2}{(2+\cos\theta)^2}$$
$$= \frac{8\cos\theta + 4 - 4 - \cos^2\theta - 4\cos\theta}{(2+\cos\theta)^2}$$
$$= \frac{4\cos\theta - \cos^2\theta}{(2+\cos\theta)^2}$$
$$\frac{dy}{d\theta} = \frac{\cos\theta(4-\cos\theta)}{(2+\cos\theta)^2}$$

$\because$ $-1 \le -\cos\theta \le 1$

$3 \le 4 - \cos\theta \le 5$

$\Rightarrow$ $4 - \cos\theta > 0$

Hence, $\dfrac{4-\cos\theta}{(2+\cos\theta)^2} > 0$

$\because$ y is increasing.

$\therefore$ $\dfrac{dy}{d\theta} \ge 0$

$\Rightarrow \quad \dfrac{\cos\theta(4-\cos\theta)}{(2+\cos\theta)^2} > 0$

$\Rightarrow \quad \cos\theta > 0 \quad \left[\because \dfrac{4-\cos\theta}{(2+\cos\theta)^2} > 0\right]$

We know that $\cos\theta$ is positive when it lies in first quadrant.

$\therefore \quad \theta \in \left[0, \dfrac{\pi}{2}\right]$

Note *Since, it is a continuous function (i) for increasing function, $f'(x) \geq 0$. (ii) for strictly increasing function, $f'(x) > 0$.*

20 (*d*) (a) Let $f(x) = \cos x$, then $f'(x) = -\sin x$. In interval $\left(0, \dfrac{\pi}{2}\right)$, $f'(x) < 0$

Therefore, $f(x)$ is strictly decreasing on $\left(0, \dfrac{\pi}{2}\right)$.

(b) Let $g(x) = \cos 2x$

$\Rightarrow g'(x) = -2\sin 2x$. In interval $\left(0, \dfrac{\pi}{2}\right)$, $f'(x) < 0$

Because $\sin 2x$ will either lie in the first or second quadrant which will give a positive value. Therefore, $g(x)$ is strictly decreasing on $\left(0, \dfrac{\pi}{2}\right)$.

(c) Let $h(x) = \cos 3x$

$\Rightarrow h'(x) = -3\sin 3x$. In interval $\left(0, \dfrac{\pi}{3}\right)$, $f'(x) < 0$

Because $\sin 3x$ will either lie in the first or second quadrant which will give a positive value. Therefore, $h(x)$ is strictly decreasing on $\left(0, \dfrac{\pi}{3}\right)$.

When $x \in \left(\dfrac{\pi}{3}, \dfrac{\pi}{2}\right)$, then $f'(x) > 0$

Because $\sin 3x$ will lie in the third quadrant.

Therefore, $f(x)$ is not strictly decreasing on $\left(0, \dfrac{\pi}{2}\right)$.

(d) Let $l(x) = \tan x$

$\Rightarrow l'(x) = \sec^2 x$. In interval $x \in \left(0, \dfrac{\pi}{2}\right)$, $f'(x) > 0$

Therefore, $l(x)$ is not strictly decreasing on $\left(0, \dfrac{\pi}{2}\right)$.

21 (*d*) Given, $f(x) = x^{100} + \sin x - 1$

$\Rightarrow \quad f'(x) = 100x^{99} + \cos x$

(a) In interval (0, 1), $\cos x > 0$ and $100x^{99} > 0$

$\therefore \quad f'(x) > 0$

$\left[\because \text{In} \left(0, \dfrac{\pi}{2}\right), \cos x > 0 \text{ i.e. In } (0, 1.57), \cos x > 0\right.$

$\left.\therefore (0, 1), \cos x > 0\right]$

Thus, function f is strictly increasing in interval (0, 1).

(b) In interval $\left(\dfrac{\pi}{2}, \pi\right)$, $\cos x < 0$ and $100x^{99} > 0$.

Also, $100x^{99} > \cos x$

$\therefore \quad f'(x) > 0$ in $\left(\dfrac{\pi}{2}, \pi\right)$

Thus, function f is strictly increasing in interval $\left(\dfrac{\pi}{2}, \pi\right)$.

(c) In interval $\left(0, \dfrac{\pi}{2}\right)$, $\cos x > 0$ and $100x^{99} > 0$.

$\therefore \quad 100x^{99} + \cos x > 0$

$\Rightarrow \quad f'(x) > 0$ in $\left(0, \dfrac{\pi}{2}\right)$

Thus, f is strictly increasing in interval $\left(0, \dfrac{\pi}{2}\right)$.

Hence, function f is not strictly decreasing in the given intervals.

The correct answer is (d).

22 (*b*) We find $f'(x)$, then for $1 < x < 2$, put $f'(x) > 0$ and find the required least value of a.

Given, $\quad f(x) = x^2 + ax + 1$

$f'(x) = 2x + a$

In interval (1, 2), $1 < x < 2$

$\Rightarrow \quad 2 < 2x < 4$

$\Rightarrow \quad (2 + a) < (2x + a) < (4 + a)$

Since, $f(x)$ is strictly increasing function, then

$(2 + a) > 0$

[for this $f'(x) > 0$ and $(2x + a) > (2 + a)$]

$\therefore \quad (2 + a) > 0$

$\Rightarrow \quad a > -2.$

Hence, the least value of $a = -2$

23 (*b*) Given, $f(x) = x + \dfrac{1}{x}$

$\Rightarrow \quad f'(x) = 1 - \dfrac{1}{x^2} = \dfrac{x^2 - 1}{x^2}$ [differentiate w.r.t. x]

If $x < -1$, then $f'(x) > 0$. If $x > 1$, then $f'(x) > 0$

$\therefore f(x)$ is strictly increasing on interval / disjoint from [–1, 1].

24 (*a*) Given, $f(x) = \log(\cos x)$

$\Rightarrow f'(x) = \dfrac{1}{\cos x}.(-\sin x) = -\tan x$ [differentiate w.r.t. x]

In interval $\left(0, \dfrac{\pi}{2}\right)$, $\tan x > 0$

$\Rightarrow \quad -\tan x < 0$ [$\because \tan x$ is in Ist quadrant]

$\therefore \quad f'(x) < 0$ in $\left(0, \dfrac{\pi}{2}\right)$

Hence, f is strictly decreasing in $\left(0, \dfrac{\pi}{2}\right)$.

Also, in interval $\left(\frac{\pi}{2}, \pi\right)$, $\tan x < 0$

[$\because$ $\tan x$ is in IInd quadrant]

$\Rightarrow -\tan x > 0$

$\therefore \quad f'(x) > 0$ in $\left(\frac{\pi}{2}, \pi\right)$

25 (*a*) Given,

$$f(x) = x^3 - 3x^2 + 3x - 100$$

$$\Rightarrow f'(x) = 3x^2 - 6x + 3$$

[differentiate w.r.t. x]

$$= 3(x^2 - 2x + 1) = 3(x-1)^2$$

For any $x \in R$, $(x-1)^2 \geq 0$, since a perfect square cannot be negative.

Then, $f'(x) \geq 0$.

Hence, the given function f is an increasing function on R.

26 (*d*) Given,

$$y = x^2 e^{-x}$$

$$\Rightarrow \frac{dy}{dx} = x^2 e^{-x}(-1) + e^{-x}(2x)$$

$$= x e^{-x}(-x+2)$$

$$= x(2-x)e^{-x}$$

For increasing function, $\frac{dy}{dx} > 0$

$$\Rightarrow \quad xe^{-x}(2-x) > 0$$

Case I

$\Rightarrow x > 0$ and $2 - x > 0$

$\Rightarrow x > 0$ and $x < 2$

$\Rightarrow 0 < x < 2$

Case II

$\Rightarrow x < 0$ and $2 - x < 0$

$\Rightarrow x < 0$ and $x > 2$

27 (*a*) $f(x) = \tan x - 4x$

$\Rightarrow f'(x) = \sec^2 x - 4$

When $\frac{-\pi}{3} < x < \frac{\pi}{3}$,

$$1 < \sec x < 2$$

Therefore, $1 < \sec^2 x < 4$

$$\Rightarrow \quad -3 < (\sec^2 x - 4) < 0$$

Thus, for $\frac{-\pi}{3} < x < \frac{\pi}{3}$, $f'(x) < 0$

Hence, f is strictly decreasing on $\left(\frac{-\pi}{3}, \frac{\pi}{3}\right)$.

28 (*a*) We have,

$$f(x) = x - e^x + \tan\left(\frac{2\pi}{7}\right)$$

$$\Rightarrow \quad f'(x) = 1 - e^x$$

For $f(x)$ to be increasing, we must have

$$f'(x) > 0$$

$$\Rightarrow \quad 1 - e^x > 0$$

$$\Rightarrow \quad e^x < 1$$

$$\Rightarrow \quad x < 0$$

$$\Rightarrow \quad x \in (-\infty, 0)$$

29 (*b*) Given, $f(x) = \dfrac{e^{2x} - 1}{e^{2x} + 1}$

$$\therefore \quad f(-x) = \frac{e^{-2x} - 1}{e^{-2x} + 1} = -f(x)$$

$\therefore f(x)$ is an odd function.

Now, $f'(x) = \dfrac{4e^{2x}}{(1 + e^{2x})^2} > 0, \forall x \in R$

$\Rightarrow f(x)$ is an increasing function.

30 (*d*) Since, $f(x) = xe^{1-x}$

$$f'(x) = -xe^{1-x} + e^{1-x}$$

$$= e^{1-x}(1-x)$$

$$\Rightarrow \quad f'(x) < 0, \forall (1, \infty)$$

Hence, $f(x)$ is strictly decreasing in $(1, \infty)$.

31 (*b*) Since, $f(x) = \tan^{-1}(\sin x + \cos x)$

$$\Rightarrow \quad f'(x) = \frac{1}{1 + (\sin x + \cos x)^2}(\cos x - \sin x)$$

$$= \frac{\sqrt{2}\cos\left(x + \frac{\pi}{4}\right)}{1 + (\sin x + \cos x)^2}$$

For $f(x)$ to be increasing,

$$-\frac{\pi}{2} < x + \frac{\pi}{4} < \frac{\pi}{2}$$

$$\Rightarrow \quad -\frac{3\pi}{4} < x < \frac{\pi}{4}$$

Hence, option (b) is correct which lies in the above interval.

32 (*d*) $\because f(x) = -x^3 + 4ax^2 + 2x - 5$

$$\therefore \quad f'(x) = -3x^2 + 8ax + 2$$

Since, $f(x)$ is decreasing, $\forall x$.

Therefore $f'(x) < 0$

$$\Rightarrow -3x^2 + 8ax + 2 < 0$$

$$\Rightarrow \quad 3x^2 - 8ax - 2 > 0$$

Now, $D = (-8a)^2 - 4(3)(-2) < 0$

$$\Rightarrow \quad 64a^2 + 24 < 0$$

$$\Rightarrow \quad a^2 < -\frac{3}{8}$$

Hence, no real value of a exist.

33 (*b*) $\because f(x) = 2x^3 + 9x^2 + 12x - 1$

$$\therefore \quad f'(x) = 6x^2 + 18x + 12$$

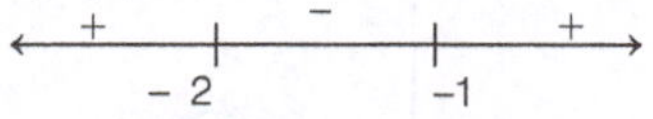

$$= 6(x^2 + 3x + 2)$$

For decreasing function,

$$f'(x) \leq 0$$

$$\Rightarrow 6(x+1)(x+2) \leq 0$$

$\therefore \quad f(x)$ is decreasing in $[-2, -1]$.

34 (*b*) $\because f(x) = 4\sin^3 x - 6\sin^2 x + 12\sin x + 100$

$$\Rightarrow \quad f'(x) = 12\sin^2 x \cdot \cos x - 12\sin x \cdot \cos x + 12\cos x + 0$$

$$= 12\cos x(\sin^2 x - \sin x + 1)$$

Since, in second quadrant $\sin x$ is positive and the $\cos x$ is negative.

So, $f'(x) < 0, \forall x \in \left(\frac{\pi}{2}, \pi\right)$

35 (*c*) $\because f(x) = \cos x$

$$\Rightarrow f'(x) = -\sin x < 0, \forall x \in \left(0, \frac{\pi}{2}\right)$$

So, $f(x) = \cos x$ is decreasing in $\left(0, \frac{\pi}{2}\right)$.

36 (*c*) $\because f(x) = (x+2)e^{-x}$

$$\Rightarrow \quad f'(x) = -(x+2)e^{-x} + e^{-x}$$

$$= -(x+1)e^{-x}$$

(a) f is increasing.

$$\Rightarrow \quad f'(x) \geq 0$$

$$\Rightarrow -(x+1)e^{-x} \geq 0$$

$$\Rightarrow \quad (x+1) \leq 0 \quad [\because e^{-x} > 0]$$

$$\Rightarrow \quad x \leq -1$$

$$\Rightarrow \quad x \in (-\infty, -1]$$

(b) For decreasing, $f'(x) \leq 0$

$$\Rightarrow -(x+1)e^{-x} \leq 0$$

$$\Rightarrow \quad (x+1)e^{-x} \geq 0$$

$$\Rightarrow \quad x \geq -1 \quad [\because e^{-x} > 0]$$

$\therefore f$ is decreasing on $[-1, \infty)$

Maxima and Minima

1 (*d*) Let f be a function defined on an interval I.

Then, f said to have a maximum value in I, if there exists a point c in I such that

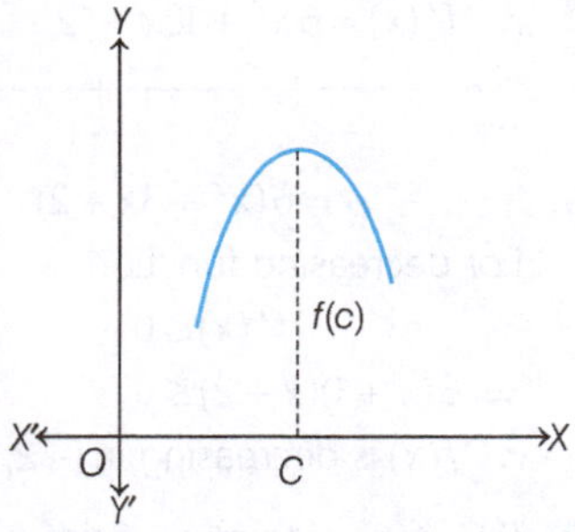

$f(c) > f(x), \forall x \in I$.

The number $f(c)$ is called the maximum value of f in I and the point c is called a point of maximum value of f in I.

2 (*a*) Let f be a function defined on an interval I.

Then, f is said to have a minimum value in I, if there exists a point c in I such that

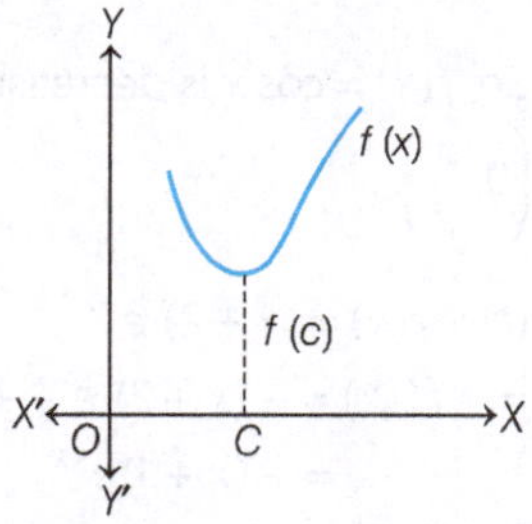

$f(c) < f(x), \forall x \in I$.

The number $f(c)$, in this case, is called the minimum value of f in I and the point c, in this case, is called a point of minimum value of f in I.

3 (*d*) We can find maximum/minimum value of a function at a point at which it is not even differentiable.

From the graphs shown below all are representing a differentiable function.

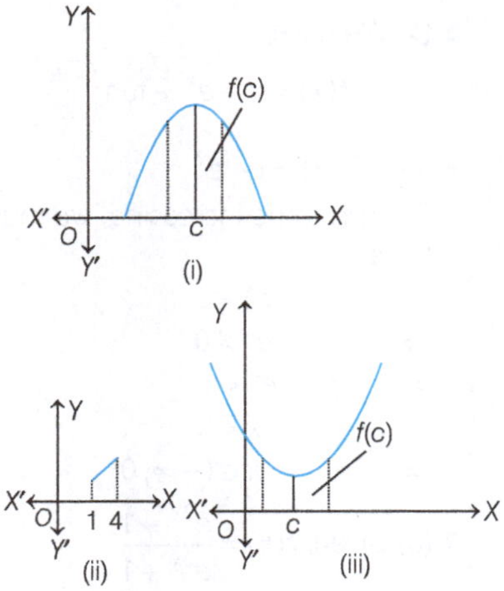

4 (*d*) From the graph of the given function, we have $f(x) = 0$ if $x = 0$. Also $f(x) \geq 0, \forall x \in R$

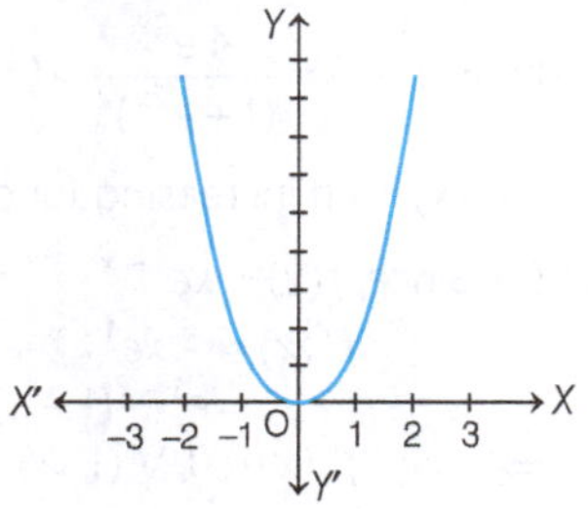

Therefore, the minimum value of f is 0 and the point of minimum value of f is $x = 0$. Further, it may be observed from the graph of the function that f has no maximum value and hence no point of maximum value of f in R.

Note *If we restrict the domain of f to* [–2, 1] *only, then f will have maximum value* $(-2)^2 = 4$ *at* $x = -2$.

5 (*b*) From the graph of the given function note that $f(x) \geq 0, \forall x \in R$ and $f(x) = 0$, if $x = 0$.

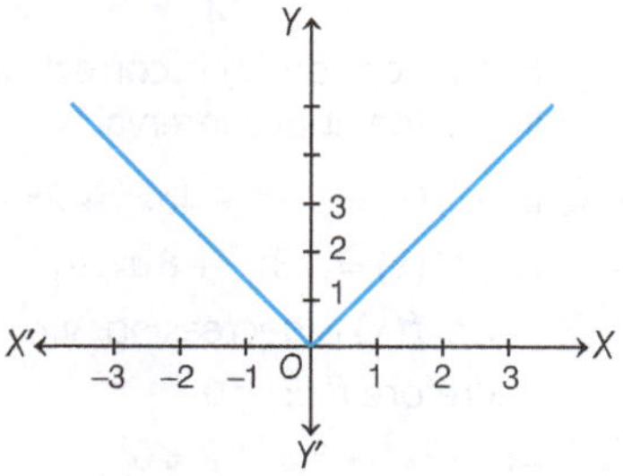

Therefore, the function f has a minimum value 0 and the point of minimum value of f is $x = 0$. Also, the graph clearly shows that f has no maximum value in R and hence no point of maximum value in R.

Note

(i) *If we restrict the domain of f to* [–2, 1] *only, then f will have maximum value* $|-2| = 2$.

(ii) *One may note that the function* $f(x) = |x|$ *is not differentiable at* $x = 0$.

6 (*d*) The given function is an increasing (strictly) function in the given interval (0, 1). From the graph of the function f, it seems that it should have the minimum value at a point closest to 0 on its right and the maximum value at a point closest to 1 on its left. Are such points available? Of course, not. It is not possible to locate such points. Infact, if a point x_0 is closest to 0, then we find $\frac{x_0}{2} < x_0, \forall x_0 \in (0, 1)$.

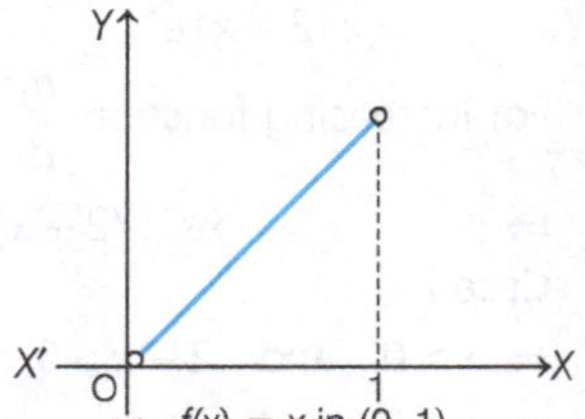

$f(x) = x$ in (0, 1)

Therefore, the given function has neither the maximum value nor the minimum value in the interval (0, 1).

Remark If we include the points 0 and 1 in the domain of f, i.e. if we extend the domain of f to [0, 1], then the function f has minimum value 0 at $x = 0$ and maximum value 1 at $x = 1$. Infact, we have the following results.

Every monotonic function assumes its maximum/minimum value at the end points of the domain of definition of the function.

A more general result – Every continuous function on a closed interval has a maximum and a minimum value.

7 (*a*) A point at which the derivative vanishes need not be a point of local maxima or local minima. For example, if $f(x) = x^3$, then $f'(x) = 3x^2$ and $f'(0) = 0$. But 0 is neither a point of local maxima nor a point of local minima. (see the figure given below)

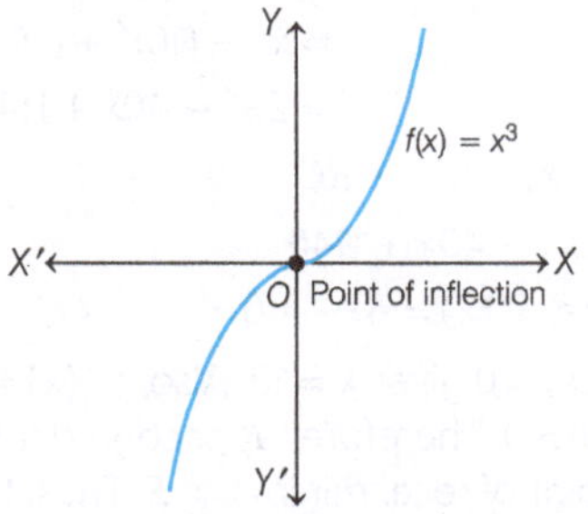

Note *At maxima and minima derivative of $f(x)$ is equal to zero i.e. $f'(x) = 0$. Converse of this result need not to be true.*

8 (*a*) A point *c* in the domain of a function *f* at which either $f'(c) = 0$ or *f* is not differentiable is called a critical point of *f*.

Note that if *f* is continuous at *c* and $f'(c) = 0$, then there exists a $h > 0$ such that *f* is differentiable in the interval $(c - h, c + h)$.

9 (*d*) We have, $f(x) = x^3 - 3x + 3$

or $f'(x) = 3x^2 - 3 = 3(x-1)(x+1)$

or $f'(x) = 0$ at $x = 1$ and $x = -1$

Thus, $x = \pm 1$ are the only critical points which could possibly be the points of local maxima and/or local minima of *f*. Let us first examine the point $x = 1$.

Note that for values close to 1 and to the right of 1, $f'(x) > 0$ and for values close to 1 and to the left of 1, $f'(x) < 0$. Therefore, by first derivative test, $x = 1$ is a point of local minima and local minimum value is $f(1) = 1$. In the case of $x = -1$, note that $f'(x) > 0$, for values close to and to the left of -1 and $f'(x) < 0$, for values close to and to the right of -1. Therefore, by first derivative test, $x = -1$ is a point of local maxima and local maximum value is $f(-1) = 5$.

Values of x	Sign of $f'(x) = 3(x-1)(x+1)$
Close to 1	
to the right (say 1.1 etc.)	>0
to the left (say 0.9 etc.)	<0
Close to -1	
to the right (say -0.9 etc.)	<0
to the left (say -1.1 etc.)	>0

10 (*d*) We have, $f(x) = 2x^3 - 6x^2 + 6x + 5$

or $f'(x) = 6x^2 - 12x + 6 = 6(x-1)^2$

or $f'(x) = 0$ at $x = 1$

Thus, $x = 1$ is the only critical point of *f*. We shall now examine this point for local maxima and/or local minima of *f*. Observe that $f'(x) \geq 0, \forall x \in R$ and in particular $f'(x) > 0$, for values close to 1 and to the left and to the right of 1.

Therefore, by first derivative test, the point $x = 1$ is neither a point of local maxima nor a point of local minima. Hence, $x = 1$ is a point of inflection.

Remark One may note that since $f'(x)$ never changes its sign on *R*, graph of *f* has no turning point and hence no point of local maxima or local minima.

11 (*c*) Note that the given function is not differentiable at $x = 0$. So, second derivative test fails. Let us try first derivative test.

Note *That 0 is a critical point of f. Now to the left of 0, $f(x) = 3 - x$ and so $f'(x) = -1 < 0$. Also to the right of 0, $f(x) = 3 + x$ and so, $f'(x) = 1 > 0$. Therefore, by first derivative test, $x = 0$ is a point of local minima of f and local minimum value of f is $f(0) = 3$.*

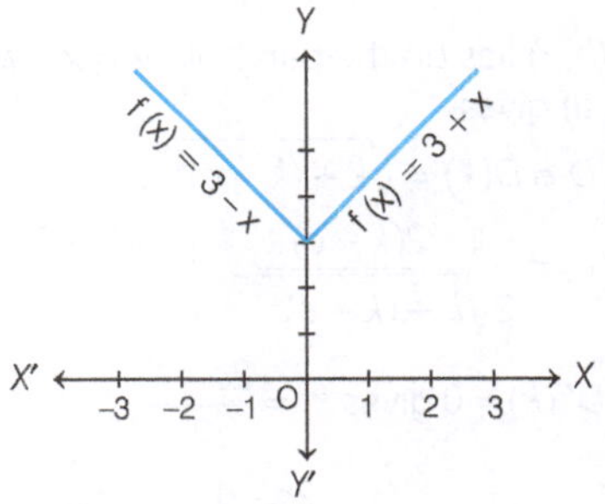

12 (*c*) We have,

$$f(x) = 3x^4 + 4x^3 - 12x^2 + 12$$

or $f'(x) = 12x^3 + 12x^2 - 24x = 12x(x-1)(x+2)$

$f'(x) = 0$ at $x = 0, x = 1$ and $x = -2$

Now, $f''(x) = 36x^2 + 24x - 24 = 12(3x^2 + 2x - 1)$

or $\begin{cases} f''(0) = -12 < 0 \\ f''(1) = 48 > 0 \\ f''(-2) = 84 > 0 \end{cases}$

Therefore, by second derivative test, $x = 0$ is a point of local maxima and local maximum value of *f* at $x = 0$ is $f(0) = 12$ while $x = 1$ and $x = -2$ are the points of local minima and local minimum values of *f* at $x = -1$ and -2 are $f(1) = 7$ and $f(-2) = -20$, respectively.

13 (c) Let one of the numbers be x. Then, the other number is $(15-x)$. Let $S(x)$ denote the sum of the squares of these numbers. Then,

$$S(x) = x^2 + (15-x)^2 = 2x^2 - 30x + 225$$

or $$\begin{cases} S'(x) = 4x - 30 \\ S''(x) = 4 \end{cases}$$

Now, $S'(x) = 0$ give $x = \frac{15}{2}$. Also, $S''\left(\frac{15}{2}\right) = 4 > 0$.

Therefore, by second derivative test, $x = \frac{15}{2}$ is the point of local minima of S. Hence, the sum of squares of numbers is minimum when the numbers are $\frac{15}{2}$ and $15 - \frac{15}{2} = \frac{15}{2}$.

Remark Proceeding as in above example, one may prove that the two positive numbers whose sum is k and the sum of whose squares is minimum, are $\frac{k}{2}$ and $\frac{k}{2}$.

14 (b) Let (h, k) be any point on the parabola $y = x^2$. Let D be the required distance between (h, k) and $(0, c)$. Then,

$$D = \sqrt{(h-0)^2 + (k-c)^2}$$
$$= \sqrt{h^2 + (k-c)^2} \quad \text{...(i)}$$

Since, (h, k) lies on the parabola $y = x^2$, we have, $k = h^2$. So, Eq. (i) gives

$$D \equiv D(k) = \sqrt{k + (k-c)^2}$$
$$D'(k) = \frac{1 + 2(k-c)}{2\sqrt{k + (k-c)^2}}$$

Now, $D'(k) = 0$ gives $k = \frac{2c-1}{2}$

Observe that when $k < \frac{2c-1}{2}$, then $2(k-c) + 1 < 0$ i.e. $D'(k) < 0$. Also, when $k > \frac{2c-1}{2}$, then $D'(k) > 0$. So, by first derivative test, $D(k)$ is minimum at $k = \frac{2c-1}{2}$. Hence, the required shortest distance is given by

$$D\left(\frac{2c-1}{2}\right) = \sqrt{\frac{2c-1}{2} + \left(\frac{2c-1}{2} - c\right)^2} = \frac{\sqrt{4c-1}}{2}$$

15 (b)

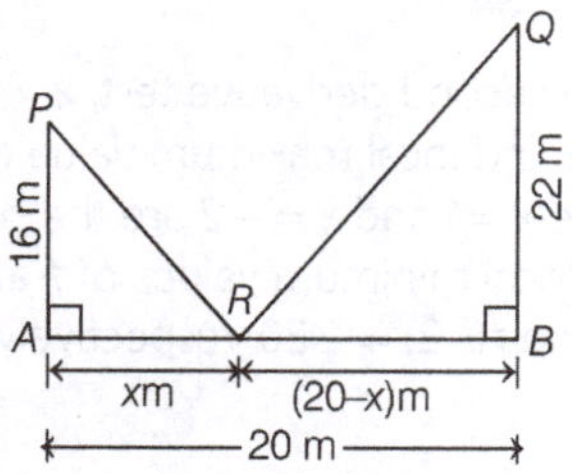

Let R be a point on AB such that $AR = x$ m. Then, $RB = (20-x)$ m (as $AB = 20$ m). From figure, we have

$$RP^2 = AR^2 + AP^2$$

and $$RQ^2 = RB^2 + BQ^2$$

Therefore, $RP^2 + RQ^2 = AR^2 + AP^2 + RB^2 + BQ^2$
$$= x^2 + (16)^2 + (20-x)^2 + (22)^2$$
$$= 2x^2 - 40x + 1140$$

Let $S \equiv S(x) = RP^2 + RQ^2$
$$= 2x^2 - 40x + 1140$$

Therefore, $S'(x) = 4x - 40$

Now $S'(x) = 0$ gives $x = 10$. Also, $S''(x) = 4 > 0, \forall x$ and so $S''(10) > 0$. Therefore, by second derivative test, $x = 10$ is the point of local minima of S. Thus, the distance of R from A on AB is $AR = x = 10$ m.

16 (b) Let $OC = r$ be the radius of the cone and $OA = h$ be its height. Let a cylinder with radius $OE = x$ inscribed in the given cone. The height QE of the cylinder is given by

$$\frac{QE}{OA} = \frac{EC}{OC} \quad [\because \Delta QEC \sim \Delta AOC]$$

or $$\frac{QE}{h} = \frac{r-x}{r}$$

or $$QE = \frac{h(r-x)}{r}$$

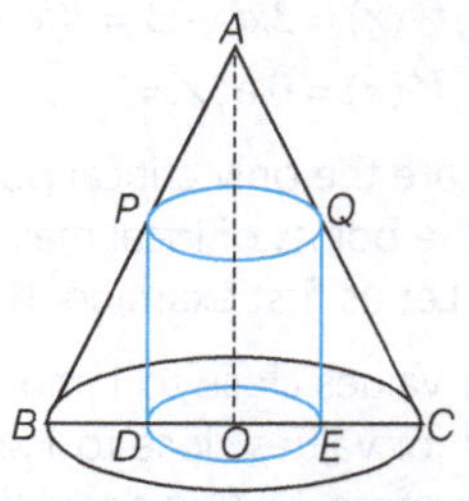

Let S be the curved surface area of the given cylinder. Then,

$$S \equiv S(x) = \frac{2\pi x h(r-x)}{r}$$
$$= \frac{2\pi h}{r}(rx - x^2)$$

or $$\begin{cases} S'(x) = \frac{2\pi h}{r}(r - 2x) \\ S''(x) = \frac{-4\pi h}{r} \end{cases}$$

Now, $S'(x) = 0$ gives $x = \frac{r}{2}$. Since,

$S''(x) < 0 \, \forall x$, $S''\left(\frac{r}{2}\right) < 0$. So, $x = \frac{r}{2}$ or $\frac{x}{r} = \frac{1}{2}$ is a point of maxima of S. Hence, the radius of the cylinder of greatest curved surface area which can be inscribed in a given cone is half of that of the cone.

17 (c) For the function f be given as $f(x) = x + 2, x \in (0, 1)$

We see that the function is continuous on (0, 1) and neither has a maximum value nor has a minimum value. Further, we may note that the function even has neither a local maximum value nor a local minimum value.

18 (d) The given function $f(x) = x + 2$ may not have a local maximum (minimum) values but it certainly does have maximum value $3 = f(1)$ and minimum value $2 = f(0)$. The maximum value 3 of f at $x = 1$ is called absolute maximum value (global maximum or greatest value) of f on the interval [0, 1].

Similarly, the minimum value 2 of f at $x = 0$ is called the absolute minimum value (global minimum or least value) of f on [0, 1].

19 (c) The given graph of a continuous function is defined on a closed interval $[a, d]$. We see that the function f has a local minima at $x = b$ and local minimum value as $f(b)$. The function also has a local maxima at $x = c$ and local maximum value is $f(c)$.

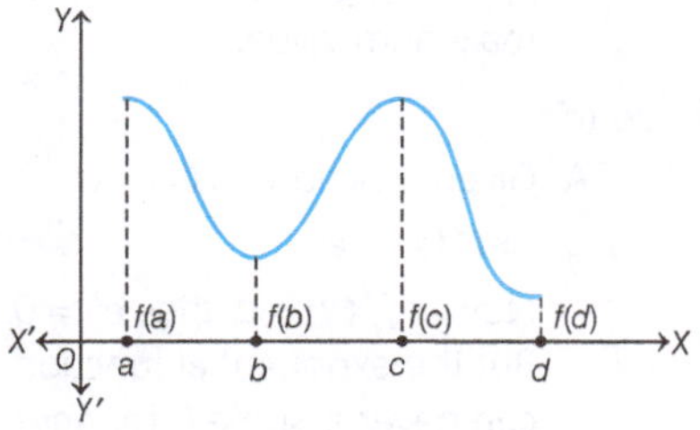

Also, from the graph, it is evident that f has absolute maximum value $f(a)$ and absolute minimum value $f(d)$. Further note that the absolute maximum (minimum) value of f is different from local maximum (minimum) value of f.

20 (d) Regarding absolute maximum and absolute minimum values of a function on a closed interval I, we get the following theorem that states as

Let f be a continuous function on an interval $I = [a, b]$. Then, f has the absolute maximum value and f attains it atleast once in I. Also, f has the absolute minimum value and attains it atleast once in I.

Thus, we can say that option (d) is correct.

21 (c) This problem can be understood with the following theorem stated as

Let f be a differentiable function on a closed interval I and let c be any interior point of I. Then,

(i) $f'(c) = 0$, if f attains its absolute maximum value at c.

(ii) $f'(c) = 0$, if f attains its absolute minimum value at c.

22 (c) We have,

$$f(x) = 2x^3 - 15x^2 + 36x + 1$$

$$\text{or } f'(x) = 6x^2 - 30x + 36 = 6(x-3)(x-2)$$

Note that $f'(x) = 0$ gives $x = 2$ and $x = 3$.

To find absolute maximum and minimum value we shall now evaluate the value of f at these points and at the end points of the interval [1, 5] i.e. $x = 1$, $x = 2$, $x = 3$ and at $x = 5$. So,

$$f(1) = 2(1)^3 - 15(1)^2 + 36(1) + 1 = 24$$
$$f(2) = 2(2)^3 - 15(2)^2 + 36(2) + 1 = 29$$
$$f(3) = 2(3)^3 - 15(3)^2 + 36(3) + 1 = 28$$
$$f(5) = 2(5)^3 - 15(5)^2 + 36(5) + 1 = 56$$

Thus, we conclude that absolute maximum value of f on [1, 5] is 56, occurring at $x = 5$ and absolute minimum value of f on [1, 5] is 24 which occurs at $x = 1$.

23 (b) For each value of x, the helicopter's position is at point $(x, x^2 + 7)$. Therefore, the distance between the helicopter and the soldier placed at (3, 7), is

$$\sqrt{(x-3)^2 + (x^2 + 7 - 7)^2}$$

i.e. $\sqrt{(x-3)^2 + x^4}$.

Let $f(x) = (x-3)^2 + x^4$

$$\text{or } f'(x) = 2(x-3) + 4x^3 = 2(x-1)(2x^2 + 2x + 3)$$

Thus $f'(x) = 0$ gives $x = 1$ or $2x^2 + 2x + 3 = 0$ for which there are no real root. Also, there are no end points of the interval to be added to the set for which $f(x)$ is zero, i.e. there is only one point namely $x = 1$. The value of f at this point is given by $f(1) = (1-3)^2 + (1)^4 = 5$. Thus, the distance between the solider and the helicopter is $\sqrt{f(1)} = \sqrt{5}$.

Note that $\sqrt{5}$ is either a maximum value or minimum value. Since,

$$\sqrt{f(0)} = \sqrt{(0-3)^2 + (0)^4} = 3 > \sqrt{5}$$

It follows that $\sqrt{5}$ is the minimum value of $\sqrt{f(x)}$. Hence, $\sqrt{5}$ is the minimum distance between the soldier and the helicopter.

24 (b)

A. Given function is

$$f(x) = (2x-1)^2 + 3$$

It can be observed that

$(2x-1)^2 \geq 0$ for every $x \in R$

[since, it is perfect square for any real number]

Therefore,

$f(x) = (2x-1)^2 + 3 \geq 3$ for every $x \in R$.

The minimum value of f is attained when $2x - 1 = 0$

i.e. $2x - 1 = 0$

$\Rightarrow \quad x = \frac{1}{2}$

$\therefore$ Minimum value of

$$f = f\left(\frac{1}{2}\right) = \left(2 \times \frac{1}{2} - 1\right)^2 + 3 = 3$$

For any value of x, value of $f(x)$ will always be greater than 3. Hence, function f does not have particular maximum value.

B. Given function is

$$f(x) = 9x^2 + 12x + 2 = 9x^2 + 12x + 4 - 2$$

[we add and subtract 2 for making it perfect square]

$= (9x^2 + 6x + 6x + 4) - 2$

$= [3x(3x + 2) + 2(3x + 2)] - 2$

$= [(3x + 2)(3x + 2)] - 2$

$= (3x + 2)^2 - 2$

It can be observed that $(3x + 2)^2 \geq 0$ for every $x \in R$.

Therefore, $f(x) = (3x + 2)^2 - 2 \geq -2$ for every $x \in R$.

The minimum value of f is attained when

$3x + 2 = 0$

i.e. $3x + 2 = 0$

$\Rightarrow \quad x = \frac{-2}{3}$

$\therefore$ Minimum value of

$f = f\left(\frac{-2}{3}\right)$

$= \left(3 \times \frac{-2}{3} + 2\right)^2 - 2 = -2$

For any value of x, $f(x) \geq -2$, hence function f does not have a particular maximum value.

C. Given, function is $f(x) = -(x-1)^2 + 10$.

It can be observed that $(x-1)^2 \geq 0, \forall x \in R$

$\Rightarrow -(x-1)^2 \leq 0$ for every $x \in R$

Therefore, $f(x) = -(x-1)^2 + 10 \leq 10$ for every $x \in R$.

The maximum value of f is attained when $(x-1) = 0$

i.e. $(x-1) = 0 \Rightarrow x = 1$

$\therefore$ Maximum value of

$f = f(1) = -(1-1)^2 + 10 = 10$

For any value of x, $f(x) \leq 10$, hence function f does not have a particular minimum value.

D. Given function is $f(x) = x^3 + 1$

We observe that the value of $f(x)$ increases when the value of x increase and $f(x)$ can be made as large as we please by giving large value to x. So, $f(x)$ does not have the maximum value. Similarly, $f(x)$ can be made as small as we please by giving smaller value to x. So, $f(x)$ does not have the minimum value.

Alternate Method

Here, $f(x) = x^3 + 1$,

$f'(x) = 3x^2, \; f''(x) = 6x$

For maxima or minima, put $f'(x) = 0$

$\Rightarrow \quad 3x^2 = 0 \Rightarrow x = 0$

At $\quad x = 0, f''(0) = 6 \times 0 = 0$

25 (a)

A. Given function is $f(x) = |x+2| - 1$

We know that $|x+2| \geq 0 \, \forall x \in R$.

Therefore, $f(x) = |x+2| - 1 \geq -1$ for every $x \in R$.

The minimum value of f is attained when $|x+2| = 0$.

i.e. $\quad |x+2| = 0 \Rightarrow x = -2$

$\therefore$ Minimum value of

$f = f(-2) = |-2+2| - 1$

$= 0 - 1 = -1$

Hence, $f(x)$ has minimum value -1 at $x = 2$, but $f(x)$ has no maximum value.

Note *The modulus value of a function is always* ≥ 0.

B. Given function is $g(x) = -|x+1| + 3$.

We know that

$|x+1| \geq 0, \forall x \in R$.

$\Rightarrow -|x+1| \leq 0, \forall x \in R$

$\Rightarrow -|x+1| + 3 \leq 3, \forall x \in R$

The maximum value of g is attained when $|x+1| = 0$.

i.e. $\quad |x+1| = 0 \Rightarrow x = -1$

$\therefore$ Maximum value of

$g = g(-1) = -|-1+1| + 3 = 3$.

Hence, $g(x)$ has maximum value 3 at $x = -1$, but $g(x)$ has no minimum value.

C. Given function is $h(x) = \sin 2x + 5$.

We know that $-1 \leq \sin x \leq 1$

$\Rightarrow \quad -1 \leq \sin 2x \leq 1$

$\Rightarrow \; -1 + 5 \leq \sin 2x + 5 \leq 1 + 5$

$\Rightarrow \quad 4 \leq \sin 2x + 5 \leq 6$

Hence, maximum value of $h(x)$ is 6 and minimum value of $h(x)$ is 4.

D. Given function is $f(x) = |\sin 4x + 3|$

We know that $-1 \leq \sin 4x \leq 1$

$\Rightarrow 3 - 1 \leq \sin 4x + 3 \leq 1 + 3$

$\Rightarrow \quad 2 \leq \sin 4x + 3 \leq 4$

$\Rightarrow \quad 2 \leq |\sin 4x + 3| \leq 4$

Hence, maximum value of $f(x)$ is 4 and minimum value of $f(x)$ is 2.

E. Given function is $h(x) = x + 1, -1 < x < 1$.

Now, $\quad -1 < x < 1$

$\Leftrightarrow \quad -1 + 1 < x + 1 < 1 + 1$

$\Leftrightarrow \quad 0 < x + 1 < 2$

Here, in the interval (0,2), f has neither a maximum value nor a minimum value.

Alternate Method

$h'(x) = 1$ exists at all $x \in (-1, 1)$.

Also, $h'(x) \neq 0$ for any $x \in (-1, 1)$.

Further $h(x)$ is defined on an open interval.

So, there is no point for which $f(x)$ may have a minimum or a maximum value.

26 (d)

A. Given function is $f(x) = e^x$

$\Rightarrow f'(x) = e^x$.

Now, if $f'(x) = 0$, then $e^x = 0$.

But the exponential function can never assume 0 for any value of x.

Therefore, there does not exist any $x \in R$ such that $f'(x) = 0$

Hence, function f does not have maxima or minima.

B. Given function is $g(x) = \log x$

$\Rightarrow g'(x) = \frac{1}{x}$.

Since, $\log x$ is defined for a positive number x, then $g'(x) > 0$ for any x.

Therefore, there does not exist any $x \in R$ such that $g'(x) = 0$.

Hence, function g does not have maxima or minima.

C. Given function is

$$h(x) = x^3 + x^2 + x + 1$$

$$\Rightarrow \quad h'(x) = 3x^2 + 2x + 1$$

Now, put $h'(x) = 0$,

$$3x^2 + 2x + 1 = 0$$

$$\Rightarrow x = \frac{-2 \pm \sqrt{4 - 4 \times 3 \times 1}}{6}$$

$$= \frac{-2 \pm \sqrt{-8}}{6}$$

$$\left[\text{using } x = \frac{-b \pm \sqrt{b^2 - 4ac}}{2a}\right]$$

$$\Rightarrow x = \frac{-2 \pm 2\sqrt{2}\,i}{6} = \frac{2(-1 \pm \sqrt{2}\,i)}{6}$$

$$= \frac{-1 \pm \sqrt{2}\,i}{3} \notin R$$

Therefore, there does not exist any $x \in R$ such that $h'(x) = 0$.

Hence, function h does not have maxima or minima.

27 (*a*)

A. Given function is $f(x) = x^3$

$$\Rightarrow \quad f'(x) = 3x^2.$$

For maxima or minima, put $f'(x) = 0$.

$$\therefore \quad 3x^2 = 0$$

$$\Rightarrow \quad x = 0 \in [-2, 2]$$

Now, we evaluate the value of f at critical point $x = 0$ and at end points of the interval $[-2, 2]$.

At $x = 0$, $f(0) = 0^3 = 0$

At $x = -2$, $f(-2) = (-2)^3 = -8$

At $x = 2$, $f(2) = (2)^3 = 8$

Thus, absolute maximum value is 8 at $x = 2$ and absolute minimum value is –8 at $x = -2$.

B. Given function is

$$f(x) = \sin x + \cos x$$

$$\Rightarrow \quad f'(x) = \cos x - \sin x$$

For maxima or minima, put $f'(x) = 0$.

$$\Rightarrow \quad \cos x - \sin x = 0$$

$$\Rightarrow \quad \frac{\sin x}{\cos x} = 1 \Rightarrow \tan x = 1$$

$$\Rightarrow \quad x = \frac{\pi}{4} \in [0, \pi]$$

Now, we evaluate the value of f at critical point $x = \frac{\pi}{4}$ and at the end points of the interval $[0, \pi]$.

At $x = \frac{\pi}{4}$,

$$f\left(\frac{\pi}{4}\right) = \sin\frac{\pi}{4} + \cos\frac{\pi}{4}$$

$$= \frac{1}{\sqrt{2}} + \frac{1}{\sqrt{2}} = \sqrt{2}$$

At $x = 0$,

$f(0) = \sin 0 + \cos 0 = 0 + 1 = 1$

At $x = \pi$,

$f(\pi) = \sin\pi + \cos\pi = 0 - 1 = -1$

Thus, absolute maximum value is $\sqrt{2}$ at $x = \frac{\pi}{4}$ and absolute minimum value is –1 at $x = \pi$.

C. Given function is

$$f(x) = 4x - \frac{1}{2}x^2$$

$$\Rightarrow \quad f'(x) = 4 - \frac{1}{2}(2x) = 4 - x$$

For maxima or minima put $f'(x) = 0$.

$$\therefore \quad 4 - x = 0$$

$$\Rightarrow \quad x = 4 \in \left[-2, \frac{9}{2}\right]$$

Now, we evaluate the value of f at critical point $x = 4$ and at the end points of the interval $\left[-2, \frac{9}{2}\right]$.

At $x = 4$,

$$f(4) = 4(4) - \frac{1}{2}(4)^2 = 16 - 8 = 8$$

At $x = -2$,

$$f(-2) = 4(-2) - \frac{1}{2}(-2)^2$$

$$= -8 - 2 = -10$$

At $x = \frac{9}{2}$,

$$f\left(\frac{9}{2}\right) = 4\left(\frac{9}{2}\right) - \frac{1}{2}\left(\frac{9}{2}\right)^2$$

$$= 18 - \frac{81}{8} = \frac{63}{8} = 7.875$$

Thus, absolute maximum value is 8 at $x = 4$ and absolute minimum value is –10 at $x = -2$.

D. Given function is

$f(x) = (x - 1)^2 + 3$.

$$\therefore \quad f'(x) = 2(x - 1)$$

For maxima or minima, put $f'(x) = 0$

$$\therefore \quad 2(x - 1) = 0$$

$$\Rightarrow \quad x = 1$$

Now, we evaluate the value of f at critical point $x = 1$ and at the end points of the interval $[-3, 1]$.

At $x = 1$, $f(1) = (1 - 1)^2 + 3 = 3$

At $x = -3$,

$f(-3) = (-3 - 1)^2 + 3 = 19$

Thus, absolute maximum value is 19 at $x = -3$ and absolute minimum value is 3 at $x = 1$.

28 (*c*) The profit function is given as $p(x) = 41 - 72x - 18x^2$.

On differentiating w.r.t. x, we get

$$p'(x) = -72 - 36x$$

$$= -36(2 + x)$$

and again on differentiating w.r.t. x,

$$p''(x) = -36$$

For maxima or minima, put

$$p'(x) = 0$$

$$\therefore \quad -36(2 + x) = 0$$

$$\Rightarrow \quad x + 2 = 0$$

$$\Rightarrow \quad x = -2$$

At $x = -2$, $p''(-2) = -36 < 0$

$\therefore$ $x = -2$ is a point of maxima.

Maximum profit,

$$p(-2) = 41 - 72(-2) - 18(-2)^2$$

$$= 41 + 144 - 72 = 113$$

29 (*a*) Let $f(x) = \sin 2x$

$$\Rightarrow \quad f'(x) = 2\cos 2x$$

For maxima or minima, put

$$f'(x) = 0$$

$$\therefore \quad 2\cos 2x = 0$$

$$\Rightarrow \quad \cos 2x = 0$$

$$\Rightarrow \quad 2x = \frac{\pi}{2}, \frac{3\pi}{2}, \frac{5\pi}{2}, \frac{7\pi}{2}$$

$$\Rightarrow \quad x = \frac{\pi}{4}, \frac{3\pi}{4}, \frac{5\pi}{4}, \frac{7\pi}{4}$$

Thus, we evaluate the values of f at critical points $x=\frac{\pi}{4},\frac{3\pi}{4},\frac{5\pi}{4},\frac{7\pi}{4}$ and at the end points of the interval $[0, 2\pi]$.

At $x=0$, $f(0)=\sin(2\times 0)=0$

At $x=2\pi$, $f(2\pi)=\sin(2\times 2\pi)=0$

At $x=\frac{\pi}{4}$,

$$f\left(\frac{\pi}{4}\right)=\sin\left(2\times\frac{\pi}{4}\right)=\sin\frac{\pi}{2}=1$$

At $x=\frac{3\pi}{4}$,

$$f\left(\frac{3\pi}{4}\right)=\sin\left(2\times\frac{3\pi}{4}\right)=\sin\frac{3\pi}{2}=\sin\left(\pi+\frac{\pi}{2}\right)=-\sin\frac{\pi}{2}=-1$$

At $x=\frac{5\pi}{4}$,

$$f\left(\frac{5\pi}{4}\right)=\sin\left(2\times\frac{5\pi}{4}\right)=\sin\frac{5\pi}{2}=\sin\left(2\pi+\frac{\pi}{2}\right)=\sin\frac{\pi}{2}=1$$

At $x=\frac{7\pi}{4}$,

$$f\left(\frac{7\pi}{4}\right)=\sin\left(2\times\frac{7\pi}{4}\right)=\sin\frac{7\pi}{2}=\sin\left(2\pi+\frac{3\pi}{2}\right)=\sin\frac{3\pi}{2}=-1$$

Hence, we can conclude that absolute maximum value of f on $[0, 2\pi]$ is 1 occurring at $x=\frac{\pi}{4}$ and $x=\frac{5\pi}{4}$.

30 (c)

(a) Given function is

$$f(x)=x^3-6x^2+9x+15$$

$\Rightarrow f'(x)=3x^2-12x+9$

and $f''(x)=6x-12$

For maxima or minima, put

$$f'(x)=0$$

$\Rightarrow 3x^2-12x+9=0$

$\Rightarrow 3(x^2-4x+3)=0$

$\Rightarrow 3(x^2-3x-x+3)=0$

$\Rightarrow 3[x(x-3)-1(x-3)]=0$

$\Rightarrow 3(x-1)(x-3)=0$

$\Rightarrow x=1$ or $x=3$

At $x=1$,

$f''(1)=6\times 1-12=6-12=-6<0$

$\therefore x=1$ is a point of maxima.

Maximum value

$=f(1)=(1)^3-6(1)^2+9(1)+15$

$=1-6+9+15=19$

At $x=3$, $f''(3)=6\times 3-12=18-12=6>0$

$\therefore x=3$ is a point of minima.

$\therefore$ Minimum value

$=f(3)=3^3-6\times 3^2+9\times 3+15$

$=27-54+27+15=15$

(b) Given function is $g(x)=\frac{x}{2}+\frac{2}{x}$, $x>0$

$\Rightarrow g'(x)=\frac{1}{2}+2\left(-\frac{1}{x^2}\right)=\frac{1}{2}-\frac{2}{x^2}$

and $g''(x)=-2(-2)x^{-3}=\frac{4}{x^3}$

For maxima or minima, put $g'(x)=0$.

$\therefore \frac{1}{2}-\frac{2}{x^2}=0$

$\Rightarrow \frac{1}{2}=\frac{2}{x^2}\Rightarrow x^2=4$

$\Rightarrow x=2$ $[\because x>0 \text{ (given)}]$

At $x=2$,

$g''(2)=\frac{4}{2^3}=\frac{4}{8}=\frac{1}{2}>0$

$\therefore x=2$ is a point of minima.

Minimum value,

$g(2)=\frac{2}{2}+\frac{2}{2}=1+1=2$

(c) Given function is $g(x)=\frac{1}{x^2+2}$.

Now, $g(x)=(x^2+2)^{-1}$

$\Rightarrow g'(x)=-1(x^2+2)^{-1-1}\times 2x=\frac{-2x}{(x^2+2)^2}$

$$g''(x)=\frac{(x^2+2)^2\cdot(-2)-(-2x)\cdot 2(x^2+2)\cdot 2x}{(x^2+2)^4}$$

$$=\frac{-2(x^2+2)^2+8x^2(x^2+2)}{(x^2+2)^4}$$

$$=\frac{(x^2+2)[-2x^2-4+8x^2]}{(x^2+2)^4}$$

$$=\frac{6x^2-4}{(x^2+2)^3}=\frac{2(3x^2-2)}{(x^2+2)^3}$$

For maxima or minima, put

$$g'(x)=0$$

$\therefore \frac{-2x}{(x^2+2)^2}=0$

$\Rightarrow -2x=0$

$\Rightarrow x=0$

At $x=0$, $g''(0)=\frac{2[3(0)^2-2]}{[(0)^2+2]^3}=\frac{-4}{8}=-\frac{1}{2}<0$

$\therefore x=0$ is a point of maxima.

Maximum value,

$g(0)=\frac{1}{(0)^2+2}=\frac{1}{2}$

(d) Given function is $f(x)=x\sqrt{1-x}$

$\Rightarrow f'(x)=\frac{x(-1)}{2\sqrt{1-x}}+\sqrt{1-x}$

$=\frac{-x+2(1-x)}{2\sqrt{1-x}}=\frac{2-3x}{2\sqrt{1-x}}$

$$f''(x)=\frac{1}{2}\left[\frac{\sqrt{1-x}(-3)-(2-3x)\left(\frac{-1}{2\sqrt{1-x}}\right)}{(1-x)}\right]$$

$$=\frac{\sqrt{1-x}(-3)-(2-3x)\left(\frac{-1}{2\sqrt{1-x}}\right)}{2(1-x)}$$

$$=\frac{-6(1-x)+(2-3x)}{4(1-x)^{3/2}}$$

$$=\frac{3x-4}{4(1-x)^{3/2}}$$

For maxima or minima, put

$$f'(x)=0$$

$\therefore \frac{2-3x}{2\sqrt{1-x}}=0$

$\Rightarrow 2-3x=0$

$\Rightarrow x=\frac{2}{3}$

At $x = \frac{2}{3}$, $f''\left(\frac{2}{3}\right) = \frac{3\left(\frac{2}{3}\right) - 4}{4\left(1 - \frac{2}{3}\right)^{3/2}}$

$= \frac{2-4}{4\left(\frac{1}{3}\right)^{3/2}} = \frac{-1}{2\left(\frac{1}{3}\right)^{3/2}} < 0$

$\therefore$ $x = \frac{2}{3}$ is a point of maxima.

Maximum value

$= f\left(\frac{2}{3}\right) = \frac{2}{3}\sqrt{1 - \frac{2}{3}} = \frac{2}{3} \times \sqrt{\frac{1}{3}}$

$= \frac{2}{3\sqrt{3}} = \frac{2\sqrt{3}}{9}$

31 (*b*) Let $f(x) = \sin x + \cos x$

$\Rightarrow$ $f'(x) = \cos x - \sin x$

and $f''(x) = -\sin x - \cos x$
$= -(\sin x + \cos x)$

For maxima or minima, put

$f'(x) = 0$

$\therefore$ $\cos x - \sin x = 0$

$\Rightarrow$ $\sin x = \cos x$

$\Rightarrow$ $\frac{\sin x}{\cos x} = 1$

$\Rightarrow$ $\tan x = 1$

$\Rightarrow$ $x = \frac{\pi}{4}, \frac{5\pi}{4}, \ldots,$

Now, $f''(x)$ will be negative when $(\sin x + \cos x)$ is positive i.e. when $\sin x$ and $\cos x$ are both positive. Also, we know that $\sin x$ and $\cos x$ both are positive in the first quadrant.

Then, $f''(x)$ will be negative when $x \in \left(0, \frac{\pi}{2}\right)$.

Thus, we consider $x = \frac{\pi}{4}$.

$f''\left(\frac{\pi}{4}\right) = -\left(\sin\frac{\pi}{4} + \cos\frac{\pi}{4}\right)$

$= -\left(\frac{1}{\sqrt{2}} + \frac{1}{\sqrt{2}}\right)$

$= -\frac{2}{\sqrt{2}} = -\sqrt{2} < 0$

By second derivative test, f will be maximum at $x = \frac{\pi}{4}$ and the maximum value of f is

$f\left(\frac{\pi}{4}\right) = \sin\frac{\pi}{4} + \cos\frac{\pi}{4} = \frac{1}{\sqrt{2}} + \frac{1}{\sqrt{2}}$

$= \frac{2}{\sqrt{2}} = \sqrt{2}$

32 (*d*) Let $f(x) = x^4 - 62x^2 + ax + 9$

$\Rightarrow$ $f'(x) = 4x^3 - 124x + a$

It is given that function f attains its maximum value on the interval $[0, 2]$ at $x = 1$.

$\therefore$ $f'(1) = 0$

$\Rightarrow$ $4 \times 1^3 - 124 \times 1 + a = 0$

$\Rightarrow$ $4 - 124 + a = 0$

$\Rightarrow$ $a = 120$

Hence, the value of a is 120.

33 (*b*) Let $f(x) = x + \sin 2x$,

$f'(x) = 1 + 2\cos 2x$

For maxima or minima, put

$f'(x) = 0$

$\therefore$ $1 + 2\cos 2x = 0$

$\Rightarrow$ $\cos 2x = -\frac{1}{2}$

$\Rightarrow$ $\cos 2x = -\cos\frac{\pi}{3} = \cos\frac{2\pi}{3}$

$\Rightarrow$ $\cos 2x = \cos\left(\pi - \frac{\pi}{3}\right)$,

$\cos\left(\pi + \frac{\pi}{3}\right), \cos\left(3\pi - \frac{\pi}{3}\right),$

$\cos\left(3\pi + \frac{\pi}{3}\right)$

[$\because$ we know that $\cos x$ is negative in second and third quadrant]

$\Rightarrow$ $2x = \frac{2\pi}{3}, \frac{4\pi}{3}, \frac{8\pi}{3}, \frac{10\pi}{3}$

$\Rightarrow$ $x = \frac{\pi}{3}, \frac{2\pi}{3}, \frac{4\pi}{3}, \frac{5\pi}{3} \in [0, 2\pi]$

Then, we evaluate the value of f at critical points

$x = \frac{\pi}{3}, \frac{2\pi}{3}, \frac{4\pi}{3}, \frac{5\pi}{3}$

and at the end points of the interval $[0, 2\pi]$.

At $x = 0$, $f(0) = 0 + \sin 0 = 0$

At $x = \frac{\pi}{3}$,

$f\left(\frac{\pi}{3}\right) = \frac{\pi}{3} + \sin\frac{2\pi}{3} = \frac{\pi}{3} + \sin\frac{\pi}{3}$

$= \frac{\pi}{3} + \frac{\sqrt{3}}{2}$

At $x = \frac{2\pi}{3}$,

$f\left(\frac{2\pi}{3}\right) = \frac{2\pi}{3} + \sin\frac{4\pi}{3} = \frac{2\pi}{3} - \sin\frac{\pi}{3}$

$= \frac{2\pi}{3} - \frac{\sqrt{3}}{2}$

At $x = \frac{4\pi}{3}$,

$f\left(\frac{4\pi}{3}\right) = \frac{4\pi}{3} + \sin\frac{8\pi}{3} = \frac{4\pi}{3} + \sin\frac{2\pi}{3}$

$= \frac{4\pi}{3} + \frac{\sqrt{3}}{2}$

At $x = \frac{5\pi}{3}$,

$f\left(\frac{5\pi}{3}\right) = \frac{5\pi}{3} + \sin\frac{10\pi}{3} = \frac{5\pi}{3} - \sin\frac{2\pi}{3}$

$= \frac{5\pi}{3} - \frac{\sqrt{3}}{2}$

At $x = 2\pi$,

$f(2\pi) = 2\pi + \sin 4\pi = 2\pi + 0 = 2\pi$

Thus, maximum value is 2π at $x = 2\pi$ and minimum value is 0 at $x = 0$.

34 (*d*) Let one number be x. Then, the other number is $(24 - x)$.

[$\because$ sum of the two numbers is 24]

Let y denotes the product of the two numbers. Thus, we have

$y = x(24 - x) = 24x - x^2$

On differentiating twice w.r.t. x, we get

$\frac{dy}{dx} = 24 - 2x$

and $\frac{d^2y}{dx^2} = -2$

Now, put $\frac{dy}{dx} = 0$

$\Rightarrow$ $24 - 2x = 0$

$\Rightarrow$ $x = 12$

At $x = 12$, $\frac{d^2y}{dx^2} = -2 < 0$

By second derivative test, $x = 12$ is the point of local maxima of y. Thus, the product of the numbers is maximum when the numbers are 12 and $24 - 12 = 12$.

Hence, the numbers are 12 and 12.

35 (*d*) Let the two numbers be x, y and $P = xy^3$

Given, $x + y = 60 \Rightarrow x = 60 - y$

On putting this value in $P = xy^3$, we get

$$P = (60 - y)y^3$$

$$\Rightarrow \quad P = 60y^3 - y^4$$

On differentiating twice w.r.t. y, we get

$$\frac{dP}{dy} = 180y^2 - 4y^3$$

and $$\frac{d^2P}{dy^2} = 360y - 12y^2$$

For maxima, we must have $\frac{dP}{dy} = 0$.

$\therefore \quad 180y^2 - 4y^3 = 0$

$\Rightarrow \quad 4y^2(45 - y) = 0 \Rightarrow y = 0, 45$

But $y \neq 0$, so $y = 45$

At $y = 45$,

$$\left(\frac{d^2P}{dy^2}\right)_{y=45} = 360 \times 45 - 12 \times (45)^2$$

$$= 16200 - 24300 = -8100 < 0$$

$\Rightarrow P$ has a local maxima at $y = 45$.

By second derivative test, $y = 45$ is a point of local maxima of P. Thus, function xy^3 is maximum when $y = 45$ and $x = 60 - 45 = 15$.

Hence, the required numbers are 15 and 45.

36 (*b*) Let the side of the square to be cut off be x cm $(0 < x < 9)$. Then, the length and the breadth of the box will be $(18 - 2x)$ cm each and the height of the box is x cm.

Let V be the volume of the open box formed by folding up the flaps. Then,

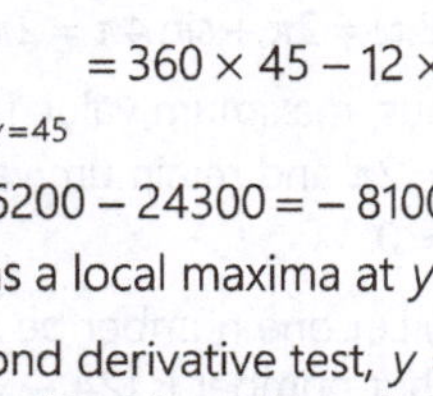

$$V = x(18 - 2x)(18 - 2x)$$

$$= 4x(9 - x)^2 = 4x(81 + x^2 - 18x)$$

$$= 4(x^3 - 18x^2 + 81x)$$

On differentiating twice w.r.t. x, we get

$$\frac{dV}{dx} = 4(3x^2 - 36x + 81)$$

$$= 12(x^2 - 12x + 27)$$

and $$\frac{d^2V}{dx^2} = 12(2x - 12) = 24(x - 6)$$

For maxima, put $\frac{dV}{dx} = 0$.

$\Rightarrow 12(x^2 - 12x + 27) = 0$

$\Rightarrow \quad x^2 - 12x + 27 = 0$

$\Rightarrow \quad (x - 3)(x - 9) = 0 \Rightarrow x = 3, 9$

But $x = 9$ is not possible.

$\therefore \quad 2x = 2 \times 9 = 18$

Which is equal to side of square piece.

At $x = 3$,

$$\left(\frac{d^2V}{dx^2}\right)_{x=3} = 24(3 - 6) = -72 < 0$$

$\therefore$ By second derivative test, $x = 3$ is the point of maxima.

Hence, if we cut off the side 3 cm from each corner of the square tin and make a box from the remaining sheet, then the volume of the box obtained is the largest possible.

37 (*d*) Let the side of the square to be cut off be x cm.

Then, the height of the box is x cm, the length is $45 - 2x$ and the breadth is $24 - 2x$.

Let V be the volume of the box.

Then, $V = x(24 - 2x)(45 - 2x)$

$\Rightarrow \quad V = x(4x^2 - 138x + 1080)$

$$= 4x^3 - 138x^2 + 1080x$$

On differentiating twice w.r.t. x, we get

$$\frac{dV}{dx} = 12x^2 - 276x + 1080$$

and $$\frac{d^2V}{dx^2} = 24x - 276$$

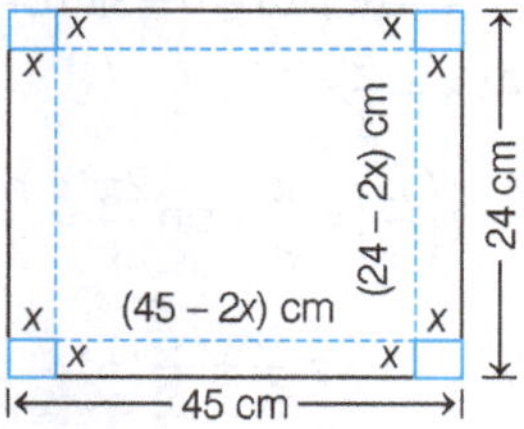

For maxima, put $\frac{dV}{dx} = 0$.

$\therefore 12x^2 - 276x + 1080 = 0$

$\Rightarrow \quad x^2 - 23x + 90 = 0$

$\Rightarrow \quad (x - 18)(x - 5) = 0$

$\Rightarrow \quad x = 5, 18$

It is not possible to cutoff a square of side 18 cm from each corner of the rectangular sheet. Thus, x cannot be equal to 18.

At $x = 5$, $$\left(\frac{d^2V}{dx^2}\right)_{x=5} = 24 \times 5 - 276$$

$$= 120 - 276 = -156 < 0$$

By second derivative test, $x = 5$ is the point of maxima.

Hence, the side of the square to be cut-off to make the volume of the box maximum possible is 5 cm.

38 (*c*) Let *EBCD* be a rectangle inscribed in the given circle of radius r having centre at O.

Let $\angle CEB = \theta$. Then, $EC = 2r$, $EB = 2r\cos\theta$ and $BC = 2r\sin\theta$

Let A be the area of rectangle *BCDE*.

Then, $A = EB \times BC = 4r^2 \sin\theta\cos\theta$

$$= 2r^2 \sin 2\theta$$

Thus, $A = 2r^2 \sin 2\theta$

where, r is constant.

$$\therefore \quad \frac{dA}{d\theta} = 4r^2 \cos 2\theta$$

$$\frac{d^2A}{d\theta^2} = -8r^2 \sin 2\theta$$

Now, put $\frac{dA}{d\theta} = 0$

$\Rightarrow \quad 4r^2 \cos 2\theta = 0 \Rightarrow \cos 2\theta = 0$

$\Rightarrow \quad 2\theta = \frac{\pi}{2}$ i.e. $\theta = \frac{\pi}{4}$

At $\theta = \frac{\pi}{4}$,

$$\left(\frac{d^2A}{d\theta^2}\right)_{\theta=\frac{\pi}{4}} = -8r^2 \sin\frac{\pi}{2} = -8r^2 < 0$$

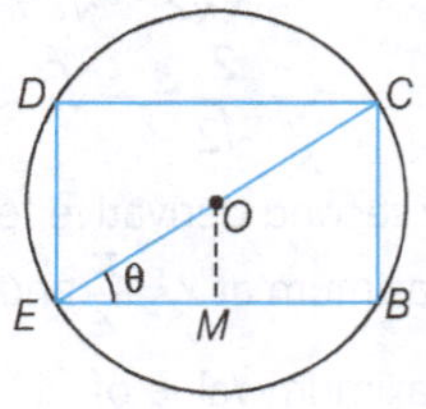

$\therefore\ \theta = \frac{\pi}{4}$ is a point of maxima.

Thus, area is maximum when $\theta = \frac{\pi}{4}$.

In this case, $EB = 2r\cos\frac{\pi}{4} = r\sqrt{2}$

and $BC = 2r\sin\frac{\pi}{4} = r\sqrt{2}$

Thus, $EB = BC$ and therefore, $BCDE$ is a square.

39 (*a*) Let r be the radius of base and h be the height of the cylindrical can. Let its volume be V and S its total surface area.

Then, $V = 100\text{ cm}^3$

$\Rightarrow \pi r^2 h = 100$ [given]

$\Rightarrow h = \frac{100}{\pi r^2}$ ...(i)

Also, $S = 2\pi r^2 + 2\pi rh$ ...(ii)

In Eq. (ii), there are two independent variables r and h. We eliminate h, on putting the value of h in Eq. (ii) from Eq. (i), we get

$$S = 2\pi r^2 + 2\pi r\left(\frac{100}{\pi r^2}\right)$$

$$= 2\pi r^2 + \frac{200}{r} \quad ...(iii)$$

On differentiating Eq. (iii) w.r.t. r, we get

$$\frac{dS}{dr} = 4\pi r - \frac{200}{r^2} \quad ...(iv)$$

Now, for maxima or minima put

$$\frac{dS}{dr} = 0$$

$$\therefore\ 4\pi r = \frac{200}{r^2}$$

$$\Rightarrow r^3 = \frac{200}{4\pi} \Rightarrow r = \left(\frac{50}{\pi}\right)^{1/3}$$

On differentiating Eq. (iv) w.r.t. r, we get

$$\frac{d^2S}{dr^2} = 4\pi + \frac{400}{r^3}$$

At $r = \left(\frac{50}{\pi}\right)^{1/3}$,

$$\frac{d^2S}{dr^2} = \frac{400}{\left(\frac{50}{\pi}\right)} + 4\pi$$

$$= \frac{400}{50} \times \pi + 4\pi$$

$$= 8\pi + 4\pi = 12\pi > 0$$

By second derivative test, the surface area is minimum when the radius of the cylinder is $\left(\frac{50}{\pi}\right)^{1/3}$.

Hence, S is minimum when $r = \left(\frac{50}{\pi}\right)^{1/3}$.

On putting the value of r in Eq. (i), we get

$$h = \frac{100}{\pi\left(\frac{50}{\pi}\right)^{2/3}}$$

$$= 2\left(\frac{50}{\pi}\right)\left(\frac{50}{\pi}\right)^{-2/3} = 2\left(\frac{50}{\pi}\right)^{1/3}\text{ cm}$$

40 (*c*) Let the length of the piece bent into the shape of a circle be x (units) so that the length of the other piece bent into the shape of a square is $(28 - x)$ units.

Now, radius of the circle

$$= \frac{\text{Circumference}}{2\pi} = \frac{x}{2\pi}$$

Area of the circle

$$= \pi\,(\text{radius})^2 = \pi\left(\frac{x}{2\pi}\right)^2 = \frac{x^2}{4\pi}$$

Also, the length of each side of the square

$$= \frac{\text{Perimeter}}{4} = \frac{28 - x}{4}$$

Area of the square

$$= (\text{side})^2 = \left(\frac{28 - x}{4}\right)^2$$

$$= \frac{(28 - x)^2}{16}$$

Let $f(x)$ be the sum of the areas of the two figures. Then,

$$f(x) = \frac{x^2}{4\pi} + \frac{(28 - x)^2}{16} \quad ...(i)$$

On differentiating Eq. (i) twice w.r.t. x, we get

$$f'(x) = \frac{2x}{4\pi} + \frac{2\,(28 - x)(-1)}{16}$$

$$= \frac{x}{2\pi} - \frac{28 - x}{8}$$

and $f''(x) = \frac{1}{2\pi} - \frac{(-1)}{8} = \frac{1}{2\pi} + \frac{1}{8}$

Now, put $f'(x) = 0$

$$\Rightarrow \frac{x}{2\pi} - \frac{28 - x}{8} = 0$$

$$\Rightarrow 4x - \pi\,(28 - x) = 0$$

$$\Rightarrow 4x + \pi x - 28\pi = 0$$

$$\Rightarrow x\,(4 + \pi) = 28\pi$$

$$\Rightarrow x = \frac{28\pi}{4 + \pi}$$

and for this value of x,

$$f''(x) = \frac{1}{2\pi} + \frac{1}{8} > 0$$

$\therefore f(x)$ has a local minima at

$$x = \frac{28\pi}{4 + \pi}$$

Since, f is continuous in (0, 28) and has only one extreme point at $\frac{28\pi}{4 + \pi} \in (0, 28)$.

Therefore, $f(x)$ is absolutely minimum for $x = \frac{28\pi}{4 + \pi}$.

Hence, the length of circular piece

$$= \frac{28\pi}{4 + \pi}\text{ m}$$

and square piece

$$= 28 - \frac{28\pi}{4 + \pi} = \frac{112}{4 + \pi}\text{ m}.$$

41 (*c*) Let r be the radius of the base, h be the height, V be the volume and S be the curved surface area of the cone. Then,

$$V = \frac{1}{3}\pi r^2 h$$

$$\Rightarrow 3V = \pi r^2 h$$

$$\Rightarrow 9V^2 = \pi^2 r^4 h^2$$

$$\Rightarrow h^2 = \frac{9V^2}{\pi^2 r^4} \quad ...(i)$$

and $S = \pi rl$

$$\Rightarrow S = \pi r\sqrt{r^2 + h^2}$$

$[\because l = \sqrt{h^2 + r^2}]$

$$\Rightarrow S^2 = \pi^2 r^2 (r^2 + h^2)$$

$$= \pi^2 r^2\left(\frac{9V^2}{\pi^2 r^4} + r^2\right)$$

[using Eq. (i)]

$\Rightarrow \quad S^2 = \dfrac{9V^2}{r^2} + \pi^2 r^4$ ...(ii)

Now, $\dfrac{d}{dr}(S^2) = -\dfrac{18V^2}{r^3} + 4\pi^2 r^3$ ...(iii)

For minima, put $\dfrac{d}{dr}(S^2) = 0$

$\Rightarrow -\dfrac{18V^2}{r^3} + 4\pi^2 r^3 = 0$

$\Rightarrow \quad 18V^2 = 4\pi^2 r^6$

$\Rightarrow \quad 9V^2 = 2\pi^2 r^6$ ...(iv)

Again, on differentiating Eq. (iii) w.r.t. r, we get

$$\frac{d^2}{dr^2}(S^2) = \frac{54V^2}{r^4} + 12\pi^2 r^2$$

At $9V^2 = 2\pi^2 r^6$,

$$\frac{d^2}{dr^2}(S^2) = \frac{54}{r^4}\left(\frac{2\pi^2 r^6}{9}\right) + 12\pi^2 r^2$$

$$= \frac{12\pi^2 r^6}{r^4} + 12\pi^2 r^2$$

$$= 24\pi^2 r^2 > 0$$

Hence, S^2 and therefore S is minimum when

$$9V^2 = 2\pi^2 r^6$$

On putting $9V^2 = 2\pi^2 r^6$ in Eq. (i), we get

$$2\pi^2 r^6 = \pi^2 r^4 h^2$$

$\Rightarrow \quad 2r^2 = h^2$

$\Rightarrow \quad h = \sqrt{2}r$

Hence, altitude of right circular cone is $\sqrt{2}$ times the radius of the base.

42 (*a*) Let d be the distance of the point (x, y) on $x^2 = 2y$ from the point (0, 5), then

$$d = \sqrt{(x-0)^2 + (y-5)^2}$$

$= \sqrt{x^2 + (y-5)^2}$ ...(i)

$= \sqrt{2y + (y-5)^2}$ [putting $x^2 = 2y$]

$$= \sqrt{y^2 - 8y + 25}$$

$$= \sqrt{y^2 - 8y + 4^2 + 9}$$

$$= \sqrt{(y-4)^2 + 9}$$

d is least when $(y-4)^2 = 0$ i.e. when $y = 4$

When $y = 4$, then $x^2 = 2 \times 4$

$\Rightarrow x = \pm\sqrt{8} = \pm 2\sqrt{2}$

$\therefore$ The points $(2\sqrt{2}, 4)$ and $(-2\sqrt{2}, 4)$ on the given curve are nearest to the point (0, 5). So, (a) is the correct option.

43 (*d*) Let $y = \dfrac{1 - x + x^2}{1 + x + x^2}$

On differentiating w.r.t. x, we get

$$\frac{dy}{dx} = \frac{(1 + x + x^2)(-1 + 2x) - (1 - x + x^2)(1 + 2x)}{(1 + x + x^2)^2}$$

$$= \frac{-1 + 2x - x + 2x^2 - x^2 + 2x^3 - 1 - 2x + x + 2x^2 - x^2 - 2x^3}{(1 + x + x^2)^2}$$

$$= \frac{-2 + 4x^2 - 2x^2}{(1 + x + x^2)^2} = \frac{2x^2 - 2}{(1 + x + x^2)^2} = \frac{2(x^2 - 1)}{(1 + x + x^2)^2}$$

Put $\dfrac{dy}{dx} = 0$

$\Rightarrow \quad x^2 = 1 \Rightarrow x = \pm 1$

Now, $\dfrac{d^2y}{dx^2}$

$$= \frac{2[(1 + x + x^2)^2(2x) - (x^2 - 1)(2)(1 + x + x^2)(1 + 2x)]}{(1 + x + x^2)^4}$$

$$= \frac{4(1 + x + x^2)[(1 + x + x^2)x - (x^2 - 1)(1 + 2x)]}{(1 + x + x^2)^4}$$

$$= \frac{4[x + x^2 + x^3 - x^2 - 2x^3 + 1 + 2x]}{(1 + x + x^2)^3} = \frac{4(1 + 3x - x^3)}{(1 + x + x^2)^3}$$

At $x = 1$, $\left(\dfrac{d^2y}{dx^2}\right)_{x=1} = \dfrac{4[1 + 3(1) - 1^3]}{(1 + 1 + 1^2)^3} = \dfrac{4(3)}{3^3} = \dfrac{4}{9} > 0$

At $x = -1$, $\left(\dfrac{d^2y}{dx^2}\right)_{x=-1} = \dfrac{4[1 + 3(-1) - (-1)^3]}{[1 + (-1) + (-1)^2]^3} = \dfrac{4(1 - 3 + 1)}{(1 - 1 + 1)^3}$

$$= 4(-1) = -4 < 0$$

$\therefore$ By second derivative test, f is minimum at $x = 1$ and the minimum value is given by $y = \dfrac{1 - 1 + 1}{1 + 1 + 1} = \dfrac{1}{3}$

44 (*c*) Let $f(x) = [x(x-1) + 1]^{1/3}$, $0 \le x \le 1 = (x^2 - x + 1)^{1/3}$

On differentiating w.r.t. x, we get

$$f'(x) = \frac{1}{3}(x^2 - x + 1)^{\frac{1}{3} - 1}(2x - 1) = \frac{1(2x-1)}{3(x^2 - x + 1)^{2/3}}$$

Now, put $f'(x) = 0 \Rightarrow 2x - 1 = 0$

$\Rightarrow \quad x = \dfrac{1}{2} \in [0, 1].$

So, $x = \dfrac{1}{2}$ is a critical point.

Now, we evaluate the value of f at critical point $x = \dfrac{1}{2}$ and at the end points of the interval [0, 1].

At $x = 0$, $f(0) = (0 - 0 + 1)^{1/3} = 1$

At $x=1$, $f(1)=(1-1+1)^{1/3}=1$

At $x=\frac{1}{2}$,

$$f\left(\frac{1}{2}\right)=\left(\frac{1}{4}-\frac{1}{2}+1\right)^{1/3}=\left(\frac{3}{4}\right)^{1/3}$$

$\therefore$ Maximum value of $f(x)$ is 1 at $x=0,1$.

Hence, (c) is the correct option.

45 (c) Here, $f(x)=e^{(x^4-x^3+x^2)}$

Also, $x^4-x^3+x^2=x^2(x^2-x+1)$

$$=x^2\left[\left(x-\frac{1}{2}\right)^2+\frac{3}{4}\right]$$

$\therefore$ $f(x)=e^{x^4-x^3+x^2}$ will attain minimum at $x=0$

$\Rightarrow$ Minimum of $f(x)=1$

46 (a) Let $y=a\sec\theta-b\tan\theta$

$$\Rightarrow \frac{dy}{d\theta}=a\sec\theta\tan\theta-b\sec^2\theta$$

$$\Rightarrow \frac{dy}{d\theta}=\sec^2\theta(a\sin\theta-b)$$

Put $\frac{dy}{d\theta}=0$

$\Rightarrow$ $\sec^2\theta(a\sin\theta-b)=0$

$\Rightarrow$ $\sin\theta=\frac{b}{a}$ [$\because \sec\theta\neq 0$]

Now, $\frac{d^2y}{d\theta^2}>0$, at $\sin\theta=\frac{b}{a}$

$\therefore$ Minimum value is

$$y=a.\frac{a}{\sqrt{a^2-b^2}}-b.\frac{b}{\sqrt{a^2-b^2}}$$

$$=\sqrt{a^2-b^2}$$

47 (b) $f(x)=e^x\sin x$

$f'(x)=e^x\cos x+e^x\sin x$

$f''(x)=-e^x\sin x+\cos xe^x+e^x\cos x+e^x\sin x$

$=2e^x\cos x$

For maximum slope,

$f''(x)=0$

$\Rightarrow$ $2e^x\cos x=0$

$\Rightarrow$ $\cos x=0$

$\Rightarrow$ $x=\frac{\pi}{2},\frac{3\pi}{2},\forall x\in[0,2\pi]$

$f'''(x)=2[-e^x\sin x+e^x\cos x]$

at $x=\frac{\pi}{2}, f'''(x)<0$

and at $x=\frac{3\pi}{2}$ $f'''(x)>0$

$\therefore$ Slope is maximum at $x=\frac{\pi}{2}$

48 (c) $f(x)=4x^3-18x^2+27x-7$

$f'(x)=12x^2-36x+27$

$=3(4x^2-12x+9)$

$=3(2x-3)^2$

$f'(x)=0$

$\Rightarrow$ $x=\frac{3}{2}$ [critical point]

Since, $f'(x)>0$ for all $x<\frac{3}{2}$ and for all $x>\frac{3}{2}$

Hence, $x=\frac{3}{2}$ is a point of inflexion i.e. neither a point of maxima nor a point of minima.

$x=\frac{3}{2}$ is the only critical point and f has neither maxima nor minima.

49 (d) Given,

$f(x)=x^3+ax^2+bx+c, a^2\leq 3b$.

On differentiating w.r.t. x, we get

$f'(x)=3x^2+2ax+b$

Put $f'(x)=0$

$\Rightarrow$ $3x^2+2ax+b=0$

$$\Rightarrow x=\frac{-2a\pm\sqrt{4a^2-12b}}{2\times 3}$$

$$=\frac{-2a\pm 2\sqrt{a^2-3b}}{6}$$

Since, $a^2\leq 3b$,

$\therefore$ x has an imaginary value.

Hence, no extreme value of x exist.

50 (c) Given, $y=\frac{\sin(x+a)}{\sin(x+b)}$

$$\Rightarrow \frac{dy}{dx}=\frac{\sin(x+b)\cos(x+a)-\sin(x+a)\cos(x+b)}{\sin^2(x+b)}$$

$$\Rightarrow \frac{dy}{dx}=\frac{\sin(b-a)}{\sin^2(x+b)}$$

For maxima or minima, put $\frac{dy}{dx}=0$

$\sin(b-a)=0$

but $b-a\neq 0$ [$\because b\neq a$]

It means no value of x i.e. y have neither maxima nor minima.

51 (b) $f'(x)=-3x^3-24x^2-45x$

$=-3x(x^2+8x+15)$

$=-3x(x+5)(x+3)$

$f'(x)=0$

$\Rightarrow$ $x=-5, x=-3$ and $x=0$

$f''(x)=-9x^2-48x-45$

$=-3(3x^2+16x+15)$

$f''(0)=-45<0$

Therefore, $x=0$ is a point of local maxima.

$f''(-3)=18>0$

Therefore, $x=-3$ is a point of local minima.

$f''(-5)=-30<0$

Therefore $x=-5$ is a point of local maxima.

52 (a) Given, $f(x)=\sin x(1+\cos x)$

$$\Rightarrow f(x)=\sin x+\frac{1}{2}\sin 2x$$

On differentiating w.r.t. x, we get

$f'(x)=\cos x+\cos 2x$

Put $f'(x)=0$

$\cos x+\cos 2x=0$

$$\Rightarrow 2\cos\left(\frac{3x}{2}\right)\cos\left(\frac{x}{2}\right)=0$$

$$\Rightarrow \cos\frac{x}{2}=0, \cos\frac{3x}{2}=0$$

$$\Rightarrow x=\pi, x=\frac{\pi}{3}$$

Now, $f''(x)=-\sin x-2\sin 2x$

At $x=\frac{\pi}{3}$, $f''\left(\frac{\pi}{3}\right)=-\sin\frac{\pi}{3}-2\sin\frac{2\pi}{3}$

$$=-\frac{\sqrt{3}}{2}-\sqrt{3}<0$$

Hence, $x=\frac{\pi}{3}$ is a point of maxima.

$\therefore$ Maximum value of f

$$=f\left(\frac{\pi}{3}\right)=\sin\left(\frac{\pi}{3}\right)\left(1+\cos\frac{\pi}{3}\right)$$

$$=\frac{\sqrt{3}}{2}\left(1+\frac{1}{2}\right)=\frac{3\sqrt{3}}{4}=\frac{3^{3/2}}{4}$$

53 (*d*) Let $y = x + \frac{1}{x} \Rightarrow \frac{dy}{dx} = 1 - \frac{1}{x^2}$

Now, $\frac{dy}{dx} = 0 \Rightarrow x^2 = 1 \Rightarrow x = \pm 1.$

$\frac{d^2y}{dx^2} = +\frac{2}{x^3}$, therefore

$\frac{d^2y}{dx^2}$ (at $x = 1) > 0$

and $\frac{d^2y}{dx^2}$ (at $x = -1) < 0$.

Hence, local maximum value of y is at $x = -1$ and the local maximum value $= -2$.

Local minimum value of y is at $x = 1$ and local minimum value $= 2$.

Therefore, local maximum value -2 is less than local minimum value 2.

54 (*d*) Let $y = \frac{\ln x}{x}$

$$\frac{dy}{dx} = \frac{x.\frac{1}{x} - \ln x.1}{x^2} = \frac{1 - \log x}{x^2}$$

For maxima, put $\frac{dy}{dx} = 0$

$\Rightarrow \frac{1 - \ln x}{x^2} = 0 \Rightarrow x = e$

Now,

$$\frac{d^2y}{dx^2} = \frac{x^2\left(-\frac{1}{x}\right) - (1 - \ln x)\,2x}{(x^2)^2}$$

At $x = e, \frac{d^2y}{dx^2} < 0,$

$\therefore$ The maximum value at $x = e$ is

$$y = \frac{1}{e}$$

55 (*b*) Given, $y = e^{(2x^2 - 2x + 1)\sin^2 x}$

For minimum or maximum, put

$$\frac{dy}{dx} = 0$$

$\therefore e^{(2x^2 - 2x + 1)\sin^2 x}[(4x - 2)\sin^2 x$

$+ 2(2x^2 - 2x + 1)\sin x \cos x] = 0$

$\Rightarrow (4x - 2)\sin^2 x + 2(2x^2 - 2x + 1)$

$\sin x \cos x = 0$

$\Rightarrow 2\sin x\,[(2x - 1)\sin x$

$+ (2x^2 - 2x + 1)\cos x] = 0$

$\Rightarrow \quad \sin x = 0$

$\therefore \quad y$ is minimum for $\sin x = 0$

Thus, minimum value of

$$y = e^{(2x^2 - 2x + 1)(0)} = e^0 = 1$$

Alternate Method

Let $f(x) = e^{(2x^2 - 2x + 1)\sin^2 x}$

Since, $\sin^2 x \geq 0$

and $2x^2 - 2x + 1 \geq \frac{4(2)(1) - 2^2}{4(2)}$

$$\left[\because \text{minima} = \frac{4ac - b^2}{4a}\right]$$

$\Rightarrow \quad 2x^2 - 2x + 1 \geq \frac{1}{2}$

$\therefore \quad (2x^2 - 2x + 1)\sin^2 x \geq 0$

$\Rightarrow \quad e^{(2x^2 - 2x + 1)\sin^2 x} \geq e^0$

$\therefore \quad f(x)_{\min} = e^0 = 1$

56 (*d*) Let x and y be two parts.

Then, $\quad x + y = 12$

Let $\quad P = x^2y^4$

$\Rightarrow \quad \sqrt{P} = xy^2 = L \quad$ [say]

$\Rightarrow \quad L = x(12 - x)^2$

$\Rightarrow \frac{dL}{dx} = (12 - x)^2 - 2x(12 - x)$

For maxima, put $\frac{dL}{dx} = 0$

$\Rightarrow (12 - x)[12 - 3x] = 0$

$\Rightarrow \quad x = 12, x = 4$

At $x = 4$, it is maximum $\quad [\because x \neq 12]$

Hence, it is maximum when the parts are 4, 8.

57 (*b*) Given, $y = a\log x + bx^2 + x$

$\Rightarrow \frac{dy}{dx} = \frac{a}{x} + 2bx + 1$

At $x = -1$ and $x = 2$, y has its extreme.

$\therefore \quad -a - 2b + 1 = 0 \Rightarrow a + 2b = 1 \quad$ ...(i)

and $\quad \frac{a}{2} + 4b + 1 = 0$

$\Rightarrow \quad a + 8b = -2 \quad$ ...(ii)

On solving Eqs. (i) and (ii), we get

$$a = 2, b = -\frac{1}{2}$$

58 (*b*) Let $f(x) = x^3 - px + q$

Then, $f'(x) = 3x^2 - p$

Put $\quad f'(x) = 0 \Rightarrow x = \sqrt{\frac{p}{3}}, -\sqrt{\frac{p}{3}}$

Now, $\quad f''(x) = 6x,$

$\therefore$ At $x = \sqrt{\frac{p}{3}}, f''(x) = 6\sqrt{\frac{p}{3}} > 0,$

minima

and at $x = -\sqrt{\frac{p}{3}}, f''(x) < 0,$

maxima

59 (*c*) Let $ABCD$ be the rectangle of maximum area with sides $AB = 2x$ and $BC = 2y$, where $C(x, y)$ is a point on the ellipse $\frac{x^2}{a^2} + \frac{y^2}{b^2} = 1$ as shown in the figure. The area A of the rectangle is $4xy$ i.e. $A = 4xy$ which gives $A^2 = 16x^2y^2 = s$ (say)

Therefore, $s = 16x^2\left(1 - \frac{x^2}{a^2}\right).b^2$

$$= \frac{16b^2}{a^2}(a^2x^2 - x^4)$$

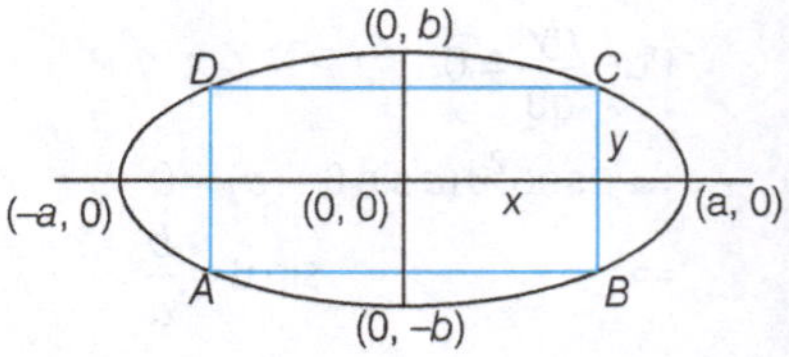

$\Rightarrow \quad \frac{ds}{dx} = \frac{16b^2}{a^2}.[2a^2x - 4x^3]$

Again, $\frac{ds}{dx} = 0 \Rightarrow x = \frac{a}{\sqrt{2}}$

and $\quad y = \frac{b}{\sqrt{2}}$

Now, $\frac{d^2s}{dx^2} = \frac{16b^2}{a^2}[2a^2 - 12x^2]$

At $x = \frac{a}{\sqrt{2}}, \frac{d^2s}{dx^2} = \frac{16b^2}{a^2}[2a^2 - 6a^2]$

$$= \frac{16b^2}{a^2}(-4a^2) < 0$$

Thus at $x = \frac{a}{\sqrt{2}}, y = \frac{b}{\sqrt{2}}$, s is maximum and hence the area A is maximum.

Maximum area

$= 4xy = 4\frac{a}{\sqrt{2}}\frac{b}{\sqrt{2}} = 2ab$ sq units.

60 (*b*) Given,

$$f(x) = 2x^3 - 9ax^2 + 12a^2x + 1$$

attains maximum and minimum at p and q respectively.

$\therefore \quad f'(p) = 0, f'(q) = 0$

$f''(p) < 0$ and $f''(q) > 0$

Since, $f'(p) = 0$ and $f'(q) = 0$

$\Rightarrow \quad 6p^2 - 18ap + 12a^2 = 0$

and $\quad 6q^2 - 18aq + 12a^2 = 0$

$\Rightarrow \quad p^2 - 3ap + 2a^2 = 0$

and $\quad q^2 - 3aq + 2a^2 = 0$

$\Rightarrow \quad p = a, 2a; q = a, 2a \quad$ ...(i)

Now, $f''(p) < 0$

$\Rightarrow \quad 12p - 18a < 0 \Rightarrow p < \dfrac{3}{2}a \quad$ ...(ii)

and $f''(q) > 0 \Rightarrow 12q - 18a > 0$

$\Rightarrow \quad q > \dfrac{3}{2}a \quad$ ...(iii)

From Eqs. (i), (ii) and (iii), we get

$p = a, q = 2a$

Now, $\quad p^2 = q$

$\Rightarrow \quad a^2 = 2a \Rightarrow a = 0, 2$

But for $a = 0$, $f(x) = 2x^3 + 1$ which does not attains a maximum or minimum for any value of x.

Hence, $a = 2$

61 (*a*) Let $y = \sin^3 x + \cos^3 x$

$\dfrac{dy}{dx} = 3\sin^2 x \cos x - 3\cos^2 x \sin x$

$= 3 \sin x \cos x (\sin x - \cos x)$

Put $\dfrac{dy}{dx} = 0$

$\sin x \cos x (\sin x - \cos x) = 0$

$\Rightarrow x = 0, \dfrac{\pi}{2}$ or $\dfrac{\pi}{4}$

Now, y has its maximum value at $x = 0$ or $\dfrac{\pi}{2}$ and $y_{max} = 1$.

62 (*b*) $\quad f(x) = \sin 2x - x$

$\Rightarrow \quad f'(x) = 2\cos 2x - 1$

Therefore,

$f'(x) = 0 \Rightarrow \cos 2x = \dfrac{1}{2} \Rightarrow 2x$ is

$\Rightarrow \dfrac{\pi}{3}$ or $-\dfrac{\pi}{3} \Rightarrow x = -\dfrac{\pi}{6}$ or $\dfrac{\pi}{6}$

$\Rightarrow f\left(-\dfrac{\pi}{2}\right) = \sin(-\pi) + \dfrac{\pi}{2} = \dfrac{\pi}{2}$

$\Rightarrow f\left(-\dfrac{\pi}{6}\right) = \sin\left(-\dfrac{2\pi}{6}\right) + \dfrac{\pi}{6}$

$= -\dfrac{\sqrt{3}}{2} + \dfrac{\pi}{6}$

$\Rightarrow f\left(\dfrac{\pi}{6}\right) = \sin\left(\dfrac{2\pi}{6}\right) - \dfrac{\pi}{6} = \dfrac{\sqrt{3}}{2} - \dfrac{\pi}{6}$

$\Rightarrow f\left(\dfrac{\pi}{2}\right) = \sin(\pi) - \dfrac{\pi}{2} = -\dfrac{\pi}{2}$

Clearly, $\dfrac{\pi}{2}$ is the greatest value and $-\dfrac{\pi}{2}$ is the least.

Therefore, difference $= \dfrac{\pi}{2} + \dfrac{\pi}{2} = \pi$

63 (*b*) Given, $f(x) = x^{25}(1-x)^{75}$

$\Rightarrow f'(x) = 25x^{24}(1-x)^{75} - 75x^{25}(1-x)^{74}$

$= 25x^{24}(1-x)^{74}(1-4x)$

Put, $\quad f'(x) = 0 \Rightarrow x = 0, 1, \dfrac{1}{4}$

If $x < \dfrac{1}{4}$, then

$f'(x) = 25x^{24}(1-x)^{74}(1-4x) > 0$

and if $x > \dfrac{1}{4}$, then

$f'(x) = 25x^{24}(1-x)^{74}(1-4x) < 0$

Thus, $f'(x)$ changes its sign from positive to negative as x passes through $1/4$ from left to right.

Hence, $f(x)$ attains its maximum at $x = 1/4$.

64 (*d*) Given, $y = x^{1/x}$

$$\ln y = \frac{1}{x}\ln x = f(x)$$

$\therefore \quad f'(x) = \dfrac{1 - \ln x}{x^2}$

For maxima and minima,

$$\frac{1 - \ln x}{x^2} = 0$$

$\Rightarrow \quad 1 - \ln x = 0 \quad \Rightarrow \quad x = e$

Now, $\quad f''(x) = \dfrac{-x - 2(1 - \ln x)x}{(x^2)^2}$

At $x = e$,

$f''(x) = \text{negative} < 0$

Hence, at $x = e$

$f(x)$ is maximum and maximum value of $x^{1/x} = e^{1/e}$.

Miscellaneous Exercise

1 (*a*) Let v be the velocity of the car at t s.

Now, $\quad x = t^2\left(2 - \dfrac{t}{3}\right)$

Therefore,

$$v = \frac{dx}{dt} = 4t - t^2 = t(4 - t)$$

Thus, $v = 0$ gives $t = 0$ and $t = 4$.

Now, $v = 0$ at P as well as at Q and at $P, t = 0$. So, at $Q, t = 4$. Thus, the car will reach the point Q after 4 s. Also, the distance travelled in 4 s is given by

$$[x]_{t=4} = 4^2\left(2 - \frac{4}{3}\right) = 16\left(\frac{2}{3}\right) = \frac{32}{3}\text{ m}$$

2 (*d*) Let r, h and α be as in figure.

Then, $\tan\alpha = \dfrac{r}{h}$.

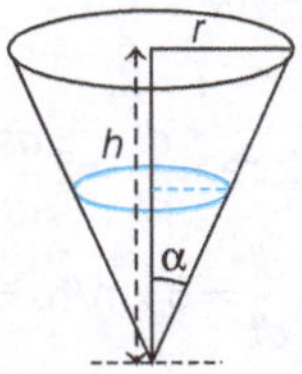

So, $\quad \alpha = \tan^{-1}\left(\dfrac{r}{h}\right)$.

But $\quad \alpha = \tan^{-1}(0.5) \quad$ [given]

$\Rightarrow \quad \dfrac{r}{h} = 0.5 \quad$ or $\quad r = \dfrac{h}{2}$

Let V be the volume of the cone. Then,

$$V = \frac{1}{3}\pi r^2 h = \frac{1}{3}\pi\left(\frac{h}{2}\right)^2 h = \frac{\pi h^3}{12}$$

Therefore, $\dfrac{dV}{dt} = \dfrac{d}{dh}\left(\dfrac{\pi h^3}{12}\right) \cdot \dfrac{dh}{dt}$

[by chain rule]

$= \dfrac{\pi}{4}h^2\dfrac{dh}{dt}$

Now, rate of change of volume, i.e. $\dfrac{dV}{dt} = 5\text{ m}^3/\text{h}$ and $h = 4$ m.

Therefore, $5 = \dfrac{\pi}{4}(4)^2 \cdot \dfrac{dh}{dt}$

$\Rightarrow \quad \dfrac{dh}{dt} = \dfrac{5}{4\pi} = \dfrac{35}{88}\text{ m/h}\left[\pi = \dfrac{22}{7}\right]$

Thus, the rate of change of water level is $\dfrac{35}{88}$ m/h.

3 (*b*) In figure, let AB be the lamp-post the lamp being at the position B and let MN be the man at a particular time t and let $AM = l$ m. Then, MS is the shadow of the man. Let $MS = s$ m.

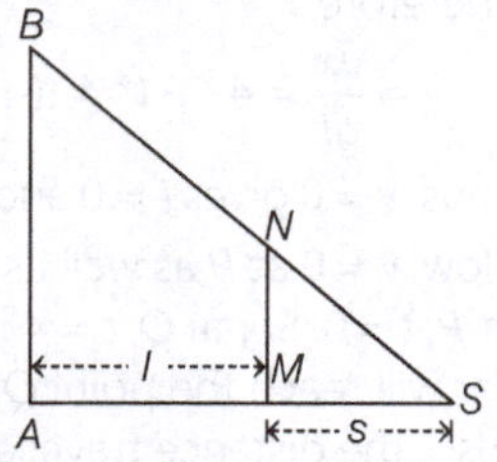

Note that $\Delta MSN \sim \Delta ASB$

$$\Rightarrow \frac{MS}{AS} = \frac{MN}{AB} \Rightarrow AS = 3s$$

(as $MN = 2$ and $AB = 6$) [given]

Thus, $AM = 3s - s = 2s.$

But $AM = l$

So, $l = 2s$

Therefore, $\frac{dl}{dt} = 2\frac{ds}{dt}$

Since, $\frac{dl}{dt} = 5$ km/h. Hence, the length of the shadow increases at the rate $\frac{5}{2}$ km/h.

4 (*d*) We have,

$$f(x) = \frac{3}{10}x^4 - \frac{4}{5}x^3 - 3x^2 + \frac{36}{5}x + 11$$

Therefore,

$$f'(x) = \frac{3}{10}(4x^3) - \frac{4}{5}(3x^2) - 3(2x) + \frac{36}{5}$$

$$= \frac{6}{5}(x-1)(x+2)(x-3)$$

[on simplification]

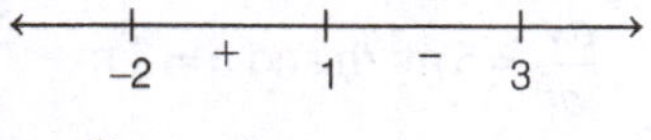

Now, $f'(x) = 0$ gives $x = 1, x = -2$ or $x = 3$. The points $x = 1, -2$ and 3 divide the real line into four disjoint intervals namely $(-\infty, -2), (-2, 1), (1, 3)$ and $(3, \infty)$.

Consider the interval $(-\infty, -2)$, i.e. when $-\infty < x < -2$.

In this case, we have $x - 1 < 0, x + 2 < 0$ and $x - 3 < 0$.

(In particular, observe that for $x = -3$,

$$f'(x) = (x-1)(x+2)(x-3)$$
$$= (-4)(-1)(-6) < 0)$$

Therefore, $f'(x) < 0$ when $-\infty < x < -2$.

Thus, the function f is strictly decreasing in $(-\infty, -2)$.

Consider the interval $(-2, 1)$ i.e. when $-2 < x < 1$.

In this case, we have $x - 1 < 0, x + 2 > 0$ and $x - 3 < 0$

(In particular, observe that for $x = 0$, $f'(x) = (x-1)(x+2)(x-3)$

$$= (-1)(2)(-3) = 6 > 0)$$

So, $f'(x) > 0$ when $-2 < x < 1$.

Thus, f is strictly increasing in $(-2, 1)$.

Now, consider the interval $(1, 3)$ i.e. when $1 < x < 3$. In this case, we have $x - 1 > 0, x + 2 > 0$ and $x - 3 < 0$.

So, $f'(x) < 0$, when $1 < x < 3$.

Thus, f is strictly decreasing in $(1, 3)$.

Finally, consider the interval $(3, \infty)$, i.e. when $x > 3$. In this case, we have $x - 1 > 0, x + 2 > 0$ and $x - 3 > 0$. So, $f'(x) > 0$ when $x > 3$.

Thus, f is strictly increasing in the interval $(3, \infty)$.

5 (*b*) We have,

$$f(x) = \tan^{-1}(\sin x + \cos x), x > 0$$

Therefore,

$$f'(x) = \frac{1}{1 + (\sin x + \cos x)^2}(\cos x - \sin x)$$

$$= \frac{\cos x - \sin x}{1 + \sin^2 x + \cos^2 x + 2\sin x \cos x}$$

$$= \frac{\cos x - \sin x}{2 + \sin 2x}$$

$[\because \sin^2\theta + \cos^2\theta = 1]$

Note that $2 + \sin 2x > 0, \forall x$ in $\left(0, \frac{\pi}{4}\right)$.

Therefore,

$f'(x) > 0$ if $\cos x - \sin x > 0$

or $f'(x) > 0$ if $\cos x > \sin x$

or $\cot x > 1$

Now, $\cot x > 1$ if $\tan x < 1$

i.e. if $0 < x < \frac{\pi}{4}$

Thus, $f'(x) > 0$ in $\left(0, \frac{\pi}{4}\right)$

Hence, f is strictly increasing function in $\left(0, \frac{\pi}{4}\right)$.

6 (*a*) Let r be the radius of the given disc and A be its area. Then

$$A = \pi r^2$$

or $\frac{dA}{dt} = 2\pi r \frac{dr}{dt}$ [by chain rule]

Now, approximate rate of increase of radius

$$= dr = \frac{dr}{dt}\Delta t$$
$$= 0.05 \text{ cm/s}.$$

Therefore, the approximate rate of increase in area is given by

$$dA = \frac{dA}{dt}(\Delta t) = 2\pi r\left(\frac{dr}{dt}\Delta t\right)$$
$$= 2\pi(3.2)(0.05)$$
$$= 0.320\pi \text{ cm}^2/\text{s}$$

$[r = 3.2 \text{ cm}]$

7 (*a*) Let x m be the length of a side of the removed squares.

Then, the height of the box is x, length is $8 - 2x$ and breadth is $3 - 2x$. If $V(x)$ is the volume of the box, then

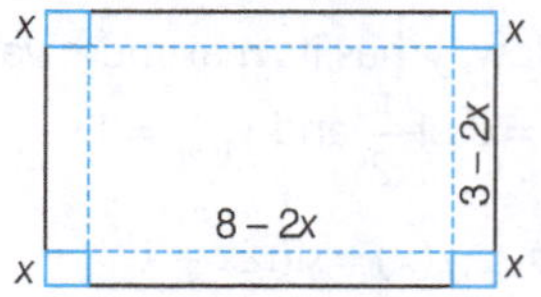

(a)

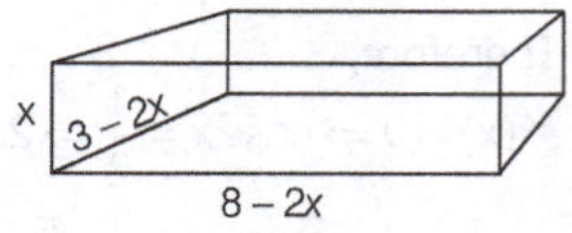

(b)

$$V(x) = x(3-2x)(8-2x)$$
$$= 4x^3 - 22x^2 + 24x$$

Therefore,

$$\begin{cases} V'(x) = 12x^2 - 44x + 24 \\ \quad = 4(x-3)(3x-2) \\ V''(x) = 24x - 44 \end{cases}$$

Now, $V'(x) = 0$ gives $x = 3, \frac{2}{3}$.

But $x \neq 3$

Thus, we have $x = \frac{2}{3}$.

Now,

$$V''\left(\frac{2}{3}\right) = 24\left(\frac{2}{3}\right) - 44 = -28 < 0.$$

Therefore, $x = \frac{2}{3}$ is the point of maxima i.e. if we remove a square of side $\frac{2}{3}$ m from each corner of the sheet and make a box from the remaining sheet, then the volume of the box such obtained will be the largest and it is given by

$$V\left(\frac{2}{3}\right) = 4\left(\frac{2}{3}\right)^3 - 22\left(\frac{2}{3}\right)^2 + 24\left(\frac{2}{3}\right) = \frac{200}{27} \text{ m}^3$$

8 (a) Let $f(x) = \frac{\log x}{x}$

On differentiating w.r.t. x, we get

$$f'(x) = \frac{x\left(\frac{1}{x}\right) - (\log x).1}{x^2} = \frac{1 - \log x}{x^2}$$

Again, on differentiating, we get

$$f''(x) = \frac{x^2\left(-\frac{1}{x}\right) - (1 - \log x).2x}{(x^2)^2}$$

$$= \frac{-x - 2x + 2x \log x}{x^4}$$

$$= \frac{x(2\log x - 3)}{x^4} = \frac{2\log x - 3}{x^3}$$

For maximum, put $f'(x) = 0$

$$\Rightarrow \quad \frac{1 - \log x}{x^2} = 0$$

$$\Rightarrow \quad \log x = 1 \Rightarrow x = e$$

At x = e, $f''(e) = \frac{2\log e - 3}{e^3}$

$$= \frac{2 \cdot 1 - 3}{e^3} = \frac{-1}{e^3} < 0$$

Therefore, by second derivative test, f is the maximum at $x = e$.

9 (d) Let ΔABC be isosceles triangle where BC is the base of fixed length b.

Let the length of two equal sides of Δ ABC be x.

Draw $AD \perp BC$ in figure.

Now, in ΔADC, by applying the Pythagoras theorem, we have

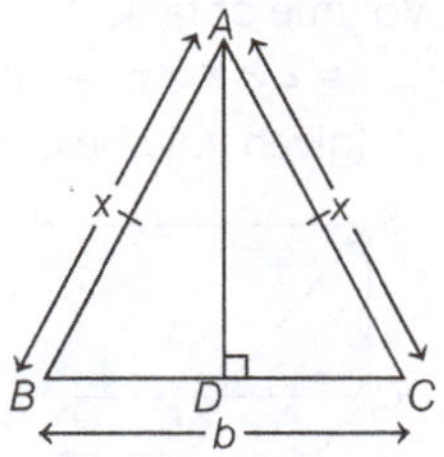

$$AD = \sqrt{x^2 - \left(\frac{b}{2}\right)^2} = \sqrt{x^2 - \frac{b^2}{4}}$$

$\therefore$ Area of triangle (A)

$$= \frac{1}{2} \times \text{Base} \times \text{Height}$$

$$= \frac{b}{2}\sqrt{x^2 - \frac{b^2}{4}}$$

The rate of change of the area A w.r.t. time t is given by

$$\frac{dA}{dt} = \frac{1}{2} b \times \frac{1}{2} \frac{2x}{\sqrt{x^2 - \frac{b^2}{4}}} \times \frac{dx}{dt}$$

$$= \frac{xb}{\sqrt{4x^2 - b^2}} \frac{dx}{dt}$$

It is given that the two equal sides of the triangle are decreasing at the rate of 3 cm/s.

$$\therefore \quad \frac{dx}{dt} = -3 \text{ cm/s}$$

[negative sign use for decreasing]

$$\therefore \quad \frac{dA}{dt} = \frac{-3xb}{\sqrt{4x^2 - b^2}} \text{cm}^2/\text{s}$$

When $x = b$, we have

$$\frac{dA}{dt} = \frac{-3b^2}{\sqrt{3b^2}} = -\sqrt{3}\, b \text{ cm}^2/\text{s}$$

Hence, if the two equal sides are equal to the base, then the area of the triangle is decreasing at the rate of $\sqrt{3}\, b \text{ cm}^2/\text{s}$.

Note *If the rate of change is increasing, we take positive sign and if the rate of change is decreasing, we take negative sign.*

10 (c) Given, $f(x) = x^3 + \frac{1}{x^3}$

On differentiating w.r.t. x, we get

$$f'(x) = 3x^2 - \frac{3}{x^4}$$

(a) $f(x)$ is increasing, if $f'(x) \geq 0$

$$\Rightarrow \quad 3x^2 - \frac{3}{x^4} \geq 0$$

$$\Rightarrow \quad x^6 \geq 1$$

$$\Rightarrow \quad (x^2)^3 \geq 1$$

$$\Rightarrow \quad x^2 \geq 1$$

$$\Rightarrow \quad x \in (-\infty, -1] \cup [1, \infty)$$

Thus, f is increasing in $(-\infty, -1] \cup [1, \infty)$

Hence f is increasing in $(-\infty, -1) \cup (1, \infty)$

(b) $f(x)$ is decreasing, if $f'(x) \leq 0$

$$\Rightarrow 3x^2 - \frac{3}{x^4} \leq 0$$

$$\Rightarrow \quad x^6 \leq 1 \Rightarrow (x^2)^3 \leq 1$$

$$\Rightarrow \quad x^2 \leq 1 \Rightarrow -1 \leq x \leq 1$$

$\therefore$ f is decreasing in $-1 < x < 1$.

11 (a) Let the equation of an ellipse be $\frac{x^2}{a^2} + \frac{y^2}{b^2} = 1$, then any point P on the ellipse is $(a\cos\theta, b\sin\theta)$.

From P, draw $PM \perp OX$ and produce it to meet the ellipse at Q, then ΔAPQ is an isosceles triangle, let S be its area, then

$$S = 2 \times \frac{1}{2} \times AM \times MP$$

$$= (OA - OM) \times MP$$

$$= (a - a\cos\theta) \cdot b\sin\theta$$

$$\Rightarrow \quad S = ab(\sin\theta - \sin\theta\cos\theta)$$

$$= ab\left(\sin\theta - \frac{1}{2}\sin 2\theta\right)$$

On differentiating w.r.t. θ, we get

$$\frac{dS}{d\theta} = ab(\cos\theta - \cos 2\theta)$$

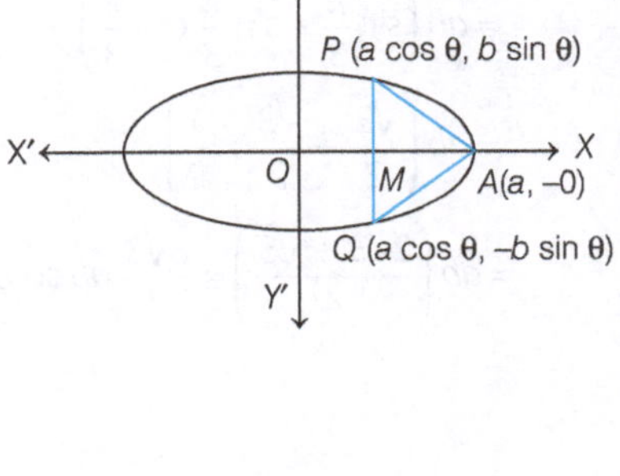

Again, on differentiating w.r.t. θ, we get

$$\frac{d^2S}{d\theta^2} = ab(-\sin\theta + 2\sin 2\theta)$$

For maxima or minima, put $\frac{dS}{d\theta} = 0$

$\Rightarrow \quad \cos\theta = \cos 2\theta$

$\Rightarrow \quad 2\theta = 2\pi - \theta$

$\Rightarrow \quad \theta = \frac{2\pi}{3}$

At $\theta = \frac{2\pi}{3}, \left(\frac{d^2S}{d\theta^2}\right)_{\theta=\frac{2\pi}{3}} = ab \left[-\sin\frac{2\pi}{3} + 2\sin\left(2 \times \frac{2\pi}{3}\right)\right]$

$$= ab\left[-\sin\left(\pi - \frac{\pi}{3}\right) + 2\sin\left(\pi + \frac{\pi}{3}\right)\right]$$

$$= ab\left(-\sin\frac{\pi}{3} - 2\sin\frac{\pi}{3}\right)$$

$$\left[\because \sin\left(\pi - \frac{\pi}{3}\right) = \sin\frac{\pi}{3} \quad \sin\left(\pi + \frac{\pi}{3}\right) = -\sin\frac{\pi}{3}\right]$$

$$= ab\left(-\frac{\sqrt{3}}{2} - \frac{2\sqrt{3}}{2}\right)$$

$$= ab\left(\frac{-3\sqrt{3}}{2}\right) = \frac{-3\sqrt{3}ab}{2} < 0$$

∴ S is maximum, when $\theta = \frac{2\pi}{3}$

and maximum value of

$$S = ab\left(\sin\frac{2\pi}{3} - \sin\frac{2\pi}{3}\cos\frac{2\pi}{3}\right)$$

$[\because \sin 2\theta = 2\sin\theta\cos\theta]$

$$= ab\left[\sin\left(\pi - \frac{\pi}{3}\right) - \sin\left(\pi - \frac{\pi}{3}\right)\cos\left(\pi - \frac{\pi}{3}\right)\right]$$

$$= ab\left(\sin\frac{\pi}{3} - \sin\frac{\pi}{3} \times \left(-\cos\frac{\pi}{3}\right)\right)$$

$$= ab\left(\sin\frac{\pi}{3} + \sin\frac{\pi}{3}\cos\frac{\pi}{3}\right)$$

$$= ab\left(\frac{\sqrt{3}}{2} + \frac{\sqrt{3}}{2} \times \frac{1}{2}\right)$$

$$= ab\left(\frac{2\sqrt{3} + \sqrt{3}}{4}\right) = \frac{3\sqrt{3}}{4} ab \text{ sq unit}$$

Thus, maximum area of isosceles triangle is $\frac{3\sqrt{3}}{4} ab$ sq unit.

12 (*a*) Let the length and breadth of the tank be x m and y m, respectively.

The depth (height) is 2 m.

∴ Volume of tank

$$= 2 \times x \times y = 2xy = 8$$

[given volume of tank = 8 m^3]

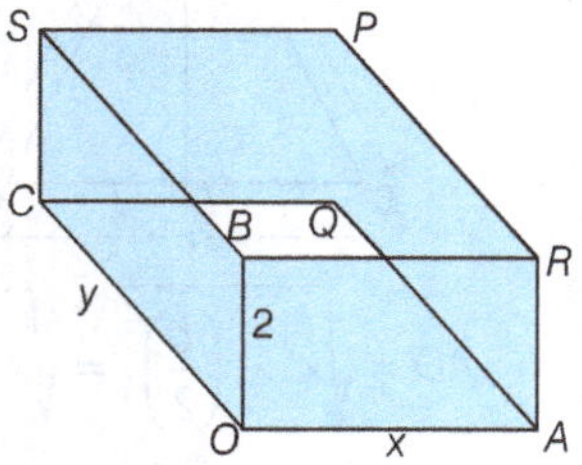

$\Rightarrow \quad xy = 4$

$\Rightarrow \quad y = \frac{4}{x}$ ...(i)

Also, area of the base

$\Rightarrow \quad xy = x \times \frac{4}{x} = 4$

and area of the four sides

$$= 2x + 2y + 2x + 2y$$

$$= 4x + 4y = 4(x + y)$$

It is given that the cost of construction for base is ₹ 70 per sq m and for side is ₹ 45 per sq m.

So, cost of construction,

$$C = ₹[70 \times xy + 45 \times 4(x + y)]$$

$$= ₹[70xy + 180(x + y)] \quad \text{...(ii)}$$

On putting value of y in Eq. (ii) from Eq. (i), we get

$$C = 70 \times 4 + 180\left(x + \frac{4}{x}\right)$$

$$= 280 + 180\left(x + \frac{4}{x}\right) \quad \text{...(iii)}$$

On differentiating w.r.t. x, we get

$$\frac{dC}{dx} = 0 + 180\left(1 - \frac{4}{x^2}\right)$$

$$= 180\left(\frac{x^2 - 4}{x^2}\right)$$

For least expense, put $\frac{dC}{dx} = 0$

$\Rightarrow \quad 180\left(\frac{x^2 - 4}{x^2}\right) = 0$

$\Rightarrow \quad x^2 = 4 \Rightarrow x = \pm 2$

$\frac{dC}{dx}$ changes sign from negative to positive at $x = 2$.

∴ C is minimum at $x = 2$

[length of the tank cannot be negative. So, $x = -2$ is not considered]

$x = 2$

and $\quad y = \frac{4}{x} = \frac{4}{2} = 2$

Thus, tank is a cube of side 2 m.

Least cost of construction is obtained on putting $x = 2$ in Eq. (iii)

i.e. $\quad = ₹\left[280 + 180\left(2 + \frac{4}{2}\right)\right]$

$$= ₹[280 + 720] = ₹1000$$

13 (*c*) Let x be the side of square and r be the radius of circle.

Perimeter of a circle = $2\pi r$ and perimeter of a square = $4x$

Given, $2\pi r + 4x = k$

$\Rightarrow \quad x = \frac{k - 2\pi r}{4}$ ...(i)

$$\therefore A = x^2 + \pi r^2 = \left[\frac{k - 2\pi r}{4}\right]^2 + \pi r^2$$

$$= \left(\frac{1}{16}\right)(k^2 - 4k\pi r + 4\pi^2 r^2) + \pi r^2$$

On differentiating w.r.t. r, we get

$$\frac{dA}{dr} = \left(\frac{1}{16}\right)(-4k\pi + 8\pi^2 r) + 2\pi r$$

Again, on differentiating w.r. t. r, we get

$$\frac{d^2A}{dr^2} = \frac{1}{16}[0 + 8\pi^2] + 2\pi$$

$$= 2\pi + \frac{\pi^2}{2} > 0$$

For maximum or minimum, put $\frac{dA}{dr} = 0$

$$\Rightarrow \quad 2\pi r - \frac{4k\pi}{16} + \frac{8\pi^2 r}{16} = 0$$

$$\Rightarrow \quad r\left(2\pi + \frac{\pi^2}{2}\right) = \frac{k\pi}{4}$$

$$\Rightarrow \quad r = \frac{\left(\frac{k\pi}{4}\right)}{2\pi + \frac{\pi^2}{2}} = \frac{k}{8+2\pi} \quad \text{...(ii)}$$

Now, $\left(\dfrac{d^2A}{dr^2}\right)_{r=\frac{k}{8+2\pi}}$ is positive.

$\therefore$ A is least when $r = \dfrac{k}{8+2\pi}$ and

put this value in Eq. (i), we get

$$x = \frac{k-2\pi r}{4} = \frac{1}{4}\left(k - 2\pi \times \frac{k}{8+2\pi}\right)$$

$$= \frac{1}{4}\left[\frac{8k+2\pi k - 2\pi k}{8+2\pi}\right]$$

$$= \frac{2k}{8+2\pi}$$

$$= 2\left(\frac{k}{8+2\pi}\right) = 2r$$

[using Eq. (ii)]

Hence, S is least when side of the square is double the radius of the circle.

14 (*c*) Let radius of semi-circle $= r$

$\therefore$ One side of rectangle $= 2r$.

Let other side $= x$

$\because P = \text{Perimeter} = 10$ [given]

$$\Rightarrow 2x + 2r + \frac{1}{2}(2\pi r) = 10$$

$$\Rightarrow \quad 2x = 10 - r(\pi + 2) \quad \text{...(i)}$$

Let A be area of the window, then

A = Area of semi-circle + Area of rectangle $= \dfrac{1}{2}\pi r^2 + 2rx$

$$\Rightarrow \quad A = \frac{1}{2}(\pi r^2) + r[10 - r(\pi+2)]$$

[using Eq. (i)]

$$= \frac{1}{2}(\pi r^2) + 10r - r^2\pi - 2r^2$$

$$= 10r - \frac{\pi r^2}{2} - 2r^2$$

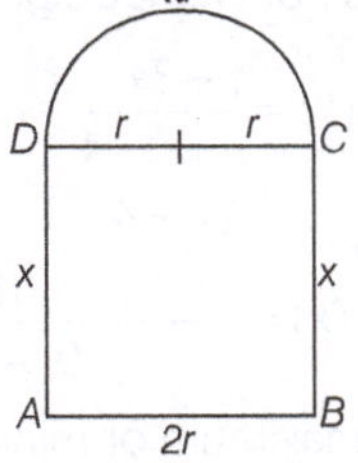

On differentiating twice w.r.t. r, we get

$$\frac{dA}{dr} = 10 - \pi r - 4r \quad \text{...(ii)}$$

and $$\frac{d^2A}{dr^2} = -\pi - 4 \quad \text{...(iii)}$$

For maxima or minima, put

$$\frac{dA}{dr} = 0$$

$$\Rightarrow 10 - \pi r - 4r = 0$$

$$\Rightarrow \quad 10 = (4+\pi)r$$

$$\Rightarrow \quad r = \frac{10}{4+\pi}$$

On putting $r = \dfrac{10}{4+\pi}$ in Eq. (iii),

we get $\dfrac{d^2A}{dr^2} < 0$

Thus, A has local maximum when

$$r = \frac{10}{4+\pi} \quad \text{...(iv)}$$

$\therefore$ Radius of semi-circle $= \dfrac{10}{4+\pi}$

and one side of rectangle

$$= 2r = \frac{2\times 10}{4+\pi}$$

$$= \frac{20}{4+\pi}$$

and other side of rectangle i.e. x from Eq. (i) is given by

$$x = \frac{1}{2}[10 - r(\pi+2)]$$

$$= \frac{1}{2}\left[10 - \left(\frac{10}{\pi+4}\right)(\pi+2)\right]$$

[from Eq. (iv)]

$$= \frac{10\pi + 40 - 10\pi - 20}{2(\pi+4)}$$

$$= \frac{20}{2(\pi+4)} = \frac{10}{\pi+4}$$

Light is maximum when area is maximum.

So, dimensions of the window are length $= 2r = \dfrac{20}{\pi+4}$, breadth $= x = \dfrac{10}{\pi+4}$.

So, both the statements are true.

15 (*b*) Let P be a point on the hypotenuse AC of right angled ΔABC,

Such that $PL \perp AB = a$

and $PM \perp BC = b$

Hence, $PL = a$

$PM = b$

Clearly, $\angle APL = \angle ACB = \theta$ [say]

$$AP = a\sec\theta,$$

$$PC = b\,\text{cosec}\,\theta$$

Let l be the length of the hypotenuse, then

$$l = AP + PC$$

$$\Rightarrow \quad l = a\sec\theta + b\,\text{cosec}\,\theta,$$

$$0 < \theta < \frac{\pi}{2}$$

On differentiating w.r.t. θ, we get

$$\frac{dl}{d\theta} = a\sec\theta\tan\theta - b\,\text{cosec}\,\theta\cot\theta$$

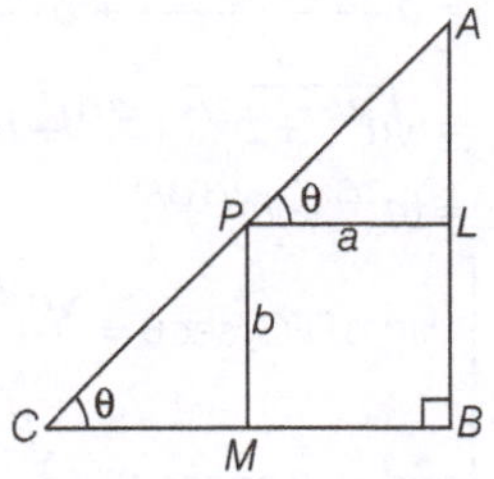

For maxima or minima, put $\dfrac{dl}{d\theta} = 0$

$$a\sec\theta\tan\theta = b\,\text{cosec}\,\theta\cot\theta$$

$$\Rightarrow \quad \frac{a\sin\theta}{\cos^2\theta} = \frac{b\cos\theta}{\sin^2\theta}$$

$$\Rightarrow \quad \frac{\sin^3\theta}{\cos^3\theta} = \frac{b}{a}$$

$$\Rightarrow \quad \tan^3\theta = \frac{b}{a}$$

$$\Rightarrow \quad \tan\theta = \left(\frac{b}{a}\right)^{1/3}$$

Now, $$\frac{d^2l}{d\theta^2} = a[\sec\theta \times \sec^2\theta + \tan\theta \times \sec\theta\tan\theta] - b[\text{cosec}\,\theta(-\text{cosec}^2\theta) + \cot\theta(-\text{cosec}\,\theta\cot\theta)]$$

$$= a\sec\theta(\sec^2\theta + \tan^2\theta) + b\,\text{cosec}\,\theta(\text{cosec}^2\theta + \cot^2\theta)$$

Since, $0 < \theta < \frac{\pi}{2}$, so trigonometric ratios are positive.

Also, $a > 0$ and $b > 0$.

$\therefore \quad \frac{d^2 l}{d\theta^2}$ is positive.

$\Rightarrow l$ is least when $\tan\theta = \left(\frac{b}{a}\right)^{1/3}$

Now, we have the following figure.

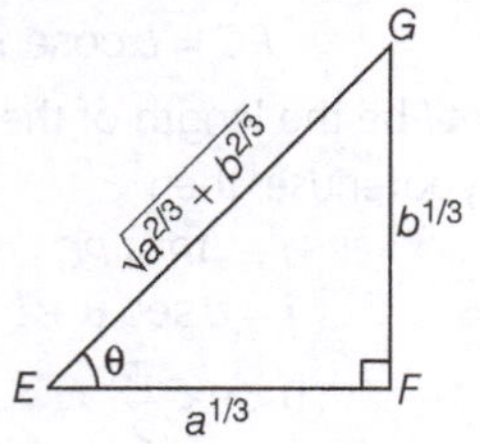

$\therefore$ Least value of

$l = a\sec\theta + b\,\text{cosec}\,\theta$

$= a\frac{\sqrt{a^{2/3}+b^{2/3}}}{a^{1/3}} + b\frac{\sqrt{a^{2/3}+b^{2/3}}}{b^{1/3}}$

$= \sqrt{a^{2/3}+b^{2/3}}\,(a^{2/3}+b^{2/3})$

$= (a^{2/3}+b^{2/3})^{3/2}$

$\left[\begin{array}{l} \because \text{in } \Delta EFG, \sec\theta = \dfrac{\sqrt{a^{2/3}+b^{2/3}}}{a^{1/3}} \\ \text{and} \quad \text{cosec}\,\theta = \dfrac{\sqrt{a^{2/3}+b^{2/3}}}{b^{1/3}} \end{array}\right]$

Numerical Type Questions

1 (8) Let A be the initial position of rider.

Then, $\quad PB = x$

$\Rightarrow \quad QB = 20 - x$

and $\quad AB = \sqrt{AP^2 + BP^2}$

$= \sqrt{6^2 + x^2}$ km

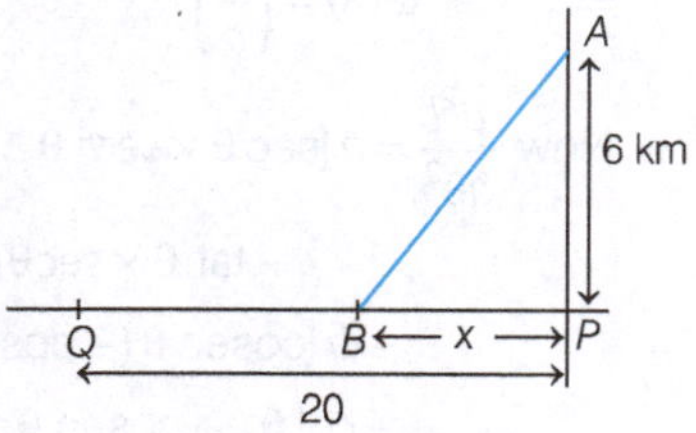

$\therefore$ Total time,

$$T = \frac{\sqrt{x^2+36}}{40} + \frac{20-x}{50}$$

For maximum and minimum value, we must have

$$\frac{dT}{dx} = 0$$

$$\Rightarrow \frac{x}{40\sqrt{x^2+36}} = \frac{1}{50}$$

or $\quad \frac{5x}{4} = \sqrt{x^2+36}$

or $\quad \frac{25x^2}{16} - x^2 = 36$

$$\Rightarrow \quad x^2 = \frac{36 \times 16}{9}$$

$$\Rightarrow \quad x = \frac{6 \times 4}{3} = 8 \text{ km}$$

2 (3) $y = \dfrac{2\sin\left(x + \frac{\pi}{6}\right)\cos x}{2\sin x \cos\left(x + \frac{\pi}{6}\right)}$

$$= \frac{\sin\left(2x + \frac{\pi}{6}\right) + \sin\frac{\pi}{6}}{\sin\left(2x + \frac{\pi}{6}\right) - \sin\frac{\pi}{6}}$$

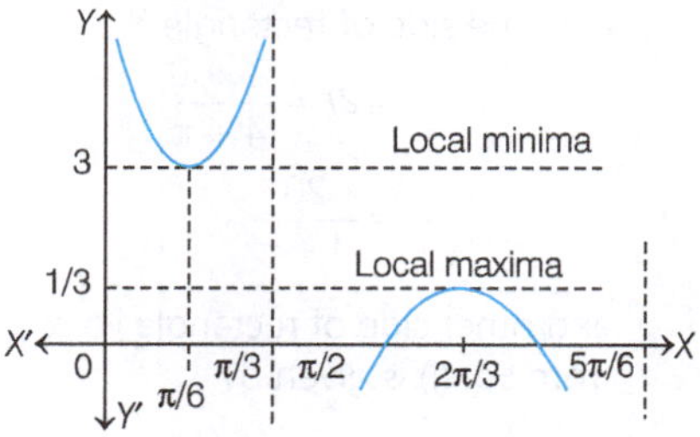

$$= 1 + \frac{1}{\sin\left(2x + \frac{\pi}{6}\right) - \sin\frac{\pi}{6}}$$

y is minimum, if $2x + \frac{\pi}{6} = \frac{\pi}{2}$

$$\Rightarrow \quad x = \frac{\pi}{6}$$

$$\Rightarrow \quad y_{\min} = 1 + 2 = 3$$

3 (9) $\dfrac{dy}{dx} = -\dfrac{4\cos x}{\sin^2 x} + \dfrac{\cos x}{(1-\sin x)^2} = 0$

gives $\sin x = \frac{2}{3}$ note that

$f(x) \to \infty$ as $x \to 0^+$ or $x \to \frac{\pi^-}{2}$

and between two maxima, we have a minima.

So, $a = \dfrac{4}{2/3} + \dfrac{1}{1-2/3} = 9$

4 (9) $\dfrac{dT}{dt} = k(T-5)^2$

$$\frac{dT}{(T-5)^2} = k\,dt$$

$$\Rightarrow \quad \frac{(T-5)^{-1}}{-1} = kt + C$$

$$\therefore \quad -(40-5)^{-1} = C \text{ i.e. } C = -\frac{1}{35}$$

$$\therefore \quad -\frac{1}{T-5} = kt - \frac{1}{35}$$

After 15 min,

$$-\frac{1}{30-5} = 15k - \frac{1}{35}$$

$$\therefore \quad k = \frac{1}{15}\left(\frac{1}{35} - \frac{1}{25}\right)$$

$$= \frac{-10}{15 \times 35 \times 25} = \frac{-2}{75 \times 35}$$

Temperature after 60 min is given by

$$-\frac{1}{T-5} = 60\left(\frac{-2}{75 \times 35}\right) - \frac{1}{35}$$

$$\Rightarrow \frac{1}{T-5} = \frac{120+75}{75 \times 35} + 5 = \frac{195}{75 \times 35}$$

$$\Rightarrow \quad T = \frac{75 \times 35}{195} + 5 = \frac{5 \times 35}{13} + 5$$

$$= \frac{175}{13} + 5$$

$\Rightarrow \quad [T] = 18$

$\therefore [T]/2 = 18/2 = 9$

5 (3)

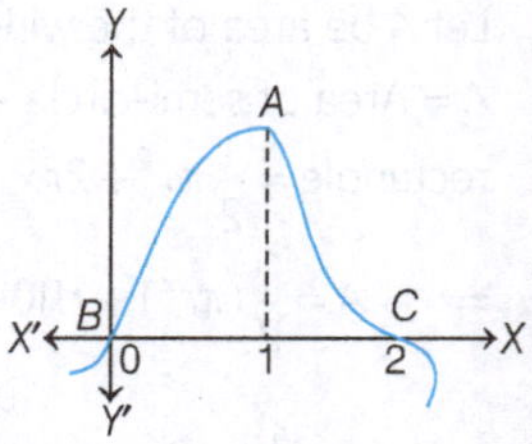

A, B, C are the 3 critical points of $y = f(x)$.

6 (0) Only at A and E, $f(x) = 0$ but does not change sign.

7 (3) $f(x) = \dfrac{t + 3x - x^2}{x-4}$,

$$f'(x) = \frac{(x-4)(3-2x) - (t+3x-x^2)}{(x-4)^2}$$

For maximum or minimum, $f'(x) = 0$

$$-2x^2 + 11x - 12 - t - 3x + x^2 = 0$$
$$-x^2 + 8x - (12 + t) = 0$$

For one M and $m, D > 0$

$$64 - 4(12 + t) > 0$$
$$16 - 12 - t > 0$$
$$\Rightarrow \quad 4 > t \text{ or } t < 4$$

Hence, the greatest value of t is 3.

8 (9) Let a be the side of a cube.

Then, we have

$$S = 6a^2 \Rightarrow \frac{dS}{dt} = 12a\frac{da}{dt}$$
$$\Rightarrow \quad 3 \cdot 6 = 12 \cdot 10\frac{da}{dt} \Rightarrow \frac{da}{dt} = \frac{3}{100}$$

Now, $V = a^3 \Rightarrow \dfrac{dV}{dt} = 3a^2 \cdot \dfrac{da}{dt}$

$$= 3 \cdot (10)^2 \cdot \frac{3}{100} = 9 \text{ cm}^3/\text{sec}$$

9 (9) Let A be the surface area of balloon.

According to the questions, we have

$$\frac{dA}{dt} = k$$

On integrating both sides, we get

$$A = kt + C$$
$$\Rightarrow \quad 4\pi^2 = kt + C \qquad \text{...(i)}$$

where r is the radius of balloon.

Now, at $t = 0, t = 3$ units

$\therefore \quad 36\pi = C$ ...(ii) [using Eq. (i)]

Also, at $t = 5$ sec, $r = 7$ units

$\therefore \quad 196\pi = 5k + 36\pi$

[using Eqs. (i) and (ii)]

$$\Rightarrow \quad k = 32\pi$$

So, from Eq. (i), we have

$$4\pi r^2 = 32\pi t + 36\pi$$
$$\Rightarrow \quad r^2 = 8t + 9$$

$\therefore$ At $t = 9$ secs, we have

$$r = \sqrt{8 \times 9 \times 9} = 9 \text{ unit}$$

10 (4) Let t be the radius of the cone when level of water is 10 m.

Given, $\dfrac{dV}{dt} = 5 \text{ m}^3/\text{min}$ and

$$\tan^{-1}\frac{1}{2} = \theta$$
$$\Rightarrow \quad \tan\theta = \frac{1}{2} = \frac{r}{h}$$
$$\therefore \quad r = \frac{h}{2}$$

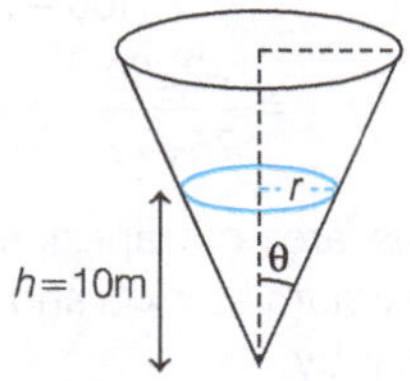

Now, $\quad V = \dfrac{1}{3}\pi r^2 h = \dfrac{1}{3}\pi\dfrac{h^3}{4}$

$$\therefore \quad \frac{dV}{dt} = \frac{\pi}{12} \cdot 3h^2\left(\frac{dh}{dt}\right)$$
$$\Rightarrow \quad 5 = \frac{\pi}{4}(100)\frac{dh}{dt}$$
$$\Rightarrow \quad \frac{dh}{dt} = \frac{1}{5\pi} \text{ m/min}$$

So, $20\pi\lambda = 20\pi \times \dfrac{1}{5\pi} = 4$

Assertion and Reason Questions

1 (a) If two variable x and y are varying w.r.t. another variable t i.e. if $x = f(t)$ and $y = g(t)$, then by chain rule $\dfrac{dy}{dx} = \dfrac{dy}{dt} / \dfrac{dx}{dt}$, if $\dfrac{dx}{dt} \neq 0$

Thus, the rate of change of y w.r.t. x can be calculated using the rule of change of y and that of x both w.r.t. t.

Hence, both the statements are true and Statement II is the correct explanation of Statement I.

2 (c) Let r be the radius of spherical balloon and V be its volume. Then, $r = 10$ cm and $V = \dfrac{4}{3}\pi r^3$

Rate of change of volume w.r.t. radius r, $\dfrac{dV}{dr} = \left(\dfrac{4}{3}\pi\right)3r^2$

[differentiating w.r.t. r]

$$= 4\pi r^2 = 4\pi(10)^2 = 400\pi$$

[$\because r = 10$ cm]

Hence, the volume of the balloon is increasing at the rate of 400π cm^3/cm.

3 (a) Here, $f(x) = 2x + \cot^{-1} x + \log(\sqrt{1 + x^2} - x)$

On differentiating both the sides w.r.t. x, we get

$$f'(x) = 2 + \frac{-1}{1 + x^2} + \frac{1}{\sqrt{1 + x^2} - x} \times \left[\frac{1}{2\sqrt{1 + x^2}} \times 2x - 1\right]$$
$$= 2 - \frac{1}{1 + x^2} + \frac{1}{\sqrt{1 + x^2} - x}\left[\frac{x - \sqrt{1 + x^2}}{\sqrt{1 + x^2}}\right]$$
$$= 2 - \frac{1}{1 + x^2} + \frac{-1}{\sqrt{1 + x^2}}$$
$$= \frac{2 + 2x^2 - 1 - 1\sqrt{1 + x^2}}{1 + x^2}$$
$$= \frac{1 + 2x^2 - \sqrt{1 + x^2}}{1 + x^2} \geq 0$$

for increasing function.

$$\Rightarrow \quad 1 + 2x^2 - \sqrt{1 + x^2} \geq 0$$

[$\because 1 + x^2 \geq 0, \forall x \in R$]

$$\Rightarrow \quad 1 + 2x^2 \geq \sqrt{1 + x^2}$$
$$\Rightarrow \quad (1 + 2x^2)^2 \geq 1 + x^2$$

[squaring both sides]

$$\Rightarrow 1 + 4x^2 + 4x^4 \geq 1 + x^2$$
$$\Rightarrow \quad 4x^4 + 3x^2 \geq 0$$
$$\Rightarrow \quad x^2(4x^2 + 3) \geq 0$$

which is true for any real value of x.

$\therefore f(x)$ is increasing in R.

So, both the statements are true and Statement II is the correct explanation of Statement I.

4 (b) $f'(x) = 6x^2 - 18x + 12$

For increasing function,

$$f'(x) \geq 0$$
$$\therefore \quad 6(x^2 - 3x + 2) \geq 0$$
$$\Rightarrow 6(x - 2)(x - 1) \geq 0$$
$$\Rightarrow x \leq 1 \quad \text{and} \quad x \geq 2$$

$\therefore f(x)$ is increasing outside the interval (1, 2), therefore it is true statement.

Now, $f'(x)<0$

$\Rightarrow \quad 6(x-2)(x-1)<0 \Rightarrow 1<x<2$

∴ A and R are both true but R is not the correct explanation of A.

5 (*a*) The required trapezium is as given in figure. Draw perpendiculars DP and CQ on AB. Let $AP = x$ cm. Note that $\Delta APD \sim \Delta BQC$.

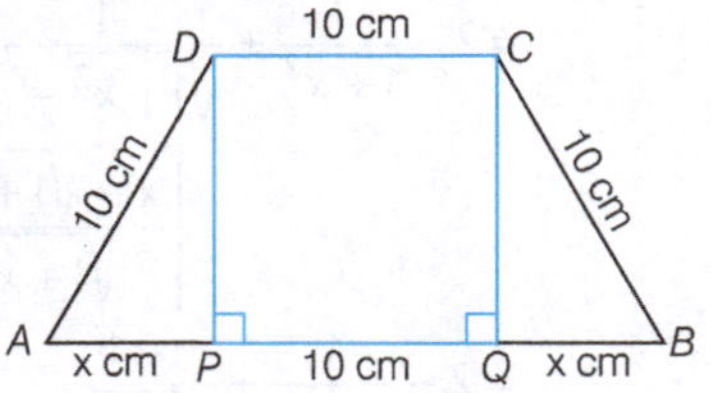

Therefore, $QB = x$ cm. Also, by Pythagoras theorem,

$DP = QC = \sqrt{100 - x^2}$.

Let A be the area of the trapezium.Then,

$$A \equiv A(x) = \frac{1}{2} \times \text{Sum of parallel sides} \times \text{Height}$$

$$= \frac{1}{2}(2x + 10 + 10)(\sqrt{100 - x^2})$$

$$= (x + 10)(\sqrt{100 - x^2})$$

or $$A'(x) = (x + 10)\frac{(-2x)}{2\sqrt{100 - x^2}} + \sqrt{100 - x^2}$$

$$= \frac{-2x^2 - 10x + 100}{\sqrt{100 - x^2}}$$

Now, $A'(x) = 0$ gives $2x^2 + 10x - 100 = 0$ i.e. $x = 5$ and $x = -10$.

Since, x represents distance, it cannot be negative.

So, $x = 5$. Now,

$$A''(x) = \frac{\left(\sqrt{100 - x^2}(-4x - 10) - (-2x^2 - 10x + 100)\dfrac{(-2x)}{2\sqrt{100 - x^2}}\right)}{100 - x^2}$$

$$= \frac{2x^3 - 300x - 1000}{(100 - x^2)^{3/2}}$$

[on simplification]

or $$A''(5) = \frac{2(5)^3 - 300(5) - 1000}{(100 - (5)^2)^{\frac{3}{2}}}$$

$$= \frac{-2250}{75\sqrt{75}} = \frac{-30}{\sqrt{75}} < 0$$

Thus, area of trapezium is maximum at $x = 5$ and the area is given by

$$A(5) = (5 + 10)\sqrt{100 - (5)^2}$$

$$= 15\sqrt{75} = 75\sqrt{3} \text{ cm}^2$$

6 (*b*) We have, $f(x) = 12x^{\frac{4}{3}} - 6x^{\frac{1}{3}}$

or $$f'(x) = 16x^{\frac{1}{3}} - \frac{2}{x^{\frac{2}{3}}} = \frac{2(8x - 1)}{x^{\frac{2}{3}}}$$

Thus, $f'(x) = 0$ gives $x = \frac{1}{8}$. Further note that $f'(x)$ is not defined at $x = 0$. So, the critical points are $x = 0$ and $x = \frac{1}{8}$. Now, evaluating the value of f at critical points $x = 0, \frac{1}{8}$ and at end points of the interval $x = -1$ and $x = 1$, we have

$$f(-1) = 12(-1)^{\frac{4}{3}} - 6(-1)^{\frac{1}{3}} = 18$$

$$f(0) = 12(0) - 6(0) = 0$$

$$f\left(\frac{1}{8}\right) = 12\left(\frac{1}{8}\right)^{\frac{4}{3}} - 6\left(\frac{1}{8}\right)^{\frac{1}{3}} = \frac{-9}{4}$$

$$f(1) = 12(1)^{\frac{4}{3}} - 6(1)^{\frac{1}{3}} = 6$$

Hence, we conclude that absolute maximum value of f is 18 that occurs at $x = -1$ and absolute minimum value of f is $\frac{-9}{4}$ that occurs at $x = \frac{1}{8}$.

7 (*a*) Let the numbers be x and y and $P = x^2y^5$, then $x + y = 35$

$\Rightarrow \quad x = 35 - y$

$\therefore \quad P = (35 - y)^2\, y^5$

On differentiating twice w.r.t. y, we get

$$\frac{dP}{dy} = (35 - y)^2\, 5y^4 + y^5 \cdot 2(35 - y)(-1)$$

$$= y^4(35 - y)[5(35 - y) - 2y]$$

$$= y^4(35 - y)(175 - 5y - 2y)$$

$$= y^4(35 - y)(175 - 7y)$$

$$= (35y^4 - y^5)(175 - 7y)$$

and $$\frac{d^2P}{dy^2} = (35y^4 - y^5)(-7) + (175 - 7y)(4 \times 35 \times y^3 - 5y^4)$$

$$= -7y^4(35 - y) + 7(25 - y) \times 5y^3(28 - y)$$

$$= -7y^4(35 - y) + 35y^3(25 - y)(28 - y)$$

For maxima, put $\frac{dP}{dy} = 0$

$\Rightarrow y^4(35 - y)(175 - 7y) = 0$

$\Rightarrow \quad y = 0,\ 35 - y = 0$

$175 - 7y = 0$

$\Rightarrow \quad y = 0,\ y = 25,\ y = 35$

When $y = 0$, $x = 35 - 0 = 35$ and the product x^2y^5 will be 0.

When $y = 35$ and $x = 35 - 35 = 0$. This will make the product x^2y^5 equal to 0.

∴ $y = 0$ and $y = 35$ cannot be the possible value of y.

When $y = 25$,

$$\left(\frac{d^2P}{dy^2}\right)_{y=25} = -7 \times (25)^4 \times (35 - 25) + 35 \times (25)^3 \times (25 - 25)(28 - 25)$$

$$= -7 \times 390625 \times 10 + 35 \times 15625 \times 0 \times 3$$

$$= -27343750 + 0$$

$$= -27343750 < 0$$

∴ By second derivative test, P will be the maximum when $y = 25$ and $x = 35 - 25 = 10$.

Hence, the required numbers are 10 and 25.

8 (*a*) Let one number is x.

Then, the other number will be $(16 - x)$.

Let the sum of the cubes of these numbers be denoted by S.

Then, $\quad S = x^3 + (16 - x)^3$

On differentiating w.r.t. x, we get

$$\frac{dS}{dx} = 3x^2 + 3(16-x)^2(-1) = 3x^2 - 3(16-x)^2$$

$$\Rightarrow \frac{d^2S}{dx^2} = 6x + 6(16-x) = 96$$

For minima, put $\frac{dS}{dx} = 0$.

$$\therefore \quad 3x^2 - 3(16-x)^2 = 0$$

$$\Rightarrow x^2 - (256 + x^2 - 32x) = 0$$

$$\Rightarrow \quad 32x = 256 \Rightarrow x = 8$$

At $x = 8$, $\left(\frac{d^2S}{dx^2}\right)_{x=8} = 96 > 0$

By second derivative test, $x = 8$ is the point of local minima of S.

Thus, the sum of the cubes of the numbers is the minimum when the numbers are 8 and $16 - 8 = 8$.

Hence, the required numbers are 8 and 8.

9 (b) We have,

$$f(x) = 2x^3 - 6x^2 + 6x + 5$$

or $\begin{cases} f'(x) = 6x^2 - 12x + 6 = 6(x-1)^2 \\ f''(x) = 12(x-1) \end{cases}$

Now, $f'(x) = 0$ gives $x = 1$.

Also, $f''(1) = 0$. Therefore, the second derivative test fails in this case. So, we shall go back to the first derivative test.

Using first derivatives test, we get $x = 1$ is neither a point of local maxima nor a point of local minima and so it is a point of inflexion.

10 (c) Let $S(x)$ be the selling price of x items and let $C(x)$ be the cost price of x items. Then, we have

$$S(x) = \left(5 - \frac{x}{100}\right)x = 5x - \frac{x^2}{100}$$

and $C(x) = \frac{x}{5} + 500$

Thus, the profit function $P(x)$ is given by

$$P(x) = S(x) - C(x) = 5x - \frac{x^2}{100} - \frac{x}{5} - 500$$

i.e. $P(x) = \frac{24}{5}x - \frac{x^2}{100} - 500$

$$\Rightarrow P'(x) = \frac{24}{5} - \frac{x}{50}$$

Now, $P'(x) = 0$ gives $x = 240$.

Also, $P''(x) = \frac{-1}{50}$

So, $P''(240) = \frac{-1}{50} < 0$

Thus, $x = 240$ is a point of maxima. Hence, the manufacturer can earn maximum profit, if he sells 240 items.

11 (b) $f(x)$ is increasing if, $f'(x) > 0$ in that interval and is decreasing if $f'(x) < 0$ in that interval.

Given, $f(x) = \frac{4\sin x - 2x - x\cos x}{2 + \cos x}$

$$= \frac{4\sin x - x(2+\cos x)}{2+\cos x} = \frac{4\sin x}{2+\cos x} - \frac{x(2+\cos x)}{2+\cos x}$$

$$= \frac{4\sin x}{2+\cos x} - x$$

On differentiating w.r.t. x, we get

$$f'(x) = 4\left\{\frac{(2+\cos x)\cos x - \sin x(0 - \sin x)}{(2+\cos x)^2}\right\} - 1$$

$$= 4\left\{\frac{2\cos x + \cos^2 x + \sin^2 x}{(2+\cos x)^2}\right\} - 1$$

$$= \frac{8\cos x + 4}{(2+\cos x)^2} - 1 \quad [\because \cos^2 x + \sin^2 x = 1]$$

$$= \frac{8\cos x + 4 - (2+\cos x)^2}{(2+\cos x)^2}$$

$$= \frac{8\cos x + 4 - 4 - \cos^2 x - 4\cos x}{(2+\cos x)^2}$$

$$= \frac{4\cos x - \cos^2 x}{(2+\cos x)^2}$$

$$= \frac{\cos x(4 - \cos x)}{(2+\cos x)^2}$$

We know that $-1 \le \cos x \le 1$

$\Rightarrow \quad 4 - \cos x > 0$

and $\quad (2+\cos x)^2 > 0$

(a) For increasing,

$f'(x) > 0$ when $\cos x > 0$

[$\because \cos x$ is positive in 1st and 4th quadrant]

$\therefore f(x)$ is increasing in the interval $\left(0, \frac{\pi}{2}\right)$ and $\left(\frac{3\pi}{2}, 2\pi\right)$.

(b) For decreasing,

$f'(x) < 0$ when $\cos x < 0$

[$\because \cos x$ is negative in 2nd and 3rd quadrant]

$\therefore f(x)$ is decreasing in the interval $\left(\frac{\pi}{2}, \frac{3\pi}{2}\right)$.

So, both the statements are true.

12 (c) We find that $x = 0$ is point of inflexion of $f(x) = x^5$. So, it is critical point of $f(x)$. The values of $f(x) = x^5$ at $x = -1$, $x = 0$ and $x = 1$ are $-1, 0, 1$, respectively. Clearly, $f(x)$ attains its maximum value at $x = 1$ not a critical point $x = 0$. So, Statement I is true.

Statement II is not true as is evident from Statement I. Hence, Statement I is true and Statement II is false.

13 (a) We have $f(x) = x^2 - 2x + 4$

$\Rightarrow f'(x) = 2x - 2 < 0, \forall x \in [-3, 1]$

So $f(x)$ is decreasing on $[-3, 1]$.

$\Rightarrow \quad M = f(-3)$ and $m = f(1)$

$\Rightarrow (m, M) = (f(1), f(-3))$

Thus, both the statements are true and Statement II is a correct explanation for Statement I.

14 (a) We have

$$f(x) = \frac{|x-1|}{x^2} = \begin{cases} \frac{1-x}{x^2}, & x < 1 \\ \frac{x-1}{x}, & x \ge 1 \end{cases}$$

We find that $f(x)$ is not differentiable at $x = 0$ and $x = 1$.

For other points, we obtain

$$f'(x) = \begin{cases} \frac{x-2}{x^3}, & x < 1 \\ \frac{-x+2}{x^3}, & x > 1 \end{cases}$$

We find $f'(x) = 0$ at $x = 2$.

So, $x = 2$ is also a critical point of $f(x)$. hence, $f(x)$ has three critical points *viz* 0, 1 and 2.

So, statement I is true, statement II is also true and it is a correct explanation for statement I.

Case or Paragraph Type Questions

Solution (Q. No. 1-3) By examine the graph of given function as shown below, we see that at points A, B, C and D on the graph, the function changes its nature from decreasing to increasing or *vice-versa*. These points may be called turning points of the given function. Further, observe that at turning points, the graph has either a little hill or a little valley. Roughly speaking, the function has minimum value in some neighbourhood (interval) of each of the points A and C which are at the bottom of their respective valleys.

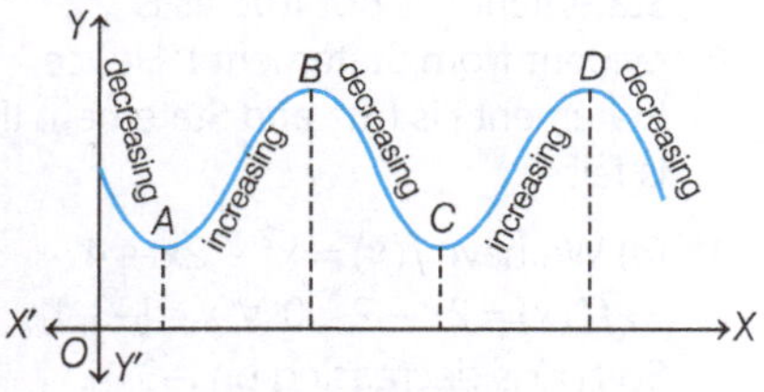

Similarly, the function has maximum value in some neighbourhood of points B and D which are at the top of their respective hills.

1 (*b*) Clearly the points A and C may be regarded as points of local minimum value (or relative minimum value).

2 (*c*) Points B and D may be regarded as points of local maximum value (or relative maximum value) for the function.

3 (*a*) The local maximum value and local minimum value of the function are referred to as local maxima and local minima, respectively of the function.

4 (*a*) Let at any time t, h cm be the height of water in the conical part of tank and r cm be the radius of base of water cone.

In $\Delta VO'A'$, we obtain

$$\tan 45° = \frac{O'A'}{VO'}$$

$$\Rightarrow \quad 1 = \frac{r}{h} \Rightarrow r = h$$

Let V be the volume of water in the conical part. Then,

$$V = \frac{1}{3}\pi r^2 h = \frac{1}{3}\pi r^3$$

$$\Rightarrow \quad \frac{dV}{dt} = \pi r^2 \frac{dr}{dt} \qquad \text{...(i)}$$

5 (*b*) It is given that water is dripping out from the tap at the bottom at the uniform rate of 2 cm^2/sec. i.e.

$$\frac{dV}{dt} = -2 \qquad \text{...(ii)}$$

From Eqs. (i) and (ii), we get

$$\pi r^2 \frac{dr}{dt} = -2$$

$$\Rightarrow \quad \frac{dr}{dt} = -\frac{2}{\pi r^2}$$

$$\Rightarrow \quad \left(\frac{dr}{dt}\right)_{r=2\sqrt{2}} = -\frac{2}{\pi \times 8}$$

$$= -\frac{1}{4\pi} \text{ cm/sec} \qquad \text{...(iii)}$$

6 (*c*) Let S be the wet surface area at time t. Then, $S = \pi rl$.

In $\Delta VO'A'$, we obtain

$$\sin 45° = \frac{r}{l}$$

$$\Rightarrow \quad \frac{1}{\sqrt{2}} = \frac{r}{l}$$

$$\Rightarrow \quad l = \sqrt{2}r$$

On substituting $l = \sqrt{2}r$ in $S = \pi rl$, we get

$$S = \sqrt{2}\pi r^2$$

$$\Rightarrow \quad \frac{dS}{dt} = 2\sqrt{2}\pi r \frac{dr}{dt}$$

$$= 2\sqrt{2}\pi r \times -\frac{1}{4\pi} = -\frac{r}{\sqrt{2}}$$

$$\left[\because \frac{dr}{dt} = -\frac{1}{4\pi}\right]$$

$$\Rightarrow \left(\frac{dS}{dt}\right)_{r=2\sqrt{2}} = -\frac{2\sqrt{2}}{\sqrt{2}}$$

$$= -2 \text{ cm}^2\text{/sec}$$

7 (*d*) We have, $l = \sqrt{2}r$ and $h = r$.
When $l = 4$, we get

$$4 = \sqrt{2}r \Rightarrow r = 2\sqrt{2}.$$

Now, $h = r$

$$\Rightarrow \quad \frac{dh}{dt} = \frac{dr}{dt}$$

$$\Rightarrow \quad \frac{dh}{dt} = -\frac{1}{4\pi} \qquad \text{[Using Eq. (iii)]}$$

$$\text{Hence, } \left(\frac{dh}{dt}\right)_{r=2\sqrt{2}} = -\frac{1}{4\pi} \text{ cm/sec}$$

8 (*a*) The volume V of the cylinder of radius r cm and height h cm is given by

$$V = \pi r^2 h \qquad \text{...(i)}$$

It is given that the metal sheet used in cylinder bore is of area 75π cm^2.

$$\therefore \quad 2\pi rh + \pi r^2 = 75\pi$$

$$\Rightarrow \quad 2rh + r^2 = 75$$

$$\Rightarrow \quad h = \frac{75 - r^2}{2r}$$

From Eqs. (i) and (ii), we get

$$V = \pi r^2 \left(\frac{75 - r^2}{2r}\right) = \frac{\pi}{2}(75r - r^3)$$

9 (*b*) $\dfrac{dV}{dr} = \dfrac{\pi}{2}(75 - 3r^2)$

and $\dfrac{d^2V}{dr^2} = -3\pi r$

10 (*c*) For maximum value of V, we must have

$$\frac{dV}{dr} = 0$$

$$\Rightarrow \quad \frac{\pi}{2}(75 - 3r^2) = 0$$

$$\Rightarrow \quad 75 = 3r^2$$

$$\Rightarrow \quad r^2 = 25 \Rightarrow r = 5$$

$$\text{Clearly, } \left(\frac{d^2V}{dr^2}\right)_{r=5} = -3\pi \times 5 < 0.$$

So, V is maximum when $r = 5$ cm.

11 (*d*) Putting $r = 5$ in Eq. (ii), we obtain $h = 5$ cm.

Thus, for maximum volume $h = r = 5$.

Past Years Questions

1 (*d*) $f(x) = \cos x - x + 1$

So, $f'(x) = -\sin x - 1$

On putting $f'(x) = 0$

$\Rightarrow -\sin x = 1 \Rightarrow \sin x = -1$

In $x \in [0, \pi]$, $\sin x = -1$ is not possible.

So, there is no critical point in $[0, \pi]$.

Now, $f(0) = 2 > 0$

$f(\pi) = -1 - \pi + 1 = -\pi < 0$

That means, $f(x)$ will have only one zero in $[0, \pi]$.

And $f(x)$ is decreasing in $[0, \pi]$.

Hence, only Statement I is correct.

2 (*c*) $f(x) = \dfrac{x}{x^2 - 6x - 16}$, $x \in R - \{-2, 8\}$

$$f'(x) = \frac{(x^2 - 6x - 16)(1) - x(2x - 6)}{(x^2 - 6x - 16)^2}$$

$$= \frac{x^2 - 6x - 16 - 2x^2 + 6x}{(x^2 - 6x - 16)^2}$$

$$= \frac{-x^2 - 16}{(x^2 - 6x - 16)^2}$$

$$= \frac{-(x^2 + 16)}{(x^2 - 6x - 16)^2} < 0$$

$\because f'(x) < 0$ for $x \in$ domain.

$\therefore$ It is a decreasing function in its domain.

$x \in (-\infty, -2) \cup (-2, 8) \cup (8, \infty)$

3 (*b*) Let S be the total surface area of a hemisphere.

$\therefore \quad S = 3\pi r^2$

On differentiating w.t. to r, we get

$$\frac{dS}{dr} = 3\pi \cdot 2r \Rightarrow \frac{dS}{dr} = 6\pi r$$

We have, $r = \sqrt[3]{1.331} = 1.1$ cm

$\Rightarrow \quad \dfrac{dS}{dr} = 6\pi \times 1.1$

$\therefore \quad \dfrac{dS}{dr} = 6.6\pi \text{ cm}^2$

4 (*a*) We have,

$$f(x) = \sin x + \frac{1}{2}\cos 2x \text{ in } \left[0, \frac{\pi}{2}\right]$$

Now, on differentiating w.r. to x, we get

$f'(x) = \cos x - \sin 2x$ ...(i)

For critical points put $f'(x) = 0$

So, $\quad \cos x - \sin 2x = 0$

$\Rightarrow \quad \cos x - 2\sin x \cos x = 0$

$\Rightarrow \quad \cos x(1 - 2\sin x) = 0$

$\Rightarrow \quad \cos x = 0$ or $1 - 2\sin x = 0$

I. $\cos x = 0$ gives $x = \dfrac{\pi}{2}$ in the interval $\left[0, \dfrac{\pi}{2}\right]$

II. $1 - 2\sin x = 0$ gives $\sin x = \dfrac{1}{2}$, which means $x = \dfrac{\pi}{6}$ in the interval $\left[0, \dfrac{\pi}{2}\right]$.

So, the critical points are $x = \dfrac{\pi}{2}$ and $x = \dfrac{\pi}{6}$.

Now, the maximum and minimum values of function.

$x = 0,$

At $x - 0$,

$$f(0) = \sin 0 + \frac{1}{2}\cos 0 = 0 + \frac{1}{2} \cdot 1 = \frac{1}{2}$$

$$\text{At } x = \frac{\pi}{6}, f\left(\frac{\pi}{6}\right) = \sin\frac{\pi}{6} + \frac{1}{2}\cos\frac{\pi}{3}$$

$$= \frac{1}{2} + \frac{1}{2} \cdot \frac{1}{2} = \frac{1}{2} + \frac{1}{4} = \frac{3}{4}$$

$$\text{At } x = \frac{\pi}{2}, f\left(\frac{\pi}{2}\right) = \sin\frac{\pi}{2} + \frac{1}{2}\cos\pi$$

$$= 1 + \frac{1}{2}(-1) = 1 - \frac{1}{2} = \frac{1}{2}$$

This is the maximum value of $f(x)$ is $\dfrac{3}{4}$, not 2 and the minimum value in the interval is $\dfrac{1}{2}$.

Hence, statement (A), (B) and (D) is correct.

5 (*c*) We have,

$$f(x) = 2\left(\tan^{-1}(e^x) - \frac{\pi}{4}\right)$$

$$\therefore \quad f(-x) = 2\left[\tan^{-1} e^{-x} - \frac{\pi}{4}\right]$$

$$= 2\left[\frac{\pi}{2} - \cot^{-1} e^{-x} - \frac{\pi}{4}\right]$$

$$= 2\left[\frac{\pi}{4} - \tan^{-1}\frac{1}{e^{-x}}\right]$$

$$= 2\left[\frac{\pi}{4} - \tan^{-1} e^x\right]$$

$$= -2\left(\tan^{-1} e^x - \frac{\pi}{4}\right)$$

$$= -f(x)$$

So, $f(x)$ is odd function.

Now, $\quad f'(x) = \dfrac{2e^x}{1 + e^{2x}}$

Since, $e^x, 1 + e^{2x} > 0$ for $x \in R$.

So, $\quad f'(x) > 0 \; \forall \; x \in R$

Hence, $f(x)$ is strictly increasing in $(-\infty, \infty)$.

6 (*a*) Given length of square sheet of side is 30 cm.

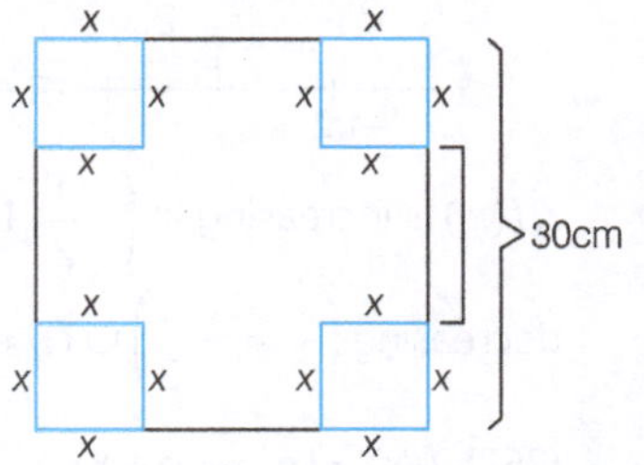

Let side of small square be x cm.

Since, a square piece of tin is to be made into a box without top by cutting square from each convex and folding up the flaps to from a box. Then, this shape framed a cuboidal shape.

Their, volume of the box (V)

$= (30 - 2x)(30 - 2x)x$

$\Rightarrow \quad V = x(30 - 2x)^2$

On differentiating both sides w.r.t. x, we get

$$\frac{dV}{dx} = (30 - 2x)^2 + x\{2(30 - 2x) \cdot (-2)\}$$

$$= (30 - 2x)^2 - 4x(30 - 2x)$$

$$= (30 - 2x)\{30 - 6x\}$$

Therefore, maximum of V, $\dfrac{dV}{dx} = 0$

$(30 - 2x)(30 - 6x) = 0$

$\Rightarrow \quad x = 15$ or $x = 5$

$\because x = 15$ is not possible $x = 5$

So, the surface area is

$= 4 \times (30 - 2x) \times x + (30 - 2x)^2$

$= 4 \times (30 - 10) \times 5 + (30 - 10)^2$ [Put $x = 5$]

$= 400 + 400 = 800$

7 (a) $f(x) = xe^{x(1-x)}$

$$\log f(x) = \log x + \log e^{x(1-x)}$$
$$\log f(x) = \log x + x(1-x)$$
$$\log f(x) = \log x + x - x^2$$

On differentiating both sides w.r.t. x, we get

$$\frac{1}{f(x)} f'(x) = \frac{1}{x} + 1 - 2x$$
$$\Rightarrow f'(x) = xe^{x(1-x)}\left[\frac{1+x-2x^2}{x}\right]$$
$$\Rightarrow f'(x) = -e^{x(1-x)}(2x^2 - x - 1)$$
$$= -e^{x(1-x)}(2x^2 - 2x + x - 1)$$
$$= -e^{x(1-x)}(2x+1)(x-1)$$
$$f'(x) = 0 \Rightarrow x = -\frac{1}{2}, 1$$

$-$ $+$ $-$
$-1/2$ 1

$\therefore f(x)$ is increasing in $\left(-\frac{1}{2}, 1\right)$ and decreasing $\left(-\infty, -\frac{1}{2}\right) \cup (1, \infty)$.

8 (252) $f(x) = (p^2 - 6p + 8)(\sin^2 2x - \cos^2 2x) + 2(2-p)x + 7$

$$f(x) = (p^2 - 6p + 8)(-\cos 4x) + 2(2-p)x + 7$$
$$f'(x) = (p^2 - 6p + 8)(\sin 4x)(4) + 2(2-p) \neq 0$$
$$\sin 4x \neq \frac{2p-4}{4(p-4)(p-2)}$$
$$\sin 4x \neq \frac{1}{2(p-4)},$$

where $p \neq 2$

$$\therefore \left|\frac{1}{2(p-4)}\right| > 1$$
$$|2(p-4)| < 1$$
$$-1 < 2(p-4) < 1$$
$$-\frac{1}{2} < p - 4 < \frac{1}{2}$$
$$\frac{7}{2} < p < \frac{9}{2}$$
$$a = \frac{7}{2}, b = \frac{9}{2}$$
$$16ab = 16 \times \frac{7}{2} \times \frac{9}{2} = 252$$

9 (4) $D = \sin^2 2\theta - 4\left(1 - \frac{\sin^2 2\theta}{2}\right)\left(1 - \frac{3}{4}\sin^2 2\theta\right)$

$$= (\sin 2\theta)^2 - 4\left(1 - \frac{5}{4}\sin^2 2\theta + \frac{3}{8}\sin^4 2\theta\right)$$
$$\Rightarrow D = -\frac{3}{2}\sin^4 2\theta + 6\sin^2 2\theta - 4 > 0$$
$$\Rightarrow 3\sin^4 2\theta - 12\sin^2 2\theta + 8 < 0$$

Critical point

$$\sin^2 2\theta = \frac{12 \pm \sqrt{(12)^2 - 4(3)(8)}}{2 \times 3}$$
$$= \frac{12 \pm 4\sqrt{3}}{6} = \frac{6 \pm 2\sqrt{3}}{3}$$
$$\sin^2 2\theta = \frac{6 \pm 2\sqrt{3}}{3} \quad [\because \sin^2 2\theta \in [0, 1]]$$
$$\therefore \sin^2 2\theta \in \left[2 - \frac{2}{\sqrt{3}}, 1\right]$$
$$\alpha = 2 - \frac{2}{\sqrt{3}}, \beta = 1$$
$$(\alpha - 2)^2 = \frac{4}{3}, (\beta - 1)^2 = 0$$
$$\therefore 3(\alpha - 2)^2 + (\beta - 1)^2 = 4$$

10 (5) Let $f(n) = \frac{n^3}{n^4 + 147}$

So, $f'(n) = \frac{3n^2(n^4 + 147) - n^3(4n^3)}{(n^4 + 147)^2}$

For maxima, $f'(n) = 0$

$\Rightarrow 3n^2(n^4 + 147) - n^3(4n^3) = 0$
$\Rightarrow n = \sqrt{21}$
$\because 4 < \sqrt{21} < 5$
$\Rightarrow f(5) > f(4)$
or $a_5 > a_4$

For $n = 5$, $f(n)$ or a_n is maximum.

$\therefore a_\alpha$ is maximum at $\alpha = 5$

11 (5)

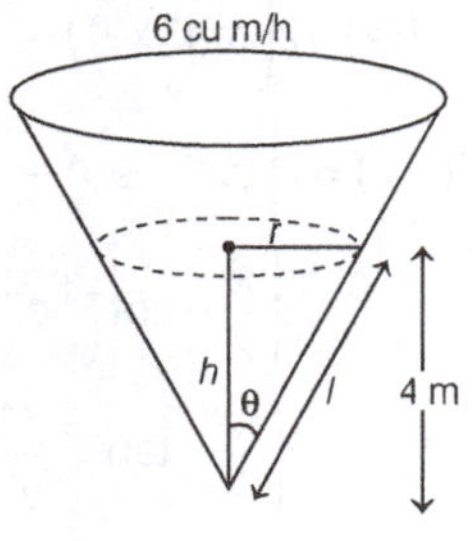

We have, $\tan\theta = \frac{3}{4} \Rightarrow \frac{r}{h} = \frac{3}{4}$

$$\therefore h = \frac{4r}{3} \quad \text{...(i)}$$
$$\Rightarrow l = \sqrt{r^2 + \frac{16r^2}{9}} = \frac{5r}{3}$$

Volume of water

$$= V = \frac{1}{3}\pi r^2 h = \frac{4\pi(r)^3}{9}$$
$$\frac{dV}{dt} = \frac{4\pi r^2}{3} \cdot \frac{dr}{dt} = 6$$
$$\therefore \frac{dr}{dt} = \frac{9}{2\pi r^2}$$

Now, curved surface area $= S = \pi r l$

$$\therefore S = \frac{5\pi r^2}{3}$$
$$\therefore \frac{dS}{dt} = \frac{10\pi r}{3}\frac{dr}{dt} = \frac{10\pi r}{3} \times \frac{9}{2\pi r^2} = \frac{15}{r}$$

Now, $h = 4$, then from Eq. (i), we get $r = 3$

$$dS/dt = 5\,\text{m}^2/\text{h}$$

Skill Boosters

1 (a) Given, $f(x) = x\sin x - \frac{1}{2}\sin^2 x$

$$\Rightarrow f'(x) = \sin x + x\cos x - \sin x \cdot \cos x$$
$$= \sin x(1 - \cos x) + x\cos x$$

Simply, we can say $f'(x) > 0$ for $x \in \left(0, \frac{\pi}{2}\right)$

Therefore, $f(x)$ is strictly increasing function for $x \in \left(0, \frac{\pi}{2}\right)$

Now, range of $f(x)$ for $x \in \left(0, \frac{\pi}{2}\right)$ is $\left(f(0), f\left(\frac{\pi}{2}\right)\right)$

$$= \left(0, \frac{\pi}{2} - \frac{1}{2}\right) = \left(0, \frac{\pi - 1}{2}\right)$$

2 (b) Given, $g(x) = (f(x))^3 - 3(f(x))^2 + 4f(x) + 5x + 3\sin x + 4\cos x$

$$\Rightarrow g'(x) = ((3(f(x))^2 - 6f(x) + 4)f'(x) + 5 + 3\cos x - 4\sin x)$$
$$= (3(f(x) - 1)^2 + 1)f'(x) + 5 + 3\cos x - 4\sin x$$

Now, we know $3(f(x) - 1)^2 + 1$ is +ve for all $x \in R$ and

$$-5 \leq 3\cos x - 4\sin x \leq 5$$

$\therefore \quad 0 \le 5 + 3\cos x - 4\sin x \le 10$

$\Rightarrow \quad g'(x) \ge 0$ when $f'(x) \ge 0$

So, $g(x)$ is increasing whenever f is increasing.

3 (a) $f(x) = x^3 - 3(a-2)x^2 + 3ax + 7$

$$f'(x) = 3x^2 - 6(a-2)x + 3a$$

$\therefore f'(x) = 0$ at $x = 1$

$$0 = 3 - 6(a-2) + 3a$$
$$3a = 15$$
$$a = 5$$

$\therefore \quad f(x) = x^3 - 9x^2 + 15x + 7$

Now $\dfrac{f(x) - 14}{(x-1)^2} = 0$

$\Rightarrow \quad \dfrac{x^3 - 9x^2 + 15x - 7}{(x-1)^2} = 0$

$\Rightarrow \quad \dfrac{(x-1)^2(x-7)}{(x-1)^2} = 0$

$\therefore \quad x = 7$

4 (a) $\dfrac{dV}{dt} = -72\pi \text{ m}^3/\text{min}$

$$V_0 = 4500\pi$$
$$V = \frac{4}{3}\pi r^3$$
$$\frac{dV}{dt} = 4\pi r^2 \frac{dr}{dt}$$

After 49 min, $V = V_0 + \left(\dfrac{dV}{dt}\right)49$

$$= 4500\pi - 49 \times 72\pi = 972\pi$$

$\Rightarrow 972\pi = \dfrac{4}{3}\pi r^3 \Rightarrow r = 9$

$\therefore \; -72\pi = 4\pi \times 81 \times \dfrac{dr}{dt}$

$\Rightarrow \quad \dfrac{dr}{dt} = -\dfrac{18}{81} = -\dfrac{2}{9}$

Thus, radius decreases at the rate of $\dfrac{2}{9}$ m/min.

5 (a) Let $f(x) = ax^4 + bx^3 + 2x^2$

$$\left[\because \lim_{x \to 0}\left(1 + \frac{f(x)}{x^2}\right) = 3\right]$$

Given, $f'(1) = f'(2) = 0$

$$f'(x) = 4ax^3 + 3bx^2 + 4x$$
$$f'(1) = 0 = 4a + 3b + 4$$

$\Rightarrow \; 4a + 3b = -4 \quad$ ...(i)

$$f'(2) = 0 = 32a + 12b + 8$$

$\Rightarrow \; 8a + 3b = -2 \quad$ ...(ii)

From Eqs. (i) and (ii), we get

$$a = \frac{1}{2}, b = -2$$

$\therefore \; f(x) = \dfrac{1}{2}x^4 - 2x^3 + 2x^2$

$$f(2) = 8 - 16 + 8 = 0$$

6 (d) $f'(x) = \begin{cases} -2, & x < -1 \\ 2, & x > -1 \end{cases}$

$f(x)$ is decreasing $(-\infty, -1)$ and increasing $(-1, \infty)$.

Therefore, $x = -1$ is the point of minima.

$$f(-1) = 1 = k + 2$$

[$\because$ we can take a possible value of $f(-1) = 1$]

$\therefore \quad k = -1$

7 (a) Let $f(x, y, z)$

$$= x^2 + 4y^2 + 3z^2 - 2x - 12y - 6z + 14$$
$$= (x-1)^2 + 4\left(y - \frac{3}{2}\right)^2 + 3(z-1)^2 + 1$$

For least value of $f(x, y, z)$

$x - 1 = 0;\; y - \dfrac{3}{2} = 0$ and $z - 1 = 0$

Hence, least value of $f(x, y, z)$ is $\left(1, \dfrac{3}{2}, 1\right) = 1.$

8 (c) Given, $\dfrac{dr}{dt} = c \quad$ [constant]

$$h = ar + b$$

Also, given $\dfrac{dh}{dt} = 3 \cdot \dfrac{dr}{dt}$

$\Rightarrow \quad a \cdot \dfrac{dr}{dt} = 3 \cdot \dfrac{dr}{dt}$

$\Rightarrow \quad a = 3$

Hence, $h = 3r + b$

When $r = 1$

$\Rightarrow \quad h = 6$

$\Rightarrow \quad b = 3$

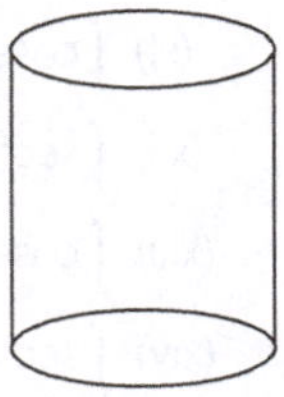

$\therefore \quad h = 3(r+1)$

$$V = \pi r^2 h = 3\pi r^2(r+1)$$
$$= 3\pi(r^3 + r^2)$$
$$\frac{dV}{dt} = 3\pi(3r^2 + 2r) \cdot \frac{dr}{dt}$$

Given, $r = 6 \Rightarrow \dfrac{dV}{dt} = 1$ c.c./s

$\therefore \quad 1 = 3\pi(108 + 12) \cdot \dfrac{dr}{dt}$

$\Rightarrow \quad 360\pi \cdot \dfrac{dr}{dt} = 1$

Again, when $r = 23$

$\Rightarrow \dfrac{dV}{dt} = n$

$$n = 3\pi[3(36)^2 + 2 \cdot (36)] \cdot \frac{dr}{dt}$$
$$= 3\pi \cdot 36 \cdot 110 \cdot \frac{1}{360\pi}$$
$$n = 33$$

$\therefore \quad \dfrac{n}{11} = 3$

9 (a) Given, $f(x) = x^{1/x}, x > 0$

$$y = f(x) = x^{1/x}$$

On taking log both sides, we get

$$\log y = \frac{1}{x}\log x$$

On differentiating both sides, we get

$$\frac{1}{y} \cdot \frac{dy}{dx} = \frac{1}{x^2} - \frac{1}{x^2}\ln x$$
$$\frac{dy}{dx} = y\left(\frac{1 - \log x}{x^2}\right)$$
$$f'(x) = \frac{x^{1/x}}{x^2}(1 - \log x)$$

Let $\quad f'(x) = 0$

$\Rightarrow \quad \log x = 1$

$\Rightarrow \quad x = e$

Again, $f''(x) = \dfrac{x^{1/x}}{x^2}\left(0 - \dfrac{1}{x}\right) + (1 - \ln x) \cdot \dfrac{d}{dx}\left(\dfrac{x^{1/x}}{x^2}\right)$

$$f''(e) < \frac{e^{1/e}}{e^2}\left(-\frac{1}{e}\right) < 0$$

$\therefore f''$ has maximum at $x = e$.

$\therefore \quad f(e) > f(\pi), \forall x > 0$

$\Rightarrow \quad e^{1/e} > \pi^{1/\pi}$

$\Rightarrow \quad e^\pi > \pi^e$

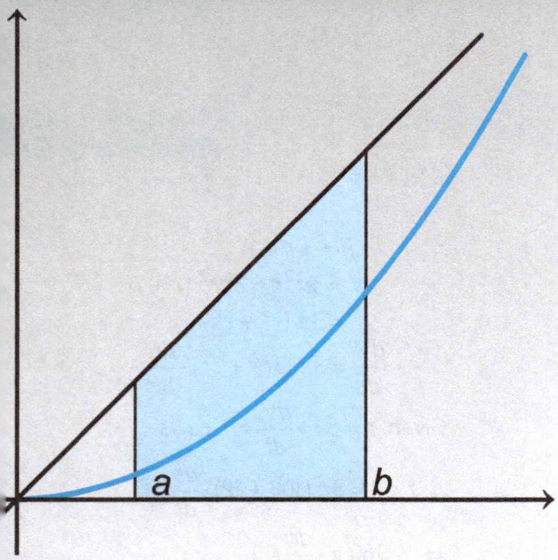

07

Integrals

Topicwise No. of Ques asked in 3 Years (JEE Main)

Topics	No. of Questions		
	2024	2023	2022
Integration as an Inverse Process of Differentiation	–	–	–
Methods of Integration	2	1	1
Integration using Trigonometric Identities	1	2	2
Integrals of Some Particular Functions	1	1	–
Integration by Partial Fractions	2	1	–
Integration by Parts	–	–	–
Integrals of Some More Types Functions	1	2	–
Definite Integral	–	–	–
Fundamental Theorem of Integral Calculus	4	3	2
Evaluation of Definite Integrals by Substitution	3	1	5
Some Properties of Definite Integrals	30	27	31

Special Type of Question Asked in last 3 Years (JEE Main)

Types	Years		
	2024	2023	2022
A-R	–	–	–
Statement Based	–	–	1
Numerical Value Type	15	16	13

Last 3 Years Weightage (JEE Main)

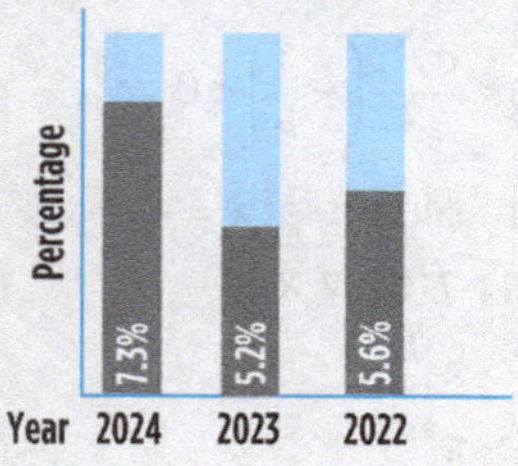

Integration as an Inverse Process of Differentiation

Indefinite Integral

Let $F(x)$ and $f(x)$ be two functions such that $\frac{d}{dx}[F(x)] = f(x)$, then $F(x)$ is called **integral of $f(x)$** or **indefinite integral** or **anti-derivative**.

Thus, $\int f(x)\,dx = F(x) + C$, where C is an arbitrary constant.

Some Standard Formulae

(i) $\int x^n dx = \frac{x^{n+1}}{n+1} + C, n \neq -1$ **[JEE Main 2024]**

(ii) $\int dx = x + C$

(iii) $\int \frac{1}{x} dx = \log|x| + C, x \neq 0$

(iv) $\int e^x dx = e^x + C$

(v) $\int a^x dx = \frac{a^x}{\log_e a} + C, a > 0, a \neq 1$ **[JEE Main 2022]**

(vi) $\int \sin x\, dx = -\cos x + C$

(vii) $\int \cos x\, dx = \sin x + C$

(viii) $\int \tan x\, dx = \log|\sec x| + C$ or $-\log|\cos x| + C$

(ix) $\int \cot x\, dx = \log|\sin x| + C$

(x) $\int \sec x\, dx = \log|\sec x + \tan x| + C = \log|\tan(\pi/4 + x/2)| + C$

(xi) $\int \text{cosec}\, x\, dx = \log|\text{cosec}\, x - \cot x| + C = \log|\tan(x/2)| + C$

(xii) $\int \sec^2 x\, dx = \tan x + C$

(xiii) $\int \text{cosec}^2 x\, dx = -\cot x + C$

(xiv) $\int \sec x \cdot \tan x\, dx = \sec x + C$

(xv) $\int \operatorname{cosec} x \cdot \cot x \, dx = -\operatorname{cosec} x + C$

(xvi) $\int \frac{1}{\sqrt{1-x^2}} dx = \sin^{-1} x + C$

(xvii) $\int \frac{1}{\sqrt{1-x^2}} dx = -\cos^{-1} x + C$

(xviii) $\int \frac{dx}{1+x^2} = \tan^{-1} x + C$

(xix) $\int \frac{1}{1+x^2} dx = -\cot^{-1} x + C$

(xx) $\int \frac{dx}{x\sqrt{x^2-1}} = \sec^{-1} x + C$

(xxi) $\int \frac{1}{x\sqrt{x^2-1}} dx = -\operatorname{cosec}^{-1} x + C$

Properties of Indefinite Integral

(i) The process of differentiation and integration are inverse of each other.

i.e. $\frac{d}{dx}\int f(x)\,dx = f(x)$ and $\int f'(x)\,dx = f(x) + C$

where, C is any arbitrary constant.

(ii) $\int \{f(x) \pm g(x)\} dx = \int f(x)\,dx \pm \int g(x)\,dx$

(iii) $\int k f(x)\,dx = k\int f(x)\,dx$

(iv) In general, if $f_1, f_2, \ldots, f_n$ are functions and $k_1, k_2, \ldots, k_n$ are numbers, then

$$\int [k_1 f_1(x) + k_2 f_2(x) + \ldots + k_n f_n(x)]\,dx$$
$$= k_1\int f_1(x)\,dx + k_2\int f_2(x)\,dx + \ldots + k_n\int f_n(x)\,dx + C$$

where, C is the constant of integration.

Methods of Integration

We have the following methods of integration.

(i) Integration by substitution.

(ii) Integration by partial function.

(iii) Integration by parts.

Integration by Substitution

The method of reducing a given integral into one of the standard integrals by proper substitution is called method of substitution. To evaluate an integral of the type $\int f\{g(x)\} \cdot g'(x)\,dx$, we substitute $g(x) = t$, so that $g'(x)\,dx = dt$.

Some Standard Substitutions

	Expression	Substitution
1.	$a^2 - x^2$ or $\sqrt{a^2 - x^2}$	$x = a\sin\theta$ or $a\cos\theta$
2.	$a^2 + x^2$ or $\sqrt{a^2 + x^2}$	$x = a\tan\theta$ or $a\cot\theta$
3.	$x^2 - a^2$ or $\sqrt{x^2 - a^2}$	$x = a\sec\theta$ or $a\operatorname{cosec}\theta$
4.	$\sqrt{\frac{a+x}{a-x}}$ or $\sqrt{\frac{a-x}{a+x}}$	$x = a\cos 2\theta$
5.	$\sqrt{\frac{x-\alpha}{\beta-x}}$ or $\sqrt{(x-\alpha)(\beta-x)}$	$x = \alpha\cos^2\theta + \beta\sin^2\theta, \beta > \alpha$
6.	$\sqrt{\frac{x}{a-x}}$ or $\sqrt{\frac{a-x}{x}}$	$x = a\sin^2\theta$ or $x = a\cos^2\theta$
7.	$\sqrt{\frac{x}{a+x}}$ or $\sqrt{\frac{a+x}{x}}$	$x = a\tan^2\theta$ or $x = a\cot^2\theta$

Integration Using Trigonometric Identities

- When the integrand involves trigonometric functions, then suitable trigonometric identities are used to evaluate the integral.
- Some useful trigonometric identities for this purpose are given below **[JEE Main 2024, 2023, 2022]**

(i) $\sin 2x = 2\sin x\cos x = \frac{2\tan x}{1+\tan^2 x}$

(ii) $\cos 2x = \cos^2 x - \sin^2 x = 2\cos^2 x - 1$
$= 1 - 2\sin^2 x = \frac{1-\tan^2 x}{1+\tan^2 x}$

(iii) $\tan 2x = \frac{2\tan x}{1-\tan^2 x}$

(iv) $\cot 2x = \frac{\cot^2 x - 1}{2\cot x}$

(v) $\sin 3x = -\sin^3 x + 3\cos^2 x\sin x = -4\sin^3 x + 3\sin x$

(vi) $\cos 3x = \cos^3 x - 3\sin^2 x\cos x = 4\cos^3 x - 3\cos x$

(vii) $\tan 3x = \frac{3\tan x - \tan^3 x}{1 - 3\tan^2 x}$

(viii) $\cot 3x = \frac{3\cot x - \cot^3 x}{1 - 3\cot^2 x}$

(ix) $\tan\frac{x}{2} = \operatorname{cosec} x - \cot x = \sqrt{\frac{1-\cos x}{1+\cos x}}$
$= \frac{\sin x}{1+\cos x} = \frac{1-\cos x}{\sin x}$

(x) $\cot\frac{x}{2} = \operatorname{cosec} x + \cot x = \sqrt{\frac{1+\cos x}{1-\cos x}}$
$= \frac{\sin x}{1-\cos x} = \frac{1+\cos x}{\sin x}$

(xi) $\sin(x+y) = \sin x\cos y + \cos x \sin y$

(xii) $\sin(x-y) = \sin x\cos y - \cos x\sin y$

(xiii) $\cos(x+y) = \cos x\cos y - \sin x\sin y$

(xiv) $\cos(x-y) = \cos x\cos y + \sin x\sin y$

(xv) $\tan(x+y) = \frac{\tan x + \tan y}{1-\tan x\tan y}$

(xvi) $\tan(x-y) = \frac{\tan x - \tan y}{1+\tan x\tan y}$

(xvii) $2\sin A\cos B = \sin(A+B) + \sin(A-B)$

(xviii) $2\cos A\sin B = \sin(A+B) - \sin(A-B)$

(xix) $2\cos A\cos B = \cos(A+B) + \cos(A-B)$

(xx) $2\sin A\sin B = \cos(A-B) - \cos(A+B)$

(xxi) $\sin A + \sin B = 2\sin\frac{A+B}{2}\cdot\cos\frac{A-B}{2}$

(xxii) $\sin A - \sin B = 2\cos\frac{A+B}{2}\cdot\sin\frac{A-B}{2}$

(xxiii) $\cos A + \cos B = 2\cos\frac{A+B}{2}\cdot\cos\frac{A-B}{2}$

(xxiv) $\cos A - \cos B = -2\sin\frac{A+B}{2}\cdot\sin\frac{A-B}{2}$

(xxv) **Inverse trigonometric functions**

(a) $\sin^{-1}(\sin x) = x$ (b) $\cos^{-1}(\cos x) = x$

(c) $\tan^{-1}(\tan x) = x$ (d) $\operatorname{cosec}^{-1}(\operatorname{cosec} x) = x$

(e) $\sec^{-1}(\sec x) = x$ (f) $\cot^{-1}(\cot x) = x$

Integrals of Some Particular Functions

(i) $\int\frac{dx}{(x^2-a^2)} = \frac{1}{2a}\log\left|\frac{x-a}{x+a}\right| + C$

(ii) $\int\frac{dx}{(a^2-x^2)} = \frac{1}{2a}\log\left|\frac{a+x}{a-x}\right| + C$

(iii) $\int\frac{dx}{(a^2+x^2)} = \frac{1}{a}\tan^{-1}\frac{x}{a} + C$

(iv) $\int\frac{dx}{\sqrt{a^2-x^2}} = \sin^{-1}\frac{x}{a} + C$

(v) $\int\frac{dx}{\sqrt{(x^2-a^2)}} = \log|x+\sqrt{x^2-a^2}| + C$

(vi) $\int\frac{dx}{\sqrt{x^2+a^2}} = \log\left|x+\sqrt{x^2+a^2}\right| + C$

(vii) **Form I** $\int\frac{1}{ax^2+bx+c}dx$ or $\int\frac{1}{\sqrt{ax^2+bx+c}}dx$

Express ax^2+bx+c as sum or difference of two squares. For this write

$$ax^2+bx+c = a\left[\left(x+\frac{b}{2}a\right)^2 + \frac{4ac-b^2}{4a^2}\right]$$

(viii) **Form II** $\int\frac{px+q}{ax^2+bx+c}dx$ or $\int\frac{px+q}{\sqrt{ax^2+bx+c}}dx$

Put $px+q = \lambda\cdot\frac{d}{dx}(ax^2+bx+c)+\mu$

Now, find values of λ and μ and then integrate it.

Some Standard Integrals and Substitutions for them

Integral	Substitution
$\int\frac{dx}{a\pm b\cos x}$	Put $\cos x = \frac{1-\tan^2\frac{x}{2}}{1+\tan^2\frac{x}{2}}$, then put $\tan\frac{x}{2} = t$
$\int\frac{dx}{a\pm b\sin x}$	Put $\sin x = \frac{2\tan\frac{x}{2}}{1+\tan^2\frac{x}{2}}$, then put $\tan\frac{x}{2} = t$
$\int\frac{dx}{a\sin x + b\cos x}$	Put $a = r\cos\theta$ and $b = r\sin\theta$ where, $r = \sqrt{a^2+b^2}$ and $\theta = \tan^{-1}\left(\frac{b}{a}\right)$
$\int\frac{dx}{a+b\sin^2 x}$, $\int\frac{dx}{a+b\cos^2 x}$, $\int\frac{dx}{a\cos^2 x + b\sin^2 x}$, $\int\frac{dx}{(a\sin x + b\cos x)^2}$ and $\int\frac{dx}{a+b\sin^2 x + c\cos^2 x}$	(a) Divide numerator and denominator by $\cos^2 x$ (b) Reduce $\sec^2 x$ in denominator as $1+\tan^2 x$ (c) Put $\tan x = t$ and proceed for perfect square
$\int\frac{dx}{(ax+b)\sqrt{px+q}}$ or $\int\frac{dx}{(ax^2+bx+c)\sqrt{px+q}}$	Put $\sqrt{px+q} = t$
$\int\frac{dx}{(px+q)(\sqrt{ax^2+bx+c})}$	Put $px+q = \frac{1}{t}$
$\int\frac{dx}{(px^2+q)\sqrt{ax^2+b}}$	Put $x = \frac{1}{t}$ and then put $\sqrt{a^2+bt^2} = u$

Integration by Partial Fractions

- Suppose, given integral is of the form $\int \frac{p(x)}{q(x)} dx$, where $p(x)$ and $q(x)$ are polynomials in x and $q(x) \neq 0$.
- To solve such integrals by partial fraction, we firstly take the given integrand $\frac{p(x)}{q(x)}$ and express it as the sum of partial fractions and then integrate each term by using suitable method.

S.No.	Form of the rational function	Form of the partial fraction
1.	$\frac{px \pm q}{(x \pm a)(x \pm b)}, a \neq b$	$\frac{A}{x \pm a} + \frac{B}{x \pm b}$
2.	$\frac{px \pm q}{(x \pm a)^2}$	$\frac{A}{(x \pm a)} + \frac{B}{(x \pm a)^2}$
3.	$\frac{px^2 \pm qx \pm r}{(x \pm a)(x \pm b)(x \pm c)}$	$\frac{A}{(x \pm a)} + \frac{B}{(x \pm b)} + \frac{C}{(x \pm c)}$
4.	$\frac{px^2 \pm qx \pm r}{(x \pm a)(x \pm b)^2}$	$\frac{A}{(x \pm a)} + \frac{B}{(x \pm b)} + \frac{C}{(x \pm b)^2}$
5.	$\frac{px^2 \pm qx \pm r}{(x \pm a)^2 (x \pm b)}$	$\frac{A}{(x \pm a)} + \frac{B}{(x \pm a)^2} + \frac{C}{(x \pm b)}$
6.	$\frac{px^2 \pm qx \pm r}{(x \pm a)^3}$	$\frac{A}{(x \pm a)} + \frac{B}{(x \pm a)^2} + \frac{C}{(x \pm a)^3}$
7.	$\frac{px^2 \pm qx \pm r}{(x \pm a)(x^2 \pm bx \pm c)}$	$\frac{A}{(x \pm a)} + \frac{Bx + C}{x^2 \pm bx \pm c}$, where $x^2 \pm bx \pm c$ cannot be factorised further.

Integration by Parts

- Let u and v be two differentiable functions of a single variable x, then the integral of the product of two functions is
$$\int \underset{\text{I}}{u} \underset{\text{II}}{v} \, dx = u \int v \, dx - \int \left(\frac{d}{dx} u \int v \, dx \right) dx.$$

Concept Master Video

- If two functions are of different types, then consider the 1st function (i.e. u) which comes first in word ILATE, where

  I : Inverse trigonometric function e.g. $\sin^{-1} x$ **[JEE Main 2023]**

  L : Logarithmic function e.g. $\log x$

  A : Algebraic function e.g. $1, x, x^2$

  T : Trigonometric function e.g. $\sin x, \cos x$

  E : Exponential function e.g. e^x
- **Integral of the type $\int e^x [f(x) + f'(x)] dx$** If the given integrand is of the form $e^x [f(x) + f'(x)]$, then we can directly write the integral as
$$\int e^x [f(x) + f'(x)] dx = e^x f(x) + C$$
[JEE Main 2024]

Integrals of Some More Types Functions

(i) $\int \sqrt{x^2 - a^2} dx = \frac{x}{2} \sqrt{x^2 - a^2} - \frac{a^2}{2} \log |x + \sqrt{x^2 - a^2}| + C$

(ii) $\int \sqrt{x^2 + a^2} dx = \frac{x}{2} \sqrt{x^2 + a^2} + \frac{a^2}{2} \log |x + \sqrt{x^2 + a^2}| + C$

(iii) $\int \sqrt{a^2 - x^2} dx = \frac{x}{2} \sqrt{a^2 - x^2} + \frac{a^2}{2} \sin^{-1} \frac{x}{a} + C$

- Integrals (i), (ii) and (iii) can be solved using trigonometric substitutions $x = a \sec \theta$ for (i), $x = a \tan\theta$ for (ii) and $x = a \sin\theta$ for (iii).

Marks Maximizer

- In integral form $\int \frac{P(x)}{ax^2 + bx + c} dx$, where $P(x)$ is a polynomial of degree 2 or more, carry out the division and express it in the form
$$\frac{P(x)}{ax^2 + bx + c} = Q(x) + \frac{R(x)}{ax^2 + bx + c},$$ where $R(x)$ is a linear expression or constant.

  Note If degree of the numerator of the integrand is equal to or greater than that of denominator, divide the numerator by the denominator until the degree of the remainder is less than that of denominator i.e.
$$\frac{\text{Numerator}}{\text{Denominator}} = \text{Quotient} + \frac{\text{Remainder}}{\text{Denominator}}$$
- $\int (px + q) \sqrt{ax^2 + bx + c} \, dx = \frac{p}{2a} \int (2ax + b) \sqrt{ax^2 + bx + c} \, dx + \left(q - \frac{pb}{2a} \right) \int \sqrt{ax^2 + bx + c} dx$
- (a) $\int a^x \cos (bx + c) \, dx = \frac{a^x}{(\log a)^2 + b^2} [(\log a) \cos(bx + c) + b \sin(bx + c)] + k$

  (b) $\int a^x \sin (bx + c) \, dx = \frac{a^x}{(\log a)^2 + b^2} [(\log a) \sin (bx + c) - b \cos(bx + c)] + k$
- (a) $\int xe^{ax} \cos(bx + c) dx = \frac{xe^{ax}}{a^2 + b^2} [a \cos(bx + c) + b \sin(bx + c)] - \frac{e^{ax}}{(a^2 + b^2)^2} [(a^2 - b^2) \cos (bx + c) + 2ab \sin (bx + c)] + k$

  (b) $\int xe^{ax} \sin (bx + c) dx = \frac{xe^{ax}}{a^2 + b^2} [a \sin(bx + c) - b \cos(bx + c)] - \frac{e^{ax}}{(a^2 + b^2)^2} [(a^2 - b^2) \sin(bx + c) - 2ab \cos(bx + c)] + k$

Definite Integral

- An integral of the form $\int_a^b f(x)\,dx$ is known as definite integral and is given by $\int_a^b f(x)\,dx = g(b) - g(a)$, where $f(x)$ is derivative of $g(x)$, a and b are **lower** and **upper limits** of a definite integral.

Fundamental Theorem of Integral Calculus

- **Theorem I** Let f be a continuous function defined on the closed interval $[a, b]$ and $A(x)$ be the area of function, i.e. $A(x) = \int_a^x f(x)\,dx$.

  Then, $A'(x) = f(x), \forall\, x \in [a, b]$.
- **Theorem II** Let f be a continuous function defined on the closed interval $[a, b]$ and F be an anti-derivative of f.

  Then, $\int_a^b f(x)\,dx = [F(x)]_a^b = F(b) - F(a)$.

Evaluation of Definite Integrals by Substitution

- To evaluate $\int_a^b f(x)\,dx$ using substitution.
  (i) Substitute $y = f(x)$ or $x = g(y)$
  (ii) Integrate the new integrand.
  (iii) Resubstitute the original variable.
  (iv) Evaluate the limits and find the difference.
- To speed up the method, after (i) and (ii) step, skip (iii) step. Instead keep the integral in the new variable and charge the limits accordingly. Then directly evaluate the integral with the new limits.

Some Properties of Definite Integrals

(i) $\int_a^b f(x)\,dx = \int_a^b f(t)\,dt$

(ii) $\int_a^b f(x)\,dx = -\int_b^a f(x)\,dx$

(iii) $\int_a^b f(x)\,dx = \int_a^c f(x)\,dx + \int_c^b f(x)\,dx$, where $a < c < b$.

(iv) $\int_a^b f(x)\,dx = \int_a^b f(a+b-x)\,dx$ **[JEE Main 2024]**

(v) $\int_0^a f(x)\,dx = \int_0^a f(a-x)\,dx$

(vi) $\int_0^{2a} f(x)\,dx = \int_0^a f(x)\,dx + \int_0^a f(2a-x)\,dx$

(vii) $\int_0^{2a} f(x)\,dx = \begin{cases} 2\int_0^a f(x)\,dx, & \text{if } f(2a-x) = f(x) \\ 0, & \text{if } f(2a-x) = -f(x) \end{cases}$

(viii) $\int_{-a}^a f(x)\,dx = \begin{cases} 2\int_0^a f(x)\,dx, & \text{if } f(-x) = f(x), \text{ i.e. even} \\ 0, & \text{if } f(-x) = -f(x), \text{ i.e. odd} \end{cases}$

[JEE Mains 2024, 22]

Marks Maximizer

- $\int_a^b \dfrac{f(x)}{f(x)+f(a+b-x)}\,dx = \dfrac{b-a}{2}$
- $\int_a^b f(x)\,dx + \int_{f(a)}^{f(b)} f^{-1}(x)\,dx = bf(b) - af(a)$
- $\int_{-a}^a f(x)\,dx = \int_0^a f(x)\,dx + \int_0^a f(-x)\,dx$
- $\int_a^b f(x)\,dx = \begin{cases} 0, & \text{if } f(a+x) = -f(b-x) \\ 2\int_a^{\frac{a+b}{2}} f(x)\,dx, & \text{if } f(a+x) = f(b-x) \end{cases}$

Caution Points

- $\int f(x)\,dx$ means integral of f with respect to x, $f(x)$ is called integrand, x is a variable of integration.
- In practice, we often skip mentioning the interval where function are defined, but in specific problems, its essential to consider the domain to ensure accurate results and avoid errors.
- If F is an anti-derivative of f, then $F + C$ (with C be any constant, belonging to R) is also an anti-derivative. A specific condition is needed to find the unique value of C.
- Ensure limits are correctly applied. If the upper limit is less than the lower limit, the integral's sign will be reversed.

PYQ Notes

1. If integral of from $\int \frac{a \sin x + b \cos x}{c \sin x + d \cos x} dx,$

   Write numerator **[JEE Main 2024]**

   $= \lambda$ (differentiation of denominator)

   $+ \mu$ (denominator)

   i.e. $a \sin x + b \cos x = \lambda (c \cos x - d \sin x) + \mu(c \sin x + d \cos x)$

   $$\int \frac{a \sin x + b \cos x}{c \sin x + d \cos x} dx = \lambda \int \frac{c \cos x - d \sin x}{c \sin x + d \cos x} dx + \mu \int \frac{c \sin x + d \cos x}{c \sin x + d \cos x} dx$$

   $= \lambda \log |c \sin x + d \cos x| + \mu x + C$

2. If integral form

   $\int \frac{px + q}{ax^2 + bx + c} dx$ or $\int \frac{px + q}{\sqrt{ax^2 + bx + c}} dx$

   or $\int (px + q)\sqrt{ax^2 + bx + c}\, dx$ **[JEE Main 2023]**

   Put $px + q = \lambda \cdot \frac{d}{dx}(ax^2 + bx + c) + \mu.$

   Now, find values of λ and μ and then integrate it.

3. $\int \frac{x^2 + 1}{x^4 + \lambda x^2 + 1} dx,$ $\int \frac{x^2 - 1}{x^4 + \lambda x^2 + 1} dx,$

   $\int \frac{1}{x^4 + \lambda x^2 + 1} dx$

   To evaluate this type of integrals we proceed as follows.

   (a) Divide numerator and denominator by x^2.

   (b) Express the denominator of integrands in the form of $\left(x + \frac{1}{x}\right)^2 \pm k^2$.

   (c) Introduce $d\left(x + \frac{1}{x}\right)$ or $d\left(x - \frac{1}{x}\right)$ or both in numerator.

   (d) Put $x + \frac{1}{x} = t$ or $x - \frac{1}{x} = t$ as the case may be.

   (e) Integral reduced to the form $\int \frac{1}{x^2 + a^2} dx$ or $\int \frac{1}{x^2 - a^2} dx.$

   [JEE Main 2024]

4. **Leibnitz Rule for Differentiation under Integral Sign**

   (a) If $\phi(x)$ and $\psi(x)$ are defined on $[a, b]$ and differentiable for (a, b) x and $f(t)$ is continuous, then

   $$\frac{d}{dx}\left[\int_{\phi(x)}^{\psi(x)} f(t)\, dt\right] = f[\psi(x)] \cdot \frac{d}{dx}[\psi(x)] - f[\phi(x)] \cdot \frac{d}{dx}[\phi(x)].$$

   (b) If $\phi(x)$ and $\psi(x)$ are defined on $[a, b]$ and differentiable for (a, b) and $f(t)$ is continuous, then

   $$\frac{d}{dx}\left[\int_{\phi(x)}^{\psi(x)} f(x, t)\, dt\right] = \left[\int_{\phi(x)}^{\psi(x)} \frac{\delta}{\delta x} f(x, t)\, dt + \frac{d\psi(x)}{dx} f\{x, \psi(x)\} - \frac{d}{dx}(\phi(x)) f\{x, \phi(x)\}\right].$$

   [JEE Main 2024]

Step by Step

Mastering NCERT

- Concept Builders
- Topical Questions
- Numerical Type Questions
- Assertion and Reason Questions
- Case or Paragraph Type Questions
- Past Years Questions
- Skill Boosters

Concept Builders

1 $\int 3^x \cdot 5^{2x}\, dx$ is ....

2 $\int e^{(2\ln 3 + \ln 2x)}$ is ....

3 $\int \dfrac{dx}{3-4x} =$ ....

4 $\int e^x\left[\tan^{-1} x + \dfrac{1}{1+x^2}\right] dx =$ ....

5 $\int_0^3 \{x\}\, dx =$ .... where $\{x\}$ is fraction part of x.

6 $\int_1^4 [x]\, dx =$ .... where $[x]$ is greatest integer function.

7 The anti-derivative of $\sec x\,(\sec x + \tan x)$ is ....

8 $\int_0^1 \dfrac{x}{1+x^2}\, dx =$ ....

9 $\int_0^3 \left(\tan^{-1}(x^2+1) + \tan^{-1}\left(\dfrac{1}{x^2+1}\right)\right) dx =$ ....

10 $\int \sqrt{1+\sin\left(\dfrac{x}{2}\right)}\, dx =$ ....

11 $\int \sec^2(2x+1)\, dx =$ ....

12 If $\dfrac{d}{dx}(f(x)) = 2x + 3x^3$ such that $f(1) = 0$, then $f(x)$ is ....

13 Find the integration of $2x^2 e^{x^3}$ is ....

14 $\int \dfrac{d\theta}{\sec^2\theta - \tan^2\theta}$ is ....

Topical Questions

Integration as an Inverse Process of Differentiation

Level I

1 Match the terms of column I with column II and choose the correct option from the codes given below. NCERT Pg. 226

	Column I (Functions)		Column II (Anti-derivatives)
A.	$\cos x$	1.	$e^x + C$
B.	x^2	2.	$\sin x + C$
C.	e^x	3.	$\dfrac{x^3}{3} + C$

Codes

	A	B	C
(a)	1	2	3
(b)	2	1	3
(c)	3	1	2
(d)	2	3	1

2 **Statement I** Anti-derivatives or integrals of the functions are unique.

Statement II There exist infinitely many anti- derivatives of each function which can be obtained by choosing a constant, C arbitrarily from the set of real numbers. NCERT Pg. 226

(a) Both statements are true.
(b) Both statements are false.
(c) Statement I is true; Statement II is false.
(d) Statement I is false; Statement II is true.

3 For any function f if F is one of its anti-derivative. Then,

Statement I Family $\{F + C, C \in R\}$ provides all possible anti-derivatives of f.

Statement II Functions with same anti-derivatives differ by a constant. NCERT Pg. 227

(a) Both statements are true.
(b) Both statements are false.
(c) Statement I is true; Statement II is false.
(d) Statement I is false; Statement II is true.

4 Match the following symbols in column I with their corresponding meaning in column II and choose the correct option from the codes given below. **NCERT Pg. 227**

	Column I		Column II
A.	$\int f(x)\,dx$	1.	Integrand
B.	'$f(x)$' in $\int f(x)\,dx$	2.	Variable of integration
C.	'x' in $\int f(x)\,dx$	3.	Integral of f with respect to x.

Codes

	A	B	C		A	B	C
(a)	2	1	3	(b)	1	2	3
(c)	3	1	2	(d)	3	2	1

5 Match the following terms/phrases in column I with their respective meaning in column II and choose the correct option from the codes given below. **NCERT Pg. 227**

	Column I		Column II
A.	Integrate	1.	Any real number C, considered as constant function.
B.	An integral of f	2.	A function F such that $F'(x) = f(x)$
C.	Integration	3.	Find the integral.
D.	Constant of integration.	4.	The process of finding the integral.

Codes

	A	B	C	D
(a)	1	2	3	4
(b)	3	4	2	1
(c)	1	2	4	3
(d)	3	2	4	1

6 **Statement I** If the derivative of function x is $\frac{d}{dx}(x) = 1$, then its anti-derivatives or integral is $\int (1)\,dx = x + C$.

Statement II If $\frac{d}{dx}\left(\frac{x^{n+1}}{n+1}\right) = x^n$, then the corresponding integral of the function is $\int x^n\,dx = \frac{x^{n+1}}{n+1} + C, n \neq -1$. **NCERT Pg. 228**

(a) Both statements are true.
(b) Both statements are false.
(c) Statement I is true; Statement II is false.
(d) Statement I is false; Statement II is true.

7 Match the following function in column I with their anti-derivatives in column II and choose the correct option from the codes given below. **NCERT Pg. 228**

	Column I		Column II
A.	$\cos x$	1.	$-\cot x + C$
B.	$\sin x$	2.	$\sin x + C$
C.	$\sec^2 x$	3.	$-\cos x + C$
D.	$\text{cosec}^2 x$	4.	$\tan x + C$

Codes

	A	B	C	D		A	B	C	D
(a)	2	3	1	4	(b)	2	3	4	1
(c)	3	2	4	1	(d)	1	2	4	3

8 If $\frac{d}{dx}(\sec x) = \sec x \tan x$, then $\int \sec x \tan x\,dx$ is **NCERT Pg. 228**

(a) $\sec x$
(b) $\log|\sec x| + C$
(c) $\sec x + C$
(d) None of these

9 **Statement II** If $\frac{d}{dx}(-\text{cosec}\, x) = \text{cosec}\, x \cot x$, then $\int \text{cosec}\, x \cot x\,dx = -\text{cosec}\, x + C$.

Statement II If we know the formulae for the derivative of many important functions, then we can write down the corresponding formulae for the integrals of these functions. **NCERT Pg. 228**

(a) Both statements are true.
(b) Both statements are false.
(c) Statement I is true; Statement II is false.
(d) Statement I is false; Statement II is true.

10 Match the following derivatives of the functions in column I with their respective anti-derivatives in column II and choose the correct option from the codes given below. **NCERT Pg. 228**

	Column I		Column II
A.	$\frac{1}{\sqrt{1-x^2}}$	1.	$\tan^{-1} x + C$
B.	$\frac{-1}{\sqrt{1-x^2}}$	2.	$\cot^{-1} x + C$
C.	$\frac{1}{1+x^2}$	3.	$\sin^{-1} x + C$
D.	$\frac{-1}{1+x^2}$	4.	$\cos^{-1} x + C$

Codes

	A	B	C	D
(a)	1	2	3	4
(b)	3	4	2	1
(c)	3	4	1	2
(d)	4	3	2	1

11 If the derivative of a function $\sec^{-1} x$ is $\dfrac{1}{x\sqrt{x^2-1}}$, then the anti-derivative of $\dfrac{1}{x\sqrt{x^2-1}}$ is **Old NCERT Pg. 291**

(a) $\sec^{-1} x$ (b) $\sec^{-1} x + C$
(c) $2\sec^{-1} x$ (d) None of these

12 Which of the following is/are correct? **Old NCERT Pg. 291**

(i) $\displaystyle\int \frac{dx}{x\sqrt{x^2-1}} = \operatorname{cosec}^{-1} x + C$

(ii) $\int e^x\,dx = \log e^x + C$

(iii) $\displaystyle\int \frac{1}{x}\,dx = \log|x| + C$

(iv) $\int a^x\,dx = a^x + C$

(a) (i) and (iii) is correct (b) All are correct
(c) Only (iii) is correct (d) All are incorrect

13 Statement I If $\dfrac{d}{dx}\int f(x)\,dx = f(x)$, then $\int f(x)\,dx = f'(x) + C$, where C is any arbitrary constant.

Statement II Process of differentiation and integration are inverses of each other. **NCERT Pg. 229**

(a) Both statements are true.
(b) Both statements are false.
(c) Statement I is true; Statement II is false.
(d) Statement I is false; Statement II is true.

14 Equivalence of the families of curves $\{\int f(x)\,dx + C_1, C_1 \in R\}$ and $\{\int g(x)\,dx + C_2, C_2 \in R\}$ is expressed as **NCERT Pg. 229**

(a) $\int f(x + C_1)\,dx = \int g(x + C_2)\,dx$
(b) $\int \{f(x) + C_1\}\,dx = \int \{g(x) + C_2\}\,dx$
(c) $\int f(x)\,dx = \int g(x)\,dx$
(d) None of the above

15 Statement I $\int [f(x) + g(x)]\,dx = \int f(x)\,dx + \int g(x)\,dx$

Statement II $\dfrac{d}{dx}[\int [f(x) + g(x)]\,dx] = f(x) + g(x)$ **NCERT Pg. 230**

(a) Both statements are true.
(b) Both statements are false.
(c) Statement I is true; Statement II is false.
(d) Statement I is false; Statement II is true.

16 Statement I For any real number k, $\int k\,f(x)\,dx = k\int f(x)$.

Statement II Process of differentiation and integration are inverse of each other. **NCERT Pg. 230**

(a) Both statements are true.
(b) Both statements are false.
(c) Statement I is true; Statement II is false.
(d) Statement I is false; Statement II is true.

17 For a finite number of functions $f_1, f_2 \ldots, f_n$ and the real numbers $k_1, k_2 \ldots k_n$ $\int [k_1 f_1(x) + k_2 f_2(x) + \ldots + k_n f_n(x)]\,dx$ can be generalised as **NCERT Pg. 231**

(a) $(k_1 + k_2 + \ldots + k_n)\int [f_1(x) + f_2(x) + \ldots + f_n(x)]\,dx$
(b) $(k_1, k_2 \ldots k_n)\int [f_1(x_1) + f_2(x) + \ldots + f_n(x)]\,dx$
(c) $k_1\int f_1(x)\,dx + k_2\int f_2(x)\,dx + \ldots + k_n\int f_n(x)\,dx$
(d) None of the above

18 The integral formula used in the integral $\int y^4\,dy = \dfrac{y^5}{5} + C$ is **NCERT Pg. 234**

(a) $\int x^n\,dx = \dfrac{x^n}{n} + C$ (b) $\int x^n\,dx = \dfrac{x^{n+1}}{n+1} + C$

(c) $\int y^n\,dx = \dfrac{y^{n+1}}{n} + C$ (d) None of these

19 Match the following functions in column I with their respective anti-derivatives in column II and choose the correct option from the codes given below. **NCERT Pg. 234**

Column I	Column II
A. $\sin 2x$	1. $\frac{1}{3}\sin 3x + C$
B. $\cos 3x$	2. $\frac{1}{3a}(ax+b)^3 + C$
C. e^{2x}	3. $-\frac{1}{2}\cos 2x + C$
D. $(ax+b)^2$	4. $\frac{1}{2}e^{2x} + C$

Codes

	A	B	C	D		A	B	C	D
(a)	1	2	4	3	(b)	3	1	4	2
(c)	3	1	2	4	(d)	1	2	3	4

20 The anti-derivative of $\sin 2x - 4e^{3x}$ is **NCERT Pg. 234**

(a) $\frac{1}{2}\cos 2x - \frac{4}{3}e^{3x} + C$ (b) $-\frac{1}{2}\cos 2x + \frac{4}{3}e^{3x} + C$

(c) $-\frac{1}{2}\cos 2x - \frac{4}{3}e^{3x} + C$ (d) None of these

21 Statement I Integral of the function $(4e^{3x} + 1)$ is $\frac{4}{3}e^{3x} + x + C$.

Statement II $\int e^{nx}\,dx = \dfrac{e^{nx}}{n} + C$ and $\int 1\,dx = x + C$. **NCERT Pg. 234**

(a) Both statements are true.
(b) Both statements are false.
(c) Statement I is true; Statement II is false.
(d) Statement I is false; Statement II is true.

22 Match the following integrals in column I with their corresponding values in column II and choose the correct option from the codes given below.

NCERT Pg. 234

Column I	Column II
A. $\int x^2\left(1-\frac{1}{x^2}\right)dx$	1. $\frac{2x^3}{3}+e^x+C$
B. $\int (ax^2+bx+c)\,dx$	2. $\frac{x^3}{3}-x+C$
C. $\int (2x^2+e^x)\,dx$	3. $\frac{x^2}{2}+\log\lvert x\rvert-2x+C$
D. $\int\left(\sqrt{x}-\frac{1}{\sqrt{x}}\right)^2 dx$	4. $\frac{ax^3}{3}+\frac{bx^2}{2}+cx+K$

Codes

	A	B	C	D		A	B	C	D
(a)	2	1	3	4	(b)	4	3	1	2
(c)	2	4	3	1	(d)	2	4	1	3

23 Value of integral $\int \frac{x^3+5x^2-4}{x^2}dx$ is

NCERT Pg. 234

(a) $x^2+5x-\frac{4}{x}+C$ (b) $\frac{x^2}{2}-5x+\frac{4}{x}+C$

(c) $\frac{x^2}{2}+5x+\frac{4}{x}+C$ (d) None of these

24 Integral of $\frac{x^3+3x+4}{\sqrt{x}}$ is

NCERT Pg. 234

(a) $\frac{2}{7}x^{5/2}+\frac{2}{3}x^{3/2}+8x^{1/2}+C$

(b) $\frac{2}{7}x^{7/2}+2x^{3/2}+8x^{1/2}+C$

(c) $\frac{1}{7}x^{7/2}+2x^{3/2}+8x^{1/2}+C$

(d) $x^{7/2}+3x^{3/2}+4x^{1/2}+C$

25 Match the following integrals in column I with their corresponding solutions in column II and choose the correct option from the codes given below.

NCERT Pg. 234, 235

Column I	Column II
A. $\int (1-x)\sqrt{x}\,dx$	1. $\frac{6}{7}x^{7/2}+\frac{4}{5}x^{5/2}+2x^{3/2}+C$
B. $\int \sqrt{x}(3x^2+2x+3)\,dx$	2. $x^2-3\sin x+e^x+C$
C. $\int (2x-3\cos x+e^x)\,dx$	3. $\frac{2}{3}x^3+\cos x+\frac{10}{3}x^{3/2}+C$
D. $\int (2x^2-3\sin x+5\sqrt{x})\,dx$	4. $\frac{2}{3}x^{3/2}-\frac{2}{5}x^{5/2}+C$

Codes

	A	B	C	D		A	B	C	D
(a)	4	1	3	2	(b)	1	2	3	4
(c)	4	1	2	3	(d)	1	3	4	2

26 The anti-derivative of $[\sec x(\sec x+\tan x)]$ is

NCERT Pg. 235

(a) $2\sec x+C$ (b) $\tan x+\sec x+C$

(c) $\sec^2 x+\sec x\tan x+C$ (d) None of these

27 **Statement I** Integral of the function $\frac{\sec^2 x}{\operatorname{cosec}^2 x}$ is $\tan x-x+C$.

Statement II $\sin^2 x=\frac{1}{\operatorname{cosec}^2 x}$ and $\cos^2 x=\frac{1}{\sec^2 x}$.

NCERT Pg. 235

(a) Both statements are true.
(b) Both statements are false.
(c) Statement I is true; Statement II is false.
(d) Statement I is false; Statement II is true.

28 The anti-derivative of $\left(\sqrt{x}+\frac{1}{\sqrt{x}}\right)$ equals

NCERT Pg. 235

(a) $\frac{1}{3}x^{\frac{1}{3}}+2x^{\frac{1}{2}}+C$ (b) $\frac{2}{3}x^{\frac{2}{3}}+\frac{1}{2}x^2+C$

(c) $\frac{2}{3}x^{\frac{3}{2}}+2x^{\frac{1}{2}}+C$ (d) $\frac{3}{2}x^{\frac{3}{2}}+\frac{1}{2}x^{\frac{1}{2}}+C$

29 If $\frac{d}{dx}f(x)=4x^3-\frac{3}{x^4}$ such that $f(2)=0$. Then, $f(x)$ is

NCERT Pg. 235

(a) $x^4+\frac{1}{x^3}-\frac{129}{8}$ (b) $x^3+\frac{1}{x^4}+\frac{129}{8}$

(c) $x^4+\frac{1}{x^3}+\frac{129}{8}$ (d) $x^3+\frac{1}{x^4}-\frac{129}{8}$

Level II

30 $\int\left(\frac{2a}{\sqrt{x}}-\frac{b}{x^2}+3c\sqrt[3]{x^2}\right)dx$ is equal to

NCERT Exemplar Pg. 146

(a) $4a\sqrt{x}-\frac{b}{x}+\frac{9}{5}Cx^{5/3}+C$ (b) $2a\sqrt{x}+\frac{b}{x}+\frac{9}{5}Cx^{5/3}+C$

(c) $4a\sqrt{x}+\frac{b}{x}+\frac{9}{5}cx^{5/3}+C$ (d) None of these

31 $\int\frac{x^3}{x+1}dx$ is equal to

NCERT Exemplar Pg. 147

(a) $x+\frac{x^2}{2}+\frac{x^3}{3}-\log\lvert 1-x\rvert+C$

(b) $x+\frac{x^2}{2}-\frac{x^3}{3}-\log\lvert 1-x\rvert+C$

(c) $x-\frac{x^2}{2}-\frac{x^3}{3}-\log\lvert 1+x\rvert+C$

(d) $x-\frac{x^2}{2}+\frac{x^3}{3}-\log\lvert 1+x\rvert+C$

32 If $\frac{d}{dx}\{f(x)\} = \frac{1}{1+x^2}$, then $\frac{d}{dx}\{f(x^3)\} =$ .... NCERT Pg. 235

(a) $\frac{3x}{1+x^3}$ (b) $\frac{3x^2}{1+x^6}$ (c) $\frac{-6x^5}{(1+x^6)^2}$ (d) $\frac{-6x^5}{1+x^6}$

33 The anti-derivative of $\frac{\sec^2 x - 7}{\sin^7 x}$ is NCERT Pg. 235

(a) $\frac{\tan x}{\sin^7 x} + C$ (b) $\frac{\cos x}{\sin^7 x} + C$

(c) $\frac{\sin x}{\cos^7 x} + C$ (d) $\frac{\sin x}{\tan^7 x} + C$

34 The value of $\int e^{\tan^{-1} x} \frac{(1+x+x^2)}{1+x^2} dx$ is NCERT Exemplar Pg. 166

(a) $\tan^{-1} x + C$ (b) $x \tan^{-1} x + e^{\tan^{-1} x} + C$

(c) $x e^{\tan^{-1} x} + C$ (d) $e^{\tan^{-1} x} - x + C$

35 If $f'(x) = x + \frac{1}{x}$, then the value of $f(x)$ is NCERT Pg. 235

(a) $x^2 + \log x + C$ (b) $\frac{x^2}{2} + \log|x| + C$

(c) $\frac{x}{2} + \log x + C$ (d) None of these

Methods of Integration

Level I

1 Which of the following statements is/are correct? NCERT Pg. 237, 238

(i) $\int \tan x \, dx = \log|\cos x| + C$

(ii) $\int \cot x \, dx = \log|\sin x| + C$

(iii) $\int \sec x \, dx = \log|\tan x| + C$

(iv) $\int \operatorname{cosec} x \, dx = -\log|\operatorname{cosec} x - \cot x| + C$

(a) (i), (ii) and (iii) are correct

(b) Only (ii) is correct

(c) (i) and (iii) are correct

(d) All are correct

2 Which of the following integration of the functions is/are correct? NCERT Pg. 240

(i) $\int \frac{2x}{1+x^2} dx = \log|x| + C$

(ii) $\int \frac{(\log x)^2}{x} dx = \frac{(\log x)^3}{3} + C$

(iii) $\int \frac{1}{x + x\log x} dx = \log|1 + \log x| + C$

(iv) $\int \sin x \sin(\cos x) \, dx = \sin(\cos x) + C$

(a) Only (iii) is correct

(b) (ii) and (iii) are correct

(c) (i), (iii) and (iv) are correct

(d) All are correct

3 $\int \sin(ax+b)\cos(ax+b)$ equal to NCERT Pg. 240

(a) $\frac{\sin(ax+b)}{2a} + C$ (b) $\frac{[\sin(ax+b)]^2}{2a} + C$

(c) $\frac{[\sin(ax+b)]^2}{2} + C$ (d) None of these

4 Match the following integrals in column I with their corresponding values in column II and choose the correct option from the codes given below. NCERT Pg. 240

Column I	Column II
A. $\int \sqrt{ax+b}\, dx$	1. $\frac{2}{5}(x+2)^{5/2} - \frac{4}{3}(x+2)^{3/2} + C$
B. $\int x\sqrt{x+2}\, dx$	2. $\frac{1}{6}(1+2x^2)^{3/2} + C$
C. $\int x\sqrt{1+2x^2}\, dx$	3. $\frac{4}{3}(x^2+x+1)^{3/2} + C$
D. $\int (4x+2)\sqrt{x^2+x+1}\, dx$	4. $\frac{2}{3a}(ax+b)^{3/2} + C$

Codes

	A	B	C	D
(a)	4	1	2	3
(b)	3	4	2	1
(c)	1	3	2	4
(d)	3	2	4	1

5 The value of $\int \frac{1}{x - \sqrt{x}} dx$ is NCERT Pg. 240

(a) $2\log\sqrt{x} + C$ (b) $2\log|\sqrt{x} - 1| + C$

(c) $\log|\sqrt{x} - 1| + C$ (d) None of these

6 $\int \frac{x}{\sqrt{x+4}} dx$ equals to NCERT Pg. 240

(a) $\frac{2}{3}(x+4)^{1/2} - 8(x+4)^{1/2} + C$

(b) $(x+4)^{3/2} - 8(x+4)^{3/2} + C$

(c) $(x+4)^{3/2} - 8(x-4)^{1/2} + C$

(d) $\frac{2}{3}(x+4)^{3/2} - 8(x+4)^{1/2} + C$

7 Which of the following integrals are correctly evaluated?

(i) $\int (x^3-1)^{1/3} x^5 dx = \frac{1}{3}(x^3-1)^{7/3} + \frac{1}{4}(x^3-1)^{4/3} + C$

(ii) $\int \frac{x^2}{(2+3x^3)^3} dx = -\frac{1}{18(2+3x^3)^2} + C$

(iii) $\int \frac{1}{x(\log x)^m} dx = \frac{(\log x)^{1-m}}{1-m} + C$

(iv) $\int \frac{x}{9-4x^2} dx = \frac{1}{8}\log\left|\frac{1}{9-4x^2}\right| + C$

NCERT Pg. 240

(a) Only (i) (b) (ii), (iii) and (iv)

(c) (iii) and (iv) (d) All of these

8 Match the following integrals in column I with their corresponding values in column II and choose the correct option from the codes given below. NCERT Pg. 240

Column I	Column II
A. $\int e^{2x+3}\,dx$	1. $e^{\tan^{-1}x}+C$
B. $\int \frac{x}{e^{x^2}}\,dx$	2. $\log\lvert e^x+e^{-x}\rvert+C$
C. $\int \frac{e^{\tan^{-1}x}}{1+x^2}\,dx$	3. $\frac{1}{2}e^{(2x+3)}+C$
D. $\int \frac{e^{2x}-1}{e^{2x}+1}\,dx$	4. $-\frac{1}{2}e^{-(x^2)}+C$

Codes

	A	B	C	D		A	B	C	D
(a)	1	2	3	4	(b)	3	4	1	2
(c)	1	3	2	4	(d)	3	1	2	4

9 The value of $\int \frac{e^{2x}-e^{-2x}}{e^{2x}+e^{-2x}}\,dx$ is NCERT Pg. 240

(a) $\frac{1}{2}\log\lvert e^x+e^{-x}\rvert+C$ (b) $2\log\lvert e^{2x}+e^{-2x}\rvert+C$
(c) $\frac{1}{2}\log\lvert e^{2x}+e^{-2x}\rvert+C$ (d) None of these

10 Consider the following statements.

Statement I The integral of $\tan^2(2x-3)$ is $\frac{\tan(2x-3)}{2}-x+C$.

Statement II Integral of $\sec^2(7-4x)$ is $-\frac{1}{4}\tan(7-4x)+C$.

Choose the correct option. NCERT Pg. 241

(a) Statement I is true.
(b) Statement II is true.
(c) Both statements are true.
(d) Both statements are false.

11 Which of the following integrals are evaluated correctly?

(i) $\int \frac{\sin^{-1}x}{\sqrt{1-x^2}}\,dx=\frac{(\sin^{-1}x)^2}{2}+C$

(ii) $\int \frac{2\cos x-3\sin x}{6\cos x+4\sin x}\,dx=\frac{1}{2}\log\lvert 3\cos x-2\sin x\rvert+C$

(iii) $\int \frac{1}{\cos^2 x(1-\tan x)^2}\,dx=\frac{1}{1-\tan x}+C$

(iv) $\int \frac{\cos\sqrt{x}}{\sqrt{x}}\,dx=2\sin x+C$ NCERT Pg. 241

(a) Only (i) (b) (ii) and (iii)
(c) (i) and (iv) (d) (i) and (iii)

12 The integral of $\sqrt{\sin 2x}\,\cos 2x$ is NCERT Pg. 241

(a) $\frac{1}{3}(\sin x)^{3/2}+C$ (b) $\frac{1}{3}(\sin x)^{1/2}+C$
(c) $\frac{1}{3}(\sin 2x)^{3/2}+C$ (d) $\frac{1}{3}(\sin 2x)^{1/2}+C$

13 Consider the following statements.

Statement I The integral of $\frac{\cos x}{\sqrt{1+\sin x}}$ is $\sqrt{1+\sin x}+C$.

Statement II The integral of $\cot x\log\sin x$ is $\frac{\log(\sin x)^2}{2}+C$.

Choose the correct option. NCERT Pg. 241

(a) Statement I is true.
(b) Statement II is true.
(c) Both statements are true.
(d) Both statements are false.

14 Match the following integrals in column I with their corresponding values in column II and choose the correct option from the codes given below. NCERT Pg. 241

Column I	Column II
A. $\int \frac{\sin x}{1+\cos x}\,dx$	1. $\frac{1}{1+\cos x}+C$
B. $\int \frac{\sin x}{(1+\cos x)^2}\,dx$	2. $\log\left\lvert\frac{1}{1+\cos x}\right\rvert+C$
C. $\int \frac{1}{1+\cot x}\,dx$	3. $\frac{1}{2}[x-\log\lvert\cos x-\sin x\rvert]+C$
D. $\int \frac{1}{1-\tan x}\,dx$	4. $\frac{1}{2}[x-\log\lvert\sin x+\cos x\rvert]+C$

Codes

	A	B	C	D
(a)	1	2	3	4
(b)	2	1	4	3
(c)	1	3	2	4
(d)	2	1	3	4

15 Which of the following integrals are evaluated correctly?

(i) $\int \frac{\sqrt{\tan x}}{\sin x\cos x}\,dx=2\sqrt{\tan x}+C$

(ii) $\int \frac{(1+\log x)^2}{x}\,dx=\frac{(1+\log x)^2}{3}+C$

(iii) $\int \frac{(x+1)(x+\log x)^2}{x}\,dx=(x+\log x)^3+C$

(iv) $\int \frac{x^3\sin(\tan^{-1}x^4)}{1+x^8}\,dx=-\frac{1}{4}\cos(\tan^{-1}x^4)+C$ NCERT Pg. 241

(a) (ii) and (iii) (b) Only (iv)
(c) (i) and (iv) (d) (i), (ii) and (iv)

16 $\int \frac{[10x^9 + 10^x \log_e 10]\, dx}{x^{10} + 10^x}$ equals

NCERT Pg. 241

(a) $10^x - x^{10} + C$ (b) $10^x + x^{10} + C$
(c) $(10^x - x^{10})^{-1} + C$ (d) $\log |10^x + x^{10}| + C$

17 $\int \frac{dx}{\sin^2 x \cos^2 x}$ equals

NCERT Pg. 241

(a) $\tan x + \cot x + C$ (b) $\tan x - \cot x + C$
(c) $\tan x \cot x + C$ (d) $\tan x - \cot 2x + C$

Level II

18 Consider the following statements.

Statement I The value of $\int (x+1)(x+2)^7 (x+3)dx$ is $\frac{(x+2)^{10}}{10} - \frac{(x+2)^8}{8} + C.$

Statement II The integral of $\int \text{cosec}\,(x-a)\,\text{cosec}\, x\, dx$ is $-\frac{1}{\sin a}[\log|\sin(x-a)\,\text{cosec} x\,] + C.$

NCERT Exemplar Pg. 167

Choose the correct option.
(a) Statement I is true (b) Statement II is true
(c) Both statements are true (d) Both statements are false

19 If $\int \frac{3e^x - 5e^{-x}}{4e^x + 5e^{-x}} dx = ax + b \log|4e^x + 5e^{-x}| + C$, then

NCERT Exemplar Pg. 159

(a) $a = \frac{-1}{8}, b = \frac{-7}{8}$ (b) $a = \frac{1}{8}, b = \frac{7}{8}$
(c) $a = \frac{-1}{8}, b = \frac{7}{8}$ (d) $a = \frac{1}{8}, b = \frac{-7}{8}$

20 $\int \frac{x^9}{(4x^2+1)^6} dx$ is equal to

NCERT Exemplar Pg. 167

(a) $\frac{1}{5x}\left(4 + \frac{1}{x^2}\right)^{-5} + C$ (b) $\frac{1}{5}\left(4 + \frac{1}{x^2}\right)^{-5} + C$
(c) $\frac{1}{10x}(1+4)^{-5} + C$ (d) $\frac{1}{10}\left(\frac{1}{x^2} + 4\right)^{-5} + C$

21 Consider the following statements.

Statement I The integral of $\frac{2x+3}{x^2+3x}$ is equal to $\log|x^2 + x| + C.$

Statement II The integral of $\frac{x}{\sqrt{x}+1}$ is $2\left[\frac{x^{3/2}}{3} - \frac{x}{2} + \sqrt{x} - \log|\sqrt{x}+1|\right] + C.$

Choose the correct option.

NCERT Exemplar Pg. 163

(a) Statement I is true
(b) Statement II is true
(c) Both statements are true
(d) Both statements are false

22 Consider the following statements.

Statement I The value of $\int \frac{1+\cos x}{x + \sin x} dx$ is $\log|x + \sin x| + C.$

Statement II The value of $\int \tan^2 x \sec^4 x\, dx$ is $\frac{1}{3}\tan^3 x + \frac{1}{5}\tan^5 x + C.$

Choose the correct option.

NCERT Exemplar Pg. 164

(a) Statement I is true (b) Statement II is true
(c) Both statements are true (d) Both statements are false

23 If $\int \frac{x^3}{\sqrt{1+x^2}} dx = a(1+x^2)^{3/2} + b\sqrt{1+x^2} + C$, then

NCERT Exemplar Pg. 168

(a) $a = \frac{1}{3}, b = 1$ (b) $a = \frac{-1}{3}, b = 1$
(c) $a = \frac{-1}{3}, b = -1$ (d) $a = \frac{1}{3}, b = -1$

24 Consider the following statements.

Statement I If $\int \frac{e^x - 1}{e^x + 1} dx = f(x) + C$, then $f(x)$ is equal to $2\log|e^x + 1| - x.$

Statement II The integral of $\frac{e^x - e^{-x}}{e^x + e^{-x}}$ is $\log|e^x + e^{-x}| - x + C.$

Choose the correct option.

NCERT Pg. 241

(a) Statement I is true (b) Statement II is true
(c) Both statements are true (d) Both statements are false

Integration using Trigonometric Identities

Level I

1 Match the following integrals in column I with their corresponding values in column II and choose the correct option from the codes given below. NCERT Pg. 243

Column I	Column II
A. $\int \sin^2(2x+5)\, dx$	1. $\frac{-\cos 7x}{14} + \frac{\cos x}{2} + C$
B. $\int \sin 3x \cos 4x\, dx$	2. $\frac{x}{2} - \frac{\sin(4x+10)}{8} + C$
C. $\int \sin^3(2x+1)\, dx$	3. $\frac{\cos^6 x}{6} - \frac{\cos^4 x}{4} + C$
D. $\int \sin^3 x \cos^3 x\, dx$	4. $\frac{-\cos(2x+1)}{2} + \frac{\cos^3(2x+1)}{6} + C$

Codes

	A	B	C	D		A	B	C	D
(a)	2	4	1	3	(b)	1	4	2	3
(c)	1	2	4	3	(d)	2	1	4	3

2 Consider the following statements.

Statement I The integral of the function $\cos 2x \cos 4x \cos 6x$ is $\frac{1}{4}\left[\frac{\sin 12x}{12}+\frac{\sin 8x}{8}+\frac{\sin 4x}{4}\right]+C.$

Statement II The integral of the function $\sin x \sin 2x \sin 3x$ is $\frac{-\cos 4x}{16}+\frac{\cos 6x}{24}-\frac{\cos 2x}{8}+C.$

Choose the correct option. **NCERT Pg. 243**

(a) Statement I is true (b) Statement II is true
(c) Both statements are true (d) Both statements are false

3 Which of the following integrals are evaluated correctly?

(i) $\int \frac{1-\cos x}{1+\cos x}dx = 2\tan\frac{x}{2} - x + C$

(ii) $\int \frac{\cos x}{1+\cos x}dx = x + \tan\frac{x}{2} + C$

(iii) $\int \cos^4 2x = \frac{x}{8} + \frac{\sin 8x}{64} + \frac{\sin 4x}{8} + C$

(iv) $\int \frac{\sin^2 x}{1+\cos x}dx = x - \sin x + C$ **NCERT Pg. 243**

(a) Only (iii) (b) (ii), (iii) and (iv)
(c) (i) and (iv) (d) All of these

4 $\int \frac{\cos 2x - \cos 2\alpha}{\cos x - \cos \alpha}dx$ is equal to **NCERT Pg. 243**

(a) $2\sin x + 2x\sin\alpha + C$ (b) $2\sin x + 2x\cos\alpha + C$
(c) $2\cos x + 2x\sin\alpha + C$ (d) $2\cos x + 2x\cos\alpha + C$

5 Match the following integrals in column I with their corresponding integrals in column II and choose the correct option from the codes given below. **NCERT Pg. 243**

Column I	Column II
A. $\int \frac{\cos x - \sin x}{1+\sin 2x}dx$	1. $\frac{1}{6}\sec^3 2x - \frac{1}{2}\sec^2 2x + C$
B. $\int \tan^3 2x \sec 2x dx$	2. $\tan x + C$
C. $\int \frac{\sin^3 x + \cos^3 x}{\sin^2 x \cos^2 x}dx$	3. $\frac{-1}{\sin x + \cos x} + C$
D. $\int \frac{\cos 2x + 2\sin^2 x}{\cos^2 x}dx$	4. $\sec x - \operatorname{cosec} x + C$

Codes

	A	B	C	D		A	B	C	D
(a)	1	2	3	4	(b)	3	1	4	2
(c)	3	4	1	2	(d)	2	1	4	3

6 Consider the following statements.

Statement I The integral of the function $\sin 4x \sin 8x$ is $\frac{1}{2}\left[\frac{\sin 4x}{4}-\frac{\sin 12x}{12}\right]+C.$

Statement II Integral of the function $\sin^4 x$ is $\left[\frac{x}{8}+\frac{\sin 4x}{32}-\frac{\sin 2x}{4}\right]+C.$

Choose the correct option. **NCERT Pg. 243**

(a) Statement I is true
(b) Statement II is true
(c) Both statements are true
(d) Both statements are false

7 The integral of the function $\tan^4 x$ is **NCERT Pg. 243**

(a) $\frac{\tan^3 x}{3} - \tan x - x + C$ (b) $\frac{\tan^3 x}{3} + \tan x - x + C$

(c) $\frac{\tan^3 x}{3} - \tan x + x + C$ (d) $\frac{\tan^3 x}{3} + \tan x + x + C$

8 Which of the following integrals are evaluated correctly?

(i) $\int \frac{1}{\sin x \cos^3 x}dx = \log|\tan x| + \tan^2 x + C$

(ii) $\int \frac{\cos 2x}{(\cos x + \sin x)^2}dx = \log|\cos x + \sin x| + C$

(iii) $\int \sin^{-1}(\cos x)dx = \frac{\pi}{2}x + \frac{x^2}{2} + C$

(iv) $\int \frac{1}{\cos(x-a)\cos(x-b)}dx = \frac{1}{\sin(b-a)}\log\left|\frac{\cos(x-b)}{\cos(x-a)}\right| + C$ **NCERT Pg. 243**

(a) Only (iii) (b) (ii) and (iv)
(c) (i) (iii) and (iv) (d) All of these

9 $\int \frac{\sin^2 x - \cos^2 x}{\sin^2 x \cos^2 x}dx$ is equal to **NCERT Pg. 243**

(a) $\tan x + \cot x + C$ (b) $\tan x + \operatorname{cosec} x + C$
(c) $-\tan x + \cot x + C$ (d) $\tan x + \sec x + C$

10 $\int \frac{e^x(1+x)}{\cos^2(e^x x)}dx$ equals **NCERT Pg. 243**

(a) $-\cot(ex^x) + C$ (b) $\tan(xe^x) + C$
(c) $\tan(e^x) + C$ (d) $\cot(e^x) + C$

Level II

11 $\int \frac{dx}{2\sin^2 x \cos^2 x}$ is equal to **NCERT Exemplar Pg. 159**

(a) $\tan x + \cot x + C$ (b) $(\tan x + \cot x)^2 + C$
(c) $\frac{\tan x}{2} - \frac{\cot x}{2} + C$ (d) $(\tan x - \cot x)^2 + C$

12 $\int \frac{\sin^6 x}{\cos^8 x}dx =$ .... **NCERT Exemplar Pg. 162**

(a) $\frac{\tan^6 x}{6} + C$ (b) $\frac{\tan^7 x}{7} + C$

(c) $\frac{\tan^8 x}{8} + C$ (d) None of these

13 Consider the following statements.

Statement I $\int \frac{\cos 5x + \cos 4x}{1 - 2\cos 3x}dx = \left[\frac{1}{2}\sin 2x + \sin x\right] + C$

Statement II $\int \frac{\sin^6 x + \cos^6 x}{\sin^2 x \cos^2 x}dx = \tan x - \cot x - 3x + C$

Choose the correct option. NCERT Exemplar Pg. 164

(a) Statement I is true
(b) Statement II is true
(c) Both statements are true
(d) Both statements are false

14 $\int \frac{dx}{\sin(x-a)\sin(x-b)}$ is equal to NCERT Exemplar Pg. 167

(a) $\sin(b-a)\log\left|\frac{\sin(x-b)}{\sin(x-a)}\right| + C$

(b) $\operatorname{cosec}(b-a)\log\left|\frac{\sin(x-a)}{\sin(x-b)}\right| + C$

(c) $\operatorname{cosec}(b-a)\log\left|\frac{\sin(x-b)}{\sin(x-a)}\right| + C$

(d) $\sin(b-a)\log\left|\frac{\sin(x-a)}{\sin(x-b)}\right| + C$

15 Which of the following integrals are correctly evaluated?

(i) $\int \frac{\sec x \operatorname{cosec} x}{2\cot x - \sec x \operatorname{cosec} x}dx = \frac{1}{2}\log|\sec 2x + \tan 2x| + C$

(ii) $\int \frac{\sec x}{\sec x + \tan x}dx = \tan x - \sec x + C$

(iii) $\int \tan(\sin^{-1} x)dx = -\sqrt{1-x^2} + C$

(iv) $\int (\sin^6 x + \cos^6 x + 3\sin^2 x \cos^2 x)dx = x + C$

NCERT Pg. 243

(a) Only (iii) (b) (ii) and (iv)
(c) (i) (iii) and (iv) (d) All of these

16 Consider the following statements.

Statement I The integral of $\frac{1}{\cos x - \sin x}$ is $\frac{1}{\sqrt{2}}\log\left|\tan\left[\frac{x}{2} - \frac{3\pi}{8}\right]\right| + C.$

Statement II The value of $\int \frac{dx}{\sin x - \cos x + \sqrt{2}}$ is $-\frac{1}{\sqrt{2}}\cot\left(\frac{x}{2} + \frac{\pi}{8}\right) + C.$

Choose the correct option. NCERT Pg. 243

(a) Statement I is true
(b) Statement II is true
(c) Both statements are true
(d) Both statements are false

17 If $\int \frac{\sin^8 x - \cos^8 x}{1 - 2\sin^2 x \cos^2 x}dx = A\sin 2x + B$, then NCERT Pg. 285

(a) $A = -\frac{1}{2}$ (b) $A = \frac{1}{2}$
(c) $A = -1$ (d) $A = 1$

Integrals of Some Particular Functions

Level I

1 Match the following integrals in column I with their corresponding values in column II and choose the correct option from the codes given below. NCERT Pg. 244

Column I	Column II
A. $\int \frac{dx}{x^2 - a^2}$	1. $\frac{1}{a}\tan^{-1}\frac{x}{a} + C$
B. $\int \frac{dx}{a^2 - x^2}$	2. $\log\lvert x + \sqrt{x^2 - a^2}\rvert + C$
C. $\int \frac{dx}{x^2 + a^2}$	3. $\log\lvert x + \sqrt{x^2 + a^2}\rvert + C$
D. $\int \frac{dx}{\sqrt{x^2 - a^2}}$	4. $\sin^{-1}\frac{x}{a} + C$
E. $\int \frac{dx}{\sqrt{a^2 - x^2}}$	5. $\frac{1}{2a}\log\left\lvert\frac{a+x}{a-x}\right\rvert + C$
F. $\int \frac{dx}{\sqrt{x^2 + a^2}}$	6. $\frac{1}{2a}\log\left\lvert\frac{x-a}{x+a}\right\rvert + C$

Codes

	A	B	C	D	E	F
(a)	5	6	4	3	1	2
(b)	6	5	1	2	4	3
(c)	1	2	5	6	3	4
(d)	3	1	5	6	2	4

2 Match the following integrals in column I with their corresponding values in column II and choose the correct option from the codes given below. NCERT Pg. 251

Column I	Column II
A. $\int \frac{3x^2}{x^6 + 1}dx$	1. $\frac{1}{2}\log\lvert 2x + \sqrt{4x^2 + 1}\rvert + C$
B. $\int \frac{1}{\sqrt{1 + 4x^2}}dx$	2. $\log\lvert(x-2) + \sqrt{(x-2)^2 + 1}\rvert + C$
C. $\int \frac{1}{\sqrt{(2-x)^2 + 1}}dx$	3. $\frac{1}{5}\sin^{-1}\left(\frac{5x}{3}\right) + C$
D. $\int \frac{1}{\sqrt{(9 - 25x^2)}}dx$	4. $\tan^{-1}(x^3) + C$

Codes

	A	B	C	D
(a)	1	3	2	4
(b)	4	2	1	3
(c)	1	2	4	3
(d)	4	1	2	3

3 Consider the following statements.

Statement I The integral of the function $\frac{3x}{1+2x^4}$ is $\frac{1}{2}\tan^{-1}(\sqrt{2}x^2)+C$.

Statement II The integral of $\frac{x^2}{1-x^6}$ is $\frac{1}{6}\log\left|\frac{1+x^3}{1-x^3}\right|+C$.

Choose the correct option. **NCERT Pg. 251**

(a) Statement I is true
(b) Statement II is true
(c) Both statements are true
(d) Both statements are false

4 Which of the following integrals are evaluated correctly?

(i) $\int \frac{x-1}{\sqrt{x^2-1}}dx = \sqrt{x^2-1}+\log|x+\sqrt{x^2+1}|+c$

(ii) $\int \frac{x^2}{\sqrt{x^6+a^6}}dx = \log|x^3+\sqrt{x^6+a^6}|+c$

(iii) $\int \frac{\sec^2 x}{\sqrt{\tan^2 x+4}}dx = \log|\tan x+\sqrt{\tan x^2+4}|+C$

(iv) $\int \frac{1}{\sqrt{x^2+2x+2}}dx = \log|(x+1)+\sqrt{x^2+2x+2}|+C$ **NCERT Pg. 251**

(a) Only (iii)
(b) (iii) and (iv)
(c) (i), (ii) and (iii)
(d) All of these

5 $\int \frac{1}{9x^2+6x+5}dx$ is equal to **NCERT Pg. 252**

(a) $\frac{1}{6}\tan^{-1}\left(\frac{3x+1}{3}\right)+C$
(b) $\sin^{-1}\left(\frac{3x+1}{2}\right)+C$
(c) $\sin^{-1}\left(\frac{3x+1}{3}\right)+C$
(d) $\frac{1}{6}\tan^{-1}\left(\frac{3x+1}{2}\right)+C$

6 The integral value of $\frac{1}{\sqrt{7-6x-x^2}}$ is **NCERT Pg. 252**

(a) $\log\left[2x+\sqrt{7-6x-x^2}\right]+C$
(b) $\frac{1}{2}\log\left|\frac{x+3}{x-3}\right|+C$
(c) $\sin^{-1}\left(\frac{x+3}{4}\right)+C$
(d) None of the above

7 **Statement I** The integral of the function $\frac{1}{\sqrt{(x-1)(x-2)}}$ is $\log\left|\left(x-\frac{3}{2}\right)+\sqrt{x^2-3x+2}\right|+C$.

Statement II The integral of the function $\frac{1}{\sqrt{(x-a)(x-b)}}$ is $\log\left|\left(x-\frac{a+b}{2}\right)+\sqrt{(x-a)(x-b)}\right|+C$. **NCERT Pg. 252**

(a) Both statements are true.
(b) Both statements are false.
(c) Statement I is true; Statement II is false.
(d) Statement I is false; Statement II is true.

8 The value of $\int \frac{1}{\sqrt{8+3x-x^2}}dx$ is equal to

(a) $\sin^{-1}\left(\frac{2x-3}{\sqrt{41}}\right)+C$
(b) $\frac{1}{\sqrt{41}}\sin^{-1}\left(\frac{2x-3}{\sqrt{41}}\right)+C$
(c) $\tan^{-1}\left(\frac{2x-3}{\sqrt{41}}\right)+C$
(d) $\frac{1}{\sqrt{41}}\tan^{-1}\left(\frac{2x-3}{\sqrt{41}}\right)+C$

9 Match the following integrals in column I with their corresponding values in column II and choose the correct option from the codes given below. **NCERT Pg. 252**

Column I	Column II
A. $\int \frac{4x+1}{\sqrt{2x^2+x-3}}dx$	1. $\frac{5}{6}\log\lvert 1+2x+3x^2\rvert - \frac{11}{3\sqrt{2}}\tan^{-1}\left(\frac{3x+1}{\sqrt{2}}\right)+C$
B. $\int \frac{x+2}{\sqrt{x^2-1}}dx$	2. $2\sqrt{2x^2+x-3}+C$
C. $\int \frac{5x-2}{1+2x+3x^2}dx$	3. $6\sqrt{x^2-9x+20}+34\log\left\lvert\left(x-\frac{9}{2}\right)+\sqrt{x^2-9x+20}\right\rvert+C$
D. $\int \frac{6x+7}{\sqrt{(x-5)(x-4)}}dx$	4. $\sqrt{x^2-1}+2\log\lvert x+\sqrt{x^2-1}\rvert+C$

Codes

	A	B	C	D		A	B	C	D
(a)	3	2	1	4	(b)	3	1	2	4
(c)	2	4	1	3	(d)	2	1	3	4

10 Which of the following integrals are evaluated correctly?

(i) $\int \frac{x+2}{\sqrt{4x-x^2}}dx = -\sqrt{4x-x^2}+4\sin^{-1}\left(\frac{x-2}{2}\right)+C$

(ii) $\int \frac{x+2}{\sqrt{x^2+2x+3}}dx = \sqrt{x^2+2x+3}+\log|x+1+\sqrt{x^2+2x+3}|+C$

(iii) $\int \frac{x+3}{x^2-2x-5}dx = \frac{1}{2}\log|x^2-2x-5|+\frac{2}{\sqrt{6}}\log\left|\frac{x-1-\sqrt{6}}{x-1+\sqrt{6}}\right|+C$

(iv) $\int \frac{5x+3}{\sqrt{x^2+4x+10}}dx = 5\sqrt{x^2+4x+10}+7\log|x+2+\sqrt{x^2+4x+10}|+C$

NCERT Pg. 252

(a) Only (i)
(b) (i), (ii) and (iii)
(c) (i) and (ii)
(d) All of these

11 $\int \frac{1}{x^2+2x+2} dx$ is equal to NCERT Pg. 252

(a) $x \tan^{-1}(x+1)+C$ (b) $\tan^{-1}(x+1)+C$

(c) $(x+1)\tan^{-1}x+C$ (d) $\tan^{-1}x+C$

12 $\int \frac{1}{\sqrt{9x-4x^2}} dx$ is equal to NCERT Pg. 252

(a) $\frac{1}{9}\sin^{-1}\left(\frac{9x-8}{8}\right)+C$ (b) $\frac{1}{2}\sin^{-1}\left(\frac{8x-9}{9}\right)+C$

(c) $\frac{1}{3}\sin^{-1}\left(\frac{9x-8}{8}\right)+C$ (d) $\frac{1}{2}\sin^{-1}\left(\frac{9x-8}{9}\right)+C$

Level II

13 Consider the following statements.

Statement I The value of $\int \frac{x^2+1}{x^4+1} dx$ is $\frac{1}{\sqrt{2}}\tan^{-1}\left(\frac{x^2-1}{\sqrt{2}x}\right)+C.$

Statement II The value of $\int \frac{x^2+4}{x^4+16} dx$ is $\frac{1}{\sqrt{2}}\tan^{-1}\left(\frac{x^2-4}{2x\sqrt{2}}\right)+C.$

Choose the correct option. NCERT Pg. 252

(a) Statement I is true
(b) Statement II is true
(c) Both statements are true
(d) Both statements are false

14 The value of $\int \frac{x^2-1}{x^4+x^2+1} dx$ is equal to NCERT Pg. 252

(a) $\frac{1}{2}\log\left|\frac{x^2+x+1}{x^2-x+1}\right|+C$ (b) $2\log\left|\frac{x^2+x+1}{x^2-x+1}\right|+C$

(c) $\frac{1}{2}\log\left|\frac{x^2-x+1}{x^2+x+1}\right|+C$ (d) None of these

15 Consider the following statements.

Statement I The value of $\int \frac{dx}{\sqrt{16-9x^2}}$ is $\frac{1}{3}\sin^{-1}\frac{3x}{4}+C.$

Statement II The value of $\int \frac{dt}{\sqrt{3t-2t^2}}$ is $\frac{1}{\sqrt{2}}\sin^{-1}\left(\frac{3-4t}{3}\right)+C.$

Choose the correct option. NCERT Exemplar Pg. 164

(a) Statement I is true
(b) Statement II is true
(c) Both statements are true
(d) Both statements are false

16 The value of $\int \frac{3x-1}{\sqrt{x^2+9}} dx$ is equal to NCERT Exemplar Pg. 164

(a) $\sqrt{x^2+9}-\log|x+\sqrt{x^2+9}|+C$

(b) $\sqrt{x^2+9}+\log|x+\sqrt{x^2+9}|+C$

(c) $3\sqrt{x^2+9}-\log|x+\sqrt{x^2+9}|+C$

(d) None of the above

17 $\int \frac{\sqrt{x}}{\sqrt{a^3-x^3}} dx$ equal to NCERT Exemplar Pg. 165

(a) $\frac{1}{3}\sin^{-1}\sqrt{\frac{x^3}{a^3}}+C$ (b) $\frac{2}{3}\sin^{-1}\sqrt{\frac{x^3}{a^3}}+C$

(c) $\frac{2}{3}\sin^{-1}\sqrt{\frac{x}{a}}+C$ (d) None of these

18 Which of the following integrals are evaluated correctly?

(i) $\int \frac{dx}{(x+1)\sqrt{4x+3}} = 2\tan^{-1}\sqrt{4x+3}+C$

(ii) $\int \frac{\sin x \cos x}{\sqrt{1-\sin^4 x}} dx = \frac{1}{2}\sin^{-1}(\cos^2 x)+C$

(iii) $\int \frac{(x^2+1)}{x^4-x^2+1} dx = \tan^{-1}\left(\frac{x}{x-1}\right)+C$

(iv) $\int \frac{dx}{x+\sqrt{x-1}} = \frac{2}{\sqrt{3}}\tan^{-1}\left(\frac{2\sqrt{x-1}+1}{\sqrt{3}}\right)+C$ NCERT Pg. 252

(a) Only (i) (b) (i), (ii) and (iv)
(c) (i) and (iv) (d) All of these

19 If $\int \frac{1}{(\sin x+4)(\sin x-1)} dx$

$= A\frac{1}{\left(\tan\frac{x}{2}-1\right)} + B\tan^{-1}[f(x)]+C_1$, then NCERT Pg. 252

(a) $A=-\frac{1}{5}, B=\frac{-2}{5\sqrt{15}}, f(x)=\frac{4\tan x+3}{\sqrt{15}}$

(b) $A=-\frac{1}{5}, B=\frac{1}{\sqrt{15}}, f(x)=\frac{4\tan\left(\frac{x}{2}\right)+1}{\sqrt{15}}$

(c) $A=\frac{2}{5}, B=-\frac{2}{5}, f(x)=\frac{4\tan x+1}{5}$

(d) $A=\frac{2}{5}, B=\frac{-2}{5\sqrt{15}}, f(x)=\frac{4\tan\left(\frac{x}{2}\right)+1}{\sqrt{15}}$

20 Let $I=\int \frac{e^x}{e^{4x}+e^{2x}+1} dx, J=\int \frac{e^{-x}}{e^{-4x}+e^{-2x}+1} dx.$

Then, for an arbitrary constanat C, the value of $J-I$ equals NCERT Pg. 252

(a) $\frac{1}{2}\log\left|\frac{e^{4x}-e^{2x}+1}{e^{4x}+e^{2x}+1}\right|+C$ (b) $\frac{1}{2}\log\left|\frac{e^{2x}-e^x+1}{e^{2x}-e^x+1}\right|+C$

(c) $\frac{1}{2}\log\left|\frac{e^{2x}-e^x+1}{e^{2x}+e^x+1}\right|+C$ (d) $\frac{1}{2}\log\left|\frac{e^{4x}+e^{2x}+1}{e^{4x}-e^{2x}+1}\right|+C$

Integration by Partial Fractions

Level I

1 Match the following form of rational function in column I with their corresponding form of partial fraction in column II and choose the correct option from the codes given below. NCERT Pg. 253

Column I	Column II
A. $\dfrac{px+q}{(x-a)(x-b)}, a \neq b$	1. $\dfrac{A}{x-a}+\dfrac{Bx+c}{x^2+bx+c}$
B. $\dfrac{px+q}{(x-a)^2}$	2. $\dfrac{A}{x-a}+\dfrac{B}{(x-a)^2}+\dfrac{c}{x-b}$
C. $\dfrac{px^2+qx+r}{(x-a)(x-b)(x-c)}$	3. $\dfrac{A}{x-a}+\dfrac{B}{x-b}$
D. $\dfrac{px^2+qx+r}{(x-a)^2(x-b)}$	4. $\dfrac{A}{x-a}+\dfrac{B}{(x-a)^2}$
E. $\dfrac{px^2+qx+r}{(x-a)(x^2+bx+c)}$, where x^2+bx+c cannot be factorised further.	5. $\dfrac{A}{(x-a)}+\dfrac{B}{(x-b)}+\dfrac{C}{(x-c)}$

Codes

	A	B	C	D	E
(a)	1	2	4	5	3
(b)	3	4	5	2	1
(c)	3	5	2	1	2
(d)	1	3	2	4	5

2 $\int \dfrac{1}{x^2-9}\,dx$ is equal to NCERT Pg. 258

(a) $\log\left|\dfrac{x-3}{x+3}\right|+C$ (b) $\dfrac{1}{6}\log\left|\dfrac{x-3}{x+3}\right|+C$

(c) $\dfrac{1}{6}\log\left|\dfrac{x+3}{x-3}\right|+C$ (d) $\log\left|\dfrac{x+3}{x-3}\right|+C$

3 Match the following integrals in column I with their correrspونding values in column II and choose the correct option from the codes given below. NCERT Pg. 258

Column I	Column II
A. $\int \dfrac{x}{(x+1)(x+2)}\,dx$	1. $\log\|x-1\|-5\log\|x-2\|+4\log\|x-3\|+C$
B. $\int \dfrac{2x}{x^2+3x+2}\,dx$	2. $\dfrac{1}{2}\log\|x-1\|-2\log\|x-2\|+\dfrac{3}{2}\log\|x-3\|+C$
C. $\int \dfrac{3x-1}{(x-1)(x-2)(x-3)}\,dx$	3. $4\log\|x+2\|-2\log\|x+1\|+C$
D. $\int \dfrac{x}{(x-1)(x-2)(x-3)}\,dx$	4. $\log\left\|\dfrac{(x+2)^2}{x+1}\right\|+C$

Codes

	A	B	C	D
(a)	3	4	2	1
(b)	1	3	2	4
(c)	4	3	1	2
(d)	4	1	2	3

4 Consider the following statements.

Statement I The integral value of $\dfrac{1-x^2}{x(1-2x)}$ is $x+\log x-\dfrac{3}{4}\log|2x-1|+C$.

Statement II The integral value of $\dfrac{x}{(x^2+1)(x-1)}$ is $\dfrac{1}{2}\log|x-1|+\dfrac{1}{4}\log|x^2+1|-\dfrac{1}{2}\tan^{-1}x+C$.

Choose the correct option. NCERT Pg. 258

(a) Statement I is true (b) Statement II is true
(c) Both statements are true (d) Both statements are false

5 Which of the following integrals are evaluated correctly?

(i) $\int \dfrac{x}{(x-1)^2(x+2)}\,dx=\dfrac{2}{9}\log\left|\dfrac{x-1}{x+2}\right|-\dfrac{1}{3}\left(\dfrac{1}{x-1}\right)+C$

(ii) $\int \dfrac{3x+5}{x^3-x^2-x+1}\,dx=\dfrac{1}{2}\log\left|\dfrac{x-1}{x+1}\right|-\dfrac{4}{x-1}+C$

(iii) $\int \dfrac{2x-3}{(x^2-1)(2x+3)}\,dx=\dfrac{5}{2}\log|x+1|-\dfrac{1}{10}\log|x-1|-\dfrac{12}{5}\log|2x+3|+C$

(iv) $\dfrac{5x}{(x+1)(x^2-4)}\,dx=\dfrac{5}{3}\log|x+1|-\dfrac{5}{2}\log|x+2|+\dfrac{5}{6}\log|x-2|+C$

NCERT Pg. 258

(a) Only (i) (b) (ii) and (iii)
(c) (i), (iii) and (iv) (d) All of these

6 Match the following integrals in column I with their corresponding values in column II and choose the correct option from the codes given below. NCERT Pg. 258

Column I	Column II
A. $\int \dfrac{x^3+x+1}{x^2-1}\,dx$	1. $-\log\|1-x\|+\dfrac{1}{2}\log(1+x^2)+\tan^{-1}x+C$
B. $\int \dfrac{2}{(1-x)(1+x^2)}\,dx$	2. $3\log\|x+2\|+\dfrac{7}{x+2}+C$
C. $\int \dfrac{3x-1}{(x+2)^2}\,dx$	3. $\dfrac{x^2}{2}+\dfrac{1}{2}\log\|x+1\|+\dfrac{3}{2}\log\|x-1\|+C$
D. $\int \dfrac{1}{x^4-1}\,dx$	4. $-\dfrac{1}{2}\tan^{-1}x+\dfrac{1}{4}\log\left\|\dfrac{x-1}{x+1}\right\|+C$

Codes

	A	B	C	D
(a)	1	3	4	2
(b)	3	1	4	2
(c)	2	4	3	1
(d)	3	1	2	4

7 Consider the following statements

Statement I The integral of $\frac{1}{x(x^n+1)}$ is $\frac{1}{n}\log\left|\frac{x^n}{x^n+1}\right|+C.$

Statement II The integral of $\frac{\cos x}{(1-\sin x)(2-\sin x)}$ is $\log\left|\frac{2-\sin x}{1-\sin x}\right|+C.$

Choose the correct option. **NCERT Pg. 258**

(a) Statement I is true
(b) Statement II is true
(c) Both statements are true
(d) Both statements are false

8 Which of the following integrals are evaluated correctly?

(i) $\int\frac{(x^2+1)(x^2+2)}{(x^2+3)(x^2+4)}dx = x-3\tan^{-1}\frac{x}{2}+\frac{2}{\sqrt{3}}\tan^{-1}\frac{x}{\sqrt{3}}+C$

(ii) $\int\frac{2x}{(x^2+1)(x^2+3)}dx=\frac{1}{2}\log\left|\frac{x^2+1}{x^2+3}\right|+C$

(iii) $\int\frac{1}{x(x^4-1)}dx=\frac{1}{4}\log\left|\frac{x^4-1}{x^4}\right|+C$

(iv) $\int\frac{1}{e^x-1}dx=\log\left|\frac{e^x-1}{e^x}\right|+C$

NCERT Pg. 259

(a) Only (i) (b) (i), (ii) and (iii)
(c) (ii) and (iii) (d) All of these

9 $\int\frac{x\,dx}{(x-1)(x-2)}$ equals **NCERT Pg. 259**

(a) $\log\left|\frac{(x-1)^2}{x-2}\right|+C$ (b) $\log\left|\frac{(x-2)^2}{x-1}\right|+C$

(c) $\log\left|\left(\frac{x-1}{x-2}\right)^2\right|+C$ (d) $\log|(x-1)(x-2)|+C$

10 $\int\frac{dx}{x(x^2+1)}$ is equals to **NCERT Pg. 259**

(a) $\log|x|-\frac{1}{2}\log(x^2+1)+C$

(b) $\log|x|+\frac{1}{2}\log(x^2+1)+C$

(c) $-\log|x|+\frac{1}{2}\log(x^2+1)+C$

(d) $\frac{1}{2}\log|x|+\log(x^2+1)+C$

Level II

11 Consider the following statements.

Statement I The value of $\int\frac{x^3}{x^4+3x^2+2}dx$ is equal to $\log\left|\frac{x^2+2}{\sqrt{x^2+1}}\right|+C.$

Statement I The value of $\int\frac{x^2}{x^4+x^2-2}dx$ is $\frac{2}{3}\tan^{-1}\frac{x}{\sqrt{2}}+\frac{1}{6}\log\left|\frac{x-1}{x+1}\right|+C.$

Choose the correct option. **NCERT Exemplar Pg. 154**

(a) Statement I is true
(b) Statement II is true
(c) Both statements are true
(d) Both statements are true

12 If $\int\frac{dx}{(x+2)(x^2+1)}=a\log|1+x^2|+b\tan^{-1}x+\frac{1}{5}\log|x+2|+C$, then

NCERT Exemplar Pg. 168

(a) $a=\frac{-1}{10}, b=\frac{-2}{5}$ (b) $a=\frac{1}{10}, b=\frac{-2}{5}$

(c) $a=\frac{-1}{10}, b=\frac{2}{5}$ (d) $a=\frac{1}{10}, b=\frac{2}{5}$

13 If $\int\frac{2x^2+3}{(x^2-1)(x^2+4)}dx=a\log\left(\frac{x-1}{x+1}\right)+b\tan^{-1}\left(\frac{x}{2}\right)+C$, then the value of a and b are

NCERT Pg. 259

(a) 1, –1 (b) –1, 1 (c) $\frac{1}{2},\frac{-1}{2}$ (d) $\frac{1}{2},\frac{1}{2}$

14 If $\int\frac{\sin x}{\cos x(1+\cos x)}dx=f(x)+C$, then $f(x)$ is equal to **NCERT Pg. 259**

(a) $\log\left|\frac{1+\cos x}{\cos x}\right|$ (b) $\log\left|\frac{\cos x}{1+\cos x}\right|$

(c) $\log\left|\frac{\sin x}{1+\sin x}\right|$ (d) $\log\left|\frac{1+\sin x}{\sin x}\right|$

15 The value of $\int\frac{e^x}{(1+e^x)(2+e^x)}dx$ is **NCERT Pg. 259**

(a) $\log\left(\frac{1+e^x}{1+2e^x}\right)+C$ (b) $\log\left(\frac{1+e^x}{2+e^x}\right)+C$

(c) $\log\left(\frac{2+e^x}{1+e^x}\right)+C$ (d) None of these

16 Consider the following statements

Statement I $\int x\sqrt{\dfrac{1-x^2}{1+x^2}}\,dx$ is equal to $\sin^{-1}x^2+\sqrt{1-x^4}+C.$

Statement II $\int \dfrac{a\,dx}{b+ce^x}$ is equal to $\dfrac{a}{b}\log\left(\dfrac{b+ce^x}{e^x}\right)+C.$

Choose the correct option. **NCERT Pg. 259**

(a) Statement I is true
(b) Statement II is true
(c) Both statements are true
(d) Both statements are false

17 The value of $\int \dfrac{dx}{(\sin x+\sin 2x)}$ is equal to **NCERT Pg. 259**

(a) $\dfrac{1}{6}\log(1-\cos x)+\dfrac{1}{2}\log(1+\cos x)-\dfrac{2}{3}\log(1+2\cos x)$
(b) $6\log(1-\cos x)+2\log(1+\cos x)+\dfrac{-2}{3}\log(1+2\cos x)+c$
(c) $6\log(1-\cos x)+\dfrac{1}{2}\log(1+\cos x)+\dfrac{2}{3}\log(1+2\cos x)+c$
(d) None of the above

Integration by Parts

Level I

1 **Statement I** Integration by parts of
$$\int x\cdot\cos x\,dx = x\sin x+\cos x+C.$$
Statement II The integral of the product of two function x and $\cos x$ is easy to find by integration by parts if we take x as first function and $\cos x$ as second function. **NCERT Pg. 260**

(a) Both statements are true.
(b) Both statements are false.
(c) Statement I is true; Statement II is false.
(d) Statement I is false; Statement II is true.

2 Which of the following integrals are written correctly?

(i) $\int \log x\,dx = x\log x - x + C$
(ii) $\int x e^{x}\,dx = xe^{x}+e^{x}+C$
(iii) $\int \dfrac{x\sin^{-1}}{\sqrt{1-x^2}}\,dx = x-\sqrt{1-x^2}\sin^{-1}x+C$
(iv) $\int e^{x}\sin x\,dx = \dfrac{e^{x}}{2}(\sin x-\cos x)+C$ **NCERT Pg. 261**

(a) Only (i) (b) (i) and (iii)
(c) (i), (iii) and (iv) (d) All of these

3 Consider the following statements.

Statement I $\int e^x\left(\tan^{-1}x+\dfrac{1}{1+x^2}\right)dx$ is $\dfrac{e^x}{1+x^2}+C.$

Statement II $\int \dfrac{(x^2+1)e^x}{(x+1)^2}\,dx$ is $\left(\dfrac{x-1}{x+1}\right)e^x+C.$

Choose the correct option. **NCERT Pg. 263**

(a) Statement I is true
(b) Statement II is true
(c) Both statements are true
(d) Both statements are false

4 Match the following integrals in column I with their corresponding values in column II and choose the correct option from the codes given below. **NCERT Pg. 263**

Column I	Column II
A. $\int x\sin x\,dx$	1. $\dfrac{-x\cos 3x}{3}+\dfrac{1}{9}\sin 3x+C$
B. $\int x\sin 3x\,dx$	2. $\dfrac{x^2}{2}\log 2x-\dfrac{1}{4}x^2+C$
C. $\int x\log x\,dx$	3. $-x\cos x+\sin x+C$
D. $\int x\log 2x\,dx$	4. $\dfrac{x^2\log x}{2}-\dfrac{1}{4}x^2+C$

Codes

	A	B	C	D
(a)	2	1	4	3
(b)	3	2	1	4
(c)	2	4	1	3
(d)	3	1	4	2

5 The value of $\int x^2e^x\,dx$ is **NCERT Pg. 263**

(a) $e^x(x^2+2x-2)+C$
(b) $e^x(x^2-2x-2)+C$
(c) $e^x(x^2-2x+2)+C$
(d) $-e^x(x^2+2x+2)+C$

6 Consider the following statements.

Statement I $\int x^2\log x\,dx$ is equal to $\dfrac{x^3}{3}\log x+\dfrac{x^3}{9}+C.$

Statement II $\int x\tan^{-1}dx$ is equal to $\left(\dfrac{x^2+1}{2}\right)\tan^{-1}x+\dfrac{1}{2}x+C.$

Choose the correct option. **NCERT Pg. 263**

(a) Statement I is true
(b) Statements II is true
(c) Both statements are true
(d) Both statements are false

7 Which of the following integrals are written correctly?

(i) $\int x\cos^{-1}x\,dx = \frac{1}{4}(2x^2-1)\cos^{-1}x + \frac{x}{4}\sqrt{1-x^2}+C$

(ii) $\int (\sin^{-1}x)^2\,dx = x(\sin^{-1}x)^2 + 2\sqrt{1-x^2}\sin^{-1}x - 2x + C$

(iii) $\int \frac{x\cos^{-1}x}{\sqrt{1-x^2}}\,dx = \sqrt{1-x^2}\cos^{-1}x + x + C$

(iv) $\int \tan^{-1}x\,dx = x\tan^{-1}x - \frac{1}{2}\log|1+x^2| + C$

NCERT Pg. 263

(a) Only (ii) (b) (ii) and (iv)
(c) (ii), (iii) and (iv) (d) All of these

8 The integral value of the function $x\sec^2 x$ is NCERT Pg. 263

(a) $x\tan - \log|\cos x| + C$ (b) $x\tan x + \log|\cos x| + C$
(c) $x\tan + \log|\sec x| + C$ (d) None of these

9 Consider the following statements.

Statement I The value of integral of the function $x(\log x)^2$ is $\frac{x^2}{2}(\log x)^2 - \frac{x^2}{2}\log x + \frac{x^2}{4} + C$.

Statement II The value of $\int (x^2+1)\log x\,dx$ is $\left(\frac{x^3}{3}+x\right)\log x + \frac{x^3}{9} + x + C$.

Choose the correct option. NCERT Pg. 263

(a) Statement I is true
(b) Statement II is true
(c) Both statements are true
(d) Both statements are false

10 The value of the integral $\int x\sin^{-1}x\,dx$ is equal to

NCERT Pg. 263

(a) $\frac{1}{2}x^2\sin^{-1}x + \frac{1}{4}x\sqrt{1-x^2} - \frac{1}{4}\sin^{-1}x + C$

(b) $\frac{1}{2}x^2\sin^{-1}x - \frac{1}{4}x\sqrt{1-x^2} - \frac{1}{4}\sin^{-1}x + C$

(c) $\frac{1}{2}x^2\sin^{-1}x + \frac{1}{4}x\sqrt{1-x^2} + \frac{1}{4}\sin^{-1}x + C$

(d) $\frac{1}{2}x^2\sin^{-1}x + \frac{1}{4}\sqrt{1-x^2} - \frac{1}{4}\sin^{-1}x + C$

11 $\int \sin^{-1}\left(\frac{2x}{1+x^2}\right)dx$ is equal to

NCERT Pg. 264

(a) $x\tan^{-1}x - \log|1+x^2| + C$

(b) $2x\tan^{-1}x + \log|1+x^2| + C$

(c) $x\tan^{-1}x + \log|1+x^2| + C$

(d) $2x\tan^{-1}x - \log|1+x^2| + C$

12 Which of the following integrals are evaluated correctly?

(i) $\int \frac{xe^x}{(1+x)^2}\,dx = \frac{e^x}{(1+x)^2} + C$

(ii) $\int e^x\left(\frac{1+\sin x}{1+\cos x}\right)dx = e^x\sec^2\frac{x}{2} + C$

(iii) $\int \frac{e^x(x-3)}{(x-1)^3}\,dx = \frac{e^x}{(x-1)^2} + C$

(iv) $\int e^{2x}\sin x\,dx = \frac{e^{2x}}{5}(\cos - 2\sin x) + C$ NCERT Pg. 264

(a) Only (iii) (b) (ii) and (iii)
(c) (i), (iii) and (iv) (d) All of these

13 Consider the following statements.

Statement I $\int e^x(\sin x + \cos x)\,dx$ is equal to $e^x\cos + C$.

Statement II $\int e^x\left(\frac{1}{x} - \frac{1}{x^2}\right)dx$ is equal to $\frac{-e^x}{x^2} + C$.

Choose the correct option. NCERT Pg. 264

(a) Statement I is true
(b) Statement II is true
(c) Both statements are true
(d) Both statements are false

14 $\int x^2 e^{x^3}\,dx$ is equal to

NCERT Pg. 264

(a) $\frac{1}{3}e^{x^3} + C$ (b) $\frac{1}{3}e^{x^2} + C$
(c) $\frac{1}{2}e^{x^3} + C$ (d) $\frac{1}{2}e^{x^2} + C$

15 $\int e^x\sec x(1+\tan x)\,dx$ equal to NCERT Pg. 264

(a) $e^x\cos x + C$ (b) $e^x\sec x + C$
(c) $e^x\sin x + C$ (d) $e^x\tan x + C$

Level II

16 $\int e^x(\cos x - \sin x)\,dx$ is equal to NCERT Exemplar Pg. 158

(a) $e^x\cos x + C$ (b) $e^x\sin x + C$
(c) $-e^x\cos x + C$ (d) $-e^x\sin x + C$

17 $\int \tan^{-1}\sqrt{x}\,dx$ is equal to NCERT Exemplar Pg. 167

(a) $(x+1)\tan^{-1}\sqrt{x} - \sqrt{x} + C$
(b) $x\tan^{-1}\sqrt{x} - \sqrt{x} + C$
(c) $\sqrt{x} - x\tan^{-1}\sqrt{x} + C$
(d) $\sqrt{x} - (x+1)\tan^{-1}\sqrt{x} + C$

18 $\int e^x\left(\frac{1-x}{1+x^2}\right)^2 dx$ is equal to

NCERT Exemplar Pg. 167

(a) $\frac{e^x}{1+x^2} + C$ (b) $\frac{-e^x}{1+x^2} + C$
(c) $\frac{e^x}{(1+x^2)^2} + C$ (d) $\frac{-e^x}{(1+x^2)^2} + C$

19 $\int \frac{x+\sin x}{1+\cos x} dx$ is equal to

NCERT Exemplar Pg. 168

(a) $\log|1+\cos x| + C$ (b) $\log|x+\sin x| + C$

(c) $x - \tan x/2 + C$ (d) $x \tan\left(\frac{x}{2}\right) + C$

20 Consider the following statements.

Statement I The value of $\int \frac{\sin^{-1} x}{(1-x^2)^{3/2}} dx$ is $\frac{x \sin^{-1} x}{\sqrt{1-x^2}} + \log\left|\sqrt{1-x^2}\right| + C.$

Statement II The value of $\int \frac{x \tan^{-1} x}{(1+x^2)^{3/2}} dx$ is $\frac{(x - \tan^{-1} x)}{\sqrt{1+x^2}} + C.$

Choose the correct option. NCERT Exemplar Pg. 164

(a) Statement I is true (b) Statement II is true

(c) Both statements are true (d) Both statements are false

21 $\int \frac{x+3}{(x+4)^2} e^x dx = \ldots\ldots\ldots$

NCERT Exemplar Pg. 169

(a) $\frac{e^x}{x+3} + C$ (b) $\frac{e^x}{(x+4)} + C$

(c) $\frac{e^x}{(x+4)^2} + C$ (d) $e^x (x+3) + C$

22 Consider the following statements.

Statement I If $\int f(x)\, dx = g(x)$, then $\int f(x)\, g(x)\, dx$ is equal to $\frac{1}{2} [g(x)]$.

Statement II If $f(x) = \frac{\sin^{-1} x}{\sqrt{1-x^2}}$ and $g(x) = e^{\sin^{-1} x}$, then $\int f(x)\, g(x)\, dx$ is equal to $e^{\sin^{-1} x} (\sin^{-1} x + 1) + C$.

Choose the correct option. NCERT Pg. 259

(a) Statement I is true (b) Statement II is true

(c) Both statements are true (d) Both statements are false

Integrals of Some More Types Functions

Level I

1 Consider the following statements.

Statement I The value of $\int \sqrt{x^2+2x+5}\, dx$ is $\frac{1}{2}(x+1)\sqrt{x^2+2x+5} + 2\log\left|x+\sqrt{x^2+2x+5}\right| + C.$

Statement II The value of $\int \sqrt{3-2x-x^2}\, dx$ is $\frac{1}{2}(x+1)\sqrt{3-2x-x^2} + 2\sin^{-1}\left(\frac{x+1}{2}\right) + C.$

Choose the correct option. NCERT Pg. 265

(a) Statement I is true

(b) Statement II is true

(c) Both statements are true

(d) Both statements are false

2 Which of the following integrals are written correctly?

(i) $\int \sqrt{4-x^2}\, dx = \frac{x}{2}\sqrt{4-x^2} + 2\sin^{-1}\frac{x}{2} + C$

(ii) $\int \sqrt{1-4x^2}\, dx = \frac{x}{2}\sqrt{1-4x^2} + \frac{1}{4}\sin^{-1}(2x) + C$

(iii) $\int \sqrt{x^2+4x+6}\, dx = \frac{x}{2}\sqrt{x^2+4x+6} + \log x + \sqrt{x^2+4x+6} + C$

(iv) $\int \sqrt{x^2+4x+1}\, dx = \frac{x+2}{2}\sqrt{x^2+4x+1} - \frac{3}{2}\log\left|(x+2)+\sqrt{x^2+4x+1}\right| + C$

(a) Only (iii) NCERT Pg. 266

(b) (iii) and (iv)

(c) (i), (ii) and (iv)

(d) All of the above

3 The value of $\int \sqrt{1-4x-x^2}$ is equal to

NCERT Pg. 266

(a) $\frac{x}{2}\sqrt{1-4x-x^2} + \frac{5}{2}\sin^{-1}\left(\frac{x+2}{\sqrt{5}}\right) + C$

(b) $\frac{x}{2}\sin^{-1}\left(\frac{x+2}{\sqrt{5}}\right) + \frac{5}{2}\sqrt{1-4x-x^2} + C$

(c) $\frac{x+2}{2}\sin^{-1}\left(\frac{x+2}{\sqrt{5}}\right) + \frac{5}{2}\sqrt{1-4x-x^2} + C$

(d) $\frac{x+2}{2}\sqrt{1-4x-x^2} + \frac{5}{2}\sin^{-1}\left(\frac{x+2}{\sqrt{5}}\right) + C$

4 Consider the following statements.

Statement I The value of $\int \sqrt{x^2+4x-5}\, dx$ is $\frac{x+2}{2}\sqrt{x^2+4x-5} - \frac{9}{2}\log\left|(x+2)+\sqrt{x^2+4x-5}\right| + C.$

Statement II The value of $\int \sqrt{1+3x-x^2}\, dx$ is $\frac{2x-3}{4}\sqrt{1+3x-x^2} + \frac{13}{8}\sin^{-1}\left(\frac{2x-3}{\sqrt{13}}\right) + C.$

Choose the correct option. NCERT Pg. 266

(a) Statement I is true

(b) Statement II is true

(c) Both statements are true

(d) Both statements are false

5 Consider the following statements.

Statement I The value of $\int \sqrt{x^2+3x}\,dx$
$= \frac{2x+3}{2}\sqrt{x^2+3x} + \frac{9}{8}\log\left|\frac{2x+3}{2} + \sqrt{x^2+3x}\right| + C$

Statement II $\int \sqrt{1+\frac{x^2}{9}}\,dx = \frac{x}{6}\sqrt{x^2+9} + \frac{3}{2}$
$\log\left|x+\sqrt{9+x^2}\right| + C$

Choose the correct option. NCERT Pg. 266

(a) Statement I is true (b) Statement II is true
(c) Both statements are true (d) Both statements are false

6 $\int \sqrt{1+x^2}\,dx$ is equal to NCERT Pg. 266

(a) $\frac{x}{2}\sqrt{1+x^2} + \frac{1}{2}\log\left|x+\sqrt{1+x^2}\right| + C$
(b) $\frac{2}{3}(1+x^2)^{3/2} + C$
(c) $\frac{2}{3}x(1+x^2)^{3/2} + C$
(d) $\frac{x^2}{2}\sqrt{1+x^2} + \frac{1}{2}x^2\log\left|x+\sqrt{1+x^2}\right| + C$

7 $\int \sqrt{x^2-8x+7}\,dx$ is equal to NCERT Pg. 266

(a) $\frac{1}{2}(x-4)\sqrt{x^2-8x+7+9}\log\left|x-4+\sqrt{x^2-8x+7}\right| + C$
(b) $\frac{1}{2}(x+4)\sqrt{x^2-8x+7} + 9\log\left|x+4+\sqrt{x^2-8x+7}\right| + C$
(c) $\frac{1}{2}(x-4)\sqrt{x^2-8x+7} - 3\sqrt{2}\log\left|x-4+\sqrt{x^2-8x+7}\right| + C$
(d) $\frac{1}{2}(x-4)\sqrt{x^2-8x+7} \frac{-9}{2}\log|x-4+\sqrt{x^2-8x+7}| + C$

8 The integral of $\sqrt{10-4x+4x^2}$ is NCERT Exemplar Pg. 153

(a) $\frac{1}{4}(2x-1)\sqrt{(2x-1)^2+9} + \frac{9}{4}\log\left|(2x-1)-\sqrt{(2x-1)^2+9}\right| + C$
(b) $\frac{1}{4}(2x-1)\sqrt{(2x-1)^2+9} + \frac{9}{4}\log|(2x-1)+\sqrt{(2x-1)^2+9}| + C$
(c) $\frac{1}{4}(2x-1)\sqrt{(2x-1)^2+9} - \frac{9}{4}\log|(2x-1)| - \sqrt{(2x-1)^2+9} + C$
(d) $-\frac{1}{4}(2x-1)\sqrt{(2x-1)^2+9} \frac{-9}{4}\log\left|(2x-1)+\sqrt{(2x-1)^2+9}\right| + C$

9 Consider the following statements.

Statement I The value of $\int \sqrt{5-2x+x^2}\,dx$ is
$\frac{(x-1)}{2}\sqrt{5-2x+x^2} + 2\log\left|(x-1)+\sqrt{5-2x+x^2}\right| + C.$

Statement II The value of $\int \sqrt{2ax-x^2}\,dx$ is
$\frac{(x-a)}{2}\sqrt{2ax-x^2} - \frac{a^2}{2}\sin^{-1}\left(\frac{x-a}{a}\right) + C.$

Choose the correct option. NCERT Exemplar Pg. 164

(a) Statement I is true (b) Statement II is true
(c) Both statements are true (d) Both statements are false

10 Consider the following statements.

Statement I $\int \cos x\sqrt{4-\sin^2 x}\,dx$ is equal to
$\frac{1}{2}\sin x\sqrt{4-\sin^2 x} + 2\sin^{-1}\left(\frac{\sin x}{2}\right) + C.$

Statement II $\int \frac{\sqrt{16+(\log x)^2}}{x}\,dx$ is equal to
$\frac{1}{2}\log x\sqrt{(\log x)^2+16} + 8\log\left|x+\sqrt{(\log x)^2+16}\right| + C.$

Choose the correct option. NCERT Pg. 264, 265

(a) Statement I is true (b) Statement II is true
(c) Both statements are true (d) Both statements are false

11 The value of $\int (x+1)\sqrt{1-x-x^2}\,dx$ is NCERT Pg. 264, 265

(a) $\frac{1}{3}(1-x-x^2)^{3/2} + \frac{1}{8}(2x+1)\sqrt{1-x-x^2} + \frac{5}{16}\sin^{-1}\left(\frac{2x+1}{\sqrt{5}}\right) + C$
(b) $\frac{1}{3}(1-x-x^2)^{3/2} - \frac{1}{8}(2x+1)\sqrt{1-x-x^2} - \frac{5}{16}\sin^{1}\left(\frac{2x+1}{\sqrt{5}}\right) + C$
(c) $\frac{-1}{3}(1-x-x^2)^{3/2} + \frac{1}{8}(2x+1)\sqrt{1-x-x^2} + \frac{5}{16}\sin^{-1}\left(\frac{2x+1}{\sqrt{5}}\right) + C$
(d) None of the above

12 Consider the following statements.

Statement I The value of $\int (3x-2)\sqrt{x^2+x+1}\,dx$ is
equal to $(x^2+x+1)^{3/2} - \frac{7}{2}\left[\frac{1}{2}\left(x+\frac{1}{2}\right)\sqrt{x^2+x+1} + \frac{3}{8}\log|x+\frac{1}{2}+\sqrt{x^2+x+1}|\right] + C$

Statement II The value of $\int (x-5)\sqrt{x^2+x}\,dx$ is equal
to $\frac{1}{3}(x^2+x)^{3/2} - \frac{11}{2}\left[\left\{\frac{2x+1}{4}\right\}\sqrt{x^2+x} - \frac{1}{8}\log\left|\left(x+\frac{1}{2}\right)+\sqrt{x^2+x}\right|\right] + C$

Choose the correct option. NCERT Pg. 264, 265
(a) Statement I is true
(b) Statement II is true
(c) Both statements are true
(d) Both statements are false

Fundamental Theorem of Calculus

Level I

1 Consider the following statements.

Statement I $y = f(x)$ is a curve and $A(x)$ is the area bounded by the curve $f(x)$, $x = a$ and $x = b$, then $A(x) = \int_a^x f(x)dx \, \forall x \in [a, b]$, if $f(x) > 0$

Statement II If $A(x) = \int_a^b f(x)dx + \left|\int_b^c f(x)dx\right|$ if $f(x) > 0$ for $x \in [a, b]$ and $f(x) < 0$ for $x \in [b, c]$

Choose the correct option. NCERT Pg. 267
(a) Statement I is true
(b) Statement II is true
(c) Both statements are true
(d) Both statements are false

2 If f be a continous function on the closed interval $[a, b]$ and A(x) be the area function, then according to first fundamental theorem of integral calculus NCERT Pg. 267
(a) $A(x) = f(x), \forall x \in [a, b]$ (b) $A'(x) = \int_a^b f(x)\,dx, \forall x \in [a, b]$
(c) $A'(x) = f(x), \forall x \in [a, b]$ (d) None of these

3 Theorem which enables us to evaluate definite integrals by making use of anti-derivative is known as NCERT Pg. 267, 268
(a) first fundamental theorem of integral calculus
(b) second fundamental theorem of integral calculus
(c) fundamental theorem of integral calculus
(d) third fundamental theorem of integral calculus

4 Which of the following statement are written correctly about second fundamental theorem of integral calculus? NCERT Pg. 268
(i) It gives us a method to calculate the definite integral easily without calculating the limit of sum.
(ii) This strengthens the relationship between differentiation and integration.
(iii) To evaluate $\int_a^b f(x)\,dx$ it is not necessary for function f to be well defined and continuous in $[a, b]$.
(a) Only (i) (b) (i) and (iii) (c) (i) and (ii) (d). All of these

5 Consider the following statements.

Statement I The value of $\int_{-1}^{1} (x + 1)\,dx$ is 2.

Statement II The value of $\int_2^3 \frac{1}{x}\,dx$ is $\log \frac{2}{3}$.

Choose the correct option. NCERT Pg. 270
(a) Statement I is true
(b) Statement II is true
(c) Both statements are true
(d) Both statements are false

6 The value of $\int_1^2 (4x^3 - 5x^2 + 6x + 9)\,dx$ equal to NCERT Pg. 270
(a) $\frac{64}{3}$ (b) 64 (c) $\frac{132}{3}$ (d) 132

7 Consider the following statements

Statement I $\int_0^{\pi/4} \sin 2x\,dx = 1$

Statement II $\int_0^{\pi/2} \cos 2x\,dx = \frac{1}{2}$

Choose the correct option. NCERT Pg. 270
(a) Statement I is true
(b) Statement II is true
(c) Both statements are true
(d) Both statements are false

8 $\int_4^5 e^x dx$ is equal to NCERT Pg. 270
(a) $e^4 (e + 1)$ (b) $e^4 \, e$ (c) $e^4 (e - 1)$ (d) $e + e^4$

9 The value of $\int_0^{\pi/4} \tan x\,dx$ is NCERT Pg. 270
(a) $\log 2$ (b) $\frac{1}{2}\log 2$
(c) $\log 2 - 2$ (d) None of these

10 Consider the following statements.

Statement I $\int_0^1 \frac{1}{\sqrt{1 - x^2}}\,dx = \frac{\pi}{2}$

Statement II $\int_0^1 \frac{1}{1 + x^2}\,dx = \frac{\pi}{4}$

Choose the correct option. NCERT Pg. 270
(a) Statement I is true (b) Statement II is true
(c) Both statements are true (d) Both statements are false

11 $\int_{\pi/6}^{\pi/4} \operatorname{cosec} x\,dx$ is equal to NCERT Pg. 270
(a) $\log\left|\frac{\sqrt{2} - 1}{2 + \sqrt{3}}\right|$ (b) $\log\left|\frac{2 - \sqrt{3}}{\sqrt{2} - 1}\right|$
(c) $\log\left|\frac{\sqrt{2} + 1}{2 - \sqrt{3}}\right|$ (d) $\log\left|\frac{\sqrt{2} - 1}{2 - \sqrt{3}}\right|$

12 Consider the following statements.

Statement I The value of $\int_2^3 \frac{dx}{x^2 - 1}$ is $\log\left(\frac{3}{2}\right)$.

Statement II The value of $\int_0^{\pi/2} \cos^2 x\,dx$ is $\frac{\pi}{4}$.

Choose the correct option. NCERT Pg. 270, 271
(a) Statement I is true (b) Statement II is true
(c) Both statements are true (d) Both statements are false

13 Which of the following integrals are written correctly?

(i) $\int_2^3 \frac{x}{x^2+1}\,dx = \frac{1}{2}\log 2$

(ii) $\int_0^1 \frac{2x+3}{5x^2+1}\,dx = \frac{1}{5}\log 6 + \frac{3}{\sqrt{5}}\tan^{-1}\sqrt{5}$

(iii) $\int_0^1 x\,e^{x^2}\,dx = \frac{1}{2}[e-1]$

(iv) $\int_1^2 \frac{5x^2}{x^2+4x+3}\,dx = 5 + \frac{5}{2}\log\left|\frac{3}{2}\right| - \frac{45}{2}\log\left|\frac{5}{4}\right|$

NCERT Pg. 271

(a) Only (iv) (b) (i) and (ii)
(c) (i), (ii) and (iii) (d) All of these

14 Match the following definite integrals in column I with their corresponding values in column II and choose the correct option from the codes given below. NCERT Pg. 271

Column I	Column II
A. $\int_0^{\pi/4} (2\sec^2 x + x^3 + 2)\,dx$	1. 0
B. $\int_0^{\pi} \left(\sin^2 \frac{x}{2} - \cos^2 \frac{x}{2}\right) dx$	2. $3\log 2 + \frac{3\pi}{8}$
C. $\int_0^2 \frac{6x+3}{x^2+4}\,dx$	3. $1 + \frac{4}{\pi} - \frac{2\sqrt{2}}{\pi}$
D. $\int_0^1 \left(xe^x + \sin\frac{\pi x}{4}\right) dx$	4. $2 + \frac{\pi}{2} + \frac{\pi^4}{1024}$

Codes

	A	B	C	D		A	B	C	D
(a)	4	1	2	3	(b)	4	2	3	1
(c)	3	1	2	4	(d)	1	4	2	3

15 $\int_1^{\sqrt{3}} \frac{dx}{1+x^2}$ is equal to NCERT Pg. 271

(a) $\frac{\pi}{3}$ (b) $\frac{2\pi}{3}$ (c) $\frac{\pi}{6}$ (d) $\frac{\pi}{12}$

16 $\int_0^{2/3} \frac{dx}{4+9x^2}$ is equal to NCERT Pg. 271

(a) $\frac{\pi}{6}$ (b) $\frac{\pi}{12}$ (c) $\frac{\pi}{24}$ (d) $\frac{\pi}{4}$

Level II

17 Consider the following statements.

Statement I The value of $\int_0^{\pi/4} \sqrt{1+\sin 2x}\,dx$ is 0.

Statement II The value of $\int_0^1 x\log(1+2x)\,dx$ is $\frac{8}{3}\log 3$.

Choose the correct option. NCERT Exemplar Pg. 152

(a) Statement I is true
(b) Statement II is true
(c) Both statements are true
(d) Both statements are false

18 $\int_{-\pi/4}^{\pi/4} \frac{dx}{1+\cos 2x}$ is equal to NCERT Exemplar Pg. 169

(a) 1 (b) 2 (c) 3 (d) 4

19 $\int_0^{\pi/2} \sqrt{1-\sin 2x}$ is equal to NCERT Exemplar Pg. 169

(a) $2\sqrt{2}$ (b) $2(\sqrt{2}+1)$ (c) 2 (d) $2(\sqrt{2}-1)$

20 Consider the following statements.

Statement I The value of $\int_0^1 \frac{x^4(1-x)^4}{1+x^2}\,dx$ is $\frac{22}{7} - \pi$.

Statement II The value of integral $\int_{-1}^1 \frac{|x+2|}{x+2}\,dx$ is 2.

Choose the correct option. NCERT Exemplar Pg. 267, 268

(a) Statement I is true
(b) Statement II is true
(c) Both statements are true
(d) Both statements are false

21 If $\int_0^a \frac{1}{1+4x^2}\,dx = \frac{\pi}{8}$, then $a = ...$ NCERT Exemplar Pg. 169

(a) $\frac{1}{4}$ (b) $\frac{1}{2}$ (c) $\frac{3}{2}$ (d) $\frac{-1}{2}$

22 If $k > 0$ and $\int_2^k (2x+1)\,dx = 6$, then k is equal to NCERT Pg. 267, 268

(a) 4 (b) −2 (c) −3 (d) 3

23 Consider the following statements.

Statement I $\int_0^{\lambda} \frac{y\,dy}{\sqrt{y+\lambda}}$ is equal to $\frac{2}{3}(2+\sqrt{2})\,\lambda\sqrt{\lambda}$.

Statement II $3a\int_0^1 \left(\frac{ax-1}{a-1}\right)^2 dx$ is equal to $(a-1)+(a-1)^2$.

Choose the correct option. NCERT Pg. 267, 268

(a) Statement I is true (b) Statement II is true
(c) Both statements are true (d) Both statements are false

Evaluation of Definite Integrals by Substitution

Level I

1 Consider the following statements.

Statement I $\int_{-1}^1 5x^4\sqrt{x^5+1}\,dx = \frac{4\sqrt{2}}{3}$

Statement II $\int_0^1 \frac{\tan^{-1} x}{1+x^2}\,dx = \frac{\pi^2}{32}$

Choose the correct option. NCERT Pg. 272

(a) Statement I is true
(b) Statement II is true
(c) Both statements are true
(d) Both statements are false

2 Which of the following definite integrals are written correctly? NCERT Pg. 273

(i) $\int_0^1 \frac{x}{x^2+1}\,dx = \frac{1}{2}\log 2$

(ii) $\int_0^{\pi/2} \sqrt{\sin\phi}\,\cos^5\phi\,d\phi = \frac{64}{231}$

(iii) $\int_0^1 \sin^{-1}\left(\frac{2x}{1+x^2}\right)dx = \frac{\pi}{2} + \log 2$

(iv) $\int_0^2 x\sqrt{x+2}\,dx = \frac{32}{15} - \frac{16\sqrt{2}}{15}$

(a) Only (iv) (b) (i) and (ii)
(c) (i), (ii) and (iii) (d) All of these

3 The value of the integral $\int_0^{\pi/2} \frac{\sin x}{1+\cos^2 x}\,dx$ is NCERT Pg. 273

(a) $\frac{\pi}{2}$ (b) $\frac{\pi}{6}$ (c) $\frac{\pi}{4}$ (d) 0

4 $\int_0^2 \frac{dx}{x+4-x^2}$ is equal to NCERT Pg. 273

(a) $\frac{1}{\sqrt{17}}\log\left|\frac{21+5\sqrt{17}}{4}\right|$

(b) $\frac{1}{\sqrt{17}}\log\left|\frac{4}{21+5\sqrt{17}}\right|$

(c) $\frac{1}{\sqrt{17}}\log\left|\frac{21-5\sqrt{17}}{4}\right|$

(d) $\frac{1}{\sqrt{17}}\log\left|\frac{5\sqrt{17}-21}{4}\right|$

5 Consider the following statements.

Statement I The value of the integral $\int_{-1}^1 \frac{1}{x^2+2x+5}\,dx$ is $\pi/4$.

Statement II The value of the integral $\int_1^2 \left(\frac{1}{x} - \frac{1}{2x^2}\right)e^{2x}\,dx$ is $\left(\frac{e^2}{2}-1\right)$.

Choose the correct option. NCERT Pg. 273

(a) Statement I is true
(b) Statement II is true
(c) Both statements are true
(d) Both statements are false

6 The value of the integral $\int_{1/3}^1 \frac{(x-x^3)^{1/3}}{x^4}\,dx$ is NCERT Pg. 273

(a) 6 (b) 0 (c) 3 (d) 9

7 If $f(x) = \int_0^x t\sin t\,dt$, then $f'(x)$ is NCERT Pg. 273

(a) $\cos x + x\sin x$ (b) $x\sin x$
(c) $x\cos x$ (d) $\sin x + x\cos x$

Level II

8 The value of $\int_0^{\pi/2} \frac{\tan x}{1+m^2\tan^2 x}\,dx$ is equal to NCERT Exemplar Pg. 165

(a) $\frac{\log m}{m^2+1}$ (b) $\frac{\log m}{m^2-1}$
(c) $\frac{\log m}{m^2}$ (d) None of these

9 If a function $f(x)$ satisfies $f'(x) = g(x)$, then the value of $\int_a^b f(x)\,g(x)\,dx$ is NCERT Pg. 271

(a) $\frac{1}{2}[(f(b))^2 - (f(a))^2]$ (b) $\frac{1}{2}[(f(b))^2 + (f(a))^2]$
(c) $\frac{1}{2}[f(b) - f(a)]^2$ (d) None of these

10 Consider the following statements.

Statement I $\int_0^\pi \frac{1}{1+\sin x}\,dx$ is equal to 2.

Statement II $\int_a^b \sqrt{(x-a)(b-x)}\,dx, (b>a)$ is equal to $\frac{\pi(b-a)^2}{8}$.

Choose the correct option. NCERT Pg. 271

(a) Statement I is true (b) Statement II is true
(c) Both statements are true (d) Both statements are false

11 Limit of $\int_0^x \left[\frac{1}{\sqrt{1+t^2}} - \frac{1}{1+t}\right]dt$ as $x \to \infty$ is NCERT Pg. 271

(a) $\log_2 e$ (b) $\log_e 2$ (c) $\log_2\left(\frac{1}{e}\right)$ (d) $\log_{1/e} 2$

12 The value of $\int_0^a \sqrt{\frac{a-x}{x}}\,dx$ is NCERT Pg. 271

(a) $\frac{a}{2}$ (b) $\frac{a}{4}$ (c) $\frac{\pi a}{2}$ (d) $\frac{\pi a}{4}$

13 If $\int_2^e \left(\frac{1}{\log x} - \frac{1}{(\log x)^2}\right)dx = a + \frac{b}{\log 2}$, then NCERT Pg. 271

(a) $a = e, b = -2$ (b) $a = e, b = 2$
(c) $a = -e, b = 2$ (d) None of these

14 Consider the following statements.

Statement I The value $\int_1^4 e^{\sqrt{x}}dx$ is $3e^2$.

Statement II The value of the integral $\int_0^{\pi/2} \sqrt{\cos x - \cos^3 x}\,dx$ is $\frac{4}{3}$.

Choose the correct option. NCERT Pg. 271

(a) Statement I is true (b) Statement II is true
(c) Both statements are true (d) Both statements are false

Some Properties of Definite Integrals

Level I

1 Which of the following definite integrals are written correctly? NCERT Pg. 280

(i) $\int_0^{\pi/2} \cos^2 x\, dx = \frac{\pi}{4}$

(ii) $\int_0^{\pi/2} \frac{\sqrt{\sin x}}{\sqrt{\sin x} + \sqrt{\cos x}} dx = \frac{\pi}{4}$

(iii) $\int_0^{\pi/2} \frac{\sin^{3/2} x}{\sin^{3/2} x + \cos^{3/2} x} dx = \frac{\pi}{2}$

(iv) $\int_0^{\pi/2} \frac{\cos^5 x}{\sin^5 x + \cos^5 x} dx = \frac{\pi}{2}$

(a) Only (i) (b) (i) and (ii)
(c) (i), (ii) and (iv) (d) All of these

2 Match the following definite integrals in column I with their corresponding values in column II and choose the correct option from the codes given below. NCERT Pg. 280

Column I		Column II
A. $\int_{-5}^{5} \lvert x+2\rvert\, dx$	1.	5
B. $\int_2^8 \lvert x-5\rvert\, dx$	2.	$\frac{16\sqrt{2}}{15}$
C. $\int_0^2 x\sqrt{2-x}\, dx$	3.	29
D. $\int_0^4 \lvert x-1\rvert\, dx$	4.	9

Codes

	A	B	C	D		A	B	C	D
(a)	2	3	1	4	(b)	3	1	2	4
(c)	3	4	2	1	(d)	2	1	3	4

3 $\int_0^1 x(1-x)^n\, dx$ is equal to NCERT Pg. 280

(a) $\frac{1}{(n+1)} + \frac{1}{(n+2)}$ (b) $\frac{1}{(n+1)(n+2)}$

(c) $(n+1)(n+2)$ (d) $\frac{(n+1)}{(n+2)}$

4 Consider the following statements.

Statement I The value of integral $\int_0^{\pi/4} \log(1+\tan x)\, dx$ is $\frac{\pi}{8}\log 2$.

Statement II The value of $\int_0^{\pi/2} (2\log \sin x - \log \sin 2x)\, dx$ is $\frac{\pi}{2}\log 2$.

Choose the correct option. NCERT Pg. 280

(a) Statement I is true (b) Statement II is true
(c) Both statements are true (d) Both statements are false

5 The value of $\int_0^a \frac{\sqrt{x}}{\sqrt{x} + \sqrt{a-x}} dx$ is NCERT Pg. 280

(a) $\frac{3a}{2}$ (b) a (c) $\frac{a}{2}$ (d) 2a

6 If f and g are defined as $f(x) = f(a-x)$ and $g(x) + g(a-x) = 4$, then $\int_0^a f(x)\, g(x)\, dx$ is equal to NCERT Pg. 280

(a) $\int_0^a f(x)\, dx$ (b) $2\int_0^a f(x)\, dx$

(c) $\int_0^a g(x)\, dx$ (d) $2\int_0^a 8(x)\, dx$

7 Which of the following definite integrals are written correctly? NCERT Pg. 280

(i) $\int_{-\pi/2}^{\pi/2} \sin^7 x\, dx = 0$

(ii) $\int_0^{2\pi} \sin^5 x\, dx = 0$

(iii) $\int_0^{\pi/2} \frac{\sin x - \cos x}{1 + \sin x \cos} dx = \frac{-\pi}{2}$

(iv) $\int_0^{\pi} \log(1+\cos x)\, dx = -\pi \log 2$

(a) Only (iii) (b) (iii) and (iv)
(c) (i), (ii) and (iv) (d) All of these

8 Consider the following statements.

Statement I The value of $\int_{-\pi/2}^{\pi/2} \sin^2 x\, dx$ is equal to $\pi/4$.

Statement II The value of $\int_0^{\pi} \frac{x}{1+\sin x} dx$ is $\pi/2$.

Choose the correct option. NCERT Pg. 280

(a) Statement I is true (b) Statement II is true
(c) Both statements are true (d) Both statements are false

9 The value of $\int_{-\pi/2}^{\pi/2} (x^3 + x\cos x + \tan^5 x + 1)\, dx$ is NCERT Pg. 280

(a) 0 (b) 2 (c) π (d) 1

10 The value of $\int_0^{\pi/2} \log\left(\frac{4+3\sin x}{4+3\cos x}\right) dx$ is NCERT Pg. 280

(a) 2 (b) $\frac{3}{4}$ (c) 0 (d) -2

Level II

11 Consider the following statements.

Statement I The value of $\int_0^{\pi/2} \frac{\tan^7 x}{\cot^7 x + \tan^7 x} dx$ is $\pi/4$.

Statement II The value of $\int_2^8 \frac{\sqrt{10-x}}{\sqrt{x} + \sqrt{10-x}} dx$ is 2.

Choose the correct option. NCERT Exemplar Pg. 151, 152

(a) Statement I is true (b) Statement II is true
(c) Both statements are true (d) Both statements are false

12 If f and g are continous functions in [0,1] satisfying $f(x) = f(a - x)$ and $g(x) + g(a - x) = a$, then $\int_0^a f(x)\, g(x)\, dx$ is equal to **NCERT Exemplar Pg. 160**

(a) $\frac{a}{2}$
(b) $\frac{a}{2}\int_0^a f(x)\, dx$
(c) $\int_0^a f(x)\, dx$
(d) $a\int_0^a f(x)\, dx$

13 $\int_{a+c}^{b+c} f(x)\, dx$ is equal to **NCERT Exemplar Pg. 160**

(a) $\int_a^b f(x - c)\, dx$
(b) $\int_a^b f(x + c)\, dx$
(c) $\int_a^b f(x)\, dx$
(d) $\int_{a-c}^{b-c} f(x)\, dx$

14 Consider the following statements.

Statement I $\int_{-100}^{100} f(x)\, dx$ is equal to $\int_{-100}^{100} f(-x)\, dx$.

Statement II $\int_0^{\pi} [\cot x]\, dx$, here $[\cdot]$ denotes the greatest integer function is equal to $\frac{\pi}{2}$.

Choose the correct option. **NCERT Pg. 274**

(a) Statement I is true
(b) Statement II is true
(c) Both statements are true
(d) Both statements are false

15 If $\int_0^{\pi} x\, f(\sin x)\, dx = A\int_0^{\pi/2} f(\sin x)\, dx$, then A is equal to **NCERT Pg. 274**

(a) 0
(b) π
(c) $\frac{\pi}{4}$
(d) 2π

16 $\int_{-3\pi/2}^{-\pi/2} [(x + \pi)^3 + \cos^2(x)]\, dx$ is equal to **NCERT Pg. 274**

(a) $\left(\frac{\pi^4}{32}\right) + \frac{\pi}{2}$
(b) $\frac{\pi}{2}$
(c) $\frac{\pi}{4} - 1$
(d) $\frac{\pi^4}{32}$

17 If $\int_{-1/2}^{1/2} \cos x \log\left(\frac{1+x}{1-x}\right) dx = k \log 2$, then k is equal to **NCERT Pg. 274**

(a) -2
(b) -1
(c) 0
(d) $\frac{1}{2}$

Miscellaneous Exercise

1 Match the following integrals in column I with their corresponding values in column II and choose the correct option from the codes given below. **NCERT Pg. 285**

Column I	Column II
A. $\int \frac{1}{x - x^3}\, dx$	1. $\frac{-2}{a}\sqrt{\frac{a-x}{x}} + C$
B. $\int \frac{1}{\sqrt{a+x} + \sqrt{x+b}}\, dx$	2. $\frac{1}{2}\log\left\lvert\frac{x^2}{1-x^2}\right\rvert + C$
C. $\int \frac{1}{x\sqrt{ax - x^2}}\, dx$	3. $-(1 + x^{-4})^{1/4} + C$
D. $\int \frac{1}{x^2(x^4+1)^{3/4}}\, dx$	4. $\frac{2}{3(a-b)}[(x+a)^{3/2} - (x+b)^{3/2}] + C$

Codes

	A	B	C	D		A	B	C	D
(a)	1	4	2	3	(b)	2	1	3	4
(c)	2	4	1	3	(d)	1	2	4	3

2 The value of $\int \frac{1}{x^{1/2} + x^{1/3}}\, dx$ is **NCERT Pg. 285**

(a) $2x^{1/2} - 3x^{1/3} + 6x^{1/6} + 6\log|x^{1/6} + 1| + C$
(b) $2x^{1/2} + 3x^{1/3} - 6x^{1/6} + 6\log|x^{1/6} + 1| + C$
(c) $2x^{1/2} - 3x^{1/3} - 6x^{1/6} - 6\log|x^{1/6} + 1| + C$
(d) $2x^{1/2} - 3x^{1/3} + 6x^{1/6} - 6\log|x^{1/6} + 1| + C$

3 Consider the following statements.

Statement I The value of integral $\int \frac{5x}{(x+1)(x^2+9)}$ is $-\frac{1}{2}\log|x+1| + \frac{1}{4}\log|x^2+9| + \frac{3}{2}\tan^{-1}\left(\frac{x}{3}\right) + C.$

Statement II The value of integral $\int \frac{\cos x}{\sqrt{4 - \sin^2 x}}\, dx$ is $\sin^{-1}\left(\frac{x}{2}\right) + C.$

Choose the correct option. **NCERT Pg. 285**

(a) Statement I is true
(b) Statement II is true
(c) Both statements are true
(d) Both statements are false

4 $\int \frac{x^3}{\sqrt{1 - x^8}}\, dx$ is equal to **NCERT Pg. 285**

(a) $\frac{1}{4}\sin^{-1}(x^4) + C$
(b) $4\sin^{-1}(x^4) + C$
(c) $\frac{1}{4}\sin^{-1}(x^2) + C$
(d) $4\sin^{-1}(x^2) + C$

5 Which of the following integrals are evaluated correctly?

(i) $\int \cos^3 x\, e^{og \sin x} dx = \frac{\cos^4 x}{4} + C$

(ii) $\int e^{3\log}(x^4 + 1)^{-1} dx = \frac{1}{4}\log|x^4 + 1| + C$

(iii) $\int \frac{1}{\sqrt{\sin^3 x \sin(x+\alpha)}} dx = \frac{-2}{\sin\alpha}\sqrt{\frac{\sin(x+\alpha)}{\sin x}} + C$

(iv) $\int \frac{\sin^{-1}\sqrt{x} - \cos^{-1}\sqrt{x}}{\sin^{-1}\sqrt{x} + \cos^{-1}\sqrt{x}} dx$

$= \frac{2}{\pi}[(2x-1)\sin^{-1}\sqrt{x} + \sqrt{x - x^2}] - x + C$ **NCERT Pg. 285**

(a) (iii) and (iv) (b) (i) and (ii)
(c) (i), (ii) and (iv) (d) All of these

6 The value of $\int f'(ax+b)[f(ax+b)]^n dx$ is **NCERT Pg. 285**

(a) $\frac{[f(ax+b)]^{n+1}}{n+1} + C$ (b) $\frac{\frac{1}{a}[f(ax+b)]^{n+1}}{n+1} + C$
(c) $\frac{a[f(ax+b)]^{n+1}}{n+1} + C$ (d) None of these

7 $\int \sqrt{\frac{1-\sqrt{x}}{1+\sqrt{x}}} dx$ is equal to **NCERT Pg. 286**

(a) $-2\sqrt{1-x} - \cos^{-1}\sqrt{x} + \sqrt{x-x^2} + C$
(b) $2\sqrt{1-x} + \cos^{-1}\sqrt{x} - \sqrt{x-x^2} + C$
(c) $-2\sqrt{1-x} + \cos^{-1}\sqrt{x} + \sqrt{x-x^2} + C$
(d) $2\sqrt{1-x} + \cos^{-1}\sqrt{x} + \sqrt{x-x^2} + C$

8 Consider the following statements.

Statement I $\int \left(\frac{2+\sin 2x}{1+\cos 2x}\right) e^x dx$ is equal to $(\tan x)e^x + C$.

Statement II $\int \frac{x^2+x+1}{(x+1)^2(x+2)} dx$ is equal to

$2\log|x+1| + \frac{1}{x+1} - 3\log|x+2| + C$.

Choose the correct option. **NCERT Pg. 286**

(a) Statement I is true
(b) Statement II is true
(c) Both statements are true
(d) Both statements are false

9 Consider the following statements.

Statement I The integral of function $\tan^{-1}\sqrt{\frac{1-x}{1+x}}$ is $\frac{1}{2}x\cos^{-1}x + \frac{1}{2}\sqrt{1-x^2} + C$.

Statement II The value of

$\int \frac{\sqrt{x^2+1}[\log(x^2+1) - 2\log x]}{x^4} dx$ is

$\frac{1}{3}\left(1+\frac{1}{x^2}\right)^{3/2}\left[\log\left(\frac{x^2+1}{x^2}\right) - \frac{2}{3}\right] + C$.

Choose the correct option. **NCERT Pg. 286**

(a) Statement I is true
(b) Statement II is true
(c) Both statements are true
(d) Both statements are false

10 Match the following definite integrals in column I with their corresponding values in column II and choose the correct option from the codes given below. **NCERT Pg. 286**

Column I	Column II
A. $\int_{\pi/2}^{\pi} e^x\left(\frac{1-\sin x}{1-\cos x}\right) dx$	1. $\frac{\pi}{6}$
B. $\int_0^{\pi/4} \frac{\sin x \cos x}{\cos^4 x + \sin^4 x} dx$	2. $e^{\pi/2}$
C. $\int_0^{\pi/2} \frac{\cos^2 x}{\cos^2 x + 4\sin^2 x} dx$	3. $\frac{\pi}{8}$
D. $\int_{\pi/6}^{\pi/3} \frac{\sin x + \cos x}{\sqrt{\sin 2x}} dx$	4. $2\sin^{-1}\left(\frac{\sqrt{3}-1}{2}\right)$

Codes

	A	B	C	D		A	B	C	D
(a)	2	3	1	4	(b)	2	3	4	1
(c)	1	2	4	3	(d)	1	4	2	3

11 Which of the following definite integrals are written correctly? **NCERT Pg. 286**

(i) $\int_0^1 \frac{dx}{\sqrt{1+x} - \sqrt{x}} = \frac{4\sqrt{2}}{3} + \frac{1}{2}$

(ii) $\int_0^{\pi/4} \frac{\sin x + \cos x}{9 + 16\sin 2x} dx = \frac{1}{40}\log 9$

(iii) $\int_0^{\pi/2} \sin 2x \tan^{-1}(\sin x) dx = \frac{\pi}{2} + 1$

(iv) $\int_0^{\pi} \frac{x\tan x}{\sec x + \tan x} dx = \frac{\pi}{2}(\pi - 2)$

(a) Only (ii) (b) (ii) and (iv)
(c) (i), (ii) and (iv) (d) All of these

12 The value of $\int_1^4 [|x-1| + |x-2| + |x-3|] dx$ is equal to **NCERT Pg. 286**

(a) 19 (b) $\frac{2}{19}$ (c) $\frac{19}{2}$ (d) $\frac{19}{3}$

13 Consider the following statements.

Statement I $\int_1^3 \frac{dx}{x^2(x+1)} = \frac{2}{3} - \log\frac{2}{3}$

Statement II $\int_0^1 xe^x dx = 1$

Choose the correct option. **NCERT Pg. 286**

(a) Statement I is true (b) Statement II is true
(c) Both statements are true (d) Both statements are false

14 Match the following definite integrals in column I with their corresponding values in column II and choose the correct option from the codes given below. NCERT Pg. 286

Column I		Column II
A. $\int_{-1}^{1} x^{17}\cos^4 x\,dx$	1.	$\frac{\pi}{2}-1$
B. $\int_0^{\pi/2} \sin^3 x\,dx$	2.	0
C. $\int_0^{\pi/4} 2\tan^3 x\,dx$	3.	$\frac{2}{3}$
D. $\int_0^1 \sin^{-1} x\,dx$	4.	$1-\log 2$

Codes

	A	B	C	D		A	B	C	D
(a)	1	3	2	4	(b)	2	3	4	1
(c)	1	2	3	4	(d)	2	4	3	1

15 If $f(a+b-x)=f(x)$, then $\int_a^b x\,f(x)\,dx$ is equal to NCERT Pg. 287

(a) $\frac{a+b}{2}\int_a^b f(b-x)\,dx$

(b) $\frac{a+b}{2}\int_a^b f(b+x)\,dx$

(c) $\frac{b-a}{2}\int_a^b f(x)\,dx$

(d) $\frac{a+b}{2}\int_a^b f(x)\,dx$

16 The value of $\int_0^1 \tan^{-1}\left(\frac{2x-1}{1+x-x^2}\right)dx$ is NCERT Pg. 286

(a) 1 (b) 0

(c) −1 (d) $\frac{\pi}{4}$

17 $\int \frac{dx}{e^x+e^{-x}}$ is equal to NCERT Pg. 286

(a) $\tan^{-1}(e^x)+C$ (b) $\tan^{-1}(e^{-x})+C$

(c) $\log(e^x-e^{-x})+C$ (d) $\log(e^x+e^{-x})+C$

18 $\int \frac{\cos 2x}{(\sin x+\cos x)^2}dx$ is equal to NCERT Pg. 286

(a) $\frac{-1}{\sin x+\cos x}+C$

(b) $\log|\sin x+\cos x|+C$

(c) $\log|\sin x-\cos x|+C$

(d) $\frac{1}{(\sin x+\cos x)^2}$

Numerical Type Questions

1 Let $f(x)=\int \frac{2\operatorname{cosec}^2 x}{(1+\cot x)^2}dx$. If $f\left(\frac{\pi}{4}\right)=4$, then $f\left(\frac{\pi}{2}\right)$ is equal to .... NCERT Pg. 285

2 $f(x)=\int 6^{x+\tan^{-1}x}\cdot\left(1+\frac{1}{x^2+1}\right)dx$. If $f(0)=\frac{1}{\log_e 6}$ then and $f(1)=\frac{\alpha^{\left(\frac{\pi+\beta}{\beta}\right)}}{\log_e \alpha}$, then $\alpha+\beta$ is .... NCERT Pg. 285

3 If $\int x^3 e^{-x^2}dx=n(x)\,e^{-x^2}+C$, where C is constant of integration, then $-2h(-3)$ is .... NCERT Pg. 285

4 If $\int \frac{4x-\sqrt{\sin^{-1}x}}{\sqrt{1-x^2}}dx=\alpha(1-x^2)^{1/2}-\beta(\sin^{-1})^{3/2}+C$, then $|\alpha/\beta|$ is .... NCERT Pg. 285

5 Let $\int(2e^{2x}+4e^x-2e^{-x}-2)\,e^{(e^x+e^{-x})}dx$ $=2h(x)\,e^{(e^x+e^{-x})}+C$ where C is constant of integration, then $\frac{h(0)}{2}=\alpha$. Then, $\alpha+2$ is .... NCERT Pg. 285

6 If $2\beta\int_{-1}^{1} e^{\beta|x|}dx=0$ then find the value of β is .... NCERT Pg. 286

7 If $\int_{-5}^{5}\frac{\cos x}{\frac{1}{2}+\left[\frac{x}{\pi}\right]}dx=r$, where $[\cdot]$ is greatest integer function. Then, find the value of $r+1$ is .... NCERT Pg. 274

8 The value of $1751\left(\frac{\int_0^1(1-x^{35})^{50}dx}{\int_0^1(1-x^{35})^{49}dx}\right)$ is .... NCERT Pg. 286

9 Find value of k such that $\int_1^2 |2x-3[x]|\,dx=k$ and where $[\cdot]$ is greatest integer function. NCERT Pg. 286

10 Find the value of integral $\int_{\pi/8}^{3\pi/8}\ln\left(\frac{5+2\sin x}{5+2\cos x}\right)dx$ is .... NCERT Pg. 286

Assertion and Reason Questions

Direction (Q. Nos. 1-8) The following questions consist of two statements, one labelled as "Assertion (A) and the other labelled as Reason (R)". You are to examine these two statements carefully true and it so, where the Reason (R) is the correct explanation a for the given Assertion (A). Select your answer from following options.

(a) Both Assertion and Reason are correct and Reason is the correct explanation of Assertion.
(b) Both Assertion and Reason are correct but Reason is not the correct explanation of Assertion.
(c) Assertion is correct but Reason is incorrect.
(d) Assertion is incorrect but Reason is correct.

1 **Assertion (A)** It is not possible to find $\int e^{-x^2} dx$ by inspection method.

Reason (R) Function is not expressible in terms of elementary functions. NCERT Pg. 235

2 **Assertion (A)** Integral of $\frac{x^3 - x^2 + x - 1}{x - 1}$ is $\frac{x^3}{3} + x + C$.

Reason (R) Factorise the numerator and cancel the common factor of numerator and denominator and then integrate it using formula

$\int x^n dx = \frac{x^{n+1}}{n+1} + C$ and $n \neq -1$. NCERT Pg. 235

3 **Assertion (A)** If the anti-derivative of a function $\frac{2 - 3\sin x}{\cos^2 x}$ is $2\sec x - 3\tan x + C$.

Reason (R) $\int \sec^2 x\, dx = \tan x + C$ and $\int \tan x \sec x\, dx = \sec x + C$. NCERT Pg. 235

4 **Assertion (A)** Method of integration by parts does not work for $\int \sqrt{x} \sin x\, dx$.

Reason (R) It is not possible to find the derivative of $\sqrt{x}$. NCERT Pg. 263

5 **Assertion (A)** We do not add any constant of integration while finding the integral of second function in integration by parts.

Reason (R) Adding a constant to the integral of the second function does not affects the final result. NCERT Pg. 260

6 **Assertion (A)** The value of $\int_a^b f(t)\, dt$ and $\int_a^b f(u)\, du$ are equal.

Reason (R) The value of definite integral of a function over any particular interval depends on the function and the interval not on the variable of integration. NCERT Pg. 268

7 **Assertion (A)** $\int_0^{2a} f(x) dx = 2\int_0^a f(x) dx$

Reason (R) $f(2a - x) = f(x)$ NCERT Pg. 274

8 **Assertion (A)** The value of $\int_0^1 e^{2-3x} dx$ is $\frac{1}{3}(e^2 - e^{-1})$.

Reason (R) $\int_a^b f(x)\, dx = \lim_{h \to 0} h\, [f(a) + f(a+h) + f(a+2h) + \ldots\ldots + f\{a + (n-1)h\}]$ NCERT Pg. 232

Case or Paragraph Type Questions

Direction (Q. No. 1-3) Ram and Shyam are friends who often discuss concept of mathematics. One day Ram ask to Shyam, if he can solve a particular math problem. Shyam, curious ask Ram to present the question Ram write the questions

$$\int e^x (g(x) + g'(x))\, dx = ?$$

After reading the questions Ram gave the answer as $e^x f(x) + c$.

On the basis of above information answer the following questions. NCERT Pg. 262

1 If $\int e^x \left(\sin^{-1} x + \frac{1}{\sqrt{1 - x^2}}\right) dx = e^x f(x) + C$. Then, find the value of $f(x)$.

(a) $\sin^{-1} 2x$ (b) $\frac{\sin^{-1} x}{\sqrt{1 - x^2}}$ (c) $\sin^{-1} x$ (d) $\frac{1}{\sqrt{1 - x^2}}$

2 Find the value of $\int e^x \sec x (1 + \tan x)\, dx$.

(a) $e^x \sec x + C$ (b) $e^x \tan x + C$
(c) $e^x \sec x \cdot \tan x + C$ (d) $e^x \sec^2 x + C$

3 Find the value of $\int e^x \left(\tan^{-1} x + \frac{1}{1+x^2}\right) dx$.

(a) $e^x \tan^{-1} x + C$ (b) $e^x \tan^{-1} 2x + C$

(c) $\frac{e^x}{1+x^2} + C$ (d) $\frac{e^x \cdot \tan^{-1} x}{1+x^2} + C$

Direction (Q. No. 4-6 Graphs of two function $g(x) = \cos x$ and $h(x) = \sin x$.

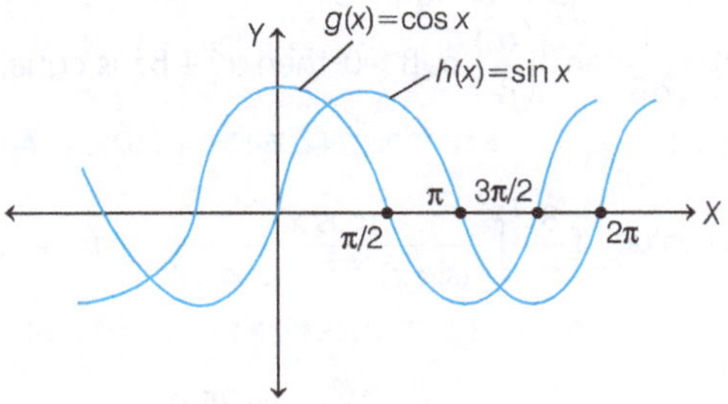

Based on the above information answer the following questions. NCERT Pg. 270

4 The value of $\int_0^{\pi/4} \cos x \, dx$ is

(a) $1 - \frac{1}{\sqrt{2}}$ (b) $\frac{1}{\sqrt{2}}$

(c) $1 + \frac{1}{\sqrt{2}}$ (d) $\sqrt{2}$

5 The value of $\int_{\pi/4}^{\pi/2} \sin x \, dx$ is

(a) $1 + \frac{1}{\sqrt{2}}$ (b) $1 - \frac{1}{\sqrt{2}}$

(c) $\frac{1}{\sqrt{2}}$ (d) $2 + \sqrt{2}$

6 The value of $\int_0^{\pi/4} (\cos x + \sin x) \, dx$ is

(a) 1 (b) 2 (c) 0 (d) $2\sqrt{2}$

Past Years Questions

Single Correct Type

1 Let $\int \frac{2 - \tan x}{3 + \tan x} dx = \frac{1}{2}(\alpha x + \log_e |\beta \sin x + \gamma \cos x|) + C$, where C is the constant of integration. Then, $\alpha + \frac{\gamma}{\beta}$ is equal to NCERT Pg. 285, JEE Main 2024, 9 April Shift-I

(a) 1 (b) 3 (c) 7 (d) 4

2 For $x \in \left(-\frac{\pi}{2}, \frac{\pi}{2}\right)$, if

$$y(x) = \int \frac{\operatorname{cosec} x + \sin x}{\operatorname{cosec} x \sec x + \tan x \sin^2 x} dx$$

and $\lim_{x \to \left(\frac{\pi}{2}\right)^-} y(x) = 0$, then $y\left(\frac{\pi}{4}\right)$ is equal to

NCERT Pg. 285, JEE Main 2024, 29 Jan Shift-I

(a) $\frac{1}{2} \tan^{-1}\left(\frac{1}{\sqrt{2}}\right)$ (b) $\frac{1}{\sqrt{2}} \tan^{-1}\left(-\frac{1}{2}\right)$

(c) $\tan^{-1}\left(\frac{1}{\sqrt{2}}\right)$ (d) $-\frac{1}{\sqrt{2}} \tan^{-1}\left(\frac{1}{\sqrt{2}}\right)$

3 The value of $k \in N$ for which the integral $I_n = \int_0^1 (1 - x^k)^n \, dx$, $n \in N$, satisfies $147 I_{20} = 148 I_{21}$ is

NCERT Pg. 286, JEE Main 2024, 8 April Shift-I

(a) 14 (b) 7 (c) 10 (d) 8

4 $\int \frac{\pi}{x^{n+1} - x} dx =$ NCERT Pg. 240, CUET 2024, 16 May

(a) $\frac{\pi}{n} \log_e \left|\frac{x^n - 1}{x^n}\right| + C$ (b) $\log_e \left|\frac{x^n + 1}{x^n - 1}\right| + C$

(c) $\frac{\pi}{n} \log_e \left|\frac{x^n + 1}{x^n}\right| + C$ (d) $\pi \log_e \left|\frac{x^n}{x^n - 1}\right| + C$

5 $\int e^x \left(\frac{2x + 1}{2\sqrt{x}}\right) dx =$ NCERT Pg. 263, CUET 2024, 16 May

(a) $\frac{1}{2\sqrt{x}} e^x + C$ (b) $-e^x \sqrt{x} + C$

(c) $-\frac{1}{2\sqrt{x}} e^x + C$ (d) $e^x \sqrt{x} + C$

6 $\int_0^{\frac{\pi}{2}} \frac{1 - \cot x}{\operatorname{cosec} x + \cos x} dx =$ NCERT Pg. 280, CUET 2024, 16 May

(a) 0 (b) $\frac{\pi}{4}$ (c) ∞ (d) $\frac{\pi}{12}$

7 Let $I(x) = \int \frac{x^2 (x \sec^2 x + \tan x)}{(x \tan x + 1)^2} dx$. If $I(0) = 0$, then $I\left(\frac{\pi}{4}\right)$ is equal to NCERT Pg. 285, JEE Main 2023, 6 April Shift-I

(a) $\log_e \frac{(\pi + 4)^2}{16} - \frac{\pi^2}{4(\pi + 4)}$ (b) $\log_e \frac{(\pi + 4)^2}{16} + \frac{\pi^2}{4(\pi + 4)}$

(c) $\log_e \frac{(\pi + 4)^2}{32} + \frac{\pi^2}{4(\pi + 4)}$ (d) $\log_e \frac{(\pi + 4)^2}{32} - \frac{\pi^2}{4(\pi + 4)}$

8 Let $f(x)$ be a function satisfying $f(x) + f(\pi - x) = \pi^2$, $\forall x \in R$. Then, $\int_0^{\pi} f(x) \sin x \, dx$ is equal to NCERT Pg. 286, JEE Main 2023, 6 April Shift-II

(a) $\frac{\pi^2}{2}$ (b) $2\pi^2$ (c) π^2 (d) $\frac{\pi^2}{4}$

9 The value of the integral $\int_{1/2}^{2} \frac{\tan^{-1} x}{x} dx$ is equal to

NCERT Pg. 286, JEE Main 2023, 29 Jan Shift-II

(a) $\frac{1}{2}\log_e 2$ (b) $\frac{\pi}{2}\log_e 2$
(c) $\frac{\pi}{4}\log_e 2$ (d) $\pi \log_e 2$

10 Let $R \to R$ be function defined as $f(x) = a\sin\left(\frac{\pi[x]}{2}\right) + [2 - x], a \in R$, where $[t]$ is the greatest integer less than or equal to t. If $\lim_{x \to -1} f(x)$ exists, then the value of $\int_0^4 f(x)dx$ is equal to

NCERT Pg. 285, JEE Main 2022, 27 July Shift-I

(a) –1 (b) –2 (c) 1 (d) 2

Numerical Value Type

11 If $\int (\sqrt{\sec 2x} - 1)\, dx = \alpha \log_e \left| \cos 2x + \beta + \sqrt{\cos 2x \left(1 + \cos \frac{1}{\beta} x\right)} \right|$ + constant, then $\beta - \alpha$ is equal to .... NCERT Pg. 285, JEE Main 2023, 15 April Shift-I

12 If $\int \text{cosec}^5 x\, dx = \alpha \cot x \,\text{cosec}\, x \left(\text{cosec}^2 x + \frac{3}{2}\right) + \beta \log_6 \left|\tan \frac{x}{2}\right| + C$, where $\alpha, \beta \in R$ and C is the constant of integration, then the value of $8(\alpha + \beta)$ equals ....

NCERT Pg. 259, JEE Main 2024, 4 April Shift-II

13 Let $f(x) = \int \frac{dx}{(3 + 4x^2)\sqrt{4 - 3x^2}}, |x| < \frac{2}{\sqrt{3}}$. If $f(0) = 0$ and $f(1) = \frac{1}{\alpha\beta}\tan^{-1}\left(\frac{\alpha}{\beta}\right)$, $\alpha, \beta > 0$, then $\alpha^2 + \beta^2$ is equal to ....

NCERT Pg. 244, JEE Main 2023, 15 April Shift-I

14 The value of $\frac{8}{\pi}\int_0^{\pi/2} \frac{(\cos x)^{2023}}{(\sin x)^{2023} + (\cos x)^{2023}} dx$ is ....

NCERT Pg. 278, JEE Main 2023, 24 Jan Shift-I

15 The value of the integral $\int_0^{\pi/2} 60 \frac{\sin(6x)}{\sin x} dx$ is equal to ....

NCERT Pg. 277, JEE Main 2022, 28 July Shift-II

Skill Boosters

1 If $g\left(\frac{x+2}{x+3}\right) = 3x + 2, x \in R - \left\{3, \frac{1}{3}\right\}$, then $\int g(x)\, dx$ is equal to (where, C is a constant of integration)

(a) $-6x - 3\log|(1 - x)| + C$
(b) $-7x - 3\log|(1 - x)| + C$
(c) $-7x + 3\log|(1 - x)| + C$
(d) $7x - 3\log|(1 - x)| + C$

2 The value of $\int_0^{\sqrt{2}} x e^{[x^2]} dx$, where $[a]$ is greatest integer $1 \leq a$ is

(a) $\left(\frac{1-e}{2}\right)$ (b) $\left(\frac{1+e}{2}\right)$ (c) $\frac{1}{2} + e$ (d) $\left(\frac{1+e}{2}\right)^2$

3 Which of the following statements is correct for the function $f(\alpha)$ for $\alpha \in R$, such that

$$f(\alpha) = \int_{\pi/6}^{\pi/3} \frac{\sec^\alpha x\, dx}{\sec^\alpha x + \text{cosec}^\alpha x}$$

(a) $f(\alpha)$ is an even function.
(b) $f(0) = 0$
(c) $f(\alpha)$ is strictly decreasing function.
(d) $f(\alpha)$ is strictly increasing function.

4 The integral $\int \sin(\log_e x)\, dx$ is equal to (where C is a constant of integration).

(a) $\frac{x}{2}\sin(\log_e x) - \cos(\log_e x) + C$
(b) $\frac{x}{2}(\sin(\log_e x) + \cos(\log_e x)) + C$
(c) $\frac{x}{2}(\cos(\log_e x) - \sin(\log_e x)) + C$
(d) $\frac{x}{2}(\cos(\log_e x) + \sin(\log_e x)) + C$

5 $\int \frac{1}{(x+6)^{5/4}(x+2)^{3/4}} dx$ is equal to

(a) $\frac{1}{4}\left(\frac{x+2}{x+6}\right)^{1/4} + C$ (b) $\frac{1}{4}\left(\frac{x+6}{x+2}\right)^{1/4} + C$
(c) $\left(\frac{x+2}{x+6}\right)^{1/4} + C$ (d) $\left(\frac{x+6}{x+2}\right)^{1/4} + C$

6 If $\int_0^x f(t)\, dt = x^3 + \int_x^3 t^3 f(t)\, dt$, then $f'(1)$ is

(a) $\frac{16}{3}$ (b) $\frac{3}{16}$ (c) $\frac{3}{15}$ (d) 3

Correct Codes

Topical Questions

Integration as an Inverse Process of Differentiation

1 (d)	2 (d)	3 (a)	4 (c)	5 (d)	6 (a)	7 (b)	8 (c)	9 (a)	10 (c)
11 (b)	12 (c)	13 (d)	14 (c)	15 (a)	16 (a)	17 (c)	18 (b)	19 (b)	20 (c)
21 (a)	22 (d)	23 (c)	24 (b)	25 (c)	26 (b)	27 (a)	28 (c)	29 (a)	30 (c)
31 (d)	32 (b)	33 (a)	34 (c)	35 (b)					

Methods of Integration

1 (b)	2 (b)	3 (b)	4 (a)	5 (b)	6 (d)	7 (b)	8 (b)	9 (c)	10 (c)
11 (d)	12 (c)	13 (d)	14 (b)	15 (c)	16 (d)	17 (b)	18 (a)	19 (c)	20 (d)
21 (b)	22 (c)	23 (d)	24 (a)						

Integration using Trigonometric Identities

1 (d)	2 (b)	3 (c)	4 (b)	5 (b)	6 (a)	7 (c)	8 (b)	9 (a)	10 (b)
11 (c)	12 (b)	13 (b)	14 (c)	15 (d)	16 (b)	17 (a)			

Integrals of Some Particular Functions

1 (b)	2 (d)	3 (b)	4 (b)	5 (d)	6 (c)	7 (a)	8 (a)	9 (c)	10 (b)
11 (b)	12 (b)	13 (a)	14 (c)	15 (a)	16 (c)	17 (b)	18 (a)	19 (d)	20 (c)

Integration by Partial Fractions

1 (b)	2 (b)	3 (c)	4 (d)	5 (c)	6 (d)	7 (c)	8 (d)	9 (b)	10 (a)
11 (a)	12 (c)	13 (d)	14 (a)	15 (b)	16 (d)	17 (a)			

Integration by Parts

1 (a)	2 (c)	3 (b)	4 (d)	5 (c)	6 (d)	7 (b)	8 (b)	9 (a)	10 (a)
11 (d)	12 (a)	13 (d)	14 (a)	15 (b)	16 (a)	17 (a)	18 (a)	19 (d)	20 (c)
21 (b)	22 (d)								

Integrals of Some More Types Functions

1 (b)	2 (c)	3 (d)	4 (c)	5 (b)	6 (a)	7 (d)	8 (b)	9 (a)	10 (a)
11 (c)	12 (c)								

Fundamental Theorem of Calculus

1 (c)	2 (c)	3 (b)	4 (c)	5 (a)	6 (a)	7 (d)	8 (c)	9 (b)	10 (c)
11 (d)	12 (b)	13 (d)	14 (a)	15 (d)	16 (c)	17 (d)	18 (a)	19 (d)	20 (c)
21 (b)	22 (d)	23 (d)							

Evaluation of Definite Integrals by Substitution

1 (c)	2 (b)	3 (c)	4 (a)	5 (d)	6 (a)	7 (b)	8 (b)	9 (a)	10 (c)
11 (b)	12 (c)	13 (a)	14 (d)						

Some Properties of Definite Integrals

1 (b) **2** (c) **3** (b) **4** (a) **5** (c) **6** (b) **7** (c) **8** (d) **9** (c) **10** (c)
11 (a) **12** (b) **13** (b) **14** (a) **15** (b) **16** (b) **17** (c)

Miscellaneous Exercise

1 (c) **2** (d) **3** (c) **4** (a) **5** (a) **6** (b) **7** (c) **8** (a) **9** (d) **10** (a)
11 (b) **12** (c) **13** (b) **14** (b) **15** (d) **16** (b) **17** (a) **18** (b)

Numerical Type Questions

1 (5) **2** (10) **3** (10) **4** (6) **5** (3) **6** (0) **7** (1) **8** (1750) **9** (1) **10** (0)

Assertion and Reason Questions

1 (a) **2** (a) **3** (d) **4** (c) **5** (a) **6** (a) **7** (b) **8** (a)

Case or Paragraph Type Questions

1 (c) **2** (a) **3** (a) **4** (b) **5** (c) **6** (a)

Past Years Questions

1 (d) **2** (b) **3** (b) **4** (a) **5** (d) **6** (a) **7** (d) **8** (c) **9** (b) **10** (b)
11 (1) **12** (1) **13** (28) **14** (2) **15** (104)

Skill Boosters

1 (b) **2** (b) **3** (a) **4** (a) **5** (c) **6** (b)

Step by Step

Decoding the Questions

Concept Builders

1 $\int 3^x \cdot 5^{2x} dx$

$= \int 3^x \cdot (5^2)^x \, dx$

$= \int 3^x \cdot 25^x dx$

$= \int 75^x \, dx = \dfrac{(75)^x}{\log_e 75} + C$

2 $\int e^{(2\ln 3 + \ln 2x)} \, dx = \int e^{(\ln 3^2 + \ln 2x)} dx$

$= \int 9 \cdot 2x \, dx$

$= \int 18x \, dx = 9x^2 + C$

3 $\left(\dfrac{-1}{4} \ln|3 - 4x| + C\right)$

4 $\int e^x \left(\tan^{-1} x + \dfrac{1}{1+x^2}\right) dx$

Using concept,

$\int e^x (f(x) + f'(x)) \, dx = e^x f(x) + C$

$\int e^x \left(\tan^{-1} x + \dfrac{1}{1+x^2}\right) dx$

$= e^x \tan^{-1}(x) + C$

5 $\int_0^3 \{x\} \, dx = \int_0^3 (x - [x]) \, dx$

$= \int_0^3 x \, dx - \int_0^3 [x] \, dx$

$= \left(\dfrac{x^2}{2}\right)_0^3$

$- \left(\int_0^1 [x] \, dx + \int_1^2 [x] \, dx + \int_2^3 [x] \, dx\right)$

$= \dfrac{9}{2} - \int_0^1 0 \, dx - \int_1^2 1 \, dx - \int_2^3 2dx$

$= \dfrac{9}{2} - (1 + 2)$

$= \dfrac{3}{2}$

6 $\int_1^4 [x] \, dx = \int_1^2 [x] \, dx + \int_2^3 [x] \, dx + \int_3^4 [x] \, dx$

$= \int_1^2 1dx + \int_2^3 2dx + \int_3^4 3dx$

$= (2 - 1) + 2(3 - 2) + 3(4 - 3)$

$= 1 + 2 + 3 = 6$

7 $\int \sec x (\sec x + \tan x) \, dx$

$= \int (\sec^2 x + \sec x \cdot \tan x) \, dx$

$= \tan x + \sec x + C$

8 $\int_0^1 \dfrac{x}{1+x^2} dx$

Put $x^2 = t \Rightarrow 2x \, dx = dt$

When $x \to 0$, then $t \to 0$

When $x \to 1$, then $t \to 1$

$\dfrac{1}{2} \int_0^1 \dfrac{1}{1+t} dt = \dfrac{1}{2} [\log|1 + t|]_0^1$

$= \dfrac{1}{2} [\log|2| - \log|1|]$

$= \dfrac{1}{2} \log|2| \; [\because \log|1| = 0]$

9 $\int_0^3 \left(\tan^{-1}(x^2 + 1) + \tan^{-1}\left(\dfrac{1}{x^2+1}\right)\right) dx$

$= \int_0^3 \tan^{-1}(x^2 + 1) + \cot^{-1} (x^2 + 1) \, dx$

$= \int_0^3 \dfrac{\pi}{2} dx = \dfrac{\pi}{2}(3 - 0) = \dfrac{3\pi}{2}$

10 $\int \sqrt{1 + \sin\left(\dfrac{x}{2}\right)} \, dx$

$= \int \sqrt{\left(\cos\dfrac{x}{4} + \sin\dfrac{x}{4}\right)^2} \, dx$

$= \int \left(\cos\dfrac{x}{4} + \sin\dfrac{x}{4}\right) dx$

$= 4\left(\sin\dfrac{x}{4} - \cos\left(\dfrac{x}{4}\right)\right) + C$

11 $\int \sec^2 (2x + 1) \, dx = \dfrac{\tan(2x + 1)}{2} + C$

12 $\dfrac{d}{dx}(f(x)) = 2x + 3x^3$

$\Rightarrow \quad f(x) = \int (2x + 3x^3) dx$

$= x^2 + \dfrac{3}{4} x^4 + C$

$f(1) = 0$

$\Rightarrow 1 + \dfrac{3}{4} + C = 0 \Rightarrow C = \dfrac{-7}{4}$

$\therefore \quad f(x) = x^2 + \dfrac{3}{4} x^4 - \dfrac{7}{4}$

13 $\int 2x^2 e^{x^3} \, dx = \dfrac{2}{3} \int 3x^2 e^{x^3} \, dx$

Put $x^3 = t$

$\Rightarrow 3x^2 \, dx = dt$

$\dfrac{2}{3} \int e^t \, dt = \dfrac{2}{3} e^{x^3} + C$

14 $\int \dfrac{d\theta}{\sec^2\theta - \tan^2\theta}$

$= \int d\theta$

$= \theta + C$

Topical Questions

Integration as an Inverse Process of Differentiation

1 (*d*) We known that,

$\dfrac{d}{dx}(\sin x) = \cos x$ ...(i)

$\dfrac{d}{dx}\left(\dfrac{x^3}{3}\right) = x^2$ ...(ii)

and $\dfrac{d}{dx}(e^x) = e^x$ ...(iii)

We observe that in (i) the function $\cos x$ is the derived function of $\sin x$. We say that $\sin x$ is an anti-derivative (or an integrals) of $\cos x$. Similarly, in Eqs. (ii) and (iii), $\dfrac{x^3}{3}$ and e^x are the anti-derivatives (or integrals) of x^2 and e^x, respectively.

Again, we note that for any real number C, treated as constant function, its derivative is zero and hence, we can write Eqs. (i), (ii) and (iii) as follows

$\dfrac{d}{dx}(\sin x + C) = \cos x,$

$\dfrac{d}{dx}\left(\dfrac{x^3}{3} + C\right) = x^2$

and $\dfrac{d}{dx}(e^x + C) = e^x$

2 (*d*) Anti-derivatives (or integrals) of the functions are not unique. Actually, there exist infinitely many anti-derivatives of each of the function which can be obtained by choosing C arbitrarily from the set of real numbers. For this reason C is customarily referred to as **arbitrary constant**. In fact, C is the **parameter** by varying which one gets different anti-derivatives (or integrals) of the given function.

3 (*a*) Functions with same derivatives differ by a constant. To show this, let g and h be two functions having the same derivatives on an interval I.

Consider the function $f = g - h$ defined by $f(x) = g(x) - h(x)$, $\forall x \in I$.

Then, $\frac{df}{dx} = f' = g' - h'$ giving

$f'(x) = g'(x) - h'(x) \forall x \in I$.

or $f'(x) = 0$, $\forall x \in I$

by hypothesis, *i.e.* the rate of change of f with respect to x is zero on I and hence f is constant.

Thus, the family $\{F + C, C \in R\}$ provides all possible anti-derivatives of f.

4 (*c*)

Symbols	Meaning
A. $\int f(x)\,dx$	Integral of f with respect to x
B. $f(x)$ in $\int f(x)\,dx$	Integrand
C. x in $\int f(x)\,dx$	Variable of integration

5 (*d*)

Terms/Phrases	Meaning
A. Integrate	Find the integral
B. An integral of f	A function F such that $F'(x) = f(x)$
C. Integration	The process of finding the integral
D. Constant of integration	Any real number C, considered as constant function

6 (*a*)

Derivatives	Integrals (Anti-derivatives)
$\frac{d}{dx}\left(\frac{x^{n+1}}{n+1}\right) = x^n$	$\int x^n\,dx = \frac{x^{n+1}}{n+1} + C$
Particularly, we note that	$; n \neq -1$
$\frac{d}{dx}x = 1$	$\int dx = x + C$

7 (*b*)

Derivatives	Anti-derivatives
A. $\frac{d}{dx}(\sin x) = \cos x$;	$\int \cos x\,dx = \sin x + C$
B. $\frac{d}{dx}(-\cos x) = \sin x$;	$\int \sin x\,dx = -\cos x + C$
C. $\frac{d}{dx}(\tan x) = \sec^2 x$;	$\int \sec^2 dx = \tan x + C$
D. $\frac{d}{dx}(-\cot x) = \operatorname{cosec}^2 x$;	$\int \operatorname{cosec}^2 x\,dx = -\cot x + C$

8 (*c*) If $\frac{d}{dx}(\sec x) = \sec x \tan x$, then

$$\int \sec x \tan x\,dx = \sec x + C$$

9 (*a*) It is correct to say that we can write the corresponding formulae for the integrals of the functions if we know the formulae of its derivatives.

$\therefore$ If $\frac{d}{dx}(-\operatorname{cosec} x) = \operatorname{cosec} x \cot x$,

then

$$\int \operatorname{cosec} x \cot x\,dx = -\operatorname{cosec} x + C$$

10 (*c*) The functions in column I are derived functions of column II, then we say that each function of column II is an anti-derivative of each function in column I.

A. $\frac{d}{dx}(\sin^{-1} x) = \frac{1}{\sqrt{1-x^2}}$

$\int \frac{dx}{\sqrt{1-x^2}} = \sin^{-1} x + C$

B. $\frac{d}{dx}(\cos^{-1} x) = \frac{-1}{\sqrt{1-x^2}}$;

$\int \frac{-dx}{\sqrt{1-x^2}} = +\cos^{-1} x + C$

C. $\frac{d}{dx}(\tan^{-1} x) = \frac{1}{1+x^2}$;

$\int \frac{dx}{1+x^2} = \tan^{-1} x + C$

D. $\frac{d}{dx}(\cot^{-1} x) = \frac{-1}{1+x^2}$;

$\int \frac{-dx}{1+x^2} = +\cot^{-1} x + C$

11 (*b*) Given that,

$\frac{d}{dx}(\sec^{-1} x) = \frac{1}{x\sqrt{x^2-1}}$

Therefore,

$\int \frac{dx}{x\sqrt{x^2-1}} = \sec^{-1} x + C$

12 (*c*) (i) $\frac{d}{dx}(-\operatorname{cosec}^{-1} x) = \frac{1}{x\sqrt{x^2-1}}$;

$\int \frac{dx}{x\sqrt{x^2-1}} = -\operatorname{cosec}^{-1} x + C$

(ii) $\frac{d}{dx}(e^x) = e^x$; $\int e^x\,dx = e^x + C$

(iii) $\frac{d}{dx}(\log|x|) = \frac{1}{x}$;

$\int \frac{1}{x}\,dx = \log|x| + C$

(iv) $\frac{d}{dx}\left(\frac{a^x}{\log a}\right) = a^x$;

$\int a^x dx = \frac{a^x}{\log a} + C$

13 (*d*) The process of differentiation and integration are inverses of each other in sense of the following results

$$\frac{d}{dx}\int f(x)\,dx = f(x)$$

and $\int f'(x)\,dx = f(x) + C$, where C is any arbitrary constant

Let F be any anti-derivative of f,

i.e. $\frac{d}{dx}F(x) = f(x)$

Then, $\int f(x)\,dx = F(x) + C$

Therefore,

$$\frac{d}{dx}\int f(x)\,dx = \frac{d}{dx}(F(x)+C)$$
$$= \frac{d}{dx}F(x) = f(x)$$

Similarly, we know that

$$f'(x) = \frac{d}{dx}f(x)$$

and hence $\int f'(x)\,dx = f(x)+C$

where, C is arbitrary constant called constant of integration.

14 (c) The equivalence of the families $\{\int f(x)\,dx + C_1, C_1 \in R\}$ and $\{\int g(x)\,dx + C_2, C_2 \in R\}$ is customarily expressed by writing $\int f(x)\,dx = \int g(x)\,dx$, without mentioning the parameter.

15 (a) We need to prove

$$\int [f(x)+g(x)]\,dx = \int f(x)\,dx + \int g(x)\,dx$$

We know that, process of differentiation and integration are inverse of each other

$$\frac{d}{dx}[\int f(x)+g(x)]\,dx] = f(x)+g(x) \quad ...(i)$$

On the otherhand, we find that

$$\frac{d}{dx}[\int f(x)\,dx + \int g(x)\,dx]$$
$$= \frac{d}{dx}\int f(x)\,dx + \frac{d}{dx}\int g(x)\,dx$$
$$= f(x)+g(x) \quad ...(ii)$$

Also, two indefinite integrals with same derivatives lead to the same family of curves and so they are equivalent.

$\therefore$ From Eqs. (i) and (ii), we get

$$\int [f(x)+g(x)]\,dx = \int f(x)\,dx + \int g(x)\,dx$$

16 (a) We know that, process of differentiation and integration are inverse of each other.

$$\therefore \frac{d}{dx}\int k f(x)\,dx = k f(x)$$

Also, $\frac{d}{dx}[k\int f(x)\,dx]$

$$= k\frac{d}{dx}\{\int f(x)\,dx\} = k f(x)$$

Also, two indefinite integrals with same derivatives lead to the same family of curves and so they are equivalent

$$\therefore \int k f(x)\,dx = k\int f(x)\,dx$$

17 (c) We know that,

$$\int [f(x)+g(x)]\,dx = \int f(x)dx + \int g(x)\,dx$$

and $\int k f(x)\,dx = k\int f(x)\,dx$

Therefore, this be generalised to a finite number of functions $f_1, f_2, ..., f_n$ and the real number, $k_1\ k_2 ...., k_n$ giving

$$\int [k_1 f_1(x) + k_2 f_2(x) + ... + k_n f_n(x)]\,dx$$
$$= k_1\int f_1(x)\,dx + k_2\int f_2(x)\,dx + ... + k_n\int f_n(x)\,dx$$

18 (b) When the variable of integration is denoted by a variable other than x, the integral formulae are modified accordingly. For given integral y,

$$\int y^4\,dy = \frac{y^{4+1}}{4+1}+C = \frac{1}{5}y^5+C$$

We use the integral formula,

$$\int x^n\,dx = \frac{x^{n+1}}{n+1}+C$$

19 (b)

A. $\int \sin 2x\,dx = -\frac{1}{2}\cos 2x + C$

$$\left[\because \frac{d}{dx}(-\frac{1}{2}\cos 2x + C) = -\frac{1}{2}(-\sin 2x)2 = \sin 2x\right]$$

B. $\int \cos 3x\,dx = \frac{1}{3}\sin 3x + C$

$$\left[\because \frac{d}{dx}\left(\frac{1}{3}\sin 3x + C\right) = \frac{1}{3}(\cos 3x)3 = \cos 3x\right]$$

C. $\int e^{2x}\,dx = \frac{1}{2}e^{2x}+C$

$$\left[\because \frac{d}{dx}\left(\frac{1}{2}e^{2x}+C\right) = \frac{1}{2}e^{2x}.2 = e^{2x}\right]$$

D. $\int (ax+b)^2\,dx = \frac{1}{3a}(ax+b)^3$

$$\left[\because \frac{d}{dx}\left(\frac{1}{3a}(ax+b)^3+C\right) = \frac{1}{3a}.3(ax+b)^2 a = (ax+b)^2\right]$$

20 (c) We have, $\sin 2x - 4e^{3x}$.

$$\int (\sin 2x - 4e^{3x})\,dx$$
$$= \int \sin 2x\,dx - 4\int e^{3x}\,dx = \frac{-\cos 2x}{2} - 4\frac{e^{3x}}{3}+C$$
$$= -\frac{1}{2}\cos 2x - \frac{4}{3}e^{3x}+C$$

$$\left[\because \frac{d}{dx}\left(-\frac{1}{2}\cos 2x\right) = -\frac{1}{2}(-\sin 2x)2 = \sin 2x \text{ and } \frac{d}{dx}\left(\frac{4}{3}e^{3x}\right) = \frac{4}{3}(e^{3x}3) = 4e^{3x}\right]$$

21 (a) A. We have $\int (4e^{3x}+1)\,dx$.

$$\int (4e^{3x}+1)\,dx = 4\int e^{3x}\,dx + \int 1\,dx$$
$$= \frac{4e^{3x}}{3}+x+C$$
$$\left[\because \int e^{nx}\,dx = \frac{e^{nx}}{n}+C\right]$$

22 (d) A.

$$\int x^2\left(1-\frac{1}{x^2}\right)dx = \int\left(x^2-\frac{x^2}{x^2}\right)dx$$
$$= \int (x^2-1)\,dx$$
$$= \int x^2 dx - \int 1\,dx$$
$$= \frac{x^3}{3} - x + C$$

B. $\int (ax^2+bx+c)\,dx$

$$= \int ax^2\,dx + \int bx\,dx + c\int 1\,dx$$
$$= \frac{ax^3}{3}+\frac{bx^2}{2}+cx+K,$$

where K is a constant of integration.

C. $\int (2x^2+e^x)\,dx$

$$= 2\int x^2\,dx + \int e^x\,dx$$
$$= \frac{2x^3}{3}+e^x+C$$

D. $\int\left(\sqrt{x}-\frac{1}{\sqrt{x}}\right)^2 dx$

$=\int\left[(\sqrt{x})^2+\left(\frac{1}{\sqrt{x}}\right)^2-2\sqrt{x}\times\frac{1}{\sqrt{x}}\right]dx$

$[\because (a-b)^2=a^2+b^2-2ab]$

$=\int\left(x+\frac{1}{x}-2\right)dx$

$=\int x\,dx+\int\frac{1}{x}dx-2\int 1\,dx$

$=\frac{x^2}{2}+\log|x|-2x+C$

23 (c) $\int\frac{x^3+5x^2-4}{x^2}dx.$

Here, the integrand cannot be integrated directly, so we will break the integrand into three terms by taking x^2 as denominator of each term of numerator and then integrate each term separately.

$\int\frac{x^3+5x^2-4}{x^2}dx$

$=\int\frac{x^3}{x^2}dx+5\int\frac{x^2}{x^2}dx-4\int\frac{1}{x^2}dx$

$=\int x\,dx+5\int 1\cdot dx-4\int x^{-2}dx$

$=\frac{x^2}{2}+5x-4\left(\frac{x^{-2+1}}{-2+1}\right)+C$

$=\frac{x^2}{2}+5x-4\left(\frac{x^{-1}}{-1}\right)+C$

$=\frac{x^2}{2}+5x+\frac{4}{x}+C$

24 (b) $\int\frac{x^3+3x+4}{\sqrt{x}}dx.$

It is not directly integrable. We split the integrand into three terms and then integrate each term separately.

$\int\frac{x^3+3x+4}{\sqrt{x}}dx$

$=\int\frac{x^3}{\sqrt{x}}dx+3\int\frac{x}{\sqrt{x}}dx+4\int\frac{1}{\sqrt{x}}dx$

$=\int x^3\cdot x^{-1/2}dx+3\int x^{1/2}dx+4\int x^{-1/2}dx$

$=\int x^{(6-1)/2}dx+3\int x^{1/2}dx+4\int x^{-1/2}dx$

$=\int x^{5/2}dx+3\int x^{1/2}dx+4\int x^{-1/2}dx$

$=\frac{x^{(5/2)+1}}{(5/2)+1}+\frac{3x^{(1/2)+1}}{(1/2)+1}+\frac{4x^{(-1/2)+1}}{(-1/2)+1}+C$

$\left[\because \int x^n dx=\frac{x^{n+1}}{n+1}\right]$

$=\frac{x^{7/2}}{7/2}+\frac{3x^{3/2}}{3/2}+\frac{4x^{1/2}}{1/2}+C$

$=\frac{2}{7}x^{7/2}+2\cdot x^{3/2}+8x^{1/2}+C.$

25 (c)

A. $\int(1-x)\sqrt{x}\,dx=\int\left(\sqrt{x}-x^{\frac{3}{2}}\right)dx$

$=\frac{x^{(1/2)+1}}{(1/2)+1}-\frac{x^{(3/2)+1}}{(3/2)+1}+C$

$=\frac{x^{(3/2)}}{(3/2)}-\frac{x^{(5/2)}}{(5/2)}+C$

$\left[\because \int x^n dx=\frac{x^{n+1}}{n+1}\right]$

$=\frac{2}{3}x^{3/2}-\frac{2}{5}x^{5/2}+C$

B. $\int\sqrt{x}(3x^2+2x+3)\,dx$

$=3\int x^{5/2}dx+2\int x^{3/2}dx+3\int x^{1/2}dx$

$=\frac{3\cdot x^{(5/2)+1}}{(5/2)+1}+\frac{2\cdot x^{(3/2)+1}}{(3/2)+1}+\frac{3\cdot x^{(1/2)+1}}{(1/2)+1}+C$

$=\frac{3x^{7/2}}{7/2}+\frac{2x^{5/2}}{5/2}+\frac{3x^{3/2}}{3/2}+C$

$=\frac{6}{7}x^{7/2}+\frac{4}{5}x^{5/2}+2x^{3/2}+C$

C. $\int(2x-3\cos x+e^x)\,dx$

$=2\int x\,dx-3\int\cos x\,dx+\int e^x\,dx$

$=\frac{2x^2}{2}-3\sin x+e^x+C$

$=x^2-3\sin x+e^x+C$

D. $\int(2x^2-3\sin x+5\sqrt{x})\,dx$

$=2\int x^2\,dx-3\int\sin x\,dx+5\int x^{1/2}dx$

$=\frac{2x^3}{3}-3(-\cos x)+5\frac{x^{(1/2)+1}}{(1/2)+1}+C$

$=\frac{2}{3}x^3+3\cos x+\frac{5\cdot 2}{3}x^{3/2}+C$

$=\frac{2}{3}x^3+3\cos x+\frac{10}{3}x^{3/2}+C$

26 (b) We have,

$\int\sec x(\sec x+\tan x)\,dx.$

$\therefore \int\sec x(\sec x+\tan x)\,dx$

$=\int(\sec^2 x+\sec x\cdot\tan x)\,dx$

$=\int\sec^2 x\,dx+\int\sec x\cdot\tan x\,dx$

$=\tan x+\sec x+C$

27 (a) Here, we can convert given integrand into simple form by using trigonometric ratios and then integrate it easily.

$\therefore \int\frac{\sec^2 x}{\text{cosec}^2 x}dx$

$=\int\frac{\sin^2 x}{\cos^2 x}dx=\int\tan^2 x\,dx$

$=\int(\sec^2 x-1)\,dx$

$\left[\because \frac{1}{\text{cosec}^2 x}=\sin^2 x \text{ and } \sec^2 x=\frac{1}{\cos^2 x}\right]$

$=\int\sec^2 x\,dx-\int 1\,dx$

$=\tan x-x+C$

28 (c) $\int\left(\sqrt{x}+\frac{1}{\sqrt{x}}\right)dx$

$=\int\sqrt{x}\,dx+\int\frac{1}{\sqrt{x}}dx$

$=\int x^{1/2}dx+\int x^{-1/2}dx$

$=\frac{x^{3/2}}{3/2}+\frac{x^{1/2}}{1/2}+C$

$=\frac{2}{3}x^{3/2}+2x^{1/2}+C$

29 (*a*) Given, $\frac{d}{dx}f(x) = 4x^3 - \frac{3}{x^4}$

$\Rightarrow$ Anti-derivative of

$$\left(4x^3 - \frac{3}{x^4}\right) = f(x)$$

$$\therefore \quad f(x) = \int\left(4x^3 - \frac{3}{x^4}\right)dx$$

$$= 4\int x^3 dx - 3\int x^{-4} dx$$

$$\Rightarrow \quad f(x) = 4\left(\frac{x^4}{4}\right) - 3\left(\frac{x^{-3}}{-3}\right) + C$$

$$= x^4 + \frac{1}{x^3} + C$$

Also, $f(2) = 0$.

$$\therefore \quad f(2) = (2)^4 + \frac{1}{(2)^3} + C$$

$$\Rightarrow 16 + \frac{1}{8} + C = 0$$

$$\Rightarrow \quad C = -\left(16 + \frac{1}{8}\right) \Rightarrow C = -\frac{129}{8}$$

$$\therefore f(x) = x^4 + \frac{1}{x^3} - \frac{129}{8}.$$

30 (*c*) $\int\left(\frac{2a}{\sqrt{x}} - \frac{b}{x^2} + 3c\sqrt[3]{x^2}\right)dx$

$$= \int 2a\,(x)^{\frac{-1}{2}}\, dx - \int bx^{-2}\, dx + \int 3c\, x^{2/3}\, dx$$

$$= 4a\sqrt{x} + \frac{b}{x} + \frac{9cx^{\frac{5}{3}}}{5} + C$$

31 (*d*) We have, $I = \int \frac{x^3}{x+1}dx$

Since, power of x in numerator is greater than denominator, So, we divide numerator by the denominator.

$$\begin{array}{r|l} x+1 & x^3 \quad (x^2 - x + 1 \\ & x^3 + x^2 \\ & - \quad - \\ \hline & -x^2 \\ & -x^2 - x \\ & + \quad + \\ \hline & x \\ & x + 1 \\ & - \quad - \\ \hline & -1 \end{array}$$

$$\therefore \quad I = \int\left[(x^2 - x + 1) - \frac{1}{x+1}\right]dx$$

$$= \frac{x^3}{3} - \frac{x^2}{2} + x - \log|x+1| + C$$

32 (*b*) We have,

$$\frac{d}{dx}\{f(x)\} = \frac{1}{1+x^2}$$

On integrating both sides, we get

$$f(x) = \tan^{-1}x + C$$

$$\left[\because \int\frac{1}{1+x^2}dx = \tan^{-1}x\right]$$

$$\therefore \quad \frac{d}{dx}f(x^3) = \frac{d}{dx}(\tan^{-1}x^3) + C$$

$$= \frac{1}{1+(x^3)^2}\cdot 3x^2 + 0$$

$$\left[\because \frac{d}{dx}\tan^{-1}x = \frac{1}{1+x^2}\right]$$

$$= \frac{3x^2}{1+x^6}$$

33 (*a*) Here, $I = \int\frac{\sec^2 x - 7}{\sin^7 x}dx$

$$= \int\frac{\sin^7 x\sec^2 x - 7\sin^7 x}{(\sin^7 x)^2}dx$$

[On multiply $\sin^7 x$ in numerator and denominator]

$$= \int\frac{d}{dx}\left(\frac{\tan x}{\sin^7 x}\right)dx$$

[using inspection method]

$$= \frac{\tan x}{\sin^7 x} + C$$

34 (*c*) We have,

$$I = \int e^{\tan^{-1}x}\frac{(1+x+x^2)}{1+x^2}dx$$

$$= \int e^{\tan^{-1}x}\left[\frac{x}{1+x^2} + 1\right]dx$$

$$= \int e^{\tan^{-1}x}dx + \int e^{\tan^{-1}x}\frac{x}{(1+x^2)}dx$$

$$= \int\left[\frac{d}{dx}(x\,e^{\tan^{-1}x})\right]dx$$

$$= xe^{\tan^{-1}x} + C$$

35 (*b*) Given that, $f'(x) = x + \frac{1}{x}$

On integrating both sides, we get

$$f(x) = \int x\,dx + \int\frac{1}{x}dx$$

$$f(x) = \frac{x^2}{2} + \log|x| + C$$

Methods of Integration

1 (*b*) (i) $\int\tan x\,dx = \log|\sec x| + C$

We have,

$$\int\tan x\,dx = \int\frac{\sin x}{\cos x}dx$$

Put $\cos x = t$, so that $\sin x\,dx = -dt$.

Then,

$$\int\tan x\,dx = -\int\frac{dt}{t} = -\log|t| + C$$

$$= -\log|\cos x| + C$$

or $\int\tan x\,dx = \log|\sec x| + C$

(ii) $\int\cot x\,dx = \log|\sin x| + C$

We have, $\int\cot x\,dx = \int\frac{\cos x}{\sin x}dx$

Put $\sin x = t$, so that $\cos x\,dx = dt$

Then,

$$\int\cot x\,dx = \int\frac{dt}{t} = \log|t| + C$$

$$= \log|\sin x| + C$$

(iii) $\int\sec x\,dx = \log|\sec x + \tan x| + C$

We have,

$$\int\sec x\,dx = \int\frac{\sec x(\sec x + \tan x)}{\sec x + \tan x}dx$$

Put $\sec x + \tan x = t$, so that $\sec x(\tan x + \sec x)\,dx = dt$.

Therefore,

$$\int\sec x\,dx = \int\frac{dt}{t} = \log|t| + C$$

$$= \log|\sec x + \tan x| + C$$

(iv) $\int\text{cosec}\,x\,dx = \log|\text{cosec}\,x - \cot x| + C$

We have, $\int\text{cosec}\,x\,\,dx$

$$= \int\frac{\text{cosec}\,x\,(\text{cosec}\,x + \cot x)}{(\text{cosec}\,x + \cot x)}dx$$

Put $\text{cosec}\,x + \cot x = t$, so that

$$-\text{cosec}\,x\,(\text{cosec}\,x + \cot x)\,dx = dt$$

So, $\int\text{cosec}\,x\,dx = -\int\frac{dt}{t}$

$$= -\log|t| + C$$

$= -\log|\text{cosec } x + \cot x| + C$

$= -\log\left|\dfrac{\text{cosec}^2 x - \cot^2 x}{\text{cosec } x - \cot x}\right| + C$

$= \log|\text{cosec } x - \cot x| + C$

2 (b) (i) Let $I = \int \dfrac{2x}{1+x^2} dx$

Let $1 + x^2 = t$

On differentiating w.r.t. x, we get

$2x\, dx = dt$

$\Rightarrow dx = \dfrac{dt}{2x}$

$\therefore I = \int \dfrac{2x}{t} \dfrac{dt}{2x}$

$= \int \dfrac{1}{t} dt = \log|t| + C$

$= \log|1 + x^2| + C$

(ii) Let $I = \int \dfrac{(\log x)^2}{x} dx$

Let $\log x = t$

On differentiating w.r.t. x, we get

$\dfrac{1}{x} = \dfrac{dt}{dx} \Rightarrow dx = x\, dt$

$\therefore I = \int \dfrac{t^2}{x} x\, dt = \int t^2 dt = \dfrac{t^3}{3} + C$

$= \dfrac{(\log x)^3}{3} + C$

(iii) Let $I = \int \dfrac{1}{x(1+\log x)} dx$

Let $1 + \log x = t$

On differentiating w.r.t. x, we get

$\dfrac{1}{x} = \dfrac{dt}{dx} \Rightarrow dx = x\, dt$

$\therefore I = \int \dfrac{1}{xt} x\, dt$

$= \int \dfrac{1}{t} dt = \log|t| + C$

$= \log|1 + \log x| + C$

(iv) Let $I = \int \sin x \sin(\cos x)\, dx$

Let $\cos x = t$

On differentiating w.r.t. x, we get

$-\sin x = \dfrac{dt}{dx}$

$\Rightarrow dx = \dfrac{dt}{-\sin x}$

$\therefore I = \int \sin x \sin(t) \dfrac{dt}{-\sin x}$

$= -\int \sin t\, dt$

$= -[-\cos t] + C$

$= \cos(\cos x) + C$

3 (b) Let $I = \int \sin(ax+b)\cos(ax+b)\, dx$

Let $\sin(ax + b) = t$

On differentiating w.r.t. x, we get

$a\cos(ax+b) = \dfrac{dt}{dx}$

$\Rightarrow dx = \dfrac{dt}{a\cos(ax+b)}$

$\therefore I = \int t\cos(ax+b) \dfrac{dt}{a\cos(ax+b)}$

$= \dfrac{1}{a}\int t\,dt = \dfrac{1}{a}\cdot\dfrac{t^2}{2} + C$

$= \dfrac{[\sin(ax+b)]^2}{2a} + C$

4 (a) A. $\int \sqrt{ax+b}\, dx = \int (ax+b)^{1/2} dx$

$\left[\because \int (ax+b)^n dx = \dfrac{(ax+b)^{n+1}}{a(n+1)}\right]$

$= \dfrac{(ax+b)^{(1/2)+1}}{a\left(\dfrac{1}{2}+1\right)} + C$

$= \dfrac{(ax+b)^{3/2}}{a\left(\dfrac{3}{2}\right)} + C$

$= \dfrac{2}{3a}(ax+b)^{3/2} + C$

B. $\int x\sqrt{x+2}\, dx$

$= \int (x+2-2)\sqrt{x+2}\, dx$

$= \int (x+2)\sqrt{x+2}\, dx - 2\int\sqrt{x+2}\, dx$

$= \int (x+2)^{3/2} dx - 2\int (x+2)^{1/2} dx$

$= \dfrac{(x+2)^{(3/2)+1}}{(3/2)+1} - 2\dfrac{(x+2)^{(1/2)+1}}{(1/2)+1} + C$

$\left[\because \int x^n dx = \dfrac{x^{n+1}}{n+1}\right]$

$= \dfrac{2}{5}(x+2)^{5/2} - \dfrac{2\times 2}{3}(x+2)^{3/2} + C$

$= \dfrac{2}{5}(x+2)^{5/2} - \dfrac{4}{3}(x+2)^{3/2} + C$

C. Let $I = \int x\sqrt{1+2x^2}\, dx$

Let $1 + 2x^2 = t$

On differentiating w.r.t. x, we get $4x = \dfrac{dt}{dx} \Rightarrow dx = \dfrac{dt}{4x}$

$\therefore I = \int x\sqrt{t}\dfrac{dt}{4x} = \dfrac{1}{4}\int\sqrt{t}\, dt$

$= \dfrac{1}{4}\int t^{1/2} dt = \dfrac{1}{4}\dfrac{t^{(1/2)+1}}{(1/2)+1} + C$

$= \dfrac{1}{6}(1+2x^2)^{3/2} + C$

D. Let $I = \int (4x+2)\sqrt{x^2+x+1}\, dx$

Let $x^2 + x + 1 = t$

On differentiating w.r.t. x, we get

$2x + 1 = \dfrac{dt}{dx} \Rightarrow dx = \dfrac{dt}{(2x+1)}$

$\therefore I = \int (4x+2)\sqrt{t}\dfrac{dt}{(2x+1)}$

$= \int 2(2x+1)\sqrt{t}\dfrac{dt}{(2x+1)}$

$= 2\int\sqrt{t}\, dt$

$= 2\dfrac{t^{(1/2)+1}}{(1/2)+1} + C$

$= \dfrac{4}{3}(x^2+x+1)^{3/2} + C$

5 (b) $\int \dfrac{1}{x-\sqrt{x}} dx = \int \dfrac{1}{\sqrt{x}(\sqrt{x}-1)} dx$

Let $\sqrt{x} - 1 = t$

$\Rightarrow \dfrac{1}{2\sqrt{x}} = \dfrac{dt}{dx} \Rightarrow dx = 2\sqrt{x}\, dt$

$\therefore \int \dfrac{1}{\sqrt{x}(\sqrt{x}-1)} dx = \int \dfrac{1}{\sqrt{x}\,t} 2\sqrt{x}\, dt$

$= \int \dfrac{2}{t} dt = 2\cdot\log|t| + C$

$= 2\log|\sqrt{x}-1| + C$

6 (d) $\int \dfrac{x}{\sqrt{x+4}} dx = \int \dfrac{x+4-4}{\sqrt{x+4}} dx$

$= \int \dfrac{x+4}{\sqrt{x+4}} dx - 4\int \dfrac{1}{\sqrt{x+4}} dx$

$= \int (x+4)^{1/2} dx - 4\int (x+4)^{-1/2} dx$

$= \dfrac{(x+4)^{(1/2)+1}}{(1/2)+1} - 4\dfrac{(x+4)^{(-1/2)+1}}{(-1/2)+1} + C$

$= \dfrac{2}{3}(x+4)^{3/2} - 8(x+4)^{1/2} + C$

7 (*b*)

(i) $\int (x^3-1)^{1/3} x^5 dx$

$$= \int (x^3-1)^{1/3} x^3 \cdot x^2 dx$$

Let $x^3 - 1 = t$

$\Rightarrow \quad x^3 = t+1$

Differentiating w.r.t. x, we get

$$3x^2 = \frac{dt}{dx}$$

$$\Rightarrow \quad dx = \frac{dt}{3x^2}$$

$$\therefore \int (x^3-1)^{1/3} x^3 \cdot x^2 dx$$

$$= \int t^{1/3}(t+1)x^2 \frac{dt}{3x^2}$$

$$= \frac{1}{3}\int (t^{4/3} + t^{1/3})\, dt$$

$$= \frac{1}{3}\left[\frac{t^{7/3}}{\frac{7}{3}} + \frac{t^{4/3}}{\frac{4}{3}}\right] + C$$

$$= \frac{1}{3}\left[\frac{3}{7}t^{7/3} + \frac{3}{4}t^{4/3}\right] + C$$

$$= \frac{1}{7}t^{7/3} + \frac{1}{4}t^{4/3} + C$$

$$= \frac{1}{7}(x^3-1)^{7/3} + \frac{1}{4}(x^3-1)^{4/3} + C$$

(ii) $\int \frac{x^2}{(2+3x^3)^3} dx$

Let $2 + 3x^3 = t$

$$\Rightarrow \quad 9x^2 = \frac{dt}{dx} \Rightarrow dx = \frac{dt}{9x^2}$$

$$\therefore \int \frac{x^2}{(2+3x^3)^3} dx = \int \frac{x^2}{t^3}\frac{dt}{9x^2}$$

$$= \frac{1}{9}\int \frac{1}{t^3} dt$$

$$= \frac{1}{9}\int t^{-3} dt = \frac{1}{9}\left(\frac{t^{-3+1}}{-3+1}\right) + C$$

$$= \frac{1}{9} \times \frac{1}{-2}t^{-2} + C = \frac{-1}{18t^2} + C$$

$$= \frac{-1}{18(2+3x^3)^2} + C$$

(iii) $\int \frac{1}{x(\log x)^m} dx$

Let $\log x = t$

$$\Rightarrow \quad \frac{1}{x} = \frac{dt}{dx} \Rightarrow dx = x\, dt$$

$$\therefore \int \frac{1}{x(\log x)^m} dx = \int \frac{1}{x(t)^m} x\, dt$$

$$= \int t^{-m} dt$$

$$= \frac{t^{-m+1}}{-m+1} + C$$

$$= \frac{(\log x)^{1-m}}{1-m} + C$$

(iv) $\int \frac{x}{9-4x^2} dx$

Let $9 - 4x^2 = t$

$$\Rightarrow \quad -8x = \frac{dt}{dx} \Rightarrow dx = \frac{dt}{-8x}$$

$$\therefore \int \frac{x}{9-4x^2} dx = \int \frac{x}{t}\frac{dt}{-8x}$$

$$= \frac{1}{-8}\int \frac{1}{t} dt = \frac{1}{-8}\log|t| + C$$

$$= -\frac{1}{8}\log|9-4x^2| + C$$

$$= \frac{1}{8}\log\left|\frac{1}{9-4x^2}\right| + C$$

$$\left[\because -a\log b = a\log b^{-1} = a\log\frac{1}{b}\right]$$

8 (*b*) A. $\int e^{(2x+3)} dx$

Let $2x + 3 = t$

$$\Rightarrow \quad 2 = \frac{dt}{dx} \quad \Rightarrow \quad dx = \frac{dt}{2}$$

$$\therefore \int e^{(2x+3)} dx = \int e^t \frac{dt}{2} = \frac{1}{2}\int e^t dt$$

$$= \frac{1}{2}e^t + C = \frac{1}{2}e^{(2x+3)} + C$$

B. $\int \frac{x}{e^{x^2}} dx$

Let $x^2 = t$

$$\Rightarrow \quad 2x = \frac{dt}{dx} \quad \Rightarrow \quad dx = \frac{dt}{2x}$$

$$\therefore \int \frac{x}{e^{x^2}} dx = \int \frac{x}{e^t}\frac{dt}{2x}$$

$$= \frac{1}{2}\int e^{-t} dt = -\frac{1}{2}e^{-t} + C$$

$$= -\frac{1}{2}e^{-(x^2)} + C$$

C. $\int \frac{e^{\tan^{-1} x}}{1+x^2} dx$

Let $\tan^{-1} x = t$

$$\Rightarrow \quad \frac{1}{1+x^2} = \frac{dt}{dx}$$

$$\Rightarrow \quad dx = (1+x^2)\, dt$$

$$\therefore \int \frac{e^{\tan^{-1} x}}{1+x^2} dx = \int \frac{e^t}{1+x^2}(1+x^2) dt$$

$$= \int e^t dt = e^t + C = e^{\tan^{-1} x} + C$$

D. $\int \frac{e^{2x}-1}{e^{2x}+1} dx = \int \frac{(e^x \cdot e^x - 1)}{(e^x \cdot e^x + 1)} dx$

$$= \int \frac{e^x\left(e^x - \frac{1}{e^x}\right)}{e^x\left(e^x + \frac{1}{e^x}\right)} dx$$

$$= \int \frac{(e^x - e^{-x})}{(e^x + e^{-x})} dx$$

Let $e^x + e^{-x} = t$

$$\Rightarrow \quad e^x - e^{-x} = \frac{dt}{dx}$$

$$\Rightarrow \quad dx = \frac{dt}{e^x - e^{-x}}$$

$$\Rightarrow \int \frac{e^{2x}-1}{e^{2x}+1} dx = \int \frac{(e^x - e^{-x})}{t}\frac{dt}{e^x - e^{-x}}$$

$$= \int \frac{1}{t} dt = \log|t| + C$$

$$= \log|e^x + e^{-x}| + C$$

9 (*c*) $\int \frac{e^{2x} - e^{-2x}}{e^{2x} + e^{-2x}} dx$

Let $e^{2x} + e^{-2x} = t$

$$\Rightarrow \quad 2e^{2x} - 2e^{-2x} = \frac{dt}{dx}$$

$$\Rightarrow \quad dx = \frac{dt}{2(e^{2x} - e^{-2x})}$$

$$\therefore \int \frac{e^{2x} - e^{-2x}}{e^{2x} + e^{-2x}} dx$$

$$= \int \frac{e^{2x} - e^{-2x}}{t}\frac{dt}{2[e^{2x} - e^{-2x}]}$$

$$= \frac{1}{2}\int \frac{1}{t} dt$$

$$= \frac{1}{2}\log|t| + C$$

$$= \frac{1}{2}\log|e^{2x} + e^{-2x}| + C$$

10 (c)

I. $\int \tan^2(2x-3)\,dx$

$= \int \sec^2(2x-3)\,dx - \int 1 dx$

$[\because \tan^2 x = \sec^2 x - 1]$

Let $2x - 3 = t$

$\Rightarrow 2dx = dt \Rightarrow dx = \frac{1}{2}dt$

$\therefore \int \sec^2(2x-3)\,dx - \int dx$

$= \frac{1}{2}\int (\sec^2 t)\,dt - \int 1 dx$

$= \frac{1}{2}\tan t - x + C$

$= \frac{1}{2}\tan(2x-3) - x + C$

$= \frac{\tan(2x-3)}{2} - x + C$

II. $\int \sec^2(7-4x)\,dx$

Let $7 - 4x = t$

$\Rightarrow -4 = \frac{dt}{dx} \Rightarrow dx = \frac{dt}{-4}$

$\therefore \int \sec^2(7-4x)\,dx$

$= \int \sec^2 t \cdot \frac{dt}{-4}$

$= -\frac{1}{4}\tan t + C$

$= -\frac{1}{4}\tan(7-4x) + C$

11 (d) (i) Let $I = \int \frac{\sin^{-1} x}{\sqrt{1-x^2}}dx$

Let $\sin^{-1} x = t$

$\Rightarrow \frac{1}{\sqrt{1-x^2}} = \frac{dt}{dx}$

$\Rightarrow dx = \sqrt{1-x^2}dt$

$\therefore \int \frac{t}{\sqrt{1-x^2}}\sqrt{1-x^2}dt$

$= \int t\,dt = \frac{t^2}{2} + C = \frac{(\sin^{-1} x)^2}{2} + C$

(ii) $\int \frac{2\cos x - 3\sin x}{6\cos x + 4\sin x}dx$

$= \int \frac{2\cos x - 3\sin x}{2(3\cos x + 2\sin x)}dx$

Let $3\cos x + 2\sin x = t$

$\Rightarrow -3\sin x + 2\cos x = \frac{dt}{dx}$

$\Rightarrow dx = \frac{dt}{2\cos x - 3\sin x}$

$\therefore \int \frac{2\cos x - 3\sin x}{2(3\cos x + 2\sin x)}dx$

$= \int \frac{2\cos x - 3\sin x}{2(t)} \cdot \frac{dt}{2\cos x - 3\sin x}$

$= \frac{1}{2}\int \frac{1}{t}dt = \frac{1}{2}\log|t| + C$

$= \frac{1}{2}\log|3\cos x + 2\sin x| + C$

(iii) $\int \frac{1}{\cos^2 x(1-\tan x)^2}dx$

$= \int \frac{\sec^2 x}{(1-\tan x)^2}dx$

Let $1 - \tan x = t$

$\Rightarrow -\sec^2 x = \frac{dt}{dx}$

$\Rightarrow dx = \frac{dt}{-\sec^2 x}$

$\therefore \int \frac{\sec^2 x}{(1-\tan x)^2}dx$

$= \int \frac{\sec^2 x}{t^2} \frac{dt}{(-\sec^2 x)}$

$= -\int t^{-2}\,dt = -\left(\frac{-t^{-2+1}}{-2+1}\right) + C$

$= \frac{1}{t} + C = \frac{1}{1-\tan x} + C$

(iv) $\int \frac{\cos\sqrt{x}}{\sqrt{x}}dx$

Let $\sqrt{x} = t$

$\Rightarrow \frac{1}{2\sqrt{x}} = \frac{dt}{dx}$

$\Rightarrow dx = 2\sqrt{x}\,dt$

$\therefore \int \frac{\cos\sqrt{x}}{\sqrt{x}}dx = \int \frac{\cos t}{\sqrt{x}}2\sqrt{x}\,dt$

$= 2\int \cos t\,dt$

$= 2\sin t + C = 2\sin\sqrt{x} + C$

12 (c) $\int \sqrt{\sin 2x}\cos 2x\,dx$

Let $\sin 2x = t$

$\Rightarrow 2\cos 2x = \frac{dt}{dx}$

$\Rightarrow dx = \frac{dt}{2\cos 2x}$

$\therefore \int \sqrt{\sin 2x}\cos 2x\,dx$

$= \int \sqrt{t}\cos 2x \frac{dt}{2\cos 2x} = \frac{1}{2}\int \sqrt{t}\,dt$

$= \frac{1}{2}\frac{t^{1/2+1}}{\left(\frac{1}{2}+1\right)} + C$

$= \frac{1}{3}t^{3/2} + C = \frac{1}{3}(\sin 2x)^{3/2} + C$

13 (d)

I. $\int \frac{\cos x}{\sqrt{1+\sin x}}dx$

$= \int (1+\sin x)^{-1/2}\cos x\,dx$

Let $1 + \sin x = t$

$\Rightarrow \cos x = \frac{dt}{dx} \Rightarrow dx = \frac{dt}{\cos x}$

$\therefore \int (1+\sin x)^{-1/2}\cos x\,dx$

$= \int (t)^{-1/2}\cos x \frac{dt}{\cos x}$

$= \frac{t^{-1/2+1}}{\left(-\frac{1}{2}+1\right)} + C$

$= 2t^{1/2} + C = 2\sqrt{1+\sin x} + C$

II. $\int \cot x \log \sin x\,dx$

Let $\log \sin x = t$

$\Rightarrow \frac{1}{\sin x}\cdot\cos x = \frac{dt}{dx}$

$\Rightarrow \cot x = \frac{dt}{dx} \Rightarrow dx = \frac{dt}{\cot x}$

$\therefore \int \cot x \log \sin x\,dx$

$= \int \cot x \cdot t \frac{dt}{\cot x}$

$= \int t\,dt = \frac{t^2}{2} + C$

$= \frac{(\log \sin x)^2}{2} + C$

14 (b)

A. Let $I = \int \frac{\sin x}{1+\cos x}dx$

Let $1 + \cos x = t$

$\Rightarrow -\sin x = \frac{dt}{dx}$

$\Rightarrow dx = \frac{dt}{-\sin x}$

$\therefore I = \int \frac{\sin x}{t} \times \frac{dt}{-\sin x} = -\int \frac{1}{t}dt$

$= -\log|t| + C$

$= -\log|1+\cos x| + C$

$= \log\left|\dfrac{1}{1+\cos x}\right| + C$

$\left[\because -\log a = \log\dfrac{1}{a}\right]$

B. Let $I = \int \dfrac{\sin x}{(1+\cos x)^2}dx$

Let $1+\cos x = t$

$\Rightarrow \quad -\sin x = \dfrac{dt}{dx}$

$\Rightarrow \quad dx = \dfrac{dt}{-\sin x}$

$\therefore I = \int \dfrac{\sin x}{(1+\cos x)^2}dx$

$= \int \dfrac{\sin x}{t^2} \times \dfrac{dt}{-\sin x} = -\int \dfrac{1}{t^2}dt$

$= -\int t^{-2}dt = \dfrac{-t^{-2+1}}{-2+1} + C = \dfrac{1}{t} + C$

$= \dfrac{1}{1+\cos x} + C$

C. Let

$I = \int \dfrac{1}{(1+\cot x)}dx = \int \dfrac{1}{1+\dfrac{\cos x}{\sin x}}dx$

$= \int \dfrac{1}{\dfrac{\sin x+\cos x}{\sin x}}dx$

$= \int \dfrac{\sin x}{(\sin x+\cos x)}dx$

$= \dfrac{1}{2}\int \dfrac{2(\sin x)}{\sin x+\cos x}dx$

$= \dfrac{1}{2}\int \dfrac{\sin x+\sin x+\cos x-\cos x}{\sin x+\cos x}dx$

[add and subtract $\cos x$ in numerator]

$= \dfrac{1}{2}\int \dfrac{(\sin x+\cos x)+(\sin x-\cos x)}{(\sin x+\cos x)}dx$

$= \dfrac{1}{2}\left[\int \dfrac{(\sin x+\cos x)}{(\sin x+\cos x)}dx + \int \dfrac{(\sin x-\cos x)}{(\sin x+\cos x)}dx\right]$

$= \dfrac{1}{2}\left[\int 1dx + \int \dfrac{(\sin x-\cos x)}{(\sin x+\cos x)}dx\right]$

Let $\sin x+\cos x = t$

$\Rightarrow \quad \cos x - \sin x = \dfrac{dt}{dx}$

$\Rightarrow dx = \dfrac{dt}{-[\sin x-\cos x]}$

$\therefore I = \dfrac{1}{2}\left[\int 1dx + \int \dfrac{(\sin x-\cos x)}{t}\dfrac{dt}{-[\sin x-\cos x]}\right]$

$= \dfrac{1}{2}\left[\int 1dx - \int \dfrac{1}{t}dt\right]$

$= \dfrac{1}{2}[x - \log|t|] + C$

$= \dfrac{1}{2}[x - \log|\sin x + \cos x|] + C$

D. Let $I = \int \dfrac{1}{1-\tan x}dx$

$= \int \dfrac{1}{1-\dfrac{\sin x}{\cos x}}dx = \int \dfrac{1}{\dfrac{\cos x-\sin x}{\cos x}}dx$

$= \dfrac{1}{2}\int \dfrac{2(\cos x)dx}{(\cos x-\sin x)}$

$= \dfrac{1}{2}\int \dfrac{\cos x+\cos x+\sin x-\sin x}{(\cos x-\sin x)}dx$

[add and subtract $\sin x$ in numerator]

$= \dfrac{1}{2}\left[\int \dfrac{(\cos x-\sin x)}{(\cos x-\sin x)}dx + \int \dfrac{(\cos x+\sin x)}{(\cos x-\sin x)}dx\right]$

$= \dfrac{1}{2}\left[\int 1dx + \int \dfrac{(\cos x+\sin x)}{(\cos x-\sin x)}dx\right]$

Let $\cos x - \sin x = t$

$\Rightarrow \quad -\sin x - \cos x = \dfrac{dt}{dx}$

$\Rightarrow -[\sin x+\cos x] = \dfrac{dt}{dx}$

$\Rightarrow \quad dx = \dfrac{dt}{-[\sin x+\cos x]}$

$\therefore I = \dfrac{1}{2}\left[\int 1dx + \int \dfrac{\cos x+\sin x}{t}\dfrac{dt}{-[\sin x+\cos x]}\right]$

$= \dfrac{1}{2}\left[\int 1dx - \int \dfrac{1}{t}dt\right]$

$= \dfrac{1}{2}[x - \log|t|] + C$

$= \dfrac{1}{2}[x - \log|\cos x - \sin x|] + C$

15 (c)

(i) $\int \dfrac{\sqrt{\tan x}}{\sin x\cos x}dx$

$= \int \dfrac{\sqrt{\tan x}}{\sin x\cos x \times \dfrac{\cos x}{\cos x}}dx$

[multiplying numerator and denominator by cosx]

$= \int \dfrac{\sqrt{\tan x}}{\tan x \cdot \cos^2 x}dx$

$= \int \dfrac{\sqrt{\tan x}}{\tan x}\cdot \sec^2 x\,dx$

Let $\quad \tan x = t$

$\Rightarrow \quad \sec^2 x = \dfrac{dt}{dx}$

$\Rightarrow \quad dx = \dfrac{dt}{\sec^2 x}$

$\therefore \int \dfrac{\sqrt{\tan x}}{\tan x}\cdot \sec^2 x\,dx$

$= \int \dfrac{\sqrt{t}}{t}\cdot \sec^2 x\,\dfrac{dt}{\sec^2 x}$

$= \int \dfrac{1}{\sqrt{t}}dt = \int t^{-1/2}dt$

$= \dfrac{t^{-1/2+1}}{\left(-\dfrac{1}{2}+1\right)} + C$

$= 2\sqrt{t} + C = 2\sqrt{\tan x} + C$

(ii) $\int \dfrac{(1+\log x)^2}{x}dx$

Let $1+\log x = t$

$\Rightarrow \quad \dfrac{1}{x} = \dfrac{dt}{dx}$

$\Rightarrow \quad dx = x\,dt$

$\therefore \int \dfrac{(1+\log x)^2}{x}dx$

$= \int \dfrac{t^2}{x}x\,dt$

$= \int t^2dt = \dfrac{t^3}{3} + C$

$= \dfrac{(1+\log x)^3}{3} + C$

(iii) $\int \frac{(x+1)(x+\log x)^2}{x} dx$

$= \int (x+\log x)^2 \left(\frac{x+1}{x}\right) dx$

$= \int (x+\log x)^2 \left(1+\frac{1}{x}\right) dx$

Let $x + \log x = t$

$\Rightarrow \left(1+\frac{1}{x}\right) dx = dt$

$\therefore \int \left(1+\frac{1}{x}\right)(x+\log x)^2 dx$

$= \int t^2 dt = \frac{t^3}{3} + C$

$= \frac{(x+\log x)^3}{3} + C$

(iv) Let $I = \int \frac{x^3 \sin(\tan^{-1} x^4)}{(1+x^8)} dx$

Let $\tan^{-1} x^4 = t$

$\Rightarrow \frac{1}{1+x^8} . 4x^3 = \frac{dt}{dx}$

$\Rightarrow dx = \frac{(1+x^8)}{4x^3} dt$

$\therefore I = \int \frac{x^3 \sin t}{(1+x^8)} \cdot \frac{1+x^8 dt}{4x^3}$

$= \frac{1}{4} \int \sin t \, dt$

$= -\frac{1}{4} \cos t + C$

$= -\frac{1}{4} \cos(\tan^{-1} x^4) + C$

16 (*d*) $\int \left(\frac{10x^9 + 10^x \log_e 10}{x^{10} + 10^x}\right) dx$

Let $x^{10} + 10^x = t$

$\Rightarrow (10x^9 + 10^x \log_e 10) dx = dt$

$\Rightarrow dx = \frac{dt}{10x^9 + 10^x \log_e 10}$

$\therefore \int \left(\frac{10x^9 + 10^x \log_e 10}{x^{10} + 10^x}\right) dx$

$= \int \frac{10x^9 + 10^x \log_e 10}{t} \times \frac{dt}{10x^9 + 10^x \log_e 10}$

$= \int \frac{dt}{t} = \log|t| + C$

$= \log|10^x + x^{10}| + C$

17 (*b*) $\int \frac{dx}{\sin^2 x \cos^2 x}$

$= \int \frac{\sin^2 x + \cos^2 x}{\sin^2 x \cdot \cos^2 x} dx$

$[\because \sin^2 x + \cos^2 x = 1]$

$= \int \frac{\sin^2 x}{\sin^2 x \cdot \cos^2 x} dx + \int \frac{\cos^2 x}{\sin^2 x \cdot \cos^2 x} dx$

$= \int \frac{1}{\cos^2 x} dx + \int \frac{1}{\sin^2 x} dx$

$= \int \sec^2 x \, dx + \int \text{cosec}^2 x \, dx$

$= \tan x - \cot x + C$

18 (*a*)

I. We have,

$I = \int (x+1)(x+2)^7 (x+3) \, dx$

$I = \int (x+2)^7 [(x+2)^2 - 1] \, dx$

$[\because (x+1)(x+3) = (x+2-1)(x+2+1) = (x+2)^2 - 1]$

$\therefore I = \int \{(x+2)^9 - (x+2)^7\} \, dx$

$= \int (x+2)^9 \, dx - \int (x+2)^7 \, dx$

$= \frac{(x+2)^{10}}{10} - \frac{(x+2)^8}{8} + C$

$[\because \text{let } x+2 = t \Rightarrow dx = dt]$

II. $I = \int \text{cosec}(x-a) \, \text{cosec} \, x \, dx$

$= \int \frac{\sin a}{\sin a \sin(x-a) \sin x} dx$

$= -\frac{1}{\sin a} \int \frac{\sin[(x-a) - x]}{\sin(x-a) \sin x} dx$

$= -\frac{1}{\sin a} \int \frac{\sin(x-a)\cos x - \cos(x-a)\sin x}{\sin(x-a)\sin x} dx$

$= -\frac{1}{\sin a} \int [\cot x - \cot(x-a)] \, dx$

$= -\frac{1}{\sin a} [\log|\sin x| - \log|\sin(x-a)|] + C$

$[\because \int \cot\theta \, d\theta = \log|\sin\theta| + C]$

$= \frac{-1}{\sin a} [\log|\sin x \, \text{cosec}(x-a)|] + C$

19 (*c*) We have, $\int \frac{3e^x - 5e^{-x}}{4e^x + 5e^{-x}} dx$

$= ax + b \log|4e^x + 5e^{-x}| + C$

On differentiating both sides, we get

$\frac{3e^x - 5e^{-x}}{4e^x + 5e^{-x}} = a + b \frac{(4e^x - 5e^{-x})}{4e^x + 5e^{-x}}$

$\therefore 3e^x - 5e^{-x} = a(4e^x + 5e^{-x}) + b(4e^x - 5e^{-x})$

Comparing coefficients on both sides, we get

$3 = 4a + 4b$ ...(i)

$-5 = 5a - 5b$ ...(ii)

On solving Eqs. (i) and (ii), we get

$a = -\frac{1}{8}$ and $b = \frac{7}{8}$

20 (*d*) Let $I = \int \frac{x^9}{(4x^2+1)^6} dx$

$= \int \frac{x^9}{x^{12}\left(4+\frac{1}{x^2}\right)^6} dx$

$= \int \frac{1}{x^3\left(4+\frac{1}{x^2}\right)^6} dx$

Put $4 + \frac{1}{x^2} = t$

$\Rightarrow -\frac{2}{x^3} dx = dt \Rightarrow \frac{dx}{x^3} = -\frac{1}{2} dt$

$\therefore \quad I = -\frac{1}{2} \int \frac{dt}{t^6}$

$I = -\frac{1}{2} \times \frac{t^{-5}}{-5} + C$

$I = \frac{1}{10} t^{-5} + C$

$I = \frac{1}{10}\left(\frac{1}{x^2} + 4\right)^{-5} + C$

21 (*b*)

I. Let $I = \int \frac{2x+3}{x^2+3x} dx$

Put $x^2 + 3x = t$

$\therefore (2x+3) \, dx = dt$

$\therefore \quad I = \int \frac{dt}{t} \Rightarrow I = \log|t| + C$

Substitute the value of t, we get

$I = \log|x^2 + 3x| + C$

II. Here, $I=\int \frac{x}{\sqrt{x}+1}dx$

Put, $\sqrt{x}=t$

$\Rightarrow \frac{1}{2\sqrt{x}}dx=dt$

$\Rightarrow dx=2\sqrt{x}\,dt$

$\Rightarrow dx=2t\,dt$

$\therefore I=\int \frac{t^2\cdot 2t}{t+1}dt$

$I=2\int \frac{t^3}{t+1}dt$

Since, power in numerator is greater than denominator, so we divide numerator by denominator.

$$\begin{array}{r|l} t+1 & t^3 \ (t^2-t+1 \\ & t^3+t^2 \\ & - \quad - \\ & -t^2 \\ & -t^2-t \\ & + \quad + \\ & t \\ & t+1 \\ & - \quad - \\ & -1 \end{array}$$

$\therefore I=2\int\left(t^2-t+1-\frac{1}{t+1}\right)dt$

$I=2\left[\frac{t^3}{3}-\frac{t^2}{2}+t-\log|t+1|\right]+C$

$I=2\left[\frac{x^{3/2}}{3}-\frac{x}{2}+\sqrt{x}-\log|\sqrt{x}+1|\right]+C$

22 (c)

I. Here, $I=\int \frac{(1+\cos x)}{x+\sin x}dx$

Put $x+\sin x=t$

$(1+\cos x)\,dx=dt$

$\therefore I=\int \frac{dt}{t}$

$I=\log|t|+C$

$I=\log|x+\sin x|+C$

II. Here, $I=\int \tan^2 x\sec^4 x\,dx$

$=\int \tan^2 x\sec^2 x\sec^2 dx$

Put $\tan x=t$

$\Rightarrow \sec^2 x\,dx=dt$

$\Rightarrow I=\int t^2(1+t^2)\,dt$ $[\because \sec^2=1+\tan^2 x]$

$=\int (t^2+t^4)\,dt$

$=\frac{t^3}{3}+\frac{t^5}{5}+C$

$=\frac{1}{3}\tan^3 x+\frac{1}{5}\tan^5 x+C$

23 (d) Here, $I=\int \frac{x^3}{\sqrt{1+x^2}}dx$

$=\int \frac{x^2\cdot x}{\sqrt{1+x^2}}dx$

Put, $1+x^2=t^2$

$\Rightarrow 2x\,dx=2t\,dt$

$\Rightarrow x\,dx=t\,dt$

$I=\int \frac{(t^2-1)\,t}{\sqrt{t^2}}dt$

$I=\int \frac{(t^2-1)\,t}{t}dt$

$I=\int (t^2-1)\,dt$

$I=\frac{t^3}{3}-t+C$

$I=\frac{(1+x^2)^{3/2}}{3}-\sqrt{1+x^2}+C$

Thus, $\frac{(1+x^2)^{3/2}}{3}-\sqrt{1+x^2}+C$

$=a(1+x^2)^{3/2}+b\sqrt{1+x^2}+C$

On comparing both sides, we get

$a=\frac{1}{3}$ and $b=-1$

24 (a)

I. Let, $I=\int \frac{e^x-1}{e^x+1}dx$

$I=\int\left(\frac{2e^x}{e^x+1}-1\right)dx$

$I=2\int \frac{e^x}{e^x+1}dx-\int 1\,dx$

$I=2I_1-x+C$

Here, $I_1=\int \frac{e^x}{e^x+1}dx$

Put, $e^x+1=t$

$\Rightarrow e^x dx=dt$

$\Rightarrow I_1=\int \frac{1}{t}dt$

$\Rightarrow I_1=\log|t|$

$\Rightarrow I_1=\log|e^x+1|$

$\therefore I=2\log|e^x+1|-x+C$ ...(i)

Given that, $I=f(x)+C$ ...(ii)

From Eqs. (i) and Eqs (ii), we get

$f(x)=2\log|e^x+1|-x$

II. $I=\int \frac{e^x-e^{-x}}{e^x+e^{-x}}dx$

Put, $e^x+e^{-x}=t$

$\Rightarrow (e^x-e^{-x})\,dx=dt$

$\therefore I=\int \frac{dt}{t}$

$=\log|t|+C$

$=\log|e^x+e^{-x}|+C$

Integration Using Trigonometric Identitites

1 (d)

A. $\int \sin^2(2x+5)\,dx$

$=\int \frac{1-\cos 2(2x+5)}{2}dx$

$=\int \frac{1-\cos(4x+10)}{2}dx$ $\left[\because \sin^2 x=\frac{1-\cos 2x}{2}\right]$

$=\int \frac{1}{2}dx-\frac{1}{2}\int \cos(4x+10)\,dx$

$=\frac{1}{2}x-\frac{1}{2}\frac{\sin(4x+10)}{4}+C$

$\left[\because \int \cos(ax+b)\,dx=\frac{\sin(ax+b)}{a}\right]$

$=\frac{1}{2}x-\frac{\sin(4x+10)}{8}+C$

B. $\int \sin 3x\cos 4x\,dx$

$=\frac{1}{2}\int 2\sin 3x\cos 4x\,dx$

$=\frac{1}{2}\int\{\sin(3x+4x)+\sin(3x-4x)\}\,dx$

$[\because 2\sin A\cos B=\sin(A+B)+\sin(A-B)]$

$= \frac{1}{2}\int \{\sin 7x - \sin x)\}\, dx$ $\quad [\because \sin(-\theta) = -\sin\theta]$

$= \frac{1}{2}\left(\frac{-\cos 7x}{7} + \cos x\right) + C \quad \left[\because \int \sin ax\, dx = \frac{-\cos ax}{a}\right]$

$= \frac{-\cos 7x}{14} + \frac{\cos x}{2} + C$

C. $\int \sin^3 (2x+1)\, dx$

$= \int \sin^2 (2x+1).\sin(2x+1)\, dx$

$= \int [1 - \cos^2 (2x+1)] \sin(2x+1)\, dx \quad [\because \sin^2 x = 1 - \cos^2 x]$

Let $\cos(2x+1) = t$

$\Rightarrow -2\sin(2x+1)\, dx = dt$

$\Rightarrow \sin(2x+1)\, dx = -\frac{dt}{2}$

$\therefore \int \sin^3 (2x+1)\, dx = \frac{-1}{2}\int (1-t^2)\, dt = \frac{-1}{2}\left(t - \frac{t^3}{3}\right) + C$

$= \frac{-1}{2}\left(\cos(2x+1) - \frac{\cos^3(2x+1)}{3}\right) + C$

$= \frac{-\cos(2x+1)}{2} + \frac{\cos^3(2x+1)}{6} + C$

D. $\int \sin^3 x \cdot \cos^3 x\, dx$

Let $\cos x = t$

$\Rightarrow -\sin x = \frac{dt}{dx}$

$\Rightarrow dx = \frac{dt}{-\sin x}$

$\therefore \int \sin^3 x \cos^3 x\, dx$

$= \int \sin^3 x \cdot t^3 \frac{dt}{-\sin x}$

$= -\int \sin^2 x . t^3 dt$

$= -\int t^3 (1 - \cos^2 x)\, dt$

$= -\int t^3 \cdot (1 - t^2)\, dt$

$= -\int [t^3 - t^5]\, dt = -\left[\frac{t^4}{4} - \frac{t^6}{6}\right] + C$

$= \frac{\cos^6 x}{6} - \frac{\cos^4 x}{4} + C$

2 (b)

I. $\int \cos 2x \cos 4x \cos 6x\, dx$

$= \int \cos 2x \frac{1}{2}[\cos(4x+6x) + \cos(4x-6x)]dx$

$[\because 2\cos A \cos B = \cos(A+B) + \cos(A-B)]$

$= \frac{1}{2}\int \{\cos 2x \cos 10x + \cos 2x \cos(-2x)]\, dx$

$= \frac{1}{2}\int [\cos 2x \cos 10x + \cos^2 2x]\, dx$

$= \frac{1}{2}\int \left[\frac{1}{2}\{\cos(2x+10x) + \cos(2x-10x)\} + \left(\frac{1+\cos 4x}{2}\right)\right] dx$

$[\because \cos 2\theta = 2\cos^2\theta - 1]$

$= \frac{1}{4}\int [\cos 12x + \cos 8x + 1 + \cos 4x]\, dx$

$= \frac{1}{4}\left[\frac{\sin 12x}{12} + \frac{\sin 8x}{8} + \frac{\sin 4x}{4} + x\right] + C$

II. $\int \sin x \sin 2x \sin 3x\, dx$

$= \frac{1}{2}\int (2\sin 3x \sin x) \sin 2x\, dx$

$= \frac{1}{2}\int \{\cos 2x - \cos 4x\} \sin 2x\, dx$

$[\because 2\sin A \sin B = \cos(A-B) - \cos(A+B)]$

$= \frac{1}{4}\int \{2\sin 2x \cos 2x - 2\cos 4x \sin 2x\}\, dx$

$= \frac{1}{4}\int \{(\sin 4x + \sin 0) - (\sin 6x - \sin 2x)\}\, dx$

$\left[\begin{array}{l}\because 2\sin A \cos B = \sin(A+B) + \sin(A-B) \\ 2\cos A \sin B = \sin(A+B) - \sin(A-B)\end{array}\right]$

$= \frac{1}{4}\int (\sin 4x - \sin 6x + \sin 2x)\, dx$

$= \frac{1}{4}\left\{\left[\frac{-\cos 4x}{4} - \frac{(-\cos 6x)}{6} + \frac{(-\cos 2x)}{2}\right]\right\} + C$

$\left[\because \int \sin ax\, dx = -\frac{\cos ax}{a}\right]$

$= \frac{-\cos 4x}{16} + \frac{\cos 6x}{24} - \frac{\cos 2x}{8} + C$

3 (c)

(i) $\int \frac{(1-\cos x)}{(1+\cos x)} dx$

$= \int \frac{2\sin^2 \frac{x}{2}}{2\cos^2 \frac{x}{2}} dx = \int \tan^2 \frac{x}{2} dx$

$\left[\because 1 - \cos x = 2\sin^2 \frac{x}{2} \text{ and } 1 + \cos x = 2\cos^2 \frac{x}{2}\right]$

$= \int \left(\sec^2 \frac{x}{2} - 1\right) dx \quad [\because \tan^2\theta = \sec^2\theta - 1]$

$= \int \sec^2 \frac{x}{2} dx - \int 1\, dx$

$= \frac{\tan \frac{x}{2}}{\frac{1}{2}} - x + C \quad \left[\because \int \sec^2 ax\, dx = \frac{\tan ax}{a}\right]$

$= 2\tan \frac{x}{2} - x + C$

(ii) $\int \frac{\cos x}{1+\cos x} dx = \int \frac{1 - 1 + \cos x}{1 + \cos x} dx$

[add and subtract 1 in numerator]

$= \int \frac{1+\cos x}{1+\cos x} dx - \int \frac{1}{1+\cos x} dx$

$= \int 1\, dx - \int \frac{1}{2\cos^2 \frac{x}{2}} dx$

$= \int 1\, dx - \frac{1}{2}\int \sec^2 \frac{x}{2} dx$

$= x - \frac{1}{2} \cdot 2\tan \frac{x}{2} + C$

$= x - \tan \frac{x}{2} + C \quad \left[\because \int \sec^2 ax\, dx = \frac{\tan ax}{a}\right]$

(iii) $\int \cos^4 2x\, dx = \int (\cos^2 2x)^2\, dx$

$= \int \left(\frac{1+\cos 4x}{2}\right)^2 dx$

$= \frac{1}{4}\int (1+\cos 4x)^2\, dx = \frac{1}{4}\int (1 + \cos^2 4x + 2\cos 4x)\, dx$

$= \frac{1}{4}[\int 1\, dx + \int \cos^2 4x\, dx + 2\int \cos 4x\, dx]$

$$= \frac{1}{4}\left[\int 1\,dx + \int \frac{1+\cos 8x}{2}\,dx + 2\int \cos 4x\,dx\right]$$

$$\left[\because \cos^2 x = \frac{1+\cos 2x}{2}\right]$$

$$= \frac{1}{4}\left[\int 1\,dx + \frac{1}{2}\{\int 1\,dx + \int \cos 8x\,dx\} + 2\int \cos 4x\,dx\right]$$

$$= \frac{1}{4}\left[x + \frac{1}{2}\left\{x + \frac{\sin 8x}{8}\right\} + \frac{2\sin 4x}{4}\right] + C$$

$$= \frac{1}{4}x + \frac{x}{8} + \frac{\sin 8x}{64} + \frac{\sin 4x}{8} + C$$

$$= \left[\frac{3x}{8} + \frac{\sin 8x}{64} + \frac{\sin 4x}{8}\right] + C$$

(iv) $\int \frac{\sin^2 x}{(1+\cos x)}\,dx$

$$= \int \frac{(1-\cos^2 x)}{(1+\cos x)}\,dx \quad [\because \sin^2 x = 1-\cos^2 x]$$

$$= \int \frac{(1+\cos x)(1-\cos x)}{(1+\cos x)}\,dx$$

$$= \int (1-\cos x)\,dx$$

$$= \int 1\,dx - \int \cos x\,dx$$

$$= x - \sin x + C$$

4 (b) $\int \frac{\cos 2x - \cos 2\alpha}{\cos x - \cos \alpha}\,dx$

$$= \int \frac{(2\cos^2 x - 1) - (2\cos^2 \alpha - 1)}{(\cos x - \cos \alpha)}\,dx \quad [\because \cos 2x = 2\cos^2 x - 1]$$

$$= \int \frac{2\cos^2 x - 1 - 2\cos^2 \alpha + 1}{(\cos x - \cos \alpha)}\,dx$$

$$= \int \frac{2(\cos^2 x - \cos^2 \alpha)}{(\cos x - \cos \alpha)}\,dx$$

$$= 2\int \frac{(\cos x - \cos \alpha)(\cos x + \cos \alpha)}{(\cos x - \cos \alpha)}\,dx \quad [\because a^2 - b^2 = (a+b)(a-b)]$$

$$= 2\,[\int \cos x\,dx + \cos \alpha \int 1\,dx]$$

$$= 2[\sin x + \cos \alpha \cdot x] + C$$

$$= 2\sin x + 2x\cos \alpha + C$$

5 (b)

A. Let $I = \int \frac{\cos x - \sin x}{1+\sin 2x}\,dx$

$$= \int \frac{\cos x - \sin x}{\sin^2 x + \cos^2 x + 2\sin x \cos x}\,dx \quad \left[\because \sin^2 x + \cos^2 x = 1;\ \sin 2x = 2\sin x \cos x\right]$$

$$= \int \frac{\cos x - \sin x}{(\sin x + \cos x)^2}\,dx$$

Let $\cos x + \sin x = t$

$$\Rightarrow -\sin x + \cos x = \frac{dt}{dx}$$

$$\Rightarrow dx = \frac{dt}{(\cos x - \sin x)}$$

$$\therefore I = \int \frac{\cos x - \sin x}{t^2} \cdot \frac{dt}{(\cos x - \sin x)}$$

$$= \int \frac{1}{t^2}\,dt = \int t^{-2}\,dt$$

$$= \frac{t^{-2+1}}{-2+1} + C$$

$$= \frac{-1}{\cos x + \sin x} + C$$

B. $\int \tan^3 2x \sec 2x\,dx$

Let $\sec 2x = t$

$$\Rightarrow 2\sec 2x \tan 2x = \frac{dt}{dx}$$

$$\Rightarrow dx = \frac{dt}{2\sec 2x \cdot \tan 2x}$$

$$\therefore \int \tan^3 2x \sec 2x\,dx = \int \tan^3 2x \sec 2x \frac{dt}{2\sec 2x \cdot \tan 2x}$$

$$= \frac{1}{2}\int \tan^2 2x\,dt$$

$$= \frac{1}{2}\int [\sec^2 2x - 1]\,dt \quad [\because \tan^2 x = \sec^2 x - 1]$$

$$= \frac{1}{2}\int [(t^2 - 1)\,dt] = \frac{1}{2}\left[\frac{t^3}{3} - t\right] + C$$

$$= \frac{1}{2}\left[\frac{\sec^3 2x}{3} - \sec 2x\right] + C$$

$$= \frac{1}{6}\sec^3 2x - \frac{1}{2}\sec 2x + C$$

C. $\int \frac{\sin^3 x + \cos^3 x}{\sin^2 x \cos^2 x}\,dx$

$$= \int \frac{\sin^3 x}{\sin^2 x \cos^2 x}\,dx + \int \frac{\cos^3 x}{\sin^2 x \cos^2 x}\,dx$$

$$= \int \frac{\sin x}{\cos x \cos x}\,dx + \int \frac{\cos x}{\sin x \sin x}\,dx$$

$$= \int \tan x \cdot \sec x\,dx + \int \cot x \cdot \operatorname{cosec} x\,dx$$

$$= \sec x - \operatorname{cosec} x + C$$

D. $\int \frac{\cos 2x + 2\sin^2 x}{\cos^2 x}\,dx$

$$= \int \frac{1 - 2\sin^2 x + 2\sin^2 x}{\cos^2 x}\,dx \quad [\because \cos 2x = 1 - 2\sin^2 x]$$

$$= \int \frac{1}{\cos^2 x}\,dx$$

$$= \int \sec^2 x\,dx$$

$$= \tan x + C$$

6 (a)

I. $\int \sin 4x \sin 8x\,dx = \frac{1}{2}\int 2\sin 8x \sin 4x\,dx$

$$= \frac{1}{2}\int (\cos 4x - \cos 12x)\,dx \quad [\because 2\sin A \sin B = \cos(A-B) - \cos(A+B)]$$

$$= \frac{1}{2}\left\{\frac{\sin 4x}{4} - \frac{\sin 12x}{12}\right\} + C$$

II. $\int \sin^4 x\,dx = \int (\sin^2 x)^2\,dx$

$$= \int \left(\frac{1-\cos 2x}{2}\right)^2 dx \quad \left[\because \sin^2 x = \frac{1-\cos 2x}{2}\right]$$

$$= \frac{1}{4}\int (1-\cos 2x)^2 dx$$

$$= \frac{1}{4}\int 1 + \cos^2 2x - 2\cos 2x\,dx$$

$$= \frac{1}{4}[\int 1\,dx + \int \cos^2 2x\,dx - 2\int \cos 2x\,dx]$$

$= \frac{1}{4}\left[\int 1\,dx + \int \frac{1+\cos 4x}{2}\,dx - 2\int \cos 2x\,dx\right]$

$\left[\because \cos^2 x = \frac{1+\cos 2x}{2}\right]$

$= \frac{1}{4}\left[\int 1\,dx + \frac{1}{2}\{\int 1\,dx + \int \cos 4x\,dx\} - 2\int \cos 2x\,dx\right]$

$= \frac{1}{4}\left[x + \frac{1}{2}\left\{x + \frac{\sin 4x}{4}\right\} - \frac{2\sin 2x}{2}\right] + C$

$= \frac{1}{4}x + \frac{x}{8} + \frac{\sin 4x}{32} - \frac{\sin 2x}{4} + C$

$= \left(\frac{2x+x}{8}\right) + \frac{\sin 4x}{32} - \frac{\sin 2x}{4} + C$

$= \left[\frac{3x}{8} + \frac{\sin 4x}{32} - \frac{\sin 2x}{4}\right] + C$

7 (*c*) Let

$I = \int \tan^4 x\,dx = \int (\tan^2 x)^2\,dx$

$\Rightarrow \quad I = \int (\tan^2 x)(\tan^2 x)\,dx$

$= \int (\sec^2 x - 1)(\tan^2 x)\,dx$

$= \int \sec^2 x \tan^2 x\,dx - \int \tan^2 x\,dx$

$= \int \sec^2 x \tan^2 x\,dx - \int [\sec^2 x - 1]\,dx$

$= \int \sec^2 x \tan^2 x dx - [\int \sec^2 x\,dx - \int 1\,dx]$

Now, let $I_1 = \int \sec^2 x \tan^2 x\,dx$ and $I_2 = \int \sec^2 x\,dx - \int 1 dx$

Then, $\quad I = I_1 - I_2 \qquad$ ...(i)

Putting $\tan x = t \Rightarrow \sec^2 x = \frac{dt}{dx}$

$\Rightarrow dx = \frac{dt}{\sec^2 x}$

$\therefore I_1 = \int \sec^2 x\, t^2 . \frac{dt}{\sec^2 x}$

$\Rightarrow I_1 = \int t^2 dt = \frac{t^3}{3} + C_1 = \frac{\tan^3 x}{3} + C_1$

$I_2 = \int \sec^2 x\,dx - \int 1\,dx$

$= \tan x - x + C_2$

$\therefore$ Putting the values of I_1 and I_2 in Eq. (i), we get

$I = \frac{\tan^3 x}{3} + C_1 - (\tan x - x + C_2)$

$\Rightarrow I = \frac{\tan^3 x}{3} - \tan x + x + C$

$[\because C_1 - C_2 = C]$

8 (*b*)

(i) Let $I = \int \frac{1}{\sin x \cos^3 x}\,dx$

$= \int \frac{\cos x}{\sin x}\sec^4 x\,dx$

$\int \frac{\sec^2 x \sec^2 x}{\tan x}\,dx$

$= \int \frac{(1+\tan^2 x)\sec^2 x}{\tan x}\,dx$

$[\because \sec^2 x = 1 + \tan^2 x]$

Putting $\tan x = t$

$\Rightarrow \quad \sec^2 x = \frac{dt}{dx}$

$\Rightarrow \quad dx = \frac{dt}{\sec^2 x}$

$\therefore \quad I = \int \left[\frac{1+t^2}{t}\right]\sec^2 x \frac{dt}{\sec^2 x}$

$= \int \frac{1+t^2}{t}\,dt$

$= \int \left[\frac{1}{t} + t\right] dt$

$= \log|t| + \frac{t^2}{2} + C$

$= \log|\tan x| + \frac{\tan^2 x}{2} + C$

(ii) Let $I = \int \frac{\cos 2x}{(\cos x + \sin x)^2}\,dx$

$= \int \frac{\cos^2 x - \sin^2 x}{(\cos x + \sin x)^2}\,dx$

$[\because \cos 2x = \cos^2 x - \sin^2 x]$

$= \int \frac{(\cos x - \sin x)(\cos x + \sin x)}{(\cos x + \sin x)^2}\,dx$

$= \int \frac{\cos x - \sin x}{\cos x + \sin x}\,dx$

$[\because (a^2 - b^2) = (a-b)(a+b)]$

Putting $\cos x + \sin x = t$

$\Rightarrow \quad -\sin x + \cos x = \frac{dt}{dx}$

$\Rightarrow \quad dx = \frac{dt}{\cos x - \sin x}$

$\therefore \quad I = \int \frac{\cos x - \sin x}{t} \cdot \frac{dt}{\cos x - \sin x}$

$= \int \frac{1}{t}\,dt = \log|t| + C$

$= \log|\cos x + \sin x| + C$

(iii) $\int \sin^{-1}(\cos x)\,dx$

$= \int \left\{\frac{\pi}{2} - \cos^{-1}(\cos x)\right\} dx$

$\left[\because \sin^{-1} t + \cos^{-1} t = \frac{\pi}{2} \text{ for } |t| \le 1\right]$

$= \int \left(\frac{\pi}{2} - x\right) dx = \frac{\pi}{2}x - \frac{x^2}{2} + C$

(iv) $\int \frac{1}{\cos(x-a)\cos(x-b)}\,dx$

$= \frac{1}{\sin(b-a)} \int \frac{\sin\{(x-a)-(x-b)\}}{\cos(x-a)\cos(x-b)}\,dx$

Multiply by $\sin(b-a)$ in numerator and denominator and put $\sin(b-a) = \sin[(x-a)-(x-b)]$ in numerator.

$= \frac{1}{\sin(b-a)} \int \frac{\sin(x-a)\cos(x-b) - \cos(x-a)\sin(x-b)}{\cos(x-a)\cos(x-b)}\,dx$

$[\because \sin(C-D) = \sin C \cos D - \cos C \sin D]$

$= \frac{1}{\sin(b-a)} \int \left[\frac{\sin(x-a)\cos(x-b)}{\cos(x-a)\cos(x-b)} - \frac{\cos(x-a)\sin(x-b)}{\cos(x-a)\cos(x-b)}\right] dx$

$= \frac{1}{\sin(b-a)} \int \{\tan(x-a) - \tan(x-b)\}\,dx$

$= \frac{1}{\sin(b-a)} . \{-\log|\cos(x-a)| + \log|\cos(x-b)|\} + C$

$[\because \int \tan x\,dx = -\log|\cos x|]$

$= \frac{1}{\sin(b-a)} \log\left|\frac{\cos(x-b)}{\cos(x-a)}\right| + C$

9 (a) $\int \frac{\sin^2 x - \cos^2 x}{\sin^2 x \cos^2 x} dx$

$= \int \left(\frac{1}{\cos^2 x} - \frac{1}{\sin^2 x} \right) dx$

$= \int (\sec^2 x - \text{cosec}^2 x)\, dx$

$= \tan x + \cot x + C$

10 (b) $\int \frac{e^x (1+x)}{\cos^2 (e^x x)} dx$

Let $xe^x = t$

$\Rightarrow \quad (xe^x + e^x) = \frac{dt}{dx}$

$\Rightarrow \quad dx = \frac{dt}{e^x (x+1)}$

$\therefore \int \frac{e^x (1+x)}{\cos^2 (e^x x)} dx = \int \frac{e^x (1+x)}{\cos^2 t} \times \frac{dt}{e^x (1+x)}$

$= \int \frac{1}{\cos^2 t} dt = \int \sec^2 t\, dt$

$= \tan t + C = \tan (xe^x) + C$

11 (c) We have,

$I = \int \frac{dx}{2 \sin^2 x \cos^2 x}$

$= \int \frac{(\sin^2 x + \cos^2 x)}{2 \sin^2 x \cos^2 x} dx$

$= \frac{1}{2} \int \sec^2 x\, dx + \frac{1}{2} \int \text{cosec}^2 x\, dx$

$= \frac{\tan x}{2} - \frac{\cot x}{2} + C$

12 (b) We have,

$I = \int \frac{\sin^6 x}{\cos^8 x} dx$

$I = \int \left(\frac{\sin x}{\cos x} \right)^6 \left(\frac{1}{\cos^2 x} \right) dx$

$I = \int \tan^6 x \sec^2 x\, dx$

Put, $\tan x = t$

$\Rightarrow \sec^2 x\, dx = dt$

$\therefore \quad I = \int t^6\, dt$

$I = \frac{t^7}{7} + C$

$I = \frac{\tan^7 x}{7} + C$

13 (b)

I. Let $I = \int \frac{\cos 5x + \cos 4x}{1 - 2\cos 3x} dx$

$= \int \frac{2 \cos \frac{9x}{2} \cos \frac{x}{2}}{1 - 2\left(2 \cos^2 \frac{3x}{2} - 1\right)} dx$

$= \int \frac{2 \cos \frac{9x}{2} \cos \frac{x}{2}}{3 - 4 \cos^2 \frac{3x}{2}} dx$

$= \int \frac{2 \cos \frac{9x}{2} \cos \frac{x}{2} \cos \frac{3x}{2}}{3 \cos \frac{3x}{2} - 4 \cos^3 \frac{3x}{2}} dx$

[multiply $\cos \frac{3x}{2}$ numerator and denomenator]

$= \int \frac{2 \cos \frac{9x}{2} \cos \frac{x}{2} \cos \frac{3x}{2}}{- \cos 3 \left(\frac{3x}{2} \right)} dx$

$[\because \cos 3\theta = 4 \cos^3 \theta - 3 \cos \theta]$

$= \int -2 \cos \left(\frac{x}{2} \right) \cos \left(\frac{3x}{2} \right) dx$

$= - \int \left[\cos \left(\frac{x}{2} + \frac{3x}{2} \right) + \cos \left(\frac{3x}{2} - \frac{x}{2} \right) \right] dx$

$= \int (-\cos 2x - \cos x)\, dx$

$= -\frac{1}{2} \sin 2x - \sin x + C$

$= -\left[\frac{1}{2} \sin 2x + \sin x \right] + C$

II. $I = \int \frac{\sin^6 x + \cos^6 x}{\sin^2 x \cos^2 x} dx$

$= \int \frac{(\sin^2 x)^3 + (\cos^2 x)^3}{\sin^2 x \cos^2 x} dx$

$= \int \frac{(\sin^2 x + \cos^2 x)(\sin^4 x + \cos^4 x - \sin^2 x \cos^2 x)}{\sin^2 x \cos^2 x} dx$

$= \int \frac{\sin^4 x + \cos^4 x - \sin^2 x \cos^2 x}{\sin^2 x \cos^2 x} dx$

$= \int \frac{\sin^4 x}{\sin^2 x \cos^2 x} dx + \int \frac{\cos^4 x}{\sin^2 x \cos^2 x} dx - \int 1\, dx$

$= \int \tan^2 x\, dx + \int \cot^2 x\, dx - \int dx$

$= \int (\sec^2 x - 1)\, dx + \int (\text{cosec}^2 x - 1)\, dx - \int dx$

$= \tan x - x + (-\cot x - x) - x + C$

$= \tan x - \cot x - 3x + C$

14 (c) Let, $I = \int \frac{dx}{\sin(x-a)\sin(x-b)}$

$= \frac{1}{\sin(b-a)} \int \frac{\sin(b-a)}{\sin(x-a)\sin(x-b)} dx$

$= \frac{1}{\sin(b-a)} \int \frac{\sin(x-a-x+b)}{\sin(x-a)\sin(x-b)} dx$

$= \frac{1}{\sin(b-a)} \int \frac{\sin[(x-a)-(x-b)]}{\sin(x-a)\sin(x-b)} dx$

$= \frac{1}{\sin(b-a)} \int \frac{\sin(x-a)\cos(x-b) - \sin(x-b)\cos(x-a)}{\sin(x-a)\sin(x-b)} dx$

$= \frac{1}{\sin(b-a)} \int \left\{ \frac{\cos(x-b)}{\sin(x-b)} - \frac{\cos(x-a)}{\sin(x-a)} \right\} dx$

$= \frac{1}{\sin(b-a)} [\log |\sin(x-b)| - \log |\sin(x-a)|] + C$

$= \frac{1}{\sin(b-a)} \log \left| \frac{\sin(x-b)}{\sin(x-a)} \right| + C$

$= \text{cosec}(b-a) \log \left| \frac{\sin(x-b)}{\sin(x-a)} \right| + C$

15 (d)

(i) Let,

$I = \int \frac{\sec x \,\text{cosec}\, x}{2 \cot x - \sec x \,\text{cosec}\, x} dx$

$= \int \frac{\frac{1}{\cos x \sin x}}{\frac{2 \cos x}{\sin x} - \frac{1}{\sin x \cos x}} dx$

$$= \int \frac{dx}{2\cos^2 x - 1}$$
$$= \int \frac{dx}{\cos 2x} = \int \sec 2x \, dx$$
$$= \frac{1}{2}\log|\sec 2x + \tan 2x| + C$$

(ii) Let, $I = \int \frac{\sec x}{\sec x + \tan x} dx$
$$= \int \frac{\sec x (\sec x - \tan x)}{\sec^2 x - \tan^2 x} dx$$
$$= \int (\sec^2 x - \sec x \tan x)\, dx \quad [\because 1 + \tan^2\theta = \sec^2\theta]$$
$$= \tan x - \sec x + C$$

(iii) Let, $I = \int \tan(\sin^{-1} x)\, dx$
$$= \int \tan\left(\tan^{-1}\frac{x}{\sqrt{1-x^2}}\right) dx$$
$$= \int \frac{x}{\sqrt{1-x^2}} dx$$
Put, $1 - x^2 = t^2$
$\Rightarrow -2x\,dx = 2t\,dt$
$\therefore \quad I = -\int \frac{t\,dt}{t} = -\int dt$
$$= -t + C = -\sqrt{1-x^2} + C$$

(iv) Let, $I = \int (\sin^6 x + \cos^6 x + 3\sin^2 x \cos^2 x)\, dx$
$$= \int \{(\sin^2 x)^3 + (\cos^2 x)^3 + 3\sin^2 x \cos^2 x\} dx$$
$$= \int [(\sin^2 x + \cos^2 x)(\sin^4 x + \cos^4 x - \sin^2 x \cos^2 x) + 3\sin^2 x\cos^2 x]\, dx$$
$$= \int [(\sin^2 x + \cos^2 x)^2 - 3\sin^2 x \cos^2 x + 3\sin^2 x \cos^2 x]\, dx$$
$$= \int 1\, dx = x + C$$

16 (b)

I. $I = \int \frac{dx}{\cos x - \sin x}$
$$= \frac{1}{\sqrt{2}} \int \frac{dx}{\left(\frac{1}{\sqrt{2}}\cos x - \frac{1}{\sqrt{2}}\sin x\right)}$$
$$= \frac{1}{\sqrt{2}} \int \frac{dx}{\cos\left(x + \frac{\pi}{4}\right)}$$
$$= \frac{1}{\sqrt{2}} \int \sec\left(x + \frac{\pi}{4}\right) dx$$
$$= \frac{1}{\sqrt{2}} \log\left|\tan\left(\frac{\pi}{4} + \frac{x}{2} + \frac{\pi}{8}\right)\right| + C$$
$$= \frac{1}{\sqrt{2}} \log\left|\tan\left(\frac{x}{2} + \frac{3\pi}{8}\right)\right| + C$$

II. Let, $I = \int \frac{dx}{\sin x - \cos x + \sqrt{2}}$
$$= \int \frac{dx}{\sin x \frac{\sqrt{2}}{\sqrt{2}} - \cos x \frac{\sqrt{2}}{\sqrt{2}} + \sqrt{2}}$$
$$= \int \frac{dx}{\sqrt{2}\left(\sin x \sin\frac{\pi}{4} - \cos x \cos\frac{\pi}{4} + 1\right)}$$
$$= \frac{1}{\sqrt{2}} \int \frac{dx}{1 - \cos\left(x + \frac{\pi}{4}\right)}$$
$$= \frac{1}{\sqrt{2}} \int \frac{dx}{1 - \cos 2\left(\frac{x}{2} + \frac{\pi}{8}\right)}$$
$$= \frac{1}{\sqrt{2}} \int \frac{dx}{2\sin^2\left(\frac{x}{2} + \frac{\pi}{8}\right)}$$
$$= \frac{1}{2\sqrt{2}} \int \operatorname{cosec}^2\left(\frac{x}{2} + \frac{\pi}{8}\right) dx$$
$$= \frac{1}{2\sqrt{2}} \cdot \frac{-\cot\left(\frac{x}{2} + \frac{\pi}{8}\right)}{\frac{1}{2}} + C$$
$$= -\frac{1}{\sqrt{2}} \cot\left(\frac{x}{2} + \frac{\pi}{8}\right) + C$$

17 (a) Let $I = \int \frac{\sin^8 x - \cos^8 x}{1 - 2\sin^2 x \cos^2 x} dx$
$$I = \int \frac{(\sin^4 x - \cos^4 x)(\sin^4 x + \cos^4 x)}{(1 - 2\sin^2 x \cos^2 x)} dx$$
$$I = \int \frac{(\sin^2 x - \cos^2 x)(\sin^2 x + \cos^2 x) \times [(\sin^2 x + \cos^2 x)^2 - 2\sin^2 x \cos^2 x]\, dx}{1 - 2\sin^2 x \cos^2 x}$$
$$I = -\int \frac{\cos 2x\,(1 - 2\sin^2 x \cos^2 x)}{1 - 2\sin^2 x \cos^2 x} dx$$
$$I = -\int \cos 2x\, dx$$
$$I = -\frac{1}{2}\sin 2x + C \quad \text{... (i)}$$
Given that, $I = A\sin 2x + B \quad \text{...(ii)}$
From Eqs. (i) and (ii), we get
$$A = -\frac{1}{2}$$

Integration of Some Particular Function

1 (b)

A. We have,
$$\frac{1}{x^2 - a^2} = \frac{1}{(x-a)(x+a)}$$
$$= \frac{1}{2a}\left[\frac{(x+a) - (x-a)}{(x-a)(x+a)}\right]$$
$$= \frac{1}{2a}\left[\frac{1}{x-a} - \frac{1}{x+a}\right]$$
Therefore,
$$\int \frac{dx}{x^2 - a^2} = \frac{1}{2a}\left[\int \frac{dx}{x-a} - \int \frac{dx}{x+a}\right]$$
$$= \frac{1}{2a}[\log|(x-a)| - \log|(x+a)|] + C$$
$$= \frac{1}{2a}\log\left|\frac{x-a}{x+a}\right| + C$$

B. In view of (A) above, we have
$$\frac{1}{a^2 - x^2} = \frac{1}{2a}\left[\frac{(a+x) + (a-x)}{(a+x)(a-x)}\right]$$
$$= \frac{1}{2a}\left[\frac{1}{a-x} + \frac{1}{a+x}\right]$$
Therefore,
$$\int \frac{dx}{a^2 - x^2} = \frac{1}{2a}\left[\int \frac{dx}{a-x} + \int \frac{dx}{a+x}\right]$$
$$= \frac{1}{2a}[-\log|a-x| + \log|a+x|] + C$$
$$= \frac{1}{2a}\log\left|\frac{a+x}{a-x}\right| + C$$

C. Put $x = a\tan\theta$.
Then $dx = a\sec^2\theta\, d\theta$.
Therefore,
$$\int \frac{dx}{x^2 + a^2} = \int \frac{a\sec^2\theta\, d\theta}{a^2\tan^2\theta + a^2}$$
$$= \frac{1}{a}\int d\theta = \frac{1}{a}\theta + C$$
$$= \frac{1}{a}\tan^{-1}\frac{x}{a} + C$$

D. Let $x = a\sec\theta$.
Then, $dx = a\sec\theta\tan\theta\, d\theta$.

Therefore,

$$\int \frac{dx}{\sqrt{x^2-a^2}} = \int \frac{a\sec\theta\tan\theta\, d\theta}{\sqrt{a^2\sec^2\theta - a^2}}$$

$$= \int \sec\theta\, d\theta$$

$$= \log|\sec\theta + \tan\theta| + C_1$$

$$= \log\left|\frac{x}{a} + \sqrt{\frac{x^2}{a^2} - 1}\right| + C_1$$

$$= \log|x + \sqrt{x^2-a^2}| - \log|a| + C_1$$

$$= \log|x + \sqrt{x^2-a^2}| + C,$$

where $C = C_1 - \log|a|$

E. Let $x = a\sin\theta$.

Then, $dx = a\cos\theta\, d\theta$.

Therefore,

$$\int \frac{dx}{\sqrt{a^2-x^2}} = \int \frac{a\cos\theta\, d\theta}{\sqrt{a^2 - a^2\sin^2\theta}}$$

$$= \int d\theta = \theta + C$$

$$= \sin^{-1}\frac{x}{a} + C$$

F. Let $x = a\tan\theta$.

Then $dx = a\sec^2\theta\, d\theta$.

Therefore,

$$\int \frac{dx}{\sqrt{x^2+a^2}} = \int \frac{a\sec^2\theta\, d\theta}{\sqrt{a^2\tan^2\theta + a^2}}$$

$$= \int \sec\theta\, d\theta$$

$$= \log|(\sec\theta + \tan\theta)| + C_1$$

$$= \log\left|\frac{x}{a} + \sqrt{\frac{x^2}{a^2} + 1}\right| C_1$$

$$= \log|x + \sqrt{x^2+a^2}| - \log|a| + C_1$$

$$= \log|x + \sqrt{x^2+a^2}| + C,$$

where $C = C_1 - \log|a|$

2 (*d*)

A. $$\int \frac{3x^2}{x^6+1}dx = \int \frac{3x^2}{(x^3)^2+1}dx$$

Let $x^3 = t$

$$\Rightarrow \quad 3x^2 = \frac{dt}{dx} \Rightarrow dx = \frac{dt}{3x^2}$$

$$\therefore \int \frac{3x^2}{(x^3)^2+1}dx$$

$$= \int \frac{3x^2}{t^2+1}\cdot\frac{dt}{3x^2} = \int \frac{dt}{t^2+1}$$

$$= \frac{1}{1}\tan^{-1}\left(\frac{t}{1}\right) + C$$

$$= \tan^{-1}(x^3) + C$$

B. $$\int \frac{dx}{\sqrt{1+4x^2}} = \int \frac{dx}{\sqrt{4\left(\left(\frac{1}{2}\right)^2 + x^2\right)}}$$

$$= \frac{1}{2}\int \frac{dx}{\sqrt{x^2 + \left(\frac{1}{2}\right)^2}}$$

$$= \frac{1}{2}\log\left|x + \sqrt{x^2 + \left(\frac{1}{2}\right)^2}\right| + C_1$$

$$\left[\because \int \frac{1}{\sqrt{x^2+a^2}}dx = \log|x + \sqrt{x^2+a^2}|\right]$$

$$= \frac{1}{2}\log\left|x + \frac{\sqrt{4x^2+1}}{2}\right| + C_1$$

$$= \frac{1}{2}\log|2x + \sqrt{4x^2+1}| - \frac{1}{2}\log 2 + C_1$$

$$\left[\because \log\left(\frac{m}{n}\right) = \log m - \log n\right]$$

$$= \frac{1}{2}\log|2x + \sqrt{4x^2+1}| + C$$

$$\left(C = \frac{-1}{2}\log 2 + C_1\right)$$

C. $$\int \frac{1}{\sqrt{(2-x)^2+1}}dx$$

$$= \int \frac{1}{\sqrt{(x-2)^2+1}}dx$$

$$= \log|(x-2) + \sqrt{(x-2)^2+1}| + C$$

$$\left[\because \int \frac{dx}{\sqrt{x^2+a^2}} = \log|x + \sqrt{x^2+a^2}|\right]$$

D. $$\int \frac{1}{\sqrt{9-25x^2}}dx$$

$$= \int \frac{1}{\sqrt{25\left[\left(\frac{3}{5}\right)^2 - x^2\right]}}dx$$

$$= \frac{1}{5}\int \frac{1}{\sqrt{\left[\left(\frac{3}{5}\right)^2 - x^2\right]}}dx$$

$$= \frac{1}{5}\sin^{-1}\left(\frac{x}{\frac{3}{5}}\right) + C$$

$$\left[\because \int \frac{dx}{\sqrt{a^2-x^2}} = \sin^{-1}\left(\frac{x}{a}\right)\right]$$

$$= \frac{1}{5}\sin^{-1}\left(\frac{5x}{3}\right) + C$$

3 (*b*)

I. $$\int \frac{3x}{1+2x^4}dx = \frac{3}{2}\int \frac{x\,dx}{\frac{1}{2} + x^4}$$

$$= \frac{3}{2}\int \frac{x\,dx}{\frac{1}{2} + (x^2)^2}$$

Let $x^2 = t$

$$\Rightarrow \quad 2x = \frac{dt}{dx} \Rightarrow dx = \frac{dt}{2x}$$

$$\therefore \frac{3}{2}\int \frac{x\,dx}{\frac{1}{2} + (x^2)^2} = \frac{3}{2}\int \frac{x}{\frac{1}{2} + (t)^2}\frac{dt}{2x}$$

$$= \frac{3}{4}\int \frac{dt}{t^2 + \left(\frac{1}{\sqrt{2}}\right)^2}$$

$$= \frac{3}{4} \times \frac{1}{\frac{1}{\sqrt{2}}}\tan^{-1}\left(\frac{t}{\frac{1}{\sqrt{2}}}\right) + C$$

$$\left[\because \int \frac{dx}{a^2+x^2} = \frac{1}{a}\tan^{-1}\left(\frac{x}{a}\right)\right]$$

$$= \frac{3}{2\sqrt{2}}\tan^{-1}(\sqrt{2}x^2) + C$$

$$[\because t = x^2]$$

II. Let $$I = \int \frac{x^2}{1-x^6}dx = \int \frac{x^2}{1-(x^3)^2}dx$$

Let $x^3 = t$

$$\Rightarrow 3x^2 = \frac{dt}{dx} \Rightarrow dx = \frac{dt}{3x^2}$$

$$\therefore \quad I = \int \frac{x^2}{1-t^2}\frac{dt}{3x^2} = \frac{1}{3}\int \frac{dt}{1-t^2}$$

$$= \frac{1}{3}\cdot\frac{1}{2}\log\left|\frac{1+t}{1-t}\right| + C$$

$$\left[\because \int \frac{dx}{a^2-x^2} = \frac{1}{2a}\log\left|\frac{a+x}{a-x}\right|\right]$$

$$= \frac{1}{6}\log\left|\frac{1+x^3}{1-x^3}\right| + C \quad [\because t = x^3]$$

4 (b)

(i) Let $I=\int \frac{x-1}{\sqrt{x^2-1}}dx$

$=\int \frac{x}{\sqrt{x^2-1}}dx-\int \frac{1}{\sqrt{x^2-1}}dx$

$=I_1-I_2$ ...(i)

Now, $I_1=\int \frac{x}{\sqrt{x^2-1}}dx$

Let $x^2-1=t \Rightarrow 2x=\frac{dt}{dx}$

$\Rightarrow dx=\frac{dt}{2x}$

$\therefore I_1=\int \frac{x}{\sqrt{t}}\frac{dt}{2x}=\frac{1}{2}\int \frac{dt}{\sqrt{t}}$

$=\frac{1}{2}\int t^{-\frac{1}{2}}dt=\frac{1}{2}\left[\frac{t^{\frac{1}{2}}}{1/2}\right]+C_1$

$=\sqrt{t}+C_1=\sqrt{x^2-1}+C_1$

$[\because t=x^2-1]$

Now, $I_2=\int \frac{1}{\sqrt{x^2-1}}dx$

$=\log|x+\sqrt{x^2-1}|+C_2$

$\left[\because \int \frac{dx}{\sqrt{x^2-a^2}}=\log|x+\sqrt{x^2-a^2}|\right]$

On putting the values of I_1 and I_2 in eq. (i), we get

$\int \frac{x-1}{\sqrt{x^2-1}}dx=\sqrt{x^2-1}-\log|x+\sqrt{x^2-1}|+C$

(where, $C=C_1-C_2$)

(ii) $\int \frac{x^2}{\sqrt{x^6+a^6}}dx=\int \frac{x^2}{\sqrt{(x^3)^2+a^6}}dx$

Let $x^3=t$

$\Rightarrow 3x^2=\frac{dt}{dx}$

$\Rightarrow dx=\frac{dt}{3x^2}$

$\therefore \int \frac{x^2}{\sqrt{(x^3)^2+a^6}}dx$

$=\int \frac{x^2}{\sqrt{t^2+a^6}}\frac{dt}{3x^2}$

$=\frac{1}{3}\int \frac{dt}{\sqrt{t^2+a^6}}=\frac{1}{3}\log|t+\sqrt{t^2+a^6}|+C$

$\left[\because \int \frac{dx}{\sqrt{x^2+a^2}}=\log|x+\sqrt{x^2+a^2}|\right]$

$=\frac{1}{3}\log|x^3+\sqrt{x^6+a^6}|+C$

$[\because t=x^3]$

(iii) $\int \frac{\sec^2 x}{\sqrt{\tan^2 x+4}}dx$

Let $\tan x=t$

$\Rightarrow \sec^2 x=\frac{dt}{dx}\Rightarrow dx=\frac{dt}{\sec^2 x}$

$\therefore \int \frac{\sec^2 x}{\sqrt{\tan^2 x+4}}dx$

$=\int \frac{\sec^2 x}{\sqrt{t^2+4}}\frac{dt}{\sec^2 x}$

$=\int \frac{dt}{\sqrt{t^2+2^2}}$

$=\log|t+\sqrt{t^2+4}|+C$

$\left[\because \int \frac{dx}{\sqrt{x^2+a^2}}=\log|x+\sqrt{x^2+a^2}|\right]$

$=\log|\tan x+\sqrt{\tan^2 x+4}|+C$

$[\because t=\tan x]$

(iv) Let $I=\int \frac{1}{\sqrt{x^2+2x+2}}dx$

$=\int \frac{1}{\sqrt{(x^2+2x+1)+1}}dx$

$=\int \frac{1}{\sqrt{(x+1)^2+1}}dx$

Let $x+1=t \Rightarrow dx=dt$

$\therefore I=\int \frac{1}{\sqrt{t^2+1}}dt$

$=\log|t+\sqrt{t^2+1}|+C$

$\left[\because \int \frac{dx}{\sqrt{x^2+a^2}}=\log|x+\sqrt{x^2+a^2}|\right]$

$=\log|(x+1)+\sqrt{(x+1)^2+1}|+C$

$=\log|(x+1)+\sqrt{x^2+2x+2}|+C$

$[\because t=x+1]$

5 (d) $\int \frac{1}{9x^2+6x+5}dx$

$=\frac{1}{9}\int \frac{1}{x^2+\frac{2}{3}x+\frac{5}{9}}dx$

$=\frac{1}{9}\int \frac{1}{x^2+2\cdot\frac{1}{3}\cdot x+\left(\frac{1}{3}\right)^2+\frac{5}{9}-\left(\frac{1}{3}\right)^2}dx$

$=\frac{1}{9}\int \frac{1}{x^2+\frac{2}{3}x+\left(\frac{1}{3}\right)^2+\frac{5}{9}-\frac{1}{9}}dx$

$=\frac{1}{9}\int \frac{1}{\left(x+\frac{1}{3}\right)^2+\left(\frac{2}{3}\right)^2}dx$

$=\frac{1}{9}\left(\frac{1}{\frac{2}{3}}\right)\tan^{-1}\left(\frac{x+\frac{1}{3}}{\frac{2}{3}}\right)+C$

$\left[\because \int \frac{dx}{a^2+x^2}=\frac{1}{a}\tan^{-1}\left(\frac{x}{a}\right)\right]$

$=\frac{1}{6}\tan^{-1}\left(\frac{3x+1}{2}\right)+C$

6 (c) Let $I=\int \frac{1}{\sqrt{7-6x-x^2}}dx$

$=\int \frac{1}{\sqrt{7-(x^2+6x)}}dx$

$=\int \frac{1}{\sqrt{7-[x^2+2\times 3x+(3)^2-(3)^2]}}dx$

$=\int \frac{1}{\sqrt{7-[x^2+6x+3^2-9]}}dx$

$=\int \frac{1}{\sqrt{7-[(x+3)^2-9]}}dx$

$=\int \frac{1}{\sqrt{4^2-(x+3)^2}}dx$

Let $x+3=t \Rightarrow dx=dt$

$\therefore I=\int \frac{1}{\sqrt{4^2-t^2}}dt=\sin^{-1}\left(\frac{t}{4}\right)+C$

$\left[\because \int \frac{dx}{\sqrt{a^2-x^2}}=\sin^{-1}\left(\frac{x}{a}\right)\right]$

$=\sin^{-1}\left(\frac{x+3}{4}\right)+C$

$[\because t=x+3]$

7 (*a*)

I. Let $I=\int \frac{1}{\sqrt{(x-1)(x-2)}}dx$

$=\int \frac{1}{\sqrt{x^2-3x+2}}dx$

$=\int \frac{1}{\sqrt{x^2-3x+\left(\frac{3}{2}\right)^2-\left(\frac{3}{2}\right)^2+2}}dx$

$=\int \frac{1}{\sqrt{\left(x-\frac{3}{2}\right)^2+\frac{-9+8}{4}}}$

$=\int \frac{1}{\sqrt{\left(x-\frac{3}{2}\right)^2-\left(\frac{1}{2}\right)^2}}dx$

Let $x-\frac{3}{2}=t \Rightarrow dx=dt$

$\therefore \quad I=\int \frac{1}{\sqrt{t^2-\left(\frac{1}{2}\right)^2}}dt$

$=\log\left|t+\sqrt{t^2-\frac{1}{4}}\right|+C$

$\left[\because \int \frac{dx}{\sqrt{x^2-a^2}}=\log|x+\sqrt{x^2-a^2}|\right]$

$=\log\left|x-\frac{3}{2}+\sqrt{\left(x-\frac{3}{2}\right)^2-\frac{1}{4}}\right|+C$

$=\log\left|\left(x-\frac{3}{2}\right)+\sqrt{x^2-3x+2}\right|+C$

II. Let $I=\int \frac{1}{\sqrt{(x-a)(x-b)}}dx$

$=\int \frac{1}{\sqrt{x^2-(a+b)x+ab}}dx$

$=\int \frac{1}{\sqrt{\left[x^2-(a+b)x+\left(\frac{a+b}{2}\right)^2-\left(\frac{a+b}{2}\right)^2+ab\right]}}dx$

$=\int \frac{1}{\sqrt{\left[x-\left(\frac{a+b}{2}\right)\right]^2+ab-\left(\frac{a+b}{2}\right)^2}}dx$

$=\int \frac{1}{\sqrt{\left[x-\left(\frac{a+b}{2}\right)\right]^2+ab-\left(\frac{a^2+b^2+2ab}{4}\right)}}dx$

$=\int \frac{1}{\sqrt{\left[x-\left(\frac{a+b}{2}\right)\right]^2+\frac{4ab-a^2-b^2-2ab}{4}}}dx$

$=\int \frac{1}{\sqrt{\left[x-\left(\frac{a+b}{2}\right)\right]^2+\frac{2ab-a^2-b^2}{4}}}dx$

$=\int \frac{1}{\sqrt{\left[x-\left(\frac{a+b}{2}\right)\right]^2-\left(\frac{a^2+b^2-2ab}{4}\right)}}dx$

$=\int \frac{1}{\sqrt{\left(x-\frac{a+b}{2}\right)^2-\left(\frac{a-b}{2}\right)^2}}dx$

Let $x-\frac{a+b}{2}=t \Rightarrow dx=dt$

$\therefore \quad I=\int \frac{1}{\sqrt{t^2-\left(\frac{a-b}{2}\right)^2}}dt$

$=\log\left|t+\sqrt{t^2-\left(\frac{a-b}{2}\right)^2}\right|+C$

$\left[\because \int \frac{dx}{\sqrt{x^2-a^2}}=\log|x+\sqrt{x^2-a^2}|\right]$

$=\log\left|\left(x-\frac{a+b}{2}\right)+\sqrt{\left(x-\frac{a+b}{2}\right)^2-\left(\frac{a-b}{2}\right)^2}\right|+C$

$\left[\because t=x-\frac{(a+b)}{2}\right]$

$=\log\left|\left(x-\frac{a+b}{2}\right)+\sqrt{(x-a)(x-b)}\right|+C$

8 (*a*) Let $I=\int \frac{1}{\sqrt{8+3x-x^2}}dx$

$=\int \frac{1}{\sqrt{8-\left[x^2-3x+\left(\frac{3}{2}\right)^2-\left(\frac{3}{2}\right)^2\right]}}dx$

$=\int \frac{1}{\sqrt{8-\left[\left(x-\frac{3}{2}\right)^2-\frac{9}{4}\right]}}dx$

$=\int \frac{1}{\sqrt{8+\frac{9}{4}-\left(x-\frac{3}{2}\right)^2}}dx$

$=\int \frac{1}{\sqrt{\left(\frac{\sqrt{41}}{2}\right)^2-\left(x-\frac{3}{2}\right)^2}}dx$

Let $x-\frac{3}{2}=t \Rightarrow dx=dt$

$\therefore \quad I=\int \frac{1}{\sqrt{\left(\frac{\sqrt{41}}{2}\right)^2-t^2}}dt$

$=\sin^{-1}\left(\frac{t}{\frac{\sqrt{41}}{2}}\right)+C$

$\left[\because \int \frac{dx}{\sqrt{a^2-x^2}}=\sin^{-1}\left(\frac{x}{a}\right)\right]$

$=\sin^{-1}\left(\frac{x-\frac{3}{2}}{\frac{\sqrt{41}}{2}}\right)+C$

$=\sin^{-1}\left(\frac{2x-3}{\sqrt{41}}\right)+C$

$\left[\because t=x-\frac{3}{2}\right]$

9 (c)

A. Let $2x^2+x-3=t$

$\Rightarrow 4x+1=\frac{dt}{dx} \Rightarrow dx=\frac{dt}{4x+1}$

$\therefore \int \frac{4x+1}{\sqrt{2x^2+x-3}}dx$

$=\int \frac{4x+1}{\sqrt{t}}\times\frac{dt}{4x+1}=\int \frac{1}{\sqrt{t}}dt$

$=2\sqrt{t}+C$

$=2\sqrt{2x^2+x-3}+C$

$[\because t=2x^2+x-3]$

B. $\int \frac{x+2}{\sqrt{x^2-1}}dx$

$= \int \frac{x}{\sqrt{x^2-1}}dx + \int \frac{2}{\sqrt{x^2-1}}dx$

$= I_1 + I_2$ ...(i)

Now, $I_1 = \int \frac{x}{\sqrt{x^2-1}}dx.$

Let $x^2-1=t \Rightarrow 2x\,dx = dt$

$\Rightarrow \quad dx = \frac{dt}{2x}$

$\therefore \quad I_1 = \int \frac{x}{\sqrt{t}} \times \frac{dt}{2x} = \frac{1}{2}\int \frac{dt}{\sqrt{t}}$

$= \frac{1}{2}\int t^{-1/2}dt = \frac{1}{2}[2\,t^{1/2}]$

$= \sqrt{t} = \sqrt{x^2-1}+C_1$

$[\because t = x^2-1]$

Now, $I_2 = 2\int \frac{1}{\sqrt{x^2-1}}dx$

$= 2\log|x+\sqrt{x^2-1}|+C_2$

$\left[\because \int \frac{dx}{\sqrt{x^2-a^2}} = \log|x+\sqrt{x^2-a^2}|\right]$

On putting the values of I_1 and I_2 in Eq. (i), we get

$I = \sqrt{x^2-1}+2\log|x+\sqrt{x^2-1}|$
$+C$

where, $C = C_1 + C_2$

C. $\int \frac{5x-2}{1+2x+3x^2}dx$

Let $5x-2 = A\frac{d}{dx}(1+2x+3x^2)$
$+B$

$\Rightarrow \quad 5x-2 = A(2+6x)+B$

$\Rightarrow \quad 5x-2 = 6Ax+(2A+B)$

On equating the coefficient of x and constant on both sides, we get

$5 = 6A \Rightarrow A = \frac{5}{6}$

and $2A+B = -2 \Rightarrow B = -\frac{11}{3}$

$\therefore \quad 5x-2 = \frac{5}{6}(2+6x)+\left(-\frac{11}{3}\right)$

$\therefore I = \int \frac{5x-2}{1+2x+3x^2}dx$

$= \int \frac{\frac{5}{6}(2+6x)-\frac{11}{3}}{1+2x+3x^2}dx$

$= \frac{5}{6}\int \frac{2+6x}{1+2x+3x^2}dx$

$-\frac{11}{3}\int \frac{1}{1+2x+3x^2}dx$

Let $I_1 = \int \frac{2+6x}{1+2x+3x^2}dx$

and $I_2 = \int \frac{1}{1+2x+3x^2}dx$

$\therefore \quad I = \frac{5}{6}I_1 - \frac{11}{3}I_2$ ...(i)

Now, $I_1 = \int \frac{2+6x}{1+2x+3x^2}dx$

Let $1+2x+3x^2 = t$

$\Rightarrow \quad (2+6x)\,dx = dt$

$\therefore \quad I_1 = \int \frac{dt}{t} = \log|t|+C_1$

$\Rightarrow I_1 = \log|1+2x+3x^2|+C_1$
...(ii)

Also, $I_2 = \int \frac{1}{1+2x+3x^2}dx$

$1+2x+3x^2$ can be written as

$1+3\left(x^2+\frac{2}{3}x\right)$

Therefore,

$1+3\left(x^2+\frac{2}{3}x\right) = 1+3$

$\left(x^2+\frac{2}{3}x+\frac{1}{9}-\frac{1}{9}\right)$

$= 1+3\left(x+\frac{1}{3}\right)^2 - \frac{1}{3} = \frac{2}{3}$

$+3\left(x+\frac{1}{3}\right)^2$

$= 3\left[\left(x+\frac{1}{3}\right)^2+\frac{2}{9}\right]$

$= 3\left[\left(x+\frac{1}{3}\right)^2+\left(\frac{\sqrt{2}}{3}\right)^2\right]$

$\therefore \quad I_2 = \frac{1}{3}\int \frac{dx}{\left[\left(x+\frac{1}{3}\right)^2+\left(\frac{\sqrt{2}}{3}\right)^2\right]}$

$= \frac{1}{3}\left[\frac{1}{\frac{\sqrt{2}}{3}}\tan^{-1}\left(\frac{x+\frac{1}{3}}{\frac{\sqrt{2}}{3}}\right)\right]+C_2$

$\left[\because \int \frac{dx}{a^2+x^2} = \frac{1}{a}\tan^{-1}\left(\frac{x}{a}\right)\right]$

$= \frac{1}{3}\left[\frac{3}{\sqrt{2}}\tan^{-1}\left(\frac{3x+1}{\sqrt{2}}\right)\right]+C_2$

$= \frac{1}{\sqrt{2}}\tan^{-1}\left(\frac{3x+1}{\sqrt{2}}\right)+C_2$ ...(iii)

On substituting the values of I_1 and I_2 from Eqs.(ii) and (iii) in Eq. (i), we get

$I = \frac{5}{6}[\log|1+2x+3x^2|]$

$-\frac{11}{3}\left[\frac{1}{\sqrt{2}}\tan^{-1}\left(\frac{3x+1}{\sqrt{2}}\right)\right]+C$

$\left[\because \frac{5}{6}C_1 - \frac{11}{3}C_2 = C\right]$

$= \frac{5}{6}\log|1+2x+3x^2| - \frac{11}{3\sqrt{2}}$

$\tan^{-1}\left(\frac{3x+1}{\sqrt{2}}\right)+C$

D. $\int \frac{6x+7}{\sqrt{(x-5)(x-4)}}dx$

$= \int \frac{6x+7}{\sqrt{x^2-9x+20}}dx$

Let $6x+7 = A\frac{d}{dx}(x^2-9x$
$+20)+B$

$\Rightarrow 6x+7 = A(2x-9)+B$

$\Rightarrow 6x+7 = 2Ax+(-9A+B)$

On equating the coefficients of x and constant term on both sides, we get

$2A = 6 \Rightarrow A = 3$

and $-9A+B = 7 \Rightarrow B = 34$

$\Rightarrow 6x+7 = 3(2x-9)+34$

$\therefore \quad \int \frac{6x+7}{\sqrt{x^2-9x+20}}dx$

$= \int \frac{3(2x-9)+34}{\sqrt{x^2-9x+20}}dx$

$= 3\int \frac{2x-9}{\sqrt{x^2-9x+20}}dx$

$+34\int \frac{1}{\sqrt{x^2-9x+20}}dx$

Let $I_1 = \int \frac{2x-9}{\sqrt{x^2-9x+20}}dx$

and $I_2 = \int \frac{1}{\sqrt{x^2-9x+20}}dx$

$\therefore \int \frac{6x+7}{\sqrt{x^2-9x+20}}dx = 3I_1 + 34I_2$ ...(i)

Now, $I_1 = \int \frac{2x-9}{\sqrt{x^2-9x+20}}dx$

Let $x^2-9x+20=t$

$\Rightarrow (2x-9)\,dx = dt$

$\therefore I_1 = \int \frac{dt}{\sqrt{t}} = 2\sqrt{t} + C_1$

$= 2\sqrt{x^2-9x+20} + C_1$ ...(ii)

And $I_2 = \int \frac{1}{\sqrt{x^2-9x+20}}dx$

$x^2-9x+20$ can be written as

$x^2-9x+20+\frac{81}{4}-\frac{81}{4}$

Therefore,

$x^2-9x+20+\frac{81}{4}-\frac{81}{4}$

$= \left(x-\frac{9}{2}\right)^2 - \frac{1}{4}$

$= \left(x-\frac{9}{2}\right)^2 - \left(\frac{1}{2}\right)^2$

$\therefore I_2 = \int \frac{1}{\sqrt{\left(x-\frac{9}{2}\right)^2-\left(\frac{1}{2}\right)^2}}dx$

$= \log\left|\left(x-\frac{9}{2}\right)+\sqrt{\left(x-\frac{9}{2}\right)^2-\frac{1}{4}}\right| + C_2$

$\left[\because \int \frac{dx}{\sqrt{x^2-a^2}} = \log|x+\sqrt{x^2-a^2}|\right]$

$= \log\left|\left(x-\frac{9}{2}\right)+\sqrt{x^2-9x+20}\right| + C_2$ ...(iii)

On substituting the values of I_1 and I_2 from Eqs.(ii) and (iii) in Eq. (i), we get

$\int \frac{6x+7}{\sqrt{x^2-9x+20}}dx$

$= 3\,[2\sqrt{x^2-9x+20}] + 34\log$

$\left|\left(x-\frac{9}{2}\right)+\sqrt{x^2-9x+20}\right| + C$

$[\because 3C_1 + 34C_2 = C]$

$= 6\sqrt{x^2-9x+20} + 34\log$

$\left|\left(x-\frac{9}{2}\right)+\sqrt{x^2-9x+20}\right| + C$

10 (*b*) (i) Let $x+2 = A\frac{d}{dx}(4x-x^2)+B$

$\Rightarrow x+2 = A(4-2x)+B$

$\Rightarrow x+2 = -2Ax+4A+B$

On equating the coefficients of x and constant term on both sides, we get

$-2A = 1 \Rightarrow A = -\frac{1}{2}$

and $4A+B=2 \Rightarrow B=4$

$\Rightarrow (x+2) = -\frac{1}{2}(4-2x)+4$

$\therefore \int \frac{x+2}{\sqrt{4x-x^2}}dx$

$= \int \frac{-\frac{1}{2}(4-2x)+4}{\sqrt{4x-x^2}}dx$

$= -\frac{1}{2}\int \frac{4-2x}{\sqrt{4x-x^2}}dx + 4\int \frac{dx}{\sqrt{4x-x^2}}$

Let $I_1 = \int \frac{4-2x}{\sqrt{4x-x^2}}dx$

and $I_2 = \int \frac{dx}{\sqrt{4x-x^2}}$

Then $\int \frac{x+2}{\sqrt{4x-x^2}}dx$

$= -\frac{1}{2}I_1 + 4I_2$ ...(i)

Now, $I_1 = \int \frac{4-2x}{\sqrt{4x-x^2}}dx$

Let $4x-x^2=t$

$\Rightarrow (4-2x)\,dx = dt$

$\Rightarrow I_1 = \int \frac{dt}{\sqrt{t}} = 2\sqrt{t}+C_1$

$= 2\sqrt{4x-x^2}+C_1$ ...(ii)

And $I_2 = \int \frac{dx}{\sqrt{4x-x^2}}$

$[\because 4x-x^2 = -(x^2-4x)$

$= -\{(x-2)^2-4\} = [(2)^2-(x-2)^2]$

$\therefore I_2 = \int \frac{1}{\sqrt{(2)^2-(x-2)^2}}dx$

$= \sin^{-1}\left(\frac{x-2}{2}\right)+C_2$ ...(iii)

$\left[\because \int \frac{dx}{\sqrt{a^2-x^2}} = \sin^{-1}\left(\frac{x}{a}\right)\right]$

On substituting the values of I_1 and I_2 from Eqs. (ii) and (iii) in Eq. (i), we get

$\int \frac{x+2}{\sqrt{4x-x^2}}dx = -\frac{1}{2}[2\sqrt{4x-x^2}]$

$+ 4\sin^{-1}\left(\frac{x-2}{2}\right)+C$

$\left[\because -\frac{1}{2}C_1 + 4C_2 = C\right]$

$= -\sqrt{4x-x^2} + 4\sin^{-1}\left(\frac{x-2}{2}\right) + C$

(ii) Let

$x+2 = A\frac{d}{dx}(x^2+2x+3)+B$

$\Rightarrow x+2 = A(2x+2)+B$

$\Rightarrow x+2 = 2Ax+(2A+B)$

On equating the coefficient of x and constant term on both sides, we get

$2A = 1$

$\Rightarrow A = \frac{1}{2}$

and $2A+B=2$

$\Rightarrow 2\times\frac{1}{2}+B=2$

$\Rightarrow B = 2-1 = 1$

$\Rightarrow x+2 = \frac{1}{2}(2x+2)+1$

$\therefore \int \frac{x+2}{\sqrt{x^2+2x+3}}dx$

$= \int \frac{\frac{1}{2}(2x+2)+1}{\sqrt{x^2+2x+3}}dx$

$= \frac{1}{2}\int \frac{2x+2}{\sqrt{x^2+2x+3}}dx + \int \frac{dx}{\sqrt{x^2+2x+3}}$

Let $I_1 = \int \frac{2x+2}{\sqrt{x^2+2x+3}} dx$

and $I_2 = \int \frac{dx}{\sqrt{x^2+2x+3}}$

Then $\int \frac{x+2}{\sqrt{x^2+2x+3}} dx$

$= \frac{1}{2} I_1 + I_2$ ...(i)

Now, $I_1 = \int \frac{2x+2}{\sqrt{x^2+2x+3}} dx$

Let $x^2+2x+3 = t$

$\Rightarrow (2x+2)\, dx = dt$

$\therefore I_1 = \int \frac{dt}{\sqrt{t}} = \int t^{-1/2} dt$

$= \frac{t^{(-1/2)+1}}{-\frac{1}{2}+1} + C_1$

$= 2\sqrt{t} + C_1 = 2\sqrt{x^2+2x+3} + C_1$

and $I_2 = \int \frac{dx}{\sqrt{x^2+2x+3}}$

$= \int \frac{dx}{\sqrt{x^2+2x+(1)^2+3-(1)^2}}$

$= \int \frac{dx}{\sqrt{(x+1)^2+(\sqrt{2})^2}}$

Let $x+1 = t \Rightarrow dx = dt$

$I_2 = \int \frac{dt}{\sqrt{t^2+(\sqrt{2})^2}}$

$= \log|t+\sqrt{t^2+2}| + C_2$

$\left[\because \int \frac{dx}{\sqrt{x^2+a^2}} = \log|x+\sqrt{x^2+a^2}|\right]$

$= \log|x+1+\sqrt{(x+1)^2+2}| + C_2$

$= \log|x+1+\sqrt{x^2+2x+3}| + C_2$

On putting the values of I_1 and I_2 in Eq. (i), we get

$\int \frac{x+2}{\sqrt{x^2+2x+3}} dx = \frac{1}{2}$

$[2\sqrt{x^2+2x+3}] + \log|x+1$

$+\sqrt{x^2+2x+3}| + C$

$\left[\because \frac{1}{2}C_1 + C_2 = C\right]$

$= \sqrt{x^2+2x+3} + \log|x+1$

$+\sqrt{x^2+2x+3}| + C$

(iii) Let

$(x+3) = A\frac{d}{dx}(x^2-2x-5) + B$

$\Rightarrow (x+3) = A(2x-2) + B$

$\Rightarrow x+3 = 2Ax - 2A + B$

On equating the coefficients of x and constant term on both sides, we get

$2A = 1 \Rightarrow A = \frac{1}{2}$

and $-2A + B = 3 \Rightarrow B = 4$

$\Rightarrow (x+3) = \frac{1}{2}(2x-2) + 4$

$\therefore \int \frac{x+3}{x^2-2x-5} dx$

$= \int \frac{\frac{1}{2}(2x-2)+4}{x^2-2x-5} dx$

$= \frac{1}{2}\int \frac{(2x-2)}{x^2-2x-5} dx$

$+ 4\int \frac{1}{x^2-2x-5} dx$

Let $I_1 = \int \frac{2x-2}{x^2-2x-5} dx$

and $I_2 = \int \frac{1}{x^2-2x-5} dx$

$\therefore \int \frac{x+3}{x^2-2x-5} dx = \frac{1}{2} I_1 + 4I_2$

...(i)

Now, $I_1 = \int \frac{2x-2}{x^2-2x-5} dx$

Let $x^2-2x-5 = t$

$\Rightarrow (2x-2)\, dx = dt$

$\therefore I_1 = \int \frac{dt}{t} = \log|t| + C_1$

$= \log|x^2-2x-5| + C_1$ ...(ii)

and $I_2 = \int \frac{1}{x^2-2x-5} dx$

$= \int \frac{1}{(x^2-2x+1)-6} dx$

$= \int \frac{1}{(x-1)^2-(\sqrt{6})^2} dx$

$= \frac{1}{2\sqrt{6}} \log\left|\frac{x-1-\sqrt{6}}{x-1+\sqrt{6}}\right|$ ...(iii)

$\left[\because \int \frac{dx}{x^2-a^2} = \frac{1}{2a}\log\left|\frac{x-a}{x+a}\right|\right]$

On substituting the values I_1 and I_2 from Eqs. (ii) and (iii) in Eq. (i), we get

$\int \frac{x+3}{x^2-2x-5} dx$

$= \frac{1}{2}\log|x^2-2x-5|$

$+ 4\left[\frac{1}{2\sqrt{6}}\log\left|\frac{x-1-\sqrt{6}}{x-1+\sqrt{6}}\right|\right] + C$

$\left[\because \frac{1}{2}C_1 + 4C_2 = C\right]$

$= \frac{1}{2}\log|x^2-2x-5|$

$+ \frac{2}{\sqrt{6}}\log\left|\frac{x-1-\sqrt{6}}{x-1+\sqrt{6}}\right| + C$

(iv) Let

$5x+3 = A\frac{d}{dx}(x^2+4x+10) + B$

$\Rightarrow 5x+3 = A(2x+4) + B$

$\Rightarrow 5x+3 = 2Ax + 4A + B$

On equating the coefficients of x and constant term on both sides, we get

$2A = 5 \Rightarrow A = \frac{5}{2}$

and $4A + B = 3 \Rightarrow B = -7$

$\Rightarrow 5x+3 = \frac{5}{2}(2x+4) - 7$

$\therefore \int \frac{5x+3}{\sqrt{x^2+4x+10}} dx$

$= \int \frac{\frac{5}{2}(2x+4)-7}{\sqrt{x^2+4x+10}} dx$

$= \frac{5}{2}\int \frac{2x+4}{\sqrt{x^2+4x+10}} dx$

$-7\int \frac{1}{\sqrt{x^2+4x+10}} dx$

Let $I_1 = \int \frac{2x+4}{\sqrt{x^2+4x+10}} dx$

and $I_2 = \int \frac{1}{\sqrt{x^2+4x+10}} dx$

$$\therefore \int \frac{5x+3}{\sqrt{x^2+4x+10}}dx = \frac{5}{2}I_1 - 7I_2 \quad \text{...(i)}$$

Now, $I_1 = \int \frac{2x+4}{\sqrt{x^2+4x+10}}dx$

Let $x^2+4x+10 = t$

$\Rightarrow (2x+4)\,dx = dt$

$\Rightarrow dx = \frac{dt}{2x+4}$

$$\therefore \quad I_1 = \int \frac{2x+4}{\sqrt{t}} \times \frac{dt}{2x+4}$$

$$= \int \frac{dt}{\sqrt{t}}$$

$$= 2\sqrt{t} + C_1$$

$$= 2\sqrt{x^2+4x+10} + C_1 \quad \text{...(ii)}$$

And $I_2 = \int \frac{1}{\sqrt{x^2+4x+10}}dx$

$$= \int \frac{1}{\sqrt{(x^2+4x+4)+6}}dx$$

$$= \int \frac{1}{\sqrt{(x+2)^2+(\sqrt{6})^2}}dx$$

$$= \log|(x+2)+\sqrt{(x+2)^2+6}| + C_2$$

$$\left[\because \int \frac{dx}{\sqrt{x^2+a^2}} = \log|x+\sqrt{x^2+a^2}|\right]$$

$$= \log|x+2+\sqrt{x^2+4x+10}| + C_2$$

On substituting the values of I_1 and I_2 from Eqs. (ii) and (iii) in Eq. (i), we get

$$\int \frac{5x+3}{\sqrt{x^2+4x+10}}dx = \frac{5}{2}[2\sqrt{x^2+4x+10}] - 7\log|x+2 + \sqrt{x^2+4x+10}| + C$$

$$\left[\because \frac{5}{2}C_1 - 7C_2 = C\right]$$

$$= 5\sqrt{x^2+4x+10} - 7\log|x+2 + \sqrt{x^2+4x+10}| + C$$

11 (*b*) Let $I = \int \frac{1}{x^2+2x+2}dx$

$$= \int \frac{1}{(x+1)^2+1^2}dx$$

Let $x+1 = t \Rightarrow dx = dt$

$$\therefore \quad I = \int \frac{1}{t^2+1^2}dt = \frac{1}{1}\tan^{-1}\left(\frac{t}{1}\right) + C$$

$$\left[\because \int \frac{dx}{a^2+x^2} = \frac{1}{a}\tan^{-1}\left(\frac{x}{a}\right)\right]$$

$$= \tan^{-1}\left(\frac{x+1}{1}\right) + C$$

$$= \tan^{-1}(x+1) + C$$

Hence, the option (b) is correct.

12 (*b*) $\int \frac{1}{\sqrt{9x-4x^2}}dx$

$$= \frac{1}{\sqrt{4}}\int \frac{1}{\sqrt{\frac{9}{4}x - x^2}}dx$$

$$= \frac{1}{2}\int \frac{1}{\sqrt{-\left[x^2 - \frac{9}{4}x + \left(\frac{9}{8}\right)^2\right] + \left(\frac{9}{8}\right)^2}}dx$$

$$= \frac{1}{2}\int \frac{1}{\sqrt{\left(\frac{9}{8}\right)^2 - \left(x-\frac{9}{8}\right)^2}}dx$$

$$= \frac{1}{2}\sin^{-1}\left(\frac{x-\frac{9}{8}}{\frac{9}{8}}\right) + C$$

$$\left[\because \int \frac{dx}{\sqrt{a^2-x^2}} = \sin^{-1}\left(\frac{x}{a}\right)\right]$$

$$= \frac{1}{2}\sin^{-1}\left(\frac{8x-9}{9}\right) + C$$

13 (*a*)

I. Let, $I = \int \frac{x^2+1}{x^4+1}dx$

On dividing the numerator and denominator by x^2, we get

$$I = \frac{1+\frac{1}{x^2}}{x^2+\frac{1}{x^2}}dx$$

$$\Rightarrow \quad I = \int \frac{1+\frac{1}{x^2}}{\left(x-\frac{1}{x}\right)^2+2}dx$$

Let, $x - \frac{1}{x} = t$

$$\Rightarrow \left(1+\frac{1}{x^2}\right)dx = dt$$

$$\therefore \quad I = \int \frac{dt}{t^2+(\sqrt{2})^2}$$

$$= \frac{1}{\sqrt{2}}\tan^{-1}\left(\frac{t}{\sqrt{2}}\right) + C$$

$$= \frac{1}{\sqrt{2}}\tan^{-1}\left(\frac{\frac{x^2-1}{x}}{\sqrt{2}}\right) + C$$

$$= \frac{1}{\sqrt{2}}\tan^{-1}\left(\frac{x^2-1}{\sqrt{2}x}\right) + C$$

II. We have,

$$I = \int \frac{x^2+4}{x^4+16}dx$$

On dividing the numerator and denominator by x^2, we get

$$I = \int \frac{1+\frac{4}{x^2}}{x^2+\frac{16}{x^2}}dx$$

$$\Rightarrow I = \int \frac{1+\frac{4}{x^2}}{x^2+\left(\frac{4}{x}\right)^2 - 8 + 8}dx$$

$$\Rightarrow \quad I = \int \frac{\left(1+\frac{4}{x^2}\right)}{\left(x-\frac{4}{x}\right)^2+8}dx$$

Let, $x - \frac{4}{x} = t.$

$$\Rightarrow \left(1+\frac{4}{x^2}\right)dx = dt$$

$$\therefore \quad I = \int \frac{dt}{t^2+(2\sqrt{2})^2}$$

$$\Rightarrow \quad I = \frac{1}{2\sqrt{2}}\tan^{-1}\left(\frac{t}{2\sqrt{2}}\right) + C$$

$$\Rightarrow \quad I = \frac{1}{2\sqrt{2}}\tan^{-1}\left(\frac{x-\frac{4}{x}}{2\sqrt{2}}\right) + C$$

$$\Rightarrow \quad I = \frac{1}{2\sqrt{2}}\tan^{-1}\left(\frac{x^2-4}{2\sqrt{2}x}\right) + C$$

14 (c) Let, $I = \int \frac{x^2-1}{x^4+x^2+1}\,dx$

On dividing numerator and denominator by x^2, we get

$$I = \int \frac{1-\frac{1}{x^2}}{x^2+1+\frac{1}{x^2}}\,dx$$

$$I = \int \frac{1-\frac{1}{x^2}}{\left(x+\frac{1}{x}\right)^2-1}\,dx$$

Let, $x+\frac{1}{x} \Rightarrow \left(1-\frac{1}{x^2}\right)dx = dt$

$$\therefore \quad I = \int \frac{dt}{t^2-1}$$

$$\Rightarrow \quad I = \frac{1}{2(1)}\log\left|\frac{t-1}{t+1}\right| + C$$

$$\Rightarrow \quad I = \frac{1}{2}\log\left|\frac{x+\frac{1}{x}-1}{x+\frac{1}{x}+1}\right| + C$$

$$\Rightarrow \quad I = \frac{1}{2}\log\left|\frac{x^2-x+1}{x^2+x+1}\right| + C$$

15 (a) I. We have, $I = \int \frac{dx}{\sqrt{16-9x^2}}$

$$= \frac{1}{3}\int \frac{dx}{\sqrt{\left(\frac{4}{3}\right)^2 - x^2}} = \frac{1}{3}\sin^{-1}\left(\frac{x}{\frac{4}{3}}\right) + C$$

$$\left[\because \int \frac{1}{\sqrt{a^2-x^2}}\,dx = \sin^{-1}\frac{x}{a} + C\right]$$

$$= \frac{1}{3}\sin^{-1}\left(\frac{3x}{4}\right) + C$$

II. We have, $I = \int \frac{dt}{\sqrt{3t-2t^2}}$

$$= \frac{1}{\sqrt{2}}\int \frac{dt}{\sqrt{-\left[(t^2)-\frac{3}{2}t+\left(\frac{3}{4}\right)^2-\left(\frac{3}{4}\right)^2\right]}}$$

$$= \frac{1}{\sqrt{2}}\int \frac{dt}{\sqrt{\left(\frac{3}{4}\right)^2-\left(t-\frac{3}{4}\right)^2}}$$

$$= \frac{1}{\sqrt{2}}\sin^{-1}\left(\frac{t-3/4}{3/4}\right)$$

$$= \frac{1}{\sqrt{2}}\sin^{-1}\left(\frac{4t-3}{3}\right) + C$$

16 (c) We have, $I = \int \frac{3x-1}{\sqrt{x^2+9}}\,dx$

By putting numerator,

$$3x-1 = A\frac{d}{dx}(x^2+9)+B$$

$$3x-1 = A(2x)+B$$

$$3x-1 = 2Ax+B$$

On comparing the coefficients of x and constant term on both sides, we get

$$2A = 3 \text{ and } B = -1$$

$$\Rightarrow \quad A = \frac{3}{2} \text{ and } B = -1$$

$$\therefore I = \frac{3}{2}\int \frac{2x}{\sqrt{x^2+9}}\,dx - \int \frac{1}{\sqrt{x^2+9}}\,dx$$

$$= \frac{3}{2}\times 2\sqrt{x^2+9} - \log|x + \sqrt{x^2+9}| + C$$

$$\left[\because \int \frac{f'(x)}{\sqrt{f(x)}}\,dx = 2\sqrt{f(x)} + C\right]$$

$$= 3\sqrt{x^2+9} - \log|x+\sqrt{x^2+9}| + C$$

17 (b) We have, $I = \int \frac{\sqrt{x}}{\sqrt{a^3-x^3}}\,dx$

$$I = \int \frac{\sqrt{x}}{\sqrt{(a^{3/2})^2 - \left(x^{\frac{3}{2}}\right)^2}}\,dx$$

Put, $x^{\frac{3}{2}} = t$

$$\Rightarrow \quad \frac{3}{2}x^{\frac{1}{2}}\,dx = dt$$

$$\Rightarrow \quad \sqrt{x}\,dx = \frac{2}{3}dt$$

$$\therefore \quad I = \frac{2}{3}\int \frac{dt}{\sqrt{\left(a^{\frac{3}{2}}\right)^2 - t^2}}$$

$$= \frac{2}{3}\sin^{-1}\left(\frac{t}{a^{\frac{3}{2}}}\right) + C$$

$$= \frac{2}{3}\sin^{-1}\left(\frac{x^{\frac{3}{2}}}{a^{\frac{3}{2}}}\right) + C$$

$$= \frac{2}{3}\sin^{-1}\sqrt{\frac{x^3}{a^3}} + C$$

18 (a)

(i) Let, $I = \int \frac{dx}{(x+1)\sqrt{4x+3}}$

Put, $4x+3 = t^2$

$$\Rightarrow \quad 4\,dx = 2t\,dt$$

$$\therefore \quad I = \frac{1}{2}\int \frac{t\,dt}{\left(\frac{t^2-3}{4}+1\right)t}$$

$$I = 2\int \frac{dt}{(t^2-3+4)}$$

$$I = 2\int \frac{dt}{t^2+1}$$

$$I = 2\tan^{-1}t + C$$

$$I = 2\tan^{-1}\sqrt{(4x+3)} + C$$

(ii) Let, $I = \int \frac{\sin x\cos x}{\sqrt{1-\sin^4 x}}\,dx$

Put, $\sin^2 x = t$

$$\Rightarrow \quad 2\sin x\cos x\,dx = dt$$

$$\therefore \quad I = \int \frac{dt}{2\sqrt{1-t^2}}$$

$$= \frac{1}{2}\sin^{-1}t + C$$

$$= \frac{1}{2}\sin^{-1}(\sin^2 x) + C$$

(iii) Let, $I = \int \frac{x^2+1}{x^4-x^2+1}\,dx$

$$I = \int \frac{1+\frac{1}{x^2}}{x^2+\frac{1}{x^2}-1}\,dx$$

$$I = \int \frac{1+\frac{1}{x^2}}{\left(x-\frac{1}{x}\right)^2+1}\,dx$$

Put, $\left(x-\frac{1}{x}\right) = t$

$$\Rightarrow \quad \left(1+\frac{1}{x^2}\right)dx = dt$$

$$\therefore \quad I = \int \frac{dt}{t^2+1}$$

$$I = \tan^{-1}t + C$$

$$I = \tan^{-1}\left(x-\frac{1}{x}\right) + C$$

$$I = \tan^{-1}\left(\frac{x^2-1}{x}\right) + C$$

(iv) Let, $I=\int \frac{dx}{x+\sqrt{x-1}}$

Put, $x=t^2+1$

$\Rightarrow dx=2t\,dt$

$\therefore I=\int \frac{2t}{t^2+t+1}dt$

$=\int \frac{2t+1}{t^2+t+1}-\int \frac{1}{t^2+t+1}dt$

$=\log(t^2+t+1)-\int \frac{1}{\left(t+\frac{1}{2}\right)^2+\left(\frac{\sqrt{3}}{2}\right)^2}dt$

$=\log(t^2+t+1)-\frac{2}{\sqrt{3}}\tan^{-1}\left(\frac{2t+1}{\sqrt{3}}\right)+C$

$=\log(x+\sqrt{x-1})-\frac{2}{\sqrt{3}}\tan^{-1}\left(\frac{2\sqrt{x-1}+1}{\sqrt{3}}\right)+C$

19 (*d*) We have,

$I=\int \frac{1}{(\sin x+4)(\sin x-1)}dx$

$=\frac{1}{5}\int \frac{(\sin x+4)-(\sin x-1)}{(\sin x+4)(\sin x-1)}dx$

$=\frac{1}{5}\int \frac{1}{\sin x-1}dx-\frac{1}{5}\int \frac{1}{\sin x+4}dx$

$=\frac{1}{5}\int \frac{\sec^2\frac{x}{2}}{2\tan\frac{x}{2}-1-\tan^2\frac{x}{2}}dx$

$-\frac{1}{5}\int \frac{\sec^2\frac{x}{2}}{2\tan\frac{x}{2}+4+4\tan^2\frac{x}{2}}dx$

Put, $\tan\frac{x}{2}=t$

$\Rightarrow \sec^2\frac{x}{2}dx=2\,dt$

$\therefore \quad I=\frac{1}{5}\int \frac{2\,dt}{2t-1-t^2}$

$-\frac{1}{5}\int \frac{2\,dt}{[2t+4(1+t^2)]}$

$\therefore \quad I=-\frac{2}{5}\int \frac{dt}{t^2-2t+1}-\frac{1}{10}\int \frac{dt}{t^2+\frac{1}{2}t+1}$

$=\frac{-2}{5}\int \frac{1}{(t-1)^2}dt$

$-\frac{1}{10}\int \frac{dt}{\left(t+\frac{1}{4}\right)^2+\left(\frac{\sqrt{15}}{4}\right)^2}$

$=\frac{2}{5}\cdot\frac{1}{t-1}-\frac{2}{5\sqrt{15}}\tan^{-1}\left(\frac{4t+1}{\sqrt{15}}\right)+C$

$=\frac{2}{5}\frac{1}{\tan\frac{x}{2}-1}$

$-\frac{2}{5\sqrt{15}}\tan^{-1}\left(\frac{4\tan\frac{x}{2}+1}{\sqrt{15}}\right)+C$ ...(i)

But, given that

$I=A\frac{1}{\left(\tan\frac{x}{2}-1\right)}+B\tan^{-1}[f(x)]+C$ ...(ii)

From Eqs. (i) and (ii), we get

$A=\frac{2}{5}, B=\frac{-2}{5\sqrt{15}}$

and $\quad f(x)=\frac{4\tan\left(\frac{x}{2}\right)+1}{\sqrt{15}}$

20 (*c*) We have,

$J=\int \frac{e^{3x}}{1+e^{2x}+e^{4x}}dx$

[by dividing numerator and denominator with e^{-4x}]

$\therefore J-I=\int \frac{e^{3x}-e^{x}}{1+e^{2x}+e^{4x}}dx$

$=\int \frac{u^2-1}{1+u^2+u^4}du$ [put $u=e^x$]

$=\int \frac{1-\frac{1}{u^2}}{1+\frac{1}{u^2}+u^2}du$

$=\int \frac{1-\frac{1}{u^2}}{\left(u+\frac{1}{u}\right)^2-1}du$

Put, $\quad u+\frac{1}{u}=t$

$\Rightarrow \left(1-\frac{1}{u^2}\right)du=dt$

$\therefore \quad J-I=\int \frac{dt}{t^2-1}$

$=\frac{1}{2}\log\left|\frac{t-1}{t+1}\right|+C$

$=\frac{1}{2}\log\left|\frac{u^2-u+1}{u^2+u+1}\right|+C$

$=\frac{1}{2}\log\left|\frac{e^{2x}-e^{x}+1}{e^{2x}+e^{x}+1}\right|+C$

Integration by Partial Fractions

1 (*b*) The following table indicates the types of simpler partial fractions that are to be associated with various kind of rational functions.

Form of the rational function	Form of the partial fraction
$\frac{px+q}{(x-a)(x-b)}$, $a\neq b$	$\frac{A}{x-a}+\frac{B}{x-b}$
$\frac{px+q}{(x-a)^2}$	$\frac{A}{x-a}+\frac{B}{(x-a)^2}$
$\frac{px^2+qx+r}{(x-a)(x-b)(x-c)}$	$\frac{A}{(x-a)}+\frac{B}{(x-b)}+\frac{C}{(x-b)}$
$\frac{px^2+qx+r}{(x-a)^2\,(x-b)}$	$\frac{A}{(x-a)}+\frac{B}{(x-a)^2}+\frac{C}{(x-b)}$
$\frac{px^2+qx+r}{(x-a)(x^2+bx+c)}$	$\frac{A}{x-a}+\frac{Bx+C}{x^2+bx+c}$
Where, x^2+bx+c cannot be factorised further.	

In the above table, *A*, *B* and *C* are real numbers to be determined suitably.

2 (*b*) $\int \frac{1}{x^2-9}dx=\int \frac{1}{x^2-3^2}dx$

$=\int \frac{1}{(x+3)(x-3)}dx$

Let $\quad \frac{1}{(x+3)(x-3)}=\frac{A}{(x+3)}+\frac{B}{(x-3)}$

$$1 = A(x-3) + B(x+3)$$

$$\Rightarrow \quad 1 = x(A+B) + (-3A+3B)$$

On equating the coefficients of x and constant term on both sides, we get

$$A+B=0 \text{ and } -3A+3B=1$$

On solving, we get

$$A = -\frac{1}{6} \text{ and } B = \frac{1}{6}$$

$$\therefore \int \frac{1}{(x+3)(x-3)} dx = \int \frac{(-1)}{6(x+3)} dx + \int \frac{1}{6(x-3)} dx$$

$$= -\frac{1}{6}\log|x+3| + \frac{1}{6}\log|x-3| + C$$

$$= \frac{1}{6}\log\left|\frac{x-3}{x+3}\right| + C$$

$$\left[\because \log b - \log a = \log\frac{b}{a}\right]$$

Alternatively apply this formula,

$$\int \frac{1}{x^2-a^2} dx = \frac{1}{2a}\log\left|\frac{x-a}{x+a}\right| + C$$

3 (c)

A. $\int \frac{x}{(x+1)(x+2)} dx.$

Let $\frac{x}{(x+1)(x+2)} = \frac{A}{(x+1)} + \frac{B}{(x+2)}$

$$\Rightarrow \frac{x}{(x+1)(x+2)} = \frac{A(x+2)+B(x+1)}{(x+1)(x+2)}$$

$$\Rightarrow x = Ax + 2A + Bx + B$$

$$\Rightarrow x = x(A+B) + 2A + B$$

On equating the coefficients of x and constant term on both sides, we get

$$A + B = 1 \quad \text{...(i)}$$

and $\quad 2A + B = 0 \quad$ ...(ii)

On subtracting Eq. (ii) form Eq.(i) we get

$$-A = 1 \Rightarrow A = -1$$

Now, on putting the value of A in Eq.(i), we get

$$-1 + B = 1 \Rightarrow B = 2$$

$$\therefore \int \frac{x}{(x+1)(x+2)} dx = \int \frac{(-1)}{x+1} dx + \int \frac{2}{x+2} dx$$

$$= -\log(x+1) + 2\log(x+2) + C$$

$$= -\log(x+1) + \log(x+2)^2 + C$$

$$= \log\left|\frac{(x+2)^2}{x+1}\right| + C$$

$$\left[\because \log b - \log a = \log\frac{b}{a}\right]$$

B. Let $= \frac{2x}{x^2+3x+2}$

$$= \frac{2x}{x^2+2x+x+2}$$

$$= \frac{2x}{x(x+2)+1(x+2)}$$

$$= \frac{2x}{(x+2)(x+1)}$$

Let $\frac{2x}{(x+2)(x+1)} = \frac{A}{(x+2)} + \frac{B}{(x+1)}$

$$\Rightarrow \frac{2x}{(x+2)(x+1)} = \frac{A(x+1)+B(x+2)}{(x+2)(x+1)}$$

$$\Rightarrow 2x = Ax + A + Bx + 2B$$

$$\Rightarrow 2x = x(A+B) + (A+2B)$$

On comparing the coefficients of x and constant term on both sides, we get

$$A + B = 2 \quad \text{... (i)}$$

and $\quad A + 2B = 0 \quad$ ...(ii)

On subtracting Eq. (ii) form Eq. (i), we get $-B = 2$

$$\Rightarrow \quad B = -2$$

On putting the value of B in Eq. (i), we get

$$A - 2 = 2$$

$$\Rightarrow \quad A = 4$$

$$\therefore \int \frac{2x}{(x+2)(x+1)} dx = \int \frac{A}{(x+2)} dx + \int \frac{B}{(x+1)} dx$$

$$= \int \frac{4}{(x+2)} dx + \int \frac{(-2)}{(x+1)} dx$$

$$= 4\log|x+2| - 2\log|x+1| + C$$

C. Let

$$\frac{3x-1}{(x-1)(x-2)(x-3)} = \frac{A}{(x-1)} + \frac{B}{(x-2)} + \frac{C}{(x-3)}$$

$$\Rightarrow \frac{3x-1}{(x-1)(x-2)(x-3)} = \frac{A(x-2)(x-3)+B(x-1)(x-3)+C(x-1)(x-2)}{(x-1)(x-2)(x-3)}$$

$$\Rightarrow 3x - 1 = A[x^2-5x+6] + B[x^2-4x+3] + C[x^2-3x+2]$$

$$\Rightarrow 3x - 1 = x^2(A+B+C) + x(-5A-4B-3C) + (6A+3B+2C)$$

On equating the coefficients of x^2, x and constant term on both sides, we get

$$A + B + C = 0 \quad \text{...(i)}$$

$$-5A - 4B - 3C = 3 \quad \text{...(ii)}$$

and $\quad 6A + 3B + 2C = -1 \quad$ ...(iii)

From Eq. (i), we get

$$A = -(B+C)$$

On putting the value of A in Eqs. (ii) and (iii), we get

$$-5\{-(B+C)\} - 4B - 3C = 3$$

$$\Rightarrow \quad 5B + 5C - 4B - 3C = 3$$

$$\Rightarrow \quad B + 2C = 3 \quad \text{...(iv)}$$

and $\quad 6\{-(B+C)\} + 3B + 2C = -1$

$$\Rightarrow \quad -6B - 6C + 3B + 2C = -1$$

$$\Rightarrow \quad -3B - 4C = -1 \quad \text{...(v)}$$

On solving Eqs. (iv) and (v), we get

$$\Rightarrow \quad C = 4$$

On putting the value of C in Eq. (iv), we get $B + 2 \times 4 = 3$

$$\Rightarrow \quad B = -5$$

Putting the value of B and C in Eq. (i), we get

$$A + (-5) + 4 = 0 \Rightarrow A = 1$$

$\therefore A = 1, B = -5, C = 4$

Now, $\int \frac{3x-1}{(x-1)(x-2)(x-3)} dx$

$= \int \left(\frac{A}{(x-1)} + \frac{B}{(x-2)} + \frac{C}{(x-3)} \right) dx$

$= \int \frac{1}{(x-1)} dx + \int \frac{(-5)}{(x-2)} dx + \int \frac{4}{(x-3)} dx$

$= \log|x-1| - 5\log|x-2| + 4\log|x-3| + C$

$\left[\because \int \frac{1}{x} dx = \log x \right]$

D. $\int \frac{x}{(x-1)(x-2)(x-3)} dx$

Let $\frac{x}{(x-1)(x-2)(x-3)} = \frac{A}{(x-1)} + \frac{B}{(x-2)} + \frac{C}{(x-3)}$

$= \frac{x}{(x-1)(x-2)(x-3)}$

$= \frac{A(x-2)(x-3) + B(x-1)(x-3) + C(x-1)(x-2)}{(x-1)(x-2)(x-3)}$

$\Rightarrow x = A[x^2 - 2x - 3x + 6] + B[x^2 - 4x + 3] + C[x^2 - x - 2x + 2]$

$\Rightarrow x = x^2(A + B + C) + x(-5A - 4B - 3C) + (6A + 3B + 2C)$

On comparing the coefficients of x^2, x and constant term on both sides, we get

$A + B + C = 0$

$\Rightarrow A = -(B + C)$ ...(i)

$-5A - 4B - 3C = 1$ ...(ii)

and $6A + 3B + 2C = 0$ ...(iii)

On putting the value of A in Eqs. (ii) and (iii), we get

$-5\{-(B + C)\} - 4B - 3C = 1$

$\Rightarrow 5B + 5C - 4B - 3C = 1$

$\Rightarrow B + 2C = 1$ ...(iv)

and $6\{-(B + C)\} + 3B + 2C = 0$

$\Rightarrow -3B - 4C = 0$ ...(v)

Multiplying by 3 in Eq. (iv) and then adding in Eq. (v), we get

$C = \frac{3}{2}$

On putting the value of C in Eq. (iv), we get $B + 2 \times \frac{3}{2} = 1$

$\Rightarrow B = -2.$

Now, put the values of B and C in Eq. (i), we get

$A - 2 + \frac{3}{2} = 0$

$\Rightarrow A = \frac{4-3}{2} = \frac{1}{2}$

$\therefore A = \frac{1}{2}$

$B = -2$ and $C = \frac{3}{2}$

Now, $\int \frac{x}{(x-1)(x-2)(x-3)} dx$

$= \int \frac{A}{(x-1)} dx + \int \frac{B}{(x-2)} dx + \int \frac{C}{(x-3)} dx$

$= \frac{1}{2} \int \frac{1}{(x-1)} dx - 2 \int \frac{1}{(x-2)} dx + \frac{3}{2} \int \frac{1}{(x-3)} dx$

$= \frac{1}{2} \log|x-1| - 2\log|x-2| + \frac{3}{2} \log|x-3| + C$

4 (*d*)

I. Let $I = \int \frac{1-x^2}{x(1-2x)} dx.$

Here, degree of numerator is equal to degree of denominator, so divide the numerator by denominator.

Thus, $\frac{1-x^2}{x(1-2x)} = \frac{x^2-1}{2x^2-x}$

$= \frac{1}{2} + \frac{\frac{1}{2}x - 1}{2x^2 - x}$

$\therefore I = \int \frac{1}{2} dx + \int \frac{\frac{1}{2}x - 1}{(2x^2 - x)} dx$

$\Rightarrow I = I_1 + I_2$ ...(i)

where, $I_1 = \int \frac{1}{2} dx$

and $I_2 = \int \frac{\frac{1}{2}x - 1}{(2x^2 - x)} dx$

Now, $I_1 = \int \frac{1}{2} dx$

$= \frac{1}{2}x + C_1$

and $I_2 = \int \frac{\frac{1}{2}x - 1}{2x^2 - x} dx$

Let $\frac{\frac{1}{2}x - 1}{(2x^2 - x)} = \frac{A}{x} + \frac{B}{(2x-1)}$

$\Rightarrow = \frac{\frac{1}{2}x - 1}{(2x^2 - x)}$

$= \frac{A(2x-1) + Bx}{x(2x-1)}$

$\Rightarrow \frac{1}{2}x - 1 = 2Ax - A + Bx$

$\Rightarrow \frac{1}{2}x - 1 = x(2A + B) - A$

On comparing the coefficient of x and constant term on both sides, we get

$2A + B = \frac{1}{2}$ ...(i)

and $-A = -1 \Rightarrow A = 1$ ...(ii)

From Eq. (i), $2 \times 1 + B = \frac{1}{2}$

$\Rightarrow B = \frac{1}{2} - 2 = \frac{-3}{2}$

$\therefore I_2 = \int \left[\frac{1}{x} - \frac{3}{2(2x-1)} \right] dx$

$= \int \frac{1}{x} dx - \frac{3}{2} \int \frac{1}{2x-1} dx$

$\Rightarrow I_2 = \log x - \frac{3}{2} \frac{\log|2x-1|}{2} + C_2$

On putting the values of I_1 and I_2 in Eq (i), we get

$I = \frac{1}{2}x + \log x - \frac{3}{4}\log|2x-1| + C$

$[\because C_1 + C_2 = C]$

II. $\int \frac{x}{(x^2+1)(x-1)}dx$

First, we resolve the given integrand into partial fractions.

Let $\frac{x}{(x^2+1)(x-1)}$

$$= \frac{A}{x-1} + \frac{Bx+C}{x^2+1} \quad \text{...(i)}$$

$$\Rightarrow x = A(x^2+1) + (Bx+C)(x-1) \quad \text{...(ii)}$$

Substituting $x=1$ and 0 in Eq. (ii), we get

$$1 = A(2) \text{ and } 0 = A - C$$

$$\Rightarrow A = \frac{1}{2} \text{ and } C = A = \frac{1}{2}$$

On equating the coefficient of x^2 on the both sides in Eq. (ii), we get

$$0 = A + B \Rightarrow B = -A = -\frac{1}{2}$$

$$\therefore \int \frac{x}{(x^2+1)(x-1)}dx$$

$$= \int \left\{ \frac{\frac{1}{2}}{x-1} + \frac{\left(-\frac{1}{2}x + \frac{1}{2}\right)}{x^2+1} \right\} dx$$

$$= \frac{1}{2}\int \frac{1}{x-1}dx + \frac{1}{2}\int \frac{(-x+1)}{x^2+1}dx$$

$$= \frac{1}{2}\int \frac{1}{x-1}dx - \frac{1}{2}\int \frac{x}{x^2+1}dx + \frac{1}{2}\int \frac{1}{x^2+1}dx$$

$$= \frac{1}{2}\log|x-1| - \frac{1}{4}I_1 + \frac{1}{2}\tan^{-1}x + C_1 \quad \text{....(iii)}$$

where, $I_1 = \int \frac{2x}{x^2+1}dx.$

Let $(x^2+1) = t$

$$\Rightarrow 2x\,dx = dt$$

$$\therefore I_1 = \int \frac{dt}{t} = \log|t| + C_2$$

$$= \log|x^2+1| + C_2$$

On putting these values in Eq. (iii), we get

$$\int \frac{x}{(x^2+1)(x-1)}dx$$

$$= \frac{1}{2}\log|x-1| - \frac{1}{4}\log|x^2+1|$$

$$+ \frac{1}{2}\tan^{-1}x + C \quad [\text{here, } C = C_1 + C_2]$$

5 (c)

(i) $\frac{x}{(x-1)^2(x+2)} = \frac{A}{x-1} + \frac{B}{(x-1)^2} + \frac{C}{x+2}$ ...(i)

$$\Rightarrow x = A(x-1)(x+2) + B(x+2) + C(x-1)^2 \quad \text{...(ii)}$$

On substituting $x=1$, and -2 respectively in Eq. (ii), we get

$$1 = B(1+2) \Rightarrow B = \frac{1}{3}$$

and $-2 = C(-2-1)^2$

and $C = \frac{-2}{9}$

On equating the coefficient of x^2 on both sides in Eq. (ii), we get

$$0 = A + C$$

$$\Rightarrow A = -C = \frac{2}{9}$$

$$\therefore \int \frac{x}{(x-1)^2(x+2)}dx$$

$$= \int \left\{ \frac{\frac{2}{9}}{x-1} + \frac{\frac{1}{3}}{(x-1)^2} + \frac{\left(-\frac{2}{9}\right)}{x+2} \right\} dx \quad [\text{from Eq. (i)}]$$

$$\Rightarrow \int \frac{x}{(x-1)^2(x+2)}dx$$

$$= \frac{2}{9}\int \frac{1}{x-1}dx + \frac{1}{3}\int \frac{1}{(x-1)^2}dx - \frac{2}{9}\int \frac{1}{x+2}dx$$

$$= \frac{2}{9}\log|x-1| + \frac{1}{3}\frac{(x-1)^{-2+1}}{(-2+1)} - \frac{2}{9}\log|x+2| + C$$

$$= \frac{2}{9}\log\left|\frac{x-1}{x+2}\right| - \frac{1}{3}\left(\frac{1}{x-1}\right) + C$$

$$\left[\because \log b - \log a = \log\left(\frac{b}{a}\right)\right]$$

(ii) $\int \frac{3x+5}{x^3-x^2-x+1}dx$

$$= \int \frac{3x+5}{(x^2-1)(x-1)}dx$$

$$= \int \frac{3x+5}{(x-1)(x+1)(x-1)}dx$$

$$= \int \frac{3x+5}{(x-1)^2(x+1)}dx$$

Let $\frac{3x+5}{(x-1)^2(x+1)} = \frac{A}{x-1} + \frac{B}{(x-1)^2} + \frac{C}{x+1}$

$$\Rightarrow \frac{3x+5}{(x-1)^2(x+1)} = \frac{A(x-1)(x+1) + B(x+1) + C(x-1)^2}{(x-1)^2(x+1)}$$

$$\Rightarrow 3x+5 = A(x^2-1) + Bx + B + C(x^2+1-2x)$$

$$\Rightarrow 3x+5 = x^2(A+C) + x(B-2C) + (-A+B+C)$$

On comparing the coefficients of x^2, x and constant term on both sides, we get

$$A + C = 0 \Rightarrow A = -C \quad \text{...(i)}$$

$$B - 2C = 3 \quad \text{...(ii)}$$

and $-A + B + C = 5$ ...(iii)

On putting the value of A from Eq. (i) in Eq. (iii), we get

$$-(-C) + B + C = 5$$

$$\Rightarrow B + 2C = 5 \quad \text{...(iv)}$$

On adding Eq. (ii) and Eq. (iv), we get

$$2B = 8 \Rightarrow B = 4$$

On putting the value of B in Eq. (ii), we get $4 - 2C = 3$

$$\Rightarrow 1 = 2C \Rightarrow C = \frac{1}{2}$$

Also, $A = -C = -\frac{1}{2}$

$$\therefore \int \frac{3x+5}{(x-1)^2(x+1)}dx$$

$$= \int \left(\frac{-\frac{1}{2}}{x-1} + \frac{4}{(x-1)^2} + \frac{\frac{1}{2}}{x+1} \right) dx$$

$$= -\frac{1}{2}\int \frac{1}{x-1}dx + 4\int \frac{1}{(x-1)^2}dx + \frac{1}{2}\int \frac{1}{x+1}dx$$

$$= -\frac{1}{2}\log|x-1| + 4\frac{(x-1)^{-2+1}}{(-2+1)} + \frac{1}{2}\log|x+1| + C$$

$$= \frac{1}{2}\log\left|\frac{x+1}{x-1}\right| - \frac{4}{x-1} + C$$

$$\left[\because \log b - \log a = \log\left(\frac{b}{a}\right)\right]$$

(iii) $\int \frac{2x-3}{(x^2-1)(2x+3)}dx$

$$= \int \frac{2x-3}{(x-1)(x+1)(2x+3)}dx$$

Let $\frac{2x-3}{(x-1)(x+1)(2x+3)} = \frac{A}{(x-1)} + \frac{B}{(x+1)} + \frac{C}{(2x+3)}$

$$\Rightarrow \frac{2x-3}{(x-1)(x+1)(2x+3)} = \frac{A(2x+3)(x+1) + B(x-1)(2x+3) + C(x-1)(x+1)}{(x-1)(x+1)(2x+3)}$$

$\Rightarrow 2x-3 = A(2x^2+3x+2x+3) + B(2x^2-2x+3x-3) + C(x^2-1)$

$\Rightarrow 2x-3 = x^2(2A+2B+C) + x(5A+B) + (3A-3B-C)$

On comparing the coefficients of x^2, x and constant term on both sides, we get

$2A + 2B + C = 0$ ...(i)

$5A + B = 2$

$\Rightarrow B = 2 - 5A$ ...(ii)

and $3A - 3B - C = -3$ ...(iii)

On putting the value of B in Eqs. (i) and (iii), we get

$2A + 2(2-5A) + C = 0$

$\Rightarrow 2A + 4 - 10A + C = 0$

$\Rightarrow -8A + C = -4$ ...(iv)

and $3A - 3(2-5A) - C = -3$

$\Rightarrow 3A - 6 + 15A - C = -3$

$\Rightarrow 18A - C = 3$ ...(v)

On adding Eqs. (iv) and (v), we get

$10A = -1$

$\Rightarrow A = \frac{-1}{10}$

On putting the value of A in Eq. (ii), we get

$B = 2 - 5\left(-\frac{1}{10}\right)$

$\Rightarrow B = 2 + \frac{1}{2} = \frac{5}{2}$

On putting the values of A and B in Eq. (i), we get

$2\left(-\frac{1}{10}\right) + 2\left(\frac{5}{2}\right) + C = 0$

$\Rightarrow -\frac{1}{5} + 5 + C = 0$

$\Rightarrow C = -\frac{24}{5}$

$\therefore A = -\frac{1}{10}, B = \frac{5}{2}$

and $C = -\frac{24}{5}$

$$\therefore \int \frac{2x-3}{(x^2-1)(2x+3)}dx = \int \frac{(-1)}{10(x-1)}dx + \frac{5}{2}\int \frac{1}{x+1}dx - \frac{24}{5}\int \frac{1}{2x+3}dx$$

$$= -\frac{1}{10}\log|x-1| + \frac{5}{2}\log|x+1| - \frac{24}{5}\frac{\log|2x+3|}{2} + C$$

$$= \frac{5}{2}\log|x+1| - \frac{1}{10}\log|x-1| - \frac{12}{5}\log|2x+3| + C$$

(iv) $\int \frac{5x}{(x+1)(x^2-4)}dx$

$$= \int \frac{5x}{(x+1)(x+2)(x-2)}dx$$

Let

$\frac{5x}{(x+1)(x-2)(x+2)} = \frac{A}{(x+1)} + \frac{B}{(x+2)} + \frac{C}{(x-2)}$ ...(i)

$$= \frac{A(x+2)(x-2) + B(x+1)(x-2) + C(x+1)(x+2)}{(x+1)(x+2)(x-2)}$$

$\Rightarrow 5x = A(x^2-4) + B(x^2+x-2x-2) + C(x^2+x+2x+2)$

$\Rightarrow 5x = x^2(A+B+C) + (-B+3C) + (-4A-2B+2C)$

On comparing the coefficients of x^2, x and constant term on both sides, we get

$A + B + C = 0$ ...(ii)

$-B + 3C = 5$ ...(iii)

and $-4A - 2B + 2C = 0$ ...(iv)

Multiply by 4 in Eq. (ii) and then adding with Eq. (iv), we get

$2(B + 3C) = 0$ ...(v)

On adding Eqs. (iii) and (v), we get $C = \frac{5}{6}$

On putting the value of C in Eq. (v), we get $B = -\frac{5}{2}$

On putting the values of B and C in Eq. (ii), we get $A = \frac{5}{3}$

$$\therefore \int \frac{5x}{(x+1)(x-2)(x+2)}dx = \int \frac{5}{3(x+1)}dx - \int \frac{5}{2(x+2)}dx + \int \frac{5}{6(x-2)}dx$$

$$= \frac{5}{3}\int \frac{1}{(x+1)}dx - \frac{5}{2}\int \frac{1}{(x+2)}dx + \frac{5}{6}\int \frac{1}{(x-2)}dx$$

$$= \frac{5}{3}\log|x+1| - \frac{5}{2}\log|x+2| + \frac{5}{6}\log|x-2| + C$$

6 (d)

A. $\int \frac{x^3+x+1}{x^2-1}dx$

$= \int x\,dx + \int \frac{2x+1}{x^2-1}dx$

$\left[\because \frac{x^3+x+1}{x^2-1} = x + \frac{2x+1}{x^2-1}\right]$

$= \int x\,dx + \int \frac{2x+1}{(x+1)(x-1)}dx$

Let $\frac{2x+1}{(x+1)(x-1)} = \frac{A}{(x+1)} + \frac{B}{(x-1)}$

$\Rightarrow \frac{2x+1}{(x+1)(x-1)} = \frac{A(x-1)+B(x+1)}{(x+1)(x-1)}$

$\Rightarrow 2x+1 = x(A+B) - A + B$

On comparing the coefficients of x and constant term on both sides, we get

$A+B=2$ and $-A+B=1$

On adding above equations, we get

$2B = 3 \Rightarrow B = \frac{3}{2}$ and then $A = \frac{1}{2}$

$\therefore \int \frac{x^2+x+1}{x^2-1}dx = \int x\,dx + \int \frac{A}{(x+1)}dx + \int \frac{B}{(x-1)}dx$

$= \int x\,dx + \frac{1}{2}\int \frac{1}{(x+1)}dx + \frac{3}{2}\int \frac{1}{(x-1)}dx$

$= \frac{x^2}{2} + \frac{1}{2}\log|x+1| + \frac{3}{2}\log|x-1| + C$

B. Let $\frac{2}{(1-x)(1+x^2)} = \frac{A}{1-x} + \frac{Bx+C}{1+x^2}$

$\therefore \frac{2}{(1-x)(1+x^2)} = \frac{A(1+x^2)+(Bx+C)(1-x)}{(1-x)(1+x^2)}$

$\Rightarrow 2 = A + Ax^2 + Bx + C - Bx^2 - Cx$

$\Rightarrow 2 = x^2(A-B) + x(B-C) + (A+C)$

On comparing the coefficients of x^2, x and constant term on both sides, we get

$A - B = 0 \Rightarrow A = B$ ...(i)

$B - C = 0 \Rightarrow B = C$ ...(ii)

and $A + C = 2$ ...(iii)

From Eqs. (i) and (ii), we get $A = C$ put this value in Eq. (iii), we get $2A = 2 \Rightarrow A = 1$

Put the value of A in Eqs. (i) and (iii), we get $B = 1$ and $C = 1$

$\therefore \int \frac{2}{(1-x)(1+x^2)}dx$

$= \int\left\{\frac{1}{1-x} + \frac{x+1}{x^2+1}\right\}dx$

$= \int \frac{1}{1-x}dx + \frac{1}{2}\int \frac{2x}{x^2+1}dx + \int \frac{1}{x^2+1}dx$

$= -\log|1-x| + \frac{1}{2}\log(1+x^2) + \tan^{-1}x + C$

(Let $x^2+1 = t \Rightarrow 2x\,dx = dt$

$\therefore \int \frac{2x}{x^2+1}dx = \int \frac{1}{t}dt = \log t$)

C. Let $\frac{3x-1}{(x+2)^2} = \frac{A}{(x+2)} + \frac{B}{(x+2)^2}$

$\Rightarrow 3x - 1 = A(x+2) + B$

On equating the coefficients of x and constant term on both sides, we get $A = 3$

and $2A + B = -1$

$\Rightarrow 2(3) + B = -1 \Rightarrow B = -7$

$\therefore \frac{3x-1}{(x+2)^2} = \frac{3}{(x+2)} - \frac{7}{(x+2)^2}$

$\therefore \int \frac{3x-1}{(x+2)^2} = 3\int \frac{1}{(x+2)}dx - 7\int \frac{1}{(x+2)^2}dx$

$= 3\log|x+2| - 7\left(\frac{-1}{x+2}\right) + C$

$= 3\log|x+2| + \frac{7}{x+2} + C$

D. $\int \frac{1}{(x^4-1)}dx$

$= \int \frac{1}{(x^2-1)(x^2+1)}dx$

$[\because a^2 - b^2 = (a+b)(a-b)]$

We have, $\int \frac{1}{(x^2-1)(x^2+1)}dx$

On putting $x^2 = t$, we get

$\frac{1}{(t-1)(t+1)} = \frac{A}{(t-1)} + \frac{B}{(t+1)}$

[by partial fraction] ...(i)

$\Rightarrow \frac{1}{(t-1)(t+1)} = \frac{A(t+1)+B(t-1)}{(t-1)(t+1)}$

$\Rightarrow 1 = At + A + Bt - B$

$\Rightarrow 1 = t(A+B) + (A-B)$

On comparing the coefficients of t and constant term on both sides, we get

$A + B = 0$ ...(ii)

$A - B = 1$ ...(iii)

On adding Eqs. (ii) and (iii), we get

$A = \frac{1}{2}$, and from Eq. (iii), $B = -\frac{1}{2}$

On putting the values of A and B in Eq. (i), we get

$\frac{1}{(t-1)(t+1)} = \frac{\frac{1}{2}}{t-1} + \frac{-\frac{1}{2}}{t+1}$

$\Rightarrow \frac{1}{(x^2-1)(x^2+1)} = \frac{1}{2} \times \frac{1}{x^2-1} - \frac{1}{2} \times \frac{1}{x^2+1}$

[on putting $t = x^2$]

$\therefore \int \frac{dx}{(x^2-1)(x^2+1)}$

$= -\frac{1}{2}\int \frac{1}{x^2+1}dx + \frac{1}{2}\int \frac{1}{x^2-1}dx$

$= -\frac{1}{2}\tan^{-1}x + \frac{1}{2}\cdot\frac{1}{2}\log\left|\frac{x-1}{x+1}\right| + C$

$= -\frac{1}{2}\tan^{-1}x + \frac{1}{4}\log\left|\frac{x-1}{x+1}\right| + C$

7 (c)

I. Let $I = \int \frac{1}{x(x^n+1)} dx$

$= \int \frac{x^{n-1}}{x^n(x^n+1)} dx$

Put $x^n = t$

$\Rightarrow \quad nx^{n-1}dx = dt$

$\Rightarrow \quad x^{n-1}dx = \frac{1}{n}dt$

$\therefore \quad I = \int \frac{x^{n-1}}{x^n(x^n+1)} dx$

$= \frac{1}{n}\int \frac{1}{t(t+1)} dt \quad$ ...(i)

Now, $\frac{1}{t(t+1)} = \frac{A}{t} + \frac{B}{(t+1)}$

$\Rightarrow \quad 1 = A(1+t) + Bt$ ...(ii)

On substituting $t = 0, -1$ in Eq. (ii), we get $A = 1$ and $B = -1$

$\therefore \frac{1}{t(t+1)} = \frac{1}{t} - \frac{1}{(t+1)}$

$\therefore \quad I = \frac{1}{n}\int \left(\frac{1}{t} - \frac{1}{(t+1)}\right)dt$

[from Eq. (i)]

$= \frac{1}{n}[\log|t| - \log|t+1|] + C$

$= \frac{1}{n}[\log|x^n|$

$- \log|x^n+1|] + C$ [put $t = x^n$]

$= \frac{1}{n}\log\left|\frac{x^n}{x^n+1}\right| + C$

II. Let $I = \int \frac{\cos x}{(1-\sin x)(2-\sin x)} dx$

Put $\quad \sin x = t$

$\Rightarrow \quad \cos x = \frac{dt}{dx}$

$\Rightarrow dx = \frac{dt}{\cos x}$

$\therefore \quad I = \int \frac{\cos x}{(1-t)(2-t)} \frac{dt}{\cos x}$

$= \int \frac{1}{(1-t)(2-t)} dt$

$= \int \left[\frac{A}{1-t} + \frac{B}{2-t}\right] dt \quad$ ...(i)

$\therefore \frac{1}{(1-t)(2-t)}$

$= \frac{A(2-t) + B(1-t)}{(1-t)(2-t)}$

$\Rightarrow \quad 1 = 2A - tA + B - Bt$

$\Rightarrow \quad 1 = 1(2A + B) + t(-A - B)$

On comparing the coefficients of t and constant term on both sides, we get

$2A + B = 1$ and $-A - B = 0$

On adding above equations, we get

$A = 1$ and then $B = -1$

$\therefore \quad I = \int \left(\frac{1}{1-t} - \frac{1}{2-t}\right) dt$

[from Eq. (i)]

$= \int \frac{1}{(1-t)} dt - \int \frac{1}{(2-t)} dt$

$= \frac{\log|1-t|}{(-1)} - \frac{\log|2-t|}{(-1)} + C$

$= \log\left|\frac{2-t}{1-t}\right| + C$

$= \log\left|\frac{2-\sin x}{1-\sin x}\right| + C$

[put $t = \sin x$]

8 (d)

(i) Here, the degree of numerator and denominator are 4 , so we convert it into simple form by putting $x^2 = t$.

$\frac{(x^2+1)(x^2+2)}{(x^2+3)(x^2+4)} = \frac{(t+1)(t+2)}{(t+3)(t+4)}$

$= \frac{t^2+3t+2}{t^2+7t+12}$

Since, degree of numerator and denominator is same, so it can be written as

$1 - \frac{4t+10}{t^2+7t+12}$

Now, $\int \frac{(x^2+1)(x^2+2)}{(x^2+3)(x^2+4)} dx$

$= \int 1dx - \int \frac{(4x^2+10)}{x^4+7x^2+12} dx$

$= \int 1dx - \int \frac{4t+10}{(t+3)(t+4)} dx$

....(i)

Let

$\frac{4t+10}{(t+4)(t+3)} = \frac{A}{(t+4)} + \frac{B}{(t+3)}$

$\Rightarrow \quad \frac{4t+10}{(t+3)(t+4)}$

$= \frac{A(t+3) + B(t+4)}{(t+4)(t+3)}$

$\Rightarrow \quad 4t + 10 = At + 3A + Bt + 4B$

$\Rightarrow 4t + 10 = t(A + B) + (3A + 4B)$

On comparing the coefficients of t and constant term on both sides, we get

$A + B = 4$

$\Rightarrow \quad 3A + 3B = 12 \quad$ ...(ii)

and $\quad 3A + 4B = 10 \quad$ ...(iii)

On subtracting Eq. (iii) from Eq. (ii), we get

$-B = 2 \Rightarrow B = -2$

and $\quad A = 6$

$\therefore \quad \frac{4t+10}{(t+4)(t+3)}$

$= \frac{6}{t+4} - \frac{2}{t+3}$

On putting this value in Eq. (i) we get

$\int \frac{(x^2+1)(x^2+2)}{(x^2+3)(x^2+4)} dx$

$= \int 1dx - \int \left(\frac{6}{(x^2+4)} - \frac{2}{(x^2+3)}\right)$

dx (put $t = x^2$)

$\Rightarrow \int \frac{(x^2+1)(x^2+2)}{(x^2+3)(x^2+4)} dx = \int 1dx$

$- \int \left(\frac{6}{x^2+2^2} - \frac{2}{x^2+(\sqrt{3})^2}\right) dx$

$\Rightarrow \int \frac{(x^2+1)(x^2+2)}{(x^2+3)(x^2+4)} dx$

$= x - 6\left(\frac{1}{2}\tan^{-1}\frac{x}{2}\right)$

$+ 2\left(\frac{1}{\sqrt{3}}\tan^{-1}\frac{x}{\sqrt{3}}\right) + C$

$\left[\because \int \frac{1}{a^2+x^2} dx = \frac{1}{a}\tan^{-1}\frac{x}{a}\right]$

$= x - 3\tan^{-1}\frac{x}{2}$

$+ \frac{2}{\sqrt{3}}\tan^{-1}\frac{x}{\sqrt{3}} + C$

(ii) Let $I=\int \frac{2x}{(x^2+1)(x^2+3)}dx$

Put $x^2=t$

$\Rightarrow 2x=\frac{dt}{dx} \Rightarrow dx=\frac{dt}{2x}$

$\therefore I=\int \frac{2x}{(t+1)(t+3)}\frac{dt}{2x}$

$=\int \frac{1}{(t+1)(t+3)}dt$

Let $\frac{1}{(t+1)(t+3)}=\frac{A}{t+1}+\frac{B}{t+3}$

$\Rightarrow \frac{1}{(t+1)(t+3)}$

$=\frac{At+3A+Bt+B}{(t+1)(t+3)}$

$\Rightarrow 1=(A+B)t+(3A+B)$

On comparing the coefficients of t and constant terms on both sides, we get

$A+B=0$ ...(i)

and $3A+B=1$ ...(ii)

On subtracting Eq. (ii) from Eq. (i), we get

$2A=1 \Rightarrow A=\frac{1}{2}$

On putting the value of A in Eq. (i), we get $B=-\frac{1}{2}$

$\therefore I=\frac{1}{2}\int \frac{1}{t+1}dt$

$-\frac{1}{2}\int \frac{1}{t+3}dt=\frac{1}{2}\log|t+1|$

$-\frac{1}{2}\log|t+3|+C$

$=\frac{1}{2}\log\left|\frac{t+1}{t+3}\right|+C$

$=\frac{1}{2}\log\left|\frac{x^2+1}{x^2+3}\right|+C$

[put $t=x^2$]

(iii) Let $I=\int \frac{1}{x(x^4-1)}dx$

$=\int \frac{x^3}{x^4(x^4-1)}dx$

$=\frac{1}{4}\int \frac{4x^3}{x^4(x^4-1)}dx$

Put $x^4=t$

$\Rightarrow 4x^3=\frac{dt}{dx}$

$\Rightarrow dx=\frac{dt}{4x^3}$

$\therefore I=\frac{1}{4}\int \frac{4x^3}{t(t-1)}\frac{dt}{4x^3}$

$=\frac{1}{4}\int \frac{dt}{t(t-1)}$

Let $\frac{1}{t(t-1)}=\frac{A}{t}+\frac{B}{(t-1)}$

$\Rightarrow 1=A(t-1)+Bt$ ...(i)

On substituting $t=0$ and 1 in Eq. (i), we get

$A=-1$ and $B=1$

$\therefore \frac{1}{t(t-1)}=\frac{-1}{t}+\frac{1}{t-1}$

$\therefore I=\frac{1}{4}\int\left(-\frac{1}{t}+\frac{1}{t-1}\right)dt$

$=\frac{1}{4}\{-\log|t|+\log|t-1|\}+C$

$=\frac{1}{4}\log\left|\frac{t-1}{t}\right|+C$

$=\frac{1}{4}\log\left|\frac{x^4-1}{x^4}\right|+C$

[put $t=x^4$]

(iv) Let $I=\int \frac{1}{e^x-1}dx$

On multiplying numerator and denominator by e^{-x}, we get

$I=\int \frac{e^{-x}}{1-e^{-x}}dx$

Put $1-e^{-x}=t$

$\Rightarrow -e^{-x}(-1)=\frac{dt}{dx}$

$\Rightarrow dx=\frac{dt}{e^{-x}}$

$\Rightarrow e^{-x}dx=dt$

$\therefore I=\int \frac{dt}{t}=\log|t|+C$

$=\log|1-e^{-x}|+C$

$=\log\left|\frac{e^x-1}{e^x}\right|+C$

9 (*b*) Let $\frac{x}{(x-1)(x-2)}$

$=\frac{A}{(x-1)}+\frac{B}{(x-2)}$

$\Rightarrow x=A(x-2)+B(x-1)$ ...(i)

On substituting $x=1$ and 2 in Eq. (i), we get $A=-1$ and $B=2$

$\therefore \frac{x}{(x-1)(x-2)}=-\frac{1}{(x-1)}+\frac{2}{(x-2)}$

$\therefore \int \frac{x}{(x-1)(x-2)}dx$

$=\int \frac{(-1)}{x-1}dx+\int \frac{2}{x-2}dx$

$=-\log|x-1|+2\log|x-2|+C$

$=-\log|x-1|+\log|x-2|^2+C$

$=\log\left|\frac{(x-2)^2}{x-1}\right|+C$

$\left[\because \log b-\log a=\log\frac{b}{a}\right]$

10 (*a*) Let $\frac{1}{x(x^2+1)}=\frac{A}{x}+\frac{Bx+C}{x^2+1}$

$\Rightarrow 1=A(x^2+1)+(Bx+C)x$

On equating the coefficients of x^2, x and constant term on both sides, we get

$A+B=0, C=0$ and $A=1$

On solving these equations, we get

$A=1, B=-1$ and $C=0$

$\therefore \frac{1}{x(x^2+1)}=\frac{1}{x}+\frac{-x}{x^2+1}$

$\therefore \int \frac{1}{x(x^2+1)}dx=\int\left\{\frac{1}{x}-\frac{x}{x^2+1}dx\right\}$

$=\log|x|-\frac{1}{2}\log(x^2+1)+C$

$\left[x^2+1=t \Rightarrow 2xdx=dt \Rightarrow x\,dx=\frac{dt}{2},\right.$

$\therefore \int \frac{x}{x^2+1}dx=\int \frac{1}{t}\frac{dt}{2}=\frac{1}{2}\log t$

$\left.=\frac{1}{2}\log(x^2+1)\right]$

11 (*a*)

I. Put $x^2=t$ then $2x\,dx=dt$.

Now $I=\int \frac{x^3dx}{x^4+3x^2+2}$

$=\frac{1}{2}\int \frac{t\,dt}{t^2+3t+2}$

Consider

$$\frac{t}{t^2+3t+2}=\frac{A}{t+1}+\frac{B}{t+2}$$

$\Rightarrow\ t=A(t+2)+B(t+1)$

$\Rightarrow\ t=(A+B)t+2A+B$

Comparing coefficient, we get

$A=-1$ and $B=2$

Then $I=\frac{1}{2}\left[2\int\frac{dt}{t+2}-\int\frac{dt}{t+1}\right]$

$=\frac{1}{2}[2\log|t+2|-\log|t+1|]+C$

$=\frac{1}{2}[2\log|x^2+2|-\log|x^2+1|]+C$

$=\log|x^2+2|-\frac{1}{2}\log|x^2+1|+C$

$=\log\left|\frac{x^2+2}{\sqrt{x^2+1}}\right|+C$

II. Let $x^2=t$. Then

$$\frac{x^2}{x^4+x^2-2}=\frac{t}{t^2+t-2}$$

$$=\frac{t}{(t+2)(t-1)}=\frac{A}{t+2}+\frac{B}{t-1}$$

So $t=A(t-1)+B(t+2)$

Comparing coefficient, we get

$A=\frac{2}{3}, B=\frac{1}{3}$.

So $\frac{x^2}{x^4+x^2-2}=\frac{2}{3}\frac{1}{x^2+2}+\frac{1}{3}\frac{1}{x^2-1}$

Therefore,

$$\int\frac{x^2}{x^4+x^2-2}dx=\frac{2}{3}\int\frac{1}{x^2+2}dx+\frac{1}{3}\int\frac{dx}{x^2-1}$$

$$=\frac{2}{3}\frac{1}{\sqrt{2}}\tan^{-1}\frac{x}{\sqrt{2}}+\frac{1}{6}\log\left|\frac{x-1}{x+1}\right|+C$$

12 (c) Let, $I=\int\frac{dx}{(x+2)(x^2+1)}$

By partial fraction method, write

$$\frac{1}{(x+2)(x^2+1)}=\frac{A}{x+2}+\frac{Bx+C}{x^2+1}$$

$$=\frac{Ax^2+A+Bx^2+Cx+2Bx+2C}{(x+2)(x^2+1)}$$

$$=\frac{x^2(A+B)+x(C+2B)+(A+2C)}{(x+2)(x^2+1)}$$

On comparing the coefficients of x^2, x and the constant on both sides, we get

$A+B=0\Rightarrow A=-B$

$2B+C=0$

$A+2C=1$

$-2A+C=0$

$2A+4C=2$

$5C=2$

$\Rightarrow\quad C=\frac{2}{5}$

$\therefore\ A=1-2C=1-2\times\frac{2}{5}=1-\frac{4}{5}=\frac{1}{5}$

$\Rightarrow\quad B=-A=-\frac{1}{5}$

$$\therefore\ I=\frac{1}{5}\int\frac{1}{x+2}dx+\frac{-1}{5}\int\frac{x}{x^2+1}dx+\frac{2}{5}\int\frac{dx}{x^2+1}$$

$$=\frac{1}{5}\log|x+2|+\frac{-1}{10}\log|x^2+1|+\frac{2}{5}\tan^{-1}x+C$$

On comparing with

$a\log|1+x^2|+b\tan^{-1}x+\frac{1}{5}\log|x+2|+C$, we get

$a=\frac{-1}{10}$ and $b=\frac{2}{5}$

13 (d) We have,

$$I=\int\frac{2x^2+3}{(x^2-1)(x^2+4)}dx$$

Let, $x^2=t$

$$\frac{2t+3}{(t-1)(t+4)}=\frac{A}{t-1}+\frac{B}{t+4}\quad\text{...(i)}$$

[put $x^2=t$]

$\Rightarrow\ 2t+3=A(t+4)+B(t-1)$

$\Rightarrow\ 2t+3=(A+B)t+4A-B$

On comparing the coefficients of t and constant term on both the sides, we get

$A+B=2$ and $4A-B=3$

On solving the above equations, we get

$A=1$ and $B=1$

On putting the values of A and B in Eq. (i), we get

$$\frac{2t+3}{(t-1)(t+4)}=\frac{1}{t-1}+\frac{1}{t+4}$$

$$\therefore\ I=\int\frac{dt}{x^2-1}+\int\frac{dt}{x^2+4}$$

[put $t=x^2$]

$$=\frac{1}{2}\log\left|\frac{x-1}{x+1}\right|+\frac{1}{2}\tan^{-1}\frac{x}{2}+C$$

But, $I=a\log\left|\frac{x-1}{x+1}\right|+b\tan^{-1}\frac{x}{2}+C$

$\therefore\ a=\frac{1}{2}, b=\frac{1}{2}$

14 (a) We have,

$$I=\int\frac{\sin x}{\cos x(1+\cos x)}dx$$

Put, $\cos x=t$

$\Rightarrow\ -\sin x\,dx=dt$

$\therefore\quad I=\int\frac{-dt}{t(1+t)}$

Let, $\frac{-1}{t(t+1)}=\frac{A}{t}+\frac{B}{t+1}$ ...(i)

$\Rightarrow\ -1=A(t+1)+Bt$

$\Rightarrow\ -1=(A+B)t+A$

On comparing the coefficient of t term and constant term on both the sides, we get

$A+B=0$ and $A=-1$

$\Rightarrow\ B=1$ and $A=-1$

On putting the values of A and B in Eq (i), we get

$$\frac{-1}{t(t+1)}=\frac{-1}{t}+\frac{1}{t+1}$$

$$\therefore\ I=-1\int\left[\frac{1}{t}-\frac{1}{t+1}\right]dt$$

$=-\log|t|+\log|t+1|+C$

$=\log\left|\frac{t+1}{t}\right|+C$

$=\log\left|\frac{1+\cos x}{\cos x}\right|+C=f(x)+C$ [given]

$\therefore\ f(x)=\log\left|\frac{1+\cos x}{\cos x}\right|$

15 (*b*) We have,

$$I=\int \frac{e^x}{(2+e^x)(e^x+1)}dx$$

Put $e^x=t$

$\Rightarrow e^x dx = dt$

$$\therefore \quad I=\int \frac{dt}{(2+t)(t+1)}$$

$$=\int\left[\frac{1}{1+t}-\frac{1}{t+2}\right]dt$$

$$\left[\begin{array}{l}\because \frac{1}{(1+t)(t+2)}=\frac{A}{t+1}+\frac{B}{t+2}\\ \Rightarrow \quad 1=(A+B)t+2A+B\\ \Rightarrow A+B=0 \text{ and } 2A+B=1\\ \Rightarrow \quad A=1 \text{ and } B=-1\end{array}\right]$$

$$=\log|1+t|-\log|t+2|+C$$

$$=\log\left|\frac{1+t}{t+2}\right|+C$$

$$=\log\left(\frac{1+e^x}{2+e^x}\right)+C$$

16 (*d*)

I. We have,

$$I=\int x\sqrt{\frac{1-x^2}{1+x^2}}dx$$

$$I=\int \frac{x(1-x^2)}{\sqrt{1-x^4}}dx$$

[Multiplying numerator and denominator by $(1-x^2)^{1/2}$]

$$I=\int\frac{(x-x^3)}{\sqrt{1-x^4}}dx$$

$$I=\int\frac{x}{\sqrt{1-x^4}}dx-\int\frac{x^3}{\sqrt{1-x^4}}dx$$

$$I=I_1-I_2$$

So, $I_1=\int\frac{x}{\sqrt{1-x^4}}dx$

Put $x^2=t$

$\Rightarrow 2x\,dx=dt$

$$\therefore \quad I_1=\frac{1}{2}\int\frac{dt}{\sqrt{1-t^2}}$$

$$=\frac{1}{2}\sin^{-1}t$$

$$=\frac{1}{2}\sin^{-1}(x^2)$$

Also, $I_2=\int\frac{x^3}{\sqrt{1-x^4}}dx$

Put $1-x^4=t$

$\Rightarrow -4x^3dx=dt$

$$\therefore \quad I_2=\frac{-1}{4}\int\frac{dt}{\sqrt{t}}=\frac{-1}{2}\sqrt{t}+C$$

$$=\frac{-1}{2}\sqrt{1-x^4}+C$$

$$\Rightarrow I=\frac{1}{2}[\sin^{-1}(x)^2+\sqrt{1-x^4}]+C$$

II. We have,

$$I=\int\frac{a\,dx}{b+ce^x}dx$$

$$I=\frac{ae^xdx}{be^x+ce^{2x}}$$

[Multiplying numerator and denominator by e^x]

Now, put $e^x=t$

$\Rightarrow \quad e^xdx=dt$

$$\therefore \quad I=a\int\frac{dt}{bt+ct^2}$$

$$I=a\int\frac{dt}{t(b+ct)} \quad \text{...(i)}$$

Let, $\frac{1}{t(bt+ct)}=\frac{A}{t}+\frac{B}{(b+ct)}$ ...(ii)

$\Rightarrow \quad 1=Ab+(Ac+B)t$

$\Rightarrow \quad Ab=1$

and $Ac+B=0$

$\Rightarrow \quad A=\frac{1}{b}$

and $\quad B=-\frac{c}{b}$

On putting the values of A and B in Eq (ii), we get

$$\frac{1}{t(b+ct)}=\frac{1}{b}\left[\frac{1}{t}-\frac{c\times 1}{b+ct}\right]$$

$$\therefore \quad I=a\int-\frac{1}{b}\left\{\frac{c}{ct+b}-\frac{1}{t}\right\}dt$$

$$=\frac{a}{b}\log\left|\frac{t}{b+ct}\right|+C$$

$$=\frac{a}{b}\log\left|\frac{e^x}{b+ce^x}\right|+C$$

17 (*a*) Here, we have

$$I=\int\frac{dx}{\sin x+\sin 2x}$$

$$I=\int\frac{dx}{\sin x+2\sin x\cos x}$$

$$I=\int\frac{\sin x\,dx}{\sin^2 x(1+2\cos x)}$$

Now, put $\cos x=t$

$\Rightarrow \quad -\sin x\,dx=dt$

$$\therefore \quad I=-\int\frac{dt}{(1-t)(1+t)(1+2t)} \quad \text{...(i)}$$

$$\left[\begin{array}{l}\because \sin^2 x=1-\cos^2 x\\ =(1-\cos x)(1+\cos x)\end{array}\right]$$

Let, $\frac{-1}{(1-t)(1+t)(1+2t)}=\frac{A}{1-t}+\frac{B}{1+t}+\frac{C}{1+2t}$

$\Rightarrow -1=A(1+t)(1+2t)+B(1-t)(1+2t)+C(1-t)(1+t)$ ...(ii)

On putting, $t=1$, we get

$$A=-\frac{1}{6}$$

On putting, $t=-1$, we get

$$B=\frac{1}{2}$$

On putting, $t=0$, we get

$$A+B+C=-1\Rightarrow C=\frac{-4}{3}$$

Putting the values of A, B and C in Eq (i), we get

$$\frac{-1}{(1-t)(1+t)(1+2t)}=\frac{-1}{6(1-t)}+\frac{1}{2}\frac{1}{(1+t)}-\frac{4}{3}\frac{1}{(1+2t)}$$

$$\therefore I=-\int\frac{1}{6(1-t)}dt+\int\frac{1}{2(1+t)}dt-\frac{4}{3}\int\frac{1}{1+2t}dt$$

$$=\frac{1}{6}\log(1-t)+\frac{1}{2}\log(1+t)-\frac{2}{3}\log(1+2t)+C$$

$$=\frac{1}{6}\log(1-\cos x)+\frac{1}{2}\log(1+\cos x)-\frac{2}{3}\log(1+2\cos x)+C$$

Integration by Parts

1 (*a*) Put $f(x) = x$ (first function) and $g(x) = \cos x$ (second function).

Then, integration by parts gives

$$\int x\cos x\,dx = x\int \cos x\,dx - \int\left[\frac{d}{dx}(x)\int \cos x\,dx\right]dx$$

$$= x\sin x - \int \sin x\,dx$$

$$= x\sin x + \cos x + C$$

Suppose, we take $f(x) = \cos x$ and $g(x) = x$.

Then $\int x\cos x\,dx = \cos x\int x\,dx - \int\left[\frac{d}{dx}(\cos x)\int x\,dx\right]dx$

$$= (\cos x)\frac{x^2}{2} + \int \sin x\frac{x^2}{2}\,dx$$

Thus, it shows that the integral $\int x\cos x\,dx$ is reduced to the comparatively more complicated integral having more power of x. Therefore, the proper choice of the first function and the second function is significant.

2 (*c*)

(i) To start with, we are unable to guess a function whose derivative is $\log x$. We take $\log x$ as the first function and the constant function 1 as the second function. Then, the integral of the second function is x.

Hence,

$$\int(\log x.1)\,dx = \log x\int 1\,dx - \int\left[\frac{d}{dx}(\log x)\int 1\,dx\right]dx$$

$$= (\log x)\cdot x - \int\frac{1}{x}x\,dx$$

$$= x\log x - x + C$$

(ii) Take first function as x and second function as e^x. The integral of the second function is e^x.

Therefore,

$$\int x e^x\,dx = x e^x - \int 1\cdot e^x\,dx$$

$$= xe^x - e^x + C$$

(iii) Let first function be $\sin^{-1}x$ and second function be $\frac{x}{\sqrt{1-x^2}}$.

First we find the integral of the second function, i.e. $\int\frac{x\,dx}{\sqrt{1-x^2}}$.

Put $t = 1 - x^2$.

Then, $dt = -2x\,dx$

Therefore, $\int\frac{x\,dx}{\sqrt{1-x^2}}$

$$= -\frac{1}{2}\int\frac{dt}{\sqrt{t}}$$

$$= -\sqrt{t} = -\sqrt{1-x^2}$$

Hence, $\int\frac{x\sin^{-1}x}{\sqrt{1-x^2}}\,dx$

$$= (\sin^{-1}x)(-\sqrt{1-x^2}) - \int\frac{1}{\sqrt{1-x^2}}(-\sqrt{1-x^2})\,dx$$

$$= -\sqrt{1-x^2}\sin^{-1}x + x + C.$$

$$= x - \sqrt{1-x^2}\sin^{-1}x + C$$

Alternatively, this integral can also be worked out by making substitution $\sin^{-1}x = \theta$ and then integrating by parts.

(iv) Take e^x as the first function and $\sin x$ as second function. Then, integrating by parts, we have

$$I = \int e^x\sin x\,dx = e^x(-\cos x) + \int e^x\cos x\,dx$$

$$= -e^x\cos x + I_1 \text{ (say)} \quad \text{...(i)}$$

Taking e^x and $\cos x$ as the first and second functions, respectively, in I_1, we get

$$I_1 = e^x\sin x - \int e^x\sin x\,dx$$

Substituting the value of I_1 in (i), we get

$$I = -e^x\cos x + e^x\sin x - I$$

or $2I = e^x(\sin x - \cos x)$

Hence, $I = \int e^x\sin x\,dx$

$$= \frac{e^x}{2}(\sin x - \cos x) + C$$

Alternate Method

Above integral can also be determined by taking $\sin x$ as the first function and e^x the second function.

3 (*b*)

I. We have

$$I = \int e^x\left(\tan^{-1}x + \frac{1}{1+x^2}\right)dx$$

Consider $f(x) = \tan^{-1}x$, then

$$f'(x) = \frac{1}{1+x^2}$$

Thus, the given integrand is of the form $e^x[f(x) + f'(x)]$.

Therefore,

$$I = \int e^x\left(\tan^{-1}x + \frac{1}{1+x^2}\right)dx$$

$$= e^x\tan^{-1}x + C$$

II. We have $I = \int\frac{(x^2+1)e^x}{(x+1)^2}\,dx$

$$= \int e^x\left[\frac{x^2-1+1+1}{(x+1)^2}\right]dx$$

$$= \int e^x\left[\frac{x^2-1}{(x+1)^2} + \frac{2}{(x+1)^2}\right]dx$$

$$= \int e^x\left[\frac{x-1}{x+1} + \frac{2}{(x+1)^2}\right]dx$$

Consider $f(x) = \frac{x-1}{x+1}$, then

$$f'(x) = \frac{2}{(x+1)^2}$$

Thus, the given integrand is of the form $e^x[f(x + f'(x)]$.

Therefore,

$$\int\frac{x^2+1}{(x+1)^2}e^x\,dx = \frac{x-1}{x+1}e^x + C.$$

4 (*d*) A. Let $I = \int \sin x\cdot x\,dx$

On taking x as first function and $\sin x$ as second function and integrating by parts, we get

$$I = x\int \sin x\,dx - \int\left[\frac{d}{dx}(x)\int \sin x\,dx\right]dx$$

$$= -x\cos x + \int 1\cdot\cos x\,dx$$

$$\Rightarrow I = -x\cos x + \sin x + C$$

B. Let $I = \int x\sin 3x\,dx$

On taking x as first function and $\sin 3x$ as second function and integrating by parts, we get

$$I = x\int \sin 3x\,dx - \int\left[\frac{d}{dx}(x)\int \sin 3x\,dx\right]dx$$

$= \frac{-x\cos 3x}{3} + \int \frac{\cos 3x}{3} dx$

$\left[\because \int \sin ax\, dx = \frac{-\cos ax}{a}\right]$

$\Rightarrow I = \frac{-x\cos 3x}{3} + \frac{1}{9}\sin 3x + C$

C. Let $I = \int x \log x dx$

On taking log x as first function and x as second function and integrating by parts, we get

[∵ log function comes before algebraic function in ILATE]

$I = \log x \int x\, dx - \int \left[\frac{d}{dx}(\log x) \int x\, dx\right] dx$

$= \frac{x^2 \log x}{2} - \frac{1}{2}\int \frac{1}{x} x^2\, dx$

$= \frac{x^2 \log x}{2} - \frac{1}{2}\int x dx$

$\Rightarrow I = \frac{x^2 \log x}{2} - \frac{1}{4}x^2$

D. On taking log 2x as first function and x as second function and integrating by parts, we get

[∵ log function comes before algebraic function in ILATE]

$I = \int x \log 2x\, dx = \log 2x \int x\, dx - \int \left[\frac{d}{dx}(\log 2x) \int x\, dx\right] dx$

$= \frac{x^2}{2}\log 2x - \int \left[\frac{1}{2x} \times 2 \times \frac{x^2}{2}\, dx\right]$

$= \frac{x^2 \log 2x}{2} - \frac{1}{2}\int x\, dx$

$\Rightarrow I = \frac{x^2}{2}\log 2x - \frac{1}{4}x^2 + C$

5 (c) Let $I = \int x^2 e^x dx$

On taking x^2 as first function and e^x as second function and integrating by parts, we get

$I = x^2 \int e^x dx - \int \left[\frac{d}{dx}(x^2) \int e^x dx\right] dx$

$= x^2 e^x - \int [2xe^x]\, dx$

Again, integrating by parts, we get

$I = x^2 e^x - \left\{2x \int e^x dx - 2\int \left[\frac{d}{dx}(x) \int e^x dx\right] dx\right\}$

$= x^2 e^x - 2xe^x + 2\int e^x dx$

$= x^2 e^x - 2xe^x + 2e^x + C$

$\Rightarrow I = e^x (x^2 - 2x + 2) + C$

6 (d)

I. On taking log x as first function and x^2 as second function and integrating by parts, we get

(∵ log function comes before algebraic function in ILATE)

$I = \int x^2 \log x\, dx = \log x \int x^2 dx - \int \left[\frac{d}{dx}(\log x) \int x^2 dx\right] dx$

$= \frac{x^3}{3}\log x - \int \left[\frac{1}{x} \cdot \frac{x^3}{3}\right] dx$

$= \frac{x^3}{3}\log x - \frac{1}{3}\int x^2 dx$

$= \frac{x^3}{3}\log x - \frac{x^3}{9} + C$

II. Let $I = \int x \tan^{-1} x\, dx$

On taking $\tan^{-1} x$ as first function and x as second function and integrating by parts, we get

[∵ Inverse functions comes before algebraic functions in ILATE]

$\therefore \quad I = \tan^{-1} x \int x\, dx - \int \left[\frac{d}{dx}(\tan^{-1} x) \int x\, dx\right] dx$

$= \tan^{-1} x \cdot \frac{x^2}{2} - \int \left[\frac{1}{1+x^2} \cdot \frac{x^2}{2}\right] dx$

$= \frac{x^2}{2} \cdot \tan^{-1} x - \frac{1}{2}\int \left[\frac{x^2 + 1 - 1}{1+x^2}\right] dx$

[add and subtract 1 in numerator of second term]

$= \frac{x^2}{2} \cdot \tan^{-1} x - \frac{1}{2}\left[\int \frac{1+x^2}{1+x^2} dx - \int \frac{1}{1+x^2} dx\right]$

$= \frac{x^2}{2}\tan^{-1} x - \frac{1}{2}\left[\int 1\, dx - \int \frac{1}{1+x^2} dx\right]$

$= \frac{x^2}{2} \cdot \tan^{-1} x - \frac{1}{2}x + \frac{1}{2}\tan^{-1} x + C$

$= \left(\frac{x^2+1}{2}\right)\tan^{-1} x - \frac{1}{2}x + C$

7 (b)

(i) Let $I = \int x \cos^{-1} x\, dx$

Put $\cos^{-1} x = t$

$\Rightarrow \quad x = \cos t$

$\Rightarrow \quad dx = -\sin t\, dt$

$\therefore \quad I = \int x \cos^{-1} x\, dx$

$= -\int t \cos t \cdot \sin t\, dt$

$= -\frac{1}{2}\int t \cdot 2 \sin t \cos t\, dt$

$= -\frac{1}{2}\int t \cdot \sin 2t\, dt$

$[\because 2 \sin x \cos x = \sin 2x]$

On taking t as first function and $\sin 2t$ as second function and integrating by parts, we get

$I = -\frac{1}{2}\left[t \int \sin 2t\, dt - \int \left\{\frac{d}{dt}(t) \cdot \int \sin 2t\, dt\right\} dt\right]$

$= -\frac{1}{2}\left[t\frac{(-\cos 2t)}{2} + \int 1 \cdot \frac{\cos 2t}{2} dt\right]$

$= \frac{1}{4}t \cos 2t - \frac{1}{4}\int \cos 2t\, dt$

$= \frac{1}{4}t \cos 2t - \frac{1}{4}\frac{\sin 2t}{2} + C$

$= \frac{1}{4}t \cos 2t - \frac{1}{8}\sin 2t + C$

$= \frac{1}{4}t(2\cos^2 t - 1) - \frac{1}{8} \cdot 2 \sin t \cos t + C$

$[\because \cos 2x = 2\cos^2 x - 1 \text{ and } \sin 2x = 2 \sin x \cos x]$

$= \frac{1}{4}t(2\cos^2 t - 1) - \frac{1}{4}(1 - \cos^2 t)^{1/2} \cos t + C$

$[\because \sin^2 x + \cos^2 x = 1 \Rightarrow \sin x = \sqrt{1 - \cos^2 x}]$

$\therefore \int x \cos^{-1} x\, dx = \frac{1}{4}\cos^{-1} x (2x^2 - 1) - \frac{1}{4}(1 - x^2)^{1/2} x + C$

[put $\cos^{-1} x = t$ and $\cos t = x$]

$= \frac{1}{4}(2x^2 - 1)\cos^{-1} x - \frac{1}{4}x\sqrt{1 - x^2} + C$

Note *Here, if we take $\cos^{-1} x$ as first function, then the integration becomes complicated. So, we convert inverse trigonometric function into trigonometric function to avoid the complication.*

(ii) Let $I = \int (\sin^{-1} x)^2 dx$

Put $\sin^{-1} x = \theta$

$\Rightarrow x = \sin\theta$

$\Rightarrow dx = \cos\theta\, d\theta$

$\therefore I = \int (\sin^{-1} x)^2 dx = \int \theta^2 \cos\theta\, d\theta$

On taking θ^2 as first function and $\cos\theta$ as second function and integrating by parts, we get

$$= \theta^2 \int \cos\theta\, d\theta - \int \left[\frac{d}{d\theta}(\theta^2) \int \cos\theta\, d\theta\right] d\theta$$

$$= \theta^2 \sin\theta - \int 2\theta \sin\theta\, d\theta$$

Again, integrating by parts, we get

$$I = \theta^2 \sin\theta - 2[\theta(-\cos\theta) - \int 1(-\cos\theta)\, d\theta] + C$$

$$= \theta^2 \sin\theta + 2\theta\cos\theta - 2\int \cos\theta\, d\theta + C$$

$$= \theta^2 \sin\theta + 2\theta\cos\theta - 2\sin\theta + C$$

$$= (\sin^{-1} x)^2\, x + 2\sin^{-1} x \sqrt{1-\sin^2\theta} - 2x + C$$

[put $\theta = \sin^{-1} x$ and $\sin\theta = x$]

$$= x(\sin^{-1} x)^2 + 2\sqrt{1-x^2}\, \sin^{-1} x - 2x + C$$

(iii) Let $I = \int \frac{x \cos^{-1} x}{\sqrt{1-x^2}} dx$

$$\Rightarrow I = \int \cos^{-1} x \cdot \frac{x}{\sqrt{1-x^2}} dx$$

Consider $\cos^{-1} x$ as first function and $\frac{x}{\sqrt{1-x^2}}$ as second function and integrating by parts, we get

$$I = \cos^{-1} x \int \frac{x}{\sqrt{1-x^2}} dx - \int \left[\frac{d}{dx}(\cos^{-1} x) \int \frac{x}{\sqrt{1-x^2}} dx\right] dx$$

Let $1 - x^2 = t^2 \Rightarrow -2x = 2t\frac{dt}{dx}$

$$\Rightarrow dx = -\frac{t}{x} dt$$

$$\therefore I = \cos^{-1} x \int \frac{x}{t}\left(\frac{-t}{x}\right) dt - \int \left[\frac{d}{dx}(\cos^{-1} x) \int \frac{x}{t}\left(\frac{-t}{x}\right) dt\right] dx$$

$$= \cos^{-1} x(-t) - \int \left[\frac{(-1)}{\sqrt{1-x^2}}(-t)\, dt\right] dx$$

$$= -\sqrt{1-x^2} \cdot \cos^{-1} x - \int \left[\frac{\sqrt{1-x^2}}{\sqrt{1-x^2}}\right] dx$$

$[\because 1 - x^2 = t^2 \Rightarrow t = \sqrt{1-x^2}]$

$$= -\sqrt{1-x^2} \cdot \cos^{-1} x - \int 1\, dx$$

$$= -\sqrt{1-x^2} \cdot \cos^{-1} x - x + C$$

(iv) Let $I = \int 1 \cdot \tan^{-1} x\, dx$

$$\Rightarrow I = \tan^{-1} x \int 1\, dx - \int \left[\frac{d}{dx}(\tan^{-1} x) \int 1\, dx\right] dx$$

$$= x \tan^{-1} x - \int \frac{1}{1+x^2} \cdot x\, dx$$

Let $1 + x^2 = t \Rightarrow 2x = \frac{dt}{dx}$

$$\Rightarrow dx = \frac{dt}{2x}$$

$$\therefore I = x\tan^{-1} x - \int \frac{x}{t} \cdot \frac{dt}{2x}$$

$$= x\tan^{-1} x - \frac{1}{2}\int \frac{1}{t} dt$$

$$= x\tan^{-1} x - \frac{1}{2}\log|t| + C$$

$$= x\tan^{-1} x - \frac{1}{2}\log|1 + x^2| + C$$

8 (b) Let $I = \int x \sec^2 x\, dx$.

On taking x as first function and $\sec^2 x$ as second function and integrating by parts, we get

$$I = x\int \sec^2 x\, dx - \int \left[\frac{d}{dx}(x) \int \sec^2 x\, dx\right] dx$$

$$= x\tan x - \int \tan x\, dx = x\tan x - \log|\sec x| + C$$

$$\Rightarrow I = x\tan x + \log|\cos x| + C$$

$\left[\log|\sec x| = \log\left|\frac{1}{\cos x}\right| = \log 1 - \log|\cos x| = -\log|\cos x|\right]$

$[\because \log 1 = 0]$

9 (a) I. Let $I = \int x(\log x)^2 dx$

On taking $(\log x)^2$ as first function and x as second function and integrating by parts, we get

$$I = (\log x)^2 \int x\, dx - \int \left[\frac{d}{dx}(\log x)^2 \int x\, dx\right] dx$$

$$= (\log x)^2 \cdot \frac{x^2}{2} - \int \left[\frac{2\log x}{x} \cdot \frac{x^2}{2}\right] dx$$

$$= \frac{x^2}{2}(\log x)^2 - \int x \log x\, dx$$

Again, integrating by parts, we get

$$I = \frac{x^2}{2}(\log x)^2 - \left[\log x \int x\, dx - \int \left\{\left(\frac{d}{dx}\log x\right) \int x\, dx\right\} dx\right] + C$$

$$= \frac{x^2}{2}(\log x)^2 - \left[\frac{x^2}{2}\log x - \int \frac{1}{x} \cdot \frac{x^2}{2} dx\right] + C$$

$$= \frac{x^2}{2}(\log x)^2 - \frac{x^2}{2}\log x + \frac{1}{2}\int x\, dx + C$$

$$= \frac{x^2}{2}(\log x)^2 - \frac{x^2}{2}\log x + \frac{x^2}{4} + C$$

II. Let $I = \int (x^2 + 1)\log x\, dx$

On taking $\log x$ as first function and $(x^2 + 1)$ as second function and integrating by parts, we get

$$I = \log x \int (x^2 + 1)\, dx - \int \left[\frac{d}{dx}(\log x) \int (x^2 + 1)\, dx\right] dx$$

$$\Rightarrow I = \log x\left(\frac{x^3}{3} + x\right) - \int \frac{1}{x} \cdot \left(\frac{x^3}{3} + x\right) dx$$

$$\Rightarrow I = \left(\frac{x^3}{3} + x\right)\log x - \int \left(\frac{x^2}{3} + 1\right) dx$$

$$= \left(\frac{x^3}{3} + x\right)\log x - \frac{x^3}{9} - x + C$$

10 (a) Let $I = \int x \sin^{-1} x dx$

$$\Rightarrow I = \sin^{-1} x \frac{x^2}{2} - \int \frac{1}{\sqrt{1-x^2}} \cdot \frac{x^2}{2} dx$$

$$\Rightarrow I = \frac{x^2}{2} \sin^{-1} x + \frac{1}{2} \int \frac{-x^2}{\sqrt{1-x^2}} dx$$

$$= \frac{x^2}{2} \sin^{-1} x + \frac{1}{2} \int \frac{1-x^2-1}{\sqrt{1-x^2}} dx$$

$$= \frac{x^2}{2} \sin^{-1} x + \frac{1}{2} \left\{ \int \frac{1-x^2}{\sqrt{1-x^2}} dx - \int \frac{1}{\sqrt{1-x^2}} dx \right\}$$

$$\Rightarrow I = \frac{x^2}{2} \sin^{-1} x + \frac{1}{2} \left\{ \int \sqrt{1-x^2}\, dx - \int \frac{1}{\sqrt{1-x^2}} dx \right\}$$

$$= \frac{x^2}{2} \sin^{-1} x + \frac{1}{2} \left[\left\{ \frac{1}{2} x \sqrt{1-x^2} + \frac{1}{2} \sin^{-1} x \right\} - \sin^{-1} x \right] + C$$

$$\Rightarrow I = \frac{1}{2} x^2 \sin^{-1} x + \frac{1}{4} x \sqrt{1-x^2} - \frac{1}{4} \sin^{-1} x + C$$

11 (d) Let $I = \int \sin^{-1} \left(\frac{2x}{1+x^2} \right) dx$

On putting $x = \tan\theta$, we get

$$I = \int \sin^{-1} \left(\frac{2\tan\theta}{1+\tan^2\theta} \right) dx$$

$$= \int \sin^{-1} (\sin 2\theta)\, dx \quad \left[\because \sin 2\theta = \frac{2\tan\theta}{1+\tan^2\theta} \right]$$

$$= 2 \int \theta\, dx = 2 \int \tan^{-1} x\, dx \quad [\because x = \tan\theta \Rightarrow \theta = \tan^{-1} x]$$

$$= 2 \int \underset{\text{II}}{1} \cdot \underset{\text{I}}{\tan^{-1} x}\, dx$$

$$= 2 \tan^{-1} x \int 1 dx - 2 \int \left[\frac{d}{dx} \tan^{-1} x \int 1 dx \right] dx$$

[using integration by parts]

$$\Rightarrow I = 2 \tan^{-1} x \cdot x - 2 \int \left[\frac{1}{1+x^2} \cdot x \right] dx$$

Put $1 + x^2 = t$

$$\Rightarrow 2x = \frac{dt}{dx} \Rightarrow dx = \frac{dt}{2x}$$

$$\therefore I = 2x \tan^{-1} x - 2 \int \left[\frac{x}{t} \cdot \frac{dt}{2x} \right]$$

$$= 2x \tan^{-1} x - \int \frac{1}{t} dt = 2x \tan^{-1} x - \log|t| + C$$

$$\Rightarrow I = 2x \tan^{-1} x - \log|1+x^2| + C$$

12 (a)

(i) Let $I = \int \frac{xe^x}{(1+x)^2} dx$

$$= \int e^x \frac{(x+1)-1}{(1+x)^2} dx$$

$$= \int e^x \left[\frac{1}{(1+x)} - \frac{1}{(1+x)^2} \right] dx$$

Let $f(x) = \frac{1}{1+x}$

$$\Rightarrow f'(x) = -\frac{1}{(1+x)^2}$$

We know that

$$\int e^x (f(x) + f'(x))\, dx = e^x f(x)$$

$$\Rightarrow I = \int e^x \left\{ \frac{1}{1+x} - \frac{1}{(1+x)^2} \right\} dx$$

$$= \frac{e^x}{1+x} + C$$

(ii) $\int e^x \left(\frac{1}{1+\cos x} + \frac{\sin x}{1+\cos x} \right) dx$

$$= \int e^x \left(\frac{1}{2\cos^2 \frac{x}{2}} + \frac{2\sin\frac{x}{2}\cos\frac{x}{2}}{2\cos^2\frac{x}{2}} \right) dx$$

$[\because \cos 2x = 2\cos^2 x - 1$ and $\sin 2x = 2 \sin x \cos x]$

$$= \int e^x \left(\frac{\sec^2 \frac{x}{2}}{2} + \tan\frac{x}{2} \right) dx$$

$$= \int e^x \left(\tan\frac{x}{2} + \frac{1}{2}\sec^2 \frac{x}{2} \right) dx$$

Let $f(x) = \tan\frac{x}{2} \Rightarrow f'(x) = \frac{\sec^2 \frac{x}{2}}{2}$

$$\therefore \int e^x \left(\tan\frac{x}{2} + \frac{\sec^2\frac{x}{2}}{2} \right) dx = e^x \tan\frac{x}{2} + C$$

$[\because \int e^x [f(x) + f'(x)]\, dx = e^x f(x)]$

(iii) Let $I = \int \frac{x-3}{(x-1)^3} e^x dx$

$$= \int \frac{x-1-2}{(x-1)^3} e^x dx$$

$$= \int e^x \left(\frac{x-1}{(x-1)^3} - \frac{2}{(x-1)^3} \right) dx$$

$$= \int e^x \left(\frac{1}{(x-1)^2} - \frac{2}{(x-1)^3} \right) dx$$

Let $f(x) = \frac{1}{(x-1)^2}$

$$\Rightarrow f'(x) = \frac{-2}{(x-1)^3}$$

$$\therefore I = \frac{e^x}{(x-1)^2} + C$$

$[\because \int e^x (f(x) + f'(x))\, dx = e^x f(x)]$

(iv) Let $I = \int e^{2x} \sin x\, dx$

On taking $\sin x$ as first function and e^{2x} as second function and integrating by parts, we get

$$\int e^{2x} \sin x\, dx = \sin x \cdot \int e^{2x} dx - \int \left[\frac{d}{dx}(\sin x) \cdot \int e^{2x} dx \right] dx$$

$$= \sin x \cdot \frac{e^{2x}}{2} - \int \cos x \cdot \frac{e^{2x}}{2} dx$$

$$= \sin x \cdot \frac{e^{2x}}{2} - \frac{1}{2} \int e^{2x} \cos x dx$$

$$\Rightarrow \int e^{2x} \sin x\, dx = \sin x \cdot \frac{e^{2x}}{2} - \frac{1}{2} I_1 \quad \text{...(i)}$$

where, $I_1 = \int e^{2x} \cos x\, dx$

On taking $\cos x$ as first function and e^{2x} as second function and integrating by parts, we get

$$I_1 = \cos x \cdot \int e^{2x} dx - \int \left[\frac{d}{dx}(\cos x) \cdot \int e^{2x} dx \right] dx$$

$$= \cos x \cdot \frac{e^{2x}}{2} - \int (-\sin x) \cdot \frac{e^{2x}}{2} dx + C_1$$

$$= \frac{e^{2x} \cos x}{2} + \frac{1}{2} \int e^{2x} \sin x\, dx + C_1$$

Putting value of I_1 in Eq. (i), we get

$$\int e^{2x} \sin x dx = \frac{e^{2x} \sin x}{2} - \frac{1}{2} \left[\frac{e^{2x} \cos x}{2} + \frac{1}{2} \int e^{2x} \sin x dx + C_1 \right]$$

$$\Rightarrow \int e^{2x}\sin x\,dx = \frac{e^{2x}\sin x}{2} - \frac{e^{2x}\cos x}{4} - \frac{1}{4}\int e^{2x}\sin x\,dx - \frac{1}{2}C_1$$

$$\Rightarrow \int e^{2x}\sin x\,dx + \frac{1}{4}\int e^{2x}\sin x\,dx = \frac{e^{2x}\sin x}{2} - \frac{e^{2x}\cos x}{4} - \frac{1}{2}C_1$$

$$\Rightarrow \frac{5}{4}\int e^{2x}\sin x\,dx = \frac{e^{2x}\sin x}{2} - \frac{e^{2x}\cos x}{4} - \frac{1}{2}C_1$$

$$\Rightarrow \int e^{2x}\sin x\,dx = \frac{4}{5}\left[\frac{e^{2x}\sin x}{2} - \frac{e^{2x}\cos x}{4} - \frac{1}{2}C_1\right]$$

$$= \frac{2}{5}e^{2x}\sin x - \frac{1}{5}e^{2x}\cos x - \frac{2}{5}C_1$$

$$= \frac{2}{5}e^{2x}\sin x - \frac{1}{5}e^{2x}\cos x + C$$

where, $C = -\frac{2}{5}C_1$

$$= \frac{e^{2x}}{5}(2\sin x - \cos x) + C$$

13 (*d*)

I. Let $I = \int e^x(\sin x + \cos x)\,dx$

Let $f(x) = \sin x$

$\Rightarrow f'(x) = \cos x$

$$I = \int e^x[f(x) + f'(x)]\,dx$$

We know that,

$$\int e^x(f(x) + f'(x))\,dx = e^x f(x) + C$$

$\therefore \quad I = e^x \sin x + C$

II. $\int e^x\left(\frac{1}{x} - \frac{1}{x^2}\right)dx$

Let $\quad I = \int e^x\left(\frac{1}{x} - \frac{1}{x^2}\right)dx$

Let $f(x) = \frac{1}{x} \Rightarrow f'(x) = -\frac{1}{x^2}$

Here, given integral is of the form $\int e^x[f(x) + f'(x)]\,dx = e^x f(x) + C$

$\therefore \quad I = \frac{e^x}{x} + C$

14 (*a*) Let $I = \int x^2 e^{x^3}\,dx$

Put $\quad x^3 = t \Rightarrow 3x^2 = \frac{dt}{dx}$

$\Rightarrow \quad dx = \frac{dt}{3x^2}$

$\therefore \quad I = \frac{1}{3}\int e^t\,dt$

$\Rightarrow \quad I = \frac{1}{3}e^t + C = \frac{1}{3}e^{x^3} + C$

15 (*b*) Let $I = \int e^x \sec x(1 + \tan x)\,dx$

$\Rightarrow I = \int e^x \sec x\,dx + \int e^x \sec x \tan x\,dx$ ...(i)

Now, $\int e^x \sec x dx = \sec x \int e^x\,dx - \int\left[\frac{d}{dx}\sec x \int e^x\,dx\right]dx$

$= e^x \sec x - \int \sec x \tan x\, e^x\,dx$ ...(ii)

On putting the value from Eq. (ii) in Eq. (i), we get

$I = e^x \sec x - \int e^x \sec x \tan x\,dx + \int \sec x \tan x\, e^x\,dx + C$

$\Rightarrow \quad I = e^x \sec x + C$

16 (*a*) We have,

$$I = \int e^x(\cos x - \sin x)\,dx$$

Here, $\quad f(x) = \cos x$

$\quad f'(x) = -\sin x$

$\therefore$ By using $\int e^x[f(x) + f'(x)]\,dx = e^x f(x) + C$, we get

$I = e^x \cos x + C$

17 (*a*) Let, $I = \int \underset{\text{I}}{\tan^{-1}\sqrt{x}}\,\underset{\text{II}}{(1)}\,dx$

$$= \tan^{-1}\sqrt{x}\int 1dx - \left[\int \frac{d}{dx}(\tan^{-1}\sqrt{x})\int (1)\,dx\right]dx$$

$$= \tan^{-1}\sqrt{x}\cdot x - \int \frac{1}{1+x}\times\frac{1}{2\sqrt{x}}\cdot x\,dx$$

$$= x\tan^{-1}\sqrt{x} - \frac{1}{2}\int \frac{x}{(1+x)\sqrt{x}}\,dx$$

Put, $x = t^2 \Rightarrow dx = 2t\,dt$

$$I_1 = \frac{1}{2}\int \frac{x}{(1+x)\sqrt{x}}$$

$$\therefore \quad I_1 = \frac{1}{2}\int \frac{t^2\cdot 2t}{(1+t^2)\cdot t}\,dt$$

$$I_1 = \frac{t^2}{1+t^2}\,dt$$

$$= x\tan^{-1}\sqrt{x} - \int \frac{t^2+1-1}{1+t^2}\,dt$$

$$= x\tan^{-1}\sqrt{x} - \int\left(1 - \frac{1}{1+t^2}\right)dt$$

$$= x\tan^{-1}\sqrt{x} - t + \tan^{-1}t + C$$

$$= x\tan^{-1}\sqrt{x} - \sqrt{x} + \tan^{-1}\sqrt{x} + C$$

$$= (x+1)\tan^{-1}\sqrt{x} - \sqrt{x} + C$$

18 (*a*) Let, $I = \int e^x\left(\frac{1-x}{1+x^2}\right)^2 dx$

$$= \int e^x \frac{1 + x^2 - 2x}{(1+x^2)^2}\,dx$$

$$= \int e^x\left(\frac{1}{1+x^2} - \frac{2x}{(1+x^2)^2}\right)dx$$

$$= \frac{e^x}{1+x^2} + C$$

[Using $\int e^x[f(x) + f'(x)]\,dx = e^x f(x) + C$]

19 (*d*) Let $I = \int \frac{x + \sin x}{1 + \cos x}\,dx$

$$\int \frac{x}{2\cos^2 x/2}\,dx + \int \frac{2\sin x/2\cos x/2}{2\cos^2 x/2}\,dx$$

$$= \frac{1}{2}\int \underset{\text{I}}{x}\,\underset{\text{II}}{\sec^2\frac{x}{2}}\,dx + \int \tan\frac{x}{2}\,dx$$

$$= \frac{1}{2}\left[x\int \sec^2\frac{x}{2}\,dx - \int\left[\frac{d}{dx}(x)\int \sec^2\frac{x}{2}\,dx\right]dx\right] + \int \tan\frac{x}{2}\,dx$$

$$= \frac{1}{2}\left[x\tan\frac{x}{2}\cdot 2 - 2\int \tan\frac{x}{2}\,dx\right] + \int \tan\frac{x}{2}\,dx$$

$$= x\tan\frac{x}{2} - \int \tan\frac{x}{2}\,dx + \int \tan\frac{x}{2}\,dx$$

$$= x\tan\left(\frac{x}{2}\right) + C$$

20 (*c*)

I. Let $I = \int \frac{\sin^{-1}x}{(1-x^2)^{3/2}}\,dx$

$$= \int \frac{\sin^{-1}x}{(1-x^2)\sqrt{1-x^2}}$$

Put $\sin^{-1} x = t$

$\Rightarrow \frac{1}{\sqrt{1-x^2}} dx = dt$

$\therefore \quad I = \int \frac{t}{(1-\sin^2 t)} dt$

$I = \int \frac{t}{\cos^2 t} dt$

$I = \int \underset{\text{I}}{t} \underset{\text{II}}{\sec^2 t}\, dt$

$= t \int \sec^2 t\, dt - \int \left[\frac{d}{dt}(t) \int \sec^2 t\, dt\right] dt$

$= t \cdot \tan t - \int \tan t\, dt$

$= t \cdot \tan t + \log|\cos t| + C$

$= \sin^{-1} x \cdot \frac{x}{\sqrt{1-x^2}} + \log|\sqrt{1-x^2}| + C$

$\left[\because \tan t = \frac{\sin t}{\cos t} = \frac{\sin t}{\sqrt{1-\sin^2 t}} = \frac{x}{\sqrt{1-x^2}}\right]$

$= \frac{x \sin^{-1} x}{\sqrt{1-x^2}} + \log|\sqrt{1-x^2}| + C$

II. Let, $I = \int \frac{x \tan^{-1} x}{(1+x^2)^{3/2}} dx$

Put, $x = \tan\theta \Rightarrow dx = \sec^2\theta\, d\theta$

$\therefore \quad I = \int \frac{\tan\theta \tan^{-1}(\tan\theta)}{(1+\tan^2\theta)^{3/2}} \sec^2\theta\, d\theta$

$I = \int \frac{\theta \tan\theta \sec^2\theta}{\sec^3\theta} d\theta$

$I = \int \underset{\text{I}}{\theta} \underset{\text{II}}{\sin\theta}\, d\theta$

$I = \theta \int (\sin\theta)\, d\theta - \int \left[\frac{d}{d\theta}(\theta) \int (\sin\theta)\, d\theta\right] d\theta$

$I = \theta(-\cos\theta) - \int (-\cos\theta)\, d\theta$

$I = -\theta\cos\theta + \int \cos\theta\, d\theta$

$I = -\theta\cos\theta + \sin\theta + C$

$\Rightarrow I = -\tan^{-1} x \cdot \frac{1}{\sqrt{1+x^2}} + \frac{x}{\sqrt{1+x^2}} + C$

$\left[\because \cos\theta = \frac{1}{\sec\theta} = \frac{1}{\sqrt{1+\tan^2\theta}} = \frac{1}{\sqrt{1+x^2}} \text{ and } \sin\theta = \tan\theta\cos\theta = \frac{x}{\sqrt{1+x^2}}\right]$

$\Rightarrow I = \frac{(x - \tan^{-1} x)}{\sqrt{1+x^2}} + C$

21 (*b*) Let $I = \int \frac{x+3}{(x+4)^2} e^x\, dx$

$I = \int \frac{(x+4)-1}{(x+4)^2} e^x\, dx$

$I = \int \left(\frac{1}{x+4} - \frac{1}{(x+4)^2}\right) e^x\, dx$

Here, $f(x) = \frac{1}{x+4}$

and $f'(x) = \frac{-1}{(x+4)^2}$

$\therefore$ By $\int e^x [f(x) + f'(x)]$, $= e^x f(x) + C$, we get

$I = \frac{e^x}{x+4} + C$

22 (*d*)

I. Given, $\int f(x)\, dx = g(x)$

$\therefore \int \underset{\text{II}}{f(x)}\, \underset{\text{I}}{g(x)}\, dx = g(x) \int f(x)\, dx - \int [g'(x) \int f(x) dx]\, dx$

[using integration by parts]

$= g(x) g(x) - \int g'(x) g(x)\, dx$

$[\because \int f(x)\, dx = g(x)]$

$= [g(x)]^2 - \int f(x) g(x)\, dx$

$2 \int f(x) g(x)\, dx = [g(x)]^2$

$\Rightarrow \int f(x) g(x)\, dx = \frac{1}{2}[g(x)]^2$

II. $\int f(x) g(x)\, dx = \int \frac{\sin^{-1} x}{\sqrt{1-x^2}} e^{\sin^{-1} x}\, dx$

Put, $\sin^{-1} x = t$

$\Rightarrow \frac{1}{\sqrt{1-x^2}} dx = dt$

$\therefore \int f(x) g(x)\, dx = \int t e^t dt$

$= t \int e^t dt - \int \left[\frac{d}{dt}(t) \int e^t dt\right] dt$

$= te^t - \int e^t\, dt$

$= te^t - e^t + C$

$= e^{\sin^{-1} x} \sin^{-1} x - e^{\sin^{-1} x} + C$

$= e^{\sin^{-1} x} (\sin^{-1} x - 1) + C$

Integrals of Some More Types Functions

1 (*b*)

I. $\int \sqrt{x^2 + 2x + 5}\, dx = \int \sqrt{(x+1)^2 + 4}\, dx$

Put $x + 1 = y$, so that $dx = dy$. Then

$\int \sqrt{x^2 + 2x + 5}\, dx = \int \sqrt{y^2 + 2^2}\, dy$

$= \frac{1}{2} y \sqrt{y^2 + 4} + \frac{4}{2} \log\left| y + \sqrt{y^2 + 4}\right| + C$

$= \frac{1}{2}(x+1)\sqrt{x^2 + 2x + 5} + 2 \log\left| x + 1 + \sqrt{x^2 + 2x + 5}\right| + C$

II. $\int \sqrt{3 - 2x - x^2}\, dx = \int \sqrt{4 - (x+1)^2}\, dx$

Put $x + 1 = y$ so that $dx = dy$.

Thus, $\int \sqrt{3 - 2x - x^2}\, dx = \int \sqrt{4 - y^2}\, dy$

$= \frac{1}{2} y \sqrt{4 - y^2} + \frac{4}{2} \sin^{-1} \frac{y}{2} + C$

$= \frac{1}{2}(x+1)\sqrt{3 - 2x - x^2} + 2 \sin^{-1}\left(\frac{x+1}{2}\right) + C$

2 (c)

(i) We have, $I = \int \sqrt{4 - x^2}\, dx$

$= \int \sqrt{(2)^2 - (x)^2}\, dx$

$= \frac{x}{2} \sqrt{4 - x^2} + \frac{4}{2} \sin^{-1} \frac{x}{2} + C$

$\left[\because \int \sqrt{a^2 - x^2}\, dx = \frac{x}{2}\sqrt{a^2 - x^2} + \frac{a^2}{2} \sin^{-1} \frac{x}{a} + C\right]$

$\Rightarrow I = \frac{x}{2}\sqrt{4 - x^2} + 2 \sin^{-1} \frac{x}{2} + C$

(ii) Let $I = \int \sqrt{1 - 4x^2}\, dx$

$= \int \sqrt{4\left(\frac{1}{4} - x^2\right)}\, dx$

$$= 2\int \sqrt{\left(\left(\frac{1}{2}\right)^2 - x^2\right)}\, dx$$

$$= 2 \cdot \frac{x}{2}\sqrt{\frac{1}{4} - x^2} + \frac{1}{4}\cdot\frac{2}{2}\sin^{-1}\frac{x}{1/2} + C$$

$$\left[\because \int \sqrt{a^2 - x^2}\, dx = \frac{x}{2}\sqrt{a^2 - x^2} + \frac{a^2}{2}\sin^{-1}\frac{x}{a} + C\right]$$

$$\Rightarrow I = \frac{x}{2}\sqrt{1 - 4x^2} + \frac{1}{4}\sin^{-1}(2x) + C$$

(iii) Let $I = \int \sqrt{x^2 + 4x + 6}\, dx$

$$= \int \sqrt{x^2 + 4x + 2^2 + 6 - 4}\, dx$$

$$= \int \sqrt{(x+2)^2 + (\sqrt{2})^2}\, dx$$

$$= \frac{x+2}{2}\sqrt{x^2 + 4x + 6} + \frac{2}{2}\log|(x+2) + \sqrt{x^2 + 4x + 6}| + C$$

$$\Rightarrow \quad I = \frac{x+2}{2}\sqrt{x^2 + 4x + 6} + \log|(x+2) + \sqrt{x^2 + 4x + 6}| + C$$

$$\left[\because \int \sqrt{x^2 + a^2}\, dx = \frac{x}{2}\sqrt{x^2 + a^2} + \frac{a^2}{2}\log|x + \sqrt{x^2 + a^2}|\right]$$

(iv) Let $I = \int \sqrt{x^2 + 4x + 1}\, dx$

$$= \int \sqrt{x^2 + 4x + 1 - 2^2 + 2^2}\, dx$$

$$= \int \sqrt{(x+2)^2 - (\sqrt{3})^2}\, dx$$

$$\Rightarrow I = \frac{x+2}{2}\sqrt{x^2 + 4x + 1} - \frac{3}{2}\log|(x+2) + \sqrt{x^2 + 4x + 1}| + C$$

$$\left[\because \int \sqrt{x^2 - a^2}\, dx = \frac{x}{2}\sqrt{x^2 - a^2} - \frac{a^2}{2}\log|x + \sqrt{x^2 - a^2}|\right]$$

3 (*d*) Let $I = \int \sqrt{1 - 4x - x^2}\, dx$

$$= \int \sqrt{-(x^2 + 4x - 1 - 2^2 + 2^2)}\, dx$$

$$= \int \sqrt{-[(x+2)^2 - (\sqrt{5})^2]}\, dx$$

$$= \int \sqrt{(\sqrt{5})^2 - (x+2)^2}\, dx$$

$$\Rightarrow \quad I = \frac{x+2}{2}\sqrt{1 - 4x - x^2} + \frac{5}{2}\sin^{-1}\frac{(x+2)}{\sqrt{5}} + C$$

$$\left[\because \int \sqrt{a^2 - x^2}\, dx = \frac{x}{2}\sqrt{a^2 - x^2} + \frac{a^2}{2}\sin^{-1}\frac{x}{a} + C\right]$$

4 (*c*)

I. Let

$$I = \int \sqrt{x^2 + 4x - 5 - 2^2 + 2^2}\, dx$$

$$= \int \sqrt{(x+2)^2 - 5 - 4}\, dx$$

$$= \int \sqrt{(x+2)^2 - (3)^2}\, dx$$

$$\Rightarrow I = \frac{x+2}{2}\sqrt{x^2 + 4x - 5} - \frac{9}{2}\log|(x+2) + \sqrt{x^2 + 4x - 5}| + C$$

$$\left[\because \int \sqrt{x^2 - a^2}\, dx = \frac{x}{2}\sqrt{x^2 - a^2} - \frac{a^2}{2}\log|x + \sqrt{x^2 - a^2}|\right]$$

II. Let $I = \int \sqrt{1 + 3x - x^2}\, dx$

$$= \int \sqrt{-(x^2 - 3x - 1)}\, dx$$

$$= \int \sqrt{-\left(x^2 - 3x + \left(\frac{3}{2}\right)^2 - \left(\frac{3}{2}\right)^2 - 1\right)}\, dx$$

$$= \int \sqrt{-\left(\left(x - \frac{3}{2}\right)^2 - \frac{9}{4} - 1\right)}\, dx$$

$$= \int \sqrt{-\left(\left(x - \frac{3}{2}\right)^2 - \frac{9+4}{4}\right)}\, dx$$

$$= \int \sqrt{-\left(\left(x - \frac{3}{2}\right)^2 - \frac{13}{4}\right)}\, dx$$

$$= \int \sqrt{\left(\frac{\sqrt{13}}{2}\right)^2 - \left(x - \frac{3}{2}\right)^2}\, dx$$

$$\therefore I = \frac{x - \frac{3}{2}}{2}\sqrt{1 + 3x - x^2} + \frac{13}{4 \times 2}\sin^{-1}\left(\frac{x - \frac{3}{2}}{\frac{\sqrt{13}}{2}}\right) + C$$

$$\left[\because \int \sqrt{a^2 - x^2}\, dx = \frac{x}{2}\sqrt{a^2 - x^2} + \frac{a^2}{2}\sin^{-1}\frac{x}{a} + C\right]$$

$$\Rightarrow \quad I = \frac{2x - 3}{4}\sqrt{1 + 3x - x^2} + \frac{13}{8}\sin^{-1}\left(\frac{2x - 3}{\sqrt{13}}\right) + C$$

5 (*b*)

I. Let $I = \int \sqrt{x^2 + 3x}\, dx$

$$= \int \sqrt{x^2 + 3x - \left(\frac{3}{2}\right)^2 + \left(\frac{3}{2}\right)^2}\, dx$$

$$= \int \sqrt{\left(x + \frac{3}{2}\right)^2 - \left(\frac{3}{2}\right)^2}\, dx$$

$$\Rightarrow I = \frac{x + \frac{3}{2}}{2}\sqrt{\left(x + \frac{3}{2}\right)^2 - \left(\frac{3}{2}\right)^2} - \frac{9}{4 \times 2}\log\left|\left(x + \frac{3}{2}\right) + \sqrt{x^2 + 3x}\right| + C$$

$$\left[\because \int \sqrt{x^2 - a^2}\, dx = \frac{x}{2}\sqrt{x^2 - a^2} - \frac{a^2}{2}\log|x + \sqrt{x^2 - a^2}|\right]$$

$$\Rightarrow I = \frac{2x + 3}{4}\sqrt{x^2 + 3x} - \frac{9}{8}\log\left|\left(\frac{2x + 3}{2}\right) + \sqrt{x^2 + 3x}\right| + C$$

II. Let $I = \int \sqrt{1 + \frac{x^2}{9}}\, dx$

$$= \int \sqrt{\frac{9 + x^2}{9}}\, dx$$

$$= \frac{1}{3}\int \sqrt{(3)^2 + x^2}\, dx$$

$$= \frac{1}{3}\cdot\frac{x}{2}\sqrt{(3)^2 + x^2} + \frac{9}{2 \times 3}\log|x + \sqrt{9 + x^2}| + C$$

$$\left[\because \int \sqrt{a^2 + x^2}\, dx = \frac{1}{2}x\sqrt{a^2 + x^2} + \frac{1}{2}a^2\log\left|x + \sqrt{a^2 + x^2}\right| + C\right]$$

$$= \frac{x}{6}\sqrt{x^2 + 9} + \frac{3}{2}\log|x + \sqrt{9 + x^2}| + C$$

6 (a) Let $I = \int \sqrt{1+x^2}\, dx$

$\Rightarrow \quad I = \frac{x}{2}\sqrt{1+x^2} + \frac{1}{2}\log|x+\sqrt{1+x^2}| + C$

$\left[\because \int \sqrt{x^2+a^2}\, dx = \frac{x}{2}\sqrt{x^2+a^2} + \frac{a^2}{2}\log|x+\sqrt{x^2+a^2}|\right]$

7 (d) Let $I = \int \sqrt{x^2-8x+7}\, dx$

$\Rightarrow I = \int \sqrt{x^2-8x+7+(4)^2-(4)^2}\, dx$

$= \int \sqrt{(x-4)^2+7-16}\, dx$

$= \int \sqrt{(x-4)^2-(3)^2}\, dx$

$\left[\because \int \sqrt{x^2-a^2}\, dx = \frac{x}{2}\sqrt{x^2-a^2} - \frac{a^2}{2}\log|x+\sqrt{x^2-a^2}|\right]$

$\Rightarrow \quad I = \frac{x-4}{2}\sqrt{x^2-8x+7} - \frac{9}{2}\log|x-4+\sqrt{x^2-8x+7}| + C$

8 (b) We have

$I = \sqrt{10-4x+4x^2}\, dx$

$= \sqrt{(2x-1)^2+(3)^2}\, dx$

Put $t = 2x-1$, then $dt = 2dx$

Therefore, $I = \frac{1}{2}\int \sqrt{t^2+(3)^2}\, dt$

$= \frac{1}{2}t\frac{\sqrt{t^2+9}}{2} + \frac{9}{4}\log\left|t+\sqrt{t^2+9}\right| + C$

$= \frac{1}{4}(2x-1)\sqrt{(2x-1)^2+9} + \frac{9}{4}\log\left|(2x-1)+\sqrt{(2x-1)^2+9}\right| + C$

9 (a)

I. Let, $I = \int \sqrt{5-2x+x^2}dx$

$= \int \sqrt{x^2-2x+1+4}\, dx$

$= \int \sqrt{(x-1)^2+(2)^2}dx$

$= \left(\frac{x-1}{2}\right)\sqrt{(x-1)^2+4} + \frac{(2)^2}{2}\times\log\left|(x-1)+\sqrt{(x-1)^2+2^2}\right| + C$

$= \left(\frac{x-1}{2}\right)\sqrt{5-2x+x^2} + 2\log\left|(x-1)+\sqrt{5-2x+x^2}\right| + C$

II. Let, $I = \int \sqrt{2ax-x^2}\, dx$

$= \int \sqrt{-(x^2-2ax+a^2-a^2)}\, dx$

$= \int \sqrt{a^2-(x-a)^2}\, dx$

$= \left(\frac{x-a}{2}\right)\sqrt{a^2-(x-a)^2} + \frac{(a)^2}{2}\sin^{-1}\left(\frac{x-a}{a}\right) + C$

$= \left(\frac{x-a}{2}\right)\sqrt{2ax-x^2} + \frac{(a)^2}{2}\sin^{-1}\left(\frac{x-a}{a}\right) + C$

10 (a)

I. Let, $I = \int \cos x\sqrt{4-\sin^2 x}\, dx$

Put, $\sin x = t$

$\Rightarrow \cos x\, dx = dt$

$\therefore \quad I = \int \sqrt{(2)^2-(t)^2}dt$

$= \frac{1}{2}t\sqrt{(2)^2-t^2} + \frac{1}{2}\times(2)^2\sin^{-1}\left(\frac{t}{2}\right) + C$

$\left[\because \int (a^2-x^2)\, dx = \frac{1}{2}x\sqrt{a^2-x^2} + \frac{1}{2}a^2\sin^{-1}\left(\frac{x}{a}\right) + C\right]$

$= \frac{1}{2}t\sqrt{4-t^2} + 2\sin^{-1}\left(\frac{t}{2}\right) + C$

$= \frac{\sin x}{2}\sqrt{4-\sin^2 x} + 2\sin^{-1}\left(\frac{\sin x}{2}\right) + C$

II. Let $I = \int \frac{\sqrt{(4)^2+(\log x)^2}}{x}\, dx$

Put, $\log x = t \quad \Rightarrow \quad \frac{1}{x}dx = dt$

$\therefore \quad I = \int \sqrt{(4)^2+t^2}\, dt$

$= \frac{1}{2}t\sqrt{(4)^2+t^2} + \frac{1}{2}(4)^2\log\left|t+\sqrt{(4)^2+t^2}\right| + C$

$= \frac{1}{2}t\sqrt{16+t^2} + 8\log|t+\sqrt{16+t^2}| + C$

$= \frac{\log x}{2}\sqrt{16+(\log x)^2} + 8\log\left|\log x+\sqrt{16+(\log x)^2}\right| + C$

11 (c) Let,

$x+1 = A\cdot\frac{d}{dx}(1-x-x^2) + B$

$x+1 = A(-1-2x) + B$

$x+1 = -2Ax - A + B$

Comparing the coefficients of like power of x, we get

$-2A = 1$ and $-A+B = 1$

$A = \frac{-1}{2}$ and $B = 1-\frac{1}{2} = \frac{1}{2}$

$\therefore \quad I = \int (x+1)\sqrt{1-x-x^2}\, dx$

$= \int \left\{\frac{-1}{2}(-1-2x)+\frac{1}{2}\right\}\sqrt{1-x-x^2}dx$

$= \frac{-1}{2}\int (-1-2x)\sqrt{1-x-x^2}\, dx + \frac{1}{2}\int \sqrt{1-x-x^2}\, dx$

$I = \frac{-1}{2}I_1 + \frac{1}{2}I_2$ ...(i)

Consider,

$I_1 = \int (-1-2x)\sqrt{1-x-x^2}\, dx$

Put, $1-x-x^2 = t$

$\Rightarrow \quad (-1-2x)\, dx = dt$

$\therefore \quad I_1 = \int t^{1/2}\, dt = \frac{2}{3}t^{3/2}dt$

$= \frac{2}{3}(1-x-x^2)^{3/2} + C_1$

Further consider,

$I_2 = \int \sqrt{1-x-x^2}\, dx$

$= \int \sqrt{\left\{1-\left(x^2+x+\frac{1}{4}-\frac{1}{4}\right)\right\}}\, dx$

$= \int \sqrt{\left(\frac{\sqrt{5}}{2}\right)^2-\left(x+\frac{1}{2}\right)^2}\, dx$

$= \frac{1}{2}\left(x+\frac{1}{2}\right)\sqrt{1-x-x^2} + \frac{1}{2}\times\frac{5}{4}\sin^{-1}\left\{\frac{(x+1/2)}{\sqrt{5}/2}\right\} + C_2$

$$= \frac{1}{2}\left(x+\frac{1}{2}\right)\sqrt{1-x-x^2} + \frac{5}{8}\sin^{-1}\left\{\frac{(x+1/2)}{\sqrt{5}/2}\right\} + C_2$$

Put, values of I_1 and I_2 in Eq. (i), we get

$$I = \frac{-1}{3}(1-x-x^2)^{3/2} + \frac{1}{8}(2x+1)\sqrt{1-x-x^2} + \frac{5}{16}\sin^{-1}\left(\frac{2x+1}{\sqrt{5}}\right) + C$$

where, $C = \frac{C_2 - C_1}{2}$ is another arbitrary constant.

12 (c)

I. Let, $(3x-2) = A\frac{d}{dx}[(x^2+x+1)] + B$

$\Rightarrow \quad 3x - 2 = A(2x+1) + B$

Comparing the coefficients of like power of x we get

$2A = 3$ and $A + B = -2$

$A = \frac{3}{2}$ and $B = \frac{-7}{2}$

$$\therefore \quad I = \int (3x-2)\sqrt{x^2+x+1}\,dx$$

$$I = \int \left\{\frac{3}{2}(2x+1) - \frac{7}{2}\right\}\sqrt{x^2+x+1}\,dx$$

$$I = \frac{3}{2}\int (2x+1)\sqrt{x^2+x+1}\,dx - \frac{7}{2}\int \sqrt{x^2+x+1}\,dx$$

$$I = \frac{3}{2}I_1 - \frac{7}{2}I_2 \qquad \text{...(i)}$$

Consider,

$$I_1 = \int (2x+1)\sqrt{x^2+x+1}\,dx$$

Put, $x^2 + x + 1 = t$

$\Rightarrow \quad (2x+1)\,dx = dt$

$$\therefore \quad I_1 = \int t^{1/2}\,dt = \frac{2}{3}t^{3/2} + C$$

$$= \frac{2}{3}(x^2+x+1)^{3/2} + C$$

Further consider,

$$I_2 = \int \sqrt{x^2+x+1}\,dx$$

$$= \int \sqrt{\left(x+\frac{1}{2}\right)^2 + \left(\frac{\sqrt{3}}{2}\right)^2}\,dx$$

$$= \frac{1}{2}\left(x+\frac{1}{2}\right)\sqrt{x^2+x+1} + \left(\frac{\sqrt{3}}{2}\right)^2\cdot\frac{1}{2}\log\left|x+\frac{1}{2}+\sqrt{x^2+x+1}\right| + C$$

Putting the values of I_1 and I_2 in Eq. (i) , we get

$$I = (x^2+x+1)^{3/2} - \frac{7}{2}\left[\frac{1}{2}\left(x+\frac{1}{2}\right)\sqrt{x^2+x+1} + \frac{3}{8}\log\left|x+\frac{1}{2}+\sqrt{x^2+x+1}\right|\right] + C$$

II. Let, $x - 5 = A\left[\frac{d}{dx}(x^2+x)\right] + B$

$x - 5 = A\,(2x+1) + B$

Comparing the coefficients of like power of x on both sides, we get

$1 = 2A$ and $A + B = -5$

$A = \frac{1}{2}$ and $B = \frac{-11}{2}$

$$\therefore \; I = \int (x-5)\sqrt{x^2+x}\,dx$$

$$= \int \left\{\frac{1}{2}(2x+1) - \frac{11}{2}\right\}\sqrt{x^2+x}\,dx$$

$$= \frac{1}{2}\int (2x+1)\sqrt{x^2+x}\,dx - \frac{11}{2}\int \sqrt{x^2+x}\,dx$$

$$I = \frac{1}{2}I_1 - \frac{11}{2}I_2 \qquad \text{...(i)}$$

Consider,

$$I_1 = \int (2x+1)\sqrt{x^2+x}\,dx$$

Put, $\quad x^2 + x = t$

$\Rightarrow \quad (2x+1)\,dx = dt$

$$\therefore \quad I_1 = \int t^{1/2}\,dt$$

$$= \frac{2}{3}t^{3/2} + C$$

$$= \frac{2}{3}(x^2+x)^{3/2} + C$$

Further consider ,

$$I_2 = \int \sqrt{x^2+x}\,dx$$

$$I_2 = \int \sqrt{\left(x+\frac{1}{2}\right)^2 - \left(\frac{1}{2}\right)^2}\,dx$$

$$= \frac{1}{2}\left(x+\frac{1}{2}\right)\sqrt{\left(x+\frac{1}{2}\right)^2 - \left(\frac{1}{2}\right)^2} - \frac{1}{2}\left(\frac{1}{2}\right)^2\log\left|\left(x+\frac{1}{2}\right)+\sqrt{\left(x+\frac{1}{2}\right)^2 - \left(\frac{1}{2}\right)^2}\right| + C$$

$$= \frac{2x+1}{4}\sqrt{x^2+x} - \frac{1}{8}\log\left|\left(x+\frac{1}{2}\right)+\sqrt{x^2+x}\right| + C$$

Putting values of I_1 and I_2 in Eq. (i), we get

$$I = \frac{1}{3}(x^2+x)^{3/2} - \frac{11}{2}\left[\left\{\frac{2x+1}{4}\sqrt{x^2+x} - \frac{1}{8}\log\left|\left(x+\frac{1}{2}\right)+\sqrt{x^2+x}\right|\right\}\right] + C$$

Fundamental Theorem of Integral Calculus

1 (c) $\int_a^b f(x)\,dx$ is the area of the region bounded by the curve $y = f(x)$, the line $x = a$ and $x = b$ and x – axis.

Let x be a given point in $[a, b]$. Then $\int_a^x f(x)\,dx$ represents the area of the light shaded region in figure [Here it is assumed that $f(x) > 0$ for $x \in [a, b]$, the assertion made below is equally true for other functions as well].

The area of this shaded region depends upon the value of x.

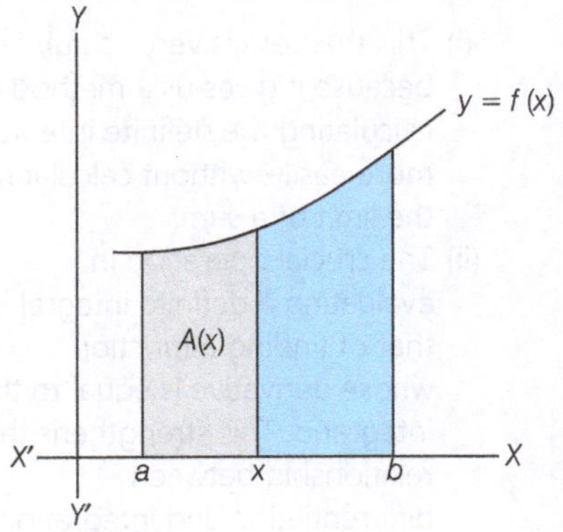

In other words, the area of this shaded region is a function of x. We denote this function of x by $A(x)$. We call the function $A(x)$ as area function and is given by

$$A(x)=\int_a^x f(x)\,dx$$

If a curve lies below x-axis we take its absolute value.

$\therefore$ Statement II $A(x)$

$$=\int_a^b f(x)\,dx+\left|\int_b^c f(x)\,dx\right| \text{ is true.}$$

When $f(x)>0$ for $x\in[a,b]$ and $f(x)<0$ for $x\in[b,c]$.

2 (c) Let f be a continuous function on the closed interval $[a, b]$ and let $A(x)$ be the area function. Then $A'(x)=f(x)$, for all $x\in[a,b]$.

Here, $A'(x)=\dfrac{d}{dx}(A(x))$

This is called first fundamental theorem of integral calculus.

3 (b) An important theorem which enables us to evaluate definite integrals by making use of anti derivative is

"Let f be continuous function defined on the closed interval $[a, b]$ and F be an anti-derivative of f. Then,

$$\int_a^b f(x)\,dx=[F(x)]_a^b=F(b)-F(a).\text{"}$$

or, it tell us that $\int_a^b f(x)\,dx=$ (value of the anti derivative F of f at the upper limit b– value of the same anti derivative at the lower limit a).

This is known as second fundamental theorem of integral calculus.

4 (c)

(i) This theorem is very useful, because it gives us a method of calculating the definite integral more easily, without calculating the limit of a sum.

(ii) The crucial operation in evaluating a definite integral is that of finding a function whose derivative is equal to the integrand. This strengthens the relationship between differentiation and integration.

(iii) In $\int_a^b f(x)\,dx$, the function f needs to be well defined and continuous in $[a, b]$.

For instance, the consideration of definite integral

$\int_{-2}^3 x(x^2-1)^{\frac{1}{2}}\,dx$ is erroneous since the function f expressed by $f(x)=x(x^2-1)^{\frac{1}{2}}$ is not defined in a portion $-1<x<1$ of the closed interval $[-2,3]$.

5 (a)

I. Let $I=\int_{-1}^1 (x+1)\,dx$

$$=\left[\frac{x^2}{2}+x\right]_{-1}^1$$

$$=\left[\frac{1^2}{2}+1\right]-\left[\frac{(-1)^2}{2}-1\right]$$

$$I=\frac{3}{2}+\frac{1}{2}=\frac{4}{2}=2$$

II. Let $I=\int_2^3 \frac{1}{x}\,dx=[\log x]_2^3$

$$=\log 3-\log 2=\log\frac{3}{2}$$

6 (a) $I=\int_1^2 (4x^3-5x^2+6x+9)\,dx$

$$=\left[\frac{4x^4}{4}-\frac{5x^3}{3}+\frac{6x^2}{2}+9x\right]_1^2$$

$$=\left[x^4-\frac{5x^3}{3}+3x^2+9x\right]_1^2$$

$$=\left[2^4-\frac{5(2)^3}{3}+3(2)^2+9(2)\right]-\left[(1)^4-\frac{5(1)^3}{3}+3(1)^2+9(1)\right]$$

$$=\left[16-\frac{40}{3}+12+18\right]-\left[1-\frac{5}{3}+3+9\right]$$

$$=\left[46-\frac{40}{3}\right]-\left[13-\frac{5}{3}\right]$$

$$=\left[\frac{138-40}{3}\right]-\left[\frac{39-5}{3}\right]$$

$$=\frac{98}{3}-\frac{34}{3}=\frac{64}{3}$$

7 (d)

I. Let $I=\int_0^{\pi/4} \sin 2x\,dx$

$$=\int_0^{\pi/4} 2\sin x\cos x\,dx$$

$[\because \sin 2x=2\sin x\cos x]$

Put $\sin x=t \Rightarrow \cos x=\dfrac{dt}{dx}$

$\Rightarrow \quad dx=\dfrac{dt}{\cos x}$

Upper limit, at $x=\dfrac{\pi}{4}$

$\Rightarrow \quad t=\sin\dfrac{\pi}{4}=\dfrac{1}{\sqrt{2}}$

Lower limit, at

$x=0 \Rightarrow t=\sin 0=0$

$$\therefore \quad I=2\int_0^{1/\sqrt{2}} t\cos x\,\frac{dt}{\cos x}$$

$$=2\int_0^{1/\sqrt{2}} t\,dt=2\left[\frac{t^2}{2}\right]_0^{1/\sqrt{2}}$$

$$=\left(\frac{1}{\sqrt{2}}\right)^2=\frac{1}{2}$$

II. $\int_0^{\pi/2} \cos 2x\,dx=\left[\dfrac{\sin 2x}{2}\right]_0^{\pi/2}$

$$\left[\because \int \cos ax\,dx=\frac{\sin ax}{a}\right]$$

$$=\frac{1}{2}[\sin 2x]_0^{\pi/2}$$

$$=\frac{1}{2}\left[\left(\sin 2\times\frac{\pi}{2}\right)-\sin(0)\right]$$

$$=\frac{1}{2}[0-0]=0$$

8 (c) $\int_4^5 e^x\,dx=[e^x]_4^5$

$$=[e^5-e^4]$$

$$=e^4[e-1]$$

9 (b) $\int_0^{\pi/4} \tan x\,dx$

$$=[-\log|\cos x|]_0^{\pi/4}$$

$$=-\log\left|\cos\frac{\pi}{4}\right|-(-\log|\cos 0|)$$

$$=-\log\frac{1}{\sqrt{2}}+\log 1$$

$$=-\log 2^{-1/2}+0$$

$$=\frac{1}{2}\log 2$$

$[\because \log 1=0 \text{ and } \log m^n=n\log m]$

10 (c)

I. $\int_0^1 \frac{1}{\sqrt{1-x^2}} dx = [\sin^{-1} x]_0^1$

$\left[\because \int \frac{dx}{\sqrt{1-x^2}} = \sin^{-1} x\right]$

$= \sin^{-1} 1 - \sin^{-1} 0 = \frac{\pi}{2} - 0 = \frac{\pi}{2}$

II. $\int_0^1 \frac{1}{1+x^2} dx = [\tan^{-1} x]_0^1$

$\left[\because \int \frac{dx}{1+x^2} = \tan^{-1} x\right]$

$= \tan^{-1} 1 - \tan^{-1} 0 = \frac{\pi}{4}$

11 (d) $I = \int_{\pi/6}^{\pi/4} \text{cosec} x \, dx$

$= [\log|\text{cosec} x - \cot x|]_{\pi/6}^{\pi/4}$

$= \log\left|\text{cosec}\frac{\pi}{4} - \cot\frac{\pi}{4}\right|$

$- \log\left|\text{cosec}\frac{\pi}{6} - \cot\frac{\pi}{6}\right|$

$= \log|\sqrt{2}-1| - \log|2-\sqrt{3}|$

$= \log\left|\frac{\sqrt{2}-1}{2-\sqrt{3}}\right|$

$\left[\because \log a - \log b = \log \frac{a}{b}\right]$

12 (b)

I. $\int_2^3 \frac{1}{x^2-1} dx = \left[\frac{1}{2}\log\left|\frac{x-1}{x+1}\right|\right]_2^3$

$\left[\because \int \frac{dx}{x^2-a^2} = \frac{1}{2a}\log\left|\frac{x-a}{x+a}\right|\right]$

$= \frac{1}{2}\log\left|\frac{3-1}{3+1}\right| - \frac{1}{2}\log\left|\frac{2-1}{2+1}\right|$

$= \frac{1}{2}\log\left|\frac{2}{4}\right| - \frac{1}{2}\log\left|\frac{1}{3}\right|$

$= \frac{1}{2}$ [log (1) – log (2)

– log(1) + log(3)]

$\left[\because \log\left(\frac{a}{b}\right) = \log a - \log b\right]$

$= \frac{1}{2}\log\left(\frac{3}{2}\right)$

II. $\int_0^{\pi/2} \cos^2 x \, dx$

$= \int_0^{\pi/2} \left(\frac{\cos 2x + 1}{2}\right) dx$

$[\because \cos 2x = 2\cos^2 x - 1]$

$= \frac{1}{2}\int_0^{\pi/2} \cos 2x \, dx + \frac{1}{2}\int_0^{\pi/2} 1 \, dx$

$= \frac{1}{2}\left[\frac{\sin 2x}{2}\right]_0^{\pi/2} + \frac{1}{2}[x]_0^{\pi/2}$

$= \frac{1}{2}\left[\left(\frac{\sin \pi}{2} - \frac{\sin 0}{2}\right) + \left(\frac{\pi}{2} - 0\right)\right]$

$= \frac{\pi}{4}.$

13 (d)

(i) Let $I = \int_2^3 \frac{x}{x^2+1} dx$

Put $x^2 + 1 = t \Rightarrow 2x = \frac{dt}{dx}$

$\Rightarrow \quad dx = \frac{dt}{2x}$

$\therefore \quad I = \int \frac{x}{t} \frac{dt}{2x} = \frac{1}{2}\int \frac{1}{t} dt$

$= \frac{1}{2}[\log|t|]$

$= \frac{1}{2}[\log|x^2+1|]_2^3 \quad [\because t = x^2+1]$

$= \frac{1}{2}[\log|3^2+1| - \log|2^2+1|]$

$= \frac{1}{2}[\log|10| - \log|5|]$

$= \frac{1}{2}\log\left|\frac{10}{5}\right| = \frac{1}{2}\log 2$

$\left[\because \log a - \log b = \log \frac{a}{b}\right]$

(ii) Let $I = \int_0^1 \frac{2x+3}{(5x^2+1)} dx$

$= \int_0^1 \frac{2x}{(5x^2+1)} dx$

$+ 3\int_0^1 \frac{1}{(5x^2+1)} dx$

Put $5x^2 + 1 = t$

$\Rightarrow 10x = \frac{dt}{dx} \Rightarrow dx = \frac{dt}{10x}$

$\therefore \quad I = \int_0^1 \frac{2x}{t}\frac{dt}{10x}$

$+ \frac{3}{5}\int_0^1 \frac{1}{x^2 + \left(\frac{1}{\sqrt{5}}\right)^2} dx$

$= \frac{1}{5}\int_0^1 \frac{1}{t} dt$

$+ \frac{3}{5}\int_0^1 \frac{1}{x^2 + \left(\frac{1}{\sqrt{5}}\right)^2} dx$

$= \frac{1}{5}[\log t]_0^1 + \frac{3}{5} \times \frac{1}{\frac{1}{\sqrt{5}}}\left[\tan^{-1}\frac{x}{\frac{1}{\sqrt{5}}}\right]_0^1$

$\left[\because \int \frac{dx}{a^2+x^2} = \frac{1}{a}\tan^{-1}\frac{x}{a}\right]$

$= \frac{1}{5}[\log|5x^2+1|]_0^1 + \frac{3}{5}\sqrt{5}$ $[\tan^{-1}\sqrt{5}x]_0^1$

$= \frac{1}{5}[\log|5+1| - \log|0+1|]$

$+ \frac{3}{\sqrt{5}}[\tan^{-1}\sqrt{5}(1) - \tan^{-1}\sqrt{5}(0)]$

$= \frac{1}{5}\log 6 + \frac{3}{\sqrt{5}}\tan^{-1}\sqrt{5}$

$[\because \log 1 = 0 \text{ and } \tan^{-1}(0) = 0]$

(iii) Let $I = \int_0^1 xe^{x^2} dx$

Put $\quad x^2 = t$

$\Rightarrow \quad 2x = \frac{dt}{dx}$

$\Rightarrow \quad dx = \frac{dt}{2x}$

Limits when $x = 0 \Rightarrow t = 0$

and when $x = 1 \Rightarrow t = 1$

$\therefore \quad I = \int_0^1 xe^t \frac{dt}{2x} = \frac{1}{2}\int_0^1 e^t \, dt$

$= \frac{1}{2}[e^t]_0^1 = \frac{1}{2}[e^1 - e^0]$

$= \frac{1}{2}[e-1]$

(iv) Let $I = \int_1^2 \frac{5x^2}{x^2+4x+3} dx$

Here, the degree of numerator and denominator is same, so on dividing numerator by denominator, we get

$\frac{5x^2}{x^2+4x+3} = 5 - \frac{20x+15}{x^2+4x+3}$

$\therefore I = \int_1^2 \left[5 - \frac{20x+15}{x^2+4x+3}\right] dx$

$= \int_1^2 5 \, dx$

$- \int_1^2 \frac{20x+15}{(x+1)(x+3)} dx \quad \text{...(i)}$

Let $\frac{20x+15}{(x+1)(x+3)}dx = \frac{A}{(x+1)} + \frac{B}{(x+3)}$

$\Rightarrow 20x+15 = A(x+3)+B(x+1)$

$\Rightarrow 20x+15 = Ax+3A+Bx+B$

On equating the coefficients of x and constant term on both sides, we get

$20 = A+B$ ...(ii)

and $15 = 3A+B$ ...(iii)

On solving Eqs. (ii) and (iii), we get

$A = -\frac{5}{2}, B = \frac{45}{2}$

$\therefore \quad I = 5\int_1^2 dx + \frac{5}{2}\int_1^2 \frac{1}{(x+1)}dx - \frac{45}{2}\int_1^2 \frac{1}{(x+3)}dx$ [from Eq. (i)]

$= \left[5x + \frac{5}{2}\log|x+1| - \frac{45}{2}\log|x+3|\right]_1^2$

$= \left[10 + \frac{5}{2}\log|3| - \frac{45}{2}\log|5| - 5 - \frac{5}{2}\log|2| + \frac{45}{2}\log|4|\right]$

$\Rightarrow I = 5 + \frac{5}{2}\log\left|\frac{3}{2}\right| - \frac{45}{2}\log\left|\frac{5}{4}\right|$

$\left[\because m\log a - m\log b = m\log\left(\frac{a}{b}\right)\right]$

14 (a)

A. $\int_0^{\pi/4}(2\sec^2 x + x^3 + 2)dx$

$= 2\int_0^{\pi/4}\sec^2 x\,dx + \int_0^{\pi/4} x^3\,dx + 2\int_0^{\pi/4} 1\,dx$

$= 2[\tan x]_0^{\pi/4} + \frac{1}{4}[x^4]_0^{\pi/4} + 2[x]_0^{\pi/4}$

$= 2\tan\frac{\pi}{4} + \frac{1}{4}\left(\frac{\pi}{4}\right)^4 + 2\left(\frac{\pi}{4}\right)$

$= 2 + \frac{\pi}{2} + \frac{\pi^4}{1024}$

B. $\int_0^{\pi}\left(\sin^2\frac{x}{2} - \cos^2\frac{x}{2}\right)dx$

$= -\int_0^{\pi}\left(\cos^2\frac{x}{2} - \sin^2\frac{x}{2}\right)dx$

$= -\int_0^{\pi}\cos x\,dx$ $[\because \cos 2x = \cos^2 x - \sin^2 x]$

$= -[\sin x]_0^{\pi} = -[\sin\pi - \sin 0] = 0$

C. Let $I = \int_0^2 \frac{6x+3}{x^2+4}dx$

$= \int_0^2 \frac{6x}{x^2+4}dx + \int_0^2 \frac{3}{x^2+4}dx$

Put $x^2+4 = t$

$\Rightarrow \quad 2x = \frac{dt}{dx}$

$\Rightarrow \quad dx = \frac{dt}{2x}$

Lower limit, when $x = 0$, $t = 0+4 = 4$

Upper limit, when $x = 2, t = 4+4 = 8$

$\therefore I = \int_4^8 \frac{6x}{t}\frac{dt}{2x} + \int_0^2 \frac{3}{x^2+4}dx$

$= 3\int_4^8 \frac{1}{t}dt + 3\int_0^2 \frac{1}{x^2+2^2}dx$

$= 3[\log t]_4^8 + \frac{3}{2}\left[\tan^{-1}\frac{x}{2}\right]_0^2$

$\left[\because \int \frac{dx}{a^2+x^2} = \frac{1}{a}\tan^{-1}\frac{x}{a}\right]$

$= 3[\log(8) - \log(4)] + \frac{3}{2}\left[\tan^{-1}\frac{2}{2}\right]$

$= 3\log\left(\frac{8}{4}\right) + \frac{3}{2}\times\frac{\pi}{4}$

$\left[\because \log b - \log a = \log\frac{b}{a}\right]$

$= 3\log 2 + \frac{3\pi}{8}$

D. $\int_0^1\left(xe^x + \sin\frac{\pi\cdot x}{4}\right)dx$

$= \int_0^1 xe^x\,dx + \int_0^1 \sin\left(\frac{\pi\cdot x}{4}\right)dx$

$= [xe^x - \int 1\cdot e^x\,dx]_0^1 + \left[\frac{-\cos\frac{\pi\cdot x}{4}}{\frac{\pi}{4}}\right]_0^1$

First integral solved by using the integration by parts and for second $\left(\int \sin ax\,dx = -\frac{\cos ax}{a}\right)$

$= [xe^x - e^x]_0^1 - \frac{4}{\pi}\left[\cos\left(\frac{\pi\cdot x}{4}\right)\right]_0^1$

$= (e-e) - (0-e^0) - \frac{4}{\pi}\left(\cos\frac{\pi}{4} - \cos 0\right)$

$= 0-(-1) - \frac{4}{\pi}\left(\frac{1}{\sqrt{2}} - 1\right)$

$= 1 - \frac{4}{\pi}\left(\frac{1-\sqrt{2}}{\sqrt{2}}\right)\times\frac{\sqrt{2}}{\sqrt{2}}$

$= 1 + \frac{2}{\pi}(2-\sqrt{2}) = 1 + \frac{4}{\pi} - \frac{2\sqrt{2}}{\pi}$

15 (d) $\int_1^{\sqrt{3}} \frac{1}{1+x^2}dx = \int_1^{\sqrt{3}} \frac{1}{x^2+1^2}dx$

$= \left[\frac{1}{1}\tan^{-1}\left(\frac{x}{1}\right)\right]_1^{\sqrt{3}} = \tan^{-1}\sqrt{3} - \tan^{-1}1 \left[\because \int \frac{dx}{1+x^2} = \tan^{-1}x\right]$

$= \frac{\pi}{3} - \frac{\pi}{4} \Rightarrow \frac{4\pi - 3\pi}{12} = \frac{\pi}{12}$.

16 (c) $\int_0^{2/3} \frac{1}{4+9x^2}dx$

$= \frac{1}{9}\int_0^{2/3} \frac{1}{\frac{4}{9}+x^2}dx$

$= \frac{1}{9}\int_0^{2/3} \frac{1}{\left(\frac{2}{3}\right)^2 + x^2}dx$

$= \frac{1}{9}\cdot\frac{1}{2/3}\left[\tan^{-1}\left(\frac{x}{2/3}\right)\right]_0^{2/3}$

$\left[\because \int \frac{dx}{a^2+x^2} = \frac{1}{a}\tan^{-1}\frac{x}{a}\right]$

$= \frac{1}{6}\left[\tan^{-1}\left(\frac{3x}{2}\right)\right]_0^{2/3}$

$= \frac{1}{6}\left[\tan^{-1}\left(\frac{3}{2}\cdot\frac{2}{3}\right) - \tan^{-1}0\right]$

$= \frac{1}{6}(\tan^{-1}1 - 0)$

$= \frac{1}{6}\cdot\frac{\pi}{4} = \frac{\pi}{24}$

17 (*d*)

I. We have, $I = \int_0^{\pi/4} \sqrt{1+\sin 2x}\, dx$

$= \int_0^{\pi/4} \sqrt{(\sin x + \cos x)^2}\, dx$

$= \int_0^{\pi/4} (\sin x + \cos x)\, dx$

$= [-\cos x + \sin x]_0^{\pi/4}$

$= \left[\left(\frac{-1}{\sqrt{2}} + \frac{1}{\sqrt{2}}\right) - (-1+0)\right] = 1$

II. Let $I = \int_0^1 x \log(1+2x)\, dx$
 II I

$= \left[\log(1+2x) \cdot \frac{x^2}{2}\right]_0^1 - \int_0^1 \frac{2}{1+2x} \times \frac{x^2}{2} dx$

$= \left[\log(3) \cdot \frac{1}{2} - 0\right] - \int_0^1 \frac{x^2}{2x+1} dx$

$= \frac{1}{2}\log 3 - \int_0^1 \left(\frac{1}{2}x - \frac{1}{4} + \frac{1}{4} \times \frac{1}{2x+1}\right) dx$

$= \frac{1}{2}\log 3 - \frac{1}{4}[x^2]_0^1 + \frac{1}{4}[x]_0^1 - \frac{1}{8}[\log(2x+1)]_0^1$

$= \frac{1}{2}\log 3 - \frac{1}{4}[1^2 - 0^2] + \frac{1}{4}[1-0] - \frac{1}{8}[\log 3 - \log 1]$

$= \frac{1}{2}\log 3 - \frac{1}{4} + \frac{1}{4} - \frac{1}{8}\log 3$

$= \frac{3}{8}\log 3$

18 (*a*) Let $I = \int_{-\pi/4}^{\pi/4} \frac{dx}{1+\cos 2x}$

$= \int_{-\pi/4}^{\pi/4} \frac{dx}{2\cos^2 x}$

$[\because 1 + \cos 2\theta = 2\cos^2\theta]$

$= \frac{1}{2}\int_{-\pi/4}^{\pi/4} \sec^2 x dx = \frac{1}{2}[\tan x]_{-\pi/4}^{\pi/4}$

$= \frac{1}{2}\left[\tan\left(\frac{\pi}{4}\right) - \tan\left(\frac{-\pi}{4}\right)\right]$

$= \frac{1}{2}\left[\tan\frac{\pi}{4} + \tan\frac{\pi}{4}\right] = \frac{1}{2}[1+1]$

$= \frac{1}{2} \times 2 = 1$

19 (*d*) Let, $I = \int_0^{\pi/2} \sqrt{1 - \sin 2x}\, dx$

$= \int_0^{\pi/4} \sqrt{(\cos x - \sin x)^2}\, dx + \int_{\pi/4}^{\pi/2} \sqrt{(\sin x - \cos x)^2}\, dx$

$\left[\because \cos x - \sin x > 0 \text{ when } x \in \left(0, \frac{\pi}{4}\right)\right.$ and $\cos x - \sin x < 0$ when $\left. x \in (\pi/4, \pi/2)\right]$

$= \int_0^{\pi/4} (\cos x - \sin x)\, dx + \int_{\pi/4}^{\pi/2} (\sin x - \cos x) dx$

$= [\sin x + \cos x]_0^{\pi/4} + [-\cos x - \sin x]_{\pi/4}^{\pi/2}$

$= \left[\left(\sin\frac{\pi}{4} + \cos\frac{\pi}{4}\right) - (\sin 0 + \cos 0)\right] + \left[\left(-\cos\frac{\pi}{2} - \sin\frac{\pi}{2}\right) - \left(-\cos\frac{\pi}{4} - \sin\frac{\pi}{4}\right)\right]$

$= \left[\left(\frac{1}{\sqrt{2}} + \frac{1}{\sqrt{2}} - 1\right) + -1 - \left(-\frac{1}{\sqrt{2}} - \frac{1}{\sqrt{2}}\right)\right]$

$= \left[\frac{2}{\sqrt{2}} - 1\right] + [-1 + \sqrt{2}]$

$= (\sqrt{2} - 1) + (-1 + \sqrt{2})$

$= 2(\sqrt{2} - 1)$

20 (*c*)

I. Let, $\int_0^1 \frac{x^4(1-x)^4}{1+x^2} dx$

$= \int_0^1 \frac{(x^4 - 1)(1-x)^4 + (1-x)^4}{(1+x^2)} dx$

$= \int_0^1 (x^2 - 1)(1-x)^4 dx + \int_0^1 \frac{(1 + x^2 - 2x)^2}{(1+x^2)} dx$

$= \int_0^1 \left\{(x^2 - 1)(1-x)^4 + (1+x^2) - 4x + \frac{4x^2}{(1+x^2)}\right\} dx$

$= \int_0^1 \left((x^2 - 1)(1-x)^4 + (1+x^2) - 4x + 4 - \frac{4}{1+x^2}\right) dx$

$= \int_0^1 \left(x^6 - 4x^5 + 5x^4 - 4x^2 + 4 - \frac{4}{1+x^2}\right) dx$

$= \left[\frac{x^7}{7} - 4\frac{x^6}{6} + \frac{5x^5}{5} - \frac{4x^3}{3} + 4x - 4\tan^{-1} x\right]_0^1$

$= \frac{1}{7} - \frac{4}{6} + \frac{5}{5} - \frac{4}{3} + 4 - 4\left(\frac{\pi}{4} - 0\right)$

$= \frac{22}{7} - \pi$

II. Let $I = \int_{-1}^1 \frac{|x+2|}{x+2} dx$

For $-1 \le x \le 1, |x+2| = 2 + x$

$\therefore \ I = \int_{-1}^1 \frac{x+2}{x+2} dx = \int_{-1}^1 1\, dx$

$= [x]_{-1}^1 = 1 - (-1) = 2$

21 (*b*) Let $I = \int_0^a \frac{1}{1+4x^2} dx$

$= \int_0^a \frac{1}{1+(2x)^2} dx = \frac{1}{2}[\tan^{-1}(2x)]_0^a$

$= \frac{1}{2}[\tan^{-1} 2a - \tan^{-1} 0]$

$= \frac{1}{2}\tan^{-1} 2a = \frac{\pi}{8}$ [given]

$\therefore \quad \tan^{-1} 2a = \pi / 4$

$\Rightarrow 2a = \tan \pi / 4 \Rightarrow a = \frac{1}{2}$

22 (*d*) Let $I = \int_2^k (2x+1) dx$

$= \left[\frac{2x^2}{2} + x\right]_2^k$

$= [k^2 + k - 4 - 2]$

$= k^2 + k - 6$

Given, $I = 6$

$\therefore \quad k^2 + k - 6 = 6$

$\Rightarrow \quad k^2 + k - 12 = 0$

$\Rightarrow \quad k^2 + 4k - 3k - 12 = 0$

$\Rightarrow \quad k(k+4) - 3(k+4) = 0$

$\Rightarrow \quad (k-3)(k+4) = 0$

$\Rightarrow \quad k = 3, -4$

$\Rightarrow \quad k = 3 \quad [\because k > 2]$

23 (*d*)

I. Let $I = \int_0^\lambda \frac{y\, dy}{\sqrt{y+\lambda}}$

$= \int_0^\lambda \left[\frac{y + \lambda - \lambda}{\sqrt{y+\lambda}}\right] dy$

$= \int_0^\lambda \left[\sqrt{y+\lambda} - \frac{\lambda}{\sqrt{y+\lambda}}\right] dy$

$$= \int_0^{\lambda}(y+\lambda)^{1/2}dy - \int_0^{\lambda}\frac{\lambda}{\sqrt{y+\lambda}}\,dy$$

$$= \left[\frac{(y+\lambda)^{3/2}}{3/2}\right]_0^{\lambda} - \left[\frac{\lambda\sqrt{y+\lambda}}{1/2}\right]_0^{\lambda}$$

$$= \frac{2}{3}[(2\lambda)^{3/2} - \lambda^{3/2}] - 2\lambda[(2\lambda)^{1/2} - (\lambda)^{1/2}]$$

$$= 2\lambda\sqrt{\lambda}\left[\frac{2\sqrt{2}-1}{3} - (\sqrt{2}-1)\right]$$

$$= \frac{2}{3}\lambda\sqrt{\lambda}\,(2-\sqrt{2})$$

II. Let, $I = 3a\int_0^1\left(\frac{ax-1}{a-1}\right)^2 dx$

$$= \frac{3a}{(a-1)^2}\left[\frac{(ax-1)^3}{3}\times\frac{1}{a}\right]_0^1$$

$$= \frac{1}{(a-1)^2}[(a-1)^3+1]$$

$$= (a-1) + (a-1)^{-2}$$

Evaluation of Definite Integrals by Substitution

1 (c) I. Put $t = x^5 + 1$, then

$dt = 5x^4 dx$.

Therefore, $\int 5x^4\sqrt{x^5+1}\,dx$

$$= \int \sqrt{t}\,dt = \frac{2}{3}t^{\frac{3}{2}} = \frac{2}{3}(x^5+1)^{\frac{3}{2}}$$

Hence,

$$\int_{-1}^{1} 5x^4\sqrt{x^5+1}\,dx = \frac{2}{3}\left[(x^5+1)^{\frac{3}{2}}\right]_{-1}^{1}$$

$$= \frac{2}{3}\left[(1^5+1)^{\frac{3}{2}} - ((-1)^5+1)^{\frac{3}{2}}\right]$$

$$= \frac{2}{3}\left[2^{\frac{3}{2}} - 0^{\frac{3}{2}}\right] = \frac{2}{3}(2\sqrt{2}) = \frac{4\sqrt{2}}{3}$$

Alternate Method

First we transform the integral and then evaluate the transformed integral with new limits.

Let $t = x^5 + 1$. Then $dt = 5\,x^4 dx$.

Note that, when $x = -1, t = 0$ and when $x = 1, t = 2$

Thus, as x varies from -1 to 1, t varies from 0 to 2

Therefore,

$$\int_{-1}^{1} 5x^4\sqrt{x^5+1}\,dx = \int_0^2 \sqrt{t}\;\;dt$$

$$= \frac{2}{3}\left[t^{\frac{3}{2}}\right]_0^2 = \frac{2}{3}\left[2^{\frac{3}{2}} - 0^{\frac{3}{2}}\right]$$

$$= \frac{2}{3}(2\sqrt{2}) = \frac{4\sqrt{2}}{3}$$

II. Let $t = \tan^{-1} x$, then $dt = \frac{1}{1+x^2}dx$. The new limits are, when $x = 0, t = 0$ and when $x = 1, t = \frac{\pi}{4}$. Thus, as x varies from 0 to 1, t varies from 0 to $\frac{\pi}{4}$.

Therefore,

$$\int_0^1 \frac{\tan^{-1}x}{1+x^2}dx = \int_0^{\frac{\pi}{4}} t\;dt = \left[\frac{t^2}{2}\right]_0^{\frac{\pi}{4}}$$

$$= \frac{1}{2}\left[\frac{\pi^2}{16} - 0\right] = \frac{\pi^2}{32}$$

2 (b)

(i) Let $I = \int_0^1 \frac{x}{x^2+1}dx$

Put $x^2 + 1 = t \Rightarrow 2x = \frac{dt}{dx}$

$\Rightarrow \quad dx = \frac{dt}{2x}$

For limit, when $x = 0 \Rightarrow t = 1$ and when $x = 1 \Rightarrow t = 2$

$[\because t = x^2 + 1]$

$$\therefore \quad I = \int_1^2 \frac{x}{t}\frac{dt}{2x} = \frac{1}{2}\int_1^2 \frac{1}{t}dt$$

$$= \frac{1}{2}[\log|t|]_1^2$$

$$= \frac{1}{2}[\log|2| - \log|1|]$$

$$= \frac{1}{2}\log 2 \qquad [\because \log 1 = 0]$$

(ii) $\int_0^{\pi/2}\sqrt{\sin\phi}\cos^5\phi\,d\phi$

$$= \int_0^{\pi/2}\sqrt{\sin\phi}\,(1-\sin^2\phi)^2\cos\phi\,d\phi$$

$[\because \cos^2\theta + \sin^2\theta = 1]$

Put $\sin\phi = t$

$\Rightarrow \quad \cos\phi = \frac{dt}{d\phi}$

$\Rightarrow \quad d\phi = \frac{dt}{\cos\phi}$

For limit when $\phi = 0 \Rightarrow t = 0$ and when $\phi = \frac{\pi}{2} \Rightarrow t = 1$

$$\therefore I = \int_0^1 \sqrt{t}(1-t^2)^2 dt$$

$$= \int_0^1 \sqrt{t}(t^4 + 1 - 2t^2)dt$$

$$= \int_0^1 (t^{9/2} + t^{1/2} - 2t^{5/2})dt$$

$$= \left[\frac{t^{\frac{9}{2}+1}}{\left(\frac{9}{2}+1\right)} + \frac{t^{\frac{1}{2}+1}}{\frac{1}{2}+1} - 2\left(\frac{t^{\frac{5}{2}+1}}{\frac{5}{2}+1}\right)\right]_0^1$$

$$= \left[\frac{2}{11} + \frac{2}{3} - \frac{4}{7}\right] - 0$$

$$= \frac{42 + 154 - 132}{11\times 3\times 7} = \frac{64}{231}$$

(iii) Let $I = \int_0^1 \sin^{-1}\left(\frac{2x}{1+x^2}\right)dx$

Put $\tan\theta = x$

$\Rightarrow \quad \sec^2\theta\,d\theta = dx$ or $\theta = \tan^{-1}x$

For limit 0, when $x = 0 \Rightarrow \theta = 0$ and when $x = 1 \Rightarrow \theta = \frac{\pi}{4}$

$[\because \theta = \tan^{-1}x]$

$$\therefore \quad I = \int_0^{\pi/4}\sin^{-1}\left(\frac{2\tan\theta}{1+\tan^2\theta}\right)\sec^2\theta\,d\theta$$

$$= \int_0^{\pi/4}\sin^{-1}(\sin 2\theta)\sec^2\theta\,d\theta$$

$$\left[\because \sin 2\theta = \frac{2\tan\theta}{1+\tan^2\theta}\right]$$

$$= 2\int_0^{\pi/4}\underset{\text{I}}{\theta}\,\underset{\text{II}}{\sec^2\theta}\,d\theta$$

Now, applying rule of integration by parts taking θ as the first function and $\sec^2\theta$ as second function, we get

$$I = 2\left[\theta\int\sec^2\theta\,d\theta - \int\left\{\left(\frac{d}{d\theta}\theta\right)\right\}\int\sec^2\theta\,d\theta\right]_0^{\pi/4}$$

$$= 2[\theta\tan\theta - \int 1\tan\theta\,d\theta]_0^{\pi/4}$$

$[\because \int\sec^2\theta d\theta = \tan\theta]$

$$= 2[\theta\tan\theta + \log|\cos\theta|]_0^{\pi/4}$$

$[\because \int\tan\theta\,d\theta = -\log\,\cos\theta]$

$$= 2\left\{\left(\frac{\pi}{4}\tan\frac{\pi}{4} + \log\left|\cos\frac{\pi}{4}\right|\right) - (|0 + \log|\cos 0|\,|)\right\}$$

$= \frac{\pi}{2} + 2\log\frac{1}{\sqrt{2}} - 0$ $[\because \log 1 = 0]$

$= \frac{\pi}{2} + 2\log 2^{-1/2} = \frac{\pi}{2} - 2\times\frac{1}{2}\log 2$

$[\because \log m^n = n\log m]$

$= \frac{\pi}{2} - \log 2$

(iv) $\int_0^2 x\sqrt{x+2}\,dx$

$= \int_0^2 \{(x+2)-2\}\sqrt{x+2}\,dx$

[add and subtract 2]

$= \int_0^2 \{(x+2)^{3/2} - 2(x+2)^{1/2}\}dx$

$= \left[\frac{(x+2)^{(3/2+1)}}{(3/2)+1} - \frac{2(x+2)^{1/2+1}}{(1/2)+1}\right]_0^2$

$= \frac{2}{5}[(x+2)^{5/2}]_0^2 - \frac{4}{3}[(x+2)^{3/2}]_0^2$

$= \frac{2}{5}[4^{5/2} - 2^{5/2}] - \frac{4}{3}[4^{3/2} - 2^{3/2}]$

$= \frac{2}{5}[2^5 - 2^{5/2}] - \frac{4}{3}[2^3 - 2^{3/2}]$

$= \frac{2}{5}[32 - 4\sqrt{2}] - \frac{4}{3}[8 - 2\sqrt{2}]$

$= \frac{8}{5}[8 - \sqrt{2}] - \frac{8}{3}[4 - \sqrt{2}]$

$= \left(\frac{64}{5} - \frac{32}{3}\right) + \left(\frac{8\sqrt{2}}{3} - \frac{8\sqrt{2}}{5}\right)$

$= \frac{32}{15} + \frac{16\sqrt{2}}{15}$

3 (c) Let $I = \int_0^{\pi/2} \frac{\sin x}{1+\cos^2 x}dx$

Put $\cos x = t$

$\Rightarrow -\sin x\,dx = dt \Rightarrow dx = \frac{dt}{-\sin x}$

For limit when

$x = 0 \Rightarrow t = \cos 0 = 1$

$[\because t = \cos x]$

and when

$x = \frac{\pi}{2} \Rightarrow t = \cos\frac{\pi}{2} = 0$

$\therefore \quad I = \int_1^0 \frac{\sin x}{1+t^2}\frac{dt}{(-\sin x)}dx$

$= -\int_1^0 \frac{1}{1+t^2}dt$

$= -\left[\frac{1}{1}\tan^{-1}\left(\frac{t}{1}\right)\right]_1^0$

$\left[\because \int\frac{1}{a^2+x^2}dx = \frac{1}{a}\tan^{-1}\frac{x}{a}\right]$

$= -[\tan^{-1} t]_1^0$

$= -[\tan^{-1}(0) - \tan^{-1}(1)]$

$= -\left(0 - \frac{\pi}{4}\right) = \frac{\pi}{4}$

4 (a) $\int_0^2 \frac{1}{x+4-x^2}dx$

$= \int_0^2 \frac{1}{x+4-x^2-\left(\frac{1}{2}\right)^2+\left(\frac{1}{2}\right)^2}dx$

$= \int_0^2 \frac{1}{4+\frac{1}{4}-\left(x^2-x+\frac{1}{4}\right)}dx$

$= \int_0^2 \frac{1}{4+\frac{1}{4}-\left(x-\frac{1}{2}\right)^2}dx$

$= \int_0^2 \frac{1}{\left(\frac{\sqrt{17}}{2}\right)^2-\left(x-\frac{1}{2}\right)^2}dx$

$= \frac{1}{2\cdot\frac{\sqrt{17}}{2}}\left[\log\left|\frac{\frac{\sqrt{17}}{2}+x-\frac{1}{2}}{\frac{\sqrt{17}}{2}-x+\frac{1}{2}}\right|\right]_0^2$

$\left[\because \int\frac{dx}{a^2-x^2} = \frac{1}{2a}\log\left|\frac{a+x}{a-x}\right|\right]$

$= \frac{1}{\sqrt{17}}\left[\log\left|\frac{\sqrt{17}+2x-1}{\sqrt{17}-2x+1}\right|\right]_0^2$

$= \frac{1}{\sqrt{17}}\left[\log\left|\frac{\sqrt{17}+3}{\sqrt{17}-3}\right| - \log\left|\frac{\sqrt{17}-1}{\sqrt{17}+1}\right|\right]$

$= \frac{1}{\sqrt{17}}\log\left|\frac{\sqrt{17}+3}{\sqrt{17}-3} \div \frac{\sqrt{17}-1}{\sqrt{17}+1}\right|$

$\left[\because \log m - \log n = \log\frac{m}{n}\right]$

$= \frac{1}{\sqrt{17}}\log\left|\frac{(\sqrt{17}+3)(\sqrt{17}+1)}{(\sqrt{17}-3)(\sqrt{17}-1)}\right|$

$= \frac{1}{\sqrt{17}}\log\left|\frac{20+4\sqrt{17}}{20-4\sqrt{17}}\right|$

$= \frac{1}{\sqrt{17}}\log\left|\frac{5+\sqrt{17}}{5-\sqrt{17}}\times\frac{5+\sqrt{17}}{5+\sqrt{17}}\right|$

[rationalising the denominator]

$= \frac{1}{\sqrt{17}}\log\left|\frac{(5+\sqrt{17})^2}{(5)^2-(\sqrt{17})^2}\right|$

$[\because (a-b)(a+b) = a^2 - b^2]$

$= \frac{1}{\sqrt{17}}\log\left|\frac{25+17+10\sqrt{17}}{25-17}\right|$

$= \frac{1}{\sqrt{17}}\log\left|\frac{42+10\sqrt{17}}{8}\right|$

$= \frac{1}{\sqrt{17}}\log\left|\frac{21+5\sqrt{17}}{4}\right|$

5 (d)

I. $\int_{-1}^1 \frac{1}{x^2+2x+5}dx$

$= \int_{-1}^1 \frac{1}{(x^2+2x+1)+4}dx$

$= \int_{-1}^1 \frac{1}{(x+1)^2+2^2}dx$

$= \frac{1}{2}\left[\tan^{-1}\frac{x+1}{2}\right]_{-1}^1$

$\left[\because \int\frac{dx}{a^2+x^2} = \frac{1}{a}\tan^{-1}\frac{x}{a}\right]$

$= \frac{1}{2}\left[\tan^{-1}\left(\frac{2}{2}\right) - \tan^{-1}\left(\frac{0}{2}\right)\right]$

$= \frac{1}{2}[\tan^{-1} 1]$

$= \frac{1}{2}\times\frac{\pi}{4} = \frac{\pi}{8}$

II. Let $I = \int_1^2\left(\frac{1}{x} - \frac{1}{2x^2}\right)e^{2x}dx$

$= \int_1^2 \frac{1}{x}e^{2x}dx - \int_1^2 \frac{1}{2x^2}e^{2x}dx$

Evaluate the first integral by rule of integration by parts taking $\frac{1}{x}$ as the first function, we get

$I = \left[\frac{1}{x}\cdot\frac{e^{2x}}{2}\right]_1^2 + \int_1^2 \frac{1}{x^2}\cdot\frac{e^{2x}}{2}dx - \int_1^2 \frac{1}{2x^2}e^{2x}dx$

$= \left[\frac{1}{x}\frac{e^{2x}}{2}\right]_1^2 = \frac{e^4}{4} - \frac{e^2}{2}$

$= \frac{e^2}{2}\left(\frac{e^2}{2} - 1\right)$

6 (*a*) Let $I=\int_{1/3}^{1}\frac{(x-x^3)^{\frac{1}{3}}}{x^4}dx$

$$=\int_{1/3}^{1}\frac{(x^3)^{1/3}\left(\frac{x}{x^3}-\frac{x^3}{x^3}\right)^{1/3}}{x^4}dx$$

[multiply and divide the numerator by $(x^3)^{1/3}$]

$$=\int_{1/3}^{1}\frac{\left(\frac{1}{x^2}-1\right)^{1/3}}{x^3}dx$$

Put $\frac{1}{x^2}=t \Rightarrow \frac{-2}{x^3}dx=dt$

$\Rightarrow \frac{dx}{x^3}=\frac{dt}{(-2)}$

For limit, when $x=1\Rightarrow t=1$ and when $x=\frac{1}{3}\Rightarrow t=3^2=9$ $\left[\because t=\frac{1}{x^2}\right]$

$\therefore \quad I=\int_9^1(t-1)^{1/3}\frac{dt}{(-2)}$

$$=-\frac{1}{2}\left[\frac{(t-1)^{\frac{1}{3}+1}}{\frac{1}{3}+1}\right]_9^1$$

$$=-\frac{1}{2}\times\frac{3}{4}\left[(t-1)^{\frac{4}{3}}\right]_9^1$$

$$=-\frac{3}{8}\left[(1-1)^{\frac{4}{3}}-(9-1)^{\frac{4}{3}}\right]$$

$$=-\frac{3}{8}\left[0-(2^3)^{\frac{4}{3}}\right]$$

$$=-\frac{3}{8}\times(-16)=6$$

7 (*b*) Given, $f(x)=\int_0^x t\sin t\,dt$

On integrating by parts, we get

$$f(x)=t\int_0^x\sin t\,dt-\int_0^x\left[\left(\frac{d}{dt}t\right)\int\sin t\,dt\right]dt$$

$$=[t(-\cos t)]_0^x-\int_0^x(-\cos t)\,dt$$

$$=[-t\cos t+\sin t]_0^x$$

$\Rightarrow f(x)=-x\cos x+\sin x$

Now, differentiating w.r.t. *x*, we get

$$f'(x)=-[\{x(-\sin x)\}+\cos x]+\cos x$$

$$=x\sin x-\cos x+\cos x$$

$$=x\sin x$$

[using the product rule $\frac{d}{dx}(u\cdot v)=u\frac{dv}{dx}+v\frac{du}{dx}$]

8 (*b*) We have,

$$I=\int_0^{\pi/2}\frac{\tan x}{1+m^2\tan^2 x}dx$$

$$=\int_0^{\pi/2}\frac{\frac{\sin x}{\cos x}}{1+m^2\frac{\sin^2 x}{\cos^2 x}}dx$$

$$=\int_0^{\pi/2}\frac{\sin x\cos x}{\cos^2 x+m^2\sin^2 x}dx$$

$$=\int_0^{\pi/2}\frac{\sin x\cos x}{1-\sin^2 x+m^2\sin^2 x}dx$$

$$=\int_0^{\pi/2}\frac{\sin x\cos x}{1-\sin^2 x(1-m^2)}dx$$

Put $\sin^2 x=t\Rightarrow 2\sin x\cos x\,dx=dt$

If $x=0$, $t=0$

If $x=\frac{\pi}{2}$, then $t=1$

$$\therefore I=\frac{1}{2}\int_0^1\frac{dt}{1-t(1-m^2)}$$

$$=\frac{1}{2}\left[-\log|1-t(1-m^2)|\times\frac{1}{1-m^2}\right]_0^1$$

$$=\frac{1}{2}\left[\frac{1}{m^2-1}\{\log|1-(1-m^2)-\log(1)|\}\right]$$

$$=\frac{1}{2}\times\frac{1}{m^2-1}\log|m^2|=\frac{2\log m}{2(m^2-1)}$$

$$=\frac{\log m}{m^2-1}$$

9 (*a*) Given that, $f'(x)=g(x)$

$\Rightarrow \int_a^b f(x)\,g(x)\,dx=\int_a^b f(x)\,f'(x)\,dx$

Put, $\quad f(x)=t$

$\Rightarrow \quad f'(x)\,dx=dt$

$\Rightarrow \int f(x)g(x)\,dx=\int t\,dt$

$$=\frac{t^2}{2}=\frac{[f(x)]^2}{2}$$

$\Rightarrow \int_a^b f(x)\,g(x)\,dx=\left[\frac{(f(x))^2}{2}\right]_a^b$

$$=\frac{1}{2}[(f(b))^2-(f(a))^2]$$

10 (*c*) I. Let, $I=\int_0^{\pi}\frac{1}{1+\sin x}dx$

$$=\int_0^{\pi}\frac{1}{1+\frac{2\tan\frac{x}{2}}{1+\tan^2\frac{x}{2}}}dx$$

$$=\int_0^{\pi}\frac{\sec^2 x/2}{(1+\tan x/2)^2}dx$$

Put, $\tan x/2=t$

$\Rightarrow \frac{1}{2}\sec^2 x/2\,dx=dt$

$\therefore \int_0^{\infty}\frac{2dt}{(1+t)^2}=\left[\frac{-2}{1+t}\right]_0^{\infty}=2$

II. Let $\quad I=\int_a^b\sqrt{(x-a)(b-x)}\,dx$

Put, $x=a\cos^2\theta+b\sin^2\theta$

$\Rightarrow dx=(-2a\cos\theta\sin\theta+2b\sin\theta\cos\theta)\,d\theta$

$\Rightarrow dx=\sin 2\theta(b-a)\,d\theta$

$$\therefore I=\int_0^{\pi/2}\sqrt{(b-a)\sin^2\theta(b-a)\cos^2\theta}\,\sin 2\theta(b-a)\,d\theta$$

$$=\int_0^{\pi/2}\frac{(b-a)^2}{2}\sin^2 2\theta\,d\theta$$

$$=\frac{(b-a)^2}{2}\int_0^{\pi/2}\left[\frac{1-\cos 4\theta}{2}\right]d\theta$$

$$=\frac{(b-a)^2}{4}\left[\theta-\frac{\sin 4\theta}{4}\right]_0^{\pi/2}$$

$$=\frac{(b-a)^2}{4}\left[\frac{\pi}{2}-0\right]=\frac{\pi(b-a)^2}{8}$$

11 (*b*) Let, $f(x)=\int_0^x\left[\frac{1}{\sqrt{1+t^2}}-\frac{1}{1+t}\right]dt$

$$=\left[\log|t+\sqrt{1+t^2}|-\log|1+t|\right]_0^x$$

$$=\left[\log\left|\frac{t+\sqrt{1+t^2}}{1+t}\right|\right]_0^x=\log\left|\frac{x+\sqrt{1+x^2}}{1+x}\right|$$

$$\lim_{x\to\infty}f(x)=\lim_{x\to\infty}\log\left(\frac{\sqrt{1+x^2}+x}{1+x}\right)$$

$$=\log\lim_{x\to\infty}\left(\frac{\sqrt{\frac{1}{x^2}+1}+1}{\frac{1}{x}+1}\right)$$

$$=\log_e 2 \qquad \left[\because \lim_{x\to\infty}\frac{1}{x}=0\right]$$

12 (c) Let $I=\int_0^a \sqrt{\frac{a-x}{x}}\,dx$

Put $x=a\sin^2\theta$

$\Rightarrow dx=2a\sin\theta\cos\theta\,d\theta$

$I=\int_0^{\pi/2}\sqrt{\frac{\cos^2\theta}{\sin^2\theta}}\cdot 2a\sin\theta\cos\theta\,d\theta$

$I=\int_0^{\pi/2}\left(\frac{\cos\theta}{\sin\theta}\right)2a\sin\theta\cos\theta\,d\theta$

$=2a\int_0^{\pi/2}\cos^2\theta\,d\theta$

$=a\int_0^{\pi/2}(1+\cos2\theta)\,d\theta$

$=a\left(\theta+\frac{\sin2\theta}{2}\right)_0^{\pi/2}$

$=a(\pi/2+0)-(0+0)$

$=\pi a/2$

13 (a) Given,

$\int_2^e\left(\frac{1}{\log x}-\frac{1}{(\log x)^2}\right)dx=a+\frac{b}{\log 2}$

Put $\log x=z \Rightarrow x=e^z$

$\Rightarrow \quad dx=e^z dz$

$\therefore \int_2^e\left(\frac{1}{\log x}-\frac{1}{(\log x)^2}\right)dx$

$=\int_{\log 2}^1\left(\frac{1}{z}-\frac{1}{z^2}\right)e^z dz$

$=\int_{\log 2}^1 e^z\left(\frac{1}{z}+d\left(\frac{1}{z}\right)\right)dz$

$=\left[e^z\cdot\frac{1}{z}\right]_{\log 2}^1=e-\frac{2}{\log 2}$

$[\because \int e^x(f(x)+f'(x))\,dx=e^x\cdot f(x)]$

$\therefore \quad a=e$

and $\quad b=-2$

14 (d) I. Let $I=\int_1^4 e^{\sqrt{x}}dx$

Put $x=t^2 \Rightarrow dx=2t\,dt$

$\therefore \ I=\int_1^2 2e^t t\,dt=2[te^t-e^t]_1^2$

$=2[(2e^2-e^2)-e+e]=2e^2$

II. Let $I=\int_0^{\pi/2}\sqrt{\cos x-\cos^3 x}\,dx$

$I=\int_0^{\pi/2}\sqrt{\cos x}|\sin x|\,dx$

$I=\int_0^{\pi/2}\sqrt{\cos x}\sin x\,dx$

Put $\cos x=t \Rightarrow -\sin x\,dx=dt$

$I=-\int_1^0\sqrt{t}\,dt=-\frac{2}{3}[t^{3/2}]_1^0=\frac{2}{3}$

Some Properties of Definite Integrals

1 (b) (i) Let $I=\int_0^{\pi/2}\cos^2 x\,dx$ ...(i)

$\Rightarrow \quad I=\int_0^{\pi/2}\cos^2\left(\frac{\pi}{2}-x\right)dx$

$\left[\because \int_0^a f(x)\,dx=\int_0^a f(a-x)\,dx\right]$

$\Rightarrow \ I=\int_0^{\pi/2}\sin^2 x\,dx$ ...(ii)

On adding Eqs. (i) and (ii), we get

$2I=\int_0^{\pi/2}(\sin^2 x+\cos^2 x)\,dx$

$=\int_0^{\pi/2}1\,dx$

$[\because \sin^2 x+\cos^2 x=1]$

$2I=[x]_0^{\pi/2}=\frac{\pi}{2}-0 \Rightarrow I=\frac{\pi}{4}$

(ii) Let

$I=\int_0^{\pi/2}\frac{\sqrt{\sin x}}{\sqrt{\sin x}+\sqrt{\cos x}}dx$ ...(i)

Then,

$I=\int_0^{\pi/2}\frac{\sqrt{\sin\left(\frac{\pi}{2}-x\right)}}{\sqrt{\sin\left(\frac{\pi}{2}-x\right)}+\sqrt{\cos\left(\frac{\pi}{2}-x\right)}}dx$

$\left[\because \int_0^a f(x)\,dx=\int_0^a f(a-x)\,dx\right]$

$\Rightarrow \ I=\int_0^{\pi/2}\frac{\sqrt{\cos x}}{\sqrt{\cos x}+\sqrt{\sin x}}dx$ ...(ii)

$\left[\because \sin\left(\frac{\pi}{2}-x\right)=\cos x \text{ and } \cos\left(\frac{\pi}{2}-x\right)=\sin x\right]$

On adding Eqs. (i) and (ii), we get

$2I=\int_0^{\pi/2}\frac{\sqrt{\sin x}+\sqrt{\cos x}}{\sqrt{\sin x}+\sqrt{\cos x}}dx$

$\Rightarrow 2I=\int_0^{\pi/2}1\,dx=[x]_0^{\pi/2}$

$=\frac{\pi}{2}-0 \Rightarrow I=\frac{\pi}{4}$

(iii) Let

$I=\int_0^{\pi/2}\frac{\sin^{3/2}x}{\sin^{3/2}x+\cos^{3/2}x}dx$ ...(i)

$\Rightarrow I=\int_0^{\pi/2}\frac{\sin^{3/2}\left(\frac{\pi}{2}-x\right)}{\sin^{3/2}\left(\frac{\pi}{2}-x\right)+\cos^{3/2}\left(\frac{\pi}{2}-x\right)}dx$

$\left[\because \int_0^a f(x)dx=\int_0^a f(a-x)\,dx\right]$

$=\int_0^{\pi/2}\frac{\cos^{3/2}x}{\cos^{3/2}x+\sin^{3/2}x}dx$ ...(ii)

$\left[\because \sin\left(\frac{\pi}{2}-x\right)=\cos x \text{ and } \cos\left(\frac{\pi}{2}-x\right)=\sin x\right]$

On adding Eqs. (i) and (ii), we get

$2I=\int_0^{\pi/2}\frac{\sin^{3/2}x+\cos^{3/2}x}{\sin^{3/2}x+\cos^{3/2}x}dx$

$=\int_0^{\pi/2}1\,dx=[x]_0^{\pi/2}=\frac{\pi}{2}-0$

$\Rightarrow \quad I=\frac{\pi}{4}$

(iv) Let $I=\int_0^{\pi/2}\frac{\cos^5 x}{\sin^5 x+\cos^5 x}dx$ ...(i)

$\Rightarrow \ I=\int_0^{\pi/2}\frac{\cos^5\left(\frac{\pi}{2}-x\right)}{\sin^5\left(\frac{\pi}{2}-x\right)+\cos^5\left(\frac{\pi}{2}-x\right)}dx$

$\left[\because \int_0^a f(x)dx=\int_0^a f(a-x)\,dx\right]$

$=\int_0^{\pi/2}\frac{\sin^5 x}{\cos^5 x+\sin^5 x}dx$ ...(ii)

On adding Eqs. (i) and (ii), we get

$2I=\int_0^{\pi/2}\frac{\cos^5 x+\sin^5 x}{\cos^5 x+\sin^5 x}dx$

$=\int_0^{\pi/2}1\,dx=[x]_0^{\pi/2}$

$=\frac{\pi}{2}-0 \Rightarrow I=\frac{\pi}{4}$

2 (c) A. Let $I=\int_{-5}^5|x+2|\,dx$

It can be seen that $(x+2)\le 0$ on $[-5,-2]$ and $(x+2)\ge 0$ on $[-2,5]$.

$\therefore \quad I=\int_{-5}^{-2}-(x+2)\,dx+\int_{-2}^5(x+2)\,dx$

$\left[\because \int_a^b f(x)\,dx=\int_a^c f(x)\,dx+\int_c^b f(x)\,dx\right]$

$$\Rightarrow \quad I = -\left[\frac{x^2}{2} + 2x\right]_{-5}^{-2} + \left[\frac{x^2}{2} + 2x\right]_{-2}^{5}$$

$$= -\left[\frac{(-2)^2}{2} + 2(-2) - \frac{(-5)^2}{2} - 2(-5)\right] + \left[\frac{(5)^2}{2} + 2(5) - \frac{(-2)^2}{2} - 2(-2)\right]$$

$$= -\left[2 - 4 - \frac{25}{2} + 10\right] + \left[\frac{25}{2} + 10 - 2 + 4\right]$$

$$= -2 + 4 + \frac{25}{2} - 10 + \frac{25}{2} + 10 - 2 + 4 = 29$$

B. Let $I = \int_2^8 |x - 5| dx$

It can be seen that $(x - 5) \le 0$ on $[2, 5]$ and $(x - 5) \ge 0$ on $[5, 8]$.

$$\because \int_a^b f(x)dx = \int_a^c f(x)dx + \int_c^b f(x)dx$$

$$\therefore \quad I = \int_2^5 \{-(x-5)\} dx + \int_5^8 (x-5) dx$$

$$= \left[5x - \frac{x^2}{2}\right]_2^5 + \left[\frac{x^2}{2} - 5x\right]_5^8$$

$$= \left(25 - \frac{25}{2}\right) - \left(10 - \frac{4}{2}\right) + \left(\frac{64}{2} - 40\right) - \left(\frac{25}{2} - 25\right)$$

$$= \frac{25}{2} - 8 - 8 + \frac{25}{2} = 25 - 16 = 9$$

C. Let $I = \int_0^2 x\sqrt{2-x}\, dx$ ...(i)

Also, $I = \int_0^2 (2-x)\sqrt{2-(2-x)}\, dx$

$$\left[\because \int_0^a f(x)dx = \int_0^a f(a-x)dx\right]$$

$$= \int_0^2 (2-x)\sqrt{x}\, dx$$

$$= \int_0^2 (2x^{1/2} - x^{3/2}) dx$$

$$= \left[\frac{2x^{(1/2)+1}}{(1/2)+1} - \frac{x^{(3/2)+1}}{(3/2)+1}\right]_0^2$$

$$= \left[\frac{4}{3}x^{3/2} - \frac{2}{5}x^{5/2}\right]_0^2$$

$$= \frac{4}{3} \cdot 2^{3/2} - \frac{2}{5} \cdot 2^{5/2} - 0$$

$$= \frac{4}{3} 2\sqrt{2} - \frac{2}{5} 4\sqrt{2}$$

$$= \left(\frac{8}{3} - \frac{8}{5}\right)\sqrt{2} = \left(\frac{40-24}{15}\right)\sqrt{2}$$

$$= \frac{16\sqrt{2}}{15}$$

D. Let $I = \int_0^4 |x - 1| dx$

It can be seen that, $(x-1) \le 0$ when $0 \le x \le 1$ and $(x-1) \ge 0$ when $1 \le x \le 4$

$$\therefore I = \int_0^1 |x-1| dx + \int_1^4 |x-1| dx$$

$$\left[\because \int_a^b f(x)dx = \int_a^c f(x)dx + \int_c^b f(x)dx\right]$$

$$= \int_0^1 (1-x)dx + \int_1^4 (x-1)dx$$

$$= \left[x - \frac{x^2}{2}\right]_0^1 + \left[\frac{x^2}{2} - x\right]_1^4$$

$$= \left(1 - \frac{1}{2}\right) - 0 + \left(\frac{4^2}{2} - 4\right) - \left(\frac{1}{2} - 1\right)$$

$$= \frac{1}{2} + 4 + \frac{1}{2} = 5$$

3 (*b*) Let $I = \int_0^1 x(1-x)^n dx$

$$\Rightarrow \quad I = \int_0^1 (1-x)\{1-(1-x)\}^n dx$$

$$\left[\because \int_0^a f(x)dx = \int_0^a f(a-x)dx\right]$$

$$= \int_0^1 (1-x)x^n\, dx$$

$$= \int_0^1 (x^n - x^{n+1}) dx$$

$$= \left[\frac{x^{n+1}}{n+1} - \frac{x^{n+2}}{n+2}\right]_0^1$$

$$= \left[\frac{1}{n+1} - \frac{1}{n+2}\right] - 0$$

$$= \frac{(n+2)-(n+1)}{(n+1)(n+2)}$$

$$= \frac{1}{(n+1)(n+2)}$$

4 (*a*)

I. Let $I = \int_0^{\pi/4} \log(1 + \tan x) dx$ ...(i)

$$\Rightarrow I = \int_0^{\pi/4} \log\left[1 + \tan\left(\frac{\pi}{4} - x\right)\right] dx$$

$$\left[\because \int_0^a f(x)dx = \int_0^a f(a-x)dx\right]$$

$$= \int_0^{\pi/4} \log\left(1 + \frac{1-\tan x}{1+\tan x}\right) dx$$

$$\left[\because \tan(A-B) = \frac{\tan A - \tan B}{1 + \tan A \tan B},\right]$$

here $A = \pi/4, B = x$

$$= \int_0^{\pi/4} \log\left(\frac{2}{1+\tan x}\right) dx$$

$$= \int_0^{\pi/4} \{\log 2 - \log(1 + \tan x)\} dx \quad \text{...(ii)}$$

$$\left[\because \log\left(\frac{m}{n}\right) = \log m - \log n\right]$$

On adding Eqs. (i) and (ii), we get

$$2I = \int_0^{\pi/4} \log 2\, dx$$

$$= \log 2 \int_0^{\pi/4} 1\, dx = \log 2\, [x]_0^{\pi/4}$$

$$= (\log 2)\left(\frac{\pi}{4} - 0\right)$$

$$\Rightarrow \quad 2I = \frac{\pi}{4}\log 2 \Rightarrow I = \frac{\pi}{8}\log 2$$

II. Let $I = \int_0^{\pi/2} (2\log \sin x - \log \sin 2x) dx$

$$= \int_0^{\pi/2} (\log \sin^2 x - \log \sin 2x) dx$$

$$[\because m \log n = \log n^m]$$

$$= \int_0^{\pi/2} \log\left(\frac{\sin^2 x}{\sin 2x}\right) dx$$

$$\left[\because \log m - \log n = \log \frac{m}{n}\right]$$

$$= \int_0^{\pi/2} \log\left(\frac{\sin^2 x}{2\sin x \cos x}\right) dx$$

$$[\because \sin 2x = 2\sin x \cos x]$$

$$= \int_0^{\pi/2} \log\left(\frac{\tan x}{2}\right) dx$$

$= \int_0^{\pi/2} \log(\tan x) - \log 2\, dx$

$= \int_0^{\pi/2} \log(\tan x)\, dx - \int_0^{\pi/2} \log 2\, dx$

$\Rightarrow I = I_1 - (\log 2)[x]_0^{\pi/2}$

$= I_1 - \left(\frac{\pi}{2} - 0\right)\log 2$ ...(i)

where,

$I_1 = \int_0^{\pi/2} \log(\tan x)\, dx$ ...(ii)

$\Rightarrow I_1 = \int_0^{\pi/2} \log\left[\tan\left(\frac{\pi}{2} - x\right)\right] dx$

$\left[\because \int_0^a f(x)\, dx = \int_0^a f(a-x)\, dx\right]$

$\Rightarrow I_1 = \int_0^{\pi/2} \log(\cot x)\, dx$ ...(iii)

On adding Eqs. (ii) and (iii), we get

$2I_1 = \int_0^{\pi/2} (\log(\tan x) + \log(\cot x))\, dx$

$= \int_0^{\pi/2} \log(\tan x \cot x)\, dx$

$[\because \log m + \log n = \log(mn)]$

$= \int_0^{\pi/2} \log 1\, dx = 0$

$\Rightarrow I_1 = 0$ $\left[\because \tan x = \frac{1}{\cot x}\right]$

On putting the value of I_1 in Eq. (i), we get

$I = 0 - \frac{\pi}{2}\log 2 = -\frac{\pi}{2}\log 2$

5 (c) Let $I = \int_0^a \frac{\sqrt{x}}{\sqrt{x} + \sqrt{a-x}}\, dx$ ...(i)

$I = \int_0^a \frac{\sqrt{a-x}}{\sqrt{a-x} + \sqrt{a-(a-x)}}\, dx$

$\left[\because \int_0^a f(x)\, dx = \int_0^a f(a-x)\, dx\right]$

$= \int_0^a \frac{\sqrt{a-x}}{\sqrt{a-x} + \sqrt{x}}\, dx$ ...(ii)

On adding Eqs. (i) and (ii), we get

$\Rightarrow 2I = \int_0^a \frac{\sqrt{x} + \sqrt{a-x}}{\sqrt{a-x} + \sqrt{x}}\, dx,$

$2I = \int_0^a 1\, dx$

$= [x]_0^a = a - 0 = a$

$\Rightarrow I = \frac{a}{2}$

6 (b) We have, $f(x) = f(a-x)$ and $g(x) + g(a-x) = 4$.

Let $I = \int_0^a f(x) g(x)\, dx$ ...(i)

$\Rightarrow I = \int_0^a f(a-x) g(a-x)\, dx$

$\left[\because \int_0^a f(x)\, dx = \int_0^a f(a-x)\, dx\right]$

$\Rightarrow I = \int_0^a f(x)\{4 - g(x)\}\, dx$ ...(ii)

$[\because f(x) = f(a-x)$ and $g(x) + g(a-x) = 4$ (given)$]$

On adding Eqs. (i) and (ii), we get

$2I = \int_0^a 4 f(x)\, dx$

$\Rightarrow I = 2\int_0^a f(x)\, dx.$

7 (c) (i) Let $I = \int_{-\pi/2}^{\pi/2} \sin^7 x\, dx$

Here, $f(x) = \sin^7 x$

$f(-x) = \sin^7(-x)$

$= [-\sin x]^7 = -\sin^7 x$

$\therefore f(-x) = -f(x)$

So, $f(x)$ is an odd function.

$\int_{-\pi/2}^{\pi/2} \sin^7 x\, dx = 0$

$\left[\because \int_{-a}^a f(x)\, dx = 0\right.$ if $f(x)$ is an odd function$]$

Note $\int_{-a}^a f(x) dx = \begin{cases} 2\int_0^a f(x)\, dx, & \text{if } f(x) \text{ is even.} \\ 0, & \text{if } f(x) \text{ is odd.} \end{cases}$

(ii) Let $I = \int_0^{2\pi} \sin^5 x\, dx$

Let $f(x) = \sin^5 x$

Now $f(2\pi - x) = \sin^5(2\pi - x)$

$= -\sin^5 x = -f(x)$

We know that,

$\int_0^{2a} f(x) dx = \begin{cases} 2\int_0^a f(x)\, dx & \text{if } f(2a-x) = f(x) \\ 0, & \text{if } f(2a-x) = [-f(x)] \end{cases}$

$\therefore I = \int_0^{2\pi} \sin^5 x\, dx = 0$

(iii) Let

$I = \int_0^{\pi/2} \frac{\sin x - \cos x}{1 + \sin x \cos x}\, dx$ ...(i)

$\Rightarrow I = \int_0^{\pi/2} \frac{\sin\left(\frac{\pi}{2} - x\right) - \cos\left(\frac{\pi}{2} - x\right)}{1 + \sin\left(\frac{\pi}{2} - x\right)\cos\left(\frac{\pi}{2} - x\right)}\, dx$

$\left[\because \int_0^a f(x)\, dx = \int_0^a f(a-x)\, dx\right]$

$= \int_0^{\pi/2} \frac{\cos x - \sin x}{1 + \cos x \sin x}\, dx$ ...(ii)

$\left[\because \sin\left(\frac{\pi}{2} - x\right) = \cos x \text{ and } \cos\left(\frac{\pi}{2} - x\right) = \sin x\right]$

On adding Eqs. (i) and (ii), we get

$2I = \int_0^{\pi/2} \frac{0}{1 + \sin x \cos x}\, dx = 0$

$\Rightarrow I = 0$

(iv) Let $I = \int_0^{\pi} \log(1 + \cos x)\, dx$ ...(i)

$\Rightarrow I = \int_0^{\pi} \log\{1 + \cos(\pi - x)\}\, dx$

$\left[\because \int_0^a f(x)\, dx = \int_0^a f(a-x)\, dx\right]$

$= \int_0^{\pi} \log(1 - \cos x)\, dx$

$[\because \cos(\pi - x) = -\cos x]$ ...(ii)

$= \int_0^{\pi} \log\left[2\sin^2\left(\frac{x}{2}\right)\right] dx$

$\left[\because 1 - \cos x = 2\sin^2\frac{x}{2}\right]$

$= \int_0^{\pi} \left[\log 2 + 2\log\left(\sin\frac{x}{2}\right)\right] dx$

$[\because \log(mn^2) = \log m + 2\log n]$

$= \int_0^{\pi} \log 2\, dx + 2\int_0^{\pi} \log\left(\sin\frac{x}{2}\right) dx$

In the second integral, put $\frac{x}{2} = t$

$\Rightarrow dx = 2dt,$

and limits when $x = 0, t = 0$ and when $x = \pi, t = \pi/2$

$\therefore I = \log 2\,[x]_0^{\pi} + 2\int_0^{\pi/2} \log(\sin t)\, 2\,dt$

$= (\log 2)(\pi - 0) + 4\left(-\frac{\pi}{2}\log 2\right)$

$\left[\because \int_0^{\pi/2} \log \sin x\, dx = -\frac{\pi}{2}\log 2\right]$

$= -\pi \log 2$

8 (*d*)

I. Let $I = \int_{-\pi/2}^{\pi/2} \sin^2 x\, dx$

Here, $f(x) = \sin^2 x$

$f(-x) = \sin^2(-x) = [\sin(-x)]^2$
$= (-\sin x)^2 = \sin^2 x = f(x)$

$\therefore$ $f(x)$ is an even function.

$I = \int_{-\pi/2}^{\pi/2} \sin^2 x\, dx$

$= 2\int_0^{\pi/2} \sin^2 x\, dx$

$\left[\because \int_{-a}^{a} f(x)dx = 2\int_0^a f(x)dx, \text{ if } f(x) \text{ is even}\right]$

$= 2\int_0^{\pi/2} \left[\frac{1-\cos 2x}{2}\right] dx$

$[\because \cos 2x = 1 - 2\sin^2 x]$

$= \int_0^{\pi/2} (1 - \cos 2x)\, dx$

$= \left[x - \frac{\sin 2x}{2}\right]_0^{\pi/2}$

$= \left[\frac{\pi}{2} - \frac{\sin \pi}{2}\right] - (0 - 0)$

$= \frac{\pi}{2} - 0 = \frac{\pi}{2}$

II. Let $I = \int_0^{\pi} \frac{x}{1+\sin x} dx$ ...(i)

Then, $I = \int_0^{\pi} \frac{\pi - x}{1 + \sin(\pi - x)} dx$

$\left[\because \int_0^a f(x)dx = \int_0^a f(a-x)dx\right]$

$\Rightarrow I = \int_0^{\pi} \frac{\pi - x}{1+\sin x} dx$ ...(ii)

$[\because \sin(\pi - x) = \sin x]$

On adding Eqs. (i) and (ii), we get

$2I = \int_0^{\pi} \frac{\pi}{(1+\sin x)} dx$

$= \pi\int_0^{\pi} \frac{1}{(1+\sin x)} dx$

$= \pi\int_0^{\pi} \frac{1-\sin x}{(1+\sin x)(1-\sin x)} dx$

[(multiply numerator and denominator by $(1-\sin x)$]

$\Rightarrow 2I = \pi\int_0^{\pi} \frac{1-\sin x}{1-\sin^2 x} dx$

$= \pi\int_0^{\pi} \frac{1}{\cos^2 x} dx - \pi\int \frac{\sin x}{\cos^2 x} dx$

$[\because \sin^2 x + \cos^2 x = 1]$

$\Rightarrow 2I = \pi\int_0^{\pi} \sec^2 x\, dx - \pi\int_0^{\pi} \sec x \cdot \tan x\, dx$

$\Rightarrow 2I = \pi\,[\tan x - \sec x]_0^{\pi}$

$\Rightarrow 21 = \pi[\tan \pi - \sec \pi - (\tan 0 - \sec 0)]$

$\Rightarrow 2I = \pi\,[0 + 1 - 0 + 1]$

$\Rightarrow 2I = 2\pi \Rightarrow I = \pi$

9 (*c*) Let $I = \int_{-\pi/2}^{\pi/2} (x^3 + x\cos x + \tan^5 x + 1)dx$

$\Rightarrow I = \int_{-\pi/2}^{\pi/2} x^3 dx + \int_{-\pi/2}^{\pi/2} x\cos x\, dx + \int_{-\pi/2}^{\pi/2} \tan^5 x dx + \int_{-\pi/2}^{\pi/2} 1 dx$

We know that,

$\int_{-a}^{a} f(x)dx = \begin{cases} 2\int_0^a f(x)dx, & \text{if } f(x) \text{ is even} \\ 0, & \text{if } f(x) \text{ is odd} \end{cases}$

$\therefore$ $I = 0 + 0 + 0 + 2\int_0^{\pi/2} 1 dx.$

$[\because x^3, x\cos x$ and $\tan^5(x)$ are odd functions]

$\therefore$ $I = 2\,[x]_0^{\pi/2} = \frac{2\pi}{2} = \pi$

10 (*c*) Let

$I = \int_0^{\pi/2} \log\left(\frac{4+3\sin x}{4+3\cos x}\right) dx$ ...(i)

$\Rightarrow I = \int_0^{\pi/2} \log\left(\frac{4+3\sin(\pi/2 - x)}{4+3\cos(\pi/2 - x)}\right) dx$

$\left[\because \int_0^a f(x)dx = \int_0^a f(a-x)dx\right]$

$\Rightarrow I = \int_0^{\pi/2} \log\left(\frac{4+3\cos x}{4+3\sin x}\right) dx$ ...(ii)

$\left[\because \sin\left(\frac{\pi}{2} - x\right) = \cos x \text{ and } \cos\left(\frac{\pi}{2} - x\right) = \sin x\right]$

On adding Eqs. (i) and (ii), we get

$2I = \int_0^{\pi/2} \left[\log\left(\frac{4+3\sin x}{4+3\cos x}\right) + \log\left(\frac{4+3\cos x}{4+3\sin x}\right)\right] dx$

$\Rightarrow 2I = \int_0^{\pi/2} \log\left(\frac{4+3\sin x}{4+3\cos x} \times \frac{4+3\cos x}{4+3\sin x}\right) dx$

$[\because \log m + \log n = \log mn]$

$\Rightarrow 2I = \int_0^{\pi/2} \log 1\, dx$

$\Rightarrow 2I = \int_0^{\pi/2} 0\, dx$ $[\because \log 1 = 0]$

$\Rightarrow I = 0$

11 (*a*)

I. We have,

$I = \int_0^{\pi/2} \frac{\tan^7 x}{\cot^7 x + \tan^7 x} dx$ ...(i)

$= \int_0^{\pi/2} \frac{\tan^7\left(\frac{\pi}{2} - x\right)}{\cot^7\left(\frac{\pi}{2} - x\right) + \tan^7\left(\frac{\pi}{2} - x\right)} dx$

$\left[\because \int_0^a f(x)dx = \int_0^a f(a-x)dx\right]$

$= \int_0^{\pi/2} \frac{\cot^7 x}{\cot^7 x + \tan^7 x} dx$ ...(ii)

Adding Eqs. (i) and (ii), we get

$2I = \int_0^{\frac{\pi}{2}} \left(\frac{\cot^7 x + \tan^7 x}{\tan^7 x + \cot^7 x}\right) dx$

$= \int_0^{\frac{\pi}{2}} dx$

which give $I = \frac{\pi}{4}$

II. We have,

$I = \int_2^8 \frac{\sqrt{10-x}}{\sqrt{x} + \sqrt{10-x}} dx$ ... (i)

$= \int_2^8 \frac{\sqrt{10-(10-x)}}{\sqrt{10-x} + \sqrt{10-(10-x)}} dx$

$= \int_2^8 \frac{\sqrt{x}\, dx}{\sqrt{10-x} + \sqrt{x}}$ ... (ii)

$\left[\because \int_a^b f(x)dx = \int_a^b f(a+b-x)dx\right]$

Adding Eqs. (i) and (ii), we get

$2I = \int_2^8 1 dx$

$= 8 - 2 = 6$

Hence, $I = 3$

12 (*b*) Since, $I = \int_0^a f(x) \cdot g(x)\,dx$

$$= \int_0^a f(a-x)\,g(a-x)\,dx$$

$$= \int_0^a f(x)(a-g(x))dx$$

$$= a\int_0^a f(x)\,dx - \int_0^a f(x)\cdot g(x)\,dx$$

$$= a\int_0^a f(x)\,dx - \text{I}$$

$$I = \frac{a}{2}\int_0^a f(x)\,dx$$

13 (*b*) Since, by putting $x = t + c$, we get

$$I = \int_a^b f(c+t)\,dt = t = \int_a^b f(x+c)\,dx$$

14 (*a*)

I. Put $x = -t \Rightarrow dx = -dt$

$$\therefore \int_{100}^{-100} f(-t)\,dt$$

$$= -\int_{-100}^{100} f(-t)\,dt$$

$$= \int_{-100}^{100} f(-x)\,dx$$

II. Let $I = \int_0^\pi [\cot x]\,dx$ ...(i)

$$\Rightarrow I = \int_0^\pi [\cot(\pi - x)]\,dx$$

$$= \int_0^\pi [-\cot x]\,dx \quad \text{...(ii)}$$

On adding Eqs. (i) and (ii), we get

$$2I = \int_0^\pi [\cot x]\,dx + \int_0^\pi [-\cot x]\,dx$$

$$= \int_0^\pi (-1)\,dx$$

$[\because [x] + [-x] = -1$, if $x \notin Z$ and $[x] + [-x] = 0$, if $x \in Z]$

$$= [-x]_0^\pi = -x$$

$$\therefore I = -\frac{\pi}{2}$$

15 (*b*) Let $I = \int_0^\pi x\,f(\sin x)\,dx$

$$= \int_0^\pi (\pi - x) f[\sin(\pi - x)]\,dx$$

$$\Rightarrow I = \int_0^\pi (\pi - x) f(\sin x)\,dx$$

On adding Eqs. (i) and (ii), we get

$$2I = \int_0^\pi \pi\,f(\sin x)\,dx$$

$$= 2\pi\int_0^{\pi/2} f(\sin x)\,dx$$

$$\Rightarrow I = \pi\int_0^{\pi/2} f(\sin x)\,dx$$

$$= A\int_0^{\pi/2} f(\sin x)\,dx$$

$$\therefore A = \pi$$

16 (*b*) Let

$$I = \int_{-3\pi/2}^{-\pi/2} [(x+\pi)^3 + \cos^2 x]\,dx \quad \text{...(i)}$$

$$I = \int_{-3\pi/2}^{-\pi/2} \left(-\frac{\pi}{2} - \frac{3\pi}{2} - x + \pi\right)^3 + \cos^2\left(-\frac{\pi}{2} - \frac{3\pi}{2} - x\right)$$

$$\Rightarrow I = \int_{-3\pi/2}^{-\pi/2} [-(x+\pi)^3 + \cos^2 x]\,dx \quad \text{...(ii)}$$

On adding Eqs. (i) and (ii), we get

$$2I = \int_{-3\pi/2}^{-\pi/2} 2\cos^2 x\,dx$$

$$= \int_{-3\pi/2}^{-\pi/2} (1 + \cos 2x)\,dx$$

$$= \left[x + \frac{\sin 2x}{2}\right]_{-3\pi/2}^{-\pi/2}$$

$$2I = \left\{-\frac{\pi}{2} + \frac{\sin(-\pi)}{2} - \left[\left(\frac{-3\pi}{2}\right) + \frac{\sin(-3\pi)}{2}\right]\right\} = \pi$$

$$\Rightarrow I = \frac{\pi}{2}$$

17 (*c*) $\cos x \log\left(\frac{1+x}{1-x}\right)$ is an odd function.

$$\therefore \int_{-1/2}^{1/2} \cos x \log\left(\frac{1+x}{1-x}\right)dx = 0$$

$$\therefore k = 0$$

Miscellaneous Exercise

1 (*c*) A. $\int \frac{1}{x - x^3}\,dx = \int \frac{1}{x(1-x^2)}\,dx$

$$= \int \frac{1}{x(1-x)(1+x)}\,dx \quad \text{...(i)}$$

Let $\frac{1}{x(1-x)(1+x)}$

$$= \frac{A}{x} + \frac{B}{(1-x)} + \frac{C}{(1+x)}$$

$$\Rightarrow 1 = A(1-x)(1+x) + B(x)(1+x) + C(x)(1-x)$$

$$\Rightarrow 1 = A(1-x^2) + B(x + x^2) + C(x - x^2)$$

$$\Rightarrow 1 = x^2(B - A - C) + x(B + C) + A$$

On equating the coefficients of x^2, x and constant term on both sides, we get

$-A + B - C = 0$, $B + C = 0$

and $A = 1$

On solving these equations, we get

$$A = 1, B = \frac{1}{2} \text{ and } C = -\frac{1}{2}$$

From Eq. (i), we get

$$\int \frac{1}{x(1-x^2)}\,dx = \int \frac{1}{x}\,dx + \frac{1}{2}\int \frac{1}{1-x}\,dx - \frac{1}{2}\int \frac{1}{1+x}\,dx$$

$$= \log|x| - \frac{1}{2}\log|1-x| - \frac{1}{2}\log|1+x| + C$$

$$= \log|x| - \frac{1}{2}\log\{|1+x|\,|1-x|\} + C$$

$$= \frac{1}{2}\log|x|^2 - \frac{1}{2}\log|1-x^2| + C$$

$$= \frac{1}{2}\log\left|\frac{x^2}{1-x^2}\right| + C$$

B. $\int \frac{1}{\sqrt{x+a} + \sqrt{x+b}}\,dx$

$$= \int \frac{1}{\sqrt{x+a} + \sqrt{x+b}} \times \frac{\sqrt{x+a} - \sqrt{x+b}}{\sqrt{x+a} - \sqrt{x+b}}\,dx$$

$$= \int \frac{\sqrt{x+a} - \sqrt{x+b}}{(x+a) - (x+b)}\,dx$$

$$= \frac{1}{a-b}\int [(x+a)^{1/2} - (x+b)^{1/2}]\,dx$$

$$= \frac{1}{a-b}\left[\frac{(x+a)^{(1/2)+1}}{\frac{1}{2}+1} - \frac{(x+b)^{(1/2)+1}}{\frac{1}{2}+1}\right] + C$$

$$= \frac{1}{a-b}\left[\frac{(x+a)^{3/2}}{3/2} - \frac{(x+b)^{3/2}}{3/2}\right] + C$$

$$= \frac{2}{3(a-b)}[(x+a)^{3/2} - (x+b)^{3/2}] + C$$

C. Let $I = \int \frac{1}{x\sqrt{ax-x^2}}dx$

Put $x = \frac{a}{t} \Rightarrow dx = \frac{-a\,dt}{t^2}$

$$\therefore\ I = \int \frac{1}{\frac{a}{t}\sqrt{a\left(\frac{a}{t}\right) - \frac{a^2}{t^2}}}\left(\frac{-a}{t^2}\right)dt$$

$$= \int \frac{-a}{a\cdot a\sqrt{t-1}}dt$$

$$= -\frac{1}{a}\int (t-1)^{-1/2}dt$$

$$= -\frac{1}{a}\cdot\frac{(t-1)^{(-1/2)+1}}{-(1/2)+1} + C$$

$$= -\frac{2}{a}\sqrt{t-1} + C$$

$$= -\frac{2}{a}\sqrt{\frac{a}{x} - 1} + C$$

$$\left[\because x = \frac{a}{t} \Rightarrow t = \frac{a}{x}\right]$$

$$= -\frac{2}{a}\sqrt{\frac{a-x}{x}} + C$$

D. Let $I = \int \frac{1}{x^2(x^4+1)^{3/4}}dx$

$$= \int \frac{1}{x^2\left\{x^4\left(1+\frac{1}{x^4}\right)\right\}^{3/4}}dx$$

$$= \int \frac{1}{x^2.x^3\left(1+\frac{1}{x^4}\right)^{3/4}}dx$$

$$= \int \frac{1}{x^5\left(1+\frac{1}{x^4}\right)^{3/4}}dx$$

Put $1 + \frac{1}{x^4} = t$

$$\Rightarrow -\frac{4}{x^5}dx = dt \Rightarrow \frac{1}{x^5}dx = -\frac{dt}{4}$$

$$\therefore\ I = \frac{1}{-4}\int \frac{1}{t^{3/4}}dt$$

$$= -\frac{1}{4}\left[\frac{t^{1/4}}{1/4}\right] + C$$

$$= -(1+x^{-4})^{1/4} + C$$

2 (*d*) Let $I = \int \frac{1}{x^{1/2} + x^{1/3}}dx$

Put $x^{1/6} = t \Rightarrow x = t^6$

$$\Rightarrow dx = 6t^5 dt$$

$$\therefore\ I = \int \frac{6t^5}{(t^6)^{1/2} + (t^6)^{1/3}}dt$$

$$= 6\int \frac{t^5}{t^3 + t^2}dt$$

$$= 6\int \frac{t^5}{t^2(t+1)}dt = 6\int \frac{t^3}{(t+1)}dt$$

$$= 6\int \left(\frac{t^3+1-1}{t+1}\right)dt$$

$$= 6\int \left[\frac{(t+1)(t^2-t+1)}{t+1} - \frac{1}{t+1}\right]dt$$

$$= 6\int \left\{t^2 - t + 1 + \frac{-1}{t+1}\right\}dt$$

$$= 6\left\{\frac{t^3}{3} - \frac{t^2}{2} + t - \log|t+1|\right\} + C$$

$$= 6\left\{\frac{(x^{1/6})^3}{3} - \frac{(x^{1/6})^2}{2} + (x^{1/6}) - \log|x^{1/6}+1|\right\} + C$$

$[\because t = x^{1/6}]$

$$= 2x^{1/2} - 3x^{1/3} + 6x^{1/6} - 6\log|x^{1/6}+1| + C$$

3 (*c*)

I. $\int \frac{5x}{(x+1)(x^2+9)}dx$

Let $\frac{5x}{(x+1)(x^2+9)} = \frac{A}{x+1} + \frac{Bx+C}{x^2+9}$

$$\Rightarrow 5x = A(x^2+9) + (Bx+C)(x+1)$$

$$\Rightarrow 5x = Ax^2 + 9A + Bx^2 + Bx + Cx + C$$

On equating the coefficients of x^2, x and constant term on both sides, we get

$$A + B = 0,\quad B + C = 5,\quad 9A + C = 0$$

On solving these equations, we get

$$A = -\frac{1}{2}, B = \frac{1}{2} \text{ and } C = \frac{9}{2}$$

$$\therefore \int \frac{5x}{(x+1)(x^2+9)}dx$$

$$= \int \frac{\left(-\frac{1}{2}\right)}{(x+1)}dx + \int \frac{\frac{1}{2}x + \frac{9}{2}}{x^2+9}dx$$

$$= -\frac{1}{2}\int \frac{1}{x+1}dx + \frac{1}{2}\int \left(\frac{x+9}{x^2+9}\right)dx$$

$$= -\frac{1}{2}\log|x+1| + \frac{1}{2}\cdot\frac{1}{2}\int \frac{2x}{x^2+9}dx + \frac{9}{2}\int \frac{1}{x^2+9}dx$$

$$= -\frac{1}{2}\log|x+1| + \frac{1}{4}\log|x^2+9| + \frac{9}{2}\cdot\frac{1}{3}\tan^{-1}\left(\frac{x}{3}\right) + C$$

$$\left[\because \int \frac{dx}{a^2+x^2} = \frac{1}{a}\tan^{-1}\left(\frac{x}{a}\right)\right]$$

$$= -\frac{1}{2}\log|x+1| + \frac{1}{4}\log|x^2+9| + \frac{3}{2}\tan^{-1}\left(\frac{x}{3}\right) + C$$

II. Let $I = \int \frac{\cos x}{\sqrt{4-\sin^2 x}}dx$

Put $\sin x = t \Rightarrow \cos x\,dx = dt$

$$\therefore\ I = \int \frac{\cos x}{\sqrt{4-t^2}}\frac{dt}{\cos x}$$

$$= \int \frac{1}{\sqrt{4-t^2}}dt = \sin^{-1}\left(\frac{t}{2}\right) + C$$

$$\left[\because \int \frac{dx}{\sqrt{a^2-x^2}} = \sin^{-1}\left(\frac{x}{a}\right)\right]$$

$$= \sin^{-1}\left(\frac{\sin x}{2}\right) + C$$

4 (*a*) Let $I = \int \frac{x^3}{\sqrt{1-x^8}}dx$

Put $x^4 = t \Rightarrow 4x^3 dx = dt$

$$\Rightarrow dx = \frac{dt}{4x^3}$$

$$\therefore\quad I = \int \frac{x^3}{\sqrt{1-t^2}}\frac{dt}{4x^3}$$

$$= \frac{1}{4}\int \frac{1}{\sqrt{1-t^2}}dt$$

$$= \frac{1}{4}\sin^{-1}t + C$$

$$\left[\because \int \frac{dx}{\sqrt{a^2-x^2}} = \sin^{-1}\left(\frac{x}{a}\right)\right]$$

$$= \frac{1}{4}\sin^{-1}(x^4) + C$$

5 (a) (i) Let $I=\int \cos^3 x e^{\log \sin x}\, dx$

$= \int (\cos x)^3 \sin x\, dx$ $[\because e^{\log x} = x]$

$= -\int (\cos x)^3(-\sin x)\, dx$

Put $\cos x = t \Rightarrow -\sin x\, dx = dt$

$\therefore \quad I = -\int t^3 dt = -\dfrac{t^4}{4} + C$

$= -\dfrac{\cos^4 x}{4} + C$

(ii) Let $I = \int e^{3\log x}(x^4+1)^{-1} dx$

$= \int \dfrac{e^{\log x^3}}{(x^4+1)} dx = \int \dfrac{x^3}{(x^4+1)} dx$ $[\because e^{\log x} = x]$

Put $x^4 + 1 = t$

$\Rightarrow \quad 4x^3 dx = dt$

$\Rightarrow \quad dx = \dfrac{dt}{4x^3}$

$\therefore \quad I = \int \dfrac{x^3}{t} \dfrac{dt}{4x^3} = \dfrac{1}{4}\int \dfrac{1}{t} dt$

$= \dfrac{1}{4} \log |t| + C$

$= \dfrac{1}{4} \log |x^4 + 1| + C$

(iii) Let $I = \int \dfrac{1}{\sqrt{\sin^3 x \sin(x+\alpha)}} dx$

$= \int \dfrac{1}{\sqrt{\sin^3 x(\sin x \cos\alpha + \cos x \sin\alpha)}} dx$

$[\because \sin(A+B) = \sin A \cos B + \cos A \sin B]$

$= \int \dfrac{1}{\sqrt{\sin^4 x(\cos\alpha + \cot x \sin\alpha)}} dx$

$= \int \dfrac{1}{\sin^2 x\sqrt{\cos\alpha + \cot x \sin\alpha}} dx$

$= \int \dfrac{\operatorname{cosec}^2 x}{\sqrt{\cos\alpha + \cot x \sin\alpha}} dx$

Put $\cos\alpha + \cot x \sin\alpha = t$

$\Rightarrow -\operatorname{cosec}^2 x \sin\alpha\, dx = dt$

$\Rightarrow dx = \dfrac{dt}{-\operatorname{cosec}^2 x \sin\alpha}$

$\therefore I = \dfrac{-1}{\sin\alpha}\int \dfrac{dt}{\sqrt{t}} = \dfrac{-1}{\sin\alpha}[2\sqrt{t}] + C$

$= \dfrac{-1}{\sin\alpha}[2\sqrt{\cos\alpha + \cot x \sin\alpha}] + C$

$= \dfrac{-2}{\sin\alpha}\sqrt{\cos\alpha + \dfrac{\cos x \sin\alpha}{\sin x}} + C$

$= \dfrac{-2}{\sin\alpha}\sqrt{\dfrac{\sin x \cos\alpha + \cos x \sin\alpha}{\sin x}} + C$

$= -\dfrac{2}{\sin\alpha}\sqrt{\dfrac{\sin(x+\alpha)}{\sin x}} + C$

$[\because \sin(A+B) = \sin A \cos B + \cos A \sin B]$

(iv) Let $I = \int \dfrac{\sin^{-1}\sqrt{x} - \cos^{-1}\sqrt{x}}{\sin^{-1}\sqrt{x} + \cos^{-1}\sqrt{x}} dx$

We know that,

$\sin^{-1}\sqrt{x} + \cos^{-1}\sqrt{x} = \dfrac{\pi}{2}$

$\Rightarrow \cos^{-1}\sqrt{x} = \dfrac{\pi}{2} - \sin^{-1}\sqrt{x}$

$\therefore I = \int \dfrac{\sin^{-1}\sqrt{x} - \left(\dfrac{\pi}{2} - \sin^{-1}\sqrt{x}\right)}{\dfrac{\pi}{2}} dx$

$= \int \dfrac{2\sin^{-1}\sqrt{x} - \dfrac{\pi}{2}}{\dfrac{\pi}{2}} dx$

$= \dfrac{2}{\pi}\int \left(2\sin^{-1}\sqrt{x} - \dfrac{\pi}{2}\right) dx$

$= \dfrac{4}{\pi}\int \sin^{-1}\sqrt{x}\, dx - \int 1\, dx$

$= \dfrac{4}{\pi}\int \sin^{-1}\sqrt{x}\, dx - x$

$\Rightarrow \quad I = \dfrac{4}{\pi} I_1 - x + C \quad$ ... (i)

where, $I_1 = \int \sin^{-1}\sqrt{x}\, dx$

Put $\sqrt{x} = t \Rightarrow x = t^2$

$\Rightarrow \quad dx = 2t\, dt$

$I_1 = \int \sin^{-1} t\, 2t\, dt$

$= 2\int \underset{\text{I}}{\sin^{-1} t} \cdot \underset{\text{II}}{t}\, dt$

$= 2\left[\sin^{-1} t \cdot \dfrac{t^2}{2} - \int \dfrac{1}{\sqrt{1-t^2}} \cdot \dfrac{t^2}{2} dt\right]$

[using intergration by part I,

$\int uv\, dx = u\int v\, dx - \int\left(\dfrac{d}{dx} u \int v\, dx\right) dx$]

$= t^2 \sin^{-1} t - \int \dfrac{t^2}{\sqrt{1-t^2}} dt$

$= t^2 \sin^{-1} t - \int \dfrac{-(1-t^2)+1}{\sqrt{1-t^2}} dt$

$= t^2 \sin^{-1} t + \int \sqrt{1-t^2}\, dt - \int \dfrac{1}{\sqrt{1-t^2}} dt$

$= t^2 \sin^{-1} t + \dfrac{t\sqrt{1-t^2}}{2} + \dfrac{1}{2}\sin^{-1} t - \sin^{-1} t$

$= \left(t^2 - \dfrac{1}{2}\right)\sin^{-1} t + \dfrac{1}{2} t\sqrt{1-t^2}$

$= \dfrac{1}{2}[(2x-1)\sin^{-1}\sqrt{x} + \sqrt{x}\sqrt{1-x}]$

$= \dfrac{1}{2}[(2x-1)\sin^{-1}\sqrt{x} + \sqrt{x-x^2}]$

On putting the value of I_1 in Eq.(i), we get

$\int \dfrac{\sin^{-1}\sqrt{x} - \cos^{-1}\sqrt{x}}{\sin^{-1}\sqrt{x} + \cos^{-1}\sqrt{x}} dx$

$= \dfrac{2}{\pi}[(2x-1)\sin^{-1}\sqrt{x} + \sqrt{x-x^2}] - x + C$

6 (b) Let $I = \int f'(ax+b)\,[f(ax+b)]^n dx$

Put $\quad f(ax+b) = t$

$\Rightarrow \quad f'(ax+b)\, a\, dx = dt$

$\Rightarrow \quad dx = \dfrac{dt}{af'(ax+b)}$

$I = \int f'(ax+b)\, t^n \dfrac{dt}{f'(ax+b)a}$

$= \dfrac{1}{a}\int t^n\, dt = \dfrac{1}{a}\left(\dfrac{t^{n+1}}{n+1}\right) + C$

$= \dfrac{1}{a} \cdot \dfrac{[f(ax+b)]^{n+1}}{n+1} + C$

7 (c) Let $I = \int \sqrt{\dfrac{1-\sqrt{x}}{1+\sqrt{x}}} dx$

Put $\sqrt{x} = \cos t \Rightarrow \cos^{-1}\sqrt{x} = t$

$\Rightarrow \quad x = \cos^2 t$

$\Rightarrow \quad dx = 2\cos t(-\sin t)\, dt$

$\therefore \quad I = \int \sqrt{\dfrac{1-\cos t}{1+\cos t}}(-2\sin t \cos t)\, dt$

$\Rightarrow I = -2\int \sqrt{\dfrac{2\sin^2 \dfrac{t}{2}}{2\cos^2 \dfrac{t}{2}}} \cdot 2\sin\dfrac{t}{2} \cos\dfrac{t}{2} \cdot \cos t\, dt$

$$= -4\int \sin^2 \frac{t}{2}\cdot \cos t\,dt$$
$$= -4\int \frac{1-\cos t}{2}\cdot \cos t\,dt$$
$$= -2\int (\cos t - \cos^2 t)\,dt$$
$$= -2\int \left(\cos t - \frac{1+\cos 2t}{2}\right) dt$$
$$= -2\sin t + t + \frac{1}{2}\sin 2t + C$$
$$= -2\sin t + t + \frac{1}{2}\times 2\sin t\cdot \cos t + C$$
$$= -2\sqrt{1-\cos^2 t} + t + \frac{1}{2}[2\sqrt{1-\cos^2 t}\cdot \cos t] + C$$
$$= -2\sqrt{1-x} + \cos^{-1}\sqrt{x} + \sqrt{x}\sqrt{1-x} + C$$
$$= -2\sqrt{1-x} + \cos^{-1}\sqrt{x} + \sqrt{x-x^2} + C$$

8 (*a*)

I. Let $I = \int \frac{2+\sin 2x}{1+\cos 2x} e^x dx$

$$= \int \left[\frac{2}{1+\cos 2x} + \frac{\sin 2x}{1+\cos 2x}\right]\cdot e^x dx$$
$$= \int \left[\frac{2}{2\cos^2 x} + \frac{2\sin x\cos x}{2\cos^2 x}\right]\cdot e^x dx$$
$\left[\because 1+\cos 2x = 2\cos^2 x \text{ and } \sin 2x = 2\sin x\cos x\right]$
$$= \int \left(\frac{1}{\cos^2 x} + \tan x\right) e^x dx$$
$$= \int (\tan x + \sec^2 x) e^x dx$$

Put $f(x) = \tan x$

$\Rightarrow f'(x) = \sec^2 x$

$\{\because \int [f(x) + f'(x)] e^x dx = e^x f(x) + C\}$

$\therefore \quad I = e^x \tan x + C$

II. We have, $\int \frac{x^2+x+1}{(x+1)^2(x+2)} dx$

The integrand $\frac{x^2+x+1}{(x+1)^2(x+2)}$ is a proper rational function.

$$\therefore \frac{x^2+x+1}{(x+1)^2(x+2)} = \frac{A}{x+1} + \frac{B}{(x+1)^2} + \frac{C}{(x+2)} \quad \text{...(i)}$$

$\Rightarrow x^2+x+1 = A(x+1)(x+2) + B(x+2) + C(x+1)^2$

$\Rightarrow x^2+x+1 = A(x^2+3x+2) + B(x+2) + C(x^2+2x+1)$

$\Rightarrow x^2+x+1 = (A+C)x^2 + (3A+B+2C)x + (2A+2B+C)$

On comparing the coefficients of like powers on both sides, we get

$A + C = 1, \quad 3A + B + 2C = 1$

and $\quad 2A + 2B + C = 1$

On solving these equations, we get

$A = -2, B = 1$ and $C = 3$

From Eq. (i), we get

$$\frac{x^2+x+1}{(x+1)^2(x+2)} = \frac{-2}{x+1} + \frac{1}{(x+1)^2} + \frac{3}{(x+2)}$$
$$\therefore \int \frac{x^2+x+1}{(x+1)^2(x+2)} dx = -2\int \frac{dx}{x+1} + \int \frac{dx}{(x+1)^2} + 3\int \frac{dx}{(x+2)}$$
$$= -2\log|x+1| - \frac{1}{(x+1)} + 3\log|x+2| + C$$

9 (*d*)

I. Let $I = \int \tan^{-1}\sqrt{\frac{1-x}{1+x}}\, dx$

Put $\quad x = \cos\theta \Rightarrow \theta = \cos^{-1} x$

$\Rightarrow \quad dx = -\sin\theta\, d\theta$

$$\therefore \quad I = \int \tan^{-1}\sqrt{\frac{1-\cos\theta}{1+\cos\theta}}\,(-\sin\theta)\,d\theta$$
$$= \int \tan^{-1}\sqrt{\frac{2\sin^2\left(\frac{\theta}{2}\right)}{2\cos^2\left(\frac{\theta}{2}\right)}}\,(-\sin\theta)\,d\theta$$
$$= \int \tan^{-1}\left(\tan\frac{\theta}{2}\right)(-\sin\theta)\,d\theta$$
$$= \frac{1}{2}\int \underset{\text{I}}{\theta}\,(-\underset{\text{II}}{\sin\theta})\,d\theta$$
$[\because \tan^{-1}(\tan\theta) = \theta]$
$$= \frac{1}{2}\{\theta\cos\theta - \int 1\cos\theta\,d\theta\} + C$$
$$= \frac{1}{2}\theta\cos\theta - \frac{1}{2}\sin\theta + C$$
[using integration by parts]
$$= \frac{1}{2}(\cos^{-1} x)x - \frac{1}{2}\sqrt{1-\cos^2\theta} + C$$
$$= \frac{1}{2}x\cos^{-1} x - \frac{1}{2}\sqrt{1-x^2} + C$$

II. Let $I = \int \frac{\sqrt{x^2+1}\,[\log(x^2+1) - 2\log x]}{x^4} dx$

$$= \int \frac{\sqrt{x^2+1}}{x^4}[\log(x^2+1) - \log x^2]\,dx$$
$$= \int \frac{\sqrt{x^2+1}}{x^4}\left[\log\left(1+\frac{1}{x^2}\right)\right] dx$$
$$= \int \frac{1}{x^3}\sqrt{\frac{x^2+1}{x^2}}\left[\log\left(1+\frac{1}{x^2}\right)\right] dx$$

Put $\frac{x^2+1}{x^2} = t \Rightarrow 1 + \frac{1}{x^2} = t$

$$\Rightarrow -\frac{2}{x^3}dx = dt \Rightarrow dx = \frac{-x^3}{2}dt$$
$$\therefore \quad I = \int \sqrt{t}\log t.\frac{1}{x^3}\left(-\frac{x^3 dt}{2}\right)$$
$$= -\frac{1}{2}\int (t)^{1/2}\log t\,dt$$

On integrating by parts, we get

$$I = -\frac{1}{2}\left[\log t\cdot \int t^{1/2}dt - \int\left\{\left(\frac{d}{dt}\log t\right)\int t^{1/2}dt\right\}dt\right]$$
$$= -\frac{1}{2}\left[\log t\cdot \frac{t^{3/2}}{\frac{3}{2}} - \int \frac{1}{t}\cdot\frac{t^{3/2}}{\frac{3}{2}}dt\right]$$
$$= -\frac{1}{2}\left[\frac{2}{3}\log t\cdot t^{3/2} - \frac{2}{3}\int t^{1/2}dt\right]$$
$$= -\frac{1}{2}\times\frac{2}{3}[\log t\cdot t^{3/2} - \int t^{1/2}dt]$$
$$= -\frac{1}{3}\left[\log t\cdot t^{3/2} - \frac{t^{3/2}}{\frac{3}{2}}\right] + C$$
$$= -\frac{1}{3}t^{3/2}\left[\log t - \frac{2}{3}\right] + C$$
$$= -\frac{1}{3}\left(1+\frac{1}{x^2}\right)^{3/2}\left[\log\left(\frac{x^2+1}{x^2}\right) - \frac{2}{3}\right] + C$$

10 (*a*)

A. Let $I=\int_{\pi/2}^{\pi} e^x\left(\frac{1-\sin x}{1-\cos x}\right)dx$

$$=\int_{\pi/2}^{\pi} e^x\left[\frac{1-2\sin\left(\frac{x}{2}\right)\cos\left(\frac{x}{2}\right)}{2\sin^2\left(\frac{x}{2}\right)}\right]dx$$

$\left[\because \sin x=2\sin\frac{x}{2}\cos\frac{x}{2} \text{ and } 1-\cos x=2\sin^2\frac{x}{2}\right]$

$$=\int_{\pi/2}^{\pi} e^x\left(\frac{1}{2}\operatorname{cosec}^2\frac{x}{2}-\cot\frac{x}{2}\right)dx$$

$$=\int_{\pi/2}^{\pi} e^x\left(-\cot\frac{x}{2}+\frac{1}{2}\operatorname{cosec}^2\frac{x}{2}\right)dx$$

[here, $\frac{d}{dx}\left(-\cot\frac{x}{2}\right)=\frac{1}{2}\operatorname{cosec}^2\frac{x}{2}$
it is the form of
$\therefore \int e^x\{f(x)+f'(x)\}dx=e^x f(x)$]

$$I=\left[e^x\left(-\cot\frac{x}{2}\right)\right]_{\pi/2}^{\pi}$$

$$=-e^{\pi}\cot\left(\frac{\pi}{2}\right)-\left[-e^{\pi/2}\cot\left(\frac{\pi}{4}\right)\right]$$

$$=-e^{\pi}\cdot 0+e^{\pi/2}\cdot 1=e^{\pi/2}$$

B. Let $I=\int_0^{\pi/4}\frac{\sin x\cos x}{\cos^4 x+\sin^4 x}dx$

$$=\int_0^{\pi/4}\frac{\sin x\cos x}{(1-\sin^2 x)^2+(\sin^2 x)^2}dx$$

$[\because \cos^2 x=1-\sin^2 x]$

Put $\sin^2 x=t$

$\Rightarrow \quad 2\sin x\cos x\,dx=dt$

For limit when $x=0\Rightarrow t=0$ and when $x=\frac{\pi}{4}\Rightarrow t=\frac{1}{2}$

$$\therefore I=\int_0^{1/2}\frac{\sin x\cos x}{(1-t)^2+t^2}\cdot\frac{dt}{2\sin x\cos x}$$

$$=\frac{1}{2}\int_0^{1/2}\frac{1}{(1-t)^2+t^2}dt$$

$$=\frac{1}{2}\int_0^{1/2}\frac{1}{2t^2-2t+1}dt$$

$$=\frac{1}{2}\cdot\frac{1}{2}\int_0^{1/2}\frac{1}{t^2-t+\frac{1}{2}}dt$$

$$=\frac{1}{4}\int_0^{1/2}\frac{1}{t^2-t+\left(\frac{1}{2}\right)^2-\left(\frac{1}{2}\right)^2+\frac{1}{2}}dt$$

$$=\frac{1}{4}\int_0^{1/2}\frac{1}{\left(t-\frac{1}{2}\right)^2+\left(\frac{1}{2}\right)^2}dt$$

$$=\frac{1}{4}\cdot\frac{1}{\frac{1}{2}}\left[\tan^{-1}\left(\frac{t-\frac{1}{2}}{\frac{1}{2}}\right)\right]_0^{1/2}$$

$$=\frac{1}{2}[\tan^{-1}0-\tan^{-1}(-1)]=\frac{1}{2}\cdot\frac{\pi}{4}$$

$[\because \tan(-\theta)=-\tan\theta]$

$$=\frac{\pi}{8}$$

C. Let $I=\int_0^{\pi/2}\frac{\cos^2 x}{\cos^2 x+4\sin^2 x}dx$ ...(i)

$$=\int_0^{\pi/2}\frac{\cos^2 x}{4-3\cos^2 x}dx$$

$[\because \sin^2 x=1-\cos^2 x]$

$$=-\frac{1}{3}\int_0^{\pi/2}\frac{4-3\cos^2 x-4}{4-3\cos^2 x}dx$$

$$=-\frac{1}{3}\int_0^{\pi/2}\left(1-\frac{4}{4-3\cos^2 x}\right)dx$$

$$=-\frac{1}{3}[x]_0^{\pi/2}+\frac{4}{3}\int_0^{\pi/2}\frac{\sec^2 x}{4\sec^2 x-3}dx$$

[divide numerator and denominator in second integral by $\cos^2 x$]

$$=-\frac{\pi}{6}+\frac{4}{3}\int_0^{\pi/2}\frac{\sec^2 x}{4(1+\tan^2 x)-3}dx$$

$[\because 1+\tan^2 x=\sec^2 x]$

Put $\tan x=t\Rightarrow \sec^2 x\,dx=dt$

When, $x=0, t=0$ and when $x=\left(\frac{\pi}{2}\right), t=\infty$

$$\therefore I=-\frac{\pi}{6}+\frac{4}{3}\int_0^{\infty}\frac{dt}{4(1+t^2)-3}$$

$$=-\frac{\pi}{6}+\frac{4}{3}\int_0^{\infty}\frac{dt}{4t^2+1}$$

$$=-\frac{\pi}{6}+\frac{4}{3}\times\frac{1}{4}\int_0^{\infty}\frac{dt}{t^2+\left(\frac{1}{2}\right)^2}$$

$$=-\frac{\pi}{6}+\frac{1}{3}\cdot 2\left[\tan^{-1}\frac{t}{\frac{1}{2}}\right]_0^{\infty}$$

$\left[\because \int\frac{dx}{a^2+x^2}=\frac{1}{a}\tan^{-1}\left(\frac{x}{a}\right)\right]$

$$=-\frac{\pi}{6}+\frac{2}{3}[\tan^{-1}2t]_0^{\infty}$$

$$=-\frac{\pi}{6}+\frac{2}{3}[\tan^{-1}\infty-\tan^{-1}0]$$

$$=-\frac{\pi}{6}+\frac{2}{3}\left[\frac{\pi}{2}-0\right]$$

$$=-\frac{\pi}{6}+\frac{\pi}{3}=\frac{\pi}{6}$$

D. $\int_{\pi/6}^{\pi/3}\frac{\sin x+\cos x}{\sqrt{\sin 2x}}dx$

We know that,

$(\sin x-\cos x)^2=\sin^2 x+\cos^2 x-2\sin x\cos x$

$\Rightarrow (\sin x-\cos x)^2=1-\sin 2x$

$[\because \sin^2 x+\cos^2 x=1$ and $2\sin x\cos x=\sin 2x]$

$\Rightarrow \sin 2x=1-(\sin x-\cos x)^2$

Put $\quad \sin x-\cos x=t$ ...(i)

$\Rightarrow (\cos x+\sin x)\,dx=dt$

$\Rightarrow dx=\frac{dt}{\cos x+\sin x}$

For limit when $x=\frac{\pi}{6}$,

$\Rightarrow \quad t=\sin\frac{\pi}{6}-\cos\frac{\pi}{6}=\frac{1}{2}-\frac{\sqrt{3}}{2}$

when $x=\frac{\pi}{3}$,

$t=\sin\frac{\pi}{3}-\cos\frac{\pi}{3}=\frac{\sqrt{3}}{2}-\frac{1}{2}$

$$\therefore I=\int_{\frac{1-\sqrt{3}}{2}}^{\frac{\sqrt{3}-1}{2}}\frac{\sin x+\cos x}{\sqrt{1-t^2}}\cdot\frac{dt}{\cos x+\sin x}=\int_{\frac{1-\sqrt{3}}{2}}^{\frac{\sqrt{3}-1}{2}}\frac{dt}{\sqrt{1-t^2}}$$

From here, we can solve it in two ways.

Ist method

$$\int_{\frac{1-\sqrt{3}}{2}}^{\frac{\sqrt{3}-1}{2}} \frac{1}{\sqrt{1-t^2}} dt = [\sin^{-1} t]_{\frac{1-\sqrt{3}}{2}}^{\frac{\sqrt{3}-1}{2}}$$

$$= \left[\sin^{-1}\left(\frac{\sqrt{3}-1}{2}\right) - \sin^{-1}\left\{-\left(\frac{\sqrt{3}-1}{2}\right)\right\}\right]$$

$$= \left[\sin^{-1}\left(\frac{\sqrt{3}-1}{2}\right) + \sin^{-1}\left(\frac{\sqrt{3}-1}{2}\right)\right]$$

$[\because \sin^{-1}(-\theta) = -\sin^{-1}\theta]$

$$= 2\sin^{-1}\left(\frac{\sqrt{3}-1}{2}\right)$$

IInd method

$$\int_{\frac{1-\sqrt{3}}{2}}^{\frac{\sqrt{3}-1}{2}} \frac{1}{\sqrt{1-t^2}} dt = \int_{-\left(\frac{\sqrt{3}-1}{2}\right)}^{\frac{\sqrt{3}-1}{2}} \frac{1}{\sqrt{1-t^2}} dt$$

As $\frac{1}{\sqrt{1-(-t)^2}} = \frac{1}{\sqrt{1-t^2}}$, therefore $\frac{1}{\sqrt{1-t^2}}$ is an even function.

And we know that, if $f(x)$ is an even function, then

$$\int_{-a}^{a} f(x)\,dx = 2\int_0^a f(x)\,dx$$

$$\therefore \quad I = 2\int_0^{\frac{\sqrt{3}-1}{2}} \frac{dt}{\sqrt{1-t^2}} = [2\sin^{-1} t]_0^{\frac{\sqrt{3}-1}{2}} = 2\sin^{-1}\left(\frac{\sqrt{3}-1}{2}\right)$$

11 (b)

(i) $\int_0^1 \frac{1}{\sqrt{1+x}-\sqrt{x}}dx$

$$= \int_0^1 \frac{(\sqrt{1+x}+\sqrt{x})}{(\sqrt{1+x}-\sqrt{x})(\sqrt{1+x}+\sqrt{x})} dx$$

[multiply numerator and denominator by $(\sqrt{1+x}+\sqrt{x})$]

$$= \int_0^1 \frac{(\sqrt{1+x}+\sqrt{x})}{1+x-x}dx$$

$$= \int_0^1 [(1+x)^{1/2} + x^{1/2}]\,dx$$

$$= \left[\frac{(1+x)^{\frac{1}{2}+1}}{\frac{1}{2}+1} + \frac{x^{\frac{1}{2}+1}}{\frac{1}{2}+1}\right]_0^1$$

$$= \frac{2}{3}\left[(1+x)^{\frac{3}{2}} + x^{\frac{3}{2}}\right]_0^1$$

$$= \frac{2}{3}\left[2^{\frac{3}{2}} + 1^{\frac{3}{2}} - \left(1^{\frac{3}{2}} + 0\right)\right]$$

$$= \frac{2}{3}(2\sqrt{2})$$

$$= \frac{4\sqrt{2}}{3}$$

(ii) $I = \int_0^{\pi/4} \frac{\sin x + \cos x}{9 + 16\sin 2x}dx$

We know that,

$(\sin x - \cos x)^2 = \sin^2 x + \cos^2 x - 2\sin x\cos x$

$\Rightarrow (\sin x - \cos x)^2 = 1 - \sin 2x$

$[\because \sin^2 x + \cos^2 x = 1$ and $2\sin x \cos x = \sin 2x]$

$\Rightarrow \sin 2x = 1 - (\sin x - \cos x)^2$

Put $\sin x - \cos x = t$

$\Rightarrow \quad \cos x + \sin x = \frac{dt}{dx}$ ...(i)

$\Rightarrow \quad dx = \frac{dt}{\cos x + \sin x}$

When $x = 0, t = 0 - \cos 0 = -1$,

when $x = \frac{\pi}{4}$,

$t = \sin\frac{\pi}{4} - \cos\frac{\pi}{4} = 0$

$$\therefore \; I = \int_{-1}^{0} \frac{\sin x + \cos x}{9 + 16(1-t^2)} \frac{dt}{\cos x + \sin x}$$

$$= \int_{-1}^{0} \frac{1}{9+16(1-t^2)}dt$$

$$= \int_{-1}^{0} \frac{1}{9+16-16t^2}dt$$

$$= \int_{-1}^{0} \frac{1}{25-16t^2}dt$$

$$= \frac{1}{16}\int_{-1}^{0} \frac{1}{\left(\frac{5}{4}\right)^2 - t^2}dt$$

$$= \frac{1}{16}\cdot\frac{1}{2.\frac{5}{4}}\left[\log\left|\frac{\frac{5}{4}+t}{\frac{5}{4}-t}\right|\right]_{-1}^{0}$$

$$\left[\because \int \frac{1}{a^2-x^2}dx = \frac{1}{2a}\log\left|\frac{a+x}{a-x}\right|\right]$$

$$= \frac{1}{40}\left[\log\left|\frac{5+4t}{5-4t}\right|\right]_{-1}^{0}$$

$$= \frac{1}{40}\left[\log 1 - \log\frac{1}{9}\right]$$

$$= \frac{1}{40}[\log 1 - (\log 1 - \log 9)]$$

$$= \frac{1}{40}\log 9$$

$$\left[\because \log\left(\frac{m}{n}\right) = \log m - \log n\right]$$

(iii) Let $I = \int_0^{\pi/2} \sin 2x \tan^{-1}(\sin x)\,dx$

$$= \int_0^{\pi/2} 2\sin x\cos x \tan^{-1}(\sin x)\,dx$$

$[\because \sin 2x = 2\sin x\cos x]$

Put $\sin x = t \cos x\, dx = dt$

$\Rightarrow \quad dx = \frac{dt}{\cos x}$

when, $x = 0,\; t = 0$ and when $x = \frac{\pi}{2}, t = \sin\frac{\pi}{2} = 1$

$$\therefore \; I = \int_0^1 2t\cos x \tan^{-1} t \frac{dt}{\cos x}$$

$$= 2\int_0^1 \underset{\text{II}}{t}\cdot \underset{\text{I}}{\tan^{-1} t}\,dt$$

$$= 2\left(\left[(\tan^{-1} t)\frac{t^2}{2}\right]_0^1 - \int_0^1 \frac{1}{1+t^2}\cdot\frac{t^2}{2}dt\right)$$

[using intergration by parts]

$$= 2\left[\frac{\tan^{-1}1}{2} - 0\right] - \int_0^1 \frac{t^2}{1+t^2}dt$$

$$= 2\left(\frac{\pi}{8}\right) - \int_0^1 \frac{(1+t^2)-1}{1+t^2}dt$$

$$= \frac{\pi}{4} - \int_0^1 \left(1 - \frac{1}{1+t^2}\right)dt$$

$$= \frac{\pi}{4} - [t - \tan^{-1} t]_0^1$$

$$= \frac{\pi}{4} - [1 - \tan^{-1} 1 - (0-0)]$$

$$= \frac{\pi}{4} - 1 + \frac{\pi}{4} = \frac{\pi}{2} - 1$$

(iv) Let $I=\int_0^{\pi}\frac{x\tan x}{\sec x+\tan x}dx$ ...(i)

$\Rightarrow I=\int_0^{\pi}\frac{(\pi-x)\tan(\pi-x)}{\sec(\pi-x)+\tan(\pi-x)}dx$

$\left[\because \int_0^a f(x)\,dx=\int_0^a f(a-x)\,dx\right]$

$\Rightarrow \quad I=\int_0^{\pi}\frac{(\pi-x)\tan x}{\sec x+\tan x}dx$ ...(ii)

[$\because \tan(\pi-x)=-\tan x$ and $\sec(\pi-x)=-\sec x$]

On adding Eqs. (i) and (ii), we get

$2I=\int_0^{\pi}\frac{\pi\tan x}{\sec x+\tan x}dx$

$=\pi\int_0^{\pi}\frac{\tan x}{\sec x+\tan x}dx$

$=\pi\int_0^{\pi}\frac{\frac{\sin x}{\cos x}}{\frac{1}{\cos x}+\frac{\sin x}{\cos x}}dx$

$=\pi\int_0^{\pi}\frac{\sin x}{1+\sin x}dx$

$=\pi\int_0^{\pi}\frac{\sin x(1-\sin x)}{(1+\sin x)(1-\sin x)}dx$

$=\pi\int_0^{\pi}\frac{\sin x(1-\sin x)}{1-\sin^2 x}dx$

[$\because \sin^2 x+\cos^2 x=1$]

$=\pi\int_0^{\pi}\frac{\sin x-\sin^2 x}{\cos^2 x}dx$

$=\pi\int_0^{\pi}\left(\frac{\sin x}{\cos^2 x}-\frac{\sin^2 x}{\cos^2 x}\right)dx$

$=\pi\int_0^{\pi}(\sec x\tan x-\tan^2 x)\,dx$

$=\pi\int_0^{\pi}\{\sec x\tan x-(\sec^2 x-1)\}\,dx$

[$\because 1+\tan^2 x=\sec^2 x$]

$=\pi[\sec x-\tan x+x]_0^{\pi}$

$=\pi\{\sec\pi-\tan\pi+\pi-(\sec 0-\tan 0+0)\}$

$=\pi(-1+\pi-1)$

$\therefore I=\frac{\pi}{2}(\pi-2)$

12 (c) $\int_1^4\{|x-1|+|x-2|+|x-3|\}\,dx$

$=\int_1^2(|x-1|+|x-2|+|x-3|)\,dx$

$+\int_2^3\{|x-1|+|x-2|+|x-3|\}\,dx$

$+\int_3^4\{|x-1|+|x-2|+|x-3|\}\,dx$

$=\int_1^2\{x-1-(x-2)-(x-3)\}\,dx$

$+\int_2^3\{x-1+x-2-(x-3)\}\,dx$

$+\int_3^4(x-1+x-2+x-3)\,dx$

$=\int_1^2(-x+4)\,dx+\int_2^3 x\,dx+\int_3^4(3x-6)\,dx$

$=\left[-\frac{x^2}{2}+4x\right]_1^2+\left[\frac{x^2}{2}\right]_2^3+\left[\frac{3x^2}{2}-6x\right]_3^4$

$=\left(\frac{-2^2}{2}+8\right)-\left(\frac{-1}{2}+4\right)+\frac{1}{2}(3^2-2^2)$

$+\left(\frac{3}{2}\times4^2-6\times4\right)-\left(\frac{3}{2}\times3^2-6\times3\right)$

$=6-\frac{7}{2}+\frac{5}{2}+(24-24)-\left(-\frac{9}{2}\right)$

$=\frac{12-7+5}{2}+0+\frac{9}{2}=\frac{19}{2}$

13 (b)

I. $\int_1^3\frac{1}{x^2(x+1)}dx=\frac{2}{3}+\log\frac{2}{3}$

By using partial fraction method,

Let $\frac{1}{x^2(x+1)}=\frac{A}{x}+\frac{B}{x^2}+\frac{C}{x+1}$ ...(i)

$\Rightarrow 1=Ax(x+1)+B(x+1)+Cx^2$ ...(ii)

Substituting $x=0,-1$ in Eq. (ii), we get

$1=B(0+1)$ and $1=C(-1)^2$

$\Rightarrow \quad B=1$ and $C=1$

On equating the coefficients of x^2 on both sides of Eq. (ii), we get

$0=A+C\Rightarrow A=-C=-1$

$\therefore \int_1^3\frac{1}{x^2(x+1)}dx$

$=\int_1^3\left(-\frac{1}{x}+\frac{1}{x^2}+\frac{1}{x+1}\right)dx$

$=\left[-\log|x|-\frac{1}{x}+\log|x+1|\right]_1^3$

$=\left[\log\left|\frac{x+1}{x}\right|-\frac{1}{x}\right]_1^3$

$=\left(\log\left|\frac{4}{3}\right|-\frac{1}{3}\right)-\left(\log\left|\frac{2}{1}\right|-\frac{1}{1}\right)$

$=\left(\log\frac{4}{3}-\log 2\right)+\left(1-\frac{1}{3}\right)$

$\left[\because \log\left(\frac{m}{n}\right)=\log m-\log n\right]$

$=\log\left(\frac{4}{3}\times\frac{1}{2}\right)+\frac{2}{3}=\log\frac{2}{3}+\frac{2}{3}$

Hence proved.

II. $\int_0^1 xe^x dx$

Applying rule of integration by parts taking x as the first function and e^x as the second function, we get

$=[x\int e^x dx-\int 1.e^x dx]_0^1$

$=[xe^x-e^x]_0^1=[e^x(x-1)]_0^1$

$=[e(1-1)-e^0(0-1)]=0+1=1$

Hence proved.

14 (b)

A. Let $f(x)=x^{17}\cos^4 x$,

$\Rightarrow f(-x)=(-x)^{17}\cos^4(-x)$

$=-x^{17}\cos^4 x$

$=-f(x)$

Therefore, $f(x)$ is an odd function.

We know that, if $f(x)$ is an odd function, then $\int_{-a}^{a}f(x)\,dx=0$

$\therefore \quad \int_{-1}^{1}x^{17}\cos^4 x\,dx=0.$

Note *If $f(x)$ is odd, then* $\int_{-a}^{a}f(x)\,dx=0$

B. Let $I=\int_0^{\pi/2}\sin^3 x\,dx$

$=\int_0^{\pi/2}\sin^2 x\cdot\sin x\,dx$

$=\int_0^{\pi/2}(1-\cos^2 x)\sin x\,dx$

[$\because \sin^2 x=1-\cos^2 x$]

Put, $\cos x=t\Rightarrow -\sin x\,dx=dt$

When, $x=0\Rightarrow t=\cos 0=1$,

when $x=\frac{\pi}{2}$

$\Rightarrow \quad t=\cos\frac{\pi}{2}=0$

$\therefore \quad I=\int_0^{\pi/2}(1-\cos^2 x)\sin x\,dx$

$=\int_1^0(1-t^2)(-dt)$

$=-\left[t-\frac{t^3}{3}\right]_1^0$

$=-\left\{(0-0)-\left(1-\frac{1}{3}\right)\right\}=\frac{2}{3}$

C. Let $I=\int_0^{\pi/4}2\tan^3 x\,dx$

$=2\int_0^{\pi/4}\tan^2 x\cdot\tan x\,dx$

$=2\int_0^{\pi/4}(\sec^2 x-1)\tan x\,dx$

$[\because 1+\tan^2 x=\sec^2 x]$

$=2\left[\int_0^{\pi/4}\sec^2 x\tan x\,dx-\int_0^{\pi/4}\tan x\,dx\right]$

$=2\int_0^{\pi/4}(\tan x)\sec^2 x\,dx$

$-2[-\log|\cos x|]_0^{\pi/4}$

$\left[\begin{array}{l}\because \text{Let } I_1=\int(\tan x)\sec^2 x\,dx\\ \text{put } \tan x=t\Rightarrow\sec^2 x\,dx=dt\\ \therefore I_1=\int t\,dt=\frac{t^2}{2}=\frac{\tan^2 x}{2}\end{array}\right]$

$=2\left[\frac{\tan^2 x}{2}\right]_0^{\pi/4}$

$+2\left[\log\left|\cos\frac{\pi}{4}\right|-\log|\cos 0|\right]$

$=\tan^2\left(\frac{\pi}{4}\right)-0+2\left[\log\left(\frac{1}{\sqrt{2}}\right)-\log 1\right]$

$=1+2\log 2^{-1/2}-0\quad[\because\log 1=0]$

$=1-2\times\frac{1}{2}\log 2=1-\log 2.$

D. Let

$I=\int_0^1\sin^{-1}x\,dx=\int_0^1\sin^{-1}x\cdot 1\,dx$

Applying rule of integration by parts taking $\sin^{-1}x$ as the first function and 1 as second function, we get

$I=[(\sin^{-1}x)x]_0^1-\int_0^1\frac{x}{\sqrt{1-x^2}}dx$

Put $1-x^2=t\Rightarrow -2x\,dx=dt$

When, $x=0$

$\Rightarrow t=1$ and when $x=1$

$\Rightarrow \quad t=0$

$\therefore I=[x\sin^{-1}x]_0^1+\frac{1}{2}\int_1^0\frac{dt}{\sqrt{t}}$

$=[x\sin^{-1}x]_0^1+\frac{1}{2}\left[\frac{t^{1/2}}{1/2}\right]_1^0$

$=1\sin^{-1}(1)+[-\sqrt{1}]=\frac{\pi}{2}-1$

15 (d) Let $I=\int_a^b x f(x)\,dx$ ...(i)

Then, by a property of definite integrals

$I=\int_a^b(a+b-x)f(a+b-x)\,dx$

$=\int_a^b(a+b-x)f(x)\,dx$ ...(ii)

$[\because \text{given } f(a+b-x)=f(x)]$

On adding Eqs. (i) and (ii), we get

$2I=\int_a^b(a+b)f(x)\,dx$

$\Rightarrow \quad I=\frac{a+b}{2}\int_a^b f(x)\,dx$

16 (b) Let $I=\int_0^1\tan^{-1}\left(\frac{2x-1}{1+x-x^2}\right)dx$

$=\int_0^1\tan^{-1}\left(\frac{x+(x-1)}{1-x(x-1)}\right)dx$

$=\int_0^1\{\tan^{-1}x+\tan^{-1}(x-1)\}\,dx$

$\left[\because \tan^{-1}A+\tan^{-1}B=\tan^{-1}\left(\frac{A+B}{1-AB}\right)\right]$

$\Rightarrow I=\int_0^1\{\tan^{-1}x-\tan^{-1}(1-x)\}\,dx$ ...(i)

Also, $I=\int_0^1\{\tan^{-1}(1-x)-\tan^{-1}(1-(1-x))\}\,dx$

$\left[\because\int_0^a f(x)\,dx=\int_0^a f(a-x)\,dx\right]$

$\Rightarrow I=\int_0^1[\tan^{-1}(1-x)-\tan^{-1}(x)]\,dx$ ...(ii)

On adding Eqs. (i) and (ii), we get

$2I=0\Rightarrow I=0$

17 (a) $I=\int\frac{1}{e^x+e^{-x}}dx=\int\frac{1}{e^x+\frac{1}{e^x}}dx$

$=\int\frac{e^x}{(e^x)^2+1}dx$

Put $e^x=t\Rightarrow e^x dx=dt$

$\left[\because\int\frac{dx}{1+x^2}=\tan^{-1}x\right]$

$\therefore \quad I=\int\frac{e^x}{t^2+1}\frac{dt}{e^x}=\tan^{-1}(t)+C$

$=\tan^{-1}e^x+C.$

18 (b) Let $I=\int\frac{\cos 2x}{(\sin x+\cos x)^2}dx$

$=\int\frac{\cos^2 x-\sin^2 x}{(\sin x+\cos x)^2}dx$

$[\because \cos 2x=\cos^2 x-\sin^2 x]$

$=\int\frac{(\cos x-\sin x)(\cos x+\sin x)}{(\sin x+\cos x)(\sin x+\cos x)}dx$

$=\int\frac{\cos x-\sin x}{\sin x+\cos x}dx$

Put $\sin x+\cos x=t$

$\Rightarrow \quad (\cos x-\sin x)\,dx=dt$

$\therefore \quad I=\int\frac{\cos x-\sin x}{t}\,\frac{dt}{\cos x-\sin x}$

$=\int\frac{1}{t}dt=\log|t|+C$

$=\log|\sin x+\cos x|+C$

Numerical Type Questions

1 (5) $f(x)=\int\frac{2\,\text{cosec}^2 x\,dx}{(1+\cot x)^2}$

Put $1+\cot x=t$

On differentiating both side with respect to 'x'.

$-\text{cosec}^2 x\,dx=dt$

$f(z)=\int\frac{-2\,dt}{t^2}=\frac{2}{t}+C$

$=\frac{2}{(1+\cot x)}+C$

Given that $f\left(\frac{\pi}{4}\right)=4$

$4=\frac{2}{1+\cot\frac{\pi}{4}}+C$

$\Rightarrow \quad C+\frac{2}{1+1}=4$

$\Rightarrow \quad C=3$

Now, $f\left(\frac{\pi}{2}\right)=\frac{2}{1+\cot\frac{\pi}{2}}+3$

$=2+3=5$

2 (10) $f(x) = \int 6^{x+\tan^{-1}(x)} \cdot \left(1 + \frac{1}{1+x^2}\right) dx$

and $f(0) = \frac{1}{\log_e 6}$

Let $x + \tan^{-1} x = t$

On differentiating both side with respect to 'x'.

$$\left(1 + \frac{1}{1+x^2}\right) dx = dt$$

$$f(x) = \int 6^t\, dt = \frac{6^t}{\log_e 6} + C$$

$$= \frac{6^{x+\tan^{-1} x}}{\log_e 6} + C$$

$$f(0) = \frac{1}{\log_e 6}$$

Then, $\frac{1}{\log_e 6} = \frac{6^0}{\log_e 6} + C$

$\Rightarrow \quad C = 0$

$\therefore \quad f(x) = \frac{6^{x+\tan^{-1} x}}{\log_e 6}$

$$f(1) = \frac{6^{1+\pi/4}}{\log_e} = \frac{(6)^{\left(\frac{4+\pi}{4}\right)}}{\log_e 6}$$

$\alpha = 6$ and $\beta = 4$

$\therefore \quad \alpha + \beta = 10$

3 (10) Let $I = \int x^3 e^{-x^2} dx$

Put $x^2 = t \Rightarrow 2x\, dx = dt$

$$I = \frac{1}{2}\int te^{-t}\, dt$$

$$= \frac{1}{2}\{-e^{-t} \cdot t - \int 1 \cdot (-e^{-t})\, dt\}$$

$$= \frac{-te^{-t}}{2} - \frac{e^{-t}}{2} + C$$

$$= \frac{-x^2 e^{-x^2} - e^{-x^2}}{2} + C$$

$$= \frac{-(x^2+1)}{2} e^{-x^2} + C$$

Given that

$$\int x^3 e^{-x^2} dx = h(x) e^{-x^2} + C$$

$\Rightarrow \quad h(x) = \frac{-(x^2+1)}{2}$

$$h(-3) = \frac{-10}{2} = -5$$

$$-2h(-3) = 10$$

4 (6) Let $I = \int \frac{4x - \sqrt{\sin^{-1} x}}{\sqrt{1-x^2}} dx$

$$= -2\underbrace{\int \frac{-2x}{\sqrt{1-x^2}} dx}_{I_1} - \underbrace{\int \frac{\sqrt{\sin^{-1} x}}{\sqrt{1-x^2}} dx}_{I_2}$$

$I_2 = -2I_1 - I_2$ ...(i)

$$I_1 = \int \frac{-2x\, dx}{\sqrt{1-x^2}}$$

Put $1 - x^2 = t \Rightarrow -2x\, dx = dt$

$$I_1 = \int \frac{dt}{\sqrt{t}} = 2\sqrt{t} + C$$

$$= 2\sqrt{1-x^2} + C$$

and $I_2 = \int \frac{\sqrt{\sin^{-1} x}}{\sqrt{1-x^2}} dx$

Put $\sin^{-1} x = t \Rightarrow \frac{1}{\sqrt{1-x^2}} dx = dt$

$$= \int \sqrt{t}\, dt = \frac{2}{3} t^{3/2} + C$$

$$= \frac{2}{3}(\sin^{-1} x)^{3/2} + C$$

Put the value of I_1 and I_2 in Eq. (i)

$$I = -2 \cdot 2\sqrt{1-x^2} - \frac{2}{3}(\sin^{-1} x)^{3/2} + C$$

$$I = -4\sqrt{1-x^2} - \frac{2}{3}(\sin^{-1} x)^{3/2} + C$$

It is given

$$\int \frac{4x - \sqrt{\sin^{-1} x}}{\sqrt{1-x^2}} dx = \alpha(1-x^2)^{1/2} - \beta(\sin^{-1})^{3/2} + C$$

$\Rightarrow \quad \alpha = -4$ and $\beta = \frac{2}{3}$

$\therefore \quad \frac{\alpha}{\beta} = \frac{-4}{\left(\frac{2}{3}\right)} = -6$

$$\frac{\alpha}{\beta} = -6 \Rightarrow \left|\frac{\alpha}{\beta}\right| = 6$$

5 (3) $\int (2e^{2x} + 4e^x - 2e^{-x} - 2)\, e^{(e^x + e^{-x})} dx$

$$= 2h(x)\, e^{(e^x+e^{-x})} + C$$

Consider,

$$2\left(\int (e^{2x} + 2e^x - e^{-x} - 1)\, e^{(e^x+e^{-x})} dx\right)$$

Put $e^x = t \Rightarrow e^x\, dx = dt$

$$dx = \frac{dt}{e^x} \Rightarrow dx = \frac{dt}{t}$$

$$2\left(\int \left(t^2 + 2t - \frac{1}{t} - 1\right) e^{(t+1/t)} \frac{dt}{t}\right)$$

$$= 2\left(\int \left(t + 2 - \frac{1}{t^2} - \frac{1}{t}\right) e^{(t+1/t)}\, dt\right)$$

$$= 2\left[\int \left((1+t)\left(1 - \frac{1}{t^2}\right) + 1\right) e^{(t+1/t)}\, dt\right]$$

$$= 2\left[\int (1+t)\left(1 - \frac{1}{t^2}\right) e^{(t+1/t)}\, dt + \int e^{t+1/t} dt\right]$$

$$= 2\left[(1+t)\, e^{(t+1/t)} - \int e^{(t+1/t)}\, dt + \int e^{(t+1/t)}\, dt\right]$$

$$= 2(1+t)\, e^{(t+1/t)} + C$$

$$= 2(1+e^x)\, e^{(e^x+e^{-x})} + C$$

It is given that

$$\int (2e^{2x} + 4e^x - 2e^{-x} - 2)\, e^{(e^x+e^{-x})} dx$$

$$= 2h(x) e^{(e^x+e^{-x})} + C$$

$$\Rightarrow 2h(x)\, e^{(e^x+e^{-x})} + C$$

$$= 2(1+e^x)\, e^{(e^x+e^{-x})} + C$$

$\Rightarrow \quad h(x) = (1 + e^x)$

$h(0) = 2$

$\frac{h(0)}{2} = \frac{2}{2} = 1$

$\Rightarrow \alpha = 1$ and $\alpha + 2 = 1 + 2 = 3$

6 (0) Given $2\beta \int_{-1}^{1} e^{\beta|x|} dx = 0$

$$\Rightarrow 2\beta\left[\int_{-1}^{0} e^{-\beta x} dx + \int_{0}^{1} e^{\beta x} dx\right] = 0$$

$$\Rightarrow \beta\left(\left(\frac{-e^{-\beta x}}{\beta}\right)_{-1}^{0} + \left(\frac{e^{\beta x}}{\beta}\right)_{0}^{1}\right) = 0$$

$\Rightarrow \quad (-1 + e^{\beta}) + (e^{\beta} - 1) = 0$

$\Rightarrow \quad 2e^{\beta} - 2 = 0$

$\Rightarrow \quad 2e^{\beta} = 2$

$\Rightarrow \quad e^{\beta} = e^0$

$\beta = 0$

7 (1) Let $\int_{-5}^{5} \frac{\cos x\, dx}{\frac{1}{2} + \left[\frac{x}{\pi}\right]} = r$

Here $f(x) = \frac{\cos x}{\frac{1}{2} + \left[\frac{x}{\pi}\right]}$

Then $f(-x) = \frac{\cos(-x)}{\frac{1}{2} + \left[\frac{-x}{\pi}\right]}$

$$\therefore\ [-x] = \begin{cases} -[x], & \text{if } x \in I \\ -1-[x], & \text{if } x \notin I \end{cases}$$

$$= \frac{\cos(x)}{\frac{1}{2} + -1 - \left[\frac{x}{\pi}\right]}$$

$$f(-x) = -\frac{\cos x}{\left(\frac{1}{2} + \left[\frac{x}{\pi}\right]\right)} = -f(x)$$

$\Rightarrow f(x)$ is an odd function.

$$\therefore\ \int_{-5}^{5} \frac{\cos x\,dx}{\frac{1}{2} + \left[\frac{x}{\pi}\right]} dx = 0$$

$\Rightarrow r = 0$, then $r + 1 = 1$.

8 (1750) Let $I_n = \int_0^1 (1 - x^{35})^n\,dx$

Integrating by parts, we get

$$I_n = [(1 - x^{35})^n \cdot x]_0^1 + \int_0^1 x\,35n\,(1 - x^{35})^{n-1} \cdot x^{34}\,dx$$

$$= 0 + 35n \int_0^1 x^{35}\,(1 - x^{35})^{n-1}\,dx$$

$$= -35n \int_0^1 [(1 - x^{35}) - 1]\,(1 - x^{35})^{n-1}\,dx$$

$$= -35n \left[\int_0^1 (1 - x^{35})^n dx - \int_0^1 (1 - x^{35})^{n-1}\,dx\right]$$

$$= -35n\,(I_n - I_{n-1})$$

$$\Rightarrow\ I_n = -35n\,I_n + 35n\,I_{n-1}$$

$$(1 + 35n)\,I_n = 35n\,I_{n-1}$$

$$\frac{I_n}{I_{n-1}} = \frac{35n}{1 + 35n}$$

At $n = 50$,

$$\frac{I_{50}}{I_{49}} = \frac{35 \times 50}{35 \times 50 + 1} = \frac{1750}{1751}$$

$$1751\left(\frac{\int_0^1 (1 - x^{35})^{50} dx}{\int_0^1 (1 - x^{35})^{49} dx}\right) = 1751\left(\frac{1750}{1751}\right) = 1750$$

9 (1) $I = \int_1^2 |2x - [3x]|\,dx$

$$= \int_1^{4/3} |2x - 3|\,dx + \int_{4/3}^{5/3} |2x - 4|\,dx + \int_{5/3}^{2} |2x - 5|\,dx$$

$$= \int_1^{4/3} (3 - 2x)\,dx + \int_{4/3}^{5/4} (4 - 2x)dx + \int_{5/3}^{2} (5 - 2x)\,dx$$

$$= (3x - x^2)_1^{4/3} + (4x - x^2)_{4/3}^{5/3} + (5x - x^2)_{5/3}^{2}$$

$$= \left(4 - \frac{16}{9} - 3 + 1\right) + \left(\frac{20}{3} - \frac{25}{9} - \frac{16}{3} + \frac{16}{9}\right) + \left(10 - 4 - \frac{25}{3} + \frac{25}{9}\right)$$

$$= (2 + 6) + \left(\frac{20}{3} - \frac{16}{3} - \frac{25}{3}\right) + \left(\frac{-16}{9} - \frac{25}{9} + \frac{16}{9} + \frac{25}{9}\right)$$

$$= 8 - \frac{21}{3} = 8 - 7 = 1$$

$\therefore$ Given that $\int_1^2 |2x - [3x]|\,dx = k$

$\therefore \qquad k = 1$

10 (0) $\int_{\pi/8}^{3\pi/8} \ln\left(\frac{5 + 2\sin x}{5 + 2\cos x}\right) dx$

$$I = \int_{\pi/8}^{3\pi/8} \ln\left(\frac{5 + 2\sin\left(\frac{3\pi}{8} + \frac{\pi}{8} - x\right)}{5 + 2\cos\left(\frac{3\pi}{8} + \frac{\pi}{8} - x\right)}\right) dx$$

$$I = \int_{\pi/8}^{3\pi/8} \ln\left(\frac{5 + 2\sin\left(\frac{\pi}{2} - x\right)}{5 + 2\cos\left(\frac{\pi}{2} - x\right)}\right) dx$$

$$I = \int_{\pi/8}^{3\pi/8} \ln\left(\frac{5 + 2\cos x}{5 + 2\sin x}\right) dx$$

$$2I = \int_{\pi/8}^{3\pi/8} \left(\ln\left(\frac{5 + 2\cos x}{5 + 2\sin x}\right) + \ln\left(\frac{5 + 2\sin x}{5 + 2\cos x}\right)\right) dx$$

$$= \int_{\pi/8}^{3\pi/8} \ln\left(\left(\frac{5 + 2\cos x}{5 + 2\sin x}\right) \cdot \left(\frac{5 + 2\sin x}{5 + 2\cos x}\right)\right) dx$$

$$= \int_{\pi/8}^{3\pi/8} \ln(1)\,dx = 0$$

$$I = 0$$

$$\Rightarrow \int_{\pi/8}^{3\pi/8} \ln\left(\frac{5 + 2\sin x}{5 + 2\cos x}\right) dx = 0$$

Assertion and Reason Questions

1 (*a*) Sometimes, function is not expressible in terms of elementary functions viz., polynomial, logarithmic, exponential, trigonometric functions and their inverses etc.

We are therefore blocked for finding $\int f(x)\,dx$. Therefore, it is not possible of find $\int e^{-x^2} dx$ by inspection since we can not find a function whose derivative is e^{-x^2}.

2 (*a*) We have, $\int \frac{x^3 - x^2 + x - 1}{(x - 1)} dx$

Here, we factorise the numerator and cancel the common term from numerator and denominator and then integrate it.

$$\int \frac{x^3 - x^2 + x - 1}{(x - 1)} dx = \int \frac{x^2(x - 1) + 1(x - 1)}{(x - 1)} dx = \int \frac{(x^2 + 1)(x - 1)}{(x - 1)} dx$$

$$= \int (x^2 + 1)\,dx = \frac{x^3}{3} + x + C$$

3 (*d*) $\int \frac{2 - 3\sin x}{\cos^2 x} dx.$

$$\therefore \int \frac{2 - 3\sin x}{\cos^2 x} dx = \int \frac{2}{\cos^2 x} dx - 3\int \frac{\sin x}{\cos^2 x} dx$$

$$= 2\int \sec^2 x\,dx - 3\int \tan x \cdot \sec x\,dx$$

$$= 2\tan x - 3\sec x + C$$

4 (*c*) It is worth mentioning that integration by parts is not applicable to product of functions in all cases, For instance, the method does not work for $\int \sqrt{x}\sin x\,dx$.

The reason is that there does not exist any function whose derivative is $\sqrt{x}\sin x$.

5 (*a*) Observe that while finding the integral of the second function. we did not add any constant of integration. If we write the integral of the second function $\cos x$ as $\sin x + k$, where k is any constant, then

$$\int x \cos x \, dx = x(\sin x + k) - \int (\sin x + k)\, dx$$
$$= x(\sin x + k) - \int \sin x \, dx - \int k \, dx$$
$$= x(\sin x + k) + \cos x - kx + C$$
$$= x \sin x + \cos x + C$$

This shows that adding a constant to the integral of the second function is superfluous so far as the final result is concerned while applying the method of integration by parts.

6 (*a*) The value of definite integral of a function over any particular interval depends on the function and the interval, but not on the variable of intergration that we choose the represent the independent variable. If the independent variable is denoted by t or u instead of x, we simply write the integral as $\int_a^b f(t)\, dt$ or $\int_a^b f(u)\, du$ instead of $\int_a^b f(x) dx$. Hence, the variable of integration is a called is dummy variable.

7 (*b*) Using

$$\int_0^{2a} f(x) dx = \int_0^a f(x) dx + \int_0^a f(2a - x) dx \quad ...(i)$$

Now, If $f(2a - x) = f(x)$, then Eq. (i) becomes

$$\int_0^{2a} f(x) dx = \int_0^a f(x) dx + \int_0^a f(x) dx,$$
$$= 2\int_0^a f(x) dx$$

and if $f(2a - x) = -f(x)$, then (1) becomes

$$\int_0^{2a} f(x) dx = \int_0^a f(x) dx - \int_0^a f(x) dx = 0$$

8 (*a*) Let $f(x) = e^{2-3x}$, then

$$\int_0^1 e^{2-3x} dx = \int_0^1 f(x)\, dx$$

We know that,

$$\int_a^b f(x)\, dx = \lim_{h \to 0} h\,[f(a) + f(a+h) + f(a+2h) + \ldots + f\{a + (n-1)h\}]$$

where, $h = \dfrac{b-a}{n}$

Here, $a = 0, b = 1$ and $nh = 1$

and $f(x) = e^{2-3x}$

$\therefore$ $f(0) = e^2; f(0 + h) = e^{2-3h}$ and so on.

$$\therefore \int_0^1 e^{2-3x}\, dx$$
$$= \lim_{h \to 0} h\{f(0) + f(0+h) + f(0+2h) + \ldots + f(0 + (n-1)\, h)\}$$
$$= \lim_{h \to 0} h\{e^2 + e^{2-3h} + e^{2-6h} + \ldots + e^{2-3(n-1)h}\}$$
$$= \lim_{h \to 0} he^2\{1 + e^{-3h} + e^{-6h} + \ldots e^{-3(n-1)h}\}$$
$$= \lim_{h \to 0} \frac{he^2\{1 - (e^{-3h})^n\}}{1 - e^{-3h}} \quad \text{(where, } nh = 1)$$

(this is a GP series, where $a = 1$, $r = |e^{-3h}| < 1$)

$$= \lim_{h \to 0} \frac{e^2\{1 - (e^{-3(1)})\}}{\dfrac{1 - e^{-3h}}{-3h}(-3)} \quad [\because nh = 1]$$
$$= \frac{e^2(1 - e^{-3})}{3 \lim\limits_{h \to 0} \dfrac{e^{-3h} - 1}{-3h}}$$
$$= \frac{1}{3}(e^2 - e^{-1}) \quad \left[\because \lim_{x \to 0} \frac{e^x - 1}{x} = 1\right]$$

Case or Paragraph Type Questions

1 (c) $\int e^x \left(\sin^{-1} x + \dfrac{1}{\sqrt{1 - x^2}}\right)$

Here $\dfrac{d}{dx}(\sin^{-1} x) = \dfrac{1}{\sqrt{1 - x^2}}$

By $\int e^x (f(x) + f'(x))\, dx = e^x f(x) + C$

$$\therefore \int e^x\left(\sin^{-1} x + \frac{1}{\sqrt{1-x^2}}\right) dx = e^x \cdot \sin^{-1} x + C$$

$\Rightarrow f(x) = \sin^{-1} x$

(c) is the correct option.

2 (*a*) $\int e^x \sec x(1 + \tan x)\, dx$

$$\Rightarrow \int e^x(\sec x + \sec x \tan x)\, dx = e^x \sec x + c$$

(a) is the correct option.

3 (*a*) $\int e^x \left(\tan^{-1} x + \dfrac{1}{1+x^2}\right) dx = e^x \tan^{-1} x + C$

(a) is the correct option.

4 (*b*) $\int_0^{\pi/4} \cos x dx = (\sin x)_0^{\pi/4}$

$$= \left(\frac{1}{\sqrt{2}} - 0\right) = \frac{1}{\sqrt{2}}$$

(b) is the correct option.

5 (c) $\int_{\pi/4}^{\pi/2} \sin x\, dx = (-\cos x)_{\pi/4}^{\pi/2}$

$$= \left(-0 + \frac{1}{\sqrt{2}}\right) = \frac{1}{\sqrt{2}}$$

(c) is the correct option.

6 (*a*) $\int_0^{\pi/4} (\cos x + \sin x)\, dx$

$$= (\sin x - \cos x)_0^{\pi/4}$$
$$= \left(\left(\frac{1}{\sqrt{2}} - \frac{1}{\sqrt{2}}\right) - (0 - 1)\right)$$
$$= 1$$

(a) is the correct option.

Past Years Questions

1 (*d*) $\int \dfrac{2 - \tan x}{3 + \tan x} dx$

$$= \int \frac{2\cos x - \sin x}{3\cos x + \sin x} dx$$

$$2\cos x - \sin x = A(3\cos x + \sin x) + B(\cos x - 3\sin x)$$

On comparing coefficient of $\sin x$ and $\cos x$ from both sides, we get

$$3A + B = 2 \quad ...(i)$$
$$A - 3B = -1 \quad ...(ii)$$

On solving Eqs. (i) and (ii), we get

$$A = \frac{1}{2}, B = \frac{1}{2}$$

So, $\int \frac{2\cos x - \sin x}{3\cos x + \sin x} dx$

$= \frac{x}{2} + \frac{1}{2} \ln|3\cos x + \sin x| + C$

$= \frac{1}{2}(x + \ln|3\cos x + \sin x|) + C$

$= \frac{1}{2}(\alpha x + \ln|\beta \sin x + \gamma \cos x| + C$

$\alpha = 1, \beta = 1, \gamma = 3$

$\therefore \alpha + \frac{\gamma}{\beta} = 1 + \frac{3}{1} = 4$

2 (b) Given,

$y(x) = \int \frac{\operatorname{cosec} x + \sin x}{\operatorname{cosec} x \sec x + \tan x \sin^2 x} dx$

$= \int \frac{(1+\sin^2 x)\cos x}{1+\sin^4 x} dx$

On putting, $\sin x = t$

$\Rightarrow \cos x\, dx = dt = \int \frac{1+t^2}{t^4+1} dt$

$= \frac{1}{\sqrt{2}} \tan^{-1} \frac{\left(t - \frac{1}{t}\right)}{\sqrt{2}} + C$

When, $x = \frac{\pi}{2}$, then $t = 1$

$\therefore \quad c = 0$

$\therefore \quad y\left(\frac{\pi}{4}\right) = \frac{1}{\sqrt{2}} \tan^{-1}\left(-\frac{1}{2}\right)$

3 (b) $I_n = \int_0^1 (1-x^k)^n dx$

and $147 I_{20} = 148 I_{21}$

Let $I_{21} = \int_0^1 (1-x^k)^{21} \times 1 \cdot dx$

Using integration by parts, we get

$I_{21} = [(1-x^k)^{21} \cdot x]_0^1$
$+ 21k \int_0^1 (1-x^k)^{20} \cdot x^{k-1} \cdot x \cdot dx$

$= 0 + 21k \int_0^1 (1-x^k)^{20}(x^k - 1 + 1) dx$

$= 21k \int_0^1 -(1-x^k)^{21} dx + \int (1-x^k)^{20} dx$

$I_{21} = 21k[-I_{21} + I_{20}]$

$\Rightarrow I_{21} = -21k\, I_{21} + 21k\, I_{20}$

Comparing with $148 I_{21} = 147 I_{20}$,

we get $k = 7$

4 (a) Let $I = \int \frac{\pi}{x^{n+1} - x} dx$

$= \pi \int \frac{1}{x(x^n - 1)} dx$

$= \pi \int \frac{x^{n-1}}{x^n(x^n-1)} dx$

Put $x^n = t \Rightarrow nx^{n-1} dx = dt$

$\therefore \quad I = \frac{\pi}{n} \int \frac{dt}{t(t-1)}$

$= \frac{\pi}{n} \int \left(\frac{1}{t-1} - \frac{1}{t}\right) dt$

$= \frac{\pi}{n} [\log_e(t-1) - \log_e t] + C$

$= \frac{\pi}{n} \log_e \left|\frac{t-1}{t}\right| + C$

$= \frac{\pi}{n} \log_e \left|\frac{x^n - 1}{x^n}\right| + C$

5 (d) Let $I = \int e^x \left(\frac{2x+1}{2\sqrt{x}}\right) dx$

$= \frac{1}{2} \int e^x \left(\frac{2x+1}{\sqrt{x}}\right) dx$

$= \frac{1}{2} \int e^x \left(2\sqrt{x} + \frac{1}{\sqrt{x}}\right) dx$

$= \frac{1}{2}\left[\int 2e^x \sqrt{x} dx + \int e^x \cdot \frac{1}{\sqrt{x}} dx\right]$

$= \frac{1}{2}\left[2e^x\sqrt{x} - \int 2e^x \cdot \frac{1}{2\sqrt{x}} dx + C + \int e^x \cdot \frac{1}{\sqrt{x}} dx\right]$

$= \frac{1}{2}\left[2e^x\sqrt{x} - \int e^x \frac{1}{\sqrt{x}} dx + C + \int e^x \cdot \frac{1}{\sqrt{x}} dx\right]$

$= \frac{1}{2}[2e^x\sqrt{x}] + C \Rightarrow I = e^x\sqrt{x} + C$

6 (a) Let $I = \int_0^{\frac{\pi}{2}} \frac{1 - \cot x}{\operatorname{cosec} x + \cos x} dx$

$I = \int_0^{\frac{\pi}{2}} \frac{\sin x - \cos x}{1 + \sin x \cos x} dx$ ...(i)

Since, $\int_a^b f(x) dx = \int_a^b f(a+b-x) dx$

So, $I = \int_0^{\frac{\pi}{2}} \frac{\sin\left(\frac{\pi}{2} - x\right) - \cos\left(\frac{\pi}{2} - x\right)}{1 + \sin\left(\frac{\pi}{2} - x\right)\cos\left(\frac{\pi}{2} - x\right)}$

$I = \int_0^{\frac{\pi}{2}} \frac{\cos x - \sin x}{1 + \sin x \cos x} dx$

$I = -\int_0^{\frac{\pi}{2}} \frac{\sin x - \cos x}{1 + \sin x \cos x} dx$ ...(ii)

On adding Eqs. (i) and (ii), we get

$2I = 0$

$\therefore \quad I = 0$

7 (d) We have,

$I(x) = \int \frac{x^2(x\sec^2 x + \tan x)}{(x\tan x + 1)^2} dx$

Integration by parts,

$x^2 \int \frac{x\sec^2 x + \tan x}{(x\tan x + 1)^2} dx$

$- \int \left\{\frac{d}{dx}(x^2) \int \frac{x\sec^2 x + \tan x}{(x\tan x + 1)^2}\right\} dx$

$= x^2 \left(\frac{-1}{x\tan x + 1}\right) + \int \frac{2x}{x\tan x + 1} dx$

Now, let $I_1 = 2\int \frac{x}{x\tan x + 1} dx$

$I_1 = 2\int \frac{x\cos x}{x\sin x + \cos x} dx$

On putting $x\sin x + \cos x = t$

$\Rightarrow (x\cos x + \sin x - \sin x) dx = dt$

$\Rightarrow x\cos x\, dx = dt$

$\therefore \quad I_1 = 2\int \frac{dt}{t} = 2\log t + c$

$= 2\log(x\sin x + \cos x) + c$

$\therefore \quad I(x) = \frac{-x^2}{x\tan x + 1}$
$+ 2\log(x\sin x + \cos x) + c$ ...(i)

When $x = 0$,

then $I(0) = 0 + 2\log(1) + c = 0$

$\Rightarrow \quad c = 0$

$\therefore \quad I(x) = \frac{-x^2}{x\tan x + 1}$
$+ 2\log(x\sin x + \cos x)$

$\Rightarrow I\left(\frac{\pi}{4}\right) = \frac{-\frac{\pi^2}{16}}{\frac{\pi}{4} + 1}$
$+ 2\log\left(\frac{\pi}{4} \times \frac{1}{\sqrt{2}} + \frac{1}{\sqrt{2}}\right)$

$= \log\left(\frac{(\pi+4)^2}{32}\right) - \frac{\pi^2}{4(\pi+4)}$

8 (c) Let $I=\int_0^{\pi} f(x)\sin x\,dx$ ...(i)

$I=\int_0^{\pi} f(\pi-x)\sin(\pi-x)\,dx$

$I=\int_0^{\pi} f(\pi-x)\sin x\,dx$ ...(ii)

On adding Eqs. (i) and (ii), we get

$2I=\int_0^{\pi}[f(x)+f(\pi-x)]\sin x\,dx$

$\Rightarrow 2I=\int_0^{\pi}\pi^2\sin x\,dx$

$=\pi^2\int_0^{\pi}\sin x\,dx$

$=\pi^2(-\cos x)_0^{\pi}=-\pi^2(-1-1)$

$=2\pi^2$

$\Rightarrow I=\pi^2$

9 (b) Let $I=\int_{1/2}^{2}\frac{\tan^{-1}x}{x}dx$ ...(i)

Put $x=\frac{1}{t}$, then $dx=\frac{-1}{t^2}dt$

$\therefore I=\int_{2}^{1/2}\frac{\tan^{-1}\left(\frac{1}{t}\right)}{\left(\frac{1}{t}\right)}\left(-\frac{1}{t^2}\right)dt$

$=\int_{1/2}^{2}\frac{\tan^{-1}\left(\frac{1}{t}\right)}{t}dt=\int_{1/2}^{2}\frac{\cot^{-1}t}{t}dt$ ...(ii)

$\therefore$ Adding Eqs. (i) and (ii), we get

$2I=\int_{1/2}^{2}\frac{\tan^{-1}x+\cot^{-1}x}{x}dx$

$=\int_{1/2}^{2}\frac{\left(\frac{\pi}{2}\right)}{x}dx$

$\Rightarrow 2I=\frac{\pi}{2}[\log x]_{\frac{1}{2}}^{2}=\frac{\pi}{2}(\log 2+\log 2)$

$\Rightarrow I=\frac{\pi}{2}\log_e 2$

10 (b) We have, $f:R\to R$

$f(x)=a\sin\left(\frac{\pi[x]}{2}\right)+[2-x],\,a\in R$

At $x=-1$

$\text{LHL}=a\sin\left(\frac{-2\pi}{2}\right)+3$

$\text{RHL}=a\sin\left(-\frac{\pi}{2}\right)+2$

Now, LHL = RHL

$\Rightarrow\quad 3=-a+2$

$\Rightarrow\quad a=-1$

Now, $\int_0^4 f(x)dx=\int_0^1(-\sin(0)+1)dx$

$+\int_1^2(-1+0)dx+\int_2^3(0-1)dx$

$+\int_3^4(1-2)dx$

$=1-1-1-1=-2$

11 (1) $I=\int\sqrt{\sec 2x-1}\,dx$

$=\int\sqrt{\frac{1-\cos 2x}{\cos 2x}}\,dx$

$=\int\frac{\sqrt{2}\sin x}{\sqrt{2\cos^2x-1}}dx$

Let $\quad\sqrt{2}\cos x=t$

$\Rightarrow\quad -\sqrt{2}\sin x\cdot dx=dt$

Then, $\quad I=\int\frac{-1}{\sqrt{t^2-1}}dt$

$=-\ln|t+\sqrt{t^2-1}|+C$

Put $t=\sqrt{2}\cos x$

$=-\ln|\sqrt{2}\cos x+\sqrt{2\cos^2x-1}|+C$

$=-\frac{1}{2}\ln|(\sqrt{2}\cos x+\sqrt{\cos 2x})^2|+C$

$=-\frac{1}{2}\ln\Big|2\cos^2x+\cos 2x$

$+2\sqrt{2}\sqrt{\cos 2x}\sqrt{\frac{1+\cos 2x}{2}}\Big|+C$

$=-\frac{1}{2}\ln|1+\cos 2x+\cos 2x$

$+2\sqrt{\cos 2x(1+\cos 2x)}|+C$

$=-\frac{1}{2}\log_e\left|\cos 2x+\frac{1}{2}+\sqrt{\cos 2x(1+\cos 2x)}\right|$

$+C$

Comparing to the given solution

So, $\alpha=-\frac{1}{2},\beta=\frac{1}{2}$

$\beta-\alpha=\frac{1}{2}-\left(-\frac{1}{2}\right)=1$

12 (1) $I=\int\operatorname{cosec}^5x\,dx$

$=\int\operatorname{cosec}^3x\cdot\operatorname{cosec}^2x\,dx$

Using by parts

$I=\operatorname{cosec}^3x\int\operatorname{cosec}^2x$

$-\int(3\operatorname{cosec}^2x\cdot(-\operatorname{cosec}x\cot x)$

$\int\operatorname{cosec}^2x\,dx)\,dx$

$\Rightarrow I=-\operatorname{cosec}^3x\cdot\cot x$

$-\int 3\operatorname{cosec}^3x\cot^2x\,dx$

$\Rightarrow I=-\operatorname{cosec}^3x\cdot\cot x$

$-3\int\operatorname{cosec}^3x(\operatorname{cosec}^2x-1)$

$\Rightarrow I=-\operatorname{cosec}^3x\cdot\cot x$

$-3\int\operatorname{cosec}^5x+3\int\operatorname{cosec}^3x$ ...(i)

$\Rightarrow I=-\operatorname{cosec}^3x\cdot\cot x-3I$

$+3\int\operatorname{cosec}x\cdot\operatorname{cosec}^2x\,dx$

$\Rightarrow 4I=-\operatorname{cosec}^3x\cdot\cot x$

$+3\operatorname{cosec}x\cdot(-\cot x)$

$-3\int(-\operatorname{cosec}x\cot x)\cdot(-\cot x)\,dx$

$\Rightarrow 4I=-\operatorname{cosec}^3x\cdot\cot x-3\operatorname{cosec}x$

$\cot x-3\int\operatorname{cosec}x(\operatorname{cosec}^2x-1)$

$\Rightarrow 4I=-\operatorname{cosec}^2x\cot x-3\operatorname{cosec}x$

$\cdot\cot x-3\int\operatorname{cosec}^3x\,dx$

$+3\int\operatorname{cosec}x\,dx$

$\Rightarrow 4I=-\operatorname{cosec}^3x\cot x-3\operatorname{cosec}x$

$\cdot\cot x-[I+\operatorname{cosec}^3x\cot x+3I)]$

$+3\ln\left|\operatorname{cosec}\frac{x}{2}+\cot\frac{x}{2}\right|+C$

[by Eq. (i)]

$\Rightarrow 8I=-2\operatorname{cosec}^3x\cot x$

$-3\operatorname{cosec}x\cdot\cot x$

$+3\ln\left|\tan\frac{x}{2}\right|+C$

$\Rightarrow I=-\frac{1}{4}\operatorname{cosec}x\cdot\cot x$

$\left(\operatorname{cosec}^2x+\frac{3}{2}\right)+\frac{3}{8}\ln\left|\tan\frac{x}{2}\right|+C$

$\alpha=-\frac{1}{4},\beta=\frac{3}{8}$

$\therefore 8(\alpha+\beta)\Rightarrow 8\alpha+8\beta=-2+3=1$

13 (28) Given,

$$f(x)=\int\frac{dx}{(3+4x^2)\sqrt{4-3x^2}},$$

$$|x|<\frac{2}{\sqrt{3}}$$

Put $x=\frac{1}{t}$

$$\Rightarrow dx=-\frac{1}{t^2}dt$$

$$\therefore f(x)=\int\frac{\left(-\frac{1}{t^2}\right)dt}{\left(3+\frac{4}{t^2}\right)\sqrt{4-\frac{3}{t^2}}}$$

$$=\int\frac{-t\,dt}{(3t^2+4)\sqrt{4t^2-3}}$$

Put $4t^2-3=z^2$

$$\Rightarrow \quad 8t\,dt=2z\,dz$$

$$\Rightarrow \quad t\,dt=\frac{1}{4}z\,dz$$

$$=\int\frac{\left(-\frac{1}{4}z\,dz\right)}{\left[3\left(\frac{z^2+3}{4}\right)+4\right]z}$$

$$=-\frac{1}{4}\int\frac{4\,dz}{3z^2+25}$$

$$=-\int\frac{dz}{3\left\{z^2+\frac{25}{3}\right\}}$$

$$=-\frac{1}{3}\int\frac{dz}{(z)^2+\left(\frac{5}{\sqrt{3}}\right)^2}$$

$$=-\frac{1}{3}\cdot\frac{\sqrt{3}}{5}\tan^{-1}\left(\frac{z}{5/\sqrt{3}}\right)+C$$

$$=\frac{-1}{5\sqrt{3}}\tan^{-1}\left(\frac{\sqrt{3}}{5}\sqrt{4t^2-3}\right)+C$$

$$\therefore f(x)=-\frac{1}{5\sqrt{3}}\tan^{-1}\left(\frac{\sqrt{3}}{5}\sqrt{\frac{4-3x^2}{x^2}}\right)+C$$

Since, $f(0)=0$

$$\Rightarrow \quad C=\frac{\pi}{10\sqrt{3}}$$

$$\therefore \quad f(x)=-\frac{1}{5\sqrt{3}}\tan^{-1}\left(\frac{\sqrt{3}}{5}\frac{\sqrt{4-3x^2}}{x}\right)+\frac{\pi}{10\sqrt{3}}$$

$$\therefore f(1)=-\frac{1}{5\sqrt{3}}\tan^{-1}\left(\frac{\sqrt{3}}{5}\right)+\frac{\pi}{10\sqrt{3}}$$

$$=\frac{1}{5\sqrt{3}}\left(\frac{\pi}{2}-\tan^{-1}\left(\frac{\sqrt{3}}{5}\right)\right)$$

$$=\frac{1}{5\sqrt{3}}\cot^{-1}\left(\frac{\sqrt{3}}{5}\right)$$

$$f(1)=\frac{1}{5\sqrt{3}}\tan^{-1}\left(\frac{5}{\sqrt{3}}\right)$$

$$=\frac{1}{\alpha\beta}\tan^{-1}\left(\frac{\alpha}{\beta}\right) \quad \text{[given]}$$

So, $\alpha=5,\beta=\sqrt{3}$ $\quad [\because \alpha,\beta>0]$

$$\therefore \quad \alpha^2+\beta^2=(5)^2+(\sqrt{3})^2$$

$$=25+3=28$$

14 (2) **Key Idea** *Use property of definite integral*

$$\int_0^{2a}f(x)dx=\begin{cases}2\int_0^a f(x)dx, & \text{If } f(2a-x)=f(x)\\ 0, & \text{If } f(2a-x)=-f(x)\end{cases}$$

Let

$$I=\frac{8}{\pi}\int_0^{\pi/2}\frac{(\cos x)^{2023}}{(\sin x)^{2023}+(\cos x)^{2023}}dx \quad \text{...(i)}$$

As we know that

$$\int_0^a f(x)\,dx=\int_0^a f(a-x)dx$$

$$\text{So, } I=\frac{8}{\pi}\int_0^{\frac{\pi}{2}}\frac{\left[\cos\left(\frac{\pi}{2}-x\right)\right]^{2023}}{\left[\sin\left(\frac{\pi}{2}-x\right)\right]^{2023}+\left[\cos\left(\frac{\pi}{2}-x\right)\right]^{2023}}dx$$

$$\Rightarrow I=\frac{8}{\pi}\int_0^{\frac{\pi}{2}}\frac{(\sin x)^{2023}}{(\cos x)^{2023}+(\sin x)^{2023}}dx \quad \text{...(ii)}$$

On adding Eqs. (i) and (ii), we get

$$2I=\frac{8}{\pi}\left[\int_0^{\frac{\pi}{2}}\frac{(\cos x)^{2023}+(\sin x)^{2023}}{(\sin x)^{2023}+(\cos x)^{2023}}dx\right]$$

$$\Rightarrow \quad 2I=\frac{8}{\pi}\int_0^{\pi/2}1\cdot dx$$

$$\Rightarrow \quad I=\frac{4}{\pi}[x]_0^{\frac{\pi}{2}}$$

$$\Rightarrow \quad I=\frac{4}{\pi}\left[\frac{\pi}{2}-0\right]$$

$$\Rightarrow \quad I=2$$

15 (104) Let $I=60\int_0^{\frac{\pi}{2}}\frac{\sin 6x}{\sin x}dx$

$$=60\times 2\int_0^{\frac{\pi}{2}}\frac{\sin 3x\cos 3x}{\sin x}dx$$

$$=120\int_0^{\frac{\pi}{2}}\frac{(3\sin x-4\sin^3 x)(4\cos^3 x-3\cos x)dx}{\sin x}$$

$$=120\int_0^{\frac{\pi}{2}}(3-4\sin^2 x)(4\cos^2 x-3)\cos x\,dx$$

$$=120\int_0^{\frac{\pi}{2}}(3-4\sin^2 x)(4(1-\sin^2 x)-3)\cos x\,dx$$

$$=120\int_0^{\frac{\pi}{2}}(3-4\sin^2 x)(1-4\sin^2 x)\cos x\,dx$$

Let $\sin x=t$, then $\cos x\,dx=dt$

When, $x\to 0$, then $t\to 0$

When, $x\to\frac{\pi}{2}$, then $t\to 1$

$$=120\int_0^1(3-4t^2)(1-4t^2)dt$$

$$=120\int_0^1(3-16t^2+16t^4)\,dt$$

$$=120\left[3t-\frac{16t^3}{3}+\frac{16t^5}{5}\right]_0^1$$

$$=120\left[3-\frac{16}{3}+\frac{16}{5}\right]$$

$$=120\left[\frac{45-80+48}{15}\right]$$

$$=8\times 13=104$$

Skill Boosters

1 (b) $g\left(\frac{x+2}{x+3}\right)=3x+2$ ...(i)

for $x \in R-\left\{3, \frac{1}{3}\right\}$

Put $\frac{x+2}{x+3}=t \Rightarrow x+2=xt+3t$

$\Rightarrow x(1-t)=3t-2 \Rightarrow x=\frac{3t-2}{1-t}$

$\Rightarrow g(t)=3\left(\frac{3t-2}{1-t}\right)+2$

$=\frac{9t-6}{1-t}+2=\frac{9t-6+2-2t}{1-t}$

$g(t)=\frac{7t-4}{1-t} \Rightarrow g(x)=\frac{7x-4}{1-x}$ ...(ii)

On integrating both sides of equation (ii), we get

$\int g(x)\,dx=\int \frac{7x-4}{1-x}\,dx$

$=\int \frac{7x}{1-x}\,dx-4\int \frac{dx}{1-x}$

$=-7\int \frac{-x\,dx}{(1-x)}-4\int \frac{dx}{1-x}$

$=-7\int \frac{(1-x)-1}{(1-x)}\,dx-4\int \frac{dx}{(1-x)}$

$=-7\int dx+7\int \frac{dx}{1-x}-4\int \frac{dx}{(1-x)}$

$=-7\int dx+3\int \frac{dx}{1-x}$

$\int g(x)\,dx=-7x-3\log|1-x|+C$

(b) is the correct option.

2 (b) Given $\int_0^{\sqrt{2}} x e^{[x^2]}\,dx$

Let $I=\int_0^{\sqrt{2}} x e^{[x^2]}dx$

$[x^2]=\begin{cases}0, & 0 \le x<1 \\ 1, & 1 \le x<\sqrt{2}\end{cases}$

Now $I=\int_0^1 x e^0\,dx+\int_1^{\sqrt{2}} xe\,dx$

$=\left(\frac{x^2}{2}\right)_0^2+e\cdot\left(\frac{x^2}{2}\right)_1^{\sqrt{2}}$

$=\frac{1}{2}+e\left(\frac{2}{2}-\frac{1}{2}\right)=\frac{1}{2}+e-\frac{e}{2}$

$I=\left(\frac{1+e}{2}\right)$

$\therefore \int_0^{\sqrt{2}} x e^{[x^2]}\,dx=\left(\frac{1+e}{2}\right)$

(b) is the correct option.

3 (a) $f(\alpha)=\int_{\pi/6}^{\pi/3} \frac{\sec^\alpha x}{\sec^\alpha x+\operatorname{cosec}^\alpha x}\,x$ ...(i)

On using the

$\int_a^b f(x)\,dx=\int_a^b f(a+b-x)dx$

$f(\alpha)=\int_{\pi/6}^{\pi/3} \frac{\sec^\alpha\left(\frac{\pi}{2}-x\right)dx}{\sec^\alpha\left(\frac{\pi}{2}-x\right)+\operatorname{cosec}^\alpha\left(\frac{\pi}{2}-x\right)}$

$=\int_{\pi/6}^{\pi/3} \frac{\operatorname{cosec}^\alpha x\,dx}{\sec^\alpha x+\operatorname{cosec}^\alpha x}$ ...(ii)

Adding Eqs. (i) and (ii), we get

$2f(\alpha)=\int_{\pi/6}^{\pi/3} \frac{\sec^\alpha x+\operatorname{cosec}^\alpha x\,dx}{(\sec^\alpha x+\operatorname{cosec}^\alpha x)}$

$2f(\alpha)=\int_{\pi/6}^{\pi/3} 1\,dx$

$f(\alpha)=\frac{1}{2}\left(\frac{\pi}{3}-\frac{\pi}{6}\right)$

$f(\alpha)=\frac{1}{2}\left(\frac{\pi}{6}\right) \Rightarrow f(\alpha)=\frac{\pi}{12}$

Here $f(x)$ is constant function.

$\therefore f(\alpha)$ is even function.

$f(0)=\frac{\pi}{12} \neq 0$

Hence (a) is the correct option.

4 (a) $I=\int \sin(\log_e x)\,dx$

By applying integration by parts.

$=x\sin(\log_e x)-\int \frac{\cos(\log_e x)}{x}\cdot x\,dx$

$=x\sin(\log_e x)-\int \cos(\log_e x)\,dx$

$=x\sin(\log_e x)-\left(x\cos(\log_e x)-\int \frac{-\sin(\log_e x)}{x}\cdot x\,dx\right)$

$I=x\sin(\log_e x)-x\cos(\log_e)-I$

$2I=x(\sin(\log_e x)-\cos(\log_e x))$

$I=\frac{x}{2}(\sin(\log_e x)-\cos(\log_e x))+C$

(a) is correct option.

5 (c) Let $I=\int \frac{dx}{(x+6)^{5/4}(x+2)^{3/4}}$

$=\int \frac{dx}{(x+6)^{5/4}(x+6)^{3/4}\left(\frac{x+2}{x+6}\right)^{3/4}}$

$=\int \frac{dx}{(x+6)^2\left(\frac{x+2}{x+6}\right)^{3/4}}$

Put $\frac{x+2}{(x+6)}=t$

Differentiating bothside with respect to 'x'.

$\left(\frac{(x+6)-(x+2)}{(x+6)^2}\right)dx=dt$

$\frac{4\,dx}{(x+6)^2}=dt \Rightarrow \frac{dx}{(x+6)^2}=\frac{dt}{4}$

$\therefore I=\int \frac{dx}{(x+6)^{5/4}\cdot(x+2)^{3/4}}$

$=\frac{1}{4}\int \frac{dt}{t^{3/4}}=\frac{1}{4}\int t^{-3/4}\,dt$

$=\frac{1}{4}\left(\frac{t^{\frac{-3}{4}+1}}{\frac{-3}{4}+1}\right)+C$

$=\frac{1}{4}\left(\frac{t^{1/4}}{1/4}\right)+C$

$=\left(\frac{x+2}{x+6}\right)^{1/4}+C$

$\therefore \int \frac{dx}{(x+6)^{5/4}(x+2)^{3/4}}=\left(\frac{x+2}{x+6}\right)^{1/4}+C$

(c) is the correct option.

6 (b) $\int_0^x f(t)\,dt=x^3+\int_x^3 t^3 f(t)\,dt$

On differentiating both side w.r.t 'x', we get

$f(x)=3x^2-x^3f(x)$

$f(x)(1+x^3)=3x^2$

$f(x)=\frac{3x^2}{(1+x^3)}$

Again Differentiating both side w.r.t. 'x'

$f'(x)=\frac{6x(1+x^3)-3x^2(3x^2)}{(1+x^3)^2}$

$f'(x)=\frac{6x+6x^4-9x^4}{(1+x^3)^2}$

$f'(x)=\frac{6x-3x^4}{(1+x^3)^2}$

$f'(1)=\frac{6-3}{(1+1)^4}=\frac{3}{16} \Rightarrow f'(1)=\frac{3}{16}$

(b) is the correct option.

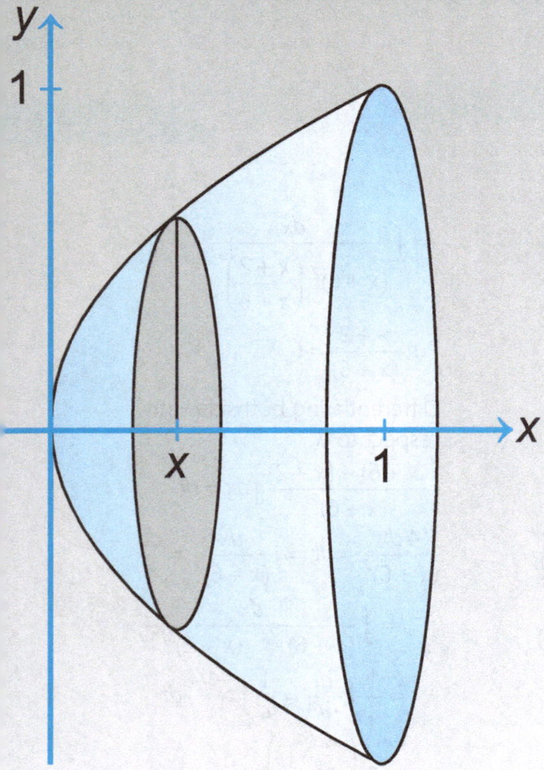

08

Application of Integrals

Topicwise No. of Ques asked in 3 Years (JEE Main)

Topics	No. of Questions		
	2024	2023	2022
Area Under Simple Curves	2	2	5

Special Type of Ques asked in 3 Years (JEE Main)

Types	Years		
	2024	2023	2022
A-R	–	–	–
Statement Based	–	–	–
Numerical Value Type	1	2	

Last 3 Years Weightage (JEE Main)

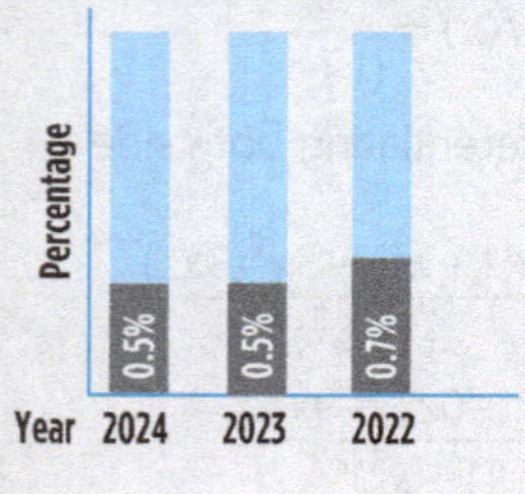

Area Under Simple Curves

Concept Master Video

1. If the curve $y = f(x)$ lies above X-axis, then the area bounded by the curve $y = f(x)$. The X-axis and the lines at $x = a$ and $x = b$, is given by $\int_a^b y\,dx$.

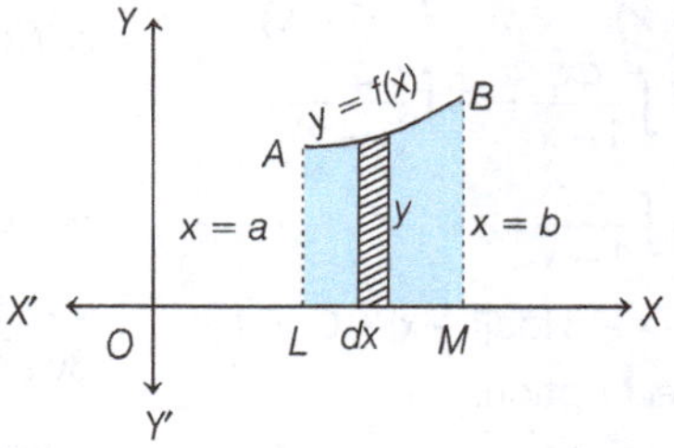

2. If the curve $x = f(y)$ lies to right of Y-axis, then the area bounded by the curve $x = f(y)$, the Y-axis and the lines at $y = c$ and $y = d$, is given by $\int_c^d x\,dy$.

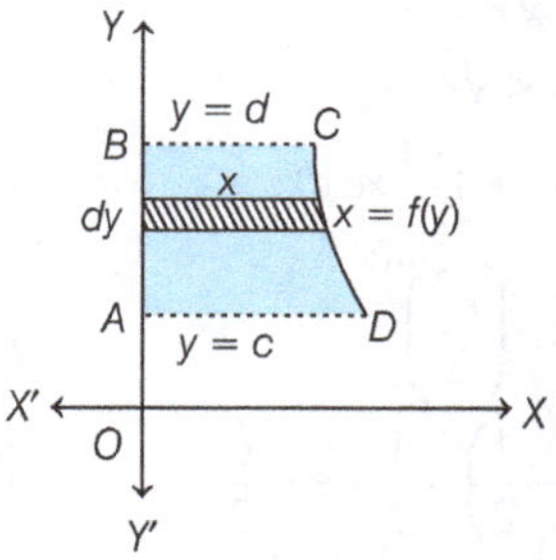

3. If the curve $y = f(x)$ lies below the X-axis, then area bounded by the curve $y = f(x)$, X-axis and the lines at $x = a$ and $x = b$, is given by $\left|\int_a^b y\,dx\right|$.

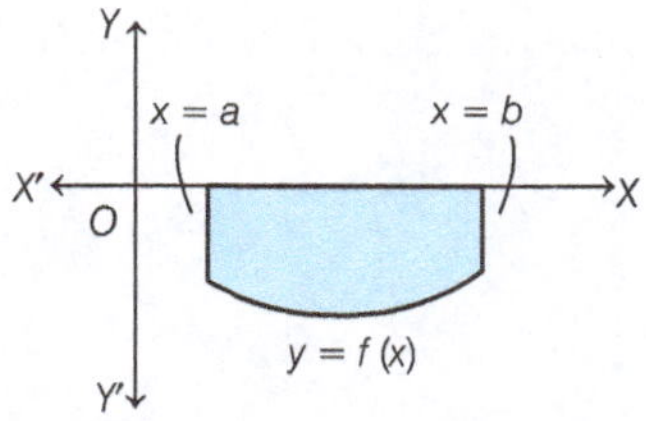

4. Generally, it may happen that some position of the curve is above X-axis and some is below the X-axis which is shown in the figure. The area A bounded by the curve $y = f(x)$, X-axis and the lines at $x = a$ and $x = b$ is given by $A = |A_2| + A_1$.

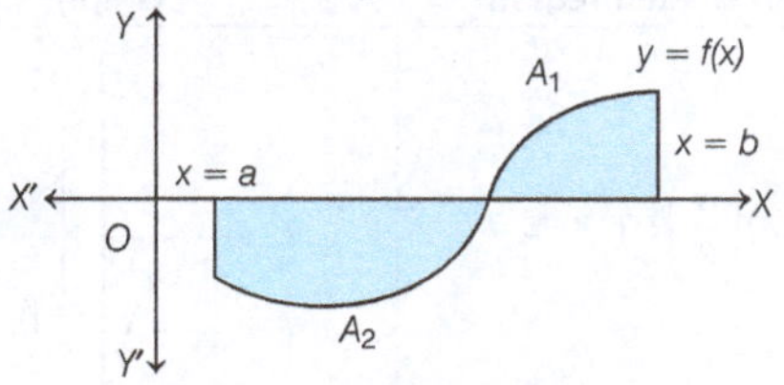

5. If the curve between the lines $y = c$, $y = d$ left to the Y-axis, then the area is given by

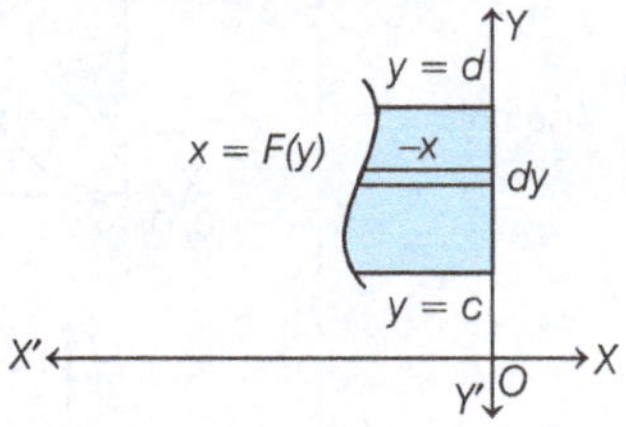

$$\left|\int_c^d (-x)\,dy\right| = \left|-\int_c^d x\,dy\right| = \left|-\int_c^d F(y)\,dy\right|$$

6. Area bounded by two curves $y = F(x)$ and $y = G(x)$ between $x = a$ and $x = b$ is given by

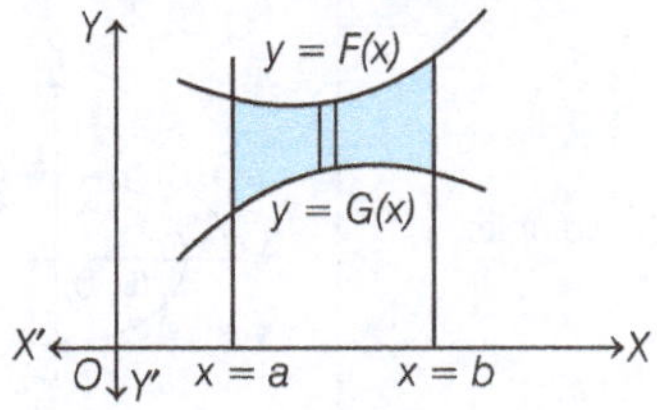

$$\int_a^b \{F(x) - G(x)\}\,dx$$

7. Area bounded by two curves $x = F(y)$ and $x = G(y)$ between $y = c$ and $y = d$ is given by

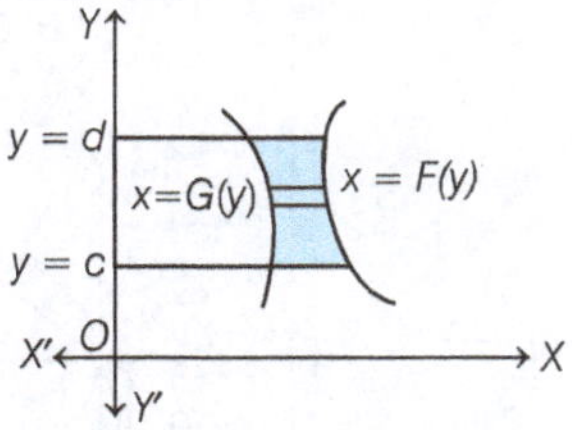

$$\int_c^d [F(y) - G(y)]\,dy$$

8. If $F(x) \geq G(x)$ in $[a, c]$ and $F(x) \leq G(x)$ in $[c, b]$, where $a < c < b$, then area of the region bounded by the curves is given as

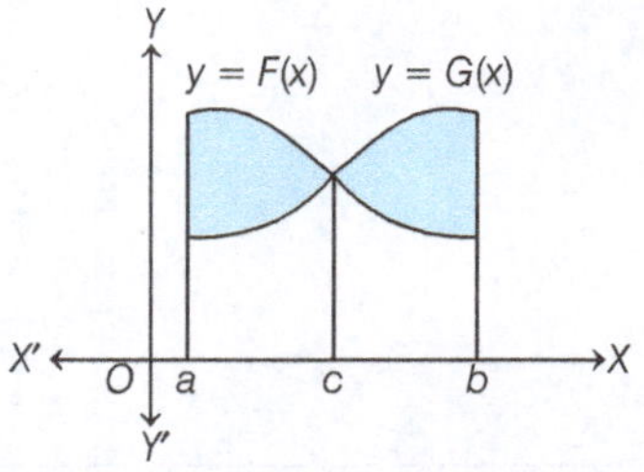

$$\text{Area} = \int_a^c \{F(x) - G(x)\}\,dx + \int_c^b \{G(x) - F(x)\}\,dx$$

Shapes of Some Curves

S.No.	Equation	Curve
(i)	$ay^2 = x^3$ (Semi-cubical parabola)	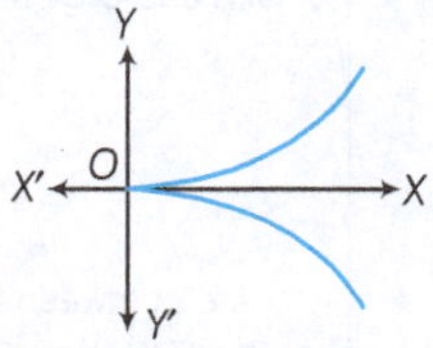
(ii)	$y = x^3$ (Cubical parabola)	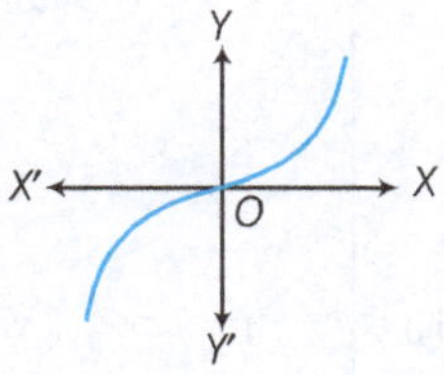
(iii)	$(x^2 + 4a^2)y = 8a^3$	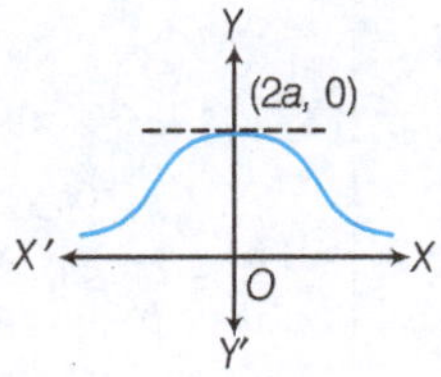
(iv)	$ay^2 = x^2(a - x)$	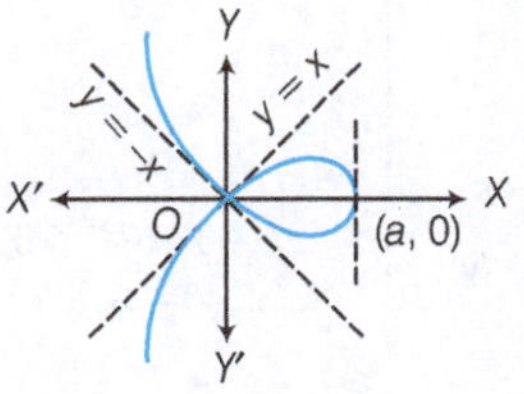
(v)	$a^2y^2 = x^2(a^2 - x^2)$	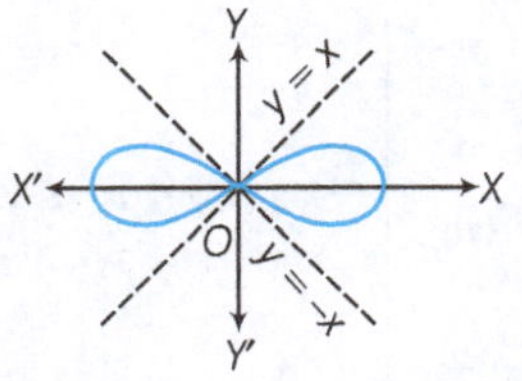

Marks Maximizer

- Area enclosed by a parabola $y^2 = 4ax$ and a rectangle $OABC$ is $\frac{2}{3}$ ar $(OABC)$.

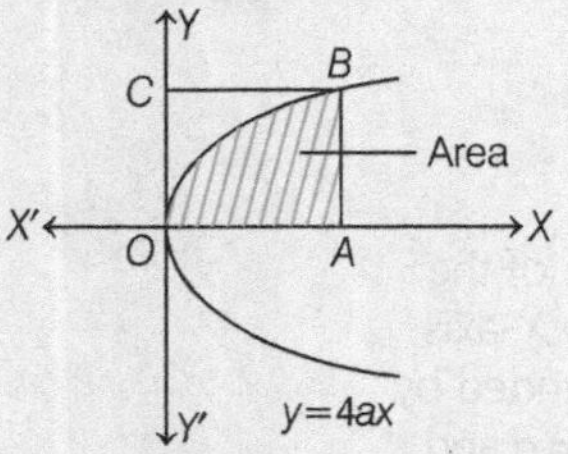

S.No.	Equation	Intersection points	Area of shaded region	Graph
(i)	If $\alpha, \beta > 0, \alpha > \beta$, then area bounded by the curve $xy = p^2$, X-axis and ordinate $x = \alpha, x = \beta$	—	$p^2 \log\left(\frac{\alpha}{\beta}\right)$ sq units	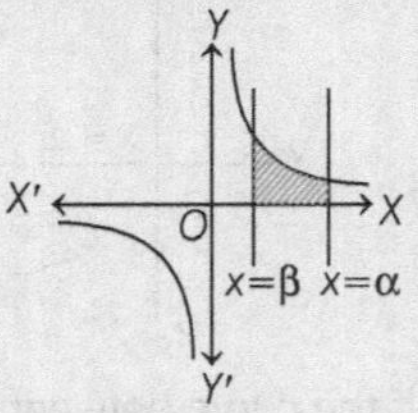
(ii)	Area between the curve $y = c^2x^2$, Y-axis and line $y = a, y = b$	$O\,(0,0), A\left(\frac{\sqrt{a}}{c}, a\right), B\left(\frac{\sqrt{b}}{c}, b\right)$	$\frac{2(b^{3/2} - a^{3/2})}{3c}$ sq units	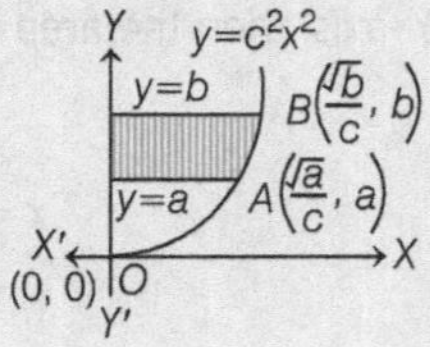
(iii)	$y = k\cos 3x,\ \forall 0 \le x \le \frac{\pi}{6}$	when $0 \le x \le \frac{\pi}{6}$, then $0 \le 3x \le \frac{\pi}{2}$	$\frac{k}{3}$ sq units	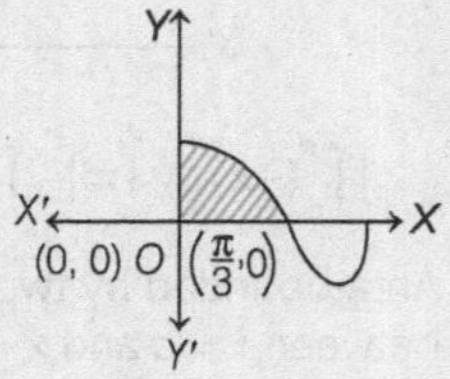
(iv)	$f(x, y);$ $\frac{x^2}{a^2} + \frac{y^2}{b^2} \le 1,\ \frac{x}{a} + \frac{y}{b} \ge 1$ or $\frac{x^2}{a^2} + \frac{y^2}{b^2} \le 1 \le \frac{x}{a} + \frac{y}{b}$	$A(a, 0), B\,(0, b)$	$ab \cdot \frac{(\pi - 2)}{4}$ sq units	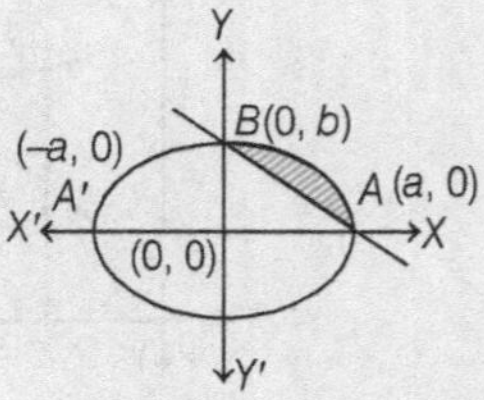
(v)	$f(x, y); ax^2 \le y \le mx$ $\therefore y = ax^2, y = mx$	$B(0, 0),\ A\left(\frac{m}{a}, \frac{m^2}{a}\right)$	$\frac{1}{6} \cdot \frac{m^3}{a^2}$ sq units	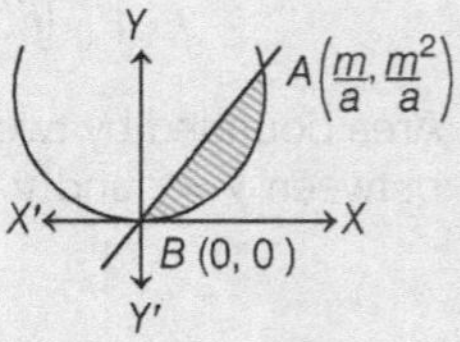
(vi)	$f(x, y); ax^2 \le y \le mx$ $\therefore y = ax^2, y = mx$	$O(0, 0),\ A\left(\frac{4a}{m^2}, \frac{4a}{m}\right)$	$\frac{8a^2}{3m^3}$ sq units	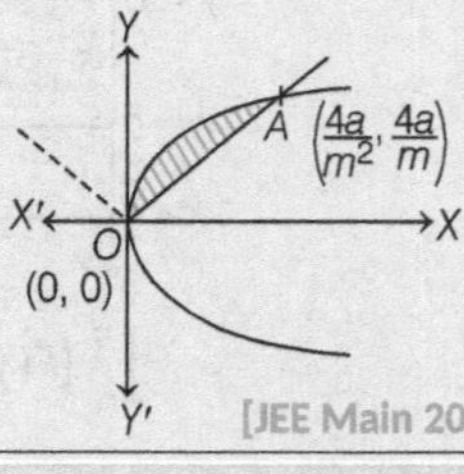 [JEE Main 2022]

Caution Points

- Make sure you correctly determine the limits of integration, as these define the range over which you are performing the integration. Misidentifying these can lead to incorrect results.
- Keep in mind that integrating from a lower limit to a higher limit results in a positive area, whereas doing it in the opposite direction yields a negative but area is never negative.
- The function should be continuos over the integration interval.
- Utilise symmetry to simplify calculations when applicable.

PYQ Notes

1. The area between a horizontal parabola and a line is $\dfrac{(y_2 - y_1)^3}{6 \times LR}$, where LR is latusrectum.
   If $(y-k)^2 = 4a(x-h)$, then $LR = 4a$

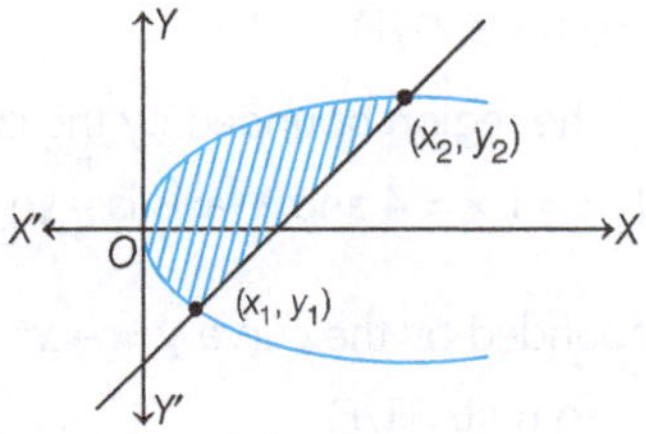

[JEE Main 2024]

2. The area between a vertical parabola and a line is $\dfrac{(x_2 - x_1)^3}{6 \times LR}$

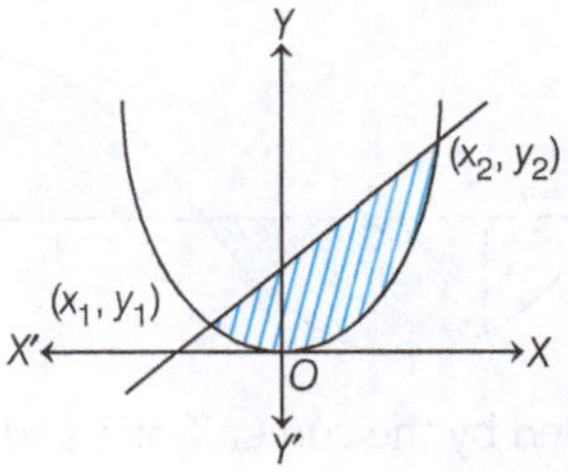

[JEE Main 2023]

Step by Step

Mastering NCERT

- Concept Builders
- Topical Questions
- Numerical Type Questions
- Assertion and Reason Questions
- Case or Paragraph Type Questions
- Past Years Questions
- Skill Boosters

Concept Builders

1 If some portion of the curve is above X-axis and some below the X-axis as shown below.

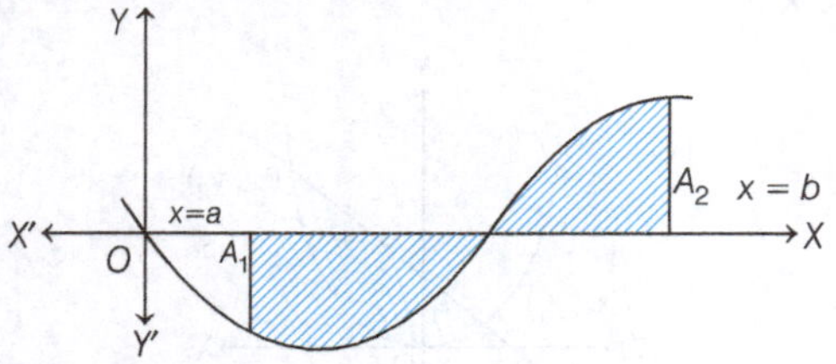

Area bounded by the curve, X-axis and ordinate is given by $A = |A_1| + A_2$. (T/F)

2 The area of the region bounded by the ellipse $\frac{x^2}{4} + \frac{y^2}{9} = 1$ is 6π sq units. (T/F)

3 Area lying in the first quadrant and bounded by the circle $x^2 + y^2 = 4$ and the lines $x = 0$ and $x = 2$ is $\frac{\pi}{2}$ sq units. (T/F)

4 Area of the region bounded by $y^2 = 2x$, Y-axis and the line $y = 1$ is $\frac{1}{6}$ sq units. (T/F)

5 The area bounded by the curve $y = x^2$ and the line $y = 9$ is 12 sq units. (T/F)

6 The area of the region bounded by the curve $y = |x - 2|$, $x = 1$, $x = 4$ and X-axis is $\frac{5}{2}$ sq units. (T/F)

7 The area bounded by the curve $y = -x^2 - x + 6$ and $y = 0$ is $\frac{125}{6}$ sq units. (T/F)

8 The area bounded by the curve $a^2y = x^2 (x + a)$ and X-axis, is ....

9 The total area enclosed by the lines $y = |x|$, $y = 0$ and $|x| = 1$ is ....

Topical Questions

Area under Simple Curves

Level I

1 Consider the following statements.

Statement I The area A of the region bounded by the curve $y = f(x)$, X-axis and ordinates $x = a$, $x = b$ is given by

$$A = \int_a^b f(x)\, dy$$

Statement II The area A of the region bounded by the curve $x = g(y)$, Y-axis and the lines $y = c$, $y = d$ is given by

$$A = \int_c^d g(y)\, dx$$

Choose the correct option. NCERT Pg. 292, 293

(a) Both statements are true.
(b) Both statements are false.
(c) Statement I is true; Statement II is false.
(d) Statement I is false; Statement II is true.

2 Area lying in the first quadrant and bounded by the circle $x^2 + y^2 = 4$ and the lines $x = 0$ and $x = 2$ is NCERT Pg. 296

(a) π sq units (b) $\frac{\pi}{2}$ sq units
(c) $\frac{\pi}{3}$ sq units (d) $\frac{\pi}{4}$ sq units

3 Area of the region bounded by the curve $y^2 = 4x$, Y-axis and the line $y = 3$ is NCERT Pg. 296

(a) 2 sq units (b) $\frac{9}{4}$ sq units
(c) $\frac{9}{3}$ sq units (d) $\frac{9}{2}$ sq units

4 Which of the following is/are true? NCERT Pg. 296, Old NCERT Pg. 366

I. The area of the region bounded by the ellipse $\frac{x^2}{16}+\frac{y^2}{9}=1$ is 24π sq units.

II. The area of the region bounded by the ellipse $\frac{x^2}{4}+\frac{y^2}{9}=1$ is 6π sq units.

III. The area of the region in the first quadrant enclosed by X-axis and $x=\sqrt{3}y$ and the circle $x^2+y^2=4$ is $\frac{\pi}{3}$ sq units.

IV. The area of the smaller part of the circle $x^2+y^2=a^2$ cut-off by the line $x=\frac{a}{\sqrt{2}}$ is $\frac{a^2}{2}\left(\frac{\pi}{2}+1\right)$ sq units.

(a) Only II is true (b) Only II and III are true
(c) Only II, III and IV are true (d) All are true

5 The area (in sq units) bounded by the ellipse $\frac{x^2}{a^2}+\frac{y^2}{b^2}=1$ and the ordinates $x=0$ and $x=ae$, where $b^2=a^2(1-e^2)$ and $e<1$, is Old NCERT Pg. 365

(a) $ab[e\sqrt{1-e^2}-\sin^{-1}e]$ (b) $ab[e\sqrt{1+e^2}+\sin^{-1}e]$
(c) $ab[e\sqrt{1-e^2}+\sin^{-1}e]$ (d) $ab[\sin^{-1}e-e\sqrt{1-e^2}]$

6 Match the following area of the region bounded by the curve and the lines in column I with their corresponding values in column II and choose the correct option from the codes given below. Old NCERT Pg. 365, 366

Column I	Column II
A. Area of the region bounded by the curve $y^2=x$ and the lines $x=1$, $x=4$ and the X-axis.	1. $4[4-\sqrt{2}]$ sq units
B. Area of the region bounded by $y^2=9x$, $x=2$, $x=4$ and the X-axis in the first quadrant.	2. $\frac{8}{3}[4-\sqrt{2}]$ sq units
C. Area of the region bounded by $x^2=4y$, $y=2$, $y=4$ and the Y-axis in the first quadrant.	3. $\frac{14}{3}$ sq units

Codes

	A	B	C		A	B	C
(a)	3	2	1	(b)	2	3	1
(c)	3	1	2	(d)	2	1	3

7 If the area between $x=y^2$ and $x=4$ is divided into two equal parts by the line $x=a$, then the value of a is Old NCERT Pg. 366

(a) $(4)^{1/3}$ (b) $(4)^{4/3}$
(c) $(4)^{2/3}$ (d) None of these

8 The area of the region bounded by the parabola $y=x^2$ and $y=|x|$ is Old NCERT Pg. 366

(a) $\frac{2}{3}$ sq units (b) $\frac{4}{3}$ sq units
(c) $\frac{5}{3}$ sq units (d) $\frac{1}{3}$ sq unit

9 Consider the following statements

Statement I The area of the region bounded by the curve $y^2=4x$ and the line $x=3$ is $8\sqrt{3}$ sq units.

Statement II The area of the region bounded by the curve $x^2=4y$ and the line $x=4y-2$ is $\frac{9}{8}$ sq units.

Choose the correct option. Old NCERT Pg. 366

(a) Statement I is true
(b) Statement II is true
(c) Both statements are true
(d) Both statements are false

Level II

10 Area of the region bounded by the curve $y=\cos x$ between $x=0$ and $x=\pi$ is NCERT Exemplar Pg. 178

(a) 2 sq units (b) 4 sq units
(c) 3 sq units (d) 1 sq unit

11 Consider the following statements.

Statement I The area of the curve $y=\sin x$ between 0 and π is 2 sq units.

Statement II The area of the region bounded by the curve $ay^2=x^3$, the Y-axis and the lines $y=a$ and $y=2a$ is $\frac{3}{5}a^2|2\cdot 2^{2/3}-1|$ sq units.

Choose the correct option. NCERT Exemplar Pg. 170, 171

(a) Both statements are true.
(b) Both statements are false.
(c) Statement I is true; Statement II is false.
(d) Statement I is false; Statement II is true.

12 The area of the region bounded by the parabola $y^2=2x$ and the straight line $x-y=4$ is NCERT Exemplar Pg. 171

(a) 18 sq units
(b) 9 sq units
(c) 27 sq units
(d) 6 sq units

13 The area (in sq units) of the region bounded by the curve $y=x^2$ and the line $y=16$ is NCERT Exemplar Pg. 176

(a) $\frac{32}{3}$ sq units (b) $\frac{256}{3}$ sq units
(c) $\frac{64}{3}$ sq units (d) $\frac{128}{3}$ sq units

14 If we draw a rough sketch of the curve $y = \sqrt{x-1}$ in the interval [1, 5], then the area under the curve and between the lines $x = 1$ and $x = 5$ is NCERT Exemplar Pg. 177

(a) $\frac{16}{9}$ sq units (b) $\frac{8}{3}$ sq units
(c) $\frac{16}{3}$ sq units (d) None of these

15 Consider the following statements.

Statement I The area bounded by the curve $y = \sin x$ between $x = 0$ and $x = 2\pi$ is 2 sq units.

Statement II The area bounded by the curve $y = 2\cos x$ and the X-axis from $x = 0$ to $x = 2\pi$ is 8 sq units.

Choose the correct option. NCERT Pg. 298, NCERT Exemplar Pg. 177

(a) Both statements are true.
(b) Both statements are false.
(c) Statement I is true; Statement II is false.
(d) Statement I is false; Statement II is true.

16 The area of the region bounded by the curve $y = \sqrt{16 - x^2}$ and X-axis is NCERT Exemplar Pg. 177

(a) 8π sq units (b) 20π sq units
(c) 16π sq units (d) 256π sq units

17 The area (in sq units) of the region bounded by $y^2 = 2x + 1$ and $x - y = 1$ is NCERT Pg. 296

(a) $\frac{2}{3}$ (b) $\frac{4}{3}$ (c) $\frac{8}{3}$ (d) $\frac{16}{3}$

18 The area (in sq units) of the region bounded by the curves $2x = y^2 - 1$ and $x = 0$ is NCERT Pg. 296

(a) $\frac{1}{3}$ (b) $\frac{2}{3}$ (c) 1 (d) 2

19 The area of the region bounded by the curves $y = |x - 2|$, $x = 1$, $x = 3$ and X-axis is NCERT Pg. 298

(a) 1 sq unit (b) 2 sq units
(c) 3 sq units (d) 4 sq units

20 Consider the following statements.

Statement I The area bounded by the parabola $y^2 = 4ax$ and the line $x = a$ and $x = 4a$ is $\frac{56a^2}{3}$ sq units.

Statement II The area bounded by the curves $y = 3x$ and $y = x^2$ is 9.5 sq units.

Choose the correct option. NCERT Pg. 298

(a) Both statements are true.
(b) Both statements are false.
(c) Statement I is true; Statement II is false.
(d) Statement I is false; Statement II is true.

21 The area bounded by $y = -x^2 + 2x + 3$ and $y = 0$ is NCERT Pg. 298

(a) 32 sq units (b) $\frac{32}{3}$ sq units
(c) $\frac{1}{32}$ sq unit (d) $\frac{1}{3}$ sq unit

22 The area (in sq units) bounded by the curves $y = \sqrt{x}$, $2y - x + 3 = 0$ and X-axis lying in the first quadrant is NCERT Exemplar Pg. 177

(a) 9 (b) 36 (c) 18 (d) $\frac{27}{4}$

23 The area of the region enclosed by the curves $y = x$, $x = e$, $y = \frac{1}{x}$ and the positive X-axis is NCERT Pg. 298

(a) 1 sq unit (b) $\frac{3}{2}$ sq units
(c) $\frac{5}{2}$ sq units (d) $\frac{1}{2}$ sq unit

Miscellaneous Exercise

1 The area of the region bounded by the line $y = 3x + 2$, the X-axis and the ordinates $x = -1$ and $x = 1$ is NCERT Pg. 296

(a) $\frac{26}{3}$ sq units (b) $\frac{19}{3}$ sq units
(c) $\frac{13}{3}$ sq units (d) None of these

2 The area of the region $\{(x, y): 0 \le y \le x^2 + 1, 0 \le y \le x + 1, 0 \le x \le 2\}$ is Old NCERT Pg. 374

(a) $\frac{26}{7}$ sq units (b) $\frac{23}{6}$ sq units
(c) $\frac{23}{3}$ sq units (d) None of these

3 Match the following area under given curves and given lines in column I with their corresponding values in column II and choose the correct option from the codes given below. NCERT Pg. 298

	Column I		Column II
A.	$y = x^2$; $x = 1$, $x = 2$ and X-axis	1.	$\frac{3124}{5}$ sq units
B.	$y = x^4$; $x = 1$, $x = 5$ and X-axis	2.	$\frac{1}{6}$ sq unit
C.	$y = x$ and $y = x^2$	3.	4 sq units
D.	$y = \sin x$, $x = 0$ and $x = 2\pi$	4.	$\frac{7}{3}$ sq units

Codes

	A	B	C	D		A	B	C	D
(a)	4	2	3	1	(b)	2	1	3	4
(c)	4	1	2	3	(d)	2	3	4	1

4 The area bounded by the curve $y = |x+3|$ between $x = 0$ and $x = -6$ is **NCERT Pg. 298**

(a) $\frac{9}{2}$ sq units (b) 9 sq units

(c) 18 sq units (d) $\frac{7}{2}$ sq units

5 The area enclosed between the parabola $y^2 = 4ax$ and the line $y = mx$ is **Old NCERT Pg. 375**

(a) $\frac{3a^2}{8m^2}$ sq units (b) $\frac{8a^2}{3m^2}$ sq units

(c) $\frac{8a^2}{3m^3}$ sq units (d) $\frac{3a^2}{8m^3}$ sq units

6 Consider the following statements.

Statement I The area of the region lying in the first quadrant and bounded by $y = 4x^2$, $x = 0$, $y = 1$ and $y = 4$ is $\frac{8}{7}$ sq units.

Statement II The area enclosed by the parabola $4y = 3x^2$ and the line $2y = 3x + 12$ is 18 sq units.

Choose the correct option. **Old NCERT Pg. 375**

(a) Both statements are true.
(b) Both statements are false.
(c) Statement I is true; Statement II is false.
(d) Statement I is false; Statement II is true.

7 Which of the following is/are true? **Old NCERT Pg. 375, 376**

I. The area of the region enclosed by the parabola $x^2 = y$, the line $y = x + 2$ and the X-axis is $\frac{9}{2}$ sq units.

II. The area bounded by the curve $|x| + |y| = 1$ is 3 sq units.

III. The area bounded by the curves $\{(x, y) : y \geq x^2$ and $y \leq |x|\}$ is $\frac{1}{3}$ sq unit.

IV. The area of the ΔABC, coordinates of whose vertices are $A(2, 0)$, $B(4, 5)$ and $C(6, 3)$, is 7 sq units.

(a) Only I is true (b) Both II and III are true
(c) I, III and IV are true (d) All are true

8 Consider the following statements.

Statement I The area of the region bounded by lines $2x + y = 4$, $3x - 2y = 6$ and $x - 3y + 5 = 0$ is $\frac{7}{2}$ sq units.

Statement II The area of the region $\{(x, y) : y^2 \leq 4x,$ $4x^2 + 4y^2 \leq 9\}$ is $\frac{9\pi}{8} + \frac{1}{3\sqrt{2}} - \frac{9}{4}\sin^{-1}\left(\frac{1}{3}\right)$.

Choose the correct option. **Old NCERT Pg. 376**

(a) Both statements are true.
(b) Both statements are false.
(c) Statement I is true; Statement II is false.
(d) Statement I is false; Statement II is true.

9 Area bounded by the curve $y = x^3$, the X-axis and the coordinates $x = -2$ and $x = 1$ is **NCERT Pg. 298**

(a) -9 sq units (b) $\frac{-15}{4}$ sq units

(c) $\frac{15}{4}$ sq units (d) $\frac{17}{4}$ sq units

10 The area bounded by the curve $y = x|x|$, X-axis and the coordinates $x = -1$ and $x = 1$ is given by **NCERT Pg. 298**

(a) 0 sq unit (b) $\frac{1}{3}$ sq unit

(c) $\frac{2}{3}$ sq units (d) $\frac{4}{3}$ sq units

11 The area of the circle $x^2 + y^2 = 16$ exterior to the parabola $y^2 = 6x$ is **Old NCERT Pg. 376**

(a) $\frac{4}{3}(4\pi - \sqrt{3})$ sq units

(b) $\frac{4}{3}(4\pi + \sqrt{3})$ sq units

(c) $\frac{4}{3}(8\pi - \sqrt{3})$ sq units

(d) $\frac{4}{3}(8\pi + \sqrt{3})$ sq units

12 Match the following area of the regions in column I with their corresponding values in column II and choose the correct option from the codes given below. **NCERT Exemplar Pg. 176, 177**

Column I	Column II
A. The area bounded by the curves $y = \cos x$ and $y = \sin x$ between the ordinates $x = 0$ and $x = \frac{3\pi}{2}$ is	1. 9 sq units
B. The area of the region bounded by the parabola $(y-2)^2 = x - 1$, the tangent to the parabola at the point (2, 3) and the X-axis is	2. 4 sq units
C. The area bounded by the curves $y = \sqrt{5 - x^2}$ and $y = \lvert x - 1\rvert$ is	3. $(4\sqrt{2} - 2)$ sq units
D. The area bounded by $y = \lvert\sin x\rvert$, X-axis and the line $\lvert x\rvert = \pi$ is	4. $\left(\frac{5\pi - 2}{4}\right)$ sq units

Codes

	A	B	C	D		A	B	C	D
(a)	3	2	4	1	(b)	4	1	2	3
(c)	2	4	1	3	(d)	3	1	4	2

13 The figure below shows a ΔAOB and the parabola $y = x^2$. The ratio of the area of the ΔAOB to the area of the region AOB of the parabola $y = x^2$ is equal to **Old NCERT Pg. 368**

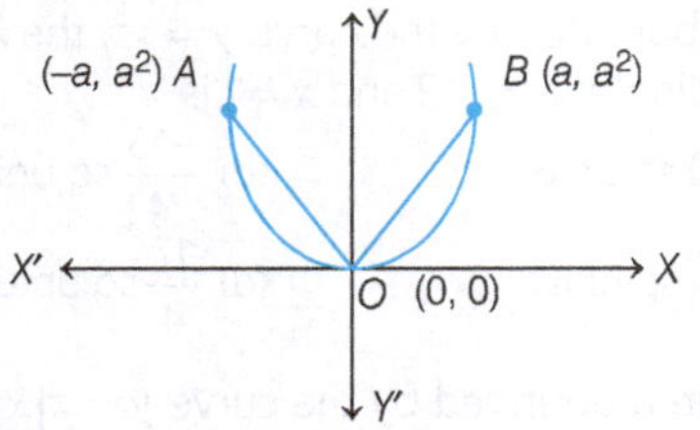

(a) $\frac{3}{5}$ (b) $\frac{3}{4}$ (c) $\frac{7}{8}$ (d) $\frac{5}{6}$

14 Area enclosed by the curve $\pi[4(x-\sqrt{2})^2+y^2]=8$ is NCERT Pg. 295

(a) π sq units (b) 2 sq units
(c) 3π sq units (d) 4 sq units

15 Consider the following statements

Statement I The area of the region bounded by the curves $y=e^x$, $y=\log_e x$ and lines $x=1$, $x=2$ is $(e^2-e-2\log_e 2+1)$ sq units.

Statement II The area bounded by $x=\sin y$, $x=\frac{1}{\sqrt{2}}$ and X-axis is $\left(\frac{\pi}{4\sqrt{2}}+\frac{1}{\sqrt{2}}+1\right)$ sq units.

Choose the correct option. Old NCERT Pg. 367

(a) Both statements are true.
(b) Both statements are false.
(c) Statement I is true; Statement II is false.
(d) Statement I is false; Statement II is true.

16 The area enclosed between the curve $y=\log_e(x+e)$ and the coordinates axes is NCERT Pg. 298

(a) 4 sq units (b) 3 sq units
(c) 2 sq units (d) 1 sq unit

17 If A is the area of the region bounded by the curve $y=\sqrt{3x+4}$, X-axis and the lines $x=-1$, $x=4$ and B is that area bounded by the curve $y^2=3x+4$, X-axis and the lines $x=-1$, $x=4$, then $A:B$ is equal to Old NCERT Pg. 375

(a) 1 : 1 (b) 2 : 1
(c) 1 : 2 (d) None of these

18 Consider the following statements

Statement I Area bounded by the curve $x=4-y^2$ and the Y-axis is $\frac{16}{3}$ sq units.

Statement II Area of the region bounded by the curve $y=\tan x$, tangent drawn to the curve at $x=\frac{\pi}{4}$ and the X-axis is $\left(\log\sqrt{2}-\frac{1}{4}\right)$ sq units.

Choose the correct option. NCERT Pg. 296

(a) Both statements are true.
(b) Both statements are false.
(c) Statement I is true; Statement II is false.
(d) Statement I is false; Statement II is true.

19 If the area above the X-axis bounded by the curves $y=2^{kx}$ and $x=0$ and $x=2$ is $\frac{3}{\log 2}$, then the value of k is NCERT Pg. 298

(a) $\frac{1}{2}$ (b) –1 (c) 1 (d) 2

20 If the ordinate $x=a$ divides the area bounded by the curve $y=\left(1+\frac{8}{x^2}\right)$, X-axis and the ordinates $x=2$, $x=4$ into two equal parts, then the value of a is NCERT Pg. 298

(a) $2a$ (b) $2\sqrt{2}$
(c) $\frac{a}{2}$ (d) None of these

21 Consider the following statements

Statement I The area bounded by the curves $x^2+y^2=25$, $4y=|4-x^2|$ and $x=0$ above the X-axis is $25\sin^{-1}\left(\frac{4}{5}\right)$.

Statement II The area bounded by the curves $y=\sqrt{x}$, $2y+3=x$ and X-axis in the first quadrant is $\frac{9}{2}$ sq units.

Choose the correct option. Old NCERT Pg. 370

(a) Both statements are true.
(b) Both statements are false.
(c) Statement I is true; Statement II is false.
(d) Statement I is false; Statement II is true.

22 Area of the region bounded by the curve $y=|x+1|+1$, $x=-3$, $x=3$ and $y=0$ is NCERT Exemplar Pg. 177

(a) 8 sq units (b) 16 sq units
(c) 32 sq units (d) None of these

23 Consider the following statements

Statement I The area bounded by $y=\log x$, X-axis and ordinates $x=1$, $x=2$ is $\log\left(\frac{4}{e}\right)$.

Statement II Area bounded by the curve $y=\log_e x$, $x=0$, $y\le 0$ and X-axis is 1 sq unit.

Choose the correct option. NCERT Pg. 296

(a) Both statements are true.
(b) Both statements are false.
(c) Statement I is true; Statement II is false.
(d) Statement I is false; Statement II is true.

24 Area bounded by the curve $y^2=16x$ and the line $y=mx$ is $\frac{2}{3}$, then m is equal to Old NCERT Pg. 372

(a) 3 (b) 4 (c) 1 (d) 2

25 Consider the following statements.

Statement I The area bounded by the curves $y^2 = 4a^2(x-1)$ and lines $x = 1$ and $y = 4a$ is $\frac{8a}{3}$ sq units.

Statement II The area enclosed between the parabola $y = x^2 - x + 2$ and the line $y = x + 2$ is $\frac{8}{3}$ sq units.

Choose the correct option. NCERT Pg. 296

(a) Both statements are true.
(b) Both statements are false.
(c) Statement I is true; Statement II is false.
(d) Statement I is false; Statement II is true.

26 If the area bounded by $y = x^2 + 2x - 3$ and the line $y = kx + 1$ is least, then its least area is Old NCERT Pg. 371

(a) $\frac{64}{3}$ sq units (b) $\frac{32}{3}$ sq units
(c) $\frac{25}{3}$ sq units (d) None of these

27 The area of the region bounded by the X-axis and the curves defined by $y = \tan x, -\frac{\pi}{3} \le x \le \frac{\pi}{3}$ and $y = \cot x, \frac{\pi}{6} \le x \le \frac{3\pi}{2}$ is NCERT Pg. 297

(a) $\log\frac{3}{2}$ sq units (b) $\log 2$ sq units
(c) $\log 3$ sq units (d) None of these

28 The area of the region bounded by the curves $y = |x-1|$ and $y = 3 - |x|$ is NCERT Pg. 298

(a) 2 sq units (b) 3 sq units
(c) 4 sq units (d) 6 sq units

Numerical Type Questions

1 Let the area of the region enclosed by the curve $y = \min\{\sin x, \cos x\}$ and the X-axis between $x = -\pi$ to $x = \pi$ be A. Then, A^3 is equal to .... Old NCERT Pg. 376

2 Let A be the area bounded by the curve $y = x|x-2|$, the X-axis and the ordinates $x = -1$ and $x = 2$. Then, 15 A is equal to .... NCERT Pg. 298

3 The area A bounded by the curve $y = |x-2|$ and $x = 0$, $x = 4$ and the X-axis is .... NCERT Pg. 298

4 Let α be the area of the larger region bounded by the curve $y^2 = 8x$ and the lines $y = x$ and $x = 2$, which lies in the first quadrant. Then, the value of 6α is equal to .... NCERT Pg. 296

5 Let a and b respectively be the points of local maximum and local minimum of the function $f(x) = 2x^3 - 3x^2 - 12x$. If A is the total area of the region bounded by $y = f(x)$, the X-axis and the lines $x = a$ and $x = b$, then $8A$ is equal to .... NCERT Pg. 293

6 If the area of the triangle formed by the X-axis, the normal and the tangent to the circle $(x-2)^2 + (y-3)^2 = 25$ at the point (5, 7) is A, then $36A$ is equal to .... Old NCERT Pg. 368

7 The area bounded by the curve $|x| + y = 1$ and X-axis, is given by .... Old NCERT Pg. 375

8 The area bounded by $y = |\sin x|$, X-axis and the line $|x| = \pi$, is .... Old NCERT Pg. 375

Assertion and Reason Questions

Directions (Q. Nos. 1-8) In the questions given below are to statements labelled as Assertion (A) and Reason (R). In the context on the two statements, which one of the following is correct?

(a) Both Assertion and Reason are correct and Reason is the correct explanation of Assertion.
(b) Both Assertion and Reason are correct but Reason is not the correct explanation of Assertion.
(c) Assertion is correct but Reason is incorrect.
(d) Assertion is incorrect but Reason is correct.

1 If the portion of the curve under consideration is below the X-axis i.e. $f(x) < 0$ from $x = a$ to $x = b$.

Assertion (A) The area bounded by the curve, X-axis and the ordinates $x = a$ and $x = b$ come out to be negative.

Reason (R) If the area is negative, then we take its absolute value. NCERT Pg. 293

2 Assertion (A) The area of the smaller region bounded by the ellipse $\frac{x^2}{9} + \frac{y^2}{4} = 1$ and the line $\frac{x}{3} + \frac{y}{2} = 1$ is $\frac{3}{2}(\pi - 2)$ sq units.

Reason (R) Formula to calculate the area of the smaller region bounded by the ellipse $\frac{x^2}{a^2} + \frac{y^2}{b^2} = 1$ and the line $\frac{x}{a} + \frac{y}{b} = 1$ is $\frac{ab}{4}(\pi - 2)$ sq units. Old NCERT Pg. 375

3 Assertion (A)

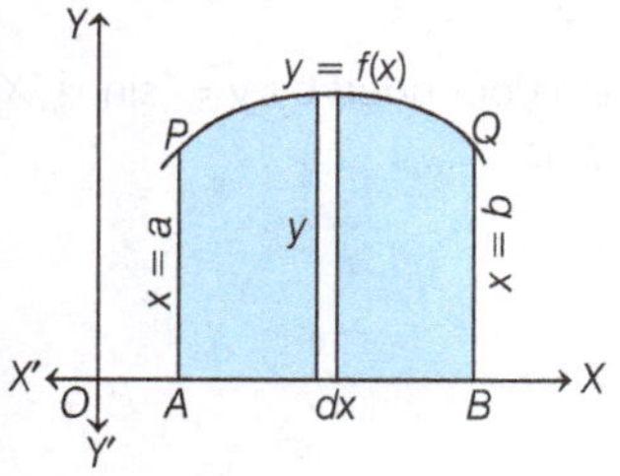

The area of region $ABQP = \int_a^b y\,dx = \int_a^b f(x)\,dx$

Reason (R)

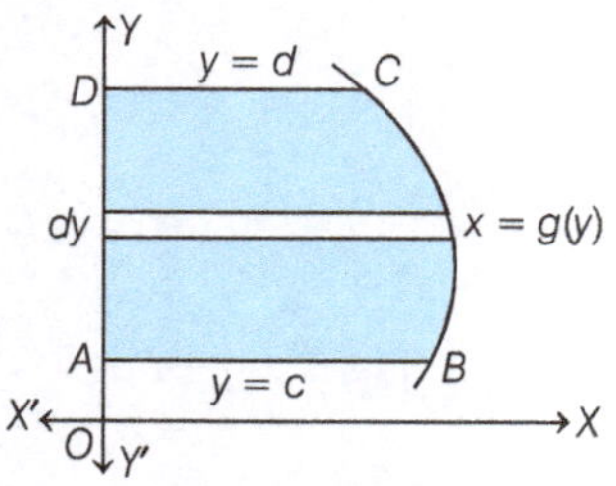

The area of region $ABCD = \int_c^d x\,dy$. NCERT Pg. 292, 293

4 Assertion (A)

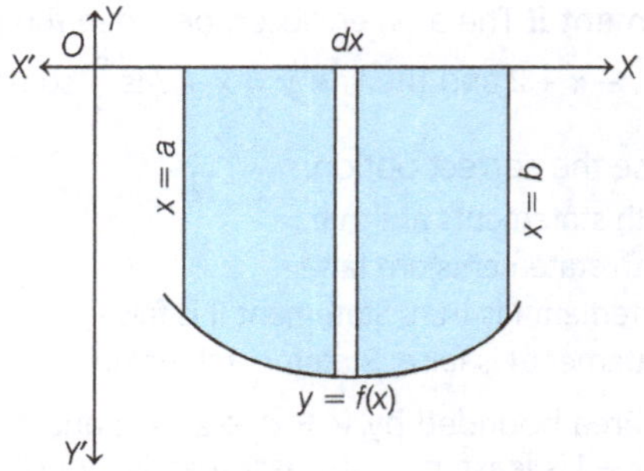

$$\text{Area} = \left| \int_a^b f(x)\,dx \right|.$$

Reason (R) If the curve under consideration lies below X-axis, then $f(x) < 0$ from $x = a$ to $x = b$, the area bounded by the curve $y = f(x)$ and the ordinates $x = a$, $x = b$ and X-axis is negative.

But, if the numerical value of the area is to be taken into consideration, then

$$\text{Area} = \left| \int_a^b f(x)\,dx \right|$$

NCERT Pg. 293

5 Assertion (A) Area bounded by $\max\{|x - y|, |x + y|\} \le 2$ is 8 sq units.

Reason (R) Area of the square of side length 4 is 16 sq units. Old NCERT Pg. 375

6 Assertion (A) the area of the curve $y = \sin^2 x$ from 0 to π will be more than that of the curve $y = \sin x$ from 0 to π.

Reason (R) $x^2 > x$, if $x > 1$. NCERT Pg. 298

7 Assertion (A) The area enclosed by the curve $|x| + |y| = 2$ is 8 units.

Reason (R) $|x| + |y| = 2$ represents a square of side length $\sqrt{8}$ units. Old NCERT Pg. 375

8 Assertion (A) The area enclosed between the parabolas $y^2 - 2y + 4x + 5 = 0$ and $x^2 + 2x - y + 2 = 0$ is same as that of bounded by curves $y^2 = -4x$ and $x^2 = y$.

Reason (R) Shifting of origin to point (h, k) does not change the bounded area. Old NCERT Pg. 368

Case or Paragraph Type Questions

Direction (Q. No. 1-4) A mirror is in the shape of an ellipse represented by $\frac{x^2}{16}+\frac{y^2}{9}=1$ was hanging on the wall. Aman and his sister were playing with ball inside the house, even their mother refused to do so. All of a sudden, ball hit the mirror and got a scratch in the shape of line represented by $\frac{x}{4}+\frac{y}{3}=1$.

Based on the above information, answer the following questions. Old NCERT Pg. 375

1 Points of intersection of ellipse and scratch (straight line) is (are)

(a) (0, 3) and (4, 0) (b) (3, 0) and (0, 4)
(c) (0, 3) and (4, 0) (d) (3, 0) and (4, 0)

2 The value of $\frac{3}{4}\int_0^4 \sqrt{16-x^2}\,dx$ is

(a) 2π (b) π (c) 3π (d) 4π

3 The value of $3\int_0^4 \left(1-\frac{x}{4}\right)dx$ is

(a) 6 (b) 18 (c) 12 (d) 21

4 Area of smaller region bounded by mirror and scratch is

(a) $(\pi-2)$ (b) $(\pi+2)$
(c) $3(\pi+2)$ (d) $3(\pi-2)$

Direction (Q. No. 5-8) A child cut a pizza with a knife. Pizza is circular in shape which is represented by $x^2+y^2=4$ and sharp edge of knife represents a straight line given by $x=\sqrt{3}y$.

Based on the above information, answer the following questions. Old NCERT Pg. 368

5 The points of intersection of the edge of knife (line) and pizza shown in the figure is (are)

(a) $(\sqrt{3}, 1)$ and $(-\sqrt{3}, -1)$ (b) $(1, -\sqrt{3})$ and $(-1, \sqrt{3})$
(c) $(-1, \sqrt{2})$ and $(-\sqrt{2}, 1)$ (d) $(\sqrt{2}, 1)$ and $(-\sqrt{2}, -1)$

6 Value of area of the region bounded by circular pizza edge and Y-axis of knife in first quadrant is

(a) $\frac{2\pi}{3}$ (b) $\frac{\pi}{3}$
(c) $\frac{4\pi}{3}$ (d) $\frac{3\pi}{2}$

7 Area of each slice of pizza which child cut into 4 equal pieces is

(a) 2π (b) π (c) $\frac{3\pi}{2}$ (d) $\frac{\pi}{2}$

8 Area of whole pizza is

(a) 4π (b) 2π
(c) π (d) 3π

Past Years Questions

Single Correct Type

1 The area (in sq. units) of the region described by $\{(x, y): y^2 \le 2x$ and $y \ge 4x-1\}$ is
Old NCERT Pg. 374, JEE Main 2024, 4 April Shift-II

(a) $\frac{11}{12}$ (b) $\frac{9}{32}$ (c) $\frac{8}{9}$ (d) $\frac{11}{32}$

2 The area (in sq units) of the region enclosed by the ellipse $x^2+3y^2=18$ in the first quadrant below the line $y=x$ is Old NCERT Pg. 369, JEE Main 2024, 9 April Shift-II

(a) $\sqrt{3}\pi$ (b) $\sqrt{3}\pi-\frac{3}{4}$
(c) $\sqrt{3}\pi+\frac{3}{4}$ (d) $\sqrt{3}\pi+1$

3 The area of the region in the first quadrant inside the circle $x^2+y^2=8$ and outside the parabola $y^2=2x$ is equal to Old NCERT Pg. 376, JEE Main 2024, 8 April Shift-II

(a) $\pi-\frac{2}{3}$ (b) $\frac{\pi}{2}-\frac{2}{3}$ (c) $\frac{\pi}{2}-\frac{1}{3}$ (d) $\pi-\frac{1}{3}$

4 If the area of the region $\left\{(x, y): \frac{a}{x^2} \le y \le \frac{1}{x}, 1 \le x \le 2, 0<a<1\right\}$ is $(\log_e 2)-\frac{1}{7}$, then the value of $7a-3$ is equal to
Old NCERT Pg. 376, JEE Main 2024, 6 April Shift-II

(a) 1 (b) 0
(c) 2 (d) −1

5 The area of the region enclosed between the curves $4x^2=y$ and $y=4$ is NCERT Pg. 298, CUET 2024

(a) 16 sq. units (b) $\frac{32}{3}$ sq. units
(c) $\frac{8}{3}$ sq. units (d) $\frac{16}{3}$ sq. units

6 The area bounded by the curves $y=|x-1|+|x-2|$ and $y=3$ is equal to
Old NCERT Pg. 375, JEE Main 2023, 6 April Shift-I

(a) 4 (b) 5
(c) 6 (d) 3

7 The area of the region bounded by the lines $x+2y=12$, $x=2$, $x=6$ and X-axis is NCERT Pg. 292

(a) 34 sq units (b) 20 sq units
(c) 24 sq units (d) 16 sq units

8 Area of the region $\{(x, y): x^2+(y-2)^2 \leq 4, x^2 \geq 2y\}$ is Old NCERT Pg. 376, JEE Main 2023, 11 April Shift-I

(a) $\pi-\frac{8}{3}$ (b) $2\pi+\frac{16}{3}$ (c) $2\pi-\frac{16}{3}$ (d) $\pi+\frac{8}{3}$

9 The area of the region $\{(x, y): x^2 \leq y \leq 8-x^2, y \leq 7\}$ is Old NCERT Pg. 376, JEE Main 2023, 8 April Shift-I

(a) 21 (b) 20 (c) 18 (d) 24

10 The odd natural number a, such that the area of the region bounded by $y=1$, $y=3$, $x=0$, $x=y^a$ is $364/3$, is equal to Old NCERT Pg. 375, JEE Main 2022, 26 July Shift-I

(a) 3 (b) 5 (c) 7 (d) 9

11 Let the locus of the centre (α, β), $\beta>0$, of the circle which touches the circle $x^2+(y-1)^2=1$ externally and also touches the X-axis be L. Then, the area bounded by L and the line $y=4$ is Old NCERT Pg. 363, JEE Main 2022, 25 July Shift-I

(a) $\frac{32\sqrt{2}}{3}$ (b) $\frac{40\sqrt{2}}{3}$ (c) $\frac{64}{3}$ (d) $\frac{32}{3}$

Numerical Value Type

12 Let the area of the region enclosed by the curve $y=\min\{\sin x, \cos x\}$ and the X-axis between $x=-\pi$ to $x=\pi$ be A. Then, A^2 is equal to .... Old NCERT Pg. 376, JEE Main 2024, 8 April Shift-I

13 The area (in sq. units) of the part of the circle $x^2+y^2=169$ which is below the line $5x-y=13$ is $\frac{\pi\alpha}{2\beta}-\frac{65}{2}+\frac{\alpha}{\beta}\sin^{-1}\left(\frac{12}{13}\right)$, where α, β are coprime numbers. Then, $\alpha+\beta$ is equal to .... . NCERT Pg. 296, JEE Main 2024, 29 Jan Shift-I

14 Let A be the area bounded by the curve $y=x|x-3|$, the X-axis and the ordinates $x=-1$ and $x=2$. Then, $12A$ is equal to .... NCERT Pg. 298, JEE Main 2023, 1 Feb Shift-I

15 The area (in sq units) of the region enclosed between the parabola $y^2=2x$ and the line $x+y=4$ is .... NCERT Pg. 296, JEE Main 2022, 24 June Shift-II

Skill Boosters

1 The area of the region bounded by the curves $y=|x-4|$, $x=3$, $x=5$ and the X-axis is ....

(a) 1 (b) 2
(c) 3 (d) 4

2 If $f(x)$ is a non-negative continuous function such that the area bounded by the curve $y=f(x)$, X-axis and the ordinates $x=\frac{\pi}{4}$ and $x=\beta>\frac{\pi}{4}$ is $\left(\beta\sin\beta+\frac{\pi}{4}\cos\beta+\sqrt{2}\beta\right)$. Then, $f\left(\frac{\pi}{3}\right)$ is equal to

(a) $\left(\frac{\sqrt{3}}{2}-\frac{\sqrt{3}\pi}{8}+\sqrt{2}\right)$

(b) $\left(\frac{\sqrt{3}}{2}-\frac{\sqrt{3}}{8}+\sqrt{\frac{1}{2}}\right)$

(c) $\left(\frac{\sqrt{3}}{2}+\frac{\sqrt{3}}{4}+\frac{\sqrt{1}}{\sqrt{2}}\right)$

(d) $\left(\frac{\sqrt{3}}{2}-\frac{\sqrt{3}}{4}-\sqrt{\frac{1}{2}}\right)$

3 The area enclosed between the curve $y=\log_e(x+e)$ and the coordinate axes is

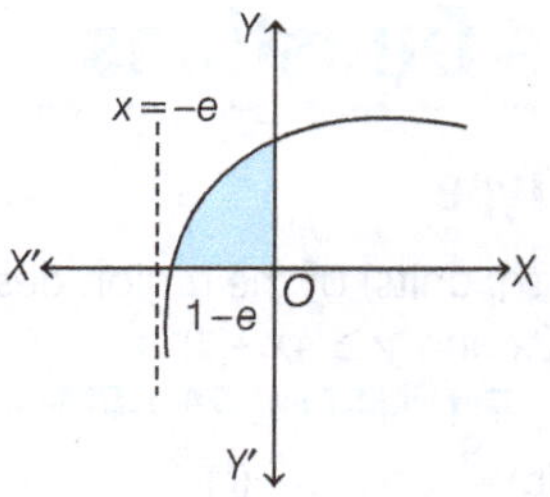

(a) e (b) 1 (c) 0 (d) $\frac{1}{e}$

4 The area of the region bounded by the parabola $y^2=2x$ and the straight line $x-y=4$ is

(a) 16 (b) 18 (c) 12 (d) 10

5 If we draw a rough sketch of the curve $y=\sqrt{x-1}$ in the interval [2, 5], then the area under the curve and between the lines $x=2$ and $x=5$ is ....

(a) $\frac{16}{3}$ (b) $\frac{19}{3}$ (c) $\frac{14}{3}$ (d) $\frac{26}{3}$

6 The value of $c+2$ for which the area of the figure bounded by the curve $y=8x^2-x^5$, the straight lines $x=1$, $x=c$ and X-axis is equal to $\frac{16}{3}$, is ....

(a) 2 (b) 3 (c) 0 (d) 1

Correct Codes

Topical Questions

Area Under Simple Curve

1 (b)	2 (a)	3 (b)	4 (b)	5 (c)	6 (c)	7 (c)	8 (d)	9 (c)	10 (a)
11 (a)	12 (a)	13 (b)	14 (c)	15 (d)	16 (a)	17 (d)	18 (b)	19 (a)	20 (c)
21 (b)	22 (a)	23 (b)							

Miscellaneous Exercise

1 (c)	2 (b)	3 (c)	4 (b)	5 (c)	6 (b)	7 (c)	8 (a)	9 (d)	10 (c)
11 (c)	12 (d)	13 (b)	14 (d)	15 (c)	16 (d)	17 (c)	18 (d)	19 (c)	20 (b)
21 (b)	22 (b)	23 (a)	24 (b)	25 (b)	26 (b)	27 (b)	28 (c)		

Numerical Type Questions

1 (64)	2 (30)	3 (4)	4 (44)	5 (228)	6 (3675)	7 (1)	8 (4)

Assertion and Reason Questions

1 (b)	2 (a)	3 (b)	4 (a)	5 (b)	6 (d)	7 (a)	8 (a)

Case or Paragraph Type Questions

1 (a)	2 (c)	3 (a)	4 (d)	5 (a)	6 (b)	7 (b)	8 (a)

Past Years Questions

1 (b)	2 (a)	3 (a)	4 (d)	5 (d)	6 (a)	7 (d)	8 (b)	9 (b)	10 (b)
11 (c)	12 (9)	13 (171)	14 (62)	15 (18)					

Skill Boosters

1 (a)	2 (a)	3 (b)	4 (b)	5 (c)	6 (d)

Step by Step

Decoding the Questions

Concept Builders

1 (True) Generally it may happen that some portion of the curve is above X-axis and some is below X-axis as shown in the figure. Here, $A_1 < 0$ and $A_2 > 0$. Therefore, the area bounded by the curve $y = f(x)$, X-axis and the ordinate $x = a$ and $x = b$ is given by $A = |A_1| + A_2$.

2 (True) The given curve is an ellipse with centre at (0, 0) and symmetrical about X-axis and Y-axis.

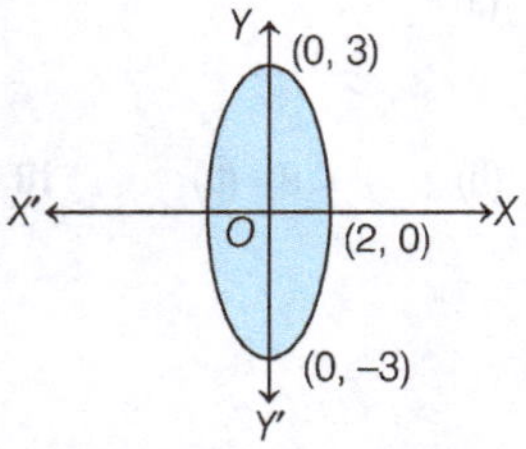

Area bounded by the ellipse

= 4 × (Area of shaded region in the first quadrant only) (by symmetry)

$= 4 \times \int_{x=a}^{x=b} |y|\, dx$

$= 4 \int_0^2 \frac{3}{2}\sqrt{4 - x^2}\, dx$

$\left[\because \frac{x^2}{4} + \frac{y^2}{9} = 1 \Rightarrow |y| = \frac{3}{2}\sqrt{4 - x^2}\right]$

$= 6 \int_0^2 \sqrt{2^2 - x^2}\, dx$

$= 6\left[\frac{x}{2}\sqrt{4 - x^2} + \frac{2^2}{2}\sin^{-1}\left(\frac{x}{2}\right)\right]_0^2$

$\left[\because \int \sqrt{a^2 - x^2}\, dx = \frac{x}{2}\sqrt{a^2 - x^2} + \frac{a^2}{2}\sin^{-1}\left(\frac{x}{a}\right)\right]$

$= 6\,[0 + 2\sin^{-1}(1) - 0] = 6 \times 2 \times \frac{\pi}{2}$

$= 6\pi$ sq. units

3 (False) The area bounded by the circle and the line $x = 0$ and $x = 2$ in the first quadrant is represented in the figure by shaded region.

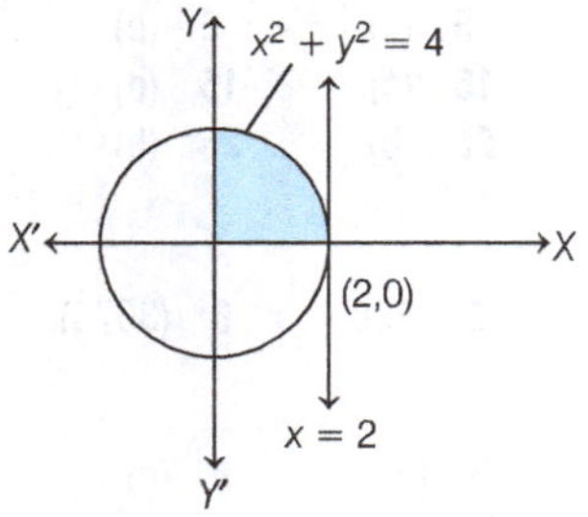

∴ Required area

$= \int_0^2 |y|\, dx = \int_0^2 \sqrt{4 - x^2}\, dx$

$= \left[\frac{x}{2}\sqrt{4 - x^2} + \frac{4}{2}\sin^{-1}\left(\frac{x}{2}\right)\right]_0^2$

$= 0 + 2\sin^{-1}(1) - 0$

$= 2 \times \frac{\pi}{2} = \pi$ sq. units

4 (True) The area bounded by the curve $y^2 = 2x$, Y-axis and $y = 1$ is represented in the figure by shaded region

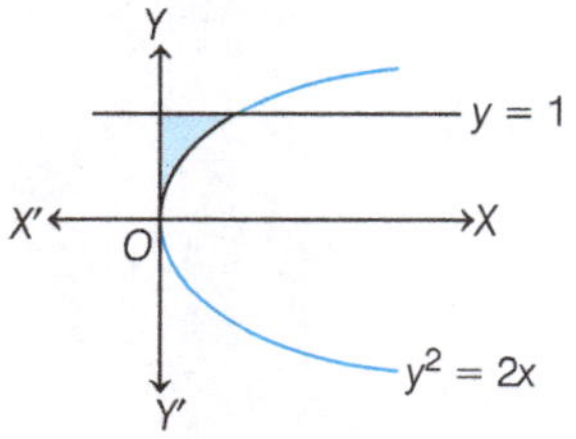

∴ Required area $= \int_0^1 |x|\, dy$

$= \int_0^1 \frac{y^2}{2}\, dy$

$= \frac{1}{2}\left[\frac{y^3}{3}\right]_0^1 = \frac{1}{6}$ sq. units

5 (False) Area of region

$= 2\int_0^9 \sqrt{y}\, dy$

[puting $y = 9$ in $y = x^2$, we get $x = \pm 3$]

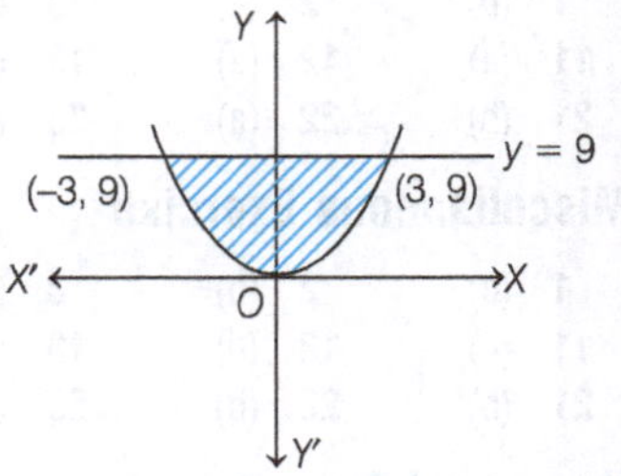

$= 2\left[\frac{y^{3/2}}{3/2}\right]_0^9 = \frac{2}{3} \times 2\,[9^{3/2} - 0]$

$= \frac{4 \times 27}{3} = 36$ sq. units

6 (True)

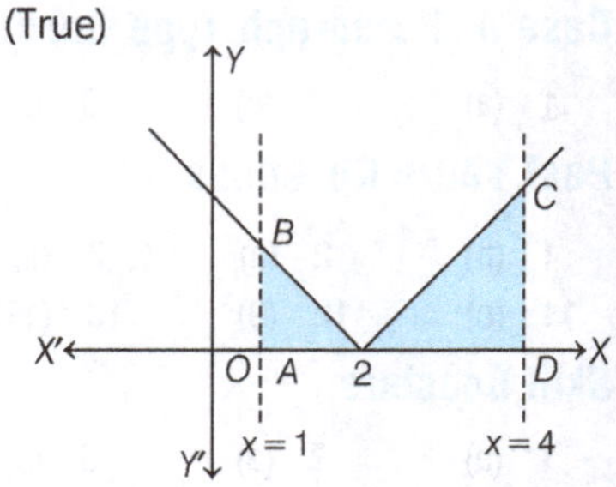

∴ Required area $= \int_1^4 |x - 2|\, dx$

$= \int_1^2 (2 - x)\, dx + \int_2^4 (x - 2)\, dx$

$= \left[2x - \frac{x^2}{2}\right]_1^2 + \left[\frac{x^2}{2} - 2x\right]_2^4$

$= \left[(4 - 2) - \left(2 - \frac{1}{2}\right)\right] + \left[\left(\frac{16}{2} - 8\right) - \left(\frac{4}{2} - 4\right)\right]$

$= 2 - \frac{3}{2} + 0 + 2 = \frac{5}{2}$ sq unit

7 (True) Intersection points of given curves with X-axis are (–3, 0) and (2, 0).

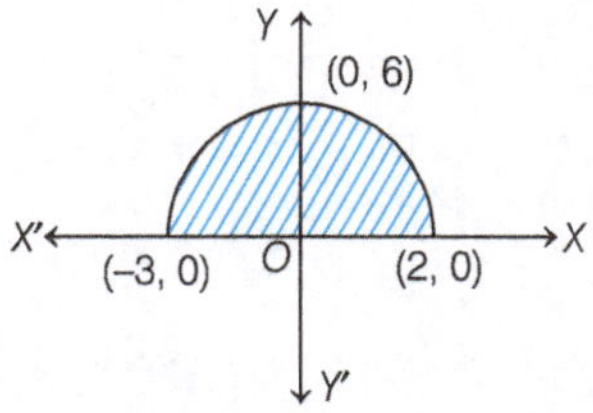

$\therefore$ Required area $= \int_{-3}^{2} (-x^2 - x + 6)\, dx$

$$= \left[-\frac{x^3}{3} - \frac{x^2}{2} + 6x\right]_{-3}^{2}$$

$$= \left(-\frac{8}{3} - \frac{4}{2} + 12\right) - \left(-\frac{(-27)}{3} - \frac{9}{2} - 18\right)$$

$$= \frac{44}{6} - \left(\frac{-81}{6}\right) = \frac{125}{6} \text{ sq units}$$

8 $\left(\frac{a^2}{12} \text{ sq unit}\right)$ The curve is $y = \frac{x^2(x+a)}{a^2}$, which is a cubic polynomial. Since, $\frac{x^2(x+a)}{a^2} = 0$ has repeated root $x = 0$, so it touches X-axis at (0, 0) and intersects at $(-a, 0)$.

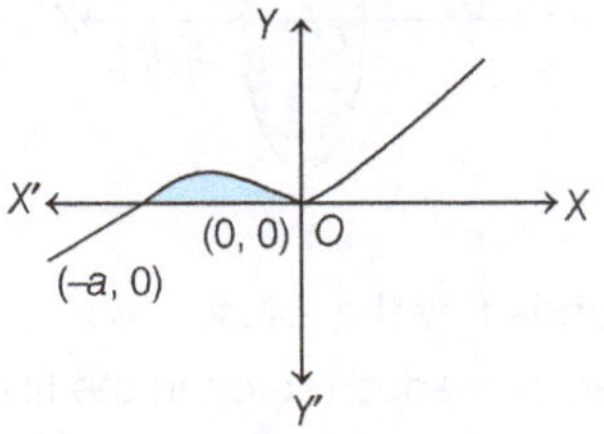

$\therefore$ Required area $= \int_{-a}^{0} y\, dx = \int_{-a}^{0} \left[\frac{x^2(x+a)}{a^2}\right] dx$

$$= \frac{a^2}{12} \text{ sq unit}$$

9 (1) Required area $= 2\int_0^1 y\, dx$, where $y = x$

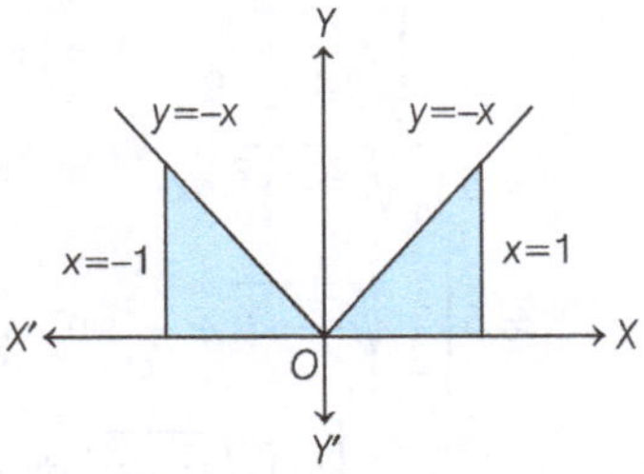

$$= 2\int_0^1 x\, dx = 2\left[\frac{x^2}{2}\right]_0^1 = 1 \text{ sq unit}$$

Topical Questions

Area under Simple Curves

1 (b)

I. We consider the easy and intuitive way of finding the area bounded by the curve $y = f(x)$, X-axis and the ordinates $x = a$ and $x = b$. From figure (i), we can think of area under the curve as composed of large number of very thin vertical strips. Consider an arbitrary strip of height y and width dx, then dA (area of the elementary strip) $= ydx$, where $y = f(x)$.

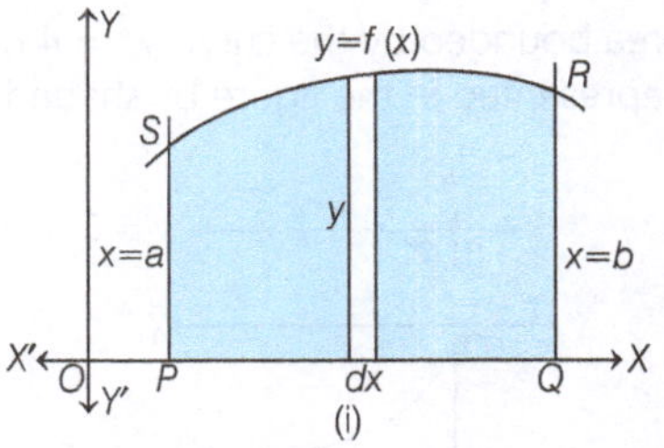

(i)

This area is called the elementary area which is located at an arbitrary position within the region which is specified by some value of x between a and b. We can think of the total area A of the region between X-axis, ordinates $x = a$, $x = b$ and the curve $y = f(x)$ as the result of adding up the elementary areas of thin strips across the region $PQRSP$. Symbolically, we express

$$A = \int_a^b dA = \int_a^b ydx = \int_a^b f(x)\, dx$$

II. The area A of the region bounded by the curve $x = g(y)$, Y-axis and the lines $y = c$ and $y = d$ is given by

$$A = \int_c^d xdy = \int_c^d g(y)\, dy$$

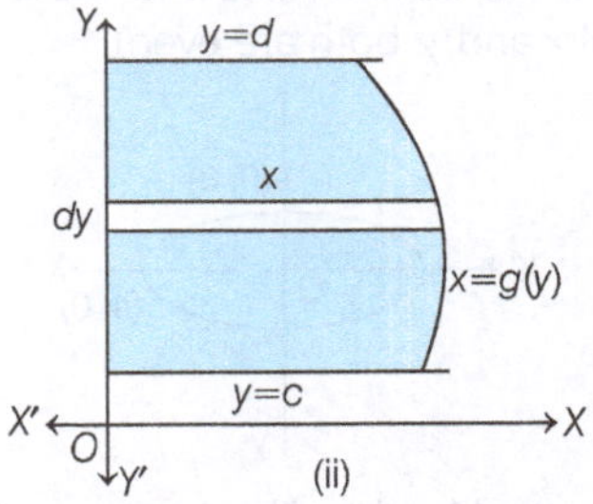

(ii)

Here, we consider horizontal strips as shown in the figure (ii).

2 (a) The area bounded by the circle and the lines $x = 0$ and $x = 2$ in the first quadrant is represented in the figure by shaded region.

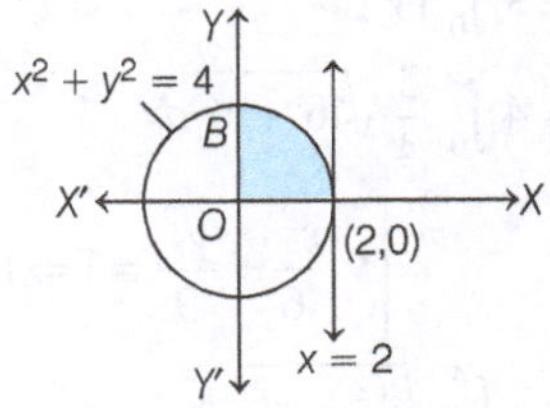

Required area $= \int_0^2 |y|\, dx = \int_0^2 \sqrt{4 - x^2}\, dx$

$$= \left[\frac{x}{2}\sqrt{4 - x^2} + \frac{4}{2}\sin^{-1}\left(\frac{x}{2}\right)\right]_0^2$$

$$= 0 + 2\sin^{-1}(1) - 0$$

$$= 2 \times \frac{\pi}{2} = \pi \text{ sq units}$$

Thus, the correct option is (a).

3 (*b*) The area bounded by the curve $y^2 = 4x$, Y-axis and $y = 3$ is represented in the figure by shaded region.

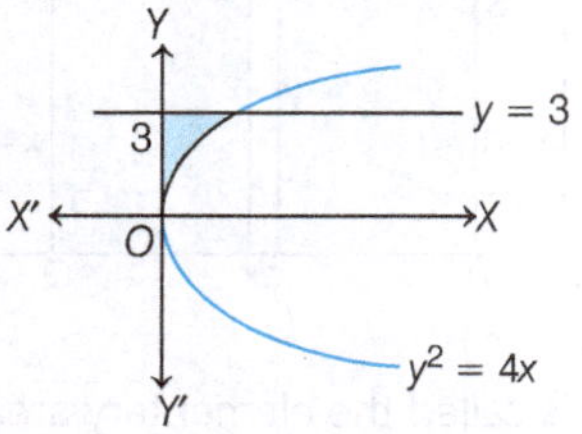

$\therefore$ Required area $= \int_0^3 |x|\,dy$

$$= \int_0^3 \frac{y^2}{4}\,dy = \frac{1}{4}\left[\frac{y^3}{3}\right]_0^3$$

$$= \frac{1}{12}(3^3 - 0)$$

$$= \frac{1}{12}(27) = \frac{9}{4} \text{ sq units}$$

Thus, the correct option is (b).

4 (*b*)

I. The given curve is an ellipse with centre at (0, 0) and is symmetrical about X-axis and Y-axis (since, the power of x and y both are even).

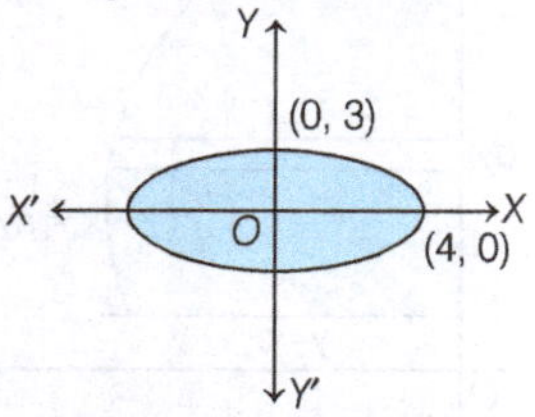

Area bounded by the ellipse = 4 ×

(Area of shaded region in the first quadrant only) [by symmetry]

$$= 4 \times \int_{x=a}^{x=b} |y|\,dx$$

$$= 4\int_0^4 |y|\,dx$$

$$= 4\int_0^4 \frac{3}{4}\sqrt{16 - x^2}\,dx$$

$$\left[\because \frac{x^2}{16} + \frac{y^2}{9} = 1 \Rightarrow |y| = \frac{3}{4}\sqrt{16 - x^2}\right]$$

$$= 3\int_0^4 \sqrt{4^2 - x^2}\,dx$$

$$= 3\left[\frac{x}{2}\sqrt{4^2 - x^2} + \frac{4^2}{2}\sin^{-1}\left(\frac{x}{4}\right)\right]_0^4$$

$$\left[\because \int \sqrt{a^2 - x^2}\,dx = \frac{x}{a}\sqrt{a^2 - x^2} + \frac{a^2}{2}\sin^{-1}\left(\frac{x}{a}\right)\right]$$

$$= 3[2\sqrt{16 - 16} + 8\sin^{-1}(1) - 0 - 8\sin^{-1}(0)]$$

$$= 3[0 + 8\sin^{-1}(1) - 0]$$

$$= 3 \times 8 \times \left(\frac{\pi}{2}\right)$$

$$= 12\pi \text{ sq units}$$

Therefore, area bounded by the ellipse is 12π sq units.

Note *If we take elementary strip about either X-axis or Y-axis, in both cases the area should be same.*

II. The given curve is an ellipse with centre at (0, 0) and symmetrical about X-axis and Y-axis.

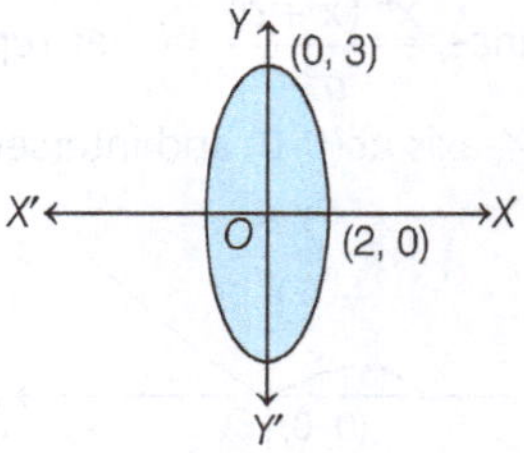

Area bounded by the ellipse = 4 ×

(Area of shaded region in the first quadrant only) [by symmetry]

$$= 4 \times \int_{x=a}^{x=b} |y|\,dx$$

$$= 4\int_0^2 |y|\,dx$$

$$= 4\int_0^2 \frac{3}{2}\sqrt{4 - x^2}\,dx$$

$$\left[\because \frac{x^2}{4} + \frac{y^2}{9} = 1 \Rightarrow |y| = \frac{3}{2}\sqrt{4 - x^2}\right]$$

$$= 6\int_0^2 \sqrt{2^2 - x^2}\,dx$$

$$= 6\left[\frac{x}{2}\sqrt{4 - x^2} + \frac{2^2}{2}\sin^{-1}\left(\frac{x}{2}\right)\right]_0^2$$

$$\left[\because \int \sqrt{a^2 - x^2}\,dx = \frac{x}{2}\sqrt{a^2 - x^2} + \frac{a^2}{2}\sin^{-1}\left(\frac{x}{a}\right)\right]$$

$$= 6[0 + 2\sin^{-1}(1) - 0]$$

$$= 6 \times 2 \times \left(\frac{\pi}{2}\right)$$

$$= 6\pi \text{ sq units}$$

III. Given equation of circle is $x^2 + y^2 = 4$ and $x = \sqrt{3}y$ or $y = \frac{1}{\sqrt{3}}x$ represents a line through the origin.

The line $y = \frac{1}{\sqrt{3}}x$ intersects the circle, so it will satisfy the equation of circle.

$\therefore \quad x^2 + \left(\frac{1}{\sqrt{3}}x\right)^2 = 4$

$\Rightarrow \quad \frac{4}{3}x^2 = 4$

$\Rightarrow \quad x^2 = \frac{4 \times 3}{4} = 3$

$\Rightarrow \quad x = \pm\sqrt{3}$

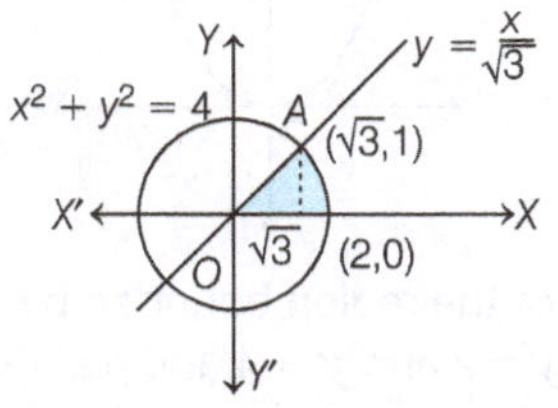

when $x = \sqrt{3}$, then $y = \frac{1}{\sqrt{3}}(\sqrt{3}) = 1$

[for first quadrant, we take $x = \sqrt{3}$ and neglect $x = -\sqrt{3}$]

$\therefore$ The line and the circle meet at the point $(\sqrt{3}, 1)$.

Required area (shaded region in first quadrant)

= (Area under the line $y = \frac{1}{\sqrt{3}}x$ from $x = 0$ to $x = \sqrt{3}$)

+ (Area under the circle from $x = \sqrt{3}$ to $x = 2$)

$= \int_0^{\sqrt{3}} \frac{1}{\sqrt{3}} x\,dx + \int_{\sqrt{3}}^{2} \sqrt{4 - x^2}\,dx$

$[\because x^2 + y^2 = 4 \Rightarrow y = \sqrt{4 - x^2}]$

$= \frac{1}{\sqrt{3}} \cdot \left[\frac{x^2}{2}\right]_0^{\sqrt{3}} + \left[\frac{x}{2}\sqrt{4 - x^2} + \frac{2^2}{2}\sin^{-1}\left(\frac{x}{2}\right)\right]_{\sqrt{3}}^{2}$

$= \frac{1}{2\sqrt{3}}[(\sqrt{3})^2 - 0^2]$

$+ \left[0 + 2\sin^{-1}(1) - \frac{\sqrt{3}}{2}\sqrt{4 - 3} - 2\sin^{-1}\left(\frac{\sqrt{3}}{2}\right)\right]$

$= \frac{\sqrt{3}}{2} + 2\left(\frac{\pi}{2}\right) - \frac{\sqrt{3}}{2} - 2\left(\frac{\pi}{3}\right) = \pi - \frac{2\pi}{3}$

$= \frac{\pi}{3}$ sq units

IV. Given line is $x = \frac{a}{\sqrt{2}}$ ...(i)

and circle is $x^2 + y^2 = a^2$ ...(ii)

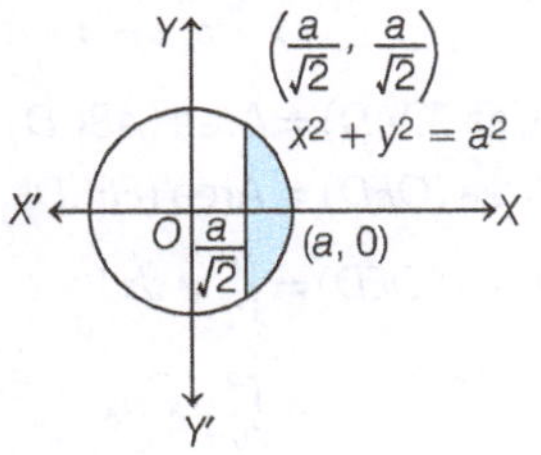

Required area = 2 (Area of shaded region in first quadrant only)

$= 2\int_{a/\sqrt{2}}^{a} |y|\,dx = 2\int_{a/\sqrt{2}}^{a} \sqrt{a^2 - x^2}\,dx$

$= 2\left[\frac{x}{2}\sqrt{a^2 - x^2} + \frac{a^2}{2}\sin^{-1}\left(\frac{x}{a}\right)\right]_{a/\sqrt{2}}^{a}$

$\left[\because \int \sqrt{a^2 - x^2}\,dx = \frac{x}{2}\sqrt{a^2 - x^2} + \frac{a^2}{2}\sin^{-1}\left(\frac{x}{a}\right)\right]$

$= 2\left[0 + \frac{a^2}{2}\sin^{-1}(1) - \frac{a}{2\sqrt{2}}\sqrt{a^2 - \frac{a^2}{2}} - \frac{a^2}{2}\sin^{-1}\left(\frac{1}{\sqrt{2}}\right)\right]$

$= 2\left[\frac{a^2}{2}\left(\frac{\pi}{2}\right) - \frac{a}{2\sqrt{2}} \cdot \frac{a}{\sqrt{2}} - \frac{a^2}{2}\left(\frac{\pi}{4}\right)\right]$

$= 2\left[\frac{a^2\pi}{4} - \frac{\pi a^2}{8} - \frac{a^2}{4}\right]$

$= \left(\frac{a^2\pi}{4} - \frac{a^2}{2}\right)$

$= \frac{a^2}{2}\left(\frac{\pi}{2} - 1\right)$ sq units

Therefore, the area of smaller part of the circle $x^2 + y^2 = a^2$ cut-off by the line $x = \frac{a}{\sqrt{2}}$ is $\frac{a^2}{2}\left(\frac{\pi}{2} - 1\right)$ sq units

5 (c)The required area of the region *BOB′-RFSB* is enclosed by the ellipse and the lines $x = 0$ and $x = ae$.

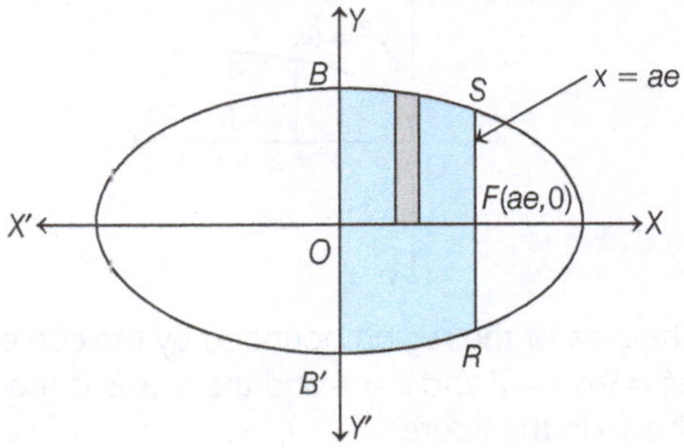

Note that the area of the region *BOB′ RFSB*

$= 2\int_0^{ae} y\,dx = 2\frac{b}{a}\int_0^{ae} \sqrt{a^2 - x^2}\,dx$

$= \frac{2b}{a}\left[\frac{x}{2}\sqrt{a^2 - x^2} + \frac{a^2}{2}\sin^{-1}\frac{x}{a}\right]_0^{ae}$

$= \frac{2b}{2a}\left[ae\sqrt{a^2 - a^2e^2} + a^2\sin^{-1}e\right]$

$= ab\left[e\sqrt{1 - e^2} + \sin^{-1}e\right]$

6 (c)

A. The area of the region bounded by the curve $y^2 = x$, the lines $x = 1$ and $x = 4$ and the X-axis is shown in the figure.

Here, $a = 1, b = 4$

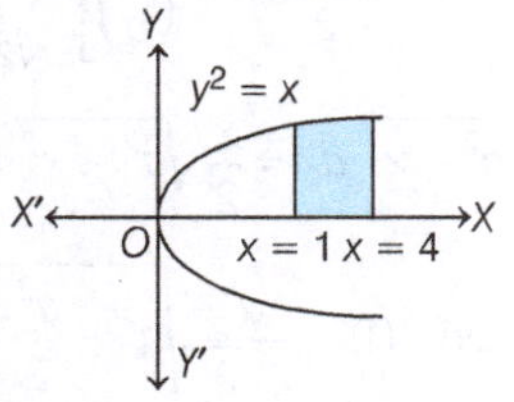

Since, the given curve $y^2 = x$ is parabola which is symmetrical about X-axis (as it contains even power of y) and passes through the origin.

$\therefore$ Required area (shaded region) $= \int_a^b |y|\,dx$

$$= \int_1^4 |y|\,dx = \int_1^4 \sqrt{x}\,dx \qquad [\because y^2 = x \Rightarrow |y| = \sqrt{x}]$$

$$= \left[\frac{x^{3/2}}{\frac{3}{2}}\right]_1^4 = \frac{2}{3}[4^{3/2} - 1^{3/2}] \qquad \left[\because \int x^n\,dx = \frac{x^{n+1}}{n+1}\right]$$

$$= \frac{2}{3}[(2^2)^{3/2} - 1] = \frac{2}{3}[8 - 1] = \frac{14}{3} \text{ sq units}$$

Note *We can solve these questions without drawing the curve.*

B. Since, the given curve $y^2 = 9x$ is a parabola which is symmetrical about X-axis (as the power of y is even) and passes through the origin.

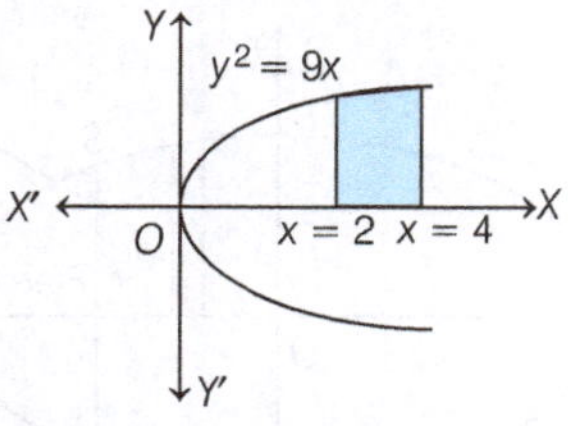

The area of the region bounded by the curve $y^2 = 9x$, $x = 2$ and $x = 4$ and the X-axis is the area shown in the figure.

$\therefore$ Required area (shaded region)

$$= \int_2^4 |y|\,dx = \int_2^4 3\sqrt{x}\,dx$$

$$[\because y^2 = 9x \Rightarrow |y| = 3\sqrt{x}]$$

$$= 3\left[\frac{x^{3/2}}{\frac{3}{2}}\right]_2^4 = \frac{3 \times 2}{3}[4^{3/2} - 2^{3/2}]$$

$$= 2[4\sqrt{4} - 2\sqrt{2}] = 2[8 - 2\sqrt{2}]$$

$$= 4[4 - \sqrt{2}] \text{ sq unit}$$

C. The given curve $x^2 = 4y$ is a parabola which is symmetrical about Y-axis (since, it contains even power of x only) and passes through the origin.

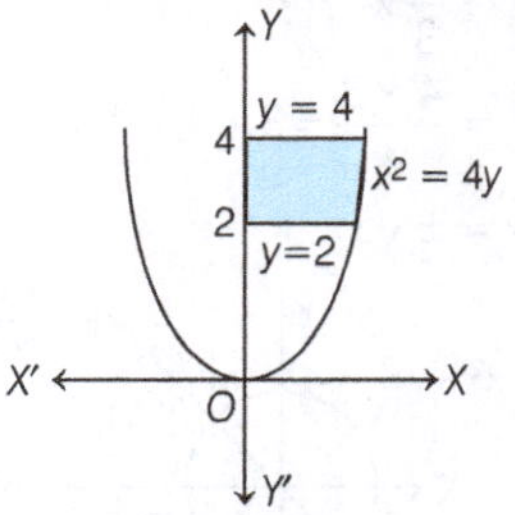

The area of the region bounded by the curve $x^2 = 4y$, $y = 2$ and $y = 4$ and the Y-axis is shown in the figure.

$\therefore$ Required area (shaded region) $= \int_{y=a}^{y=b} |x|\,dy$

Here, $|x| = \sqrt{4y}$

and $a = 2, b = 4$

$$= \int_2^4 |x|\,dy$$

[considering the elementary strip on Y-axis]

$$= \int_2^4 2\sqrt{y}\,dy \qquad [\because x^2 = 4y \Rightarrow |x| = 2\sqrt{y}]$$

$$= 2\left[\frac{y^{3/2}}{3/2}\right]_2^4$$

$$= \frac{4}{3}[4^{3/2} - 2^{3/2}]$$

$$= \frac{4}{3}[8 - 2\sqrt{2}]$$

$$= \frac{8}{3}[4 - \sqrt{2}] \text{ sq units}$$

7 (c) Given curve $x = y^2$ is a parabola symmetrical about X-axis and passing through the origin.

The line $x = a$ divides the area bounded by the parabola and $x = 4$ into two equal parts.

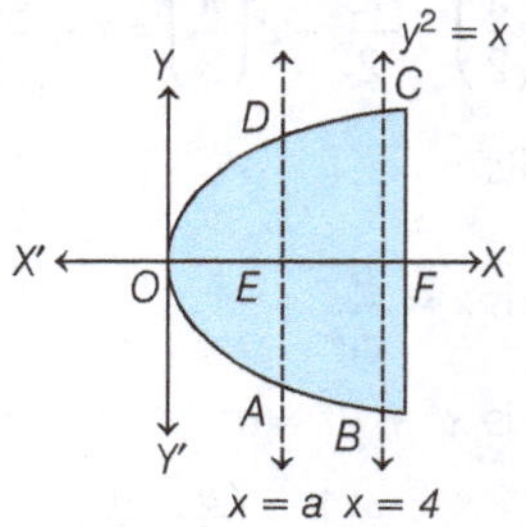

$$\text{Area } (OAD) = \text{Area } (ABCD)$$

$\therefore$ Area (OED) = Area $(EFCD)$

$\Rightarrow$ Area $(OED) = \int_0^a y\,dx$

$$= \int_0^a \sqrt{x}\,dx$$

Area of $EFCD = \int_a^4 \sqrt{x}\,dx$

$[\because y^2 = x \Rightarrow |y| = \sqrt{x}]$

$\Rightarrow \int_0^a \sqrt{x}\,dx = \int_a^4 \sqrt{x}\,dx$

$\Rightarrow \left[\frac{x^{3/2}}{3/2}\right]_0^a = \left[\frac{x^{3/2}}{3/2}\right]_a^4$

$\Rightarrow \frac{2}{3}[a^{3/2} - 0] = \frac{2}{3}[4^{3/2} - a^{3/2}]$

$\Rightarrow a^{3/2} = 4^{3/2} - a^{3/2}$

$\Rightarrow 2a^{3/2} = 8 \Rightarrow a^{3/2} = 4$

$\therefore a = (4)^{2/3}$

Therefore, the value of a is $(4)^{2/3}$.

8 (*d*) Given parabola $y = x^2$ which is symmetrical about Y-axis and passes through $(0, 0)$ and the curve $y = |x|$.

On putting $x = -x$, we get

$y = |-x| = |x|$

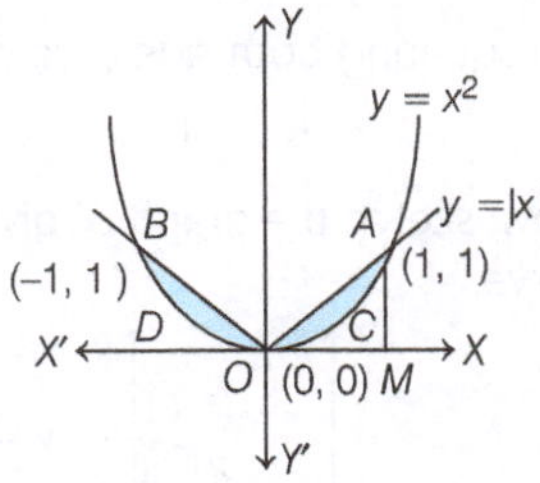

$\therefore$ Curve $y = |x|$ is symmetrical about Y-axis and passes through origin.

The area bounded by the parabola $y = x^2$ and the line $y = |x|$ or $y = \pm x$ can be represented in the figure.

The point of intersection of parabola $x^2 = y$ and line $y = x$ in first quadrant is $A(1, 1)$.

The given area is symmetrical about Y-axis.

$\therefore$ Area $(OACO)$ = Area $(ODBO)$

$\therefore$ Required area

= 2 (Area of shaded region in the first quadrant only)

$= 2\int_0^1 (y_2 - y_1)\,dx$

$= 2\int_0^1 (x - x^2)\,dx$

[$\because$ the curve $y = |x|$ lies above the curve $y = x^2$ in $[0, 1]$, so we take $y_2 = x$ and $y_1 = x^2$]

$= 2\left[\int_0^1 x\,dx - \int_0^1 x^2\,dx\right]$

$= 2\left(\left[\frac{x^2}{2}\right]_0^1 - \left[\frac{x^3}{3}\right]_0^1\right)$

$= 2\left\{\left(\frac{1}{2} - 0\right) - \left(\frac{1}{3} - 0\right)\right\}$

$= \frac{1}{3}$ sq unit

Therefore, required area is $\frac{1}{3}$ sq unit.

9 (*c*)

I. The given curve is $y^2 = 4x$, which represents a right hand parabola with vertex at $(0, 0)$ and axis along X-axis and the equation of line is $x = 3$.

Required area = 2 × (Area of shaded region in the first quadrant only)

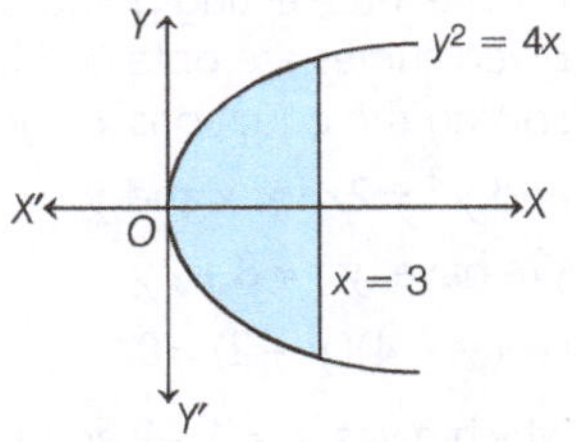

$= 2\int_0^3 |y|\,dx = 2\int_0^3 2\sqrt{x}\,dx$

$[\because y^2 = 4x \Rightarrow y = 2\sqrt{x}]$

$= 4\left[\frac{x^{3/2}}{3/2}\right]_0^3 = \frac{8}{3}[3^{3/2} - 0]$

$= \frac{8}{3}(3\sqrt{3})$

$= 8\sqrt{3}$ sq units

Therefore, the required area is $8\sqrt{3}$ sq units.

II. Given curve is

$x^2 = 4y \Rightarrow y = \frac{x^2}{4}$ ...(i)

which represents an upward parabola with vertex $(0, 0)$ and axis along Y-axis and the equation of straight line

$x = 4y - 2 \Rightarrow y = \frac{x+2}{4}$ ...(ii)

For intersection point, put the value of $4y$ from Eq. (i) in Eq. (ii), we get

$x^2 = x + 2$

$\Rightarrow x^2 - x - 2 = 0$

$\Rightarrow (x - 2)(x + 1) = 0$

$\Rightarrow x = 2, -1$

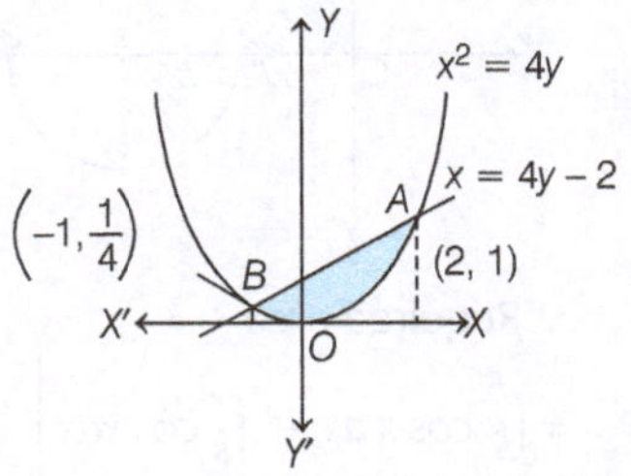

When $x = 2$, then from Eq. (ii), we get

$4y = 2 + 2 \Rightarrow y = 1$

When $x = -1$, then from Eq. (ii), we get

$4y = 2 - 1 = 1 \Rightarrow y = \frac{1}{4}$

$\therefore$ The line meets the parabola at the points $B\left(-1, \frac{1}{4}\right)$ and $A(2, 1)$.

Required area

= (Area under the line $x = 4y - 2$)

– (Area under the parabola $x^2 = 4y$)

$= \int_{-1}^{2}\left(\frac{x+2}{4}\right)dx - \int_{-1}^{2}\frac{x^2}{4}dx$

[from Eqs. (i) and (ii)]

$= \frac{1}{4}\left[\frac{x^2}{2} + 2x\right]_{-1}^{2} - \frac{1}{4}\left[\frac{x^3}{3}\right]_{-1}^{2}$

$= \frac{1}{4}\left\{\frac{2^2}{2} + 2 \times 2 - \left(\frac{1}{2} - 2\right)\right\} - \frac{1}{12}[2^3 - (-1)^3]$

$= \frac{1}{4}\left(6 + \frac{3}{2}\right) - \frac{1}{12} \times 9$

$= \frac{15}{8} - \frac{3}{4} = \frac{9}{8}$ sq units

Therefore, required area is $\frac{9}{8}$ sq units.

10 (*a*) We have, $y = \cos x$ and lines $x = 0, x = \pi$

Draw the rough sketch of the function $\cos x$.

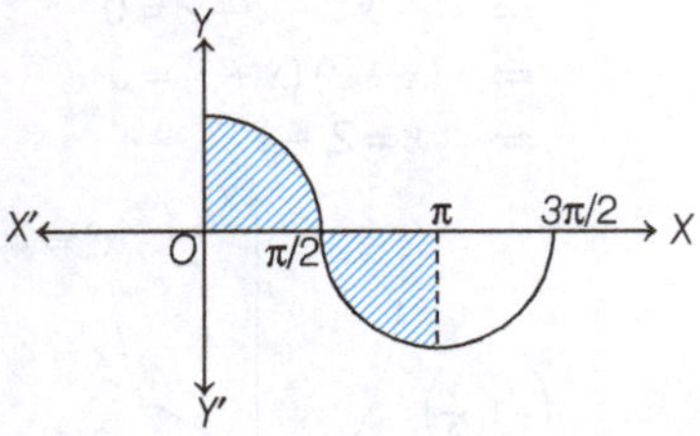

$\therefore$ Required area

$$= \int_0^{\frac{\pi}{2}} \cos x\, dx + \left| \int_{\frac{\pi}{2}}^{\pi} \cos x dx \right|$$

$$= [\sin x]_0^{\pi/2} + |[\sin x]_{\pi/2}^{\pi}|$$

$$= \left[\sin\frac{\pi}{2} - \sin 0\right] + \left|\left[\sin \pi - \sin\frac{\pi}{2}\right]\right|$$

$$= [1 - 0] + |0 - 1| = 1 + 1$$

$= 2$ sq units

11 (*a*)

I. Let us draw the rough sketch of the curve $y = \sin x$ between 0 to π.

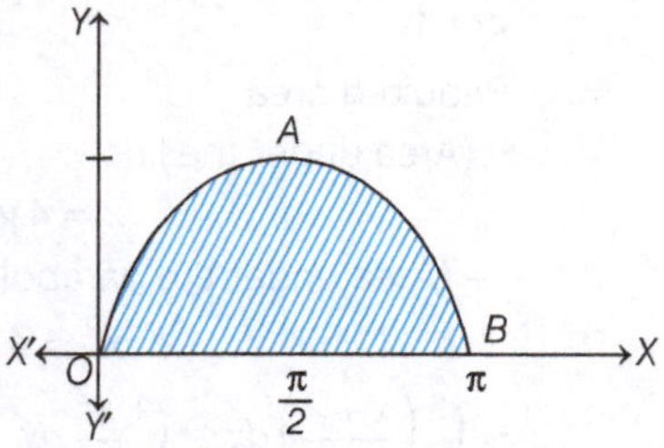

$$\therefore \text{ Area } (OAB) = \int_0^{\pi} y\, dx$$

$$= \int_0^{\pi} \sin x\, dx$$

$$= |-\cos|_0^{\pi}$$

$$= \cos 0 - \cos \pi$$

$= 2$ sq units

II. First draw the rough sketch of the curve.

$$\therefore \text{ Area } (BMNC) = \int_a^{2a} x\, dy$$

$$= \int_a^{2a} a^{\frac{1}{3}} y^{\frac{2}{3}} dy$$

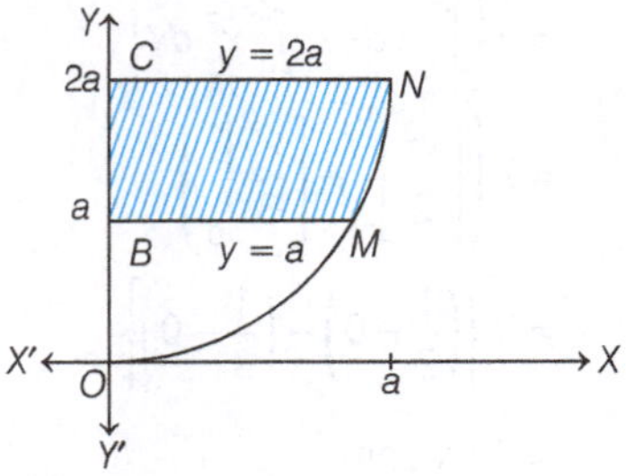

$$= \frac{3a^{\frac{1}{3}}}{5} \left| y^{\frac{5}{3}} \right|_a^{2a}$$

$$= \frac{3a^{\frac{1}{3}}}{5} \left| (2a)^{\frac{5}{3}} - a^{\frac{5}{3}} \right|$$

$$= \frac{3}{5} a^{\frac{1}{3}} a^{\frac{5}{3}} \left| (2)^{\frac{5}{3}} - 1 \right|$$

$$= \frac{3}{5} a^2 \left| 2 \cdot 2^{\frac{2}{3}} - 1 \right| \text{ sq units}$$

12 (*a*) The intersecting points of the given curves are obtained by solving the equations $x - y = 4$ and $y^2 = 2x$ for x and y.

We have, $y^2 = 8 + 2y$

i.e. $(y - 4)(y + 2) = 0$

which gives $y = 4, -2$ and $x = 8, 2$.

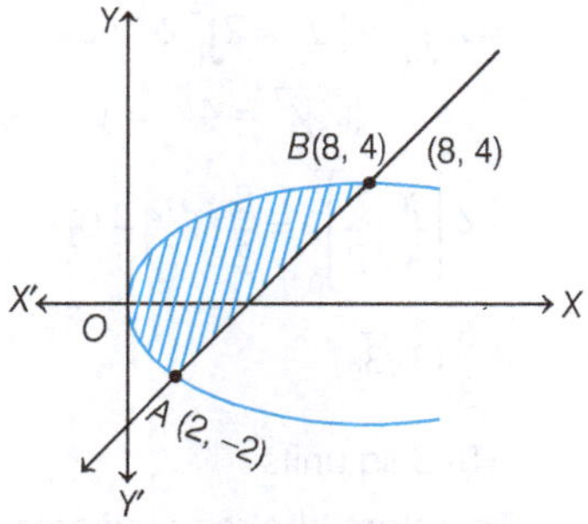

Thus, the points of intersection are (8, 4) and (2, – 2).

$$\therefore \quad \text{Area} = \int_{-2}^{4} \left(4 + y - \frac{1}{2} y^2\right) dy$$

$$= \left| 4y + \frac{y^2}{2} - \frac{1}{6} y^3 \right|_{-2}^{4}$$

$= 18$ sq units

13 (*b*) Area of region $= 2\int_0^{16} \sqrt{y}\, dy$

(putting $y = 16$ in $y = x^2$, we get $x = \pm 4$)

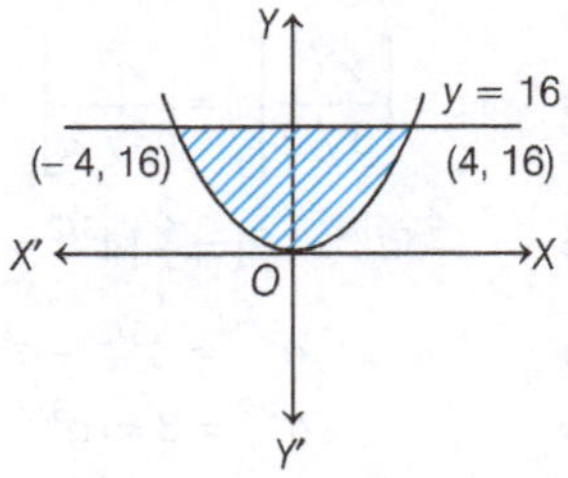

$$= 2\left[\frac{y^{3/2}}{3/2}\right]_0^{16} = \frac{2}{3} \times 2\,[16^{3/2} - 0]$$

$$= \frac{4 \times 64}{3} = \frac{256}{3} \text{ sq units}$$

14 (*c*) We have,

equation of the curve

$$y = \sqrt{x - 1}$$

On squaring both sides, we get

$$y^2 = x - 1$$

Now, sketch the graph of given curve.

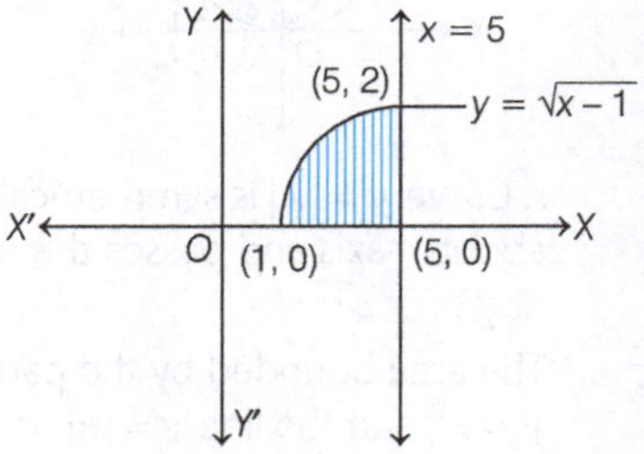

$\therefore$ Area of the shaded region

$$= \int_1^5 \sqrt{x - 1}\, dx$$

$$= \left[\frac{(x-1)^{3/2}}{3/2}\right]_1^5 = \frac{2}{3} [(x-1)^{3/2}]_1^5$$

$$= \frac{2}{3} [(4)^{3/2} - 0]$$

$$= \frac{2}{3} \times 8 = \frac{16}{3} \text{ sq units}$$

15 (*d*)

I. We have, $y = \sin x$

Let us draw a graph of $\sin x$ between 0 to 2π.

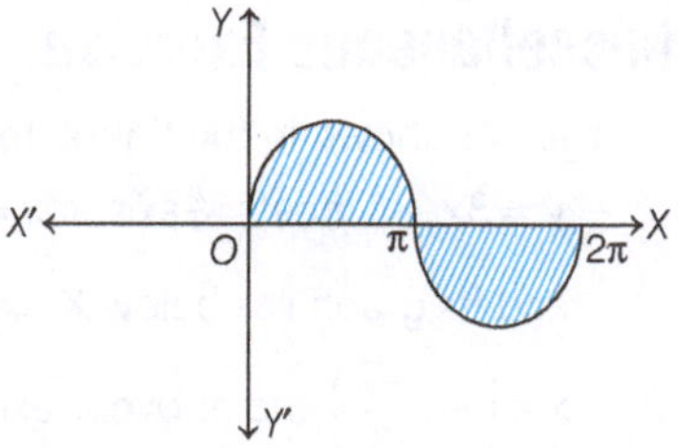

$\therefore$ Area of shaded region

$= \int_0^{\pi} \sin x dx + \left| \int_{\pi}^{2\pi} \sin x \, dx \right|$

$= [-\cos x]_0^{\pi} + |[-\cos x]_{\pi}^{2\pi}|$

$= [-\cos \pi + \cos 0] + |-\cos 2\pi + \cos \pi|$

$= |1 + 1| + |-1 - 1|$

$= 2 + 2$

$= 4$ sq units

II. We have,

$y = 2\cos x$

Let us draw the graph of $2\cos x$ between 0 to 2π.

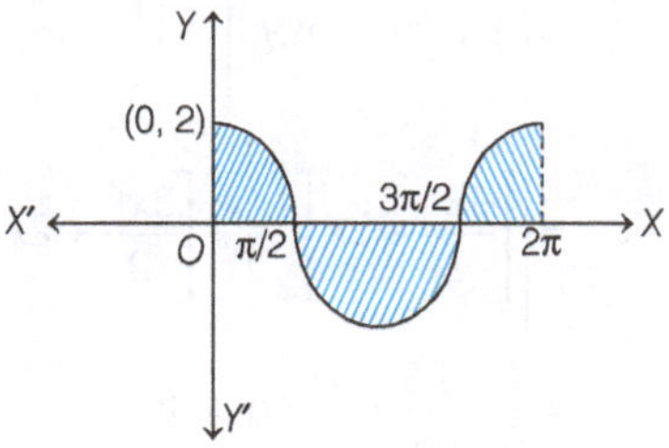

$\therefore$ Area of shaded region

$= \int_0^{\pi/2} 2\cos x \, dx + \left| \int_{\pi/2}^{3\pi/2} 2\cos x \, dx \right| + \int_{3\pi/2}^{2\pi} 2\cos x \, dx$

$= 2[\sin x]_0^{\pi/2} + |[2\sin x]_{\pi/2}^{3\pi/2}| + [2\sin x]_{3\pi/2}^{2\pi}$

$= 2\left[\sin \frac{\pi}{2} - 0\right] + \left| 2\left[\sin \frac{3\pi}{2} - \sin \frac{\pi}{2}\right] \right| + 2\left[\sin 2\pi - \sin \frac{3\pi}{2}\right]$

$= 2 + 2 \times 2 + 2$

$= 2 + 4 + 2$

$= 8$ sq units

16 (*a*) We have, $y = \sqrt{16 - x^2}$

On squaring both sides, we get

$y^2 = 16 - x^2$

$x^2 + y^2 = 16$

Let us sketch the figure of the curve which represents a circle. $(y \geq 0)$

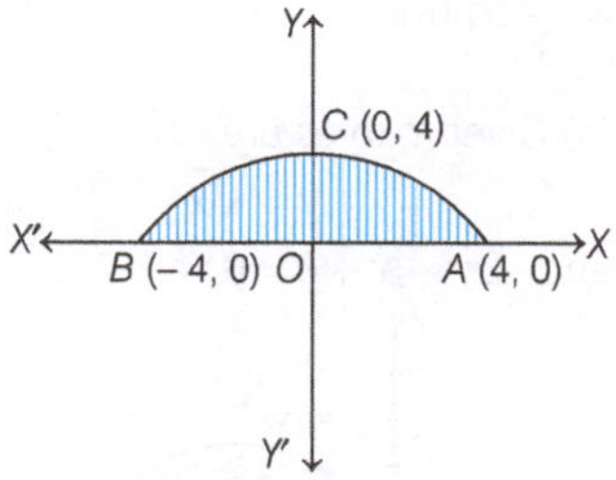

$\therefore$ Area of shaded region

= Area $(BOACB)$

$= \int_{-4}^{4} \sqrt{16 - x^2} dx$

$= \int_{-4}^{4} \sqrt{(4)^2 - x^2} dx$

$= \left[\frac{x}{2}\sqrt{16 - x^2} + 8\sin^{-1}\left(\frac{x}{4}\right) \right]_{-4}^{4}$

$= \left[\left\{ \frac{4}{2}\sqrt{16 - 16} + 8\sin^{-1}\left(\frac{4}{4}\right) \right\} - \left\{ \frac{-4}{2}\sqrt{16 - (-4)^2} + 8\sin^{-1}\left(\frac{-4}{4}\right) \right\} \right]$

$= \left[2 \times 0 + 8 \times \frac{\pi}{2} + 8 \times \frac{\pi}{2} \right]$

$= 8\pi$ sq units

17 (*d*) Given curves are

$y^2 = 2x + 1$

and $x - y = 1$

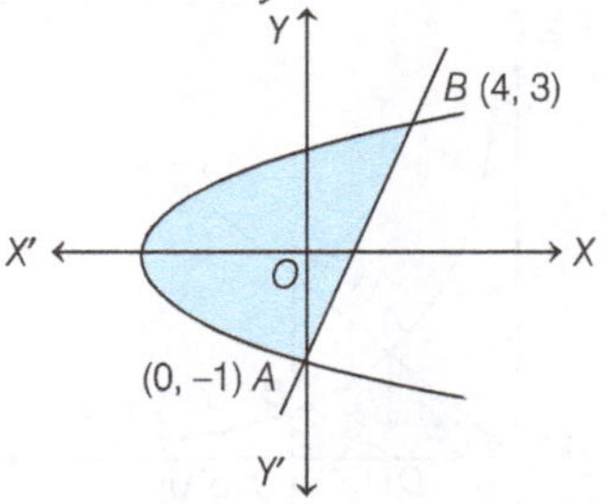

Points of intersection are $A(0, -1)$ and $B(4, 3)$.

$\therefore$ Area

$= \int_{-1}^{3} (1 + y) \, dy - \int_{-1}^{3} \left(\frac{y^2 - 1}{2} \right) dy$

$= \left[y + \frac{y^2}{2} \right]_{-1}^{3} - \left[\frac{1}{2}\left(\frac{y^3}{3} - y \right) \right]_{-1}^{3}$

$= \left[3 + \frac{9}{2} - \left(-1 + \frac{1}{2} \right) \right] - \frac{1}{2}\left[9 - 3 - \left(-\frac{1}{3} + 1 \right) \right]$

$= 8 - \frac{8}{3} = \frac{16}{3}$

18 (*b*) Given curve can be rewritten as

$y^2 = 2\left(x + \frac{1}{2} \right)$

[$\because$ put $y = 0$, $x = -\frac{1}{2}$ which is the vertex of parabola]

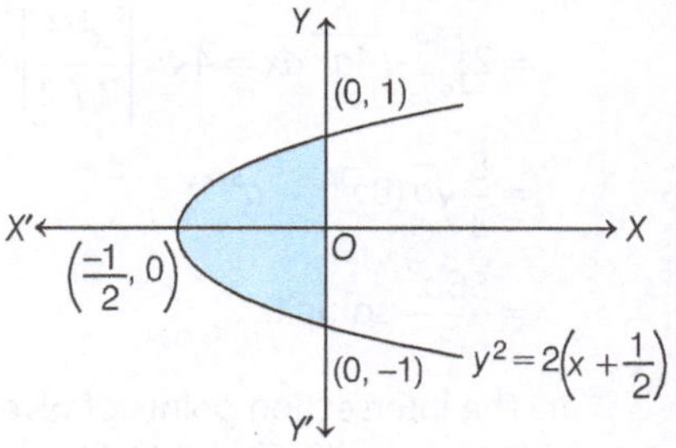

$\therefore$ Required area $= \left| \int_{-1}^{1} x dy \right|$

$= \left| 2\int_0^1 \frac{y^2 - 1}{2} dy \right|$

$= \left| \left[\frac{y^3}{3} - y \right]_0^1 \right| = \frac{2}{3}$ sq unit

19 (*a*) Required area $= \int_1^3 |x - 2| dx$

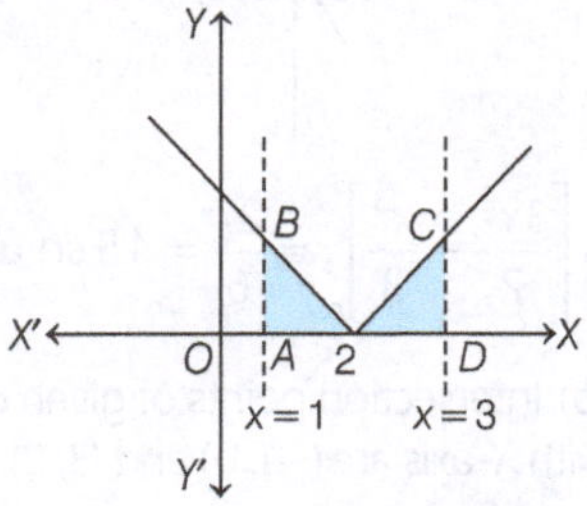

$= \int_1^2 (2 - x) dx + \int_2^3 (x - 2) dx$

$= \left[2x - \frac{x^2}{2} \right]_1^2 + \left[\frac{x^2}{2} - 2x \right]_2^3$

$= 2 - \frac{3}{2} - \frac{3}{2} + 2 = 1$ sq unit

Alternate Method

Area = Area of ΔAOB + Area of ΔODC

$= \frac{1}{2} \times 1 \times 1 + \frac{1}{2} \times 1 \times 1$

$= 1$ sq unit

20 (c)

I. Required area = 2 × Area of curve *PSRQP*

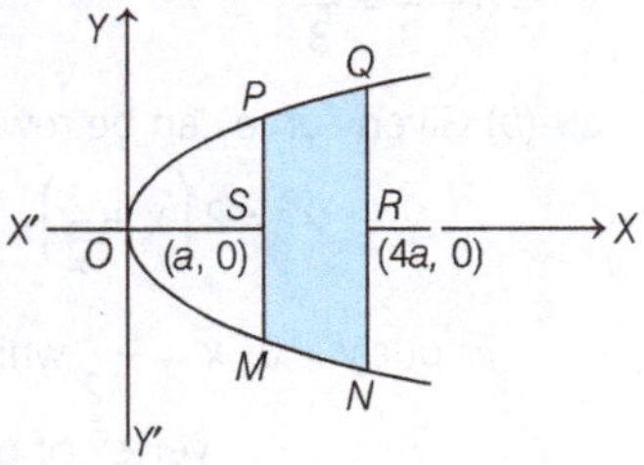

$$= 2\int_a^{4a} \sqrt{4ax}\, dx = 4\sqrt{a}\left[\frac{x^{3/2}}{3/2}\right]_a^{4a}$$

$$= \frac{8}{3}\sqrt{a}\,(8a^{3/2} - a^{3/2})$$

$$= \frac{56a^2}{3} \text{ sq units}$$

II. The intersection points of given curves are (0, 0) and (3, 9).

∴ Required area

$$= \int_0^3 (3x - x^2)dx$$

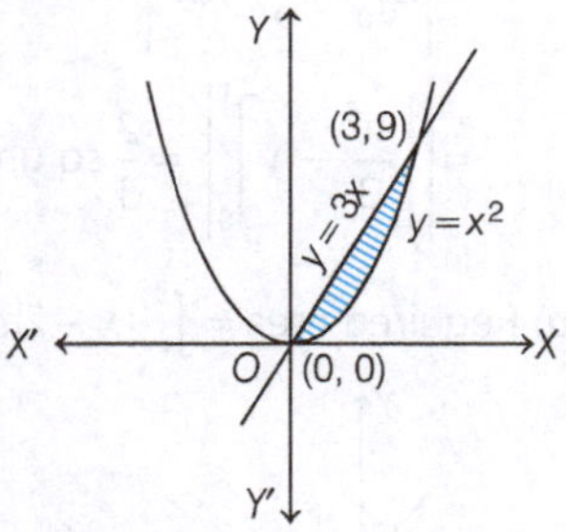

$$= \left[\frac{3x^2}{2} - \frac{x^3}{3}\right]_0^3 = \frac{27}{6} = 4.5 \text{ sq units}$$

21 (b) Intersection points of given curves with *X*-axis are (−1, 0) and (3, 0).

∴ Required area

$$= \int_{-1}^{3} (-x^2 + 2x + 3)\, dx$$

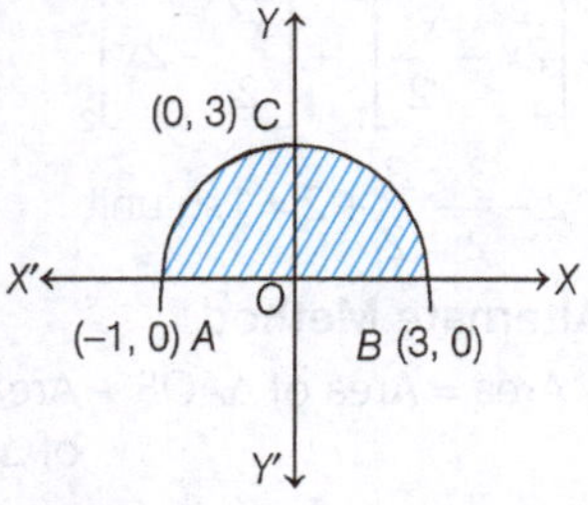

$$= \left[-\frac{x^3}{3} + \frac{2x^2}{2} + 3x\right]_{-1}^{3}$$

$$= \left[-9 + 9 + 9 - \left(\frac{1}{3} + 1 - 3\right)\right]$$

$$= \frac{32}{3} \text{ sq units}$$

22 (a) Given curves are

$$y = \sqrt{x} \qquad \text{...(i)}$$

and $2y - x + 3 = 0$ ...(ii)

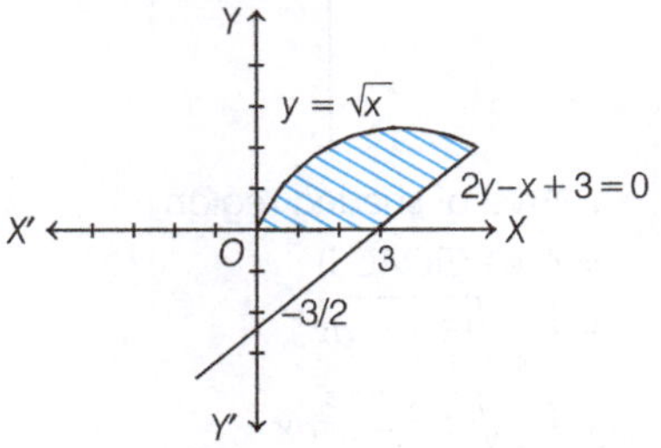

On solving Eqs. (i) and (ii), we get

$$2\sqrt{x} - (\sqrt{x})^2 + 3 = 0$$

$$\Rightarrow \quad (\sqrt{x})^2 - 2\sqrt{x} - 3 = 0$$

$$\Rightarrow \quad (\sqrt{x} - 3)(\sqrt{x} + 1) = 0$$

$$\Rightarrow \quad \sqrt{x} = 3$$

[∵ $\sqrt{x} = -1$ is not possible]

∴ $y = 3$

∴ Required area $= \int_0^3 (x_2 - x_1)\, dy$

$$= \int_0^3 \{(2y + 3) - y^2\} dy$$

$$= \left[y^2 + 3y - \frac{y^3}{3}\right]_0^3 = 9 + 9 - 9 = 9$$

23 (b) Given, $y = x$, $x = e$ and $y = \frac{1}{x}$, $x \ge 0$

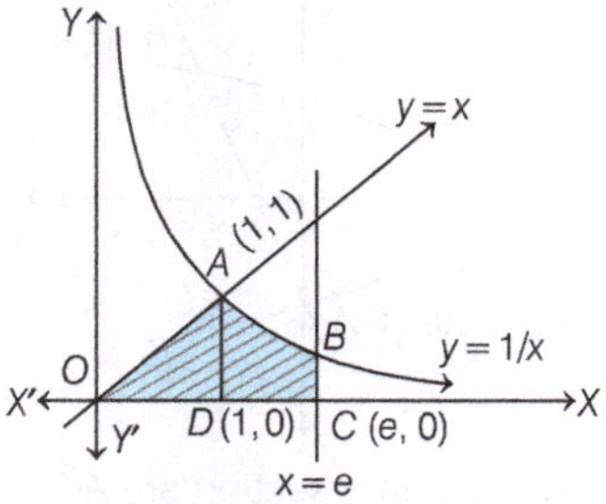

Since, $y = x$ and $x \ge 0 \Rightarrow y \ge 0$

∴ Area to be calculated in first quadrant shown in figure.

∴ Area = Area of ΔODA + Area of *DABCD*

$$= \frac{1}{2}(1 \times 1) + \int_1^e \frac{1}{x} dx = \frac{1}{2} + [\log|x|]_1^e$$

$$= \frac{1}{2} + [\log|x|]_1^e = \frac{1}{2} + 1 = \frac{3}{2} \text{ sq units}$$

Miscellaneous Exercise

1 (c) As shown in the figure, the line $y = 3x + 2$ meets *X*-axis at $x = \frac{-2}{3}$ and its graph lies below *X*-axis for $x \in \left(-1, \frac{-2}{3}\right)$ and above *X*-axis for $x \in \left(\frac{-2}{3}, 1\right)$.

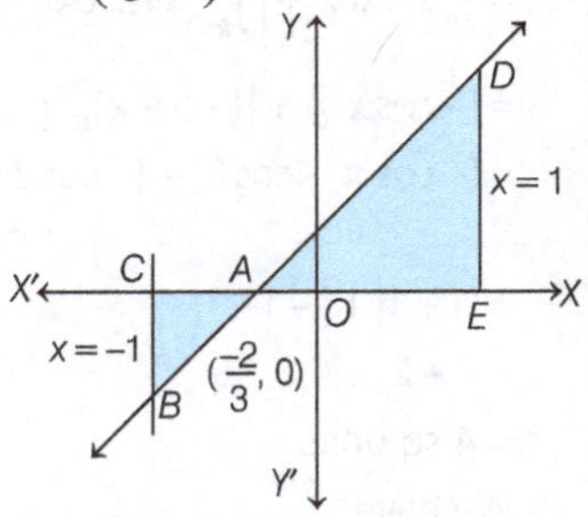

The required area = Area of the region *ACBA* + Area of the region *ADEA*

$$= \left|\int_{-1}^{\frac{-2}{3}} (3x + 2)\, dx\right| + \int_{\frac{-2}{3}}^{1} (3x + 2)\, dx$$

$$= \left|\left[\frac{3x^2}{2} + 2x\right]_{-1}^{\frac{-2}{3}}\right| + \left[\frac{3x^2}{2} + 2x\right]_{\frac{-2}{3}}^{1}$$

$$= \frac{1}{6} + \frac{25}{6} = \frac{13}{3} \text{ sq units}$$

2 (b) Let us first sketch the region whose area is to be found out. This region is the intersection of the following regions

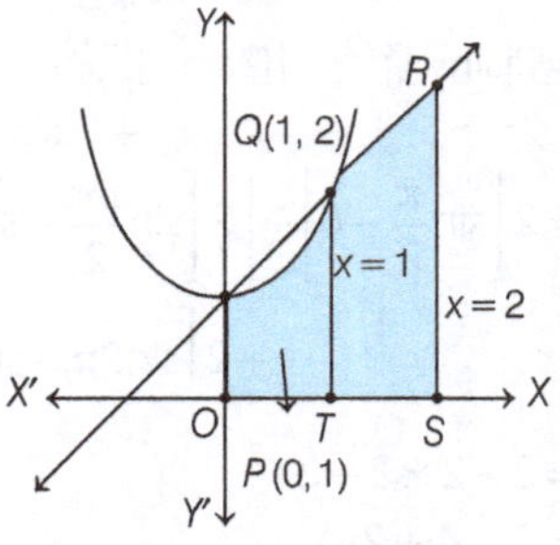

$$A_1 = \{(x, y) : x \le y \le x^2 + 1\}$$

$$A_2 = \{(x, y) : 0 \le y \le x + 1\}$$

$$A_3 = \{(x, y) : 0 \le x \le 2\}$$

The points of intersection of $y = x^2 + 1$ and $y = x + 1$ are points

$P(0, 1)$ and $Q(1, 2)$. From the figure, the required region is the shaded region $OPQRSTO$ whose area is Area of the region $OTQPO$ + Area of the region $TSRQT$

$= \int_0^1 (x^2 + 1)\, dx + \int_1^2 (x + 1)\, dx$

$= \left[\left(\frac{x^3}{3} + x\right)\right]_0^1 + \left[\left(\frac{x^2}{2} + x\right)\right]_1^2$

$= \left[\left(\frac{1}{3} + 1\right) - 0\right] + \left[(2 + 2) - \left(\frac{1}{2} + 1\right)\right]$

$= \frac{23}{6}$ sq units

3 (c)

A. The given curve $y = x^2$ represents an upward parabola with vertex (0, 0) and axis along Y-axis.

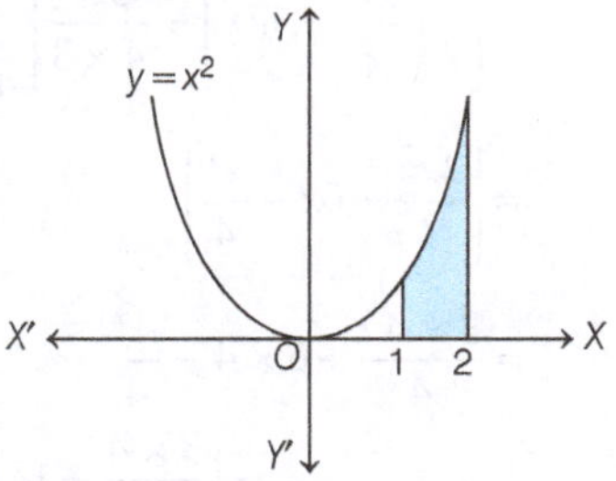

$\therefore$ Required area (shown in shaded region)

= [Area under the curve $y = x^2$, X-axis and $x = 1$, $x = 2$]

$= \int_1^2 y\, dx = \int_1^2 x^2\, dx$

$= \left[\frac{x^3}{3}\right]_1^2 = \frac{1}{3}[2^3 - 1^3]$

$= \frac{8}{3} - \frac{1}{3} = \frac{7}{3}$ sq units

B. Given, $y = x^4$

Here, x is even, so curve is symmetrical about Y-axis and passes through origin (0, 0).

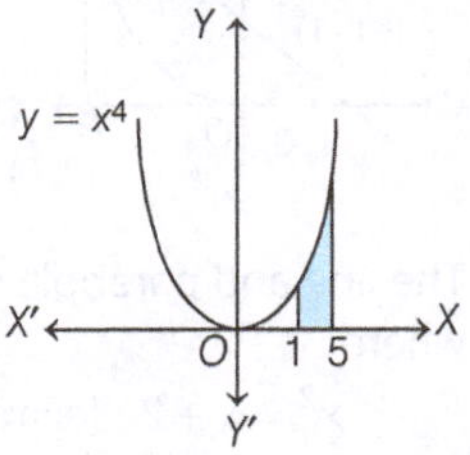

$\therefore$ Required area = [Area under the curve $y = x^4$, X-axis and $x = 1$, $x = 5$]

$= \int_1^5 x^4 dx = \left[\frac{x^5}{5}\right]_1^5 = \frac{1}{5}[5^5 - 1]$

$= \frac{1}{5}(3125 - 1) = \frac{3124}{5}$ sq units

C. Given curve represents an upward parabola with vertex (0, 0), is

$x^2 = y$ ...(i)

and equation of the line is

$y = x$ ...(ii)

For intersection point, $x^2 = x$ [from Eqs.(i) and (ii)]

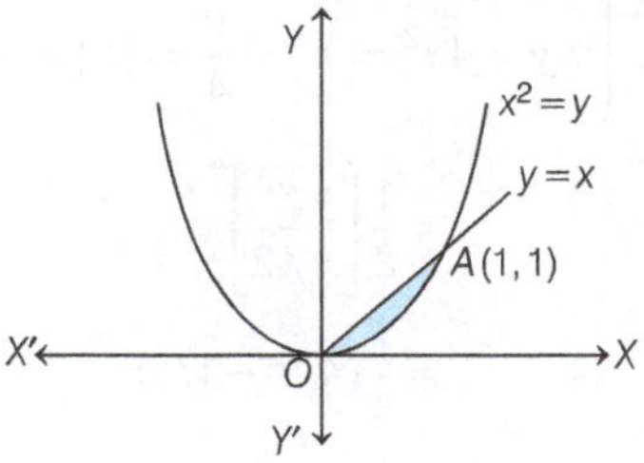

$\Rightarrow x(x - 1) = 0$

$\Rightarrow x = 0, 1$

When $x = 0$, then $y = 0$

and when $x = 1$, then $y = 1$

Thus, point of intersection of parabola and line are (0, 0) and (1, 1).

$\therefore$ Required area

$= \int_0^1 (y_2 - y_1)\, dx = \int_0^1 (x - x^2)\, dx$

$= \left[\frac{x^2}{2} - \frac{x^3}{3}\right]_0^1$

$= \left(\frac{1}{2} - \frac{1}{3}\right) - 0 = \frac{1}{6}$ sq unit

D. The graph of $y = \sin x$ can be drawn as

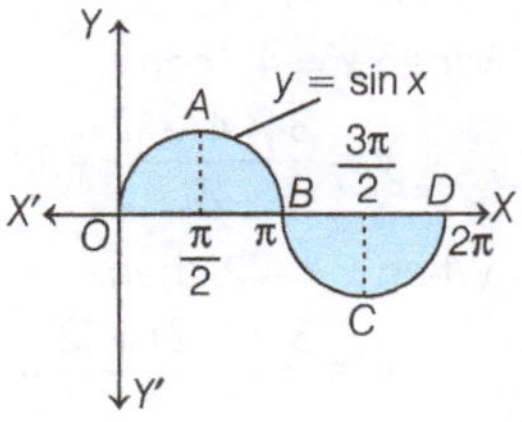

$\therefore$ Required area = Area $(OABO)$ + Area $(BCDB)$

$= \int_0^{\pi} |\sin x|\, dx + \int_{\pi}^{2\pi} |\sin x|\, dx$

$= \int_0^{\pi} \sin x\, dx + \int_{\pi}^{2\pi} (-\sin x)\, dx$

($\because \sin x \ge 0$ for $x \in [0, \pi]$ and $\sin x \le 0$ for $x \in [\pi, 2\pi]$)

$= [-\cos x]_0^{\pi} + [\cos x]_{\pi}^{2\pi}$

$= -\cos \pi + \cos 0 + \cos 2\pi - \cos \pi$

$= -(-1) + 1 + 1 - (-1)$

$= 4$ sq units

4 (b) $y = |x + 3|$

$= \begin{cases} -(x + 3), & \text{for } x < -3 \\ x + 3, & \text{for } x \ge -3 \end{cases}$

When $x < -3$, then $y = -x - 3$

x	−4	−5	−6
y	1	2	3

When $x \ge -3$, then $y = x + 3$

x	−1	−2	−3
y	2	1	0

Draw these points on the graph paper and get the required figure.

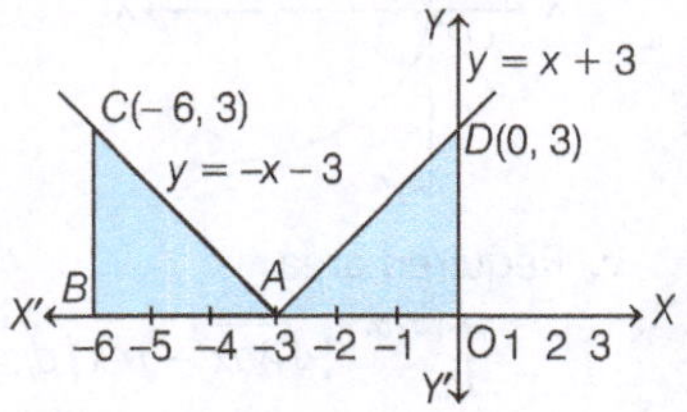

$\therefore$ Required area = Area of region ABC + Area of region OAD

$= \int_{-6}^{-3} |x + 3|\, dx + \int_{-3}^{0} |x + 3|\, dx$

$= \int_{-6}^{-3} (-x - 3)\, dx + \int_{-3}^{0} (x + 3)\, dx$

$= \left[\frac{-x^2}{2} - 3x\right]_{-6}^{-3} + \left[\frac{x^2}{2} + 3x\right]_{-3}^{0}$

$= \left[\left(\frac{-(-3)^2}{2} - 3 \times (-3)\right) - \left(\frac{-(-6)^2}{2} - 3 \times (-6)\right)\right] + \left[0 - \left(\frac{(-3)^2}{2} + 3 \times (-3)\right)\right]$

$$= \left[\left(\frac{-9}{2}+9\right)-(-18+18)\right]+\left[\frac{9}{2}\right]$$

$$= \frac{9}{2}+\frac{9}{2} = 9 \text{ sq units}$$

5 (c) Given, the curve, represents a parabola with vertex (0, 0), is

$$y^2 = 4ax \quad \text{...(i)}$$

and equation of line is

$$y = mx \quad \text{...(ii)}$$

From Eqs. (i) and (ii), we get

$$(mx)^2 = 4ax$$

$$\Rightarrow \quad x(m^2x - 4a) = 0$$

$$\Rightarrow \quad x = 0 \text{ or } x = \frac{4a}{m^2}$$

When $x = 0$, then $y = m \times 0 = 0$

When $x = \frac{4a}{m^2}$, then

$$y = m \times \frac{4a}{m^2} = \frac{4a}{m}$$

$\therefore$ The points of intersection of both the curves are (0, 0) and $\left(\frac{4a}{m^2}, \frac{4a}{m}\right)$.

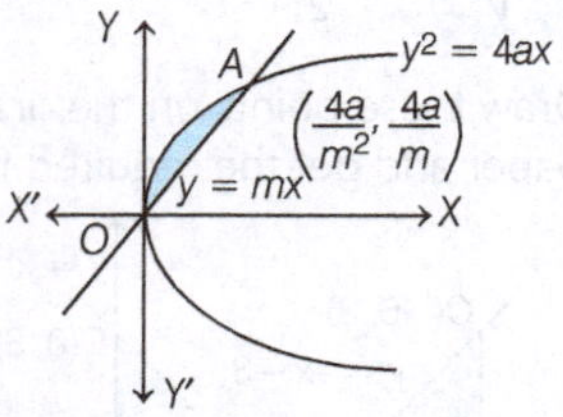

$\therefore$ Required area

$$= \int_0^{4a/m^2} (\sqrt{4ax} - mx)\, dx$$

$[\because y^2 = 4ax$, so $y = \sqrt{4ax}$ in the first quadrant$]$

$$= 2\sqrt{a}\left[\frac{x^{3/2}}{3/2}\right]_0^{4a/m^2} - \left[m\frac{x^2}{2}\right]_0^{4a/m^2}$$

$$= \frac{4}{3}\sqrt{a}\left(\frac{4a}{m^2}\right)^{3/2} - \frac{m}{2}\left(\frac{4a}{m^2}\right)^2$$

$$= \frac{4}{3}\sqrt{a}\cdot\left(\frac{4a}{m^2}\right)\sqrt{\frac{4a}{m^2}} - \frac{m(16a^2)}{2m^4}$$

$$= \frac{32}{3}\cdot\frac{a^2}{m^3} - \frac{8a^2}{m^3}$$

$$= \frac{8a^2}{3m^3} \text{ sq units}$$

6 (b)

I. The area in the first quadrant bounded by $y = 4x^2$, $y = 4$, $x = 0$ and $y = 1$ is represented by the shaded region.

$\therefore$ Required area (shown in shaded region) $= \int_1^4 |x|\, dy$

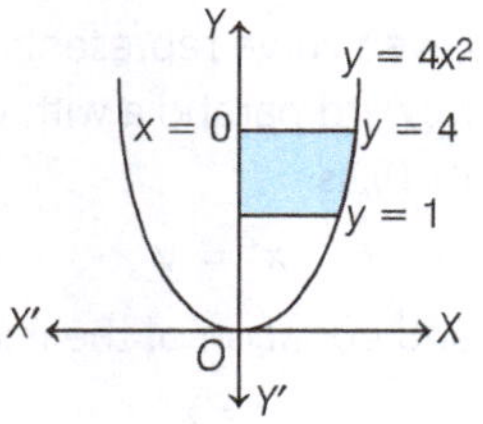

$$= \int_1^4 \frac{1}{2}\sqrt{y}\, dy$$

$$\left[\because y = 4x^2 \Rightarrow x^2 = \frac{y}{4} \Rightarrow |x| = \frac{\sqrt{y}}{2}\right]$$

$$= \frac{1}{2}\left[\frac{y^{3/2}}{3/2}\right]_1^4$$

$$= \frac{1}{3}(4^{3/2} - 1^{3/2})$$

$$= \frac{1}{3}[(2^2)^{3/2} - 1]$$

$$= \frac{1}{3}(8-1) = \frac{7}{3} \text{ sq units}$$

II. Given, the curve, represents an upward parabola with vertex (0, 0), is

$$4y = 3x^2 \quad \text{...(i)}$$

and equation of line is

$$2y = 3x + 12 \quad \text{...(ii)}$$

For intersection point, from Eqs. (i) and (ii), we get

$$2(3x+12) = 3x^2$$

$$\Rightarrow \quad 3x^2 - 6x - 24 = 0$$

$$\Rightarrow \quad x^2 - 2x - 8 = 0$$

$$\Rightarrow \quad (x-4)(x+2) = 0$$

$$\Rightarrow \quad x = 4, -2$$

When $x = 4$, then

$$y = \frac{3\times 4 + 12}{2} = 12$$

When $x = -2$, then

$$y = \frac{3\times(-2)+12}{2} = 3$$

Thus, intersection points are (−2, 3) and (4, 12).

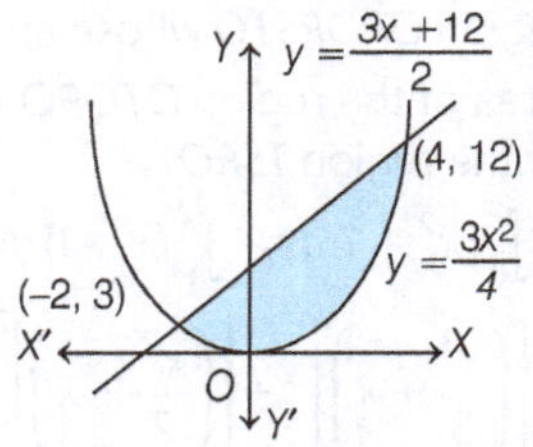

$\therefore$ Required area (shown in shaded region)

= (Area under the line between $x = -2$ and $x = 4$) − (Area under the parabola between $x = -2$ and $x = 4$)

$$= \int_{-2}^{4}\left(\frac{3x+12}{2} - \frac{3x^2}{4}\right)dx$$

$$= \left[\frac{1}{2}\left(\frac{3x^2}{2}+12x\right) - \frac{3x^3}{4\times 3}\right]_{-2}^{4}$$

$$= \left[\frac{3x^2}{4} + 6x - \frac{x^3}{4}\right]_{-2}^{4}$$

$$= \frac{3\times 4^2}{4} + 6\times 4 - \frac{4^3}{4} - \left[\frac{3\times 4}{4} - 12 + \frac{8}{4}\right]$$

$$= 12 + 24 - 16 - 3 + 12 - 2$$

$$= 27 \text{ sq units}$$

7 (c)

I. Given curve, represents an upward parabola with vertex (0, 0), is

$$y = x^2 \quad \text{...(i)}$$

and equation of the line is

$$y = x + 2 \quad \text{...(ii)}$$

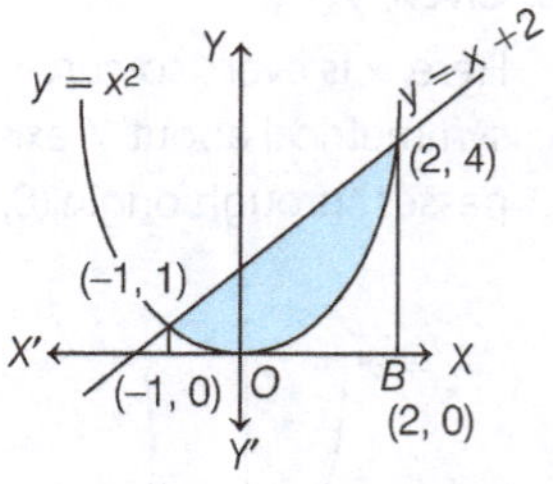

The line and parabola meet where

$$x^2 = x + 2 \quad \text{[eliminating } y]$$

$\therefore \quad x^2 - x - 2 = 0$

$\Rightarrow \quad (x-2)(x+1) = 0$

$\Rightarrow \quad x = 2 \text{ or } -1$

When $x = 2$, then

$y = 2 + 2 = 4$

When $x = -1$, then

$y = (-1) + 2 = 1$

Thus, the points of intersection of the parabola and line are $(-1, 1)$ and $(2, 4)$.

$\therefore$ Required area

= (Area under the line $y = x + 2$ between $x = -1$ and $x = 2$)

− (Area under the curve $x^2 = y$ between $x = -1$ and $x = 2$)

$$= \int_{-1}^{2} (x+2)\,dx - \int_{-1}^{2} x^2 dx$$

$$= \left[\frac{x^2}{2} + 2x\right]_{-1}^{2} - \left[\frac{x^3}{3}\right]_{-1}^{2}$$

$$= \left[\frac{2^2}{2} + 2 \times 2\right] - \left[\frac{(-1)^2}{2} + 2(-1)\right] - \frac{1}{3}(2^3 - (-1)^3)$$

$$= 6 - \frac{1}{2} + 2 - 3 = \frac{9}{2} \text{ sq units}$$

II. The given curve is $|x| + |y| = 1$.
In first quadrant, $(x > 0, y > 0)$.
Then, the line AB is $x + y = 1$.
In second quadrant, $(x < 0, y > 0)$.
Then, the line BC is $-x + y = 1$.
In third quadrant, $(x < 0, y < 0)$.
Then, the line CD is $-x - y = 1$.
In fourth quadrant, $(x > 0, y < 0)$.
Then, the line DA is $x - y = 1$.
Since, $ABCD$ is a square.

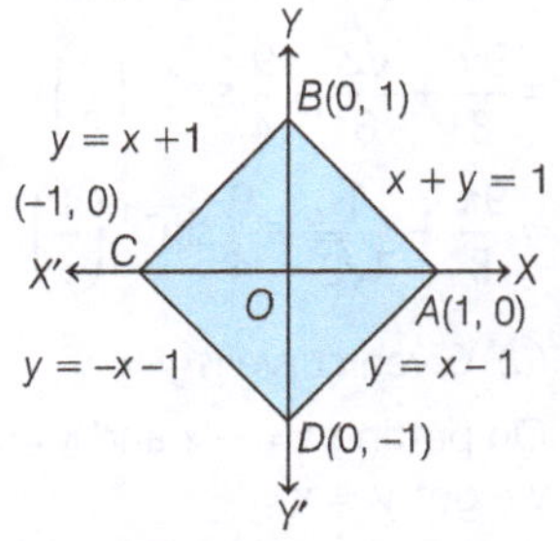

$\therefore$ Required area

= 4 × (Area of shaded region in the first quadrant)

$$= 4\int_0^1 (1-x)\,dx \quad [\because x + y = 1 \Rightarrow y = 1 - x]$$

$$= 4\left[x - \frac{x^2}{2}\right]_0^1 = 4\left[\left(1 - \frac{1}{2}\right) - 0\right]$$

= 2 sq units

III. The given curve is $y = x^2$ ...(i)
and equation of line is
$y = |x|$ ...(ii)
In first quadrant, the equation of the line is $y = x$ and in second quadrant, the equation of line is $y = -x$.
The points of intersection of the parabola and line are $(-1, 1)$ and $(1, 1)$. As the area to be found is symmetrical about Y-axis.

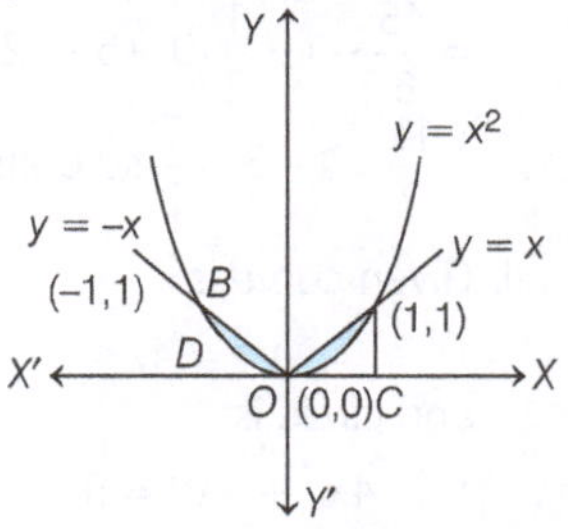

$\therefore$ Required area = 2 × (Area of shaded region in the first quadrant)

$$= 2\int_0^1 (x - x^2)\,dx$$

$$= 2\left[\int_0^1 x\,dx - \int_0^1 x^2 dx\right]$$

$$= 2\left(\left[\frac{x^2}{2}\right]_0^1 - \left[\frac{x^3}{3}\right]_0^1\right)$$

$$= 2\left[\left(\frac{1}{2} - 0\right) - \left(\frac{1}{3} - 0\right)\right]$$

$$= 2\left[\frac{1}{2} - \frac{1}{3}\right] = 2\left[\frac{1}{6}\right] = \frac{1}{3} \text{ sq unit}$$

IV. The given points are $A(2, 0)$, $B(4, 5)$ and $C(6, 3)$.
Equation of line AB is

$$y - 0 = \frac{5-0}{4-2}(x-2)$$

$$\left[\text{using } y - y_1 = \frac{y_2 - y_1}{x_2 - x_1}(x - x_1)\right]$$

$$\Rightarrow \quad y = \frac{5}{2}x - 5$$

Equation of line BC is

$$y - 5 = \frac{3-5}{6-4}(x-4)$$

$$\Rightarrow \quad y = -x + 9$$

Equation of line AC is

$$y - 0 = \frac{3-0}{6-2}(x-2)$$

$$\Rightarrow \quad y = \frac{3}{4}x - \frac{3}{2}$$

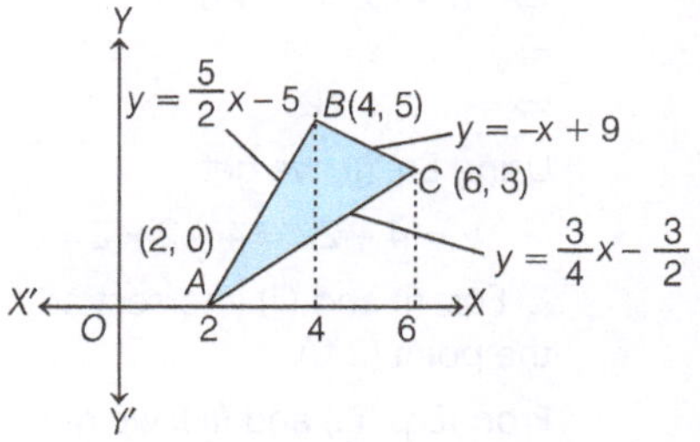

$\therefore$ Required area = (Area under line segment AB) + (Area under line segment BC) − (Area under line segment AC)

$$= \int_2^4 \left(\frac{5}{2}x - 5\right)dx + \int_4^6 (-x + 9)\,dx - \int_2^6 \left(\frac{3}{4}x - \frac{3}{2}\right)dx$$

$$= \left[\frac{5x^2}{4} - 5x\right]_2^4 + \left[\frac{-x^2}{2} + 9x\right]_4^6 - \left[\frac{3x^2}{8} - \frac{3}{2}x\right]_2^6$$

$$= \left(\frac{5 \times 4^2}{4} - 5 \times 4\right) - \left(\frac{5 \times 2^2}{4} - 5 \times 2\right) + \left(\frac{-6^2}{2} + 9 \times 6\right) - \left(\frac{-4^2}{2} + 9 \times 4\right) - \left(\frac{3 \times 6^2}{8} - \frac{3}{2} \times 6\right) + \left(\frac{3 \times 2^2}{8} - \frac{3}{2} \times 2\right)$$

$$= (20 - 20) - (5 - 10) + (-18 + 54) - (-8 + 36) - \left(\frac{27}{2} - 9\right) + \left(\frac{3}{2} - 3\right)$$

$$= 5 + 36 - 28 - \frac{9}{2} - \frac{3}{2}$$

= 7 sq units

8 (*a*)

I. The given lines are

$$2x + y = 4 \quad \text{...(i)}$$
$$3x - 2y = 6 \quad \text{...(ii)}$$
$$x - 3y + 5 = 0 \quad \text{...(iii)}$$

From Eqs. (i) and (ii), we get

$$4 - 2x = \frac{3x - 6}{2} \quad \text{[eliminating } y]$$

$\Rightarrow \quad 8 - 4x = 3x - 6$

$\Rightarrow \quad 7x = 14$

$\Rightarrow \quad x = 2$

Using Eq. (i), we get

$$y = 4 - 2x = 4 - 2 \times 2 = 0$$

$\therefore$ Eqs. (i) and (ii) intersect at the point $(2, 0)$.

From Eqs. (ii) and (iii), we get

$$\frac{3x - 6}{2} = \frac{x + 5}{3}$$

$\Rightarrow 9x - 18 = 2x + 10$

$\Rightarrow \quad 7x = 28 \Rightarrow x = 4$

Using Eq. (ii), we get

$$y = \frac{3 \times 4 - 6}{2} = 3$$

$\therefore$ Eqs. (ii) and (iii) intersect at the point $(4, 3)$.

From Eqs. (i) and (iii), we get

$$4 - 2x = \frac{x + 5}{3}$$

$\Rightarrow \quad 7x = 7 \Rightarrow x = 1$

Using Eq. (i), we get

$$y = 4 - 2x = 4 - 2 \times 1 = 2$$

$\therefore$ Eqs. (i) and (iii) intersect at the point $(1, 2)$.

$\therefore$ Required area = (Area under line segment BA) − (Area under line segment BC) − (Area under line segment AC)

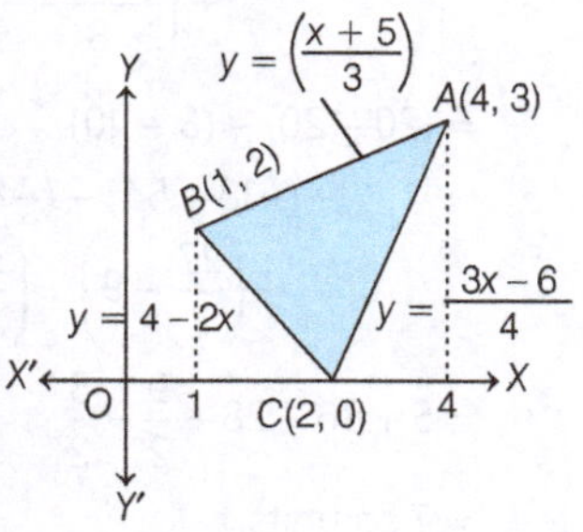

$$= \int_1^4 \left(\frac{x + 5}{3}\right) dx - \int_1^2 (4 - 2x)\, dx - \int_2^4 \left(\frac{3x - 6}{2}\right) dx$$

$$= \frac{1}{3}\left[\frac{(x + 5)^2}{2}\right]_1^4 - [4x - x^2]_1^2 - \frac{1}{2}\left[\frac{3x^2}{2} - 6x\right]_2^4$$

$$= \frac{1}{6}[9^2 - 6^2] - [(8 - 4) - (4 - 1)] - \frac{1}{2}\left[\left(\frac{3 \times 4^2}{2} - 6 \times 4\right) - \left(3 \times \frac{2^2}{2} - 6 \times 2\right)\right]$$

$$= \frac{45}{6} - 1 - \frac{1}{2}(0 - 6 + 12)$$

$$= \frac{15}{2} - 1 - 3 = \frac{7}{2} \text{ sq units}$$

II. Given curve is

$$y^2 = 4x \quad \text{...(i)}$$

and circle is

$$4x^2 + 4y^2 = 9 \quad \text{...(ii)}$$

which represents a circle whose centre is $(0, 0)$ and radius $\frac{3}{2}$.

For intersecting points of parabola and circle, putting the value of y^2 from Eq. (i) in Eq. (ii), we get

$$4x^2 + 16x = 9$$

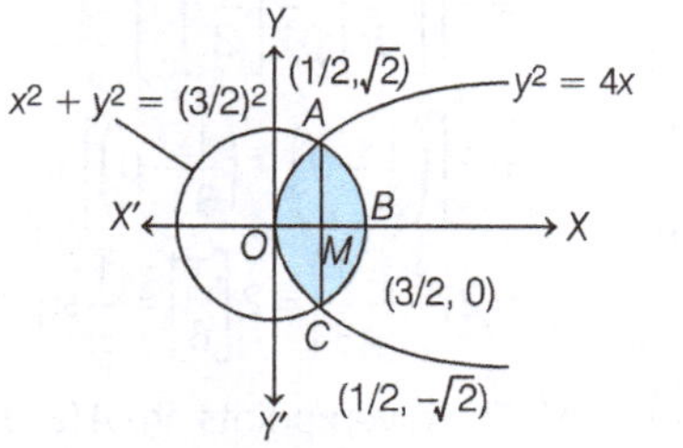

$\Rightarrow \quad 4x^2 + 16x - 9 = 0$

$\Rightarrow \quad 4x^2 + 18x - 2x - 9 = 0$

$\Rightarrow \quad 2x(2x + 9) - 1(2x + 9) = 0$

$\Rightarrow \quad (2x + 9)(2x - 1) = 0$

$\Rightarrow \quad x = -\frac{9}{2}, \frac{1}{2}$

$\Rightarrow \quad x = \frac{1}{2}$

$\left(x \neq -\frac{9}{2}, \text{ because it does not satisfy the given inequality}\right)$

On putting $x = \frac{1}{2}$ in Eq. (i), we get

$$y = \pm\sqrt{2}$$

Thus, the points of intersection of both the curves are $A\left(\frac{1}{2}, \sqrt{2}\right)$ and $C\left(\frac{1}{2}, -\sqrt{2}\right)$.

Since, the shaded region is symmetrical about X-axis.

$\therefore$ Required area

$= 2 \times$ (Area $OABO$)

$$= 2\left[\int_0^{1/2} \sqrt{4x}\, dx + \int_{1/2}^{3/2} \sqrt{\frac{9 - 4x^2}{4}}\, dx\right]$$

$$= 2 \times 2\left[\frac{x^{3/2}}{3/2}\right]_0^{1/2} + 2\int_{1/2}^{3/2} \sqrt{\left(\frac{3}{2}\right)^2 - x^2}\, dx$$

$$= \frac{8}{3}\left[\left(\frac{1}{2}\right)^{3/2} - 0\right] + 2\left[\frac{x}{2}\sqrt{\frac{9}{4} - x^2} + \frac{9}{8}\sin^{-1}\left(\frac{x}{3/2}\right)\right]_{1/2}^{3/2}$$

$$= \frac{8}{3} \cdot \frac{1}{2\sqrt{2}} + 2\left[0 + \frac{9}{8}\sin^{-1}(1) - \frac{1}{4}\sqrt{\frac{9}{4} - \frac{1}{4}} - \frac{9}{8}\sin^{-1}\left(\frac{1}{3}\right)\right]$$

$$= \frac{2\sqrt{2}}{3} + \frac{9}{4} \cdot \frac{\pi}{2} - \frac{\sqrt{2}}{2} - \frac{9}{4}\sin^{-1}\left(\frac{1}{3}\right)$$

$$= \frac{9\pi}{8} + \frac{\sqrt{2}}{6} - \frac{9}{4}\sin^{-1}\left(\frac{1}{3}\right)$$

$$= \frac{9\pi}{8} + \frac{1}{3\sqrt{2}} - \frac{9}{4}\sin^{-1}\left(\frac{1}{3}\right)$$

9 (*d*) Given curve is $y = x^3$

On putting $x = -x$ and $y = -y$, we get $y = x^3$

Therefore, the curve is symmetrical in opposite quadrant and passes through $(0, 0)$.

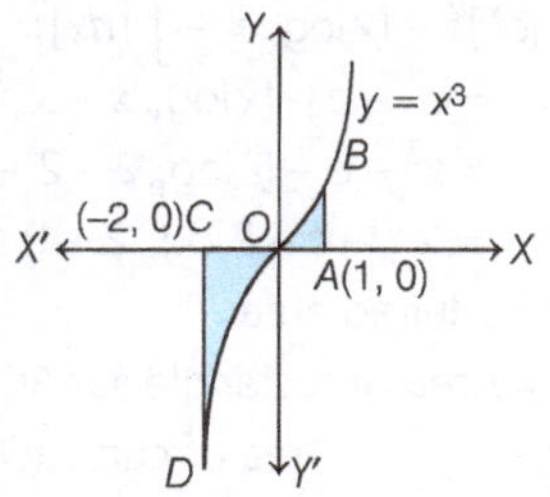

∴ Required area

$= \int_{-2}^{1} |x^3|\, dx = \int_{-2}^{0} |x^3|\, dx + \int_0^1 |x^3|\, dx$

$= \int_{-2}^{0} (-x^3)\, dx + \int_0^1 x^3\, dx$

$\left[\because |x^3| = \begin{cases} x^3, & \text{if } x \ge 0 \\ -x^3, & \text{if } x < 0 \end{cases}\right]$

$= -\left[\frac{x^4}{4}\right]_{-2}^{0} + \left[\frac{x^4}{4}\right]_0^1$

$= -\left[0 - \frac{(-2)^4}{4}\right] + \left[\frac{1}{4} - 0\right]$

$= -(-4) + \left(\frac{1}{4}\right) = \frac{17}{4}$ sq units

So, the correct option is (d).

10 (c) Given, $y = x|x| = \begin{cases} x^2, x \ge 0 \\ -x^2, x < 0 \end{cases}$

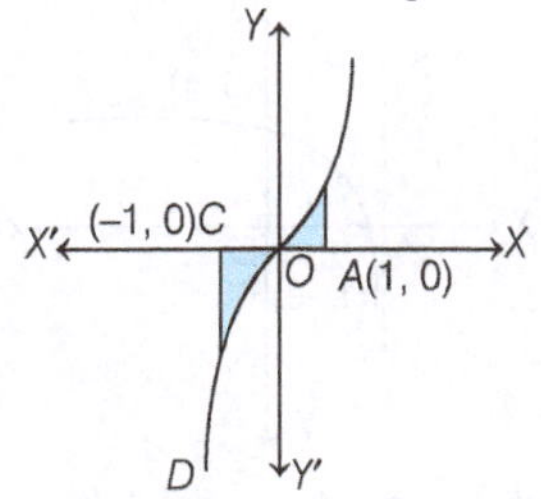

∴ Required area = 2 × (Area under the curve $y = x^2$ between $x = 0$ and $x = 1$)

[∵ the curve is symmetrical in opposite quadrant]

$= 2\int_0^1 x|x| = 2\int_0^1 x^2 dx$

$= 2\left[\frac{x^3}{3}\right]_0^1 = \frac{2}{3}(1^3 - 0^3)$

$= \frac{2}{3}$ sq unit

So, the correct option is (c).

11 (c) The circle $x^2 + y^2 = 16$ and the parabola $y^2 = 6x$ meet where

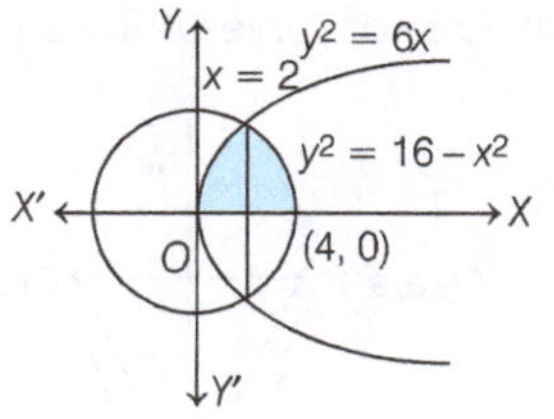

$x^2 + 6x = 16$ [eliminating y]

$\Rightarrow \quad x^2 + 6x - 16 = 0$

$\Rightarrow (x + 8)(x - 2) = 0$

$\Rightarrow \quad x = -8, 2$

∴ Required area = Area of the circle – 2 × Area shown in the shaded region

$= \pi(4)^2 - 2\left[\int_0^2 \sqrt{6x} + \int_2^4 \sqrt{16 - x^2}\, dx\right]$

$= 16\pi - 2\sqrt{6}\left[\frac{x^{3/2}}{3/2}\right]_0^2 - 2\left[\frac{x}{2}\sqrt{16 - x^2} + \frac{16}{2}\sin^{-1}\left(\frac{x}{4}\right)\right]_2^4$

$= 16\pi - \frac{4\sqrt{6}}{3}(2^{3/2} - 0) - 2\left[0 + 8\sin^{-1}(1) - \sqrt{16 - 4} - 8\sin^{-1}\left(\frac{1}{2}\right)\right]$

$= 16\pi - \frac{4\sqrt{6} \times 2\sqrt{2}}{3} - 2\left[8 \times \frac{\pi}{2} - \sqrt{12} - 8 \times \frac{\pi}{6}\right]$

$= 16\pi - \frac{16\sqrt{3}}{3} - \frac{16\pi}{3} + 4\sqrt{3}$

$= \frac{32\pi}{3} - \frac{4\sqrt{3}}{3}$

$= \frac{4}{3}(8\pi - \sqrt{3})$ sq units

So, the correct option is (c).

12 (d)

A. Required area

$= \int_0^{\pi/4} (\cos x - \sin x)\, dx + \int_{\pi/4}^{5\pi/4} (\sin x - \cos x)\, dx + \int_{5\pi/4}^{3\pi/2} (\cos x - \sin x)\, dx$

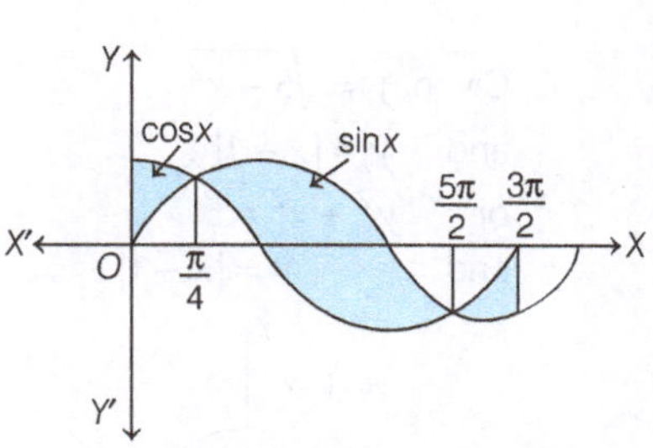

$= [\sin x + \cos x]_0^{\pi/4} + [-\cos x - \sin x]_{\pi/4}^{5\pi/4} + [\sin x + \cos x]_{5\pi/4}^{3\pi/2}$

$= \left[\frac{1}{\sqrt{2}} + \frac{1}{\sqrt{2}}\right] - [1] + \left[\frac{1}{\sqrt{2}} + \frac{1}{\sqrt{2}} - \left(\frac{-1}{\sqrt{2}} - \frac{1}{\sqrt{2}}\right)\right] + \left[-1 - \left(\frac{-1}{\sqrt{2}} - \frac{1}{\sqrt{2}}\right)\right]$

$= (\sqrt{2} - 1) + (\sqrt{2} + \sqrt{2}) + (-1 + \sqrt{2})$

$= (4\sqrt{2} - 2)$ sq units

B. The equation of tangent at (2, 3) to the given parabola is

$y - y_1 = \left(\frac{dy}{dx}\right)(x - x_1)$

$\therefore \quad 2(y - 2)\frac{dy}{dx} = 1$

$\Rightarrow \quad \left(\frac{dy}{dx}\right)_{2,3} = \frac{1}{2}$

$\therefore \quad y - 3 = \frac{1}{2}(x - 2)$

$2y - 6 = x - 2$

$x - 2y = -4$

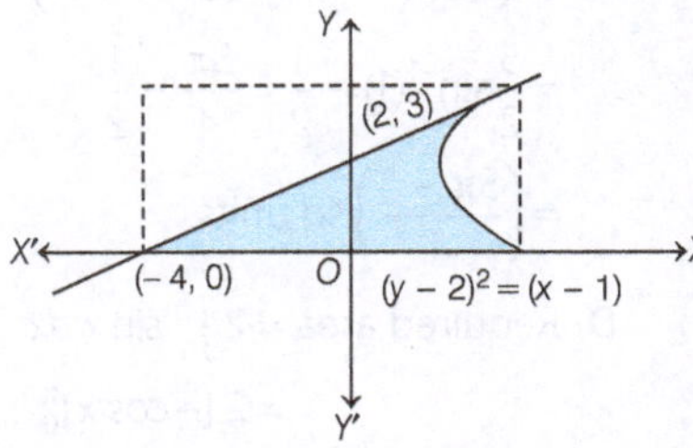

∴ Required area

$= \int_0^3 \{(y - 2)^2 + 1 - 2y + 4\}\, dy$

$= \left[\frac{(y - 2)^3}{3} - y^2 + 5y\right]_0^3$

$= \frac{1}{3} - 9 + 15 + \frac{8}{3}$

$= 9$ sq units

C. Given, $y=\sqrt{5-x^2}$

and $y=|x-1|$

or $y^2+x^2=5$

and $y=|x-1|$

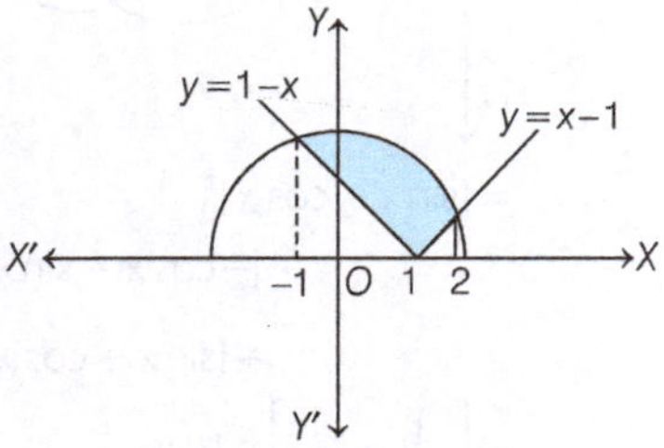

$\therefore$ Required area

$$=\int_{-1}^{2}\sqrt{5-x^2}\,dx-\int_{-1}^{1}(1-x)\,dx-\int_{1}^{2}(x-1)\,dx$$

$$=\left[\frac{x}{2}\sqrt{5-x^2}+\frac{5}{2}\sin^{-1}\left(\frac{x}{\sqrt{5}}\right)\right]_{-1}^{2}-\left[x-\frac{x^2}{2}\right]_{-1}^{1}-\left[\frac{x^2}{2}-x\right]_{1}^{2}$$

$$=\left[1+\frac{5}{2}\sin^{-1}\left(\frac{2}{\sqrt{5}}\right)+1+\frac{5}{2}\sin^{-1}\left(\frac{1}{\sqrt{5}}\right)\right]-\left[1-\frac{1}{2}-\left(-1-\frac{1}{2}\right)\right]-\left[2-2-\left(\frac{1}{2}-1\right)\right]$$

$$=2+\frac{5}{2}\sin^{-1}\left(\frac{2}{\sqrt{5}}\sqrt{1-\frac{1}{5}}+\frac{1}{\sqrt{5}}\sqrt{1-\frac{4}{5}}\right)-\frac{5}{2}$$

$$=\frac{5}{2}\sin^{-1}(1)-\frac{1}{2}=\frac{5\pi}{4}-\frac{1}{2}$$

$$=\left(\frac{5\pi-2}{4}\right)\text{ sq units}$$

D. Required area $=2\int_{0}^{\pi}\sin x\,dx$

$$=2\,[-\cos x]_{0}^{\pi}$$

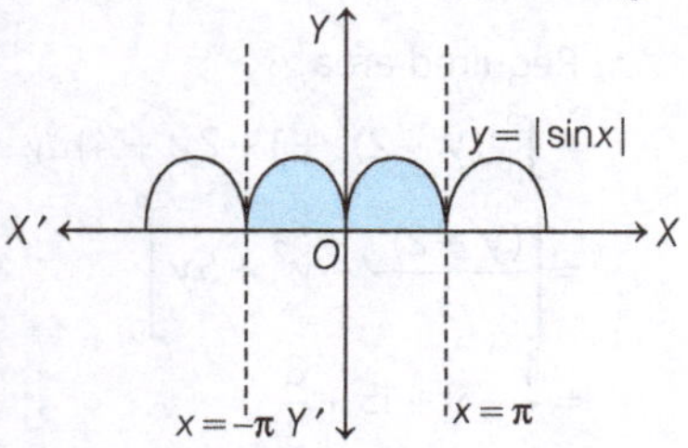

$$=2\,[1+1]=4\text{ sq units}$$

13 (*b*) Area of curve $OAB=2\int_{0}^{a^2}x\,dy$

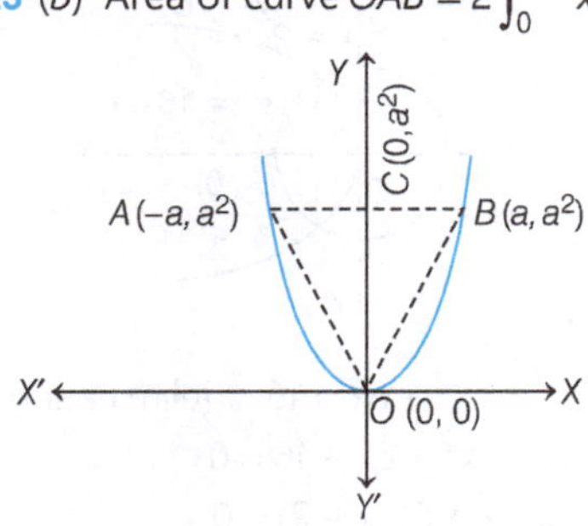

$$=2\int_{0}^{a^2}\sqrt{y}\,dy=2\left[\frac{y^{3/2}}{3/2}\right]_{0}^{a^2}=\frac{4}{3}[a^3]$$

Now, area of $\Delta OAB=\frac{1}{2}\times AB\times OC$

$$=\frac{1}{2}\times 2a\times a^2=a^3$$

$$\therefore\quad\frac{\text{Area of }\Delta AOB}{\text{Area of curve }AOB}=\frac{a^3}{\frac{4}{3}a^3}=\frac{3}{4}$$

14 (*d*) Students are advised to memorise that the area enclosed by $\frac{x^2}{a^2}+\frac{y^2}{b^2}=1$ is πab sq unit. For use in objective question, the solution below is done using this formula. The given equation can be rewritten as

$$\frac{(x-\sqrt{2})^2}{2/\pi}+\frac{y^2}{8/\pi}=1$$

which represents an ellipse.

Here, $a=\sqrt{\frac{2}{\pi}}$ and $b=\sqrt{\frac{8}{\pi}}$

$\therefore$ Area enclosed by an ellipse $=\pi ab$

$$=\pi\sqrt{\frac{2}{\pi}}\sqrt{\frac{8}{\pi}}=4\text{ sq units}$$

15 (*c*) I. Required area

$$=\int_{1}^{2}(e^x-\log_e x)\,dx$$

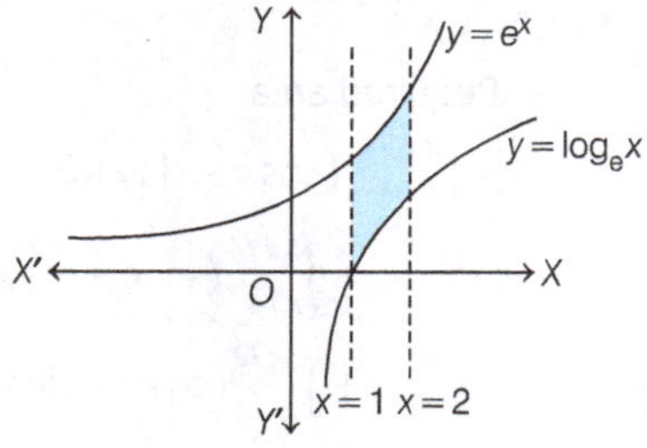

$$[e^x]_1^2-[x\log_e x-\int 1\,dx]_1^2$$

$$=e^2-e-[x\log_e x-x]_1^2$$

$$=e^2-e-[2\log_e 2-2-(0-1)]$$

$$=(e^2-e-2\log_e 2+1)\text{ sq units}$$

II. Required area

= Area of rectangle $(OABC)$ − Area of curve $(OBCO)$

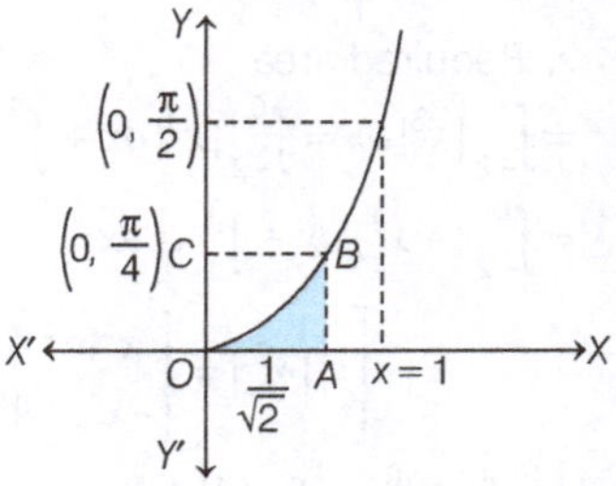

$$=\frac{\pi}{4\sqrt{2}}-\int_{0}^{\pi/4}\sin y\,dy$$

$$=\frac{\pi}{4\sqrt{2}}+[\cos y]_{0}^{\pi/4}$$

$$=\left[\frac{\pi}{4\sqrt{2}}+\left(\frac{1}{\sqrt{2}}-1\right)\right]\text{ sq unit}$$

16 (*d*) Required area,

$$A=\int_{1-e}^{0}\log_e(x+e)\,dx$$

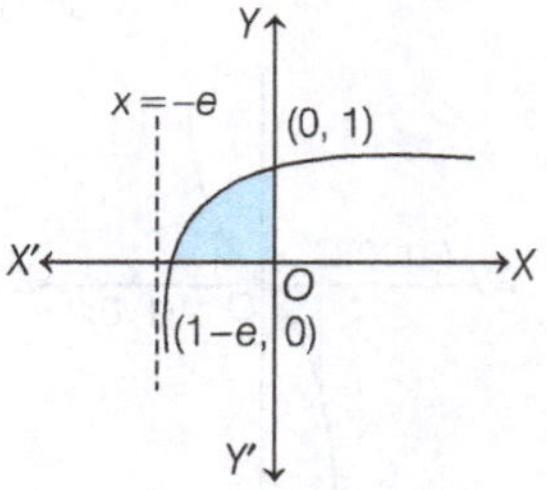

Put $x+e=t\Rightarrow dx=dt$

$$\therefore A=\int_{1}^{e}\log_e t\,dt$$

$$=[t\log_e t-t]_1^e=(e-e-0+1)$$

$$=1\text{ sq unit}$$

17 (*c*) Let area bounded by the curve $y=\sqrt{3x+4}$, X-axis and the lines $x=-1$ and $x=4$ be A and area bounded by the curve $y^2=\sqrt{3x+4}$ i.e. $y=\pm(3x+4)^{1/2}$, X-axis and the lines $x=-1$ and $x=4$ is B.

$\therefore\quad B=2A$

[since, it is the area of both sides about X-axis]

Now, $A:B = A:2A = 1:2$

For subjective (Board) approach first calculate

$$A = \int_{-1}^{4} \sqrt{3x+4}\, dx$$

and then $B = 2\int_{-1}^{4} \sqrt{3x+4}\, dx.$

Thus, show $A : B = 1 : 2$.

18 (*d*) I.

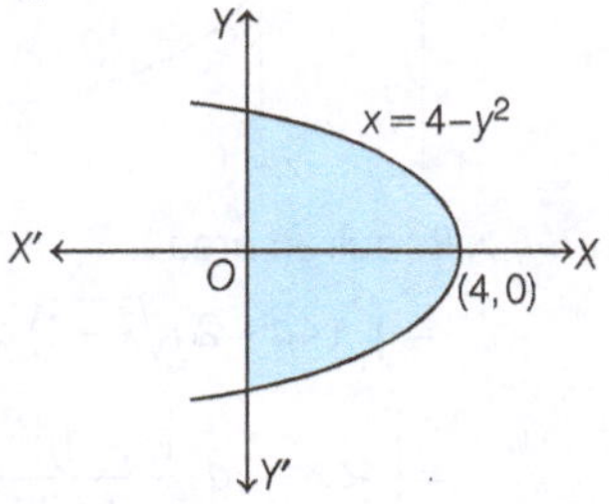

Required area

$$= 2 \times \int_{o}^{4} \sqrt{4-x}\, dx$$

$$= 2\left[-\frac{(4-x)^{3/2}}{3/2}\right]_0^4$$

$$= 2\left[-\frac{2}{3} \times 0 + \frac{2}{3}(4)^{3/2}\right]$$

$$= \frac{32}{3} \text{ sq units}$$

II. When $x = \frac{\pi}{4}$, then $y = \tan\frac{\pi}{4} = 1$

$$\frac{dy}{dx} = \sec^2 x \quad [\because y = \tan x]$$

$$\Rightarrow \left[\frac{dy}{dx}\right]_{x=\pi/4} = 2$$

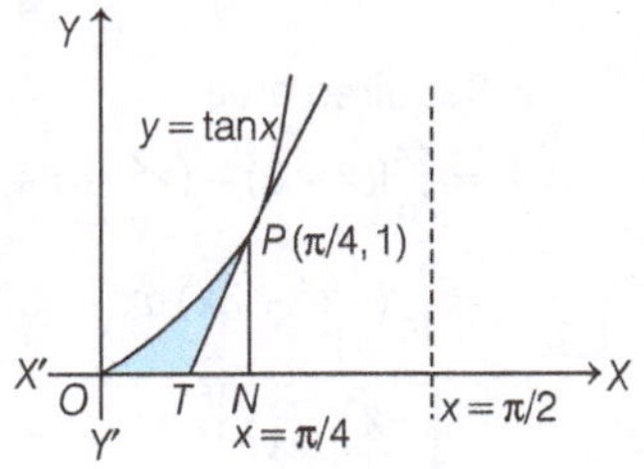

Equation of tangent at $P\left(\frac{\pi}{4}, 1\right)$ is $y - 1 = 2\left(x - \frac{\pi}{4}\right)$

$$\Rightarrow \quad y = 2x + 1 - \frac{\pi}{2}$$

It meets X-axis at $T\left(\frac{\pi-2}{4}, 0\right)$.

$\therefore$ Required area

$$= \int_0^{\pi/4} \tan x\, dx - \frac{1}{2} TN \cdot PN$$

$$= [\log \sec x]_0^{\pi/4} - \frac{1}{2}\cdot\frac{1}{2}\cdot 1$$

$$\left[\because TN = ON - OT = \frac{\pi}{4} - \frac{\pi-2}{4} = \frac{1}{2}\right]$$

$$= \log\sqrt{2} - 0 - \frac{1}{4}$$

$$= \left(\log\sqrt{2} - \frac{1}{4}\right) \text{ sq unit}$$

19 (*c*) Given, area $= \int_0^2 2^{kx}\, dx = \frac{3}{\log 2}$

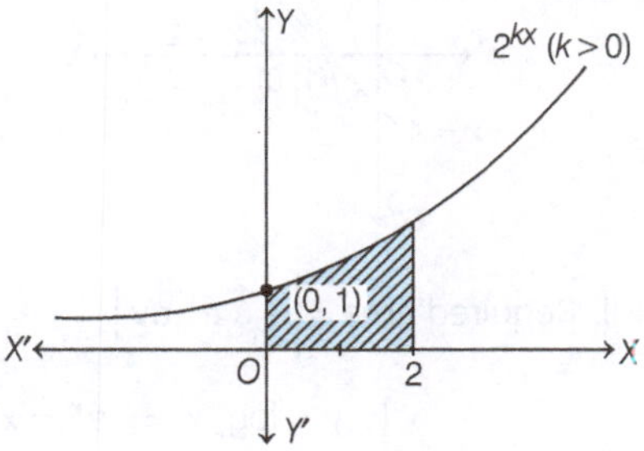

$$\Rightarrow \quad \frac{1}{k}\left[\frac{2^{kx}}{\log_e 2}\right]_0^2 = \frac{3}{\log 2}$$

$$\Rightarrow \quad \frac{1}{k}\left[\frac{2^{2k}}{\log_e 2} - \frac{1}{\log_e 2}\right] = \frac{3}{\log 2}$$

$$\Rightarrow \quad 2^{2k} - 1 = 3k$$

$$\therefore \quad k = 1$$

20 (*b*) Area of curve

$$MNBA = \int_2^4 \left(1 + \frac{8}{x^2}\right) dx$$

$$= \left[x - \frac{8}{x}\right]_2^4 = 4 \qquad \text{...(i)}$$

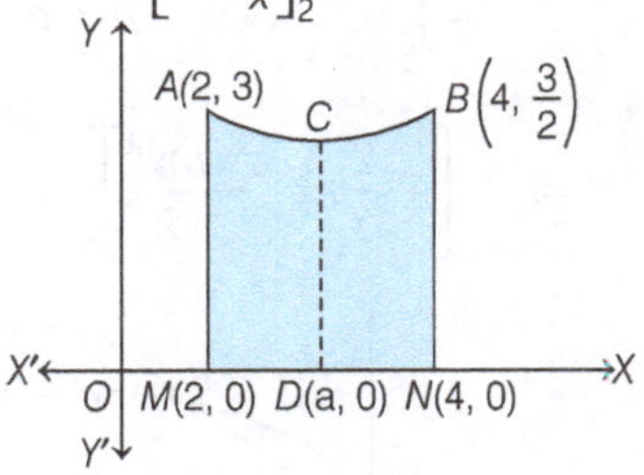

Area of curve

$$ACDM = \int_2^a \left(1 + \frac{8}{x^2}\right) dx$$

$$= \left[x - \frac{8}{x}\right]_2^a$$

$$= a - \frac{8}{a} - [2 - 4]$$

$$= a - \frac{8}{a} + 2 \qquad \text{...(ii)}$$

From Eqs. (i) and (ii), we get

$$a - \frac{8}{a} + 2 = \frac{1}{2}(4)$$

$$\Rightarrow \quad a^2 - 8 = 0$$

$$\Rightarrow \quad a = 2\sqrt{2} \qquad [\because a > 0]$$

21 (*b*)

I. Required area

$$= 2\left[\int_0^4 \sqrt{(25 - x^2)}\, dx - \int_0^2 \frac{4 - x^2}{4} dx - \int_2^4 \frac{x^2 - 4}{4} dx\right]$$

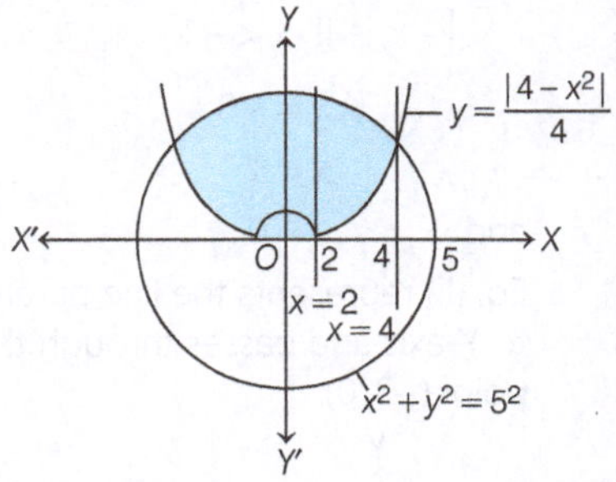

$$= 2\left\{\left[\frac{x}{2}\sqrt{25 - x^2} + \frac{25}{2}\sin^{-1}\left(\frac{x}{5}\right)\right]_0^4 - \frac{1}{4}\left[4x - \frac{x^3}{3}\right]_0^2 - \frac{1}{4}\left[\frac{x^3}{3} - 4x\right]_2^4\right\}$$

$$= 2\left\{\left[2 \times 3 + \frac{25}{2}\sin^{-1}\left(\frac{4}{5}\right)\right] - \frac{1}{4}\left(\frac{64}{3} - 16\right) + \frac{1}{4}\left(\frac{8}{3} - 8\right)\right\}$$

$$= \frac{20}{3} + 25\sin^{-1}\left(\frac{4}{5}\right)$$

II. Required area ($OABO$)

$$= \int_0^9 \sqrt{x}\, dx - \int_3^9 \left(\frac{x-3}{2}\right) dx$$

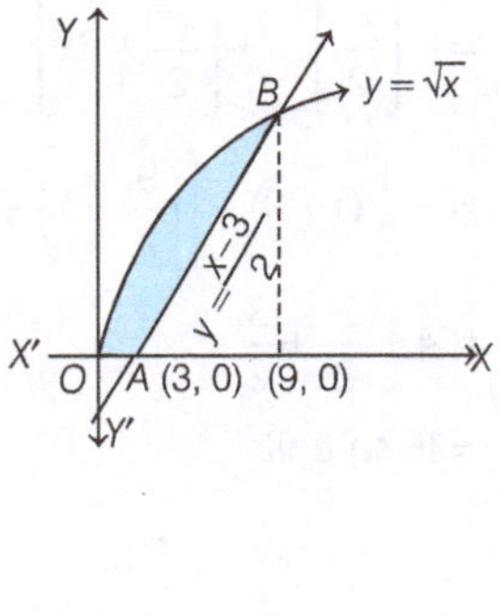

$$=\left(\frac{x^{3/2}}{3/2}\right)_0^9-\frac{1}{2}\left(\frac{x^2}{2}-3x\right)_3^9$$

$$=\left(\frac{2}{3}\cdot 27\right)$$

$$-\frac{1}{2}\left\{\left(\frac{81}{2}-27\right)-\left(\frac{9}{2}-9\right)\right\}$$

$= 9$ sq units

22 (*b*) Given equations of the curves are

$$y=|x+1|+1$$

$$=\begin{cases}(x+1)+1, & \text{if } x+1\geq 0\\ -(x+1)+1, & \text{if } x+1<0\end{cases}$$

$$=\begin{cases}x+2, & \text{if } x\geq -1\\ -x, & \text{if } x<-1\end{cases} \quad \text{...(i)}$$

$$x=-3 \quad \text{...(ii)}$$

$$x=3 \quad \text{...(iii)}$$

and $\quad y=0 \quad$ ...(iv)

Eq. (ii) represents the line parallel to *Y*-axis and passes through the point $(-3, 0)$.

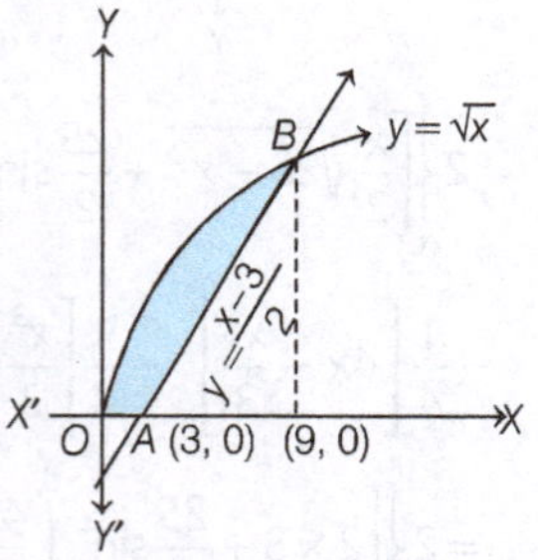

Eq. (iii) represents the line parallel to *Y*-axis and passes through the point $(3, 0)$.

Eq. (iv) represents *X*-axis.

∴ Required area

$$=\int_{-3}^{-1} y\,dx+\int_{-1}^{3} y\,dx$$

$$=\int_{-3}^{-1}(-x)\,dx+\int_{-1}^{3}(x+2)\,dx$$

$$=-\left[\frac{x^2}{2}\right]_{-3}^{-1}+\left[\frac{x^2}{2}+2x\right]_{-1}^{3}$$

$$=-\frac{1}{2}(1-9)+\left[\left(\frac{9}{2}+6\right)-\left(\frac{1}{2}-2\right)\right]$$

$$=4+\frac{21}{2}+\frac{3}{2}$$

$= 16$ sq units

23 (*a*)

I. Required area

$$=\int_1^2 \log x\,dx$$

$$=[x\log x-x]_1^2=2\log 2-1$$

$$=\log 4-\log e=\log\left(\frac{4}{e}\right)$$

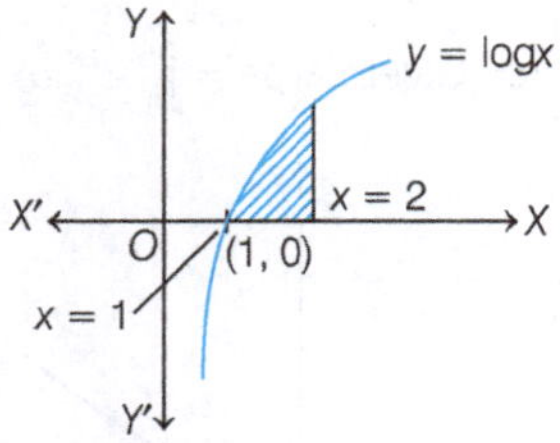

II. Required area $=\left|\int_0^{-\infty} e^y\,dy\right|$

$$[\because y=\log_e x \Rightarrow e^y=x]$$

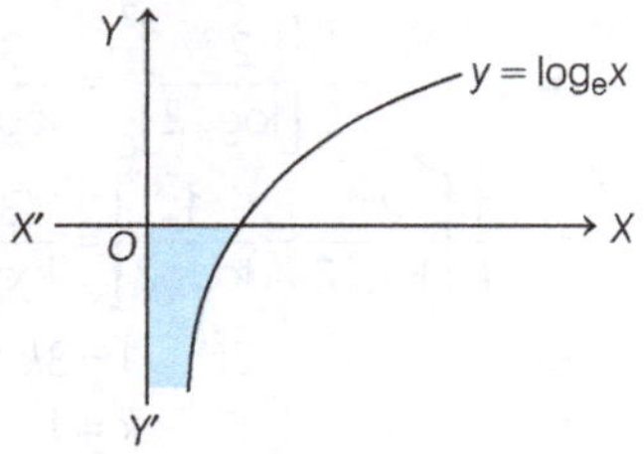

$$=|[e^y]_0^{-\infty}|$$

$= 1$ sq unit

24 (*b*) Area

$$=\int_0^{16/m^2}(\sqrt{16x}-mx)\,dx=\frac{2}{3}$$

$$\Rightarrow \left[4\cdot\frac{2}{3}x^{3/2}-\frac{mx^2}{2}\right]_0^{16/m^2}=\frac{2}{3}$$

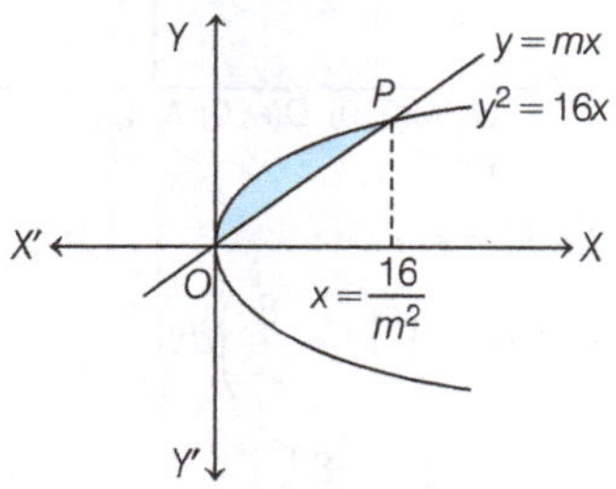

$$\Rightarrow \frac{1}{m^3}\left[\frac{512}{3}-\frac{256}{2}\right]=\frac{2}{3}$$

$$\Rightarrow m^3=\frac{128}{3}\times\frac{3}{2}=64$$

$$\therefore \quad m=4$$

25 (*b*)

I. On solving $y^2=4a^2(x-1)$ and $y=4a$, we get $x=5$

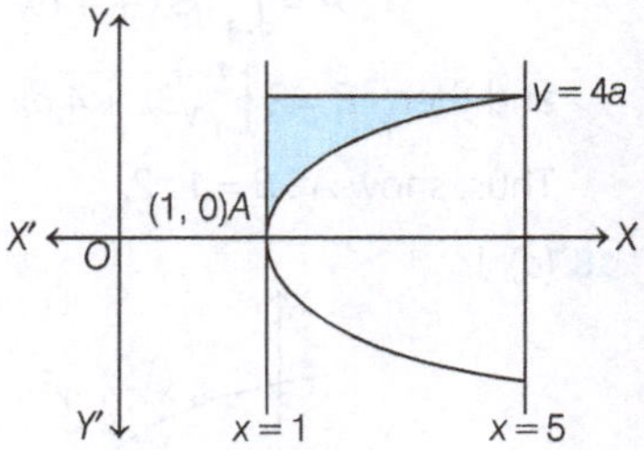

∴ Required area

$$=\int_1^5(4a-2a\sqrt{x-1})\,dx$$

$$=\left[4ax-2a\cdot\frac{(x-1)^{3/2}}{3/2}\right]_1^5$$

$$=\frac{16a}{3} \text{ sq units}$$

II. Given equation of parabola can be rewritten as

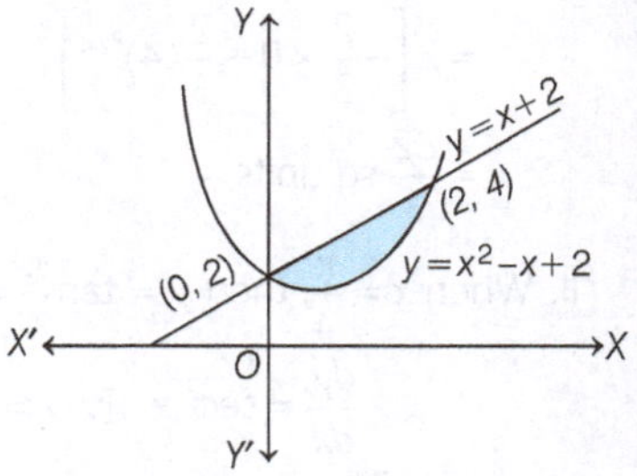

$$\left(x-\frac{1}{2}\right)^2=y-\frac{7}{4}$$

∴ Required area

$$=\int_0^2[(x+2)-(x^2-x+2)]\,dx$$

$$=\int_0^2(-x^2+2x)\,dx$$

$$=\left[\frac{-x^3}{3}+x^2\right]_0^2$$

$$=-\frac{8}{3}+4$$

$$=\frac{4}{3} \text{ sq units}$$

26 (*b*) x_1 and x_2 are the roots of the equation

$$x^2+2x-3=kx+1$$

$$\Rightarrow x^2+(2-k)x-4=0$$

$$x_1+x_2=k-2 \Rightarrow x_1x_2=-4$$

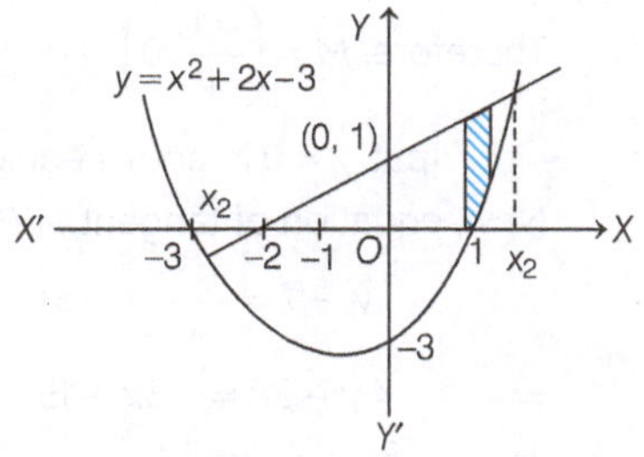

Required area,

$$A=\int_{x_1}^{x_2}[(kx+1)-(x^2+2x-3)]\,dx$$

$$=\left[(k-2)\frac{x^2}{2}-\frac{x^3}{3}+4x\right]_{x_1}^{x_2}$$

$$=\left[(k-2)\frac{x_2^2-x_1^2}{2}-\frac{1}{3}(x_2^3-x_1^3)+4(x_2-x_1)\right]$$

$$=(x_2-x_1)\left[\frac{(k-2)^2}{2}-\frac{1}{3}\{(x_2+x_1)^2-x_1x_2\}+4\right]$$

$$=\sqrt{(x_2+x_1)^2-4x_1x_2}\left[\frac{(k-2)^2}{2}-\frac{1}{3}\{(k-2)^2+4\}+4\right]$$

$$=\sqrt{(k-2)^2+16}\left[\frac{1}{6}(k-2)^2+\frac{8}{3}\right]$$

$$=\frac{[(k-2)^2+16]^{3/2}}{6}$$

$\Rightarrow$ A is minimum, if $k=2$.

Hence, $A_{min}=\dfrac{32}{3}$ sq units

27 (*b*) Given curves are

$$y=\tan x,\ -\frac{\pi}{3}\le x\le\frac{\pi}{3}$$

and $\quad y=\cot x,\ \dfrac{\pi}{6}\le x\le\dfrac{3\pi}{2}$

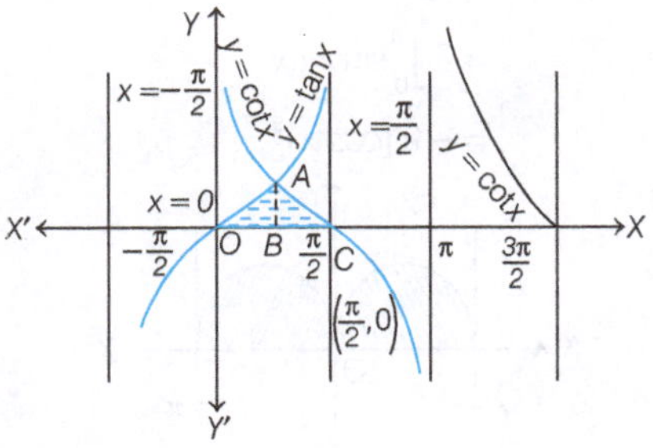

$\therefore$ Required area = Area $(OABO)$ + Area $(BACB)$

$$=\int_0^{\pi/4}\tan x\,dx+\int_{\pi/4}^{\pi/2}\cot x\,dx$$

$$=[\log\sec x]_0^{\pi/4}+[\log\sin x]_{\pi/4}^{\pi/2}$$

$$=\log\sqrt{2}-\log 1+\log 1-\log\frac{1}{\sqrt{2}}$$

$$=\log\sqrt{2}-\log\frac{1}{\sqrt{2}}$$

$$=\log\sqrt{2}-(\log 1-\log\sqrt{2})$$

$$=2\log\sqrt{2}=\log(\sqrt{2})^2$$

$=\log 2$ sq units

28 (*c*) Since,

$$y=|x-1|=\begin{cases}x-1, & x>1\\ -x+1, & x\le 1\end{cases}$$

and $\quad y=3-|x|=\begin{cases}3+x, & x\le 0\\ 3-x, & x>0\end{cases}$

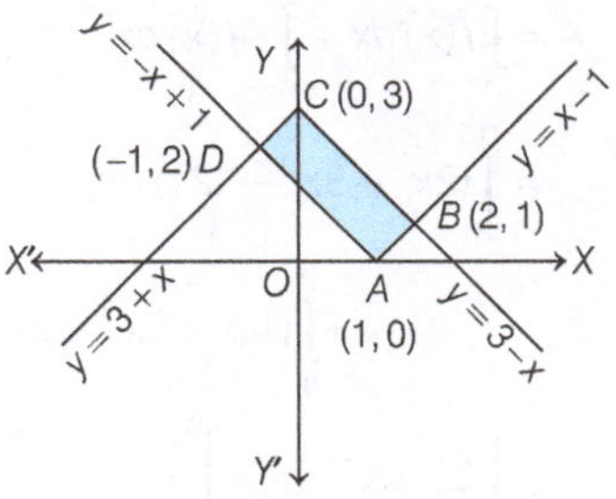

On solving $y=x-1$ and $y=3-x$, we get

$$x-1=3-x$$

$\Rightarrow \quad x=2$

and $\quad y=3-2$

$\Rightarrow \quad y=1$

Now, $\quad AB^2=(2-1)^2+(1-0)^2$

$$=1+1=2$$

$\Rightarrow \quad AB=\sqrt{2}$

and $\quad BC^2=(0-2)^2+(3-1)^2$

$$=4+4=8$$

$\Rightarrow \quad BC=2\sqrt{2}$

Area of rectangle

$$ABCD=AB\times BC$$

$$=\sqrt{2}\times 2\sqrt{2}$$

$=4$ sq units

Note *The above approach is objective approach, for board (school) exams find area using integration.*

Numerical Type Questions

1 (64) $y=\min\{\sin x,\cos x\}$ and $x\in[-\pi,\pi]$

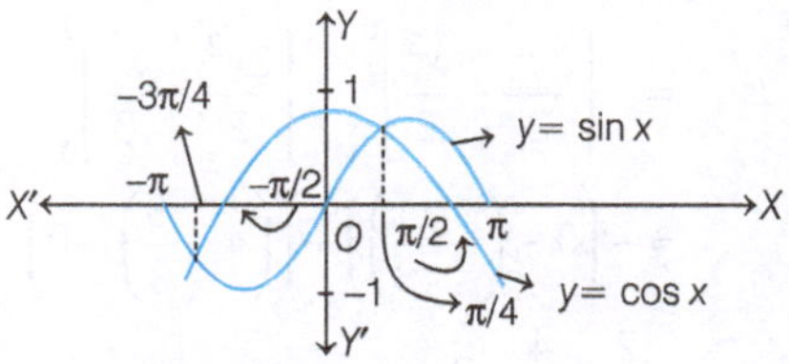

So, $\min\{\sin x,\cos x\}$

$$=\begin{cases}\cos x, & -\pi\le x<-\dfrac{3\pi}{4}\\ \sin x, & -\dfrac{3\pi}{4}<x<\dfrac{\pi}{4}\\ \cos x, & \dfrac{\pi}{4}\le x<\pi\end{cases}$$

Therefore, the region enclosed

$$A=\int_{-\pi}^{-3\pi/4}-\cos x\cdot dx+\int_{-3\pi/4}^{0}-\sin x\cdot dx+\int_0^{\pi/4}\sin x\cdot dx+\int_{\pi/4}^{\pi/2}\cos x\cdot dx+\int_{\pi/2}^{\pi}-\cos x\cdot dx$$

$$=[-\sin x]_{-\pi}^{-\frac{3\pi}{4}}+[\cos x]_{-\frac{3\pi}{4}}^{0}+[-\cos x]_0^{\pi/4}+[\sin x]_{\pi/4}^{\pi/2}+[-\sin x]_{\pi/2}^{\pi}$$

$$=\left(\frac{1}{\sqrt{2}}-1\right)+\left(1+\frac{1}{\sqrt{2}}\right)+\left(-\frac{1}{\sqrt{2}}+1\right)+\left(1-\frac{1}{\sqrt{2}}\right)+(-0+1)$$

$$=-1+1+1+1+1+1=4$$

So, $A^3=64$

2 (30) We have, $y=x|x-2|$

$$=\begin{cases}-x(x-2), & x<2\\ x(x-2), & x\ge 2\end{cases}$$

$$=\begin{cases}2x-x^2, & x<2\\ x^2-2x, & x\ge 2\end{cases}$$

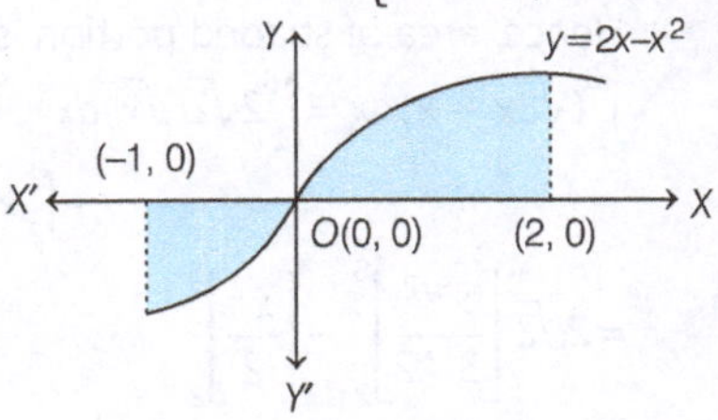

∴ Required area,

$A = \int_{-1}^{0} -(2x - x^2)\,dx + \int_0^2 (2x - x^2)\,dx$

$= -\left[\frac{2x^2}{2} - \frac{x^3}{3}\right]_{-1}^{0} + \left[\frac{2x^2}{2} - \frac{x^3}{3}\right]_0^2$

$= -\left(0 - \left(1 - \frac{1}{3}\right)\right) + \left(\left(4 - \frac{8}{3}\right) - 0\right)$

$= \frac{2}{3} + \frac{4}{3} = 2$

∴ $15A = 15 \times 2 = 30$

3 (4) $y = \begin{cases} x - 2, & \text{if } x > 2 \\ 0 & \text{if } x = 0 \\ 2 - x & \text{if } x < 2 \end{cases}$

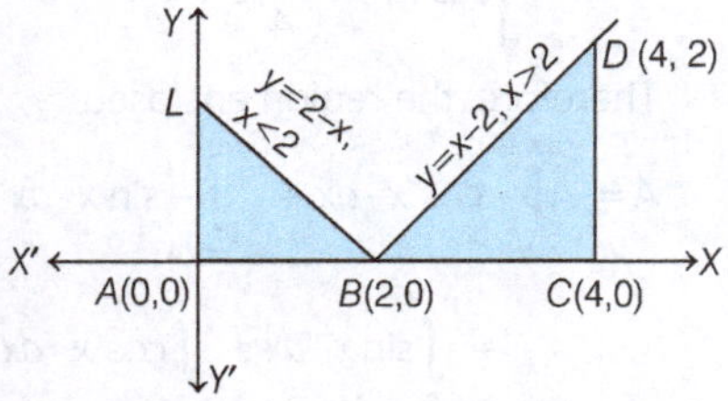

∴ Required area = Area of ΔLAB + Area of ΔBCD

$= \frac{1}{2}[AL \times AB] + \frac{1}{2}[CD \times BC]$

$= \frac{1}{2}[2 \times 2] + \frac{1}{2}[2 \times 2] = 4$ sq. units

4 (44) Given equation of curves are

$y^2 = 8x$ ...(i)

$y = x$ ...(ii)

and $x = 2$ ...(iii)

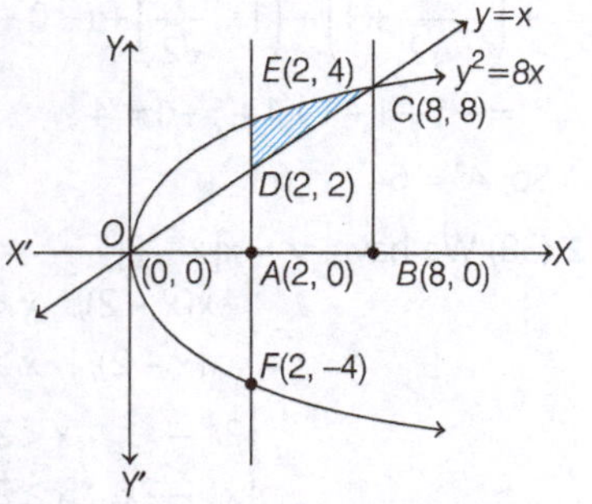

Hence, area of shaded portion is

$\int_2^8 (\sqrt{8x} - x)\,dx = \int_2^8 2\sqrt{2}\sqrt{x}\,dx - \int_2^8 x\,dx$

$= 2\sqrt{2}\left[\frac{x^{3/2}}{3/2}\right]_2^8 - \left[\frac{x^2}{2}\right]_2^8$

$= \frac{4\sqrt{2}}{3}[(8)^{3/2} - (2)^{3/2}] - \frac{1}{2}[(8)^2 - (2)^2]$

$= \frac{22}{3} = \alpha$ [Given]

Hence, $6\alpha = 6 \times \frac{22}{3} = 44$

5 (228) We have,

$f(x) = 2x^3 - 3x^2 - 12x$

∴ $f'(x) = 6x^2 - 6x - 12$

$= 6(x^2 - x - 2)$

$= 6(x + 1)(x - 2)$

$f'(x) = 0 \Rightarrow x = -1$ and 2

∴ $x = -1$ and 2 are critical points

∴ $a = -1$ and $b = 2$

Now, required area,

$A = \int_{-1}^{0} f(x)\,dx + \int_0^2 -f(x)\,dx$

$= \int_{-1}^{0} (2x^3 - 3x^2 - 12x)\,dx + \int_0^2 (12x + 3x^2 - 2x^3)\,dx$

$= \left[\frac{x^4}{2} - x^3 - 6x^2\right]_{-1}^{0} + \left[6x^2 + x^3 - \frac{x^4}{2}\right]_0^2 = \frac{114}{4}$

Hence, $8 \times \frac{114}{4} = 228$

6 (3675) Given, circle

$(x - 2)^2 + (y - 3)^2 = 5^2$

$c = (2, 3)$ $r = 5$

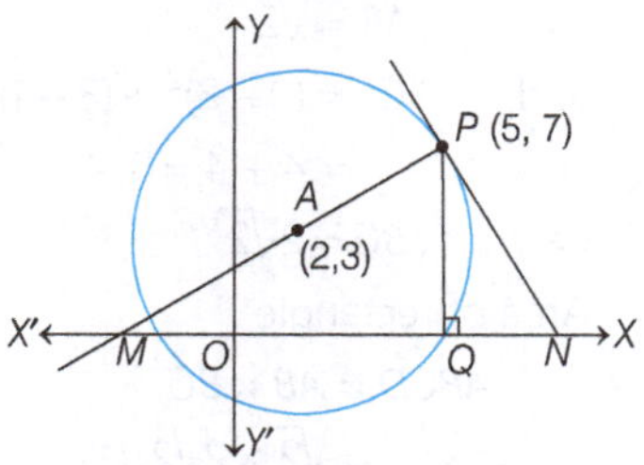

Equation of normal at P (i.e. PA line)

$\Rightarrow (y - 7) = \left(\frac{7 - 3}{5 - 2}\right)(x - 5)$

$\Rightarrow 3y - 21 = 4x - 20$

$\Rightarrow 4x - 3y + 1 = 0$

Therefore, $M = \left(\frac{-1}{4}, 0\right)$

[put $y = 0$ in above equation]

Now, equation of tangent at P,

$y - 7 = \frac{-3}{4}(x - 5)$

$\Rightarrow 4y - 28 = -3x + 15$

$\Rightarrow 3x + 4y = 43$

Therefore, $N = \left(\frac{43}{3}, 0\right)$

∴ Area $(A) = \frac{1}{2} \times MN \times PQ$

$= \frac{1}{2} \times \left(\frac{43}{3} + \frac{1}{4}\right) \times 7 = \frac{1}{2} \times \frac{175}{12} \times 7$

∴ $36A = 36 \times \frac{1}{2} \times \frac{175}{12} \times 7 = 3675$

7 (1) Required area

$= \int_{-1}^{0} y\,dx + \int_0^1 y\,dx$

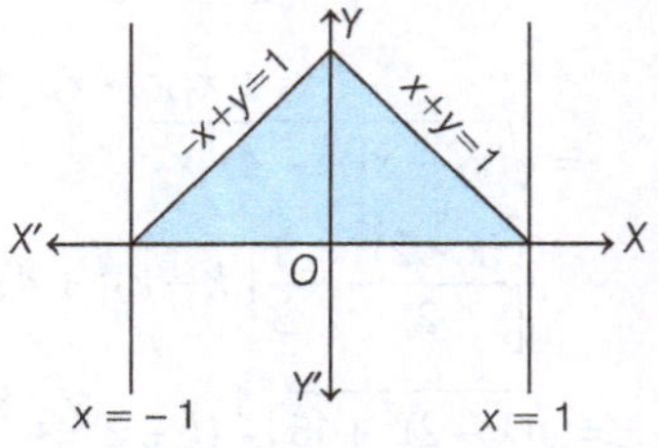

$= \int_{-1}^{0} (x + 1)\,dx + \int_0^1 (1 - x)\,dx$

$= \left[\frac{x^2}{2} + x\right]_{-1}^{0} + \left[x - \frac{x^2}{2}\right]_0^1$

$= \left[0 - \left(\frac{1}{2} - 1\right)\right] + \left[\left(1 - \frac{1}{2}\right) - 0\right]$

$= \frac{1}{2} + \frac{1}{2} = 1$ sq unit

8 (4) Required area

$= \int_{-\pi}^{\pi} |\sin x|\,dx$

$= 2\int_0^{\pi} \sin x\,dx$

$= -2\,[\cos x]_0^{\pi}$

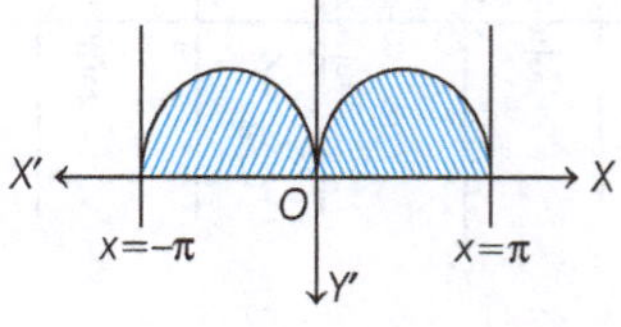

$= -2(\cos \pi - \cos 0)$

$= 4$ sq units

Assertion and Reason Questions

1 (*b*) If the portion of the curve under consideration is below the X-axis, then since $f(x) < 0$ from $x = a$ to $x = b$, as shown in figure, the area bounded by the curve, X-axis and the ordinates $x = a$ and $x = b$ comes out to be negative. But, it is only the numerical value of the area which is taken into consideration. Thus, if the area is negative, we take its absolute value i.e. $\left|\int_a^b f(x)\,dx\right|$.

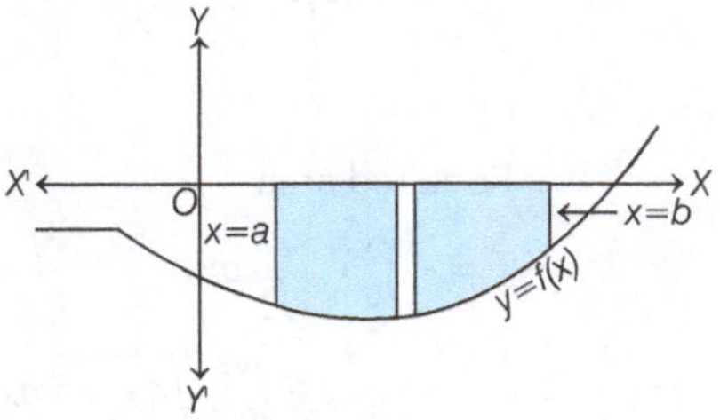

2 (*a*) **Assertion** (A) Given curve, represents an ellipse with centre at (0, 0), is

$$\frac{x^2}{9} + \frac{y^2}{4} = 1 \quad \text{...(i)}$$

and equation of line is

$$\frac{x}{3} + \frac{y}{2} = 1 \quad \text{...(ii)}$$

For the points of intersection of ellipse and line, put the value of x from Eq. (ii) in Eq. (i), we get

$$\left(\frac{y}{2} - 1\right)^2 + \frac{y^2}{4} = 1$$

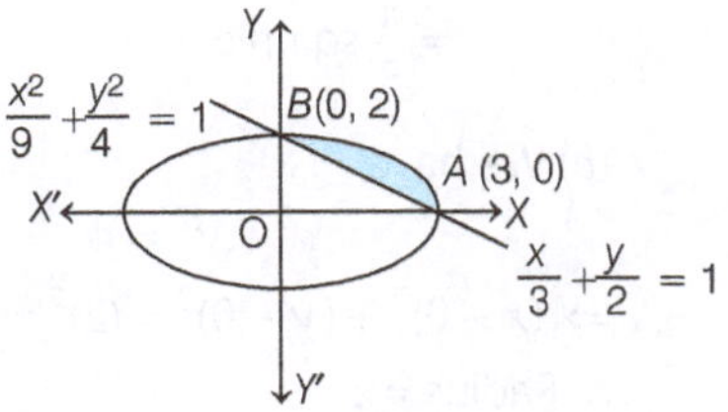

$$\Rightarrow \quad \frac{y^2}{4} + 1 - y + \frac{y^2}{4} = 1$$

$$\Rightarrow \quad y^2 - 2y = 0$$

$$\Rightarrow \quad y = 0, 2$$

When $y = 0$, then $x = 3$ and when $y = 2$, then $x = 0$

Thus, intersection points are $A(3, 0)$ and $B(0, 2)$.

$\therefore$ Required area

= (Area under the curve $\frac{x^2}{9} + \frac{y^2}{4} = 1$ between $x = 0$ and $x = 3$)

− (Area under the line $\frac{x}{3} + \frac{y}{2} = 1$ between $x = 0$ and $x = 3$)

$$= \int_0^3 2\sqrt{1 - \frac{x^2}{9}}\,dx - \int_0^3 2\left(1 - \frac{x}{3}\right)dx$$

$$= \frac{2}{3}\int_0^3 \sqrt{3^2 - x^2}\,dx - \frac{2}{3}\int_0^3 (3 - x)\,dx$$

$$= \frac{2}{3}\left[\frac{x}{2}\sqrt{3^2 - x^2} + \frac{9}{2}\sin^{-1}\frac{x}{3}\right]_0^3 - \frac{2}{3}\left[3x - \frac{x^2}{2}\right]_0^3$$

$$\left[\because \int \sqrt{a^2 - x^2}\,dx = \frac{x}{2}\sqrt{a^2 - x^2} + \frac{a^2}{2}\sin^{-1}\frac{x}{a}\right]$$

$$= \frac{2}{3}\left[0 + \frac{9}{2}\sin^{-1}(1) - 0\right] - \frac{2}{3}\left[9 - \frac{9}{2} - 0\right]$$

$$= 3\left(\frac{\pi}{2}\right) - (3) = 3\left(\frac{\pi}{2} - 1\right)$$

$$= \frac{3}{2}(\pi - 2) \text{ sq units}$$

Reason (R) Given, the curve is

$$\frac{x^2}{a^2} + \frac{y^2}{b^2} = 1 \quad \text{...(i)}$$

and equation of line is

$$\frac{x}{a} + \frac{y}{b} = 1 \quad \text{...(ii)}$$

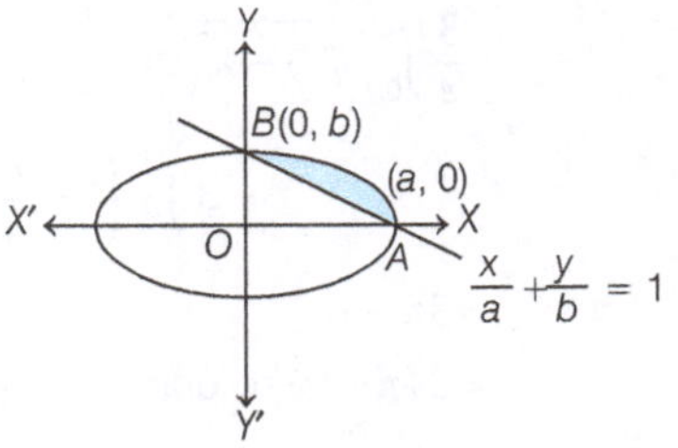

On putting the value of $\frac{x}{a}$ from Eq. (ii) in Eq. (i), we get

$$\left(1 - \frac{y}{b}\right)^2 + \frac{y^2}{b^2} = 1$$

$$\Rightarrow \quad 1 + 2\left(\frac{y^2}{b^2}\right) - \frac{2y}{b} = 1$$

$$\Rightarrow \quad \frac{2y}{b}\left(\frac{y}{b} - 1\right) = 0$$

When $y = 0$ and $y = b$, then $x = a$ and $x = 0$, respectively.

Thus, the intersection points are $A(a, 0)$ and $B(0, b)$.

The required area is shown in the shaded figure. For the ellipse,

$$\frac{y^2}{b^2} = 1 - \frac{x^2}{a^2}$$

$$\Rightarrow \quad |y| = \frac{b}{a}\sqrt{a^2 - x^2}$$

Now, area of $\Delta AOB = \frac{1}{2}|OA| \cdot |OB| = \frac{1}{2}ab$ sq unit

Also, area under the ellipse in the first quadrant

$$= \int_0^a y\,dx = \int_0^a \frac{b}{a}\sqrt{a^2 - x^2}\,dx$$

$$= \frac{b}{a}\left[\frac{x\sqrt{a^2 - x^2}}{2} + \frac{a^2}{2}\sin^{-1}\frac{x}{a}\right]_0^a$$

$$= \frac{b}{2a}[(0 + a^2\sin^{-1}(1)) - (0 + a^2\sin^{-1}(0))]$$

$$= \frac{b}{2a}\left[a^2 \cdot \frac{\pi}{2} - a^2 \cdot 0\right]$$

$$= \frac{\pi ab}{4} \text{ sq unit}$$

$\therefore$ Required area = Area of shaded region = Area of curve $OABO$ − Area of ΔOAB

$$= \frac{\pi ab}{4} - \frac{1}{2}ab = \frac{(\pi - 2)ab}{4}$$

$$= \frac{ab}{4}(\pi - 2) \text{ sq unit}$$

If we put $a = 3$ and $b = 2$ in above area, then area enclosed by $\frac{x^2}{9} + \frac{y^2}{4} = 1$ and $\frac{x}{3} + \frac{y}{2} = 1$ is $\frac{6}{4}(\pi - 2)$ i.e. $\frac{3}{2}(\pi - 2)$ sq units

Both Assertion and Reason are correct and Reason is the correct explanation of Assertion.

3 (*b*) Both Assertion and Reason are correct but Reason (R) is not the correct explanation of Assertion (A).

4 (*a*) Both Assertion (A) and Reason (R) are correct and Reason (R) is the correct explanation of Assertion (A).

5 (*b*) We have, max

$$\{|x-y|, |x+y|\} \le 2$$

$\Rightarrow |x-y| \le 2$ and $|x+y| \le 2$, which form a square of diagonal length 4 units.

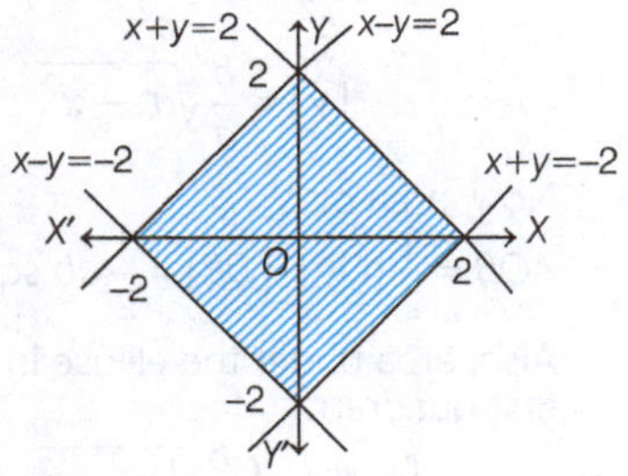

$\therefore$ Area of the region $= \dfrac{1}{2} \times 4 \times 4$

$= 8$ sq units, which is equal to the area of square of side length $2\sqrt{2}$.

6 (*d*) $\because \sin^2 x \le \sin x, \forall x \in (0, \pi)$

Therefore, area of $y = \sin^2 x$ will be lesser from area of $y = \sin x$.

Statement II is obviously true.

Hence, (d) is the correct answer.

7 (*a*) Clearly, $|x| + |y| = 2$ represents a square of $\sqrt{8}$ units and area of square is equal to square of the side length.

Hence, (a) is the correct answer.

8 (*a*) Given curves are

$$y^2 - 2y + 4x + 5 = 0$$

and $\quad x^2 + 2x - y + 2 = 0$

or $\quad (y-1)^2 = -4(x+1)$

and $\quad (x+1)^2 = y - 1$

Shifting origin to $(-1, 1)$, equation of given curves changes to $Y^2 = -4X$ and $X^2 = Y$.

Hence, Assertion and Reason are true, Reason is the correct explanation for Assertion.

Case or Paragraph Type Questions

1 (*a*) Point $(0, 3)$ and $(4, 0)$ pass through both line and ellipse.

2 (*c*)

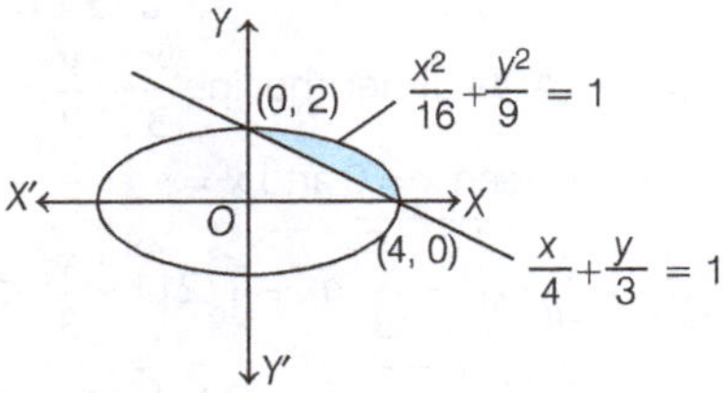

$$\frac{3}{4}\int_0^4 \sqrt{16-x^2}\,dx$$

$$= \frac{3}{4}\int_0^4 \sqrt{4^2-x^2}\,dx$$

$$= \frac{3}{4}\left[\frac{x}{2}\sqrt{16-x^2} + \frac{16}{2}\sin^{-1}\left(\frac{x}{4}\right)\right]_0^4$$

$$= \frac{3}{4}\left[\frac{4}{2}\sqrt{0} + 8\sin^{-1}(1) - 0\right]$$

$$= \frac{3}{4}\left[8 \times \frac{\pi}{2}\right]$$

$$= 3\pi$$

3 (*a*) $3\displaystyle\int_0^4 \left(1 - \frac{x}{4}\right)dx$

$$= 3\left[x - \frac{x^2}{8}\right]_0^4$$

$$= 3\left[4 - \frac{16}{8} - 0\right]$$

$$= 3[4-2] = 6$$

4 (*d*) Area of smaller region bounded by the mirror and scratch

$$= \frac{3}{4}\int_0^4 \sqrt{16-x^2}\,dx - 3\int_0^4\left(1-\frac{x}{4}\right)dx$$

$$= 3\pi - 6$$

$$= 3(\pi - 2) \text{ sq units}$$

5 (*a*) We have,

$$x^2 + y^2 = 4 \quad \text{...(i)}$$

and $\quad x = \sqrt{3}y \quad$ ...(ii)

From Eqs. (i) and (ii), we get

$$3y^2 + y^2 = 4 \Rightarrow 4y^2 = 4$$

$$\Rightarrow \quad y^2 = 1 \Rightarrow y = \pm 1$$

From Eq. (ii), $x = \sqrt{3}, -\sqrt{3}$

$\therefore$ Point of intersection of pizza and edge of knife are $(\sqrt{3}, 1), (-\sqrt{3}, -1)$.

6 (*b*)

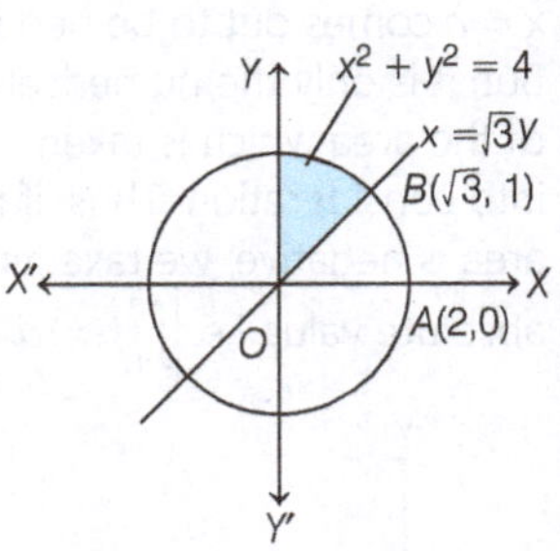

$\therefore$ Required area

$$= -\int_0^{\sqrt{3}} \frac{x}{\sqrt{3}}\,dx + \int_0^{\sqrt{3}} \sqrt{4-x^2}\,dx$$

$$= -\frac{1}{\sqrt{3}}\left[\frac{x^2}{2}\right]_0^{\sqrt{3}} + \left[\frac{x}{2}\sqrt{4-x^2} + \frac{4}{2}\sin^{-1}\left(\frac{x}{2}\right)\right]_{\sqrt{3}}^2$$

$$= \frac{1}{\sqrt{3}}\left[\frac{3}{2} - 0\right] + \left[2\sin^{-1}(1) - \left(\frac{\sqrt{3}}{2} + 2\sin^{-1}\left(\frac{\sqrt{3}}{2}\right)\right)\right]$$

$$= \frac{\sqrt{3}}{2} + \frac{2\pi}{2} - \frac{\sqrt{3}}{2} - \frac{2\pi}{3}$$

$$= \frac{\pi}{3} \text{ sq units}$$

7 (*b*) We have,

$$x^2 + y^2 = 4$$

$$\Rightarrow (x-0)^2 + (y-0)^2 = (2)^2$$

$\therefore$ Radius $= 2$

Area of $\dfrac{1}{4}$th slice of pizza

$$= \frac{1}{4}\pi(2)^2 = \pi \text{ sq units}$$

8 (*a*) Area of whole pizza $= \pi(2)^2$

$$= 4\pi \text{ sq. units.}$$

Past Years Questions

1 (*b*) $y^2 \le 2x, y \ge 4x - 1$

Point of intersection

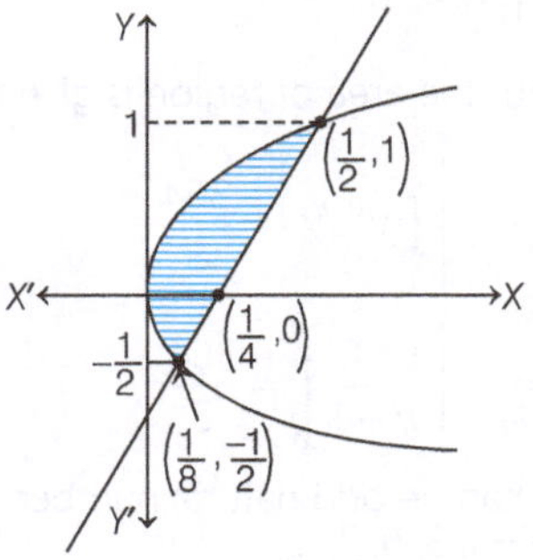

$$y^2 = 2x \text{ and } y = 4x - 1$$

$$y = 2y^2 - 1$$

$\Rightarrow \quad 2y^2 - y - 1 = 0$

$\Rightarrow \quad 2y^2 - 2y + y - 1 = 0$

$\Rightarrow \quad 2y(y-1) + 1(y-1) = 0$

$\Rightarrow \quad (y-1)(2y+1) = 0$

$\Rightarrow \quad y = 1, -\frac{1}{2} \Rightarrow x = \frac{1}{2}, \frac{1}{8}$

$\therefore$ Point of intersection

$$\left(\frac{1}{2},1\right), \left(\frac{1}{8}, -\frac{1}{2}\right)$$

$\therefore$ Required area

$$= \int_{-1/2}^{1} (x_1 - x_2)\, dy$$

$$= \int_{-1/2}^{1} \left(\frac{y+1}{4}\right) - \left(\frac{y^2}{2}\right) dy$$

$$= \left[\frac{(y+1)^2}{8} - \frac{y^3}{6}\right]_{-1/2}^{1}$$

$$= \left(\frac{4}{8} - \frac{1}{6}\right) - \left(\frac{1}{32} + \frac{1}{48}\right)$$

$$= \left(\frac{2}{6}\right) - \left(\frac{5}{96}\right)$$

$$= \frac{32-5}{96} = \frac{27}{96} = \frac{9}{32}$$

2 (*a*) Equation of ellipse : $\frac{x^2}{18} + \frac{y^2}{6} = 1$

Line : $y = x$

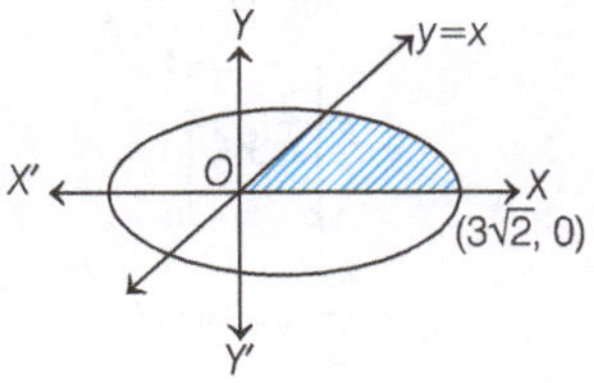

Since, $y = x$, we have

$$\frac{x^2}{18} + \frac{x^2}{6} = 1 \Rightarrow \frac{4x^2}{18} = 1$$

$$x = \frac{3}{\sqrt{2}} = y$$

$\therefore$ Required area

$$= \frac{1}{2} \times \frac{3}{\sqrt{2}} \times \frac{3}{\sqrt{2}} + \int_{3/\sqrt{2}}^{3\sqrt{2}} \frac{\sqrt{18 - x^2}}{\sqrt{3}} dx$$

$$= \frac{9}{4} + \frac{1}{\sqrt{3}} \left(\frac{x\sqrt{18-x^2}}{2} + \frac{18}{2} \sin^{-1} \frac{x}{3\sqrt{2}} \right)_{3/\sqrt{2}}^{3\sqrt{2}}$$

$$= \frac{9}{4} + \frac{1}{\sqrt{3}} \left[\left(0 + \frac{18}{2} \sin^{-1} \frac{3\sqrt{2}}{3\sqrt{2}}\right) - \frac{\frac{3}{\sqrt{2}} \cdot \frac{3\sqrt{3}}{\sqrt{2}}}{2} - \frac{18}{2} \sin^{-1} \frac{\frac{3}{\sqrt{2}}}{3\sqrt{2}} \right]$$

$$= \frac{9}{4} + \frac{1}{\sqrt{3}} \left(9 \times \frac{\pi}{2} - \frac{9\sqrt{3}}{4} - 9 \times \frac{\pi}{6} \right)$$

$$= \frac{9}{4} + \frac{1}{\sqrt{3}} \left(\frac{9\pi}{2} - \frac{3\pi}{2} - \frac{9\sqrt{3}}{4} \right)$$

$$= \frac{9}{4} + \frac{1}{\sqrt{3}} \times 3\pi - \frac{9}{4} = \sqrt{3}\pi$$

3 (*a*) $x^2 + y^2 = 8$

$\Rightarrow x^2 + y^2 = (2\sqrt{2})^2$ and $y^2 = 2x$

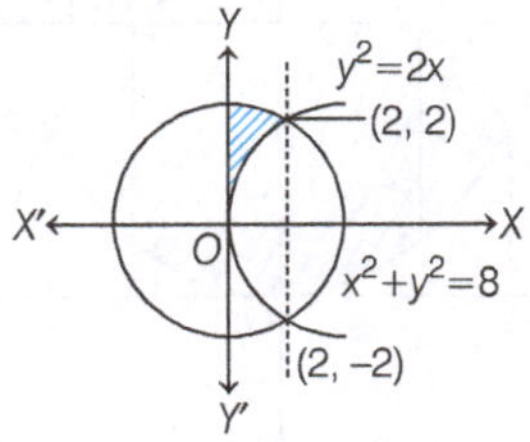

$\therefore$ Required area

$$= \int_0^2 \sqrt{8 - x^2} \cdot dx - \int_0^2 \sqrt{2x} \cdot dx$$

$$= \left[\frac{x}{2}\sqrt{8 - x^2} + \frac{8}{2} \sin^{-1}\left(\frac{x}{2\sqrt{2}}\right)\right]_0^2 - \left[\frac{2\sqrt{2}}{3}(x\sqrt{x})\right]_0^2$$

$$= \left[2 + 4 \sin^{-1}\left(\frac{1}{\sqrt{2}}\right) - 0\right] - \frac{8}{3}$$

$$= 2 + 4 \cdot \frac{\pi}{4} - \frac{8}{3} = \pi - \frac{2}{3}$$

4 (*d*) Given, $\frac{a}{x^2} \le y \le \frac{1}{x}$,

$$1 \le x \le 2 \text{ and } 0 < a < 1$$

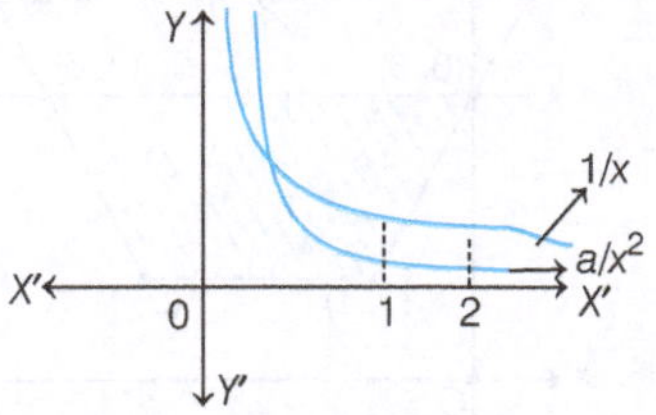

According to the question,

$$\int_1^2 \left(\frac{1}{x} - \frac{a}{x^2}\right) dx = \log_e 2 - \frac{1}{7}$$

$\Rightarrow \quad \left[\ln|x| + \frac{a}{x}\right]_1^2 = \ln 2 - \frac{1}{7}$

$\Rightarrow \ln 2 - \ln 1 + \frac{a}{2} - a = \ln 2 - \frac{1}{7}$

$\Rightarrow \quad -\frac{a}{2} = -\frac{1}{7} \Rightarrow a = \frac{2}{7}$

$\therefore$ The value of $7a - 3 = 7 \times \frac{2}{7} - 3$

$$= 2 - 3 = -1$$

5 (*d*) Given, curves are $4x^2 = y$ and $y = 4$

Now, to find intersection points of the given curve by putting $y = 4$ in the first curve.

$$4x^2 = y$$

$\Rightarrow \quad 4x^2 = 4 \Rightarrow x^2 = 1$

$\therefore \quad x = \pm 1$

Thus, the required area

$$= \int_{-1}^{1} (4 - 4x^2) dx$$

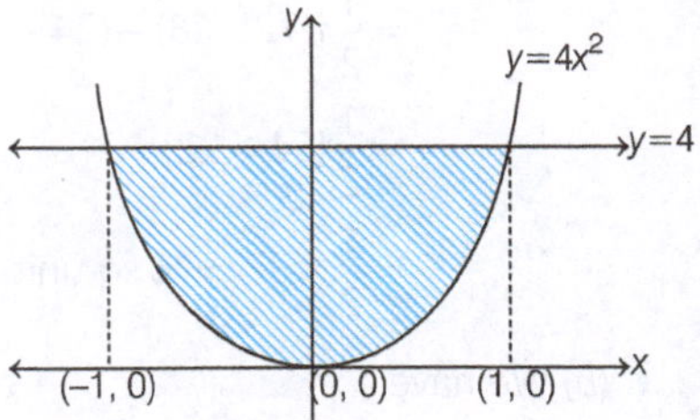

$$= \left(4x - \frac{4x^3}{3}\right)_{-1}^{1}$$

$$= \left(4 - \frac{4}{3}\right) - \left(-4 + \frac{4}{3}\right)$$

$$= 8 - \frac{8}{3} = \frac{16}{3} \text{ sq. unit}$$

6 (*a*) Given equation of curves are
$y = |x-1| + |x-2|$ and $y = 3$

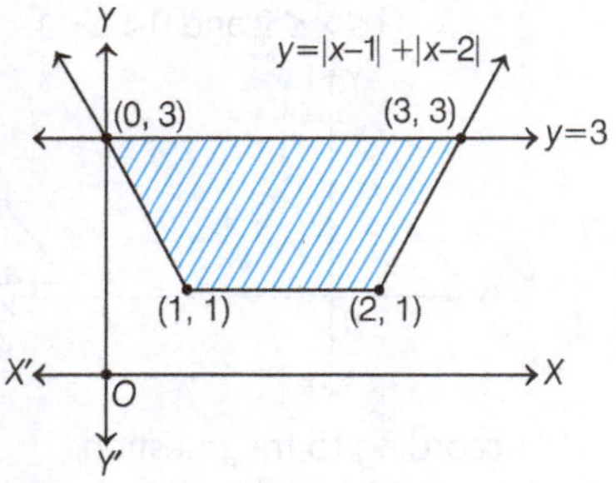

Now, the required area
= Area of trapezium
$= \frac{1}{2}(1+3) \times 2 = 4$

7 (*d*) We have,
$x + 2y = 12$, $x = 2$, $x = 6$, X-axis

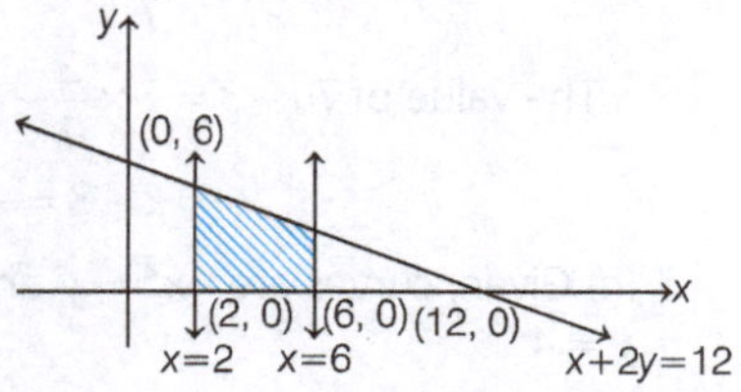

∴ Required area

$$= \int_2^6 y_{\text{line}}\, dx$$

$$= \int_2^6 \left(\frac{12-x}{2}\right) dx$$

$$= \frac{1}{2}\left[12x - \frac{x^2}{2}\right]_2^6$$

$$= \frac{1}{2}[(72-18)-(24-2)]$$

$$= \frac{1}{2}[54-22]$$

$$= \frac{1}{2} \times 32 = 16 \text{ sq unit}$$

8 (*b*) We have,
$x^2 + (y-2)^2 \le 2^2$ and $x^2 \ge 2y$
Solving the given equation of parabola and circle, we get
$2y + (y-2)^2 = 4 \Rightarrow y = 0$ or 2
If $y = 0$, then $x = 0$ and
If $y = 2$, then $x = \pm 2$
The intersecting point of circle and parabola are $(0,0), (-2,2), (2,2)$.

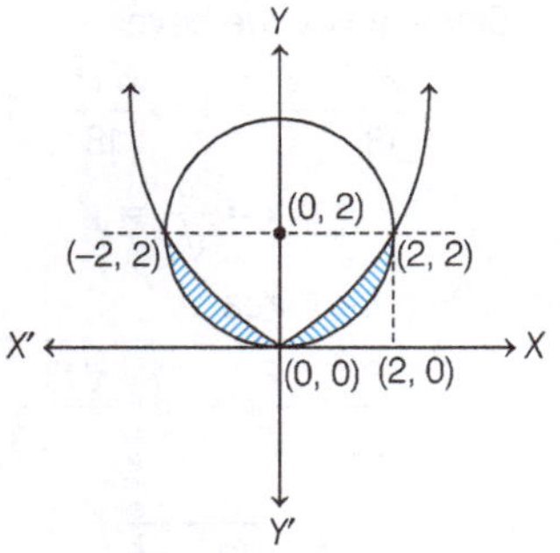

Area of the shaded region

$$= 2\int_0^2 \left|\left[\frac{x^2}{2} - (\sqrt{4-x^2} + 2)\right]\right| dx$$

$$= 2\left|\left[\frac{x^3}{6} - \frac{x}{2}\sqrt{4-x^2} - 2\sin^{-1}\left(\frac{x}{2}\right) - 2x\right]_0^2\right|$$

$$= 2\left|\left[\frac{8}{6} - 2 \times \frac{\pi}{2} - 4\right]\right|$$

$$= 2\left|\left[\frac{4}{3} - \pi - 4\right]\right|$$

$$= 2\pi + \frac{16}{3} \text{ sq units}$$

9 (*b*) Given region is,

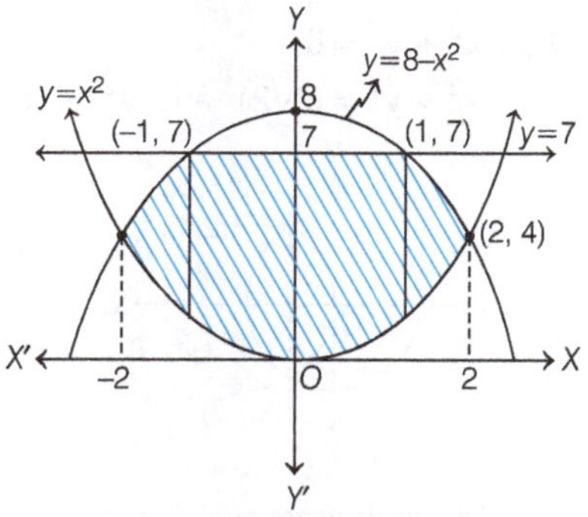

∴ Required area

$$= 2\int_0^1 (7 - x^2)\, dx + 2\int_1^2 (8 - x^2 - x^2)\, dx$$

$$= 2\left[7x - \frac{x^3}{3}\right]_0^1 + 2\left[8x - \frac{2x^3}{3}\right]_1^2$$

$$= 2\left(\frac{20}{3}\right) + 2\left(\frac{10}{3}\right)$$

$$\Rightarrow \frac{40}{3} + \frac{20}{3} = \frac{60}{3} = 20$$

10 (*b*) Area bounded by the curve
$x = y^a$, $x = 0$, $y = 1$, $y = 3$ is
$\left|\int_1^3 y^a dy\right|$.

But the area of region is given $\frac{364}{3}$

$$\Rightarrow \left|\int_1^3 y^a dy\right| = \frac{364}{3}$$

$$\Rightarrow \left[\frac{y^{a+1}}{a+1}\right]_1^3 = \frac{364}{3}$$

a can be odd natural number when $a = 1, 3, 5, 7, \ldots$
By hit and trial method,

$$\frac{3^{5+1}-1}{5+1} = \frac{3^6-1}{6} = \frac{729-1}{6}$$

$$= \frac{728}{6} = \frac{364}{3}$$

Hence, $a = 5$

11 (*c*) Since, the locus of the centre $(\alpha, \beta), \beta > 0$ of the circle which touches the circle $x^2 + (y-1)^2 = 1$ externally and also touches the X-axis be L.
Thus, $\alpha^2 + (\beta - 1)^2 = (|\beta| + 1)^2$
$\Rightarrow \alpha^2 + \beta^2 - 2\beta + 1 = \beta^2 + 1 + 2|\beta|$
$\Rightarrow \qquad \alpha^2 = 4\beta$ as $\beta > 0$
Thus, the locus L is

$$x^2 = 4y, y > 0$$

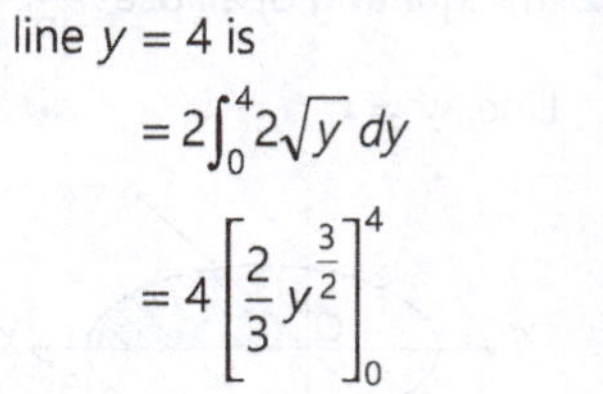

Hence, the area bounded by L and the line $y = 4$ is

$$= 2\int_0^4 2\sqrt{y}\, dy$$

$$= 4\left[\frac{2}{3}y^{\frac{3}{2}}\right]_0^4$$

$$= \frac{64}{3} \text{ sq units}$$

12 (9) $y = \min\{\sin x, \cos x\}$
and $x \in [-\pi, \pi]$

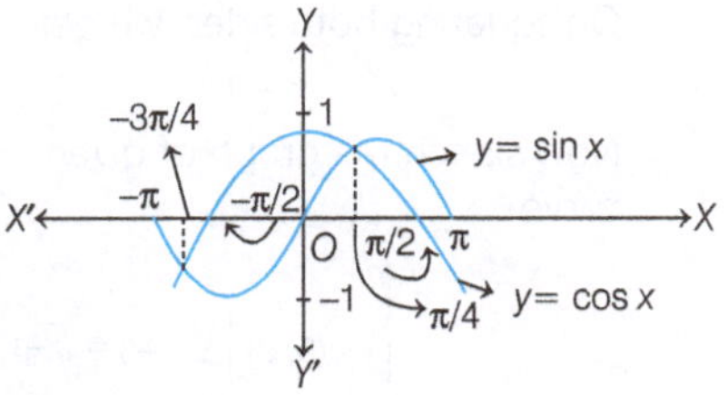

So, $\min\{\sin x, \cos x\}$

$$= \begin{cases} \cos x, & -\pi \le x < -\dfrac{3\pi}{4} \\ \sin x, & -\dfrac{3\pi}{4} < x < \dfrac{\pi}{4} \\ \cos x, & \dfrac{\pi}{4} < x < \pi \end{cases}$$

Therefore, the region enclosed

$$A = \int_{-\pi}^{-3\pi/4} -\cos x \cdot dx + \int_{-3\pi/4}^{0} -\sin x \cdot dx + \int_{0}^{\pi/4} \sin x \cdot dx + \int_{\pi/4}^{\pi/2} \cos x \cdot dx + \int_{\pi/2}^{\pi} -\cos x \cdot dx$$

$$= [-\sin x]_{-\pi}^{-\frac{3\pi}{4}} + [\cos x]_{-\frac{3\pi}{4}}^{0} + [-\cos x]_0^{\pi/4} + [\sin x]_{\pi/4}^{\pi/2} + [-\sin x]_{\pi/2}^{\pi}$$

$$= \left(\frac{1}{\sqrt{2}} - 1\right) + \left(1 + \frac{1}{\sqrt{2}}\right) + \left(-\frac{1}{\sqrt{2}} + 1\right) + \left(1 - \frac{1}{\sqrt{2}}\right) + (-0 + 1)$$

$$= -1 + 1 + 1 + 1 + 1 = 3$$

So, $A^2 = 9$

13 (171) Given, equation of circle,

$$x^2 + y^2 = 169$$

Centre $= (0, 0)$ and Radius $= 13$

$\therefore$ Intersecting point of circle and line is $(5, 12)$

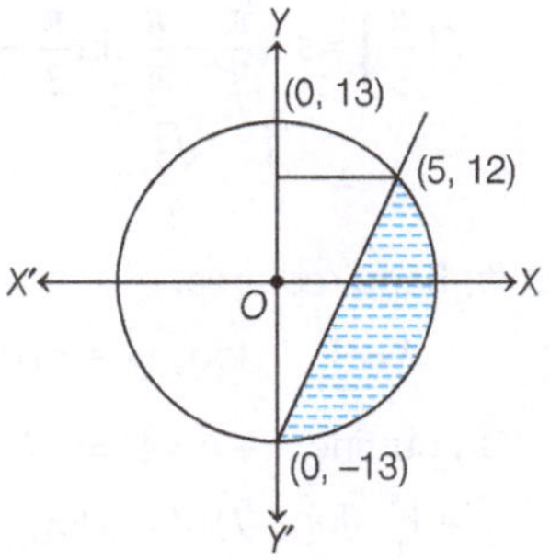

$\therefore$ Required area

$$= \frac{\pi(13)^2}{2} - \left[\frac{1}{2} \times 25 \times 5 + \int_{12}^{13} \sqrt{(169 - y^2)}\, dy\right]$$

$$= \frac{169\pi}{2} - \left[\frac{125}{2} + \left\{\frac{y}{2}\sqrt{169 - y^2} + \frac{169}{2}\sin^{-1}\left(\frac{y}{13}\right)\right\}_{12}^{13}\right]$$

$$= \frac{169\pi}{2} - \frac{125}{2} - \left[\frac{169}{2} \times \frac{\pi}{2} - 6 \times 5 - \frac{169}{2}\sin^{-1}\frac{12}{13}\right]$$

$$= \frac{169\pi}{4} - \frac{65}{2} + \frac{169}{2}\sin^{-1}\frac{12}{13}$$

$\therefore \quad \alpha = 169, \beta = 2$

$\therefore \alpha + \beta = 171$

14 (62) We have,

$$y = x|x - 3|$$

$$= \begin{cases} -x(x-3), & x < 3 \\ x(x-3), & x \ge 3 \end{cases}$$

$$= \begin{cases} 3x - x^2, & x < 3 \\ x^2 - 3x, & x \ge 3 \end{cases}$$

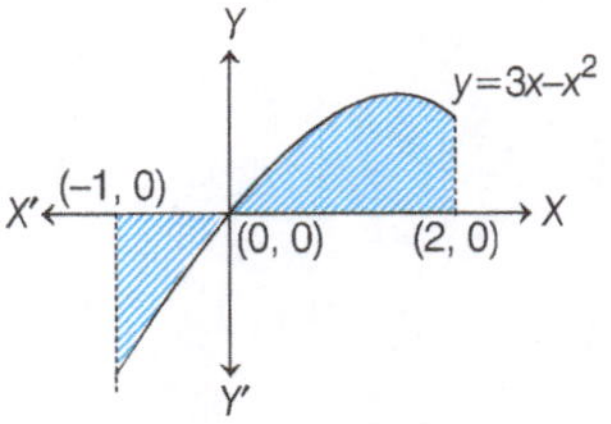

$\therefore$ Required area,

$$A = \int_{-1}^{0} -(3x - x^2)dx + \int_0^2 (3x - x^2)\, dx$$

$$= -\left[\frac{3x^2}{2} - \frac{x^3}{3}\right]_{-1}^{0} + \left[\frac{3x^2}{2} - \frac{x^3}{3}\right]_0^2$$

$$= -\left[0 - \left(\frac{3}{2} + \frac{1}{3}\right)\right] + \left[\left(6 - \frac{8}{3}\right) - 0\right]$$

$$= \frac{3}{2} + \frac{1}{3} + 6 - \frac{8}{3}$$

$$= \frac{9 + 2 + 36 - 16}{6}$$

$$= \frac{31}{6}$$

$$\therefore 12A = 12 \times \frac{31}{6} = 62$$

15 (18) Given that,

Equation of the parabola $y^2 = 2x$ and equation of the line $x + y = 4$

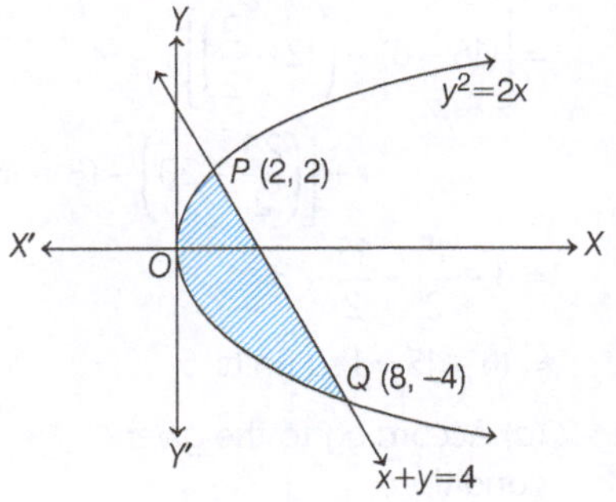

Now solving above two equations $y^2 = 2x$ and $x + y = 4$ to get intersecting points $P(2, 2)$ and $Q(8, -4)$.

Thus, the required area is

$$= \int_{-4}^{2} \left((4 - y) - \frac{y^2}{2}\right) dy$$

$$= \left[4y - \frac{y^2}{2} - \frac{y^3}{6}\right]_{-4}^{2}$$

$$= \left(8 - 2 - \frac{4}{3}\right) - \left(-16 - 8 + \frac{32}{3}\right)$$

$$= 18$$

Skill Boosters

1 (*a*)

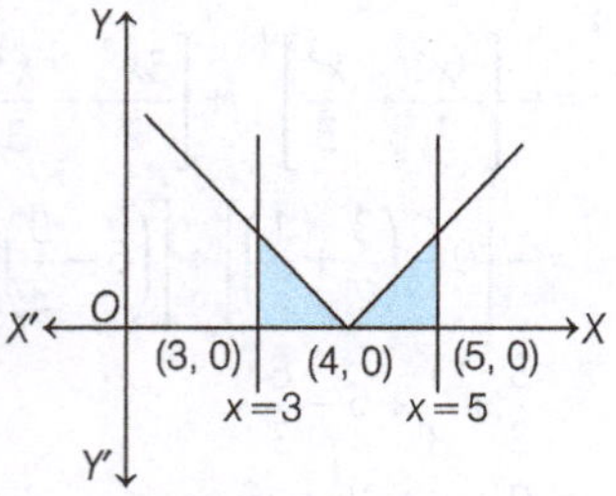

$\therefore$ Required area

$= \int_3^5 |x-4|\,dx$

$= \int_3^4 -(x-4)\,dx + \int_4^5 (x-4)\,dx$

$= \int_3^4 (4-x)\,dx + \int_4^5 (x-4)\,dx$

$= \left[4x - \frac{x^2}{2}\right]_3^4 + \left[\frac{x^2}{2} - 4x\right]_4^5$

$= \left[(16-8) - \left(12 - \frac{9}{2}\right)\right] + \left[\left(\frac{25}{2} - 20\right) - (8-16)\right]$

$= 8 - \frac{15}{2} - \frac{15}{2} + 8$

$= 16 - 15 = 1$ sq units

2 (*a*) According to the given condition,

$\int_{\pi/4}^{\beta} f(x)\,dx = \beta\sin\beta + \frac{\pi}{4}$
$\cos\beta + \sqrt{2}\beta$

On differentiating both sides, w.r.t. β, we get

$f(\beta) = \sin\beta - \frac{\pi}{4}\sin\beta + \sqrt{2}$

$\therefore f\left(\frac{\pi}{3}\right) = \sin\frac{\pi}{3} - \frac{\pi}{4}\sin\frac{\pi}{3} + \sqrt{2}$

$= \frac{\sqrt{3}}{2} - \frac{\sqrt{3}}{8}\pi + \sqrt{2}$

3 (*b*) Required area,

$A = \int_{1-e}^{0} \log_e (x+e)\,dx$

On putting $x + e = t \Rightarrow dx = dt$

$\therefore A \int_1^e (\log_e (t)\,dt = [t\log_e t - t]_1^e$

$= e - e - 0 + 1 = 1$ sq unit

4 (*b*) The intersecting points of the given curves are obtained by solving the equations $x - y = 4$ and $y^2 = 2x$ for x and y,

we have, $y^2 = 2(4+y)$

$\Rightarrow \quad y^2 = 8 + 2y$

$\Rightarrow \quad (y-4)(y+2) = 0$

which gives $y = 4, -2$ and $x = 8, 2$

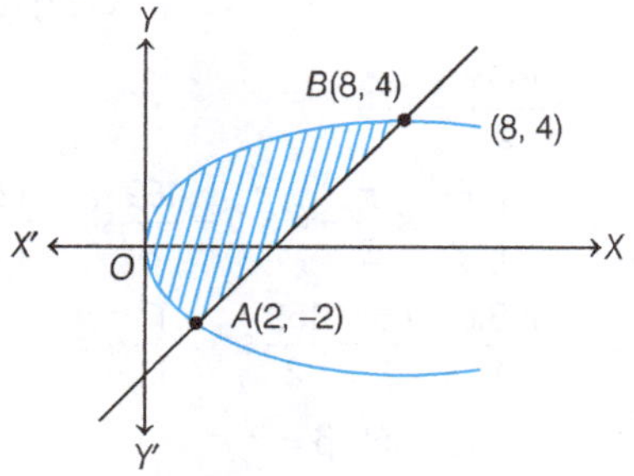

Thus, the points of intersection are (8, 4) and (2, – 2)

$\therefore$ Area $= \int_{-2}^{4} \left(4 + y - \frac{1}{2}y^2\right) dy$

$= \left| 4y + \frac{y^2}{2} - \frac{1}{2}y^3 \right|_{-2}^{4}$

= 18 sq units

5 (*c*) We have

Equation of the curve $y = \sqrt{x-1}$

On squaring both sides, we get

$y^2 = x - 1$

Now sketch the graph of given curve

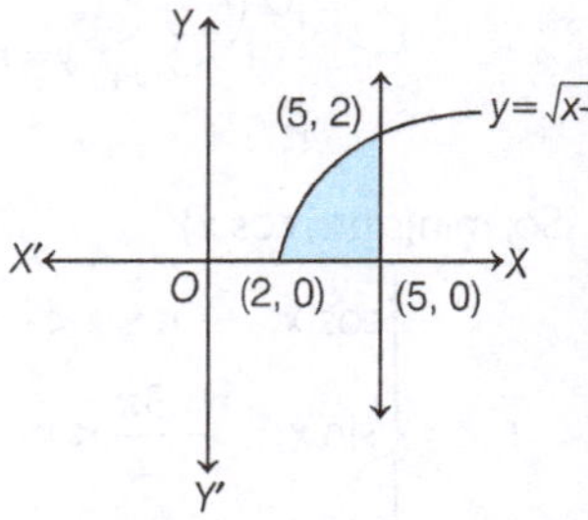

$\therefore$ Area of the shaded region

$= \int_2^5 \sqrt{x-1}\,dx$

$= \left[\frac{(x-1)^{3/2}}{3/2}\right]_2^5$

$= \frac{2}{3}[8-1] = \frac{14}{3}$ sq units

6 (*d*) For $c < 1$, $\int_c^1 (8x^2 - x^5)\,dx = \frac{16}{3}$

$\Rightarrow \quad \frac{8}{3} - \frac{1}{6} - \frac{8c^3}{3} - \frac{c^6}{6} = \frac{16}{3}$

$\Rightarrow \; -c^3\left[\frac{8}{3} + \frac{c^3}{6}\right] = \frac{16}{3} - \frac{8}{3} + \frac{1}{6} = \frac{17}{6}$

$\Rightarrow \quad c = -1$

Again, for $c \geq 1$, none of the values of satisfy the required condition that

$\int_1^c (8x^2 - x^5)\,dx = \frac{16}{3}$

$\therefore \quad c + 2 = -1 + 2 = 1$

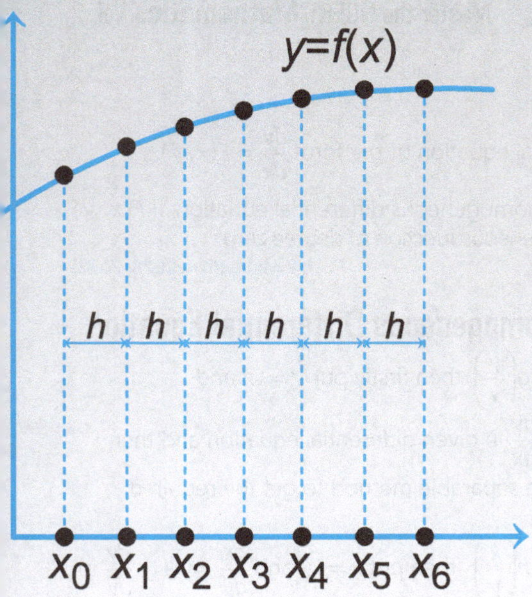

09

Differential Equations

Topicwise No. of Ques asked in 3 Years (JEE Main)

Topics	Number of Questions		
	2024	2023	2022
Basic Concepts	2	–	2
General and Particular Solutions of a Differential Equation	–	–	–
Differential Equations with Variables Separable	13	1	6
Homogeneous Differential Equations	4	4	4
Linear Differential Equations	13	18	18

Special Types of Question Asked in last 3 Years (JEE Main)

Types	Years		
	2024	2023	2022
A-R	–	–	–
Statement Based	–	–	–
Numerical Value Type	15	6	8

Last 3 Years Weightage (JEE Main)

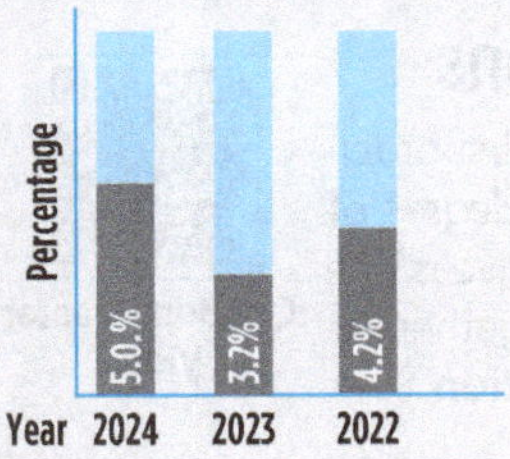

Basic Concepts

1. **Differential Equation** An equation involving independent variable(s), dependent variable(s) and derivative(s) of dependent variable with respect to independent variable(s), is called a differential equation.
2. **Order of a Differential Equation** The order of the highest order derivative of dependent variable with respect to independent variable occurring in the differential equation, is called the order of differential equation.
3. **Degree of a Differential Equation** The highest power (positive integral index) of the highest order derivative involved in a differential equation, when it is written as a polynomial equation in derivatives, is called degree of a differential equation.
4. Order and degree (if defined) of a differential equation are always positive integers.
5. The order of a differential equation representing a family of curves is same as the number of arbitrary constants present in the equation.

General and Particular Solutions of a Differential Equation

1. **General Solution of a Differential Equation** A solution of a differential equation which contains as many arbitrary constants as the order of the differential equation, is called the general solution or primitive solution of the differential equation.

2. **Particular Solution of a Differential Equation**
The solution obtained by giving particular values to the arbitrary constants in general solution, is called a particular solution of the differential equation. In other words, the solution free from arbitrary constants is called particular solution.

Methods of Solving First Order-First Degree Differential Equations

Differential Equations with Variable Separable

1. Suppose a first order and first degree differential equation $\frac{dy}{dx} = f(x, y)$, such that $f(x, y)$ can be written as

$$g(x) \cdot h(y) \quad \text{...(i)}$$

Then, expressed the given differential equation as

$$\frac{dy}{dx} = h(y) \cdot g(x). \quad \text{...(ii)}$$

2. If $h(y) \neq 0$, then separating the variables.
Eq. (ii) can be written as $\frac{1}{h(y)} dy = g(x) dx$.

On integrating both sides, we get the required solution of given differential equation. **[JEE Main 2024, 2023, 2022]**

Marks Maximizer

- **Differential Equation Reducible to Variables Separable Form**

A differential equation of the form $\frac{dy}{dx} = f(ax + by + c)$ can be reduced to variables separable form by substituting

$$ax + by + c = z \Rightarrow a + b\frac{dy}{dx} = \frac{dz}{dx}$$

The given equation becomes

$$\frac{1}{b}\left(\frac{dz}{dx} - a\right) = f(z) \Rightarrow \frac{dz}{dx} = a + b\,f(z)$$

$$\Rightarrow \quad \frac{dz}{a + bf(z)} = dx$$

Hence, the variables are separated in terms of z and x.

Homogeneous Differential Equations

1. A function $F(x, y)$ is said to be homogeneous function of degree n, if

$$F(x, y) = x^n g\left(\frac{y}{x}\right) \text{ or } y^n h\left(\frac{x}{y}\right).$$

2. A differential equation of the form $\frac{dy}{dx} = F(x, y)$ is called a homogeneous differential equation, if $F(x, y)$ is a homogeneous function of degree zero. **[JEE Main 2024, 2023, 2022]**

Solution of Homogeneous Differential Equation

1. If $F(x, y) = g\left(\frac{y}{x}\right)$, then firstly put $y = vx$ and $\frac{dy}{dx} = v + x\frac{dv}{dx}$ in given differential equation and then use variable separable method to get the required solution.

2. If $F(x, y) = h\left(\frac{x}{y}\right)$, then put $x = vy$ and $\frac{dx}{dy} = v + y\frac{dv}{dy}$ in the given differential equation. **[JEE Main 2024, 2023, 2022]**

Marks Maximizer

- **Differential Equations Reducible to Homogeneous Form**

The differential equation of the form

$$\frac{dy}{dx} = \frac{a_1x + b_1y + c_1}{a_2x + b_2y + c_2},$$

where $a_1b_2 - a_2b_1 \neq 0$ i.e. $\frac{a_1}{a_2} \neq \frac{b_1}{b_2}$ ...(i)

can be reduced to homogeneous form by substituting

$$x = X + h \text{ and } y = Y + k$$

$$\therefore \quad \frac{dY}{dX} = \frac{a_1X + b_1Y + (a_1h + b_1k + c_1)}{a_2X + b_2Y + (a_2h + b_2k + c_2)} \quad \text{...(ii)}$$

For finding h and k, put $a_1h + b_1k + c_1 = 0$ and $a_2h + b_2k + c_2 = 0$.

On solving, we get

$$\frac{h}{b_1c_2 - b_2c_1} = \frac{k}{c_1a_2 - c_2a_1} = \frac{1}{a_1b_2 - a_2b_1}$$

$$\Rightarrow \quad h = \frac{b_1c_2 - b_2c_1}{a_1b_2 - a_2b_1} \text{ and } k = \frac{c_1a_2 - c_2a_1}{a_1b_2 - a_2b_1}$$

Then, Eq. (ii) reduces to $\frac{dY}{dX} = \frac{a_1X + b_1Y}{a_2X + b_2Y}$, which is a homogeneous form and can be solved easily.

Linear Differential Equations

Concept Master Video

1. **Linear Differential Equation** A first order differential equation in which the degree of dependent variable and its derivative is one and they do not get multiplied together, is called a **linear differential equation**.

(i) **Type I** A differential equation of the form $\frac{dy}{dx} + Py = Q$, where P and Q are constants or functions of x only, is called linear differential equation, whose solution is given by
$y \cdot (\text{IF}) = \int Q \cdot (\text{IF})\, dx + C$, where $\text{IF} = e^{\int P\, dx}$.

(ii) **Type II** A differential equation of the form $\frac{dx}{dy} + Px = Q$, where P and Q are constants or functions of y only, is called linear differential equation, whose solution is given by
$x \cdot (\text{IF}) = \int Q \cdot (\text{IF})\, dy + C$, where $\text{IF} = e^{\int P\, dy}$.
[JEE Main 2024, 2023, 2022]

2. **Differential Equation Reducible to the Linear Form**
Equation of the form $f'(y)\frac{dy}{dx} + f(y)P = Q$, where P and Q are functions of x only or constants, can be reduced to linear form by substituting

i.e. $$f(y) = u \Rightarrow f'(y) \cdot \frac{dy}{dx} = \frac{du}{dx}$$

This will reduce the given differential equation to $\frac{du}{dx} + uP = Q$,

which is in linear differential equation form and can be solved in the usual manner.

Caution Points

- Always check that your solution satisfies given initial conditions.
- When integrating, especially in cases involving non-standard forms or substitutions, ensure all constants of integration are accounted for and correctly applied.
- Be aware of special solutions or cases (such as singular solutions) that might not be immediately apparent. These can sometimes be over looked in the general solution.
- Ensure that all terms in the differential equation are dimensionally consistent.
- For solving linear differential equation, ensure that the integrating factor is correctly calculated and applied.

PYQ Notes

1. If the differential equation can be written as
$f[f_1(x, y)]\, d\{f_1(x, y)\} + \phi\, [f_2(x, y)]\, d\, \{f_2(x, y)\} + \dots = 0$
then, each form can be integrated separately.
For this, remember the following results.

(i) $\frac{x\, dy - y\, dx}{x^2} = d\left(\frac{y}{x}\right)$ **[JEE Main 2024, 2022]**

(ii) $xdy + y\, dx = d(xy)$ **[JEE Main 2022]**

Step by Step Mastering NCERT

- Concept Builders
- Topical Questions
- Numerical Type Questions
- Assertion and Reason Questions
- Case or Paragraph Type Questions
- Past Years Questions
- Skill Boosters

Concept Builders

1 The order of the differential equation $y = \frac{a}{\frac{dy}{dx}} + \frac{dy}{dx}$ is ....

2 The degree of the differential equation $\frac{d^2y}{dx^2} = 2 + \sqrt{\frac{dy}{dx}}$ is ....

3 The order and degree of the differential equation $y + \frac{dy}{dx} = \frac{1}{2}\int y\,dx$ are ...*A*... and ...*B*..., respectively. Then the value of *A* and *B* are ....

4 The solution of the differential equation $\frac{dy}{dx} = \frac{1}{y^2 + \cos y}$ is $x = \frac{y^3}{3} + \sin y + C$. (T/F)

5 The solution of the differential equation $\frac{dy}{dx} = \sin^2 y$ is $x + \cot y = C$. (T/F)

6 The solution of the differential equation $e^x \sqrt{1-y^2}\,dx + \frac{y}{x}dy = 0$ is $xe^x + e^x = \sqrt{1-y^2} + C$. (T/F)

7 The solution of the differential equation $\log\left(\frac{dy}{dx}\right) = ax - by$ is $\frac{e^{by}}{b} = \frac{e^{ax}}{a} + C$. (T/F)

8 A function $f(x, y) = x^2 + y^2 + 3xy$ is a homogeneous function of degree ....

Topical Questions

Basic Concepts

Level I

1 Consider the following equations

I. $x^2 - 3x + 3 = 0$ II. $\sin x + \cos x = 0$

III. $x + y = 7$ IV. $x\frac{dy}{dx} + y = 0$

Then, the equation which involves derivative of dependent variable is/are NCERT Pg. 300

(a) I and II (b) I and IV

(c) III and IV (d) Only IV

2 The equation of the form

$$2\frac{d^2y}{dx^2} + \left(\frac{dy}{dx}\right)^3 = 0$$

is a /an NCERT Pg. 301

(a) cubic equation

(b) quadratic equation

(c) ordinary differential equation

(d) None of the above

3 Match the terms of column I with the terms of column II and choose the correct option from the codes given below. NCERT Pg. 302

	Column I (Differential equation)		Column II (Degree)
A.	$\frac{dy}{dx} = e^x$	1.	1
B.	$\frac{d^2y}{dx^2} + y = 0$	2.	2
C.	$\frac{d^3y}{dx^3} + x^2\left(\frac{d^2y}{dx^2}\right)^3 = 0$	3.	Not defined
D.	$\frac{d^3y}{dx^3} + 2\left(\frac{d^2y}{dx^2}\right)^2 - \frac{dy}{dx} + y = 0$	4.	3
E.	$\left(\frac{dy}{dx}\right)^2 + \left(\frac{dy}{dx}\right) - \sin^2 y = 0$		
F.	$\frac{dy}{dx} + \sin\left(\frac{dy}{dx}\right) = 0$		

Codes

	A	B	C	D	E	F
(a)	2	2	4	3	1	1
(b)	1	1	1	1	2	3
(c)	3	4	1	1	2	3
(d)	1	1	1	3	4	2

4 The order and degree (if defined) of a differential equation are always **NCERT Pg. 302**

(a) negative integers (b) rational numbers
(c) real numbers (d) positive integers

5 The order and degree of the differential equation $\frac{d^4y}{dx^4} + \sin(y''') = 0$ are respectively **NCERT Pg. 303**

(a) 4 and 1
(b) 1 and 2
(c) 4 and 4
(d) 4 and not defined

6 Which of the following is incorrect? **NCERT Pg. 303**

(a) The order and degree of the differential equation $y' + 5y = 0$ are respectively 1 and 1.

(b) For the differential equation $\left(\frac{ds}{dt}\right)^4 + 3s\frac{d^2s}{dt^2} = 0$, its order is 2 and degree is 1.

(c) If the differential equation is given by $\left(\frac{d^2y}{dx^2}\right)^2 + \cos\left(\frac{dy}{dx}\right) = 0$, then its order is 2 and degree is 2.

(d) The order of the differential equation $\frac{d^2y}{dx^2} = \cos 3x + \sin 3x$ is 2 and its degree is 1.

7 Match the terms of column I with the terms of column II and choose the correct option from the codes given below. **NCERT Pg. 303**

	Column I (Differential equation)		Column II (Order and degree respectively)
A.	$(y''')^2 + (y'')^3 + (y')^4 + y^5 = 0$	1.	2, 1
B.	$y''' + 2y'' + y' = 0$	2.	1,1
C.	$y' + y = e^x$	3.	3,1
D.	$y'' + (y')^2 + 2y = 0$	4.	3, 2
		5.	1, not defined

Codes

	A	B	C	D		A	B	C	D
(a)	5	4	1	3	(b)	2	4	1	3
(c)	4	2	3	1	(d)	4	3	2	1

8 The degree of the differential equation

$$\left(\frac{d^2y}{dx^2}\right)^3 + \left(\frac{dy}{dx}\right)^3 + \sin\left(\frac{dy}{dx}\right) + 1 = 0 \text{ is}$$

NCERT Pg. 304

(a) 3 (b) 2
(c) 1 (d) not defined

9 The order of the differential equation

$$2x^2\frac{d^2y}{dx^2} - 3\frac{dy}{dx} + y = 0 \text{ is}$$

NCERT Pg. 304

(a) 2 (b) 1
(c) 0 (d) not defined

10 The order and degree of the differential equation $y'' + 2y' + \sin y = 0$ are respectively **NCERT Pg. 304**

(a) 1 and 2 (b) 2 and 1 (c) 2 and 2 (d) 1 and 2

Level II

11 The order and degree of the differential equation

$$\left(1 + \left(\frac{dy}{dx}\right)^2\right)^{3/4} = \left(\frac{d^2y}{dx^2}\right)^{1/3} \text{ are respectively}$$

NCERT Pg. 302

(a) 2 and 4 (b) 2 and 3
(c) 6 and 4 (d) 6 and 9

12 The degree of the equation $e^x\frac{d^2y}{dx^2} + \sin\left(\frac{dy}{dx}\right) = 3$ is **NCERT Pg. 302**

(a) 2 (b) 0
(c) not defined (d) 1

13 The order and degree of the differential equation

$$x^3 + y = \log_2\left|\frac{dy}{dx} + 3\right| - \log_4\left(\frac{d^2y}{dx^2} + 2\frac{dy}{dx} + 4\right) \text{ are}$$

respectively **NCERT Pg. 302**

(a) 2 and 1 (b) 1 and 2
(c) 1 and 1 (d) 2 and 2

14 Consider the following statements

I. The order and degree of the differential equation $\frac{d^2y}{dx^2} + 5x\left(\frac{dy}{dx}\right)^2 - 6y = \log x$ are respectively 2 and 1.

II. If the differential equation is given by

$$\left(\frac{dy}{dx}\right)^3 - 4\left(\frac{dy}{dx}\right)^2 + 7y = \sin x$$

Then, its order is 1 and degree is 2.

Choose the correct option. **NCERT Pg. 302**

(a) Only I is true
(b) Only I is true
(c) Both I and II are true
(d) Neither I nor II is true

15 The degree of the differential equation

$$y = x\frac{dy}{dx} + a\sqrt{1+\left(\frac{dy}{dx}\right)^2} \text{ is}$$

NCERT Pg. 302

(a) 2 (b) 1
(c) 0 (d) not defined

16 The order and degree of the differential equation $\sqrt{\sin x}\cdot(dx+dy) = \sqrt{\cos x}\cdot(dx-dy)$ are respectively NCERT Pg. 302

(a) 1 and 2 (b) 2 and 2 (c) 1 and 1 (d) 2 and 1

General and Particular Solutions of a Differential Equation

Level I

1 The number of arbitrary constants in the general solution of a differential equation of fourth order is NCERT Pg. 306

(a) 0 (b) 2
(c) 3 (d) 4

2 The number of arbitrary constants in the particular solution of a differential equation of third order is NCERT Pg. 306

(a) 3 (b) 2
(c) 1 (d) 0

3 The function $y = \sqrt{a^2 - x^2}, x \in (-a, a)$ is the solution of the differential equation NCERT Pg. 306

(a) $x + y\frac{dy}{dx} = 0\ (y \neq 0)$ (b) $y + x\frac{dy}{dx} = 0\ (x \neq 0)$
(c) $x - y\frac{dy}{dx} = 0\ (y \neq 0)$ (d) $y - x\frac{dy}{dx} = 0\ (x \neq 0)$

4 Consider the following statements

I. $x + y = \tan^{-1} y$ is the solution of the differential equation $y^2y' + y^2 + 1 = 0$.
II. $y - \cos y = x$ is the solution of the differential equation $(y \sin y + \cos y + x)\, y' = y$.

Choose the correct option NCERT Pg. 306

(a) Only I is true (b) Only II is true
(c) Both I and II are true (d) Neither I nor II is true

5 The function $xy = \log y + C$ is the solution of the differential equation NCERT Pg. 306

(a) $y' = \frac{y^2}{1-xy}\ (xy \neq 1)$ (b) $y' = \frac{-y^2}{1-xy}\ (x, y \neq 1)$
(c) $y' = \frac{y^2}{1+xy}\ (xy \neq -1)$ (d) None of these

6 Match the terms of column I with the terms of column II and choose the correct option from the codes given below. NCERT Pg. 306

	Column I (Solutions)		Column II (Differential equations)
A.	$y = e^x + 1$	1.	$y' + \sin x = 0$
B.	$y = x^2 + 2x + C$	2.	$xy' = y + x\sqrt{x^2 - y^2}$ ($x \neq 0$ and $x > y$ or $x < -y$)
C.	$y = \cos x + C$	3.	$y'' - y' = 0$
D.	$y = \sqrt{1+x^2}$	4.	$xy' = y\ (x \neq 0)$
E.	$y = Ax$	5.	$y' - 2x - 2 = 0$
F.	$y = x \sin x$	6.	$y' = \frac{xy}{1+x^2}$

Codes

	A	B	C	D	E	F
(a)	2	1	4	3	6	5
(b)	2	1	4	6	5	3
(c)	5	6	1	4	3	2
(d)	3	5	1	6	4	2

Level II

7 If $x^2 + y^2 = 1$, then NCERT Pg. 304

(a) $yy'' - (2y')^2 + 1 = 0$ (b) $yy'' + (y')^2 + 1 = 0$
(c) $yy'' - (y')^2 - 1 = 0$ (d) $yy'' + 2(y')^2 + 1 = 0$

8 $y = cx - c^2$ is the general solution of the differential equation NCERT Pg. 304

(a) $(y')^2 - xy' + y = 0$ (b) $y'' = 0$
(c) $y' = c$ (d) $(y')^2 + xy' + y = 0$

9 Consider the following statements

I. $y = ae^x + be^{-x} + x^2$ is the solution of the differential equation $x\frac{d^2y}{dx^2} + 2\frac{dy}{dx} - xy + x^2 - 2 = 0$.
II. $y = e^x(a\cos x + b\sin x)$ is the solution of the differential equation $\frac{d^2y}{dx^2} - 2\frac{dy}{dx} + 2y = 0$.

Choose the correct option NCERT Pg. 334

(a) Only I is true (b) Only II is true
(c) Both I and II are true (d) Neither I nor II is true

10 If $y = e^{-x}(A\cos x + B\sin x)$, then y is a solution of NCERT Exemplar Pg. 195

(a) $\frac{d^2y}{dx^2} + 2\frac{dy}{dx} = 0$ (b) $\frac{d^2y}{dx^2} - 2\frac{dy}{dx} + 2y = 0$
(c) $\frac{d^2y}{dx^2} + 2\frac{dy}{dx} + 2y = 0$ (d) $\frac{d^2y}{dx^2} + 2y = 0$

11 If C_1, C_2, C_3, C_4, C_5 and C_6 are constants, then the order of the differential equation whose general solution is given by $y = C_1\cos(x + C_2) + C_3\sin(x + C_4) + C_5e^x + C_6$, is NCERT Pg. 304

(a) 6 (b) 5 (c) 4 (d) 3

12 $y = 2e^{2x} - e^{-x}$ is the solution of the differential equation
NCERT Pg. 304

(a) $y'' + y' + 2y = 0$ (b) $y'' - y' + 2y = 0$
(c) $y'' + y' = 0$ (d) $y'' - y' - 2y = 0$

Differential Equations with Variables Separable

Level I

1 The equation of the curve passing through the point (1, 1), whose differential equation is $x\,dy = (2x^2 + 1)\,dx$ $(x \neq 0)$ is
NCERT Pg. 308

(a) $x^2 = y + \log|x|$ (b) $y = x^2 + \log|x|$
(c) $y^2 = x + \log|x|$ (d) $y = x + \log|x|$

2 The equation of a curve passing through the point (−2, 3) having the slope of tangent to the curve at any point as $\frac{2x}{y^2}$ is
NCERT Pg. 309

(a) $y = (3x^2 + 15)$ (b) $y^3 = 3x^2 - 15$
(c) $y = (3x^2 + 15)^{1/3}$ (d) $y^{1/3} = 3x^2 + 15$

3 In a bank, principal increases continuously at the rate of 5% per year. In how many years ₹ 1000 double itself?
NCERT Pg. 310

(a) 2 (b) 20
(c) $20 \log_e 2$ (d) $2 \log_e 20$

4 Match the terms of column I with the terms of column II and choose the correct option from the codes given below
NCERT Pg. 311

	Column I (Differential equation)		Column II (General solution)
A.	$\frac{dy}{dx} = \frac{1-\cos x}{1+\cos x}$	1.	$y = 2\sin(x + C)$
B.	$\frac{dy}{dx} = \sqrt{4 - y^2}$, $(-2 < y < 2)$	2.	$y = 2\tan\frac{x}{2} - x + C$
C.	$\frac{dy}{dx} + y = 1, (y \neq 1)$	3.	$\tan x \tan y = C$
D.	$\sec^2 x \tan y\,dx + \sec^2 y \tan x\,dy = 0$	4.	$y = 1 + Ae^{-x}$
E.	$(e^x + e^{-x})\,dy - (e^x - e^{-x})\,dx = 0$	5.	$\tan^{-1} y = x + \frac{x^3}{3} + C$
F.	$\frac{dy}{dx} = (1 + x^2)(1 + y^2)$	6.	$y = \log(e^x + e^{-x}) + C$

Codes

	A	B	C	D	E	F
(a)	4	3	1	2	6	5
(b)	2	1	4	3	6	5
(c)	5	6	4	3	1	2
(d)	6	5	4	3	2	1

5 The general solution of the differential equation $y \log y\,dx - x\,dy = 0$ is
NCERT Pg. 311

(a) $y = -e^{Cx}$ (b) $y = x$ (c) $y = Ce^x$ (d) $y = e^{Cx}$

6 The general solution of the differential equation $x^5 \frac{dy}{dx} = -y^5$ is
NCERT Pg. 311

(a) $x^{-4} + y^{-4} = C$ (b) $x^4 + y^{-4} = C$
(c) $x^{-4} + y^4 = C$ (d) $x^4 + y^4 = C$

7 Consider the following statements

I. The general solution of the differential equation $\frac{dy}{dx} = \sin^{-1} x$ is $y = x\sin^{-1} x + \sqrt{1 - x^2} + C$.

II. The general solution of the differential equation $e^x \tan y\,dx + (1 - e^x)\sec^2 y\,dy = 0$ is $\tan y = C(1 - e^x)$.

Choose the correct option
NCERT Pg. 311

(a) Only I is true (b) Only II is true
(c) Both I and II are true (d) Neither I nor II is true

8 The equation of a curve passing through the point (0, − 2) given that at any point (x, y) on curve, the product of the slope of its tangent and y-coordinate of the point is equal to the x-coordinate of the point, is
NCERT Pg. 311

(a) $y^2 + x^2 = 4$ (b) $x^2 - y^2 = 4$
(c) $y^2 - x^2 = 4$ (d) $x^2 + y^2 = -4$

9 At any point (x, y) of a curve, the slope of tangent is twice the slope of the line segment joining the point of contact to the point (−4, − 3). The equation of the curve given that it passes through (−2, 1), is
NCERT Pg. 311

(a) $x + 4 = (y + 3)^2$ (b) $(x + 4)^2 = (y - 3)$
(c) $x - 4 = (y - 3)^2$ (d) $(x + 4)^2 = |y + 3|$

10 Match the terms of column I with the terms of column II and choose the correct option from the codes given below.
NCERT Pg. 311

	Column I (Differential equation)		Column II (Particular solutions)
A.	$(x^3 + x^2 + x + 1)\frac{dy}{dx} = 2x^2 + x$; $y = 1$ when $x = 0$	1.	$y = \sec x$
B.	$x(x^2 - 1)\frac{dy}{dx} = 1$; $y = 0$ when $x = 2$	2.	$\cos\left(\frac{y-2}{x}\right) = a$
C.	$\cos\left(\frac{dy}{dx}\right) = a\,(a \in R)$, $y = 2$ when $x = 0$	3.	$y = \frac{1}{2}\log\left\lvert\left(\frac{x^2-1}{x^2}\right)\right\rvert - \frac{1}{2}\log\left(\frac{3}{4}\right)$
D.	$\frac{dy}{dx} = y\tan x$; $y = 1$ when $x = 0$	4.	$y = \frac{1}{4}\log[(x+1)^2(x^2+1)^3] - \frac{1}{2}\tan^{-1} x + 1$

Codes

	A	B	C	D		A	B	C	D
(a)	2	1	4	3	(b)	4	3	2	1
(c)	3	2	4	1	(d)	2	1	3	4

11 The volume of spherical balloon being inflated changes at a constant rate. If initially its radius is 3 units and after 3 s, it is 6 units, then the radius of balloon after t seconds is **NCERT Pg. 311**

(a) $(63t+27)^{1/3}$ (b) $(63t-27)^{1/3}$
(c) $(63t+27)^3$ (d) $(63t-27)^3$

12 Consider the following statements

I. The equation of a curve passing through the point (0, 0) and whose differential equation is $y' = e^x \sin x$, is $y - x + 2 = \log[(x^2(y+2)^2)]$.

II. For the differential equation $xy\dfrac{dy}{dx} = (x+2)(y+2)$, the solution curve passing through the point $(1, -1)$ is $2y - 1 = e^x(\sin x - \cos x)$.

Choose the correct option **NCERT Pg. 311**

(a) Only I is true (b) Only II is true
(c) Both I and II are true (d) Neither I nor II is true

13 The general solution of the differential equation $\dfrac{dy}{dx} = e^{x+y}$ is **NCERT Pg. 312**

(a) $e^x + e^{-y} = C$ (b) $e^x + e^y = C$
(c) $e^{-x} + e^y = C$ (d) $e^{-x} + e^{-y} = C$

14 In a bank, principal increases continuously at the rate of r% per year. If ₹ 100 double itself in 10 yr, then the value of r is ($\log_e 2 = 0.6931$) **NCERT Pg. 312**

(a) 6.9% (b) 6.93% (c) 6.81% (d) 6.83%

15 In a bank, principal increases continuously at the rate of 5% per year. An amount of ₹ 1000 is deposited with this bank. How much will it worth after 10 yr? ($e^{0.5} = 1.648$) **NCERT Pg. 312**

(a) ₹ 1468 (b) ₹ 1680
(c) ₹ 6480 (d) ₹ 1648

16 In a culture, the bacteria count is 100000. The number is increased by 10% in 2 h. In how many hours, will the count reach 200000, if the rate of growth of bacteria is proportional to the number present? **NCERT Pg. 312**

(a) $\dfrac{2\log 2}{\log\left(\dfrac{11}{10}\right)}$ (b) $\dfrac{\log 2}{\log 11}$ (c) $\dfrac{\log 2}{\log 10}$ (d) $\dfrac{\log 2}{\log\dfrac{11}{10}}$

Level II

17 The particular solution of the differential equation $\log\left(\dfrac{dy}{dx}\right) = 3x + 4y$ given that $y = 0$ when $x = 0$, is **NCERT Pg. 330**

(a) $4e^{3x} + 3e^{-4y} - 7 = 0$ (b) $3e^{3x} + 4e^{4y} + 7 = 0$
(c) $4e^{3x} - 3e^{4y} - 7 = 0$ (d) $3e^{3x} + 4e^{4y} - 7 = 0$

18 Solution of the differential equation $x\,dy - y\,dx = 0$ represents **NCERT Exemplar Pg. 197**

(a) parabola (b) circle
(c) hyperbola (d) straight line

19 The solution of differential equation $\cos y \dfrac{dy}{dx} = e^{x+\sin y} + x^2 e^{\sin y}$ is **NCERT Pg. 307**

(a) $e^x - e^{-\sin y} + \dfrac{x^3}{3} = C$ (b) $e^{-x} - e^{-\sin y} + \dfrac{x^3}{3} = C$
(c) $e^x + e^{-\sin y} + \dfrac{x^3}{3} = C$ (d) $e^x - e^{\sin y} - \dfrac{x^3}{3} = C$

20 The solution of differential equation $\dfrac{dy}{dx} = 1 + y + y^2 + x + xy + xy^2$ is **NCERT Pg. 307**

(a) $4\tan^{-1}\left(\dfrac{2y+1}{\sqrt{3}}\right) = \sqrt{3}(2x + x^2) + C$

(b) $\tan^{-1}\left(\dfrac{2y+1}{\sqrt{3}}\right) = x + x^2 + C$

(c) $\sqrt{3}\tan^{-1}\left(\dfrac{3y+1}{3}\right) = 4(1 + x + x^2) + C$

(d) $\tan^{-1}\left(\dfrac{2y+1}{3}\right) = 4(2x + x^2) + C$

21 The equation of a curve whose tangent at any point on it different from origin has slope $y + \dfrac{y}{x}$, is **NCERT Exemplar Pg. 182**

(a) $y = e^x$ (b) $y = kx\cdot e^x$
(c) $y = kx$ (d) $y = x\cdot e^{x^2}$

22 The population of a village increases continuously at the rate proportional to the number of its inhabitants present at any time. If the population of the village was 20000 in 1999 and 25000 in the year 2004, the population of the village in 2009 is **NCERT Pg. 312**

(a) 31250 (b) 26000 (c) 31000 (d) 31520

23 The equation of curve through the point (1, 0), if the slope of the tangent to the curve at any point (x, y) is $\dfrac{y-1}{x^2+x}$, is **NCERT Exemplar Pg. 194**

(a) $(y+1)(x-1) + 2x = 0$ (b) $(y+1)(x-1) - 2x = 0$
(c) $(y-1)(x-1) + 2x = 0$ (d) $(y-1)(x+1) + 2x = 0$

24 A curve whose slope of tangent at some point is two times the slope of the straight line joining the same point to the origin, is a/an **NCERT Exemplar Pg. 197**

(a) circle (b) ellipse
(c) parabola (d) hyperbola

25 The solution of the differential equation $e^{-x}(y+1)\,dy + (\cos^2 x - \sin 2x)\,y\,dx = 0$ subjected to the condition $y = 1$, when $x = 0$ is **NCERT Pg. 307**

(a) $y + \log y + e^x \cos^2 x = 2$
(b) $\log(y+1) + e^x \cos^2 x = 1$
(c) $y + \log y = e^x \cos^2 x$
(d) $(y+1) + e^x \cos^2 x = 2$

26 The solution of the differential equation $x\left(\frac{dy}{dx}\right)^2 + 2\sqrt{xy}\,\frac{dy}{dx} + y = 0$ is **NCERT Pg. 307**

(a) $x + y = C$ (b) $\sqrt{x} - \sqrt{y} = \sqrt{C}$
(c) $x^2 + y^2 = C^2$ (d) $\sqrt{x} + \sqrt{y} = C$

27 It is given that radium decomposes at a rate proportional to the amount present. If p% of the original amount of radium disappears in l years, then what percentage of it will remain after $2l$ years? **NCERT Pg. 312**

(a) $\left(10 - \frac{p}{10}\right)^2$ (b) $\left(10 + \frac{p}{10}\right)^2$
(c) $\left(10 - \frac{p}{10}\right)$ (d) $\left(10 + \frac{p}{10}\right)$

Homogeneous Differential Equations

Level I

1 The family of curves for which the slope of the tangent at any point (x, y) is $\frac{x^2 + y^2}{2xy}$, is given by **NCERT Pg. 314**

(a) $x^2 + y^2 = Cx$ (b) $x^2 - y^2 = Cx$
(c) $x^2 + y^2 = Cy$ (d) $x^2 - y^2 = Cy$

2 Which of the following is a homogeneous differential equation? **NCERT Pg. 313**

(a) $(4x + 6y + 5)\,dy - (3y + 2x + 4)\,dx = 0$
(b) $(xy)\,dx - (x^3 + y^3)\,dy = 0$
(c) $(x^3 + 2y^2)\,dx + 2xy\,dy = 0$
(d) $y^2 dx + (x^2 - xy - y^2)\,dy = 0$

3 The solution of the differential equation **NCERT Pg. 321**

$$\left\{x\cos\left(\frac{y}{x}\right) + y\sin\left(\frac{y}{x}\right)\right\} y\,dx = \left\{y\sin\left(\frac{y}{x}\right) - x\cos\left(\frac{y}{x}\right)\right\} x\,dy \text{ is}$$

(a) $xy\cos\left|\frac{y}{x}\right| = A$ (b) $xy\cos\left|\frac{x}{y}\right| = A$
(c) $x\cos y = A$ (d) $y\cos x = A$

4 If the differential equation in column I are homogeneous then match the terms of column I with the terms of column II and choose the correct option from the codes given below. **NCERT Pg. 321**

	Column I (Differential equation)		Column II (Solutions)
A.	$(x^2 + xy)\,dy = (x^2 + y^2)\,dx$	1.	$y + \sqrt{x^2 + y^2} = Cx^2$
B.	$y' = \frac{x + y}{x}$	2.	$\frac{1}{2\sqrt{2}}\log\left\lvert\frac{x + \sqrt{2}y}{x - \sqrt{2}y}\right\rvert = \log\lvert x\rvert + C$
C.	$(x - y)\,dy - (x + y)\,dx = 0$	3.	$x^2 + y^2 = Cx$
D.	$(x^2 - y^2)\,dx + 2xy\,dy = 0$	4.	$\tan^{-1}\left(\frac{y}{x}\right) = \frac{1}{2}\log(x^2 + y^2) + C$
E.	$x^2\frac{dy}{dx} = x^2 - 2y^2 + xy$	5.	$y = x\log\lvert x\rvert + Cx$
F.	$x\,dy - y\,dx = \sqrt{x^2 + y^2}\,dx$	6.	$(x - y)^2 = Cxe^{-\frac{y}{x}}$

Codes

	A	B	C	D	E	F
(a)	4	3	2	1	5	6
(b)	4	3	6	5	2	1
(c)	6	5	4	3	2	1
(d)	6	5	1	2	4	5

5 The solution of the differential equation $x\frac{dy}{dx} - y + x\sin\left(\frac{y}{x}\right) = 0$ is **NCERT Pg. 321**

(a) $x\left[1 - \cos\left(\frac{y}{x}\right)\right] = C\sin\left(\frac{y}{x}\right)$
(b) $y\left[1 - \cos\left(\frac{y}{x}\right)\right] = C\sin\left(\frac{y}{x}\right)$
(c) $x\left[1 + \cos\left(\frac{y}{x}\right)\right] = C\sin\left(\frac{x}{y}\right)$
(d) $y\left[1 - \cos\left(\frac{x}{y}\right)\right] = C\sin\left(\frac{x}{y}\right)$

6 The solution of the differential equation $y\,dx + x\log\left(\frac{y}{x}\right)dy - 2x\,dy = 0$ is **NCERT Pg. 321**

(a) $Cx = \log\left|\frac{y}{x}\right| - 1$
(b) $Cy = \log\left|\frac{y}{x}\right| - 1$
(c) $Cx = \log\left|\frac{x}{y}\right| - 1$
(d) $Cy = \log\left|\frac{x}{y}\right| - 1$

7 The solution of the differential equation $(1+e^{\frac{x}{y}})\,dx + e^{\frac{x}{y}}\left(1-\frac{x}{y}\right)dy = 0$ is **NCERT Pg. 321**

(a) $ye^{x} + x = C$ (b) $xe^{y} + y = C$

(c) $ye^{\frac{y}{x}} + y = C$ (d) $ye^{\frac{x}{y}} + x = C$

8 The particular solution of the differential equation $2xy + y^2 - 2x^2\frac{dy}{dx} = 0$; $y = 2$ when $x = 1$, is **NCERT Pg. 321**

(a) $y = \frac{2x}{1-\log|x|}$; $(x \neq 0, x \neq e)$

(b) $x = \frac{2y}{1-\log|y|}$; $(y \neq 0, y \neq e)$

(c) $y = \frac{2x}{1+\log|x|}$; $(x \neq e)$

(d) None of the above

9 Match the terms of column I with the terms of column II and choose the correct option from the codes given below. **NCERT Pg. 321**

	Column I (Differential equation)		Column II (Solutions)
A.	$(x+y)\,dy + (x-y)\,dx = 0$; $y = 1$ when $x = 1$	1.	$y + 2x = 3x^2y$
B.	$x^2dy + (xy + y^2)\,dx = 0$; $y = 1$ when $x = 1$	2.	$\log(x^2+y^2) + 2\tan^{-1}\frac{y}{x} = \frac{\pi}{2} + \log 2$
C.	$\left[x\sin^2\left(\frac{y}{x}\right) - y\right]dx + x\,dy = 0$; $y = \frac{\pi}{4}$ when $x = 1$	3.	$\cos\left(\frac{y}{x}\right) = \log\lvert ex\rvert$
D.	$\frac{dy}{dx} - \frac{y}{x} + \operatorname{cosec}\left(\frac{y}{x}\right) = 0$; $y = 0$ when $x = 1$	4.	$\cot\left(\frac{y}{x}\right) = \log\lvert ex\rvert$

Codes

	A	B	C	D		A	B	C	D
(a)	3	4	2	1	(b)	3	1	2	4
(c)	4	3	2	1	(d)	2	1	4	3

Level II

10 The general solution of the differential equation $(x^3 - 3xy^2)\,dx = (y^3 - 3x^2y)\,dy$ is **NCERT Pg. 321**

(a) $x^2 - y^2 = C(x^2+y^2)^2$

(b) $x^2 + y^2 = C(x^2-y^2)^2$

(c) $(x^2-y^2)^2 = C(x^2+y^2)$

(d) $(x^2-y^2)^2 = C(x^2+y^2)^2$

11 The solution of the differential equation $xy^2dy - (x^3+y^3)\,dx = 0$ is **NCERT Pg. 320**

(a) $y^3 = 3x^3 + C$ (b) $y^3 = 3x^3\log(Cx)$

(c) $y^3 = 3x^2 + \log(Cx)$ (d) $y^3 + 3x^3 = \log(Cx)$

12 If the perpendicular distance of the origin from the normal at any point $P(x, y)$ of the curve is equal to the distance of P from X-axis, then the equation of a curve passing through the point (1, 1) is **NCERT Exemplar Pg. 183**

(a) $x^2 - y^2 - 2x = 0$ (b) $x^2 + y^2 + 2x = 0$

(c) $x^2 + y^2 - 2x = 0$ (d) $x^2 - y^2 + 2x = 0$

13 If the slope of the tangent to the curve at any point $P(x, y)$ is $\frac{y}{x} - \cos^2\frac{y}{x}$, then the equation of a curve passing through $\left(1, \frac{\pi}{4}\right)$ is **NCERT Exemplar Pg. 184**

(a) $\tan\left(\frac{y}{x}\right) + \log x = 1$ (b) $\tan\left(\frac{y}{x}\right) + \log y = 1$

(c) $\tan\left(\frac{x}{y}\right) + \log x = 1$ (d) $\tan\left(\frac{x}{y}\right) + \log y = 1$

14 The general solution of $y^2dx + (x^2 - xy + y^2)\,dy = 0$ is **NCERT Pg. 322**

(a) $\tan^{-1}\left(\frac{x}{y}\right) + \log|y| = C$ (b) $\tan^{-1}\left(\frac{x}{y}\right) - \log|y| = C$

(c) $\tan^{-1}\left(\frac{y}{x}\right) + \log|x| = C$ (d) $\tan^{-1}\left(\frac{y}{x}\right) - \log|y| = C$

15 If $\frac{dy}{dx} = \frac{y + x\tan\frac{y}{x}}{x}$, then $\sin\frac{y}{x}$ is equal to **NCERT Pg. 322**

(a) Cx^2 (b) Cx (c) Cx^3 (d) Cx^4

16 If $dx + dy = (x+y)(dx - dy)$, then $\log(x+y)$ is equal to **NCERT Pg. 322**

(a) $x + y + C$ (b) $x + 2y + C$

(c) $x - y + C$ (d) $2x + y + C$

17 If $\frac{dy}{dx} = \frac{xy}{x^2+y^2}$, $y(1) = 1$, then one of the values of x_0 satisfying $y(x_0) = e$ is given by **NCERT Pg. 322**

(a) $e\sqrt{2}$ (b) $e\sqrt{3}$ (c) $e\sqrt{5}$ (d) $\frac{e}{\sqrt{2}}$

18 The slope of the tangent to a curve at any point (x, y) is given by $\frac{y}{x} - \cot\frac{y}{x}\cdot\cos\frac{y}{x}$ $(x > 0, y > 0)$ and the curve passes through the point $\left(1, \frac{\pi}{4}\right)$, then the equation of the curve is **NCERT Pg. 322**

(a) $\sec\left(\frac{y}{x}\right) = \log|x| + \sqrt{2}$ (b) $\sec\left(\frac{y}{x}\right) = \log|x| - \sqrt{2}$

(c) $\sec\left(\frac{y}{x}\right) = -\log|x| - \sqrt{2}$ (d) $\sec\left(\frac{y}{x}\right) = -\log|x| + \sqrt{2}$

Linear Differential Equations

Level I

1 The general solution of the differential equation $\frac{dy}{dx} - y = \cos x$ is **NCERT Pg. 324**

(a) $y = \left(\frac{\sin x + \cos x}{2}\right) + Ce^x$

(b) $y = \left(\frac{\sin x - \cos x}{2}\right) + Ce^x$

(c) $y = \left(\frac{\sin x - \cos x}{2}\right) + Ce^{-x}$

(d) $y = \left(\frac{\sin x + \cos x}{2}\right) + Ce^{-x}$

2 The general solution of the differential equation $x\frac{dy}{dx} + 2y = x^2 \ (x \neq 0)$ is **NCERT Pg. 325**

(a) $y = \frac{x^2}{4} - Cx^2$ (b) $y = \frac{x^2}{4} - Cx^{-2}$

(c) $y = \frac{x^2}{4} + Cx^{-2}$ (d) $y = \frac{x}{3} + Cx^{-2}$

3 The general solution of the differential equation $y\,dx - (x + 2y^2)\,dy = 0$ is **NCERT Pg. 326**

(a) $x = 2y^2 + C$ (b) $y = 2x^2 + Cx$

(c) $y = 2x^2 + C$ (d) $x = 2y^2 + Cy$

4 The particular solution of the differential equation $\frac{dy}{dx} + y\cot x = 2x + x^2 \cot x, (x \neq 0)$ given that $y = 0$ when $x = \frac{\pi}{2}$, is **NCERT Pg. 326**

(a) $y = x^2 - \frac{\pi^2}{4 \sin x}, (\sin x \neq 0)$

(b) $y = x^2 + \frac{\pi^2}{4 \sin x}, (\sin x \neq 0)$

(c) $y = x^2 - \frac{\pi^2}{\sin x}, (\sin x \neq 0)$

(d) None of the above

5 If the slope of the tangent to the curve at any point (x, y) is equal to the sum of the x-coordinate (abscissa) and the product of the x-coordinate and y-coordinate (ordinate) of that point, then the equation of a curve passing through the point (0, 1) is **NCERT Pg. 327**

(a) $y = 1 - 2e^{\frac{x^2}{2}}$ (b) $y = -1 + 2e^{\frac{x^2}{2}}$

(c) $x = 1 - 2e^{\frac{y^2}{2}}$ (d) $x = -1 + 2e^{\frac{y^2}{2}}$

6 Match the terms of column I with the terms of column II and choose the correct option from the codes given below. **NCERT Pg. 328**

Column I (Differential equation)	Column II (Solutions)
A. $\frac{dy}{dx} + 2y = \sin x$	1. $y = (\tan x - 1) + Ce^{-\tan x}$
B. $\frac{dy}{dx} + 3y = e^{-2x}$	2. $y = \frac{x^2}{16}(4\log\|x\| - 1) + Cx^2$
C. $\frac{dy}{dx} + \frac{y}{x} = x^2$	3. $xy = \frac{x^4}{4} + C$
D. $\frac{dy}{dx} + (\sec x)\,y = \tan x, \left(0 \le x < \frac{\pi}{2}\right)$	4. $y(\sec x + \tan x) = \sec x + \tan x - x + C$
E. $\cos^2 x \frac{dy}{dx} + y = \tan x \left(0 \le x < \frac{\pi}{2}\right)$	5. $y = \frac{1}{5}(2\sin x - \cos x) + Ce^{-2x}$
F. $x\frac{dy}{dx} + 2y = x^2 \log x$	6. $y = e^{-2x} + Ce^{-3x}$

Codes

	A	B	C	D	E	F
(a)	6	4	1	3	5	2
(b)	3	1	4	5	2	6
(c)	5	6	3	4	1	2
(d)	6	5	4	3	2	1

7 The general solution of the differential equation $x\log x\frac{dy}{dx} + y = \frac{2}{x}\log x$ is **NCERT Pg. 328**

(a) $y\log x = -\frac{2}{x}(1 + \log|x|) + C$

(b) $x\log y = -\frac{2}{x}(1 + \log|x|) + C$

(c) $y\log x = \frac{2}{x}(1 + \log|x|) + C$

(d) $x\log y = \frac{2}{x}(1 - \log|x|) + C$

8 The general solution of the differential equation $(1 + x^2)\,dy + 2xy\,dx = \cot x\,dx, (x \neq 0)$ is **NCERT Pg. 328**

(a) $y = (1 + x^2)^{-1}\log|\sin x| + C(1 + x^2)^{-1}$

(b) $y = (1 - x^2)^{-1}\log|\sin x| + C(1 + x^2)^{-1}$

(c) $y = (1 + x^2)^{-1}\log|\sin x| + C(1 - x^2)^{-1}$

(d) $y = (1 - x^2)^{-1}\log|\sin x| + C(1 - x^2)^{-1}$

9 The integrating factor of the differential equation $x\frac{dy}{dx} - y = 2x^2$ is **NCERT Pg. 329**

(a) e^{-x} (b) e^{-y} (c) $\frac{1}{x}$ (d) x

10 The integrating factor of the differential equation $(1-y^2)\dfrac{dx}{dy}+yx=ay(-1<y<1)$ is NCERT Pg. 329

(a) $\dfrac{1}{y^2-1}$ (b) $\dfrac{1}{\sqrt{y^2-1}}$ (c) $\dfrac{1}{1-y^2}$ (d) $\dfrac{1}{\sqrt{1-y^2}}$

11 If the sum of the coordinates of any point on the curve exceeds the magnitude of the slope of the tangent to the curve at that point by 5, then the equation of a curve passing through the point (0, 2) is NCERT Pg. 329

(a) $y=4-x-2e^x$ (b) $y=4+x+2e^x$
(c) $y=4-x+2e^x$ (d) $y=4+x-2e^x$

12 Match the terms of column I with the terms of column II and choose the correct option from the codes given below. NCERT Pg. 329

	Column I (Differential equation)		Column II (Solutions)
A.	$\dfrac{dy}{dx}+2y\tan x=\sin x$ $y=0$ when $x=\dfrac{\pi}{3}$	1.	$y(1+x^2)=\tan^{-1}x-\dfrac{\pi}{4}$
B.	$(1+x^2)\dfrac{dy}{dx}+2xy=\dfrac{1}{1+x^2}$ $y=0$, when $x=1$	2.	$y=4\sin^3 x-2\sin^2 x$
C.	$\dfrac{dy}{dx}-3y\cot x=\sin 2x$ $y=2$ when $x=\dfrac{\pi}{2}$	3.	$y=\cos x-2\cos^2 x$

Codes

	A	B	C		A	B	C
(a)	2	1	3	(b)	3	2	1
(c)	3	1	2	(d) None of these			

13 Consider the following statements

I. The general solution of the differential equation $x\dfrac{dy}{dx}+y-x+xy\cot x=0,(x\neq 0)$ is $y=\dfrac{1}{x}-\cot x+\dfrac{C}{x\sin x}$.

II. The general solution of the differential equation $(x+y)\dfrac{dy}{dx}=1$ is $(x+y+1)=Ce^y$.

Choose the correct option. NCERT Pg. 329

(a) Only I is true (b) Only II is true
(c) Both I and II are true (d) Neither I nor II is true

14 The equation of a curve passing through the origin such that the slope of the tangent to the curve at any point (x, y) is equal to the sum of the coordinates of the point, is NCERT Pg. 329

(a) $x+y+1=e^x$ (b) $x+y+1=e^{-x}$
(c) $x-y+1=e^x$ (d) $x+y-1=e^{-x}$

15 The general solution of the differential equation $y\,dx+(x-y^2)\,dy=0$ is NCERT Pg. 329

(a) $y=\dfrac{x^2}{3}+\dfrac{C}{x}$ (b) $y=\cos x-2\cos^2 x$
(c) $x=\dfrac{y^2}{3}+\dfrac{C}{y}$ (d) $x=\dfrac{y^3}{3}-\dfrac{C}{y}$

16 The general solution of the differential equation $(x+3y^2)\dfrac{dy}{dx}=y(y>0)$ is NCERT Pg. 329

(a) $x=3y^2+Cy$ (b) $x=3y-Cy^2$
(c) $y=3x^2+Cy$ (d) $y=3x-Cx^2$

Level II

17 The general solution of the differential equation $(\tan^{-1}y-x)\,dy=(1+y^2)\,dx$ is NCERT Pg. 333

(a) $x=(\tan^{-1}y+1)+Ce^{-\tan^{-1}y}$
(b) $x=(\tan^{-1}y-1)+Ce^{-\tan^{-1}y}$
(c) $y=(\tan^{-1}x-1)+Ce^{-\tan^{-1}x}$
(d) $y=(\tan^{-1}x+1)+Ce^{-\tan^{-1}x}$

18 The general solution of the differential equation of the type $\dfrac{dx}{dy}+P_1x=Q_1$ is NCERT Pg. 335

(a) $ye^{\int P_1dy}=\int(Q_1e^{\int P_1dy})\,dy+C$
(b) $y\cdot e^{\int P_1dx}=\int(Q_1e^{\int P_1dx})\,dx+C$
(c) $xe^{\int P_1dy}=\int(Q_1e^{\int P_1dy})\,dy+C$
(d) $xe^{\int P_1dy}=\int(Q_1e^{\int P_1dx})\,dx+C$

19 The solution of the differential equation $x\dfrac{dy}{dx}+2y=x^2$ is NCERT Pg. 325

(a) $y=\dfrac{x^2+C}{4x^2}$ (b) $y=\dfrac{x^2}{4}+C$
(c) $y=\dfrac{x^4+C}{x^2}$ (d) $y=\dfrac{x^4+C}{4x^2}$

20 The solution of $\dfrac{dy}{dx}+y=e^{-x}$, $y(0)=0$ is NCERT Pg. 324

(a) $y=e^x(x-1)$ (b) $y=xe^{-x}$
(c) $y=xe^{-x}+1$ (d) $y=(x+1)e^{-x}$

21 The equation of one of the curve whose slope at any point is equal to $y+2x$, is NCERT Pg. 324

(a) $y=2(e^x+x-1)$ (b) $y=2(e^x-x-1)$
(c) $y=2(e^x-x+1)$ (d) $y=2(e^x+x+1)$

22 The solution of the differential equation $\cos x\,dy=y(\sin x-y)\,dx, 0<x<\dfrac{\pi}{2}$ is NCERT Pg. 324

(a) $\sec x=(\tan x+C)\,y$ (b) $y\sec x=\tan x+C$
(c) $y\tan x=\sec x+C$ (d) $\tan x=(\sec x+C)\,y$

23 The solution of differential equation

$$\left(\frac{e^{-2\sqrt{x}}}{\sqrt{x}} - \frac{y}{\sqrt{x}}\right)\frac{dx}{dy} = 1, x \neq 0 \text{ is}$$

NCERT Exemplar Pg. 190

(a) $ye^{2\sqrt{x}} = 2\sqrt{x} + C$ (b) $ye^{\sqrt{x}} = \sqrt{x} + C$
(c) $ye^{2\sqrt{x}} = \sqrt{x} + C$ (d) $ye^{2\sqrt{x}} = 2\sqrt{x} + C$

24 The particular solution of the differential equation $\frac{dy}{dx} + y\cot x = 4x \operatorname{cosec} x, (x \neq 0)$ given that $y = 0$ when $x = \frac{\pi}{2}$, is

NCERT Pg. 324

(a) $y \sin x = 2x^2 + \frac{\pi^2}{2}$ (b) $y \sin x = 2x^2 - \frac{\pi^2}{2}$
(c) $y \sin^2 x = 2x^2 - \frac{\pi^2}{2}$ (d) None of these

25 The solution of the differential equation $(1 + y^2) + (x - e^{\tan^{-1} y})\frac{dy}{dx} = 0$ is

NCERT Exemplar Pg. 194

(a) $2xe^{\tan^{-1} y} = e^{2\tan^{-1} y} + C$ (b) $xe^{\tan^{-1} y} = \tan^{-1} y + C$
(c) $xe^{2\tan^{-1} y} = e^{\tan^{-1} y} + C$ (d) $(x - 2) = e^{-\tan^{-1} y} + C$

26 The integrating factor of the differential equation $\frac{dy}{dx} + \frac{y}{(1 - x)\sqrt{x}} = 1 - \sqrt{x}$ is

NCERT Pg. 324

(a) $\frac{1 - \sqrt{x}}{1 + \sqrt{x}}$ (b) $\frac{1 + \sqrt{x}}{1 - \sqrt{x}}$
(c) $\frac{1 - x}{1 + x}$ (d) $\frac{\sqrt{x}}{1 - \sqrt{x}}$

27 If $y(t)$ is a solution of $(1 + t)\frac{dy}{dt} - ty = 1$ and $y(0) = -1$, then $y(1)$ is equal to

NCERT Exemplar Pg. 193

(a) $-\frac{1}{2}$ (b) $e + \frac{1}{2}$ (c) $e - \frac{1}{2}$ (d) $\frac{1}{2}$

Miscellaneous Exercise

1 The order and degree of the differential equation $\frac{d^4y}{dx^4} - \sin\left(\frac{d^3y}{dx^3}\right) = 0$ are respectively

NCERT Pg. 303

(a) 4, 1 (b) 3, 1
(c) 1, 4 (d) 4, not defined

2 Consider the following statements

I. The function $y = x \sin 3x$ is a solution of the differential equation $\frac{d^2y}{dx^2} + 9y - 6\cos 3x = 0$.

II. The function $x^2 = 2y^2 \log y$ is a solution of the differential equation $(x^2 + y^2)\frac{dy}{dx} - xy = 0$.

Choose the correct option. NCERT Pg. 334

(a) Only I is true (b) Only II is true
(c) Both I and II are true (d) Neither I nor II is true

3 If p and q are the order and degree of the differential equation $y\frac{dy}{dx} + x^3\frac{d^2y}{dx^2} + xy = \cos x$, then

NCERT Pg. 302

(a) $p < q$ (b) $p = q$
(c) $p > q$ (d) None of these

4 The degree of the differential equation

$$x = 1 + \left(\frac{dy}{dx}\right) + \frac{1}{2!}\left(\frac{dy}{dx}\right)^2 + \frac{1}{3!}\left(\frac{dy}{dx}\right)^3 + \ldots \text{ is}$$

NCERT Pg. 302

(a) 3 (b) 2
(c) 1 (d) not defined

5 The differential equation whose solution is $Ax^2 + By^2 = 1$, where A and B are arbitrary constants, is of

NCERT Exemplar Pg. 194

(a) first order and second degree
(b) first order and first degree
(c) second order and first degree
(d) second order and second degree

6 The solution of the differential equation $x\,dy - y\,dx = \sqrt{x^2 + y^2}$ is

NCERT Pg. 312

(a) $y + \sqrt{x^2 + y^2} = Cx^2$ (b) $y^2 + \sqrt{x^2 + y^2} = Cx$
(c) $y + \sqrt{x^2 - y^2} = Cx^2$ (d) $y^2 - \sqrt{x^2 - y^2} = Cx$

7 The general solution of the differential equation $(1 + y^2)\,dx + (1 + x^2)\,dy = 0$ is

NCERT Pg. 306

(a) $x - y = C(1 - xy)$ (b) $x - y = C(1 + xy)$
(c) $x + y = C(1 - xy)$ (d) $x + y = C(1 + xy)$

8 The solution of the differential equation $\frac{dy}{dx} = \frac{x + y}{x}$ satisfying the condition $y(1) = 1$ is

NCERT Pg. 322

(a) $y = x\log x + x$ (b) $y = \log x + x$
(c) $y = x\log x + x^2$ (d) $y = xe^{(x-1)}$

9 Consider the following statements

I. The particular solution of the differential equation $(x - y)(dx + dy) = dx - dy$ given that $y = -1$, when $x = 0$, is $\log|x + y| = x + y + 1$.

NCERT Pg. 335

II. The particular solution of the differential equation $(x + 1)\frac{dy}{dx} = 2e^{-y} - 1$, given $y = 0$ when $x = 0$, is $y = \log\left|\frac{2x + 1}{x + 1}\right|, x \neq -1$.

NCERT Pg. 306

Choose the correct option.

(a) Only I is true (b) Only II is true
(c) Both I and II are true (d) Neither I nor II is true

10 The general solution of the differential equation $e^x dy + (ye^x + 2x)\,dx = 0$ is **NCERT Pg. 322**

(a) $xe^y + x^2 = C$ (b) $xe^y + y^2 = C$
(c) $ye^x + x^2 = C$ (d) $ye^y + x^2 = C$

11 The differential equation of the family of circles passing through the fixed points $(a, 0)$ and $(-a, 0)$, is **Old NCERT Pg. 391**

(a) $y_1(y^2 - x^2) + 2xy + a^2 = 0$
(b) $y_1y^2 + xy + a^2x^2 = 0$
(c) $y_1(y^2 - x^2 + a^2) + 2xy = 0$
(d) $y_1(y^2 + x^2) - 2xy + a^2 = 0$

12 The differential equation of the system of all circles of radius r in the XY-plane is **Old NCERT Pg. 391**

(a) $\left[1+\left(\frac{dy}{dx}\right)^3\right]^2 = r^2\left(\frac{d^2y}{dx^2}\right)^2$

(b) $\left[1+\left(\frac{dy}{dx}\right)^3\right]^2 = r^2\left(\frac{d^2y}{dx^2}\right)^3$

(c) $\left[1+\left(\frac{dy}{dx}\right)^2\right]^3 = r^2\left(\frac{d^2y}{dx^2}\right)^2$

(d) $\left[1+\left(\frac{dy}{dx}\right)^2\right]^3 = r^2\left(\frac{d^2y}{dx^2}\right)^3$

13 The equation of the curve through the point $(1, 0)$ and whose slope is $\frac{y-1}{x^2+x}$, is **Old NCERT Pg. 391**

(a) $2x + (y-1)(x+1) = 0$ (b) $2x - (y-1)(x+1) = 0$
(c) $2x + (y-1)(x-1) = 0$ (d) None of these

14 Match the terms of column I with the terms of column II and choose the correct option from the codes given below. **NCERT Pg. 334**

Column I (Differential equation)	Column II (Solutions)
A. $\frac{dy}{dx} + \sqrt{\frac{1-y^2}{1-x^2}} = 0$	1. $y = Cx$
B. $\frac{dy}{dx} + \frac{y^2+y+1}{x^2+x+1} = 0$	2. $e^{\frac{x}{y}} = y + C$
C. $ye^{\frac{x}{y}}dx = (xe^{\frac{x}{y}} + y^2)\,dy$ $(y \neq 0)$	3. $(x+y+1) = A(1-x-y-2xy)$
D. $\frac{y\,dx - x\,dy}{y} = 0$	4. $\sin^{-1} y + \sin^{-1} x = C$

Codes

	A	B	C	D		A	B	C	D
(a)	2	1	3	4	(b)	3	4	2	1
(c)	4	3	2	1	(d)	2	4	3	1

15 The solution of the differential equation $(x^2 - yx^2)\frac{dy}{dx} + y^2 + xy^2 = 0$ is **NCERT Pg. 306**

(a) $\log\left(\frac{x}{y}\right) = \frac{1}{x} + \frac{1}{y} + C$ (b) $\log\left(\frac{y}{x}\right) = \frac{1}{x} + \frac{1}{y} + C$
(c) $\log(xy) = \frac{1}{x} + \frac{1}{y} + C$ (d) $\log(xy) + \frac{1}{x} + \frac{1}{y} = C$

16 Which of the following is a second order differential equation? **NCERT Pg. 304**

(a) $(y')^2 + x = y^2$ (b) $y'y'' + y = \sin x$
(c) $y''' + (y'')^2 + y = 0$ (d) $y' = y^2$

17 The equation of the curve satisfying the equation $(xy - x^2)\frac{dy}{dx} = y^2$ and passing through the point $(-1, 1)$, is **NCERT Pg. 312**

(a) $y = (\log y - 1)\,x$ (b) $y = (\log y + 1)\,x$
(c) $x = (\log x - 1)\,y$ (d) $x = (\log x + 1)\,y$

18 The differential equation of the family of circles in the first quadrant which touch the coordinate axes, is **Old NCERT Pg. 389**

(a) $(x - yy')^2 = (x-y)^2\,(1 + (y')^2)$
(b) $(x + yy')^2 = (x-y)^2\,(1 + (y')^2)$
(c) $(x + yy')^2 = (x+y)^2\,(1 + (y')^2)$
(d) None of the above

19 The equation of the curve passing through the point $\left(0, \frac{\pi}{4}\right)$ whose differential equation is $\sin x \cos y\,dx + \cos x \sin y\,dy = 0$, is **NCERT Pg. 334**

(a) $\sec y = \frac{\cos x}{\sqrt{2}}$ (b) $\cos x = -\frac{\sec y}{\sqrt{2}}$
(c) $\sec y = \sqrt{\ }\cos x$ (d) $\cos y = \frac{\sec x}{\sqrt{2}}$

20. The degree and order of the differential equation whose solution is a parabola and axis is X-axis, are respectively **NCERT Pg. 304**

(a) 1, 1 (b) 1, 2 (c) 1, 0 (d) 2, 1

21 The solution of the differential equation $\frac{dy}{dx} = x \log x$ is **NCERT Pg. 306**

(a) $y = x^2 \log x - \frac{x^2}{2} + C$ (b) $y = \frac{x^2}{2}\log x - \frac{x^2}{4} + C$
(c) $y = \frac{x^2}{2} + \frac{x^2}{2}\log x + C$ (d) None of these

22 The general solution of the differential equation $(e^x + 1)\,y\,dy = (y+1)\,e^x dx$ is **NCERT Pg. 306**

(a) $y + 1 = k(e^x + 1)$ (b) $y + 1 = e^x + 1 + k$
(c) $y = \log|k(y+1)(e^x+1)|$ (d) $y = \log\left|\frac{e^x+1}{y+1}\right| + k$

23 The differential equation obtained by eliminating arbitrary constants from $y = ae^{bx}$ is **NCERT Pg. 304**

(a) $y\frac{d^2y}{dx^2} + \frac{dy}{dx} = 0$ (b) $y\frac{d^2y}{dx^2} - \frac{dy}{dx} = 0$

(c) $y\frac{d^2y}{dx^2} - \left(\frac{dy}{dx}\right)^2 = 0$ (d) $y\frac{d^2y}{dx^2} + \left(\frac{dy}{dx}\right)^2 = 0$

24 The differential equation representing the family of curves given by $(x-a)^2 + 2y^2 = a^2$, where a is an arbitrary constant, is **NCERT Pg. 304**

(a) $y' = \frac{2y^2 - x^2}{4xy}$ (b) $y' = \frac{2y^2 + x^2}{4xy}$

(c) $y' = \frac{2x^2 - y^2}{4xy}$ (d) $y' = \frac{2x^2 + y^2}{4xy}$

25 The particular solution of the differential equation $(1+e^{2x})\,dy + (1+y^2)\,e^x dx = 0$ given that $y = 1$ when $x = 0$, is **NCERT Pg. 306**

(a) $\tan^{-1} y - \tan^{-1}(e^x) = \frac{\pi}{2}$

(b) $\tan^{-1}(e^x) - \tan^{-1}(y) = \frac{\pi}{2}$

(c) $\tan^{-1} y + \tan^{-1}(e^x) = \frac{\pi}{2}$

(d) None of the above

Numerical Type Questions

1 The number of arbitrary constants in the general solution of a differential equation of third order is .... **NCERT Pg. 304**

2 The number of arbitrary constants in the particular solution of fourth order is .... **NCERT Pg. 304**

3 The sum of the order and degree of the differential equation $\frac{d^3y}{dx^3} + \left(\frac{dy}{dx}\right)^2 = \sin x$ is .... **NCERT Pg. 302**

4 If f is a differential function such that $x^2 f(x) - x = 4\int_0^x t\,f(t)\,dt$, $f(1) = \frac{2}{3}$. Then, $9f(3)$ is .... **NCERT Pg. 322**

5 Let $\alpha x = \exp(x^\beta y^\gamma)$ be the solution of the differential equation $2x^2 y\,dy - (1 - xy^2)\,dx = 0, x > 0$ $y(2) = \sqrt{\log_e 2}$. Then, $\alpha - \beta + \gamma$ equals .... **NCERT Pg. 322**

6 If $\sin\left(\frac{y}{x}\right) = \log_e|x| + \frac{\alpha}{2}$ is the solution of the differential equation $x\cos\left(\frac{y}{x}\right)\frac{dy}{dx} = y\cos\left(\frac{y}{x}\right) + x$ and $y(1) = \frac{\pi}{4}$, then α^2 is equal to ....

7 Let $f : [0, 1] \to R$ be such that $f(x, y) = f(x)\,f(g)$; for all $x, y \in [0, 1]$ and $f(0) \neq 0$. If $y = y(x)$ satisfies the differential equation, $\frac{dy}{dx} = f(x)$ with $y(0) = 2$, then $y\left(\frac{1}{3}\right) + y\left(\frac{2}{3}\right)$ is equal to .... **NCERT Pg. 335**

8 Let $\alpha\,|X| = |\,y\,|\,e^{xy-\beta}$, $\alpha, \beta \in N$ be the solution of the differential eqution $xdy - ydx + xy\,(xdy + ydx) = 0$, $y\,(1) = 2$, then $\alpha - \beta$ is equal to .... **NCERT Pg. 306**

9 Let the solution $y = y(x)$ of differential equation $\frac{dy}{dx} - y = 1 + 4\sin x$ satisfy $y(\pi) = 1$. Then, $y\left(\frac{\pi}{2}\right) + 20$ is equal to .... **NCERT Pg. 322**

10 If the solution of the curve $y = y(x)$ of the differential equation $(1+y^2)(1+\log_e x)\,dx + xdy = 0, x > 0$ passes through the point $(1, 1)$ and $y(e) = \frac{\alpha - \tan\left(\frac{3}{2}\right)}{\beta + \tan\left(\frac{3}{2}\right)}$, then $3\alpha + 2\beta$ is .... **NCERT Pg. 322**

Assertion and Reason Questions

Direction (Q. No. 1-7) The following questions consist of two statements, one labelled as "Assertion (A) and the other labelled as Reason (R)". You are to examine these two statements carefully true and it so, where the Reason (R) is the correct explanation a for the given Assertion (A). Select your answer from following options.

(a) Both Assertion and Reason are correct and Reason is the correct explanation of Assertion.

(b) Both Assertion and Reason are correct but Reason is not the correct explanation of Assertion.

(c) Assertion is correct but Reason is incorrect.

(d) Assertion is incorrect but Reason is correct.

1 **Assertion (A)** The degree of the differential equation $\frac{d^3y}{dx^3}+2\left(\frac{d^2y}{dx^2}\right)^2-\frac{dy}{dx}+y=0$ can be defined.

Reason (R) The degree of a differential equation can be defined, if it is a polynomial equation in derivatives. NCERT Pg. 302

2 **Assertion (A)** The degree of the differential equation $\frac{d^2y}{dx^2}+3\left(\frac{dy}{dx}\right)^2=x^2\log\left(\frac{d^2y}{dx^2}\right)$ is not defined.

Reason (R) If the differential equation is a polynomial in terms of its derivatives, then its degree is defined. NCERT Pg. 302

3 **Assertion (A)** The differential equation $x^2=y^2+xy\frac{dy}{dx}$ is an ordinary differential equation.

Reason (R) An ordinary differential equation involves derivatives of the dependent variable with respect to only one independent variable. NCERT Pg. 301

4 The solution of the differential equation $\frac{d^2y}{dx^2}+y=0$ is $y=\phi(x)=a\sin(x+b)$.

Assertion (A) The function $y=\phi(x)$ is called general solution.

Reason (R) The solution which contains arbitrary constants, is called general solution. NCERT Pg. 305

5 For the differential equation $\frac{d^2y}{dx^2}+y=0$, let its solution be $y=\phi_1(x)=2\sin\left(x+\frac{\pi}{4}\right)$.

Assertion (A) The function $y=\phi_1(x)$ is called the particular solution.

Reason (R) The solution which is free from arbitrary constant, is called a particular solution. NCERT Pg. 305

6 **Assertion (A)** The differential equations $\frac{dx}{dy}+x=\cos y$ and $\frac{dx}{dy}+\frac{-2x}{y}=y^2e^{-y}$ are first order linear differential equations.

Reason (R) The differential equation of the form $\frac{dx}{dy}+P_1x=Q_1$ NCERT Pg. 322
where, P_1 and Q_1 are constants or functions of y only, is called first order linear differential equation.

7 Consider the differential equation $\frac{dy}{dx}-\frac{\tan y}{x}=\frac{\tan y\sin y}{x^2}$

Assertion (A) Its solution is $\frac{x}{\sin y}+\log x=C$.

Reason (R) Its solution is x. NCERT Pg. 322

Case or Paragraph Type Questions

Direction (Q. No. 1-3) If the equation is of the form $\frac{dy}{dx}=\frac{f(x,y)}{g(x,y)}$ or $\frac{dy}{dx}=F\left(\frac{y}{x}\right)$, where $f(x,y)$, $g(x,y)$ are homogeneous functions of the some degree in x and y, the put $y+vx$ and $\frac{dy}{dx}=v+x\frac{dv}{dx}$ so that the dependent variable y is changed to another variable v and then apply variable separable method.

Based on the above information, answer the following questions. NCERT Pg. 313

1 The general solution of $x^2\frac{dy}{dx}=x^2+xy+y^2$ is

(a) $\tan^{-1}\left(\frac{y}{x}\right)=\log|x|+C$ (b) $\tan^{-1}\left(\frac{x}{y}\right)=\log|x|+C$

(c) $\tan^{-1}\left(\frac{x}{y}\right)=\log|2x|+C$ (d) $\tan^{-1}\left(\frac{x}{y}\right)=2\log|x|+C$

2 Solution of the defferential equation $2xy\frac{dy}{dx}=x^2+3y^2$ is

(a) $x^2+2y^2=x^3C$
(b) $x^2+y^2=x^3C$
(c) $2x^3+y^2=x^3C$
(d) $x^2+3y^3=x^3C$

3 Solution of the differential equation $(x^2+3xy+y^2)\,dx-x^2dy=0$ is

(a) $2\log x+\frac{x}{x+y}=C$

(b) $\log x+\frac{x}{x-y}=C$

(c) $\log x+\frac{x}{x+y}=C$

(d) $\log x+\frac{2x}{x-y}=C$

Direction (Q. No. 4-6) **Order** The order of a differential equation is the order of the highest order derivative appering in the differential equation.

Degree The degree of differential equation is the power of the highest order derivative, when differential coefficients are made freee from radicals and fractions. Also, differential equation must be a polynomial equation in derivatives for the degree to be defined.

Based on the above information, answer the following questions. NCERT Pg. 302

4 Find the degree of the differential equation

$$2\frac{d^2y}{dx^2}+3\sqrt{1-\left(\frac{dy}{dx}\right)^2}-y=0$$

(a) 2 (b) 3
(c) 4 (d) 1

5 Order and degree of the differential equation $y\frac{dy}{dx}=\frac{x}{\frac{dy}{dx}+\left(\frac{dy}{dx}\right)^3}$ are respectively.

(a) 1 and 3 (b) 1 and 4
(c) 2 and 3 (d) 2 and 4

6 Find order and degree of the equation $y'''+y^2+e^{y'}=0$

(a) 2 and not defined (b) 3 and not defined
(c) not defined and 3 (d) 4 and not defined

Past Years Questions

Single Correct Type

1 The solution curve of the differential equation $2y\frac{dy}{dx}+3=5\frac{dy}{dx}$ passing through the point (0, 1) is a conic, whose vertex lies on the line.

NCERT Pg. 306, JEE Main 2024, 9 April Shift-I

(a) $2x+3y=9$ (b) $2x+3y=-9$
(c) $2x+3y=6$ (d) $2x+3y=-6$

2 Let $y=y(x)$ be the solution of the differential equation $(1+y^2)e^{\tan x}dx+\cos^2 x(1+e^{2\tan x})dy=0$, $y(0)=1$. Then, $y\left(\frac{\pi}{4}\right)$ is equal to

NCERT Pg. 306, JEE Main 2024, 8 April Shift-I

(a) $\frac{2}{e}$ (b) $\frac{2}{e^2}$ (c) $\frac{1}{e^2}$ (d) $\frac{1}{e}$

3 The temperature $T(t)$ of a body at time $t=0$ is 160°F and it decreases continuously as per the differential equation $\frac{dT}{dt}=-K(T-80)$, where K is a positive constant. If $T(15)=120°F$, then $T(45)$ is equal to

NCERT Pg. 306, JEE Main 2024, 31 Jan Shift-II

(a) 85°F (b) 95°F (c) 80°F (d) 90°F

4 Let $y=y(x)$ be a solution curve of the differential equation $(1-x^2y^2)dx=ydx+xdy$.

If the line $x=1$ intersects the curve $y=y(x)$ at $y=2$ and the line $x=2$ intersects the curve $y=y(x)$ at $y=\alpha$, then a value of α is NCERT Pg. 306, JEE Main 2023, 11 April Shift-I

(a) $\frac{3e^2}{2(3e^2+1)}$ (b) $\frac{3e^2}{2(3e^2-1)}$
(c) $\frac{1-3e^2}{2(3e^2+1)}$ (d) $\frac{1+3e^2}{2(3e^2-1)}$

5 If the solution curve of the differential equation $\frac{dy}{dx}=\frac{x+y-2}{x-y}$ passes through the point (2, 1) and $(k+1, 2)$, $k>0$, then

NCERT Pg. 312, JEE Main 2022, 29 July Shift-II

(a) $2\tan^{-1}\left(\frac{1}{k}\right)=\log_e(k^2+1)$

(b) $\tan^{-1}\left(\frac{1}{k}\right)=\log_e(k^2+1)$

(c) $2\tan^{-1}\left(\frac{1}{k+1}\right)=\log_e(k^2+2k+2)$

(d) $2\tan^{-1}\left(\frac{1}{k}\right)=\log_e\left(\frac{k^2+1}{k^2}\right)$

6 Let $y=y(x)$, $y>0$, be a solution curve of the differential equation $(1+x^2)\,dy=y(x-y)\,dx$.
If $y(0)=1$ and $y(2\sqrt{2})=\beta$, then

NCERT Pg. 322, JEE Main 2023, 12 April Shift-I

(a) $e^{\beta^{-1}}=e^{-2}(5+\sqrt{2})$ (b) $e^{\beta^{-1}}=e^{-2}(3+2\sqrt{2})$
(c) $e^{3\beta^{-1}}=e(3+2\sqrt{2})$ (d) $e^{3\beta^{-1}}=e(5+\sqrt{2})$

7 Let $y=y(x)$ be the solution curve of the differential equation $\frac{dy}{dx}=\frac{y}{x}(1+xy^2(1-\log_e x))$, $x>0$, $y(1)=3$.

Then, $\frac{y^2(x)}{9}$ is equal to

NCERT Pg. 322, JEE Main 2023, 25 Jan Shift-I

(a) $\frac{x^2}{3x^3(1+\log_e x^2)-2}$ (b) $\frac{x^2}{2x^3(2+\log_e x^3)-3}$
(c) $\frac{x^2}{5-2x^3(2+\log_e x^3)}$ (d) $\frac{x^2}{7-3x^3(2+\log_e x^2)}$

8 The degree of the differential equation

$$\left(1-\left(\frac{dy}{dx}\right)^2\right)^{\frac{3}{2}}=\frac{d^2y}{dx^2} \text{ is}$$

NCERT Pg. 302, CUET 2024

(a) 1 (b) 2 (c) 3 (d) $\frac{3}{2}$

9 Match List-I with List-II.

	List-I		List-II
A.	Integrating factor of $xdy-(y+2x^2)dx=0$	(i)	$\frac{1}{x}$
B.	Integrating factor of $(2x^2-3y)dx=xdy$	(ii)	x
C.	Integrating factor of $(2y+3x^2)dx+xdy=0$	(iii)	x^2
D.	Integrating factor of $2xdy+(3x^3+2y)dx=0$	(iv)	x^3

Choose the correct answer from the options given below: NCERT Pg. 322 and 323, CUET 2024

	A	B	C	D		A	B	C	D
(a)	(i)	(iii)	(iv)	(ii)	(b)	(i)	(iv)	(iii)	(ii)
(c)	(ii)	(i)	(iii)	(iv)	(d)	(iii)	(iv)	(ii)	(i)

10 For the differential equation

$$(x\log_e x)dy=(\log_e x-y)dy$$

A. Degree of the given differential equation is 1.
B. It is a homogeneous differential equation.
C. Solution is $2y\log_e x+A=(\log_e x)^2$, where A is an arbitrary constant.
D. Solution is $2y\log_e x+A=\log_e(\log_e x)$, where A is an arbitrary constant.

Choose the correct answer from the options given below. NCERT Pg. 322 and 323, CUET 2024

(a) A and C (b) A, B and C
(c) A, B and D (d) A and D

Numerical Value Type

11 Let $y=y(x)$, $x>1$, be the solution of the differential equation

$$(x-1)\frac{dy}{dx}+2xy=\frac{1}{x-1} \text{ with } y(2)=\frac{1+e^4}{2e^4}.$$

If $y(3)=\frac{e^\alpha+1}{\beta e^\alpha}$, then the value of $\alpha+\beta$ is equal to ....

NCERT Pg. 322, JEE Main 2023, 12 April Shift-I

12 If $x=x(t)$ is the solution of the differential equation $(t+1)dx=(2x+(t+1)^4)\,dt$, $x(0)=2$, then, $x(1)$ equals ....

NCERT Pg. 322 JEE Main 2024, 1 Feb Shift-I

13 Let $y=y(x)$ the solution of the differential equation

$$\frac{dy}{dx}+\frac{2x}{(1+x^2)^2}y=xe^{\left(\frac{1}{1+x^2}\right)};\ y(0)=0$$

Then, the area enclosed by the curve $f(x)=y(x)e^{-\frac{1}{(1+x^2)}}$ and the line $y-x=4$ is ....

NCERT Pg. 335, JEE Main 2024, 5 April Shift-II

14 If the solution curve of the differential equation $(y-2\log_e x)dx+(x\log_e x^2)dy=0$, $x>1$ passes through the points $\left(e,\frac{4}{3}\right)$ and (e^4,α), then α is equal to ....

NCERT Pg. 335, JEE Main 2023, 8 April Shift-I

15 Suppose, $y=y(x)$ be the solution curve to the differential equation $\frac{dy}{dx}-y=2-e^{-x}$ such that $\lim_{x\to\infty} y(x)$ is finite. If a and b are respectively the x and y-intercepts of the tangent to the curve at $x=0$, then the value of $a-4b$ is equal to ....

NCERT Pg. 335, JEE Main 2022, 26 July Shift-II

Skill Boosters

1 The order and degree of the differential equation $\left(2+5\frac{dy}{dx}\right)^{2/3}=3\frac{d^3y}{dx^3}$ are

(a) (2, 2) (b) (3, 3) (c) (2, 5) (d) (4, 2)

2 Let $y = f(x)$ be the solution of the differential equation $y(x-1)\,dx - x^2\,dy = 0$, $y(1) = e$. Then, $\lim\limits_{x\to 0^+} f(x)$ is equal to ....

(a) 4 (b) 1 (c) 0 (d) 2

3 Let $y = y(x)$ be the solution of the differential equation $x\,dy = (y + x^3 \cos x)\,dx$ with $y(\pi) = 1$, then $y\left(\frac{\pi}{2}\right)$ is equal to ....

(a) $\frac{\pi^2}{4}+\frac{\pi}{2}+\frac{1}{2}$ (b) $\frac{\pi^2}{4}+\pi$

(c) $\frac{\pi^2}{2}+\pi+2$ (d) $\frac{\pi^2}{4}-\pi+1$

4 Let the solution curve of the differential equation $x\,dy = (\sqrt{x^2+y^2}+y)\,dx$, $x>0$, intersect the line $x=1$ at $y=0$ and the line $x=3$ at $y=\alpha$. Then, the value of α is ....

(a) 1 (b) 4 (c) 0 (d) 7

5 Let $y = y(x)$ be the solution of the differential equation $\frac{dy}{dx} = 2(y + 2\sin x + 5)\,x - 2\cos x$ such that $y(0) = -3$. Then, $y(\pi)$ is equal to ....

(a) $e^{\frac{\pi^2}{4}}-7$ (b) $3e^{\frac{\pi^2}{4}}$ (c) $2e^{\frac{\pi^2}{4}}+7$ (d) $2e^{\frac{\pi^2}{4}}-7$

6 If $\cos x\frac{dy}{dx} - y\sin x = 6x$, $\left(0<x<\frac{x}{2}\right)$ and $y\left(\frac{\pi}{3}\right)=0$, then $y(\pi)$ is equal to ....

(a) $\frac{8\pi^2}{2}$ (b) $\frac{8\pi^2}{7}$ (c) $\frac{-8\pi^2}{3}$ (d) $\frac{5\pi^2}{2}$

Correct Codes

Topical Questions

Basic Concepts

1 (d)	2 (c)	3 (b)	4 (d)	5 (d)	6 (c)	7 (d)	8 (d)	9 (a)	10 (b)
11 (a)	12 (c)	13 (a)	14 (a)	15 (a)	16 (c)				

General and Particular Solutions of a Differential Equation

1 (d)	2 (d)	3 (a)	4 (c)	5 (a)	6 (d)	7 (b)	8 (a)	9 (b)	10 (c)
11 (c)	12 (d)								

Methods of Solving First Order, First Degree Differential Equation

1 (b)	2 (c)	3 (c)	4 (b)	5 (d)	6 (a)	7 (c)	8 (c)	9 (d)	10 (b)
11 (a)	12 (d)	13 (a)	14 (b)	15 (d)	16 (a)	17 (a)	18 (d)	19 (c)	20 (a)
21 (b)	22 (a)	23 (d)	24 (c)	25 (a)	26 (d)	27 (a)			

Homogeneous Differential Equations

1 (b)	2 (d)	3 (a)	4 (c)	5 (a)	6 (b)	7 (d)	8 (a)	9 (d)	10 (a)
11 (b)	12 (c)	13 (a)	14 (a)	15 (b)	16 (c)	17 (b)	18 (d)		

Linear Differential Equations

1 (b)	2 (c)	3 (d)	4 (a)	5 (b)	6 (c)	7 (a)	8 (a)	9 (c)	10 (d)
11 (a)	12 (c)	13 (c)	14 (a)	15 (c)	16 (a)	17 (b)	18 (c)	19 (d)	20 (b)
21 (b)	22 (a)	23 (a)	24 (b)	25 (a)	26 (b)	27 (a)			

Miscellaneous Exercise

1 (d)	2 (c)	3 (c)	4 (c)	5 (c)	6 (a)	7 (c)	8 (a)	9 (b)	10 (c)
11 (c)	12 (c)	13 (a)	14 (c)	15 (a)	16 (b)	17 (a)	18 (b)	19 (d)	20 (b)
21 (b)	22 (c)	23 (c)	24 (a)	25 (c)					

Numerical Type Questions

1 (3)	2 (0)	3 (4)	4 (80)	5 (3)	6 (2)	7 (5)	8 (0)	9 (17)	10 (5)

Assertion and Reason Questions

1 (a)	2 (a)	3 (a)	4 (a)	5 (a)	6 (a)	7 (c)

Case or Paragraph Type Questions

1 (a)	2 (b)	3 (c)	4 (a)	5 (b)	6 (b)

Past Years Questions

1 (a)	2 (d)	3 (d)	4 (d)	5 (a)	6 (c)	7 (c)	8 (b)	9 (b)	10 (a)
11 (14)	12 (14)	13 (18)	14 (3)	15 (3)					

Skill Boosters

1 (b)	2 (c)	3 (a)	4 (b)	5 (d)	6 (c)

Step by Step

Decoding the Questions

Concept Builders

1 (1) The given differential equation can be written as

$$\left(\frac{dy}{dx}\right)^2 - y\frac{dy}{dx} + a = 0$$

The highest order derivative is $\frac{dy}{dx}$, therefore the order of the given differential equation is 1.

2 (2) The given differential equation can be written as

$$\left(\frac{d^2y}{dx^2}\right)^2 - 4\frac{d^2y}{dx^2} - \frac{dy}{dx} + 4 = 0$$

Here, the highest order derivative is $\frac{d^2y}{dx^2}$, whose power is 2.

Therefore, the degree is 2.

3 (2 and 1) Given differential equation is

$$y + \frac{dy}{dx} = \frac{1}{2}\int y\, dx$$

On differentiating w.r.t. x, we get

$$\frac{dy}{dx} + \frac{d^2y}{dx^2} = \frac{1}{2}y$$

Here, the highest order derivative is $\frac{d^2y}{dx^2}$, whose power is 1.

Therefore, the order is 2 and degree is 1.

4 (True) We have, $\frac{dy}{dx} = \frac{1}{y^2 + \cos y}$

$$\Rightarrow \quad \frac{dx}{dy} = y^2 + \cos y$$

$$\Rightarrow \quad dx = (y^2 + \cos y)\, dy$$

On integrating both sides, we get

$$\int dx = \int (y^2 + \cos y)\, dy$$

$$\Rightarrow \quad x = \frac{y^3}{3} + \sin y + C$$

5 (True) Given differential equation is

$$\frac{dy}{dx} = \sin^2 y$$

$$\Rightarrow \quad \frac{dy}{\sin^2 y} = dx$$

$$\Rightarrow \quad \text{cosec}^2\, y\, dy = dx$$

On integrating both sides, we get

$$-\cot y + C = x \Rightarrow x + \cot y = C$$

6 (False) Given differential equation is

$$e^x\sqrt{1-y^2}\, dx + \frac{y}{x}dy = 0$$

$$\Rightarrow \quad e^x\sqrt{1-y^2}\, dx = -\frac{y}{x}dy$$

$$\Rightarrow \quad xe^x\, dx = -\frac{y}{\sqrt{1-y^2}}dy$$

On integrating both sides, we get

$$\Rightarrow \quad \int xe^x\, dx = \int \frac{-y}{\sqrt{1-y^2}}dy$$

$$\Rightarrow \quad xe^x - \int e^x\, dx = \frac{1}{2}\int \frac{dt}{\sqrt{t}},$$

where $t = 1 - y^2$

$$\Rightarrow \quad xe^x - e^x = \frac{1}{2}\left(\frac{t^{1/2}}{\frac{1}{2}}\right) + C$$

$$\Rightarrow \quad xe \quad - e^x = \sqrt{t} + C$$

$$\Rightarrow \quad xe^x - e^x = \sqrt{1-y^2} + C,$$

7 (True) Given differential equation is

$$\log\left(\frac{dy}{dx}\right) = ax - by$$

$$\Rightarrow \quad \frac{dy}{dx} = e^{ax-by}$$

$$\Rightarrow \quad \frac{dy}{dx} = e^{ax}\, e^{-by}$$

$$\Rightarrow \quad dy = e^{ax}\, e^{-by}\, dx$$

$$\Rightarrow \quad e^{by}dy = e^{ax}\, dx$$

On integrating both sides, we get

$$\int e^{by}\, dy = \int e^{ax} dx$$

$$\Rightarrow \quad \frac{e^{by}}{b} = \frac{e^{ax}}{a} + C$$

8 (2) Given function,

$$f(x, y) = x^2 + y^2 + 3xy$$

$$f(\lambda x, \lambda y) = (\lambda x)^2 + (\lambda y)^2 + 3(\lambda x)(\lambda y)$$

$$= \lambda^2 x^2 + \lambda^2 y^2 + 3\lambda^2 xy$$

$$= \lambda^2 (x^2 + y^2 + 3xy)$$

Hence, $f(x, y) = x^2 + y^2 + 3xy$ is a homogeneous function of degree 2.

Topical Questions

Basic Concepts

1 (*d*) $x^2 - 3x + 3 = 0$ ...(i)

$\sin x + \cos x = 0$ ...(ii)

$x + y = 7$ ...(iii)

$x\frac{dy}{dx} + y = 0$ ...(iv)

We see that Eqs. (i), (ii) and (iii) involve independent and/or dependent variable (variables) only but Eq. (iv) involves variables as well as derivative of the dependent variable y with respect to the independent variable x. Such an equation is called a differential equation.

2 (*c*) $2\frac{d^2y}{dx^2} + \left(\frac{dy}{dx}\right)^3 = 0$ is an ordinary differential equation.

3 (*b*) The degree of the differential equation

$$\frac{dy}{dx} = e^x, \frac{d^2y}{dx^2} + y = 0,$$

$$\left(\frac{d^3y}{dx^3}\right) + x^2\left(\frac{d^2y}{dx^2}\right)^3 = 0$$

and $\frac{d^3y}{dx^3} + 2\left(\frac{d^2y}{dx^2}\right)^2 - \frac{dy}{dx} + y = 0$

is 1, since the highest power of highest order derivative is 1.

The degree of the differential equation

$$\left(\frac{dy}{dx}\right)^2 + \left(\frac{dy}{dx}\right) - \sin^2 y = 0$$

is 2, since the highest power of highest order derivative is 2.

The degree of the differential equation $\frac{dy}{dx} + \sin\left(\frac{dy}{dx}\right) = 0$ cannot be defined, since this differential equation is not a polynomial equation in $y', y'', y''', \ldots$ etc.

4 (d) Order and degree (if defined) of a differential equation are always positive integers.

5 (d) $\frac{d^4y}{dx^4} + \sin(y''') = 0$

$\Rightarrow y'''' + \sin(y''') = 0$

The highest order derivative which occurs in the given differential equation is y'''', therefore its order is 4.

As the given differential equation is not a polynomial equation in derivatives of y w.r.t. x (i.e. y'''), therefore its degree is not defined.

6 (c) (a) The highest order derivative which occurs in the given differential equation is y' and index of highest power is one, therefore the given differential equation is of order 1 and degree 1.

(b) The highest order derivative present in the given differential equation is $\frac{d^2s}{dt^2}$. Therefore, the index of its highest power is one, hence the given differential equation is of order 2 and degree 1.

(c) The highest order derivative present in the given differential equation is $\frac{d^2y}{dx^2}$, therefore its order is 2.

But the given differential equation is not a polynomial equation in $\frac{dy}{dx}$. Hence, its degree is not defined.

(d) The highest order derivative which occurs in the given differential equation is $\frac{d^2y}{dx^2}$.

Therefore, its order is two. It is a polynomial equation in $\frac{d^2y}{dx^2}$ and the power raised to $\frac{d^2y}{dx^2}$ is 1.

Hence, its degree is one.

7 (d)

A. The highest order derivative which occurs in the given differential equation is y'''. Therefore, its order is three. The given differential equation is a polynomial equation in y''', y'' and y'.

The highest power raised to y''' is 2. Hence, its degree is 2.

B. The highest order derivative which occurs in the given differential equation is y'''. Therefore, its order is three. It is a polynomial equation in y''', y'' and y'. The highest power raised to y''' is 1. Hence, its degree is 1.

C. The highest order derivative present in the given differential equation is y'. Therefore, its order is one. The given differential equation is a polynomial equation in y'. The highest power raised to y' is 1. Hence, its degree is 1.

D. The highest order derivative, present in the differential equation is y''. Therefore, its order is two. The given differential equation is a polynomial equation in y'' and y' and the highest power raised to y'' is 1. Hence, its degree is 1.

8 (d) The given differential equation is not a polynomial equation in $\frac{dy}{dx}$.

Therefore, its degree is not defined.

9 (a) The highest order derivative present in the given differential equation is $\frac{d^2y}{dx^2}$. Therefore, its order is two.

10 (b) The highest order derivative present in the differential equation is y''. Therefore, its order is two. This is a polynomial equation in y'' and y' and the highest power raised to y'' is one. Hence, its degree is one.

11 (a) Given differential equation can be rewritten as

$$\left[1 + \left(\frac{dy}{dx}\right)^2\right]^{\frac{3}{4} \times 12} = \left(\frac{d^2y}{dx^2}\right)^{\frac{1}{3} \times 12}$$

$$\Rightarrow \left[1 + \left(\frac{dy}{dx}\right)^2\right]^9 = \left(\frac{d^2y}{dx^2}\right)^4$$

Here, we see that order of highest derivative is 2 and degree is 4.

12 (c) The given differential equation is $e^x \frac{d^2y}{dx^2} + \sin\left(\frac{dy}{dx}\right) = 3$.

Since, this differential equation is not a polynomial equation in terms of its derivatives.

$\therefore$ Its degree is not defined.

13 (a) The given differential equation is

$$x^3 + y = \log_2\left|\frac{dy}{dx} + 3\right| - \log_4\left(\frac{d^2y}{dx^2} + 2\frac{dy}{dx} + 4\right)$$

$$\Rightarrow x^3 + y = \log_2\left|\frac{dy}{dx} + 3\right| - \log_{2^2}\left(\frac{d^2y}{dx^2} + \frac{2dy}{dx} + 4\right)$$

$$= \log_2\left|\frac{dy}{dx} + 3\right| - \frac{1}{2}\log_2\left(\frac{d^2y}{dx^2} + 2\frac{dy}{dx} + 4\right)$$

$$\left(\because \log_{a^b} x = \frac{1}{b}\log_a x\right)$$

$$= \log_2 \left| \frac{dy}{dx} + 3 \right| - \log_2 \left(\frac{d^2y}{dx^2} + 2\frac{dy}{dx} + 4 \right)^{1/2}$$

$[\because \log x^a = a \log x]$

$$\Rightarrow x^3 + y = \log_2 \frac{\left| \frac{dy}{dx} + 3 \right|}{\left(\frac{d^2y}{dx^2} + 2\frac{dy}{dx} + 4 \right)^{1/2}}$$

$\left[\because \log a - \log b = \log \frac{a}{b}\right]$

$$\Rightarrow 2^{y + x^3} = \frac{\left| \frac{dy}{dx} + 3 \right|}{\left(\frac{d^2y}{dx^2} + 2\frac{dy}{dx} + 4 \right)^{1/2}}$$

$[\because \log_k a = b \Rightarrow k^b = a]$

$$\Rightarrow (2^{y + x^3})^2 \left(\frac{d^2y}{dx^2} + 2\frac{dy}{dx} + 4 \right) = \left(\frac{dy}{dx} + 3 \right)^2$$

Hence, its order is 2 and degree is 1.

14 (*a*)

I. The given differential equation is

$$\frac{d^2y}{dx^2} + 5x\left(\frac{dy}{dx}\right)^2 - 6y = \log x$$

$$\Rightarrow \frac{d^2y}{dx^2} + 5x\left(\frac{dy}{dx}\right)^2 - 6y - \log x = 0$$

As the highest order derivative that occurs in the given differential equation is $\frac{d^2y}{dx^2}$. Thus, its order is 2.

Also, index of the highest order derivative $\frac{d^2y}{dx^2}$ is one. Hence, degree of the given differential equation is 1.

II. The given differential equation is $\left(\frac{dy}{dx}\right)^3 - 4\left(\frac{dy}{dx}\right)^2 + 7y = \sin x$

$$\Rightarrow \left(\frac{dy}{dx}\right)^3 - 4\left(\frac{dy}{dx}\right)^2 + 7y - \sin x = 0$$

As the highest order derivative that occurs in the given differential equation is $\frac{dy}{dx}$, thus order of the given differential equation is 1 and its degree is 3.

15 (*a*) The given differential equation is

$$y = x\frac{dy}{dx} + a\sqrt{1 + \left(\frac{dy}{dx}\right)^2}$$

$$\Rightarrow y - x\frac{dy}{dx} = a\sqrt{1 + \left(\frac{dy}{dx}\right)^2}$$

$$\Rightarrow \left(y - x\frac{dy}{dx}\right)^2 = a^2\left(1 + \left(\frac{dy}{dx}\right)^2\right)$$

The order of the highest order derivative is 1 and its degree is 2.

16 (*c*) The given differential equation is $\sqrt{\sin x}\,(dx + dy) = \sqrt{\cos x}\,(dx - dy)$

$$\Rightarrow \sqrt{\sin x}\left(1 + \frac{dy}{dx}\right) = \sqrt{\cos x}\left(1 - \frac{dy}{dx}\right)$$

$$\Rightarrow \frac{dy}{dx} = \frac{\sqrt{\cos x} - \sqrt{\sin x}}{\sqrt{\cos x} + \sqrt{\sin x}}$$

Thus, the order of the differential equation is 1 and its degree is 1.

General and Particular Solutions of a Differential Equation

1 (*d*) We know that the number of constants in the general solution of a differential equation of order n is equal to its order i.e. n.

Therefore, the number of constants in the general equation of fourth order differential equation is four.

2 (*d*) In the particular solution of a differential equation of third order, there is no arbitrary constant because in the particular solution of any differential equation we removes all the arbitrary constants by substituting some particular values.

3 (*a*) Consider, $y = \sqrt{a^2 - x^2}$.

On differentiating both sides w.r.t. x, we get

$$\frac{dy}{dx} = y' = \frac{d}{dx}\sqrt{a^2 - x^2}$$

$$\Rightarrow y' = \frac{1}{2}(a^2 - x^2)^{\frac{1}{2} - 1}\frac{d}{dx}(a^2 - x^2)$$

$$\Rightarrow y' = \frac{1}{2\sqrt{a^2 - x^2}}(-2x)$$

$$= \frac{-x}{\sqrt{a^2 - x^2}}$$

On substituting the value of y' in equation $x + y\frac{dy}{dx} = 0$, we get

$$\text{LHS} = x + yy'$$

$$= x + \sqrt{a^2 - x^2} \times \frac{-x}{\sqrt{a^2 - x^2}}$$

$[\because y = \sqrt{a^2 - x^2}]$

$$= x - x = 0$$

$$\Rightarrow x + yy' = 0$$

$\therefore$ $y = \sqrt{a^2 - x^2}$ is a solution of the differential equation $x + y\frac{dy}{dx} = 0$.

4 (*c*)

I. Given, $x + y = \tan^{-1} y$. ...(i)

On differentiating both sides w.r.t. x, we get

$$\frac{d}{dx}(x + y) = \frac{d}{dx}\tan^{-1} y$$

$$\Rightarrow 1 + y' = \frac{1}{1 + y^2}(y')$$

$\left[\because \frac{dy}{dx} = y'\right]$

$$\Rightarrow (1 + y')(1 + y^2) = y'$$

$$\Rightarrow 1 + y^2 + y' + y^2y' = y'$$

$$\Rightarrow 1 + y^2 + y^2y' = 0$$

Hence, $x + y = \tan^{-1} y$ is a solution of the given differential equation.

II. Given, $y - \cos y = x$. ...(i)

On differentiating both sides w.r.t. x, we get

$$y' - \frac{d}{dx}(\cos y) = \frac{d}{dx}x$$

$$\Rightarrow y' - (-\sin y)\,y' = 1 \qquad \left[\because \frac{dy}{dx} = y'\right]$$

$$\Rightarrow y'(1 + \sin y) = 1$$

$$\Rightarrow y' = \frac{1}{1 + \sin y}$$

But we have to verify,

$(y \sin y + \cos y + x)\,y' = y$ ...(ii)

On substituting the values of y' in Eq. (ii), we get

$$\text{LHS} = (y \sin y + \cos y + x)\,y'$$

$$= (y \sin y + y) \times \frac{1}{1 + \sin y} \qquad [\because y = x + \cos y]$$

$$= y(1 + \sin y) \times \frac{1}{1 + \sin y}$$

$$= y = \text{RHS}$$

Hence, $y - \cos y = x$ is a solution of the given differential equation.

5 (a) Given, $xy = \log y + C$. ...(i)

On differentiating both sides w.r.t. x, we get

$$\frac{d}{dx}(xy) = \frac{d}{dx}(\log y + C)$$

$$\Rightarrow y\frac{d}{dx}x + xy' = \frac{1}{y}y'$$

[using product rule of differentiation in LHS]

$$\Rightarrow xy' + y = \frac{1}{y}y'$$

$$\Rightarrow xy'y + y^2 = y'$$

$$\Rightarrow y^2 = y'(1 - xy)$$

$$\Rightarrow y' = \frac{y^2}{1 - xy}$$

Hence, $xy = \log y + C$ is a solution of the differential equation

$$y' = \frac{y^2}{1 - xy},\ xy \neq 1.$$

6 (d)

A. Given, $y = e^x + 1$. ...(i)

On differentiating both sides of this equation w.r.t. x, we get

$$y' = \frac{d}{dx}(e^x + 1) = e^x \qquad \text{...(ii)}$$

Again, on differentiating both sides w.r.t. x, we get

$$y'' = \frac{d}{dx}(e^x) = e^x$$

$$\Rightarrow y'' = e^x$$

$$\Rightarrow y'' - y' = e^x - e^x = 0$$

Hence, $y = e^x + 1$ is a solution of the different equation $y'' - y' = 0$.

B. Given, $y = x^2 + 2x + C$. ...(i)

On differentiating both sides w.r.t. x, we get

$$\frac{dy}{dx} = y' = \frac{d}{dx}(x^2 + 2x + C)$$

$$\Rightarrow y' = 2x + 2$$

$$\Rightarrow y' - 2x - 2 = 0$$

Hence, $y = x^2 + 2x + C$ is a solution of the differential equation $y' - 2x - 2 = 0$.

C. Given, $y = \cos x + C$ ...(i)

On differentiating both sides w.r.t. x, we get

$$y' = -\sin x$$

$$\Rightarrow y' + \sin x = 0$$

Hence, $y = \cos x + C$ is a solution of the differential equation $y' + \sin x = 0$.

D. Given, $y = \sqrt{1 + x^2}$. ...(i)

On differentiating both sides of Eq. (i) w.r.t. x, we get

$$y' = \frac{d}{dx}(\sqrt{1 + x^2})$$

$$\Rightarrow y' = \frac{1}{2}(1 + x^2)^{-\frac{1}{2}}(2x)$$

$$\Rightarrow y' = \frac{2x}{2\sqrt{1 + x^2}}$$

$$\Rightarrow y' = \frac{x}{\sqrt{1 + x^2}}$$

$$= \frac{xy}{\sqrt{1 + x^2} \cdot \sqrt{1 + x^2}}$$

$$y' = \frac{xy}{(1 + x^2)}$$

Hence, $y = \sqrt{1 + x^2}$ is the solution of the differential equation $y' = \dfrac{xy}{(1 + x^2)}$.

E. The given function is

$$y = Ax \qquad \text{...(i)}$$

On differentiating both sides, we get

$$y' = A$$

$$\Rightarrow y' = \frac{y}{x} \qquad [\because y = Ax,\ x \neq 0]$$

$$\Rightarrow xy' = y$$

Hence, $y = Ax$ is the solution of the differential equation $xy' = y\ (x \neq 0)$.

F. Given, $y = x \sin x$. ...(i)

On differentiating both sides w.r.t. x, we get

$$\frac{dy}{dx} = y' = \frac{d}{dx}(x \sin x)$$

$$\Rightarrow y' = \sin x.\frac{d}{dx}x + x\frac{d}{dx}(\sin x)$$

[using product rule of differentiation]

$$\Rightarrow y' = x\cos x + \sin x$$

On substituting the values of y and y' in the equation $xy' = y + x\sqrt{x^2 - y^2}$, we get

$$\text{LHS} = xy' = x(x\cos x + \sin x)$$

$$= x^2 \cos x + x \sin x$$

$$= x^2\sqrt{1 - \sin^2 x} + y$$

$$[\because \cos^2 x = 1 - \sin^2 x \text{ and } x \sin x = y]$$

$$= x^2\sqrt{1 - \left(\frac{y}{x}\right)^2} + y$$

$$= x\sqrt{x^2 - y^2} + y = \text{RHS}$$

Hence, $y = x \sin x$ is a solution of the differential equation

$$xy' = y + x\sqrt{x^2 - y^2}$$

$$(x \neq 0,\ x > y \text{ or } x < -y)$$

7 (*b*) Given, $x^2 + y^2 = 1$.

On differentiating w.r.t. x, we get

$$2x + 2yy' = 0$$

$$\Rightarrow \quad x + yy' = 0$$

Again, on differentiating w.r.t. x, we get

$$1 + yy'' + (y')^2 = 0$$

8 (*a*) We have, $y = cx - c^2$. ...(i)

On differentiating w.r.t. x, we get

$$y' = c$$

On putting this value in Eq. (i), we get

$$y = x(y') - (y')^2$$

$$\Rightarrow \quad (y')^2 - xy' + y = 0$$

9 (*b*) I. Given, $x\frac{d^2y}{dx^2} + 2\frac{dy}{dx} - xy + x^2 - 2 = 0$ ...(i)

and $y = ae^x + be^{-x} + x^2$ ...(ii)

On differentiating both sides of Eq. (ii) w.r.t. x, we get

$$\frac{dy}{dx} = ae^x - be^{-x} + 2x$$

Again, on differentiating both sides w.r.t. x, we get

$$\frac{d^2y}{dx^2} = ae^x + be^{-x} + 2$$

Now, on substituting the values of $y, \frac{dy}{dx}$ and $\frac{d^2y}{dx^2}$ in Eq. (i), we get

$$\text{LHS} = x\frac{d^2y}{dx^2} + 2\frac{dy}{dx} - xy + x^2 - 2$$

$$= x(ae^x + be^{-x} + 2) + 2(ae^x - be^{-x} + 2x) - x(ae^x + be^{-x} + x^2) + x^2 - 2$$

$$= (ax\,e^x + bx\,e^{-x} + 2x) + (2ae^x - 2be^{-x} + 4x) - (ax\,e^x + bx\,e^{-x} + x^3) + x^2 - 2$$

$$= ax\,e^x + bxe^{-x} + 2x + 2ae^x - 2be^{-x} + 4x - axe^x - bx\,e^{-x} - x^3 + x^2 - 2$$

$$= 2a\,e^x - 2b\,e^{-x} - x^3 + x^2 + 6x - 2 \neq 0$$

LHS $\neq$ RHS

Hence, the given function is not a solution of the corresponding differential equation.

II. Given, $y = e^x (a\cos x + b\sin x)$.

On dividing by e^x both sides, we get

$$e^{-x}\, y = a\cos x + b\sin x \quad \text{...(i)}$$

On differentiating both sides w.r.t. x, we get

$$e^{-x}\frac{dy}{dx} - ye^{-x} = -a\sin x + b\cos x$$

Again, on differentiating both sides w.r.t. x, we get

$$e^{-x}\frac{d^2y}{dx^2} - \frac{dy}{dx}e^{-x} - \left\{-ye^{-x} + e^{-x}\frac{dy}{dx}\right\} = -a\cos x - b\sin x$$

$$\Rightarrow e^{-x}\frac{d^2y}{dx^2} - \frac{dy}{dx}e^{-x} + ye^{-x} - e^{-x}\frac{dy}{dx} = -(a\cos x + b\sin x)$$

$$\Rightarrow e^{-x}\frac{d^2y}{dx^2} - 2e^{-x}\frac{dy}{dx} + y\,e^{-x} = -ye^{-x} \quad \text{[from Eq. (i)]}$$

$$\Rightarrow \quad e^{-x}\frac{d^2y}{dx^2} - 2e^{-x}\frac{dy}{dx} + 2y\,e^{-x} = 0$$

$$\Rightarrow e^{-x}\left\{\frac{d^2y}{dx^2} - 2\frac{dy}{dx} + 2y\right\} = 0$$

$$\Rightarrow \quad \frac{d^2y}{dx^2} - 2\frac{dy}{dx} + 2y = 0$$

Hence, the given function is a solution of the corresponding differential equation.

10 (*c*) Given that,

$$y = e^{-x}(A\cos x + B\sin x) \quad \text{...(i)}$$

On differentiating both sides w.r.t. x, we get

$$\frac{dy}{dx} = e^{-x}(-A\sin x + B\cos x) - e^{-x}(A\cos x + B\sin x)$$

$$= e^{-x}[-A\sin x + B\cos x] - y \quad \text{...(ii)}$$

[using Eq. (i)]

Again, differentiating both sides w.r.t. x, we get

$$\frac{d^2y}{dx^2} = e^{-x}[-A\cos x - B\sin x] - e^{-x}[-A\sin x + B\cos x] - \frac{dy}{dx}$$

$$\Rightarrow \frac{d^2y}{dx^2} = (-y) - \left(\frac{dy}{dx} + y\right) - \frac{dy}{dx}$$

[using Eqs. (i) and (ii)]

$$\Rightarrow \quad \frac{d^2y}{dx^2} = -y - \frac{dy}{dx} - y - \frac{dy}{dx}$$

$$\Rightarrow \quad \frac{d^2y}{dx^2} + 2y + 2\frac{dy}{dx} = 0$$

$$\Rightarrow \quad \frac{d^2y}{dx^2} + 2\frac{dy}{dx} + 2y = 0$$

11 (*c*) Given,

$$y = C_1\cos(x + C_2) + C_3\sin(x + C_4) + C_5e^x + C_6$$

$$y = C_1[\cos x\cos C_2 - \sin x\sin C_2] + C_3[\sin x\cos C_4 + \cos x\sin C_4] + C_5e^x + C_6$$

$$= \cos x(C_1\cos C_2 + C_3\sin C_4) + \sin x(-C_1\sin C_2 + C_3\cos C_4) + C_5e^x + C_6$$

$$= A\cos x + B\sin x + Ce^x + D,$$

where $A = C_1\cos C_2 + C_3\sin C_4$,

$B = -C_1\sin C_2 + C_3\cos C_4$,

$C = C_5$ and $D = C_6$

Hence, order is 4.

[$\because$ number of arbitrary constants is 4]

12 (*d*) Given,

$$y = 2e^{2x} - e^{-x}.$$

$$\Rightarrow \quad y' = 4e^{2x} + e^{-x}$$

$$\Rightarrow \quad y'' = 8e^{2x} - e^{-x}$$

$$\Rightarrow \quad y'' = 4e^{2x} + e^{-x} + 4e^{2x} - 2e^{-x}$$

$$\Rightarrow \quad y'' = y' + 2(2e^{2x} - e^{-x})$$

$$\Rightarrow \quad y'' = y' + 2y$$

$$\Rightarrow \quad y'' - y' - 2y = 0$$

Differential Equations with Variables Separable

1 (*b*) The given differential equation can be expressed as

$$dy = \frac{2x^2+1}{x}dx$$

or $$dy = \left(2x + \frac{1}{x}\right)dx \quad \text{...(i)}$$

On integrating both sides of Eq. (i), we get

$$\int dy = \int\left(2x + \frac{1}{x}\right)dx$$

$$\Rightarrow \quad y = x^2 + \log|x| + C \quad \text{...(ii)}$$

Eq. (ii) represents the family of solution curves of the given differential equation but we are interested in finding the equation of a particular member of the family which passes through the point (1, 1). Therefore, substituting $x = 1, y = 1$ in Eq. (ii), we get

$$C = 0$$

Now, substituting the value of C in Eq. (ii), we get the equation of the required curve as $y = x^2 + \log|x|$.

2 (*c*) We know that, the slope of the tangent to a curve is given by $\frac{dy}{dx}$.

So, $$\frac{dy}{dx} = \frac{2x}{y^2} \quad \text{...(i)}$$

On separating the variables, Eq. (ii) can be written as

$$y^2dy = 2x\,dx \quad \text{...(ii)}$$

On integrating both sides of Eq. (ii), we get

$$\int y^2dy = \int 2x\,dx$$

$$\Rightarrow \quad \frac{y^3}{3} = x^2 + C \quad \text{...(iii)}$$

On substituting $x = -2, y = 3$ in Eq. (iii), we get $C = 5$

On substituting the value of C in Eq. (iii), we get the equation of the required curve as

$$\frac{y^3}{3} = x^2 + 5$$

or $$y = (3x^2+15)^{\frac{1}{3}}$$

3 (*c*) Let P be the principal at any time T.

According to the given problem,

$$\frac{dP}{dt} = \left(\frac{5}{100}\right) \times P \Rightarrow \frac{dP}{dt} = \frac{P}{20} \quad \text{...(i)}$$

On separating the variables in Eq. (i), we get

$$\frac{dP}{P} = \frac{dt}{20} \quad \text{...(ii)}$$

On integrating both sides of Eq. (ii), we get

$$\log P = \frac{t}{20} + C_1$$

$$\Rightarrow \quad P = e^{\frac{t}{20}} \cdot e^{C_1}$$

$$\Rightarrow \quad P = Ce^{\frac{t}{20}},$$

[where $e^{C_1} = C$] ...(iii)

Now, $P = 1000$, when $t = 0$

On substituting the values of P and t in Eq. (iii), we get $C = 1000$.

Therefore, Eq. (iii), gives

$$P = 1000\,e^{\frac{t}{20}}$$

Let t years be the time required to double the principal.

Then, $2000 = 1000\,e^{\frac{t}{20}}$

$$\Rightarrow \quad t = 20\log_e 2$$

4 (*b*)

A. Given, $\frac{dy}{dx} = \frac{1-\cos x}{1+\cos x}$.

On separating the variables and integrating, we get

$$\int dy = \int \frac{1-\cos x}{1+\cos x}dx$$

$$\Rightarrow \quad y = \int \frac{2\sin^2(x/2)}{2\cos^2(x/2)}dx$$

$[\because 1-\cos x = 2\sin^2(x/2)$ and $1+\cos x = 2\cos^2(x/2)]$

$$y = \int \tan^2(x/2)\,dx$$

$$\Rightarrow \quad y = \int (\sec^2(x/2) - 1)\,dx$$

$$\left[\because 1 + \tan^2\frac{x}{2} = \sec^2\frac{x}{2}\right]$$

$$\Rightarrow \quad y = \int \sec^2(x/2)\,dx - \int 1\,dx$$

$$\Rightarrow \quad y = 2\tan\frac{x}{2} - x + C.$$

$[\because \int \sec^2 x\,dx = \tan x]$

which is the required general solution.

B. Given, $\frac{dy}{dx} = \sqrt{4-y^2}$.

On separating the variables, we get $dx = \frac{dy}{\sqrt{4-y^2}}$

On integrating, we get

$$\int \frac{dy}{\sqrt{2^2-y^2}} = \int dx$$

$$\Rightarrow \quad \sin^{-1}\frac{y}{2} = x + C$$

$$\left[\because \int \frac{1}{\sqrt{a^2-x^2}}dx = \sin^{-1}\frac{x}{a}\right]$$

$$\Rightarrow \quad \frac{y}{2} = \sin(x+C)$$

$$\Rightarrow \quad y = 2\sin(x+C),$$

which is the required general solution.

C. Given, $\frac{dy}{dx} + y = 1$.

On separating the variables, we get

$$dy + y\,dx = dx$$

$$\Rightarrow \quad dy = dx - y\,dx$$

$$\Rightarrow \quad dy = dx(1-y)$$

$$\Rightarrow \quad dx = \frac{dy}{1-y}$$

On integrating both sides, we get

$$\int \frac{dy}{(1-y)} = \int dx$$

$$\Rightarrow \quad -\log|1-y| = x - C$$

$$\Rightarrow \quad -x + C = \log|1-y|$$

$$\Rightarrow \quad |1-y| = e^{-x+C}$$

$[\because \log_e x = m \Rightarrow e^m = x]$

$$\Rightarrow \quad y - 1 = (\pm e^C)e^{-x}$$

$$\Rightarrow \quad y = 1 + Ae^{-x},$$

[where $A = \pm e^C$]

which is the required general solution of the given differential equation.

D. Given, $\sec^2 x \tan y dx + \sec^2 y \tan x dy = 0$.

On separating the variables, we get

$\sec^2 x \tan y \, dx = -\sec^2 y \tan x \, dy$

$$\Rightarrow \frac{\sec^2 x}{\tan x} dx = -\frac{\sec^2 y}{\tan y} dy$$

On integrating both sides, we get

$$\int \frac{\sec^2 x}{\tan x} dx = -\int \frac{\sec^2 y}{\tan y} dy$$

Let $\tan x = u$

$$\Rightarrow \sec^2 x = \frac{du}{dx}$$

$$\Rightarrow dx = \frac{du}{\sec^2 x}$$

and $\tan y = v$

$$\Rightarrow \sec^2 y = \frac{dv}{dy}$$

$$\Rightarrow dy = \frac{dv}{\sec^2 y}$$

$$\int \frac{\sec^2 x}{u} \frac{du}{\sec^2 x} = -\int \frac{\sec^2 y}{v} \frac{dv}{\sec^2 y}$$

$$\Rightarrow \int \frac{du}{u} = -\int \frac{dv}{v}$$

$\Rightarrow \log|u| = -\log|v| + \log|C|$

$\Rightarrow \log|\tan x| = -\log|\tan y| + \log|C|$

$\Rightarrow \log|\tan x \tan y| = \log|C|$

[$\because \log m + \log n = \log mn$]

$\Rightarrow \tan x \cdot \tan y = C$

[$\because \log m = \log n \Rightarrow m = n$]

which is the required general solution.

E. Given,

$(e^x + e^{-x}) dy - (e^x - e^{-x}) dx = 0$

$\Rightarrow (e^x + e^{-x}) dy = (e^x - e^{-x}) dx$

On separating the variables, we get

$$dy = \left(\frac{e^x - e^{-x}}{e^x + e^{-x}}\right) dx$$

On integrating, we get

$$\int dy = \int \left(\frac{e^x - e^{-x}}{e^x + e^{-x}}\right) dx$$

Let $e^x + e^{-x} = t$

$$\Rightarrow e^x - e^{-x} = \frac{dt}{dx}$$

$$\Rightarrow dx = \frac{dt}{e^x - e^{-x}}$$

$$\therefore \int dy = \int \frac{e^x - e^{-x}}{t} \frac{dt}{e^x - e^{-x}}$$

$$= \int \frac{1}{t} dt$$

$\Rightarrow y = \log|t| + C$

$\Rightarrow y = \log|e^x + e^{-x}| + C$,

which is the required general solution.

F. Given, $\frac{dy}{dx} = (1 + x^2)(1 + y^2)$.

On separating the variables, we get

$$\frac{dy}{1 + y^2} = dx(1 + x^2)$$

$$\Rightarrow \frac{dy}{1 + y^2} = 1 dx + x^2 dx$$

On integrating, we get

$$\int \frac{dy}{1 + y^2} = \int dx + \int x^2 dx$$

$$\Rightarrow \tan^{-1} y = x + \frac{x^3}{3} + C,$$

which is the required general solution.

5 (d) Given, $y \log y \, dx - x \, dy = 0$.

On separating the variables, we get

$y \log y \, dx = x \, dy$

$$\Rightarrow \frac{1}{x} dx = \frac{1}{y \log y} dy$$

On integrating, we get

$$\int \frac{1}{x} dx = \int \frac{1}{y \log y} dy$$

Let $\log y = t$

$$\Rightarrow \frac{1}{y} = \frac{dt}{dy} \Rightarrow dy = y \, dt$$

$$\therefore \int \frac{1}{x} dx = \int \frac{1}{yt} y dt$$

$\Rightarrow \log|x| = \log|t| - \log|C|$

$\Rightarrow \log|xC| = \log|\log y|$

$\Rightarrow Cx = \log y$

[$\because \log m + \log n = \log mn$ and $\log m = \log n \Rightarrow m = n$]

$\Rightarrow y = e^{Cx}$

[$\because \log_e x = m \Rightarrow e^m = x$]

which is the required general solution.

6 (a) Given, $x^5 \frac{dy}{dx} = -y^5$.

On separating the variables, we get

$$\frac{dy}{y^5} = -\frac{dx}{x^5}$$

On integrating, we get

$$\int \frac{dy}{y^5} = -\int \frac{dx}{x^5}$$

$$\Rightarrow \int y^{-5} dy = -\int x^{-5} dx$$

$$\Rightarrow \frac{y^{-5+1}}{(-5+1)} = -\frac{x^{-5+1}}{(-5+1)} + C_1$$

$$\left[\because \int x^n dx = \frac{x^{n+1}}{n+1}\right]$$

$$\Rightarrow \frac{y^{-4}}{-4} = -\frac{x^{-4}}{(-4)} + C_1$$

$\Rightarrow x^{-4} + y^{-4} = -4C_1$

$\Rightarrow x^{-4} + y^{-4} = C$, (where $C = -4C_1$)

which is the required general solution.

7 (c)

I. Given, $\frac{dy}{dx} = \sin^{-1} x$.

On separating the variables, we get $dy = \sin^{-1} x \, dx$

On integrating, we get

$$\int dy = \int \sin^{-1} x \, dx$$

$$\Rightarrow y = \sin^{-1} x \int 1 dx - \int \left[\frac{d}{dx}(\sin^{-1} x) \int 1 dx\right] dx$$

[using integration by parts]

$$\Rightarrow y = x \sin^{-1} x - \int \left[\frac{x}{\sqrt{1 - x^2}}\right] dx$$

Let $1-x^2=t$.

$\Rightarrow -2x=\dfrac{dt}{dx}\Rightarrow dx=\dfrac{dt}{-2x}$

$\therefore \quad y=x\sin^{-1}x+\int \dfrac{x}{\sqrt{t}}\dfrac{dt}{2x}$

$\Rightarrow \quad y=x\sin^{-1}x+\dfrac{1}{2}\cdot\dfrac{t^{-1/2+1}}{-1/2+1}+C$

$\Rightarrow y=x\sin^{-1}x+\dfrac{2}{2}\sqrt{t}+C$

$\Rightarrow y=x\sin^{-1}x+\sqrt{1-x^2}+C$

which is the required general solution.

II. $e^x\tan y\,dx+(1-e^x)\sec^2 y\,dy=0$

On separating the variables, we get

$e^x\tan y\,dx=-(1-e^x)\sec^2 y\,dy$

$\Rightarrow \quad \dfrac{e^x}{(e^x-1)}dx=\dfrac{\sec^2 y}{\tan y}dy$

On integrating, we get

$\int\dfrac{e^x}{(e^x-1)}dx=\int\dfrac{\sec^2 y}{\tan y}dy$

Let $\quad e^x-1=t$.

$\Rightarrow \quad e^x=\dfrac{dt}{dx}$

$\Rightarrow \quad dx=\dfrac{dt}{e^x}$

and let $\tan y=v$.

$\Rightarrow \sec^2 y=\dfrac{dv}{dy}\Rightarrow dy=\dfrac{dv}{\sec^2 y}$

$\therefore \int\dfrac{e^x}{t}\dfrac{dt}{e^x}=\int\dfrac{\sec^2 y}{v}\dfrac{dv}{\sec^2 y}$

$\Rightarrow \log|t|=\log|v|-\log|C'|$

$\Rightarrow \log|e^x-1|=\log|\tan y|-\log|C'|$

$\Rightarrow \log|C'(e^x-1)|=\log|\tan y|$

$[\because \log m+\log n=\log mn]$

$\Rightarrow \quad C'(e^x-1)=\tan y$

$[\because \log m=\log n\Rightarrow m=n]$

$\Rightarrow \quad \tan y=C(1-e^x)$

(where $C=-C'$)

which is the required general solution.

8 (c) Let x and y be the x-coordinate and y-coordinate of the curve, respectively.

We know that, the slope of a tangent to the curve in the coordinate axis is given by the relation $\dfrac{dy}{dx}$.

According to given question,

Product of the slope of tangent with y-coordinate = x-coordinate

$$y\cdot\frac{dy}{dx}=x \quad \text{...(i)}$$

On separating the variables, we get

$$y\,dy=x\,dx$$

On integrating both sides, we get

$$\int y\,dy=\int x\,dx$$

$\Rightarrow \quad \dfrac{y^2}{2}=\dfrac{x^2}{2}+C \quad$ ...(ii)

Now, the curve passes through the point $(0,-2)$. Therefore,

$$\frac{(-2)^2}{2}=0+C$$

$\Rightarrow \quad C=\dfrac{4}{2}=2$

On substituting this value of C in Eq. (ii), we get

$$\frac{y^2}{2}=\frac{x^2}{2}+2$$

$\Rightarrow x^2-y^2+4=0\Rightarrow y^2-x^2=4$

which is the required equation of the curve.

9 (d) It is given that, (x,y) is the point of contact of the curve and its tangent.

The slope of the line segment joining the points $(x_2,y_2)\equiv(x,y)$ and $(x_1,y_1)\equiv(-4,-3)$

$$=\frac{y-(-3)}{x-(-4)}=\frac{y+3}{x+4}$$

$\left[\because \text{slope of tangent}=\dfrac{y_2-y_1}{x_2-x_1}\right]$

According to the question,

Slope of tangent is twice the slope of the line.

$\therefore \quad \dfrac{dy}{dx}=2\left(\dfrac{y+3}{x+4}\right)$

Now, separating the variables, we get

$$\frac{dy}{y+3}=\left(\frac{2}{x+4}\right)dx$$

On integrating both sides, we get

$$\int\frac{dy}{y+3}=\int\left(\frac{2}{x+4}\right)dx$$

$\Rightarrow \log|y+3|=2\log|x+4|+\log|C|$

$\Rightarrow \log|y+3|=\log|x+4|^2+\log|C|$

$\Rightarrow \log\dfrac{|y+3|}{|x+4|^2}=\log|C|$

$\left[\because \log m-\log n=\log\dfrac{m}{n}\right]$

$\Rightarrow \quad \dfrac{|y+3|}{|x+4|^2}=C \quad$ ...(ii)

The curve passes through the point $(-2,1)$, therefore

$\Rightarrow \quad \dfrac{|1+3|}{|-2+4|^2}=C\Rightarrow C=1$

On substituting $C=1$ in Eq. (ii), we get

$$\frac{|y+3|}{|x+4|^2}=1$$

$\Rightarrow \quad |y+3|=(x+4)^2$

which is the required equation of curve.

10 (b)

A. Given,

$$(x^3+x^2+x+1)\frac{dy}{dx}=2x^2+x$$

On separating the variables, we get $dy=\dfrac{2x^2+x}{(x^3+x^2+x+1)}dx$

On integrating both sides, we get

$$\int dy=\int\frac{2x^2+x}{(x^3+x^2+x+1)}dx$$

$\Rightarrow\int dy=\int\dfrac{2x^2+x}{x^2(x+1)+1(x+1)}dx$

$\Rightarrow\int dy=\int\dfrac{2x^2+x}{(x+1)(x^2+1)}dx$

$\Rightarrow y=\int\dfrac{2x^2+x}{(x+1)(x^2+1)}dx \quad$ ...(i)

Let $\dfrac{2x^2+x}{(x+1)(x^2+1)}=\dfrac{A}{(x+1)}+\dfrac{Bx+C}{(x^2+1)}$ ...(ii)

[by partial fraction]

$\Rightarrow \dfrac{2x^2+x}{(x+1)(x^2+1)}=\dfrac{A(x^2+1)+(Bx+C)(x+1)}{(x+1)(x^2+1)}$

$\Rightarrow 2x^2+x=Ax^2+A+Bx^2+Bx+Cx+C$

$\Rightarrow 2x^2+x=x^2(A+B)+x(B+C)+(A+C)$

On comparing the coefficients of x^2, x and constant terms on both sides, we get

$A+B=2,$

$B+C=1$

and $A+C=0$

On solving these equations, we get

$A=\dfrac{1}{2}, B=\dfrac{3}{2}$ and $C=-\dfrac{1}{2}$

On substituting the values of A, B and C in Eq.(ii), we get

$$\frac{2x^2+x}{(x+1)(x^2+1)}=\frac{1}{2(x+1)}+\frac{\frac{3}{2}x-\frac{1}{2}}{x^2+1}$$

$$\therefore \int\frac{2x^2+x}{(x^2+1)(x+1)}dx=\frac{1}{2}\int\frac{1}{(x+1)}dx+\int\frac{\frac{3}{2}x-\frac{1}{2}}{(x^2+1)}dx$$

Then, from Eq. (i), we get

$$y=\frac{1}{2}\log|x+1|+\frac{3}{2}\int\frac{x}{(x^2+1)}dx-\frac{1}{2}\int\frac{1}{(x^2+1)}dx$$

$$\Rightarrow y=\frac{1}{2}\log|x+1|+\frac{3}{2}\int\frac{x}{(x^2+1)}dx-\frac{1}{2}\tan^{-1}x$$

Let $x^2+1=t.$

$\Rightarrow \quad 2x=\dfrac{dt}{dx}\Rightarrow dx=\dfrac{dt}{2x}$

$$\therefore \quad y=\frac{1}{2}\log|x+1|+\frac{3}{2}\int\frac{x}{t}\frac{dt}{2x}-\frac{1}{2}\tan^{-1}x$$

$$\Rightarrow y=\frac{1}{2}\log|x+1|+\frac{3}{4}\int\frac{1}{t}dt-\frac{1}{2}\tan^{-1}x$$

$$\Rightarrow y=\frac{1}{2}\log|x+1|+\frac{3}{4}\log|t|-\frac{1}{2}\tan^{-1}x+C$$

$$\Rightarrow y=\frac{1}{2}\log|x+1|+\frac{3}{4}\log|x^2+1|-\frac{1}{2}\tan^{-1}x+C$$

$$\Rightarrow y=\frac{1}{4}[2\log|x+1|+3\log|x^2+1|]-\frac{1}{2}\tan^{-1}x+C$$

$$\Rightarrow y=\frac{1}{4}[\log\{(x+1)^2(x^2+1)^3\}]-\frac{1}{2}\tan^{-1}x+C \text{ ...(iii)}$$

$[\because \log m^n=n\log m]$

When $x=0$, then $y=1$.

On putting these values in Eq. (iii), we get

$$1=\frac{1}{4}\log(1)-\frac{1}{2}\tan^{-1}(0)+C$$

$$\Rightarrow 1=\frac{1}{4}\times0-\frac{1}{2}\times0+C\Rightarrow C=1$$

On putting $C=1$ in Eq. (iii), we get

$$y=\frac{1}{4}[\log\{(x+1)^2(x^2+1)^3\}]-\frac{1}{2}\tan^{-1}x+1$$

which is the required particular solution.

B. Given, $x(x^2-1)\dfrac{dy}{dx}=1.$

On separating the variables, we get

$$dy=\frac{1}{x(x^2-1)}dx$$

$$\Rightarrow dy=\frac{1}{x(x-1)(x+1)}dx$$

On integrating both sides, we get

$$\int dy=\int\frac{1}{x(x-1)(x+1)}dx \text{ ...(i)}$$

Let $\dfrac{1}{x(x-1)(x+1)}=\dfrac{A}{x}+\dfrac{B}{x-1}+\dfrac{C}{x+1}$ ...(ii)

[by partial fraction]

$$\Rightarrow \frac{1}{x(x-1)(x+1)}=\frac{A(x-1)(x+1)+Bx(x+1)+Cx(x-1)}{x(x-1)(x+1)}$$

$\therefore 1=A(x^2-1)+B(x)(x+1)+C(x)(x-1)$

$\Rightarrow 1=Ax^2-A+Bx^2+Bx+Cx^2-Cx$

$\Rightarrow \quad 1=x^2(A+B+C)+x(B-C)+(-A)$

On comparing the coefficients of x^2, x and constant terms on both sides, we get

$A+B+C=0$ ...(iii)

$B-C=0$ ...(iv)

and $-A=1$ ...(v)

On putting the value of A in Eq. (iii), we get

$B+C=1$ ...(vi)

On adding Eqs. (iv) and (vi), we get

$2B=1 \quad\Rightarrow\quad B=\dfrac{1}{2}$

Then, from Eq. (iv), $C=\dfrac{1}{2}$

On putting the values of A, B and C in Eq. (ii), we get

$$\frac{1}{x(x-1)(x+1)}=\frac{-1}{x}+\frac{1}{2(x-1)}+\frac{1}{2(x+1)}$$

$$\Rightarrow\int dy=-\int\frac{1}{x}dx+\frac{1}{2}\int\frac{1}{x-1}dx+\frac{1}{2}\int\frac{1}{x+1}dx$$

Now, from Eq. (i), we get

$$y = -\log|x| + \frac{1}{2}\log|(x-1)| + \frac{1}{2}\log|(x+1)| + C$$

$$\Rightarrow y = -\frac{1}{2}\log(x^2) + \frac{1}{2}\log|(x-1)| + \frac{1}{2}\log|(x+1)| + C$$

$$\Rightarrow y = \frac{1}{2}\left[\log\left(\frac{(x-1)(x+1)}{x^2}\right)\right] + C$$

$$\left[\because \log l + \log m - \log n = \log\frac{lm}{n}\right]$$

$$\Rightarrow y = \frac{1}{2}\left[\log\left|\left(\frac{x^2-1}{x^2}\right)\right|\right] + C \quad \text{...(vii)}$$

On putting $y = 0$ and $x = 2$ in Eq. (vii), we get

$$0 = \frac{1}{2}\left[\log\left|\left(\frac{2^2-1}{2^2}\right)\right|\right] + C$$

$$\Rightarrow C = -\frac{1}{2}\log\left(\frac{3}{4}\right)$$

On substituting the value of C in Eq. (vii), we get

$$y = \frac{1}{2}\log\left|\left(\frac{x^2-1}{x^2}\right)\right| - \frac{1}{2}\log\left(\frac{3}{4}\right)$$

which is the required particular solution.

C. Given, $\cos\left(\frac{dy}{dx}\right) = a$.

$$\Rightarrow \frac{dy}{dx} = \cos^{-1} a$$

On separating the variables, we get $dy = (\cos^{-1} a)\,dx$

On integrating both sides, we get $\int dy = \cos^{-1} a \int dx$

$$\Rightarrow y = (\cos^{-1} a)(x) + C \quad \text{...(i)}$$

On putting $y = 2$ and $x = 0$, we get

$$2 = \cos^{-1}(a) \times 0 + C$$

$$\Rightarrow C = 2$$

On substituting $C = 2$ in Eq. (i), we get

$$y = x\cos^{-1} a + 2$$

$$\Rightarrow \frac{y-2}{x} = \cos^{-1} a$$

$$\Rightarrow \cos\left(\frac{y-2}{x}\right) = a,$$

which is the required particular solution.

D. Given, $\frac{dy}{dx} = y\tan x$.

On separating the variables, we get

$$\frac{1}{y}dy = \tan x\,dx$$

On integrating both sides, we get

$$\int \frac{1}{y}dy = \int \tan x\,dx$$

$$\Rightarrow \log|y| = \log|(\sec x)| + \log|C|$$

$$\Rightarrow \log y = \log|(C\sec x)|$$

$$[\because \log m + \log n = \log mn]$$

$$\Rightarrow y = C\sec x$$

$$[\because \log m = \log n \Rightarrow m = n] \quad \text{...(i)}$$

Now, put $y = 1$ and $x = 0$, we get

$$1 = C\sec 0$$

$$\Rightarrow 1 = C \times 1 \Rightarrow C = 1$$

On substituting $C = 1$ in Eq. (i), we get $y = \sec x$, which is the required particular solution.

11 (*a*) Let the rate of change of the volume of the balloon be k (where k is constant)

$$\because \frac{d}{dt}(\text{volume}) = \text{constant}$$

$$\Rightarrow \frac{d}{dt}\left(\frac{4}{3}\pi r^3\right) = k$$

$$\left[\because \text{volume of sphere} = \frac{4}{3}\pi r^3\right]$$

$$\Rightarrow \left(\frac{4}{3}\pi\right)\left(3r^2\frac{dr}{dt}\right) = k$$

On separating the variables, we get

$$4\pi r^2\,dr = k\,dt \quad \text{...(i)}$$

On integrating both sides, we get

$$4\pi\int r^2 dr = k\int dt$$

$$\Rightarrow 4\pi\frac{r^3}{3} = kt + C$$

$$\Rightarrow 4\pi r^3 = 3(kt + C) \quad \text{...(ii)}$$

Now, at $t = 0$, $r = 3$.

$$\therefore 4\pi(3)^3 = 3(k \times 0 + C)$$

$$\Rightarrow 108\pi = 3C \Rightarrow C = 36\pi$$

Also, when $t = 3$, $r = 6$.

Then, from Eq. (ii),

$$4\pi(6)^3 = 3(k \times 3 + C)$$

$$\Rightarrow 864\pi = 3(3k + 36\pi)$$

$$\Rightarrow 3k = 288\pi - 36\pi = 252\pi$$

$$\Rightarrow k = 84\pi$$

On substituting the values of k and C in Eq. (ii), we get

$$4\pi r^3 = 3[84\pi t + 36\pi]$$

$$\Rightarrow 4\pi r^3 = 4\pi(63t + 27)$$

$$\Rightarrow r^3 = 63t + 27$$

$$\Rightarrow r = (63t + 27)^{1/3}$$

which is the required radius of the balloon at time t.

12 (*d*)

I. The given differential equation of the curve is

$$y' = e^x \sin x \text{ or } \frac{dy}{dx} = e^x \sin x$$

On separating the variables, we get

$$dy = e^x \sin x\,dx$$

On integrating both sides, we get

$$\int dy = \int e^x \sin x\,dx \quad \text{...(i)}$$

$$\text{Let } I = \int e^x \sin x\,dx \quad \text{...(ii)}$$

$$\Rightarrow I = \sin x\int e^x dx - \int\left(\frac{d}{dx}(\sin x)\int e^x dx\right)dx$$

[using integration by parts]

$$= \sin x\int e^x dx - \int \cos x \cdot e^x dx$$

$$= \sin x.e^x - \left[\cos x.\int e^x dx - \int\left(\frac{d}{dx}(\cos x)\cdot\int e^x dx\right)dx\right]$$

[again using integration by parts]

$$\Rightarrow I = \sin x.e^x - [\cos x.e^x - \int(-\sin x).e^x dx]$$

$$= \sin x.e^x - e^x.\cos x - \int e^x.\sin x.dx$$

$\Rightarrow I = \sin x . e^x - \cos x . e^x - I$ [from Eq. (ii)]

$\Rightarrow 2I = e^x(\sin x - \cos x)$

$\Rightarrow I = \dfrac{e^x(\sin x - \cos x)}{2}$

On substituting this value in Eq. (i), we get

$$y = \frac{e^x(\sin x - \cos x)}{2} + C \quad ...(iii)$$

Now, the curve passes through the point (0, 0) or we can say $x = 0, y = 0$.

$\therefore \quad 0 = \dfrac{e^0(\sin 0 - \cos 0)}{2} + C$ [from Eq. (iii)]

$\Rightarrow \quad 0 = \dfrac{1(0-1)}{2} + C \Rightarrow C = \dfrac{1}{2}$

On substituting $C = \dfrac{1}{2}$ in Eq. (iii), we get

$$y = \frac{e^x(\sin x - \cos x)}{2} + \frac{1}{2}$$

$\Rightarrow 2y = e^x(\sin x - \cos x) + 1$

$\Rightarrow 2y - 1 = e^x(\sin x - \cos x)$

Hence, the equation of the curve is

$$2y - 1 = e^x(\sin x - \cos x).$$

II. The given curve is

$$xy\frac{dy}{dx} = (x+2)(y+2) \quad ...(i)$$

On separating the variables, we get

$$\frac{y}{y+2}dy = \frac{x+2}{x}dx$$

On integrating both sides, we get

$$\int \frac{y}{y+2}dy = \int \frac{x+2}{x}dx$$

$\Rightarrow \int \left(\dfrac{y+2-2}{y+2}\right)dy = \int \dfrac{x+2}{x}dx$

$\Rightarrow \int \dfrac{y+2}{y+2}dy - \int \dfrac{2}{y+2}dy = \int \dfrac{x}{x}dx + \int \dfrac{2}{x}dx$

$\Rightarrow \int dy - 2\int \dfrac{1}{y+2}dy = \int dx + 2\int \dfrac{1}{x}dx$

$\Rightarrow \quad y - 2\log|y+2| = x + 2\log|x| + C \quad ...(ii)$

Now, the curve passes through the point (1, – 1).

So, put $x = 1$ and $y = -1$.

$-1 - 2\log|-1+2| = 1 + 2\log 1 + C$

$\Rightarrow -1 - 2\log 1 = 1 + 2\log 1 + C$

$\Rightarrow \quad C = -2$ [$\because \log 1 = 0$]

Hence, from Eq. (ii) we get

$y - 2\log|y+2| = x + 2\log|x| - 2$

$\Rightarrow \quad y - x + 2 = 2\log|x(y+2)|$ [$\because \log m + \log n = \log mn$]

$\Rightarrow \quad y - x + 2 = \log[x^2(y+2)^2]$ [$\because \log m^n = n\log m$]

Hence, the equation of the curve is

$$y - x + 2 = \log(x^2(y+2)^2)$$

13 (*a*) Given, $\dfrac{dy}{dx} = e^{x+y}$.

$\Rightarrow \quad \dfrac{dy}{dx} = e^x e^y$

Now, separating the variables, we get

$$e^{-y}dy = e^x dx$$

On integrating both sides, we get

$$\int e^{-y}dy = \int e^x dx$$

$\Rightarrow \quad \dfrac{e^{-y}}{-1} = e^x + A$

$\Rightarrow \quad e^x + e^{-y} = -A$

$\Rightarrow \quad e^x + e^{-y} = C$ [where $C = -A$]

14 (*b*) Let P, t and r represents the principal, time and rate of interest, respectively.

It is given that the principal increases continuously at the rate of r% per year.

$\therefore \quad \dfrac{dP}{dt} = r\%$ of P

$\Rightarrow \quad \dfrac{dP}{dt} = \dfrac{rP}{100} \Rightarrow \dfrac{dP}{P} = \dfrac{r}{100}dt$ [by separating the variables]

On integrating both sides, we obtain

$$\int \frac{dP}{P} = \int \frac{r}{100}dt$$

$\Rightarrow \quad \log|P| = \dfrac{r}{100}t + C \quad ...(i)$

When $t = 0$, let $P = P_0$, then

$\log|P_0| = 0 + C$

$\Rightarrow \quad C = \log|P_0|$

On substituting the value of C in Eq. (i), we get

$$\log|P| = \frac{r}{100}t + \log|P_0|$$

$\Rightarrow \log|P| - \log|P_0| = \dfrac{r}{100}t$

$\Rightarrow \quad \log\left|\dfrac{P}{P_0}\right| = \dfrac{r}{100}t \quad ...(ii)$

It is given that, when $t = 10$, then $P = 2P_0$. Put in Eq. (ii), we get

$\log 2 = \dfrac{r(10)}{100}$

$\Rightarrow \quad r = 10\log 2 = 10 \times 0.6931$

$\Rightarrow \quad r = 6.931$

Hence, the value of r is 6.93%.

15 (*d*) Let P and t be the principal and time, respectively.

It is given that the principal increases continuously at the rate of 5% per year.

So, $\dfrac{dP}{dt} = 5\%$ of $P \Rightarrow \dfrac{dP}{dt} = \dfrac{5}{100}P$

On separating the variables, we get

$$\frac{dP}{P} = \frac{1}{20}dt$$

On integrating, we get

$$\int \frac{dP}{P} = \int \frac{1}{20}dt$$

$\Rightarrow \quad \log|P| = \dfrac{1}{20}t + C \quad ...(i)$

When $t = 0$, $P = 1000$.

$\Rightarrow \quad \log 1000 = C \quad ...(ii)$

Put the value of C in Eq. (i), we get

$$\log|P| = \frac{1}{20}t + \log 1000$$

$\Rightarrow \quad \log\left|\left(\dfrac{P}{1000}\right)\right| = \dfrac{1}{20}t$ $\left[\because \log m - \log n = \log\dfrac{m}{n}\right]$

When $t = 10$, then

$$\log\left|\frac{P}{1000}\right| = \frac{1}{20} \times 10$$

$$\Rightarrow \quad \frac{P}{1000} = e^{1/2}$$

$[\because \log_e x = m \Rightarrow e^m = x]$

$$\Rightarrow \quad \frac{P}{1000} = e^{0.5} = 1.648$$

$$\Rightarrow \quad P = 1000 \times 1.648$$

$$\Rightarrow \quad P = 1648$$

Hence, after 10 yr, the amount will worth ₹ 1648.

16 (*a*) Let y be the count of the bacteria at the end of t hours, then

$$\frac{dy}{dt} \propto y \Rightarrow \frac{dy}{dt} = ky,$$

where k is constant of proportionality.

Now, separating the variables, we get

$$\frac{dy}{y} = k\,dt$$

On integrating, we get

$$\int \frac{dy}{y} = \int k\,dt$$

$$\Rightarrow \quad \log|y| = kt + C \quad \text{...(i)}$$

When $t = 0$, $y = 100000$ (initially), then

$$\log 100000 = C \quad \text{...(ii)}$$

and when $t = 2$, $y = 110000$, then

$$\log 110000 = 2k + C \quad \text{...(iii)}$$

On subtracting Eqs. (ii) from Eqs. (iii), we get

$$\log 110000 - \log 100000 = 2k$$

$$\Rightarrow \quad \log \frac{110000}{100000} = 2k$$

$$\Rightarrow \quad k = \frac{1}{2} \log\left(\frac{11}{10}\right)$$

On substituting the value of k and C in Eq. (i), we get

$$\log y = \frac{1}{2}\log\left(\frac{11}{10}\right)t + \log 100000$$

When $y = 200000$, then

$$\log 200000 = \frac{1}{2}\log\left(\frac{11}{10}\right)t + \log 100000$$

$$\Rightarrow \log\left(\frac{200000}{100000}\right) = \frac{1}{2}\log\left(\frac{11}{10}\right)t$$

$$\Rightarrow \quad 2\log(2) = \log\left(\frac{11}{10}\right)t$$

$$\Rightarrow \quad t = \frac{2\log 2}{\log\left(\frac{11}{10}\right)}$$

Hence, in $\dfrac{2\log 2}{\log\left(\frac{11}{10}\right)}$ h, the number of bacteria increases from 100000 to 200000.

17 (*a*) The given differential equation can be written as

$$\frac{dy}{dx} = e^{(3x + 4y)}$$

or $$\frac{dy}{dx} = e^{3x} \cdot e^{4y} \quad \text{...(i)}$$

On separating the variables, we get

$$\frac{dy}{e^{4y}} = e^{3x}dx$$

Therefore, $\int e^{-4y}dy = \int e^{3x}dx$

$$\Rightarrow \quad \frac{e^{-4y}}{-4} = \frac{e^{3x}}{3} + C$$

or $4e^{3x} + 3e^{-4y} + 12C = 0 \quad \text{...(ii)}$

On substituting $x = 0$ and $y = 0$ in Eq. (ii), we get

$$4 + 3 + 12C = 0 \text{ or } C = \frac{-7}{12}$$

On substituting the value of C in Eq. (ii), we get

$$4e^{3x} + 3e^{-4y} - 7 = 0$$

which is the required particular solution of the given differential equation.

18 (*d*) Given differential equation is

$$x\,dy = y\,dx$$

$$\Rightarrow \quad \frac{dy}{y} = \frac{dx}{x}$$

$$\Rightarrow \quad \int \frac{dy}{y} = \int \frac{dx}{x}$$

$$\Rightarrow \quad \log_e y = \log_e x + \log_e C$$

$$\Rightarrow \quad y = Cx$$

which is a straight line.

19 (*c*) Given,

$$\cos y \frac{dy}{dx} = e^{x + \sin y} + x^2 e^{\sin y}$$

$$\Rightarrow \quad \cos y\,dy = e^{\sin y}(e^x + x^2)\,dx$$

$$\Rightarrow \quad \int \frac{\cos y}{e^{\sin y}}dy = \int (e^x + x^2)\,dx$$

Put $\sin y = t$ in LHS.

$$\Rightarrow \cos y\,dy = dt$$

$$\because \quad \int \frac{dt}{e^t} = \int (e^x + x^2)\,dx$$

$$\Rightarrow \quad -e^{-t} = e^x + \frac{x^3}{3} + C$$

$$\Rightarrow \quad e^x + e^{-\sin y} + \frac{x^3}{3} = C$$

20 (*a*) The given differential equation is

$$\frac{dy}{dx} = 1 + y + y^2 + x + xy + xy^2$$

$$= (1 + y + y^2) + x(1 + y + y^2)$$

$$\Rightarrow \frac{dy}{dx} = (1 + x)(1 + y + y^2)$$

$$\Rightarrow \quad \frac{1}{1 + y + y^2}dy = (1 + x)\,dx$$

On integrating both sides, we get

$$\int \frac{dy}{\left(y + \frac{1}{2}\right)^2 + \left(\frac{\sqrt{3}}{2}\right)^2} = \int (1 + x)\,dx$$

$$\Rightarrow \frac{1}{\frac{\sqrt{3}}{2}} \tan^{-1}\left(\frac{y + \frac{1}{2}}{\frac{\sqrt{3}}{2}}\right) = x + \frac{x^2}{2} + \frac{C}{2}$$

$$\Rightarrow 4\tan^{-1}\left(\frac{2y + 1}{\sqrt{3}}\right) = \sqrt{3}(2x + x^2) + C$$

21 (*b*) According to the question,

$$\frac{dy}{dx} = y + \frac{y}{x} = y\left(1 + \frac{1}{x}\right)$$

$$\Rightarrow \quad \frac{dy}{y} = \left(1 + \frac{1}{x}\right)dx$$

On integrating both sides, we get

$$\int \frac{dy}{y} = \int \left(1 + \frac{1}{x}\right)dx$$

$$\Rightarrow \quad \log y = x + \log x + C$$

$$\Rightarrow \quad \log\left(\frac{y}{x}\right) = x + C$$

$\Rightarrow \quad \dfrac{y}{x} = e^{x+C}$

$= e^x \cdot e^C$

$\Rightarrow \quad \dfrac{y}{x} = ke^x$

$\Rightarrow \quad y = kx \cdot e^x$, where $k = e^C$.

22 (*a*) Let y be the population at time t, then $\dfrac{dy}{dt} \propto y$

$\Rightarrow \dfrac{dy}{dt} = ky$, where k is constant

$\Rightarrow \dfrac{dy}{y} = k\,dt$

On integrating both sides, we get

$$\log y = kt + C \quad \text{...(i)}$$

In the year 1999, $t = 0$, $y = 20000$.

From Eq. (i),

$$\log 20000 = k(0) + C$$

$\Rightarrow \quad \log 20000 = C \quad$ ...(ii)

In the year 2004,

$$t = 5,\ y = 25000.$$

So from Eq. (i),

$$\log 25000 = k(5) + C$$

$\Rightarrow \quad \log 25000 = 5k + \log 20000$ [using Eq. (iii)]

$\Rightarrow \quad 5k = \log\left(\dfrac{25000}{20000}\right) = \log\left(\dfrac{5}{4}\right)$

$\Rightarrow \quad k = \dfrac{1}{5}\log\dfrac{5}{4}$

For year 2009, $t = 10$ yr.

Now, substituting the values of t, k and C in Eq. (i), we get

$$\log y = 10 \times \frac{1}{5}\log\left(\frac{5}{4}\right) + \log(20000)$$

$\Rightarrow \quad \log y = \log\left[20000 \times \left(\dfrac{5}{4}\right)^2\right]$

[$\because \log m + \log n = \log mn$]

$\Rightarrow \quad y = 20000 \times \dfrac{5}{4} \times \dfrac{5}{4}$

$\Rightarrow \quad y = 31250$

Hence, the population of the village in 2009 will be 31250.

23. (*d*) Here, the slope of the tangent to the curve at any point (x, y) is $\dfrac{y-1}{x^2+x}$.

$\therefore \quad \dfrac{dy}{dx} = \dfrac{y-1}{x^2+x}$

$\Rightarrow \quad \dfrac{dy}{y-1} = \dfrac{dx}{x^2+x}$

On integrating both sides, we get

$$\int \frac{dy}{y-1} = \int \frac{dx}{x(x+1)}$$

$\Rightarrow \log(y-1) = \int\left(\dfrac{1}{x} - \dfrac{1}{x+1}\right)dx$

$\Rightarrow \log(y-1) = \log x - \log(x+1) + \log C$

$\Rightarrow \log(y-1) = \log\left(\dfrac{x}{x+1}\right) + \log C$

$\Rightarrow \log(y-1) = \log\left(\dfrac{xC}{x+1}\right)$

$\Rightarrow \quad (y-1) = \dfrac{xC}{x+1}$

$\Rightarrow \quad (y-1)(x+1) = xC$

Since, the above curve passes through (1, 0).

$\Rightarrow \quad (-1)(2) = 1 \cdot C \Rightarrow C = -2$

$\therefore$ Required equation of the curve is

$$(y-1)(x+1) = -2x$$

$\Rightarrow \quad (y-1)(x+1) + 2x = 0$

24 (*c*) The equation of a line passing through origin is

$$y = mx \Rightarrow m = \frac{y}{x}$$

Hence, slope of the line is $\dfrac{y}{x}$.

According to the given condition,

$$\frac{dy}{dx} = 2\left(\frac{y}{x}\right) \Rightarrow \frac{dy}{y} = 2\frac{dx}{x}$$

On integrating both sides, we get

$$\int \frac{dy}{y} = 2\int \frac{dx}{x}$$

$\Rightarrow \quad \log y = 2\log x + \log C$

$\Rightarrow \quad \log y = \log Cx^2$

$\therefore \quad y = Cx^2$

which represents a parabola of the form $x^2 = 4ay$.

25 (*a*) The given differential equation is $e^{-x}(y+1)\,dy + (\cos^2 x - \sin 2x)\,y\,dx = 0$

$\Rightarrow \quad \left(1 + \dfrac{1}{y}\right)dy = -e^x(\cos^2 x - \sin 2x)\,dx$

On integrating both sides, we get

$$\int\left(1 + \frac{1}{y}\right)dy = \int -e^x(\cos^2 x - \sin 2x)\,dx$$

$\Rightarrow \quad y + \log y = -e^x\cos^2 x + \int e^x \sin 2x\,dx - \int e^x \sin 2x\,dx + C$

$\Rightarrow \quad y + \log y = -e^x\cos^2 x + C$

At $x = 0$, $y = 1$.

$\Rightarrow 1 + \log 1 = -e^0\cos 0 + C \Rightarrow C = 2$

$\therefore$ The solution of the given differential equation is

$$y + \log y + e^x\cos^2 x = 2$$

26 (*d*) The given differential equation is

$$x\left(\frac{dy}{dx}\right)^2 + 2\sqrt{xy}\,\frac{dy}{dx} + y = 0$$

$\Rightarrow \quad \left(\sqrt{x}\dfrac{dy}{dx} + \sqrt{y}\right)^2 = 0$

$\Rightarrow \quad \sqrt{x}\dfrac{dy}{dx} + \sqrt{y} = 0$

$\Rightarrow \quad \dfrac{1}{\sqrt{y}}dy + \dfrac{1}{\sqrt{x}}dx = 0$

On integrating, both sides we get

$$\int \frac{1}{\sqrt{y}}\,dy + \int \frac{1}{\sqrt{x}}\,dx = 0$$

$\Rightarrow \quad 2\sqrt{y} + 2\sqrt{x} = C_1$

$\Rightarrow \quad \sqrt{x} + \sqrt{y} = C$

$\left[\text{where, } C = \dfrac{C_1}{2}\right]$

27 (*a*) Let A_0 be the original amount of radium and A be the amount of radium at any time t. Then,

$\dfrac{dA}{dt} \propto A$ [given]

$\Rightarrow \quad \dfrac{dA}{dt} = -\lambda A$

[λ is a positive constant]

$\Rightarrow \quad \dfrac{dA}{A} = -\lambda\,dt$

On integrating both sides, we get

$$\int \frac{dA}{A} = -\lambda \int 1\,dt$$

$$\Rightarrow \quad \log A = -\lambda t + C \quad \text{...(i)}$$

At $t = 0$, $\quad A = A_0$

$$\Rightarrow \quad C = \log A_0$$

So, from Eq. (i), we get

$$\log A = -\lambda t + \log A_0$$

$$\Rightarrow \quad \log\left(\frac{A}{A_0}\right) = -\lambda t \quad \text{...(ii)}$$

It is given that $p\%$ of the original amount of radium disappears in l years.

$$\Rightarrow \quad A = A_0 - \frac{A_0 p}{100}$$

i.e. $\quad \dfrac{A}{A_0} = 1 - \dfrac{p}{100}$

So, from Eq. (ii), we get

$$\log\left(1 - \frac{p}{100}\right) = -\lambda l$$

$$\Rightarrow \quad \lambda = -\frac{1}{l}\log\left(1 - \frac{p}{100}\right)$$

On putting the value of λ in Eq. (ii), we get

$$\log\left(\frac{A}{A_0}\right) = \frac{t}{l}\log\left(1 - \frac{p}{100}\right)$$

When $t = 2l$, then we get

$$\log\left(\frac{A}{A_0}\right) = 2\log\left(1 - \frac{p}{100}\right)$$

$$\Rightarrow \quad \frac{A}{A_0} = \left(1 - \frac{p}{100}\right)^2$$

$$\Rightarrow \quad \frac{A}{A_0} \times 100 = \left(1 - \frac{p}{100}\right)^2 \times 100$$

$$= \left(10 - \frac{p}{10}\right)^2$$

Hence, required percent is $\left(10 - \dfrac{p}{10}\right)^2$.

Homogeneous Differential Equations

1 (*b*) We know that, the slope of the tangent at any point on a curve is $\dfrac{dy}{dx}$.

Therefore, $\dfrac{dy}{dx} = \dfrac{x^2 + y^2}{2xy}$

or $\quad \dfrac{dy}{dx} = \dfrac{1 + \dfrac{y^2}{x^2}}{\dfrac{2y}{x}} \quad \text{...(i)}$

Clearly, Eq. (i) is a homogeneous differential equation. To solve it we make substitution

$$y = vx$$

On differentiating $y = vx$ w.r.t. x, we get

$$\frac{dy}{dx} = v + x\frac{dv}{dx}$$

$$\Rightarrow \quad v + x\frac{dv}{dx} = \frac{1 + v^2}{2v}$$

$$\Rightarrow \quad x\frac{dv}{dx} = \frac{1 - v^2}{2v}$$

$$\Rightarrow \quad \frac{2v}{1 - v^2}dv = \frac{dx}{x}$$

$$\Rightarrow \quad \frac{2v}{v^2 - 1}dv = -\frac{dx}{x}$$

Therefore,

$$\int \frac{2v}{v^2 - 1}dv = \int -\frac{1}{x}dx$$

$\Rightarrow \log|v^2 - 1| = -\log|x| + \log|C_1|$

$\Rightarrow \log|(v^2 - 1)(x)| = \log|C_1|$

$$\Rightarrow \quad (v^2 - 1)x = \pm C_1$$

On replacing v by $\dfrac{y}{x}$, we get

$$\left(\frac{y^2}{x^2} - 1\right)x = \pm C_1$$

$$\Rightarrow \quad (y^2 - x^2) = \pm C_1 x$$

or $\quad x^2 - y^2 = Cx$

2 (*d*)

(a) Given equation $(4x + 6y + 5)\,dy - (3y + 2x + 4)\,dx = 0$ can be rewritten as

$$\frac{dy}{dx} = \frac{3y + 2x + 4}{4x + 6y + 5}$$

$$\Rightarrow \quad \frac{dy}{dx} = \frac{x\left(3\cdot\dfrac{y}{x} + 2 + \dfrac{4}{x}\right)}{x\left(4 + 6\dfrac{y}{x} + \dfrac{5}{x}\right)}$$

This equation is not homogeneous.

(b) Given equation is

$xy\,dx - (x^3 + y^3)\,dy = 0$

On separating the variables, we get

$$(x^3 + y^3)\,dy = xy\,dx$$

$$\Rightarrow \quad \frac{dy}{dx} = \frac{xy}{x^3 + y^3}$$

$$\Rightarrow \quad \frac{dy}{dx} = \frac{\dfrac{y}{x^2}}{1 + \left(\dfrac{y}{x}\right)^3}$$

This equation is not homogeneous equation.

(c) Given equation is

$(x^3 + 2y^2)\,dx + 2xy\,dy = 0$

$2xy\,dy = -(x^3 + 2y^2)\,dx$

On separating the variables, we get

$$\frac{dy}{dx} = -\frac{(x^3 + 2y^2)}{2xy}$$

$$\Rightarrow \quad \frac{dy}{dx} = -\frac{\left(1 + \dfrac{2y^2}{x^3}\right)}{\dfrac{2y}{x^2}}$$

This equation is not homogeneous equation.

(d) Given equation is

$y^2\,dx + (x^2 - xy - y^2)\,dy = 0$

On separating the variables, we get

$(x^2 - xy - y^2)\,dy = -y^2\,dx$

$$\Rightarrow \quad \frac{dy}{dx} = -\frac{y^2}{x^2 - xy - y^2}$$

$$\Rightarrow \quad \frac{dy}{dx} = -\frac{\left(\dfrac{y}{x}\right)^2}{\left(1 - \dfrac{y}{x} - \left(\dfrac{y}{x}\right)^2\right)}$$

This equation is homogeneous equation.

3 (*a*) Given,

$$\left\{x\cos\left(\frac{y}{x}\right) + y\sin\left(\frac{y}{x}\right)\right\}y\,dx$$

$$= \left\{y\sin\left(\frac{y}{x}\right) - x\cos\left(\frac{y}{x}\right)\right\}x\,dy$$

$$\Rightarrow \frac{dy}{dx} = \frac{y\left\{x\cos\frac{y}{x} + y\sin\frac{y}{x}\right\}}{x\left\{y\sin\frac{y}{x} - x\cos\frac{y}{x}\right\}}$$

$$= g\left(\frac{y}{x}\right) \quad \text{...(i)}$$

Thus, the given differential equation is homogeneous.

So, put $y = vx$

$$\Rightarrow \frac{dy}{dx} = v + x\frac{dv}{dx}$$

$$\therefore v + x\frac{dv}{dx} = \frac{vx\{x\cos v + vx\sin v\}}{x\{vx\sin v - x\cos v\}}$$

$$\Rightarrow v + x\frac{dv}{dx} = \frac{v\{\cos v + v\sin v\}}{v\sin v - \cos v}$$

$$\Rightarrow x\frac{dv}{dx} = \frac{v\cos v + v^2\sin v}{v\sin v - \cos v} - v$$

$$\Rightarrow x\frac{dv}{dx} = \frac{v\cos v + v^2\sin v - v^2\sin v + v\cos v}{v\sin v - \cos v}$$

$$\Rightarrow x\frac{dv}{dx} = \frac{2v\cos v}{v\sin v - \cos v}$$

$$\Rightarrow \left(\frac{v\sin v - \cos v}{v\cos v}\right)dv = \frac{2}{x}dx$$

$$\Rightarrow \left(\tan v - \frac{1}{v}\right)dv = \frac{2}{x}dx$$

On integrating both sides, we get

$$\int\left(\tan v - \frac{1}{v}\right)dv = \int\frac{2\,dx}{x}$$

$$\Rightarrow \int \tan v\,dv - \int\frac{1}{v}dv = 2\int\frac{1}{x}dx$$

$$\Rightarrow -\log|\cos v| - \log|v| = 2\log|x| + C$$

$$\Rightarrow \log|v\cos v| + 2\log|x| = -C$$

$$[\because \log m + \log n = \log mn]$$

$$\Rightarrow \log[(v\cos v)x^2] = -C$$

$$\Rightarrow (v\cos v)x^2 = e^{-C}$$

$$[\because \log_e x = m \Rightarrow e^m = x]$$

$$\Rightarrow x^2 v\cos|v| = A \quad [\text{where } A = e^{-C}]$$

$$\Rightarrow x^2\frac{y}{x}\cos\left|\frac{y}{x}\right| = A \quad \left[\because y = \frac{v}{x}\right]$$

$$\Rightarrow xy\cos\left|\frac{y}{x}\right| = A$$

This is the required solution of the given differential equation.

4 (c)

A. The given differential equation is $(x^2 + xy)\,dy = (x^2 + y^2)\,dx$

$$\Rightarrow \frac{dy}{dx} = \frac{x^2 + y^2}{x^2 + xy} \quad \text{...(i)}$$

This is of the form $\frac{dy}{dx} = F(x, y)$,

where $F(x, y) = \frac{x^2 + y^2}{x^2 + xy}$

$$= \frac{1 + \left(\frac{y}{x}\right)^2}{1 + \left(\frac{y}{x}\right)} = g\left(\frac{y}{x}\right)$$

$$\therefore \frac{dy}{dx} = g\left(\frac{y}{x}\right)$$

The given differential equation is a homogeneous differential equation.

Now, let $y = vx$

$$\Rightarrow \frac{dy}{dx} = v + x\frac{dv}{dx}$$

On putting the values of $\frac{dy}{dx}$ and y in Eq. (i), we get

$$v + x\frac{dv}{dx} = \frac{x^2 + x^2v^2}{x^2 + vx^2}$$

$$\Rightarrow v + x\frac{dv}{dx} = \frac{x^2(1 + v^2)}{x^2(1 + v)}$$

$$\Rightarrow x\frac{dv}{dx} = \frac{1 + v^2}{1 + v} - v$$

$$\Rightarrow x\frac{dv}{dx} = \frac{1 + v^2 - v - v^2}{1 + v} = \frac{1 - v}{1 + v}$$

$$\Rightarrow \frac{1 + v}{1 - v}dv = \frac{dx}{x}$$

$$\Rightarrow \frac{2 - 1 + v}{1 - v}dv = \frac{dx}{x}$$

$$\Rightarrow \left(\frac{2}{1 - v} - \frac{1 - v}{1 - v}\right)dv = \frac{dx}{x}$$

$$\Rightarrow \left(\frac{2}{1 - v} - 1\right)dv = \frac{dx}{x}$$

On integrating both sides, we get

$$\int\frac{2}{1 - v}dv - \int 1\,dv = \int\frac{1}{x}dx$$

$$\Rightarrow -2\log(1 - v) - v = \log x - \log C$$

$$\Rightarrow -v - 2\log(1 - v) - \log x = -\log C$$

$$\Rightarrow v + 2\log(1 - v) + \log x = \log C$$

Put $v = \frac{y}{x}$

$$\Rightarrow \frac{y}{x} + 2\log\left(1 - \frac{y}{x}\right) + \log x = \log C$$

$$\Rightarrow \frac{y}{x} + \log\left(\frac{x - y}{x}\right)^2 + \log x = \log C$$

$$\Rightarrow \frac{y}{x} + \log(x - y)^2 - \log x^2 + \log x = \log C$$

$$\Rightarrow \frac{y}{x} + \log(x - y)^2 - 2\log x + \log x = \log C$$

$$\Rightarrow \frac{y}{x} + \log(x - y)^2 - \log x = \log C$$

$$\Rightarrow \frac{y}{x} + \log\frac{(x - y)^2}{x} - \log C = 0$$

$$\Rightarrow \log\left(\frac{(x - y)^2}{x}\cdot\frac{1}{C}\right) = -\frac{y}{x}$$

$$\Rightarrow (x - y)^2 = Cxe^{-\frac{y}{x}}$$

This is the required solution of the given differential equation.

B. The given differential equation is

$$y' = \frac{x + y}{x} \quad \text{...(i)}$$

$$\Rightarrow \frac{dy}{dx} = F(x, y),$$

where $F(x, y) = \frac{x + y}{x}$

Now, for non-zero constant λ,

$$F(\lambda x, \lambda y) = \frac{\lambda x + \lambda y}{\lambda x}$$

$$= \frac{\lambda(x + y)}{\lambda x} = \frac{x + y}{x}$$

$$\Rightarrow F(\lambda x, \lambda y) = \lambda^0\left(\frac{x + y}{x}\right)$$

$\because F(x, y)$ is a homogeneous function of degree 0.

$\therefore$ The differential Eq. (i) is a homogeneous differential equation.

So, put $y = vx$

$$\Rightarrow \frac{dy}{dx} = v + x\frac{dv}{dx}$$

On putting values of $\frac{dy}{dx}$ and y in Eq. (i), we get

$$\therefore \quad v + x\frac{dv}{dx} = \frac{x + vx}{x}$$

$$\Rightarrow \quad v + x\frac{dv}{dx} = 1 + v$$

$$\Rightarrow \frac{dv}{dx} = \frac{1}{x} \Rightarrow dv = \frac{dx}{x}$$

On integrating both sides, we get

$$\int dv = \int \frac{1}{x}dx$$

$$\Rightarrow \quad v = \log|x| + C$$

$$\Rightarrow \quad \frac{y}{x} = \log|x| + C \ [\because v = y/x]$$

$$\Rightarrow \quad y = x\log|x| + Cx.$$

This is the required solution of the given differential equation.

C. The given differential equation is

$$(x - y)\,dy - (x + y)\,dx = 0$$

$$\Rightarrow \frac{dy}{dx} = \frac{x + y}{x - y} \quad \text{...(i)}$$

This can be written as

$$\frac{dy}{dx} = \frac{1 + \frac{y}{x}}{1 - \frac{y}{x}} = g\left(\frac{y}{x}\right)$$

$$\Rightarrow \quad \frac{dy}{dx} = g\left(\frac{y}{x}\right)$$

The given differential equation is a homogeneous differential equation.

So, put $y = vx$

$$\Rightarrow \frac{dy}{dx} = v + x\frac{dv}{dx}$$

On putting values of $\frac{dy}{dx}$ and y in Eq. (i), we get

$$v + x\frac{dv}{dx} = \frac{x + vx}{x - vx}$$

$$\Rightarrow v + x\frac{dv}{dx} = \frac{1 + v}{1 - v}$$

$$\Rightarrow \quad x\frac{dv}{dx} = \frac{1 + v}{1 - v} - v$$

$$\Rightarrow \quad x\frac{dv}{dx} = \frac{1 + v - v + v^2}{1 - v}$$

$$\Rightarrow \frac{1 - v}{1 + v^2}dv = \frac{dx}{x}$$

On integrating both sides, we get

$$\int \frac{1 - v}{1 + v^2}dv = \int \frac{dx}{x}$$

$$\Rightarrow \int \frac{1}{1 + v^2}dv - \int \frac{v}{1 + v^2}dx = \log|x| + C$$

Let $1 + v^2 = t$

$$\Rightarrow \quad 2v = \frac{dt}{dv}$$

$$\Rightarrow \quad dv = \frac{dt}{2v},$$

$$\therefore \tan^{-1} v - \int \frac{v}{t} \times \frac{dt}{2v} = \log|x| + C$$

$$\Rightarrow \tan^{-1} v - \frac{1}{2}\log|t| = \log|x| + C$$

$$\Rightarrow 2\tan^{-1} v - [\log(1 + v^2) + 2\log(x)] = 2C \quad [\text{put } t = 1 + v^2]$$

$$\Rightarrow 2\tan^{-1} v - \log[(1 + v^2)x^2] = 2C$$

$$\Rightarrow 2\tan^{-1}\frac{y}{x} - \log\left[\left(\frac{x^2 + y^2}{x^2}\right)x^2\right] = 2C \quad \left[\text{put } v = \frac{y}{x}\right]$$

$$\Rightarrow 2\tan^{-1}\frac{y}{x} - \log(x^2 + y^2) = 2C$$

$$\Rightarrow \tan^{-1}\frac{y}{x} - \frac{1}{2}\log(x^2 + y^2) = C$$

This is the required solution of the given differential equation.

D. The given differential equation is

$$(x^2 - y^2)\,dx + 2xy\,dy = 0$$

$$\Rightarrow \frac{dy}{dx} = \frac{y^2 - x^2}{2xy} \quad \text{...(i)}$$

$$= \frac{\frac{y^2}{x^2} - 1}{2\frac{y}{x}} = \frac{\left(\frac{y}{x}\right)^2 - 1}{2\left(\frac{y}{x}\right)}$$

$$= g\left(\frac{y}{x}\right)$$

$$\because \frac{dy}{dx} = g\left(\frac{y}{x}\right)$$

$\therefore$ Eq. (i) is a homogeneous differential equation.

So, put $y = vx$

$\Rightarrow \frac{dy}{dx} = v + x\frac{dv}{dx}$, then Eq. (i) becomes

$$v + x\frac{dv}{dx} = \frac{v^2x^2 - x^2}{2x^2v}$$

$$\Rightarrow \quad v + x\frac{dv}{dx} = \frac{v^2 - 1}{2v}$$

$$\Rightarrow \quad x\frac{dv}{dx} = \frac{v^2 - 1}{2v} - v$$

$$\Rightarrow \quad x\frac{dv}{dx} = \frac{-1 - v^2}{2v}$$

$$\Rightarrow \quad \frac{2v}{v^2 + 1}dv = -\frac{dx}{x}$$

On integrating both sides, we get

$$\int \frac{2v}{v^2 + 1}dv + \int \frac{dx}{x} = 0$$

Let $v^2 + 1 = t \Rightarrow 2v = \frac{dt}{dv}$

$$\Rightarrow \quad dv = \frac{dt}{2v}.$$

$$\therefore \quad \int \frac{2v}{t} \times \frac{dt}{2v} + \int \frac{dx}{x} = 0$$

$$\Rightarrow \log|t| + \log|x| = \log C$$

$$\Rightarrow \log|(v^2 + 1)x| = \log C \quad [\because t = 1 + v^2]$$

$$\Rightarrow \log\left[\left(\frac{y^2 + x^2}{x^2}\right)x\right] = \log C$$

$$\Rightarrow \quad \frac{y^2 + x^2}{x} = C \quad [\because v = y/x]$$

$$\Rightarrow \quad x^2 + y^2 = Cx.$$

This is the required solution of the given differential equation.

E. The given differential equation is $x^2 \frac{dy}{dx} = x^2 - 2y^2 + xy$

$\Rightarrow \frac{dy}{dx} = \frac{x^2 - 2y^2 + xy}{x^2}$

$= \frac{1 - 2\left(\frac{y}{x}\right)^2 + \frac{y}{x}}{1} = g\left(\frac{y}{x}\right)$

$\because \frac{dy}{dx} = g\left(\frac{y}{x}\right)$

$\therefore$ Eq. (i) is the homogeneous differential equation.

So, put $y = vx$

$\Rightarrow \frac{dy}{dx} = v + x\frac{dv}{dx}$

Then, Eq. (i) becomes

$v + x\frac{dv}{dx} = \frac{x^2 - 2x^2v^2 + x^2v}{x^2}$

$\Rightarrow v + x\frac{dv}{dx} = 1 - 2v^2 + v$

$\Rightarrow x\frac{dv}{dx} = 1 - 2v^2$

$\Rightarrow \frac{1}{1-2v^2} dv = \frac{1}{x} dx$

On integrating both sides, we get

$\int \frac{1}{1-2v^2} dv = \int \frac{dx}{x}$

$\Rightarrow \frac{1}{2}\int \frac{1}{\left(\frac{1}{\sqrt{2}}\right)^2 - v^2} dv = \int \frac{dx}{x}$

$\Rightarrow \frac{1}{2} \cdot \frac{1}{2 \cdot \frac{1}{\sqrt{2}}} \log \left| \frac{\frac{1}{\sqrt{2}} + v}{\frac{1}{\sqrt{2}} - v} \right| = \log|x| + C$

$\left[\because \int \frac{dx}{a^2 - x^2} = \frac{1}{2a} \log \left|\frac{a+x}{a-x}\right| + C\right]$

$\Rightarrow \frac{1}{2\sqrt{2}} \log \left|\frac{1+\sqrt{2}v}{1-\sqrt{2}v}\right| = \log|x| + C$

$\Rightarrow \frac{1}{2\sqrt{2}} \log \left|\frac{1+\sqrt{2}\frac{y}{x}}{1-\sqrt{2}\frac{y}{x}}\right| = \log|x| + C \quad \left[\text{put } v = \frac{y}{x}\right]$

$\Rightarrow \frac{1}{2\sqrt{2}} \log \left|\frac{x+\sqrt{2}y}{x-\sqrt{2}y}\right| = \log|x| + C$

This is the required solution of given differential equation.

F. The given differential equation is

$x\,dy - y\,dx = \sqrt{x^2 + y^2}\,dx$

$\Rightarrow \frac{dy}{dx} = \frac{y + \sqrt{x^2+y^2}}{x}$ ...(i)

$= \frac{\frac{y}{x} + \sqrt{1 + \left(\frac{y}{x}\right)^2}}{1} = g\left(\frac{y}{x}\right)$

$\because \frac{dy}{dx} = g\left(\frac{y}{x}\right)$

$\therefore$ Eq.(i) is the homogeneous differential equation.

So, put $y = vx \Rightarrow \frac{dy}{dx} = v + x\frac{dv}{dx}$,

then Eq. (i) becomes

$v + x\frac{dv}{dx} = \frac{vx + \sqrt{x^2 + x^2v^2}}{x}$

$\Rightarrow v + x\frac{dv}{dx} = \frac{x[v + \sqrt{1+v^2}]}{x}$

$\Rightarrow v + x\frac{dv}{dx} = v + \sqrt{1+v^2}$

$\Rightarrow \frac{1}{\sqrt{1+v^2}} dv = \frac{1}{x} dx$

On integrating both sides, we get

$\int \frac{1}{\sqrt{1+v^2}} dv = \int \frac{dx}{x}$

$\Rightarrow \log(v + \sqrt{1+v^2}) = \log x + C$

$\left[\because \int \frac{dx}{\sqrt{x^2+a^2}} = \log|x + \sqrt{x^2+a^2}| + C\right]$

$\Rightarrow \log\left[\frac{y}{x} + \sqrt{1 + \left(\frac{y}{x}\right)^2}\right] = \log x + \log C \quad \left[\text{put } v = \frac{y}{x}\right]$

$\Rightarrow \log\left[\frac{y}{x} + \sqrt{\frac{x^2+y^2}{x^2}}\right] = \log(x\,C)$

$[\because \log m + \log n = \log mn]$

$\Rightarrow \frac{y}{x} + \frac{\sqrt{x^2+y^2}}{x} = Cx$

$[\because \log m = \log n \Rightarrow m = n]$

$\Rightarrow y + \sqrt{x^2+y^2} = Cx^2$

which is the required solution.

5 (*a*) The given differential equation is

$x\frac{dy}{dx} - y + x\sin\left(\frac{y}{x}\right) = 0$

$\Rightarrow \frac{dy}{dx} = \frac{y}{x} - \sin\left(\frac{y}{x}\right)$ ...(i)

[by dividing x]

$= g\left(\frac{y}{x}\right)$

$\therefore$ Eq.(i) is the homogeneous differential equation.

So, put $\frac{y}{x} = v \Rightarrow y = vx$

$\Rightarrow \frac{dy}{dx} = v + x\frac{dv}{dx}$

Then, Eq. (i) becomes

$v + x\frac{dv}{dx} = v - \sin v$

$\Rightarrow \operatorname{cosec} v\,dv = -\frac{1}{x}dx$

On integrating both sides, we get

$\int \operatorname{cosec} v\,dv = -\int \frac{dx}{x}$

$\Rightarrow \log|\operatorname{cosec} v - \cot v| = -\log|x| + A$

$[\because \int \operatorname{cosec} x\,dx = \log|\operatorname{cosec} x - \cot x|]$

$\Rightarrow \log|(\operatorname{cosec} v - \cot v)| + \log|x| = A$

$\Rightarrow \log|(\operatorname{cosec} v - \cot v)\,x| = A$

$\Rightarrow |x(\operatorname{cosec} v - \cot v)| = e^A$

$\Rightarrow x\left(\frac{1}{\sin v} - \frac{\cos v}{\sin v}\right) = e^A$

$\Rightarrow x\left(\frac{1 - \cos v}{\sin v}\right) = e^A$

$\Rightarrow x(1 - \cos v) = e^A \sin v$

$\Rightarrow x\left[1 - \cos\left(\frac{y}{x}\right)\right] = C\sin\left(\frac{y}{x}\right)$

$\left[\text{put } C = e^A \text{ and } v = \frac{y}{x}\right]$

This is the required solutions of given differential equation.

6 (*b*) The given differential equation is

$$y\,dx + x\log\left(\frac{y}{x}\right)dy - 2x\,dy = 0$$

$$\Rightarrow \quad \frac{dy}{dx} = \frac{\frac{y}{x}}{2-\log\left(\frac{y}{x}\right)} \quad \text{...(i)}$$

$$= g\left(\frac{y}{x}\right)$$

$$\because \quad \frac{dy}{dx} = g\left(\frac{y}{x}\right)$$

∴ Eq. (i) is the homogeneous differential equation.

So, put $\frac{y}{x} = v$ i.e. $y = vx$

$$\Rightarrow \quad \frac{dy}{dx} = v + x\frac{dv}{dx}$$

Then, Eq. (i) becomes

$$v + x\frac{dv}{dx} = \frac{v}{2-\log v}$$

$$\Rightarrow \quad x\frac{dv}{dx} = \frac{v}{2-\log v} - v$$

$$\Rightarrow \quad x\frac{dv}{dx} = \frac{v - 2v + v\log v}{2-\log v}$$

$$\Rightarrow \quad x\frac{dv}{dx} = \frac{v\log v - v}{2-\log v}$$

$$\Rightarrow \quad \frac{2-\log v}{v\log v - v}dv = \frac{1}{x}dx$$

$$\Rightarrow \quad \frac{1-(\log v - 1)}{v(\log v - 1)}dv = \frac{1}{x}dx$$

$$\Rightarrow \left(\frac{1}{v(\log v - 1)} - \frac{(\log v - 1)}{v(\log v - 1)}\right)dv = \frac{1}{x}dx$$

On integrating both sides, we get

$$\int\left(\frac{1}{v(\log v - 1)} - \frac{1}{v}\right)dv = \int\frac{dx}{x}$$

$$\Rightarrow \int\frac{1}{v(\log v - 1)}dv - \int\frac{1}{v}dv = \int\frac{dx}{x}$$

Let $\log v - 1 = t$

$$\Rightarrow \quad \frac{1}{v}dv = dt$$

$$\therefore \int\frac{dt}{t} - \int\frac{1}{v}dv = \int\frac{dx}{x}$$

$$\Rightarrow \log|t| - \log|v| = \log|x| + \log C$$

$$\Rightarrow \log|\log v - 1| - \log|v| = \log|x| + \log C \quad [\because t = \log v - 1]$$

$$\Rightarrow \log|\log v - 1| - \log|v| - \log|x| = \log C$$

$$\Rightarrow \log\left|\frac{\log v - 1}{vx}\right| = \log C$$

$$\left[\because \log\frac{m}{n} = \log m - \log n\right]$$

$$\Rightarrow \quad \left|\frac{\log v - 1}{vx}\right| = C$$

$$\Rightarrow \quad \frac{\log v - 1}{vx} = C$$

$$\Rightarrow \quad \frac{\log\left|\frac{y}{x}\right| - 1}{y} = C \quad [\because v = y/x]$$

$$\Rightarrow \log\left|\frac{y}{x}\right| - 1 = Cy$$

7 (*d*) The given differential equation is

$$(1 + e^{\frac{x}{y}})\,dx + e^{\frac{x}{y}}\left(1 - \frac{x}{y}\right)dy = 0$$

$$\frac{dx}{dy} = \frac{e^{\frac{x}{y}}\left(\frac{x}{y} - 1\right)}{(e^{x/y} + 1)} \quad \text{...(i)}$$

$$= g\left(\frac{x}{y}\right)$$

$$\because \quad \frac{dx}{dy} = g\left(\frac{x}{y}\right)$$

∴ Eq. (i) is the homogeneous differential equation.

So, put $\frac{x}{y} = v$

i.e. $x = vy \Rightarrow \frac{dx}{dy} = v + y\frac{dv}{dy}$

Then, Eq. (i) becomes

$$v + y\frac{dv}{dy} = \frac{e^v(v-1)}{e^v + 1}$$

$$\Rightarrow \quad y\frac{dv}{dy} = \frac{e^v(v-1)}{e^v + 1} - v$$

$$\Rightarrow \quad y\frac{dv}{dy} = \frac{ve^v - e^v - ve^v - v}{e^v + 1}$$

$$\Rightarrow \quad \frac{e^v + 1}{e^v + v}dv = -\frac{1}{y}dy$$

On integrating both sides, we get

$$\int\frac{e^v + 1}{e^v + v}dv = -\int\frac{1}{y}dy$$

Put $e^v + v = t$

$$\Rightarrow \quad e^v + 1 = \frac{dt}{dv} \Rightarrow dv = \frac{dt}{e^v + 1}$$

$$\therefore \int\frac{e^v + 1}{t}\,\frac{dt}{e^v + 1} = -\log|y| + \log C$$

$$\Rightarrow \quad \log|t| + \log|y| = \log C$$

$$\Rightarrow \log|e^v + v| + \log|y| = \log C$$

$$[\because t = e^v + v]$$

$$\Rightarrow \log|(e^v + v)\,y| = \log C$$

$$\Rightarrow \quad |(e^v + v)y| = C$$

$$\Rightarrow \quad (e^v + v)\,y = C$$

So, put $v = \frac{x}{y}$, we get

$$\left(e^{x/y} + \frac{x}{y}\right)y = C$$

$$\Rightarrow \quad ye^{x/y} + x = C$$

This is the required solution of the given differential equation.

8 (*a*) The given differential equation is

$$2xy + y^2 - 2x^2\frac{dy}{dx} = 0$$

$$\Rightarrow \quad \frac{dy}{dx} = \frac{2xy + y^2}{2x^2} \quad \text{...(i)}$$

So, put $\frac{y}{x} = v$ i.e. $y = vx$

$$\Rightarrow \quad \frac{dy}{dx} = v + x\frac{dv}{dx}$$

Then, Eq. (i) becomes

$$v + x\frac{dv}{dx} = \frac{2x^2v + x^2v^2}{2x^2}$$

$$\Rightarrow \quad v + x\frac{dv}{dx} = \frac{x^2(2v + v^2)}{2x^2}$$

$$\Rightarrow \quad v + x\frac{dv}{dx} = v + \frac{1}{2}v^2$$

$$\Rightarrow \quad x\frac{dv}{dx} = \frac{1}{2}v^2$$

$$\Rightarrow \quad \frac{2}{v^2}dv = \frac{1}{x}dx$$

On integrating both sides, we get

$$2\int v^{-2}dv = \int\frac{dx}{x}$$

$$\Rightarrow \quad 2\left(\frac{v^{-2+1}}{-2+1}\right) = \log|x| + C$$

$$\Rightarrow \quad 2\left(\frac{v^{-1}}{-1}\right) = \log|x| + C$$

$$\Rightarrow \quad -\frac{2}{v} = \log|x| + C$$

$$\Rightarrow \quad -\frac{2x}{y} = \log|x| + C \quad \text{...(ii)}$$

$$\left[\because v = \frac{y}{x}\right]$$

When $x = 1$, then $y = 2$, therefore

$$\frac{-2\times 1}{2} = \log 1 + C$$

$$\Rightarrow \quad -1 = 0 + C$$

On putting the value of C in Eq. (ii), we get

$$-\frac{2x}{y} = \log|x| - 1$$

$$\Rightarrow \quad y = \frac{2x}{1-\log|x|}$$

9 (*d*)

A. The given differential equation is

$$(x+y)\,dy + (x-y)\,dx = 0$$

$$\Rightarrow \quad \frac{dy}{dx} = \frac{y-x}{x+y} \quad \text{...(i)}$$

So, put $\frac{y}{x} = v$

i.e. $y = vx \Rightarrow \frac{dy}{dx} = v + x\frac{dv}{dx}$

Then, Eq. (i) becomes

$$v + x\frac{dv}{dx} = \frac{vx - x}{x + vx}$$

$$\Rightarrow \quad v + x\frac{dv}{dx} = \frac{x(v-1)}{x(1+v)}$$

$$\Rightarrow \quad v + x\frac{dv}{dx} = \frac{v-1}{1+v}$$

$$\Rightarrow \quad x\frac{dv}{dx} = \frac{v-1}{1+v} - v$$

$$\Rightarrow \quad x\frac{dv}{dx} = \frac{v-1-v-v^2}{1+v}$$

$$\Rightarrow \quad -x\frac{dv}{dx} = \frac{1+v^2}{1+v}$$

$$\Rightarrow \quad \frac{(v+1)}{1+v^2}dv = -\frac{1}{x}dx$$

On integrating both sides, we get

$$\int \frac{(v+1)}{1+v^2}dv = -\int \frac{dx}{x}$$

$$\Rightarrow \int \frac{v}{1+v^2}dv + \int \frac{1}{1+v^2}dv = -\int \frac{dx}{x}$$

In first integral, put

$$v^2 + 1 = t \Rightarrow 2v = \frac{dt}{dv}$$

$$\Rightarrow \quad dv = \frac{dt}{2v}$$

$$\therefore \int \frac{v}{t}\times\frac{dt}{2v} + \int \frac{1}{1+v^2}dv = -\int \frac{dx}{x}$$

$$\Rightarrow \frac{1}{2}\int \frac{1}{t}dt + \int \frac{1}{1+v^2}dv = -\int \frac{dx}{x}$$

$$\Rightarrow \quad \frac{1}{2}\log|t| + \tan^{-1} v = -\log|x| + C$$

$$\left[\because \int \frac{1}{1+x^2}dx = \tan^{-1} x\right]$$

$$\Rightarrow \quad \frac{1}{2}\log|v^2+1| + \tan^{-1} v = -\log|x| + C$$

$$[\because t = v^2 + 1]$$

$$\Rightarrow \frac{1}{2}\log\left(\frac{y^2+x^2}{x^2}\right) + \log|x| + \tan^{-1}\left(\frac{y}{x}\right) = C \quad \left[\text{put } v = \frac{y}{x}\right]$$

$$\Rightarrow \quad \log\left(\frac{y^2+x^2}{x^2}\right) + 2\log|x| + 2\tan^{-1}\left(\frac{y}{x}\right) = 2C$$

$$\Rightarrow \log\left(\frac{y^2+x^2}{x^2}\right) + \log x^2 + 2\tan^{-1}\left(\frac{y}{x}\right) = 2C$$

$$\Rightarrow \quad \log\frac{(y^2+x^2)x^2}{x^2} + 2\tan^{-1}\left(\frac{y}{x}\right) = 2C$$

$$\Rightarrow \log(x^2+y^2) + 2\tan^{-1}\left(\frac{y}{x}\right) = A \quad \text{...(ii)}$$

[put $2C = A$]

We are given that when $x = 1$, $y = 1$

$$\log 2 + \left(2\times\frac{\pi}{4}\right) = A$$

$$\left[\because \tan^{-1}(1) = \frac{\pi}{4}\right]$$

On putting the value of A in Eq. (ii), we get

$$\log(x^2+y^2) + 2\tan^{-1}\left(\frac{y}{x}\right) = \frac{\pi}{2} + \log 2$$

This is the required solution of the given differential equation.

B. The given differential equation is

$$x^2 dy + (xy + y^2)\,dx = 0$$

$$\Rightarrow \quad \frac{dy}{dx} = -\left(\frac{xy+y^2}{x^2}\right) \quad \text{...(i)}$$

So, put $\frac{y}{x} = v$ i.e. $y = vx$

$$\Rightarrow \quad \frac{dy}{dx} = v + x\frac{dv}{dx}$$

Then, Eq. (i) becomes

$$v + x\frac{dv}{dx} = -\frac{x^2 v + x^2 v^2}{x^2}$$

$$\Rightarrow \quad v + x\frac{dv}{dx} = -\frac{x^2(v+v^2)}{x^2}$$

$$\Rightarrow \quad v + x\frac{dv}{dx} = -(v+v^2)$$

$$\Rightarrow \quad x\frac{dv}{dx} = -(2v+v^2)$$

$$\Rightarrow \quad \frac{dv}{v^2+2v} = -\frac{1}{x}dx$$

On integrating both sides, we get

$$\int \frac{dv}{v^2+2v} = -\int \frac{dx}{x}$$

$$\Rightarrow \int \frac{1}{v^2+2v+1-1}dv = -\int \frac{dx}{x}$$

$$\Rightarrow \quad \int \frac{1}{(v+1)^2-1}dv = -\int \frac{dx}{x}$$

Let $v + 1 = t \Rightarrow dv = dt$

$$\therefore \quad \int \frac{1}{t^2-1}dt = -\int \frac{dx}{x}$$

$$\Rightarrow \frac{1}{2}\log\left|\frac{t-1}{t+1}\right| = -\log|x| + C$$

$$\left[\because \int \frac{dx}{x^2-a^2} = \frac{1}{2a}\log\left|\frac{x-a}{x+a}\right| + C\right]$$

$$\Rightarrow \frac{1}{2}\log\left|\frac{v+1-1}{v+1+1}\right| = -\log|x| + \log C \quad [\because t = v+1]$$

$$\Rightarrow \frac{1}{2}\log\left|\frac{v}{v+2}\right| + \log|x| = \log C$$

$$\Rightarrow \log\left|\frac{v}{v+2}\right| + 2\log|x| = 2\log C$$

$$\Rightarrow \log\left|\left(\frac{v}{v+2}\right)x^2\right| = \log C^2$$

$$\Rightarrow \log\left|\left(\frac{\frac{y}{x}}{\frac{y}{x}+2}\right)x^2\right| = \log C^2 \quad \left[\text{put } v = \frac{y}{x}\right]$$

$$\Rightarrow \frac{x^2 y}{2x+y} = A \quad \text{...(ii)}$$

[let $C^2 = A$ and $\log m = \log n \Rightarrow m = n$]

When $x = 1$, then $y = 1$

$$\therefore \frac{1}{2+1} = A \Rightarrow A = \frac{1}{3}$$

On putting the value of A in Eq. (ii), we get

$$\frac{x^2 y}{2x+y} = \frac{1}{3} \Rightarrow 3x^2 y = 2x + y$$

This is the required solution of the given differential equation.

C. The given differential equation is

$$\left[x\sin^2\left(\frac{y}{x}\right) - y\right]dx + x\,dy = 0$$

$$\Rightarrow \frac{dy}{dx} = \frac{y}{x} - \sin^2\left(\frac{y}{x}\right) \quad \text{...(i)}$$

So, put $\frac{y}{x} = v$

i.e. $y = vx$

$$\Rightarrow \frac{dy}{dx} = v + x\frac{dv}{dx}$$

Then, Eq. (i) becomes

$$v + x\frac{dv}{dx} = v - \sin^2 v$$

$$\Rightarrow x\frac{dv}{dx} = -\sin^2 v$$

$$\Rightarrow \operatorname{cosec}^2 v\,dv = -\frac{1}{x}dx$$

On integrating both sides, we get

$$\int \operatorname{cosec}^2 v\,dv = -\int \frac{dx}{x}$$

$$\Rightarrow -\cot v = -\log|x| + C$$

$$\Rightarrow \log|x| - \cot v = C$$

$$\Rightarrow \log|x| - \cot\left(\frac{y}{x}\right) = C \quad \left[\text{put } v = \frac{y}{x}\right] \text{...(ii)}$$

When $x = 1$, then $y = \frac{\pi}{4}$,

therefore $\log|1| - \cot\frac{\pi}{4} = C$

$$\Rightarrow C = 0 - 1 = -1$$

On putting the value of C in Eq. (ii), we get

$$\log|x| - \cot\left(\frac{y}{x}\right) = -1$$

$$\Rightarrow \log|x| - \cot\left(\frac{y}{x}\right) = -\log e \quad [\because 1 = \log e]$$

$$\Rightarrow \cot\left(\frac{y}{x}\right) = \log|ex| \quad [\because \log m + \log n = \log mn]$$

This is the required solution of the given differential equation.

D. The given differential equation is

$$\frac{dy}{dx} - \frac{y}{x} + \operatorname{cosec}\left(\frac{y}{x}\right) = 0$$

$$\Rightarrow \frac{dy}{dx} = \frac{y}{x} - \operatorname{cosec}\left(\frac{y}{x}\right) \quad \text{...(i)}$$

So, put $\frac{y}{x} = v$ i.e. $y = vx$

$$\Rightarrow \frac{dy}{dx} = v + x\frac{dv}{dx}$$

Then, Eq. (i) becomes

$$v + x\frac{dv}{dx} = v - \operatorname{cosec} v$$

$$\Rightarrow x\frac{dv}{dx} = -\operatorname{cosec} v$$

$$\Rightarrow \sin v\,dv = -\frac{1}{x}dx$$

On integrating both sides, we get

$$\int \sin v\,dv = -\int \frac{dx}{x}$$

$$\Rightarrow -\cos v = -\log|x| + C$$

$$\Rightarrow \log|x| - \cos\left(\frac{y}{x}\right) = C \quad \text{...(ii)}$$

When $x = 1$, then $y = 0$

Therefore, $\log 1 - \cos 0 = C$

$$\Rightarrow C = 0 - 1 = -1$$

On putting the value of C in Eq. (ii), we get

$$\log|x| - \cos\left(\frac{y}{x}\right) = -1$$

$$\Rightarrow \log|x| + 1 = \cos\frac{y}{x}$$

$$\Rightarrow \log|x| + \log e = \cos\left(\frac{y}{x}\right) \quad [\because \log e = 1]$$

$$\Rightarrow \log|ex| = \cos\left(\frac{y}{x}\right)$$

This is the required solution of the given differential equation.

10 (a) The given differential equation is

$$(x^3 - 3xy^2)\,dx = (y^3 - 3x^2 y)\,dy$$

$$\frac{dy}{dx} = \frac{x^3 - 3xy^2}{y^3 - 3x^2 y} \quad \text{...(i)}$$

So, put $y = vx$

$$\Rightarrow \frac{dy}{dx} = v + x\frac{dv}{dx}$$

Then, Eq. (i) becomes

$$v + x\frac{dv}{dx} = \frac{x^3 - 3x(vx)^2}{(vx)^3 - 3x^2(vx)}$$

$$\Rightarrow v + x\frac{dv}{dx} = \frac{1 - 3v^2}{v^3 - 3v}$$

$$\Rightarrow x\frac{dv}{dx} = \frac{1 - 3v^2}{v^3 - 3v} - v$$

$$\Rightarrow x\frac{dv}{dx} = \frac{1 - 3v^2 - v^4 + 3v^2}{v^3 - 3v}$$

$$\Rightarrow x\frac{dv}{dx} = \frac{1 - v^4}{v^3 - 3v}$$

$$\Rightarrow \left(\frac{v^3 - 3v}{1 - v^4}\right)dv = \frac{dx}{x}$$

On integrating both sides, we get

$$\int\left(\frac{v^3-3v}{1-v^4}\right)dv=\int\frac{dx}{x}$$

$$\Rightarrow \int\left(\frac{v^3-3v}{1-v^4}\right)dv=\log x+\log C_1 \quad ...(ii)$$

Now, $\int\left(\frac{v^3-3v}{1-v^4}\right)dv=\int\frac{v^3}{1-v^4}dv-3\int\frac{v}{1-v^4}dv$

$$\Rightarrow \int\left(\frac{v^3-3v}{1-v^4}\right)dv=I_1-3I_2 \quad ...(iii)$$

where $I_1=\int\frac{v^3}{1-v^4}dv$

and $I_2=\int\frac{v}{1-v^4}dv$

Put $1-v^4=t \Rightarrow -4v^3=\frac{dt}{dv}$

$$\Rightarrow v^3\,dv=-\frac{dt}{4}$$

$$\therefore \quad I_1=\int\frac{-dt}{4t}=-\frac{1}{4}\log t$$

$$=-\frac{1}{4}\log(1-v^4)$$

and $I_2=\int\frac{vdv}{1-v^4}=\int\frac{vdv}{1-(v^2)^2}$

Put $v^2=z$

$$\Rightarrow vdv=\frac{dz}{2}\Rightarrow I_2=\frac{1}{2}\int\frac{dz}{1-z^2}$$

$$=\frac{1}{2\times 2}\log\left|\frac{1+z}{1-z}\right|$$

$$=\frac{1}{4}\log\left|\frac{1+v^2}{1-v^2}\right| \quad [\because z=v^2]$$

$$\left[\because \int\frac{dx}{a^2-x^2}=\frac{1}{2a}\log\left|\frac{a+x}{a-x}\right|\right]$$

On substituting the values of I_1 and I_2 in Eq. (iii), we get

$$\int\left(\frac{v^3-3v}{1-v^4}\right)dv=-\frac{1}{4}\log(1-v^4)-\frac{3}{4}\log\left|\frac{1+v^2}{1-v^2}\right|$$

Therefore, Eq. (ii) becomes

$$-\frac{1}{4}\log(1-v^4)-\frac{3}{4}\log\left|\frac{1+v^2}{1-v^2}\right|=\log x+\log C_1$$

$$\Rightarrow -\frac{1}{4}\log\left[(1-v^4)\left(\frac{1+v^2}{1-v^2}\right)^3\right]=\log C_1x$$

$$\Rightarrow -\frac{1}{4}\log\left[(1-v^2)(1+v^2)\times\frac{(1+v^2)^3}{(1-v^2)^3}\right]=\log C_1x$$

$$\Rightarrow \log\left[\frac{(1+v^2)^4}{(1-v^2)^2}\right]^{-\frac{1}{4}}=\log C_1x$$

$$\Rightarrow \left[\frac{(1+v^2)^4}{(1-v^2)^2}\right]^{-\frac{1}{4}}=C_1x$$

$$\Rightarrow \frac{(1+v^2)^4}{(1-v^2)^2}=(C_1x)^{-4}$$

$$\Rightarrow \frac{\left(1+\frac{y^2}{x^2}\right)^4}{\left(1-\frac{y^2}{x^2}\right)^2}=\frac{1}{C^4x^4}$$

$$\Rightarrow \frac{(x^2+y^2)^4}{x^4(x^2-y^2)^2}=\frac{1}{C_1^4x^4} \quad [\because v=y/x]$$

$$\Rightarrow (x^2-y^2)^2=C_1^4(x^2+y^2)^4$$

$$\Rightarrow x^2-y^2=C(x^2+y^2)^2 \quad [\text{where } C=C_1^2]$$

11 (*b*) The given differential equation is

$$xy^2dy-(x^3+y^3)\,dx=0$$

$$\Rightarrow \frac{dy}{dx}=\frac{x^3+y^3}{xy^2} \quad ...(i)$$

$$=\frac{1+\left(\frac{y}{x}\right)^3}{\left(\frac{y}{x}\right)^2}=g\left(\frac{y}{x}\right) \quad ...(ii)$$

$$\because \quad \frac{dy}{dx}=g\left(\frac{y}{x}\right)$$

$\therefore$ From Eq. (i) is the homogeneous differential equation.

Now, put $y=vx$

$$\Rightarrow \frac{dy}{dx}=v+x\frac{dv}{dx} \quad ...(iii)$$

$$\Rightarrow x\frac{dv}{dx}+v=\frac{1+v^3}{v^2} \quad [\text{from (iii)}]$$

$$\Rightarrow v^2dv=\frac{dx}{x}$$

$$\Rightarrow \frac{v^3}{3}=\log x+\log C \quad [\text{integrating}]$$

$$\Rightarrow \frac{1}{3}\left(\frac{y}{x}\right)^3=\log x+\log C$$

$$\Rightarrow y^3=3x^3\log Cx$$

12 (*c*) Let the equation of normal at $P(x, y)$ be $Y-y=\frac{-dx}{dy}(X-x)$, i.e.

$$Y+X\frac{dx}{dy}-\left(y+x\frac{dx}{dy}\right)=0 \quad ...(i)$$

Therefore, the length of perpendicular from origin to Eq. (i) is

$$\frac{y+x\frac{dx}{dy}}{\sqrt{1+\left(\frac{dx}{dy}\right)^2}} \quad ...(ii)$$

Also, distance between P and X-axis is $|y|$. Thus, we get

$$\frac{y+x\frac{dx}{dy}}{\sqrt{1+\left(\frac{dx}{dy}\right)^2}}=|y|$$

or $\left(y+x\frac{dx}{dy}\right)^2=y^2\left[1+\left(\frac{dx}{dy}\right)^2\right]$

$$\Rightarrow \frac{dx}{dy}\left[\frac{dx}{dy}(x^2-y^2)+2xy\right]=0$$

$$\Rightarrow \frac{dx}{dy}=0$$

or $\frac{dx}{dy}=\frac{2xy}{y^2-x^2}$

***Case* I** $\frac{dx}{dy}=0$

$$\Rightarrow dx=0$$

On integrating both sides, we get $x=k$, then substituting $x=1$, we get

$$k=1$$

Therefore, $x=1$ is the equation of curve (not possible, so rejected).

Case II $\dfrac{dx}{dy}=\dfrac{2xy}{y^2-x^2}$

$\Rightarrow \dfrac{dy}{dx}=\dfrac{y^2-x^2}{2xy}$

On substituting $y = vx$, we get

$$v+x\frac{dv}{dx}=\frac{v^2x^2-x^2}{2vx^2}$$

$$\Rightarrow x\cdot\frac{dv}{dx}=\frac{v^2-1}{2v}-v=\frac{-(1+v^2)}{2v}$$

$$\Rightarrow \frac{2v}{1+v^2}dv=\frac{-dx}{x}$$

On integrating both sides, we get

$$\log(1+v^2)=-\log x+\log C$$

$$\Rightarrow \log(1+v^2)(x)=\log C$$

$$\Rightarrow (1+v^2)x=C$$

$$\Rightarrow x^2+y^2=Cx$$

On substituting $x=1$, $y=1$, we get

$$C=2$$

Therefore, $x^2+y^2-2x=0$ is the required solution.

13 (*a*) According to the condition,

$$\frac{dy}{dx}=\frac{y}{x}-\cos^2\frac{y}{x} \quad \text{...(i)}$$

This is a homogeneous differential equation.

Substituting $y = vx$, we get

$$v+x\frac{dv}{dx}=v-\cos^2 v$$

$$\Rightarrow x\frac{dv}{dx}=-\cos^2 v$$

$$\Rightarrow \sec^2 v\,dv=-\frac{dx}{x}$$

$$\Rightarrow \tan v=-\log x+C$$

$$\Rightarrow \tan\frac{y}{x}+\log x=C \quad \text{...(ii)}$$

On substituting $x=1$, $y=\dfrac{\pi}{4}$, we get $C = 1$. Thus, we get

$$\tan\left(\frac{y}{x}\right)+\log x=1$$

which is the required solution.

14 (*a*) The given differential equation is

$$y^2dx+(x^2-xy+y^2)dy=0$$

$$\Rightarrow \frac{dx}{dy}=-\left(\frac{x^2-xy+y^2}{y^2}\right) \quad \text{...(i)}$$

$$=-\left(\frac{x}{y}\right)^2+\left(\frac{x}{y}\right)-1$$

Now, put $\dfrac{x}{y}=v$

$$\Rightarrow x=vy \Rightarrow \frac{dx}{dy}=v+y\frac{dv}{dy}$$

$$\therefore v+y\frac{dv}{dy}=-v^2+v-1$$

$$\Rightarrow y\frac{dv}{dy}=-v^2+v-1-v$$

$$=-(v^2+1)$$

$$\Rightarrow y\frac{dv}{dy}=-(v^2+1)$$

$$\Rightarrow \frac{dv}{v^2+1}=-\frac{dy}{y}$$

On integrating both sides, we get

$$\int\frac{dv}{v^2+1}=-\int\frac{dy}{y}$$

$$\Rightarrow \tan^{-1}v=-\log|y|+C$$

$$\Rightarrow \tan^{-1}\left(\frac{x}{y}\right)=-\log|y|+C$$

$$\Rightarrow \tan^{-1}\left(\frac{x}{y}\right)+\log|y|=C$$

15 (*b*) The given differential equation is

$$\frac{dy}{dx}=\frac{y+x\tan\dfrac{y}{x}}{x} \quad \text{...(i)}$$

So, put $y = vx$

$$\Rightarrow \frac{dy}{dx}=v+x\frac{dv}{dx}$$

$$\therefore v+x\frac{dv}{dx}=\frac{vx+x\tan\left(\dfrac{vx}{x}\right)}{x}$$

$$\Rightarrow x\frac{dv}{dx}=v+\tan v-v$$

$$\Rightarrow \int\cot v\,dv=\int\frac{dx}{x}$$

$$\Rightarrow \log\sin v=\log x+\log C$$

$$\Rightarrow \sin\frac{y}{x}=Cx$$

16 (*c*) The given differential equation is

$$dx+dy=(x+y)(dx-dy)$$

$$\Rightarrow \frac{dy}{dx}=\frac{x+y-1}{x+y+1} \quad \text{...(i)}$$

Put $x+y=t$

$$\Rightarrow 1+\frac{dy}{dx}=\frac{dt}{dx}$$

$$\Rightarrow \frac{dy}{dx}=\frac{dt}{dx}-1$$

So, from Eq. (i), we get

$$\frac{dt}{dx}-1=\frac{t-1}{t+1}$$

$$\Rightarrow \frac{dt}{dx}=\frac{t-1}{t+1}+1\Rightarrow\frac{dt}{dx}=\frac{t-1+t+1}{t+1}$$

$$\Rightarrow \frac{1}{2}\left(1+\frac{1}{t}\right)dt=dx$$

On integrating both sides, we get

$$\int\frac{1}{2}\left(1+\frac{1}{t}\right)dt=\int dx$$

$$\Rightarrow \frac{1}{2}\cdot(t+\log t)=x+\frac{C}{2}$$

$$\Rightarrow t+\log t=2x+C$$

$$\Rightarrow x+y+\log(x+y)=2x+C$$

$$\Rightarrow \log(x+y)=x-y+C$$

17 (*b*) The given differential equation is

$$\frac{dy}{dx}=\frac{xy}{x^2+y^2} \quad \text{...(i)}$$

$$=\frac{y/x}{1+\left(\dfrac{y}{x}\right)^2}=g\left(\frac{y}{x}\right)$$

$$\left[\because \frac{dy}{dx}=g\left(\frac{y}{x}\right)\right]$$

$\therefore$ Eq. (i) is the homogeneous differential equation.

So, put $y = vx$

$$\Rightarrow \frac{dy}{dx}=v+x\frac{dv}{dx}$$

$$\therefore v+x\frac{dv}{dx}=\frac{x^2v}{x^2(1+v^2)}$$

$$\Rightarrow \int\frac{1+v^2}{v^3}dv=-\int\frac{dx}{x}$$

$$\Rightarrow -\frac{1}{2v^2}+\log v=-\log x+\log C$$

$$\Rightarrow -\frac{1}{2}\cdot\frac{x^2}{y^2}+\log|y|=\log C$$

$$\because y(1)=1 \Rightarrow -\frac{1}{2}=\log C$$

$$\therefore -\frac{1}{2}\cdot\frac{x^2}{y^2}+\log|y|=-\frac{1}{2}$$

$$\Rightarrow \log_e|y|+\frac{1}{2}=\frac{x^2}{2y^2}$$

Again, when $x=x_0$, then $y=e$

$$1+\frac{1}{2}=\frac{x_0^2}{2e^2}\Rightarrow x_0=\sqrt{3}e$$

18 (*d*) Let $y = f(x)$ be the given curve.

Then, the slope of the tangent at $P(x, y)$ is $\frac{dy}{dx}$.

Thus, according to the question,

$$\frac{dy}{dx} = \frac{y}{x} - \cot\frac{y}{x}\cdot\cos\frac{y}{x} \quad ...(i)$$

$$= g\left(\frac{y}{x}\right)$$

$$\because \quad \frac{dy}{dx} = g\left(\frac{y}{x}\right)$$

$\therefore$ Eq. (i) is the homogeneous differential equation.

So, put

$$y = vx$$

$$\Rightarrow \quad \frac{dy}{dx} = v + x\frac{dv}{dx}$$

So, from Eq. (i), we get

$$v + x\frac{dv}{dx} = v - \cot v \cdot \cos v$$

$$\Rightarrow \quad x\frac{dv}{dx} = -\cot v \cdot \cos v$$

$$\Rightarrow \quad \sec v \cdot \tan v \, dv = -\frac{dx}{x}$$

On integrating both sides, we get

$$\int \sec v \tan v \cdot dv = -\int \frac{dx}{x}$$

$$\Rightarrow \quad \sec v = -\log|x| + C$$

$$\Rightarrow \quad \sec\left(\frac{y}{x}\right) = -\log|x| + C \quad ...(ii)$$

The curve passes through $\left(1, \frac{\pi}{4}\right)$.

$$\therefore \quad \sec\frac{\pi}{4} = -\log 1 + C$$

$$\Rightarrow \quad C = \sqrt{2}$$

So, from Eq. (ii), we get

the equation of the required curve is

$$\sec\left(\frac{y}{x}\right) = -\log|x| + \sqrt{2}$$

Linear Differential Equations

1 (*b*) Given differential equation is of the form

$$\frac{dy}{dx} + Py = Q$$

where, $P = -1$

and $\quad Q = \cos x$

Therefore, $\text{IF} = e^{\int -1\,dx} = e^{-x}$

On multiplying both sides of equation by IF, we get

$$e^{-x}\frac{dy}{dx} - e^{-x}y = e^{-x}\cos x$$

or $\quad \frac{dy}{dx}(ye^{-x}) = e^{-x}\cos x$

On integrating both sides w.r.t. x, we get

$$ye^{-x} = \int e^{-x}\cos x\,dx + C \quad ...(i)$$

Let $\quad I = \int e^{-x}\cos x\,dx$

$$= \cos x\left(\frac{e^{-x}}{-1}\right) - \int(-\sin x)(-e^{-x})\,dx$$

$$= -\cos x\,e^{-x} - \int \sin x\,e^{-x}\,dx$$

$$= -\cos x\,e^{-x} - [\sin x(-e^{-x}) - \int \cos x(-e^{-x})\,dx]$$

$$= -\cos x\,e^{-x} + \sin x.e^{-x} - \int \cos x.e^{-x}\,dx$$

$$\Rightarrow \quad I = -e^{-x}\cos x + \sin x\,e^{-x} - I$$

$$\Rightarrow \quad 2I = (\sin x - \cos x)\,e^{-x}$$

$$\Rightarrow \quad I = \frac{(\sin x - \cos x)\,e^{-x}}{2}$$

Substituting the value of I in Eq. (i), we get

$$ye^{-x} = \left(\frac{\sin x - \cos x}{2}\right)e^{-x} + C$$

$$\Rightarrow \quad y = \left(\frac{\sin x - \cos x}{2}\right) + Ce^{x}$$

which is the general solution of the given differential equation.

2 (*c*) The given differential equation is $x\frac{dy}{dx} + 2y = x^2 \quad ...(i)$

On dividing both sides of Eq. (i) by x, we get

$$\frac{dy}{dx} + \frac{2}{x}y = x$$

which is a linear differential equation of the type $\frac{dy}{dx} + Py = Q$,

where $P = \frac{2}{x}$ and $Q = x$

So, $\text{IF} = e^{\int \frac{2}{x}dx} = e^{2\log x} = e^{\log x^2} = x^2$

[as $e^{\log f(x)} = f(x)$]

Therefore, solution of the given equation is given by

$$y \cdot x^2 = \int (x)(x^2)\,dx + C$$

$$= \int x^3 dx + C$$

$$\Rightarrow \quad y = \frac{x^2}{4} + Cx^{-2}$$

which is the general solution of the given differential equation.

3 (*d*) The given differential equation can be written as

$$\frac{dx}{dy} - \frac{x}{y} = 2y$$

This is a linear differential equation of the type $\frac{dx}{dy} + P_1x = Q_1$, where

$P_1 = -\frac{1}{y}$ and $Q_1 = 2y$.

Therefore, $\text{IF} = e^{\int -\frac{1}{y}dy} = e^{-\log y}$

$$= e^{\log(y)^{-1}} = \frac{1}{y}$$

Hence, the solution of the given differential equation is

$$x\frac{1}{y} = \int (2y)\left(\frac{1}{y}\right)dy + C$$

$$\Rightarrow \quad \frac{x}{y} = \int (2dy) + C$$

$$\Rightarrow \quad \frac{x}{y} = 2y + C \Rightarrow x = 2y^2 + Cy$$

which is a general solution of the given differential equation.

4 (a) The given equation is a linear differential equation of the type $\frac{dy}{dx}+Py=Q$, where $P=\cot x$ and $Q=2x+x^2\cot x$. Therefore,

$$\text{IF}=e^{\int \cot x\,dx}=e^{\log \sin x}=\sin x$$

Hence, the solution of the differential equation is given by

$$y\cdot\sin x=\int (2x+x^2\cot x)\sin x\,dx+C$$

$$\Rightarrow y\sin x=\int 2x\sin x\,dx+\int x^2\cos x\,dx+C$$

$$\Rightarrow y\sin x=\sin x\left(\frac{2x^2}{2}\right)-\int \cos x\left(\frac{2x^2}{2}\right)dx+\int x^2\cos x\,dx+C$$

$$\Rightarrow y\sin x=x^2\sin x-\int x^2\cos x\,dx+\int x^2\cos x\,dx+C$$

$$\Rightarrow y\sin x=x^2\sin x+C \quad \text{...(i)}$$

On substituting $y=0$ and $x=\frac{\pi}{2}$ in Eq. (i), we get

$$0=\left(\frac{\pi}{2}\right)^2\sin\left(\frac{\pi}{2}\right)+C \text{ or } C=\frac{-\pi^2}{4}$$

On substituting the value of C in Eq. (i), we get

$$y\sin x=x^2\sin x-\frac{\pi^2}{4}$$

$$\Rightarrow \quad y=x^2-\frac{\pi^2}{4\sin x} \quad [\sin x\neq 0]$$

which is the particular solution of the given differential equation.

5 (b)

A. We know that the slope of the tangent to the curve is $\frac{dy}{dx}$.

Therefore,

$$\frac{dy}{dx}=x+xy \text{ or } \frac{dy}{dx}-xy=x \quad \text{...(i)}$$

This is a linear differential equation of the type $\frac{dy}{dx}+Py=Q$, where $P=-x$ and $Q=x$.

Therefore, $\text{IF}=e^{\int -x\,dx}=e^{\frac{-x^2}{2}}$

Hence, the solution of equation is given by

$$y\cdot e^{\frac{-x^2}{2}}=\int (x)\left(e^{\frac{-x^2}{2}}\right)dx+C \quad \text{...(ii)}$$

Let $\quad I=\int (x)\,e^{\frac{-x^2}{2}}\,dx$

Let $\frac{-x^2}{2}=t$

Then, $-x\,dx=dt$ or $x\,dx=-dt$

Therefore,

$$I=-\int e^t dt=-e^t=-e^{\frac{-x^2}{2}}$$

On substituting the value of I in Eq. (ii), we get

$$ye^{\frac{-x^2}{2}}=-e^{\frac{-x^2}{2}}+C$$

or $\quad y=-1+Ce^{\frac{x^2}{2}} \quad$ ...(iii)

Now, Eq. (iii) represents the equation of family of curves. But we are interested in finding a particular member of the family passing through (0, 1).

On substituting $x=0$ and $y=1$ in Eq. (iii), we get

$$1=-1+C\cdot e^0 \text{ or } C=2$$

On substituting the value of C in equation (iii), we get

$y=-1+2e^{\frac{x^2}{2}}$ which is the equation of the required curve.

6 (c)

A. The given differential equation is $dy/dx+2y=\sin x$.

Comparing with the form $dy/dx+Py=Q$, we get

$$P=2$$

and $\quad Q=\sin x$

$\therefore \quad \text{IF}=e^{\int P dx}\Rightarrow e^{2\int 1 dx}$

$\Rightarrow \quad \text{IF}=e^{2x}$

Hence, the solution is given by

$$y\cdot\text{IF}=\int(Q\times\text{IF})\,dx+C$$

$$\Rightarrow y\times e^{2x}=\int \sin x\cdot e^{2x}\,dx+C \quad \text{...(i)}$$

Let $\quad I=\int \sin x\, e^{2x}$

$$\therefore \quad I=\sin x\int e^{2x}dx-\int\left[\frac{d}{dx}\sin x\int e^{2x}dx\right]dx$$

[integrating by parts]

$$\Rightarrow I=\sin x\,\frac{e^{2x}}{2}-\frac{1}{2}\int \cos x\,e^{2x}dx$$

$$\Rightarrow I=\sin x\,\frac{e^{2x}}{2}-\frac{1}{2}\cos x\,\frac{e^{2x}}{2}+\frac{1}{2}\int\left[\frac{d}{dx}\cos x\int e^{2x}dx\right]dx$$

$$\Rightarrow I=\sin x\,\frac{e^{2x}}{2}-\frac{1}{4}\cos x\,e^{2x}+\frac{1}{4}\int(-\sin x)\,e^{2x}dx$$

$$\Rightarrow I=\sin x\,\frac{e^{2x}}{2}-\frac{1}{4}\cos x\,e^{2x}-\frac{1}{4}I$$

$$\Rightarrow \frac{5I}{4}=\frac{e^{2x}}{4}(2\sin x-\cos x)$$

$$\Rightarrow I=\frac{e^{2x}}{5}(2\sin x-\cos x)$$

Therefore, Eq. (i) becomes

$$y\times e^{2x}=\frac{e^{2x}}{5}(2\sin x-\cos x+C)$$

$$\Rightarrow y=\frac{1}{5}(2\sin x-\cos x)+e^{-2x}C$$

B. The given differential equation is $\frac{dy}{dx}+3y=e^{-2x}$.

On comparing with the form $\frac{dy}{dx}+Py=Q$, we get

$$P=3 \text{ and } Q=e^{-2x}$$

$\therefore \quad \text{IF}=e^{\int P\cdot dx}$

$\Rightarrow \quad e^{\int 3\cdot dx}\Rightarrow \text{IF}=e^{3x}$

The solution of the given differential equation is given by

$$y\cdot\text{IF}=\int(Q\times\text{IF})\,dx+C$$

$$\Rightarrow y\times e^{3x}=\int e^{-2x}\cdot e^{3x}\,dx+C$$

$$\Rightarrow \quad ye^{3x}=\int e^x\,dx+C$$

$$\Rightarrow \quad ye^{3x}=e^x+C$$

$$\Rightarrow \quad y=e^{-2x}+Ce^{-3x}$$

C. The given differential equation is $\frac{dy}{dx}+\frac{y}{x}=x^2$.

On comparing with the form $\frac{dy}{dx}+Py=Q$, we get

$$P=\frac{1}{x} \text{ and } Q=x^2$$

$\therefore \quad IF=e^{\int P\cdot dx}=e^{\int\frac{1}{x}dx}$

$\Rightarrow \quad IF=e^{\log|x|}=x\, [\because e^{\log x}=x]$

The solution of the given differential equation is given by

$$y\cdot IF=\int(Q\times IF)\,dx+C$$

$\Rightarrow \quad yx=\int x^3\,dx+C$

$\Rightarrow \quad yx=\frac{x^4}{4}+C$

D. The given differential equation is $\frac{dy}{dx}+y\sec x=\tan x$.

On comparing with the form $\frac{dy}{dx}+Py=Q$, we get $P=\sec x$ and $Q=\tan x$.

$\therefore \quad IF=e^{\int P\cdot dx}=e^{\int\sec x\,dx}$

$\Rightarrow IF=e^{\log|\sec x+\tan x|}=\sec x+\tan x \quad$ ...(i)

The general solution of the given differential equation is given by

$$y\cdot IF=\int(Q\times IF)\,dx+C$$

$\Rightarrow y\,(\sec x+\tan x)$

$=\int\tan x\,(\sec x+\tan x)\,dx+C$

$\Rightarrow y(\sec x+\tan x)=\int\tan x\sec x\,dx+\int\tan^2 x\,dx+C$

$\Rightarrow y\,(\sec x+\tan x)=\sec x+\int\sec^2 x\,dx-\int 1\,dx+C$

$[\because \tan^2 x=\sec^2 x-1]$

$\Rightarrow y\,(\sec x+\tan x)$

$=\sec x+\tan x-x+C$

E. Given, $\cos^2 x\frac{dy}{dx}+y=\tan x$

On dividing by $\cos^2 x$ both sides, we get

$$\frac{dy}{dx}+y\sec^2 x=\tan x\sec^2 x$$

On comparing with the form $\frac{dy}{dx}+Py=Q$, we get $P=\sec^2 x$

and $\quad Q=\tan x\sec^2 x$

$\therefore \quad IF=e^{\int P\,dx}=e^{\int\sec^2 x\,dx}$

$\Rightarrow \quad IF=e^{\tan x} \quad$ ...(i)

The general solution of the given differential equation is given by

$$y\cdot IF=\int(Q\times IF)\,dx+C$$

$\Rightarrow \quad ye^{\tan x}=\int e^{\tan x}\cdot\tan x\sec^2 x\,dx$

Put $\quad \tan x=t$

$\Rightarrow \quad \sec^2 x=\frac{dt}{dx}\Rightarrow dx=\frac{dt}{\sec^2 x}$

$\therefore \ ye^{\tan x}=\int e^t\cdot t\sec^2 x\,\frac{dt}{\sec^2 x}$

$\Rightarrow \quad ye^{\tan x}=\int e^t\cdot t\,dt$

$\Rightarrow \quad ye^{\tan x}=e^t\cdot t-\int\left[\frac{d}{dt}(t)\cdot\int e^t\,dt\right]dt$

$\Rightarrow \quad ye^{\tan x}=e^t\cdot t-\int e^t\,dt$

$\Rightarrow y\,e^{\tan x}=e^t\,t-e^t+C$

$\Rightarrow \quad ye^{\tan x}=(\tan x-1)\,e^{\tan x}+C$

$\Rightarrow \quad y=\tan x-1+Ce^{-\tan x}$

F. Given, $x\frac{dy}{dx}+2y=x^2\log x$

On dividing by x both sides, we get $\frac{dy}{dx}+2\frac{y}{x}=x\log x$

On comparing with the form $\frac{dy}{dx}+Py=Q$, we get

$$P=\frac{2}{x} \text{ and } Q=x\log x$$

$\therefore \quad IF=e^{\int P\,dx}=e^{2\int\frac{1}{x}dx}$

$\Rightarrow \quad IF=e^{2\log|x|}=x^2$

The general solution of the given differential equation is given by

$$y\cdot IF=\int(Q\times IF)\,dx+C$$

$\Rightarrow x^2y=\int x^2\cdot x\log x\,dx+C$

$\Rightarrow \quad x^2y=\int \underset{\text{I}}{x^3}\,\underset{\text{II}}{\log x}\,dx+C$

$\Rightarrow \quad x^2y=\log x\cdot\int x^3-\int\left[\frac{d}{dx}\log x\int x^3\,dx\right]dx+C$

$\Rightarrow \quad x^2y=\log x\cdot\frac{x^4}{4}-\int\left[\frac{d}{dx}\log x\int x^3\,dx\right]dx+C$

$\Rightarrow x^2y=\log x\cdot\frac{x^4}{4}-\int\left[\frac{1}{x}\times\frac{x^4}{4}\right]dx+C$

$\Rightarrow x^2y=\log x\cdot\frac{x^4}{4}-\int\frac{x^3}{4}\,dx+C$

$\Rightarrow x^2y=\frac{x^4}{4}\log x-\frac{x^4}{16}+C$

$\Rightarrow \quad y=\frac{x^2}{16}(4\log x-1)+Cx^{-2}$

7 (*a*) Given, $x\log x\frac{dy}{dx}+y=\frac{2}{x}\log x$

On dividing by $x\log x$, both sides, we get

$$\frac{dy}{dx}+\frac{y}{x\log x}=\frac{2}{x^2}$$

On comparing with the form $\frac{dy}{dx}+Py=Q$, we get

$$P=\frac{1}{x\log x} \text{ and } Q=\frac{2}{x^2}$$

$\therefore \quad IF=e^{\int P\,dx}=e^{\int\frac{1\,dx}{x\log x}}$

Let $\log x=t \Rightarrow \frac{1}{x}=\frac{dt}{dx}$

$\Rightarrow \quad dx=x\,dt$

$\therefore \quad IF=e^{\int\frac{1}{t}dt}=e^{\log|t|}=t=\log x$

$[\because t=\log x]$

The general solution of the given differential equation is given by

$$y\cdot IF=\int(Q\times IF)\,dx+C$$

$\Rightarrow y\cdot\log x=\int\frac{2}{x^2}\log x\,dx+C$

$\Rightarrow y\log x=2\int\left(\log x\cdot\frac{1}{x^2}\right)dx+C$

$=2\left[\log x\int\frac{1}{x^2}dx-\int\left(\frac{d}{dx}(\log x)\int\frac{1}{x^2}dx\right)dx\right]+C$

[integrating by parts]

$$= 2\left[\log x\left(-\frac{1}{x}\right) - \int\left\{\frac{1}{x}\cdot\left(-\frac{1}{x}\right)\right\}dx\right] + C$$

$$= 2\left[-\frac{\log x}{x} + \int\frac{1}{x^2}dx\right] + C$$

$$= 2\left[-\frac{\log x}{x} - \frac{1}{x}\right] + C$$

$$\therefore\ y\log x = -\frac{2}{x}(1 + \log x) + C$$

8 (a) Given,

$$(1 + x^2)\,dy + 2xy\,dx = \cot x\,dx$$

$$\Rightarrow\ (1 + x^2)\,dy = dx\,(\cot x - 2xy)$$

$$\Rightarrow\ \frac{dy}{dx} = \frac{\cot x - 2xy}{1 + x^2}$$

$$\Rightarrow\ \frac{dy}{dx} + \frac{2xy}{1 + x^2} = \frac{\cot x}{1 + x^2}$$

On comparing with the form $\frac{dy}{dx} + Py = Q$, we get

$$P = \frac{2x}{1 + x^2} \text{ and } Q = \frac{\cot x}{1 + x^2}$$

$$\therefore\ \text{IF} = e^{\int P\,dx} = e^{\int \frac{2x}{1+x^2}dx}$$

Let $1 + x^2 = t$

$$\Rightarrow\ 2x = \frac{dt}{dx} \Rightarrow dx = \frac{dt}{2x}$$

$$\therefore\ \text{IF} = e^{\int \frac{2x}{t}\times\frac{dt}{dx}}$$

$$\Rightarrow\ \text{IF} = e^{\log|t|} = t = 1 + x^2 \quad \text{...(i)}$$

The general solution of the given differential equation is given by

$$y\cdot\text{IF} = \int (Q \times \text{IF})\,dx + C$$

$$\Rightarrow\ (1 + x^2)\,y = \int\left((1 + x^2)\frac{\cot x}{(1 + x^2)}\right)dx + C$$

$$\Rightarrow\ (1 + x^2)\,y = \log|\sin x| + C$$

$$\Rightarrow\ y = \log|\sin x|(1 + x^2)^{-1} + C(1 + x^2)^{-1}$$

9 (c) Given differential equation is

$$x\frac{dy}{dx} - y = 2x^2$$

$$\Rightarrow\ \frac{dy}{dx} + \left(-\frac{1}{x}\right)y = 2x$$

It is a linear differential equation of the form $\frac{dy}{dx} + Py = Q$.

$$\therefore\ P = -\frac{1}{x} \text{ and } Q = 2x$$

and $\text{IF} = e^{\int P\cdot dx}$

$$\Rightarrow\ \text{IF} = e^{\int\left(-\frac{1}{x}\right)dx}$$

$$\Rightarrow\ \text{IF} = e^{-\log|x|}$$

$$\Rightarrow\ \text{IF} = e^{\log|x|^{-1}} = \frac{1}{x}$$

An integrating factor for the given equation is $\frac{1}{x}$ (assuming $x > 0$).

10 (d) The given differential equation is $(1 - y^2)\frac{dx}{dy} + yx = ay, -1 < y < 1$.

On dividing by $(1 - y^2)$ both sides in the above equation, we get

$$\Rightarrow\ \frac{dx}{dy} + \left(\frac{y}{1 - y^2}\right)x = \frac{ay}{1 - y^2}$$

Here, $P = \frac{y}{1 - y^2}, Q = \frac{ay}{1 - y^2}$

and $\text{IF} = e^{\int \frac{y}{1-y^2}dy}$

$$\Rightarrow\ \text{IF} = e^{-\frac{1}{2}\int\frac{-2y}{1-y^2}dy}$$

$$\Rightarrow\ \text{IF} = e^{\frac{-1}{2}\log(1 - y^2)}$$

$$\Rightarrow\ \text{IF} = e^{\log(1 - y^2)^{-1/2}} = (1 - y^2)^{-1/2} = \frac{1}{\sqrt{1 - y^2}}$$

11 (a) According to the question, we have

$$x + y = \frac{dy}{dx} + 5$$

or $$\frac{dy}{dx} + (-1)\,y = x - 5 \quad \text{...(i)}$$

It is a linear differential equation of the form $\frac{dy}{dx} + Py = Q$.

$$\therefore\ P = -1 \text{ and } Q = x - 5$$

and $\text{IF} = e^{\int P\cdot dx}$

$$\Rightarrow\ \text{IF} = e^{\int(-1)\,dx} \Rightarrow \text{IF} = e^{-x}$$

The general equation of the curve is given by

$$y\cdot\text{IF} = \int (Q \times \text{IF})\,dx + C$$

$$\Rightarrow\ y\cdot e^{-x} = \int (x - 5)\,e^{-x}\,dx + C$$

$$\Rightarrow\ y\cdot e^{-x} = (x - 5)\int e^{-x}\,dx - \int\left[\frac{d}{dx}(x - 5)\cdot\int e^{-x}\,dx\right]dx + C$$

$$\Rightarrow\ y\cdot e^{-x} = (x - 5)(-e^{-x})$$

$$\Rightarrow\ y\cdot e^{-x} = (5 - x)\,e^{-x} - e^{-x} + C \quad \text{...(ii)}$$

The curve passes through the point (0, 2).

Therefore,

$$2e^{-0} = (5 - 0)\,e^{-0} - e^0 + C$$

$$\Rightarrow\ 2 = 5 - 1 + C$$

$$\Rightarrow\ C = 2 - 4 = -2$$

On putting the value of C in equation (ii), we get

$$e^{-x}\,y = (5 - x)\,e^{-x} - e^{-x} - 2$$

$$\Rightarrow\ y = 4 - x - 2\,e^x$$

which is the required equation of the curve.

12 (c)

A. Given, $\frac{dy}{dx} + 2y\tan x = \sin x$

On comparing with the form $\frac{dy}{dx} + Py = Q$, we get

$$P = 2\tan x, Q = \sin x$$

$$\therefore\ \text{IF} = e^{2\int\tan x\,dx} = e^{2\log|\sec x|}$$

$$\Rightarrow\ \text{IF} = \sec^2 x$$

The general solution is given by

$$y\cdot\text{IF} = \int (Q \times \text{IF})\,dx + C \quad \text{...(i)}$$

$$\Rightarrow y\sec^2 x = \int(\sin x\cdot\sec^2 x)\,dx + C$$

$$\Rightarrow y\sec^2 x = \int\sin x\cdot\frac{1}{\cos^2 x}\,dx + C$$

$$\Rightarrow y\sec^2 x = \int\tan x\sec x\,dx + C$$

$$\Rightarrow\ y\sec^2 x = \sec x + C \quad \text{...(ii)}$$

On putting, $y = 0$ and $x = \frac{\pi}{3}$ in Eq. (ii), we get

$$0 \times \sec^2\frac{\pi}{3} = \sec\frac{\pi}{3} + C$$

$$\Rightarrow\ 0 = 2 + C$$

$$\Rightarrow\ C = -2$$

On putting the value of C in Eq. (ii), we get

$$y\sec^2 x = \sec x - 2$$

$$\Rightarrow \quad y = \cos x - 2\cos^2 x$$

Hence, the required solution of the given differential equation is $y = \cos x - 2\cos^2 x$.

B. Given, $(1+x^2)\dfrac{dy}{dx} + 2xy = \dfrac{1}{1+x^2}$

On dividing by $(1+x^2)$ both sides, we get

$$\frac{dy}{dx} + \frac{2xy}{1+x^2} = \frac{1}{(1+x^2)^2}$$

On comparing with the form $\dfrac{dy}{dx} + Py = Q$, we get

$$P = \frac{2x}{1+x^2} \text{ and } Q = \frac{1}{(1+x^2)^2}$$

$$\therefore \quad \text{IF} = e^{\int \frac{2x}{1+x^2} dx}$$

Put $1+x^2 = t \Rightarrow 2x = \dfrac{dt}{dx}$

$$\Rightarrow \quad dx = \frac{dt}{2x}$$

$$\therefore \quad \text{IF} = e^{\int \frac{2x}{t} \times \frac{dt}{2x}}$$

$$\Rightarrow \quad \text{IF} = e^{\log|t|} = t$$

$$\Rightarrow \quad \text{IF} = 1 + x^2 \quad \text{...(i)}$$

The general solution of the given equation is given by

$$y \cdot \text{IF} = \int (Q \times \text{IF})\, dx + C$$

$$\Rightarrow y(1+x^2) = \int \left(\frac{1}{(1+x^2)^2} \times (1+x^2) \right) dx + C$$

$$\Rightarrow y(1+x^2) = \int \frac{1}{1+x^2} dx + C$$

$$\Rightarrow y(1+x^2) = \tan^{-1} x + C \quad \text{...(ii)}$$

Now, $y = 0$ and $x = 1$

Then, $0(1+1) = \tan^{-1}(1) + C$

$$\Rightarrow \quad 0 = \frac{\pi}{4} + C \Rightarrow C = -\frac{\pi}{4}$$

On putting the value of C in Eq. (ii), we get

$$(1+x^2)\,y = \tan^{-1} x - \frac{\pi}{4}$$

which is the required solution of the given differential equation.

C. Given, $\dfrac{dy}{dx} - 3y\cot x = \sin 2x$

On comparing with the form $\dfrac{dy}{dx} + Py = Q$, we get

$$P = -3\cot x, Q = \sin 2x$$

$$\therefore \quad \text{IF} = e^{-3\int \cot x\, dx}$$

$$= e^{-3\log|\sin x|}$$

$$= e^{\log|\sin x|^{-3}}$$

$$\Rightarrow \quad \text{IF} = \frac{1}{\sin^3 x} \quad \text{...(i)}$$

The general solution of the given differential equation is given by

$$y \times \text{IF} = \int (Q \times \text{IF})\, dx + C$$

$$\Rightarrow y \times \frac{1}{\sin^3 x} = \int \frac{1}{\sin^3 x} \sin 2x\, dx$$

$$\Rightarrow y \times \frac{1}{\sin^3 x} = 2\int \frac{\sin x \cos x}{\sin^3 x} dx + C$$

$$\Rightarrow \frac{1}{\sin^3 x} \times y = 2\int \frac{\cos x}{\sin^2 x} dx + C$$

$$\Rightarrow \frac{y}{\sin^3 x} = 2\int \cot x \operatorname{cosec} x\, dx + C$$

$$\Rightarrow \frac{y}{\sin^3 x} = -2\operatorname{cosec} x + C$$

$$\Rightarrow y = -2\left(\frac{1}{\sin x} \times \sin^3 x\right) + C\sin^3 x$$

$$\Rightarrow y = -2\sin^2 x + C\sin^3 x \quad \text{...(ii)}$$

Given, $y = 2$ when $x = \dfrac{\pi}{2}$.

Then, from Eq. (ii), we get

$$2 = -2\sin^2\left(\frac{\pi}{2}\right) + C\sin^3\left(\frac{\pi}{2}\right)$$

$$\Rightarrow 2 = -2 + C \Rightarrow C = 4$$

On putting the value of C in Eq. (ii), we get

$$y = -2\sin^2 x + 4\sin^3 x$$

$$\Rightarrow y = 4\sin^3 x - 2\sin^2 x$$

13 (c)

I. Given,

$$x\frac{dy}{dx} + y - x + xy\cot x = 0$$

$$\Rightarrow x\frac{dy}{dx} + y(1 + x\cot x) = x$$

On dividing by x both sides, we get

$$\frac{dy}{dx} + \frac{y(1 + x\cot x)}{x} = 1$$

On comparing with the form $\dfrac{dy}{dx} + Py = Q$, we get

$$P = \frac{1 + x\cot x}{x}$$

and $Q = 1$

$$\therefore \quad \text{IF} = e^{\int P\, dx} = e^{\int \left(\frac{1}{x} + \cot x\right) dx}$$

$$= e^{\log x + \log|\sin x|}$$

$$= e^{\log(x\sin x)}$$

$$\Rightarrow \text{IF} = x\sin x \quad [\because e^{\log ax} = ax] \quad \text{...(i)}$$

The general solution of the differential equation is given by

$$y \cdot \text{IF} = \int (Q \times \text{IF})\, dx + C$$

$$\Rightarrow y(x\sin x) = \int x\sin x\, dx + C$$

$$\Rightarrow y(x\sin x) = -x\cos x + \int \cos x\, dx + C$$

[integrating by parts]

$$\Rightarrow y(x\sin x) = -x\cos x + \sin x + C$$

$$\Rightarrow y = \frac{-x\cos x}{x\sin x} + \frac{\sin x}{x\sin x} + \frac{C}{x\sin x}$$

$$\Rightarrow y = \frac{1}{x} - \cot x + \frac{C}{x\sin x}$$

II. $(x+y)\dfrac{dy}{dx} = 1$

$$\Rightarrow \quad \frac{dx}{dy} = (x+y)$$

$$\Rightarrow \quad \frac{dx}{dy} - x = y$$

On comparing with the form $\frac{dx}{dy} + Px = Q$, we get

$$P = -1 \text{ and } Q = y$$

$\therefore \quad \text{IF} = e^{\int P \cdot dy} = e^{-\int 1\, dy}$

$\Rightarrow \quad \text{IF} = e^{-y}$ ...(i)

The general solution of the given differential equation is given by,

$$x\,\text{IF} = \int (Q \times \text{IF})\, dy + C$$

$\Rightarrow xe^{-y} = \int e^{-y} \cdot y\, dy + C$

$\Rightarrow xe^{-y} = y \int e^{-y}\, dy - \int \left[\frac{d}{dy} y \int e^{-y}\, dy\right] dy + C$

[integrating by parts]

$\Rightarrow xe^{-y} = -y\,(e^{-y}) + \int e^{-y} dy + C$

$\Rightarrow xe^{-y} = -ye^{-y} - e^{-y} + C$

$\Rightarrow \quad x = -y - 1 + e^{y}C$

$\Rightarrow x + y + 1 = Ce^{y}.$

14 (a) According to the question, the differential equation is

$$\frac{dy}{dx} = x + y \Rightarrow \frac{dy}{dx} - y = x$$

On comparing with the form $\frac{dy}{dx} + Py = Q$, we get

$$P = -1 \text{ and } Q = x$$

$\therefore \quad \text{IF} = e^{-\int 1\, dx} \Rightarrow \text{IF} = e^{-x}$

The general solution of the given differential equation is given by

$$y \cdot \text{IF} = \int (Q \times \text{IF})\, dx + C$$

$\Rightarrow \quad ye^{-x} = \int e^{-x} \cdot x\, dx + C$

$\Rightarrow \quad y\,e^{-x} = x \int e^{-x}\, dx - \int \left[\frac{d}{dx}(x) \int e^{-x}\, dx\right] dx + C$

[integrating by parts]

$\Rightarrow ye^{-x} = -xe^{-x} + \int e^{-x}\, dx + C$

$\Rightarrow e^{-x}\, y = -xe^{-x} - e^{-x} + C$ ...(ii)

Since, the curve passing through the origin, so put $x = 0$ and $y = 0$ in Eq. (ii), we get

$$(0)\,e^{-0} = -0(e^{-0}) - e^{-0} + C \Rightarrow C = 1$$

On putting the value of C in Eq. (ii), we get

$\Rightarrow \quad e^{-x}\, y = -xe^{-x} - e^{-x} + 1$

$\Rightarrow \quad y = -x - 1 + e^{x}$

$\Rightarrow \quad x + y + 1 = e^{x}$

which is the required equation of curve.

15 (c) Given, $y\, dx + (x - y^2)\, dy = 0$

$\Rightarrow \quad y\, dx = (y^2 - x)\, dy$

$\Rightarrow \quad \frac{dx}{dy} + \frac{x}{y} = y$

On comparing with the form $\frac{dx}{dy} + Px = Q$, we get

$$P = \frac{1}{y} \text{ and } Q = y$$

$\therefore \quad \text{IF} = e^{\int \frac{1}{y} dy}$

$\Rightarrow \quad \text{IF} = e^{\log|y|} = y$ ...(i)

The general solution of the given differential equation is given by

$$x \cdot \text{IF} = \int (Q \times \text{IF})\, dy + C$$

$\Rightarrow \quad xy = \int (y \times y)\, dy + C$

$\Rightarrow \quad xy = \int y^2\, dy + C$

$\Rightarrow \quad xy = \frac{y^3}{3} + C \Rightarrow x = \frac{y^2}{3} + \frac{C}{y}$

16 (a) Given, $(x + 3y^2)\frac{dy}{dx} = y$

$\Rightarrow \quad y\frac{dx}{dy} = x + 3y^2$

On dividing by y both sides, we get

$$\frac{dx}{dy} = \frac{x}{y} + 3y$$

$\Rightarrow \quad \frac{dx}{dy} - \frac{x}{y} = 3y$

On comparing with the form $\frac{dx}{dy} + Px = Q$, we get

$$P = -\frac{1}{y} \text{ and } Q = 3y$$

$\therefore \quad \text{IF} = e^{-\int \frac{1}{y} dy}$

$\Rightarrow \quad \text{IF} = e^{-\log y} = e^{\log(y)^{-1}}$

$= y^{-1} = \frac{1}{y}$ ...(i)

The general solution of the given differential equation is given by

$$x \cdot \text{IF} = \int (Q \times \text{IF})\, dy + C$$

$\Rightarrow \quad x \cdot \frac{1}{y} = \int \frac{1}{y} \times 3y\, dy + C$

$\Rightarrow \quad \frac{x}{y} = 3y + C$

$\Rightarrow \quad x = 3y^2 + Cy$

17 (b) The given differential equation can be written as

$$\frac{dx}{dy} + \frac{x}{1 + y^2} = \frac{\tan^{-1} y}{1 + y^2} \quad \text{...(i)}$$

Now, Eq. (i) is a linear differential equation of the form $\frac{dx}{dy} + P_1 x = Q_1$

where, $P_1 = \frac{1}{1 + y^2}$

and $\quad Q_1 = \frac{\tan^{-1} y}{1 + y^2}$

Therefore, $\text{IF} = e^{\int \frac{1}{1+y^2} dy} = e^{\tan^{-1} y}$

Thus, the solution of the given differential equation is given by

$$xe^{\tan^{-1} y} = \int \left(\frac{\tan^{-1} y}{1 + y^2}\right) e^{\tan^{-1} y}\, dy + C \quad \text{...(ii)}$$

Let $\quad I = \int \left(\frac{\tan^{-1} y}{1 + y^2}\right) e^{\tan^{-1} y}\, dy$

On substituting $\tan^{-1} y = t$ so that $\left(\frac{1}{1 + y^2}\right) dy = dt$, we get

$$I = \int te^{t} dt = te^{t} - \int 1 \cdot e^{t} dt$$

$$= te^{t} - e^{t} = e^{t}(t - 1)$$

or $\quad I = e^{\tan^{-1} y}(\tan^{-1} y - 1)$

On substituting the value of I in Eq. (ii), we get

$$x \cdot e^{\tan^{-1} y} = e^{\tan^{-1} y}(\tan^{-1} y - 1) + C$$

or $\quad x = (\tan^{-1} y - 1) + Ce^{-\tan^{-1} y}$

which is the general solution of the given differential equation.

18 (*c*) The integrating factor of the given differential equation

$\frac{dx}{dy} + P_1 x = Q_1$ is $e^{\int P_1 dy}$.

The general solution of the differential equation is given by

$$x \cdot \text{IF} = \int (Q \times \text{IF})\, dy + C$$

$$\therefore x e^{\int P_1 dy} = \int (Q_1 e^{\int P_1 dy})\, dy + C$$

19 (*d*) The given differential equation is

$$x\frac{dy}{dx} + 2y = x^2 \Rightarrow \frac{dy}{dx} + \frac{2}{x}y = x$$

Here, $P = \frac{2}{x}$ and $Q = x$

$$\therefore \text{IF} = e^{\int \frac{2}{x}dx} = e^{2\log x} = e^{\log x^2} = x^2$$

$\therefore$ The solution is

$$yx^2 = \int x^2 \cdot x\, dx + C$$

$$\Rightarrow \quad yx^2 = \frac{x^4}{4} + C$$

$$\therefore \quad y = \frac{x^4 + C}{4x^2}$$

20 (*b*) The given differential equation is

$$\frac{dy}{dx} + y = e^{-x}$$

Here, $P = 1$ and $Q = e^{-x}$

$$\therefore \quad \text{IF} = e^{\int 1 \cdot dx} = e^x$$

$\therefore$ Solution of the differential equation is

$$ye^x = \int e^{-x} \cdot e^x dx$$

$$\Rightarrow \quad ye^x = x + C$$

Also, given that at $x = 0$, $y = 0$

$$\therefore \quad c = 0$$

$\therefore$ The solution of the differential equation is

$$ye^x = x$$

$$\Rightarrow \quad y = xe^{-x}$$

21 (*b*) According to the given condition,

$$\frac{dy}{dx} = y + 2x$$

$$\Rightarrow \quad \frac{dy}{dx} - y = 2x$$

$$\text{IF} = e^{\int -1\, dx} = e^{-x}$$

$\therefore$ Solution of the differential equation is

$$y \cdot e^{-x} = 2\int xe^{-x}dx$$

$$= 2(-xe^{-x} - e^{-x}) + C$$

$$\Rightarrow \quad y = 2e^x(-xe^{-x} - e^{-x}) + Ce^x$$

$$\Rightarrow \quad y = -2x - 2 + Ce^x$$

For $c = 2$, we get

$$y = 2(e^x - x - 1)$$

22 (*a*) Since,

$$\cos x\, dy = y \sin x\, dx - y^2 dx$$

$$\Rightarrow \quad \frac{1}{y^2}\frac{dy}{dx} - \frac{1}{y}\tan x = -\sec x$$

Put $\quad -\frac{1}{y} = z$

$$\Rightarrow \quad \frac{1}{y^2}\frac{dy}{dx} = \frac{dz}{dx}$$

$$\Rightarrow \quad \frac{dz}{dx} + (\tan x)\, z = -\sec x$$

This is a linear differential equation. Therefore,

$$\text{IF} = e^{\int \tan x\, dx} = e^{\log \sec x} = \sec x$$

Hence, the solution is

$$z \cdot (\sec x) = \int -\sec x \cdot \sec x\, dx + C_1$$

$$\Rightarrow \quad -\frac{1}{y}\sec x = -\tan x + C_1$$

$$\Rightarrow \quad \sec x = y(\tan x + C)$$

23 (*a*) The given differential equation is

$$\left(\frac{e^{-2\sqrt{x}}}{\sqrt{x}} - \frac{y}{\sqrt{x}}\right)\frac{dx}{dy} = 1 \quad \text{...(i)}$$

$$\Rightarrow \quad \frac{dy}{dx} = \frac{e^{-2\sqrt{x}}}{\sqrt{x}} - \frac{y}{\sqrt{x}}$$

$$\Rightarrow \quad \frac{dy}{dx} + \frac{1}{\sqrt{x}}y = \frac{e^{-2\sqrt{x}}}{\sqrt{x}} \quad \text{...(ii)}$$

On comparing with the form

$\frac{dy}{dx} + Py = Q$, we get

$$P = \frac{1}{\sqrt{x}} \text{ and } Q = \frac{e^{-2\sqrt{x}}}{\sqrt{x}}$$

$$\therefore \quad \text{IF} = e^{\int \frac{1}{\sqrt{x}}dx}$$

$$\Rightarrow \text{IF} = e^{2x^{1/2}} = e^{2\sqrt{x}}$$

The general solution of the given differential equation is given by

$$y \cdot \text{IF} = \int (Q \times \text{IF})\, dx + C$$

$$\Rightarrow \quad ye^{2\sqrt{x}} = \int e^{2\sqrt{x}} \times \frac{e^{-2\sqrt{x}}}{\sqrt{x}}\, dx + C$$

$$\Rightarrow \quad ye^{2\sqrt{x}} = \int \frac{1}{\sqrt{x}}\, dx + C$$

$$\Rightarrow \quad ye^{2\sqrt{x}} = 2\sqrt{x} + C$$

24 (*b*) Given differential equation is

$$\frac{dy}{dx} + y\cot x = 4x \operatorname{cosec} x \quad \text{...(i)}$$

On comparing with the form

$\frac{dy}{dx} + Py = Q$, we get

$$P = \cot x \text{ and } Q = 4x \operatorname{cosec} x$$

$$\therefore \quad \text{IF} = e^{\int P \cdot dx}$$

$$\Rightarrow \quad \text{IF} = e^{\int \cot x\, dx}$$

$$\Rightarrow \quad \text{IF} = e^{\log|\sin x|} = \sin x$$

The general solution of the given differential equation is given by

$$y \cdot \text{IF} = \int (Q \times \text{IF})\, dx + C$$

$$\Rightarrow y \sin x = \int (4x \operatorname{cosec} x)(\sin x)\, dx + C$$

$$\Rightarrow \quad y \sin x = \int 4x\, dx + C$$

$$\Rightarrow \quad y \sin x = 4 \cdot \frac{x^2}{2} + C$$

$$\Rightarrow \quad y \sin x = 2x^2 + C \quad \text{...(ii)}$$

Now, at $x = \frac{\pi}{2}$, $y = 0$

$$\therefore 0 \times \sin\frac{\pi}{2} = 2\left(\frac{\pi}{2}\right)^2 + C \Rightarrow C = -\frac{\pi^2}{2}$$

On putting the value of C in Eq. (ii), we get

$$y \sin x = 2x^2 - \frac{\pi^2}{2}$$

25 (*a*) Given differential equation is

$$(1 + y^2) + (x - e^{\tan^{-1} y})\frac{dy}{dx} = 0$$

$$\Rightarrow \quad (1 + y^2)\frac{dx}{dy} = -x + e^{\tan^{-1} y}$$

$$\Rightarrow \quad \frac{dx}{dy} + \frac{x}{1 + y^2} = \frac{e^{\tan^{-1} y}}{1 + y^2}$$

which is a linear differential equation.

Here, $P = \frac{1}{1+y^2}$ and $Q = \frac{e^{\tan^{-1} y}}{1+y^2}$

$\therefore \text{IF} = e^{\int P \cdot dy} = e^{\int \frac{1}{1+y^2} dy} = e^{\tan^{-1} y}$

Required solution is

$$x \cdot \text{IF} = \int (Q \cdot \text{IF})\, dy + C$$

$$xe^{\tan^{-1} y} = \int \frac{e^{\tan^{-1} y}}{1+y^2} \cdot e^{\tan^{-1} y}\, dy + \frac{C}{2}$$

$$\Rightarrow \quad xe^{\tan^{-1} y} = \frac{e^{2\tan^{-1} y}}{2} + \frac{C}{2}$$

$$\therefore \quad 2xe^{\tan^{-1} y} = e^{2\tan^{-1} y} + C$$

26 (*b*) Given, $\frac{dy}{dx} + \frac{y}{(1-x)\sqrt{x}} = 1 - \sqrt{x}$

$\therefore \quad \text{IF} = e^{\int \frac{1}{(1-x)\sqrt{x}} dx}$

Put $\sqrt{x} = t$

$\Rightarrow \frac{1}{2\sqrt{x}} dx = dt$

$\therefore \quad \text{IF} = e^{\int \frac{2}{1-t^2} dt}$

$$= e^{\frac{2}{2}\log\left(\frac{1+t}{1-t}\right)} = \frac{1+t}{1-t} = \frac{1+\sqrt{x}}{1-\sqrt{x}}$$

27 (*a*) Given that, $y(t)$ is the solution of the differential equation

$(1+t)\frac{dy}{dt} - ty = 1$ and $y(0) = -1$

Now, the given differential equation can be written as

$$\frac{dy}{dt} - \left(\frac{t}{1+t}\right) y = \frac{1}{(1+t)}$$

and $\quad y(0) = -1$

$\therefore \text{IF} = e^{\int -\left(\frac{t}{1+t}\right) dt} = e^{-\int \left(1 - \frac{1}{1+t}\right) dt}$

$$= e^{-t + \log(1+t)} = e^{-t}(1+t)$$

$\therefore$ Required solution is

$$ye^{-t}(1+t) = \int \frac{1}{1+t} e^{-t}(1+t)\, dt + C$$

$$= \int e^{-t} dt + C$$

$$\Rightarrow \quad ye^{-t}(1+t) = -e^{-t} + C$$

Since, $\quad y(0) = -1 \Rightarrow c = 0$

$$\therefore \quad y = -\frac{1}{(1+t)} \Rightarrow y(1) = -\frac{1}{2}$$

Miscellaneous Exercise

1 (*d*) The given differential equation is $\frac{d^4y}{dx^4} - \sin\left(\frac{d^3y}{dx^3}\right) = 0.$

Since, the highest order derivative which occurs in the given differential equation is $\frac{d^4y}{dx^4}$.

Thus, order of the given equation is 4, as $\sin\left(\frac{d^3y}{dx^3}\right)$ occurs in the equation, it is not a polynomial equation.

Hence, degree is not defined.

2 (*c*)

I. Given, $\quad y = x\sin 3x \quad$ ...(i)

On differentiating both sides w.r.t. x, we get

$$\frac{dy}{dx} = x\frac{d}{dx}(\sin 3x) + \sin 3x \frac{d}{dx}(x)$$

[using product rule of differentiation]

$$\frac{dy}{dx} = x\cos 3x \times 3 + \sin 3x$$

Again, differentiating both sides w.r.t. x, we get

$$\frac{d^2y}{dx^2} = 3\left[x\frac{d}{dx}\cos 3x + \cos 3x \frac{d}{dx}(x)\right] + \frac{d}{dx}(\sin 3x)$$

$$\Rightarrow \frac{d^2y}{dx^2} = 3\,[x(-\sin 3x)\cdot(3) + \cos 3x] + (\cos 3x)\cdot(3)$$

$$\Rightarrow \frac{d^2y}{dx^2} = -9x\sin 3x + 3\cos 3x + 3\cos 3x$$

$$\Rightarrow \frac{d^2y}{dx^2} = -9x\sin 3x + 6\cos 3x$$

$$\Rightarrow \frac{d^2y}{dx^2} = -9y + 6\cos 3x$$

[using Eq. (i)]

$$\Rightarrow \frac{d^2y}{dx^2} + 9y - 6\cos 3x = 0$$

Hence, the given function is a solution of the corresponding differential equation.

II. Given, $x^2 = 2y^2 \log y \quad$ ...(i)

On differentiating both sides w.r.t. x, we get

$$2x = 2\left[y^2 \times \frac{1}{y}\frac{dy}{dx} + \log y \times 2y\frac{dy}{dx}\right]$$

$$\Rightarrow 2x = 2\{y + 2y\log y\}\frac{dy}{dx}$$

$$\Rightarrow \quad x = (y + 2y\log y)\frac{dy}{dx}$$

On multiplying both sides by y, we get

$$xy = (y^2 + 2y^2\log y)\frac{dy}{dx}$$

$$\Rightarrow \quad xy = (y^2 + x^2)\frac{dy}{dx}$$

[using Eq. (i)]

$$\Rightarrow \quad (x^2 + y^2)\frac{dy}{dx} - xy = 0$$

Hence, the given function is a solution of the corresponding differential equation.

3 (*c*) The given differential equation is

$$y\frac{dy}{dx} + x^3\frac{d^2y}{dx^2} + xy = \cos x$$

Its order is 2 and its degree is 1.

$\therefore \quad p = 2$ and $q = 1$

Hence, $\quad p > q$

4 (*c*) The given differential equation is

$$x = 1 + \left(\frac{dy}{dx}\right) + \frac{1}{2!}\left(\frac{dy}{dx}\right)^2 + \frac{1}{3!}\left(\frac{dy}{dx}\right)^3 + \ldots$$

$$\Rightarrow \quad x = e^{\frac{dy}{dx}}$$

$$\left[\because e^x = 1 + x + \frac{x^2}{2!} + \frac{x^3}{3!} + \ldots\right]$$

$$\therefore \quad \log_e x = \frac{dy}{dx}$$

Hence, the degree of the differential equation is 1.

5 (c) The given equation is

$$Ax^2 + By^2 = 1$$

$$\Rightarrow \quad 2Ax + 2By\frac{dy}{dx} = 0 \quad \text{...(i)}$$

$$\Rightarrow 2A + 2B\left\{\left(\frac{dy}{dx}\right)^2 + y\frac{d^2y}{dx^2}\right\} = 0 \quad \text{...(ii)}$$

On eliminating A and B from Eqs. (i) and (ii), we get

$$y\frac{d^2y}{dx^2} + \left(\frac{dy}{dx}\right)^2 - \frac{y}{x}\cdot\frac{dy}{dx} = 0$$

Hence, order = 2 and degree = 1

6 (a) Given equation can be written as $x\,dy = (\sqrt{x^2+y^2} + y)\,dx$,

i.e. $$\frac{dy}{dx} = \frac{\sqrt{x^2+y^2}+y}{x} \quad \text{...(i)}$$

Clearly, RHS of equation (i) is a homogeneous function of degree zero. Therefore, the given equation is a homogeneous differential Eq. Substituting $y = vx$, we get, from Eq. (i)

$$v + x\frac{dv}{dx} = \frac{\sqrt{x^2+v^2x^2}+vx}{x}$$

i.e. $$v + x\frac{dv}{dx} = \sqrt{1+v^2} + v$$

$$\Rightarrow \quad x\frac{dv}{dx} = \sqrt{1+v^2}$$

$$\Rightarrow \quad \frac{dv}{\sqrt{1+v^2}} = \frac{dx}{x} \quad \text{...(ii)}$$

On integrating both sides of Eq. (ii), we get

$$\log(v + \sqrt{1+v^2}) = \log x + \log C$$

$$\Rightarrow \quad v + \sqrt{1+v^2} = Cx$$

$$\Rightarrow \quad \frac{y}{x} + \sqrt{1+\frac{y^2}{x^2}} = Cx$$

$$\Rightarrow \quad y + \sqrt{x^2+y^2} = Cx^2$$

7 (c) The given differential equation is

$$(1+y^2)\,dx + (1+x^2)\,dy = 0$$

$$\Rightarrow \quad \frac{dx}{1+x^2} + \frac{dy}{1+y^2} = 0$$

On integrating, we get

$$\int\frac{1}{1+x^2}dx + \int\frac{1}{1+y^2}dy = 0$$

$$\Rightarrow \quad \tan^{-1}x + \tan^{-1}y = \tan^{-1}C$$

$$\Rightarrow \quad \tan^{-1}\left(\frac{x+y}{1-xy}\right) = \tan^{-1}C$$

$$\therefore \quad x + y = C(1-xy)$$

8 (a) Given equation can be rewritten as

$$\frac{dy}{dx} - \frac{1}{x}\cdot y = 1$$

$$\therefore \quad \text{IF} = e^{-\int\frac{1}{x}dx} = e^{-\log x} = \frac{1}{x}$$

$\therefore$ Required solution is

$$y\left(\frac{1}{x}\right) = \int\frac{1}{x}dx = \log x + C$$

Since, $y(1) = 1$ and $C = 1$

$$\therefore \quad y = x\log x + x$$

9 (b)

I. Given differential equation is

$$(x-y)(dx+dy) = dx - dy$$

$$\Rightarrow \quad dx + dy = \frac{dx-dy}{x-y}$$

On integrating both sides, we get

$$\int(dx+dy) = \int\frac{dx-dy}{x-y}$$

Let $\quad x - y = t$

$$\Rightarrow \quad dx - dy = dt$$

$$\therefore \int dx + dy = \int\frac{dx+dy}{x-y} = \int\frac{dt}{t}$$

$$= \log|t| + C = \log|x-y| + C$$

$$\Rightarrow x + y = \log|x-y| + C \quad \text{...(i)}$$

It is given that when

$$x = 0,\ y = -1$$

$$\therefore \quad 0 + (-1) = \log(0+1) + C$$

$$\Rightarrow \quad C = -1$$

On substituting this value in Eq. (i), we get the required particular solution as

$$x + y = \log|x-y| - 1$$

$$\Rightarrow \log|x-y| = x + y + 1$$

II. Given differential equation is

$$(x+1)\frac{dy}{dx} = 2e^{-y} - 1 \quad \text{...(i)}$$

On separating the variables,

$$\Rightarrow \quad \frac{dy}{2e^{-y}-1} = \frac{dx}{x+1}$$

$$\Rightarrow \quad \frac{e^y\,dy}{2-e^y} = \frac{dx}{x+1}$$

On integrating both sides, we get

$$\int\frac{e^y\,dy}{2-e^y} = \int\frac{dx}{x+1} \quad \text{...(ii)}$$

Put $2 - e^y = t$

$$\Rightarrow \quad -e^y = \frac{dt}{dy}$$

$$\Rightarrow \quad e^y\,dy = -dt$$

Eq. (ii) becomes,

$$\int\frac{-dt}{t} = \int\frac{dx}{x+1}$$

$$\Rightarrow -\log|t| = \log|x+1| + \log C$$

$$\Rightarrow -\log|2-e^y| = \log|C(x+1)|$$

$$\Rightarrow \quad \frac{1}{2-e^y} = C(x+1)$$

$$[\because -\log x = \log x^{-1}]$$

$$\Rightarrow \quad 2 - e^y = \frac{1}{C(x+1)} \quad \text{...(iii)}$$

Now, at $x = 0$, $y = 0$

$$\therefore \quad 2 - 1 = \frac{1}{C} \Rightarrow C = 1$$

On putting the value of C in Eq. (iii), we get

$$2 - e^y = \frac{1}{(x+1)}$$

$$\Rightarrow \quad e^y = 2 - \frac{1}{x+1}$$

$$\Rightarrow \quad e^y = \frac{2x+2-1}{x+1}$$

$$\Rightarrow \quad e^y = \frac{2x+1}{x+1}$$

$$\Rightarrow \; y = \log\left|\frac{2x+1}{x+1}\right|,\ (x \neq -1)$$

$$[\because \text{if } \log_e x = m \Rightarrow e^m = x]$$

10 (c) Given differential equation is

$$e^x\,dy + (ye^x + 2x)\,dx = 0$$

$$\Rightarrow \quad e^x\frac{dy}{dx} + ye^x + 2x = 0$$

$$\Rightarrow \quad \frac{dy}{dx} + y = -2x\,e^{-x}$$

This is a linear differential equation of the form

$$\frac{dy}{dx} + Py = Q$$

On comparing,

$$P = 1$$

and $\quad Q = -2xe^{-x}$

$$\therefore \quad \text{IF} = e^{\int 1\,dx} = e^x$$

The general solution of the given differential equation is given by

$$y \cdot \text{IF} = \int (-2xe^{-x} \times e^x)\,dx + C$$

$$\Rightarrow \quad ye^x = -\int 2x\,dx + C$$

$$\Rightarrow \quad ye^x = -x^2 + C$$

$$\Rightarrow \quad ye^x + x^2 = C.$$

11 (c) The equation of circle passing through given points is

$$x^2 + y^2 - 2fy = a^2$$

$$\Rightarrow \quad 2x + 2yy_1 - 2fy_1 = 0 \quad \text{...(i)}$$

[on differentiating]

$$\Rightarrow \quad x = y_1(f - y)$$

$$\Rightarrow \quad x = y_1\left(\frac{x^2 + y^2 - a^2}{2y} - y\right)$$

[from Eq. (i)]

$$\Rightarrow \quad y_1(y^2 - x^2 + a^2) + 2xy = 0$$

12 (c) The equation of the family of circles of radius r is

$$(x - a)^2 + (y - b)^2 = r^2 \quad \text{...(i)}$$

where, a and b are arbitrary constants.

$$\Rightarrow \quad 2(x - a) + 2(y - b)\frac{dy}{dx} = 0$$

$$\Rightarrow \quad (x - a) + (y - b)\frac{dy}{dx} = 0 \quad \text{...(ii)}$$

$$\Rightarrow 1 + (y - b)\frac{d^2y}{dx^2} + \left(\frac{dy}{dx}\right)^2 = 0$$

$$\Rightarrow \quad (y - b) = -\frac{1 + \left(\frac{dy}{dx}\right)^2}{\left(\frac{d^2y}{dx^2}\right)} \quad \text{...(iii)}$$

From Eq. (ii),

$$(x - a) = \frac{\left[1 + \left(\frac{dy}{dx}\right)^2\right]\frac{dy}{dx}}{\frac{d^2y}{dx^2}} \quad \text{...(iv)}$$

On putting the value of $(y - b)$ and $(x - a)$ in Eq. (i), we get

$$\frac{\left[1 + \left(\frac{dy}{dx}\right)^2\right]^2\left(\frac{dy}{dx}\right)^2}{\left(\frac{d^2y}{dx^2}\right)^2} + \frac{\left[1 + \left(\frac{dy}{dx}\right)^2\right]^2}{\left(\frac{d^2y}{dx^2}\right)^2} = r^2$$

$$\Rightarrow \quad \left[1 + \left(\frac{dy}{dx}\right)^2\right]^3 = r^2\left[\frac{d^2y}{dx^2}\right]^2$$

13 (a) According to the question,

$$\frac{dy}{dx} = \frac{y - 1}{x^2 + x}$$

$$\Rightarrow \quad \frac{dy}{y - 1} = \frac{dx}{x^2 + x}$$

$$\Rightarrow \quad \int \frac{dy}{y - 1} = \int \left(\frac{1}{x} - \frac{1}{x + 1}\right)dx$$

$$\Rightarrow \log(y - 1) = \log x - \log(x + 1) + \log C$$

$$\Rightarrow \quad y - 1 = \frac{xC}{(x + 1)} \quad \text{...(i)}$$

Since, curve passes through (1, 0).

$$\therefore \quad 0 - 1 = \frac{C}{2} \Rightarrow C = -2$$

$\therefore$ From Eq. (i), we get

$$2x + (y - 1)(x + 1) = 0$$

14 (c) A. Given differential equation is

$$\frac{dy}{dx} + \sqrt{\frac{1 - y^2}{1 - x^2}} = 0$$

$$\Rightarrow \quad \frac{dy}{dx} = -\frac{\sqrt{1 - y^2}}{\sqrt{1 - x^2}}$$

$$\Rightarrow \quad \frac{1}{\sqrt{1 - y^2}}\,dy = -\frac{1}{\sqrt{1 - x^2}}\,dx$$

On integrating both sides, we get

$$\int \frac{1}{\sqrt{1 - y^2}}\,dy = -\int \frac{1}{\sqrt{1 - x^2}}\,dx$$

$$\Rightarrow \quad \sin^{-1} y = -\sin^{-1} x + C$$

$$\Rightarrow \sin^{-1} x + \sin^{-1} y = C$$

which is the required general solution.

B. Given differential equation is

$$\frac{dy}{dx} + \frac{y^2 + y + 1}{x^2 + x + 1} = 0$$

$$\Rightarrow \frac{dy}{y^2 + y + 1} + \frac{dx}{x^2 + x + 1} = 0$$

On integrating both sides, we get

$$\int \frac{dy}{y^2 + y + 1} + \int \frac{dx}{x^2 + x + 1} = C$$

$$\Rightarrow \int \frac{dy}{y^2 + y + 1 + \left(\frac{1}{2}\right)^2 - \left(\frac{1}{2}\right)^2} + \int \frac{dx}{x^2 + x + 1 + \left(\frac{1}{2}\right)^2 - \left(\frac{1}{2}\right)^2} = C$$

$$\Rightarrow \int \frac{dy}{\left(y + \frac{1}{2}\right)^2 + \left(1 - \frac{1}{4}\right)} + \int \frac{dx}{\left(x + \frac{1}{2}\right)^2 + \left(1 - \frac{1}{4}\right)} = C$$

$$\Rightarrow \int \frac{dy}{\left(y + \frac{1}{2}\right)^2 + \left(\frac{\sqrt{3}}{2}\right)^2} + \int \frac{dx}{\left(x + \frac{1}{2}\right)^2 + \left(\frac{\sqrt{3}}{2}\right)^2} = C$$

$$\Rightarrow \frac{2}{\sqrt{3}}\tan^{-1}\left(\frac{y+\frac{1}{2}}{\frac{\sqrt{3}}{2}}\right)+\frac{2}{\sqrt{3}}\tan^{-1}\left(\frac{x+\frac{1}{2}}{\frac{\sqrt{3}}{2}}\right)=C$$

$$\left[\because \int \frac{1}{a^2+x^2}dx=\frac{1}{a}\tan^{-1}\frac{x}{a}\right]$$

$$\Rightarrow \tan^{-1}\left(\frac{2y+1}{\sqrt{3}}\right)+\tan^{-1}\left(\frac{2x+1}{\sqrt{3}}\right)=\frac{\sqrt{3}\,C}{2}=k \text{ [say]}$$

$$\Rightarrow \tan^{-1}\left[\frac{\frac{2y+1}{\sqrt{3}}+\frac{2x+1}{\sqrt{3}}}{1-\left(\frac{2y+1}{\sqrt{3}}\right)\left(\frac{2x+1}{\sqrt{3}}\right)}\right]=k$$

$$\left[\because \tan^{-1}x+\tan^{-1}y=\tan^{-1}\left(\frac{x+y}{1-xy}\right)\right]$$

$$\Rightarrow \tan^{-1}\left[\frac{\frac{2y+1+2x+1}{\sqrt{3}}}{1-\left(\frac{4xy+2x+2y+1}{3}\right)}\right]=k$$

$$\Rightarrow \frac{2\sqrt{3}\,(x+y+1)}{3-(4xy+2x+2y+1)}=\tan k$$

$$\Rightarrow \frac{2\sqrt{3}\,(x+y+1)}{2\,(1-x-y-2xy)}=\tan k$$

$$\Rightarrow x+y+1=\frac{1}{\sqrt{3}}\tan k\,(1-x-y-2xy)$$

Let $A=\frac{1}{\sqrt{3}}\tan k$ is an arbitrary constant.

$$\Rightarrow x+y+1=A\,(1-x-y-2xy)$$

C. Given differential equation is

$$ye^{\frac{x}{y}}\,dx=\left(xe^{\frac{x}{y}}+y^2\right)dy$$

$$\Rightarrow e^{\frac{x}{y}}\frac{dx}{dy}=\frac{x}{y}e^{\frac{x}{y}}+y$$

$$\Rightarrow e^{\frac{x}{y}}\frac{dx}{dy}-\frac{x}{y}e^{\frac{x}{y}}=y \quad \text{...(i)}$$

On putting $\frac{x}{y}=v \Rightarrow x=vy$

$$\Rightarrow \frac{dx}{dy}=v+y\frac{dv}{dy}$$

Eq. (i) becomes

$$e^v\left(v+y\frac{dv}{dy}\right)-ve^v=y$$

$$\Rightarrow e^v y\frac{dv}{dy}=y$$

$$\Rightarrow e^v\frac{dv}{dy}=1$$

$$\Rightarrow e^v\,dv=dy$$

On integrating both sides, we get

$$\int e^v\,dv=\int 1dy$$

$$\Rightarrow e^v=y+C$$

$$\Rightarrow e^{\frac{x}{y}}=y+C$$

D. Given differential equation is

$$\frac{y\,dx-x\,dy}{y}=0$$

$$\Rightarrow y\,dx-x\,dy=0$$

$$\Rightarrow \frac{1}{x}dx-\frac{1}{y}dy=0$$

On integrating both sides, we get

$$\log|x|-\log|y|=\log k$$

$$\Rightarrow \log\left|\frac{x}{y}\right|=\log k \Rightarrow \frac{x}{y}=k$$

$$\Rightarrow y=\frac{1}{k}x$$

$$\Rightarrow y=Cx \quad \left[\text{let } \frac{1}{k}=C\right]$$

15 (*a*) The given differential equation can be rewritten as

$$\Rightarrow \left(\frac{1}{y^2}-\frac{1}{y}\right)dy=-\left(\frac{1}{x^2}+\frac{1}{x}\right)dx$$

$$\Rightarrow -\frac{1}{y}-\log y=-\left(-\frac{1}{x}+\log x\right)+C \text{ [integrating]}$$

$$\Rightarrow \log\left(\frac{x}{y}\right)=\frac{1}{x}+\frac{1}{y}+C$$

16 (*b*) The differential equation $(y')^2+x=y^2$ is of order 1

$y'y''+y=\sin x$ is of order 2.

The order of $y'''+(y'')^2+y=0$ is 3 and order of $y'=y^2$ is 1.

17 (*a*) We have, $(xy-x^2)\frac{dy}{dx}=y^2$

$$\Rightarrow y^2\frac{dx}{dy}=xy-x^2$$

$$\Rightarrow \frac{1}{x^2}\frac{dx}{dy}-\frac{1}{x}\cdot\frac{1}{y}=-\frac{1}{y^2}$$

Put $\frac{1}{x}=v \Rightarrow -\frac{1}{x^2}\frac{dx}{dy}=\frac{dv}{dy}$

$\therefore \frac{dv}{dy}+\frac{v}{y}=\frac{1}{y^2}$, which is linear differential equation.

$$\therefore \text{IF}=e^{\int\frac{1}{y}dy}=e^{\log y}=y$$

$\therefore$ The solution is

$$vy=\int\frac{1}{y^2}\cdot y\,dy+C$$

$$\Rightarrow \frac{y}{x}=\log y+C$$

$$\Rightarrow y=x(\log y+C)$$

This passes through the point (–1, 1).

$\therefore\ 1=-1(\log 1+C)$ i.e. $C=-1$

Thus, the equation of the curve is

$$y=x(\log y-1)$$

18 (*b*) Let the radius of circle be a, then centre of the circle is (a, a). Hence, the equation of the circle is

$$(x-a)^2+(y-a)^2=a^2 \quad \text{...(i)}$$

$$\Rightarrow x^2+y^2-2ax-2ay+a^2=0$$

On differentiating Eq. (i) w.r.t. x, we get

$$2x+2yy'-2a-2ay'=0$$

$$\Rightarrow x+yy'-a(1+y')=0$$

$$\Rightarrow a=\frac{x+yy'}{1+y'}$$

On substituting this value of a in Eq. (i), we get

$$\left(x-\frac{x+yy'}{1+y'}\right)^2+\left(y-\frac{x+yy'}{1+y'}\right)^2=\left(\frac{x+yy'}{1+y'}\right)^2$$

$\Rightarrow (xy' - yy')^2 + (y - x)^2 = (x + yy')^2$

$\Rightarrow (x - y)^2 (y')^2 + (x - y)^2 = (x + yy')^2$

$\Rightarrow (x - y)^2 [1 + (y')^2] = (x + yy')^2$

which is the required differential equation.

19 (*d*) The differential equation of the given curve is

$\sin x \cos y \, dx + \cos x \sin y \, dy = 0$

$\Rightarrow \quad \dfrac{\sin x}{\cos x} dx + \dfrac{\sin y}{\cos y} dy = 0$

$\Rightarrow \quad \tan x \, dx + \tan y \, dy = 0$

On integrating both sides, we get

$\int \tan x \, dx + \int \tan y \, dy = \log C$

$\Rightarrow \log(\sec x) + \log(\sec y) = \log C$

$\Rightarrow \quad \sec x \cdot \sec y = C \quad$ ...(i)

The curve passes through the point $\left(0, \dfrac{\pi}{4}\right)$, therefore put

$x = 0, y = \dfrac{\pi}{4}$, we get

$\sec 0 \sec \dfrac{\pi}{4} = C \Rightarrow C = \sqrt{2}$

On putting the value of C in Eq. (i), we get

$\sec x \cdot \sec y = \sqrt{2}$

$\Rightarrow \quad \sec x \cdot \dfrac{1}{\cos y} = \sqrt{2}$

$\therefore \quad \cos y = \dfrac{\sec x}{\sqrt{2}}$.

Hence, the required equation of the curve is $\cos y = \dfrac{\sec x}{\sqrt{2}}$.

20 (*b*) The general equation of parabola whose axis is X-axis, is

$y^2 = 4a(x - h)$

$\Rightarrow \quad 2y \dfrac{dy}{dx} = 4a \Rightarrow y \dfrac{dy}{dx} = 2a$

$\Rightarrow \quad \left(\dfrac{dy}{dx}\right)^2 + y \dfrac{d^2y}{dx^2} = 0$

Hence, degree = 1 and order = 2

21 (*b*) The given differential equation is

$\dfrac{dy}{dx} = x \log x$

$\Rightarrow \quad dy = x \log x \, dx$

$\Rightarrow \quad y = \dfrac{x^2}{2} \log x - \int \dfrac{x}{2} dx$

[integrating by parts]

$\Rightarrow \quad y = \dfrac{x^2}{2} \log x - \dfrac{x^2}{4} + C$

22 (*c*) The given differential equation is

$(e^x + 1) \, y \, dy = (y + 1) \, e^x dx$

$\Rightarrow \quad \dfrac{y}{y+1} dy = \dfrac{e^x}{e^x + 1} dx$

On integrating both sides, we get

$\Rightarrow \int \dfrac{y}{y+1} dy = \int \dfrac{e^x}{e^x + 1} dx$

$\Rightarrow \int \left(1 - \dfrac{1}{y+1}\right) dy = \int \dfrac{e^x}{e^x + 1} dx$

$\Rightarrow y - \log|y + 1| = \log|e^x + 1| + \log k$

$\Rightarrow \quad y = \log|e^x + 1| + \log|y + 1| + \log k$

$\Rightarrow \quad y = \log|k(e^x + 1)(y + 1)|$

23 (*c*) The given equation is

$y = ae^{bx}$

$\Rightarrow \quad \dfrac{dy}{dx} = abe^{bx} \quad$ ...(i)

$\Rightarrow \quad \dfrac{d^2y}{dx^2} = ab^2e^{bx} \quad$ ...(ii)

$\Rightarrow ae^{bx} \dfrac{d^2y}{dx^2} = a^2b^2e^{2bx}$

$\Rightarrow \quad y \dfrac{d^2y}{dx^2} = \left(\dfrac{dy}{dx}\right)^2 \quad$ [from Eq. (ii)]

$\Rightarrow \quad y \dfrac{d^2y}{dx^2} - \left(\dfrac{dy}{dx}\right)^2 = 0$

24 (*a*) Given family of curves is $(x - a)^2 + 2y^2 = a^2$ and a being an arbitrary constant.

$\therefore \quad x^2 - 2ax + 2y^2 = 0 \quad$ ...(i)

On differentiating both sides w.r.t. x, we get

$2x - 2a + 4y \dfrac{dy}{dx} = 0 \quad$ ...(ii)

On multiplying Eq. (ii) by x and then subtracting Eq. (i) from it, we get

$x\left(2x - 2a + 4y \dfrac{dy}{dx}\right) - (x^2 - 2ax + 2y^2) = 0$

$\Rightarrow 2x^2 - 2ax + 4xy \dfrac{dy}{dx} - x^2 + 2ax - 2y^2 = 0$

$\Rightarrow 4xy \dfrac{dy}{dx} + x^2 - 2y^2 = 0$

$\Rightarrow \quad \dfrac{dy}{dx} = \dfrac{2y^2 - x^2}{4xy}$

which is the required differential equation.

25 (*c*) Given differential equation is

$(1 + e^{2x}) \, dy + (1 + y^2) \, e^x \, dx = 0$

Separating the variables, we get

$\dfrac{dy}{1 + y^2} + \dfrac{e^x \, dx}{1 + e^{2x}} = 0$

On integrating both sides, we get

$\int \dfrac{dy}{1 + y^2} + \int \dfrac{e^x \, dx}{1 + e^{2x}} = C$

Put $t = e^x \quad \Rightarrow e^x \, dx = dt$

$\Rightarrow \quad \tan^{-1} y + \int \dfrac{dt}{1 + t^2} = C$

$\Rightarrow \quad \tan^{-1} y + \tan^{-1} t = C$

$\Rightarrow \quad \tan^{-1} y + \tan^{-1} e^x = C \quad$ ...(i)

Now, put $x = 0, y = 1$

$\therefore \quad \tan^{-1} 1 + \tan^{-1} e^0 = C$

$\Rightarrow \quad \dfrac{\pi}{4} + \dfrac{\pi}{4} = C \Rightarrow C = \dfrac{\pi}{2}$

On putting the value of C in Eq. (i), we get

$\tan^{-1} y + \tan^{-1} e^x = \dfrac{\pi}{2}$

which is the required particular solution.

Numerical Type Questions

1 (3) We know that the number of arbitrary constants in the general solution of a differential equation of order n is equal to its order.

$\therefore$ The number of arbitrary constants in the general solution of a differential equation of third order is 3.

2 (0) The number of arbitrary constants in the particular solution of a differential is zero.

3 (4) Given differential equation is

$\dfrac{d^3y}{dx^3} + \left(\dfrac{d^2y}{dx^2}\right)^2 = \sin x$

Here, the highest derivative is $\dfrac{d^3y}{dx^3}$, whose power is 1.

So, order is 3 and degree is 1.

$\therefore$ Required sum $= 3 + 1 = 4$

4 (80) Given that

$$x^2f(x)-x=4\int_0^x tf(t)\,dt$$

On differentiating both sides, we get

$$2xf(x)+x^2f'(x)-1=4xf(x)$$

$$\Rightarrow x^2f'(x)-2xf(x)-1=0$$

$$\Rightarrow \quad x^2\frac{dy}{dx}-2xy=1$$

[let $y=f(x)$]

On comparing above equation with $\frac{dy}{dx}+Py=Q$.

where $P=\frac{-2}{x}$, $Q=\frac{1}{x^2}$

Now, $\text{IF}=e^{\int(-2/x)\,dx}=e^{-2\log x}=\frac{1}{x^2}$

Solution is

$$y\cdot\left(\frac{1}{x^2}\right)=\int\left(\frac{1}{x^2}\right)\frac{1}{x^2}dx$$

$$\Rightarrow \quad \frac{y}{x^2}=\int\frac{1}{x^4}dx=\frac{-1}{3x^3}+C$$

$$\Rightarrow \quad y=\frac{-1}{3x}+Cx^2$$

Given, $f(1)=\frac{2}{3}$

So, $\quad \frac{2}{3}=\frac{-1}{3}+C\Rightarrow C=1$

Thus, $y=f(x)=\frac{-1}{3x}+x^2$

$$\therefore \quad 9f(3)=9\left\{9-\frac{1}{9}\right\}$$

$$=9\times\frac{80}{9}=80$$

5 (3) We have,

$$2x^2y\,dy-(1-xy^2)\,dx=0$$

$$\Rightarrow \quad 2x^2y\,dy=(1-xy^2)\,dx$$

$$\Rightarrow \quad 2x^2y\frac{dy}{dx}=1-xy^2$$

$$\Rightarrow \quad 2y\frac{dy}{dx}+\frac{1}{x}y^2=\frac{1}{x^2}$$

Let $y^2=v=2y\frac{dy}{dx}=\frac{dv}{dx}$

$$\therefore \quad \frac{dv}{dx}+\frac{1}{x}v=\frac{1}{x^2}$$

which is a linear differential equation.

$$\therefore \quad \text{IF}=e^{\int\frac{1}{x}dx}=e^{\log_e x}=x$$

Now, solution is

$$vx=\int\frac{1}{x^2}\cdot x\,dx+C$$

$$\Rightarrow \quad vx=\int\frac{1}{x}dx+C$$

$$\Rightarrow y^2x=\log x+C$$

Now, we have $y(2)=\sqrt{\log 2}$

$$\therefore \quad 2\log 2=\log 2+C$$

$$\Rightarrow \quad C=\log 2$$

$\therefore$ Solution is $y^2x=\log x+\log 2$

$$\Rightarrow \quad y^2x=\log 2x\Rightarrow 2x=e^{xy^2}$$

But solution given is $\alpha x=e^{x^\beta y^\gamma}$

$$\therefore \quad \alpha=2,\beta=1,\gamma=2$$

So, $\alpha-\beta+\gamma=2-1+2=3$

6 (2) $\sin\frac{y}{x}=\ln x+\frac{\alpha}{2}$

$$\because \quad y(1)=\frac{\pi}{4}$$

$$\therefore \quad \sin\left(\frac{\pi}{4}\right)=\ln(1)+\frac{\alpha}{2}$$

$\left[\because x=1 \text{ and } y=\frac{\pi}{4}\right]$

$$\Rightarrow \quad \frac{1}{\sqrt{2}}=0+\frac{\alpha}{2}$$

$$\Rightarrow \quad \alpha=\sqrt{2}$$

So, $\quad \alpha^2=(\sqrt{2})^2=2$

7 (5) $f(x,y)=f(x)\cdot f(y)$

Put $x=0$, $y=0$

$$f(0)=(f(0))^2$$

$$\Rightarrow \quad f(0)=1 \text{ as } f(0)\neq 0$$

Now, put $y=0$

$$f(0)=f(x)\cdot f(0)\Rightarrow f(x)=1$$

As given, $\frac{dy}{dx}=f(x)$

$$\Rightarrow \quad y=\int f(x)\,dx=\int 1\,dx$$

$$\Rightarrow \quad y=x+C$$

At $x=0$, $y(0)=2\Rightarrow C=2$

$$\therefore \quad y(x)=x+2$$

So, $y\left(\frac{1}{3}\right)+y\left(\frac{2}{3}\right)=\frac{1}{3}+2+\frac{2}{3}+2=5$

8 (0) $\alpha|x|=|y|e^{xy-\beta}$, $\alpha,\beta\in N$

$$x\,dy-y\,dx+xy\,(x\,dy+y\,dx)=0$$

$$\Rightarrow \quad \frac{dy}{y}-\frac{dx}{x}+(x\,dy+y\,dx)=0$$

$$\Rightarrow \quad \ln|y|-\ln|x|+xy=C$$

$$\because \quad y(1)=2$$

So, $\ln(2)-0+2=C\Rightarrow C=2+\ln(2)$

Then, $\ln|y|-\ln|x|+xy=2+\ln 2$

$$\Rightarrow \quad \ln|x|=\ln\left|\frac{y}{2}\right|-2+xy$$

$$\Rightarrow \quad |x|=\left|\frac{y}{2}\right|e^{xy-2}$$

$$\Rightarrow \quad 2|x|=|y|e^{xy-2}$$

Comparing with $\alpha|x|=|y|e^{xy-\beta}$,

we get $\alpha=2,\beta=2$

Therefore, $\alpha-\beta=2-2=0$

9 (17) Given differential equation is

$$\frac{dy}{dx}-y=1+4\sin x$$

$$\text{IF}=e^{\int(-1)\,dx}=e^{-x}$$

So, its solution is

$$y\times\text{IF}=\int Q\times\text{IF}\,dx$$

$$\Rightarrow y\times e^{-x}=\int(e^{-x}+4e^{-x}\sin x)\,dx$$

$$\Rightarrow -e^{-x}-2\,(e^{-x}\sin x+e^{-x}\cos x)+C$$

$$\Rightarrow y=-1-2\,(\sin x+\cos x)+Ce^x$$

$\because \quad y(\pi)=1$, so $C=0$

Hence, $y\left(\frac{\pi}{2}\right)=-1-2=-3$

and thus $y\left(\frac{\pi}{2}\right)+20=3+20=17$

10 (5) We have,

$$(1+y^2)\,(1+\log_e x)\,dx+x\,dy=0$$

$$\Rightarrow (1+y^2)\left(\frac{1}{x}+\frac{\log x}{x}\right)dx+dy=0$$

$$\Rightarrow \int\left(\frac{1}{x}+\frac{\log x}{x}\right)dx+\int\frac{dy}{1+y^2}=0$$

$$\Rightarrow \log x+\frac{(\log x)^2}{2}+\tan^{-1}y=C$$

On putting $x=y=1$, we get

$$C=\frac{\pi}{4}$$

$$\therefore \log x+\frac{(\log x)^2}{2}+\tan^{-1}y=\frac{\pi}{4}$$

At $x=e$, $y=\tan\left(\frac{\pi}{4}-\frac{3}{2}\right)=\frac{1-\tan\frac{3}{2}}{1+\tan\frac{3}{2}}$

$$\therefore \quad \alpha=1,\beta=1$$

$$\therefore \quad 3\alpha+2\beta=3+2=5$$

Assertion and Reason Questions

1 (*a*) To study the degree of a differential equation the key point is that the differential equation must be a polynomial equation in derivatives, i.e. y', y'', y''' etc. The given differential equation is

$$\frac{d^3y}{dx^3} + 2\left(\frac{d^2y}{dx^2}\right)^2 - \frac{dy}{dx} + y = 0$$

This is a polynomial equation in y''', y'' and y'.

$\therefore$ Its degree can be defined.

2 (*a*) The given differential equation is

$$\frac{d^2y}{dx^2} + 3\left(\frac{dy}{dx}\right)^2 = x^2 \log\left(\frac{d^2y}{dx^2}\right)$$

This is not a polynomial equation in terms of its derivatives.

$\therefore$ Its degree is not defined.

3 (*a*) The given differential equation is

$$x^2 = y^2 + xy\frac{dy}{dx}$$

Since, this equation involves the derivative of the dependent variable *y* with respect to only one independent variable *x*.

$\therefore$ It is an ordinary differential equation.

4 (*a*) The solution which contains arbitrary constants is called the general solution (primitive) of the differential equation.

Here, function ϕ consists of two arbitrary constants (parameters) *a* and *b* and it is called general solution of the given differential equation.

5 (*a*) The solution free from arbitrary constants, i.e. the solution obtained from the general solution by giving particular values to the arbitrary constants is called a particular solution of the differential equation.

Here, function ϕ_1 contains no arbitrary constants but only the particular values of the parameters *a* and *b* and hence is called a particular solution of the given differential equation.

6 (*a*) Another form of first order linear differential equation is

$$\frac{dx}{dy} + P_1x = Q_1$$

where, P_1 and Q_1 are constants or functions of *y* only. This type of differential equation are

$$\frac{dx}{dy} + x = \cos y$$

$$\frac{dx}{dy} + \frac{-2x}{y} = y^2e^{-y}$$

7 (*c*) Given, $\frac{dy}{dx} - \frac{\tan y}{x} = \frac{\tan y \sin y}{x^2}$

$$\Rightarrow \cot y \operatorname{cosec} y \frac{dy}{dx} - \frac{\operatorname{cosec} y}{x} = \frac{1}{x^2} \quad \text{...(i)}$$

Put $-\operatorname{cosec} y = t$

$$\Rightarrow \cot y \operatorname{cosec} y \frac{dy}{dx} = \frac{dt}{dx}$$

$$\therefore \frac{dt}{dx} + \frac{t}{x} = \frac{1}{x^2} \quad \text{[from Eq. (i)]}$$

$$\therefore \text{IF} = e^{\int P\,dx} = e^{\int \frac{1}{x}dx} = x$$

$$\therefore \text{Solution is } tx = \int x \cdot \frac{1}{x^2}dx - C$$

$$\Rightarrow -\operatorname{cosec} y \cdot x = \log x - C$$

$$\Rightarrow \frac{x}{\sin y} + \log x = C$$

Case or Paragraph Type Questions

1 (*a*) We have,

$$\frac{dy}{dx} = \frac{x^2 + xy + y^2}{x^2}$$

Put $y = vx$ and $\frac{dy}{dx} = v + x\frac{dv}{dx}$

$$\therefore v + x\frac{dv}{dx} = \frac{x^2 + xvx + v^2x^2}{x^2}$$

$$= 1 + v + v^2$$

$$\Rightarrow x\frac{dv}{dx} = 1 + v^2$$

$$\Rightarrow \int \frac{dv}{1+v^2} = \int \frac{dx}{x} + C$$

$$\Rightarrow \tan^{-1} v = \log|x| + C$$

$$\Rightarrow \tan^{-1} \frac{y}{x} = \log|x| + C$$

2 (*b*) We have,

$$2xy\frac{dy}{dx} = x^2 + 3y^2$$

$$\Rightarrow \frac{dy}{dx} = \frac{x^2 + 3y^2}{2xy}$$

Put $y = vx$ and $\frac{dy}{dx} = v + x\frac{dv}{dx}$

$$\therefore v + x\frac{dv}{dx} = \frac{x^2 + 3v^2x^2}{2vx^2}$$

$$\Rightarrow x\frac{dv}{dx} = \frac{1+3v^2}{2v} - v$$

$$\Rightarrow x\frac{dv}{dx} = \frac{1+v^2}{2v}$$

$$\Rightarrow \int \frac{2v}{1+v^2}dv = \int \frac{dx}{x} + \log C$$

$$\Rightarrow \log|1+v^2| = \log|x| + \log|C|$$

$$\Rightarrow \log|v^2+1| = \log|xC|$$

$$\Rightarrow v^2 + 1 = xC$$

$$\Rightarrow \frac{y^2}{x^2} + 1 = xC$$

$$\Rightarrow x^2 + y^2 = x^3C$$

3 (*c*) We have,

$$(x^2 + 3xy + y^2)\,dx - x^2dy = 0$$

$$\Rightarrow \frac{x^2 + 3xy + y^2}{x^2} = \frac{dy}{dx}$$

Put $y = vx$ and $\frac{dy}{dx} = v + x\frac{dv}{dx}$

$$\frac{x^2 + 3x^2v + x^2v^2}{x^2} = v + x\frac{dv}{dx}$$

$$1 + 3v + v^2 = v + x\frac{dv}{dx}$$

$$1 + 2v + v^2 = x\frac{dv}{dx}$$

$$\Rightarrow \frac{dx}{x} - \int (v+1)^2\,dv = C$$

$$\Rightarrow \log x + \frac{1}{v+1} = C$$

$$\Rightarrow \log x + \frac{x}{x+y} = C$$

4 (*a*) We have, $2\frac{d^2y}{dx^2} + 3\sqrt{1 - \left(\frac{dy}{dx}\right)^2} - y = 0$

$$\therefore 2\frac{d^2y}{dx^2} = -3\sqrt{1 - \left(\frac{dy}{dx}\right)^2} - y$$

On squaring both sides, we get

$$4\left(\frac{d^2y}{dx^2}\right)^2 = 9\left[1-\left(\frac{dy}{dx}\right)^2 - y\right]$$

Here, highest order derivative is $\frac{d^2y}{dx^2}$ and its power is 2.

So, its degree is 2.

5 (b) We have,

$$y\frac{dy}{dx} = \frac{x}{\frac{dy}{dx}+\left(\frac{dy}{dx}\right)^3}$$

$$\Rightarrow y\left(\frac{dy}{dx}\right)^2 + y\left(\frac{dy}{dx}\right)^4 = x$$

$\Rightarrow$ Here, highest order derivative is $\frac{dy}{dx}$.

So, its order is 1 and degree is 4.

6 (b) We have,

$$y''' + y^2 + e^{y'} = 0$$

$$\frac{d^3y}{dx^3} + y^2 + e^{\left(\frac{dy}{dx}\right)} = 0$$

Highest order derivative is $\frac{d^3y}{dx^3}$.

So, its order is 3.

Also, given differential cannot be expressed as a polynomial.

So, its degree is not defined.

Past Years Questions

1 (a) Given, differential equation is

$$2y\frac{dy}{dx} + 3 = 5\frac{dy}{dx}$$

$$\Rightarrow \quad (2y-5)\frac{dy}{dx} = -3$$

$$\Rightarrow \quad (2y-5)dy = -3dx$$

On integrating, we get

$$2\cdot\frac{y^2}{2} - 5y = -3x + C \quad \text{...(i)}$$

$\because$ Curve passes through (0, 1) i.e. putting $x = 0$ and $y = 1$ in Eq. (i)

$\therefore$ $c = -4$

From Eq. (i), $y^2 - 5y = -3x - 4$

$$\Rightarrow y^2 - 2\left(\frac{5}{2}\right)y + \frac{25}{4} = -3x - 4 + \frac{25}{4}$$

$$\Rightarrow \left(y-\frac{5}{2}\right)^2 = -3\left(x-\frac{3}{4}\right)$$ which is the equation of shifted parabola whose vertex is $\left(\frac{3}{4},\frac{5}{2}\right)$ and this vertex satisfies the equation $2x + 3y = 9$.

2 (d) $(1+y^2)e^{\tan x}\,dx + \cos^2 x\,(1+e^{2\tan x})dy = 0$

$$\Rightarrow -\frac{1}{1+y^2}\cdot dy = \frac{e^{\tan x}\cdot\sec^2 x}{1+(e^{\tan x})^2}\cdot dx$$

On integrating both sides, we get

$$\int\frac{1}{1+y^2}dy = -\int\frac{e^{\tan x}}{1+(e^{\tan x})^2}\sec^2 x\cdot dx$$

Let $\tan x = t \Rightarrow \sec^2 x\cdot dx = dt$

$$\Rightarrow \tan^{-1}(y) = -\int\frac{e^t}{1+(e^t)^2}\cdot dt$$

Let $e^t = u$, $e^t\cdot dt = du$

$$\Rightarrow \tan^{-1}(y) = -\int\frac{1}{1+u^2}dx$$

$$\Rightarrow \tan^{-1}(y) = -\tan^{-1}(u) + C$$

$$\Rightarrow \tan^{-1}(y) = -\tan^{-1}(e^{\tan x}) + C$$

$\because \quad y(0) = 1$

$$\Rightarrow \quad \frac{\pi}{4} = -\tan^{-1}(1) + C$$

$$\Rightarrow \quad C = \frac{\pi}{4}+\frac{\pi}{4} = \frac{\pi}{2}$$

So, $y = \tan\left(\frac{\pi}{2} - \tan^{-1}(e^{\tan x})\right)$

$$= \cot(\tan^{-1}(e^{\tan x}))$$

At $x = \frac{\pi}{4}$, $y\left(\frac{\pi}{4}\right) = \cot(\tan^{-1}(e))$

$$= \cot\left(\cot^{-1}\left(\frac{1}{e}\right)\right) = \frac{1}{e}$$

3 (d) Given, $\frac{dT}{dt} = -K(T-80)$

$$\int_{160}^{T}\frac{dT}{T-80} = \int_0^t -K\,dt$$

$$\Rightarrow \quad [\ln|T-80|]_{160}^{T} = -K[t]_0^t$$

$$\Rightarrow \ln|T-80| - \ln(80) = -K(t-0)$$

$$\Rightarrow \quad \ln\left|\frac{T-80}{80}\right| = -Kt$$

$$\Rightarrow \quad \frac{T-80}{80} = e^{-Kt}$$

$$T = 80 + 80e^{-Kt}$$

Given, $T(15) = 120°$ F

$$120 = 80 + 80e^{-15K}$$

$$\Rightarrow \quad 40 = 80e^{-15K}$$

$$\Rightarrow \quad e^{-15K} = \frac{1}{2}$$

At $t = 45$, $T = 80 + 80e^{-45K}$

$$T = 80 + 80(e^{-15K})^3$$

$$= 80 + 80\left(\frac{1}{2}\right)^3 = 90°\text{F}$$

4 (d) We have,

$(1-x^2y^2)dx = ydx + xdy$, $y(1) = 2$

$$\Rightarrow \quad dx = \frac{ydx + xdy}{1-(xy)^2}$$

On integrating both sides, we get

$$\int dx = \int\frac{d(xy)}{1-(xy)^2}$$

$$x = \frac{1}{2}\log\left|\frac{1+xy}{1-xy}\right| + C$$

As $y(1) = 2$,

$$1 = \frac{1}{2}\log\left|\frac{1+2}{1-2}\right| + C$$

$$\Rightarrow \quad C = 1 - \frac{1}{2}\log 3$$

Now, substituting $x = 2$ as $y(2) = \alpha$

$$2 = \frac{1}{2}\log\left|\frac{1+2\alpha}{1-2\alpha}\right| + 1 - \frac{1}{2}\log 3$$

$$\Rightarrow 1 + \frac{1}{2}\log 3 = \frac{1}{2}\log\left|\frac{1+2\alpha}{1-2\alpha}\right|$$

$$\Rightarrow \quad 2 + \log 3 = \log\left|\frac{1+2\alpha}{1-2\alpha}\right|$$

$$\Rightarrow \quad \left|\frac{1+2\alpha}{1-2\alpha}\right| = 3e^2$$

$$\Rightarrow \quad \frac{1+2\alpha}{1-2\alpha} = \pm\frac{3e^2}{1}$$

$$\Rightarrow \quad \frac{1}{2\alpha} = \frac{\pm 3e^2+1}{\pm 3e^2-1}$$

$$\Rightarrow \quad 2\alpha = \frac{\pm 3e^2-1}{\pm 3e^2+1}$$

$$\Rightarrow \quad \alpha = \frac{1}{2}\left(\frac{\pm 3e^2-1}{1\pm 3e^2}\right)$$

$$\therefore \quad \alpha = \frac{3e^2-1}{2(1+3e^2)} \text{ or } \frac{3e^2+1}{2(3e^2-1)}$$

5 (a) $\frac{dy}{dx}=\frac{x+y-2}{x-y}=\frac{(x-1)+(y-1)}{(x-1)-(y-1)}$

On putting $x-1=X,\ y-1=Y$

$$\frac{dY}{dX}=\frac{X+Y}{X-Y} \quad \text{...(i)}$$

Now, this is a homogeneous differential function.

Put $Y=VX$

On differentiating w.r.t. X, we get

$$\frac{dY}{dX}=V+X\frac{dV}{dX}$$

On putting in Eq (i), we get

$$V+X\frac{dV}{dX}=\frac{X+VX}{X-VX}=\frac{1+V}{1-V}$$

$$\Rightarrow X\frac{dV}{dX}=\frac{1+V-V+V^2}{1-V}$$

$$\Rightarrow \frac{1-V}{1+V^2}dV=\frac{dX}{X}$$

$$\Rightarrow \int\frac{1}{1+V^2}dV-\int\frac{1}{2}\frac{2V}{1+V^2}dV=\int\frac{dX}{X}$$

$$\tan^{-1}V-\frac{1}{2}\ln(1+V^2)=\ln X+c$$

On putting $V=Y/X$,

$$\tan^{-1}\frac{Y}{X}-\frac{1}{2}\ln\left(1+\frac{Y^2}{X^2}\right)=\ln X+C$$

On putting $Y=y-1,\ X=x-1$

$$\tan^{-1}\left(\frac{y-1}{x-1}\right)-\frac{1}{2}\ln\left(1+\frac{(y-1)^2}{(x-1)^2}\right)=\ln(x-1)+c$$

Given that curve passes through (2, 1)

$$\tan^{-1}(0)-\frac{1}{2}\ln(1+0)=\ln 1+c$$

$$0-0=0+c\Rightarrow c=0$$

So, curve is

$$\tan^{-1}\left(\frac{y-1}{x-1}\right)-\frac{1}{2}\ln\left(1+\frac{(y-1)^2}{(x-1)^2}\right)=\ln(x-1)$$

Curve also passes through $(k+1, 2),\ k>0$

$$\tan^{-1}\left(\frac{1}{k}\right)-\frac{1}{2}\ln\left(1+\frac{1}{k^2}\right)=\ln k$$

$$\Rightarrow 2\tan^{-1}\left(\frac{1}{k}\right)=\ln\left(\frac{k^2+1}{k^2}\right)+2\ln k$$

$$\Rightarrow 2\tan^{-1}\left(\frac{1}{k}\right)=\ln(1+k^2)$$

6 (c) We have,

$$(1+x^2)\,dy=y(x-y)dx \quad \text{...(i)}$$

Let $y=\frac{1}{t}\Rightarrow dy=\frac{-1}{t^2}dt$

So, Eq. (i) becomes

$$\frac{-(1+x^2)}{t^2}dt=\frac{1}{t}\left(x-\frac{1}{t}\right)dx$$

$$\Rightarrow \frac{-(1+x^2)}{t^2}dt=\frac{1}{t^2}(tx-1)dx$$

$$\Rightarrow \frac{dt}{dx}+\frac{tx}{1+x^2}=\frac{1}{1+x^2} \quad \text{...(ii)}$$

Let $P(x)=\frac{x}{1+x^2}$

$$\Rightarrow \int P(x)dx=\frac{1}{2}\int\frac{2x\,dx}{1+x^2}=\frac{1}{2}\ln(1+x^2)=\ln\sqrt{1+x^2}$$

Now, integrating factor in Eq. (ii) is

$$e^{\int P(x)dx}=e^{\ln\sqrt{1+x^2}}=\sqrt{1+x^2}$$

$\therefore$ Solution of Eq. (ii) is

$$t\cdot\sqrt{1+x^2}=\int\frac{1}{1+x^2}\cdot\sqrt{1-x^2}\,dx$$

$$\Rightarrow t\cdot\sqrt{1+x^2}=\int\frac{1}{\sqrt{1+x^2}}dx \quad \text{...(iii)}$$

$$\Rightarrow \frac{\sqrt{1+x^2}}{y}=\ln|x+\sqrt{1+x^2}|+C$$

Now, $y(0)=1$

$$\frac{\sqrt{1+0^2}}{1}=\ln|0+\sqrt{1+0^2}|+C$$

$$\Rightarrow C=1$$

$$\therefore y=\frac{\sqrt{1+x^2}}{\ln|x+\sqrt{1+x^2}+1|}$$

Now, $y(2\sqrt{2})=\beta$

$$\Rightarrow \beta=\frac{\sqrt{1+(2\sqrt{2})^2}}{\ln|2\sqrt{2}+\sqrt{1+(2\sqrt{2})^2}|+1}=\frac{3}{\ln|3+2\sqrt{2}|+1}$$

$$\Rightarrow \ln|3+2\sqrt{2}|+1=3\beta^{-1}$$

$$\Rightarrow \ln(3+2\sqrt{2})+\ln e=3\beta^{-1}$$

$$\Rightarrow \ln[(e)(3+2\sqrt{2})]=3\beta^{-1}$$

$$\Rightarrow e^{3\beta^{-1}}=e(3+2\sqrt{2})$$

7 (c) **Key Idea** *Convert the given differential equation in the standard form of linear differential equation, $\frac{dy}{dx}+Py=Q$, where P and Q are function of x, then solve the linear differential equation using integration.*

$$\frac{dy}{dx}=\frac{y}{x}(1+xy^2(1+\log x_e)),\ x>0,$$

$$y(1)=3$$

$$\frac{dy}{dx}-\frac{y}{x}=y^3(1+\log_e x)$$

$$\frac{1}{y^3}\frac{dy}{dx}-\frac{1}{y^2}\frac{1}{x}=1+\log_e x$$

Let $-\frac{1}{y^2}=t$

On differentiating w.r.t. x, we get

$$\frac{2}{y^3}\frac{dy}{dx}=\frac{dt}{dx}$$

$$\Rightarrow \frac{1}{y^3}\frac{dy}{dx}=\frac{1}{2}\frac{dt}{dx}$$

Differential equation becomes,

$$\frac{1}{2}\frac{dt}{dx}+\frac{t}{x}=1+\log_e x$$

$$\Rightarrow \frac{dt}{dx}+\frac{2}{x}t=2(1+\log_e x)$$

On comparing with standard equation of linear differential equation,

$$\frac{dy}{dx}+Py=Q$$

$$P=\frac{2}{x},\ Q=2(1+\log_e x)$$

$\Rightarrow$ Integrating factor,

$$\text{IF}=e^{\int P\,dx}=e^{2\int\frac{1}{x}dx}$$

$$\text{IF}=e^{2\ln x}=e^{\ln x^2}=x^2$$

General solution

$$t\cdot\text{IF}=\int Q\cdot\text{IF}\,dx$$

$$t\cdot x^2=\int 2(1+\log_e x)\,x^2dx$$

$$\Rightarrow \frac{-x^2}{y^2}=2\left[(1+\log_e x)\frac{x^3}{3}-\int\frac{1}{x}\cdot\frac{x^3}{3}dx\right]$$

$$\Rightarrow \frac{-x^2}{y^2}=\frac{2}{3}[x^3(1+\log_e x)-\int x^2dx]$$

$$\Rightarrow \frac{-x^2}{y^2} = \frac{2}{3}\left[x^3(1+\log_e x) - \frac{x^3}{3}\right] + C$$

Given, $y(1) = 3$

$$\frac{-1}{9} = \frac{2}{3}\left[1(1+\log_e 1) - \frac{1}{3}\right] + C$$

$$\Rightarrow \quad \frac{-1}{9} = \frac{4}{9} + C \Rightarrow C = \frac{-5}{9}$$

Solution becomes,

$$-\frac{x^2}{y^2} = \frac{2}{3}\left[x^3(1+\log_e x) - \frac{x^3}{3}\right] - \frac{5}{9}$$

$$\Rightarrow -\frac{x^2}{y^2} = \frac{2x^3}{9}[2+\log_e x^3] - \frac{5}{9}$$

$$\Rightarrow \frac{9}{y^2} = -2x[2+\log_e x^3] + \frac{5}{x^2}$$

$$\Rightarrow \frac{9}{y^2} = \frac{5 - 2x^3[2+\log_e x^3]}{x^2}$$

$$\Rightarrow \frac{y^2}{9} = \frac{x^2}{5 - 2x^3(2+\log_e x^3)}$$

8 (b) Given, $\left[1 - \left(\frac{dy}{dx}\right)^2\right]^{\frac{3}{2}} = \frac{d^2y}{dx^2}$

On squaring both sides, we get

$$\left[1 - \left(\frac{dy}{dx}\right)^2\right]^3 = \left(\frac{d^2y}{dx^2}\right)^2$$

Hence, the degree of differential equation is 2.

9 (b) A. $xdy - (y + 2x^2)dx = 0$

$$\Rightarrow \quad \frac{dy}{dx} - \frac{1}{x}y = 2x$$

$$\text{IF} = e^{-\int \frac{1}{x}dx} = e^{-\ln x} = e^{\ln \frac{1}{x}} = \frac{1}{x}$$

So, IF $= \frac{1}{x}$

B. $(2x^2 - 3y)dx = xdy$

$$\Rightarrow \frac{dy}{dx} + \frac{3}{x}y = 2x$$

$$\text{IF } e^{\int \frac{3}{x}dx} = e^{3\int \frac{1}{x}dx} = e^{3\ln x}$$

$$= e^{\ln x^3} = x^3$$

So, IF $= x^3$

C. $(2y + 3x^2)dx + xdy = 0$

$$\Rightarrow \frac{dy}{dx} + \frac{2}{x}y = -3x$$

$$\text{IF} = e^{\int \frac{2}{x}dx} = e^{2\int \frac{1}{x}dx}$$

$$= e^{2\ln x} = e^{\ln x^2} = x^2$$

So, IF $= x^2$

D. $2xdy + (3x^3 + 2y)dx = 0$

$$\Rightarrow \quad \frac{dy}{dx} + \frac{1}{x}y = -\frac{3}{2}x^2$$

$$\text{IF} = e^{\int \frac{1}{x}dx} = e^{\ln x} = x$$

So, IF $= x$

Thus, A-(i), B-(iv), C-(iii), D-(ii).

10 (a) Given, differential equation is

$(x\log_e x)dy = (\log_e x - y)dx$

$$\Rightarrow \quad \frac{dy}{dx} = \frac{\log_e x - y}{x\log_e x}$$

A. Degree of the differential equation

Since, here $\frac{dy}{dx}$ appears linearly (to the first power), so the degree of the differential equation is 1.

So, statement (a) is correct.

B. Homogeneity of the differential equation.

To determine if the differential equation is homogeneous, let's check if it can be expressed in terms of $\frac{y}{x}$.

If we substitute $x \to kx$ and $y \to ky$.

$$\frac{dy}{dx} = \frac{\log_e(kx) - ky}{kx\log_e(kx)}$$

$$= \frac{\log_e k + \log_e x - ky}{kx(\log_e k + \log_e x)}$$

This does not simplify to a function of $\frac{y}{x}$ alone. Therefore, it is not a homogeneous differential equation.

So, statement (b) is correct.

C. Solution of the differential equation,

$$\frac{dy}{dx} = \frac{\log_e x - y}{x\log_e x}$$

$$\Rightarrow \frac{dy}{dx} + \frac{1}{x\log_e x}y = \frac{1}{x}$$

Which is linear differential equation.

Now, IF $= e^{\int \frac{1}{x\log_e x}dx}$

$= e^{\log(\log x)} = \log x$

So, solution is given by

$$(\log_e x)\cdot y = \int (\log_e x)\frac{1}{x}dx$$

$$(\log_e x)y = \frac{(\log_e x)^2}{2} + C$$

$$\Rightarrow 2y\cdot\log_e x + A = (\log_e x)^2$$

Where A = an arbitrary constant.

So, statement (c) is correct.

11 (14) Given,

$$(x-1)\frac{dy}{dx} + 2xy = \frac{1}{x-1} \quad \text{... (i)}$$

$$y(2) = \frac{1+e^4}{2e^4} \text{ and } y(3) = \frac{e^\alpha + 1}{\beta e^\alpha}$$

From Eq. (i),

$$\frac{dy}{dx} + \frac{2x.y}{(x-1)} = \frac{1}{(x-1)^2}$$

$$\text{IF} = e^{\int \frac{2x}{x-1}.dx} = e^{2\int \frac{x-1+1}{x-1}.dx}$$

$$= e^{2\int 1 + \frac{1}{x-1}dx} = e^{2x + 2\ln(x-1)}$$

$$= e^{2x}\cdot e^{\ln(x-1)^2} = (x-1)^2\cdot e^{2x}$$

$\therefore$ Solution is

$$y\cdot(x-1)^2e^{2x} = \int \frac{1}{(x-1)^2}(x-1)^2e^{2x}dx + c$$

$$\Rightarrow y(x-1)^2e^{2x} = \frac{e^{2x}}{2} + c \quad \text{... (ii)}$$

On putting $x = 2$, $y = \frac{1+e^4}{2e^4}$ in Eq. (ii), we get

$$\left(\frac{1+e^4}{2e^4}\right)\cdot(1)\cdot(e^4) = \frac{e^4}{2} + C$$

$$\Rightarrow \quad C = \frac{1}{2}$$

$$\therefore \quad y(x-1)^2e^{2x} = \frac{e^{2x}}{2} + \frac{1}{2}$$

On putting $x = 3$ in above equation

$$y(2)^2e^6 = \frac{e^6}{2} + \frac{1}{2}$$

$$\Rightarrow \quad y = \frac{e^6+1}{8e^6} = \frac{e^\alpha + 1}{\beta e^\alpha}$$

$$\Rightarrow \quad \alpha + \beta = 14$$

12 (14) **Key Idea** *First, form linear differential equation in x. Then, conclude the solution of differential equation by* $x \times \text{IF} = \int Q \times \text{IF}\, dx$

$$\frac{dx}{dt} = \frac{2x}{(t+1)} + (t+1)^3$$

$$\Rightarrow \frac{dx}{dt} - \frac{2x}{t+1} = (t+1)^3 \text{ [LDE]}$$

$$\text{IF} \Rightarrow e^{-2\int \frac{dt}{t+1}} = e^{-2\ln(t+1)} = \frac{1}{(t+1)^2}$$

$$\Rightarrow x \cdot \frac{1}{(1+t)^2} = \int (t+1)^3 \cdot \frac{1}{(t+1)^2} dt$$

$$\Rightarrow \frac{x}{(t+1)^2} = \frac{(t+1)^2}{2} + C$$

$$\Rightarrow \quad = \frac{(t+1)^4}{2} + C(t+1)^2$$

Put $t = 0, x = 2$

$$2 = \frac{1}{2} + C \Rightarrow C = \frac{3}{2}$$

$$\Rightarrow x = \frac{(t+1)^4}{2} + \frac{3}{2}(t+1)^2$$

Put $t = 1$, $x = \frac{16}{2} + \frac{3}{2} \cdot 4 = 14$

13 (18) $\frac{dy}{dx} + \frac{2x}{(1+x^2)^2} y = x e^{\frac{1}{1+x^2}}$

$$P = \frac{2x}{(1+x^2)^2}, Q = x e^{\frac{1}{1+x^2}}$$

$$\text{IF} = e^{\int \frac{2x}{(1+x^2)^2} dx} = e^{\frac{-1}{1+x^2}}$$

∴ Solution is

$$y(\text{IF}) = \int Q \cdot (\text{IF})\, dx + C$$

$$y\left(e^{\frac{-1}{1+x^2}}\right) = \int x e^{\frac{1}{1+x^2}} \cdot e^{\frac{-1}{1+x^2}} \cdot dx + C$$

$$\frac{y}{e^{\frac{1}{1+x^2}}} = \frac{x^2}{2} + C$$

∴ $y(0) = 0 \Rightarrow 0 = 0 + C \Rightarrow C = 0$

$$\therefore \quad y = \frac{x^2}{2} e^{\frac{1}{1+x^2}}$$

$$f(x) = \frac{x^2}{2} e^{\left(\frac{1}{1+x^2}\right)} e^{\left(\frac{-1}{1+x^2}\right)} = \frac{x^2}{2}$$

$f(x) = \frac{x^2}{2}$ and line $y - x = 4$

$$A = \int_{-2}^{4} (x+4) - \frac{x^2}{2}$$

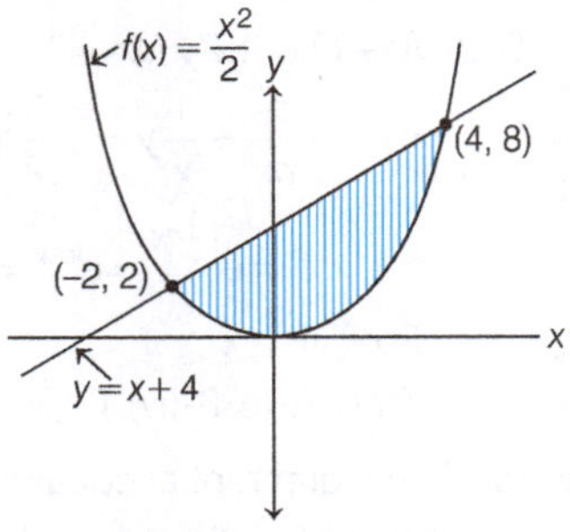

$= 18$ sq units.

14 (3) Given, differential equation

$$(y - 2\log_e x)\, dx + (x \log_e x^2)\, dy = 0$$

$$\Rightarrow 2x \log x \frac{dy}{dx} + y = 2\log_e x$$

$$\Rightarrow \frac{dy}{dx} + \frac{y}{2x \log_e x} = \frac{1}{x}$$

$$\text{IF} = e^{\int \frac{1}{2x \log_e x} dx} = e^{\frac{1}{2}\log(\log x)} = \sqrt{\log x}$$

∴ Solution of differential equation

$$y \cdot \sqrt{\log_e x} = \int \frac{1}{x} \sqrt{\log x}\, dx + C$$

$$y\sqrt{\log_e x} = \frac{(\log x)^{3/2}}{3/2} + C$$

It passes through $\left(e, \frac{4}{3}\right)$

$$\Rightarrow \quad \frac{4}{3} = \frac{2}{3} + C \Rightarrow C = \frac{2}{3}$$

It also passes through (e^4, α),

$$\therefore \quad \alpha \cdot (2) = \frac{16}{3} + \frac{2}{3} = 6$$

$$\Rightarrow \quad \alpha = 3$$

15 (3) Given, differential equation

$\frac{dy}{dx} - y = 2 - e^{-x}$, which is of the first order linear differential equation.

Here, $P = -1, Q = 2 - e^{-x}$

$$\therefore \quad \text{IF} = e^{\int P dx} = e^{\int -1\, dx} = e^{-x}$$

Now, solution is given by

$$y \cdot \text{IF} = \int Q \times \text{IF}\, dx + C$$

$$\Rightarrow y \times e^{-x} = \int (2 - e^{-x})e^{-x} + C$$

$$\Rightarrow \quad ye^{-x} = \int (2e^{-x} - e^{-2x})dx + C$$

$$\Rightarrow \quad ye^{-x} = -2e^{-x} + \frac{e^{-2x}}{2} + C$$

$$\Rightarrow \quad y = -2 + \frac{e^{-x}}{2} + ce^{x}$$

$\lim_{x \to \infty} y(x)$ is finite, then

$\lim_{x \to \infty} \left(-2 + \frac{e^{-x}}{2} + ce^{-x}\right)$ is finite

This is possible when $c = 0$

$$y = -2 + \frac{e^{-x}}{2} \Rightarrow \frac{dy}{dx} = -\frac{e^{-x}}{2}$$

$$\left.\frac{dy}{dx}\right|_{x=0} = -\frac{1}{2}$$

∴ Slope $= -\frac{1}{2}$

When $x = 0$, then $y = -2 + \frac{1}{2} = -\frac{3}{2}$

Equation of tangent

$$y + \frac{3}{2} = -\frac{1}{2}(x - 0)$$

$$\Rightarrow \quad 2y + 3 = -x$$

$$\Rightarrow \quad x + 2y = -3$$

$$\frac{x}{-3} + \frac{y}{-\frac{3}{2}} = 1$$

$$\therefore \quad a = -3, b = -\frac{3}{2}$$

Now, $a - 4b = -3 - 4\left(-\frac{3}{2}\right)$

$$= -3 + 6 = 3$$

Skill Boosters

1 (b) The given differential equation can be rewritten as

$$\left(2 + 5\frac{dy}{dx}\right)^2 = 27\left(\frac{d^3y}{dx^3}\right)^3$$

This shows that the order and degree of given equation are 3 and 3, respectively.

2 (c) We have, $y(x - 1)\, dx = x^2\, dy$

$$\Rightarrow \quad \frac{x-1}{x^2} dx = \frac{dy}{y}$$

On integrating both sides, we get

$$\log x + \frac{1}{x} = \log y + C$$

When $x = 1, y = e$

$\Rightarrow \quad C = 0 + 1 - 1 = 0$

$\therefore \quad \log y = \log x - \frac{1}{x} + 0$

$\Rightarrow \quad \log y = \log x - \frac{1}{x} \Rightarrow y = xe^{\frac{-1}{x}}$

$\therefore \quad \lim_{x \to 0^+} y = 0 \times e^{-\infty} = 0$

3 (*a*) Given differential equation

$x\,dy = (y + x^3 \cos x)\,dx$

$\Rightarrow \quad x\,dy = y\,dx + x^3 \cos x\,dx$

$\Rightarrow \quad x\,dy - y\,dx = x^3 \cos x\,dx$

$\Rightarrow \quad \frac{x\,dy - y\,dx}{x^2} = x \cos x\,dx$

$\Rightarrow \quad \frac{d}{dx}\left(\frac{y}{x}\right) = \int x \cos x dx$

$\Rightarrow \quad \frac{y}{x} = x \sin x - \int 1 \cdot \sin x\,dx$

$\Rightarrow \quad \frac{y}{x} = x \sin x + \cos x + C$

At $x = \pi$ and $y = 1$

$\frac{1}{\pi} = -1 + C = C = \frac{1 + \pi}{\pi}$

On substituting the value of C in Eq. (i), we get

$\frac{y}{x} = x \sin x + \cos x + \left(\frac{1 + \pi}{\pi}\right)$

$\Rightarrow y = x^2 \sin x + x \cos x + \left(\frac{1 + \pi}{\pi}\right) x$

At $x = \frac{\pi}{2}$

$\Rightarrow y\left(\frac{\pi}{2}\right) = \frac{\pi^2}{4}(1) + 0 + \left(\frac{1 + \pi}{\pi}\right)\frac{\pi}{2}$

$= \frac{\pi^2}{4} + \frac{\pi}{2} + \frac{1}{2}$

4 (*b*) Given, $x\,dy = \sqrt{x^2 + y^2}\,dx + y\,dx$

$\Rightarrow x\,dy - y\,dx = \sqrt{x^2 + y^2}\,dx$

$\Rightarrow \frac{x\,dy - y\,dx}{x^2} = \frac{\sqrt{x^2 + y^2}}{x^2}\,dx$

$d\left(\frac{y}{x}\right) = x\frac{\sqrt{1 + y^2}}{x^2}\,dx$

$\Rightarrow \quad d\left(\frac{y}{x}\right) = \sqrt{1 + \left(\frac{y}{x}\right)^2} \cdot \frac{dx}{x}$

$\Rightarrow \quad \frac{d\left(\frac{y}{x}\right)}{\sqrt{1 + \left(\frac{y}{x}\right)^2}} = \frac{dx}{x}$

On integrating both sides, we get

$\ln\left(\frac{y}{x} + \sqrt{1 + \left(\frac{y}{x}\right)^2}\right) = \ln(x) + \ln C$

$\because$ Using $\int \frac{dx}{\sqrt{1 + x^2}} = \ln(x + \sqrt{1 + x^2})$

$\Rightarrow \quad \ln\left(\frac{y}{x} + \frac{\sqrt{x^2 + y^2}}{x}\right) = \ln(Cx)$

$\Rightarrow \quad y + \sqrt{x^2 + y^2} = Cx \quad \text{...(i)}$

According to given condition, when $x = 1$, then $y = 0$

From Eq. (i), $0 + \sqrt{1 + 0} = C \times (1)^2$

$\Rightarrow \quad C = 1$

So, equation of curve is

$y + \sqrt{x^2 + y^2} = x^2$ [from Eq. (i)]

Now, when $x = 3$, then $y = \alpha$ [given]

So, $\quad \alpha + \sqrt{9 + \alpha^2} = 9$

$\Rightarrow \quad 9 + \alpha^2 = 81 + \alpha^2 - 18\alpha$

$\Rightarrow \quad 18\alpha = 72 \Rightarrow \alpha = 4$

5 (*d*) Given, $\frac{dy}{dx} = 2(y + 2\sin x + 5)x$

$- 2\cos x, y(0) = -3$

$\Rightarrow \quad \frac{dy}{dx} + 2\cos x$

$= 2(y + 2\sin x + 5) \quad \text{...(i)}$

Let $y + 2\sin x + 5 = t$

$\Rightarrow \quad \frac{dy}{dx} + 2\cos x = \frac{dt}{dx}$

Then, Eq. (i) becomes

$\frac{dt}{dx} = 2tx \Rightarrow \frac{dt}{t} = 2x\,dx$

On integrating both sides, we get

$\ln t = x^2 + C$

$\Rightarrow \ln(y + 2\sin x - 5) = x^2 + C \quad \text{...(ii)}$

Given, $y(0) = -3$

$\Rightarrow \ln(-3 + 0 + 5) = 0 + C \Rightarrow C = \ln 2$

$\therefore$ From Eq. (ii),

$\ln(y + 2\sin x + 5) = x^2 + \ln 2$

Now, at $x = \frac{\pi}{2}$

$\ln\left(y\left(\frac{\pi}{2}\right) + 2\sin\frac{\pi}{2} + 5\right) = \frac{\pi^2}{4} + \ln 2$

$\Rightarrow \quad \ln\left(y\left(\frac{\pi}{2}\right) + 7\right) = \frac{\pi^2}{4} + \ln 2$

$\Rightarrow \quad y\left(\frac{\pi}{2}\right) + 7 = e^{\frac{\pi^2}{4} + \ln 2}$

$\Rightarrow \quad y\left(\frac{\pi}{2}\right) = 2e^{\frac{\pi^2}{4}} - 7$

6 (*c*) Given differential equation

$\cos x \frac{dy}{dx} - (\sin x)\, y = 6x$

$\Rightarrow \quad \frac{dy}{dx} - (\tan x)\, y = \frac{6x}{\cos x},$

which is the linear differential equation of the form

$\frac{dy}{dx} + Px = Q$

So, IF $= e^{-\int \tan x\,dx}$

$= e^{-\log(\sec x)} = \cos x,$

$\therefore$ Required solution of differential equation is

$y(\cos x) = \int (6x)\frac{\cos x}{\cos x}\,dx + C$

$= \frac{6x^2}{2} + C = 3x^2 + C$

Given, $y\left(\frac{\pi}{3}\right) = 0$

So, $\quad 0 = 3\left(\frac{\pi}{3}\right)^2 + C \Rightarrow C = \frac{-\pi^2}{3}$

$\therefore \quad y(\cos x) = 3x^2 - \frac{\pi^2}{3}$

Now, at $x = \pi$

$y(-1) = 3\pi^2 - \frac{\pi^2}{3} \Rightarrow y = -\frac{8\pi^2}{3}$

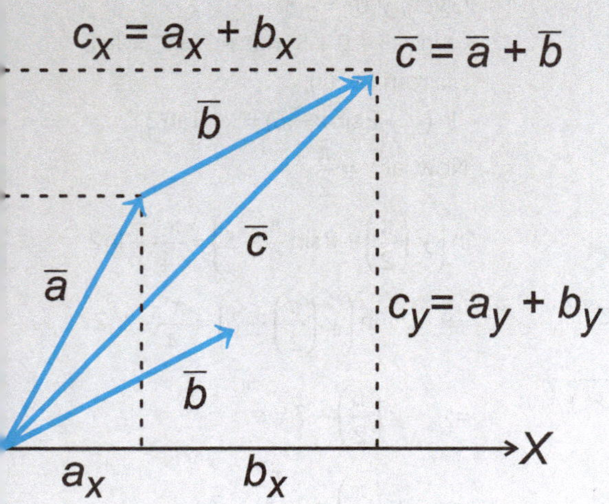

10

Vector Algebra

Topicwise No. of Ques asked in 3 Years (JEE Main)

Topics	No. of Questions		
	2024	2023	2022
Some Basic Concepts and Types of Vectors	–	–	–
Addition of Vectors and Multiplication of a Vector by a Scalar	4	5	2
Scalar (or dot) Product of Two Vectors	9	3	2
Vector (or cross) Product of Two Vectors	26	20	13

Special Type of Ques Asked in Last 3 Years (JEE Main)

Types	Years		
	2024	2023	2022
A-R	–	–	–
Statement Based	1	0	1
Numerical Value Type	8	8	4

Last 3 Years Weightage (JEE Main)

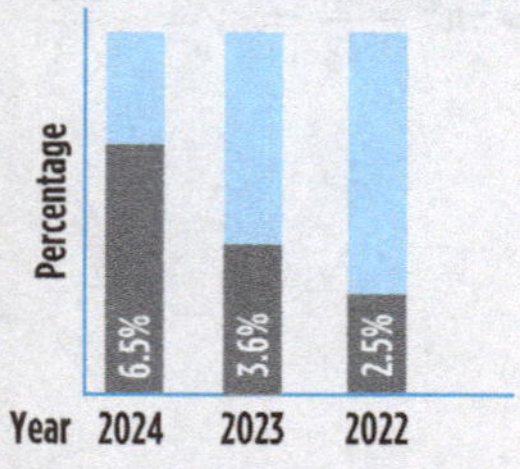

Some Basic Concepts

- **Scalars** A quantity which has magnitude but no direction, is called a scalar.
- **Vectors** A quantity which has magnitude as well as direction, is called a vector.
- **Magnitude of a Vector** The length of the vector **AB** or **a** is called the magnitude of **AB** or **a** and it is represented by |**AB**| or |**a**|.
- If $\mathbf{a} = x\,\hat{\mathbf{i}} + y\,\hat{\mathbf{j}} + z\hat{\mathbf{k}}$, then $|\mathbf{a}| = \sqrt{x^2 + y^2 + z^2}$.
- Since, the length is never negative, so the notation $|\mathbf{a}| < 0$ has no meaning.

Types of Vectors

(i) **Zero or Null Vector** A vector, whose magnitude is zero or whose initial and terminal points coincide, is called a null vector or zero vector, **0**.

(ii) **Unit Vector** A vector, whose magnitude is one unit ($|\hat{\mathbf{a}}| = 1$). The unit vector in the direction of **a** is represented by $\hat{\mathbf{a}}$. The unit vectors along X-axis, Y-axis and Z-axis are represented by $\hat{\mathbf{i}}$, $\hat{\mathbf{j}}$ and $\hat{\mathbf{k}}$, respectively.

(iii) **Coinitial Vectors** Two or more vectors having the same initial point are called coinitial vectors.

(iv) **Collinear or Parallel Vectors** The vectors, which have same or parallel support are called collinear vectors. [JEE Main 2024]

(v) **Equal Vectors** Two vectors are equal, if they have same magnitude and direction.

(vi) **Negative of a Vector** A vector, whose magnitude is same as that of given vector but the direction is opposite, is called negative vector of the given vector. e.g. Let **AB** be a vector, then −**AB** or **BA** is a negative vector.

(vii) **Coplanar Vectors** A system of vectors is said to be coplanar, if they are parallel to the same plane.

- If the initial point of a vector is not specified, then it is called a **free vector**.

Let O be any point called the origin of reference or say simply origin and a point P in space, having coordinates (x, y, z) w.r.t. origin $O(0, 0, 0)$, then vector **OP**(= **r**) having O and P as its initial and terminal point respectively, is called the position vector of the point P w.r.t. O.

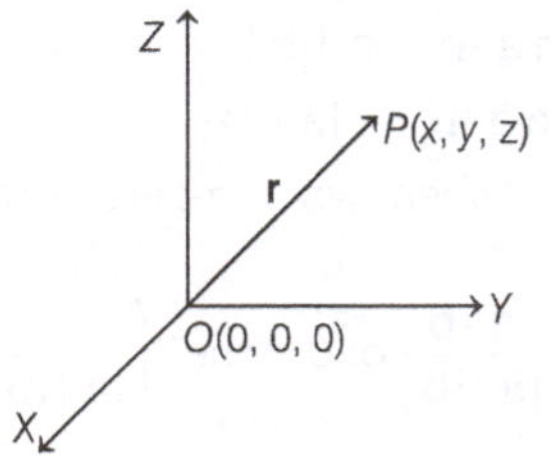

The magnitude of **OP** or **r** is given by

$$|\mathbf{OP}| = |\mathbf{r}| = \sqrt{x^2 + y^2 + z^2}$$

Addition of Vectors and Multiplication of a Vector by a Scalar

Addition of Vectors

(i) Triangle Law of Vector Addition

If two vectors are represented along two sides of a triangle taken in order, then their resultant is represented by the third side taken in opposite direction i.e. in ΔABC, by triangle law of vector addition, we have **AB** + **BC** = **AC**.

Concept Master Video

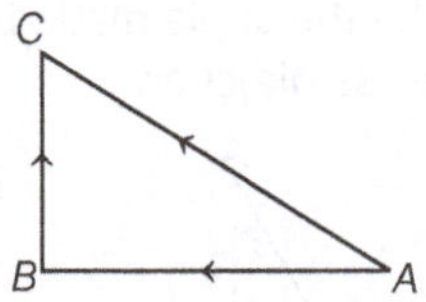

(ii) Parallelogram Law of Vector Addition

If two vectors are represented along the two adjacent sides of a parallelogram, then their resultant is represented by the diagonal of the parallelogram, which is coinitial with the given vectors. If the sides OA and OC of parallelogram $OABC$ represents **OA** and **OC** respectively, then we get

OA + **OC** = **OB** or **OA** + **AB** = **OB** [∵ **AB** = **OC**]

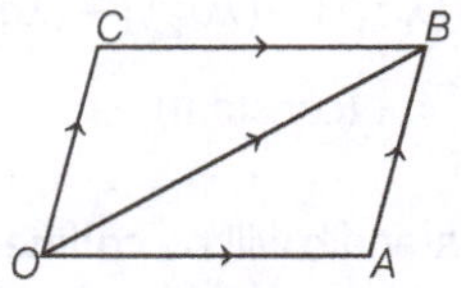

- We may say that the two laws of vectors addition are equivalent to each other.

Properties of Vector Addition

(i) For any two vectors **a** and **b**,

$$\mathbf{a} + \mathbf{b} = \mathbf{b} + \mathbf{a} \qquad \text{[commutative law]}$$

(ii) For any three vectors **a**, **b** and **c**,

$$\mathbf{a} + (\mathbf{b} + \mathbf{c}) = (\mathbf{a} + \mathbf{b}) + \mathbf{c} \qquad \text{[associative law]}$$

(iii) For any vector **a**, we have

$$\mathbf{a} + \mathbf{0} = \mathbf{0} + \mathbf{a} = \mathbf{a}.$$

The zero vector **0** is called the **additive identity** for the vector addition.

Multiplication of a Vector by Scalar

Let **a** be a given vector and λ be a scalar. Then, the product of the vector **a** by the scalar λ, denoted by λ **a**, is called the multiplication of vector **a** by the scalar λ.

Properties of Multiplication of a Vector by a Scalar

Let **a** and **b** be any two vectors and k and m be any scalars. Then,

(i) $k\mathbf{a} + m\mathbf{a} = (k + m)\mathbf{a}$ (ii) $k(\mathbf{a} + \mathbf{b}) = k\mathbf{a} + k\mathbf{b}$

(iii) $k(m\mathbf{a}) = (km)\mathbf{a}$

Components of a Vector

If $\mathbf{a} = a_1\hat{\mathbf{i}} + a_2\hat{\mathbf{j}} + a_3\hat{\mathbf{k}}$, then we can say that the scalar components of **a** along X-axis, Y-axis and Z-axis are a_1, a_2 and a_3, respectively.

Important Results in Component Form

If **a** and **b** are any two vectors given in the component form as $\mathbf{a} = a_1\hat{\mathbf{i}} + a_2\hat{\mathbf{j}} + a_3\hat{\mathbf{k}}$ and $\mathbf{b} = b_1\hat{\mathbf{i}} + b_2\hat{\mathbf{j}} + b_3\hat{\mathbf{k}}$.

Then, (a_1, a_2, a_3) and (b_1, b_2, b_3) are called **direction ratios** of **a** and **b**, respectively.

(i) The sum (or resultant) of the vectors **a** and **b** is given by

$$\mathbf{a} + \mathbf{b} = (a_1 + b_1)\hat{\mathbf{i}} + (a_2 + b_2)\hat{\mathbf{j}} + (a_3 + b_3)\hat{\mathbf{k}}$$

(ii) The difference of the vectors **a** and **b** is given by

$$\mathbf{a} - \mathbf{b} = (a_1 - b_1)\hat{\mathbf{i}} + (a_2 - b_2)\hat{\mathbf{j}} + (a_3 - b_3)\hat{\mathbf{k}}$$

(iii) The vectors **a** and **b** are equal, iff

$$a_1 = b_1, a_2 = b_2 \text{ and } a_3 = b_3$$

(iv) The multiplication of vector **a** by any scalar λ is given by $\lambda\mathbf{a} = (\lambda a_1)\hat{\mathbf{i}} + (\lambda a_2)\hat{\mathbf{j}} + (\lambda a_3)\hat{\mathbf{k}}$

(v) If $\frac{b_1}{a_1} = \frac{b_2}{a_2} = \frac{b_3}{a_3} = k$ (constant).

Then, vectors **a** and **b** will be **collinear**. [JEE Main 2024]

(vi) If it is given that l, m and n are direction cosines of a vector, then

$$l\hat{\mathbf{i}} + m\hat{\mathbf{j}} + n\hat{\mathbf{k}} = (\cos\alpha)\hat{i} + (\cos\beta)\hat{\mathbf{j}} + (\cos\gamma)\hat{\mathbf{k}}$$

is the unit vector in the direction of that vector, where α, β and γ are the angles which the vector makes with X, Y and Z-axes, respectively.

Vector Joining Two Points

If $P_1(x_1, y_1, z_1)$ and $P_2(x_2, y_2, z_2)$ are any two points on the plane, then vector joining P_1 and P_2 is [JEE Main 2024]

$$\mathbf{P_1P_2} = \mathbf{OP_2} - \mathbf{OP_1}$$
$$= (x_2\hat{\mathbf{i}} + y_2\hat{\mathbf{j}} + z_2\hat{\mathbf{k}}) - (x_1\hat{\mathbf{i}} + y_1\hat{\mathbf{j}} + z_1\hat{\mathbf{k}})$$
$$= (x_2 - x_1)\hat{\mathbf{i}} + (y_2 - y_1)\hat{\mathbf{j}} + (z_2 - z_1)\hat{\mathbf{k}}$$

Section Formulae

- Let A and B be two points with position vectors **a** and **b**, respectively and P be a point which divides AB internally in the ratio $m : n$.

  Then, position vector of $\mathbf{P} = \frac{m\mathbf{b} + n\mathbf{a}}{m + n}$.

- If P divides AB **externally** in the ratio $m : n$.

  Then, position vector of $\mathbf{P} = \frac{m\mathbf{b} - n\mathbf{a}}{m - n}$.

Marks Maximizer

- The necessary and sufficient condition that three points with position vectors **a**, **b** and **c** are collinear iff there exists three scalars x, y, z not all zero such that $x\mathbf{a} + y\mathbf{b} + z\mathbf{c} = 0$, together with $x + y + z = 0$. [JEE Main 2023]
- The bisector of the angle between two non-collinear vectors **a** and **b** is given by $\lambda(\hat{\mathbf{a}} + \hat{\mathbf{b}})$ or $\lambda\left(\frac{\mathbf{a}}{|a|} \pm \frac{\mathbf{b}}{|b|}\right)$
- **Position Vector of Different Centres of a Triangle**

If **a**, **b** and **c** are PV's of the vertices A, B and C of a ΔABC respectively,

(i) Then the PV of the centroid G of the triangle is $\frac{\mathbf{a} + \mathbf{b} + \mathbf{c}}{3}$.

(ii) The PV of incentre of ΔABC is $\frac{(BC)\mathbf{a} + (CA)\mathbf{b} + (AB)\mathbf{c}}{BC + CA + AB}$

(iii) The PV of orthocentre of ΔABC is

$$\frac{\mathbf{a}(\tan A) + \mathbf{b}(\tan B) + \mathbf{c}(\tan C)}{\tan A + \tan B + \tan C}$$ [JEE Main 2023]

Scalar (or dot) Product of Two Vectors

Let **a** and **b** be the two non-zero vectors inclined at an angle θ. Then, the scalar product or dot product of **a** and **b** is represented by $\mathbf{a} \cdot \mathbf{b}$ and it is defined as $\mathbf{a} \cdot \mathbf{b} = |\mathbf{a}||\mathbf{b}|\cos\theta$, where $0 \le \theta \le \pi$.

Important Results Based on Scalar Product

(i) $\mathbf{a} \perp \mathbf{b} \Leftrightarrow \mathbf{a} \cdot \mathbf{b} = 0$ [JEE Main 2024, 2023]

(ii) $\hat{\mathbf{i}} \cdot \hat{\mathbf{i}} = \hat{\mathbf{j}} \cdot \hat{\mathbf{j}} = \hat{\mathbf{k}} \cdot \hat{\mathbf{k}} = 1$ and $\hat{\mathbf{i}} \cdot \hat{\mathbf{j}} = \hat{\mathbf{j}} \cdot \hat{\mathbf{k}} = \hat{\mathbf{k}} \cdot \hat{\mathbf{i}} = 0$

(iii) If $\theta = 0$, then $\mathbf{a} \cdot \mathbf{b} = |\mathbf{a}||\mathbf{b}|$

If $\theta = \pi$, then $\mathbf{a} \cdot \mathbf{b} = -|\mathbf{a}||\mathbf{b}|$

(iv) The angle between two non-zero vectors **a** and **b** is given by

$$\cos\theta = \frac{\mathbf{a} \cdot \mathbf{b}}{|\mathbf{a}||\mathbf{b}|} \text{ or } \theta = \cos^{-1}\left(\frac{\mathbf{a} \cdot \mathbf{b}}{|\mathbf{a}||\mathbf{b}|}\right)$$ [JEE Main 2024]

Properties of Scalar Product

(i) $\mathbf{a} \cdot \mathbf{b} = \mathbf{b} \cdot \mathbf{a}$ [commutative]

(ii) $\mathbf{a} \cdot (\mathbf{b} + \mathbf{c}) = \mathbf{a} \cdot \mathbf{b} + \mathbf{a} \cdot \mathbf{c}$ [left distributivity]

(iii) $\mathbf{a} \cdot \mathbf{a} = |\mathbf{a}|^2 = a^2$

where, a represents magnitude of vector **a**.

(iv) $(\mathbf{a} + \mathbf{b}) \cdot (\mathbf{a} - \mathbf{b}) = a^2 - b^2$, where a and b represent the magnitude of vectors **a** and **b**.

(v) $(\lambda\mathbf{a}) \cdot \mathbf{b} = \lambda(\mathbf{a} \cdot \mathbf{b})$

- If α, β and γ are the direction angles of vector $\mathbf{a} = a_1\hat{\mathbf{i}} + a_2\hat{\mathbf{j}} + a_3\hat{\mathbf{k}}$, then its DC's is given as

$$\cos\alpha = \frac{a_1}{|\mathbf{a}|},\ \cos\beta = \frac{a_2}{|\mathbf{a}|},\ \cos\gamma = \frac{a_3}{|\mathbf{a}|}$$

Projection of a Vector

Let **a** and **b** be two vectors represented by **OA** and **OB**, respectively and let θ be the angle made by **a** with directed line l in the anti-clockwise direction.

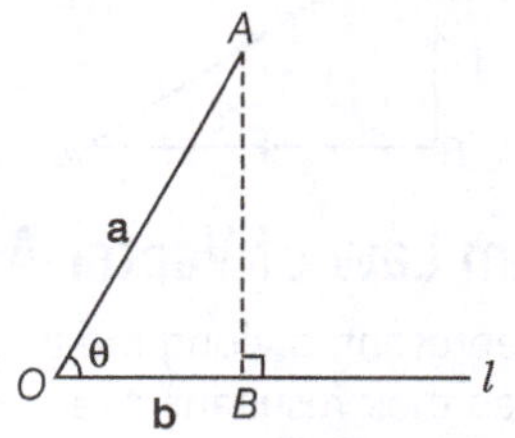

Then, the projection of **OA** on the line l is **OB**, which is given by $|\mathbf{OA}|\cos\theta$ and the direction of **b**, called **projection vector**, being the same (or opposite) to that of the line l, depending upon whether $\cos\theta$ is positive or negative.

- $\mathbf{b} = |\mathbf{OA}|\cos\theta \cdot \hat{\mathbf{b}} = |\mathbf{a}|\cos\theta \cdot \hat{\mathbf{b}}$

$\therefore$ Projection of $\mathbf{a}$ on $\mathbf{b} = \frac{\mathbf{a}\cdot\mathbf{b}}{|\mathbf{b}|}$ and projection of $\mathbf{b}$ on $\mathbf{a} = \frac{\mathbf{a}\cdot\mathbf{b}}{|\mathbf{a}|}$

Marks Maximizer

- Important results of dot product
  - (i) $m\mathbf{a}\cdot\mathbf{b} = m(\mathbf{a}\cdot\mathbf{b}) = \mathbf{a}\cdot m\mathbf{b}$, for any scalar m.
  - (ii) If $|\mathbf{a}+\mathbf{b}| = |\mathbf{a}| + |\mathbf{b}|$, then $\mathbf{a}$ is parallel to $\mathbf{b}$.
  - (iii) If $|\mathbf{a}-\mathbf{b}| = |\mathbf{a}| - |\mathbf{b}|$, then $\mathbf{a}$ is perpendicular to $\mathbf{b}$.
  - (iv) $|\mathbf{a}\pm\mathbf{b}|^2 = |\mathbf{a}|^2 + |\mathbf{b}|^2 \pm 2|\mathbf{a}\cdot\mathbf{b}|$
  - (v) $\mathbf{a}\cdot\mathbf{b} > 0$, iff θ is acute.
  - (vi) $\mathbf{a}\cdot\mathbf{b} < 0$, iff θ is obtuse. [JEE Main 2024]
  - (vii) $|\mathbf{a}+\mathbf{b}|^2 + |\mathbf{a}-\mathbf{b}|^2 = 2(|\mathbf{a}|^2 + |\mathbf{b}|^2)$
  - (viii) $|\mathbf{a}+\mathbf{b}|^2 - |\mathbf{a}-\mathbf{b}|^2 = 4|\mathbf{a}|\cdot|\mathbf{b}|$
  - (ix) $(\mathbf{a}\cdot\mathbf{b})^2 \le |\mathbf{a}|^2\cdot|\mathbf{b}|^2$
- If $\mathbf{a}, \mathbf{b}, \mathbf{c}$ are three vectors, then $\mathbf{a}\cdot\mathbf{b} = a_1b_1 + a_2b_2 + a_3b_3$
  $|\mathbf{a}+\mathbf{b}+\mathbf{c}|^2 = |\mathbf{a}|^2 + |\mathbf{b}|^2 + |\mathbf{c}|^2 + 2(\mathbf{a}\cdot\mathbf{b} + \mathbf{b}\cdot\mathbf{c} + \mathbf{c}\cdot\mathbf{a})$
- Projection vector of $\mathbf{a}$ on $\mathbf{b} = \left\{\frac{\mathbf{a}\cdot\mathbf{b}}{|\mathbf{b}|^2}\right\}\hat{\mathbf{b}} = \left\{\frac{\mathbf{a}\cdot\mathbf{b}}{|\mathbf{b}|^2}\right\}\mathbf{b}$

Vector (or cross) Product of Two Vectors

Let θ be the angle between two non-zero vectors $\mathbf{a}$ and $\mathbf{b}$, then the vector or cross product of $\mathbf{a}$ and $\mathbf{b}$ is represented by $\mathbf{a}\times\mathbf{b}$ and defined as $\mathbf{a}\times\mathbf{b} = |\mathbf{a}||\mathbf{b}|\sin\theta\,\hat{\mathbf{n}}$, where, $\hat{\mathbf{n}}$ is a unit vector perpendicular to the plane of $\mathbf{a}$ and $\mathbf{b}$.

Properties of Cross Product

(i) $(\mathbf{a}\times\mathbf{b}) = -(\mathbf{b}\times\mathbf{a})$ [not commutative]

(ii) $\mathbf{a}\times(\mathbf{b}+\mathbf{c}) = \mathbf{a}\times\mathbf{b} + \mathbf{a}\times\mathbf{c}$ [distributive property]

(iii) $\lambda(\mathbf{a}\times\mathbf{b}) = (\lambda\mathbf{a})\times\mathbf{b} = \mathbf{a}\times(\lambda\mathbf{b})$

Important Results Based on Cross Product

(i) A unit vector perpendicular to both $\mathbf{a}$ and $\mathbf{b}$ is given by $\hat{\mathbf{n}} = \frac{(\mathbf{a}\times\mathbf{b})}{|\mathbf{a}\times\mathbf{b}|}$.

(ii) $\mathbf{a}\,||\,\mathbf{b} \Leftrightarrow \mathbf{a}\times\mathbf{b} = \mathbf{0}$

(iii) $\mathbf{a}\times\mathbf{a} = \mathbf{0}$

(iv) $\hat{\mathbf{i}}\times\hat{\mathbf{i}} = \mathbf{0}, \hat{\mathbf{j}}\times\hat{\mathbf{j}} = \mathbf{0}, \hat{\mathbf{k}}\times\hat{\mathbf{k}} = \mathbf{0}$

(v) $\hat{\mathbf{i}}\times\hat{\mathbf{j}} = \hat{\mathbf{k}}, \hat{\mathbf{j}}\times\hat{\mathbf{k}} = \hat{\mathbf{i}}, \hat{\mathbf{k}}\times\hat{\mathbf{i}} = \hat{\mathbf{j}}$;
$\hat{\mathbf{j}}\times\hat{\mathbf{i}} = -\hat{\mathbf{k}}, \hat{\mathbf{k}}\times\hat{\mathbf{j}} = -\hat{\mathbf{i}}, \hat{\mathbf{i}}\times\hat{\mathbf{k}} = -\hat{\mathbf{j}}$

(vi) If $\mathbf{a} = a_1\hat{\mathbf{i}} - a_2\hat{\mathbf{j}} + a_3\hat{\mathbf{k}}$ and $\mathbf{b} = b_1\hat{\mathbf{i}} + b_2\hat{\mathbf{j}} + b_3\hat{\mathbf{k}}$, then

$$\mathbf{a}\times\mathbf{b} = \begin{vmatrix} \hat{\mathbf{i}} & \hat{\mathbf{j}} & \hat{\mathbf{k}} \\ a_1 & a_2 & a_3 \\ b_1 & b_2 & b_3 \end{vmatrix}$$

[JEE Main 2023]

(vii) Area of a parallelogram with sides $\mathbf{a}$ and $\mathbf{b} = |\mathbf{a}\times\mathbf{b}|$

(viii) Area of a parallelogram with diagonals $\mathbf{d}_1$ and $\mathbf{d}_2 = \frac{1}{2}|\mathbf{d}_1\times\mathbf{d}_2|$

[JEE Main 2024]

Marks Maximizer

- Important results of cross product
  - (i) If $a\times b = 0$, then $a = 0, b = 0$ or a and b are parallel or collinear.
  - (ii) If $\mathbf{a}, \mathbf{b}$ and $\mathbf{c}$ are the PV's of the vertices A, B and C of ΔABC, then

    Area of $\Delta ABC = \frac{1}{2}|\mathbf{a}\times\mathbf{b} + \mathbf{b}\times\mathbf{c} + \mathbf{c}\times\mathbf{a}|$

    Length of the perpendicular from c on AB
    $= \frac{|\mathbf{a}\times\mathbf{b} + \mathbf{b}\times\mathbf{c} + \mathbf{c}\times\mathbf{a}|}{|\mathbf{b}-\mathbf{a}|}$
  - (iii) The points, whose PV's $\mathbf{a}, \mathbf{b}$ and $\mathbf{c}$ are collinear, if and only if $\mathbf{a}\times\mathbf{b} + \mathbf{b}\times\mathbf{c} + \mathbf{c}\times\mathbf{a} = 0$.

Caution Points

- A vector have both magnitude and direction.
- The dot product is commutative, $\mathbf{a}\cdot\mathbf{b} = \mathbf{b}\cdot\mathbf{a}$
- The dot product can be interpreted as the projection of one vector onto another, multiplied by the magnitude of the other vector.
- The cross product is not commutative, $\mathbf{a}\times\mathbf{b} = -(\mathbf{b}\times\mathbf{a})$
- If $\mathbf{a}\times\mathbf{b} = 0$, either the vectors are parallel or one of them is the zero vector.

PYQ Notes

1. The area of quadrilateral $ABCD$ equal to $\frac{1}{2}|\mathbf{AC}\times\mathbf{BD}|$. [JEE Main 2024]
2. If A, B, C are the three vertices of triangle, then

   Area of a $\Delta ABC = \frac{1}{2}|\mathbf{AB}\times\mathbf{AC}|$ [JEE Main 2024]

   $= \frac{1}{2}|\mathbf{BC}\times\mathbf{BA}|$

   $= \frac{1}{2}|\mathbf{CB}\times\mathbf{CA}|$

Step by Step

Mastering NCERT

- Concept Builders
- Topical Questions
- Numerical Type Questions
- Assertion and Reason Questions
- Case or Paragraph Type Questions
- Past Years Questions
- Skill Boosters

Concept Builders

1 Dot product of two vectors holds commutive property. (T/F)

2 Vector product of two vectors is holds commutative property. (T/F)

3 If **a** and **b** are two vectors inclined at an angle θ, then $\cos\theta$ is equal to ....

4 If **a** and **b** are two vectors and the scalar product of **a** and **b** is 0, then **a** is .... to **b.**

5 If two vectors is orthogonal, then angle between them is ....

6 The magnitude of $\mathbf{a} = \hat{i} + \hat{j} - \hat{k}$ is ....

7 If θ is an angle between two vectors **a** and **b** such that $\theta \in \left[0, \frac{\pi}{2}\right]$. Then, $\mathbf{a} \cdot \mathbf{b}$ is .... (greater/less) than 0.

8 If **a** and **b** are parallel, then $\mathbf{a} \times \mathbf{b}$ is equal to ....

9 The value of $\hat{j} \cdot \hat{k} + \hat{k} \cdot \hat{i} + \hat{j} \cdot \hat{i}$ is equal to ....

10 If **a** and **b** are any vector and angle between **a** and **b** is π, then $\mathbf{a} \cdot \mathbf{b}$ is equal to ....

11 If two vectors are collinear, then $\mathbf{a} \times \mathbf{b}$ is equal to ....

12 If **a** and **b** are two non-zero vectors, then $\mathbf{a} \times \mathbf{b}$ is equal to ....

13 If **a**, **b** and **c** are any three non-zero vector, then $\mathbf{a} \times (\mathbf{b} \times \mathbf{c})$ is equal to ....

14 If **a** and **b** are any two non-zero vector then the value of $[\mathbf{a} \ \ \mathbf{b} \ \ \mathbf{b}]$ is equal to ....

Topical Questions

Some Basic Concepts and Types of Vectors

Level I

1 Consider the following figures (i), (ii) and (iii) given below.

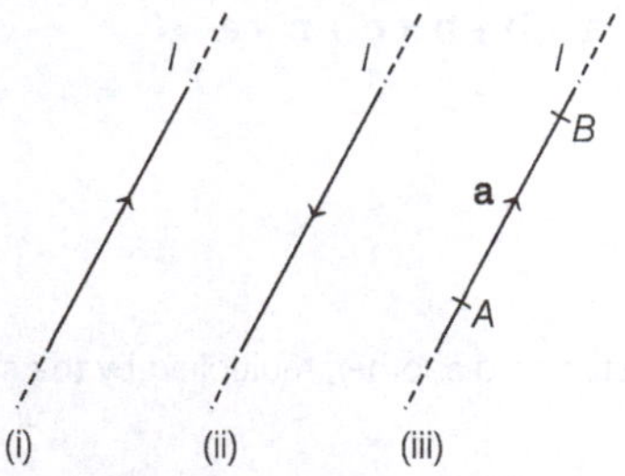

Here, l is representing any straight line in plane or three dimensional space. **NCERT Pg. 339**

Based on above figures, which of the following is depicting correct information?

(a) Figures (i) and (ii) are representing a directed line.
(b) Figure (iii) is representing a directed line segment.
(c) A directed line segment has magnitude as well as direction.
(d) All of the above

2 Suppose there is a point P in space having coordinates (x, y, z) with respect to the origin $(0, 0, 0)$, then which of the following is true? **NCERT Pg. 339**

(a) The vector **OP**, having its initial point as P and terminal point as O, is called the position vector of the point P with respect to O.
(b) The magnitude of **OP** (or **r**) is given by $|\mathbf{OP}| = \sqrt{x^2 + y^2 + z^2}$
(c) The position vectors of points A, B, C etc; with respect to origin O are denoted by **a**, **b**, **c**, etc, respectively.
(d) All are true.

3 Consider the figure given below.

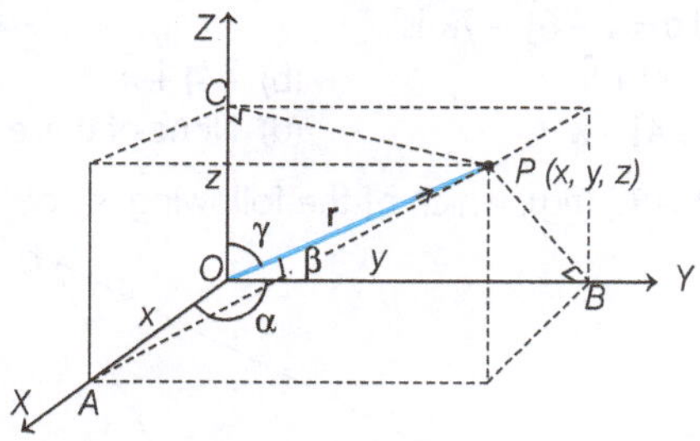

Here, position vector **OP** (or **r**) of a point $P(x, y, z)$ is given such that it is making α, β and γ with the positive directions of X, Y and Z-axes, respectively.

Based on above the information, which among the following is/are true? **NCERT Pg. 340**

I. α, β and γ are direction angles of the vector **r**.

II. l, m and n are direction cosines of vector **r** such that $l = \cos\alpha$, $m = \cos\beta$ and $n = \cos\gamma$.

III. The coordinates of point P are (lr, mr, nr). (r stands for $|\mathbf{r}|$)

IV. Direction ratios of vector **r** in general are denoted as a, b and c, respectively.

(a) Only III is true. (b) II and III are true.
(c) I and IV are true. (d) All are true.

4 If $P(x, y, z)$ be a point in space such that $\mathbf{r} = \mathbf{OP}$ and the direction cosines of OP are l, m, n, then $l^2 + m^2 + n^2$ is **NCERT Pg. 341**

(a) 1 (b) 0 (c) 2 (d) 3

5 Which of the following is/are true? **NCERT Pg. 341**

I. In a zero vector, initial and terminal points coincide.

II. Zero vector is denoted as **0**.

III. Zero vector has zero magnitude.

(a) Only II is true. (b) I and III are true.
(c) II and III are true. (d) All are true.

6 If two vectors **a** and **b** are such that **a** = **b**, then **NCERT Pg. 341**

(a) they have same magnitude and direction regardless of the positions of their initial points.
(b) they have same magnitude and different directions.
(c) Both (a) and (b) are true.
(d) Both (a) and (b) are false.

7 A vector, whose magnitude is the same as that of a given vector, but direction is opposite to that of it, is called **NCERT Pg. 341**

(a) negative of the given vector.
(b) equal vector.
(c) null vector.
(d) collinear vector.

8 Consider the figure (a square) given below.

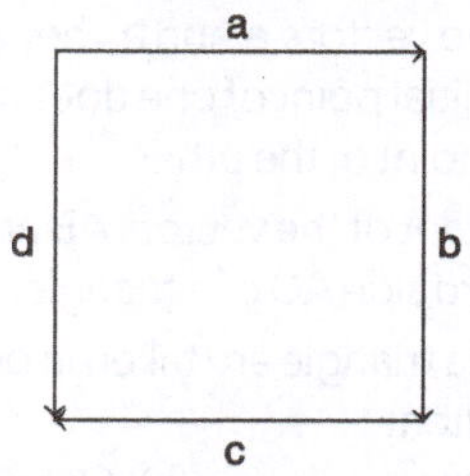

Based on above figure, which of the following is true? **NCERT Pg. 342**

(a) **a** and **d** are coinitial vectors.
(b) **b** and **d** are coinitial vectors.
(c) **a** and **c** are equal vectors.
(d) None of the above

Level II

9 Which among the following is incorrect statement?

(a) **AA** and **BB** are examples of zero vector. **NCERT Pg. 341**
(b) Magnitude of unit vector is 1.
(c) **BA** = − **AB**
(d) If two or more vectors are parallel to the same line, irrespective of their magnitudes and directions are called coinitial vectors.

10 If two vectors **A** and **B** have same magnitudes, then the necessary condition that they will have opposite direction is **NCERT Pg. 341**

(a) **A** = − **B** (b) **A** = **B** (c) **A** = 2**B** (d) None of these

11 Vectors, whose initial points are not specified are called **NCERT Pg. 341**

(a) null vectors (b) free vectors
(c) parallel vectors (d) non-collinear vectors

Addition of Vectors and Multiplication of a Vector by a Scalar

Level I

1 A vector **AB** simply means **NCERT Pg. 343**

(a) the distance from a point A to the point B
(b) the distance from a point B to the point A
(c) the displacement from a point A to the point B
(d) the displacement from a point B to the point A

2 If a girl moves from A to B and then from B to C (as shown). Then, net displacement made by the girl from A to C, is **NCERT Pg. 343**

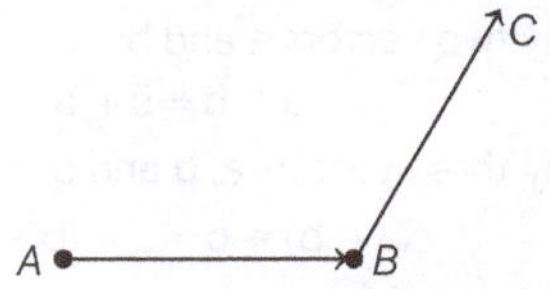

(a) **AB** − **BC** = **AC** (b) **AC** = **AB** − **BC**
(c) **AC** = **AB** + **BC** (d) None of these

3 Which of the following is/are true? NCERT Pg. 343

I. To add two vectors **a** and **b**, they are positioned such that the initial point of one does not coincide with the terminal point of the other.

II. The resultant of the vectors **AB** and **BC** is represented by the third side **AC** of a triangle.

III. If sides of a triangle are taken in order, then it leads to zero resultant.

(a) Only I is true (b) Only II is true
(c) Both II and III are true (d) All are true

4 Consider the figure given below.

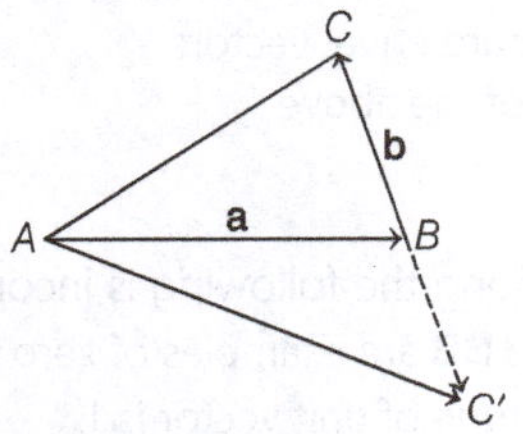

Here, it is shown that a vector **BC′** is having same magnitude as the vector **BC**, but its direction is opposite to that of it.
Based on the above information, which of the following is true? NCERT Pg. 343

(a) $\mathbf{AC'} = \mathbf{a} + \mathbf{b}$
(b) $\mathbf{AC'} = \mathbf{a} - \mathbf{b}$
(c) Difference of **a** and **b** is **AC**
(d) None of the above

5 If two vectors **a** and **b** are represented by two adjacent sides of a parallelogram in magnitude and direction, then **a** + **b** is represented as NCERT Pg. 344

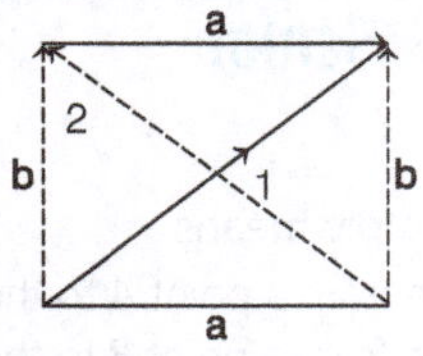

(a) diagonal 1 (as shown)
(b) diagonal 2 (as shown)
(c) sides opposite to either of the side
(d) None of the above

6 Which of the following statements(s) is/are true?

(a) For any two vectors **a** and **b** NCERT Pg. 345
$$\mathbf{a} + \mathbf{b} = \mathbf{b} + \mathbf{a}$$
(b) For any three vectors **a**, **b** and **c**
$$(\mathbf{a} + \mathbf{b}) + \mathbf{c} = \mathbf{a} + (\mathbf{b} + \mathbf{c})$$
(c) Both (a) and (b) are true.
(d) Both (a) and (b) are false.

7 The sum of the vectors $\mathbf{a} = \hat{i} - 2\hat{j} + \hat{k}$, $\mathbf{b} = -2\hat{i} + 4\hat{j} + 5\hat{k}$ and $\mathbf{c} = \hat{i} - 6\hat{j} - 7\hat{k}$ is NCERT Pg. 345

(a) $-3\hat{j} + \hat{k}$ (b) $-4\hat{j} + \hat{k}$
(c) $-4\hat{j} - \hat{k}$ (d) None of these

8 In ΔABC (fig), which of the following is not true?

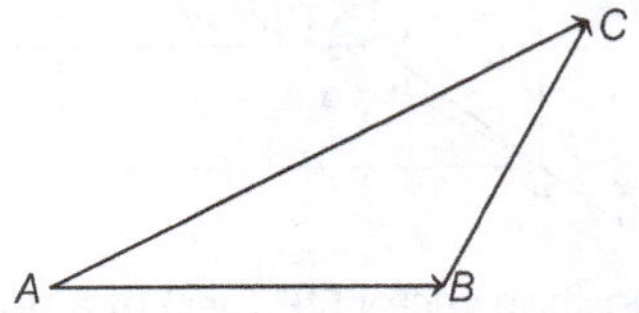

NCERT Pg. 345

(a) $\mathbf{AB} + \mathbf{BC} + \mathbf{CA} = \mathbf{0}$ (b) $\mathbf{AB} + \mathbf{BC} - \mathbf{AC} = \mathbf{0}$
(c) $-\mathbf{AB} + \mathbf{BC} + \mathbf{CA} = \mathbf{0}$ (d) $\mathbf{AB} - \mathbf{CB} + \mathbf{CA} = \mathbf{0}$

9 If **a** be a given vector and λ be a scalar, then which of the following is true? NCERT Pg. 346

(a) $\lambda\mathbf{a}$ is not a vector.
(b) $\lambda\mathbf{a}$ has the same direction to that of vector **a**.
(c) $\lambda\mathbf{a}$ has opposite direction to that of vector **a**.
(d) The magnitude of vector $|\lambda\mathbf{a}|$ is $|\lambda|$ times the magnitude of the vector **a** i.e. $|\lambda\mathbf{a}| = |\lambda||\mathbf{a}|$.

10 If a vector with the direction is as shown below.

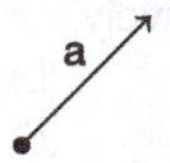

then, which of the following is a correct geometric visualization of multiplication of above vector by a scalar?

(i) 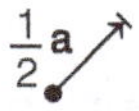

(ii) 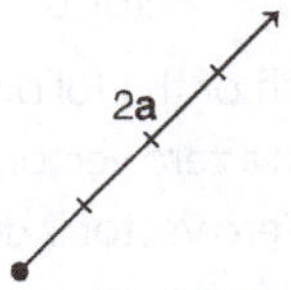

(iii) 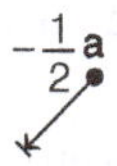

(iv) 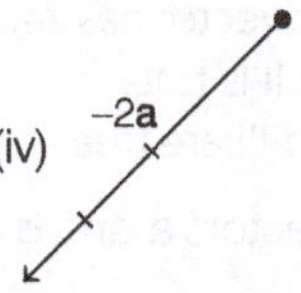

NCERT Pg. 346

(a) (ii) and (iii) are correct. (b) Only (ii) is correct.
(c) (i) and (ii) are correct. (d) All are correct.

11 For $\lambda\mathbf{a}$, which of the following cannot be true? NCERT Pg. 346

(a) For $\lambda = -1$, we get the additive inverse of vector **a**.
(b) For $\lambda = \frac{1}{|a|}$, $\mathbf{a} \neq 0$, $\lambda\mathbf{a}$ represents the unit vector in the direction of **a**.
(c) For $\lambda = \frac{1}{|a|}$, $\mathbf{a} \neq 0$, $\lambda\mathbf{a}$ represents the unit vector in the opposite direction of **a**.
(d) $\lambda 0 = 0$

12 Which of the following statement(s) is/are true? **NCERT Pg. 347**

(a) $\hat{\mathbf{i}}$, $\hat{\mathbf{j}}$ and $\hat{\mathbf{k}}$ are unit vectors along the axis OX, OY and OZ, respectively.
(b) Magnitude of each of the vectors $\hat{\mathbf{i}}$, $\hat{\mathbf{j}}$ and $\hat{\mathbf{k}}$ is 1 unit.
(c) Both (a) and (b) are true.
(d) Both (a) and (b) are false.

13 Consider the position vector **OP** of a point $P(x, y, z)$ as in figure shown below.

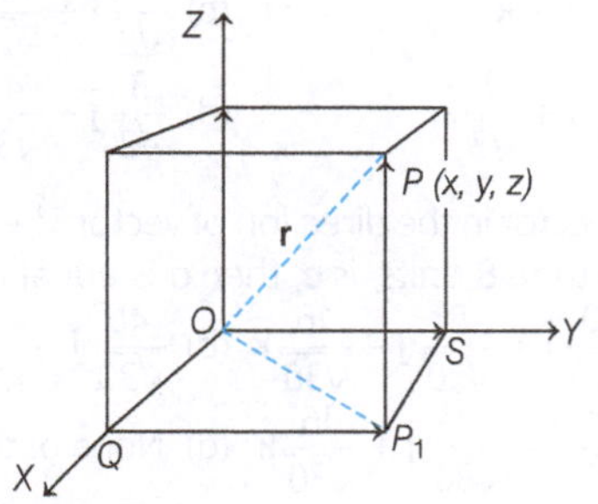

If P_1 is the foot of perpendicular from the point P on the plane XOY, then which of the following option is not true? **NCERT Pg. 347**

(a) Component form of vector **OP** (or **r**) $= x\hat{\mathbf{i}} + y\hat{\mathbf{j}} + z\hat{\mathbf{k}}$.
(b) x, y and z are called scalar components of **OP** or (**r**).
(c) $x\hat{\mathbf{i}}$, $y\hat{\mathbf{j}}$ and $z\hat{\mathbf{k}}$ are called the vector components of **r** along the respective axis.
(d) The length of any vector $\mathbf{r} = x\hat{\mathbf{i}} + y\hat{\mathbf{j}} + z\hat{\mathbf{k}}$ is given by $|\mathbf{r}| = \sqrt{x^2 - y^2 + z^2}$.

14 If **a** and **b** are any two vectors given in the component form $a_1\hat{\mathbf{i}} + a_2\hat{\mathbf{j}} + a_3\hat{\mathbf{k}}$ and $b_1\hat{\mathbf{i}} + b_2\hat{\mathbf{j}} + b_3\hat{\mathbf{k}}$ respectively, then which of the following is correct? **NCERT Pg. 348**

(a) The sum (or resultant) of the vectors **a** and **b** is given by $\mathbf{a} + \mathbf{b} = (a_1 + a_2)\hat{\mathbf{i}} + (b_1 + b_2)\hat{\mathbf{j}} + (a_3 + b_3)\hat{\mathbf{k}}$.
(b) $\mathbf{a} - \mathbf{b} = (a_1 - b_1)\hat{\mathbf{i}} + (a_2 - b_2)\hat{\mathbf{j}} + (a_3 - b_3)\hat{\mathbf{k}}$.
(c) Both (a) and (b) are correct.
(d) Both (a) and (b) are incorrect.

15 If **a** and **b** are any two vectors given in the component form $a_1\hat{\mathbf{i}} + a_2\hat{\mathbf{j}} + a_3\hat{\mathbf{k}}$ and $b_1\hat{\mathbf{i}} + b_2\hat{\mathbf{j}} + b_3\hat{\mathbf{k}}$ respectively, then which of the following is incorrect? **NCERT Pg. 348**

I. The vectors **a** and **b** are equal, if and only if $a_1 = a_2 = a_3$ and $b_1 = b_2 = b_3$.
II. The vectors **a** and **b** are equal, if and only if $a_1 = b_1$, $a_2 = b_2$ and $a_3 = b_3$.
III. $\lambda\mathbf{a} = (\lambda a_1)\hat{\mathbf{i}} + (\lambda a_2)\hat{\mathbf{j}} + (\lambda a_3)\hat{\mathbf{k}}$, where λ is a scalar.

(a) Only I is incorrect.
(b) Only II is incorrect.
(c) I and II are incorrect.
(d) Only III is incorrect.

16 If **a** and **b** are any two vectors and k and m are any scalars, then which of the following is correct? **NCERT Pg. 349**

(a) $k\mathbf{a} + m\mathbf{a} = (k + m)\mathbf{a}$
(b) $k(m\mathbf{a}) = (km)\mathbf{a}$
(c) $k(\mathbf{a} + \mathbf{b}) = k\mathbf{a} + k\mathbf{b}$
(d) All of the above

17 Which of the following is true? **NCERT Pg. 349**

(a) $\lambda\mathbf{a}$ is always collinear to the vector a, where λ is a scalar.
(b) If the vectors **a** and **b** are given in the component form, then the two vectors are collinear, if and only if $\frac{b_1}{a_1} = \frac{b_2}{a_2} = \frac{b_3}{a_3} = \lambda$.
(c) Both (a) and (b) are true.
(d) Both (a) and (b) are false.

18 If $\mathbf{a} = a_1\hat{\mathbf{i}} + a_2\hat{\mathbf{j}} + a_3\hat{\mathbf{k}}$, then direction ratios of **a** are **NCERT Pg. 349**

(a) a_1, a_2, a_3
(b) $\frac{a_1}{\sqrt{3}}, \frac{2a_2}{\sqrt{3}}, \frac{a_3}{\sqrt{3}}$
(c) $\frac{a_1}{2}, \frac{a_2}{3}, \frac{a_3}{4}$
(d) None of the above

19 If l, m and n are the direction cosines of a vector, and α, β and γ are the angles, which the vector makes with X, Y and Z-axes respectively, then the unit vector in the direction of that vector is **NCERT Pg. 349**

(a) $l\hat{\mathbf{i}} + m\hat{\mathbf{j}} + n\hat{\mathbf{k}} = \frac{\hat{\mathbf{i}}}{\cos\alpha} + \frac{\hat{\mathbf{j}}}{\cos\beta} + \frac{\hat{\mathbf{k}}}{\cos\gamma}$
(b) $l\hat{\mathbf{i}} + m\hat{\mathbf{j}} + n\hat{\mathbf{k}} = (\cos\alpha)\hat{\mathbf{i}} + (\cos\beta)\hat{\mathbf{j}} + (\cos\gamma)\hat{\mathbf{k}}$
(c) $l\hat{\mathbf{i}} + m\hat{\mathbf{j}} + n\hat{\mathbf{k}} = (l\cos\alpha)\hat{\mathbf{i}} + (m\cos\beta)\hat{\mathbf{j}} + (n\cos\gamma)\hat{\mathbf{k}}$
(d) None of the above

20 The unit vector in the direction of the sum of the vectors, $\mathbf{a} = 2\hat{\mathbf{i}} + 2\hat{\mathbf{j}} - 5\hat{\mathbf{k}}$ and $\mathbf{b} = 2\hat{\mathbf{i}} + \hat{\mathbf{j}} + 3\hat{\mathbf{k}}$ is **NCERT Pg. 350**

(a) $\frac{4}{\sqrt{29}}\hat{\mathbf{i}} + \frac{3}{\sqrt{29}}\hat{\mathbf{j}} - \frac{2}{\sqrt{29}}\hat{\mathbf{k}}$
(b) $\frac{4}{\sqrt{29}}\hat{\mathbf{i}} - \frac{3}{\sqrt{29}}\hat{\mathbf{j}} + \frac{2}{\sqrt{29}}\hat{\mathbf{k}}$
(c) $\frac{3}{\sqrt{29}}\hat{\mathbf{i}} + \frac{4}{\sqrt{29}}\hat{\mathbf{j}} - \frac{2}{\sqrt{29}}\hat{\mathbf{k}}$
(d) None of the above

21 If $P_1(x_1, y_1, z_1)$ and $P_2(x_2, y_2, z_2)$ are any two points, and the vector joining P_1 and P_2 is the vector $\mathbf{P_1P_2}$, then **NCERT Pg. 351**

(a) $\mathbf{P_1P_2} = \mathbf{OP_2} - \mathbf{OP_1}$
(b) $\mathbf{P_1P_2} = (x_2 - x_1)\hat{\mathbf{i}} + (y_2 - y_1)\hat{\mathbf{j}} + (z_2 - z_1)\hat{\mathbf{k}}$
(c) $|\mathbf{P_1P_2}| = \sqrt{(x_2 - x_1)^2 + (y_2 - y_1)^2 + (z_2 - z_1)^2}$
(d) All of the above

22 The vector joining the points $P(2, 3, 0)$ and $Q(-1, -2, -4)$ directed from P to Q is **NCERT Pg. 352**
(a) $3\hat{i} - 5\hat{j} + 4\hat{k}$
(b) $-3\hat{i} - 5\hat{j} - 4\hat{k}$
(c) $-5\hat{i} - 3\hat{j} + 4\hat{k}$
(d) None of the above

23 If a line segment joining the points P and Q, whose position vectors are **a** and **b** respectively, then the position vector of a point R, which divides the line segment in the ratio $m:n$.
I. Internally, is given by $\dfrac{m\mathbf{b}+n\mathbf{a}}{m+n}$
II. Externally, is given by $\dfrac{m\mathbf{b}-n\mathbf{a}}{m-n}$
Choose the correct option. **NCERT Pg. 352**
(a) Only I is true. (b) Only II is true.
(c) Both I and II are true. (d) Both I and II are false.

24 If $\mathbf{a} = \hat{i} + \hat{j} + \hat{k}$, $\mathbf{b} = 2\hat{i} - 7\hat{j} - 3\hat{k}$ and $\mathbf{c} = \dfrac{1}{\sqrt{3}}\hat{i} + \dfrac{1}{\sqrt{3}}\hat{j} - \dfrac{1}{\sqrt{3}}\hat{k}$. Then, magnitude of vectors **a**, **b**, **c** are, respectively **NCERT Pg. 354**
(a) $1, \sqrt{3}, \sqrt{62}$ (b) $\sqrt{3}, 1, 62$
(c) $\sqrt{3}, \sqrt{62}, 1$ (d) None of these

25 Which of the following is an example of two different vectors with same magnitude? **NCERT Pg. 354**
(a) $(2\hat{i} + 3\hat{j} + \hat{k})$ and $(2\hat{i} + 3\hat{j} - \hat{k})$
(b) $(3\hat{i} + 5\hat{j} + \hat{k})$ and $(3\hat{i} + 4\hat{j} + \hat{k})$
(c) $(\hat{j} + \hat{k})$ and $(2\hat{j} + 3\hat{k})$
(d) None of the above

26 Which of the following is an example of two different vectors having same direction? **NCERT Pg. 354**
(a) $(\hat{i} + \hat{j} + \hat{k})$ and $(2\hat{i} + 2\hat{j} + 3\hat{k})$
(b) $(2\hat{i} + \hat{j} + \hat{k})$ and $(4\hat{i} + 5\hat{j} + 7\hat{k})$
(c) $(\hat{i} + \hat{j} + \hat{k})$ and $(2\hat{i} + 2\hat{j} + 2\hat{k})$
(d) None of the above

27 The values of x and y, so that the vectors $2\hat{i} + 3\hat{j}$ and $x\hat{i} + y\hat{j}$ are equal, are respectively **NCERT Pg. 354**
(a) 3, 2 (b) 4, 2 (c) 2, 3 (d) 2, 2

28 The unit vector in the direction of the vector $\mathbf{a} = \hat{i} + \hat{j} + 2\hat{k}$ is **NCERT Pg. 354**
(a) $\dfrac{1}{\sqrt{6}}\hat{i} + \dfrac{1}{\sqrt{6}}\hat{j} + \dfrac{1}{\sqrt{6}}\hat{k}$
(b) $\dfrac{2}{\sqrt{6}}\hat{i} + \dfrac{3}{\sqrt{6}}\hat{j} + \dfrac{1}{\sqrt{6}}\hat{k}$
(c) $\dfrac{1}{\sqrt{6}}\hat{i} + \dfrac{1}{\sqrt{6}}\hat{j} + \dfrac{2}{\sqrt{6}}\hat{k}$
(d) None of the above

29 The unit vector in the direction of vector **PQ**, where P and Q are the points (1, 2, 3) and (4, 5, 6) respectively, is **NCERT Pg. 354**
(a) $\dfrac{1}{\sqrt{3}}\hat{i} + \dfrac{1}{\sqrt{3}}\hat{j} + \dfrac{2}{\sqrt{3}}\hat{k}$ (b) $\dfrac{1}{\sqrt{3}}\hat{i} + \dfrac{1}{\sqrt{3}}\hat{j} + \dfrac{1}{\sqrt{3}}\hat{k}$
(c) $\dfrac{1}{\sqrt{3}}\hat{i} + \dfrac{1}{\sqrt{5}}\hat{j} + \dfrac{1}{\sqrt{7}}\hat{k}$ (d) None of these

30 If $\mathbf{a} = 2\hat{i} - \hat{j} + 2\hat{k}$ and $\mathbf{b} = -\hat{i} + \hat{j} - \hat{k}$, then the unit vector in the direction of the vector $\mathbf{a} + \mathbf{b}$ is **NCERT Pg. 354**
(a) $\dfrac{1}{2}\hat{i} + \dfrac{1}{3}\hat{k}$ (b) $\dfrac{1}{\sqrt{2}}\hat{i} + \dfrac{1}{\sqrt{2}}\hat{k}$
(c) $\dfrac{1}{\sqrt{2}}\hat{i} + \dfrac{2}{\sqrt{3}}\hat{k}$ (d) $\dfrac{3}{\sqrt{2}}\hat{j} + \dfrac{4}{\sqrt{3}}\hat{k}$

31 If the vector in the direction of vector $5\hat{i} - \hat{j} + 2\hat{k}$, which has magnitude 8 units, is **c**, then **c** is equal to **NCERT Pg. 354**
(a) $\dfrac{40}{\sqrt{30}}\hat{i} + \dfrac{8}{\sqrt{30}}\hat{j} - \dfrac{16}{\sqrt{30}}\hat{k}$ (b) $\dfrac{40}{\sqrt{30}}\hat{i} - \dfrac{8}{\sqrt{30}}\hat{j} + \dfrac{16}{\sqrt{30}}\hat{k}$
(c) $\dfrac{10}{\sqrt{15}}\hat{i} - \dfrac{8}{\sqrt{30}}\hat{j} + \dfrac{16}{\sqrt{30}}\hat{k}$ (d) None of these

32 The direction cosines of the vector $\hat{i} + 2\hat{j} + 3\hat{k}$ are **NCERT Pg. 354**
(a) $\dfrac{1}{\sqrt{14}}, \dfrac{2}{\sqrt{14}}, \dfrac{3}{\sqrt{14}}$ (b) $\dfrac{2}{\sqrt{14}}, \dfrac{3}{\sqrt{14}}, \dfrac{4}{\sqrt{14}}$
(c) $\dfrac{11}{\sqrt{14}}, \dfrac{13}{\sqrt{14}}, \dfrac{21}{\sqrt{14}}$ (d) None of these

33 The direction cosines of the vector joining the points $A(1, 2, -3)$ and $B(-1, -2, 1)$, directed from A to B are **NCERT Pg. 354**
(a) $-\dfrac{1}{\sqrt{3}}, -\dfrac{2}{\sqrt{3}}, \dfrac{2}{\sqrt{3}}$ (b) $\dfrac{-1}{3}, \dfrac{-2}{3}, \dfrac{2}{3}$
(c) $\dfrac{1}{\sqrt{3}}, \dfrac{2}{\sqrt{3}}, \dfrac{2}{\sqrt{3}}$ (d) None of these

34 The position vector of the mid-point of the vector joining the points $P(2, 3, 4)$ and $Q(4, 1, -2)$ is **NCERT Pg. 355**
(a) $3\hat{i} + 2\hat{j} + \hat{k}$ (b) $3\hat{i} - 2\hat{j} + \hat{k}$
(c) $\hat{i} + 2\hat{j} + \hat{k}$ (d) $2\hat{i} + 3\hat{j} + \hat{k}$

35 If **a** and **b** are two collinear vectors, then which of the following is/are incorrect?
I. $\mathbf{b} = \lambda\mathbf{a}$, for some scalars λ, $\lambda \neq 0$.
II. $\hat{\mathbf{a}} = \pm\hat{\mathbf{b}}$
III. The respective components of **a** and **b** are not proportional.
IV. Both the vectors **a** and **b** have same direction, but different magnitude. **NCERT Pg. 355**
(a) Only I is incorrect.
(b) Both III and IV are incorrect.
(c) Only III is incorrect.
(d) Both I and II are incorrect.

Level II

36 If m_1, m_2, m_3 and m_4 are respectively the magnitudes of the vectors $\mathbf{a}_1 = 2\hat{i} - \hat{j} + \hat{k}$, $\mathbf{a}_2 = 3\hat{i} - 4\hat{j} - 4\hat{k}$, $\mathbf{a}_3 = \hat{i} + \hat{j} - \hat{k}$ and $\mathbf{a}_4 = -\hat{i} + 3\hat{j} + \hat{k}$, then the correct order of m_1, m_2, m_3 and m_4 is **NCERT Pg. 354**

(a) $m_3 < m_1 < m_4 < m_2$ (b) $m_3 < m_1 < m_2 < m_4$
(c) $m_3 < m_4 < m_1 < m_2$ (d) $m_3 < m_4 < m_2 < m_1$

37 If $\mathbf{a}$ is a vector of magnitude 50, collinear with the vector $\mathbf{b} = 6\hat{i} - 8\hat{j} - \frac{15}{2}\hat{k}$ and makes an acute angle with the positive direction of Z-axis, then $\mathbf{a}$ is equal to **NCERT Pg. 341**

(a) $-24\hat{i} + 32\hat{j} + 30\hat{k}$ (b) $24\hat{i} - 32\hat{j} - 30\hat{k}$
(c) $-12\hat{i} + 16\hat{j} - 15\hat{k}$ (d) $12\hat{i} - 16\hat{j} - 15\hat{k}$

38 If $2\mathbf{a} + 3\mathbf{b} - 5\mathbf{c} = 0$, then the ratio in which $\mathbf{c}$ divides $\mathbf{AB}$ is **NCERT Pg. 352**

(a) 3 : 2 internally (b) 3 : 2 externally
(c) 2 : 3 internally (d) 2 : 3 externally

39 If P is any point with in a ΔABC, then $\mathbf{PA} + \mathbf{CP}$ is equal to

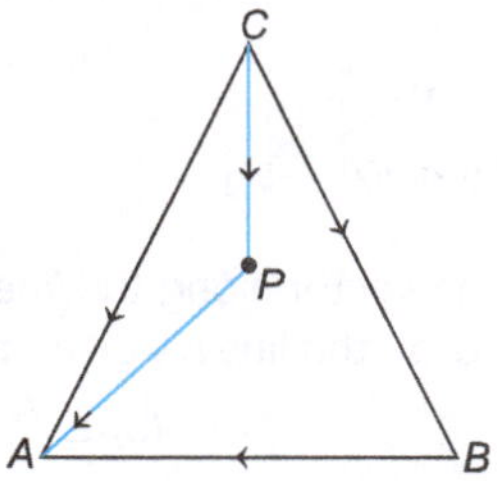

NCERT Pg. 344

(a) $\mathbf{AC} + \mathbf{CB}$ (b) $\mathbf{BC} + \mathbf{BA}$
(c) $\mathbf{CB} + \mathbf{AB}$ (d) $\mathbf{CB} + \mathbf{BA}$

40 The ratio in which $\hat{i} + 2\hat{j} + 3\hat{k}$ divides the join of $-2\hat{i} + 3\hat{j} + 5\hat{k}$ and $7\hat{i} - \hat{k}$ is **NCERT Pg. 352**

(a) 1 : 2 (b) 1 : 4
(c) 2 : 3 (d) 3 : 4

41 If $ABCD$ is a parallelogram and M is the point of intersection of the diagonals, if O is any point, then $\mathbf{OA} + \mathbf{OB} + \mathbf{OC} + \mathbf{OD}$ is equal to **NCERT Pg. 344**

(a) 3 $\mathbf{OM}$ (b) 2 $\mathbf{OM}$ (c) 4 $\mathbf{OM}$ (d) $\mathbf{OM}$

42 Let $ABCD$ be the parallelogram, whose sides AB and AD are represented by the vectors $2\hat{i} + 4\hat{j} - 5\hat{k}$ and $\hat{i} + 2\hat{j} + 3\hat{k}$, respectively. Then, if $\mathbf{a}$ is a unit vector parallel to $\mathbf{AC}$, then $\mathbf{a}$ is equal to **NCERT Pg. 354**

(a) $(3\hat{i} - 6\hat{j} - 2\hat{k})/3$ (b) $(3\hat{i} + 6\hat{j} + 2\hat{k})/3$
(c) $(3\hat{i} - 6\hat{j} - 3\hat{k})/7$ (d) $(3\hat{i} + 6\hat{j} - 2\hat{k})/7$

43 The position vectors of the points A and B with respect to O are $2\hat{i} + 2\hat{j} + \hat{k}$ and $2\hat{i} + 4\hat{j} + 4\hat{k}$. The length of the internal bisector of $\angle BOA$ of ΔAOB is **NCERT Pg. 354**

(a) $\frac{\sqrt{136}}{9}$ (b) $\frac{\sqrt{136}}{3}$ (c) $\frac{20}{3}$ (d) $\frac{\sqrt{217}}{9}$

44 If $ABCDEF$ is a regular hexagon with $\mathbf{AB} = \mathbf{a}$ and $\mathbf{BC} = \mathbf{b}$, then $\mathbf{CE}$ is equal to **NCERT Pg. 343**

(a) $\mathbf{b} - \mathbf{a}$ (b) $-\mathbf{b}$ (c) $\mathbf{b} - 2\mathbf{a}$ (d) None of these

45 Let $\mathbf{a}, \mathbf{b}$ and $\mathbf{c}$ be three non-zero vectors such that no two of these are collinear. If the vector $\mathbf{a} + 2\mathbf{b}$ is collinear with $\mathbf{c}$ and $\mathbf{b} + 3\mathbf{c}$ is collinear with $\mathbf{a}$ (λ being some non-zero scalar), then $\mathbf{a} + 2\mathbf{b} + 6\mathbf{c}$ is equal to **NCERT Pg. 341**

(a) $\lambda\mathbf{a}$ (b) $\lambda\mathbf{b}$ (c) $\lambda\mathbf{c}$ (d) $\mathbf{0}$

46 The position vectors of P and Q are respectively $\mathbf{a}$ and $\mathbf{b}$. If R is a point on $\mathbf{PQ}$ such that $\mathbf{PR} = 5\mathbf{PQ}$, then the position vector of R is **NCERT Pg. 354**

(a) $5\mathbf{b} - 4\mathbf{a}$ (b) $5\mathbf{b} + 4\mathbf{a}$ (c) $4\mathbf{b} - 5\mathbf{a}$ (d) $4\mathbf{b} + 5\mathbf{a}$

47 Let $\mathbf{a}$ and $\mathbf{b}$ be non-zero and non-collinear vectors, if there exists scalars α, β such that $\alpha\mathbf{a} + \beta\mathbf{b} = \mathbf{0}$, then

(a) $\alpha = \beta \neq 0$ (b) $\alpha + \beta = 0$ **NCERT Pg. 354**
(c) $\alpha = \beta = 0$ (d) $\alpha \neq \beta$

48 If $4\hat{i} + 7\hat{j} + 8\hat{k}$, $2\hat{i} + 3\hat{j} + 4\hat{k}$ and $2\hat{i} + 5\hat{j} + 7\hat{k}$ are the position vectors of the vertices A, B and C respectively of ΔABC, then the position vector of the point, where the bisector of angle A meets BC is **NCERT Pg. 352**

(a) $\frac{2}{3}(6\hat{i} + 2\hat{j} - 8\hat{k})$ (b) $\frac{1}{3}(6\hat{i} + 13\hat{j} + 18\hat{k})$
(c) $\frac{1}{3}(-6\hat{i} - 8\hat{j} - 9\hat{k})$ (d) $\frac{2}{3}(-6\hat{i} - 12\hat{j} + 8\hat{k})$

49 Consider points A, B, C and D with position vectors $7\hat{i} - 4\hat{j} + 7\hat{k}$, $\hat{i} - 6\hat{j} + 10\hat{k}$, $-\hat{i} - 3\hat{j} + 4\hat{k}$ and $5\hat{i} - \hat{j} + 5\hat{k}$, respectively. Then, $ABCD$ is **NCERT Pg. 354**

(a) square (b) rhombus
(c) rectangle (d) None of these

50 A unit vector $\mathbf{a}$ makes an angle $\frac{\pi}{4}$ with Z-axis, if $\hat{\mathbf{a}} + \hat{i} + \hat{j}$ is a unit vector, then $\mathbf{a}$ is equal to **NCERT Pg. 340**

(a) $\frac{\hat{i}}{2} + \frac{\hat{j}}{2} + \frac{\hat{k}}{2}$ (b) $\frac{\hat{i}}{2} + \frac{\hat{j}}{2} - \frac{\hat{k}}{\sqrt{2}}$
(c) $-\frac{\hat{i}}{2} - \frac{\hat{j}}{2} + \frac{\hat{k}}{\sqrt{2}}$ (d) $\frac{\hat{i}}{2} - \frac{\hat{j}}{2} - \frac{\hat{k}}{\sqrt{2}}$

51 The non-zero vectors, $\mathbf{a}, \mathbf{b}$ and $\mathbf{c}$ are related by $\mathbf{a} = 8\mathbf{b}$ and $\mathbf{c} = -7\mathbf{b}$, then the angle between $\mathbf{a}$ and $\mathbf{c}$ is **NCERT Pg. 354**

(a) π (b) 0 (c) $\frac{\pi}{4}$ (d) $\frac{\pi}{2}$

52 $ABCD$ is a parallelogram. If L and M be the mid-points of BC and CD respectively, then $\mathbf{AL} + \mathbf{AM}$ is equal to **NCERT Pg. 343**

(a) $\mathbf{AC}$ (b) $2\mathbf{AC}$ (c) $\frac{\mathbf{AC}}{2}$ (d) $\frac{3}{2}\mathbf{AC}$

53 $ABCDEF$ is a regular hexagon with centre at origin such that $\mathbf{AD} + \mathbf{EB} + \mathbf{FC} = \lambda\mathbf{ED}$, then λ is equal to **NCERT Pg. 343**

(a) 2 (b) 4 (c) 6 (d) 3

Scalar (or dot) Product of Two Vectors

Level I

1 Multiplication of two vectors is defined in two ways, namely **NCERT Pg. 355**

(a) scalar product and dot product
(b) vector product and cross product
(c) scalar product and vector product
(d) None of the above

2 The scalar product of two non-zero vectors **a** and **b**, denoted by $\mathbf{a}\cdot\mathbf{b}$ is defined as $\mathbf{a}\cdot\mathbf{b} =$ **NCERT Pg. 355**

(a) $|\mathbf{a}||\mathbf{b}|\sin\theta$ (b) $|\mathbf{a}||\mathbf{b}|\cos\theta$
(c) $|\mathbf{a}||\mathbf{b}|$ (d) None of these

3 If either $\mathbf{a}=\mathbf{0}$ or $\mathbf{b}=\mathbf{0}$, then **NCERT Pg. 356**

(a) $\mathbf{a}\cdot\mathbf{b}=1$ (b) $\mathbf{a}\cdot\mathbf{b}=-1$ (c) $\mathbf{a}\cdot\mathbf{b}=\pm 1$ (d) $\mathbf{a}\cdot\mathbf{b}=0$

4 Which of the following is not true? **NCERT Pg. 356**

I. $\mathbf{a}\cdot\mathbf{b}$ is a real number.
II. $\mathbf{a}\cdot\mathbf{b}=0 \Leftrightarrow \mathbf{a} \,||\, \mathbf{b}; \mathbf{a}\neq 0, \mathbf{b}\neq 0$
III. $\mathbf{a}\cdot\mathbf{a}=|\mathbf{a}|^2$
IV. $\mathbf{a}\cdot(-\mathbf{a})=|\mathbf{a}|^2$

(a) II and IV are not true. (b) II and III are not true.
(c) Only III is not true. (d) Only I is not true.

5 Which of the following is true? **NCERT Pg. 356**

(a) $\hat{\mathbf{i}}\cdot\hat{\mathbf{i}}=\hat{\mathbf{j}}\cdot\hat{\mathbf{j}}=\hat{\mathbf{k}}\cdot\hat{\mathbf{k}}=0$
(b) $\hat{\mathbf{i}}\cdot\hat{\mathbf{j}}=\hat{\mathbf{j}}\cdot\hat{\mathbf{k}}=\hat{\mathbf{k}}\cdot\hat{\mathbf{i}}=1$
(c) Both (a) and (b) are true.
(d) Both (a) and (b) are false.

6 The angle between two non-zero vectors **a** and **b** is given by **NCERT Pg. 356**

(a) $\theta=\cos^{-1}\dfrac{\mathbf{a}\cdot\mathbf{b}}{|\mathbf{a}||\mathbf{b}|}$ (b) $\theta=\sin^{-1}\dfrac{\mathbf{a}\cdot\mathbf{b}}{|\mathbf{a}|\cdot|\mathbf{b}|}$

(c) $\theta=\tan^{-1}\dfrac{\mathbf{a}\cdot\mathbf{b}}{|\mathbf{a}|\cdot|\mathbf{b}|}$ (d) None of these

7 Which of the following is incorrect? **NCERT Pg. 356**

(a) If **a**, **b** and **c** be any three vectors, then $\mathbf{a}\cdot(\mathbf{b}+\mathbf{c})=\mathbf{a}\cdot\mathbf{b}+\mathbf{a}\cdot\mathbf{c}$
(b) If **a** and **b** be any two vectors and λ be any scalar, then $(\lambda\mathbf{a})\cdot\mathbf{b}=\lambda(\mathbf{a}\cdot\mathbf{b})$
(c) If two vectors **a** and **b** in component form, then $\mathbf{a}\cdot\mathbf{b}=(a_1\,a_2-b_1\,b_2-a_3\,b_3)$, if $\mathbf{a}=(a_1\hat{\mathbf{i}}+a_2\hat{\mathbf{j}}+a_3\hat{\mathbf{k}})$ and $\mathbf{b}=(b_1\hat{\mathbf{i}}+b_2\hat{\mathbf{j}}+b_3\hat{\mathbf{k}})$
(d) If **a** and **b** be any two vectors and λ be any scalar, then $(\lambda\mathbf{a})\cdot\mathbf{b}=\mathbf{a}\cdot(\lambda\mathbf{b})$

8 Consider the figure given below.

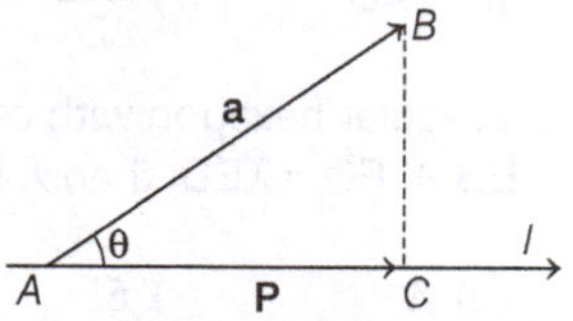

Here, a vector **AB** is making an angle θ with the given directed line. A vector **P** (say) on line l is as shown. Here, $0°<\theta<90°$.

Based on the above information, which among the following is true? **NCERT Pg. 357**

(a) The projection of **AB** on l is a vector **P** (as shown).
(b) **P** has magnitude $|\mathbf{AB}||\cos\theta|$.
(c) Direction of **P** is in the direction of line l.
(d) All are true.

9 Which among the following figure correctly represents projection of **AB** on a line l? **NCERT Pg. 357**

(a)
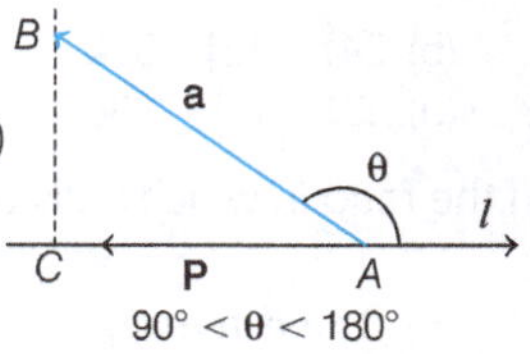

(b)
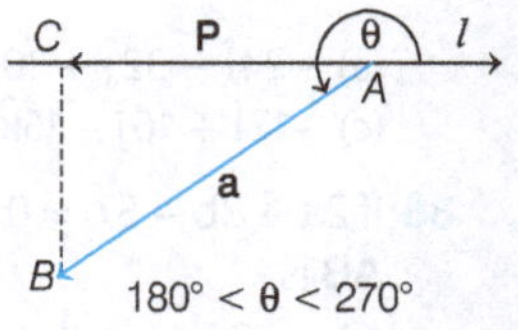

(c)
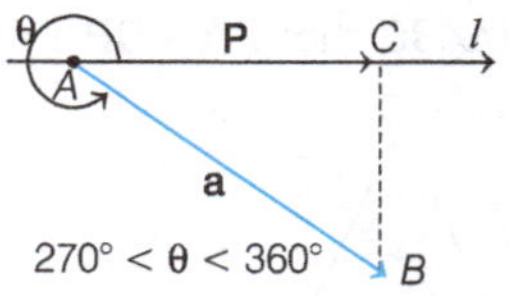

(d) All of these

10 If $\hat{\mathbf{P}}$ is the unit vector along the line l, then the projection of a vector **a** on the line l is given by **NCERT Pg. 358**

(a) $\dfrac{\mathbf{a}}{|\mathbf{a}|}\cdot\hat{\mathbf{P}}$ (b) $\mathbf{a}\cdot\hat{\mathbf{P}}$

(c) $\dfrac{1}{|\mathbf{a}|}\hat{\mathbf{P}}$ (d) None of these

11 Projection of vector **a** on other vector **b**, is equal to **NCERT Pg. 358**

(a) $\mathbf{a}\cdot\hat{\mathbf{b}}$ (b) $\mathbf{a}\cdot\left(\dfrac{\mathbf{b}}{|\mathbf{b}|}\right)$

(c) $\dfrac{1}{|\mathbf{b}|}(\mathbf{a}\cdot\mathbf{b})$ (d) All of these

12 If $\theta=0°$, then the projection vector of **AB** will be β and if $\theta=\pi$, then the projection vector of **AB** will be α. Here, β and α refers to **NCERT Pg. 358**

(a) **AB** and **BA** respectively.
(b) **AB** and **AB** respectively.
(c) Both (a) and (b) are true.
(d) Both (a) and (b) are false.

13 If $\theta=\dfrac{\pi}{2}$ or $\theta=\dfrac{3\pi}{2}$, then the projection vector of **AB** will be **NCERT Pg. 358**

(a) unit vector
(b) null vector
(c) collinear vector
(d) None of the above

14 If α, β and γ are the direction angles of vector $\mathbf{a} = a_1\hat{i} + a_2\hat{j} + a_3\hat{k}$. Based on above information, which of the following is incorrect? NCERT Pg. 358

(a) Direction cosines are $\cos\alpha = \frac{a_1}{|\mathbf{a}|}$, $\cos\beta = \frac{a_2}{|\mathbf{a}|}$ and $\cos\gamma = \frac{a_3}{|\mathbf{a}|}$

(b) The scalar components a_1, a_2 and a_3 of the vector **a**, are precisely the projections of **a** along *X*, *Y* and *Z*-axes, respectively

(c) If **a** is a unit vector, then $\mathbf{a} = \frac{\hat{i}}{\cos\alpha} + \frac{\hat{j}}{\cos\beta} + \frac{\hat{k}}{\cos\gamma}$

(d) Projection of **a** along *OX*, *OY* and *OZ* are $|\mathbf{a}|\cos\alpha$, $|\mathbf{a}|\cos\beta$, $|\mathbf{a}|\cos\gamma$, respectively.

15 Representation of a unit vector **a**, in terms of its direction cosines are NCERT Pg. 358

(a) $\mathbf{a} = \sin\alpha\hat{i} + \sin\beta\hat{j} + \sin\gamma\hat{k}$

(b) $\mathbf{a} = \cos\alpha\hat{i} + \cos\beta\hat{j} + \cos\gamma\hat{k}$

(c) Both (a) and (b) are true.

(d) Both (a) and (b) are false.

16 **Statement I** The projection of the vector $\mathbf{a} = 2\hat{i} + 3\hat{j} + 2\hat{k}$ on the vector $\mathbf{b} = \hat{i} + 2\hat{j} + \hat{k}$ is $\frac{5}{3}\sqrt{6}$.

Statement II The projection of vector **a** on vector **b** is $\frac{1}{|\mathbf{a}|}(\mathbf{a}\cdot\mathbf{b})$. NCERT Pg. 359

(a) Statement I and II are true; Statement II is a correct explanation for Statement I.

(b) Statement I and II are true; Statement II is not a correct explanation for Statement I.

(c) Statement I is true but Statement II is false.

(d) Statement I is false but Statement II is true.

17 If two vectors **a** and **b** are such that $|\mathbf{a}| = 2$, $|\mathbf{b}| = 3$ and $\mathbf{a}\cdot\mathbf{b} = 4$, then $|\mathbf{a} - \mathbf{b}|$ is equal to NCERT Pg. 359

(a) $\sqrt{3}$ (b) $\sqrt{5}$
(c) $\sqrt{7}$ (d) $2\sqrt{2}$

18 If **a** is a unit vector and $(\mathbf{x} - \mathbf{a})\cdot(\mathbf{x} + \mathbf{a}) = 8$, then the value of $|\mathbf{x}|$ is equal to NCERT Pg. 360

(a) 3 (b) 4 (c) 5 (d) 6

19 The points $A(-2\mathbf{i} + 3\mathbf{j} + 5\mathbf{k})$, $B(\mathbf{i} + 2\mathbf{j} + 3\mathbf{k})$ and $C(7\mathbf{i} - \mathbf{k})$ are NCERT Pg. 361

(a) non-collinear (b) collinear
(c) representing a triangle (d) None of these

20 The angle between two vectors **a** and **b** with magnitudes $\sqrt{3}$ and 2, respectively having $\mathbf{a}\cdot\mathbf{b} = \sqrt{6}$ is NCERT Pg. 361

(a) $\frac{\pi}{2}$ (b) $\frac{\pi}{3}$ (c) $\frac{\pi}{4}$ (d) $\frac{\pi}{6}$

21 The angle between the vectors $\hat{i} - 2\hat{j} + 3\hat{k}$ and $3\hat{i} - 2\hat{j} + \hat{k}$ is NCERT Pg. 361

(a) $\cos^{-1}\left(\frac{7}{5}\right)$ (b) $\sin^{-1}\left(\frac{7}{5}\right)$
(c) $\cos^{-1}\left(\frac{5}{7}\right)$ (d) $\sin^{-1}\left(\frac{5}{7}\right)$

22 The projection of the vector $\hat{i} - \hat{j}$ on the vector $\hat{i} + \hat{j}$ is NCERT Pg. 361

(a) 0 (b) 1
(c) −1 (d) None of these

23 Consider the three vectors given below.

$\frac{1}{7}(2\hat{i} + 3\hat{j} + 6\hat{k})$, $\frac{1}{7}(3\hat{i} - 6\hat{j} + 2\hat{k})$, $\frac{1}{7}(6\hat{i} + 2\hat{j} - 3\hat{k})$.

Based on above vectors, which among the following is true? NCERT Pg. 361

(a) Each of the vectors is a unit vector.

(b) All the vectors are mutually perpendicular to each other.

(c) Both (a) and (b) are true.

(d) Both (a) and (b) are false.

24 If $(\mathbf{a} + \mathbf{b})\cdot(\mathbf{a} - \mathbf{b}) = 8$ and $|\mathbf{a}| = 8|\mathbf{b}|$, then NCERT Pg. 362

(a) $|\mathbf{a}| = \frac{16}{3}\sqrt{\frac{2}{7}}$

(b) $|\mathbf{b}| = \frac{2}{3}\sqrt{\frac{2}{7}}$

(c) Both (a) and (b) are true

(d) Both (a) and (b) are not true

25 The product $(3\mathbf{a} - 5\mathbf{b})\cdot(2\mathbf{a} + 7\mathbf{b})$ is equal to NCERT Pg. 362

(a) $6|\mathbf{a}|^2 + 11(\mathbf{a}\cdot\mathbf{b}) - 35|\mathbf{b}|^2$

(b) $3|\mathbf{a}|^2 + 11(\mathbf{a}\cdot\mathbf{b}) - 35|\mathbf{b}|^2$

(c) $6|\mathbf{a}|^2 + 11(\mathbf{a}\cdot\mathbf{b}) + 35|\mathbf{b}|^2$

(d) None of the above

26 The magnitude of two vectors **a** and **b**, if both have the same magnitude, the angle between them is 60° and their scalar product is 1/2, is NCERT Pg. 362

(a) 1 (b) 2 (c) 3 (d) 4

27 For a unit vector **a**, if $(x - \mathbf{a})\cdot(x + \mathbf{a}) = 12$, then $|\mathbf{x}|$ is equal to NCERT Pg. 362

(a) $\sqrt{11}$ (b) $\sqrt{13}$ (c) $\sqrt{14}$ (d) $\sqrt{5}$

28 If $\mathbf{a} = 2\hat{i} + 2\hat{j} + 3\hat{k}$, $\hat{\mathbf{b}} = -\hat{i} + 2\hat{j} + \hat{k}$ and $\mathbf{c} = 3\hat{i} + \hat{j}$ such that $\mathbf{a} + \lambda\mathbf{b}$ is perpendicular to **c**, then the value of λ is NCERT Pg. 362

(a) 5 (b) 6
(c) 7 (d) 8

29 If **a**, **b**, **c** are unit vectors such that $\mathbf{a} + \mathbf{b} + \mathbf{c} = \mathbf{0}$, then the value of $\mathbf{a}\cdot\mathbf{b} + \mathbf{b}\cdot\mathbf{c} + \mathbf{c}\cdot\mathbf{a}$ is equal to NCERT Pg. 362

(a) $\frac{3}{2}$ (b) $\frac{-3}{2}$ (c) $\frac{1}{2}$ (d) $\frac{-1}{2}$

30 If the vertices A, B, C of a ΔABC are (1, 2, 3), (–1, 0, 0), (0, 1, 2) respectively, then $\angle ABC$ is equal to($\angle ABC$ is the angle between the vectors **BA** and **BC**) NCERT Pg. 362

(a) $\cos^{-1}\left(\frac{10}{\sqrt{114}}\right)$ (b) $\cos^{-1}\left(\frac{10}{\sqrt{102}}\right)$

(c) $\cos^{-1}\left(\frac{10}{7}\right)$ (d) None of these

31 Points $A(1, 2, 7), B(2, 6, 3), C(3, 10, -1)$ are NCERT Pg. 362

(a) the vertices of an equilateral triangle.
(b) the vertices of a right angled triangle.
(c) the vertices of an isosceles triangle.
(d) None of the above

32 The vectors $2\hat{i}-\hat{j}+\hat{k}$, $\hat{i}-3\hat{j}-5\hat{k}$ and $3\hat{i}-4\hat{j}-4\hat{k}$ are NCERT Pg. 362

(a) collinear.
(b) the vertices of a right angled triangle.
(c) the vertices of an equilateral triangle.
(d) None of the above

33 If **a** is a non-zero vector of magnitude 'a' and λ is non-zero scalar, then λ**a** is unit vector, if NCERT Pg. 362

(a) $\lambda = 1$ (b) $\lambda = -1$

(c) $a = |\lambda|$ (d) $a = \frac{1}{|\lambda|}$

Level II

34 If $\mathbf{a} = 2\hat{i}-\hat{j}+\hat{k}$, $\mathbf{b} = \hat{i}+\hat{j}-2\hat{k}$ and $\mathbf{c} = \hat{i}+3\hat{j}-\hat{k}$ then the value of λ, such that **a** is perpendicular to $\lambda\mathbf{b}+\mathbf{c}$ is NCERT Exemplar Pg. 209

(a) –1 (b) –2

(c) 2 (d) 1

35 The value of λ, for which the two vectors $2\hat{i}-\hat{j}+2\hat{k}$ and $3\hat{i}+\lambda\hat{j}+\hat{k}$ are perpendicular, is NCERT Pg. 356

(a) 2 (b) 4

(c) 6 (d) 8

36 If **a** and **b** are unit vectors, then what is the angle between **a** and **b** for $\sqrt{3}\mathbf{a}-\mathbf{b}$ to be a unit vector? NCERT Pg. 356

(a) 30° (b) 45°

(c) 60° (d) 90°

37 Let P, Q, R and S be the points on the plane with position vectors $-2\hat{i}-\hat{j}$, $4\hat{i}$, $3\hat{i}+3\hat{j}$ and $-3\hat{i}+2\hat{j}$, respectively. The quadrilateral $PQRS$ must be a NCERT Pg. 362

(a) parallelogram, which is neither a rhombus nor a rectangle.
(b) square.
(c) rectangle but not a square.
(d) rhombus but not a square.

38 If **p**, **q** and **r** are perpendicular to $\mathbf{q}+\mathbf{r}$, $\mathbf{r}+\mathbf{p}$ and $\mathbf{p}+\mathbf{q}$, respectively and if $|\mathbf{p}+\mathbf{q}| = 6$, $|\mathbf{q}+\mathbf{r}| = 4\sqrt{3}$ and $|\mathbf{r}+\mathbf{p}| = 4$, then $|\mathbf{p}+\mathbf{q}+\mathbf{r}|$ is NCERT Pg. 356

(a) $5\sqrt{2}$ (b) 10 (c) 5 (d) 15

39 If the scalar product of the vector $\hat{i}+\hat{j}+2\hat{k}$ with the unit vector along $m\hat{i}+2\hat{j}+3\hat{k}$ is equal to 2, then one of the values of m is NCERT Pg. 362

(a) 3 (b) 4

(c) 6 (d) 7

40 It is given that $\mathbf{a} = \lambda\hat{i}-7\hat{j}+3\hat{k}$, $\mathbf{b} = \lambda\hat{i}+\hat{j}++2\lambda\hat{k}$. If the angle between **a** and **b** is greater than 90°, then λ satisfies the inequality NCERT Pg. 356

(a) $-7 < \lambda < 1$ (b) $\lambda > 1$

(c) $1 < \lambda < 7$ (d) $-5 < \lambda < 1$

41 A unit vector in xy- plane makes an angle of 45° with the vector $\hat{i}+\hat{j}$ and an angle of 60° with the vector $3\hat{i}-4\hat{j}$ is NCERT Pg. 356

(a) $\frac{13}{7}\hat{i}+\frac{1}{7}\hat{j}$ (b) $\frac{7}{13}\hat{i}+\frac{7}{15}\hat{j}$

(c) $\frac{13}{14}\hat{i}++\frac{1}{14}\hat{j}$ (d) None of these

42 A parallelogram is constructed on the vectors $\mathbf{a} = 3\alpha-\beta$, $\mathbf{b} = \alpha+3\beta$, If $|\alpha| = |\beta| = 2$ and angle between α and β is $\frac{\pi}{3}$, then length of a diagonal of the parallelogram is NCERT Pg. 356

(a) $4\sqrt{5}$ (b) $3\sqrt{2}$

(c) $4\sqrt{3}$ (d) $5\sqrt{3}$

43 If $|\mathbf{a}| = |\mathbf{b}| = 1$ and $|\mathbf{a}+\mathbf{b}| = \sqrt{3}$, then the value of $(3\mathbf{a}-4\mathbf{b})\cdot(2\mathbf{a}+5\mathbf{b})$ is equal to NCERT Pg. 355

(a) –21 (b) $\frac{-21}{13}$

(c) –11 (d) None of these

Vector (or Cross) Product of Two Vectors

Level I

1 A right handed screw will advance in the direction of the positive Z-axis, if NCERT Pg. 363

(a) the positive X-axis is rotated counter clockwise into the positive Y-axis.
(b) the positive X-axis is rotated counter clockwise into the positive Z-axis.
(c) Both (a) and (b) are true.
(d) Both (a) and (b) are false.

2 The vector product of two non-zero vectors **a** and **b**, is denoted by $\mathbf{a}\times\mathbf{b}$ and is equal to NCERT Pg. 363

(a) $|\mathbf{a}||\mathbf{b}|\cos\theta$ (b) $|\mathbf{a}||\mathbf{b}|\sin\theta\hat{n}$

(c) $|\mathbf{a}||\mathbf{b}|\cos\theta\hat{n}$ (d) None of these

3 If either $\mathbf{a} = \mathbf{0}$ or $\mathbf{b} = \mathbf{0}$, then $\mathbf{a}\times\mathbf{b}$ is defined as NCERT Pg. 363

(a) $|\mathbf{a}||\mathbf{b}|$ (b) null vector

(c) unit vector (d) None of these

4 Which of the following is not true? NCERT Pg. 363
(a) $\mathbf{a} \times \mathbf{b}$ is a vector
(b) for two non-zero vectors **a** and **b**, If $\mathbf{a} \times \mathbf{b} = \mathbf{0}$, then **a** and **b** are perpendicular each other.
(c) $\mathbf{a} \times \mathbf{b} = \mathbf{0}$ is possible for two non-zero vectors **a** and **b**
(d) $\mathbf{a} \times (-\mathbf{a}) = \mathbf{0}$ for non-zero vector **a**

5 Which of the following is correct? NCERT Pg. 364
(a) If $\theta = \frac{\pi}{2}$, then $|\mathbf{a} \times \mathbf{b}| = |\mathbf{a}| \cdot |\mathbf{b}|$
(b) $\hat{i} \times \hat{i} = \hat{j} \times \hat{j} = \hat{k} \times \hat{k} = 0$
(c) $\hat{i} \times \hat{j} = \hat{k}, \hat{j} \times \hat{k} = \hat{i}, \hat{k} \times \hat{i} = \hat{j}$
(d) All are correct

6 The angle between two vectors **a** and **b** in terms of vector product is NCERT Pg. 364
(a) $\sin\theta = \frac{|\mathbf{a} \times \mathbf{b}|}{|\mathbf{a}||\mathbf{b}|}$ (b) $\cos\theta = \frac{|\mathbf{a} \times \mathbf{b}|}{|\mathbf{a}||\mathbf{b}|}$
(c) $\sin\theta = \frac{|\mathbf{a}||\mathbf{b}|}{|\mathbf{a} \times \mathbf{b}|}$ (d) $\cos\theta = \frac{|\mathbf{a}||\mathbf{b}|}{|\mathbf{a} \times \mathbf{b}|}$

7 **Statement I** $\mathbf{a} \times \mathbf{b} = -\mathbf{b} \times \mathbf{a}$ i.e. vector product is not commutative.

Statement II If we assume **a** and **b** to lie in the plane of the paper and If $\mathbf{a} \times \mathbf{b} = |\mathbf{a}||\mathbf{b}|\sin\theta\,\hat{\mathbf{n}}$, $\mathbf{b} \times \mathbf{a} = |\mathbf{b}||\mathbf{a}|\sin\theta\,\hat{\mathbf{n}}$ then $\hat{\mathbf{n}}$ and $\hat{\mathbf{n}}_1$ both will be parallel to the plane of paper. NCERT Pg. 364
(a) Statement I and II are true; Statement II is a correct explanation for statement I.
(b) Statement I and II are true; Statement II is not a correct explanation for statement I.
(c) Statement I is true but Statement II is false.
(d) Statement I is false but Statement II is true.

8 Which of the following is true? NCERT Pg. 364
(a) $\hat{j} \times \hat{i} = \hat{k}$ (b) $\hat{k} \times \hat{j} = \hat{i}$
(c) $\hat{i} \times \hat{k} = -\hat{j}$ (d) All of these

9 If **a** and **b** represent the adjacent sides of a parallelogram *ABCD* and θ is the angle between these sides, then area of parallelogram is equal to NCERT Pg. 365
(a) $|\mathbf{a} \times \mathbf{b}|$ (b) $|\mathbf{b}|\,|\mathbf{a}|\sin\theta$
(c) Both (a) and (b) (d) $\frac{1}{2}|\mathbf{a} \times \mathbf{b}|$

10 For any three vectors **a**, **b** and **c** and λ be a scalar, which of the following is incorrect ? NCERT Pg. 365
(a) $\mathbf{a} \times (\mathbf{b} + \mathbf{c}) = \mathbf{a} \times \mathbf{b} + \mathbf{a} \times \mathbf{c}$
(b) $\lambda(\mathbf{a} \times \mathbf{b}) = (\lambda\mathbf{a}) \times \mathbf{b}$,
(c) $\lambda(\mathbf{a} \times \mathbf{b}) = \mathbf{a} \times (\lambda\mathbf{b})$
(d) $\lambda(\mathbf{a} \times \mathbf{b}) = (\lambda\mathbf{a}) \times (\lambda\mathbf{b})$

11 If **a** and **b** are two vectors in their component form as $a_1\hat{i} + a_2\hat{j} + a_3\hat{k}$ and $b_1\hat{i} + b_2\hat{j} + b_3\hat{k}$, then NCERT Pg. 366
(a) $\mathbf{a} \times \mathbf{b} = \begin{vmatrix} \hat{i} & \hat{j} & \hat{k} \\ a_1 & a_2 & a_3 \\ b_1 & b_2 & b_3 \end{vmatrix}$
(b) $\mathbf{a} \times \mathbf{b} = (a_2b_3 - a_3b_2)\hat{i} - (a_1b_3 - a_3b_1)\hat{j} + (a_1b_2 - a_2b_1)\hat{k}$
(c) Both (a) and (b) are true
(d) Both (a) and (b) are false

12 If $\mathbf{a} = \hat{i} - 7\hat{j} + 7\hat{k}$ and $\mathbf{b} = 3\hat{i} - 2\hat{j} + 2\hat{k}$, then $|\mathbf{a} \times \mathbf{b}| = ?$ NCERT Pg. 368
(a) $19\sqrt{3}$ (b) $\sqrt{3}$
(c) $19\sqrt{2}$ (d) $20\sqrt{3}$

13 If $\mathbf{a} = 3\hat{i} + 2\hat{j} + 2\hat{k}$ and $\mathbf{b} = \hat{i} + 2\hat{j} - 2\hat{k}$, then the unit vector perpendicular to each of the vector $\mathbf{a} + \mathbf{b}$ and $\mathbf{a} - \mathbf{b}$ are NCERT Pg. 368
(a) $\pm\frac{1}{3}(2\hat{i} - 2\hat{j} - \hat{k})$ (b) $\pm\frac{2}{3}\hat{i} \pm \frac{2}{3}\hat{j} \pm \frac{2}{3}\hat{k}$
(c) $\pm\frac{3}{2}\hat{i} \mp \frac{2}{3}\hat{j} \mp \frac{1}{3}\hat{k}$ (d) None of these

14 Cross product of $(\mathbf{a} - \mathbf{b}) \times (\mathbf{a} + \mathbf{b})$ is equal to NCERT Pg. 368
(a) $\frac{2}{3}(\mathbf{a} \times \mathbf{b})$ (b) $(\mathbf{a} \times \mathbf{b})$
(c) $2(\mathbf{a} \times \mathbf{b})$ (d) None of these

15 If $(2\hat{i} + 6\hat{j} + 27\hat{k}) \times (\hat{i} + \lambda\hat{j} + \mu\hat{k}) = \mathbf{0}$, then NCERT Pg. 368
(a) $\lambda = 3, \mu = 27$ (b) $\mu = \frac{27}{2}$ and $\lambda = 3$
(c) $\lambda = 27$ and $\mu = 3$ (d) $\lambda = 4$ and $\mu = 27$

16 If $\mathbf{a} \cdot \mathbf{b} = 0$ and $\mathbf{a} \times \mathbf{b} = \mathbf{0}$, then NCERT Pg. 368
(a) $|\mathbf{a}| = 0$ (b) $|\mathbf{b}| = 0$
(c) Both (a) and (b) are true (d) Either $|\mathbf{a}| = 0$ or $|\mathbf{b}| = 0$

17 The area of the triangle with vertices *A* (1,1,2,), *B* (2, 3, 5) and *C* (1,5,5) is NCERT Pg. 368
(a) $\frac{\sqrt{31}}{2}$ (b) $\frac{\sqrt{34}}{2}$ (c) $\frac{\sqrt{61}}{2}$ (d) $\frac{\sqrt{47}}{4}$

18 The area of the parallelogram whose adjacent sides are determined by the vectors $\mathbf{a} = \hat{i} - \hat{j} + 3\hat{k}$ and $\mathbf{b} = 2\hat{i} - 7\hat{j} + \hat{k}$ is NCERT Pg. 369
(a) $15\sqrt{3}$ (b) $15\sqrt{2}$ (c) $31\sqrt{2}$ (d) $34\sqrt{3}$

19 If the vectors **a** and **b** be such that $|\mathbf{a}| = 3$ and $|\mathbf{b}| = \frac{\sqrt{2}}{3}$, then $\mathbf{a} \times \mathbf{b}$ is a unit vector, if the angle between **a** and **b** is NCERT Pg. 369
(a) $\frac{\pi}{6}$ (b) $\frac{\pi}{4}$ (c) $\frac{\pi}{3}$ (d) $\frac{\pi}{2}$

20 Area of a rectangle having vertices *A*, *B*, *C* and *D* with position vectors $-\hat{i} + \frac{1}{2}\hat{j} + 4\hat{k}$, $\hat{i} + \frac{1}{2}\hat{j} + 4\hat{k}$, $\hat{i} - \frac{1}{2}\hat{j} + 4\hat{k}$ and $-\hat{i} - \frac{1}{2}\hat{j} + 4\hat{k}$ respectively, is NCERT Pg. 369
(a) $\frac{1}{2}$ (b) 1 (c) 2 (d) 4

Level II

21 The unit vector perpendicular to the vectors $\hat{i}-\hat{j}$ and $\hat{i}+\hat{j}$ forming a right handed system is NCERT Exemplar Pg. 214

(a) $\hat{k}$ (b) $-2\hat{k}$

(c) $\frac{\hat{i}-\hat{j}}{\sqrt{2}}$ (d) $\frac{\hat{i}+\hat{j}}{\sqrt{2}}$

22 The moment about the point $\hat{i}+2\hat{j}+3\hat{k}$ of a force represented by $\hat{i}+\hat{j}+\hat{k}$ acting through the point $2\hat{i}+3\hat{j}+\hat{k}$ is NCERT Pg. 362

(a) $3\hat{i}+3\hat{j}$ (b) $3\hat{i}+\hat{j}$

(c) $-\hat{i}+\hat{j}$ (d) $3\hat{i}-3\hat{j}$

23 If **a**, **b**, **c**, be three vectors such that $\mathbf{a}+\mathbf{b}+\mathbf{c}=\mathbf{0}$, then $\mathbf{a}\times\mathbf{b}=\mathbf{b}\times\mathbf{c}=\mathbf{c}\times\mathbf{a}$ and its deduction is NCERT Exemplar Pg. 215

(a) sine rule (b) cosine rule

(c) Both (a) and (b) (d) None of these

24 If $\mathbf{a}\times\mathbf{b}=\mathbf{c}\times\mathbf{d}$ and $\mathbf{a}\times\mathbf{c}=\mathbf{b}\times\mathbf{d}$, then $\mathbf{a}-\mathbf{d}$ ($\mathbf{a}\neq\mathbf{d}$ and $\mathbf{b}\neq\mathbf{c}$) is, parallel to NCERT Pg. 362

(a) $\mathbf{b}-\mathbf{c}$ (b) $\mathbf{c}+\mathbf{a}$

(c) $\mathbf{c}+\mathbf{b}$ (d) None of these

25 The moment of the couple consisting of the force $\mathbf{F}=3\hat{i}+2\hat{j}-\hat{k}$ acting through the point $\hat{i}-\hat{j}+\hat{k}$ and $-\mathbf{F}$ acting through the point $2\hat{i}-3\hat{j}-\hat{k}$ is NCERT Pg. 362

(a) $\sqrt{5}$ (b) $5\sqrt{5}$

(c) $\sqrt{51}$ (d) None of these

26 Let $\mathbf{u}=\hat{i}+\hat{j}$, $\mathbf{v}=\hat{i}-\hat{j}$ and $\mathbf{w}=\hat{i}+2\hat{j}+3\hat{k}$. If $\hat{\mathbf{n}}$ is a unit vector such that $\mathbf{u}\cdot\hat{\mathbf{n}}=\mathbf{0}$ and $\mathbf{v}\cdot\hat{\mathbf{n}}=0$, then $|\mathbf{w}\cdot\mathbf{n}|$ is equal to NCERT Pg. 363

(a) 3 (b) 0 (c) 1 (d) 2

27 A unit vector **d** is equally inclined at an angle α with the vectors $\mathbf{a}=\cos\theta\cdot\hat{i}+\sin\theta\cdot\hat{j}$, $\mathbf{b}=-\sin\theta\cdot\hat{i}+\cos\theta\cdot\hat{j}$ and $\mathbf{c}=\hat{k}$. Then, α is equal to NCERT Pg. 363

(a) $\cos^{-1}\frac{1}{\sqrt{2}}$ (b) $\cos^{-1}\frac{1}{\sqrt{3}}$

(c) $\cos^{-1}\frac{1}{3}$ (d) $\frac{\pi}{2}$

Miscellaneous Exercise

1 If all the unit vectors in *xy*-plane is written as **r**, then **r** is equal to NCERT Pg. 369

(a) $\cos\theta\hat{i}+\sin\theta\hat{j}$ (b) $\sin\theta\hat{i}+\cos\theta\hat{j}$

(c) $\cos\theta\hat{i}-\sin\theta\hat{j}$ (d) $\sin\theta\hat{i}-\cos\theta\hat{j}$

2 If **a**, **b** and **c** be three vectors such that $|\mathbf{a}|=3$, $|\mathbf{a}|=4$, $|\mathbf{c}|=5$ and each one of them being perpendicular to the sum of the other two, then $|\mathbf{a}+\mathbf{b}+\mathbf{c}|$ is equal to NCERT Pg. 370

(a) 5 (b) $\sqrt{2}$ (c) 3 (d) $5\sqrt{2}$

3 Three vectors **a**, **b** and **c** are such that $\mathbf{a}+\mathbf{b}+\mathbf{c}=0$.

If $|\mathbf{a}|=1$, $|\mathbf{b}|=4$ and $|\mathbf{c}|=2$ and $\mu=\mathbf{a}\cdot\mathbf{b}+\mathbf{b}\cdot\mathbf{c}+\mathbf{c}\cdot\mathbf{a}$, then the value of μ is equal to NCERT Pg. 371

(a) 21 (b) $\frac{-21}{2}$

(c) $\frac{-11}{2}$ (d) -11

4 With reference to the right handed system of mutually perpendicular unit vectors $\hat{i}$, $\hat{j}$ and $\hat{k}$. It is given that $\alpha=3\hat{i}-\hat{j}$, $\beta=2\hat{i}+\hat{j}-3\hat{k}$.

If $\beta=\beta_1+\beta_2$, where β_1 is parallel to α and β_2 is perpendicular to α, then β_1 and β_2 are respectively NCERT Pg. 371

(a) $\frac{1}{2}\hat{i}+\frac{3}{2}\hat{j}-3\hat{k}$ and $\frac{3}{2}\hat{i}-\frac{1}{2}\hat{j}$

(b) $\frac{3}{2}\hat{i}-\frac{1}{2}\hat{j}$ and $\frac{1}{2}\hat{i}+\frac{3}{2}\hat{j}-3\hat{k}$

(c) $\hat{i}+\frac{1}{2}\hat{j}$ and $\hat{i}+\frac{1}{2}\hat{j}-3\hat{k}$

(d) $\hat{i}+\frac{1}{2}\hat{j}-3\hat{k}$ and $\hat{i}+\frac{1}{2}\hat{j}$

5 The unit vector in *xy*-plane, making an angle of 30° is anticlockwise direction with the positive direction of *X*-axis, is NCERT Pg. 372

(a) $\frac{1}{2}\hat{i}+\frac{\sqrt{3}}{2}\hat{j}$ (b) $\frac{1}{2}\hat{i}+\frac{2}{\sqrt{3}}\hat{j}$

(c) $\frac{\sqrt{3}}{2}\hat{i}+\frac{1}{2}\hat{j}$ (d) None of these

6 Magnitude of the vector joining the points $P(x_1, y_1, z_1)$ and $Q(x_2, y_2, z_2)$ is NCERT Pg. 372

(a) $(x_2-x_1)+(y_2-y_1)+(z_2-z_1)$

(b) $(x_2+y_2+z_2)(x_1+y_1+z_1)$

(c) $\sqrt{(x_2-x_1)^2+(y_2-y_1)^2}$

(d) None of the above

7 A girl walks 4 km towards West. Then, she walks 3 km in a direction 30° East to North and stops. The girls displacement from her initial point of departure is NCERT Pg. 372

(a) $-\frac{3}{2}\hat{i}+\frac{3\sqrt{3}}{2}\hat{j}$ (b) $-\frac{5}{2}\hat{i}+\frac{3}{2}\hat{j}$

(c) $-\frac{5}{2}\hat{i}+\frac{3\sqrt{3}}{2}\hat{j}$ (d) None of these

8 The value of *x*, for which $\mathbf{x}(\hat{i}+\hat{j}+\hat{k})$ is a unit vector, is NCERT Pg. 372

(a) $\pm\sqrt{3}$ (b) $\pm\sqrt{2}$ (c) $\pm\frac{1}{\sqrt{2}}$ (d) $\pm\frac{1}{\sqrt{3}}$

9 A vector having its magnitude 5 units and parallel to the resultant of the vectors $\mathbf{a}=2\hat{i}+3\hat{j}-\hat{k}$ and $\mathbf{b}=\hat{i}-2\hat{j}+\hat{k}$, is NCERT Pg. 372

(a) $\pm\frac{\sqrt{10}}{2}\hat{i}+\frac{3\sqrt{10}}{2}\hat{j}$ (b) $\pm\frac{3\sqrt{10}}{2}\hat{i}\pm\frac{\sqrt{10}}{2}\hat{j}$

(c) $\pm\frac{3\sqrt{10}}{2}\hat{i}\mp\frac{\sqrt{10}}{2}\hat{j}$ (d) None of these

10 If $\mathbf{a}=\hat{i}+\hat{j}+\hat{k}$, $\mathbf{b}=2\hat{i}-\hat{j}+3\hat{k}$ and $\mathbf{c}=\hat{i}-2\hat{j}+\hat{k}$, then the unit vector parallel to the vector $2\mathbf{a}-\mathbf{b}+3\mathbf{c}$ is **NCERT Pg. 372**

(a) $\frac{3}{\sqrt{21}}\hat{i}-\frac{3}{\sqrt{21}}\hat{j}-\frac{2}{\sqrt{21}}\hat{k}$ (b) $\frac{3}{\sqrt{22}}\hat{i}+\frac{3}{\sqrt{22}}\hat{j}+\frac{2}{\sqrt{22}}\hat{k}$

(c) $\frac{3}{\sqrt{22}}\hat{i}-\frac{3}{\sqrt{22}}\hat{j}+\frac{2}{\sqrt{22}}\hat{k}$ (d) None of these

11 If θ be the angle between two vectors **a** and **b**, then $\mathbf{a}\cdot\mathbf{b}\geq\mathbf{0}$ only when **NCERT Pg. 372**

(a) $0<\theta<\frac{\pi}{2}$ (b) $0\leq\theta\leq\frac{\pi}{2}$

(c) $0\leq\theta\leq\pi$ (d) $0\leq\theta\leq\pi$

12 If **a** and **b** be two unit vectors and θ is the angle between them, then $\mathbf{a}+\mathbf{b}$ is a unit vector, if **NCERT Pg. 373**

(a) $\theta=\frac{\pi}{4}$ (b) $\theta=\frac{\pi}{3}$

(c) $\theta=\frac{\pi}{2}$ (d) $\theta=\frac{2\pi}{3}$

13 The value of $\hat{i}\cdot(\hat{j}\times\hat{k})+\hat{j}\cdot(\hat{k}\times\hat{i})+\hat{k}\cdot(\hat{i}\times\hat{j})$ is **NCERT Pg. 373**

(a) zero (b) –1

(c) 1 (d) 3

14 The direction cosines of a vector equally inclined to the axes *OX*, *OY* and *OZ* are **NCERT Pg. 372**

(a) $\frac{1}{\sqrt{3}},\frac{1}{\sqrt{3}},\frac{1}{\sqrt{3}}$ (b) $\frac{1}{\sqrt{2}},\frac{1}{\sqrt{2}},\frac{1}{\sqrt{2}}$

(c) 1, 1, 1 (d) None of these

15 If $\mathbf{a}=\hat{i}+4\hat{j}+2\hat{k}$, $\mathbf{b}=3\hat{i}-2\hat{j}+7\hat{k}$ and $\mathbf{c}=2\hat{i}-\hat{j}+4\hat{k}$, then a vector **d** which is perpendicular to both **a** and **b**, and $\mathbf{c}\cdot\mathbf{d}=15$, is **NCERT Pg. 372**

(a) $\frac{1}{3}[160\hat{i}+5\hat{j}+70\hat{k}]$ (b) $\frac{2}{3}[32\hat{i}-\hat{j}-14\hat{k}]$

(c) $\frac{1}{3}[160\hat{i}-5\hat{j}-70\hat{k}]$ (d) None of these

16 If θ is the angle between any two vectors **a** and **b**, then $|\mathbf{a}\cdot\mathbf{b}|=|\mathbf{a}\times\mathbf{b}|$, when θ is equal to **NCERT Pg. 373**

(a) zero (b) $\frac{\pi}{4}$ (c) $\frac{\pi}{2}$ (d) π

17 If the scalar product of the vector $\hat{i}+\hat{j}+\hat{k}$ with a unit vector along the sum of vectors $2\hat{i}+4\hat{j}-5\hat{k}$ and $\lambda\hat{i}+2\hat{j}+3\hat{k}$ is equal to one then the value of λ is **NCERT Pg. 372**

(a) 0 (b) –1

(c) $\frac{1}{2}$ (d) None of these

18 If $(\mathbf{a}+\mathbf{b})\cdot(\mathbf{a}+\mathbf{b})=|\mathbf{a}|^2+|\mathbf{b}|^2$ given $\mathbf{a}\neq\mathbf{0},\mathbf{b}\neq\mathbf{0}$, then

(a) **a**, **b** are perpendicular

(b) **a**, **b** are parallel

(c) **a** and **b** are either parallel or perpendicular

(d) $\mathbf{a}=2\mathbf{b}$ **NCERT Pg. 373**

Numerical Type Questions

1 Let **a**, **b** and **c** are non-zero vectors such that $\mathbf{a}=2\mathbf{b}$ and $\mathbf{c}=-5\mathbf{b}$. If the angle between **a** and **c** is α then $\frac{\alpha}{\pi}$ is .... **NCERT Pg. 356**

2 If $\mathbf{A}=(\mu+2)\,\mathbf{a}+\mathbf{b}$ and $\mathbf{B}=(2\mu-1)\,\mathbf{a}+\mathbf{b}$ be two given vector where **a** and **b** are non-collinear. Then, for what value of μ vector **A** and **B** are collinear is .... **NCERT Pg. 341**

3 In ΔABC, if $|\mathbf{AB}|=5$ and $|\mathbf{BC}|=3$ and $|\mathbf{AC}|=4$. Then the projection of the vector **AB** on **BC** is equal to .... **NCERT Pg. 357**

4 Let **a** and **b** be two vectors such that $|2\mathbf{a}+3\mathbf{b}|=|3\mathbf{a}+\mathbf{b}|$ and the angle between **a** and **b** is 60°. If $\frac{a}{8}$ is a unit vector, then $|\mathbf{b}|$ is .... **NCERT Pg. 355**

5 Let **a**, **b** and **c** be three vectors such that $|\mathbf{a}|=4$, $|\mathbf{b}|=5$ and $|\mathbf{c}|=2$ and each one of them being perpendicular to the sum of the other two, find $\frac{|\mathbf{a}+\mathbf{b}+\mathbf{c}|}{\sqrt{5}}$ is .... **NCERT Pg. 356**

6 If $\mathbf{a}=3\hat{i}+2\hat{j}+\hat{k}$ and $\mathbf{b}=8\hat{i}+3\hat{j}+4\hat{k}$ and **c** be a vector such that $(2\mathbf{a}+\mathbf{b})\times\mathbf{c}=\mathbf{c}\times(\mathbf{a}+2\mathbf{b})$ and $(3\mathbf{a}+2\mathbf{b})\cdot\mathbf{c}=1170$, then $|\mathbf{c}|^2$ is equal to .... **NCERT Pg. 362**

7 If $\mathbf{a}=3\hat{i}+\hat{j}+\hat{k}$ and $\mathbf{b}=-\hat{i}+2\hat{j}+3\hat{k}$ and $\mathbf{c}=3\hat{i}-2\hat{j}+\hat{k}$. Such that $\mathbf{r}\times\mathbf{a}+\mathbf{a}\times\mathbf{c}=0$ and $\mathbf{r}\cdot\mathbf{b}=0$ then $|\mathbf{r}\cdot\mathbf{c}|$ is .... **NCERT Pg. 355, 362**

8 If $|\mathbf{a}|=3$, $|\mathbf{b}|=4$ and $|\mathbf{a}\cdot\mathbf{b}|=6$, then $|\mathbf{a}\times\mathbf{b}|^2$ is equal to .... **NCERT Exemplar Pg. 219**

Assertion and Reason Questions

Direction (Q. Nos. 1-8) The following questions consist of two statements, one labelled as "Assertion (A) and the other labelled as Reason (R)". You are to examine these two statements carefully and decide if Assertion (A) and Reason (R) are individually true and the Reason (R) is the correct explanation a for the given Assertion (A). Select your answer from following options.

(a) Both Assertion and Reason are correct and Reason is the correct explanation of Assertion.
(b) Both Assertion and Reason are correct but Reason is not the correct explanation of Assertion.
(c) Assertion is correct but Reason is incorrect.
(d) Reason is correct but Assertion is incorrect.

1 Assertion (A) The vectors $2\hat{i}-3\hat{j}+4\hat{k}$ and $-4\hat{i}+6\hat{j}-8\hat{k}$ are collinear.

Reason (R) Two vectors are collinear, if they are parallel to the same line, irrespective of their magnitude and directions. **NCERT Pg. 341**

2 Assertion (A) The points *A*, *B* and *C* with position vectors, $\mathbf{a}=3\hat{i}-4\hat{j}-4\hat{k}$, $\mathbf{b}=2\hat{i}-\hat{j}+\hat{k}$ and $\mathbf{c}=\hat{i}-3\hat{j}-5\hat{j}$ respectively, form the vertices of a right angled triangle.

Reason (R) Three points *A*, *B* and *C* form a right angled triangle, then sum of squares of magnitudes of any two vectors (corresponding to sides) equals to square of magnitude of third vector (corresponding to the third side). **NCERT Pg. 341**

3 Assertion (A) Scalar product is commutative.

Reason (R) $\mathbf{a}\cdot\mathbf{b}=|\mathbf{a}||\mathbf{b}|\cos\theta$. **NCERT Pg. 356**

4 Assertion (A) The projection of the vector $\mathbf{a}=2\hat{i}+3\hat{j}+2\hat{k}$ on the vector $\mathbf{b}=\hat{i}+2\hat{j}+\hat{k}$ is $\frac{5}{3}\sqrt{6}$.

Reason (R) The projection of vector **a** on vector **b** is $\frac{1}{|\mathbf{a}|}(\mathbf{a}\cdot\mathbf{b})$. **NCERT Pg. 357**

5 Assertion (A) The projection of the vector $\hat{i}+3\hat{j}+7\hat{k}$ on the vector $7\hat{i}-\hat{j}+8\hat{k}$ is $\frac{60}{\sqrt{114}}$.

Reason (R) The projection of vector **a** on **b** is $\frac{\mathbf{a}\cdot\mathbf{b}}{|\mathbf{b}|}$. **NCERT Pg. 358**

6 Assertion (A) $\mathbf{a}\times\mathbf{b}=-\mathbf{b}\times\mathbf{a}$ i.e. vector product is not commutative.

Reason (R) If we assume **a** and **b** to lie in the plane of the paper and If $\mathbf{a}\times\mathbf{b}=|\mathbf{a}||\mathbf{b}|\sin\theta\,\hat{n}$, $\mathbf{b}\times\mathbf{a}=|\mathbf{b}||\mathbf{a}|\sin\theta\,\hat{n}$, then $\hat{n}$ and $\hat{n}_1$ both will be parallel to the plane of paper. **NCERT Pg. 364**

7 Assertion (A) If adjacent sides of a parallelogram are given by the vectors.

$\mathbf{a}=3\hat{i}+\hat{j}+4\hat{k}$ and $\mathbf{b}=\hat{i}-\hat{j}+\hat{k}$, then the area of the parallelogram is $\sqrt{43}$.

Reason (R) The area of a parallelogram with **a** and **b** as its adjacent sides is $|\mathbf{a}\times\mathbf{b}|$. **NCERT Pg. 365**

Case or Paragraph Type Questions

Direction (Q. Nos. 1-4) Consider the figure (regular hexagon) given below

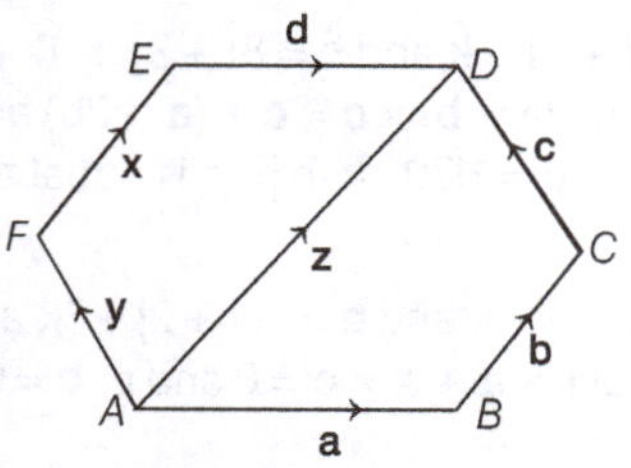

Based on above figure, answer the following questions. **NCERT Pg. 341**

1 Example of collinear vectors are

(a) a, d (b) b, x, z
(c) c, y (d) All of these

2 Which of the following is not an example of equal vectors?

(a) b, x (b) a, d (c) c, y (d) a, c

3 From the figure, coinitial vectors are

(a) a, y, z
(b) x, d
(c) Both (a) and (b) are true
(d) Both (a) and (b) are false

4 Which among the following is example of collinear vectors but not equal vectors?

(a) b, z
(b) x, z
(c) Both (a) and (b) are true
(d) Both (a) and (b) are false

Direction (Q. Nos. 5-7) Ram purchased an air plant holder which is in the shape of tetrahedron.

Let P, Q, R, and S are the coordinates of the air plant holder where $P=(2,2,2)$, $Q=(1,2,3)$, $R=(3,2,1)$ and $S=(2,3,4)$.

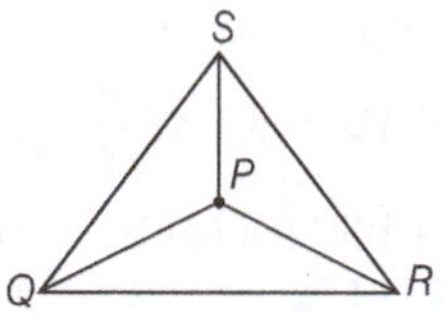

Based on the above information, answer the following questions. NCERT Pg. 339, 341

5 Find the position vector of **PQ**.
(a) $-\hat{i}+\hat{k}$ (b) $-\hat{i}-\hat{k}$
(c) $\hat{j}+\hat{k}$ (d) $-\hat{i}-\hat{j}$

6 Find the magnitude of **PR**.
(a) $\sqrt{3}$ (b) $\sqrt{2}$ (c) $\frac{1}{\sqrt{2}}$ (d) $2\sqrt{2}$

7 Find the unit vector along **PS**.
(a) $\frac{\hat{i}+2\hat{k}}{\sqrt{5}}$ (b) $\frac{\hat{j}+\hat{k}}{\sqrt{2}}$
(c) $\frac{\hat{j}+2\hat{k}}{\sqrt{5}}$ (d) $\frac{2\hat{j}+\hat{k}}{\sqrt{5}}$

Past Years Questions

Single Correct Type

1 Let **a**, **b** and **c** be three non-zero vectors such that **b** and **c** are non-collinear. If **a** + 5**b** is collinear with **c**, **b** + 6**c** is collinear with **a** and $\mathbf{a}+\alpha\mathbf{b}+\beta\mathbf{c}=\mathbf{0}$, then $\alpha+\beta$ is equal to NCERT Pg. 341, JEE Main 2024, 29 Jan Shift-I
(a) −25 (b) 35
(c) 30 (d) −30

2 Let O be the origin and the position vectors of A and B be $2\hat{i}+2\hat{j}+\hat{k}$ and $2\hat{i}+4\hat{j}+4\hat{k}$, respectively. If the internal bisector of $\angle AOB$ meets the line AB at C, then the length of OC is NCERT Pg. 352, JEE Main 2024, 29 Jan Shift-I
(a) $\frac{3}{2}\sqrt{34}$ (b) $\frac{2}{3}\sqrt{34}$
(c) $\frac{3}{2}\sqrt{31}$ (d) $\frac{2}{3}\sqrt{31}$

3 The position vectors of the vertices A, B and C of a triangle are $2\hat{i}-3\hat{j}+3\hat{k}$, $2\hat{i}+2\hat{j}+3\hat{k}$ and $-\hat{i}+\hat{j}+3\hat{k}$, respectively. Let l denotes the length of the angle bisector AD of $\angle BAC$, where D is on the line segment BC, then $2l^2$ equals NCERT Pg. 352, JEE Main 2024, 27 Jan Shift-II
(a) 49 (b) 42 (c) 45 (d) 50

4 Let the position vectors of the vertices A, B and C of a triangle be $2\hat{i}+2\hat{j}+\hat{k}$, $\hat{i}+2\hat{j}+2\hat{k}$ and $2\hat{i}+\hat{j}+2\hat{k}$, respectively. Let l_1, l_2 and l_3 be the lengths of perpendiculars drawn from the orthocenter of the triangle on the sides AB, BC and CA respectively, then $l_1^2+l_2^2+l_3^2$ equals NCERT Pg. 351, JEE Main 2024, 27 Jan Shift-II
(a) $\frac{1}{5}$ (b) $\frac{1}{4}$ (c) $\frac{1}{3}$ (d) $\frac{1}{2}$

5 Let $ABCD$ be a quadrilateral. If E and F are the mid-points of the diagonals AC and BD respectively and $(\mathbf{AB}-\mathbf{BC})+(\mathbf{AD}-\mathbf{DC})=k\mathbf{FE}$, then k is equal to NCERT Pg. 353, JEE Main 2023, 15 April Shift-I
(a) 4 (b) −4 (c) −2 (d) 2

6 For any vector $\mathbf{a}=a_1\hat{i}+a_2\hat{j}+a_3\hat{k}$, with $10|a_i|<1$, $i=1,2,3$, consider the following statements
(A) $\max\{|a_1|,|a_2|,|a_3|\}\le|\mathbf{a}|$
(B) $|\mathbf{a}|\le 3\max\{|a_1|,|a_2|,|a_3|\}$
NCERT Pg. 360, JEE Main 2023, 11 April Shift-I
(a) Neither (A) nor (B) is true
(b) Both (A) and (B) are true
(c) Only (B) is true
(d) Only (A) is true

7 If the points P and Q are respectively the circumcenter and the orthocentre of a ΔABC, then **PA** + **PB** + **PC** is equal to NCERT Pg. 353, JEE Main 2023, 10 April Shift-II
(a) **PQ** (b) 2 **QP**
(b) **QP** (d) 2 **PQ**

8 Let $\mathbf{a}=\hat{i}+\hat{j}+2\hat{k}$, $\mathbf{b}=2\hat{i}-3\hat{j}+\hat{k}$ and $\mathbf{c}=\hat{i}-\hat{j}+\hat{k}$ be three given vectors. Let **v** be a vector in the plane of **a** and **b** whose projection on **c** is $\frac{2}{\sqrt{3}}$, if $\mathbf{v}\cdot\hat{j}=7$, then $\mathbf{v}\cdot(\hat{i}+\hat{k})$ is equal to
NCERT Pg. 352, JEE Main 2022, 26 June Shift-II
(a) 6 (b) 7 (c) 8 (d) 9

9 If $(\mathbf{a}-\mathbf{b})\cdot(\mathbf{a}+\mathbf{b})=27$ and $|\mathbf{a}|=2|\mathbf{b}|$, then $|\mathbf{b}|$ is
NCERT Pg. 362, CUET 2024, 16 May
(a) 3 (b) 2 (c) $\frac{5}{6}$ (d) 6

10 The unit vector perpendicular to each of the vectors **a** + **b** and **a** − **b**, where $\mathbf{a}=\hat{i}+\hat{j}+\hat{k}$ and $\mathbf{b}=\hat{i}+2\hat{j}+3\hat{k}$ is
NCERT Pg. 367, CUET 2024, 16 May
(a) $\frac{1}{\sqrt{6}}\hat{i}+\frac{2}{\sqrt{6}}\hat{j}+\frac{1}{\sqrt{6}}\hat{k}$ (b) $-\frac{1}{\sqrt{6}}\hat{i}+\frac{1}{\sqrt{6}}\hat{j}-\frac{1}{\sqrt{6}}\hat{k}$
(c) $-\frac{1}{\sqrt{6}}\hat{i}+\frac{2}{\sqrt{6}}\hat{j}+\frac{2}{\sqrt{6}}\hat{k}$ (d) $-\frac{1}{\sqrt{6}}\hat{i}+\frac{2}{\sqrt{6}}\hat{j}-\frac{1}{\sqrt{6}}\hat{k}$

Numerical Value Type

11 The least positive integral value of α, for which the angle between the vectors $\alpha\hat{i} - 2\hat{j} + 2\hat{k}$ and $\alpha\hat{i} + 2\alpha\hat{j} - 2\hat{k}$ is acute, is ....
NCERT Pg. 356, JEE Main 2024, 27 Jan Shift-I

12 Let $\mathbf{a} = 9\hat{i} - 13\hat{j} + 25\hat{k}$, $\mathbf{b} = 3\hat{i} + 7\hat{j} - 13\hat{k}$ and $\mathbf{c} = 17\hat{i} - 2\hat{j} + \hat{k}$ be three given vectors. If $\mathbf{r}$ is a vector such that $\mathbf{r} \times \mathbf{a} = (\mathbf{b} \times \mathbf{c}) \times \mathbf{a}$ and $\mathbf{r} \cdot (\mathbf{b} - \mathbf{c}) = 0$, then $\dfrac{|593\mathbf{r} + 67\mathbf{a}|^2}{(593)^2}$ is equal to ....
NCERT Pg. 362, JEE Main 2024, 8 April Shift-I

13 Let $\mathbf{a} = \hat{i} + 2\hat{j} + 3\hat{k}$ and $\mathbf{b} = \hat{i} + \hat{j} - \hat{k}$. If $\mathbf{c}$ is a vector such that $\mathbf{a} \cdot \mathbf{c} = 11$, $\mathbf{b} \cdot (\mathbf{a} \times \mathbf{c}) = 27$ and $\mathbf{b} \cdot \mathbf{c} = -\sqrt{3}|\mathbf{b}|$, then $|\mathbf{a} \times \mathbf{c}|^2$ is equal to ....
NCERT Pg. 355, 362 JEE Main 2023, 11 April Shift-II

14 Let θ be the angle between the vectors $\mathbf{a}$ and $\mathbf{b}$ where $|\mathbf{a}| = 4$, $|\mathbf{b}| = 3$, $\theta \in \left(\dfrac{\pi}{4}, \dfrac{\pi}{3}\right)$. Then, $|(\mathbf{a} - \mathbf{b}) \times (\mathbf{a} + \mathbf{b})|^2 + 4(\mathbf{a} \cdot \mathbf{b})^2$ is equal to ....
NCERT Pg. 355, 362 JEE Main 2022, 25 June Shift-I

Skill Boosters

1 Let $|\mathbf{a}| = 3$ and $|\mathbf{b}| = 4$ and the angle between the vectors $\mathbf{a}$ and $\mathbf{b}$ be $\dfrac{\pi}{2}$. Then, $|(\mathbf{a} + 2\mathbf{b}) \times (\mathbf{a} - \mathbf{b})|^2$ is equal to
(a) 1296 (b) 1180
(c) 1298 (d) 1294

2 Let $\mathbf{a} = 2\hat{i} + 3\hat{j} + \hat{k}$ and $\mathbf{b} = \hat{i} + 3\hat{j} - 4\hat{k}$ be two vectors. If a vector perpendicular to both the vectors $\mathbf{a} + \mathbf{b}$ and $\mathbf{a} - \mathbf{b}$ has the magnitude $2\sqrt{35}$, then one such vector is
(a) $3(5\hat{i} - 3\hat{j} + \hat{k})$ (b) $3(5\hat{i} - 3\hat{j} - \hat{k})$
(c) $2(5\hat{i} - 3\hat{j} - \hat{k})$ (d) $2(5\hat{i} - 3\hat{j} + \hat{k})$

3 If $\mathbf{a}$ and $\mathbf{b}$ are unit vectors and θ is the acute angle between them, then $3\mathbf{a} \times 2\mathbf{b}$ is a unit vector for
(a) Exactly two values of θ
(b) More than two values of θ
(c) No value of θ
(d) Exactly one value of θ

4 In cartesian co-ordinates the point P is (a_1, b_1) where $a_1 = 2$ on the curve $y = x^2 + x$. The tangent at P cuts the X-axis at θ. the value of $\mathbf{OP} \cdot \mathbf{PQ}$ is
(a) −41 (b) −42 (c) 40 (d) 42

5 If $\mathbf{a} + \mathbf{b} + \mathbf{c} = 0$, $|\mathbf{a}| = 3$, $|\mathbf{b}| = 5$ and $|\mathbf{c}| = 7$ find the angle between $\mathbf{a}$ and $\mathbf{c}$
(a) $\cos^{-1}\left(\dfrac{14}{11}\right)$ (b) $\cos^{-1}\left(\dfrac{11}{12}\right)$
(c) $\cos^{-1}\left(\dfrac{12}{11}\right)$ (d) $\cos^{-1}\left(\dfrac{11}{14}\right)$

6 Let $\mathbf{a} = 3\hat{i} + \alpha\hat{j} + 2\hat{k}$, $\mathbf{b} = 3\hat{i} + 2\hat{j} + \beta\hat{k}$ and $\mathbf{c} = \hat{i} + 3\hat{j} + 3\hat{k}$ where $\alpha, \beta \in R$, be three vectors. If the projection of $\mathbf{a}$ on $\mathbf{c}$ is $\dfrac{12}{\sqrt{19}}$ and $\mathbf{b} \times \mathbf{c} = -12\hat{i} - 3\hat{j} + 7\hat{k}$, then the value of $\alpha \cdot \beta$ is
(a) 2 (b) 6 (c) 4 (d) 3

Correct Codes

Topical Questions

Some Basic Concepts and Types of Vectors

1 (d)	2 (d)	3 (d)	4 (a)	5 (d)	6 (a)	7 (a)	8 (a)	9 (d)	10 (a)
11 (b)									

Addition of Vectors and Multiplication of a Vector by a Scalar

1 (c)	2 (c)	3 (c)	4 (b)	5 (a)	6 (c)	7 (c)	8 (c)	9 (d)	10 (d)
11 (c)	12 (c)	13 (d)	14 (b)	15 (a)	16 (d)	17 (c)	18 (a)	19 (b)	20 (a)
21 (d)	22 (b)	23 (c)	24 (c)	25 (a)	26 (c)	27 (c)	28 (c)	29 (b)	30 (b)
31 (b)	32 (a)	33 (b)	34 (a)	35 (b)	36 (a)	37 (a)	38 (a)	39 (d)	40 (a)
41 (c)	42 (d)	43 (b)	44 (c)	45 (d)	46 (a)	47 (c)	48 (b)	49 (d)	50 (c)
51 (a)	52 (d)	53 (b)							

Scalar (or dot) Product of Two Vectors

1 (c)	2 (b)	3 (d)	4 (a)	5 (d)	6 (a)	7 (c)	8 (d)	9 (d)	10 (b)
11 (d)	12 (a)	13 (b)	14 (c)	15 (b)	16 (c)	17 (b)	18 (a)	19 (b)	20 (c)
21 (c)	22 (a)	23 (c)	24 (c)	25 (a)	26 (a)	27 (b)	28 (d)	29 (b)	30 (b)
31 (d)	32 (b)	33 (d)	34 (b)	35 (d)	36 (a)	37 (a)	38 (a)	39 (c)	40 (a)
41 (c)	42 (c)	43 (d)							

Vector (or cross) Product of Two Vectors

1 (a)	2 (b)	3 (b)	4 (b)	5 (d)	6 (a)	7 (c)	8 (c)	9 (c)	10 (d)
11 (c)	12 (c)	13 (a)	14 (c)	15 (b)	16 (d)	17 (c)	18 (b)	19 (b)	20 (c)
21 (a)	22 (d)	23 (a)	24 (a)	25 (b)	26 (a)	27 (b)			

Miscellaneous Exercise

1 (a)	2 (d)	3 (b)	4 (b)	5 (c)	6 (d)	7 (c)	8 (d)	9 (b)	10 (c)
11 (b)	12 (d)	13 (d)	14 (a)	15 (c)	16 (b)	17 (d)	18 (a)		

Numberical Type Questions

1 (1)	2 (3)	3 (4)	4 (5)	5 (3)	6 (1539)	7 (18)	8 (108)

Assertion and Reason Questions

1 (a)	2 (a)	3 (a)	4 (c)	5 (a)	6 (c)	7 (d)

Case or Paragraph Type Questions

1 (d)	2 (d)	3 (a)	4 (c)	5 (a)	6 (b)	7 (c)

Past Years Questions

1 (b)	2 (b)	3 (c)	4 (d)	5 (b)	6 (b)	7 (d)	8 (d)	9 (a)	10 (d)
11 (5)	12 (569)	13 (285)	14 (576)						

Skill Boosters

1 (a)	2 (c)	3 (d)	4 (b)	5 (d)	6 (b)

Step by Step

Decoding the Questions

Concept Builders

1 True

2 False

3 $\dfrac{\mathbf{a}\cdot\mathbf{b}}{|\mathbf{a}||\mathbf{b}|}$

4 Perpendicular

5 90°

6 $\sqrt{3}$

7 greater than

8 0

9 0

10 $-|\mathbf{a}||\mathbf{b}|$

11 0

12 $|\mathbf{a}||\mathbf{b}|\sin\theta\cdot\hat{\mathbf{n}}$

13 $(\mathbf{a}\cdot\mathbf{c})\,\mathbf{b}-(\mathbf{a}\cdot\mathbf{b})\,\mathbf{c}$

14 0

Topical Questions

Some Basic Concepts and Types of Vectors

1 (*d*) Given that l is any straight line in plane or three dimensional space. This line can be given two directions by means of arrowheads. A line with one of these directions prescribed is called a directed line [Fig (i), (ii)].

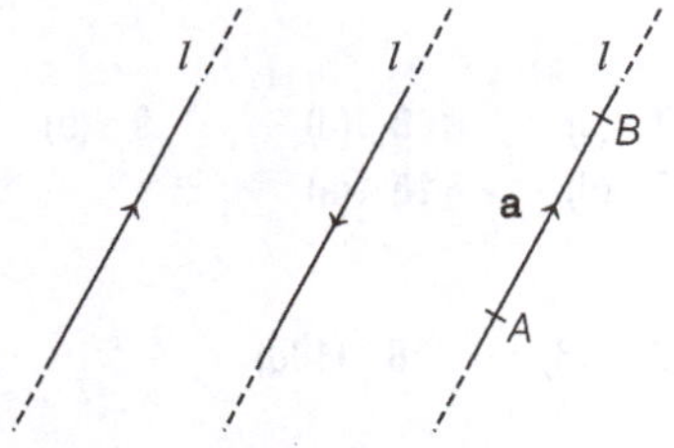

(i) (ii) (iii)

Now, observe that on restricting the line l to the line segment AB, a magnitude is prescribed on the line l with one of the two directions, so that we obtain a directed line segment [Fig (iii)]. Thus, a directed line segment has magnitude as well as direction.

So, all the given options are correct.

2 (*d*) We know that in three dimensional right handed rectangular coordinate systems [Fig. (i)], if a point P in space, having coordinates (x, y, z) with respect to the origin O (0, 0, 0). Then , the vector **OP** having O and P as its initial and terminal points, respectively, is called the position vector of the point P with respect to O. Using distance formula, the magnitude of **OP** (or **r**) is given by

$$|\mathbf{OP}|=\sqrt{x^2+y^2+z^2}$$

In practice, the position vectors of points A, B and C, etc., with respect to the origin O are denoted by **a**,**b** and **c** etc., respectively [Fig. (ii)].

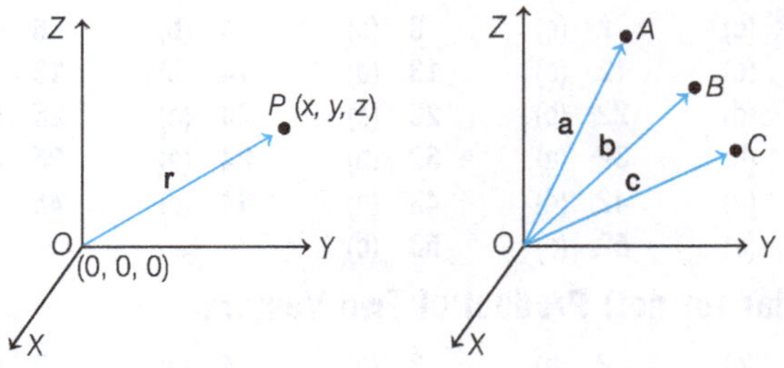

(i) (ii)

So, option (d) is correct.

3 (*d*) Consider the position vector **OP** or **r** of a point $P(x, y, z)$ as in given figure. The angles α, β and γ made by the vector **r** with the positive directions of x, y and z-axes respectively, are called its direction angles. The cosine values of these angles, i.e. $\cos\alpha$, $\cos\beta$ and $\cos\gamma$ are called its direction cosines of the vector **r** and usually denoted by l, m and n, respectively.

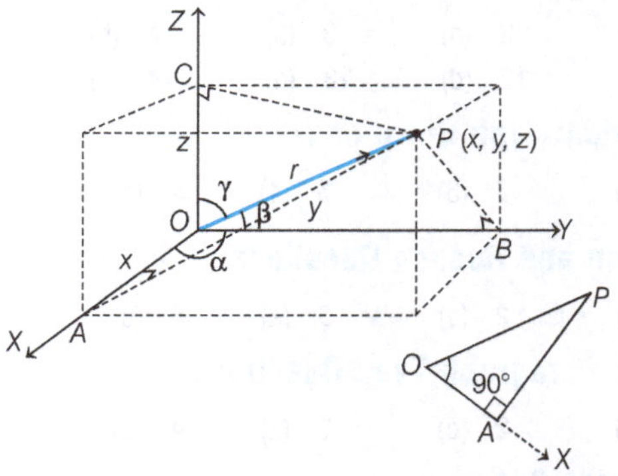

From the figure one may note that the ΔOAP is right angled, and in it we have $\cos\alpha=\dfrac{x}{r}$ (r stands for $|\mathbf{r}|$).

Similarly, from the right angled triangles OBP and OCP, we may write $\cos\beta=\dfrac{y}{r}$ and $\cos\gamma=\dfrac{z}{r}$.

Thus, the coordinates of the point P may also be expressed as (lr, mr, nr). The numbers lr, mr and nr, proportional to the direction cosines are called as direction ratios of vector **r** and denoted as a, b and c, respectively.

4 (*a*) $OP = |\mathbf{r}| \Rightarrow \sqrt{x^2 + y^2 + z^2} = |\mathbf{r}|$

$$\Rightarrow \quad x^2 + y^2 + z^2 = |\mathbf{r}|^2$$

$$\Rightarrow \quad l^2|\mathbf{r}|^2 + m^2|\mathbf{r}|^2 + n^2|\mathbf{r}|^2 = |\mathbf{r}|^2$$

$$[\because x = l|\mathbf{r}|, y = m|\mathbf{r}|, z = n|\mathbf{r}|]$$

$$\Rightarrow \quad l^2 + m^2 + n^2 = 1$$

Note $a^2 + b^2 + c^2 \neq 1$ *where a, b and c are direction ratios.*

5 (*d*) A vector, whose initial and terminal points coincide, is called a zero vector (or null vector) and denoted as **0**. Zero vector cannot be assigned a definite direction as it has zero magnitude or alternatively otherwise, it may be regarded as having any direction. The vectors **AA**, **BB** represent the zero vector.

6 (*a*) Two vectors **a** and **b** are said to be equal vectors, if they have the same magnitude and direction regardless of the positions of their initial points and written as **a** = **b**.

7 (*a*) A vector whose magnitude is the same as that of a given vector (say, **AB**), but direction is opposite to that of it, is called negative of the given vector.

e.g. vector **BA** is negative of the vector **AB** and written as **BA** = – **AB**.

8 (*a*)

(i) Vectors **a** and **d** are coinitial because they have the same initial point.

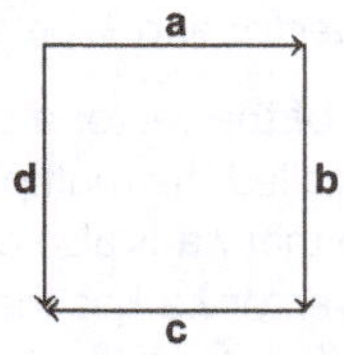

(ii) Vectors **b** and **d** are not coinitial vectors.

(iii) Vectors **a** and **c** are collinear but not equal. Although they are parallel, this is because their directions are not same.

9 (*d*) It two or more vectors are parallel to the same line, irrespective of their magnitudes and directions, are called cointial vectors.

10 (*a*) We know that, if two vectors have same magnitude, then they will be of opposite sign if they are in opposite direction, i.e. **A** = – **B**.

11 (*b*) Vectors, whose initial points are not specified, are called free vectors.

Addition of Vectors and Multiplication of a Vector by a Scalar

1 (*c*) A vector **AB** simply means the displacement from a point *A* to the point *B*.

2 (*c*) If a girl moves from *A* to *B* and then from *B* to *C* (see the fig.). The net displacement made by the girl from point *A* to the point *C*, is given by vector **AC** and expressed as **AC** = **AB** + **BC**.

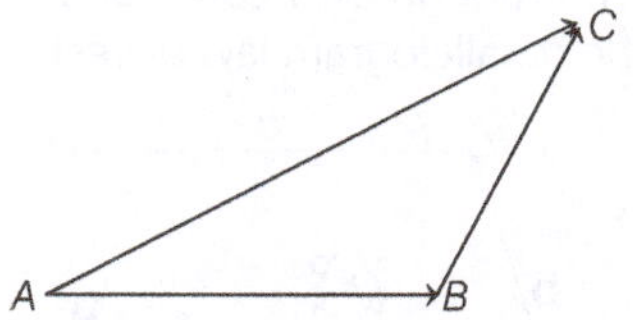

This is known as the triangle law of vector addition.

3 (*c*) If two vectors **a** and **b** are given [Fig. (i)], then to add them, they are positioned so that the initial point of one coincides with the terminal point of the other [(Fig. (ii)].

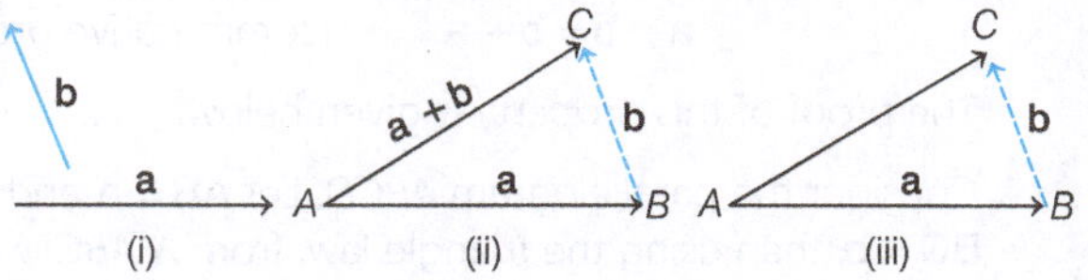

For example, in Fig. (ii), we have shifted vector b without changing its magnitude and direction, so that it's initial point coincides with the terminal point of **a**. Then the vector **a** + **b**, represented by the third side **AC** of the ΔABC, gives us the sum (or resultant) of the vectors **a** and **b** i.e. in ΔABC [Fig. (ii)], we have

$$\mathbf{AC} = \mathbf{AB} + \mathbf{BC}$$

Now again, since **AC** = – **CA** from the above equation, we have

$$\mathbf{AB} + \mathbf{BC} + \mathbf{CA} = \mathbf{AA} = 0$$

This means that when the sides of a triangle are taken in order, it leads to zero resultant as the initial and terminal points get coincides [Fig. (iii)].

4 (*b*) A vector **BC′** is given such that its magnitude is same as the vector **BC**, but its direction is opposite to that of it

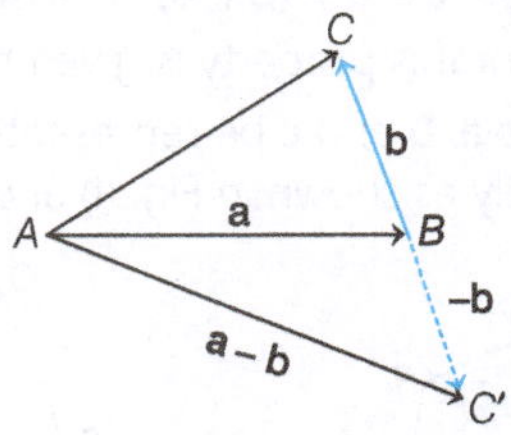

$$\mathbf{BC'} = -\,\mathbf{BC}$$

Then, on applying triangle law from the figure, we have

$$\mathbf{AC'} = \mathbf{AB} + \mathbf{BC'} = \mathbf{AB} + (-\,\mathbf{BC}) = \mathbf{a} - \mathbf{b}$$

The vector **AC′** is said to represent the difference of **a** and **b**.

So, only option (b) is correct.

5 (*a*) If we have two vectors **a** and **b** represented by the two adjacent sides of a parallelogram in magnitude and direction then their sum **a** + **b** is represented in magnitude and direction by the diagonal of the parallelogram through their common point. This is known as the parallelogram law of vector addition.

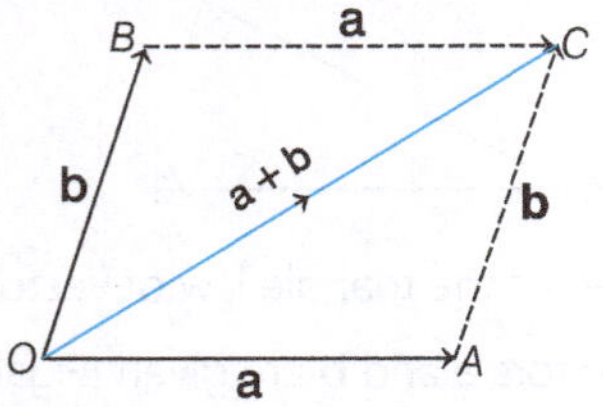

6 (*c*) (a) For any two vectors **a** and **b**,

$$\mathbf{a}+\mathbf{b}=\mathbf{b}+\mathbf{a} \quad \text{(commutative property)}$$

The proof of this property is given below.

Consider the parallelogram *ABCD*. Let **AB** = **a** and **BC** = **b**, then using the triangle law, from Δ *ABC*, we have

$$\mathbf{AC}=\mathbf{a}+\mathbf{b}$$

Now, since the opposite sides of a parallelogram are equal and parallel, from figure. we have **AD** = **BC** = **b** and **DC** = **AB** = **a**. Again using triangle law, from Δ *ADC*, we have

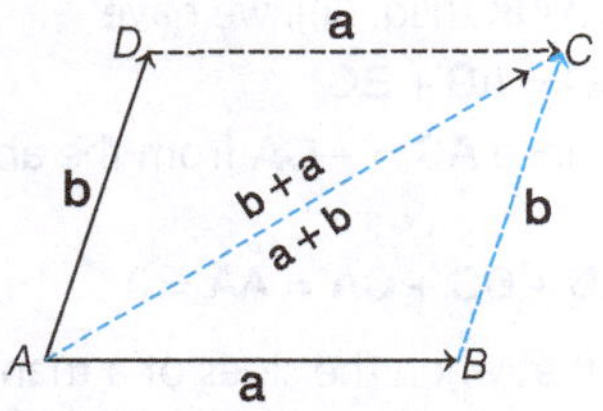

$$\mathbf{AC}=\mathbf{AD}+\mathbf{DC}=\mathbf{b}+\mathbf{a}$$

Hence, $\mathbf{a}+\mathbf{b}=\mathbf{b}+\mathbf{a}$

(b) For any three vectors **a**,**b** and **c**

$$(\mathbf{a}+\mathbf{b})+\mathbf{c}=\mathbf{a}+(\mathbf{b}+\mathbf{c}) \quad \text{(associative property)}$$

The proof of this property is given below.

Let the vectors **a**, **b** and **c** be represented by **PQ**, **QR** and **RS**, respectively as shown in Fig. (i) and (ii).

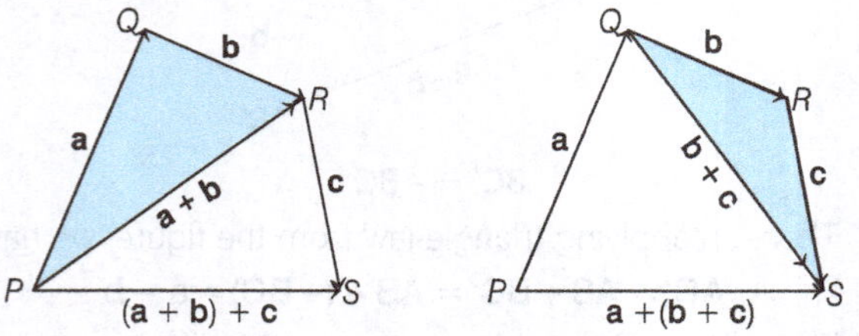

(a + b) + c (i)   a + (b + c) (ii)

Then, $\mathbf{a}+\mathbf{b}=\mathbf{PQ}+\mathbf{QR}=\mathbf{PR}$

and $\mathbf{b}+\mathbf{c}=\mathbf{QR}+\mathbf{RS}=\mathbf{QS}$

So, $(\mathbf{a}+\mathbf{b})+\mathbf{c}=\mathbf{PR}+\mathbf{RS}=\mathbf{PS}$

and $\mathbf{a}+(\mathbf{b}+\mathbf{c})=\mathbf{PQ}+\mathbf{QS}=\mathbf{PS}$

Hence, $(\mathbf{a}+\mathbf{b})+\mathbf{c}=\mathbf{a}+(\mathbf{b}+\mathbf{c})$

So, both (a) and (b) are correct.

7 (*c*) To find the sum of different vectors, components ($\hat{\mathbf{i}}$, $\hat{\mathbf{j}}$ and $\hat{\mathbf{k}}$) are added separately.

Here, given

$$\mathbf{a}=\hat{\mathbf{i}}-2\hat{\mathbf{j}}+\hat{\mathbf{k}},\ \mathbf{b}=-2\hat{\mathbf{i}}+4\hat{\mathbf{j}}+5\hat{\mathbf{k}},\ \mathbf{c}=\hat{\mathbf{i}}-6\hat{\mathbf{j}}-7\hat{\mathbf{k}}$$

Sum of these vectors can be calculated by adding their $\hat{\mathbf{i}}$, $\hat{\mathbf{j}}$ and $\hat{\mathbf{k}}$ components.

∴

$$\mathbf{a}+\mathbf{b}+\mathbf{c}=(\hat{\mathbf{i}}-2\hat{\mathbf{j}}+\hat{\mathbf{k}})+(-2\hat{\mathbf{i}}+4\hat{\mathbf{j}}+5\hat{\mathbf{k}})+(\hat{\mathbf{i}}-6\hat{\mathbf{j}}-7\hat{\mathbf{k}})$$

$$=(\hat{\mathbf{i}}-2\hat{\mathbf{i}}+\hat{\mathbf{i}})+(-2\hat{\mathbf{j}}+4\hat{\mathbf{j}}-6\hat{\mathbf{j}})+(\hat{\mathbf{k}}+5\hat{\mathbf{k}}-7\hat{\mathbf{k}})$$

$$=0\hat{\mathbf{i}}-4\hat{\mathbf{j}}-\hat{\mathbf{k}}=-4\hat{\mathbf{j}}-\hat{\mathbf{k}}$$

8 (*c*) By triangle law of vector addition,

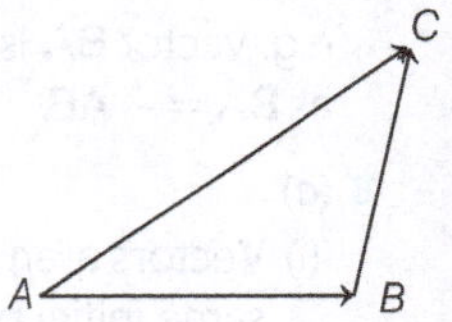

$$\mathbf{AB}+\mathbf{BC}=\mathbf{AC}$$

or $\mathbf{AB}+\mathbf{BC}=-\mathbf{CA}$

$\Rightarrow \mathbf{AB}+\mathbf{BC}+\mathbf{CA}=\mathbf{0}$

So, option (c) is incorrect.

9 (*d*) If **a** is a given vector and λ be a scalar.

Then, the product of the vector **a** by the scalar λ, denoted as λ**a**, is called the multiplication of vector **a** by the scalar λ , Note that λ**a** is also a vector, collinear to the vector **a**. The vector λ**a** has the direction same (or opposite) to that of vector **a** according as the value of λ is positive (or negative). Also, the magnitude of vector λ**a** is |λ| times the magnitude of the vector ā. i.e. $|\lambda\mathbf{a}|=|\lambda||\mathbf{a}|$

10 (*d*) A geometric visualization of multiplication of a vector by a scalar is given below.

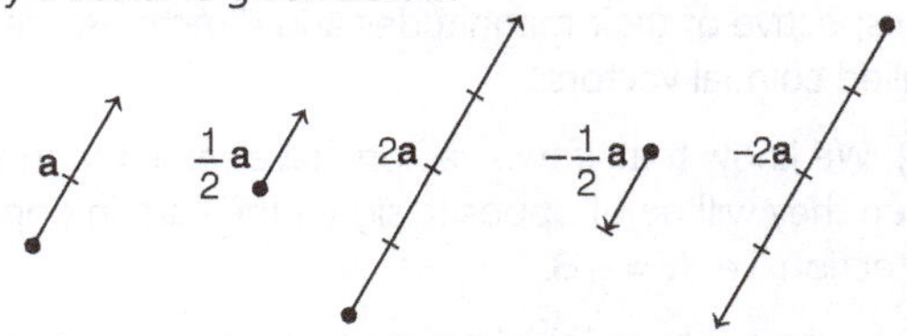

So, option (d) is correct.

11 (*c*) (a) When λ = – 1, then λ**a** = – **a**, which is a vector having magnitude equal to the magnitude of **a** and direction opposite to that of the direction of **a**. The vector – **a** is called the negative (or additive inverse) of vector **a** and we always have

$$\mathbf{a}+(-\mathbf{a})=(-\mathbf{a})+\mathbf{a}=\mathbf{0}$$

(b) Also, if $\lambda = \frac{1}{|\mathbf{a}|}$, provided $\mathbf{a} \neq 0$, i.e. **a** is not a null vector, then $|\lambda\mathbf{a}| = |\lambda||\mathbf{a}| = \frac{1}{|\mathbf{a}|}|\mathbf{a}| = 1$

So, $\lambda\mathbf{a}$ represents the unit vector in the direction of **a**.

We write it as $\mathbf{a} = \frac{1}{|\mathbf{a}|}\mathbf{a}$

(d) For any scalar k, $k\mathbf{0} = \mathbf{0}$.

So, only option (c) is not true.

12 (c) If we take the points **A** (1, 0, 0), **B** (0, 1, 0) and **C** (0, 0, 1) on the *x*-axis, *y*-axis and *z*-axis, respectively. Then, clearly

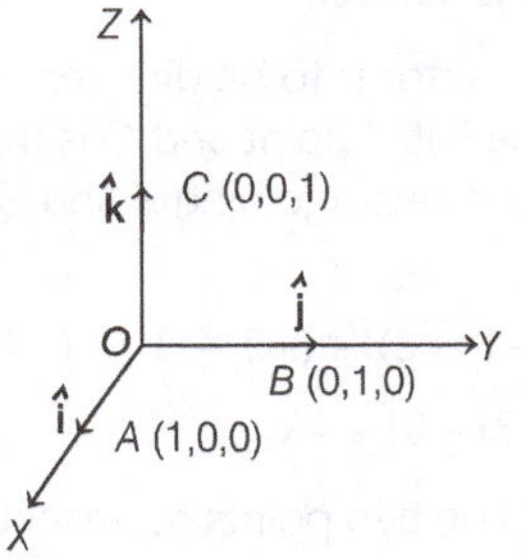

$$|\mathbf{OA}| = 1, |\mathbf{OB}| = 1 \text{ and } |\mathbf{OC}| = 1$$

The vectors **OA**, **OB** and **OC**, each having magnitude 1, are called unit vectors along the axes OX, OY and OZ, respectively, and denoted by $\hat{\mathbf{i}}$, $\hat{\mathbf{j}}$ and $\hat{\mathbf{k}}$, respectively.

So, both (a) and (b) are true.

13 (d) Considering the position vector **OP** of a point *P* (*x*, *y*, *z*) as in figure where P_1 be the foot of the perpendicular from *P* on the plane *XOY*. We, thus, see that $\mathbf{P_1 P}$ is

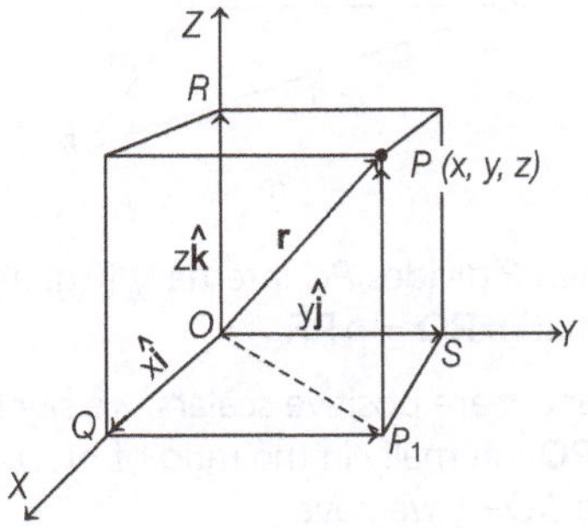

parallel to *Z*-axis. As $\hat{\mathbf{i}}$, $\hat{\mathbf{j}}$ and $\hat{\mathbf{k}}$ are the unit vectors along the *X*, *Y* and *Z*-axes, respectively and by the definition of the coordinates of **P**, we have $\mathbf{P_1P} = \mathbf{OR} = z\hat{\mathbf{k}}$.

Similarly, $\mathbf{QP_1} = \mathbf{OS} = y\hat{\mathbf{j}}$ and $\mathbf{OQ} = x\hat{\mathbf{i}}$.

Therefore, it follows that $\mathbf{OP_1} = \mathbf{OQ} + \mathbf{QP_1} = x\hat{\mathbf{i}} + y\hat{\mathbf{j}}$

and $\mathbf{OP} = \mathbf{OP_1} + \mathbf{P_1P} = x\hat{\mathbf{i}} + y\hat{\mathbf{j}} + z\hat{\mathbf{k}}$

Hence, the position vector of P with reference to O is given by

$$\mathbf{OP} \text{ (or } \mathbf{r}) = x\hat{\mathbf{i}} + y\hat{\mathbf{j}} + z\hat{\mathbf{k}}$$

This form of any vector is called its component form. Here *x*, *y* and *z* are called as the scalar components of r and $x\hat{\mathbf{i}}$, $y\hat{\mathbf{j}}$ and $z\hat{\mathbf{k}}$ are called the vector components of r along the respective axes. Sometimes *x*, *y* and *z* are also termed as rectangular components.

The length of any vector $\mathbf{r} = x\hat{\mathbf{i}} + y\hat{\mathbf{j}} + z\hat{\mathbf{k}}$, is readily determined by applying the Pythagoras theorem twice. We note that in the right angle ΔOQP_1 (fig.)

$$|\mathbf{OP_1}| = \sqrt{|\mathbf{OQ}|^2 + |\mathbf{QP_1}|^2} = \sqrt{x^2 + y^2}$$

and in the right angle ΔOP_1P. we have

$$\mathbf{OP} = \sqrt{|\mathbf{OP_1}|^2 + |\mathbf{P_1P}|^2} = \sqrt{(x^2 + y^2) + z^2}$$

Hence, the length of any vector $\mathbf{r} = x\hat{\mathbf{i}} + y\hat{\mathbf{j}} + z\hat{\mathbf{k}}$ is given by

$$|\mathbf{r}| = |x\hat{\mathbf{i}} + y\hat{\mathbf{j}} + z\hat{\mathbf{k}}| = \sqrt{x^2 + y^2 + z^2}$$

So, only option (d) is incorrect.

14 (b) If **a** and **b** are any two vectors given in the components form $a_1\hat{\mathbf{i}} + a_2\hat{\mathbf{j}} + a_3\hat{\mathbf{k}}$ and $b_1\hat{\mathbf{i}} + b_2\hat{\mathbf{j}} + b_3\hat{\mathbf{k}}$, respectively, then

A. The sum (or resultant) of the vectors **a** and **b** is given by

$$\mathbf{a} + \mathbf{b} = (\mathbf{a_1} + \mathbf{b_1})\hat{\mathbf{i}} + (\mathbf{a_2} + \mathbf{b_2})\hat{\mathbf{j}} + (\mathbf{a_3} + \mathbf{b_3})\hat{\mathbf{k}}$$

B. The difference of the vector **a** and **b** is given by

$$\mathbf{a} - \mathbf{b} = (\mathbf{a_1} - \mathbf{b_1})\hat{\mathbf{i}} + (\mathbf{a_2} - \mathbf{b_2})\hat{\mathbf{j}} + (\mathbf{a_3} - \mathbf{b_3})\hat{\mathbf{k}}$$

So, only (b) is correct.

15 (a) If **a** and **b** are any two vectors given in the components from

$a_1\hat{\mathbf{i}} + a_2\hat{\mathbf{j}} + a_3\hat{\mathbf{k}}$ and $b_1\hat{\mathbf{i}} + b_2\hat{\mathbf{j}} + b_3\hat{\mathbf{k}}$ respectively, then

A. The vectors **a** and **b** are equal, if and only if

$$a_1 = b_1, a_2 = b_2 \text{ and } a_3 = b_3$$

B. The multiplication of vector **a** by any scalar λ is given by

$$\lambda\mathbf{a} = (\lambda a_1)\hat{\mathbf{i}} + (\lambda a_2)\hat{\mathbf{j}} + (\lambda a_3)\hat{\mathbf{k}}$$

So, only I is incorrect.

16 (d) The addition of vectors and the multiplication of a vector by a scalar together give the following distributive laws.

Let **a** and **b** be any two vectors, and *k* and *m* be any scalars. Then,

(i) $k\mathbf{a} + m\mathbf{a} = (k + m)\mathbf{a}$

(ii) $k(m\mathbf{a}) = (km)\mathbf{a}$

(iii) $k(\mathbf{a} + \mathbf{b}) = k\mathbf{a} + k\mathbf{b}$

So, option (d) is correct.

17 (c) One may observe that whatever be the value of λ, the vector $\lambda\mathbf{a}$ is always collinear to the vector $\mathbf{a}$. Infact, two vectors $\mathbf{a}$ and $\mathbf{b}$ are collinear, if and only if there exists a non-zero scalar λ such that $\mathbf{b} = \lambda\mathbf{a}$. If the vectors a and b are given in the component form, i.e. $\mathbf{a} = a_1\hat{\mathbf{i}} + a_2\hat{\mathbf{j}} + a_3\hat{\mathbf{k}}$ and $\mathbf{b} = b_1\hat{\mathbf{i}} + b_2\hat{\mathbf{j}} + b_3\hat{\mathbf{k}}$, then the two vectors are collinear, if and only if

$$b_1\hat{\mathbf{i}} + b_2\hat{\mathbf{j}} + b_3\hat{\mathbf{k}} = \lambda(a_1\hat{\mathbf{i}} + a_2\hat{\mathbf{j}} + a_3\hat{\mathbf{k}})$$

$$\Leftrightarrow \quad b_1\hat{\mathbf{i}} + b_2\hat{\mathbf{j}} + b_3\hat{\mathbf{k}} = (\lambda a_1)\hat{\mathbf{i}} + (\lambda a_2)\hat{\mathbf{j}} + (\lambda a_3)\hat{\mathbf{k}}$$

$$\Leftrightarrow \quad b_1 = \lambda a_1,\ b_2 = \lambda a_2,\ b_3 = \lambda a_3$$

$$\Leftrightarrow \quad \frac{b_1}{a_1} = \frac{b_2}{a_2} = \frac{b_3}{a_3} = \lambda$$

So, both (a) and (b) are true.

18 (a) If $\mathbf{a} = a_1\hat{\mathbf{i}} + a_2\hat{\mathbf{j}} + a_3\hat{\mathbf{k}}$, then a_1, a_2, a_3 are also called direction ratios of $\mathbf{a}$.

So, option (a) is correct.

19 (b) In case if it is given that l, m, n are direction cosines of a vector, then $l\hat{\mathbf{i}} + m\hat{\mathbf{j}} + n\hat{\mathbf{k}} = (\cos\alpha)\hat{\mathbf{i}} + (\cos\beta)\hat{\mathbf{j}} + (\cos\gamma)\hat{\mathbf{k}}$ is the unit vector in the direction of that vector where α, β and γ are the angles, which of the vector makes with X, Y and Z-axes, respectively.

So, option (b) is correct.

20 (a) The sum of the given vectors is

$$\mathbf{a} + \mathbf{b} = \mathbf{c} \text{ (say)} = 4\hat{\mathbf{i}} + 3\hat{\mathbf{j}} - 2\hat{\mathbf{k}}$$

and $$|\mathbf{c}| = \sqrt{4^2 + 3^2 + (-2)^2} = \sqrt{29}$$

Thus, the required unit vector is

$$\hat{\mathbf{c}} = \frac{1}{|\mathbf{c}|}\mathbf{c} = \frac{1}{\sqrt{29}}(4\hat{\mathbf{i}} + 3\hat{\mathbf{j}} - 2\hat{\mathbf{k}}) = \frac{4}{\sqrt{29}}\hat{\mathbf{i}} + \frac{3}{\sqrt{29}}\hat{\mathbf{j}} - \frac{2}{\sqrt{29}}\hat{\mathbf{k}}$$

21 (d) If $P_1(x_1, y_1, z_1)$ and $P_2(x_2, y_2, z_2)$ are any two points, the vector joining P_1 and P_2 is the vector $\mathbf{P_1P_2}$.

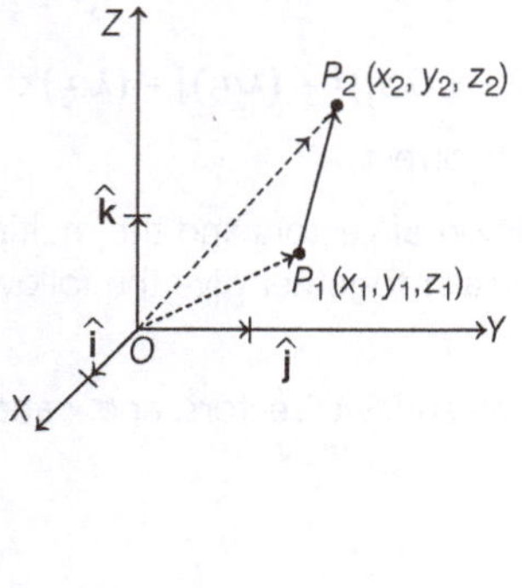

Joining the points P_1 and P_2 with the origin O and applying triangle law, from the triangle OP_1P_2, we have

$$\mathbf{OP_1} + \mathbf{P_1P_2} = \mathbf{OP_2}$$

Using the properties of vector addition, the above equation becomes

$$\mathbf{P_1P_2} = \mathbf{OP_2} - \mathbf{OP_1}$$

i.e. $$\mathbf{P_1P_2} = (x_2\hat{\mathbf{i}} + y_2\hat{\mathbf{j}} + z_2\hat{\mathbf{k}}) - (x_1\hat{\mathbf{i}} + y_1\hat{\mathbf{j}} + z_1\hat{\mathbf{k}})$$
$$= (x_2 - x_1)\hat{\mathbf{i}} + (y_2 - y_1)\hat{\mathbf{j}} + (z_2 - z_1)\hat{\mathbf{k}}$$

The magnitude of vector $\mathbf{P_1P_2}$ is given by

$$P_1P_2 = \sqrt{(x_2 - x_1)^2 + (y_2 - y_1)^2 + (z_2 - z_1)^2}$$

So, option (d) is correct.

22 (b) Since, the vector is to be directed from P to Q. Clearly, P is the initial point and Q is the terminal point. So, the required vector joining P and Q is the vector $\mathbf{PQ}$ given by

$$\mathbf{PQ} = (-1 - 2)\hat{\mathbf{i}} + (-2 - 3)\hat{\mathbf{j}} + (-4 - 0)\hat{\mathbf{k}}$$
$$\mathbf{PQ} = -3\hat{\mathbf{i}} - 5\hat{\mathbf{j}} - 4\hat{\mathbf{k}}$$

23 (c) Let P and Q be two points represented by the position vectors $\mathbf{OP}$ and $\mathbf{OQ}$, respectively with respect to the origion O. Then, the line segment joining the points P and Q may be divided by a third point, say R in two ways– internally [Fig (i)] and externally [Fig (ii)]. Here, we intend to find the position vector $\mathbf{OR}$ for the point R with respect to the origin O. We take the two cases one by one.

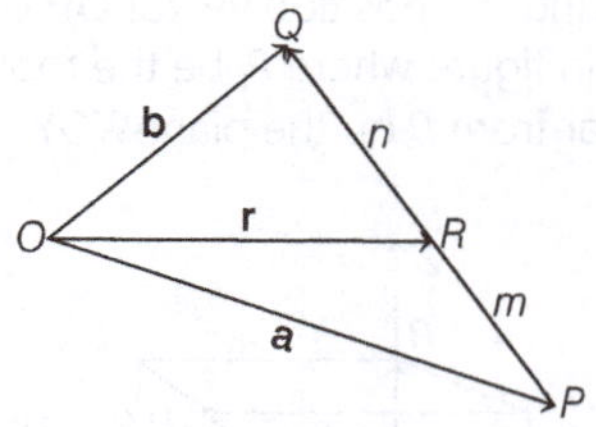

Fig (i)

Case I When R divides PQ internally [Fig. (i)]. If R divides $\mathbf{PQ}$ such that $m\,\mathbf{RQ} = n\,\mathbf{PR}$,

where m and n are positive scalars, we say that the point R divides $\mathbf{PQ}$ internally in the ratio of $m : n$. Now, from ΔORQ and ΔOPR, we have

$$\mathbf{RQ} = \mathbf{OQ} - \mathbf{OR} = \mathbf{b} - \mathbf{r}$$

and $$\mathbf{PR} = \mathbf{OR} - \mathbf{OP} = \mathbf{r} - \mathbf{a},$$

Therefore, we have $m(\mathbf{b} - \mathbf{r}) = n(\mathbf{r} - \mathbf{a})$

or $$\mathbf{r} = \frac{m\mathbf{b} + n\mathbf{a}}{m + n} \quad \text{[on simplification]}$$

Hence, the position vector of the point R, which divides P and Q internally in the ratio of $m : n$ is given by

$$\mathbf{OR} = \frac{m\mathbf{b} + n\mathbf{a}}{m + n}$$

Case II When R divides the line segment PQ externally in the ratio $m : n$.

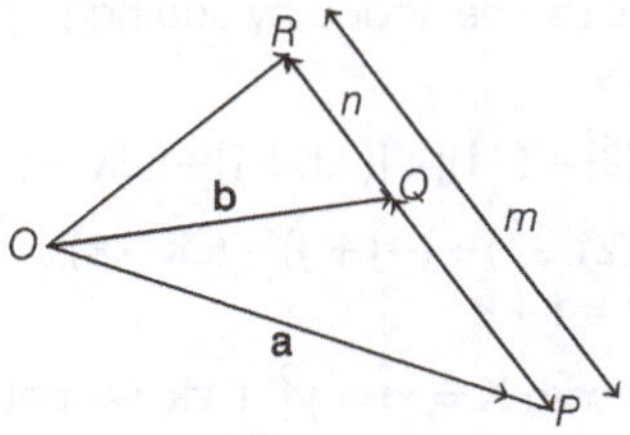

Fig. (ii)

i.e. $$\frac{\mathbf{PR}}{\mathbf{QR}} = \frac{m}{n}$$

$$\frac{\mathbf{PR}}{\mathbf{QR}} = \frac{m}{n}$$

$$\Rightarrow \quad \frac{\mathbf{OR} - \mathbf{OP}}{\mathbf{OR} - \mathbf{OQ}} = \frac{m}{n}$$

$$\Rightarrow \quad \frac{\mathbf{r} - \mathbf{a}}{\mathbf{r} - \mathbf{b}} = \frac{m}{n}$$

$$\Rightarrow \quad n\mathbf{r} - n\mathbf{a} = m\mathbf{r} - m\mathbf{b}$$

$$m\mathbf{r} - n\mathbf{r} = m\mathbf{b} - n\mathbf{a}$$

$$\mathbf{r}\,(m - n) = m\mathbf{b} - n\mathbf{a}$$

$$\mathbf{r} = \frac{m\mathbf{b} - n\mathbf{a}}{m - n}$$

$$\mathbf{OR} = \frac{m\mathbf{b} - n\mathbf{a}}{m - n}$$

So, option (c) is correct.

24 (c) Given, vector $\mathbf{a} = \hat{\mathbf{i}} + \hat{\mathbf{j}} + \hat{\mathbf{k}}$.

On comparing with

$$\mathbf{a} = x\,\hat{\mathbf{i}} + y\hat{\mathbf{j}} + z\hat{\mathbf{k}},$$

we get $x = 1,\ y = 1,\ z = 1$.

The magnitude of given vector is

$$|\mathbf{a}| = |x\hat{\mathbf{i}} + y\hat{\mathbf{j}} + z\hat{\mathbf{k}}| = \sqrt{x^2 + y^2 + z^2}$$

$$= \sqrt{1^2 + 1^2 + 1^2} = \sqrt{3}$$

Similarly, magnitude of

$$\mathbf{b} = |\mathbf{b}| = |2\hat{\mathbf{i}} - 7\hat{\mathbf{j}} - 3\hat{\mathbf{k}}|$$

$$= \sqrt{2^2 + (-7)^2 + (-3)^2}$$

$$= \sqrt{4 + 49 + 9} = \sqrt{62}$$

and $$|\mathbf{c}| = \left|\frac{1}{\sqrt{3}}\hat{\mathbf{i}} + \frac{1}{\sqrt{3}}\hat{\mathbf{j}} - \frac{1}{\sqrt{3}}\hat{\mathbf{k}}\right|$$

$$= \sqrt{\left(\frac{1}{\sqrt{3}}\right)^2 + \left(\frac{1}{\sqrt{3}}\right)^2 + \left(-\frac{1}{\sqrt{3}}\right)^2}$$

$$= \sqrt{\frac{1}{3} + \frac{1}{3} + \frac{1}{3}} = 1$$

So, option (c) is correct.

25 (a) Two vectors can have same magnitude, if the sum of the squares of coefficient of $\hat{\mathbf{i}}$, $\hat{\mathbf{j}}$ and $\hat{\mathbf{k}}$ is same. The vectors $\mathbf{a} = (2\hat{\mathbf{i}} + 3\hat{\mathbf{j}} + \hat{\mathbf{k}})$ and $\mathbf{b} = (2\hat{\mathbf{i}} + 3\hat{\mathbf{j}} - \hat{\mathbf{k}})$ are different vectors having the same magnitudes.

Magnitude of Ist vector

$$= \sqrt{(2)^2 + (3)^2 + (1)^2}$$

$$= \sqrt{4 + 9 + 1} = \sqrt{14}$$

and magnitude of IInd vector

$$= \sqrt{(2)^2 + (1)^2 + (-3)^2} = \sqrt{4 + 1 + 9} = \sqrt{14}$$

i.e. they have same magnitude.

26 (c) Two vectors can have the same directions, if their direction cosines (l, m, n) are same. Direction cosines for a vector $\mathbf{A} = x\hat{\mathbf{i}} + y\hat{\mathbf{j}} + z\hat{\mathbf{k}}$ are given by

$$l = \frac{x}{\sqrt{x^2 + y^2 + z^2}}$$

$$m = \frac{y}{\sqrt{x^2 + y^2 + z^2}}$$

$$n = \frac{z}{\sqrt{x^2 + y^2 + z^2}}$$

Let $\quad \mathbf{a} = (\hat{\mathbf{i}} + \hat{\mathbf{j}} + \hat{\mathbf{k}})$

and $\quad \mathbf{b} = (2\hat{\mathbf{i}} + 2\hat{\mathbf{j}} + 2\hat{\mathbf{k}})$.

For Ist vector, $\mathbf{a} = \hat{\mathbf{i}} + \hat{\mathbf{j}} + \hat{\mathbf{k}}$

Comparing with $\mathbf{A} = x\,\hat{\mathbf{i}} + y\,\hat{\mathbf{j}} + z\,\hat{\mathbf{k}}$, we get $x = 1, y = 1, z = 1$

The direction cosines of $\mathbf{a}$ are given by

$$l = \frac{1}{\sqrt{1^2 + 1^2 + 1^2}} = \frac{1}{\sqrt{3}},$$

$$m = \frac{1}{\sqrt{1^2 + 1^2 + 1^2}} = \frac{1}{\sqrt{3}}$$

and $$n = \frac{1}{\sqrt{1^2 + 1^2 + 1^2}} = \frac{1}{\sqrt{3}}$$

Similarly, the direction cosines of $\mathbf{b}$ are given by

$$l=\frac{2}{\sqrt{2^2+2^2+2^2}}=\frac{2}{2\sqrt{3}}=\frac{1}{\sqrt{3}},$$

$$m=\frac{2}{\sqrt{2^2+2^2+2^2}}=\frac{2}{2\sqrt{3}}=\frac{1}{\sqrt{3}}$$

and $n=\frac{2}{\sqrt{2^2+2^2+2^2}}=\frac{2}{2\sqrt{3}}=\frac{1}{\sqrt{3}}$

Here, we see that both have same direction cosines.

27 (*c*) Two vectors are equal, if both have the same coefficients of $\hat{\mathbf{i}}$, $\hat{\mathbf{j}}$ and $\hat{\mathbf{k}}$ along with the sign.

Let $\mathbf{a}=2\hat{\mathbf{i}}+3\hat{\mathbf{j}}$ and $\mathbf{b}=x\hat{\mathbf{i}}+y\hat{\mathbf{j}}$ be two given vectors. Comparing coefficients of $\hat{\mathbf{i}}$ and $\hat{\mathbf{j}}$ of both **a** and **b**, we get

$\Rightarrow \quad x=2$ and $y=3$

28 (*c*) Unit vector in the direction of given vector can be calculated by formula $\hat{\mathbf{a}}=\frac{\mathbf{a}}{|\mathbf{a}|}$

where, $|\mathbf{a}|$ = magnitude of given vector **a**.

Given, $\mathbf{a}=\hat{\mathbf{i}}+\hat{\mathbf{j}}+2\hat{\mathbf{k}}$ comparing with $\mathbf{x}=a\hat{\mathbf{i}}+b\hat{\mathbf{j}}+c\hat{\mathbf{k}}$, we get $a=1, b=1, c=2$

Magnitude of vector

$$\mathbf{a}=|\mathbf{a}|=\sqrt{a^2+b^2+c^2}$$
$$=\sqrt{1^2+1^2+2^2}=\sqrt{6}$$

$\therefore$ The unit vector $\hat{\mathbf{a}}$ in the direction of vector $\mathbf{a}=\hat{\mathbf{i}}+\hat{\mathbf{j}}+2\hat{\mathbf{k}}$ is given by $\hat{\mathbf{a}}=\frac{\mathbf{a}}{|\mathbf{a}|}=\frac{1}{\sqrt{6}}(\hat{\mathbf{i}}+\hat{\mathbf{j}}+2\hat{\mathbf{k}})$

$$=\frac{1}{\sqrt{6}}\hat{\mathbf{i}}+\frac{1}{\sqrt{6}}\hat{\mathbf{j}}+\frac{2}{\sqrt{6}}\hat{\mathbf{k}}$$

29 (*b*) A vector with initial point (x_1, y_1, z_1) and terminal point (x_2, y_2, z_2) is given by

$$(x_2-x_1)\hat{\mathbf{i}}+(y_2-y_1)\hat{\mathbf{j}}+(z_2-z_1)\hat{\mathbf{k}}$$

The given points are $P(1, 2, 3)$ and $Q(4, 5, 6)$.

$\therefore \ x_1=1, y_1=2, z_1=3$ and $x_2=4, y_2=5, z_2=6$

So, vector $\mathbf{PQ}=(x_2-x_1)\hat{\mathbf{i}}+(y_2-y_1)\hat{\mathbf{j}}+(z_2-z_1)\hat{\mathbf{k}}$
$$=(4-1)\hat{\mathbf{i}}+(5-2)\hat{\mathbf{j}}+(6-3)\hat{\mathbf{k}}$$
$=3\hat{\mathbf{i}}+3\hat{\mathbf{j}}+3\hat{\mathbf{k}}$

$\therefore$ Magnitude of given vector

$$|\mathbf{PQ}|=\sqrt{3^2+3^2+3^2}=\sqrt{9+9+9}=\sqrt{27}=3\sqrt{3}$$

Hence, the unit vector in the direction of **PQ**,

$$\frac{\mathbf{PQ}}{|\mathbf{PQ}|}=\frac{3\hat{\mathbf{i}}+3\hat{\mathbf{j}}+3\hat{\mathbf{k}}}{3\sqrt{3}}=\frac{3}{3\sqrt{3}}(\hat{\mathbf{i}}+\hat{\mathbf{j}}+\hat{\mathbf{k}})$$
$$=\frac{1}{\sqrt{3}}\hat{\mathbf{i}}+\frac{1}{\sqrt{3}}\hat{\mathbf{j}}+\frac{1}{\sqrt{3}}\hat{\mathbf{k}}$$

30 (*b*) Firstly, determine **a** + **b** and then unit vector
$$=\frac{\mathbf{a}+\mathbf{b}}{|\mathbf{a}+\mathbf{b}|}$$

The given vectors are $\mathbf{a}=2\hat{\mathbf{i}}-\hat{\mathbf{j}}+2\hat{\mathbf{k}}$ and $\mathbf{b}=-\hat{\mathbf{i}}+\hat{\mathbf{j}}-\hat{\mathbf{k}}$

$\therefore \quad \mathbf{a}+\mathbf{b}=(2\hat{\mathbf{i}}-\hat{\mathbf{j}}+2\hat{\mathbf{k}})+(-\hat{\mathbf{i}}+\hat{\mathbf{j}}-\hat{\mathbf{k}})$

Two vectors can be added by adding $\hat{\mathbf{i}}$, $\hat{\mathbf{j}}$ and $\hat{\mathbf{k}}$ components.

$\therefore \ \mathbf{a}+\mathbf{b}=[2\hat{\mathbf{i}}+(-\hat{\mathbf{i}})]+[(-\hat{\mathbf{j}})+\hat{\mathbf{j}}]+[(2\hat{\mathbf{k}})+(-\hat{\mathbf{k}})]$
$$=(2\hat{\mathbf{i}}-\hat{\mathbf{i}})+(-\hat{\mathbf{j}}+\hat{\mathbf{j}})+(2\hat{\mathbf{k}}-\hat{\mathbf{k}})$$
$=\hat{\mathbf{i}}+0\hat{\mathbf{j}}+\hat{\mathbf{k}}=\hat{\mathbf{i}}+\hat{\mathbf{k}}$

Comparing with $\mathbf{X}=x\hat{\mathbf{i}}+y\hat{\mathbf{j}}+z\hat{\mathbf{k}}$, we get $x=1, y=0, z=1$

$\therefore$ Magnitude $|\mathbf{a}+\mathbf{b}|=\sqrt{x^2+y^2+z^2}=\sqrt{1^2+0^2+1^2}=\sqrt{2}$

Hence, the unit vector in the direction of $(\mathbf{a}+\mathbf{b})$,

$$\frac{(\mathbf{a}+\mathbf{b})}{|\mathbf{a}+\mathbf{b}|}=\frac{(\hat{\mathbf{i}}+\hat{\mathbf{k}})}{\sqrt{2}}=\frac{1}{\sqrt{2}}\hat{\mathbf{i}}+\frac{1}{\sqrt{2}}\hat{\mathbf{k}}$$

31 (*b*) To find a vector in the direction of given vector, first of all we have to find unit vector in the direction of given vector.

Let $\quad \mathbf{a}=5\hat{\mathbf{i}}-\hat{\mathbf{j}}+2\hat{\mathbf{k}}$

Comparing with $\mathbf{X}=x\hat{\mathbf{i}}+y\hat{\mathbf{j}}+z\hat{\mathbf{k}}$, we get
$$x=5, y=-1, z=2$$

$\therefore$ Magnitude $|\mathbf{a}|=\sqrt{x^2+y^2+z^2}=\sqrt{5^2+(-1)^2+2^2}$
$$=\sqrt{25+1+4}=\sqrt{30}$$

$\therefore$ Unit vector in the direction of given vector

$$\hat{\mathbf{a}}=\frac{\mathbf{a}}{|\mathbf{a}|}=\frac{5\hat{\mathbf{i}}-\hat{\mathbf{j}}+2\hat{\mathbf{k}}}{\sqrt{30}}$$

Hence, the vector in the direction of vector $5\hat{\mathbf{i}}-\hat{\mathbf{j}}+2\hat{\mathbf{k}}$, which has magnitude 8 units is given by (multiplying the unit vector by 8, we have the vector with magnitude 8 as the magnitude of unit vector is 1).

$$8\hat{\mathbf{a}}=8\left(\frac{5\hat{\mathbf{i}}-\hat{\mathbf{j}}+2\hat{\mathbf{k}}}{\sqrt{30}}\right)=\frac{40}{\sqrt{30}}\hat{\mathbf{i}}-\frac{8}{\sqrt{30}}\hat{\mathbf{j}}+\frac{16}{\sqrt{30}}\hat{\mathbf{k}}$$

32 (*a*) To find the direction of a given vector, we have to find the unit vector in the direction of given vector.

Let $\quad \mathbf{a}=\hat{\mathbf{i}}+2\hat{\mathbf{j}}+3\hat{\mathbf{k}}$

Then, $\quad |\mathbf{a}|=\sqrt{1^2+2^2+3^2}=\sqrt{14}$

$\therefore \quad \hat{\mathbf{a}}=\frac{\mathbf{a}}{|\mathbf{a}|} \Rightarrow \hat{\mathbf{a}}=\frac{1}{\sqrt{14}}(\hat{\mathbf{i}}+2\hat{\mathbf{j}}+3\hat{\mathbf{k}})$

$\Rightarrow \quad \hat{\mathbf{a}}=\frac{1}{\sqrt{14}}\hat{\mathbf{i}}+\frac{2}{\sqrt{14}}\hat{\mathbf{j}}+\frac{3}{\sqrt{14}}\hat{\mathbf{k}}$

Hence, direction cosines of the given vector are $\frac{1}{\sqrt{14}}, \frac{2}{\sqrt{14}}, \frac{3}{\sqrt{14}}$. [$\because$ direction cosines are the coefficients of $\hat{i}, \hat{j}, \hat{k}$ of unit vector]

33 (*b*) The given points are $A(1, 2, -3)$ and $B(-1, -2, 1)$.

i.e. $x_1 = 1, y_1 = 2, z_1 = -3$

and $x_2 = -1, y_2 = -2, z_2 = 1$

Vector $\mathbf{AB} = (x_2 - x_1)\hat{i} + (y_2 - y_1)\hat{j} + (z_2 - z_1)\hat{k}$
$= (-1-1)\hat{i} + (-2-2)\hat{j} + [1-(-3)]\hat{k}$
$= -2\hat{i} - 4\hat{j} + 4\hat{k}$

On comparing with $\mathbf{X} = x\hat{i} + y\hat{j} + z\hat{k}$, we get

$$x = -2, y = -4, z = 4$$

Now, magnitude

$$|\mathbf{AB}| = \sqrt{x^2 + y^2 + z^2} = \sqrt{(-2)^2 + (-4)^2 + 4^2}$$
$$= \sqrt{4 + 16 + 16} = \sqrt{36} = 6$$

Direction cosines of a vector $\mathbf{X} = x\hat{i} + y\hat{j} + z\hat{k}$ are

$$\frac{x}{|\mathbf{X}|}, \frac{y}{|\mathbf{X}|}, \frac{z}{|\mathbf{X}|}$$

$\therefore$ Direction cosines of **AB** are $\frac{-2}{6}, \frac{-4}{6}, \frac{4}{6}$ or $-\frac{1}{3}, -\frac{2}{3}, \frac{2}{3}$.

34 (*a*) The position vector of mid-point of the vector joining the points $P(2, 3, 4)$ and $Q(4, 1, -2)$ is given by

PV of the mid-point of $(PQ) = \frac{1}{2}(PV \text{ of } P + PV \text{ of } Q)$

$$= \frac{1}{2}[(2\hat{i} + 3\hat{j} + 4\hat{k}) + (4\hat{i} + \hat{j} - 2\hat{k})]$$
$$= \frac{1}{2}(6\hat{i} + 4\hat{j} + 2\hat{k}) = 3\hat{i} + 2\hat{j} + \hat{k}$$

35 (*b*) Considering each statement.

Statement I $b = \lambda a, \lambda \neq 0$ is correct, it is the condition for collinearity of two vectors.

Statement II $\hat{\mathbf{a}} = \pm\hat{\mathbf{b}}$ is also correct, it shows that unit vectors in the direction of given vectors are either in the same direction or in opposite. [$\because$ **a** and **b** are collinear]

Statement III is incorrect, if for two vectors the respective components are proportional, then their magnitude will be different but they will be collinear.

Statement IV is incorrect, because if the two vectors are collinear, then they may have same directions or opposite directions.

36 (*a*) Given, $m_1 = |\mathbf{a}_1| = \sqrt{2^2 + (-1)^2 + (1)^2} = \sqrt{6}$

$$m_2 = |\mathbf{a}_2| = \sqrt{3^2 + (-4)^2 + (-4)^2} = \sqrt{41}$$
$$m_3 = |\mathbf{a}_3| = \sqrt{1^2 + 1^2 + (-1)^2} = \sqrt{3}$$

and $m_4 = |\mathbf{a}_4| = \sqrt{(-1)^2 + (3)^2 + (1)^2} = \sqrt{11}$

$\therefore$ $m_3 < m_1 < m_4 < m_2$

37 (*a*) Since, $\mathbf{a} = m\mathbf{b}$ for some scalars m

i.e. $\mathbf{a} = m\left(6\hat{i} - 8\hat{j} - \frac{15}{2}\hat{k}\right)$

$\Rightarrow$ $|\mathbf{a}| = |m|\sqrt{36 + 64 + \frac{225}{4}} \Rightarrow 50 = \frac{25}{2}|m|$

$\Rightarrow$ $|m| = 4 \Rightarrow m = \pm 4$

Since, **a** makes an acute angle with the positive direction of *Z*-axis, so its *z* component must be positive and hence, *m* must be -4.

$\therefore$ $\mathbf{a} = -4\left(6\hat{i} - 8\hat{j} - \frac{15}{2}\hat{k}\right) = -24\hat{i} + 32\hat{j} + 30\hat{k}$

38 (*a*) Given, $2\mathbf{a} + 3\mathbf{b} - 5\mathbf{c} = 0$

$\Rightarrow$ $\frac{2\mathbf{a} + 3\mathbf{b}}{5} = \mathbf{c}$

$\Rightarrow$ $\frac{2\mathbf{a} + 3\mathbf{b}}{2+3} = \mathbf{c}$

$\Rightarrow$ $\frac{\mathbf{a} + \frac{3}{2}\mathbf{b}}{1 + \frac{3}{2}} = \mathbf{c}$ ...(i)

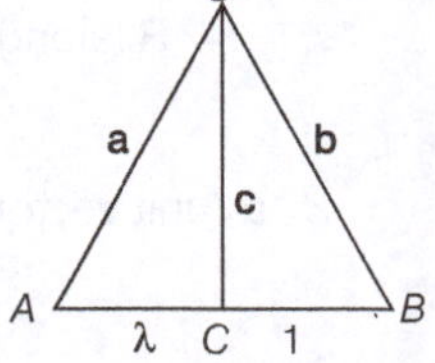

Let c divides **AB** in the ratio $\lambda : 1$

Then, $\mathbf{c} = \frac{\mathbf{a} + \lambda\mathbf{b}}{1 + \lambda}$ ...(ii)

On comparing Eqs. (i) and (ii), we get $\lambda = \frac{3}{2}$

$\therefore$ Required ratio is 3 : 2 internally.

39 (*d*) $\mathbf{CP} + \mathbf{PA} = \mathbf{CA}$

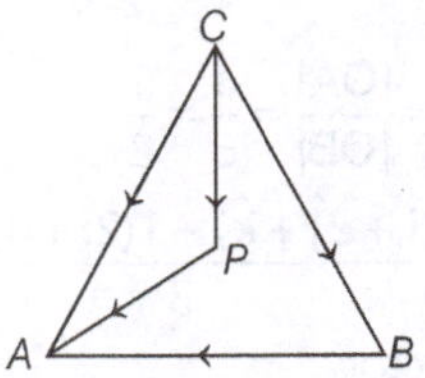

By triangle law, $\mathbf{CA} = \mathbf{CB} + \mathbf{BA}$

$\therefore$ $\mathbf{CP} + \mathbf{PA} = \mathbf{CB} + \mathbf{BA}$

40 (*a*) Let the line joining the points with position vectors $-2\hat{i} + 3\hat{j} + 5\hat{k}$ and $7\hat{i} - \hat{k}$ be divided in the ratio $\lambda : 1$ by $\hat{i} + 2\hat{j} + 3\hat{k}$.

$\therefore$ $\frac{\lambda(7\hat{i} - \hat{k}) + (-2\hat{i} + 3\hat{j} + 5\hat{k})}{\lambda + 1} = \hat{i} + 2\hat{j} + 3\hat{k}$

$\Rightarrow (7\lambda - 2)\hat{i} + 3\hat{j} + (5 - \lambda)\hat{k} = (\lambda + 1)\hat{i} + 2(\lambda + 1)\hat{j} + 3(\lambda + 1)\hat{k}$

On equating the coefficient of $\hat{i}$, we get

$$7\lambda - 2 = \lambda + 1 \Rightarrow \lambda = \frac{1}{2}$$

Hence, required ratio $= \lambda : 1 = 1 : 2$

41 (*c*) We know that the diagonals of a parallelogram bisect each other. Therefore, M is the mid-point of AC and BD both.

$\therefore \quad \mathbf{OA}+\mathbf{OC}=2\,\mathbf{OM}$

and $\quad \mathbf{OB}+\mathbf{OD}=2\,\mathbf{OM}$

$\Rightarrow \quad \mathbf{OA}+\mathbf{OB}+\mathbf{OC}+\mathbf{OD}=4\,\mathbf{OM}$

42 (*d*) Let $\mathbf{R}_1 = 2\hat{\mathbf{i}}+4\hat{\mathbf{j}}-5\hat{\mathbf{k}}$

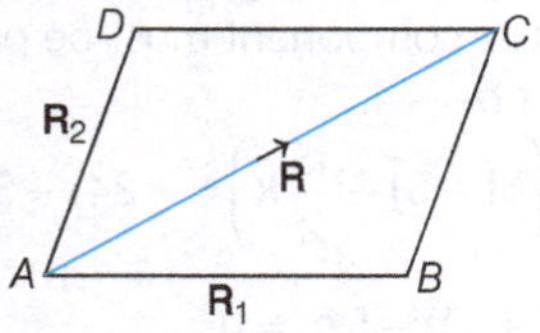

and $\quad \mathbf{R}_2=\hat{\mathbf{i}}+2\hat{\mathbf{j}}+3\hat{\mathbf{k}}$

$\therefore \quad \mathbf{R}\text{ (along } \mathbf{AC}) = \mathbf{R}_1+\mathbf{R}_2 = 3\hat{\mathbf{i}}+6\hat{\mathbf{j}}-2\hat{\mathbf{k}}$

$\therefore \quad \mathbf{a}\text{ (unit vector along } AC) = \dfrac{\mathbf{R}}{|\mathbf{R}|} = \dfrac{3\hat{\mathbf{i}}+6\hat{\mathbf{j}}-2\hat{\mathbf{k}}}{\sqrt{9+36+4}} = \dfrac{1}{7}(3\hat{\mathbf{i}}+6\hat{\mathbf{j}}-2\hat{\mathbf{k}})$

43 (*b*) $\quad |\mathbf{OA}| = \sqrt{4+4+1} = 3$

and $\quad |\mathbf{OB}| = \sqrt{4+16+16} = 6$

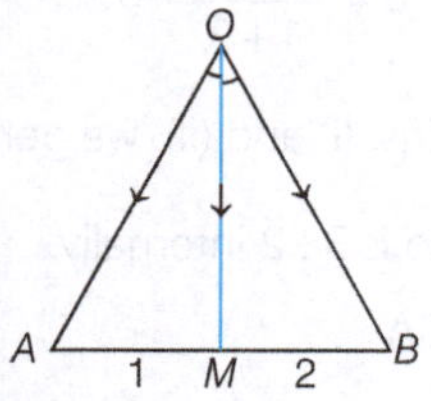

We know, $\dfrac{AM}{MB} = \dfrac{|\mathbf{OA}|}{|\mathbf{OB}|} = \dfrac{3}{6} = \dfrac{1}{2}$

$\therefore PV \text{ of } M = \dfrac{2(2\hat{\mathbf{i}}+2\hat{\mathbf{j}}+\hat{\mathbf{k}})+1(2\hat{\mathbf{i}}+4\hat{\mathbf{j}}+4\hat{\mathbf{k}})}{3} = \dfrac{6\hat{\mathbf{i}}+8\hat{\mathbf{j}}+6\hat{\mathbf{k}}}{3}$

$\therefore$ Length of bisector

$$|\mathbf{OM}| = \sqrt{\frac{1}{9}(36+64+36)} = \frac{\sqrt{136}}{3} \text{ units}$$

$\therefore$ Required length of a vector is $\dfrac{\sqrt{136}}{3}$.

44 (*c*) In ΔABC, $\mathbf{AB}+\mathbf{BC}=\mathbf{AC}$

$\Rightarrow \quad \mathbf{AC}=\mathbf{a}+\mathbf{b}$

AD is parallel to BC and $AD = 2BC$

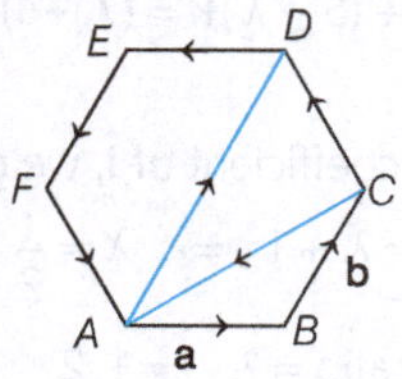

$\therefore \quad \mathbf{AD}=2\mathbf{b}$

In ΔACD, $\mathbf{AC}+\mathbf{CD}=\mathbf{AD}$

$\Rightarrow \mathbf{CD}=2\mathbf{b}-(\mathbf{a}+\mathbf{b})=\mathbf{b}-\mathbf{a}$

Now, $\mathbf{CE}=\mathbf{CD}+\mathbf{DE}=\mathbf{b}-\mathbf{a}-\mathbf{a} = \mathbf{b}-2\mathbf{a}$

45 (*d*) If $\mathbf{a}+2\mathbf{b}$ is collinear with $\mathbf{c}$, then

$$\mathbf{a}+2\mathbf{b}=t\mathbf{c} \quad \text{...(i)}$$

Also, if $\mathbf{b}+3\mathbf{c}$ is collinear with $\mathbf{a}$, then $\mathbf{b}+3\mathbf{c}=\lambda\,\mathbf{a}$

$$\Rightarrow \quad \mathbf{b}=\lambda\,\mathbf{a}-3\,\mathbf{c} \quad \text{...(ii)}$$

On putting the value of $\mathbf{b}$ in Eq. (i), we get

$\mathbf{a}+2(\lambda\mathbf{a}-3\,\mathbf{c})=t\mathbf{c}$

$\Rightarrow \quad (\mathbf{a}-6\mathbf{c})=t\,\mathbf{c}-2\lambda\mathbf{a}$

On comparing, we get $1=-2\lambda$ and $-6=t$

$\Rightarrow \quad \lambda=-\dfrac{1}{2}$

and $\quad t=-6$

From Eq. (i)

$\mathbf{a}+2\mathbf{b}=-6\mathbf{c}$

$\Rightarrow \mathbf{a}+2\mathbf{b}+6\mathbf{c}=\mathbf{0}$

46 (*a*) Given, $\mathbf{PR}=5\,\mathbf{PQ}$

It means R divides PQ externally in the ratio 5 : 4.

$\therefore$ Position vector of $R = \dfrac{5\,\mathbf{b}-4\,\mathbf{a}}{5-4} = 5\,\mathbf{b}-4\,\mathbf{a}$

47 (*c*) If $\mathbf{a}$ and $\mathbf{b}$ are non-zero and non-collinear vectors and there exists α and β such that $\alpha\,\mathbf{a}+\beta\,\mathbf{b}=0$, then $\alpha=\beta=0$.

48 (*b*) $\mathbf{AB}=2\hat{\mathbf{i}}+3\hat{\mathbf{j}}+4\hat{\mathbf{k}}-4\hat{\mathbf{i}}-7\hat{\mathbf{j}}-8\hat{\mathbf{k}} = -2\hat{\mathbf{i}}-4\hat{\mathbf{j}}-4\hat{\mathbf{k}}$

and $\mathbf{AC}=2\hat{\mathbf{i}}+5\hat{\mathbf{j}}+7\hat{\mathbf{k}}-4\hat{\mathbf{i}}-7\hat{\mathbf{j}}-8\hat{\mathbf{k}} = -2\hat{\mathbf{i}}-2\hat{\mathbf{j}}-\hat{\mathbf{k}}$

$\therefore \quad |\mathbf{AB}|=6$ and $|\mathbf{AC}|=3$

We know, $\dfrac{BM}{MC}=\dfrac{|\mathbf{AB}|}{|\mathbf{AC}|}=\dfrac{6}{3}$

$\therefore$ Position vector of required bisector

$$= \frac{6(2\hat{\mathbf{i}}+5\hat{\mathbf{j}}+7\hat{\mathbf{k}})+3(2\hat{\mathbf{i}}+3\hat{\mathbf{j}}+4\hat{\mathbf{k}})}{6+3} = \frac{1}{3}(6\hat{\mathbf{i}}+13\hat{\mathbf{j}}+18\hat{\mathbf{k}})$$

49 (*d*) $|\mathbf{AB}| = \sqrt{(7-1)^2+(-4+6)^2+(7-10)^2} = 7$

$|\mathbf{BC}| = \sqrt{(1+1)^2+(-6+3)^2+(10-4)^2} = 7$

$|\mathbf{CD}| = \sqrt{(-1-5)^2+(-3+1)^2+(4-5)^2} = \sqrt{41}$

and $|\mathbf{DA}| = \sqrt{(5-7)^2 + (-1+4)^2 + (5-7)^2} = \sqrt{17}$

So, *ABCD* is neither a square and nor a rhombus. Also, it is not a rectangle.

50 (c) Let $\mathbf{a} = l\hat{\mathbf{i}} + m\hat{\mathbf{j}} + n\hat{\mathbf{k}}$ makes an angle $\frac{\pi}{4}$ with *Z*-axis

Also, $l^2 + m^2 + n^2 = 1$

Here, $n = \cos\frac{\pi}{4} = \frac{1}{\sqrt{2}}, l^2 + m^2 = \frac{1}{2}$ ...(i)

$\therefore \quad \mathbf{a} = l\hat{\mathbf{i}} + m\hat{\mathbf{j}} + \frac{\hat{\mathbf{k}}}{\sqrt{2}}$

$\Rightarrow \therefore \ \mathbf{a} + \hat{\mathbf{i}} + \hat{\mathbf{j}} = (l+1)\,\hat{\mathbf{i}} + (m+1)\,\hat{\mathbf{j}} + \frac{\hat{\mathbf{k}}}{\sqrt{2}}$

$\Rightarrow |\mathbf{a} + \hat{\mathbf{i}} + \hat{\mathbf{j}}| = \sqrt{(l+1)^2 + (m+1)^2 + \left(\frac{1}{\sqrt{2}}\right)^2}$

$\Rightarrow 1 = l^2 + m^2 + 2 + 2l + 2m + \frac{1}{2}$

$\Rightarrow \quad l + m = -1$ [from Eq. (i)]

$\Rightarrow \quad l^2 + m^2 + 2lm = 1$

$\Rightarrow \quad 2lm = \frac{1}{2}$

$\Rightarrow \quad l = m = -\frac{1}{2}$

$\left[\because l = m = \frac{1}{2} \text{ is not satisfied the given equation}\right]$

$\therefore \quad \mathbf{a} = -\frac{\hat{\mathbf{i}}}{2} - \frac{\hat{\mathbf{j}}}{2} + \frac{\hat{\mathbf{k}}}{\sqrt{2}}$

51 (*a*) Since, $\mathbf{a} = 8\,\mathbf{b}$ and $\mathbf{c} = -7\mathbf{b}$

a is parallel to **b** and **c** is anti-parallel to **b**.

$\Rightarrow$ **a** and **c** are anti-parallel.

$\Rightarrow$ Angle between **a** and **c** is π.

52 (*d*) From the figure,

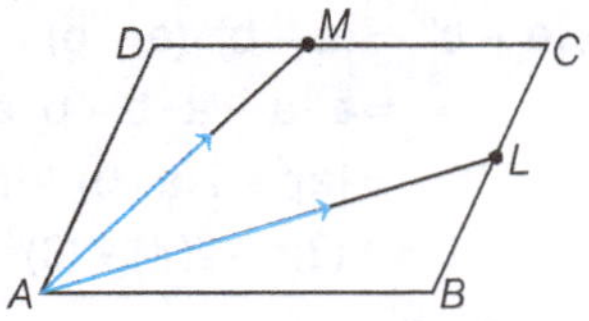

$$\mathbf{AL} = \mathbf{AB} + \mathbf{BL} = \mathbf{AB} + \frac{1}{2}\mathbf{BC} = \mathbf{AB} + \frac{1}{2}\mathbf{AD}$$

and $\quad \mathbf{AM} = \mathbf{AD} + \mathbf{DM} = \mathbf{AD} + \frac{1}{2}\mathbf{DC} = \mathbf{AD} + \frac{1}{2}\mathbf{AB}$

$\therefore \ \mathbf{AL} + \mathbf{AM} = \frac{3}{2}(\mathbf{AB} + \mathbf{AD}) = \frac{3}{2}(\mathbf{AB} + \mathbf{BC})$

$= \left(\frac{3}{2}\mathbf{AC}\right)$

53. (*b*) Given, $\mathbf{AD} + \mathbf{EB} + \mathbf{FC} = \lambda\mathbf{ED}$

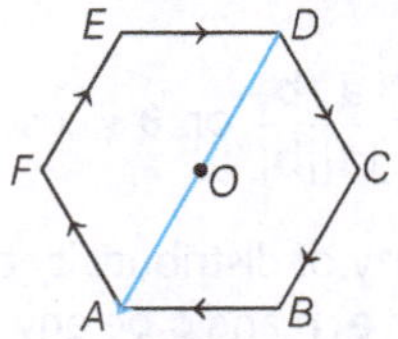

$\Rightarrow (\mathbf{AE} + \mathbf{ED}) + (\mathbf{ED} + \mathbf{DB}) + 2\mathbf{ED} = \lambda\mathbf{ED}$

$\Rightarrow \quad 4\,\mathbf{ED} + (\mathbf{AE} + \mathbf{DB}) = \lambda\mathbf{ED}$

$\Rightarrow \quad 4\,\mathbf{ED} = \lambda\,\mathbf{ED} \quad [\because \mathbf{AE} = -\mathbf{DB}]$

$\lambda = 4$

Alternate Method

Now, $\quad \mathbf{AD} + \mathbf{EB} + \mathbf{FC} = 2(\mathbf{OD} + \mathbf{EO} + \mathbf{ED})$

$= 2(\mathbf{ED} + \mathbf{ED}) = 4\,\mathbf{ED}$

$\therefore \quad \lambda = 4$

Scalar (or dot) Product of Two Vectors

1 (*c*) Multiplication of two vectors is defined in two ways, namely, scalar (or dot) product where the result is a scalar and vector (or cross) product where the result is a vector. Based upon these two types of products for vectors, they have found various applications in geometry, mechanics and engineering.

2 (*b*) The scalar product of two non-zero vectors **a** and **b**, denoted by $\mathbf{a}\cdot\mathbf{b}$, is defined as $\mathbf{a}\cdot\mathbf{b} = |\mathbf{a}||\mathbf{b}|\cos\theta$,

where, θ is the angle between **a** and **b**, $0 \le \theta \le \pi$.

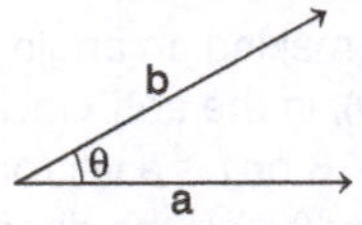

3 (*d*) If either $\mathbf{a} = \mathbf{0}$ or $\mathbf{b} = \mathbf{0}$, then θ is not defined and in this case we define $\mathbf{a}\cdot\mathbf{b} = 0$

4 (*a*) If **a** and **b** are two vector then $\mathbf{a}\cdot\mathbf{b} = |\mathbf{a}||\mathbf{b}|\cos\theta$. By this we can conclude that.

(i) $\mathbf{a}\cdot\mathbf{b}$ is a real number.

(ii) If **a** and **b** be two non-zero vectors, then $\mathbf{a}\cdot\mathbf{b} = 0$, if and only if **a** and **b** are perpendicular to each other, i.e. $\mathbf{a}\cdot\mathbf{b} = \mathbf{0} \Leftrightarrow \mathbf{a} \perp \mathbf{b}$.

(iii) If $\theta = 0°$, then $\mathbf{a}\cdot\mathbf{b} = |\mathbf{a}||\mathbf{b}|$. In particular, $\mathbf{a}\cdot\mathbf{a} = |\mathbf{a}|^2$, as θ in this case is 0.

(iv) If $\theta = \pi$, then $\mathbf{a}\cdot\mathbf{b} = -|\mathbf{a}||\mathbf{b}|$ in particular, $\mathbf{a}\cdot\mathbf{a} = -|\mathbf{a}|^2$ as θ in this case is π.

So, we see that option (a) is correct.

5 (*d*) Since, $\hat{\mathbf{i}}, \hat{\mathbf{j}}$ and $\hat{\mathbf{k}}$ are mutually perpendicular unit vectors, so we have

$\hat{\mathbf{i}}\cdot\hat{\mathbf{i}} = \hat{\mathbf{j}}\cdot\hat{\mathbf{j}} = \hat{\mathbf{k}}\cdot\hat{\mathbf{k}} = 1$

and $\quad \hat{\mathbf{i}}\cdot\hat{\mathbf{j}} = \hat{\mathbf{j}}\cdot\hat{\mathbf{k}} = \hat{\mathbf{k}}\cdot\hat{\mathbf{i}} = 0$

6 (*a*) The angle between two non-zero vectors **a** and **b** is given by

$$\cos\theta = \frac{\mathbf{a}\cdot\mathbf{b}}{|\mathbf{a}||\mathbf{b}|} \text{ or } \theta = \cos^{-1}\left(\frac{\mathbf{a}\cdot\mathbf{b}}{|\mathbf{a}||\mathbf{b}|}\right)$$

7 (*c*) (a) By property of distributivity of scalar product over addition. Let **a**, **b** and **c** be any three vectors, then

$$\mathbf{a}\cdot(\mathbf{b}+\mathbf{c}) = \mathbf{a}\cdot\mathbf{b}+\mathbf{a}\cdot\mathbf{c}$$

So, option (a) is correct.

(b) and (d) If **a** and b be any two vectors, and λ be any scalar. Then,

$$(\lambda\mathbf{a})\cdot\mathbf{b} = (\lambda\mathbf{a})\cdot\mathbf{b} = \mathbf{a}\cdot(\lambda\mathbf{b})$$

So, option (b) and (d) are correct.

(c) If two vectors **a** and **b** are given in component form as $a_1\hat{i}+a_2\hat{j}+a_3\hat{k}$ and $b_1\hat{i}+b_2\hat{j}+b_3\hat{k}$, then, their scalar product is given as

$$\begin{aligned}\mathbf{a}\cdot\mathbf{b} &= (a_1\hat{i}+a_2\hat{j}+a_3\hat{k})\cdot(b_1\hat{i}+b_2\hat{j}+b_3\hat{k})\\ &= a_1\hat{i}\cdot(b_1\hat{i}+b_2\hat{j}+b_3\hat{k})+a_2\hat{j}\cdot(b_1\hat{i}+b_2\hat{j}+b_3\hat{k})\\ &\quad + a_3\hat{k}\cdot(b_1\hat{i}+b_2\hat{j}+b_3\hat{k})\\ &= a_1b_1(\hat{i}\cdot\hat{i})+a_1b_2(\hat{i}\cdot\hat{j})+a_1b_3(\hat{i}\cdot\hat{k})+a_2b_1(\hat{j}\cdot\hat{i})\\ &\quad + a_2b_2(\hat{j}\cdot\hat{j})+a_2b_3(\hat{j}\cdot\hat{k})\\ &\quad + a_3b_1(\hat{k}\cdot\hat{i})+a_3b_2(\hat{k}\cdot\hat{j})+a_3b_3(\hat{k}\cdot\hat{k})\\ &= a_1b_1+a_2b_2+a_3b_3\end{aligned}$$

$$[\because \hat{i}\cdot\hat{j}=\hat{j}\cdot\hat{k}=\hat{k}\cdot\hat{i}=0 \text{ and } \hat{i}\cdot\hat{i}=\hat{j}\cdot\hat{j}=\hat{k}\cdot\hat{k}=1]$$

Thus, $\mathbf{a}\cdot\mathbf{b} = a_1b_1+a_2b_2+a_3b_3$

So, we can say that option (c) is incorrect.

8. (*d*) A vector **AB** is making an angle θ with the given directed line *l* (say), in the anti-clockwise direction (Fig.) the projection of **AB** on *l* is a vector **P** (say) with magnitude $|\mathbf{AB}|\cos\theta$, and the direction of **P** being the same (or opposite) to that of the line *l*, depending upon whether $\cos\theta$ is positive or negative. The vector **P** is called projection vector, and its magnitude $|\mathbf{P}|$ is simply called as the projection of the vector **AB** on the directed line *l*.

9 (*d*)

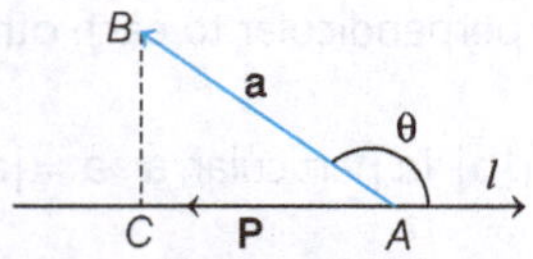

(90° < θ < 180°)

(i)

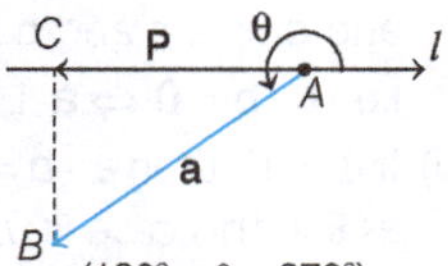

(180° < θ < 270°)

(ii)

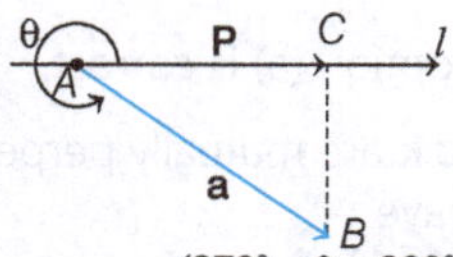

(270° < θ < 360°)

(iii)

For example, in each of the above figures (figure) (i) to (iii), projection vector of **AB** along the line *l* is vector **AC**.

10 (*b*) If $\hat{\mathbf{P}}$ is the unit vector along a line *l*, then the projection of a vector a on the line *l* is given by $\mathbf{a}\cdot\hat{\mathbf{P}}$.

11 (*d*) Projection of a vector **a** on other vector **b**, is given by

$$\mathbf{a}\cdot\hat{\mathbf{b}} \text{ or } \mathbf{a}\cdot\left(\frac{\mathbf{b}}{|\mathbf{b}|}\right) \text{ or } \frac{1}{|\mathbf{b}|}(\mathbf{a}\cdot\mathbf{b})$$

12 (*a*) If $\theta = 0°$, then the projection vector of **AB** will be **AB** itself and if $\theta = \pi$, then the projection vector of **AB** will be **BA**.

13. (*b*) If $\theta = \frac{\pi}{2}$ or $\theta = \frac{3\pi}{2}$, then the projection vector of AB will be zero vector (or null vector).

14 (*c*) If α, β and γ are the direction angles of vector $\mathbf{a} = a_1\hat{i}+a_2\hat{j}+a_3\hat{k}$, then its direction cosines are

$$\cos\alpha = \frac{\mathbf{a}\cdot\hat{i}}{|\mathbf{a}||\hat{i}|} = \frac{a_1}{|\mathbf{a}|} \text{ similarly, } \cos\beta = \frac{a_2}{|\mathbf{a}|} \text{ and } \cos\gamma = \frac{a_3}{|\mathbf{a}|}$$

Since, **a** is a unit vector.

$\cos\alpha = a_1, \cos\beta = a_2, \cos\gamma = a_3$

Thus, $\mathbf{a} = \cos\alpha\,\hat{i}+\cos\beta\,\hat{j}+\cos\gamma\,\hat{k}$

15 (*b*) As we know that $|\mathbf{a}|\cos\alpha$, $|\mathbf{a}|\cos\beta$ and $|\mathbf{a}|\cos\gamma$ are, respectively the projections of **a** along *OX*, *OY* and *OZ*. i.e. the scalar components a_1, a_2 and a_3 of the vector **a**, are precisely the projections of **a** along *X*-axis, *Y*-axis and *Z*-axis, respectively. If **a** is a unit vector, then it may be expressed in terms of its direction cosines as

$$\mathbf{a} = \cos\alpha\hat{i}+\cos\beta\hat{j}+\cos\gamma\hat{k}$$

16 (*c*) The projection of vector **a** on the vector **b** is given by

$$\frac{(\mathbf{a}\cdot\mathbf{b})}{|\mathbf{b}|} = \frac{(2\times1+3\times2+2\times1)}{\sqrt{(1)^2+(2)^2+(1)^2}} = \frac{10}{\sqrt{6}} = \frac{5}{3}\sqrt{6}$$

17 (*b*) We have, $|\mathbf{a}-\mathbf{b}|^2 = (\mathbf{a}-\mathbf{b})\cdot(\mathbf{a}-\mathbf{b})$

$$\begin{aligned}&= \mathbf{a}\cdot\mathbf{a}-\mathbf{a}\cdot\mathbf{b}-\mathbf{b}\cdot\mathbf{a}+\mathbf{b}\cdot\mathbf{b}\\ &= |\mathbf{a}|^2-2(\mathbf{a}\cdot\mathbf{b})+|\mathbf{b}|^2\\ &= (2)^2-2(4)+(3)^2\end{aligned}$$

Therefore, $|\mathbf{a}-\mathbf{b}| = \sqrt{5}$

18 (*a*) Since, **a** is a unit vector, $|\mathbf{a}| = 1$. Also,

$$(\mathbf{x}-\mathbf{a})\cdot(\mathbf{x}+\mathbf{a}) = 8$$

or $\mathbf{x}\cdot\mathbf{x}+\mathbf{x}\cdot\mathbf{a}-\mathbf{a}\cdot\mathbf{x}-\mathbf{a}\cdot\mathbf{a} = 8$

or $|\mathbf{x}|^2-1 = 8$

i.e. $|\mathbf{x}|^2 = 9$

Therefore, $|\mathbf{x}| = 3$ (as magnitude of vector is non negative).

19 (*b*) We have,

$$\mathbf{AB} = (1+2)\hat{\mathbf{i}} + (2-3)\hat{\mathbf{j}} + (3-5)\hat{\mathbf{k}} = 3\hat{\mathbf{i}} - \hat{\mathbf{j}} - 2\hat{\mathbf{k}}$$

$$\mathbf{BC} = (7-1)\hat{\mathbf{i}} + (0-2)\hat{\mathbf{j}} + (-1-3)\hat{\mathbf{k}} = 6\hat{\mathbf{i}} - 2\hat{\mathbf{j}} - 4\hat{\mathbf{k}},$$

$$\mathbf{AC} = (7+2)\hat{\mathbf{i}} + (0-3)\hat{\mathbf{j}} + (-1-5)\hat{\mathbf{k}} = 9\hat{\mathbf{i}} - 3\hat{\mathbf{j}} - 6\hat{\mathbf{k}}$$

$$|\mathbf{AB}| = \sqrt{14}, |\mathbf{BC}| = 2\sqrt{14} \text{ and } |\mathbf{AC}| = 3\sqrt{14}$$

Therefore, $|\mathbf{AC}| = |\mathbf{AB}| + |\mathbf{BC}|$

Hence, the points A, B and C are collinear.

Note *One may note that although* $\mathbf{AB} + \mathbf{BC} + \mathbf{CA} = 0$ *but the points A, B and C do not form the vertices of a triangle.*

20 (*c*) To determine the angle between **a** and **b**, we can use the formula

$$\cos\theta = \frac{\mathbf{a}\cdot\mathbf{b}}{|\mathbf{a}|\ |\mathbf{b}|}$$

It is given that $|\mathbf{a}| = \sqrt{3}, |\mathbf{b}| = 2$ and $\mathbf{a}\cdot\mathbf{b} = \sqrt{6}$

Let θ be the required angle, then

$$\cos\theta = \frac{\mathbf{a}\cdot\mathbf{b}}{|\mathbf{a}|\ |\mathbf{b}|} = \frac{\sqrt{6}}{\sqrt{3}\times 2} = \frac{1}{\sqrt{2}}$$

$$\Rightarrow \quad \theta = \cos^{-1}\left(\frac{1}{\sqrt{2}}\right) = \cos^{-1}\left(\cos\frac{\pi}{4}\right) = \frac{\pi}{4}$$

Hence, the angle between the given vectors a and b is $\pi/4$.

21 (*c*) The angle between the two vectors **a** and **b** is given by $\cos\theta = \frac{\mathbf{a}\cdot\mathbf{b}}{|\mathbf{a}||\mathbf{b}|}$. Here, we are not given $\mathbf{a}\cdot\mathbf{b}$ (dot product) and magnitude $|\mathbf{a}|$ and $|\mathbf{b}|$, so first of all we have to find these required factors.

Let $\quad \mathbf{a} = \hat{\mathbf{i}} - 2\hat{\mathbf{j}} + 3\hat{\mathbf{k}}$ and $\mathbf{b} = 3\hat{\mathbf{i}} - 2\hat{\mathbf{j}} + \hat{\mathbf{k}}$

Magnitude of **a**,

$$|\mathbf{a}| = \sqrt{1^2 + (-2)^2 + 3^2} = \sqrt{1+4+9} = \sqrt{14}$$

Magnitude of b,

$$|\mathbf{b}| = \sqrt{3^2 + (-2)^2 + 1^2} = \sqrt{9+4+1} = \sqrt{14}$$

Now, $\mathbf{a}\cdot\mathbf{b} = (\hat{\mathbf{i}} - 2\hat{\mathbf{j}} + 3\hat{\mathbf{k}})\cdot(3\hat{\mathbf{i}} - 2\hat{\mathbf{j}} + \hat{\mathbf{k}})$

$$= 1\cdot 3 + (-2)\cdot(-2) + 3\cdot 1$$

$$= 3 + 4 + 3 = 10$$

[dot product of two vectors is equal to the sum of the products of their corresponding components]

Let θ be the required angle between a and b, then

$$\cos\theta = \frac{\mathbf{a}\cdot\mathbf{b}}{|\mathbf{a}|\ |\mathbf{b}|} = \frac{10}{\sqrt{14}\sqrt{14}} = \frac{10}{14} = \frac{5}{7}$$

$$\Rightarrow \quad \theta = \cos^{-1}\left(\frac{5}{7}\right)$$

22 (*a*) Let $\mathbf{a} = \hat{\mathbf{i}} - \hat{\mathbf{j}}, \mathbf{b} = \hat{\mathbf{i}} + \hat{\mathbf{j}}$.

Projection of **a** on **b** is given by,

$$\frac{\mathbf{a}\cdot\mathbf{b}}{|\mathbf{b}|} = \frac{(\hat{\mathbf{i}}-\hat{\mathbf{j}})\cdot(\hat{\mathbf{i}}+\hat{\mathbf{j}})}{\sqrt{1^2+1^2}} = \frac{1\times 1 + (-1)\times 1}{\sqrt{2}} = 0$$

Hence, the projection of vector **a** on **b** is 0.

23 (*c*) To prove that a vector is a unit vector we have to prove that its magnitude is unit i.e., 1. Two vectors **a** and **b** are perpendicular, if $\mathbf{a}\cdot\mathbf{b} = 0$.

Let $\quad \mathbf{a} = \frac{1}{7}(2\hat{\mathbf{i}} + 3\hat{\mathbf{j}} + 6\hat{\mathbf{k}}) = \frac{2}{7}\hat{\mathbf{i}} + \frac{3}{7}\hat{\mathbf{j}} + \frac{6}{7}\hat{\mathbf{k}}$

$$\mathbf{b} = \frac{1}{7}(3\hat{\mathbf{i}} - 6\hat{\mathbf{j}} + 2\hat{\mathbf{k}}) = \frac{3}{7}\hat{\mathbf{i}} - \frac{6}{7}\hat{\mathbf{j}} + \frac{2}{7}\hat{\mathbf{k}}$$

and $\quad \mathbf{c} = \frac{1}{7}(6\hat{\mathbf{i}} + 2\hat{\mathbf{j}} - 3\hat{\mathbf{k}}) = \frac{6}{7}\hat{\mathbf{i}} + \frac{2}{7}\hat{\mathbf{j}} - \frac{3}{7}\hat{\mathbf{k}}$

Then, magnitude of **a**,

$$|\mathbf{a}| = \sqrt{\left(\frac{2}{7}\right)^2 + \left(\frac{3}{7}\right)^2 + \left(\frac{6}{7}\right)^2} = \sqrt{\frac{49}{49}} = 1$$

magnitude of **b**,

$$|\mathbf{b}| = \sqrt{\left(\frac{3}{7}\right)^2 + \left(\frac{-6}{7}\right)^2 + \left(\frac{2}{7}\right)^2} = \sqrt{\frac{49}{49}} = 1$$

and magnitude of **c**,

$$|\mathbf{c}| = \sqrt{\left(\frac{6}{7}\right)^2 + \left(\frac{2}{7}\right)^2 + \left(\frac{-3}{7}\right)^2} = \sqrt{\frac{49}{49}} = 1$$

Thus, each of the given three vectors is a unit vector.

Now, $\mathbf{a}\cdot\mathbf{b} = \left(\frac{2}{7}\hat{\mathbf{i}} + \frac{3}{7}\hat{\mathbf{j}} + \frac{6}{7}\hat{\mathbf{k}}\right)\cdot\left(\frac{3}{7}\hat{\mathbf{i}} - \frac{6}{7}\hat{\mathbf{j}} + \frac{2}{7}\hat{\mathbf{k}}\right)$

$$= \frac{2}{7}\times\frac{3}{7} + \frac{3}{7}\times\left(\frac{-6}{7}\right) + \frac{6}{7}\times\frac{2}{7}$$

$$= \frac{6}{49} - \frac{18}{49} + \frac{12}{49} = \frac{6-18+12}{49} = \frac{0}{49} = 0$$

i.e. **a** and **b** are perpendicular to each other.

$$\mathbf{b}\cdot\mathbf{c} = \left(\frac{3}{7}\hat{\mathbf{i}} - \frac{6}{7}\hat{\mathbf{j}} + \frac{2}{7}\hat{\mathbf{k}}\right)\cdot\left(\frac{6}{7}\hat{\mathbf{i}} + \frac{2}{7}\hat{\mathbf{j}} - \frac{3}{7}\hat{\mathbf{k}}\right)$$

$$= \frac{3}{7}\times\frac{6}{7} + \left(\frac{-6}{7}\right)\times\frac{2}{7} + \frac{2}{7}\times\left(\frac{-3}{7}\right)$$

$$= \frac{18}{49} - \frac{12}{49} - \frac{6}{49} = \frac{18-12-6}{49} = \frac{0}{49} = 0$$

i.e. **b** and **c** are perpendicular to each other.

$$\mathbf{c}\cdot\mathbf{a} = \left(\frac{6}{7}\hat{\mathbf{i}} + \frac{2}{7}\hat{\mathbf{j}} - \frac{3}{7}\hat{\mathbf{k}}\right)\cdot\left(\frac{2}{7}\hat{\mathbf{i}} + \frac{3}{7}\hat{\mathbf{j}} + \frac{6}{7}\hat{\mathbf{k}}\right)$$

$$= \frac{6}{7} \times \frac{2}{7} + \frac{2}{7} \times \frac{3}{7} + \left(\frac{-3}{7}\right) \times \frac{6}{7}$$

$$= \frac{12}{49} + \frac{6}{49} - \frac{18}{49} = \frac{12+6-18}{49} = \frac{0}{49} = 0$$

i.e. **c** and **a** are perpendicular to each other.

Hence, the given three vectors are mutually perpendicular to each other.

24 (*c*) Given, $(\mathbf{a} + \mathbf{b}) \cdot (\mathbf{a} - \mathbf{b}) = 8$ and $|\mathbf{a}| = 8|\mathbf{b}|$

$\Rightarrow \quad \mathbf{a} \cdot \mathbf{a} - \mathbf{a} \cdot \mathbf{b} + \mathbf{b} \cdot \mathbf{a} - \mathbf{b} \cdot \mathbf{b} = 8$

$\Rightarrow \quad |\mathbf{a}|^2 - |\mathbf{b}|^2 = 8$ [$\because \mathbf{a} \cdot \mathbf{a} = |\mathbf{a}|^2$ and $\mathbf{a} \cdot \mathbf{b} = \mathbf{b} \cdot \mathbf{a}$]

$\Rightarrow \quad (8|\mathbf{b}|)^2 - |\mathbf{b}|^2 = 8$

$\Rightarrow \quad 63|\mathbf{b}|^2 = 8$ [given, $|\mathbf{a}| = 8|\mathbf{b}|$]

$\Rightarrow \quad |\mathbf{b}| = \sqrt{\frac{8}{63}} = \frac{2}{3}\sqrt{\frac{2}{7}}$

Also, $\quad |\mathbf{a}| = 8|\mathbf{b}| = 8\left(\frac{2}{3}\sqrt{\frac{2}{7}}\right) = \frac{16}{3}\sqrt{\frac{2}{7}}$

25 (*a*) To find the product, use $\mathbf{a} \cdot \mathbf{a} = |\mathbf{a}|^2$, $\mathbf{b} \cdot \mathbf{b} = |\mathbf{b}|^2$ and $\mathbf{a} \cdot \mathbf{b} = \mathbf{b} \cdot \mathbf{a}$.

We have, $(3\mathbf{a} - 5\mathbf{b}) \cdot (2\mathbf{a} + 7\mathbf{b})$

$= (3\mathbf{a}) \cdot (2\mathbf{a} + 7\mathbf{b}) - (5\mathbf{b}) \cdot (2\mathbf{a} + 7\mathbf{b})$

$= 6(\mathbf{a} \cdot \mathbf{a}) + 21(\mathbf{a} \cdot \mathbf{b}) - 10(\mathbf{b} \cdot \mathbf{a}) - 35(\mathbf{b} \cdot \mathbf{b})$

$= 6|\mathbf{a}|^2 + 11(\mathbf{a} \cdot \mathbf{b}) - 35|\mathbf{b}|^2$

[$\because \mathbf{a} \cdot \mathbf{a} = |\mathbf{a}|^2$ and $\mathbf{a} \cdot \mathbf{b} = \mathbf{b} \cdot \mathbf{a}$]

26 (*a*) Both vectors have same magnitude i.e. $|\mathbf{a}| = |\mathbf{b}|$ and scalar product of vectors, $\mathbf{a} \cdot \mathbf{b} = \frac{1}{2}$ (given).

Let θ be the angle between two vectors **a** and **b**, then

$$\cos\theta = \frac{\mathbf{a} \cdot \mathbf{b}}{|\mathbf{a}|\ |\mathbf{b}|}$$

$\Rightarrow \quad \cos 60^\circ = \dfrac{\frac{1}{2}}{|\mathbf{a}||\mathbf{a}|}$ [$\because |\mathbf{a}| = |\mathbf{b}|$]

$\Rightarrow \quad \frac{1}{2} = \frac{1}{2|\mathbf{a}|^2} \Rightarrow |\mathbf{a}|^2 = 1$

$\Rightarrow \quad |\mathbf{a}| = 1$

Thus, $\quad |\mathbf{a}| = |\mathbf{b}| = 1$

27 (*b*) Given, $|\mathbf{a}| = 1$

[$\because$ It is a unit vector, magnitude of a unit vector is 1.]

and $\quad (\mathbf{x} - \mathbf{a}).(\mathbf{x} + \mathbf{a}) = 12$

$\Rightarrow \quad \mathbf{x} \cdot \mathbf{x} + \mathbf{x} \cdot \mathbf{a} - \mathbf{a} \cdot \mathbf{x} - \mathbf{a} \cdot \mathbf{a} = 12$

[$\because \mathbf{a} \cdot \mathbf{a} = |\mathbf{a}|^2$ and $\mathbf{a} \cdot \mathbf{b} = \mathbf{b} \cdot \mathbf{a}$]

$\Rightarrow \quad |\mathbf{x}|^2 - |\mathbf{a}|^2 = 12$

$\Rightarrow \quad |\mathbf{x}|^2 - 1^2 = 12$ [$\because |\mathbf{a}| = 1$ as **a** is a unit vector]

$\Rightarrow \quad |\mathbf{x}|^2 = 13$

$\Rightarrow \quad |\mathbf{x}| = \sqrt{13}$

28 (*d*) The given vectors are $\mathbf{a} = 2\hat{\mathbf{i}} + 2\hat{\mathbf{j}} + 3\hat{\mathbf{k}}$, $\mathbf{b} = -\hat{\mathbf{i}} + 2\hat{\mathbf{j}} + \hat{\mathbf{k}}$ and $\mathbf{c} = 3\hat{\mathbf{i}} + \hat{\mathbf{j}}$.

Now, $\quad (\mathbf{a} + \lambda\mathbf{b}) \perp \mathbf{c}$ [given]

$\Rightarrow \quad (\mathbf{a} + \lambda\mathbf{b}) \cdot \mathbf{c} = 0$

[$\because$ scalar product of two perpendicular vectors is zero]

$\Rightarrow \quad [(2\hat{\mathbf{i}} + 2\hat{\mathbf{j}} + 3\hat{\mathbf{k}}) + \lambda(-\hat{\mathbf{i}} + 2\hat{\mathbf{j}} + \hat{\mathbf{k}})] \cdot (3\hat{\mathbf{i}} + \hat{\mathbf{j}}) = 0$

$\Rightarrow \quad [(2-\lambda)\hat{\mathbf{i}} + (2+2\lambda)\hat{\mathbf{j}} + (3+\lambda)\hat{\mathbf{k}}] \cdot (3\hat{\mathbf{i}} + \hat{\mathbf{j}}) = 0$

$\Rightarrow \quad (2-\lambda)3 + (2+2\lambda)1 + (3+\lambda)0 = 0$

$\Rightarrow \quad 6 - 3\lambda + 2 + 2\lambda = 0$

$\Rightarrow \quad 8 - \lambda = 0$

$\Rightarrow \quad \lambda = 8$

Hence, the required value of λ is 8.

29 (*b*) As **a**, **b** and **c** are unit vectors, so use $|\mathbf{a}| = |\mathbf{b}| = |\mathbf{c}| = 1$ and expand $(\mathbf{a} + \mathbf{b} + \mathbf{c}) \cdot (\mathbf{a} + \mathbf{b} + \mathbf{c})$ to get the value of $\mathbf{a} \cdot \mathbf{b} + \mathbf{b} \cdot \mathbf{c} + \mathbf{c} \cdot \mathbf{a}$.

Given, $\quad |\mathbf{a}| = |\mathbf{b}| = |\mathbf{c}| = 1$ and $\mathbf{a} + \mathbf{b} + \mathbf{c} = \mathbf{0}$

We have, $\quad (\mathbf{a} + \mathbf{b} + \mathbf{c}) \cdot (\mathbf{a} + \mathbf{b} + \mathbf{c}) = 0$

$\Rightarrow \quad \mathbf{a} \cdot (\mathbf{a} + \mathbf{b} + \mathbf{c}) + \mathbf{b} \cdot (\mathbf{a} + \mathbf{b} + \mathbf{c}) + \mathbf{c} \cdot (\mathbf{a} + \mathbf{b} + \mathbf{c}) = 0$

$\Rightarrow \mathbf{a} \cdot \mathbf{a} + \mathbf{a} \cdot \mathbf{b} + \mathbf{a} \cdot \mathbf{c} + \mathbf{b} \cdot \mathbf{a} + \mathbf{b} \cdot \mathbf{b} + \mathbf{b}.\mathbf{c}$
$+ \mathbf{c} \cdot \mathbf{a} + \mathbf{c} \cdot \mathbf{b} + \mathbf{c} \cdot \mathbf{c} = 0$

$\Rightarrow \quad |\mathbf{a}|^2 + |\mathbf{b}|^2 + |\mathbf{c}|^2 + 2(\mathbf{a} \cdot \mathbf{b} + \mathbf{b} \cdot \mathbf{c} + \mathbf{c} \cdot \mathbf{a}) = 0$

[$\because \mathbf{a} \cdot \mathbf{a} = |\mathbf{a}|^2$ and $\mathbf{a} \cdot \mathbf{b} = \mathbf{b} \cdot \mathbf{a}$]

$\Rightarrow \quad 1 + 1 + 1 + 2(\mathbf{a} \cdot \mathbf{b} + \mathbf{b} \cdot \mathbf{c} + \mathbf{c} \cdot \mathbf{a}) = 0$

[$\because |\mathbf{a}| = |\mathbf{b}| = |\mathbf{c}| = 1$]

$\Rightarrow \quad 3 + 2(\mathbf{a} \cdot \mathbf{b} + \mathbf{b} \cdot \mathbf{c} + \mathbf{c} \cdot \mathbf{a}) = 0$

$\Rightarrow \quad \mathbf{a} \cdot \mathbf{b} + \mathbf{b} \cdot \mathbf{c} + \mathbf{c} \cdot \mathbf{a} = -\frac{3}{2}$

30 (*b*) Here, we have to find $\angle ABC$ *i.e.*, angle between **BA** and **BC**, so first of all we have to calculate both these vectors after that we can find the angle between them by $\cos\theta = \dfrac{(\mathbf{BA}) \cdot (\mathbf{BC})}{|\mathbf{BA}||\mathbf{BC}|}$

We are given the points $A(1, 2, 3)$, $B(-1, 0, 0)$ and $C(0, 1, 2)$.

Also, it is given that $\angle ABC$ is the angle between the vectors **BA** and **BC**.

Here, $\mathbf{BA} = PV$ of $A - PV$ of B

$= (\hat{\mathbf{i}} + 2\hat{\mathbf{j}} + 3\hat{\mathbf{k}}) - (-\hat{\mathbf{i}} + 0\hat{\mathbf{j}} + 0\hat{\mathbf{k}})$

$= [\hat{\mathbf{i}} - (-\hat{\mathbf{i}}) + (2\hat{\mathbf{j}} - 0) + (3\hat{\mathbf{k}} - 0)] = 2\hat{\mathbf{i}} + 2\hat{\mathbf{j}} + 3\hat{\mathbf{k}}$

$$|\mathbf{BA}|=\sqrt{(2)^2+(2)^2+(3)^2}=\sqrt{4+4+9}=\sqrt{17}$$

$$\mathbf{BC}=PV \text{ of } C-PV \text{ of } B=(0\hat{i}+1\hat{j}+2\hat{k})-(-\hat{i}+0\hat{j}+0\hat{k})$$
$$=[0-(-\hat{i})+(1\hat{j}-0)+(2\hat{k}-0)]=\hat{i}+\hat{j}+2\hat{k}$$
$$|\mathbf{BC}|=\sqrt{(1)^2+(1)^2+(2)^2}=\sqrt{1+1+4}=\sqrt{6}$$

Now, $\mathbf{BA}\cdot\mathbf{BC}=(2\hat{i}+2\hat{j}+3\hat{k})\cdot(\hat{i}+\hat{j}+2\hat{k})$
$$=2\times1+2\times1+3\times2=10$$
$$\cos\theta=\frac{\mathbf{BA}\cdot\mathbf{BC}}{|\mathbf{BA}||\mathbf{BC}|}$$
$$\Rightarrow \cos(\angle ABC)=\frac{10}{\sqrt{17}\sqrt{6}}$$
$$\Rightarrow \angle ABC=\cos^{-1}\left(\frac{10}{\sqrt{102}}\right)$$

31 (*d*) The given points are $A(1,2,7)$, $B(2,6,3)$ and $C(3,10,-1)$.

$\therefore$ $\mathbf{AB}=PV$ of $B-PV$ of A
$$=(2\hat{i}+6\hat{j}+3\hat{k})-(1\hat{i}+2\hat{j}+7\hat{k})$$
$$=(2-1)\hat{i}+(6-2)\hat{j}+(3-7)\hat{k}$$
$$=\hat{i}+4\hat{j}-4\hat{k}$$

Magnitude of **AB**,
$$|\mathbf{AB}|=\sqrt{(1)^2+(4)^2+(-4)^2}=\sqrt{1+16+16}=\sqrt{33}$$

$\mathbf{BC}=PV$ of $C-PV$ of B
$$=(3\hat{i}+10\hat{j}-1\hat{k})-(2\hat{i}+6\hat{j}+3\hat{k})$$
$$=(3-2)\hat{i}+(10-6)\hat{j}+(-1-3)\hat{k}$$
$$=\hat{i}+4\hat{j}-4\hat{k}$$

Magnitude of **BC**,
$$|\mathbf{BC}|=\sqrt{(1)^2+(4)^2+(-4)^2}=\sqrt{1+16+16}=\sqrt{33}$$

$\mathbf{AC}=PV$ of $C-PV$ of A
$$=(3\hat{i}+10\hat{j}-1\hat{k})-(1\hat{i}+2\hat{j}+7\hat{k})$$
$$=(3-1)\hat{i}+(10-2)\hat{j}+(-1-7)\hat{k}$$
$$=2\hat{i}+8\hat{j}-8\hat{k}$$

Magnitude of **AC**,
$$|\mathbf{AC}|=\sqrt{2^2+8^2+(-8)^2}=\sqrt{4+64+64}$$
$$=\sqrt{132}=2\sqrt{33}=\sqrt{33}+\sqrt{33}$$

$\therefore$ $|\mathbf{AC}|=|\mathbf{AB}|+|\mathbf{BC}|$. Hence, the given points A, B and C are collinear.

32 (*b*) Let $\mathbf{OA}=2\hat{i}-\hat{j}+\hat{k}$, $\mathbf{OB}=\hat{i}-3\hat{j}-5\hat{k}$

and $\mathbf{OC}=3\hat{i}-4\hat{j}-4\hat{k}$

$\therefore$ Side $\mathbf{AB}=PV$ of $B-PV$ of A
$$=(\hat{i}-3\hat{j}-5\hat{k})-(2\hat{i}-\hat{j}+\hat{k})$$
$$=\hat{i}-3\hat{j}-5\hat{k}-2\hat{i}+\hat{j}-\hat{k}=-\hat{i}-2\hat{j}-6\hat{k}$$
$$|\mathbf{AB}|=\sqrt{(-1)^2+(-2)^2+(-6)^2}$$
$$=\sqrt{1+4+36}=\sqrt{41}$$

$\mathbf{BC}=PV$ of $C-PV$ of B
$$=(3\hat{i}-4\hat{j}-4\hat{k})-(\hat{i}-3\hat{j}-5\hat{k})$$
$$=3\hat{i}-4\hat{j}-4\hat{k}-\hat{i}+3\hat{j}+5\hat{k}=2\hat{i}-\hat{j}+\hat{k}$$
$$|\mathbf{BC}|=\sqrt{2^2+(-1)^2+1^2}=\sqrt{4+1+1}=\sqrt{6}$$

and $\mathbf{AC}=PV$ of $C-PV$ of A
$$=(3\hat{i}-4\hat{j}-4\hat{k})-(2\hat{i}-\hat{j}+\hat{k})$$
$$=3\hat{i}-4\hat{j}-4\hat{k}-2\hat{i}+\hat{j}-\hat{k}=\hat{i}-3\hat{j}-5\hat{k}$$

and $|\mathbf{AC}|=\sqrt{1^2+(-3)^2+(-5)^2}$
$$=\sqrt{1+9+25}=\sqrt{35}$$

Now, $|\mathbf{BC}|^2+|\mathbf{AC}|^2=6+35=41=|\mathbf{AB}|^2$

which shows that ABC is a right angled triangle.

33 (*d*) Vector λ **a** is a unit vector, if $|\lambda\,\mathbf{a}|=1$

Now, $|\lambda\,\mathbf{a}|=1 \Rightarrow |\lambda||\mathbf{a}|=1$

$\Rightarrow$ $|\lambda||\mathbf{a}|=1 \Rightarrow |\mathbf{a}|=\dfrac{1}{|\lambda|}$ $[\because \lambda\neq 0]$

$\Rightarrow$ $a=\dfrac{1}{|\lambda|}$ [given $|\mathbf{a}|=a$]

34 (*b*) We have, $\lambda\mathbf{b}+\mathbf{c}=\lambda(\hat{i}+\hat{j}-2\hat{k})+(\hat{i}+3\hat{j}-\hat{k})$
$$=(\lambda+1)\,\hat{i}+(\lambda+3)\hat{j}-(2\lambda+1)\hat{k}$$

Since, $\mathbf{a}\perp(\lambda\mathbf{b}+\mathbf{c}) \Rightarrow \mathbf{a}\cdot(\lambda\mathbf{b}+\mathbf{c})=0$

$\Rightarrow$ $(2\hat{j}-\hat{j}+\hat{k})\cdot[(\lambda+1)\hat{i}+(\lambda+3)\hat{j}-(2\lambda+1)\hat{k}]=0$

$\Rightarrow$ $2(\lambda+1)-(\lambda+3)-(2\lambda+1)=0$

$\Rightarrow$ $\lambda=-2$

35 (*d*) For being perpendicular,
$$(2\hat{i}-\hat{j}+2\hat{k})\cdot(3\hat{i}+\lambda\hat{j}+\hat{k})=0$$
$$\Rightarrow 6-\lambda+2=0$$
$$\Rightarrow \lambda=8$$

36 (*a*) We have,
$$(\sqrt{3}\,\mathbf{a}-\mathbf{b})^2=3\mathbf{a}^2+\mathbf{b}^2-2\sqrt{3}\,\mathbf{a}\cdot\mathbf{b}=1$$
$$3+1-2\sqrt{3}\,\mathbf{a}\cdot\mathbf{b}=1$$ [$\because$ **a** and **b** are unit vectors]

Thus, $a^2=b^2=1$
$$3=2\sqrt{3}\,\mathbf{a}\cdot\mathbf{b}$$
$$\mathbf{a}\cdot\mathbf{b}=\frac{\sqrt{3}}{2}$$
$$|\mathbf{a}||\mathbf{b}|\cos\theta=\frac{\sqrt{3}}{2}$$
$$\Rightarrow \cos\theta=\frac{\sqrt{3}}{2}$$
$$\Rightarrow \theta=30^\circ$$

37 (*a*)
$$\mathbf{PQ} = 6\hat{i} + \hat{j}$$
$$\mathbf{QR} = -\hat{i} + 3\hat{j}$$
$$\mathbf{RS} = -6\hat{i} - \hat{j}$$
$$\mathbf{SP} = \hat{i} - 3\hat{j}$$
$$|\mathbf{PQ}| = \sqrt{37} = |\mathbf{RS}|$$
$$|\mathbf{QR}| = \sqrt{10} = |\mathbf{SP}|$$
$$\mathbf{PQ}\cdot\mathbf{QR} = -6+3 = -3 \neq 0$$

PQ is parallel to **RS** and their magnitudes are equal.

⇒ Quadrilateral *PQRS* must be a parallelogram, which is neither rhombus nor rectangle.

38 (*a*) $\mathbf{p} \perp \mathbf{q}+\mathbf{r},\ \mathbf{q} \perp \mathbf{r}+\mathbf{p}$ and $\mathbf{r} \perp \mathbf{p}+\mathbf{q}$

$$\therefore \quad \mathbf{p}\cdot(\mathbf{q}+\mathbf{r}) = 0$$
$$\mathbf{q}\cdot(\mathbf{r}+\mathbf{p}) = 0$$
$$\mathbf{r}\cdot(\mathbf{p}+\mathbf{q}) = 0$$
$$\mathbf{p}\cdot\mathbf{q}+\mathbf{p}\cdot\mathbf{r} = 0$$
$$\mathbf{q}\cdot\mathbf{r}+\mathbf{q}\cdot\mathbf{p} = 0$$
$$\mathbf{r}\cdot\mathbf{p}+\mathbf{r}\cdot\mathbf{q} = 0$$

On adding, we get
$$2(\mathbf{p}\cdot\mathbf{q}+\mathbf{q}\cdot\mathbf{r}+\mathbf{r}\cdot\mathbf{p}) = 0$$

Also, $|\mathbf{p}+\mathbf{q}| = 6$
$$\Rightarrow \quad |\mathbf{p}+\mathbf{q}|^2 = 36$$
$$\Rightarrow \quad p^2+q^2+2\mathbf{p}\cdot\mathbf{q} = 36$$

Similarly, $q^2+r^2+2\mathbf{q}\cdot\mathbf{r} = 48$

and $r^2+p^2+2\mathbf{r}\cdot\mathbf{p} = 16$

Adding all, we get
$$2(p^2+q^2+r^2+\mathbf{p}\cdot\mathbf{q}+\mathbf{q}\cdot\mathbf{r}+\mathbf{r}\cdot\mathbf{p})$$
$$\Rightarrow \quad 2(p^2+q^2+r^2) = 100 \quad [\because \mathbf{p}\cdot\mathbf{q}+\mathbf{q}\cdot\mathbf{r}+\mathbf{r}\cdot\mathbf{p} = 0]$$
$$\Rightarrow \quad p^2+q^2+r^2 = 50$$
$$\Rightarrow \quad |\mathbf{p}+\mathbf{q}+\mathbf{r}|^2 = 50$$
$$|\mathbf{p}+\mathbf{q}+\mathbf{r}| = 5\sqrt{2}$$

39 (*c*)
$$(\hat{i}+\hat{j}+2\hat{k})\cdot\left(\frac{m\hat{i}+2\hat{j}+3\hat{k}}{\sqrt{13+m^2}}\right) = 2$$
$$\Rightarrow \quad m+2+6 = 2\sqrt{13+m^2}$$
$$\Rightarrow \quad (m+8)^2 = 4(13+m^2)$$
$$\Rightarrow \quad m^2+16m+64 = 4m^2+52$$
$$\Rightarrow \quad 3m^2-16m-12 = 0$$
$$\Rightarrow \quad (3m+2)(m-6) = 0$$
$$\Rightarrow \quad m = 6, -\frac{2}{3}$$

40 (*a*) Given, $\mathbf{a} = \lambda\hat{i}-7\hat{j}+3\hat{k}$,
$$\mathbf{b} = \lambda\hat{i}+\hat{j}+2\lambda\hat{k}$$

$$\therefore \quad \cos\theta = \frac{\mathbf{a}\cdot\mathbf{b}}{|\mathbf{a}||\mathbf{b}|} = \frac{\lambda^2-7+6\lambda}{\sqrt{\lambda^2+49+9}\sqrt{\lambda^2+1+4\lambda^2}} < 0$$
$$\Rightarrow \quad (\lambda+7)(\lambda-1) < 0$$
$$\Rightarrow \quad -7 < \lambda < 1$$

41 (*c*) Let the required unit vector be $\mathbf{r} = a\hat{i}+b\hat{j}$.

Then, $|\mathbf{r}| = 1$
$$\Rightarrow \quad a^2+b^2 = 1 \qquad \text{...(i)}$$

Since, **r** makes an angle of 45° with $\hat{i}+\hat{j}$ and an angle of 60° with $3\hat{i}-4\hat{j}$. Therefore,
$$\cos\frac{\pi}{4} = \frac{\mathbf{r}\cdot(\hat{i}+\hat{j})}{|\mathbf{r}||\hat{i}+\hat{j}|}$$
and
$$\cos\frac{\pi}{3} = \frac{\mathbf{r}\cdot(3\hat{i}-4\hat{j})}{|\mathbf{r}||3\hat{i}-4\hat{j}|}$$
$$\Rightarrow \quad \frac{1}{\sqrt{2}} = \frac{a+b}{\sqrt{2}}$$
and
$$\frac{1}{2} = \frac{3a-4b}{5}$$
$$\Rightarrow \quad a+b = 1$$
and
$$a-4b = \frac{5}{2}$$
$$\Rightarrow \quad a = \frac{13}{14},\ b = \frac{1}{14}$$
$$\therefore \quad \mathbf{r} = \frac{13}{14}\hat{i}+\frac{1}{14}\hat{j}$$

42 (*c*) Let $\mathbf{AB} = \mathbf{a} = 3\alpha-\beta$,
$$\mathbf{BC} = \mathbf{b} = \alpha+3\beta$$

Diagonal $\mathbf{AC} = \mathbf{AB}+\mathbf{BC} = \mathbf{a}+\mathbf{b}$
$$\Rightarrow \quad |\mathbf{AC}| = |\mathbf{a}+\mathbf{b}|$$
$$\Rightarrow \quad |\mathbf{AC}| = |4\alpha+2\beta|$$
$$\Rightarrow |\mathbf{AC}|^2 = 16\alpha^2+4\beta^2+16\alpha\cdot\beta$$
$$\Rightarrow |\mathbf{AC}|^2 = 64+16+16|\alpha||\beta|\cos\frac{\pi}{3}$$
$$= 64+16+16\times4\times\frac{1}{2}$$
$$\Rightarrow |\mathbf{AC}|^2 = 80+16\times4\times\frac{1}{2} = 112$$
$$\Rightarrow \quad |\mathbf{AC}| = 4\sqrt{7}$$

Other diagonal is $|\mathbf{BD}| = |\mathbf{a}-\mathbf{b}|$
$$\Rightarrow \quad |\mathbf{BD}|^2 = |2\alpha-4\beta|^2 = 4|\alpha|^2+16|\beta|^2-16|\alpha||\beta|\cos\frac{\pi}{3}$$
$$|\mathbf{BD}|^2 = 16+64-64\left(\frac{1}{2}\right)$$
$$\Rightarrow \quad |\mathbf{BD}| = \sqrt{48} = 4\sqrt{3}$$

43 (*d*) $|\mathbf{a}+\mathbf{b}|=\sqrt{3}$

$\Rightarrow |\mathbf{a}|^2+|\mathbf{b}|^2+2\mathbf{a}\cdot\mathbf{b}=3$

$\Rightarrow \qquad \mathbf{a}\cdot\mathbf{b}=\frac{1}{2} \qquad \text{...(i)}$

$[\because |\mathbf{a}|=|\mathbf{b}|=1, \text{ given}]$

$\therefore (3\mathbf{a}-4\mathbf{b})\cdot(2\mathbf{a}+5\mathbf{b})$

$=6+7\mathbf{a}\cdot\mathbf{b}-20$

$\left[\begin{array}{l}\because \mathbf{a}\cdot\mathbf{a}=|\mathbf{a}|^2=1\\ \text{and } \mathbf{b}\cdot\mathbf{b}=|\mathbf{b}|^2=1\end{array}\right]$

$=6+\frac{7}{2}-20$

$=-\frac{21}{2} \qquad$ [from Eq. (i)]

Vector (or cross) Product of Two vectors

1 (*a*) When the positive *X*-axis is rotated counter clockwise into the positive *Y*-axis, a right handed (standard) screw would advance in the direction of the positive *Z*-axis.

In a right handed coordinate system, the thumb of the right hand points in the direction of the positive *Z*-axis when the fingers are curled in the direction away from the positive *X*-axis toward the positive *Y*-axis.

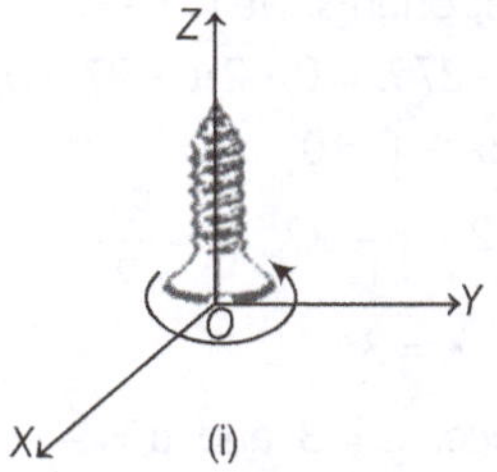

(i)

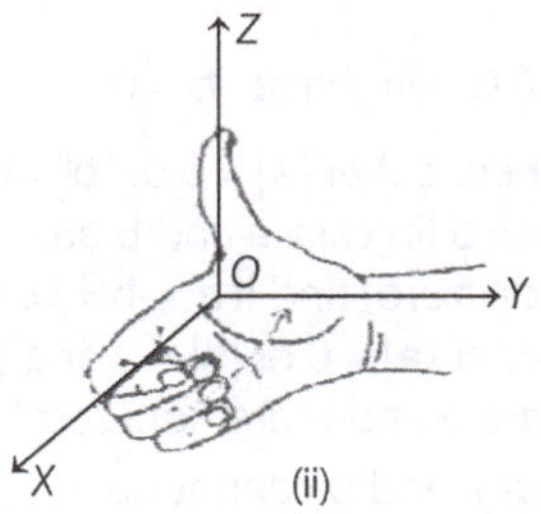

(ii)

2 (*b*) The vector product of two non-zero vectors a and b, is denoted by **a**, **b** and defined as

$$\mathbf{a}\times\mathbf{b}=|\mathbf{a}||\mathbf{b}|\sin\theta\,\hat{\mathbf{n}}$$

where, θ is the angle between **a** and **b**, $0\le\theta\le\pi$ and $\hat{\mathbf{n}}$ is a unit vector perpendicular to both **a** and **b**, such that **a**, **b** and $\hat{\mathbf{n}}$ form a right handed system i.e. the right handed system rotated from **a** to **b** moves in the direction of $\hat{\mathbf{n}}$.

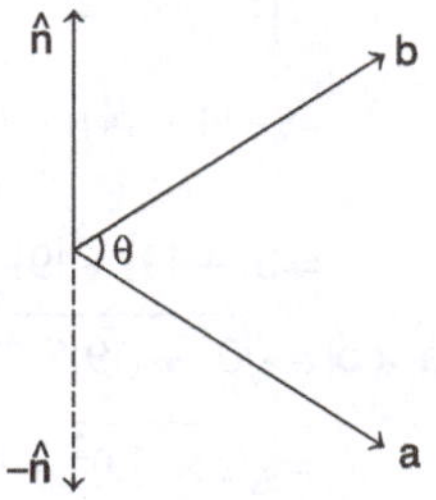

3 (*b*) If either $\mathbf{a}=\mathbf{0}$ or $\mathbf{b}=\mathbf{0}$, then θ is not defined and in this case, we define $\mathbf{a}\times\mathbf{b}=\mathbf{0}$ null vector).

4 (*b*) $\mathbf{a}\times\mathbf{b}$ is a vector.

If a and b be two non-zero vectors, then $\mathbf{a}\times\mathbf{b}=\mathbf{0}$, if and only if a and b are parallel (or collinear) to each other i.e.

$\mathbf{a}\times\mathbf{b}=\mathbf{0} \Leftrightarrow \mathbf{a}\,||\,\mathbf{b}$

In particular, $\mathbf{a}\times\mathbf{a}=\mathbf{0}$ and $\mathbf{a}\times(-\mathbf{a})=\mathbf{0}$, since in the first situation $\theta=0$ and in the second one, $\theta=\pi$, making the value of $\sin\theta$ to be 0.

5 (*d*) If $\theta=\frac{\pi}{2}$, then $|\mathbf{a}\times\mathbf{b}|=|\mathbf{a}|\cdot|\mathbf{b}|$

For mutually perpendicular unit vectors $\hat{\mathbf{i}},\hat{\mathbf{j}}$ and $\hat{\mathbf{k}}$, we have

$\hat{\mathbf{i}}\times\hat{\mathbf{i}}=\hat{\mathbf{j}}\times\hat{\mathbf{j}}=\hat{\mathbf{k}}\times\hat{\mathbf{k}}=0$

and $\quad \hat{\mathbf{i}}\times\hat{\mathbf{j}}=\hat{\mathbf{k}},\ \hat{\mathbf{j}}\times\hat{\mathbf{k}}=\hat{\mathbf{i}},\ \hat{\mathbf{k}}\times\hat{\mathbf{i}}=\hat{\mathbf{j}}$

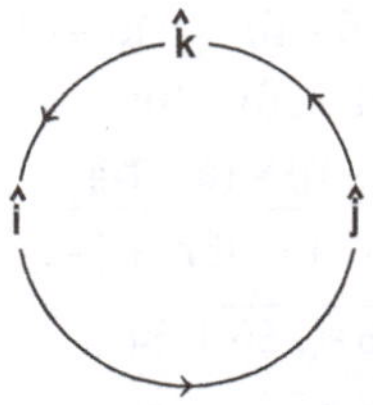

6 (*a*) In terms of vector product, the angle between two vectors a and b may be given as

$$\sin\theta=\frac{|\mathbf{a}\times\mathbf{b}|}{|\mathbf{a}||\mathbf{b}|}$$

7 (*c*) It is always true that the vector product is not commutative, $\mathbf{a}\times\mathbf{b}=-\mathbf{b}\times\mathbf{a}$.

Indeed, $\mathbf{a}\times\mathbf{b}=|\mathbf{a}||\mathbf{b}|\sin\theta\,\hat{\mathbf{n}}$, where **a**, **b** and $\hat{\mathbf{n}}$ form a right handed system, i.e. θ is traversed from **a** to **b**. While $\mathbf{b}\times\mathbf{a}=|\mathbf{a}||\mathbf{b}|\sin\theta\,\hat{\mathbf{n}}_1$, where b, a and $\hat{\mathbf{n}}_1$ form a left handed system i.e. θ is traversed from b to a [fig (ii)].

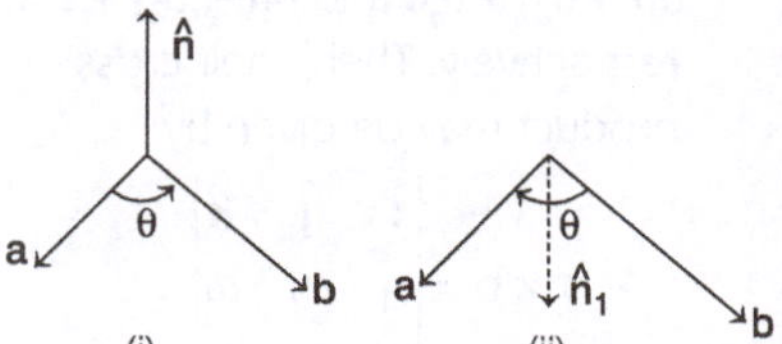

(i) (ii)

Thus, if we assume a and b to lie in the plane of the paper, then $\hat{\mathbf{n}}$ and $\hat{\mathbf{n}}_1$ both will be perpendicular to the plane of the paper. But, $\hat{\mathbf{n}}$ being directed above the paper while $\hat{\mathbf{n}}_1$ directed below the paper. i.e. $\hat{\mathbf{n}}_1=-\hat{\mathbf{n}}$.

Hence, $\mathbf{a}\times\mathbf{b}=|\mathbf{a}||\mathbf{b}|\sin\theta\,\hat{\mathbf{n}}$

$=-|\mathbf{b}||\mathbf{a}|\sin\theta\,\hat{\mathbf{n}}_1$

$=-\mathbf{b}\times\mathbf{a}$

So, only statement I is true.

8 (c) We know that,

$\mathbf{A}\times\mathbf{B}=-\mathbf{B}\times\mathbf{A}$

$\hat{\mathbf{i}}\times\hat{\mathbf{j}}=\hat{\mathbf{k}}$ then $\hat{\mathbf{j}}\times\hat{\mathbf{i}}=-\hat{\mathbf{k}}$

$\hat{\mathbf{k}}\times\hat{\mathbf{i}}=\hat{\mathbf{j}}$ then $\hat{\mathbf{i}}\times\hat{\mathbf{k}}=-\hat{\mathbf{j}}$

$\hat{\mathbf{j}}\times\hat{\mathbf{k}}=\hat{\mathbf{i}}$ then $\hat{\mathbf{k}}\times\hat{\mathbf{j}}=-\hat{\mathbf{i}}$

9 (*c*) If a and b represent the adjacent sides of a parallelogram, then its area is given by $|\mathbf{a}\times\mathbf{b}|$.

From figure, we have area of parallelogram$ABCD=AB\cdot DE$

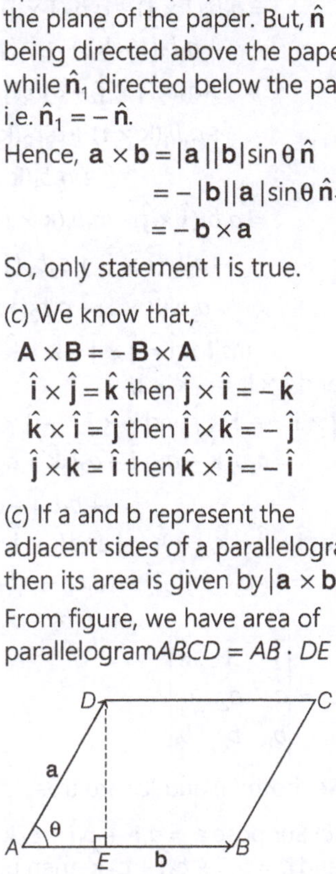

But $AB=|\mathbf{b}|$ (as given), and $DE=|\mathbf{a}|\sin\theta$

Thus, Area of parallelogram $ABCD=|\mathbf{b}||\mathbf{a}|\sin\theta=|\mathbf{a}\times\mathbf{b}|$.

10 (*d*) By the property of distributivity of vector product over addition, if a, b and c are any three vectors and λ be a scalar, then

(i) $\mathbf{a} \times (\mathbf{b} + \mathbf{c}) = \mathbf{a} \times \mathbf{b} + \mathbf{a} \times \mathbf{c}$

(ii) $\lambda(\mathbf{a} \times \mathbf{b}) = (\lambda \mathbf{a}) \times \mathbf{b} = \mathbf{a} \times (\lambda \mathbf{b})$

So, only option (d) is incorrect.

11 (*c*) If a and b are two vectors given in component form as $a_1\hat{i} + a_2\hat{j} + a_3\hat{k}$ and $b_1\hat{i} + b_2\hat{j} + b_3\hat{k}$, respectively. Then, their cross product may be given by

$$\mathbf{a} \times \mathbf{b} = \begin{vmatrix} \hat{i} & \hat{j} & \hat{k} \\ a_1 & a_2 & a_3 \\ b_1 & b_2 & b_3 \end{vmatrix}$$

We have, $\mathbf{a} \times \mathbf{b} = (a_1\hat{i} + a_2\hat{j} + a_3\hat{k}) \times (b_1\hat{i} + b_2\hat{j} + b_3\hat{k})$

$$= a_1b_1(\hat{i} \times \hat{i}) + a_1b_2(\hat{i} \times \hat{j}) + a_1b_3(\hat{i} \times \hat{k}) + a_2b_1(\hat{j} \times \hat{i}) + a_2b_2(\hat{j} \times \hat{j}) + a_2b_3(\hat{j} \times \hat{k}) + a_3b_1(\hat{k} \times \hat{i}) + a_3b_2(\hat{k} \times \hat{j}) + a_3b_3(\hat{k} \times \hat{k})$$

$$= a_1b_2(\hat{i} \times \hat{j}) - a_1b_3(\hat{k} \times \hat{i}) - a_2b_1(\hat{i} \times \hat{j}) + a_2b_3(\hat{j} \times \hat{k}) + a_3b_1(\hat{k} \times \hat{i}) - a_3b_2(\hat{j} \times \hat{k})$$

(as $\hat{i} \times \hat{i} = \hat{j} \times \hat{j} = \hat{k} \times \hat{k} = 0$ and $\hat{i} \times \hat{k} = -\hat{k} \times \hat{i}$, $\hat{j} \times \hat{i} = -\hat{i} \times \hat{j}$ and $\hat{k} \times \hat{j} = -\hat{j} \times \hat{k}$)

$$= a_1b_2\hat{k} - a_1b_3\hat{j} - a_2b_1\hat{k} + a_2b_3\hat{i} + a_3b_1\hat{j} - a_3b_2\hat{i}$$

[as $\hat{i} \times \hat{j} = \hat{k}$, $\hat{j} \times \hat{k} = \hat{i}$ and $\hat{k} \times \hat{i} = \hat{j}$]

$$= (a_2b_3 - a_3b_2)\hat{i} - (a_1b_3 - a_3b_1)\hat{j} + (a_1b_2 - a_2b_1)\hat{k}$$

$$= \begin{vmatrix} \hat{i} & \hat{j} & \hat{k} \\ a_1 & a_2 & a_3 \\ b_1 & b_2 & b_3 \end{vmatrix}$$

So, both (a) and (b) are true.

12 (*c*) Suppose $\mathbf{a} = a_1\hat{i} + b_1\hat{j} + c_1\hat{k}$ and $\mathbf{b} = a_2\hat{i} + b_2\hat{j} + c_2\hat{k}$, then use

$$\mathbf{a} \times \mathbf{b} = \begin{vmatrix} \hat{i} & \hat{j} & \hat{k} \\ a_1 & b_1 & c_1 \\ a_2 & b_2 & c_2 \end{vmatrix}.$$

We can find the value by expanding this determinant.

It is given that $\mathbf{a} = \hat{i} - 7\hat{j} + 7\hat{k}$ and $\mathbf{b} = 3\hat{i} - 2\hat{j} + 2\hat{k}$

$$\therefore \mathbf{a} \times \mathbf{b} = \begin{vmatrix} \hat{i} & \hat{j} & \hat{k} \\ 1 & -7 & 7 \\ 3 & -2 & 2 \end{vmatrix}$$

$$= (-14 + 14)\hat{i} - (2 - 21)\hat{j} + (-2 + 21)\hat{k}$$

$$= 0\hat{i} + 19\hat{j} + 19\hat{k}$$

$$\Rightarrow |\mathbf{a} \times \mathbf{b}| = \sqrt{0^2 + (19)^2 + (19)^2}$$

$$= \sqrt{2 \times (19)^2} = 19\sqrt{2}$$

13 (*a*) Unit vector perpendicular to two vectors **A** and **B** is given by

$$\hat{n} = \frac{\mathbf{A} \times \mathbf{B}}{|\mathbf{A} \times \mathbf{B}|}$$

Then, determine **a** + **b** and **a** − **b**, then unit vector perpendicular to both (**a** + **b**) and (**a** − **b**) is given by

$$\pm\frac{(\mathbf{a} + \mathbf{b}) \times (\mathbf{a} - \mathbf{b})}{|(\mathbf{a} + \mathbf{b}) \times (\mathbf{a} - \mathbf{b})|}.$$

Given that $\mathbf{a} = 3\hat{i} + 2\hat{j} + 2\hat{k}$ and $\mathbf{b} = \hat{i} + 2\hat{j} - 2\hat{k}$

$$\therefore \mathbf{a} + \mathbf{b} = (3\hat{i} + 2\hat{j} + 2\hat{k}) + (\hat{i} + 2\hat{j} - 2\hat{k})$$

$$= 4\hat{i} + 4\hat{j} + 0\hat{k}$$

and $\mathbf{a} - \mathbf{b} = (3\hat{i} + 2\hat{j} + 2\hat{k}) - (\hat{i} + 2\hat{j} - 2\hat{k})$

$$= 2\hat{i} + 4\hat{k}$$

Now, $(\mathbf{a} + \mathbf{b}) \times (\mathbf{a} - \mathbf{b}) = \begin{vmatrix} \hat{i} & \hat{j} & \hat{k} \\ 4 & 4 & 0 \\ 2 & 0 & 4 \end{vmatrix}$

$$= \hat{i}(16 - 0) - \hat{j}(16 - 0) + \hat{k}(0 - 8)$$

$$= 16\hat{i} - 16\hat{j} - 8\hat{k}$$

$$\Rightarrow |(\mathbf{a} + \mathbf{b}) \times (\mathbf{a} - \mathbf{b})|$$

$$= \sqrt{(16)^2 + (-16)^2 + (-8)^2}$$

$$= \sqrt{256 + 256 + 64}$$

$$= \sqrt{576} = 24$$

$\therefore$ A unit vector, perpendicular to both (**a** + **b**) and (**a** − **b**) is

$$\pm\frac{(\mathbf{a} + \mathbf{b}) \times (\mathbf{a} - \mathbf{b})}{|(\mathbf{a} + \mathbf{b}) \times (\mathbf{a} - \mathbf{b})|}$$

$$= \pm\frac{16\hat{i} - 16\hat{j} - 8\hat{k}}{24}$$

$$= \pm\frac{8(2\hat{i} - 2\hat{j} - 1\hat{k})}{24}$$

$$= \pm\frac{1}{3}(2\hat{i} - 2\hat{j} - \hat{k})$$

$\therefore$ Required vector is either

$$\frac{2}{3}\hat{i} - \frac{2}{3}\hat{j} - \frac{1}{3}\hat{k}$$

or $$-\frac{2}{3}\hat{i} + \frac{2}{3}\hat{j} + \frac{1}{3}\hat{k}$$

14 (*c*) $(\mathbf{a} - \mathbf{b}) \times (\mathbf{a} + \mathbf{b})$

$$= \mathbf{a} \times \mathbf{a} + \mathbf{a} \times \mathbf{b} - \mathbf{b} \times \mathbf{a} - \mathbf{b} \times \mathbf{b}$$

$$= 0 + \mathbf{a} \times \mathbf{b} + \mathbf{a} \times \mathbf{b} - 0$$

$[\because \mathbf{a} \times \mathbf{a} = 0 \text{ and } \mathbf{a} \times \mathbf{b} = -\mathbf{b} \times \mathbf{a}]$

$$= 2(\mathbf{a} \times \mathbf{b})$$

15 (*b*) Given,

$$(2\hat{i} + 6\hat{j} + 27\hat{k}) \times (\hat{i} + \lambda\hat{j} + \mu\hat{k}) = \mathbf{0}$$

$$\Rightarrow \begin{vmatrix} \hat{i} & \hat{j} & \hat{k} \\ 2 & 6 & 27 \\ 1 & \lambda & \mu \end{vmatrix} = \mathbf{0}$$

$$\Rightarrow \hat{i}(6\mu - 27\lambda) - \hat{j}(2\mu - 27) + \hat{k}(2\lambda - 6) = 0\hat{i} + 0\hat{j} + 0\hat{k}$$

On comparing the corresponding components, we have

$$6\mu - 27\lambda = 0, -2\mu + 27 = 0, 2\lambda - 6 = 0$$

$$\Rightarrow 2\mu = -9\lambda, \mu = \frac{27}{2}$$

and $\lambda = 3$

Hence, $\lambda = 3$ and $\mu = \frac{27}{2}$

16 (*d*) Given that $\mathbf{a} \cdot \mathbf{b} = 0$

Then, either $|\mathbf{a}| = 0$ or $|\mathbf{b}| = 0$ or $\mathbf{a} \perp \mathbf{b}$ (in case a and b are non-zero) and if $\mathbf{a} \times \mathbf{b} = \mathbf{0}$, then either $|\mathbf{a}| = 0$ or $|\mathbf{b}| = 0$ or $\mathbf{a} \parallel \mathbf{b}$ (in case a and b are non-zero)

But a and b cannot be perpendicular and parallel simultaneously.

Hence, either $|\mathbf{a}| = 0$ or $|\mathbf{b}| = 0$

17 (*c*) To determine the area of triangle, use formula

$$\Delta = \frac{1}{2}|\mathbf{AB} \times \mathbf{AC}|.$$

The vertices of ΔABC are given as $A(1,1,2), B(2,3,5)$ and $C(1,5,5)$.

First, we find vectors **AB** and **AC**.

Now, $\mathbf{AB} = PV$ of $B - PV$ of A

$$= (2\hat{i} + 3\hat{j} + 5\hat{k}) - (\hat{i} + \hat{j} + 2\hat{k})$$
$$= (2-1)\hat{i} + (3-1)\hat{j} + (5-2)\hat{k}$$
$$= \hat{i} + 2\hat{j} + 3\hat{k}$$

and $\mathbf{AC} = PV$ of $C - PV$ of A

$$= (\hat{i} + 5\hat{j} + 5\hat{k}) - (\hat{i} + \hat{j} + 2\hat{k})$$
$$= (1-1)\hat{i} + (5-1)\hat{j} + (5-2)\hat{k}$$
$$= 4\hat{j} + 3\hat{k}$$

$$\therefore \mathbf{AB} \times \mathbf{AC} = \begin{vmatrix} \hat{i} & \hat{j} & \hat{k} \\ 1 & 2 & 3 \\ 0 & 4 & 3 \end{vmatrix}$$

$$= \hat{i}(6-12) - \hat{j}(3-0) + \hat{k}(4-0)$$
$$= -6\hat{i} - 3\hat{j} + 4\hat{k}$$

Comparing with

$\mathbf{X} = x\hat{i} + y\hat{j} + z\hat{k}$, we get

$x = -6, y = -3, z = 4$

$$\therefore |\mathbf{AB} \times \mathbf{AC}| = \sqrt{x^2 + y^2 + z^2}$$
$$= \sqrt{(-6)^2 + (-3)^2 + (4)^2}$$
$$= \sqrt{36 + 9 + 16} = \sqrt{61}$$

Area of $\Delta ABC = \frac{1}{2}|\mathbf{AB} \times \mathbf{AC}|$

$$= \frac{1}{2} \times \sqrt{61} = \frac{\sqrt{61}}{2} \text{ sq units.}$$

Hence, the area of ΔABC is $\frac{\sqrt{61}}{2}$ sq units.

18 (*b*) The area of the parallelogram whose adjacent sides are a and b, is $|\mathbf{a} \times \mathbf{b}|$.

Adjacent sides are given as

$$\mathbf{a} = \hat{i} - \hat{j} + 3\hat{k}$$

and $\mathbf{b} = 2\hat{i} - 7\hat{j} + \hat{k}$

$$\therefore \mathbf{a} \times \mathbf{b} = \begin{vmatrix} \hat{i} & \hat{j} & \hat{k} \\ 1 & -1 & 3 \\ 2 & -7 & 1 \end{vmatrix}$$

$$= \hat{i}(-1+21) - \hat{j}(1-6) + \hat{k}(-7+2)$$
$$= 20\hat{i} + 5\hat{j} - 5\hat{k}$$

On comparing with

$\mathbf{X} = x\hat{i} + y\hat{j} + z\hat{k}$, we get

$x = 20, y = 5, z = -5$

$\therefore$ Area of the parallelogram

$$= |\mathbf{a} \times \mathbf{b}|$$
$$\Rightarrow |\mathbf{a} \times \mathbf{b}| = \sqrt{x^2 + y^2 + z^2}$$
$$= \sqrt{(20)^2 + 5^2 + (-5)^2}$$
$$= \sqrt{450} = \sqrt{225 \times 2}$$
$$= 15\sqrt{2} \text{ sq units}$$

Hence, the area of the given parallelogram is $15\sqrt{2}$ sq units.

19 (b) It is given that

$$|\mathbf{a}| = 3 \text{ and } |\mathbf{b}| = \frac{\sqrt{2}}{3}.$$

Let θ be the angle between a and b, given $|\mathbf{a} \times \mathbf{b}| = 1$

$$\Rightarrow |\mathbf{a}||\mathbf{b}|\sin\theta = 1$$
$$\Rightarrow 3 \times \frac{\sqrt{2}}{3} \times \sin\theta = 1$$
$$\Rightarrow \sin\theta = \frac{1}{\sqrt{2}}$$
$$\Rightarrow \theta = \frac{\pi}{4}$$

Hence, $\mathbf{a} \times \mathbf{b}$ is a unit vector, if the angle between **a** and **b** is $\frac{\pi}{4}$.

20 (*c*) To determine the area of rectangle, use the relation that if a and b are the adjacent sides of a parallelogram, then area of parallelogram $= |\mathbf{a} \times \mathbf{b}|$.

The position vectors of vertices A, B, C and D of rectangle $ABCD$ are given.

First, we compute vectors AB and AD.

Now, $AB = PV$ of $B - PV$ of A

$$= \left(\hat{i} + \frac{1}{2}\hat{j} + 4\hat{k}\right) - \left(-\hat{i} + \frac{1}{2}\hat{j} + 4\hat{k}\right)$$
$$= [1 - (-1)]\hat{i} + \left(\frac{1}{2} - \frac{1}{2}\right)\hat{j} + (4-4)\hat{k} = 2\hat{i}$$

and $AD = PV$ of $D - PV$ of A

$$= \left(-\hat{i} - \frac{1}{2}\hat{j} + 4\hat{k}\right) - \left(-\hat{i} + \frac{1}{2}\hat{j} + 4\hat{k}\right)$$
$$= [-1 - (-1)]\hat{i} + \left(-\frac{1}{2} - \frac{1}{2}\right)\hat{j} + (4-4)\hat{k} = -\hat{j}$$

$$\therefore \mathbf{AB} \times \mathbf{AD} = \begin{vmatrix} \hat{i} & \hat{j} & \hat{k} \\ 2 & 0 & 0 \\ 0 & -1 & 0 \end{vmatrix} = -2\hat{k}$$

Area of rectangle

$$ABCD = |\mathbf{AB} \times \mathbf{AD}|$$
$$= \sqrt{(-2)^2} = 2 \text{ sq units}$$

Hence, the area of the rectangle is $|\mathbf{AB} \times \mathbf{AD}| = 2$ sq units.

21 (*a*) Required unit vector is

$$\pm\frac{(\hat{i} - \hat{j}) \times (\hat{i} + \hat{j})}{|(\hat{i} - \hat{j}) \times (\hat{i} + \hat{j})|} = \pm\frac{2\hat{k}}{2} = \pm\hat{k}$$

22 (*d*) Here,

$$\mathbf{r} = (2\hat{i} + 3\hat{j} + \hat{k}) - (\hat{i} + 2\hat{j} + 3\hat{k})$$
$$\Rightarrow \mathbf{r} = \hat{i} + \hat{j} - 2\hat{k}$$

and $\mathbf{F} = \hat{i} + \hat{j} + \hat{k}$

Then, the required moment is given by

$$\mathbf{r} \times \mathbf{F} = (\hat{i} + \hat{j} - 2\hat{k}) \times (\hat{i} + \hat{j} + \hat{k})$$
$$= \begin{vmatrix} \hat{i} & \hat{j} & \hat{k} \\ 1 & 1 & -2 \\ 1 & 1 & 1 \end{vmatrix} = 3\hat{i} - 3\hat{j}$$

$\therefore$ Moment about given point

$$= 3\hat{i} - 3\hat{j}$$

23 (*a*) Let **BC**, **CA** and **AB** represent the vectors, **a**, **b** and **c** respectively,

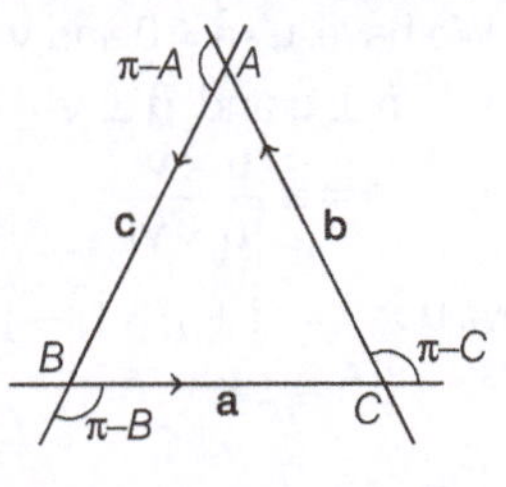

We have, $\mathbf{a} + \mathbf{b} + \mathbf{c} = 0$

$$\Rightarrow \mathbf{c} = -(\mathbf{a} + \mathbf{b})$$
$$\Rightarrow \mathbf{b} \times \mathbf{c} = \mathbf{b} \times (-\mathbf{a} - \mathbf{b})$$
$$= -\mathbf{b} \times \mathbf{a} = \mathbf{a} \times \mathbf{b}$$

Similarly, $\mathbf{c} \times \mathbf{a} = \mathbf{a} \times \mathbf{b}$

Hence, $\mathbf{b} \times \mathbf{c} = \mathbf{c} \times \mathbf{a} = \mathbf{a} \times \mathbf{b}$

$$|\mathbf{b} \times \mathbf{c}| = |\mathbf{c} \times \mathbf{a}| = |\mathbf{a} \times \mathbf{b}|$$

$\Rightarrow \mathbf{bc}\sin(\pi - A) = \mathbf{ac}\sin(\pi - B)$
$= \mathbf{ab}\sin(\pi - C)$

$\Rightarrow \mathbf{bc}\sin A = \mathbf{ca}\sin B = \mathbf{ab}\sin C$

$\Rightarrow \dfrac{\sin A}{\mathbf{a}} = \dfrac{\sin B}{\mathbf{b}} = \dfrac{\sin C}{\mathbf{c}}$

[divide by **abc**]

24 (*a*) $(\mathbf{a} - \mathbf{d}) \times (\mathbf{b} - \mathbf{c}) = 0$

$\Rightarrow \mathbf{a} \times \mathbf{b} - \mathbf{a} \times \mathbf{c} - \mathbf{d} \times \mathbf{b} + \mathbf{d} \times \mathbf{c} = 0$

Using, $\mathbf{a} \times \mathbf{b} = \mathbf{c} \times \mathbf{d}$

and $\mathbf{a} \times \mathbf{c} = \mathbf{b} \times \mathbf{d}$

we get,

$\mathbf{c} \times \mathbf{d} - \mathbf{b} \times \mathbf{d} - \mathbf{d} \times \mathbf{b} + \mathbf{d} \times \mathbf{c} = 0$

$\Rightarrow \mathbf{d} \times \mathbf{c} + \mathbf{d} \times \mathbf{b} - \mathbf{d} \times \mathbf{b} + \mathbf{d} \times \mathbf{c} = 0$

[as $\mathbf{a} \times \mathbf{b} = -\mathbf{b} \times \mathbf{a}$]

$\Rightarrow 0 = 0$

$\therefore (\mathbf{a} - \mathbf{d}) \times (\mathbf{b} - \mathbf{c}) = 0$

which shows $(\mathbf{a} - \mathbf{d})$ is parallel to $(\mathbf{b} - \mathbf{c})$, when $\mathbf{a} \neq \mathbf{b}$ and $\mathbf{b} \neq \mathbf{c}$

25 (*b*) Let *A* and *B* be the points having position vectors $\hat{\mathbf{i}} - \hat{\mathbf{j}} + \hat{\mathbf{k}}$ and $2\hat{\mathbf{i}} - 3\hat{\mathbf{j}} - \hat{\mathbf{k}}$ respectively. Then

$\mathbf{r} = \mathbf{BA} = (\hat{\mathbf{i}} - \hat{\mathbf{j}} + \hat{\mathbf{k}}) - (2\hat{\mathbf{i}} - 3\hat{\mathbf{i}} - \hat{\mathbf{k}})$
$= -\hat{\mathbf{i}} + 2\hat{\mathbf{j}} + 2\hat{\mathbf{k}}$

$\therefore$ Moment of couple

$$= |\mathbf{r} \times \mathbf{F}| = \begin{vmatrix} \hat{\mathbf{i}} & \hat{\mathbf{j}} & \hat{\mathbf{k}} \\ -1 & 2 & 2 \\ 3 & 2 & -1 \end{vmatrix}$$

$= |-6\hat{\mathbf{i}} + 5\hat{\mathbf{j}} - 8\hat{\mathbf{k}}|$
$= \sqrt{36 + 25 + 64} = 5\sqrt{5}$

26 (*a*) We have, $\mathbf{u} \cdot \hat{\mathbf{n}} = 0$ and $\mathbf{v} \cdot \hat{\mathbf{n}} = 0$

$\Rightarrow \hat{\mathbf{n}} \perp \mathbf{u}$ and $\hat{\mathbf{n}} \perp \mathbf{v}$

$\Rightarrow \hat{\mathbf{n}} = \pm \dfrac{\mathbf{u} \times \mathbf{v}}{|\mathbf{u} \times \mathbf{v}|}$

Now, $\mathbf{u} \times \mathbf{v} = (\hat{\mathbf{i}} + \hat{\mathbf{j}}) \times (\hat{\mathbf{i}} - \hat{\mathbf{j}}) = -2\hat{\mathbf{k}}$

$\hat{\mathbf{n}} = \pm \hat{\mathbf{k}}$

Hence,

$|\mathbf{w} \cdot \hat{\mathbf{n}}| = |(\hat{\mathbf{i}} + 2\hat{\mathbf{i}} + 3\hat{\mathbf{k}}) \cdot (\pm \hat{\mathbf{k}})| = 3$

27 (*b*) Let $\mathbf{d} \cdot \mathbf{a} = \mathbf{d} \cdot \mathbf{b} = \mathbf{d} \cdot \mathbf{c} = \cos\alpha$

$\Rightarrow \mathbf{d} \cdot (\mathbf{a} - \hat{\mathbf{k}}) = 0$

and $\mathbf{d} \cdot (\mathbf{b} - \hat{\mathbf{k}}) = 0$

$\Rightarrow \mathbf{d}$ is perpendicular to $(\mathbf{a} - \hat{\mathbf{k}})$ and $(\mathbf{b} - \hat{\mathbf{k}})$.

Hence, **d** is parallel to

$$(\mathbf{a} - \hat{\mathbf{k}}) \times (\mathbf{b} - \hat{\mathbf{k}}) = \begin{vmatrix} \hat{\mathbf{i}} & \hat{\mathbf{j}} & \hat{\mathbf{k}} \\ \cos\theta & \sin\theta & -1 \\ -\sin\theta & \cos\theta & -1 \end{vmatrix}$$

$$\therefore \mathbf{d} = \frac{(\cos\theta - \sin\theta)\hat{\mathbf{i}} + (\cos\theta + \sin\theta)\hat{\mathbf{j}} + \hat{\mathbf{k}}}{\sqrt{3}}$$

$\cos\alpha = \mathbf{d} \cdot \hat{\mathbf{k}} = \dfrac{1}{\sqrt{3}}$

$\Rightarrow \alpha = \cos^{-1}\left(\dfrac{1}{\sqrt{3}}\right)$

Miscellaneous Exercise

1 (*a*) Let $\mathbf{r} = x\,\hat{\mathbf{i}} + y\,\hat{\mathbf{j}}$ be a unit vector in *xy*-plane (figure). Then, from the figure, we have $x = \cos\theta$ and $y = \sin\theta$ (Since, $|\mathbf{r}| = 1$). So, we may write the vector r as

$\mathbf{r} = (\mathbf{OP}) = \cos\theta\,\hat{\mathbf{i}} + \sin\theta\,\hat{\mathbf{j}}$ ... (i)

Clearly, $|\mathbf{r}| = \sqrt{\cos^2\theta + \sin^2\theta} = 1$

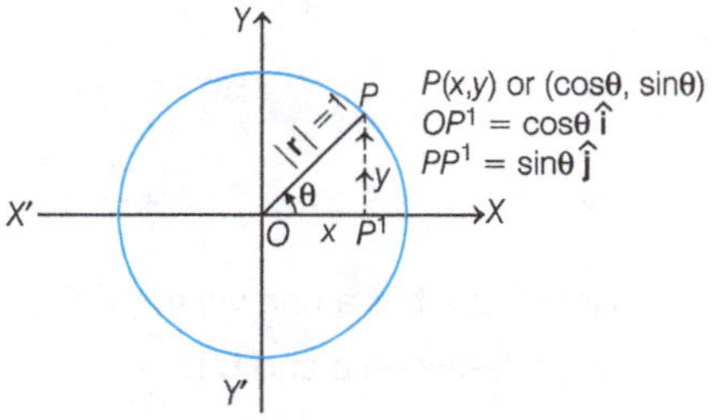

Also, as θ various from 0 to 2π, the point *P* (figure) traces the circle $x^2 + y^2 = 1$ counterclockwise, and this covers all possible directions. So, (i) gives every unit vector in the *XY*-plane.

2 (*d*) Given, $\mathbf{a} \cdot (\mathbf{b} + \mathbf{c}) = 0$,

$\mathbf{b} \cdot (\mathbf{c} + \mathbf{a}) = 0$,

$\mathbf{c} \cdot (\mathbf{a} + \mathbf{b}) = 0$

Now, $(\mathbf{a} + \mathbf{b} + \mathbf{c}) = (\mathbf{a} + \mathbf{b} + \mathbf{c})^2$

$= (\mathbf{a} + \mathbf{b} + \mathbf{c}) \cdot (\mathbf{a} + \mathbf{b} + \mathbf{c})$

$= \mathbf{a} \cdot \mathbf{a} + \mathbf{a} \cdot (\mathbf{b} + \mathbf{c}) + \mathbf{b} \cdot \mathbf{b} + \mathbf{b} \cdot (\mathbf{a} + \mathbf{c}) + \mathbf{c} \cdot (\mathbf{a} + \mathbf{b}) + \mathbf{c} \cdot \mathbf{c}$

$= |\mathbf{a}|^2 + |\mathbf{b}|^2 + |\mathbf{c}|^2$

$= 9 + 16 + 25 = 50$

Therefore, $|\mathbf{a} + \mathbf{b} + \mathbf{c}| = \sqrt{50} = 5\sqrt{2}$

3 (*b*) Since. $\mathbf{a} + \mathbf{b} + \mathbf{c} = 0$, we have

$\mathbf{a} \cdot (\mathbf{a} + \mathbf{b} + \mathbf{c}) = 0$

or $\mathbf{a} \cdot \mathbf{a} + \mathbf{a} \cdot \mathbf{b} + \mathbf{a} \cdot \mathbf{c} = 0$

Therefore,

$\mathbf{a} \cdot \mathbf{b} + \mathbf{a} \cdot \mathbf{c} = -|\mathbf{a}|^2 = -1$ ...(i)

Again, $\mathbf{b} \cdot (\mathbf{a} + \mathbf{b} + \mathbf{c}) = 0$

or $\mathbf{a} \cdot \mathbf{b} + \mathbf{b} \cdot \mathbf{c} = -|\mathbf{b}|^2 = -16$ ...(ii)

Similarly, $\mathbf{a} \cdot \mathbf{c} + \mathbf{b} \cdot \mathbf{c} = -4$ ...(iii)

adding Eqs. (i), (ii) and (iii), we have

$2(\mathbf{a} \cdot \mathbf{b} + \mathbf{b} \cdot \mathbf{c} + \mathbf{a} \cdot \mathbf{c}) = -21$

$2\mu = -21$

i.e. $\mu = \dfrac{-21}{2}$

4 (*b*) β_1 is parallel to α

$\therefore$ Let, $\beta_1 = \lambda\alpha$, λ is a scalar, ie.

$\beta_1 = 3\lambda\,\hat{\mathbf{i}} - \lambda\,\hat{\mathbf{j}}$

Now, $\beta_2 = \beta - \beta_1 = (2 - 3\lambda)\,\hat{\mathbf{i}} + (1 + \lambda)\,\hat{\mathbf{j}} - 3\,\hat{\mathbf{k}}$

Now, since β_2 is to be perpendicular to α, we should have $\alpha . \beta_2 = 0$ i.e.

$3(2 - 3\lambda) - (1 + \lambda) = 0$

or $\lambda = \dfrac{1}{2}$

Therefore, $\beta_1 = \dfrac{3}{2}\hat{\mathbf{i}} - \dfrac{1}{2}\hat{\mathbf{j}}$

and $\beta_2 = \dfrac{1}{2}\hat{\mathbf{i}} + \dfrac{3}{2}\hat{\mathbf{j}} - 3\hat{\mathbf{k}}$

5 (*c*) Let **OP** make 30° with *X*-axis, 60° with *Y*-axis and 90° with *Z*-axis and it lies in *xy*-plane.

$\therefore$ Direction cosines of **OP** are cos 30°, cos 60° and cos 90°

i.e. $\dfrac{\sqrt{3}}{2}, \dfrac{1}{2}, 0.$

Thus, **OP** is $\dfrac{\sqrt{3}}{2}\hat{\mathbf{i}} + \dfrac{1}{2}\hat{\mathbf{j}}$,

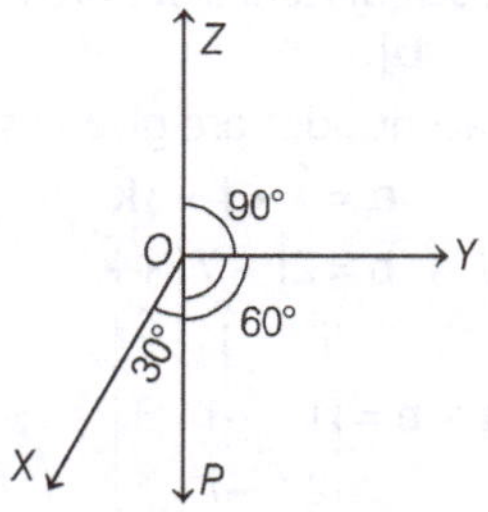

$$|\mathbf{OP}| = \sqrt{\left(\frac{\sqrt{3}}{2}\right)^2 + \left(\frac{1}{2}\right)^2}$$
$$= \sqrt{\frac{3}{4} + \frac{1}{4}} = \sqrt{1} = 1$$

which is required unit vector in XY-plane.

6 (*d*) The vector joining the points $P(x_1, y_1, z_1)$ and $Q(x_2, y_2, z_2)$ can be obtained by,

$\mathbf{PQ} = PV$ of $Q - PV$ of P

$$\mathbf{PQ} = (x_2\,\hat{\mathbf{i}} + y_2\,\hat{\mathbf{j}} + z_2\,\hat{\mathbf{k}}) - (x_1\,\hat{\mathbf{i}} + y_1\,\hat{\mathbf{j}} + z_1\,\hat{\mathbf{k}})$$
$$\mathbf{PQ} = (x_2 - x_1)\,\hat{\mathbf{i}} + (y_2 - y_1)\,\hat{\mathbf{j}} + (z_2 - z_1)\,\hat{\mathbf{k}}$$

$\therefore$ Scalar components of PQ are $x_2 - x_1, y_2 - y_1, z_2 - z_1$.

$\therefore$ Magnitude of PQ,

$$|PQ| = \sqrt{(x_2 - x_1)^2 + (y_2 - y_1)^2 + (z_2 - z_1)^2}$$

7 (c) Let O and B be the initial and final positions of the girl respectively.

Then, the girls's position can be shown as in the figure. Now, we have $\mathbf{OA} = -4\hat{\mathbf{i}}$

$$\mathbf{AB} = \hat{\mathbf{i}}\,|\mathbf{AB}|\cos 60° + \hat{\mathbf{j}}\,|\mathbf{AB}|\sin 60°$$

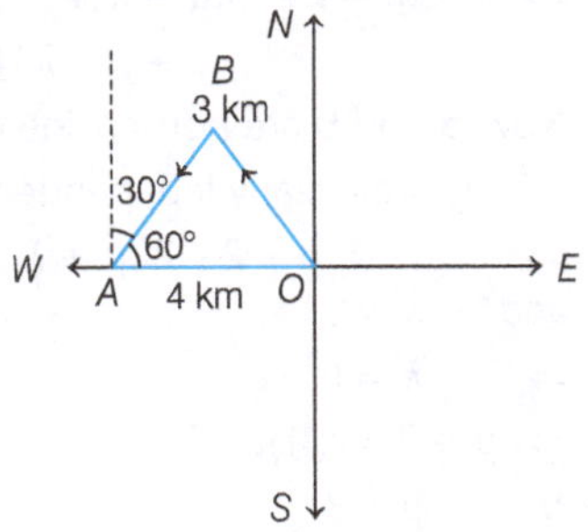

($AB\cos 60°$ is component of AB along X-axis and $AB\sin 60°$ is component of AB along Y-axis)

$$= \hat{\mathbf{i}}\left(3 \times \frac{1}{2}\right) + \hat{\mathbf{j}}\left(3 \times \frac{\sqrt{3}}{2}\right)$$
$$= \frac{3}{2}\,\hat{\mathbf{i}} + \frac{3\sqrt{3}}{2}\,\hat{\mathbf{j}}$$

By the triangle law of vector addition, we have

$$\mathbf{OB} = \mathbf{OA} + \mathbf{AB}$$
$$= (-4\,\hat{\mathbf{i}}) + \left(\frac{3}{2}\,\hat{\mathbf{i}} + \frac{3\sqrt{3}}{2}\,\hat{\mathbf{j}}\right)$$
$$= \left(-4 + \frac{3}{2}\right)\hat{\mathbf{i}} + \frac{3\sqrt{3}}{2}\,\hat{\mathbf{j}}$$
$$= \left(\frac{-8+3}{2}\right)\hat{\mathbf{i}} + \frac{3\sqrt{3}}{2}\,\hat{\mathbf{j}}$$
$$= \frac{-5}{2}\,\hat{\mathbf{i}} + \frac{3\sqrt{3}}{2}\,\hat{\mathbf{j}}$$

Hence, the girl's displacement from her initial point of departure is $\frac{-5}{2}\,\hat{\mathbf{i}} + \frac{3\sqrt{3}}{2}\,\hat{\mathbf{j}}$.

8 (*d*) Given, $x\,(\hat{\mathbf{i}} + \hat{\mathbf{j}} + \hat{\mathbf{k}})$ is a unit vector, therefore $|x\,(\hat{\mathbf{i}} + \hat{\mathbf{j}} + \hat{\mathbf{k}})| = 1$

$$\Rightarrow \quad |x\hat{\mathbf{i}} + x\hat{\mathbf{j}} + x\hat{\mathbf{k}})| = 1$$
$$\Rightarrow \quad \sqrt{x^2 + x^2 + x^2} = 1$$
$$\Rightarrow \sqrt{3x^2} = 1 \Rightarrow \pm\sqrt{3}x = 1$$
$$\Rightarrow \pm\sqrt{3}x = 1 \Rightarrow x = \pm\frac{1}{\sqrt{3}}$$

Hence, the required values of x are $\pm\frac{1}{\sqrt{3}}$.

9 (*b*) Determine the resultants of vectors **a** and **b**, vector $\mathbf{c} = \mathbf{a} + \mathbf{b}$ and then find the direction of **c** by finding unit vector in its direction and than multiplying it by 5, we can find the required vector.

Given vectors $\mathbf{a} = 2\hat{\mathbf{i}} + 3\hat{\mathbf{j}} - \hat{\mathbf{k}}$ and $\mathbf{b} = \hat{\mathbf{i}} - 2\hat{\mathbf{j}} + \hat{\mathbf{k}}$.

Let c be the resultant of **a** and **b**.

$$\therefore \mathbf{c} = \mathbf{a} + \mathbf{b} = (2\hat{\mathbf{i}} + 3\hat{\mathbf{j}} - \hat{\mathbf{k}}) + (\hat{\mathbf{i}} - 2\hat{\mathbf{j}} + \hat{\mathbf{k}})$$
$$\Rightarrow \mathbf{c} = 3\hat{\mathbf{i}} + \hat{\mathbf{j}} + 0\hat{\mathbf{k}}$$

Comparing with $\mathbf{X} = x\hat{\mathbf{i}} + y\hat{\mathbf{j}} + z\hat{\mathbf{k}}$

$$\therefore \quad |\mathbf{c}| = \sqrt{x^2 + y^2 + z^2} = \sqrt{3^2 + 1^2}$$
$$= \sqrt{9+1} = \sqrt{10}$$

$\therefore$ Unit vector in the direction of **c**,

$$\mathbf{c} = \frac{\mathbf{c}}{|\mathbf{c}|} = \frac{3\hat{\mathbf{i}} + \hat{\mathbf{j}}}{\sqrt{10}}$$

Hence, the vector of magnitude 5 units and parallel to the resultant of vectors **a** and **b** is

$$\pm 5\,\hat{\mathbf{c}} = \pm 5\frac{1}{\sqrt{10}}(3\hat{\mathbf{i}} + \hat{\mathbf{j}})$$
$$= \pm\frac{3\sqrt{10}}{2}\,\hat{\mathbf{i}} \pm \frac{\sqrt{10}}{2}\,\hat{\mathbf{j}}$$

10 (*c*) We have,

$$\mathbf{a} = \hat{\mathbf{i}} + \hat{\mathbf{j}} + \hat{\mathbf{k}}, \mathbf{b} = 2\hat{\mathbf{i}} - \hat{\mathbf{j}} + 3\hat{\mathbf{k}}$$

and $\quad \mathbf{c} = \hat{\mathbf{i}} - 2\hat{\mathbf{j}} + \hat{\mathbf{k}}$

Let $\quad \mathbf{v} = 2\mathbf{a} - \mathbf{b} + 3\mathbf{c} = 2(\hat{\mathbf{i}} + \hat{\mathbf{j}} + \hat{\mathbf{k}}) - (2\hat{\mathbf{i}} - \hat{\mathbf{j}} + 3\hat{\mathbf{k}}) + 3(\hat{\mathbf{i}} - 2\hat{\mathbf{j}} + \hat{\mathbf{k}}) = 3\hat{\mathbf{i}} - 3\hat{\mathbf{j}} + 2\hat{\mathbf{k}}$

Now, $|\mathbf{v}| = |3\hat{\mathbf{i}} - 3\hat{\mathbf{j}} + 2\hat{\mathbf{k}}|$

$$= \sqrt{3^2 + (-3)^2 + 2^2} = \sqrt{22}$$

Hence, the unit vector along **v** is

$$\hat{\mathbf{v}} = \frac{\mathbf{v}}{|\mathbf{v}|} = \frac{3\hat{\mathbf{i}} - 3\hat{\mathbf{j}} + 2\hat{\mathbf{k}}}{\sqrt{22}}$$
$$= \left(\frac{3}{\sqrt{22}}\hat{\mathbf{i}} - \frac{3}{\sqrt{22}}\hat{\mathbf{j}} + \frac{2}{\sqrt{22}}\hat{\mathbf{k}}\right)$$

11 (*b*) It is given that $\mathbf{a}\,.\,\mathbf{b} \ge 0$

Since, $\quad \mathbf{a}\,.\,\mathbf{b} = |\mathbf{a}|.|\mathbf{a}|\cos\theta \ge 0$

$$\Rightarrow \quad \cos\theta \ge 0$$
$$\Rightarrow \quad 0 \le \theta \le \frac{\pi}{2}$$

12 (*d*) Let **a** and **b** be two unit vectors and θ be the angle between them.

Then, $\quad |\mathbf{a}| = |\mathbf{b}| = 1$

Now, $(\mathbf{a} + \mathbf{b})$ is a unit vector if

$$|\mathbf{a} + \mathbf{b}| = 1$$
$$\Rightarrow` \quad (\mathbf{a} + \mathbf{b})^2 = 1$$
$$\Rightarrow (\mathbf{a} + \mathbf{b}) \cdot (\mathbf{a} + \mathbf{b}) = 1$$
$$\Rightarrow \mathbf{a} \cdot \mathbf{a} + \mathbf{a} \cdot \mathbf{b} + \mathbf{b} \cdot \mathbf{a} + \mathbf{b} \cdot \mathbf{b} = 1$$
$$\Rightarrow |\mathbf{a}|^2 + |\mathbf{b}|^2 + 2\mathbf{a} \cdot \mathbf{b} = 1 \quad [\because \mathbf{a} \cdot \mathbf{b} = \mathbf{b} \cdot \mathbf{a}]$$
$$\Rightarrow 1^2 + 1^2 + 2\mathbf{a} \cdot \mathbf{b} = 1$$
$$\Rightarrow \quad \mathbf{a} \cdot \mathbf{b} = -\frac{1}{2}$$
$$\Rightarrow \quad |\mathbf{a}||\mathbf{b}|\cos\theta = -\frac{1}{2}$$
$$\Rightarrow \quad 1 \times 1 \times \cos\theta = -\frac{1}{2}$$
$$\Rightarrow \cos\theta = -\frac{1}{2} \Rightarrow \theta = \frac{2\pi}{3}$$

13 (*d*) We have,

$$\hat{\mathbf{i}}\cdot(\hat{\mathbf{j}}\times\hat{\mathbf{k}})+\hat{\mathbf{j}}\cdot(\hat{\mathbf{k}}\times\hat{\mathbf{i}})+\hat{\mathbf{k}}\cdot(\hat{\mathbf{i}}\times\hat{\mathbf{j}})$$
$$=\hat{\mathbf{i}}\cdot\hat{\mathbf{i}}+\hat{\mathbf{j}}\cdot\hat{\mathbf{j}}+\hat{\mathbf{k}}\cdot\hat{\mathbf{k}}$$
$$[\because \hat{\mathbf{j}}\times\hat{\mathbf{k}}=\hat{\mathbf{i}},\ \hat{\mathbf{k}}\times\hat{\mathbf{i}}=\hat{\mathbf{j}},\ \hat{\mathbf{i}}\times\hat{\mathbf{j}}=\hat{\mathbf{k}}]$$
$$=1+1+1$$
$$[\because \hat{\mathbf{i}}\cdot\hat{\mathbf{i}}=\hat{\mathbf{j}}\cdot\hat{\mathbf{j}}=\hat{\mathbf{k}}\cdot\hat{\mathbf{k}}=1]$$
$$=3$$

14 (*a*) Let a vector be equally inclined to OX, OY and OZ and let it make an angle α with each of these three, then the direction cosines are $\cos\alpha$, $\cos\alpha$ and $\cos\alpha$.

$$\Rightarrow \cos^2\alpha+\cos^2\alpha+\cos^2\alpha=1 \quad [\because l^2+m^2+n^2=1]$$
$$3\cos^2\alpha=1$$
$$\Rightarrow \cos^2\alpha=\frac{1}{3}$$
$$\Rightarrow \cos\alpha=\pm\frac{1}{\sqrt{3}}$$

Hence, the direction cosines of the vector which is equally inclined to the axes are either $\frac{1}{\sqrt{3}},\frac{1}{\sqrt{3}},\frac{1}{\sqrt{3}}$ or $-\frac{1}{\sqrt{3}},-\frac{1}{\sqrt{3}},-\frac{1}{\sqrt{3}}$.

15 (*c*) The vector which is perpendicular to both **a** and **b** must be parallel to **a** × **b**.

$$\text{Now, } \mathbf{a}\times\mathbf{b}=\begin{vmatrix}\hat{\mathbf{i}} & \hat{\mathbf{j}} & \hat{\mathbf{k}}\\ 1 & 4 & 2\\ 3 & -2 & 7\end{vmatrix}$$
$$=\hat{\mathbf{i}}(28+4)-\hat{\mathbf{j}}(7-6)+\hat{\mathbf{k}}(-2-12)$$
$$=32\hat{\mathbf{i}}-\hat{\mathbf{j}}-14\hat{\mathbf{k}}$$

Let $\mathbf{d}=\lambda(\mathbf{a}\times\mathbf{b})$

$$=\lambda(32\hat{\mathbf{i}}-\hat{\mathbf{j}}-14\hat{\mathbf{k}})$$

Also, $\mathbf{c}\cdot\mathbf{d}=15$

$$\Rightarrow (2\hat{\mathbf{i}}-\hat{\mathbf{j}}+4\hat{\mathbf{k}})\cdot\lambda(32\hat{\mathbf{i}}-\hat{\mathbf{j}}-14\hat{\mathbf{k}})=15$$
$$\Rightarrow 2\times(32\lambda)+(-1)\times(-\lambda)+4\times(-14\lambda)=15$$
$$64\lambda+\lambda-56\lambda=15$$
$$\Rightarrow 9\lambda=15$$
$$\Rightarrow \lambda=\frac{15}{9}=\frac{5}{3}$$

∴ Required vector,

$$\mathbf{d}=\frac{5}{3}(32\hat{\mathbf{i}}-\hat{\mathbf{j}}-14\hat{\mathbf{k}}).$$
$$=\frac{1}{3}(160\hat{\mathbf{i}}-5\hat{\mathbf{j}}-70\hat{\mathbf{k}})$$

16 (*b*) We have, $|\mathbf{a}\cdot\mathbf{b}|=|\mathbf{a}\times\mathbf{b}|$

$$\Rightarrow |\mathbf{a}||\mathbf{b}|\cos\theta=|\mathbf{a}||\mathbf{b}|\sin\theta$$
$$\Rightarrow \cos\theta=\sin\theta$$
$$\Rightarrow \tan\theta=1$$
$$\Rightarrow \theta=\frac{\pi}{4}$$

17 (*d*) Let $\mathbf{a}=\hat{\mathbf{i}}+\hat{\mathbf{j}}+\hat{\mathbf{k}}$,

$$\mathbf{b}=2\hat{\mathbf{i}}+4\hat{\mathbf{j}}-5\hat{\mathbf{k}}$$
$$\text{and } \mathbf{c}=\lambda\hat{\mathbf{i}}+2\hat{\mathbf{j}}+3\hat{\mathbf{k}}$$

Now,

$$\mathbf{b}+\mathbf{c}=2\hat{\mathbf{i}}+4\hat{\mathbf{j}}-5\hat{\mathbf{k}}+\lambda\hat{\mathbf{i}}+2\hat{\mathbf{j}}+3\hat{\mathbf{k}}$$
$$=(2+\lambda)\hat{\mathbf{i}}+6\hat{\mathbf{j}}-2\hat{\mathbf{k}}$$
$$\therefore |\mathbf{b}+\mathbf{c}|=\sqrt{(2+\lambda)^2+(6)^2+(-2)^2}$$
$$=\sqrt{4+\lambda^2+4\lambda+36+4}$$
$$=\sqrt{\lambda^2+4\lambda+44}$$

The unit vector along (**b** + **c**), i.e.

$$\frac{\mathbf{b}+\mathbf{c}}{|\mathbf{b}+\mathbf{c}|}=\frac{(2+\lambda)\hat{\mathbf{i}}+6\hat{\mathbf{j}}-2\hat{\mathbf{k}}}{\sqrt{\lambda^2+4\lambda+44}}$$

Scalar product of $(\hat{\mathbf{i}}+\hat{\mathbf{j}}+\hat{\mathbf{k}})$ with this unit vector is 1.

$$\therefore (\hat{\mathbf{i}}+\hat{\mathbf{j}}+\hat{\mathbf{k}})\cdot\frac{\mathbf{b}+\mathbf{c}}{|\mathbf{b}+\mathbf{c}|}=1$$
$$\Rightarrow (\hat{\mathbf{i}}+\hat{\mathbf{j}}+\hat{\mathbf{k}})\cdot\frac{(2+\lambda)\hat{\mathbf{i}}+6\hat{\mathbf{j}}-2\hat{\mathbf{k}}}{\sqrt{\lambda^2+4\lambda+44}}=1$$
$$\Rightarrow \frac{1(2+\lambda)+1(6)+1(-2)}{\sqrt{\lambda^2+4\lambda+44}}=1$$
$$\Rightarrow \frac{(2+\lambda)+6-2}{\sqrt{\lambda^2+4\lambda+44}}=1$$
$$\Rightarrow \lambda+6=\sqrt{\lambda^2+4\lambda+44}$$
$$\Rightarrow (\lambda+6)^2=\lambda^2+4\lambda+44$$
$$\Rightarrow \lambda^2+12\lambda+36=\lambda^2+4\lambda+44$$
$$\Rightarrow 8\lambda=8 \Rightarrow \lambda=1.$$

Hence, the value of λ is 1.

18 (*a*) To expand $(\mathbf{a}+\mathbf{b})\cdot(\mathbf{a}+\mathbf{b})$ use

$$\mathbf{a}\cdot\mathbf{a}=|\mathbf{a}|^2$$
$$\text{and} \quad \mathbf{b}\cdot\mathbf{b}=|\mathbf{b}|^2,$$
$$\mathbf{a}\cdot\mathbf{b}=\mathbf{b}\cdot\mathbf{a}$$

Given, $(\mathbf{a}+\mathbf{b})\cdot(\mathbf{a}+\mathbf{b})=|\mathbf{a}|^2+|\mathbf{b}|^2$

$$\Rightarrow \mathbf{a}\cdot(\mathbf{a}+\mathbf{b})+\mathbf{b}\cdot(\mathbf{a}+\mathbf{b})=|\mathbf{a}|^2+|\mathbf{b}|^2$$
$$\Rightarrow \mathbf{a}\cdot\mathbf{a}+\mathbf{a}\cdot\mathbf{b}+\mathbf{b}\cdot\mathbf{a}+\mathbf{b}\cdot\mathbf{b}=|\mathbf{a}|^2+|\mathbf{b}|^2$$
$$\Rightarrow |\mathbf{a}|^2+2\mathbf{a}\cdot\mathbf{b}+|\mathbf{b}|^2=|\mathbf{a}|^2+|\mathbf{b}|^2$$
$$2\mathbf{a}\cdot\mathbf{b}=0 \quad [\because \mathbf{a}\cdot\mathbf{b}=\mathbf{b}\cdot\mathbf{a}]$$

[scalar product is commutative]

$$\Rightarrow \mathbf{a}\cdot\mathbf{b}=0$$

∴ **a** and **b** are perpendicular. [given $\mathbf{a}\neq 0, \mathbf{b}\neq 0$]

Numerical Type Questions

1 (1) Since, $\mathbf{a}=2\mathbf{b}$ and $\mathbf{c}=-5\mathbf{b}$

So, **a** is parallel to **b** and **c** is anti-parallel to **b**

⇒ **a** and **c** are anti-parallel.

So, angle between **a** and **c** is π.

$$\Rightarrow \alpha=\pi, \text{ then } \frac{\alpha}{\pi}=1.$$

2 (3) Two vectors are said to be collinear. If $\mathbf{a}=\lambda\mathbf{b}$ where λ is non-zero scalar.

Let the vectors $\mathbf{A}=(\mu+2)\,\mathbf{a}+\mathbf{b}$ and $\mathbf{B}=(2\mu-1)\,\mathbf{a}+\mathbf{b}$ are collinear, where **a** and **b** are non-collinear.

∴ $A=\lambda B$ where λ is non-zero

$$(\mu+2)\,a+b=\lambda\,(2\mu-1)\,a+\lambda b$$
$$\Rightarrow (\mu+2-2\lambda\mu+\lambda)\,\mathbf{a}+(1-\lambda)\,\mathbf{b}=0$$

Now, **a** and **b** are non-collinear.

∴ They are linearly independent

$$\Rightarrow \mu+2-2\lambda\mu+\lambda=0$$

and $1-\lambda=0$

$$\Rightarrow \lambda=1$$
$$\Rightarrow \mu+2=2(1)\,\mu-1$$
$$\therefore \mu=3$$

3 (4) Given, ΔABC, $|\mathbf{AB}|=5$ and $|\mathbf{BC}|=3$ and $|\mathbf{AC}|=4$

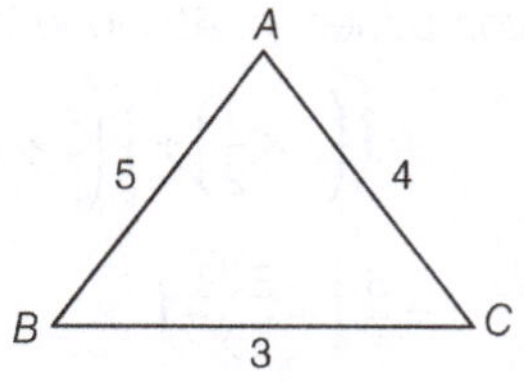

Now, projection of **AB** on **BC**

$$= \frac{\mathbf{AB}\cdot\mathbf{BC}}{|\mathbf{BC}|} = \frac{|\mathbf{AB}|\cdot|\mathbf{BC}|\cos B}{|\mathbf{BC}|}$$

$$\cos B = \frac{(5)^2+(4)^2-9}{2\times5\times4}$$

$$= \frac{25+16-9}{2\times5\times4} = \frac{32}{2\times5\times4} = \frac{4}{5}$$

$$= \frac{4}{5}|\mathbf{AB}| = \frac{4}{5}\times5 = 4$$

∴ Projection of **AB** on **BC** = 4.

4 (5) $|2\mathbf{a}+3\mathbf{b}| = |3\mathbf{a}+\mathbf{b}|$

On squaring, both sides,

$\Rightarrow \quad 4|\mathbf{a}|^2 + 9|\mathbf{b}|^2 + 12\mathbf{a}\cdot\mathbf{b}$

$= 9|\mathbf{a}|^2 + |\mathbf{b}|^2 + 6\mathbf{a}\cdot\mathbf{b}$

$\Rightarrow \quad 5|\mathbf{a}|^2 - 6\mathbf{a}\cdot\mathbf{b} - 8|\mathbf{b}|^2 = 0$

$\frac{a}{8}$ is a unit vector.

So, $|a| = 8$.

and $\quad 5(8)^2 - \frac{6}{2}(8)|\mathbf{b}| - 8|\mathbf{b}|^2 = 0$

$[\because \theta = 60^\circ]$

and $\quad 5\times64 - \frac{6}{2}8|\mathbf{b}| - 8|\mathbf{b}|^2 = 0$

$\Rightarrow \quad |\mathbf{b}|^2 + 3|\mathbf{b}| - 40 = 0$

$\Rightarrow \quad (|\mathbf{b}|+8)(|\mathbf{b}|-5) = 0$

$\Rightarrow \quad |\mathbf{b}| = 5$

and $|b| = -8$ is not possible.

5 (3) Given $\mathbf{a}\cdot(\mathbf{b}+\mathbf{c}) = 0$,

$\mathbf{b}\cdot(\mathbf{c}+\mathbf{a}) = 0$ and $\mathbf{c}\cdot(\mathbf{a}+\mathbf{b}) = 0$

Now, $|\mathbf{a}+\mathbf{b}+\mathbf{c}|^2$

$= (\mathbf{a}+\mathbf{b}+\mathbf{c})^2 = (\mathbf{a}+\mathbf{b}+\mathbf{c})\cdot(\mathbf{a}+\mathbf{b}+\mathbf{c})$

$= \mathbf{a}\cdot\mathbf{a} + \mathbf{a}\cdot(\mathbf{b}+\mathbf{c}) + \mathbf{b}\cdot\mathbf{b} + \mathbf{b}\cdot(\mathbf{a}+\mathbf{c}) + \mathbf{c}\cdot(\mathbf{a}+\mathbf{b}) + \mathbf{c}\cdot\mathbf{c}$

$= |\mathbf{a}|^2 + |\mathbf{b}|^2 + |\mathbf{c}|^2 = 16+25+4$

$|\mathbf{a}+\mathbf{b}+\mathbf{c}|^2 = 45$

$|\mathbf{a}+\mathbf{b}+\mathbf{c}| = \sqrt{45} = 3\sqrt{5}$

Then, $\quad \frac{|(\mathbf{a}+\mathbf{b}+\mathbf{c})|}{\sqrt{5}} = 3$

6 (1539) $\mathbf{a} = 3\hat{i}+2\hat{j}+\hat{k}$

and $\mathbf{b} = 8\hat{i}+3\hat{j}+4\hat{k}$

$(2\mathbf{a}+\mathbf{b})\times\mathbf{c} = \mathbf{c}\times(\mathbf{a}+2\mathbf{b})$

$\Rightarrow (2\mathbf{a}+\mathbf{b})\times\mathbf{c} - \mathbf{c}\times(\mathbf{a}+2\mathbf{b}) = 0$

$\Rightarrow (2\mathbf{a}+\mathbf{b})\times\mathbf{c} + (\mathbf{a}+2\mathbf{b})\times\mathbf{c} = 0$

$\Rightarrow \quad (2\mathbf{a}+\mathbf{b}+\mathbf{a}+2\mathbf{b})\times\mathbf{c} = 0$

$\Rightarrow \quad (3\mathbf{a}+3\mathbf{b})\times\mathbf{c} = 0$

$\mathbf{c} = \mu(3\mathbf{a}+3\mathbf{b})$

$\mathbf{c} = \mu(3(3\hat{i}+2\hat{j}+\hat{k}) + 3(8\hat{i}+3\hat{j}+4\hat{k}))$

$= \mu\,(9\hat{i}+6\hat{j}+3\hat{k}+24\hat{i}+9\hat{j}+12\hat{k})$

$\mathbf{c} = \mu(33\hat{i}+15\hat{j}+15\hat{k})$

Now, $(3\mathbf{a}+2\mathbf{b})\cdot\mathbf{c} = 1170$

$(3(3\hat{i}+2\hat{j}+\hat{k}) + 2(8\hat{i}+3\hat{j}+4\hat{k}))\cdot\mu\,(33\hat{i}+15\hat{j}+15\hat{k})\,\mu = 1170$

$(9\hat{i}+6\hat{j}+3\hat{k}+16\hat{i}+6\hat{j}+8\hat{k})\cdot(33\hat{i}+15\hat{j}+15\hat{k})\,\mu = 1170$

$(25\hat{i}+12\hat{j}+11\hat{k})\cdot(33\hat{i}+15\hat{j}+15\hat{k})\,\mu = 1170$

$1170\mu = 1170$

$\therefore \quad \mu = 1$

So, $\quad \mathbf{c} = 33\hat{i}+15\hat{j}+15\hat{k}$

$|\mathbf{c}|^2 = (\sqrt{(33)^2+(15)^2+(15)^2})^2$

$= (\sqrt{1089+225+225})^2 = 1539$

$\Rightarrow |\mathbf{c}|^2 = 1539$

7 (18) $\mathbf{a} = 3\hat{i}+\hat{j}+\mathbf{k}$, $\mathbf{b} = -\hat{i}+2\hat{j}+3\hat{k}$ and $\mathbf{c} = 3\hat{i}-2\mathbf{j}+\mathbf{k}$

Given that $\mathbf{r}\times\mathbf{a} + \mathbf{a}\times\mathbf{c} = 0$

$\Rightarrow \quad \mathbf{r}\times\mathbf{a} - \mathbf{c}\times\mathbf{a} = 0$

$\Rightarrow \quad (\mathbf{r}-\mathbf{c})\times\mathbf{a} = 0$

$\Rightarrow \quad (\mathbf{r}-\mathbf{c}) = \mu\mathbf{a}$

$\Rightarrow \quad \mathbf{r} = \mathbf{c}+\mu\mathbf{a}$

$\mathbf{r}\cdot\mathbf{b} = 0$

$\Rightarrow \quad (\mathbf{c}+\mu\mathbf{a})\cdot\mathbf{b} = 0$

$\Rightarrow \quad \mathbf{c}\cdot\mathbf{a} + \mu\mathbf{a}\cdot\mathbf{b} = 0$

$\Rightarrow \quad (3\hat{i}-2\hat{j}+\hat{k})\cdot(3\hat{i}+\hat{j}+\hat{k}) + \mu(3\hat{i}+\hat{j}+\hat{k})\cdot(-\hat{i}+2\hat{j}+3\hat{k}) = 0$

$\Rightarrow \quad 9-2+1+\mu(-3+2+3) = 0$

$\Rightarrow \quad 8+\mu(2) = 0$

$\mu = -4$

$\Rightarrow \quad \mathbf{r}\cdot\mathbf{c} = (\mathbf{c}+\mu\mathbf{a})\cdot\mathbf{c}$

$= \mathbf{c}\cdot\mathbf{c} + \mu\mathbf{a}\cdot\mathbf{c}$

$= |\mathbf{c}|^2 + -4(3\hat{i}+\hat{j}+\hat{k})\cdot(3\hat{i}-2\hat{j}+\hat{k})$

$= 14 - 4\,(9-2+1)$

$= 14 - 4(8) = 14 - 32$

$\mathbf{r}\cdot\mathbf{c} = -18$

$\therefore \quad |\mathbf{r}\cdot\mathbf{c}| = 18$

8 (108) $|\mathbf{a}| = 3$ and $|\mathbf{b}| = 4$ and $|\mathbf{a}\cdot\mathbf{b}| = 6$

We need to find $|\mathbf{a}\times\mathbf{b}|$

Apply Lagrange's indentity.

If $\mathbf{a}\cdot\mathbf{b}$ be any 2 vector, then

$|\mathbf{a}\times\mathbf{b}|^2 + |\mathbf{a}\cdot\mathbf{b}|^2 = |\mathbf{a}|^2\,|\mathbf{b}|^2$

$\Rightarrow |\mathbf{a}\times\mathbf{b}|^2 = |\mathbf{a}|^2\,|\mathbf{b}|^2 - |\mathbf{a}\cdot\mathbf{b}|^2$

$= (3)^2\cdot(4)^2 - (6)^2$

$= 9\cdot16 - 36$

$= 144 - 36$

$|\mathbf{a}\times\mathbf{b}|^2 = 108$

Assertion and Reason Questions

1 (a) To prove that the given two vectors **a**, **b** to be collinear, we have to prove $\mathbf{a} = \lambda\mathbf{b}$, where λ is a numerical value scalar.

Let $\quad \mathbf{a} = 2\hat{i} - 3\hat{j} + 4\hat{k}$

and $\quad \mathbf{b} = -4\hat{i} + 6\hat{j} - 8\hat{k}$

It is observed that

$\mathbf{b} = -4\hat{i} + 6\hat{j} - 8\hat{k}$

$= -2\,(2\hat{i} - 3\hat{j} + 4\hat{k}) = -2\mathbf{a}$

$\therefore \quad \mathbf{b} = \lambda\mathbf{a}$, where $\lambda = -2$

Therefore, they are collinear.

So, Assertion (A) is true.

Reason (R) is also true and also justify Assertion (A).

2 (a) If three points A, B, C form a right angle triangle, then $|\mathbf{AB}|^2 + |\mathbf{CA}|^2 = |\mathbf{BC}|^2$.

Position vectors of points A, B and C are respectively given as

$\mathbf{a} = 3\hat{i} - 4\hat{j} - 4\hat{k}$, $\mathbf{b} = 2\hat{i} - \hat{j} + \hat{k}$ and $\mathbf{c} = \hat{i} - 3\hat{j} - 5\hat{k}$

Now, $\mathbf{AB} = \mathbf{b} - \mathbf{a}$

$= (PV \text{ of } B - PV \text{ of } A)$

$\Rightarrow \mathbf{b}-\mathbf{a} = [(2\hat{i}-\hat{j}+\hat{k}) - (3\hat{i}-4\hat{j}-4\hat{k})]$

$= -\hat{i}+3\hat{j}+5\hat{k}$

Comparing with $\mathbf{X} = x\hat{i} + y\hat{j} + z\hat{k}$, we get

$x = -1, y = 3, z = 5$

Magnitude of **AB**,

$|\mathbf{AB}| = \sqrt{x^2+y^2+z^2}$

$= \sqrt{(-1)^2+(3)^2+(5)^2}$

$= \sqrt{1+9+25} = \sqrt{35}$

$\therefore |\mathbf{AB}|^2 = 35$

Similarly,

$\mathbf{BC} = \mathbf{c} - \mathbf{b} = (PV \text{ of } C - PV \text{ of } B)$

$\Rightarrow \mathbf{c} - \mathbf{b} = (\hat{i} - 3\hat{j} - 5\hat{k}) - (2\hat{i} - \hat{j} + \hat{k})$

$= -\hat{i} - 2\hat{j} - 6\hat{k}$

Similarly,

$$|\mathbf{BC}| = \sqrt{(-1)^2 + (-2)^2 + (-6)^2}$$

$\Rightarrow |\mathbf{BC}|^2 = 41$

and $\mathbf{CA} = \mathbf{a} - \mathbf{c}$

$= (PV \text{ of } A - PV \text{ of } C)$

$\Rightarrow \mathbf{a} - \mathbf{c} = (3\hat{i} - 4\hat{j} - 4\hat{k}) - (\hat{i} - 3\hat{j} - 5\hat{k})$

$= 2\hat{i} - \hat{j} + \hat{k}$

$|\mathbf{CA}| = \sqrt{(2)^2 + (-1)^2 + (1)^2}$

$= \sqrt{4+1+1} = \sqrt{6} \Rightarrow |\mathbf{CA}|^2 = 6$

Now, we find $|\mathbf{AB}|^2 + |\mathbf{CA}|^2$

$= 35 + 6 = 41 = |\mathbf{BC}|^2$

Therefore, ΔABC is a right angled triangle with right angle at A.

3 (*a*) The scalar product is commutative is $\mathbf{a} \cdot \mathbf{b} = \mathbf{b} \cdot \mathbf{a}$

[since, $\mathbf{a} \cdot \mathbf{b} = |\mathbf{a}||\mathbf{b}|\cos\theta = ab\cos\theta$ and $\mathbf{b} \cdot \mathbf{a} = |\mathbf{b}||\mathbf{a}|\cos\theta = ab\cos\theta$, so both are same]

So, both the statements are true and Reason (R) is the correct explanation of Assertion (A).

4 (*c*) The projection of vector a on the vector b is given by

$$\frac{(\mathbf{a} \cdot \mathbf{b})}{|\mathbf{b}|} = \frac{(2 \times 1 + 3 \times 2 + 2 \times 1)}{\sqrt{(1)^2 + (2)^2 + (1)^2}}$$

$$= \frac{10}{\sqrt{6}} = \frac{5}{3}\sqrt{6}$$

5 (*a*) Let $\mathbf{a} = \hat{i} + 3\hat{j} + 7\hat{k}$ and $\mathbf{b} = 7\hat{i} - \hat{j} + 8\hat{k}$, then projection of $\mathbf{a}$ on $\mathbf{b}$ is given by

$$\frac{\mathbf{a} \cdot \mathbf{b}}{|\mathbf{b}|} = \left(\frac{(\hat{i} + 3\hat{j} + 7\hat{k}) \cdot (7\hat{i} - \hat{j} + 8\hat{k})}{\sqrt{7^2 + (-1)^2 + 8^2}}\right)$$

$$= \left(\frac{1 \times 7 + 3 \times (-1) + 7 \times 8}{(\sqrt{49 + 1 + 64})}\right)$$

$$= \frac{7 - 3 + 56}{\sqrt{114}} = \frac{60}{\sqrt{114}}$$

Hence, the projection of vector $(\hat{i} + 3\hat{j} + 7\hat{k})$ on $(7\hat{i} - \hat{j} + 8\hat{k})$ is $\frac{60}{\sqrt{114}}$.

6 (*c*) It is always true that the vector product is not commutative,

$\mathbf{a} \times \mathbf{b} = -\mathbf{b} \times \mathbf{a}$.

Indeed, $\mathbf{a} \times \mathbf{b} = |\mathbf{a}||\mathbf{b}|\sin\theta\,\hat{\mathbf{n}}$, where a, b and $\hat{\mathbf{n}}$ form a right handed system, i.e. θ is traversed from a to $\mathbf{b}$. While $\mathbf{b} \times \mathbf{a} = |\mathbf{a}||\mathbf{b}|\sin\theta\,\hat{\mathbf{n}}_1$, where $\mathbf{b}$, $\mathbf{a}$ and $\hat{\mathbf{n}}_1$ form a left handed system i.e. θ is traversed from b to a [fig (ii)].

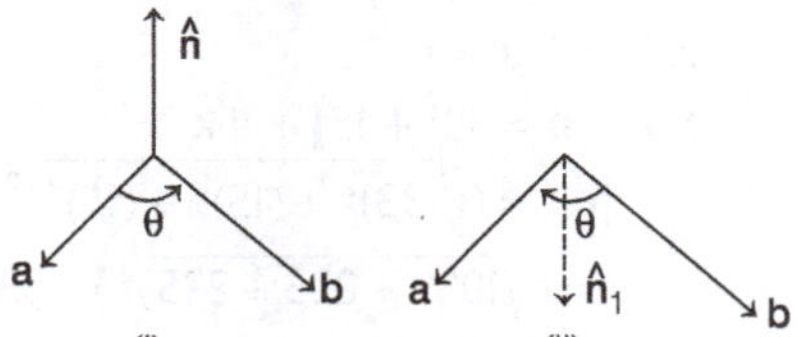

(i) (ii)

Thus, if we assume a and b to lie in the plane of the paper, then $\hat{\mathbf{n}}$ and $\hat{\mathbf{n}}_1$ both will be perpendicular to the plane of the paper. But, $\hat{\mathbf{n}}$ being directed above the paper while $\hat{\mathbf{n}}_1$ directed below the paper. i.e. $\hat{\mathbf{n}}_1 = -\hat{\mathbf{n}}$.

Hence, $\mathbf{a} \times \mathbf{b} = |\mathbf{a}||\mathbf{b}|\sin\theta\,\hat{\mathbf{n}}$

$= -|\mathbf{b}||\mathbf{a}|\sin\theta\,\hat{\mathbf{n}}_1$

$= -\mathbf{b} \times \mathbf{a}$

So, Reason (R) is not true.

$\therefore$ (c) is the correct option.

7 (*d*) The area of a parallelogram with a and b as its adjacent sides is given by $|\mathbf{a} \times \mathbf{b}|$.

Now,

$$\mathbf{a} \times \mathbf{b} = \begin{vmatrix} \hat{i} & \hat{j} & \hat{k} \\ 3 & 1 & 4 \\ 1 & -1 & 1 \end{vmatrix} = 5\hat{i} + \hat{j} - 4\hat{k}$$

Therefore,

$$|\mathbf{a} \times \mathbf{b}| = \sqrt{25 + 1 + 16} = \sqrt{42}$$

Hence, the required area is $\sqrt{42}$.

Reason (R) is true since, area of parallelogram whose adjacent sides are $\mathbf{a}$ and $\mathbf{b}$ is $|\mathbf{a} \times \mathbf{b}|$.

Case or Paragraph Type Questions

Solution (Q. Nos. 1-4)

1 (*d*) Example of collinear vectors are $\mathbf{a}, \mathbf{d}; \mathbf{b}, \mathbf{x}, \mathbf{z}$ and $\mathbf{c}, \mathbf{y}$.

2 (*d*) $\mathbf{a}, \mathbf{c}$ is not an example of equal vectors.

3 (*a*) Coinitial vectors are $\mathbf{a}, \mathbf{y}, \mathbf{z}$.

4 (*c*) Example of collinear vectors but not equal vectors are $\mathbf{b}, \mathbf{z}$ and $\mathbf{x}, \mathbf{z}$.

Solution (Q. Nos. 5-7) $P = (2, 2, 2)$ and $Q = (1, 2, 3)$, $R = (3, 2, 1)$ and $S = (2, 3, 4)$

5 (*a*) $\mathbf{PQ} = \mathbf{Q} - \mathbf{P}$

$= (1-2)\hat{i} + (2-2)\hat{j} + (3-2)\hat{k}$

$\mathbf{PQ} = -\hat{i} + \hat{k}$

6 (*b*) $\mathbf{PR} = \mathbf{R} - \mathbf{P}$

$= (3-2)\hat{i} + (2-2)\hat{j} + (1-2)\hat{k}$

$\hat{i} - \hat{k}$

$|\mathbf{PR}| = \sqrt{1+1} = \sqrt{2}$

$|\mathbf{PR}| = \sqrt{2}$

7 (*c*) $\mathbf{PS} = \mathbf{S} - \mathbf{P}$

$= (2-2)\hat{i} + (3-2)\hat{j} + (4-2)\hat{k}$

$\mathbf{PS} = \mathbf{j} + 2\mathbf{k}$

$$\mathbf{PS} = \frac{\mathbf{PS}}{|\mathbf{PS}|} = \frac{\hat{j} + 2k}{\sqrt{5}}$$

Past Years Questions

1 (*b*) We have,

$\mathbf{a} + 5\mathbf{b} = \lambda\mathbf{c}$ ...(i)

and $\mathbf{b} + 6\mathbf{c} = \mu\mathbf{a}$ ...(ii)

From Eq. (i), we have,

$\mathbf{a} = \lambda\mathbf{c} - 5\mathbf{b}$

$\therefore \mathbf{b} + 6\mathbf{c} = \mu(\lambda\mathbf{c} - 5\mathbf{b})$ [from Eq. (ii)]

$\Rightarrow \frac{\mathbf{b}}{\mu} + \frac{6}{\mu}\mathbf{c} = \lambda\mathbf{c} - 5\mathbf{a}$

$\therefore \frac{6}{\mu} = \lambda$ and $\frac{1}{\mu} = -5$

$\Rightarrow \mu = -\frac{1}{5} \Rightarrow \lambda = -30$

$\therefore \mathbf{a} + 5\mathbf{b} + 30\mathbf{c} = 0$

$\Rightarrow \alpha = 5$ and $\beta = 30$

$\therefore \alpha + \beta = 5 + 30 = 35$

2 (*b*) We have,

$$\mathbf{OA} = 2\hat{\mathbf{i}} + 2\hat{\mathbf{j}} + \hat{\mathbf{k}}$$

and $\mathbf{OB} = 2\hat{\mathbf{i}} + 4\hat{\mathbf{j}} + 4\hat{\mathbf{k}}$

$$|\mathbf{OA}| = \sqrt{4+4+1} = \sqrt{9} = 3$$

$$|\mathbf{OB}| = \sqrt{4+16+16} = 6$$

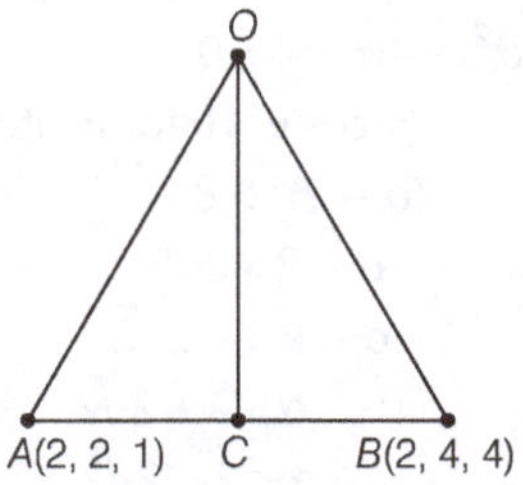

$$\Rightarrow \frac{\mathbf{OA}}{\mathbf{OB}} = \frac{3}{6} = \frac{1}{2} \Rightarrow \frac{\mathbf{AC}}{\mathbf{BC}} = \frac{1}{2}$$

$$\therefore \quad \mathbf{OC} = \frac{1 \times (2\hat{\mathbf{i}} + 4\hat{\mathbf{j}} + 4\hat{\mathbf{k}}) + 2(2\hat{\mathbf{i}} + 2\hat{\mathbf{j}} + \hat{\mathbf{k}})}{1+2}$$

$$= \frac{6\hat{\mathbf{i}} + 8\hat{\mathbf{j}} + 6\hat{\mathbf{k}}}{3}$$

$$\therefore \quad |\mathbf{OC}| = \frac{\sqrt{36+64+36}}{3}$$

$$= \frac{\sqrt{136}}{3} = \frac{2\sqrt{34}}{3}$$

3 (*c*) Given position vectors of the vertices A, B, C of ΔABC are $2\hat{\mathbf{i}} - 3\hat{\mathbf{j}} + 3\hat{\mathbf{k}}, 2\hat{\mathbf{i}} + 2\hat{\mathbf{j}} + 3\hat{\mathbf{k}}$ and $-\hat{\mathbf{i}} + \hat{\mathbf{j}} + 3\hat{\mathbf{k}}$ respectively.

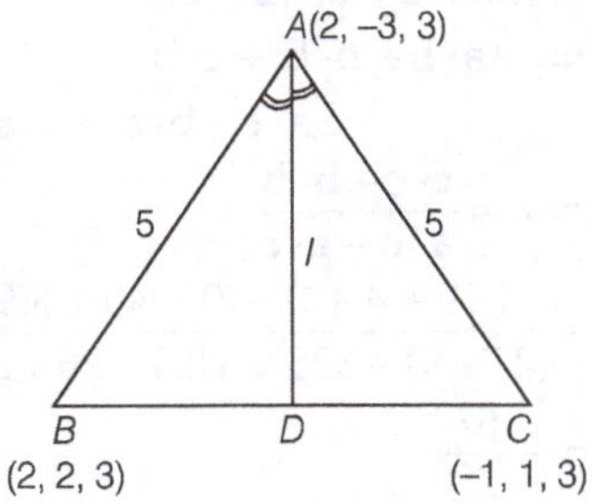

So, coordinates of $A \equiv (2, -3, 3)$,

$$B \equiv (2, 2, 3)$$

and $\quad C \equiv (-1, 1, 3)$

Now, $AB = 5$ and $AC = 5$

As we know that

$$\frac{BD}{DC} = \frac{AB}{AC} \Rightarrow \frac{BD}{DC} = \frac{5}{5} = \frac{1}{1}$$

$$\Rightarrow \quad BD = DC$$

i.e. D is mid-point of BC.

Now, $\quad D \equiv \left(\frac{2-1}{2}, \frac{2+1}{2}, \frac{3+3}{2}\right)$

$$\equiv \left(\frac{1}{2}, \frac{3}{2}, 3\right)$$

Hence, $\quad l = AD$

$$= \sqrt{\left(2-\frac{1}{2}\right)^2 + \left(-3-\frac{3}{2}\right)^2 + (3-3)^2}$$

$$= \sqrt{\frac{9}{4} + \frac{81}{4}} = \sqrt{\frac{90}{4}} = \sqrt{\frac{45}{2}}$$

$$\therefore \quad 2l^2 = 2 \times \frac{45}{2} = 45$$

4 (*d*) Given position vectors of the vertices A, B, C are $2\hat{\mathbf{i}} + 2\hat{\mathbf{j}} + \hat{\mathbf{k}}$, $\hat{\mathbf{i}} + 2\hat{\mathbf{j}} + 2\hat{\mathbf{k}}$ and $2\hat{\mathbf{i}} + \hat{\mathbf{j}} + 2\hat{\mathbf{k}}$, respectively.

So, coordinates of $A \equiv (2, 2, 1)$,

$$B \equiv (1, 2, 2) \text{ and } C \equiv (2, 1, 2)$$

l_1 : Length of perpendicular drawn from orthocentre of ΔABC on AB.

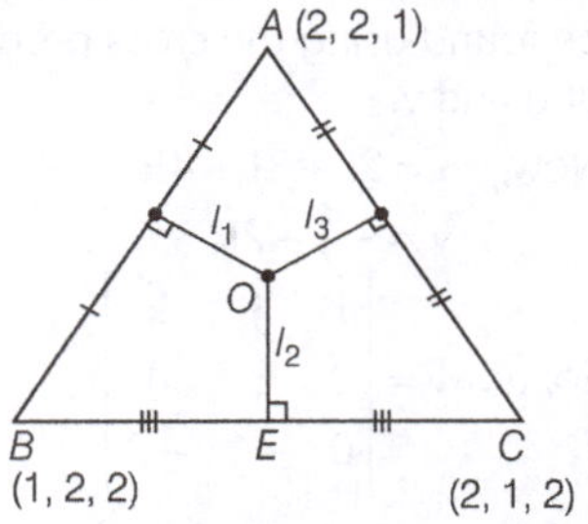

l_2 : Length of perpendicular drawn from orthocentre of ΔABC on BC.

l_3 : Length of perpendicular drawn from orthocentre of ΔABC on CA.

Now,

$$AB = \sqrt{(2-1)^2 + (2-2)^2 + (1-2)^2}$$

$$= \sqrt{1+0+1} = \sqrt{2}$$

$$BC = \sqrt{(1-2)^2 + (2-1)^2 + (2-2)^2}$$

$$= \sqrt{1+1+0} = \sqrt{2}$$

$$CA = \sqrt{(2-2)^2 + (1-2)^2 + (2-1)^2}$$

$$= \sqrt{0+1+1} = \sqrt{2}$$

This represents ΔABC is an equilateral triangle.

As we known that in an equilateral triangle, orthocentre and centroid will be same [coincide].

So, $\quad$ centroid $\equiv \left(\frac{5}{3}, \frac{5}{3}, \frac{5}{3}\right)$

Let D be the mid-point of

$$AB = \left(\frac{3}{2}, 2, \frac{3}{2}\right)$$

$$\therefore \quad l_1 = \sqrt{\frac{1}{36} + \frac{1}{9} + \frac{1}{36}}$$

$$= \frac{1}{\sqrt{6}} = l_2 = l_3$$

Hence, $l_1^2 + l_2^2 + l_3^2 = \frac{1}{6} + \frac{1}{6} + \frac{1}{6}$

$$= 3\left(\frac{1}{6}\right) = \frac{1}{2}$$

5 (*b*) Let the position vectors of vertices A, B, C and D of quadrilateral $ABCD$ be **a**, **b**, **c** and **d**, respectively.

E is the mid point of AC

$\therefore$ Position vector of $E = \frac{1}{2}(\mathbf{a} + \mathbf{c})$

F is the mid-point of BD

$\therefore$ Position vector of $F = \frac{1}{2}(\mathbf{b} + \mathbf{d})$

$\therefore$ **EF** = (position vector of F) − (position vector of E)

$$= \frac{1}{2}(\mathbf{b} + \mathbf{d}) - \frac{1}{2}(\mathbf{a} + \mathbf{c})$$

$$= \frac{1}{2}(\mathbf{b} + \mathbf{d} - \mathbf{a} - \mathbf{c})$$

Now, $\mathbf{AB} + \mathbf{AD} + \mathbf{CB} + \mathbf{CD}$

$$= (\mathbf{b} - \mathbf{a}) + (\mathbf{d} - \mathbf{a}) + (\mathbf{b} - \mathbf{c}) + (\mathbf{d} - \mathbf{c})$$

$$= 2(\mathbf{b} + \mathbf{d} - \mathbf{a} - \mathbf{c}) = 2 \times 2\mathbf{EF}$$

$$\mathbf{AB} + \mathbf{AD} + \mathbf{CB} + \mathbf{CD} = 4\mathbf{EF}$$

$$\mathbf{AB} + (-\mathbf{BC}) + \mathbf{AD} + (-\mathbf{DC}) = 4\mathbf{EF}$$

$$= -4\mathbf{FE}$$

$$(\mathbf{AB} - \mathbf{BC}) + (\mathbf{AD} - \mathbf{DC})$$

$$= -4\mathbf{FE} = k\mathbf{FE}$$

$$\Rightarrow \quad k = -4$$

6 (*b*) We have, $10|a_i| < 1, i = 1, 2, 3$

Let $\quad |a_1| \ge |a_2| \ge |a_3|$

$$|\mathbf{a}| = \sqrt{a_1^2 + a_2^2 + a_3^2} \ge \sqrt{a_1^2}$$

$\therefore$ $|\mathbf{a}| \ge |a_1|$ or $\max\{|a_1|, |a_2|, |a_3|\}$

Hence, (A) is true.

$$|\mathbf{a}| = \sqrt{a_1^2 + a_2^2 + a_3^2} \le \sqrt{a_1^2 + a_1^2 + a_1^2}$$

$$= \sqrt{3}|a_1|$$

$$\therefore \quad |\mathbf{a}| = \sqrt{3}|a_1| < 3|a_1|$$

$$\therefore \quad |\mathbf{a}| < 3\max\{|a_1|, |a_2|, |a_3|\}$$

7 (*d*)

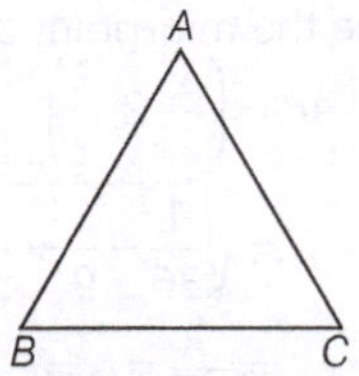

Let position vector of *A*, *B* and *C* are **a**, **b** and **c**, respectively.

P and *Q* are respectively circumcentre and orthocentre of ΔABC, whose position vector are **p** and **q**.

Let *G* be the centroid of triangle whose position vector is

$$\mathbf{G} = \frac{\mathbf{a}+\mathbf{b}+\mathbf{c}}{3} \quad ...(i)$$

Centroid divides the line joining the circumcenter and orthocenter in the ratio 2 : 1.

$$\mathbf{G} = \frac{2\mathbf{q}+\mathbf{p}}{3} \quad ...(ii)$$

On comparing Eqs. (i) and (ii), we get

$$2\mathbf{q}+\mathbf{p} = \mathbf{a}+\mathbf{b}+\mathbf{c} \quad ...(iii)$$

Now, $\mathbf{PA}+\mathbf{PB}+\mathbf{PC} = \mathbf{a}-\mathbf{p}+\mathbf{b}-\mathbf{p}+\mathbf{c}-\mathbf{p}$

$= 2\mathbf{q}+\mathbf{p}-3\mathbf{p}$ [From Eq. (iii)]

$= 2\mathbf{PQ}$

8 (d) Let $\mathbf{v} = \lambda\mathbf{a}+\mu\mathbf{b}$

$\mathbf{v} = \lambda(1, 1, 2)+\mu(2, -3, 1)$

$\mathbf{v} = (\lambda+2\mu, \lambda-3\mu, 2\lambda+\mu)$

$\mathbf{v}\cdot\hat{\mathbf{j}} = 7$ and $\mathbf{v}\cdot\dfrac{\mathbf{c}}{|\mathbf{c}|} = \dfrac{2}{\sqrt{3}}$

$\Rightarrow \quad \lambda-3\mu = 7 \quad ...(i)$

and $\quad \mathbf{v}\cdot\dfrac{\mathbf{c}}{\sqrt{3}} = \dfrac{2}{\sqrt{3}} \Rightarrow \mathbf{v}\cdot\mathbf{c} = 2$

$\Rightarrow (\lambda+2\mu, \lambda-3\mu, 2\lambda+\mu)\cdot(1, -1, 1) = 2$

$\Rightarrow \lambda+2\mu-\lambda+3\mu+2\lambda+\mu = 2$

$\Rightarrow 2\lambda+6\mu = 2 \Rightarrow \lambda+3\mu = 1 \quad ...(ii)$

and $\quad \lambda-3\mu = 7$ [From Eq. (i)]

$\therefore \quad 2\lambda = 8 \Rightarrow \lambda = 4$

and $\quad \mu = -1$

Thus, $\mathbf{v} = (2, 7, 7)$

Hence, $\mathbf{v}\cdot(\hat{\mathbf{i}}+\hat{\mathbf{k}})$

$= (2, 7, 7)\cdot(1, 0, 1) = 2+7 = 9$

9 (*a*) Given, $(\mathbf{a}-\mathbf{b})\cdot(\mathbf{a}+\mathbf{b}) = 27$

$\Rightarrow \mathbf{a}\cdot\mathbf{a}+\mathbf{a}\cdot\mathbf{b}-\mathbf{b}\cdot\mathbf{a}-\mathbf{b}\cdot\mathbf{b} = 27$

$\Rightarrow \quad |\mathbf{a}^2|-|\mathbf{b}|^2 = 27$

{Since, $\mathbf{a}\cdot\mathbf{b} = \mathbf{b}\cdot\mathbf{a}$}

Also, given that $|\mathbf{a}| = 2|\mathbf{b}|$, we get

$\Rightarrow \quad (2|\mathbf{b}|^2)-|\mathbf{b}|^2 = 27$

$\Rightarrow \quad 4|\mathbf{b}|^2-|\mathbf{b}|^2 = 27$

$\Rightarrow \quad 3|\mathbf{b}|^2 = 27$

$\Rightarrow \quad |\mathbf{b}|^2 = 9$

$\therefore \quad |\mathbf{b}| = 3$

Hence, $\quad |\mathbf{b}| = 3$

10 (*d*) Suppose $\mathbf{u} = \mathbf{a}+\mathbf{b}$

$\mathbf{v} = \mathbf{a}-\mathbf{b}$

and given: $\mathbf{a} = \hat{\mathbf{i}}+\hat{\mathbf{j}}+\hat{\mathbf{k}}$

$\mathbf{b} = \hat{\mathbf{i}}+2\hat{\mathbf{j}}+3\hat{\mathbf{k}}$

Since, the unit vector that is perpendicular to both u and v can be found using the cross product of u and v.

Now, $\quad \mathbf{u} = 2\hat{\mathbf{i}}+3\hat{\mathbf{j}}+4\hat{\mathbf{k}}$

$\mathbf{v} = -\hat{\mathbf{j}}-2\hat{\mathbf{k}}$

So, $\mathbf{u}\times\mathbf{v} = \begin{vmatrix} \hat{\mathbf{i}} & \hat{\mathbf{j}} & \hat{\mathbf{k}} \\ 2 & 3 & 4 \\ 0 & -1 & -2 \end{vmatrix}$

$\mathbf{u}\times\mathbf{v} = -2\hat{\mathbf{i}}+4\hat{\mathbf{j}}-2\hat{\mathbf{k}}$

Now,

$|\mathbf{u}\times\mathbf{v}| = \sqrt{(-2)^2+(4)^2+(-2)^2}$

$= \sqrt{4+16+4}$

$= \sqrt{24} = 2\sqrt{6}$

The required unit vector

$= \dfrac{\mathbf{u}\times\mathbf{v}}{|\mathbf{u}\times\mathbf{v}|}$

$= \dfrac{-2\hat{\mathbf{i}}+4\hat{\mathbf{j}}-2\hat{\mathbf{k}}}{2\sqrt{6}}$

$= -\dfrac{1}{\sqrt{6}}\hat{\mathbf{i}}+\dfrac{2}{\sqrt{6}}\hat{\mathbf{j}}-\dfrac{1}{\sqrt{6}}\hat{\mathbf{k}}$

11 (5) Let θ be the acute angle between the vectors $\alpha\hat{\mathbf{i}}-2\hat{\mathbf{j}}+2\hat{\mathbf{k}}$ and $\alpha\hat{\mathbf{i}}+2\alpha\hat{\mathbf{j}}-2\hat{\mathbf{k}}$.

Now,

$$\cos\theta = \frac{(\alpha\hat{\mathbf{i}}-2\hat{\mathbf{j}}+2\hat{\mathbf{k}})\cdot(\alpha\hat{\mathbf{i}}+2\alpha\hat{\mathbf{j}}-2\hat{\mathbf{k}})}{\sqrt{\alpha^2+4+4}\sqrt{\alpha^2+4\alpha^2+4}}$$

$\Rightarrow \cos\theta$

$= \dfrac{\alpha^2-4\alpha-4}{\sqrt{\alpha^2+4+4}\sqrt{\alpha^2+4\alpha^2+4}}$

$\Rightarrow \cos\theta = \dfrac{\alpha^2-4\alpha-4}{\sqrt{\alpha^2+8}\sqrt{5\alpha^2+4}}$

$\Rightarrow \alpha^2-4\alpha-4 > 0$

[$\because \cos\theta > 0$ for acute angle]

$\Rightarrow \quad (\alpha-2)^2 > 8$

$\Rightarrow \quad \alpha-2 > 2\sqrt{2}$

or $\quad \alpha-2 < -2\sqrt{2}$

$\Rightarrow \quad \alpha > 2+2\sqrt{2}$

or $\quad \alpha < 2-2\sqrt{2}$

$\Rightarrow x \in (-\infty, -0.82) \cup (4.82, \infty)$

Hence, least positive integral value of $\alpha = 5$.

12 (569) $\quad \mathbf{a} = 9\hat{\mathbf{i}}-13\hat{\mathbf{j}}+25\hat{\mathbf{k}}$,

$\mathbf{b} = 3\hat{\mathbf{i}}+7\hat{\mathbf{j}}-13\hat{\mathbf{k}}$

and $\quad \mathbf{c} = 17\hat{\mathbf{i}}-2\hat{\mathbf{j}}+\hat{\mathbf{k}}$

$\therefore \quad \mathbf{b}+\mathbf{c} = 20\hat{\mathbf{i}}+5\hat{\mathbf{j}}-12\hat{\mathbf{k}}$

and $\mathbf{b}-\mathbf{c} = -14\hat{\mathbf{i}}+9\hat{\mathbf{j}}-14\hat{\mathbf{k}}$

$\because \quad \mathbf{r}\times\mathbf{a} = (\mathbf{b}+\mathbf{c})\times\mathbf{a}$

$\Rightarrow \quad [\mathbf{r}-(\mathbf{b}+\mathbf{c})]\times\mathbf{a} = 0$

$\Rightarrow \quad \mathbf{r}-(\mathbf{b}+\mathbf{c}) = \lambda\mathbf{a}$

$\Rightarrow \quad \mathbf{r} = \lambda\mathbf{a}+\mathbf{b}+\mathbf{c} \quad ...(i)$

Also, $\quad \mathbf{r}\cdot(\mathbf{b}-\mathbf{c}) = 0$

$\Rightarrow (\lambda\mathbf{a}+\mathbf{b}+\mathbf{c})\cdot(\mathbf{b}-\mathbf{c}) = 0$

$\Rightarrow \quad \lambda\mathbf{a}\cdot\mathbf{b}+\mathbf{b}\cdot\mathbf{b}+\mathbf{c}\cdot\mathbf{b}$

$-\lambda\mathbf{a}\cdot\mathbf{c}-\mathbf{b}\cdot\mathbf{c}-\mathbf{c}\cdot\mathbf{c} = 0$

$\Rightarrow \lambda = \dfrac{\mathbf{c}\cdot\mathbf{c}-\mathbf{b}\cdot\mathbf{b}}{\mathbf{a}\cdot\mathbf{b}-\mathbf{a}\cdot\mathbf{c}}$

$= \dfrac{(289+4+1)-(9+49+169)}{(27-91-325)-(153+26+25)}$

$= -\dfrac{67}{593}$

$\therefore \mathbf{r}-(\mathbf{b}+\mathbf{c}) = \dfrac{-67}{593}\mathbf{a}$

$\Rightarrow 593\mathbf{r}+67\mathbf{a} = 593(\mathbf{b}+\mathbf{c})$

So, $\dfrac{|593\mathbf{r}+67\mathbf{a}|^2}{(593)^2} = \dfrac{(593)^2|\mathbf{b}+\mathbf{c}|^2}{(593)^2}$

$= |\mathbf{b}+\mathbf{c}|^2 = 20^2+5^2+12^2 = 569$

13 (285) Given: $\mathbf{a} = \hat{\mathbf{i}}+2\hat{\mathbf{j}}+3\hat{\mathbf{k}}$,

$\mathbf{b} = \hat{\mathbf{i}}+\hat{\mathbf{j}}-\hat{\mathbf{k}}$

$\mathbf{a}\cdot\mathbf{c} = 11, \mathbf{b}\cdot(\mathbf{a}\times\mathbf{c}) = 27,$

$$\mathbf{b}\cdot\mathbf{c} = -\sqrt{3}\,|b|$$

$\Rightarrow \quad \mathbf{b}\cdot\mathbf{c} = -\sqrt{3}\times\sqrt{3}$

$[\because \ |b| = \sqrt{1^2+1^2+(-1)^2} = \sqrt{3}]$

$\Rightarrow \quad \mathbf{b}\cdot\mathbf{c} = -3$

Let $\quad \mathbf{c} = x\hat{\mathbf{i}} + y\hat{\mathbf{j}} + z\hat{\mathbf{k}}$

Then, using $\mathbf{a}\cdot\mathbf{c} = 11$

$\Rightarrow \ x + 2y + 3z = 11 \quad$ ...(i)

and Using $\mathbf{b}\cdot\mathbf{c} = -3$

$\Rightarrow \quad x + y - z = -3 \quad$ ...(ii)

and Using $\mathbf{b}\cdot(\mathbf{a}\times\mathbf{c}) = 27$

$\Rightarrow (\mathbf{a}\times\mathbf{b})\cdot\mathbf{c} = 27$

$$\therefore \ \mathbf{a}\times\mathbf{b} = \begin{vmatrix}\hat{\mathbf{i}} & \hat{\mathbf{j}} & \hat{\mathbf{k}}\\ 1 & 2 & 3\\ 1 & 1 & -1\end{vmatrix} = -5\hat{\mathbf{i}} + 4\hat{\mathbf{j}} - \hat{\mathbf{k}}$$

$\Rightarrow \quad -5x + 4y - z = -27$

$\Rightarrow \quad 5x - 4y + z = 27 \quad$ ...(iii)

On adding Eqs. (ii) and (iii), we get

$6x - 3y = 24$

$\Rightarrow \quad 2x - y = 8$

$\Rightarrow \quad y = 2x - 8 \quad$ ...(iv)

On multiplying Eq. (i) with 2 times of Eq. (ii), we get

$4x + 5y = 2$

Using Eq. (iv), we get

$4x + 5(2x - 8) = 2 \Rightarrow x = 3$

From Eq. (iv), $y = 2\times 3 - 8 = -2$

Now, from Eq. (i),

$3 + 2(-2) + 3z = 11$

$\Rightarrow \quad z = 4$

So, $\quad \mathbf{c} = 3\hat{\mathbf{i}} - 2\hat{\mathbf{j}} + 4\hat{\mathbf{k}}$

Now, $|\mathbf{a}\times\mathbf{c}|^2 = -(\mathbf{a}\cdot\mathbf{c})^2 + \mathbf{a}^2\mathbf{c}^2$

$= -(3 - 4 + 12)^2 + 14\times 29$

$= -121 + 406 = 285$

14 (576) $|(\mathbf{a}-\mathbf{b})\times(\mathbf{a}+\mathbf{b})|^2 + 4(\mathbf{a}\cdot\mathbf{b})^2$

$= |\mathbf{a}\times\mathbf{a} - \mathbf{b}\times\mathbf{a} + \mathbf{a}\times\mathbf{b} - \mathbf{b}\times\mathbf{b}|^2 + 4(\mathbf{a}\cdot\mathbf{b})^2$

$= |2\mathbf{a}\times\mathbf{b}|^2 + 4(\mathbf{a}\cdot\mathbf{b})^2$

$[\because \mathbf{a}\times\mathbf{a} = 0 \text{ and } \mathbf{b}\times\mathbf{a} = -(\mathbf{a}\times\mathbf{b})]$

$= 4|\mathbf{a}|^2|\mathbf{b}|^2\sin^2\theta = 4|\mathbf{a}|^2|\mathbf{b}|^2 + 4|\mathbf{a}|^2|\mathbf{b}|^2\cos^2\theta$

$[\sin^2\theta + \cos^2\theta]$

$= 4\times 4^2\times 3^2$

$= 4\times 16\times 9$

$= 576$

Skill Boosters

1 (*a*) $|\mathbf{a}| = 3$ and $|\mathbf{b}| = 4$ and $\theta = \dfrac{\pi}{2}$

$|(\mathbf{a}+2\mathbf{b})\times(\mathbf{a}-\mathbf{b})|^2$

$= |\mathbf{a}\times\mathbf{a} + 2\mathbf{b}\times\mathbf{a} - \mathbf{a}\times\mathbf{b} - 2\mathbf{b}\times\mathbf{b}|$

$= |2(\mathbf{b}\times\mathbf{a}) + (\mathbf{b}\times\mathbf{a})|^2$

$= |3(\mathbf{b}\times\mathbf{a})|^2 = |3\times|\mathbf{b}||\mathbf{a}|\sin\pi/2|^2$

$= |3\times 3\times 4|^2 = (36)^2 = 1296$

$\therefore \ |(\mathbf{a}+2\mathbf{b})\times(\mathbf{a}-\mathbf{b})|^2 = 1296$

2 (*c*) $\mathbf{a} = 2\hat{\mathbf{i}} + 3\hat{\mathbf{j}} + \hat{\mathbf{k}}$

and $\quad \mathbf{b} = \hat{\mathbf{i}} + 3\hat{\mathbf{j}} - 4\hat{\mathbf{k}}$

and $\mathbf{a}+\mathbf{b} = 3\hat{\mathbf{i}} + 6\hat{\mathbf{j}} - 3\hat{\mathbf{k}}$

and $\mathbf{a}-\mathbf{b} = \hat{\mathbf{i}} + 5\mathbf{k}$

$\therefore$ *A* vector which is perpendicular to both the vectors $\mathbf{a}+\mathbf{b}$ and $\mathbf{a}-\mathbf{b}$ is

$$(\mathbf{a}+\mathbf{b})\times(\mathbf{a}-\mathbf{b}) = \begin{vmatrix}\hat{\mathbf{i}} & \hat{\mathbf{j}} & \hat{\mathbf{k}}\\ 3 & 6 & -3\\ 1 & 0 & 5\end{vmatrix}$$

$= \hat{\mathbf{i}}(30) - \mathbf{j}(15+3) + \mathbf{k}(-6)$

$= 30\hat{\mathbf{i}} - 18\mathbf{j} - 6\hat{\mathbf{k}}$

$= 6(5\hat{\mathbf{i}} - 3\hat{\mathbf{j}} - \hat{\mathbf{k}})$

Then, the required vector along $(\mathbf{a}+\mathbf{b})\times(\mathbf{a}-\mathbf{b})$ having magnitude $4\sqrt{35}$ is

$$= \frac{\pm 2\sqrt{35}\,(6(5\hat{\mathbf{i}} - 3\hat{\mathbf{j}} - \mathbf{k}))}{6\sqrt{25+9+1}}$$

$= 2(5\hat{\mathbf{i}} - 3\hat{\mathbf{j}} - \hat{\mathbf{k}})$

3 (*d*) Since, $3\mathbf{a}\times 2\mathbf{b}$ is a unit vector.

$\Rightarrow \quad |3\mathbf{a}\times 2\mathbf{b}| = 1$

$\Rightarrow \quad 6|\mathbf{a}||\mathbf{b}|\,|\sin\theta| = 1$

$\Rightarrow \quad \sin\theta = \dfrac{1}{6}$

Since, θ is an acute angle, then there is exactly one value of θ for which $3\mathbf{a}\times 2\mathbf{b}$ is a unit vector.

4 (*b*) Given curve is $y = x^2 + x$ when

$x = 2 \quad$ ...(i)

$y = (2)^2 + 2 = 6$

$\therefore P(2, 6)$

$\therefore \quad \mathbf{OP} = 2\hat{\mathbf{i}} + 6\hat{\mathbf{j}}$

From Eq. (i), $\dfrac{dy}{dx} = 2x + 1$,

$\left(\dfrac{dy}{dx}\right)_{(1,6)} = 3.$

Equation of tangent at *A* is

$$y - 6 = \left(\frac{dy}{dx}\right)_{(1,6)}(x - 1)$$

$\Rightarrow \quad y - 6 = 3(x - 1)$

$\Rightarrow \quad y = 3x + 3$

This tangent cuts *X*-axis (i.e. $y = 0$) at $(-1, 0)$

$\therefore \quad Q = (-1, 0)$

$\mathbf{PQ} = \mathbf{Q} - \mathbf{P} = (-1-2)\,\hat{\mathbf{i}} + (-6)\hat{\mathbf{j}}$

$\mathbf{PQ} = -3\hat{\mathbf{i}} - 6\hat{\mathbf{j}}$

$\mathbf{OP}\cdot\mathbf{PQ} = (2\hat{\mathbf{i}} + 6\hat{\mathbf{j}})\cdot(-3\hat{\mathbf{i}} - 6\hat{\mathbf{j}})$

$= -6 - 36$

$\mathbf{OP}\cdot\mathbf{PQ} = -42$

5 (*d*) We have, $\mathbf{a}+\mathbf{b}+\mathbf{c} = 0$

$\mathbf{a}+\mathbf{c} = -\mathbf{b}$

On squaring both sides,

$(\mathbf{a}+\mathbf{c})^2 = (-\mathbf{b})^2$

$|\mathbf{a}|^2 + |\mathbf{c}|^2 + 2\mathbf{a}\cdot\mathbf{c} = |\mathbf{b}|^2$

$|\mathbf{a}|^2 + |\mathbf{c}|^2 + 2|\mathbf{a}||\mathbf{c}|\cos\theta = |\mathbf{b}|^2$

$9 + 49 + 2\times 3\times 7\cos\theta = 25$

$\cos\theta = \dfrac{33}{2\times 3\times 7}$

$\Rightarrow \quad \cos\theta = \dfrac{11}{14}$

$\theta = \cos^{-1}\left(\dfrac{11}{14}\right)$

6 (*b*) Projection of $\mathbf{a}$ on $\mathbf{c}$ is $\dfrac{12}{\sqrt{19}}$

$\dfrac{\mathbf{a}\cdot\mathbf{c}}{|\mathbf{c}|} = \dfrac{12}{\sqrt{19}}$

$\dfrac{3 + 3\alpha + 6}{\sqrt{19}} = \dfrac{12}{\sqrt{19}}$

$3\alpha = 3 \Rightarrow \alpha = 1$

$$|\mathbf{b}\times\mathbf{c}| = \begin{vmatrix}\hat{\mathbf{i}} & \hat{\mathbf{j}} & \hat{\mathbf{k}}\\ 3 & 2 & \beta\\ 1 & 3 & 3\end{vmatrix} = -12\hat{\mathbf{i}} - 3\hat{\mathbf{j}} + 7\hat{\mathbf{k}}$$

$\hat{\mathbf{i}}(6 - 3\beta) - \hat{\mathbf{j}}(9 - \beta) + \hat{\mathbf{k}}(9 - 2) = -12\hat{\mathbf{i}} - 3\hat{\mathbf{j}} + 7\hat{\mathbf{k}}$

$\hat{\mathbf{i}}(6 - 3\beta) + \hat{\mathbf{j}}(\beta - 9) + \hat{\mathbf{k}}(7) = -12\hat{\mathbf{i}} - 3\hat{\mathbf{j}} + 7\hat{\mathbf{k}}$

$6 - 3\beta = -12$

$3\beta = 18 \Rightarrow \beta = 6$

$\beta - 9 = -3$

$\beta = 6$

Now, $\quad \alpha\cdot\beta = 1\times 6 = 6$

11

Three Dimensional Geometry

Topicwise No. of Ques asked in 3 Years (JEE Main)

Topics	No. of Questions		
	2024	2023	2022
Direction Cosine and Direction Ratios of a Line	–	–	2
Equation of a Line in Space	14	8	5
Angle between Two Lines	3	–	11
Shortest Distance between Two Skew-Lines	8	7	3

Special Type of Ques Asked in 3 Years (JEE Main)

Types	Years		
	2024	2023	2022
A-R	–	–	–
Statement Based	–	–	–
Numerical Value Type	13	8	6

Last 3 Years Weightage (JEE Main)

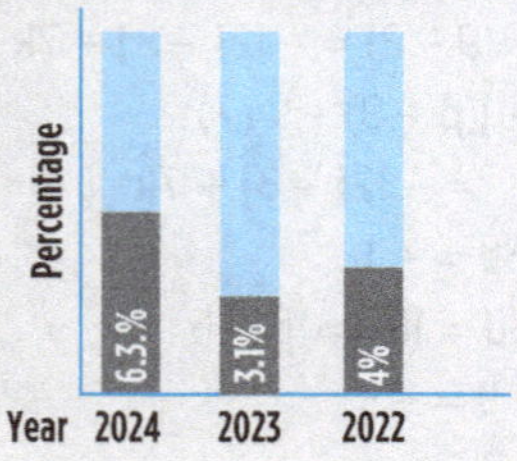

Direction Cosines and Direction Ratios of a Line

1. If a line makes angles α, β and γ with X-axis, Y-axis and Z-axis, respectively, then $l = \cos\alpha$, $m = \cos\beta$ and $n = \cos\gamma$ are called the **direction cosines** of the line.

   The relation between direction cosines of a line is, $l^2 + m^2 + n^2 = 1$.

2. Numbers proportional to the direction cosines of a line are called the **direction ratios** of the line. If a, b and c are the direction ratios of a line, then

$$l = \frac{\pm a}{\sqrt{a^2 + b^2 + c^2}},$$

$$m = \frac{\pm b}{\sqrt{a^2 + b^2 + c^2}}$$

and
$$n = \frac{\pm c}{\sqrt{a^2 + b^2 + c^2}}$$

3. For any line, direction cosines are unique but direction ratios are not unique.

4. The direction cosines and direction ratios of the line passing through the points $P(x_1, y_1, z_1)$ and $Q(x_2, y_2, z_2)$ are respectively given by

$$\frac{x_2 - x_1}{PQ}, \frac{y_2 - y_1}{PQ}, \frac{z_2 - z_1}{PQ}$$

and $(x_2 - x_1, y_2 - y_1, z_2 - z_1)$

where, $PQ = \sqrt{(x_2 - x_1)^2 + (y_2 - y_1)^2 + (z_2 - z_1)^2}$

Equation of a Line in Space

Equation of a line Passing Through a given Point and Parallel to a given Vector

1. **Vector Equation** The equation of a line through a given point A with position vector $\mathbf{a}$ and parallel to a given vector $\mathbf{b}$ is given by $\mathbf{r} = \mathbf{a} + \lambda\mathbf{b}$, where λ is a scalar.
2. **Cartesian Equation** The equation of a line passing through a point $A(x_1, y_1, z_1)$ and having direction ratios a, b and c is

$$\frac{x - x_1}{a} = \frac{y - y_1}{b} = \frac{z - z_1}{c}$$

If l, m and n are the direction cosines of the line, then equation of the line is

$$\frac{x - x_1}{l} = \frac{y - y_1}{m} = \frac{z - z_1}{n}$$

Equation of a Line Passing Through Two given points

1. **Vector Equation** The vector equation of a line passing through two points with position vectors $\mathbf{a}$ and $\mathbf{b}$ is given by

$\mathbf{r} = \mathbf{a} + \lambda\,(\mathbf{b} - \mathbf{a})$, where λ is a scalar.

2. **Cartesian Equation** The equation of a line passing through two points $A(x_1, y_1, z_1)$ and $B(x_2, y_2, z_2)$ is

$$\frac{x - x_1}{x_2 - x_1} = \frac{y - y_1}{y_2 - y_1} = \frac{z - z_1}{z_2 - z_1}$$

Angle between Two Lines

Concept Master Video

1. **Vector form** $\cos\theta = \left|\dfrac{\mathbf{b}_1 \cdot \mathbf{b}_2}{|\mathbf{b}_2||\mathbf{b}_2|}\right|$.
2. **Cartesian form** $\cos\theta = \left|\dfrac{a_1a_2 + b_1b_2 + c_1c_2}{\sqrt{a_1^2 + b_1^2 + c_1^2}\sqrt{a_2^2 + b_2^2 + c_2^2}}\right|$.

[JEE Main 2024, 2022]

Shortest Distance Between Two Skew-Lines

1. The shortest distance between two skew-lines is the length of line-segment perpendicular to both the lines.

In vector form Shortest distance between the skew-lines $\mathbf{r} = \mathbf{a}_1 + \lambda\mathbf{b}_1$ and $\mathbf{r} = \mathbf{a}_2 + \mu\mathbf{b}_2$ is given by

$$SD = \left|\frac{|(\mathbf{a}_2 - \mathbf{a}_1)\cdot(\mathbf{b}_1 \times \mathbf{b}_2)|}{|\mathbf{b}_1 \times \mathbf{b}_2|}\right|$$

2. The shortest distance between the parallel lines $\mathbf{r} = \mathbf{a}_1 + \lambda\mathbf{b}$ and $\mathbf{r} = \mathbf{a}_2 + \mu\mathbf{b}$ is given by

$$SD = \left|\frac{\mathbf{b} \times (\mathbf{a}_2 - \mathbf{a}_1)}{|\mathbf{b}|}\right|$$

3. **In cartesian form** The shortest distance between the lines

$\dfrac{x - x_1}{a_1} = \dfrac{y - y_1}{b_1} = \dfrac{z - z_1}{c_1}$ and $\dfrac{x - x_2}{a_2} = \dfrac{y - y_2}{b_2} = \dfrac{z - z_2}{c_2}$ is

$$\left|\frac{\begin{vmatrix} x_2 - x_1 & y_2 - y_1 & z_2 - z_1 \\ a_1 & b_1 & c_1 \\ a_2 & b_2 & c_2 \end{vmatrix}}{\sqrt{(b_1c_2 - b_2c_1)^2 + (c_1a_2 - c_2a_1)^2 + (a_1b_2 - a_2b_1)^2}}\right|$$

[JEE Main 2024, 2023, 2022]

Caution Points

- Ensure all coordinates are correctly applied in your calculation to avoid errors in distance or intersection points.
- Know the difference between parametric, symmetric and vector form of line equations.
- If line are parallel, there won't be an intersection point, which affects distance calculations.
- For shortest distance, use perpendicular projections to ensure the correct distance. Calculation between skew lines.

PYQ Notes

1. Area of triangle ABC, $\Delta = \dfrac{1}{2}|\mathbf{AB} \times \mathbf{AC}|$
2. Two lines $r = a_1 + \lambda\, b_1$ and $r = a_2 + \lambda b_2$ are intersecting when $(\mathbf{b}_1 \times \mathbf{b}_2)\cdot(\mathbf{a}_2 - \mathbf{a}_1) = 0$
3. The length of the perpendicular from a point $P(\alpha)$ on the line

$r = \mathbf{a} + \lambda\mathbf{b}$ is given by $\sqrt{\sqrt{|\alpha - \mathbf{a}|^2} - \left\{\dfrac{(\alpha - \mathbf{a})\cdot\mathbf{b}}{|\mathbf{b}|}\right\}^2}$

Step by Step

Mastering NCERT

- Concept Builders
- Topical Questions
- Numerical Type Questions
- Assertion and Reason Questions
- Case or Paragraph Type Questions
- Past Years Questions
- Skill Boosters

Concept Builders

1 If l, m, n are the direction cosines, then $l^2 + m^2 + n^2 =$ ....

2 The direction ratio of the line $2x - 2 = y + 1 = 3z - 2$, is ....

3 The angle between $\frac{x-1}{3} = \frac{y+2}{5} = \frac{z-3}{2}$ and $\frac{x-1}{1} = \frac{y+2}{3} = \frac{z+3}{3}$, is

4 Lines $\frac{x}{2} = \frac{y}{3} = \frac{z}{4}$ and $\frac{x+2}{2} = \frac{y-2}{3} = \frac{3-z}{-4}$ are .... lines

5 Find carteisian equation of line passing through origin and parallel to Z-axis ....

6 The equation of Z-axis in space is ....

7 If $r = \mathbf{a}_1 + \mu \mathbf{b}_1$ is $r = \mathbf{a}_2 + \mu \mathbf{b}_2$ are the equations of two lines, then $\cos \theta =$ ....

Topical Questions

Direction Cosines and Direction Ratios of a Line

Level I

1 Consider the following statements

Statement I If a line in a space does not pass through the origin, then direction cosines of the line does not exist.

Statement II Two parallel lines have same set of direction cosines.

Choose the correct option. NCERT Pg. 378

(a) Statement I is true
(b) Statement II is true
(c) Both statements are true
(d) Both statements are false

2 Any three numbers which are proportional to the direction cosines of a line, are called ...X... . Here, X refers to NCERT Pg. 378

(a) direction angles
(b) direction ratios
(c) another set of direction cosines
(d) None of the above

3 In the figure, $RS \parallel OP$ and l, m, n are the direction cosines of RS. Then, NCERT Pg. 378

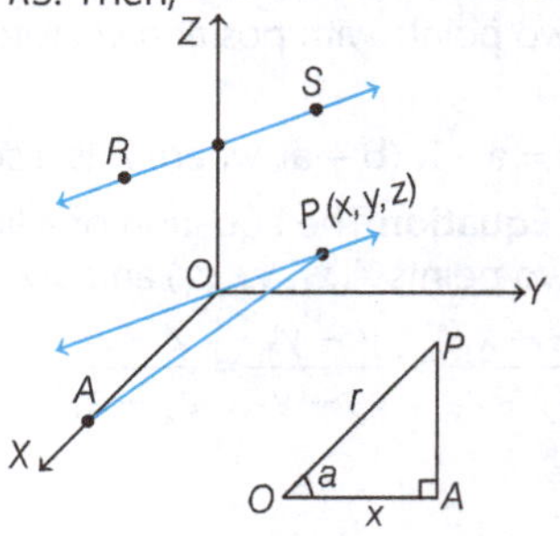

(a) $l^2 + m^2 + n^2 = 0$
(b) $l^2 + m^2 + n^2 = -1$
(c) $l^2 + m^2 + n^2 = 1$
(d) None of the above

4 If a, b, c are the direction ratios of a line and l, m, n are the direction cosines of the line, then NCERT Pg. 378, 379

(a) $l = \pm a(a^2 + b^2 + c^2)$, $m = \pm b(a^2 + b^2 + c^2)$, $n = \pm c(a^2 + b^2 + c^2)$

(b) $l = \pm \frac{a}{a^2 + b^2 + c^2}$, $m = \pm \frac{b}{a^2 + b^2 + c^2}$, $n = \pm \frac{c}{a^2 + b^2 + c^2}$

(c) $l = \pm \frac{\sqrt{a}}{\sqrt{a^2+b^2+c^2}}, m = \pm \frac{\sqrt{b}}{\sqrt{a^2+b^2+c^2}}, n = \pm \frac{\sqrt{c}}{\sqrt{a^2+b^2+c^2}}$

(d) $l = \pm \frac{a}{\sqrt{a^2+b^2+c^2}}, m = \pm \frac{b}{\sqrt{a^2+b^2+c^2}}, n = \pm \frac{c}{\sqrt{a^2+b^2+c^2}}$

5 Which of the following are true? NCERT Pg. 379

I. If a, b and c are the direction ratios of a line, then ka, kb and kc is also a set of direction ratios.

II. The two sets of direction ratios of a line are in proportion.

III. There exists two sets of direction ratios of a line.

(a) I and II are true (b) II and III are true
(c) I and II are true (d) All are true

6 The direction cosines of a line passing through two points $P(x_1, y_1, z_1)$ and $Q(x_2, y_2, z_2)$ are NCERT Pg. 379, 380

(a) $(x_2 - x_1), (y_2 - y_1), (z_2 - z_1)$
(b) $(x_2 + x_1), (y_2 + y_1), (z_2 + z_1)$
(c) $\frac{x_2 - x_1}{PQ}, \frac{y_2 - y_1}{PQ}, \frac{z_2 - z_1}{PQ}$
(d) $\frac{x_2 + x_1}{PQ}, \frac{y_2 + y_1}{PQ}, \frac{z_2 + z_1}{PQ}$

7 The direction ratios of the line segment joining $P(x_1, y_1, z_1)$ and $Q(x_2, y_2, z_2)$ are NCERT Pg. 380

(a) $x_2 - x_1, y_2 - y_1, z_2 - z_1$
(b) $x_1 - x_2, y_1 - y_2, z_1 - z_2$
(c) Both (a) and (b)
(d) None of the above

8 Match the terms of column I with the terms of column II and choose the correct option from the codes given below. NCERT Pg. 381

Column I (Lines)		Column II (Direction cosines)
A. A line makes angles 90°, 135°, 45° with the X, Y and Z-axes, respectively.	1.	$\frac{1}{\sqrt{3}}, \frac{1}{\sqrt{3}}, \frac{1}{\sqrt{3}}$
B. A line which makes equal angles with coordinate axes.	2.	$\frac{-9}{11}, \frac{6}{11}, \frac{-2}{11}$
C. A line has the direction ratios −18, 12 and −4.	3.	$0, \frac{-1}{\sqrt{2}}, \frac{1}{\sqrt{2}}$

Codes

	A	B	C		A	B	C
(a)	1	3	2	(b)	2	3	1
(c)	3	1	2	(d)	2	1	3

9 If $A(3, 5, -4)$, $B(-1, 1, 2)$ and $C(-5, -5, -2)$ are the vertices of a ΔABC, then NCERT Pg. 381

(a) direction cosines of AB are $\frac{-2}{\sqrt{17}}, \frac{-2}{\sqrt{17}}, \frac{3}{\sqrt{17}}$
(b) direction cosines of AC are $\frac{4}{\sqrt{42}}, \frac{5}{\sqrt{42}}, \frac{-1}{\sqrt{42}}$
(c) direction cosines of BC are $\frac{-2}{\sqrt{17}}, \frac{-3}{\sqrt{17}}, \frac{-2}{\sqrt{17}}$
(d) All of the above

Level II

10 If a line makes angles of 30° and 45° with X-axis and Y-axis, then the angle made by it with Z-axis is NCERT Pg. 380

(a) 45° (b) 60°
(c) 120° (d) None of these

11 Consider the following statements

Statement I If the direction ratios of a line are 1, 1 and 2, then the direction cosines of the line are $\frac{1}{\sqrt{6}}, \frac{1}{\sqrt{6}}$ and $\frac{2}{\sqrt{6}}$.

Statement II The direction cosines of the line passing through the points $P(2, 3, 5)$ and $Q(-1, 2, 4)$ are $\frac{-3}{\sqrt{11}}, \frac{-1}{\sqrt{11}}$ and $\frac{-1}{\sqrt{11}}$.

Choose the correct option. NCERT Pg. 380

(a) Statement I is true
(b) Statement II is true
(c) Both statements are true
(d) Both statements are false

12 If α, β, γ be the direction angles of a vector and $\cos\alpha = \frac{14}{15}$, $\cos\beta = \frac{1}{3}$, then $\cos\gamma = \ldots K \ldots$. Here, K refers to NCERT Pg. 380

(a) $\pm\frac{2}{15}$ (b) $\frac{1}{5}$
(c) $\pm\frac{1}{15}$ (d) None of these

13 If the points $(-1, 3, 2)$, $(-4, 2, -2)$ and $(5, 5, \lambda)$ are collinear, then λ is equal to NCERT Pg. 381

(a) −10 (b) 5 (c) −5 (d) 10

14 Consider the following statements

Statement I The points (1, 2, 3), (−2, 3, 4) and (7, 0, 1) are collinear.

Statement II If a line makes angles $\frac{\pi}{2}, \frac{3\pi}{4}$ and $\frac{\pi}{4}$ with X, Y and Z-axes respectively, then its direction cosines are $0, \frac{-1}{\sqrt{2}}$ and $\frac{1}{\sqrt{2}}$.

Choose the correct option. NCERT Pg. 381

(a) Statement I is true.
(b) Statement II is true.
(c) Both statements are true.
(d) Both statements are false.

15 A line makes angles α, β and γ with the co-ordinate axes. If $\alpha + \beta = 90°$, then γ is equal to NCERT Pg. 381

(a) 0 (b) 90°
(c) 180° (d) None of these

16 If a line makes the angles α, β and γ with three dimensional coordinate axes respectively, then the value of $\cos 2\alpha + \cos 2\beta + \cos 2\gamma$ is NCERT Pg. 380

(a) –2 (b) –1 (c) 3 (d) 2
(e) –3

17 If O is the origin and $OP = 3$ with direction ratios –1, 2 and –2, then coordinates of P are NCERT Pg. 381

(a) (1, 2, 2) (b) (–1, 2, –2)
(c) (–3, 6, 9) (d) $\left(-\frac{1}{3}, \frac{2}{3}, \frac{-2}{3}\right)$

Equation *of* a Line in Space

Level I

1 Consider the following statements

Statement I A line is uniquely determined, if it is passes through a given point.

Statement II A line is uniquely determined, if it passes through two given points.

Choose the correct option. NCERT Pg. 381

(a) Statement I is true
(b) Statement II is true
(c) Both statements are true
(d) Both statements are false

2 Consider the following statements

Statement I The vector equation of a line passing through two points whose position vectors are **a** and **b**, is $\mathbf{r} = \mathbf{a} + \lambda(\mathbf{b} - \mathbf{a}) \ \forall \ \lambda \in R$.

Statement II The cartesian equation of a line passing through two points (x_1, y_1, z_1) and (x_2, y_2, z_2) is

$$\frac{x - x_1}{x_2 - x_1} = \frac{y - y_1}{y_2 - y_1} = \frac{z - z_1}{z_2 - z_1}$$

Choose the correct option. NCERT Pg. 382

(a) Statement I is true
(b) Statement II is true
(c) Both statements are true
(d) Both statements are false

3 If l, m and n are the direction cosines of line L, then equation of the line is NCERT Pg. 382

(a) $\frac{x - x_1}{l} = \frac{y - y_1}{m} = \frac{z - z_1}{n}$

(b) $\left(\frac{x - x_1}{l}\right)\left(\frac{y - y_1}{m}\right) = \left(\frac{z - z_1}{n}\right)$

(c) $\frac{x + x_1}{l} = \frac{y + y_1}{m} = \frac{z + z_1}{n}$

(d) None of the above

4 The vector and cartesian equations of the line through the point (5, 2, –4) and which is parallel to the vector $3\hat{\mathbf{i}} + 2\hat{\mathbf{j}} - 8\hat{\mathbf{k}}$, are NCERT Pg. 382, 383

(a) $\mathbf{r} = (3\hat{\mathbf{i}} + 2\hat{\mathbf{j}} - 8\hat{\mathbf{k}}) + \lambda(5\hat{\mathbf{i}} + 2\hat{\mathbf{j}} - 4\hat{\mathbf{k}})$; $\frac{x - 3}{5} = \frac{y - 2}{2} = \frac{z + 8}{-4}$

(b) $\mathbf{r} = (5\hat{\mathbf{i}} + 2\hat{\mathbf{j}} - 4\hat{\mathbf{k}}) + \lambda(3\hat{\mathbf{i}} + 2\hat{\mathbf{j}} - 8\hat{\mathbf{k}})$; $\frac{x - 3}{5} = \frac{y - 2}{2} = \frac{z + 8}{-1}$

(c) $\mathbf{r} = (5\hat{\mathbf{i}} + 2\hat{\mathbf{j}} - 4\hat{\mathbf{k}}) + \lambda(3\hat{\mathbf{i}} + 2\hat{\mathbf{j}} - 8\hat{\mathbf{k}})$; $\frac{x - 5}{3} = \frac{y - 2}{2} = \frac{z + 4}{-8}$

(d) $\mathbf{r} = (3\hat{\mathbf{i}} + 2\hat{\mathbf{j}} - 8\hat{\mathbf{k}}) + \lambda(5\hat{\mathbf{i}} + 2\hat{\mathbf{j}} - 4\hat{\mathbf{k}})$; $\frac{x - 5}{3} = \frac{y - 2}{2} = \frac{z + 4}{-8}$

5 The equation of the line in vector and cartesian form that passes through the point with position vector $2\hat{\mathbf{i}} - \hat{\mathbf{j}} + 4\hat{\mathbf{k}}$ and is in the direction $\hat{\mathbf{i}} + 2\hat{\mathbf{j}} - \hat{\mathbf{k}}$ are NCERT Pg. 382, 383

(a) $\mathbf{r} = (2\hat{\mathbf{i}} - \hat{\mathbf{j}} + 4\hat{\mathbf{k}}) + \lambda(\hat{\mathbf{i}} + 2\hat{\mathbf{j}} - \hat{\mathbf{k}})$; $\frac{x - 1}{2} = \frac{y - 2}{-1} = \frac{z + 1}{-4}$

(b) $\mathbf{r} = (\hat{\mathbf{i}} + 2\hat{\mathbf{j}} - \hat{\mathbf{k}}) + \lambda(2\hat{\mathbf{i}} - \hat{\mathbf{j}} + 4\hat{\mathbf{k}})$; $\frac{x - 1}{2} = \frac{y - 2}{-1} = \frac{z + 1}{4}$

(c) $\mathbf{r} = (\hat{\mathbf{i}} + 2\hat{\mathbf{j}} - \hat{\mathbf{k}}) + \lambda(2\hat{\mathbf{i}} - \hat{\mathbf{j}} + 4\hat{\mathbf{k}})$; $\frac{x - 2}{1} = \frac{y + 1}{2} = \frac{z - 4}{-1}$

(d) $\mathbf{r} = (2\hat{\mathbf{i}} - \hat{\mathbf{j}} + 4\hat{\mathbf{k}}) + \lambda(\hat{\mathbf{i}} + 2\hat{\mathbf{j}} - \hat{\mathbf{k}})$; $\frac{x - 2}{1} = \frac{y + 1}{2} = \frac{z - 4}{-1}$

6 Consider the following statements

Statement I The cartesian equation of the line which passes through the point (–2, 4 –5) and parallel to the line given by $\frac{x + 3}{3} = \frac{y - 4}{5} = \frac{z + 8}{6}$ is $\frac{x + 3}{-2} = \frac{y - 4}{4} = \frac{z + 8}{-5}$.

Statement II If the cartesian equation of a line is $\frac{x - 5}{3} = \frac{y + 4}{7} = \frac{z - 6}{2}$, then its vector form is $\mathbf{r} = 5\hat{\mathbf{i}} + 4\hat{\mathbf{j}} + 6\hat{\mathbf{k}} + \lambda(3\hat{\mathbf{i}} + 7\hat{\mathbf{j}} + 2\hat{\mathbf{k}})$.

Choose the correct option. NCERT Pg. 382, 383

(a) Statement I is true
(b) Statement II is true
(c) Both statements are true
(d) Both statements are false

7 The vector and the cartesian equations of the line that passes through the origin and (5, −2, 3) are ...A... and ...B... . Here, A and B refer to NCERT Pg. 382, 383

(a) $\mathbf{r} = 5\hat{i} - 2\hat{j} + 3\hat{k};\quad 5x = -2y = 3z$
(b) $\mathbf{r} = \lambda(5\hat{i} - 2\hat{j} + 3\hat{k});\ 5x = -2y = 3z$
(c) $\mathbf{r} = \lambda(5\hat{i} - 2\hat{j} + 3\hat{k});\ \frac{x}{5} = \frac{y}{-2} = \frac{z}{3}$
(d) None of the above

8 The vector and cartesian equations of the line that passes through the points (3, −2, −5) and (3, −2, 6) are NCERT Pg. 382, 383

(a) $\mathbf{r} = 3\hat{i} - 2\hat{j} - 5\hat{k};\ x - 3 = y + 2 = \frac{z+5}{11}$
(b) $\mathbf{r} = 3\hat{i} - 2\hat{j} - 5\hat{k};\ \frac{x-3}{0} = \frac{y+2}{0} = \frac{z+5}{11}$
(c) $\mathbf{r} = 3\hat{i} - 2\hat{j} - 5\hat{k} + \lambda(11\hat{k});\ x - 3 = y + 2 = \frac{z+5}{11}$
(d) $\mathbf{r} = 3\hat{i} - 2\hat{j} - 5\hat{k} + \lambda(11\,\hat{k});\ \frac{x-3}{0} = \frac{y+2}{0} = \frac{z+5}{11}$

Level II

9 The point of intersection of the lines $\frac{x-4}{5} = \frac{y-1}{2} = \frac{z}{1}$ and $\frac{x-1}{2} = \frac{y-2}{3} = \frac{z-3}{4}$ is NCERT Pg. 389

(a) (−1, −1, −1) (b) (−1, −1, 1)
(c) (1, −1, −1) (d) (−1, 1, −1)

10 The equation of a line passing through the point (−3, 2, −4) and equally inclined to the axes are NCERT Pg. 382

(a) $x - 3 = y + 2 = z - 4$
(b) $x + 3 = y - 2 = z + 4$
(c) $\frac{x+3}{1} = \frac{y-2}{2} = \frac{z+4}{3}$
(d) None of the above

11 The symmetric equation of the lines $3x + 2y + z - 5 = 0$ and $x + y - 2z - 3 = 0$ is NCERT Pg. 382

(a) $\frac{x-1}{5} = \frac{y-4}{7} = \frac{z-0}{1}$ (b) $\frac{x+1}{5} = \frac{y+4}{7} = \frac{z-0}{1}$
(c) $\frac{x+1}{-5} = \frac{y-4}{7} = \frac{z-0}{1}$ (d) $\frac{x-1}{-5} = \frac{y-4}{7} = \frac{z-0}{1}$

12 The equation of straight line passing through the point (a, b, c) and parallel to Z-axis is NCERT Pg. 382, 383

(a) $\frac{x-a}{1} = \frac{y-b}{1} = \frac{z-c}{0}$ (b) $\frac{x-a}{0} = \frac{y-b}{1} = \frac{z-c}{1}$
(c) $\frac{x-a}{1} = \frac{y-b}{0} = \frac{z-c}{0}$ (d) $\frac{x-a}{0} = \frac{y-b}{0} = \frac{z-c}{1}$

13 The equation of the line passing through the point (1, 2, −4) and perpendicular to the two lines

$$\frac{x-8}{3} = \frac{y+19}{-16} = \frac{z-10}{7}$$

and $\frac{x-15}{3} = \frac{y-29}{8} = \frac{z-5}{-5}$ will be NCERT Pg. 391

(a) $\frac{x-1}{2} = \frac{y-2}{3} = \frac{z+4}{6}$ (b) $\frac{x-1}{-2} = \frac{y-2}{3} = \frac{z+4}{8}$
(c) $\frac{x-1}{3} = \frac{y-2}{2} = \frac{z+4}{8}$ (d) None of the above

14 The coordinates of a point on the line $\frac{x+2}{3} = \frac{y+1}{2} = \frac{z-3}{2}$ at a distance of $\frac{6}{\sqrt{2}}$ from the point (1, 2, 3) is NCERT Pg. 384

(a) (56, 43, 111) (b) $\left(\frac{56}{17}, \frac{43}{17}, \frac{111}{17}\right)$
(c) (2, 1, 3) (d) (−2, −1, −3)

Angle between Two Lines

Level I

1 Consider the following statements

Statement I The cosine of the angle between two lines is given by

$$\cos\theta = \left|\frac{a_1a_2 + b_1b_2 + c_1c_2}{\sqrt{a_1^2 + b_1^2 + c_1^2}\sqrt{a_2^2 + b_2^2 + c_2^2}}\right|$$

Where, a_1, b_1, c_1 and a_2, b_2, c_2 are the direction ratios of two lines, respectively.

Statement II The sine of the angle between two lines is given by

$$\sin\theta = \frac{(a_1b_2 - a_2b_1)^2 + (b_1c_2 - b_2c_1)^2 + (c_1a_2 - c_2a_1)^2}{\sqrt{a_1^2 + b_1^2 + c_1^2}\sqrt{a_2^2 + b_2^2 + c_2^2}}$$

where a_1, b_1, c_1 and a_2, b_2, c_2 are the direction ratios of two lines, respectively.

Choose the correct option. NCERT Pg. 383, 384

(a) Statement I is true
(b) Statement II is true
(c) Both statements are true
(d) Both statements are false

2 The angle between two lines, if l_1, m_1, n_1 and l_2, m_2, n_2 are their direction cosines respectively, is given by NCERT Pg. 384

(a) $\cos\theta = |l_1l_2 + m_1m_2 + n_1n_2|$
(b) $\sin\theta = \sqrt{(l_1m_2 - l_2m_1)^2 + (m_1n_2 - m_2n_1)^2 + (n_1l_2 - n_2l_1)^2}$
(c) Both (a) and (b)
(d) None of the above

3 If $\mathbf{r} = \mathbf{a}_1 + \lambda\mathbf{b}_1$ and $\mathbf{r} = \mathbf{a}_2 + \mu\mathbf{b}_2$ are the equations of two lines, then $\cos\theta$ = ...X... Here, X refers to NCERT Pg. 384

(a) $\left|\frac{\mathbf{a}_1 \cdot \mathbf{a}_2}{|\mathbf{a}_1||\mathbf{a}_2|}\right|$ (b) $\left|\frac{\mathbf{b}_1 \cdot \mathbf{b}_2}{|\mathbf{b}_1||\mathbf{b}_2|}\right|$
(c) $\left|\frac{\mathbf{a}_1 \cdot \mathbf{a}_2}{|\mathbf{b}_1||\mathbf{b}_2|}\right|$ (d) $\left|\frac{\mathbf{b}_1 \cdot \mathbf{b}_2}{|\mathbf{a}_1||\mathbf{a}_2|}\right|$

4 If $\frac{x-x_1}{a_1}=\frac{y-y_1}{b_1}=\frac{z-z_1}{c_1}$ and $\frac{x-x_2}{a_2}=\frac{y-y_2}{b_2}=\frac{z-z_2}{c_2}$ are the equations of two lines, then $\cos\theta =$ ...*Y*... . Here, *Y* refers to **NCERT Pg. 384**

(a) $\left|\frac{a_1+b_1+c_1}{\sqrt{a_1^2+b_1^2+c_1^2}}\right|$ (b) $\left|\frac{a_2+b_2+c_2}{\sqrt{a_2^2+b_2^2+c_2^2}}\right|$

(c) $\left|\frac{a_1a_2+b_1b_2+c_1c_2}{\sqrt{a_1^2+b_1^2+c_1^2}\sqrt{a_2^2+b_2^2+c_2^2}}\right|$

(d) None of the above

5 The angle between the lines $\frac{x-5}{7}=\frac{y+2}{-5}=\frac{z}{1}$ and $\frac{x}{1}=\frac{y}{2}=\frac{z}{3}$ is **NCERT Pg. 384, 385**

(a) 0 (b) $\frac{\pi}{2}$ (c) $\frac{\pi}{3}$ (d) $\frac{\pi}{4}$

6 Consider the following statements

Statement I The three lines with direction cosines $\frac{12}{13}, \frac{-3}{13}, \frac{-4}{13}; \frac{4}{13}, \frac{12}{13}, \frac{3}{13}; \frac{3}{13}, \frac{-4}{13}, \frac{12}{13}$ are mutually perpendicular.

Statement II The line through the points (1, –1, 2) and (3, 4, –2) is perpendicular to the line through the points (0, 3, 2) and (3, 5, 6).

Choose the correct option. **NCERT Pg. 389**

(a) Statement I is true
(b) Statement II is true
(c) Both statements are true
(d) Both statements are false

7 The angle between the lines through the points (4, 7, 8), (2, 3, 4) and (–1, –2, 1), (1, 2, 5) is **NCERT Pg. 389**

(a) 0 (b) $\frac{\pi}{2}$ (c) $\frac{\pi}{4}$ (d) $\frac{\pi}{6}$

8 Match the angles between the pair of lines in column I with the values in column II and choose the correct option from the codes given below.

Column I	Column II
A. $\mathbf{r}=2\hat{i}-5\hat{j}+\hat{k}+\lambda(3\hat{i}+2\hat{j}+6\hat{k})$ and $\mathbf{r}=7\hat{i}-6\hat{k}+\mu(\hat{i}+2\hat{j}+2\hat{k})$	1. $\cos^{-1}\left(\frac{8}{5\sqrt{3}}\right)$
B. $\mathbf{r}=3\hat{i}+\hat{j}-2\hat{k}+\lambda(\hat{i}-\hat{j}-2\hat{k})$ and $\mathbf{r}=2\hat{i}-\hat{j}-56\hat{k}+\mu(3\hat{i}-5\hat{j}-4\hat{k})$	2. $\cos^{-1}\left(\frac{2}{3}\right)$
C. $\frac{x-2}{2}=\frac{y-1}{5}=\frac{z+3}{-3}$ and $\frac{x+2}{-1}=\frac{y-4}{8}=\frac{z-5}{4}$	3. $\cos^{-1}\left(\frac{19}{21}\right)$
D. $\frac{x}{2}=\frac{y}{2}=\frac{z}{1}$ and $\frac{x-5}{4}=\frac{y-2}{1}=\frac{z-3}{8}$	4. $\cos^{-1}\left(\frac{26}{9\sqrt{38}}\right)$

Codes **NCERT Pg. 390**

	A	B	C	D		A	B	C	D
(a)	2	1	4	3	(b)	3	1	4	2
(c)	4	1	2	3	(d)	4	3	2	1

9 The value of *p*, so that the lines $\frac{1-x}{3}=\frac{7y-14}{2p}=\frac{z-3}{2}$ and $\frac{7-7x}{3p}=\frac{y-5}{1}=\frac{6-z}{5}$ are at right angle, is **NCERT Pg. 390**

(a) $\frac{10}{11}$ (b) $\frac{70}{11}$ (c) $\frac{10}{7}$ (d) $\frac{70}{9}$

Level II

10 Consider the following statements

Statement I If the coordinates of the points *A*, *B*, *C*, *D* be (1, 2, 3), (4, 5, 7), (–4, 3, –6) and (2, 9, 2) respectively, then the angle between the lines *AB* and *CD* is $\frac{\pi}{6}$.

Statement II The straight lines $\frac{x-1}{1}=\frac{y-2}{2}=\frac{z-3}{3}$ and $\frac{x-1}{2}=\frac{y-2}{2}=\frac{z-3}{-2}$ are parallel.

Choose the correct option. **NCERT Pg. 384, 385**

(a) Statement I is true
(b) Statement II is true
(c) Both statements are true
(d) Both statements are false

11 The angle between the lines whose direction cosines are connected by the relations $l+m+n=0$ and $2lm+2nl-mn=0$, is **NCERT Pg. 385**

(a) $\frac{\pi}{6}$ (b) $\frac{2\pi}{3}$
(c) π (d) None of these

12 The coordinates of the foot of perpendicular drawn from the point (2, 5, 7) on the *X*-axis are given by **NCERT Pg. 385**

(a) (2, 0, 0) (b) (0, 5, 0)
(c) (0, 0, 7) (d) (0, 5, 7)

13 The lines $x=py+q$, $z=ry+s$ and $x=p'y+q'$, $z=r'y+s'$ are perpendicular, if **NCERT Pg. 385**

(a) $pr+p'r'+1=0$ (b) $pp'+rr'+1=0$
(c) $pr+p'r'=0$ (d) $pp'+rr'=0$

14 The straight line $\frac{x-3}{3}=\frac{y-2}{1}=\frac{z-1}{0}$ is ...*A*.... Here, *A* refers to **NCERT Pg. 385**

(a) parallel to *X*-axis
(b) parallel to *Y*-axis
(c) parallel to *Z*-axis
(d) perpendicular to *Z*-axis

15 If the lines $\frac{x-1}{-3}=\frac{y-2}{2k}=\frac{z-3}{2}$ and $\frac{x-1}{3k}=\frac{y-5}{1}=\frac{z-6}{-5}$ are at right angle, then k is equal to NCERT Pg. 391

(a) -10 (b) $\frac{10}{7}$ (c) $\frac{-10}{7}$ (d) $\frac{-7}{10}$

Shortest Distance between Two Skew-Lines

Level I

1 Consider the following statements

Statement I If two lines in a space intersect at a point, then the shortest distance between them is zero.

Statement II If two lines in space are parallel, then shortest distance between them will be the perpendicular distance.

Choose the correct option. NCERT Pg. 385

(a) Statement I is true (b) Statement II is true
(c) Both statements are true (d) Both statements are false

2 The lines in a space which are neither intersecting nor parallel, are called ...*A*... . Here, *A* refers to NCERT Pg. 385

(a) concurrent lines (b) intersecting lines
(c) skew lines (d) parallel lines

3 Which of the following is/are true? NCERT Pg. 386

I. By the shortest distance between two lines, we mean the length of segment between lines is the smallest.
II. For skew lines, the line of the shortest distance will not perpendicular to any of the line.

(a) Only I is true (b) Only II is true
(c) Both I and II are true (d) Neither I nor II is true

4 Shortest distance between two skew lines can be evaluated by the formula, where lines are given by $\mathbf{r}=\mathbf{a}_1+\lambda\mathbf{b}_1$ and $\mathbf{r}=\mathbf{a}_2+\mu\mathbf{b}_2$. NCERT Pg. 386

(a) $d=\left|\frac{(\mathbf{b}_1-\mathbf{b}_2)\cdot(\mathbf{a}_1\times\mathbf{a}_2)}{|\mathbf{a}_1\times\mathbf{a}_2|}\right|$ (b) $d=\left|\frac{(\mathbf{b}_1\cdot\mathbf{b}_2)\times(\mathbf{a}_2-\mathbf{a}_1)}{|\mathbf{b}_1||\mathbf{b}_2|}\right|$

(c) $d=\left|\frac{(\mathbf{b}_1\times\mathbf{b}_2)\cdot(\mathbf{a}_2-\mathbf{a}_1)}{|\mathbf{b}_1\times\mathbf{b}_2|}\right|$ (d) $d=\left|\frac{(\mathbf{b}_1\times\mathbf{b}_2)\cdot(\mathbf{a}_1\times\mathbf{a}_2)}{|\mathbf{b}_1\times\mathbf{b}_2||\mathbf{a}_1\times\mathbf{b}_2|}\right|$

5 The shortest distance between the lines $\frac{x-x_1}{a_1}=\frac{y-y_1}{b_1}=\frac{z-z_1}{c_1}$ and $\frac{x-x_2}{a_2}=\frac{y-y_2}{b_2}=\frac{z-z_2}{c_2}$ is $\frac{\begin{vmatrix}x_2-x_1 & y_2-y_1 & z_2-z_1\\ a_1 & b_1 & c_1\\ a_2 & b_2 & c_2\end{vmatrix}}{..A..}$.

Here, A refers to NCERT Pg. 387

(a) $(b_1c_2-b_2c_1)^2-(c_1a_2-c_2a_1)^2+(a_1b_2-a_2b_1)^2$
(b) $(b_1c_2-b_2c_1)^2+(c_1a_2-c_2a_1)^2+(a_1b_2-a_2b_1)^2$
(c) $\sqrt{(b_1c_2-b_2c_1)^2+(c_1a_2-c_2a_1)^2+(a_1b_2-a_2b_1)^2}$
(d) None of the above

6 The distance between two parallel lines can be taken out by the formula NCERT Pg. 387, 388

(a) $d=\left|\frac{\mathbf{b}\cdot(\mathbf{a}_2-\mathbf{a}_1)}{|\mathbf{b}|}\right|$ (b) $d=\left|\frac{\mathbf{b}\cdot(\mathbf{a}_2-\mathbf{a}_1)}{|\mathbf{a}_2-\mathbf{a}_1|}\right|$

(c) $d=\left|\frac{\mathbf{b}\times(\mathbf{a}_2-\mathbf{a}_1)}{|\mathbf{a}_2-\mathbf{a}_1|}\right|$ (d) $d=\left|\frac{\mathbf{b}\times(\mathbf{a}_2-\mathbf{a}_1)}{|\mathbf{b}|}\right|$

7 Match the terms of column I with the terms of column II and choose the correct option from the codes given below. NCERT Pg. 386, 387

Column I (Pair of lines)	Column II (Distance between them)
A. $\mathbf{r}=(\hat{\mathbf{i}}+2\hat{\mathbf{j}}+\hat{\mathbf{k}})+\lambda(\hat{\mathbf{i}}-\hat{\mathbf{j}}+\hat{\mathbf{k}})$ and $\mathbf{r}=(2\hat{\mathbf{i}}-\hat{\mathbf{j}}-\hat{\mathbf{k}})+\mu(2\hat{\mathbf{i}}+\hat{\mathbf{j}}+2\hat{\mathbf{k}})$	1. $2\sqrt{29}$
B. $\frac{x+1}{7}=\frac{y+1}{-6}=\frac{z+1}{1}$ and $\frac{x-3}{1}=\frac{y-5}{2}=\frac{z-7}{1}$	2. $\frac{8}{\sqrt{29}}$
C. $\mathbf{r}=(\hat{\mathbf{i}}+2\hat{\mathbf{j}}+3\hat{\mathbf{k}})+\lambda(\hat{\mathbf{i}}-3\hat{\mathbf{j}}+2\hat{\mathbf{k}})$ and $\mathbf{r}=4\hat{\mathbf{i}}+5\hat{\mathbf{j}}+6\hat{\mathbf{k}}+\mu(2\hat{\mathbf{i}}+3\hat{\mathbf{j}}+\hat{\mathbf{k}})$	3. $\frac{3\sqrt{2}}{2}$
D. $\mathbf{r}=(1-t)\hat{\mathbf{i}}+(t-2)\hat{\mathbf{j}}+(3-2t)\hat{\mathbf{k}}$ and $\mathbf{r}=(s+1)\hat{\mathbf{i}}+(2s-1)\hat{\mathbf{j}}-(2s+1)\hat{\mathbf{k}}$	4. $\frac{3}{\sqrt{19}}$

Codes

	A	B	C	D		A	B	C	D
(a)	3	1	4	2	(b)	2	3	4	1
(c)	3	4	1	2	(d)	4	3	2	1

Level II

8 The shortest distance between the lines given by $\mathbf{r}=(8+3\lambda)\hat{\mathbf{i}}-(9+16\lambda)\hat{\mathbf{j}}+(10+7\lambda)\hat{\mathbf{k}}$ and $\mathbf{r}=15\hat{\mathbf{i}}+29\hat{\mathbf{j}}+5\hat{\mathbf{k}}+\mu(3\hat{\mathbf{i}}+8\hat{\mathbf{j}}-5\hat{\mathbf{k}})$ is NCERT Pg. 388

(a) 84 (b) 14 (c) 21 (d) 16

9 The shortest distance between the lines $\frac{x-3}{3}=\frac{y-8}{-1}=\frac{z-3}{1}$ and $\frac{x+3}{-3}=\frac{y+7}{2}=\frac{z-6}{4}$ is NCERT Pg. 387

(a) $\sqrt{30}$ (b) $2\sqrt{30}$ (c) $5\sqrt{30}$ (d) $3\sqrt{30}$

10 The two lines $\frac{x+1}{3}=\frac{y+3}{5}=\frac{z+5}{7}$ and $\frac{x-2}{1}=\frac{y-4}{3}=\frac{z-6}{5}$ NCERT Pg. 387

(a) intersect (b) do not intersect
(c) are parallel (d) None of these

11 The distance between the lines given by $\mathbf{r} = \hat{i} + \hat{j} + \lambda(\hat{i} - 2\hat{j} + 3\hat{k})$ and $\mathbf{r} = (2\hat{i} - 3\hat{k}) + \mu(\hat{i} - 2\hat{j} + 3\hat{k})$ is **NCERT Pg. 388, 389**

(a) $\sqrt{\frac{59}{14}}$ (b) $\sqrt{\frac{59}{7}}$ (c) $\sqrt{\frac{118}{7}}$ (d) $\frac{\sqrt{59}}{7}$

12 The distance between the lines $\frac{x-4}{5} = \frac{y+1}{2} = \frac{z}{1}$ and $\frac{x-1}{5} = \frac{y-2}{2} = \frac{z-3}{1}$ is **NCERT Pg. 391**

(a) $5\sqrt{129}$ (b) $\frac{\sqrt{129}}{5}$
(c) $\sqrt{\frac{129}{10}}$ (d) $\sqrt{\frac{129}{5}}$

13 Consider the following statements

Statement I The distance between the lines $\frac{x-5}{3} = \frac{y-7}{-1} = \frac{z+4}{1}$ and $\frac{x+3}{-36} = \frac{y-3}{2} = \frac{z-6}{4}$ is $\frac{\sqrt{10}}{3}$.

Statement II The lines $\frac{x-5}{3} = \frac{y-7}{-1} = \frac{z+4}{1}$ and $\frac{x+3}{-36} = \frac{y-3}{2} = \frac{z-6}{4}$ intersect each other.

Choose the correct option. **NCERT Pg. 387**

(a) Statement I is true
(b) Statement II is true
(c) Both statements are true
(d) Both statements are false

Miscellaneous Exercise

1 Consider the following statements

Statement I The line joining the origin to the point (2, 1, 1) is perpendicular to the line determined by the points (3, 5, – 1) and (4, 3, – 1).

Statement II If l_1, m_1, n_1 and l_2, m_2, n_2 are the direction cosines of two mutually perpendicular lines, then the direction cosines of the line perpendicular to both of these are $m_1 n_2 - m_2 n_1; n_1 l_2 - n_2 l_1; l_1 m_2 - l_2 m_1$.

Choose the correct option. **NCERT Pg. 389**

(a) Statement I is true
(b) Statement II is true
(c) Both statements are true
(d) Both statements are false

2 The angle between the lines whose direction ratios are a, b, c and $b-c, c-a, a-b$, is **NCERT Pg. 390**

(a) $\frac{\pi}{4}$ (b) $\frac{\pi}{2}$ (c) 0 (d) $\frac{\pi}{3}$

3 The equation of a line parallel to X-axis and passing through origin is **NCERT Pg. 390**

(a) $\frac{x}{1} = \frac{y}{0} = \frac{z}{0}$ (b) $\frac{x}{0} = \frac{y}{1} = \frac{z}{1}$
(c) $\frac{x}{0} = \frac{y}{-1} = \frac{z}{-1}$ (d) $\frac{x}{1} = \frac{y}{-1} = \frac{z}{-1}$

4 The coordinates of the point, where the line through (5, 1, 6) and (3, 4, 1) crosses the yz-plane, is **NCERT Pg. 380**

(a) $\left(0, \frac{17}{2}, \frac{-13}{2}\right)$ (b) $\left(0, \frac{17}{3}, \frac{13}{3}\right)$
(c) $\left(0, \frac{17}{2}, \frac{13}{2}\right)$ (d) $\left(0, \frac{17}{3}, \frac{-13}{3}\right)$

5 Which of the following is/are true? **NCERT Pg. 391**

I. The vector equation of the line passing through the point (1, 2, – 4) and perpendicular to the two lines $\frac{x-8}{3} = \frac{y+19}{-16} = \frac{z-10}{7}$ and $\frac{x-15}{3} = \frac{y-29}{8} = \frac{z-5}{-5}$ is

$$\mathbf{r} = (\hat{i} + 2\hat{j} - 4\hat{k}) + \lambda(2\hat{i} + 3\hat{j} + 6\hat{k})$$

II. If a plane has intercepts a, b, c and is at a distance of p units from the origin, then $p^2 = a^2 + b^2 + c^2$.

(a) Only I is true (b) Only II is true
(c) Both I and II are true (d) Neither I nor II is true

6 A line makes angles α, β, γ and δ with the diagonals of a cube. Then, $\cos^2\alpha + \cos^2\beta + \cos^2\gamma + \cos^2\delta$ is equal to **NCERT Pg. 383**

(a) $\frac{1}{3}$ (b) $\frac{3}{4}$ (c) $\frac{4}{3}$ (d) $\frac{8}{3}$

7 The angle between the lines whose direction cosines are given by the equations $3l + m + 5n = 0$ and $6mn - 2nl + 5lm = 0$, is **NCERT Pg. 383**

(a) $\cos^{-1}\left(\frac{1}{\sqrt{6}}\right)$ (b) $\cos^{-1}\left(\frac{1}{3}\right)$
(c) $\cos^{-1}\left(\frac{-1}{6}\right)$ (d) $\cos^{-1}\left(\frac{-2}{3}\right)$

8 The equations of two lines through the origin, which intersect the line $\frac{x-3}{2} = \frac{y-3}{1} = \frac{z}{1}$ at angles of $\frac{\pi}{3}$ each, are **NCERT Pg. 391**

(a) $\frac{x}{1} = \frac{y}{2} = \frac{z}{1}; \frac{x}{1} = \frac{y}{1} = \frac{z}{2}$
(b) $\frac{x}{1} = \frac{y}{2} = \frac{z}{-1}; \frac{x}{-1} = \frac{y}{1} = \frac{z}{-2}$
(c) $\frac{x}{1} = \frac{y}{2} = \frac{z}{-1}; \frac{x}{1} = \frac{y}{-1} = \frac{z}{-2}$
(d) None of the above

Numerical Type Questions

1 A line PQ in three-dimensional space makes an angles 60° and 45° with the positive x-axis and the positive y-axis. If PQ makes an acute angle θ with positive z-axis, then $6\cos\theta$ is .... NCERT Pg. 378

2 If the lines $\frac{x-1}{2}=\frac{y+1}{3}=\frac{z-1}{4}$ and $\frac{x-3}{1}=\frac{y-k}{2}=\frac{z}{1}$ intersect, then the value of $2k$ is .... NCERT Pg. 390

3 If the image of the point $P(2, 4, 4)$ in the line $\frac{x}{1}=\frac{y-1}{1}=\frac{z-2}{3}$ is Q. Then find length $|PQ|^2$ is NCERT Pg. 385

4 Find the product of $(\sqrt{6})$ and the shortest distance between the lines

$\mathbf{r}=(\hat{\mathbf{i}}+2\hat{\mathbf{j}}+5\hat{\mathbf{k}})+\mu(2\hat{\mathbf{i}}+3\hat{\mathbf{j}}+4\hat{\mathbf{k}})$ and

$\mathbf{r}=(2\hat{\mathbf{i}}+4\hat{\mathbf{j}}+5\hat{\mathbf{k}})+\mu(3\hat{\mathbf{i}}+4\hat{\mathbf{j}}+5\hat{\mathbf{k}})$ is NCERT Pg. 388

5 If the angle between line $\frac{x-5}{2}=\frac{y-3}{7}=\frac{z-1}{4}$ and $\frac{x-1}{1}=\frac{y-3}{-2}=\frac{z-4}{3}$ is α. Then $\frac{4\alpha}{\pi}$ is NCERT Pg. 385

6 Let C be the the point on the line passing through the points $A(2, 3, 4)$ and $B(5, 2, 4)$. Further from the origin and at a distance of $\sqrt{10}$ unit from the A be (a, b, c). Then $a+b+c$ is

7 If the line $\frac{x-2}{3}=\frac{y-2}{2+\Omega}=\frac{z-4}{2}$ and $\frac{x+3}{2}=\frac{y-2}{3}=\frac{z-5}{\mu}$ are orthogonal to each other then $|2\mu+3\Omega|$ is NCERT Pg. 385

8 The shortest distance between the lines are $\mathbf{r}=(3\hat{\mathbf{i}}-15\hat{\mathbf{j}}+9\hat{\mathbf{k}})+\Omega(2\hat{\mathbf{i}}-7\hat{\mathbf{j}}+5\hat{\mathbf{k}})$ and $\mathbf{r}=(-\hat{\mathbf{i}}+\hat{\mathbf{j}}+9\hat{\mathbf{k}})+\mu(2\hat{\mathbf{i}}+\hat{\mathbf{j}}-3\hat{\mathbf{k}})$ is α, then find $\frac{\alpha}{\sqrt{3}}$ is NCERT Pg. 388

Assertion and Reason Questions

Direction (Q. Nos. 1-8) The following questions consist of two statements, one labelled as "Assertion (A) and the other labelled as Reason (R)". You are to examine these two statements carefully true and it so, where the Reason (R) is the correct explanation a for the given Assertion (A). Select your answer from following options.

(a) Both Assertion and Reason are correct and Reason is the correct explanation of Assertion.
(b) Both Assertion and Reason are correct but Reason is not the correct explanation of Assertion.
(c) Assertion is correct but Reason is incorrect.
(d) Assertion is incorrect but Reason is correct.

1 **Assertion (A)** Two lines are perpendicular, if $a_1a_2+b_1b_2+c_1c_2=0$, where a_1, b_1, c_1 and a_2, b_2, c_2 are the direction ratios of two lines.

Reason (R) Two lines are parallel, if $\frac{a_1}{a_2}=\frac{b_1}{b_2}=\frac{c_1}{c_2}$ where a_1, b_1, c_1 and a_2, b_2, c_2 are the direction ratios of two lines. NCERT Pg. 384

2 **Assertion (A)** The pair of lines given by $\mathbf{r}=\hat{\mathbf{i}}-\hat{\mathbf{j}}+\lambda(2\hat{\mathbf{i}}+\hat{\mathbf{k}})$ and $\mathbf{r}=2\hat{\mathbf{i}}-\hat{\mathbf{k}}+\mu(\hat{\mathbf{i}}+\hat{\mathbf{j}}-\hat{\mathbf{k}})$ intersect.

Reason (R) Two lines intersect each other, if they are not parallel. NCERT Pg. 384

3 **Assertion (A)** if a line makes angle α, β and γ with the co-ordinate axes then $\cos 2\alpha+\cos 2\beta+\cos 2\gamma=-1$

Reason (R) If l, m, n are direction cosines of a line. Then $l^2+m^2+n^2=1$. NCERT Pg. 378

4 **Assertion (A)** If a line makes an angle α, β and γ with co-ordinate axes, then $\sin^2\alpha+\sin^2\beta+\sin^2\gamma=1$.

Reason (R) If l, m, n are direction cosines of a line. Then $l^2+m^2+n^2=1$. NCERT Pg. 378

5 **Assertion (A)** The lines $\mathbf{r}=\mathbf{a}_1+\mu\mathbf{b}_1$ and $\mathbf{r}=\mathbf{a}_2+\mu\mathbf{b}_2$ are perpendicular, then $\mathbf{b}_1\cdot\mathbf{b}_1=0$.

Reason (R) The angle θ between the lines is 90°. NCERT Pg. 384

6 **Assertion (A)** The equation of the line passing through the points $(\hat{\mathbf{i}}+2\hat{\mathbf{j}}+3\hat{\mathbf{k}})$ and $(3\hat{\mathbf{i}}-\hat{\mathbf{j}}-3\hat{\mathbf{k}})$ is

$\mathbf{r}=(\hat{\mathbf{i}}+2\hat{\mathbf{j}}+3\hat{\mathbf{k}})+\lambda(2\hat{\mathbf{i}}+3\hat{\mathbf{j}}+3\hat{\mathbf{k}})$

Reason (R) The equation of line passing through the points $\mathbf{a}$ and $\mathbf{b}$ is $\mathbf{r}=\mathbf{a}+\mu(\mathbf{b}-\mathbf{a})$ NCERT Pg. 381, 382

7 **Assertion (A)** A line through the points $P(2, 3, 4)$ and $Q(4, 7, 8)$ is parallel to a line through the points $R(-1, -2, 1)$ and $S(1, 2, 5)$

Reason (R) Lines $\mathbf{r}=\mathbf{a}_1+\mu\mathbf{b}_2$ and $\mathbf{r}=\mathbf{a}_2+\mu\mathbf{b}_2$ are parallel if $\mathbf{b}_2\cdot\mathbf{b}_2=0$. NCERT Pg. 384

8 Assertion (A) The equation of line $\frac{x-1}{2}=\frac{y-2}{3}=\frac{z-4}{5}$ then (2, 3, 5) are the direction ratio of given line.

Reason (R) If a, b, c ar the direction ratio of line and line passing through (x_1, y_1, z_1) then equation of line is $\frac{x-x_1}{a}=\frac{y-y_1}{b}+\frac{z-z_1}{c}$ NCERT Pg. 382

Case or Paragraph Type Questions

Direction (Q. No. 1-4) Two motor cycles P and Q are running at the speed more then allowed speed on the road along the lines $\mathbf{r}=(\hat{i}+\hat{j}+2\hat{k})+\lambda(\hat{i}+2\hat{j}-\hat{k})$ and $\mathbf{r}=3\hat{i}+3\hat{j}+\mu(2\hat{i}+\hat{j}+\hat{k})$ respectively.

Based on the above information answer the following questions.

1 The cartesian equation of the line along which motorcycle P is running is NCERT Pg. 382

(a) $\frac{x-1}{1}=\frac{y-1}{2}=\frac{z-2}{-1}$ (b) $\frac{x-3}{2}=\frac{y-3}{1}=\frac{z}{1}$

(c) $\frac{x-1}{2}=\frac{y-1}{1}=\frac{z-1}{-1}$ (d) $\frac{x-1}{2}=\frac{y-3}{1}=\frac{z-1}{1}$

2 The direction cosines of line along which motor cycle P is running are NCERT Pg. 380

(a) $\left(\frac{1}{\sqrt{6}}, \frac{-2}{\sqrt{6}}, \frac{1}{\sqrt{6}}\right)$ (b) $\left(\frac{-1}{\sqrt{6}}, \frac{-2}{\sqrt{6}}, \frac{1}{\sqrt{6}}\right)$

(c) $\left(\frac{1}{\sqrt{6}}, \frac{2}{\sqrt{6}}, \frac{-1}{\sqrt{6}}\right)$ (d) $\left(\frac{-1}{\sqrt{6}}, \frac{2}{\sqrt{6}}, \frac{1}{\sqrt{6}}\right)$

3 The cartesian equation of line along which motor cyclic Q is running is NCERT Pg. 382

(a) $\frac{x-3}{2}=\frac{y-3}{1}=\frac{z-1}{1}$ (b) $\frac{x-3}{2}=\frac{y-3}{1}=\frac{z}{1}$

(c) $\frac{x-3}{2}=\frac{y-3}{2}=\frac{z}{1}$ (d) $\frac{x-2}{2}=\frac{y-3}{1}=\frac{z-1}{1}$

4 The direction ratios of line along which motor cyclic Q is running are NCERT Pg. 380

(a) (2, 2, 1) (b) (2, 1, 2)
(c) (2, 2, 3) (d) (2, 1, 1)

Direction (Q. No. 5-7) In the figure, **a** be the position vector of the point A with respect to the origin O. l is a line parallel to **a** *vector* **b**.

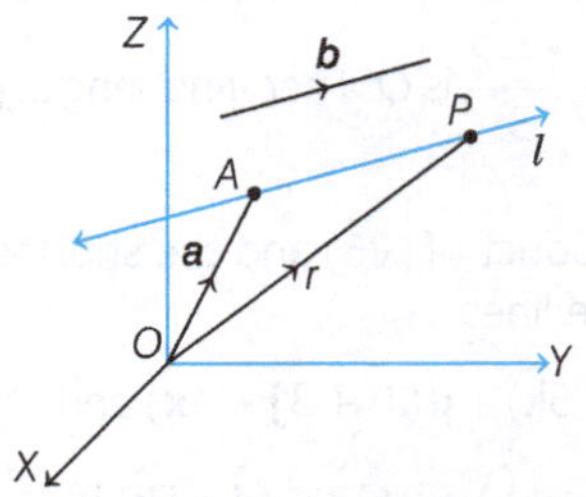

5 The vector equation of the line l is NCERT Pg. 381, 382

(a) $\mathbf{r}=\lambda(\mathbf{a}\times\mathbf{b})$ (b) $\mathbf{r}=\lambda\mathbf{a}-\mathbf{b}$
(c) $\mathbf{r}=\mathbf{a}+\lambda\mathbf{b}$ (d) $\mathbf{r}=\lambda(\mathbf{a}\cdot\mathbf{b})$

6 If a, b and c are the direction ratios of the line l, then NCERT Pg. 382

(a) $\mathbf{b}=a\hat{i}+a\hat{j}+a\hat{k}$ (b) $\mathbf{b}=b\hat{i}+b\hat{j}+b\hat{k}$
(c) $\mathbf{b}=c\hat{i}+c\hat{j}++c\hat{k}$ (d) $\mathbf{b}=a\hat{i}+b\hat{j}+c\hat{k}$

7 The cartesian equation of the line l when it passes through the point (x_1, y_1, z_1) and parallel to the vector $\mathbf{b}=a\hat{i}+b\hat{j}+c\hat{k}$, is NCERT Pg. 382

(a) $x-x_1=y-y_1=z-z_1$
(b) $x+x_1=y+y_1=z-z_1$
(c) $\frac{x+x_1}{a}=\frac{y+y_1}{b}=\frac{z+z_1}{c}$
(d) $\frac{x-x_1}{a}=\frac{y-y_1}{b}=\frac{z-z_1}{c}$

Past Years Questions

Single Correct Type

1 The shortest distance between the lines $\frac{x-3}{4}=\frac{y+7}{-11}=\frac{z-1}{5}$ and $\frac{x-5}{3}=\frac{y-9}{-6}=\frac{z+2}{1}$ is

NCERT Pg. 390, JEE Main 2024, 9 April Shift-I

(a) $\frac{178}{\sqrt{563}}$ (b) $\frac{185}{\sqrt{563}}$ (c) $\frac{179}{\sqrt{563}}$ (d) $\frac{187}{\sqrt{563}}$

2 If the shortest distance between the lines

$L_1 : \mathbf{r} = (2+\lambda)\hat{\mathbf{i}} + (1-3\lambda)\hat{\mathbf{j}} + (3+4\lambda)\hat{\mathbf{k}}, \lambda \in R$

$L_2 : \mathbf{r} = 2(1+\mu)\hat{\mathbf{i}} + 3(1+\mu)\hat{\mathbf{j}} + (5+\mu)\hat{\mathbf{k}}, \mu \in R$

is $\frac{m}{\sqrt{n}}$, where $gcd(m, n) = 1$, then the value of $m+n$ is equal to

NCERT Pg. 390, JEE Main 2024, 9 April Shift-I

(a) 387 (b) 377 (c) 384 (d) 390

3 The shortest distance between the lines $\frac{x-3}{2}=\frac{y+15}{-7}=\frac{z-9}{5}$ and $\frac{x+1}{2}=\frac{y-1}{1}=\frac{z-9}{-3}$ is

NCERT Pg. 390, JEE Main 2024, 6 April Shift-I

(a) $5\sqrt{3}$ (b) $4\sqrt{3}$
(c) $8\sqrt{3}$ (d) $6\sqrt{3}$

4 Let (α, β, γ) be the image of the point (8, 5, 7) in the line $\frac{x-1}{2}=\frac{y+1}{3}=\frac{z-2}{5}$. Then, $\alpha+\beta+\gamma$ is equal to

NCERT Pg. 385, JEE Main 2024, 5 April Shift-II

(a) 16 (b) 14 (c) 18 (d) 20

5 The shortest distance between the lines $\frac{x-1}{2}=\frac{y+8}{-7}=\frac{z-4}{5}$ and $\frac{x-1}{2}=\frac{y-2}{1}=\frac{z-6}{-3}$ is

NCERT Pg. 390, JEE Main 2023, 29 Jan Shift-II

(a) $5\sqrt{3}$ (b) $3\sqrt{3}$
(c) $4\sqrt{3}$ (d) $2\sqrt{3}$

6 The distance of the point $P(4, 6, -2)$ from the line passing through the point $(-3, 2, 3)$ and parallel to a line with direction ratios 3, 3, – 1 is equal to

NCERT Pg. 391, JEE Main 2023, 25 Jan Shift-I

(a) $\sqrt{14}$ (b) 3
(c) $2\sqrt{3}$ (d) $\sqrt{6}$

7 If the length of the perpendicular drawn from the point $P(a, 4, 2)$, $a > 0$ on the line $\frac{x+1}{2}=\frac{y-3}{3}=\frac{z-1}{-1}$ is $2\sqrt{6}$ units and $Q(\alpha_1, \alpha_2, \alpha_3)$ is the image of the point P in this line, then $a+\sum_{i=1}^{3}\alpha_i$ is equal to

NCERT Pg. 385, JEE Main 2022, 27 July Shift-II

(a) 7 (b) 8 (c) 12 (d) 14

8 The angle between two lines whose direction ratios are proportional to 1, 1, – 2 and $(\sqrt{3}-1), (-\sqrt{3}-1), -4$ is

NCERT Pg. 383, CUET 2024

(a) $\frac{\pi}{3}$ (b) π (c) $\frac{\pi}{6}$ (d) $\frac{\pi}{2}$

9 Consider the lines L_1 and L_2 given by

$L_1 : \frac{x-1}{2}=\frac{y-3}{1}=\frac{z-2}{2}$; $L_2 : \frac{x-2}{1}=\frac{y-2}{2}=\frac{z-3}{3}$

A line L_3 having direction ratios 1, – 1, – 2, intersects L_1 and L_2 at the points P and Q, respectively. Then, the length of line segment PQ is

NCERT Pg. 319, JEE Main 2023, 25 Jan Shift-I

(a) $4\sqrt{3}$ (b) 4 (c) $2\sqrt{6}$ (d) $3\sqrt{2}$

10 Which of the following cannot be the direction ratios of the straight line $\frac{x-3}{2}=\frac{2-y}{3}=\frac{z+4}{-1}$?

NCERT Pg. 383, CUET 2024

(a) 2, – 3, – 1 (b) – 2, 3, 1
(c) 2, 3, – 1 (d) 6, – 9, – 3

11 The shortest distance between the lines $\frac{x-3}{2}=\frac{y-2}{3}=\frac{z-1}{-1}$ and $\frac{x+3}{2}=\frac{y-6}{1}=\frac{z-5}{3}$ is

NCERT Pg. 390, JEE Main 2022, 27 June Shift-II

(a) $\frac{18}{\sqrt{5}}$ (b) $\frac{22}{3\sqrt{5}}$ (c) $\frac{46}{3\sqrt{5}}$ (d) $6\sqrt{3}$

12 If the shortest distance between the lines $\frac{x-1}{2}=\frac{y-2}{3}=\frac{z-3}{\lambda}$ and $\frac{x-2}{1}=\frac{y-4}{4}=\frac{z-5}{5}$ is $\frac{1}{\sqrt{3}}$, then the sum of all possible values of λ is

NCERT Pg. 390, JEE Main 2022, 24 June Shift-II

(a) 16 (b) 6 (c) 12 (d) 15

Numerical Value Type

13 A line with direction ratios 2, 1, 2 meets the lines $x = y + 2 = z$ and $x + 2 = 2y = 2z$ respectively at the points P and Q. If the length of the perpendicular from the point (1, 2, 12) to the line PQ is l, then l^2 is.

NCERT Pg. 379, JEE Main 2024, 29 Jan Shift-I

14 If the shortest distance between the lines $\frac{x-\lambda}{3} = \frac{y-2}{-1} = \frac{z-1}{1}$ and $\frac{x+2}{-3} = \frac{y+5}{2} = \frac{z-4}{4}$ is $\frac{44}{\sqrt{30}}$, then the largest possible value of $|\lambda|$ is equal to ....

NCERT Pg. 387, JEE Main 2024, 6 April Shift-II

15 Let a line L pass through the point $P(2, 3, 1)$ and be parallel to the line $x + 3y - 2z - 2 = 0 = x - y + 2z$. If the distance of L from the point (5,3,8) is α, then $3\alpha^2$ is equal to ....

NCERT Pg. 382, JEE Main 2023, 30 Jan Shift-II

16 Let Q and R be two points on the line $\frac{x+1}{2} = \frac{y+2}{3} = \frac{z-1}{2}$ at a distance $\sqrt{26}$ from the point $P(4, 2, 7)$. Then, the square of the area of the ΔPQR is ....

NCERT Pg. 382, JEE Main 2022, 26 July Shift-I

Skill Boosters

1 The projection of a vector on the three co-ordinate axes are $-3, 2, 6$ respectively. The direction cosines of the vector are

(a) 6, −3, 2
(b) $\frac{-3}{7}, \frac{2}{7}, \frac{6}{7}$
(c) $\frac{-3}{7}, \frac{6}{7}, \frac{2}{7}$
(d) $\frac{3}{7}, \frac{6}{7}, \frac{2}{7}$

2 The equation of the line through the point (1, 2, 3) and perpendicular to the line $\frac{x+1}{2} = \frac{y-1}{3} = \frac{z-1}{2}$ is

(a) $\frac{x-1}{\frac{-12}{17}} = \frac{y-2}{\frac{16}{17}} = \frac{z-3}{\frac{-12}{17}}$

(b) $\frac{x-1}{\frac{12}{17}} = \frac{y-2}{\frac{16}{17}} = \frac{z-3}{\frac{-12}{17}}$

(c) $\frac{x-1}{\frac{-12}{17}} = \frac{y-2}{\frac{-16}{17}} = \frac{z-3}{\frac{12}{17}}$

(d) $\frac{x-1}{\frac{12}{17}} = \frac{y-2}{\frac{-16}{17}} = \frac{z-3}{\frac{-12}{17}}$

3 Find the shortest distance between the lines $\mathbf{r} = 3\hat{i} + 8\hat{j} + 3\hat{k} + \lambda(3\hat{i} - 2\hat{j} + \hat{k})$ and $\mathbf{r} = -3\hat{i} + 7\hat{j} - 6\hat{k} + \mu(3\hat{i} - 2\hat{j} - 4\hat{k})$ is

(a) $\frac{87}{\sqrt{365}}$
(b) $\frac{87}{\sqrt{366}}$
(c) $\frac{87}{\sqrt{369}}$
(d) $\frac{87}{\sqrt{350}}$

4 If a line makes an angle of $\frac{\pi}{3}$ with positive directions of each of y-axis and z-axis, then angle that the line makes with the positive direction of the x-axis is

(a) $\frac{\pi}{6}$
(b) $\frac{\pi}{4}$
(c) $\frac{\pi}{3}$
(d) $\frac{\pi}{2}$

5 Find the angle between the lines $\frac{x-2}{2} = \frac{y+2}{7} = \frac{z+3}{-1}$ and $\frac{x-2}{3} = \frac{2y-8}{4} = \frac{z-5}{4}$

(a) $\cos^{-1}\left(\frac{10}{\sqrt{242}}\right)$
(b) $\cos^{-1}\left(\frac{10}{\sqrt{250}}\right)$
(c) $\cos^{-1}\left(\frac{10}{\sqrt{240}}\right)$
(d) $\cos^{-1}\left(\frac{10}{\sqrt{246}}\right)$

Correct Codes

Topical Questions

Direction Cosines and Direction Ratio of a Line

1 (b)	2 (b)	3 (c)	4 (d)	5 (a)	6 (c)	7 (c)	8 (c)	9 (d)	10 (d)
11 (c)	12 (a)	13 (d)	14 (c)	15 (b)	16 (b)	17 (b)			

Equation of a Line in Space

1 (b)	2 (c)	3 (a)	4 (c)	5 (d)	6 (d)	7 (c)	8 (d)	9 (a)	10 (b)
11 (c)	12 (d)	13 (a)	14 (b)						

Angle between Two Lines

1 (a)	2 (c)	3 (b)	4 (c)	5 (b)	6 (c)	7 (a)	8 (b)	9 (b)	10 (d)
11 (b)	12 (a)	13 (b)	14 (d)	15 (c)					

Shortest Distance between Two Skew-Lines

1 (c)	2 (c)	3 (a)	4 (c)	5 (c)	6 (d)	7 (a)	8 (b)	9 (d)	10 (a)
11 (b)	12 (d)	13 (a)							

Miscellaneous Exercise

1 (c)	2 (b)	3 (a)	4 (a)	5 (a)	6 (c)	7 (c)	8 (b)

Numerical Type Questions

1 (3)	2 (9)	3 (24)	4 (3)	5 (2)	6 (11)	7 (12)	8 (4)

Assertion and Reason Questions

1 (b)	2 (c)	3 (a)	4 (d)	5 (a)	6 (d)	7 (c)	8 (a)

Case or Paragraph Type Questions

1 (a)	2 (c)	3 (b)	4 (d)	5 (c)	6 (d)	7 (d)

Past Years Questions

1 (d)	2 (a)	3 (b)	4 (b)	5 (c)	6 (a)	7 (b)	8 (a)	9 (c)	10 (a)
11 (a)	12 (a)	13 (65)	14 (43)	15 (158)	16 (153)				

Skill Boosters

1 (b)	2 (a)	3 (c)	4 (b)	5 (d)

Step by Step

Decoding the Questions

Concept Builders

1 1

2 $\left(\frac{1}{2}, -1, \frac{1}{3}\right)$

3 $\cos^{-1}\left(\frac{24}{\sqrt{38}\sqrt{19}}\right)$

4 Parallel

5 $\frac{x}{0} = \frac{y}{0} = \frac{z}{1}$

6 $x = y = 0$

7 $\left|\frac{\mathbf{b}_1 \cdot \mathbf{b}_2}{|\mathbf{b}_1||\mathbf{b}_2|}\right|$

Topical Questions

Direction Cosine and Direction Ratio of a Line

1 (*b*) If the given line in space does not pass through the origin, then in order to find its direction cosines, we draw a line through the origin and parallel to the given line.

Now, take one of the directed lines from the origin and find its direction cosines as two parallel line have same set of direction cosines.

2 (*b*) Any three numbers which are proportional to the direction cosines of a line, are called the direction ratios of the line. If l, m and n are direction cosines and a, b and c are direction ratios of a line, then $a = \lambda l$, $b = \lambda m$ and $c = \lambda n$ for any non-zero $\lambda \in R$.

3 (*c*) Given, $OP = r$.

Then, $\cos\alpha = \frac{OA}{OP} = \frac{x}{r}$. This gives $x = lr$.

[$\because RS \parallel OP \Rightarrow$ direction cosines of RS and OP are same]

Similarly, $y = mr$ and $z = nr$

Thus,

$$x^2 + y^2 + z^2 = r^2(l^2 + m^2 + n^2)$$

But $x^2 + y^2 + z^2 = r^2$

Hence, $l^2 + m^2 + n^2 = \frac{r^2}{r^2} = 1$

4 (*d*) Let a, b and c be direction ratios of a line and l, m and n be the direction cosines (DC's) of the line. Then,

$$\frac{l}{a} = \frac{m}{b} = \frac{n}{c} = k \quad \text{(say)},$$

k being a constant.

Therefore, $l = ak$, $m = bk$,

$$n = ck \quad \text{...(i)}$$

But $l^2 + m^2 + n^2 = 1$

Therefore, $k^2(a^2 + b^2 + c^2) = 1$

or $k = \pm\frac{1}{\sqrt{a^2 + b^2 + c^2}}$

Hence, from Eq. (i), the DC's of the line are

$$l = \pm\frac{a}{\sqrt{a^2 + b^2 + c^2}},$$

$$m = \pm\frac{b}{\sqrt{a^2 + b^2 + c^2}},$$

$$n = \pm\frac{c}{\sqrt{a^2 + b^2 + c^2}}$$

Where, depending on the desired sign of k, either a positive or a negative sign is to be taken for l, m and n.

5 (*a*) For any line, if a, b and c are direction ratios of a line, then ka, kb, kc; $k \neq 0$ is also a set of direction ratios. So, any two sets of direction ratios of a line are also proportional. Also, for any line there are infinitely many sets of direction ratios.

6 (*c*) Since, one and only one line passes through two given points, we can determine the direction cosines of a line passing through the given points $P(x_1, y_1, z_1)$ and $Q(x_2, y_2, z_2)$ as follows.

Let l, m and n be the direction cosines of the line PQ and let it makes angles α, β and γ with the X, Y *and* Z-axes, respectively.

Draw perpendiculars from P and Q to xy-plane to meet at R and S. Draw a perpendicular from P to QS to meet at N.

Now, in right angled ΔPNQ, $\angle PQN = \gamma$ from (figure).

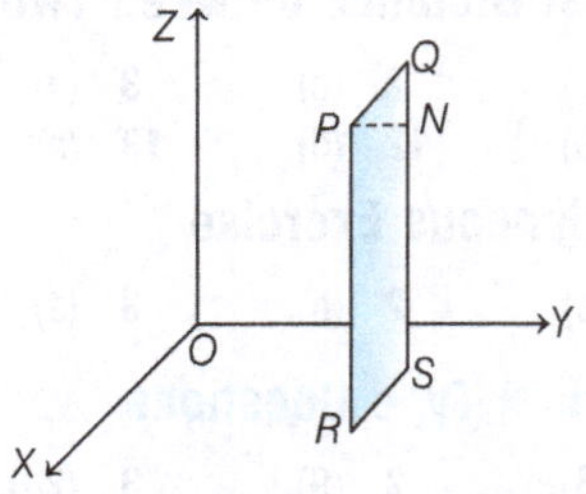

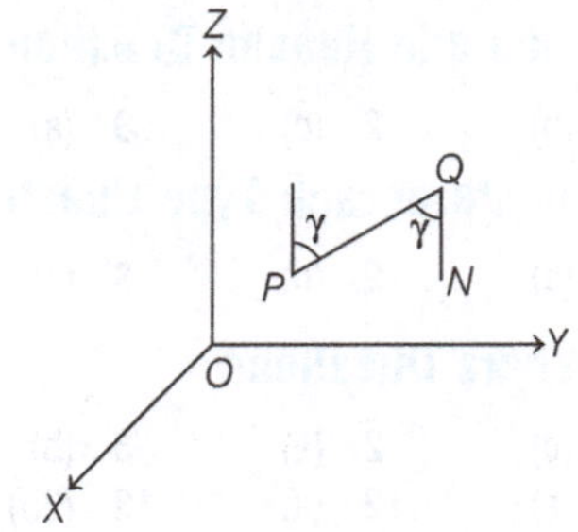

Therefore, $\cos\gamma = \frac{NQ}{PQ} = \frac{z_2 - z_1}{PQ}$

Similarly, $\cos\alpha = \frac{x_2 - x_1}{PQ}$

and $\cos\beta = \frac{y_2 - y_1}{PQ}$

Hence, the direction cosines of the line segment joining the points $P(x_1, y_1, z_1)$ and $Q(x_2, y_2, z_2)$ are

$$\frac{x_2 - x_1}{PQ}, \frac{y_2 - y_1}{PQ}, \frac{z_2 - z_1}{PQ}$$

Where,

$$PQ = \sqrt{(x_2 - x_1)^2 + (y_2 - y_1)^2 + (z_2 - z_1)^2}$$

7 (*c*) The direction ratios of the line segment joining $P(x_1, y_1, z_1)$ and $Q(x_2, y_2, z_2)$ may be taken as

$$x_2 - x_1, y_2 - y_1, z_2 - z_1$$

or $$x_1 - x_2, y_1 - y_2, z_1 - z_2$$

8 (*c*)

A. Let direction cosines of the line be l, m and n with the X, Y, and Z-axes respectively and given that

$$\alpha = 90°, \beta = 135° \text{ and } \gamma = 45°$$

Then, $l = \cos\alpha = \cos 90° = 0$

$$m = \cos\beta = \cos 135° = \frac{-1}{\sqrt{2}}$$

and $n = \cos\gamma = \cos 45° = \dfrac{1}{\sqrt{2}}$

Therefore, the direction cosines of the line are $0, -\dfrac{1}{\sqrt{2}}$ and $\dfrac{1}{\sqrt{2}}$.

B. Let the line makes an angle α with each of the three coordinate axes. Then its direction cosines are

$$l = \cos\alpha,\ m = \cos\alpha,$$
$$n = \cos\alpha$$

We know that $l^2 + m^2 + n^2 = 1$

$$\Rightarrow \cos^2\alpha + \cos^2\alpha + \cos^2\alpha = 1$$
$$[\because l = m = n = \cos\alpha]$$
$$\Rightarrow 3\cos^2\alpha = 1$$
$$\Rightarrow \cos^2\alpha = \frac{1}{3}$$
$$\Rightarrow \cos\alpha = \pm\frac{1}{\sqrt{3}}$$

$\therefore$ Direction cosines of the line are either $\dfrac{1}{\sqrt{3}}, \dfrac{1}{\sqrt{3}}, \dfrac{1}{\sqrt{3}}$ or $-\dfrac{1}{\sqrt{3}}, -\dfrac{1}{\sqrt{3}}, -\dfrac{1}{\sqrt{3}}$.

C. Given, direction ratios are –18, 12 and –4.

Here, $a = -18, b = 12$ and $c = -4$.

Then, direction cosines of a line are

$$\left(\frac{a}{\sqrt{a^2+b^2+c^2}}, \frac{b}{\sqrt{a^2+b^2+c^2}}, \frac{c}{\sqrt{a^2+b^2+c^2}}\right)$$

$$\left[\because \text{if } a, b, c \text{ are direction ratios, then direction cosines are } \frac{a}{\sqrt{a^2+b^2+c^2}}, \frac{b}{\sqrt{a^2+b^2+c^2}}, \frac{c}{\sqrt{a^2+b^2+c^2}}\right]$$

$$= \left(\frac{-18}{\sqrt{(-18)^2+(12)^2+(-4)^2}}, \frac{12}{\sqrt{(-18)^2+(12)^2+(-4)^2}}, \frac{-4}{\sqrt{(-18)^2+(12)^2+(-4)^2}}\right)$$

$$= \left(\frac{-18}{\sqrt{484}}, \frac{12}{\sqrt{484}}, \frac{-4}{\sqrt{484}}\right)$$

$$= \left(\frac{-18}{22}, \frac{12}{22}, \frac{-4}{22}\right) = \left(\frac{-9}{11}, \frac{6}{11}, \frac{-2}{11}\right)$$

Thus, the direction cosines are $-\dfrac{9}{11}, \dfrac{6}{11}$ and $\dfrac{-2}{11}$.

9 (*d*) Let the vertices of the triangle be $A(3, 5, -4)$, $B(-1, 1, 2)$ and $C(-5, -5, -2)$, respectively.

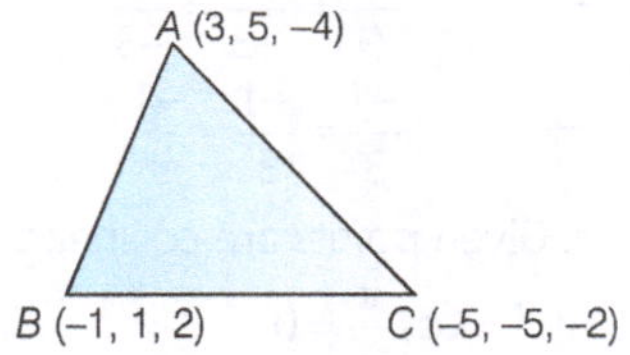

The direction ratios of side AB are

$$(-1-3, 1-5, 2-(-4))$$
$$\Rightarrow (-4, -4, 2+4)$$
$$\Rightarrow (-4, -4, 6).$$

$[\because$ If $A(x_1, y_1, z_1)$ and $B(x_2, y_2, z_2)$ then DR's of $AB = (x_2 - x_1, y_2 - y_1, z_2 - z_1)]$

Then, magnitude of AB,

$$|AB| = \sqrt{(-4)^2+(-4)^2+(6)^2}$$
$$= \sqrt{16+16+36} = \sqrt{68} = 2\sqrt{17}$$

Therefore, the direction cosines of AB are

$$\frac{-4}{2\sqrt{17}}, \frac{-4}{2\sqrt{17}}, \frac{6}{2\sqrt{17}}$$
$$\Rightarrow \frac{-2}{\sqrt{17}}, \frac{-2}{\sqrt{17}}, \frac{3}{\sqrt{17}}$$

Similarly, the direction ratios of side BC are $(-5-(-1)), (-5-1)$ and $(-2-2)$ i.e. $(-4, -6, -4)$.

Magnitude of BC,

$$|BC| = \sqrt{(-4)^2+(-6)^2+(-4)^2}$$
$$= \sqrt{68} = 2\sqrt{17}$$

Therefore, the direction cosines of BC are

$$\frac{-4}{2\sqrt{17}}, \frac{-6}{2\sqrt{17}}, \frac{-4}{2\sqrt{17}}$$
$$\Rightarrow \frac{-2}{\sqrt{17}}, \frac{-3}{\sqrt{17}}, \frac{-2}{\sqrt{17}}$$

The direction ratios of side CA are $(-5-3), (-5-5)$ and $(-2+4)$ i.e. $(-8, -10, 2)$ or $(8, 10, -2)$.

$$|CA| = \sqrt{(-8)^2+(-10)^2+(2)^2}$$
$$= \sqrt{64+100+4}$$
$$= \sqrt{168} = 2\sqrt{42}$$

Therefore, the direction cosines of AC are

$$\frac{8}{2\sqrt{42}}, \frac{10}{2\sqrt{42}}, \frac{-2}{2\sqrt{42}}$$
$$\Rightarrow \frac{4}{\sqrt{42}}, \frac{5}{\sqrt{42}}, \frac{-1}{\sqrt{42}}$$

10 (*d*) Given, $\alpha = 30°, \beta = 45°, \gamma = ?$

$$l = \cos\alpha = \cos 30° = \frac{\sqrt{3}}{2}$$
$$m = \cos\beta = \cos 45° = \frac{1}{\sqrt{2}}$$
$$n = \cos\gamma$$
$$\because \quad l^2 + m^2 + n^2 = 1$$
$$\Rightarrow \frac{3}{4} + \frac{1}{2} + \cos^2\gamma = 1$$
$$\Rightarrow \cos^2\gamma = 1 - \frac{3}{4} - \frac{1}{2}$$
$$= \frac{4-3-2}{4} = \frac{-1}{4}$$

which is not possible. $[\because \cos^2\gamma > 0]$

11 (*c*) The direction cosines are given by

$$l = \frac{a}{\sqrt{a^2+b^2+c^2}},$$
$$m = \frac{b}{\sqrt{a^2+b^2+c^2}}$$

and $n = \dfrac{c}{\sqrt{a^2 + b^2 + c^2}}$

Here, a, b, c are 1, 1, 2 respectively.

Therefore, $l = \dfrac{1}{\sqrt{1^2 + 1^2 + 2^2}}$,

$$m = \frac{1}{\sqrt{1^2 + 1^2 + 2^2}},$$

$$n = \frac{2}{\sqrt{1^2 + 1^2 + 2^2}}$$

i.e. $l = \dfrac{1}{\sqrt{6}}, m = \dfrac{1}{\sqrt{6}}, n = \dfrac{1}{\sqrt{6}}$

i.e. $\pm\left(\dfrac{1}{\sqrt{6}}, \dfrac{1}{\sqrt{6}}, \dfrac{2}{\sqrt{6}}\right)$ are DC's of the line.

The direction cosines of a line passing through the points $P(x_1, y_1, z_1)$ and $Q(x_2, y_2, z_2)$ are $\dfrac{x_2 - x_1}{PQ}, \dfrac{y_2 - y_1}{PQ}, \dfrac{z_2 - z_1}{PQ}$

Here,

$$PQ = \sqrt{(x_2 - x_1)^2 + (y_2 - y_1)^2 + (z_2 - z_1)^2}$$

$$= \sqrt{(-1-2)^2 + (2-3)^2 + (4-5)^2}$$

$$= \sqrt{9+1+1} = \sqrt{11}$$

Hence, DC's are $\pm\left(\dfrac{-3}{\sqrt{11}}, \dfrac{-1}{\sqrt{11}}, \dfrac{-1}{\sqrt{11}}\right)$.

12 (a) We know that

$$l^2 + m^2 + n^2 = 1$$

$$\Rightarrow \cos^2\alpha + \cos^2\beta + \cos^2\gamma = 1$$

$$\Rightarrow \left(\frac{14}{15}\right)^2 + \left(\frac{1}{3}\right)^2 + \cos^2\gamma = 1$$

$$\Rightarrow \frac{196}{225} + \frac{1}{9} + \cos^2\gamma = 1$$

$$\Rightarrow \cos^2\gamma = 1 - \frac{196}{225} - \frac{1}{9}$$

$$\Rightarrow \cos^2\gamma = \frac{225 - 196 - 25}{225}$$

$$\Rightarrow \cos^2\gamma = \frac{4}{225}$$

$$\therefore \cos\gamma = \pm\frac{2}{15}$$

13 (d) Three points (x_1, y_1, z_1), (x_2, y_2, z_2) and (x_3, y_3, z_3) are collinear if

$$\frac{x_2 - x_1}{x_3 - x_1} = \frac{y_2 - y_1}{y_3 - y_2} = \frac{z_2 - z_1}{z_3 - z_2}$$

$$\Rightarrow \frac{-4-(-1)}{5-(-4)} = \frac{2-3}{5-2} = \frac{-2-2}{\lambda+2}$$

$$\Rightarrow \frac{-3}{9} = \frac{-1}{3} = \frac{-4}{\lambda+2}$$

$$\Rightarrow \frac{-1}{3} = \frac{-4}{\lambda+2}$$

$$\Rightarrow \lambda + 2 = 12 \Rightarrow \lambda = 10$$

14 (c) I. We have, $x_1 = 1, y_1 = 2, z_1 = 3$

$$x_2 = -2, y_2 = 3, z_2 = 4$$

$$x_3 = 7, y_3 = 0, z_3 = 1$$

$$\Rightarrow \frac{x_2 - x_1}{x_3 - x_2} = \frac{y_2 - y_1}{y_3 - y_2} = \frac{z_2 - z_1}{z_3 - z_2}$$

$$\Rightarrow \frac{-2-1}{7-(-2)} = \frac{3-2}{0-3} = \frac{4-3}{1-4}$$

$$\Rightarrow \frac{-3}{9} = \frac{1}{-3} = \frac{1}{-3}$$

$$\Rightarrow \frac{-1}{3} = \frac{-1}{3} = \frac{-1}{3}$$

$\therefore$ Given points are collinear.

II. $l = \cos\dfrac{\pi}{2} = 0$

$$m = \cos\frac{3\pi}{4} = \cos\left(\pi - \frac{\pi}{4}\right)$$

$$= -\cos\frac{\pi}{4} = \frac{-1}{\sqrt{2}}$$

$$n = \cos\frac{\pi}{4} = \frac{1}{\sqrt{2}}$$

$\therefore$ Direction cosines are $0, \dfrac{-1}{\sqrt{2}}, \dfrac{1}{\sqrt{2}}$.

15 (b) $\cos^2\alpha + \cos^2\beta + \cos^2\gamma = 1$

$$\Rightarrow \cos^2\alpha + \cos^2(90° - \alpha) + \cos^2\gamma = 1$$

$$[\because \alpha + \beta = 90° \Rightarrow \beta = 90° - \alpha]$$

$$\Rightarrow \cos^2\alpha + \sin^2\alpha + \cos^2\gamma = 1$$

$$\Rightarrow 1 + \cos^2\gamma = 1$$

$$\Rightarrow \cos^2\gamma = 0$$

$$\Rightarrow \cos\gamma = 0$$

$$\therefore \gamma = \frac{\pi}{2} = 90°$$

16 (b) $\cos 2\alpha + \cos 2\beta + \cos 2\gamma$

$$= (2\cos^2\alpha - 1) + (2\cos^2\beta - 1) + (2\cos^2\gamma - 1)$$

$$= 2(\cos^2\alpha + \cos^2\beta + \cos^2\gamma) - 3$$

$$= 2 - 3 \quad [\because \cos^2\alpha + \cos^2\beta + \cos^2\gamma = 1]$$

$$= -1$$

17 (b) Let the coordinate of P be (x_1, y_1, z_1)

$\therefore$ Direction ratios of OP are $(x_1 - 0, y_1 - 0, z_1 - 0)$ *i.e.*, (x_1, y_1, z_1).

Hence, coordinates of P are $(-1, 2, -2)$.

Equation of a Line in Space

1 (b) A line is uniquely determined, if

(i) it passes through a given point and has given direction or

(ii) it passes through two given points.

2 (c)

I. Let **a** and **b** be the position vectors of two points $A(x_1, y_1, z_1)$ and $B(x_2, y_2, z_2)$, respectively that are lying on a line

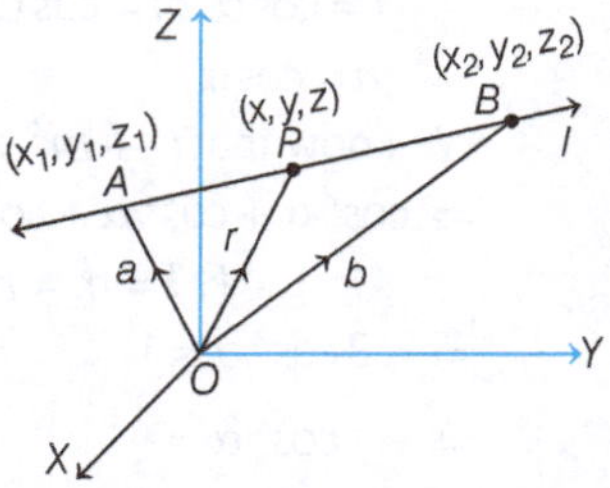

Let **r** be the position vector of an arbitrary point $P(x, y, z)$, then P is a point on the line if and only if $\mathbf{AP} = \mathbf{r} - \mathbf{a}$ and $\mathbf{AB} = \mathbf{b} - \mathbf{a}$ are collinear vectors. Therefore, P is on the line if and only if

$$\mathbf{r} - \mathbf{a} = \lambda(\mathbf{b} - \mathbf{a})$$

or $\mathbf{r} = \mathbf{a} + \lambda(\mathbf{b} - \mathbf{a}), \lambda \in R$ ...(i)

This is the vector equation of the line.

II. We have,

$$\mathbf{r} = x\,\hat{\mathbf{i}} + y\,\hat{\mathbf{j}} + z\,\hat{\mathbf{k}}$$

$$\mathbf{a} = x_1\,\hat{\mathbf{i}} + y_1\,\hat{\mathbf{j}} + z_1\,\hat{\mathbf{k}}$$

and $\mathbf{b} = x_2\,\hat{\mathbf{i}} + y_2\,\hat{\mathbf{j}} + z_2\,\hat{\mathbf{k}}$

On substituting these values in Eq. (i), we get

$$x\hat{i} + y\hat{j} + z\hat{k} = x_1\hat{i} + y_1\hat{j} + z_1\hat{k} + \lambda[(x_2 - x_1)\hat{i} + (y_2 - y_1)\hat{j} + (z_2 - z_1)\hat{k}]$$

Equating the like coefficients of $\hat{i}$, $\hat{j}$ and $\hat{k}$, we get

$$x = x_1 + \lambda(x_2 - x_1)$$
$$y = y_1 + \lambda(y_2 - y_1)$$
$$z = z_1 + \lambda(z_2 - z_1)$$

On eliminating λ, we obtain

$$\frac{x - x_1}{x_2 - x_1} = \frac{y - y_1}{y_2 - y_1} = \frac{z - z_1}{z_2 - z_1} \quad \text{...(ii)}$$

which is the equation of the line in cartesian form.

3 (*a*) If l, m, n are the direction cosines of the line, the equation of the line which passes through (x_1, y_1, z_1) is

$$\frac{x - x_1}{l} = \frac{y - y_1}{m} = \frac{z - z_1}{n} \quad \left[\because \frac{a}{l} = \frac{b}{m} = \frac{c}{n}\right]$$

4 (*c*) We have,

$$\mathbf{a} = 5\hat{i} + 2\hat{j} - 4\hat{k}$$
and $$\mathbf{b} = 3\hat{i} + 2\hat{j} - 8\hat{k}$$

Therefore, the vector equation of the line is

$$\mathbf{r} = 5\hat{i} + 2\hat{j} - 4\hat{k} + \lambda(3\hat{i} + 2\hat{j} - 8\hat{k})$$

Now, $\mathbf{r}$ is the position vector of any point $P(x, y, z)$ on the line.

Therefore, $x\hat{i} + y\hat{j} + z\hat{k}$

$$= 5\hat{i} + 2\hat{j} - 4\hat{k} + \lambda(3\hat{i} + 2\hat{j} - 8\hat{k})$$
$$= (5 + 3\lambda)\hat{i} + (2 + 2\lambda)\hat{j} + (-4 - 8\lambda)\hat{k}$$

Eliminating λ, we get

$$\frac{x - 5}{3} = \frac{y - 2}{2} = \frac{z + 4}{-8}$$

which is the equation of the line in cartesian form.

5 (*d*) It is given that the line passes through the point with position vector $\mathbf{a} = 2\hat{i} - \hat{j} + 4\hat{k}$ and $\mathbf{b} = \hat{i} + 2\hat{j} - \hat{k}$.

It is known that a line through a point with position vector **a** and parallel to **b** i.e. in direction of **b** is given by the equation, $\mathbf{r} = \mathbf{a} + \lambda\mathbf{b}$.

$$\therefore \mathbf{r} = 2\hat{i} - \hat{j} + 4\hat{k} + \lambda(\hat{i} + 2\hat{j} - \hat{k})$$

This is the required equation of the line in vector form.

Let $\mathbf{r} = x\hat{i} + y\hat{j} + z\hat{k}$

$$\therefore x\hat{i} + y\hat{j} + z\hat{k} = (\lambda + 2)\hat{i} + (2\lambda - 1)\hat{j} + (-\lambda + 4)\hat{k}$$

Eliminating λ, we obtain the cartesian form equation as

$$\frac{x - 2}{1} = \frac{y + 1}{2} = \frac{z - 4}{-1}$$

This is the required equation of the given line in cartesian form.

6 (*d*) I. It is given that the line passes through the point $(-2, 4, -5)$ and is parallel to

$$\frac{x + 3}{3} = \frac{y - 4}{5} = \frac{z + 8}{6}$$

The direction ratios of the line $\frac{x + 3}{3} = \frac{y - 4}{5} = \frac{z + 8}{6}$ are (3, 5, 6).

The required line is parallel to $\frac{x + 3}{3} = \frac{y - 4}{5} = \frac{z + 8}{6}$.

It is known that the equation of the line passes through the point (x_1, y_1, z_1) and with direction ratios a, b, c is given by

$$\frac{x - x_1}{a} = \frac{y - y_1}{b} = \frac{z - z_1}{c}$$

Also, the line passes through $(-2, 4, -5)$ and having direction ratios (3, 5, 6). Therefore, the equation of the line (in cartesian form) is

$$\frac{x - (-2)}{3} = \frac{y - 4}{5} = \frac{z - (-5)}{6}$$
$$\Rightarrow \frac{x + 2}{3} = \frac{y - 4}{5} = \frac{z + 5}{6}$$

which is the equation of required line.

II. The given cartesian equation is

$$\frac{x - 5}{3} = \frac{y + 4}{7} = \frac{z - 6}{2}.$$

The above line passes through the point $(5, -4, 6)$. The position vector of this point is $\mathbf{a} = 5\hat{i} - 4\hat{j} + 6\hat{k}$.

Also, the direction ratios of the given line are 3, 7 and 2. This means that the line is in the direction of vector, $\mathbf{b} = 3\hat{i} + 7\hat{j} + 2\hat{k}$.

It is known that the line through position vector **a** and in the direction of the vector **b** is given by the equation, $\mathbf{r} = \mathbf{a} + \lambda\mathbf{b}, \lambda \in R$.

$$\therefore \mathbf{r} = 5\hat{i} - 4\hat{j} + 6\hat{k} + \lambda(3\hat{i} + 7\hat{j} + 2\hat{k})$$

This is the required equation of the given line in vector form.

7 (*c*) Let **a** and **b** be the position vectors of points (0, 0, 0) and $(5, -2, 3)$, respectively.

$$\therefore \mathbf{a} = 0\hat{i} + 0\hat{j} + 0\hat{k}$$
and $$\mathbf{b} = 5\hat{i} - 2\hat{j} + 3\hat{k}$$

We know that, the vector equation of a line passing through the points having position vectors **a** and **b** is $\mathbf{r} = \mathbf{a} + \lambda(\mathbf{b} - \mathbf{a})$.

$$\therefore \mathbf{r} = 0 + \lambda(5\hat{i} - 2\hat{j} + 3\hat{k} - 0)$$
$$\Rightarrow \mathbf{r} = \lambda(5\hat{i} - 2\hat{j} + 3\hat{k}) \quad \text{...(i)}$$

(which is vector equation)

Putting $\mathbf{r} = x\hat{i} + y\hat{j} + z\hat{k}$ in Eq. (i), we have

$$x\hat{i} + y\hat{j} + z\hat{k} = \lambda(5\hat{i} - 2\hat{j} + 3\hat{k})$$
$$\Rightarrow x\hat{i} + y\hat{j} + z\hat{k} = 5\lambda\hat{i} - 2\lambda\hat{j} + 3\lambda\hat{k}$$

Comparing coefficient of $\hat{i}$, $\hat{j}$ and $\hat{k}$ on both sides, we have

$$x = 5\lambda, y = -2\lambda \text{ and } z = 3\lambda$$

$$\therefore \frac{x}{5} = \frac{y}{-2} = \frac{z}{3} = \lambda$$

which is cartesian form of required line.

8 (*d*) Let **a** and **b** be the position vectors of points $(3, -2, -5)$ and $(3, -2, 6)$, respectively.

$$\therefore \mathbf{a} = 3\hat{i} - 2\hat{j} - 5\hat{k}$$
and $$\mathbf{b} = 3\hat{i} - 2\hat{j} + 6\hat{k}$$

We know that the vector equation of a line passing through the points having position vectors **a** and **b** is $\mathbf{r} = \mathbf{a} + \lambda(\mathbf{b} - \mathbf{a})$

$\therefore\ \mathbf{r} = 3\hat{i} - 2\hat{j} - 5\hat{k} + \lambda[(3\hat{i} - 2\hat{j} + 6\hat{k}) - (3\hat{i} - 2\hat{j} - 5\hat{k})]$

$\Rightarrow \mathbf{r} = 3\hat{i} - 2\hat{j} - 5\hat{k} + \lambda[3\hat{i} - 2\hat{j} + 6\hat{k} - 3\hat{i} + 2\hat{j} + 5\hat{k}]$

$\Rightarrow \mathbf{r} = 3\hat{i} - 2\hat{j} - 5\hat{k} + \lambda(11\hat{k})$ ...(i)

[which is vector equation]

Putting $\mathbf{r} = x\hat{i} + y\hat{j} + z\hat{k}$, in Eq. (i), we have

$x\hat{i} + y\hat{j} + z\hat{k} = 3\hat{i} - 2\hat{j} + (11\lambda - 5)\hat{k}$

Comparing coefficients of $\hat{i}$, $\hat{j}$ and $\hat{k}$ on both sides, we have

$x = 3,\ y = -2$

and $z = 11\lambda - 5$

$\therefore\ \dfrac{x-3}{0} = \dfrac{y+2}{0} = \dfrac{z+5}{11}$ $\left[\because \text{here}, \dfrac{x-3}{0} \neq \infty \text{ and } \dfrac{y+2}{0} \neq \infty\right]$

which is the cartesian form of required line.

9 (*a*) We have,

$\dfrac{x-4}{5} = \dfrac{y-1}{2} = \dfrac{z}{1} = \lambda$ (let)

$\Rightarrow x = 5\lambda + 4,\ y = 2\lambda + 1,\ z = \lambda$

So, the coordinates of any point on this line are $(5\lambda + 4, 2\lambda + 1, \lambda)$

Equation of second line

$\dfrac{x-1}{2} = \dfrac{y-2}{3} = \dfrac{z-3}{4} = \mu$ (let)

$\Rightarrow\ x = 2\mu + 1,\ y = 3\mu + 2,$

$z = 4\mu + 3$

So, the coordinates of any point on this line are $(2\mu + 1, 3\mu + 2, 4\mu + 3)$.

If the lines intersect, then they have a common point.

So, $5\lambda + 4 = 2\mu + 1$ ...(i)

$2\lambda + 1 = 3\mu + 2$ ...(ii)

$\lambda = 4\mu + 3$ ...(iii)

On solving Eqs. (ii) and (iii), we get

$\lambda = -1,\ \mu = -1$

Since, $\lambda = -1,\ \mu = -1$ satisfy Eq. (i). So, the given line intersect.

Substituting $\lambda = -1$ in $(5\lambda + 4, 2\lambda + 1, \lambda)$, we get the point of intersection $(-1, -1, -1)$.

10 (*b*) Since, line equally inclined with the axes.

$\therefore\ l = m = n$ ...(i)

The required equation of line is

$\dfrac{x-x_1}{l} = \dfrac{y-y_1}{m} = \dfrac{z-z_1}{n}$

$\dfrac{x+3}{l} = \dfrac{y-2}{l} = \dfrac{z+4}{l}$ [by Eq. (i)]

$\Rightarrow \dfrac{x+3}{1} = \dfrac{y-2}{1} = \dfrac{z+4}{1}$

$\Rightarrow x + 3 = y - 2 = z + 4$

11 (*c*) Let *a*, *b*, *c* be the DR's of required line

$\therefore\ 3a + 2b + c = 0$

and $a + b - 2c = 0$

$\Rightarrow \dfrac{a}{\begin{vmatrix} 2 & 1 \\ 1 & -2 \end{vmatrix}} = \dfrac{b}{\begin{vmatrix} 1 & 3 \\ -2 & 1 \end{vmatrix}} = \dfrac{c}{\begin{vmatrix} 3 & 2 \\ 1 & 1 \end{vmatrix}}$

$\Rightarrow \dfrac{a}{-4-1} = \dfrac{b}{1-(-6)} = \dfrac{c}{3-2}$

$\Rightarrow \dfrac{a}{-5} = \dfrac{b}{7} = \dfrac{c}{1}$

Now, we have to find a point on the line for this put $z = 0$ in given equations, we get

$3x + 2y = 5$

and $x + y = 3$

Solving these two equations, we get

$x = -1,\ y = 4$

$\therefore$ Coordinate of point on the line are $(-1, 4, 0)$.

Hence, the required equation of line is $\dfrac{x+1}{-5} = \dfrac{y-4}{7} = \dfrac{z-0}{1}$

12 (*d*) The equation of line passing through (*a*, *b*, *c*) is

$\dfrac{x-a}{l} = \dfrac{y-b}{m} = \dfrac{z-c}{n} = \lambda$ (let)...(i)

Since, the line is parallel to *Z*-axis, therefore any point on this line will be of the form (a, b, z_1).

Now, from Eq. (i) any point on the line is $(\lambda l + a, \lambda m + b, \lambda n + c)$

$\therefore\ \lambda l + a = a \Rightarrow l = 0, \lambda = 0$

$\Rightarrow \lambda m + b = b \Rightarrow m = 0, \lambda = 0$

$\Rightarrow \lambda n + c = z_1 \Rightarrow z_1 = c$ $[\because \lambda = 0]$

$\Rightarrow\ l^2 + m^2 + n^2 = 1$

$\Rightarrow\ 0 + 0 + n^2 = 1$

$\Rightarrow\ n = 1$

Hence, the equation of line is

$\dfrac{x-a}{0} = \dfrac{y-b}{0} = \dfrac{z-c}{1}$

13 (*a*) Given lines are

$\dfrac{x-8}{3} = \dfrac{y+19}{-16} = \dfrac{z-10}{7}$ ...(i)

and $\dfrac{x-15}{3} = \dfrac{y-29}{8} = \dfrac{z-5}{-5}$ ...(ii)

Both lines are in the form

$\dfrac{x-x_1}{a} = \dfrac{y-y_1}{b} = \dfrac{z-z_1}{c}$

$\therefore\ a_1 = 3,\ b_1 = -16,\ c_1 = 7$

$a_2 = 3,\ b_2 = 8,\ c_2 = -5$

Now, $\mathbf{b}_1 = a_1\hat{i} + b_1\hat{j} + c_1\hat{k}$

$= 3\hat{i} - 16\hat{j} + 7\hat{k}$

and $\mathbf{b}_2 = a_2\hat{i} + b_2\hat{j} + c_2\hat{k}$

$= 3\hat{i} + 8\hat{j} - 5\hat{k}$

The vector perpendicular to both Eqs. (i) and (ii) is given by

$\mathbf{b} = \mathbf{b}_1 \times \mathbf{b}_2$

$= \begin{vmatrix} \hat{i} & \hat{j} & \hat{k} \\ 3 & -16 & 7 \\ 3 & 8 & -5 \end{vmatrix}$

$= \hat{i}(80 - 56) - \hat{j}(-15 - 21) + \hat{k}(24 + 48)$

$\mathbf{b}_1 \times \mathbf{b}_2 = 24\hat{i} + 36\hat{j} + 72\hat{k}$

Hence, the required equation of line is

$\dfrac{x-1}{24} = \dfrac{y-2}{36} = \dfrac{z+4}{72}$

i.e. $\dfrac{x-1}{2} = \dfrac{y-2}{3} = \dfrac{z+4}{6}$

14 (*b*) Given equation of line is

$$\frac{x+2}{3}=\frac{y+1}{2}=\frac{z-3}{2}=\lambda \quad \text{(let)}$$

$$\Rightarrow \quad x=3\lambda-2,$$

$$y=2\lambda-1,\; z=2\lambda+3 \quad \text{...(i)}$$

∴ Coordinates of any point on the line are $(3\lambda-2, 2\lambda-1, 2\lambda+3)$

The distance between this point and (1, 2, 3) is $\frac{6}{\sqrt{2}}$

$$\therefore \sqrt{(3\lambda-2-1)^2+(2\lambda-1-2)^2+(2\lambda+3-3)^2}=\frac{6}{\sqrt{2}}$$

$$\Rightarrow (3\lambda-3)^2+(2\lambda-3)^2+(2\lambda)^2=\frac{36}{2}$$

[squaring on both sides]

$$\Rightarrow 9\lambda^2+9-18\lambda+4\lambda^2+9-12\lambda+4\lambda^2=18$$

$$\Rightarrow \quad 17\lambda^2-30\lambda=0$$

$$\Rightarrow \quad \lambda(17\lambda-30)=0 \Rightarrow \lambda=0, \frac{30}{17}$$

Substituting the values of λ in Eq. (i) we get the required point

$$(-2,-1,3) \text{ or } \left(\frac{56}{17}, \frac{43}{17}, \frac{111}{17}\right).$$

Angle between Two Lines

1 (*a*) Let L_1 and L_2 be two lines passing through the origin and with direction ratios a_1, b_1, c_1 and a_2, b_2, c_2, respectively. Let *P* be a point on L_1 and Q be a point on L_2. Consider the directed lines *OP* and *OQ* as given in figure. Let θ be the acute angle between *OP* and *OQ*. Now, recall that the directed line segments *OP* and *OQ* are vectors with components a_1, b_1, c_1 and a_2, b_2, c_2, respectively. Therefore, the angle θ between them is given by

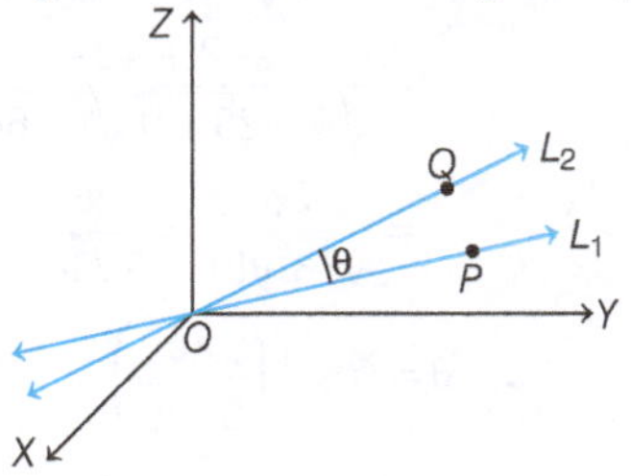

$$\cos\theta=\left|\frac{a_1a_2+b_1b_2+c_1c_2}{\sqrt{a_1^2+b_1^2+c_1^2}\sqrt{a_2^2+b_2^2+c_2^2}}\right| \quad \text{...(i)}$$

The angle between the lines in terms of sin θ is given by

$$\sin\theta=\sqrt{1-\cos^2\theta}$$

$$=\sqrt{1-\frac{(a_1a_2+b_1b_2+c_1c_2)^2}{(a_1^2+b_1^2+c_1^2)(a_2^2+b_2^2+c_2^2)}}$$

$$=\frac{\sqrt{(a_1^2+b_1^2+c_1^2)(a_2^2+b_2^2+c_2^2)-(a_1a_2+b_1b_2+c_1c_2)^2}}{\sqrt{(a_1^2+b_1^2+c_1^2)}\sqrt{(a_2^2+b_2^2+c_2^2)}}$$

$$=\frac{\sqrt{(a_1b_2-a_2b_1)^2+(b_1c_2-b_2c_1)^2+(c_1a_2-c_2a_1)^2}}{\sqrt{a_1^2+b_1^2+c_1^2}\sqrt{a_2^2+b_2^2+c_2^2}} \quad \text{...(ii)}$$

Note *In case, the lines L_1 and L_2 do not pass through the origin, we may take lines L'_1 and L'_2 which are parallel to L_1 and L_2 respectively and pass through the origin.*

2 (*c*) If instead of direction ratios for the lines L_1 and L_2 direction cosines, namely, l_1, m_1, n_1 for L_1 and l_2, m_2, n_2 for L_2 are given, then Eqs. (i) and (ii) in above takes the following form

$$\cos\theta=|l_1l_2+m_1m_2+n_1n_2|$$

$$[\because l_1^2+m_1^2+n_1^2=l_2^2+m_2^2+n_2^2=1]$$

$$\text{and } \sin\theta=\sqrt{(l_1m_2-l_2m_1)^2+(m_1n_2-m_2n_1)^2+(n_1l_2-n_2l_1)^2}$$

3 (*b*) We find the angle between two lines when their equations are given. If θ is the acute angle between the lines

$\mathbf{r}=\mathbf{a}_1+\lambda\mathbf{b}_1$ and $\mathbf{r}=\mathbf{a}_2+\mu\mathbf{b}_2$,

then $\cos\theta=\left|\frac{\mathbf{b}_1\cdot\mathbf{b}_2}{|\mathbf{b}_1|\,|\mathbf{b}_2|}\right|$

4 (*c*) In cartesian form, if θ is the angle between the lines

$$\frac{x-x_1}{a_1}=\frac{y-y_1}{b_1}=\frac{z-z_1}{c_1} \quad \text{...(i)}$$

$$\text{an} \quad \frac{x-x_2}{a_2}=\frac{y-y_2}{b_2}=\frac{z-z_2}{c_2} \quad \text{...(ii)}$$

Where, a_1, b_1, c_1 and a_2, b_2, c_2, are the direction ratios of the lines (i) and (ii), respectively, then

$$\cos\theta=\left|\frac{a_1a_2+b_1b_2+c_1c_2}{\sqrt{a_1^2+b_1^2+c_1^2}\sqrt{a_2^2+b_2^2+c_2^2}}\right|$$

5 (*b*) The equations of the given lines are $\frac{x-5}{7}=\frac{y+2}{-5}=\frac{z}{1}$ and $\frac{x}{1}=\frac{y}{2}=\frac{z}{3}$.

Direction ratios of the given lines are respectively 7, −5, 1 and 1, 2, 3.

$$\therefore a_1a_2+b_1b_2+c_1c_2$$

$$=(7)(1)+(-5)(2)+(1)(3)$$

$$=7-10+3=0$$

Therefore, the given lines are perpendicular.

6 (*c*)

I. For first two lines with direction cosines $\frac{12}{13}, \frac{-3}{13}, \frac{-4}{13}$ and $\frac{4}{13}, \frac{12}{13}, \frac{3}{13}$, we obtain

$$l_1l_2+m_1m_2+n_1n_2=\frac{12}{13}\times\frac{4}{13}+\left(\frac{-3}{13}\right)\times\frac{12}{13}+\left(\frac{-4}{13}\right)\times\frac{3}{13}$$

$$=\frac{48}{169}-\frac{36}{169}-\frac{12}{169}=0$$

Therefore, the lines are perpendicular.

For second and third lines with direction cosines $\frac{4}{13}, \frac{12}{13}, \frac{3}{13}$ and $\frac{3}{13}, \frac{-4}{13}, \frac{12}{13}$, we obtain

$$l_1l_2+m_1m_2+n_1n_2=\frac{4}{13}\times\frac{3}{13}+\frac{12}{13}\times\left(\frac{-4}{13}\right)+\frac{3}{13}\times\frac{12}{13}$$

$$= \frac{12}{169} - \frac{48}{169} + \frac{36}{169} = 0$$

Therefore, the lines are perpendicular.

For third and first lines with directions cosines $\frac{3}{13}, \frac{-4}{13}, \frac{12}{13}$ and $\frac{12}{13}, \frac{-3}{13}, \frac{-4}{13}$, we obtain

$$l_1l_2 + m_1m_2 + n_1n_2 = \frac{3}{13} \times \frac{12}{13} + \left(\frac{-4}{13}\right) \times \left(\frac{-3}{13}\right) + \frac{12}{13} \times \left(\frac{-4}{13}\right)$$

$$= \frac{36}{169} + \frac{12}{169} - \frac{48}{169}$$

$$= \frac{36}{169} - \frac{36}{169} = 0$$

Therefore, the lines are perpendicular.

Hence, all the lines are mutually perpendicular.

II. The given points are $A(1, -1, 2)$, $B(3, 4, -2)$, $C(0, 3, 2)$ and $D(3, 5, 6)$ direction ratios of AB are

$(3 - 1, 4 - (-1), -2 - 2)$

$= (2, 4 + 1, -4) = (2, 5, -4)$

and direction ratios of CD are $(3 - 0, 5 - 3, 6 - 2)$ or $(3, 2, 4)$

We know that, two lines AB and CD with direction ratios, a_1, b_1, c_1 and a_2, b_2, c_2 are perpendicular, if $a_1a_2 + b_1b_2 + c_1c_2 = 0$

$$= 2 \times 3 + 5 \times 2 + (-4) \times 4$$

$$= 6 + 10 - 16 = 0$$

Therefore, the lines AB and CD are at right angles.

7 (a) Let the given points be $A(4, 7, 8)$, $B(2, 3, 4)$, $C(-1, -2, 1)$ and $D(1, 2, 5)$.

Direction ratios of AB (a_1, b_1, c_1) are $(2 - 4), (3 - 7), (4 - 8)$

i.e. $(-2, -4, -4)$

$\therefore \quad a_1 = -2, b_1 = -4, c_1 = -4$

Direction ratios of CD (a_2, b_2, c_2) are $(1 + 1), (2 + 2), (5 - 1)$ i.e. $(2, 4, 4)$

$\therefore \quad a_2 = 2, b_2 = 4, c_2 = 4$

We have,

$$\frac{a_1}{a_2} = \frac{-2}{2} = -1, \frac{b_1}{b_2} = \frac{-4}{4} = -1$$

and $\frac{c_1}{c_2} = \frac{-4}{4} = -1$

$$\therefore \quad \frac{a_1}{a_2} = \frac{b_1}{b_2} = \frac{c_1}{c_2}$$

[$\because$ two lines with DR's (a_1, b_1, c_1) and (a_2, b_2, c_2) are parallel, if $\frac{a_1}{a_2} = \frac{b_1}{b_2} = \frac{c_1}{c_2}$]

Thus, $AB \parallel CD$

Hence, angle between the line is 0.

8 (b) A. Let θ be the acute angle between the given lines, then

$$\cos\theta = \left|\frac{\mathbf{b}_1 \cdot \mathbf{b}_2}{|\mathbf{b}_1|\,|\mathbf{b}_2|}\right|$$

The given lines are respectively parallel to the vectors

$$\mathbf{b}_1 = 3\hat{\mathbf{i}} + 2\hat{\mathbf{j}} + 6\hat{\mathbf{k}}$$

and $\mathbf{b}_2 = \hat{\mathbf{i}} + 2\hat{\mathbf{j}} + 2\hat{\mathbf{k}}$

$$\therefore \quad |\mathbf{b}_1| = \sqrt{(3^2 + 2^2 + 6^2)} = \sqrt{9 + 4 + 36} = \sqrt{49} = 7$$

$$|\mathbf{b}_2| = \sqrt{(1^2 + 2^2 + 2^2)} = \sqrt{1 + 4 + 4} = \sqrt{9} = 3$$

and $\mathbf{b}_1 \cdot \mathbf{b}_2 = (3\hat{\mathbf{i}} + 2\hat{\mathbf{j}} + 6\hat{\mathbf{k}}) \cdot (\hat{\mathbf{i}} + 2\hat{\mathbf{j}} + 2\hat{\mathbf{k}})$

$$= 3 \times 1 + 2 \times 2 + 6 \times 2$$

$$= 3 + 4 + 12 = 19$$

$$\therefore \cos\theta = \left|\frac{\mathbf{b}_1 \cdot \mathbf{b}_2}{|\mathbf{b}_1|\,|\mathbf{b}_2|}\right| = \frac{19}{7 \times 3}$$

$$= \frac{19}{21} \Rightarrow \cos^{-1}\left(\frac{19}{21}\right)$$

B. Let θ be the acute angle between the given lines, then

$$\cos\theta = \left|\frac{\mathbf{b}_1 \cdot \mathbf{b}_2}{|\mathbf{b}_1|\,|\mathbf{b}_2|}\right|$$

The given lines are respectively parallel to the vectors

$$\mathbf{b}_1 = \hat{\mathbf{i}} - \hat{\mathbf{j}} - 2\hat{\mathbf{k}}$$

and $\mathbf{b}_2 = 3\hat{\mathbf{i}} - 5\hat{\mathbf{j}} - 4\hat{\mathbf{k}}$

$$|\mathbf{b}_1| = \sqrt{(1)^2 + (-1)^2 + (-2)^2} = \sqrt{1 + 1 + 4} = \sqrt{6}$$

$$|\mathbf{b}_2| = \sqrt{(3)^2 + (-5)^2 + (-4)^2} = \sqrt{9 + 25 + 16} = \sqrt{50} = 5\sqrt{2}$$

and $\mathbf{b}_1 \cdot \mathbf{b}_2 = (\hat{\mathbf{i}} - \hat{\mathbf{j}} - 2\hat{\mathbf{k}}) \cdot (3\hat{\mathbf{i}} - 5\hat{\mathbf{j}} - 4\hat{\mathbf{k}})$

$$= 1 \times 3 - 1 \times (-5) - 2 \times (-4)$$

$$= 3 + 5 + 8 = 16$$

$$\therefore \cos\theta = \left|\frac{\mathbf{b}_1 \cdot \mathbf{b}_2}{|\mathbf{b}_1|\,|\mathbf{b}_2|}\right| = \frac{16}{\sqrt{6} \times 5\sqrt{2}} = \frac{16}{10\sqrt{3}} = \frac{8}{5\sqrt{3}}$$

$$\therefore \quad \theta = \cos^{-1}\left(\frac{8}{5\sqrt{3}}\right)$$

C. Here, the equation of given lines are

$$\frac{x - 2}{2} = \frac{y - 1}{5} = \frac{z + 3}{-3}$$

and $\frac{x + 2}{-1} = \frac{y - 4}{8} = \frac{z - 5}{4}$

[$\because$ if $\frac{x - x_1}{a_1} = \frac{y - y_1}{b_1} = \frac{z - z_1}{c_1}$ be a line, then its DR' are (a_1, b_1, c_1)]

$\therefore$ Direction ratios of two lines are $(2, 5, -3)$ and $(-1, 8, 4)$.

Let θ be the acute angle between the given lines.

Then,

$$\cos\theta = \frac{a_1a_2 + b_1b_2 + c_1c_2}{\sqrt{a_1^2 + b_1^2 + c_1^2}\sqrt{a_2^2 + b_2^2 + c_2^2}}$$

$$\Rightarrow \cos\theta = \frac{2 \times (-1) + 5 \times 8 + (-3) \times 4}{\sqrt{2^2 + 5^2 + (-3)^2}\sqrt{(-1)^2 + 8^2 + 4^2}}$$

$$= \frac{-2 + 40 - 12}{\sqrt{4 + 25 + 9}\sqrt{1 + 64 + 16}}$$

$$= \frac{26}{\sqrt{38}\sqrt{81}} = \frac{26}{9\sqrt{38}}$$

$$\therefore \quad \theta = \cos^{-1}\left(\frac{26}{9\sqrt{38}}\right)$$

D. Here, the equation of given lines are

$$\frac{x}{2}=\frac{y}{2}=\frac{z}{1}$$

and $\frac{x-5}{4}=\frac{y-2}{1}=\frac{z-3}{8}$

$\therefore$ Direction ratios of two lines are (2, 2, 1) and (4, 1, 8).

Let θ be the acute angle between the given lines. Then,

$$\cos\theta=\frac{a_1a_2+b_1b_2+c_1c_2}{\sqrt{a_1^2+b_1^2+c_1^2}\sqrt{a_2^2+b_2^2+c_2^2}}$$

$$\Rightarrow \cos\theta=\frac{2\times4+2\times1+1\times8}{\sqrt{2^2+2^2+1^2}\sqrt{4^2+1^2+8^2}}$$

$$=\frac{8+2+8}{\sqrt{4+4+1}\sqrt{16+1+64}}$$

$$=\frac{18}{\sqrt{9}\sqrt{81}}=\frac{18}{3\times9}=\frac{2}{3}$$

$$\therefore\ \theta=\cos^{-1}\left(\frac{2}{3}\right)$$

9 (*b*) Equation of the given lines can be written as standard form

$$\frac{x-1}{-3}=\frac{y-2}{\frac{2p}{7}}=\frac{z-3}{2}$$

and $\frac{x-1}{-\frac{3p}{7}}=\frac{y-5}{1}=\frac{z-6}{-5}$

Direction ratios of these lines are respectively $-3, \frac{2p}{7}, 2$ and $\frac{-3p}{7}, 1, -5$.

Two lines with direction ratios a_1, b_1, c_1 and a_2, b_2, c_2 are perpendicular to each other, if $a_1a_2+b_1b_2+c_1c_2=0$.

$$\therefore\ (-3)\left(\frac{-3p}{7}\right)+\left(\frac{2p}{7}\right)(1)+(2)(-5)=0$$

$$\Rightarrow \frac{9p}{7}+\frac{2p}{7}-10=0$$

$$\Rightarrow \frac{11p}{7}=10 \Rightarrow p=\frac{70}{11}.$$

Thus, the value of p is $\frac{70}{11}$.

Note *For making a line in standard form, we ensure that coefficient of variable should be non-negative and coefficient of variable should be 1.*

10 (*d*) I. $\mathbf{AB}=\mathbf{OB}-\mathbf{OA}$

$$=(4\hat{\mathbf{i}}+5\hat{\mathbf{j}}+7\hat{\mathbf{k}})-(\hat{\mathbf{i}}+2\hat{\mathbf{j}}+3\hat{\mathbf{k}})$$

$$=3\hat{\mathbf{i}}+3\hat{\mathbf{j}}+4\hat{\mathbf{k}}$$

$\mathbf{CD}=\mathbf{OD}-\mathbf{OC}$

$$=(2\hat{\mathbf{i}}+9\hat{\mathbf{j}}+2\hat{\mathbf{k}})-(-4\hat{\mathbf{i}}+3\hat{\mathbf{j}}-6\hat{\mathbf{k}})$$

$$=6\hat{\mathbf{i}}+6\hat{\mathbf{j}}+8\hat{\mathbf{k}}$$

$$\because\ \cos\theta=\left|\frac{\mathbf{AB}\cdot\mathbf{CD}}{|\mathbf{AB}||\mathbf{CD}|}\right|$$

$$\cos\theta=\left|\frac{(3\hat{\mathbf{i}}+3\hat{\mathbf{j}}+4\hat{\mathbf{k}})\cdot(6\hat{\mathbf{i}}+6\hat{\mathbf{j}}+8\hat{\mathbf{k}})}{\sqrt{3^2+3^2+4^2}\sqrt{6^2+6^2+8^2}}\right|$$

$$=\left|\frac{18+18+32}{\sqrt{34}\sqrt{136}}\right|$$

$$=\left|\frac{68}{2\times34}\right|=1$$

$$\therefore\ \theta=\cos^{-1}1=0$$

Hence, statement I is false.

II. Given $a_1=1, b_1=2, c_1=3$

$a_2=2, b_2=2, c_2=-2$

$\frac{a_1}{a_2}=\frac{1}{2}, \frac{b_1}{b_2}=\frac{2}{2}$

$\because\ \frac{a_1}{a_2}\neq\frac{b_1}{b_2}$

Hence, given lines are not parallel.

Therefore, statement II is false.

11 (*b*) Given, $l+m+n=0$ ...(i)

$2lm+2nl-mn=0$ ...(ii)

$m=-l-n$ [from Eq.(i)]

On substituting the value of m in Eq. (ii), we get

$$2l(-l-n)+2nl-(-l-n)n=0$$

$$\Rightarrow -2l^2-2ln+2nl+ln+n^2=0$$

$$\Rightarrow n^2+ln-2l^2=0$$

$$\Rightarrow n^2+2ln-ln-2l^2=0$$

$$\Rightarrow n(n+2l)-l(n+2l)=0$$

$$\Rightarrow (n+2l)(n-l)=0$$

$$\therefore\ n=l, n=-2l$$

When $n=l, m=-2l$

When, $n=-2l, m=l$

Therefore, direction ratios of two lines are

1, 1, –2 and 1, –2, 1

$$\text{Now, }\cos\theta=\frac{a_1a_2+b_1b_2+c_1c_2}{\sqrt{a_1^2+b_1^2+c_1^2}\sqrt{a_2^2+b_2^2+c_2^2}}$$

$$=\frac{1-2-2}{\sqrt{1^2+1^2+(-2)^2}\sqrt{1^2+(-2)^2+1^2}}$$

$$=\frac{-3}{\sqrt{6}\sqrt{6}}$$

$$=\frac{-3}{6}=\frac{-1}{2}$$

$$\therefore\ \theta=\cos^{-1}\left(-\frac{1}{2}\right)=\pi-\cos^{-1}\left(\frac{1}{2}\right)$$

$$=\pi-\frac{\pi}{3}=\frac{2\pi}{3}$$

12 (*a*) Since, the foot of the perpendicular lie on X-axis. So, it is of the form $(a, 0, 0)$. The coordinates of the point where the perpendicular has to be drawn are (2, 5, 7).

$$\therefore\ a=2$$

Hence, the required point is (2, 0, 0).

13 (*b*) Given lines are

$$x=py+q, z=ry+s$$

$$\Rightarrow \frac{x-q}{p}=y=\frac{z-s}{r}$$

and $x=p'y+q', z=r'y+s'$

$$\Rightarrow \frac{x-q'}{p'}=y=\frac{z-s'}{r'}$$

Two lines

$$\frac{x-x_1}{a_1}=\frac{y-y_1}{b_1}=\frac{z-z_1}{c_1}$$

and $\frac{x-x_2}{a_2}=\frac{y-y_2}{b_2}=\frac{z-z_2}{c_2}$

are perpendicular, if

$a_1a_2+b_1b_2+c_1c_2=0$

$\therefore$ Given lines are perpendicular, if

$$pp'+1+rr'=0$$

14 (*d*) Given line is

$$\frac{x-3}{3}=\frac{y-2}{1}=\frac{z-1}{0}$$

Direction ratios of the line are 3,1, 0.

Direction ratios of Z-axis are 0, 0, 1.

$$a_1a_2+b_1b_2+c_1c_2$$
$$=(3)(0)+(1)(0)+(0)(1)=0$$

Hence, given line is perpendicular to Z-axis.

15 (*c*) Given, $a_1=-3,\ b_1=2k,\ c_1=2$

$$a_2=3k,\ b_2=1,\ c_2=-5$$

Since, given line is perpendicular, then

$$a_1a_2+b_1b_2+c_1c_2=0$$
$$\Rightarrow -3(3k)+2k(1)+2(-5)=0$$
$$\Rightarrow \quad -9k+2k-10=0$$
$$\Rightarrow \quad -7k=10$$
$$\therefore \quad k=\frac{-10}{7}$$

Shortest Distance between Two Skew-Lines

1 (*c*) If two lines in space intersect at a point, then the shortest distance between them is zero.

Also, if two lines in space are parallel, then the shortest distance between them will be the perpendicular distance, i.e. the length of the perpendicular drawn from a point on one line to the other line.

2 (*c*) In a space, there are lines which are neither intersecting nor parallel. Infact, such pair of lines are non-coplanar and are called skew-lines.

3 (*a*) By the shortest distance between two lines we mean the joining of a point in one line with one point on the other line so that the length of the segment so obtained is the smallest.

For skew-lines, the line of the shortest distance will be perpendicular to both the lines.

4 (*c*) Let l_1 and l_2 be two skew-lines with equations

$$\mathbf{r}=\mathbf{a}_1+\lambda\mathbf{b}_1 \quad \text{...(i)}$$
$$\text{and} \quad \mathbf{r}=\mathbf{a}_2+\mu\mathbf{b}_2 \quad \text{...(ii)}$$

Take any point S on l_1 with position vector $\mathbf{a}_1$ and T on l_2 with position vector $\mathbf{a}_2$. Then, the magnitude of the shortest distance vector will be equal to that of the projection of **ST** along the direction of the line of shortest distance.

If **PQ** is the shortest distance vector between l_1 and l_2, then it being perpendicular to both $\mathbf{b}_1$ and $\mathbf{b}_2$, the unit vector $\hat{\mathbf{n}}$ along **PQ** would therefore be

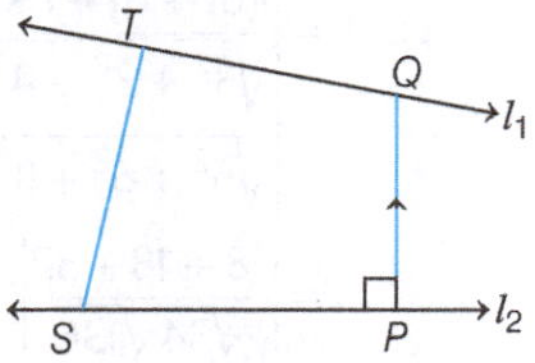

$$\hat{\mathbf{n}}=\frac{\mathbf{b}_1\times\mathbf{b}_2}{|\mathbf{b}_1\times\mathbf{b}_2|} \quad \text{...(iii)}$$

Then, $\mathbf{PQ}=d\hat{\mathbf{n}}$

Where, d is the magnitude of the shortest distance vector. Let θ be the angle between **ST** and **PQ**. Then, $\mathbf{PQ}=\mathbf{ST}|\cos\theta|$

$$\text{But } \cos\theta=\left|\frac{\mathbf{PQ}\cdot\mathbf{ST}}{|\mathbf{PQ}||\mathbf{ST}|}\right|$$

$$\cos\theta=\left|\frac{d\hat{\mathbf{n}}\cdot(\mathbf{a}_2-\mathbf{a}_1)}{d\,\mathbf{ST}}\right|$$

$$[\because \mathbf{ST}=\mathbf{a}_2-\mathbf{a}_1]$$

$$\cos\theta=\left|\frac{(\mathbf{b}_1\times\mathbf{b}_2)\cdot(\mathbf{a}_2-\mathbf{a}_1)}{\mathbf{ST}|\mathbf{b}_1\times\mathbf{b}_2|}\right|$$

[from Eq. (iii)]

Hence, the required shortest distance is

$$d=PQ=ST|\cos\theta|$$

$$\text{or} \quad d=\left|\frac{(\mathbf{b}_1\times\mathbf{b}_2)\cdot(\mathbf{a}_2-\mathbf{a}_1)}{|\mathbf{b}_1\times\mathbf{b}_2|}\right|$$

5 (*c*) The shortest distance between the lines

$$\frac{x-x_1}{a_1}=\frac{y-y_1}{b_1}=\frac{z-z_1}{c_1}$$

$$\text{and } \frac{x-x_2}{a_2}=\frac{y-y_2}{b_2}=\frac{z-z_2}{c_2}$$

in cartesian form is

$$\frac{\left|\begin{vmatrix} x_2-x_1 & y_2-y_1 & z_2-z_1 \\ a_1 & b_1 & c_1 \\ a_2 & b_2 & c_2 \end{vmatrix}\right|}{\sqrt{(b_1c_2-b_2c_1)^2+(c_1a_2-c_2a_1)^2+(a_1b_2-a_2b_1)^2}}$$

6 (*d*) If two lines l_1 and l_2 are parallel, then they are coplanar. Let the lines be given by

$$\mathbf{r}=\mathbf{a}_1+\lambda\mathbf{b} \quad \text{...(i)}$$
$$\text{and} \quad \mathbf{r}=\mathbf{a}_2+\mu\mathbf{b} \quad \text{...(ii)}$$

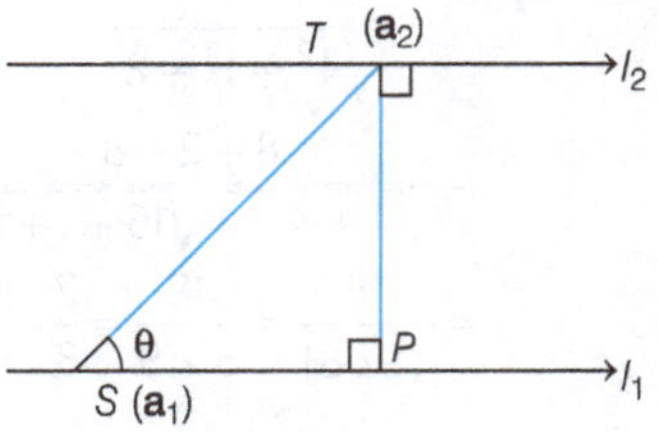

Where, $\mathbf{a}_1$ is the position vector of a point S on l_1 and $\mathbf{a}_2$ is the position vector of a point T on l_2. As l_1, l_2 are coplanar, if the foot of the perpendicular from T on the line l_1 is P, then the distance between the lines, l_1 and $l_2=|\mathbf{TP}|$.

Let θ be the angle between the vector **ST** and **b**.

Then, $\mathbf{b}\times\mathbf{ST}=(|\mathbf{b}||\mathbf{ST}|\sin\theta)\hat{\mathbf{n}}$ ...(iii)

where $\hat{\mathbf{n}}$ is the unit vector perpendicular to the plane of the line l_1 and l_2

But $\quad \mathbf{ST}=\mathbf{a}_2-\mathbf{a}_1$

Therefore, from Eq. (iii), we get

$$\mathbf{b}\times(\mathbf{a}_2-\mathbf{a}_1)=|\mathbf{b}|\mathbf{PT}\hat{\mathbf{n}}$$

$$[\because \mathbf{PT}=\mathbf{ST}\sin\theta]$$

i.e. $|\mathbf{b}\times(\mathbf{a}_2-\mathbf{a}_1)|=|\mathbf{b}|\,PT\cdot 1$

$$[\text{as } |\hat{\mathbf{n}}|=1]$$

Hence, the distance between the given parallel lines is

$$d=|\mathbf{PT}|=\left|\frac{\mathbf{b}\times(\mathbf{a}_2-\mathbf{a}_1)}{|\mathbf{b}|}\right|$$

7 (a)

A. The given equations are

$$\mathbf{r} = \hat{i} + 2\hat{j} + \hat{k} + \lambda\,(\hat{i} - \hat{j} + \hat{k})$$

and

$$\mathbf{r} = 2\hat{i} - \hat{j} - \hat{k} + \mu\,(2\hat{i} + \hat{j} + 2\hat{k})$$

which is of the form

$$\mathbf{r} = \mathbf{a}_1 + \lambda\,\mathbf{b}_1$$

and $\mathbf{r} = \mathbf{a}_2 + \mu\,\mathbf{b}_2$

Where, $\mathbf{a}_1 = \hat{i} + 2\hat{j} + \hat{k}$,

$\mathbf{b}_1 = \hat{i} - \hat{j} + \hat{k}$

and $\mathbf{a}_2 = 2\hat{i} - \hat{j} - \hat{k}$,

$\mathbf{b}_2 = 2\hat{i} + \hat{j} + 2\hat{k}$

Now, $\mathbf{a}_2 - \mathbf{a}_1 = (2\hat{i} - \hat{j} - \hat{k}) - (\hat{i} + 2\hat{j} + \hat{k})$

$= \hat{i} - 3\hat{j} - 2\hat{k}$

and $\mathbf{b}_1 \times \mathbf{b}_2 = \begin{vmatrix} \hat{i} & \hat{j} & \hat{k} \\ 1 & -1 & 1 \\ 2 & 1 & 2 \end{vmatrix}$

$= \hat{i}(-2-1) - \hat{j}(2-2) + \hat{k}(1+2)$

$= -3\hat{i} + 3\hat{k}$

$\Rightarrow \quad |\mathbf{b}_1 \times \mathbf{b}_2| = \sqrt{(-3)^2 + (3)^2}$

$= \sqrt{9+9}$

$= \sqrt{18} = 3\sqrt{2}$

Substituting all the values in equation, we obtain

Shortest distance

$$= \left|\frac{(\mathbf{b}_1 \times \mathbf{b}_2)\cdot(\mathbf{a}_2 - \mathbf{a}_1)}{|\mathbf{b}_1 \times \mathbf{b}_2|}\right|$$

$$= \frac{|(-3\hat{i} + 3\hat{k})\cdot(\hat{i} - 3\hat{j} - 2\hat{k})|}{3\sqrt{2}}$$

$$= \frac{|(-3)\times 1 + 0\times(-3) + 3\times(-2)|}{3\sqrt{2}}$$

$$= \frac{9}{3\sqrt{2}} = \frac{3\times\sqrt{2}}{\sqrt{2}\times\sqrt{2}} = \frac{3\sqrt{2}}{2} \text{ units}$$

Therefore, the shortest distance between the two lines is $\frac{3\sqrt{2}}{2}$ units.

B. The given lines are

$$\frac{x+1}{7} = \frac{y+1}{-6} = \frac{z+1}{1}$$

and $\dfrac{x-3}{1} = \dfrac{y-5}{-2} = \dfrac{z-7}{1}$

For line 1st DR's = (7, – 6, 1) and passes through (–1, – 1, – 1), then equation of given lines (in vector form) is

$\Rightarrow \mathbf{r}_1 = -\hat{i} - \hat{j} - \hat{k} + \lambda\,(7\hat{i} - 6\hat{j} + \hat{k})$

Similarly,

$\mathbf{r}_2 = 3\hat{i} + 5\hat{j} + 7\hat{k} + \mu\,(\hat{i} - 2\hat{j} + \hat{k})$

which are of the form

$\mathbf{r}_1 = \mathbf{a}_1 + \lambda\,\mathbf{b}_1$ and $\mathbf{r}_2 = \mathbf{a}_2 + \mu\,\mathbf{b}_2$

where, $\mathbf{a}_1 = -\hat{i} - \hat{j} - \hat{k}$,

$\mathbf{b}_1 = 7\hat{i} - 6\hat{j} + \hat{k}$

and $\mathbf{a}_2 = 3\hat{i} + 5\hat{j} + 7\hat{k}$,

$\mathbf{b}_2 = \hat{i} - 2\hat{j} + \hat{k}$

Now, $\mathbf{a}_2 - \mathbf{a}_1 = (3\hat{i} + 5\hat{j} + 7\hat{k}) - (-\hat{i} - \hat{j} - \hat{k})$

$= 4\hat{i} + 6\hat{j} + 8\hat{k}$

and $\mathbf{b}_1 \times \mathbf{b}_2 = \begin{vmatrix} \hat{i} & \hat{j} & \hat{k} \\ 7 & -6 & 1 \\ 1 & -2 & 1 \end{vmatrix}$

$= \hat{i}\,(-6+2) - \hat{j}\,(7-1) + \hat{k}\,(-14+6)$

$= -4\hat{i} - 6\hat{j} - 8\hat{k}$

$|\mathbf{b}_1 \times \mathbf{b}_2| = \sqrt{(-4)^2 + (-6)^2 + (-8)^2}$

$= \sqrt{16+36+64} = \sqrt{116} = 2\sqrt{29}$

$\therefore$ SD between the given lines

$$d = \left|\frac{(\mathbf{b}_1 \times \mathbf{b}_2)\,.\,(\mathbf{a}_2 - \mathbf{a}_1)}{|\mathbf{b}_1 \times \mathbf{b}_2|}\right|$$

$$= \frac{|(-4\hat{i} - 6\hat{j} - 8\hat{k})\,.\,(4\hat{i} + 6\hat{j} + 8\hat{k})|}{2\sqrt{29}}$$

$$= \frac{|(-4)\times 4 + (-6)\times 6 + (-8)\times 8|}{2\sqrt{29}}$$

$$= \frac{|-16-36-64|}{2\sqrt{29}} = \frac{116}{2\sqrt{29}}$$

$$= \frac{58}{\sqrt{29}} = 2\sqrt{29} \text{ units}$$

C. The given lines are

$\mathbf{r} = \hat{i} + 2\hat{j} + 3\hat{k} + \lambda\,(\hat{i} - 3\hat{j} + 2\hat{k})$

and

$\mathbf{r} = 4\hat{i} + 5\hat{j} + 6\hat{k} + \mu\,(2\hat{i} + 3\hat{j} + \hat{k})$.

It is known that the shortest distance between the lines $\mathbf{r} = \mathbf{a}_1 + \lambda\mathbf{b}_1$ and $\mathbf{r} = \mathbf{a}_2 + \mu\mathbf{b}_2$ is given by

$$d = \left|\frac{(\mathbf{b}_1 \times \mathbf{b}_2)\,.\,(\mathbf{a}_2 - \mathbf{a}_1)}{|\mathbf{b}_1 \times \mathbf{b}_2|}\right|$$

Comparing the given equations with $\mathbf{r} = \mathbf{a}_1 + \lambda\mathbf{b}_1$ and $\mathbf{r} = \mathbf{a}_2 + \mu\mathbf{b}_2$, we obtain

$\mathbf{a}_1 = \hat{i} + 2\hat{j} + 3\hat{k}$,

$\mathbf{b}_1 = \hat{i} - 3\hat{j} + 2\hat{k}$

and $\mathbf{a}_2 = 4\hat{i} + 5\hat{j} + 6\hat{k}$,

$\mathbf{b}_2 = 2\hat{i} + 3\hat{j} + \hat{k}$

Here, $\mathbf{a}_2 - \mathbf{a}_1 = (4\hat{i} + 5\hat{j} + 6\hat{k}) - (\hat{i} + 2\hat{j} + 3\hat{k})$

$= 3\hat{i} + 3\hat{j} + 3\hat{k}$

Also, $\mathbf{b}_1 \times \mathbf{b}_2 = \begin{vmatrix} \hat{i} & \hat{j} & \hat{k} \\ 1 & -3 & 2 \\ 2 & 3 & 1 \end{vmatrix}$

$= \hat{i}\,(-3-6) - \hat{j}\,(1-4) + \hat{k}\,(3+6)$

$= -9\hat{i} + 3\hat{j} + 9\hat{k}$

$\Rightarrow |\mathbf{b}_1 \times \mathbf{b}_2| = \sqrt{(-9)^2 + (3)^2 + (9)^2}$

$= \sqrt{81+9+81} = \sqrt{171} = 3\sqrt{19}$

$\therefore$ Required shortest distance

$$d = \left|\frac{(\mathbf{b}_1 \times \mathbf{b}_2)\,.\,(\mathbf{a}_2 - \mathbf{a}_1)}{|\mathbf{b}_1 \times \mathbf{b}_2|}\right|$$

$$= \frac{|(-9\hat{i} + 3\hat{j} + 9\hat{k})\,.\,(3\hat{i} + 3\hat{j} + 3\hat{k})|}{3\sqrt{19}}$$

$$= \frac{|-9\times 3 + 3\times 3 + 9\times 3|}{3\sqrt{19}}$$

$$= \frac{-27+9+27}{3\sqrt{19}} = \frac{9}{3\sqrt{19}} = \frac{3}{\sqrt{19}}$$

Therefore, the shortest distance between the two given lines is $\frac{3}{\sqrt{19}}$ unit.

D. Equation of the given lines of the form

$\mathbf{r} = (\hat{i} - 2\hat{j} + 3\hat{k}) + t(-\hat{i} + \hat{j} - 2\hat{k})$

and

$\mathbf{r} = (\hat{i} - \hat{j} - \hat{k}) + s(\hat{i} + 2\hat{j} - 2\hat{k})$

Compare these with

$\mathbf{r} = \mathbf{a}_1 + t\mathbf{b}_1$ and $\mathbf{r} = \mathbf{a}_2 + s\mathbf{b}_2$

$\mathbf{a}_1 = \hat{i} - 2\hat{j} + 3\hat{k}$

$\mathbf{b}_1 = -\hat{\mathbf{i}} + \hat{\mathbf{j}} - 2\hat{\mathbf{k}}$

and $\mathbf{a}_2 = \hat{\mathbf{i}} - \hat{\mathbf{j}} - \hat{\mathbf{k}}$

$\mathbf{b}_2 = \hat{\mathbf{i}} + 2\hat{\mathbf{j}} - 2\hat{\mathbf{k}}$

Now, $\mathbf{a}_2 - \mathbf{a}_1 = (\hat{\mathbf{i}} - \hat{\mathbf{j}} - \hat{\mathbf{k}}) - (\hat{\mathbf{i}} - 2\hat{\mathbf{j}} + 3\hat{\mathbf{k}}) = \hat{\mathbf{j}} - 4\hat{\mathbf{k}}$

and $\mathbf{b}_1 \times \mathbf{b}_2 = \begin{vmatrix} \hat{\mathbf{i}} & \hat{\mathbf{j}} & \hat{\mathbf{k}} \\ -1 & 1 & -2 \\ 1 & 2 & -2 \end{vmatrix}$

$= (-2+4)\hat{\mathbf{i}} - (2+2)\hat{\mathbf{j}} + (-2-1)\hat{\mathbf{k}}$

$= 2\hat{\mathbf{i}} - 4\hat{\mathbf{j}} - 3\hat{\mathbf{k}}$

$\Rightarrow |\mathbf{b}_1 \times \mathbf{b}_2| = \sqrt{(2)^2 + (-4)^2 + (-3)^2}$

$= \sqrt{4+16+9} = \sqrt{29}$

$\therefore$ Required shortest distance

$$d = \left|\frac{(\mathbf{b}_1 \times \mathbf{b}_2)\cdot(\mathbf{a}_2 - \mathbf{a}_1)}{|\mathbf{b}_1 \times b_2|}\right|$$

$$= \frac{|(2\hat{\mathbf{i}} - 4\hat{\mathbf{j}} - 3\hat{\mathbf{k}})\cdot(\hat{\mathbf{j}} - 4\hat{\mathbf{k}})|}{\sqrt{29}}$$

$$= \frac{|-4+12|}{\sqrt{29}} = \frac{8}{\sqrt{29}}$$

8 (*b*) Given equations of lines

$\mathbf{r} = (8+3\lambda)\hat{\mathbf{i}} - (9+16\lambda)\hat{\mathbf{j}} + (10+7\lambda)\hat{\mathbf{k}}$

i.e. $\mathbf{r} = 8\hat{\mathbf{i}} - 9\hat{\mathbf{j}} + 10\hat{\mathbf{k}} + \lambda(3\hat{\mathbf{i}} - 16\hat{\mathbf{j}} + 7\hat{\mathbf{k}})$

and $\mathbf{r} = 15\hat{\mathbf{i}} + 29\hat{\mathbf{j}} + 5\hat{\mathbf{k}} + \mu(3\hat{\mathbf{i}} + 8\hat{\mathbf{j}} - 5\hat{\mathbf{k}})$

Here, $\mathbf{a}_1 = 8\hat{\mathbf{i}} - 9\hat{\mathbf{j}} + 10\hat{\mathbf{k}}$

$\mathbf{b}_1 = 3\hat{\mathbf{i}} - 16\hat{\mathbf{j}} + 7\hat{\mathbf{k}}$

$\mathbf{a}_2 = 15\hat{\mathbf{i}} + 29\hat{\mathbf{j}} + 5\hat{\mathbf{k}}$

$\mathbf{b}_2 = 3\hat{\mathbf{i}} + 8\hat{\mathbf{j}} - 5\hat{\mathbf{k}}$

$\mathbf{a}_2 - \mathbf{a}_1 = (15\hat{\mathbf{i}} + 29\hat{\mathbf{j}} + 5\hat{\mathbf{k}}) - (8\hat{\mathbf{i}} - 9\hat{\mathbf{j}} + 10\hat{\mathbf{k}})$

$= 7\hat{\mathbf{i}} + 38\hat{\mathbf{j}} - 5\hat{\mathbf{k}}$

$\mathbf{b}_1 \times \mathbf{b}_2 = \begin{vmatrix} \hat{\mathbf{i}} & \hat{\mathbf{j}} & \hat{\mathbf{k}} \\ 3 & -16 & 7 \\ 3 & 8 & -5 \end{vmatrix}$

$= \hat{\mathbf{i}}(80-56) - \hat{\mathbf{j}}(-15-21) + \hat{\mathbf{k}}(24+48)$

$= (24\hat{\mathbf{i}} + 36\hat{\mathbf{j}} + 72\hat{\mathbf{k}})$

$\therefore$ Shortest distance

$$d = \left|\frac{(\mathbf{a}_2 - \mathbf{a}_1)\cdot(\mathbf{b}_1 \times \mathbf{b}_2)}{|\mathbf{b}_1 \times \mathbf{b}_2|}\right|$$

$$= \left|\frac{(7\hat{\mathbf{i}} + 38\hat{\mathbf{j}} - 5\hat{\mathbf{k}})\cdot(24\hat{\mathbf{i}} + 36\hat{\mathbf{j}} + 72\hat{\mathbf{k}})}{\sqrt{(24)^2 + (36)^2 + (72)^2}}\right|$$

$$= \left|\frac{168 + 1368 - 360}{\sqrt{576 + 1296 + 5184}}\right|$$

$$= \left|\frac{1176}{\sqrt{7056}}\right| = \frac{1176}{84} = 14$$

9 (*d*) Given lines are

$$\frac{x-3}{3} = \frac{y-8}{-1} = \frac{z-3}{1}$$

and $$\frac{x+3}{-3} = \frac{y+7}{2} = \frac{z-6}{4}$$

i.e. $$\frac{x-(-3)}{-3} = \frac{y-(-7)}{2} = \frac{z-6}{4}$$

Here, $\mathbf{a}_1 = 3\hat{\mathbf{i}} + 8\hat{\mathbf{j}} + 3\hat{\mathbf{k}}$,

$\mathbf{b}_1 = 3\hat{\mathbf{i}} - \hat{\mathbf{j}} + \hat{\mathbf{k}}$

$\mathbf{a}_2 = -3\hat{\mathbf{i}} - 7\hat{\mathbf{j}} + 6\hat{\mathbf{k}}$,

$\mathbf{b}_2 = -3\hat{\mathbf{i}} + 2\hat{\mathbf{j}} + 4\hat{\mathbf{k}}$

$\mathbf{a}_2 - \mathbf{a}_1 = (-3\hat{\mathbf{i}} - 7\hat{\mathbf{j}} + 6\hat{\mathbf{k}}) - (3\hat{\mathbf{i}} + 8\hat{\mathbf{j}} + 3\hat{\mathbf{k}})$

$= -6\hat{\mathbf{i}} - 15\hat{\mathbf{j}} + 3\hat{\mathbf{k}}$

$\mathbf{b}_1 \times \mathbf{b}_2 = \begin{vmatrix} \hat{\mathbf{i}} & \hat{\mathbf{j}} & \hat{\mathbf{k}} \\ 3 & -1 & 1 \\ -3 & 2 & 4 \end{vmatrix}$

$= \hat{\mathbf{i}}(-4-2) - \hat{\mathbf{j}}(12+3) + \hat{\mathbf{k}}(6-3)$

$= -6\hat{\mathbf{i}} - 15\hat{\mathbf{j}} + 3\hat{\mathbf{k}}$

$|\mathbf{b}_1 \times \mathbf{b}_2| = \sqrt{(-6)^2 + (-15)^2 + (3)^2}$

$= \sqrt{36 + 225 + 9}$

$= \sqrt{270}$

$$\text{SD} = \left|\frac{(\mathbf{a}_2 - \mathbf{a}_1)\cdot(\mathbf{b}_1 \times \mathbf{b}_2)}{|\mathbf{b}_1 \times \mathbf{b}_2|}\right|$$

$$= \left|\frac{(-6\hat{\mathbf{i}} - 15\hat{\mathbf{j}} + 3\hat{\mathbf{k}})\cdot(-6\hat{\mathbf{i}} - 15\hat{\mathbf{j}} + 3\hat{\mathbf{k}})}{\sqrt{270}}\right|$$

$$= \left|\frac{36 + 225 + 9}{\sqrt{270}}\right|$$

$$= \frac{270}{\sqrt{270}} = \sqrt{270} = 3\sqrt{30}$$

10 (*a*) Given lines are

$$\frac{x+1}{3} = \frac{y+3}{5} = \frac{z+5}{7}$$

i.e. $$\frac{x-(-1)}{3} = \frac{y-(-3)}{5} = \frac{z-(-5)}{7}$$

and $$\frac{x-2}{1} = \frac{y-4}{3} = \frac{z-6}{5}$$

Here, $\mathbf{a}_1 = -\hat{\mathbf{i}} - 3\hat{\mathbf{j}} - 5\hat{\mathbf{k}}$,

$\mathbf{b}_1 = 3\hat{\mathbf{i}} + 5\hat{\mathbf{j}} + 7\hat{\mathbf{k}}$

$\mathbf{a}_2 = 2\hat{\mathbf{i}} + 4\hat{\mathbf{j}} + 6\hat{\mathbf{k}}$,

$\mathbf{b}_2 = \hat{\mathbf{i}} + 3\hat{\mathbf{j}} + 5\hat{\mathbf{k}}$

Clearly, given lines are not parallel.

Now, $\mathbf{a}_2 - \mathbf{a}_1 = (2\hat{\mathbf{i}} + 4\hat{\mathbf{j}} + 6\hat{\mathbf{k}}) - (-\hat{\mathbf{i}} - 3\hat{\mathbf{j}} - 5\hat{\mathbf{k}})$

$= 3\hat{\mathbf{i}} + 7\hat{\mathbf{j}} + 11\hat{\mathbf{k}}$

$\mathbf{b}_1 \times \mathbf{b}_2 = \begin{vmatrix} \hat{\mathbf{i}} & \hat{\mathbf{j}} & \hat{\mathbf{k}} \\ 3 & 5 & 7 \\ 1 & 3 & 5 \end{vmatrix}$

$= \hat{\mathbf{i}}(25-21) - \hat{\mathbf{j}}(15-7) + \hat{\mathbf{k}}(9-5)$

$= (4\hat{\mathbf{i}} - 8\hat{\mathbf{j}} + 4\hat{\mathbf{k}})$

$|\mathbf{b}_1 \times \mathbf{b}_2| = \sqrt{4^2 + (-8)^2 + 4^2}$

$= \sqrt{16 + 64 + 16} = \sqrt{96} = 4\sqrt{6}$

$$\text{SD} = \left|\frac{(\mathbf{a}_2 - \mathbf{a}_1)\cdot(\mathbf{b}_1 \times \mathbf{b}_2)}{|\mathbf{b}_1 \times \mathbf{b}_2|}\right|$$

$$= \left|\frac{(3\hat{\mathbf{i}} + 7\hat{\mathbf{j}} + 11\hat{\mathbf{k}})\cdot(4\hat{\mathbf{i}} - 8\hat{\mathbf{j}} + 4\hat{\mathbf{k}})}{4\sqrt{6}}\right|$$

$$= \left|\frac{12 - 56 + 44}{4\sqrt{6}}\right| = 0$$

Hence, given lines intersect.

11 (*b*) Here, $\mathbf{a}_1 = \hat{\mathbf{i}} + \hat{\mathbf{j}}$, $\mathbf{a}_2 = 2\hat{\mathbf{i}} - 3\hat{\mathbf{k}}$

$\mathbf{b} = \hat{\mathbf{i}} - 2\hat{\mathbf{j}} + 3\hat{\mathbf{k}}$

Distance $$d = \left|\frac{\mathbf{b} \times (\mathbf{a}_2 - \mathbf{a}_1)}{|\mathbf{b}|}\right|$$

Now, $\mathbf{a}_2 - \mathbf{a}_1 = (2\hat{\mathbf{i}} - 3\hat{\mathbf{k}}) - (\hat{\mathbf{i}} + \hat{\mathbf{j}})$

$= \hat{\mathbf{i}} - \hat{\mathbf{j}} - 3\hat{\mathbf{k}}$

$\mathbf{b} \times (\mathbf{a}_2 - \mathbf{a}_1) = \begin{vmatrix} \hat{\mathbf{i}} & \hat{\mathbf{j}} & \hat{\mathbf{k}} \\ 1 & -2 & 3 \\ 1 & -1 & -3 \end{vmatrix}$

$= \hat{\mathbf{i}}(6+3) - \hat{\mathbf{j}}(-3-3) + \hat{\mathbf{k}}(-1+2)$

$= 9\hat{\mathbf{i}} + 6\hat{\mathbf{j}} + \hat{\mathbf{k}}$

$|\mathbf{b}| = \sqrt{1^2 + (-2)^2 + 3^2}$

$= \sqrt{1+4+9} = \sqrt{14}$

$\therefore$ Distance, $d = \left|\frac{9\hat{i}+6\hat{j}+\hat{k}}{\sqrt{14}}\right|$

$= \frac{1}{\sqrt{14}}\sqrt{(9)^2+(6)^2+(1)^2}$

$= \frac{1}{\sqrt{14}}\sqrt{81+36+1}$

$= \sqrt{\frac{118}{14}} = \sqrt{\frac{59}{7}}$

12 (*d*) Given lines are

$\frac{x-4}{5} = \frac{y+1}{2} = \frac{z}{1}$

i.e. $\frac{x-4}{5} = \frac{y-(-1)}{2} = \frac{z}{1}$

and $\frac{x-1}{5} = \frac{y-2}{2} = \frac{z-3}{1}$

Here, $\mathbf{a}_1 = 4\hat{i} - \hat{j}, \mathbf{a}_2 = \hat{i} + 2\hat{j} + 3\hat{k}$

$\mathbf{b} = 5\hat{i} + 2\hat{j} + \hat{k}$

$\mathbf{a}_2 - \mathbf{a}_1 = (\hat{i}+2\hat{j}+3\hat{k}) - (4\hat{i}-\hat{j})$

$= -3\hat{i} + 3\hat{j} + 3\hat{k}$

$\mathbf{b} \times (\mathbf{a}_2 - \mathbf{a}_1) = \begin{vmatrix} \hat{i} & \hat{j} & \hat{k} \\ 5 & 2 & 1 \\ -3 & 3 & 3 \end{vmatrix}$

$= \hat{i}(6-3) - \hat{j}(15+3) + \hat{k}(15+6)$

$= 3\hat{i} - 18\hat{j} + 21\hat{k}$

$|\mathbf{b}| = \sqrt{5^2+2^2+1^2}$

$= \sqrt{25+4+1} = \sqrt{30}$

$\therefore$ Distance $d = \left|\frac{\mathbf{b} \times (\mathbf{a}_2 - \mathbf{a}_1)}{|\mathbf{b}|}\right|$

$= \frac{1}{\sqrt{30}}|3\hat{i} - 18\hat{j} + 21\hat{k}|$

$= \frac{1}{\sqrt{30}}\sqrt{3^2+(-18)^2+21^2}$

$= \frac{1}{\sqrt{30}}\sqrt{9+324+441}$

$= \sqrt{\frac{774}{30}} = \sqrt{\frac{129}{5}}$

13 (*a*) Given lines are

$\frac{x-5}{3} = \frac{y-7}{-1} = \frac{z+4}{1}$

i.e. $\frac{x-5}{3} = \frac{y-7}{-1} = \frac{z-(-4)}{1}$

and $\frac{x+3}{-36} = \frac{y-3}{2} = \frac{z-6}{4}$

i.e. $\frac{x-(-3)}{-36} = \frac{y-3}{2} = \frac{z-6}{4}$

Here, $\mathbf{a}_1 = 5\hat{i} + 7\hat{j} - 4\hat{k}$,

$\mathbf{b}_1 = 3\hat{i} - \hat{j} + \hat{k}$

$\mathbf{a}_2 = -3\hat{i} + 3\hat{j} + 6\hat{k}$

$\mathbf{b}_2 = -36\hat{i} + 2\hat{j} + 4\hat{k}$

Clearly, given lines are not parallel.

$\mathbf{a}_2 - \mathbf{a}_1 = (-3\hat{i} + 3\hat{j} + 6\hat{k}) - (5\hat{i} + 7\hat{j} - 4\hat{k})$

$= -8\hat{i} - 4\hat{j} + 10\hat{k}$

$\mathbf{b}_1 \times \mathbf{b}_2 = \begin{vmatrix} \hat{i} & \hat{j} & \hat{k} \\ 3 & -1 & 1 \\ -36 & 2 & 4 \end{vmatrix}$

$= \hat{i}(-4-2) - \hat{j}(12+36) + \hat{k}(6-36)$

$= -6\hat{i} - 48\hat{j} - 30\hat{k}$

$SD = \left|\frac{(\mathbf{a}_2 - \mathbf{a}_1)\cdot(\mathbf{b}_1 \times \mathbf{b}_2)}{|\mathbf{b}_1 \times \mathbf{b}_2|}\right|$

$= \left|\frac{(-8\hat{i} - 4\hat{j} + 10\hat{k})\cdot(-6\hat{i} - 48\hat{j} - 30\hat{k})}{\sqrt{(-6)^2+(-48)^2+(-30)^2}}\right|$

$= \left|\frac{48+192-300}{\sqrt{36+2304+900}}\right|$

$= \left|\frac{60}{\sqrt{3240}}\right| = \left|\frac{60}{18\sqrt{10}}\right| = \frac{1}{3}\sqrt{10} \neq 0$

Hence, given lines do not intersect.

Miscellaneous Exercise

1 (*c*)

(i) Direction ratios of the line joining the origin (0, 0, 0) to the point (2, 1, 1) are ((2 – 0), (1 – 0), (1 – 0)) $\Rightarrow$ (2, 1, 1).

Direction ratios of the line determined by the points (3, 5, –1) and (4, 3, –1) are (4 – 3), (3 –5), (–1 + 1) $\Rightarrow$ (1, –2, 0)

Condition for perpendicular,

$a_1a_2 + b_1b_2 + c_1c_2 = 0$

$\therefore\ 2\times1 + 1\times(-2) + 1\times0 = 0$

$\Rightarrow\ 0 = 0$

Therefore, the lines in reference are perpendicular to each other.

(ii) Given lines are respectively parallel to unit vector

$\mathbf{b}_1 = l_1\hat{i} + m_1\hat{j} + n_1\hat{k}$ ...(i)

and $\mathbf{b}_2 = l_2\hat{i} + m_2\hat{j} + n_2\hat{k}$ ...(ii)

Now, $\mathbf{b}_1 \times \mathbf{b}_2$ is a vector which is at right angles to both $\mathbf{b}_1$ and $\mathbf{b}_2$ and is of magnitude unity.

Hence, components of $\mathbf{b}_1 \times \mathbf{b}_2$ are direction cosines of a line which is at right angles to both $\mathbf{b}_1$ and $\mathbf{b}_2$. So, we compute $\mathbf{b}_1 \times \mathbf{b}_2$.

$\mathbf{b}_1 \times \mathbf{b}_2 = \begin{vmatrix} \hat{i} & \hat{j} & \hat{k} \\ l_1 & m_1 & n_1 \\ l_2 & m_2 & n_2 \end{vmatrix}$

$= (m_1n_2 - m_2n_1)\hat{i} - (n_2l_1 - n_1l_2)\hat{j} + (l_1m_2 - l_2m_1)\hat{k}$

$= (m_1n_2 - m_2n_1)\hat{i} + (n_1l_2 - n_2l_1)\hat{j} + (l_1m_2 - l_2m_1)\hat{k}$

Thus, the direction consines of the required line are

$m_1n_2 - m_2n_1, n_1l_2 - n_2l_1, l_1m_2 - l_2m_1$.

2 (*b*) The direction ratios of the two lines are (*a*, *b*, *c*) and (*b* – *c*, *c* – *a*, *a* – *b*).

Let θ be the acute angle between the two lines, then

$\cos\theta = \left|\frac{a(b-c)+b(c-a)+c(a-b)}{\sqrt{a^2+b^2+c^2}\sqrt{(b-c)^2+(c-a)^2+(a-b)^2}}\right|$

$\left[\because \cos\theta = \left|\frac{a_1a_2+b_1b_2+c_1c_2}{\sqrt{a_1^2+b_1^2+c_1^2}\sqrt{a_2^2+b_2^2+c_2^2}}\right|\right]$

$= \left|\frac{ab-ac+bc-ab+ca-bc}{\sqrt{a^2+b^2+c^2}\sqrt{(b-c)^2+(c-a)^2+(a-b)^2}}\right| = 0$

$\Rightarrow\ \cos\theta = 0 \Rightarrow \theta = \frac{\pi}{2} = 90°$

Thus, the angle between the lines is 90°.

3 (*a*) Let *A* be a point on *X*-axis. Therefore, the coordinates of *A* are given by $(a, 0, 0)$, where $a \in R$.

Direction ratios of *OA* are $(a-0), 0, 0 = a, 0, 0$

The equation of *OA* is given by,

$$\frac{x-0}{a} = \frac{y-0}{0} = \frac{z-0}{0}$$

$$\Rightarrow \quad \frac{x}{1} = \frac{y}{0} = \frac{z}{0} = a$$

4 (*a*) It is known that equation of *YZ*-plane is $x = 0$.

The equation of the line joining $(5, 1, 6)$ and $(3, 4, 1)$ is $\frac{x-5}{3-5} = \frac{y-1}{4-1} = \frac{z-6}{1-6}$

$$\Rightarrow \quad \frac{x-5}{-2} = \frac{y-1}{3} = \frac{z-6}{-5} = \lambda \text{ (say)}$$

Any point on this line is

$$(5-2\lambda, 1+3\lambda, 6-5\lambda) \quad \text{...(i)}$$

Since, the line passes through *YZ*-plane $(x = 0)$

∴ From Eq. (i),

$$5 - 2\lambda = 0 \Rightarrow \lambda = \frac{5}{2}$$

∴ Required point of intersection of plane and line is

$$\left(5 - 2\times\frac{5}{2}, 1 + 3\times\frac{5}{2}, 6 - 5\times\frac{5}{2}\right) = \left(0, \frac{17}{2}, \frac{-13}{2}\right).$$

5 (*a*) I. Any line through $(1, 2, -4)$ can be written as

$$\frac{x-1}{a} = \frac{y-2}{b} = \frac{z+4}{c} \quad \text{...(i)}$$

Where, *a*, *b*, *c* are the direction ratios of line (i).

Now, the line (i) be perpendicular to the lines

$$\frac{x-8}{3} = \frac{y+19}{-16} = \frac{z-10}{7}$$

$$\text{and } \frac{x-15}{3} = \frac{y-29}{8} = \frac{z-5}{-5}$$

In above lines direction ratios are $(3, -16, 7)$ and $(3, 8, -5)$ respectively, which is perpendicular with the Eq. (i).

$$\therefore \quad 3a - 16b + 7c = 0 \quad \text{...(ii)}$$

$$\text{and} \quad 3a + 8b - 5c = 0 \quad \text{...(iii)}$$

By cross-multiplication, we have

$$\frac{a}{80-56} = \frac{b}{21+15} = \frac{c}{24+48}$$

$$\Rightarrow \quad \frac{a}{24} = \frac{b}{36} = \frac{c}{72}$$

$$\Rightarrow \quad \frac{a}{2} = \frac{b}{3} = \frac{c}{6} = \lambda \quad \text{(say)}$$

$$\therefore \quad a = 2\lambda, b = 3\lambda \text{ and } c = 6\lambda$$

The equation of required line which passes through the point $(1, 2, -4)$ and parallel to vector $2\hat{i} + 3\hat{j} + 6\hat{k}$ is $\mathbf{r} = (\hat{i} + 2\hat{j} - 4\hat{k}) + \lambda(2\hat{i} + 3\hat{j} + 6\hat{k})$.

II. The equation of a plane having intercepts *a*, *b*, *c*, with *X*, *Y* and *Z*-axes respectively, is given by

$$\frac{x}{a} + \frac{y}{b} + \frac{z}{c} = 1$$

$$\Rightarrow \left(\frac{1}{a}\right)x + \left(\frac{1}{b}\right)y + \left(\frac{1}{c}\right)z - 1 = 0$$

Distance of this plane from the origin (0, 0, 0,) is given to be *p*.

$$\therefore \quad p = \frac{\left|\frac{1}{a}\cdot 0 + \frac{1}{b}\cdot 0 + \frac{1}{c}\cdot 0 - 1\right|}{\sqrt{\left(\frac{1}{a}\right)^2 + \left(\frac{1}{b}\right)^2 + \left(\frac{1}{c}\right)^2}}$$

$$\Rightarrow \frac{1}{p} = \sqrt{\frac{1}{a^2} + \frac{1}{b^2} + \frac{1}{c^2}}$$

On squaring both sides, we get

$$\frac{1}{p^2} = \frac{1}{a^2} + \frac{1}{b^2} + \frac{1}{c^2}$$

∴ (ii) is false.

6 (*c*) A cube is a rectangular parallelopiped having equal length, breadth and height. Let *OADBFEGC* be the cube with each side of length *a* units.

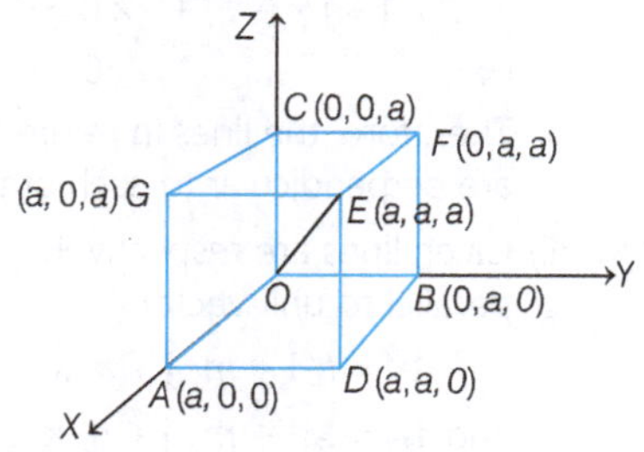

The four diagonals are *OE*, *AF*, *BG* and *CD*.

The direction cosines of the diagonal *OE* which is the line joining two points *O* and *E* are

$$\frac{a-0}{\sqrt{a^2+a^2+a^2}}, \frac{a-0}{\sqrt{a^2+a^2+a^2}}, \frac{a-0}{\sqrt{a^2+a^2+a^2}} \text{ i.e. } \frac{1}{\sqrt{3}}, \frac{1}{\sqrt{3}}, \frac{1}{\sqrt{3}}$$

Similarly, the direction cosines of *AF*, *BG* and *CD* are $\frac{-1}{\sqrt{3}}, \frac{1}{\sqrt{3}}, \frac{1}{\sqrt{3}}$; $\frac{1}{\sqrt{3}}, \frac{-1}{\sqrt{3}}, \frac{1}{\sqrt{3}}$ and $\frac{1}{\sqrt{3}}, \frac{1}{\sqrt{3}}, \frac{-1}{\sqrt{3}}$, respectively.

Let *l*, *m*, *n* be the direction cosines of the given line which makes angles $\alpha, \beta, \gamma, \delta$ with *OE*, *AF*, *BG*, *CD*, respectively.

Then, $\cos\alpha = \frac{1}{\sqrt{3}}(l+m+n)$;

$$\cos\beta = \frac{1}{\sqrt{3}}(-l+m+n);$$

$$\cos\gamma = \frac{1}{\sqrt{3}}(l-m+n);$$

$$\cos\delta = \frac{1}{\sqrt{3}}(l+m-n)$$

Squaring and adding, we get

$$\cos^2\alpha + \cos^2\beta + \cos^2\gamma + \cos^2\delta$$

$$= \frac{1}{3}[(l+m+n)^2 + (-l+m+n)^2 + (l-m+n)^2 + (l+m-n)^2]$$

$$= \frac{1}{3}[4(l^2+m^2+n^2)] = \frac{4}{3}$$

$$[\because l^2 + m^2 + n^2 = 1]$$

7 (*c*) Eliminating *m* from the given equations, we get

$$2n^2 + 3ln + l^2 = 0$$

$$\Rightarrow \quad (n+l)(2n+l) = 0$$

$\Rightarrow$ Either $n = -l$ or $l = -2n$

Now, if $l = -n$, then $m = -2n$

and if $l = -2n$, then $m = n$.

Thus, the direction ratios of two lines are proportional to $-n, -2n, n$ and $-2n, n, n$

i.e. $\quad 1, 2, -1$ and $-2, 1, 1$.

So, vectors parallel to these lines are $\mathbf{a} = \hat{\mathbf{i}} + 2\hat{\mathbf{j}} - \hat{\mathbf{k}}$ and $\mathbf{b} = -2\hat{\mathbf{i}} + \hat{\mathbf{j}} + \hat{\mathbf{k}}$, respectively.

If θ is the angle between the lines, then

$$\cos\theta = \frac{\mathbf{a}\cdot\mathbf{b}}{|\mathbf{a}||\mathbf{b}|}$$

$$= \frac{(\hat{\mathbf{i}} + 2\hat{\mathbf{j}} - \hat{\mathbf{k}})\cdot(-2\hat{\mathbf{i}} + \hat{\mathbf{j}} + \hat{\mathbf{k}})}{\sqrt{1^2 + 2^2 + (-1)^2}\sqrt{(-2)^2 + 1^2 + 1^2}}$$

$$= -\frac{1}{6}$$

Hence, $\theta = \cos^{-1}\left(-\frac{1}{6}\right)$.

8 (*b*) Given equations of line is

$$\frac{x-3}{2} = \frac{y-3}{1} = \frac{z}{1}$$

$\Rightarrow$ DR's of the given line are 2, 1, 1

$\Rightarrow$ DC's of the given line are $\frac{2}{\sqrt{6}}, \frac{1}{\sqrt{6}}, \frac{1}{\sqrt{6}}$.

Since, required lines make an angle $\frac{\pi}{3}$ with the given line.

The DC's of the required lines are $\frac{1}{\sqrt{6}}, \frac{2}{\sqrt{6}}, \frac{-1}{\sqrt{6}}$ and $\frac{-1}{\sqrt{6}}, \frac{1}{\sqrt{6}}, \frac{-2}{\sqrt{6}}$, respectively.

Also, both the required lines pass through the origin.

$\therefore$ Equation of required lines are

$$\frac{x}{1} = \frac{y}{2} = \frac{z}{-1}$$

and $\frac{x}{-1} = \frac{y}{1} = \frac{z}{-2}$.

Numerical Type Questions

1 (3) We know that

$$\cos^2 60° + \cos^2 45° + \cos^2\theta = 1$$

$$\frac{1}{4} + \frac{1}{2} + \cos^2\theta = 1$$

$$\frac{3}{4} + \cos^2\theta = 1$$

$$\cos^2\alpha = 1 - \frac{3}{4} = \frac{1}{4}$$

$$\cos\theta = \frac{1}{2}$$

Since, θ is acute angle

$\therefore \quad \cos\theta = \frac{1}{2}$

Now, $6\cos\theta = 3$

2 (9) $\frac{x-1}{2} = \frac{y+1}{3} = \frac{z-1}{4} = \Omega$

and $\frac{x-3}{1} = \frac{y-k}{2} = \frac{z}{1} = \mu$

Then, for some Ω and μ have point of introduction, when

$(2\Omega + 1, 3\Omega - 1, 4\Omega + 1)$

$= (\mu + 3, 2\mu + k, \mu)$

$2\Omega + 1 = \mu + 3$

$2\Omega - \mu = 2$ ...(i)

$4\Omega - \mu = -1$ ...(ii)

$3\Omega - 1 = 2\mu + k$ ...(iii)

solving (i) and (ii) we get $\Omega = \frac{-3}{2}$

and $\mu = -5$

The given lines intersect.

$\therefore$ (Ω and μ) satisfy the Eq. (iii)

$$3\left(\frac{-3}{2}\right) - 1 = 2(-5) + k$$

$$\frac{-9}{2} - 1 = -10 + k$$

$$k = 10 - \frac{11}{2}$$

$$k = \frac{9}{2}$$

$\therefore \quad 2k = 9$

3 (24) Let P be the given point and let L be the foot of perpendicular from P to the given line.

The coordinates of a general point on the given line are given by

$$\frac{x-0}{1} = \frac{y-1}{1} = \frac{z-2}{3} = \Omega$$

i.e. $x = \Omega, y = \Omega + 1, z = 3\Omega + 2$

let the co-ordinates of L be $(\Omega, (\Omega + 1), (3\Omega + 2))$

So, direction ratio of PL are $(\Omega - 2, \Omega - 3, 3\Omega - 2)$.

Direction ratios of the given line are (1, 1, 3) which is perpendicular to PL.

$$(\Omega - 2)\cdot 1 + (\Omega - 3)\cdot 1 + (3\Omega - 2) \times 3 = 0$$

$$\Omega - 2 + \Omega - 3 + 9\Omega - 6 = 0$$

$$11\Omega = 11$$

$$\Omega = 1$$

So, coordinate of L are (1, 2, 5).

Let $Q(x_1, y_1, z_1)$ be the image of $P(2, 4, 4)$ on given line where L is the mid-point of PQ.

$$\frac{2 + x_1}{2} = 1 \Rightarrow x_1 = 0$$

$$\frac{4 + y_1}{2} = 2 \Rightarrow y_1 = 0$$

$$\frac{4 + z_1}{2} = 5$$

$$z_1 = 6$$

$\Rightarrow$ Image of $P(2, 4, 4)$ in the given line (0, 0, 6)

$\therefore |PQ|$

$$= \sqrt{(2-0)^2 + (4-0)^2 + (4-6)^2}$$

$$= \sqrt{4 + 16 + 4}$$

$\therefore \quad |PQ|^2 = 24$

4 (3) We know that shortest distance between the lines $\mathbf{r} = \mathbf{a}_1 + \Omega\mathbf{b}_1$ and $\mathbf{r} = \mathbf{a}_2 + \mu\mathbf{b}_2$ is

$$d = \left|\frac{(\mathbf{a}_2 - \mathbf{a}_1)\cdot(\mathbf{b}_1 \times \mathbf{b}_2)}{|\mathbf{b}_1 \times \mathbf{b}_2|}\right|$$

$$\mathbf{b}_1 \times \mathbf{b}_2 = \begin{vmatrix} \hat{\mathbf{i}} & \hat{\mathbf{j}} & \hat{\mathbf{k}} \\ 2 & 3 & 4 \\ 3 & 4 & 5 \end{vmatrix}$$

$$= \hat{\mathbf{i}}(15 - 16) - \hat{\mathbf{j}}(10 - 12) + \hat{\mathbf{k}}(8 - 9)$$

$$\mathbf{b}_1 \times \mathbf{b}_2 = -\hat{\mathbf{i}} + 2\hat{\mathbf{j}} - \hat{\mathbf{k}}$$

and $(\mathbf{b}_1 \times \mathbf{b}_2) = \sqrt{6}$.

$$(\mathbf{a}_2 - \mathbf{a}_1) = (\hat{\mathbf{i}} + 2\hat{\mathbf{j}})$$

$$(\mathbf{a}_2 - \mathbf{a}_1)\cdot(\mathbf{b}_1 \times \mathbf{b}_2)$$

$$= (\hat{\mathbf{i}} + 2\hat{\mathbf{j}})\cdot(-\hat{\mathbf{i}} + 2\hat{\mathbf{j}} - \hat{\mathbf{k}})$$

$$= -1 + 4 = 3$$

$\therefore$ Shortest distance

$$= \left|\frac{(\mathbf{a}_2 - \mathbf{a}_2)\cdot(\mathbf{b}_1 - \mathbf{b}_2)}{|\mathbf{b}_1 - \mathbf{b}_2|}\right|$$

$$= \left|\frac{3}{\sqrt{6}}\right| = \frac{3}{\sqrt{6}}$$

$\therefore \sqrt{6} \times \frac{3}{\sqrt{6}} = 3$

5 (2) $\frac{x-5}{2}=\frac{y-3}{7}=\frac{z-1}{4}$ and

$\frac{x-1}{1}=\frac{y+3}{-2}=\frac{z-4}{3}$

We know that angle between the lines are

$$\cos\theta=\frac{a_1a_2+b_1b_2+c_1c_2}{\sqrt{a_1^2+b_1^2+c_1^2}\sqrt{a_2^2+b_2^2+c_2^2}}$$

$$\cos\theta=\frac{2\cdot(1)+7(-2)+4(3)}{\sqrt{4+49+16}\sqrt{1+4+9}}$$

$$\cos\theta=\frac{2-14+12}{\sqrt{69}\sqrt{14}}$$

$$\theta=\frac{\pi}{2}=\alpha$$

$$\alpha=\frac{\pi}{2}$$

$$\alpha=\frac{\pi}{2}, \text{ then } \frac{4\alpha}{\pi}=\frac{4}{\pi}\times\frac{\pi}{2}=2$$

$$\frac{4\alpha}{\pi}=2$$

6 (11) Equation of line *AB* is

$$\frac{x-2}{3}=\frac{y-3}{1}=\frac{z-4}{0}=\Omega \quad \text{(say)}$$

so, co-ordinates of point is $(3\Omega+2, \Omega+3, 4)$

Now, $(\text{Distance})^2=9\Omega^2+\Omega^2$

$$10\Omega^2=(\sqrt{10})^2$$

$$\Rightarrow \quad 10\Omega^2=10$$

$$\Omega=\pm 1$$

So, the coordinates of point is (5, 2, 4) lines $a=5$, $b=2$ and $c=4$

Then $a+b+c=5+2+4=11$.

$$a+b+c=11$$

7 (12) Given lines are

$$\frac{x-2}{3}=\frac{y-2}{2+\Omega}=\frac{z-4}{2} \quad \text{...(i)}$$

and $\frac{x+3}{2}=\frac{y-2}{3}=\frac{z-5}{\mu}$ ...(ii)

Since, lines (i) and (ii) are orthogonal to each other i.e. both lines are perpendicular to each other.

$$(3)(2)+(2+\Omega)(3)+(2)(\mu)=0$$

$$6+6+3\Omega+2\mu=0$$

$$|2\mu+3\Omega|=12$$

8 (4) $\mathbf{r}=(3\hat{i}-15\hat{j}+9\hat{k})+\Omega(2\hat{i}-7\hat{j}+5\hat{k})$

and $\mathbf{r}=(-\hat{i}+\hat{j}+9\hat{k})+\mu(2\hat{i}+\hat{j}-3\hat{k})$

We know that if $\mathbf{r}_1=\mathbf{a}_1+\Omega\mathbf{b}_1$ and $\mathbf{r}_2=\mathbf{a}_2+\mu\mathbf{b}_2$ is

Then shortest distance

$$=\left|\frac{(\mathbf{a}_2-\mathbf{a}_1)\cdot(\mathbf{b}_1\times\mathbf{b}_2)}{|\mathbf{b}_1\times\mathbf{b}_2|}\right|$$

$$(\mathbf{a}_2-\mathbf{a}_1)=-4\hat{i}+16\hat{j}$$

$$(\mathbf{b}_1\times\mathbf{b}_2)=\begin{vmatrix}\hat{i}&\hat{j}&\hat{k}\\2&-7&5\\2&1&-3\end{vmatrix}$$

$$=16\hat{i}+16\hat{j}+16\hat{k}$$

$$(\mathbf{b}_1\times\mathbf{b}_2)=16\sqrt{3}$$

$$d=\frac{(-4\hat{i}+16\hat{j})\cdot16(\hat{i}+\hat{j}+\hat{k})}{16\sqrt{3}}$$

$$=\left|\frac{-4+16}{\sqrt{3}}\right|$$

$$=\frac{12}{\sqrt{3}}$$

$$\therefore \quad \frac{\alpha}{\sqrt{3}}=\frac{12}{\sqrt{3}\cdot\sqrt{3}}=\frac{12}{3}=4$$

$$\frac{\alpha}{\sqrt{3}}=4$$

Assertion and Reason Questions

1 (*b*) Two lines with direction ratios a_1, b_1, c_1 and a_2, b_2, c_2 are

(i) Perpendicular *i.e.*, if $\theta=90°$ by

$$\cos\theta=\frac{a_1a_2+b_1b_2+c_1c_2}{\sqrt{a_1^2+b_1^2+c_1^2}\sqrt{a_2^2+b_2^2+c_2^2}}$$

$$a_1a_2+b_1b_2+c_1c_2=0$$

(ii) Parallel i.e. if $\theta=0$ by

$$\sin\theta=\sqrt{\frac{(a_1b_2-a_2b_1)^2+(b_1c_2-b_2c_1)^2+(c_1a_2-c_2a_1)^2}{(a_1^2+b_1^2+c_1^2)(a_2^2+b_2^2+c_2^2)}}$$

$$\frac{a_1}{a_2}=\frac{b_1}{b_2}=\frac{c_1}{c_2}$$

2 (*c*) Here, $\mathbf{a}_1=\hat{i}-\hat{j}$, $\mathbf{b}_1=2\hat{i}+\hat{k}$

$\mathbf{a}_2=2\hat{i}-\hat{k}$, $\mathbf{b}_2=\hat{i}+\hat{j}-\hat{k}$

$\because$ $\mathbf{b}_1\neq\lambda\mathbf{b}_2$, for any scalar λ

$\therefore$ Given lines are not parallel.

$$\mathbf{a}_2-\mathbf{a}_1=(2\hat{i}-\hat{k})-(\hat{i}-\hat{j})$$

$$=\hat{i}+\hat{j}-\hat{k}$$

$$\mathbf{b}_1\times\mathbf{b}_2=\begin{vmatrix}\hat{i}&\hat{j}&\hat{k}\\2&0&1\\1&1&-1\end{vmatrix}$$

$$=\hat{i}(0-1)-\hat{j}(-2-1)+\hat{k}(2-0)$$

$$=-\hat{i}+3\hat{j}+2\hat{k}$$

$$|\mathbf{b}_1\times\mathbf{b}_2|=\sqrt{(-1)^2+(3)^2+(2)^2}$$

$$=\sqrt{1+9+4}=\sqrt{14}$$

$$SD=\left|\frac{(\mathbf{a}_2-\mathbf{a}_1)\cdot(\mathbf{b}_1\times\mathbf{b}_2)}{|\mathbf{b}_1\times\mathbf{b}_2|}\right|$$

$$=\left|\frac{(\hat{i}+\hat{j}-\hat{k})\cdot(-\hat{i}+3\hat{j}+2\hat{k})}{\sqrt{14}}\right|$$

$$=\left|\frac{-1+3-2}{\sqrt{14}}\right|=0$$

Hence, two lines intersect each other.

$\therefore$ A is correct.

Two lines intersect each other, if they are not parallel and shortest distance = 0.

So, the information given in R is not complete. Hence, R is incorrect.

3 (*a*) Given that $l=\cos\alpha\cdot m=\cos\beta$ and $n=\cos\gamma$.

$$\therefore \; l^2+m^2+n^2=1$$

$$\cos^2\alpha+\cos^2\beta+\cos^2\gamma=1$$

$$\frac{1+\cos2\alpha}{2}+\frac{1+\cos2\beta}{2}+\frac{1+\cos2\gamma}{2}=1$$

$$\cos2\alpha+\cos2\beta+\cos2\gamma=-1$$

Hence, Assertion (A) is true.

$l^2+m^2+n^2=1$ is standard result.

So, Reason (R) is true.

and (a) is the correct option.

4 (*d*) If $l, m\, n$ be direction cosines of line making angles α, β and γ with co-ordinate axes.

Then, $l = \cos\alpha$, $m = \cos\beta$

and $n = \cos\gamma$

$\Rightarrow \cos^2\alpha + \cos^2\beta + \cos^2\gamma = 1$

$\Rightarrow 1 - \sin^2\alpha + 1 - \sin^2\beta + 1 - \sin^2\gamma = 1$

$\Rightarrow \quad \sin^2\alpha + \sin^2\beta + \sin^2\gamma = 2$

$\therefore$ Assertion (A) is not true.

and Reason (R) is true.

(d) is the correct option.

5 (*a*) The angle between the lines $\mathbf{r} = \mathbf{a}_1 + \Omega\mathbf{b}_1$ and $\mathbf{r} = \mathbf{a}_2 + \mu\mathbf{b}_2$ is the angle between parallel vector $\mathbf{b}_1$ and $\mathbf{b}_2$ is given by

$$\cos\theta = \frac{\mathbf{b}_1 \cdot \mathbf{b}_2}{|\mathbf{b}_1||\mathbf{b}_2|}, \text{ if } \theta = 90^\circ$$

$$\cos\theta = \frac{\mathbf{b}_1 \cdot \mathbf{b}_2}{|\mathbf{b}_1||\mathbf{b}_2|}$$

$\Rightarrow \mathbf{b}_1 \cdot \mathbf{b}_2 = 0$

So, Assertion (A) and Reason (R) both are true.

(a) is the correct option.

6 (*d*) Reason (R) is true.

The equation of line passing through $\mathbf{a} = \hat{\mathbf{i}} + 2\hat{\mathbf{j}} + 3\hat{\mathbf{k}}$ and $\mathbf{b} = 3\hat{\mathbf{i}} - \hat{\mathbf{j}} + 3\hat{\mathbf{k}}$ are $\mathbf{r} = \mathbf{a} + \Omega(\mathbf{b} - \mathbf{a})$

$\Rightarrow \mathbf{r} = (\hat{\mathbf{i}} + 2\hat{\mathbf{j}} + 3\hat{\mathbf{k}}) + \Omega(3-1)\hat{\mathbf{i}} + (-1-2)\hat{\mathbf{j}} + (3-3)\hat{\mathbf{k}}$

$\Rightarrow \mathbf{r} = (\hat{\mathbf{i}} + 2\hat{\mathbf{j}} + 3\hat{\mathbf{k}}) + \Omega\, 2(\hat{\mathbf{i}} - 3\hat{\mathbf{j}})$

So, Assertion (A) is not true.

Hence, (d) is the correct option.

7 (*c*) Line through points P and Q is parallel to the vector

$\mathbf{b}_1 = \mathbf{PQ} = -2\hat{\mathbf{i}} - 4\hat{\mathbf{j}} - 4\hat{\mathbf{k}}$ and

The line through $P(-1, -2, 1)$ and $Q(1, 2, 5)$ is parallel to

$\mathbf{b}_2 = 2\hat{\mathbf{i}} - 4\hat{\mathbf{j}} + 4\hat{\mathbf{k}}$.

Clearly, $\mathbf{b}_2 = -\mathbf{b}_1$ so, given lines are parallel.

Hence, Assertion (A) is true.

Reason (R) is not true because $\mathbf{b}_1 \cdot \mathbf{b}_2 = 0$ lines are perpendicular.

(c) is the correct option.

8 (*a*) Assertion and Reason both are correct.

(a) is the correct answer.

Case or Paragraph Type Questions

1 (*a*) The line along which motorcycle is running is

$\mathbf{r} = (\hat{\mathbf{i}} + \hat{\mathbf{j}} + 2\hat{\mathbf{k}}) + \lambda(\hat{\mathbf{i}} + 2\hat{\mathbf{j}} - \hat{\mathbf{k}})$

$\Rightarrow (x\hat{\mathbf{i}} + y\hat{\mathbf{j}} + z\hat{\mathbf{k}}) - (\hat{\mathbf{i}} + \hat{\mathbf{j}} + 2\hat{\mathbf{k}}) = \lambda(\hat{\mathbf{i}} + 2\hat{\mathbf{j}} - \hat{\mathbf{k}})$

$(x-1)\hat{\mathbf{i}} + (y-1)\hat{\mathbf{j}} + (z-2)\hat{\mathbf{k}} = \lambda(\hat{\mathbf{i}} + 2\hat{\mathbf{j}} - \hat{\mathbf{k}})$

$$\Rightarrow \frac{(x-1)}{1} = \frac{y-1}{2} = \frac{z-2}{-1} = \lambda$$

$\therefore$ Required cartesian equation is

$$\frac{x-1}{1} = \frac{y-1}{2} = \frac{z-2}{-1}$$

2 (*c*) Direction ratio of P is $(1, 2, -1)$

$\therefore$ Direction cosine is

$$= \frac{1}{\sqrt{1+4+1}}, \frac{-1}{\sqrt{1+4+1}}$$

$$= \left(\frac{1}{\sqrt{6}}, \frac{2}{\sqrt{6}}, \frac{-1}{\sqrt{6}}\right)$$

3 (*b*) The line along which motor cycle Q is running is

$\mathbf{r} = 3\hat{\mathbf{i}} + 3\hat{\mathbf{j}} + \mu(2\hat{\mathbf{i}} + \hat{\mathbf{j}} + \hat{\mathbf{k}})$

$\Rightarrow (x-3)\hat{\mathbf{i}} + (y-3)\hat{\mathbf{j}} + z\hat{\mathbf{k}} = \mu(2\hat{\mathbf{i}} + \hat{\mathbf{j}} + \hat{\mathbf{k}})$

$$\frac{x-3}{2} = \frac{y-2}{1} = \frac{2}{1} = \mu$$

$\therefore$ Required correction equation is

$$\frac{x-3}{2} = \frac{y-3}{1} = \frac{z}{1}$$

4 (*d*) The driection ratio of motor cycle Q is $(2, 1, 1)$

(d) is the correct option.

5 (*c*) From the figure (see in question)

AP is parallel to the vector **b**, i.e.

$\mathbf{AP} = \lambda\mathbf{b}$, where λ is some real number.

But $\quad \mathbf{AP} = \mathbf{OP} - \mathbf{OA}$

i.e. $\quad \lambda\mathbf{b} = \mathbf{r} - \mathbf{a}$

Conversely, for each value of the parameter λ, this equation gives the position vector of a point P on the line. Hence, the vector equation of the line is given by

$$\mathbf{r} = \mathbf{a} + \lambda\mathbf{b}$$

6 (*d*) If $\mathbf{b} = a\hat{\mathbf{i}} + b\hat{\mathbf{j}} + c\hat{\mathbf{k}}$, then a, b, c are direction ratios of the line and conversely, if a, b, c are direction ratios of a line then, $\mathbf{b} = a\hat{\mathbf{i}} + b\hat{\mathbf{j}} + c\hat{\mathbf{k}}$ will be the parallel to the line. Here, b should not be confused with $|\mathbf{b}|$.

7 (*d*) The coordinates of the given point A be (x_1, y_1, z_1) and the direction ratios of the line be a, b, c. Consider the coordinates of any point P be (x, y, z). Then,

$\mathbf{r} = x\hat{\mathbf{i}} + y\hat{\mathbf{j}} + z\hat{\mathbf{k}}$

$\mathbf{a} = x_1\hat{\mathbf{i}} + y_1\hat{\mathbf{j}} + z_1\hat{\mathbf{k}}$

and $\quad \mathbf{b} = a\hat{\mathbf{i}} + b\hat{\mathbf{j}} + c\hat{\mathbf{k}}$

On substituting these values in $\mathbf{r} = \mathbf{a} + \lambda\mathbf{b}$ and equating the coefficients of $\hat{\mathbf{i}}$, $\hat{\mathbf{j}}$ and $\hat{\mathbf{k}}$, we get

$x = x_1 + \lambda a$; $y = y_1 + \lambda b$;

$z = z_1 + \lambda c \quad$ ...(i)

These are parametric equations of the line. Eliminating the parameter λ from Eq. (i), we get

$$\frac{x - x_1}{a} = \frac{y - y_1}{b} = \frac{z - z_1}{c} \quad \text{...(ii)}$$

This is the cartesian equation of the line.

Past Years Questions

1 (*d*) Given equation of lines are

$$\frac{x-3}{4} = \frac{y+7}{-11} = \frac{z-1}{5}$$

and $$\frac{x-5}{3} = \frac{y-9}{-6} = \frac{z+2}{1}$$

From figure,

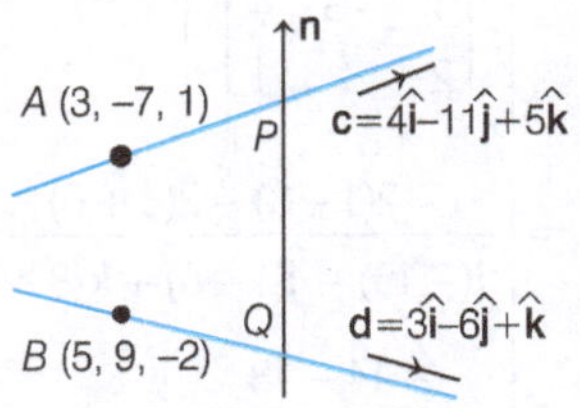

$n = c \times d$

$$= \begin{vmatrix} \hat{\mathbf{i}} & \hat{\mathbf{j}} & \hat{\mathbf{k}} \\ 4 & -11 & 5 \\ 3 & -6 & 1 \end{vmatrix}$$

$= 19\hat{\mathbf{i}} + 11\hat{\mathbf{j}} + 9\hat{\mathbf{k}}$

∴ Shortest distance

(SD) = Projection of **AB** on **n**

$$= \left|\frac{\mathbf{AB}\cdot\mathbf{n}}{|\mathbf{n}|}\right|$$

$$= \left|\frac{(2\hat{i}+16\hat{j}-3\hat{k})\cdot(19\hat{i}+11\hat{j}+9\hat{k})}{\sqrt{361+121+81}}\right|$$

$$= \frac{38+176-27}{\sqrt{563}} = \frac{187}{\sqrt{563}}$$

2 (*a*) **Key Idea** *If* $\mathbf{r} = \mathbf{a}_1 + \lambda\mathbf{b}_1$ *and* $\mathbf{r} = \mathbf{a}_2 + \mu\mathbf{b}_2$ *be two skew lines, then the shortest distance between two lines is*

$$d = \left|\frac{(\mathbf{a}_2 - \mathbf{a}_1)\cdot(\mathbf{b}_1 \times \mathbf{b}_2)}{|\mathbf{b}_1 \times \mathbf{b}_2|}\right|$$

$$L_1 : \mathbf{r} = (2+\lambda)\hat{i} + (1-3\lambda)\hat{j} + (3+4\lambda)\hat{k}$$

$$L_2 : \mathbf{r} = 2(1+\mu)\hat{i} + 3(1+\mu)\hat{j} + (5+\mu)\hat{k}$$

$$= (2+2\mu)\hat{i} + (3+3\mu)\hat{j} + (5+\mu)\hat{k}$$

Shortest distance (d)

$$= \left|\frac{\begin{vmatrix} x_2-x_1 & y_2-y_1 & z_2-z_1 \\ a_1 & b_1 & c_1 \\ a_2 & b_2 & c_2 \end{vmatrix}}{\begin{vmatrix} \hat{i} & \hat{j} & \hat{k} \\ a_1 & a_2 & a_3 \\ b_1 & b_2 & b_3 \end{vmatrix}}\right|$$

$$= \left|\frac{\begin{vmatrix} 0 & -2 & -2 \\ 1 & -3 & 4 \\ 2 & 3 & 1 \end{vmatrix}}{\begin{vmatrix} \hat{i} & \hat{j} & \hat{k} \\ 1 & -3 & 4 \\ 2 & 3 & 1 \end{vmatrix}}\right|$$

$$= \left|\frac{2(1-8)-2(3+6)}{\hat{i}(-15)-\hat{j}(1-8)+\hat{k}(3+6)}\right|$$

$$= \left|\frac{-14-18}{-15\hat{i}+7\hat{j}+9\hat{k}}\right|$$

$$= \frac{32}{\sqrt{(-15)^2+7^2+9^2}}$$

$$= \frac{32}{\sqrt{225+49+81}}$$

$$= \frac{32}{\sqrt{355}} = \frac{m}{\sqrt{n}}$$

So, $m = 32$ and $n = 355$

Therefore, $m + n = 32 + 355 = 387$

3 (*b*) **Key Idea** *First write the given equation of lines in the form of* $\mathbf{r}_1 = \mathbf{a}_1 + \lambda\mathbf{b}_1$ *and* $\mathbf{r}_2 = \mathbf{a}_2 + \mu\mathbf{b}_2$, *then use formula of shortest distance,*

$$d = \left|\frac{(a_2-a_1)\cdot(b_1\times b_2)}{|b_1\times b_2|}\right|$$

Given lines are,

$$\frac{x\ 3}{2} = \frac{y+15}{-7} = \frac{z-9}{5}$$

and $$\frac{x+1}{2} = \frac{y-1}{1} = \frac{z-9}{-3}$$

So, $\mathbf{a}_1 = 3\hat{i} - 15\hat{j} + 9\hat{k}$

$a_2 = -1\hat{i} + \hat{j} + 9\hat{k}$

and $b_1 = 2\hat{i} - 7\hat{j} + 5\hat{k}$

$b_2 = 2\hat{i} + \hat{j} - 3\hat{k}$

Now, $a_2 - a_1 = -4\hat{i} + 16\hat{j}$

$$(b_1 \times b_2) = \begin{vmatrix} \hat{i} & \hat{j} & \hat{k} \\ 2 & -7 & 5 \\ 2 & 1 & -3 \end{vmatrix}$$

$$= 16\hat{i} + 16\hat{j} + 16\hat{k}$$

$$|\mathbf{b}_1 \times \mathbf{b}_2| = 16\sqrt{3}$$

$$d = \left|\frac{(-4\hat{i}+16\hat{j})\cdot 16(\hat{i}+\hat{j}+\hat{k})}{16\sqrt{3}}\right|$$

$$= \left|\frac{-4+16}{\sqrt{3}}\right| = \frac{12}{\sqrt{3}} = 4\sqrt{3}$$

4 (*b*) Let $R = 2\lambda+1, 3\lambda-1, 5\lambda+2$

$PR \perp b$

$$(2\lambda+1-8)\,2 + (3\lambda-1-5)\,3 + (5\lambda+2-7)\,5 = 0$$

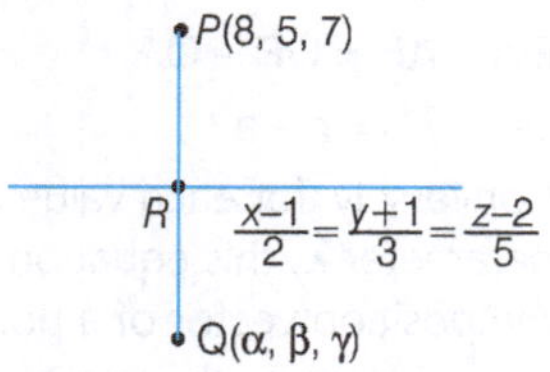

$$\lambda = \frac{57}{38} = \frac{3}{2}$$

$$\because \quad \frac{\alpha+8}{2} = 2\lambda + 1$$

$$\Rightarrow \quad \alpha = 4\lambda + 2 - 8$$

$$\frac{\beta+5}{2} = 3\lambda - 1$$

$$\Rightarrow \quad \beta = 6\lambda - 2 - 5$$

$$\frac{\gamma+7}{2} = 5\lambda + 2$$

$$\Rightarrow \quad \gamma = 10\lambda + 4 - 7$$

$$\alpha + \beta + \gamma = 20\lambda - 16$$

$$= 20 \times \frac{3}{2} - 16 = 14$$

5 (*c*) $L_1 : \frac{x-1}{2} = \frac{y+8}{-7} = \frac{(z-4)}{5}$

$\Rightarrow a_1 = \hat{i} - 8\hat{j} + 4\hat{k};$

$b_1 = 2\hat{i} - 7\hat{j} + 5\hat{k}$

$L_2 : \frac{x-1}{2} = \frac{y-2}{1} = \frac{z-6}{-3}$

$\Rightarrow a_2 = \hat{i} + 2\hat{j} + 6\hat{k};\ \ b_2 = 2\hat{i} + \hat{j} - 3\hat{k}$

$$b_1 \times b_2 = \begin{vmatrix} \hat{i} & \hat{j} & \hat{k} \\ 2 & -7 & 5 \\ 2 & 1 & -3 \end{vmatrix}$$

$$= \hat{i}(21-5) - \hat{j}(-6-10) + \hat{k}(2+14)$$

$$= 16\hat{i} + 16\hat{j} + 16\hat{k}$$

$$\therefore (a_2 - a_1)\cdot(b_1 \times b_2) = (10\hat{j} + 2\hat{k}) \cdot 16(\hat{i}+\hat{j}+\hat{k})$$

$$= 32(5\hat{j}+\hat{k})\cdot(\hat{i}+\hat{j}+\hat{k})$$

$$= 32(5+1) = 192$$

∴ Shortest distance

$$= \left|\frac{(a_2-a_1)\cdot(b_1\times b_2)}{|b_1\times b_2|}\right|$$

$$= \frac{192}{16\sqrt{3}} = \frac{12}{\sqrt{3}} = 4\sqrt{3}$$

6 (*a*) Equation of line passing through(– 3, 2, 3) and parallel to a line with direction ratios 3, 3, – 1

$$L : \frac{x+3}{3} = \frac{y-2}{3} = \frac{z-3}{-1} = \lambda$$

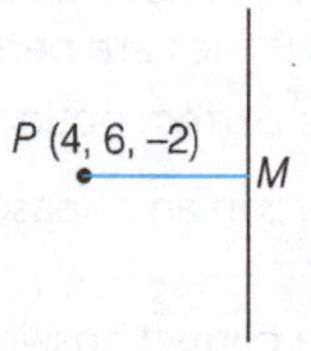

$L: x = 3\lambda - 3,\ y = 3\lambda + 2,$
$z = -\lambda + 3$

Let $M(3\lambda - 3, 3\lambda + 2, -\lambda + 3)$

Direction ratio of line

$PM: (3\lambda - 3 - 4, 3\lambda + 2 - 6, -\lambda + 3 + 2)$

$\equiv (3\lambda - 7, 3\lambda - 4, -\lambda + 5)$

Direction ratio of line L: 3, 3, -1

We know that if two lines are perpendicular, then

$$a_1a_2 + b_1b_2 + c_1c_2 = 0$$

Here, $PM \perp L$

$\Rightarrow 3(3\lambda - 7) + 3(3\lambda - 4) - 1(-\lambda + 5) = 0$

$19\lambda - 38 = 0 \Rightarrow \lambda = 2$

So, point $M(3, 8, 1)$

Distance

$PM = \sqrt{(3-4)^2 + (8-6)^2 + (1+2)^2}$

$= \sqrt{1 + 4 + 9} = \sqrt{14}$

7 (*b*) Let R be $(2k - 1, 3k + 3, -k + 1)$.

Direction ratios of PR are
$< 2k - 1 - a, 3k - 1, -k - 1 >$

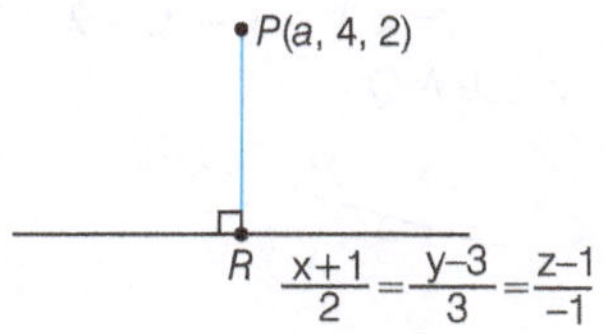

as PR perpendicular to the given line (2) $(2k - 1 - a) + (3)(3k - 1) + (-1)(-k - 1) = 0$

$\Rightarrow 14k - 4 - 2a = 0 \Rightarrow a = 7k - 2$

$PR = \sqrt{(2k-1-a)^2 + (3k-1)^2 + (-k-1)^2} = 2\sqrt{6}$

$\Rightarrow 25k^2 - 10k + 1 + 9k^2 - 6k + 1 + k^2 + 2k + 1 = 24$

$\Rightarrow \quad 35k^2 - 14k - 21 = 0$

$\Rightarrow \quad 5k^2 - 2k - 3 = 0$

$\Rightarrow k = 1 \text{ or } k = \frac{-3}{5} \Rightarrow a = 5$

or $\quad a = \frac{-31}{5} \Rightarrow a = 5$

$P \equiv (5, 4, 2), R \equiv (1, 6, 0)$

$Q \equiv (-3, 8, -2)$

$\therefore \quad a + \sum_{i=1}^{3} \alpha_i = 5 - 3 + 8 - 2 = 8$

8 (*a*) Given, the direction ratios are, $<1, 1, -2>$

and $<\sqrt{3} - 1, -\sqrt{3} - 1, -4>$.

$\because \cos\theta$

$$= \frac{l_1l_2 + m_1m_2 + n_1n_2}{\sqrt{l_1^2 + m_1^2 + n_1^2}\sqrt{l_2^2 + m_2^2 + n_2^2}}$$

Where, l_1, m_1, n_1 and l_2, m_2, n_2 are direction ratios of two lines.

So,

$$\cos\theta = \frac{1(\sqrt{3} - 1) + 1(-\sqrt{3} - 1) + (-2)(-4)}{\sqrt{1^2 + 1^2 + (-2)^2} \cdot \sqrt{(\sqrt{3} - 1)^2 + (-\sqrt{3} - 1)^2 + (-4)^2}}$$

$$= \frac{\sqrt{3} - 1 - \sqrt{3} - 1 + 8}{\sqrt{6}\sqrt{24}} = \frac{6}{12} = \frac{1}{2}$$

$\Rightarrow \cos\theta = \frac{1}{2} = \cos\frac{\pi}{3}$

$\therefore \quad \theta = \frac{\pi}{3}$

9 (*c*)

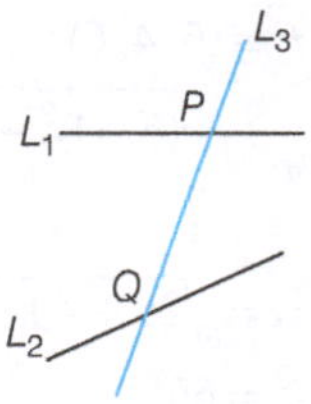

We have,

$L_1: \frac{x-1}{2} = \frac{y-3}{1} = \frac{z-2}{2} = \lambda$

$x = 2\lambda + 1, y = \lambda + 3, z = 2\lambda + 2$

Let $P(2\lambda + 1, \lambda + 3, 2\lambda + 2)$

$L_2: \frac{x-2}{1} = \frac{y-2}{2} = \frac{z-3}{3} = \mu$

$x = \mu + 2, y = 2\mu + 2, z = 3\mu + 3$

Let $Q(\mu + 2, 2\mu + 2, 3\mu + 3)$

Direction ratio of line PQ

$= (2\lambda + 1 - \mu - 2, \lambda + 3 - 2\mu - 2, 2\lambda + 2 - 3\mu - 3)$

$= (2\lambda - \mu - 1, \lambda - 2\mu + 1, 2\lambda - 3\mu - 1)$

Given, direction ratio of L_3: 1, -1, -2 and L_3 and PQ are same line

So, $\frac{2\lambda - \mu - 1}{1} = \frac{\lambda - 2\mu + 1}{-1}$

$= \frac{2\lambda - 3\mu - 1}{-2}$

On taking, $\frac{2\lambda - \mu - 1}{1} = \frac{\lambda - 2\mu + 1}{-1}$

$2\lambda - \mu - 1 = -\lambda + 2\mu - 1$

$3\lambda = 3\mu \Rightarrow \lambda = \mu \quad$ ...(i)

On taking, $\frac{\lambda - 2\mu + 1}{-1} = \frac{2\lambda - 3\mu - 1}{-2}$

$2\lambda - 4\mu + 2 = 2\lambda - 3\mu - 1$

$\mu = 3$

From Eq. (i), $\lambda = \mu = 3$

Now, $P(7, 6, 8)$ and $Q(5, 8, 12)$

Length of segment

$PQ = \sqrt{(7-5)^2 + (6-8)^2 + (8-12)^2}$

$= \sqrt{4 + 4 + 16} = \sqrt{24} = 2\sqrt{6}$

10 (*c*) We have, equation of line

$\frac{x-3}{2} = \frac{2-y}{3} = \frac{z+4}{-1}$

$\Rightarrow \quad \frac{x-3}{2} = \frac{y-2}{-3} = \frac{z+4}{-1}$

So, the direction ratios of line are $< 2, -3, -1 >$

Now, $< 2, -3, -1 > = < -2, 3, 1 >$, $< 6, -9, -3 >$

So, $< 2, 3, -1 >$ cannot be the direction ratios of given line.

11 (*a*) Vector form of the given equations are

$\mathbf{r} = (3\hat{\mathbf{i}} + 2\hat{\mathbf{j}} + \hat{\mathbf{k}}) + \lambda(2\hat{\mathbf{i}} + 3\hat{\mathbf{j}} - \hat{\mathbf{k}})$

and $\mathbf{r} = (-3\hat{\mathbf{i}} + 6\hat{\mathbf{j}} + 5\hat{\mathbf{k}}) + \mu(2\hat{\mathbf{i}} + \hat{\mathbf{j}} + 3\hat{\mathbf{k}})$

$\therefore$ Shortest distance between the two lines is

$$\frac{(|\{(-3\hat{\mathbf{i}} + 6\hat{\mathbf{j}} + 5\hat{\mathbf{k}}) - (3\hat{\mathbf{i}} + 2\hat{\mathbf{j}} + \hat{\mathbf{k}})\} \cdot \{(2\hat{\mathbf{i}} + 3\hat{\mathbf{j}} - \hat{\mathbf{k}}) \times (2\hat{\mathbf{i}} + \hat{\mathbf{j}} + 3\hat{\mathbf{k}})\}|)}{|(2\hat{\mathbf{i}} + 3\hat{\mathbf{j}} - \hat{\mathbf{k}}) \times (2\hat{\mathbf{i}} + \hat{\mathbf{j}} + 3\hat{\mathbf{k}})|}$$

Now, $(2\hat{\mathbf{i}} + 3\hat{\mathbf{j}} - \hat{\mathbf{k}}) \times (2\hat{\mathbf{i}} + \hat{\mathbf{j}} + 3\hat{\mathbf{k}})$

$$= \begin{vmatrix} \hat{\mathbf{i}} & \hat{\mathbf{j}} & \hat{\mathbf{k}} \\ 2 & 3 & -1 \\ 2 & 1 & 3 \end{vmatrix}$$

$= (10\hat{\mathbf{i}} - 8\hat{\mathbf{j}} - 4\hat{\mathbf{k}})$

$\therefore$ Shortest distance

$$= \frac{|(-6\hat{i} + 4\hat{j} + 4\hat{k}) \cdot (10\hat{i} - 8\hat{j} - 4\hat{k})}{|10\hat{i}i - 8\hat{j} - 4\hat{k}|}$$

$$= \frac{|-60 - 32 - 16|}{\sqrt{10^2 + 8^2 + 4^2}} = \frac{108}{\sqrt{180}} = \frac{18}{\sqrt{5}}$$

12 (*a*) Let $a_1 = \hat{i} + 2\hat{j} + 3\hat{k}$

and $\mathbf{a}_2 = 2\hat{i} + 4\hat{j} + 5\hat{k}$

$\mathbf{b}_1 = 2\hat{i} + 3\hat{j} + \lambda\hat{k}$, $\mathbf{b}_2 = \hat{i} + 4\hat{j} + 5\hat{k}$

$$\therefore b_1 \times b_2 = \begin{vmatrix} \hat{i} & \hat{j} & \hat{k} \\ 2 & 3 & \lambda \\ 1 & 4 & 5 \end{vmatrix}$$

$$= \hat{i}(15 - 4\lambda) - \hat{j}(10 - \lambda) + 5\hat{k}$$

and $a_2 - a_1 = \hat{i} + 2\hat{j} + 2\hat{k}$

$\therefore$ Shortest distance

$$= \left|\frac{(a_2 - a_1) \cdot (b_1 \times b_2)}{|b_1 \times b_2|}\right| = \frac{1}{\sqrt{3}} \text{ [Given]}$$

$$\Rightarrow \left|\frac{(15 - 4\lambda) - 2(10 - \lambda) + 10}{\sqrt{(15 - 4\lambda)^2 + (10 - \lambda)^2 + 25}}\right| = \frac{1}{\sqrt{3}}$$

$$\Rightarrow \left|\frac{-2\lambda + 5}{\sqrt{(15 - 4\lambda)^2 + (10 - \lambda)^2 + 25}}\right| = \frac{1}{\sqrt{3}}$$

On squaring both sides, we get

$3(5 - 2\lambda)^2$

$= (15 - 4\lambda)^2 + (10 - \lambda)^2 + 25$

$\Rightarrow \quad 5\lambda^2 - 80\lambda + 275 = 0$

$\Rightarrow \quad \lambda^2 - 16\lambda + 55 = 0$

$\Rightarrow \quad (\lambda - 5)(\lambda - 11) = 0$

$\Rightarrow \quad \lambda = 5, 11$

$\therefore$ Sum of the value of λ is 16.

13 (65) Given lines are $x = y + 2 = z$

$$\Rightarrow \frac{x}{1} = \frac{y - (-2)}{1} = \frac{z}{1} = t \text{ (let)} \quad \dots \text{(i)}$$

Let any point on the line (i) be

$P(t, t - 2, t)$

and any point on the

$x + 2 = 2y = 2z$ is $Q(2s - 2, s, s)$

$\therefore$ Direction ratio of PQ is

$2s - 2 - t, s - t + 2, s - t$

$$\therefore \frac{2s - 2 - t}{2} = \frac{s - t + 2}{1} = \frac{s - t}{2}$$

$\Rightarrow \quad t = 6$ and $s = 2$

$\therefore \quad P = (6, 4, 6)$ and $Q = (2, 2, 2)$

Equation of line PQ is

$$\frac{x - 2}{2} = \frac{y - 2}{1} = \frac{z - 2}{2} = \lambda \quad \dots \text{(ii)}$$

Let any point on the line (ii) be $F(2\lambda + 2, \lambda + 2, 2\lambda + 2)$ and let $A(1, 2, 12)$.

$\therefore$ Direction ratio of AF is

$2\lambda + 1, \lambda, 2\lambda - 10$

Here, $\quad \mathbf{AF} \cdot \mathbf{PQ} = 0$

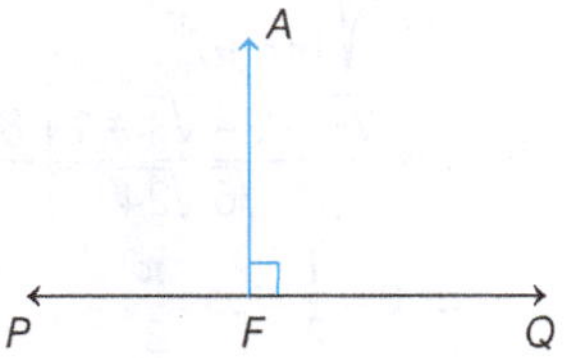

$\Rightarrow \quad 4\lambda + 2 + \lambda + 4\lambda - 20 = 0$

$\Rightarrow \quad 9\lambda = 18 \Rightarrow \lambda = 2$

$F \equiv (6, 4, 6)$

$$\therefore \quad AF = \sqrt{(6 - 1)^2 + (4 - 2)^2 + (6 - 12)^2}$$

$$\Rightarrow \quad l = \sqrt{25 + 4 + 36} = \sqrt{65}$$

$\therefore \quad l^2 = 65$

14 (43) Firstly convert the given equation of lines in the form of $\mathbf{r}_1 = \mathbf{a}_1 + \lambda\mathbf{b}_1$ and $\mathbf{r}_2 = \mathbf{a}_2 + \mu\mathbf{b}_2$, then use formula for shortest distance

$$d = \left|\frac{(\mathbf{a}_2 - \mathbf{a}_1) \cdot (\mathbf{b}_1 \times \mathbf{b}_2)}{|\mathbf{b}_1 \times \mathbf{b}_2|}\right|$$

$\mathbf{a}_1 = \lambda\hat{i} + 2\hat{j} + \hat{k}$

$\mathbf{a}_2 = -2\hat{i} - 5\hat{j} + 4\hat{k}$

$\mathbf{b}_1 = 3\hat{i} - \hat{j} + \hat{k}$

$\mathbf{b}_2 = -3\hat{i} + 2\hat{j} + 4\hat{k}$

$\Rightarrow \mathbf{a}_1 - \mathbf{a}_2 = (\lambda + 2)\hat{i} + 7\hat{j} - 3\hat{k}$

$$\Rightarrow \mathbf{b}_1 \times \mathbf{b}_2 = \begin{vmatrix} \hat{i} & \hat{j} & \hat{k} \\ 3 & -1 & 1 \\ -3 & 2 & 4 \end{vmatrix}$$

$$= -6\hat{i} - 15\hat{j} + 3\hat{k}$$

Now, $\quad d = \left|\frac{(a_2 - a_1) \cdot (b_1 \times b_2)}{|b_1 \times b_2|}\right|$

$$\frac{44}{\sqrt{30}} = \frac{|6\lambda + 126|}{3\sqrt{30}}$$

$\Rightarrow \quad 132 = |6\lambda + 126|$

$\Rightarrow \quad \lambda = 1, \lambda = -43$

$\therefore \quad |\lambda| = 43$

15 (158) We have to find direction ratio of line

$$\begin{vmatrix} \hat{i} & \hat{j} & \hat{k} \\ 1 & 3 & -2 \\ 1 & -1 & 2 \end{vmatrix} = \hat{i}(6 - 2) - \hat{j}(2 + 2) + \hat{k}(-1 - 3)$$

$$= 4\hat{i} - 4\hat{j} - 4\hat{k}$$

Then, equation of line

$$\frac{x - 2}{1} = \frac{y - 3}{-1} = \frac{z - 1}{-1} = \lambda$$

Let $M(\lambda + 2, -\lambda + 3, -\lambda + 1)$

Direction ratio of

$MQ = <\lambda + 2 - 5, -\lambda + 3 - 3, -\lambda + 1 - 8>$

$= <\lambda - 3, -\lambda, -\lambda - 7>$

$\because L \perp MQ$

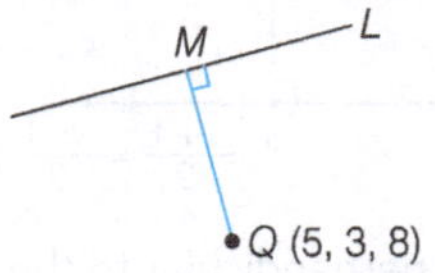

Then, $(\lambda - 3)(1) + (-\lambda)(-1) + (-\lambda - 7)(-1) = 0$

$\Rightarrow \quad \lambda - 3 + \lambda + \lambda + 7 = 0$

$\Rightarrow 3\lambda = -4 \Rightarrow \lambda = -4/3$

$$\therefore \quad M = \left(-\frac{4}{3} + 2, \frac{4}{3} + 3, \frac{4}{3} + 1\right)$$

$$= \left(\frac{2}{3}, \frac{13}{3}, \frac{7}{3}\right)$$

and $MQ = a$, then

$$3a^2 = 3\left[\left(5 - \frac{2}{3}\right)^2 + \left(3 - \frac{13}{3}\right)^2 + \left(8 - \frac{7}{3}\right)^2\right]$$

$$= 3\left[\frac{169}{9} + \frac{16}{9} + \frac{289}{9}\right]$$

$$= 3\left(\frac{474}{9}\right) = \frac{474}{3} = 158$$

16 (153) Given, equation of line is

$$\frac{x+1}{2}=\frac{y+2}{3}=\frac{z-1}{2}$$

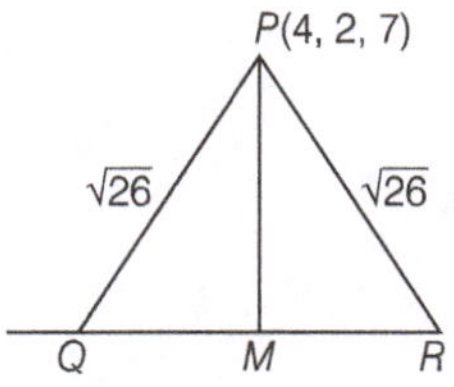

$$\frac{x+1}{2}=\frac{y+2}{3}=\frac{z-1}{2}=k$$

Let co-ordinate of M be $(2k-1, 3k-2, 2k+1)$.

As PQR is an isosceles triangle, so $PM \perp QR$, where M is mid-point of QR.

Direction ratios of $QR = 2, 3, 2$

Direction ratios of $PM = 2k-1-4, 3k-2-2, 2k+1-7$

$= 2k-5, 3k-4, 2k-6$

As $QR \perp PM$

$2(2k-5)+3(3k-4)+2(2k-6)=0$

$\Rightarrow \quad 4k-10+9k-12+4k-12=0$

$\Rightarrow \quad 17k-34=0 \Rightarrow k=2$

Coordinate of M is $(2\times 2-1, 3\times 2-2, 2\times 2+1) \Rightarrow M\,(3, 4, 5)$

$PM=\sqrt{(3-4)^2+(4-2)^2+(5-7)^2}$

$=\sqrt{1+4+4}=3$

$\Rightarrow \quad \frac{x+1}{2}=\frac{y+2}{3}=\frac{z-1}{2}=\lambda$

$x=2\lambda-1, y=3\lambda-2, z=2\lambda+1$

$\because \quad (PQ)^2=(PR)^2=26$

$\therefore \quad (2\lambda-1-4)^2+(3\lambda-2-2)^2+(2\lambda+1-7)^2=26$

$\Rightarrow (2\lambda-5)^2+(3\lambda-4)^2+(2\lambda-6)^2=26$

$\Rightarrow 17\lambda^2-68\lambda+51=0$

$\Rightarrow \quad \lambda^2-4\lambda+3=0 \Rightarrow \lambda=1, 3$

$\therefore$ Coordinate of Q is (1, 1, 3) and R is (5, 7, 7).

$QR=\sqrt{(5-1)^2+(7-1)^2+(7-3)^2}$

$=\sqrt{16+36+16}=\sqrt{68}=2\sqrt{17}$

Area of $\Delta PQR=\frac{1}{2}\times PM\times QR$

$=\frac{1}{2}\times 3\times 2\sqrt{17}=3\sqrt{17}$

Square of area of ΔPQR

$=9\times 17=153$

Skill Boosters

1 (*b*) Projection of a vector on co-ordinate axes are

$x_2-x_1, y_2-y_1, z_2, -z_1$

Now, $\sqrt{(x_2-x_1)^2+(y_2-y_1)^2+(z_2-z_1)^2}$

$=\sqrt{9+4+36}=49$

So, the direcdtion cosines of the vector are $\left(\frac{-3}{7}, \frac{2}{7}, \frac{6}{7}\right)$

2 (*a*) Given line

$$\frac{x+1}{2}=\frac{y-1}{3}=\frac{z-1}{2}=\Omega \quad \text{(let)}$$

Any point on this line is $B(2\Omega-1, 3\Omega+1, 2\Omega+1)$

Let the given point be $A(1, 2, 3)$ then the direction ratio of AB is

$(2\Omega-1, 3\Omega+1-2, 2\Omega+1-3)$

$=(2\Omega-2, 3\Omega-1, 2\Omega-2)$

Since both lines are perpendicular to each other

$\therefore d_1\cdot d_2=0$

$2(2\Omega-2)+3(3\Omega-1)+2(2\Omega-2)=0$

$4\Omega-4+9\Omega-3+4\Omega-4=0$

$17\Omega=11 \Rightarrow \Omega=\frac{11}{17}$

$\therefore$ Required direction ratio of line is

$\left(2\frac{11}{17}-2, 3\times\frac{11}{17}-1, 2\times\frac{11}{17}-2\right)$

$\left(\frac{22-34}{17}, \frac{33-17}{17}, \frac{22-34}{17}\right)$

$=\left(\frac{-12}{17}, \frac{16}{17}, \frac{-12}{17}\right)$

This line passes through (1, 2, 3)

$\therefore$ Required equation of line

$$\frac{x-1}{\frac{-12}{17}}=\frac{y-2}{\frac{16}{17}}=\frac{z-3}{\frac{-12}{17}}$$

3 (*c*) $\mathbf{r}=3\hat{\mathbf{i}}+8\hat{\mathbf{j}}+3\hat{\mathbf{k}}+\lambda(3\hat{\mathbf{i}}-2\hat{\mathbf{j}}+\hat{\mathbf{k}})$ and

$\mathbf{r}=-3\hat{\mathbf{i}}+7\hat{\mathbf{j}}-6\hat{\mathbf{k}}+\mu(3\hat{\mathbf{i}}-2\hat{\mathbf{j}}-4\hat{\mathbf{k}})$

$(\mathbf{a}_2-\mathbf{a}_1)=(-3-3, 7-8, -6-3)$

Shortest Distance

$$D=\left|\frac{(a_2-a_1)\cdot(b_1\times b_2)}{|b_1\times b_2|}\right|$$

$=(-6\hat{\mathbf{i}}-\hat{\mathbf{j}}-9\hat{\mathbf{k}})$

$$\therefore \quad b_1\times b_2=\begin{vmatrix}\hat{\mathbf{i}} & \hat{\mathbf{j}} & \hat{\mathbf{k}}\\ 3 & -2 & 1\\ 3 & -2 & -4\end{vmatrix}$$

$=\hat{\mathbf{i}}(8+2)-\hat{\mathbf{j}}(-12-3)+\hat{\mathbf{k}}(-6+6)$

$b_1\times b_2=12\hat{\mathbf{i}}+15\hat{\mathbf{j}}$

$|b_1\times b_2|=\sqrt{144+225}=\sqrt{369}$

$\therefore \ \text{SD}=\left|\frac{(-6\hat{\mathbf{i}}+\hat{\mathbf{j}}-9\hat{\mathbf{k}})\cdot(12\hat{\mathbf{i}}+15\hat{\mathbf{j}})}{\sqrt{369}}\right|$

$=\left|\frac{-72-15}{\sqrt{369}}\right|=\frac{87}{\sqrt{369}}$

4 (*b*) Since, a line makes an angle of $\frac{\pi}{3}$ with positive direction of each of Y-axis and Z-axis, therefore

$\beta=\frac{\pi}{3}$ and $\gamma=\frac{\pi}{3}$

We know that

$\cos^2\alpha+\cos^2\beta+\cos^2\gamma=1$

$\therefore \cos^2\alpha+\cos^2\left(\frac{\pi}{3}\right)+\cos^2\left(\frac{\pi}{3}\right)=1$

$\cos^2\alpha+\frac{1}{4}+\frac{1}{4}=1$

$\cos^2\alpha=\frac{1}{2}\Rightarrow\cos\alpha=\frac{1}{\sqrt{2}}$

$\therefore \quad \alpha=\frac{\pi}{4}$

5 (*d*) $\frac{x-2}{2}=\frac{y+2}{7}=\frac{z+3}{-1}$

and $\frac{x-2}{3}=\frac{2y-8}{4}=\frac{z-5}{4}$

Here, $\cos\theta$

$$=\left|\frac{a_1a_2+b_1b_2+c_1c_2}{\sqrt{a_1^2+b_1^2+c_1^2}\sqrt{a_2^2+b_2^2+c_2^2}}\right|$$

$\cos\theta=\left|\frac{2\cdot 3+7\cdot 4+(-1)\cdot 4}{\sqrt{4+49+1}\sqrt{9+16+16}}\right|$

$\cos\theta=\left|\frac{6+28-4}{\sqrt{54}\sqrt{41}}\right|$

$\cos\theta=\frac{30}{3\sqrt{246}}=\frac{10}{\sqrt{246}}$

$\theta=\cos^{-1}\left(\frac{10}{\sqrt{246}}\right)$

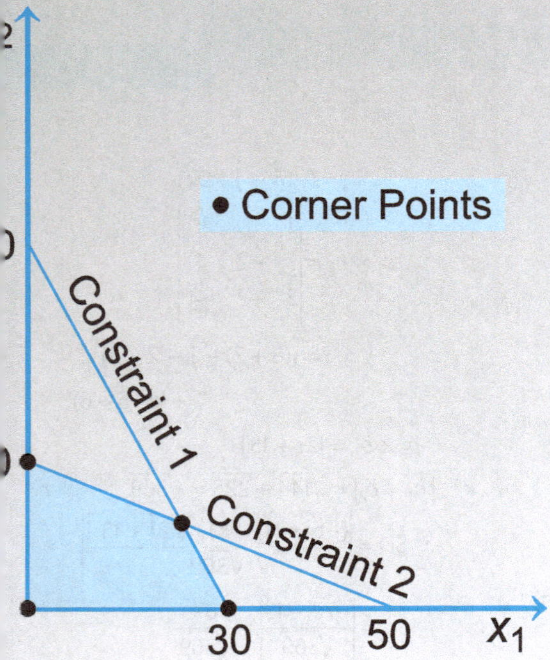

12

Linear Programming

Topicwise No. of Ques asked in 3 Years (JEE Main)

Topics	No. of Questions		
	2024	2023	2022
Linear Programming Problem and Its Mathematical Formulation	–	–	–

Special Type of Ques Asked in 3 Years (JEE Main)

Types	Years		
	2024	2023	2022
A-R	–	–	–
Statement Based	–	–	–
Numerical Value Type	–	–	–

Last 3 Years Weightage (JEE Main)

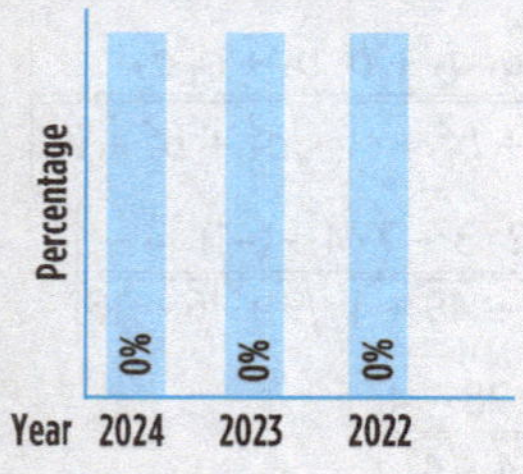

Linear Programming Problem and Its Mathematical Formulation

Linear Programming Problem (LPP)

A linear programming problem is one that is concerned with finding the optimal value (maximum or minimum value) of a linear function (called objective function) of several variables (say x and y called decision variables), subject to the constraints that the variables are non-negative and satisfy a set of linear inequalities (called linear constraints).

Mathematical Form of LPP

- The general mathematical form of a linear programming problem may be written as
  Maximise or Minimise $Z = c_1x + c_2y$ subject to constraints are $a_1x + b_1y \le d_1, a_2x + b_2y \le d_2$, etc. and non-negative restrictions are $x \ge 0, y \ge 0$.

Some Terms Related to LPP

- **Constraints** The linear inequations or inequalities or restrictions on the variables of a linear programming problem are called **constraints**. The conditions $x \ge 0$, $y \ge 0$ are called **non-negative restrictions**.
- **Optimisation Problem** A problem which seeks to maximise or minimise a linear function subject to certain constraints determined by a set of linear inequalities is called an **optimisation problem**. Linear programming problems are special type of optimisation problems.

- **Objective Function** A linear function of two or more variables which has to be maximised or minimised under the given restrictions in the form of linear inequations or linear constraints is called the objective function.The variables used in the **objective function** are called **decision variables**.
- **Optimal Values** The maximum or minimum value of an objective function is known as its **optimal value**.
- **Feasible and Infeasible Regions** The common region determined by all the constraints including non-negative constraints $x, y \geq 0$ of a linear programming problem is called the **feasible region** or **solution region**. Each point in this region represents a feasible choice. The region other than feasible region is called an **infeasible region**.
- **Bounded and Unbounded Regions** A feasible region of a system of linear inequalities is said to be **bounded**, if it can be enclosed within a circle. Otherwise, it is said to be **unbounded region**.
- **Feasible and Infeasible Solutions** Any solution to the given linear programming problem which also satisfies the non-negative restrictions of the problem is called a **feasible solution**.
- Any point outside the feasible region is called an **infeasible solution**.
- **Optimal Solution** A feasible solution at which the objective function has optimal value is called the **optimal solution** of the linear programming problem.
- **Optimisation Technique** The process of obtaining the optimal solution is called **optimisation technique**.

Important Theorems

(i) **Theorem 1** Let R be the feasible region (convex polygon) for a linear programming problem and $Z = ax + by$ be the objective function.

- When Z has an optimal value (maximum or minimum), where the variables x and y are subject to constraints described by linear inequalities, this optimal value must occur at a corner point (vertex) of the feasible region.
- A corner point of a feasible region is a point of intersection of two boundary lines in the region.

(ii) **Theorem 2** Let R be the feasible region for a linear programming problem and $Z = ax + by$ be the objective function. If R is bounded, then the objective function Z has both a maximum and a minimum value on R and each of these occurs at a corner point (vertex) of R.

- Maximum or minimum value of the objective function may or may not exist, if the feasible region is unbounded.

Graphical Method of Solving LPP

The following steps are given below

Concept Master Video

Step I Find the feasible region of the linear programming problem and determine its corner points (vertices) either by inspection or by solving the two equations of the lines intersecting at that point.

Step II Evaluate the objective function $Z = ax + by$ at each corner point. Let M and m respectively denote the largest and smallest values of these points.

Step III When the feasible region is bounded, M and m are the maximum and minimum values of Z.

Step IV When the feasible region is unbounded, then

- M is the maximum value of Z, if the open half plane determined by $ax + by > M$ has no point in common with the feasible region. Otherwise, Z has no maximum value.
- Similarly, m is the minimum value of Z, if the open half plane determined by $ax + by < m$ has no point in common with the feasible region. Otherwise, Z has no minimum value.

Caution Points

- Ensure that the objective function and constraints are correctly formulated based on the problem statement. Misformulation can lead to incorrect solution.
- Verify that the feasible region, defined by the constraints, is correctly identified. An infeasible region or incorrect boundaries can invalidate the results.
- After solving the problem confirms that the solution meets all compatibility conditions.
- Verify your calculations throughly and ensure that all steps adhere to LPP principles for accuracy.

Step by Step

Mastering NCERT

- Concept Builders
- Topical Questions
- Numerical Type Questions
- Assertion and Reason Questions
- Case or Paragraph Type Questions
- Skill Boosters

Concept Builders

1 The feasible region is always a concave region. (T/F)

2 The maximum (or minimum) solution of the objective function occurs at the vertex of the feasible region. (T/F)

3 If two corner points produce the same maximum (or minimum) value of the objective function, then every point on the line segment joining these points will also give the same maximum (or minimum) value. (T/F)

4 Maximise the objective function $Z = -x + 2y$, subject to the constraints $x \geq 3$, $x + y \geq 5$, $x + 2y \geq 6$, $x, y \geq 0$ has no maximum value. (T/F)

5 If the feasible region of an LPP is unbounded, then maximum or minimum value of the objective function $Z = ax + by$ may or may not exist. (T/F)

6 Maximum value of the objective function $Z = ax + by$ in an LPP always occurs at only corner point of the feasible region. (T/F)

7 In an LPP, the objective function is always ....

8 A feasible region of a system of linear inequalities is said to be .... , if it can be enclosed within a circle.

9 The corner points of the feasible region of an LPP are (0, 0), (0, 8), (2, 7), (5, 4) and (6, 0). The maximum profit $P = 3x + 2y$ occurs at the point ....

10 A corner point of a feasible region is a point in the region which is the .... of two boundary lines.

11 The maximum value of $Z = 4x + 2y$ subject to the constraints $2x + 3y \leq 18$, $x + y \leq 10$, $x \geq 0$, $y \geq 0$ is ....

12 In an LPP, the linear inequalities or restrictions on the variables are called ....

13 In an LPP, the linear function which has to be maximised or minimised is called a linear .... function.

14 The common region determined by all the linear constraints of an LPP is called the .... region.

15 The minimum of the objective function $Z = 2x + 10y$ for linear constraints $x - y \geq 0$, $x - 5y \leq -5$, $x \geq 0$, $y \geq 0$ is ....

Topical Questions

Introduction of Linear Programming Problem and Its Mathematical Formulation

Level I

1 A furniture dealer deals in only two items–tables and chairs. He has ₹ 50000 to invest and has storage space of at most 60 pieces. A table costs ₹ 2500 and a chair ₹ 500. Then the constraints of the above problem are (where, x is number of tables and y is number of chairs) **NCERT Pg. 395**

(a) $x \geq 0, y \geq 0$ (b) $5x + y \leq 100$
(c) $x + y \leq 60$ (d) All of these

2 A linear programming problem is one that is concerned with finding the ...*A*... of a linear function called ...*B*... function of several variables (say x and y), subject to the conditions that the variables are ...*C*... *and satisfy set of linear inequalities called linear constraints.*

Here, *A*, *B* and *C* are respectively **NCERT Pg. 396**

(a) objective, optimal value, negative
(b) optimal value, objective, negative
(c) optimal value, objective, non-negative
(d) objective, optimal value, non-negative

3 If a furniture dealer estimates that from the sale of one table he can make a profit of ₹ 250 and from the sale of one chair of a profit of ₹ 75 and if x is the number of chairs and y is the number of tables, then its linear objective function is **NCERT Pg. 396**

(a) $Z = 75x + 250y$ (b) $Z = 75x + 25y$
(c) $Z = 250x + 75y$ (d) $Z = 25x + 75y$

4 Let x and y are the number of tables and chairs respectively, on which a furniture dealer wants to make profit for the constraints

Maximise $Z = 250x + 75y$

Subject to $5x + y \leq 100$

$x + y \leq 60$

$x \geq 0 \Rightarrow y \geq 0$

Consider the following graph

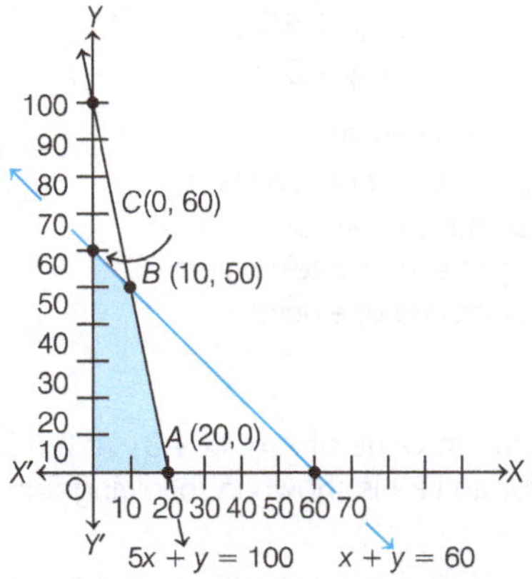

Then, the maximum profit to the dealer results from buying **NCERT Pg. 397**

(a) 10 tables and 50 chairs
(b) 50 tables and 10 chairs
(c) 0 table and 60 chairs
(d) 20 tables and 40 chairs

5 Let R be the feasible region (convex polygon) for a linear programming problem and $Z = ax + by$ be the objective function. **NCERT Pg. 398**

Then, which of the following statements is false?

(a) When Z has an optimal value, where the variables x and y are subject to constraints described by linear inequalities, this optimal value must occur at a corner point (vertex) of the feasible region
(b) If R is bounded, then the objective function Z has both a maximum and a minimum value on R and each of these occurs at a corner point of R
(c) If R is unbounded, then a maximum or a minimum value of the objective function may not exist
(d) If R is unbounded and a maximum or a minimum value of the objective function exists, then it does not occur at a corner point

6 The corner point method for bounded feasible region comprises of the following steps

I. When the feasible region is bounded, M and m are the maximum and minimum values of Z.
II. Find the feasible region of the linear programming problem and determine its corner points.
III. Evaluate the objective function $Z = ax + by$ at each corner point. Let M and m, respectively be the largest and smallest values of these points.

The correct order of these above steps is **NCERT Pg. 399**

(a) III, I, II (b) II, III, I
(c) II, I, III (d) I, III, II

7 Let the feasible region of the linear programming problem with the objective function $Z = ax + by$ is unbounded and let M and m be the maximum and minimum value of Z, respectively.

Now consider the following statements

I. M is the maximum value of Z, if the open half plane determined by $ax + by > M$ has no point in common with the feasible region. Otherwise, Z has no maximum value.
II. m is the minimum value of Z, if the open half plane determined by $ax + by < m$ has no point in common with the feasible region. Otherwise, Z has no minimum value.

Choose the correct option. **NCERT Pg. 399**

(a) Only I is true
(b) Only II is true
(c) Both I and II are true
(d) Neither I nor II is true

8 The minimum and maximum values of Z for the problem,

minimise and maximise $Z = 3x + 9y$ ...(i)

subject to the constraints

$x + 3y \leq 60$ ...(ii)

$x + y \geq 10$ ...(iii)

$x \leq y$ ...(iv)

$x \geq 0,\ y \geq 0$ ...(v)

are respectively **NCERT Pg. 401**

(a) 60 and 180 (b) 180 and 60
(c) 50 and 190 (d) 190 and 50

9 Minimise the linear programming problem

$Z = 3x + 2y$

subject to the constraints

$x + y \geq 8$

$3x + 5y \leq 15$

$x \geq 0,\ y \geq 0$ has **NCERT Pg. 403**

(a) one solution (b) no feasible solution
(c) two solutions (d) infinitely many solutions

10 The maximum value of the objective function

$$Z = 3x + 4y$$

subject to the constraints

$$x + y \leq 4$$
$$x \geq 0,\ y \geq 0 \text{ is}$$

NCERT Pg. 403

(a) 16 (b) 18 (c) 20 (d) 25

11 Match the terms of column I with the terms of column II and choose correct option from the codes given below. NCERT Pg. 404

	Column I (Linear programming problem)		Column II (Solution)
A.	Minimise $Z = -3x + 4y$ subject to $x + 2y \leq 8$, $3x + 2y \leq 12$, $x \geq 0, y \geq 0$	1.	$\frac{235}{19}$
B.	Maximise $Z = 5x + 3y$, subject to $3x + 5y \leq 15$, $5x + 2y \leq 10$, $x \geq 0, y \geq 0$	2.	-12
C.	Minimise $Z = 3x + 5y$, such that $x + 3y \geq 3$, $x + y \geq 2$, $x, y \geq 0$	3.	18
D.	Maximise $Z = 3x + 2y$, subject to $x + 2y \leq 10$, $3x + y \leq 15$, $x, y \geq 0$	4.	7
		5.	No solution

Codes

	A	B	C	D		A	B	C	D
(a)	4	5	3	2	(b)	2	5	3	1
(c)	2	1	4	3	(d)	3	5	2	1

12 The minimum value of the objective function $Z = x + 2y$ subject to the constraints

$$2x + y \geq 3,\ x + 2y \geq 6$$
$$x, y \geq 0 \text{ occurs}$$

NCERT Pg. 404

(a) at every point on the line $x + 2y = 6$
(b) at every point on the line $2x + y = 3$
(c) at every point on the line $x + 2y = 3$
(d) at every point on the line $2x + y = 6$

13 The minimum and maximum values of the objective function

$$Z = 5x + 10y$$

subject to $x + 2y \leq 120$
$$x + y \geq 60$$
$$x - 2y \geq 0$$
$$x, y \geq 0$$

are respectively NCERT Pg. 404

(a) 300 and 500 (b) 300 and 600
(c) 600 and 700 (d) 300 and 400

14 The maximum and minimum values of the objective function

$$Z = x + 2y$$

subject to the constraints

$$x + 2y \geq 100$$
$$2x - y \leq 0$$
$$2x + y \leq 200$$
$$x, y \geq 0$$

occurs respectively at NCERT Pg. 404

(a) one point and three points
(b) two points and one point
(c) one point and infinitely points
(d) one point and one point

Level II

15 The maximum value of $Z = 4x + 3y$, if the feasible region for an LPP is shown in following figure, is

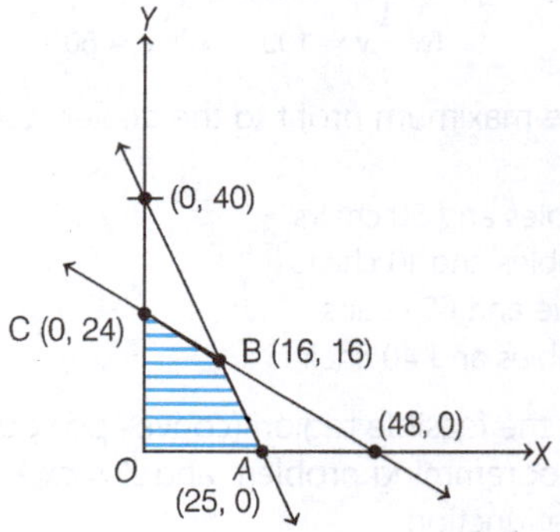

NCERT Exemplar Pg. 242, 243

(a) 112 (b) 100
(c) 72 (d) 110

16 The corner points of the feasible region determined by the stystem of linear constraints are (0, 0), (0, 40), (20, 40), (60, 20), (60, 0). The objective function is $Z = 4x + 3y$. NCERT Exemplar Pg. 254

Compare the quantities in column A and column B.

Column A	Column B
Maximum of Z	325

(a) The quantity in column A is greater.
(b) The quantity in column B is greater.
(c) The two quantities are equal.
(d) The relationship cannot be determined on the basis of the given information.

17 The maximum and minimum values of the objective function

$$Z = 3x - 4y$$

subject to the constraints

$$x - 2y \leq 0$$
$$-3x + y \leq 4$$
$$x - y \leq 6$$
$$x, y \geq 0$$

are respectively **NCERT Exemplar Pg. 254**

(a) 12, 10 (b) 10, 12
(c) 12, does not exist (d) 5, 12

18 The corner points of the feasible region determined by the system of linear constraints are (0, 10), (5, 5) (15, 15), (0, 20). Let $Z = px + qy$, where $p, q > 0$. Then, the condition on p and q so that the maximum of Z occurs at both the points (15, 15) and (0, 20), is **NCERT Exemplar Pg. 248**

(a) $p = q$ (b) $p = 2q$
(c) $q = 2p$ (d) $q = 3p$

Numerical Type Questions

1 Reshma wishes to mix two types of food P and Q in such a way that the vitamin contents of the mixture contain atleast 8 units of vitamin A and 11 units of vitamin B. Food P costs ₹ 60/kg and food Q costs ₹ 80/kg. Food P contains 3 units/kg of vitamin A and 5 units/kg of vitamin B, while food Q contains 4 units/kg of vitamin A and 2 units/kg of vitamin B. Then, the minimum cost of the mixture is in ₹ .... **Old NCERT Pg. 519**

2 One kind of cake requires 200g of flour and 25g of fat and another kind of cake requires 100g of flour and 50g of fat. Then, the maximum number of cakes which can be made from 5kg of flour and 1kg of fat assuming that there is no storage of the other ingredients used in making the cakes, is .... **Old NCERT Pg. 519**

3 A factory manufactures two types of screws, A and B. Each type of screw requires the use of two machines, an automatic and a hand operated. It takes 4 min on the automatic and 6 min on hand operated machines to get of screws A, while it takes 6 min on automatic and 3 min on the hand operated machines to manufacture a package to screws B.

Each machine is available for atmost 4 h on any day. The manufacturer can sell a package of screws A at a profit of ₹7 and screws B at a profit of ₹10. Assuming that he can sell all the screws he manufactures, the maximum profit is in ₹ .... **Old NCERT Pg. 519**

4. A diet is to contain atleast 80 units of vitamin A and 100 units of minerals. Two foods F_1 and F_2 are available. Food F_1 costs ₹ 4 per unit and food F_2 costs ₹ 6 per unit. One unit of food F_1 contains 3 units of vitamin A and 4 units of minerals. One unit of food F_2 contains 6 units of vitamin A and 3 units of minerals. Then, the minimum cost for diet that consists of mixture of these two foods and also meets the minimal nutritional requirements, is in ₹ .... **Old NCERT Pg. 520**

5 A farmer mixes two brands P and Q of cattle feed. Brand P, costing ₹ 250 per bag, contains 3 units of nutritional element A, 2.5 units of element B and 2 units of element C. Brand Q costing ₹ 200 per bag contains 1.5 units of nutritional element A, 11.25 units of element B, and 3 units of element C. The minimum requirements of nutrients A, B and C are 18 units, 45 units and 24 units, respectively. Then, the minimum cost is in ₹ .... **Old NCERT Pg. 526**

6 A manufacturer has three machines I, II and III installed in his factory. Machines I and II are capable of being operated for atmost 12 h whereas machine III must be operated for atleast 5 h a day. She produces only two items M and N each requiring the use of all the three machines.

The number of hours required for producing 1 unit of each of M and N on the three machines are given in the following table **Old NCERT Pg. 522**

Items	Number of hours required on machines		
	I	II	III
M	1	2	1
N	2	1	1.25

She makes a profit of ₹ 600 and ₹ 400 on items M and N, respectively.

Then, to maximise the profit, number of units of item M, the manufacturer has to produce, is in ....

7 If the given constraints are

$$5x + 4y \geq 2$$
$$x \leq 6$$
$$y \leq 7$$
$$x, y \geq 0$$

Then, the maximum value of the function $Z = x + 2y$ is **NCERT Pg. 404**

Assertion and Reason Questions

Direction (Q. Nos. 1-5) The following questions consist of two statements, one labelled as "Assertion (A) and the other labelled as Reason (R)". You are to examine these two statements carefully true and it so, where the Reason (R) is the correct explanation for the given Assertion (A). Select your answer from following options.

(a) Both Assertion and Reason are correct and Reason is the correct explanation of Assertion.

(b) Both Assertion and Reason are correct but Reason is not the correct explanation of Assertion.

(c) Assertion is correct but Reason is incorrect.

(d) Assertion is incorrect but Reason is correct.

For Q. Nos. (1-3) Consider the graph of constrants stated as linear inequalities as below

$$5x + y \leq 100 \quad \text{...(i)}$$
$$x + y \leq 60 \quad \text{...(ii)}$$
$$x \geq 0 \quad \text{...(iii)}$$
$$y \geq 0 \quad \text{...(iv)}$$

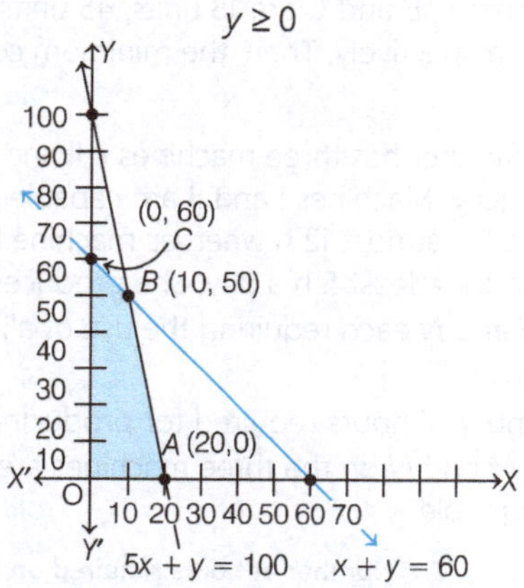

1 Assertion (A) The region *OABCO* is the feasible region for the problem.

Reason (R) The common region determined by all the constraints including non-negative constraints $x, y \geq 0$ of a linear programming problem. NCERT Pg. 397

2 Assertion (A) The points (10, 50), (0, 60) or (20, 0) are feasible solutions.

Reason (R) Points within and on the boundary of the feasible region represent feasible solutions of the constraints. NCERT Pg. 397

3 Assertion (A) (25, 40) is an infeasible solution of the problem.

Reason (R) Any point inside the feasible region is called an infeasible solution. NCERT Pg. 397

4 Assertion (A) The objective function

$$Z = -50x + 20y$$

subject to the constraints

$$2x - y \geq -5$$
$$3x + y \geq 3$$
$$2x - 3y \leq 12$$
$$x \geq 0, y \geq 0$$

has no minimum value.

Reason (R) If the open half plane determined by $ax + by < m$, where m is the minimum value of Z, has a point in common with feasible region, then Z has no minimum value. NCERT Pg. 399, 402, 403

5 Assertion (A) The maximum value of

$$Z = 11x + 7y$$

subject to the constraints

$$2x + y \leq 6$$
$$x \leq 2$$
$$x \geq 0, y \geq 0$$

occurs at the corner point (0, 6).

Reason (R) If the feasible region of the given LPP is bounded, then the maximum and minimum value of the objective function occurs at corner points.

NCERT Exemplar Pg. 250

Case or Paragraph Type Questions

Direction (Q. Nos. 1-4) A furniture dealer deals in only two items tables and chairs. He has ₹ 50000 to invest and has storage space of atmost 60 pieces. A table costs ₹ 2500 and a chair ₹ 500. He estimates that from the sale of one table, he can make a profit of ₹ 250 and that from the sale of one chair a profit of ₹ 75. He wants to know how many tables and chairs he should buy from the available money so as to maximise his total profit, assuming that he can sell all the items which he buys.

On the basis of the above information, answer the following questions. NCERT Pg. 394, 395 & 396

1 The above stated optimisation problem is an example of
(a) linear programming problem
(b) functional programming problem
(c) computer programming problem
(d) None of the above

2 Which of the following are constraints for the given problem?
(a) Maximum investment is ₹ 50000 and storage space is for maximum of 60 pieces
(b) Minimum investment is ₹ 50000 and storage space is for minimum of 60 pieces
(c) Maximum investment is ₹ 50000 and storage space is for minimum of 60 pieces
(d) None of the above

3 If he buys tables only, then his profit will be
(a) ₹ 500 (b) ₹ 5000 (c) ₹ 7500 (d) ₹ 2500

4 Suppose he chooses to buy chairs only. Then, his maximum profit is
(a) ₹ 4500 (b) ₹ 7500 (c) ₹ 4000 (d) ₹ 5700

Direction (Q. Nos. 5-8) *Consider the graph of constraints stated as linear inequalities as below*

$$5x + y \le 100 \quad ...(i)$$
$$x + y \le 60 \quad ...(ii)$$
$$x \ge 0 \quad ...(iii)$$
$$y \ge 0 \quad ...(iv)$$

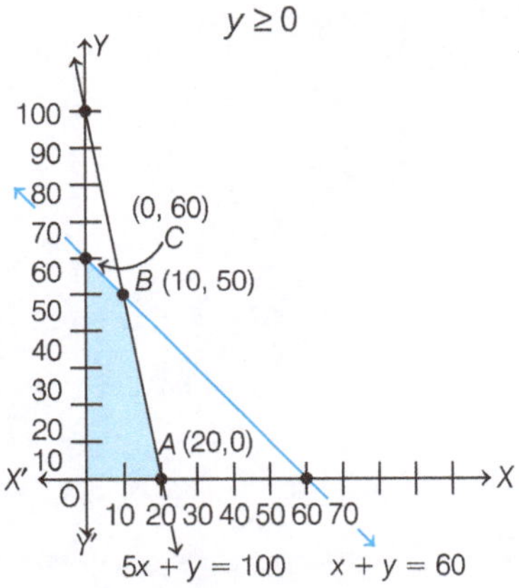

where, x and y are number of tables and chairs on which a furniture dealer wants to make his profit. NCERT Pg. 397 & 398

5 The shaded region in the graph is called
(a) feasible region (b) critical region
(c) non-feasible region (d) None of these

6 Every point in the feasible region is called
(a) no solution
(b) unbounded solution
(c) feasible solution
(d) non-feasible solution

7 Any point in the feasible region that gives the optimal value (maximum or minimum) of the objective function is called a/an
(a) optimal solution (b) no solution
(c) finite solution (d) None of these

8 There is/are ...D... point(s) in the feasible region *OABCO* that satisfy all the constraints given in (i) to (iv).
Here, D refers to
(a) only 1 (b) only 2
(c) finitely many (d) infinitely many

Direction (Q. Nos. 9-11) *The feasible solution for a LPP is shown as below* NCERT Exemplar Pg. 255

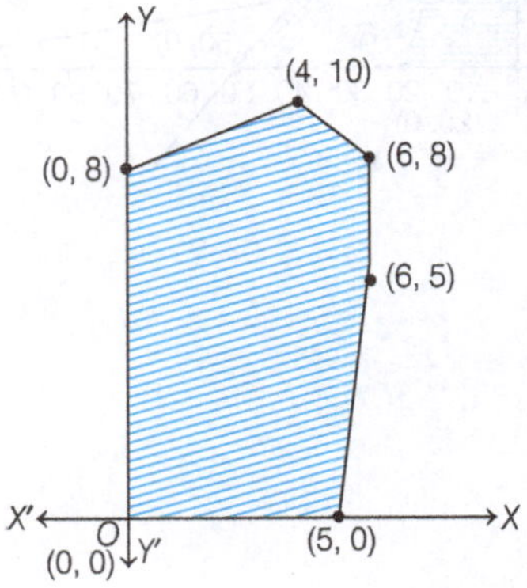

Let $Z = 3x - 4y$ be the objective function. Then,

9 Minimum of Z occurs at
(a) (0, 0) (b) (0, 8)
(c) (5, 0) (d) (4, 10)

10 Maximum of Z occurs at
(a) (5, 0) (b) (6, 5)
(c) (6, 8) (d) (4, 10)

11 (Maximum value of Z + Minimum value of Z) is equal to
(a) 13 (b) 1
(c) – 13 (d) – 17

Past Years Questions

Single Correct Type

1 An objective function $Z = ax + by$ is maximum at points (8, 2) and (4, 6). If $a \geq 0$ and $b \geq 0$ and $ab = 25$, then the maximum value of the function is equal to
NCERT Pg. 398, CUET 2024
(a) 60 (b) 50 (c) 40 (d) 80

2 The corner points of the feasible region determined by $x + y \leq 8, 2x + y \geq 8, x \geq 0, y \geq 0$ are $A(0, 8)$, $B(4, 0)$ and $C(8, 0)$. If the objective function $Z = ax + by$ has its maximum value on the line segment AB, then the relation between a and b is **NCERT Pg. 398, CUET 2024**
(a) $8a + 4 = b$ (b) $a = 2b$
(c) $b = 2a$ (d) $8b + 4 = a$

3 The feasible region represented by the constraints $4x + y \geq 80$, $x + 5y \geq 115$, $3x + 2y \leq 150$, $x, y \geq 0$ of an LPP is **NCERT Pg. 397, CUET 2024**

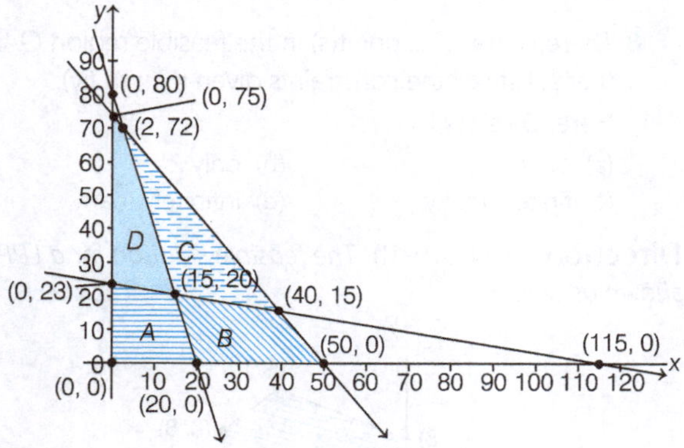

(a) Region A
(b) Region B
(c) Region C
(d) Region D

4 Which one of the following represents the correct feasible region determined by the following constraints of an LPP ?

$$x + y \geq 10, 2x + 2y \leq 25, x \geq 0, y \geq 0$$

NCERT Pg. 397, CUET 2024

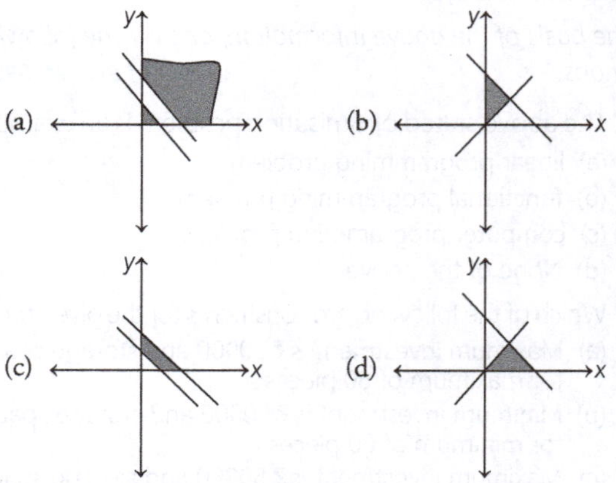

Skill Boosters

1 A factory makes tennis rackets and cricket bats. A tennis racket takes 1.5 h of machine time and 3 h of craftman's time in its making, while a cricket bat takes 3 h of machine time and 1 h of craftman's time in a day, the factory has the availability of not more than 42 h of machine time and 24 h of craftsman's time.

Now, consider the following statements

I. If the factory is to work at full capacity, then the number of rackets and bats must be made, are respectively 4 and 12.

II. If the profit on a racket and on a bat is ₹ 20 and ₹ 10 respectively, then the maximum profit of the factory when it works at full capacity, is ₹ 200

Choose the correct option.

(a) Only I is true (b) Only II is true
(c) Both I and II are true (d) Neither I nor II is true

2 A manufacturing company makes two types of television sets; one is black and white and the other is colour. The company has resources to make atmost 300 sets per week. It takes ₹ 1800 to make a black and white set and ₹ 2700 to make a coloured set. The company can spend not more than ₹ 648000 per week to make television sets. If it makes a profit of ₹ 510 per black and white set and ₹ 675 per coloured set, how many sets of each type should be produced, so that the company has maximum profit?

(a) 120 black and white and 180 colour television sets
(b) 300 black and white television sets
(c) 240 colour television sets
(d) 180 black and white and 120 colour television sets

3 A manufacturer of electronic circuits has a stock of 200 resistors, 120 transistors and 150 capacitors and is required to produce two types of circuits *A* and *B*. Type *A* requires 20 resistors, 10 transistors and 10 capacitors. Type *B* requires 10 resistors, 20 transistors and 30 capacitors. If the profit on type *A* circuit is ₹ 50 and that on type *B* circuit is ₹ 60, then which of the following constraint does not hold for the given problem?

(a) $2x + y \le 20$ (b) $x + 2y \ge 12$
(c) $x + 3y \le 15$ (d) All of these

4 There is a factory located at each of the two places *P* and *Q*. From these location, a certain commodity is delivered to each of the three depots situated at *A*, *B* and *C*. The weekly requirements of the depots are respectively 5, 5 and 4 units commodity, while of the production capacity of the factories at *P* and *Q* are 8 and 6 units respectively. The cost of transportation per unit is given below.

To/From	Cost (in ₹)		
	A	*B*	*C*
P	16	10	15
Q	10	12	10

Formulate the LPP, so that the units transported from each factory to each depot in such an order that the transportation cost is minimum.

(a) Minimise $Z = x - 7y + 190$
subject to the constraints
$$x + y \le 8$$
$$x + y \ge 4$$
$$x \le 5$$
$$y \le 5$$
$$x, y \ge 0$$

(b) Minimise $Z = x + 7y + 190$
subject to the constraints
$$x + y \le 8$$
$$x + y \le 5$$
$$x, y \ge 0$$

(c) Minimise $Z = x + 7y + 90$
subject to the constraints
$$x + y \le 8$$
$$x + y \le 4$$
$$x \le 5$$
$$y \le 5$$
$$x, y \ge 0$$

(d) None of the above

5 Anil wants to invest atmost ₹ 12000 in bonds *A* and *B*. According to the rules, he has to invest atleast ₹ 2000 in bond *A* and atleast ₹ 4000 in bond *B*. If the rate of interest in bond *A* is 8% per annum and on bond *B* is 10% per annum, then to maximise the interest, the investment in bond *A* and *B* are respectively

(a) ₹ 10000 and ₹ 2000 (b) ₹ 2000 and ₹ 10000
(c) ₹ 6000 and ₹ 6000 (d) None of these

6 The corner points of the feasible region determined by the following system of linear inequalities $2x + y \le 10$, $x + 3y \le 15$, $x, y \ge 0$ are (0, 0) (5, 0) (3, 4) and (0, 5). Let $Z = px + qy$, where $p, q > 0$. Condition on *p* and *q*, so that the maximum of *Z* occurs at both (3, 4) and (0, 5), is

(a) $p = q$ (b) $p = 2q$
(c) $p = 3q$ (d) $q = 3p$

Correct Codes

Topical Questions

Introduction and Linear Programming Problem and Its Mathematical Formulation

1 (d)	2 (c)	3 (c)	4 (a)	5 (d)	6 (b)	7 (c)	8 (a)	9 (b)	10 (a)
11 (c)	12 (a)	13 (b)	14 (c)	15 (a)	16 (b)	17 (c)	18 (d)		

Numerical Type Questions

1 (160)	2 (30)	3 (410)	4 (104)	5 (1950)	6 (4)	7 (20)

Assertion and Reason Questions

1 (a)	2 (a)	3 (c)	4 (a)	5 (a)

Case or Paragraph Type Questions

1 (a)	2 (a)	3 (b)	4 (a)	5 (a)	6 (c)	7 (a)	8 (d)	9 (b)	10 (a)
11 (d)									

Past Years Questions

1 (b)	2 (b)	3 (c)	4 (c)

Skill Boosters

1 (c)	2 (d)	3 (b)	4 (a)	5 (b)	6 (d)

Step by Step

Decoding the Questions

Concept Builders

1 (False) 2 (True)
3 (True) 4 (True)
5 (True) 6 (False)
7 (linear) 8 (bounded)
9 (5, 4) 10 (Intersection)
11 (36)
12 (linear constraints)
13 (Objective) 14 (feasible)
15 (15)

Introduction and Linear Programming Problem and Its Mathematical Formulation

1 (*d*) The constraints in the given problem are

$$x \geq 0,\ y \geq 0,$$
$$2500x + 500y \leq 50000$$
or $$5x + y \leq 100$$
$$x + y \leq 60$$

2 (*c*) A linear programming problem is one that is concerned with finding the optimal value (maximum or minimum value) of a linear function (called objective function) of several variables (say x and y), subject to the conditions that the variables are non-negative and satisfy a set of linear inequalities (called linear constraints).

3 (*c*) $Z = 250x + 75y$ is the linear objective function for the given problem.

4 (*a*) The graph of the given constraints is

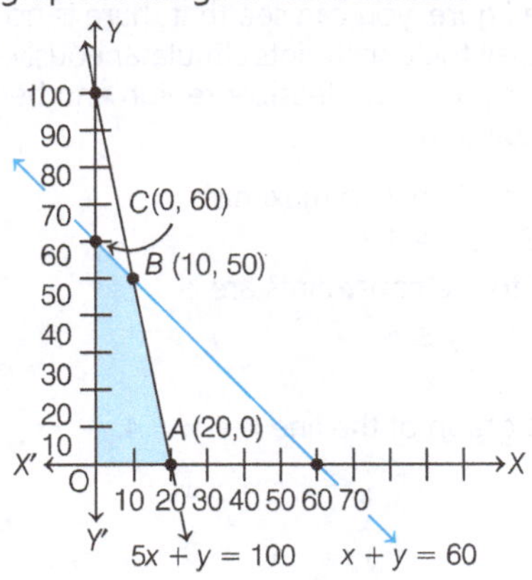

The corner points (vertices) of the bounded (feasible) region are O, A, B and C and it is easy to find their coordinates as (0, 0), (20, 0), (10, 50) and (0, 60). respectively. Let us now compute the values of Z at these points.

We have,

Vertex of the feasible region	Corresponding value of Z (in ₹)	
O (0, 0)	0	
C (0, 60)	4500	
B (10, 50)	**6250**	⟵ Maximum
A (20, 0)	5000	

We observe that the maximum profit to the dealer results from the investment strategy (10, 50), i.e. buying 10 tables and 50 chairs.

This method of solving linear programming problem is referred as corner point method.

5 (*d*) (a) Let R be the feasible region (convex polygon) for a linear programming problem and let $Z = ax + by$ be the objective function. When Z has an optimal value (maximum or minimum), where the variables x and y are subject to constraints described by linear inequalities, this optimal value must occur at a corner point (vertex) of the feasible region.

(b) Let R be the feasible region for a linear programming problem and let $Z = ax + by$ be the objective function. If R is bounded, then the objective function Z has both a maximum and a minimum value on R and each of these occurs at a corner point (vertex) of R.

(c) If R is unbounded, then a maximum or a minimum value of the objective function may not exist.

(d) If R is unbounded and a maximum or a minimum value of Z exists, it must occur at a corner point of R.

6 (*b*) The corner point method for bounded feasible region comprises of the following steps

I. Find the feasible region of the linear programming problem and determine its corner points (vertices) either by inspection or by solving the two equations of the lines intersecting at that point.

II. Evaluate the objective function $Z = ax + by$ at each corner point. Let M and m, respectively denote the largest and smallest values of these points.

III. When the feasible region is bounded, M and m are the maximum and minimum values of Z.

7 (c) In case, the feasible region is unbounded, we have

I. M is the maximum value of Z, if the open half plane determined by $ax + by > M$ has no point in common with the feasible region. Otherwise, Z has no maximum value.

II. Similarly, m is the minimum value of Z, if the open half plane determined by $ax + by < m$ has no point in common with the feasible region. Otherwise, Z has no minimum value.

8 (a) Given that,

Minimise and Maximise $Z = 3x + 9y$ ...(i)

Subject to the constraints are

$$x + 3y \le 60 \quad \text{...(ii)}$$
$$x + y \ge 10 \quad \text{...(iii)}$$
$$x \le y \quad \text{...(iv)}$$
$$x \ge 0,\ y \ge 0 \quad \text{...(v)}$$

First of all, let us graph the feasible region of the system of linear inequalities (ii) to (v). The feasible region $ABCD$ is shown in the figure. Note that the region is bounded. The coordinates of the corner points A, B, C and D are (0, 10), (5, 5), (15, 15) and (0, 20), respectively.

Corner point	Corresponding value of $Z = 3x + 9y$	
A (0, 10)	90	
B (5, 5)	**60**	← Minimum
C (15, 15)	180	← Maximum (multiple optimal solutions)
D (0, 20)	180	

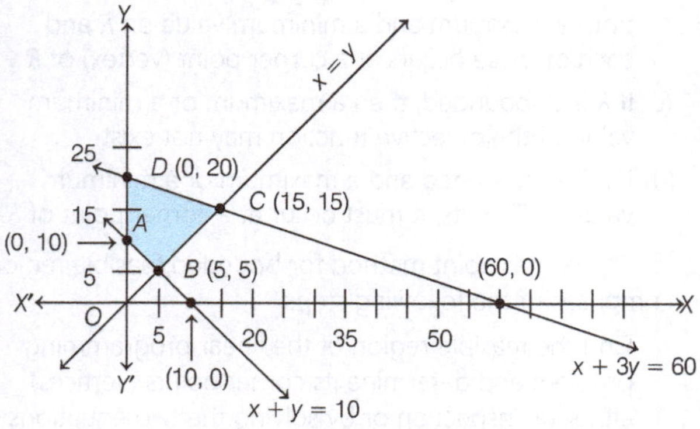

We, now find the minimum and maximum value of Z. From the table, we find that the minimum value of Z is 60 at the point B (5, 5) of the feasible region.

The maximum value of Z on the feasible region occurs at the two corner points C (15, 15) and D (0, 20) and it is 180 in each case.

Remark Observe that in the above example, the problem has multiple optimal solutions at the corner points C and D, i.e., the both points produce same maximum value 180. In such cases, you can see that every point on the line segment CD joining the two corner points C and D also give the same maximum value. Same is also true in the case, if the two points produce same minimum value.

9 (b) Given that,

Minimise $\quad Z = 3x + 2y$

Subject to the constraints are

$$x + y \ge 8 \quad \text{...(i)}$$
$$3x + 5y \le 15 \quad \text{...(ii)}$$
$$x \ge 0,\ y \ge 0 \quad \text{...(iii)}$$

Let us graph the inequalities (i) to (iii).

From figure, you can see that there is no point satisfying all the constraints simultaneously. Thus, the problem is having no feasible region and hence no feasible solution.

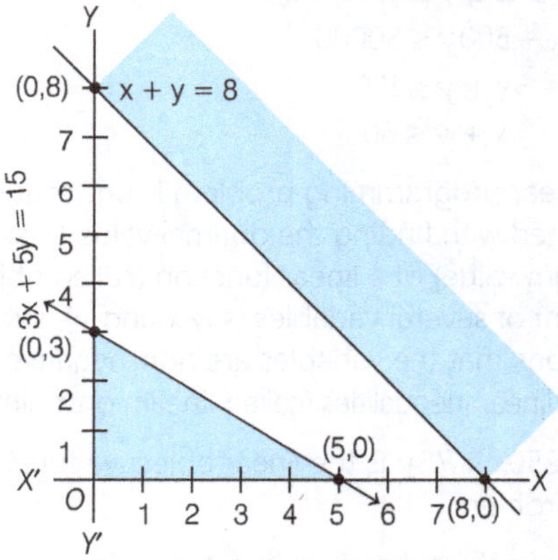

From the figure, you can see that there is no point satisfying all the constraints simulataneously. Thus, the problem is having no feasible region and hence no feasible solution.

10 (a) Our problem is to maximise

$$Z = 3x + 4y \quad \text{...(i)}$$

Subject to the constraints are

$$x + y \le 4 \quad \text{...(ii)}$$
$$x \ge 0, y \ge 0 \quad \text{...(iii)}$$

Draw the graph of the line $x + y = 4$.

x	0	4
y	4	0

Putting (0, 0) in the inequality $x + y \le 4$, we have

$0 + 0 \le 4 \Rightarrow 0 \le 4$ (which is true)

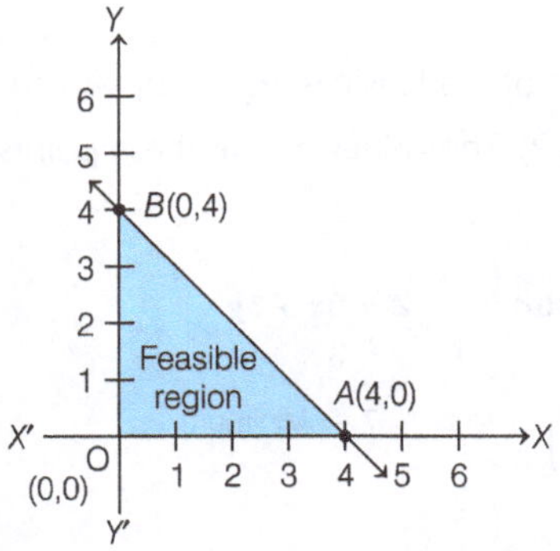

So, the half plane is towards the origin. Since, $x, y \geq 0$.

So, the feasible region lies in the first quadrant.

$\therefore$ Feasible region is *OABO*.

The corner points of the feasible region are *O*(0, 0), *A*(4,0) and *B*(0, 4). The values of *Z* at these points are as follows

Corner point	$Z = 3x + 4y$
O(0, 0)	0
A(4, 0)	12
B(0, 4)	16 $\rightarrow$ Maximum

Therefore, the maximum value of *Z* is 16 at the point *B*(0, 4).

11 (c) A. Our problem is to minimise

$$Z = -3x + 4y \qquad ...(i)$$

Subject to the constraints are

$$x + 2y \leq 8 \qquad ...(ii)$$

$$3x + 2y \leq 12 \qquad ...(iii)$$

$$x \geq 0, y \geq 0 \qquad ...(iv)$$

In the line $x + 2y = 8$ if $x = 0$, then $y = 4$ and if $y = 0$ then, $x = 8$

x	0	8
y	4	0

Putting (0, 0) in the inequality $x + 2y \leq 8$, we have

$$0 + 0 \leq 8 \Rightarrow 0 \leq 8 \text{ (which is true)}$$

So, the half plane is towards the origin.

Since, $x, y \geq 0$

So, the feasible region lies in the first quadrant.

In the line $3x + 2y = 12$, if $x = 0$, then $y = 6$ and if $y = 0$, then $x = 4$.

x	0	4
y	6	0

Putting (0, 0) in the inequality $3x + 2y \leq 12$, we have

$$3 \times 0 + 2 \times 0 \leq 12$$

$$\Rightarrow \qquad 0 \leq 12 \text{ (which is true)}$$

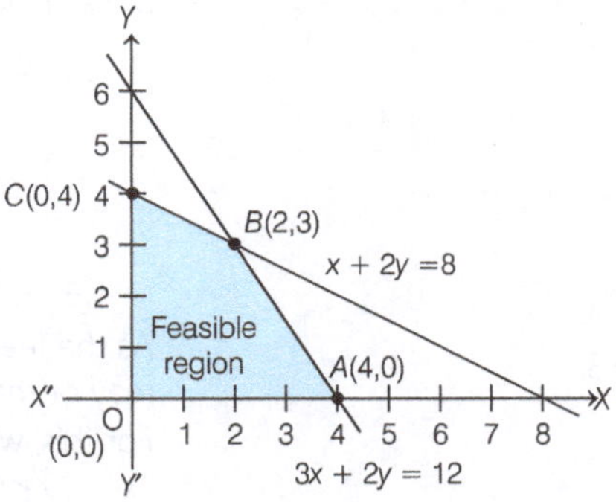

So, the half plane is towards the origin.

$\therefore$ Feasible region is *OABCO*.

On solving equations $x + 2y = 8$ and $3x + 2y = 12$, we get

$$x = 2 \text{ and } y = 3$$

$\therefore$ Intersection point *B* is (2, 3).

The corner points of the feasible region are *O*(0, 0), *A*(4, 0), *B*(2, 3) and *C*(0, 4). The values of *Z* at these points are as follows

Corner point	$Z = -3x + 4y$
O(0, 0)	0
A(4, 0)	**−12** $\rightarrow$ Minimum
B(2, 3)	6
C(0, 4)	16

Therefore, the minimum value of *Z* is −12 at the point *A*(4, 0).

B. Our problem is to maximise

$$Z = 5x + 3y \qquad ...(i)$$

Subject to the constraints are

$$3x + 5y \leq 15 \qquad ...(ii)$$

$$5x + 2y \leq 10 \qquad ...(iii)$$

$$x \geq 0, y \geq 0 \qquad ...(iv)$$

Draw the graph of the line $3x + 5y = 15$.

x	0	5
y	3	0

Putting (0, 0) in the inequality $3x + 5y \leq 15$, we have

$$3 \times 0 + 5 \times 0 \leq 15$$

$$\Rightarrow \qquad 0 \leq 15 \text{ (which is true)}$$

So, the half plane is towards the origin. Since, $x, y \geq 0$.

So, the feasible region lies in the first quadrant.

Draw the graph of the line $5x + 2y = 10$.

x	0	2
y	5	0

Putting (0, 0) in the inequality $5x + 2y \leq 10$, we have

$$5 \times 0 + 2 \times 0 \leq 10$$

$$\Rightarrow \qquad 0 \leq 10 \qquad \text{(which is true)}$$

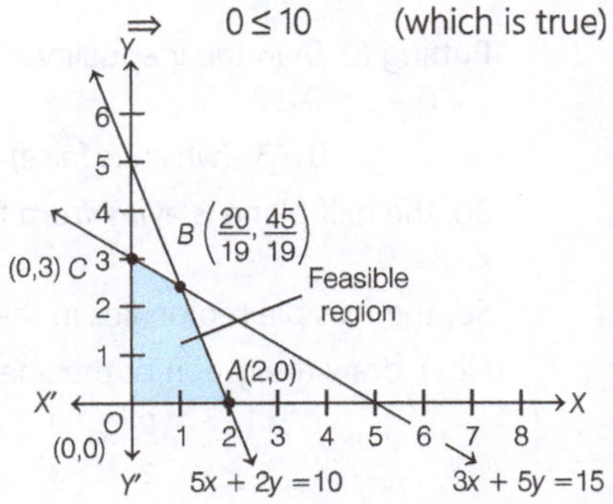

So, the half plane is towards the origin.

On solving given equations,

$$3x + 5y = 15$$

and $5x + 2y = 10$,

we get $x = \dfrac{20}{19}$, $y = \dfrac{45}{19}$

Coordinates of point *B* is $\left(\dfrac{20}{19}, \dfrac{45}{19}\right)$.

$\therefore$ Feasible region is *OABCO*.

The corner points of the feasible region are *O*(0, 0), *A*(2, 0), $B\left(\dfrac{20}{19}, \dfrac{45}{19}\right)$ and *C*(0, 3).

The values of *Z* at these points are as follows

Corner point	$Z = 5x + 3y$
O(0, 0)	0
A(2, 0)	10
C(0, 3)	9
$B\left(\frac{20}{19}, \frac{45}{19}\right)$	$\mathbf{\frac{235}{19}}$ $\rightarrow$ Maximum

Therefore, the maximum value of Z is $\frac{235}{19}$ at the point $B\left(\frac{20}{19}, \frac{45}{19}\right)$.

C. Our problem is to minimise

$$Z = 3x + 5y \quad \text{...(i)}$$

Subject to the constraints are

$$x + 3y \geq 3 \quad \text{...(ii)}$$
$$x + y \geq 2 \quad \text{...(iii)}$$
$$x \geq 0, y \geq 0 \quad \text{...(iv)}$$

Draw the graph of the line $x + 3y = 3$.

x	0	3
y	1	0

Putting (0, 0) in the inequality $x + 3y \geq 3$, we have

$$0 + 3 \times 0 \geq 3$$

$\Rightarrow \quad 0 \geq 3$ (which is false)

So, the half plane is away from the origin. Since, $x, y \geq 0$

So, the feasible region lies in the first quadrant.

Now, draw the graph of the line $x + y = 2$.

x	0	2
y	2	0

Putting (0, 0) in the inequality $x + y \geq 2$, we have

$$0 + 0 \geq 2$$

$\Rightarrow \quad 0 \geq 2$ (which is false)

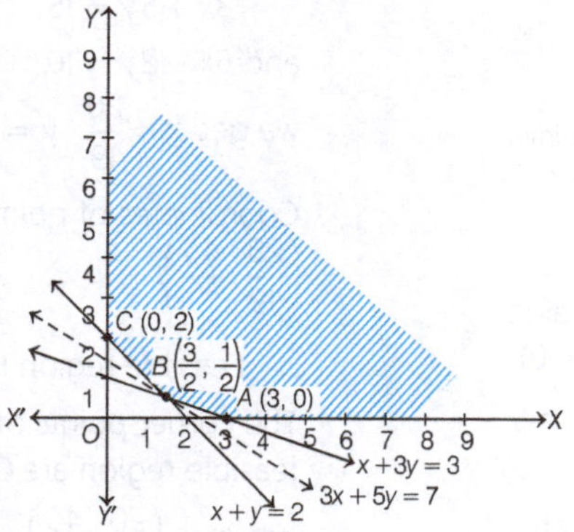

So, the half plane is away from the origin.

It can be seen that the feasible region is unbounded.

On solving equations $x + y = 2$ and $x + 3y = 3$, we get

$$x = \frac{3}{2} \quad \text{and} \quad y = \frac{1}{2}$$

$\therefore$ Intersection point B is $\left(\frac{3}{2}, \frac{1}{2}\right)$.

The corner points of the feasible region are $A(3, 0)$, $B\left(\frac{3}{2}, \frac{1}{2}\right)$ and $C(0, 2)$. The values of Z at these points are as follows

Corner point	$Z = 3x + 5y$
$A(3, 0)$	9
$B\left(\frac{3}{2}, \frac{1}{2}\right)$	7 → Minimum
$C(0, 2)$	10

As the feasible region is unbounded. Therefore, 7 may or may not be the minimum value of Z.

For this, we draw the graph of the inequality $3x + 5y < 7$ and check whether the resulting half plane has points in common with the feasible region or not.

It can be seen that the feasible region has no common point with $3x + 5y < 7$.

Therefore, the minimum value of Z is 7 at $B\left(\frac{3}{2}, \frac{1}{2}\right)$.

D. Our problem is to maximise

$$Z = 3x + 2y \quad \text{...(i)}$$

Subject to the constraints are

$$x + 2y \leq 10 \quad \text{...(ii)}$$
$$3x + y \leq 15 \quad \text{...(iii)}$$
$$x \geq 0, y \geq 0 \quad \text{...(iv)}$$

Draw the graph of the line $x + 2y = 10$.

x	0	10
y	5	0

Putting (0, 0) in the inequality $x + 2y \leq 10$, we have

$$0 + 2 \times 0 \leq 10$$

$\Rightarrow \quad 0 \leq 10$ (which is true)

So, the half plane is towards the origin. Since, $x, y \geq 0$.

So, the feasible region lies in the first quadrant.

Draw the graph of the line $3x + y = 15$.

x	0	5
y	15	0

Putting (0, 0) in the inequality $3x + y \leq 15$, we have

$$3 \times 0 + 0 \leq 15$$

$\Rightarrow \quad 0 \leq 15$ (which is true)

So, the half plane is towards the origin.

On solving equations $x + 2y = 10$ and $3x + y = 15$, we get

$$x = 4 \text{ and } y = 3$$

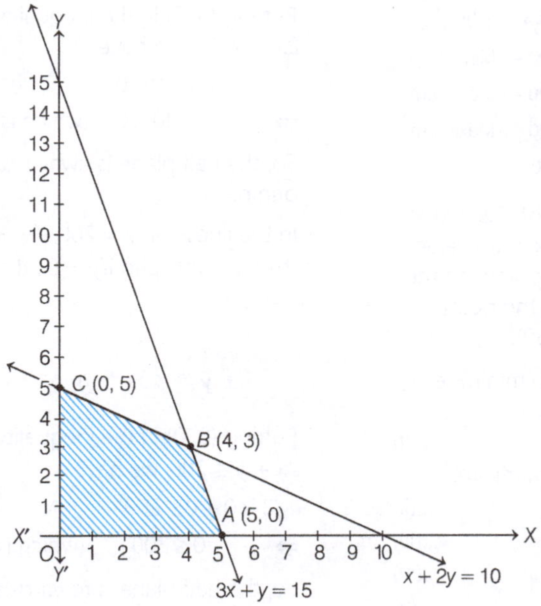

∴ Intersection point B is (4, 3).

∴ Feasible region is $OABCO$.

The corner points of the feasible region are O (0, 0), A(5, 0), B(4, 3) and C(0, 5). The values of Z at these points are as follows

Corner point	$Z = 3x + 2y$
O(0, 0)	0
A(5, 0)	15
B(4, 3)	**18** → Maximum
C(0, 5)	10

Therefore, the maximum value of Z is 18 at the point B(4, 3).

12 (*a*) Our problem is to minimise

$$Z = x + 2y \quad \text{...(i)}$$

Subject to the constraints are

$$2x + y \geq 3 \quad \text{...(ii)}$$
$$x + 2y \geq 6 \quad \text{...(iii)}$$
$$x \geq 0,\ y \geq 0 \quad \text{...(iv)}$$

In the line $2x + y = 3$, if $x = 0$, then $y = 3$ and if $y = 0$, then $x = \frac{3}{2}$.

x	0	3/2
y	3	0

Putting (0, 0) in the inequality $2x + y \geq 3$, we have

$$2 \times 0 + 0 \geq 3$$
$$\Rightarrow \quad 0 \geq 3 \quad \text{(which is false)}$$

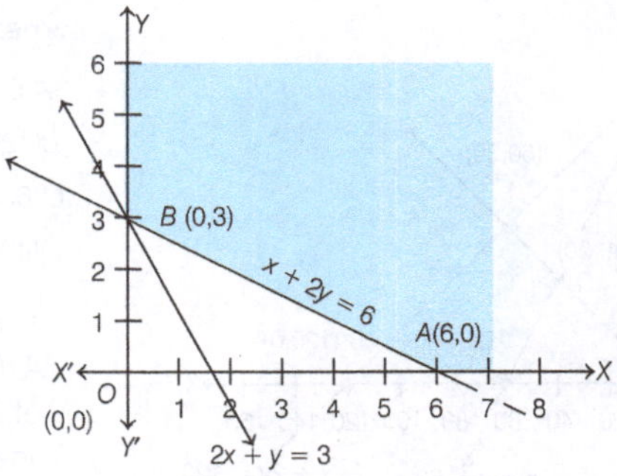

So, the half plane is away from the origin. Since, $x, y \geq 0$. So, the feasible region lies in the first quadrant.

In the line $x + 2y = 6$, if $x = 0$ then $y = 3$ and if $y = 0$, then $x = 6$.

x	0	6
y	3	0

Putting (0, 0) in the inequality $x + 2y \geq 6$, we have

$$0 + 2 \times 0 \geq 6 \Rightarrow 0 \geq 6 \quad \text{(which is false)}$$

So, the half plane is away from the origin.

The intersection point of the lines $x + 2y = 6$ and $2x + y = 3$ is B(0, 3).

The corner points of the feasible region are A(6, 0) and B(0, 3). The values of Z at these points are as follows

Corner point	$Z = x + 2y$
A(6, 0)	6
B(0, 3)	6

It can be seen that the value of Z at points A and B are same. If we take any other point such as (2, 2) on line $x + 2y = 6$, then $Z = 6$. Thus, the minimum value of Z occurs for more than 2 points. $Z = 6$ may or may not be the minimum value of the objective function because region is unbounded, so we draw a line $x + 2y < 6$. Clearly the open half plane of this line does not lie in the feasible region. Therefore, $Z = 6$ is the minimum value.

13 (*b*) Our problem is to minimise and maximise

$$Z = 5x + 10y \quad \text{...(i)}$$

Subject to the constraints are

$$x + 2y \leq 120 \quad \text{...(ii)}$$
$$x + y \geq 60 \quad \text{...(iii)}$$
$$x - 2y \geq 0 \quad \text{...(iv)}$$
$$x, y \geq 0 \quad \text{...(v)}$$

In the line $x + 2y = 120$, if $x = 0$, then $y = 60$ and if $y = 0$, then $x = 120$.

x	0	120
y	60	0

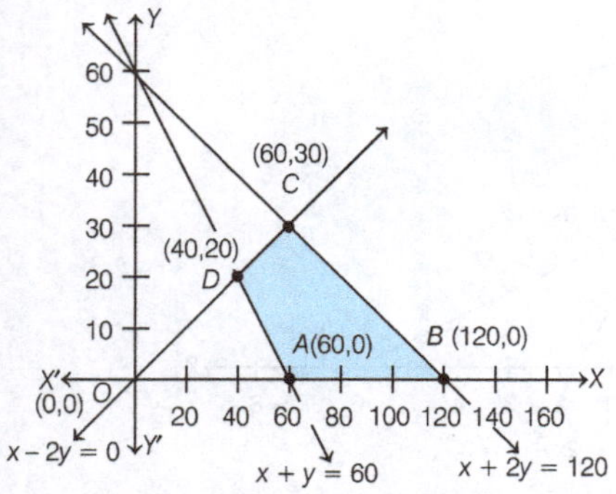

Putting (0, 0) in the inequality $x+2y\le 120$, we have

$$0+2\times 0\le 120$$

$\Rightarrow \quad 0\le 120$ (which is true)

So, the half plane is towards the origin.

In the line $x+y=60$, if $x=0$, then $y=60$ and if $y=0$, then $x=60$.

x	0	60
y	60	0

Putting (0, 0) in the inequality $x+y\ge 60$, we have

$$0+0\ge 60$$

$\Rightarrow \quad 0\ge 60$ (which is false)

So, the half plane is away from the origin.

In the line $x-2y=0$, if $x=0$, then $y=0$ and if $y=5$, then $x=10$.

x	0	10
y	0	5

Putting (5, 0) in the inequality $x-2y\ge 0$, we have

$$5-2\times 0\ge 0$$

$\Rightarrow \quad 5\ge 0$ (which is true)

So, the half plane is towards the X-axis. Since, $x, y\ge 0$.

So, the feasible region lies in the first quadrant.

$\therefore$ Feasible region is $ABCDA$.

On solving equations $x-2y=0$ and $x+y=60$, we get D (40, 20) and on solving equations $x-2y=0$ and $x+2y=120$, we get C(60, 30).

The corner points of the feasible region are A(60, 0), B(120, 0), C(60, 30) and D(40, 20). The values of Z at these points are as follows

Corner point	$Z=5x+10y$
A(60, 0)	**300** $\rightarrow$ Minimum
B(120, 0)	**600** $\rightarrow$ Maximum
C(60, 30)	**600** $\rightarrow$ Maximum
D(40, 20)	400

The minimum value of Z is 300 at A (60, 0) and the maximum value of Z is 600 at all the points on the line segment joining the points B (120, 0) and C (60, 30).

14 (c) Our problem is to minimise and maximise

$$Z=x+2y \quad \text{...(i)}$$

Subject to the constraints are

$$x+2y\ge 100 \quad \text{...(ii)}$$

$$2x-y\le 0 \quad \text{...(iii)}$$

$$2x+y\le 200 \quad \text{...(iv)}$$

$$x\ge 0, y\ge 0 \quad \text{...(v)}$$

In the line $x+2y=100$, if $x=0$, then $y=50$ and if $y=0$, then $x=100$.

x	0	100
y	50	0

Putting (0, 0) in the inequality $x+2y\ge 100$, we have

$$0+2\times 0\ge 100$$

$\Rightarrow \quad 0\ge 100$ (which is false)

So, the half plane is away from the origin.

In the line $2x-y=0$, if $x=0$, then $y=0$ and if $x=10$, then $y=20$.

x	0	10
y	0	20

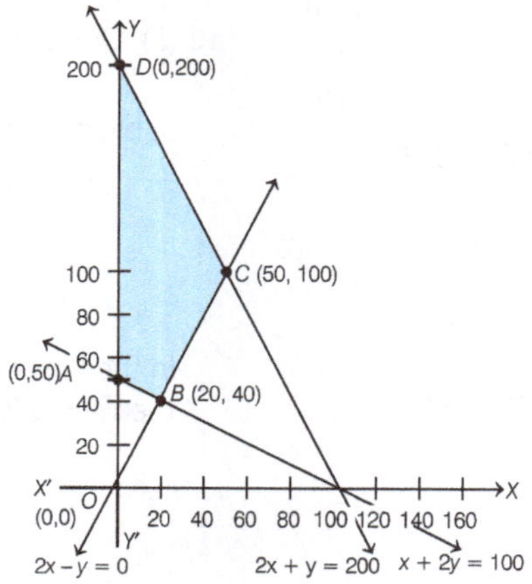

Putting (5, 0) in the inequality $2x-y\le 0$, we have

$$2\times 5-0\le 0$$

$\Rightarrow \quad 10\le 0$ (which is false)

So, the half plane is away from origin.

In the line $2x+y=200$, if $x=0$, then $y=200$ and if $y=0$, then $x=100$.

x	0	100
y	200	0

Putting (0, 0) in the inequality $2x+y\le 200$, we have

$$2\times 0+0\le 200$$

$\Rightarrow \quad 0\le 200$ (which is true)

So, the half plane is towards the origin. Since, $x, y\ge 0$

So, the feasible region lies in the first quadrant.

On solving equations $2x-y=0$ and $x+2y=100$, we get B(20, 40) and on solving the equations $2x-y=0$ and $2x+y=200$, we get C(50, 100).

$\therefore$ Feasible region is $ABCDA$.

The corner points of the feasible region are A(0, 50), B(20, 40), C(50, 100) and D(0, 200).

The values of Z at these points are as follows

Corner point	$Z=x+2y$
A(0, 50)	**100** $\rightarrow$ Minimum
B(20, 40)	**100** $\rightarrow$ Minimum
C(50,100)	250
D(0, 200)	**400** $\rightarrow$ Maximum

The maximum value of Z is 400 at D(0, 200) and the minimum value of Z is 100 at all the points on the line segment joining A(0, 50) and B(20, 40), i.e. at infinite point.

15 (a) The feasible region is bounded. Therefore, maximum of Z must occurs at the corner points of the feasible region

Corner Point	Value of Z
$O(0, 0)$	$4(0) + 3(0) = 0$
$A(25, 0)$	$4(25) + 3(0) = 100$
$B(16, 16)$	$4(16) + 3(16) = \mathbf{112} \leftarrow$ Maximum
$C(0, 24)$	$4(0) + 3(24) = 72$

Hence, the maximum value of Z is 112.

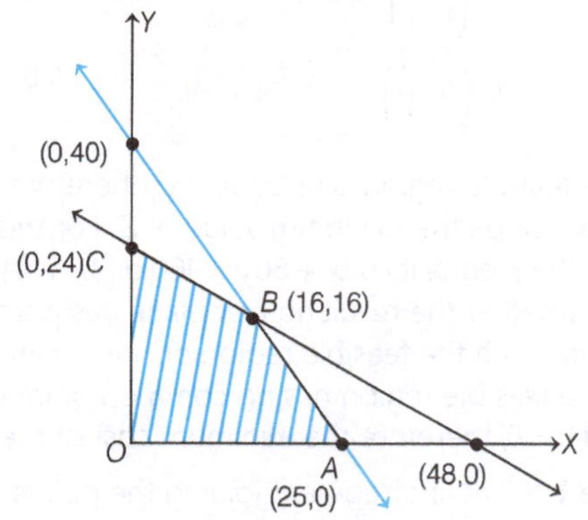

16 (*b*) The corner points of the feasible region determined by the system of linear constraints are (0, 0), (0, 40), (20, 40) (60, 20), (60, 0).

The objective function is $Z = 4x + 3y$. The values of Z at these corner points is given by

Corner point	Corresponding value of Z
(0, 0)	0
(0, 40)	120
(20, 40)	200
(60, 20)	300
(60, 0)	240

The maximum value of Z is $300 < 325$.

$\therefore$ The quantity of column B is greater.

17 (*c*) The given LPP is

Maximise and minimise $Z = 3x - 4y$

Subject to the constraints are

$$x - 2y \le 0$$
$$-3x + y \le 4$$
$$x - y \le 6$$
$$x, y \ge 0$$

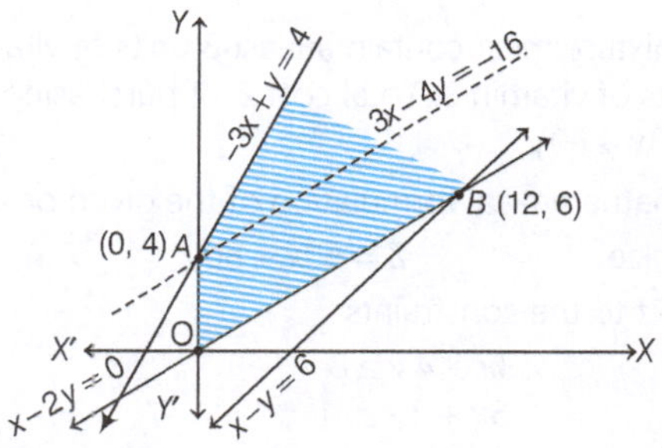

The shaded region is the feasible region which is unbounded.

The feasible unbounded region is AOB and the corner points are $O(0,0)$, $A(0,4)$, $B(12, 6)$. The values of Z at these corner points are given by

Corner point	Corresponding value of Z
$O(0, 0)$	0
$A(0, 4)$	-16
$B(12, 6)$	12

$\therefore$ The maximum value of Z is 12 at $B(12, 6)$. Also, to check for the minimum value of Z, we draw the graph of $3x - 4y = -16$.

Since, the open half plane $3x - 4y < -16$ cuts the feasible region at the point (0, 4) and has common area with feasible region.

$\therefore$ The given LPP has no minimum solution.

18 (*d*) The corner points of the feasible region are (0, 10), (5, 5), (15, 15), (0, 20).

The given objective function is $Z = px + qy\ , p, q > 0$

It is given that the maximum value of Z occurs at the points (15, 15) and (0, 20).

$\therefore$ We have, $p \cdot 15 + q \cdot 15 = p \cdot 0 + q \cdot 20$

$\Rightarrow \quad (p + q)\,15 = q \cdot 20 \Rightarrow 3(p + q) = 4q$

$\therefore \quad 3p = q$

Numerical Type Questions

1 (160) Let Reshma mixes x kg of food P and y kg of food Q. Construct the following table

Food	Quantity	Vitamin A	Vitamin B	Cost (₹ per kg)
P	x kg	$3x$	$5x$	$60x$
Q	y kg	$4y$	$2y$	$80y$
Total		$3x + 4y$	$5x + 2y$	$60x + 80y$
Requirement		Atleast 8	Atleast 11	

The mixture must contain atleast 8 units of vitamin A and 11 units of vitamin B. Total cost Z of purchasing food is $Z = 60x + 80y$,

The mathematical formulation of the given problem is

Minimize $\qquad Z = 60x + 80y \qquad$ ...(i)

Subject to the constraints

$3x + 4y \geq 8 \qquad$ ...(ii)

$5x + 2y \geq 11 \qquad$ ...(iii)

$x \geq 0,\ y \geq 0 \qquad$ ...(iv)

In the line $3x + 4y = 8$, if $x = 0$, then $y = 2$ and if $y = 0$, then $x = \frac{8}{3}$.

x	0	8/3
y	2	0

Putting (0, 0) in the inequality $3x + 4y \geq 8$, we have

$3 \times 0 + 4 \times 0 \geq 8 \Rightarrow 0 \geq 8$ (which is false)

So, the half plane is away from the origin.

Since, $x, y \geq 0$

So, the feasible region lies in the first quadrant.

In the line $5x + 2y = 11$, if $x = 0$, then $y = \frac{11}{2}$ and if $y = 0$, then $x = \frac{11}{5}$.

x	0	11/5
y	11/2	0

Putting (0, 0) in the inequality $5x + 2y \geq 11$, we have

$5 \times 0 + 2 \times 0 \geq 11 \Rightarrow 0 \geq 11$ (which is false)

So, the half plane is away from the origin.

It can be seen that the feasible region is unbounded.

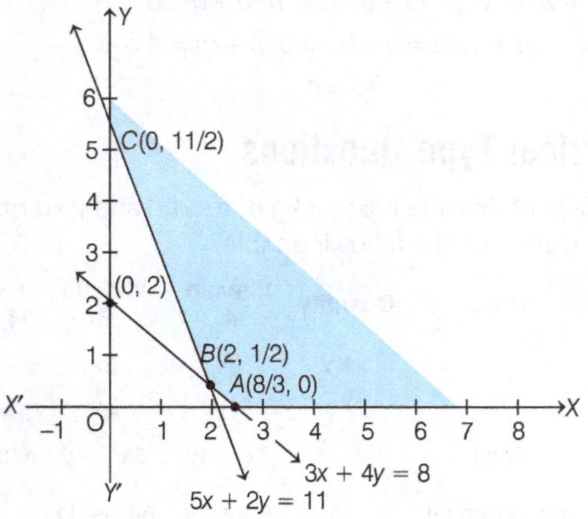

On solving equations $3x + 4y = 8$ and $5x + 2y = 11$, we get $B\left(2, \frac{1}{2}\right)$.

The corner points of the feasible region are $A\left(\frac{8}{3}, 0\right)$, $B\left(2, \frac{1}{2}\right)$ and $C\left(0, \frac{11}{2}\right)$.

The values of Z at these points are as follows

Corner point	$Z = 60x + 80y$
$A\left(\frac{8}{3}, 0\right)$	160 → Minimum
$B\left(2, \frac{1}{2}\right)$	160 → Minimum
$C\left(0, \frac{11}{2}\right)$	440

As the feasible region is unbounded, therefore 160 may or may not be the minimum value of Z. For this, we graph the inequality $60x + 80y < 160$ or $3x + 4y < 8$ and check whether the resulting half plane has points in common with the feasible region or not. It can be seen that the feasible region has no common point with $3x + 4y < 8$, therefore the minimum cost of the mixture will be ₹ 160 at line segment joining the points $A\left(\frac{8}{3}, 0\right)$ and $B\left(2, \frac{1}{2}\right)$.

2 (30) Let x be the number of cakes of one kind and y be the number of cakes of other kind. Construct the following table

Kind	Number of cakes	Flour required (in g)	Fat required (in g)
I	x	$200x$	$25x$
II	y	$100y$	$50y$
Total	$x + y$	$200x + 100y$	$25x + 50y$
Requirement		5000	1000

Our problem is to maximise $Z = x + y$ ...(i)

Subject to constraints are

$200x + 100y \leq 5000 \Leftrightarrow 2x + y \leq 50$ ...(ii)

$25x + 50y \leq 1000 \Leftrightarrow x + 2y \leq 40$ ...(iii)

and $\qquad x, y \geq 0$ ...(iv)

In the line $2x + y = 50$, if $x = 0$, then $y = 50$ and if $y = 0$, then $x = 25$.

x	0	25
y	50	0

Putting (0, 0) in the inequality $2x + y \leq 50$, we have

$2 \times 0 + 0 \leq 50 \Rightarrow 0 \leq 50$ (which is true)

So, the half plane is towards the origin.

In the line $x + 2y = 40$, if $x = 0$, then $y = 20$ and if $y = 0$, then $x = 40$.

x	0	40
y	20	0

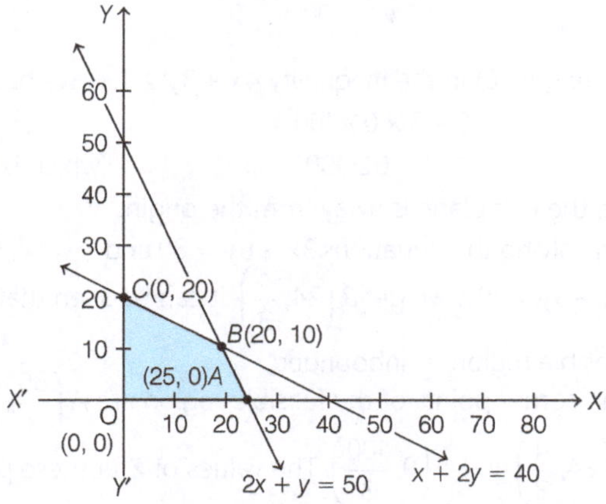

Putting (0, 0) in the inequality $x + 2y \le 40$, we have

$0 + 2 \times 0 \le 40 \Rightarrow 0 \le 40$ (which is true)

So, the half plane is towards the origin.

Since, $x, y \ge 0$

So, the feasible region lies in the first quadrant.

On solving equations $2x + y = 50$ and $x + 2y = 40$, we get $B(20, 10)$

$\therefore$ Feasible region is $OABCO$.

The corner points of the feasible region are $O(0, 0)$, $A(25, 0)$, $B(20, 10)$ and $C(0, 20)$. The values of Z at these points are as follows

Corner point	**$Z = x + y$**
$O(0, 0)$	0
$A(25, 0)$	25
$B(20, 10)$	**30** → Maximum
$C(0, 20)$	20

Thus, the maximum number of cakes that can be made is 30 i.e. 20 of one kind and 10 of the other kind.

3 (410) Let the manufacturer produces x package of screws A and y package of screws B. We construct the following table

Types of screw	**Number of packages**	**Time on automatic machine (in min)**	**Time on hand machine (in min)**	**Profit (in ₹)**
A	x	$4x$	$6x$	$7x$
B	y	$6y$	$3y$	$10y$
Total	$x + y$	$4x + 6y$	$6x + 3y$	$7x + 10y$
Availability		$4 \times 60 = 240$	$4 \times 60 = 240$	

The profit on a package of screws A is ₹ 7 and on the package of screws B is ₹ 10.

Our problem is to maximise $Z = 7x + 10y$ ...(i)

Subject to constraints are

$4x + 6y \le 240 \Leftrightarrow 2x + 3y \le 120$ ...(ii)

$6x + 3y \le 240 \Leftrightarrow 2x + y \le 80$ ...(iii)

and $x \ge 0, y \ge 0$ ...(iv)

In the line $2x + 3y = 120$, if $x = 0$, then $y = 40$ and if $y = 0$, then $x = 60$.

x	0	60
y	40	0

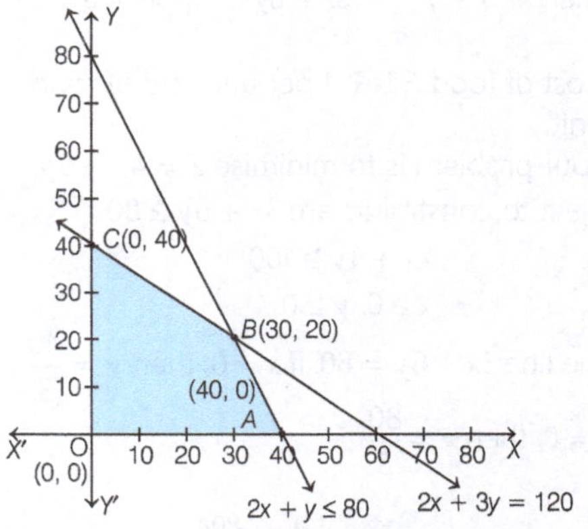

Putting (0, 0) in the inequality $2x + 3y \le 120$, we have

$2 \times 0 + 3 \times 0 \le 120 \Rightarrow 0 \le 120$ (which is true)

So, the half plane is towards the origin.

In the line $2x + y = 80$, if $x = 0$, then $y = 80$ and if $y = 0$, then $x = 40$.

x	40	0
y	0	80

Putting (0, 0) in the inequality $2x + y \le 80$, we have

$2 \times 0 + 0 \le 80 \Rightarrow 0 \le 80$ (which is true)

So, the half plane is towards the origin. Since, $x, y \ge 0$.

So, the feasible region lies in the first quadrant.

On solving equations $2x + 3y = 120$ and $2x + y = 80$, we get $B(30, 20)$.

$\therefore$ Feasible region is $OABCO$.

The corner points of the feasible region are $O(0, 0)$, $A(40, 0)$, $B(30, 20)$ and $C(0, 40)$. The values of Z at these points are as follows

Corner point	**$Z = 7x + 10y$**
$O(0, 0)$	0
$A(40, 0)$	280
$B(30, 20)$	**410** → Maximum
$C(0, 40)$	400

The maximum value of Z is ₹ 410 at $B(30, 20)$.

Thus, the factory should produce 30 packages of screws A and 20 packages of screws B to get the maximum profit of ₹ 410.

4 (104) Let the diet contains x units of food F_1 and y units of food F_2. We construct the following table

Type	Number	Vitamin A per unit	Minerals per unit	Cost (in ₹)
F_1	x	$3x$	$4x$	$4x$
F_2	y	$6y$	$3y$	$6y$
Total	$x+y$	$3x+6y$	$4x+3y$	$4x+6y$

The cost of food F_1 is ₹ 4 per unit and of food F_2 is ₹ 6 per unit.

So, our problem is to minimise $Z = 4x + 6y$ ...(i)

Subject to constraints are $3x + 6y \geq 80$ ...(ii)

$$4x + 3y \geq 100 \quad \text{...(iii)}$$

$$x \geq 0,\ y \geq 0 \quad \text{...(iv)}$$

In the line $3x + 6y = 80$, if $x = 0$, then $y = \frac{40}{3}$ and if $y = 0$, then $x = \frac{80}{3}$.

x	0	80/3
y	40/3	0

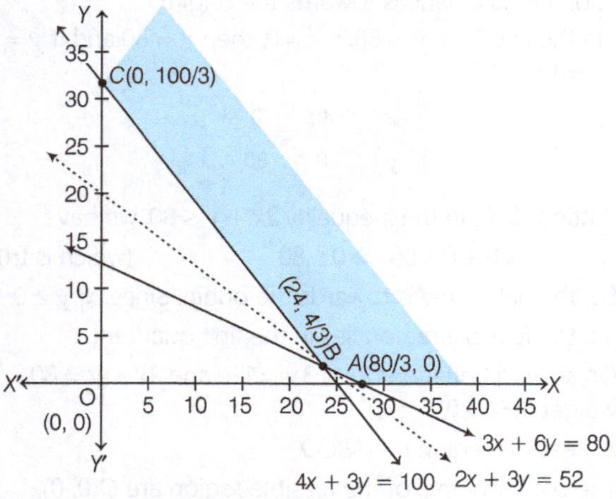

Putting (0, 0) in the inequality $3x + 6y \geq 80$, we have

$$3 \times 0 + 6 \times 0 \geq 80$$

$\Rightarrow$ $0 \geq 80$ (which is false)

So, the half plane is away from the origin.

Since, $x, y \geq 0$

So, the feasible region lies in the first quadrant.

In the line $4x + 3y = 100$, if $x = 0$, then $y = \frac{100}{3}$ and if $y = 0$, then $x = 25$.

x	0	25
y	100/3	0

Putting (0, 0) in the inequality $4x + 3y \geq 100$, we have

$$4 \times 0 + 3 \times 0 \geq 100$$

$\Rightarrow$ $0 \geq 100$ (which is false)

So, the half plane is away from the origin.

On solving the equations $3x + 6y = 80$ and $4x + 3y = 100$, we get $B\left(24, \frac{4}{3}\right)$. It can be seen that the feasible region is unbounded.

The corner points of the feasible region are $A\left(\frac{80}{3}, 0\right)$, $B\left(24, \frac{4}{3}\right)$ and $C\left(0, \frac{100}{3}\right)$. The values of Z at these points are as follows

Corner point	Z = 4x + 6y
$A\left(\frac{80}{3}, 0\right)$	$\frac{320}{3} = 106.67$
$B\left(24, \frac{4}{3}\right)$	104 → Minimum
$C\left(0, \frac{100}{3}\right)$	200

As the feasible is unbounded, therefore 104 may or may not be the minimum value of Z.

For this, we draw a graph of the inequality, $4x + 6y < 104$ or $2x + 3y < 52$ and check, whether the resulting half plane has points in common with the feasible region or not.

It can be seen that the feasible region has no common point with

$$2x + 3y < 52$$

Therefore, the minimum cost of the mixture will be ₹ 104.

5 (1950) So, our problem is minimise $Z = 250x + 200y$ ...(i)

Subject to constraints are

$$3x + 1.5y \geq 18 \Leftrightarrow 2x + y \geq 12 \quad \text{...(ii)}$$

$$2.5x + 11.25y \geq 45 \Leftrightarrow 2x + 9y \geq 36 \quad \text{...(iii)}$$

$$2x + 3y \geq 24 \quad \text{...(iv)}$$

$$x \geq 0,\ y \geq 0 \quad \text{...(v)}$$

In the line $3x + 1.5y = 18$, if $x = 6$, then $y = 0$ and if $y = 12$, then $x = 0$.

x	6	0
y	0	12

Putting (0, 0) in the inequality $3x + 1.5y \geq 18$, we have

$3 \times 0 + 1.5 \times 0 \geq 18 \Rightarrow 0 \geq 18$ (which is false)

So, the half plane is away from the origin.

In the line $2.5x + 11.25y = 45$, if $x = 18$, then $y = 0$ and if $y = 4$ then $x = 0$.

x	18	0
y	0	4

Putting (0, 0) in the inequality $2.5x + 11.25y \geq 45$, we have
$2.5 \times 0 + 11.25 \times 0 \geq 45 \Rightarrow 0 \geq 45$ (which is false)

So, the half plane is away from the origin.

In the line $2x + 3y = 24$, if $x = 0$, then $y = 8$ and if $y = 0$, then $x = 12$.

x	0	12
y	8	0

Putting (0, 0) in the inequality $2x + 3y \geq 24$, we have
$2 \times 0 + 3 \times 0 \geq 24 \Rightarrow 0 \geq 24$ (which is false)

So, the half plane is away from the origin. Since, $x, y \geq 0$

So, the feasible region lies in the first quadrant.

On solving equations $3x + 1.5y = 18$ and $2x + 3y = 24$, we get $C(3, 6)$.

Similarly, on solving equations $2.5x + 11.25y = 45$ and $2x + 3y = 24$, we get $B(9, 2)$.

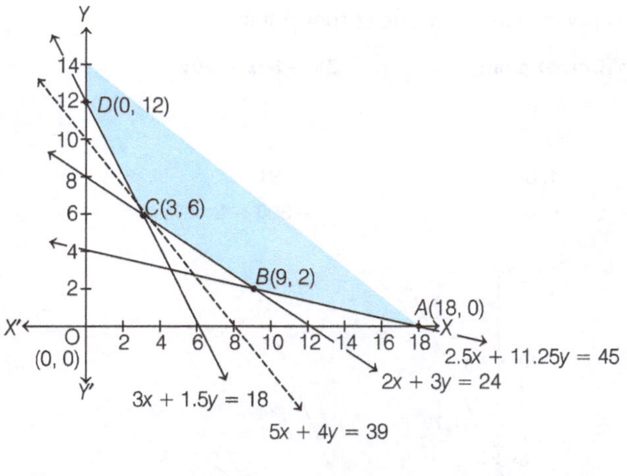

The corner points of the feasible region are $A(18, 0)$, $B(9, 2)$, $C(3, 6)$ and $D(0, 12)$. The values of Z at these points are as follows.

Corner point	$Z = 250x + 200y$
$A(18, 0)$	4500
$B(9, 2)$	2650
$C(3, 6)$	**1950** → Minimum
$D(0, 12)$	2400

As the feasible region is unbounded, therefore 1950 may or may not be the minimum value of Z.

For this, we draw a graph of the inequality $250x + 200y < 1950$ or $5x + 4y < 39$ and check, whether the resulting half plane has points in common with the feasible region or not.

It can be seen that the feasible region has no common point with $5x + 4y < 39$.

Therefore, the minimum value of Z is 1950 at $C(3, 6)$.

Thus, 3 bags of brand P and 6 bags of brand Q should be used in the mixture to minimise the cost to ₹ 1950.

6 (4) Let x and y be the number of items M and N, respectively.

Total profit on the production = ₹ $(600x + 400y)$

Mathematical formulation of the given problem is as follows

Maximise $Z = 600x + 400y$

Subject to the constraints are

$x + 2y \leq 12$ (constraint on machine I) ...(i)

$2x + y \leq 12$ (constraint on machine II) ...(ii)

$x + \frac{5}{4}y \geq 5$ (constraint on machine III) ...(iii)

$x \geq 0, y \geq 0$ ...(iv)

Let us draw the graph of constraints (i) to (iv). *ABCDE* is the feasible region (shaded) as shown in figure determined by the constraints (i) to (iv). Observe that the feasible region is bounded, coordinates of the corner points A, B, C, D and E are (5, 0) (6, 0), (4, 4), (0, 6) and (0, 4) respectively.

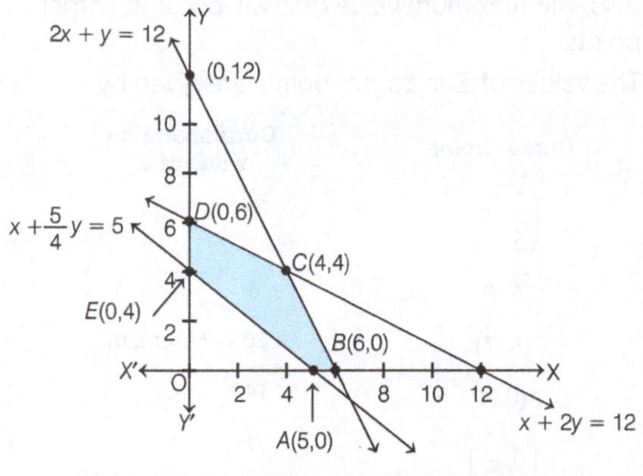

Let us evaluate $Z = 600x + 400y$ at these corner points.

Corner point	$Z = 600x + 400y$
(5, 0)	3000
(6, 0)	3600
(4, 4)	**4000** ← Maximum
(0, 6)	2400
(0, 4)	1600

We see that the point (4, 4) is giving the maximum value of Z. Hence, the manufacturer has to produce 4 units of each item to get the maximum profit of ₹ 4000.

7 (20) The given LPP is

Maximise $Z = x + 2y$

Subject to the constraints are

$$5x + 4y \geq 2$$
$$x \leq 6$$
$$y \leq 7$$
$$x, y \geq 0$$

The graph of the above LPP is

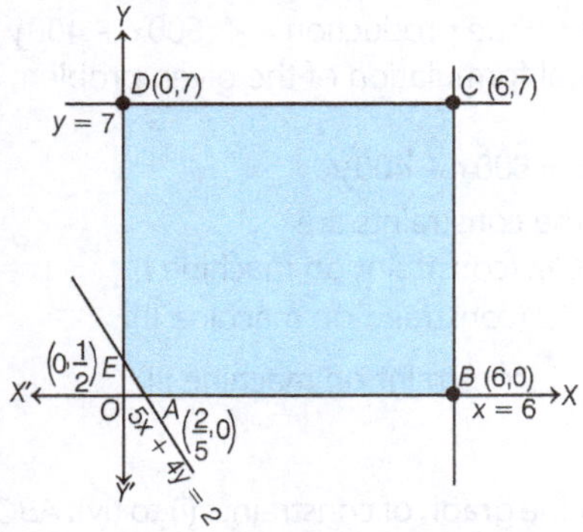

From the above graph we see that the shaded region is the feasible region $ABCDE$ which is bounded.

Also, the maximum value of Z will occur at corner points.

The values of Z at corner points are given by

Corner point	Corresponding value of Z
$\left(\frac{2}{5}, 0\right)$	2/5
(6, 0)	6
(6, 7)	**20** ← Maximum
(0,7)	14
$\left(0, \frac{1}{2}\right)$	1

From the above table, we see that the maximum value of Z is 20 which occurs at (6, 7).

Assertion and Reason Questions

1 (*a*) **Feasible region** The common region determined by all the constraints including non-negative constraints $x, y \geq 0$ of a linear programming problem is called the feasible region (or solution region) for the problem. In the given figure, the region $OABCO$ (shaded) is the feasible region for the problem. The region other than feasible region is called an infeasible region.

2 (*a*) **Feasible solutions** Points within and on the boundary of the feasible region represent feasible solutions of the constraints. In the given figure, every point within and on the boundary of the feasible region $OABCO$ represents feasible solution to the problem. For example, the point (10, 50) is a feasible solution of the problem and so are the points (0,60), (20, 0) etc.

3 (*c*) Any point outside the feasible region is called an infeasible solution. For example, the point (25, 40) is an infeasible solution of the problem.

4 (*a*) Given that,

$$Z = -50x + 20y \quad \text{...(i)}$$

Subject to the constraints are

$$2x - y \geq -5 \quad \text{...(ii)}$$
$$3x + y \geq 3 \quad \text{...(iii)}$$
$$2x - 3y \leq 12 \quad \text{...(iv)}$$
$$x \geq 0, y \geq 0 \quad \text{...(v)}$$

First of all, let us graph the feasible region of the system of inequalities (ii) to (v). The feasible region (shaded) is shown in the figure. Observe that the feasible region is unbounded.

We now evaluate Z at the corner points.

Corner point	$Z = -50x + 20y$
(0, 5)	100
(0, 3)	60
(1, 0)	– 50
(6, 0)	**– 300** ← Smallest

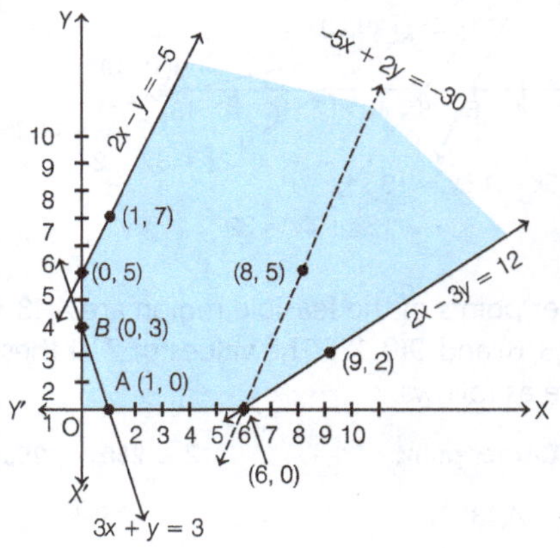

From this table, we find that –300 is the smallest value of Z at the corner point (6, 0). Can we say that minimum value of Z is –300. Note that, if the region would have been bounded, this smallest value of Z is the minimum value of Z but here we see that the feasible region is unbounded. Therefore, –300 may or may not be the minimum value of Z. To decide this issue, we grap the inequality

$$-50x + 20y < -300$$

i.e. $-5x + 2y < -30$

and check whether the resulting open half plane has points in common with feasible region or not. If it has common points, then –300 will not be the minimum value of Z. Otherwise, –300 will be the minimum value of Z.

As shown in the figure, it has common points. Therefore, $Z = -50x + 20y$ has no minimum value subject to the given constraints.

Note *In the above example, can you say whether* $z = -50x + 20y$ *has the maximum value 100 at (0, 5)? For this, check whether the graph of* $-50x + 20y > 100$ *has points in common with the feasible region.*

5 (*a*) The given LPP is

Maximise $Z = 11x + 7y$

Subject to the constraints are

$$2x + y \le 6$$
$$x \le 2$$
$$x \ge 0, y \ge 0$$

The corresponding graph of the above LPP is

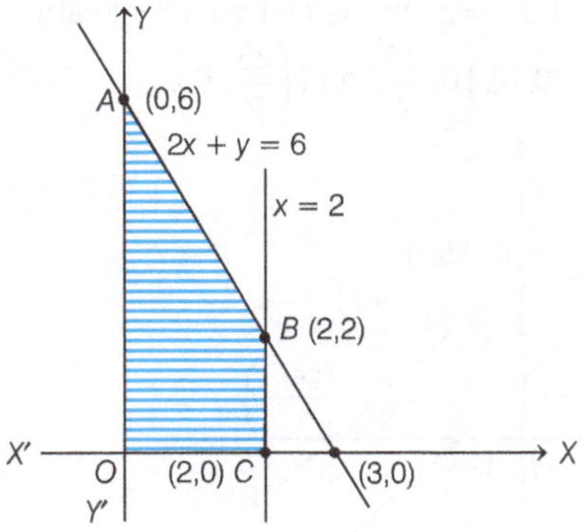

From the above graph, we see that the shaded region is the feasible region $OABCO$ which is bounded.

$\therefore$ The maximum value of the objective function Z occurs at the corner points.

The corner points are O (0, 0), A (0, 6), B (2, 2), C (2, 0).

The values of Z at these corner points are given by

Corner point	Corresponding value of $Z = 11x + 7y$
(0, 0)	0
(0, 6)	42 ← Maximum
(2, 2)	36
(2, 0)	22

Thus, the maximum value of Z is 42 which occurs at the point (0, 6).

Case or Paragraph Type Questions

1 (*a*) The stated optimisation problem is an example of linear programming problem.

2 (*a*) The dealer can invest his money in buying tables or chairs or combination thereof. Further, he would earn different profits by following different investment strategies. There are certain overriding conditions or constraints *viz.*, his investment is limited to a maximum of ₹ 50000 and so is his storage space which is for a maximum of 60 pieces.

3 (*b*) Suppose he decides to buy tables only and no chairs, so he can buy 50000 ÷ 2500, i.e. 20 tables. His profit in this case will be ₹ (250 × 20), i.e. ₹ 5000.

4 (*a*) Suppose he chooses to buy chairs only and no tables, With his capital of ₹ 50000, he can buy 50000 ÷ 500, i.e. 100 chairs. But he can store only 60 pieces. Therefore, he is forced to buy only 60 chairs which will give him a total profit of ₹ (60 × 75), i.e. ₹ 4500.

5 (*a*) Constraints are

$$5x + y \le 100 \quad \text{...(i)}$$
$$x + y \le 60 \quad \text{...(ii)}$$
$$x \ge 0 \quad \text{...(iii)}$$
$$y \ge 0 \quad \text{...(iv)}$$

Their graph is

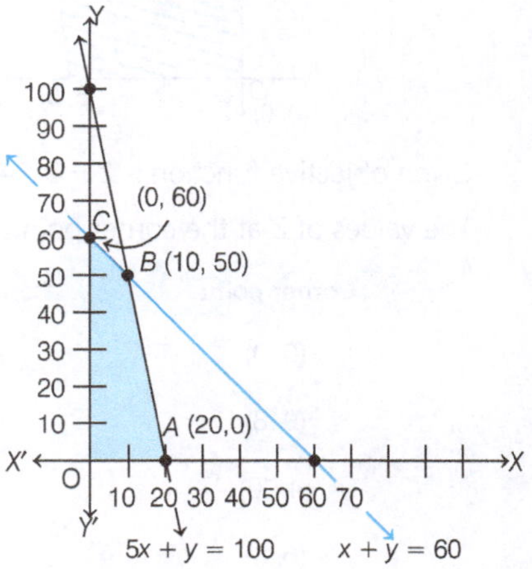

The graph of this system (shaded region) consists of the points common to all half planes determined by the inequalities (i) to (iv). Each point in this region represents a feasible choice open to the dealer for investing in tables and chairs. The region, therefore, is called the feasible region for the problem.

6 (*c*) Every point in the feasible region is called a feasible solution to the problem.

7 (*a*) Optimal (feasible) solution Any point in the feasible region that gives the optimal value (maximum or minimum) of the objective function is called an optimal solution.

8 (*d*) Every point in the feasible region $OABCO$ satisfies all the constraints as given in question.

$\therefore$ There are infinitely many points.

Solution. (Q.Nos. 9-11) The feasible solution is

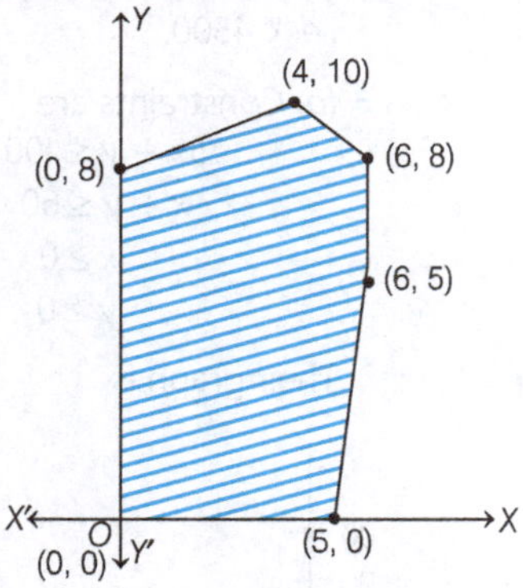

Given objective function is $Z = 3x - 4y$.

The values of Z at the corner points are given by

Corner point	Corresponding value of Z
(0, 0)	0
(0, 8)	–32
(4, 10)	–28
(6, 8)	–14
(6, 5)	–2
(5, 0)	15

9 (*b*) From the above table, the minimum value of Z is –32 which occurs at (0, 8).

10 (*a*) The maximum value of Z is 15 which occurs at (5, 0).

11 (*d*) Maximum value of Z + Minimum value of Z

$$= 15 - 32 = -17$$

Past Years Questions

1 (*b*) We have,

$$Z = ax + by,$$

Since, Z has maximum value at (8, 2) and (4, 6)

$\therefore \quad Z \text{ (at } (8, 2)) = Z \text{ (at } (4, 6))$

$\Rightarrow \quad 8a + 2b = 4a + 6b$

$\Rightarrow \quad 4a = 4b$

$\Rightarrow \quad a = b$

But, $\quad ab = 25$

$\Rightarrow \quad a^2 = 25$

$\Rightarrow \quad a = 5 \qquad [\because a \geq 0, b \geq 0]$

So, $\quad a = b = 5$

$\therefore \quad Z = 5x + 5y$

So, $\quad Z_{max} = 5 \times 8 + 5 \times 2 = 50$

2 (*b*) Given that, $Z = ax + by$ has its maximum value on the line segment AB, where $A = (0, 8)$ and $B = (4, 0)$.

$\therefore \quad a \times 0 + b \times 8 = a \times 4 + b \times 0$

$\Rightarrow \quad 8b = 4a$

$\therefore \quad a = 2b$

3 (*c*)

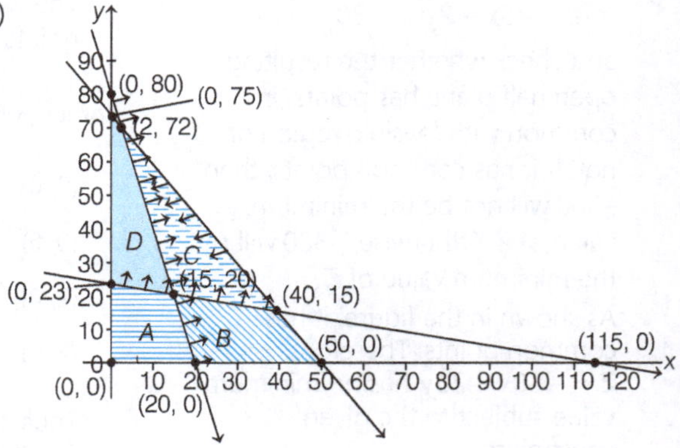

Since, Region C satisfies all the given constraints. So, Region C is feasible region.

4 (*c*) The given LPP is,

$$x + y \geq 10$$

$$2x + 2y \leq 25$$

$$x \geq 0, y \geq 0$$

The vertex of $x + y = 10$ is (0, 10) and (10, 0)

The vertex of $2x + 2y = 25$ is $\left(0, \frac{25}{2}\right)$ and $\left(\frac{25}{2}, 0\right)$

From $x + y \geq 10$ the feasible region is above the line $x + y = 10$

From $2x + 2y \leq 25$ the feasible region is below the line $2x + 2y \leq 25$.

So, that find feasible region is bounded by the lines $x + y = 10$ and $2x + 2y = 25$ in the first quadrant with vertices at (0, 10), (10, 0), $\left(0, \frac{25}{2}\right)$ and $\left(\frac{25}{2}, 0\right)$

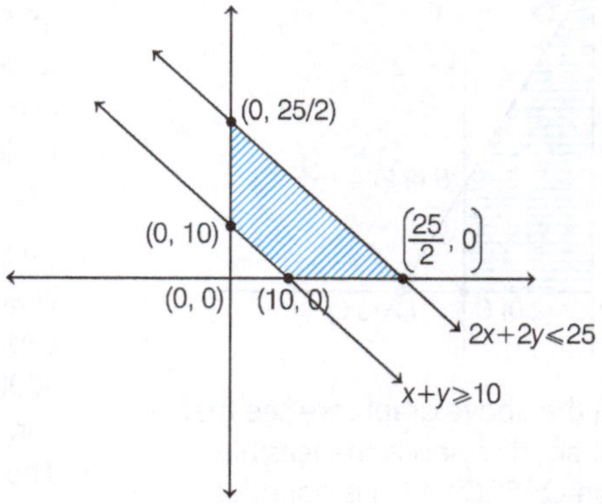

Thus, the option (c) is correct.

Skill Boosters

1 (c) Let the number of rackets and the number of cricket bats to be made in a day be x and y, respectively.
Construct the following table

Item	Number	Machine time (in h)	Craftsman's time (in h)	Profit (in ₹)
Tennis rackets	x	$1.5x$	$3x$	$20x$
Cricket bats	y	$3y$	$1y$	$10y$
Total	$x+y$	$1.5x+3y$	$3x+y$	$20x+10y$
Availability		42	24	

The machine time is not available for more than 42 h.

$\therefore \quad 1.5x+3y \le 42$

The craftman's time is not available for more than 24 h.

$\therefore \quad 3x+y \le 24$

The profit on rackets is ₹ 20 and on bats is ₹ 10.

$\therefore$ Maximum $\quad Z = 20x+10y \quad$ ...(i)

Subject to constraints are $1.5x+3y \le 42 \quad$ ...(ii)

$3x+y \le 24 \quad$ ...(iii)

$x \ge 0,\ y \ge 0 \quad$ ...(iv)

In the line $1.5x+3y=42$, if $x=0$, then $y=14$ and if $y=0$, then $x=28$.

x	0	28
y	14	0

Putting (0, 0) in the inequality $1.5x+3y=42$, we have

$1.5\times 0+3\times 0 \le 42 \Rightarrow 0 \le 42$
(which is true)

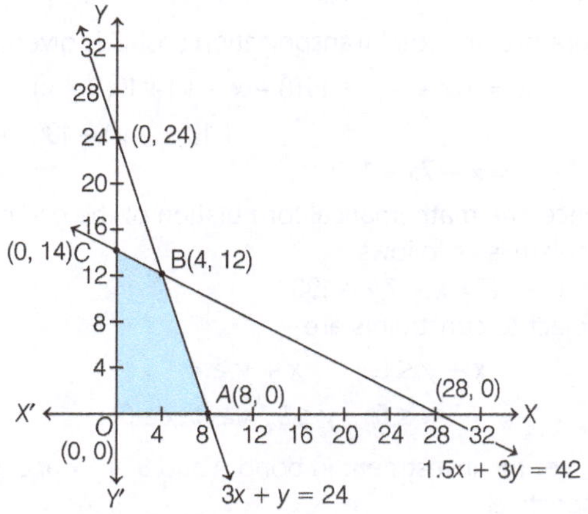

So, the half plane is towards the origin.

Since, $\quad x, y \ge 0$

So, the feasible region lies in the first quadrant.

In the line $3x+y=24$, if $x=0$, then $y=24$ and if $y=0$, then $x=8$.

x	0	8
y	24	0

Putting (0, 0) in the inequality $3x+y \le 24$, we have

$3\times 0+0 \le 24 \quad$ (which is true)

So, the half plane is towards the origin.

On solving equations $1.5x+3y=42$ and $3x+y=24$, we get $B(4, 12)$.

$\therefore$ Feasible region is $OABCO$.

The corner points of the feasible region are $O(0, 0)$, $A(8, 0)$, $B(4, 12)$ and $C(0, 14)$. The values of Z at these points are as follows

Corner point	$Z = 20x + 10y$
$O(0, 0)$	0
$A(8, 0)$	160
$B(4, 12)$	**200** $\rightarrow$ Maximum
$C(0, 14)$	140

Thus, the maximum profit of the factory when it works to its full capacity is ₹ 200.

2 (d) Let x and y denote, respectively, the number of black and white sets and coloured sets made each week. Thus,

$x \ge 0,\ y \ge 0$

Since, the company can make atmost 300 sets a week, therefore, $x+y \le 300$

Weekly cost (in ₹) of manufacturing the set is

$1800x+2700y$

and the company can spend upto ₹ 648000. Therefore,

$1800x+2700y \le 648000$, i.e. or $2x+3y \le 720$

The total profit on x black and white sets and y colour sets is ₹ $(510x+675y)$. Let $Z=510x+675y$. This is the objective function.

Thus, the mathematical formulation of the problem is

Maximise $Z=510x+675y$

Subject to the constraints are $\left.\begin{array}{r} x+y \le 300 \\ 2x+3y \le 720 \\ x \ge 0,\ y \ge 0 \end{array}\right\}$

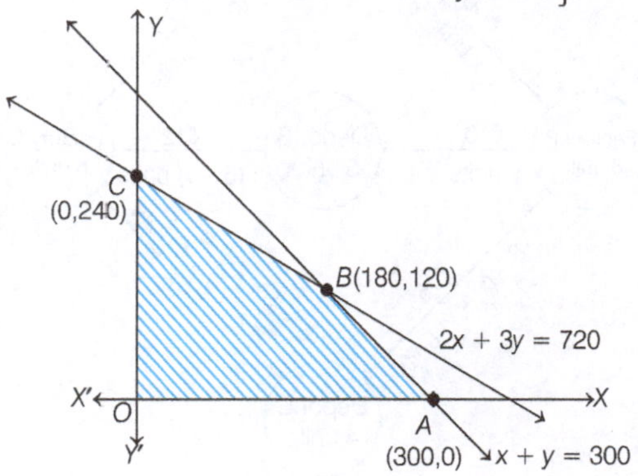

The feasible region $OABCO$ is shown in the figure.

Since, the feasible region is bounded, therefore maximum of Z must occur at the corner point of $OABC$.

Corner point	Value of Z	
$O(0, 0)$	$510(0) + 675(0) = 0$	
$A(300, 0)$	$510(300) + 675(0) = 153000$	
$B(180, 120)$	$510(180) + 675(120) = \mathbf{172800}$	← Maximum
$C(0, 240)$	$510(0) + 675(240) = 162000$	

Thus, maximum Z is 172800 at the point (180, 120), i.e. the company should produce 180 black and white television sets and 120 coloured television sets to get maximum profit.

3 (*b*) Let the manufacturer produces x units of type A circuits and y units of type B circuits.

Given that, x units of type A circuits require 20 resistors and y units of type B circuits require 10 resistors and since a manufacturer of electronic circuit has a stock of 200 resistors.

We have, $20x + 10y \le 200 \Rightarrow 2x + y \le 20$

Similarly, for 120 transistors, we have

$$10x + 20y \le 120 \Rightarrow x + 2y \le 12$$

and for 150 capacitors, we have

$$10x + 30y \le 150 \Rightarrow x + 3y \le 15$$

Clearly, x and y are non-negative integers

$\therefore \quad x \ge 0, y \ge 0$

Thus, the constraints of the LPP are

$$2x + y \le 20; \quad x + 2y \le 12$$
$$x + 3y \le 15; \quad x \ge 0, y \ge 0$$

4 (*a*) The given information, can be expressed diagramatically as follows

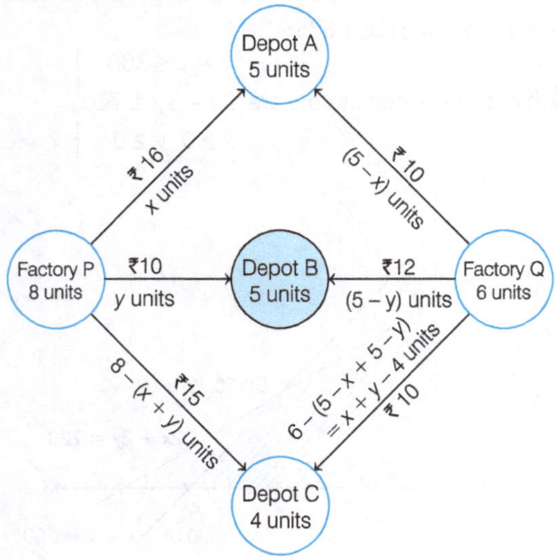

Let the factory at P transports x units of commodity to depot at A and y units to depot at B. Since, the factory at P has the capacity of 8 units of the commodity. Therefore, the left out $(8 - x - y)$ units will be transported to depot at C.

Since, the requirements are always non-negative quantities, therefore we have

$$x \ge 0, y \ge 0$$

and $\quad 8 - x - y \ge 0$

$\Rightarrow \quad x \ge 0, y \ge 0$

and $\quad x + y \le 8$

Since, weekly requirements of the depot at A is 5 units of the commodity and x units are transported from the factory at P. Therefore, the remaining $5 - x$ units are to be transported from the factory at Q.

Similarly, $5 - y$ units of the commodity will be transported from the factory at Q to the depot at B.

But the factory at Q has the capacity of 6 units only, therefore the remaining $6 - (5 - x + 5 - y) = x + y - 4$ units will be transported to the depot at C.

As, the requirements at the depots at A, B and C are always non-negative.

$\therefore \quad 5 - x \ge 0, 5 - y \ge 0$

and $\quad x + y - 4 \ge 0$

$\Rightarrow \quad x \le 5, \; y \le 5$

and $\quad x + y \ge 4$

The transportation cost from the factory at P to the depots at A, B and C are respectively, ₹ $16x$, ₹ $10y$ and ₹ $15(8 - x - y)$. Similarly, the transportation cost from the factory at Q to the depots at A, B and C are respectively ₹ $10(5 - x)$, ₹ $12(5 - y)$ and ₹ $10(x + y - 4)$.

Therefore, the total transportation cost Z is given by

$$Z = 16x + 10y + 15(8 - x - y) + 10(5 - x) + 12(5 - y) + 10(x + y - 4)$$
$$= x - 7x + 190$$

Hence, the mathematical formulation of the given problem is as follows.

Minimise $Z = x - 7y + 190$

Subject to constraints are

$$x + y \le 8, \qquad x + y \ge 4$$
$$x \le 5, \quad y \le 5, \; x \ge 0, y \ge 0$$

5 (*b*) Let the investment in bond A and B are x and y respectively.

Then, our problem is to

Maximise $Z = 0.08x + 0.10x$

Subject to constraints are

$$x + y \le 12000, \quad x \ge 2000, \quad y \ge 4000, \quad y \ge 0$$

The graph of the above inequality is given by

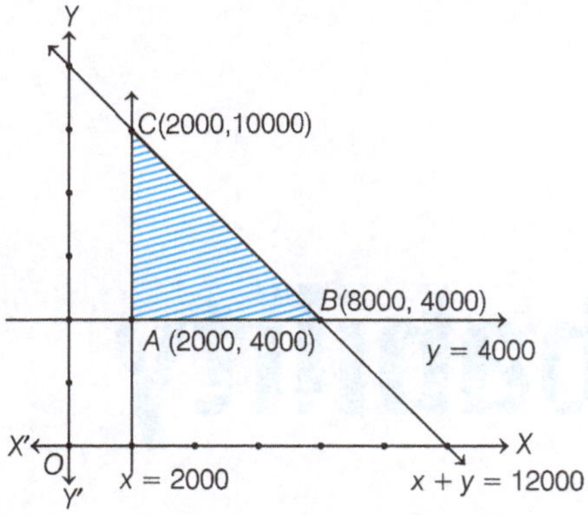

In the above graph shaded region is the feasible bounded region *ABCA*.

Now, the values of *Z* the the corner points are given by

Corner point	Value of *Z*
(2000, 4000)	560
(8000, 4000)	1040
(2000, 10000)	**1160** ← Maximum

From the above table, we see that the maximum value of *Z* is 1160 which occurs at the point (2000, 10000).

Hence, to maximise the interest ₹ 2000 and ₹ 10000 must be invested in bond *A* and *B*, respectively.

6 (*d*) The maximum value of *Z* is unique.

It is given that the maximum value of *Z* occurs at two points (3, 4) and (0, 5). Value of *Z* at (3, 4) = Value of *Z* at (0, 5)

$\Rightarrow \quad p(3) + q(4) = p(0) + q(5),$

$$3p + 4q = 5q \Rightarrow 3p = q$$

13 Probability

Topicwise No. of Ques asked in 3 Years (JEE Main)

Topics	No. of Questions		
	2024	2023	2022
Conditional Probability	3	3	5
Multiplication Theorem on Probability	2	4	3
Independent Events	–	–	2
Bayes' Theorem	2	1	0
Random Variables and its Probability Distributions	6	7	8

Special Type of Ques Asked in 3 Years (JEE Main)

Types	Years		
	2024	2023	2022
A-R	–	–	–
Statement Based	–	–	1
Numerical Value Type	5	3	1

Last 3 Years Weightage (JEE Main)

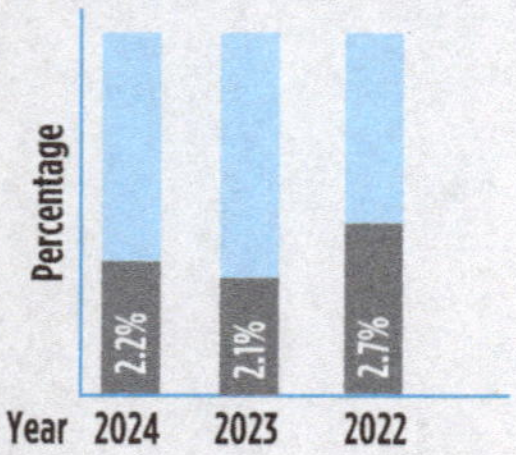

Conditional Probability

Let E and F be two events associated with a random experiment. Then, probability of occurrence of event E, when the event F has already occurred, is called conditional probability of event E over F and is denoted by $P(E / F)$.

$$P(E / F) = \frac{P(E \cap F)}{P(F)}, \text{ where } P(F) \neq 0.$$

Properties of Conditional Probability

Let A, B and C be the events of a sample space S. Then,

(i) $P(S/A) = P(A/A) = 1$

(ii) $P\{(A \cup B)/C\} = P(A/C) + P(B/C) - P\{(A \cap B)/C\}; P(C) \neq 0$

(iii) $P(A'/B) = 1 - P(A/B)$, where A' is complement of A.

Multiplication Theorem of Probability

Let A and B be two events associated with a random experiment, then

$$P(A \cap B) = \begin{cases} P(A) \cdot P(B/A), \text{ where } P(A) \neq 0 \\ P(B) \cdot P(A/B), \text{ where } P(B) \neq 0 \end{cases}$$

Multiplication Theorem for More than Two Events

Let E, F and G be three events of sample space S, then

$$P(E \cap F \cap G) = P(E) \cdot P\left(\frac{F}{E}\right) \cdot P\left(\frac{G}{E \cap F}\right)$$

Independent Events

- Two events A and B are said to be independent, if the occurrence or non-occurrence of one event does not affect the occurrence or non-occurrence of another event.
- Two events E and F are said to be independent, if

$$P(F/E) = P(F),\ P(E) \neq 0$$

and

$$P(E/F) = P(E),\ P(F) \neq 0.$$

- If E and F are independent events, then

$$P(E \cap F) = P(E) \cdot P(F)$$

Marks Maximizer

- Three events A, B and C are said to be mutually independent, if $P(A \cap B) = P(A) \cdot P(B)$, $P(A \cap C) = P(A) \cdot P(C)$, $P(B \cap C) = P(B) \cdot P(C)$ and $P(A \cap B \cap C) = P(A) \cdot P(B) \cdot P(C)$.
- Mutually independent events are pairwise independent, but the converse may not be true.

Bayes' Theorem

Concept Master Video

- Let S be the sample space and $E_1, E_2, \dots, E_n$ be n mutually exclusive and exhaustive events associated with a random experiment.

  If A is any event which occurs with $E_1, E_2, \dots, E_n$, then probability of occurrence of E_i, when A occurred,

$$P(E_i/A) = \frac{P(E_i)\,P(A/E_i)}{\sum_{i=1}^{n} P(E_i)\,P(A/E_i)},\ i = 1, 2, \dots, n$$

- **Theorem of Total Probability** Let S be the sample space and $E_1, E_2, E_3, \dots, E_n$ be n mutually exclusive and exhaustive events associated with a random experiment.

  If E is any event which occurs with $E_1, E_2, E_3, \dots, E_n$.

  Then, $P(E) = P(E_1) \cdot P(E/E_1) + P(E_2) \cdot P(E/E_2)$
  $+ P(E_3) \cdot P(E/E_3) + \dots + P(E_n) \cdot P(E/E_n)$

  or $$P(E) = \sum_{i=1}^{n} P(E_i) \cdot P\left(\frac{E}{E_i}\right)$$

- A random variable is a real valued function, whose domain is the sample space of a random experiment. Generally, it is denoted by capital letter X.
- The system in which the value of a random variable are given along with their corresponding probability is called probability distribution.
- If X is a random variable and takes the value $x_1, x_2, x_3, \dots, x_n$ with respective probabilities $p_1, p_2, p_3, \dots, p_n$. Then, the probability distribution of X is represented by

X	x_1	x_2	x_3	...	x_n
P(X)	p_1	p_2	p_3	...	p_n

where, $p_i > 0$ such that $\Sigma p_i = 1, i = 1, 2, 3, \dots, n$.

- **Mean** of X denoted by μ is the number $\sum_{i=1}^{n} x_i p_i$. It is also called the expectation of X, denoted by $E(X)$.
- If x_i is one of the possible values of a random variable X, the statement $X = x_i$ is true only at some point(s) of the sample space. Hence, the probability that X takes value x_i is always non-zero, i.e. $P(X = x_i) \neq 0$.

Caution Points

- Carefully read and interpret the problem. Misunderstanding the problem can lead to incorrect application of probability principles.
- Be aware of whether events are independents or mutually exclusive. Miscalculating intersection or unions of events can lead to incorrect answers.
- Ensure that you correctly identify the sample space and its comprehensive. Incorrect sample space can distort the probability calculations.
- Always double check your work and verify calculations to ensure accuracy.

PYQ Notes

1. Probability of atmost 'r' successes in n trails $= \sum_{r=0}^{r} {}^nC_r\, p^r\, q^{n-r}$.
2. Probability of at least 'r' successes in 'n' trials $= \sum_{r=r}^{n} {}^nC_r\, p^r q^{n-r}$.
3. Probability of having 1st successes at the rth trial $= p \cdot q^{r-1}$.

Step by Step

Mastering NCERT

- Concept Builders
- Topical Questions
- Numerical Type Questions
- Assertion and Reason Questions
- Case or Paragraph Type Questions
- Past Years Questions
- Skill Boosters

Concept Builders

1 The number of exhaustive cases of throwing n dice simultaneously is ....

2 If $P(A)=1$, then event A is a ....

3 If A, B and C are mutually exclusive events, then $P(A\cap B\cap C)$ ....

4 If A and B are two independent events, then $P(A)\times P(B)$ ....

5 The sum of the probability of all elementary events of an experiment is ....

6 If $P(A)=0.4$, $P(B)=0.5$ and A and B are mutually exclusive events, then $P(A\cup B)$ is ....

7 The conditional probability $P\left(\frac{A}{B}\right)$ is defined as ....

8 The sum of the probabilities of a sure event and an impossible event is ....

9 If the events A and B are independent events, then A' and B' are ....

10 A random variable can be either .... or ....

11 The mean of a random variable X is also called the .... of X.

12 The events E_i and E_j are pairwise disjoint and $\bigcap_{i=1}^{n} E_i=S$, then events $E_1, E_2, \ldots, E_n$ are called .... and ....

13 The probability of impossible events is ....

14 If A and B are independent events, then $P\left(\frac{A}{B}\right)$ is ....

15 If A and B are mutually exclusive event, then $P(A\cap B)=0$. (T/F)

Topical Questions

Conditional Probability

Level I

1 Consider the experiment of tossing three fair coins. Let E be the event 'atleast two heads appear' and F be the event 'first coin shows tail'. Then, $P(E\cap F)$ is **NCERT Pg. 407**

(a) $\frac{1}{4}$ (b) $\frac{1}{5}$

(c) $\frac{1}{8}$ (d) $\frac{1}{2}$

2 Consider the experiment of tossing three fair coins. The sample space of the experiment is

$S=\{HHH, HHT, HTH, THH, HTT, THT, TTH, TTT\}$.

Let E be the event 'atleast two heads appear' and F be the event 'first coin shows tail'. Then,

$$E=\{HHH, HHT, HTH, THH\}$$

and $$F=\{THH, THT, TTH, TTT\}.$$

Then, the probability of event E given that F has already occurred, is **NCERT Pg. 407**

(a) $\frac{1}{2}$ (b) $\frac{1}{4}$ (c) $\frac{1}{8}$ (d) $\frac{1}{5}$

3 Let E and F be the events associated with a sample space S of an experiment, such that $P\left(\frac{S}{F}\right)=1$. Then, $P\left(\frac{E'}{F}\right)$ is equal to **NCERT Pg. 409**

(a) $1-P\left(\frac{E}{F}\right)$ (b) $P\left(\frac{E}{F}\right)$

(c) $1-P\left(\frac{F}{E}\right)$ (d) None of these

4 If $P(A)=\frac{7}{13}$, $P(B)=\frac{9}{13}$ and $P(A\cap B)=\frac{4}{13}$, then $P(A/B)$ is equal to **NCERT Pg. 409**

(a) $\frac{2}{9}$ (b) $\frac{4}{9}$ (c) $\frac{5}{9}$ (d) $\frac{1}{9}$

5 Given that E and F are events such that $P(E) = 0.6$, $P(F) = 0.3$ and $P(E \cap F) = 0.2$. Then, $P(E/F)$ and $P(F/E)$ are respectively **NCERT Pg. 413**

(a) $\frac{1}{2}, \frac{2}{3}$ (b) $\frac{2}{5}, \frac{1}{3}$

(c) $\frac{1}{5}, \frac{2}{5}$ (d) $\frac{2}{3}, \frac{1}{3}$

6 If $P(B) = 0.5$ and $P(A \cap B) = 0.32$, then $P(A/B)$ is equal to **NCERT Pg. 413**

(a) $\frac{15}{23}$ (b) $\frac{16}{25}$

(c) $\frac{16}{27}$ (d) $\frac{16}{23}$

7 If $P(A) = 0.8$, $P(B) = 0.5$ and $P(B/A) = 0.4$, then match the terms of column I with the terms of column II and choose the correct option from the codes given below. **NCERT Pg. 413**

Column I		Column II	
A.	$P(A \cap B)$	1.	0.64
B.	$P(A/B)$	2.	0.98
C.	$P(A \cup B)$	3.	0.32

Codes

	A	B	C
(a)	1	2	3
(b)	3	1	2
(c)	2	3	1
(d)	1	2	3

8 If $2P(A) = P(B) = \frac{5}{13}$ and $P(A/B) = \frac{2}{5}$, then $P(A \cup B)$ is equal to **NCERT Pg. 413**

(a) $\frac{11}{26}$ (b) $\frac{13}{25}$

(c) $\frac{11}{24}$ (d) $\frac{11}{21}$

9 If $P(A) = \frac{6}{11}$, $P(B) = \frac{5}{11}$ and $P(A \cup B) = \frac{7}{11}$, then match the terms of column I with the terms of column II and choose the correct option from the codes given below. **NCERT Pg. 413**

Column I		Column II	
A.	$P(A \cap B)$	1.	$\frac{2}{3}$
B.	$P(A/B)$	2.	$\frac{4}{11}$
C.	$P(B/A)$	3.	$\frac{4}{5}$

Codes

	A	B	C		A	B	C
(a)	1	2	3	(b)	2	3	1
(c)	3	1	2	(d)	1	2	3

10 A coin is tossed three times. Then, match the terms of column I with the terms of column II and choose the correct option from the codes given below. **NCERT Pg. 413**

Column I		Column II	
A.	If E : head on third toss and F : heads on first two tosses, then $P(E/F)$ is	1.	$\frac{3}{7}$
B.	If E : atleast two heads and F : atmost two heads, then $P(E/F)$ is	2.	$\frac{6}{7}$
C.	If E : atmost two tails and F : atleast one tail, then $P(E/F)$ is	3.	$\frac{1}{2}$

Codes

	A	B	C		A	B	C
(a)	3	2	1	(b)	2	3	1
(c)	1	2	3	(d)	3	1	2

11 Mother, father and son line up at random for a family picture. If E : son on one end and F : father in middle, then $P(E/F)$ is ...K... . Here, K refers to **NCERT Pg. 414**

(a) $\frac{2}{3}$ (b) $\frac{1}{3}$

(c) 1 (d) $\frac{4}{3}$

12 A fair die is rolled. Consider events $E = \{1, 3, 5\}$, $F = \{2, 3\}$ and $G = \{2, 3, 4, 5\}$. Then, match the terms of column I with the terms of column II and choose the correct option from the codes given below. **NCERT Pg. 414**

Column I		Column II	
A.	$P(E/F)$ and $P(F/E)$	1.	$\frac{3}{4}$ and $\frac{1}{4}$
B.	$P(E/G)$ and $P(G/E)$	2.	$\frac{1}{2}$ and $\frac{1}{3}$
C.	$P((E \cup F)/G)$ and $P((E \cap F)/G)$	3.	$\frac{1}{2}$ and $\frac{2}{3}$

Codes

	A	B	C		A	B	C
(a)	2	3	1	(b)	1	2	3
(c)	2	1	3	(d)	3	1	2

13 Assume that each born child is equally likely to be a boy or a girl. If a family has two children, then the conditional probabilities that both are girls given that

(i) the youngest is a girl,

(ii) atleast one is a girl,

are respectively **NCERT Pg. 414**

(a) $\frac{1}{3}, \frac{1}{2}$ (b) $\frac{1}{2}, \frac{1}{3}$

(c) $\frac{1}{3}, \frac{1}{4}$ (d) $\frac{2}{3}, \frac{2}{5}$

14 An instructor has a question bank consisting of 300 easy true/false questions, 200 difficult true/false questions, 500 easy multiple choice questions and 400 difficult multiple choice questions. If a question is selected at random from the question bank, then the probability that it will be an easy question given that it is a multiple choice question, is **NCERT Pg. 414**

(a) $\frac{2}{9}$ (b) $\frac{1}{9}$ (c) $\frac{4}{9}$ (d) $\frac{5}{9}$

15 If $P(A)=\frac{1}{2}$, $P(B)=0$, then $P(A/B)$ is **NCERT Pg. 414**

(a) 0 (b) $\frac{1}{2}$

(c) Not defined (d) 1

16 If A and B are events such that $P(A/B)=P(B/A)$, then **NCERT Pg. 415**

(a) $A\subset B$ but $A\neq B$ (b) $A=B$

(c) $A\cap B=\phi$ (d) $P(A)=P(B)$

Level II

17 10% of the bulbs produced in a factory are of red colour and 2% are red and defective. If one bulb is picked up at random, the probability of its being defective, if it is red, is **NCERT Exemplar Pg. 262**

(a) $\frac{1}{5}$ (b) $\frac{1}{3}$ (c) $\frac{1}{7}$ (d) $\frac{1}{2}$

18 Let A and B be two events. If $P(A)=0.2$, $P(B)=0.4$ and $P(A\cup B)=0.6$, then $P(A/B)$ is equal to **NCERT Exemplar Pg. 269**

(a) 0.8 (b) 0.5 (c) 0.3 (d) 0

19 If $P(A)=\frac{3}{10}$, $P(B)=\frac{2}{5}$ and $P(A\cup B)=\frac{3}{5}$, then $P(B/A)+P(A/B)$ is equal to **NCERT Exemplar Pg. 279**

(a) $\frac{1}{4}$ (b) $\frac{1}{3}$ (c) $\frac{5}{12}$ (d) $\frac{7}{12}$

20 Given that A and B are two events such that $P(B)=\frac{3}{5}$, $P(A/B)=\frac{1}{2}$ and $P(A\cup B)=\frac{4}{5}$. Then, $P(A)$ is equal to **NCERT Exemplar Pg. 280**

(a) $\frac{3}{10}$ (b) $\frac{1}{5}$ (c) $\frac{1}{2}$ (d) $\frac{3}{5}$

21 Given that A and B are two events such that $P(B)=\frac{3}{5}$, $P(A/B)=\frac{1}{2}$ and $P(A\cup B)=\frac{4}{5}$, then $P\left(\frac{B}{A'}\right)$ is equal to **NCERT Exemplar Pg. 280**

(a) $\frac{1}{5}$ (b) $\frac{2}{5}$ (c) $\frac{3}{5}$ (d) $\frac{2}{3}$

22 Let A and B be two events such that $P(A)=\frac{3}{8}$, $P(B)=\frac{5}{8}$ and $P(A\cup B)=\frac{3}{4}$. Then, $P(A/B)\cdot P(A'/B)$ is equal to **NCERT Exemplar Pg. 281**

(a) $\frac{2}{5}$ (b) $\frac{3}{8}$ (c) $\frac{3}{20}$ (d) $\frac{6}{25}$

23 It is given that the events A and B are such that $P(A)=\frac{1}{4}$, $P(A/B)=\frac{1}{2}$ and $P(B/A)=\frac{2}{3}$. Then, $P(B)$ is **NCERT Pg. 413**

(a) $\frac{1}{2}$ (b) $\frac{1}{6}$ (c) $\frac{1}{3}$ (d) $\frac{2}{3}$

24 Suppose that E_1 and E_2 are two events of a random experiment such that $P(E_1)=\frac{1}{4}$, $P\left(\frac{E_2}{E_1}\right)=\frac{1}{2}$ and $P\left(\frac{E_1}{E_2}\right)=\frac{1}{4}$. Then, match the terms of column I with the terms of column II and choose the correct option from the codes given below. **NCERT Pg. 413**

Column I		Column II	
A.	$P(E_2)$	1.	1/4
B.	$P(E_1\cup E_2)$	2.	5/8
C.	$P(\bar{E}_1/\bar{E}_2)$	3.	1/2
D.	$P(E_1/\bar{E}_2)$	4.	3/4

Codes

	A	B	C	D
(a)	3	2	4	1
(b)	2	3	1	4
(c)	4	2	3	1
(d)	1	2	3	4

25 Two dice are thrown. If it is known that the sum of numbers on the dice was less than 6, the probability of getting a sum 3, is **NCERT Pg. 408**

(a) $\frac{1}{18}$ (b) $\frac{5}{18}$ (c) $\frac{1}{5}$ (d) $\frac{2}{5}$

26 In a college, 30% students fail in Physics, 25% fail in Mathematics and 10% fail in both. One student is chosen at random. The probability that she fails in Physics, if she has failed in Mathematics, is **NCERT Exemplar Pg. 285**

(a) $\frac{1}{10}$ (b) $\frac{2}{5}$ (c) $\frac{9}{20}$ (d) $\frac{1}{3}$

27 If A and B are two events such that $P(A/B)=p$, $P(A)=p$, $P(B)=1/3$ and $P(A\cup B)=5/9$, then p is equal to **NCERT Pg. 408**

(a) $\frac{1}{2}$ (b) $\frac{2}{3}$ (c) $\frac{1}{3}$ (d) $\frac{2}{5}$

28 A signal, which can be green or red with probability 4/5 and 1/5 respectively, is received by station A and then transmitted to station B. The probability of each station receiving the signal correctly is 3/4. If the signal received at station B is given, then the probability that the original signal is green, is **NCERT Pg. 412**

(a) $\frac{3}{5}$ (b) $\frac{6}{7}$ (c) $\frac{20}{23}$ (d) $\frac{9}{20}$

Multiplication Theorem on Probability

Level I

1 The set $E \cap F$ denotes the event that **NCERT Pg. 415**
(a) Both E and F occured
(b) Both E and F have not occured
(c) E has occured but F has not occured
(d) None of the above

2 By the rule of multiplication of probability, $P(E \cap F)$ is equal to **NCERT Pg. 415**
(a) $P(E) \cdot P(F/E)$ (b) $P(F) \cdot P(E/F)$
(c) Both (a) and (b) (d) None of these

3 An urn contains 10 black and 5 white balls. Two balls are drawn from the urn one after the other without replacement, then the probability that both drawn balls are black, is **NCERT Pg. 415**
(a) $\frac{2}{7}$ (b) $\frac{1}{7}$ (c) $\frac{5}{7}$ (d) $\frac{3}{7}$

Level II

4 If three events of a sample space are E, F and G, then $P(E \cap F \cap G)$ is equal to **NCERT Pg. 416**
(a) $P(E)\ P(F/E)\ P(G/(E \cap F))$
(b) $P(E)\ P(F/E)\ P(G/EF)$
(c) Both (a) and (b)
(d) None of the above

5 Three cards drawn successively, without replacement from a pack of 52 well shuffled cards, then the probability that first two cards are kings and the third card drawn is an ace, is **NCERT Pg. 416**
(a) $\frac{2}{5525}$ (b) $\frac{1}{5525}$ (c) $\frac{2}{5527}$ (d) $\frac{1}{5527}$

Independent Events

Level I

1 If E and F be two independent events associated with the same random experiment, then $P(E \cap F)$ is equal to **NCERT Pg. 418**
(a) $P(E) \cdot P(F)$ (b) $P(E) + P(F)$
(c) $P(E) - P(F)$ (d) None of these

2 If three mutually independent events are A, B and C, then **NCERT Pg. 418**
(a) $P(A \cap B) = P(A) \cdot P(B)$, $P(A \cap C) = P(A) \cdot P(C)$
(b) $P(B \cap C) = P(B) \cdot P(C)$
(c) $P(A \cap B \cap C) = P(A) \cdot P(B) \cdot P(C)$
(d) All of the above

3 A box of oranges is inspected by examining three randomly selected oranges drawn without replacement. If all the three oranges are good, the box is approved for sale, otherwise, it is rejected. Then, the probability that a box containing 15 oranges out of, which 12 are good and 3 are bad ones will be approved for sale, is **NCERT Pg. 421**
(a) $\frac{44}{91}$ (b) $\frac{40}{49}$
(c) $\frac{41}{91}$ (d) $\frac{42}{91}$

4 A fair coin and an unbiased die are tossed. Let A be the event 'head appears on the coin' and B be the event '3 on the die'. Then, **NCERT Pg. 421**
(a) A and B are independent.
(b) A and B are dependent.
(c) A and B are mutually exclusive.
(d) None of the above

5 Given that the events A and B are such that $P(A) = \frac{1}{2}$, $P(A \cup B) = \frac{3}{5}$ and $P(B) = p$. Then, probabilities of B, if they are **NCERT Pg. 422**
(i) mutually exclusive
(ii) independent
are, respectively
(a) $\frac{1}{2}, \frac{1}{3}$ (b) $\frac{1}{5}, \frac{1}{3}$ (c) $\frac{2}{3}, \frac{1}{3}$ (d) $\frac{1}{10}, \frac{1}{5}$

6 Let A and B be independent events with $P(A) = 0.3$ and $P(B) = 0.4$. Then, match the terms of column I with their respective values in column II and choose the correct option from the codes given below. **NCERT Pg. 422**

	Column I		Column II
A.	$P(A \cap B)$	1.	0.4
B.	$P(A \cup B)$	2.	0.3
C.	$P(A/B)$	3.	0.58
D.	$P(B/A)$	4.	0.12

Codes

	A	B	C	D
(a)	4	2	3	1
(b)	4	3	2	1
(c)	4	3	1	2
(d)	2	1	4	3

7 Given, two independent events A and B such that $P(A) = 0.3$, $P(B) = 0.6$. Then, match the terms of column I with their respective values in column II and choose the correct option from the codes given below. **NCERT Pg. 422**

Column I		Column II
A. $P(A \text{ and } B)$	1.	0.28
B. $P(A \text{ and not } B)$	2.	0.72
C. $P(A \text{ or } B)$	3.	0.12
D. $P(\text{neither } A \text{ nor } B)$	4.	0.18

Codes

	A	B	C	D		A	B	C	D
(a)	4	3	1	2	(b)	4	2	1	3
(c)	1	2	3	4	(d)	4	3	2	1

8 A die is tossed thrice. Then, the probability of getting an odd number atleast once is **NCERT Pg. 422**

(a) $\frac{1}{8}$ (b) $\frac{3}{8}$
(c) $\frac{7}{8}$ (d) $\frac{5}{8}$

9 Two balls are drawn at random with replacement from a box containing 10 black and 8 red balls. Then, match the probability of events in column I with their respective values in column II and choose the correct option from the codes given below. **NCERT Pg. 422**

Column I		Column II
A. Both balls are red	1.	$\frac{40}{81}$
B. First ball is black and second is red	2.	$\frac{20}{81}$
C. One of them is black and other is red	3.	$\frac{16}{81}$

Codes

	A	B	C		A	B	C
(a)	3	2	1	(b)	1	2	3
(c)	3	1	2	(d)	1	3	2

10 Probability of solving specific problem independently by A and B are $\frac{1}{2}$ and $\frac{1}{3}$, respectively. If both try to solve the problem independently, then the probabilities that

(i) the problem is solved
(ii) exactly one of them solve the problem

are, respectively **NCERT Pg. 422**

(a) $\frac{1}{3}, \frac{2}{3}$ (b) $\frac{2}{3}, \frac{1}{2}$
(c) $\frac{1}{5}, \frac{1}{3}$ (d) $\frac{1}{2}, \frac{2}{3}$

11 One card is drawn at random from a well-shuffled deck of 52 cards.

(i) E :'the card drawn is a spade'
F :'the card drawn is an ace'
(ii) E :'the card drawn is black'
F :'the card drawn is a king'
(iii) E :'the card drawn is a king or queen'
F :'the card drawn is a queen or jack'

Which of the following option is correct? **NCERT Pg. 422**

(a) In (i), E and F are independent.
(b) In (ii), E and F are independent.
(c) In (iii), E and F are not independent.
(d) All of the above

12 In a hostel, 60% of the students read Hindi newspaper, 40% read English newspaper and 20% read both Hindi and English newspapers. A student is selected at random. Then, match the terms of column I with their respective values in column II and choose the correct option from the codes given below. **NCERT Pg. 423**

Column I		Column II
A. The probability that she reads neither Hindi nor English newspapers.	1.	$\frac{1}{3}$
B. If she reads Hindi newspaper, then the probability that she reads English newspaper.	2.	$\frac{1}{2}$
C. If she reads English newspaper, then the probability that she reads Hindi newspaper.	3.	$\frac{1}{5}$

Codes

	A	B	C		A	B	C
(a)	3	1	2	(b)	1	2	3
(c)	2	3	1	(d)	3	2	1

13 The probability of obtaining an even prime number on each die, when a pair of dice is rolled, is **NCERT Pg. 423**

(a) 0 (b) $\frac{1}{3}$ (c) $\frac{1}{12}$ (d) $\frac{1}{36}$

14 Two events A and B will be independent, if

(a) A and B are mutually exclusive. **NCERT Pg. 423**
(b) $P(A'B') = [1 - P(A)][1 - P(B)]$
(c) $P(A) = P(B)$
(d) $P(A) + P(B) = 1$

Level II

15 If A, B and C are three independent events such that $P(A) = P(B) = P(C) = p$, then P(atleast two of A, B, C occur) is equal to **NCERT Exemplar Pg. 286**

(a) $p^3 - 3p$ (b) $3p - 2p^2$
(c) $3p^2 - 2p^3$ (d) $3p^2$

16 Let A and B be two events such that $P(A) = 0.6$, $P(B) = 0.2$, and $P(A/B) = 0.5$. Then, $P(A'/B')$ is equal to **NCERT Exemplar Pg. 269**

(a) $\frac{1}{10}$ (b) $\frac{3}{10}$
(c) $\frac{3}{8}$ (d) $\frac{6}{7}$

17 If A and B are independent events such that $0 < P(A) < 1$ and $0 < P(B) < 1$, then which of the following is not correct? **NCERT Exemplar Pg. 270**

(a) A and B are mutually exclusive.
(b) A and B' are independent.
(c) A' and B are independent.
(d) A' and B' are independent.

18 If A and B are independent events such that $P(A) = p$, $P(B) = 2p$ and $P(\text{exactly one of } A, B) = \frac{5}{9}$, then $p = ...K...$. Here, K refers to **NCERT Exemplar Pg. 270**

(a) $\frac{1}{5}, \frac{5}{12}$ (b) $\frac{2}{5}, \frac{1}{3}$ (c) $\frac{1}{3}, \frac{5}{12}$ (d) $\frac{1}{8}, \frac{1}{5}$

19 Two events E and F are independent. If $P(E) = 0.3$, $P(E \cup F) = 0.5$, then $P(E/F) - P(F/E)$ equals ...K... . Here, K refers to **NCERT Pg. 417**

(a) $\frac{2}{7}$ (b) $\frac{3}{35}$
(c) $\frac{1}{70}$ (d) $\frac{1}{7}$

20 For a loaded die, the probabilities of outcomes are given as under; $P(1) = P(2) = 0.2$, $P(3) = P(5) = P(6) = 0.1$ and $P(4) = 0.3$.

The dice is thrown two times. Let A and B be the events, 'same number each time', and 'a total score is 10 or more', respectively. Then, match the terms of column I with their respective values in column II and choose the correct option from the codes given below. **NCERT Exemplar Pg. 271**

Column I	Column II
A. $P(A)$	1. Independent
B. $P(B)$	2. 0.02
C. $P(A \cap B)$	3. 0.10
D. Events A and B are	4. 0.20
	5. Dependent

Codes

	A	B	C	D		A	B	C	D
(a)	4	3	2	1	(b)	4	3	1	5
(c)	4	1	3	5	(d)	2	4	1	3

21 Three persons A, B and C, fire at a target in turn, starting with A. Their probability of hitting the target are 0.4, 0.3 and 0.2, respectively. The probability of two hits is **NCERT Pg. 417**

(a) 0.024 (b) 0.188
(c) 0.336 (d) 0.452

22 A die is thrown and a card is selected at random from a deck of 52 playing cards. The probability of getting an even number on the die and a spade card is **NCERT Pg. 417**

(a) $\frac{1}{2}$ (b) $\frac{1}{4}$
(c) $\frac{1}{8}$ (d) $\frac{3}{4}$

23 A problem in Mathematics is given to three students A, B and C, and their respective probability of solving the problem is $\frac{1}{2}, \frac{1}{3}$ and $\frac{1}{4}$. Probability that the problem is solved, is **NCERT Pg. 417**

(a) $\frac{3}{4}$ (b) $\frac{1}{2}$ (c) $\frac{2}{3}$ (d) $\frac{1}{3}$

24 Let A, B and C be pairwise independent events with $P(C) > 0$ and $P(A \cap B \cap C) = 0$. Then, $P(A^C \cap B^C | C)$ is equal to **NCERT Pg. 417**

(a) $P(A^C) - P(B)$ (b) $P(A) - P(B^C)$
(c) $P(A^C) + P(B^C)$ (d) $P(A^C) - P(B^C)$

25 Let A and B be two events such that $P(\overline{A \cup B}) = \frac{1}{6}$, $P(A \cap B) = \frac{1}{4}$ and $P(\bar{A}) = \frac{1}{4}$, where $\bar{A}$ stands for complement of event A. Then, events A and B are

(a) mutually exclusive and independent. **NCERT Pg. 417**
(b) independent but not equally likely.
(c) equally likely but not independent.
(d) equally likely and mutually exclusive.

26 The probability that A speaks truth is 4/5 while this probability for B is 3/4. The probability that they contradict each other when asked to speak on a fact, is **NCERT Pg. 417**

(a) $\frac{3}{20}$ (b) $\frac{1}{5}$ (c) $\frac{7}{20}$ (d) $\frac{4}{5}$

Bayes' Theorem

Level I

1 The method to find the reverse probability of any problem by using conditional probability is knowns as **NCERT Pg. 423**

(a) Baye's theorem (b) Multiplication theorem
(c) Bernoulli trials (d) None of these

2 The events $E_1, E_2, ..., E_n$ represent a partition of the sample space S, if **NCERT Pg. 423**

(a) $E_i \cap E_j = \phi, i \neq j, i, j = 1, 2, 3, ..., n$

(b) $E_1 \cup E_2 \cup ... \cup E_n = S$

(c) $P(E_i) > 0$ for all $i = 1, 2, 3, ..., n$

(d) All of the above

3 Let $\{E_1, E_2, ..., E_n\}$ be a partition of the sample space S, and suppose that each of the events $E_1, E_2, ..., E_n$ has non-zero probability of occurrence. Let A be any event associated with S, then **NCERT Pg. 424**

(a) $P(A) = P(E_1)P(A/E_1) + P(E_2)P(A/E_2) + \cdots + P(E_n)P(A/E_n)$

(b) $P(A) = \sum_{j=1}^{n} P(E_j)P(A/E_j)$

(c) Both (a) and (b)

(d) None of the abvoe

4 A person has undertaken a construction job. The probabilities are 0.65 that there will be strike, 0.80 that the construction job will be completed on time if there is no strike, and 0.32 that the construction job will be completed on time if there is a strike. Then, the probability that the construction job will be completed on time is **NCERT Pg. 425**

(a) 0.614 (b) 0.488

(c) 0.128 (d) 0.288

5 If $E_1, E_2, ..., E_n$ are n non empty events which constitute a partition of sample space S, *i.e.*, $E_1, E_2, ..., E_n$ are pairwise disjoint and $E_1 \cup E_2 \cup ... \cup E_n = S$ and A is any event of non-zero probability, then $P(E_i/A)$ is equal to ...K... . Here, K refers to **NCERT Pg. 425**

(a) $\dfrac{P(E_i)P(A/E_i)}{\sum_{j=1}^{n} P(E_j)P(A/E_j)}$ for any $i = 1, 2, 3, ..., n$

(b) $\dfrac{P(E_i)P(E_i/A)}{\sum_{j=1}^{n} P(E_j)P(A/E_j)}$ for any $i = 1, 2, 3, ..., n$

(c) $\dfrac{P(E_i)P(E_i/A)}{P(A)}$

(d) None of the above

6 Suppose that the reliability of a HIV test is specified as follows.

Of people having HIV, 90% of the test detect the disease but 10% go undetected. Of people free of HIV, 99% of the test are judged HIV–ive but 1% are diagnosed as showing HIV+ive. From a large population of which only 0.1% have HIV, one person is selected at random, given the HIV test, and the pathologist reports him/her as HIV+ive. Then, the probability that the person actually has HIV, is **NCERT Pg. 427**

(a) 0.081 (b) 0.082

(c) 0.084 (d) 0.083

7 In a factory which manufactures bolts, machines A, B and C manufacture, respectively 25%, 35% and 40% of the bolts. Of their outputs, 5, 4 and 2 percent are, respectively defective bolts. A bolt is drawn at random from the product and is found to be defective. Then, the probability that it is manufactured by the machine B is ...K... . Here, K refers to **NCERT Pg. 428**

(a) $\frac{28}{69}$ (b) $\frac{27}{68}$

(c) $\frac{28}{71}$ (d) $\frac{27}{64}$

8 A doctor is to visit a patient. From the past experience, it is known that the probabilities that he will come by train, bus, scooter or by other means of transport are, respectively $\frac{3}{10}, \frac{1}{5}, \frac{1}{10}$ and $\frac{2}{5}$. The probabilities that he will be late are $\frac{1}{4}, \frac{1}{3}$ and $\frac{1}{12}$, if he comes by train, bus and scooter respectively, but if he comes by other means of transport, then he will not be late. When he arrives, he is late. Then, the probability that he comes by train is **NCERT Pg. 429**

(a) $\frac{1}{3}$ (b) $\frac{1}{5}$

(c) $\frac{1}{6}$ (d) $\frac{1}{2}$

9 A man is known to speak truth 3 out of 4 times. He throws a dice and reports that it is a six. Then, the probability that it is actually a six, is ...K... . Here, K refers to **NCERT Pg. 430**

(a) $\frac{5}{8}$ (b) $\frac{1}{8}$

(c) $\frac{3}{8}$ (d) $\frac{7}{8}$

10 Of the students in a college, it is known that 60% reside in hostel and 40% are day scholars (not residing in hostel). Previous year results report that 30% of all students, who reside in hostel attain A grade and 20% of day scholars attain A grade in their annual examination. At the end of the year, one student is chosen at random from the college and he has an A grade. Then, the probability that the student is a hostlier is **NCERT Pg. 431**

(a) $\frac{9}{13}$ (b) $\frac{1}{13}$

(c) $\frac{3}{13}$ (d) $\frac{2}{13}$

11 In answering a question on a multiple choice test, a student either knows the answer or guesses. Let $\frac{3}{4}$ be the probability that he knows the answer and $\frac{1}{4}$ be the probability that he guesses. Assuming that a student, who guesses at the answer will be correct with probability $\frac{1}{4}$. Then, the probability that the student knows the answer given that he answered it correctly is **NCERT Pg. 431**

(a) $\frac{11}{13}$ (b) $\frac{12}{13}$
(c) $\frac{10}{13}$ (d) $\frac{1}{13}$

12 A laboratory blood test is 99% effective in detecting a certain disease when it is in fact, present. However, the test also yields a false positive result for 0.5% of the healthy person tested (i.e. if a healthy person is tested, then, with probability 0.005, the test will imply he has the disease). If 0.1 per cent of the population actually has the disease, then the probability that a person has the disease given that his test result is positive is **NCERT Pg. 431**

(a) $\frac{22}{135}$ (b) $\frac{22}{129}$
(c) $\frac{22}{133}$ (d) $\frac{22}{131}$

13 A factory has two machines A and B. Past record shows that machine A produced 60% of the items of output and machine B produced 40% of the items. Further, 2% of the items produced by machine A and 1% produced by machine B were defective. All the items are put into one stockpile and then one item is chosen at random from this and is found to be defective. Then, the probability that it was produced by machine B is **NCERT Pg. 432**

(a) $\frac{1}{5}$ (b) $\frac{1}{2}$ (c) $\frac{1}{3}$ (d) $\frac{1}{4}$

14 Two groups are competing for the position of the board of directors of a corporation. The probabilities that the first and the second groups will win are 0.6 and 0.4, respectively. Further, if the first group wins, the probability of introducing a new product is 0.7 and the corresponding probability is 0.3, if the second group wins. The probability that the new product introduced was by the second group is **NCERT Pg. 432**

(a) $\frac{1}{3}$ (b) $\frac{1}{9}$
(c) $\frac{2}{9}$ (d) $\frac{2}{3}$

15 Match the terms of column I with the terms of column II and choose the correct option from the codes given below. **NCERT Pg. 432**

Column I	Column II (Probability)
A. Suppose a girl throws a die. If she gets a 5 or 6, she tosses a coin three times and notes the number of heads. If she gets 1, 2, 3 or 4, she tosses a coin once and notes whether a head or tail is obtained. If she obtained exactly one head, then the probability that she threw 1, 2, 3 or 4 with the die is	1. $\frac{5}{34}$
B. A manufacturer has three machine operators A, B and C. The first operator A produces 1% defective items, where as the other two operators B and C produce 5% and 7% defective items, respectively. A is on the job for 50% of the time, B is on the job for 30% of the time and C is on the job for 20% of the time. A defective item is produced, then the probability that it was produced by A.	2. $\frac{11}{50}$
C. A card from a pack of 52 cards is lost. From the remaining cards of the pack, two cards are drawn and are found to be both diamonds. Then, the probability of the lost card being a diamond.	3. $\frac{8}{11}$

Codes

	A	B	C		A	B	C
(a)	3	1	2	(b)	1	2	3
(c)	2	1	3	(d)	3	2	1

16 Probability that A speaks truth is $\frac{4}{5}$. A coin is tossed. A reports that a head appears. The probability that actually there was head as **NCERT Pg. 432**

(a) $\frac{4}{5}$ (b) $\frac{1}{2}$ (c) $\frac{1}{5}$ (d) $\frac{2}{5}$

17 If A and B are two events such that $A \subset B$ and $P(B) \neq 0$, then which of the following is correct? **NCERT Pg. 433**

(a) $P(A/B) = \frac{P(B)}{P(A)}$ (b) $P(A/B) < P(A)$
(c) $P(A/B) \geq P(A)$ (d) None of these

Level II

18 A car manufacturing factory has two plants, X and Y. Plant X manufactures 70% of cars and plant Y manufactures 30%. 80% of the cars at plant X and 90% of the cars at plant Y are rated of standard quality. A car is chosen at random and is found to be of standard quality. The probability is from plant X, is **NCERT Exemplar Pg. 268**

(a) $\frac{56}{73}$ (b) $\frac{56}{84}$ (c) $\frac{56}{83}$ (d) $\frac{56}{79}$

19 A bag contains 5 red marbles and 3 black marbles. Three marbles are drawn one by one without replacement. Then, the probability that atleast one of the three marbles drawn be black, if the first marble is red, is **NCERT Exemplar Pg. 271**

(a) $\frac{15}{32}$ (b) $\frac{23}{36}$ (c) $\frac{21}{37}$ (d) $\frac{25}{56}$

20 A bag contains 4 white and 5 black balls. Another bag contains 9 white and 7 black balls. A ball is transferred from the first bag to the second and then a ball is drawn at random from the second bag. Then, the probability that the ball drawn is white is ...*K*... . Here, *K* refers to **NCERT Exemplar Pg. 273**

(a) $\frac{85}{152}$ (b) $\frac{85}{151}$ (c) $\frac{85}{153}$ (d) $\frac{85}{181}$

21 Suppose you have two coins, which appear identical in your pocket. You know that one is fair and other is 2-headed. If you take one out, toss it and get a head, then the probability that it was a fair coin, is **NCERT Exemplar Pg. 275**

(a) $\frac{2}{5}$ (b) $\frac{2}{3}$ (c) $\frac{1}{5}$ (d) $\frac{1}{3}$

22 Suppose that 6% of the people with blood group O are left handed and 10% of those with other blood groups are left handed. 30% of the people have blood group O. If a left handed person is selected at random, then the probability that he/she will have blood group O is **NCERT Exemplar Pg. 275**

(a) $\frac{9}{44}$ (b) $\frac{5}{44}$

(c) $\frac{3}{44}$ (d) $\frac{1}{44}$

23 An urn contains *m* white and *n* black balls. A ball is drawn at random and is put back into the urn along with *k* additional balls of the same colour as that of the ball drawn. A ball is again drawn at random. Then, the probability of drawing a white ball now, is **NCERT Exemplar Pg. 276**

(a) $\frac{km}{n}$ (b) $\frac{(m-n)}{k(m+1)}$

(c) $\frac{km}{m+n}$ (d) independent of k

24 A letter is known to have come either from TATA NAGAR or from CALCUTTA. On the envelope, just two consecutive letter TA are visible. Then, the probability that the letter came from TATA NAGAR is **NCERT Exemplar Pg. 277**

(a) $\frac{3}{11}$ (b) $\frac{2}{11}$ (c) $\frac{7}{11}$ (d) $\frac{1}{11}$

25 There are two bags, one of which contains 3 black and 4 white balls while the other contains 4 black and 3 white balls. A die is thrown. If it shows up 1 or 3, a ball is taken from the Ist bag; but if it shows up any other number, a ball is chosen from the second bag. Then, the probability of choosing a black ball is **NCERT Exemplar Pg. 277**

(a) $\frac{10}{21}$ (b) $\frac{1}{21}$ (c) $\frac{5}{21}$ (d) $\frac{11}{21}$

26 By examining the chest X-ray, the probability that TB is detected when a person is actually suffering is 0.99. The probability of an healthy person diagnosed to have TB is 0.001. In a certain city, 1 in 1000 people suffers from TB. *A* person is selected at random and is diagnosed to have TB. Then, the probability that he actually has TB is ...*K*... . Here, *K* refers to **NCERT Exemplar Pg. 277**

(a) $\frac{110}{221}$ (b) $\frac{2}{223}$ (c) $\frac{110}{223}$ (d) $\frac{1}{221}$

Random Variables *and* Its Probability Distributions

Level I

1 The variable obtained by assigning each outcome of the experiment to a single real number is **Old NCERT Pg. 558**

(a) random variable (b) Bernoulli's trial
(c) not a random variable (d) None of these

2 A real valued function whose domain is the sample space of a random experiment is called **Old NCERT Pg. 558**

(a) random function (b) random variable
(c) random experiment (d) None of these

3 Consider the experiment of tossing a coin two times in succession. Let *X* denotes the number of heads obtained, then **Old NCERT Pg. 558**

(a) $X(HH)=2, X(HT)=1$ (b) $X(TH)=1, X(TT)=0$
(c) Only (a) (d) Both (a) and (b)

4 A description giving the values of the random variable along with the corresponding probabilities is called ...*K*... of the random variable *X*. Here, *K* refers to **Old NCERT Pg. 560**

(a) conditional probability
(b) probability distribution
(c) mean
(d) None of the above

5 The probability distribution of a random variable *X* is the system of numbers is defined as **Old NCERT Pg. 560**

$X: x_1\ x_2 ... x_n,\ P(x): p_1\ p_2 ... p_n$, where

(a) $p_i > 0$ (b) $\sum_{i=1}^{n} p_i = 1, i = 1, 2, ..., n$

(c) Both (a) and (b) (d) None of these

6 Let X denote the number of hours, you study during a randomly selected school day. The probability that X can take the values x, has the following form, where k is some unknown constant.

$$P(X=x)=\begin{cases}0.1, \text{ if } x=0\\ kx, \text{ if } x=1 \text{ or } 2\\ k(5-x), \text{ if } x=3 \text{ or } 4\\ 0, \text{ otherwise}\end{cases}$$

Then, match the terms of column I with their respective values in column II and choose the correct option from the codes given below. **Old NCERT Pg. 563**

	Column I		Column II
A.	The value of k	1.	0.55
B.	P (you study atleast two hours)	2.	0.3
C.	P (you study exactly two hours)	3.	0.75
D.	P (you study atmost two hours)	4.	0.15

Codes

	A	B	C	D
(a)	1	4	3	2
(b)	4	3	1	2
(c)	4	2	3	1
(d)	4	3	2	1

7 A measure of location or central tendency that locates a middle or average value of the random variable is called ...K... . Here, K refers to **Old NCERT Pg. 563**

(a) mode
(b) mean
(c) median
(d) None of these

8 The variance of random variable X *i.e.*, σ_x^2 or var(X) is equal to **Old NCERT Pg. 567**

(a) $E(X^2)+[E(X^2)]^2$
(b) $E(X)-[E(X^2)]$
(c) $E(X^2)-[E(X)]^2$
(d) None of these

9 Which of the following is the probability distribution of a random variable? **Old NCERT Pg. 569**

(i)

X	0	1	2
P(X)	0.4	0.4	0.2

(ii)

X	0	1	2	3	4
P(X)	0.1	0.5	0.2	−0.1	0.3

(iii)

Y	−1	0	1
P(Y)	0.6	0.1	0.2

(iv)

Z	3	2	1	0	−1
P(Z)	0.3	0.2	0.4	0.1	0.05

(a) Only (i)
(b) Only (ii)
(c) Both (iii) and (iv)
(d) None of the above

10 Match the probability distributions of column I with their respective values in column II and choose the correct option from the codes given below. **Old NCERT Pg. 570**

	Column I		Column II					
A.	Number of heads in two tosses of a coin.	1.	X	0	1	2	3	4
			$P(X)$	$\frac{1}{16}$	$\frac{1}{4}$	$\frac{3}{8}$	$\frac{1}{4}$	$\frac{1}{16}$
B.	Number of tails in the simultaneous tosses of three coins.	2.	X	0	1	2		
			$P(X)$	$\frac{1}{4}$	$\frac{1}{2}$	$\frac{1}{4}$		
C.	Number of heads in four tosses of a coin.	3.	X	0	1	2	3	
			$P(X)$	$\frac{1}{8}$	$\frac{3}{8}$	$\frac{3}{8}$	$\frac{1}{8}$	

Codes

	A	B	C
(a)	1	2	3
(b)	3	1	2
(c)	2	3	1
(d)	1	2	3

11 The probability distributions of the number of successes in two tosses of a die, where a success is defined as

(i) number greater than 4 **Old NCERT Pg. 570**

(ii) six appears on atleast one die, respectively are

(a)

X	0	1	2
P(X)	$\frac{4}{9}$	$\frac{4}{9}$	$\frac{1}{9}$

X	0	1
P(X)	$\frac{25}{36}$	$\frac{11}{36}$

(b)

X	0	1	2
P(X)	$\frac{1}{9}$	$\frac{4}{9}$	$\frac{4}{9}$

X	0	1
P(X)	$\frac{11}{36}$	$\frac{25}{36}$

(c)

X	0	1	2
P(X)	$\frac{1}{9}$	$\frac{1}{9}$	$\frac{2}{9}$

X	0	1
P(X)	$\frac{2}{19}$	$\frac{1}{19}$

(d) None of the above

12 A random variable X has the following probability distribution. **Old NCERT Pg. 570**

X	0	1	2	3	4	5	6	7
P(X)	0	k	$2k$	$2k$	$3k$	k^2	$2k^2$	$7k^2+k$

Then, match the terms of column I with their respective values in column II and choose the correct option from the codes given below.

Column I	Column II
A. The value of k	1. $\frac{17}{100}$
B. $P(X<3)$	2. $\frac{3}{10}$
C. $P(X>6)$	3. $\frac{1}{10}$
D. $P(0<X<3)$	

Codes

	A	B	C	D
(a)	3	1	1	3
(b)	3	2	2	1
(c)	3	2	1	2
(d)	1	2	3	1

13 The random variable X has a probability distribution $P(X)$ of the following form, where k is some number.

$$P(X)=\begin{cases}k, \text{ if } x=0\\ 2k, \text{ if } x=1\\ 3k, \text{ if } x=2\\ 0, \text{ otherwise}\end{cases}$$

Then, match the terms of column I with their respective values in column II and choose the correct option from the codes given below. **Old NCERT Pg. 571**

Column I	Column II
A. The value of k	1. $\frac{1}{2}$
B. $P(X<2)$	2. 1
C. $P(X\le 2)$	3. $\frac{1}{2}$
D. $P(X\ge 2)$	4. $\frac{1}{6}$

Codes

	A	B	C	D
(a)	4	2	3	1
(b)	4	3	2	1
(c)	3	1	4	2
(d)	4	2	1	3

14 A class has 15 students, whose ages in years are 14, 17, 15, 14, 21, 17, 19, 20, 16, 18, 20, 17, 16, 19 and 20. One student is selected in such a manner that each has the same chance of being chosen and the age X of the selected student is recorded.

Then, match the terms of column I with their respective values in column II and choose the correct option from the codes given below. **Old NCERT Pg. 571**

Column I	Column II
A. Probability distribution of X	1. 2.19
B. Mean of X	2. 4.8
C. Variance of X	3. 17.53
D. Standard deviation of X	4. (table below)

X	14	15	16	17	18	19	20	21
Number of students	2	1	2	3	1	2	3	1
P(X)	$\frac{2}{15}$	$\frac{1}{15}$	$\frac{2}{15}$	$\frac{3}{15}$	$\frac{1}{15}$	$\frac{2}{15}$	$\frac{3}{15}$	$\frac{1}{15}$

Codes

	A	B	C	D
(a)	4	3	2	1
(b)	4	2	3	1
(c)	4	3	1	2
(d)	4	1	2	3

15 In a meeting, 70% of the members favour and 30% oppose a certain proposal. A member is selected at random and we take $X=0$, if he opposed and $X=1$, if he is in favour. Then, $E(X)$ and $\text{Var}(X)$ are respectively **Old NCERT Pg. 571**

(a) $\frac{3}{7}, \frac{5}{17}$ (b) $\frac{13}{15}, \frac{2}{15}$
(c) $\frac{7}{10}, \frac{21}{100}$ (d) $\frac{7}{10}, \frac{23}{100}$

16 The mean of the numbers obtained on throwing a die having written 1 on three faces, 2 on two faces and 5 on one face is **Old NCERT Pg. 571**

(a) 1 (b) 2 (c) 5 (d) $\frac{8}{3}$

17 Suppose that two cards are drawn at random from a deck of cards. Let X be the number of aces obtained. Then, the value of $E(X)$ is **Old NCERT Pg. 571**

(a) $\frac{37}{221}$ (b) $\frac{5}{13}$ (c) $\frac{1}{13}$ (d) $\frac{2}{13}$

Level II

18 Let X be discrete random variable. The probability distribution of X is given below. **NCERT Exemplar Pg. 277**

X	30	10	–10
P(X)	$\frac{1}{5}$	$\frac{3}{10}$	$\frac{1}{2}$

Then, $E(X)$ is equal to

(a) 6 (b) 4 (c) 3 (d) –5

19 The random variable X can take only the values 0, 1, 2. Given that $P(X=0)=P(X=1)=p$ and that $E(X^2)=E[X]$, find the value of p. Old NCERT Pg. 565

(a) $\frac{1}{5}$ (b) $\frac{3}{10}$

(c) $\frac{2}{5}$ (d) $\frac{1}{2}$

20 The variance and standard deviation of the number of heads in three tosses of a coin are respectively Old NCERT Pg. 565

(a) $\frac{3}{4}, \frac{\sqrt{3}}{2}$ (b) $\frac{1}{4}, \frac{1}{2}$

(c) $\frac{3}{4}, \frac{\sqrt{3}}{4}$ (d) None of these

21 In a dice game, a player pays a stake of ₹ 1 for each throw of a die. She receives ₹ 5, if the die shows a 3, ₹ 2 if the die shows a 1 or 6 and nothing otherwise. Then, the player's expected profit per throw over a long series of throws is Old NCERT Pg. 571

(a) $\frac{2}{3}$ (b) $\frac{1}{2}$

(c) $\frac{1}{5}$ (d) $\frac{1}{3}$

22 Suppose 10000 tickets are sold in a lottery each for ₹ 1. First prize is of ₹ 3000 and the second prize is of ₹ 2000. There are three third prizes of ₹ 500 each. If you buy one ticket, then your expectation is Old NCERT Pg. 563

(a) ₹ 0.61 (b) ₹ 0.60

(c) ₹ 0.65 (d) ₹ 0.64

23. The probability distribution of a random variable X is given below. NCERT Exemplar Pg. 274

X	0	1	2	3
$P(X)$	k	$\frac{k}{2}$	$\frac{k}{4}$	$\frac{k}{8}$

Then, match the terms column I with their respective values in column II and choose the correct option from the codes given below.

Column I		Column II
A. The value of k	1.	$\frac{14}{15}$
B. $P(X \le 2)$	2.	1
C. $P(X \le 2) + P(X > 2)$	3.	$\frac{8}{15}$

Codes

	A	B	C
(a)	3	1	2
(b)	1	2	3
(c)	3	2	1
(d)	2	1	3

24 For the following probability distribution, the standard deviation of the random variable X is NCERT Exemplar Pg. 274

X	2	3	4
$P(X)$	0.2	0.5	0.3

(a) 0.5 (b) 0.6 (c) 0.61 (d) 0.7

Miscellaneous Exercise

1 A and B throw a pair of dice alternately. A wins the game, if he gets a total of 6 and B wins, if she gets a total of 7. If A starts the game, then the probability of winning the game by A in third throw of the pair of dice is NCERT Pg. 434

(a) $\frac{775}{7776}$ (b) $\frac{773}{7776}$

(c) $\frac{770}{7779}$ (d) None of these

2 A bag contains 5 red and 3 blue balls. If 3 balls are drawn at random without replacement, the probability of getting exactly one red ball is NCERT Pg. 417

(a) $\frac{45}{196}$ (b) $\frac{135}{392}$

(c) $\frac{15}{56}$ (d) $\frac{15}{29}$

3 Coloured balls are distributed in four boxes as shown in the following table.

Box	Colour			
	Black	White	Red	Blue
I	3	4	5	6
II	2	2	2	2
III	1	2	3	1
IV	4	3	1	5

A box is selected at random and then a ball is randomly drawn from the selected box. The colour of the ball is black. The probability that ball drawn is from the box III, is NCERT Pg. 423

(a) 0.161 (b) 0.162

(c) 0.165 (d) 0.104

4 The mean of the binomial distribution $B\left(4, \frac{1}{3}\right)$ is ...K... .

Here, K refers to Old NCERT Pg. 579

(a) $\frac{5}{3}$ (b) $\frac{2}{3}$

(c) $\frac{1}{3}$ (d) $\frac{4}{3}$

5 The probability of a shooter hitting a target is $\frac{3}{4}$. The minimum number of times must he/she fire so that the probability of hitting the target atleast once is more than 0.99 is ...K... . Here, K refers to **Old NCERT Pg. 580**

(a) 4 (b) 3 (c) 5 (d) 2

6 A and B throw a die alternatively till one of them gets a '6' and wins the game. Then, probabilities of winning B, if A starts first, is **Old NCERT Pg. 581**

(a) $\frac{2}{11}$ (b) $\frac{5}{11}$ (c) $\frac{3}{11}$ (d) $\frac{1}{11}$

7 If a machine is correctly set up, it produces 90% acceptable items. If it is incorrectly set up, it produces only 40% acceptable items. Past experience shows that 80% of the setups are correctly done. If after a certain set up, the machine produces 2 acceptable items, then the probability that the machine is correctly set up is **Old NCERT Pg. 582**

(a) 0.91 (b) 0.94 (c) 0.92 (d) 0.95

8 Suppose that 5% of men and 0.25% of women have grey hair. A grey haired person is selected at random. Then, the probability of this person being male. Assuming that there are equal number of males and females is **Old NCERT Pg. 582**

(a) $\frac{19}{21}$ (b) $\frac{15}{22}$ (c) $\frac{22}{21}$ (d) $\frac{20}{21}$

Numerical Type Questions

1 A bag contains 4 red and 6 black balls. A ball is drawn at random from the bag, its colour is observed and this ball along with two additional balls of the same colour are returned to the bag. If now a ball is drawn of random from the bag, then the probability that this drawn ball is red is k, then the value of $5k+1$ is .... **NCERT Pg. 424**

2 A random variable X has the following probability distribution.

X	1	2	3	4	5
$P(X)$	$3k$	$2k^2$	k	k	$4k^2$

Then, $P(X>3)$ is equal to $\frac{\alpha}{\beta}$, then value of $(\beta-\alpha)$ is .... **Old NCERT Pg. 558**

3 Three urns A, B and C contains 7 red, 4 black, 5 red 6 black and 6 red, 5 black balls, respectively. One of the urn is selected at random and a ball is drawn from it. If the ball drawn is black, then the probability that it is drawn from urn B is $\alpha/5$, then α is .... **NCERT Pg. 425**

4 One ticket is selected at random from 50 tickets numbered 00, 01, 02, ..., 49. Then, the probability that the sum of the digits on the selected ticket is 8, given that the product of these digits is zero, is $\frac{k_1}{k_2}$, then value of (k_1+k_2) is .... **NCERT Pg. 406**

5 The probability that in a year of 22nd century chosen at random, there will be 53 Sundays is $\frac{k}{28}$, then value of k is **NCERT Pg. 424**

6 Of the three independent events E_1, E_2 and E_3, the probability that only E_1 occurs is α, only E_2 occurs is β and only E_3 occurs is γ. If the probability p that none of events E_1, E_2 or E_3 occurs satisfy the equations $(\alpha-2\beta)\,p=\alpha\beta$ and $(\beta-3\gamma)\,p=2\beta\gamma$. All the given probabilities are assumed to lie in the interval (0, 1), then the $\frac{P(E_1)}{P(E_3)}$ is .... **NCERT Pg. 417**

Assertion and Reason Questions

Direction (Q. Nos. 1-10) The following questions consist of two statements Assertion (A) and Reason (R). Answer these questions by selecting the appropriate option given below.

(a) Both A and R are true and R is the correct explanation of A.

(b) Both A and R are true but R is not the correct explanation of A.

(c) A is true but R is false.

(d) A is false but R is true.

1 Two coins are tossed once.

Assertion (A) If E : tail appears on one coin and F : one coin shows head, then $P(E/F)$ is 1.

Reason (R) If E : no tail appears and F : no head appears, then $P(E/F)$ is 0. **NCERT Pg. 406**

2 A black and a red dice are rolled.

Assertion (A) The conditional probability of obtaining a sum greater than 9, given that the black die resulted in a 5, is $\frac{1}{3}$.

Reason (R) The conditional probability of obtaining the sum 8, given that the red die resulted in a number less than 4, is $\frac{1}{9}$.

NCERT Pg. 406

3 **Assertion (A)** Given that, the two numbers appearing on throwing two dice are different. Then, the probability of the event 'the sum of numbers on the dice is 4' is $\frac{1}{15}$.

Reason (R) Consider the experiment of throwing a die, if a multiple of 3 comes up, throw the die again and if any other number comes, toss a coin. Then, the conditional probability of the event 'the coin shows a tail', given that 'atleast one die shows a 3' is $\frac{1}{14}$.

NCERT Pg. 406

4 **Assertion (A)** The mean of a random variable X is also called the expectation of X, denoted by $E(X)$.

Reason (R) The mean or expectation of a random variable X is not sum of the products of all possible values of X by their respective probabilities. Old NCERT Pg. 557

5 **Assertion (A)** A dice marked 1, 2, 3 in red and 4, 5, 6 in green is tossed. Let A be the event, 'the number is even' and B be the event, 'the number is red'. Then, A and B are not independent.

Reason (R) Let E and F be events with $P(E)=\frac{3}{5}$, $P(F)=\frac{3}{10}$ and $P(E\cap F)=\frac{1}{5}$. Then, E and F are independent.

NCERT Pg. 417

6 **Assertion (A)** A box has 5 blue and 4 red balls. One ball is drawn at random and not replaced. Its colour is also not noted. Then, another ball is drawn at random. The probability of second ball being blue is $\frac{5}{9}$.

Reason (R) Four cards are successively drawn without replacement from a deck of 52 playing cards. The probability that all the four cards are king is $\frac{1}{270725}$.

NCERT Pg. 424

7 Three bags contain a number of red and white balls as follows.

Bag 1 : 3 red balls, Bag 2 : 2 red balls and 1 white ball, Bag 3 : 3 white balls.

The probability that bag i will be chosen and a ball is selected from it is $\frac{i}{6}$, $i=1, 2, 3$. Then,

Assertion (A) The probability that a red ball will be selected is $\frac{7}{18}$.

Reason (R) The probability that a white ball will be selected is $\frac{11}{18}$.

NCERT Pg. 424

8 **Assertion (A)** If A and B are two events such that $P(A)=\frac{1}{4}$, $P(B)=\frac{1}{2}$ and $P(A\cap B)=\frac{1}{8}$, then $P(\text{not } A \text{ and not } B)$ is $\frac{3}{8}$.

Reason (R) Events A and B are such that $P(A)=\frac{1}{2}$, $P(B)=\frac{7}{12}$ and $P(\text{not } A \text{ or not } B)=\frac{1}{4}$, then A and B are independent. NCERT Pg. 417

9 **Assertion (A)** The variance of X i.e. $V(X)$ or σ^2_x is equal to $\sum_{i=1}^{n}(x_i-\mu)^2p(x_i)$, where $\mu=E(X)$ be the mean of X.

Reason (R) $\sigma_x=\sqrt{\text{var}(X)}=\sqrt{\sum_{i=1}^{n}(x_i-\mu)^2p(x_i)}$ is called the standard deviation of the random variable X.

Old NCERT Pg. 565

10 **Assertion (A)** An urn contains 5 red and 2 black balls. Two balls are randomly drawn. Let X represent the number of black balls. Then, the possible values of X are 0, 1 and 2 and X is a random variable.

Reason (R) Let X represent the difference between the number of heads and the number of tails obtained when a coin is tossed 6 times. Then, the possible values of X are 0, 2, 4 and 6. Old NCERT Pg. 568

Case or Paragraph Type Questions

Direction (Q. Nos. 1-4) A factory has three machines A, B and C to manufacture bolts. Machine A manufacture 30%, machine B manufacture 20% and machine C manufacture 50% of the bolts, respectively. Out of their respective outputs 5%, 2% and 4 % are defective. A bolt is drawn at random from total production and it is found to be defective.

Based on the above information, answer the following questions.

NCERT Pg. 428

1 Probability that defective bolt drawn is manufactured by machine *A*, is

(a) $\frac{4}{13}$ (b) $\frac{5}{13}$
(c) $\frac{6}{13}$ (d) $\frac{9}{13}$

2 Probability that defective bolt drawn is manufactured by machine *B*, is

(a) 0.1 (b) 0.3 (c) 0.2 (d) 0.4

3 Probability that defective bolt is not manufactured by machine *B*, is

(a) $\frac{35}{39}$ (b) $\frac{61}{39}$
(c) $\frac{41}{39}$ (d) None of these

4 Probability that defective bolt is not manufactured by machine C, is

(a) 0.03 (b) 0.09
(c) 0.48 (d) 0.9

Direction (Q. Nos. 5-8) Box I contains 1 white, 3 black and 2 red balls. Box II contains 2 white, 1 black and 3 red balls. Box III contains 3 white, 2 black and 1 red balls. One box is chosen at random and two balls are drawn with replacement. If E_1, E_2, E_3 be the events that the balls drawn from box I, box II and box III, respectively and *A* be the event that balls drawn are one white and one red, then answer the following questions. **NCERT Pg. 431**

5 Probability of occurrence of event *A* given that the balls drawn are from box I, is

(a) $\frac{1}{9}$ (b) $\frac{2}{6}$ (c) $\frac{3}{5}$ (d) $\frac{1}{7}$

6 Probability of occurrence of event *A*, given that the balls drawn are from box II, is

(a) $\frac{1}{3}$ (b) $\frac{1}{4}$ (c) $\frac{3}{4}$ (d) $\frac{3}{5}$

7 Probability of occurrence of event *A*, given that balls drawn are from box III, is

(a) $\frac{1}{12}$ (b) $\frac{3}{11}$ (c) $\frac{1}{6}$ (d) $\frac{4}{11}$

8 The probability that the balls drawn are from box II, given that event *A* has already occurred, is

(a) $\frac{1}{11}$ (b) $\frac{6}{11}$
(c) $\frac{5}{11}$ (d) None of these

Past Years Questions

Single Correct Type

1 A company has two plants *A* and *B* to manufacture motorcycles. 60% motorcycles are manufactured at plant *A* and the remaining are manufactured at plant *B*. 80% of the motorcycles manufactured at plant *A* are rated of the standard quality, while 90% of the motorcycles manufactured at plant *B* are rated of the standard quality. A motorcycle picked up randomly from the total production is found to be of the standard quality. If *p* is the probability that it was manufactured at plant *B*, then 126*p* is **NCERT Pg. 423, JEE Main 2024, 6 April Shift-I**

(a) 66 (b) 56 (c) 64 (d) 54

2 A bag contains 8 balls, whose colours are either white or black. 4 balls are drawn at random without replacement and it was found that 2 balls are white and other 2 balls are black. The probability that the bag contains equal number of white and black balls is

NCERT Pg. 423, JEE Main 2024, 1 Feb Shift-I

(a) $\frac{2}{7}$ (b) $\frac{1}{5}$
(c) $\frac{2}{5}$ (d) $\frac{1}{7}$

3 Bag *A* contains 3 white, 7 red balls and Bag *B* contains 3 white, 2 red balls. One bag is selected at random and a ball is drawn from it. The probability of drawing the ball from the bag *A*, if the ball drawn is white, is

NCERT Pg. 423, JEE Main 2024, 30 Jan Shift-II

(a) $\frac{1}{4}$ (b) $\frac{1}{3}$
(c) $\frac{3}{10}$ (d) $\frac{1}{9}$

4 Let a die be rolled *n* times. Let the probability of getting odd numbers seven times be equal to the probability of getting odd numbers nine times. If the probability of getting even numbers twice is $\frac{k}{2^{15}}$, then *k* is equal to

Old NCERT Pg. 576, JEE Main 2023, 10 April Shift-II

(a) 90 (b) 60 (c) 30 (d) 15

5 A pair of dice is thrown 5 times. For each throw, a total of 5 is considered a success. If the probability of at least 4 successes is $\frac{k}{3^{11}}$, then *k* is equal to

Old NCERT Pg. 573, JEE Main 2023, 6 April Shift-I

(a) 75 (b) 123 (c) 164 (d) 82

6 In a binomial distribution $B(n, p)$ the sum and the product of the mean and the variance are 5 and 6 respectively, then $6(n+p-q)$ is equal to

Old NCERT Pg. 573, JEE Main 2023, 1 Feb Shift-I

(a) 53 (b) 50 (c) 51 (d) 52

7 A die is rolled thrice. What is the probability of getting a number greater than 4 in the first and the second throw of dice and a number less than 4 in the third throw ?

NCERT Pg. 413, CUET 2024, 16 May

(a) $\frac{1}{3}$ (b) $\frac{1}{6}$ (c) $\frac{1}{9}$ (d) $\frac{1}{18}$

8 If the random variable X has the following distribution.

X	0	1	2	otherwise
$P(X)$	k	$2k$	$3k$	0

Match List-I with List-II.

	List-I		List-II
A.	k	(i)	$\frac{5}{6}$
B.	$P(X<2)$	(ii)	$\frac{4}{3}$
C.	$E(X)$	(iii)	$\frac{1}{2}$
D.	$P(1 \le X \le 2)$	(iv)	$\frac{1}{6}$

Choose the correct answer from the options given below:

NCERT Pg. 421, CUET 2024, 16 May

	A	B	C	D
(a)	(i)	(ii)	(iii)	(iv)
(b)	(iv)	(iii)	(ii)	(i)
(c)	(i)	(ii)	(iv)	(iii)
(d)	(iii)	(iv)	(i)	(ii)

9 Let X denote the number of hours you play during a randomly selected day. The probability that, X can take values x has the following form, where c is some constant.

$$P(X=x)=\begin{cases} 0.1, & \text{if } x=0 \\ cx, & \text{if } x=1 \text{ or } x=2 \\ c(5-x), & \text{if } x=3 \text{ or } x=4 \\ 0, & \text{otherwise} \end{cases}$$

Match List-I with List-II.

	List-I		List-II
A.	c	(i)	0.75
B.	$P(X \le 2)$	(ii)	0.3
C.	$P(X=2)$	(iii)	0.55
D.	$P(X \ge 2)$	(iv)	0.15

Choose the correct answer from the options given below:

NCERT Pg. 422, CUET 2024, 16 May

	A	B	C	D
(a)	(i)	(ii)	(iii)	(iv)
(b)	(iv)	(iii)	(ii)	(i)
(c)	(i)	(ii)	(iv)	(iii)
(d)	(iii)	(iv)	(i)	(ii)

10 There are two bags, Bag-1 contains 4 white and 6 black balls and Bag-2 contains 5 white and 5 black balls. A die is rolled, if it shows a number divisible by 3, a ball is drawn from Bag-I, else a ball is drawn from Bag-2. If the ball drawn is not black in colour, the probability that it was not drawn from Bag-2 is

NCERT Pg. 422, CUET 2024, 16 May

(a) $\frac{4}{9}$ (b) $\frac{3}{8}$

(c) $\frac{2}{7}$ (d) $\frac{4}{19}$

Numerical Value Type

11 Three balls are drawn at random from a bag containing 5 blue and 4 yellow balls. Let the random variables X and Y, respectively denote the number of blue and yellow balls. If $\overline{X}$ and $\overline{Y}$ are the means of X and Y respectively. Then, $7\overline{X}+4\overline{Y}$ is equal to ....

Old NCERT Pg. 565, JEE Main 2024, 8 April Shift-I

12 Let the mean and the standard deviation of the probability distribution

X	α	1	0	-3
$P(X)$	$\frac{1}{3}$	K	$\frac{1}{6}$	$\frac{1}{4}$

be μ and α, respectively. If $\sigma-\mu=2$, then $\sigma+\mu$ is equal to ....

Old NCERT Pg. 567, JEE Main 2024, 5 April Shift-II

13 Let the probability of getting head for a biased coin be $\frac{1}{4}$. It is tossed repeatedly until a head appears. Let N be the number of tosses required. If the probability that the equation $64x^2+5Nx+1=0$ has no real root is $\frac{p}{q}$, where p and q are co-prime, then $q-p$ is equal to ....

Old NCERT Pg. 573, JEE Main 2023, 11 April Shift-II

14 25% of the population are smokers. A smoker has 27 times more chances to develop lung cancer than a non smoker. A person is diagnosed with lung cancer and the probability that this person is a smoker is $k/10$. Then, the value of k is ....

NCERT Pg. 576, JEE Main 2023, 25 Jan Shift-II

Skill Boosters

1 A bag contains $n+1$ coins. It is know that one of these coins shows heads on both sides, whereas the other coins are fair. One coin is selected at random and tossed. If the probability that toss result in head is $\frac{11}{20}$, then value of n is

(a) 9 (b) 6 (c) 4 (d) 3

2 Two number are selected randomly from the $S=\{1, 2, 3, 4, 5, 6\}$ without replacement one by one. The probability that the minimum of two numbers is less than 4 is

(a) $\frac{2}{5}$ (b) $\frac{3}{5}$ (c) $\frac{4}{5}$ (d) $\frac{1}{5}$

3 If two cards are drawn successively with replacement from a well shuffled deck of 52 cards, then mean of the number of ace is

(a) $\frac{2}{13}$ (b) $\frac{4}{13}$
(c) $\frac{1}{13}$ (d) $\frac{5}{13}$

4 Three students appear in an examination of Mathematics. The probabilities of their success are $\frac{1}{3}, \frac{1}{4}$ and $\frac{1}{5}$, respectively. If the probability of success of atleast two is $\frac{\lambda}{12}$, then the value of λ is

(a) 3 (b) 4
(c) 2 (d) 1

5 A signal which can be green or red with probability $\frac{4}{5}$ and $\frac{1}{5}$ respectively, is received by station A and then transmitted to station B. The probability of each station receiving the signal correctly is $\frac{3}{4}$. If the signal received at station B is green, then the probability that the original signal was green, is

(a) $\frac{22}{23}$ (b) $\frac{21}{23}$ (c) $\frac{20}{23}$ (d) $\frac{19}{23}$

Correct Codes

Topical Questions

Conditional Probability

1 (c)	2 (b)	3 (a)	4 (b)	5 (d)	6 (b)	7 (b)	8 (a)	9 (b)	10 (d)
11 (c)	12 (a)	13 (b)	14 (d)	15 (c)	16 (d)	17 (a)	18 (d)	19 (d)	20 (c)
21 (c)	22 (d)	23 (c)	24 (a)	25 (c)	26 (b)	27 (c)	28 (c)		

Multiplication Theorem on Probability

1 (a)	2 (c)	3 (d)	4 (c)	5 (a)

Independent Events

1 (a)	2 (d)	3 (a)	4 (a)	5 (d)	6 (b)	7 (d)	8 (c)	9 (a)	10 (b)
11 (d)	12 (a)	13 (d)	14 (b)	15 (c)	16 (c)	17 (a)	18 (c)	19 (c)	20 (a)
21 (b)	22 (c)	23 (a)	24 (a)	25 (b)	26 (c)				

Bayes' Theorem

1 (a)	2 (d)	3 (c)	4 (b)	5 (a)	6 (d)	7 (a)	8 (d)	9 (c)	10 (a)
11 (b)	12 (c)	13 (d)	14 (c)	15 (a)	16 (a)	17 (c)	18 (c)	19 (d)	20 (c)
21 (d)	22 (a)	23 (d)	24 (c)	25 (d)	26 (a)				

Random Variables and Its Probability Distributions

1 (a)	2 (b)	3 (d)	4 (b)	5 (c)	6 (d)	7 (b)	8 (c)	9 (a)	10 (c)
11 (a)	12 (c)	13 (b)	14 (a)	15 (c)	16 (b)	17 (d)	18 (b)	19 (d)	20 (a)
21 (b)	22 (c)	23 (a)	24 (d)						

Miscellaneous Exercise

1 (a)	2 (c)	3 (c)	4 (d)	5 (a)	6 (b)	7 (d)	8 (d)	9 (d)	10 (a)
11 (d)	12 (a)	13 (c)	14 (a)	15 (a)	16 (c)	17 (b)			

Numerical Type Questions

1 (3)	2 (13)	3 (2)	4 (15)	5 (5)	6 (6)

Assertion and Reason Questions

1 (b)	2 (b)	3 (c)	4 (c)	5 (c)	6 (b)	7 (b)	8 (c)	9 (b)	10 (b)

Case or Paragraph Type Questions

1 (b)	2 (a)	3 (a)	4 (c)	5 (a)	6 (a)	7 (c)	8 (b)

Past Years Questions

1 (d)	2 (a)	3 (b)	4 (b)	5 (b)	6 (d)	7 (d)	8 (b)	9 (b)	10 (c)
11 (17)	12 (5)	13 (27)	14 (479)						

Skill Boosters

1 (a)	2 (c)	3 (a)	4 (c)	5 (c)

Step by Step

Decoding the Questions

Concept Builders

1 6^n

2 Sure event

3 0

4 $P(A \cap B)$

5 1

6 0.9

7 $P(A \cap B) / P(B)$

8 1

9 Independent events

10 Discrete, continuous

11 Expectation

12 Mutually exclusive, exhaustive events

13 0

14 $P(A)$

15 True

Topical Questions

Conditional Probability

1 (*c*) Consider the experiment of tossing three fair coins. The sample space of the experiment is $S = \{HHH, HHT, HTH, THH, HTT, THT, TTH, TTT\}$.

Since, the coins are fair. So, we can assign the portability $\frac{1}{8}$ to each sample point. Let E be the event 'atleast two heads appear' and F be the event 'first coin shows tail'.

Then, $E = \{HHH, HHT, HTH, THH\}$

and $F = \{THH, THT, TTH, TTT\}$

Therefore,

$$P(E) = P(\{HHH\}) + P(\{HHT\}) + P(\{HTH\}) + P(\{THH\})$$
$$= \frac{1}{8} + \frac{1}{8} + \frac{1}{8} + \frac{1}{8} = \frac{1}{2}$$
$$P(F) = P(\{THH\}) + P(\{THT\}) + P(\{TTH\}) + P(\{TTT\})$$
$$= \frac{1}{8} + \frac{1}{8} + \frac{1}{8} + \frac{1}{8} = \frac{1}{2}$$

Also, $E \cap F = \{THH\}$

with $P(E \cap F) = P(\{THH\}) = \frac{1}{8}$

2 (*b*) Suppose we are given that the first coin shows tail i.e. F occurs with the information of occurrence of F, we are sure that the cases in which first coin does not result into a tail should not be considered while finding the probability of E. This information reduces our sample space from the set S to its subset F for the event E. In other words, the additional information really amounts to telling us that the situation may be considered as being that of a new random experiment for which the sample space consists of all those outcomes only which are favourable to the occurrence of the event F.

Now, the sample point of F which is favourable to event E, is THH.

Thus, the probability of E considering F as the sample space $= \frac{1}{4}$ or probability of E given that the event F has occurred $= \frac{1}{4}$.

This probability of the event E is called the conditional probability of E given that F has already occurred and is denoted by $P\left(\frac{E}{F}\right)$.

Thus, $P\left(\frac{E}{F}\right) = \frac{1}{4}$

3 (*a*) We know,

$$P\left(\frac{S}{F}\right) = 1$$
$$\Rightarrow P\frac{(E \cup E')}{F} = 1 \quad [\because S = E \cup E']$$
$$\Rightarrow P\left(\frac{E}{F}\right) + P\left(\frac{E'}{F}\right) = 1$$

[$\because$ E and E' are disjoint events]

Thus, $P\left(\frac{E'}{F}\right) = 1 - P\left(\frac{E}{F}\right)$

4 (*b*) We have,

$$P\left(\frac{A}{B}\right) = \frac{P(A \cap B)}{P(B)} = \frac{\frac{4}{13}}{\frac{9}{13}} = \frac{4}{9}$$

5 (*d*) It is given that $P(E) = 0.6$, $P(F) = 0.3$ and $P(E \cap F) = 0.2$.

We know that,

$$P\left(\frac{E}{F}\right) = \frac{P(E \cap F)}{P(F)} = \frac{0.2}{0.3} = \frac{2}{3}$$

and $P\left(\frac{F}{E}\right) = \frac{P(F \cap E)}{P(E)} = \frac{0.2}{0.6} = \frac{1}{3}$

6 (*b*) It is given that $P(B) = 0.5$ and $P(A \cap B) = 0.32$.

$$\therefore P\left(\frac{A}{B}\right) = \frac{P(A \cap B)}{P(B)} = \frac{0.32}{0.5}$$
$$= \frac{32}{50} = \frac{16}{25}$$

7 (*b*)

A. Given, $P(A) = 0.8, P(B) = 0.5$ and $P\left(\frac{B}{A}\right) = 0.4$

$$\Rightarrow \frac{P(A \cap B)}{P(A)} = 0.4$$
$$\left[\because P\left(\frac{B}{A}\right) = \frac{P(A \cap B)}{P(A)}\right]$$
$$\Rightarrow \frac{P(A \cap B)}{0.8} = 0.4$$
$$\Rightarrow P(A \cap B) = 0.8 \times 0.4$$
$$= 0.32$$

B. $P\left(\frac{A}{B}\right) = \frac{P(A \cap B)}{P(B)} = \frac{0.32}{0.5}$

$$= \frac{32}{50} = 0.64$$

C. From the relation,

$$P(A \cup B) = P(A) + P(B) - P(A \cap B)$$
$$= 0.8 + 0.5 - 0.32$$
$$= 1.3 - 0.32 = 0.98$$

8 (*a*) Given, $2P(A) = P(B) = \frac{5}{13}$

$\Rightarrow P(A) = \frac{5}{26}$ and $P(B) = \frac{5}{13}$

Now, $P\left(\frac{A}{B}\right) = \frac{P(A \cap B)}{P(B)}$

$\Rightarrow \frac{2}{5} = \frac{P(A \cap B)}{\frac{5}{13}}$

$\Rightarrow P(A \cap B) = \frac{2}{5} \times \frac{5}{13} = \frac{2}{13}$

Again, $P(A \cup B) = P(A) + P(B) - P(A \cap B)$

$= \frac{5}{26} + \frac{5}{13} - \frac{2}{13}$

$= \frac{5 + 10 - 4}{26} = \frac{11}{26}$

9 (*b*)

A. Given, $P(A \cup B) = \frac{7}{11}$, $P(A) = \frac{6}{11}$ and $P(B) = \frac{5}{11}$.

We know that

$P(A \cup B) = P(A) + P(B) - P(A \cap B)$

$\Rightarrow \frac{7}{11} = \frac{6}{11} + \frac{5}{11} - P(A \cap B)$

$\Rightarrow P(A \cap B) = \frac{6}{11} + \frac{5}{11} - \frac{7}{11} = \frac{4}{11}$

B. We know that

$P\left(\frac{A}{B}\right) = \frac{P(A \cap B)}{P(B)}$

$\Rightarrow P\left(\frac{A}{B}\right) = \frac{\frac{4}{11}}{\frac{5}{11}} = \frac{4}{11} \times \frac{11}{5} = \frac{4}{5}$

$\left[\because P(B) = \frac{5}{11}, \text{ given}\right]$

C. We know that

$P\left(\frac{B}{A}\right) = \frac{P(B \cap A)}{P(A)}$

$\Rightarrow P\left(\frac{B}{A}\right) = \frac{\frac{4}{11}}{\frac{6}{11}} = \frac{4}{11} \times \frac{11}{6} = \frac{4}{6} = \frac{2}{3}$

$[\because P(A \cap B) = P(B \cap A)]$

10 (*d*) When a coin is tossed three times, the sample space S contains $2^3 = 8$ equally likely sample points.

$\therefore S = \{HHH, HHT, HTH, HTT, THH, THT, TTH, TTT\}$

A. Here, E : Set of events in which head occurs on third toss and F : Set of events in which heads occur on first two tosses.

$\therefore E = \{HHH, THH, HTH, TTH\}$

and $F = \{HHH, HHT\}$

$\Rightarrow E \cap F = \{HHH\}$

Hence,

$P(E) = \frac{\text{Number of favourable outcomes}}{\text{Total number of outcomes}}$

$= \frac{4}{8} = \frac{1}{2}$

Similarly, $P(F) = \frac{2}{8} = \frac{1}{4}$

and $P(E \cap F) = \frac{1}{8}$

$\therefore P\left(\frac{E}{F}\right) = \frac{P(E \cap F)}{P(F)}$

$= \frac{\frac{1}{8}}{\frac{1}{4}} = \frac{1}{8} \times \frac{4}{1} = \frac{1}{2}$

B. Here, E : Set of events in which atleast two heads occur and F : Set of events in which atmost two heads occur.

$\therefore E = \{HHH, HHT, HTH, THH\}$

[here, we consider the cases of two and three heads, as the condition given is atleast not atmost]

and $F = \{TTT, THT, TTH, HTT, HHT, HTH, THH\}$

$\Rightarrow (E \cap F) = \{HHT, HTH, THH\}$

Hence,

$P(E) = \frac{\text{Number of favourable outcomes}}{\text{Total number of outcomes}}$

$= \frac{4}{8} = \frac{1}{2}$

Similarly, $P(F) = \frac{7}{8}$

and $P(E \cap F) = \frac{3}{8}$

$\therefore P\left(\frac{E}{F}\right) = \frac{P(E \cap F)}{P(F)}$

$= \frac{\frac{3}{8}}{\frac{7}{8}} = \frac{3}{8} \times \frac{8}{7}$

$= \frac{3}{7}$

C. Here, E : Set of events in which atmost two tails occur and F : Set of events in which atleast one tail occurs.

$\therefore E = \{HHH, HHT, HTH, THH, HTT, THT, TTH\}$

[Here, we can consider the cases of two tails, one tail and no tail because the condition is atmost not atleast]

and $F = \{TTT, THT, TTH, HTT, HHT, HTH, THH\}$

[Here, we can consider the cases of one or more tails because the condition given is atleast not atmost]

$\Rightarrow (E \cap F) = \{HHT, HTH, THH, HTT, THT, TTH\}$

Now,

$P(E) = \frac{\text{Number of favourable outcomes}}{\text{Total number of outcomes}}$

$= \frac{7}{8}$

Similarly, $P(F) = \frac{7}{8}$

and $P(E \cap F) = \frac{6}{8}$

$\therefore P\left(\frac{E}{F}\right) = \frac{P(E \cap F)}{P(F)}$

$= \frac{6/8}{7/8} = \frac{6}{7}$

11 (c) If mother (m), father (f) and son (s) line up for the family picture, then the sample space will be

$S = \{mfs, msf, fms, fsm, smf, sfm\}$

$\Rightarrow n(S) = 6$, which contains 6 equally likely sample events.

Here, E: Set of events having son on one end

and F: Set of events having father in the middle.

$E = \{mfs, fms, smf, sfm\}$

and $F = \{mfs, sfm\}$

$\therefore E \cap F = \{mfs, sfm\}$

$\Rightarrow n(E) = 4, n(F) = 2$

and $n(E \cap F) = 2$

Now,

$$P(E) = \frac{\text{Number of favourable outcomes}}{\text{Total number of outcomes}} = \frac{4}{6} = \frac{2}{3}$$

Similarly, $P(F) = \frac{2}{6} = \frac{1}{3}$

and $P(E \cap F) = \frac{2}{6} = \frac{1}{3}$

Thus, $P\left(\frac{E}{F}\right) = \frac{P(E \cap F)}{P(F)} = \frac{\frac{1}{3}}{\frac{1}{3}} = 1$

12 (a) Here, the sample space is

$S = \{1, 2, 3, 4, 5, 6\}$

Given, $E = \{1, 3, 5\}, F = \{2, 3\}$

and $G = \{2, 3, 4, 5\}$

$\Rightarrow E \cap F = \{3\}, E \cap G = \{3, 5\},$

$E \cup F = \{1, 2, 3, 5\},$

$(E \cup F) \cap G = \{2, 3, 5\}$

and $(E \cap F) \cap G = \{3\}$

$\Rightarrow n(S) = 6, n(E) = 3,$

$n(F) = 2$ and $n(G) = 4$

$n(E \cap F) = 1, n(E \cap G) = 2,$

and $n(E \cup F) = 4$

$\Rightarrow n[(E \cup F) \cap G] = 3$

and $n[(E \cap F) \cap G] = 1$

$\therefore$ By the formula,

$$\text{Probability} = \frac{\text{Number of favourable outcomes}}{\text{Total number of outcomes}}$$

We have, $P(E) = \frac{3}{6} = \frac{1}{2},$

$P(F) = \frac{2}{6} = \frac{1}{3}$

and $P(G) = \frac{4}{6} = \frac{2}{3}$

$P(E \cap F) = \frac{1}{6}$

and $P(E \cap G) = \frac{2}{6} = \frac{1}{3}$

$P[(E \cup F) \cap G] = \frac{3}{6} = \frac{1}{2}$

and $P[(E \cap F) \cap G] = \frac{1}{6}$

A. $P\left(\frac{E}{F}\right) = \frac{P(E \cap F)}{P(F)} = \frac{1/6}{1/3} = \frac{1}{2}$

and $P\left(\frac{F}{E}\right) = \frac{P(F \cap E)}{P(E)}$

$= \frac{1/6}{1/2} = \frac{1}{3}$

B. $P\left(\frac{E}{G}\right) = \frac{P(E \cap G)}{P(G)} = \frac{1/3}{2/3} = \frac{1}{2}$

and $P\left(\frac{G}{E}\right) = \frac{P(G \cap E)}{P(E)}$

$= \frac{1/3}{1/2} = \frac{2}{3}$

C. $P\left(\frac{E \cup F}{G}\right) = \frac{P[(E \cup F) \cap G]}{P(G)}$

$= \frac{1/2}{2/3} = \frac{3}{4}$

and

$P\left(\frac{E \cap F}{G}\right) = \frac{P[(E \cap F) \cap G]}{P(G)}$

$= \frac{1/6}{2/3} = \frac{1}{4}$

13 (b) Let b and g represent the boy and the girl child, respectively. If a family has two children, then the sample space will be

$S = \{bb, bg, gb, gg\}$

which contains four equally likely sample points i.e. $n(S) = 4$.

Let E : Both children are girls. Then,

$E = \{gg\} \Rightarrow n(E) = 1$

I. Let F : The youngest is a girl. Then,

$F = \{bg, gg\}$

$\Rightarrow n(F) = 2$

$\Rightarrow E \cap F = \{gg\}$

$\Rightarrow n(E \cap F) = 1$

$P(E) = \frac{1}{4},$

$P(F) = \frac{2}{4} = \frac{1}{2}$

and $P(E \cap F) = \frac{1}{4}$

$\therefore$ Required probability is,

$P\left(\frac{E}{F}\right) = \frac{P(E \cap F)}{P(F)}$

$= \frac{1/4}{2/4} = \frac{1}{2}$

II. Let F : Atleast one is a girl. Then,

$F = \{bg, gb, gg\}$

$\Rightarrow E \cap F = \{gg\} = E$

$\Rightarrow n(F) = 3$ and $n(E \cap F) = 1$

$\therefore$ Required probability is,

$P\left(\frac{E}{F}\right) = \frac{P(E \cap F)}{P(F)}$

$= \frac{P(E)}{P(F)} = \frac{1/4}{3/4} = \frac{1}{3}$

14 (d) Total number of questions

$= 300 + 200 + 500 + 400$

$= 1400$

Let E be the event that selected question is an easy question.

Then, $n(E) = 500 + 300 = 800$

$$\therefore P(E) = \frac{\text{Number of favourable outcomes}}{\text{Total number of outcomes}}$$

$= \frac{800}{1400} = \frac{4}{7}$

Let F be the event that selected question is a multiple choice question.

Then, $n(F) = 500 + 400 = 900$

$$\therefore \quad P(F) = \frac{\text{Number of multiple choice questions}}{\text{Total number of questions}}$$

$$= \frac{900}{1400} = \frac{9}{14}$$

$$\therefore \ P(E \cap F) = \frac{500}{1400} = \frac{5}{14}$$

$$\therefore \quad P\left(\frac{E}{F}\right) = \frac{P(E \cap F)}{P(F)} = \frac{5/14}{9/14} = \frac{5}{9}$$

15 (c) It is given that $P(A) = \frac{1}{2}$

and $P(B) = 0$.

Then, $P\left(\frac{A}{B}\right) = \frac{P(A \cap B)}{P(B)}$

$$= \frac{P(A \cap B)}{0} = \infty$$

Therefore, $P\left(\frac{A}{B}\right)$ is not defined.

16 (d) Here, $P\left(\frac{A}{B}\right) = P\left(\frac{B}{A}\right)$

$$\therefore \quad \frac{P(A \cap B)}{P(B)} = \frac{P(B \cap A)}{P(A)}$$

$$\Rightarrow \quad P(A) = P(B)$$

$[\because P(A \cap B) = P(B \cap A)]$

17 (a) Let A and B be the events that the bulb is red and defective, respectively.

Then, $P(A) = \frac{10}{100} = \frac{1}{10}$

and $P(A \cap B) = \frac{2}{100} = \frac{1}{50}$

$$\therefore \quad P\left(\frac{B}{A}\right) = \frac{P(A \cap B)}{P(A)}$$

$$= \frac{\frac{1}{50}}{\frac{1}{10}} = \frac{10}{50} = \frac{1}{5}$$

18 (d) From the given data,

$P(A) + P(B) = P(A \cup B)$.

This shows that $P(A \cap B) = 0$

$[\because P(A \cap B) = P(A) + P(B) - P(A \cup B)]$

Thus, $P(A/B) = \frac{P(A \cap B)}{P(B)} = 0$

19 (d) Given that $P(A) = \frac{3}{10}$, $P(B) = \frac{2}{5}$

and $P(A \cup B) = \frac{3}{5}$

Now, $P(A \cup B) = P(A) + P(B) - P(A \cap B)$

$$\Rightarrow \quad \frac{3}{5} = \frac{3}{10} + \frac{2}{5} - P(A \cap B)$$

$$\Rightarrow \ P(A \cap B) = \frac{3}{10} + \frac{2}{5} - \frac{3}{5}$$

$$= \frac{3 + 4 - 6}{10} = \frac{7 - 6}{10} = \frac{1}{10}$$

$$\therefore \quad P\left(\frac{B}{A}\right) = \frac{P(A \cap B)}{P(A)}$$

$$= \frac{\frac{1}{10}}{\frac{3}{10}} = \frac{10}{3 \times 10} = \frac{1}{3}$$

$$P\left(\frac{A}{B}\right) = \frac{P(A \cap B)}{P(B)} = \frac{\frac{1}{10}}{\frac{2}{5}} = \frac{1}{4}$$

$$\Rightarrow \ P\left(\frac{B}{A}\right) + P\left(\frac{A}{B}\right) = \frac{1}{3} + \frac{1}{4} = \frac{4+3}{12}$$

$$= \frac{7}{12}$$

20 (c) Let $P(A) = x$.

Given that, $P(B) = \frac{3}{5}$, $P\left(\frac{A}{B}\right) = \frac{1}{2}$

and $P(A \cup B) = \frac{4}{5}$

$$\because \quad P\left(\frac{A}{B}\right) = \frac{P(A \cap B)}{P(B)}$$

$$\therefore \quad \frac{1}{2} = \frac{P(A \cap B)}{\frac{3}{5}}$$

$$\Rightarrow \quad P(A \cap B) = \frac{1 \times 3}{2 \times 5}$$

$$\Rightarrow \quad P(A \cap B) = \frac{3}{10}$$

$\because \quad P(A \cup B) = P(A) + P(B) - P(A \cap B)$

$$\therefore \quad \frac{4}{5} = x + \frac{3}{5} - \frac{3}{10}$$

$$\Rightarrow \quad x = \frac{4}{5} - \frac{3}{5} + \frac{3}{10}$$

$$= \frac{8 - 6 + 3}{10} = \frac{5}{10} = \frac{1}{2}$$

21 (c) Given that,

$$P(B) = \frac{3}{5}, \ P\left(\frac{A}{B}\right) = \frac{1}{2}$$

and $P(A \cup B) = \frac{4}{5}$

$$\because \quad P\left(\frac{A}{B}\right) = \frac{P(A \cap B)}{P(B)}$$

$$\therefore \quad \frac{1}{2} = \frac{P(A \cap B)}{\frac{3}{5}}$$

$$\Rightarrow \quad P(A \cap B) = \frac{3}{10}$$

$\because \ P(A \cup B) = P(A) + P(B) - P(A \cap B)$

$$\therefore \quad \frac{4}{5} = P(A) + \frac{3}{5} - \frac{3}{10}$$

$$\Rightarrow \quad P(A) = \frac{1}{2}$$

Now, $P\left(\frac{B}{A'}\right) = \frac{P(B \cap A')}{P(A')}$

$$= \frac{P(B) - P(A \cap B)}{1 - P(A)}$$

$$= \frac{\frac{3}{5} - \frac{3}{10}}{1 - \frac{1}{2}} = \frac{\frac{3}{10}}{\frac{1}{2}} = \frac{3}{5}$$

22 (d) Given that $P(A) = \frac{3}{8}$, $P(B) = \frac{5}{8}$

and $P(A \cup B) = \frac{3}{4}$

$\therefore \quad P(A \cap B) = P(A) + P(B) - P(A \cup B)$

$$= \frac{3}{8} + \frac{5}{8} - \frac{3}{4} = 1 - \frac{3}{4} = \frac{4-3}{4} = \frac{1}{4}$$

Now, $P\left(\frac{A}{B}\right) = \frac{P(A \cap B)}{P(B)} = \frac{\frac{1}{4}}{\frac{5}{8}} = \frac{2}{5}$

$$P\left(\frac{A'}{B}\right) = \frac{P(A' \cap B)}{P(B)}$$

$$= \frac{P(B) - P(A \cap B)}{P(B)}$$

$$= \frac{\frac{5}{8} - \frac{1}{4}}{\frac{5}{8}} = \frac{\frac{5-2}{8}}{\frac{5}{8}} = \frac{\frac{3}{8}}{\frac{5}{8}} = \frac{3}{5}$$

$$\therefore \quad P\left(\frac{A}{B}\right) \cdot P\left(\frac{A'}{B}\right) = \frac{2}{5} \times \frac{3}{5} = \frac{6}{25}$$

23 (c) Given that,

$$P(A) = \frac{1}{4},$$

$$P\left(\frac{A}{B}\right) = \frac{1}{2}$$

and $$P\left(\frac{B}{A}\right) = \frac{2}{3}$$

We know that,

$$P\left(\frac{A}{B}\right) = \frac{P(A \cap B)}{P(B)} \quad \text{...(i)}$$

and $$P\left(\frac{B}{A}\right) = \frac{P(B \cap A)}{P(A)} \quad \text{...(ii)}$$

$$\therefore \quad P(B) = \frac{P\left(\frac{B}{A}\right) . P(A)}{P\left(\frac{A}{B}\right)}$$

$$= \frac{\left(\frac{2}{3}\right)\left(\frac{1}{4}\right)}{\left(\frac{1}{2}\right)}$$

$$= \frac{2}{3} \times \frac{1}{4} \times \frac{2}{1} = \frac{1}{3}$$

24 (a)

A. Given, $P\left(\frac{E_2}{E_1}\right) = \frac{1}{2}$

$$\Rightarrow \frac{P(E_2 \cap E_1)}{P(E_1)} = \frac{1}{2}$$

$$\Rightarrow P(E_2 \cap E_1) = \frac{1}{2} \times P(E_1)$$

$$\therefore \quad P(E_2 \cap E_1) = \frac{1}{8}$$

$$\left[\because P(E_1) = \frac{1}{4}\right]$$

Also, given that $P\left(\frac{E_1}{E_2}\right) = \frac{1}{4}$

$$\Rightarrow \frac{P(E_1 \cap E_2)}{P(E_2)} = \frac{1}{4}$$

$$\Rightarrow \frac{1}{8\,P(E_2)} = \frac{1}{4}$$

$$\Rightarrow P(E_2) = \frac{1}{2}$$

B. $P(E_1 \cup E_2) = P(E_1) + P(E_2) - P(E_1 \cap E_2)$

$$= \frac{1}{4} + \frac{1}{2} - \frac{1}{8} = \frac{5}{8}$$

C. $$P\left(\frac{\bar{E}_1}{\bar{E}_2}\right) = \frac{P(\bar{E}_1 \cap \bar{E}_2)}{P(\bar{E}_2)}$$

$$= \frac{1 - P(E_1 \cup E_2)}{1 - P(E_2)}$$

$$= \frac{1 - \frac{5}{8}}{1 - \frac{1}{2}} = \frac{3}{4}$$

D. $$P\left(\frac{E_1}{\bar{E}_2}\right) = \frac{P(E_1 \cap \bar{E}_2)}{P(\bar{E}_2)}$$

$$= \frac{P(E_1) - P(E_1 \cap E_2)}{1 - P(E_2)}$$

$$= \frac{\frac{1}{4} - \frac{1}{8}}{1 - \frac{1}{2}} = \frac{\frac{1}{8}}{\frac{1}{2}} = \frac{1}{4}$$

25 (c) When two dice are thrown, then the number of events in the sample space = 36

Let A : Sum of the numbers on the dice was less than 6

and B : Getting a sum equals to 3.

Then, $A = \{(1, 1), (1, 2), (1, 3), (1, 4), (2, 1), (2, 2), (2, 3), (3, 1), (3, 2), (4, 1)\}$,

$B = \{(1, 2), (2, 1)\}$

and $A \cap B = \{(1, 2), (2, 1)\}$

$$\therefore \quad P(A \cap B) = \frac{2}{36} = \frac{1}{18}$$

and $$P(A) = \frac{10}{36} = \frac{5}{18}$$

Now, $$P\left(\frac{B}{A}\right) = \frac{P(A \cap B)}{P(A)}$$

$$= \frac{\frac{1}{18}}{\frac{5}{18}} = \frac{1}{5}$$

26 (b) Let A : The student fails in Physics and B : The student fails in Mathematics.

$$\therefore \quad P(A) = \frac{30}{100}, \; P(B) = \frac{25}{100}$$

and $$P(A \cap B) = \frac{10}{100}$$

Now, $$P\left(\frac{A}{B}\right) = \frac{P(A \cap B)}{P(B)}$$

$$= \frac{\frac{10}{100}}{\frac{25}{100}}$$

$$= \frac{10}{100} \times \frac{100}{25}$$

$$= \frac{10}{25} = \frac{2}{5}$$

27 (c) Given that, $P(A \cup B) = \frac{5}{9}$,

$$P(A) = p \text{ and } P(B) = \frac{1}{3}$$

We know that

$$P(A \cap B) = P(A) + P(B) - P(A \cup B)$$

$$= p + \frac{1}{3} - \frac{5}{9}$$

$$= p + \frac{3 - 5}{9}$$

$$= p + \left(\frac{-2}{9}\right) = p - \frac{2}{9}$$

Now, $P\left(\frac{A}{B}\right) = \frac{P(A \cap B)}{P(B)} = p$ [given]

$$\Rightarrow \frac{p - \frac{2}{9}}{\frac{1}{3}} = p \Rightarrow \frac{9p - 2}{3} = p$$

$$\Rightarrow \quad 9p - 2 = 3p \Rightarrow 6p = 2$$

$$\Rightarrow \quad p = \frac{1}{3}$$

28 (c) From the tree diagram, it follows that

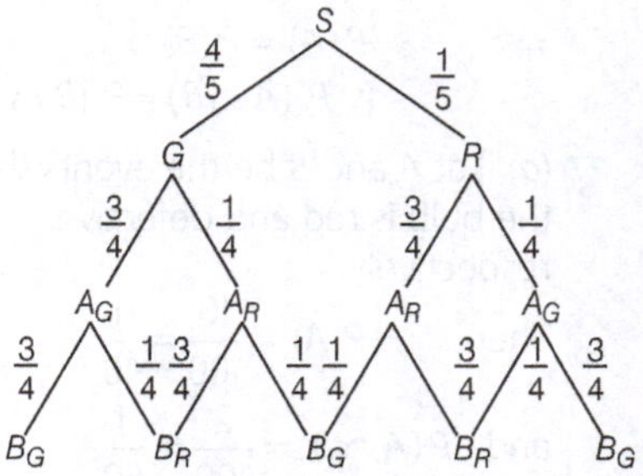

$$P(B_G) = \frac{46}{80}, \; P(G) = \frac{4}{5}$$

and $$P(B_G / G) = \frac{10}{16} = \frac{5}{8}$$

$$\therefore \quad P(B_G \cap G) = \frac{5}{8} \times \frac{4}{5} = \frac{1}{2}$$

$$\left[\because P(B_G \cap G) = P\left(\frac{B_G}{G}\right) \times P(G)\right]$$

Now, $$P(G / B_G) = \frac{P(B_G \cap G)}{P(B_G)}$$

$$= \frac{1}{2} \times \frac{80}{46} = \frac{20}{23}$$

Multiplication Theorem on Probability

1 (*a*) Let E and F be two events associated with a sample space S. Clearly, the set $E \cap F$ denotes the event that both E and F have occurred. In other words, $E \cap F$ denotes the simultaneous occurrence of the events E and F. The event $E \cap F$ is also written as EF.

2 (*c*) We know that conditional probability of event E given that F has occurred is denoted by $P(E/F)$ and is given by

$$P(E/F) = \frac{P(E \cap F)}{P(F)}, P(F) \neq 0$$

From this result, we can write

$$P(E \cap F) = P(F) \cdot P(E/F) \quad \text{...(i)}$$

Also, we know that

$$P(F/E) = \frac{P(F \cap E)}{P(E)}, P(E) \neq 0$$

$$P(F/E) = \frac{P(E \cap F)}{P(E)}$$

$$[\because E \cap F = F \cap E]$$

Thus, $P(E \cap F) = P(E) \cdot P(F/E)$ ...(ii)

On combining Eqs. (i) and (ii), we find that

$$P(E \cap F) = P(E) \cdot P(F/E) = P(F)\, P(E/F)$$

provided $P(E) \neq 0$ and $P(F) \neq 0$.

The above result in known as the multiplication rule of probability.

3 (*d*) Let E and F denote respectively the events that first and second ball drawn are black.

We have to find $P(E \cap F)$ or $P(EF)$.

Now, $P(E) = P$ (black ball in first drawn) $= \frac{10}{15}$

Also, given that the first ball drawn is black i.e. event E has occurred. Now, there are 9 black balls and 5 white balls left in the urn.

Therefore, the probability that the second ball drawn is black, given that the ball in the first drawn is black, is nothing but the conditional probability of F given that E has occurred

i.e. $P(F/E) = \frac{9}{14}$

By multiplication rule of probability, we get

$$P(E \cap F) = P(E) \cdot P(F/E) = \frac{10}{15} \times \frac{9}{14} = \frac{3}{7}$$

4 (*c*) If E, F and G are three events of sample space, then we have

$$P(E \cap F \cap G) = P(E)\, P(F/E)\, P(G/(E \cap F)) = P(E)\, P(F/E)\, P(G/EF)$$

Similarly, the multiplication rule of probability can be extended for four or more events.

5 (*a*) Let K denote the event that the card drawn is king and A be the event that the card drawn is an ace.

Clearly, we have to find $P(KKA)$.

Now, $P(K) = \frac{4}{52}$

Also, $P(K/K)$ is the probability of second king with the condition that one king has already been drawn. Now, there are 3 kings in $(52 - 1) = 51$ cards.

Therefore, $P(K/K) = \frac{3}{51}$

Lastly, $P(A/KK)$ is the probability of third drawn card to be an ace, with the condition that two kings have already been drawn. Now, there are 4 aces in left 50 cards.

Therefore, $P(A/KK) = \frac{4}{50}$

By multiplication law of probability, we get

$$P(KKA) = P(K) \cdot P(K/K) \cdot P(A/KK) = \frac{4}{52} \times \frac{3}{51} \times \frac{4}{50} = \frac{2}{5525}$$

Independent Events

1 (*a*) Two events E and F are said to be independent, if

$P(F/E) = P(F)$, provided $P(E) \neq 0$ and $P(E/F) = P(E)$, provided $P(F) \neq 0$.

Thus, in this definition, we have $P(E) \neq 0$ and $P(F) \neq 0$.

Now, by the multiplication rule of probability, we get

$$P(E \cap F) = P(E) \cdot P(F/E) \quad \text{... (i)}$$

If E and F are independent, then Eq. (i) becomes

$$P(E \cap F) = P(E) \cdot P(F) \quad \text{...(ii)}$$

Thus, using Eq. (ii), the independence of two events is also defined as follows.

Let E and F be two events associated with the same random experiment. Then, E and F are said to be independent, if

$$P(E \cap F) = P(E) \cdot P(F)$$

Note *Two events E and F are said to be dependent if they are not independent, i.e. if*

$$P(E \cap F) \neq P(E) \cdot P(F)$$

2 (*d*) Three events A, B and C are said to be mutually independent if

$$P(A \cap B) = P(A)\, P(B)$$

$$\Rightarrow \quad P(A \cap C) = P(A)\, P(C)$$

$$\Rightarrow \quad P(B \cap C) = P(B)\, P(C)$$

and $P(A \cap B \cap C) = P(A)\, P(B)\, P(C)$

If atleast one of the above is not true for three given events, we say that events are not independent.

3 (*a*) Let A, B and C be the respective events that the first, second and third drawn orange is good.

Therefore, probability that first drawn orange is good,

$$P(A) = \frac{12}{15}$$

Therefore, probability of getting second orange is good,

$$P(B)=\frac{11}{14}$$

[∵ the oranges are not replaced, so number of good oranges left is 11]

Similarly, probability of getting third orange is good,

$$P(C)=\frac{10}{13}$$

[∵ the oranges are not replaced, so number of good oranges left is 10]

The box is approved for sale, if all the three oranges are good.

Thus, probability of getting all the three oranges good

$$=\frac{12}{15}\times\frac{11}{14}\times\frac{10}{13}$$

Therefore, the probability that the box is approved for sale $=\frac{44}{91}$

4 (*a*) If a fair coin and an unbiased die are tossed, then the sample space is given by,

$$S=\left\{\begin{matrix}(H,1),(H,2),(H,3),\\(H,4),(H,5),(H,6),\\(T,1),(T,2),(T,3),\\(T,4),(T,5),(T,6)\end{matrix}\right\}$$

$\Rightarrow n(S)=12$

Also, A : Head appears on the coin and B : 3 appears on the die.

$\therefore$ A = Set of outcomes having head on the coin

$=\{(H,1),(H,2),(H,3),(H,4),(H,5),(H,6)\}$

B = Set of outcomes having 3 on the die $=\{(H,3),(T,3)\}$

$\Rightarrow A\cap B=\{(H,3)\}$

$\Rightarrow n(A)=6,\ n(B)=2$

and $n(A\cap B)=1$

Hence, $P(A)=\frac{6}{12}=\frac{1}{2}$,

$P(B)=\frac{2}{12}=\frac{1}{6}$ and $P(A\cap B)=\frac{1}{12}$

Now, $P(A)\times P(B)=\frac{1}{2}\times\frac{1}{6}$

$=\frac{1}{12}=P(A\cap B)$

Therefore, A and B are independent events.

5 (*d*) (i) When A and B are mutually exclusive, then

$$A\cap B=\phi$$

$\Rightarrow P(A\cap B)=0$

$\because P(A\cup B)=P(A)+P(B)-P(A\cap B)$

$\Rightarrow \frac{3}{5}=\frac{1}{2}+p-0$

$\Rightarrow p=\frac{3}{5}-\frac{1}{2}=\frac{6-5}{10}=\frac{1}{10}$

(ii) When A and B are independent events, then

$P(A\cap B)=P(A)\cdot P(B)=\frac{1}{2}p$

$\left[\because P(A)=\frac{1}{2}\text{ and } P(B)=p,\text{ given}\right]$

Now, $P(A\cup B)=P(A)+P(B)-P(A)\times P(B)$

$\Rightarrow \frac{3}{5}=\frac{1}{2}+p-\frac{1}{2}p$

$\Rightarrow \frac{3}{5}-\frac{1}{2}=\frac{2p-p}{2}$

$\Rightarrow \frac{p}{2}=\frac{6-5}{10}$

$\Rightarrow p=\frac{2}{10}=\frac{1}{5}$

6 (*b*) It is given that $P(A)=0.3$ and $P(B)=0.4$.

A. If A and B are independent events, then

$P(A\cap B)=P(A)\times P(B)$

$=0.3\times0.4=0.12$

B. We know that

$P(A\cup B)=P(A)+P(B)-P(A\cap B)$

$=P(A)+P(B)-P(A)\,P(B)$

$=0.3+0.4-0.3\times0.4$

$=0.7-0.12=0.58$

C. We know that

$P\left(\frac{A}{B}\right)=\frac{P(A\cap B)}{P(B)}=\frac{P(A)\,P(B)}{P(B)}$

$\Rightarrow P\left(\frac{A}{B}\right)=P(A)=0.3$

D. We know that,

$P\left(\frac{B}{A}\right)=\frac{P(B\cap A)}{P(A)}=\frac{P(B)\,P(A)}{P(A)}$

$\Rightarrow P\left(\frac{B}{A}\right)=P(B)=0.4$

7 (*d*) If A and B are two independent events, then A' and B, A and B', A' and B' are all independent events.

It is given that $P(A)=0.3$ and $P(B)=0.6$

Also, A and B are independent events.

A. $P(A \text{ and } B)$

$=P(A\cap B)=P(A)\times P(B)$

$=0.3\times0.6=0.18$

[∵ A and B are independent]

B. $P(A\text{ and not }B)=P(A\cap B')$

$=P(A)\times P(B')$

$\left[\begin{matrix}\because A\text{ and }B\text{ are independent.}\\ \therefore A\text{ and }B'\text{ are also independent}\end{matrix}\right]$

$=(0.3)\,[1-P(B)]$

$=(0.3)\,(1-0.6)$

$=0.3\times0.4$

$=0.12$

C. $P(A\text{ or }B)=P(A\cup B)$

$=P(A)+P(B)-P(A\cap B)$

$=P(A)+P(B)-P(A)\times P(B)$

$=0.3+0.6-0.3\times0.6$

$=0.9-0.18=0.72$

D. P (neither A nor B)

$=P(A'\text{ and }B')$

$=P(A'\cap B')=P(A\cup B)'$

[$\because P(A'\cap B')=P(A\cup B)'$]

$=1-P(A\cup B)$

$=1-0.72=0.28$ [using part (C)]

Alternate Method

P (neither A nor B)

$=P(A'\cap B')=P(A')\,P(B')$

$\left[\begin{matrix}\because A\text{ and B are independent.}\\ \therefore A'\text{ and }B'\text{ are also independent}\end{matrix}\right]$

$=[1-P(A)]\,[1-P(B)]$

$=(1-0.3)\,(1-0.6)$

$=0.7\times0.4$

$=0.28$

8 (c) Probability of getting an odd number atleast once
$= 1 -$ probability of getting an odd number in none of the throws.
When a die is thrown, then are 3 odd numbers on the die out of 6 numbers.
$\therefore$ Probability of getting an odd number

$$= \frac{\text{Number of favourable cases}}{\text{Total number of cases}}$$

$$= \frac{3}{6} = \frac{1}{2}$$

Probability of getting an even number $= 1 -$ Probability of getting an odd number $= 1 - \frac{1}{2} = \frac{1}{2}$

Probability of getting an even number when the die is tossed thrice,

$$P(E) = \frac{1}{2} \times \frac{1}{2} \times \frac{1}{2} = \frac{1}{8}$$

Therefore, Probability of getting an odd number atleast once
$= 1 -$ Probability of getting an odd number in none of the throws

$$= 1 - P(E) = 1 - \frac{1}{8} = \frac{7}{8}$$

9 (a) Total number of balls $= 18$,
number of red balls $= 8$
and number of black balls $= 10$
$\therefore$ Probability of drawing a red ball

$$= \frac{\text{Number of red balls}}{\text{Total number of balls}} = \frac{8}{18}$$

Similarly, Probability of drawing a black ball

$$= \frac{\text{Number of black balls}}{\text{Total number of balls}} = \frac{10}{18}$$

A. Probability of getting both red balls $= P$ (both balls are red)
$= P$ (a red ball is drawn at first draw and again a red ball at second draw)

$$= \frac{8}{18} \times \frac{8}{18} = \frac{16}{81}$$

B. P (probability of getting first ball is black and second is red)

$$= \frac{10}{18} \times \frac{8}{18} = \frac{20}{81}$$

C. Probability of getting one black and other red ball
$= P$(first ball is black and second is red)
$+ P$ (first ball is red and second is black)

$$= \frac{10}{18} \times \frac{8}{18} + \frac{8}{18} \times \frac{10}{18} = \frac{40}{81}$$

10 (b) Probability of solving the problem by A

i.e. $P(A) = \frac{1}{2}$

Probability of solving the problem by B

i.e. $P(B) = \frac{1}{3}$

Probability of not solving the problem by A

$$= P(A') = 1 - P(A) = 1 - \frac{1}{2} = \frac{1}{2}$$

and probability of not solving the problem by B

$$= P(B') = 1 - P(B) = 1 - \frac{1}{3} = \frac{2}{3}$$

I. P (the problem is solved)
$= 1 - P$ (none of them solve the problem)

$$= 1 - P(A' \cap B')$$

$$= 1 - P(A')\,P(B')$$

[$\because$ A and B are independent.
$\therefore$ A' and B' are independent]

$$= 1 - \left(\frac{1}{2} \times \frac{2}{3}\right) = 1 - \frac{1}{3} = \frac{2}{3}$$

II. P (exactly one of them solve the problem)

$$= P(A)\,P(B') + P(A')\,P(B)$$

$$= \frac{1}{2} \times \frac{2}{3} + \frac{1}{2} \times \frac{1}{3} = \frac{1}{3} + \frac{1}{6}$$

$$= \frac{2+1}{6} = \frac{3}{6} = \frac{1}{2}$$

11 (d)

(i) In a deck of 52 cards, 13 cards are spades and 4 cards are aces.
Given, E: The card drawn is a spade
$\Rightarrow \quad n(E) = 13$
and F: The card drawn is an ace
$\Rightarrow \quad n(F) = 4$ and $n(S) = 52$
Here, $P(E) = P$ (card drawn is spade)

$$= \frac{n(E)}{n(S)} = \frac{13}{52} = \frac{1}{4}$$

$P(F) = P$ (card drawn is an ace)

$$= \frac{n(F)}{n(S)} = \frac{4}{52} = \frac{1}{13}$$

Also, $E \cap F$: The deck of cards, only 1 card is an ace of spades.

$$\Rightarrow P(E \cap F) = \frac{n(E \cap F)}{n(S)} = \frac{1}{52}$$

Now, $P(E) \times P(F) = \frac{1}{4} \times \frac{1}{13}$

$$= \frac{1}{52} = P(E \cap F)$$

Therefore, the events E and F are independent.

(ii) In a deck of 52 cards, 26 cards are black and 4 cards are kings.
Given, E: The card drawn is black
$\Rightarrow \quad n(E) = 26$
F: The card drawn is king
$\Rightarrow \quad n(F) = 4$
Also, $\quad n(S) = 52$
$P(E) = P$ (card drawn is black)

$$= \frac{n(E)}{n(S)} = \frac{26}{52} = \frac{1}{2}$$

and $P(F) = P$ (card drawn is a king)

$$= \frac{n(F)}{n(S)} = \frac{4}{52} = \frac{1}{13}$$

Also, $E \cap F$: Card drawn is a black king

$$\Rightarrow \quad P(E \cap F) = \frac{n(E \cap F)}{n(S)}$$

$$= \frac{2}{52} = \frac{1}{26}$$

Now, $P(E) \times P(F) = \frac{1}{2} \times \frac{1}{13}$

$$= \frac{1}{26} = P(E \cap F)$$

$$\Rightarrow \quad P(E \cap F) = P(E)P(F)$$

Therefore, the events E and F are independent.

(iii) In a deck of 52 cards, 4 cards are kings, 4 cards are queens and 4 cards are jacks.

$P(E) = P$ (card drawn is a king or a queen)

$= P$ (king) $+ P$ (queen)

$= \frac{4}{52} + \frac{4}{52} = \frac{8}{52} = \frac{2}{13}$

and $P(F) = P$ (cards drawn is a queen or a jack)

$= P$ (queen) $+ P$ (jack)

$= \frac{4}{52} + \frac{4}{52} = \frac{8}{52} = \frac{2}{13}$

Also, $E \cap F$: Card drawn is a queen

$\Rightarrow \quad P(E \cap F) = \frac{4}{52} = \frac{1}{13}$

Now, $P(E) \times P(F) = \frac{2}{13} \times \frac{2}{13}$

$= \frac{4}{169} \neq P(E \cap F)$

$\Rightarrow \quad P(E \cap F) \neq P(E)\, P(F)$

Therefore, the events E and F are not independent.

12 (*a*) Let H : Set of students reading Hindi newspaper

and E : Set of students reading English newspaper.

Let $n(S) = 100$. Then, $n(H) = 60$

$n(E) = 40$ and $n(H \cap E) = 20$

$\therefore \quad P(H) = \frac{n(H)}{n(S)} = \frac{60}{100} = \frac{3}{5},$

$P(E) = \frac{n(E)}{n(S)} = \frac{40}{100} = \frac{2}{5}$

and $P(H \cap E) = \frac{n(H \cap E)}{n(S)}$

$= \frac{20}{100} = \frac{1}{5}$

A. Required probability

$= P$ (student reads neither Hindi nor English newspaper)

$= P(H' \cap E') = P(H \cup E)'$

$= 1 - P(H \cup E)$

$= 1 - [P(H) + P(E) - P(H \cap E)]$

$= 1 - \left[\frac{3}{5} + \frac{2}{5} - \frac{1}{5}\right] = \frac{1}{5}$

B. Required probability

$= P$(a randomly chosen student reads English newspaper, if she reads Hindi newspaper).

$\therefore \quad P\left(\frac{E}{H}\right) = \frac{P(E \cap H)}{P(H)} = \frac{\frac{1}{5}}{\frac{3}{5}} = \frac{1}{3}$

C. Required probability

$= P$ (student reads Hindi newspaper when it is given that she reads English newspaper)

$\therefore \quad P\left(\frac{H}{E}\right) = \frac{P(H \cap E)}{P(E)} = \frac{\frac{1}{5}}{\frac{2}{5}} = \frac{1}{2}$

13 (*d*) When a pair of dice is rolled once, then the sample space contains $6 \times 6 = 36$ elements

i.e. $\quad n(S) = 36$

The only even prime number is 2.

Let E be the event of getting an even prime number on each die. Then, $= (2, 2)$ i.e. $n(E) = 1$

Required probability

$= P$ (an even prime on each die)

$= \frac{n(E)}{n(S)} = \frac{1}{36}$

[$\because$ (2, 2) is the only favourable outcome]

14 (*b*) A and B are independent if

$P(A \cap B) = P(A)\, P(B)$

$\therefore \quad P(A' \cap B') = P(A \cup B)'$

$= 1 - P(A \cup B)$

$[\because P(A \cup B)' = 1 - P(A \cup B)]$

$= 1 - [P(A) + P(B) - P(A \cap B)]$

$= 1 - P(A) - P(B) + P(A)\, P(B)$

$= [1 - P(A)]\, [1 - P(B)]$

Therefore, the correct answer is (b).

15 (*c*) P (atleast two of A, B, C occur)

$= P(A)\, P(B)\, P(C) + P(A)\, P(\overline{B})\, P(C) + P(A)P(B)\, P(\overline{C}) + P(\overline{A})\, P(B)\, P(C)$

$= p \cdot p \cdot p + p \cdot (1 - p) \cdot p + p \cdot p \cdot (1 - p) + (1 - p) \cdot p \cdot p$

$= p^3 + p^2 - p^3 + p^2 - p^3 + p^2 - p^3$

$= 3p^2 - 2p^3$

16 (*c*) Given that,

$P(A) = 0.6, P(B) = 0.2$

and $\quad P(A/B) = 0.5$

Now, $P(A \cap B) = P(A / B) \cdot P(B)$

$= (0.5)\,(0.2) = 0.1$

$\therefore \quad P(A'/B') = \frac{P(A' \cap B')}{P(B')}$

$= \frac{P[(A \cup B)']}{P(B')}$

$= \frac{1 - P(A \cup B)}{1 - P(B)}$

$= \frac{1 - P(A) - P(B) + P(A \cap B)}{1 - 0.2} = \frac{3}{8}$

17 (*a*) We know that two events are independent if the probability of occurrence of one does not effect the probability of occurrence of others.

Also, mutually exclusive events are those events in which occurrence of one event prevents the occurrence of the other events.

In other words, two independent events having non-zero probabilities of occurrence cannot be mutually exclusive and conversely i.e. two mutually exclusive events having non-zero probabilities of occurrence cannot be independent.

18 (*c*) Given that $P(A) = p, P(B) = 2p$

$\Rightarrow \quad P$ (exactly one of A, B) $= \frac{5}{9}$

$\Rightarrow \quad P(A'B + AB') = \frac{5}{9}$

$\Rightarrow [(1 - p)\,(2p) + p(1 - 2p)] = \frac{5}{9}$

$\Rightarrow \quad [2p - 2p^2 + p - 2p^2] = \frac{5}{9}$

$\Rightarrow \quad [-4p^2 + 3p] = \frac{5}{9}$

$\Rightarrow \quad 36p^2 - 27p + 5 = 0$

$\Rightarrow \quad 36p^2 - 15p - 12p + 5 = 0$

$\Rightarrow 3p(12p - 5) - 1(12p - 5) = 0$

$\Rightarrow \quad (3p - 1)\,(12p - 5) = 0$

$\Rightarrow \quad 3p - 1 = 0$

$\Rightarrow \quad p = 1/3$

and $\quad 12p - 5 = 0$

$\Rightarrow \quad p = 5/12$

19 (c) Let $P(F) = x$.

We know that,

$$P(E \cup F) = P(E) + P(F) - P(E \cap F)$$

$$\Rightarrow P(E \cup F) = P(E) + P(F) - P(E) \cdot P(F)$$

$$\Rightarrow 0.5 = 0.3 + x - 0.3 \times x$$

$$\Rightarrow 0.5 - 0.3 = 0.7x$$

$$\Rightarrow 0.2 = 0.7x$$

$$\Rightarrow x = \frac{2}{7}$$

Now, $P\left(\frac{E}{F}\right) - P\left(\frac{F}{E}\right)$

$$= \frac{P(E \cap F)}{P(F)} - \frac{P(E \cap F)}{P(E)}$$

$$= \frac{0.3 \times \frac{2}{7}}{\frac{2}{7}} - \frac{0.3 \times \frac{2}{7}}{0.3}$$

$$= \frac{0.6}{2} - \frac{2}{7} = \frac{3}{10} - \frac{2}{7}$$

$$= \frac{21 - 20}{70} = \frac{1}{70}$$

20 (a) Here, $P(1) = P(2) = 0.2$,

$$P(3) = P(5) = P(6) = 0.1$$

and $P(4) = 0.3$

Let A be the event that same number each time and B be the event that a total score is 10 or more.

A. $P(A) = P(1, 1) + P(2, 2) + P(3, 3) + P(4, 4) + P(5, 5) + P(6, 6)$

$$= P(1) \cdot P(1) + P(2) \cdot P(2) + P(3) \cdot P(3) + P(4) \cdot P(4) + P(5) \cdot P(5) + P(6) \cdot P(6)$$

$$= (0.2)^2 + (0.2)^2 + (0.1)^2 + (0.3)^2 + (0.1)^2 + (0.1)^2$$

$$= 0.04 + 0.04 + 0.01 + 0.09 + 0.01 + 0.01$$

$$= 0.20$$

B. $P(B) = P(4, 6) + P(5, 5) + P(6, 4) + P(5, 6) + P(6, 5) + P(6, 6)$

$$= P(4) \cdot P(6) + P(5) \cdot P(5) + P(6) \cdot P(4) + P(5) \cdot P(6) + P(6) \cdot P(5) + P(6) \cdot P(6)$$

$$= 0.3 \times 0.1 + 0.1 \times 0.1 + 0.1 \times 0.3 + 0.1 \times 0.1 + 0.1 \times 0.1 + 0.1 \times 0.1$$

$$= 0.03 + 0.01 + 0.03 + 0.01 + 0.01 + 0.01$$

$$= 0.10$$

C. $P(A \cap B) = P(5, 5) + P(6, 6)$

$$= P(5) \cdot P(5) + P(6) \cdot P(6)$$

$$= 0.1 \times 0.1 + 0.1 \times 0.1$$

$$= 0.01 + 0.01$$

$$= 0.02$$

D. Since, $P(A) \times P(B)$

$$= 0.20 \times 0.10$$

$$= 0.020 = 0.02 = P(A \cap B).$$

Therefore, the events are independent.

21 (b) Given that

$$P(A) = 0.4,\ P(B) = 0.3$$

and $P(C) = 0.2$

$\therefore$ $P(\bar{A}) = 1 - P(A) = 1 - 0.4 = 0.6,$

$$P(\bar{B}) = 1 - P(B) = 1 - 0.3 = 0.7$$

and $P(\bar{C}) = 1 - P(C) = 1 - 0.2 = 0.8$

Now, P (two hits)

$$= P(A)\, P(B)\, P(\bar{C}) + P(A)\, P(\bar{B})\, P(C) + P(\bar{A})\, P(B)\, P(C)$$

$$= 0.4 \times 0.3 \times 0.8 + 0.4 \times 0.7 \times 0.2 + 0.6 \times 0.3 \times 0.2$$

$$= 0.096 + 0.056 + 0.036$$

$$= 0.188$$

22 (c) Let A : An even number on the die

Let B : A spade card is drawn.

Then, $P(A \cap B) = P(A)\, P(B)$

[$\because$ A and B are independent]

$$P(A) = \frac{3}{6}$$

and $P(B) = \dfrac{13}{52}$

$$\therefore \quad P(A \cap B) = \frac{3}{6} \times \frac{13}{52} = \frac{3}{24} = \frac{1}{8}$$

23 (a) Since, the probabilities of solving the problem by A, B and C are $\frac{1}{2}, \frac{1}{3}$ and $\frac{1}{4}$, respectively.

$\therefore$ Probability that the problem is not solved

$$= P(\bar{A})\, P(\bar{B})\, P(\bar{C})$$

$$= \left(1 - \frac{1}{2}\right)\left(1 - \frac{1}{3}\right)\left(1 - \frac{1}{4}\right)$$

$$= \frac{1}{2} \times \frac{2}{3} \times \frac{3}{4} = \frac{1}{4}$$

Hence, the probability that the problem is solved

$$= 1 - \frac{1}{4} = \frac{3}{4}$$

24 (a) $P\left(\dfrac{A^C \cap B^C}{C}\right) = \dfrac{P(A^C \cap B^C \cap C)}{P(C)}$

$$= \frac{P(C) - P(A \cap C) - P(B \cap C) + P(A \cap B \cap C)}{P(C)} \quad \text{...(i)}$$

Given, $P(A \cap B \cap C) = 0$ and A, B, C are pairwise independent.

$\therefore$ $P(A \cap C) = P(A) \cdot P(C)$

and $P(B \cap C) = P(B) \cdot P(C)$

$\therefore$ $P\left(\dfrac{A^C \cap B^C}{C}\right)$

$$= \frac{P(C) - P(A) \cdot P(C) - P(B) \cdot P(C) + 0}{P(C)}$$

[from Eq. (i)]

$$= 1 - P(A) - P(B)$$

$$= P(A^C) - P(B)$$

25 (b) Given that,

$$P(A \cap B) = \frac{1}{4},\ P(\bar{A}) = \frac{1}{4}$$

and $P(\overline{A \cup B}) = \dfrac{1}{6}$

$$\Rightarrow 1 - P(A \cup B) = \frac{1}{6}$$

$$\Rightarrow 1 - P(A) - P(B) + P(A \cap B) = \frac{1}{6}$$

$$\Rightarrow P(\bar{A}) - P(B) + \frac{1}{4} = \frac{1}{6}$$

$$\Rightarrow P(B) = \frac{1}{4} + \frac{1}{4} - \frac{1}{6}$$

$$\Rightarrow P(B) = \frac{1}{3}$$

and $P(A) = \dfrac{3}{4}$

Now, $P(A \cap B) = \dfrac{1}{4} = \dfrac{3}{4} \times \dfrac{1}{3}$

$$= P(A)\, P(B)$$

Hence, the events A and B are independent events but not equally likely.

26 (c) Given probabilities of speaking truth are

$$P(A) = \frac{4}{5} \text{ and } P(B) = \frac{3}{4}$$

and their corresponding probabilities of not speaking truth are

$$P(\bar{A}) = \frac{1}{5}$$

and $$P(\bar{B}) = \frac{1}{4}$$

∴ Required probability

$$= P(A) \times P(\bar{B}) + P(\bar{A}) \times P(B)$$
$$= \frac{4}{5} \times \frac{1}{4} + \frac{1}{5} \times \frac{3}{4}$$
$$= \frac{1}{5} + \frac{3}{20} = \frac{7}{20}$$

Bayes' Theorem

1 (a) Consider that there are two bags I and II. Bag I contains 2 white and 3 red balls and bag II contains 4 white and 5 red balls. One ball is drawn at random from one of the bags.We can find the probability of selecting any of the bags $\left(\text{i.e. } \frac{1}{2}\right)$ or probability of drawing a ball of a particular colour (say white) from a particular bag (say bag I). In other words, we can find the probability that the ball drawn is of a particular colour, if we are given the bag from which the ball is drawn. But, can we find the probability that the ball drawn is from a particular bag (say bag II), if the colour of the ball drawn is given.

Here, we have to find the reverse probability of bag II to be selected when an event occurred after it is known. Famous mathematician, John Bayes' solved the problem of finding reverse probability using conditional probability. The formula developed by him is known as 'Baye's theorem' which was published posthumously in 1763.

2 (d) A set of events $E_1, E_2, ..., E_n$ represents a partition of the sample space S, if

(a) $E_i \cap E_j = \phi, i \neq j, i, j = 1, 2, 3,..., n$

(b) $E_1 \cup E_2 \cup ... \cup E_n = S$ and

(c) $P(E_i) > 0$ for all $i = 1, 2, ..., n$

In other words, the events $E_1, E_2, ..., E_n$ represent a partition of the sample space S, if they are pairwise disjoint, exhaustive and have non-zero probabilities.

As an example, we see that any non-empty event E and its complement E' form a partition of the sample space S, since they satisfy $E \cap E' = \phi$ and $E \cup E' = S$.

From the Venn diagram in figure, one can easily observe that if E and F are any two events associated with a sample space S, then the set $\{E \cap F', E \cap F, E' \cap F, E' \cap F'\}$ is a partition of the sample space S. It may be mentioned that the partition of a sample space is not unique. There can be several partitions of the same sample space.

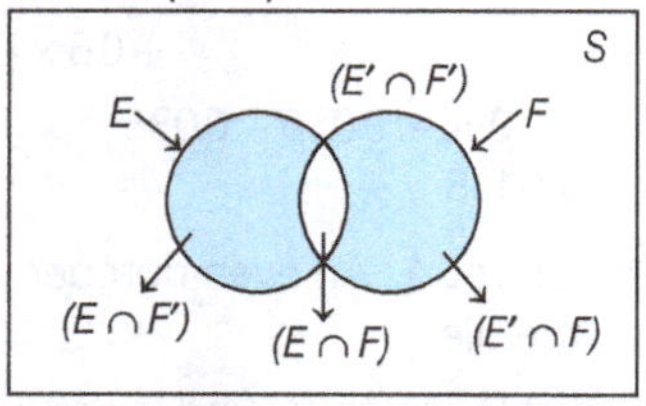

3 (c) Given, the events $E_1, E_2, ..., E_n$ represent is a partition of the sample space S. Therefore,

$$S = E_1 \cup E_2 \cup ... \cup E_n$$

and $E_i \cap E_j = \phi, i \neq j, i, j = 1, 2, ..., n$

Now, we know that for any event A,

$$A = A \cap S$$
$$= A \cap (E_1 \cup E_2 \cup ... \cup E_n)$$
$$= (A \cap E_1) \cup (A \cap E_2) \cup ... \cup (A \cap E_n)$$

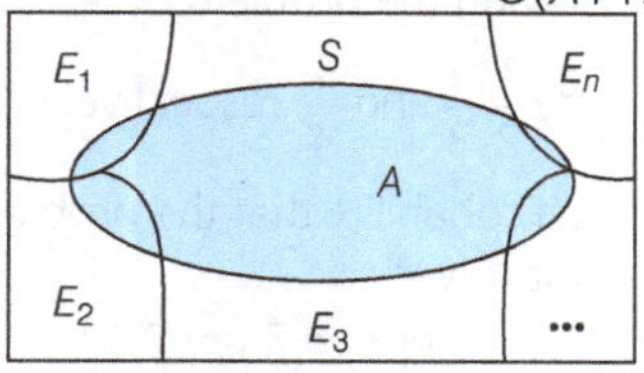

Also, $A \cap E_i$ and $A \cap E_j$ are respectively the subsets of E_i and E_j. We know that E_i and E_j are disjoint, for $i \neq j$. Therefore, $A \cap E_i$ and $A \cap E_j$ are also disjoint for all $i \neq j, i, j = 1, 2, ..., n$.

Thus, $P(A) = P[(A \cap E_1) \cup (A \cap E_2) \cup .... \cup (A \cap E_n)]$

$$= P(A \cap E_1) + P(A \cap E_2) + ... + P(A \cap E_n)$$

Now, by multiplication rule of probability, we get

$P(A \cap E_i) = P(E_i)P(A/E_i)$ as $P(E_i) \neq 0, \forall i = 1, 2, ..., n$

Therefore,

$$P(A) = P(E_i)P(A/E_1) + P(E_2)P(A/E_2) + ... + P(E_n)P(A/E_n)$$

or $$P(A) = \sum_{j=1}^{n} P(E_j)\, P(A/E_j)$$

4 (b) Let A be the event that the construction job will be completed on time and B be the event that there will be a strike. We have to find $P(A)$.

We have, $P(B) = 0.65$.

$$P(\text{no strike}) = P(B') = 1 - P(B) = 1 - 0.65 = 0.35$$

$$P(A/B) = 0.32,\ P(A/B') = 0.80$$

Since, events B and B' form a partition of the sample space S. Therefore, by theorem on total probability, we get

$$P(A) = P(B)P(A/B) + P(B')P(A/B')$$
$$= 0.65 \times 0.32 + 0.35 \times 0.8$$
$$= 0.208 + 0.28 = 0.488$$

Thus, the probability that the construction job will be completed on time is 0.488.

5 (a) By formula of conditional probability, we get

$$P(E_i/A) = \frac{P(A \cap E_i)}{P(A)} = \frac{P(E_i)P(A/E_i)}{P(A)}$$

[by multiplication rule of probability]

$$= \frac{P(E_i)P(A/E_i)}{\sum_{j=1}^{n} P(E_j)P(A/E_j)}$$

[by the result of theorem of total probability]

Note *The following terminology is generally used when Bayes' theorem is applied.*
The events $E_1, E_2, \ldots, E_n$ are called hypothesis. The probability $P(E_i)$ is called the priori probability of the hypothesis E_i.
The conditional probability $P(E_i/A)$ is called a posterior probability of the hypothesis E_i.

6 (*d*) Let E denote the event that the person selected is actually having HIV and A be the event that the person's HIV test is diagnosed as positive. We need to find $P(E/A)$. Also, E' denotes the event that the person selected is actually not having HIV.

Clearly, $\{E, E'\}$ is a partition of the sample space of all people in the population.

$$P(E) = 0.1\% = \frac{0.1}{100} = 0.001$$

and $P(E') = 1 - P(E) = 0.999$

$P(A/E) = P$(person tested as HIV positive given that he/she is actually having HIV)

$$= 90\% = \frac{90}{100} = 0.9$$

and $P(A/E') = P$(person tested as HIV positive given that he/she is actually not having HIV)

$$= 1\% = \frac{1}{100} = 0.01$$

Now, by Bayes' theorem,

$P(E/A)$

$$= \frac{P(E)P(A/E)}{P(E)P(A/E) + P(E')P(A/E')}$$

$$= \frac{0.001 \times 0.9}{0.001 \times 0.9 + 0.999 \times 0.01} = \frac{90}{1089}$$

$= 0.083$ approx.

Thus, the probability that a person selected at random is actually having HIV given that he/she is tested HIV positive is 0.083.

7 (*a*) Let events B_1, B_2 and B_3 be the following.

B_1 : The bolt is manufactured by machine A.

B_2 : The bolt is manufactured by machine B.

B_3 : The bolt is manufactured by machine C.

Clearly, B_1, B_2, B_3, are mutually exclusive and exhaustive events and hence they represent a partition of the sample space.

Let the event E be 'the bolt is defective'.

The event E occurs with B_1 or with B_2 or with B_3.

Given that $P(B_1) = 25\% = 0.25$,

$P(B_2) = 0.35$

and $P(B_3) = 0.40$

Again, $P(E/B_1)$ = Probability that the bolt drawn is defective given that it is manufactured by machine $A = 5\% = 0.05$

Similarly, $P(E/B_2) = 0.04$

and $P(E/B_3) = 0.02$

Hence, by Bayes' theorem, we get

$$P(B_2/E) = \frac{P(B_2)\,P(E/B_2)}{P(B_1)\,P(E/B_1) + P(B_2)\,P(E/B_2) + P(B_3)\,P(E/B_3)}$$

$$= \frac{0.35 \times 0.04}{0.25 \times 0.05 + 0.35 \times 0.04 + 0.40 \times 0.02}$$

$$= \frac{0.0140}{0.0345} = \frac{28}{69}$$

8 (*d*) Let E be the event that the doctor visits the patient late and let T_1, T_2, T_3 and T_4 be the events that the doctor comes by train, bus, scooter and other means of transport, respectively.

Then, $P(T_1) = \frac{3}{10}$, $P(T_2) = \frac{1}{5}$,

$P(T_3) = \frac{1}{10}$ and $P(T_4) = \frac{2}{5}$ [given]

$P(E/T_1)$ = Probability that the doctor arriving late comes by train $= \frac{1}{4}$.

Similarly, $P(E/T_2) = \frac{1}{3}$, $P(E/T_3) = \frac{1}{12}$

and $P(E/T_4) = 0$. Since, he is not late if he comes by other means of transport.

Therefore, by Bayes' theorem, we get

$P(T_1/E)$ = Probability that the doctor comes by train, given that he arrives late

$$= \frac{P(T_1)P(E/T_1)}{P(T_1)P(E/T_1) + P(T_2)P(E/T_2) + P(T_3)P(E/T_3) + P(T_4)P(E/T_4)}$$

$$= \frac{\frac{3}{10} \times \frac{1}{4}}{\frac{3}{10} \times \frac{1}{4} + \frac{1}{5} \times \frac{1}{3} + \frac{1}{10} \times \frac{1}{12} + \frac{2}{5} \times 0}$$

$$= \frac{3}{40} \times \frac{120}{18} = \frac{1}{2}$$

Hence, the required probability is $\frac{1}{2}$.

9 (*c*) Let E be the event that the man report that six occurs in the throwing of the die and let S_1 be the event that six occurs and S_2 be the event that six does not occur.

Then, $P(S_1)$ = Probability that six occurs $= \frac{1}{6}$ and $P(S_2)$ = Probability that six does not occur $= \frac{5}{6}$

$P(E/S_1)$ = Probability that the man reports that six occurs when six has actually occurred on the die = Probability that the man speaks the truth $= \frac{3}{4}$

and $P(E/S_2)$ = Probability that the man reports that six occurs when six has not actually occurred on the die = Probability that the man does not speak the truth

$$= 1 - \frac{3}{4} = \frac{1}{4}$$

Thus, by Bayes' theorem, we get

$P(S_1/E)$ = Probability that the report of the man that six has occurred is actually a six

$$= \frac{P(S_1)P(E/S_1)}{P(S_1)P(E/S_1) + P(S_2)P(E/S_2)}$$

$$= \frac{\frac{1}{6} \times \frac{3}{4}}{\frac{1}{6} \times \frac{3}{4} + \frac{5}{6} \times \frac{1}{4}} = \frac{1}{8} \times \frac{24}{8} = \frac{3}{8}$$

Hence, the required probability is $\frac{3}{8}$.

10 (*a*) Let E_1 : The event that the student is residing in hostel and E_2 : The event that the student is not residing in the hostel.

Let E : A student attains A grade.

Then, E_1 and E_2 are mutually exclusive and exhaustive.

Moreover,

$$P(E_1) = 60\% = \frac{60}{100} = \frac{3}{5}$$

and $P(E_2) = 40\% = \frac{40}{100} = \frac{2}{5}$

Then, $P\left(\frac{E}{E_1}\right) = 30\% = \frac{30}{100} = \frac{3}{10}$

and $P\left(\frac{E}{E_2}\right) = 20\% = \frac{20}{100} = \frac{2}{10}$

By Bayes' theorem, we get

$$P\left(\frac{E_1}{E}\right) = \frac{P\left(\frac{E}{E_1}\right)P(E_1)}{P\left(\frac{E}{E_1}\right)P(E_1) + P\left(\frac{E}{E_2}\right)P(E_2)}$$

$$= \frac{\frac{3}{10}\times\frac{3}{5}}{\frac{3}{10}\times\frac{3}{5}+\frac{2}{10}\times\frac{2}{5}} = \frac{9}{9+4} = \frac{9}{13}$$

11 (*b*) Let E_1 : The event that the student knows the answer and E_2 : The event that the student guesses the answer.

Therefore, E_1 and E_2 are mutually exclusive and exhaustive.

$\therefore \quad P(E_1) = \frac{3}{4}$

and $\quad P(E_2) = \frac{1}{4}$

Let E : the answer is correct.

The probability that the student answered correctly, given that he knows the answer, is 1

i.e. $P\left(\frac{E}{E_1}\right) = 1$

Probability that the students answered correctly, given that he guessed, is $\frac{1}{4}$ i.e. $P\left(\frac{E}{E_2}\right) = \frac{1}{4}$

By Bayes' theorem, we obtain

$$P\left(\frac{E_1}{E}\right) = \frac{P\left(\frac{E}{E_1}\right)P(E_1)}{P\left(\frac{E}{E_1}\right)P(E_1) + P\left(\frac{E}{E_2}\right)P(E_2)}$$

$$= \frac{1\times\frac{3}{4}}{1\times\frac{3}{4}+\frac{1}{4}\times\frac{1}{4}} = \frac{\frac{3}{4}}{\frac{3}{4}+\frac{1}{16}} = \frac{\frac{3}{4}}{\frac{12+1}{16}}$$

$$= \frac{3}{4}\times\frac{16}{13} = \frac{12}{13}$$

Note *If two events are not mutually exclusive/exhaustive, then do not use Bayes' theorem.*

12 (*c*) Let E_1 : The event that the person has disease and E_2 : The event that the person is healthy.

Then, E_1 and E_2 are mutually exclusive and exhaustive.

Moreover,

$$P(E_1) = 0.1\% = \frac{0.1}{100} = 0.001$$

and $\quad P(E_2) = 1 - 0.001 = 0.999$

Let E : The event that test is positive.

Then, $P\left(\frac{E}{E_1}\right) = P$ (result is positive given the person has disease)

$$= 99\% = \frac{99}{100} = 0.99$$

Probability that a person does not have disease and test result is positive.

$\therefore \quad P\left(\frac{E}{E_2}\right) = 0.5\% = \frac{0.5}{100} = 0.005$

By Bayes' theorem, we get

$$P\left(\frac{E_1}{E}\right) = \frac{P\left(\frac{E}{E_1}\right)P(E_1)}{P\left(\frac{E}{E_1}\right)P(E_1) + P\left(\frac{E}{E_2}\right)P(E_2)}$$

$$= \frac{0.001\times 0.99}{0.001\times 0.99 + 0.999\times 0.005}$$

$$= \frac{0.00099}{0.00099 + 0.004995}$$

$$= \frac{0.00099}{0.005985} = \frac{990}{5985} = \frac{110}{665} = \frac{22}{133}$$

13 (*d*) Let E_1 : The event that the item is produced by machine A and E_2 : The event that the item is produced by machine B.

Then, E_1 and E_2 are mutually exclusive and exhaustive events.

Moreover,

$$P(E_1) = 60\% = \frac{60}{100} = \frac{3}{5}$$

and $\quad P(E_2) = 40\% = \frac{40}{100} = \frac{2}{5}$

Let E : The event that the item chosen is defective.

$\therefore \quad P\left(\frac{E}{E_1}\right) = P$ (machine A produced defective items)

$$= 2\% = \frac{2}{100}$$

and $P\left(\frac{E}{E_2}\right) = P$ (machine B produced defective items)

$$= 1\% = \frac{1}{100}$$

The probability that the randomly selected item was from machine B, given that it is defective, is given by $P\left(\frac{E_2}{E}\right)$.

By Bayes' theorem, we obtain

$$P\left(\frac{E_2}{E}\right) = \frac{P\left(\frac{E}{E_2}\right)P(E_2)}{P\left(\frac{E}{E_1}\right)P(E_1) + P\left(\frac{E}{E_2}\right)P(E_2)}$$

$$= \frac{\frac{1}{100}\times\frac{2}{5}}{\frac{2}{100}\times\frac{3}{5}+\frac{1}{100}\times\frac{2}{5}} = \frac{\frac{2}{500}}{\frac{6}{500}+\frac{2}{500}}$$

$$= \frac{2}{6+2} = \frac{1}{4}$$

14 (*c*) Let E_1 : The event that the first group wins and E_2 : The event that the second group wins.

Then, E_1 and E_2 are mutually exclusive and exhaustive events.

$\therefore \quad P(E_1) = 0.6 = \frac{6}{10}$

and $\quad P(E_2) = 0.4 = \frac{4}{10}$

Let E : The event that the new product is introduced.

$P\left(\frac{E}{E_1}\right) = P$ (introducing a new product, if the first group wins)

$= 0.7 = \frac{7}{10}$

$\therefore\ P\left(\frac{E}{E_2}\right) = P$ (introducing a new product, if the second group wins)

$= 0.3 = \frac{3}{10}$

The probability that the new product is introduced by the second group is given by $P\left(\frac{E_2}{E}\right)$.

By Bayes' theorem, we obtain

$$P\left(\frac{E_2}{E}\right) = \frac{P\left(\frac{E}{E_2}\right)P(E_2)}{P\left(\frac{E}{E_1}\right)P(E_1) + P\left(\frac{E}{E_2}\right)P(E_2)}$$

$$= \frac{\frac{3}{10}\times\frac{4}{10}}{\frac{7}{10}\times\frac{6}{10}+\frac{3}{10}\times\frac{4}{10}} = \frac{12}{42+12}$$

$$= \frac{12}{54} = \frac{2}{9}$$

15 (*a*) A. Let E_1 : The event that 5 or 6 is shown on die

and E_2 : The event that 1, 2, 3, or 4 is shown on die.

Then, E_1 and E_2 are mutually exclusive and exhaustive events

and $n(E_1) = 2, n(E_2) = 4$

Also, $n(S) = 6$

$\therefore\ P(E_1) = \frac{2}{6} = \frac{1}{3}$ and $P(E_2) = \frac{4}{6} = \frac{2}{3}$

Let E : The event that exactly one head shows up.

$\therefore\ P\left(\frac{E}{E_1}\right) = P$ (exactly one head shows up when coin is tossed thrice)

$= P\{HTT, THT, TTH\} = \frac{3}{8}$

[$\because$ total number of events $= 2^3 = 8$]

$P\left(\frac{E}{E_2}\right) = P$ (head shows up when coin is tossed once)

$= \frac{1}{2}$

The probability that the girl threw, 1, 2, 3 or 4 with the die, if she obtained exactly one head, is given by $P\left(\frac{E_2}{E}\right)$.

By Bayes' theorem, we get

$$P\left(\frac{E_2}{E}\right) = \frac{P\left(\frac{E}{E_2}\right)P(E_2)}{P\left(\frac{E}{E_1}\right)P(E_1) + P\left(\frac{E}{E_2}\right)P(E_2)}$$

$$= \frac{\frac{1}{2}\times\frac{2}{3}}{\frac{1}{2}\times\frac{2}{3}+\frac{3}{8}\times\frac{1}{3}} = \frac{\frac{1}{3}}{\frac{1}{3}+\frac{1}{8}}$$

$$= \frac{8}{8+3} = \frac{8}{11}$$

B. Let E_1 : The event that item is produced by machine A,

E_2 : The event that item is produced by machine B

and E_3 : The event that item is produced by machine C.

Here, E_1, E_2 and E_3 are mutually exclusive and exhaustive events. Moreover,

$P(E_1) = 50\% = \frac{50}{100}$,

$P(E_2) = 30\% = \frac{30}{100}$

and $P(E_3) = 20\% = \frac{20}{100}$

Let E : The event that item chosen is found to be defective.

$\therefore\ P\left(\frac{E}{E_1}\right) = \frac{1}{100}$,

$P\left(\frac{E}{E_2}\right) = \frac{5}{100}$

and $P\left(\frac{E}{E_3}\right) = \frac{7}{100}$.

By Bayes' theorem, we get

$$P\left(\frac{E_1}{E}\right) = \frac{P\left(\frac{E}{E_1}\right)P(E_1)}{P\left(\frac{E}{E_1}\right)P(E_1) + P\left(\frac{E}{E_2}\right)P(E_2) + P\left(\frac{E}{E_3}\right)P(E_3)}$$

$$= \frac{\frac{1}{100}\times\frac{50}{100}}{\frac{1}{100}\times\frac{50}{100}+\frac{5}{100}\times\frac{30}{100}+\frac{7}{100}\times\frac{20}{100}}$$

$$= \frac{50}{50+150+140} = \frac{50}{340} = \frac{5}{34}$$

C. Let E_1 : The event that lost card is a diamond

$\Rightarrow \quad n(E_1) = 13$

E_2 : Lost card is not a diamond

$\Rightarrow \quad n(E_2) = 52 - 13 = 39$

And $n(S) = 52$

Then, E_1 and E_2 are mutually exclusive and exhaustive events.

$\therefore \quad P(E_1) = \frac{13}{52} = \frac{1}{4}$

and $P(E_2) = \frac{39}{52} = \frac{3}{4}$

Let E : The events that two cards drawn from the remaining pack are diamonds. When one diamond card is lost. There are 12 diamond cards out of 51 cards.

The cards can be drawn out of 12 diamond cards in ${}^{12}C_2$ ways. Similarly, 2 diamond cards can be drawn out of 51 cards in ${}^{51}C_2$ ways. The probability of getting two cards, when one diamond card is lost, is given by $P\left(\frac{E}{E_1}\right)$.

$$\therefore\ P\left(\frac{E}{E_1}\right) = \frac{{}^{12}C_2}{{}^{51}C_2} = \frac{\frac{12\times 11}{1\times 2}}{\frac{51\times 50}{1\times 2}}$$

$$= \frac{12\times 11}{51\times 50}$$

and $P\left(\frac{E}{E_2}\right)=\frac{{}^{13}C_2}{{}^{51}C_2}=\frac{\frac{13\times12}{1\times2}}{\frac{51\times50}{1\times2}}$

$=\frac{13\times12}{51\times50}$

By Bayes' theorem, we get

$$P\left(\frac{E_1}{E}\right)=\frac{P\left(\frac{E}{E_1}\right)P(E_1)}{P\left(\frac{E}{E_1}\right)P(E_1)+P\left(\frac{E}{E_2}\right)P(E_2)}$$

$$=\frac{\frac{12\times11}{51\times50}\times\frac{1}{4}}{\frac{12\times11}{51\times50}\times\frac{1}{4}+\frac{13\times12}{51\times50}\times\frac{3}{4}}$$

$$=\frac{12\times11}{12\times11+13\times12\times3}$$

$$=\frac{132}{132+468}=\frac{132}{600}=\frac{11}{50}$$

16 (*a*) Let E_1 : The event that coin comes up with a head and E_2 : The event that coin comes up with a tail.

Then, E_1 and E_2 are mutually exclusive and exhaustive events.

Moreover, $P(E_1)=P(E_2)=\frac{1}{2}$

E : The event that A reports that a head appears.

$\therefore\ P\left(\frac{E}{E_1}\right)=P$ (head comes up and A speaks truth) $=\frac{4}{5}$

$P\left(\frac{E}{E_2}\right)=P$ (tail comes up and A speaks lie) $=\frac{1}{5}$

The probability that there is actually a head is given by $P\left(\frac{E_1}{E}\right)$.

By Bayes' theorem, we get

$$P\left(\frac{E_1}{E}\right)=\frac{P\left(\frac{E}{E_1}\right)P(E_1)}{P\left(\frac{E}{E_1}\right)P(E_1)+P\left(\frac{E}{E_2}\right)P(E_2)}$$

$$=\frac{\frac{4}{5}\times\frac{1}{2}}{\frac{4}{5}\times\frac{1}{2}+\frac{1}{5}\times\frac{1}{2}}=\frac{4}{4+1}=\frac{4}{5}$$

17 (*c*) If $A\subset B$, then $A\cap B=A$.

$\therefore\quad P(A\cap B)=P(A)$

We know that

$$P\left(\frac{A}{B}\right)=\frac{P(A\cap B)}{P(B)}=\frac{P(A)}{P(B)}$$

But $\quad P(B)\le1$

$\therefore\quad P\left(\frac{A}{B}\right)\ge P(A).$

18 (*c*) Let E be the event that the car is of standard quality. Let B_1 and B_2 be the events that the car is manufactured in plants X and Y, respectively.

Now, $P(B_1)=\frac{70}{100}=\frac{7}{10}$

and $\quad P(B_2)=\frac{30}{100}=\frac{3}{10}$

$P(E/B_1)=$ Probability that the car is manufactured in plant X, given that it is of standard quality

$=\frac{80}{100}=\frac{8}{10}$

and $\quad P(E/B_2)=\frac{90}{100}=\frac{9}{10}$

$P(B_1/E)=$ Probability that the car is manufactured in plant X, given that it is of standard quality

$$=\frac{P(B_1)\times P(E/B_1)}{P(B_1)\cdot P(E/B_1)+P(B_2)\cdot P(E/B_2)}$$

$$=\frac{\frac{7}{10}\times\frac{8}{10}}{\frac{7}{10}\times\frac{8}{10}+\frac{3}{10}\times\frac{9}{10}}=\frac{56}{83}$$

Hence, the required probability is $\frac{56}{83}$.

19 (*d*) Let A be the event that the first marble is red.

Let B be the event that the second marble is black.

Let C be the event that the second marble is red.

Let D be the event that the third marble is black and

Let E be the event that the third marble is red.

$\therefore$ The required probability

$=P(A)\times P(B/A)\times P(D/A\cap B)$
$+P(A)\times P(C/A)\times P(D/A\cap C)$
$+P(A)\times P(B/A)\times P(E/A\cap B)$

$=\frac{5}{8}\times\frac{3}{7}\times\frac{2}{6}+\frac{5}{8}\times\frac{4}{7}\times\frac{3}{6}+\frac{5}{8}\times\frac{3}{7}\times\frac{4}{6}$

$=\frac{30}{336}+\frac{60}{336}+\frac{60}{336}=\frac{30+60+60}{336}$

$=\frac{150}{336}=\frac{25}{56}$

20 (*c*) Let A denote the event that the ball transferred from the first bag is white.

Let B denote the event that the ball transferred from the first bag is black.

Let E denote the event that the ball drawn from the second bag is white.

$P(E/A)=\frac{10}{17}$ and $P(E/B)=\frac{9}{17}$

$P(A)=\frac{4}{9}$ and $P(B)=\frac{5}{9}$

$\therefore$ Required probability,

$\therefore\quad P(E)=P(A)\times P(E/A)+P(B)\times P(E/B)$

$\Rightarrow\quad P(E)=\frac{4}{9}\times\frac{10}{17}+\frac{5}{9}\times\frac{9}{17}$

$=\frac{40}{153}+\frac{45}{153}=\frac{40+45}{153}=\frac{85}{153}$

21 (*d*) Let A denote the event that fair coin is drawn.

Let B denote the event that 2 headed coin is drawn.

Let E denote the event that tossed coin resulted in head.

Now, we can get

$P(A)=\frac{1}{2},\ P(B)=\frac{1}{2}$

$P(E/A)=\frac{1}{2},\ P(E/B)=1$

$\therefore$ By Bayes' theorem,

$P(A/E)$

$$=\frac{P(A)\times P(E/A)}{P(A)\times P(E/A)+P(B)\times P(E/B)}$$

$$=\frac{\frac{1}{2}\times\frac{1}{2}}{\frac{1}{2}\times\frac{1}{2}+\frac{1}{2}\times 1}=\frac{\frac{1}{4}}{\frac{1}{4}+\frac{1}{2}}$$

$$=\frac{\frac{1}{4}}{\frac{3}{4}}=\frac{4\times 1}{4\times 3}=\frac{1}{3}$$

22 (a) Let A : The people has blood group O.

Let B : The people has blood group other than O.

Let E : The people is left handed.

$$P(A)=\frac{30}{100},\ P(B)=\frac{70}{100},$$

$$P(E/A)=\frac{6}{100} \text{ and } P(E/B)=\frac{10}{100}$$

Now, by Baye's theorem

$P(A/E)$

$$=\frac{P(A)\times P(E/A)}{P(A)\times P(E/A)+P(B)\times P(E/B)}$$

$$=\frac{\frac{30}{100}\times\frac{6}{100}}{\frac{30}{100}\times\frac{6}{100}+\frac{70}{100}\times\frac{10}{100}}$$

$$=\frac{\frac{180}{10000}}{\frac{180}{10000}+\frac{700}{10000}}=\frac{180}{880}=\frac{9}{44}$$

23 (d) Let A : The first ball drawn is white.

Let B : The first ball drawn is black.

Let E : The second ball drawn is white.

Number of white balls $= m$, number of black balls $= n$

$\therefore$ Total number of balls $= m+n$

$$\therefore\ P(A)=\frac{m}{m+n} \text{ and } P(B)=\frac{n}{m+n}$$

$$P(E/A)=\frac{m+k}{m+n+k}$$

$$\text{and } P(E/B)=\frac{m}{m+n+k}$$

Now, $P(E)=P(A)\times P(E/A)+P(B)\times P(E/B)$

$$=\frac{m}{m+n}\times\frac{m+k}{m+n+k}+\frac{n}{m+n}\times\frac{m}{m+n+k}$$

$$=\frac{m(m+k)+mn}{(m+n)(m+n+k)}$$

$$=\frac{m(m+k+n)}{(m+n)(m+n+k)}=\frac{m}{m+n}$$

which is independent of k.

$\therefore$ The probability of drawing a white ball now does not depend on k.

24 (c) Let E_1, E_2 and E be the events defined as follows.

E_1 = Letter (i.e. envelope) has come from CALCUTTA

E_2 = Letter (i.e. envelope) has come from TATANAGAR.

E = Two consecutive letters (i.e. alphabets) TA are visible on envelope.

$$P(E_1)=\frac{1}{2},\ P(E_2)=\frac{1}{2}$$

$$P\left(\frac{E}{E_1}\right)=\frac{n(E\cap E_1)}{n(E_1)}=\frac{1}{7}$$

[$\because$ 7 pairs of consecutive letters are CA, AL, LC, CU, UT, TT, TA]

$$P\left(\frac{E}{E_2}\right)=\frac{n(E\cap E_2)}{n(E_2)}=\frac{2}{8}$$

[$\because$ 8 pairs of consecutive letters are TA, AT, TA, AN, NA, AG, GA, AR]

$$\therefore\ P\left(\frac{E_2}{E}\right)=\frac{P(E_2)\,P\left(\frac{E}{E_2}\right)}{P(E_1)\,P\left(\frac{E}{E_1}\right)+P(E_2)\,P\left(\frac{E}{E_2}\right)}$$

$$=\frac{\left(\frac{1}{2}\right)\left(\frac{2}{8}\right)}{\left(\frac{1}{2}\right)\left(\frac{1}{7}\right)+\left(\frac{1}{2}\right)\left(\frac{2}{8}\right)}$$

$$=\frac{\frac{2}{16}}{\frac{8+14}{2\times 7\times 8}}=\frac{2\times 7}{22}=\frac{7}{11}$$

Hence, required probability is $\frac{7}{11}$.

25 (d) Let A: First bag is chosen.

Let B : Second bag is chosen.

Let E denote the event of choosing a black ball.

$\because$ A die is thrown and if it shows up 1 or 3, a ball is taken from the first bag.

$$\therefore\ P(A)=\frac{2}{6}=\frac{1}{3}$$

Since, the second bag is chosen when the die shows any of the numbers 2, 4, 5, 6.

$$\text{Therefore, } P(B)=\frac{4}{6}=\frac{2}{3}$$

Bag I contains 3 black and 4 white balls.

$$\text{Therefore, } P\left(\frac{E}{A}\right)=\frac{3}{7}$$

Similarly, bag II contains 4 black and 3 white balls.

$$\text{Therefore, } P\left(\frac{E}{B}\right)=\frac{4}{7}$$

Now, probability of choosing a black ball is given by

$$P(E)=P(A)\times P\left(\frac{E}{A}\right)+P(B)\times P\left(\frac{E}{B}\right)$$

$$=\frac{1}{3}\times\frac{3}{7}+\frac{2}{3}\times\frac{4}{7}=\frac{3}{21}+\frac{8}{21}=\frac{11}{21}$$

26 (a) Let A denote the event that the person has TB.

Let B denote the event that the person has not TB.

Let E denote the event that the person is diagonsed to have TB.

$$\therefore\ P(A)=\frac{1}{1000} \text{ and } P(B)=\frac{999}{1000}$$

$$P\left(\frac{E}{A}\right)=0.99 \text{ and } P\left(\frac{E}{B}\right)=0.001$$

The required probability is given by

$$P\left(\frac{A}{E}\right)=\frac{P(A)\times P\left(\frac{E}{A}\right)}{P(A)\times P\left(\frac{E}{A}\right)+P(B)\times P\left(\frac{E}{B}\right)}$$

$$=\frac{\frac{1}{1000}\times 0.99}{\frac{1}{1000}\times 0.99+\frac{999}{1000}\times 0.001}$$

$$=\frac{0.99}{0.99+0.001\times 0.999}=\frac{0.99}{0.99+0.999}$$

$$=\frac{990}{990+999}=\frac{990}{1989}=\frac{110}{221}$$

Random Variables and Its Probability Distributions

1 (*a*) To answer this, let us consider the following examples/ experiments.

(i) In tossing two dice, we may be interested in the sum of the numbers on the two dice.

(ii) In tossing a coin 50 times, we may want the number of heads obtained.

(iii) In the experiment of taking out four articles (one after the other) at random from a lot of 20 articles in which 6 are defective, we want to know the number of defectives in the sample of four and not in the particular sequence of defective and non-defective articles.

In all of the above experiments, we have a rule which assigns to each outcome of the experiment a single real number. This single real number may vary with different outcomes of the experiment. Hence, it is a variable. Also, its value depends upon the outcome of a random experiment and hence is called random variable. A random variable is usually denoted by X.

2 (*b*) The random variable X is a function whose domain is the set of outcomes (or sample space) of a random experiment. A random variable can take any real value. Therefore, its codomain is the set of real numbers. Hence, a random variable can be defined as follows.

A random variable is a real valued function whose domain is the sample space of a random experiment.

3 (*d*) The experiment of tossing a coin two times in succession. The sample space of the experiment is

$$S = \{HH, HT, TH, TT\}.$$

If X denotes the number of heads obtained, then X is a random variable and for each outcome, its value is as given below

$$X(HH) = 2, X(HT) = 1,$$
$$X(TH) = 1 \text{ and } X(TT) = 0$$

Note *More than one random variables can be defined on the same sample space.*

e.g. let Y denote the number of heads minus the number of tails for each outcome of the above sample space S.

Then, $Y(HH) = 2, Y(HT) = 0,$

$$Y(TH) = 0 \text{ and } Y(TT) = -2$$

Thus, X and Y are two different random variables defined on the same sample space S.

4 (*b*) Let us look at the experiment of selecting one family out of ten families $f_1, f_2, \ldots, f_{10}$ in such a manner that each family is equally likely to be selected. Let the families $f_1, f_2, \ldots, f_{10}$ have 3, 4, 3, 2, 5, 4, 3, 6, 4, 5 members, respectively.

Let us select a family and note down the number of members in the family denoting X. Clearly, X is random variable defined as below

$$X(f_1) = 3, X(f_2) = 4,$$
$$X(f_3) = 3, X(f_4) = 2, X(f_5) = 5,$$
$$X(f_6) = 4, \; X(f_7) = 3, X(f_8) = 6,$$
$$X(f_9) = 4 \text{ and } X(f_{10}) = 5$$

Thus, X can take any value 2, 3, 4, 5 or 6 depending upon which family is selected.

Now, X will take the value 2 when the family f_4 is selected. X can take the value 3 when anyone of the families f_1, f_3, f_7 is selected.

Similarly, $X = 4$, when family f_2, f_6 or f_9 is selected,

$X = 5$, when family f_5 or f_{10} is selected

and $X = 6$, when family f_8 is selected.

Since, we had assumed that each family is equally likely to be selected. The probability that family f_4 is selected is $\frac{1}{10}$.

Thus, the probability that X can take the value 2, is $\frac{1}{10}$. We write

$$P(X = 2) = \frac{1}{10}$$

Also, the probability that any one of the families f_1, f_3 or f_7 is selected, is $P(\{f_1, f_3, f_7\}) = \frac{3}{10}$.

Thus, the probability that X can take the value 3 is $\frac{3}{10}$

We write $P(X = 3) = \frac{3}{10}$

Similarly, we get

$$P(X = 4) = P(\{f_2, f_6, f_9\}) = \frac{3}{10},$$
$$P(X = 5) = P(\{f_5, f_{10}\}) = \frac{2}{10}$$
and $$P(X = 6) = P(\{f_8\}) = \frac{1}{10}$$

Such a description giving the values of the random variable along with the corresponding probabilities is called the probability distribution of the random variable X.

5 (*c*) The probability distribution of a random variable X is the system of numbers is defined as

X	x_1	x_2	...	x_n
P(X)	p_1	p_2	...	p_n

where $p_i > 0, \sum_{i=1}^{n} p_i = 1, i = 1, 2, \ldots, n$

The real numbers $x_1, x_2, \ldots, x_n$ are the possible values of the random variable X and $p_i (i = 1, 2, \ldots, n)$ is the probability of the random variable X taking the value x_i

i.e. $\quad P(X = x_i) = p_i$

Note *If x_i is one of the possible values of a random variable X, then the statement $X = x_i$ is true only at some point(s) of the sample space. Hence, the probability that X takes value x_i is always non-zero, i.e. $P(X = x_i) \neq 0$.*

Also, for all possible values of the random variable X, all elements of the sample space are covered. Hence, the sum of all the probabilities in a probability distribution must be one.

6 (*d*) The probability distribution of X is as follows

X	0	1	2	3	4
$P(X)$	0.1	k	$2k$	$2k$	k

A. We know that $\sum_{i=1}^{n} p_i = 1$

Therefore,

$0.1 + k + 2k + 2k + k = 1$

i.e. $k = 0.15$

B. P(you study for atleast two hours) $= P(X \geq 2)$

$= P(X = 2) + P(X = 3) + P(X = 4)$

$= 2k + 2k + k = 5k = 5 \times 0.15$

$= 0.75$

C. P(you study exactly two hours)

$= P(X = 2)$

$= 2k = 2 \times 0.15 = 0.3$

D. P(you study atmost two hours)

$= P(X \leq 2)$

$= P(X = 0) + P(X = 1) + P(X = 2)$

$= 0.1 + k + 2k = 0.1 + 3k$

$= 0.1 + 3 \times 0.15 = 0.55$

7 (*b*) Mean is a measure of location or central tendency in the sense that it roughly locates a middle or average value of the random variable.

8 (*c*) We know that

$$\text{Var}(X) = \sum_{i=1}^{n} (x_i - \mu)^2 p(x_i)$$

$$= \sum_{i=1}^{n} (x_i^2 + \mu^2 - 2\mu x_i) p(x_i)$$

$$= \sum_{i=1}^{n} x_i^2 p(x_i) + \sum_{i=1}^{n} \mu^2 p(x_i) - \sum_{i=1}^{n} 2\mu x_i p(x_i)$$

$$= \sum_{i=1}^{n} x_i^2 p(x_i) + \mu^2 \sum_{i=1}^{n} p(x_i) - 2\mu \sum_{i=1}^{n} x_i p(x_i)$$

$$= \sum_{i=1}^{n} x_i^2 p(x_i) + \mu^2 - 2\mu^2$$

$$\left[\because \sum_{i=1}^{n} p(x_i) = 1 \text{ and } \mu = \sum_{i=1}^{n} x_i p(x_i)\right]$$

$$= \sum_{i=1}^{n} x_i^2 p(x_i) - \mu^2$$

or $\text{Var}(X) = \sum_{i=1}^{n} x_i^2 p(x_i) - \left(\sum_{i=1}^{n} x_i p(x_i)\right)^2$

or $\text{Var}(X) = E(X^2) - [E(X)]^2$,

where $E(X^2) = \sum_{i=1}^{n} x_i^2 p(x_i)$

9 (*a*) A distribution is a probability distribution of a random variable X.

(i) $\Sigma P(X) = 1$

(ii) $0 < P(X) \leq 1$

We will check both the conditions for each probability distribution.

We know that the sum of all the probabilities in a probability distribution is 1.

(i) Sum of the probabilities

$= 0.4 + 0.4 + 0.2 = 1$

Therefore, the given table is a probability distribution of a random variable.

(ii) It can be seen that for

$X = 3, P(X) = -0.1$

It is known that probability of any observation is not negative. Therefore, the given table is not a probability distribution of random variable.

(iii) Here, all the probabilities are positive but the sum of probabilities

$= 0.6 + 0.1 + 0.2$

$= 0.9 < 1$

Thus, the given distribution is not a probability distribution.

(iv) Here, all the probabilities are positive but the sum of probabilities

$= 0.3 + 0.2 + 0.4 + 0.1 + 0.05$

$= 1.05 > 1$

Thus, the given distribution is not a probability distribution.

10 (*c*) Write sample space for each case. Then, find the possible number of heads and tails that can be obtained in each case.

At last, find their probabilities and arrange in a distribution.

A. When one coin is tossed twice, the sample space is

$S = \{HH, HT, TH, TT\}$

Let X denote the number of heads in any outcome in S.

$X(HH) = 2, X(HT) = 1, X(TH) = 1$ and $X(TT) = 0$

Therefore, X can take the value of 0, 1 or 2. It is known that

$P(HH) = P(HT) = P(TH)$

$= P(TT) = \frac{1}{4}$

$\therefore$ $P(X = 0) = P$ (tail occurs on both tosses)

$= P(\{TT\}) = \frac{1}{4}$

$P(X = 1) = P$ (one head and one tail occurs)

$= P(\{TH, HT\})$

$= \frac{2}{4} = \frac{1}{2}$

and $P(X = 2) = P$ (head occurs on both tosses)

$= P(\{HH\})$

$= \frac{1}{4}$

Thus, the required probability distribution is as follows

X	0	1	2
P(X)	$\frac{1}{4}$	$\frac{1}{2}$	$\frac{1}{4}$

B. When three coins are tossed thrice, then the sample space is

$$S = \{HHH, HHT, HTH, HTT, THH, THT, TTH, TTT\}$$

which contains eight equally likely sample points.

Let X represent the number of tails.

Then, X can take values 0, 1, 2 and 3.

$P(X=0) = P$ (no tail)

$= P(\{HHH\}) = \frac{1}{8}$,

$P(X=1) = P$ (one tail and two heads show up)

$= P(\{HHT, HTH, THH\}) = \frac{3}{8}$,

$P(X=2) = P$ (two tails and one head show up)

$= P(\{HTT, THT, TTH\}) = \frac{3}{8}$

and $P(X=3) = P$ (three tails show up) $= P(\{TTT\}) = \frac{1}{8}$

Thus, the probability distribution is as follows

X	0	1	2	3
P(X)	$\frac{1}{8}$	$\frac{3}{8}$	$\frac{3}{8}$	$\frac{1}{8}$

C. When a coin is tossed four times, the sample space is

$$S = \begin{Bmatrix} HHHH, HHHT, HHTH, HTHT, HTTH, \\ HTTT, THHH, HTHH, THHT, THTH, HHTT, \\ TTHH, TTHT, TTTH, THTT, TTTT \end{Bmatrix}$$

which contains 16 equally likely sample points.

Let X be the random variable, which represents the number of heads. It can be seen that X can take the values 0, 1, 2, 3 or 4.

$P(X=0) = P$ (no head shows up)

$= P\{TTTT\} = \frac{1}{16}$

$P(X=1) = P$ (one head and three tails show up)

$= P\{HTTT, THTT, TTHT, TTTH\} = \frac{4}{16} = \frac{1}{4}$,

$P(X=2) = P$ (two heads and two tails show up)

$= P(\{HHTT, HTHT, HTTH, THHT, THTH, TTHH\})$

$= \frac{6}{16} = \frac{3}{8}$

$P(X=3) = P$ (three heads and one tail show up)

$= P(\{HHHT, HHTH, HTHH, THHH\}) = \frac{4}{16} = \frac{1}{4}$

and $P(X=4) = P$ (four heads show up)

$= P(\{HHHH\}) = \frac{1}{16}$

Thus, the probability distribution is as follows

X	0	1	2	3	4
P(X)	$\frac{1}{16}$	$\frac{1}{4}$	$\frac{3}{8}$	$\frac{1}{4}$	$\frac{1}{16}$

11 (a) When a die is tossed two times, we obtain $(6 \times 6) = 36$ number of sample points.

(i) Let X be the random variable which denote the number of successes in two tosses of a die. So, X may have values 0, 1 or 2.

Now, $P(X=0) = P$ (number less than or equal to 4 on both the tosses) $= \frac{4}{6} \times \frac{4}{6} = \frac{16}{36} = \frac{4}{9}$,

$P(X=1) = P$ (number less than or equal to 4 on first toss and greater than 4 on second toss) $+ P$ (number greater than 4 on first toss and less than or equal to 4 on second toss)

$= \frac{4}{6} \times \frac{2}{6} + \frac{4}{6} \times \frac{2}{6} = \frac{16}{36} = \frac{4}{9}$

and $P(X=2) = P$ (number greater than 4 on both the tosses) $= \frac{2}{6} \times \frac{2}{6} = \frac{4}{36} = \frac{1}{9}$

Probability distribution of X i.e. number of successes is as follows

X	0	1	2
P(X)	$\frac{4}{9}$	$\frac{4}{9}$	$\frac{1}{9}$

(ii) Let X be the random variable which denote the failure or success of the event (six appears on atleast one die). So, X may have values 0 or 1.

$P(X=0) = P$ (six does not appear on any of the die)

$= \frac{5}{6} \times \frac{5}{6} = \frac{25}{36}$

$P(X=1) = P$ (six appears on atleast one of the die)

$= \frac{11}{36}$

Thus, the required probability distribution is as follows

X	0	1
P(X)	$\frac{25}{36}$	$\frac{11}{36}$

12 (c) A. It is known that the sum of a probability distribution of random variable is one i.e. $\Sigma P(X) = 1$, therefore

$P(0) + P(1) + P(2) + P(3) + P(4) + P(5) + P(6) + P(7) = 1$

$$\Rightarrow \quad 0 + k + 2k + 2k + 3k + k^2 + 2k^2 + 7k^2 + k = 1$$
$$\Rightarrow \quad 10k^2 + 9k - 1 = 0$$
$$\Rightarrow \quad 10k^2 + 10k - k - 1 = 0$$
$$\Rightarrow \quad 10k(k+1) - 1(k+1) = 0$$
$$\Rightarrow \quad (k+1)(10k-1) = 0$$
$$\Rightarrow \quad k + 1 = 0 \text{ or } 10k - 1 = 0$$
$$\Rightarrow \quad k = -1 \text{ or } k = \frac{1}{10}$$

$k = -1$ is not possible as the probability of an event is never negative.

$$\therefore \quad k = \frac{1}{10}$$

B. $P(X < 3) = P(0) + P(1) + P(2) = 0 + k + 2k$

$$= 0 + \frac{1}{10} + \frac{2}{10} = \frac{3}{10} \qquad \left[\text{put, } k = \frac{1}{10}\right]$$

C. $P(X > 6) = P(7) = 7k^2 + k$

$$= \frac{7}{100} + \frac{1}{10} = \frac{17}{100} \qquad \left[\text{put, } k = \frac{1}{10}\right]$$

D. $P(0 < X < 3) = P(1) + P(2) = k + 2k$

$$= \frac{1}{10} + \frac{2}{10} = \frac{3}{10} \qquad \left[\text{put, } k = \frac{1}{10}\right]$$

13 (b) Given distribution of X is

X	0	1	2	otherwise
P(X)	k	$2k$	$3k$	0

A. Since, $\Sigma P(X) = 1$.

$\therefore P(0) + P(1) + P(2) + P(\text{otherwise}) = 1$

$$\Rightarrow \quad k + 2k + 3k + 0 = 1 \Rightarrow 6k = 1$$
$$\Rightarrow \quad k = \frac{1}{6}$$

B. $P(X < 3) = P(0) + P(1)$

$$= k + 2k = 3k = 3 \times \frac{1}{6} = \frac{1}{2}$$

C. $P(X \le 2) = P(0) + P(1) + P(2)$

$$= k + 2k + 3k = 6k = 6 \times \frac{1}{6} = 1$$

D. $P(X \ge 2) = P(2) + P(\text{otherwise}) = 3k + 0 = 3 \times \frac{1}{6} = \frac{1}{2}$

14 (a) Here, total students = 15.

The ages of students in ascending order are 14, 14, 15, 16, 16, 17, 17, 17, 18, 19, 19, 20, 20, 20, 21.

Now, $P(X = 14) = \frac{2}{15}$, $P(X = 15) = \frac{1}{15}$,

$P(X = 16) = \frac{2}{15}$, $P(X = 17) = \frac{3}{15}$,

$P(X = 18) = \frac{1}{15}$, $P(X = 19) = \frac{2}{15}$, $P(X = 20) = \frac{3}{15}$

and $P(X = 21) = \frac{1}{15}$

A. Thus, the probability distribution of random variable X is as follows

X	14	15	16	17	18	19	20	21
Number of students	2	1	2	3	1	2	3	1
P(X)	$\frac{2}{15}$	$\frac{1}{15}$	$\frac{2}{15}$	$\frac{3}{15}$	$\frac{1}{15}$	$\frac{2}{15}$	$\frac{3}{15}$	$\frac{1}{15}$

B. The third row gives the probability distribution of X.

Mean of $X = \Sigma X\, P(X)$

$$= \frac{\begin{bmatrix} 14 \times 2 + 15 \times 1 + 16 \times 2 + 17 \times 3 + 18 \times 1 \\ + 19 \times 2 + 20 \times 3 + 21 \times 1 \end{bmatrix}}{15}$$

$$= \frac{28 + 15 + 32 + 51 + 18 + 38 + 60 + 21}{15}$$

$$= \frac{263}{15} = 17.53$$

C. Variance of $X = \Sigma X^2 P(X) - (\text{Mean})^2$

$$= \frac{\begin{bmatrix} (14)^2 \times 2 + (15)^2 \times 1 + (16)^2 \times 2 + (17)^2 \times 3 \\ + (18)^2 \times 1 + (19)^2 \times 2 + (20)^2 \times 3 + (21)^2 \times 1 \end{bmatrix}}{15} - \left(\frac{263}{15}\right)^2$$

$$= \frac{4683}{15} - \left(\frac{263}{15}\right)^2 = 312.2 - 307.4 = 4.8$$

D. SD of $X = \sqrt{\text{Variance}} = \sqrt{4.8} = 2.19$

15 (c) It is given that $P(X = 0) = 30\% = \frac{30}{100} = \frac{3}{10}$

and $\qquad P(X = 1) = 70\% = \frac{70}{100} = \frac{7}{10}$

Therefore, the probability distribution is as follows

X	0	1
P(X)	$\frac{3}{10}$	$\frac{7}{10}$

$\therefore$ Mean of $X = E(X) = \Sigma X\, P(X)$

$$= 0 \times \frac{3}{10} + 1 \times \frac{7}{10} = \frac{7}{10}$$

Variance of $X = \Sigma X^2 P(X) - (\text{Mean})^2$

$$= 0^2 \times \frac{3}{10} + 1^2 \times \frac{7}{10} - \left(\frac{7}{10}\right)^2$$

$$= \frac{7}{10} - \frac{49}{100} = \frac{21}{100}$$

16 (*b*) Let X be the random variable representing a number on the die.

The total number of observations is 6.

$$P(X=1) = \frac{3}{6} = \frac{1}{2},\ P(X=2) = \frac{2}{6} = \frac{1}{3} \text{ and } P(X=5) = \frac{1}{6}$$

Thus, required probability distribution of X is as follows

X	1	2	5
P(X)	$\frac{1}{2}$	$\frac{1}{3}$	$\frac{1}{6}$

Mean $(x) = \sum X\,P(X)$

$$= 1 \times \frac{1}{2} + 2 \times \frac{1}{3} + 5 \times \frac{1}{6}$$

$$= \frac{3+4+5}{6} = \frac{12}{6} = 2$$

17 (*d*) Firstly, make the probability distribution and then use the formula $E(X) = \Sigma\, X\,P(X)$.

Let X denote the number of aces obtained. Therefore, X can take any of the value of 0, 1 or 2.

In a deck of 52 cards, 4 cards are aces. Therefore, there are 48 non-ace cards.

$\therefore\quad P(X=0) = P$ (no ace is drawn)

$$= \frac{^{48}C_2}{^{52}C_2} = \frac{48 \times 47}{52 \times 51} = \frac{188}{221},$$

$P(X=1) = P$ (one ace and one non-ace are drawn)

$$= \frac{^4C_1 \times {^{48}C_1}}{^{52}C_2} = \frac{4 \times 48}{\frac{52 \times 51}{2!}} = \frac{32}{221}$$

and $\quad P(X=2) = P$ (two aces are drawn)

$$= \frac{^4C_2}{^{52}C_2} = \frac{4 \times 3}{52 \times 51} = \frac{1}{221}$$

$\therefore$ Thus, the probability distribution of X is as follows

X	0	1	2
P(X)	$\frac{188}{221}$	$\frac{32}{221}$	$\frac{1}{221}$

$$\therefore\quad E(X) = \Sigma X\,P(X) = 0 \times \frac{188}{221} + 1 \times \frac{32}{221} + 2 \times \frac{1}{221}$$

$$= \frac{34}{221} = \frac{2}{13}$$

18 (*b*) Given that,

X	30	10	−10
P(X)	$\frac{1}{5}$	$\frac{3}{10}$	$\frac{1}{2}$

$$E(X) = 30 \times \frac{1}{5} + 10 \times \frac{3}{10} + (-10) \times \frac{1}{2}$$

$$= 6 + 3 - 5 = 9 - 5 = 4$$

19 (*d*) Given that $\quad P(X=0) = p$

and $\quad P(X=1) = p$

Let $\quad P(X=2) = x$

$\because\quad \Sigma P(X) = 1$

$\therefore\quad p + p + x = 1$

$\Rightarrow\quad x = 1 - 2p \quad$ ...(i)

Also, $\quad E(X) = \Sigma X P(X) = 0 \times p + 1 \times p + 2 \times x$

$= p + 2x$

$= p + 2(1 - 2p) \quad$ [using Eq. (i)]

$= p + 2 - 4p$

$= 2 - 3p$

$E(X^2) = \Sigma X^2 P(X) = 0 + 1 \times p + 4 \times x$

$= p + 4x = p + 4(1 - 2p) \quad$ [using Eq. (i)]

$= 4 - 7p$

$\because\quad E(X^2) = E(X)$

$\therefore\quad 4 - 7p = 2 - 3p$

$\Rightarrow\quad 2 = 4p \Rightarrow p = \frac{1}{2}$

20 (*a*) Let X denote the number of heads tossed. So, X can take the values 0, 1, 2, 3. When a coin is tossed three times, we get

Sample space, $S = \{HHH, HHT, HTH, HTT, THH, THT, TTH, TTT\}$

$P(X=0) = P(\text{no head}) = P(TTT) = \frac{1}{8},$

$P(X=1) = P(\text{one head}) = P(HTT, THT, TTH) = \frac{3}{8},$

$P(X=2) = P(\text{two heads}) = P(HHT, HTH, THH) = \frac{3}{8}$

and $P(X=3) = P(\text{three heads}) = P(HHH) = \frac{1}{8}$

Thus, the probability distribution of X is as follows

X	0	1	2	3
P(X)	$\frac{1}{8}$	$\frac{3}{8}$	$\frac{3}{8}$	$\frac{1}{8}$

Variance of $X = \sigma^2 = \Sigma x_i^2 p_i - \mu^2 \quad$ ...(i)

where μ is the mean of X given by

$$\mu = \Sigma x_i p_i = 0 \times \frac{1}{8} + 1 \times \frac{3}{8} + 2 \times \frac{3}{8} + 3 \times \frac{1}{8} = \frac{3}{2} \quad \text{...(ii)}$$

Now, $\Sigma x_i^2 p_i = 0^2 \times \frac{1}{8} + 1^2 \times \frac{3}{8} + 2^2 \times \frac{3}{8} + 3^2 \times \frac{1}{8} = 3$ ...(iii)

From Eqs. (i), (ii) and (iii), we get

$$\sigma_x^2 = 3 - \left(\frac{3}{2}\right)^2 = \frac{3}{4}$$

Standard deviation $\sqrt{\sigma_x^2} = \sqrt{\frac{3}{4}} = \frac{\sqrt{3}}{2}$

21 (*b*) Let X denote a random variable of profits the player can have.

$\therefore X$ can take values -1, 1 or 4.

$$P(X = -1) = \frac{3}{6} = \frac{1}{2},$$

$$P(X = 1) = \frac{2}{6} = \frac{1}{3}$$

and $$P(X = 4) = \frac{1}{6}$$

$$E(X) = \sum x\,P(X) = -1 \times \frac{1}{2} + 1 \times \frac{1}{3} + 4 \times \frac{1}{6}$$

$$= -\frac{1}{2} + \frac{1}{3} + \frac{2}{3}$$

$$= \frac{-3 + 2 + 4}{6} = \frac{3}{6} = \frac{1}{2}$$

22 (*c*) Let X denote the random variable of the prizes.

$\therefore X$ can take values 3000, 2000, 500.

$$P(X = 3000) = \frac{1}{10000},$$

$$P(X = 2000) = \frac{1}{10000}$$

and $$P(X = 500) = \frac{3}{10000}$$

Now, $E(X) = \Sigma XP(X)$

$$= 3000 \times \frac{1}{10000} + 2000 \times \frac{1}{10000} + 500 \times \frac{3}{10000}$$

$$= \frac{3000 + 2000 + 1500}{10000} = \frac{6500}{10000} = 0.65$$

23 (*a*) Given that,

X	0	1	2	3
$P(X)$	k	$\frac{k}{2}$	$\frac{k}{4}$	$\frac{k}{8}$

$\because$ $$\Sigma P(X) = 1$$

$\Rightarrow$ $$k + \frac{k}{2} + \frac{k}{4} + \frac{k}{8} = 1$$

$\Rightarrow$ $$\frac{8k + 4k + 2k + k}{8} = 1$$

$\Rightarrow$ $$\frac{15k}{8} = 1$$

$\therefore$ $$k = \frac{8}{15}$$

Now, $P(X \le 2) = P(X = 0) + P(X = 1) + P(X = 2)$

$$= k + \frac{k}{2} + \frac{k}{4}$$

$$= \frac{4k + 2k + k}{4}$$

$$= \frac{7k}{4} = \frac{7}{4} \times \frac{8}{15} = \frac{14}{15}$$

and $P(X > 2) = P(X = 3)$

$$= \frac{k}{8} = \frac{8}{8 \times 15} = \frac{1}{15}$$

$\therefore$ $P(X \le 2) + P(X > 2) = \frac{14}{15} + \frac{1}{15} = \frac{15}{15} = 1$

A. $k = \frac{8}{15}$

B. $P(X \le 2) = \frac{14}{15}$

C. $P(X < 2) + P(X > 2) = 1$

24 (*d*) Given that,

X	2	3	4
$P(X)$	0.2	0.5	0.3

X	$P(X)$	$XP(X)$	$X^2P(X)$
2	0.2	0.4	0.8
3	0.5	1.5	4.5
4	0.3	1.2	4.8
		$\Sigma XP(X) = 3.1$	$\Sigma X^2P(X) = 10.1$

$$\mu = \Sigma \times P(X) = 3.1$$

$$\text{var } X = \Sigma X^2 P(X) - \mu^2 = 10.1 - (3.1)^2$$

$$= 10.1 - 9.61 = 0.49$$

$\therefore$ Standard deviation $= \sqrt{V(X)}$

$$= \sqrt{0.49} = 0.7$$

Miscellaneous Exercise

1 (*a*) Since, A wins the game if he gets a total of six.

Total of six will be in five cases

$= \{1, 5\}, \{2, 4\}, \{3, 3\}, \{4, 2\}, \{5, 1\}$

$\therefore$ $P(A) = \frac{5}{36}$ and $P(\bar{A}) = 1 - \frac{5}{36} = \frac{31}{36}$

$\because$ B wins the game if she gets a total of seven.

Total of seven will be in six cases

$= \{1, 6\}, \{2, 5\}, \{3, 4\}, \{4, 3\}, \{5, 2\}, \{6, 1\}$

$\therefore \quad P(B) = \frac{6}{36}$ and $P(\bar{B}) = 1 - \frac{6}{36} = \frac{30}{36} = \frac{5}{6}$

P(winning the game by A in the third throw)

$$= P(\bar{A}\bar{B}A)$$
$$= P(\bar{A})P(\bar{B})P(A)$$
$$= \frac{31}{36} \times \frac{5}{6} \times \frac{5}{36} = \frac{775}{7776}$$

2 (c) Given that red balls = 5 and blue balls = 3

Total number of balls = 5 + 3 = 8

$$P(\text{red}) = \frac{5}{8}$$

and $$P(\text{blue}) = \frac{3}{8}$$

Required probability is given by

$$P(\text{red}) = P(\text{red})\,P(\text{blue})\,P(\text{blue}) + P(\text{blue})\,P(\text{red})P(\text{blue}) + P(\text{blue})P(\text{blue})P(\text{red})$$
$$= \frac{5}{8} \times \frac{3}{7} \times \frac{2}{6} + \frac{3}{8} \times \frac{5}{7} \times \frac{2}{6} + \frac{3}{8} \times \frac{2}{7} \times \frac{5}{6}$$
$$= \frac{30}{336} + \frac{30}{336} + \frac{30}{336}$$
$$= \frac{90}{336} = \frac{15}{56}$$

3 (c) Let A, E_1, E_2, E_3 and E_4 be the events as defined below.

A : A black ball is selected $\quad E_1$: Box I is selected

E_2 : Box II is selected $\quad E_3$: Box III is selected

E_4 : Box IV is selected

Since, the boxes are chosen at random.

Therefore, $P(E_1) = P(E_2) = P(E_3) = P(E_4) = \frac{1}{4}$

Also, $P(A/E_1) = \frac{3}{18}$, $P(A/E_2) = \frac{2}{8}$, $P(A/E_3) = \frac{1}{7}$

and $P(A/E_4) = \frac{4}{13}$

P(box III is selected, given that the drawn ball is black)

$$= P(E_3/A)$$

By Bayes' theorem,

$$P(E_3/A) = \frac{P(E_3)P(A/E_3)}{P(E_1)P(A/E_1) + P(E_2)P(A/E_2) + P(E_3)\,P(A/E_3) + P(E_4)P(A/E_4)}$$

$$= \frac{\frac{1}{4} \times \frac{1}{7}}{\frac{1}{4} \times \frac{3}{18} + \frac{1}{4} \times \frac{1}{4} + \frac{1}{4} \times \frac{1}{7} + \frac{1}{4} \times \frac{4}{13}} = 0.165$$

4 (d) Let X be the random variable whose probability distribution is $B\left(4, \frac{1}{3}\right)$.

Here, $n = 4$, $p = \frac{1}{3}$ and $q = 1 - \frac{1}{3} = \frac{2}{3}$.

We know that $P(X = x) = {}^4C_x \left(\frac{2}{3}\right)^{4-x} \left(\frac{1}{3}\right)^x$, $x = 0, 1, 2, 3, 4$

i.e. the distribution of X is as follows

x_i	$P(x_i)$	$x_i P(x_i)$
0	${}^4C_0 \left(\frac{2}{3}\right)^4$	0
1	${}^4C_1 \left(\frac{2}{3}\right)^3 \left(\frac{1}{3}\right)$	${}^4C_1 \left(\frac{2}{3}\right)^3 \left(\frac{1}{3}\right)$
2	${}^4C_2 \left(\frac{2}{3}\right)^2 \left(\frac{1}{3}\right)^2$	$2 \cdot {}^4C_2 \left(\frac{2}{3}\right)^2 \left(\frac{1}{3}\right)^2$
3	${}^4C_3 \left(\frac{2}{3}\right) \left(\frac{1}{3}\right)^3$	$3 \cdot {}^4C_3 \left(\frac{2}{3}\right) \left(\frac{1}{3}\right)^3$
4	${}^4C_4 \left(\frac{1}{3}\right)^4$	$4 \cdot {}^4C_4 \left(\frac{1}{3}\right)^4$

Now, mean $(\mu) = \sum_{i=1}^{4} x_i P(x_i)$

$$= 0 + {}^4C_1 \left(\frac{2}{3}\right)^3 \left(\frac{1}{3}\right) + 2 \cdot {}^4C_2 \left(\frac{2}{3}\right)^2 \left(\frac{1}{3}\right)^2 + 3 \cdot {}^4C_3 \left(\frac{2}{3}\right) \left(\frac{1}{3}\right)^3 + 4 \cdot {}^4C_4 \left(\frac{1}{3}\right)^4$$

$$= 4 \times \frac{2^3}{3^4} + 2 \times 6 \times \frac{2^2}{3^4} + 3 \times 4 \times \frac{2}{3^4} + 4 \times 1 \times \frac{1}{3^4}$$

$$= \frac{32 + 48 + 24 + 4}{3^4} = \frac{108}{81} = \frac{4}{3}$$

5 (a) Let the shooter fire n times. Obviously, n fires are n Bernoulli trails. In each trial,

P = Probability of hitting the target $= \frac{3}{4}$

and q = Probability of not hitting the target $= \frac{1}{4}$.

Then, $$P(X = x) = {}^nC_x\, q^{n-x} p^x$$
$$= {}^nC_x \left(\frac{1}{4}\right)^{n-x} \left(\frac{3}{4}\right)^x = {}^nC_x \frac{3^x}{4^n}$$

Now, given that

P(hitting the target atleast once) > 0.99

i.e. $\quad P(x \geq 1) > 0.99$

Therefore, $1 - P(x = 0) > 0.99$

$\Rightarrow \quad 1 - {}^nC_0 \dfrac{1}{4^n} > 0.99$

$\Rightarrow \quad {}^nC_0 \dfrac{1}{4^n} < 0.01$ i.e. $\dfrac{1}{4^n} < 0.01$

$\Rightarrow \quad 4^n > \dfrac{1}{0.01} = 100$ ...(i)

The minimum value of n to satisfy the inequality (i) is 4. Thus, the shooter must fire 4 times.

6 (*b*) Let S denote the success (geting a '6') and F denote the failure (not getting a '6').

Thus, $P(S) = \dfrac{1}{6}, P(F) = \dfrac{5}{6}$

$P(A \text{ wins in the first throw}) = P(S) = \dfrac{1}{6}$

A gets the third throw, when the first throw by A and second throw by B result into failures.

Therefore, $P(A$ wins in the 3rd throw)

$$= P(FFS) = P(F)P(F)P(S)$$

$$= \frac{5}{6} \cdot \frac{5}{6} \cdot \frac{1}{6} = \left(\frac{5}{6}\right)^2 \times \frac{1}{6}$$

$P(A \text{ wins in the 5th throw}) = P(FFFFS) = \left(\dfrac{5}{6}\right)^4 \times \dfrac{1}{6}$ and so on.

Hence, $P(A \text{ wins}) = \dfrac{1}{6} + \left(\dfrac{5}{6}\right)^2 \cdot \dfrac{1}{6} + \left(\dfrac{5}{6}\right)^4 \cdot \dfrac{1}{6} + \ldots$

$$= \frac{\frac{1}{6}}{1 - \frac{25}{36}} = \frac{6}{11}$$

$$P(B \text{ wins}) = 1 - P(A \text{ wins}) = 1 - \frac{6}{11} = \frac{5}{11}$$

Note *If* $a + ar + ar^2 + \ldots + ar^{n-1} + \ldots$, *where* $|r| < 1$, *then sum of this infinite GP is given by* $\dfrac{a}{1-r}$.

7. (*d*) Let A be the event that the machine produces 2 acceptable items. Also, let B_1 represent the event of correct set up and let B_2 represent the event of incorrect setup.

Now, $P(B_1) = 0.8$ and $P(B_2) = 0.2$

$P(A / B_1) = 0.9 \times 0.9$ and $P(A / B_2) = 0.4 \times 0.4$

Therefore, $P(B_1 / A) = \dfrac{P(B_1)\, P(A / B_1)}{P(B_1)\, P(A / B_1) + P(B_2)\, P(A / B_2)}$

$$= \frac{0.8 \times 0.9 \times 0.9}{0.8 \times 0.9 \times 0.9 + 0.2 \times 0.4 \times 0.4}$$

$$= \frac{648}{680} = 0.95$$

8 (*d*) Let E_1 : The event that selected person is a male and E_2: The event that selected person is a female.

E_1 and E_2 are mutually exclusive and exhaustive events.

Moreover, $P(E_1) = P(E_2) = \dfrac{1}{2}$

Let E : The event that selected person is grey haired.

$\therefore \quad P\left(\dfrac{E}{E_1}\right) = \dfrac{5}{100} = \dfrac{1}{20}$ and $P\left(\dfrac{E}{E_2}\right) = \dfrac{0.25}{100} = \dfrac{1}{400}$

By Bayes' theorem,

Required probability,

$$P\left(\frac{E_1}{E}\right) = \frac{P\left(\frac{E}{E_1}\right) P(E_1)}{P\left(\frac{E}{E_1}\right) P(E_1) + P\left(\frac{E}{E_2}\right) P(E_2)}$$

$$= \frac{\frac{1}{20} \times \frac{1}{2}}{\frac{1}{20} \times \frac{1}{2} + \frac{1}{400} \times \frac{1}{2}} = \frac{\frac{1}{20}}{\frac{1}{20} + \frac{1}{400}} = \frac{\frac{1}{20}}{\frac{21}{400}} = \frac{20}{21}$$

Numerical Type Questions

1 (3) Let E_1 be the event that first ball drawn is red, E_2 be the event that second ball drawn is black and A be the event that second ball drawn is red.

$$P(E_1) = \frac{4}{10} \text{ and } P\left(\frac{A}{E_1}\right) = \frac{6}{12}$$

$\Rightarrow \quad P(E_2) = \dfrac{6}{10}$ and $\left(\dfrac{A}{E_2}\right) = \dfrac{4}{12}$

By law of total probability,

$$P(A) = P(E_1) \times P\left(\frac{A}{E_1}\right) + P(E_2) \times P\left(\frac{A}{E_2}\right)$$

$$= \frac{4}{10} \times \frac{6}{12} + \frac{6}{10} \times \frac{4}{12} = \frac{24}{120} + \frac{24}{120} = \frac{2}{5} = k$$

$$k = \frac{2}{5}$$

Thus, $\quad 5k = 5 \times \dfrac{2}{5} = 2$

$\Rightarrow \quad 5k + 1 = 3$

2 (13) Given probability distribution for a random variable X is

X	1	2	3	4	5
P(X)	$3k$	$2k^2$	k	k	$4k^2$

Then, $P(X > 3) = 1 - \{P(X = 1) + P(X = 2) + P(X = 3)\}$

$$= 1 - \{3k + 2k^2 + k\}$$

$$= 1 - 2k^2 - 4k$$

$\therefore \sum_{x=1}^{5} P(X)=1$

$\Rightarrow 6k(k+1)-1(k+1)=0$

$\Rightarrow \quad k=\frac{1}{6},-1 \quad [\because P(X)\ge 0, \text{ so } k\le 0]$

$k=\frac{1}{6}$

$\therefore \; P(X>3)=1-\frac{1}{18}-\frac{4}{6}=\frac{18-1-12}{18}=\frac{5}{18}$

$\Rightarrow \quad \frac{\alpha}{\beta}=\frac{5}{18} \Rightarrow (\beta-\alpha)=(18-5)=13$

3 (2)

A	B	C
7 red 4 black	5 red 6 black	6 red 5 black

Now, if ball drawn is black, then the probability that it is chosen from

$$\text{urn } B=\frac{\frac{1}{3}\times\frac{6}{11}}{\frac{1}{3}\times\frac{4}{11}+\frac{1}{3}\times\frac{6}{11}+\frac{1}{3}\times\frac{5}{11}}=\frac{\frac{2}{11}}{\frac{4}{33}+\frac{6}{33}+\frac{5}{33}}=\frac{\frac{2}{11}}{\frac{15}{33}}=\frac{2}{5}$$

$\Rightarrow \frac{\alpha}{5}=\frac{2}{5}$

$\therefore \; \alpha=2$

4 (15) We have, $S=\{00, 01, 02, \ldots, 49\}$

Let E_1 be the event that sum of the digits on the selected ticket is Q. Then, $E_1=\{08, 17, 26, 35, 44\}$ and let E_2 be the event that the product of the digit is zero.

$\therefore \; E_2=\{00, 01, 02, \ldots, 09, 10, 20, 30, 40\}$

$\therefore \; E_1\cap E_2=\{08\}$

$\therefore$ Required probability $=P\left(\frac{E_1}{E_2}\right)=\frac{P(E_1\cap E_2)}{P(E_2)}$

$=\frac{1/50}{14/50}=\frac{1}{14}$

$\therefore \quad (k_1+k_2)=1+14=15$

5 (5) In the 22nd century there are 25 leap years as 2100, 2104, ... , 2196 and 75 non-leap years.

Let E_1 be the event selecting a leap year and E_2 be the event selecting a non-leap year. E be the event that there are 53 sundays in a year of 22nd century.

$\therefore \quad P(E_1)=\frac{25}{100}$ and $P(E_2)=\frac{75}{100}$

$P\left(\frac{E}{E_1}\right)=\frac{2}{7}$ and $P\left(\frac{E}{E_2}\right)=\frac{1}{7}$

$\therefore \quad P(E)=P(E_1)\,P\left(\frac{E}{E_1}\right)+P(E_2)\,P\left(\frac{E_1}{E_2}\right)$

$=\frac{25}{100}\times\frac{2}{7}+\frac{75}{100}\times\frac{1}{7}=\frac{5}{28}$

$\therefore \quad k=5$

6 (6) Let x, y and z be probabilities of E_1, E_2 and E_3, respectively

$\therefore \quad \alpha=x(1-y)(1-z)$ ...(i)

$\beta=(1-x)\,y\,(1-z)$ ...(ii)

$\gamma=(1-x)(1-y)\,z$ ...(iii)

Given, $(\alpha-2\beta)\,p=\alpha\beta$ and $(\beta-3\gamma)\,p=2\beta\gamma$

$p=(1-x)(1-y)(1-z)$ ...(iv)

$\therefore$ From the above Eqs. (i), (ii), (iii) and (iv),

$x=2y$ and $y=3z$

$\therefore \quad x=6z \Rightarrow \frac{x}{z}=6$

Assertion and Reason Questions

1 (*b*) If two coins are tossed once, then the sample space,

$S=\{HH, HT, TH, TT\}$

I. E = Set of events having tail on one coin $=\{HT, TH\}$,

F = Set of events having one coin showing head $=\{HT, TH\}$ and $E\cap F=\{HT, TH\}$

$\Rightarrow \quad P(E)=\frac{2}{4}=\frac{1}{2}$

$P(F)=\frac{2}{4}=\frac{1}{2}$

and $\; P(E\cap F)=\frac{2}{4}=\frac{1}{2}$

$\therefore \quad P\left(\frac{E}{F}\right)=\frac{P(E\cap F)}{P(F)}=\frac{\frac{1}{2}}{\frac{1}{2}}=1$

II. E = Set of events having no tail $=\{HH\}$,

F = Set of events having no head $=\{TT\}$

and $\; E\cap F=\phi$

$\Rightarrow \quad P(E)=\frac{1}{4}, P(F)=\frac{1}{4}$ and $P(E\cap F)=\frac{0}{4}=0.$

$\therefore \quad P\left(\frac{E}{F}\right)=\frac{P(E\cap F)}{P(F)}=\frac{0}{1/4}=0$

2 (*b*) Let the first observation be from the black die and second from the red die.

When two dice (one black and another red) are rolled, then Sample space, $S=6\times 6=36$ (equally likely sample events)

I. Let E : Set of events in which sum greater than 9 and F : Set of events in which black die resulted in a 5

$E=\{(6, 4), (4, 6), (5, 5), (5, 6), (6, 5), (6, 6)\}$

$\Rightarrow \quad n(E)=6$

and $\quad F=\{(5, 1), (5, 2), (5, 3), (5, 4), (5, 5), (5, 6)\}$

$\Rightarrow \quad n(F)=6$

$\therefore \quad E\cap F=\{(5, 5), (5, 6)\}$

$\Rightarrow n(E\cap F)=2$

The conditional probability of obtaining a sum greater than 9, given that the black die resulted in a 5, is given by $P\left(\frac{E}{F}\right)$.

Now, $P(E) = \frac{\text{Number of favourable outcomes}}{\text{Total number of outcomes}}$

$= \frac{6}{36} = \frac{1}{6}$

Similarly, $P(F) = \frac{6}{36} = \frac{1}{6}$ and $P(E \cap F) = \frac{2}{36} = \frac{1}{18}$

$\therefore \quad P\left(\frac{E}{F}\right) = \frac{P(E \cap F)}{P(F)} = \frac{1/18}{1/6} = \frac{1}{18} \times \frac{6}{1} = \frac{1}{3}$

II. Let E : Set of events having 8 as the sum of the observations

and F : Set of events in which red die resulted in a number less than 4.

$\therefore \quad E = \{(2,6),(3,5),(4,4),(5,3),(6,2)\}$

$\Rightarrow \quad n(E) = 5$

and $\quad F = \begin{Bmatrix} (1,1),(1,2),(1,3),(2,1),(2,2),(2,3), \\ (3,1),(3,2),(3,3),(4,1),(4,2),(4,3), \\ (5,1),(5,2),(5,3),(6,1),(6,2),(6,3) \end{Bmatrix}$

$\Rightarrow \quad n(F) = 18$

$\therefore \quad E \cap F = \{(5,3),(6,2)\}$

$\Rightarrow n(E \cap F) = 2$

Now, $\quad P(E) = \frac{\text{Number of favourable outcomes}}{\text{Total number of outcomes}}$

$= \frac{5}{36}$

Similarly, $\quad P(F) = \frac{18}{36} = \frac{1}{2}$

and $\quad P(E \cap F) = \frac{2}{36} = \frac{1}{18}$

$\therefore$ Required probability is

$$P\left(\frac{E}{F}\right) = \frac{P(E \cap F)}{P(F)} = \frac{\frac{1}{18}}{\frac{1}{2}} = \frac{1}{18} \times \frac{2}{1} = \frac{1}{9}$$

3 (c)

I. When a die is thrown, then number of observations in the sample space is $S = 6 \times 6 = 36$ (equally likely sample events) i.e. $n(S) = 36$

Let E : Set of numbers in which the sum of the numbers on the dice is 4

and F : Set of numbers in which numbers appearing on the two dice are different.

Then, $\quad E = \{(1,3),(2,2),(3,1)\}$

$\Rightarrow \quad n(E) = 3$

$F = \begin{Bmatrix} (1,2),(1,3),(1,4),(1,5),(1,6), \\ (2,1),(2,3),(2,4),(2,5),(2,6), \\ (3,1),(3,2),(3,4),(3,5),(3,6), \\ (4,1),(4,2),(4,3),(4,5),(4,6), \\ (5,1),(5,2),(5,3),(5,4),(5,6), \\ (6,1),(6,2),(6,3),(6,4),(6,5) \end{Bmatrix}$

$\Rightarrow \quad n(F) = 30$

Here, F contains all points of S except $\{(1,1),(2,2),(3,3),(4,4),(5,5),(6,6)\}$

$\therefore \quad E \cap F = \{(1,3),(3,1)\}$

$\therefore \quad P(E) = \frac{\text{Number of favourable outcomes}}{\text{Total number of outcomes}}$

$= \frac{3}{36} = \frac{1}{12}$

Similarly, $\quad P(F) = \frac{30}{36} = \frac{5}{6}$ and $P(E \cap F) = \frac{2}{36} = \frac{1}{18}$

Hence, the required probability is

$$P\left(\frac{E}{F}\right) = \frac{P(E \cap F)}{P(F)} = \frac{\frac{1}{18}}{\frac{5}{6}} = \frac{1}{15}$$

II. The outcomes of the given experiment can be represented by the following set.

The sample space of the experiment is

$S = \begin{Bmatrix} (3,1),(3,2),(3,3),(3,4),(3,5),(3,6), \\ (6,1),(6,2),(6,3),(6,4),(6,5),(6,6), \\ (1,H),(1,T),(2,H),(2,T),(4,H), \\ (4,T),(5,H),(5,T) \end{Bmatrix}$

$\Rightarrow \quad n(S) = 20$

Let E : The coin shows a tail

and F : Atleast one die shows up a 3.

$E = \{(1,T),(2,T),(4,T),(5,T)\}$

$\Rightarrow \quad n(E) = 4$

$F = \{(3,1),(3,2),(3,3),(3,4),(3,5),(3,6),(6,3)\}$

$\Rightarrow \quad n(F) = 7$

$\Rightarrow E \cap F = \phi$ because here is no common element.

$\therefore \quad P(E) = \frac{\text{Favourable outcomes}}{\text{Total number of outcomes}} = \frac{n(E)}{n(S)}$

$= \frac{4}{20} = \frac{1}{5}$

Similarily, $\quad P(F) = \frac{n(F)}{n(S)} = \frac{7}{20}$

and $\quad P(E \cap F) = \frac{n(E \cap F)}{n(S)} = \frac{0}{20} = 0$

Hence, the required probability is

$$P\left(\frac{E}{F}\right)=\frac{P(E\cap F)}{P(F)}=\frac{0}{\frac{7}{20}}=0$$

4 (c) Let X be a random variable whose possible values $x_1, x_2, x_3, \ldots, x_n$ occur with probabilities $p_1, p_2, p_3, \ldots, p_n$, respectively.

The mean of X, denoted by μ, is the number $\sum_{i=1}^{n} x_i p_i$ i.e. the mean of X is the weighted average of the possible values of X, each value being weighted by its probability with which is occurs.

The mean of a random variable X is also called the expectation of X, denoted by $E(X)$.

Thus, $E(X)=\mu=\sum_{i=1}^{n} x_i p_i = x_1p_1+x_2p_2+\ldots+x_np_n$

In other words, the mean or expectation of a random variable X is the sum of the products of all possible values of X by their respective probabilities.

5 (c)

I. When a die is thrown, then the sample space, $S=\{1,2,3,4,5,6\}$.

Also, A : number is even and B : number is red

$\therefore$ $A=\{2,4,6\}, B=\{1,2,3\}$ and $A\cap B=\{2\}$

$\Rightarrow$ $n(A)=3, n(B)=3$ and $n(A\cap B)=1$

Now, $P(A)=\frac{3}{6}=\frac{1}{2}, P(B)=\frac{3}{6}=\frac{1}{2}, \quad P(A\cap B)=\frac{1}{6}$

and $P(A)\times P(B)=\frac{1}{2}\times\frac{1}{2}=\frac{1}{4}\neq\frac{1}{6}=P(A\cap B)$

$\Rightarrow$ $P(A\cap B)\neq P(A)\,P(B)$

Thus, A and B are not independent events.

II. It is given that $P(E)=\frac{3}{5}, P(F)=\frac{3}{10}$

and $P(E\cap F)=\frac{1}{5}$

Now, $P(E)\cdot P(F)=\frac{3}{5}\times\frac{3}{10}=\frac{9}{50}\neq\frac{1}{5}$

$=P(E\cap F)$

Therefore, E and F are not independent events.

6 (b)

I. Let A denote the event that the first ball drawn is blue.

Let B denote the event that the first ball drawn is red

and let E denote the event that the second ball drawn is blue.

Number of red balls = 4

and number of blue balls = 5

Now, total balls = 5 + 4 = 9

$\therefore$ $P(A)=\frac{5}{9}$

$\Rightarrow$ $P(B)=\frac{4}{9}$

$\Rightarrow$ $P(E/A)=\frac{4}{8}$

$\Rightarrow$ $P(E/B)=\frac{5}{8}$

Now, $P(E)=P(A)\times P(E/A)+P(B)\times P(E/B)$

$$=\frac{5}{9}\times\frac{4}{8}+\frac{4}{9}\times\frac{5}{8}$$

$$=\frac{20}{72}+\frac{20}{72}=\frac{40}{72}$$

$$=\frac{10}{18}=\frac{5}{9}$$

II. Let A denote the event that the first card is king.

Let B denote the event that the second card is king.

Let C denote the event that the third card is king.

Let D denote the event that the fourth card is king.

Now, $P(A\cap B\cap C\cap D)=P(A)\times P(B/A)$
$\times P(C/(A\cap B))\times P(D/(A\cap B\cap C))$

$$=\frac{4}{52}\times\frac{3}{51}\times\frac{2}{50}\times\frac{1}{49}$$

$$=\frac{1}{13}\times\frac{1}{17}\times\frac{1}{25}\times\frac{1}{49}$$

$$=\frac{1}{270725}$$

7 (b) Let A : bag 1 is selected.

Let B : bag 2 is selected.

Let C : bag 3 is selected.

In bag 1, red balls = 3

In bag 2, red balls = 2 and white balls = 1

In bag 3, white balls = 3

$\therefore$ $P(A)=\frac{1}{6}, P(B)=\frac{2}{6}$ and $P(C)=\frac{3}{6}$

I. Let E be the event of selecting a red ball.

Then, $P\left(\frac{E}{A}\right)=\frac{P(E\cap A)}{P(A)}$

$\therefore$ $P\left(\frac{E}{A}\right)=1, P\left(\frac{E}{B}\right)=\frac{2}{3}$ and $P\left(\frac{E}{C}\right)=0$

Now, $P(E)=P(A)\times P(E/A)+P(B)\times P(E/B)$
$+P(C)\times P(E/C)$

$$=\frac{1}{6}\times1+\frac{2}{6}\times\frac{2}{3}+\frac{3}{6}\times0=\frac{1}{6}+\frac{2}{9}+0=\frac{3+4}{18}=\frac{7}{18}$$

II. Let F denote that a white ball is selected.

$\therefore \quad P\left(\frac{F}{A}\right)=0,\ P\left(\frac{F}{B}\right)=\frac{1}{3}$ and $P\left(\frac{F}{C}\right)=1$

Now, $P(F)=P(A)\times P\left(\frac{F}{A}\right)+P(B)\times P\left(\frac{F}{B}\right)+P(1)\times P\left(\frac{F}{C}\right)$

$$=0+\frac{2}{6}\times\frac{1}{3}+\frac{3}{6}\times 1=\frac{1}{9}+\frac{1}{2}=\frac{2+9}{18}=\frac{11}{18}$$

8 (c)

I. We have, $P(A)=\frac{1}{4}, P(B)=\frac{1}{2}$ and $P(A\cap B)=\frac{1}{8}$

$\Rightarrow \quad P(A')=1-P(A)=1-\frac{1}{4}=\frac{3}{4}$

and $\quad P(B')=1-P(B)=1-\frac{1}{2}=\frac{1}{2}$

Also, $P(A\cap B)=\frac{1}{8}=\frac{1}{4}\times\frac{1}{2}=P(A)\times P(B).$

Therefore, A and B are independent events.

$\therefore$ A' and B' are also independent events

$\Rightarrow \quad P(A'\cap B')=P(A')\,P(B')$

$\therefore \quad P$ (not A and not B)

$$=P(A'\cap B')=P(A')P(B')=\frac{3}{4}\times\frac{1}{2}=\frac{3}{8}$$

Note *If A and B are independent events, then $A'\cdot B$, $A\cdot B'$ and $A'\cdot B'$ are also independent events.*

II. Given, P (not A or not B) $=\frac{1}{4}$

$\Rightarrow \quad P(A' \text{ or } B')=\frac{1}{4}\Rightarrow P(A'\cup B')=\frac{1}{4}$

$\Rightarrow \quad P[(A\cap B)']=\frac{1}{4} \quad [\because P(A'\cup B')=P(A\cap B)']$

$\Rightarrow \quad 1-P(A\cap B)=\frac{1}{4}\Rightarrow P(A\cap B)=1-\frac{1}{4}=\frac{3}{4}$ ...(i)

Also, $\quad P(A)\times P(B)=\frac{1}{2}\times\frac{7}{12}=\frac{7}{24}\neq\frac{3}{4}$

$$\left[\because P(A)=\frac{1}{2}, P(B)=\frac{7}{12}\right]$$

$\Rightarrow \quad P(A)\times P(B)\neq P(A\cap B)$

$\therefore$ A and B are not independent events.

9 (b)

I. The mean of a random variable does not give us information about the variability in the values of the random variable. Infact, if the variance is small, then the values of the random variable are close to the mean. Also, random variables with different probability distributions can have equal means, as shown in the following distributions of X and Y.

X	1	2	3	4
$P(X)$	$\frac{1}{8}$	$\frac{2}{8}$	$\frac{3}{8}$	$\frac{2}{8}$

Y	-1	0	4	5	6
$P(Y)$	$\frac{1}{8}$	$\frac{2}{8}$	$\frac{3}{8}$	$\frac{1}{8}$	$\frac{1}{8}$

Clearly, $E(X)=1\times\frac{1}{8}+2\times\frac{2}{8}+3\times\frac{3}{8}+4\times\frac{2}{8}$

$$=\frac{22}{8}=2.75$$

and $\quad E(Y)=-1\times\frac{1}{8}+0\times\frac{2}{8}+4\times\frac{3}{8}+5\times\frac{1}{8}+6\times\frac{1}{8}$

$$=\frac{22}{8}=2.75$$

The variables X and Y are different, however their means are same. It is also easily observable from the diagrammatic representation of these distributions.

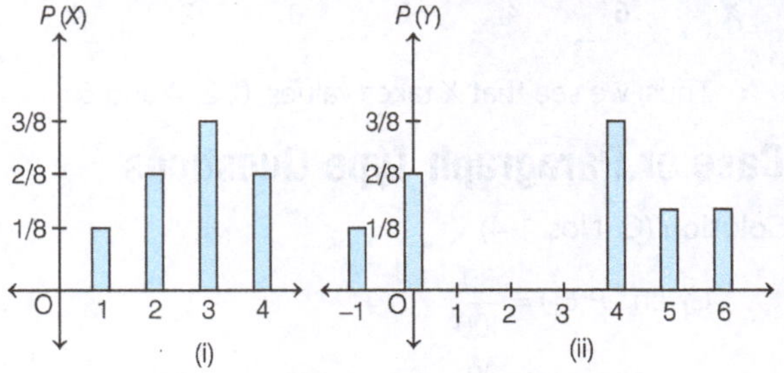

To distinguish X from Y, we require a measure of the extend to which the values of the random variables spread out. In Statistics, we have studied that the variance is a measure of the spread or scatter in data. Likewise, the variability or spread in the values of a random variable may be measured by variance.

II. Let X be a random variable whose possible values $x_1, x_2, \ldots, x_n$ occur with probabilities $p(x_1), p(x_2), \ldots, p(x_n)$, respectively.

Let $\mu=E(X)$ be the mean of X. The variance of X, denoted by Var(X) or σ_x^2 is defned as

$$\sigma_x^2=\text{Var}(X)=\sum_{i=1}^{n}(x_i-\mu)^2 p(x_i)$$

or equivalently $\sigma_x^2=E(X-\mu)^2$

The non-negative number $\sigma_x=\sqrt{\text{Var}(X)}$

$$=\sqrt{\sum_{i=1}^{n}(x_i-\mu)^2 p(x_i)}$$

is called the standard deviation of the random variable X.

10 (*b*)

I. The two balls are selected can be represented as *BB*, *BR*, *RB*, *RR*, where *B* represents a black ball and *R* represents a red ball and *X* represents the number of black balls.

$$X(BB)=2,\ X(BR)=1,\ X(RB)=1 \text{ and } X(RR)=0$$

Therefore, the possible values of *X* are 0, 1 and 2.

Thus, *X* is a random variable.

II. Let *M* denote the number of heads and *N* denote the number of tails when a coin is tossed 6 times.

Given, X = difference between M and $N = |M-N|$.

Here, both *M* and *N* can take values 0, 1, 2, 3, 4, 5, 6 but $M+N$ is always equal to 6.

Look at the following table

M	0	1	2	3	4	5	6
N	6	5	4	3	2	1	0
X	6	4	2	0	2	4	6

Thus, we see that *X* takes values, 0, 2, 4 and 6.

Case or Paragraph Type Questions

Solution (Q. Nos. 1-4)

Given, $P(E_1)=\frac{30}{100}$,

$$P(E_2)=\frac{20}{100}$$

and $P(E_3)=\frac{50}{100}$

1 (*b*) $P(A)=\frac{30}{100}\times\frac{5}{100}+\frac{20}{100}\times\frac{2}{100}+\frac{50}{100}\times\frac{4}{100}$

$$\Rightarrow \quad P(A)=\frac{150+40+200}{10000}=\frac{390}{10000}$$

$$P\left(\frac{E_1}{A}\right)=\frac{150}{390}=\frac{5}{13}$$

2 (*a*) $P\left(\frac{E_2}{A}\right)=\frac{40}{390}=\frac{4}{39}=0.1$

3 (*a*) $1-P\left(\frac{E_2}{A}\right)=1-\frac{4}{39}=\frac{35}{39}$

4 (*c*) $1-P\left(\frac{E_3}{A}\right)=1-\frac{20}{39}=\frac{19}{39}=0.48 \quad \left[\because P\left(\frac{E_3}{A}\right)=\frac{200}{390}=\frac{20}{39}\right]$

Solution (Q. Nos. 5-8)

$$P(E_1)=P(E_2)=P(E_3)=\frac{1}{3}$$

5 (*a*) $P\left(\frac{A}{E_1}\right)=\overset{W}{\frac{1}{6}}\times\overset{R}{\frac{2}{6}}+\overset{R}{\frac{2}{6}}\times\overset{W}{\frac{1}{6}}$

$$=\frac{1}{18}+\frac{1}{18}=\frac{1}{9}$$

6 (*a*) $P\left(\frac{A}{E_2}\right)=\overset{W}{\frac{2}{6}}\times\overset{R}{\frac{3}{6}}+\overset{R}{\frac{3}{6}}\times\overset{W}{\frac{2}{6}}$

$$=\frac{12}{36}=\frac{1}{3}$$

7 (*c*) $P\left(\frac{A}{E_3}\right)=\overset{W}{\frac{3}{6}}\times\overset{R}{\frac{1}{6}}+\overset{R}{\frac{1}{6}}\times\overset{W}{\frac{3}{6}}$

$$=\frac{6}{36}=\frac{1}{6}$$

8 (*b*) $P\left(\frac{E_2}{A}\right)=\frac{\frac{1}{3}\times\frac{1}{3}}{\frac{1}{3}\times\frac{1}{9}+\frac{1}{3}\times\frac{1}{3}+\frac{1}{3}\times\frac{1}{6}}=\frac{6}{11}$

Past Years Questions

1. (*d*) Let $E_1 \rightarrow$ Motorcycle produced by company *A*,
$E_2 \rightarrow$ Motorcycle produced by company *B*
and $A \rightarrow$ Motorcycle of standard quality.
So, according to the question,

$$P(E_1)=0.6 \text{ and } P(E_2)=0.4$$

$$P(A/E_1)=0.8 \text{ and } P(A/E_2)=0.9$$

So, by Baye's theorem, probability of motorcycle produced at *B* and of standard quality

$$P(E_2/A)=\frac{P(E_2)\,P(A/E_2)}{P(E_1)\,P(A/E_1)+P(E_2)\,P(A/E_2)}$$

$$=\frac{0.4\times0.9}{0.6\times0.8+0.4\times0.9}=\frac{36}{84}=\frac{3}{7}$$

$$\therefore \quad p=\frac{3}{7}$$

and $126p=126\times\frac{3}{7}=54$

2 (*a*) $E_1=2$ black, 6 white,

$E_2=3$ black, 5 white,

$E_3=4$ black, 4 white,

$E_4=5$ black, 3 white,

$E_5=6$ black, 2 white

$A=2$ white, 2 black balls drawn

$$P(E_1)=P(E_2)=P(E_3)=P(E_4)$$

$$=P(E_5)=\frac{1}{5}$$

$$P\left(\frac{A}{E_1}\right)=\frac{^2C_2\times{}^6C_2}{^8C_4},$$

$$P\left(\frac{A}{E_2}\right)=\frac{^3C_2\times{}^5C_2}{^8C_4},$$

$$P\left(\frac{A}{E_3}\right)=\frac{^4C_2\times{}^4C_2}{^8C_4}$$

$$P\left(\frac{A}{E_4}\right)=\frac{^5C_2\times{}^3C_2}{^8C_4}$$

and $P\left(\frac{A}{E_5}\right)=\frac{^6C_2\times{}^2C_2}{^8C_4}$

Required proabality $= P\left(\frac{E_3}{A}\right)$

$$=\frac{\frac{1}{5}\times\frac{^4C_2\times{}^4C_2}{^8C_4}}{\frac{1}{5}\left(\frac{^2C_2\times{}^6C_2}{^8C_4}+\frac{^3C_2\times{}^5C_2}{^8C_4}+\frac{^4C_2\times{}^4C_2}{^8C_4}+\frac{^5C_2\times{}^3C_2}{^8C_4}+\frac{^6C_2\times{}^3C_2}{^8C_4}\right)}$$

$$=\frac{36}{15+30+36+30+15}$$

$$=\frac{36}{126}=\frac{2}{7}$$

3 (*b*) Use having formula,

$$P(E_i / A)=\frac{P(E_i)P(A/E_i)}{\sum_{i=1}^{n}P(E_i)P(A/E_i)},$$

$i=1, 2, \ldots, n$

E_1 = Bag A is selected

and E_2 = Bag B is selected.

3W 7R	3W 2R
A	B

E = Drawing ball from bag is white.

According to the question,

we have to find $P\left(\frac{E_1}{E}\right)$.

Using Bayes' theorem,

$$P\left(\frac{E_1}{E}\right)=\frac{P(E_1)\cdot P\left(\frac{E}{E_1}\right)}{P(E_1)\cdot P\left(\frac{E}{E_1}\right)+P(E_2)\cdot P\left(\frac{E}{E_2}\right)}$$

$$=\frac{\frac{1}{2}\times\frac{3}{10}}{\frac{1}{2}\times\frac{3}{10}+\frac{1}{2}\times\frac{3}{5}}=\frac{3}{3+6}=\frac{1}{3}$$

4 (*b*) Here, $p=\frac{1}{2}$ and $q=\frac{1}{2}$

We have, P (getting an odd number 7 times)

$= P$ (getting an odd numbers nine time)

$$\Rightarrow {}^nC_7\left(\frac{1}{2}\right)^7\left(\frac{1}{2}\right)^{n-7}={}^nC_9\left(\frac{1}{2}\right)^9\left(\frac{1}{2}\right)^{n-9}$$

$$\Rightarrow {}^nC_7={}^nC_9$$

$$\Rightarrow n=7+9=16 \quad [\because 7\neq 9]$$

P (getting an even number twice) $=\frac{k}{2^{15}}$

$$^{16}C_2\times\left(\frac{1}{2}\right)^2\times\left(\frac{1}{2}\right)^{16-2}=\frac{k}{2^{15}}$$

$$\frac{16\times 15}{1\times 2}\times\frac{1}{2^{16}}=\frac{k}{2^{15}}$$

$$\Rightarrow k=60$$

5 (*b*) Given, a pair of dice is thrown once, then number of outcomes $=6\times 6=36$. A total of 5 are $\{(1, 4), (2, 3), (4, 1), (3, 2)\}$

$$\therefore p=P\,(\text{success})=\frac{4}{36}=\frac{1}{9}$$

$$q=1-\frac{1}{9}=\frac{8}{9}$$

Let X represent the number of success.

$\therefore$ P (at least 4 success)

$=P(X=4)+P(X=5)$

$={}^5C_4\,p^4q+{}^5C_5p^5q^{5-5}$

$=5\left(\frac{1}{9}\right)^4\left(\frac{8}{9}\right)+\left(\frac{1}{9}\right)^5$

$=\frac{40+1}{(3^2)^5}=\frac{41}{3^{10}}$

$=\frac{41\times 3}{3^{11}}=\frac{123}{3^{11}}$

$\Rightarrow \quad k=123$

6 (*d*) Let mean be a and variance be b. Then, according to the question, $a+b=5$ and $ab=6$

$\therefore \quad a=2, b=3$ or $a=3, b=2$

Now, when $a=2, b=3$,

then $np=2$ and $npq=3$

$\therefore \quad 2q=3\Rightarrow q=\frac{3}{2}$

which is not possible.

Again, when $a=3, b=2$,

then $np=3$ and $npq=2$

$\therefore \quad 3q=2$

$\Rightarrow \quad q=\frac{2}{3}$

Also, $p=1-q=1-\frac{2}{3}=\frac{1}{3}$

Again, $\quad np=3$

$\Rightarrow \quad n\times\frac{1}{3}=3\Rightarrow n=9$

So, $6(n+p-q)=6\left(9+\frac{1}{3}-\frac{2}{3}\right)$

$=54+2-4=52$

7 (*d*) Since, there are 6 possible outcomes when rolling a die.

There are 2 numbers greater than 4 on a die (5 and 6).

So, the probability of getting an number greater than 4 in throw is $\frac{2}{6}$.

$\because$ There are 3 numbers less than 4 on a die (1, 2 and 3).

So that, the probability of getting a number less than 4 in throw is $\frac{3}{6}$.

Now, according to the question,

The events of getting a number greater than 4 in the first and the second throw and a number less than 4 in the third throw are independent.

Hence, required probability

$$=\frac{2}{6}\cdot\frac{2}{6}\cdot\frac{3}{6}=\frac{1}{18}$$

8 (*b*) A. Since, the sum of all probabilities in a probability distribution is equal to 1.

$\therefore \quad \Sigma P(X) = 1$

$\Rightarrow k + 2k + 3k + 0 = 1 \Rightarrow 6k = 1$

$\therefore \quad k = \frac{1}{6}$

B. For $P(X < 2)$

$P(X < 2) = P(X = 0) + P(X = 1)$

$= k + 2k = 3k = 3 \times \frac{1}{6} = \frac{1}{2}$

Thus, $P(X < 2) = \frac{1}{2}$

C. Since, $E(X) = \Sigma[X \cdot P(X)]$

$= 0 \cdot k + 1 \times 2k + 2 \times 3k + 3 \cdot 0$

$= 0 \cdot \frac{1}{6} + 1 \cdot 2 \cdot \frac{1}{6} + 2 \cdot 3 \cdot \frac{1}{6} + 0$

$= 0 + \frac{1}{3} + 1 + 0$

$\therefore \quad E(X) = \frac{4}{3}$

D. For $P(1 \le X \le 2)$

$P(1 \le X \le 2) = P(X = 1) + P(X = 2)$

$= 2k + 3k$

$= 2 \cdot \frac{1}{6} + 3 \cdot \frac{1}{6} = \frac{1}{3} + \frac{1}{2}$

$P(1 \le X \le 2) = \frac{5}{6}$

Therefore, the required values are,

$k = \frac{1}{6}, P(X < 2) = \frac{1}{2}, E(X) = \frac{4}{3},$

$P(1 \le X \le 2) = \frac{5}{6}$

Thus, A-(iv), B-(iii), C-(ii), D-(i)

9 (*b*) We know that, $\Sigma P(x) = 1$

A. $P(X = 0) + P(X = 1) + P(X = 2)$

$+ P(X = 3) + P(X = 4)$

$+ P(X = X) = 1$

$\Rightarrow 0.1 + c + 2c + 2c + c + 0 = 1$

$\Rightarrow \quad 6c = 0.9 \quad \therefore c = 0.15$

B. $P(X \le 2) = P(X = 0) + P(X = 1)$

$+ P(X = 2)$

$= 0.1 + c + 2c$

$= 0.1 + 0.15 + 0.30 = 0.55$

C. $P(X = 2) = 2c = 0.30$

D. $P(X \ge 2) = P(X = 2) + P(X = 3)$

$+ P(X = 4)$

$= 2c + 2c + c$

$= 0.30 + 0.30 + 0.15 = 0.75$

Thus, A-(iv), B-(iii), C-(ii), D-(i)

Hence, the correct option is (b).

10 (*c*) Let,

E_1 : Event that Bag-1 is selected

E_2 : Event that Bag-2 is selected

A : Drawn ball is white.

Now, $P(E_1) = P$ (die shown multiple of 3)

$= \frac{2}{6} = \frac{1}{3}$

$P(E_2) = 1 - P(E_1) = 1 - \frac{1}{3} = \frac{2}{3}$

Again, $P\left(\frac{A}{E_1}\right) = \frac{4}{10} = \frac{2}{5}$

and $P\left(\frac{A}{E_2}\right) = \frac{5}{10} = \frac{1}{2}$

Now, required probability

= Probability that ball is not drawn from Bag-2, if it is not of black colour

= Probability that ball is drawn from Bag-1, if it is of white colour.

$$= P\left(\frac{E_1}{A}\right) = \frac{P(E_1)\,P\left(\frac{A}{E_1}\right)}{P(E_1)\,P\left(\frac{A}{E_1}\right) + P(E_2)\,P\left(\frac{A}{E_2}\right)}$$

$$= \frac{\frac{1}{3} \times \frac{2}{5}}{\frac{1}{3} \times \frac{2}{5} + \frac{2}{3} \times \frac{1}{2}} = \frac{\left(\frac{2}{5}\right)}{\frac{2}{5} + 1} = \frac{\left(\frac{2}{5}\right)}{\left(\frac{7}{5}\right)} = \frac{2}{7}$$

11 (17)

Blue balls	Probability
$\frac{^5C_0 \cdot {^4C_1}}{^9C_3}$	0
$\frac{^5C_1 \cdot {^4C_2}}{^9C_3}$	1
$\frac{^5C_2 \cdot {^4C_1}}{^9C_3}$	2
$\frac{^5C_3 \cdot {^4C_0}}{^9C_3}$	3
0	4
0	5

$$7\overline{X} = \frac{(^5C_0 \cdot {^4C_1} \times 0) + {^5C_1} \cdot {^4C_2} + {^5C_2} \cdot {^4C_1} \times 2 + {^5C_3} \cdot {^4C_0} \times 3}{^9C_3} \times 7$$

$$= \frac{30 + 80 + 30}{84} \times 7 = \frac{35}{3}$$

Yellow	Probability
$^5C_3 \cdot {^4C_0}$	0
$^5C_2 \cdot {^4C_1}$	1
$^5C_1 \cdot {^4C_2}$	2
$^5C_0 \cdot {^4C_3}$	3
0	4

$$4\overline{Y} = \frac{0 + {^5C_2} \cdot {^4C_1} + {^5C_1} \cdot {^4C_2} \times 2 + {^5C_0} \cdot {^4C_3} \times 3}{^9C_3} \times 4$$

$$= \frac{40 + 60 + 12}{84} \times 4 = \frac{112}{21} = \frac{16}{3}$$

Then, $7\overline{X} + 4\overline{Y} = \frac{35}{3} + \frac{16}{3} = 17$

12 (5)

X	α	1	0	−3
$P(X)$	$\frac{1}{3}$	k	$\frac{1}{6}$	$\frac{1}{4}$

$\Sigma P_i = 1$

$\frac{1}{3} + k + \frac{1}{6} + \frac{1}{4} = 1$

$\Rightarrow \quad k = \frac{1}{4}$

Mean $= \Sigma P_i x_i = \frac{\alpha}{3} + k + 0 - \frac{3}{4}$

$= \frac{\alpha}{3} + \frac{1}{4} - \frac{3}{4} = \frac{\alpha}{3} - \frac{1}{2}$

Variance $= \Sigma P_i x_i^2 - (\Sigma P_i x_i)^2$

$= \left(\frac{\alpha^2}{3} + k + 0 + \frac{9}{4}\right) - \left(\frac{\alpha}{3} - \frac{1}{2}\right)^2$

$\sigma^2 = \frac{\alpha^2}{3} + \frac{1}{4} + \frac{9}{4} - \frac{\alpha^2}{9} + \frac{\alpha}{3} - \frac{1}{4}$

$\sigma^2 = \frac{2\alpha^2}{9} + \frac{\alpha}{3} + \frac{9}{4}$

Now, $\sigma - \mu = 2$

$\sigma = \mu + 2$

$\sigma^2 = (\mu + 2)^2$

$$\frac{2\alpha^2}{9}+\frac{\alpha}{3}+\frac{9}{4}=\left(\frac{\alpha}{3}+\frac{3}{2}\right)^2$$

$$\frac{\alpha^2}{9}-\frac{2\alpha}{3}=0$$

$$\alpha = 0 \text{ (reject) or } 6$$

$$\therefore \sigma+\mu=\mu+2+\mu=2\mu+2$$

$$=\frac{2\alpha}{3}-1+2$$

$$=\frac{2\times 0}{3}+1=5$$

13 (27) Given, $P(H)=\frac{1}{4}$ then,

$$P(T)=1-\frac{1}{4}=\frac{3}{4}$$

If N = number of tosses required when the process is repeated until a head appears.

Then, probability

$$=\frac{1}{4}+\left(\frac{3}{4}\right)\left(\frac{1}{4}\right)+\left(\frac{3}{4}\right)^2\left(\frac{1}{4}\right)+\ldots+\left(\frac{3}{4}\right)^{N-1}\left(\frac{1}{4}\right)$$

$$P=\frac{1}{4}\left[1+\frac{3}{4}+\left(\frac{3}{4}\right)^2+\ldots+\left(\frac{3}{4}\right)^{N-1}\right]$$

$$P=\frac{1}{4}\left\{\frac{1\cdot\left\{1-\left(\frac{3}{4}\right)^N\right\}}{1-\frac{3}{4}}\right\}$$

$$\Rightarrow \quad P=1-\left(\frac{3}{4}\right)^N$$

Now, quadratic equation

$64x^2+5Nx+1=0$ has no real root

$$\Rightarrow \quad D<0$$

$$25N^2-4\times 64<0$$

$$\Rightarrow \quad (5N)^2<(16)^2$$

$$\Rightarrow \quad 5N<16$$

$$\Rightarrow \quad N<\frac{16}{5}$$

$$\Rightarrow \quad N<3.2$$

Then, $p=1-\left(\frac{3}{4}\right)^3$; $p=1-\frac{27}{64}=\frac{37}{64}$

Hence, $p=37, q=64$

$$q-p=64-37=27$$

14 (479) Required probability

$$={}^4C_2\left(\frac{3}{4}\right)^2\left(\frac{1}{4}\right)^2\left(\frac{1}{4}\right)^6+{}^6C_2\left(\frac{3}{4}\right)^2\left(\frac{1}{4}\right)^4\left(\frac{3}{4}\right)^4+{}^4C_1\,{}^6C_1\left(\frac{3}{4}\right)\left(\frac{1}{4}\right)\left(\frac{3}{4}\right)^3\left(\frac{1}{4}\right)^5$$

$$=\frac{1}{4^{10}}[6\times 9+15\times 9^3+24\times 9^2]$$

$$=\frac{27}{4^{10}}\times 479=\frac{27}{4^{10}}k$$

Thus, the value of k is 479.

Skill Boosters

1 (a) Let E_1 be the event that coin with two heads,

E_2 be the event that coin is fair and A be the event that toss result in heads,

$$\therefore \quad P(E_1)=\frac{1}{n+1} \text{ and } P(E_2)=\frac{n}{n+1}$$

$$P\left(\frac{A}{E_1}\right)=1$$

and $\quad P\left(\frac{A}{E_2}\right)=\frac{1}{2}$

$$\therefore P(A)=P(E_1)\,P\left(\frac{A}{E_1}\right)+P(E_2)\,P\left(\frac{A}{E_2}\right)$$

$$\Rightarrow \quad \frac{11}{20}=\frac{1}{n+1}\times 1+\frac{n}{n+1}\times\frac{1}{2}$$

$$\Rightarrow \quad \frac{11}{20}=\frac{2+n}{2(n+1)}$$

$$\Rightarrow \quad 11n+11=20+10n$$

$$\Rightarrow \quad n=9$$

2 (c) Let A_i denote the event that the number selected in ith draw is less than 4, where $i=1,2$.

$\therefore$ Required probability

$$=P(A_1\cup A_2)=1-P(\overline{A_1}\cap\overline{A_2})$$

$$=1-P(\overline{A_1})\,P\left(\frac{\overline{A_2}}{\overline{A_1}}\right)$$

$$=1-P(A_1)\,P(\overline{A_2}\,\overline{A}/\overline{A_1})$$

$$=1-\frac{3}{6}\times\frac{2}{5}=\frac{4}{5}$$

3 (a) Let X denote the number of aces. Then, probability of selecting aces,

$$p=\frac{4}{52}=\frac{1}{13}$$

and probability of not selecting aces,

$$q=1-\frac{1}{13}=\frac{12}{13}$$

and $P(X=1)=2\times\frac{1}{13}\times\frac{12}{13}=\frac{24}{169}$

and $P(X=2)=\left(\frac{1}{13}\right)^2\times\left(\frac{12}{13}\right)^0=\frac{1}{169}$

$$\therefore \text{ Mean}=\sum p_iX_i=\frac{24}{169}+\frac{2}{169}=\frac{2}{13}$$

4 (c) Let E_1, E_2 and E_3 be the events that first, second and third student get success.

$$\therefore \quad P(E_1)=\frac{1}{3},$$

$P(E_2)=\frac{1}{4}$ and $P(E_3)=\frac{1}{5}$

Given, probability of success of atleast two $=\frac{\lambda}{12}$

$$\Rightarrow P(E_1\cap E_2\cap \overline{E_3})+P(\overline{E_1}\cap E_2\cap E_3)$$
$$+P(E_1\cap \overline{E_2}\cap E_3)+P(E_1\cap E_2\cap E_3)=\frac{\lambda}{12}$$

$$\Rightarrow P(E_1)\,P(E_2)\,P(\overline{E_3})+P(\overline{E_1})\,P(E_2)\,P(E_3)+P(E_1)\,P(\overline{E_2})\,P(E_3)+P(E_1)\,P(E_2)\,P(E_3)=\frac{\lambda}{12}$$

$$\Rightarrow \frac{1}{3}\times\frac{1}{4}\times\frac{4}{5}+\frac{2}{3}\times\frac{1}{4}\times\frac{1}{5}+\frac{1}{3}\times\frac{3}{4}\times\frac{1}{5}+\frac{1}{3}\times\frac{1}{4}\times\frac{1}{5}=\frac{\lambda}{12}$$

$$\Rightarrow \frac{10}{60}=\frac{\lambda}{12}\Rightarrow \lambda=2$$

5 (c) Let E_1 denote original signal is green, E_2 denote original signal is red and E denote signal received at station B is green,

$$\therefore P\left(\frac{E_1}{E}\right)=\frac{P(E_1)\,P\left(\frac{E}{E_1}\right)}{P(E_1)\,P\left(\frac{E}{E_1}\right)+P(E_2)\,P\left(\frac{E}{E_2}\right)}$$

$$=\frac{4}{5}\left[\left(\frac{3}{4}\right)^2+\left(\frac{1}{4}\right)^2\right]+\frac{1}{5}$$

$$=\frac{4}{5}\left[\left(\frac{3}{4}\right)^2\times\left(\frac{1}{4}\right)^2\right]+\frac{1}{5}\left[\frac{3}{4}\times\frac{1}{4}+\frac{1}{4}\times\frac{3}{4}\right]$$

$$=\frac{\frac{4}{5}\left(\frac{10}{16}\right)}{\frac{4}{5}\times\frac{10}{16}+\frac{1}{5}\times\frac{6}{16}}$$

$$=\frac{20}{23}$$